The
Harcourt
ANTHOLOGY
of DRAMA
Brief Edition

W. B. WORTHEN
University of California, Berkeley

HARCOURT COLLEGE PUBLISHERS

Fort Worth   Philadelphia   San Diego   New York   Orlando   Austin   San Antonio
Toronto   Montreal   London   Sydney   Tokyo

Publisher	Earl McPeek
Acquisitions Editor	Bill Hoffman
Market Strategist	Katrina Byrd
Developmental Editor	Camille Adkins
Project Editor	Jon Davies
Art Director	April Eubanks
Production Manager	Cindy Young

Cover design and scratchboard/digital illustrations by Lamberto Alvarez.

ISBN: 0-15-506395-2

Library of Congress Catalog Card Number: 00-111784

Address for Domestic Orders
Harcourt College Publishers
6277 Sea Harbor Drive
Orlando, FL 32887-6777
800-782-4479

Address for International Orders
International Customer Service
Harcourt, Inc.
6277 Sea Harbor Drive
Orlando, FL 32887-6777
407-345-3800
(fax) 407-345-4060
(e-mail) hbintl@harcourt.com

Address for Editorial Correspondence
Harcourt College Publishers
301 Commerce Street, Suite 3700
Fort Worth, TX 76102

Web Site Address
http://www.harcourtcollege.com

Harcourt College Publishers will provide complimentary supplements or supplement packages to those adopters qualified under our adoption policy. Please contact your sales representative to learn how you qualify. If as an adopter or potential user you receive supplements you do not need, please return them to your sales representative or send them to: Attn: Returns Department, Troy Warehouse, 465 South Lincoln Drive, Troy, MO 63379.

Printed in the United States of America

1 2 3 4 5 6 7 8 9 0   043   9 8 7 6 5 4 3 2 1

Harcourt College Publishers

PREFACE

Studying drama is more than reading plays. It requires us to study the theaters where the plays were produced, the cultures that framed those theaters, and the critical and performance history that has framed the meanings of drama over time. *The Harcourt Anthology of Drama*, Brief Edition, presents drama in these two important contexts: in the play's original theater and the society that sustained it, and in *our* culture, where the play continues to live both as literature and as theatrical performance.

Based on the full-length *Harcourt Brace Anthology of Drama*, the brief edition offers a convenient collection of classic and contemporary plays from Europe, the Americas, Africa, and Asia. Designed to be used in a variety of drama and theater courses, in general surveys of drama and theater, in courses on tragedy and/or comedy, or in classes on modern theater, the brief edition offers a useful selection of classic theater and a rich selection of contemporary drama drawn from around the world.

The brief anthology builds on the strengths and success of the full-length *Harcourt Brace Anthology of Drama*, and provides many of the important elements of that anthology in a more streamlined form. It is divided into seven units, each focused on a significant period in the history of drama and theater: Athens in the fifth century BCE (three plays); feudal Japan (two plays); England in the late Middle Ages and Renaissance (three plays); France, Spain, England, and the Americas in the seventeenth and eighteenth centuries (four plays); Europe from 1850 through the twentieth century (six plays); the United States (seven plays); and contemporary stages around the world (six plays). As in the full-length anthology, each unit of the brief edition begins with an extensive introduction, placing drama in the context of a specific historical era and using illustrations of theater design to develop a precise sense of stage practice. Each play is accompanied by a brief biography of the playwright and a short introduction to the play. Each unit concludes with a selection of critical readings drawn from the period and essays on performance. *The Harcourt Anthology of Drama*, Brief Edition, emphasizes the diversity of drama and theater throughout history, both in its selection of plays and essays and in the issues and ideas raised for discussion as well.

The brief edition draws from the strengths of the third edition of *The Harcourt Brace Anthology of Drama*: It shares that volume's commitment to representing the scope of drama and theater in history and across the spectrum of contemporary performance, but in a smaller and more select volume. The brief edition retains plays by Sophocles, Euripides, Aristophanes, Shakespeare, Calderón, Molière, Ibsen, Chekhov, Shaw, Brecht, Beckett, Churchill, Glaspell, Valdez, Wilson, Hwang, Kushner, Soyinka, Friel, and

Highway. *The Harcourt Brace Anthology of Drama*, Brief Edition, also includes:

- a unit, "World Stages," focusing on postcolonial drama and theater, including plays from modern Martinique, Nigeria, Northern Ireland, South Africa, and Canada
- a section in each unit, "Critical Contexts," featuring critical or theoretical essays from the period as well as essays on the history and theory of performance
- a large selection of plays by women (five)
- a large selection of comedies (nine)
- a Kabuki play *The Forty-Seven Samurai*
- a brief play on the impact of religion on the indigenous peoples of the Americas, written by the greatest writer of colonial Mexico, Sor Juan Inés de la Cruz's *Loa* to *The Divine Narcissus*
- American drama in one unit, now including Suzan-Lori Parks's brilliant recent play on African Americans in history, *The America Play*
- one play by Native playwright Tomson Highway, *Dry Lips Oughta Move to Kapuskasing*
- two plays from contemporary South African theater, one from the apartheid era, Maishe Maponya's *Gangsters*, and one from the post-apartheid era, Athol Fugard's *Valley Song*
- "Aside" sections in each unit-opening essay devoted to topics of special importance: Roman drama and theater, Sanskrit drama and theater, the masque, the new Shakespeare's Globe Theatre in London, *commedia dell' arte*, melodrama, the Federal Theater Project, performance art, and intercultural performance
- two student essays in the "Writing about Drama and Theater" section, focusing on different approaches to Caryl Churchill's *Cloud Nine*

The brief edition retains many of the critical essays of the third full-length edition, such as selections by Aristotle, Friedrich Nietzsche, Zeami Motokiyo, Sir Philip Sidney, John Dryden, Katharine Eisaman Maus, Émile Zola, Bertolt Brecht, Antonin Artaud, Arthur Miller, and Henry Louis Gates Jr. The brief edition also includes several important essays devoted to performance practice and theory, including essays by Niall Slater, Louis Montrose, Constantin Stanislavski, and Helen Gilbert and Joanne Tompkins. In addition, the book includes a landmark essay in postcolonial theory by Frantz Fanon. The brief edition continues its effort to enable students and teachers to explore the issues of representation in the theater and the ways that culture shapes identity, gender and sexuality, power, and race.

The Harcourt Anthology of Drama, Brief Edition, is designed for both beginning and advanced students but is particularly addressed to courses at the introductory level. An introduction to writing about drama and theater furnishes beginning students with an outline of the formal and rhetorical practices used in writing about plays. The book also includes a useful glossary of dramatic, theatrical, and literary terms as well as an extensive bibliography of drama and theater history and theory and of works about plays and playwrights included in the volume. The book concludes with a selected list of video, film, and sound recordings. For the instructor, a thorough Instructor's Manual by Sharon Mazer of the University of Canterbury (New Zealand) offers an overview and reading suggestions for each unit as well as a summary, a commentary, and study, discussion, and writing questions for each play. The brief edition provides a wide-ranging survey of drama and theater, one that presents both traditional issues and the materials to interrogate those traditions.

ACKNOWLEDGMENTS

My thanks to the editorial staff of Harcourt who have brought *The Harcourt Anthology of Drama,* Brief Edition, to fruition. I am especially grateful to Bill Hoffman for his involvement in this project, and to Camille Adkins for her advice on how the volume could be improved. My thanks, too, to Jon Davies, Michele Jone, and Charles Naylor for their careful editing of the manuscript, and for many valuable ideas, suggestions, and corrections; to Susan Holtz for her work on securing permissions, photographs, and artwork; to Lamberto Alvarez for his cooperation—and inspiration—on the artwork for the unit openings; to April Eubanks for her coordination of the art program; to Sue Hart for her design; and to Cindy Young for overseeing the book's production.

I would also like to thank the many instructors and scholars who commented on the second edition, suggesting ways we might improve the third edition:

David Adamson (University of North Carolina, Chapel Hill)
Gilbert L. Bloom (Ball State University)
Brian Boney (University of Texas)
Cynthia Bowers (Loyola University)
Karen Buckley (University of Wisconsin, Whitewater)
Susan Carlson (Iowa State University)
Allen Chesler (Northern Illinois University)
Barbara Clayton (University of Wisconsin, Madison)
Kathleen Colligan Cleary (Clark State Community College)
Jill Dolan (City University of New York)
David S. Escoffery (University of Pittsburgh)
Anthony Graham-White (University of Illinois at Chicago)
John E. Hallwas (Western Illinois University)
L. W. Harrison (Santa Rosa Junior College)

Anne-Charlotte Harvey (San Diego State University)
Gregory Kable (University of North Carolina, Chapel Hill)
Lawrence Kinsman (New Hampshire College)
Ann Klautsch (Boise State University)
Margaret Knapp (Arizona State University)
Josephine Lee (University of Minnesota)
Michael J. Longrie (University of Wisconsin, Whitewater)
Kim Marra (University of Iowa)
Carla McDonough (Eastern Illinois University)
John F. O'Malley (DePaul University)
Michael Peterson (Millikin University)
Carol Rocamora (NYU Tisch School of the Arts)
Hans Rudnick (Southern Illinois University)
Terry Donovan Smith (University of Washington)
Tramble Turner (Penn State University)
Jon W. Tuttle (Francis Marion University)
Timothy Wiles (Indiana University)
Barry Yzereef (University of Calgary)

I would also like to thank those who responded to the survey for the third edition:

George Adams (University of Wisconsin, Whitewater)
Ruth Anderson (San Diego State University)
Cynthia Bowers (Loyola University)
Ruth Contrell (New Mexico State University)
Kenneth Cox (Oklahoma State University)
Mary Emery (University of Wisconsin, Whitewater)
Tom Empy (Casper College)
Lawrence Fink (Ohio State University)
James Fisher (Wabash College)
Kay Forston (Phillips University)
Melissa Gibson (University of Pittsburgh)
Marsha Morrison (Genesee Community College)
Chris Mullen (University of North Carolina, Chapel Hill)
Lurana O'Malley (University of Hawai'i)
Gwendolyn Orel (University of Pittsburgh)
Eva Patton (Fordham University)
Richard Schauer (University of Wisconsin, Whitewater)
John Terhes (Chemeketa Community College)
Charles Trainer (Siena College)
Tramble Turner (Penn State University)

I would also like to thank reviewers for the second edition: George R. Adams (University of Wisconsin, Whitewater), Bonnie M. Anderson (San Diego State University), Karen Buckley (University of Wisconsin, Whitewater), Kathleen Colligan Cleary (Clark State Community College), Mary Ann Emery (University of Wisconsin, Whitewater), Lawrence E. Fink (Ohio State University), Melissa Gibson (University of Pittsburgh), Kiki Gounaridou (University of

Pittsburgh), Anne-Charlotte Harvey (San Diego State University), Dennis Kennedy (Trinity College, Dublin), Chris Mullen (University of North Carolina, Chapel Hill), Lurana O'Malley (University of Hawai'i), Gwen Orel (University of Pittsburgh), Angela Peckenpaugh (University of Wisconsin, Whitewater), Ruth Schauer (University of Wisconsin, Whitewater). In addition, I am grateful to the following reviewers of the manuscript of the second edition for their valuable revision suggestions: Anne Brannen (Duquesne University), Bradley Boney (University of Texas, Austin), Susan Carlson (Iowa State University), S. Alan Chesler (Northern Illinois University), Jill Dolan (City University of New York), Anthony J. Fichera (University of North Carolina, Chapel Hill), L. W. Harrison (Santa Rosa Junior College), Margaret Knapp (Arizona State University), Josephine Lee (University of Minnesota), Michael Longrie (University of Wisconsin, Whitewater), Michael Peterson (University of Wisconsin, Madison), Eula Thompson (Jefferson State Community College), Jon Tuttle (Francis Marion University).

My thanks to the people who read and commented on the manuscript of the first edition, making it more accurate and useful for instructors: Stanton B. Garner Jr. (University of Tennessee), Josephine Lee (University of Minnesota), Don Moore (Louisiana State University), Cyndia Susan Clegg (Pepperdine University).

I am again indebted to Sharon Mazer for writing and revising the Instructor's Manual and for her many helpful suggestions about the contents and orientation of the anthology. I remain grateful to Stephen T. Jordan for originally proposing this project, to Oscar G. Brockett of the University of Texas at Austin for allowing me to think out loud about what a book like this one might accomplish, and to Shannon Steen for sharing her ideas on the project.

Finally, I would like to encourage anyone using this book to feel free to drop me a line with ideas and suggestions for later editions. To the many students and colleagues who have called, sent me a note to correct my oversights and omissions, or have graciously spoken to me about the book at professional meetings and conferences, my sincere thanks for your attention and kindness. The flaws and faults that remain are, of course, entirely my own doing.

—W. B. W.

CONTENTS

UNIT IV
EARLY MODERN EUROPE 267

UNIT V
MODERN EUROPE 401

UNIT **VII**
WORLD STAGES 777

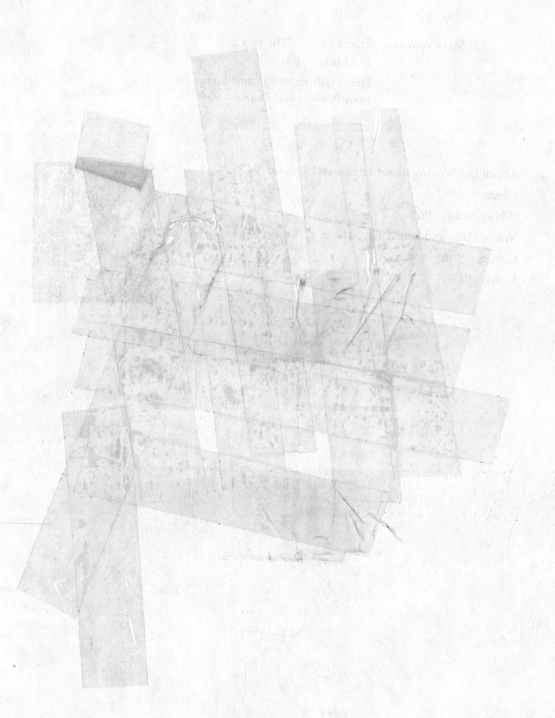

INTRODUCTION: DRAMA, THEATER, AND CULTURE

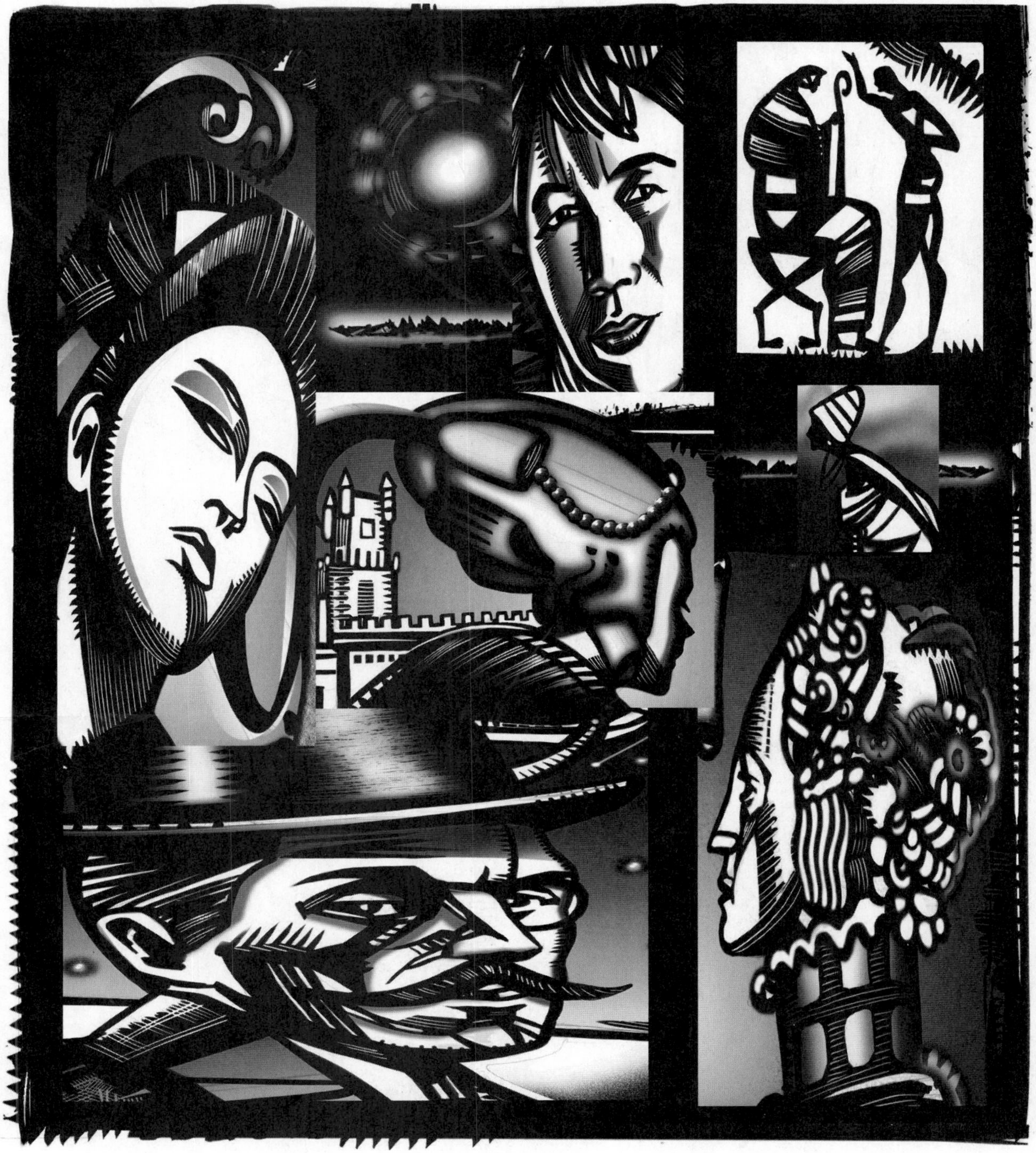

✠ ✠ ✠

OF THE MANY KINDS OF LITERATURE, DRAMA IS PERHAPS THE MOST IMMEDIATELY involved in the life of its community. Drama shares with such other literary modes as lyric poetry, the novel, the epic, and romance the ability to represent and challenge social, political, philosophical, and esthetic attitudes. But unlike most literature, drama has generally been composed for performance, confronting the audience in the public, sociable confines of a theater.

To understand DRAMA, we need to understand THEATER, because the theater forges the active interplay between drama and its community.[1] On a practical level, for instance, the community must determine where drama will take place, and it is in the theater that a space is carved out for dramatic performance. Not surprisingly, the place of the theater in a city's social and physical geography often symbolizes drama's place in the culture at large. In classical Athens, the theater adjoined a sacred precinct, and plays were part of an extensive religious and civic festival. Greek drama accordingly engages questions of moral, political, and religious authority. In seventeenth-century Paris, the close affiliation between the theater and the court of Louis XIV is embodied in drama's concern with power, authority, and the regulation of rebellious passions. In the United States today, most live theater takes place either in the privileged setting of colleges and universities, or in the "theater districts" of major cities, competing for an audience alongside movie theaters, nightclubs, and other entertainments. Drama also seems to be struggling to define itself as part of an established cultural tradition reaching back to Aeschylus and as part of the lively diversity of contemporary popular culture. Social attitudes are reflected in the theater in other ways, too; during performance, the theater constructs its own "society" of performers and spectators. Staging a play puts it immediately into a dynamic social exchange: the interaction between dramatic characters, between characters and the actors who play them, between the performers and the audience, between the drama onstage and the drama of life outside the theater.

The Greek word for "theater," *theatron,* means "seeing place," and plays performed in the theater engage their audiences largely through visual means. Less than a century ago, live plays could be seen only on the stage; today, most of us see drama in a variety of media: on film and television as well as in the theater. Yet for the past five hundred years or so we have also had access to plays in another, nontheatrical venue: by reading them in books. To see a play performed and to read it in a book are two very different activities, but these distinct experiences of drama can enrich one another in a number of ways.

In the theater, a dramatic text is fashioned into an event, something existing in space and time. The space of the stage, with whatever setting is devised, becomes the place of the drama. The characters are embodied by specific individuals. How a given actor interprets a role tends to shape the audience's sense of that dramatic character; for the duration of the play, it is difficult to imagine another kind of performance—a different Oedipus, Lear, or Miss Julie than the one standing before us in the flesh. The drama onstage is also bound by the temporal exigencies of performance. The process of performance is irreversible; for the

READING DRAMA AND SEEING THEATER

---

[1]Terms in bold small caps are defined in the **Glossary.**

3

duration of the performance, each moment becomes significant and yet unrecoverable—we can't flip back a few pages to an earlier scene, or rewind the videotape. When a company puts a play into stage production, it inevitably confronts these material facts of the theater: a specific cast of actors, a given theatrical space, a certain amount of money to spend, and the necessity of transforming the rich possibilities offered by the play into a clear and meaningful performance. To make the drama active and concrete, theatrical production puts a specific interpretation of the play on the stage. Whether or not to play Caliban in Shakespeare's *The Tempest* as a native of the West Indies; whether to play Torvald Helmer in Ibsen's *A Doll House* as a patriarchal autocrat or as someone bewildered by a changing world; whether to set *Tartuffe* in a classical, neoclassical, or a modern setting; whether to use cross-gender or intercultural casting in *The Cherry Orchard*—these are some of the kinds of questions that a production must face, and how the production decides such issues inevitably leads the audience toward a particular sense of the play. Everything that happens onstage becomes meaningful for an audience, something to interpret. Even apparently irrelevant facts—a short actor cast to play Hamlet in Shakespeare's play, or a beautiful actress playing Brecht's *Mother Courage*—become part of the audience's experience of the play, particularizing the play, lending it a definite flavor and meaning.

Reading a play presents us with a different experience of the drama. Reading plays is, first of all, a relatively recent phenomenon. In early theaters, like those of classical Athens and Rome, medieval Europe, and even Renaissance Europe of the sixteenth century, drama was almost entirely a theatrical event, rather than a mode of literature. Although the texts of plays were written down, by and large, audiences came into contact with drama primarily through theatrical performance. By the late sixteenth century, though, the status of drama began to change. The recovery and prestige of Greek and Latin literature led to pervasive familiarity with classical texts, including plays. Throughout Europe, schooling was conducted mainly in Latin, and the plays of Roman playwrights like Plautus, Terence, and Seneca were frequently used to teach Latin grammar and rhetoric; these plays were widely imitated by playwrights writing drama in vernacular languages for emerging secular, commercial theaters. Printing made it possible to disseminate texts more widely, and plays slowly came to be regarded as worthy of publication and preservation in book form. By the late nineteenth century, widespread literacy created a large reading public and a great demand for books; continued improvements in printing technology provided the means to meet the demand. Playwrights often published their plays as books before they could be produced onstage, with some profound effects. The detailed narrative stage directions in plays by Bernard Shaw, Eugene O'Neill, or Henrik Ibsen, for instance, are useful to a stage director and set designer, but they principally fill in a kind of novelistic background for the reading audience who will experience the play only on the page.

Theater audiences are bound to the temporality and specificity of the stage, but readers have the freedom to compose the play in much more varied ways. A reader can pause over a line, teasing out possible meanings, in effect stopping the progress of the play. Readers are not bound by the linear progress of the play's action, in that they can flip back and forth in the play, looking for clues, confirmations, or connections. Nor are readers bound by the stringent physical economy of the stage, the need to embody the characters with individual actors, to specify the dramatic locale as a three-dimensional space. While actors and directors must decide on a specific interpretation of each moment and every character in the play, readers can keep several competing interpretations alive in the imagination at the same time.

Both ways of thinking about drama are demanding, and students of drama should try to develop a sensitivity to both approaches. Treating the play like a novel or poem, decomposing and recomposing it critically, leads to a much fuller sense of the play's potential meanings, its gaps and inconsistencies; it allows us to question the text without the need to come to definite conclusions. Treating the play as a design for the stage forces us to make commitments, to articulate and defend a particular version of the play, and to find ways of making those meanings active onstage, visible in performance. As readers, one way to develop a sense of the reciprocity between stage and page is to think of the play as constructed mainly of actions, not of words. Think of seeing a play in an unknown language: the *action* of the play would still emerge in its larger outlines, carried by the deeds of the characters. Not knowing the words would not prevent the audience from understanding what a character is doing onstage—threatening, lying, persuading, boasting.

When reading a play, it is easy to be seduced by the text, to think of the play's language as mainly narrative, describing the attitudes of the character. For performers onstage, however, speech—language in action—is always a way of doing something. One way for readers to attune themselves to this active quality of dramatic writing is to ask questions of the text from the point of view of performers or characters. What do I—Lysistrata, Everyman, Miranda—want in this speech? How can I use this speech to help me get it? What am I trying to do by speaking in this way? Although questions like these are still removed from the actual practice of performance, they can help readers unfamiliar with drama begin to read plays in theatrical terms.

Another way to enrich the reading experience of drama is to imagine staging the play: How could the design of the set, the movements of the actors, the pacing of the scenes affect the play's meaning, make the play mean something in particular? Questions of this kind can help to make the play seem more concrete, but they have one important limitation. When asking questions like these, it is tempting to imagine the play being performed in today's theaters, according to our conventions of acting and stagecraft, and within the social and cultural context that frames the theater now. To imagine the play on our stage is, of course, to produce it in our contemporary idiom, informed by our notions both of theater and of the world our theater represents. However, while envisioning performance, we should also imagine the play in the circumstances of its original theater, a theater located in a different culture and possibly sharing few practices of stagecraft with the modern theater. How would Hamlet's advice to the players have appeared on the Globe theater's empty platform stage in 1601? Are there ways in which the text capitalizes on the similarities between Shakespeare's company of actors and those Hamlet addresses fictively in the play? In a theater where a complete, "realistic" illusion was not possible (and, possibly, not even desirable), how does Shakespeare's play turn the conditions of theatrical performance to dramatic advantage? Both reading drama and staging drama involve a complex double-consciousness, inviting us to see the plays with contemporary questions in mind, while at the same time imagining them on their original stages. In this doubleness lies an important dramatic principle: Plays can speak to us in our theater but perhaps always retain something of their original accents.

DRAMA AND THEATER IN HISTORY

Throughout its development, dramatic art has changed as the theater's place in the surrounding society has changed. The categories that we apply to drama and theater today—art versus entertainment, popular versus classic, literary versus theatrical—are categories of relatively recent vintage. They imply ways of thinking about drama and theater that are foreign to the function of theater in many other cultures. Much as drama and theater today emerge in relation to other media of dramatic performance like film and television, so in earlier eras the theater defined itself in relation to other artistic, social, and religious institutions. Placed in a different sphere of culture, drama and theater gained a different kind of significance than they have in the United States today.

Drama and theater often arise in relation to religious observance. In ancient Egypt, for instance, religious rituals involved the imitation of events in a god's or goddess's life. In Greece, drama may have had similar origins; by the sixth century BCE, the performance of plays had become part of a massive religious festival celebrating the god Dionysus. The plays performed in this theater—including those of Sophocles, Euripides, and Aristophanes gathered here—were highly wrought and intellectually, morally, and esthetically complex and demanding works. Aristotle classified drama among other forms of poetry, but in classical Athens these plays occupied a very different position in the spectrum of culture than do drama or "art" today, precisely because of their central role in the City Dionysia. The Roman theater set drama in the context of a much greater variety of performance—chariot racing, juggling, gladiatorial shows—and while plays were performed on religious holidays, drama was more clearly related to secular entertainments than it had been in Athens. Theater waned in Europe with the decline of the Roman Empire and the systematic efforts of the Catholic church to prevent theatrical performance. Yet, when theater was revived in the late Middle Ages, it emerged with the support of the church itself. By the year 1000, brief dramatizations illustrated the liturgy of the Catholic Mass; by the fourteenth century, a full range of dramatic forms—plays dramatizing the lives of saints, morality plays, narrative plays on Christian history—was used to illustrate Christian doctrine and to celebrate important days in the Christian year. Like plays in classical Athens, these plays were produced through community effort rather than by specialized "theaters" in the modern sense. Although we now regard medieval drama as extraordinarily rich and complex "literature," in its own era it was part of a different strand of culture, sharing space with other forms of pageantry and religious celebration, rather than being read with the poetry of Chaucer or Dante.

Similarly, in feudal Japan, the Buddhists developed a form of theater to illustrate the central concepts of their faith. Throughout the twelfth and thirteenth centuries, an increasing number of professional players came to imitate these dramatic performances on secular occasions, and for secular audiences. By the fourteenth century, it became conventional for the great samurai lords—or SHOGUNS—to patronize a theatrical company, giving rise to the classical era of the Noh theater. The social history of theater in Japan was complicated by other factors as well. The aristocratic NOH theater was rivaled by the popular, often quite contemporary, KABUKI theater. Government restrictions on the professions (which tended to make acting a family business, passed on through generations), and Japan's militant isolationism (coming to an end only in the mid-nineteenth century), have contributed to making Japan's classical theater survive in many ways unchanged.

Secular performance did, of course, also take place in classical and medieval Europe, including improvised farces on contemporary life, fairground shows, puppetry, mimes, and other quasi-dramatic events. Many plays were performed only on religious occasions, though, and their performers were usually itinerant, lacking the social and institutional support that would provide them with lasting and continuous existence. Only in the Renaissance of the fifteenth and sixteenth centuries did the Western theater begin to assume the function it has today: a fully secular, profit-making, commercial enterprise. Although Renaissance theaters continually vied with religious and state officials for the freedom to practice their trade, by the sixteenth century, the European theater was part of a secular entertainment market, competing with bear-baiting, animal shows, athletic contests, public executions, royal and civic pageants, public preaching, and many other attractions to draw a paying public. The theater emerged in this period as a distinct institution, supported by its own income; the theater became a trade, a profession, a business, rather than a necessary function of the state or of religious worship. Indeed, if drama in classical Athens was conceived more as religious ritual than as "art" in a modern sense, drama in Renaissance London was classed mainly as popular "entertainment." The theater only gradually became recognized as an arena for "literary" accomplishment, for literary status in this period was reserved mainly for skill demonstrated in forms like the sonnet, the prose romance, or the epic, forms that could win the authors a measure of aristocratic prestige and patronage. As part of the motley, vulgar world of the public theater, plays were not considered serious, permanent literature.

However, the desire to transform drama from ephemeral theatrical "entertainment" into permanent literary "art" begins to be registered in the Renaissance. The poet and playwright Ben Jonson included plays in the 1616 edition of his *Works,* insisting on the literary importance of the volume by publishing it in the large, FOLIO format generally reserved for classical authors. In 1623, seven years after his death, William Shakespeare's friends and colleagues published a similar, folio-sized collection of his plays, a book that was reprinted several times throughout the seventeenth century. By the 1660s and 1670s, writers at the court of Louis XIV in Paris could achieve both literary and social distinction as dramatists; Jean Racine's reputation as a playwright, in part at least, helped to win his appointment as Louis's royal historiographer. Yet, despite many notable exceptions, the theatrical origins of drama prevented contemporary plays from being regarded as "literature," although plays from earlier eras were increasingly republished and gradually seen to have "literary" merit. Indeed, by the nineteenth century, contemporary plays often achieved "literary" recognition by avoiding the theater altogether. English poets like Lord Byron and Percy Bysshe Shelley, for instance, wrote plays that were in many ways unstageable, and so preserved them from degrading contact with the tawdry stage. The English critic Charles Lamb remarked in a famous essay that he preferred reading Shakespeare's plays to seeing them in the theater; for Lamb, the practical mechanics of acting and the stage intruded on the experience of the drama's poetic dimension. In fact, the great playwrights of the late nineteenth century—Henrik Ibsen, Anton Chekhov, August Strindberg, and even the young Bernard Shaw—carved a space for themselves as dramatists by writing plays *in opposition* to the values of their contemporary audiences and to the practice of their contemporary theater, a strategy that would have seemed unimaginable to Sophocles, Shakespeare, or even Molière. To bring their plays successfully to the stage, new theaters and new theater practices had to be devised, and a new audience had to be found, or made.

This split between the "literary drama" and the "popular theater" has become the condition of twentieth-century drama and theater: plays of the artistic AVANT-GARDE are more readily absorbed into the CANON of literature, while more conventional entertainments—television screenplays, for instance—remain outside it. The major modern playwrights from Ibsen to Luigi Pirandello to Samuel Beckett first wrote for small theaters and were produced by experimental companies playing to coterie audiences on the fringes of the theatrical "mainstream." This sense of modernist "art" as opposed to the values of bourgeois culture was not confined to drama and theater. Modernist fiction and poetry—cubist and abstract painting and sculpture, modern dance, and modern music—all developed a new formal complexity, thematic abstraction, and critical self-consciousness in opposition to the sentimental superficiality they found in conventional art forms. This modernist tendency has itself produced a kind of reaction, a desire to bring the devices of popular culture and mass culture into drama, as a way of altering the place of the theater in society and changing the relationship between the spectators and the stage. Bertolt Brecht's ALIENATION EFFECT, Samuel Beckett's importation of circus and film clowns into absurdist theater, Suzan-Lori Parks's PASTICHE of American history in her POSTMODERN *America Play,* or Wole Soyinka's interweaving of African ritual and realism in *Death and the King's Horseman* are all examples of this reaction. The theater has been challenged by film and television to define its space in contemporary culture, and, given the pervasive availability of other media, theater has increasingly seemed to occupy a place akin to that of opera, among the privileged, elite forms of "high culture." As a result, innovation in today's theater often takes place on the margins or fringes of mainstream theater and culture: in smaller companies experimenting with new performance forms, in subversive theaters confronting political oppression in many parts of the world, and in theaters working to form a new audience and a new sense of theater by conceiving new forms of drama.

DRAMATIC GENRES

Perhaps because its meaning must emerge rapidly and clearly in performance, drama tends to be compressed and condensed; its characters tend toward types, and its action tends toward certain general patterns as well. It is conventional to speak of these kinds of drama as GENRES, each with its own identifying formal structure and typical themes. Following Aristotle's *Poetics,* for example, TRAGEDY is usually considered to concern the fate of an individual hero, singled out from the community through circumstances and through his or her own actions. In the course of the drama, the hero's course of action entwines with events and circumstances beyond his or her control. As a result, the hero's final downfall—usually, but not always, involving death—seems at once both chosen and inevitable. COMEDY, on the other hand, focuses on the fortunes of the community itself. While the hero of tragedy is usually unique, the heroes of comedy often come in pairs: the lovers who triumph over their parents in romantic comedies, the dupe and the trickster at the center of more ironic or satirical comic modes. While tragedy points toward the hero's downfall or death, comedy generally points toward some kind of broader reform or remaking of society, usually signaled by a wedding or other celebration at the end of the play.

To speak of genre in this way, though, is to suggest that these ideal critical abstractions actually exist in some form, exemplified more or less adequately by particular plays. Yet, as the very different genres of Japanese theater suggest, terms like *tragedy* and *comedy,* or MELODRAMA, TRAGICOMEDY, FARCE, and others, arise from our efforts to find continuities between extraordinarily different kinds of drama: between plays written in different theaters, for different purposes, to please different audiences, under different historical pressures. When we impose these terms in a prescriptive way, we usually find that the drama eludes them or even calls them into question. Aristotle's brilliant sense of Greek tragedy in the *Poetics,* for instance, hardly "applies" with equal force to Greek plays as different as *Oedipus the King* and *Medea,* or Kan'ami's elegant Noh drama, *Matsukaze,* let alone later plays like *Hamlet* or *Endgame.* In his essay, "Tragedy and the Common Man," Arthur Miller tries to preserve "tragedy" for modern drama by redefining Aristotle's description of the hero of tragedy. Instead of Aristotle's hero—a man (not a woman) of an elevated social station—Miller argues that the modern hero should be an average, "common" man (not a woman), precisely because the "best families" do not seem normative to us or representative of our basic values. Our exemplary characters are taken from the middle classes. Yet to redefine the hero in this way calls Aristotle's other qualifications—the notion of the hero's character and actions, the meaning of the tragic "fall"—into question as well, forcing us to redefine Aristotelian tragedy in ways that make it something entirely new, something evocative in modern terms.

In approaching the question of genre, then, it is often useful to avoid asking how a play exemplifies the universal and unchanging features of tragedy or comedy. Instead, one could ask how a play or a theater *invents* tragedy or comedy for its contemporary audience. What terms does the drama present, what formal features does it use, to represent human experience? How do historically "local" genres—Renaissance REVENGE TRAGEDY, French NEOCLASSICAL DRAMA, modern THEATER OF THE ABSURD—challenge, preserve, or redefine broader notions of genre?

DRAMATIC FORM

In about 335 BCE, Aristotle's *Poetics* set down the formal elements of drama, and the influence of Aristotle's description has been massive: Today we still speak of dramatic form in terms of its PLOT, CHARACTERS, LANGUAGE, THEME, and its performative elements, what Aristotle called MUSIC and SPECTACLE. Any student of drama can profit by thinking about how these formal elements function in a given play. How are the incidents of the play—its plot—arranged? What effects are achieved by *this* ordering, rather than by another? How does the plot relate to the play's narrative story, which includes events dating from before the play begins? How does the plot, the structure of the events—for instance, Nora Helmer's first act in *A Doll House* is to enter the house, and her last act is to leave it—develop the play's themes? We might then ask how the play defines its characters. What elements of human experience—family history, psychological motivation, public action—seem to be most prominent in a play's conception of "character"? How do the formal conventions of characterization—blank verse in Shakespeare's plays; the densely poetic language of Noh theater—affect our reading of the characters and our understanding of them as representations of human beings?

Although Aristotle presents these elements of drama as distinct, in practice they are mutually defining, making it very difficult to speak of them separately. A play's language, for example, can be analyzed purely for its verbal and rhetorical features, but it is more interesting to ask how the language affects our understanding of the characters or invests the play with certain thematic possibilities. Similarly, while we may regard a play's themes as inside the play, they actually arise only in our interpretation of the play. The themes are something we create by asking certain questions about the play's plotting, its characterization, its use of language. The artificiality of separating these features becomes especially clear when we turn to a play's performative or theatrical dimension. Although Aristotle suggests that a play's literary and theatrical dimensions are independent, to get a real sense of drama we must see the play both as literature and as theater. We must assess how an audience's sense of the play's plot, characters, and themes are shaped by the kinds of spectacle demanded by the play and provided by the theater. The "meaning" of Greek drama cannot be separated from its conditions of performance: the religious festival, the huge amphitheater, the masked actors, the singing, dancing chorus. The barren "sterile promontory" of *Hamlet,* cross-dressed performance in Calderón de la Barca's *Life is a Dream* or Churchill's *Cloud Nine:* These elements of the theatrical spectacle are not outside the meaning of the drama; they are its means, the vehicle for achieving that meaning on the stage.

THE STAGE IN CRITICAL PRACTICE

In a book like this one, indeed, in any book, it is difficult to convey a real sense of the power of theater. It is possible, though, to imagine this experience and to discuss it through the materials collected here: dramatic texts, descriptions of stage practices, illustrations of theaters, photographs, essays. However, an obstacle to understanding arises from a split between the disciplines we use to understand drama and theater. At many colleges and universities, this split is represented in the geography of the campus itself, where the English or Literature departments, which teach dramatic literature, are housed in one building, and the Theater or Drama department, which teaches acting, directing, design, and which actually stages the plays, is housed in another. "Literary" approaches to drama focus our attention initially, sometimes exclusively, on the text of a play and train the complex strategies of poetics and poetic interpretation on it. Such interpretation regards the dramatic text as incomplete and specifies the text's range of possible meanings by placing it in various textual and cultural contexts; in a sense, the negotiation between the text and these contexts determines what we can say the play *means.*

"Theatrical" approaches to drama tend to see a play in terms of stage practice, both in the terms of the play's original production and in the light of performance practice today. This approach interrogates the play's staging: how it can be set, what obstacles it presents to acting and casting, what the dramatic effects of costume and design will be. "Theatrical" interpretation regards the dramatic text as an incomplete design for performance and trains the complex machinery of stage representation—directing, acting, design, costuming on the task of fleshing the script out as performed action. The meaning of the play in this regard emerges from what we can make the play *do*.

The literary and theatrical approaches to drama and theater share the assumption that plays are not fully meaningful in themselves; they share the sense that the meaning of drama emerges from the kinds of questions we ask of it, the contexts—literary, historical, theoretical, theatrical—in which we can make it perform, and make it mean something in particular. Although each approach can seem needlessly mysterious, involving its own specialized language and critical practice, its own set of "right" questions and "right" answers, this book has been assembled with the belief that the literary and the theatrical approaches are necessary complements to each other.

In the units that follow, each introductory essay attempts to provide an overview of the dense implication of drama and theater in its culture and how dramatic literature and theatrical practices have been revived, engaged, or transformed by succeeding generations. Each essay, in other words, introduces the social, political, and cultural milieu of the theater; the theater's physical and symbolic position in the landscape of its culture; the theater's representation of gendered, sexual, and racial identities; the physical design of theaters, and the practices of acting and staging; and the dynamic impact of literary innovation on the work of performance. Although these issues are treated differently, given different prominence in each essay, this constellation of questions stems from a single conviction: that thinking about drama requires that we think about how plays perform as literature, in culture and history, and on the stage.

✠ ✠ ✠

GREAT DRAMA ARISES WHERE THE THEATER OCCUPIES AN IMPORTANT PLACE IN THE life of the community. In many respects, Western understanding of drama originated in fifth-century (500–400) BCE classical Athens, where the theater played a central role in politics, religion, and society. The Athenian stage invented forms of TRAGEDY and COMEDY that persist to the present day. In tragedy, the Greeks dramatized climactic events in the lives of legendary heroes from prehistory and myth, bringing ethical problems of motive and action to the stage. In comedy, the theater staged satiric portraits of the life of the *POLIS* (the city-state), vividly depicting the energetic conflicts of contemporary Athens in matters of politics, war, education—even the art of drama. Playwrights through the long history of the theater have continued to find in Greek drama both a model and a point of resistance against which to practice their own craft—see, for example, Bernard Shaw's *Major Barbara* in this volume. And we need only recall Sigmund Freud's understanding of the "Oedipus complex" to sense the influence of models of action derived from the Greek theater on later Western culture.

Athens and Sparta were dominant rival powers in fifth-century Greece, which comprised many small independent city-states, each with its own political and cultural institutions, form of government, and alliances. Dramatic performances took place under a variety of circumstances in all Greek cities, but drama as we know it developed in Athens. Dramatic performance in Athens was part of citywide religious festivals honoring the god Dionysus, the most important being the CITY DIONYSIA. Plays were produced as contests, in which playwrights, actors, and choruses competed for prizes and for distinction among their fellow citizens. These contests, held in an outdoor amphitheater adjoining the sacred temple of the god, followed several days of religious parades and sacrifices. This connection between early drama and religion suggests that the essential nature of Greek drama lies in its supposed "origins" in religious ritual. But the City Dionysia was also a massive civic spectacle that went far beyond religious worship, emphasizing the theater's implication in other areas of public life. Dramatic performance contributed to this celebration of Athens' economic power, cultural accomplishment, and military might. The City Dionysia united religion and politics, enabling Athenians to celebrate both Dionysus and the achievements of their *polis.*

The City Dionysia was the most prominent of four religious festivals held in Athens and the surrounding province of Attica between December and April; it took place in the month of Elaphebolion (March–April), one month after the previous festival. Although its purpose was primarily a religious one, the City Dionysia was structured around a series of contests between individual citizens and between major Athenian social groups—the ten (later twelve to fifteen) "tribes" that formed the city's basic political and military units. Dramatic performance was introduced into the City Dionysia during the sixth century BCE and became the centerpiece of the elaborate festival. Each year a city magistrate, or *ARCHON,* honored selected wealthy citizens by choosing them to finance one of the three principal tragic dramatists competing for a prize at the festival. Each sponsor, called a *CHOREGOS,* was responsible for hiring the CHORUS of young men who sang and danced in the plays. He also hired musicians and provided costumes and other support for the

THE CITY DIONYSIA

playwright to whom he was assigned. Later in the period, the state also assigned the leading actor to the *choregos* as well, and this actor also competed for a prize. The playwright was responsible for training the chorus and the actors, and for some of the acting himself, and he shared his prize with the *choregos*. Serving as a *choregos* was both a civic duty and an important honor, equivalent to other tasks imposed on the wealthy—maintaining a battleship for a year, or training athletes for the Olympic games.

Taking place over several days, the City Dionysia opened with a display of actors and choruses to the city; on the next day there was a lavish parade of religious officials through the city, followed by religious observances and sacrifices held in the theater. Athens also received its annual tribute of goods, money, and slaves from subject and allied states at this time, and war orphans raised at state expense also were displayed to the audience. After this display of religious worship and civic pride, two days were then devoted to contests of DITHYRAMBS, hymns sung and danced by a large chorus. Each of Athens' tribes sponsored two choruses: one consisting of fifty men, another consisting of fifty boys. The city's politics revolved around the tribes, and their contribution to the festival was prominent in this contest, too. The dithyrambic contest involved a thousand Athenian citizens directly in the performance, a significant portion of the adult male citizens. (Athens in the fifth century is estimated to have had a total population of about 300,000: 100,000 slaves, 30,000 noncitizen foreigners, and 30,000–40,000 adult, male citizens; women and children were not citizens.) Following the dithyrambs, the main dramatic contest began. The competing playwrights each produced a TRILOGY of tragedies, staged over three days. A trilogy could take a single theme or series of events as its subject (like the three plays of Aeschylus' *Oresteia,* 458 BCE), or present three distinct, unrelated dramas. A rugged farce called a SATYR PLAY followed the performance of each complete trilogy and was considered part of it; these plays parodied a god's activities using actors dressed as satyrs—half-man, half-goat. After 486 BCE, comedies were also awarded prizes, but it is unclear whether the comedies were performed on a single day or spread over several days. Prominent citizens representing each of the tribes served as judges and awarded prizes to the playwrights, their *choregoi,* and the actors.

THE THEATER OF DIONYSUS

The Greek theater was a public spectacle, a kind of cross between Inauguration Day, the Super Bowl, the Academy Awards, Memorial Day, and a major religious holiday. Plays were first produced in the *AGORA* (marketplace), which often served as a performance place for festivals in Athens and elsewhere. The size and importance of the City Dionysia, however, required a separate site, and a theater was built on the slope of the Acropolis, near the precinct of Dionysus. The original theater, a ring of wooden seats facing a circular floor, was later refined, enlarged, and constructed of stone. By the time of Aeschylus, Euripides, Sophocles, and Aristophanes, the Athenian theater had achieved its basic design: a circular floor for dancing and acting, ringed by a hillside AMPHITHEATER and backed by a low, rectangular building.

The focus of the classical amphitheater—which seated about 14,000 people—was the round ORCHESTRA ("dancing place"), containing the central altar of Dionysus, at which the festival sacrifices were performed. The dithyrambic choruses performed their ecstatic dances in the orchestra, and the bulk of the action of the plays took place there as well. Facing the orchestra, the hillside was divided into wedge-shaped seating areas. The citizens sat on wooden benches with their tribes: leaders and priests in the front of the sections, women perhaps toward the rear or possibly in a separate section. *Metics* (resident aliens) and visitors were probably seated in a separate area. Special front and center seats—called *prohedria*—were reserved for the judges and the priests of Dionysus.

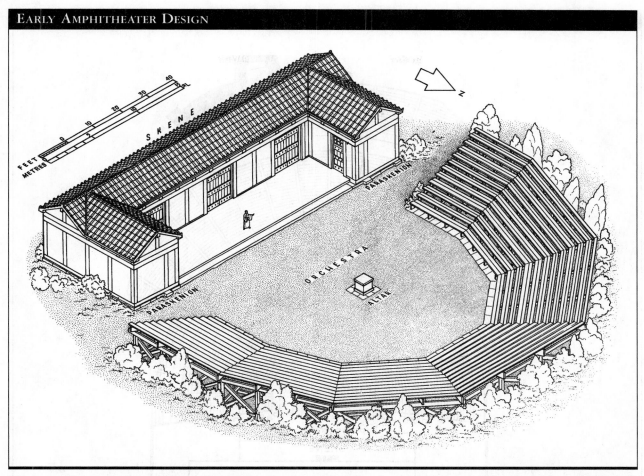

EARLY AMPHITHEATER DESIGN

This is an artist's reconstruction of an early theater in Eretria, Greece. Notice that the seating is constructed of wooden benches and the skene *is a temporary structure.*

Behind the *orchestra*, a low building called the SKENE faced the audience. Although the *skene* became a permanent stone structure in the fourth century BCE, in the fifth century it was a temporary wooden building, used for changing masks and possibly also for changing costumes. Playwrights quickly found the theatrical potential latent in the *skene*'s facade and set of doors; through these doors the audience heard Agamemnon being murdered in his bath, or saw eyeless Oedipus return to confront the Chorus and his future in exile. In Aeschylus' *Agamemnon,* the Watchman awaits the signal fires on the palace roof, and in performance he may have waited on the roof of the *skene.* The theater also used some machinery for scenic effects: a rolling platform (the *EKKYKLYMA*) used to bring objects or bodies from the *skene* into the orchestra; a crane (*MACHINA*) to raise or lower characters the gods, for instance, from the orchestra over the roof of the skene; and possibly painted panels to indicate the play's setting or location.

The experience of theater in classical Athens was in some ways akin to participation in other institutions of civic life. Athens was a participatory democracy for its citizens, though citizenship was restricted to adult male Athenians: women, foreigners, slaves,

**THEATER AND
SOCIAL LIFE**

THEATER OF DIONYSUS

ORCHESTRA

PARODOS   PARODOS

PROSKENION

SKENE

OLD TEMPLE

NEW TEMPLE

ALTAR

N

S

0   5   10M

This ground plan is of the sacred precinct of Dionysus in Athens, fourth century BCE. Notice that the theater is much larger than the earlier theater at provincial Eretria. The large and permanent skene was constructed after the fifth century BCE.

freed slaves, and children were not citizens. Citizens sat in the assembly to discuss and vote on matters of state policy, and they were eligible to serve in all public and military offices as well. Attendance at the City Dionysia was, then, like other aspects of Athenian public life, a privilege and an obligation mainly reserved for citizens. Citizens received tickets to the festival from officials in their neighborhood, or *DEME;* tickets may have been awarded on the basis of participation in other civic obligations—serving in the courts, the assembly, the army. At the theater, citizens sat together with members of their tribe. In a sense, the theater offered a visual map of the organization of Athenian society, for the tribes formed the basis of political participation outside the theater: The Athenian Assembly and the army were similarly arranged by tribe. Organized by tribes, with precedence given to religious officials and with inferior status or nonparticipation accorded to noncitizens such as women, slaves, and foreigners, the theater of Dionysus mirrored the structure of Athenian society.

The fifth century BCE was the era of Athens' greatest political power and cultural vitality and an era of intense reciprocity between Athenian theater and society. Yet the tension manifest in Greek drama perhaps points to the precarious stability of the Athenian *polis.* The Athenian maritime empire, forged after the defeat of massive Persian forces in 479, was resisted by the smaller Greek states and opposed by Athens' chief rival, the military state of Sparta. Following a long period of hostility and skirmishing, Athens and Sparta declared war against each other in 431 BCE, resulting in Athens' utter defeat in 404. Athenian democracy was replaced by an oppressive oligarchy, the Thirty Tyrants. Although the tyrants were rapidly overthrown and democracy restored, Athens never regained the dynamic cultural life and political power it enjoyed during the fifth century. And although dramatic performance continued after the restoration of democracy, the theater's central role in the *polis* seems to have declined after the Spartan victory. Yet, the theater became one of Greece's most widely disseminated cultural products. When Alexander the Great conquered Greece, the Near East, and northern Africa, he took Greek culture—including theater and drama—with him throughout his empire. And when the Roman Empire later absorbed Alexander's former dominions, it appropriated Greek dramatic traditions, the design of Greek theaters, and the arts and religion of Greece, as well.

DRAMA AND PERFORMANCE

In his *Poetics,* Aristotle suggests that drama originated in the singing of the dithyrambic choruses; a masked actor was first used to respond to the chorus as an individualized "character" in the mid-sixth century BCE, an innovation attributed to the playwright Thespis, about whom little else is known. Aeschylus was the first to use two actors, probably taking one of the parts himself; in the 460s, Sophocles introduced a third actor and was successfully imitated by Aeschylus in his *Oresteia* in 458 BCE. In general, classical tragedy can be performed with three actors, and comedy with four, though each actor may play several parts. All of the performers in the Greek theater—the dramatists, actors, musicians, and chorus members—were male citizens of Athens, as was the bulk of the audience. The dramatic choruses were perhaps composed of young men between the age of seventeen, when military training began, and twenty-one, when Athenian men entered into adulthood.

The chorus of tragedy both sang and danced, and it was expected to perform with grace and precision. Actors and choruses wore full-head masks made of painted linen or lightweight wood. The main characters' masks were individualized, but the members of the chorus all wore identical masks, giving a special force to the conflict between the unique claims of the protagonist and the more diffuse claims of his society. Costuming in comedy was somewhat more complex. Aristophanes' plays suggest that the chorus at times wore animal masks. The comic protagonists' masks, though, were again individualized; since Aristophanes often put his contemporaries in his plays (Socrates in *Clouds,* for

CHORUS OF SATYRS

These actors, apparently in a satyr play, appear on a vase painting. Notice that the central seated figure of Dionysus (holding the polelike thyrsus) is surrounded by actors holding their masks. The older, bearded actor to the right of Dionysus, wearing the lion skin over his shoulder, is apparently playing Hercules, the protagonist

instance, or Euripides in *Frogs*)—the masks probably resembled these citizens quite closely. Comic actors often sported a leather PHALLUS, clearly visible in statues depicting comic actors and of much dramatic use in plays like *Lysistrata*.

In reading Greek drama, we should remember that its leading parts—both the leading character and the chorus—were designed for competition, as instruments for the actor and chorus to win prizes. The literary brilliance of the plays is, in this sense, a means to enable a particular virtuosity in performance.

WOMEN IN THE ATHENIAN THEATER

In Athenian tragedy and comedy, female characters were played by men. Not only did men sponsor and write the plays, but the "women" onstage were literally men in disguise. Yet, many plays throw the theatrical convention of men playing women into relief. In Euripides' play *The Bacchae*, Pentheus is possessed by Dionysus when he dresses up as a woman and admires his good looks; in *Lysistrata*, the Spartan woman Lampito is closely and physically examined by Lysistrata and the other women in ways that focus the audience's attention precisely on the fact that the woman is being played by a man. Drama, then, participated fully in Athens' denial of equality to women. Athena says as much in Aeschylus' *The Eumenides* when she judges Orestes' murder of his mother as a lesser crime than Clytaemnestra's murder of her husband. Looking closely at both the drama and its performance can help us to see how justice, power, and gender came to be arranged in Athenian society.

Yet although the theater, like Athenian society, was a male-dominated institution, Greek drama repeatedly inquires into the nature of gendered behavior and uses female characters to focus some of its most challenging questions. Given the absence of women from

of the play. The other, younger and beardless figures may compose the chorus. While Hercules holds an individualized mask, the chorus members all hold masks similar to each other, and they wear costumes suggestive of satyrs.

the stage and their marginal status in the theater and in the state, it is fascinating to note how many plays turn on the action of female characters. Women were not themselves citizens of Athens, and their prerogatives—which were considerable—in the *polis* were defined only through marriage to a citizen. Yet many of the plays raise critical moral, ethical, and political problems through the actions of women—Medea in Euripides' *Medea,* and the women of Aristophanes' *Lysistrata* and *Assembly of Women.* Although Aristotle probably voices his contemporaries' views when he remarks in his *Poetics* that "a woman can be good, or a slave, although one of these classes [women] is inferior and the other, as a class, worthless," the theater stages women in ways that implicitly challenge the authority of this "natural" connection between the good, the legitimate, and the masculine. As a category that troubles the "natural" linkage between masculinity and humanity itself, women in Greek drama often appear to stage a crisis in how the state imagines and justifies itself.

Formally, Greek tragedy is organized somewhat differently than modern plays are, for Greek drama is based on the singing and dancing of the chorus, for whom many of the plays were named. Most plays begin with a PROLOGUE, followed by the *PARODOS* (entrance) of the singing and dancing chorus. Several EPISODES follow, in which the central characters engage one another and the chorus; the chorus itself often sings (and dances) several ODES, which are used to enunciate and enlarge on the play's pivotal issues, and the Chorus often becomes a decisive character in the play, as it does in Aeschylus' *The Eumenides* or Euripides' *The Bacchae.* The choral odes are written in lyric meters different from the meters used for the characters' speeches. The play's *CATASTROPHE,* literally its

FORMS OF GREEK DRAMA

ALTHOUGH MANY OF THEIR TRADITIONS were absorbed from Greece, the Romans developed a distinctive theater, quite different from the Athenian stage. From its beginnings, Roman theater was more varied than the Greek stage, including acrobatics, juggling, athletic events, gladiatorial combats, and skits. In the sixth and seventh centuries BCE, Rome was a relatively unimportant town, ruled by the Etruscan kingdoms of northern Italy. In 509, the Romans drove out the Etruscans and founded a republic; the republic expanded its influence throughout the fourth century BCE and eventually came to control many territories once governed by the Greeks and by Alexander. Much as the Romans absorbed other Greek cultural institutions, they also absorbed Greek theater and drama, which were first performed in Rome in the mid-third century, in 240 BCE. As Rome's political influence expanded, particularly under the Roman Empire (27 BCE–476 CE), the Romans disseminated their characteristic cultural institutions—including theater and drama—throughout Europe, North Africa, and the Middle East.

Like the Greeks, the Romans associated the drama with festivals, but the Romans not only produced plays on festival occasions throughout the year, they also developed a much wider variety of theatrical entertainments, of which drama was only a small part. Some of the Roman entertainments descended from the sixth-century BCE *ludi Romani,* which included chariot racing, boxing, and other athletic contests, and Greek drama was first performed in Rome at these games. Moreover, Greek drama not only competed with other nondramatic entertainment, it also was rivaled by an indigenous dramatic form, known as ATELLAN FARCE. Associated with the town of Atella (near present-day Naples), these farces were probably improvised comic skits, involving stock characters and played by masked actors.

After the introduction of tragedy and comedy to the *ludi Romani* in 240 BCE, dramatic performances were introduced to several other festivals, and by 179 BCE, drama was being performed at major religious festivals throughout the year: at the *ludi Romani* honoring Jupiter in September, at a second festival consecrated to Jupiter in November, at festivals honoring Flora and the Great Mother in April, and at a festival honoring Apollo in July. Dramatic performances, though still associated with festivals, were much more common in Rome than in fifth-century Athens, not only because special celebrations sometimes included theatrical performance, but also because any disruption in the rituals connected with the festivals required that the entire festival be repeated, including the dramatic performances.

Given the variety of entertainments offered in Rome—including the chariot races and gladiatorial combats that became increasingly popular in the later Empire, especially after 300 CE—it is not surprising that the Romans built several different kinds of entertainment buildings, stadiums and racecourses as well as theaters. Yet until 55 BCE, theaters in Rome were temporary, built and taken down for each festival. In the first century BCE, the Romans began to build permanent theaters with some regularity. Like their Greek predecessors, the Roman theaters were outdoor amphitheaters, but the Romans built their theaters on level ground, and their superior engineering, particularly the Romans' use of arches in construction, enabled them to build much more massive buildings. Roman theaters were generally three stories in height. A rectangular stage house, or SCAENA stood like the Greek *skene* behind the semicircular orchestra and faced a steeply tiered semicircular auditorium. The facade of the *scaena* was elaborately ornamented with columns and porticos. The Romans built theaters of stone and built them throughout the Empire; many of the Greek theaters that remain today were refurbished and redesigned by the Romans.

Although the Romans continued to perform plays from the Greek theater, they also developed a native strain of drama represented in the

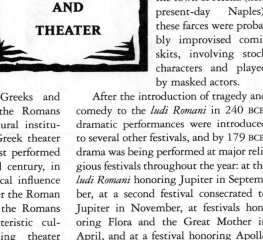

(A S I D E)

ROMAN DRAMA AND THEATER

"down turn," marks some change in the hero's status and is followed by the departure of the characters from the stage and the *EXODOS,* or final song, dance, and departure of the chorus. Comedy—at least for Aristophanes, whose plays are the only surviving comedies from the period—is structured similarly, though Aristophanes' plays usually include a long *PARABASIS,* a choral ode delivered to the audience discussing political issues, and a final *KOMOS,* a scene of choral dancing and revelry.

This formal description, however, hardly accounts for the real and continued power of Greek drama, which arises from an intense and economical relationship between (1) a situation, usually at the point of climax as the play opens, (2) a complex of characters, each plays of Plautus, Terence, and Seneca. Titus Maccius Plautus (c. 254–c. 184 BCE) is probably the most influential Roman comic playwright. His earliest surviving plays date from 205 BCE, or about thirty-five years after Greek drama was first introduced to Rome; Plautus is thought to have based many of his comedies on Greek New Comedy, but none of these prototypes survive. Plautus is thought to have written more than one hundred comedies, many of which—*Amphitryon, The Braggart Warrior, The Rope,* and *The Menaechmus Twins,* for example—established the formal conventions of later comedy. Publius Terentius Afer (c. 195–159 BCE)—usually called Terence—was probably born in Carthage and brought to Rome as a slave. Unlike the prolific Plautus, Terence wrote only six comedies, all of which survive, and strove throughout his career to adapt Greek originals to the Roman stage: *The Woman of Andros, Mother-in-Law, Self-Tormentor, Eunuch, Phormio,* and *The Brothers.* The plays of Plautus and Terence have been particularly influential on the form and structure of later European comedy; not only did they establish many of the forms and character types developed by later playwrights, but in the late Middle Ages and Renaissance, their plays were often used to teach Latin in the schools, giving rise to generations of playwrights—including William Shakespeare and Molière—who found in Roman drama a form for their own contemporary plays.

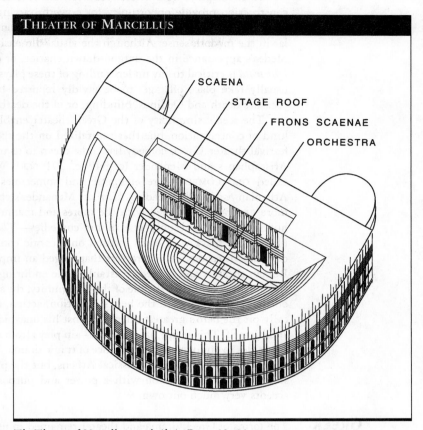

THEATER OF MARCELLUS

SCAENA
STAGE ROOF
FRONS SCAENAE
ORCHESTRA

The Theater of Marcellus was built in Rome, 13–11 BCE.

The only surviving Roman tragedies were written by Lucius Annaeus Seneca (5 BCE–65 CE). Seneca's tragedies were adapted from Greek plays but tend to be more sensational and violent; indeed, it is doubtful if they were performed in the theater. Although only nine of Seneca's plays survive—*The Trojan Women, Medea, Oedipus, Phaedra, Thyestes, Hercules on Oeta, Hercules Mad, The Phoenecian Women, Agamemnon*—Senecan tragedy also exerted an important influence on later drama, especially in the English Renaissance, where Senecan tragedy provided a prototype for the nascent English drama of the sixteenth century.

with distinctive goals and motives, (3) a chorus used both as a character and as a commentator on the action, and (4) a series of incidents that precipitates a crisis and brings the meaning of the PROTAGONIST'S actions into focus. Aristotle termed this crisis the *PERIPETEIA,* or "reversal," in the external situation or fortunes of the main character, and he argued that it should be accompanied by an act of *ANAGNORISIS,* or "recognition," in which the character responds to this change. Indeed, Aristotle argued that when the pressure of the tragic action produces a close relationship between reversal and recognition, it instills in the audience intense feelings of fear and pity and then effects *CATHARSIS,* a purgation of these emotions.

Since the plays were written for a contest, it is not surprising that their language and construction provide opportunity for powerful acting, particularly since the plays were judged only in performance. And yet the stage action of Greek drama is hardly spectacular in the modern sense. Although the visual dimension of blind and bloody Oedipus, or Medea's appearance in the dragon-drawn chariot, or even the aching gait of the men in *Lysistrata* is critical to any understanding of these plays, scenes of murder, suicide, or battle usually take place offstage, to be vividly reported by messengers, as in the reports of Jocasta's death and Oedipus' blinding, or of the death of Jason's young bride in *Medea*.

The scenic simplicity of the Greek theater enabled playwrights to achieve a special kind of concentration, one that capitalized on the special circumstances of the open-air, festival theater. Greek comedy has come down to us in the work of only two playwrights, Aristophanes and Menander (c. 342–c. 291 BCE). While Aristophanes' plays—usually called OLD COMEDY—are energetic and sometimes ribald comedies lampooning the Athenian *polis* and its leading citizens, Menander's comedies—called NEW COMEDY—are more generally concerned with the mores and manners. Menander wrote more than one hundred plays, but only one of his comedies—*The Grouch*—survives in its entirety. Menander's plays were often focused on a comic conflict between parents and children, devising situations and characters that forged an important link between the Greek and Roman theaters and helped to establish the enduring traditions of stage comedy. While the comedies center on the life of the community, the stage action of Greek tragedy focuses on the relation between the hero's intention, action, and consequence in ways that typically pit the hero's greatest talents against his unavoidable destiny, his society, his family, and himself. This recipe has provided—in plays from the era of Aeschylus, Sophocles, and Euripides to our own—the substance of tragic drama. The characteristic concerns of Greek drama speak undeniably of classical Athens, but the plays also represent trials of decision, suffering, and desperation with a power and purpose that continue to speak to us in accents very much our own.

GREEK DRAMA IN PERFORMANCE HISTORY

The forms of Greek drama and theater remained in use after the fall of Athens to Sparta; indeed, they were both exported to Rome, Egypt, and the Middle East by Alexander. Yet while tragedy and comedy continued to be written and performed throughout the Greek Mediterranean throughout the Hellenistic period (fourth and third centuries BCE) and beyond, and theater design continued to develop and refine the classical amphitheater, in an important sense the tradition of dramatic writing and performance inaugurated in fifth-century Athens were confined to the Greek provinces; although the modes of Greek drama and (to a lesser extent) performance survived somewhat longer in the eastern reaches of the Roman Empire, in the west they gradually disappeared under the influence of Roman culture. Moreover, while the manuscripts of Greek drama—and of important collateral texts, like Aristotle's *Poetics*—continued to be copied for students and readers, they fell out of public circulation. The few texts that have survived of the plays of Aeschylus, Sophocles, Euripides, and Aristophanes are based on copies made for teachers and scholars in Byzantium, dating from the third and fourth centuries CE. Not only have the bulk of their plays been lost (Sophocles is said to have written 123 plays, of which we have seven; Aeschylus is thought to have written over seventy, of which seven remain; Euripides' nineteen plays are all that remain of over ninety), but the entire dramatic output of seven hundred years of theater as well—the names of Agathon, Thespis, Chairemon, Theodektes, Philokles, Ariastas, and others are all that remain of their work—was lost as well. Moreover, since these manuscripts were collected in scholarly or monastic libraries, they have been subject to the destructive forces of history. Many Greek plays were lost in the burning of the library at Alexandria during Caesar's invasion of Egypt; the crusaders sacked Constantinople (previously known as Byzantium) in 1204, and in the process destroyed a city which had joined eastern and western cultures for centuries.

However, for all their violence, the Crusades also reopened cultural contact with the Islamic Middle East; many of the texts of Greek and Roman culture had been translated into Arabic, or had been preserved by Islamic scholars and libraries. With the reopening of European trading and military contacts in the fourteenth, fifteenth, and sixteenth centuries, Europe was able to rediscover the literature of classical Greece, sometimes in Latin translations, sometimes only through commentaries on still-lost texts (such as Aristotle's *Poetics*). In many respects, though, this recovery was principally of Roman theater and drama. The prestige, and availability, of texts by Latin authors like Plautus, Terence, and Seneca meant that these playwrights were widely taught in schools, convents (like Gandersheim, where the canoness Hrosvitha [953–973 CE] wrote six comedies modeled on Terence's plays), and universities, where their plays were often performed; the influence of these playwrights can be felt everywhere in European drama of the sixteenth century, most familiarly in Shakespeare's early comedies (like *A Comedy of Errors,* based on Plautus' *The Menaechmus Twins*) and in the vogue for violent tragedies reminiscent of Seneca's unstaged dramas, plays like Shakespeare's *Titus Andronicus.* The rediscovery of Vitruvius' first-century book on Roman architecture, *De Architectura,* in 1414 (it was printed—a new technology—in 1486) also led a generation of fifteenth- and sixteenth-century architects to design and build theaters on what they took to be a Roman model.

In many respects, though, Greek drama only became widely known in Europe in the later seventeenth and eighteenth centuries, where Greek plays often provided the models for contemporary playwrights, such as Jean Racine as well as for the first operas. And it was only in the nineteenth and twentieth centuries that the restoration of classical amphitheaters, and the historical and archaeological recovery of the theatrical practices of classical Athens began to make possible experiments in staging classical Greek drama in ways that attempted to approximate the circumstances of classical theater, or that attempted to translate those circumstances into a more effective modern idiom. Since the late nineteenth century, for example, the amphitheater at Epidaurus has often been used to stage classical Greek plays, in ways that attempt to approximate the traditions of fifth-century Athenian performance.

Clearly, of course, much has changed in the last 2,500 years, and performing classical drama poses a series of challenges to modern performers. First, the chorus—both its singing/dancing performance style, and its function in the drama—has posed a critical problem for modern companies and audiences: The German director Max Reinhardt staged a production of *The Oresteia* in 1919 that was among the first of his productions to experiment with large crowds onstage; later productions have tended to make the chorus smaller, and more energetic, in an attempt to recapture the exciting movement of the classical chorus. Beyond that, the use of masks in classical theater is no longer conventional on the modern stage, although many modern playwrights—Eugene O'Neill, for example, in *Strange Interlude* (1928)—have experimented with masks in an attempt to render psychological complexity with what they take to be "classical" decorum. The 1981 National Theatre (London) production of *The Oresteia,* directed by Sir Peter Hall, used an entirely male cast and performed the play in masks; this production was the first English language production of a Greek tragedy to be performed in the classical theater at Epidaurus. But while this effort to "recover" the initial circumstances and flavor of Greek performance has driven many performances, Greek drama has also provided the framework for a number of important AVANT-GARDE theatrical experiments in the modern era. Of course, Racine's adaptation of Euripides in *Phaedra* might be considered an "updating" of this kind, but in the modern era, stage practices have often been used not so much to recover the classical past as to restage the plays in a modern idiom. Josef Svoboda's brilliant 1963 production of *Oedipus the King* in Prague, for example, took place on a thirty-foot-wide staircase that rose from the bottom of the orchestra pit to beyond the top of the proscenium. The French director Ariane Mnouchkine staged a production of Euripides' *Iphigeneia at Aulis* as an introduction to her staging of *The Oresteia* in 1990 (under the overall title, *Les Atrides*); this brilliant production used makeup, costume, movement, and dance idioms from classical Indian and Indonesian theater, implying that a contemporary staging of the Greek classics might well turn to another tradition of "classical" performance to find a still-living stage language. Both for directors—Peter Sellars's 1993 staging of Aeschylus' *The Persians* framed the play with allusions to the Gulf War—and for writers, such as Heiner Müller (*Medeamaterial*), Charles Mee, Jr. *(Orestes)*, Caryl Churchill (*A Mouthful of Birds,* based on Euripides' *The Bacchae,* and written with David Lan), Timberlake Wertenbaker (who has translated several Greek plays), Wole Soyinka (*The Bacchae of Euripides*), and others, the theater and drama of classical Athens continue to provide a way to see and understand ourselves.

SOPHOCLES

Like Aeschylus, Sophocles (c. 496–406 BCE) had an important career in the civic life of Athens as well as in the theater. He was treasurer for the Athenian imperial league, and served as one of ten generals who led a campaign against Samos, an island threatening to secede from the Athenian alliance. In 411 BCE, he was appointed to a committee called to examine Athens's disastrous military campaign in Sicily. Sophocles' greatest achievements, though, were in the theater. Sophocles is responsible for introducing a third actor into dramatic performance, an innovation rapidly imitated by other playwrights, including Aeschylus and Euripides. He also enlarged the size of the chorus from twelve to fifteen men. Sophocles won his first victory, against Aeschylus, in 468 BCE: he was victorious twenty-four times in his career and never finished lower than second in the dramatic competition. Of the 120 plays attributed to Sophocles, only seven survive: *Ajax, Trachiniae, Antigone, Oedipus the King, Electra, Philoctetes,* and *Oedipus at Colonus.* Fragments of a satyr play, *The Trackers,* also remain. The three "Theban" plays—*Antigone, Oedipus the King,* and *Oedipus at Colonus*—are thematically related, but, unlike *The Oresteia* of Aeschylus, were not composed as a single trilogy. *Antigone,* a play about Oedipus' daughters after his banishment from Thebes, was composed around the year 441 BCE; *Oedipus the King* was first produced sometime shortly after the declaration of war with Sparta in 431 BCE; and *Oedipus at Colonus* was first produced after Sophocles' death and Athens' defeat.

OEDIPUS THE KING

Oedipus the King is framed by two acts of identification, recognition, and acknowledgment. The action of the play is about the deepening and horrible understanding of what it means for the hero to recognize who he is, what it means to *be* Oedipus.

In his *Poetics,* written nearly a century later (about 335 BCE), Aristotle frequently refers to *Oedipus the King* as a definitive example of the form and purpose of tragedy. Modern audiences, though, sometimes find the play baffling, in part because the prophecy delivered to Oedipus' parents, Laius and Jocasta—that their son will murder his father and marry his mother—seems to rob Oedipus of the ability to act, to decide his fate through his own deeds. The tension between destiny and discovery is central to the play, and to understand it, we should pay attention to the function of the oracle at Delphi both in the Greek world and in *Oedipus the King.* The Greeks consulted the oracle at Delphi on a variety of matters, ranging from personal decisions to problems of state. In the play, Laius and Jocasta, for example, have consulted the oracle to learn the future of their child, and Oedipus turns to Delphi to find out whether Polybus is actually his father; at the same time, the oracle also speaks on important public issues: about the cause of the plague afflicting Thebes and about what should be done with Oedipus after his blinding. Sophocles lived in an era of increasing skepticism, when political conflict and the rise of rhetorical training raised questions about the nature and significance of truth, even the truth of oracular revelation. It is not surprising that characters in *Oedipus the King* frequently question such prophecy or have difficulty learning how to accept and interpret it—as when Oedipus flees Corinth to avoid murdering his father.

Critical as the prophecy is to Oedipus' life, Oedipus' deeds are really at issue in *Oedipus the King.* Sophocles chose to begin and end his drama on the day of Oedipus' discovery of his own identity. The play focuses less on the prophecy than on the course and meaning of Oedipus' actions, on how he comes to recognize himself as the criminal he seeks. Oedipus arrives at this recognition only through an extraordinary effort of action and decision: Oedipus calls for the exile of Laius' murderer; he insults Tiresias when the prophet tries to evade his questions; he accuses Creon; he threatens the old shepherd with torture in order to learn the truth of his birth. The oracle says that Oedipus will commit his terrible crimes of murder and incest, but Oedipus chooses the relentless, brutal pursuit of the truth himself, even to the point of his own incrimination and destruction. The tragedy of *Oedipus the King* lies in the fearsome turn of events caused by Oedipus' inflexible compulsion to discover the truth.

Aristotle considers the hero of tragedy at some length, in terms that are at once compelling and confusing, particularly in the case of Oedipus. Aristotle suggests in his *Poetics* that the hero of tragedy should be "a man who is neither a paragon of virtue and justice nor undergoes the change to misfortune through any real badness or wickedness but because of some mistake," a description that leads some to look for the cause of this error within Oedipus' character, in a so-called "tragic flaw." But, in fact, when he says that the character's "mistake"—or *HAMARTIA*—is not the result of "any real badness or wickedness," Aristotle seems to deny that the hero's downfall is the effect of any moral "flaw" at all. It might help us to remember that to his audience, Oedipus may have seemed to share some typically "Athenian" characteristics. Oedipus' passion for inquiry, his abrupt decisiveness, and his impulsive desire to act were seen as the stereotypical traits of Athenian citizens and of Athens as a city. Far from being "flaws," these are just the qualities that made Oedipus (and Athens) successful. What is "tragic" about Oedipus' fate in *Oedipus the King* is the way that his own surest strengths, the aggressive, pragmatic qualities that enabled him to outwit the Sphinx, lead, on this one occasion, to his destruction. Oedipus' "mistake" is neither a moral failing nor a deed that he might have avoided; it is simply that he is Oedipus and acts like Oedipus—intelligent, masterful, assertive, impatient, impulsive. The tragedy lies in the way that acting like Oedipus leads him, as it has always led him in the past, to the discovery of the truth he seeks, this time with ruinous consequences.

OEDIPUS THE KING

Sophocles

TRANSLATED BY ROBERT FAGLES

———— CHARACTERS ————

OEDIPUS, *king of Thebes*
A PRIEST *of Zeus*
CREON, *brother of Jocasta*
A CHORUS *of Theban citizens*
and their LEADER
TIRESIAS, *a blind prophet*
JOCASTA, *the queen, wife of*
Oedipus

A MESSENGER *from Corinth*
A SHEPHERD
A MESSENGER *from inside the*
palace
ANTIGONE, ISMENE, *daughters*
of Oedipus and Jocasta
GUARDS *and* ATTENDANTS
PRIESTS *of Thebes*

TIME AND SCENE: *The royal house of Thebes. Double doors dominate*
the façade; a stone altar stands at the center of the stage.

Many years have passed since OEDIPUS *solved the riddle of the Sphinx*
and ascended the throne of Thebes, and now a plague has struck the
city. A procession of PRIESTS *enters; suppliants, broken and despondent,*
they carry branches wound in wool and lay them on the altar.

The doors open. GUARDS *assemble.* OEDIPUS *comes forward, majestic*
but for a telltale limp, and slowly views the condition of his people.

OEDIPUS: Oh my children, the new blood of ancient Thebes,
why are you here? Huddling at my altar,
praying before me, your branches wound in wool.
Our city reeks with the smoke of burning incense,
rings with cries for the Healer and wailing for the dead.   5
I thought it wrong, my children, to hear the truth
from others, messengers. Here I am myself—
you all know me, the world knows my fame:
I am Oedipus.

(Helping a PRIEST *to his feet.)*

                Speak up, old man. Your years,
your dignity—you should speak for the others.   10
Why here and kneeling, what preys upon you so?
Some sudden fear? some strong desire?
You can trust me. I am ready to help,
I'll do anything. I would be blind to misery
not to pity my people kneeling at my feet.   15
PRIEST: O Oedipus, king of the land, our greatest power!
You see us before you now, men of all ages
clinging to your altars. Here are boys,
still too weak to fly from the nest,
and here the old, bowed down with the years,   20
the holy ones—a priest of Zeus myself—and here
the picked, unmarried men, the young hope of Thebes.
And all the rest, your great family gathers now,
branches wreathed, massing in the squares,
kneeling before the two temples of queen Athena   25
or the river-shrine where the embers glow and die
and Apollo sees the future in the ashes.
                Our city—
look around you, see with your own eyes—
our ship pitches wildly, cannot lift her head
from the depths, the red waves of death . . .   30
Thebes is dying. A blight on the fresh crops
and the rich pastures, cattle sicken and die,

and the women die in labor, children stillborn,
and the plague, the fiery god of fever hurls down
on the city, his lightning slashing through us—   35
raging plague in all its vengeance, devastating
the house of Cadmus! And black Death luxuriates
in the raw, wailing miseries of Thebes.

Now we pray to you. You cannot equal the gods,
your children know that, bending at your altar.   40
But we do rate you first of men,
both in the common crises of our lives
and face-to-face encounters with the gods.
You freed us from the Sphinx, you came to Thebes
and cut us loose from the bloody tribute we had paid   45
that harsh, brutal singer. We taught you nothing,
no skill, no extra knowledge, still you triumphed.
A god was with you, so they say, and we believe it—
you lifted up our lives.
                So now again,
Oedipus, king, we bend to you, your power—   50
we implore you, all of us on our knees:
find us strength, rescue! Perhaps you've heard
the voice of a god or something from other men,
Oedipus . . . what do you know?
The man of experience—you see it every day—   55
his plans will work in a crisis, his first of all.

Act now—we beg you, best of men, raise up our city!
Act, defend yourself, your former glory!
Your country calls you savior now
for your zeal, your action years ago.   60
Never let us remember of your reign:
you helped us stand, only to fall once more.
Oh raise up our city, set us on our feet.
The omens were good that day you brought us joy—
be the same man today!   65
Rule our land, you know you have the power,
but rule a land of the living, not a wasteland.
Ship and towered city are nothing, stripped of men
alive within it, living all as one.
OEDIPUS: My children,
I pity you. I see—how could I fail to see   70
what longings bring you here? Well I know
you are sick to death, all of you,
but sick as you are, not one is sick as I.

Your pain strikes each of you alone, each
75 in the confines of himself, no other. But my spirit
grieves for the city, for myself and all of you.
I wasn't asleep, dreaming. You haven't wakened me—
I have wept through the nights, you must know that,
groping, laboring over many paths of thought.
80 After a painful search I found one cure:
I acted at once. I sent Creon,
my wife's own brother, to Delphi—
Apollo the Prophet's oracle—to learn
what I might do or say to save our city.

85 Today's the day. When I count the days gone by
it torments me . . . what is he doing?
Strange, he's late, he's gone too long.
But once he returns, then, then I'll be a traitor
if I do not do all the god makes clear.
90 PRIEST: Timely words. The men over there
are signaling—Creon's just arriving.
OEDIPUS: (*Sighting* CREON, *then turning to the altar.*) Lord Apollo,
let him come with a lucky word of rescue,
shining like his eyes!
PRIEST: Welcome news, I think—he's crowned, look,
95 and the laurel wreath is bright with berries.
OEDIPUS: We'll soon see. He's close enough to hear—

(*Enter* CREON *from the side; his face is shaded with a wreath.*)

Creon, prince, my kinsman, what do you bring us?
What message from the god?
CREON: Good news.
I tell you even the hardest things to bear,
100 if they should turn out well, all would be well.
OEDIPUS: Of course, but what were the god's *words?* There's
no hope
and nothing to fear in what you've said so far.
CREON: If you want my report in the presence of these
people . . .

(*Pointing to the* PRIESTS *while drawing* OEDIPUS *toward the palace.*)

I'm ready now, or we might go inside.
OEDIPUS: Speak out,
105 speak to us all. I grieve for these, my people,
far more than I fear for my own life.
CREON: Very well,
I will tell you what I heard from the god.
Apollo commands us—he was quite clear—
"Drive the corruption from the land,
110 don't harbor it any longer, past all cure,
don't nurse it in your soil—root it out!"
OEDIPUS: How can we cleanse ourselves—what rites?
What's the source of the trouble?
CREON: Banish the man, or pay back blood with blood.
115 Murder sets the plague-storm on the city.
OEDIPUS: Whose murder?
Whose fate does Apollo bring to light?
CREON: Our leader,
my lord, was once a man named Laius,
before you came and put us straight on course.
OEDIPUS: I know—
or so I've heard. I never saw the man myself.

CREON: Well, he was killed, and Apollo commands us now—   120
he could not be more clear,
"Pay the killers back—whoever is responsible."
OEDIPUS: Where on earth are they? Where to find it now,
the trail of the ancient guilt so hard to trace?
CREON: "Here in Thebes," he said.   125
Whatever is sought for can be caught, you know,
whatever is neglected slips away.
OEDIPUS: But where,
in the palace, the fields or foreign soil,
where did Laius meet his bloody death?
CREON: He went to consult an oracle, Apollo said,   130
and he set out and never came home again.
OEDIPUS: No messenger, no fellow-traveler saw what
happened?
Someone to cross-examine?
CREON: No,
they were all killed but one. He escaped,
terrified, he could tell us nothing clearly,   135
nothing of what he saw—just one thing.
OEDIPUS: What's that?
One thing could hold the key to it all,
a small beginning give us grounds for hope.
CREON: He said thieves attacked them—a whole band,
not single-handed, cut King Laius down.   140
OEDIPUS: A thief,
so daring, so wild, he'd kill a king? Impossible,
unless conspirators paid him off in Thebes.
CREON: We suspected as much. But with Laius dead
no leader appeared to help us in our troubles.
OEDIPUS: Trouble? Your *king* was murdered—royal blood!   145
What stopped you from tracking down the killer
then and there?
CREON: The singing, riddling Sphinx.
She . . . persuaded us to let the mystery go
and concentrate on what lay at our feet.
OEDIPUS: No,
I'll start again—I'll bring it all to light myself!   150
Apollo is right, and so are you, Creon,
to turn our attention back to the murdered man.
Now you have *me* to fight for you, you'll see:
I am the land's avenger by all rights,
and Apollo's champion too.   155
But not to assist some distant kinsman, no,
for my own sake I'll rid us of this corruption.
Whoever killed the king may decide to kill me too,
with the same violent hand—by avenging Laius
I defend myself.   160

(*To the* PRIESTS.)

                    Quickly, my children.
Up from the steps, take up your branches now.

(*To the* GUARDS.)

One of you summon the city here before us,
tell them I'll do everything. God help us,
we will see our triumph—or our fall.

(OEDIPUS *and* CREON *enter the palace, followed by the* GUARDS.)

165 PRIEST: Rise, my sons. The kindness we came for
    Oedipus volunteers himself.
    Apollo has sent his word, his oracle—
    Come down, Apollo, save us, stop the plague.

(The PRIESTS *rise, remove their branches and exit to the side. Enter a* CHORUS, *the citizens of Thebes, who have not heard the news that* CREON *brings. They march around the altar, chanting.)*

CHORUS: Zeus!
    Great welcome voice of Zeus, what do you bring?
170 What word from the gold vaults of Delphi
    comes to brilliant Thebes? Racked with terror—
                       terror shakes my heart
    and I cry your wild cries, Apollo, Healer of Delos
    I worship you in dread . . . what now, what is your price?
175 some new sacrifice? some ancient rite from the past
    come round again each spring?—
                what will you bring to birth?
    Tell me, child of golden Hope
        warm voice that never dies!

180 You are the first I call, daughter of Zeus
    deathless Athena—I call your sister Artemis,
    heart of the market place enthroned in glory,
                  guardian of our earth—
    I call Apollo, Archer astride the thunderheads of heaven—
185 O triple shield against death, shine before me now!
    If ever, once in the past, you stopped some ruin
    launched against our walls
          you hurled the flame of pain
    far, far from Thebes—you gods
190   come now, come down once more!
                        No, no
    the miseries numberless, grief on grief, no end—
    too much to bear, we are all dying
    O my people . . .
        Thebes like a great army dying
195 and there is no sword of thought to save us, no
    and the fruits of our famous earth, they will not ripen
    no and the women cannot scream their pangs to birth—
    screams for the Healer, children dead in the womb
          and life on life goes down
200   you can watch them go
    like seabirds winging west, outracing the day's fire
    down the horizon, irresistibly
           streaking on to the shores of Evening
                              Death
    so many deaths, numberless deaths on deaths, no end—
205 Thebes is dying, look, her children
    stripped of pity . . .
        generations strewn on the ground
    unburied, unwept, the dead spreading death
    and the young wives and gray-haired mothers with them
210 cling to the altars, trailing in from all over the city—
    Thebes, city of death, one long cortege
          and the suffering rises
                  wails for mercy rise
    and the wild hymn for the Healer blazes out
215 clashing with our sobs our cries of mourning—

O golden daughter of god, send rescue
    radiant as the kindness in your eyes!
    Drive him back!—the fever, the god of death
           that raging god of war
    not armored in bronze, not shielded now, he burns me,   220
    battle cries in the onslaught burning on—
    O rout him from our borders!
    Sail him, blast him out to the Sea-queen's chamber
                the black Atlantic gulfs
        or the northern harbor, death to all   225
    where the Thracian surf comes crashing.
    Now what the night spares he comes by day and kills—
    the god of death.

          O lord of the stormcloud,
    you who twirl the lightning, Zeus, Father,
    thunder Death to nothing!   230

Apollo, lord of the light, I beg you—
        whip your longbow's golden cord
    showering arrows on our enemies—shafts of power
    champions strong before us rushing on!

Artemis, Huntress,   235
    torches flaring over the eastern ridges—
           ride Death down in pain!

God of the headdress gleaming gold, I cry to you—
    your name and ours are one, Dionysus—
        come with your face aflame with wine   240
                  your raving women's cries
        your army on the march! Come with the lightning
    come with torches blazing, eyes ablaze with glory!
    Burn that god of death that all gods hate!

*(*OEDIPUS *enters from the palace to address the* CHORUS, *as if addressing the entire city of Thebes.)*

OEDIPUS: You pray to the gods? Let me grant your prayers.   245
    Come, listen to me—do what the plague demands:
    you'll find relief and lift your head from the depths.

I will speak out now as a stranger to the story,
    a stranger to the crime. If I'd been present then,
    there would have been no mystery, no long hunt   250
    without a clue in hand. So now, counted
    a native Theban years after the murder,
    to all of Thebes I make this proclamation:
    if any one of you knows who murdered Laius,
    the son of Labdacus, I order him to reveal   255
    the whole truth to me. Nothing to fear,
    even if he must denounce himself,
    let him speak up
    and so escape the brunt of the charge—
    he will suffer no unbearable punishment,   260
    nothing worse than exile, totally unharmed.

*(*OEDIPUS *pauses, waiting for a reply.)*

                       Next,
    if anyone knows the murderer is a stranger,
    a man from alien soil, come, speak up.
    I will give him a handsome reward, and lay up
    gratitude in my heart for him besides.   265

(Silence again, no reply.)

But if you keep silent, if anyone panicking,
trying to shield himself or friend or kin,
rejects my offer, then hear what I will do.
I order you, every citizen of the state
270   where I hold throne and power: banish this man—
whoever he may be—never shelter him, never
speak a word to him, never make him partner
to your prayers, your victims burned to the gods.
Never let the holy water touch his hands.
275   Drive him out, each of you, from every home.
He is the plague, the heart of our corruption,
as Apollo's oracle has just revealed to me.
So I honor my obligations:
I fight for the god and for the murdered man.

280   Now my curse on the murderer. Whoever he is,
a lone man unknown in his crime
or one among many, let that man drag out
his life in agony, step by painful step—
I curse myself as well . . . if by any chance
285   he proves to be an intimate of our house,
here at my hearth, with my full knowledge,
may the curse I just called down on him strike me!

These are your orders: perform them to the last.
I command you, for my sake, for Apollo's, for this country
290   blasted root and branch by the angry heavens.
Even if god had never urged you on to act,
how could you leave the crime uncleansed so long?
A man so noble—your king, brought down in blood—
you should have searched. But I am the king now,
295   I hold the throne that he held then, possess his bed
and a wife who shares our seed . . . why, our seed
might be the same, children born of the same mother
might have created blood-bonds between us
if his hope of offspring had not met disaster—
300   but fate swooped at his head and cut him short.
So I will fight for him as if he were my father,
stop at nothing, search the world
to lay my hands on the man who shed his blood,
the son of Labdacus descended of Polydorus,
305   Cadmus of old and Agenor, founder of the line:
their power and mine are one.
                              Oh dear gods,
my curse on those who disobey these orders!
Let no crops grow out of the earth for them—
shrivel their women, kill their sons,
310   burn them to nothing in this plague
that hits us now, or something even worse.
But you, loyal men of Thebes who approve my actions,
may our champion, Justice, may all the gods
be with us, fight beside us to the end!
315   LEADER: In the grip of your curse, my king, I swear
I'm not the murderer, I cannot point him out.
As for the search, Apollo pressed it on us—
he should name the killer.
OEDIPUS: Quite right,
but to force the gods to act against their will—
320   no man has the power.

LEADER: Then if I might mention
the next best thing . . .
OEDIPUS: The third best too—
don't hold back, say it.
LEADER: I still believe . . .
Lord Tiresias sees with the eyes of Lord Apollo.
Anyone searching for the truth, my king,
might learn it from the prophet, clear as day.   325
OEDIPUS: I've not been slow with that. On Creon's cue
I sent the escorts, twice, within the hour.
I'm surprised he isn't here.
LEADER: We need him—
without him we have nothing but old, useless rumors.
OEDIPUS: Which rumors? I'll search out every word.   330
LEADER: Laius was killed, they say, by certain travelers.
OEDIPUS: I know—but no one can find the murderer.
LEADER: If the man has a trace of fear in him
he won't stay silent long,
not with your curses ringing in his ears.   335
OEDIPUS: He didn't flinch at murder,
he'll never flinch at words.

(Enter TIRESIAS, *the blind prophet, led by a boy with escorts in attendance. He remains at a distance.)*

LEADER: Here is the one who will convict him, look,
they bring him on at last, the seer, the man of god.
The truth lives inside him, him alone.   340
OEDIPUS: O Tiresias,
master of all the mysteries of our life,
all you teach and all you dare not tell,
signs in the heavens, signs that walk the earth!
Blind as you are, you can feel all the more
what sickness haunts our city. You, my lord,   345
are the one shield, the one savior we can find.

We asked Apollo—perhaps the messengers
haven't told you—he sent his answer back:
"Relief from the plague can only come one way.
Uncover the murderers of Laius,   350
put them to death or drive them into exile."
So I beg you, grudge us nothing now, no voice,
no message plucked from the birds, the embers
or the other mantic ways within your grasp.
Rescue yourself, your city, rescue me—   355
rescue everything infected by the dead.
We are in your hands. For a man to help others
with all his gifts and native strength:
that is the noblest work.
TIRESIAS: How terrible—to see the truth
when the truth is only pain to him who sees!   360
I knew it well, but I put it from my mind,
else I never would have come.
OEDIPUS: What's this? Why so grim, so dire?
TIRESIAS: Just send me home. You bear your burdens,
I'll bear mine. It's better that way,   365
please believe me.
OEDIPUS: Strange response . . . unlawful,
unfriendly too to the state that bred and reared you—
you withhold the word of god.

TIRESIAS: I fail to see
that your own words are so well-timed.

370 I'd rather not have the same thing said of me . . .

OEDIPUS: For the love of god, don't turn away,
not if you know something. We beg you,
all of us on our knees.

TIRESIAS: None of you knows—
and I will never reveal my dreadful secrets,

375 not to say your own.

OEDIPUS: What? You know and you won't tell?
You're bent on betraying us, destroying Thebes?

TIRESIAS: I'd rather not cause pain for you or me.
So why this . . . useless interrogation?

380 You'll get nothing from me.

OEDIPUS: Nothing! You,
you scum of the earth, you'd enrage a heart of stone!
You won't talk? Nothing moves you?
Out with it, once and for all!

TIRESIAS: You criticize my temper . . . unaware

385 of the one *you* live with, you revile me.

OEDIPUS: Who could restrain his anger hearing you?
What outrage—you spurn the city!

TIRESIAS: What will come will come.
Even if I shroud it all in silence.

390 OEDIPUS: What will come? You're bound to *tell* me that.

TIRESIAS: I will say no more. Do as you like, build your anger
to whatever pitch you please, rage your worst—

OEDIPUS: Oh I'll let loose, I have such fury in me—
now I see it all. You helped hatch the plot,

395 you did the work, yes, short of killing him
with your own hands—and given eyes I'd say
you did the killing single-handed!

TIRESIAS: Is that so!
I charge you, then, submit to that decree
you just laid down: from this day onward

400 speak to no one, not these citizens, not myself.
You are the curse, the corruption of the land!

OEDIPUS: You, shameless—
aren't you appalled to start up such a story?
You think you can get away with this?

TIRESIAS: I have already.

405 The truth with all its power lives inside me.

OEDIPUS: Who primed you for this? Not your prophet's
trade.

TIRESIAS: You did, you forced me, twisted it out of me.

OEDIPUS: What? Say it again—I'll understand it better.

TIRESIAS: Didn't you understand, just now?

410 Or are you tempting me to talk?

OEDIPUS: No, I can't say I grasped your meaning.
Out with it, again!

TIRESIAS: I say you are the murderer you hunt.

OEDIPUS: That obscenity, twice—by god, you'll pay.

415 TIRESIAS: Shall I say more, so you can really rage?

OEDIPUS: Much as you want. Your words are nothing—
futile.

TIRESIAS: You cannot imagine . . . I tell you,
you and your loved ones live together in infamy,
you cannot see how far you've gone in guilt.

420 OEDIPUS: You think you can keep this up and never suffer?

TIRESIAS: Indeed, if the truth has any power.

OEDIPUS: It does
but not for you, old man. You've lost your power,
stone-blind, stone-deaf—senses, eyes blind as stone!

TIRESIAS: I pity you, flinging at me the very insults
each man here will fling at you so soon. 425

OEDIPUS: Blind,
lost in the night, endless night that nursed you!
You can't hurt me or anyone else who sees the light—
you can never touch me.

TIRESIAS: True, it is not your fate
to fall at my hands. Apollo is quite enough,
and he will take some pains to work this out. 430

OEDIPUS: Creon! Is this conspiracy his or yours?

TIRESIAS: Creon is not your downfall, no, you are your own.

OEDIPUS: O power—
wealth and empire, skill outstripping skill
in the heady rivalries of life,
what envy lurks inside you! Just for this, 435
the crown the city gave me—I never sought it,
they laid it in my hands—for this alone, Creon,
the soul of trust, my loyal friend from the start
steals against me . . . so hungry to overthrow me
he sets this wizard on me, this scheming quack, 440
this fortune-teller peddling lies, eyes peeled
for his own profit—seer blind in his craft!

Come here, you pious fraud. Tell me,
when did you ever prove yourself a prophet?
When the Sphinx, that chanting Fury kept her 445
deathwatch here,
why silent then, not a word to set our people free?
There was a riddle, not for some passer-by to solve—
it cried out for a prophet. Where were you?
Did you rise to the crisis? Not a word,
you and your birds, your gods—nothing. 450
No, but I came by, Oedipus the ignorant,
I stopped the Sphinx! With no help from the birds,
the flight of my own intelligence hit the mark.

And this is the man you'd try to overthrow?
You think you'll stand by Creon when he's king? 455
You and the great mastermind—
you'll pay in tears, I promise you, for this,
this witch-hunt. If you didn't look so senile
the lash would teach you what your scheming means!

LEADER: I would suggest his words were spoken in anger, 460
Oedipus . . . yours too, and it isn't what we need.
The best solution to the oracle, the riddle
posed by god—we should look for that.

TIRESIAS: You are the king no doubt, but in one respect,
at least, I am your equal: the right to reply. 465
I claim that privilege too.
I am not your slave. I serve Apollo.
I don't need Creon to speak for me in public.

So,
you mock my blindness? Let me tell you this.
You with your precious eyes, 470
you're blind to the corruption of your life,
to the house you live in, those you live with—
who *are* your parents? Do you know? All unknowing
you are the scourge of your own flesh and blood,

475   the dead below the earth and the living here above,
and the double lash of your mother and your father's curse
will whip you from this land one day, their footfall
treading you down in terror, darkness shrouding
your eyes that now can see the light!
                                        Soon, soon
480   you'll scream aloud—what haven won't reverberate?
What rock of Cithaeron won't scream back in echo?
That day you learn the truth about your marriage,
the wedding-march that sang you into your halls,
the lusty voyage home to the fatal harbor!
485   And a crowd of other horrors you'd never dream
will level you with yourself and all your children.

There. Now smear us with insults—Creon, myself
and every word I've said. No man will ever
be rooted from the earth as brutally as you.
490   OEDIPUS: Enough! Such filth from him? Insufferable—
what, still alive? Get out—
faster, back where you came from—vanish!
TIRESIAS: I would never have come if you hadn't called me here.
OEDIPUS: If I thought you would blurt out such absurdities,
495   you'd have died waiting before I'd had you summoned.
TIRESIAS: Absurd, am I! To you, not to your parents:
the ones who bore you found me sane enough.
OEDIPUS: Parents—who? Wait . . . who is my father?
TIRESIAS: This day will bring your birth and your destruction.
500   OEDIPUS: Riddles—all you can say are riddles, murk and
darkness.
TIRESIAS: Ah, but aren't you the best man alive at solving riddles?
OEDIPUS: Mock me for that, go on, and you'll reveal my
greatness.
TIRESIAS: Your great good fortune, true, it was your ruin.
OEDIPUS: Not if I saved the city—what do I care?
505   TIRESIAS: Well then, I'll be going.

(*To his* ATTENDANT.)

                                        Take me home, boy.
OEDIPUS: Yes, take him away. You're a nuisance here.
Out of the way, the irritation's gone.

(*Turning his back on* TIRESIAS, *moving toward the palace.*)

TIRESIAS: I will go,
once I have said what I came here to say.
I will never shrink from the anger in your eyes—
510   you can't destroy me. Listen to me closely:
the man you've sought so long, proclaiming,
cursing up and down, the murderer of Laius—
he is here. A stranger,
you may think, who lives among you,
515   he soon will be revealed a native Theban
but he will take no joy in the revelation.
Blind who now has eyes, beggar who now is rich,
he will grope his way toward a foreign soil,
a stick tapping before him step by step.

(OEDIPUS *enters the palace.*)

520   Revealed at last, brother and father both
to the children he embraces, to his mother

son and husband both—he sowed the loins
his father sowed, he spilled his father's blood!

Go in and reflect on that, solve that.
And if you find I've lied   525
from this day onward call the prophet blind.

(TIRESIAS *and the boy exit to the side.*)

CHORUS: Who—
who is the man the voice of god denounces
resounding out of the rocky gorge of Delphi?
        The horror too dark to tell,
whose ruthless bloody hands have done the work?   530
His time has come to fly
        to outrace the stallions of the storm
                        his feet a streak of speed—
Cased in armor, Apollo son of the Father
lunges on him, lightning-bolts afire!   535
And the grim unerring Furies
                        closing for the kill.
                                        Look,
the word of god has just come blazing
flashing off Parnassus' snowy heights!
        That man who left no trace—   540
after him, hunt him down with all our strength!
Now under bristling timber
        up through rocks and caves he stalks
                        like the wild mountain bull—
cut off from men, each step an agony, frenzied, racing blind   545
but he cannot outrace the dread voices of Delphi
ringing out of the heart of Earth,
        the dark wings beating around him shrieking doom
                        the doom that never dies, the terror—
The skilled prophet scans the birds and shatters me with   550
        terror!
I can't accept him, can't deny him, don't know what to say,
I'm lost, and the wings of dark foreboding beating—
I cannot see what's come, what's still to come . . .
and what could breed a blood feud between
        Laius' house and the son of Polybus?   555
I know of nothing, not in the past and not now,
no charge to bring against our king, no cause
to attack his fame that rings throughout Thebes—
        not without proof—not for the ghost of Laius,
        not to avenge a murder gone without a trace.   560

Zeus and Apollo know, they know, the great masters
        of all the dark and depth of human life.
But whether a mere man can know the truth,
whether a seer can fathom more than I—
there is no test, no certain proof   565
        though matching skill for skill
a man can outstrip a rival. No, not till I see
these charges proved will I side with his accusers.
We saw him then, when the she-hawk swept against him,
saw with our own eyes his skill, his brilliant triumph—   570
        there was the test—he was the joy of Thebes!
        Never will I convict my king, never in my heart.

(*Enter* CREON *from the side.*)

CREON: My fellow-citizens, I hear King Oedipus
    levels terrible charges at me. I had to come.
575 I resent it deeply. If, in the present crisis,
    he thinks he suffers any abuse from me,
    anything I've done or said that offers him
    the slightest injury, why, I've no desire
    to linger out this life, my reputation in ruins.
580 The damage I'd face from such an accusation
    is nothing simple. No, there's nothing worse:
    branded a traitor in the city, a traitor
    to all of you and my good friends.
LEADER: True,
    but a slur might have been forced out of him,
585 by anger perhaps, not any firm conviction.
CREON: The charge was made in public, wasn't it?
    I put the prophet up to spreading lies?
LEADER: Such things were said . . .
    I don't know with what intent, if any.
590 CREON: Was his glance steady, his mind right
    when the charge was brought against me?
LEADER: I really couldn't say, I never look
    to judge the ones in power.

(The doors open. OEDIPUS *enters.)*

                 Wait,
    here's Oedipus now.
OEDIPUS: You—here? You have the gall
595 to show your face before the palace gates?
    You, plotting to kill me, kill the king—
    I see it all, the marauding thief himself
    scheming to steal my crown and power!
                      Tell me,
    in god's name, what did you take me for,
600 coward or fool, when you spun out your plot?
    Your treachery—you think I'd never detect it
    creeping against me in the dark? Or sensing it,
    not defend myself? Aren't you the fool,
    you and your high adventure. Lacking numbers,
605 powerful friends, out for the big game of empire—
    you need riches, armies to bring that quarry down!
CREON: Are you quite finished? It's your turn to listen
    for just as long as you've . . . instructed me.
    Hear me out, then judge me on the facts.
610 OEDIPUS: You've a wicked way with words, Creon,
    but I'll be slow to learn—from you.
    I find you a menace, a great burden to me.
CREON: Just one thing, hear me out in this.
OEDIPUS: Just one thing,
    don't tell *me* you're not the enemy, the traitor.
615 CREON: Look, if you think crude, mindless stubbornness
    such a gift, you've lost your sense of balance.
OEDIPUS: If you think you can abuse a kinsman,
    then escape the penalty, you're insane.
CREON: Fair enough, I grant you. But this injury
620 you say I've done you, what is it?
OEDIPUS: Did you induce me, yes or no,
    to send for that sanctimonious prophet?
CREON: I did. And I'd do the same again.
OEDIPUS: All right then, tell me, how long is it now
625   since Laius . . .

CREON: Laius—what did *he* do?
OEDIPUS: Vanished,
    swept from sight, murdered in his tracks.
CREON: The count of the years would run you far back . . .
OEDIPUS: And that far back, was the prophet at his trade?
CREON: Skilled as he is today, and just as honored.
OEDIPUS: Did he ever refer to me then, at that time?   630
CREON: No,
    never, at least, when I was in his presence.
OEDIPUS: But you did investigate the murder, didn't you?
CREON: We did our best, of course, discovered nothing.
OEDIPUS: But the great seer never accused me then—why
    not?
CREON: I don't know. And when I don't, *I* keep quiet.   635
OEDIPUS: You do know this, you'd tell it too—
    if you had a shred of decency.
CREON: What?
    If I know, I won't hold back.
OEDIPUS: Simply this:
    if the two of you had never put heads together,
    we would never have heard about *my* killing Laius.   640
CREON: If that's what he says . . . well, you know best.
    But now I have a right to learn from you
    as you just learned from me.
OEDIPUS: Learn your fill,
    you never will convict me of the murder.
CREON: Tell me, you're married to my sister, aren't you?   645
OEDIPUS: A genuine discovery—there's no denying that.
CREON: And you rule the land with her, with equal power?
OEDIPUS: She receives from me whatever she desires.
CREON: And I am the third, all of us are equals?
OEDIPUS: Yes, and it's there you show your stripes—   650
    you betray a kinsman.
CREON: Not at all.
Not if you see things calmly, rationally,
as I do. Look at it this way first:
who in his right mind would rather rule
and live in anxiety than sleep in peace?   655
Particularly if he enjoys the same authority.
Not I, I'm not the man to yearn for kingship,
not with a king's power in my hands. Who would?
No one with any sense of self-control.
Now, as it is, you offer me all I need,   660
not a fear in the world. But if I wore the crown . . .
there'd be many painful duties to perform,
hardly to my taste.
                How could kingship
please me more than influence, power
without a qualm? I'm not that deluded yet,   665
to reach for anything but privilege outright,
profit free and clear.
    Now all men sing my praises, all salute me,
now all who request your favors curry mine.
I am their best hope: success rests in me.   670
Why give up that, I ask you, and borrow trouble?
A man of sense, someone who sees things clearly
would never resort to treason.
No, I have no lust for conspiracy in me,
nor could I ever suffer one who does.   675

Do you want proof? Go to Delphi yourself,
examine the oracle and see if I've reported
the message word-for-word. This too:
if you detect that I and the clairvoyant
680   have plotted anything in common, arrest me,
execute me. Not on the strength of one vote,
two in this case, mine as well as yours.
But don't convict me on sheer unverified surmise.
How wrong it is to take the good for bad,
685   purely at random, or take the bad for good.
But reject a friend, a kinsman? I would as soon
tear out the life within us, priceless life itself.
You'll learn this well, without fail, in time.
Time alone can bring the just man to light—
690   the criminal you can spot in one short day.
LEADER: Good advice,
my lord, for anyone who wants to avoid disaster.
Those who jump to conclusions may go wrong.
OEDIPUS: When my enemy moves against me quickly,
plots in secret, I move quickly too, I must,
695   I plot and pay him back. Relax my guard a moment,
waiting his next move—he wins his objective,
I lose mine.
CREON: What do you want?
You want me banished?
OEDIPUS: No, I want you dead.
CREON: Just to show how ugly a grudge can . . .
OEDIPUS: So,
700   still stubborn? you don't think I'm serious?
CREON: I think you're insane.
OEDIPUS: Quite sane—in my behalf.
CREON: Not just as much in mine?
OEDIPUS: You—my mortal enemy?
CREON: What if you're wholly wrong?
OEDIPUS: No matter—I must rule.
CREON: Not if you rule unjustly.
OEDIPUS: Hear him, Thebes, my city!
705 CREON: My city too, not yours alone!
LEADER: Please, my lords.

(Enter JOCASTA *from the palace.)*

                  Look, Jocasta's coming,
and just in time too. With her help
you must put this fighting of yours to rest.
JOCASTA: Have you no sense? Poor misguided men,
710   such shouting—why this public outburst?
Aren't you ashamed, with the land so sick,
to stir up private quarrels?

(To OEDIPUS.)

Into the palace now. And Creon, you go home.
Why make such a furor over nothing?
715 CREON: My sister, it's dreadful . . . Oedipus, your husband,
he's bent on a choice of punishments for me,
banishment from the fatherland or death.
OEDIPUS: Precisely. I caught him in the act, Jocasta,
plotting, about to stab me in the back.
720 CREON: Never—curse me, let me die and be damned
if I've done you any wrong you charge me with.

JOCASTA: Oh god, believe it, Oedipus,
honor the solemn oath he swears to heaven.
Do it for me, for the sake of all your people.

(The CHORUS *begins to chant.)*

CHORUS: Believe it, be sensible   725
give way, my king, I beg you!
OEDIPUS: What do you want from me, concessions?
CHORUS: Respect him—he's been no fool in the past
and now he's strong with the oath he swears to god.
OEDIPUS: You know what you're asking?   730
CHORUS: I do.
OEDIPUS: Then out with it!
CHORUS: The man's your friend, your kin, he's under oath—
don't cast him out, disgraced
branded with guilt on the strength of hearsay only.
OEDIPUS: Know full well, if that is what you want
you want me dead or banished from the land.   735
CHORUS: Never—
no, by the blazing Sun, first god of the heavens!
    Stripped of the gods, stripped of loved ones,
let me die by inches if that ever crossed my mind.
But the heart inside me sickens, dies as the land dies
and now on top of the old griefs you pile this,   740
your fury—both of you!
OEDIPUS: Then let him go,
even if it does lead to my ruin, my death
or my disgrace, driven from Thebes for life.
It's you, not him I pity—your words move me.
He, wherever he goes, my hate goes with him.   745
CREON: Look at you, sullen in yielding, brutal in your rage—
you will go too far. It's perfect justice:
natures like yours are hardest on themselves.
OEDIPUS: Then leave me alone—get out!
CREON: I'm going.
You're wrong, so wrong. These men know I'm right.   750

(Exit to the side. The CHORUS *turns to* JOCASTA.)

CHORUS: Why do you hesitate, my lady
why not help him in?
JOCASTA: Tell me what's happened first.
CHORUS: Loose, ignorant talk started dark suspicions
and a sense of injustice cut deeply too.   755
JOCASTA: On both sides?
CHORUS: Oh yes.
JOCASTA: What did they say?
CHORUS: Enough, please, enough! The land's so racked already
or so it seems to me . . .
End the trouble here, just where they left it.
OEDIPUS: You see what comes of your good intentions now?   760
And all because you tried to blunt my anger.
CHORUS: My king,
I've said it once, I'll say it time and again—
    I'd be insane, you know it,
senseless, ever to turn my back on you.
You who set our beloved land—storm-tossed, shattered— 765
straight on course. Now again, good helmsman,
steer us through the storm!

(The CHORUS *draws away, leaving* OEDIPUS *and* JOCASTA *side by side.)*

JOCASTA: For the love of god,
    Oedipus, tell me too, what is it?
    Why this rage? You're so unbending.
770 OEDIPUS: I will tell you. I respect you, Jocasta,
    much more than these men here . . .

(Glancing at the CHORUS.*)*

    Creon's to blame, Creon schemes against me.
    JOCASTA: Tell me clearly, how did the quarrel start?
    OEDIPUS: He says *I* murdered Laius—I am guilty.
775 JOCASTA: How does he know? Some secret knowledge
        or simple hearsay?
    OEDIPUS: Oh, he sent his prophet in
    to do his dirty work. You know Creon,
    Creon keeps his own lips clean.
    JOCASTA: A prophet?
    Well then, free yourself of every charge!
780 Listen to me and learn some peace of mind:
    no skill in the world,
    nothing human can penetrate the future.
    Here is proof, quick and to the point.

    An oracle came to Laius one fine day
785 (I won't say from Apollo himself
    but his underlings, his priests) and it declared
    that doom would strike him down at the hands of a son,
    our son, to be born of our own flesh and blood. But Laius,
    so the report goes at least, was killed by strangers,
790 thieves, at a place where three roads meet . . . my son—
    he wasn't three days old and the boy's father
    fastened his ankles, had a henchman fling him away
    on a barren, trackless mountain.
                        There, you see?
    Apollo brought neither thing to pass. My baby
795 no more murdered his father than Laius suffered—
    his wildest fear—death at his own son's hands.
    That's how the seers and all their revelations
    mapped out the future. Brush them from your mind.
    Whatever the god needs and seeks
800 he'll bring to light himself, with ease.
    OEDIPUS: Strange,
    hearing you just now . . . my mind wandered,
    my thoughts racing back and forth.
    JOCASTA: What do you mean? Why so anxious, startled?
    OEDIPUS: I thought I heard you say that Laius
805 was cut down at a place where three roads meet.
    JOCASTA: That was the story. It hasn't died out yet.
    OEDIPUS: Where did this thing happen? Be precise.
    JOCASTA: A place called Phocis, where two branching roads,
        one from Daulia, one from Delphi,
810 come together—a crossroads.
    OEDIPUS: When? How long ago?
    JOCASTA: The heralds no sooner reported Laius dead
        than you appeared and they hailed you king of Thebes.
    OEDIPUS: My god, my god—what have you planned to do to me?
815 JOCASTA: What, Oedipus? What haunts you so?
    OEDIPUS: Not yet.
    Laius—how did he look? Describe him.
    Had he reached his prime?

JOCASTA: He was swarthy,
    and the gray had just begun to streak his temples,
    and his build . . . wasn't far from yours.
OEDIPUS: Oh no no,
    I think I've just called down a dreadful curse   820
    upon myself—I simply didn't know!
JOCASTA: What are you saying? I shudder to look at you.
OEDIPUS: I have a terrible fear the blind seer can see.
    I'll know in a moment. One thing more—
JOCASTA: Anything,
    afraid as I am—ask, I'll answer, all I can.   825
OEDIPUS: Did he go with a light or heavy escort,
    several men-at-arms, like a lord, a king?
JOCASTA: There were five in the party, a herald among them,
    and a single wagon carrying Laius.
OEDIPUS: Ai—
    now I can see it all, clear as day.   830
    Who told you all this at the time, Jocasta?
JOCASTA: A servant who reached home, the lone survivor.
OEDIPUS: So, could he still be in the palace—even now?
JOCASTA: No indeed. Soon as he returned from the scene
    and saw you on the throne with Laius dead and gone,   835
    he knelt and clutched my hand, pleading with me
    to send him into the hinterlands, to pasture,
    far as possible, out of sight of Thebes.
    I sent him away. Slave though he was,
    he'd earned that favor—and much more.   840
OEDIPUS: Can we bring him back, quickly?
JOCASTA: Easily. Why do you want him so?
OEDIPUS: I am afraid,
    Jocasta, I have said too much already.
    That man—I've got to see him.
JOCASTA: Then he'll come.
    But even I have a right, I'd like to think,   845
    to know what's torturing you, my lord.
OEDIPUS: And so you shall—I can hold nothing back from you,
    now I've reached this pitch of dark foreboding.
    Who means more to me than you? Tell me,
    whom would I turn toward but you   850
    as I go through all this?

    My father was Polybus, king of Corinth.
    My mother, a Dorian, Merope. And I was held
    the prince of the realm among the people there,
    till something struck me out of nowhere,   855
    something strange . . . worth remarking perhaps,
    hardly worth the anxiety I gave it.
    Some man at a banquet who had drunk too much
    shouted out—he was far gone, mind you—
    that I am not my father's son. Fighting words!   860
    I barely restrained myself that day
    but early the next I went to mother and father,
    questioned them closely, and they were enraged
    at the accusation and the fool who let it fly.
    So as for my parents I was satisfied,   865
    but still this thing kept gnawing at me,
    the slander spread—I had to make my move.
                        And so,
    unknown to mother and father I set out for Delphi,
    and the god Apollo spurned me, sent me away

870   denied the facts I came for,
      but first he flashed before my eyes a future
      great with pain, terror, disaster—I can hear him cry,
      "You are fated to couple with your mother, you will bring
      a breed of children into the light no man can bear to see—
875   you will kill your father, the one who gave you life!"
      I heard all that and ran. I abandoned Corinth,
      from that day on I gauged its landfall only
      by the stars, running, always running
      toward some place where I would never see
880   the shame of all those oracles come true.
      And as I fled I reached that very spot
      where the great king, you say, met his death.

      Now, Jocasta, I will tell you all.
      Making my way toward this triple crossroad
885   I began to see a herald, then a brace of colts
      drawing a wagon, and mounted on the bench . . . a man,
      just as you've described him, coming face-to-face,
      and the one in the lead and the old man himself
      were about to thrust me off the road—brute force—
890   and the one shouldering me aside, the driver,
      I strike him in anger!—and the old man, watching me
      coming up along his wheels—he brings down
      his prod, two prongs straight at my head!
      I paid him back with interest!
895   Short work, by god—with one blow of the staff
      in this right hand I knock him out of his high seat,
      roll him out of the wagon, sprawling headlong—
      I killed them all—every mother's son!

      Oh, but if there is any blood-tie
900   between Laius and this stranger . . .
      what man alive more miserable than I?
      More hated by the gods? *I* am the man
      no alien, no citizen welcomes to his house,
      law forbids it—not a word to me in public,
905   driven out of every hearth and home.
      And all these curses I—no one but I
      brought down these piling curses on myself!
      And you, his wife, I've touched your body with these,
      the hands that killed your husband cover you with blood.

910   Wasn't I born for torment? Look me in the eyes!
      I am abomination—heart and soul!
      I must be exiled, and even in exile
      never see my parents, never set foot
      on native ground again. Else I am doomed
915   to couple with my mother and cut my father down . . .
      Polybus who reared me, gave me life.

                              But why, why?
      Wouldn't a man of judgment say—and wouldn't he be
          right—
      some savage power has brought this down upon my head?

      Oh no, not that, you pure and awesome gods,
920   never let me see that day! Let me slip
      from the world of men, vanish without a trace
      before I see myself stained with such corruption,
      stained to the heart.
   LEADER: My lord, you fill our hearts with fear.
925   But at least until you question the witness,
      do take hope.

OEDIPUS: Exactly. He is my last hope—
      I am waiting for the shepherd. He is crucial.
JOCASTA: And once he appears, what then? Why so urgent?
OEDIPUS: I will tell you. If it turns out that his story
      matches yours, I've escaped the worst.   930
JOCASTA: What did I say? What struck you so?
OEDIPUS: You said
      thieves—
      he told you a whole band of them murdered Laius.
      So, if he still holds to the same number,
      I cannot be the killer. One can't equal many.
      But if he refers to one man, one alone,   935
      clearly the scales come down on me:
      I am guilty.
JOCASTA: Impossible. Trust me,
      I told you precisely what he said,
      and he can't retract it now;
      the whole city heard it, not just I.   940
      And even if he should vary his first report
      by one man more or less, still, my lord,
      he could never make the murder of Laius
      truly fit the prophecy. Apollo was explicit:
      my son was doomed to kill my husband . . . my son,   945
      poor defenseless thing, he never had a chance
      to kill his father. They destroyed him first.

      So much for prophecy. It's neither here nor there.
      From this day on. I wouldn't look right or left.
OEDIPUS: True, true. Still, that shepherd,   950
      someone fetch him—now!
JOCASTA: I'll send at once. But do let's go inside.
      I'd never displease you, least of all in this.

(OEDIPUS *and* JOCASTA *enter the palace.*)

CHORUS: Destiny guide me always
      Destiny find me filled with reverence   955
          pure in word and deed.
      Great laws tower above us, reared on high
      born for the brilliant vault of heaven—
          Olympian Sky their only father,
      nothing mortal, no man gave them birth,
      their memory deathless, never lost in sleep: 960
      within them lives a mighty god, the god does not
          grow old.

      Pride breeds the tyrant
      violent pride, gorging, crammed to bursting
          with all that is overripe and rich with ruin—   965
      clawing up to the heights, headlong pride
      crashes down the abyss—sheer doom!
          No footing helps, all foothold lost and gone.
      But the healthy strife that makes the city strong—
      I pray that god will never end that wrestling: 970
      god, my champion, I will never let you go.

      But if any man comes striding, high and mighty
          in all he says and does,
      no fear of justice, no reverence
      for the temples of the gods—   975
          let a rough doom tear him down,
      repay his pride, breakneck, ruinous pride!
      If he cannot reap his profits fairly

980   cannot restrain himself from outrage—
        mad, laying hands on the holy things untouchable!

        Can such a man, so desperate, still boast
        he can save his life from the flashing bolts of god?
        If all such violence goes with honor now
        why join the sacred dance?

985   Never again will I go reverent to Delphi,
        the inviolate heart of Earth
        or Apollo's ancient oracle at Abae
        or Olympia of the fires—
        unless these prophecies all come true
990   for all mankind to point toward in wonder.
        King of kings, if you deserve your titles
        Zeus, remember, never forget!
        You and your deathless, everlasting reign.

        They are dying, the old oracles sent to Laius,
995   now our masters strike them off the rolls.
        Nowhere Apollo's golden glory now—
        the gods, the gods go down.

(Enter JOCASTA *from the palace, carrying a suppliant's branch wound in wool.)*

JOCASTA: Lords of the realm, it occurred to me,
    just now, to visit the temples of the gods,
1000   so I have my branch in hand and incense too.

    Oedipus is beside himself. Racked with anguish,
    no longer a man of sense, he won't admit
    the latest prophecies are hollow as the old—
    he's at the mercy of every passing voice
1005   if the voice tells of terror.
    I urge him gently, nothing seems to help,
    so I turn to you, Apollo, you are nearest.

(Placing her branch on the altar, while an old herdsman enters from the side, not the one just summoned by the King but an unexpected MESSENGER *from Corinth.)*

    I come with prayers and offerings . . . I beg you,
    cleanse us, set us free of defilement!
1010   Look at us, passengers in the grip of fear,
    watching the pilot of the vessel go to pieces.
MESSENGER: *(Approaching* JOCASTA *and the* CHORUS.*)* Strangers,
    please, I wonder if you could lead us
    to the palace of the king . . . I think it's Oedipus.
    Better, the man himself—you know where he is?
1015 LEADER: This is his palace, stranger. He's inside.
    But here is his queen, his wife and mother
    of his children.
MESSENGER: Blessings on you, noble queen,
    queen of Oedipus crowned with all your family—
    blessings on you always!
1020 JOCASTA: And the same to you, stranger, you deserve it . . .
    such a greeting. But what have you come for?
    Have you brought us news?
MESSENGER: Wonderful news—
    for the house, my lady, for your husband too.
JOCASTA: Really, what? Who sent you?
MESSENGER: Corinth.
1025   I'll give you the message in a moment.

    You'll be glad of it—how could you help it?—
    though it costs a little sorrow in the bargain.
JOCASTA: What can it be, with such a double edge?
MESSENGER: The people there, they want to make your Oedipus
    king of Corinth, so they're saying now.   1030
JOCASTA: Why? Isn't old Polybus still in power?
MESSENGER: No more. Death has got him in the tomb.
JOCASTA: What are you saying? Polybus, dead?—dead?
MESSENGER: If not,
    if I'm not telling the truth, strike me dead too.
JOCASTA: *(To a* SERVANT.*)* Quickly, go to your master, tell him
    this!   1035

    You prophecies of the gods, where are you now?
    This is the man that Oedipus feared for years,
    he fled him, not to kill him—and now he's dead,
    quite by chance, a normal, natural death,
    not murdered by his son.   1040
OEDIPUS: *(Emerging from the palace.)*
              Dearest,
    what now? Why call me from the palace?
JOCASTA: *(Bringing the* MESSENGER *closer.)* Listen to *him,* see for
    yourself what all
    those awful prophecies of god have come to.
OEDIPUS: And who is he? What can he have for me?
JOCASTA: He's from Corinth, he's come to tell you   1045
    your father is no more—Polybus—he's dead!
OEDIPUS: *(Wheeling on the* MESSENGER.*)* What? Let me have it
    from your lips.
MESSENGER: Well,
    if that's what you want first, then here it is:
    make no mistake, Polybus is dead and gone.
OEDIPUS: How—murder? sickness?—what? what killed him?   1050
MESSENGER: A light tip of the scales can put old bones to rest.
OEDIPUS: Sickness then—poor man, it wore him down.
MESSENGER: That,
    and the long count of years he'd measured out.
OEDIPUS: So!
    Jocasta, why, why look to the Prophet's hearth,
    the fires of the future? Why scan the birds   1055
    that scream above our heads? They winged me on
    to the murder of my father, did they? That was my doom?
    Well look, he's dead and buried, hidden under the earth,
    and here I am in Thebes, I never put hand to sword—
    unless some longing for me wasted him away,   1060
    then in a sense you'd say I caused his death.
    But now, all those prophecies I feared—Polybus
    packs them off to sleep with him in hell!
    They're nothing, worthless.
JOCASTA: There.
    Didn't I tell you from the start?   1065
OEDIPUS: So you did. I was lost in fear.
JOCASTA: No more, sweep it from your mind forever.
OEDIPUS: But my mother's bed, surely I must fear—
JOCASTA: Fear?
    What should a man fear? It's all chance,
    chance rules our lives. Not a man on earth   1070
    can see a day ahead, groping through the dark.
    Better to live at random, best we can.
    And as for this marriage with your mother—
    have no fear. Many a man before you,

1075 in his dreams, has shared his mother's bed.
Take such things for shadows, nothing at all—
Live, Oedipus,
as if there's no tomorrow!
OEDIPUS: Brave words,
and you'd persuade me if mother weren't alive.
1080 But mother lives, so for all your reassurances
I live in fear, I must.
JOCASTA: But your father's death,
that, at least, is a great blessing, joy to the eyes!
OEDIPUS: Great, I know . . . but I fear *her*—she's still alive.
MESSENGER: Wait, who is this woman, makes you so afraid?
1085 OEDIPUS: Merope, old man. The wife of Polybus.
MESSENGER: The queen? What's there to fear in her?
OEDIPUS: A dreadful prophecy, stranger, sent by the gods.
MESSENGER: Tell me, could you? Unless it's forbidden
other ears to hear.
OEDIPUS: Not at all.
1090 Apollo told me once—it is my fate—
I must make love with my own mother,
shed my father's blood with my own hands.
So for years I've given Corinth a wide berth,
and it's been my good fortune too. But still,
1095 to see one's parents and look into their eyes
is the greatest joy I know.
MESSENGER: You're afraid of that?
That kept you out of Corinth?
OEDIPUS: My *father*, old man—
so I wouldn't kill my father.
MESSENGER: So that's it.
Well then, seeing I came with such good will, my king,
1100 why don't I rid you of that old worry now?
OEDIPUS: What a rich reward you'd have for that!
MESSENGER: What do you think I came for, majesty?
So you'd come home and I'd be better off.
OEDIPUS: Never, I will never go near my parents.
1105 MESSENGER: My boy, it's clear, you don't know what you're
doing.
OEDIPUS: What do you mean, old man? For god's sake, explain.
MESSENGER: If you ran from *them*, always dodging home . . .
OEDIPUS: Always, terrified Apollo's oracle might come true—
MESSENGER: And you'd be covered with guilt, from both your
parents.
1110 OEDIPUS: That's right, old man, that fear is always
with me.
MESSENGER: Don't you know? You've really nothing to fear.
OEDIPUS: But why? If I'm their son—Merope, Polybus?
MESSENGER: Polybus was nothing to you, that's why, not in
blood.
OEDIPUS: What are you saying—Polybus was not my father?
1115 MESSENGER: No more than I am. He and I are equals.
OEDIPUS: My father—
how can my father equal nothing? You're nothing to me!
MESSENGER: Neither was he, no more your father than I am.
OEDIPUS: Then why did he call me his son?
MESSENGER: You were a gift,
years ago—know for a fact he took you
1120 from my hands.
OEDIPUS: No, from another's hands?
Then how could he love me so? He loved me, deeply . . .

MESSENGER: True, and his early years without a child
made him love you all the more.
OEDIPUS: And you, did you . . .
buy me? find me by accident?
MESSENGER: I stumbled on you,
down the woody flanks of Mount Cithaeron.   1125
OEDIPUS: So close,
what were you doing here, just passing through?
MESSENGER: Watching over my flocks, grazing them on the
slopes.
OEDIPUS: A herdsman, were you? A vagabond, scraping for
wages?
MESSENGER: Your savior too, my son, in your worst hour.
OEDIPUS: Oh—
when you picked me up, was I in pain? What exactly?   1130
MESSENGER: Your ankles . . . they tell the story. Look at them.
OEDIPUS: Why remind me of that, that old affliction?
MESSENGER: Your ankles were pinned together. I set you free.
OEDIPUS: That dreadful mark—I've had it from the cradle.
MESSENGER: And you got your name from that misfortune too,   1135
the name's still with you.
OEDIPUS: Dear god, who did it?—
mother? father? Tell me.
MESSENGER: I don't know.
The one who gave you to me, he'd know more.
OEDIPUS: What? You took me from someone else?
You didn't find me yourself?   1140
MESSENGER: No sir,
another shepherd passed you on to me.
OEDIPUS: Who? Do you know? Describe him.
MESSENGER: He called himself a servant of . . .
if I remember rightly—Laius.

(JOCASTA *turns sharply.*)

OEDIPUS: The king of the land who ruled here long ago?   1145
MESSENGER: That's the one. That herdsman was *his* man.
OEDIPUS: Is he still alive? Can I see him?
MESSENGER: They'd know best, the people of these parts.

(OEDIPUS *and the* MESSENGER *turn to the* CHORUS.)

OEDIPUS: Does anyone know that herdsman,
the one he mentioned? Anyone seen him   1150
in the fields, here in the city? Out with it!
The time has come to reveal this once for all.
LEADER: I think he's the very shepherd you wanted to see,
a moment ago. But the queen, Jocasta,
she's the one to say.   1155
OEDIPUS: Jocasta,
you remember the man we just sent for?
Is *that* the one he means?
JOCASTA: That man . . .
why ask? Old shepherd, talk, empty nonsense,
don't give it another thought, don't even think—
OEDIPUS: What—give up now, with a clue like this?   1160
Fail to solve the mystery of my birth?
Not for all the world!
JOCASTA: Stop—in the name of god,
if you love your own life, call off this search!
My suffering is enough.

OEDIPUS: Courage!
1165   Even if my mother turns out to be a slave,
        and I a slave, three generations back,
        you would not seem common.
JOCASTA: Oh no,
        listen to me, I beg you, don't do this.
OEDIPUS: Listen to you? No more. I must know it all,
1170   must see the truth at last.
JOCASTA: No, please—
        for your sake—I want the best for you!
OEDIPUS: Your best is more than I can bear.
JOCASTA: You're doomed—
        may you never fathom who you are!
OEDIPUS: (*To a servant.*) Hurry, fetch me the herdsman, now!
1175   Leave her to glory in her royal birth.
JOCASTA: Aieeeeee—
                    man of agony—
        that is the only name I have for you,
        that, no other—ever, ever, ever!

(*Flinging through the palace doors. A long, tense silence follows.*)

LEADER: Where's she gone, Oedipus?
1180   Rushing off, such wild grief . . .
        I'm afraid that from this silence
        something monstrous may come bursting forth.
OEDIPUS: Let it burst! Whatever will, whatever must!
        I must know my birth, no matter how common
1185   it may be—I must see my origins face-to-face.
        She perhaps, she with her woman's pride
        may well be mortified by my birth,
        but I, I count myself the son of Chance,
        the great goddess, giver of all good things—
1190   I'll never see myself disgraced. She is my mother!
        And the moons have marked me out, my blood-brothers,
        one moon on the wane, the next moon great with power.
        That is my blood, my nature—I will never betray it,
        never fail to search and learn my birth!
1195 CHORUS: Yes—if I am a true prophet
            if I can grasp the truth,
            by the boundless skies of Olympus,
            at the full moon of tomorrow, Mount Cithaeron
            you will know how Oedipus glories in you—
1200   you, his birthplace, nurse, his mountain-mother!
        And we will sing you, dancing out your praise—
        you lift our monarch's heart!
            Apollo, Apollo, god of the wild cry
                may our dancing please you!
                            Oedipus—
1205   son, dear child, who bore you?
        Who of the nymphs who seem to live forever
        mated with Pan, the mountain-striding Father?
        Who was your mother? who, some bride of Apollo
        the god who loves the pastures spreading toward the sun?
1210   Or was it Hermes, king of the lightning ridges?
        Or Dionysus, lord of frenzy, lord of the barren peaks—
        did he seize you in his hands, dearest of all his lucky
            finds?—
            found by the nymphs, their warm eyes dancing, gift
        to the lord who loves them dancing out his joy!

(OEDIPUS *strains to see a figure coming from the distance. Attended by*
palace GUARDS, *an old* SHEPHERD *enters slowly, reluctant to approach*
the king.)

OEDIPUS: I never met the man, my friends . . . still,   1215
        if I had to guess, I'd say that's the shepherd,
        the very one we've looked for all along.
        Brothers in old age, two of a kind,
        he and our guest here. At any rate
        the ones who bring him in are my own men,   1220
        I recognize them.

(*Turning to the* LEADER.)

                But you know more than I,
        you should, you've seen the man before.
LEADER: I know him, definitely. One of Laius' men,
        a trusty shepherd, if there ever was one.
OEDIPUS: You, I ask you first, stranger,   1225
        you from Corinth—is this the one you mean?
MESSENGER: You're looking at him. He's your man.
OEDIPUS: (*To the* SHEPHERD.) You, old man, come over here—
        look at me. Answer all my questions.
        Did you ever serve King Laius?   1230
SHEPHERD: So I did . . .
        a slave, not bought on the block though,
        born and reared in the palace.
OEDIPUS: Your duties, your kind of work?
SHEPHERD: Herding the flocks, the better part of my life.
OEDIPUS: Where, mostly? Where did you do your grazing?   1235
SHEPHERD: Well,
        Cithaeron sometimes, or the foothills round about.
OEDIPUS: This man—you know him? ever see him there?
SHEPHERD: (*Confused, glancing from the* MESSENGER *to the king.*)
        Doing what?—what man do you mean?
OEDIPUS: (*Pointing to the* MESSENGER.) This one here—ever
        have dealings with him?
SHEPHERD: Not so I could say, but give me a chance,   1240
        my memory's bad . . .
MESSENGER: No wonder he doesn't know me, master.
        But let me refresh his memory for him.
        I'm sure he recalls old times we had
        on the slopes of Mount Cithaeron;   1245
        he and I, grazing our flocks, he with two
        and I with one—we both struck up together,
        three whole seasons, six months at a stretch
        from spring to the rising of Arcturus in the fall,
        then with winter coming on I'd drive my herds   1250
        to my own pens, and back he'd go with his
        to Laius' folds.

(*To the* SHEPHERD.)

                Now that's how it was,
        wasn't it—yes or no?
SHEPHERD: Yes, I suppose . . .
        it's all so long ago.
MESSENGER: Come, tell me,
        you gave me a child back then, a boy, remember?   1255
        A little fellow to rear, my very own.
SHEPHERD: What? Why rake up that again?

MESSENGER: Look, here he is, my fine old friend—
    the same man who was just a baby then.
1260 SHEPHERD: Damn you, shut your mouth—quiet!
OEDIPUS: Don't lash out at him, old man—
    you need lashing more than he does.
SHEPHERD: Why,
    master, majesty—what have I done wrong?
OEDIPUS: You won't answer his question about the boy.
1265 SHEPHERD: He's talking nonsense, wasting his breath.
OEDIPUS: So, you won't talk willingly—
    then you'll talk with pain.

(The GUARDS *seize the* SHEPHERD.*)*

SHEPHERD: No, dear god, don't torture an old man!
OEDIPUS: Twist his arms back, quickly!
SHEPHERD: God help us, why?—
1270   what more do you need to know?
OEDIPUS: Did you give him that child? He's asking.
SHEPHERD: I did . . . I wish to god I'd died that day.
OEDIPUS: You've got your wish if you don't tell the truth.
SHEPHERD: The more I tell, the worse the death I'll die.
1275 OEDIPUS: Our friend here wants to stretch things out,
    does he?

(Motioning to his men for torture.)

SHEPHERD: No, no, I gave it to him—I just said so.
OEDIPUS: Where did you get it? Your house? Someone else's?
SHEPHERD: It wasn't mine, no, I got it from . . . someone.
OEDIPUS: Which one of them?

(Looking at the citizens.)

                    Whose house?
SHEPHERD: No—
1280   god's sake, master, no more questions!
OEDIPUS: You're a dead man if I have to ask again.
SHEPHERD: Then—the child came from the house . . .
    of Laius.
OEDIPUS: A slave? or born of his own blood?
SHEPHERD: Oh no,
1285   I'm right at the edge, the horrible truth—I've got to say it!
OEDIPUS: And I'm at the edge of hearing horrors, yes, but I
    must hear!
SHEPHERD: All right! His son, they said it was—his son!
    But the one inside, your wife,
    she'd tell it best.
OEDIPUS: My wife—
1290   *she* gave it to you?
SHEPHERD: Yes, yes, my king.
OEDIPUS: Why, what for?
SHEPHERD: To kill it.
OEDIPUS: Her own child,
1295   how could she?
SHEPHERD: She was afraid—
    frightening prophecies.
OEDIPUS: What?
SHEPHERD: They said—
    he'd kill his parents.
1300 OEDIPUS: But you gave him to this old man—why?

SHEPHERD: I pitied the little baby, master,
    hoped he'd take him off to his own country,
    far away, but he saved him for this, this fate.
    If you are the man he says you are, believe me,
    you were born for pain.   1305
OEDIPUS: O god—
    all come true, all burst to light!
    O light—now let me look my last on you!
    I stand revealed at last—
    cursed in my birth, cursed in marriage,
    cursed in the lives I cut down with these hands!   1310

(Rushing through the doors with a great cry. The Corinthian MESSEN-
GER, *the* SHEPHERD, *and* ATTENDANTS *exit slowly to the side.)*

CHORUS: O the generations of men
    the dying generations—adding the total
    of all your lives I find they come to nothing . . .
             does there exist, is there a man on earth
    who seizes more joy than just a dream, a vision?   1315
    And the vision no sooner dawns than dies
    blazing into oblivion.

    You are my great example, you, your life
    your destiny, Oedipus, man of misery—
    I count no man blest.   1320

             You outranged all men!
        Bending your bow to the breaking-point
    you captured priceless glory, O dear god,
    and the Sphinx came crashing down,
             the virgin, claws hooked
    like a bird of omen singing, shrieking death—   1325
    like a fortress reared in the face of death
    you rose and saved our land.

    From that day on we called you king
    we crowned you with honors, Oedipus, towering over all—
    mighty king of the seven gates of Thebes.   1330
    But now to hear your story—is there a man more agonized?
    More wed to pain and frenzy? Not a man on earth,
    the joy of your life ground down to nothing
    O Oedipus, name for the ages—
        one and the same wide harbor served you   1335
                  son and father both
    son and father came to rest in the same bridal chamber.
    How, how could the furrows your father plowed
    bear you, your agony, harrowing on
    in silence O so long?   1340

             But now for all your power
    Time, all-seeing Time has dragged you to the light,
    judged your marriage monstrous from the start—
    the son and the father tangling, both one—
    O child of Laius, would to god
        I'd never seen you, never never!   1345
        Now I weep like a man who wails the dead
    and the dirge comes pouring forth with all my heart!
    I tell you the truth, you gave me life
    my breath leapt up in you
    and now you bring down night upon my eyes.   1350

(Enter a MESSENGER *from the palace.)*

MESSENGER: Men of Thebes, always first in honor,
what horrors you will hear, what you will see,
what a heavy weight of sorrow you will shoulder . . .
if you are true to your birth, if you still have
1355 some feeling for the royal house of Thebes.
I tell you neither the waters of the Danube
nor the Nile can wash this palace clean.
Such things it hides, it soon will bring to light—
terrible things, and none done blindly now,
1360 all done with a will. The pains
we inflict upon ourselves hurt most of all.
LEADER: God knows we have pains enough already.
What can you add to them?
MESSENGER: The queen is dead.
LEADER: Poor lady—how?
1365 MESSENGER: By her own hand. But you are spared the worst,
you never had to watch . . . I saw it all,
and with all the memory that's in me
you will learn what that poor woman suffered.

Once she'd broken in through the gates,
1370 dashing past us, frantic, whipped to fury,
ripping her hair out with both hands—
straight to her rooms she rushed, flinging herself
across the bridal-bed, doors slamming behind her—
once inside, she wailed for Laius, dead so long,
1375 remembering how she bore his child long ago,
the life that rose up to destroy him, leaving
its mother to mother living creatures
with the very son she'd borne.
Oh how she wept, mourning the marriage-bed
1380 where she let loose that double brood—monsters—
husband by her husband, children by her child.
                                        And then—
but how she died is more than I can say. Suddenly
Oedipus burst in, screaming, he stunned us so
we couldn't watch her agony to the end,
1385 our eyes were fixed on him. Circling
like a maddened beast, stalking, here, there,
crying out to us—
                    Give him a sword! His wife,
no wife, his mother, where can he find the mother earth
that cropped two crops at once, himself and all his
children?
1390 He was raging—one of the dark powers pointing the way,
none of us mortals crowding around him, no,
with a great shattering cry—someone, something leading
him on—
he hurled at the twin doors and bending the bolts back
out of their sockets, crashed through the chamber.
1395 And there we saw the woman hanging by the neck,
cradled high in a woven noose, spinning,
swinging back and forth. And when he saw her,
giving a low, wrenching sob that broke our hearts,
slipping the halter from her throat, he eased her down,
1400 in a slow embrace he laid her down, poor thing . . .
then, what came next, what horror we beheld!

He rips off her brooches, the long gold pins
holding her robes—and lifting them high,
looking straight up into the points,

he digs them down the sockets of his eyes, crying, "You, 1405
you'll see no more the pain I suffered, all the pain I caused!
Too long you looked on the ones you never should have seen,
blind to the ones you longed to see, to know! Blind
from this hour on! Blind in the darkness—blind!"
His voice like a dirge, rising, over and over 1410
raising the pins, raking them down his eyes.
And at each stroke blood spurts from the roots,
splashing his beard, a swirl of it, nerves and clots—
black hail of blood pulsing, gushing down.

These are the griefs that burst upon them both, 1415
coupling man and woman. The joy they had so lately,
the fortune of their old ancestral house
was deep joy indeed. Now, in this one day,
wailing, madness and doom, death, disgrace,
all the griefs in the world that you can name, 1420
all are theirs forever.
LEADER: Oh poor man, the misery—
has he any rest from pain now?

(A voice within, in torment.)

MESSENGER: He's shouting,
"Loose the bolts, someone, show me to all of Thebes!
My father's murderer, my mother's—"
No, I can't repeat it, it's unholy. 1425
Now he'll tear himself from his native earth,
not linger, curse the house with his own curse.
But he needs strength, and a guide to lead him on.
This is sickness more than he can bear.

(The palace doors open.)

                                        Look,
he'll show you himself. The great doors are opening— 1430
you are about to see a sight, a horror
even his mortal enemy would pity.

(Enter OEDIPUS, blinded, led by a boy. He stands at the palace steps,
as if surveying his people once again.)

CHORUS: Oh, the terror—
the suffering, for all the world to see,
the worst terror that ever met my eyes.
What madness swept over you? What god, 1435
what dark power leapt beyond all bounds,
beyond belief, to crush your wretched life?—
godforsaken, cursed by the gods!
I pity you but I can't bear to look.
I've much to ask, so much to learn, 1440
so much fascinates my eyes,
but you . . . I shudder at the sight.
OEDIPUS: Oh, Ohh—
the agony! I am agony—
where am I going? where on earth?
                    where does all this agony hurl me? 1445
where's my voice?—
                    winging, swept away on a dark tide—
My destiny, my dark power, what a leap you made!
CHORUS: To the depths of terror, too dark to hear, to see.

1450 OEDIPUS: Dark, horror of darkness
           my darkness, drowning, swirling around me
           crashing wave on wave—unspeakable, irresistible
                    headwind, fatal harbor! Oh again,
           the misery, all at once, over and over
1455   the stabbing daggers, stab of memory
       raking me insane.
       CHORUS: No wonder you suffer
           twice over, the pain of your wounds,
           the lasting grief of pain.
       OEDIPUS: Dear friend, still here?
           Standing by me, still with a care for me,
1460   the blind man? Such compassion,
                    loyal to the last. Oh it's you,
           I know you're here, dark as it is
           I'd know you anywhere, your voice—
       it's yours, clearly yours.
       CHORUS: Dreadful, what you've done . . .
1465   how could you bear it, gouging out your eyes?
           What superhuman power drove you on?
       OEDIPUS: Apollo, friends, Apollo—
           he ordained my agonies—these, my pains on pains!
           But the hand that struck my eyes was mine,
1470   mine alone—no one else—
                    I did it all myself!
           What good were eyes to me?
           Nothing I could see could bring me joy.
       CHORUS: No, no, exactly as you say.
       OEDIPUS: What can I ever see?
1475   What love, what call of the heart
           can touch my ears with joy? Nothing, friends.
           Take me away, far, far from Thebes,
           quickly, cast me away, my friends—
       this great murderous ruin, this man cursed to heaven,
1480   the man the deathless gods hate most of all!
       CHORUS: Pitiful, you suffer so, you understand so much . . .
           I wish you had never known.
       OEDIPUS: Die, die—
           whoever he was that day in the wilds
           who cut my ankles free of the ruthless pins,
1485   he pulled me clear of death, he saved my life
           for this, this kindness—
                    Curse him, kill him!
           If I'd died then, I'd never have dragged myself,
           my loved ones through such hell.
       CHORUS: Oh if only . . . would to god.
1490   OEDIPUS: I'd never have come to
       this,
           my father's murderer—never been branded
           mother's husband, all men see me now! Now,
           loathed by the gods, son of the mother I defiled
           coupling in my father's bed, spawning lives in
           the loins
1495   that spawned my wretched life. What grief can crown
           this grief?
                    It's mine alone, my destiny—I am Oedipus!
       CHORUS: How can I say you've chosen for the best?
           Better to die than be alive and blind.
       OEDIPUS: What I did was best—don't lecture me,
1500   no more advice. I, with *my* eyes,
           how could I look my father in the eyes

when I go down to death? Or mother, so abused . . .
I have done such things to the two of them,
crimes too huge for hanging.
                    Worse yet,
the sight of my children, born as they were born,   1505
how could I long to look into their eyes?
No, not with these eyes of mine, never.
Not this city either, her high towers,
the sacred glittering images of her gods—
I am misery! I, her best son, reared   1510
as no other son of Thebes was ever reared,
I've stripped myself, I gave the command myself.
All men must cast away the great blasphemer,
the curse now brought to light by the gods,
the son of Laius—I, my father's son!   1515

Now I've exposed my guilt, horrendous guilt,
could I train a level glance on you, my countrymen?
Impossible! No, if I could just block off my ears,
the springs of hearing, I would stop at nothing—
I'd wall up my loathsome body like a prison,   1520
blind to the sound of life, not just the sight.
Oblivion—what a blessing . . .
for the mind to dwell a world away from pain.

O Cithaeron, why did you give me shelter?
Why didn't you take me, crush my life out on the spot?   1525
I'd never have revealed my birth to all mankind.

O Polybus, Corinth, the old house of my fathers,
so I believed—what a handsome prince you raised—
under the skin, what sickness to the core.
Look at me! Born of outrage, outrage to the core.   1530
O triple roads—it all comes back, the secret,
dark ravine, and the oaks closing in
where the three roads join . . .
You drank my father's blood, my own blood
spilled by my own hands—you still remember me?   1535
What things you saw me do? Then I came here
and did them all once more!
                    Marriages! O marriage,
you gave me birth, and once you brought me into the
    world
you brought my sperm rising back, springing to light
fathers, brothers, sons—one murderous breed—   1540
brides, wives, mothers. The blackest things
a man can do, I have done them all!
                    No more—
it's wrong to name what's wrong to do. Quickly,
for the love of god, hide me somewhere,
kill me, hurl me into the sea   1545
where you can never look on me again.

(Beckoning to the CHORUS *as they shrink away.)*

                              Closer,
it's all right. Touch the man of grief.
Do. Don't be afraid. My troubles are mine
and I am the only man alive who can sustain them.

(Enter CREON *from the palace, attended by palace* GUARDS.*)*

1550 LEADER: Put your requests to Creon. Here he is,
        just when we need him. He'll have a plan, he'll act.
        Now that he's the sole defense of the country
        in your place.
   OEDIPUS: Oh no, what can I say to him?
        How can I ever hope to win his trust?
1555   I wronged him so, just now, in every way.
        You must see that—I was so wrong, so wrong.
   CREON: I haven't come to mock you, Oedipus,
        or to criticize your former failings.

(Turning to the GUARDS.*)*

                              You there,
        have you lost all respect for human feelings?
1560   At least revere the Sun, the holy fire
        that keeps us all alive. Never expose a thing
        of guilt and holy dread so great it appalls
        the earth, the rain from heaven, the light of day!
        Get him into the halls—quickly as you can.
1565   Piety demands no less. Kindred alone
        should see a kinsman's shame. This is obscene.
   OEDIPUS: Please, in god's name . . . you wipe my fears away,
        coming so generously to me, the worst of men.
        Do one thing more, for your sake, not mine.
1570 CREON: What do you want? Why so insistent?
   OEDIPUS: Drive me out of the land at once, far from sight,
        where I can never hear a human voice.
   CREON: I'd have done that already, I promise you.
        First I wanted the god to clarify my duties.
1575 OEDIPUS: The god? His command was clear, every word:
        death for the father-killer, the curse—
        he said destroy me!
   CREON: So he did. Still, in such a crisis
        it's better to ask precisely what to do.
   OEDIPUS: So miserable—
1580   you would consult the god about a man like me?
   CREON: By all means. And this time, I assume,
        even you will obey the god's decrees.
   OEDIPUS: I will,
        I will. And you, I command you—I beg you . . .
        the woman inside, bury her as you see fit.
1585   It's the only decent thing,
        to give your own the last rites. As for me,
        never condemn the city of my fathers
        to house my body, not while I'm alive, no,
        let me live on the mountains, on Cithaeron,
1590   my favorite haunt, I have made it famous.
        Mother and father marked out that rock
        to be my everlasting tomb—buried alive.
        Let me die there, where they tried to kill me.

        Oh but this I know: no sickness can destroy me,
1595   nothing can. I would never have been saved
        from death—I have been saved
        for something great and terrible, something strange.
        Well let my destiny come and take me on its way!
        About my children, Creon, the boys at least,
1600   don't burden yourself. They're men,
        wherever they go, they'll find the means to live.
        But my two daughters, my poor helpless girls,

        clustering at our table, never without me
        hovering near them . . . whatever I touched,
        they always had their share. Take care of them,   1605
        I beg you. Wait, better—permit me, would you?
        Just to touch them with my hands and take
        our fill of tears. Please . . . my king.
        Grant it, with all your noble heart.
        If I could hold them, just once, I'd think   1610
        I had them with me, like the early days
        when I could see their eyes.

*(*ANTIGONE *and* ISMENE, *two small children, are led in from the palace by a nurse.*)*

                              What's that?
        O god! Do I really hear you sobbing?—
        my two children. Creon, you've pitied me?
        Sent me my darling girls, my own flesh and blood!   1615
        Am I right?
   CREON: Yes, it's my doing.
        I know the joy they gave you all these years,
        the joy you must feel now.
   OEDIPUS: Bless you, Creon!
        May god watch over you for this kindness,
        better than he ever guarded me.   1620

                              Children, where are you?
        Here, come quickly—

(Groping for ANTIGONE *and* ISMENE, *who approach their father cautiously, then embrace him.*)*

                              Come to these hands of mine,
        your brother's hands, your own father's hands
        that served his once bright eyes so well—
        that made them blind. Seeing nothing, children,
        knowing nothing, I became your father,   1625
        I fathered you in the soil that gave me life.

        How I weep for you—I cannot see you now . . .
        just thinking of all your days to come, the bitterness,
        the life that rough mankind will thrust upon you.
        Where are the public gatherings you can join,   1630
        the banquets of the clans? Home you'll come,
        in tears, cut off from the sight of it all,
        the brilliant rites unfinished.
        And when you reach perfection, ripe for marriage,
        who will he be, my dear ones? Risking all   1635
        to shoulder the curse that weighs down my parents,
        yes and you too—that wounds us all together.
        What more misery could you want?
        Your father killed his father, sowed his mother,
        one, one and the selfsame womb sprang you—   1640
        he cropped the very roots of his existence.

        Such disgrace, and you must bear it all!
        Who will marry you then? Not a man on earth.
        Your doom is clear: you'll wither away to nothing,
        single, without a child.   1645

(Turning to CREON.*)*

                              Oh Creon,
        you are the only father they have now . . .

we who brought them into the world
are gone, both gone at a stroke—
Don't let them go begging, abandoned,
1650   women without men. Your own flesh and blood!
Never bring them down to the level of my pains.
Pity them. Look at them, so young, so vulnerable,
shorn of everything—you're their only hope.
Promise me, noble Creon, touch my hand!

(Reaching toward CREON, who draws back.)

1655   You, little ones, if you were old enough
to understand, there is much I'd tell you.
Now, as it is, I'd have you say a prayer.
Pray for life, my children,
live where you are free to grow and season.
1660   Pray god you find a better life than mine,
the father who begot you.
CREON: Enough.
You've wept enough. Into the palace now.
OEDIPUS: I must, but I find it very hard.
CREON: Time is the great healer, you will see.
1665   OEDIPUS: I am going—you know on what condition?
CREON: Tell me. I'm listening.
OEDIPUS: Drive me out of Thebes, in exile.
CREON: Not I. Only the gods can give you that.
OEDIPUS: Surely the gods hate me so much—

CREON: You'll get your wish at once.   1670
OEDIPUS: You consent?
CREON: I try to say what I mean; it's my habit.
OEDIPUS: Then take me away. It's time.
CREON: Come along, let go of the children.
OEDIPUS: No—
don't take them away from me, not now! No no no!

(Clutching his daughters as the GUARDS wrench them loose and take
them through the palace doors.)

CREON: Still the king, the master of all things?   1675
No more: here your power ends.
None of your power follows you through life.

(Exit OEDIPUS and CREON to the palace. The CHORUS comes forward
to address the audience directly.)

CHORUS: People of Thebes, my countrymen, look on Oedipus.
He solved the famous riddle with his brilliance,
he rose to power, a man beyond all power.   1680
Who could behold his greatness without envy?
Now what a black sea of terror has overwhelmed him.
Now as we keep our watch and wait the final day,
count no man happy till he dies, free of pain at last.

(Exit in procession.)

EURIPIDES

Euripides (c. 484–406 BCE) was the youngest of the three tragic playwrights whose plays remain today. Although he first competed in the City Dionysia in 455 BCE, and won his first victory in 441 BCE, he won only four victories in his lifetime and left Athens about the year 408 BCE for the court of King Archileus of Macedon, where he died. We do not know why Euripides won so infrequently, but his tragedies are much more bitter and ironic than those of Aeschylus or Sophocles, brilliantly unfolding the selfish capriciousness of gods and heroes alike. Of the roughly ninety plays Euripides is thought to have written, eighteen survive, and most of these were written and produced during the war with Sparta: *Alcestis, Medea, Heracleidae, Hippolytus, Cyclops* (a satyr play), *Heracles, Iphigeneia in Tauris, Helen, Hecuba, Andromache, The Trojan Women, Ion, The Suppliant Women, Orestes, Electra, The Phoenician Women.* Three additional plays—*Iphigeneia at Aulis, The Bacchae,* and *Alcmaeon at Corinth* (now lost)—were written in Macedon and brought to Athens by the playwright's son Euripides the Younger. This trilogy, produced after Euripides' death, won him his final prize at the City Dionysia.

MEDEA

Although many Greek tragedies center on female characters, Euripides was famous in Athens for centering his tragedies so frequently on women. Euripides was hardly a feminist in any modern sense, yet more than his contemporaries, he used his tragic heroines to explore the relationship between gender and the other conceptual, political, social, and esthetic categories organizing Athenian life.

Like all roles in the Athenian theater, the role of Medea was played by a male actor; nonetheless, in many ways *Medea* illustrates Euripides' skeptical and ironic regard for conventional attitudes, and his tendency toward a more sensational form of tragic action. Like Shakespeare's *Hamlet, Medea* is a tragedy of revenge, in which Medea poisons her husband Jason's newly married wife and her father, Creon, and in the play's climactic moment executes her own children from her marriage with Jason. What sometimes seems most monstrous to modern readers and audiences is that Medea herself—in one of Euripides' most striking uses of the *machina*—flees Corinth alive at the end of the play, rising above the *skene* in a dragon-drawn chariot, draped in the bodies of her dead children, taunting and reviling the impotent Jason. That is, modern audiences sometimes feel that Medea herself should die at the play's close if *Medea* is to be a truly tragic drama, as though by dying Medea would be "punished" for her revenge in some appalling vision of tragic "justice." But Euripides seems uninterested in such a moralized version of tragedy. Indeed, as Aristotle implies in *Poetics,* tragedy is a deeply dialectical, contradictory way of representing human experience: tragedy arises from the unresolvable tension between pity and fear, from the relationship between the hero's actions (remembering that the tragic hero is neither a "paragon of virtue" nor inherently wicked) and their terrible, somehow fitting consequences. And while Aristotle praises Sophocles' *Oedipus the King* as the best-constructed tragedy, he also remarks that Euripides "is felt by the audience to be the most tragic, at least, of the poets." To grasp Euripides' sense of tragedy means placing Medea's execution of the children within the context of the action as a whole, an act that brings her history to bear in one exacting deed, an act like Oedipus' blistering interrogation of the ancient shepherd.

At the play's opening, Medea is an outcast, a foreign exile in Corinth, and the play repeatedly stresses Medea's otherness—she is an Eastern exotic, she has little respect for

Greek culture and its institutions, and she is a sorceress as well. Medea is consistently shown to be a figure of willful passion, brought into exile through her love for Jason. Falling in love with Jason when he went to Colchis in search of the Golden Fleece, Medea used her sorcery to help Jason gain the Fleece, betraying her father and killing her brother in the bargain. When the play opens, Jason has returned to Greece with Medea and their children; in Corinth, however, Jason decides to marry the daughter of King Creon. Creon, no doubt recognizing that Medea and her children will pose a constant threat to his own line of succession, has ruled that Medea and her children must again be sent into exile.

Yet as Medea suggests to the Chorus, the indignity that Jason has thrust upon her—being doubly exiled, from her country and from her marriage—is in an important sense merely an extension of the state of all women in Greek culture. For once women "buy a husband and take for our bodies / A master," they are exiled from their own homes, and from the mastery of their own lives. Inasmuch as women are represented as creatures of passion, they are "exiled" as well from the organizing principles of the Greek state: reason, the law, and legitimate society are identified in the play as the preserve of men. Euripides makes Jason the spokesman for these values. When Jason first confronts Medea, he takes pride in his talents as a speaker, listing his arguments in support of taking a new wife almost as though he were arguing in the courtroom or conducting a philosophical demonstration. But while Oedipus, for instance, uses the strategies of philosophic inquiry to discover the truth, Jason's arguments seem to conceal the truth—he is betraying Medea and their children, after all—behind a smokescreen of sophistic rhetoric. Having brought Medea into exile, Jason argues that she is fortunate merely to "inhabit a Greek land and understand our ways / How to live by law instead of the sweet will of force." Yet the law that Jason praises seems designed to enable him to act out his own "sweet will"—taking a second wife—while it prevents Medea from acting on hers. And the more Jason insists that he is acting reasonably, the more unreasonable his arguments become; he becomes increasingly irritable, and finally insulting: "you women have got into such a state of mind / That, if your life at night is good, you think you have / Everything." Euripides' treatment of Jason is typical of his tendency to present an ironic view of the heroes of Greek mythology. Here, in making Jason the representative of Greek values of reason, law, and justice, Euripides suggests the limits of those values. For the Chorus clearly sees Jason's "reason" as a self-indulgent pretense: "though you have made this speech of yours look well, / [. . .] / You have betrayed your wife and are acting badly."

As Medea comes to recognize, both Jason and the masculine laws of Corinth are willing to betray her, to call her fidelity and love merely irrational, to force her again into exile. Having poisoned Creon and his daughter, Medea first claims to kill the children in order that they not be slain "by another hand less kindly to them." But it is also clear that in killing the children, Medea revenges herself on Jason in the only way open to her; he has little regard for her love for him, but the children are his property, an extension of himself, of his identity. More importantly, the children are his successors, representing his continued presence in the world. For as Jason laments, Medea has contrived a punishment for him that no Greek woman would have dared: in leaving him childless, Medea transforms Jason into an exile like herself, prophesying that he will die "without distinction."

Medea's acts epitomize the ethical ambiguity that drives Greek tragedy. Agamemnon strides on the blood-red carpet, magisterially desecrating the honor of his family as he had once done in sacrificing Iphigeneia; Oedipus sentences the hidden criminal to exile, only to discover that he is the criminal he seeks. To force Jason into a childless exile, Medea commits the kind of crime that Jason has repeatedly drawn her to enact: she murders what she loves in order to insist on the priority and power of her love for him. As in other classical tragedies, the hero chooses to act in a way that is not only consistent with her past, but a self-conscious reenactment of it. The *peripeteia,* the reversal that defines the tragic action, seems in many ways to be a kind of restoration as well, revealing destructive consequences that have been latent in the action from the beginning.

It should be clear that while Euripides interrogates the relationship between reason and passion, culture and nature, the rational and the irrational, science and magic, *Medea* does not finally disrupt or overturn this relationship. Nor does the play finally question the way that Greek culture gendered these categories as masculine and feminine, expressing the conceptual and political hierarchies of its own making as the "natural" outgrowth of some essential gender difference. Euripides exposes the destructive tension lurking in Greek conceptions of gender, power, and identity, but the language of tragedy is not the language of revolution. For although tragedy frequently exposes the values of its world as contradictory and destructive, it also accepts those values as somehow inevitable, unavoidable. Medea flees Corinth and the abusive Jason, but only by destroying herself in the same way she destroys Jason; Medea triumphs over Jason, but only by destroying her family and becoming an exile yet again. The only alternative that *Medea* offers to the way that Medea—and, she argues, all women—is positioned as an outsider, an "exile" to the governing categories of Greek life, is a deeper, more permanent isolation.

MEDEA

Euripides

TRANSLATED BY REX WARNER

───── CHARACTERS ─────

MEDEA, *princess of Colchis*
and wife of
JASON, *son of Aeson,*
king of Iolcus
TWO CHILDREN *of Medea and*
Jason
CREON, *king of Corinth*

AEGEUS, *king of Athens*
NURSE *to Medea*
TUTOR *to Medea's children*
MESSENGER
CHORUS *of Corinthian women*
ATTENDANTS

SCENE: *In front of* MEDEA's *house in Corinth.*

Enter from the house Medea's NURSE.

NURSE: How I wish the Argo never had reached the land
  Of Colchis, skimming through the blue Symplegades,
  Nor ever had fallen in the glades of Pelion
  The smitten fir-tree to furnish oars for the hands
5 Of heroes who in Pelias' name attempted
  The Golden Fleece! For then my mistress Medea
  Would not have sailed for the towers of the land of Iolcus,
  Her heart on fire with passionate love for Jason;
  Nor would she have persuaded the daughters of Pelias
10 To kill their father, and now be living here
  In Corinth with her husband and children. She gave
  Pleasure to the people of her land of exile,
  And she herself helped Jason in every way.
  This is indeed the greatest salvation of all—
15 For the wife not to stand apart from the husband.
  But now there's hatred everywhere, Love is diseased.
  For, deserting his own children and my mistress,
  Jason has taken a royal wife to his bed,
  The daughter of the ruler of this land, Creon.
20 And poor Medea is slighted, and cries aloud on the
  Vows they made to each other, the right hands clasped
  In eternal promise. She calls upon the gods to witness
  What sort of return Jason has made to her love.
  She lies without food and gives herself up to suffering,
25 Wasting away every moment of the day in tears.
  So it has gone since she knew herself slighted by him.
  Not stirring an eye, not moving her face from the ground,
  No more than either a rock or surging sea water
  She listens when she is given friendly advice.
30 Except that sometimes she twists back her white neck and
  Moans to herself, calling out on her father's name,
  And her land, and her home betrayed when she came away
    with
  A man who now is determined to dishonor her.
  Poor creature, she has discovered by her sufferings
35 What it means to one not to have lost one's own country.
  She has turned from the children and does not like to see them.

─────

1 **Argo** Jason's ship on the expedition of the Argonauts, sent by
Pelias, king of Iolcus in Thessaly (Jason's uncle, who had usurped the
throne), to Colchis on the Black Sea. The Symplegades were clashing
rocks, one of the obstacles along the way. Pelion is a mountain in
Thessaly. Medea was a princess of Colchis who fell in love with Jason
and followed him back to Greece

I am afraid she may think of some dreadful thing,
For her heart is violent. She will never put up with
The treatment she is getting. I know and fear her
Lest she may sharpen a sword and thrust to the heart, 40
Stealing into the palace where the bed is made,
Or even kill the king and the new-wedded groom,
And thus bring a greater misfortune on herself.
She's a strange woman. I know it won't be easy
To make an enemy of her and come off best. 45
But here the children come. They have finished playing.
They have no thought at all of their mother's trouble.
Indeed it is not usual for the young to grieve.

(Enter from the right the slave who is the TUTOR *to Medea's two small*
children. The CHILDREN *follow him.)*

TUTOR: You old retainer of my mistress' household,
  Why are you standing here all alone in front of the 50
  Gates and moaning to yourself over your misfortune?
  Medea could not wish you to leave her alone.
NURSE: Old man, and guardian of the children of Jason,
  If one is a good servant, it's a terrible thing
  When one's master's luck is out; it goes to one's heart. 55
  So I myself have got into such a state of grief
  That a longing stole over me to come outside here
  And tell the earth and air of my mistress' sorrows.
TUTOR: Has the poor lady not yet given up her crying?
NURSE: Given up? She's at the start, not halfway through her 60
  tears.
TUTOR: Poor fool—if I may call my mistress such a name—
  How ignorant she is of trouble more to come.
NURSE: What do you mean, old man? You needn't fear to speak.
TUTOR: Nothing. I take back the words which I used just now.
NURSE: Don't, by your beard, hide this from me, your 65
  fellow-servant.
  If need be, I'll keep quiet about what you tell me.
TUTOR: I heard a person saying, while I myself seemed
  Not to be paying attention, when I was at the place
  Where the old draught-players sit, by the holy fountain,
  That Creon, ruler of the land, intends to drive 70
  These children and their mother in exile from Corinth.
  But whether what he said is really true or not
  I do not know. I pray that it may not be true.
NURSE: And will Jason put up with it that his children
  Should suffer so, though he's no friend to their mother? 75
TUTOR: Old ties give place to new ones. As for Jason, he
  No longer has a feeling for this house of ours.

NURSE: It's black indeed for us, when we add new to old
    Sorrows before even the present sky has cleared.
80 TUTOR: But you be silent, and keep all this to yourself.
    It is not the right time to tell our mistress of it.
NURSE: Do you hear, children, what a father he is to you?
    I wish he were dead—but no, he is still my master.
    Yet certainly he has proved unkind to his dear ones.
85 TUTOR: What's strange in that? Have you only just
        discovered
    That everyone loves himself more than his neighbor?
    Some have good reason, others get something out of it.
    So Jason neglects his children for the new bride.
NURSE: Go indoors, children. That will be the best thing.
90   And you, keep them to themselves as much as possible.
    Don't bring them near their mother in her angry mood.
    For I've seen her already blazing her eyes at them
    As though she meant some mischief and I am sure that
    She'll not stop raging until she has struck at someone.
95   May it be an enemy and not a friend she hurts!

(MEDEA is heard inside the house.)

MEDIA: Ah, wretch! Ah, lost in my sufferings,
    I wish, I wish I might die.
NURSE: What did I say, dear children? Your mother
    Frets her heart and frets it to anger.
100   Run away quickly into the house.
    And keep well out of her sight.
    Don't go anywhere near, but be careful
    Of the wildness and bitter nature
    Of that proud mind.
105   Go now! Run quickly indoors.
    It is clear that she soon will put lightning
    In that cloud of her cries that is rising
    With a passion increasing. O, what will she do,
    Proud-hearted and not to be checked on her course,
110   A soul bitten into with wrong?

(The TUTOR takes the CHILDREN into the house.)

MEDEA: Ah, I have suffered
    What should be wept for bitterly. I hate you,
    Children of a hateful mother. I curse you
    And your father. Let the whole house crash.
115 NURSE: Ah, I pity you, you poor creature.
    How can your children share in their father's
    Wickedness? Why do you hate them? Oh children,
    How much I fear that something may happen!
    Great people's tempers are terrible, always
120   Having their own way, seldom checked.
    Dangerous they shift from mood to mood.
    How much better to have been accustomed
    To live on equal terms with one's neighbors.
    I would like to be safe and grow old in a
125   Humble way. What is moderate sounds best,
    Also in practice *is* best for everyone.
    Greatness brings no profit to people.
    God indeed, when in anger, brings
    Greater ruin to great men's houses.

(Enter, on the right, a CHORUS of Corinthian women. They have come
to inquire about MEDEA and to attempt to console her.)

CHORUS: I heard the voice, I heard the cry   130
    Of Colchis' wretched daughter.
    Tell me, mother, is she not yet
    At rest? Within the double gates
    Of the court I heard her cry. I am sorry
    For the sorrow of this home. O, say, what has happened?   135
NURSE: There is no home. It's over and done with.
    Her husband holds fast to his royal wedding,
    While she, my mistress, cries out her eyes
    There in her room, and takes no warmth from
    Any word of any friend.   140
MEDEA: O, I wish
    That lightning from heaven would split my head open.
    Oh, what use have I now for life?
    I would find my release in death
    And leave hateful existence behind me.   145
CHORUS: O God and Earth and Heaven!
    Did you hear what a cry was that
    Which the sad wife sings?
    Poor foolish one, why should you long.
    For that appalling rest?   150
    The final end of death comes fast.
    No need to pray for that.
    Suppose your man gives honor
    To another woman's bed.
    It often happens. Don't be hurt.   155
    God will be your friend in this.
    You must not waste away
    Grieving too much for him who shared your bed.
MEDEA: Great Themis, lady Artemis, behold
    The things I suffer, though I made him promise,   160
    My hateful husband. I pray that I may see him,
    Him and his bride and all their palace shattered
    For the wrong they dare to do me without cause.
    Oh, my father! Oh, my country! In what dishonor
    I left you, killing my own brother for it.   165
NURSE: Do you hear what she says, and how she cries
    On Themis, the goddess of Promises, and on Zeus,
    Whom we believe to be the Keeper of Oaths?
    Of this I am sure, that no small thing
    Will appease my mistress' anger.   170
CHORUS: Will she come into our presence?
    Will she listen when we are speaking
    To the words we say?
    I wish she might relax her rage
    And temper of her heart.   175
    My willingness to help will never
    Be wanting to my friends.
    But go inside and bring her
    Out of the house to us,
    And speak kindly to her: hurry,   180
    Before she wrongs her own.
    This passion of hers moves to something great.
NURSE: I will, but I doubt if I'll manage
    To win my mistress over.

---

159 **Themis . . . Artemis** goddesses: Themis was the goddess of
justice; the virgin Artemis would be sensitive to the plight of
women   165 **brother** during the escape from Colchis, to delay
her father's pursuit

185   But still I'll attempt it to please you.
      Such a look she will flash on her servants
      If any comes near with a message.
      Like a lioness guarding her cubs,
      It is right, I think, to consider
190   Both stupid and lacking in foresight
      Those poets of old who wrote songs
      For revels and dinners and banquets.
      Pleasant sounds for men living at ease;
      But none of them all has discovered
195   How to put to an end with their singing
      Or musical instruments grief,
      Bitter grief, from which death and disaster
      Cheat the hopes of a house. Yet how good
      If music could cure men of this! But why raise
200   To no purpose the voice at a banquet? For *there* is
      Already abundance of pleasure for men
      With a joy of its own.

(*The* NURSE *goes into the house.*)

CHORUS: I heard a shriek that is laden with sorrow,
        Shrilling out her hard grief she cries out
205   Upon him who betrayed both her bed and her marriage.
        Wronged, she calls on the gods,
        On the justice of Zeus, the oath sworn,
        Which brought her away
        To the opposite shore of the Greeks
210   Through the gloomy salt straits to the gateway
        Of the salty unlimited sea.

(MEDEA, *attended by servants, comes out of the house.*)

MEDEA: Women of Corinth, I have come outside to you
       Lest you should be indignant with me; for I know
       That many people are overproud, some when alone,
215   And others when in company. And those who live
       Quietly, as I do, get a bad reputation.
       For a just judgment is not evident in the eyes
       When a man at first sight hates another, before
       Learning his character, being in no way injured;
220   And a foreigner especially must adapt himself.
       I'd not approve of even a fellow-countryman
       Who by pride and want of manners offends his neighbors.
       But on me this thing has fallen so unexpectedly.
       It has broken my heart. I am finished. I let go
225   All my life's joy. My friends, I only want to die.
       It was everything to me to think well of one man,
       And he, my own husband, has turned out wholly vile.
       Of all things which are living and can form a judgment
       We women are the most unfortunate creatures.
230   Firstly, with an excess of wealth it is required
       For us to buy a husband and take for our bodies
       A master; for not to take one is even worse.
       And now the question is serious whether we take
       A good or bad one; for there is no easy escape
235   For a woman, nor can she say no to her marriage.
       She arrives among new modes of behavior and manners.
       And needs prophetic power, unless she has learned at home,
       How best to manage him who shares the bed with her.
       And if we work out all this well and carefully.

       And the husband lives with us and lightly bears his yoke.   240
       Then life is enviable. If not, I'd rather die.
       A man, when he's tired of the company in his home,
       Goes out of the house and puts an end to his boredom
       And turns to a friend or companion of his own age.
       But we are forced to keep our eyes on one alone.   245
       What they say of us is that we have a peaceful time
       Living at home, while they do the fighting in war.
       How wrong they are! I would very much rather stand
       Three times in the front of battle than bear one child.
       Yet what applies to me does not apply to you.   250
       You have a country. Your family home is here.
       You enjoy life and the company of your friends.
       But I am deserted, a refugee, thought nothing of
       By my husband—something he won in a foreign land.
       I have no mother or brother, nor any relation   255
       With whom I can take refuge in this sea of woe.
       This much then is the service I would beg from you:
       If I can find the means or devise any scheme
       To pay my husband back for what he has done to me—
       Him and his father-in-law and the girl who married him—   260
       Just to keep silent. For in other ways a woman
       Is full of fear, defenseless, dreads the sight of cold
       Steel; but, when once she is wronged in the matter of love,
       No other soul can hold so many thoughts of blood.
CHORUS: This I will promise. You are in the right, Medea,   265
        In paying your husband back. I am not surprised at you
        For being sad.
                    But look! I see our King Creon
        Approaching. He will tell us of some new plan.

(*Enter, from the right,* CREON, *with attendants.*)

CREON: You, with that angry look, so set against your husband.
       Medea, I order you to leave my territories   270
       An exile, and take along with you your two children,
       And not to waste time doing it. It is my decree,
       And I will see it done. I will not return home
       Until you are cast from the boundaries of my land.
MEDEA: Oh, this is the end for me. I am utterly lost.   275
       Now I am in the full force of the storm of hate
       And have no harbor from ruin to reach easily.
       Yet still, in spite of it all, I'll ask the question:
       What is your reason, Creon, for banishing me?
CREON: I am afraid of you—why should I dissemble it?—   280
       Afraid that you may injure my daughter mortally.
       Many things accumulate to support my feeling.
       You are a clever woman, versed in evil arts.
       And are angry at having lost your husband's love.
       I hear that you are threatening, so they tell me,   285
       To do something against my daughter and Jason
       And me, too. I shall take my precautions first.
       I tell you, I prefer to earn your hatred now
       Than to be soft-hearted and afterward regret it.
MEDEA: This is not the first time, Creon. Often previously   290
       Through being considered clever I have suffered much.
       A person of sense ought never to have his children
       Brought up to be more clever than the average.
       For, apart from cleverness bringing them no profit,
       It will make them objects of envy and ill-will.   295

If you put new ideas before the eyes of fools
They'll think you foolish and worthless into the bargain;
And if you are thought superior to those who have
Some reputation for learning, you will become hated.
300 I have some knowledge myself of how this happens;
For being clever, I find that some will envy me,
Others object to me. Yet all my cleverness
Is not so much.
                    Well, then, are you frightened, Creon,
That I should harm you? There is no need. It is not
305 My way to transgress the authority of a king.
How have you injured me? You gave your daughter away
To the man you wanted. Oh, certainly I hate
My husband, but you, I think, have acted wisely;
Nor do I grudge it you that your affairs go well.
310 May the marriage be a lucky one! Only let me
Live in this land. For even though I have been wronged,
I will not raise my voice, but submit to my betters.
CREON: What you say sounds gentle enough. Still in my heart
I greatly dread that you are plotting some evil,
315 And therefore I trust you even less than before.
A sharp-tempered woman, or, for that matter, a man,
Is easier to deal with than the clever type
Who holds her tongue. No. You must go. No need
    for more
Speeches. The thing is fixed. By no manner of means
320 Shall you, an enemy of mine, stay in my country.
MEDEA: I beg you. By your knees, by your new-wedded girl.
CREON: Your words are wasted. You will never persuade me.
MEDEA: Will you drive me out, and give no heed to my prayers?
CREON: I will, for I love my family more than you.
325 MEDEA: O my country! How bitterly now I remember you!
CREON: I love my country too—next after my children.
MEDEA: O what an evil to men is passionate love!
CREON: That would depend on the luck that goes along with it.
MEDEA: O God, do not forget who is the cause of this!
330 CREON: Go. It is no use. Spare me the pain of forcing you.
MEDEA: I'm spared no pain. I lack no pain to be spared me.
CREON: Then you'll be removed by force by one of my men.
MEDEA: No. Creon, not that! But do listen, I beg you.
CREON: Woman, you seem to want to create a disturbance.
335 MEDEA: I *will* go into exile. *This* is not what I beg for.
CREON: Why then this violence and clinging to my hand?
MEDEA: Allow me to remain here just for this one day,
So I may consider where to live in my exile,
And look for support for my children, since their father
340 Chooses to make no kind of provision for them.
Have pity on them! You have children of your own.
It is natural for you to look kindly on them.
For myself I do not mind if I go into exile.
It is the children being in trouble that I mind.
345 CREON: There is nothing tyrannical about my nature,
And by showing mercy I have often been the loser.
Even now I know that I am making a mistake.
All the same you shall have your will. But this I tell you,
That if the light of heaven tomorrow shall see you,
350 You and your children in the confines of my land,
You die. This word I have spoken is firmly fixed.
But now, if you must stay, stay for this day alone.
For in it you can do none of the things I fear.

(Exit CREON, with his attendants.)

CHORUS: Oh, unfortunate one! Oh, cruel!
    Where will you turn? Who will help you?   355
    What house or what land to preserve you
    From ill can you find?
    Medea, a god has thrown suffering
    Upon you in waves of despair.
MEDEA: Things have gone badly every way. No doubt of that   360
But not these things this far, and don't imagine so.
There are still trials to come for the new-wedded pair,
And for their relations pain that will mean something.
Do you think that I would ever have fawned on that man
Unless I had some end to gain or profit in it?   365
I would not even have spoken or touched him with my hands.
But he has got to such a pitch of foolishness
That, though he could have made nothing of all my plans
By exiling me, he has given me this one day
To stay here, and in this I will make dead bodies   370
Of three of my enemies—father, the girl, and my husband.
I have many ways of death which I might suit to them,
And do not know, friends, which one to take in hand;
Whether to set fire underneath their bridal mansion,
Or sharpen a sword and thrust it to the heart.   375
Stealing into the palace where the bed is made.
There is just one obstacle to this. If I am caught
Breaking into the house and scheming against it,
I shall die, and give my enemies cause for laughter.
It is best to go by the straight road, the one in which   380
I am most skilled, and make away with them by poison.
So be it then.
And now suppose them dead. What town will receive me?
What friend will offer me a refuge in his land,
Or the guaranty of his house and save my own life?   385
There is none. So I must wait a little time yet,
And if some sure defense should then appear for me,
In craft and silence I will set about this murder.
But if my fate should drive me on without help,
Even though death is certain, I will take the sword   390
Myself and kill, and steadfastly advance to crime.
It shall not be—I swear it by her, my mistress,
Whom most I honor and have chosen as partner,
Hecate, who dwells in the recesses of my hearth—
That any man shall be glad to have injured me.   395
Bitter I will make their marriage for them and mournful,
Bitter the alliance and the driving me out of the land.
Ah, come, Medea, in your plotting and scheming
Leave nothing untried of all those things which you know.
Go forward to the dreadful act. The test has come   400
For resolution. You see how you are treated. Never
Shall you be mocked by Jason's Corinthian wedding,
Whose father was noble, whose grandfather Helius.
You have the skill. What is more, you were born a woman,
And women, though most helpless in doing good deeds,   405
Are of every evil the cleverest of contrivers.
CHORUS: Flow backward to your sources, sacred rivers,
And let the world's great order be reversed.
It is the thoughts of *men* that are deceitful,

---

394 **Hecate** a goddess of the night   403 **Helius** sun god

410   *Their* pledges that are loose.
    Story shall now turn my condition to a fair one,
    Women are paid their due.
    No more shall evil-sounding fame be theirs.

    Cease now, you muses of the ancient singers,
415   To tell the tale of my unfaithfulness;
    For not on us did Phoebus, lord of music,
    Bestow the lyre's divine
    Power, for otherwise I should have sung an answer
    To the other sex. Long time
420   Has much to tell of us, and much of them.

    You sailed away from your father's home,
    With a heart on fire you passed
    The double rocks of the sea.
    And now in a foreign country
425   You have lost your rest in a widowed bed,
    And are driven forth, a refugee
    In dishonor from the land.

    Good faith has gone, and no more remains
    In great Greece a sense of shame.
430   It has flown away to the sky.
    No father's house for a haven
    Is at hand for you now, and another queen
    Of your bed has dispossessed you and
    Is mistress of your home.

(Enter JASON, *with attendants.)*

435 JASON: This is not the first occasion that I have noticed
    How hopeless it is to deal with a stubborn temper.
    For, with reasonable submission to our ruler's will,
    You might have lived in this land and kept your home.
    As it is you are going to be exiled for your loose speaking.
440   Not that I mind myself. You are free to continue
    Telling everyone that Jason is a worthless man.
    But as to your talk about the king, consider
    Yourself most lucky that exile is your punishment.
    I, for my part, have always tried to calm down
445   The anger of the king, and wished you to remain.
    But you will not give up your folly, continually
    Speaking ill of him, and so you are going to be banished.
    All the same, and in spite of your conduct, I'll not desert
    My friends, but have come to make some provision for you,
450   So that you and the children may not be penniless
    Or in need of anything in exile. Certainly
    Exile brings many troubles with it. And even
    If you hate me, I cannot think badly of you.
MEDEA: O coward in every way—that is what I call you,
455   With bitterest reproach for your lack of manliness,
    You have come, you, my worst enemy, have come to me!
    It is not an example of overconfidence
    Or of boldness thus to look your friends in the face,
    Friends you have injured—no, it is the worst of all
460   Human diseases, shamelessness. But you did well
    To come, for I can speak ill of you and lighten
    My heart, and you will suffer while you are listening.

    And first I will begin from what happened first.
    I saved your life, and every Greek knows I saved it.
    Who was a shipmate of yours aboard the Argo.   465
    When you were sent to control the bulls that breathed fire
    And yoke them, and when you would sow that deadly field.
    Also that snake, who encircled with his many folds
    The Golden Fleece and guarded it and never slept,
    I killed, and so gave you the safety of the light.   470
    And I myself betrayed my father and my home,
    And came with you to Pelias' land of Iolcus.
    And then, showing more willingness to help than wisdom,
    I killed him, Pelias, with a most dreadful death
    At his own daughters' hands, and took away your fear.   475
    This is how I behaved to you, you wretched man,
    And you forsook me, took another bride to bed,
    Though you had children; for, if that had not been,
    You would have had an excuse for another wedding.
    Faith in your word has gone. Indeed, I cannot tell   480
    Whether you think the gods whose names you swore by then
    Have ceased to rule and that new standards are set up,
    Since you must know you have broken your word to me.
    O my right hand, and the knees which you often clasped
    In supplication, how senselessly I am treated   485
    By this bad man, and how my hopes have missed their mark!
    Come, I will share my thoughts as though you were a
        friend—
    You! Can I think that you would ever treat me well?
    But I will do it, and these questions will make you
    Appear the baser. Where am I to go? To my father's?   490
    Him I betrayed and his land when I came with you.
    To Pelias' wretched daughters? What a fine welcome
    They would prepare for me who murdered their father!
    For this is my position—hated by my friends
    At home, I have, in kindness to you, made enemies   495
    Of others whom there was no need to have injured.
    And how happy among Greek women you have made me
    On your side for all this! A distinguished husband
    I have—for breaking promises. When in misery
    I am cast out of the land and go into exile,   500
    Quite without friends and all alone with my children,
    That will be a fine shame for the new-wedded groom,
    For his children to wander as beggars and she who saved
        him.
    O God, you have given to mortals a sure method
    Of telling the gold that is pure from the counterfeit;   505
    Why is there no mark engraved upon men's bodies,
    By which we could know the true ones from the false ones?
CHORUS: It is a strange form of anger, difficult to cure,
    When two friends turn upon each other in hatred.
JASON: As for me, it seems I must be no bad speaker.   510
    But, like a man who has a good grip of the tiller,
    Reef up his sail, and so run away from under
    This mouthing tempest, woman, of your bitter tongue.
    Since you insist on building up your kindness to me.
    My view is that Cypris was alone responsible   515
    Of men and gods for the preserving of my life.
    You are clever enough—but really I need not enter

---

416 **Phoebus** Apollo

515 **Cypris** Aphrodite, goddess of love

Into the story of how it was love's inescapable
Power that compelled you to keep my person safe.
520 On this I will not go into too much detail.
In so far as you helped me, you did well enough.
But on this question of saving me, I can prove
You have certainly got from me more than you gave.
Firstly, instead of living among barbarians,
525 You inhabit a Greek land and understand our ways,
How to live by law instead of the sweet will of force.
And all the Greeks considered you a clever woman.
You were honored for it; while, if you were living at
The ends of the earth, nobody would have heard of you.
530 For my part, rather than stores of gold in my house
Or power to sing even sweeter songs than Orpheus,
I'd choose the fate that made me a distinguished man.
There is my reply to your story of my labors.
Remember it was you who started the argument.
535 Next for your attack on my wedding with the princess:
Here I will prove that, first, it was a clever move,
Secondly, a wise one, and, finally, that I made it
In your best interests and the children's. Please keep calm.
When I arrived here from the land of Iolcus,
540 Involved, as I was, in every kind of difficulty,
What luckier chance could I have come across than this,
An exile to marry the daughter of the king?
It was not—the point that seems to upset you—that I
Grew tired of your bed and felt the need of a new bride;
545 Nor with any wish to outdo your number of children.
We have enough already. I am quite content.
But—this was the main reason—that we might live well,
And not be short of anything. I know that all
A man's friends leave him stone-cold if he becomes poor.
550 Also that I might bring my children up worthily
Of my position, and, by producing more of them
To be brothers of yours, we would draw the families
Together and all be happy. You need no children.
And it pays me to do good to those I have now
555 By having others. Do you think this a bad plan?
You wouldn't if the love question hadn't upset you.
But you women have got into such a state of mind
That, if your life at night is good, you think you have
Everything; but, if in that quarter things go wrong,
560 You will consider your best and truest interests
Most hateful. It would have been better far for men
To have got their children in some other way, and women
Not to have existed. Then life would have been good.
CHORUS: Jason, though you have made this speech of yours
look well,
565 Still I think, even though others do not agree,
You have betrayed your wife and are acting badly.
MEDEA: Surely in many ways I hold different views
From others, for I think that the plausible speaker
Who is a villain deserves the greatest punishment.
570 Confident in his tongue's power to adorn evil,
He stops at nothing. Yet he is not really wise.
As in your case. There is no need to put on the airs
Of a clever speaker, for one word will lay you flat.
If you were not a coward, you would not have married
575 Behind my back, but discussed it with me first.

JASON: And you, no doubt, would have furthered the proposal,
If I had told you of it, you who even now
Are incapable of controlling your bitter temper.
MEDEA: It was not that. No, you thought it was not respectable
As you got on in years to have a foreign wife. 580
JASON: Make sure of this: it was not because of a woman
I made the royal alliance in which I now live.
But, as I said before, I wished to preserve you
And breed a royal progeny to be brothers
To the children I have now, a sure defense to us. 585
MEDEA: Let me have no happy fortune that brings pain with it,
Or prosperity which is upsetting to the mind!
JASON: Change your ideas of what you want, and show more
sense.
Do not consider painful what is good for you.
Nor, when you are lucky, think yourself unfortunate. 590
MEDEA: You can insult me. You have somewhere to turn to.
But I shall go from this land into exile, friendless.
JASON: It was what you chose yourself. Don't blame others for it.
MEDEA: And how did I choose it? Did I betray my husband?
JASON: You called down wicked curses on the king's family. 595
MEDEA: A curse, that is what I am become to your house too.
JASON: I do not propose to go into all the rest of it;
But, if you wish for the children or for yourself
In exile to have some of my money to help you,
Say so, for I am prepared to give with open hand, 600
Or to provide you with introductions to my friends
Who will treat you well. You are a fool if you do not
Accept this. Cease your anger and you will profit.
MEDEA: I shall never accept the favors of friends of yours,
Nor take a thing from you, so you need not offer it. 605
There is no benefit in the gifts of a bad man.
JASON: Then, in any case, I call the gods to witness that
I wish to help you and the children in every way,
But you refuse what is good for you. Obstinately
You push away your friends. You are sure to suffer for it. 610
MEDEA: Go! No doubt you hanker for your virginal bride,
And are guilty of lingering too long out of her house.
Enjoy your wedding. But perhaps—with the help of God—
You will make the kind of marriage that you will regret.

(JASON goes out with his attendants.)

CHORUS: When love is in excess 615
It brings a man no honor
Nor any worthiness.
But if in moderation Cypris comes,
There is no other power at all so gracious.
O goddess, never on me let loose the unerring 620
Shaft of your bow in the poison of desire.

Let my heart be wise.
It is the gods' best gift.
On me let mighty Cypris
Inflict no wordy wars or restless anger 625
To urge my passion to a different love.
But with discernment may she guide women's weddings,
Honoring most what is peaceful in the bed.

O country and home,
Never, never may I be without you, 630

Living the hopeless life,
Hard to pass through and painful,
Most pitiable of all.
Let death first lay me low and death
635   Free me from this daylight,
There is no sorrow above
The loss of a native land.

I have seen it myself,
Do not tell of a secondhand story.
640   Neither city nor friend
Pitied you when you suffered
The worst of sufferings.
O let him die ungraced whose heart
Will not reward his friends,
645   Who cannot open an honest mind
No friend will he be of mine.

(*Enter* AEGEUS, *king of Athens, an old friend of* MEDEA.)

AEGEUS: Medea, greeting! This is the best introduction
Of which men know for conversation between friends.
MEDEA: Greeting to you too, Aegeus, son of King Pandion.
650   Where have you come from to visit this country's soil?
AEGEUS: I have just left the ancient oracle of Phoebus.
MEDEA: And why did you go to earth's prophetic center?
AEGEUS: I went to inquire how children might be born to me.
MEDEA: Is it so? Your life still up to this point is childless?
655   AEGEUS: Yes. By the fate of some power we have no children.
MEDEA: Have you a wife, or is there none to share your bed?
AEGEUS: There is. Yes, I am joined to my wife in marriage.
MEDEA: And what did Phoebus say to you about children?
AEGEUS: Words too wise for a mere man to guess their meaning.
660   MEDEA: It is proper for me to be told the god's reply?
AEGEUS: It is. For sure what is needed is cleverness.
MEDEA: Then what was his message? Tell me, if I may hear.
AEGEUS: I am not to loosen the hanging foot of the wineskin . . .
MEDEA: Until you have done something, or reached some country?
665   AEGEUS: Until I return again to my hearth and house.
MEDEA: And for what purpose have you journeyed to this land?
AEGEUS: There is a man called Pittheus, king of Troezen.
MEDEA: A son of Pelops, they say, a most righteous man.
AEGEUS: With him I wish to discuss the reply of the god.
670   MEDEA: Yes. He is wise and experienced in such matters.
AEGEUS: And to me also the dearest of all my spear-friends.
MEDEA: Well, I hope you have good luck, and achieve your will.
AEGEUS: But why this downcast eye of yours, and this pale cheek?
MEDEA: O Aegeus, my husband has been the worst of all to me.
675   AEGEUS: What do you mean? Say clearly what has caused this
grief.
MEDEA: Jason wrongs me, though I have never injured him.
AEGEUS: What has he done? Tell me about it in clearer words.
MEDEA: He has taken a wife to his house, supplanting me.
AEGEUS: Surely he would not dare to do a thing like that.
680   MEDEA: Be sure he has. Once dear, I now am slighted by him.
AEGEUS: Did he fall in love? Or is he tired of your love?
MEDEA: He was greatly in love, this traitor to his friends.
AEGEUS: Then let him go, if, as you say, he is so bad.
MEDEA: A passionate love—for an alliance with the king.
685   AEGEUS: And who gave him his wife? Tell me the rest of it.
MEDEA: It was Creon, he who rules this land of Corinth.
AEGEUS: Indeed, Medea, your grief was understandable.

MEDEA: I am ruined. And there is more to come: I am banished.
AEGEUS: Banished? By whom? Here you tell me of a new wrong.
MEDEA: Creon drives me an exile from the land of Corinth.   690
AEGEUS: Does Jason consent? I cannot approve of this.
MEDEA: He pretends not to, but he will put up with it.
Ah, Aegeus, I beg and beseech you, by your beard
And by your knees I am making myself your suppliant,
Have pity on me, have pity on your poor friend,   695
And do not let me go into exile desolate,
But receive me in your land and at your very hearth.
So may your love, with God's help, lead to the bearing
Of children, and so may you yourself die happy.
You do not know what a chance you have come on here.   700
I will end your childlessness, and I will make you able
To beget children. The drugs I know can do this.
AEGEUS: For many reasons, woman, I am anxious to do
This favor for you. First, for the sake of the gods,
And then for the birth of children which you promise,   705
For in that respect I am entirely at my wits' end.
But this is my position: if you reach my land,
I, being in my rights, will try to befriend you.
But this much I must warn you of beforehand:
I shall not agree to take you out of this country;   710
But if you by yourself can reach my house, then you
Shall stay there safely. To none will I give you up
But from this land you must make your escape yourself,
For I do not wish to incur blame from my friends.
MEDEA: It shall be so. But, if I might have a pledge from you   715
For this, then I would have from you all I desire.
AEGEUS: Do you not trust me? What is it rankles with you?
MEDEA: I trust you, yes. But the house of Pelias hates me,
And so does Creon. If you are bound by this oath,
When they try to drag me from your land, you will not   720
Abandon me; but if our pact is only words,
With no oath to the gods, you will be lightly armed,
Unable to resist their summons. I am weak,
While they have wealth to help them and a royal house.
AEGEUS: You show much foresight for such negotiations.   725
Well, if you will have it so, I will not refuse.
For, both on my side this will be the safest way
To have some excuse to put forward to your enemies,
And for you it is more certain. You may name the gods.
MEDEA: Swear by the plain of Earth, and Helius, father   730
Of my father, and name together all the gods . . .
AEGEUS: That I will act or not act in what way? Speak.
MEDEA: That you yourself will never cast me from your land,
Nor, if any of my enemies should demand me,
Will you, in your life, willingly hand me over.   735
AEGEUS: I swear by the Earth, by the holy light of Helius,
By all the gods, I will abide by this you say.
MEDEA: Enough. And, if you fail, what shall happen to you?
AEGEUS: What comes to those who have no regard for heaven.
MEDEA: Go on your way. Farewell. For I am satisfied.   740
And I will reach your city as soon as I can,
Having done the deed I have to do and gained my end.

(AEGEUS *goes out.*)

CHORUS: May Hermes, god of travelers,
Escort you, Aegeus, to your home!
And may you have the things you wish   745

So eagerly; for you
Appear to me to be a generous man.
MEDEA: God, and God's daughter, justice, and light of Helius!
Now, friends, has come the time of my triumph over
750 My enemies, and now my foot is on the road.
Now I am confident they will pay the penalty.
For this man, Aegeus, has been like a harbor to me
In all my plans just where I was most distressed.
To him I can fasten the cable of my safety
755 When I have reached the town and fortress of Pallas.
And now I shall tell to you the whole of my plan.
Listen to these words that are not spoken idly.
I shall send one of my servants to find Jason
And request him to come once more into my sight.
760 And when he comes, the words I'll say will be soft ones.
I'll say that I agree with him, that I approve
The royal wedding he has made, betraying me.
I'll say it was profitable, an excellent idea.
But I shall beg that my children may remain here:
765 Not that I would live in a country that hates me
Children of mine to feel their enemies' insults,
But that by a trick I may kill the king's daughter.
For I will send the children with gifts in their hands
To carry to the bride, so as not to be banished—
770 A finely woven dress and a golden diadem.
And if she takes them and wears them upon her skin
She and all who touch the girl will die in agony;
Such poison will I lay upon the gifts I send.
But there, however, I must leave that account paid.
775 I weep to think of what a deed I have to do
Next after that; for I shall kill my own children.
My children, there is none who can give them safety.
And when I have ruined the whole of Jason's house,
I shall leave the land and flee from the murder of my
780 Dear children, and I shall have done a dreadful deed.
For it is not bearable to be mocked by enemies.
So it must happen. What profit have I in life?
I have no land, no home, no refuge from my pain.
My mistake was made the time I left behind me
785 My father's house, and trusted the words of a Greek,
Who, with heaven's help, will pay me the price for that.
For those children he had from me he will never
See alive again, nor will he on his new bride
Beget another child, for she is to be forced
790 To die a most terrible death by these my poisons.
Let no one think me a weak one, feeble-spirited,
A stay-at-home, but rather just the opposite,
One who can hurt my enemies and help my friends;
For the lives of such persons are most remembered.
795 CHORUS: Since you have shared the knowledge of your plan
           with us,
I both wish to help you and support the normal
Ways of mankind, and tell you not to do this thing.
MEDEA: I can do no other thing. It is understandable
For you to speak thus. You have not suffered as I have.
800 CHORUS: But can you have the heart to kill your flesh and blood?
MEDEA: Yes, for this is the best way to wound my husband.
CHORUS: And you, too. Of women you will be most unhappy.

MEDEA: So it must be. No compromise is possible.

(*She turns to the* NURSE.)

Go, you, at once, and tell Jason to come to me.
You I employ on all affairs of greatest trust.   805
Say nothing of these decisions which I have made.
If you love your mistress, if you were born a woman.
CHORUS: From of old the children of Erechtheus are
Splendid, the sons of blessed gods. They dwell
In Athens' holy and unconquered land,   810
Where famous Wisdom feeds them and they pass gaily
Always through that most brilliant air where once, they say,
That golden Harmony gave birth to the nine
Pure Muses of Pieria.

And beside the sweet flow of Cephisus' stream,   815
Where Cypris sailed, they say, to draw the water,
And mild soft breezes breathed along her path,
And on her hair were flung the sweet-smelling garlands
Of flowers of roses by the Lovers, the companions
Of Wisdom, her escort, the helpers of men   820
In every kind of excellence.

How then can these holy rivers
Or this holy land love you,
Or the city find you a home,
You, who will kill your children,   825
You, not pure with the rest?
O think of the blow at your children
And think of the blood that you shed.
O, over and over I beg you,
By your knees I beg you do not   830
Be the murderess of your babes!

O where will you find the courage
Or the skill of hand and heart,
When you set yourself to attempt
A deed so dreadful to do?   835
How, when you look upon them,
Can you tearlessly hold the decision
For murder? You will not be able,
When your children fall down and implore you,
You will not be able to dip   840
Steadfast your hand in their blood.

(*Enter* JASON, *with attendants.*)

JASON: I have come at your request. Indeed, although you are
Bitter against me, this you shall have: I will listen
To what new thing you want, woman, to get from me.
MEDEA: Jason, I beg you to be forgiving toward me   845
For what I said. It is natural for you to bear with
My temper, since we have had much love together.
I have talked with myself about this and I have
Reproached myself. "Fool" I said, "why am I so mad?
Why am I set against those who have planned wisely?   850
Why make myself an enemy of the authorities
And of my husband, who does the best thing for me
By marrying royalty and having children who
Will be as brothers to my own? What is wrong with me?

---

755 **fortress of Pallas** Athens, the town of Athena

808 **children of Erechtheus** the Athenians   815 **beside . . .
stream** at Athens

855   Let me give up anger, for the gods are kind to me.
    Have I not children, and do I not know that we
    In exile from our country must be short of friends?"
    When I considered this I saw that I had shown
    Great lack of sense, and that my anger was foolish.
860   Now I agree with you. I think that you are wise
    In having this other wife as well as me, and I
    Was mad. I should have helped you in these plans of yours,
    Have joined in the wedding, stood by the marriage bed,
    Have taken pleasure in attendance on your bride.
865   But we women are what we are—perhaps a little
    Worthless; and you men must not be like us in this,
    Nor be foolish in return when we are foolish.
    Now, I give in, and admit that then I was wrong.
    I have come to a better understanding now.

(She turns toward the house.)

870   Children, come here, my children, come outdoors to us!
    Welcome your father with me, and say goodbye to him,
    And with your mother, who just now was his enemy,
    Join again in making friends with him who loves us.

(Enter the CHILDREN, *attended by the* TUTOR.)

    We have made peace, and all our anger is over.
875   Take hold of his right hand—O God, I am thinking
    Of something which may happen in the secret future.
    O children, will you just so, after a long life,
    Hold out your loving arms at the grave? O children,
    How ready to cry I am, how full of foreboding!
880   I am ending at last this quarrel with your father,
    And, look my soft eyes have suddenly filled with tears.
    CHORUS: And the pale tears have started also in my eyes.
    O may the trouble not grow worse than now it is!
    JASON: I approve of what you say. And I cannot blame you
885   Even for what you said before. It is natural
    For a woman to be wild with her husband when he
    Goes in for secret love. But now your mind has turned
    To better reasoning. In the end you have come to
    The right decision, like the clever woman you are.
890   And of you, children, your father is taking care.
    He has made, with God's help, ample provision for you.
    For I think that a time will come when you will be
    The leading people in Corinth with your brothers.
    You must grow up. As to the future, your father
895   And those of the gods who love him will deal with that.
    I want to see you, when you have become young men,
    Healthy and strong, better men than my enemies.
    Medea, why are your eyes all wet with pale tears?
    Why is your cheek so white and turned away from me?
900   Are not these words of mine pleasing for you to hear?
    MEDEA: It is nothing. I was thinking about these children.
    JASON: You must be cheerful. I shall look after them well.
    MEDEA: I will be. It is not that I distrust your words,
    But a woman is a frail thing, prone to crying.
905   JASON: But why then should you grieve so much for these
        children?
    MEDEA: I am their mother. When you prayed that they might live
    I felt unhappy to think that these things will be.
    But come, I have said something of the things I meant

    To say to you, and now I will tell you the rest.
    Since it is the king's will to banish me from here—   910
    And for me, too, I know that this is the best thing,
    Not to be in your way by living here or in
    The king's way, since they think me ill-disposed to them—
    I then am going into exile from this land;
    But do you, so that you may have the care of them,   915
    Beg Creon that the children may not be banished.
JASON: I doubt if I'll succeed, but still I'll attempt it.
MEDEA: Then you must tell your wife to beg from her father
    That the children may be reprieved from banishment.
JASON: I will, and with her I shall certainly succeed.   920
MEDEA: If she is like the rest of us women, you will.
    And I, too, will take a hand with you in this business,
    For I will send her some gifts which are far fairer,
    I am sure of it, than those which now are in fashion,
    A finely woven dress and a golden diadem,   925
    And the children shall present them. Quick, let one of you
    Servants bring here to me that beautiful dress.

(One of her attendants goes into the house.)

    She will be happy not in one way, but in a hundred,
    Having so fine a man as you to share her bed,
    And with this beautiful dress which Helius of old,   930
    My father's father, bestowed on his descendants.

(Enter attendant carrying the poisoned dress and diadem.)

    There, children, take these wedding presents in your hands.
    Take them to the royal princess, the happy bride,
    And give them to her. She will not think little of them.
JASON: No, don't be foolish, and empty your hands of these.   935
    Do you think the palace is short of dresses to wear?
    Do you think there is no gold there? Keep them, don't
        give them
    Away. If my wife considers me of any value,
    She will think more of me than money, I am sure of it.
MEDEA: No, let me have my way. They say the gods themselves   940
    Are moved by gifts, and gold does more with men than words.
    Hers is the luck, her fortune that which god blesses;
    She is young and a princess; but for my children's reprieve
    I would give my very life, and not gold only.
    Go children, go together to that rich palace,   945
    Be suppliants to the new wife of your father,
    My lady, beg her not to let you be banished.
    And give her the dress—for this is of great importance,
    That she should take the gift into her hand from yours.
    Go, quick as you can. And bring your mother good news   950
    By your success of those things which she longs to gain.

(JASON goes out with his attendants, followed by the TUTOR *and the* CHILDREN *carrying the poisoned gifts.)*

CHORUS: Now there is no hope left for the children's lives.
    Now there is none. They are walking already to murder.
    The bride, poor bride, will accept the curse of the gold,
    Will accept the bright diadem.   955
    Around her yellow hair she will set that dress
    Of death with her own hands.

    The grace and the perfume and glow of the golden robe
    Will charm her to put them upon her and wear the wreath,

960 And now her wedding will be with the dead below,
Into such a trap she will fall,
Poor thing, into such a fate of death and never
Escape from under that curse.

You, too, O wretched bridegroom, making your match
with kings,
965 You do not see that you bring
Destruction on your children and on her,
Your wife, a fearful death.
Poor soul, what a fall is yours!

In your grief, too, I weep, mother of little children,
970 You who will murder your own,
In vengeance for the loss of married love
Which Jason has betrayed
As he lives with another wife.

(Enter the TUTOR *with the* CHILDREN.*)*

TUTOR: Mistress, I tell you that these children are reprieved,
975 And the royal bride has been pleased to take in her hands
Your gifts. In that quarter the children are secure.
But come,
Why do you stand confused when you are fortunate?
Why have you turned round with your cheek away from me?
980 Are not these words of mine pleasing for you to hear?
MEDEA: Oh! I am lost!
TUTOR: That word is not in harmony with my tidings.
MEDEA: I am lost, I am lost!
TUTOR: Am I in ignorance telling you
Of some disaster, and not the good news I thought?
985 MEDEA: You have told what you have told. I do not blame you.
TUTOR: Why then this downcast eye, and this weeping of tears?
MEDEA: Oh, I am forced to weep, old man. The gods and I,
I in a kind of madness, have contrived all this.
TUTOR: Courage! You, too, will be brought home by your
children.
990 MEDEA: Ah, before that happens I shall bring others home.
TUTOR: Others before you have been parted from their
children.
Mortals must bear in resignation their ill luck.
MEDEA: That is what I shall do. But go inside the house,
And do for the children your usual daily work.

(The TUTOR *goes into the house.* MEDEA *turns to her* CHILDREN.*)*

995 O children, O my children, you have a city,
You have a home, and you can leave me behind you,
And without your mother you may live there forever.
But I am going in exile to another land
Before I have seen you happy and taken pleasure in you,
1000 Before I have dressed your brides and made your marriage
beds
And held up the torch at the ceremony of wedding.
Oh, what a wretch I am in this my self-willed thought!
What was the purpose, children, for which I reared you?
For all my travail and wearing myself away?
1005 They were sterile, those pains I had in the bearing of you.
Oh surely once the hopes in you I had, poor me,
Were high ones: you would look after me in old age,
And when I died would deck me well with your own hands;

A thing which all would have done. Oh but now it is gone,
That lovely thought. For, once I am left without you, 1010
Sad will be the life I'll lead and sorrowful for me.
And you will never see your mother again with
Your dear eyes, gone to another mode of living.
Why, children, do you look upon me with your eyes?
Why do you smile so sweetly that last smile of all? 1015
Oh, Oh, what can I do? My spirit has gone from me,
Friends, when I saw that bright look in the children's eyes.
I cannot bear to do it. I renounce my plans
I had before. I'll take my children away from
This land. Why should I hurt their father with the pain 1020
They feel, and suffer twice as much of pain myself?
No, no, I will not do it. I renounce my plans.
Ah, what is wrong with me? Do I want to let go
My enemies unhurt and be laughed at for it?
I must face this thing. Oh, but what a weak woman 1025
Even to admit to my mind these soft arguments.
Children, go into the house. And he whom law forbids
To stand in attendance at my sacrifices,
Let him see to it. I shall not mar my handiwork.
Oh! Oh! 1030
Do not, O my heart, you must not do these things!
Poor heart, let them go, have pity upon the children.
If they live with you in Athens they will cheer you.
No! By Hell's avenging furies it shall not be—
This shall never be, that I should suffer my children 1035
To be the prey of my enemies' insolence.
Every way is it fixed. The bride will not escape.
No, the diadem is now upon her head, and she,
The royal princess, is dying in the dress, I know it.
But—for it is the most dreadful of roads for me 1040
To tread, and them I shall send on a more dreadful still—
I wish to speak to the children.

(She calls the CHILDREN *to her.)*

                                        Come, children, give
Me your hands, give your mother your hands to kiss them.
Oh the dear hands, and O how dear are these lips to me,
And the generous eyes and the bearing of my children! 1045
I wish you happiness, but not here in this world.
What is here your father took. Oh how good to hold you!
How delicate the skin, how sweet the breath of children!
Go, go! I am no longer able, no longer
To look upon you. I am overcome by sorrow. 1050

(The CHILDREN *go into the house.)*

I know indeed what evil I intend to do,
But stronger than all my afterthoughts is my fury,
Fury that brings upon mortals the greatest evils.

(She goes out to the right, toward the royal palace.)

CHORUS: Often before
I have gone through more subtle reasons, 1055
And have come upon questionings greater
Than a woman should strive to search out.
But we too have a goddess to help us
And accompany us into wisdom.
Not all of us. Still you will find 1060

Among many women a few,
And our sex is not without learning.
This I say, that those who have never
Had children, who know nothing of it,
1065   In happiness have the advantage
Over those who are parents.
The childless, who never discover
Whether children turn out as a good thing
Or as something to cause pain, are spared
1070   Many troubles in lacking this knowledge.
And those who have in their homes
The sweet presence of children, I see that their lives
Are all wasted away by their worries.
First they must think how to bring them up well and
1075   How to leave them something to live on.
And then after this whether all their toil
Is for those who will turn out good or bad,
Is still an unanswered question.
And of one more trouble, the last of all,
1080   That is common to mortals I tell.
For suppose you have found them enough for their living,
Suppose that the children have grown into youth
And have turned out good, still, if God so wills it,
Death will away with your children's bodies,
1085   And carry them off into Hades.
What is our profit, then, that for the sake of
Children the gods should pile upon mortals
After all else
This most terrible grief of all?

(Enter MEDEA, *from the spectators' right.*)

1090   MEDEA: Friends, I can tell you that for long I have waited
For the event. I stare toward the place from where
The news will come. And now, see one of Jason's servants
Is on his way here, and that labored breath of his
Shows he has tidings for us, and evil tidings.

(Enter, *also from the right, the* MESSENGER.)

1095   MESSENGER: Medea, you who have done such a dreadful thing,
So outrageous, run for your life, take what you can,
A ship to bear you hence or chariot on land.
MEDEA: And what is the reason deserves such flight as this?
MESSENGER: She is dead, only just now, the royal princess,
1100   And Creon dead, too, her father, by your poisons.
MEDEA: The finest words you have spoken. Now and hereafter
I shall count you among my benefactors and friends.
MESSENGER: What! Are you right in the mind? Are you not mad,
Woman? The house of the king is outraged by you.
1105   Do you enjoy it? Not afraid of such doings?
MEDEA: To what you say I on my side have something too
To say in answer. Do not be in a hurry, friend,
But speak. How did they die? You will delight me twice
As much again if you say they died in agony.
1110   MESSENGER: When those two children, born of you, had
entered in,
Their father with them, and passed into the bride's house,
We were pleased, we slaves who were distressed by your
wrongs.
All through the house we were talking of but one thing,
How you and your husband had made up your quarrel.

Some kissed the children's hands and some their yellow hair,   1115
And I myself was so full of my joy that I
Followed the children into the women's quarters.
Our mistress, whom we honor now instead of you,
Before she noticed that your two children were there,
Was keeping her eye fixed eagerly on Jason.   1120
Afterwards, however, she covered up her eyes,
Her cheek paled, and she turned herself away from him,
So disgusted was she at the children's coming there.
But your husband tried to end the girl's bad temper,
And said "You must not look unkindly on your friends.   1125
Cease to be angry. Turn your head to me again.
Have as your friends the same ones as your husband has.
And take these gifts, and beg your father to reprieve
These children from their exile. Do it for my sake."
She, when she saw the dress, could not restrain herself.   1130
She agreed with all her husband said, and before
He and the children had gone far from the palace,
She took the gorgeous robe and dressed herself in it,
And put the golden crown around her curly locks,
And arranged the set of the hair in a shining mirror,   1135
And smiled at the lifeless image of herself in it.
Then she rose from her chair and walked about the room,
With her gleaming feet stepping most soft and delicate,
All overjoyed with the present. Often and often
She would stretch her foot out straight and look along it.   1140
But after that it was a fearful thing to see.
The color of her face changed, and she staggered back,
She ran, and her legs trembled, and she only just
Managed to reach a chair without falling flat down.
An aged woman servant who, I take it, thought   1145
This was some seizure of Pan or another god,
Cried out "God bless us," but that was before she saw
The white foam breaking through her lips and her rolling
The pupils of her eyes and her face all bloodless.
Then she raised a different cry from that "God bless us,"   1150
A huge shriek, and the women ran, one to the king,
One to the newly wedded husband to tell him
What had happened to his bride; and with frequent sound
The whole of the palace rang as they went running.
One walking quickly round the course of a race-track   1155
Would now have turned the bend and be close to the goal,
When she, poor girl, opened her shut and speechless eye,
And with a terrible groan she came to herself.
For a twofold pain was moving up against her.
The wreath of gold that was resting around her head   1160
Let forth a fearful stream of all-devouring fire,
And the finely woven dress your children gave to her,
Was fastening on the unhappy girl's fine flesh.
She leapt up from the chair, and all on fire she ran,
Shaking her hair now this way and now that, trying   1165
To hurl the diadem away; but fixedly
The gold preserved its grip, and, when she shook her hair,
Then more and twice as fiercely the fire blazed out.
Till, beaten by her fate, she fell down to the ground,
Hard to be recognized except by a parent.   1170
Neither the setting of her eyes was plain to see,
Nor the shapeliness of her face. From the top of
Her head there oozed out blood and fire mixed together.
Like the drops on pine-bark, so the flesh from her bones
Dropped away, torn by the hidden fang of the poison.   1175

It was a fearful sight; and terror held us all
From touching the corpse. We had learned from what had
    happened.
But her wretched father, knowing nothing of the event,
Came suddenly to the house, and fell upon the corpse,
1180 And at once cried out and folded his arms about her,
And kissed her and spoke to her, saying, "O my poor child,
What heavenly power has so shamefully destroyed you?
And who has set me here like an ancient sepulcher,
Deprived of you? O let me die with you, my child!"
1185 And when he had made an end of his wailing and crying,
Then the old man wished to raise himself to his feet;
But, as the ivy clings to the twigs of the laurel,
So he stuck to the fine dress, and he struggled fearfully.
For he was trying to lift himself to his knee,
1190 And she was pulling him down, and when he tugged hard
He would be ripping his aged flesh from his bones.
At last his life was quenched, and the unhappy man
Gave up the ghost, no longer could hold up his head.
There they lie close, the daughter and the old father,
1195 Dead bodies, an event he prayed for in his tears.
As for your interests, I will say nothing of them,
For you will find your own escape from punishment.
Our human life I think and have thought a shadow,
And I do not fear to say that those who are held
1200 Wise among men and who search the reasons of things
Are those who bring the most sorrow on themselves.
For mortals there is no one who is happy.
If wealth flows in upon one, one may be perhaps
Luckier than one's neighbor, but still not happy.

(Exit.)

1205 CHORUS: Heaven, it seems, on this day has fastened many
Evils on Jason, and Jason has deserved them.
Poor girl, the daughter of Creon, how I pity you
And your misfortunes, you who have gone quite away
To the house of Hades because of marrying Jason.
1210 MEDEA: Women, my task is fixed: as quickly as I may
To kill my children, and start away from this land,
And not, by wasting time, to suffer my children
To be slain by another hand less kindly to them.
Force every way will have it they must die, and since
1215 This must be so, then I, their mother, shall kill them.
Oh, arm yourself in steel, my heart! Do not hang back
From doing this fearful and necessary wrong.
Oh, come, my hand, poor wretched hand, and take the sword.
Take it, step forward to this bitter starting point,
1220 And do not be a coward, do not think of them,
How sweet they are, and how you are their mother. Just for
This one short day be forgetful of your children,
Afterward weep; for even though you will kill them,
They were very dear—Oh, I am an unhappy woman!

(With a cry she rushes into the house.)

1225 CHORUS: O Earth, and the far shining
Ray of the Sun, look down, look down upon
This poor lost woman, look, before she raises
The hand of murder against her flesh and blood.
Yours was the golden birth from which
1230 She sprang, and now I fear divine

Blood may be shed by men.
O heavenly light, hold back her hand,
Check her, and drive from out the house
The bloody Fury raised by fiends of Hell.
1235 Vain waste, your care of children;
Was it in vain you bore the babes you loved,
After you passed the inhospitable strait
Between the dark blue rocks, Symplegades?
O wretched one, how has it come,
1240 This heavy anger on your heart,
This cruel bloody mind?
For God from mortals asks a stern
Price for the stain of kindred blood
In like disaster falling on their homes.

(A cry from ONE OF THE CHILDREN *is heard.)*

CHORUS: Do you hear the cry, do you hear the children's cry? 1245
O you hard heart, O woman fated for evil!
ONE OF THE CHILDREN: *(From within.)* What can I do and how
escape my mother's hands?
ANOTHER CHILD: *(From within.)* O my dear brother, I cannot tell.
We are lost.
CHORUS: Shall I enter the house? Oh, surely I should
Defend the children from murder. 1250
A CHILD: *(From within.)* O help us, in God's name, for now we
need your help.
Now, now we are close to it. We are trapped by the sword.
CHORUS: O your heart must have been made of rock or steel,
You who can kill
With your own hand the fruit of your own womb. 1255
Of one alone I have heard, one woman alone
Of those of old who laid her hands on her children,
Ino, sent mad by heaven when the wife of Zeus
Drove her out from her home and made her wander;
And because of the wicked shedding of blood 1260
Of her own children she threw
Herself, poor wretch, into the sea and stepped away
Over the sea-cliff to die with her two children.
What horror more can be? O women's love,
So full of trouble, 1265
How many evils have you caused already!

(Enter JASON, *with attendants.)*

JASON: You women, standing close in front of this dwelling,
Is she, Medea, she who did this dreadful deed,
Still in the house, or has she run away in flight?
For she will have to hide herself beneath the earth, 1270
Or raise herself on wings into the height of air,
If she wishes to escape the royal vengeance.
Does she imagine that, having killed our rulers,
She will herself escape uninjured from this house?
But I am thinking not so much of her as for 1275
The children—her the king's friends will make to suffer
For what she did. So I have come to save the lives
Of my boys, in case the royal house should harm them
While taking vengeance for their mother's wicked deed.
CHORUS: O Jason, if you but knew how deeply you are 1280
Involved in sorrow, you would not have spoken so.
JASON: What is it? That she is planning to kill me also?
CHORUS: Your children are dead, and by their own mother's hand.
JASON: What! That is it? O woman, you have destroyed me!

1285 CHORUS: You must make up your mind your children are no more.

JASON: Where did she kill them? Was it here or in the house?

CHORUS: Open the gates and there you will see them murdered.

JASON: Quick as you can unlock the doors, men, and undo
 The fastenings and let me see this double evil,
1290 My children dead and her—Oh her I will repay.

(His attendants rush to the door. MEDEA *appears above the house in a chariot drawn by dragons. She has the dead bodies of the* CHILDREN *with her.)*

MEDEA: Why do you batter these gates and try to unbar them,
 Seeking the corpses and for me who did the deed?
 You may cease your trouble, and, if you have need of me,
 Speak, if you wish. You will never touch me with your hand,
1295 Such a chariot has Helius, my father's father,
 Given me to defend me from my enemies.

JASON: You hateful thing, you woman most utterly loathed
 By the gods and me and by all the race of mankind,
 You who have had the heart to raise a sword against
1300 Your children, you, their mother, and left me childless—
 You have done this, and do you still look at the sun
 And at the earth, after these most fearful doings?
 I wish you dead. Now I see it plain, though at that time
 I did not, when I took you from your foreign home
1305 And brought you to a Greek house, you, an evil thing,
 A traitress to your father and your native land.
 The gods hurled the avenging curse of yours on me.
 For your own brother you slew at your own hearthside,
 And then came aboard that beautiful ship, the Argo.
1310 And that was your beginning. When you were married
 To me, your husband, and had borne children to me,
 For the sake of pleasure in the bed you killed them.
 There is no Greek woman who would have dared such deeds,
 Out of all those whom I passed over and chose you
1315 To marry instead, a bitter destructive match,
 A monster, not a woman, having a nature
 Wilder than that of Scylla in the Tuscan sea.
 Ah! no, not if I had ten thousand words of shame
 Could I sting you. You are naturally so brazen.
1320 Go, worker in evil, stained with your children's blood.
 For me remains to cry aloud upon my fate,
 Who will get no pleasure from my newly wedded love,
 And the boys whom I begot and brought up, never
 Shall I speak to them alive. Oh, my life is over!

1325 MEDEA: Long would be the answer which I might have made to
 These words of yours, if Zeus the father did not know
 How I have treated you and what you did to me.
 No, it was not to be that you should scorn my love,
 And pleasantly live your life through, laughing at me;
1330 Nor would the princess, nor he who offered the match,
 Creon, drive me away without paying for it.
 So now you may call me a monster, if you wish,
 A Scylla housed in the caves of the Tuscan sea.
 I too, as I had to, have taken hold of your heart.

1335 JASON: You feel the pain yourself. You share in my sorrow.

MEDEA: Yes, and my grief is gain when you cannot mock it.

JASON: O children, what a wicked mother she was to you!

MEDEA: They died from a disease they caught from their father.

JASON: I tell you it was not my hand that destroyed them.

MEDEA: But it was your insolence, and your virgin wedding. 1340

JASON: And just for the sake of that you chose to kill them.

MEDEA: Is love so small a pain, do you think, for a woman?

JASON: For a wise one, certainly. But you are wholly evil.

MEDEA: The children are dead. I say this to make you suffer.

JASON: The children, I think, will bring down curses on you. 1345

MEDEA: The gods know who was the author of this sorrow.

JASON: Yes, the gods know indeed, they know your loathsome
 heart.

MEDEA: Hate me. But I tire of your barking bitterness.

JASON: And I of yours. It is easier to leave you.

MEDEA: How then? What shall I do? I long to leave you too. 1350

JASON: Give me the bodies to bury and to mourn them.

MEDEA: No, that I will not. I will bury them myself,
 Bearing them to Hera's temple on the promontory;
 So that no enemy may evilly treat them
 By tearing up their grave. In this land of Corinth 1355
 I shall establish a holy feast and sacrifice
 Each year for ever to atone for the blood guilt.
 And I myself go to the land of Erechtheus
 To dwell in Aegeus' house, the son of Pandion.
 While you, as is right, will die without distinction, 1360
 Struck on the head by a piece of the Argo's timber,
 And you will have seen the bitter end of my love.

JASON: May a Fury for the children's sake destroy you,
 And justice, Requitor of blood.

MEDEA: What heavenly power lends an ear 1365
 To a breaker of oaths, a deceiver?

JASON: Oh, I hate you, murderess of children.

MEDEA: Go to your palace. Bury your bride.

JASON: I go, with two children to mourn for.

MEDEA: Not yet do you feel it. Wait for the future. 1370

JASON: Oh, children I loved!

MEDEA: I loved them, you did not.

JASON: You loved them, and killed them.

MEDEA: To make you feel
 pain.

JASON: Oh, wretch that I am, how I long
 To kiss the dear lips of my children!

MEDEA: Now you would speak to them, now you would kiss 1375
 them.
 Then you rejected them.

JASON: Let me, I beg you,
 Touch my boys delicate flesh.

MEDEA: I will not. Your words are all wasted.

JASON: O God, do you hear it, this persecution,
 These my sufferings from this hateful 1380
 Woman, this monster, murderess of children?
 Still what I can do that I will do:
 I will lament and cry upon heaven,
 Calling the gods to bear me witness
 How you have killed my boys and prevent me from 1385
 Touching their bodies or giving them burial.
 I wish I had never begot them to see them
 Afterward slaughtered by you.

CHORUS: Zeus in Olympus is the overseer
 Of many doings. Many things the gods 1390
 Achieve beyond our judgment. What we thought
 Is not confirmed and what we thought not god
 Contrives. And so it happens in this story.

1317 **Scylla** a monster in the *Odyssey*

ARISTOPHANES

Aristophanes (c. 450–c. 388 BCE) pursued his career as a playwright throughout the Peloponnesian War. As he observed the decline and defeat of Athens, his comedies relentlessly attacked the war and the individuals and attitudes that supported it. Aristophanes first entered the City Dionysia in 427 BCE and first won in 426 BCE with a now-lost play that satirized the policies and character of the military leader Cleon. Many of Aristophanes' plays—*Birds, Lysistrata, Assembly of Women*—use a utopian premise to criticize the war, but in other plays, Aristophanes lampoons other aspects of city life. In *Frogs,* for instance, a pompous Aeschylus and an embittered Euripides come from Hades to vie with one another once again; in *Clouds,* Aristophanes ridicules the sophists—professional teachers of rhetoric—for their ability to argue any side of an issue, and he particularly singles out Socrates for blame. The impact of Aristophanes' comedy on Athens should not be underestimated. In *Plato's Apology,* Socrates cites Aristophanes' portrayal of him in *Clouds* as one of the factors that turned Athenian sentiment against him, resulting in his trial and sentence of execution. Aristophanes' plays include *Acharnians, Knights, Clouds, Wasps, Peace, Birds, Lysistrata, Women Celebrating the Thesmophoria, Frogs, Assembly of Women,* and *Plutus.*

LYSISTRATA

Lysistrata is one of several plays critical of Athens' war with Sparta. Produced in 411 BCE, it follows shortly on a disastrous phase of the war for Athens. Two years earlier, the Athenian raid on Sicily had failed, and the navy was decimated, leaving Athens vulnerable to attack by Sparta. Although the navy was rebuilt before Sparta mounted its final assault, Athens fell to Sparta in 404 BCE.

Lysistrata explores the premise that the women of Greece—drawn from all the major city-states and regions—could unite to oppose the war. Led by the Athenian Lysistrata (her name means "disband the army"), the women barricade themselves on the Acropolis, withholding sex from the men until peace can be declared. Aristophanes provides each of his women with the physical attributes and accent typical of her region. The large and powerful Spartan woman Lampito, for example, is both an expert in the Spartan rump-kicking dance and speaks in what was—to an Athenian audience—an outlandish accent (to make this clear for English-speaking readers, this translation gives Lampito an exaggerated Southern drawl).

Lysistrata addresses the politics of its era in a variety of ways. It is, of course, a passionate plea for peace, concluding with a scene of comic feasting and dancing enjoyed by all the characters in the play, Athenians and Spartans, men and women. For modern audiences, though, the play's connection between gender and politics may seem more immediate. On one hand, the play implies an equality between men and women. The women claim that the morality of their domestic sphere is superior to the military morality pursued by the men, and to get the women back, the men are forced to compromise with them. On the other hand, although *Lysistrata* seems to provide women with political power, their power resides wholly in their sexuality; they can interrupt, but not change, the fact that they are the property of men. The Theater of Dionysus could not, of course, put women on the stage, and Lysistrata, Lampito, Kalonike, and the rest—even the naked girl Harmony—were all played by men in padded costumes. In the play and in the *polis,* women were defined principally through their relation to men. The limited influence women could exert was subordinate to the civil power that Aristophanes and his audience took to be the "natural" preserve of the male audience. Despite the play's earthy humor and apparent feminism, *Lysistrata* documents the actual status of women in classical Athens; their power is restricted to the sphere of the oikos, or home, and can be practiced only through their subservience to men, who—as citizens—finally can command women's bodies, the home, and the state as well.

LYSISTRATA

Aristophanes

TRANSLATED BY DONALD SUTHERLAND

——— CHARACTERS ———

LYSISTRATA ⎫
KALONIKE ⎬ *Athenian women*
MYRRHINA ⎭
LAMPITO, *a Spartan woman*
CHORUS OF OLD MEN
CHORUS OF WOMEN
ATHENIAN COMMISSIONER

OLD MARKET-WOMEN
CINESIAS, *an Athenian, husband*
   of Myrrhina
SPARTAN HERALD
SCYTHIAN POLICEMEN
PORTER
ATHENIAN OFFICIAL

ATHENIANS
SPARTAN AMBASSADORS
ATHENIAN AMBASSADORS
HARMONY
LADY COP

A street in Athens before daylight.

LYSISTRATA: If anyone had asked them to a festival
    of Aphrodite or of Bacchus or of Pan,
    you couldn't get through Athens for the tambourines,
    but now there's not one solitary woman here.
5   Except my next-door neighbor. Here she's coming out.
    Hello, Kalonike.
KALONIKE: Hello, Lysistrata.
    What are you so upset about? Don't scowl so, dear.
    You're less attractive when you knit your brows and glare.
LYSISTRATA: I know, Kalonike, but I am smoldering
10   with indignation at the way we women act.
    Men think we are so gifted for all sorts of crime
    that we will stop at nothing—
KALONIKE: Well, we are, by Zeus!
LYSISTRATA: —but when it comes to an appointment here
    with me
    to plot and plan for something really serious
15   they lie in bed and do not come.
KALONIKE: They'll come, my dear.
    You know what trouble women have in going out:
    one of us will be wrapped up in her husband still,
    another waking up the maid, or with a child
    to put to sleep, or give its bath, or feed its pap.
20 LYSISTRATA: But they had other more important things to do
    than those.
KALONIKE: What ever is it, dear Lysistrata?
    What have you called us women all together for?
    How much of a thing is it?
LYSISTRATA: Very big.
KALONIKE: And thick?
LYSISTRATA: Oh very thick indeed.
KALONIKE: Then *how* can we be late?
25 LYSISTRATA: That's not the way it is. Or we would all be here.
    But it is something I have figured out myself
    and turned and tossed upon for many a sleepless night.
KALONIKE: It must be something slick you've turned and
    tossed upon!
30 LYSISTRATA: So slick that the survival of all Greece depends
    upon the women.
KALONIKE: On the women? In that case
    poor Greece has next to nothing to depend upon.
LYSISTRATA: Since now it's we who must decide affairs of state:
    either there is to be no Spartan left alive—
KALONIKE: A very good thing too, if none were left,
    by Zeus!

LYSISTRATA: —and every living soul in Thebes to be destroyed— 35
KALONIKE: Except the eels! Spare the delicious eels of Thebes!
LYSISTRATA: —and as for Athens—I can't bring myself to say
    the like of that for us. But just think what I mean!
    Yet if the women meet here as I told them to
    from Sparta, Thebes, and all of their allies,   40
    and we of Athens, all together we'll save Greece.
KALONIKE: What reasonable thing could women ever do,
    or glorious, we who sit around all prettied up
    in flowers and scandalous saffron-yellow gowns,
    groomed and draped to the ground in oriental stuffs 45
    and fancy pumps?
LYSISTRATA: And those are just the very things
    I count upon to save us—wicked saffron gowns,
    perfumes and pumps and rouge and sheer transparent
    frocks.
KALONIKE: But what use can they be?
LYSISTRATA: So no man in our time
    will raise a spear against another man again— 50
KALONIKE: I'll get a dress dyed saffron-yellow, come what may!
LYSISTRATA: —nor touch a shield—
KALONIKE: I'll slip into the sheerest gown!
LYSISTRATA: —nor so much as a dagger—
KALONIKE: I'll buy a pair of pumps!
LYSISTRATA: So don't you think the women should be here
    by now?
KALONIKE: I don't. They should have *flown* and got here 55
    long ago.
LYSISTRATA: You'll see, my dear. They will, like good Athenians,
    do everything too late. But from the coastal towns
    no woman is here either, nor from Salamis.
KALONIKE: I'm certain those from Salamis have crossed the
    strait:
    they're always straddling *something* at this time of night. 60
LYSISTRATA: Not even those I was expecting would be first
    to get here, from Acharnae, from so close to town,
    not even they are here.
KALONIKE: But one of them, I know,
    is under way, and three sheets to the wind, by now.
    But look—some women are approaching over there. 65
LYSISTRATA: And over here are some, coming this way—
KALONIKE: Phew! Phew!
    Where are they from?
LYSISTRATA: Down by the marshes.
KALONIKE: Yes, by Zeus!
    It smells as if the bottoms had been all churned up!

(Enter MYRRHINA, *and others.)*

MYRRHINA: Hello Lysistrata. Are we a little late?
70   What's that? Why don't you speak?
LYSISTRATA: I don't think much of you,
     Myrrhina, coming to this business only now.
MYRRHINA: Well, I could hardly find my girdle in the dark.
     If it's so urgent, tell us what it is. We're here.
KALONIKE: Oh no. Let's wait for just a little while until
75   the delegates from Sparta and from Thebes arrive.
LYSISTRATA: You show much better judgment.

(Enter LAMPITO, *and others.)*

                              Here comes Lampito!
LYSISTRATA: Well, darling Lampito! My dearest Spartan friend!
     How very sweet, how beautiful you look! That fresh
     complexion! How magnificent your figure is!
80   Enough to crush a bull!
LAMPITO: Ah shorely think Ah could.
     Ah take mah exacise. Ah jump and thump mah butt.
KALONIKE: And really, what a handsome set of tits you have!
LAMPITO: You feel me ovah lahk a cow fo sacrafahce!
LYSISTRATA: And this other young thing—where ever is *she* from?
85 LAMPITO: She's prominent, Ah sweah, in Thebes—a delegate
     ample enough.
LYSISTRATA: By Zeus, she represents Thebes well,
     having so trim a ploughland.
KALONIKE: Yes, by Zeus, she does!
     There's not a weed of all her field she hasn't plucked.
LYSISTRATA: And who's the other girl?
LAMPITO: Theah's nothing small, Ah sweah,
90   or tahght about her folks in Corinth.
KALONIKE: No, by Zeus!—
     to judge by this side of her, nothing small or tight.
LAMPITO: But who has called togethah such a regiment
     of all us women?
LYSISTRATA: Here I am. I did.
LAMPITO: Speak up,
     just tell us what you want.
KALONIKE: Oh yes, by Zeus, my dear,
95   do let us know what the important business is!
LYSISTRATA: Let me explain it, then. And yet . . . before I do . . .
     I have one little question.
KALONIKE: Anything you like.
LYSISTRATA: Don't you all miss the fathers of your little ones,
     your husbands who have gone away to war? I'm sure
100   you all have husbands in the armies far from home.
KALONIKE: Mine's been away five months in Thrace—
     a general's guard,
     posted to see his general does not desert.
MYRRHINA: And mine has been away in Pylos seven whole
     months.
LAMPITO: And mahn, though he does get back home on leave
     sometahms,
105   no soonah has he come than he is gone again.
LYSISTRATA: No lovers either. Not a sign of one is left.
     For since our eastern allies have deserted us
     they haven't sent a single six-inch substitute
     to serve as leatherware replacement for our men.
110   Would you be willing, then, if I thought out a scheme,
     to join with me to end the war?

KALONIKE: Indeed I would,
     even if I had to pawn this very wrap-around
     and drink up all the money in one day, I would!
MYRRHINA: And so would I, even if I had to see myself
     split like a flounder, and give half of me away!   115
LAMPITO: And so would Ah! Ah'd climb up Mount
     Taÿgetos
     if Ah just had a chance of seeing peace from theah!
LYSISTRATA: Then I will tell you. I may now divulge my plan.
     Women of Greece!—if we intend to force the men
     to make a peace, we must abstain . . .   120
KALONIKE: From what? Speak out!
LYSISTRATA: But will you do it?
KALONIKE: We will, though death should be the price!
LYSISTRATA: Well then, we must abstain utterly from the prick.
     Why do you turn your backs? Where are you off to now?
     And you—why pout and make such faces, shake your heads?
     Why has your color changed? Why do you shed those tears?   125
     Will you do it or will you not? Why hesitate?
KALONIKE: I will not do it. Never. Let the war go on!
MYRRHINA: Neither will I. By Zeus, no! Let the war go on!
LYSISTRATA: How can you say so, Madam Flounder, when just
     now
     you were declaiming you would split yourself in half?   130
KALONIKE: Anything else you like, anything! If I must
     I'll gladly walk through fire. That, rather than the prick!
     Because there's nothing like it, dear Lysistrata.
LYSISTRATA: How about you?
MYRRHINA: I too would gladly walk through fire.
LYSISTRATA: Oh the complete depravity of our whole sex!   135
     It is no wonder tragedies are made of us,
     we have such unrelenting unity of mind!
     But you, my friend from Sparta, dear, if you alone
     stand by me, only you, we still might save the cause.
     Vote on my side!   140
LAMPITO: They'ah hahd conditions, mahty hahd,
     to sleep without so much as the fo'skin of one . . .
     but all the same . . . well . . . yes. We need peace just as
     bad.
LYSISTRATA: Oh dearest friend!—the one real woman of them all!
KALONIKE: And if we really should abstain from what you say—
     which Heaven forbid!—do you suppose on that account   145
     that peace might come to be?
LYSISTRATA: I'm absolutely sure.
     If we should sit around, rouged and with skins well
     creamed,
     with nothing on but a transparent negligé,
     and come up to them with our deltas plucked quite smooth,
     and, once our men get stiff and want to come to grips,   150
     we do not yield to them at all but just hold off,
     they'll make a truce in no time. There's no doubt of that.
LAMPITO: We say in Spahta that when Menelaos saw
     Helen's ba'e apples he just tossed away his swo'd.
KALONIKE: And what, please, if our husbands just toss *us* away?   155
LYSISTRATA: Well, you have heard the good old saying: Know
     Thyself.
KALONIKE: It isn't worth the candle. I hate cheap substitutes.
     But what if they should seize and drag us by brute force
     into the bedroom?
LYSISTRATA: Hang onto the doors!
KALONIKE: And if—
     they beat us?   160

LYSISTRATA: Then you must give in, but nastily,
and do it badly. There's no fun in it by force.
And then, just keep them straining. They will give it up
in no time—don't you worry. For never will a man
enjoy himself unless the woman coincides.

165 KALONIKE: If both of you are for this plan, then so are we.
LAMPITO: And we of Spahta shall persuade ouah men to keep
the peace sinceahly and with honah in all ways,
but how could anyone pe'suade the vulgah mob
of Athens not to deviate from discipline?

170 LYSISTRATA: Don't worry, we'll persuade our men. They'll keep
the peace.
LAMPITO: They won't, so long as they have battleships afloat
and endless money sto'ed up in the Pahthenon.
LYSISTRATA: But that too has been carefully provided for:
we shall take over the Acropolis today.

175 The oldest women have their orders to do that:
while we meet here, they go as if to sacrifice
up there, but really seizing the Acropolis.
LAMPITO: All should go well. What you say theah is very
smaht.
LYSISTRATA: In that case, Lampito, what are we waiting for?

180 Let's take an oath, to bind us indissolubly.
LAMPITO: Well, just you show us what the oath is. Then we'll
sweah.
LYSISTRATA: You're right. Where is that lady cop?

(To the armed LADY COP looking around for a LADY COP.)

                                    What do you think
you're looking for? Put down your shield in front of us,
there, on its back, and someone get some scraps of gut.

185 KALONIKE: Lysistrata, what in the world do you intend
to make us take an oath on?
LYSISTRATA: What? Why, on a shield,
just as they tell me some insurgents in a play
by Aeschylus once did, with a sheep's blood and guts.
KALONIKE: Oh don't, Lysistrata, don't swear upon a shield,

190 not if the oath has anything to do with peace!
LYSISTRATA: Well then, what will we swear on? Maybe we
should get
a white horse somewhere, like the Amazons, and cut
some bits of gut from it.
KALONIKE: Where would we get a horse?

LYSISTRATA: But what kind of an oath is suitable for us?
195 KALONIKE: By Zeus, I'll tell you if you like. First we put down
a big black drinking-cup, face up, and then we let
the neck of a good jug of wine bleed into it,
and take a solemn oath to—add no water in.
LAMPITO: Bah Zeus, Ah jest can't tell you how Ah lahk that
oath!

200 LYSISTRATA: Someone go get a cup and winejug from inside.

(KALONIKE goes and is back in a flash.)

KALONIKE: My dears, my dearest dears—how's this for pottery?
You feel good right away, just laying hold of it.
LYSISTRATA: Well, set it down, and lay your right hand on
this pig.
O goddess of Persuasion, and O Loving-cup,
205 accept this victim's blood! Be gracious unto us.
KALONIKE: It's not anaemic, and flows clear. Those are good signs.

LAMPITO: What an aroma, too! Bah Castah it is sweet!
KALONIKE: My dears, if you don't mind—I'll be the first to
swear.
LYSISTRATA: By Aphrodite, no! If you had drawn first place
by lot—but now let all lay hands upon the cup.   210
Yes, Lampito—and now, let one of you repeat
for all of you what I shall say. You will be sworn
by every word she says, and bound to keep this oath:
No lover and no husband and no man on earth—
KALONIKE: No lover and no husband and no man on earth—   215
LYSISTRATA: shall e'er approach me with his penis up. Repeat.
KALONIKE: shall e'er approach me with his penis up. Oh dear,
my knees are buckling under me, Lysistrata!
LYSISTRATA: and I shall lead an unlaid life alone at home,
KALONIKE: and I shall lead an unlaid life alone at home,   220
LYSISTRATA: wearing a saffron gown and groomed and beautified
KALONIKE: wearing a saffron gown and groomed and beautified
LYSISTRATA: so that my husband will be all on fire for me
KALONIKE: so that my husband will be all on fire for me
LYSISTRATA: but I will never willingly give in to him   225
KALONIKE: but I will never willingly give in to him
LYSISTRATA: and if he tries to force me to against my will
KALONIKE: and if he tries to force me to against my will
LYSISTRATA: I'll do it badly and not wiggle in response
KALONIKE: I'll do it badly and not wiggle in response   230
LYSISTRATA: nor toward the ceiling will I lift my Persian pumps
KALONIKE: nor toward the ceiling will I lift my Persian pumps
LYSISTRATA: nor crouch down as the lions on cheese-graters do
KALONIKE: nor crouch down as the lions on cheese-graters do
LYSISTRATA: and if I keep my promise, may I drink of this—   235
KALONIKE: and if I keep my promise, may I drink of this—
LYSISTRATA: but if I break it, then may water fill the cup!
KALONIKE: but if I break it, then may water fill the cup!
LYSISTRATA: Do you all swear to this with her?
ALL: We do, by Zeus!
LYSISTRATA: I'll consecrate our oath now.   240
KALONIKE: Share alike, my dear,
so we'll be friendly to each other from the start.
LAMPITO: What was that screaming?
LYSISTRATA: That's what I was telling you:
the women have already seized the Parthenon
and the Acropolis. But now, dear Lampito,
return to Sparta and set things in order there—   245
but leave these friends of yours as hostages with us—
And let us join the others in the citadel
and help them bar the gates.
KALONIKE: But don't you think the men
will rally to the rescue of the citadel,
attacking us at once?   250
LYSISTRATA: They don't worry me much:
they'll never bring against us threats or fire enough
to force open the gates, except upon our terms.
KALONIKE: Never by Aphrodite! Or we'd lose our name
for being battle-axes and unbearable!

(Exeunt. The scene changes to the Propylaea of the Acropolis. A CHORUS
OF VERY OLD MEN struggles slowly in, carrying logs and firepots.)

ONE OLD MAN: Lead on! O Drakës, step by step, although your 255
shoulder's aching
and under this green olive log's great weight
your back be breaking!

ANOTHER: Eh, life is long but always has
260   more surprises for us!
             Now who'd have thought we'd live to hear
                    this, O Strymodorus?—

             The wives we fed and looked upon
                    as helpless liabilities
265   now dare to occupy the Parthenon,
             our whole Acropolis, for once they seize
                    the Propylaea, straightway
                    they lock and bar the gateway.
CHORUS: Let's rush to the Acropolis with due precipitation
270   and lay these logs down circlewise, till presently we turn them
      into one mighty pyre to make a general cremation
      of all the women up there—eh! with our own hands we'll
             burn them,
      the leaders and the followers, without discrimination!
AN OLD MAN: They'll never have the laugh on me!
275   Though I may not look it,
                    I rescued the Acropolis
                    when the Spartans took it
                    about a hundred years ago.
             We laid a siege that kept their king
280   six years unwashed, so when I made him throw
                    his armor off, for all his blustering,
                    in nothing but his shirt he
                    looked very very dirty.
CHORUS: How strictly I besieged the man! These gates were
      all invested
285   with seventeen ranks of armored men all equally ferocious!
      Shall women—by Euripides and all the gods detested—
      not be restrained—with me on hand—from something so
             atrocious?
      They shall!—or may our trophies won at Marathon be bested!
                    But we must go a long way yet
290   up that steep and winding road
      before we reach the fortress where we want to get.
                    How shall we ever drag this load,
                    lacking pack-mules, way up there?
      I can tell you that my shoulder has caved in
      beyond repair!
295   Yet we must trudge ever higher,
                    ever blowing on the fire,
             so its coals will still be glowing when we get
      where we are going
                    Fooh! Fooh!
                    Whoo! I choke!
300   What a smoke!

             Lord Herakles! How fierce it flies
                    out against me from the pot!
      and like a rabid bitch it bites me in the eyes!
             It's female fire, or it would not
305   scratch my poor old eyes like this.
             Yet undaunted we must onward, up the high
      Acropolis
                    where Athena's temple stands
                    fallen into hostile hands.
             O my comrades! shall we ever have a greater
      need to save her?
310   Fooh! Fooh!
                    Whoo! I choke!
                    What a smoke!

FIRST OLD MAN: Well, thank the gods, I see the fire is yet alive
      and waking!
SECOND OLD MAN: Why don't we set our lumber down right
      here in handy batches,
      then stick a branch of grape-vine in the pot until it catches 315
THIRD OLD MAN: and hurl ourselves against the gate with
      battering and shaking?
FIRST OLD MAN: and if the women won't unbar at such an
      ultimatum
      we'll set the gate on fire and then the smoke will suffocate
      'em.
SECOND OLD MAN: Well, let's put down our load. Fooh fooh,
      what smoke! But blow as needed!
THIRD OLD MAN: Your ablest generals *these* days would not carry 320
      wood like *we* did.
SECOND OLD MAN: At last the lumber ceases grinding my poor
      back to pieces!
THIRD OLD MAN: These are your orders, Colonel Pot: wake up
      the coals and bid them
      report here and present to me a torch lit up and flaring.
FIRST OLD MAN: O Victory, be with us! If you quell the
      women's daring
      we'll raise a splendid trophy of how you and we undid 325
      them!

(A CHORUS OF MIDDLE-AGED WOMEN *appears in the offing.*)

A WOMAN: I think that I perceive a smoke in which appears a
      flurry
      of sparks as of a lighted fire. Women, we'll have to hurry!
CHORUS OF WOMEN: Oh fleetly fly, oh swiftly flit,
             my dears, e'er Kalykë be lit
             and with Kritylla swallowed up alive 330
                    in flames which the gales dreadfully drive
                    and deadly old men fiercely inflate!
             Yet one thing I'm afraid of: will I not arrive too late?
      for filling up my water-jug has been no easy matter
      what with the crowd at the spring in the dusk and the 335
                    clamor and pottery clatter.
                    Pushed as I was, jostled by slave-
                    women and sluts marked with a brand
                    yet with my jug firmly in hand
                    here I have come, hoping to save 340
                    my burning friends and brave,

             for certain windy, witless, old,
             and wheezy fools, so I was told,
      with wood some tons in weight crept up this path,
             not having in mind heating a bath 345
             but uttering threats, vowing they will
      consume those nasty women into cinders on grill!
      But O Athena! never may I see my friends igniting!
      Nay!—let them save all the cities of Greece and their
             people from folly and fighting! 350
      Goddess whose crest flashes with gold,
             they were so bold taking your shrine
             only for this—Goddess who holds
             Athens—for *this* noble design,
             braving the flames, calling on you 355
                    to carry water too!

(ONE OF THE OLD MEN *urinates noisily.*)

CHORUS OF WOMEN: Be still! What was that noise? Aha! Oh, wicked and degraded!
Would any good religious men have ever done what *they* did?
CHORUS OF MEN: Just look! It's a surprise-attack! Oh, dear, we're being raided
360 by swarms of them below us when we've got a swarm above us!
CHORUS OF WOMEN: Why panic at the sight of us? This is not many of us.
We number tens of thousands but you've hardly seen a fraction.
CHORUS OF MEN: O Phaidrias, shall they talk so big and we not take some action?
Oh, should we not be bashing them and splintering our lumber?

(The OLD MEN *begin to strip for combat.)*

365 CHORUS OF WOMEN: Let us, too, set our pitchers down, so they will not encumber
our movements if these gentlemen should care to offer battle.
CHORUS OF MEN: Oh someone should have clipped their jaws— twice, thrice, until they rattle—
(as once the poet put it)—then we wouldn't hear their prating.
CHORUS OF WOMEN: Well, here's your chance. Won't someone hit me? Here I stand, just waiting!
370 No other bitch will ever grab your balls, the way I'll treat you!
CHORUS OF MEN: Shut up—or I will drub you so old age will never reach you!
CHORUS OF WOMEN: Won't anyone step and lay one finger on Stratyllis?
CHORUS OF MEN: And if we pulverize her with our knuckles, will you kill us?
CHORUS OF WOMEN: No, only chew your lungs out and your innards and your eyes, sir.
375 CHORUS OF MEN: How clever is Euripides! There is no poet wiser:
he says indeed that women are the worst of living creatures.
CHORUS OF WOMEN: Now is the time, Rhodippe: let us raise our brimming pitchers.
CHORUS OF MEN: Why come up here with water, you, the gods' abomination?
CHORUS OF WOMEN: And why come here with fire, you tomb? To give yourself cremation?
380 CHORUS OF MEN: To set your friends alight upon a pyre erected for them.
CHORUS OF WOMEN: And so we brought our water-jugs. Upon your pyre we'll pour them.
CHORUS OF MEN: *You'll* put my fire out?
CHORUS OF WOMEN: Any time! You'll see there's nothing to it.
CHORUS OF MEN: I think I'll grill you right away, with just this torch to do it!
CHORUS OF WOMEN: Have you some dusting-powder? Here's your wedding-bath all ready.
385 CHORUS OF MEN: *You'll* bathe me, garbage that you are?
CHORUS OF WOMEN: Yes, bridegroom, just hold steady!
CHORUS OF MEN: Friends, you have heard her insolence—
CHORUS OF WOMEN: I'm free-born, not your slave, sir.
CHORUS OF MEN: I'll have this noise of yours restrained—

CHORUS OF WOMEN: Court's out—so be less grave, sir.
CHORUS OF MEN: Why don't you set her hair on fire?
CHORUS OF WOMEN: Oh, Water, be of service!
CHORUS OF MEN: Oh woe is me!
CHORUS OF WOMEN: Was it too hot?
CHORUS OF MEN: Oh, stop! What *is* this? Hot? Oh no!   390
CHORUS OF WOMEN: I'm watering you to make you grow.
CHORUS OF MEN: I'm withered from this chill I got!
CHORUS OF WOMEN: You've got a fire, so warm yourself. You're trembling: are you nervous?

(Enter ATHENIAN COMMISSIONER, *escorted by four* SCYTHIAN PO-LICEMEN *with bows and quivers slung on their backs.)*

COMMISSIONER: Has the extravagance of women broken out into full fury, with their banging tambourines   395
and constant wailings for their oriental gods,
and on the roof-tops their Adonis festival,
which I could hear myself from the Assembly once?
For while Demostratos—that numbskull—had the floor,
urging an expedition against Sicily,   400
his wife was dancing and we heard her crying out
"Weep for Adonis!"—so the expedition failed
with such an omen. When the same Demostratos
was urging that we levy troops from our allies
his wife was on the roof again, a little drunk: 405
"Weep for Adonis! Beat your breast!" says she. At that,
he gets more bellicose, that god-Damn-ox-tratos.
To this has the incontinence of women come!
CHORUS OF MEN: You haven't *yet* heard how outrageous they can be!
With other acts of violence, these women here   410
have showered us from their jugs, so now we are reduced
to shaking out our shirts as if we'd pissed in them.
COMMISSIONER: Well, by the God of Waters, what do you expect?
When we ourselves conspire with them in waywardness
and give them good examples of perversity   415
such wicked notions naturally sprout in them.
We go into a shop and say something like this:
"Goldsmith, about that necklace you repaired: last night
my wife was dancing, when the peg that bolts the catch
fell from its hole. I have to sail for Salamis,   420
but if you have the time, by all means try to come
towards evening, and put in the peg she needs."
Another man says to a cobbler who is young
and has no child's-play of a prick, "Cobbler," he says,
"her sandal-strap is pinching my wife's little toe,   425
which is quite delicate. So please come by at noon
and stretch it for her so it has a wider play."
Such things as that result of course in things like this:
when I, as a Commissioner, have made a deal
to fit the fleet with oars and need the money now,   430
I'm locked out by these women from the very gates.
But it's no use just standing here. Bring on the bars,
so I can keep these women in their proper place.
What are *you* gaping at, you poor unfortunate?
Where are *you* looking? Only seeing if a bar   435
is open yet downtown? Come, drive these crowbars in
under the gates on that side, pry away, and I
will pry away on this.

*(*LYSISTRATA *comes out.)*

LYSISTRATA: No need to pry at all.
I'm coming out, of my own will. What use are bars?
440   It isn't bolts and bars we need so much as brains.
COMMISSIONER: Really, you dirty slut? Where is that officer?
Arrest her, and tie both her hands behind her back.
LYSISTRATA: By Artemis, just let him lift a hand at me
and, public officer or not, you'll hear him howl.
445 COMMISSIONER: You let her scare you? Grab her round the
middle, you.
Then *you* go help him and between you get her tied.

(KALONIKE *comes out.*)

KALONIKE: By Artemis, if you just lay one hand on her
I have a mind to trample the shit out of you.
COMMISSIONER: It's out already! Look! Now where's the other
one?
450   Tie up *that* woman first. She babbles, with it all.

(MYRRHINA *comes out.*)

MYRRHINA: By Hecatë, if you just lay a hand on her
you'll soon ask for a cup—to get your swellings down!

(*The* POLICEMAN *dashes behind the* COMMISSIONER *and clings to him
for protection.*)

COMMISSIONER: What happened? Where's that bowman, now?
Hold onto *her!*

(*He moves quickly away downhill.*)

I'll see that none of you can get away through here!
455 LYSISTRATA: By Artemis, you come near her and I'll bereave
your head of every hair! You'll weep for each one, too.
COMMISSIONER: What a calamity! This one has failed me too.
But never must we let ourselves be overcome
by women. All together now, O Scythians—
460   let's march against them in formation!
LYSISTRATA: You'll find out
that inside there we have four companies
of fighting women perfectly equipped for war.
COMMISSIONER: Charge! Turn their flanks, O Scythians! and tie
their hands!
LYSISTRATA: O allies—comrades—women! Sally forth and fight!
465   O vegetable vendors, O green-grocery-
grain-garlic-bread-bean-dealers and inn-keepers all!

(*A group of fierce* OLD MARKET-WOMEN, *carrying baskets of vegetables,
spindles, etc., emerges. There is a volley of vegetables. The* SCYTHIANS
are soon routed.)

Come pull them, push them, smite them, smash them
into bits!
Rail and abuse them in the strongest words you know!
Halt, Halt! Retire in order! We'll forego the spoils!
470 COMMISSIONER: (*Tragically, like say Xerxes.*) Oh what reverses
have my bowmen undergone!
LYSISTRATA: But what did you imagine? Did you think you came
against a pack of slaves? Perhaps you didn't know
that women can be resolute?
COMMISSIONER: I know they can—
above all when they spot a bar across the way.

CHORUS OF MEN: Commissioner of Athens, you are spending   475
words unduly,
to argue with these animals, who only roar the louder,
or don't you know they showered us so coldly and so
cruelly,
and in our undershirts at that, and furnished us no powder?
CHORUS OF WOMEN: But beating up your neighbor is
inevitably bringing
a beating on yourself, sir, with your own eyes black and   480
bloody.
I'd rather sit securely like a little girl demurely
not stirring up a single straw nor harming anybody,
So long as no one robs my hive and rouses me to stinging.
CHORUS OF MEN: How shall we ever tame these brutes? We
cannot tolerate
the situation further, so we must investigate   485
this occurrence and find
with what purpose in mind
they profane the Acropolis, sieze it, and lock
the approach to this huge and prohibited rock,
to our holiest ground!   490
Cross-examine them! Never believe one word
they tell you—refute them, confound them!
We must get to the bottom of things like this
and the circumstances around them.
COMMISSIONER: Yes indeed! and I want to know first one   495
thing:
just *why* you committed this treason,
barricading the fortress with locks and bars—
I insist on knowing the reason.
LYSISTRATA: To protect all the money up there from you—
you'll have nothing to fight for without it.   500
COMMISSIONER: You think it is *money* we're fighting for?
LYSISTRATA: All the troubles we have are about it.
It was so Peisander and those in power
of his kind could embezzle the treasure
that they cooked up emergencies all the time.   505
Well, let them, if such is their pleasure,
but they'll never get into this money again,
though you men should elect them to spend it.
COMMISSIONER: And just what will *you* do with it?
LYSISTRATA: Can you ask?
Of course we shall superintend it.   510
COMMISSIONER: You will superintend the treasury, *you!?*
LYSISTRATA: And why should it strike you so funny?
when we manage our houses in everything
and it's we who look after your money.
COMMISSIONER: But it's not the same thing!   515
LYSISTRATA: Why not?
COMMISSIONER: It's war,
and *this* money must pay the expenses.
LYSISTRATA: To begin with, you needn't be waging war.
COMMISSIONER: To survive, we don't need our defenses?
LYSISTRATA: You'll survive: we shall save you.
COMMISSIONER: Who? You?
LYSISTRATA: Yes, we.
COMMISSIONER: You absolutely disgust me.   520
LYSISTRATA: You may like it or not, but you *shall* be saved.
COMMISSIONER: I protest!
LYSISTRATA: If you care to, but, trust me,
this has got to be done all the same.

COMMISSIONER: It has?
It's illegal, unjust, and outrageous!

525 LYSISTRATA: We must save you, sir.

COMMISSIONER: Yes? And if I refuse?

LYSISTRATA: You will much the more grimly engage us.

COMMISSIONER: And whence does it happen that war and peace
are fit matters for women to mention?

LYSISTRATA: I will gladly explain—

COMMISSIONER: And be quick, or else
530 you'll be howling!

LYSISTRATA: Now, just pay attention
and keep your hands to yourself, if you can!

COMMISSIONER: But I can't. You can't think how I suffer
from holding them back in my anger!

AN OLD WOMAN: Sir—
if you don't you will have it much rougher.

535 COMMISSIONER: You may croak that remark to yourself, you hag!
Will *you* do the explaining?

LYSISTRATA: I'll do it.
Heretofore we women in time of war
have endured very patiently through it,
putting up with whatever you men might do,
540 for never a peep would you let us
deliver on your unstatesmanly acts
no matter how much they upset us,
but we knew very well, while we sat at home,
when you'd handled a big issue poorly,
545 and we'd ask you then, with a pretty smile
though our heart would be grieving us sorely,
"And what were the terms for a truce, my dear,
you drew up in assembly this morning?"
"And what's it to you?" says our husband, "Shut up!"
550 —so, as ever, at this gentle warning
I of course would discreetly shut up.

KALONIKE: Not me!
You can bet I would never be quiet!

COMMISSIONER: I'll bet, if you weren't, you were beaten up.

LYSISTRATA: *I'd* shut up, and I do not deny it,
555 but when plan after plan was decided on,
so bad we could scarcely believe it,
I would say "This last is so mindless, dear,
I cannot think how you achieve it!"
And then he would say, with a dirty look,
560 "Just you think what your spindle is for, dear,
or your head will be spinning for days on end—
let the *men* attend to the war, dear."

COMMISSIONER: By Zeus, *he* had the right idea!

LYSISTRATA: You fool!
Right ideas were quite out of the question,
565 when your reckless policies failed, and yet
we never could make a suggestion.
And lately we heard you say so yourselves:
in the streets there'd be someone lamenting:
"There's not one man in the country now!"
570 —and we heard many others assenting.
After that, we conferred through our deputies
and agreed, having briefly debated,
to act in common to save all Greece
at once—for why should we have waited?
575 So now, when we women are talking sense,
if you'll only agree to be quiet

and to listen to us as we did to you,
you'll be very much edified by it.

COMMISSIONER: *You* will edify *us!* I protest!

LYSISTRATA: Shut up!

COMMISSIONER: *I'm* to shut up and listen, you scum, you?! 580
Sooner death! And a veil on your head at that!

LYSISTRATA: We'll fix that. It may really become you:
do accept this veil as a present from me.
Drape it modestly—so—round your head, do you see?
And now—*not* a word more, sir. 585

KALONIKE: Do accept this dear little wool-basket, too!
Hitch your girdle and card! Here are beans you may chew
the way all of the nicest Athenians do—
and the *women* will see to the war, sir!

CHORUS OF WOMEN: Oh women, set your jugs aside and keep 590
a closer distance:
our friends may need from us as well some resolute
assistance.

Since never shall I weary of the stepping of the dance
nor will my knees of treading, for these ladies I'll advance
anywhere they may lead,
and they're daring indeed, 595
they have wit, a fine figure, and boldness of heart,
they are prudent and charming, efficient and smart,
patriotic and brave!

But, O manliest grandmothers, onward now!
And you matronly nettles, don't waver! 600
but continue to bristle and rage, my dears,
for you've still got the wind in your favor!

(*The* CHORUS OF WOMEN *and the* OLD MARKET-WOMEN *join.*)

LYSISTRATA: But if only the spirit of tender Love
and the power of sweet Aphrodite
were to breathe down over our breasts and thighs 605
an attraction both melting and mighty,
and infuse a pleasanter rigor in men,
raising only their cudgels of passion,
then I think we'd be known throughout all of Greece
as makers of peace and good fashion. 610

COMMISSIONER: Having done just what?

LYSISTRATA: Well, first of all
we shall certainly make it unlawful
to go madly to market in armor.

AN OLD MARKET-WOMAN: Yes!
By dear Aphrodite, it's awful!

LYSISTRATA: For now, in the midst of the pottery-stalls 615
and the greens and the beans and the garlic,
men go charging all over the market-place
in full armor and beetling and warlike.

COMMISSIONER: They must do as their valor impels them to!

LYSISTRATA: But it makes a man only look funny 620
to be wearing a shield with a Gorgon's head
and be wanting sardines for less money.

OLD MARKET-WOMEN: Well, I saw a huge cavalry-captain once
on a stallion that scarcely could hold him,
pouring into his helmet of bronze a pint 625
of pea-soup an old women had sold him,
and a Thracian who, brandishing shield and spear
like some savage Euripides staged once,

when he'd frightened a vendor of figs to death,
630   gobbled up all her ripest and aged ones.
COMMISSIONER: And how, on the international scale,
      can you straighten out the enormous
      confusion among all the states of Greece?
LYSISTRATA: Very easily.
COMMISSIONER: How? Do inform us.
635 LYSISTRATA: When our skein's in a tangle we take it thus
      on our spindles, or haven't you seen us?—
      one on this side and one on the other side,
      and we work out the tangles between us.
      And that is the way we'll undo this war,
640   by exchanging ambassadors, whether
      you like it or not, one from either side,
      and we'll work out the tangles together.
COMMISSIONER: Do you really think that with wools and skeins
      and just being able to spin you
645 can end these momentous affairs, you fools?
LYSISTRATA: With any intelligence in you
      you statesmen would govern as we work wool,
      and in everything Athens would profit.
COMMISSIONER: How so? Do tell.
LYSISTRATA: First, you take raw fleece
650   and you wash the beshittedness off it:
      just so, you should first lay the city out
      on a washboard and beat out the rotters
      and pluck out the sharpers like burrs, and when
      you find tight knots of schemers and plotters
655 who are out for key offices, card them loose,
      but best tear off their heads in addition.
      Then into one basket together card
      all those of a good disposition
      be they citizens, resident aliens, friends,
660   an ally or an absolute stranger,
      even people in debt to the commonwealth,
      you can mix them all in with no danger.
      And the cities which Athens has colonized—
      by Zeus, you should try to conceive them
665 as so many shreddings and tufts of wool
      that are scattered about and not leave them
      to lie around loose, but from all of them
      draw the threads in here, and collect them
      into one big ball and then weave a coat
670   for the people, to warm and protect them.
COMMISSIONER: Now, isn't this awful? They treat the state
      like wool to be beaten and carded,
      who have nothing at all to do with war!
LYSISTRATA: Yes we do, you damnable hard-head!
675 We have none of your honors but we have more
      than double your sufferings by it.
      First of all, we bear sons whom you send to war.
COMMISSIONER: Don't bring up our old sorrows! Be quiet!
LYSISTRATA: And now, when we ought to enjoy ourselves,
680   making much of our prime and our beauty,
      we are sleeping alone because all the men
      are away on their soldierly duty.
      But never mind *us*—when young girls grow old
      in their bedrooms with no men to share them.
685 COMMISSIONER: You seem to forget that men, too, grow old.
LYSISTRATA: By Zeus, but you cannot compare them!

When a man gets back, though he be quite gray,
      he can wed a young girl in a minute,
      but the season of woman is very short:
      she must take what she can while she's in it.   690
      And you know she must, for when it's past,
      although you're not awfully astute, you're
      aware that no man will marry her then
      and she sits staring into the future.
COMMISSIONER: But he who can raise an erection still—   695
LYSISTRATA: Is there some good reason you don't drop dead?
      We'll sell you a coffin if you but will.
      Here's a string of onions to crown your head
      and I'll make a honey-cake large and round
      you can feed to Cerberus underground!   700
FIRST OLD MARKET-WOMAN: Accept these few fillets of leek
      from me!
SECOND OLD MARKET-WOMAN: Let me offer you these for your
      garland, sir!
LYSISTRATA: What now? Do you want something else you see?
      Listen! Charon's calling his passenger—
      will you catch the ferry or still delay   705
      when his other dead want to sail away?
COMMISSIONER: Is it not downright monstrous to treat *me* like
      this?
      By Zeus, I'll go right now to the Commissioners
      and show myself in evidence, just as I am!

(He begins to withdraw with dignity and his four Scythian policemen.)

LYSISTRATA: Will you accuse us of not giving you a wake?   710
      But your departed spirit will receive from us
      burnt offerings in due form, two days from now at dawn!

*(LYSISTRATA with the other women goes into the Acropolis. The COM-
MISSIONER, etc., have left. The MALE CHORUS and the mixed FEMALE
CHORUS are alone.)*

CHORUS OF MEN: No man now dare fall to drowsing, if he
      wishes to stay free!
      Men, let's strip and gird ourselves for this eventuality!

      To me this all begins to have a smell   715
      of bigger things and larger things as well:
      most of all I sniff a tyranny afoot. I'm much afraid
      certain secret agents of the Spartans may have come,
      meeting under cover here, in Cleisthenes' home,
instigating those damned women by deceit to make a raid 720
      upon our treasury and that great sum
      the city paid my pension from.

Sinister events already!—think of lecturing the state,
women as they are, and prattling on of things like shields
      of bronze,
even trying hard to get us reconciled to those we hate— 725
those of Sparta, to be trusted like a lean wolf when it
      yawns!
All of this is just a pretext, men, for a dictatorship—
but to me they shall not dictate! Watch and ward! A sword
      I'll hide
underneath a branch of myrtle; through the agora I'll slip,
following Aristogeiton, backing the tyrannicide!   730

(The OLD MEN *pair off to imitate the gestures of the famous group statue of the tyrannicides Harmodius and Aristogeiton.)*

Thus I'll take my stand beside him! Now my rage is
 goaded raw
I'm as like as not to clip this damned old woman on the jaw!
CHORUS OF WOMEN: Your own mother will not know you when
 you come home, if you do!
Let us first, though, lay our things down, O my dear old
 friends
and true.

735 For now, O fellow-citizens, we would
  consider what will do our city good.
Well I may, because it bred me up in wealth and elegance:
 letting me at seven help with the embroidering
 of Athena's mantle, and at ten with offering
740 cakes and flowers. When I was grown and beautiful I had
  my chance
 to bear her baskets, at my neck a string
 of figs, and proud as anything.

Must I not, then, give my city any good advice I can?
Need you hold the fact against me that I was not born a man,
745 when I offer better methods than the present ones, and when
I've a share in this economy, for I contribute men?
But, you sad old codgers, *yours* is forfeited on many scores:
 you have drawn upon our treasure dating from the Persian
  wars,
what they call grampatrimony, and you've paid no taxes back.
750 Worse, you've run it nearly bankrupt, and the prospect's
  pretty black.
Have you anything to answer? Say you were within the law
and I'll take this rawhide boot and clip you one across the
 jaw!

CHORUS OF MEN: Greater insolence than ever!—
    that's the method that she calls
755   "better"—if you would believe her.
But this threat must be prevented! Every man with both
 his balls
must make ready—take our shirts off, for a man must reek
 of male
outright—not wrapped up in leafage like an omelet for sale!

  Forward and barefoot: we'll do it again
760 to the death, just as when we resisted
  tyranny out at Leipsydrion, when
  we really existed!

   Now or never we must grow
   young again and, sprouting wings
765   over all our bodies, throw
   off this heaviness age brings!

For if any of us give them even just a little hold
nothing will be safe from their tenacious grasp. They are
 so bold
they will soon build ships of war and, with exorbitant intent,
770 send such navies out against us as Queen Artemisia sent.
But if they attack with horse, our knights we might as
 well delete:
nothing rides so well as woman, with so marvelous a seat,
never slipping at the gallop. Just look at those Amazons

in that picture in the Stoa, from their horses bringing bronze
axes down on men. We'd better grab *these* members of the 775
 sex
one and all, arrest them, get some wooden collars on their
 necks!

CHORUS OF WOMEN: By the gods, if you chagrin me
   or annoy me, if you dare,
   I'll turn loose the sow that's in me
till you rouse the town to help you with the way I've done 780
 your hair!
Let us too make ready, women, and our garments quickly
 doff
so we'll smell like women angered fit to bite our fingers off!

  Now I am ready: let one of the men
  come against me, and *he'll* never hanker
  after a black bean or garlic again: 785
  no woman smells ranker!

   Say a single unkind word,
   I'll pursue you till you drop,
   as the beetle did the bird.
   My revenge will never stop! 790

Yet you will not worry me so long as Lampito's alive
and my noble friends in Thebes and other cities still
 survive.
You'll not overpower us, even passing seven decrees or eight,
you, poor brutes, whom everyone and everybody's
 neighbors hate.
Only yesterday I gave a party, honoring Hecatë, 795
but when I invited in the neighbor's child to come and play,
such a pretty thing from Thebes, as nice and quiet as you
 please,
just an eel, they said she couldn't, on account of your
 decrees.
You'll go on forever passing such decrees without a check
till somebody takes you firmly by the leg and breaks your 800
 neck!

*(*LYSISTRATA *comes out. The* CHORUS OF WOMEN *addresses her in the manner of tragedy.)*

Oh Queen of this our enterprise and all our hopes,
 wherefore in baleful brooding hast thou issued forth?
LYSISTRATA: The deeds of wicked women and the female mind
 discourage me and set me pacing up and down.
CHORUS OF WOMEN: What's that? What's that you say? 805
LYSISTRATA: The truth, alas, the truth!
CHORUS OF WOMEN: What is it that's so dreadful? Tell it to
 your friends.
LYSISTRATA: A shameful thing to tell and heavy not to tell.
CHORUS OF WOMEN: Oh, never hide from me misfortune that is
 ours!
LYSISTRATA: To put it briefly as I can, we are in heat. 810
CHORUS OF WOMEN: Oh Zeus!
LYSISTRATA: Why call on Zeus? This is the
 way things are.
At least it seems I am no longer capable
of keeping them from men. They are deserting me.
This morning I caught one of them digging away
to make a tunnel to Pan's grotto down the slope, 815

another letting herself down the parapet
with rope and pulley, and another climbing down
its sheerest face, and yesterday was one I found
sitting upon a sparrow with a mind to fly
820   down to some well-equipped whoremaster's place in town.
Just as she swooped I pulled her backward by the hair.
They think of every far-fetched excuse they can
for going home. And here comes one deserter now.
You there, where are you running?

FIRST WOMAN: I want to go home,
825   because I left some fine Milesian wools at home
that must be riddled now with moths.

LYSISTRATA: Oh, damn your moths!
Go back inside.

FIRST WOMAN: But I shall come back right away,
just time enough to stretch them out upon my bed.

LYSISTRATA: Stretch nothing out, and don't you go away at all.

830   FIRST WOMAN: But shall I let my wools be ruined?

LYSISTRATA: If you must.

SECOND WOMAN: Oh miserable me! I sorrow for the flax
I left at home unbeaten and unstripped!

LYSISTRATA: One more—
wanting to leave for stalks of flax she hasn't stripped.
Come back here!

SECOND WOMAN: But, by Artemis, I only want
835   to strip my flax. Then I'll come right back here again.

LYSISTRATA: Strip me no strippings! If you start this kind of
thing
some other woman soon will want to do the same.

THIRD WOMAN: O lady Artemis, hold back this birth until
I can get safe to some unconsecrated place!

840   LYSISTRATA: What is this raving?

THIRD WOMAN: I'm about to have a child.

LYSISTRATA: But you weren't pregnant yesterday.

THIRD WOMAN: I am today.
Oh, send me home this instant, dear Lysistrata,
so I can find a midwife.

LYSISTRATA: What strange tale is this?
What is this hard thing you have here?

THIRD WOMAN: The child is male.

845   LYSISTRATA: By Aphrodite, no! You obviously have
some hollow thing of bronze. I'll find out what it is.
You silly thing!—you have Athena's helmet here—
and claiming to be pregnant!

THIRD WOMAN: So I am, by Zeus!

LYSISTRATA: In that case, what's the helmet for?

THIRD WOMAN: So if the pains
850   came on me while I'm still up here, I might give birth
inside the helmet, as I've seen the pigeons do.

LYSISTRATA: What an excuse! The case is obvious. Wait here.
I want to show this bouncing baby helmet off.

(She passes the huge helmet around the CHORUS OF WOMEN.*)*

SECOND WOMAN: But I can't even sleep in the Acropolis,
855   not for an instant since I saw the sacred snake!

FOURTH WOMAN: The owls are what are killing *me.* How can I
sleep
with their eternal whit-to-whoo-to-whit-to-whoo?

LYSISTRATA: You're crazy! Will you stop this hocus-pocus now?

No doubt you miss your husbands: don't you think that they
are missing us as much? I'm sure the nights they pass   860
are just as hard. But, gallant comrades, do bear up,
and face these gruelling hardships yet a little while.
There is an oracle that says we'll win, if we
only will stick together. Here's the oracle.

CHORUS OF WOMAN: Oh, read us what it says!   865

LYSISTRATA: Keep silence, then and hear:
"*Now when to one high place are gathered the fluttering
swallows,
Fleeing the Hawk and the Cock however hotly it follows.
Then will their miseries end, and that which is over be under:
Thundering Zeus will decide.*

A WOMAN: Will *we* lie on top now, I wonder?

LYSISTRATA: *But if the Swallows go fighting each other and*   870
springing and winging
Out of the holy and high sanctuary, then people will never
Say there was any more dissolute bitch of a bird whatsoever."

A WOMAN: The oracle is clear, by Zeus!

LYSISTRATA: By *all* the gods!
So let us not renounce the hardships we endure.
But let us go back in. Indeed, my dearest friends,   875
it would be shameful to betray the oracle.

(Exeunt into the Acropolis.)

CHORUS OF MEN: Let me tell you a story I heard one day
    when I was a child:
There was once a young fellow Melanion by name
who refused to get married and ran away   880
    to the wild.
    To the mountains he came
    and inhabited there
        in a grove
    and hunted the hare   885
    both early and late
    with nets that he wove
    and also a hound
and he never came home again, such was his hate,
    all women he found   890
    so nasty, and we
    quite wisely agree.

    Let us kiss you, dear old dears!

CHORUS OF WOMEN: With no onions, you'll shed tears!

CHORUS OF MEN: I mean, lift my leg and *kick.*   895

CHORUS OF WOMEN: My, you wear your thicket thick!

CHORUS OF MEN: Great Myronides was rough
    at the front and black enough
    in the ass to scare his foes.
        Just ask anyone who knows: 900
        it's with hair that wars are won—
        take for instance Phormion.

CHORUS OF WOMEN: Let me tell you a story in answer to
    Melanion's case.
There is now a man, Timon, who wanders around   905
in the wilderness, hiding his face from view
    in a place
    where the brambles abound
    so he looks like a chip
    off a Fur-   910

y, curling his lip.
Now Timon retired
in hatred and pure
contempt of all men
915 and he cursed them in words that were truly inspired
again and again
but women he found
delightful and sound.

Would you like your jaw repaired?
920 CHORUS OF MEN: Thank you, no. You've got me scared.
CHORUS OF WOMEN: Let me jump and kick it though.
CHORUS OF MEN: You will let your man-sack show.
CHORUS OF WOMEN: All the same you wouldn't see,
old and gray as I may be,
925 any superfluity
of unbarbered hair on me;
it is plucked and more, you scamp,
since I singe it with a lamp!

(Enter LYSISTRATA on the wall.)

LYSISTRATA: Women, O women, come here quickly, here to me!
930 WOMEN: Whatever is it? Tell me! What's the shouting for?
LYSISTRATA: I see a man approaching, shaken and possessed,
seized and inspired by Aphrodite's power.
O thou, of Cyprus, Paphos, and Cythera, queen!
continue straight along this way you have begun!
935 A WOMAN: Whoever he is, where is he?
LYSISTRATA: Near Demeter's shrine.
A WOMAN: Why yes, by Zeus, he is. Whoever can he be?
LYSISTRATA: Well, look at him. Do any of you know him?
MYRRHINA: Yes.
I do. He's my own husband, too, Cinesias.
LYSISTRATA: Then it's your duty now to turn him on a spit,
940 cajole him and make love to him and not make love,
to offer everything, short of those things of which
the wine-cup knows.
MYRRHINA: I'll do it, don't you fear.
LYSISTRATA: And I
will help you tantalize him. I will stay up here
and help you roast him slowly. But now, disappear!

(Enter CINESIAS.)

945 CINESIAS: Oh how unfortunate I am, gripped by what spasms,
stretched tight like being tortured on a wheel!
LYSISTRATA: Who's there? Who has got this far past the
sentries?
CINESIAS: I.
LYSISTRATA: A man?
CINESIAS: A man, for sure.
LYSISTRATA: Then clear away from here.
CINESIAS: Who're you, to throw me out?
LYSISTRATA: The look-out for the day.
950 CINESIAS: Then, for the gods' sake, call Myrrhina out for me.
LYSISTRATA: You don't say! Call Myrrhina out! And who are you?
CINESIAS: Her husband. I'm Cinesias Paionides.
LYSISTRATA: Well, my dear man, hello! Your name is not
unknown
among us here and not without a certain fame,
955 because your wife has it forever on her lips.

She can't pick up an egg or quince but she must say:
Cinesias would enjoy it so!
CINESIAS: How wonderful!
LYSISTRATA: By Aphrodite, yes. And if we chance to talk
of husbands, your wife interrupts and says the rest
are nothing much compared to her Cinesias.   960
CINESIAS: Go call her.
LYSISTRATA: Will you give me something if I do?
CINESIAS: Indeed I will, by Zeus, if it is what you want.
I can but offer what I have, and I have this.
LYSISTRATA: Wait there. I will go down and call her.
CINESIAS: Hurry up!
because I find no charm whatever left in life   965
since she departed from the house. I get depressed
whenever I go into it, and everything
seems lonely to me now, and when I eat my food
I find no taste in it at all—because I'm stiff.
MYRRHINA: *(offstage)* I love him, how I love him! But he   970
doesn't want
my love! *(on wall)* So what's the use of calling me to him?
CINESIAS: My sweet little Myrrhina, why do you act like that?
Come down here.
MYRRHINA: There? By Zeus, I certainly will not.
CINESIAS: Won't you come down, Myrrhina, when I'm calling
you?
MYRRHINA: Not when you call me without needing   975
anything.
CINESIAS: Not needing anything? I'm desperate with need.
MYRRHINA: I'm going now.
CINESIAS: Oh no! No, don't go yet! At least
you'll listen to the baby. Call your mammy, you.
BABY: Mammy mammy mammy!
CINESIAS: What's wrong with you? Have you no pity on your   980
child
when it is six days now since he was washed or nursed?
MYRRHINA: Oh, *I* have pity. But his father takes no care of him.
CINESIAS: Come down, you flighty creature, for the child.
MYRRHINA: Oh, what it is to be a mother! I'll come down,
for what else can I do?   985

(MYRRHINA exits to reenter below.)

CINESIAS: It seems to me she's grown
much younger, and her eyes have a more tender look.
Even her being angry with me and her scorn
are just the things that pain me with the more desire.
MYRRHINA: Come let me kiss you, dear sweet little baby mine,
with such a horrid father. Mammy loves you, though.   990
CINESIAS: But why are you so mean? Why do you listen to
those other women, giving me such pain?—And you,
you're suffering yourself.
MYRRHINA: Take your hands off of me!
CINESIAS: But everything we have at home, my things and yours,
you're letting go to pieces.   995
MYRRHINA: Little do I care!
CINESIAS: Little you care even if your weaving's pecked apart
and carried off by chickens?
MYRRHINA: *(bravely.)*   Little I care, by Zeus!
CINESIAS: You have neglected Aphrodite's rituals
for such a long time now. Won't you come back again?

1000 MYRRHINA: Not I, unless you men negotiate a truce
  and make an end of war.
CINESIAS: Well, if it's so decreed,
  we will do even that.
MYRRHINA: Well, if it's so decreed,
  I will come home again. Not now. I've sworn I won't.
CINESIAS: All right, all right. But now lie down with me once
  more.
1005 MYRRHINA: No! No!—yet I don't say I'm not in love with you.
CINESIAS: You love me? Then why not lie down, Myrrhina dear?
MYRRHINA: Don't be ridiculous! Not right before the child!
CINESIAS: By Zeus, of course not. Manes, carry him back home.
  There now. You see the baby isn't in your way.
1010   Won't you lie down?
MYRRHINA: But *where,* you rogue, just where
  is one to do it?
CINESIAS: Where? Pan's grotto's a fine place.
MYRRHINA: But how could I come back to the Acropolis
  in proper purity?
CINESIAS: Well, there's a spring below
  the grotto—you can very nicely bathe in that.

(Ekkyklema or inset-scene with grotto.)

1015 MYRRHINA: And then I'm under oath. What if I break my vows?
CINESIAS: Let me bear all the blame. Don't worry about your
  oath.
MYRRHINA: Wait here, and I'll go get a cot for us.
CINESIAS: No no,
  the ground will do.
MYRRHINA: No, by Apollo! Though you *are*
  so horrid, I can't have you lying on the ground.

(Leaves.)

1020 CINESIAS: You know, the woman loves me—*that's* as plain as day.
MYRRHINA: There. Get yourself in bed and I'll take off my
  clothes.
  Oh, what a nuisance! I must go and get a mat.
CINESIAS: What for? I don't need one.
MYRRHINA: Oh yes, by Artemis!
  On the bare cords? How ghastly!
CINESIAS: Let me kiss you now.
1025 MYRRHINA: Oh, very well.
CINESIAS: Wow! Hurry, hurry and come back.

(MYRRHINA leaves. A long wait.)

MYRRHINA: Here is the mat. Lie down now, while I get
  undressed.
  Oh, what a nuisance! You don't have a pillow, dear.
CINESIAS: But I don't need one, not one bit!
MYRRHINA: By Zeus, I do!

(Leaves.)

CINESIAS: Poor prick, the service around here is terrible!
1030 MYRRHINA: Sit up, my dear, jump up! Now I've got
  everything.
CINESIAS: Indeed you have. And now, my golden girl, come
  here.

MYRRHINA: I'm just untying my brassiere. Now don't forget:
  about that treaty—you won't disappoint me, dear?
CINESIAS: By Zeus, no! On my life!
MYRRHINA: You have no blanket, dear.
CINESIAS: By Zeus, I do not need one. I just want to screw. 1035
MYRRHINA: Don't worry, dear, you will. I'll be back right away.

(Leaves.)

CINESIAS: This number, with her bedding, means to murder me.
MYRRHINA: Now raise yourself upright.
CINESIAS: But *this* is upright now!
MYRRHINA: Wouldn't you like some perfume?
CINESIAS: By Apollo, no!
MYRRHINA: By Aphrodite, yes! You must—like it or not. 1040

(Leaves.)

CINESIAS: Lord Zeus! Just let the perfume spill! That's all I ask!
MYRRHINA: Hold out your hand. Take some of this and rub it on.
CINESIAS: This perfume, by Apollo, isn't sweet at all.
  It smells a bit of stalling—not of wedding nights!
MYRRHINA: I brought the *Rhodian* perfume! How absurd of me! 1045
CINESIAS: It's fine! Let's keep it.
MYRRHINA: You *will* have your little joke.

(Leaves.)

CINESIAS: Just let me at the man who first distilled perfumes!
MYRRHINA: Try this, in the long vial.
CINESIAS: I've got one like it, dear.
  But don't be tedious. Lie down. And please don't bring
  anything more. 1050
MYRRHINA: *(Going.)* That's what I'll do, by Artemis!
  I'm taking off my shoes. But dearest, don't forget
  you're going to vote for peace.
CINESIAS: I will consider it.
  She has destroyed me, murdered me, that woman has!
  On top of which she's got me skinned and gone away!

   What shall I do? Oh, whom shall I screw, 1055
   cheated of dear Myrrhina, the first
   beauty of all, a creature divine?
   How shall I tend this infant of mine?
   Find me a pimp: it has to be nursed!
CHORUS OF MEN: *(In tragic style, as if to Prometheus or Andromeda*
  bound.)
   In what dire woe, how heavy-hearted 1060
   I see thee languishing, outsmarted!
    I pity thee, alas I do.
   What kidney could endure such pain,
   what spirit could, what balls, what back,
   what loins, what sacroiliac, 1065
   if they came under such a strain
   and never had a morning screw?
CINESIAS: O Zeus! the twinges! Oh, the twitches!
CHORUS OF MEN: And this is what she did to you,
  that vilest, hatefullest of bitches! 1070
CINESIAS: Oh nay, by Zeus, she's dear and sweet!
CHORUS OF MEN: How can she be? She's vile, O Zeus, she's vile!
  Oh treat her, Zeus, like so much wheat—
  O God of Weather, hear my prayer—

1075   and raise a whirlwind's mighty blast
    to roll her up into a pile
    and carry her into the sky
    far up and up and then at last
    drop her and land her suddenly
1080   astride that pointed penis there!

(The ekkyklema turns, closing the inset-scene. Enter, from opposite sides, a SPARTAN HERALD *and an* ATHENIAN OFFICIAL.*)*

SPARTAN: Wheah is the Senate-house of the Athenians?
    Ah wish to see the chaihman. Ah have news fo him.
ATHENIAN: And who are you? Are you a Satyr or a man?
SPARTAN: Ah am a herald, mah young friend, yes, by the gods,
1085   and Ah have come from Sparta to negotiate.
ATHENIAN: And yet you come here with a spear under your
    arm?
SPARTAN: Not Ah, bah Zeus, not Ah!
ATHENIAN: Why do you turn around?
    Why throw your cloak out so in front? Has the long trip
    given you a swelling?
SPARTAN: Ah do think the man is queah!
1090 ATHENIAN: But you have an erection, oh you reprobate!
SPARTAN: Bah Zeus, Ah've no sech thing! And don't you fool
    around!
ATHENIAN: And what have you got there?
SPARTAN: A Spahtan scroll-stick, suh.
ATHENIAN: Well, if it is, *this* is a Spartan scroll-stick, too.
    But look, I know what's up: you can tell *me* the truth.
1095   Just how are things with you in Sparta: tell me that.
SPARTAN: Theah is uprising in all Spahta. Ouah allies
    are all erect as well. We need ouah milkin'-pails.
ATHENIAN: From where has this great scourge of frenzy fallen
    on you?
    From Pan?
SPARTAN: No, Ah think Lampito began it all,
1100   and then, the othah women throughout Spahta joined
    togethah, just lahk at a signal fo a race,
    and fought theah husbands off and drove them from theah
    cunts.
ATHENIAN: So, how're you getting on?
SPARTAN: We suffah. Through the town
    we walk bent ovah as if we were carrying
1105   lamps in the wind. The women will not let us touch
    even theah berries, till we all with one acco'd
    have made a peace among the cities of all Greece.
ATHENIAN: This is an international conspiracy
    launched by the women! Now I comprehend it all!
1110   Return at once to Sparta. Tell them they must send
    ambassadors fully empowered to make peace.
    And our Assembly will elect ambassadors
    from our side, when I say so, showing them this prick.
SPARTAN: Ah'll run! Ah'll flah! Fo all you say is excellent!
1115 CHORUS OF MEN: No wild beast is more impossible than
       woman is to fight,
    nor is fire, nor has the panther such unbridled appetite!
CHORUS OF WOMEN: Well you know it, yet you go on warring
       with me without end,
    when you might, you cross-grained creature, have me as a
       trusty friend.

CHORUS OF MEN: Listen: I will never cease from hating women
       till I die!
CHORUS OF WOMEN: Any time you like. But meanwhile is   1120
       there any reason why
    I should let you stand there naked, looking so ridiculous?
    I am only coming near you, now, to slip your coat on, thus.
CHORUS OF MEN: That was very civil of you, very kind to treat
       me so,
    when in such uncivil rage I took it off a while ago.
CHORUS OF WOMEN: Now you're looking like a man again,   1125
       and not ridiculous.
    If you hadn't hurt my feelings, I would not have made a fuss,
    I would even have removed that little beast that's in your eye.
CHORUS OF MEN: *That* is what was hurting me! Well, won't
       you take my ring to pry
    back my eyelid? Rake the beast out. When you have it, let
       me see,
    for some time now it's been at my eye and irritating me.   1130
CHORUS OF WOMEN: Very well, I will—though you were *born*
       an irritable man.
    What a monster of a gnat, by Zeus! Look at it if you can.
    Don't you see it? It's a native of great marshes, can't you tell?
CHORUS OF MEN: Much obliged, by Zeus! The brute's been
       digging at me like a well!
    So that now you have removed it, streams of tears come   1135
       welling out.
CHORUS OF WOMEN: I will dry them. You're the meanest man
       alive, beyond a doubt,
    yet I will, and kiss you, too.
CHORUS OF MEN: Don't kiss me!
CHORUS OF WOMEN: If you will or not!
CHORUS OF MEN: Damn you! Oh, what wheedling flatterers
       you all are, born and bred!
    That old proverb is quite right and not inelegantly said:
    "There's no living *with* the bitches and, without them,   1140
       even *less*"—
    so I might as well make peace with you, and from now on,
       I guess,
    I'll do nothing mean to you and, from you, suffer nothing
       wrong.
    So let's draw our ranks together now and start a little song:

    For a change, we're not preparing
    any mean remark or daring   1145
    aimed at any man in town,
   but the very opposite: we plan to do and say
  only good to everyone,
  when the ills we have already are sufficient anyway.
    Any man or woman who   1150
    wants a little money, oh
    say three minas, maybe two,
    kindly let us know.
    What we have is right in here.
    (Notice we have purses, too!)   1155
    And if ever peace appear,
    he who takes our loan today
       never need repay.

    We are having guests for supper,
    allies asked in by our upper   1160
    classes to improve the town.

There's pea-soup, and I had killed a sucking-pig of mine:
I shall see it is well done,
so you will be tasting something very succulent and fine.

1165   Come to see us, then, tonight
    early, just as soon as you
    have a bath and dress up right:
    bring your children, too.
    Enter boldly, never mind
1170   asking anyone in sight.
    Go straight in and you will find
    you are quite at home there, but
    all the doors are shut.

And here come the Spartan ambassadors,
1175   dragging beards that are really the biggest I
have ever beheld, and around their thighs
        they are wearing some sort of a pig-sty.

    Oh men of Sparta, let me bid you welcome first,
    and then you tell us how you are and why you come.
1180 SP. AMB.: What need is theah to speak to you in many words?
    Fo you may see youahself in what a fix we come.
    CHORUS OF MEN: Too bad! Your situation has become
    terribly hard and seems to be at fever-pitch.
    SP. AMB.: Unutterably so! And what is theah to say?
1185   Let someone bring us peace on any tuhms he will!
    CHORUS OF MEN: And here I see some natives of Athenian soil,
    holding their cloaks far off their bellies, like the best
    wrestlers, who sicken at the touch of cloth. It seems
    that overtraining may bring on this strange disease.
1190 ATH. AMB.: Will someone tell us where to find Lysistrata?
    We're men, and here we are, in this capacity.
    CHORUS OF MEN: This symptom and that other one sound
      much alike.
    Toward morning I expect convulsions do occur?
    ATH. AMB.: By Zeus, we are exhausted with just doing that,
1195   so, if somebody doesn't reconcile us quick,
    there's nothing for it: we'll be screwing Cleisthenes.
    CHORUS OF MEN: Be careful—put your cloaks on, or you might
      be seen
    by some young blade who knocks the phalluses off herms.
    ATH. AMB.: By Zeus, an excellent idea!
    SP. AMB.: *(Having overheard.)*   Yes, bah the gods!
1200   It altogethah is. Quick, let's put on our cloaks.

*(Both groups cover quick and then recognize each other with full
diplomatic pomp.)*

ATH. AMB.: Greetings, O men of Sparta! *(To his group.)* We have
    been disgraced!
SP. AMB.: *(To one of his group.)* Mah dearest fellah, what a
    dreadful thing fo *us,*
if these Athenians had seen ouah wo'st defeat!
ATH. AMB.: Come now, O Spartans: one must specify each point.
1205   Why have you come here?
SP. AMB.:   To negotiate a peace.
We ah ambassadahs.
ATH. AMB.:   Well put. And so are we.
Therefore, why do we not call in Lysistrata,
she who alone might get us to agree on terms?
SP. AMB.: Call her or any man, even a Lysistratus!

CHORUS OF MEN: But you will have no need, it seems, to call   1210
    her now,
    for here she is. She heard you and is coming out.
CHORUS OF MEN *and* CHORUS OF WOMEN: All hail, O manliest
    woman of all!
    It is time for you now to be turning
into something still better, more dreadful, mean,
        unapproachable, charming, discerning,   1215
    for here are the foremost nations of Greece,
        bewitched by your spells like a lover,
who have come to you, bringing you all their claims,
    and to *you* turning everything over.
LYSISTRATA: The work's not difficult, if one can catch them now   1220
    while they're excited and not making passes at
    each other. I will soon find out. Where's *HARMONY?*

(A naked maid, perhaps wearing a large ribbon reading HARMONY,
appears from inside.)

    Go take the Spartans first, and lead them over here,
    not with a rough hand nor an overbearing one,
    nor, as our husbands used to do this, clumsily,   1225
    but like a woman, in our most familiar style:
    If he won't give his hand, then lead him by the prick.
    And now, go bring me those Athenians as well,
    leading them by whatever they will offer you.
    O men of Sparta, stand right here, close by my side,   1230
    and *you* stand over there, and listen to my words.
    I am a woman, yes, but there is mind in me.
    In native judgment I am not so badly off,
    and, having heard my father and my elders talk
    often enough, I have some cultivation, too.   1235
    And so, I want to take and scold you, on both sides,
    as you deserve, for though you use a lustral urn
    in common at the altars, like blood-relatives,
    when at Olympia, Delphi, or Thermopylae—
    how many others I might name if I took time!—   1240
    yet, with barbarian hordes of enemies at hand,
    it is Greek men, it is Greek cities, you destroy.
    That is one argument so far, and it is done.
ATH. AMB.: My prick is skinned alive—that's what's destroy-
    ing *me.*
LYSISTRATA: Now, men of Sparta—for I shall address you first—   1245
    do you not know that once one of your kings came here
    and as a suppliant of the Athenians
    sat by our altars, death-pale in his purple robe,
    and begged us for an army? For Messenē then
    oppressed you, and an earthquake from the gods as well.   1250
    Then Cimon went, taking four thousand infantry,
    and saved the whole of Lacedaemon for your state.
    That is the way Athenians once treated you;
    you ravage their land now, which once received you well.
ATH. AMB.: By Zeus, these men are in the wrong, Lysistrata!   1255
SP. AMB.: *(With his eyes on* HARMONY.) We'ah wrong . . . What
    an unutterably lovely ass!
LYSISTRATA: Do you suppose I'm letting you Athenians off?
    Do you not know that once the Spartans in their turn,
    when you were wearing the hide-skirts of slavery,
    came with their spears and slew many Thessalians,   1260
    many companions and allies of Hippias?

They were the only ones who fought for you that day,
freed you from tyranny and, for the skirt of hide,
gave back your people the wool mantle of free men.
1265 SP. AMB.: Ah nevah saw a woman broadah—in her views.
ATH. AMB.: And I have never seen a lovelier little nook.
LYSISTRATA: So why, when you have done each other so much
   good,
go on fighting with no end of malevolence?
Why don't you make a peace? Tell me, what's in your way?
1270 SP. AMB.: Whah, *we* ah willin', if *they* will give up to us
that very temptin' cuhve. *(Of* HARMONY, *as hereafter.)*
LYSISTRATA: What curve, my friend?
SP. AMB.:   The bay
of Pylos, which we've wanted and felt out so long.
ATH. AMB.: No, by Poseidon, you will not get into that!
LYSISTRATA: Good friend, do let them have it.
ATH. AMB.:   No! What other town
1275 can we manipulate so well?
LYSISTRATA: Ask them for one.
ATH. AMB.: Damn, let me think! Now first suppose you cede
   to us
that bristling tip of land, Echinos, behind which
the gulf of Malia recedes, and those long walls,
the legs on which Megara reaches to the sea.
1280 SP. AMB.: No, mah deah man, not *everything,* bah Castah, no!
LYSISTRATA: Oh, give them up. Why quarrel for a pair of legs?
ATH. AMB.: I'd like to strip and get to plowing right away.
SP. AMB.: And *Ah* would lahk to push manuah, still earliah.
LYSISTRATA: When you have made a peace, then you will do
   all that.
1285 But if you want to do it, first deliberate,
go and inform your allies and consult with them.
ATH. AMB.: Oh, damn our allies, my good woman! We are stiff.
Will all of our allies not stand resolved with us—
namely, to screw?
SP. AMB.:   And so will ouahs, Ah'll guarantee.
1290 ATH. AMB.: Our mercenaries, even, will agree with us.
LYSISTRATA: Excellent. Now to get you washed and purified
so you may enter the Acropolis, where we
women will entertain you out of our supplies.
You will exchange your pledges there and vows for peace.
1295 And after that each one of you will take his wife,
departing then for home.
ATH. AMB.:   Let's go in right away.
SP. AMB.: Lead on, ma'am, anywheah you lahk.
ATH. AMB.:   Yes, and be quick.

(Exeunt into Acropolis.)

CHORUS OF MEN *and* CHORUS OF WOMEN:
         All the rich embroideries, the
         scarves, the gold accessories, the
1300   trailing gowns, the robes I own
   I begrudge to no man: let him take what things he will
   for his children or a grown
   daughter who must dress for the procession up Athena's
      hill.
         Freely of my present stocks
1305   I invite you all to take.
         There are here no seals nor locks

very hard to break.
Search through every bag and box,
look—you will find nothing there   1310
if your eyesight isn't fine—
sharper far than mine!

Are there any of you needing
food for all the slaves you're feeding,
all your little children, too?

I have wheat in tiny grains for you, the finest sort,   1315
and I also offer you
plenty of the handsome strapping grains that slaves get by the
   quart.

         So let any of the poor
         visit me with bag or sack
         which my slave will fill with more   1320
         wheat than they can pack,
         giving each his ample share.
         Might I add that at my door
         I have watch-dogs?—so beware.
         Come too close by day or night,   1325
         you will find they bite.

(Voice of drunken ATHENIANS *from inside.)*

FIRST ATHENIAN: Open the door! *(Shoves the* PORTER *aside.)*
                        And will you get out of my way?

(A second drunken ATHENIAN *follows. The first sees the* CHORUS.*)*

What are you sitting *there* for? Shall I, with this torch,
burn you alive? *(Drops character.)*
                        How vulgar! Oh, how commonplace!
I can not do it!   1330

(Starts back in. The second ATHENIAN *stops him and remonstrates
with him in a whisper. The first turns and addresses the audience.)*
                        Well, if it really must be done
   to please you, we shall face it and go through with it.
CHORUS OF MEN *and* CHORUS OF WOMEN:
   And *we* shall face it and go through with it with you.
FIRST ATHENIAN: *(In character again, extravagantly.)*
   Clear out of here! Or you'll be wailing for your hair!

*(*CHORUS OF WOMEN *scours away in mock terror.)*

Clear out of here! so that the Spartans can come out
and have no trouble leaving, after they have dined.   1335

*(*CHORUS OF MEN *scours away in mock terror.)*

SECOND ATHENIAN: I never saw a drinking-party like this
   one:
   even the Spartans were quite charming, and of course
   we make the cleverest company, when in our cups.
FIRST ATHENIAN: You're right, because when sober we are not
   quite sane.
   If I can only talk the Athenians into it,   1340
   we'll always go on any embassy quite drunk,
   for now, going to Sparta sober, we're so quick
   to look around and see what trouble we can make
   that we don't listen to a single word they say—

1345   instead we think we hear them say what they do not—
      and none of our reports on anything agree.
      But just now everything was pleasant. If a man
      got singing words belonging to another song,
      we all applauded and swore falsely it was fine!
1350   But here are those same people coming back again
      to the same spot! Go and be damned, the pack of you!

(The CHORUS OF MEN AND WOMEN, *having thrown off their masks,
put on other cloaks, and rushed back on stage, stays put.*)

SECOND ATHENIAN: Yes, damn them, Zeus! Just when the
      party's coming out!

(*The party comes rolling out.*)

A SPARTAN: (*To another.*) Mah very chahmin friend, will you
      take up youah flutes?
1355   Ah'll dance the dipody and sing a lovely song
      of us and the Athenians, of both at once!
FIRST ATHENIAN: (*As pleasantly as he can.*)
      Oh yes, take up your little reeds, by all the gods:
      I very much enjoy seeing you people dance.

SPARTAN: Memory, come,
1360   come inspiah thah young
         votaries to song,
         come inspiah theah dance!

(*Other* SPARTANS *join.*)

         Bring thah daughtah, bring the sweet
         Muse, fo well she knows
1365   us and the Athenians,
         how at Ahtemisium
         they in godlike onslaught rose
         hahd against the Puhsian fleet,
         drove it to defeat!
1370   Well she knows the Spartan waws,
         how Leonidas
         in the deadly pass
         led us on lahk baws
         whettin' shahp theah tusks, how sweat
1375   on ouah cheeks in thick foam flowahed,
         off ouah legs how thick it showahed,
         fo the Puhsian men were mo'
         than the sands along the sho'.
         Goddess, huntress, Ahtemis,
1380   slayeh of the beasts, descend:
         vuhgin goddess, come to this
         feast of truce to bind us fast
         so ouah peace may nevah end.
         Now let friendship, love, and wealth
1385   come with ouah acco'd at last.
         May we stop ouah villainous
         wahly foxy stealth!
           Come, O huntress, heah to us,
           heah, O vuhgin, neah to us!

LYSISTRATA: Come, now that all the rest has been so well
      arranged,
      you Spartans take these women home; these others, you.   1390
      Let husband stand beside his wife, and let each wife
      stand by her husband: then, when we have danced a dance
      to thank the gods for our good fortune, let's take care
      hereafter not to make the same mistakes again.
ATHENIAN: Bring on the chorus! Invite the three Graces to   1395
      follow,
      and then call on Artemis, call her twin brother,
      the leader of choruses, healer Apollo!
CHORUS OF MEN AND WOMEN: (*Joins.*) Pray for their friendliest
      favor, the one and the other.
      Call Dionysus, his tender eyes casting
      flame in the midst of his Maenads ecstatic with dancing.   1400
      Call upon Zeus, the resplendent in fire,
      call on his wife, rich in honor and ire,
      call on the powers who possess everlasting
      memory, call them to aid,
      call them to witness the kindly, entrancing   1405
      peace Aphrodite has made!
         Alalai!
         Bound, and leap high! Alalai!
         Cry, as for victory, cry
         Alalai!   1410
LYSISTRATA: Sing us a new song, Spartans, capping our new song.
SPARTANS: Leave thah favohed mountain's height,
      Spahtan Muse, come celebrate
      Amyclae's lord with us and great
      Athena housed in bronze;   1415
      praise Tyndareus' paih of sons,
      gods who pass the days in spoht
      wheah the cold Eurotas runs.

(*General dancing.*)

      Now to tread the dance,
      now to tread it light,   1420
      praising Spahta, wheah you find
        love of singing quickened bah the pounding beat
         of dancing feet,
      when ouah guhls lahk foals cavoht
      wheah the cold Eurotas runs,   1425
      when they fleetly bound and prance
        till theah haih unfilleted shakes in the wind,
      as of Maenads brandishin'
      ahvied wands and revelin',
        Leda's daughtah, puah and faiah,   1430
        leads the holy dances theah.
FULL CHORUS: (*As everyone leaves dancing.*)
      So come bind up youah haih with youah hand,
        with youah feet make a bound
      lahk a deeah; fo the chorus clap out
        an encouragin' sound,   1435
      singin' praise of the temple of bronze
        housin' her we adaw:
      sing the praise of Athena: the goddess unvanquished in
      waw!

CRITICAL CONTEXTS

Born near Macedonia, Aristotle entered the Academy in Athens at the age of seventeen to study with Plato. After Plato's death, Aristotle conducted research in natural history—mainly botany and zoology—throughout the Aegean region and served as the tutor of the young Alexander the Great in Macedon, before returning to Athens to found the Lyceum in 355 BCE.

Aristotle wrote extensively on topics ranging from ethics, rhetoric, and metaphysics to physics and natural history. In The Poetics, *he analyzes the field of poetry into different "species" or genres (epic, tragedy, comedy, dithyramb) and attempts to discover the basic features of each. The Poetics demonstrates Aristotle's extensive knowledge of drama, which he uses to refine a keen sense of the form and purpose of tragedy. We should remember that* The Poetics *was written sometime after 335 BCE, roughly a century after the height of the Athenian theater. And although* The Poetics *is the cornerstone of Western dramatic criticism, the meaning of several of Aristotle's key terms—*MIMESIS *(imitation),* CATHARSIS *(purgation),* HAMARTIA *(error)—remain controversial.*

ARISTOTLE
(384–322 BCE)

from *The Poetics*
(c. 335 BCE)

TRANSLATED BY
GERALD F. ELSE

The art of poetic composition in general and its various species, the function and effect of each of them; how the plots should be constructed if the composition is to be an artistic success; how many other component elements are involved in the process, and of what kind; and similarly all the other questions that fall under this same branch of inquiry—these are the problems we shall discuss; let us begin in the right and natural way, with basic principles.

Epic composition, then; the writing of tragedy, and of comedy also; the composing of dithyrambs; and the greater part of the making of music with flute and lyre: these are all in point of fact, taken collectively, imitative processes. They differ from each other, however, in three ways, namely by virtue of having (1) different means, (2) different objects, and (3) different methods of imitation.

**BASIC
CONSIDERATIONS**

First, in the same way that certain people imitate a variety of things by means of shapes and colors, making visible replicas of them (some doing this on the basis of art, others out of habit), while another group produces its mimicry with the voice, so in the case of the arts we just mentioned: they all carry on their imitation through the media of rhythm, speech, and melody, but with the latter two used separately or together. Thus the arts of flute and lyre music, and any others of similar nature and effect such as the art of the pan-pipe, produce their imitation using melody and rhythm alone, while there is another which does so using speeches or verses alone, bare of music, and either mixing the verses with one another or employing just one certain kind—an art which is, as it happens, nameless up to the present time. In fact we could not even assign a common name to the mimes of Sophron and Xenarchus and the Socratic discourses: nor again if somebody should compose his imitation in trimeters or elegiac couplets or certain other verses of that kind; (Except people do link up poetic composition with verse and speak of "elegiac poets," "epic poets," not treating them as poets by virtue of their imitation, but employing the term as a common appellation going along with the use of verse. And in fact the name is also applied to anyone who treats a medical or scientific topic in verses, yet Homer and Empedocles actually have nothing in common except their verse; hence the proper term for the one is "poet," for the other, "science-writer" rather than "poet.") and likewise if someone should mix all the kinds of verse together in composing his imitation, as Chaeremon composed a *Centaur* using all the verses.

**THE
DIFFERENTIATION
ACCORDING TO
MEDIUM**

Such is the disjunction we feel is called for in these cases. There are on the other hand certain arts which use all the aforesaid media, I mean such as rhythm, song, and verse. The composition of dithyrambs and of nomes does so, and both tragedy and comedy. But there is a difference in that some of these arts use all the media at once while others use them in different parts of the work.

These then are the differentiations of the poetic arts with respect to the media in which the poets carry on their imitation.

THE OBJECTS OF IMITATION

Since those who imitate men in action, and these must necessarily be either worthwhile or worthless people (for definite characters tend pretty much to develop in men of action), it follows that they imitate men either better or worse than the average, as the painters do—for Polygnotus used to portray superior and Pauson inferior men; and it is evident that each of the forms of imitation aforementioned will include these differentiations, that is, will differ by virtue of imitating objects which are different in this sense. Indeed it is possible for these dissimilarities to turn up in flute and lyre playing, and also in prose dialogues and bare verses: thus Homer imitated superior men and Hegemon of Thasos, the inventor of parody, and Nicochares, the author of the *Deiliad,* inferior ones, likewise in connection with dithyrambs and nomes, for one can make the imitation the way Timotheus and Philoxenus did their *Cyclopes.* Finally, the difference between tragedy and comedy coincides exactly with the master-difference: namely the one tends to imitate people better, the other one people worse, than the average.

THE MODES OF IMITATION

The third way of differentiating these arts is by the mode of imitation. For it is possible to imitate the same objects, and in the same media, (1) by narrating part of the time and dramatizing the rest of the time, which is the way Homer composes (mixed mode), or (2) with the same person continuing without change (straight narrative), or (3) with all the persons who are performing the imitation acting, that is, carrying on for themselves (straight dramatic mode).

JOTTINGS, CHIEFLY ON COMEDY

Poetic imitation, then, shows these three *differentiae,* as we said at the beginning: in the media, objects, and modes of imitation. So in one way Sophocles would be the same (kind of) imitator as Homer, since they both imitate worthwhile people, and in another way the same as Aristophanes, for they both imitate people engaged in action, doing things. In fact some authorities maintain that that is why plays are called dramas, because the imitation is of men acting (*drôntas,* from *drân,* 'do, act'). It is also the reason why both tragedy and comedy are claimed by the Dorians: comedy by the Megarians, both those from hereabouts, who say that it came into being during the period of their democracy, and those in Sicily, and tragedy by some of those in the Peloponnese. They use the names "comedy" and "drama" as evidence; for they say that *they* call their outlying villages *kômai* while the Athenians call theirs "demes" (*dêmoi*)—the assumption being that the participants in comedy were called *kômôidoi* not from their being revelers but because they wandered from one village to another, being degraded and excluded from the city—and that they call "doing" or "acting" *drân* while the Athenians designate it by *prattein.*

THE ORIGIN AND DEVELOPMENT OF POETRY

So much, then, for the *differentiae* of imitation, their number and identity. As to the origin of the poetic art as a whole, it stands to reason that two operative causes brought it into being, both of them rooted in human nature. Namely (1) the habit of imitating is congenital to human beings from childhood (actually man differs from the other animals in that he is the most imitative and learns his first lessons through imitation), and so is (2) the pleasure that all men take in works of imitation. A proof of this is what happens in our experience. There are things which we see with pain so far as they themselves are concerned but whose images, even when executed in very great detail, we view with pleasure. Such is the case for example with renderings of the least favored animals, or of cadavers. The cause of this also is that learning is eminently pleasurable not only to philosophers but to the rest of mankind in the same way, although their share in the pleasure is restricted. For the reason they take pleasure in seeing the images is that in the process of viewing they find themselves learning, that is, reckoning what kind a given thing belongs to: "This individual is a So-and-so." Because if the viewer happens not to have seen such a thing before, the reproduction will not produce the pleasure *qua* reproduction but through its workmanship or color or something else of that sort.

Since, then, imitation comes naturally to us, and melody and rhythm too (it is obvious that verses are segments of the respective rhythms), in the beginning it was those who were most gifted in these respects who, developing them little by little, brought the making of poetry into being out of improvisations. And the poetic enterprise split into two branches, in accordance with the two kinds of character. Namely, the soberer spirits were imitating noble actions and the actions of noble persons, while the cheaper ones were imitating those of the worthless, producing lampoons and invectives at first just as the other sort were producing hymns and encomia. (. . .) In them (i.e., the invectives), in accordance with what is suitable and fitting, iambic verse also put in its appearance; indeed that is why it is called "iambic" now, because it is the verse in which they used to "iambize," that is, lampoon, each other. And so some of the early poets became composers of epic, the others of iambic, verses.

Now it happens that we cannot name anyone before Homer as the author of that kind of poem (i.e., an iambic poem), though it stands to reason that there were many who were; but from Homer on we can do so: thus his *Margites* and other poems of that sort. However, just as on the serious side Homer was most truly a poet, since he was the only one who not only composed well but constructed dramatic imitations, so too he was the first to adumbrate the forms of comedy by producing a (1) dramatic presentation, and not of invective but of (2) the ludicrous. For as the *Iliad* stands in relation to our tragedies, so the *Margites* stands in relation to our comedies.

Once tragedy and comedy had been partially brought to light, those who were out in pursuit of the two kinds of poetic activity, in accordance with their own respective natures, became in the one case comic poets instead of iambic poets, in the other case producers of tragedies instead of epics, because these genres were higher and more esteemed than the others. Now to review the question whether even tragedy is adequate to the basic forms or not—a question which is (can be) judged both by itself, in the abstract, and in relationship to our theater audiences—that is another story. However that may be, it did spring from an improvisational beginning (both it and comedy: the one from those who led off the dithyramb, the other from those who did so for the phallic performances [?] which still remain on the program in many of our cities); it did expand gradually, each feature being further developed as it appeared; and after it had gone through a number of phases it stopped upon attaining its full natural growth. Thus Aeschylus was the first to expand the troupe of assisting actors from one to two, shorten the choral parts, and see to it that the dialogue takes first place; (. . .) at the same time the verse became iambic trimeter instead of trochaic tetrameter. For in the beginning they used the tetrameter because the form of composition was "satyr-like," that is, more given over to dancing, but when speech came along the very nature of the case turned up the appropriate verse. For iambic is the most speech-like of verses. An indication of this is that we speak more iambics than any other kind of verse in our conversation with each other, whereas we utter hexameters rarely, and when we do we abandon the characteristic tone-pattern of ordinary speech.

Further, as to plurality of episodes and the other additions which are recorded as having been made to tragedy, let our account stop here; for no doubt it would be burdensome to record them in detail.

COMEDY

Comedy is as we said it was, an imitation of persons who are inferior; not, however, going all the way to full villainy, but imitating the ugly, of which the ludicrous is one part. The ludicrous, that is, is a failing or a piece of ugliness which causes no pain or destruction; thus, to go no farther, the comic mask is something ugly and distorted but painless.

Now the stages of development of tragedy, and the men who were responsible for them, have not escaped notice, but comedy did escape notice in the beginning because it was not taken seriously. (In fact it was late in its history that the presiding magistrate officially "granted a chorus" to the comic poets; until then they were volunteers.) Thus comedy already possessed certain defining characteristics when the first "comic poets," so-called, appear in the record. Who gave it masks, or prologues, or troupes of actors and all that sort of thing, is not known. The composing of plots came originally from Sicily; of the Athenian poets, Crates was the first to abandon the lampooning mode and compose arguments, that is, plots, of a general nature.

EPIC AND TRAGEDY

Well then, epic poetry followed in the wake of tragedy up to the point of being a (1) good-sized (2) imitation (3) in verse (4) of people who are to be taken seriously; but in its having its verse unmixed with any other and being narrative in character, there they differ. Further, so far as its length is concerned tragedy tries as hard as it can to exist during a single daylight period, or to vary but little, while the epic is not limited in its time and so differs in that respect. Yet originally they used to do this in tragedies just as much as they did in epic poems.

The constituent elements are partly identical and partly limited to tragedy. Hence anybody who knows about good and bad tragedy knows about epic also; for the elements that the epic possesses appertain to tragedy as well, but those of tragedy are not all found in the epic.

TRAGEDY AND ITS SIX CONSTITUENT ELEMENTS

Our discussions of imitative poetry in hexameters, and of comedy, will come later; at present let us deal with tragedy, recovering from what has been said so far the definition of its essential nature, as it was in development. Tragedy, then, is a process of imitating an action which has serious implications, is complete, and possesses magnitude; by means of language which has been made sensuously attractive, with each of its varieties found separately in the parts; enacted by the persons themselves and not presented through narrative; through a course of pity and fear completing the purification of tragic acts which have those emotional characteristics. By "language made sensuously attractive" I mean language that has rhythm and melody, and by "its varieties found separately" I mean the fact that certain parts of the play are carried on through spoken verses alone and others the other way round, through song.

Now first of all, since they perform the imitation through action (by acting it), the adornment of their visual appearance will perforce constitute some part of the making of tragedy; and song-composition and verbal expression also, for those are the media in which they perform the imitation. By "verbal expression" I mean the actual composition of the verses, and by "song-composition" something whose meaning is entirely clear.

Next, since it is an imitation of an action and is enacted by certain people who are performing the action, and since those people must necessarily have certain traits both of character and thought (for it is thanks to these two factors that we speak of people's actions also as having a defined character, and it is in accordance with their actions that all either succeed or fail); and since the imitation of the action is the plot, for by "plot" I mean here the structuring of the events, and by the "characters" that in accordance with which we say that the persons who are acting have a defined moral character, and by "thought" all the passages in which they attempt to prove some thesis or set forth an opinion—it follows of necessity, then, that tragedy as a whole has just six constituent elements, in relation to the essence that makes it a distinct species; and they are plot, characters, verbal expression, thought, visual adornment, and song-composition. For the elements by which they imitate are two (i.e., verbal expression and song-composition), the manner in which they imitate is one (visual adornment), the things they imitate are three (plot, characters, thought), and there is nothing more beyond these. These then are the constituent forms they use.

The greatest of these elements is the structuring of the incidents. For tragedy is an imitation not of men but of a life, an action, and they have moral quality in accordance with their characters but are happy or unhappy in accordance with their actions; hence they are not active in order to imitate their characters, but they include the characters along with the actions for the sake of the latter. Thus the structure of events, the plot, is the goal of tragedy, and the goal is the greatest thing of all.

The Relative Importance of the Six Elements

Again: a tragedy cannot exist without a plot, but it can without characters: thus the tragedies of most of our modern poets are devoid of character, and in general many poets are like that; so also with the relationship between Zeuxis and Polygnotus, among the painters: Polygnotus is a good portrayer of character, while Zeuxis' painting has no dimension of character at all.

Again: if one strings end to end speeches that are expressive of character and carefully worked in thought and expression, he still will not achieve the result which we said was the aim of tragedy; the job will be done much better by a tragedy that is more deficient in these other respects but has a plot, a structure of events. It is much the same case as with painting: the most beautiful pigments smeared on at random will not give as much pleasure as a black-and-white outline picture. Besides, the most powerful means tragedy has for swaying our feelings, namely the peripeties and recognitions, are elements of the plot.

Again: an indicative sign is that those who are beginning a poetic career manage to hit the mark in verbal expression and character portrayal sooner than they do in plot construction; and the same is true of practically all the earliest poets.

So plot is the basic principle, the heart and soul, as it were, of tragedy, and the characters come second: (. . .) it is the imitation of an action and imitates the persons primarily for the sake of their action.

Third in rank is thought. This is the ability to state the issues and appropriate points pertaining to a given topic, an ability which springs from the arts of politics and rhetoric; in fact the earlier poets made their characters talk "politically," the present-day poets rhetorically. But "character" is that kind of utterance which clearly reveals the bent of a man's moral choice (hence there is no character in that class of utterances in which there is nothing at all that the speaker is choosing or rejecting), while "thought" is the passages in which they try to prove that something is so or not so, or state some general principle.

Fourth is the verbal expression of the speeches. I mean by this the same thing that was said earlier, that the "verbal expression" is the conveyance of thought through language: a statement which has the same meaning whether one says "verses" or "speeches."

The song-composition of the remaining parts is the greatest of the sensuous attractions, and the visual adornment of the dramatic persons can have a strong emotional effect but is the least artistic element, the least connected with the poetic art; in fact the force of tragedy can be felt even without benefit of public performance and actors, while for the production of the visual effect the property man's art is even more decisive than that of the poets.

GENERAL PRINCIPLES OF THE TRAGIC PLOT

With these distinctions out of the way, let us next discuss what the structuring of the events should be like, since this is both the basic and the most important element in the tragic art. We have established, then, that tragedy is an imitation of an action which is complete and whole and has some magnitude (for there is also such a thing as a whole that has no magnitude). "Whole" is that which has beginning, middle, and end. "Beginning" is that which does not necessarily follow on something else, but after it something else naturally is or happens; "end," the other way round, is that which naturally follows on something else, either necessarily or for the most part, but nothing else after it; and "middle" that which naturally follows on something else and something else on it. So, then, well-constructed plots should neither begin nor end at any chance point but follow the guidelines just laid down.

Furthermore, since the beautiful, whether a living creature or anything that is composed of parts, should not only have these in a fixed order to one another but also possess a definite size which does not depend on chance—for beauty depends on size and order; hence neither can a very tiny creature turn out to be beautiful (since our perception of it grows blurred as it approaches the period of imperceptibility) nor an excessively huge one (for then it cannot all be perceived at once and so its unity and wholeness are lost), if for example there were a creature a thousand miles long—so, just as in the case of living creatures they must have some size, but one that can be taken in in a single view, so with plots: they should have length, but such that they are easy to remember. As to a limit of the length, the one is determined by the tragic competitions and the ordinary span of attention. (If they had to compete with a hundred tragedies they would compete by the water clock, as they say used to be done [?].) But the limit fixed by the very nature of the case is: the longer the plot, up to the point of still being perspicuous as a whole, the finer it is so far as size is concerned; or to put it in general terms, the length in which, with things happening in unbroken sequence, a shift takes place either probably or necessarily from bad to good fortune or from good to bad—that is an acceptable norm of length.

But a plot is not unified, as some people think, simply because it has to do with a single person. A large, indeed an indefinite number of things can happen to a given individual, some of which go to constitute no unified event; and in the same way there can be many acts of a given individual from which no single action emerges. Hence it seems clear that those poets are wrong who have composed *Heracleïds, Theseïds,* and the like. They think that since Heracles was a single person it follows that the plot will be single too. But Homer, superior as he is in all other respects, appears to have grasped this point well also, thanks either to art or nature, for in composing an *Odyssey* he did not incorporate into it everything that happened to the hero, for example how he was wounded on Mt. Parnassus or how he feigned madness at the muster, neither of which events, by happening, made it at all necessary or probable that the other should happen. Instead, he composed the *Odyssey*—and the *Iliad* similarly—around a unified action of the kind we have been talking about.

A poetic imitation, then, ought to be unified in the same way as a single imitation in any other mimetic field, by having a single object: since the plot is an imitation of an action, the latter ought to be both unified and complete, and the component events ought to be so firmly compacted that if any one of them is shifted to another place, or removed, the whole is loosened up and dislocated; for an element whose addition or subtraction makes no perceptible extra difference is not really a part of the whole.

From what has been said it is also clear that the poet's job is not to report what has happened but what is likely to happen: that is, what is capable of happening according to the rule of probability or necessity. Thus the difference between the historian and the poet is not in their utterances being in verse or prose (it would be quite possible for Herodotus' work to be translated into verse, and it would not be any the less a history with verse than it is without it); the difference lies in the fact that the historian speaks of what has happened, the poet of the kind of thing that *can* happen. Hence also poetry is a more philosophical and serious business than history; for poetry speaks more of universals, history of particulars. "Universal" in this case is what kind of person is likely to do or say certain kinds of things, according to probability or necessity; that is what poetry aims at, although it gives its persons particular names afterward; while the "particular" is what Alcibiades did or what happened to him.

In the field of comedy this point has been grasped: our comic poets construct their plots on the basis of general probabilities and then assign names to the persons quite arbitrarily, instead of dealing with individuals as the old iambic poets did. But in tragedy they still cling to the historically given names. The reason is that what is possible is persuasive; so what has not happened we are not yet ready to believe is possible, while what has happened is, we feel, obviously possible: for it would not have happened if it were impossible. Nevertheless, it is a fact that even in our tragedies, in some cases only one or two of the names are traditional, the rest being invented, and in some others none at all. It is so, for example, in Agathon's *Antheus*—the names in it are as fictional as the events—and it gives no less pleasure because of that. Hence the poets ought not to cling at all costs to the traditional plots, around which our tragedies are constructed. And in fact it is absurd to go searching for this kind of authentication, since even the familiar names are familiar to only a few in the audience and yet give the same kind of pleasure to all.

So from these considerations it is evident that the poet should be a maker of his plots more than of his verses, insofar as he is a poet by virtue of his imitations and what he imitates is actions. Hence even if it happens that he puts something that has actually taken place into poetry, he is none the less a poet; for there is nothing to prevent some of the things that have happened from being the kind of things that can happen, and that is the sense in which he is their maker.

Among simple plots and actions the episodic are the worst. By "episodic" plot I mean one in which there is no probability or necessity for the order in which the episodes follow one another. Such structures are composed by the bad poets because they are bad poets, but by the good poets because of the actors: in composing contest pieces for them, and stretching out the plot beyond its capacity, they are forced frequently to dislocate the sequence.

Furthermore, since the tragic imitation is not only of a complete action but also of events that are fearful and pathetic, and these come about best when they come about contrary to one's expectation yet logically, one following from the other; that way they will be more productive of wonder than if they happen merely at random, by chance—because even among chance occurrences the ones people consider most marvelous are those that seem to have come about as if on purpose: for example the way the statue of Mitys at Argos killed the man who had been the cause of Mitys' death, by falling on him while he was attending the festival; it stands to reason, people think, that such things don't happen by chance—so plots of that sort cannot fail to be artistically superior.

Some plots are simple, others are complex; indeed the actions of which the plots are imitations already fall into these two categories. By "simple" action I mean one the development of which being continuous and unified in the manner stated above, the reversal comes without peripety or recognition, and by "complex" action one in which the reversal is continuous but with recognition or peripety or both. And these developments must grow out of the very structure of the plot itself, in such a way that on the basis of

SIMPLE AND COMPLEX PLOTS

what has happened previously this particular outcome follows either by necessity or in accordance with probability; for there is a great difference in whether these events happen because of those or merely after them.

"Peripety" is a shift of what is being undertaken to the opposite in the way previously stated, and that in accordance with probability or necessity as we have just been saying; as for example in the *Oedipus* the man who has come, thinking that he will reassure Oedipus, that is, relieve him of his fear with respect to his mother, by revealing who he once was, brings about the opposite; and in the *Lynceus,* as he (Lynceus) is being led away with every prospect of being executed, and Danaus pursuing him with every prospect of doing the executing, it comes about as a result of the other things that have happened in the play that *he* is executed and Lynceus is saved. And "recognition" is, as indeed the name indicates, a shift from ignorance to awareness, pointing in the direction either of close blood ties or of hostility, of people who have previously been in a clearly marked state of happiness or unhappiness.

The finest recognition is one that happens at the same time as a peripety, as is the case with the one in the *Oedipus.* Naturally, there are also other kinds of recognition: it is possible for one to take place in the prescribed manner in relation to inanimate objects and chance occurrences, and it is possible to recognize whether a person has acted or not acted. But the form that is most integrally a part of the plot, the action, is the one aforesaid; for that kind of recognition combined with peripety will excite either pity or fear (and these are the kinds of action of which tragedy is an imitation according to our definition), because both good and bad fortune will also be most likely to follow that kind of event. Since, further, the recognition is a recognition of persons, some are of one person by the other one only (when it is already known who the "other one" is), but sometimes it is necessary for both persons to go through a recognition, as for example Iphigenia is recognized by her brother through the sending of the letter, but of him by Iphigenia another recognition is required.

These then are two elements of plot: peripety and recognition; third is the *pathos.* Of these, peripety and recognition have been discussed; a *pathos* is a destructive or painful act, such as deaths on stage, paroxysms of pain, woundings, and all that sort of thing.

THE TRAGIC SIDE OF TRAGEDY: PITY AND FEAR AND THE PATTERNS OF THE COMPLEX PLOT

The "parts" of tragedy which should be used as constituent elements were mentioned earlier; (. . .) but what one should aim at and what one should avoid in composing one's plots, and whence the effect of tragedy is to come, remains to be discussed now, following immediately upon what has just been said.

Since, then, the construction of the finest tragedy should be not simple but complex, and at the same time imitative of fearful and pitiable happenings (that being the special character of this kind of poetry), it is clear first of all that (1) neither should virtuous men appear undergoing a change from good to bad fortune, for that is not fearful, nor pitiable either, but morally repugnant; nor (2) the wicked from bad fortune to good—that is the most untragic form of all, it has none of the qualities that one wants: it is productive neither of ordinary sympathy nor of pity nor of fear—nor again (3) the really wicked man changing from good fortune to bad, for that kind of structure will excite sympathy but neither pity nor fear, since the one (pity) is directed towards the man who does not deserve his misfortune and the other (fear) towards the one who is like the rest of mankind—what is left is the man who falls between these extremes. Such is a man who is neither a paragon of virtue and justice nor undergoes the change to misfortune through any real badness or wickedness but because of some mistake; one of those who stand in great repute and prosperity, like Oedipus and Thyestes: conspicuous men from families of that kind.

So, then, the artistically made plot must necessarily be single rather than double, as some maintain, and involve a change not from bad fortune to good fortune but the other way round, from good fortune to bad, and not thanks to wickedness but because of some mistake of great weight and consequence, by a man such as we have described or else on the good rather than the bad side. An indication comes from what has been happening in tragedy: at the beginning the poets used to "tick off" whatever plots came their way, but nowadays the finest tragedies are composed about a few houses: they deal with Alcmeon, Oedipus, Orestes, Meleager, Thyestes, Telephus, and whichever others have had the misfortune to do or undergo fearful things.

Thus the technically finest tragedy is based on this structure. Hence those who bring charges against Euripides for doing this in his tragedies are making the same mistake. His practice is correct in the way that has been shown. There is a very significant indication: on our stages and in the competitions, plays of this structure are accepted as the most tragic, *if* they are handled successfully, and Euripides, though he may not make his other arrangements effectively, still is felt by the audience to be the most tragic, at least, of the poets.

Second comes the kind which is rated first by certain people, having its structure double like the *Odyssey* and with opposite endings for the good and bad. Its being put first is due to the weakness of the audiences; for the poets follow along, catering to their wishes. But this particular pleasure is not the one that springs from tragedy but is more characteristic of comedy.

Now it is possible for the fearful or pathetic effect to come from the actors' appearance, but it is also possible for it to arise from the very structure of the events, and this is closer to the mark and characteristic of a better poet. Namely, the plot must be so structured, even without benefit of any visual effect, that the one who is hearing the events unroll shudders with fear and feels pity at what happens: which is what one would experience on hearing the plot of the *Oedipus*. To set out to achieve this by means of the masks and costumes is less artistic, and requires technical support in the staging. As for those who do not set out to achieve the fearful through the masks and costumes, but only the monstrous, they have nothing to do with tragedy at all; for one should not seek any and every pleasure from tragedy, but the one that is appropriate to it.

Since it is the pleasure derived from pity and fear by means of imitation that the poet should seek to produce, it is clear that these qualities must be built into the constituent events. Let us determine, then, which kinds of happening are felt by the spectator to be fearful, and which pitiable. Now such acts are necessarily the work of persons who are near and dear (close blood kin) to one another, or enemies, or neither. But when an enemy attacks an enemy there is nothing pathetic about either the intention or the deed, except in the actual pain suffered by the victim; nor when the act is done by "neutrals"; but when the tragic acts come within the limits of close blood relationship, as when brother kills or intends to kill brother or do something else of that kind to him, or son to father or mother to son or son to mother—those are the situations one should look for.

Now although it is not admissible to break up the transmitted stories—I mean for instance that Clytemestra was killed by Orestes, or Eriphyle by Alcmeon—one should be artistic both in inventing stories and in managing the ones that have been handed down. But what we mean by "artistic" requires some explanation.

It is possible, then, (1) for the act to be performed as the older poets presented it, knowingly and wittingly; Euripides did it that way also, in Medea's murder of her children. It is possible (2) to refrain from performing the deed, with knowledge. Or it is possible (3) to perform the fearful act, but unwittingly, then recognize the blood relationship later, as Sophocles' Oedipus does; in that case the act is outside the play, but it can be in the tragedy itself, as with Astydamas' Alcmeon, or Telegonus in the *Wounding of Odysseus*. A further mode, in addition to these, is (4) while intending because of ignorance to perform some black crime, to discover the relationship before one does it. And there is no

PITY AND FEAR AND THE TRAGIC ACT

other mode besides these; for one must necessarily either do the deed or not, and with or without knowledge of what it is.

Of these modes, to know what one is doing but hold off and not perform the act (no. 2) is worst: it has the morally repulsive character and at the same time is not tragic; for there is no tragic act. Hence nobody composes that way, or only rarely, as, for example, Haemon threatens Creon in the *Antigone*. Performing the act (with knowledge) (no. 1) is second (poorest). Better is to perform it in ignorance and recognize what one has done afterward (no. 3); for the repulsive quality does not attach to the act, and the recognition has a shattering emotional effect. But the best is the last (no. 4): I mean a case like the one in the *Cresphontes* where Merope is about to kill her son but does not do so because she recognizes him first; or in *Iphigenia in Tauris* the same happens with sister and brother; or in the *Helle* the son recognizes his mother just as he is about to hand her over to the enemy.

The reason for what was mentioned a while ago, namely that our tragedies have to do with only a few families, is this: It was because the poets, when they discovered how to produce this kind of effect in their plots, were conducting their search on the basis of chance, not art; hence they have been forced to focus upon those families which happen to have suffered tragic happenings of this kind.

THE TRAGIC CHARACTERS

Enough, then, concerning the structure of events and what traits the tragic plots should have. As for the characters, there are four things to be aimed at. First and foremost, that they be good. The persons will have character if in the way previously stated their speech or their action reveals the moral quality of some choice, and good character if a good choice. Good character exists, moreover, in each category of persons; a woman can be good, or a slave, although one of these classes (*sc.* women) is inferior and the other, as a class, worthless. Second, that they be appropriate; for it is possible for a character to be brave, but inappropriately to a woman. Third is likeness to human nature in general; for this is different from making the character good and appropriate according to the criteria previously mentioned. And fourth is consistency. For even if the person being imitated is inconsistent, and that kind of character has been taken as the theme, he should be inconsistent in a consistent fashion.

An example of moral depravity that accomplishes no necessary purpose is the Menelaus in Euripides' *Orestes;* of an unsuitable and inappropriate character, the lamentation of Odysseus in the *Scylla* and the speech of Melanippe; and of the inconsistent, Iphigenia at Aulis, for the girl who pleads for her life is in no way like the later one.

In character portrayal also, as in plot construction, one should always strive for either the necessary or the probable, so that it is either necessary or probable for that kind of person to do or say that kind of thing, just as it is for one event to follow the other. It is evident, then, that the dénouements of plots also should come out of the character itself, and not from the "machine" as in the *Medea* or with the sailing of the fleet in the *Aulis*. Rather the machine should be used for things that lie outside the drama proper, either previous events that a human being cannot know, or subsequent events which require advance prophecy and exposition; for we grant the gods the ability to foresee everything. But let there be no illogicality in the web of events, or if there is, let it be outside the play like the one in Sophocles' *Oedipus.*

Since tragedy is an imitation of persons who are better than average, one should imitate the good portrait painters, for in fact, while rendering likenesses of their sitters by reproducing their individual appearance, they also make them better-looking; so the poet, in imitating men who are irascible or easygoing or have other traits of that kind, should make them, while still plausibly drawn, morally good, as Homer portrayed Achilles as good yet like other men.

What recognition is generically, was stated earlier; now as to its varieties: First comes the one that is least artistic and is most used, merely out of lack of imagination, that by means of tokens. Of these some are inherited, like "the lance that all the Earth-born wear," or "stars" such as Carcinus employs in his *Thyestes;* some are acquired, and of those some are on the body, such as scars, others are external, like the well-known amulets or the recognition in the *Tyro* by means of the little ark. There are better and poorer ways of using these; for example, Odysseus was recognized in different ways by means of his scar, once by the nurse and again by the swineherds. Those that are deliberately cited for the sake of establishing an identity, and all that kind, are less artistic, while those that develop naturally but unexpectedly, like the one in the foot-washing scene, are better.

Second poorest are those that are contrived by the poet and hence are inartistic; for example the way, in the *Iphigenia,* she recognizes that it is Orestes: *she* was recognized by means of the letter, but *he* goes out of his way to say what the poet, rather than the plot, wants him to say. Thus this mode is close kin to the error mentioned above: he might as well have actually worn some tokens. Similarly, in Sophocles' *Tereus,* the "voice of the shuttle."

Third poorest is that through recollection, by means of a certain awareness that follows on seeing or hearing something, like the one in the *Cypriotes* of Dicaeogenes where the hero bursts into tears on seeing the picture, and the one in Book 8 of the *Odyssey:* Odysseus weeps when he hears the lyre-player and is reminded of the War; in both cases the recognition follows.

Fourth in ascending order is the recognition based on reasoning; for example in the *Libation-Bearers:* "Somebody like me has come; nobody is like me but Orestes; therefore he has come." And the one suggested by the sophist Polyidus in speaking of the *Iphigenia*: it would have been natural, he said, for Orestes to draw the conclusion (aloud): "My sister was executed as a sacrifice, and now it is my turn." Also in the *Tydeus* of Theodectes: "I came expecting to find my son, and instead I am being destroyed myself." Or the one in the *Daughters of Phineus:* when they see the spot they reflect that it was indeed their fate to die here; for they had been exposed here as babies also. There is also one based on mistaken inference on the part of the audience, as in *Odysseus the False Messenger.* In that play, that he and no one else can string the bow is an assumption, a premise invented by the poet, and also his saying that he would recognize the bow when in fact he had not seen it; whereas the notion that he (the poet) has made his invention for the sake of the other person who would make the recognition, that is a mistaken inference.

The best recognition of all is the one that arises from the events themselves; the emotional shock of surprise is then based on probabilities, as in Sophocles' *Oedipus* and in the *Iphigenia;* for it was only natural that she should wish to send a letter. Such recognitions are the only ones that dispense with artificial inventions and visible tokens. And second-best are those based on reasoning. . . .

Niall Slater has written widely about the performance of classical Greek and Roman theater and is the author of Plautus in Performance *(1985) and* Reading Petronius *(1990). In this essay, he describes the ways in which the public performance of classical Athenian actors dramatizes a sense of acting as a craft and as an art.*

Before actors there was drama. The actor as a conceptual category is posterior to the playing of drama before an audience. Like so much in the fifth-century theater, the emergence of the actor as a category can be discerned only dimly. Any attempt to deal with it will of necessity involve a great deal of speculation. It is nonetheless worth the effort, for I will argue that the creation of concepts of actor and acting is essential to the process whereby

---

TECHNIQUES OF RECOGNITION

NIALL W. SLATER

from "The Idea of the Actor" (1990)

the unique public enactment at a festival which we have so far been describing becomes a portable and repeatable play in very much our modern sense in the next century.

I take my title from a splendid book of the same name by William Worthen.[1] His is a study of the ethics of performance, the changes in the conception and self-conception of the actor in the Renaissance, eighteenth century, and modern theater. My concern here is with the origin of the concept of "actor" and thus is even more precisely ethical—that which is essential to the ethos of acting as opposed to any other mode of public or private performance.

This difference in essence is easily stated: it is dialogic performance. Here I may seem merely to repeat the traditional accounts that say that drama arises from an actor responding to the chorus. Note, though, that mimesis alone is not enough to create the actor. Other types of poetry, other performances had been mimetic before. When Homer has Akhilleus [Achilles] speak in the *Iliad,* that speech mimes real speech, but there is still an enormous gulf between Homer singing of characters speaking (even in dialogue with each other) and placing two physically exemplified voices onstage. In the latter situation the controlling voice of the Homeric narrative has disappeared. The two voices onstage claim an equal status—neither has by nature a better claim to speak for the poet or for any particular order. To borrow and perhaps misuse a term from Bakhtin, acting comes into being through heteroglossia.

It is at this moment that the performance of this type of poetry becomes unreproducible by the individual. Much has been written about the fusion of poetic forms, of iambic and choral meters, of dialogue and song, which creates tragedy and comedy. What has been too little acknowledged is that this is a fusion between that which can, and that which cannot, be reperformed outside its original context.

Here I ought to confront more directly the recent work of C. J. Herington.[2] In his book *Poetry into Drama,* Herington posits a song culture in ancient Greece in which all poetry is created in hopes of endless reperformance. He believes that the music to all the lyric poets and tragedy was passed down to the fourth century by a series of reperformances. He even argues for the survival of some original choreography through reperformance.

The problem with this theory is to find both an occasion and a medium for such reperformance. It is immediately apparent that much choral lyric will never have been reperformed by a chorus—as in the case of epinician poetry. It seems unlikely that there was ever an occasion to recruit and train a new chorus for further performances of a Pindaric victory ode after the first celebration. In this case it is indeed possible, as Herington invites us to do, to imagine reperformance of the work by an individual performer.

The example of a scene between Strepsiades and Pheidippides in Aristophanes' *Clouds* is relevant here, though far from unambiguous. Strepsiades asks Pheidippides to sing Simonides; then, when Pheidippides spurns that request, Strepsiades asks him to "recite" (*lexai*) some Aiskhylos [Aeschylus] (1353–67). This too Pheidippides refuses to do and then, according to the manuscripts, he "sings" a speech or *rhesis* from Euripides.[3]

Whatever Pheidippides then performs apparently came from Euripides' *Aiolos,* but it is not possible to determine whether this is a chorus or a lyric solo. Devotees might well

[1] William B. Worthen, *The Idea of the Actor: Drama and the Ethics of Performance* (Princeton, 1984).

[2] C. J. Herington, *Poetry into Drama: Early Tragedy and the Greek Poetic Tradition* (Berkeley, Los Angeles, and London, 1985).

[3] K. J. Dover in *Aristophanes: Clouds,* 2d ed. (Oxford, 1968), on verse 1371 (see also 251–53) emends the various forms of *aido* found in the manuscripts to *eg',* from *ago,* quoting a parallel from Theophrastos. Dover himself says that recitation from tragedy after dinner was not usual, and the practice from Theophrastos' day may not be that of the fifth century.

have learned lyric solo passages and sung them at symposiums. Likewise the Aiskhylos requested might have been solo or chorus. It cannot, however, have been an excerpt from the genuinely dramatic part of drama—an exchange between two or more characters. Who would ever have learned a passage of stichomythia by heart? On what occasion would such a passage be reperformed?

If I may be pardoned a modern analogy, early tragedy and comedy, with their "bad plots and laughable diction,"[4] must have been a great deal like early twentieth-century musical comedies—a series of songs stitched together with a few pennyworth of plot. The creators of these early musicals certainly hoped that the shows would promote their songs and lodge them in the public memory; they hoped for sales of sheet music and later recordings, the modern version of imperishable *kleos*. Many songs that still live in our musical memory were introduced in such shows—but the plots and dialogue have long since vanished. So too I am persuaded that the poets of early tragedy and comedy will have written their lyrics in the hope that their songs would catch the audience's imagination and live on through reperformance—but the dialogue was occasional poetry, written for a single performance. Aiskhylos could not have dreamed at the beginning of his career that anyone would want to memorize his dialogue—because on what occasion would two or three people meet to give it an oral performance?

Other evidence for private reperformance of dramatic texts in the fifth century suggests only choruses. The famous story in Plutarch's *Life of Nikias* which tells how prisoners from the Sicilian expedition won their freedom from the mines by their knowledge of Euripides again must mean ability to sing tragic choruses.[5] Nor is it surprising that so many would have such a knowledge of Euripides. John J. Winkler has persuasively argued that the choruses of tragedy were drawn yearly from the ephebes. A large number of young men fresh from military training who were shipped off to join the Sicilian debacle will have recently performed in a Euripidean chorus.[6]

Acting of course did not remain a marginal contribution to the drama. It is a commonplace that over time, the balance between acting and choral performance was reversed. The chorus in its turn became marginal. Less common is any attempt to model or explain this change other than in terms of "degeneracy" of the form. I will suggest a model with three rather loosely delimited stages: first, one in which acting is judged in relation to the myth it enacts; second, one in which actors are compared and judged in similar but not identical performances; and finally a stage in which reperformance has become possible and comparisons can be made of actors playing precisely the same roles.

Tradition tells us the poets were their own first actors, and we have no compelling reason to doubt this. Indeed it has been suggested that a poet as late as Aristophanes played in his own comedies.[7] Obviously the poet was not granted a chorus on the basis of his acting ability but for his skill in composition, and equally obviously poets will have differed in their personal histrionic skills. The *Life of Sophokles* [Sophocles] says that he was the first poet to abandon acting in his own plays because of his weak voice. If true, this would be an important milestone: not merely the quality of the poetry but the quality of the acting now makes a difference to the success of a drama. Though M. R. Lefkowitz dismisses this

---

[4]Aristotle, *Poetics* 6, 18, notes that the earlier tragic poets were much better with language and character study than with their plots.

[5]*Life of Nikias* 29. Plutarch speaks first of Euripides' *poemata* in general, but then specifies that some, wandering on the battlefield, were given food and drink for singing a *melos* of Euripides. He connects with this the story of a ship admitted to the harbor because those on board knew *asmata* of the poet.

[6]See the estimate of W. B. Sedgwick, "*The Frogs* and the Audience," *Classica et Mediaevalia* 9 (1947): 1–9, for the numbers who would have had experience singing in the chorus.

[7]C. Bailey, "Who Played Dicaeopolis?" in *Greek Poetry and Life,* ed. Bailey et al. (Oxford, 1936).

statement from the *Life* by a chain of reasoning I cannot follow,[8] it seems likely on the whole that early poets did act, while later poets did not. Dating the change to Sophokles' early career may be wrong, but it is not likely to be far out of the actual historical sequence.

From the moment the poet creates a dialogue between characters, he needs another actor for his performance. What little evidence we have suggests that poets regularly employed certain people, presumably friends, as actors. What special qualifications these would have had is unknown—they certainly do not seem to have been themselves poets by and large.[9] Again the *Life of Sophokles* (trans. Lefkowitz) reports on the authority of Ister:

> Ister also says that he discovered the white half-boots that actors and chorus members wear, and that he wrote his dramas to suit their characters.

The statement about writing the *dramata* according to *phuseis autōn* is our interest here. Does this mean that Sophokles had in mind the peculiar capacities of his performers in the composition process? Like so much of the lives of the poets, this is a laundry list, and the relation of one item to another is far from clear. Though the grammatical antecedents of *autōn* are *hypokritai* and *khoreutai*, these two statements may not have been connected in Ister—what have white boots to do with typecasting? Interpreting this way also presents us with an extreme improbability. What on earth can it mean to write a chorus according to the *phuseis* of its performers? Once again, let us remember that the pool of choristers change every year—did Sophokles walk into rehearsal, look over the pimply throng, and say, "You lads look much more like Lemnian maidens than Argive elders"? But the notion that he wrote *actors'* parts according to their performance capacities is far from improbable.

The principal objection to accepting this as a historical datum is the possibility that actors were allotted to the poets, not chosen by them, in the later fifth century, but there is no proof that allotment of actors was introduced this early, and I shall argue against it on grounds of probability below. A poet who writes according to the capacities of his actors is another important milestone, whoever that poet was. Fifty years ago, A. S. Owen argued that Sophokles was just such a poet, to the extent that he changed distribution of singing parts based on the capacities of his actors.[10]

---

[8] In *The Lives of the Greek Poets* (Baltimore, 1981), 77–78, she asserts that this detail is inserted to explain the statement that Sophokles invented the third actor. The sequence where Aiskhylos invents the second actor and Sophokles the third *is* suspicious. But the *Life* makes no causal link between Sophokles' ceasing to act and the invention of the third actor; indeed the author's statement about Sophokles' changes in the size of the choruses intervenes between the two. I can see no reason to believe that the author of the *Life* or anyone else thought Sophokles' abandonment of acting *explained* his invention of the third actor.

[9] P. Ghiron-Bistagne, *Recherches sur les acteurs dans la Grèce antique* (Paris, 1976), 136–54, summarizes what we know. The *Life of Aiskhylos* gives us the names of his customary actors, Kleandros and Mynniskos, otherwise unknown.

[10] A. S. Owen, "The Date of the *Electra* of Sophocles," in *Greek Poetry and Life,* ed. Bailey, 145–57. Lefkowitz's citation (*Lives,* 79) of this article by Owen in the course of her argument for allotment is somewhat misleading. Owen *doubts* the allotment of actors this early. The source of the notion that allotment was introduced at the same time as contest for actors seems to be A. E. Haigh, the source for *DFA* as well. In the first edition of *The Attic Theatre* (Oxford, 1889), 76, Haigh simply states that "long before the end of the fifth century" allotment of actors was introduced, and he offers as evidence an inference from silence: "Towards the end of the fifth century we no longer hear of particular poets and actors being permanently connected together." By the time of the second edition of *The Attic Theatre* (Oxford, 1898), 80, he has decided that "the change in the method of selection was probably introduced about the middle of the fifth century, when the contests in acting were established, and the position of the actors received its first official recognition." He adduces, however, no new evidence in support of this view. Finally, allotment itself need not be a bar to adapting the text to the capacities of the performers. Only if the text were fixed before the allotment and unalterable thereafter would the poet be unable to adapt his text to the performer's capacity. Texts in a working theater are never written in stone. I believe that the text of a Greek drama was quite fluid up until the moment of performance, the *arkhōn* did not grant a chorus on the basis of one of the Oxford Classical Texts in hand.

Thus in the early fifth century, actors existed primarily in relation to the piece they enacted. Their performance was not separable from the overall performance of the drama. Gradually, this began to change. We can describe a parallel evolution in which their part of the drama increased in both size and complexity without yet determining causality between the two. It is only logical to assume that, insofar as the victorious poets tended to employ the same actors, at first in subordinate roles, then later as protagonists, the actors' skills improved apace. At some point the poets ceased to act, in recognition of the fact that mimetic skill was now a significant factor in the success or failure of the piece as a whole.

The narrowing in the choice of tragic subjects which seems to begin in the course of the fifth century may be related to the developing skills of the actors. Aristotle says that some myths are better suited to tragedy than others.[11] One can only speculate that acting plays a part here. One representation of Orestes can build on another, both histrionically as well as poetically. The urn supposedly containing Orestes' ashes is as much a creation of performance as of poetry, if not more. How an actor realizes a scene onstage creates just as much an anxiety of influence for future performers as do the words of the text. Mrs. Siddons' "tender" Lady Macbeth still exerts an influence over performers today. Thus as the storehouse of myths for tragedy begins to contract ever so slightly, the actors begin to portray characters whom other actors have portrayed before. As this process accelerates, it creates the standards by which quality of acting can be judged and actors typed in their abilities to represent certain kinds of characters.

We have no direct glimpse of this process, unless the vague reference to Sophokles' writing according to his actors' *phuseis* is one. Our real evidence for the process is its result: the institution of contests for actors of tragedy at the City Dionysia almost certainly in 449, at the Lenaia perhaps in 442.

The importance of the institution of the contests cannot be overemphasized. Their existence means that acting is now conceptually separate from the drama. Actors have an ontology in and for themselves. Standards exist by which one actor's performance can be judged superior to another's. If actors do not yet have the same status as the poets, they nonetheless are seen to be doing something very different—for it is now possible for a victorious actor to play in a losing play. No doubt at the beginning the prize for acting tended to go to the protagonist of the victorious play, just as today there is some association of the Oscar for best actor or actress and best picture. Nonetheless the possibility exists that a great play can be inadequately acted or that extraordinary acting can be done in inadequate plays. We first know that this happened in 418, when we have inscriptional evidence for a victorious protagonist in a losing play.[12]

Certainly actors are part of the public consciousness by now, as some of Aristophanes' anecdotes about actors indicate. At *Peace* 781–86 he complains about the dancing of the sons of Karkinos who spoiled his production of *Wasps*.[13] In the *Frogs* (303) he has a good bit of fun at the expense of the unfortunate Hegelokhos and his famous mispronunciation in his performance of *Orestes*. If Aristophanes can have such fun at their expense, actors must now have something of the same public recognition and presence as the other public figures he attacks.

It would be a great help to know when the system of allotment for protagonists began. What we know of it comes from the *Suda,* where we also learn that the victor of one year's contest was entitled to be one of the protagonists the following year. We know nothing else

---

[11] In *Poetics* 13.7 he discusses the narrowing of the tragic canon, noting that earlier drew their plots from a wide range of sources, but later tragedians focused on the experiences of a few families.

[12] Recorded in the *didascalia, IG* H², 2319. See *DFA,* 95.

[13] See D. M. MacDowell, *Aristophanes: Wasps* (Oxford, 1971), 326–32, on 1501 ff.; M. Platnauer, *Aristophanes: Peace* (Oxford, 1964), 94–95, on 289–91; and 135 ff., on 781 ff.

of how the group of actors to be allotted was drawn up. Nor do we know how deuteragonist and tritagonist were selected, although it seems likely that the protagonist would have had some influence on their choice. There is an appeal of economy in Haigh's suggestion that allotment is contemporary with the initiation of the contests, but that seems to me specious. It presupposes an extraordinarily swift change in the status of actors in the middle of the fifth century, from nonentities to a controlled and rationed commodity. The provision that a victor has an automatic right to compete the next year also seems very suspicious this early, and the *Suda* clearly links this with allotment. One would assume that at first a victor in one year's contest would quite naturally be asked to compete the next year. A formal provision securing this right suggests a situation in which there are many more actors than slots for them at the festival. It therefore seems more probable that allotment and the right of a victor to a slot the next year came some time after the introduction of contests, when the number of available actors was large and even the chance to appear had to be fought for, a situation much more likely in the fourth century.

Large numbers of actors do not simply appear; they must be trained. As with any other *tekhnē* in ancient Greece, theater seems to have run in certain families. D. F. Sutton has just published a collection of the evidence for such families.[14] Interestingly, Sutton says that he began collecting evidence for *actors'* families only, but broadened his definition after discovering only father-son combinations among actors. Given average Greek life expectancies, it is perhaps not surprising that there are no families with three successive generations of actors. For a father to train his own son demands that he exceed the average life expectancy.

Necessarily, then, actors must have trained others beside family members. Gregory Sifakis[15] has suggested on the evidence of the Mytilene mosaics that boy apprentices were used to represent certain nonspeaking parts in the performances of New Comedy. Apprenticeship was surely the natural way to learn the craft of acting in Greece, and a system such as Sifakis suggests whereby apprentices became synagonists and finally protagonists themselves seems quite likely. Child performers certainly would have been used to represent Alkestis' children in Euripides, for example, and these might well have been boys in training.

There are certainly more actors as the century goes on, but it is only in the latter half of the century that they become visible as such in art. In vase painting earlier on, we can distinguish with certainty only choristers. The bird dancers of black-figure . . . are usually considered a theriomorphic chorus and have often been discussed, despite the wide gap in time, in connection with the *Birds* of Aristophanes. There is now at the Getty Museum in Malibu a late fifth-century krater which, according to J. R. Green,[16] may well be a contemporary illustration of the *Birds,* showing two bird choristers dancing around the flute-player . . .

As with animal choruses, so with satyrs. One can usually tell satyr performers from real satyrs; the former wear hairy shorts or trunks which support the phallus and the tail, but the heads are drawn as if they were quite realistic and not masks. Performers representing normal human characters are usually only distinguishable if they have removed or not yet assumed their masks. . . . Even in these cases, the performers are choristers. We must wait until near the end of the century to find performers who are definitely actors represented as such. Here we find a few fragmentary representations and the famous Pronomos Vase. . . .

---

[14]D. F. Sutton, "The Theatrical Families of Athens," *AJP* 108 (1987): 9–26.

[15]"Boy Actors in New Comedy," in *Arktouros,* ed. G. W. Bowersock. W. Burkert, and M.C.J. Putnam (New York and Berlin, 1979), 199–208.

[16]J. R. Green, "A Representation of the *Birds* of Aristophanes," *Greek Vases in the J. Paul Getty Museum* (Malibu, 1985), 2:95–118.

Our admittedly impressionistic survey of vase painting and the theater in the fifth century is nonetheless food for thought. It is customary to attribute these results to the conventions of vase painting. Trendall and Webster are probably right, for example, to see behind certain earlier fifth-century vases the inspiration of actors performing Aiskhylean plays, though there is nothing definite to mark the figures as actors.[17] Here the vase painter seems to accept the mimesis as reality and represents it as such in his work. But this merely begs the question—where do conventions come from? When, only gradually and toward the end of the century, the painters do choose to represent actors themselves, seen in moments at which they are separate from the drama which it is their function to enact, what is causing painting convention to change? Whence comes a consciousness of, and interest in, the process of mimesis?

Some sculptural evidence can be drawn into our study of when the actor as a category emerges. Most germane to our purpose is the famous Peiraeus actors' relief. . . . The piece dates from the very end of the fifth century and shows three actors and two figures on a banqueting couch; one figure is labelled (in an inscription which is clearly much later than the carving of the relief) Dionysos. This is a fascinating piece of evidence for the history of actors in the fifth century, but it is unfortunately easier to say what it cannot be, than what it was. This is *not* a victory dedication for any play, and certainly not the *Bakkhai* [*Bacchae*], as has been suggested.[18] We have victory dedications for plays, but they celebrate the *khorēgos.* Nor is it a victory dedication from the acting contest. That contest was only among protagonists; here the full complement of three actors is represented. Iconographically the relief is very similar to a series of banqueting hero reliefs which we know from this period. These heroes are largely anonymous but do imply some form of cult activity. The question then becomes: who are the worshippers on the Peiraeus relief, and what is their relationship to the figure on the couch?

I have elsewhere attempted to argue back from the subsequent reinscription of the piece to its original context. I will not reiterate all the details of that argument here, but only state that I would connect the reinscription with the formation of the Athenian branch of the Artists of Dionysos in the early third century BCE. I believe the figure on the couch did not originally represent Dionysos, but was one of the customary banqueting heroes.[19]

Are the three human figures then the actual dedicators of the piece or simply representative (as protagonist, deuteragonist, and tritagonist) of a larger group of actors? Both are certainly possibilities. By the end of the fifth century a protagonist may well have regularly worked with the same two synagonists in a master/journeyman relationship. Thus this could be a dedication in gratitude for the success of this partnership. I find the rededication of the piece several generations later suggestive, however. The rededication implies that it remained on display in a place of worship frequented by actors who felt some proprietary interest in the piece, such that they reinscribed it to their patron Dionysos when the new guild was formed. I suggest then that the piece was in its original use a dedication of a group, perhaps a proto-guild, of Athenian actors to their hero/patron. Worship by actors of a hero, whether as a partnership or a larger group, implies a sense of group identity, a sense if you will of professionalism. Actors now have both public recognition and self-recognition.

Thus at the end of the fifth century, actors had a public presence, though perhaps still not one equal with that of the poet. Once again we must remind ourselves that

---

[17] *IGD,* e.g., III 1, 2 (*Khoephoroi*), III 1, 8 (*Eumenides*), III 1, 13 (*Edonoi*), III 1, 24 and 25 (*Phineus*).

[18] The view of T.B.L. Webster—see my article, "Vanished Players: Two Classical Reliefs and Theatre History," *GRBS* 26 (1985): 333–44.

[19] See my "Vanished Players."

fifth-century plays were written for single performances. While a poet might then take his play to Syracuse or the court of Macedon, Athens would not see it performed at the Dionysia again. I leave out of account here plays so revised as to be new, such as Euripides' two versions of *Hippolytos* or Aristophanes' two versions of *Clouds* (whose second performance is a matter of grave doubt anyway). The sole exception to the rule of one Athenian performance per play in the fifth century is Aiskhylos, whose plays were accorded the unique right of reperformance after his death. Details of this are very sketchy. Were it not for the evidence of Aristophanes in *Akharnians* 10 where Dikaiopolis refers to his anticipation of a revival of Aiskhylos, we might suspect that the tradition of reperformances of Aiskhylos in the fifth century was a projection backward of later practice. We do not know if a revived Aiskhylos play competed with the works of the living or not. In any case this is the great exception. Thus in the fifth century an actor could not make a reputation in a particular performance. There were no legendary interpretations such as Mrs. Siddons' Lady Macbeth or Irving's Hamlet.

The decisive move to repeated performances and the development of a genuine touring circuit of performances was a phenomenon of the fourth century. While we know of dramatic performances at the theater in the Peiraeus at the end of the fifth century, there do not seem to have been theatrical performances at most celebrations of the Rural Dionysia until after the Peloponnesian War.[20] My own belief is that country inhabitants, cooped up in the hated city during the war, nonetheless took back with them to the country in the fourth century a taste for theater.

To review briefly: at the beginning of the fifth century, actors as a category of public attention simply did not exist. As performers they were not differentiated from the singers of dithyramb—volunteer amateurs participating in the city's festival. The principal actors were usually the poets, and thus were simply identified with the pieces they wrote. As the first half of the century progressed, however, acting skill began to be recognized as something apart from the poetry. Histrionic skill could make or mar. The poets gradually abandoned acting to men of more specifically performative skills. The recognition of this change comes with the establishment of acting contests in the middle of the century. Now performances are judged in relation to each other as well as to the work. At the same time the storehouse of myths suitable for dramatic representation seems to be shrinking; it is tempting to speculate that acting helps in this winnowing process as one performance builds on, and of course competes with, another. The art of the second half of the fifth century shows us actors as such for the first time, not only as the painter's eye dwells on the margins, on the transitions into and out of illusion in the theater, but also as the actors see themselves and pay to have themselves represented. Only in the fourth century do we reach the final stage where an actor like Polos can become famous for his representation of a particular role.[21] Only then are plays the repeatable texts we think of today, because a social context for a reperformance has at last been created. The actors through their skills and their assertion of their individuality are a key force in that transformation.

---

[20]Some recent discoveries of small deme theaters, as yet unpublished, may require a revision of the chronology I here argue for; these may be late fifth century. Theaters were not used solely for dramatic performances, however, and even if there were deme theaters in Attica before 403 BCE that still may not prove the existence of an already functioning touring circuit and the expectation that plays from the City Dionysia would be reperformed in such theaters.

[21]Epiktetos (*Dissertationes* frag. 11, p. 464, Schenkl, editio minor) tells us of his portrayals of Oidipous [Oedipus], both as king and as beggar. Polus also might be claimed as the inventor of method acting. Aulus Gellius, *Natura animalium* 6.5, tells us how Polus increased the power of his performance as Elektra lamenting over the supposed urn containing Orestes' ashes by using an urn containing the ashes of his own recently deceased son.

✠ ✠ ✠

THE DRAMA AND THEATER OF THE ASIAN WORLD HAS A HISTORY AS COMPLEX AND multifaceted as the histories of the many civilizations, peoples, and nations that have been said—by the West—to comprise the "Asian world." India, for example, has a literature—in SANSKRIT—over three thousand years old; although the "golden age" of Sanskrit theater took place in the fourth and fifth centuries, theater of various kinds—folk, classical, and modern—thrives in India today. The conventions of Indian theater have pervasively influenced the theater of southeast Asia; the Sanskrit epic poems *Mahabharata* and *Ramayana* provide the characters and settings, for example, for the beautiful shadow-puppet theater of Java in Indonesia—the *WAYANG KULIIT*—and related forms of performance using dolls or live actors.

The masked dance drama of Korea—called *KAMYONGUK*—is related both to Chinese and Japanese theater, and Korea, like other Asian countries, has developed an important modern theater as well.

European knowledge of China's theater probably dates from Marco Polo's visits (1254–1324); we know of more than 550 playwrights who wrote after the Mongol invasion during China's Yüan dynasty (1279–1368), part of a theatrical tradition that is recorded as early as 1000 BCE, and that developed throughout the Han (206 BCE–221 CE), Hui (589–614), T'ang (618–904), and Sung (960–1279) periods. Several plays from the Yüan theater have been adapted by European playwrights; Voltaire's *The Orphan of China* (1755), an adaptation of Chi Chünhsiang's *The House of Chao,* was the first Chinese play to become widely known in Europe, and Li Hsing's *The Story of the Chalk Circle* has been adapted several times, notably by Bertolt Brecht in *The Caucasian Chalk Circle* (1944). After the Mongols were expelled during the Ming dynasty (1368–1644), the center of theatrical activity shifted from northern China toward southern cities such as Hangchow. It was only during the eighteenth and nineteenth centuries—under the Ch'ing dynasty (1644–1912)—that the most characteristic form of modern Chinese theater, the *BEIJING OPERA,* began to take the shape that it has today, sharing the stage with both Western and Western-style plays, and with a vigorous experimental theater working in a more distinctly Chinese dramatic idiom.

Although no one theater can be said to "represent" these rich and diverse theatrical traditions, the classical theater of Japan shares many features common to other Asian theaters: it blends aristocratic and popular affiliations; it descends from social and religious ritual traditions; it coordinates acting, dance, music, and spectacle; many of its plots and characters are derived from familiar literary and historical narratives and legends; its performance conventions are elaborately stylized and refined; and its performers are often trained with a level of formality not found in Western theater. This is hardly surprising, in that the introduction of Buddhism into Japan during the sixth century coincided with an important period of Japanese cultural and political expansion; for the next two centuries, Japan was actively in contact with the vital cultures of India, China, and Korea. And while the period of "classical" Japanese theater—roughly the twelfth through the eighteenth centuries—coincides with an extended period of cultural isolation, the expansion of Japan's military, political, and economic power in the nineteenth and twentieth centuries has again brought Japanese culture into dialogue with Asia and the West.

Indeed, while Japan's imperial ambitions—the invasion of China and much of the Pacific Rim before and during World War II—were extinguished with the atomic bombing of Hiroshima and Nagasaki, Japanese theater and drama have continued to develop both in response to Western culture, and through the experimental innovation of its own traditions.

The classical Japanese theater is a product of a distinctive period in the history of Japan, extending from 1192, when the emperor gave all civil and secular power to a *SHOGUN,* a hereditary military leader, to 1868, when the emperor regained state as well as religious authority. For better than 750 years the Japanese emperors lived in Kyoto engaged in largely ceremonial duties, while the *shoguns,* based in Edo, exercised all political and judicial authority. The Genroku period (1680–1730) saw an extraordinary flowering of Japanese art and culture supported by the shogunate: this is the period of Basho, the famous *haiku* poet; of Ihara Saikaku, the novelist; and of Chikamatsu Monzaemon, Japan's greatest playwright. Although the Noh theater was in decline by the Genroku period, the three principal modes of Japanese classical theater—NOH, DOLL THEATER, and KABUKI—are in different ways the product of the elaborately hierarchical culture of feudal Japan, and of the increasing tension between the class of warriors who ruled Japan and a class of artisans and merchants—sometimes called simply *CHONIN,* or townsmen—whose economic power was centered in Japan's cities. With the rise of the shogunate, Japanese society assumed a feudal character that represented the interests and values of its ruling class of *SAMURAI* warriors. Owing their allegiance to the *shogun,* the ranks of the *samurai* were comprised of various warrior lords, or *DAIMYO,* and their attendant warriors. As in other feudal societies, in Japan it was both a right and an obligation to display the signs and behavior of one's caste; the *samurai,* for example, were expected to obey a stringent honor code, one that required their absolute loyalty to the *shogun,* to the *samurai* caste, and to its military ethos. If a *samurai* betrayed his lord, he and his followers risked becoming outcasts, called *RŌNIN* or "men adrift." The most famous Kabuki drama, *Chūshingura* (1748), takes the fortunes of such a *samurai* lord and his forty-seven followers as its subject, and *rōnin* are common figures in the Japanese theater. This organization extended throughout Japanese society; not only was Japanese society divided into major castes, but its professions—including theater and prostitution, often closely associated in the popular imagination—were strictly controlled through an elaborate guild system. In the major cities, theaters were built in specifically licensed quarters, and actors were generally required to live in or near those districts. Much as tradespeople had to make their trade known through conventions of dress (a practice common in Europe at this time as well), so actors were required in 1709 to shave their forelocks, as a public sign of their profession.

Under the Ashikaga shogunate, which began in 1338 and ended in a civil war in the late sixteenth century, not only were the values of the *samurai* dominant, but the privileges of the *samurai* relative to other castes—such as the many ranks of merchants, artisans, farmers, and peasants—were rigidly observed. The principal forms of theatrical entertainment, especially Noh (or Nō) theater, were both sponsored by and largely reserved for the elite *samurai* castes, and represented the literary and cultural values of their patrons. In 1603, Tokugawa Ieyasu (1542–1616) became the Emperor's *shogun,* and in the Tokugawa period (1603–1867; sometimes called the Edo period, after the city that was his seat, present-day Tokyo), Japan entered a period of extended peace and increasing cultural isolation. In the seventeenth century, the *shoguns* began to expel all foreigners from Japan, reserving specific enclaves in port cities like Nagasaki as protected zones where foreign trade might be undertaken. More importantly, as cities like Osaka, Tokyo, and Kyoto became significant urban centers, the merchant classes became wealthier and more powerful. While their status was lower than that of the *samurai,* many of the merchants amassed huge fortunes that far exceeded the wealth of many *samurai*. The *samurai* still exerted political authority—in 1705 the *samurai* confiscated the fortune of a merchant to whom many of them were indebted—but the merchant classes came to dominate the cultural sphere, as they became the principal audience for poetry, fiction, and theater. Although all three forms of classical Japanese theater are preserved and performed today, they first became popular in different eras of Japan's history: the Noh as it is now known was developed largely between the fourteenth and early seventeenth centuries; the doll theater's greatest popularity was in the late seventeenth century; Kabuki, which is said to have originated when Okuni, a dancer from the Izumo Shrine in Kyoto, began to perform satirical skits in Kyoto in 1603, developed largely between the late seventeenth and mid-eighteenth centuries.

Although Noh theater achieved its highly literary and ceremonial form in the fourteenth century, it is usually said to have developed from performance modes popular throughout the tenth and eleventh centuries, the SARUGAKU-NO, and a related form, DENGAKU-NO. "Noh" means "accomplishment" or "performance," and both forms of entertainment contributed elements to the development of Noh theater and drama. *Dengaku-no* may have had more explicit ritual elements, and was initially associated with the native Japanese religion of Shinto, but both forms involved acrobatics, comic role-playing, and dance. *Sarugaku* means "monkey music," which may give some idea of the exuberance of these performances. In the twelfth century, however, *sarugaku-no* was adapted by Buddhist priests to illustrate tenets of Buddhist thought and belief, and performances were given to large audiences at major temples, acted by lower-ranking priests. In time, professional players both imitated these performances outside the temples and were hired to replace the priests in temple performances; by the mid-twelfth century, guilds of performers were attached to major temples. In return for free performances during religious ceremonies and festivals, the professional guilds were given a monopoly on performing in the region of the temple.

Although the *sarugaku-no* and *dengaku-no* seem to have been energetic and spirited forms of entertainment, it was their association with the contemplative and literary elements of Buddhism that were to have the greatest effect on the formation of Noh theater. In 1374, Kan'ami Kiyotsugu (1333–1384)—a leader of one of the four main *sarugaku-no* troupes—performed before the *shogun* Yoshimitsu Ashikaga (1358–1408). Kan'ami was one of the great innovators of his era and is thought to have contributed to giving the Noh its current form: he emphasized the rhythmic nature of the musical accompaniment, developed a greater use of mime in acting, and correlated dance and musical elements more closely with a dramatic plot. These innovations might well have been lost, however, had the *shogun* not been so impressed that he took Kan'ami and his son Zeami Motokiyo (1363–1444) under his patronage; Kan'ami's troupe became the most influential in Japan, and after his father's death Zeami assumed control of the company, until he was exiled from the court in 1434 by one of Yoshimitsu's sons. Together, Kan'ami and Zeami gave the Noh drama its now-traditional ethos and shape. Kan'ami's innovations were explored and formalized by Zeami, who wrote or revised more than 100 of the 241 plays that make up the Noh repertoire, and described the philosophical, esthetic, and practical goals of Noh performance in several theoretical essays. In time, the *daimyo*, emulating the *shogun*, came to sponsor their own Noh performers. Because the performers and performances were so closely bound to the status of the *samurai* caste, however, Noh never became a popular or even very public form of theater. While *samurai* occasionally sponsored "subscription" performances of Noh for the "townsmen," these highly refined, intensely literary dramas were definitively the entertainment of the elite.

THE DEVELOPMENT OF NOH THEATER

The esthetics of Noh derive from the Buddhist emphasis on ZEN, or contemplation, an attitude of repose and withdrawal from worldly desire and distraction. Noh performance aims to induce a similar kind of attentive repose in its audience, to evoke what is called YUGEN (often translated as "grace," though for Western readers this may have irrelevant Christian connotations), a mood or state of mind responsive to the mysterious, graceful, and impermanent beauty of the performance. For this reason, perhaps, Noh drama is not really driven by the cause-and-effect narrative logic of Western drama. Noh plays are typically centered on scenes of revelation that climax in the main actor's principal dance. Rather than imitating life, a Noh play should evoke the "flower," as Zeami termed the fusion of esthetic, spiritual, and moral beauty arising from the performance.

NOH DRAMATIC FORM

A "typical" Noh play might begin with the WAKI, or secondary actor, meeting the SHITE, or principal actor, at a site of historical, legendary, or mythological importance. The *waki* enters first, and in his opening song—sometimes called the TRAVELING SONG, because he sings it while making his entrance—announces who he is (often a priest), and where he is going. The *shite* then enters, taking the role of an ordinary person. They discuss the significance of the place, perhaps where a legendary warrior was killed in battle. The characters speak a densely literary language, for part of the Noh dramatist's skill is shown in his cunning ability to borrow allusions and quotations from Japanese literature; the actors repeat and emphasize a network of phrases and images that convey the play's central theme. The chorus—kneeling stage left—also contributes to this "literary" texture, narrating some of the action and singing or reciting some of the dialogue. The *shite* then leaves the stage, and in some Noh productions a KYŌGEN (a brief farce also descended from *sarugaku*) is performed. When the *shite* returns, however, he reveals who he really is, usually a god, hero, or demon connected with the place whose destiny is troubled; he might, for example, be the ghost of the legendary warrior. In a manner of speaking, the character continues to haunt this place because he or she is unable to let go of the world, of the "character" and its investment in the world that are the essence of his or her being. The ghost is haunted by the tortuous attitude or emotion that keeps him or her connected to the world. Unlike a Greek or Shakespearean tragedy, a Noh play does not conclude with a speech of recognition or response; instead, Noh drama concludes with an intricate dance, a beautiful interplay of dialogue, dance, narration, and music for the audience's contemplation.

Since the active repertoire of Noh drama has remained more or less the same for over 400 years, it is perhaps not surprising that other elements of Noh theater and performance have become highly systematic and conventionalized. There are five types of Noh drama— plays praising the gods, plays about warriors, plays about women, plays about madness or spirits, and plays about demons—and in classical Japan, a program of Noh performance included one play from each of these categories, performed in this order, with a *kyōgen* between each Noh play. In modern Japan, it has become more common to perform only two or three plays followed by a *kyōgen,* in part because the pace of performance is much slower today. Although women at one time performed in Noh theater, in 1629 women were banned from the Japanese stage; while women do perform in the modern Japanese theater, Noh companies are now traditionally all male. Plays are performed by the *shite* who is masked, an unmasked *waki,* and actors who play the *shite*'s companions (TSURE). A chorus of six to ten men both sings and narrates from a position to the side of the stage, and musicians—a flute and two or three drums—are positioned at the rear of the stage. The drums beat rhythmically, punctuating and accentuating the actors' delivery, while the flute plays in a kind of counterpoint to their speech. The *shite*'s mask is drawn from one of five categories—old person, male, female, gods, monsters—and the clothing of the performers is similarly stylized: the actors sometimes wear elaborate headdresses, and

NOH PERFORMANCE SPACE, FIFTEENTH CENTURY

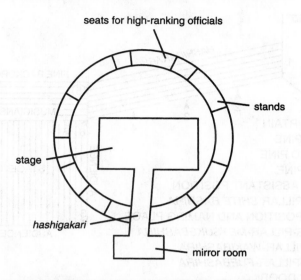

This is the ground plan of the performance space in the time of Zeami.

sumptuous silk clothing, arranged and layered in particular ways for certain roles. The chorus wears the traditional dress of the *samurai.* Attendants clothed in black are present onstage throughout the performance, helping the actors with costumes and masks, and placing and removing properties when needed; they are always senior actors of the company, since they may also need to step in to finish a performance if an actor is unable to continue. The stage is bare of sets, and hand properties are few and conventional; a bundle of firewood might be represented by a few sticks bound with flowers. Similarly, many of the properties are purely symbolic: a twig carried by a grieving woman is the sign of her madness. Throughout the performance, the actors move slowly and ceremonially; indeed, many of their actions must take place at a prescribed area of the stage.

Although the Noh stage was shaped somewhat differently in Kan'ami and Zeami's era, by 1615 it had assumed the shape it retains to this day. A stage (*BUTAI*), roughly eighteen feet square, extends into the audience area; the stage is roofed like the early shrines from which it derives, and the audience is seated in front and on the stage-right side. A painted backdrop behind the stage always pictures the Yogo Pine at the Kasuga Shrine in Nara. The stage is always of highly polished wood with sounding jars concealed beneath it to resonate with the emphatic stamping that is part of the actors' performance. The musicians are seated directly behind the main stage area on a second, narrow stage (*ATOZA*); they are in full view of the audience and are able to see the actors and adjust their playing to the actors' performance throughout the play. A small entrance, called the "HURRY DOOR," leads off the stage-left side of the *atoza,* which is used by the stage assistants, the chorus, and for the exit of dead characters. A second narrow stage runs along the stage-left side of the stage, the *WAKI-ZA,* where the chorus is seated, again in view of the audience and able to adjust their narration and singing to the pace of the actors. Finally, a long bridge, the *HASHIGAKARI,* leads from the upstage right corner of the stage out to the MIRROR ROOM,

THE NOH STAGE

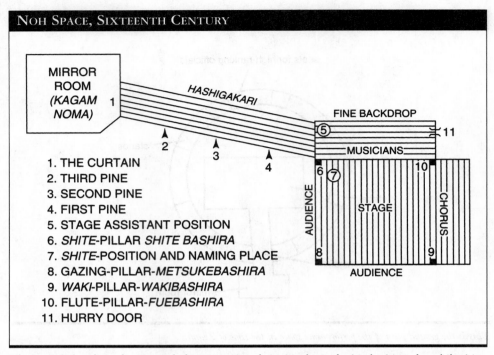

NOH SPACE, SIXTEENTH CENTURY

MIRROR ROOM *(KAGAM NOMA)*

HASHIGAKARI

FINE BACKDROP

MUSICIANS

AUDIENCE

STAGE

CHORUS

AUDIENCE

1. THE CURTAIN
2. THIRD PINE
3. SECOND PINE
4. FIRST PINE
5. STAGE ASSISTANT POSITION
6. *SHITE*-PILLAR *SHITE BASHIRA*
7. *SHITE*-POSITION AND NAMING PLACE
8. GAZING-PILLAR-*METSUKEBASHIRA*
9. *WAKI*-PILLAR-*WAKIBASHIRA*
10. FLUTE-PILLAR-*FUEBASHIRA*
11. HURRY DOOR

This ground plan shows the stage with the mirror room, the hashigakari, *the* shitebashira, *the* wakibashira, *the* metsukebashira, *and the* fuebashira, *as well as the locations for the musicians and the chorus.*

where the costumed actors have been studying themselves in order to get into the character. The *hashigakari* is six feet wide by 33 to 52 feet long; it is bordered by a narrow strip of white pebbles, on which stand three pine trees, representing heaven, earth, and man.

The four pillars that support the roof over the stage also have specific functions in the performance, and provide a sense of the ceremonial formality of Noh theater. The upstage right pillar closest to the *hashigakari* is called the SHITEBASHIRA, or *shite*'s pillar. When the shite enters the *hashigakari,* he slides his feet (which are bound in cotton cloth) slowly along the floor; reaching the *shitebashira* he pauses to announce who he is, where he is coming from, and where he is going (sometimes the *waki* will make this announcement when the *shite* reaches the *shitebashira*). The pillar down stage right is called the METSUKE-BASHIRA, the gazing or eye-fixing pillar. It is the place where the *shite* looks while delivering his speech, and which he watches through the slits in his mask to help orient his performance; given the tiny eye-openings in Noh masks, the *metsukebashira* is nearly all the *shite* can see. Down stage left, diagonally across from the *shitebashira,* is the WAKIBASHIRA, where the *waki* is often stationed when the *shite* enters. Upstage left is the FUEBASHIRA, the flute-player's pillar, where the flute-player is positioned.

As Zeami suggests in "Teachings on Style and the Flower" (see Critical Contexts), the training of a Noh actor in the fourteenth century was presumed to be life-long, more a vocation than an occupation. Under the shogunate, Noh performers were given the privileges of the *samurai* caste, and five schools for training Noh actors were founded. These schools were run by hereditary masters, and certain families of Noh performers have influenced the theater over several generations; indeed, we owe the preservation of many documents (including Zeami's treatises), properties, and masks to the unusually closed and traditional ways in which Noh training has been passed from generation to generation. Four of the five current Noh companies were founded in Zeami's lifetime. Although Japan is no longer a caste society, acting in a Noh company today still requires years of dedication and intense training, something between the priesthood and the military. Moreover, because the relatively small number of classical Noh plays was stabilized in the early seventeenth century, Noh actors have generally mastered all the roles of the repertoire and perform without rehearsal. Their intensive training in movement, song, and dance prepares the actors, chorus, musicians, and stage assistants to be closely responsive to the many subtleties of their collective performance. And given the stability of the repertoire, of training, and of performance conventions, Noh theater has been performed in an unbroken tradition from Zeami's era to the present day.

THE DEVELOPMENT OF DOLL THEATER

Like the Noh theater, the doll theater owes something to the desire of Buddhist priests to educate a wider Japanese audience in their teachings; unlike the Noh, however, the doll theater was not supported or protected directly by the shogunate, and it came to enjoy a more popular audience. The doll theater arose from the confluence of two kinds of performance: puppet shows and storytelling to music. Much like the itinerant performers of *sarugaku-no,* wandering puppeteers became associated with shrines and temples in the twelfth century. At the same time, a form of live storytelling also became popular, the singing and recitation of legends and stories to the accompaniment of the BIWA, a four-stringed, plucked instrument. One of the most popular of these narratives was *The Tale of Jōruri,* a love story about a wealthy girl named Jōruri; although the story dates from the fifteenth century, it became popular when it was performed to a musical instrument imported from the Ryukyu Islands between 1558 and 1569, the SAMISEN. The samisen, a three-stringed instrument that is both plucked and struck, has a much wider tonal and dynamic range than the *biwa.* Samisen-accompanied dialogue and narrative became so popular that this kind of performance was termed simply *JŌRURI.* In effect, the doll theater is a form of *jōruri* in which the song and spoken narrative are accompanied by puppet performance.

Although puppets had been used in Japan for several centuries, puppets were first used in conjunction with *jōruri* performances in the sixteenth century; puppet-*jōruri* performances have been recorded in Kyoto as early as 1596, and by the late seventeenth century there were important doll theaters in both Tokyo and Osaka. As in the Noh, the plays performed in the doll theaters used narrative, dialogue, music, and acting to convey the dramatic action, and in the seventeenth century playwrights writing for the doll theaters adapted plots and characters directly from Noh models. In part, however, because of their derivation from the romantic *jōruri* narratives, in part because their audiences were well-to-do merchants and citizens rather than the aristocratic *samurai,* and in part because they were competing with the more salacious Kabuki theaters for that audience, the doll theaters came to dramatize events more closely approaching contemporary life. Although the earliest doll theater plays were on historical and legendary subjects (like the Noh plays), by the late seventeenth and early eighteenth centuries, doll drama concerned stagings of current events, and romanticized portrayals of contemporary life, called "domestic plays" or *SEWAMONO.* Although the shogunate forbade the staging of current events in 1703, the shoguns were more concerned about the satirical portrayals of *samurai* common in Kabuki; playwrights continued to write about contemporary events.

The doll theater played a major role in the development of Japanese theater generally. When Gidayu Takemoto (1651–1714), a famous performer of *jōruri,* opened the Takemoto Theater in Osaka in 1684, he began a collaboration with Chikamatsu Monzaemon (1653–1725), now generally recognized as Japan's greatest dramatist. Chikamatsu wrote an important body of plays for the doll theater, on historical subjects as well as on contemporary life. His play *Love Suicides at Sonezaki* (1703) concerns the double suicide of a young merchant and a prostitute in 1703, and was renowned for the beauty of its language and the power of its performance. The genre became so popular that in 1722 the shogunate banned plays about double suicide, which were common in both the doll theater and the Kabuki theater, perhaps fearing that Chikamatsu's play would be imitated by romantic young Japanese. Not only did Chikamatsu and other playwrights—notably Chikamatsu Hanji (1725–1783) and Uemura Bunrakuken (1737–1810), for whom the current puppet theater of Japan, *BUNRAKU*, is named—produce an extraordinarily rich body of plays, but these plays were immediately mined by the Kabuki theaters, providing a source of material for living actors as well as the doll theater's elaborate puppets.

THE DOLL THEATER STAGE

The stage of the doll theater is 36 feet wide by 26 feet deep and is divided into three sections, each separated by a low screen. The three puppeteers who operate each puppet are visible throughout the performance. They are costumed in elegant traditional clothes and are seated behind the screens. The puppeteers and their dolls share the stage with several other performers: the stage assistants, dressed in black as in the Noh theater; the announcer; the narrator; and the *samisen* player. The announcer begins the performance by announcing the title of the play and introducing the narrator and the *samisen* player. The narrator is responsible for the verbal art of the play in a direct development of his role in the *jōruri:* he narrates the story of the play, speaks the dialogue of the characters and expresses their emotions as well, smiling, laughing, weeping, and so on. Later in the eighteenth century, several narrators were used, one for each of the major characters in the drama. The *samisen* is played to augment, clarify, and deepen the narrator's performance, lending it a special plangency.

As in the Noh theater, performance in the doll theater is extremely ceremonial and precise, and performers undergo years of training to achieve their craft. Although marionettes were used in the seventeenth century, hand-operated puppets became increasingly popular and by 1736 had supplanted earlier forms. The typical doll is three or four feet tall and is operated by three puppeteers. The most senior operator, dressed in a formal nineteenth-century costume, stands behind the doll and holds it up; he works a system of strings and pulleys within the head that control the doll's head, eyebrows, and eyelids, and he also operates the doll's right arm and right hand by means of hidden strings. His two assistants are clothed in black like the stage assistants, and their faces are covered; one assistant operates the left arm and hand, and the other assistant operates the legs and feet. Much as training in the Noh theater resembles that of a traditional art, so learning to operate the puppets of the doll theater entails a lifetime of commitment. Puppeteers take an apprenticeship of ten years to learn to operate the legs and feet of the dolls with sufficient grace; they then take another ten years to learn the correct operation of the left arm and hand before spending the final ten years on mastering the subtleties of the right arm, right hand, and head.

Doll theater contributed extensively to the dramatic repertoire of the Kabuki theater, and the fixed poses of the puppets are sometimes thought to contribute to the exaggerated expressive stance of the Kabuki actors, the *MIE.* But the doll theater contributed other innovations to Japanese theater, and to world theater generally. Much as the dolls increased in complexity throughout the late seventeenth century and early eighteenth century—gaining eye movement in 1730, finger joints and movements in 1733, and so on—so the stage itself became increasingly mechanized. By 1715 the doll theaters were using movable settings, and by 1727 elevator traps were used to raise and lower scenery visibly through the floor of the stage. This machinery not only was put to use in the more spectacular

Kabuki theater, but also was adapted and imitated by theaters around the world. Although the doll theater was surpassed in popularity by the Kabuki in the nineteenth century, it continues to be sponsored by the Japanese government and performed regularly in Osaka and Tokyo.

Kabuki is in many ways the most energetic and spectacular mode of classical Japanese theater, using live actors to stage intense and passionate dramas whose effect is heightened by a range of powerful performance conventions, and by an elaborately mechanized stage. Like the doll theater, Kabuki arose as a popular form of entertainment, supported by audiences outside the aristocratic sphere of Noh performance. And while Kabuki drama, like the drama of the doll theaters, was initially derived from the plays of the Noh theater, Kabuki theater rapidly developed its own dramatic style and performance esthetics.

Unlike Noh and doll theater, Kabuki did not originate in medieval performance forms like the *sarugaku-no* and the *biwa*-accompanied narratives that became *jōruri*. Instead, Kabuki began in 1603, when Okuni, who claimed to be a priestess from the Izumo Grand Shrine, set up an impromptu stage in the Kyoto riverbed, where she performed dances and satirical skits. Okuni's company was largely composed of women, and within a short time, a number of companies—some involving prostitutes, who offered performances as entertainment—were established in Kyoto and elsewhere. Although comic roles—called SARUWAKA—were always performed by men, the earliest troupes were composed mainly of women, called either ONNA KABUKI (women's Kabuki) or YŪGO KABUKI (prostitutes' Kabuki). At the same time, however, other Kabuki companies composed mainly of adolescent boys became popular.

Throughout the early period of Kabuki, its performers—both women and boys—were frequently associated with prostitution, which extended in various ways to a variety of leisure activities: to bathhouses, dances, and to the practice of GEISHA, which has its origins at this time. All of these activities, however, were distinct from the work of the YŪGO, or professional prostitute. As in other respects, the shogunate treated Kabuki like prostitution, beginning in 1624 to license companies and theater districts.

The boundary between theater and prostitution (by men, women, and boys) was difficult to police, though, and in 1652 authorities finally banned the boys' Kabuki *(WAKASHU KABUKI)* outright. Thereafter, the only Kabuki companies that were licensed to perform were the YARO KABUKI, or adult male Kabuki companies, which are now traditional.

The repertoire of Kabuki theater contains two kinds of plays, one based on historical or legendary incidents, and *sewamono*—or "domestic plays"—based on contemporary events. Okuni had once acted the role of a young *samurai* soliciting a prostitute, and plays based on the visit of a wealthy and powerful young man to the "licensed quarter" became a popular Kabuki genre, particularly in Kyoto and Osaka. Many of these plays, including *Love Letter from the Licensed Quarter* (1780), concern the fortunes of Yūgiri, a well-known courtesan of the Osaka Shinmachi quarter who died in 1678. Chikamatsu—whose *Love Suicides at Sonezaki* (1703) adapted the conventions of Kabuki to the doll stage—played a central role in this regard as well, for he worked as the house playwright for over twenty years to a famous Kabuki company. Although plays that dramatize love suicides and plays staging the scandals of the *samurai* caste were banned after 1722, playwrights continued to write about contemporary life under the guise of one of the other major genres of Kabuki theater, the history play. It quickly became apparent that by changing names and setting the drama in the past, playwrights were able to write domestic plays thinly veiled as history. For example, in 1703 the forty-seven retainers of Lord Asano took revenge on their master's disgrace at the hands of a shogunate official by killing the official and then committing *seppuku,* or ritual disembowelment. Within two weeks, a Kabuki

THE
DEVELOPMENT
OF KABUKI
THEATER

KABUKI STAGE, NINETEENTH CENTURY

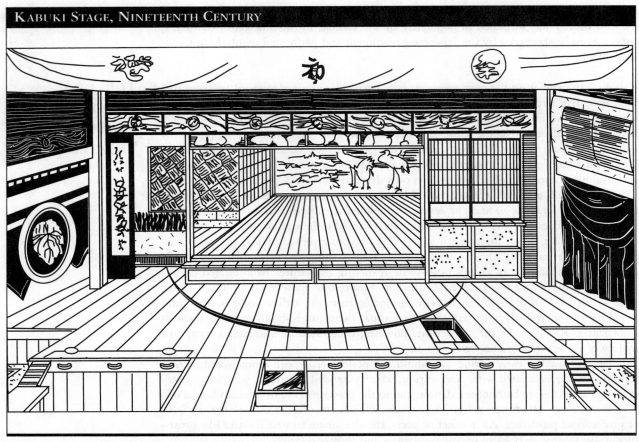

Notice the screens to the side of the stage, the hanamichi *(which attaches to the front of the stage in the lower left-center of the picture), and a revolving platform in the center of the stage.*

play alluding to the incident was staged, and then rapidly closed by the government. When Chikamatsu turned to these events in 1710, he set the play in the fourteenth century in order to sidestep the ban, and one of the most famous Kabuki plays, *Chūshingura* (1748), concerns these events as well.

THE KABUKI STAGE

Kabuki is very much a performance genre, and its plays were organized around the abilities of its actors rather than around a literary script. For this reason, even the plays written by the most influential Kabuki playwrights—Chikamatsu Monzaemon, Takedo Izumo (1691–1756), and Kawatake Mokuami (1816–1893)—began as outlines of scenes to be elaborated by a cadre of assistant playwrights. A Kabuki company contained forty to sixty actors, each of whom specialized in a certain kind of role and expected the playwright to devise scenes that would allow him to display his talents. Companies generally included a leading-man actor, or *TACHIYAKU,* and specialists in villainous men (*KATAKIYAKU*), in young men and boys (*WAKASHUGATA*), in comic roles (*DOKEKATA*), and in women's roles (*ONNAGATA*), which were also divided according to age and type.

Finally, the unusual duration of a Kabuki performance also demanded the talents of the playwright's staff of assistants. Kabuki performances originally began around three o'clock in the morning, and did not conclude until dusk; the fourteen- to fifteen-hour production was composed of a series of scenes arranged around a common theme or mood. The production usually began with a dance play, followed by a familiar play from the company's repertoire. Since the play was familiar to the company, it required little preparation. Then the company would perform one or two short practice plays, written by apprentice playwrights and performed by actors-in-training as part of their education. The main play—the HON KYŌGEN—would be performed at about seven o'clock in the morning, and lasted until dusk. This play was outlined by the house playwright in collaboration with the company's leading actor and manager, and he would write the most important sections himself; the company's second and third rank playwrights would elaborate dialogue for the rest of the play. The play was customarily divided into four sections: a history section in four to six acts (JIDAIMONO) concerning the exploits of the samurai; a dance; a sewamono (contemporary) section in one to three acts, set in the milieu of artisans, traders, and merchants; and a concluding dance drama. Kabuki performances today are generally given in two programs, lasting from eleven to four o'clock and from four-thirty until nine-thirty in the evening. Although it is rare to see a full-length Kabuki play performed today, the four-part sequence is still followed.

Kabuki is very much an actor's theater. The actors undergo a long period of training, and as in Noh theater, certain families of actors have dominated the history of Kabuki. Indeed, Kabuki actors often wear their family crest in performance, and audiences frequently compare an actor's performance in a given role with his father's or his uncle's. Originating as a form of dance, Kabuki places a premium on choreography, which accompanies gesture and speech as a means of realizing the character's essential tone or feeling in a precise and elegant image. Yet the actors play directly to the audience, and the most striking moments in the performance—the mie, a highly conventionalized posed performance of passion—are underscored as performance when the stage assistants clap two pieces of wood loudly and rhythmically together. The actors play conventional roles, and each role in the Kabuki repertoire has a conventional costume associated with it. The costumes are extremely cumbersome, so the actors are often helped by stage assistants clothed in black who position properties and move pieces of the set. The actors are not masked, but wear an elaborate and conventionalized makeup, usually of red and black lines and patterns ranged over a white base; onnagata actors generally add only eyebrow lines and rouged cheeks and lips to an otherwise white face. Given its close relationship to jōruri and doll theater, it is not surprising that Kabuki usually requires a narrator onstage as well, who not only sets the scene, but comments on the action throughout; he also occasionally speaks dialogue as well. Kabuki actors never sing, and so their songs are sung by the narrator and by an onstage chorus as well. Moreover, each play is accompanied by traditional music, played by musicians wearing the traditional samurai costume; the orchestra for Kabuki is considerably larger than that for Noh and makes use of flutes, bells, drums, cymbals, and gongs, as well as the samisen.

Although the first Kabuki companies played on impromptu stages, they soon were allowed to use Noh theaters; given their raffish character, however, Kabuki companies were not allowed to have roofed theaters until 1724. Like the doll theater, Kabuki theater quickly made use of scenic technology; the elevator stage was in use by 1736, and by the late eighteenth century it was common for Kabuki theaters to have a revolving stage, sometimes two independent turntables with one turning inside the other. Kabuki makes extensive use of scenery, though much of it is of a symbolic or ornamental nature. Like properties in this theater, which tend to be suggestive of the objects they represent, the scenery of a Kabuki performance is openly theatrical in character: the scenery is changed in view of the audience by visible assistants (who help the actors as well) and aims to suggest the locale of the scene rather than put it on the stage in a realistic way. It is a

THE CULTURES, LANGUAGES, AND THEATER of the Indian subcontinent have been transformed by three massive invasions: by the Aryans sometime between 3000 and 2000 BCE; by the Moslems, who brought both Persian and the Koran, in the tenth and eleventh centuries; and by the British, beginning in the seventeenth century. The Aryan language—Sanskrit (literally, "the perfected tongue")—became the foundation of ancient Indian culture. Sanskrit was a spoken language until early in the first millennium, when Prakit became the vernacular. Something like Latin in medieval Europe, Sanskrit was reserved for ritual, religious, and academic uses, and for India's rich literature and theater. Sanskrit is the language of the *Rgveda,* a collection of prayers and hymns composed between 1500 and 1000 BCE that is the oldest work in any Indo-European language. The two major epics of Indian culture—the *Mahabharata* and the *Ramayana*—date from around 1000 BCE, but took their current form during India's "golden age," which lasted from the second century CE into the ninth century. Although it had long been thought in the West that Sanskrit theater gradually disappeared after the Moslem invasions of the tenth and eleventh centuries, Sanskrit plays were still performed in Kerala—a state in the southwest of India—by performers who were part of a hereditary caste connected to religious temples.

Hindu belief and the caste structure of ancient Indian society inform the esthetics of Sanskrit theater and drama. Ancient India was a rigidly stratified society composed of four hereditary castes, each of which was subdivided: the *Brahmins* (priests and intellectuals), *Kshatriyas* (aristocrats, warriors), *Vaisyas* (craftsmen, farmers), and *Sudras* (unskilled workers, peasants). Although these castes were devised and perpetuated along racial and economic lines, they also translated Hindu religious beliefs into the organizing structure of society. Hindu is based on a belief in Brahman, or "world-soul." Although different aspects of Brahman are often represented as distinct gods—Brahma the creator, Siva the destroyer, Vishnu the preserver, for example—these gods are really aspects of Brahman, the only whole, perfect, and unchanging being. The created universe is arrayed hierarchically, according to the degree that each being is able to contemplate or participate in this sense of wholeness or perfection.

In performance, Sanskrit drama emblematizes this dichotomy between the distracting diversity of lived experience and the contemplation of wholeness and perfection; Sanskrit theater offers its audience a richly varied performance while inducing the audience to adopt a unifying and impersonal, even contemplative mood. Most of our understanding of Sanskrit drama derives from the second-century *Natyasastra,* or *Art of the Theater,* usually attributed to the playwright Bharata, from several other treatises, and from the twenty-five plays that remain. Much as ancient Greek plays were based on myth and legend mainly drawn from the *Iliad* and the *Odyssey,* Sanskrit plays were generally based on heroic stories taken from the *Mahabharata* and the *Ramayana,* and were divided into two groups. *RUPAKA* (major drama) and *UPA-RUPAKA* (minor drama). *Rupaka* are of various lengths, and include the plays of Bharata, Bhasa's second-century plays *The Vision of Vasavadatta* and *Carudatta,* King Sudraka's *The Clay Cart* (written sometime between the fourth and eighth centuries), Kalidasa's fifth-century *Sakuntala,* and the plays of King Harsa and Bhavabhuti (seventh century). As in the Japanese Noh, the narrative of the play is less critical than the attitude it produces, the impersonal and contemplative mood of wholeness called *RASA.* According to the *Natyasastra,* there are eight basic *rasas* or moods that a play should strive to produce—erotic, comic, pathetic, furious, heroic, terrible, odious, marvelous—and while a given play may include several *rasas,* it should be designed so that one mood dominates. Moreover, these *rasas* are related to the *BHAVA,* the emotions or feelings displayed in the play by the characters. The eight *bhavas* (desire, comic or sympathetic laughter, sadness, anger, vigor or power, fear, loathing, and wonder) are the organizing, "stable" emotions

(ASIDE)

SANSKRIT DRAMA AND THEATER

measure, though, of the relationship between the extroverted Kabuki performance and its audience that its most distinguishing feature involves the audience more directly in the production. In the early eighteenth century, Kabuki theaters added a *HANAMICHI,* or elevated bridge, extending from the rear of the auditorium to the stage. Actors made their exits and entrances here, and scenes could be played on the *hanamichi* as well. By the 1770s, a second *hanamichi* was added, and the area between the two *hanamichi* was divided into floor boxes, while other rows of seating ran along the sides of the auditorium.

staged in the play, and are complicated by thirty-three "unstable" emotions. The subtle balance and interplay of the *bhavas* should evoke a sense of harmony and perfection, the dominant *rasa* of the play.

As in Hindu philosophy, Sanskrit drama aims to produce a sense of oneness from the diversity of experience; *rasa* arises from each play's cunning interplay of the range of *bhavas*, of dialogue written in both verse and prose, of Sanskrit and Prakit, and of character types ranging from gods, kings, and heroes to servants, peasants, and children. Yet despite this diversity, Sanskrit plays have several common characteristics. Each play not only produces its main mood or *rasa*, it also illustrates the workings of *karma* or cosmic justice. For this reason, Sanskrit drama falls outside the Western understanding of tragedy, and Sanskrit playwrights are urged by the *Natyasastra* not to represent death onstage. Sanskrit is spoken by all the male Brahmin and Kshatriya characters in the play, while women, peasants, and children speak Prakit, as does the jester character who appears in most plays, often as the hero's sidekick. Although plays vary in length from one act to ten acts, each act generally takes place within a single day; the action usually takes place in several earthly and heavenly locations.

Plays were performed on a variety of occasions in ancient India—at festivals, weddings, coronations, and at other public events—and the play's *rasa* was appropriate to the occasion. The *Natyasastra* describes three kinds of theater structure—square, rectangular, and triangular—each in three different

CLASSICAL SANSKRIT PERFORMANCE

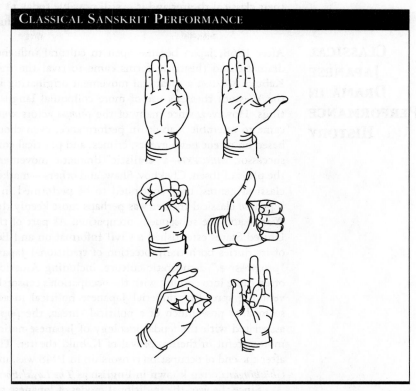

These six hand positions are used in a classical Sanskrit performance.

sizes. The rectangular theaters were divided into two equal areas. The audience area was supported by four pillars, representing both the four compass points and the four principal castes; the stage area was divided into two parts: a relatively shallow performing space divided from a backstage area by a wall.

Performances were accompanied by a variety of musical instruments, and were elaborately ceremonial in character; actors used an elaborate system of movement, gesture, and speech. Since the performers were to represent codified *bhavas*, the *Natyasastra* described the gestures appropriate to them: it describes, for instance, thirty-two different eye movements, thirty-two positions for the feet, twenty-four gestures for one hand. Both the Sanskrit drama and texts like the *Natyasastra* document the extraordinary theatrical vitality of the "golden age" of classical Indian culture.

Although the second *hanamichi* is still required for some plays, it is generally no longer in use.

The restoration of the emperor in 1868 not only brought about the collapse of the shogunate, but also ended Japan's isolation. It also dramatized the economic weakness of the *samurai* relative to the merchant class. In many respects, Japan's theater was vulnerable to extinction, especially the Noh and doll theaters, which had no truly popular audience; Kabuki was the only theater which continued to attract new plays, playwrights, and audiences in the nineteenth and twentieth centuries. But the Japanese worked to preserve their classical theater and it is still possible today to see plays from the Noh, doll theater, and Kabuki repertoire in excellent, traditional productions.

CLASSICAL JAPANESE DRAMA IN PERFORMANCE HISTORY

After 1868, Japan became open to cultural influence from the West, and a variety of dramatic and theatrical forms came to rival the traditional genres of Noh, *jōruri*, and Kabuki. *SHIMPA,* a theatrical movement originating in Osaka in the 1880s, responded to the Western theater's use of more colloquial language and contemporary dramatic settings. However, since many of the *shimpa* actors were drawn from Kabuki, it gradually came to resemble Kabuki in performance, even though its dramas were more evidently based on recent news events, crimes, and political controversies. But while *shimpa* and its successor, *SHINGEKI*—a "realistic" dramatic movement that both imported and imitated the plays of Ibsen, Chekhov, Shaw, and others—marked an important move away from the classical genres, they continued to be performed in the twentieth century. Indeed, the Japanese classical theater was perhaps most keenly threatened by Japan's defeat in World War II and the subsequent occupation. As part of the postwar occupation of Japan, the United States established a Civil Information and Education Section, which had as part of its duties both the protection of traditional Japanese culture and the importation of "progressive," democratic culture, including American literature and drama. This office often came into conflict with the occupation's censorship office, concerned as it was to prevent the spread of imperial Japanese political ideas. Although neither Noh nor *jōruri* seemed to pose much of a political threat, the popular Kabuki theater had long been associated with the feudal ideology of Japanese nationalism, and the censors were much more careful in their approval of Kabuki theater. The first Kabuki play to be produced after the end of occupation censorship in 1948 was, in fact, the great *samurai* revenge play, *Chūshingura* often known in English as *The Loyal Forty-Seven Samurai.*

Since the war, the traditional modes of Japanese theater have become popular not only in Japan, but throughout the world. Several modern playwrights—notably Mishima Yukio—have either written new Noh or Kabuki plays, or have adapted earlier dramas to modern settings. Moreover, the revival of Japanese classical theater has been part of an important resurgence of interest in traditional modes of artistic expression in Japan, which has taken place alongside Japan's emergence as a leading political, economic, and cultural power in the late twentieth century.

KAN'AMI KIYOTSUGU

Kan'ami Kiyotsugu (1333–1384) was one of the principal performers of *sarugaku-no,* and the leader of a prominent company. When he appeared before the *shogun* Yoshimitsu Ashikiga in 1374, the *shogun* was so impressed with the company that he retained them as his players. Kan'ami is generally credited with refining and systematizing the Noh for his aristocratic audience, and with writing many of the plays that became part of the standard Noh repertoire. Kan'ami's son, Zeami Motokiyo (1363–1444), succeeded his father as the leader of the company, and had a massive influence on the development of the Noh. Zeami both reworked older plays and wrote many new plays of his own; of the 241 plays in the Noh repertoire, more than one hundred are connected to Zeami. Zeami influenced the development of Noh in other respects as well, mainly in writing sixteen essays on Noh esthetics. These essays cover a range of topics, including the training of actors, the proper style of dramatic writing, and the goals of performance. Although Zeami enjoyed the favor of Yoshimitsu until the *shogun*'s death in 1408, he fared less well under the rule of Yoshimitsu's son, Yoshimochi (1386–1428), and was banished to the remote island of Sado in 1434 when Yoshimochi's younger brother Yoshinori (1394–1441) became *shogun.* The reasons for Yoshinori's hostility to Zeami are not clear, but may involve Yoshinori's preference for another playwright, On'ami. Zeami did succeed in passing his essays on to his son-in-law Komparu Zenchiku (1405–1468), who became an important Noh playwright and theoretician. Not much is known about the end of Zeami's life; legend has it that he was able to return to the mainland after Yoshinori was assassinated in 1441.

MATSUKAZE

Matsukaze was originally written by Kan'ami and extensively reworked by Zeami; it has remained in the Noh repertoire since the fifteenth century, and is performed by all Noh companies.

This elegant drama, like most Noh plays, takes place in a setting familiar from the classic literature of Japan, the Bay of Suma. Suma is principally associated with the famous poet, courtier, and scholar Ariwaka no Yukihira (818–893), whose exile at Suma was recounted in his own poetry and formed the basis for many stories and legends. It also inspired the narrative of Genji's exile at Suma in the Japanese epic *Tale of Genji.* The narrative of the play, though, seems to have been invented by Kan'ami. The play opens when the *waki*—playing a priest—enters the stage, singing a traveling song about his arrival at Suma. He asks the *kyōgen* (playing a villager) about the significance of the pine tree, and he is informed that it memorializes two fisher girls, Murasame and Matsukaze, who have long since died. Shortly thereafter Murasame—played by the *tsure*—enters, followed by the *shite,* Matsukaze. The two girls elaborately mime dipping brine into their cart with their fans, and in speeches that quote from Yukihira and from other poets, they describe their desolation. Their language here is rich with imagery, particularly of the changing sea, the hard lives of the fishermen, and of the moon, a Buddhist symbol of enlightenment. As is typical of the Noh, many of their lines are spoken by the Chorus.

Although the *shite* and his *tsure* do not leave the stage, they retire to the *shitebashira,* where they mime sitting in their small hut. The *waki*—who has observed them throughout the first scene, approaches the hut and asks for shelter, quoting one of Yukihira's poems in passing. The girls then reveal that they are the ghosts of Matsukaze and Murasame, still "steeped in longing" for the exiled poet, even in death. They had fallen in love with Yukihira during his exile at Suma, and he had given them their names, "Wind in the Pines" (*matsukaze*) and "Autumn Rain" (*murasame*), names redolent of the imagery of classical Japanese poetry. The girls were not able to follow Yukihira when he returned to court after his exile; all they have in his memory is his hunting cloak and court hat. Driven nearly to madness with her eternal grief, Matsukaze puts on Yukihira's cloak and hat for her final dance.

Matsukaze is an evocative example of the way Noh theater attempts to capture a particular mood through the collaborative interplay between each of its highly wrought arts. The beauty of the language, the delicacy of characterization, the succinct action, the music of the flute and drums, the chanting of the Chorus, and the refinement of the acting combine to capture the subtle intensity of feeling for which Noh theater is famous.

MATSUKAZE

Kan'ami Kiyotsugu

TRANSLATED BY ROYALL TYLER

─── CHARACTERS ───

AN ITINERANT PRIEST (*waki*) MATSUKAZE (*shite*) PLACE: *Suma Bay in Settsu Province*
A VILLAGER (*kyōgen*) MURASAME (*tsure*) TIME: *Autumn, the Ninth Month*

(The stage assistant places a stand with a pine sapling set into it at the front of the stage. The PRIEST *enters and stands at the naming-place. He carries a rosary.)*

PRIEST: I am a priest who travels from province to province. Lately I have been in the Capital. I visited the famous sites and ancient ruins, not missing a one. Now I intend to make a pilgrimage to the western provinces. *(He faces forward.)* I have hurried, and here I am already at the Bay of Suma in Settsu Province. *(His attention is caught by the pine tree.)* How strange! That pine on the beach has a curious look. There must be a story connected with it. I'll ask someone in the neighborhood. *(He faces the bridgeway.)* Do you live in Suma?

(The VILLAGER *comes down the bridgeway to the first pine. He wears a short sword.)*

VILLAGER: Perhaps I am from Suma; but first tell me what you want.
PRIEST: I am a priest and I travel through the provinces. Here on the beach I see a solitary pine tree with a wooden tablet fixed to it, and a poem slip hanging from the tablet. Is there a story connected with the tree? Please tell me what you know.
VILLAGER: The pine is linked with the memory of two fisher girls, Matsukaze and Murasame. Please say a prayer for them as you pass.
PRIEST: Thank you. I know nothing about them, but I will stop at the tree and say a prayer for them before I move on.
VILLAGER: If I can be of further service, don't hesitate to ask.
PRIEST: Thank you for your kindness.
VILLAGER: At your command, sir.

(The VILLAGER *exits. The* PRIEST *goes to stage center and turns toward the pine tree.)*

PRIEST: So, this pine tree is linked with the memory of two fisher girls, Matsukaze and Murasame. It is sad! Though their bodies are buried in the ground, their names linger on. This lonely pine tree lingers on also, ever green and untouched by autumn, their only memorial. Ah! While I have been chanting sutras and invoking Amida Buddha for their repose, the sun, as always on autumn days, has quickly set. That village at the foot of the mountain is a long way. Perhaps I can spend the night in this fisherman's salt shed.

(He kneels at the waki-*position. The stage assistant brings out the prop, a cart for carrying pails of brine, and sets it by the gazing-pillar. He places a pail on the cart.)*

*(*MURASAME *enters and comes down the bridgeway as far as the first pine. She wears the* tsure *mask.* MATSUKAZE *follows her and stops at the third pine. She wears the* wakaonna *mask. Each carries a water pail. They face each other.)*

MATSUKAZE AND MURASAME: A brine cart wheeled along the beach
Provides a meager livelihood:
The sad world rolls
Life by quickly and in misery!
MURASAME: Here at Suma Bay
The waves shatter at our feet, 40
And even the moonlight wets our sleeves
With its tears of loneliness.

*(*MURASAME *goes to stage center while* MATSUKAZE *moves to the* shite *position.)*

MATSUKAZE: The autumn winds are sad.
When the Middle Counselor Yukihira 45
Lived here back a little from the sea,
They inspired his poem,
"Salt winds blowing from the mountain pass. . . ."
On the beach, night after night,
Waves thunder at our door; 50
And on our long walks to the village
We've no companion but the moon.
Our toil, like all of life, is dreary,
But none could be more bleak than ours.
A skiff cannot cross the sea, 55
Nor we this dream world.
Do we exist, even?
Like foam on the salt sea,
We draw a cart, friendless and alone,
Poor fisher girls whose sleeves are wet 60
With endless spray, and tears
From our hearts' unanswered longing.
CHORUS: Our life is so hard to bear
That we envy the pure moon

---

48 "Salt . . . pass" from the poem by Yukihira, no. 876 in the *Shinkokinshū*: "The sleeves of the traveler have turned cold; the wind from Suma Bay blows through the pass." 52 **We've . . . moon** a modified quotation from the poem by Hōkyō Chūmei, no. 187 in the *Kin'yōshū*: "Pillow of grass—as I sleep on my journey I realize I have no companion but the moon." 58–59 **salt sea** the words "salt sea," which can also be translated "brine," lead to mention of the brine cart even though the cart does not logically belong in the context 64 **That . . . moon** from the poem by Fujiwara Takamitsu, no. 435 in the *Shūishū*: "In this world which seems difficult to pass through, how I envy the pure moon!"

65 Now rising with the tide.
But come, let us dip brine,
Dip brine from the rising tide!
Our reflections seem to shame us!

(They look down as if catching a glimpse of their reflections in the water. The movement of their heads "clouds" the expression on their masks, making it seem sad.)

Yes, they shame us!
70 Here, where we shrink from men's eyes,
Drawing our timorous cart;
The withdrawing tide
Leaves stranded pools behind.
How long do they remain?
75 If we were the dew on grassy fields,
We would vanish with the sun.
But we are sea tangle,
Washed up on the shore,
Raked into heaps by the fishermen,
80 Fated to be discarded, useless,
Withered and rotting,
Like our trailing sleeves,
Like our trailing sleeves.

(They look down again.)

Endlessly familiar, still how lovely
85 The twilight at Suma!
The fishermen call out in muffled voices;
At sea, the small boats loom dimly.
Across the faintly glowing face of the moon
Flights of wild geese streak,
90 And plovers flock below along the shore.
Fall gales and stiff sea winds:
These are things, in such a place,
That truly belong to autumn.
But oh, the terrible, lonely nights!

(They hide their faces.)

95 MATSUKAZE: Come, dip the brine.
MURASAME: Where the seas flood and fall,
Let us tie our sleeves back to our shoulders.
MATSUKAZE: Think only, "Dip the brine."
MURUSAME: We ready ourselves for the task,
100 MATSUKAZE: But for women, this cart is too hard.
CHORUS: While the rough breakers surge and fall,

(MURASAME moves upstage to stand beside MATSUKAZE.)

While the rough breakers surge and fall,
And cranes among the reeds
Fly up with sharp cries.
105 The four winds add their wailing.
How shall we pass the cold night?

(They look up.)

The late moon is so brilliant—
What we dip is its reflection!
Smoke from the salt fires
110 May cloud the moon—take care!

---

85 **The twilight** the following description is generally inspired by the "Exile at Suma" chapter of *The Tale of Genji*

Are we always to spend only
The sad autumns of fishermen?
At Ojima in Matsushima

(MATSUKAZE half-kneels by the brine cart and mimes dipping with her fan.)

The fisherfolk, like us,
Delight less in the moon   115
Than in the dipping of its reflection;
There they take delight in dipping
Reflections of the moon.

(MATSUKAZE returns to the shite position.)

We haul our brine from afar,
As in far-famed Michinoku   120
And at the salt kilns of Chika—
Chika, whose name means "close by."
MATSUKAZE: Humble folk hauled wood for salt fires
At the ebb tide on Akogi Shore.
CHORUS: On Ise Bay there's Twice-See Beach—   125
Oh, could I live my life again!

(MATSUKAZE looks off into the distance.)

MATSUKAZE: On days when pine groves stand hazy,
And the sea lanes draw back
From the coast at Narumi—
CHORUS: You speak of Narumi; this is Naruo,   130
Where pines cut off the moonlight
From the reed-thatched roofs of Ashinoya.
MATSUKAZE: Who is to tell of our unhappiness
Dipping brine at Nada?
With boxwood combs set in our hair,   135
From rushing seas we draw the brine,
Oh look! I have the moon in my pail!

---

113 **Ojima** is one of the islands at Matsushima, a place renowned for its scenic beauty. Both names are conventionally associated in poetry with *ama*, fisherwomen   120 **As in far-famed . . .** the following passage is a *tsukushi*, or "exhaustive enumeration," of place-names associated with the sea, including allusions and plays on words. This passage was apparently borrowed from an older work, a play called *Tōei* that was set by Ashinoya Bay. Michinoku is a general name for the northern end of the island of Honshu. Chika was another name for Shiogama ("Salt Kiln"), and sounds like the word meaning "near"   124 **Akogi** is the name of a stretch of shore on Ise Bay. The pulling in of the nets and the hauling of the wood for the salt kilns at Akogi were frequently mentioned in poetry   125 **Twice-See Beach** (Futami-ga-ura) is a word evocative of Ise and often used in poetry for the meaning of its name   129 **Narumi** was often mentioned in poetry because of its dry flats that appeared at low tide   132 **Ashinoya** (modern Ashiya) and Naruo are two places near Suma. Ashinoya means literally "reed house"   134 **Dipping . . . Nada** derived from the poem in the 87th episode of the *Ise Monogatari*: "At Nada by Ashinoya, I have no respite from boiling brine for salt; I have come without even putting a boxwood comb in my hair."   135 **With boxwood . . .** the line recalls the poem quoted in previous note, but it is used because of the pivot-word *tsuge no*, "of boxwood," and *tsuge*, "to inform." Similarly, *kushi sashi*, "Setting a comb (in the hair)," leads into *sashi-kuru nami*, "in-rushing waves"

(MURASAME *kneels before the brine cart and places her pail on it.* MATSUKAZE, *still standing, looks into her pail.*)

MATSUKAZE: In my pail too I hold the moon!
CHORUS: How lovely! A moon here too!

(MURASAME *picks up the rope tied to the cart and gives it to* MATSUKAZE, *then moves to the* shite *position.* MATSUKAZE *looks up.*)

140 MATSUKAZE: The moon above is one;
        Below it has two, no, three reflections

(*She looks into both pails.*)

        Which shine in the flood tide tonight,

(*She pulls the cart to a spot before the musicians.*)

        And on our cart we load the moon!
        No, life is not all misery
145   Here by the sea lanes.

(*She drops the rope. The stage assistant removes the cart.* MATSUKAZE *sits on a low stool and* MURASAME *kneels beside her, a sign that the two women are resting inside their hut. The* PRIEST *rises.*)

PRIEST: The owner of the salt shed has returned. I shall ask for a night's lodging. (*To* MATSUKAZE *and* MURASAME.) I beg your pardon. Might I come inside?
MURASAME: (*Standing and coming forward a little.*) Who might
150   you be?
PRIEST: A traveler, overtaken by night on my journey. I should like to ask lodging for the night.
MURASAME: Wait here. I must ask the owner. (*She kneels before* MATSUKAZE.) A traveler outside asks to come in and spend
155   the night.
MATSUKAZE: That is little enough, but our hut is so wretched we cannot ask him in. Please tell him so.
MURASAME: (*Standing, to the* PRIEST.) I have spoken to the owner. She says the house is too wretched to put anyone up.
160 PRIEST: I understand those feelings
        Perfectly, but poverty makes
        No difference at all to me.
        I am only a priest. Please
        Say I beg her to let
165   Me spend the night.
MURASAME: No, we really cannot put you up.
MATSUKAZE: (*To* MURASAME.) Wait!
        I see in the moonlight
        One who has renounced the world.
170   He will not mind a fisherman's hut,
        With its rough pine pillars and bamboo fence;
        I believe it is very cold tonight,
        So let him come in and warm himself
        At our sad fire of rushes.
175   You may tell him that.
MURASAME: Please come in.
PRIEST: Thank you very much. Forgive me for intruding.

(*He takes a few steps forward and kneels.* MURASAME *goes back beside* MATSUKAZE.)

MATSUKAZE: I wished from the beginning to invite you in, but this place is so poor I felt I must refuse.

PRIEST: You are very kind. I am a priest and a traveler, and 180
        never stay anywhere very long. Why prefer one lodging to
        another? In any case, what sensitive person would not
        prefer to live here at Suma, in the quiet solitude. Yukihira
        wrote,
        "If ever anyone   185
        Chances to ask for me,
        Say I live alone,
        Soaked by the dripping seaweed
        On the shore of Suma Bay."
(*He looks at the pine tree.*) A while ago I asked someone the 190
        meaning of that solitary pine on the beach. I was told it
        grows there in memory of two fisher girls, Matsukaze and
        Murasame. There is no connection between them and me,
        but I went to the pine anyway and said a prayer for them.
(MATSUKAZE *and* MURASAME *weep. The* PRIEST *stares at them.*) 195
        This is strange! They seem distressed at the mention of
        Matsukaze and Murasame. Why?
MATSUKAZE AND MURASAME: Truly, when a grief is hidden,
        Still, signs of it will show.
        His poem, "If ever anyone   200
        Chances to ask for me,"
        Filled us with memories which are far too fond.
        Tears of attachment to the world
        Wet our sleeves once again.
PRIEST: Tears of attachment to the world? You speak as though 205
        you are no longer of the world. Yukihira's poem overcame
        you with memories. More and more bewildering! Please,
        both of you, tell me who you are.
MATSUKAZE AND MURASAME: We would tell you our names,
        But we are too ashamed!   210
        No one, ever,
        Has chanced to ask for us,
        Long dead as we are,
        And so steeped in longing
        For the world by Suma Bay   215
        That pain has taught us nothing.
        Ah, the sting of regret!
        But having said this,
        Why should we hide our names any longer?
        At twilight you said a prayer   220
        By a mossy grave under the pine
        For two fisher girls,
        Matsukaze and Murasame.
        We are their ghosts, come to you.
        When Yukihira was here he whiled away   225
        Three years of weary exile
        Aboard his pleasure boat,
        His heart refreshed
        By the moon of Suma Bay.
        There were, among the fisher girls,   230
        Who hauled brine each evening,
        Two sisters whom he chose for his favors.
        "Names to fit the season!"
        He said, calling us
        Pine Wind and Autumn Rain.   235
        We had been Suma fisher girls,
        Accustomed to the moon,

185–89 **If ever . . . Bay** poem no. 962 in the *Kokinshū*

But he changed our salt makers' clothing
To damask robes,
240   Burnt with the scent of faint perfumes.
MATSUKAZE: Then, three years later, Yukihira
Returned to the Capital.
MURASAME: Soon, we heard he had died, oh so young!
MATSUKAZE: How we both loved him!
245   Now the message we pined for
Would never, never come.
CHORUS: Pine Wind and Autumn Rain
Both drenched their sleeves with the tears
Of hopeless love beyond their station,
250   Fisher girls of Suma.
Our sin is deep, o priest.
Pray for us, we beg of you!

(*They press their palms together in supplication.*)

Our love grew rank as wild grasses;
Tears and love ran wild.
255   It was madness that touched us.
Despite spring purification,
Performed in our old robes,
Despite prayers inscribed on paper streamers,
The gods refused us their help.
260   We were left to melt away
Like foam on the waves,
And, in misery, we died.

(MATSUKAZE *looks down, shading her mask.*)

Alas! How the past evokes our longing!
Yukihira, the Middle Counselor,

(*The stage assistant puts a man's cloak and court hat in* MATSUKAZE's
left hand.)

265   Lived three years here by Suma Bay.
Before he returned to the Capital,
He left us these keepsakes of his stay:
A court hat and a hunting cloak.
Each time we see them,

(*She looks at the cloak.*)

270   Our love grows again,
And gathers like dew
On the tip of a leaf
So that there's no forgetting,
Not for an instant.
275   Oh endless misery!

(*She places the cloak in her lap.*)

---

240 **Burnt** . . . derived from a poem by Fujiwara Tameuji, no. 361
in the *Shingo-senshū:* "The fishermen of Suma are accustomed to the
moon, spending the autumn in clothes wet with waves blown by
the salt wind."   258 **Despite prayers** . . . literally, "purification
on the day of the serpent." The ceremony was performed on the
first day of the serpent in the third month. Genji had the ceremony
performed while he was at Suma. The streamers were conventional
Shinto offerings

"This keepsake
Is my enemy now;
For without it

(*She lifts the cloak.*)

I might forget."

(*She stares at the cloak.*)

The poem says that   280
And it's true:
My anguish only deepens.

(*She weeps.*)

MATSUKAZE: "Each night before I go to sleep,
I take off the hunting cloak
CHORUS: And hang it up . . ."   285

(*The keepsakes in her hand, she stands and, as in a trance, takes a few
steps toward the gazing-pillar.*)

I hung all my hopes
On living in the same world with him,
But being here makes no sense at all
And these keepsakes are nothing.

(*She starts to drop the cloak, only to cradle it in her arms and press it
to her.*)

I drop it, but I cannot let it lie;   290
So I take it up again
To see his face before me yet once more.

(*She turns to her right and goes toward the naming-place, then stares
down the bridgeway as though something were coming after her.*)

"Awake or asleep,
From my pillow, from the foot of my bed,
Love rushes in upon me."   295
Helplessly I sink down,
Weeping in agony.

(*She sits at the* shite *position, weeping. The stage assistant helps her
take off her outer robe and replace it with the cloak. He also helps tie
on the court hat.*)

MATSUKAZE: The River of Three Fords
Has gloomy shallows
Of never-ending tears;
I found, even there,   300
An abyss of wildest love.

276–79 **This keepsake . . . forget** a slightly modified quotation
of the anonymous poem, no. 746 in the *Kokinshū*. It is also quoted
in *Lady Han*   283–85 **Each night . . . up** the first part of a poem
by Ki no Tomomori, no. 593 in the *Kokinshū*. The last two lines
run: "When I wear it there is no instant when I do not long for
him."   293–95 **"Awake . . . me"** the first part of an anonymous
poem, no. 1023 in the *Kokinshū*. The last part runs: "Helpless, I
stay in the middle of the bed."   298 **River . . . Three Fords** the
river of the afterworld

Oh joy! Look! Over there!
Yukihira has returned!

(She rises, staring at the pine tree.)

305 He calls me by my name, Pine Wind!
I am coming!

(She goes to the tree. MURASAME *hurriedly rises and follows. She catches* MATSUKAZE's *sleeve.)*

MURASAME: For shame! For such thoughts as these
You are lost in the sin of passion.
All the delusions that held you in life—
310 None forgotten!

(Both step back from the tree.)

That is a pine tree.
And Yukihira is not here.
MATSUKAZE: You are talking nonsense!

(She looks at the pine tree.)

315 This pine *is* Yukihira!
"Though we may part for a time,
If I hear you are pining for me,
I'll hurry back."
Have you forgotten those words he wrote?
MURASAME: Yes, I had forgotten!
320 He said, "Though we may part for a time,
If you pine, I will return to you."
MATSUKAZE: I have not forgotten.
And I wait for the pine wind
To whisper word of his coming.
325 MURASAME: If that word should ever come,
My sleeves for a while
Would be wet with autumn rain.
MATSUKAZE: So we await him. He will come,
Constant ever, green as a pine.
330 MURASAME: Yes, we can trust
MATSUKAZE: his poem:
CHORUS: "I have gone away

315–17 **"Though . . . back"** a paraphrase of the poem by Yuki-hira, no. 365 in the *Kokinshū*. Another paraphrase is given in the following speech by Murasame, and the poem is given in its correct form below. In Japanese *matsu* means both "pine tree" and "to wait."

*(*MURASAME, *weeping, kneels before the flute player.* MATSUKAZE *goes to the first pine on the bridgeway, then returns to the stage and dances.)*

MATSUKAZE: Into the mountains of Inaba,
Covered with pines,
But if I hear you pine,   335
I shall come back at once."
Those are the mountain pines
Of distant Inaba,

(She looks up the bridgeway.)

And these are the pines
On the curving Suma shore.   340
Here our dear prince once lived.
If Yukihira comes again,
I shall go stand under the tree

(She approaches the tree.)

Bent by the sea-wind,
And, tenderly, tell him   345

(She stands next to the tree.)

I love him still!

(She steps back a little and weeps. Then she circles the tree, her dancing suggesting madness.)

CHORUS: Madly the gale howls through the pines,
And breakers crash in Suma Bay;
Through the frenzied night
We have come to you   350
In a dream of deluded passion.
Pray for us! Pray for our rest!

(At stage center, MATSUKAZE *presses her palms together in supplication.)*

Now we take our leave. The retreating waves
Hiss far away, and a wind sweeps down
From the mountain to Suma Bay.   355
The cocks are crowing on the barrier road.
Your dream is over. Day has come.
Last night you heard the autumn rain;
This morning all that is left
Is the wind in the pines,   360
The wind in the pines.

---

336 **"I . . . once"** the poem by Yukihira mentioned in the previous note

CHŪSHINGURA:
THE FORTY-SEVEN SAMURAI

In 1701, at the court of the *shogun* in Edo, the *daimyo* of Akō Lord Asano drew his sword and slightly wounded Lord Kira, one of the *shogun*'s officials; as a consequence of drawing his sword at the court—a capital crime—Lord Asano was sentenced to *seppuku,* or ritual suicide. In the following months, Asano's *rōnin,* or retainers, felt themselves to have been dishonored and humiliated by the ruling against their lord, and plotted to take revenge. In January of 1703 they made a bold nighttime raid on Lord Kira's mansion. When they found Kira, they beheaded him, and ceremoniously marched with his head to Lord Asano's tomb. The raid on Lord Kira was, not surprisingly, a major scandal, and posed the shogunate with a difficult legal and political problem: on the one hand, Lord Asano's *rōnin* had acted with superb loyalty, risking their lives to avenge the honor of their feudal lord, upholding the values of the *samurai;* on the other hand, they had formed an illegal secret conspiracy and had carried out murder. Two months after taking revenge on Lord Kira, the *rōnin* were ordered by the *shogun* to commit *seppuku* themselves.

These are the historical events standing behind one of the *jōruri* and Kabuki theaters' most famous and enduring narratives, the tale of *The Forty-Seven Samurai.* Within weeks of the verdict, a host of plays were written and performed, mainly in the *jōruri* theaters; in most cases, however, the Tokagawa edict against staging contemporary events forced playwrights to alter the characters' names, and to set the story in an earlier historical period. In 1710, the great playwright Chikamatsu Monzaemon (1623–1725) wrote a play for the puppet theater entitled *Goban Taiheiki,* which relocated the events of contemporary Edo to the fourteenth century. Probably the first professional playwright in Japanese history, Chikamatsu (born Sugimori Nobumori) was the second son of the Sugimori *samurai* family. He moved with his family to Kyoto in his teens, and took the stage name Chikamatsu in his thirties, becoming a celebrated playwright for the *jōruri* theater, and collaborating with the most famous Kabuki actor of his era, Tojuro Sakata (1647–1709). A member of the *rōnin* himself, Chikamatsu was sympathetic with the dishonor done to Asano's retainers, and in his staging of their dramatic revenge established many of the dramatic conventions that would become standard in later versions of the story. In the next thirty years, Chikamatsu's play was one of hundreds of plays on the subject performed before the opening of the classic version of the story—*Kanadehon Chūshingura*—at the Takemoto puppet theater in 1748. Within the year, four Kabuki theaters (three in Edo and one in Kyoto) staged versions of *Chūshingura* which rapidly became part of the standard Kabuki repertory. The story of the forty-seven *samurai* has been one of the most enduring and popular of all Kabuki plays.

Although the Kabuki versions of *Chūshingura* are based on *jōruri* narratives, the genesis of plays in the Kabuki theater was quite different from that in the puppet theater. While the *jōruri* theaters closely followed the elaborately crafted dramatic text supplied by the playwright, in the Kabuki theater, the performers tended to take existing stories and refashion them in order to showcase their talents. While *Chūshingura* is one of the few plays still occasionally performed in the all-day form of *jōruri,* Kabuki performance tends to concentrate on several scenes from the narrative that have now become standard, which enables the play to be performed within the shorter duration of contemporary Kabuki theater. In this sense, the version of *Chūshingura: The Forty-Seven Samurai* printed here follows traditional Kabuki practice: it is a version of *Kanadehon Chūshingura* prepared by the professional Kabuki actor Nakamura Matagorow II, for a three-hour, English-language production at the University of Hawaii in 1979. Readers who wish to consult the entire *jōruri* text should consult Donald Keene's *Chūshingura: The Treasury of Loyal Retainers.*

CHŪSHINGURA: THE FORTY-SEVEN SAMURAI

Adaptation by Nakamura Matagorō II and James R. Brandon

TRANSLATED BY JAMES R. BRANDON, JUNKO BERBERICH, AND MICHAEL FELDMAN

——— CHARACTERS ———

TADAYOSHI, *younger brother of the shōgun*
KŌ NO MORONAO, *chief councilor of the shōgun and governor of Kamakura*
MOMONOI WAKASANOSUKE, *a young samurai*
ENYA HANGAN, *a young provincial lord*
KAOYO, *wife of Enya Hangan*
KAKOGAWA HONZŌ, *chief retainer of Wakasanosuke*
SAGISAKA BANNAI, *retainer of Moronao*
OKARU, *in love with Kampei, and later his wife*
KAMPEI, *retainer of Enya Hangan*
ISHIDŌ, *the shōgun's representative at Hangan's death*
YAKUSHIJI, *envoy from the shōgun*
GOEMON, *elderly retainer of Enya Hangan*

RIKIYA, *son of Yuranosuke*
ŌBOSHI YURANOSUKE, *chief retainer of Enya Hangan*
KUDAYŪ, *former retainer of Enya Hangan, now Moronao's spy*
HEIEMON, *older brother of Okaru*
SHIMIZU ICHIGAKU, *Moronao's bodyguard*
TAKEMORI KITAHACHI, *retainer to Enya Hangan*
PROVINCIAL LORDS
FOOTMEN
RETAINERS
LADIES-IN-WAITING
MAIDS
MALE GEISHA
FIGHTING CHORUS
SOLDIERS
STAGE ASSISTANTS
SAMISEN
NARRATOR

STAGE MANAGER
SECOND STAGE MANAGER
KIYOMOTO SINGER
JESTER

——— TIME AND PLACE OF ACTION ———

Act I   SCENE 1: Hachiman Shrine in Kamakura, 1338.
       SCENE 2: Outside the gate of the shogunal mansion in Kamakura, the next evening.
       SCENE 3: The Pine Room of the shogunal mansion in Kamakura, a few minutes later.

Act II   SCENE 1: Along the road, near Mt. Fuji, the following morning.
       SCENE 2: A reception room in Enya Hangan's mansion, the same day.
       SCENE 3: The rear gate of Enya Hangan's mansion, immediately following.

Act III SCENE 1: The Ichiriki Brothel in Kyoto, eighteen months later.
       SCENE 2: The garden of Moronao's mansion in Kamakura, several days later.

——— ACT ONE ———

SCENE I

Hachiman Shrine

Two sharp clacks of the hardwood ki *signal offstage musicians to begin slow and regular drum and flute music, "Kata Shagiri" ("Half-Shagiri"). The deliberate pace of the music gradually accelerates. The lights in the auditorium dim slightly; the audience watches the kabuki curtain of broad rust, black, and green stripes. Very slowly, the curtain is pushed open by a* STAGE ASSISTANT *walking from stage right to left. Ki clacks intersperse every eighth, every fourth, then every second drum beat. Drumming and* ki *intermingle as the tempo rapidly increases during the last few feet of the curtain opening. The scene is a ceremonial audience before Hachiman Shrine in Kamakura. The shōgun's brother,* TADAYOSHI, *is seated on the center of a broad stone platform running across the back of the stage. He wears a subdued Chinese-style court robe with bloused trousers and a gold lacquered hat. On his left sits the highest local official of the government,* KŌ NO MORONAO. *A voluminous black robe with large sleeves and trailing trousers encase his body and a high black hat increases his height. Six* PROVINCIAL LORDS *kneel behind them on the platform. Kneeling on the ground before them are two samurai officials,* MOMONOI WAKASANOSUKE *and* ENYA HANGAN *dressed, respectively, in powder blue and yellow robes of the same exaggerated cut as* MO-RONAO's, *and* HANGAN's *wife,* KAOYO. *She wears a silk embroidered kimono and outer robe of deep blue. Two* FOOTMEN *sit on the ground cross-legged to the right. The heads of all the characters are dropped forward limply on their chests, in imitation of puppets before they have been brought to life. Two* ki *clacks signal the music to stop and the action of the scene to begin.*

STAGE MANAGER: *(Rhythmic, prolonged calls from offstage right.)* Hear ye, hear ye, hear ye, hear ye, hear ye, hear ye . . . hear ye!

(Deep, thick chords of a jōruri, or puppet-style, samisen are heard from the small room above the set stage left. The team of jōruri SAMISEN PLAYER *and* NARRATOR *are not seen, but they can see the action on stage through the thin bamboo blind that hangs in front of them. The* NARRATOR *constantly shifts his vocal style between a kind of half-spoken chanting and singing. His tones are rich and full and unabashedly project the extremes of human emotion. Each syllable is precisely uttered. Sharp samisen chords punctuate the end of a chanted phrase; they become melodic under sung passages. A syllable can be clipped or staccato, or it can be prolonged into a lengthy obligato, spread over many samisen chords, so that the narrative line compresses or expands in time in order to best project the theatrical needs of the moment.)*

NARRATOR: *(Chants.)* "A banquet laid out before your eyes! Without eating of its food, never will you be able to know its taste!" Likewise, a country in peace . . . its able retainers [5] will hide their gallantry and chivalry. *(Sings.)* Take our story as an example . . . witness here and now!

SECOND STAGE MANAGER: *(Calling from offstage left.)* Hear ye, hear ye, hear ye, hear ye . . . hear ye!

STAGE MANAGER: *(Calling from offstage center.)* Hear ye, hear ye . . . [10] hear ye!

NARRATOR: *(Chants.)* Ashikaga government chief Takauji has Kyoto as the headquarters of his reign, his power expanding far. The time is the closing of February, thirteen thirty-eight. The place is Kamakura in the east, at Hachiman [15] Shrine, now completed in its awesome grandeur. *(Sings.)*

Gathered here to celebrate a battle fought and won are lords of distinction, in their solemn moments. (Chants.) Acting as government proxy, Ashikaga Tadayoshi has just arrived from the capital . . . of Kyoto!

20

(At the mention of his name, TADAYOSHI raises his head, opens his eyes, and elegantly flicks open his sleeves: puppetlike, he has been "brought to life.")

Here in Kamakura, he is received by the shōgun's official, Kō no Moronao! The officers of the reception are: Momonoi Wakasanosuke Yasuchika, Moronao's target of displeasure for his rough manners, and Hakushu's castle lord, Enya Hangan Takasada. (Sings.) Among these men, a single flower, Lady Kaoyo, wife of Hangan.

25

(Each character, as named, comes to life, showing his or her personality through the simple actions of lifting the head, opening the eyes, and adjusting the trailing kimono sleeves: MORONAO's evil nature—seven abrupt head jerks ending in a fierce mie pose with eyes crossed, arms extending aggressively forward as two loud beats of the wooden tsuke call attention to the pose; WAKASANOSUKE's impetuosity—five strong movements of the head, sudden opening of the eyes, each arm flicked out independently; HANGAN's composure—three smooth head movements, gentle eye opening, and both sleeves elegantly adjusted; KAOYO's modesty—no movement at all except for the slow raising of the head. Narrative shifts to song.)

Moronao casts amorous eyes at this rare beauty. Loyal men, bowing low . . .

(MORONAO leers openly at KAOYO. Then everyone places their hands on the floor and they make a ceremonious, deep bow to TADAYOSHI. Narrative returns to chanting.)

As Tadayoshi speaks, all listen in reverence!

(All lift their heads and listen respectfully.)

30 TADAYOSHI: (Clear, unaffected voice, looking straight ahead.) Attend, Lady Kaoyo!
KAOYO: (Bowing.) My lord.
TADAYOSHI: It is the shōgun, not I, who has summoned you here. You served the emperor Godaigo when he bestowed
35 upon the warrior Yoshisada the imperial battle crown. Now, with prayers commemorating our victory in battle, my brother the shōgun wills that this battle crown be dedicated to the shrine of Hachiman, god of war. If you can, confirm that this, and no other, is the one! Come, come! Answer me,
40 answer me!
KAOYO: (Bowing.) My lord.
NARRATOR: (Chants.) Attendants carry forth the precious battle crown, bending down to open up the heavy wooden chest. Lifting up the battle crown . . . is it the one of fame? (Sings.)
45 Though gazing closely at the battle crown held high, she will only speak when she is certain . . . and then, floating famous fragrance of the crown well known . . .

(The two FOOTMEN place a large wooden chest center and remove its lid. They bring out a samurai helmet. Its golden fittings gleam in the light. KAOYO moves forward the better to observe it, kneels, and noticing its special perfume, nods decisively.)

KAOYO: This is the very crown Yoshisada wore in battle, I can say with certainty.
NARRATOR: (Chants.) Saying these words, Kaoyo bows deep in 50 reverence.

(She bows. A FOOTMAN places the helmet at TADAYOSHI's feet. With the second FOOTMAN, he carries off the chest.)

TADAYOSHI: Enya Hangan! Momonoi Wakasanosuke! In conjunction with the dedication, all ceremonies are placed in your care. Consult Lord Moronao. Kaoyo, you may go!
KAOYO: (Bowing.) My lord. 55
NARRATOR: (Chants.) Kaoyo has now been freed of her demanding task, waiting as his lordship . . . into the palace goes!

(TADAYOSHI rises; a STAGE ASSISTANT takes off the stool he has been sitting on. Without looking to the right or left, he walks with a dignified gait down the steps. He stops and poses. Drum and flute play stately exit music. TADAYOSHI flicks open his sleeves, turns, and moves slowly off left. PROVINCIAL LORDS rise and follow, their formal court trousers trailing behind them. FOOTMEN bring up the rear. They exit. The music continues in the background as HANGAN, WAKASANOSUKE, and KAOYO play out in silence their petitions to MORONAO for permission to depart. To HANGAN's polite bow of request MORONAO nods condescendingly. HANGAN rises, and with unruffled composure, goes off left, carrying the helmet with him, to be deposited in the shrine. WAKASANOSUKE bows brusquely, scarcely bothering to conceal his contempt for MORONAO. In response, MORONAO deliberately and disdainfully averts his gaze. Moving to where he is in MORONAO's line of sight again, WAKASANOSUKE bows a second time, more brusquely still. Again MORONAO ignores him and looks away. Trembling with fury, WAKASANOSUKE moves directly in front of MORONAO and bows a third time. MORONAO looks over his head as if the young samurai were not there. WAKASANOSUKE leaps up in rage, strikes back his sleeve, and rushes off left. Music stops. MORONAO laughs soundlessly, then looks expectantly to KAOYO, who bows politely, rises, and starts to move away. MORONAO rises, a STAGE ASSISTANT removing the stool on which he has been sitting. He stops KAOYO with an unctuous, but clearly threatening, command.)

MORONAO: One moment, Lady Kaoyo! I wish to have a word with you. I believe that you and I share in common an unspoken passion, for the art of writing poetry. Will you 60 accept from me this poem, composed with loving care, your reply to which I will not be displeased to receive from your own lips, Kaoyo, my lady.
NARRATOR: (Chants.) From his sleeve to her sleeve, a love letter from Moronao! (Sings.) Saying not a single word, she throws 65 it aside.

(Crossing to her, MORONAO looks around to see that no one is watching. He passes a love letter into KAOYO's sleeve. She takes it out, and looking at the salutation, knows immediately what it is. Coldly she drops it to the ground. MORONAO scoops it up and tucks it away in the breast of his kimono.)

MORONAO: (Insinuatingly.) Casually you cast my letter to the ground, but you will not cast down my intentions that easily. Until you accept my love, I will track you, chase you, wear you down. In the palace your husband is my puppet, 70 to rise or to fall in his duties, solely on Moronao's will. Kaoyo, my lady . . . well? Do you not agree?

(He glances about again, then moves behind her and enfolds her in a rough embrace. She discreetly tries to free herself: their bodies sway back and forth.)

NARRATOR: *(Sings.)* In her heart are angry words but Kaoyo refrains. Dear Lady Kaoyo, tears in her eyes.

(Without warning WAKASANOSUKE strides on. Taking in the situation at a glance, he turns his back.)

75 WAKASANOSUKE: Ahem! Ahem! *(Furious, MORONAO breaks away. WAKASANOSUKE moves beside KAOYO.)* Lady Kaoyo, Lord Tadayoshi dismissed you long ago. If you linger, you are risking his displeasure. Go! Do not stay a moment longer!
80 KAOYO: Yes, good Lord Wakasanosuke, with your permission, I shall take my leave.
NARRATOR: *(Sings.)* Burdened with care, to her mansion . . . Kaoyo returns.

(KAOYO bows and moves quickly onto the hanamichi, the rampway which extends from the stage, through the audience, to the rear of the auditorium. She stops at the "seven-three" position, that is, the position seven-tenths of the distance from the back of the auditorium and three-tenths from the stage. She poses, puts her hands inside her kimono sleeves, then regally moves down the hanamichi. She passes out of sight as the narration ends.)

MORONAO: *(Snarling.)* No one summoned you! You are inso-
85 lent, Wakasanosuke! Kaoyo was entreating me, in private audience, to guide Hangan in his palace duties. That is how even the mighty must grovel before the shōgun's chief councilor. And who are you? A country rustic, a nobody. So low a single word from Moronao would send you tumbling
90 into the streets to beg for your food! And you call yourself a samurai? A samurai? *(MORONAO strikes WAKASANOSUKE's chest with his heavy fan.)* You . . . a sa-mu-rai? *(On the last three syllables, MORONAO strikes WAKASANOSUKE's chest, sword hilt, and chest again. WAKASANOSUKE falls back.)* B-b-block-
95 head country bumpkin!
NARRATOR: *(Chants.)* You dare to meddle, little man? Moronao's revenge! Bursting in hot anger, Wakasanosuke . . . here in the sacred shrine before his Majesty, a moment of patience is all I need! One more word decides my life, death may be my
100 fate! Wakasanosuke now holds himself in!

(To the narration: WAKASANOSUKE poses with hand on the hilt of his sword; he notices he is in a sacred shrine and falls back; his hand trembles; he nods with determination, throws his fan into the air, and lunges forward as if to draw his sword. MORONAO slaps his fan against WAKASANOSUKE's sword arm and glares at his young opponent in alarm and rage. At that moment a cry is heard from off stage announcing the return of TADAYOSHI.)

VOICES OFF: *(In unison.)* Bow down!
MORONAO: *(Snarling.)* Bow down, I say!

(MORONAO strikes WAKASANOSUKE's sword arm viciously with his closed fan. WAKASANOSUKE drops to one knee, glares at MORONAO, and poses with his hand on his sword. MORONAO rushes up the platform steps, suddenly pivots back to face WAKASANOSUKE, flips open his

sleeves, and poses in a fierce mie. MORONAO crosses his eyes and glares to two loud beats of the tsuke. WAKASANOSUKE restrains himself; his chest heaves. The curtain is run closed to accelerating ki clacks. A single ki clack marks the end of the scene and signals the offstage drum and flute to play "Sagariha" {"Departure"} as the scene is changed.)

SCENE II
Bribery and Rendezvous

Two ki clacks: the curtain is run open. Ki clacks accelerate, then fade away. The scene is the rear gate of the shōgunal mansion in Kamakura where the state ceremonies are to be held. It is night. Pale blue light floods the stage. One ki clack signals action to begin.

NARRATOR: *(Chants.)* Chief retainer of Wakasanosuke, *(Sings.)* Kakogawa Honzō comes in with a tray full of gifts, a self-assigned task.

(HONZŌ, carrying a tray of silks as a bribe for MORONAO, comes onto the hanamichi. He stops at the seven-three position, looks toward the gate, and poses.)

HONZŌ: Bannai. Master Bannai.

(BANNAI, a comic villain, enters from inside the gate. HONZŌ moves quickly onto the stage, places the gifts on the ground, and kneels respectfully before BANNAI.)

BANNAI: *(Officiously.)* Someone calls me. Who is it, who is it? 5
(Notices HONZŌ. Starts.) State your business, I am a busy man!
HONZŌ: *(Bowing obsequiously.)* I am Kakogawa Honzō, chief retainer of Momonoi Wakasanosuke.
BANNAI: *(Chuckles delightedly.)* The bluebird Wakasanosuke and 10 his friend, the yellow canary Enya Hangan, are country chickens. What a cackling they will make in the palace. Oh, my master, Lord Moronao, will pluck them clean!
HONZŌ: *(Carefully watching BANNAI's expression.)* That is the matter on which I have come, good Bannai. My master is 15 young and untutored in the intricacies of palace etiquette. Only with Lord Moronao's generous guidance will he be able to carry out his important duties. Taking this opportunity, I express my gratitude for your master's favor.

(HONZŌ bows low. BANNAI turns front with a self-satisfied smirk on his face.)

BANNAI: Everyone needs a chief councilor's favors. But your 20 Wakasanosuke was rude to my master. Go back where you came from, go back, go away! *(BANNAI strikes a pose: feet together, head up, right fist extended toward HONZŌ.)*
HONZŌ: What you say is true, still please accept these gifts on behalf of Wakasanosuke and his grateful followers. 25

(HONZŌ bows toward the gifts of silk. He looks about, to be sure they are unseen, then takes out a wrapped package of gold coins. Moving forward on his knees to BANNAI's side, he drops the package into the open kimono sleeve.)

Carry my message to Lord Moronao. Do what is necessary, good Bannai. Will you do so, Bannai? Bannai?

(HONZŌ *tugs lightly on* BANNAI's *sleeve.*)

NARRATOR: (*Chants.*) Wondering, Bannai takes it in his hand!

(BANNAI *flicks* HONZŌ's *hand away and in doing so strikes the heavy coins. He clutches his fingers in pain, then wonders what his hand hit. He sneaks a look at the coins. He reacts with delighted surprise.*)

NARRATOR: (*Sings.*) Money talks words of power!

30 BANNAI: (*Effusive, his attitude completely changed.*) Well, well, Kakogawa Honzō, how nice of you to come. (*He squats and bows to* HONZŌ.) You have come at the right moment: the ceremonial rooms are being prepared. Come, come!

(BANNAI *picks up the tray of gifts, rises, and gestures for* HONZŌ *to follow him.*)

HONZŌ: (*Bowing carefully.*) I am a person of no importance, I do
35   not dare enter the palace.
BANNAI: (*Proudly.*) If Lord Moronao is with you, who would dare object? Come, I will show you the rooms.
HONZŌ: I will enter then, most gratefully.
BANNAI: Then come along. Come along!

(BANNAI *poses.* HONZŌ *bows. They cross toward the gate: three times* BANNAI *turns back, chuckling and bowing, to beckon* HONZŌ *forward. At the gate* BANNAI *stops short.*)

40   Master Honzō, the threshold is high.
NARRATOR: (*Sings.*) Moronao is happy. Honzō bought the life of Wakasanosuke. His scheme now is accomplished. Together they go.

(BANNAI *steps carefully over the foot-high threshold of the gate and goes inside, followed by* HONZŌ.)

NARRATOR: (*A* nō *song, as if part of the entertainment inside the mansion.*)

    "At the end of the journey we have reached Takasago Bay;
45   At the end of the journey we have reached Takasago Bay."

(OKARU, *a beautiful young girl in her late teens, enters on the* hanamichi. *She wears a maiden's trailing kimono with long sleeves, in a purple arrow pattern. She holds a lacquered letter box in her right hand. She stops at the seven-three position, looks toward the gate, and poses.*)

OKARU: My Lady Kaoyo urgently sends this letter to her husband, Lord Enya Hangan. How fortunate that I, her favorite, was allowed to bring it. Dearest Kampei, I cannot bear to be apart from you a single moment.

(*Offstage musicians play* nō-*style drum and flute music in the background.* KAMPEI, *a young samurai, enters from the gate followed by a* RETAINER. *They wear black kimono under stiff vests; their divided skirts are folded up to their knees, showing that they are on guard duty.* KAMPEI *is in the service of* HANGAN *and is* OKARU's *lover.* OKARU *sees him and runs to meet him.*)

50 KAMPEI: Okaru, is it you?
OKARU: (*Coquettishly.*) Dearest Kampei, I missed you so.
KAMPEI: (*Flustered and worried about meeting her while he is on duty.*)

But why are you here at the palace gate, at night, and all alone?
OKARU: I've come for Lady Kaoyo. "Meet Kampei and tell him   55
he is to ask my husband to deliver this letter to Lord Moronao"—those were her very words.

(OKARU *passes him the letter box.*)

KAMPEI: (*Unsure.*) I am to deliver this directly to Lord Hangan?
HOKARU: Yes, dearest Kampei.

(*She smiles invitingly at him.*)

KAMPEI: Wait for me, Okaru.   60

(*He turns to go.*)

OKARU: (*She holds his sleeve.*) Kampei!
KAMPEI: I should take it to our master myself. I should be with him. It is my duty not to leave his side in the palace. I . . .

(*He is irresolute. He tries to leave; she tugs gently, persuasively at his sleeve. He looks into her pleading eyes. He decides. He turns to the* RETAINER.)

    Take this immediately to Lord Hangan.   65
RETAINER: I will.

(*The* RETAINER *takes the letter box, bows, and crosses into the gate.*)

OKARU: I want to be with you so. Now that we are here, together . . .
KAMPEI: You are flushed with excitement, Okaru!
OKARU: (*Taking his hand in hers.*) Please come. I don't care!   70
NARRATOR: (*Sings.*) Seizing fast her lover's hand . . . she leads him away!

(*She presses against him boldly, folding her arm over his. They pose: a sharp* ki *clack emphasizes the moment. Offstage drum and samisen resume in the background. They look excitedly into each other's eyes and then hurriedly cross into the darkness of the trees beyond the gate. The curtain is run quickly closed to accelerating* ki *clacks. Music ends. Soft, intermittent* ki *clacks mark time while the scene is changed.*)

SCENE III
Pine Room

Two ki *clacks: the curtain opens. The scene is a large reception room of the* shōgunal *mansion called the Pine Room because of the designs painted on the gold sliding doors extending across the full stage. A single* ki *clack: action begins.*

NARRATOR: (*Chants.*) Utter indignation, for Moronao is late! Impatiently waiting in the palace . . . Wakasanosuke!

(WAKASANOSUKE *rushes onto the* hanamichi. *He drops to one knee at the seven-three position, resolutely slaps his thigh, and poses, waiting for the arrival of* MORONAO. *A sliding door left opens. Rapid drum and flute music.* BANNAI *ushers* MORONAO *on stage, bowing obsequiously. He carries a small paper lantern to light the room. Without a word,* WAKASANOSUKE *leaps to his feet, slips his sword arm free of the restricting formal vest, and rushes to attack* MORONAO. BANNAI *momentarily is able to block* WAKASANOSUKE's *path, but then is hurled to the floor as* WAKASANOSUKE *pushes past.* MORONAO *falls to his knees. He clasps his hands together pleadingly.* BANNAI *throws his arms around* WAKASANOSUKE's *lower leg, holding him fast. Music stops.*)

MORONAO: There you are, there you are, Lord Wakasanosuke, good Wakasanosuke. Your early arrival makes me ashamed,
5 ashamed, so very ashamed. I was rude to you at Hachiman Shrine. I was. (WAKASANOSUKE *edges forward as if to draw.*) Now, now, now, you have every right to be angry. But have pity on a foolish old samurai. I throw my sword at your feet. I clasp my hands and apologize. Bannai, Bannai, you too,
10 bow, apologize to Lord Wakasanosuke.
NARRATOR: (*Sings.*) Flattering, and what is more, detestable words so sweet. Taken aback completely, Wakasanosuke wonders what has happened. There is nothing he can do . . .

(MORONAO *bows his head low to the floor.* WAKASANOSUKE *cannot believe his eyes, seeing the proud councilor abasing himself. He kicks* BANNAI *away, slips his sword arm inside his vest, and strides past* MORONAO. MORONAO *circles to avoid him, crawling on his hands and knees indecorously.* WAKASANOSUKE *turns back, spitting out his words.*)

WAKASANOSUKE: Contemptible samurai!

(*He strides off stage left.*)

15 MORONAO: I was wrong, I was wrong, I apologize, I apologize, I . . .

(*Eyes fearfully on the ground,* MORONAO *continues.* BANNAI *registers comic shock, seeing his master bowing and speaking to no one. He scurries forward on his hands and knees. He pulls* MORONAO's *sleeve. Music stops. Their eyes meet.* BANNAI *nods in the direction of* WAKASANOSUKE's *exit.* MORONAO *sees that he is alone and sighs with relief. Recovering his dignity, he sits up.*)

MORONAO: Bannai, that stupid young puppy meant, I think, to kill me. "A sword in a fool's hand makes the wise man cautious."
20 BANNAI: (*Bowing.*) Oh yes, my lord, how true.
NARRATOR: (*Chants "Jo no Mai"* ["*Slow Dance*"] *drum and flute music.*) Who has planned this mischievous fate? (*Sings.*) Enya Hangan . . . innocent of this all, proceeds to Moronao. (*Chants.*) Moronao . . . seeing his victim!

(*Simultaneously,* BANNAI *arranges his master's sword and the lantern and exits stage left while* HANGAN *appears on the* hanamichi, *carrying in his left hand the letter box given by* KAMPEI's *retainer. Nō-style "Jo no Mai" drum and flute music continues in the background.*)

25 MORONAO: (*Ominously.*) Late, late, late! You're late, Hangan!

(HANGAN *bows slightly and hurries on stage. He kneels, bowing again.*)

HANGAN: I humbly beg your pardon for being a few moments late. I come ready for your instructions. First, however, I have been asked by my wife to place this letter in your hands.

(*He moves forward on his knees, places the letter box on the floor beside* MORONAO, *moves back, and bows respectfully.*)

MORONAO: (*Feigning ignorance.*) Hmm, hmm. A letter from Lady Kaoyo? To me? (*Opens the box and removes the letter* 30 *card.*) Ah, I understand. My poetic skill is renowned. No doubt she wishes me to place the touch of my pen upon her heartfelt words, to correct any blemishes. There is time before the ceremonies. Sit and be at ease. (*He reads.*) "A woman's love does, not lie in the hopeful eye, of her be- 35 holder; not beholden to lie I, aver never to lie with you." (*Music stops.* MORONAO *again.*) "Not beholden to lie I, aver never to lie . . . with you."
NARRATOR: (*Chanting rapidly.*) After weighing the words . . . Kaoyo has rejected my love and this is the proof! This must 40 mean that Hangan has found out my intention! (*Sings.*) Anger and humiliation . . . but pretending ignorance.

(MORONAO *looks straight forward, his face frozen in humiliated rage, his right hand slowly closing into a rigid fist that crushes his brocade silk robe. Masking his emotions he turns toward* HANGAN. *Drum and flute music resume.*)

MORONAO: Hangan, was this poem shown to you?
HANGAN: (*Bows politely.*) I have not seen it until this moment, your Excellency.   45

(*Reassured that* HANGAN *is not party to* KAOYO's *insult,* MORONAO *proceeds to deliberately humiliate him.*)

MORONAO: Is that so? Well, the lord of little Hakushu castle has a clever wife. She can dash off a subtle poem like this. A woman so talented and famous for her beauty must be a source of great husbandly pride. Such a superlative creature in fact, that her infatuated husband, not bearing to be sep- 50 arated from her, finds his sacred duties at the palace . . . wearisome!

(MORONAO *casually turns his back to* HANGAN, *idly playing with his fan.*)

NARRATOR: (*Chants.*) Moronao is filled with spiteful words of insinuation. Riding on his frustration . . . any may be his prey. Hangan is perplexed at the burst of displeasure. 55 (*Sings.*) Gushing anger, he holds it down, holds it in!

(HANGAN *starts. He almost turns to confront* MORONAO, *but then suppresses his anger. He pretends to smile, as if sharing* MORONAO's *joke. Ominous drum beats continue in the background.*)

HANGAN: Ha, ha, ha, ha. I see my lordship is in a playful mood. He has, perhaps, been drinking and is feeling in good humor. Yes, surely my lord has been drinking. Ha, ha, ha, ha.   60
MORONAO: (*Dangerously, facing* HANGAN.) What is that? When have you seen me drinking? You, who have never offered me as much as a cup of wine? Whether I, Moronao, choose to drink or not, nothing keeps me from *my* duty! The one who's been drinking is you, Hangan. You've come from a 65 drinking party with your charming wife, she pouring for you, and you pouring for her! Isn't that why you come to the palace late?

(HANGAN's *face tightens.* MORONAO *notices and turns away with a malicious look in his eye.*)

70 Isn't there a story about a stay-at-home like you, helpless beyond his front door? I seem to recall . . . ah, yes, the "Tadpole in the Puddle." There once was a young tadpole that lived in a tiny puddle. He knew no other place between heaven and earth, and so he thought his puddle the most wonderful home in the world. One day a compassionate per-

75 son passed by, just like Moronao, who, taking pity, lifted him from his stagnant pool and released him in the waters of a broad river. (*Arms out,* MORONAO *deliberately strikes* HANGAN's *chest with his heavy fan.*) Well, the tadpole was out of his depth, dropped suddenly into the great world from

80 his shallow one. Completely at a loss, willy-nilly he went this way, and willy-nilly he went that way. (*Pointing with fan.*) And in the end he ran headfirst smack into a bridge-post. (*Strikes* HANGAN *full in the chest with his fan.*) And shivering and quivering, and shivering and quivering, the little

85 tadpole expired. (*Twirling his fan in limp fingers.*) The tadpole is . . . you! (*Looks full into* HANGAN's *straining face.*) Oh? I do believe the young tadpole has lost his tail and is turning into a toad. (HANGAN *turns and glares furiously at* MORONAO.) Yes, with your eyes bulging out, Hangan, you

90 look exactly like a toad. Ha, ha, ha, ha! This Moronao has lived many years, but this is the first time I've seen in the palace a toad wearing clothes. Oh, come here, come here, Bannai, Hangan's turning into a toad. Hangan *is* a toad, a sa-mu-rai toad! (*Drum beats stop. Silence.* MORONAO *deliber-*

95 *ately strikes* HANGAN's *chest, sword hilt, and chest with his fan.*) Ha, ha, ha, ha, ha!
NARRATOR: (*Chants.*) Toad! Devil talk! Demon words!

(MORONAO *rears back, points contemptuously at* HANGAN *with his fan, rotates his head, and poses in a* mie *to two loud* tsuke *beats. Music stops.*)

Hangan can no more take the vile old man!
HANGAN: (*Slowly, with dangerous, suppressed fury.*) Do you dare
100 compare Enya Hangan Takasada, castle lord of Hakushu . . . to a toad! You cannot possibly mean the words you have said! Have you gone out of your mind . . . Councilor Moronao!

(HANGAN *pivots to face* MORONAO, *slapping his thigh for emphasis.*)

MORONAO: (*Darkly.*) Watch yourself, Hangan! Remember I am
105 councilor of the shōgun. No one calls me insane. You are ludicrous!
HANGAN: You have been deliberately insulting me? Do you dare tell me that!
MORONAO: (*Insinuating.*) Indeed, I dare. And if I dare, who are
110 you to complain?
HANGAN: (*Drawn out.*) If you dare . . .
MORONAO: (*Leaning in insolently.*) If I dare . . . ?
HANGAN: Hmm!

(HANGAN's *patience snaps. He rises on one knee, his hand on his sword.* MORONAO *instantly parries* HANGAN's *sword arm with his closed fan.*)

MORONAO: (*Commandingly.*) The palace! (MORONAO *slaps*
HANGAN's *sword arm away and the two men pull back:* 115
MORONAO *fearfully,* HANGAN *furious.*) The palace! The palace! It is the palace! Don't you know the law? Draw your sword in the palace and your house will be destroyed! Don't you know that! (*Drum beats resume.* MORONAO *slaps his fan commandingly on the floor.* HANGAN, *anguished that he must re-* 120 *strain his rage, folds his arms tightly over the hilts of his swords and slowly sinks back onto his haunches.* MORONAO *notes this and is emboldened to continue his provocation.*) Hm, since you know . . . then go ahead, kill me. Well . . . draw . . . draw . . . draw your sword. Come, kill me! Kill me . . . Hangan! 125

(MORONAO *forces himself bodily against* HANGAN *and leans against* HANGAN's *swords. They pose. Burning with humiliation,* HANGAN *abases himself in order to fulfill his ceremonial duties. He backs away and bows low.*)

HANGAN: A moment, a moment, Lord Moronao, I beg your indulgence. Without thinking I spoke out of turn. I implore you, instruct me in my duties for the ceremony. I will do as you say. Humbly, I beseech you, your Excellency.

(*Music stops.* HANGAN *looks up from his bow.* MORONAO *smugly turns away, avoiding his gaze.* HANGAN's *patience snaps a second time: his hand leaps for his sword. Instantly* MORONAO *reacts.*)

MORONAO: Your hand! 130
HANGAN: My hand?
MORONAO: (*With all his authority.*) Yes, your hand!
HANGAN: This hand . . .

(*He hesitates, looks at his trembling hand, then drops his hands to the floor and bows in defeat.*)

. . . humbly begs your forgiveness.
MORONAO: (*Savoring his victory.*) So, you apologize, do you? Very 135 well, very well. Soon instructions in great detail for today's ceremony . . .
HANGAN: (*Looks up hopefully.*) . . . will be given to me?
MORONAO: (*Viciously.*) No, not to you! To Wakasanosuke! (HANGAN *is stunned, motionless. In silence* MORONAO *casually* 140 *rises, tears* KAOYO's *letter card in two, and throws the pieces in* HANGAN's *face.*) There is no educating a provincial barbarian.

(MORONAO *deliberately turns his back and kicks his left and right trailing trouser legs in* HANGAN's *face.* HANGAN *rears back. Chuckling,* MORONAO *starts to leave.*)

HANGAN: Moronao! Wait!

(HANGAN *steps on* MORONAO's *trailing trouser leg.* MORONAO *is brought up short. He tugs at the trouser; it is held fast.*)

MORONAO: (*Deadly calm.*) Be careful. You'll soil my trousers. 145 Hop. Hop, hop, hop. (MORONAO *turns to leave, but cannot move.*) So, you won't hop away, little toad? Can there be something else you want?
HANGAN: What I want is . . .
MORONAO: What you want is . . . ? 150

(HANGAN *quietly slips his sword arm free of the stiff vest.* MORONAO *turns and thrusts his sneering face toward* HANGAN.)

HANGAN: (*A scream.*) You!

(HANGAN's *short sword flashes out of its sheath and gashes* MORONAO's *forehead. Drum and flute play furious "Haya Mai" ("Fast Dance"). * MORONAO *staggers and falls.* BANNAI *rushes on to help his master flee.* HANGAN *leaps to his feet and is about to finish* MORONAO *with a second blow when* HONZŌ, *who has been hiding behind a decorative screen stage right, rushes out and seizes* HANGAN *from behind.*)

NARRATOR: "Hold me not! My foe is there!"

(Six PROVINCIAL LORDS *run on from right.* HANGAN *struggles to get free, but he is encircled and held fast. In desperation he hurls his sword after the disappearing enemy. A single sharp clack of the* ki. *The sword falls short. He reaches out with both hands after* MORONAO *and poses: his fingers curl into fists and his chest heaves with sobs of mortification. But* HONZŌ *and the* PROVINCIAL LORDS *hold him fast. To gradually accelerating* ki *clacks the curtain is run closed. Offstage musicians play "Shagiri." A single* ki *clack concludes the act.*)

—————— ACT TWO ——————

SCENE I
Fugitive Travel

The large drum beats melancholy "Yama Oto" ("Mountain Pattern"). To accelerating ki *clacks the curtain is slowly pushed open. A sky-blue curtain fills the stage. A single* ki *clack: the blue curtain drops and is whisked away by black-robed* STAGE ASSISTANTS *to reveal a colorful springtime scene in the country. Snow-covered Mt. Fuji is seen in the background, pink cherry blossoms bloom everywhere.* OKARU *and* KAMPEI *stand center, their faces hidden behind a straw hat. A temple bell tolls in the distance.* Kiyomoto *music begins from off stage.* KAMPEI *lowers the hat and we see the lovers dressed for traveling: kimono skirts raised and a bundle over* KAMPEI's *shoulder. They mime in slow dance movements to the* kiyomoto *lyrics the story of their disgrace and flight.*

KIYOMOTO SINGER: Oh, you who flee, do you not see yon green field, a veil of new green?

(*They look at the flowers at their feet, to the left and the right. They look into each other's eyes, then pose gazing into the distance. Singing ends; samisen continues in the background. Facing upstage, they pass their sandals and* KAMPEI's *hat and bundle to two* STAGE ASSISTANTS. *They turn front and kneel center stage.* KAMPEI *places his long sword on the ground beside him.*)

KAMPEI: (*Melancholy.*) Giving myself over in love to you, I
5   failed our master when he needed me, and now we are fugitives fleeing in the dead of night I know not where. When I think of it, I no longer have the heart to live. Say prayers over the grave of this dishonored samurai. Okaru . . . farewell.

(KAMPEI *takes his short sword from his sash and is about to draw the blade. Gently she seizes it and prevents him.*)

OKARU: No, I won't have you saying that again. I am to blame
10   that you were not beside Lord Hangan. I cannot live without

you. If you die then so must I. But rather than praising your spirit, people will say we died as lovers frequently do. Please, live, dearest Kampei. Live . . . in love . . . for me.

(KAMPEI *tries to draw the sword again. She pulls one way, he the other.* KAMPEI, *irresolute, allows her to take the short sword. She places it beside her, away from his reach.*)

KIYOMOTO SINGER: " 'Twas then my heart went astray. It was when you, yes, you made me love, oh, so imprudently.   15
Blame my imprudent heart that spoke to me thus: 'So easy it is to die, but you must live, live on.' "

(KAMPEI *takes up the long sword to kill himself. Again, she gently holds the scabbard so that he cannot draw. They rise and move left, then right, in a delicate struggle for the sword. Allowing himself to be persuaded, they pose with the sword held firmly in her hands. He looks away, wiping his falling tears. She takes the sword and places it out of his reach. They kneel side-by-side.*)

KAMPEI: Your tenderness overwhelms me. (*Nods with resolution.*) We will flee across the mountains to your father's home.
OKARU: (*Smiling, relieved.*) You make me so happy.   20
KAMPEI: In time I know I can find a way to atone for deserting my master. Come, let us go.
OKARU: (*Meekly.*) Yes, Kampei.
KIYOMOTO SINGER: Now for travel they prepare, but who should confront them!   25

(KAMPEI *rises and poses facing front.*)

BANNAI: (*Off, at the rear of the* hanamichi.) Hey, hey! Here we go!
FIGHTING CHORUS: (*Also off.*) Haaa!

(*Loud beats of the big drum. Strong accelerating* tsuke *pattern as* BANNAI *runs onto the* hanamichi *followed by eight of his men, the* FIGHTING CHORUS. BANNAI *has his kimono tucked up to his knees, and a cord holds back his sleeves. His makeup has become ludicrous: bat-shaped eyebrows, drooping eyes, and a tiny blue-gray mustache. The* FIGHTING CHORUS *is dressed identically in red leggings and arm coverings and red and white patterned kimono that stop at their knees. Each carries a branch of cherry blossoms as a weapon.* BANNAI *stops at the seven-three position.* KAMPEI *escorts* OKARU *to the left, out of harm's way, and stands calmly.*)

BANNAI: (*A comic challenge.*) Hey, hey! Kampei!

(*He stamps forward with two steps, each accented by two* tsuke *beats. He and his men march on stage. The men, alert for their master's call, kneel upstage in two rows.* BANNAI *faces front, with a supercilious look. He speaks in a special rhythmical pattern,* nori, *in which each dialogue phrase fits into an eight-beat samisen musical phrase. He accompanies the tale with comic gestures.*)

Your stupid master, Enya Hangan, Takasada and my honored master, Councilor Moronao, met in the palace while,   30
chittering chattering, chittering chattering, your master Hangan, flew into a snit. Taking a teensy sword, he whipped it out, he made a slash. He is a traitor, locked up in his residence, boxed up like a criminal. Ha ha ha . . . ha ha ha . . . haha haha hahaha! Hangan has been hauled away!   35
I'll catch you like a chick! I'll pluck you like a duck! I am claiming Okaru! Well? Well? Well, well? (*Accelerating.*)

Well, well, well, well, well! Kampei! Your goose is cooked!
Give her . . . to me!

(BANNAI stands on tiptoe, holds his sword hilts threateningly, and cocks his head in comic mie to two beats of the tsuke.)

40 KIYOMOTO SINGER: "Give her to me," yells Sagisaka Bannai.
Kampei bursts out with mocking laughter.
KAMPEI: *(Laughs, then speaks in rhythmic nori phrases.)* You are a
funny bird, Sagisaka Bannai, a little chirping sparrow, I
could swallow in a bite. *(Rapidly.)* Kampei's fiery gaze could
45 fry you to a crisp! But instead of eating you, I will make you
eat crow!

(KAMPEI slips his fists out of the breast of his kimono, allowing the black outer kimono to drop. An inner kimono of brilliant crimson color is revealed. He stamps aggressively forward, then poses with arms outstretched, head cocked in a mie to two tsuke beats. BANNAI tumbles to the ground terrified.)

KIYOMOTO SINGER: Glaring and with arms outstretched, Kampei
stands before him!
BANNAI: *(Weakly.)* Help!

(KIYOMOTO samisen and drums play instrumental music as the eight members of the FIGHTING CHORUS attack KAMPEI. KAMPEI waves half of them past him until he stands center in a mie position. Four men face him from either side, holding their cherry branches as if they were swords. They strike at him right, left, right. He forces them back. They fall away. They pose in a mie to two tsuke beats. KAMPEI now fights his opponents in a series of group combats that are executed in delicate, controlled dance patterns. Rhythmic drums and samisen support the action.)

50 KIYOMOTO SINGER: Cherry, cherry blossoms! A name, oh, so
beloved.

(One man on each side strikes at KAMPEI with the cherry branch. Three times KAMPEI avoids, then seizing the tips of the branches, he whirls them in a circle and presses them to their knees. He poses in a mie. Flicking the branches away, the men are hit on the forehead; they retreat. KAMPEI nonchalantly dusts off his hands.)

"No, no, you can't have her," and why should that be?

(One man on each side seizes KAMPEI's arms. They struggle right, left, right. KAMPEI flicks them forward onto their knees. They try to seize his feet, he backs up. They rush in to encircle him. He avoids, then casually taps them on the back. They do a cartwheel and fall prostrate on the ground. KAMPEI poses in a mie.)

So tender, so fine, so frail, never to be won by you!

(Four men form a square around KAMPEI. Two-by-two they attack, but he pivots to avoid them. Six men strike with their cherry branches. KAMPEI drops to his knees, deftly knocks the wind out of them with an open-hand blow, and, with a sweeping gesture, knocks them off their feet. They fall on their bottoms in unison.)

Delightful, though she's only to be seen. How can you ever
55 feel true love, if she won't play with you!

(The FIGHTING CHORUS retires upstage. BANNAI pulls OKARU by the sleeve. Foolishly flirting, he touches his cheek to her hand. KAMPEI

pushes him away, and when BANNAI tries to get past to OKARU, blocks his way. BANNAI slips under KAMPEI's sleeve, but is caught and held by the nape of the neck. BANNAI struggles free, strikes at KAMPEI, is kicked to his knees, and finally is grasped by the ear, lifted, and spun around. BANNAI is near tears in frustration and humiliation. Trying once again, he raises his fist, but KAMPEI turns and casually pushes BANNAI to the ground. KAMPEI stamps forward and poses in a strong mie to two tsuke beats.)

BANNAI: *(Plaintively.)* Take him!

(Large drum and tsuke beats. The FIGHTING CHORUS attacks in unison: KAMPEI passes them off right and left as he strides from stage left to right; he turns and passes unharmed between them as they strike at him with their cherry branches. One man, coming from hiding, strikes at KAMPEI from behind. KAMPEI kicks him to the ground, places his foot on his back, and poses in a strong mie to two beats of the tsuke. KAMPEI kicks the man away and attacks. Booming drum accelerates. The FIGHTING CHORUS retreats. They run pell-mell down the hanamichi and out of sight. KAMPEI poses in a powerful "stone-throwing" mie to two beats of the tsuke. BANNAI sneaks up.)

BANNAI: Kampei, here I come!

(BANNAI raises his sword to strike. KAMPEI catches his wrist, spins him around, forces him to his knees, and raises the sword.)

KAMPEI: *(Bantering.)* Shall I cut your ears off? *(Terrified, BANNAI covers his ears with wildly trembling hands.)* Shall I cut off your nose? *(BANNAI covers his nose.)* Or shall I simply kill you?   60
OKARU: Killing him would bring more trouble. So, please, just
let him go.
BANNAI: *(Foolishly, imitating OKARU's inflections.)* So, please, just
let him go!

(BANNAI clasps his trembling hands together in prayer.)

KIYOMOTO SINGER: Oh, how he prattles on, that bird, Sagisaka!   65
Smoothing his ruffled feathers, slowly, then faster, flirts
with death, and yet to live, away he flies!

(KAMPEI nods agreement. He casually rolls BANNAI across the stage away from OKARU. He poses facing front. BANNAI rubs his throat, then noticing KAMPEI is holding his sword, meekly gestures a request that it be returned. Contemptuously, KAMPEI tosses the sword on the ground. BANNAI leaps back in terror. Gathering his courage, he snares the sword with his foot, then suddenly turns and raises the sword as if to strike. A fierce glance from KAMPEI deflates him completely. He turns and escapes off right, lifting his legs high in the air in a "stork walk.")

KAMPEI: He deserved to die. But his death would be a crime to
add to my disloyalty.

(A cock crows in the distance. They both look up into the sky. They speak in melancholy, poetic tones.)

Already it is dawning . . .   70
OKARU: . . . on the peaks of the mountains . . .
KAMPEI: . . . the eastern light glows . . .
OKARU and KAMPEI: *(In unison.)* . . . lighting trailing clouds.

(They pose together center stage, absorbed in their own melancholy.)

KIYOMOTO SINGER: They fly away at daybreak, like the crows
75   that cry, "caw, caw." So dear to each other, in love, in love.

(*A* STAGE ASSISTANT *passes to* OKARU *the hat, bundle, and swords.
Dutifully,* OKARU *helps* KAMPEI *adjust the bundle and slide the
swords into his sash. They put on their sandals. A temple bell tolls.
They move apart, pose, then move back-to-back.*)

Though they must hasten to depart, their minds are filled
with woe. Who would doubt their loyalty if they proved
the guilt they feel? Away they go.

(*They look into each other's eyes. Restraining tears,* KAMPEI *puts on a
manly bearing, takes* OKARU *by the hand, and turns to begin their long
journey.* BANNAI *sneaks up behind them. He holds* OKARU *by the waist.*)

BANNAI: Okaru is mine, all mine!

(KAMPEI *moves to block* BANNAI, *passing* OKARU *to safety on the
hanamichi. He pushes* BANNAI *away and turns to join* OKARU.)

80 BANNAI: Kampei, wait!
    KAMPEI: (*Turning back at the seven-three position.*) Bannai, you
        want. . . . ?
    BANNAI: (*Posing.*) Kampei, I want . . .
    KAMPEI: Hmm?
85 BANNAI: (*Deflated.*) Nothing.
    KAMPEI: Simpleton!

(*A loud ki clack:* BANNAI *collapses to the ground. Drum booms
loudly.* KAMPEI *takes* OKARU's *hand and slowly they exit down the
hanamichi. Kiyomoto samisen plays plaintive chords and* ki *clacks
accelerate as the curtain begins to close.* BANNAI *is in the path of the
curtain. He retreats before it, then, realizing it is hopeless, seizes the
curtain with both hands and, grinning happily, prances across the
stage, closing the curtain and disappearing from sight. A single* ki
clack: drum and flute play lively "Shagiri" to close the scene.)

SCENE II
Hangan's Suicide

Two ki *clacks: the curtain is slowly opened to the rachetlike sound of
an old-fashioned clock. The scene is a large, formal room in* HANGAN's
*mansion. Sliding doors that make up the rear wall are painted pow-
der blue and covered with silver crests of* HANGAN's *clan. Tatami mat-
ting covers the floor.* HANGAN, *dressed in a simple kimono and vest so
pale a blue-gray that it verges on white, kneels center. He faces two envoys from the shōgun,* ISHIDŌ *and* YAKUSHIJI, *who are sitting stage left
on high stools. They wear dark kimono, vests, and trousers.* ISHIDŌ's
sympathetic manner contrasts sharply with YAKUSHIJI's *derisive attitude.* GOEMON, *a senior retainer of* HANGAN, *kneels upstage. Silence.*
ISHIDŌ *rises and faces* HANGAN. *He takes from the breast of his kimono
a large folded letter. He holds it reverently to his forehead.*

ISHIDŌ: Hear the shōgun's command. (*Removing the letter from
    its envelope, he reads.*) "Whereas, Enya Hangan Takasada,
    you have willfully committed an act of bloodshed against
    our chief councilor, Moronao, and thereby have defiled
5   the palace, know that your estates, large and small, are
    hereby confiscated and you are ordered to end your life by
    seppuku."

(ISHIDŌ *gravely holds the open letter in front of him, so* HANGAN *can
read the order with his own eyes. After glancing at it,* HANGAN *bows
respectfully.*)

HANGAN: (*With perfect control.*) In all respects I accept the
    shōgun's command.
NARRATOR: (*Chants.*) From the adjoining room, knocking on   10
    the door . . .

(*A* RETAINER *knocks on the sliding door. He speaks in a faint, muffled voice, suggesting tears.*)

RETAINER: (*Off.*) Goemon, Goemon. We, Lord Hangan's retain-
    ers, beg permission to see our master . . .
RETAINERS: (*Off, quietly in unison.*) . . . one last time.
GOEMON: (*Bowing to* HANGAN.) My lord, your retainers wish to   15
    see you.
HANGAN: Tell them not until Chief Retainer Yuranosuke has
    arrived from our province.
GOEMON: (*Facing the door.*) You heard our lord. You may enter
    when Yuranosuke arrives, not before.   20
RETAINERS: (*Scarcely audible.*) Ahhh.
NARRATOR: (*Sings.*) Their plea, not granted . . . no one dares
    utter a single word. In the room, silence prevails.

(HANGAN *rises and retires upstage, where he kneels with his back to
the audience.*)

GOEMON: (*Quietly, facing offstage right.*) Proceed.
RETAINER: (*Faintly, off.*) Yes.   25

(*In complete silence arrangements are made for* HANGAN's *death by
ritual disembowelment.* RETAINERS, *dressed in somber blue and gray
kimono, vests, and split trousers, swiftly and unobtrusively enter. They
place two tatami mats center to make a six-foot square platform. They
cover it with a pure white cloth. Sprigs of green, in small bamboo hold-
ers, are placed at the four corners. With downcast eyes, the* RETAINERS
slip quietly away. GOEMON *bows to* HANGAN *indicating that the
place of suicide is ready.* HANGAN *rises, slowly pivots front, and crosses
down to the cloth seat. Unconsciously his gaze drifts to the* hanamichi:
he is waiting for the arrival of his chief retainer, YURANOSUKE, *and
does not want to die before passing to him his last instructions. His
right foot touches the cloth. He remembers it is obligatory to step into
the place of suicide with the left foot. He glances at the envoys to see if
they have noticed: they are gazing straight ahead. He deliberately steps
onto the cloth and slowly kneels.*)

NARRATOR: (*Chants.*) Rikiya proceeds with the saddest order.
    (*Sings.*) The master's suicide blade weighing heavy on his
    heart . . .

(YURANOSUKE's *son,* RIKIYA, *enters from up left. He carries a plain
wooden tray bearing the short dagger with which* HANGAN *will kill
himself. The long sleeves of his black kimono and a delicate forelock of
hair indicate he is a youth, not yet grown to manhood. He places the
tray on the floor before the envoys for their verification. He bows.*
ISHIDŌ *and* YAKUSHIJI *look at the blade, then nod to each other that
it is satisfactory.* ISHIDŌ *nods gravely to* RIKIYA.)

NARRATOR: Before Lord Hangan he lays the blade.

(RIKIYA *places the tray on the cloth before* HANGAN, *bows low, and
then looks up for instructions.* HANGAN *looks gently into* RIKIYA's *eyes*

and with a single head movement indicates that RIKIYA *is to leave: a boy so young should not have to witness* seppuku. RIKIYA *politely shakes his head: until his father arrives, he must fulfill his father's duties.* HANGAN *repeats the order to leave; again* RIKIYA *shakes his head. Impressed by the boy's loyalty,* HANGAN *nods that he may stay.* RIKIYA *bows gratefully, rises, backs away, and takes a place beside* GOEMON.)

30   NARRATOR: *(Sings.)* Taking off, in hushed silence, his outer clothes to expose his death robe . . . securing the seat of death.

*(*HANGAN *prepares himself for death with calm deliberation. He slips off the vest, letting it drop to his waist. He tucks the ends under his legs so as to hold his body in place after he has died. He drops the outer kimono to his waist and tucks it in as well. Beneath he is wearing a pure white kimono appropriate for death, an indication to the envoys that he was prepared to die even before they brought the shōgun's command. He places his hands firmly on his thighs and looks intently down the hanamichi.)*

HANGAN: *(Softly but urgently.)* Rikiya.
RIKIYA: *(Bowing.)* Yes.
HANGAN: Yuranosuke . . . ?
35   RIKIYA: Yuranosuke . . . *(He looks down the* hanamichi *for a sign that his father has arrived.)* . . . has not as yet arrived.
NARRATOR: *(Sings.)* Proper steps for suicide, he lifts the tray and bows. *(Chants.)* Waiting no longer, the blade in his hand.

*(*HANGAN *prepares the dagger. He lifts the tray to his forehead respectfully. He ceremoniously takes the dagger in his right hand and a sheet of white paper in his left. He wraps the paper around the blade until only its tip is bare. He is now able to grasp the blade low for extra leverage. He holds the blade at ready on his thigh. The tip points to his stomach. Outwardly calm, his voice betrays his anxiety.)*

40   HANGAN: Rikiya, Rikiya!
RIKIYA: *(Bowing.)* Yes.
HANGAN: Yuranosuke . . . ?
RIKIYA: Yes! *(*RIKIYA *bows and rushes to the end of the* hanamichi. *He falls to his knees, looks to the right, the left, then straight*
45   *ahead, searching for sight of his father. His lip trembles, he is close to tears.)* Yuranosuke . . . *(He rushes back and throws himself on the floor before* HANGAN.) . . . has not as yet arrived!
HANGAN: *(Calmly.)* Tell him that I regret . . . not seeing him one last time. *(*HANGAN *nods that* RIKIYA *may retire and pivots*
50   *slightly toward* ISHIDŌ.) Lord Ishidō, I ask that you witness and report my death.
NARRATOR: *(Sings.)* Here at last the time has come, the blade is aimed. Hangan . . . thrusts it in . . . thrusts it deep!

*(*HANGAN *places the tray behind him. He rises slightly on his knees, looking one last time down the* hanamichi *for* YURANOSUKE. *He holds the dagger under the ribs on his left side. With a sudden jerk he thrusts the blade into his stomach. Involuntarily his body drops forward and his head falls. Rapid narrative shifts to chanting.)*

55   Running at a desperate speed, the awaited person comes! Here at last is Ōboshi Yuranosuke! A frantic gaze at his master: "Is he still alive?" Overcome by the sight, he falls on his knees!

*(*YURANOSUKE *bursts onto the* hanamichi, *running frantically, all decorum cast aside. He wears a formal gray kimono, vest, and trousers*

pulled up for travel. Reaching the seven-three position, he sees his master in the midst of suicide. He reels, falls back, then slowly sinks to his knees.)

ISHIDŌ: *(Rising.)* Is it Ōboshi Yuranosuke?
YURANOSUKE: It is.
ISHIDŌ: *(Urgently.)* Approach, approach quickly!

*(*YURANOSUKE *attempts to rise, but his legs will not function. He weeps unashamedly. To gain control of himself, he reaches inside the breast of his kimono to pull tight the inner cloth binding his waist. With great effort he pushes himself up from the floor and moves unsteadily to* HANGAN's *side. He falls to his knees and bows deeply.)*

NARRATOR: *(Chants.)* The men of Hangan, all, till now for-   60
bidden . . . but no longer! They come rushing in!

(Ten RETAINERS *enter swiftly from up right. They are barefooted and carry no swords. They fall to their knees in a row upstage and, following* YURANOSUKE's *lead, bow deeply to their master* HANGAN. YURANOSUKE's *eyes remain downcast and* HANGAN, *in pain, does not yet look up.)*

YURANOSUKE: Ōboshi Yuranosuke kneels before my lord.
HANGAN: *(Weakly.)* Yuranosuke?
YURANOSUKE: I am here.
HANGAN: At last you've come.   65
YURANOSUKE: All that I could ever ask is to be at your side in these last moments . . .
HANGAN: Ah, it makes me content as well. *(Slowly their gazes meet.)* You have heard, have you not . . . everything . . . everything . . . ?   70

(His voice trails off in pain. YURANOSUKE *edges closer, looking meaningfully at* HANGAN.)

YURANOSUKE: Yes!
HANGAN: *(Rousing himself.)* I am humiliated . . . !
YURANOSUKE: *(Interrupting.)* No words can express such feelings as I hold. Nothing remains now but for me to assure you a just end.   75
HANGAN: *(Meaningfully.)* One thing remains.
NARRATOR: *(Chants.)* Gripping tight the blade, cutting straight across in disembowelment. *(Sings.)* Such moments of agony . . . exhaling his breath . . .

*(*HANGAN *cuts his stomach across from left to right. Although the pain is excruciating and his lips tremble and his breathing grows labored,* HANGAN *maintains the stoic decorum expected of a samurai until the blade reaches its final point just under the right ribs. Then breath seems to leave him. His body sags. He braces his left hand on his thigh.)*

HANGAN: *(Faintly.)* Yuranosuke . . . Yuranosuke . . . come   80
close . . .
YURANOSUKE: Yes.

*(*HANGAN *is near death.* YURANOSUKE *slides forward urgently. Knowing* HANGAN *cannot speak openly because the shōgun's envoys are present, he searches his master's face for some command.)*

HANGAN: Take this blade . . . to remind you . . . do not forget. Re-ve-n . . . *(*YURANOSUKE *starts.* HANGAN *must not say "revenge" out loud.* HANGAN *catches himself.)* . . . remember me.   85

(*Weakly* HANGAN *looks into* YURANOSUKE'S *face, then down the* hanamichi. YURANOSUKE *follows* HANGAN'S *gaze. Master and retainer look deeply into each other's eyes.* YURANOSUKE *understands that in spite of his master's seeming calm acceptance of the death sentence,* HANGAN *passionately desires vengeance against the enemy outside the mansion, that is,* MORONAO.)

YURANOSUKE: (*Passionately.*) I swear!

(YURANOSUKE *slaps his chest for emphasis and bows deeply.* HANGAN *knows that* YURANOSUKE *understands. He is now free to die. He smiles.*)

HANGAN: Ha ha. Ha ha. Ha, ha, ha, ha . . .

(*The laugh fades. With ebbing strength,* HANGAN *pulls the blade from his stomach. He gasps.*)

NARRATOR: (*Chants.*) Aiming the blade at his throat . . . one slash across. Breathing his last breath, lifeless he crumples.

(*Weakened hands, trembling violently, lift the blade upward. He tilts his head. His neck is exposed. A quick slash and the jugular vein is cut. His body rises upward in three spasms of breath. His eyes flutter closed. He falls limply forward, dead. Silently* ISHIDŌ *rises. A* STAGE ASSISTANT *whisks his stool off stage.* ISHIDŌ *places the shōgun's letter on his open fan and places them on* HANGAN'S *body. He moves stage right and kneels beside* YURANOSUKE.)

90 ISHIDŌ: (*Quietly.*) Yuranosuke, Yakushiji now assumes authority over Hangan's estates. Hangan's retainers are hereby denied the rank of samurai and are disbanded. I will report to the shōgun that the death of Hangan is accomplished. You have my deepest sympathy, Yuranosuke.

95 NARRATOR: (*Sings.*) Ishidō, the envoy, expresses sympathy. His sad assignment is over.

(ISHIDŌ *rises facing the line of* RETAINERS. *He raises his arms in a gesture of condolence. The* RETAINERS *look up, then bow respectfully. Slowly* ISHIDŌ *walks to the seven-three position on the* hanamichi. *At a signal from* YURANOSUKE, RIKIYA *moves forward to see him out.* ISHIDŌ *turns back.*)

ISHIDŌ: There is no need. There is no need.
NARRATOR: He prays silently.

(ISHIDŌ *folds his hands and, with downcast eyes, walks slowly down the* hanamichi *and out of sight.*)

NARRATOR: (*Chants.*) Yakushiji holds them in contempt!

(YAKUSHIJI *rises brusquely. The* STAGE ASSISTANT *takes away his stool.*)

100 YAKUSHIJI: Now that he's dead, I'm master here! Cart the corpse away, while I settle in. Show me the way! (*He starts to go, then turns back.*) It's a sad time, isn't it! Ha, ha, ha, ha!

(YAKUSHIJI *strides off left, shown out by a* RETAINER. *Complete silence.* YURANOSUKE *moves in to attend to his master's body. He straightens the legs and brings kimono and vest up over the torso. He moves closer and tries to take the dagger from* HANGAN'S *hand. In death*

HANGAN'S *fingers hold it tightly.* YURANOSUKE *falls back weeping. He gently massages his master's hand until the fingers are warmed, softened, and the dagger slips from their grasp.* YURANOSUKE *places the dagger carefully into the breast of his kimono. He backs away. He and the* RETAINERS *bow expectantly.*)

NARRATOR: (*Singing plaintively.*) Lady Kaoyo enters from another room. Her hair so long and black, oh, so beautiful, now pitiful, it is no more. She will pray as a nun, till her end.   105

(KAOYO *and four* LADIES-IN-WAITING *enter from the left, walking with downcast eyes. They are dressed in pure white kimono and hold Buddhist rosaries. The last* LADY-IN-WAITING *carries a small tray on which rests the cloth-wrapped remains of* KAOYO'S *long hair. They kneel left. The* MAIDS *bow deeply.*)

KAOYO: (*Quietly.*) Yuranosuke. When I think of why my husband had to die, and that I was the cause . . .
YURANOSUKE: (*Firmly.*) My lady, please understand our heartfelt feelings. All of us, each retainer offers his deepest condolence.

(YURANOSUKE *bows to* KAOYO, *then nods to* GOEMON. GOEMON *and the* RETAINERS *rise and move in a circle around their master. Silently, they take up the white cloth, the tatami mats, tray, and sprigs of green. They exit upstage right.* HANGAN *moves off behind the cloth. In an instant all sign of the suicide is removed.*)

KAOYO: Yuranosuke.   110
YURANOSUKE: Yes, my lady.
KAOYO: I offer my lock of hair.

(*The* LADY-IN-WAITING *places the tray with the hair center stage.* YURANOSUKE *sees it and weeps.* KAOYO *turns to show her close-cropped head.*)

NARRATOR: (*Prolonged, melancholy singing.*) Kaoyo is left behind, her grief is so . . . o . . . o . . . She yearns to go to the temple . . .   115

(*She rises, as if to follow her husband, but* YURANOSUKE *stops her with a commanding gesture.*)

YURANOSUKE: My lady!

(*She falls back weakly. A single ki clack. They move into a pose:* YURANOSUKE *picks up the tray with one hand and forces her back with the other;* KAOYO *faces front, lifts the rosary to her eyes, and sobs silently. Ki clacks accelerate as the curtain is slowly walked closed.*)

SCENE III
Outer Gate

Two ki clacks signal drum and flute to play "Toki no Taiko" ("Time Drum"). The curtain is pushed quickly open. The scene is outside the massive outer gate of HANGAN'S *mansion. No one is on stage.*

NARRATOR: (*Chanting rapidly.*) Farewell to Hangan. Now his body lies alone. The young retainers run back from the temple! They no longer can hold the shame inside!

(*To loud, accelerating tsuke beats,* RIKIYA *leads a band of* RETAINERS *onto the* hanamichi. *They urge each other on with shouts of "Kill*

them!" "They won't have our lord's mansion!" "We'll fight them!"
"Lord Hangan was unjustly killed!" At the same time YURANOSUKE
and GOEMON *come out of a small door in the gate.* GOEMON *rushes*
up to the RETAINERS *with outstretched arms, shouting, "Stop, stop!"*
YURANOSUKE *roughly pushes* RIKIYA *to the ground.)*

5   YURANOSUKE: *(Furious.)* What, you too, Rikiya? What are you
     thinking of, trying to attack the mansion? We are no longer
     samurai. We cannot fight Yakushiji's men. *(Drops to one knee,*
     hand on the hilt of his short sword.) If you do not stop, I shall
     commit *seppuku* on this very spot! Do you want to be my
     seconds, all of you?
10   RETAINERS: No, but master . . .
     YURANOSUKE: *(Implacably.)* Then will you stop when I tell you?
     RETAINERS: Yes, but . . .
     YURANOSUKE: It will achieve nothing to die now!

(The RETAINERS *cannot disobey. Grumbling and rebellious, they begin*
to fall back.)

     NARRATOR: *(Chants.)* Behind the gate is heard . . . Yakushiji's
15   voice!
     YAKUSHIJI: *(Off.)* Hey, men, there's a sight. Newly hatched
     ex-samurai, milling around like chickens with their heads
     cut off! It's enough to make you laugh!
     YAKUSHIJI'S MEN: *(Off.)* Ha, ha, ha, ha, ha!
20   FIRST RETAINER: Do you . . .
     RETAINERS: . . . hear that?

(Furious, they turn to storm the gate, hands on the hilts of their
swords. YURANOSUKE *springs into their path and blocks the way.)*

     YURANOSUKE: Have you forgotten our late lord?
     RETAINERS: No, but . . .
     YURANOSUKE: Not now! Go back, go back! Go back I tell you!

*(*YURANOSUKE *draws himself up commandingly. He runs his hand up*
the edge of his vest and poses in a furious mie. *Two* tsuke *beats.)*

25   NARRATOR: *(Sings.)* "Go back," he commands!
     YURANOSUKE: *(Almost in a scolding tone now.)* Back, back, back.

*(*YURANOSUKE *waves them away. They fall back grudgingly, then*
turn and stride off down the hanamichi. YURANOSUKE *watches them*
leave. He is alone. Silence. He sighs with relief. The hand at his breast
slides down until it accidentally touches the dagger. He slowly drops to
his knees and takes it out. He unwraps the covering purple cloth. The
blade tip is red with HANGAN's *blood.)*

     NARRATOR: *(Sings.)* The suicide blade, red with blood, cries out
     for revenge . . . cries out for revenge! Burning tears rake his
     heart, tears . . . falling . . . falling . . . falling . . . falling . . .

(Gazing at the blade, YURANOSUKE's *chest heaves. He covers his eyes*
to hide the tears.)

30   Hangan's last words of vengeance imbedded deep in Yura-
     nosuke. *(Chanting.)* We know indeed the motive of Yura-
     nosuke, his revenge to be noted for many ages . . .
     forty-seven loyal men immortalized!

(He wipes blood from the blade onto his palm and then deliberately
brings his hand up to his mouth. He licks the blood as an oath of

vengeance. Music stops. Silence. YURANOSUKE *begins his long pan-*
tomime of departure. He carefully wraps the dagger in the purple cloth.
He holds it to his forehead respectfully. He places it in the breast of his
kimono. He rises and stands. He slaps the dust from his knees. He ad-
justs his trousers. He folds both hands inside his kimono sleeves. He
rests his hands on the hilts of his swords. He half-closes his eyes, re-
gretting deeply that he must abandon his master's mansion. A temple
bell tolls in the distance. Pensively, he begins to walk away from the
gate. The gate recedes, indicating YURANOSUKE *has covered a long*
distance. He turns back. A crow caws in the distance. He resumes the
painful separation. A crow caws a second time. A second bell tolls. He
stops, stricken with the finality of parting. Then, he moves onto the
hanamichi. Once more he turns back and, as if he has no heart to con-
tinue, slides to his knees. A temple bell tolls. Plaintive, tentative chords
of the samisen begin. He rises, begins to walk away, looks sadly over
his shoulder for one last glimpse, then resolutely turns and strides down
the hanamichi *and out of sight. Music crescendoes and* ki *clacks ac-*
celerate: the curtain is run closed. Drum and flute play rapid "Sha-
giri" to end the scene.)

——— ACT THREE ———

SCENE I
Ichiriki Brothel

Two ki *clacks: the curtain is pushed open to offstage singing of*
"Hana ni Asobaba" ("If You Play in the Flowers"). The scene is the
Ichiriki Brothel in the Gion licensed quarter in Kyoto. Two pavil-
ions are set in a garden. Lying on his side in the larger room, stage
center, is YURANOSUKE. *He is feigning sleep, his face covered with a*
half-open fan. He wears an elegant purple kimono and matching
cloak. Curtains are at the back and a stone water basin is left. Three
steps lead down into the garden. Paper-covered sliding doors conceal
the interior of the smaller pavilion, stage left. It is several feet higher
off the ground than the center pavilion.

     NARRATOR: *(Singing briskly.)* The mountains and the moon.
     From the eastern mountains, just a few miles, breathless
     from running fast, the young man . . . Rikiya.

*(*RIKIYA *enters on the* hanamichi. *A purple scarf covers his head and*
serves as a partial disguise. His black kimono is hiked up at the sides,
to free his legs for running. He stops at a garden gate set on the
hanamichi at the seven-three position. He looks back to see if he is be-
ing observed, then swiftly passes through the gate, closing it.)

     Entering the brothel garden . . . there lies Yuranosuke, pre-
     tending to be drunk. Taking caution to wake his father in 5
     secrecy, he walks softly in, stepping close to him. The sword
     guard speaks!

*(*RIKIYA *sees his father. He mounts the steps, kneels, and makes a ring-*
ing sound by striking sword guard against sheath. YURANOSUKE *ges-*
tures RIKIYA *away with a sleepy movement of the fan.* RIKIYA *crosses*
swiftly back through the gate, closes it, looks around to be certain they
are not being observed, and kneels to wait for his father. Offstage
samisen play tentative chords. YURANOSUKE *rises. He staggers as if*
drunk, ad-libbing, "That was heady wine. I need some air. Don't go
away, girls. I'll be in the garden." He looks through the curtains to see
if anyone is watching. He crosses to the gate, stumbling several times
in order to have the chance to look carefully in all directions. He stands
swaying, fan before his face. He speaks guardedly.)

YURANOSUKE: Rikiya, do I hear the sound of urgency in the echo of your sword?

10 RIKIYA: Yes, Father. I bring a secret message from Lady Kaoyo. (RIKIYA *brings out a letter from his right sleeve and passes it to* YURANOSUKE, *who puts it immediately into the breast of his kimono without examining it.*)

YURANOSUKE: (*Carefully.*) Did she say anything to you?

15 RIKIYA: (*Rising on his knees urgently.*) Soon, soon our enemy . . .

YURANOSUKE: Rikiya! "Soon at night our enemy, flees like plovers o'er the sea. . . ."

(*Music swells. To cover the slip of his son's tongue,* YURANOSUKE *sings a well-known passage from a nō play. He staggers in a circle looking to see if anyone has heard* RIKIYA's *remark. Simultaneously,* RIKIYA *pivots in the opposite direction, looking for eavesdroppers.* YURANOSUKE *gestures for* RIKIYA *to come closer;* RIKIYA *whispers* KAOYO's *message in his father's ear. The curtains in the room center part.* KUDAYŪ *peeks out. He is a gray-haired former retainer of* HANGAN, *now secretly working for* MORONAO. *He wears a plain brown kimono and cloak. He watches for a moment, then slips away.*)

YURANOSUKE: Send a palanquin for me tonight. Tell the others to be ready. Go, go!

20 NARRATOR: (*Sings.*) No time left for hesitation . . . to the eastern hills, homeward now . . .

(YURANOSUKE *sharply gestures with the fan.* RIKIYA *bows, rises, and holding firmly onto the hilts of his swords, begins to leave.*)

YURANOSUKE: Rikiya!

RIKIYA: (*Returning and bowing.*) Yes.

YURANOSUKE: Be careful while passing through the quarter.

25   Then hurry! Go now!

RIKIYA: Yes!

NARRATOR: Rikiya returns home.

(RIKIYA *realizes his mistake; he is holding his swords ready to draw, thus calling attention to himself. He hides the hilts with his sleeves. Swiftly, carefully, he hurries down the* hanamichi *out of sight. Offstage samisen play* "Odoriji Aikata" ("Dance Melody"). *Four* MAIDS *and a male* JESTER *enter through the curtain, ad-libbing,* "Yura, where are you?" "Come drink with us." "Don't leave us, Yura." YURANOSUKE *pretends drunkenness again.*)

FIRST MAID: Yura, Yura, are you here?

YURANOSUKE: Hmm. You've come to get me? I'm a lucky man.

30   Come close all of you, let's amuse ourselves. Come, sing and dance for me.

(YURANOSUKE *sits on the steps. The* MAIDS *and the* JESTER *kneel in the garden in a semicircle around him.*)

SECOND MAID: Very well . . .

ALL: . . . let's begin, let's begin!

(*Lilting music of offstage samisen, drum, and bell accompanies various dances and songs. These are extemporized by the performers from production to production.* MAIDS *and* JESTER *ad-lib comic banter throughout.*)

MAIDS: (*Clapping as they sing.*) "What will it be like, what will

35   it be like? If you don't be careful, we will make you drink. Ah, what will it be like, what will it be like?"

(JESTER *and* THIRD MAID *rise and move center. They do a game of jan-ken-po, "scissors-paper-stone." He loses. She laughingly pushes him. He falls in a heap on the ground. The* MAIDS *rise and form pairs.*)

FOURTH MAID: Come, let's dance!

ALL: "First your left foot, then your right, tap, tap, tap;
   Around we go, back again;
   Are you ready, one, two, three!"   40

(*They circle left, then right, touching palms of their outstretched hands. They turn their backs to each other and bump bottoms on the count of three. With peals of laughter they recover their balance. The* JESTER *and* YURANOSUKE *laugh and applaud.*)

YURANOSUKE: Very good, very good!

FIRST MAID: How about a game, Yura dear?

JESTER: Blind man's bluff!

SECOND MAID: You be It!

ALL: Yes, yes!   45

(YURANOSUKE *tries to wave them away, but they playfully surround him and put a cloth over his eyes. They twirl him around in the center of the garden, and move left, laughing and clapping in time to their song.*)

ALL: "Yura, Yura, over here;
   Listen to our clapping hands."

YURANOSUKE: (*Sings.*) "I'll catch you all, soon enough you'll see."

(*He stumbles in their direction. They easily avoid his outstretched arms and flee to the other side of the garden.*)

ALL: "Yura, Yura over here;
   Come and catch us if you can."   50

YURANOSUKE: "I'll catch you all, and make you drink with me."

(*They duck under his arms. When he turns back to continue pursuit, they take him by the hands and, still singing and clapping, lead him off to the inner room with his blindfold still in place. They are no sooner off than* KUDAYŪ's *head pops through the curtain on the other side of the stage. Samisen music stops.* KUDAYŪ *peers about intently. He slips into the room.*)

KUDAYŪ: That letter Rikiya gave to Yuranosuke . . . the rumor of a vendetta must be true! He has not forgotten; they are plotting, just as I thought. When I tell Moronao, what will be my great reward? If, of course, it's true. I'll spy him out!   55
   Here's a perfect place to hide.

(*He sees a hiding place. He removes a board under the veranda, opening a space for him to crawl in. He hides behind the steps.* YURANOSUKE *enters alone from upstage, pretending to be drunk.*)

YURANOSUKE: I'll be back . . . don't wait, girls . . . in a minute, I'll be back.

(*Samisen music resumes. He looks around. Seeing he is alone, he drops his pretense. He rinses his mouth with water from the stone basin. He spits it out. It falls on the unsuspecting* KUDAYŪ. *He takes out the letter from* KAOYO *and holds it respectfully to his forehead. He begins to read, slowly unrolling the letter until it reaches the ground. At the same time the paper doors slide open to reveal* OKARU *in the small room left. She wears the elaborate hairstyle and clinging kimono of a courtesan.*)

NARRATOR: (*Sings.*) Evening breeze, brings a courtesan, Kampei's
60   wife Okaru, away from her love. Someone has sent a love let-
      ter, "I wish it were for me." Okaru from a room above, tries
      to see the words. Too far in the evening dusk, the letters are
      not clear to read. Thinking of a way out, a mirror in her hand,
      she leans back . . . mirror held up high, reflection of the
65   letter. Under the floor a spy, Kudayū waits . . . the trailing
      letter glows in the moonlight. (*Chants.*) Who could know
      someone is reading words of confidence?

(*The three form a tableau:* YURANOSUKE *is engrossed in reading the
secret letter;* OKARU *views the letter backwards in a mirror; and* KU-
DAYŪ, *spectacles on his nose, reads the bottom portion, line-by-line, as
it comes down to him. Narrative shifts to singing.*)

      Okaru, unaware that her hairpin has loosened! (*Chants.*) It
      drops to the floor! Surprised by the sound above, he quickly
70   hides the letter . . . Yuranosuke! Underneath Kudayū smirk-
      ing at his game. (*Sings.*) Okaru pretends nothing has hap-
      pened here.

(YURANOSUKE *quickly resumes his drunken role. He begins to roll
up the letter, but not before* KUDAYŪ *rips off the part he has been
reading.* OKARU *puts down the mirror, picks up a fan, and turns to
YURANOSUKE.*)

OKARU: (*Languidly.*) Yura dear, is it you?
YURANOSUKE: Hmm, Okaru? So close at hand, what are you
75   doing?
OKARU: (*In poetic form of seven and five syllables.*) Yura dear, it's all
      your fault, I drank too much wine; my head is whirling
      round and I can scarcely see; I have come to sober up,
      wafted by the evening breeze.

(YURANOSUKE *reaches the end of the letter. He feels the ragged edge.
Startled, he looks quickly at the letter, then puts it away in the breast
of his kimono. He takes out a piece of tissue paper and wads it up, covering his action by improvising conversation with* OKARU.)

80   YURANOSUKE: Hmm. Wafted by the evening breeze, you say?
      Wafted by the evening breeze? Ah!

(*He drops the wad of paper to the ground.* KUDAYŪ, *thinking it is
part of the letter, snatches it and stuffs it into his kimono breast.*
YURANOSUKE *falls back, supposedly in a drunken stupor, but actually
wanting to ponder what to do next. He decides. Soft samisen plays
"Odoriji Aikata" in the background.*)

      Hm. Okaru, there is something I want to talk to you about.
      Come over here.
OKARU: (*Rises as if to leave her room.*) Very well, I'll come around
85   and visit you.
YURANOSUKE: (*Coming down into the garden.*) No, Okaru, if you
      go that way the maids will catch you. They will force on
      you more wine. Ah, a ladder. Fortune smiles. Climb down
      this way and you won't be seen. (*Places a ladder against*
90   OKARU's *pavilion. Bantering.*) Descend for me, Okaru!
OKARU: (*Coquettishly on the ladder.*) I've never climbed a ladder
      before.
YURANOSUKE: You've climbed other things.
OKARU: I'm not used to this strange position. It frightens me.

YURANOSUKE: You're past the age to be afraid of a new position.   95
      Straddle it, open your legs, it'll all go smoothly.
OKARU: Don't be naughty, Yura. I tell you it frightens me. It's
      swaying like a boat.
YURANOSUKE: Never mind, I'll throw in my anchor. That will
      hold you down. Where shall I put it? (*He tries to lift her skirt*   100
      with his fan. She brushes his hand away.)
OKARU: You mustn't peek, Yura.
YURANOSUKE: (*Singing.*) "I adore your crescent moon, glistening
      in its secret grotto." Ha, ha, ha.
OKARU: (*Pouting.*) If you talk that way, I won't come down.   105
YURANOSUKE: Don't prattle like a virgin. You're a courtesan in
      the Gion brothel. I'll take you from behind. (YURANOSUKE
      embraces her from behind.)
OKARU: Oh, stop it.
YURANOSUKE: Then come, come.   110
OKARU: I am, I am!

(*Laughing, she slips off the final rung of the ladder and moves away
from* YURANOSUKE. *She kneels right, fanning herself.* YURANOSUKE
*glances at her sharply, then resumes the drunken pose. He stoops to re-
trieve the dropped hairpin and crosses to give it to her.*)

YURANOSUKE: (*Casually.*) Just now, Okaru, did something
      catch your eye?
OKARU: I . . . nothing.
YURANOSUKE: (*Coaxing.*) Come now, didn't you see, didn't you   115
      see . . .
OKARU: . . . your interesting letter . . .
YURANOSUKE: . . . from up above?
OKARU: (*Lightly.*) Hmm, yes.
YURANOSUKE: And you read it all?   120
OKARU: Oh, you do go on.

(*Covering his concern, he pretends to stumble. He recovers his balance,
singing a nō song which both hides and expresses his feelings.*)

YURANOSUKE: "Fate conspires to bring, my life to this crisis. . . ."
      (*Mimes striking a nō drum.*) Ya, tum, tum, tum! Ha, ha, ha!
OKARU: (*Turns to him, laughing.*) What in the world do you
      mean?   125
YURANOSUKE: It means that of all the women in the world, I
      have become enamored of you. Come live with me, Okaru.
OKARU: Stop it. You're such a tease!
YURANOSUKE: (*Grandiloquently.*) I will redeem your contract
      with the master of the brothel and take you away.   130
OKARU: I don't believe it. You're making fun of me.
YURANOSUKE: I'll prove it's not a lie. Be my mistress for just
      three days, and after that, Okaru, your spirit will be free to
      go where it will.
OKARU: (*Taking him seriously for the first time.*) For three days?   135
YURANOSUKE: On my sacred oath as a samurai. Live with me
      for three days. I'll find the master and buy your contract
      now. Well, is it agreed?

(OKARU *looks carefully at him to see if it possibly can be true. They
pose. She bows low.*)

OKARU: I am grateful, Yuranosuke.
YURANOSUKE: Can it make you happy to be redeemed . . . by   140
      this Yuranosuke?
OKARU: Oh, yes!

YURANOSUKE: Such radiance shines in that happy face.

(They pose: she looks at him with gratitude; flicking open his fan, he covers his face to hide his stricken expression.)

YURANOSUKE: Don't go away now. I'll be right back.
145 OKARU: Three days? Yes, Yuranosuke. I'll be here.

(Off stage, sad "Yo ni mo Inga" ("Nighttime Fate") is sung quietly. They lightly ad-lib to cover his exit. Still pretending to be drunk, he staggers up the steps. He turns back several times. He passes through the curtains in search of the master of the house. When he is gone she kneels center stage, trembling with excitement.)

OKARU: How happy I am! I must write to dearest Kampei that I am coming home! And to Mother and Father, to tell the wonderful news!

(She hurries up the steps into the center room, brings out a writing box and roll of letter paper, kneels, and begins to write a letter home. Song ends.)

NARRATOR: *(Chants.)* Now appears . . . Heiemon!

(Offstage samisen briskly play "Odoriji Aikata." A young samurai strides on from the right into the garden. His hair is severely drawn back and his plain kimono suggests poverty. It is HEIEMON, OKARU's older brother, in search of both YURANOSUKE and OKARU. He looks around, then seeing a woman in the room, enters and sits behind her. He speaks brusquely, almost rudely.)

150 HEIEMON: Sorry to trouble you, Miss, but I am looking for a young woman, from my hometown of Yamazaki, by the name of Okaru, brought here a year ago . . .

(Hearing her name OKARU turns. They recognize each other.)

Sister!
OKARU: Heiemon! Oh! I feel ashamed for you to see me here!

(OKARU's demeanor completely changes: in the presence of a male family member who is her elder, she becomes submissive, gentle, a little girl seeking approbation. She hides her face. She rushes down the steps, and falls to her knees. HEIEMON, though stern, acts protectively toward her. He rises and poses on the steps.)

155 HEIEMON: What is there to feel ashamed of? When I returned home Mother told me you had sold yourself to this brothel, hoping that with your contract price Kampei could contribute to the vendetta against Lord Hangan's enemy. You have willingly sacrificed yourself for your husband and for
160 Lord Hangan. I am proud of you, Okaru! *(He poses at the top of the steps: right foot forward, right arm extended protectively in her direction.)*
OKARU: *(Hesitantly, looks up at him.)* Then you're not going to scold me?
165 HEIEMON: Scold you? I am filled with admiration, filled with admiration!

(He crosses down the steps and kneels. He sits proudly, sword placed on the ground beside him.)

OKARU: I'm happy that you think kindly of me. *(Becoming excited.)* Oh, there are so many things I want to ask my dear big brother. I don't know where to begin . . . how is Kam . . .
HEIEMON: *(Uneasy.)* Kam . . . ? 170

(OKARU is embarrassed to have asked about her husband first. She changes the subject.)

OKARU: Come . . . tell me, how is Mother?
HEIEMON: Set your mind at ease. Mother is well.
OKARU: And Father? Nothing troubles him, I hope?
HEIEMON: *(Uncomfortably.)* Hm . . . Father . . . he is at rest . . . he is at rest. 175
OKARU: *(Modestly.)* And what of Kampei?
HEIEMON: Kampei? Ah . . . well . . . he is as well as can be.
OKARU: You set my heart at ease. *(Bubbling.)* Oh, I forgot . . . be happy for me, Brother. Tonight, without warning, Yuranosuke offered to buy out my contract. 180
HEIEMON: Yuranosuke did that? *(Trying to understand how such a thing could be.)* Ah, then he's become your patron?
OKARU: Nonsense. We have only drunk together two or three times. And Heiemon, it's almost too good to be true. After three days he will let me come home. 185
HEIEMON: Hm? Then you told him you are Kampei's wife?
OKARU: How could I, a prostitute, tell him that and bring disgrace to Kampei and to my parents?
HEIEMON: *(Facing front.)* Hm! Then he is no more than a whoremaster! *(He slaps his thigh in anger.)* He has no intention of 190 avenging Hangan, our lord and master!
OKARU: Oh, no, Brother, he has. He has. Listen . . .
NARRATOR: *(Sings.)* In whispers, the content of the letter is revealed.

(OKARU and HEIEMON rise. He leans forward. She whispers in his ear. They pose for a moment, then break apart and kneel.)

OKARU: . . . so you see? 195
HEIEMON: *(Shocked.)* Then you read it all?
OKARU: Yes, and after reading it, his eye met mine, and flirting, he looked me up and down, up and down, and then began to talk of taking me away.

(OKARU mimes his flirting by pressing the backs of her index fingers together, right on top of left, then left on top of right. HEIEMON is puzzled. He tries to understand her words, miming as she did.)

HEIEMON: What? After reading it, flirting, he looked you up 200 and down, up and down . . . *(He slaps his thigh for emphasis.)* Ah! Now I understand!
OKARU: *(Laughing.)* You startled me.
HEIEMON: *(Facing the inner room, he bows low.)* Forgive me, Master Yuranosuke, I misjudged you! I was wrong, forgive me! 205
OKARU: Dearest Brother, what in the world are you doing?
HEIEMON: *(Turns and looks into OKARU's eyes.)* Dear Sister. There is something I must ask of you. Okaru, do now exactly as I say.
OKARU: You sound so very stiff and formal. What must you ask 210 of me?
HEIEMON: What I must ask of you is . . .
OKARU: What you must ask of me is . . . ?
HEIEMON: Okaru, let your brother take your life!

(He springs to his feet and whips out his long sword. She falls back. Rapid "Odoriji Aikata." To double beats of the tsuke, *he slashes at her right, left, right. She avoids. She rises and pushes him away. He turns to strike; she distracts him with a shower of tissue paper drawn from her breast and thrown in the air. She runs to the* hanamichi; *he follows. She closes the gate between them. They pose in a* mie *to two loud* tsuke *beats: on the ground, she holds up her hands imploringly; he stands with legs together, the sword directly overhead as if to strike. Music stops.)*

215 OKARU: *(Appealing to him.)* What am I supposed to have done wrong? You have no right to just do as you please. I have my husband and both my parents to care for. Forgive me if I have spoken out of turn. I clasp my hands and beg you to spare me!

220 NARRATOR: *(Sings.)* Seeing his sister's clasped hands . . . a brother's love overwhelms the dutiful heart. He can only cry.

(He tries to but cannot strike his sister. He falls back distraught, turns upstage to face away from her, holds the sword behind his back, and weeps unashamedly. When the narration is finished, he turns to face OKARU. *He is contrite. Slow offstage "Odoriji Aikata" resumes in the background.)*

HEIEMON: I was wrong, Okaru, not to explain. Come, come over here.

(He waves her to him. She flounces.)

OKARU: No, I will not come near you.

225 HEIEMON: *(Sternly.)* When your elder brother calls, why don't you come?

OKARU: *(Sweetly.)* If you want to know, I'll tell you why: I think you still intend to kill me, and I don't like that at all!

*(*HEIEMON *notices the long sword in his hand. He puts it on the ground and pushes it toward her.)*

HEIEMON: Ah, this. There is nothing to stop you now. So come,
230 come!

OKARU: Yes, there is. Something else.

(She points at the short sword in his sash. Annoyed, he pushes it toward her.)

HEIEMON: There, now. Come over here!

(She rises and is about to cross through the gate. She looks at him and stops.)

OKARU: Your face is so frightening.

HEIEMON: I can't help that. This is the face I was born with.

235 OKARU: Well then, please turn around.

HEIEMON: What a nuisance. Like this? Like this?

(Grumbling, he turns his back. He poses with arms stretched out to either side.)

OKARU: Now, don't look. Keep your face turned away. *(She cautiously goes through the gate, picks up the swords, and puts them out of his reach. She kneels behind him, placing her hands on his sash. Music stops. She poses.)* All right, here I am. Brother
240

dear, what is it you want? *(He turns to face her. He places his hands protectively on her shoulders. They pose.)*

HEIEMON: *(Voice filled with emotion, he speaks in poetic form of seven and five syllables.)* Once you were a samurai, now a courtesan; combing out your silken hair, while the world has 245 changed; precious Sister how pitiful, totally unaware of the life you left behind!

*(*HEIEMON *breaks away and kneels left.* OKARU *moves close.)*

OKARU: Totally unaware . . . of what, Heiemon?

HEIEMON: Soon after you left home last year, one rainy night, Father was . . . 250

OKARU: *(Frightened.)* Father was . . . ?

HEIEMON: *(Choked scream.)* . . . struck down by a robber and slain by his sword!

OKARU: *(Falls back slackly.)* That cannot be true.

HEIEMON: You must be strong, Okaru. You look forward to 255 leaving here and being with your husband . . .

OKARU: Yes . . . Kampei . . . what about Kampei?

HEIEMON: Kampei!

OKARU: Kampei . . . ?

HEIEMON: *(A terrible scream.)* Cut open his stomach and is dead! 260

(He mimes the suicide and collapses, weeping. OKARU *falls back, shocked, hardly able to breathe.)*

OKARU: Kampei . . . oh . . . no. What shall I do? What shall I do?

HEIEMON: I know, I know, I know . . .

(They speak alternately, then faster and faster, until they are speaking at the same time. Then their grief-stricken voices fade away. OKARU *crawls to her older brother and puts her head on his lap. She weeps pitiably. At last* HEIEMON *gains control of himself. He gently disengages himself.)*

HEIEMON: Don't you see? Yuranosuke is not a man to be infatuated, and he did not know you were Kampei's wife. Okaru, 265 you were wrong to have read that secret letter. Yuranosuke's loyalty is clear. He cannot risk letting you live and he intends to buy your contract . . . just to kill you! Rather than dying at someone else's hand, let me be the one to take your life. Let me prove to Yuranosuke and his followers that 270 though I am a mere foot soldier, my spirit is as loyal as theirs. Let me serve our late master. Give me your life, dear Sister!

NARRATOR: *(Sings.)* The tragedy is disclosed! Okaru is prepared!

*(*HEIEMON *is agonized by the conflict between his duty to* HANGAN *and his love for* OKARU. *He beseeches her with clasped hands.* OKARU *willingly prepares to sacrifice herself. Gently she opens his hands.)*

OKARU: It is my karma not to meet my beloved husband and 275 father again. There is no reason for me to live.

(She crosses to get the swords, returns, and places them before him.)

Brother dear, please end my life now.

(She turns her back, clasps her hands in prayer, and drops her head forward, exposing her neck to his sword.)

HEIEMON: Admirable resolve. Namu Amida Butsu. Praise Buddha the Merciful.

(He stands. He unsheaths the sword. He raises it to strike. YURA-NOSUKE's voice is heard from behind the curtain.)

280 YURANOSUKE: *(Off.)* Wait, wait! Stop at once! *(He enters.)* Your behavior is admirable, both of you. I acknowledge your loyalty. Heiemon, I hereby permit you to accompany us on our journey to the east.

(HEIEMON and OKARU move right and kneel respectfully. HEIEMON is excited by YURANOSUKE's acceptance of him into the vendetta group.)

HEIEMON: Then you are ready? And I may go with you? Okaru,
285   Sister, do you hear? I am forever grateful.

(HEIEMON bows to YURANOSUKE. YURANOSUKE comes down the steps.)

YURANOSUKE: Okaru, for your loyalty, your husband, Kampei, will be admitted to our league. And since he was unable during his life to kill even a single enemy, let your action, Okaru, serve as his apology to Lord Hangan in the afterlife . . . here
290   and now . . .

(YURANOSUKE takes HEIEMON's long sword and places it in OKARU's hands. He guides her to the veranda. They pose.)

NARRATOR: *(Chants.)* Thrusting deep through the dark of the hiding place. The hateful spy, Kudayū, a fatal blow in his shoulder, rolls and turns in deadly pain!

(They thrust the sword under the veranda. Double tsuke beats. KU-DAYŪ cries out. HEIEMON drags the mortally wounded KUDAYŪ into the garden and throws him to the ground. YURANOSUKE kneels, and holding KUDAYŪ by the scruff of the neck, strikes furiously with closed fan.)

YURANOSUKE: Kudayū, you wretch! Traitor! More than forty of
295   us day and night have shed tears of agony. We have parted from our children, deserted our parents, and sold our wives into prostitution—all in order to avenge our Lord Hangan's death. And you, who enjoyed wealth and honor in his service, have betrayed your master and become Moronao's spy!
300   Fiend! Demon! You are a monster!
NARRATOR: *(Sings.)* As if to grind him into the ground, Yuranosuke . . . his burst of anger cannot be gratified!

(He strikes him five times to sharp tsuke beats. Then contemptuously he pushes him away. Bringing his hand to his eyes, YURANOSUKE openly weeps. Just then the MAIDS cry out offstage. Rapid "Odoriji Aikata." Instantly YURANOSUKE reverts to his pose as a drunken brothel patron. He rises, staggering. The MAIDS enter and kneel in a semicircle in the center room.)

FIRST MAID: Master Yuranosuke, Master Yuranosuke . . .
SECOND MAID: . . . your palanquin has arrived.
305 YURANOSUKE: You've come for me?
ALL: We will see you out.

(YURANOSUKE crosses up the steps and stands at the top. He gestures for OKARU to join him there and for HEIEMON to pick up the nearly dead KUDAYŪ. Music stops.)

YURANOSUKE: Heiemon. Take our drunken friend to the Kamo River. Let him drown his sorrows . . . in the waters there!

(YURANOSUKE flicks open his fan and raises it overhead. OKARU kneels beside YURANOSUKE, placing her hands on his sash. HEIEMON drapes KUDAYŪ's limp body over his shoulder. A single sharp clack of the ki. They freeze in a group mie pose. Ki clacks accelerate, drum beats speed up, and offstage "Odoriji Aikata" crescendoes as the curtain is slowly pushed closed.)

SCENE II
Vendetta

Two sharp ki clacks: large drum softly beats "Yuki Oto" ("Snow Sound"). The ki clacks accelerate to accompany the opening of the curtain. The scene is the garden of MORONAO's mansion in Edo. It is night. Snow is falling. Rocks, trees, ground, and small bridge across a pond are covered with a mantle of white. Soft, rapid tsuke beats. Several WOMEN from MORONAO's household rush on from the left. They are wearing nightclothes. Frightened and confused they urge each other to flee. They disappear. Drum and tsuke beats crescendo. Two RETAINERS with drawn swords rush on from the right. They pose.

MORONAO'S RETAINER: I am Riku Handayū, retainer of Moronao. Name yourself!
HANGAN'S RETAINER: Akagaki Genzō, loyal to Enya Hangan. Let me pass!

(They pose. Another two RETAINERS run on from the left.)

MORONAO'S RETAINER: You will burn in hell before you touch   5
Lord Moronao!
HANGAN'S RETAINER: I, Katayama Genta, will take his head for Lord Hangan! Stand aside!

(Large drum pattern of triple beats, "Mitsudaiko," and loud continuous tsuke beats. The paired opponents fight: they slash and parry with their long swords. In the end HANGAN's men gain the upper hand; MORONAO's men turn and are pursued off stage. Drumming changes to quiet "Snow Sound." SHIMIZU enters on the hanamichi. He is a famous swordsman hired by MORONAO as a bodyguard. A woman's kimono is draped over his head as a disguise, to allow him to reach the side of his master without being detained by HANGAN's men. He stops at the seven-three position.)

SHIMIZU: The war drum. Yuranosuke has come at last. But he will not succeed. The moon shall see the severed heads of   10
forty-seven rōnin before it witnesses the death of Lord Moronao!

(SHIMIZU rushes on stage. He meets TAKEMORI, one of HANGAN's men. They circle each other warily. SHIMIZU's swords are seen.)

TAKEMORI: Stop! Who are you?
SHIMIZU: *(Dropping the kimono to his waist.)* I am Shimizu Ichigaku, protector of Lord Moronao.   15
TAKEMORI: And I am Takemori Kitahachi! I've come for Moronao's head!
SHIMIZU: Then you must take mine first.
TAKEMORI: Come, fight! Fight!

("Mitsudaiko" drumming, loud tsuke beats, and "Chūya Aikata" samisen music accompany the battle. TAKEMORI attacks, rushing past

SHIMIZU. SHIMIZU *throws tiny daggers at* TAKEMORI, *who falls to the ground to evade. One of* HANGAN's *spearmen rushes on from the right, forcing* SHIMIZU *away from* TAKEMORI. SHIMIZU *is attacked from both sides. He slips free and runs onto the bridge over the pond. He is attacked by spear and sword simultaneously.* TAKEMORI *reaches under his guard and stabs* SHIMIZU *in the chest. A second slash, down his back, sends* SHIMIZU *toppling into the water of the pond and out of sight. Drum crescendoes. A loud whistle is heard off left. It signals* MORONAO's *capture.* MORONAO *is dragged on by several of* HANGAN's *men. He is thrown to the ground. He wears nothing except a white sleeping kimono. He is unarmed.* YURANOSUKE, RIKIYA, GOEMON, HEIEMON, *and other* RETAINERS *enter. They surround* MORONAO, *watching him carefully.* YURANOSUKE *kneels beside* MORONAO *politely.)*

20 YURANOSUKE: We allow you to die, Moronao, by your own hand . . . with this blade.

(He unwraps HANGAN's *suicide dagger and respectfully places it before* MORONAO, *offering him the opportunity to die with honor, instead of being killed.* MORONAO *is shaking with fright. He picks up the dagger as if to kill himself, then lunges at* YURANOSUKE. *Seizing* MORONAO's *wrist,* YURANOSUKE *turns the dagger against* MORONAO *and plunges it into his breast.* MORONAO *cries out once, then falls back dead. The* RETAINERS *form a ring around* MORONAO, *hiding him from view.* TAKEMORI *raises his sword and with a single stroke cuts off* MORONAO's *head. Two loud* tsuke *beats. It is wrapped in a white cloth and held high at the end of a spear.* MORONAO *moves offstage unseen behind a black cloth held by a* STAGE ASSISTANT. *The* RETAINERS *rise triumphantly.)*

YURANOSUKE: You have fought bravely, all of you. Your years of hardship, endured without thought of self, have brought success to our cherished plan. What joy Lord Hangan's spirit must feel for your deeds. On his behalf I thank you. 25
GOEMON: And now, let us bring Moronao's head to our master!

(Spoken lightly, the lines are in poetic phrases of seven and five syllables.)

YURANOSUKE: Deep concerns like drifted snow, melt in the clear of day . . .
RIKIYA: . . . at last our long awaited, vengeance is achieved . . . 30
GOEMON: . . . together with the clearing, of the morning clouds . . .
AGAKI: . . . at the cock's crow announcing, dawn of a new day . . .
TAKEMORI: . . . our hearts filled to overflowing, rise with the 35
rising sun . . .
GOEMON: . . . as we go together to . . .
ALL: . . . our Lord Hangan's grave.
YURANOSUKE: Shout victory together! Victory!

(Single ki *clack: offstage drum and samisen play "Taka no Hara" ("Hawk Plain") slowly, gradually accelerating until the scene is over. Each person turns to those next to him, nods, wipes tears of gratitude, grips an elbow, or places a hand on a shoulder. Then their thoughts return to their master,* HANGAN, *and all of them stand silent, posed in mingled happiness and grief. The curtain closes to rapidly accelerating* ki *clacks. The offstage musicians play "Shagiri" indicating the play is over.)*

CRITICAL CONTEXTS

Although in many respects Zeami's critical writings describe the esthetics of Noh drama, Zeami was necessarily concerned with the practical training of his performers. In this essay, he treats the lifelong discipline of the classical Noh actor.

In searching for the origins of *sarugaku* and *ennen*, some say they came from India, and some say they have been handed down since the age of the gods. Yet as time moves on and those ages grow remote, any proper skill is lacking to learn the ancient ways precisely. The origin of the *nō*, which all enjoy today, goes back to the reign of the Empress Suiko, when Prince Shōtoku commanded Hata no Kōkatsu (some say for the sake of peace in the country, some say to entertain the people) to create sixty-six public entertainments, which were named *sarugaku*. From that time onward, men in every age must have used images of the beauties of nature as a means to render this entertainment more elegant. Later, the descendants of Kōkatsu inherited this art and served at the Kasuga and Hie shrines.[1] This is why, even now, those performers from Yamato and Ōmi perform rites at both temples, which are still flourishing. Therefore, while studying the old and admiring the new, the great traditions of elegance must never be slighted. A truly skillful player is one whose speech lacks no refinement and whose appearance creates a feeling of Grace. One who wishes to follow the path of the *nō* must engage himself in no other art. There is one exception: the art of poetry deserves study, for it is a means to open the actor to the profound beauties of nature and enrich his life. I will note here in general various things I have seen and heard since my youth concerning the practice of the *nō*.

—Sensual pleasures, gambling, heavy drinking represent the Three Prohibitions. Such was the precept of my late father.

—Rehearse with the greatest effort; do not be overbearing with others.

AGE SEVEN. It may be said of our art that one may begin at seven.[2] When a boy practices at this age, he will naturally of his own accord show some elements of beauty in what he does. If, by chance, he should show some special skill in dancing, movement, chanting, or in the kind of powerful gestures required for demon roles, he should be left free to perform them in his own manner, according to his own desires. He should certainly not be instructed as to what he did well and what he did poorly. If rehearsals are too strict, and if the child is admonished too much, he will lose his enthusiasm. If the *nō* becomes unpleasant for him, then his progress will cease. He should only be taught dancing, movement, and the chant. In particular, he should not be instructed in the fine points of Role Playing, even though he may show aptitude for it. He must not be permitted to perform in a *waki sarugaku*, especially on an open stage. Let him perform at a time that seems

ZEAMI
MOTOKIYO
(1363–1444)

from "Teachings
on Style and
the Flower"
(1402)
TRANSLATED BY
J. THOMAS RIMER AND
YAMAZAKI MASAKAZU

ITEMS CONCERNING
THE PRACTICE
OF THE NŌ IN
RELATION TO THE
AGE OF THE ACTOR

---

[1]The Yamato *sarugaku* troupe had an official affiliation with the Kasuga Shrine in Nara. A series of *nō* performances was included in the important Wakamiya festival held there. The Ōmi troupe had official ties with the Hie Shrine on Mount Hiei, to the north of Kyoto, the site of the great Buddhist temple complex of Enryakuji.

[2]Traditionally, ages were calculated so that a person was considered one year old at birth and two at the beginning of the next calendar year. Thus the ages given here are higher than would have been assigned to a Western actor at the same stage of development. Thus Zeami's actor at the age of seventeen or eighteen would probably be, by Western reckoning, between fourteen and sixteen.

appropriate, in the third or fourth play in the day's program, when he can be given a part he can perform with skill.

AGE OF ELEVEN OR TWELVE.   From this age onward, the voice begins to achieve its proper pitch, and the actor can begin to comprehend the *nō*. Therefore, various aspects of the art can now be explained. In the first place, a boy's appearance, no matter in what aspect, will produce the sensation of Grace. And his voice at this age will always sound charming as well. Because of those two strong points, any defects can be hidden and the good points will be made all the more evident. On the whole, it is better not to teach any fine points concerning Role Playing for a child's performance, for such knowledge would make his performances at this stage seem inappropriate and, in fact, hinder further progress in his art. Later, as he becomes more skillful, he should be allowed to practice every element of the art. With the appearance and voice of a child, a boy actor, if he shows skill in his performance, can hardly give a bad impression. Still, this Flower is not the true Flower. It is only a temporary bloom. For that reason, practice at this time is easily managed. This does not mean that, because of this one flowering, he will always appear to be so skillful. As rehearsal at this age will always allow the young actor to create the impression of the Flower through his good points, the development of his basic skills is crucial. His movements must be authentic, the words of his chanting distinct, and his positions for dancing must be well fixed. These skills must be carefully and thoroughly rehearsed.

FROM THE AGE OF SEVENTEEN OR EIGHTEEN.   This is a particularly crucial period, and not too many kinds of training can be arranged. First of all, since the actor's voice is changing, he loses his first Flower. His physical figure changes as well, and his movements become awkward. Before, his voice was full and beautiful, and it was easy for him to perform; now, realizing that the rules have changed, the actor's will falters. What is more, since the audience may look scornfully at his performance, he now feels embarrassed and discouraged. As concerns training, then, at this age, the actor, even though there are those who may point to him and laugh, must take no note, but retire to his own house, and, in a pitch comfortable to him, practice his chanting, using appropriate techniques for morning and evening.[3] Most important of all, he must vow to himself that, although he is now in a crucial period, he will truly stake his life on the *nō* and never abandon it. Should any actor give up his training at this point, his skill can never increase. In general, although the pitch of the individual voice at this age may vary, it usually lies between the *ōshiki* and the *banshiki*.[4] If the actor tries to regulate the pitch too strictly [by forcing], he risks getting into bad habits with his posture. Then too, this may be the cause of damage to the actor's voice in later life.

FROM TWENTY-FOUR OR TWENTY-FIVE.   It is in this period that the level of artistry of the performer begins to become established. The limits of the actor will be fixed by his training and his self-discipline. His voice will by now have settled, and his body will have matured. These are the strong points required in our art: voice and physical appearance. Both of these become fixed at this period. This is the time in an actor's life when the art is born that will lead to the skills of his later years. In the eyes of others, it may well

[3]Zeami's remark suggests that a certain caution must be used when exercising the voice in the morning, whereas in the evening the voice is freer and can thus be exercised more vigorously.

[4]*Ōshiki* and *banshiki* are two of the twelve pitches in the traditional Japanese musical scales. *Ōshiki* is considered to correspond roughly to the pitch A in the Western musical scale, *banshiki* to B.

appear that a new and highly skilled performer has appeared. Therefore, even though he is being judged against a performer who is already highly regarded, it may seem on the occasion of his performance that his Flower is a new and fresh one, and, should he win a competition, others may praise him beyond his due, so that the actor himself comes to believe that he is already highly skilled. I cannot stress often enough that such an attitude serves as an enemy to the actor. For such is not the true Flower. A truly novel Flower comes about because of the actor's age and experience, when his spectators can truly be surprised. Spectators of real discernment are able to make this distinction. It would indeed be a shame if this early Flower, which actually represents only the actor's first level of accomplishment, should somehow be fixed in the actor's thoughts, so that he sees this phase as the culmination of his art, and therefore indulges himself in what is a deviation from the true path. Actually, even if an actor is praised by his audience and manages to win a competition over a famous performer, he must take cognizance of the fact that his Flower is merely a temporary one; therefore, he will begin at once to study Role Playing with the utmost seriousness and will ask every detail of those who have already achieved a real reputation for their performances, so that he may rehearse all the more diligently. One who believes that this temporary Flower is the real Flower is one who has separated himself from the true way. And indeed, any performer can be taken in by this temporary Flower and so fail to realize that he is losing the real one. Such is the situation of a young actor.

Here is one point that must be considered carefully. If one has a true ability to understand his own level of perfection in his art, then he can never lose that level of the Flower. If an actor thinks he has attained a higher level of skill than he has reached, however, he will lose even the level that he has achieved. This matter must be thought over carefully.

THIRTY-FOUR OR THIRTY-FIVE YEARS.   This age represents the peak of perfection in our art. If an actor grasps the various items set down here, and masters them, he will truly be acknowledged by the public and will achieve a reputation as a great actor. If such public recognition does not come, however, and he does not obtain such a reputation, then no matter how skillful the actor may be, he must recognize the fact that he is not one who has yet found the true Flower. And if he has not obtained such a Flower by this time, his art will begin to decline when he is forty. The proof of this fact will become clear as the actor grows older. An actor is on the rise until he is thirty-four or thirty-five, and he begins to decline after forty. This fact cannot be repeated too often—those who do not achieve a reputation at this stage of their career have not actually mastered the art of the *nō*. Therefore it is in this period that the actor must perfect his self-discipline. At this time in his career, he can recall all that he has learned: it is also the moment when he is able to plan for the means to accomplish what he wishes to in the future. If such things are not mastered at this age, then, let me repeat again, it will be difficult for an actor to find success with audiences later in his career.

FORTY-FOUR, FORTY-FIVE YEARS.   From this point on, the actor must find new means of showing his skills. Even if he has achieved a fine reputation and has mastered the art of the *nō,* he must be able in turn to have in his troupe young actors who will follow him. Although his real art may not decline, yet, as his years advance, his physical presence and the beauty others find in him will be diminished. Leaving aside the exceptionally handsome performer, even a fairly good-looking actor, as he grows older, should no longer be seen playing roles that do not require a mask. Thus this former aspect of his art will now be lacking. From this point onward, it is best not to perform elaborate parts. On the whole, an actor should choose roles that are congenial to him and that can be played in a relaxed manner without physical strain. He should allow the younger actors to show off their own abilities, and he should play with them in a modest fashion, as an associate. Even if he has no young successor of a suitable caliber, an actor should not himself perform any highly complicated and strenuous roles. In any case, the audience will find no Flower in this sort of performance. If, on the other hand, an actor has not lost his Flower by this age, then it will remain truly his possession. If an actor still possesses his Flower as he approaches fifty, then he must have achieved a real reputation before the age of forty. Even an actor who has gained such a reputation however, if he is truly a master, must most of all know himself, and, therefore, work to give the young actors proper training; he will exert himself to the utmost, without performing roles that may betray his own weaknesses. One who truly knows how to see and reflect upon himself—it is he who has really grasped the nature of our art.

FIFTY YEARS OLD AND LATER. From this point onward, for the most part, there is little more that can be done. There is a saying that "even *Ch'i lin,* when old, is worse than a worn out packhorse."[5] Nevertheless, an actor who has truly mastered his art, even though he has lost his ability to perform many of his roles, and although he may manifest less and less of his art in performance, will still have something of his Flower left about him.

My late father died at the age of fifty-two on the nineteenth day of the fifth month [of 1384], and on the fourth day of that same month, he performed the *nō* in connection with religious services at the Sengen shrine in the province of Suruga.[6] The performances that day were particularly colorful, and all the spectators, high-ranking and commoner alike, praised his performances. At that time the various plays were given over to the younger actors, and he performed a few easy roles in a modest way. Yet the beauty of his Flower was all the more striking. For when an artist has achieved a real Flower, then the art of the *nō*, even if the foliage is slight and the tree grows old, still retains its blooms. This is the very proof that, even in an ancient frame, the Flower remains.

What has been written above constitutes the appropriate stages of *nō* training at various ages.

VARIOUS ITEMS CONCERNING ROLE PLAYING

It would be impossible to describe in writing all the various aspects of Role Playing. Yet as this skill forms the fundamental basis of our art, various roles must be studied with the greatest care. In general, Role Playing involves an imitation, in every particular, with nothing left out. Still, depending on the circumstances, one must know how to vary the degree of imitation involved. For example, when it comes to playing the part of a ruler or a high official, it is extremely difficult to perform with the necessary detail, since the actor cannot know the real way of life of the court nobility, or the bearing appropriate to a great lord. Still, he can study carefully their way of speaking, observe their circumstances, and ask the opinion of those noblemen who watch the performances. Next, he must imitate down to the smallest detail the various things done by persons of high profession, especially those elements related to high artistic pursuits. On the other hand, when it comes to imitating laborers and rustics, their commonplace actions should not be copied too realistically. In the case of woodcutters, grass cutters, charcoal burners, and salt workers, however, they should be imitated in detail insofar as they have traditionally been found congenial as poetic subjects. In general, men of lowly occupation should not

---

[5]*Ch'i-lin* (*kirin* in Japanese) famous in ancient Chinese historical chronicles was, rather like the Greek Pegasus, a horse with the miraculous ability to travel enormous distances very quickly.

[6]Generally identified as the Sengen Shrine in the present city of Shizuoka, a little over a hundred miles south of Tokyo.

be imitated in any meticulous fashion, nor shown to men of refined taste. Should they see such things, they will merely find them vulgar, and the performance will hold no attraction for them. The need for prudence in this matter can be fully understood. Thus the degree of imitation must vary, depending on the kind of role being performed.

WOMEN'S ROLES.   In general, a young *shite* is the most suitable actor to play the part of a woman. Nevertheless, playing such a part represents a considerable undertaking. If the actor's style of dress is unseemly, there will be nothing worth watching in the performance. When it comes to impersonating high-ranking women of the court, such as ladies-in-waiting, for example, since the actor cannot easily view their actual deportment, he must make serious, detailed inquiries concerning such matters. As for items of clothing such as the *kinu* and the *hakama,* these too cannot merely be chosen on the basis of the actor's personal preference. The actor must make a proper investigation concerning what is correct. When it comes to impersonating an ordinary woman, however, the actor will be familiar with the appropriate details, and so the task will not be difficult. If the actor dresses in an appropriate *kinu* or *kosode,* that will doubtless suffice. When performing *kusemai, shirabyōshi,* or mad women's roles, the actor should hold a fan or a sprig of flowers, for example, loosely in his hand in order to represent female gentleness. The *kinu* and the *hakama,* as well, should be long enough to conceal his steps, his hips and knees should be straight, and his bodily posture pliable. As for his head posture, if he bends backward, his face will appear coarse. If the actor looks down, on the other hand, his appearance from the back will be unseemly. Then too, if he holds his neck too stiffly, he will not look feminine. He should certainly wear a robe with long sleeves, and he should avoid showing the tips of his hands. His *obi* should be loosely tied. The fact that an actor takes great care with his costume means that he is truly anxious to perform his role as well as possible. No matter what the role, bad costuming will never be effective, and, in the case of a woman's role, proper dressing is essential.

OLD MEN.   Playing the role of an old man represents the very pinnacle of our art. These roles are crucial, since the spectators who watch can gauge immediately the real skills of the actor. There are many *shite* who have mastered the art of *nō* quite well, but who cannot achieve the appearance of an old man. When an actor plays a woodcutter, salt scooper, or a similar part that contains conspicuous gestures, it is easy enough for the spectators to be deceived and to make a false judgment too quickly concerning the performer's talents. But to play the part of an old man of high rank whose gestures involve no characteristic movement is truly difficult and requires the skills of a master actor. Unless an actor rehearses over the years until his art is at its peak, he cannot properly present this kind of role. Without a proper Flower, such a restrained performance can have nothing of interest about it.

In terms of stage deportment, most actors, thinking to appear old, bend their loins and hips, shrink their bodies, lose their Flower, and give withered, uninteresting performances. Thus there is little that is attractive in what such actors do. It is particularly important that the actor refrain from performing in a limp or weak manner, but bear himself with grace and dignity. Most crucial of all is the dancing posture chosen for the role of an old man. One must study assiduously the precept: portray an old man while still possessing the Flower. The results should resemble an old tree that puts forth flowers.

PERFORMING WITHOUT A MASK.   This too represents an important aspect of our art. As such roles are those representing ordinary persons, they may seem to be easy to perform, but, surprisingly, unless the highest level of skill in the *nō* is used, such a performance will not be worth watching. The actor must of necessity study the object of each role individually [since the face is visible]. Although it is not possible to imitate any particular individual countenance in performance, actors sometimes alter their own ordinary facial expressions in an attempt to create some particular effect. The results are always without interest. The performance should rather be constructed from the movements and general feeling of the person being portrayed. The actor must always use his own natural facial expressions and never try to alter them.

ROLES OF MAD PERSONS.   This skill represents the most fascinating aspect of our art. In this category there are many types of roles, and an actor who has truly taken up this specialty can play successfully all types of roles. I must repeat again and again that an actor must fully commit himself to rehearse and practice continuously, as I have admonished. In general, there are various types of possessed beings; for example, those inhabited by the curse of a god, a Buddha, the spirit of a living person, or of a dead person. Therefore, if the actor studies the nature of the spirit who possesses the character, he should be able to manage the part well. On the other hand, the really difficult parts involve those characters whose thoughts have become confused because their minds have become crazed—a parent searching for a lost child, for example, a wife thrown over by her husband, or a husband who lives on after his wife. Even a relatively skillful *shite* may fail to make the distinction between them, and he will create his mad gestures in the same manner, so that no emotional response is engendered in those who watch him. In the case of characters of this sort, the actor must have as his intention the manifestation of the precise feelings that can indicate the character's emotional disturbance, and make them the core of his Flower; then, if he feigns madness with all the skill he has at his command, there will certainly be many arresting elements in his performance. If an actor possesses this kind of skill, and if he can make his spectators weep, his art will represent the highest attainment possible. Reflect as fully as possible on what I have written above.

It goes without saying that a costume appropriate for the role of a mad person is essential. Still, as the character is a mad person, the costume might, depending on the occasion, be more gaudy than usual. The actor can carry in his hand a sprig of flowers appropriate to the season.

Then again, while I have spoken in terms of acting that imitates surface realities, there is another point that must be seriously considered. Although I said that the madness of the character must be performed in terms of the being who possesses that character, when it comes to playing a madwoman possessed by a warrior or a demon, for example, the circumstances are made quite difficult for the actor. Thinking to act out the true nature of the being who possesses such a character, the actor will show masculine wrath while playing a woman, and his performance will seem quite inappropriate. On the other hand, if the actor concentrates on the womanly traits of his character, there will be no logic to the possession. Similarly, when a male character is possessed by a woman, the same difficulty arises. In sum, to avoid plays with such characters represents an important secret of our art. Those who compose such texts simply do not understand the nature of our art. A writer who truly understands the art of *nō* would never compose a text that showed such a lack of harmony. To possess this truth is another secret of our art.

When it comes to playing the role of a mad person without a mask, the performance will not be complete unless the actor has truly mastered his art. For, if the expressions on the actor's face are not properly descriptive, there will be no sense of madness conveyed. If the actor changes his face without a profound understanding of his art, on the other hand, the results will be merely ugly. The deepest arts of Role Playing are required for these paradoxical circumstances.

Thus, in important performances, inexperienced actors must participate with the greatest caution. Playing without a mask is very difficult. Acting a mad role is also very difficult. To combine these two elements into one: how difficult indeed to elevate such a role to the level of the Flower. Rehearsal and study are the only methods possible.

ROLES OF BUDDHIST PRIESTS.   Although such roles exist, they are few in number and do not require so much practice. In general, when playing a gorgeously robed cleric or a priest of high rank, the actor must use the majesty and dignity of the character as the basis for his performance. When it comes to lesser-ranking priests, such as those who have abandoned the world and practice austerities, their religious pilgrimage is of paramount importance to them, and so it is crucial for the actor to create the impression that such characters are absorbed in their religious devotions. In the end, when it comes to the materials on which to build a performance, more pains may be required than might be expected.

SHURA.   Here is still another type of role. Such dead warrior roles, even when well performed, are seldom arresting. Thus they should not be performed too often. Nevertheless, when it comes to events dealing with the famous Genji or Heike warriors,[7] if the various elements are knit together with suitable elegance, so that the text is a good one, such a performance can be more moving than one of any other variety. In such plays, some spectacular moment is particularly important. The wildness of the *shura* style may well lead to the kind of behavior appropriate to a demon role. Then again, such a role risks turning entirely into a dance performance. If there is a section in the play that resembles *kusemai,* it is allowable to include some appropriate dancelike gestures. As it is customary for the actor to carry with him a bow and quiver and to wear some variety of sword, the performer should undertake a careful study of how to carry and use such objects, making efforts to exhibit the essence of this type of role. The actor must take special care to avoid both those movements appropriate to a demon role on the one hand, and the use of purely dancelike motions on the other.

ROLES OF GODS.   In general, this kind of Role Playing is related to that appropriate for the demon roles. As the appearance of such a figure is always fierce, no particular difficulties are created by playing the part in the manner of a demon, depending, of course, on the role of the god involved. However, there is one essential difference between the two types of characters. Dancelike gestures are the most appropriate for the role of a god, but they are not suitable for a demon role. Particularly in the case of a god role, the only means available to the actor to represent such a being lies in his being properly dressed, and therefore he must give particular attention to the creation of a properly noble appearance. The actor must decorate his costume correctly and adjust his clothing in an appropriate manner.

DEMON ROLES.   These roles are a particular specialty of the Yamato school. They are extremely difficult to perform successfully. True, it is simple to play effectively the demon roles of vengeful ghosts or possessed beings, as they offer visible elements of interest that can make them arresting. The performer, directing himself toward his acting partner, should use small foot and hand motions and make his movements in accordance with the

---

[7]The Genji and Heike clans were the chief rivals in the disastrous civil wars of 1185 that brought an end to the political domination by the Kyoto court. Many importnant *nō* texts by Zeami dealt with characters and incidents from those battles.

effect created by his headgear. In the case of a real demon from hell, however, even if the actor studies well, his performance is likely to be merely frightening. There are no real means to make such roles truly enjoyable for the spectators. In fact, these are such difficult roles to play that there are few actors who can perform them in an effective way, it seems.

The essence of such roles lies in forcefulness and frightfulness. Yet such qualities do not stimulate feelings of enjoyment. For this reason, the role of a demon is particularly difficult to play. Logically, the harder the actor tries to perform them, the less interesting they become. The essence of such a role is frightfulness, yet the qualities of frightfulness and enjoyment are as different as black and white. Thus, it might be said that an actor who can perform such a role in an enjoyable way would indeed be a performer of the highest talent. Indeed, an actor who strives for nothing but to play demon roles well can never really attain the Flower. Therefore, a performance by a young actor, even if it seems well done, will not really be effective. Is it not then true that an actor who only strives to play demon roles well can never actually perform them well? This paradox must be carefully studied. For the interest the spectator finds in the performance of a demon role is like a flower blooming among the rocks.

CHINESE ROLES.   As these are special kinds of characters, there is no fixed form of practice for the actor. The element of appearance is essential. In choosing a mask—even though the character is of course a human being just like anyone else—it is best for the actor to wear something with an unusual appearance so as to maintain the effect of something somehow out of the ordinary.

Such parts are effectively played by older artists with talent and experience. Still, other than costuming, there are no special techniques required. In any case, since any attempt to imitate the Chinese style directly, either in chant or in movement, will not in itself be effective, it is better to add just one representative element to an ordinary performance. The selection of just such an element, slight in itself, can serve as a means to animate the whole. Although usually such changes are not considered appropriate, there is no way truly to copy the style, and so such a slight change in gesture will add something of the Chinese flavor and can give the spectators an appropriate sensation. Such methods have been practiced for a long time.

In general, such are the various elements of Role Playing. It is difficult to express any finer details in writing. Nevertheless, an actor who has fully grasped the points enumerated above will be able by himself to grasp them.

✠ ✠ ✠

THE FIFTEENTH, SIXTEENTH, AND SEVENTEENTH CENTURIES SAW EUROPE TRANS-formed by the extraordinary cultural revolution we now call the European Renaissance. Fueled by new technology, like printing, and by new scientific, political, and religious ideas, explosive change transformed European culture. The known world expanded beyond the sea to embrace the New World; the recovery of Greek and Latin literature spurred a sweeping intellectual revolution; strong centralized monarchies in Spain, Portugal, France, and England created new empires abroad and fought to control an increasingly restive populace at home; the Protestant Reformation undermined the religious and political authority of the Catholic church, beginning a period of violent religious conflict; the "new philosophy"—modern science—of Copernicus, Bacon, and Galileo seemed to put even the physical world of heaven and earth in doubt. "'Tis all in pieces, all coherence gone," the poet John Donne wrote in 1611, voicing the profound anxiety and exhilaration of many of his contemporaries: "Prince, subject, father, son are things forgot. / For every man alone thinks that he hath got / To be a Phoenix." The changing tides of thought swept away the crumbling edifice of the medieval world—the feudal state, the universal church, scholastic philosophy, an ordered heaven, and revealed truth—and opened the way for the modern world.

This revolution also infused the theater; the Renaissance—especially in Italy, France, Spain, and England—is one of the great ages of theatrical and dramatic achievement. In England, the professional theater as we know it originated at this time: the history of the secular, profit-making, commercial theater is conventionally dated from the opening of the first theater building, The Theatre, in London in 1576. Licensed and protected as an aristocratic entertainment, the theater was also a popular institution in which commoners such as William Shakespeare, Richard Burbage, Edward Alleyn, Inigo Jones, and others, could indeed rise like the phoenix. However, to understand the revolutionary impact of theater and drama in Shakespeare's era, we need to understand their conservative inheritance, their deep indebtedness to the medieval stage that preceded them.

DRAMA AND THEATER IN MEDIEVAL ENGLAND

Dramatic performance in medieval Europe was thoroughly conditioned by the Catholic church's central role in the life of the community. Having closed the Roman theaters in the sixth century, the church maintained a vigilant opposition to the secular theater and the vices associated with it. Yet the revival of theater in Europe, beginning in the tenth century, was inspired and sponsored by the church itself. The four major dramatic forms in the late Middle Ages were connected with the church, its rituals, and its calendar of religious observances: LITURGICAL DRAMA enacted as part of the liturgy of the Catholic Mass; CYCLE PLAYS, illustrating scriptural history and performed by craft guilds on the feast of Corpus Christi; MORALITY DRAMA, enacting the symbolic structure of Christian life; and plays written and performed in schools and universities, sometimes imitating classical plays. In England, cycle and morality plays particularly influenced the later, secular drama of the sixteenth century.

LITURGICAL DRAMA

The earliest dramatic records, dating from the ninth century, are musical TROPES, brief elaborations of the authorized liturgy, written to amplify the scriptural text and enhance its impact and appeal. These compositions were set to music and sung in ANTIPHONAL PERFORMANCE (back and forth, in dialogue) between monks or boy choristers to accompany the liturgy of the Mass. In England, Ethelwold, Bishop of Winchester wrote a series of lessons concerning the conduct of the Mass, the *Regularis Concordia* (965–975), including instructions for such performances. What follows are his instructions to the priests for representing the visit of the three Marys to the tomb of Christ after the Crucifixion (translated from Latin). This trope is often called the *Quem Quaeritis,* after the Latin text spoken by the "angel," "Whom seek you?":

> While the third lesson is being chanted, let four brethren vest themselves; of whom, let one, vested in an alb, enter as if to take part in the service, and let him without being observed approach the place of the sepulchre [i.e., near the altar], and there, holding a palm in his hand, let him sit down quietly. While the third responsory is being sung, let the remaining three follow, all of them vested in copes, and carrying in their hands censers filled with incense; and slowly, in the manner of seeking something, let them come before the place of the sepulchre. These things are done in imitation of the angel seated in the monument, and of the women coming with spices to anoint the body of Jesus. When therefore that one seated shall see the three, as if straying about and seeking something, approach him, let him begin in a dulcet voice of medium pitch to sing:
>
> > *Whom seek ye in the sepulchre, O followers of Christ?*
>
> When he has sung this to the end, let the three respond in unison:
>
> > *Jesus of Nazareth, which was crucified, O celestial one.*
>
> To whom that one:
>
> > *He is not here; he is risen; just as he foretold.*
> > *Go, announce that he is risen from the dead.*
>
> At the word of this command let those three turn themselves to the choir, saying:
>
> > *Alleluia! The Lord is risen to-day.*
> > *The strong lion, the Christ, the Son of God. Give thanks to God.*
>
> This said, let the former, again seating himself, as if recalling them, sing the anthem:
>
> > *Come, and see the place where the Lord was laid. Alleluia! Alleluia!*
>
> And saying this, let him rise and let him lift the veil and show them the place bare of the cross, but only the cloths laid there with which the cross was wrapped. Seeing which, let them set down the censers which they carried into the same sepulchre, and let them take up the cloth and spread it out before the eyes of the clergy; and as if making known that the Lord had risen and was not now therein wrapped, let them sing this anthem:
>
> > *The Lord is risen from the sepulchre.*
> > *Who for us hung upon the cross.*
>
> And let them place the cloth upon the altar. The anthem being ended, let the Prior, rejoicing with them at the triumph of our King, in that, having conquered death, he arose, begin the hymn:
>
> > *We praise thee, O God.*
>
> This begun, all the bells chime out together.[1]

Despite its brevity, and the limitations imposed by the liturgy itself, this trope has the elements of drama: a progressive plot, the involvement of specific characters, conflict and resolution. Ethelwold's "stage directions" convey a subtle sense of how character can be created

---

[1] *Regularis Concordia,* in *Chief Pre-Shakespearean Dramas,* ed. Joseph Quincy Adams (Boston: Houghton Mifflin, 1924), 9–10.

by performance and a fine sense of visual spectacle as well, all within the narrow scope allowed by the Mass.

Throughout the Middle Ages and beyond, liturgical plays of this kind became increasingly common and complex. Enacted in different locations—called MANSIONS—within the church, liturgical drama provided a model for the forms of religious drama that came to be performed outside the church and outside the framework of the liturgy. In the tenth and eleventh centuries, the church sponsored dramatized scenes from the life of Christ or the lives of the saints, staged on important Christian holidays. A town, for example, might commemorate the entrance of Christ into Jerusalem on Palm Sunday with a procession to the cathedral in which townspeople enacted various roles. In addition, the church oversaw the production of cycles of plays, which became a principal mode of theatrical and dramatic innovation. These cycles were performed sixty days after Easter as part of the feast of Corpus Christi, a holiday inaugurated in the fourteenth century to celebrate the doctrine of the Eucharist. The Corpus Christi festival frequently featured the performance of a series of plays dramatizing scriptural history—the Creation, Old Testament events (Noah and the Flood, Abraham and Isaac), scenes from the New Testament (the Annunciation, Herod and the Slaughter of the Innocents), and prophetic plays concerning the Harrowing of Hell and the Last Judgment. The production of these plays could last several days or weeks and called on the services of the entire town. Each craft guild (or *mystery,* as the guilds were called; the cycles are sometimes called MYSTERY CYCLES) financed and produced a different play, often on a subject appropriate to the guild. The shipwrights' guild might undertake the Noah play, the Three Kings play might be assigned to the goldsmiths, and so on. The plays were the property of the guilds and passed through generations of guild members. In major towns with many craft guilds, the cycles often included a large number of plays. Of the English cycles, the York cycle is the longest, containing forty-eight plays, the Wakefield cycle has thirty-two, and the Chester cycle has twenty-four.

Although they were produced for a popular, largely illiterate audience, the cycle dramas are extremely sophisticated and involved the talents of trained performers. One of the cycles' most powerful and typical features is their use of ANACHRONISM—the blending of the historical past with contemporary events and characters. Many of the characters who appear in the plays are medieval English peasants, who often display an ironic, even theatrical sense of their involvement in the scriptural events of the past. One of the most telling uses of this technique occurs in the York *Crucifixion,* for one of the ways that the York playwright conveys the Roman soldiers' hardness to the message of Christ is by making them jest with him about the crucifixion they are performing:

> 1 SOLDIER: *(To* CHRIST.) Say, Sir, how likes you now
>   This work that we have wrought?
> 2 SOLDIER: We pray you say us how
>   Ye feel, or faint ye aught.
> JESUS: . . . My Father, that all bales [evils] may beet [abate].
>   Forgive these men that do me pine [pain].
>   What they work wot [know] they nought;
>   Therefore, my Father, I crave,
>   Let never their sins be sought,
>   But see their souls to save.
> 1 SOLDIER: We! Hark! he jangles like a jay.

By characterizing the jesting Roman soldiers as, in effect, contemporaries of the medieval audience, the play implies that biblical events are part of the audience's contemporary history. Seeing their neighbors enacting the biblical scenes, and seeing contemporary characters

CYCLE DRAMA

MEDIEVAL PAGEANT WAGON

One actor is playing in the street in front of the wagon.

share the stage with biblical figures, must have emphasized the immediacy of the ongoing Christian story.

MORALITY DRAMA   Like the cycle plays, morality plays dramatized elements of Christian life. Instead of staging events from scriptural history, morality drama stages a symbolic **ALLEGORY** of the Christian's spiritual journey through life. Increasingly popular throughout the fourteenth and fifteenth centuries, plays like *The Castle of Perseverance* (c. 1425), *Mankind* (c. 1470), and *Everyman*

(c. 1500) emphasized the individual's struggle with sin, while the cycle plays emphasized the larger patterns of Christian history. Later playwrights, including Shakespeare, found both models useful. The cycles provided a pattern for staging the epic sweep of secular English history, and morality drama provided a supple device for representing psychological and moral conflict. Morality plays often provided the structure for the secular plays written at schools and universities, as well, and for the INTERLUDES performed at court as a break from holiday feasting. They also provided a staple technique for characterization in the later secular drama. Christopher Marlowe's *Doctor Faustus* (1590) uses the Good and Evil Angels to externalize Faustus's moral conflict, and other playwrights frequently used the devices of morality drama to dramatize the difficulties of political choice. In John Skelton's interlude, *Magnificence* (1516) written for Henry VIII or Thomas Sackville and Thomas Norton's *Gorboduc* (1561), the monarch is shown to make his decisions framed by a host of allegorized counsellors, good and bad advisers who approximate the role played in morality drama by angels and demons.

Medieval plays were often acted on or near PAGEANT WAGONS. In some towns, it appears that the audience remained stationary at various locations, while the wagons and their plays proceeded past them; at others, the wagons were drawn in a procession of *TABLEAUX VIVANTS* (posed scenes) through the town and then arranged in an open area for the performance, allowing the audience to move from play to play. In Chester, for example, a list survives of the stations where the plays were performed, and for York it is possible to trace the route of the pageant wagons through the city. Given the size and complexity of these performances, it's not surprising to find that they were not easily performed on one day: the procession took three days at Chester, and began at 4:30 A.M. in York, lasting until past midnight. The plays combined historical and contemporary elements; in performance, the staging produced a close and powerful relationship between the dramatic characters and the audience. In the Coventry play of the Magi, for example, Herod raves when he discovers that the three kings have escaped him:

> I Stamp! I Stare! I look all about!
> Might I them take, I should them burn at a glede [fire]!
> I rant! I run! and now run I wode [mad]
> A! That these villain traitors hath marred this my mood!
> They shall be hanged, if I may come them to!

> (*Here Herod rages in the pagond* [pageant wagon] *and in the street also.*)[2]

Herod's rage was certainly one of the highlights of the medieval cycles. Shakespeare, at least, seems to refer to it in *Hamlet* (1600), when he has Hamlet remind his actors that they should be restrained and natural in their performance, for overacting "out-Herods Herod." The stage direction also suggests that Herod's frenzy carried him from the wagon and into the street, into a closer and more effective relationship to his audience. This interaction between actor and audience is characteristic of popular theater and is a feature of medieval performance carried into Renaissance acting. It also suggests that the "place" of medieval drama, the fictitious locale of the play, was not firmly localized onstage; the actors/characters could move easily back and forth between Herod's Jerusalem and the medieval audience, and even onstage places could be rapidly and easily transformed. This flexibility also allowed medieval playwrights to treat stage space symbolically. The ground plot for *The Castle of Perseverance,* for instance—with its scaffolds for various evils, its moat, and its central castle—clearly offers us a symbolic locale rather than an actual geography. The various demons on their scaffolds stand at a symbolic distance, not an actual distance, from the central castle.

STAGING
MEDIEVAL
DRAMA

---

[2]The Coventry *Magi, Herod, and the Slaughter of the Innocents,* in *Chief Pre-Shakespearean Dramas,* ed. Joseph Quincy Adams (Boston: Houghton Mifflin, 1924), 163.

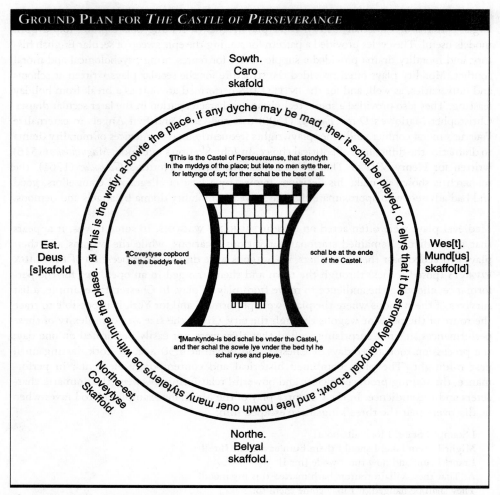

GROUND PLAN FOR *THE CASTLE OF PERSEVERANCE*

Sowth.
Caro
skafold

This is the watyr a-bowte the place, if any dyche may be mad, ther it schal be pleyed, or ellys that it be strongely barryd al a-bowt; and lete nowth over many styteleys be with-inne the plase.

¶This is the Castel of Perseueraunse, that stondyth
In the myddys of the place; but lete no men sytte ther,
for lettynge of syt; for ther schal be the best of all.

Est.
Deus
[s]kafold

¶Coveytyse copbord
be the beddys feet

schal be at the ende
of the Castel.

Wes[t].
Mund[us]
skaffo[ld]

¶Mankynde-is bed schal be vnder the Castel,
and ther schal the sowle lye vnder the bed tyl he
schal ryse and pleye.

Northe-est.
Coveytyse
Skaffold.

Northe.
Belyal
skaffold.

The ground-plot for the medieval morality play shows five scaffolds (North, Northeast, South, East, and West) arranged around a playing area, with a castle in the center. A ditch enclosed the castle to keep spectators at a distance. In the manuscript, a note beneath the drawing describes the costumes and special effects: "He that shall play Belial (a devil), look that he have gunpowder burning in pipes in his hands and in his ears, and in his arse, when he goes to battle. The four daughters should be clad in mantles; Mercy in white, Ruthwiseness in red, all together, Truth in sad green, and Peace all in black; and they shall play in the place all together until they bring up the soul."

This complex of dramatic conventions, staging practices, and audience attitudes is a legacy of the medieval theater passed on to later theater. Although the medieval stage was only one of many influences on it, the drama of the sixteenth and seventeenth centuries is reminiscent of medieval drama in many ways. Renaissance drama frequently treats secular history according to a providential design similar to that of the cycles; it often treats its characters in the symbolic terms of the medieval moralities; and it uses both acting and stage space to create an immediacy between the fictive play and its audience. These habits take on very different meanings in Renaissance London, in a city and in a state in which the Anglican Protestant church is the state religion and where signs of Catholicism—or, in fact, of any religious subject matter—in the theater could be read as an act of sedition. The medieval theater provided the forms of drama and the practices of theater that were refashioned by the political, social, and theatrical pressures of the new era.

The explosion of theatrical and dramatic activity in London can be marked by two dates: 1567, when John Brayne built the Red Lion, London's first purpose-built theater (his brother-in-law, James Burbage, built The Theatre in 1576); and 1642, when plays were suspended and theaters were closed at the outbreak of the Civil War. The theater underwent profound changes from the reign of Elizabeth I (ruled 1558–1603) to the reigns of her successors James I (1603–1625) and Charles I (1625–1642, executed 1649), and yet at the same time it endured the intense social and cultural upheavals of the period with remarkable consistency. As an institution, the new professional theater witnessed the emergence of England as a modern state; the rise of England as an important mercantile and naval power, aided by the defeat of the Spanish Armada in 1588; the expansion of English interests in the New World; the growth of the city of London to roughly 250,000 inhabitants; and the ascendance of the Puritan faction that closed the theaters and deposed and executed the king.

The professional theater—a new institution in England, though already established on the continent—necessarily reflected the political and social strains of the time. These strains are most readily visible in the many laws regulating theatrical performance. The location of theater buildings, the structure and organization of theater companies, and the entire scene of theatrical activity in Renaissance London epitomized the fundamental tensions of English society as it moved from the medieval to the modern world.

DRAMA AND THEATER IN RENAISSANCE LONDON

THE PROFESSIONAL THEATER AND ITS SOCIETY

The sixteenth century witnessed intense religious and civil controversy, dating in part from Henry VIII's divorce from Catherine of Aragon in 1532 and his consequent excommunication from the Catholic church in 1533. Once Henry established the Protestant church of England as the religion of the realm in 1535, English politics were often dictated by England's vulnerability to the massive, hostile powers of the Catholic church in Rome and Catholic states such as France and Spain. Within England, a variety of Protestant sects competed with each other, with the government, and with the Church of England for power. This was also a period of profound changes in the ordering of society, a period of growing mercantile power, of aristocratic discontent with the power of the monarchy, and of the rise of new merchants and other social groups into prominence and power. As a result, the Crown was eternally on guard to suppress civil unrest or religious nonconformity.

Given this volatile political climate, it is not surprising that the Crown sought to limit and control public assembly, including theatrical performances. Laws were frequently directed against the theater, particularly against productions identified with England's Catholic past. In 1548, for example, the English church cancelled the Feast of Corpus Christi, and the production of the cycle plays was systematically suppressed. In 1569, the York cycle was performed for the last time, and in 1575, the mayor of Chester was arrested for allowing cycle plays to be performed. The last cycle performance took place in Coventry in 1576, and the last record of any Corpus Christi play being performed in England (before the modern era) dates from 1605, in Kendal. Morality plays may have seemed less sectarian in the kind of instruction they offered; features of morality drama were more readily absorbed by the secular theater.

Yet while the Crown limited and censored the stage, it also maintained its traditional patronage of the theater as well. The population of London doubled between 1581 and 1602; the Elizabethan era was characterized by several large crop failures, a deflation in the value of currency, repeated bouts of the plague, and persistent threats of invasion from without and sedition from within. Not surprisingly, both the queen and her Privy Council, and the local city magistrates throughout England, were fearful both of itinerant travelers, and of large—potentially riotous—assemblies. The famous "Act for the punishment of Vagabonds" of 1572 is a case in point. The law prohibited itinerant players and entertainers from wandering throughout the realm, but its ultimate effect was to establish permanent theatrical companies under the protection of noble patrons. The law ordered that "all Fencers, Bearwards,

Common Players in Interludes, and Minstrels, not belonging to any Baron of this Realm, or towards any other honorable Personage of greater Degree [. . . who] wander abroad and have not License of two Justices of the Peace at the least [. . .] shall be taken adjudged and deemed Rogues Vagabonds and Sturdy Beggars." Unless they belonged to the retinue of a nobleman, players were classed with common vagrants and could be arrested and fined. Protected as servants, a company of players could receive a license to perform in public.

The statute points to the strong bond between the theater and the aristocracy, and patents granted by Elizabeth entitled noblemen to retain companies of actors as servants. These patents—granted for the Lord Chamberlain's Men (Shakespeare's company), the Lord Admiral's Men (who produced Marlowe's plays), and others—shaped the professional theater of Renaissance London. Elizabeth authorized such companies to perform "Comedies, Tragedies, Interludes, and stage plays" in public, both in London and elsewhere. Yet, in granting these privileges, the Crown made significant qualifications. Elizabeth required the companies to submit their plays to her Master of Revels for approval. She also stipulated that plays "be not published or shown in the time of common prayer, or in the time of great and common plague in our said City of London." Religious and civic officials exerted considerable authority over when and where plays could actually be performed and where theaters could legally be built, and they often closed theaters for months at a time due to plague or civil strife. In 1598, the Privy Council restricted London to two companies (the Lord Chamberlain's Men and the Lord Admiral's Men), and in 1600 restricted them to playing at the Globe and Fortune theaters.

PROFESSIONAL COMPANIES

The City of London, like many towns, had its own ordinances prohibiting plays within the city limits, and for this reason James Burbage—a member of the Earl of Leicester's company—built The Theatre to the north of the city. Within a decade theaters had been built both to the north of the city and to the south, across the Thames River.

Although they were technically "servants," the major acting companies—the most famous being the Lord Chamberlain's Men, patented in 1593 and then given royal sponsorship as the King's Men when King James I succeeded Elizabeth in 1603—were organized as stockholding, profit-making corporations, that is, as business enterprises in the modern sense. Their economic survival depended on their public performances, for their patron might command and finance only a few productions per year. Several investors, or SHARERS, put up the capital to finance the company and took a percentage of its profits. The sharers were not just investors, they were involved in all aspects of the theater. The sharers of the King's Men, for example, included Shakespeare (playwright and actor), Richard Burbage (James Burbage's son and the company's principal actor, who was the first to play Shakespeare's King Lear, Hamlet, and Macbeth), the actors John Heminges and Henry Condell (who later published Shakespeare's plays), and several others. The sharers were responsible for building or leasing a theater, for purchasing plays, for taking on boy actors as apprentices, and for hiring other actors for each production. They also were liable when legal proceedings were brought against the company.

Although several companies flourished during the theater's heyday, life for actors and playwrights was hard. Any company could be forced (by theatrical fashion, plague, or fear of unrest) to leave the relative profit and security of London to take up the dangerous life of an itinerant troupe. Playwrights, who were paid a flat fee by the company for the script of a play, hustled to scrape together a living, and even a famous dramatist like Ben Jonson could die in penury. On the other hand, the theater also provided an opportunity for advancement as well. Several actors, including Richard Burbage and Edward Alleyn, were able to amass considerable fortunes. Shakespeare used the money he received as sharer to invest in property both in London and in his home, Stratford-upon-Avon, where he purchased

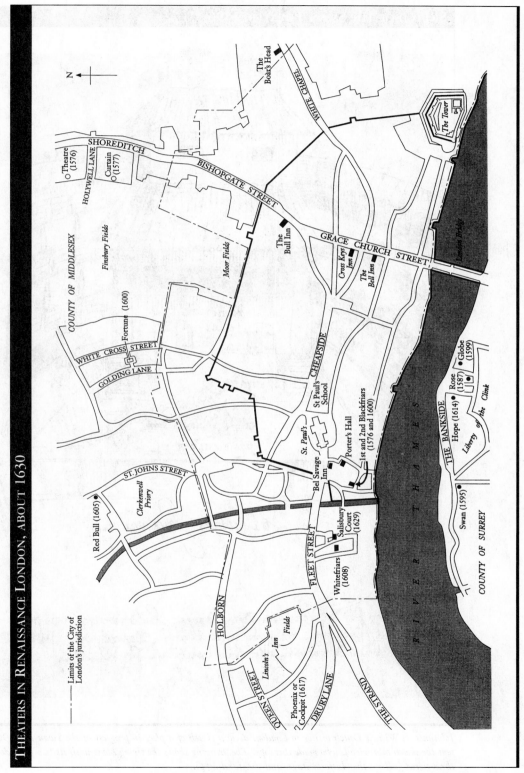

THEATERS IN RENAISSANCE LONDON, ABOUT 1630

- - - - - Limits of the City of
London's jurisdiction

N ←

SHOREDITCH

○ Theatre (1576)
HOLYWELL LANE
Curtain ○ (1577)

BISHOPGATE STREET

WHITE CHAPEL

The Boar's Head ▪

The Tower

COUNTY OF MIDDLESEX

Finsbury Fields

Moor Fields

The Bull Inn ▪

GRACE CHURCH STREET

Cross Keys Inn

The Bull Inn

London Bridge

Fortune (1600)

WHITE CROSS STREET

GOLDING LANE

CHEAPSIDE

St Paul's School

St. Paul's

Porter's Hall
1st and 2nd Blackfriars
(1576 and 1600)

Rose (1587) ●
● Globe (1599)

THE BANKSIDE
Hope (1614) ●

Liberty of the Clink

Red Bull (1605) ●

ST. JOHNS STREET

Clerkenwell Priory

Bel Savage Inn

Salisbury Court (1629)

Swan (1595) ●

COUNTY OF SURREY

R I V E R   T H A M E S

HOLBORN

FLEET STREET

Whitefriars (1608)

THE STRAND

QUEEN STREET

Lincoln's Inn Fields

Phoenix or Cockpit (1617)

DRURY LANE

A number of theaters were constructed in London after 1574. The dark line extending from The Tower (lower right) to Blackfriars in the west is the old city wall. Note that, with the exception of the first and second Blackfriars theaters, the theaters are either north of the city (the Fortune, The Theatre, the Curtain, the Red Bull) or south of the Thames River (the Swan, the Hope, the Rose, the Globe).

SKETCH OF THE SWAN THEATER, 1596

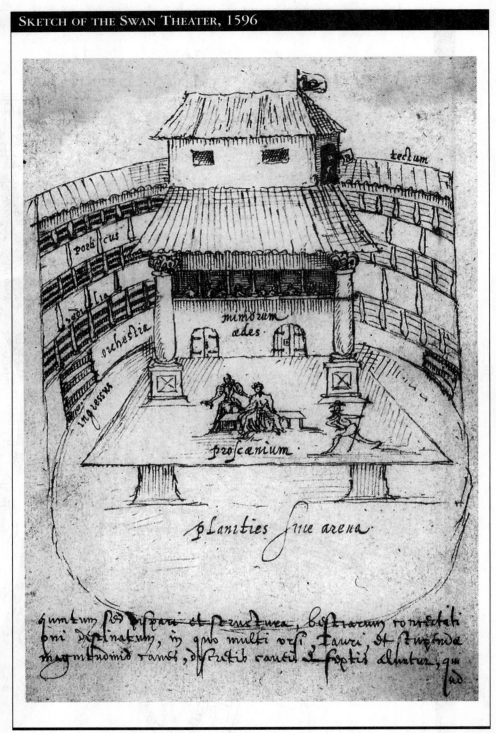

Johannes de Witt, a Dutch visitor to London, drew a sketch of a play in progress at the Swan in 1596. He sent the sketch to a friend, who made this copy. The drawing shows the tiring house with its two stage doors, a three-tiered gallery, the platform stage, and the standing pit.

MODERN RECONSTRUCTION OF THE SWAN THEATER

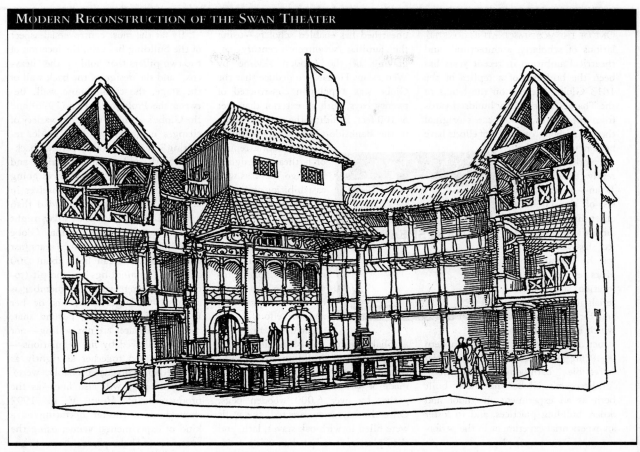

C. Walter Hodges based this reconstruction on the de Witt sketch.

a large house and land. Such careers were the exception rather than the rule, however, in an era when the theater was widely regarded as illicit and was frequently declared illegal.

English companies performed on three kinds of stage: large, open, outdoor buildings called PUBLIC THEATERS that held as many as 3,000 people; smaller, indoor, more elite PRIVATE THEATERS holding perhaps 700; and private performances at court or at the home of the patron. Public theaters, inspired both by the innyard booths where itinerant companies performed and by the circular arenas used for animal baiting, were outdoor buildings accommodating a large and diverse audience for afternoon performances. Although one theater, the Fortune, was rectangular, most public theaters were polygonal structures. The roughly circular, three-story gallery surrounded an open pit for standing audiences, into which a stage extended at about the height of five feet. The stage was partly roofed, and two doors used for entrances were set into the rear wall, or TIRING HOUSE. On the gallery level above the stage, small rooms were used for aristocratic seating, for music, and for scenes requiring action above the stage—as in the balcony scene in *Romeo and Juliet,* or when Prospero appears "aloft" in *The Tempest.* The stage had a central trapdoor (or GRAVE TRAP), and its roofed area held a pulley for raising or lowering actors or properties. The public theaters catered to a paying audience, charging one penny to enter the pit and an

THE THEATERS

ONE OF THE MOST FASCINATING CONSTEL-lations of scholarly, architectural, and theatrical ambition in recent years has been the building of a replica of the 1613 Globe Theater, on the banks of the Thames River, a few hundred yards from the site of Shakespeare's original theater. Although a variety of efforts have been made throughout the world—one is currently under way in Japan—to build models of the Globe or other English Renaissance theaters, this project has been notable for the scrupulousness of its research into the location, size, and materials of the Globe, and for the care with which it has been constructed. Within the limits of modern legal (fire laws, for example) and social (accessible bathrooms) conventions, "Shakespeare's Globe" has been built both as an experiment in Tudor and Stuart building practices, and to foster an experiential experiment in the performance of Renaissance plays.

The American actor Sam Wanamaker instigated the project, and remained its guiding force until his death in 1993. Part of Wanamaker's vision was that the theater should be both a theatrical and a scholarly endeavor, and much of the success of the final project is due to the team he assembled, including the scholar Andrew Gurr, architect Theo Crosby (who died in 1994), and artistic director Mark Rylance. The accuracy of the building was immeasurably helped by the discovery in 1989 of a section of the Globe's foundation beneath a nineteenth-century building adjacent to the Southwark bridge; although Anchor Terrace is protected as a landmark (preventing much excavation of the Globe's foundation), the section of foundation that has been

(ASIDE)

SHAKESPEARE'S GLOBE

unearthed has enabled scholars—using the familiar seventeenth-century engraving of the London skyline by Wenceslaus Hollar—to deduce that the Globe was a polygon constructed of twenty bays, with an exterior diameter of 100 feet. Building the theater as part of the Bankside Globe Center—which also includes a replica of a theater designed by Inigo Jones, as well as exhibition and other facilities—was not an easy task, however, and much of what has been learned about the Globe has been the result of scholarly investigation into Tudor building practices, and the efforts to reconstruct them.

Shakespeare's Globe is an impressively handmade building, using traditional building practices: the bays are made of oak timbers, and are held together by over 6,000 wooden pegs. Once the bays were erected, the walls were filled in with oak staves, lath, and then plastered: rather than using modern plaster, research showed that Tudor builders used a plaster made of lime and cow's hair. Since modern English cow's hair is too short, the Globe builders used a lime plaster mixed with goat hair. A fire sheet was put between each wall, and tests on the resulting lath-and-plaster showed that it could resist 1,000 degrees for three hours—long enough to empty the theater in an emergency (when the Globe burned in 1613, no injuries were reported, either). The building is also the first wood-framed building to be built in London since the great fire of 1666: its thatched roof is applied in the traditional manner and has been treated with a fire-retardant chemical, and a sprinkler system is installed just under the roofline.

By far the most controversial aspect of the building has been the location of the two pillars that hold up the "heavens," and the design of the back wall of the stage, the tiring house wall. Between the Prologue Season (1996) and the Globe's opening in 1997 a variety of changes in both have been made, resulting in a sumptuously painted backdrop with additional tapestries, and faux-marble columns. Audiences going to the Globe today find themselves in a theater somewhat less crowded than a full house in Shakespeare's day might have been: while the original Globe held 3,000, the current Globe seats just over 1,000, and can hold about 500 standing "groundlings" in the pit (today, the average audience member is about 10% larger than his or her Elizabethan predecessor; beyond that, modern audiences are not willing—nor are they allowed by fire regulations—to be jammed together as tightly as Elizabethan patrons probably were). But what they will also find—as the production of *Henry V* in 1997 showed—is a theater operating as a kind of experimental venue, using the container of Shakespeare's drama to explore how the plays might have worked in their original conditions. At the present time, the company intends to do some productions in period dress (the costumes often themselves made with Tudor clothmaking and dye techniques), but to do others in modern dress. The result of a massive and energetic combination of talents, Shakespeare's Globe is finally meant to work as a living theater.[1]

---

[1]The building of the Globe was recorded in a variety of newspaper and scholarly accounts throughout the early 1990s; students interested in learning more about Shakespeare's Globe should consult Shakespeare's Globe Education Centre, Bankside, London SE1 9DT, United Kingdom.

THE GLOBE THEATER FOUNDATION

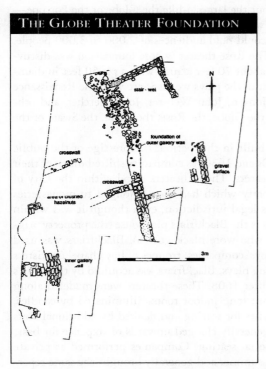

In 1989, part of the foundation of the Globe Theater was discovered. This portion of the Globe foundation extends from beneath a landmark nineteenth-century building; the remainder of the Globe foundation is beneath the building and therefore cannot be excavated. Nonetheless, this section of the inner and outer wall of the theater, and of the exterior stairwell which led to the galleries, has enabled scholars to gauge with much greater accuracy both the size and configuration of Shakespeare's theater.

DESIGNING SHAKESPEARE'S GLOBE

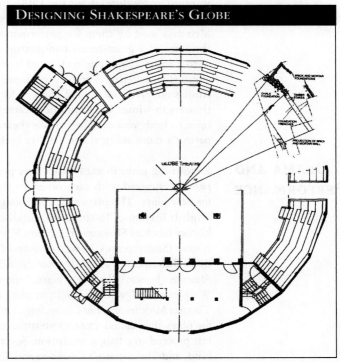

This illustration shows how the archaeological evidence of the Globe Theater foundations has been used—along with other evidence—to develop a new understanding of the theater's size and shape. The foundations, which comprise two "bays" or sections of the Globe's exterior structure, enabled Theo Crosby—the architect of the reconstructed Shakespeare's Globe Theater in London—to estimate the overall dimensions of the building (about ninety-nine feet in diameter) and also to determine that the Globe was a twenty-sided polygon.

additional penny to enter each of the galleries, where seating was provided on benches. Estimates on the size of the theaters vary, but the larges—like the Globe or the Fortune—were about 100 feet in external diameter, with a standing pit about 70 feet across, and a stage 45 feet wide and 27 feet deep; they could hold audiences of 2,000 to 3,000 people. Some theaters were considerably smaller. The Rose theater (whose foundation was discovered in 1989) was a twelve-sided building about 70 feet across, with a pit 50 feet in diameter and a stage roughly 25 by 15 feet. Most of the plays we associate with the Renaissance theater—those of Marlowe, Shakespeare, Jonson, John Webster, John Fletcher, and others—were produced in public theaters like the Globe, the Rose, the Hope, the Swan, or the Fortune.

Although a number of theaters were built in this period, the prestige of the public theaters seems to have declined in the 1620s and 1630s as companies shifted much of their attention to the more lucrative private theaters. These theaters stood within the City of London, on lands called "liberties"—property which had once belonged to monasteries and which had remained outside the city's legal jurisdiction, even though it was within the city limit. Best-known of these theaters is the Blackfriars playhouse (the property originally belonged to the Dominican friars, who wore black gowns). Blackfriars was used intermittently throughout the 1590s by boys' companies, troupes of boy chapel choristers who on occasion formed companies for acting plays. Blackfriars was acquired by the King's Men and used by them for performances after 1608. These theaters were modeled along the lines of a great-house banqueting room: long indoor rooms illuminated by candles, with a low stage at one end, faced by benches for seating and flanked by additional seats along side galleries. The private theaters generally charged upwards of sixpence for basic admission, with additional charges for special seating. Companies performed at private theaters in winter and at public theaters in summer and generally brought the same repertoire to both venues. The private theaters did develop the reputation, however, for originating a more satirical and erudite body of drama.

DRAMA AND PERFORMANCE

Performing plays in REPERTORY over perhaps as many as 200 days a year, the London companies competed with each other for their audiences and generated an enormous demand for new plays. The plays that they bought and performed are among the greatest works of English literature. In the main, English drama in this period comprises plays on English history (such as Shakespeare's *Henry V* and *Richard III,* or Marlowe's *Edward II*); on classical history (Shakespeare's *Julius Caesar* and *Coriolanus,* Ben Jonson's *Sejanus*); romantic comedies (like Shakespeare's *A Midsummer Night's Dream*); city comedies (Shakespeare's *Measure for Measure,* Jonson's *Volpone*); heroic tragedies (Shakespeare's *Hamlet* and *King Lear,* John Webster's *The Duchess of Malfi*); or plays of intrigue or satire (John Marston's *The Malcontent,* Thomas Middleton's *The Changeling*). Later in the period, audiences seemed to develop a taste for plays they called TRAGICOMEDIES, usually romantic plays that begin in the tragic vein but proceed to a happy resolution. Several of John Fletcher's plays are tragicomedies of this kind, and Shakespeare's *Cymbeline* and *The Tempest* resemble tragicomedy as well.

This list of genres suggests both the fertile range of innovation in the Renaissance theater and the drama's dependence on models drawn from the classical and medieval theaters. Roman drama—the comedies of Plautus and Terence, and the tragedies of Seneca—was widely used in schools and universities as part of the teaching of Latin, and university students often staged these plays in Latin. It is not surprising, then, that some features of classical drama made their way into the Renaissance theater. The model of Shakespearean romantic comedy—mistaken identities, separated lovers, an irascible old man or father, a wily servant—derives directly from Plautus' plays; indeed, Shakespeare's *Comedy of Errors* directly adapts Plautus' *The Menaechmus Twins.* In a similar fashion, the violence of Seneca's tragedies makes its way directly into the action of Elizabethan drama. Formally and thematically, however, Renaissance drama also differs sharply from its classical ancestors. Renaissance plays tend to be more diffuse, involving a greater variety of characters and multiple plots; in tragedy, the action is often not quite as closely focused on the fortunes of a single hero as it is in classical tragedy. In these and other ways—in the Christian providence that seems to stand behind the action of many plays, in its variety of contemporary characters, in its use of symbolic anachronism, and in the complex relationship between the dramatic world and the world of the audience—Renaissance drama bears the signs of its medieval inheritance.

Playwrights generally wrote in BLANK VERSE, an unrhymed IAMBIC PENTAMETER line (ten syllables with alternating stress), and occasionally used other verse forms as well. They often used prose, sometimes for emphasis, sometimes to develop the qualities of a particular character. Although modern editors divided the plays into five acts, in most cases Renaissance playwrights probably did not compose their plays in this form. Performance on the public theater stage was rapid and continuous. The theaters used an open stage, few large properties, and had little or no scenery onstage, so that scenes could follow one another without interruption.

Despite the absence of elaborate stage sets, performance in the Renaissance theater was nonetheless spectacular. Actors used costumes, properties, and language to transform the midafternoon stage into a dramatic locale—Prospero's desert island, Lear's heath, Faustus's study. Some larger properties could be wheeled out from the rear doors, or perhaps raised from the trap: a throne, for instance, or a bed for Desdemona in *Othello,* or the hell-mouth used at the end of *Doctor Faustus.* A cannon fired during a production of Shakespeare's *Henry VIII* in 1613 unfortunately set fire to the Globe and burned it to the ground.

The unlocalized stage of medieval drama can be seen as the forerunner of the Renaissance theater's fluid use of stage space. The open stage made for a kind of cinematic flexibility in performance, as the play could range rapidly from scene to scene, place to place. Costuming was eclectic and anachronistic: the actors wore mainly Elizabethan clothing, adding armor, royal finery, motley, or some "classical" style of gowns when needed. The actors—Burbage, Alleyn, Will Kemp, among many others—were widely praised for their power and effectiveness. Their acting style was oratorical in tragedy and extemporaneous in comedy, but there is no doubt that many were consummate performers, in command of dozens of roles that could be put into play at short notice.

WOMEN IN DRAMA AND PERFORMANCE

Boy actors played a significant part in the experience of English theater, for boy actors played the parts of women and girls onstage, including major roles like Lady Macbeth, Ophelia, and Cleopatra. Much as they did in classical Athens, "women" emerged onstage in Renaissance London only as a side-effect of masculine attitudes and performances. In the English theater, this CROSS-DRESSING came into special prominence, though, because the romantic, sexual, and political intrigue so popular in Renaissance plays was often focused on female characters and therefore on the performance of the boy actors. Indeed, the drama frequently uses cross-dressing as a way of interrogating the power and perquisites of gender, in ways that sometimes confirm and sometimes question the role of gender in English society. English society was an overtly hierarchical one, and despite the power of the "Virgin Queen," women had little access to education, most could not hold property, and they were generally subject to discrimination of many kinds. In this social economy—and in a theater in which Puritan opposition to the stage frequently criticized the theater's "effeminacy"—the absence of women from the stage became a powerful sign of their absence from other scenes of power. Much as sumptuary laws prevented individuals from

ONE OF THE PRINCIPAL OBLIGATIONS OF the professional companies was to perform at court or for their patron. Performances at court often took place during holidays and were commanded with increasing frequency by James I and Charles I. The companies performed many of their staple plays at court, but they also performed special entertainments called MASQUES, plays written in verse, usually on mythological subjects, that involved dancing, fanciful costumes, music, and special scenic machinery and effects. While the actors spoke the lines in these plays, they shared the stage with members of the court, who performed in the elaborate dances that began, ended, and punctuated the masques. The little play that Prospero puts on for Ferdinand and Miranda in Shakespeare's *The Tempest* resembles court masques in many ways, with its cast of goddesses, its formal singing and dancing, and the ceremonial quality of the occasion it celebrates.

Masques were an elaborate and expensive entertainment; some were performed on special state occasions—Jonson's *Hymenaei* (1605) celebrated the marriage of Lady Essex, and *The Masque of Oberon* (1610) was written to celebrate Prince Henry's investiture as Prince of Wales—and all had important implications for the mythology of the Stuart dynasty. Since members of the royal and aristocratic families performed in the masques, the poet was challenged to devise a setting and dramatic narrative that were elevated enough for the courtly audience. More important, each masque included several "grand masquing dances," which were performed by members of the court, often costumed as "characters" in the masque. Jonson was by far the most renowned writer of masques, though the playwrights James Shirley, William Davenant (who became

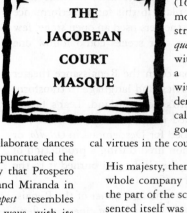

(ASIDE)

THE JACOBEAN COURT MASQUE

a critically important theater manager after the restoration of the monarchy in 1660), and others also wrote masques. Jonson, however, wrote more than a dozen masques, and in the course of his long career innovated the genre in several ways. While the earlier Stuart masques tend to have a relatively simple narrative, later masques—beginning with *The Masque of Queens* (1609) — adopted a more complicated structure. *The Masque of Queens* begins with an ANTIMASQUE, a scene involving witches, goblins, or demons who are magically transformed into goddesses or allegorical virtues in the course of the action.

His majesty, then, being set, and the whole company in full expectation, the part of the scene which first presented itself was an ugly hell, which flaming beneath, smoked unto the top of the roof. And in respect all evils are, morally said to come from hell, . . . these witches, with a kind of hollow and infernal music, came forth from thence. First one, then two, and three, and more, till their number increased to eleven, all differently attired: some with rats on their head, some on their shoulders; others with ointment pots at their girdles; all with spindles, timbrels, rattles or other venefical [having to do with witchcraft] instruments, making a confused noise, with strange gestures.

The witches dance and pronounce a series of charms until, suddenly, "with a strange and sudden music,"

they fell into a magical dance full of preposterous change and gesticulation. . . . In the heat of their dance on the sudden was heard a sound of loud music, as if many instruments

had made one blast; with which not only the hags themselves but the hell into which they ran quite vanished, and the whole face of the scene altered, scarce suffering the memory of such a thing. But in the place of it appeared a glorious and magnificent building figuring the House of Fame, in the top of which were discovered the twelve masquers sitting upon a throne triumphal erected in form of a pyramid and circled with all store of light. From whom a person, by this time descended, in the furniture of Perseus, and expressing heroic and masculine virtue began to speak.[1]

The antimasque establishes a world of demonic disorder, which suddenly vanishes when the members of the court appear in the House of Fame, among classical heroes and virtues. We can get a sense of the delicacy of Jonson's situation when we recognize that the performers of the masque included the queen herself, as well as the countesses of Arundel, Derby, Huntington, Bedford, Essex, and Montgomery, Viscountess Cranborne, and several ladies in waiting. The court was both performer and audience of this self-enclosed spectacle, which almost of necessity reflected back on its audience an idealized vision of courtly perfection. Indeed, in the last Stuart masque, *Salmacida Spolia,* written by Davenant, both the king and the queen were among the dancers.

As an ambitious writer, it is understandable that Jonson thought the masques were essentially a vehicle for his splendid poetry. But as even this brief description suggests, the masques were highly dependent on the development of new scenic technology, and on the skills of the architect and designer Inigo Jones (1573–1652). The masques were unusually expensive: one of King James's masques cost more than £4,000, and one of King Charles's cost £21,000.

[1]From *Ben Jonson: Selected Masques,* ed. Stephen Orgel (New Haven, CT: Yale University Press, 1970).

Much of this money was spent on the elaborate changeable scenery that accompanied the masques, the first changeable scenery in the English theater. Inigo Jones designed the theater space where masques were performed, the banqueting hall of Whitehall Palace. Jones had visited Italy in 1600; he may have visited again during 1607–1608, and he is known to have been in Italy from 1613 to 1615. In Italy, he came into contact with the theater designs of Andrea Palladio (1518–1580), who adapted the design of classical Roman theaters for indoor stages: Palladio's Teatro Olimpico had a curved amphitheater-like auditorium and a proscenium stage. As court architect and designer, Jones had the opportunity both to import Palladio's understanding of theatrical design, and to develop his own interest in elaborate spectacle. The stage at Whitehall was about 40 feet wide by 28 feet deep, and gently raked; although Jones's theater at Whitehall changed during his long tenure at court, it eventually consisted of staggered wings and a backdrop to convey a sense of perspective. Unlike both the public and private theaters of Renaissance London, Jones's theater was the first to use changeable scenery, and when the theaters reopened in 1660, the English companies brought this aristocratic inheritance with them: Jones's WINGS-AND-BACKDROP designs became the basic model for changeable scenery throughout the eighteenth century.

Jones's interest in spectacle was far-reaching, and he devised the instruments to execute many of Jonson's most elaborate poetic images: flying machines, a globe which opened to reveal several aristocratic dancers, and brilliant costumes to dress the masques' allegorical characters. But it was Jones's development of a perspective in the theater that was most deeply implicated in the rhetoric of court life. For at Whitehall performances, the King sat on a raised, central dais directly in front of the stage; since none of the other courtiers could be seated with their backs to the King, those closer to the stage were seated

FIERY SPIRIT

Inigo Jones created this costume for a fiery spirit in 1635.

along the side walls of the room, while others were seated behind the royal spectator. It has been argued that the king was positioned in a complex relation to the stage and to the rest of the audience: not only was he the only spectator for whom the illusion of perspective was complete (the other spectators could probably see between the wings, for example), but the rest of the audience could see that only the king had a perfect vision of the world onstage. The closer one sat to the royal seat, the more one's view of the illusion onstage approximated the king's ideal vantage. Spectators and performers, in other words, engaged in a richly hierarchical sense of illusion, in which the King's centrality—and, in a sense, his omniscience—was constantly displayed, and each spectator's distance from that sense of illusion was constantly experienced. Like Jonson, whose texts frequently betray his intense awareness of his royal

audience and aristocratic performers, Jones's perspective theater reflects the increasingly absolutist ideology of the Stuart monarchy.

The banqueting hall at Whitehall played one more ironic role in the history of performance. Charles I became increasingly hostile to Parliament—he refused to call Parliament from 1629 to 1640—and when civil war broke out in 1642, Charles fled London. The Royalist forces were concentrated in Oxford, and in 1647 Charles was defeated and captured by the Parliamentary army. In 1649, he was sentenced to death by Parliament, and he visited the Whitehall banquet hall on his way to his execution. The executioner's block was set on a large public stage outside a window of the banquet hall; Charles was led through the room where the masques' brilliant fantasies had been staged for him to his own last performance, the public stage where he was beheaded.

COSTUMES FOR SHAKESPEARE'S *TITUS ANDRONICUS*

Dating from about 1595, this drawing appears to show a scene from Titus Andronicus, *by William Shakespeare. Two of the actors wear pseudo-classical Roman costumes; the others are dressed in Elizabethan clothing.*

wearing jewels and clothing above their social station, so, too, was cross-dressing a legal offense in sixteenth-century England, punishable by whipping and a prison sentence. The license of the theater, the freedom to create magical new worlds on the stage, was, like other forms of power in the period, the prerogative of men, and the images that men created for the stage are in important ways imprinted with the signs of a specifically masculine imagination. As with all stage conventions, cross-dressing was deeply implicated in the values of the culture outside the theater, so much so that when women did perform onstage in England—a French company used actresses at Blackfriars in 1629—they met with hostility, ridicule, and rejection.

Nonetheless, women not only attended the theater, but a few—aristocratic women, who often patronized poets and other artists—also wrote plays. Queen Elizabeth is thought to have translated a passage from Seneca's *Hercules on Mount Oeta,* and other women similarly adapted or wrote plays. Mary Sidney, the countess of Pembroke and sister of Sir Philip Sidney, translated Robert Garnier's play *The Tragedy of Antonie* in the 1590s. Her niece, Lady Mary Wroth (daughter of Mary Sidney's brother Robert, and a frequent participant in Jacobean court masques), wrote a mythological play, *Love's Victory,* probably in the early 1620s. Perhaps the best known plays today are Elizabeth Cary, Viscountess of Falkland's *Tragedy of Miriam* (published 1613) and the plays published by Margaret Cavendish, Marchioness of Newcastle, in 1662 and 1668. Although these plays were not staged—aristocratic women did not traffic in theater business—they have since become a critical part of our understanding of English Renaissance drama.

The theater had an extraordinary hold on the English imagination. In their many progresses, pageants, and allegorical entertainments, the English monarchs revealed a keen sense of the power of fictive images to represent reality, or a version of it, and so to shape their subjects' understanding of royal power. Playwrights and audiences also found in the theater a magical image of human possibility. Think of Prospero summoning the storm, Ariel, and other spirits with his stagey magic; or of the playwright John Webster's description of "an excellent actor": "All men have been of his occupation, and indeed what he doth feignedly, that do others essentially: this day one plays a Monarch, the next a private person. Here one acts a Tyrant, on the morrow an Exile; a Parasite [sponger] this man tonight, tomorrow a Precisian [Puritan], and so of divers others." Acting and the theater provided a liberating image of human—or, at least, masculine—power: the power to transform oneself and the world. However, the rich, strange, transforming freedom of the theater could also seem empty and terrifying, even demonic. Rather than an image of human potential, the theater could seem to offer an image of the poverty of human action, the sterile and deceptive emptiness of the world we make and inhabit. As King Lear preaches to blinded Gloucester, "When we are born, we cry that we are come / To this great stage of fools." Puritan critics of the theater insistently reminded audiences that the stage's methods—to seduce with the vain and showy image of a false reality—were also Satan's, and that the theater subversively invited audiences to "unman, unChristian, uncreate themselves." Yet it is precisely this transforming power that lies at the heart of the Renaissance theater's fascination for its audience. For while the theater sometimes seemed to depict a world threatened with constant change and loss, it also presented the power of illusion to recreate the real.

MEDIEVAL AND RENAISSANCE DRAMA IN PERFORMANCE AND HISTORY

Although the banning of the cycle dramas in England in the sixteenth century marked an ending of the traditions of medieval drama and theater there, the same was not true on the continent, where both cycle dramas and morality dramas continued to be performed. In Spain, for example, the *AUTOS SACRAMENTALES*—morality plays on Christian themes— were produced in major cities like Madrid, and had an important influence on dramatic writing as well (see Unit 4). Similarly, staging short pageants—like the shepherd plays or *pastorelas* performed today throughout Latin America, and in many Latino communities in the United States, before Christmas—has remained a part of religious festivities in many places; perhaps the most striking of these is the processional staging of the Passion held in Oberammergau, Germany.

In many respects, though, the vivid and popular style of the cycle plays had to wait until the late nineteenth and early twentieth centuries to find an audience; when the manuscripts of the four English cycles first began to be studied seriously in the nineteenth century, their plays were seen merely as primitive precursors to the more finished, literary achievement of English Renaissance dramatists. However, this model of the "evolution" of dramatic forms from "simple" to "complex" is not really borne out by a close examination of the plays themselves, which use a popular literary and theatrical medium to undertake a drama of enormous subtlety, scope, and power. Beginning in the twentieth century, a number of efforts were made to stage medieval drama—both the cycle plays and morality plays like *Everyman*—and the force and theatrical vitality of the plays became immediately apparent. In recent years, the cycle plays have been staged frequently, both in their traditional locations (at York, for instance), and elsewhere: the University of Toronto and the Court Theater at the University of Chicago have mounted very well received versions.

Although the English theaters were closed in 1642, interrupting the practices both of playwriting and of theatrical performance, the secular drama of Renaissance England has had in many respects a more sustained tradition. When the theaters reopened in 1660, they reopened in a very different form—indoor theaters, using lights and stage machinery, replaced the outdoor public theaters of the Jacobean and Caroline periods—and to a much more narrowly circumscribed audience (see Unit 4). And while there was considerable demand for new plays, for many years some plays of the Renaissance period held the stage, and indeed provided the dramatic conventions on which new plays were mapped. But while today we tend to think of Shakespeare as the preeminent writer of his era, in the Restoration period, Shakespeare's plays were revived less frequently than those of other playwrights, notably Ben Jonson, James Shirley, and Francis Beaumont and John Fletcher; it was only within the course of the eighteenth century that Shakespeare's plays began to have something approaching their current popularity.

The history of Shakespeare in the theater, however, is a history of adaptation: the notion that Shakespeare's plays have an inner logic, and should be performed "as they were written" is a purely modern idea. Shakespeare's plays were, of course, altered in the practice of his own company, and playwrights in the later seventeenth and eighteenth centuries adapted the plays to the taste of their era. John Dryden, for example, transformed Shakespeare's erotically supercharged Antony and Cleopatra into an honorable Roman and his staid matron in his version of *Antony and Cleopatra* called *All for Love* (1677); Nahum Tate's version of Shakespeare's *King Lear* (1681) concludes with Edgar marrying Cordelia (yes, she lives), and retiring happily offstage with Lear (he lives, too) and Kent: this version of *Lear* held the stage well into the nineteenth century. Rather than regarding these revisions as quaintly misguided, we should recognize that theatrical production always rewrites the drama in the idiom of the day; to their audiences, these productions were fully "Shakespearean," just as recent films—Kenneth Branagh's setting of *Hamlet* in the nineteenth century or Baz Luhrmann's framing *Romeo and Juliet* as a gang war in a Latin American Verona—are efforts to make Shakespeare speak in ways that will be powerful to audiences today.

Indeed, today we tend to think of Shakespeare across a variety of media: in film and television and advertising as well as in a range of theatrical venues. But for the seventeenth, eighteenth, and nineteenth centuries, Shakespeare was the property of the theater, and many actors and actresses became famous for their portrayals of Shakespearean roles: Thomas Betterton (1635–1710), Charles Macklin (1700–97), Sarah Siddons (1755–1831), Edmund Kean (1789–1833), Sir Henry Irving (1838–1905) the first English actor to be knighted—and Ellen Terry (1847–1928) are just a few. In many respects, though, David Garrick (1717–79) had the greatest impact as a Shakespearean actor. In part through his celebrated performances—he was renowned as Hamlet, Macbeth, and Richard III—Garrick helped to create a new interest in Shakespeare in the theater: he had his portrait painted frequently in Shakespearean roles (Hogarth's painting of Garrick as Richard III is a famous example), and he used his popularity to advance Shakespeare's reputation, not least by staging a Shakespeare Jubilee in Stratford. Garrick was a friend of the great literary critic Samuel Johnson, and Garrick's efforts in the theater coincided with a series of attempts to produce better, more accurate editions of Shakespeare's plays. But although Garrick had the reputation of restoring "Shakespeare's" original texts to the stage, he could hardly hope to succeed in the face of a century of popular stage adaptations. Although Garrick did introduce some Shakespearean material that had previously been cut from performances, his King Lear survived the play just as Nahum Tate's did, and his Richard III bawled out—as he had ever since Colley Cibber revised the play in 1700—"Off with his head!" (Indeed, Cibber's version of *Richard III* cuts several characters and persisted onstage well into the twentieth century; it also partly informs Laurence Olivier's film of the play.)

The stage production of Shakespearean drama has always responded to the beliefs and values of its contemporary audiences. Tate's adaptation of *King Lear* was praised by Johnson, for example, for its happy ending seemed to restore justice in the theater; Johnson thought

Shakespeare's original ending fine for readers, but too bleak and destructive for the stage. Shakespeare's plays were adapted to the more melodramatic and sentimental tastes of the eighteenth century; in the nineteenth century, a vogue for historical accuracy and stage realism led to a series of splendid efforts to reconstruct the historical setting of the plays: medieval Scotland in Charles Kean's 1853 *Macbeth,* or Christian-era England in Irving's *Cymbeline* (1896). These changes in taste are reflected in acting style as well: Betterton's portrayal of Hamlet was renowned in the late seventeenth century for its gravity and grace; Betterton is said never to have raised his arms above his waist, an illustration of neoclassical decorum in performance. By the early decades of the nineteenth century, Samuel Taylor Coleridge remarked that watching Edmund Kean in performance was akin to reading Shakespeare "by flashes of lightning"; Kean's performance impressed his audiences precisely through his well-crafted *lack* of decorum, in accord with Romantic beliefs about emotional expressivity. Irving is in many ways the first modern actor in what we would recognize as a psychological tradition of acting; although his career preceded the Russian director Constantin Stanislavski's pioneering work on the style of realistic performance (see Unit 5), Irving's penchant for subtle physical details of characterization—his enemies called them mannerisms—gave his work a psychological concreteness and complexity that was powerful to an audience whose understanding of dramatic character was trained on the novels of Dickens and George Eliot.

The theater also registers its culture's changing social attitudes in its portrayal of Shakespearean roles. Charles Macklin, for example, was probably the first actor to take a more sympathetic portrayal of the Jewish moneylender Shylock in *The Merchant of Venice;* the role had traditionally been performed as a satiric stereotype. Yet even Macklin retained the comic red wig and beard with which Shylock had always been performed; Edmund Kean was the first actor to get rid of them. Henry Irving's production of the play ended after the Act IV trial scene: in his version, *The Merchant of Venice* becomes something more like "The Tragedy of Shylock." In 1994, Peter Sellars set the play in a version of Los Angeles and drew explicit parallels to the police beating of Rodney King and the uprising that followed the acquittal of the officers involved. In Sellars's production the play's Jews were all played as African Americans; the Venetians were all played as Latinos and Latinas; and Portia and her retinue were all played as Asian Americans. Although Sellars's production was deservedly controversial, it illustrates a sense that Shakespeare's drama is capable of entering into new situations unimagined by Shakespeare, and of saying new things as well.

In the twentieth century, the pictorial style favored by Victorian theaters has largely been replaced in an effort to stage the plays in the simpler style of Shakespeare's theater. The first experiments of this kind were undertaken by William Poel (1852–1934), who used his Elizabethan Stage Society to produce versions of *Twelfth Night* and other plays on an open stage, and using a text more closely approximating Shakespeare's. Poel made it possible to see Shakespeare's plays as lively and fast-moving (all those scene changes in Victorian productions had made a Shakespeare play a very long evening, requiring many cuts to compensate for all the time it took to raise and lower sets), and regardless of whether directors (a new role in the theater also dating to this period) have chosen to stage the plays in Elizabethan or other settings, the sense of a rapidly changing series of scenes, localized not by extensive sets onstage but by the language and action, informs most twentieth-century Shakespeare. Indeed, it is often said that filmic techniques—quick cutting between scenes made possible by camera work and editing—provided a means to understand how Shakespearean drama might be played differently onstage.

It's now possible to see a range of Shakespeares on the contemporary stage, not only Shakespeare performed in languages other than English, but through the eclectic range of theatrical styles characteristic of the modern stage. Some productions—the "restored" versions, like the 1997 *Henry V*, at Shakespeare's Globe in London—work hard to use Elizabethan costumes to produce the flavor of Shakespeare's theater. Other productions set the plays in a different historical era (there have been several recent *Henry V* productions set in the American Civil War, for example), in order to make the workings of the play's society visible to us in more familiar circumstances. Still others use eclectic staging, combining set and costume elements from a variety of periods to take Shakespeare out of history—in the Royal Shakespeare Company's 1991 *Troilus and Cressida,* for example, Agamemnon appeared in a breastplate and a ratty old cardigan sweater: a kind of timeless image of the doddering old general.

Of course, the ability of the modern stage to bring a great technological flexibility to Shakespeare is matched by the possibilities of film. Shakespeare plays were among the first subjects of silent filmmakers, and many of the most distinguished films of the twentieth century are versions of Shakespearean drama. Indeed, contemporary students of Shakespeare are often much more likely to see a Shakespeare film than a live Shakespeare performance, especially with the number of exciting Shakespeare films produced in the 1990s: Kenneth Branagh in *Henry V, Much Ado about Nothing,* and *Hamlet;* Ian McKellan in *Richard III;* Mel Gibson in *Hamlet;* Leonardo Di Caprio and Claire Danes in *Romeo + Juliet.* As a part of the common cultural inheritance of the West—and indeed, frequently challenged as such by resistant, postcolonial productions in India, Canada, Africa, and elsewhere—Shakespeare is produced today across the spectrum of performance.

EVERYMAN

Everyman was written late in the fifteenth century and strongly resembles a Flemish play, *Elckerlijc* ("Everyman"), which was printed in 1495. It seems likely that one of the two plays is a translation of the other, but scholars are uncertain about which is the original. Given the play's subtle treatment of the Catholic doctrine of salvation, it has sometimes been argued that *Everyman* was written by a monk or cleric. Yet *Everyman* is hardly a theological treatise; it brims with a vitality that brings the reality of impending death vividly to the stage.

In the play, God orders Death to seek out Everyman and prepare him to die. Like most people, though, Everyman is not ready to meet his end. He first tries to bribe Death and then pleads unsuccessfully for mercy. When Death does not relent, Everyman begins a kind of spiritual journey, confronting several allegorical figures and asking them to accompany him to the grave. Medieval allegory often involved the personification of moral or psychological abstractions, much like the characters that Everyman meets: Fellowship, Kindred, Goods, Good Deeds, Knowledge, and so on. In performance, however, these abstractions become vividly fleshed-out, for the playwright gives these characters traits and behaviors that make them powerfully "real" and recognizable as individuals on the stage rather than as abstract moral emblems. As Everyman proceeds toward death, he is deserted by most of his worldly attributes, but Good Deeds remains faithful to him, especially once he has repented. Although the playwright concludes *Everyman* with a moralizing sermon by the Doctor, we may well feel that the theatrical lesson of the play has at least as much to do with the humanizing of Everyman and his poignant confrontation with our common mortality.

EVERYMAN

Anonymous
TRANSLATED BY A. C. CAWLEY

—— CHARACTERS ——

GOD	COUSIN	STRENGTH
MESSENGER	GOODS	DISCRETION
DEATH	GOOD DEEDS	FIVE WITS
EVERYMAN	KNOWLEDGE	ANGEL
FELLOWSHIP	CONFESSION	DOCTOR
KINDRED	BEAUTY	

Here beginneth a treatise how the High Father of Heaven sendeth death to summon every creature to come and give account of their lives in this world, and is in manner of a moral play.

MESSENGER: I pray you all give your audience,
    And hear this matter with reverence,
    By figure a moral play:
    The *Summoning of Everyman* called it is,
5   That of our lives and ending shows
    How transitory we be all day.
    This matter is wondrous precious,
    But the intent of it is more gracious,
    And sweet to bear away.
10   The story saith: Man, in the beginning
    Look well, and take good heed to the ending,
    Be you never so gay!
    Ye think sin in the beginning full sweet,
    Which in the end causeth the soul to weep,
15   When the body lieth in clay.
    Here shall you see how Fellowship and Jollity,
    Both Strength, Pleasure, and Beauty,
    Will fade from thee as flower in May;
    For ye shall hear how our Heaven King
20   Calleth Everyman to a general reckoning:
    Give audience, and hear what he doth say.   *(Exit.)*

(GOD speaketh:)

GOD: I perceive, here in my majesty,
    How that all creatures be to me unkind,
    Living without dread in worldly prosperity:
25   Of ghostly sight the people be so blind,
    Drowned in sin, they know me not for their God;
    In worldly riches is all their mind,
    They fear not my righteousness, the sharp rod.
    My law that I showed, when I for them died,
30   They forget clean, and shedding of my blood red;
    I hanged between two, it cannot be denied;
    To get them life I suffered to be dead;
    I healed their feet, with thorns hurt was my head.
    I could do no more than I did, truly;
35   And now I see the people do clean forsake me:
    They use the seven deadly sins damnable,
    As pride, covetise, wrath, and lechery
    Now in the world be made commendable;

And thus they leave of angels the heavenly company.
Every man liveth so after his own pleasure,   40
And yet of their life they be nothing sure:
I see the more that I them forbear
The worse they be from year to year.
All that liveth appaireth fast;
Therefore I will, in all the haste,   45
Have a reckoning of every man's person;
For, and I leave the people thus alone
In their life and wicked tempests,
Verily they will become much worse than beasts;
For now one would by envy another up eat;   50
Charity they do all clean forget.
I hoped well that every man
In my glory should make his mansion,
And thereto I had them all elect;
But now I see, like traitors deject,   55
They thank me not for the pleasure that I to them meant,
Nor yet for their being that I them have lent,
I proffered the people great multitude of mercy,
And few there be that asketh it heartily.
They be so cumbered with worldly riches   60
That needs on them I must do justice,
On every man living without fear.
Where art thou, Death, thou mighty messenger?

(Enter DEATH.)

DEATH: Almighty God, I am here at your will,
    Your commandment to fulfill.   65
GOD: Go thou to Everyman,
    And show him, in my name,
    A pilgrimage he must on him take,
    Which he in no wise may escape;
    And that he bring with him a sure reckoning   70
    Without delay or any tarrying.

(GOD withdraws.)

DEATH: Lord, I will in the world go run overall,
    And cruelly outsearch both great and small;
    Every man will I beset that liveth beastly
    Out of God's laws, and dreadeth not folly.   75

---

3 **By figure** in form   6 **all day** always   8 **But . . . gracious** but the purpose of it is more devout   23 **unkind** ungrateful   25 **Of ghostly sight** in spiritual vision   32 **I . . . dead** I consented to die   37 **covetise** covetousness

41 **And . . . sure** and yet their lives are by no means obscure   44 **appaireth** degenerates   47 **and** if   48 **tempests** tumults   55 **deject** abject   59 **heartily** earnestly   72 **overall** everywhere

He that loveth riches I will strike with my dart,
His sight to blind, and from heaven to depart—
Except that alms be his good friend—
In hell for to dwell, world without end.

80   Lo, yonder I see Everyman walking.
Full little he thinketh on my coming;
His mind is on fleshly lusts and his treasure,
And great pain it shall cause him to endure
Before the Lord, Heaven King.

(Enter EVERYMAN.)

85   Everyman, stand still! Whither art thou going
Thus gaily? Hast thou thy Maker forget?
EVERYMAN: Why askest thou?
Wouldest thou wit?
DEATH: Yea, sir; I will show you:
90   In great haste I am sent to thee
From God out of his majesty.
EVERYMAN: What, sent to me?
DEATH: Yea, certainly.
Though thou have forget him here,
95   He thinketh on thee in the heavenly sphere,
As, ere we depart, thou shalt know.
EVERYMAN: What desireth God of me?
DEATH: That shall I show thee:
A reckoning he will needs have
100   Without any longer respite.
EVERYMAN: To give a reckoning longer leisure I crave;
This blind matter troubleth my wit.
DEATH: On thee thou must take a long journey;
Therefore thy book of count with thee thou bring,
105   For turn again thou cannot by no way.
And look thou be sure of thy reckoning,
For before God thou shalt answer, and show
Thy many bad deeds, and good but a few;
How thou hast spent thy life, and in what wise,
110   Before the chief Lord of paradise.
Have ado that we were in that way,
For, wit thou well, thou shalt make none attorney.
EVERYMAN: Full unready I am such reckoning to give.
I know thee not. What messenger art thou?
115 DEATH: I am Death, that no man dreadeth,
For every man I rest, and no man spareth;
For it is God's commandment
That all to me should be obedient.
EVERYMAN: O Death, thou comest when I had thee least in
mind!
120   In thy power it lieth me to save;
Yet of my good will I give thee, if thou will be kind:
Yea, a thousand pound shalt thou have,
And defer this matter till another day.
DEATH: Everyman, it may not be, by no way.
125   I set not by gold, silver, nor riches,

Ne by pope, emperor, king, duke, ne princes;
For, and I would receive gifts great,
All the world I might get;
But my custom is clean contrary.
I give thee no respite. Come hence, and not tarry.   130
EVERYMAN: Alas, shall I have no longer respite?
I may say Death giveth no warning!
To think on thee, it maketh my heart sick,
For all unready is my book of reckoning.
But twelve year and I might have abiding,   135
My counting-book I would make so clear
That my reckoning I should not need to fear.
Wherefore, Death, I pray thee, for God's mercy,
Spare me till I be provided of remedy.
DEATH: Thee availeth not to cry, weep, and pray;   140
But haste thee lightly that thou were gone that journey,
And prove thy friends if thou can,
For, wit thou well, the tide abideth no man,
And in the world each living creature
For Adam's sin must die of nature.   145
EVERYMAN: Death, if I should this pilgrimage take,
And my reckoning surely make,
Show me, for saint charity,
Should I not come again shortly?
DEATH: No, Everyman; and thou be once there,   150
Thou mayst never more come here,
Trust me verily.
EVERYMAN: O gracious God in the high seat celestial,
Have mercy on me in this most need!
Shall I have no company from this vale terrestrial   155
Of mine acquaintance, that way me to lead?
DEATH: Yea, if any be so hardy
That would go with thee and bear thee company.
Hie thee that thou were gone to God's magnificence,
Thy reckoning to give before his presence.   160
What, weenest thou thy life is given thee,
And thy worldly goods also?
EVERYMAN: I had wend so, verily.
DEATH: Nay, nay; it was but lent thee;
For as soon as thou art go,   165
Another a while shall have it, and then go therefro,
Even as thou hast done.
Everyman, thou art mad! Thou hast thy wits five,
And here on earth will not amend thy life;
For suddenly I do come.   170
EVERYMAN: O wretched caitiff, whither shall I flee,
That I might scape this endless sorrow?
Now, gentle Death, spare me till to-morrow,
That I may amend me
With good advisement.   175
DEATH: Nay, thereto I will not consent,
Nor no man will I respite;
But to the heart suddenly I shall smite
Without any advisement.
And now out of thy sight I will me hie;   180
See thou make thee ready shortly,

---

77 **depart** separate   88 **wit** know   102 **blind** obscure   104 **count**
account   105 **turn again** return   111 **Have . . . way** i.e., let's see
about making that journey   112 **none attorney** no one [your]
advocate   115 **that . . . dreadeth** who fears no man   116 **rest**
arrest   121 **good** goods   123 **And defer** if you defer   125 **set**
not by care not for

---

143 **tide** time   161 **weenest** suppose   163 **wend** supposed
165 **go** gone   166 **therefro** from it   175 **advisement** reflection

For thou mayst say this is the day
That no man living may scape away.

(*Exit* DEATH.)

EVERYMAN: Alas, I may well weep with sighs deep!
185   Now have I no manner of company
To help me in my journey, and me to keep;
And also my writing is full unready.
How shall I do now for to excuse me?
I would to God I had never be get!
190   To my soul a full great profit it had be;
For now I fear pains huge and great.
The time passeth, Lord, help, that all wrought!
For though I mourn it availeth nought.
The day passeth. and is almost ago;
195   I wot not well what for to do.
To whom were I best my complaint to make?
What and I to Fellowship thereof spake,
And showed him of this sudden chance?
For in him is all mine affiance;
200   We have in the world so many a day
Be good friends in sport and play.
I see him yonder, certainly.
I trust that he will bear me company;
Therefore to him will I speak to ease my sorrow.
205   Well met, good Fellowship, and good morrow!

(FELLOWSHIP *speaketh:*)

FELLOWSHIP: Everyman, good morrow, by this day!
Sir, why lookest thou so piteously?
If any thing be amiss, I pray thee me say,
That I may help to remedy.
210 EVERYMAN: Yea, good Fellowship, yea;
I am in great jeopardy.
FELLOWSHIP: My true friend, show to me your mind;
I will not forsake thee to my life's end,
In the way of good company.
215 EVERYMAN: That was well spoken, and lovingly.
FELLOWSHIP: Sir, I must needs know your heaviness;
I have pity to see you in any distress.
If any have you wronged, ye shall revenged be,
Though I on the ground be slain for thee—
220   Though that I know before that I should die.
EVERYMAN: Verily, Fellowship, gramercy.
FELLOWSHIP: Tush! by thy thanks I set not a straw.
Show me your grief, and say no more.
EVERYMAN: If my heart should to you break,
225   And then you to turn your mind from me,
And would not me comfort when ye hear me speak,
Then should I ten times sorrier be.
FELLOWSHIP: Sir, I say as I will do indeed.
EVERYMAN: Then be you a good friend at need:
230   I have found you true herebefore.
FELLOWSHIP: And so ye shall evermore;
For, in faith; and thou go to hell,

I will not forsake thee by the way.
EVERYMAN: Ye speak like a good friend; I believe you well.
I shall deserve it, and I may.   235
FELLOWSHIP: I speak of no deserving, by this day!
For he that will say, and nothing do,
Is not worthy with good company to go;
Therefore show me the grief of your mind,
As to your friend most loving and kind.   240
EVERYMAN: I shall show you how it is:
Commanded I am to go a journey,
A long way, hard and dangerous,
And give a strait count, without delay,
Before the high Judge, Adonai.   245
Wherefore, I pray you, bear me company,
As ye have promised, in this journey.
FELLOWSHIP: That is matter indeed. Promise is duty;
But, and I should take such a voyage on me,
I know it well, it should be to my pain;   250
Also it maketh me afeard, certain.
But let us take counsel here as well as we can,
For your words would fear a strong man.
EVERYMAN: Why, ye said if I had need
Ye would me never forsake, quick ne dead,   255
Though it were to hell, truly.
FELLOWSHIP: So I said, certainly,
But such pleasures be set aside, the sooth to say;
And also, if we took such a journey,
When should we come again?   260
EVERYMAN: Nay, never again, till the day of doom.
FELLOWSHIP: In faith, then will not I come there!
Who hath you these tidings brought?
EVERYMAN: Indeed, Death was with me here.
FELLOWSHIP: Now, by God that all hath bought,   265
If Death were the messenger,
For no man that is living to-day
I will not go that loath journey—
Not for the father that begat me!
EVERYMAN: Ye promised, otherwise, pardie.   270
FELLOWSHIP: I wot well I said so, truly;
And yet if thou wilt eat, and drink, and make good cheer,
Or haunt to women the lusty company,
I would not forsake you while the day is clear,
Trust me verily.   275
EVERYMAN: Yea, thereto ye would be ready!
To go to mirth, solace, and play,
Your mind will sooner apply,
Than to bear me company in my long journey.
FELLOWSHIP: Now, in good faith, I will not that way.   280
But and thou will murder, or any man kill,
In that I will help thee with a good will.
EVERYMAN: O, that is a simple advice indeed.
Gentle fellow, help me in my necessity!
We have loved long, and now I need;   285
And now, gentle Fellowship, remember me.

---

186 **keep** guard   187 **writing** the writing of Everyman's accounts
189 **be get** been born   194 **ago** gone   197 **and if**   199 **affiance**
trust   206 **by this day** an asseveration   216 **heaviness** sorrow
224 **break** open

235 **deserve** repay   244 **strait count** strict account   245 **Adonai**
a Hebrew name for God   248 **That . . . indeed** that is a good
reason indeed [for asking me]   253 **fear** frighten   265 **bought**
redeemed   268 **loath** loathsome   270 **pardie** by God
273 **Or . . . company** or frequent the pleasant company of
women   274 **while . . . clear** until day-break   278 **apply** attend

FELLOWSHIP: Whether ye have loved me or no,
 By Saint John, I will not with thee go.
EVERYMAN: Yet, I pray thee, take the labour, and do so much
 for me
290 To bring me forward, for saint charity,
 And comfort me till I come without the town.
FELLOWSHIP: Nay, and thou would give me a new gown,
 I will not a foot with thee go;
 But, and thou had tarried, I would not have left thee so.
295 And as now God speed thee in thy journey,
 For from thee I will depart as fast as I may.
EVERYMAN: Whither away, Fellowship? Will thou forsake me?
FELLOWSHIP: Yea, by my fay! To God I betake thee.
EVERYMAN: Farewell, good Fellowship; for thee my heart is
 sore.
300 Adieu for ever! I shall see thee no more.
FELLOWSHIP: In faith, Everyman, farewell now at the ending;
 For you I will remember that parting is mourning.

(*Exit* FELLOWSHIP.)

EVERYMAN: Alack! shall we thus depart indeed—
 Ah, Lady, help!—without any more comfort?
305 Lo, Fellowship forsaketh me in my most need.
 For help in this world whither shall I resort?
 Fellowship herebefore with me would merry make,
 And now little sorrow for me doth he take.
 It is said, 'In prosperity men friends may find,
310 Which in adversity be full unkind.'
 Now whither for succour shall I flee,
 Sith that Fellowship hath forsaken me?
 To my kinsmen I will, truly,
 Praying them to help me in my necessity;
315 I believe that they will do so,
 For kind will creep where it may not go.
 I will go say, for yonder I see them.
 Where be ye now, my friends and kinsmen?

(*Enter* KINDRED *and* COUSIN.)

KINDRED: Here be we now at your commandment.
320 Cousin, I pray you show us your intent
 In any wise, and do not spare.
COUSIN: Yea, Everyman, and to us declare
 If ye be disposed to go anywhither;
 For, wit you well, we will live and die together.
325 KINDRED: In wealth and woe we will with you hold,
 For over his kin a man may be bold.
EVERYMAN: Gramercy, my friends and kinsmen kind.
 Now shall I show you the grief of my mind:
 I was commanded by a messenger,
330 That is a high king's chief officer;
 He bade me go a pilgrimage, to my pain,

And I know well I shall never come again;
 Also I must give a reckoning strait,
 For I have a great enemy that hath me in wait,
 Which intendeth me for to hinder. 335
KINDRED: What account is that which ye must render?
 That would I know.
EVERYMAN: Of all my works I must show
 How I have lived and my days spent;
 Also of ill deeds that I have used 340
 In my time, sith life was me lent;
 And of all virtues that I have refused.
 Therefore, I pray you, go thither with me
 To help to make mine account, for saint charity.
COUSIN: What, to go thither? Is that the matter? 345
 Nay, Everyman, I had liefer fast bread and water
 All this five year and more.
EVERYMAN: Alas, that ever I was bore!
 For now shall I never be merry,
 If that you forsake me. 350
KINDRED: Ah, sir, what ye be a merry man!
 Take good heart to you, and make no moan.
 But one thing I warn you, by Saint Anne—
 As for me, ye shall go alone.
EVERYMAN: My Cousin, will you not with me go? 355
COUSIN: No, by our Lady! I have the cramp in my toe.
 Trust not to me, for, so God me speed,
 I will deceive you in your most need.
KINDRED: It availeth not us to tice.
 Ye shall have my maid with all my heart; 360
 She loveth to go to feasts, there to be nice,
 And to dance, and abroad to start:
 I will give her leave to help you in that journey,
 If that you and she may agree.
EVERYMAN: Now show me the very effect of your mind: 365
 Will you go with me, or abide behind?
KINDRED: Abide behind? Yea, that will I, and I may!
 Therefore farewell till another day.

(*Exit* KINDRED.)

EVERYMAN: How should I be merry or glad?
 For fair promises men to me make, 370
 But when I have most need they me forsake.
 I am deceived; that maketh me sad.
COUSIN: Cousin Everyman, farewell now,
 For verily I will not go with you.
 Also of mine own an unready reckoning 375
 I have to account; therefore I make tarrying.
 Now God keep thee, for now I go.

(*Exit* COUSIN.)

---

290 **bring me forward** escort me 298 **fay** faith; **betake** commend 303 **depart** part 312 **Sith** since 316 **For . . . go** For kinship will creep where it cannot walk, that is, blood is thicker than water 317 **go say** essay, try 321 **In . . . spare** without fail, and do not hold back 323 **anywhither** anywhere 325 **hold** side 326 **For . . . bold** for a man may be sure of his kinsfolk

334 **For . . . wait** a great enemy (the devil) who has me under observation 340 **used** practised 346 **I . . . water** I had rather fast on bread and water 348 **bore** born 351 **what . . . man** what a merry man you are 359 **It . . . tice** it is no use trying to entice us 361 **nice** wanton 362 **abroad to start** go out and about 365 **effect** tenor

EVERYMAN: Ah, Jesus, is all come hereto?
       Lo, fair words maketh fools fain;
380   They promise, and nothing will do, certain.
       My kinsmen promised me faithfully
       For to abide with me steadfastly,
       And now fast away do they flee:
       Even so Fellowship promised me.
385   What friend were best me of to provide?
       I lose my time here longer to abide.
       Yet in my mind a thing there is:
       All my life I have loved riches;
       If that my Good now help me might,
390   He would make my heart full light.
       I will speak to him in this distress—
       Where art thou, my Goods and riches?

(GOODS *speaks from a corner.*)

       GOODS: Who calleth me? Everyman? What! hast thou haste?
       I lie here in corners, trussed and piled so high,
395   And in chests I am locked so fast,
       Also sacked in bags. Thou mayst see with thine eye
       I cannot stir; in packs low I lie.
       What would ye have? Lightly me say.
       EVERYMAN: Come hither, Goods, in all the haste thou may,
400   For of counsel I must desire thee.
       GOODS: Sir, and ye in the world have sorrow or adversity,
       That can I help you to remedy shortly.
       EVERYMAN: It is another disease that grieveth me;
       In this world it is not, I tell thee so.
405   I am sent for, another way to go,
       To give a strait count general
       Before the highest Jupiter of all;
       And all my life I have had joy and pleasure in thee,
       Therefore, I pray thee, go with me;
410   For, peradventure, thou mayst before God Almighty
       My reckoning help to clean and purify;
       For it is said ever among
       That money maketh all right that is wrong.
       GOODS: Nay, Everyman, I sing another song.
415   I follow no man in such voyages;
       For, and I went with thee,
       Thou shouldst fare much the worse for me;
       For because on me thou did set thy mind,
       Thy reckoning I have made blotted and blind,
420   That thine account thou cannot make truly;
       And that hast thou for the love of me.
       EVERYMAN: That would grieve me full sore,
       When I should come to that fearful answer.
       Up, let us go thither together.
425   GOODS: Nay, not so! I am too brittle, I may not endure;
       I will follow no man one foot, be ye sure.
       EVERYMAN: Alas, I have thee loved, and had great pleasure
       All my life-days on good and treasure.

GOODS: That is to thy damnation, without leasing,
       For my love is contrary to the love everlasting;   430
       But if thou had me loved moderately during,
       As to the poor to give part of me,
       Then shouldst thou not in this dolour be,
       Nor in this great sorrow and care.
       EVERYMAN: Lo, now was I deceived ere I was ware,   435
       And all I may wite misspending of time.
       GOODS: What, weenest thou that I am thine?
       EVERYMAN: I had wend so.
       GOODS: Nay, Everyman, I say no.
       As for a while I was lent thee;   440
       A season thou hast had me in prosperity.
       My condition is man's soul to kill;
       If I save one, a thousand I do spill.
       Weenest thou that I will follow thee?
       Nay, not from this world, verily.   445
       EVERYMAN: I had wend otherwise.
       GOODS: Therefore to thy soul Goods is a thief;
       For when thou art dead, this is my guise—
       Another to deceive in this same wise
       As I have done thee, and all to his soul's reprief.   450
       EVERYMAN: O false Goods, cursed may thou be.
       Thou traitor to God, that hast deceived me
       And caught me in thy snare!
       GOODS: Marry, thou brought thyself in care,
       Whereof I am glad;   455
       I must needs laugh, I cannot be sad.
       EVERYMAN: Ah, Goods, thou hast had long my heartly love;
       I gave thee that which should be the Lord's above.
       But wilt thou not go with me indeed?
       I pray thee truth to say.   460
       GOODS: No, so God me speed!
       Therefore farewell, and have good day.

(*Exit* GOODS.)

EVERYMAN: O, to whom shall I make my moan
       For to go with me in that heavy journey?
       First Fellowship said he would with me gone;   465
       His words were very pleasant and gay,
       But afterward he left me alone.
       Then spake I to my kinsmen, all in despair,
       And also they gave me words fair;
       They lacked no fair speaking,   470
       But all forsook me in the ending.
       Then went I to my Goods, that I loved best,
       In hope to have comfort, but there had I least;
       For my Goods sharply did me tell
       That he bringeth many into hell.   475
       Then of myself I was ashamed,

---

385 **me . . . provide** to provide myself with   389 **Good** Goods
398 **Lightly** quickly   400 **For . . . thee** for I must entreat your
advice   403 **disease** trouble   412 **For . . . among** for it is sometimes said   419 **blind** obscure

---

429 **without leasing** without a lie, that is, truly   431–32
But . . . me but if you had loved me moderately during your lifetime, so as to give part of me to the poor   433 **dolour** distress
435 **ware** aware   436 **And . . . time** and I may blame it all on
the bad use I have made of time   438 **wend** supposed   442 **condition** nature   443 **spill** ruin   448 **guise** practice   450 **reprief**
shame   457 **heartly** heartfelt

And so I am worthy to be blamed;
Thus may I well myself hate.
Of whom shall I now counsel take?
480 I think that I shall never speed
Till that I go to my Good Deed.
But, alas, she is so weak
That she can neither go nor speak;
Yet will I venture on her now.
485 My Good Deeds, where be you?

(GOOD DEEDS *speaks from the ground.*)

GOOD DEEDS: Here I lie, cold in the ground;
Thy sins hath me sore bound,
That I cannot stir.
EVERYMAN: O Good Deeds, I stand in fear!
490 I must you pray of counsel,
For help now should come right well.
GOOD DEEDS: Everyman, I have understanding
That ye be summoned account to make
Before Messias, of Jerusalem King;
495 And you do by me, that journey with you will I take.
EVERYMAN: Therefore I come to you, my moan to make;
I pray you that ye will go with me,
GOOD DEEDS: I would full fain, but I cannot stand, verily.
EVERYMAN: Why, is there anything on you fall?
500 GOOD DEEDS: Yea, sir, I may thank you of all;
If ye had perfectly cheered me,
Your book of count full ready had be.
Look, the books of your works and deeds eke!
Behold how they lie under the feet,
505 To your soul's heaviness.
EVERYMAN: Our Lord Jesus help me!
For one letter here I cannot see.
GOOD DEEDS: There is a blind reckoning in time of distress.
EVERYMAN: Good Deeds, I pray you help me in this need,
510 Or else I am for ever damned indeed;
Therefore help me to make reckoning
Before the Redeemer of all thing,
That King is, and was, and ever shall.
GOOD DEEDS: Everyman, I am sorry of your fall,
515 And fain would I help you, and I were able.
EVERYMAN: Good Deeds, your counsel I pray you give me.
GOOD DEEDS: That shall I do verily;
Though that on my feet I may not go,
I have a sister that shall with you also,
520 Called Knowledge, which shall with you abide,
To help you to make that dreadful reckoning.

(*Enter* KNOWLEDGE.)

KNOWLEDGE: Everyman, I will go with thee, and be thy guide,
In thy most need to go by thy side.
EVERYMAN: In good condition I am now in every thing,
And am wholly content with this good thing,   525
Thanked be God my creator.
GOOD DEEDS: And when she hath brought you there
Where thou shalt heal thee of thy smart,
Then go you with your reckoning and your Good Deeds
together,
For to make you joyful at heart   530
Before the blessed Trinity.
EVERYMAN: My Good Deeds, gramercy!
I am well content, certainly,
With your words sweet.
KNOWLEDGE: Now go we together lovingly   535
To Confession, that cleansing river.
EVERYMAN: For joy I weep; I would we were there!
But, I pray you, give me cognition
Where dwelleth that holy man, Confession.
KNOWLEDGE: In the house of salvation: 540
We shall find him in that place,
That shall us comfort, by God's grace.

(KNOWLEDGE *takes* EVERYMAN *to* CONFESSION.)

Lo, this is Confession. Kneel down and ask mercy,
For he is in good conceit with God Almighty.
EVERYMAN: O glorious fountain, that all uncleanness doth clarify,   545
Wash from me the spots of vice unclean,
That on me no sin may be seen.
I come with Knowledge for my redemption,
Redempt with heart and full contrition;
For I am commanded a pilgrimage to take,   550
And great accounts before God to make.
Now I pray you, Shrift, mother of salvation,
Help my Good Deeds for my piteous exclamation.
CONFESSION: I know your sorrow well, Everyman.
Because with Knowledge ye come to me,   555
I will you comfort as well as I can,
And a precious jewel I will give thee,
Called penance, voider of adversity;
Therewith shall your body chastised be,
With abstinence and perseverance in God's service.   560
Here shall you receive that scourge of me,
Which is penance strong that ye must endure,
To remember thy Saviour was scourged for thee
With sharp scourges, and suffered it patiently;
So must thou, ere thou scape that painful pilgrimage.   565
Knowledge, keep him in this voyage,
And by that time Good Deeds will be with thee.
But in any wise be siker of mercy,
For your time draweth fast; and ye will saved be,
Ask God mercy, and he will grant truly.   570

---

483 **go** walk   484 **venture** gamble   491 **For . . . well** for help would now be very welcome   495 **And . . . me** if you do as I advise   499 **fall** befallen   500 **of** for   501 **If . . . me** if you had encouraged me fully   503 **eke** also   508 **There . . . distress** a sinful person in this hour of need finds that the account of his good deeds is dimly written and difficult to read   520 **Knowledge** the meaning of Knowledge here is acknowledgment or recognition of sins

---

528 **smart** pain   538 **cognition** knowledge   540 **In . . . salvation** in the church   544 **conceit** esteem   549 **Redempt . . . contrition** redeemed by heartfelt and full contrition   552 **Shrift** confession   553 **for . . . exclamation** in answer to my piteous cry   558 **voider** expeller   568 **siker** sure   569 **draweth fast** draws quickly to an end; **and** if

When with the scourge of penance man doth him bind,
The oil of forgiveness then shall he find.
EVERYMAN: Thanked be God for his gracious work!
For now I will my penance begin;
575   This hath rejoiced and lighted my heart,
Though the knots be painful and hard within.
KNOWLEDGE: Everyman, look your penance that ye fulfil,
What pain that ever it to you be;
And Knowledge shall give you counsel at will
580   How your account ye shall make clearly.
EVERYMAN: O eternal God, O heavenly figure,
O way of righteousness, O goodly vision,
Which descended down in a virgin pure
Because he would every man redeem,
585   Which Adam forfeited by his disobedience:
O blessed Godhead, elect and high divine,
Forgive my grievous offence;
Here I cry thee mercy in this presence.
O ghostly treasure, O ransomer and redeemer,
590   Of all the world hope and conductor,
Mirror of joy, and founder of mercy,
Which enlumineth heaven and earth thereby,
Hear my clamorous complaint, though it late be;
Receive my prayers, of thy benignity;
595   Though I be a sinner most abominable,
Yet let my name be written in Moses' table.
O Mary, pray to the Maker of all thing,
Me for to help at my ending;
And save me from the power of my enemy,
600   For Death assaileth me strongly.
And, Lady, that I may by mean of thy prayer
Of your Son's glory to be partner,
By the means of his passion, I it crave;
I beseech you help my soul to save.
605   Knowledge, give me the scourge of penance;
My flesh therewith shall give acquittance:
I will now begin, if God give me grace.
KNOWLEDGE: Everyman, God give you time and space!
Thus I bequeath you in the hands of our Saviour;
610   Now may you make your reckoning sure.
EVERYMAN: In the name of the Holy Trinity,
My body sore punished shall be:
Take this, body, for the sin of the flesh!

(Scourges himself.)

---

571 **him** himself   575 **lighted** lightened   576 **Though . . .
within** though the knots [of the scourge] be painful and hard to
my body   586 **divine** divinity   588 **in this presence** in the
presence of this company   592 **thereby** besides   596 **Yet . . .
table** medieval theologians regarded the two tables given on Sinai
as symbols of baptism and penance, respectively. Thus Everyman
is asking to be numbered among those who have escaped damnation by doing penance for their sins   599 **my enemy** the devil
601–603 **And . . . crave** and, Lady, I beg that through the medi-
ation of thy prayer I may share in your Son's glory, in consequence
of His passion   606 **acquittance** satisfaction (as a part of the
sacrament of penance)   608 **space** opportunity

Also thou delightest to go gay and fresh,
And in the way of damnation thou did me bring,   615
Therefore suffer now strokes and punishing.
Now of penance I will wade the water clear,
To save me from purgatory, that sharp fire.

(GOOD DEEDS rises from the ground.)

GOOD DEEDS: I thank God, now I can walk and go,
And am delivered of my sickness and woe.   620
Therefore with Everyman I will go, and not spare;
His good works I will help him to declare.
KNOWLEDGE: Now, Everyman, be merry and glad!
Your Good Deeds cometh now; ye may not be sad.
Now is your Good Deeds whole and sound,   625
Going upright upon the ground.
EVERYMAN: My heart is light, and shall be evermore;
Now will I smite faster than I did before.
GOOD DEEDS: Everyman, pilgrim, my special friend,
Blessed be thou without end;   630
For thee is preparate the eternal glory.
Ye have me made whole and sound,
Therefore I will bide by thee in every stound.
EVERYMAN: Welcome, my Good Deeds; now I hear thy voice,
I weep for very sweetness of love.   635
KNOWLEDGE: Be no more sad, but ever rejoice;
God seeth thy living in his throne above.
Put on this garment to thy behoof,
Which is wet with your tears,
Or else before God you may it miss,   640
When ye to your journey's end come shall.
EVERYMAN: Gentle Knowledge, what do ye it call?
KNOWLEDGE: It is a garment of sorrow:
From pain it will you borrow;
Contrition it is,   645
That geteth forgiveness;
It pleaseth God passing well.
GOOD DEEDS: Everyman, will you wear it for your heal?
EVERYMAN: Now blessed be Jesu, Mary's Son,
For now have I on true contrition.   650
And let us go now without tarrying;
Good Deeds, have we clear our reckoning?
GOOD DEEDS: Yea, indeed, I have it here.
EVERYMAN: Then I trust we need not fear;
Now, friends, let us not part in twain.   655
KNOWLEDGE: Nay, Everyman, that will we not, certain.
GOOD DEEDS: Yet must thou lead with thee
Three persons of great might.
EVERYMAN: Who should they be?
GOOD DEEDS: Discretion and Strength they hight,   660
And thy Beauty may not abide behind.
KNOWLEDGE: Also ye must call to mind
Your Five Wits as for your counsellors.
GOOD DEEDS: You must have them ready at all hours.
EVERYMAN: How shall I get them hither?   665

---

631 **preparate** prepared   633 **stound** trial   638 **behoof** advantage   644 **borrow** release   647 **passing** exceedingly   648 **heal**
salvation   660 **hight** are called   663 **Wits** senses

KNOWLEDGE: You must call them all together,
　　And they will hear you incontinent.
EVERYMAN: My friends, come hither and be present,
　　Discretion, Strength, my Five Wits, and Beauty.

(*Enter* BEAUTY, STRENGTH, DISCRETION, *and* FIVE WITS.)

670　BEAUTY: Here at your will we be all ready.
　　What will ye that we should do?
　　GOOD DEEDS: That ye would with Everyman go,
　　And help him in his pilgrimage.
　　Advise you, will ye with him or not in that voyage?
675　STRENGTH: We will bring him all thither,
　　To his help and comfort, ye may believe me.
　　DISCRETION: So will we go with him all together.
　　EVERYMAN: Almighty God, lofed may thou be!
　　I give thee laud that I have hither brought
680　Strength, Discretion, Beauty, and Five Wits. Lack
　　　　I nought.
　　And my Good Deeds, with Knowledge clear,
　　All be in my company at my will here;
　　I desire no more to my business.
　　STRENGTH: And I, Strength, will by you stand in distress,
685　Though thou would be in battle fight on the ground.
　　FIVE WITS: And though it were through the world round,
　　We will not depart for sweet ne sour.
　　BEAUTY: No more will I unto death's hour
　　Whatsoever thereof befall.
690　DISCRETION: Everyman, advise you first of all;
　　Go with a good advisement and deliberation.
　　We all give you virtuous monition
　　That all shall be well.
　　EVERYMAN: My friends, harken what I will tell:
695　I pray God reward you in his heavenly sphere.
　　Now harken, all that be here,
　　For I will make my testament
　　Here before you all present:
　　In alms half my good I will give with my hands twain
700　In the way of charity, with good intent,
　　And the other half still shall remain
　　In queth, to be returned there it ought to be.
　　This I do in despite of the fiend of hell,
　　To go quit out of his peril
705　Ever after and this day.
　　KNOWLEDGE: Everyman, harken what I say:
　　Go to priesthood, I you advise,
　　And receive of him in any wise
　　The holy sacrament and ointment together.
710　Then shortly see ye turn again hither;
　　We will all abide you here.
　　FIVE WITS: Yea, Everyman, hie you that ye ready were.

There is no emperor, king, duke, ne baron,
That of God hath commission
As hath the least priest in the world being;　715
For of the blessed sacraments pure and benign
He beareth the keys, and thereof hath the cure
For man's redemption—it is ever sure—
Which God for our soul's medicine
Gave us out of his heart with great pine.　720
Here in this transitory life, for thee and me,
The blessed sacraments seven there be:
Baptism, confirmation, with priesthood good,
And the sacrament of God's precious flesh and blood,
Marriage, the holy extreme unction, and penance;　725
These seven be good to have in remembrance,
Gracious sacraments of high divinity.
EVERYMAN: Fain would I receive that holy body,
　　And meekly to my ghostly father I will go.
FIVE WITS: Everyman, that is the best that ye can do.　730
　　God will you to salvation bring,
　　For priesthood exceedeth all other thing:
　　To us Holy Scripture they do teach,
　　And converteth man from sin heaven to reach;
　　God hath to them more power given　735
　　Than to any angel that is in heaven.
　　With five words he may consecrate,
　　God's body in flesh and blood to make,
　　And handleth his Maker between his hands.
　　The priest bindeth and unbindeth all bands,　740
　　Both in earth and in heaven.
　　Thou ministers all the sacraments seven;
　　Though we kissed thy feet, thou were worthy;
　　Thou art surgeon that cureth sin deadly:
　　No remedy we find under God　745
　　But all only priesthood.
　　Everyman, God gave priests that dignity,
　　And setteth them in his stead among us to be;
　　Thus be they above angels in degree.

(EVERYMAN *goes to the priest to receive the last sacraments.*)

KNOWLEDGE: If priests be good, it is so, surely.　750
　　But when Jesus hanged on the cross with great smart,
　　There he gave out of his blessed heart
　　The same sacrament in great torment:
　　He sold them not to us, that Lord omnipotent.
　　Therefore Saint Peter the apostle doth say　755
　　That Jesu's curse hath all they
　　Which God their Saviour do buy or sell,
　　Or they for any money do take or tell.
　　Sinful priests giveth the sinners example bad;
　　Their children sitteth by other men's fires, I have heard;　760

---

667 **incontinent** immediately　674 **Advise** consider　678 **lofed** praised　683 **to** for　687 **for . . . sour** that is, in happiness or adversity　688 **unto** until　691 **advisement** reflection　692 **monition** forewarning　701–02 **And . . . be** the meaning seems to be that Everyman's immovable property (his body) will lie at rest in the earth　704–05 **To . . . day** to go free out of his power today and ever after　708　**in any wise** without fail　712 **hie . . . were** hurry and prepare yourself

714 **commission** authority　715 **being** living　720 **pine** suffering　728 **that holy body** the sacrament　729 **ghostly** spiritual　737 **five words** *Hoc est enim corpus meum* ("This is my body")　742 **ministers** administer　746 **But . . . priesthood** except only from the priesthood　750 **it is so** that they are above the angels　755–57 **Therefore . . . sell** the reference here is to the sin of simony (Acts 8:18 ff.)　760 **Their . . . fires** their children are illegitimate

And some haunteth women's company
With unclean life, as lusts of lechery:
These be with sin made blind.

FIVE WITS: I trust to God no such may we find;
765   Therefore let us priesthood honour,
And follow their doctrine for our souls' succour.
We be their sheep, and they shepherds be
By whom we all be kept in surety.
Peace, for yonder I see Everyman come,
770   Which hath made true satisfaction.
GOOD DEEDS: Methink it is he indeed.

(Re-enter EVERYMAN.)

EVERYMAN: Now Jesu be your alder speed!
I have received the sacrament for my redemption,
And then mine extreme unction:
775   Blessed be all they that counselled me to take it!
And now, friends, let us go without longer respite;
I thank God that ye have tarried so long.
Now set each of you on this rood your hand,
And shortly follow me:
780   I go before there I would be; God be our guide!
STRENGTH: Everyman, we will not from you go
Till ye have done this voyage long.
DISCRETION: I, Discretion, will bide by you also.
KNOWLEDGE: And though this pilgrimage be never so strong,
785   I will never part you fro.
STRENGTH: Everyman, I will be as sure by thee
As ever I did by Judas Maccabee.

(EVERYMAN comes to his grave.)

EVERYMAN: Alas, I am so faint I may not stand;
My limbs under me doth fold.
790   Friends, let us not turn again to this land,
Not for all the world's gold;
For into this cave must I creep
And turn to earth, and there to sleep.
BEAUTY: What, into this grave? Alas!
795   EVERYMAN: Yea, there shall ye consume, more and less.
BEAUTY: And what, should I smother here?
EVERYMAN: Yea, by my faith, and never more appear.
In this world live no more we shall,
But in heaven before the highest Lord of all.
800   BEAUTY: I cross out all this; adieu, by Saint John!
I take my cap in my lap, and am gone.
EVERYMAN: What, Beauty, whither will ye?
BEAUTY: Peace, I am deaf; I look not behind me,
Not and thou wouldest give me all the gold in thy chest.

(Exit BEAUTY.)

---

772 **be . . . speed** be the helper of you all   778 **rood** cross
784 **strong** grievous   785 **you fro** from you   786–87 **Everyman . . . Maccabee** I will stand by you as steadfastly as ever I did by Judas Maccabaeus (I Macc. 3)   795 **consume . . . less** decay, all of you   800 **I . . . this** I cancel all this, that is, my promise to stay with you   801 **I . . . lap** I doff my cap (so low that it comes) into my lap

---

EVERYMAN: Alas, whereto may I trust?   805
Beauty goeth fast away from me;
She promised with me to live and die.
STRENGTH: Everyman, I will thee also forsake and deny;
Thy game liketh me not at all.
EVERYMAN: Why, then, ye will forsake me all?   810
Sweet Strength, tarry a little space.
STRENGTH: Nay, sir, by the rood of grace!
I will hie me from thee fast,
Though thou weep till thy heart to-brast.
EVERYMAN: Ye would ever bide by me, ye said.   815
STRENGTH: Yea, I have you far enough conveyed.
Ye be old enough, I understand,
Your pilgrimage to take on hand;
I repent me that I hither came.
EVERYMAN: Strength, you to displease I am to blame;   820
Yet promise is debt, this ye well wot.
STRENGTH: In faith, I care not.
Thou art but a fool to complain;
You spend your speech and waste your brain.
Go thrust thee into the ground!   825

(Exit STRENGTH.)

EVERYMAN: I had wend surer I should you have found.
He that trusteth in his Strength
She him deceiveth at the length.
Both Strength and Beauty forsaketh me;
Yet they promised me fair and lovingly.   830
DISCRETION: Everyman, I will after Strength be gone;
As for me, I will leave you alone.
EVERYMAN: Why, Discretion, will you forsake me?
DISCRETION: Yea, in faith, I will go from thee,
For when Strength goeth before   835
I follow after evermore.
EVERYMAN: Yet, I pray thee, for the love of the Trinity,
Look in my grave once piteously.
DISCRETION: Nay, so nigh will I not come;
Farewell, every one!   840

(Exit DISCRETION.)

EVERYMAN: O, all thing faileth, save God alone—
Beauty, Strength, and Discretion;
For when Death bloweth his blast,
They all run from me full fast.
FIVE WITS: Everyman, my leave now of thee I take;   845
I will follow the other, for here I thee forsake.
EVERYMAN: Alas, then may I wail and weep,
For I took you for my best friend.
FIVE WITS: I will no longer thee keep;
Now farewell, and there an end.   850

(Exit FIVE WITS.)

EVERYMAN: O Jesu, help! All hath forsaken me.
GOOD DEEDS: Nay, Everyman; I will bide with thee.
I will not forsake thee indeed;

---

809 **liketh** pleases   811 **space** while   814 **to-brast** break
820 **you . . . blame** I am to blame for displeasing you

Thou shalt find me a good friend at need.
855 EVERYMAN: Gramercy, Good Deeds! Now may I true friends
see.
They have forsaken me, every one;
I loved them better than my Good Deeds alone.
Knowledge, will ye forsake me also?
KNOWLEDGE: Yea, Everyman, when ye to Death shall go;
860 But not yet, for no manner of danger.
EVERYMAN: Gramercy, Knowledge, with all my heart.
KNOWLEDGE: Nay, yet I will not from hence depart
Till I see where ye shall become.
EVERYMAN: Methink, alas, that I must be gone
865 To make my reckoning and my debts pay,
For I see my time is nigh spent away.
Take example, all ye that this do hear or see,
How they that I loved best do forsake me,
Except my Good Deeds that bideth truly.
870 GOOD DEEDS: All earthly things is but vanity:
Beauty, Strength, and Discretion do man forsake,
Foolish friends, and kinsmen, that fair spake—
All fleeth save Good Deeds, and that am I.
EVERYMAN: Have mercy on me, God most mighty;
875 And stand by me, thou mother and maid, holy Mary.
GOOD DEEDS: Fear not; I will speak for thee.
EVERYMAN: Here I cry God mercy.
GOOD DEEDS: Short our end, and minish our pain;
Let us go and never come again.
880 EVERYMAN: Into thy hands, Lord, my soul I commend;
Receive it, Lord, that it be not lost,
As thou me boughtest, so me defend,
And save me from the fiend's boast,
That I may appear with that blessed host
885 That shall be saved at the day of doom.
In manus tuas, of mights most
For ever, *commendo spiritum meum.*

(He sinks into his grave.)

KNOWLEDGE: Now hath he suffered that we all shall endure;
The Good Deeds shall make all sure.
Now hath he made ending; 890
Methinketh that I hear angels sing,
And make great joy and melody
Where Everyman's soul received shall be.
ANGEL: Come, excellent elect spouse, to Jesu!
Hereabove thou shalt go 895
Because of thy singular virtue.
Now the soul is taken the body fro,
Thy reckoning is crystal-clear.
Now shalt thou into the heavenly sphere,
Unto the which all ye shall come 900
That liveth well before the day of doom.

(Enter DOCTOR.)

DOCTOR: This moral men may have in mind.
Ye hearers, take it of worth, old and young,
And forsake Pride, for he deceiveth you in the end;
And remember Beauty, Five Wits, Strength, and 905
Discretion,
They all at the last do every man forsake,
Save his Good Deeds there doth he take.
But beware, for and they be small
Before God, he hath no help at all;
None excuse may be there for every man. 910
Alas, how shall he do then?
For after death amends may no man make,
For then mercy and pity doth him forsake.
If his reckoning be not clear when he doth come,
God will say: '*Ite, maledicti, in ignem eternum.*' 915
And he that hath his account whole and sound,
High in heaven he shall be crowned;
Unto which place God bring us all thither,
That we may live body and soul together.
Thereto help the Trinity! 920
Amen, say ye, for saint charity.

---

863 where . . . become what shall become of you   878 Short . . .
pain shorten our end, and diminish our pain   886–87 In . . .
meum Into thy hands, most mighty One for ever, I commend my
spirit

---

894 spouse bride of Jesus [a common medieval metaphor to express the idea of the soul's union with God]   903 take . . . worth
value it   907 Save unless   915 Ite . . . eternum depart, ye
cursed, into everlasting fire (Matt. xxv.41)

◆ THUS ENDETH THIS MORAL PLAY OF EVERYMAN ◆

WILLIAM SHAKESPEARE

Given the fact that William Shakespeare (1564–1616) was a commoner and that he worked in the ephemeral trades of the theater, what we know about his life is extraordinarily rich and revealing, especially in comparison to the lives of other playwrights of the period like Christopher Marlowe or John Webster. William Shakespeare was born in Stratford-upon-Avon, a town to the northwest of London in Warwickshire. He was baptized on April 26, 1564, and was probably born a few days earlier—his birth date is conventionally given as April 23, the feast day of St. George, the patron saint of England, and the day on which Shakespeare died fifty-two years later in 1616, again at his home in Stratford. One of eight children, Shakespeare was the son of a glover—a tradesman who worked with a variety of leather goods. It is not known whether Shakespeare attended the local school, the King's New School, but like other schools of the period, it would have provided him with an extensive grounding in Latin grammar, rhetoric, and literature. Later in his career, Shakespeare often drew on works he could have read at such a school: plays by Terence and Plautus, the poetry of Virgil and Ovid, the writings of Caesar.

He married Anne Hathaway in November of 1582; she was twenty-six and he was eighteen. In May of 1583 they had their first daughter, Susannah, followed by twins, Hamnet and Judith, born in 1585. Although his wife and children remained in Stratford throughout his career, Shakespeare went to London sometime in the late 1580s, possibly joining one of the theater companies that passed through Stratford.

By the 1590s, Shakespeare was established in London as an up-and-coming playwright; he was associated with the Lord Chamberlain's Men; he had written several plays on English history; and he was at work on several comedies and tragedies. When plague closed the theaters in London from the summer of 1592 through the spring of 1594, Shakespeare wrote two narrative poems, *Venus and Adonis* and *The Rape of Lucrece,* which he dedicated to Henry Wriothesley, the third Earl of Southampton, in a bid for patronage. He later wrote *The Phoenix and the Turtle* and circulated a brilliant and ambitious sequence of sonnets in manuscript before publishing it in 1609. As a shareholder of the Lord Chamberlain's Men, Shakespeare would have had many duties; no doubt he acted many parts, and we know he appeared in two plays by his contemporary Ben Jonson—*Every Man in His Humour* and *Sejanus.* In 1598, the Lord Chamberlain's men tore down The Theatre, brought the timbers south of the city and used them to build a new theater, the Globe. The Globe would remain the principal public-theater venue for the rest of Shakespeare's career, complemented by court and private-theater performances.

Shakespeare became the most popular playwright in London. He profited handsomely from his efforts at the Globe and from the patronage of the court, particularly after James I came to the throne in 1603 and took on the Lord Chamberlain's company as his own King's Men. Shakespeare used his income to buy a large house—called New Place—in Stratford, and throughout his career added to his property there; he retired and returned to Stratford in 1613. He drew up a will shortly before he died in 1616, leaving property to his family and mentioning gifts for several of his friends, including members of the King's Men: Richard Burbage, John Heminges, and Henry Condell. Heminges and Condell proved true to Shakespeare, for in 1623 they took Shakespeare's plays and published them in a single large volume. In an era when plays were not regarded as "literature," this was an important event. Although many of Shakespeare's plays had been published individually during his lifetime, roughly half of Shakespeare's plays (*Macbeth, Antony and Cleopatra,* and *The Tempest,* for instance) existed only in manuscript form at Shakespeare's death and certainly would not have survived without the efforts of Heminges and Condell. This complete volume is now usually called the "First Folio" because it is printed in a large,

FOLIO-sized format (about twice the dimensions of this book). The First Folio contains thirty-six of Shakespeare's plays; two more plays all or partly by Shakespeare and published in his lifetime (*Pericles* and *The Two Noble Kinsmen*) were left out of the Folio, and it is generally thought that Shakespeare contributed to a thirty-ninth play, *Sir Thomas More*. More recently, several scholars have argued that Shakespeare collaborated on a history play, *Edward III*. Finally, although many people have advanced the thesis that someone else actually wrote the "Shakespeare" plays—Sir Francis Bacon, Francis Walsingham, the Earl of Oxford, among others—these claims belong to the realm of myth, not to the realm of history.

The range of Shakespeare's accomplishment as a playwright is astonishing. Early in his career, Shakespeare wrote two cycles of plays on English history—*Henry VI (Parts 1, 2,* and *3),* and *Richard III;* and *Richard II, Henry IV (Parts 1* and *2),* and *Henry V*—that not only established a vogue for history plays but gave the English audience an epic version of the struggles that founded the Tudor and Stuart dynasties. Shakespeare's early comedies—*The Comedy of Errors, Two Gentlemen of Verona*—are very much in the vein of Plautus. Later comedies—*A Midsummer Night's Dream, As You Like It, Twelfth Night, The Merchant of Venice*—explore a variety of complex relations between love, sexuality, adulthood, ethnic discrimination, power, politics, and money. To many audiences today, Shakespeare is most remembered for *Hamlet* and the magisterial series of tragedies that followed, including *Othello, King Lear,* and *Macbeth.* Shakespeare's achievements often began with experimentation. The major tragedies benefited from his earlier efforts in the mode of the Roman playwright Seneca in *Titus Andronicus,* in morality drama in *Richard III,* in romantic tragedy in *Romeo and Juliet,* and political intrigue–drama in *Julius Caesar.* In his final years as a playwright, Shakespeare seems to have collaborated with John Fletcher on a few occasions and to have turned his hand to plays in the vein of "tragicomedy," now generally called ROMANCE: *Pericles, Cymbeline, The Winter's Tale,* and *The Tempest.*

HAMLET

In his landmark study, *The Idea of a Theater,* the actor and scholar Francis Fergusson characterized *Hamlet* as one of the "sphinxes of literature," a play that has repeatedly drawn actors, audiences, and scholars into its labyrinthine mystery. Yet while *Hamlet,* like the brooding young prince of Denmark, may now seem like a difficult and philosophical problem, to its original audiences the play was a version of a popular genre on the Elizabethan stage, the revenge tragedy. As in many of his other plays, Shakespeare adapted his tragedy from a variety of known materials. The story of Amlethus, a disinherited Danish prince who uses feigned madness and cunning to avenge his father's murder and regain the throne from his villainous uncle, dates from the twelfth-century *Historia Danica* of the Danish historian Saxo Grammaticus; it was later adapted as a tragic narrative by François de Belleforest and included in his *Histoires tragiques* in 1576. While Shakespeare may have known these versions, it is more certain that he knew a now-lost play on the subject of Hamlet's revenge that was staged in the 1580s. This play—usually called the *Ur-Hamlet* by scholars—was possibly written by Thomas Kyd, the author of another popular revenge tragedy, *The Spanish Tragedy.* While little is known about this play, we do know that it had at least one element of Shakespeare's play; in 1596, the playwright and novelist Thomas Lodge remarked on a play in which a pale ghost "cried so miserably at the Theater, like an oyster-wife, '*Hamlet, revenge!*'"

A ghost, a sinister and deceptive family, a court full of busybodies and spies, a broken romance, an elaborate play-within-the-play, a command—sometimes from beyond the grave—to take revenge, an elaborate finale in which the stage is littered with corpses:

these devices were common in revenge tragedies preceding Shakespeare's play, such as *The Spanish Tragedy,* and common also in those that capitalized on Hamlet's success in 1601, plays like John Marston's *The Malcontent* and Cyril Tourneur's *The Revenger's Tragedy* (which opens with a man speaking to a skull) and John Webster's *The White Devil.* While *Hamlet* avails itself of all these devices, it also reflects and refracts them; the play seems to question what it means to take action, simply to *act* let alone take revenge, in a world of such complete duplicity that any behavior might seem the treacherous "actions that a man might play." In his famous essay, "The World of *Hamlet,*" Maynard Mack suggests that the play is in the "interrogative mood": not only does Hamlet repeatedly ask questions of himself and others ("To be or not to be [. . .]," "Is it not monstrous [. . .]," and so on), but much of the action of the play involves, as Polonius suggests, using theatrical "indirections" to "find directions out": Polonius sends Reynaldo to spread dishonorable rumors about Laertes, to see whether Laertes is being virtuous in Paris; Claudius and Polonius "stage" Ophelia for Hamlet, hoping to discover whether he's mad for revenge or madly in love; Hamlet hopes that the players' *Murder of Gonzago* will reveal Claudius's guilt; Polonius hides fatally behind the arras while Hamlet interrogates Gertrude; Claudius stages a "duel" between Hamlet and Laertes that is really a design for murder.

The world of *Hamlet* is a world in which appearances sometimes deceive and sometimes speak the truth: not being able to read the signs—as Ophelia, Rosencrantz and Guildenstern, and Polonius all discover—can be fatal. Indeed, the play's obsession with seeming ("Seems, madam? Nay, it is. I know not 'seems,'" Hamlet declares in his first scene in the play) perhaps explains its obsession with the arts of seeming, with acting, performance, theater. In *Hamlet,* Shakespeare undertakes an extended meditation on the purpose and limits of theater. Hamlet, of course, is quite familiar with the theater, and Shakespeare clearly characterizes the troupe of players as his audience's contemporaries: not only is the company all male, but they seem to have left the city, as many professional companies did in the late 1590s as a result of the "war of the theaters," the contemporary vogue for companies of boy-actors performing satirical plays. Moreover, Hamlet's famous advice to the players (3.2) suggests that he has a keen eye for performance. He chastens the actors not to "mouth it, as many of our players do," not to "saw the air too much with your hand," but to "Suit the action to the word, the word to the action." Yet in *Hamlet,* words and actions are more often than not suited to deception, to the extent that to Hamlet "this goodly frame, the earth, seems [. . .] a sterile promontory." Hamlet's blatant reference to the Globe itself—an actor, surrounded by the circular frame of the Globe, standing on the bare platform of the stage—suggests a skeptical regard for the theater's creation. While plays like *A Midsummer Night's Dream* or perhaps *The Tempest* suggest the theater's ability to present healing fictions, the theater in *Hamlet* is presented from a more ironic, even disaffected perspective: to be trapped in a theatrical world, a world where performance outruns truth, is to be trapped in a world of empty and sterile pretending.

Shakespeare was clearly captivated by the character of Hamlet, which is often described as the richest acting role in the theatrical repertoire. But the theatricality that besets Hamlet in the shady world of Elsinore also poses problems for Hamlet's many interpreters, not only for Polonius and Claudius—who spend much of the play trying to "read" Hamlet, figure him out—but for the generations of actors, audiences, and scholars who have attempted to "pluck out the heart of [his] mystery." The difficulties of sounding Hamlet, however, are also part of the play's elaborate design. From his opening scene in the play, in which Hamlet both wears the conventional black of mourning and chides his mother for presuming that he is seeming to be in mourning, Hamlet's performance challenges his audiences (both onstage and off) to "read" him, to interpret his character through the signs and signals of his behavior. That is, Hamlet presents the audience with the same challenges that any actor does, inviting us to interpret "that within" from the various behaviors that pass "show." And, contrary to Laurence Olivier—whose brilliant film of the play opens with a voice intoning that *Hamlet* is the story "of a man who could not make up his mind"—Hamlet seems to act decisively throughout the play; what's difficult about reading Hamlet is that it's hard to tell when he's *acting* and when he's "acting in earnest." Hamlet feigns madness in some scenes, but seems madly out of control in others, such as the "nunnery" scene with Ophelia or the scene in Gertrude's closet. He asks the player to act the part of vengeful Pyrrhus, then seems to adopt the murderous swagger of the stage revenger, and then to question his performance ("Why, what an ass am I"). He directs the players to insert a scene into *The Murder of Gonzago* in order to trick Claudius into revealing his guilt, and then can't seem to keep himself off the stage, interrupting and interpreting the play as they play it. He's so offended when Laertes stagily leaps into Ophelia's grave that he outperforms Laertes's overacting: "Nay, an thou'lt mouth, / I'll rant as well as thou." Even Hamlet's soliloquies are problematic in this regard. For although we might think that we hear the "true" Hamlet when he speaks alone onstage, how can we know that Hamlet isn't trying on another role, either for his own benefit or ours—as he seems to do when he plays the revenger in the "O what a rogue and peasant slave am I" speech? And as the play proceeds, Hamlet's soliloquies become less frequent, and less revealing: when he returns from England in Act 5—having sent his friends Rosencrantz and Guildenstern to their deaths—the play provides him with no more solo speeches; like the court, we have only Hamlet's abrupt and irritable actions to go on.

Hamlet was evidently a success when it was first performed in 1600 or 1601; a pirated version of the play (the so-called bad quarto, Q1) was published in 1603, presumably because the play's popularity suggested that a published text could make some money. A version of the play authorized by the King's Men was published in 1604 (the second quarto, Q2), and the play was later included in the 1623 Folio (F); while Q1 is the most corrupt version of the play, Q2 and F are by no means identical, and most modern texts collate elements of both versions. From its inception, *Hamlet* has been a popular play with actors and audiences, and from Richard Burbage's creation of the role, Hamlet has been a mark of distinction in the history of English acting: the Restoration actor Thomas Betterton and the great eighteenth-century actor David Garrick were both admired in the part (Henry Fielding's novel *Tom Jones* contains a memorable parody of Garrick's performance). In the late nineteenth century Sir Henry Irving, the first actor to be knighted in England, gave a celebrated performance in which Hamlet never left the stage but several other characters (Rosencrantz and Guildenstern, for instance) were cut entirely. In the twentieth century, the play has, if anything, confirmed its reputation as an obligatory test for great actors, who have given a host of brilliant performances: Sir John Gielgud and Sir Laurence Olivier both produced fine stage versions of the play, and Olivier later won a Best Film Oscar for his film version. Since World War II, Richard Burton, Jonathan Pryce, Derek Jacobi, and Michael Pennington are among the many actors to have given distinguished performances of this demanding play. The complexity of the play is something that faces actors even more immediately than readers of the play, for they will have to find a way to suit their acting to Hamlet's wild and whirling character. As Michael Pennington remarks in an essay on playing Hamlet, "to pull it off will take the actor further down into his psyche, memory and imagination, and further outwards to the limits of his technical knowledge and equipment, than he has probably been before."[1]

---

[1] Michael Pennington, "Hamlet," *Players of Shakespeare: Essays in Shakespearean Performance by Twelve Players with the Royal Shakespeare Company,* ed. Philip Brockbank (Cambridge UP, 1985), 117.

HAMLET

William Shakespeare

EDITED BY CYRUS HOY

——— CHARACTERS ———

CLAUDIUS, *King of Denmark*
HAMLET, *son to the late, and nephew to the present king*
POLONIUS, *Lord Chamberlain*
HORATIO, *friend to Hamlet*
LAERTES, *son to Polonius*
VOLTEMAND
CORNELIUS
ROSENCRANTZ } *courtiers*
GUILDENSTERN
OSRIC
A GENTLEMAN
A PRIEST
MARCELLUS } *officers*
BERNARDO

FRANCISCO, *a soldier*
REYNALDO, *servant to Polonius*
PLAYERS
TWO CLOWNS, *grave-diggers*
FORTINBRAS, *Prince of Norway*
A NORWEGIAN CAPTAIN
ENGLISH AMBASSADORS
GERTRUDE, *Queen of Denmark, and mother of Hamlet*
OPHELIA, *daughter to Polonius*
GHOST OF HAMLET'S FATHER
LORDS, LADIES, OFFICERS, SOLDIERS, SAILORS, MESSENGERS, *and* ATTENDANTS

SCENE: *Denmark.*

——— ACT ONE ———

SCENE I

Enter BERNARDO *and* FRANCISCO, *two sentinels.*

BERNARDO: Who's there?
FRANCISCO: Nay, answer me. Stand, and unfold yourself.
BERNARDO: Long live the king!
FRANCISCO: Bernardo?
5 BERNARDO: He.
FRANCISCO: You come most carefully upon your hour.
BERNARDO: 'Tis now struck twelve. Get thee to bed, Francisco.
FRANCISCO: For this relief much thanks. 'Tis bitter cold,
    And I am sick at heart.
10 BERNARDO: Have you had quiet guard?
FRANCISCO: Not a mouse stirring.
BERNARDO: Well, good night.
    If you do meet Horatio and Marcellus,
    The rivals of my watch, bid them make haste.

(Enter HORATIO *and* MARCELLUS.)

FRANCISCO: I think I hear them. Stand, ho! Who is there?
15 HORATIO: Friends to this ground.
MARCELLUS: And liegemen to the Dane.
FRANCISCO: Give you good night.
MARCELLUS: O, farewell, honest soldier!
    Who hath relieved you?
FRANCISCO: Bernardo hath my place.
    Give you good night.

(Exit FRANCISCO.)

MARCELLUS: Holla, Bernardo!
BERNARDO: Say—
    What, is Horatio there?

HORATIO: A piece of him.
BERNARDO: Welcome, Horatio. Welcome, good Marcellus.   20
HORATIO: What, has this thing appeared again to-night?
BERNARDO: I have seen nothing.
MARCELLUS: Horatio says 'tis but our fantasy,
    And will not let belief take hold of him
    Touching this dreaded sight twice seen of us.   25
    Therefore I have entreated him along
    With us to watch the minutes of this night,
    That if again this apparition come,
    He may approve our eyes and speak to it.
HORATIO: Tush, tush, 'twill not appear.   30
BERNARDO: Sit down awhile,
    And let us once again assail your ears,
    That are so fortified against our story,
    What we have two nights seen.
HORATIO: Well, sit we down,
    And let us hear Bernardo speak of this.
BERNARDO: Last night of all,   35
    When yond same star that's westward from the pole
    Had made his course t' illume that part of heaven
    Where now it burns, Marcellus and myself,
    The bell then beating one—

(Enter GHOST.)

MARCELLUS: Peace, break thee off. Look where it comes again.   40
BERNARDO: In the same figure like the king that's dead.
MARCELLUS: Thou art a scholar; speak to it, Horatio.
BERNARDO: Looks 'a not like the king? Mark it, Horatio.
HORATIO: Most like. It harrows me with fear and wonder.
BERNARDO: It would be spoke to.   45
MARCELLUS: Question it, Horatio.
HORATIO: What art thou that usurp'st this time of night

I.i. 13 **rivals** partners   15 **Dane** King of Denmark

29 **approve** confirm   36 **pole** polestar   44 **harrows** afflicts, distresses

Together with that fair and warlike form
In which the majesty of buried Denmark
Did sometimes march? By heaven I charge thee, speak.
50 MARCELLUS: It is offended.
BERNARDO: See, it stalks away.
HORATIO: Stay. Speak, speak. I charge thee, speak.

(*Exit* GHOST.)

MARCELLUS: 'Tis gone and will not answer.
BERNARDO: How now, Horatio! You tremble and look pale.
    Is not this something more than fantasy?
55   What think you on't?
HORATIO: Before my God, I might not this believe
    Without the sensible and true avouch
    Of mine own eyes.
MARCELLUS: Is it not like the king?
HORATIO: As thou art to thyself.
60   Such was the very armour he had on
    When he the ambitious Norway combated.
    So frowned he once when, in an angry parle,
    He smote the sledded Polacks on the ice.
    'Tis strange.
65 MARCELLUS: Thus twice before, and jump at this dead hour,
    With martial stalk hath he gone by our watch.
HORATIO: In what particular thought to work I know not,
    But in the gross and scope of mine opinion,
    This bodes some strange eruption to our state.
70 MARCELLUS: Good now, sit down, and tell me he that knows,
    Why this same strict and most observant watch
    So nightly toils the subject of the land,
    And why such daily cast of brazen cannon
    And foreign mart for implements of war;
75   Why such impress of shipwrights, whose sore task
    Does not divide the Sunday from the week.
    What might be toward that this sweaty haste
    Doth make the night joint-laborer with the day?
    Who is't that can inform me?
HORATIO: That can I.
80   At least, the whisper goes so. Our last king,
    Whose image even but now appeared to us,
    Was as you know by Fortinbras of Norway,
    Thereto pricked on by a most emulate pride,
    Dared to the combat; in which our valiant Hamlet
85   (For so this side of our known world esteemed him)
    Did slay this Fortinbras; who by a sealed compact
    Well ratified by law and heraldry,
    Did forfeit, with his life, all those his lands
    Which he stood seized of, to the conqueror;
90   Against the which a moiety competent

Was gagèd by our king; which had returned
To the inheritance of Fortinbras,
Had he been vanquisher; as, by the same comart
And carriage of the article designed,
His fell to Hamlet. Now, sir, young Fortinbras,   95
Of unimprovèd mettle hot and full,
Hath in the skirts of Norway here and there
Sharked up a list of lawless resolutes
For food and diet to some enterprise
That hath a stomach in't; which is no other,   100
As it doth well appear unto our state,
But to recover of us by strong hand
And terms compulsatory, those foresaid lands
So by his father lost; and this, I take it,
Is the main motive of our preparations,   105
The source of this our watch, and the chief head
Of this post-haste and romage in the land.
BERNARDO: I think it be no other but e'en so.
    Well may it sort that this portentous figure
    Comes armèd through our watch; so like the king   110
    That was and is the question of these wars.
HORATIO: A mote it is to trouble the mind's eye.
    In the most high and palmy state of Rome,
    A little ere the mightiest Julius fell,
    The graves stood tenantless and the sheeted dead   115
    Did squeak and gibber in the Roman streets;
    As stars with trains of fire, and dews of blood,
    Disasters in the sun; and the moist star,
    Upon whose influence Neptune's empire stands,
    Was sick almost to doomsday with eclipse.   120
    And even the like precurse of feared events,
    As harbingers preceding still the fates
    And prologue to the omen coming on,
    Have heaven and earth together demonstrated
    Unto our climatures and countrymen.   125

(*Enter* GHOST.)

But soft, behold, lo where it comes again!
I'll cross it though it blast me.—Stay, illusion.

([GHOST] *spreads his arms.*)

If thou hast any sound or use of voice,
Speak to me.
If there be any good thing to be done,   130
That may to thee do ease, and grace to me,
Speak to me.
If thou art privy to thy country's fate,
Which happily foreknowing may avoid,

---

48 **buried Denmark** the buried King of Denmark   49 **sometimes** formerly   57 **sensible** confirmed by one of the senses   61 **Norway** King of Norway   62 **parle** parley   63 **sledded Polacks** the Poles mounted on sleds or sledges   65 **jump** just, exactly   68 **gross and scope** general drift   72 **toils** causes to toil; **subject** people   74 **mart** traffic, bargaining   75 **impress** conscription   77 **toward** imminent, impending   83 **emulate** ambitious   87 **heraldry** the law of arms, regulating tournaments and state combats   89 **seized** possessed   90 **moiety competent** sufficient portion

---

91 **gaged** pledged   93 **comart** joint bargain   94 **carriage** import   96 **unimprovèd** unrestrained   98 **Sharked up** picked up indiscriminately   100 **stomach** spice of adventure   106 **head** fountainhead   107 **romage** turnmoil   109 **sort** suit, be in accordance   112 **mote** particle of dust   113 **palmy** flourishing   115 **sheeted** in shrouds; **moist star** the moon   121 **precurse** heralding, foreshadowing   122 **harbingers** forerunners; **still** ever   123 **omen** ominous event   125 **climatures** regions   127 **cross it** cross its path   134 **happily** haply, petchance

135 O, speak!
  Or if thou hast uphoarded in thy life
  Extorted treasure in the womb of earth,
  For which, they say, you spirits oft walk in death,

(The cock crows.)

  Speak of it. Stay, and speak. Stop it, Marcellus.
140 MARCELLUS: Shall I strike at it with my partisan?
  HORATIO: Do, if it will not stand.
  BERNARDO: 'Tis here.
  HORATIO: 'Tis here!

(Exit GHOST.*)*

  MARCELLUS: 'Tis gone!
  We do it wrong, being so majestical,
  To offer it the show of violence;
145 For it is as the air, invulnerable,
  And our vain blows malicious mockery.
  BERNARDO: It was about to speak when the cock crew.
  HORATIO: And then it started like a guilty thing
  Upon a fearful summons. I have heard
150 The cock, that is the trumpet to the morn,
  Doth with his lofty and shrill-sounding throat
  Awake the god of day and at his warning,
  Whether in sea or fire, in earth or air,
  Th' extravagant and erring spirit hies
155 To his confine; and of the truth herein
  This present object made probation.
  MARCELLUS: It faded on the crowing of the cock.
  Some say that ever 'gainst that season comes
  Wherein our Saviour's birth is celebrated,
160 The bird of dawning singeth all night long,
  And then, they say, no spirit dare stir abroad.
  The nights are wholesome, then no planets strike,
  No fairy takes, nor witch hath power to charm,
  So hallowed and so gracious is that time.
165 HORATIO: So have I heard and do in part believe it.
  But look, the morn in russet mantle clad
  Walks o'er the dew of yon high eastward hill.
  Break we our watch up, and by my advice
  Let us impart what we have seen to-night
170 Unto young Hamlet, for, upon my life
  This spirit, dumb to us, will speak to him.
  Do you consent we shall acquaint him with it,
  As needful in our loves, fitting our duty?
  MARCELLUS: Let's do't, I pray, and I this morning know
175 Where we shall find him most convenient.

(Exeunt.)

SCENE II

Flourish. Enter CLAUDIUS, KING OF DENMARK, GERTRUDE THE
QUEEN, COUNCILLORS, *{including}* POLONIUS *and his son* LAERTES,
HAMLET, *cum aliis {including* VOLTEMAND *and* CORNELIUS.*}*

---

140 **partisan** pike 154 **extravagant** straying, vagrant; **erring**
wandering 156 **probation** proof 158 **'gainst** just before 162
strike blast, destroy by malign influence 163 **takes** bewitches
I.ii. s.d. **cum aliis** with others

KING: Though yet of Hamlet our dear brother's death
  The memory be green, and that it us befitted
  To bear our hearts in grief, and our whole kingdom
  To be contracted in one brow of woe,
  Yet so far hath discretion fought with nature 5
  That we with wisest sorrow think on him,
  Together with remembrance of ourselves.
  Therefore our sometime sister, now our queen,
  Th' imperial jointress to this warlike state,
  Have we, as 'twere with a defeated joy, 10
  With an auspicious and a dropping eye,
  With mirth in funeral and with dirge in marriage,
  In equal scale weighing delight and dole,
  Taken to wife; nor have we herein barred
  Your better wisdoms, which have freely gone 15
  With this affair along. For all, our thanks.
  Now follows that you know young Fortinbras,
  Holding a weak supposal of our worth,
  Or thinking by our late dear brother's death
  Our state to be disjoint and out of frame, 20
  Colleaguèd with this dream of his advantage,
  He hath not failed to pester us with message
  Importing the surrender of those lands
  Lost by his father, with all bands of law,
  To our most valiant brother. So much for him. 25
  Now for ourself, and for this time of meeting,
  Thus much the business is: we have here writ
  To Norway, uncle of young Fortinbras—
  Who, impotent and bedrid, scarcely hears
  Of this his nephew's purpose—to suppress 30
  His further gait herein, in that the levies,
  The lists, and full proportions are all made
  Out of his subject; and we here dispatch
  You, good Cornelius, and you, Voltemand,
  For bearers of this greeting to old Norway, 35
  Giving to you no further personal power
  To business with the king, more than the scope
  Of these delated articles allow.
  Farewell, and let your haste commend your duty.
  CORNELIUS: } In that and all things will we show our duty. 40
  VOLTEMAND: }
  KING: We doubt it nothing, heartily farewell.

(Exeunt VOLTEMAND *and* CORNELIUS.*)*

  And now, Laertes, what's the news with you?
  You told us of some suit. What is't, Laertes?
  You cannot speak of reason to the Dane
  And lose your voice. What wouldst thou beg, Laertes, 45
  That shall not be my offer, not thy asking?
  The head is not more native to the heart,
  The hand more instrumental to the mouth,
  Than is the throne of Denmark to thy father.
  What wouldst thou have, Laertes? 50

---

9 **jointress** a widow who holds a jointure or life interest in an
estate 14 **barred** excluded 21 **Colleaguèd** united 31 **gait** proceeding 32 **proportions** forces or supplies for war 38 **delated**
expressly stated 44 **Dane** King of Denmark 45 **lose your
voice** speak in vain 47 **native** joined by nature 48 **instrumental** serviceable

LAERTES: My dread lord,
    Your leave and favour to return to France,
    From whence, though willingly, I came to Denmark
    To show my duty in your coronation,
    Yet now I must confess, that duty done,
55   My thoughts and wishes bend again toward France,
    And bow them to your gracious leave and pardon.
KING: Have you your father's leave? What says Polonius?
POLONIUS: He hath, my lord, wrung from me my slow leave
    By laborsome petition, and at last
60   Upon his will I sealed my hard consent.
    I do beseech you give him leave to go.
KING: Take thy fair hour, Laertes. Time be thine,
    And thy best graces spend it at thy will.
    But now, my cousin Hamlet, and my son—
65 HAMLET: (*Aside.*) A little more than kin, and less than kind.
KING: How is it that the clouds still hang on you?
HAMLET: Not so, my lord. I am too much in the sun.
QUEEN: Good Hamlet, cast thy nighted color off,
    And let thine eye look like a friend on Denmark.
70   Do not for ever with thy vailèd lids
    Seek for thy noble father in the dust.
    Thou know'st 'tis common—all that lives must die,
    Passing through nature to eternity.
HAMLET: Ay, madam, it is common.
QUEEN: If it be,
75   Why seems it so particular with thee?
HAMLET: Seems, madam? Nay, it is. I know not 'seems.'
    'Tis not alone my inky cloak, good mother,
    Nor customary suits of solemn black,
    Nor windy suspiration of forced breath,
80   No, nor the fruitful river in the eye,
    Nor the dejected haviour of the visage,
    Together with all forms, moods, shapes of grief,
    That can denote me truly. These indeed seem,
    For they are actions that a man might play,
85   But I have that within which passeth show—
    These but the trappings and the suits of woe.
KING: 'Tis sweet and commendable in your nature, Hamlet,
    To give these mourning duties to your father,
    But you must know your father lost a father,
90   That father lost, lost his, and the survivor bound
    In filial obligation for some term
    To do obsequious sorrow. But to persever
    In obstinate condolement is a course
    Of impious stubbornness. 'Tis unmanly grief.
95   It shows a will most incorrect to heaven,
    A heart unfortified, a mind impatient,
    An understanding simple and unschooled.
    For what we know must be, and is as common
    As any the most vulgar thing to sense,
100   Why should we in our peevish opposition
    Take it to heart? Fie, 'tis a fault to heaven,

A fault against the dead, a fault to nature,
To reason most absurd, whose common theme
Is death of fathers, and who still hath cried,
From the first corse till he that died to-day,   105
'This must be so.' We pray you throw to earth
This unprevailing woe, and think of us
As of a father, for let the world take note
You are the most immediate to our throne,
And with no less nobility of love   110
Than that which dearest father bears his son
Do I impart toward you. For your intent
In going back to school in Wittenberg,
It is most retrograde to our desire,
And we beseech you, bend you to remain   115
Here in the cheer and comfort of our eye,
Our chiefest courtier, cousin, and our son.
QUEEN: Let not thy mother lose her prayers, Hamlet.
    I pray thee stay with us, go not to Wittenberg.
HAMLET: I shall in all my best obey you, madam.   120
KING: Why, 'tis a loving and a fair reply.
    Be as ourself in Denmark. Madam, come.
    This gentle and unforced accord of Hamlet
    Sits smiling to my heart, in grace whereof,
    No jocund health that Denmark drinks to-day   125
    But the great cannon to the clouds shall tell,
    And the king's rouse the heaven shall bruit again,
    Respeaking earthly thunder. Come away.

(Flourish. Exeunt all but HAMLET.*)*

HAMLET: O, that this too too sallied flesh would melt,
    Thaw and resolve itself into a dew,   130
    Or that the Everlasting had not fixed
    His canon 'gainst self-slaughter. O God, God,
    How weary, stale, flat, and unprofitable
    Seem to me all the uses of this world!
    Fie on't, ah, fie, 'tis an unweeded garden   135
    That grows to seed. Things rank and gross in nature
    Possess it merely. That it should come to this,
    But two months dead, nay, not so much, not two.
    So excellent a king, that was to this
    Hyperion to a satyr, so loving to my mother,   140
    That he might not beteem the winds of heaven
    Visit her face too roughly. Heaven and earth,
    Must I remember? Why, she would hang on him
    As if increase of appetite had grown
    By what it fed on, and yet, within a month—   145
    Let me not think on't. Frailty, thy name is woman—
    A little month, or ere those shoes were old

---

56 **pardon** indulgence 60 **hard** reluctant 64 **cousin** kinsman
of any kind except parent, child, brother, or sister 65 **kin** related
as nephew; **kind** (1) affectionate (2) natural, lawful 70 **vailèd**
lowered 75 **particular** personal, individual 92 **obsequious**
dutiful in performing funeral obsequies or manifesting regard for
the dead; **persever** persevere

105 **corse** corpse 114 **retrograde** contrary 127 **rouse** full
draught of liquor; **bruit** echo 129 **sallied** sullied. "Sallied" is the
reading of *Quarto 2* (*Q2,* also *Q1*). *Folio* (*F*) reads "solid." Since
Hamlet's primary concern is with the fact of the flesh's impurity, not
with its corporeality, the choice as between *Q* and *F* clearly lies with
Q. "Sally" is a legitimate sixteenth-century form of "sully"; it occurs
in Dekker's *Patient Grissil* (1.1.12), printed in 1603, as F. T. Bowers has pointed out (in "Hamlet's 'Sullied' or 'Solid' Flesh. A Bibli-
ographical Case-History," *Shakespeare Survey* 9 [1956]: p. 44); and it
occurs as a noun at 2.1.39 of *Hamlet* 132 **canon** law 137 **merely**
entirely 140 **Hyperion** the sun god 141 **beteem** allowed

With which she followed my poor father's body
Like Niobe, all tears, why she—
150 O God, a beast that wants discourse of reason
Would have mourned longer—married with my uncle,
My father's brother, but no more like my father
Than I to Hercules. Within a month,
Ere yet the salt of most unrighteous tears
155 Had left the flushing in her gallèd eyes,
She married. O, most wicked speed, to post
With such dexterity to incestuous sheets!
It is not, nor it cannot come to good.
But break my heart, for I must hold my tongue.

(*Enter* HORATIO, MARCELLUS, *and* BERNARDO.)

160 HORATIO: Hail to your lordship!
HAMLET: I am glad to see you well.
   Horatio—or I do forget myself.
HORATIO: The same, my lord, and your poor servant ever.
HAMLET: Sir, my good friend, I'll change that name with you.
   And what make you from Wittenberg, Horatio?
165 Marcellus?
MARCELLUS: My good lord!
HAMLET: I am very glad to see you. (*To* BERNARDO.) Good
      even, sir.—
   But what, in faith, make you from Wittenberg?
HORATIO: A truant disposition, good my lord.
170 HAMLET: I would not hear your enemy say so,
   Nor shall you do my ear that violence
   To make it truster of your own report
   Against yourself. I know you are no truant.
   But what is your affair in Elsinore?
175 We'll teach you to drink deep ere you depart.
HORATIO: My lord, I came to see your father's funeral.
HAMLET: I prithee, do not mock me, fellow-student,
   I think it was to see my mother's wedding.
HORATIO: Indeed, my lord, it followed hard upon.
180 HAMLET: Thrift, thrift, Horatio. The funeral baked meats
   Did coldly furnish forth the marriage tables.
   Would I had met my dearest foe in heaven
   Or ever I had seen that day, Horatio!
   My father—methinks I see my father.
185 HORATIO: Where, my lord?
HAMLET: In my mind's eye, Horatio.
HORATIO: I saw him once, 'a was a goodly king.
HAMLET: 'A was a man, take him for all in all,
   I shall not look upon his like again.
HORATIO: My lord, I think I saw him yesternight.
190 HAMLET: Saw who?
HORATIO: My lord, the king your father.
HAMLET: The king my father?
HORATIO: Season your admiration for a while

With an attent ear, till I may deliver
Upon the witness of these gentlemen
This marvel to you.   195
HAMLET: For God's love, let me hear!
HORATIO: Two nights together had these gentlemen,
   Marcellus and Bernardo, on their watch
   In the dead waste and middle of the night
   Been thus encountered. A figure like your father,
   Armed at point exactly, cap-a-pe,   200
   Appears before them, and with solemn march
   Goes slow and stately by them. Thrice he walked
   By their oppressed and fear-surprisèd eyes
   Within his truncheon's length, whilst they, distilled
   Almost to jelly with the act of fear,   205
   Stand dumb and speak not to him. This to me
   In dreadful secrecy impart they did,
   And I with them the third night kept the watch,
   Where, as they had delivered, both in time,
   Form of the thing, each word made true and good, 210
   The apparition comes. I knew your father.
   These hands are not more like.
HAMLET: But where was this?
MARCELLUS: My lord, upon the platform where we watch.
HAMLET: Did you not speak to it?
HORATIO: My lord, I did,   215
   But answer made it none. Yet once methought
   It lifted up it head and did address
   Itself to motion, like as it would speak;
   But even then the morning cock crew loud,
   And at the sound it shrunk in haste away
   And vanished from our sight.   220
HAMLET: 'Tis very strange.
HORATIO: As I do live, my honoured lord, 'tis true,
   And we did think it writ down in our duty
   To let you know of it.
HAMLET: Indeed, sirs, but
   This troubles me. Hold you the watch to-night?
ALL: We do, my lord.   225
HAMLET: Armed, say you?
ALL: Armed, my lord.
HAMLET: From top to toe?
ALL: My lord, from head to foot.
HAMLET: Then saw you not his face.
HORATIO: O yes, my lord, he wore his beaver up.
HAMLET: What, looked he frowningly?
HORATIO: A countenance more in sorrow than in anger.   230
HAMLET: Pale or red?
HORATIO: Nay, very pale.
HAMLET: And fixed his eyes upon you?
HORATIO: Most constantly.
HAMLET: I would I had been there.
HORATIO: It would have much amazed you.
HAMLET: Very like.
   Stayed it long?   235
HORATIO: While one with moderate haste might tell a
      hundred.

---

149 **Niobe** wife of Amphion, King of Thebes, she boasted of having more children than Leto and was punished when her seven sons and seven daughters were slain by Apollo and Artemis, children of Leto; in her grief she was changed by Zeus into a stone, which continually dropped tears   150 **wants** lacks; **discourse of reason** the reasoning faculty   155 **gallèd** sore from rubbing or chafing   163 **change** exchange   164 **make** do   182 **dearest** direst   192 **Season** temper, moderate; **admiration** wonder, astonishment

---

200 **at point exactly** in every particular; **cap-a-pe** from head to foot   204 **truncheon** military leader's baton   216 **it** its   228 **beaver** the part of the helmet that was drawn down to cover the face   235 **tell** count

BOTH: Longer, longer.
HORATIO: Not when I saw't.
HAMLET: His beard was grizzled, no?
HORATIO: It was as I have seen it in his life,
   A sable silvered.
HAMLET: I will watch to-night.
240 Perchance 'twill walk again.
HORATIO: I warr'nt it will.
HAMLET: If it assume my noble father's person,
   I'll speak to it though hell itself should gape
   And bid me hold my peace. I pray you all,
   If you have hitherto concealed this sight,
245 Let it be tenable in your silence still,
   And whatsomever else shall hap to-night,
   Give it an understanding but no tongue.
   I will requite your loves. So fare you well.
   Upon the platform 'twixt eleven and twelve
250 I'll visit you.
ALL: Our duty to your honor.
HAMLET: Your loves, as mine to you. Farewell.

(Exeunt {all but HAMLET*}.)*

   My father's spirit in arms? All is not well.
   I doubt some foul play. Would the night were come!
   Till then sit still, my soul. Foul deeds will rise,
255 Though all the earth o'erwhelm them, to men's eyes.

(Exit.)

SCENE III

Enter LAERTES *and* OPHELIA *his sister.*

LAERTES: My necessaries are embarked. Farewell.
   And, sister, as the winds give benefit
   And convoy is assistant, do not sleep,
   But let me hear from you.
OPHELIA: Do you doubt that?
5 LAERTES: For Hamlet, and the trifling of his favor,
   Hold it a fashion and a toy in blood,
   A violet in the youth of primy nature,
   Forward, not permanent, sweet, not lasting,
   The perfume and suppliance of a minute,
10 No more.
OPHELIA: No more but so?
LAERTES: Think it no more.
   For nature crescent does not grow alone
   In thews and bulk, but as this temple waxes
   The inward service of the mind and soul
   Grows wide withal. Perhaps he loves you now,
15 And now no soil nor cautel doth besmirch
   The virtue of his will, but you must fear,
   His greatness weighed, his will is not his own,
   For he himself is subject to his birth.

---

237 **grizzled** grayish 239 **sable silvered** black mixed with white 245 **tenable** retained 246 **whatsomever** whatsover 253 **doubt** suspect

I.iii. 6 **fashion** the creation of a season only; **toy in blood** passing fancy 7 **primy** of the springtime 11 **crescent** growing 12 **thews** sinews, strength; **this temple** the body 15 **cautel** deceit 16 **will** desire 17 **greatness weighed** high position considered

He may not, as unvalued persons do,
Carve for himself, for on his choice depends   20
The safety and health of this whole state,
And therefore must his choice be circumscribed
Unto the voice and yielding of that body
Whereof he is the head. Then if he says he loves you,
It fits your wisdom so far to believe it   25
As he in his particular act and place
May give his saying deed, which is no further
Than the main voice of Denmark goes withal.
Then weigh what loss your honor may sustain
If with too credent ear you list his songs,   30
Or lose your heart, or your chaste treasure open
To his unmastered importunity.
Fear it, Ophelia, fear it, my dear sister,
And keep you in the rear of your affection,
Out of the shot and danger of desire.   35
The chariest maid is prodigal enough
If she unmask her beauty to the moon.
Virtue itself scapes not calumnious strokes.
The canker galls the infants of the spring
Too oft before their buttons be disclosed,   40
And in the morn and liquid dew of youth
Contagious blastments are most imminent.
Be wary then; best safety lies in fear.
Youth to itself rebels, though none else near.
OPHELIA: I shall the effect of this good lesson keep   45
   As watchman to my heart. But, good my brother,
   Do not as some ungracious pastors do,
   Show me the steep and thorny way to heaven,
   Whiles like a puffed and reckless libertine
   Himself the primrose path of dalliance treads   50
   And recks not his own rede.
LAERTES: O, fear me not.

(Enter POLONIUS.*)*

   I stay too long. But here my father comes.
   A double blessing is a double grace;
   Occasion smiles upon a second leave.
POLONIUS: Yet here, Laertes? Aboard, aboard, for shame!   55
   The wind sits in the shoulder of your sail,
   And you are stayed for. There, my blessing with thee,
   And these few precepts in thy memory
   Look thou character. Give thy thoughts no tongue,
   Nor any unproportioned thought his act.   60
   Be thou familiar, but by no means vulgar.
   Those friends thou hast, and their adoption tried,
   Grapple them to thy soul with hoops of steel,
   But do not dull thy palm with entertainment
   Of each new-hatched, unfledged courage. Beware   65
   Of entrance to a quarrel, but being in,
   Bear't that th' opposèd may beware of thee.

---

19 **unvalued persons** persons of no social importance 20 **Carve for himself** act according to his own inclination 23 **yielding assent** 30 **credent** trusting 34 **affection** feeling 39 **canker** canker-worm (which feeds on roses); **galls** injures 40 **buttons** buds 42 **blastments** blights 51 **recks** regards; **rede** counsel 59 **character** engrave 60 **unproportioned** inordinate 61 **vulgar** common 65 **courage** young blood, man of spirit

Give every man thy ear, but few thy voice;
Take each man's censure, but reserve thy judgement.
70 Costly thy habit as thy purse can buy,
But not expressed in fancy; rich not gaudy,
For the apparel oft proclaims the man,
And they in France of the best rank and station
Are of a most select and generous chief in that.
75 Neither a borrower nor a lender be,
For loan oft loses both itself and friend,
And borrowing dulls th' edge of husbandry.
This above all, to thine own self be true,
And it must follow as the night the day
80 Thou canst not then be false to any man.
Farewell. My blessing season this in thee!
LAERTES: Most humbly do I take my leave, my lord.
POLONIUS: The time invites you. Go, your servants tend.
LAERTES: Farewell, Ophelia, and remember well
85   What I have said to you.
OPHELIA: 'Tis in my memory locked,
And you yourself shall keep the key of it.
LAERTES: Farewell.

(Exit LAERTES.)

POLONIUS: What is 't, Ophelia, he hath said to you?
OPHELIA: So please you, something touching the Lord
       Hamlet.
90 POLONIUS: Marry, well bethought.
'Tis told me he hath very oft of late
Given private time to you, and you yourself
Have of your audience been most free and bounteous.
If it be so—as so 'tis put on me,
95 And that in way of caution—I must tell you,
You do not understand yourself so clearly
As it behooves my daughter and your honor.
What is between you? Give me up the truth.
OPHELIA: He hath, my lord, of late made many tenders
100   Of his affection to me.
POLONIUS: Affection? Pooh! You speak like a green girl,
Unsifted in such perilous circumstance.
Do you believe his tenders, as you call them?
OPHELIA: I do not know, my lord, what I should think.
105 POLONIUS: Marry, I will teach you. Think yourself a baby
That you have ta'en these tenders for true pay
Which are not sterling. Tender yourself more dearly,
Or (not to crack the wind of the poor phrase,
Running it thus) you'll tender me a fool.
110 OPHELIA: My lord, he hath importuned me with love
In honorable fashion.
POLONIUS: Ay, fashion you may call it. Go to, go to.
OPHELIA: And hath given countenance to his speech, my lord,
With almost all the holy vows of heaven.
115 POLONIUS: Ay, springes to catch woodcocks. I do know,
When the blood burns, how prodigal the soul
Lends the tongue vows. These blazes, daughter,
Giving more light than heat, extinct in both
Even in their promise, as it is a-making,

You must not take for fire. From this time   120
Be something scanter of your maiden presence.
Set your entreatments at a higher rate
Than a command to parle. For Lord Hamlet,
Believe so much in him that he is young,
And with a larger tether may he walk   125
Than may be given you. In few, Ophelia,
Do not believe his vows, for they are brokers,
Not of that dye which their investments show,
But mere implorators of unholy suits,
Breathing like sanctified and pious bawds,   130
The better to beguile. This is for all:
I would not, in plain terms, from this time forth
Have you so slander any moment leisure
As to give words or talk with the Lord Hamlet.
Look to't, I charge you. Come your ways.   135
OPHELIA: I shall obey, my lord.

(Exeunt.)

SCENE IV

Enter HAMLET, HORATIO, *and* MARCELLUS.

HAMLET: The air bites shrewdly; it is very cold.
HORATIO: It is a nipping and an eager air.
HAMLET: What hour now?
HORATIO: I think it lacks of twelve.
MARCELLUS: No, it is struck.
HORATIO: Indeed? I heard it not. It then draws near the season 5
Wherein the spirit held his wont to walk.

(A flourish of trumpets, and two pieces go off.)

What does this mean, my lord?
HAMLET: The king doth wake to-night and takes his rouse,
Keeps wassail, and the swagg'ring up-spring reels,
And as he drains his draughts of Rhenish down,   10
The kettledrum and trumpet thus bray out
The triumph of his pledge.
HORATIO: Is it a custom?
HAMLET: Ay, marry, is't,
But to my mind, though I am native here
And to the manner born, it is a custom   15
More honored in the breach than the observance.
This heavy-headed revel east and west
Makes us traduced and taxed of other nations.
They clepe us drunkards, and with swinish phrase
Soil our addition, and indeed it takes   20
From our achievements, though performed at height,
The pith and marrow of our attribute.
So oft it chances in particular men,
That for some vicious mole of nature in them,

---

122 **entreatments** military negotiations for surrender   127 **brokers** go-betweens   128 **investments** clothes   129 **implorators** solicitors

I.iv. 2 eager sharp   **9 wassail** carousal; **up-spring** a German dance   **18 taxed of** censured by   **19 clepe** call   **20 addition** title added to a man's name to denote his rank   **22 attribute** reputation

---

74 **chief** eminence   77 **husbandry** thriftiness   81 **season** ripen
83 **tend** attend, wait   90 **Marry** by Mary   99 **tenders** offers
102 **Unsifted** untried   115 **springes** snares

25 As, in their birth, wherein they are not guilty
    (Since nature cannot choose his origin),
    By the o'ergrowth of some complexion,
    Oft breaking down the pales and forts of reason,
    Or by some habit that too much o'er-leavens
30 The form of plausive manners—that these men,
    Carrying, I say, the stamp of one defect,
    Being nature's livery or fortune's star,
    His virtues else, be they as pure as grace,
    As infinite as man may undergo,
35 Shall in the general censure take corruption
    From that particular fault. The dram of evil
    Doth all the noble substance often doubt
    To his own scandal.

(Enter GHOST.*)*

    HORATIO: Look, my lord, it comes.
    HAMLET: Angels and ministers of grace defend us!
40 Be thou a spirit of health or goblin damned,
    Bring with thee airs from heaven or blasts from hell,
    Be thy intents wicked or charitable,
    Thou com'st in such a questionable shape
    That I will speak to thee. I'll call thee Hamlet,
45 King, father, royal Dane. O, answer me!
    Let me not burst in ignorance, but tell
    Why thy canonized bones, hearsèd in death,
    Have burst their cerements; why the sepulchre
    Wherein we saw thee quietly interred,
50 Hath oped his ponderous and marble jaws
    To cast thee up again. What may this mean
    That thou, dead corse, again in complete steel
    Revisits thus the glimpses of the moon,
    Making night hideous, and we fools of nature
55 So horridly to shake our disposition
    With thoughts beyond the reaches of our souls?
    Say, why is this? wherefore? What should we do?

*([*GHOST*] beckons.)*

    HORATIO: It beckons you to go away with it,
      As if it some impartment did desire
60   To you alone.
    MARCELLUS: Look, with what courteous action
      It waves you to a more removèd ground.
      But do not go with it.
    HORATIO: No, by no means.
    HAMLET: It will not speak; then I will follow it.
    HORATIO: Do not, my lord.
    HAMLET: Why, what should be the fear?
65   I do not set my life at a pin's fee,
      And for my soul, what can it do to that,
      Being a thing immortal as itself?
      It waves me forth again. I'll follow it.

---

26 **his** its   27 **complexion** one of the four temperaments (sanguine, melancholy, choleric, and phlegmatic)   29 **o'er-leavens** works change throughout   30 **plausive** pleasing   32 **livery** badge; **star** a person's fortune, rank, or destiny, viewed as determined by the stars   37 **doubt** put out, obliterate   38 **his** its   47 **canonized** buried according to the church's rule; **hearsèd** coffined, buried   59 **impartment** communication

HORATIO: What if it tempt you toward the flood, my lord,
  Or to the dreadful summit of the cliff   70
  That beetles o'er his base into the sea,
  And there assume some other horrible form,
  Which might deprive your sovereignty of reason
  And draw you into madness? Think of it.
  The very place puts toys of desperation,   75
  Without more motive, into every brain
  That looks so many fathoms to the sea
  And hears it roar beneath.
HAMLET: It waves me still.
  Go on. I'll follow thee.
MARCELLUS: You shall not go, my lord.   80
HAMLET: Hold off your hands.
HORATIO: Be ruled; You shall not go.
HAMLET: My fate cries out,
  And makes each petty artere in this body
  As hardy as the Nemean lion's nerve.
  Still am I called. Unhand me, gentlemen.
  By heaven, I'll make a ghost of him that lets me.   85
  I say, away—Go on. I'll follow thee.

({Exeunt} GHOST *and* HAMLET.*)*

HORATIO: He waxes desperate with imagination.
MARCELLUS: Let's follow. 'Tis not fit thus to obey him.
HORATIO: Have after. To what issue will this come?
MARCELLUS: Something is rotten in the state of Denmark.   90
HORATIO: Heaven will direct it.
MARCELLUS: Nay, let's follow him.

(Exeunt.)

SCENE V

Enter GHOST *and* HAMLET.

HAMLET: Whither wilt thou lead me? Speak. I'll go no further.
GHOST: Mark me.
HAMLET: I will.
GHOST: My hour is almost come
  When I to sulph'rous and tormenting flames
  Must render up myself.
HAMLET: Alas, poor ghost!
GHOST: Pity me not, but lend thy serious hearing   5
  To what I shall unfold.
HAMLET: Speak. I am bound to hear.
GHOST: So art thou to revenge, when thou shalt hear.
HAMLET: What?
GHOST: I am thy father's spirit,
  Doomed for a certain term to walk the night,   10
  And for the day confined to fast in fires,
  Till the foul crimes done in my days of nature
  Are burnt and purged away. But that I am forbid
  To tell the secrets of my prison house,
  I could a tale unfold whose lightest word   15
  Would harrow up thy soul, freeze thy young blood,

---

71 **beetles** juts out   73 **sovereignty of reason** state of being ruled by reason   75 **toys** fancies, impules   82 **artere** artery   83 **Nemean lion** slain by Hercules in the performance of one of his twelve labors   85 **lets** hinders

Make thy two eyes like stars start from their spheres,
Thy knotted and combinèd locks to part,
And each particular hair to stand an end,
20 Like quills upon the fretful porpentine.
But this eternal blazon must not be
To ears of flesh and blood. List, list, O, list!
If thou didst ever thy dear father love—
HAMLET: O God!
25 GHOST: Revenge his foul and most unnatural murder.
HAMLET: Murder!
GHOST: Murder most foul, as in the best it is,
But this most foul, strange, and unnatural.
HAMLET: Haste me to know't, that I, with wings as swift
30 As meditation or the thoughts of love,
May sweep to my revenge.
GHOST: I find thee apt,
And duller shouldst thou be than the fat weed
That roots itself in ease on Lethe wharf,
Wouldst thou not stir in this. Now, Hamlet, hear.
35 'Tis given out that, sleeping in my orchard,
A serpent stung me. So the whole ear of Denmark
Is by a forgèd process of my death
Rankly abused. But know, thou noble youth,
The serpent that did sting thy father's life
40 Now wears his crown.
HAMLET: O my prophetic soul!
My uncle!
GHOST: Ay, that incestuous, that adulterate beast,
With witchcraft of his wits, with traitorous gifts—
O wicked wit and gifts that have the power
45 So to seduce!—won to his shameful lust
The will of my most seeming virtuous queen.
O Hamlet, what a falling off was there,
From me, whose love was of that dignity
That it went hand in hand even with the vow
50 I made to her in marriage, and to decline
Upon a wretch whose natural gifts were poor
To those of mine!
But virtue, as it never will be moved,
Though lewdness court it in a shape of heaven,
55 So lust, though to a radiant angel linked,
Will sate itself in a celestial bed
And prey on garbage.
But soft, methinks I scent the morning air.
Brief let me be. Sleeping within my orchard,
60 My custom always of the afternoon,
Upon my secure hour thy uncle stole,
With juice of cursed hebona in a vial,
And in the porches of my ears did pour
The leperous distilment, whose effect
65 Holds such an enmity with blood of man
That swift as quicksilver it courses through
The natural gates and alleys of the body,
And with a sudden vigor it doth posset
And curd, like eager droppings into milk,

The thin and wholesome blood. So did it mine, 70
And a most instant tetter barked about
Most lazar-like with vile and loathsome crust
All my smooth body.
Thus was I sleeping by a brother's hand
Of life, of crown, of queen, at once dispatched, 75
Cut off even in the blossoms of my sin,
Unhouseled, disappointed, unaneled,
No reck'ning made, but sent to my account
With all my imperfections on my head.
O, horrible! O, horrible! most horrible! 80
If thou hast nature in thee, bear it not,
Let not the royal bed of Denmark be
A couch for luxury and damnèd incest.
But howsomever thou pursues this act,
Taint not thy mind, nor let thy soul contrive 85
Against thy mother aught. Leave her to heaven,
And to those thorns that in her bosom lodge
To prick and sting her. Fare thee well at once.
The glowworm shows the matin to be near,
And gins to pale his uneffectual fire. 90
Adieu, adieu, adieu. Remember me.

(Exit.)

HAMLET: O all you host of heaven! O earth! What else?
And shall I couple hell? O, fie! Hold, hold, my heart,
And you, my sinews, grow not instant old,
But bear me stiffly up. Remember thee? 95
Ay, thou poor ghost, whiles memory holds a seat
In this distracted globe. Remember thee?
Yea, from the table of my memory
I'll wipe away all trivial fond records,
All saws of books, all forms, all pressures past 100
That youth and observation copied there,
And thy commandment all alone shall live
Within the book and volume of my brain,
Unmixed with baser matter. Yes, by heaven!
O most pernicious woman! 105
O villain, villain, smiling, damnèd villain!
My tables—meet it is I set it down
That one may smile, and smile, and be a villain
At least I am sure it may be so in Denmark.   *(Writing.)*
So, uncle, there you are. Now to my word: 110
It is 'Adieu, adieu! Remember me,'
I have sworn't.

(Enter HORATIO *and* MARCELLUS.*)*

HORATIO: My lord, my lord!
MARCELLUS: Lord Hamlet!
HORATIO: Heavens secure him!
HAMLET: So be it!

---

71 **tetter** a skin eruption; **barked** covered as with bark   77 **Unhouseled** without having received the sacrament; **disappointed** unprepared; **unaneled** without extreme unction   83 **luxury** lust   89 **matin** morning   97 **globe** head   98 **table** writing tablet, memorandum book (as at line 107, below; here metaphorically of the mind)   99 **fond** foolish   100 **saws** sayings; **forms** concepts; **pressures** impressions

---

I.v. 19 **an** on   20 **porpentine** porcupine   21 **eternal blazon** proclamation of the secrets of eternity   33 **Lethe** the river in Hades that brings forgetfulness   37 **process** account   61 **secure** free from suspicion   62 **hebona** an imaginary poison, associated with henbane   68 **posset** curdle   69 **eager** acid

115 MARCELLUS: Illo, ho, ho, my lord!
    HAMLET: Hillo, ho, ho, boy! Come, bird, come.
    MARCELLUS: How is't, my noble lord?
    HORATIO: What news, my lord?
    HAMLET: O, wonderful!
    HORATIO: Good my lord, tell it.
    HAMLET: No, you will reveal it.
120 HORATIO: Not I, my lord, by heaven.
    MARCELLUS: Nor I, my lord.
    HAMLET: How say you then, would heart of man once think it?
        But you'll be secret?
    BOTH: Ay, by heaven, my lord.
    HAMLET: There's never a villain dwelling in all Denmark
        But he's an arrant knave.
125 HORATIO: There needs no ghost, my lord, come from the grave
        To tell us this.
    HAMLET: Why, right, you are in the right,
        And so without more circumstance at all
        I hold it fit that we shake hands and part,
        You, as your business and desire shall point you,
130   For every man has business and desire
        Such as it is, and for my own poor part,
        I will go pray.
    HORATIO: These are but wild and whirling words, my lord.
    HAMLET: I am sorry they offend you, heartily;
135   Yes, faith, heartily.
    HORATIO: There's no offence, my lord.
    HAMLET: Yes, by Saint Patrick, but there is, Horatio,
        And much offence too. Touching this vision here,
        It is an honest ghost, that let me tell you
        For your desire to know what is between us,
140   O'ermaster't as you may. And now, good friends,
        As you are friends, scholars, and soldiers,
        Give me one poor request.
    HORATIO: What is't, my lord? We will.
    HAMLET: Never make known what you have seen to-night.
145 BOTH: My lord, we will not.
    HAMLET: Nay, but swear't.
    HORATIO: In faith,
        My lord, not I.
    MARCELLUS: Nor I, my lord, in faith.
    HAMLET: Upon my sword.
    MARCELLUS: We have sworn, my lord, already.
    HAMLET: Indeed, upon my sword, indeed.

(GHOST *cries under the stage.*)

    GHOST: Swear.
    HAMLET: Ha, ha, boy, say'st thou so? Art thou there, truepenny?
150 Come on. You hear this fellow in the cellarage.
        Consent to swear.
    HORATIO: Propose the oath, my lord.
    HAMLET: Never to speak of this that you have seen,
        Swear by my sword.
    GHOST: (*Beneath.*) Swear.
155 HAMLET: Hic et ubique? Then we'll shift our ground.

---

115 **Illo, ho, ho** cry of the falconer to summon his hawk   136 **Saint
Patrick** associated, in the late middle ages, with purgatory, whence
the ghost has presumably come   149 **truepenny** honest fellow
155 **Hic et ubique** here and everywhere

Come hither, gentlemen,
        And lay your hands again upon my sword.
        Swear by my sword
        Never to speak of this that you have heard.
    GHOST: (*Beneath.*) Swear by his sword.   160
    HAMLET: Well said, old mole! Canst work i' th' earth so fast?
        A worthy pioneer! Once more remove, good friends.
    HORATIO: O day and night, but this is wondrous strange!
    HAMLET: And therefore as a stranger give it welcome.
        There are more things in heaven and earth, Horatio,   165
        Than are dreamt of in your philosophy.
        But come.
        Here as before, never, so help you mercy,
        How strange or odd some'er I bear myself
        (As I perchance hereafter shall think meet   170
        To put an antic disposition on),
        That you, at such times, seeing me, never shall,
        With arms encumbered thus, or this head-shake,
        Or by pronouncing of some doubtful phrase,
        As 'Well, well, we know,' or 'We could, and if we would' 175
        Or 'If we list to speak,' or 'There be, and if they might'
        Or such ambiguous giving out, to note
        That you know aught of me—this do swear,
        So grace and mercy at your most need help you.
    GHOST: (*Beneath.*) Swear.   180
    HAMLET: Rest, rest, perturbèd spirit! So, gentlemen,
        With all my love I do commend me to you,
        And what so poor a man as Hamlet is
        May do t' express his love and friending to you,
        God willing, shall not lack. Let us go in together,   185
        And still your fingers on your lips, I pray.
        The time is out of joint. O cursèd spite
        That ever I was born to set it right!
        Nay, come, let's go together.

(*Exeunt.*)

——— ACT TWO ———

SCENE I

Enter old POLONIUS *with his man* [REYNALDO].

POLONIUS: Give him this money and these notes. Reynaldo.
REYNALDO: I will, my lord.
POLONIUS: You shall do marvellous wisely, good Reynaldo,
        Before you visit him, to make inquire
        Of his behavior.   5
REYNALDO: My lord, I did intend it.
POLONIUS: Marry, well said, very well said. Look you, sir,
        Enquire me first what Danskers are in Paris,
        And how, and who, what means, and where they keep,
        What company, at what expense; and finding
        By this encompassment and drift of question   10
        That they do know my son, come you more nearer
        Than your particular demands will touch it.
        Take you as 'twere some distant knowledge of him,

---

162 **pioneer** miner   171 **antic** mad   173 **encumbered** folded
II.i. 7 Danskers Danes   8 **means** wealth   10 **encompass-
ment** talking round the matter

As thus, 'I know his father and his friends,
15   And in part him,' do you mark this, Reynaldo?
REYNALDO: Ay, very well, my lord.
POLONIUS: 'And in part him, but,' you may say, 'not well,
      But if't be he I mean, he's very wild,
      Addicted so and so.' And there put on him
20   What forgeries you please; marry, none so rank
      As may dishonour him. Take heed of that.
      But, sir, such wanton, wild, and usual slips
      As are companions noted and most known
      To youth and liberty.
REYNALDO: As gaming, my lord?
25 POLONIUS: Ay, or drinking, fencing, swearing, quarrelling,
      Drabbing—you may go so far.
REYNALDO: My lord, that would dishonour him.
POLONIUS: Faith, no, as you may season it in the charge.
      You must not put another scandal on him,
30   That he is open to incontinency.
      That's not my meaning. But breathe his faults so quaintly
      That they may seem the taints of liberty,
      The flash and outbreak of a fiery mind,
      A savageness in unreclaimèd blood,
35   Of general assault.
REYNALDO: But, my good lord—
POLONIUS: Wherefore should you do this?
REYNALDO: Ay, my lord,
      I would know that.
POLONIUS: Marry, sir, here's my drift,
      And I believe it is a fetch of warrant.
      You laying these slight sullies on my son,
40   As 'twere a thing a little soiled i' th' working,
      Mark you,
      Your party in converse, him you would sound,
      Having ever seen in the prenominate crimes
      The youth you breathe of guilty, be assured
45   He closes with you in this consequence,
      'Good sir', or so, or 'friend', or 'gentleman',
      According to the phrase or the addition
      Of man and country.
REYNALDO: Very good, my lord.
POLONIUS: And then, sir, does 'a this—'a does—What was I
      about to say?
50   By the mass, I was about to say something.
      Where did I leave?
REYNALDO: At 'closes in the consequence.'
POLONIUS: At 'closes in the consequence'—ay, marry,
      He closes thus: 'I know the gentleman.
55   I saw him yesterday, or th' other day,
      Or then, or then, with such, or such, and as you say,
      There was 'a gaming, there o'ertook in 's rouse;
      There falling out at tennis', or perchance
      'I saw him enter such a house of sale',
60   Videlicet, a brothel, or so forth.

See you, now—
      Your bait of falsehood takes this carp of truth,
      And thus do we of wisdom and of reach,
      With windlasses and with assays of bias,
      By indirections find directions out;   65
      So by my former lecture and advice
      Shall you my son. You have me, have you not?
REYNALDO: My lord, I have.
POLONIUS: God bye ye; fare ye well.
REYNALDO: Good my lord.
POLONIUS: Observe his inclination in yourself.   70
REYNALDO: I shall, my lord.
POLONIUS: And let him ply his music.
REYNALDO: Well, my lord.
POLONIUS: Farewell.

(*Exit* REYNALDO.)

(*Enter* OPHELIA.)

                        How now, Ophelia! what's the matter?
OPHELIA: O my lord, my lord, I have been so affrighted!
POLONIUS: With what, i' th' name of God?   75
OPHELIA: My lord, as I was sewing in my closet,
      Lord Hamlet, with his doublet all unbraced,
      No hat upon his head, his stockings fouled,
      Ungartered, and down-gyvèd to his ankle,
      Pale as his shirt, his knees knocking each other,   80
      And with a look so piteous in purport
      As if he had been loosèd out of hell
      To speak of horrors—he comes before me.
POLONIUS: Mad for thy love?
OPHELIA: My lord, I do not know,
      But truly I do fear it.   85
POLONIUS: What said he?
OPHELIA: He took me by the wrist, and held me hard,
      Then goes he to the length of all his arm,
      And with his other hand thus o'er his brow,
      He falls to such perusal of my face
      As 'a would draw it. Long stayed he so.   90
      At last, a little shaking of mine arm
      And thrice his head thus waving up and down,
      He raised a sigh so piteous and profound
      As it did seem to shatter all his bulk
      And end his being. That done, he lets me go,   95
      And with his head over his shoulder turned,
      He seemed to find his way without his eyes,
      For out adoors he went without their helps,
      And to the last bended their light on me.
POLONIUS: Come, go with me. I will go seek the king.   100
      This is the very ecstasy of love,
      Whose violent property fordoes itself,
      And leads the will to desperate undertakings
      As oft as any passion under heaven
      That does afflict our natures. I am sorry.   105
      What, have you given him any hard words of late?

---

20 **forgeries** invented wrongdoings 24 **liberty** license 26 **Drabbing** whoring 28 **season** moderate 31 **quaintly** delicately 34 **unreclaimèd** untamed 35 **Of general assault** assailing all 38 **fetch of warrant** allowable device 43 **prenominate** before-named 45 **closes** agrees; **in this consequence** as follows 47 **addition** title 60 **Videlicet** namely

63 **reach** ability 64 **windlasses** roundabout approaches; **assays of bias** indirect attempts 68 **God buy ye** God be with you 76 **closet** private room 77 **unbraced** unlaced 79 **down-gyvèd** hanging down, like gyves or fetters on a prisoner's ankles 101 **ecstasy** madness 102 **fordoes** destroys

OPHELIA: No, my good lord, but as you did command
    I did repel his letters, and denied
    His access to me.
POLONIUS: That hath made him mad.
110 I am sorry that with better heed and judgement
    I had not quoted him. I feared he did but trifle,
    And meant to wrack thee; but beshrew my jealousy.
    By heaven, it is as proper to our age
    To cast beyond ourselves in our opinions
115 As it is common for the younger sort
    To lack discretion. Come, go we to the king.
    This must be known, which being kept close, might move
    More grief to hide than hate to utter love.
    Come.

(Exeunt.)

SCENE II

Flourish. Enter KING *and* QUEEN, ROSENCRANTZ, *and* GUILDEN-
STERN *{and* ATTENDANTS*}.*

KING: Welcome, dear Rosencrantz and Guildenstern.
    Moreover that we much did long to see you,
    The need we have to use you did provoke
    Our hasty sending. Something have you heard
5 Of Hamlet's transformation—so call it,
    Sith nor th' exterior nor the inward man
    Resembles that it was. What it should be,
    More than his father's death, that thus hath put him
    So much from th' understanding of himself,
10 I cannot dream of. I entreat you both
    That, being of so young days brought up with him,
    And sith so neighboured to his youth and havior,
    That you vouchsafe your rest here in our court
    Some little time, so by your companies
15 To draw him on to pleasures, and to gather
    So much as from occasion you may glean,
    Whether aught to us unknown afflicts him thus,
    That opened, lies within our remedy.
QUEEN: Good gentlemen, he hath much talked of you,
20 And sure I am two men there is not living
    To whom he more adheres. If it will please you
    To show us so much gentry and good will
    As to expend your time with us awhile
    For the supply and profit of our hope,
25 Your visitation shall receive such thanks
    As fits a king's remembrance.
ROSENCRANTZ: Both your majesties
    Might, by the sovereign power you have of us,
    Put your dread pleasures more into command
    Than to entreaty.
GUILDENSTERN: But we both obey,
30 And here give up ourselves in the full bent
    To lay our service freely at your feet,
    To be commanded.
KING: Thanks, Rosencrantz and gentle Guildenstern.

QUEEN: Thanks, Guildenstern and gentle Rosencrantz.
    And I beseech you instantly to visit   35
    My too much changed son. Go, some of you,
    And bring these gentlemen where Hamlet is.
GUILDENSTERN: Heavens make our presence and our practices
    Pleasant and helpful to him!
QUEEN: Ay, amen!

(Exeunt ROSENCRANTZ *and* GUILDENSTERN *{with some*
ATTENDANTS*}.)*

(Enter POLONIUS.*)*

POLONIUS: Th' ambassadors from Norway, my good lord,   40
    Are joyfully returned.
KING: Thou still hast been the father of good news.
POLONIUS: Have I, my lord? I assure my good liege,
    I hold my duty as I hold my soul,
    Both to my God and to my gracious king;   45
    And I do think—or else this brain of mine
    Hunts not the trail of policy so sure
    As it hath used to do—that I have found
    The very cause of Hamlet's lunacy.
KING: O, speak of that, that do I long to hear.   50
POLONIUS: Give first admittance to th' ambassadors.
    My news shall be the fruit to that great feast.
KING: Thyself do grace to them, and bring them in.

(Exit POLONIUS.*)*

    He tells me, my dear Gertrude, he hath found
    The head and source of all your son's distemper.   55
QUEEN: I doubt it is no other but the main,
    His father's death and our o'erhasty marriage.
KING: Well, we shall sift him.

(Enter AMBASSADORS [VOLTEMAND *and* CORNELIUS], *with*
POLONIUS.*)*

                Welcome, my good friends,
    Say, Voltemand, what from our brother Norway?
VOLTEMAND: Most fair return of greetings and desires.   60
    Upon our first, he sent out to suppress
    His nephew's levies, which to him appeared
    To be a preparation 'gainst the Polack,
    But better looked into, he truly found
    It was against your highness, whereat grieved,   65
    That so his sickness, age, and impotence
    Was falsely borne in hand, sends out arrests
    On Fortinbras, which he in brief obeys,
    Receives rebuke from Norway, and in fine,
    Makes vow before his uncle never more   70
    To give th' assay of arms against your majesty.
    Whereon old Norway, overcome with joy,
    Gives him three score thousand crowns in annual fee,
    And his commission to employ those soldiers,
    So levied as before, against the Polack,   75
    With an entreaty, herein further shown,   *(Gives a paper.)*
    That it might please you to give quiet pass
    Through your dominions for this enterprise,

---

111 **quoted** observed   112 **wrack** ruin   113 **proper to** characteristic of   117 **close** secret; **move** cause
II.ii. 6 **Sith** since   18 **opened** disclosed   22 **gentry** courtesy

---

42 **still** ever   56 **doubt** suspect   63 **the Polack** the Polish
nation   67 **borne in hand** deceived   69 **in fine** in the end
71 **assay** trial

On such regards of safety and allowance
80   As therein are set down.
KING: It likes us well,
And at our more considered time we'll read,
Answer, and think upon this business.
Meantime we thank you for your well-took labor.
Go to your rest; at night we'll feast together.
85   Most welcome home!

(Exeunt AMBASSADORS.*)*

POLONIUS: This business is well ended.
My liege and madam, to expostulate
What majesty should be, what duty is,
Why day is day, night night, and time is time,
Were nothing but to waste night, day and time.
90   Therefore, since brevity is the soul of wit,
And tediousness the limbs and outward flourishes,
I will be brief. Your noble son is mad.
Mad call I it, for to define true madness,
What is't but to be nothing else but mad?
95   But let that go.
QUEEN: More matter with less art.
POLONIUS: Madam, I swear I use no art at all.
That he is mad, 'tis true: 'tis true 'tis pity.
And pity 'tis 'tis true. A foolish figure,
But farewell it, for I will use no art.
100   Mad let us grant him, then, and now remains
That we find out the cause of this effect,
Or rather say the cause of this defect,
For this effect defective comes by cause.
Thus it remains, and the remainder thus.
105   Perpend.
I have a daughter—have while she is mine—
Who in her duty and obedience, mark,
Hath given me this. Now gather, and surmise.   *(Reads.)*
'To the celestial, and my soul's idol, the most beautified
110   Ophelia'—That's an ill phrase, a vile phrase, 'beautified' is
a vile phrase. But you shall hear. Thus: *(Reads.)*
'In her excellent white bosom, these, etc.'
QUEEN: Came this from Hamlet to her?
POLONIUS: Good madam, stay awhile. I will be faithful.
(Reads Letter.)
115   'Doubt thou the stars are fire,
                Doubt that the sun doth move;
                Doubt truth to be a liar;
                But never doubt I love.

        'O dear Ophelia, I am ill at these numbers. I have not art
120   to reckon my groans, but that I love thee best, O most best,
believe it. Adieu.
                Thine evermore, most dear lady, whilst
                        this machine is to him, Hamlet.'
This in obedience hath my daughter shown me,
125   And more above, hath his solicitings,
As they fell out by time, by means and place,
All given to mine ear.

KING: But how hath she
Received his love?
POLONIUS: What do you think of me?
KING: As of a man faithful and honourable.
POLONIUS: I would fain prove so. But what might you think,   130
When I had seen this hot love on the wing,
(As I perceived it, I must tell you that,
Before my daughter told me), what might you,
Or my dear majesty your queen here, think,
If I had played the desk or table-book,   135
Or given my heart a winking, mute and dumb,
Or looked upon this love with idle sight,
What might you think? No, I went round to work,
And my young mistress thus I did bespeak:
'Lord Hamlet is a prince out of thy star.   140
This must not be'. and then I prescripts gave her,
That she should lock herself from his resort,
Admit no messengers, receive no tokens.
Which done, she took the fruits of my advice;
And he repelled, a short tale to make,   145
Fell into a sadness, then into a fast,
Thence to a watch, thence into a weakness,
Thence to a lightness, and, by this declension,
Into the madness wherein now he raves,
And all we mourn for.   150
KING: Do you think 'tis this?
QUEEN: It may be, very like.
POLONIUS: Hath there been such a time—I would fain know
        that—
That I have positively said ''Tis so,'
When it proved otherwise?
KING: Not that I know.
POLONIUS: *(Pointing to his head and shoulder.)* Take this from   155
        this, if this be otherwise:
If circumstances lead me, I will find
Where truth is hid, though it were hid indeed
Within the centre.
KING: How may we try it further?
POLONIUS: You know, sometimes he walks four hours together
Here in the lobby.   160
QUEEN: So he does, indeed.
POLONIUS: At such a time I'll loose my daughter to him.
Be you and I behind an arras then.
Mark the encounter. If he love her not,
And be not from his reason fall'n thereon,
Let me be no assistant for a state,   165
But keep a farm and carters.
KING: We will try it.

(Enter HAMLET *{reading on a book}.)*

QUEEN: But look where sadly the poor wretch comes reading.
POLONIUS: Away, I do beseech you both away,
I'll board him presently.

({Exeunt} king and queen {with attendants}.)

                O, give me leave.

---

79 **regards** considerations   90 **wit** understanding   95 **matter**
meaning, sense   105 **Perpend** consider   119 **numbers** verses
123 **machine** body

---

135 **played . . . table-book** acted as silent go-between   138 **round**
directly   147 **watch** sleeplessness   148 **lightness** lightheaded-
ness   158 **centre** centre of the earth and of the Ptlolemaic universe   169 **board** accost; **presently** immediately

170   How does my good Lord Hamlet?
        HAMLET: Well, God-a-mercy.
        POLONIUS: Do you know me, my lord?
        HAMLET: Excellent well, you are a fishmonger.
        POLONIUS: Not I, my lord.
175   HAMLET: Then I would you were so honest a man.
        POLONIUS: Honest, my lord?
        HAMLET: Ay, sir, to be honest as this world goes, is to be one
            man picked out of ten thousand.
        POLONIUS: That's very true, my lord.
180   HAMLET: For if the sun breed maggots in a dead dog, being a
            good kissing carrion—Have you a daughter?
        POLONIUS: I have, my lord.
        HAMLET: Let her not walk i' th' sun. Conception is a blessing,
            but as your daughter may conceive—friend, look to 't.
185   POLONIUS: (Aside.) How say you by that? Still harping on my
            daughter. Yet he knew me not at first. 'A said I was a fish-
            monger. 'A is far gone. And truly in my youth I suffered
            much extremity for love, very near this. I'll speak to him
            again.—What do you read, my lord?
190   HAMLET: Words, words, words.
        POLONIUS: What is the matter, my lord?
        HAMLET: Between who?
        POLONIUS: I mean the matter that you read, my lord.
        HAMLET: Slanders, sir; for the satirical rogue says here that old
195   men have grey beards, that their faces are wrinkled, their
            eyes purging thick amber and plum-tree gum, and that
            they have a plentiful lack of wit, together with most weak
            hams—all which, sir, though I most powerfully and po-
            tently believe, yet I hold it not honesty to have it thus set
200   down, for yourself, sir, shall grow old as I am, if like a crab
            you could go backward.
        POLONIUS: (Aside.) Though this be madness, yet there is
            method in 't.—Will you walk out of the air, my lord?
        HAMLET: Into my grave?
205   POLONIUS: (Aside.) Indeed, that's out of the air. How pregnant
            sometimes his replies are! a happiness that often madness
            hits on, which reason and sanity could not so prosperously
            be delivered of. I will leave him, and suddenly contrive the
            means of meeting between him and my daughter.—My
210   lord, I will take my leave of you.
        HAMLET: You cannot take from me anything that I will not
            more willingly part withal—except my life, except my life,
            except my life.

        (Enter GUILDENSTERN and ROSENCRANTZ.)

        POLONIUS: Fare you well, my lord.
215   HAMLET: These tedious old fools!
        POLONIUS: You go to seek the Lord Hamlet. There he is.
        ROSENCRANTZ: (To POLONIUS.) God save you, sir!

        (Exit POLONIUS.)

        GUILDENSTERN: My honored lord!
        ROSENCRANTZ: My most dear lord!
220   HAMLET: My excellent good friends! How dost thou,
            Guildenstern?
            Ah, Rosencrantz! Good lads, how do ye both?

        ROSENCRANTZ: As the indifferent children of the earth.
        GUILDENSTERN: Happy in that we are not over-happy;
            On Fortune's cap we are not the very button.   225
        HAMLET: Nor the soles of her shoe?
        ROSENCRANTZ: Neither, my lord.
        HAMLET: Then you live about her waist, or in the middle of her
            favors?
        GUILDENSTERN: Faith, her privates we.   230
        HAMLET: In the secret parts of Fortune? O, most true, she is a
            strumpet. What news?
        ROSENCRANTZ: None, my lord, but that the world's grown
            honest.
        HAMLET: Then is doomsday near. But your news is not true. Let 235
            me question more in particular. What have you, my good
            friends, deserved at the hands of Fortune, that she sends you
            to prison hither?
        GUILDENSTERN: Prison, my lord!
        HAMLET: Denmark's a prison.   240
        ROSENCRANTZ: Then is the world one.
        HAMLET: A goodly one, in which there are many confines,
            wards, and dungeons, Denmark being one o' th' worst.
        ROSENCRANTZ: We think not so, my lord.
        HAMLET: Why then 'tis none to you; for there is nothing either 245
            good or bad, but thinking makes it so. To me it is a prison.
        ROSENCRANTZ: Why then your ambition makes it one. 'Tis too
            narrow for your mind.
        HAMLET: O God, I could be bounded in a nutshell and count
            myself a king of infinite space, were it not that I have bad 250
            dreams.
        GUILDENSTERN: Which dreams indeed are ambition; for the
            very substance of the ambitious is merely the shadow of a
            dream.
        HAMLET: A dream itself is but a shadow.   255
        ROSENCRANTZ: Truly, and I hold ambition of so airy and light
            a quality that it is but a shadow's shadow.
        HAMLET: Then are our beggars bodies, and, our monarchs and
            outstretched heroes the beggars' shadows. Shall we to th'
            court? for, by my fay, I cannot reason.   260
        BOTH: We'll wait upon you.
        HAMLET: No such matter. I will not sort you with the rest of my
            servants; for to speak to you like an honest man, I am most
            dreadfully attended. But in the beaten way of friendship,
            what make you at Elsinore?   265
        ROSENCRANTZ: To visit you, my lord; no other occasion.
        HAMLET: Beggar that I am, I am ever poor in thanks, but I
            thank you; and sure, dear friends, my thanks are too dear a
            halfpenny. Were you not sent for? Is it your own inclining?
            Is it a free visitation? Come, come, deal justly with me.   270
            Come, come, nay speak.
        GUILDENSTERN: What should we say, my lord?
        HAMLET: Anything but to the purpose. You were sent for, and
            there is a kind of confession in your looks, which your mod-
            esties have not craft enough to color. I know the good king 275
            and queen have sent for you.
        ROSENCRANTZ: To what end, my lord?
        HAMLET: That you must teach me. But let me conjure you by
            the rights of our fellowship, by the consonancy of our

---

205 **pregnant** full of meaning   206 **happiness** aptness

223 **indifferent** average   225 **button** knob on the top of the cap
260 **fay** faith   262 **sort you with** put you in the same class with

280   youth, by the obligation of our ever-preserved love, and by
what more dear a better proposer can charge you withal be
even and direct with me whether you were sent for or no.

ROSENCRANTZ: *(Aside to* GUILDENSTERN.*)* What say you?

HAMLET: *(Aside.)* Nay, then, I have an eye of you.—If you love
285   me, hold not off.

GUILDENSTERN: My lord, we were sent for.

HAMLET: I will tell you why; so shall my anticipation prevent
your discovery, and your secrecy to the king and queen
moult no feather. I have of late—but wherefore I know
290   not—lost all my mirth, forgone all custom of exercises; and
indeed it goes so heavily with my disposition, that this
goodly frame the earth seems to me a sterile promontory,
this most excellent canopy the air, look you, this brave
o'er-hanging firmament, this majestical roof fretted with
295   golden fire, why it appeareth nothing to me but a foul and
pestilent congregation of vapors. What a piece of work is a
man, how noble in reason, how infinite in faculties, in form
and moving, how express and admirable in action, how like
an angel in apprehension, how like a god: the beauty of the
300   world, the paragon of animals. And yet to me, what is this
quintessence of dust? Man delights not me, nor woman neither, though by your smiling you seem to say so.

ROSENCRANTZ: My lord, there was no such stuff in my
thoughts.

305   HAMLET: Why did ye laugh, then, when I said 'Man delights
not me'?

ROSENCRANTZ: To think, my lord, if you delight not in man,
what lenten entertainment the players shall receive from
you. We coted them on the way, and hither are they com-
310   ing to offer you service.

HAMLET: He that plays the king shall be welcome—his majesty
shall have tribute on me; the adventurous knight shall use
his foil and target; the lover shall not sigh gratis; the humorous man shall end his part in peace; the clown shall
315   make those laugh whose lungs are tickle o' th' sere; and the
lady shall say her mind freely, or the blank verse shall halt
for 't. What players are they?

ROSENCRANTZ: Even those you were wont to take such delight
in, the tragedians of the city.

320   HAMLET: How chances it they travel? Their residence, both in
reputation and profit, was better both ways.

ROSENCRANTZ: I think their inhibition comes by the means of
the late innovation.

HAMLET: Do they hold the same estimation they did when I
was in the city? Are they so followed?   325

ROSENCRANTZ: No, indeed, are they not.

HAMLET: How comes it? Do they grow rusty?

ROSENCRANTZ: Nay, their endeavour keeps in the wonted pace;
but there is, sir, an eyrie of children, little eyases, that cry out
on the top of question, and are most tyrannically clapped   330
for't. These are now the fashion, and so berattle the common stages (so they call them) that many wearing rapiers
are afraid of goose quills and dare scarce come thither.

HAMLET: What, are they children? Who maintains 'em? How
are they escoted? Will they pursue the quality no longer   335
than they can sing? Will they not say afterwards, if they
should grow themselves to common players (as it is most
like, if their means are no better), their writers do them
wrong to make them exclaim against their own succession?

ROSENCRANTZ: 'Faith, there has been much to do on both sides;   340
and the nation holds it no sin to tarre them to controversy.
There was for a while no money bid for argument, unless
the poet and the player went to cuffs in the question.

HAMLET: Is't possible?

GUILDENSTERN: O, there has been much throwing about of   345
brains.

HAMLET: Do the boys carry it away?

ROSENCRANTZ: Ay, that they do, my lord, Hercules and his
load too.

HAMLET: It is not very strange, for my uncle is King of Den-   350
mark, and those that would make mouths at him while my
father lived give twenty, forty, fifty, a hundred ducats apiece
for his picture in little. 'Sblood, there is something in this
more than natural, if philosophy could find it out.

(A flourish.)

GUILDENSTERN: There are the players.   355

HAMLET: Gentlemen, you are welcome to Elsinore. Your hands.
Come then th' appurtenance of welcome is fashion and ceremony. Let me comply with you in this garb, lest my extent to the players, which I tell you must show fairly
outwards, should more appear like entertainment than   360
yours. You are welcome. But my uncle-father and
aunt-mother are deceived.

GUILDENSTERN: In what, my dear lord?

HAMLET: I am but mad north-north-west; when the wind is
southerly I know a hawk from a handsaw.   365

---

287 **prevent** forestall   288 **discovery** disclosure   294 **fretted**
decorated with fretwork   308 **lenten** scanty   309 **coted** passed
313 **foil and target** spear and shield   313–14 **humorous man**
the actor who plays the eccentric character dominated by one of
the four humors   315 **tickle o' th' sere** easily set off (**sere** is that
part of a gunlock which keeps the hammar at full or half cock)
316 **halt** limp   322 **inhibition** prohibition of plays by authority
(possibly with reference to decree of the Privy Council of 22 June
1600, limiting the number of London theater companies to two,
and stipulating that the two were to perform only twice a week)
323 **innovation** meaning uncertain (sometimes taken to refer to
the reintroduction, ca. 1600, on the London theatrical scene of
companies of boy actors performing in private theaters; sometimes
interpreted as "political upheaval," with special reference to Essex's
rebellion, February, 1601)

329 **eyrie** nest; **eyases** nestling hawks (here, the boys in the children's companies training as actors)   330 **on the top of question**
louder than all others on matter of dispute   331–32 **common
stages** public theaters of the **common players** (below, line 337),
organized in companies composed mainly of adult actors   333
goose quills pens (of the satiric dramatists writing for the private
theaters)   335 **escoted** maintained; **pursue the quality** continue
in the profession of acting   336 **sing** i.e., until their voices change
341 **tarre** incite   342 **argument** plot of a play   349 **load** i.e., the
world (the sign of the Globe Theatre represented Hercules bearing
the world on his shoulders)   351 **mouths** grimaces   353 **in little**
in miniature   357 **appurtenance** adjuncts   358–59 **extent** welcome   365 **hawk** mattock or pickaxe (also called "hack," here used
with a play on *hawk* as a bird); **handsaw** a saw managed with one hand
(here used with a play on some corrupt form of *hernshaw*, "heron")

(*Enter* POLONIUS.)

POLONIUS: Well be with you, gentlemen.

HAMLET: Hark you, Guildenstern—and you too—at each ear a
hearer. That great baby you see there is not yet out of his
swaddling clouts.

370 ROSENCRANTZ: Happily he is the second time come to them,
for they say an old man is twice a child.

HAMLET: I will prophesy he comes to tell me of the players.
Mark it.—You say right, sir, a Monday morning, 'twas then
indeed.

375 POLONIUS: My lord, I have news to tell you.

HAMLET: My lord, I have news to tell you. When Roscius was
an actor in Rome—

POLONIUS: The actors are come hither, my lord.

HAMLET: Buzz, buzz.

380 POLONIUS: Upon my honor—

HAMLET: Then came each actor on his ass—

POLONIUS: The best actors in the world, either for tragedy, comedy, history, pastoral, pastoral-comical, historical-pastoral,
tragical-historical, tragical-comical-historical-pastoral, scene

385 individable, or poem unlimited. Seneca cannot be too heavy
nor Plautus too light. For the law of writ and the liberty,
these are the only men.

HAMLET: O Jephthah, judge of Israel, what a treasure hadst
thou!

390 POLONIUS: What a treasure had he, my lord?

HAMLET: Why—

        'One fair daughter, and no more,
        The which he loved passing well.'

POLONIUS: (*Aside.*) Still on my daughter.

395 HAMLET: Am I not i' th' right, old Jephthah?

POLONIUS: If you call me Jephthah, my lord, I have a daughter
that I love passing well.

HAMLET: Nay, that follows not.

POLONIUS: What follows then, my lord?

400 HAMLET: Why—

        'As by lot, God wot,'

and then, you know,

        'It came to pass, as most like it was.'

The first row of the pious chanson will show you more, for

405 look where my abridgment comes.

(*Enter the* PLAYERS.)

You are welcome, masters; welcome, all.—I am glad to see
thee well.—Welcome, good friends. O, old friend! Why
thy face is valanced since I saw thee last. Come'st thou to
beard me in Denmark?—What, my young lady and mistress? By'r lady, your ladyship is nearer to heaven than when 410
I saw you last by the altitude of a chopine. Pray God, your
voice, like a piece of uncurrent gold, be not cracked within
the ring.—Masters, you are all welcome. We'll e'en to't like
French falconers, fly at any thing we see. We'll have a
speech straight. Come give us a taste of your quality, come 415
a passionate speech.

1 PLAYER: What speech, my good lord?

HAMLET: I heard thee speak me a speech once, but it was never
acted, or if it was, not above once, for the play, I remember,
pleased not the million; 'twas caviary to the general. But it 420
was—as I received it, and others whose judgements in such
matters cried in the top of mine—an excellent play, well digested in the scenes, set down with as much modesty as
cunning. I remember one said there were no sallets in the
lines to make the matter savory, nor no matter in the phrase 425
that might indict the author of affectation, but called it an
honest method, as wholesome as sweet, and by very much
more handsome than fine. One speech in't I chiefly loved.
'Twas Æneas' tale to Dido and thereabout of it especially
when he speaks of Priam's slaughter. If it live in your mem- 430
ory, begin at this line—let me see, let me see:

        'The rugged Pyrrhus, like th' Hyrcanian beast'—

'tis not so;—it begins with Pyrrhus—

        'The rugged Pyrrhus, he whose sable arms,
        Black as his purpose, did the night resemble   435
        When he lay couchèd in the ominous horse,
        Hath now this dread and black complexion smeared
        With heraldry more dismal; head to foot
        Now is he total gules, horridly tricked
        With blood of fathers, mothers, daughters, sons,   440
        Baked and impasted with the parching streets,
        That lend a tyrannous and a damnèd light
        To their lord's murder. Roasted in wrath and fire,
        And thus o'er-sizèd with coagulate gore,
        With eyes like carbuncles, the hellish Pyrrhus   445
        Old grandsire Priam seeks.'

So, proceed you.

POLONIUS: Fore God, my lord, well spoken, with good accent
and good discretion.

1 PLAYER: 'Anon he finds him   450
        Striking too short at Greeks. His antique sword,
        Rebellious to his arm, lies where it falls,

---

370 **Happily** perhaps   376 **Roscius** the greatest of Roman comic
actors, though regarded by the Elizabethans as a tragic one   384–85
scene individable i.e., a play that observes the unities of time and
place   385 **poem unlimited** a play that does not observe the unities; **Seneca** Roman writer of tragedies   386 **Plautus** Roman
comic dramatist; **law of writ and the liberty** i.e., plays according to strict classical rules, and those that ignored the unities
of time and place   388 **Jephthah** was compelled to sacrifice a
beloved daughter (Judges 2). Hamlet quotes from a contemporary
ballad titled *Jephthah, Judge of Israel* at lines 392–393, 401, and
403   404 **row** stanza

---

408 **valanced** bearded   409 **young lady** i.e., the boy who plays
female roles   411 **chopine** a shoe with high cork heel and sole
412–13 **cracked within the ring** a coin cracked within the circle
surrounding the head of the sovereign was no longer legal tender
and so *uncurrent*   415 **straight** immediately   420 **caviary**
caviare; **general** multitude   422–23 **digested** arranged   424
sallets salads, highly seasoned passages   428 **more handsome
than fine** admirable rather than appealing by mere cleverness
432 **Hyrcanian beast** tiger   436 **horse** i.e., the Trojan horse
439 **gules** heraldic term for red; **tricked** delineated   444
o'er-sizèd covered as with size: **coagulate** clotted

Repugnant to command. Unequal matched,
Pyrrhus at Priam drives, in rage strikes wide.
455 But with the whiff and wind of his fell sword
Th' unnervèd father falls. Then senseless Ilium,
Seeming to feel this blow, with flaming top
Stoops to his base, and with a hideous crash
Takes prisoner Pyrrhus' ear. For, lo! his sword,
460 Which was declining on the milky head
Of reverend Priam, seemed i' th' air to stick.
So as a painted tyrant Pyrrhus stood,
And like a neutral to his will and matter,
Did nothing.
465 But as we often see, against some storm,
A silence in the heavens, the rack stand still,
The bold winds speechless, and the orb below
As hush as death, anon the dreadful thunder
Doth rend the region; so, after Pyrrhus' pause,
470 A rousèd vengeance sets him new awork,
And never did the Cyclops' hammers fall
On Mars's armor, forged for proof eterne
With less remorse than Pyrrhus' bleeding sword
Now falls on Priam.
475 Out, out, thou strumpet, Fortune! All you gods,
In general synod take away her power,
Break all the spokes and fellies from her wheel,
And bowl the round nave down the hill of heaven
As low as to the fiends.'
480 POLONIUS: This is too long.
HAMLET: It shall to the barber's with your beard.—Prithee, say
on. He's for a jig, or a tale of bawdry, or he sleeps. Say on,
come to Hecuba.
1 PLAYER: 'But who, ah woe! had seen the mobled queen—'
485 HAMLET: 'The mobled queen'?
POLONIUS: That's good.
1 PLAYER: 'Run barefoot up and down, threat'ning the flames
With bisson rheum; a clout upon that head
Where late the diadem stood, and for a robe,
490 About her lank and all o'er-teemèd loins,
A blanket, in the alarm of fear caught up—
Who this had seen, with tongue in venom steeped,
'Gainst Fortune's state would treason have pronounced.
But if the gods themselves did see her then,
495 When she saw Pyrrhus make malicious sport
In mincing with his sword her husband's limbs,
The instant burst of clamor that she made,
Unless things mortal move them not at all,
Would have made milch the burning eyes of heaven,
500 And passion in the gods.'
POLONIUS: Look whe'r he has not turned his color, and has tears
in's eyes. Prithee no more.

HAMLET: 'Tis well. I'll have thee speak out the rest of this
soon.—Good my lord, will you see the players well bestowed? Do you hear, let them be well used, for they are the 505
abstract and brief chronicles of the time; after your death
you were better have a bad epitaph than their ill report
while you live.
POLONIUS: My lord, I will use them according to their desert.
HAMLET: God's bodkin, man, much better. Use every man after 510
his desert, and who shall 'scape whipping? Use them after
your own honor and dignity. The less they deserve, the
more merit is in your bounty. Take them in.
POLONIUS: Come, sirs.
HAMLET: Follow him, friends. We'll hear a play tomorrow. 515
(Aside to 1 PLAYER.) Dost thou hear me, old friend, can you
play the 'Murder of Gonzago'?
1 PLAYER: Ay, my lord.
HAMLET: We'll ha't tomorrow night. You could for a need study
a speech of some dozen or sixteen lines which I would set 520
down and insert in't, could you not?
1 PLAYER: Ay, my lord.
HAMLET: Very well. Follow that lord, and look you mock him
not.

(Exeunt POLONIUS and PLAYERS.)

My good friends, I'll leave you till night. You are welcome 525
to Elsinore.
ROSENCRANTZ: Good my lord!

(Exeunt {ROSENCRANTZ and GUILDENSTERN}.)

HAMLET: Ay, so God by to you. Now I am alone.
O, what a rogue and peasant slave am I!
Is it not monstrous that this player here, 530
But in a fiction, in a dream of passion,
Could force his soul so to his own conceit
That from her working all his visage wanned;
Tears in his eyes, distraction in his aspect,
A broken voice, and his whole function suiting 535
With forms to his conceit? And all for nothing,
For Hecuba!
What's Hecuba to him or he to Hecuba,
That he should weep for her? What would he do
Had he the motive and the cue for passion 540
That I have? He would drown the stage with tears,
And cleave the general ear with horrid speech,
Make mad the guilty, and appal the free,
Confound the ignorant, and amaze indeed
The very faculties of eyes and ears. 545
Yet I,
A dull and muddy-mettled rascal, peak
Like John-a-dreams, unpregnant of my cause,
And can say nothing; no, not for a king
Upon whose property and most dear life 550
A damned defeat was made. Am I a coward?
Who calls me villain, breaks my pate across,

---

453 **Repugnant** refractory   455 **fell** fierce, cruel   465 **against**
just before   466 **rack** mass of cloud   469 **region** air   471 **Cyclops** giant workmen who made armor in the smithy of Vulcan
472 **proof eterne** to be forever impenetrable   477 **fellies** the
curved pieces forming the rim of a wheel   478 **nave** hub of a
wheel   484 **mobled** muffled   488 **bisson rheum** blinding tears
490 **o'er-teemed** exhausted by many births   493 **state** government   499 **milch** moist, tearful (lit., milk, giving)

---

506 **abstract** summary account   510 **God's bodkin** by God's
dear body   532 **conceit** imagination   542 **general** public
547 **muddy-mettled** dull-spirited: **peak** mope   548 **unpregnant**
not quickened to action

Plucks off my beard and blows it in my face,
Tweaks me by the nose, gives me the lie i' th' throat
555 As deep as to the lungs? Who does me this?
Ha, 'swounds, I should take it; for it cannot be
But I am pigeon-livered and lack gall
To make oppression bitter, or ere this
I should 'a fatted all the region kites
560 With this slave's offal. Bloody, bawdy villain!
Remorseless, treacherous, lecherous, kindless villain!
Why, what an ass am I! This is most brave,
That I, the son of a dear father murdered,
Prompted to my revenge by heaven and hell,
565 Must like a whore unpack my heart with words,
And fall a-cursing like a very drab,
A scullion! Fie upon 't! foh!
About, my brains! Hum—I have heard
That guilty creatures sitting at a play,
570 Have by the very cunning of the scene
Been struck so to the soul that presently
They have proclaimed their malefactions:
For murder, though it have no tongue, will speak
With most miraculous organ. I'll have these players
575 Play something like the murder of my father
Before mine uncle. I'll observe his looks.
I'll tent him to the quick. If 'a do blench,
I know my course. The spirit that I have seen
May be the devil, and the devil hath power
580 T' assume a pleasing shape, yea, and perhaps
Out of my weakness and my melancholy,
As he is very potent with such spirits,
Abuses me to damn me. I'll have grounds
More relative than this. The play's the thing
585 Wherein I'll catch the conscience of the king.

(Exit.)

————— ACT THREE —————

SCENE I

Enter KING, QUEEN, POLONIUS, OPHELIA, ROSENCRANTZ,
GUILDENSTERN, LORDS.

KING: And can you by no drift of conference
Get from him why he puts on this confusion,
Grating so harshly all his days of quiet
With turbulent and dangerous lunacy?
5 ROSENCRANTZ: He does confess he feels himself distracted,
But from what cause 'a will by no means speak.

GUILDENSTERN: Nor do we find him forward to be sounded,
But with a crafty madness keeps aloof
When we would bring him on to some confession
Of his true state.   10
QUEEN: Did he receive you well?
ROSENCRANTZ: Most like a gentleman.
GUILDENSTERN: But with much forcing of his disposition.
ROSENCRANTZ: Niggard of question, but of our demands
Most free in his reply.
QUEEN: Did you assay him
To any pastime?   15
ROSENCRANTZ: Madam, it so fell out that certain players
We o'er-raught on the way. Of these we told him,
And there did seem in him a kind of joy
To hear of it. They are here about the court,
And as I think, they have already order   20
This night to play before him.
POLONIUS: 'Tis most true,
And he beseeched me to entreat your majesties
To hear and see the matter.
KING: With all my heart, and it doth much content me
To hear him so inclined.   25
Good gentlemen, give him a further edge,
And drive his purpose into these delights.
ROSENCRANTZ: We shall, my lord.

(Exeunt ROSENCRANTZ *and* GUILDENSTERN.*)*

KING: Sweet Gertrude, leave us too;
For we have closely sent for Hamlet hither,
That he, as 'twere by accident, may here   30
Affront Ophelia.
Her father and myself (lawful espials)
We'll so bestow ourselves that, seeing unseen,
We may of their encounter frankly judge,
And gather by him, as he is behaved,   35
If 't be th' affliction of his love or no
That thus he suffers for.
QUEEN: I shall obey you.—
And for your part, Ophelia, I do wish
That your good beauties be the happy cause
Of Hamlet's wildness. So shall I hope your virtues   40
Will bring him to his wonted way again,
To both your honors.
OPHELIA: Madam, I wish it may.

(Exit QUEEN *with* LORDS.*)*

POLONIUS: Ophelia, walk you here.—Gracious, so please you,
We will bestow ourselves.—*(To* OPHELIA.*)* Read on this book,
That show of such an exercise may color   45
Your loneliness.—We are oft to blame in this,
'Tis too much proved, that with devotion's visage
And pious action we do sugar o'er
The devil himself.

---

559 **region kites** kites of the air   561 **kindless** unnatural. Following this line, *F* adds the words "Oh Vengeance!" Their inappropriateness to the occasion is noted by Professor Harold Jenkins (in his "Playhouse Interpolations in the Folio Text of Hamlet," *Studies in Bibliography* 13 [1960]: 37). Professor Jenkins remarks that the folio text, by introducing Hamlet's "call for vengeance while he is still absorbed in self-reproaches, both anticipates and misconstrues" the crisis of his passion and of the speech, which comes in fact at line 568 ("**About, my brains**"), when "he abandons his self-reproaches and plans action"   567 **scullion** kitchen wench   571 **presently** immediately   577 **tent** probe; **blench** flinch   583 **Abuses** deludes   584 **relative** relevant

---

III.i. 7 **forward** willing   14 **assay** try to win   17 **o'er-raught** overtook   26 **give him a further edge** sharpen his inclination   29 **closely** privately   31 **Affront** meet face to face   32 **espials** spies   45 **exercise** act of devotion; **color** give an appearance of naturalness to

KING: *(Aside.)*   O, 'tis too true.
50   How smart a lash that speech doth give my conscience!
      The harlot's cheek, beautied with plast'ring art,
      Is not more ugly to the thing that helps it
      Then is my deed to my most painted word.
      O heavy burden!
55 POLONIUS: I hear him coming. Let's withdraw, my lord.

(Exeunt KING *and* POLONIUS.*)*

(Enter HAMLET.*)*

HAMLET: To be, or not to be, that is the question:
      Whether 'tis nobler in the mind to suffer
      The slings and arrows of outrageous fortune,
      Or to take arms against a sea of troubles,
60   And by opposing end them. To die, to sleep—
      No more; and by a sleep to say we end
      The heartache, and the thousand natural shocks
      That flesh is heir to: 'tis a consummation
      Devoutly to be wished. To die, to sleep—
65   To sleep, perchance to dream, ay there's the rub;
      For in that sleep of death what dreams may come
      When we have shuffled off this mortal coil
      Must give us pause. There's the respect
      That makes calamity of so long life,
70   For who would bear the whips and scorns of time,
      Th' oppressor's wrong, the proud man's contumely,
      The pangs of despised love, the law's delay,
      The insolence of office, and the spurns
      That patient merit of th' unworthy takes,
75   When he himself might his quietus make
      With a bare bodkin? Who would fardels bear,
      To grunt and sweat under a weary life,
      But that the dread of something after death,
      The undiscovered country, from whose bourn
80   No traveller returns, puzzles the will,
      And makes us rather bear those ills we have
      Than fly to others that we know not of?
      Thus conscience does make cowards of us all,
      And thus the native hue of resolution
85   Is sicklied o'er with the pale cast of thought,
      And enterprises of great pitch and moment
      With this regard their currents turn awry
      And lose the name of action. Soft you now,
      The fair Ophelia.—Nymph, in thy orisons
90   Be all my sins remembered.
OPHELIA: Good my lord,
      How does your honor for this many a day?
HAMLET: I humbly thank you, well.
OPHELIA: My lord, I have remembrances of yours
      That I have longed long to re-deliver.
95   I pray you now receive them.
HAMLET: No, not I,
      I never gave you aught.

OPHELIA: My honored lord, you know right well you did,
      And with them words of so sweet breath composed
      As made the things more rich. Their perfume lost,
      Take these again, for to the noble mind   100
      Rich gifts wax poor when givers prove unkind.
      There, my lord.
HAMLET: Ha, ha! are you honest?
OPHELIA: My lord?
HAMLET: Are you fair?   105
OPHELIA: What means your lordship?
HAMLET: That if you be honest and fair, your honesty should
      admit no discourse to your beauty.
OPHELIA: Could beauty, my lord, have better commerce than
      with honesty?   110
HAMLET: Ay, truly, for the power of beauty will sooner trans-
      form honesty from what it is to a bawd than the force of
      honesty can translate beauty into his likeness. This was
      sometime a paradox, but now the time gives it proof. I did
      love you once.   115
OPHELIA: Indeed, my lord, you made me believe so.
HAMLET: You should not have believed me, for virtue cannot so
      inoculate our old stock but we shall relish of it. I loved you
      not.
OPHELIA: I was the more deceived.   120
HAMLET: Get thee to a nunnery. Why wouldst thou be a
      breeder of sinners? I am myself indifferent honest, but yet I
      could accuse me of such things that it were better my
      mother had not borne me: I am very proud, revengeful, am-
      bitious, with more offences at my beck than I have thoughts 125
      to put them in, imagination to give them shape, or time to
      act them in. What should such fellows as I do crawling be-
      tween earth and heaven? We are arrant knaves all; believe
      none of us. Go thy ways to a nunnery. Where's your father?
OPHELIA: At home, my lord.   130
HAMLET: Let the doors be shut upon him, that he may play the
      fool nowhere but in's own house. Farewell.
OPHELIA: O, help him, you sweet heavens!
HAMLET: If thou dost marry, I'll give thee this plague for thy
      dowry: be thou as chaste as ice, as pure as snow, thou shalt 135
      not escape calumny. Get thee to a nunnery, farewell. Or if
      thou wilt needs marry, marry a fool, for wise men know well
      enough what monsters you make of them. To a nunnery, go,
      and quickly too. Farewell.
OPHELIA: Heavenly powers, restore him!   140
HAMLET: I have heard of your paintings well enough. God hath
      given you one face, and you make yourselves another. You
      jig and amble, and you lisp; you nickname God's creatures,
      and make your wantonness your ignorance. Go to, I'll no
      more on't, it hath made me mad. I say we will have no moe   145
      marriage. Those that are married already, all but one, shall
      live. The rest shall keep as they are. To a nunnery, go.

(Exit.)

OPHELIA: O, what a noble mind is here o'erthrown!
      The courtier's, soldier's, scholar's, eye, tongue, sword,

---

52 **to** compared to   65 **rub** obstacle (lit., obstruction encountered by bowler's ball)   67 **coil** bustle, turmoil   75 **quietus** settlement   76 **bodkin** dagger; **fardels** burdens   79 **bourn** realm
86 **pitch** height   87 **regard** consideration   89 **orisons** prayers

---

103 **honest** chaste   118 **inoculate** graft   122 **indifferent honest** moderately respectable   144 **make your wantonness your
ignorance** excuse your wanton behavior with the plea that you
don't know any better   145 **moe** more

150 Th' expectancy and rose of the fair state,
The glass of fashion and the mould of form,
Th' observed of all observers, quite quite down!
And I of ladies most deject and wretched,
That sucked the honey of his musiced vows,
155 Now see that noble and most sovereign reason
Like sweet bells jangled, out of time and harsh;
That unmatched form and feature of blown youth
Blasted with ecstasy. O, woe is me
T' have seen what I have seen, see what I see!

(Enter KING and POLONIUS.)

160 KING: Love? His affections do not that way tend,
Nor what he spake, though it lacked form a little,
Was not like madness. There's something in his soul,
O'er which his melancholy sits on brood,
And I do doubt the hatch and the disclose
165 Will be some danger; which for to prevent,
I have in quick determination
Thus set it down: he shall with speed to England
For the demand of our neglected tribute.
Haply the seas and countries different,
170 With variable objects, shall expel
This something-settled matter in his heart
Whereon his brains still beating puts him thus
From fashion of himself. What think you on't?
POLONIUS: It shall do well. But yet do I believe
175 The origin and commencement of his grief
Sprung from neglected love.—How now, Ophelia?
You need not tell us what Lord Hamlet said;
We heard it all.—My lord, do as you please,
But if you hold it fit, after the play
180 Let his queen-mother all alone entreat him
To show his grief. Let her be round with him,
And I'll be placed, so please you, in the ear
Of all their conference. If she find him not,
To England send him; or confine him where
185 Your wisdom best shall think.
KING: It shall be so.
Madness in great ones must not unwatched go.

(Exeunt.)

SCENE II

Enter HAMLET and three of the PLAYERS.

HAMLET: Speak the speech, I pray you, as I pronounced it to
you, trippingly on the tongue; but if you mouth it as many
of our players do, I had as lief the town-crier spoke my lines.
Nor do not saw the air too much with your hand thus, but
5   use all gently, for in the very torrent, tempest, and as I may
say, whirlwind of your passion, you must acquire and beget
a temperance that may give it smoothness. O, it offends me
to the soul to hear a robustious periwig-pated fellow tear
a passion to tatters, to very rags, to split the ears of the
groundlings, who for the most part are capable of nothing 10
but inexplicable dumb shows and noise. I would have such
a fellow whipped for o'erdoing Termagant. It out-Herods
Herod. Pray you avoid it.
1 PLAYER: I warrant your honour.
HAMLET: Be not too tame neither, but let your own discretion 15
be your tutor. Suit the action to the word, the word to the
action, with this special observance, that you o'erstep not
the modesty of nature; for any thing so o'erdone is from the
purpose of playing, whose end both at the first, and now,
was and is, to hold as 'twere the mirror up to nature, to 20
show virtue her own feature, scorn her own image, and the
very age and body of the time his form and pressure. Now
this overdone, or come tardy off, though it make the un-
skilful laugh, cannot but make the judicious grieve, the
censure of the which one must in your allowance o'erweigh 25
a whole theatre of others. O, there be players that I have
seen play—and heard others praise, and that highly—not
to speak it profanely, that neither having th' accent of
Christians, nor the gait of Christian, pagan, nor man, have
so strutted and bellowed that I have thought some of na- 30
ture's journeymen had made men, and not made them well,
they imitated humanity so abominably.
1 PLAYER: I hope we have reformed that indifferently with us.
HAMLET: O, reform it altogether. And let those that play your
clowns speak no more than is set down for them, for there 35
be of them that will themselves laugh, to set on some quantity of barren spectators to laugh too, though in the meantime some necessary question of the play be then to be
considered. That's villanous, and shows a most pitiful ambition in the fool that uses it. Go, make you ready.   40

(Exeunt PLAYERS.)

(Enter POLONIUS, GUILDENSTERN, and ROSENCRANTZ.)

How now, my lord? Will the king hear this piece of work?
POLONIUS: And the queen too, and that presently.
HAMLET: Bid the players make haste. (Exit POLONIUS.)
Will you two help to hasten them?
ROSENCRANTZ: Ay, my lord.   45

(Exeunt they two.)

HAMLET: What, ho! Horatio!

(Enter HORATIO.)

HORATIO: Here, sweet lord, at your service.
HAMLET: Horatio, thou art e'en as just a man
As e'er my conversation coped withal.
HORATIO: O my dear lord!   50
HAMLET: Nay, do not think I flatter,
For what advancement may I hope from thee,

---

150 **expectancy** hope   151 **glass** mirror   157 **blown** blooming
158 **ecstasy** madness   160 **affections** emotions   164 **doubt** fear
181 **round** plain-spoken

III.ii. 10 **groundlings** spectators who paid least and stood on the
ground   12 **Termagant** thought to be a Mohammedan deity, and
represented in medieval mystery plays as a violent and ranting personage; **Herod** represented in the mystery plays as a blustering
tyrant   25 **censure** judgment, opinion   33 **indifferently** fairly
well   49 **coped** encountered

That no revenue hast but thy good spirits
To feed and clothe thee? Why should the poor be flattered?
No, let the candied tongue lick absurd pomp,
55   And crook the pregnant hinges of the knee
Where thrift may follow fawning. Dost thou hear?
Since my dear soul was mistress of her choice
And could of men distinguish her election,
S'hath sealed thee for herself, for thou hast been
60   As one in suff'ring all that suffers nothing,
A man that Fortune's buffets and rewards
Hast ta'en with equal thanks; and blest are those
Whose blood and judgment are so well comeddled
That they are not a pipe for Fortune's finger
65   To sound what stop she please. Give me that man
That is not passion's slave, and I will wear him
In my heart's core, ay, in my heart of heart,
As I do thee. Something too much of this.
There is a play to-night before the king.
70   One scene of it comes near the circumstance
Which I have told thee of my father's death.
I prithee, when thou seest that act afoot,
Even with the very comment of thy soul
Observe my uncle. If his occulted guilt
75   Do not itself unkennel in one speech,
It is a damnèd ghost that we have seen,
And my imaginations are as foul
As Vulcan's stithy. Give him heedful note,
For I mine eyes will rivet to his face,
80   And after we will both our judgements join
In censure of his seeming.
HORATIO: Well, my lord.
If 'a steal aught the whilst this play is playing,
And 'scape detecting, I will pay the theft.

(Enter Trumpets and Kettledrums, KING, QUEEN, POLONIUS, OPHELIA,
{ROSENCRANTZ, GUILDENSTERN, *and other* LORDS *attendant}.)*

HAMLET: They are coming to the play. I must be idle.
85   Get you a place.
KING: How fares our cousin Hamlet?
HAMLET: Excellent, i' faith, of the chameleon's dish. I eat the
     air, promise-crammed. You cannot feed capons so.
KING: I have nothing with this answer, Hamlet. These words
90   are not mine.
HAMLET: No, nor mine now. *(To* POLONIUS.) My lord, you
     played once i' th' university, you say?
POLONIUS: That did I, my lord; and was accounted a good
     actor.
95   HAMLET: What did you enact?
POLONIUS: I did enact Julius Caesar. I was killed i' th' Capitol;
     Brutus killed me.
HAMLET: It was a brute part of him to kill so capital a calf there.
     Be the players ready?
100 ROSENCRANTZ: Ay, my lord, they stay upon your patience.

---

55 **pregnant** ready   56 **thrift** profit   58 **election** choice   63 **comeddled** mingled   73 **the very comment of thy soul** with a keen-
ness of observation that penetrates to the very being   74 **occulted**
hidden   75 **unkennel** reveal   78 **stithy** forge   81 **censure** opinion   84 **idle** crazy   87 **chameleon's dish** the air, on which the
chameleon was supposed to feed

QUEEN: Come hither, my dear Hamlet, sit by me.
HAMLET: No, good mother, here's metal more attractive.
POLONIUS: *(To the* KING.) O, ho! do you mark that?
HAMLET: Lady, shall I lie in your lap?

(Lying down at OPHELIA's *feet.)*

OPHELIA: No, my lord.   105
HAMLET: I mean, my head upon your lap?
OPHELIA: Ay, my lord.
HAMLET: Do you think I meant country matters?
OPHELIA: I think nothing, my lord.
HAMLET: That's a fair thought to lie between maids' legs.   110
OPHELIA: What is, my lord?
HAMLET: Nothing.
OPHELIA: You are merry, my lord.
HAMLET: Who, I?
OPHELIA: Ay, my lord.   115
HAMLET: O God, your only jig-maker! What should a man do
     but be merry? For look you how cheerfully my mother
     looks, and my father died within's two hours.
OPHELIA: Nay, 'tis twice two months, my lord.
HAMLET: So long? Nay then, let the devil wear black, for I'll   120
     have a suit of sables. O heavens! die two months ago, and
     not forgotten yet? Then there's hope a great man's memory
     may outlive his life half a year, but, by'r lady 'a must build
     churches then, or else shall 'a suffer not thinking on, with
     the hobby-horse, whose epitaph is   125

          'For O, for O, the hobby-horse is forgot!'

(The trumpets sound. Dumb Show follows.)

(Enter a KING *and a* QUEEN *{very lovingly}; the* QUEEN *embracing
him and he her. {She kneels, and makes show of protestation unto
him.} He takes her up, and declines his head upon her neck. He lies
him down upon a bank of flowers; she, seeing him asleep, leaves him.
Anon comes in another man, takes off his crown, kisses it, pours poison
in the sleeper's ears, and leaves him. The* QUEEN *returns, finds the
KING dead, makes passionate action. The* POISONER *with some three
or four come in again, seem to condole with her. The dead body is carried away. The* POISONER *woos the* QUEEN *with gifts; she seems harsh
awhile, but in the end accepts love.)*

(Exeunt.)

OPHELIA: What means this, my lord?
HAMLET: Marry, this is miching mallecho; it means mischief.
OPHELIA: Belike this show imports the argument of the play.

(Enter PROLOGUE.*)*

HAMLET: We shall know by this fellow. The players cannot keep 130
     counsel; they'll tell all.
OPHELIA: Will 'a tell us what this show meant?
HAMLET: Ay, or any show that you will show him. Be not you
     ashamed to show, he'll not shame to tell you what it means.

---

125 **hobby-horse** the figure of a horse fastened round the waist of
a morris dancer. Puritan efforts to suppress the country sports in
which the hobby-horse figured led to a popular ballad lamenting
the fact that "the hobby-horse is forgot"   128 **miching mallecho**
skulking or crafty crime

135 OPHELIA: You are naught, you are naught. I'll mark the play.
PROLOGUE:
                    For us, and for our tragedy,
                    Here stooping to your clemency,
                    We beg your hearing patiently.

(Exit.)

HAMLET: Is this a prologue, or the posy of a ring?
140 OPHELIA: 'Tis brief, my lord.
HAMLET: As woman's love.

(Enter {the PLAYER} KING and QUEEN.)

PLAYER KING: Full thirty times hath Phoebus' cart gone round
            Neptune's salt wash and Tellus' orbèd ground,
            And thirty dozen moons with borrowed sheen
145   About the world have times twelve thirties been,
            Since love our hearts and Hymen did our hands
            Unite comutual in most sacred bands.
PLAYER QUEEN: So many journeys may the sun and moon
            Make us again count o'er ere love be done!
150 But woe is me, you are so sick of late,
            So far from cheer and from your former state,
            That I distrust you. Yet though I distrust,
            Discomfort you, my lord, it nothing must.
            For women's fear and love hold quantity,
155   In neither aught, or in extremity.
            Now what my love is proof hath made you know,
            And as my love is sized, my fear is so.
            Where love is great, the littlest doubts are fear;
            Where little fears grow great, great love grows there.
160 PLAYER KING: Faith, I must leave thee, love, and shortly too;
            My operant powers their functions leave to do.
            And thou shalt live in this fair world behind,
            Honored, beloved; and haply one as kind
            For husband shalt thou—
PLAYER QUEEN: O, confound the rest!
165   Such love must needs be treason in my breast.
            In second husband let me be accurst!
            None wed the second but who killed the first.
HAMLET: That's wormwood.
PLAYER QUEEN: The instances that second marriage move
170   Are base respects of thrift, but none of love.
            A second time I kill my husband dead,
            When second husband kisses me in bed.
PLAYER KING: I do believe you think what now you speak,
            But what we do determine oft we break.
175   Purpose is but the slave to memory,
            Of violent birth, but poor validity;
            Which now, like fruit unripe, sticks on the tree,
            But fall unshaken when they mellow be.
            Most necessary 'tis that we forget
180   To pay ourselves what to ourselves is debt.

What to ourselves in passion we propose,
            The passion ending, doth the purpose lose.
            The violence of either grief or joy
            Their own enactures with themselves destroy.
            Where joy most revels, grief doth most lament;   185
            Grief joys, joy grieves, on slender accident.
            This world is not for aye, nor 'tis not strange
            That even our loves should with our fortunes change;
            For 'tis a question left us yet to prove,
            Whether love lead fortune, or else fortune love.   190
            The great man down, you mark his favorite flies;
            The poor advanced makes friends of enemies;
            And hitherto doth love on fortune tend,
            For who not needs shall never lack a friend,
            And who in want a hollow friend doth try,   195
            Directly seasons him his enemy.
            But orderly to end where I begun,
            Our wills and fates do so contrary run
            That our devices still are overthrown;
            Our thoughts are ours, their ends none of our own.   200
            So think thou wilt no second husband wed,
            But die thy thoughts when thy first lord is dead.
PLAYER QUEEN: Nor earth to me give food, nor heaven light,
            Sport and repose lock from me day and night.
            To desperation turn my trust and hope,   205
            An anchor's cheer in prison be my scope,
            Each opposite that blanks the face of joy
            Meet what I would have well, and it destroy,
            Both here and hence pursue me lasting strife,
            If once a widow, ever I be wife!   210
HAMLET: If she should break it now!
PLAYER KING: 'Tis deeply sworn. Sweet, leave me here awhile.
            My spirits grow dull, and fain I would beguile
            The tedious day with sleep.

(Sleeps.)

PLAYER QUEEN: Sleep rock thy brain.
            And never come mischance between us twain!   215

(Exit.)

HAMLET: Madam, how like you this play?
QUEEN: The lady doth protest too much, methinks.
HAMLET: O, but she'll keep her word.
KING: Have you heard the argument? Is there no offence in't?
HAMLET: No, no, they do but jest, poison in jest; no offence i' 220
th' world.
KING: What do you call the play?
HAMLET: 'The Mouse-trap.' Marry, how? Tropically. This play
is the image of a murder done in Vienna. Gonzago is the
duke's name; his wife, Baptista. You shall see anon. 'Tis a   225
knavish piece of work, but what of that? Your majesty, and
we that have free souls, it touches us not. Let the galled jade
winch, our withers are unwrung.

(Enter LUCIANUS.)

---

135 **naught** naughty, lewd   139 **posy** brief motto engraved on a
fingerring   142 **Phoebus' cart** the sun's chariot   143 **Tellus'
orbed ground** the earth (Tellus was the Roman goddess of the
earth)   146 **Hymen** god of marriage   152 **distrust** fear for
154 **hold quantity** are proportional, weigh alike   157 **as my
love is sized** according to the greatness of my love   161 **operant**
vital   169 **instances** motives   176 **validity** endurance

---

184 **enactures** enactments   187 **aye** ever   196 **seasons him**
ripens him into   206 **anchor's** anchorite's   227 **galled jade**
sorebacked horse

This is one Lucianus, nephew to the king.

230   OPHELIA: You are as good as a chorus, my lord.

HAMLET: I could interpret between you and your love, if I could
    see the puppets dallying.

OPHELIA: You are keen, my lord, you are keen.

HAMLET: It would cost you a groaning to take off mine edge.

235   OPHELIA: Still better, and worse.

HAMLET: So you mis-take your husbands.—Begin, murderer.
    Leave thy damnable faces and begin. Come, the croaking
    raven doth bellow for revenge.

LUCIANUS: Thoughts black, hands apt, drugs fit, and time
    agreeing,

240   Confederate season, else no creature seeing.
    Thou mixture rank, of midnight weeds collected,
    With Hecate's ban thrice blasted, thrice infected,
    Thy natural magic and dire property
    On wholesome life usurp immediately.

(Pours the poison in his ears.)

245   HAMLET: 'A poisons him i' th' garden for his estate. His name's
    Gonzago. The story is extant, and written in very choice
    Italian. You shall see anon how the murderer gets the love
    of Gonzago's wife.

OPHELIA: The king rises.

250   HAMLET: What, frighted with false fire?

QUEEN: How fares my lord?

POLONIUS: Give o'er the play.

KING: Give me some light. Away!

POLONIUS: Lights, lights, lights!

(Exeunt all but HAMLET and HORATIO.)

255   HAMLET: Why, let the strucken deer go weep,
            The hart ungallèd play.
        For some must watch, while some must sleep;
            Thus runs the world away.

Would not this, sir, and a forest of feathers—if the rest of

260   my fortunes turn Turk with me—with two Provincial roses
    on my razed shoes, get me a fellowship in a cry of players?

HORATIO: Half a share.

HAMLET: A whole one, I.

        For thou dost know, O Damon dear,

265   This realm dismantled was
        Of Jove himself, and now reigns here
        A very, very—pajock.

HORATIO: You might have rhymed.

HAMLET: O good Horatio, I'll take the ghost's word for a thou-

270   sand pound. Didst perceive?

HORATIO: Very well, my lord.

HAMLET: Upon the talk of the poisoning.

HORATIO: I did very well note him.

HAMLET: Ah, ha! Come, some music. Come, the recorders.

---

242 **Hecate** goddess of witchcraft; **blasted** fallen under a blight
259 **feathers** plumes for actors' costumes   260 **Provincial roses**
i.e., Provençal roses. Ribbon rosettes resembling these French
roses were used to decorate shoes   261 **razed** with ornamental
slashing; **cry** company   267 **pajock** presumably a variant form of
"patch-cock," a despicable person. Cf. 3.4.104

                            For if the king like not the comedy,   275
                            Why then, belike, he likes it not, perdy.

Come, some music.

(Enter ROSENCRANTZ *and* GUILDENSTERN.)

GUILDENSTERN: Good my lord, vouchsafe me a word with you.

HAMLET: Sir, a whole history.

GUILDENSTERN: The king, sir—   280

HAMLET: Ay, sir what of him?

GUILDENSTERN: Is in his retirement marvellous distempered.

HAMLET: With drink, sir?

GUILDENSTERN: No, my lord, with choler.

HAMLET: Your wisdom should show itself more richer to signify   285
    this to the doctor, for for me to put him to his purgation
    would perhaps plunge him into more choler.

GUILDENSTERN: Good my lord, put your discourse into some
    frame, and start not so wildly from my affair.

HAMLET: I am tame, sir. Pronounce.   290

GUILDENSTERN: The queen, your mother, in most great afflic-
    tion of spirit, hath sent me to you.

HAMLET: You are welcome.

GUILDENSTERN: Nay, good my lord, this courtesy is not of the
    right breed. If it shall please you to make me a wholesome   295
    answer, I will do your mother's commandment. If not, your
    pardon and my return shall be the end of my business.

HAMLET: Sir, I cannot.

GUILDENSTERN: What, my lord?

HAMLET: Make you a wholesome answer; my wit's diseased.   300
    But, sir, such answer as I can make, you shall command, or
    rather, as you say, my mother. Therefore no more, but to the
    matter. My mother, you say—

ROSENCRANTZ: Then thus she says: your behaviour hath struck
    her into amazement and admiration.   305

HAMLET: O wonderful son, that can so stonish a mother! But is
    there no sequel at the heels of this mother's admiration?
    Impart.

ROSENCRANTZ: She desires to speak with you in her closet ere
    you go to bed.   310

HAMLET: We shall obey, were she ten times our mother. Have
    you any further trade with us?

ROSENCRANTZ: My lord, you once did love me.

HAMLET: And do still, by these pickers and stealers.

ROSENCRANTZ: Good my lord, what is your cause of distemper?   315
    You do surely bar the door upon your own liberty, if you
    deny your griefs to your friend.

HAMLET: Sir, I lack advancement.

ROSENCRANTZ: How can that be, when you have the voice of
    the king himself for your succession in Denmark?   320

HAMLET: Ay, sir, but 'While the grass grows'—the proverb is
    something musty.

---

275 **For if . . . comedy** a seeming parody of *The Spanish Tragedy,*
4.1.197–98 ("And if the world like not this tragedy, / Hard is the
hap of old Hieronimo"), where another revenger's dramatic entertainment is referred to   287 **choler** one of the four bodily humors, an excess of which gave rise to anger   295 **wholesome**
reasonable   307 **admiration** wonder   314 **pickers and stealers** hands   321 **"while the grass grows"** a proverb ending "the
horse starves"

(Enter the PLAYERS *with recorders.)*

    O, the recorders! Let me see one. To withdraw with you—
    why do you go about to recover the wind of me, as if you
325   would drive me into a toil?
GUILDENSTERN: O, my lord, if my duty be too bold, my love is
    too unmannerly.
HAMLET: I do not well understand that. Will you play upon this
    pipe?
330 GUILDENSTERN: My lord, I cannot.
HAMLET: I pray you.
GUILDENSTERN: Believe me, I cannot.
HAMLET: I beseech you.
GUILDENSTERN: I know no touch of it, my lord.
335 HAMLET: It is easy as lying. Govern these ventages with your
    fingers and thumb, give it breath with your mouth, and it
    will discourse most eloquent music. Look you, these are the
    stops.
GUILDENSTERN: But these cannot I command to any utt'rance
340   of harmony. I have not the skill.
HAMLET: Why look you now, how unworthy a thing you make
    of me! You would play upon me, you would seem to know
    my stops, you would pluck out the heart of my mystery, you
    would sound me from my lowest note to the top of my com-
345   pass; and there is music, excellent voice, in this little organ,
    yet cannot you make it speak. 'Sblood, do you think I am
    easier to be played on than a pipe? Call me what instrument
    you will, though you can fret me, you cannot play upon me.

(Enter POLONIUS.*)*

350   God bless you, sir!
POLONIUS: My lord, the queen would speak with you, and
    presently.
HAMLET: Do you see yonder cloud that's almost in shape of a
    camel?
355 POLONIUS: By th' mass and 'tis, like a camel indeed.
HAMLET: Methinks it is like a weasel.
POLONIUS: It is backed like a weasel.
HAMLET: Or like a whale.
POLONIUS: Very like a whale.
360 HAMLET: Then I will come to my mother by and by. *(Aside.)*
    They fool me to the top of my bent.—I will come by and by.
POLONIUS: I will say so.

(Exit POLONIUS.*)*

HAMLET: 'By and by' is easily said. Leave me, friends.

(Exeunt all but HAMLET.*)*

    'Tis now the very witching time of night,
365   When churchyards yawn and hell itself breathes out
    Contagion to this world. Now could I drink hot blood,
    And do such bitter business as the day
    Would quake to look on. Soft, now to my mother.
    O heart, lose not thy nature; let not ever
370   The soul of Nero enter this firm bosom.

    Let me be cruel, not unnatural;
    I will speak daggers to her, but use none.
    My tongue and soul in this be hypocrites:
    How in my words somever she be shent,
    To give them seals never my soul consent!   375

(Exit.)

SCENE III

Enter KING, ROSENCRANTZ, *and* GUILDENSTERN.

KING: I like him not, nor stands it safe with us
    To let his madness range. Therefore prepare you.
    I your commission will forthwith dispatch,
    And he to England shall along with you.
    The terms of our estate may not endure   5
    Hazard so near's as doth hourly grow
    Out of his brows.
GUILDENSTERN: We will ourselves provide,
    Most holy and religious fear it is
    To keep those many many bodies safe
    That live and feed upon your majesty.   10
ROSENCRANTZ: The single and peculiar life is bound
    With all the strength and armor of the mind
    To keep itself from noyance, but much more
    That spirit upon whose weal depends and rests
    The lives of many. The cess of majesty   15
    Dies not alone, but like a gulf doth draw
    What's near it with it. It is a massy wheel
    Fixed on the summit of the highest mount,
    To whose huge spokes ten thousand lesser things
    Are mortised and adjoined, which when it falls,   20
    Each small annexment, petty consequence,
    Attends the boist'rous ruin. Never alone
    Did the king sigh, but with a general groan.
KING: Arm you, I pray you, to this speedy voyage,
    For we will fetters put about this fear,   25
    Which now goes too free-footed.
ROSENCRANTZ: We will haste us.

(Exeunt Gentlemen [ROSENCRANTZ *and* GUILDENSTERN].*)*

(Enter POLONIUS.*)*

POLONIUS: My lord, he's going to his mother's closet.
    Behind the arras I'll convey myself
    To hear the process. I'll warrant she'll tax him home,
    And as you said, and wisely was it said,   30
    'Tis meet that some more audience than a mother,
    Since nature makes them partial, should o'erhear
    The speech of vantage. Fare you well, my liege.
    I'll call upon you ere you go to bed,
    And tell you what I know.   35

---

374 **somever,** soever; **shent** reproved, abused

III.iii. 5 **terms of our estate** conditions required for our rule as
king   7 **brows** threatening looks that suggest the dangerous
plots Hamlet's brain is hatching   11 **peculiar** private   13 **noy-
ance** harm   15 **cess** cessation, extinction   20 **mortised** jointed
(as with mortise and tenon)   33 **of vantage** (1) in addition;
(2) from a convenient place for listening

---

323 **withdraw** step aside for private conversation   325 **toil** net,
snare   335 **ventages** holes or stops in the recorder   348 **fret** (1)
a stop on the fingerboard of a guitar (2) annoy   370 **Nero** Roman
emperor who murdered his mother

KING: Thanks, dear my lord. (*Exit* POLONIUS.)
  O, my offence is rank, it smells to heaven;
  It hath the primal eldest curse upon't,
  A brother's murder. Pray can I not,
  Though inclination be as sharp as will.
40 My stronger guilt defeats my strong intent,
  And like a man to double business bound,
  I stand in pause where I shall first begin,
  And both neglect. What if this cursèd hand
  Were thicker than itself with brother's blood,
45 Is there not rain enough in the sweet heavens
  To wash it white as snow? Whereto serves mercy
  But to confront the visage of offence?
  And what's in prayer but this twofold force,
  To be forestallèd ere we come to fall,
50 Or pardoned being down? Then I'll look up.
  My fault is past. But, O, what form of prayer
  Can serve my turn? 'Forgive me my foul murder'?
  That cannot be, since I am still possessed
  Of those effects for which I did the murder—
55 My crown, mine own ambition, and my queen.
  May one be pardoned and retain th' offence?
  In the corrupted currents of this world
  Offence's gilded hand may shove by justice,
  And oft 'tis seen the wicked prize itself
60 Buys out the law. But 'tis not so above
  There is no shuffling: there the action lies
  In his true nature, and we ourselves compelled,
  Even to the teeth and forehead of our faults,
  To give in evidence. What then? What rests?
65 Try what repentance can. What can it not?
  Yet what can it when one can not repent?
  O wretched state! O bosom black as death!
  O limèd soul, that struggling to be free
  Art more engaged! Help, angels! Make assay.
70 Bow, stubborn knees, and heart with strings of steel,
  Be soft as sinews of the new-born babe.
  All may be well.

(*He kneels.*)

(*Enter* HAMLET.)

HAMLET: Now might I do it pat, now 'a is a-praying,
  And now I'll do't—and so 'a goes to heaven,
75 And so am I revenged. That would be scanned.
  A villain kills my father, and for that,
  I, his sole son, do this same villain send
  To heaven.
  Why, this is hire and salary, not revenge.
80 'A took my father grossly, full of bread,
  With all his crimes broad blown, as flush as May;
  And how his audit stands who knows save heaven?
  But in our circumstance and course of thought
  'Tis heavy with him; and am I then revenged

  To take him in the purging of his soul,   85
  When he is fit and seasoned for his passage?
  No.
  Up, sword, and know thou a more horrid hent.
  When he is drunk asleep, or in his rage,
  Or in th' incestuous pleasure of his bed,   90
  At game a-swearing, or about some act
  That has no relish of salvation in't—
  Then trip him, that his heels may kick at heaven,
  And that his soul may be as damned and black
  As hell, whereto it goes. My mother stays.   95
  This physic but prolongs thy sickly days.

(*Exit.*)

KING: (*Rising.*) My words fly up, my thoughts remain below.
  Words without thoughts never to heaven go.

(*Exit.*)

SCENE IV

Enter [QUEEN] GERTRUDE *and* POLONIUS.

POLONIUS: 'A will come straight. Look you lay home to him.
  Tell him his pranks have been too broad to bear with,
  And that your grace hath screened and stood between
  Much heat and him. I'll silence me even here.
  Pray you be round.   5
QUEEN: I'll warrant you. Fear me not.
  Withdraw, I hear him coming.

(POLONIUS *goes behind the arras.*)

(*Enter* HAMLET.)

HAMLET: Now, mother, what's the matter?
QUEEN: Hamlet, thou hast thy father much offended.
HAMLET: Mother, you have my father much offended.
QUEEN: Come, come, you answer with an idle tongue.   10
HAMLET: Go, go, you question with a wicked tongue.
QUEEN: Why, how, now, Hamlet?
HAMLET: What's the matter now?
QUEEN: Have you forgot me?
HAMLET: No, by the rood, not so:
  You are the queen, your husband's brother's wife,
  And would it were not so, you are my mother.   15
QUEEN: Nay, then I'll set those to you that can speak.
HAMLET: Come, come, and sit you down. You shall not budge.
  You go not till I set you up a glass
  Where you may see the inmost part of you.
QUEEN: What will thou do? Thou wilt not murder me?   20
  Help, ho!
POLONIUS: (*Behind.*) What, ho! help!
HAMLET: (*Draws.*) How now! a rat?
  Dead for a ducat, dead!

(*Thrusts his sword through the arras and kills* POLONIUS.)

---

39 **will** carnal desire   61 **shuffling** doubledealing; **action** legal
action   68 **limèd** soul caught by sin as the bird by lime   69 **assay**
an effort   80 **grossly** unprepared spiritually   81 **as flush as May**
in full flower   83 **in our circumstance** considering all evidence;
course beaten way, habit

88 **hent** occasion, opportunity

III.iv. 5 Following Polonius's "Pray you be round" (which in *F*
reads "Pray you be round with him"), *F* adds the line: "*Hamlet
within.* Mother, mother, mother"   13 **rood** cross

25 POLONIUS: *(Behind.)* O, I am slain!
    QUEEN: O me, what hast thou done?
    HAMLET: Nay, I know not.
       Is it the king?
    QUEEN: O, what a rash and bloody deed is this!
    HAMLET: A bloody deed? Almost as bad, good mother,
30   As kill a king and marry with his brother.
    QUEEN: As kill a king?
    HAMLET: Ay, lady, it was my word.

(Lifts up the arras and sees the body of POLONIUS.*)*

       Thou wretched, rash, intruding fool, farewell!
       I took thee for thy better. Take thy fortune.
       Thou find'st to be too busy is some danger.—
35   Leave wringing of your hands. Peace, sit you down
       And let me wring your heart, for so I shall
       If it be made of penetrable stuff,
       If damnèd custom have not brazed it so
       That it be proof and bulwark against sense.
40 QUEEN: What have I done that thou dar'st wag thy tongue
       In noise so rude against me?
    HAMLET: Such an act
       That blurs the grace and blush of modesty,
       Calls virtue hypocrite, takes off the rose
       From the fair forehead of an innocent love,
45   And sets a blister there, makes marriage-vows
       As false as dicers' oaths. O, such a deed
       As from the body of contraction plucks
       The very soul, and sweet religion makes
       A rhapsody of words. Heaven's face does glow
50   O'er this solidity and compound mass
       With heated visage, as against the doom—
       Is thought-sick at the act.
    QUEEN: Ay me, what act,
       That roars so loud, and thunders in the index?
    HAMLET: Look here, upon this picture and on this.
55   The counterfeit presentment of two brothers.
       See what a grace was seated on this brow:
       Hyperion's curls, the front of Jove himself,
       An eye like Mars, to threaten and command,
       A station like the herald Mercury
60   New lighted on a heaven-kissing hill—
       A combination and a form indeed
       Where every god did seem to set his seal
       To give the world assurance of a man.
       This was your husband. Look you now what follows.
65   Here is your husband, like a mildewed ear
       Blasting his wholesome brother. Have you eyes?
       Could you on this fair mountain leave to feed,
       And batten on this moor? Ha! have you eyes?
       You cannot call it love, for at your age
70   The heyday in the blood is tame, it's humble,

And waits upon the judgement, and what judgement
Would step from this to this? Sense sure you have,
Else could you not have motion, but sure that sense
Is apoplexed, for madness would not err
Nor sense to ecstasy was ne'er so thralled   75
But it reserved some quantity of choice
To serve in such a difference. What devil was't
That thus hath cozened you at hoodman-blind?
Eyes without feeling, feeling without sight,
Ears without hands or eyes, smelling sans all,   80
Or but a sickly part of one true sense
Could not so mope. O shame! where is thy blush?
Rebellious hell,
If thou canst mutine in a matron's bones,
To flaming youth let virtue be as wax   85
And melt in her own fire. Proclaim no shame
When the compulsive ardor gives the charge,
Since frost itself as actively doth burn,
And reason pandars will.
QUEEN: O Hamlet, speak no more!
   Thou turn'st mine eyes into my very soul,   90
   And there I see such black and grainèd spots
   As will not leave their tinct.
HAMLET: Nay, but to live
   In the rank sweat of an enseamèd bed,
   Stewed in corruption, honeying and making love
   Over the nasty sty—   95
QUEEN: O, speak to me no more!
   These words like daggers enter in mine ears.
   No more, sweet Hamlet.
HAMLET: A murderer and a villain,
   A slave that is not twentieth part the tithe
   Of your precedent lord, a vice of kings,
   A cutpurse of the empire and the rule,   100
   That from a shelf the precious diadem stole
   And put it in his pocket—
QUEEN: No more.

(Enter GHOST.*)*

HAMLET: A king of shreds and patches—
   Save me and hover o'er me with your wings,   105
   You heavenly guards! What would your gracious figure?
QUEEN: Alas, he's mad.
HAMLET: Do you not come your tardy son to chide,
   That lapsed in time and passion lets go by
   Th' important acting of your dread command?   110
   O, say!
GHOST: Do not forget. This visitation
   Is but to whet thy almost blunted purpose.
   But look, amazement on thy mother sits.
   O, step between her and her fighting soul!   115

---

38 **brazed** plated it as with brass   39 **proof** impenetrable, as of
armor   47 **contraction** the contract of marriage   50 **this solidity and compound mass** the earth, as compounded of the four
elements   51 **doom** Judgment Day   53 **index** table of contents;
thus, indication of what is to follow   55 **counterfeit presentment** portrait   57 **front** forehead   59 **station** bearing figure
68 **batten** feed like an animal   70 **heyday** ardor

72 **Sense** the senses collectively, which according to Aristotelian
tradition are found in all creatures that have the power of loco-
motion   75 **ecstasy** madness   78 **hoodman-blind** blindman's
bluff   80 **sans** without   82 **mope** act without full use of one's wits
89 **will** desire   91 **grainèd spots** indelible stains   92 **tinct** color
93 **enseamèd** greasy   99 **vice** a character in the morality plays,
presented often as a buffoon (here, a caricature)

Conceit in weakest bodies strongest works.
Speak to her, Hamlet.
HAMLET: How is it with you, lady?
QUEEN: Alas, how is't with you,
That you do bend your eye on vacancy,
120   And with th' incorporal air do hold discourse?
Forth at your eyes your spirits wildly peep,
And as the sleeping soldiers in th' alarm,
Your bedded hair like life in excrements
Start up and stand an end. O gentle son,
125   Upon the heat and flame of thy distemper
Sprinkle cool patience. Whereon do you look?
HAMLET: On him, on him! Look you how pale he glares.
His form and cause conjoined, preaching to stones,
Would make them capable.—Do not look upon me,
130   Lest with this piteous action you convert
My stern effects. Then what I have to do
Will want true color—tears perchance for blood.
QUEEN: To whom do you speak this?
HAMLET: Do you see nothing there?
135 QUEEN: Nothing at all, yet all that is I see.
HAMLET: Nor did you nothing hear?
QUEEN: No, nothing but ourselves.
HAMLET: Why, look you there. Look, how it steals away.
My father, in his habit as he lived!
140   Look where he goes even now out at the portal.

(*Exit* GHOST.)

QUEEN: This is the very coinage of your brain.
This bodiless creation ecstasy
Is very cunning in.
HAMLET: My pulse as yours doth temperately keep time,
145   And makes us healthful music. It is not madness
That I have uttered. Bring me to the test,
And I the matter will re-word, which madness
Would gambol from. Mother, for love of grace,
Lay not that flattering unction to your soul,
150   That not your trespass but my madness speaks.
It will but skin and film the ulcerous place
Whiles rank corruption, mining all within,
Infects unseen. Confess yourself to heaven,
Repent what's past, avoid what is to come,
155   And do not spread the compost on the weeds,
To make them ranker. Forgive me this my virtue,
For in the fatness of these pursy times
Virtue itself of vice must pardon beg,
Yea, curb and woo for leave to do him good.
160 QUEEN: O Hamlet, thou hast cleft my heart in twain.
HAMLET: O, throw away the worser part of it,
And live the purer with the other half.
Good night—but go not to my uncle's bed.
Assume a virtue, if you have it not.
165   That monster custom, who all sense doth eat,

Of habits devil, is angel yet in this,
That to the use of actions fair and good
He likewise gives a frock or livery
That aptly is put on. Refrain to-night,
And that shall lend a kind of easiness   170
To the next abstinence; the next more easy;
For use almost can change the stamp of nature,
And either curb the devil, or throw him out
With wondrous potency. Once more, good night,
And when you are desirous to be blest,   175
I'll blessing beg of you. For this same lord,
I do repent; but heaven hath pleased it so,
To punish me with this, and this with me,
That I must be their scourge and minister.
I will bestow him and will answer well   180
The death I gave him. So, again, good night.
I must be cruel only to be kind.
This bad begins and worse remains behind.
One word more, good lady.
QUEEN: What shall I do?
HAMLET: Not this, by no means, that I bid you do: 185
Let the bloat king tempt you again to bed,
Pinch wanton on your cheek, call you his mouse,
And let him, for a pair of reechy kisses,
Or paddling in your neck with his damned fingers,
Make you to ravel all this matter out,   190
That I essentially am not in madness,
But mad in craft. 'Twere good you let him know,
For who that's but a queen, fair, sober, wise,
Would from a paddock, from a bat, a gib,
Such dear concernings hide? Who would so do?   195
No, in despite of sense and secrecy,
Unpeg the basket on the house's top,
Let the birds fly, and like the famous ape,
To try conclusions, in the basket creep
And break your own neck down.   200
QUEEN: Be thou assured, if words be made of breath
And breath of life, I have no life to breathe
What thou hast said to me.
HAMLET: I must to England; you know that?
QUEEN: Alack,
I had forgot. 'Tis so concluded on.   205
HAMLET: There's letters sealed, and my two school-fellows,
Whom I will trust as I will adders fanged,
They bear the mandate; they must sweep my way
And marshal me to knavery. Let it work,

---

116 **Conceit** imagination   123 **excrements** nails, hair (whatever grows out of the body)   124 **an** on   129 **capable** able to respond   132 **want** lack   148 **gambol** leap or start, as a shying horse   149 **unction** ointment; hence, soothing notion   152 **mining** undermining   157 **fatness** grossness, slackness; **pursy** corpulent   165 **who all sense doth eat** who consumes all human sense, both bodily and spiritual

166 **Of habits devil** being a devil in, or in respect of, habits (with a play on "habits," as meaning both settled practices and garments, whereby devilish practices contrast with "actions fair and good," line 167, and devilish garments contrast with the "frock or livery" of line 168, which custom in its angelic aspect provides)   183 **This** i.e., the death of Polonius (cf. line 178); **remains behind** is yet to come   188 **reechy** dirty   191 **essentially** in fact   194 **paddock** toad; **gib** tom-cat   197–200 **Unpeg the basket . . . neck down** the story is lost (in it, apparently, the ape carries a cage of birds to the top of a house, releases them by accident, and, surprised at their flight, imagines he can imitate it by first creeping into the basket and then leaping out. The moral of the story, for the queen, is not to expose herself to destruction by making public what good sense decrees should be kept secret.)

210   For 'tis the sport to have the engineer
    Hoist with his own petar; and 't shall go hard
    But I will delve one yard below their mines
    And blow them at the moon. O, 'tis most sweet
    When in one line two crafts directly meet.
215   This man shall set me packing.
    I'll lug the guts into the neighbour room.
    Mother, good night indeed. This counsellor
    Is now most still, most secret and most grave,
    Who was in life a foolish prating knave.
220   Come sir, to draw toward an end with you.
    Good night, mother.

*(Exit [*HAMLET *tugging in* POLONIUS]*.)*

——— ACT FOUR ———

SCENE I

Enter KING *{to the}* QUEEN, *with* ROSENCRANTZ *and* GUILDEN-
STERN.

KING: There's matter in these sighs, these profound heaves,
    You must translate, 'tis fit we understand them.
    Where is your son?
QUEEN: Bestow this place on us a little while.

(Exeunt ROSENCRANTZ *and* GUILDENSTERN.*)*

5   Ah, mine own lord, what have I seen to-night!
KING: What, Gertrude, how does Hamlet?
QUEEN: Mad as the sea and wind when both contend
    Which is the mightier. In his lawless fit,
    Behind the arras hearing something stir,
10   Whips out his rapier, cries 'A rat, a rat!'
    And in this brainish apprehension kills
    The unseen good old man.
KING: O heavy deed!
    It had been so with us had we been there.
    His liberty is full of threats to all—
15   To you yourself, to us, to every one.
    Alas, how shall this bloody deed be answered?
    It will be laid to us, whose providence
    Should have kept short, restrained, and out of haunt,
    This mad young man. But so much was our love,
20   We would not understand what was most fit,
    But like the owner of a foul disease,
    To keep it from divulging, let it feed
    Even on the pith of life. Where is he gone?
QUEEN: To draw apart the body he hath killed,
25   O'er whom his very madness, like some ore
    Among a mineral of metals base,
    Shows itself pure: 'a weeps for what is done.
KING: O Gertrude, come away!
    The sun no sooner shall the mountains touch
30   But we will ship him hence, and this vile deed

    We must with all our majesty and skill,
    Both countenance and excuse. Ho, Guildenstern!

(Enter ROSENCRANTZ *and* GUILDENSTERN.*)*

    Friends both, go join you with some further aid.
    Hamlet in madness hath Polonius slain,
    And from his mother's closet hath he dragged him.   35
    Go seek him out; speak fair, and bring the body
    Into the chapel. I pray you haste in this.

(Exeunt ROSENCRANTZ *and* GUILDENSTERN.*)*

    Come, Gertrude, we'll call up our wisest friends
    And let them know both what we mean to do
    And what's untimely done; so haply slander—   40
    Whose whisper o'er the world's diameter,
    As level as the cannon to his blank,
    Transports his poisoned shot—may miss our name,
    And hit the woundless air. O, come away!
    My soul is full of discord and dismay.   45

(Exeunt.)

SCENE II

Enter HAMLET.

HAMLET: Safely stowed.—But soft, what noise? who calls on
    Hamlet? O, here they come.

({Enter} ROSENCRANTZ, [GUILDENSTERN,] *and* OTHERS.*)*

ROSENCRANTZ: What have you done, my lord, with the dead
    body?
HAMLET: Compounded it with dust, whereto 'tis kin.   5
ROSENCRANTZ: Tell us where 'tis, that we may take it thence
    And bear it to the chapel.
HAMLET: Do not believe it.
ROSENCRANTZ: Believe what?
HAMLET: That I can keep your counsel and not mine own. Be-   10
    sides, to be demanded of a sponge—what replication
    should be made by the son of a king?
ROSENCRANTZ: Take you me for a sponge, my lord?
HAMLET: Ay, sir, that soaks up the king's countenance, his re-
    wards, his authorities. But such officers do the king best   15
    service in the end. He keeps them, like an apple in the cor-
    ner of his jaw, first mouthed to be last swallowed. When he
    needs what you have gleaned, it is but squeezing you and,
    sponge, you shall be dry again.
ROSENCRANTZ: I understand you not, my lord.   20
HAMLET: I am glad of it. A knavish speech sleeps in a foolish
    ear.
ROSENCRANTZ: My lord, you must tell us where the body is,
    and go with us to the king.
HAMLET: The body is with the king, but the king is not with   25
    the body.
        The king is a thing—

---

211 **petar** a bomb or charge for blowing in gates   217 **indeed** in
earnest (cf. lines 163, 174, 181)

IV.i. The action is continuous with that of the preceding scene. The
Queen does not leave the stage.   2 **translate** explain   11 **brain-
ish apprehension** frenzied delusion   18 **out of haunt** away from
society   26 **mineral** mine

---

42 **As level** as sure of aim; **blank** target

IV.ii. 1 After the words "Safely stowed," *F* adds the line: "*Gentlemen within. Hamlet, Lord Hamlet.*" Here, as at 3.4.5 "when a character speaks of hearing someone coming, *F* provides, though
Q does not, for the audience to hear it too" (Jenkins, *SB*, 13.35)
11 **replication** reply

GUILDENSTERN: A thing, my lord!

HAMLET: Of nothing. Bring me to him. Hide fox, and all after.

(Exeunt.)

SCENE III

Enter KING, *and two or three.*

KING: I have sent to seek him, and to find the body.
 How dangerous is it that this man goes loose!
 Yet must not we put the strong law on him.
 He's loved of the distracted multitude,
5 Who like not in their judgement but their eyes,
 And where 'tis so, th' offender's scourge is weighed,
 But never the offence. To bear all smooth and even,
 This sudden sending him away must seem
 Deliberate pause. Diseases desperate grown
10 By desperate appliance are relieved,
 Or not at all.

(Enter ROSENCRANTZ, [GUILDENSTERN,] *and all the rest.)*

    How now! what hath befall'n?

ROSENCRANTZ: Where the dead body is bestowed, my lord,
 We cannot get from him.

KING: But where is he?

ROSENCRANTZ: Without, my lord; guarded, to know your
 pleasure.

15 KING: Bring him before us.

ROSENCRANTZ: Ho! bring in the lord.

(They enter {with HAMLET*}.)*

KING: Now, Hamlet, where's Polonius?

HAMLET: At supper.

KING: At supper? Where?

HAMLET: Not where he eats, but where 'a is eaten. A certain
20 convocation of politic worms are e'en at him. Your worm is
 your only emperor for diet. We fat all creatures else to fat
 us, and we fat ourselves for maggots. Your fat king and your
 lean beggar is but variable service—two dishes, but to one
 table. That's the end.

25 KING: Alas, alas!

HAMLET: A man may fish with the worm that hath eat of a
 king, and eat of the fish that hath fed of that worm.

KING: What dost thou mean by this?

HAMLET: Nothing but to show you how a king may go a
30 progress through the guts of a beggar.

KING: Where is Polonius?

HAMLET: In heaven. Send thither to see. If your messenger find
 him not there, seek him i' th' other place yourself. But if,
 indeed, you find him not within this month, you shall nose
35 him as you go up the stairs into the lobby.

KING: *(To* ATTENDANTS.*)* Go seek him there.

HAMLET: 'A will stay till you come.

---

29 **Hide fox, and all after** presumably a cry in some game such
as hide-and-seek. The words, which do not occur in *Q2,* may be an
actor's addition

IV.iii. 9 **Deliberate pause** carefully considered   30 **progress** the
state journey of a ruler

(Exeunt ATTENDANTS.*)*

KING: Hamlet, this deed, for thine especial safety—
 Which we do tender, as we dearly grieve
 For that which thou hast done—must send thee hence 40
 With fiery quickness. Therefore prepare thyself.
 The bark is ready, and the wind at help,
 Th' associates tend, and everything is bent
 For England.

HAMLET: For England?

KING: Ay, Hamlet.

HAMLET: Good.

KING: So is it, if thou knew'st our purposes. 45

HAMLET: I see a cherub that sees them. But come, for
 England!
 Farewell, dear mother.

KING: Thy loving father, Hamlet.

HAMLET: My mother. Father and mother is man and wife, man
 and wife is one flesh. So, my mother. Come, for England. 50

(Exit.)

KING: Follow him at foot: tempt him with speed aboard.
 Delay it not: I'll have him hence to-night.
 Away! for every thing is sealed and done
 That else leans on th' affair. Pray you make haste.

(Exeunt all but the KING.*)*

 And, England, if my love thou hold'st at aught— 55
 As my great power thereof may give thee sense,
 Since yet thy cicatrice looks raw and red
 After the Danish sword, and thy free awe
 Pays homage to us—thou mayst not coldly set
 Our sovereign process, which imports at full 60
 By letters congruing to that effect
 The present death of Hamlet. Do it, England.
 For like the hectic in my blood he rages,
 And thou must cure me. Till I know 'tis done,
 Howe'er my haps, my joys were ne'er begun. 65

(Exit.)

SCENE IV

Enter FORTINBRAS *with his* ARMY *over the stage.*

FORTINBRAS: Go, captain, from me greet the Danish king.
 Tell him that by his license Fortinbras
 Craves the conveyance of a promised march
 Over his kingdom. You know the rendezvous.
 If that his majesty would aught with us, 5
 We shall express our duty in his eye,
 And let him know so.

CAPTAIN: I will do't, my lord.

---

39 **tender** value   46 **cherub** one of the cherubim, the watchmen
or sentinels of heaven, and thus endowed with the keenest vision
57 **cicatrice** scar, used here of memory of a defeat   59 **coldly set**
regard with indifference   60 **process** mandate   61 **congruing**
to in accordance with   63 **hectic** consumptive fever   65 **haps**
fortunes

IV.iv. 3 **conveyance** conduct   6 **eye** presence

FORTINBRAS: Go softly on.

(*Exeunt all but the* CAPTAIN.)

(*Enter* HAMLET, ROSENCRANTZ, {GUILDENSTERN,} *and* OTHERS.)

HAMLET: Good sir, whose powers are these?
10 CAPTAIN: They are of Norway, sir.
HAMLET: How purposed, sir, I pray you?
CAPTAIN: Against some part of Poland.
HAMLET: Who commands them, sir?
CAPTAIN: The nephew to old Norway, Fortinbras.
15 HAMLET: Goes it against the main of Poland, sir,
      Or for some frontier?
CAPTAIN: Truly to speak, and with no addition,
      We go to gain a little patch of ground
      That hath in it no profit but the name.
20   To pay five ducats, five, I would not farm it;
      Nor will it yield to Norway or the Pole
      A ranker rate should it be sold in fee.
HAMLET: Why, then the Polack never will defend it.
CAPTAIN: Yes, it is already garrisoned.
25 HAMLET: Two thousand souls and twenty thousand ducats
      Will not debate the question of this straw.
      This is th' imposthume of much wealth and peace,
      That inward breaks, and shows no cause without
      Why the man dies. I humbly thank you, sir.
30 CAPTAIN: God buy you, sir.

(*Exit.*)

ROSENCRANTZ: Will 't please you go, my lord?
HAMLET: I'll be with you straight. Go a little before.

(*Exeunt all but* HAMLET.)

      How all occasions do inform against me,
      And spur my dull revenge! What is a man,
      If his chief good and market of his time
35   Be but to sleep and feed? A beast, no more.
      Sure he that made us with such large discourse,
      Looking before and after, gave us not
      That capability and godlike reason
      To fust in us unused. Now, whether it be
40   Bestial oblivion, or some craven scruple
      Of thinking too precisely on th' event—
      A thought which, quartered, hath but one part wisdom
      And ever three parts coward—I do not know
      Why yet I live to say 'This thing's to do',
45   Sith I have cause, and will, and strength, and means,
      To do 't. Examples gross as earth exhort me:
      Witness this army of such mass and charge,
      Led by a delicate and tender prince,
      Whose spirit, with divine ambition puffed,
50   Makes mouths at the invisible event,
      Exposing what is mortal and unsure
      To all that fortune, death, and danger dare,

Even for an eggshell. Rightly to be great
Is not to stir without great argument,
But greatly to find quarrel in a straw   55
When honor's at the stake. How stand I then,
That have a father killed, a mother stained,
Excitements of my reason and my blood,
And let all sleep, while to my shame I see
The imminent death of twenty thousand men   60
That for a fantasy and trick of fame
Go to their graves like beds, fight for a plot
Whereon the numbers cannot try the cause,
Which is not tomb enough and continent
To hide the slain? O, from this time forth,   65
My thoughts be bloody, or be nothing worth!

(*Exit.*)

SCENE V

Enter HORATIO, {QUEEN} GERTRUDE, *and a* GENTLEMAN.

QUEEN: I will not speak with her.
GENTLEMAN: She is importunate, indeed distract.
      Her mood will needs be pitied.
QUEEN: What would she have?
GENTLEMAN: She speaks much of her father, says she hears
      There's tricks i' th' world, and hems, and beats her heart,   5
      Spurns enviously at straws, speaks things in doubt
      That carry but half sense. Her speech is nothing,
      Yet the unshaped use of it doth move
      The hearers to collection; they aim at it,
      And botch the words up fit to their own thoughts,   10
      Which, as her winks and nods and gestures yield them,
      Indeed would make one think there might be thought,
      Though nothing sure, yet much unhappily.
HORATIO: 'Twere good she were spoken with, for she may
          strew
      Dangerous conjectures in ill-breeding minds.   15
QUEEN: Let her come in. (*Exit* GENTLEMAN.)
      (*Aside.*) To my sick soul, as sin's true nature is,
      Each toy seems prologue to some great amiss.
      So full of artless jealousy is guilt,
      It spills itself in fearing to be spilt.   20

(*Enter* OPHELIA {*distracted*}.)

OPHELIA: Where is the beauteous majesty of Denmark?
QUEEN: How now, Ophelia!
OPHELIA: (*She sings.*)

---

15 **main** chief part   17 **addition** exaggeration   20 **To pay** i.e., for a yearly rental   22 **a ranker rate** a greater price; **sold in fee** sold with absolute and perpetual possession   27 **imposthume** abscess   32 **inform** take shape   34 **market** profit   36 **discourse** power of reasoning   39 **fust** grow musty   50 **Makes mouths at** makes scornful faces at, derides

---

53–56 **Rightly to be great . . . honor's at the stake** i.e., to be rightly great is *not* to refuse to act ("stir") in a dispute ("argument") because the grounds are insufficient, but to be moved to action even in trivial circumstances where a question of honor is involved   63 **try the cause** settle by combat   64 **continent** receptacle

IV.v. 6 **Spurns enviously at straws** takes exception, spitefully, to trifles   7 **nothing** nonsense   8 **unshaped use** disordered manner   9 **collection** attempts at shaping meaning; **aim** guess   13 **sure** certain   18 **toy** trifle   19 **artless jealousy** ill-concealed suspicion   20 **spills** destroys

        How should I your true love know
        From another one?
25   By his cockle hat and staff,
        And his sandal shoon.

QUEEN: Alas, sweet lady, what imports this song?
OPHELIA: Say you? Nay, pray you mark. *(Song.)*

        He is dead and gone, lady,
30   He is dead and gone;
        At his head a grass-green turf,
        At his heels a stone.

  O, ho!
QUEEN: Nay, but Ophelia—
OPHELIA: Pray you mark.

(Sings.)

35   White his shroud as the mountain snow—

(Enter KING.*)*

QUEEN: Alas, look here, my lord.
OPHELIA: *(Song.)*

       Larded all with sweet flowers;
       Which bewept to the grave did not go
       With true-love showers.

40 KING: How do you, pretty lady?
OPHELIA: Well, good dild you! They say the owl was a baker's
    daughter. Lord, we know what we are, but know not what
    we may be. God be at your table!
KING: Conceit upon her father.
45 OPHELIA: Pray let's have no words of this, but when they ask
    you what it means, say you this:

(Song.)

       To-morrow is Saint Valentine's day,
       All in the morning betime,
       And I a maid at your window,
50   To be your Valentine.
       Then up he rose, and donned his clo'es,
       And dupped the chamber-door,
       Let in the maid, that out a maid
       Never departed more.

55 KING: Pretty Ophelia—
OPHELIA: Indeed, without an oath, I'll make an end on't:

(Sings.)

       By Gis and by Saint Charity,
       Alack, and fie for shame!
       Young men will do't, if they come to't;

       By cock, they are to blame.   60
       Quoth she 'Before you tumbled me,
       You promised me to wed.'

He answers:

       'So would I a' done, by yonder sun,
       An thou hadst not come to my bed.'   65

KING: How long hath she been thus?
OPHELIA: I hope all will be well. We must be patient, but I can-
    not choose but weep, to think they would lay him i' th' cold
    ground. My brother shall know of it, and so I thank you for
    your good counsel. Come, my coach! Good night, ladies, 70
    good night. Sweet ladies, good night, good night.

(Exit.)

KING: Follow her close; give her good watch, I pray you.

(Exeunt HORATIO *and* GENTLEMEN.*)*

    O, this is the poison of deep grief; it springs
    All from her father's death, and now behold!
    O Gertrude, Gertrude,   75
    When sorrows come, they come not single spies,
    But in battalions: first, her father slain;
    Next, your son gone, and he most violent author
    Of his own just remove; the people muddied,
    Thick and unwholesome in their thoughts and whispers 80
    For good Polonius' death; and we have done but greenly
    In hugger-mugger to inter him; poor Ophelia
    Divided from herself and her fair judgement,
    Without the which we are pictures, or mere beasts;
    Last, and as much containing as all these,   85
    Her brother is in secret come from France,
    Feeds on his wonder, keeps himself in clouds,
    And wants not buzzers to infect his ear
    With pestilent speeches of his father's death,
    Wherein necessity, of matter beggared,   90
    Will nothing stick our person to arraign
    In ear and ear, O my dear Gertrude, this,
    Like to a murd'ring piece, in many places
    Gives me superfluous death. Attend,   *(A noise within.)*

(Enter a MESSENGER.*)*

    Where are my Switzers? Let them guard the door. 95
    What is the matter?
MESSENGER: Save yourself, my lord.
    The ocean, overpeering of his list,
    Eats not the flats with more impiteous haste
    Then young Laertes, in a riotous head,
    O'erbears your officers. The rabble call him lord, 100
    And as the world were now but to begin,

---

25 **cockle hat** hat bearing a cockle shell, worn by a pilgrim who had been to the shrine of St. James of Compostella, in Spain   26 **shoon** shoes   37 **Larded** garnished, strewn   41 **good dild you** God yield (requite) you   41–42 **They say the owl was a baker's daughter** allusion to a folktale in which a baker's daughter was transformed into an owl because of her ungenerous behavior (giving short measure) when Christ asked for bread in the baker's shop   44 **Conceit upon her father** i.e., obsessed with her father's death   48 **betime** early   52 **dupped** opened   57 **Gis** Jesus

60 **cock** corruption of God   79 **remove** banishment, departure; **muddied** stirred up and confused   81 **greenly** without judgment   82 **hugger-mugger** secrecy and disorder   87 **in clouds** i.e., of suspicion and rumor   88 **wants** lacks   90 **of matter beggared** lacking facts   91 **nothing stick** in no way hesitate   93 **murd'ring piece** cannon loaded with shot meant to scatter   94 F omits the King's "Attend," but substitutes, by way of drawing attention to the "noise within"   95 **Switzers** Swiss bodyguard   97 **list** boundary   99 **riotous head** turbulent mob

Antiquity forgot, custom not known,
The ratifiers and props of every word,
They cry 'Choose we, Laertes shall be king'.
105   Caps, hands, and tongues, applaud it to the clouds,
'Laertes shall be king, Laertes king!'
QUEEN: How cheerfully on the false trail they cry!

(A noise within.)

O, this is counter, you false Danish dogs!
KING: The doors are broke.

(Enter LAERTES *with* OTHERS.*)*

110   LAERTES: Where is this king?—Sirs, stand you all without.
ALL: No, let's come in.
LAERTES: I pray you give me leave.
ALL: We will, we will.

(Exeunt his followers.)

LAERTES: I thank you. Keep the door.—O thou vile king,
Give me my father!
QUEEN: Calmly, good Laertes,
115   LAERTES: That drop of blood that's calm proclaims me bastard,
Cries cuckold to my father, brands the harlot
Even here between the chaste unsmirchèd brow
Of my true mother.
KING: What is the cause, Laertes,
That thy rebellion looks so giant-like?
120   Let him go, Gertrude. Do not fear our person.
There's such divinity doth hedge a king
That treason can but peep to what it would,
Acts little of his will. Tell me, Laertes.
Why thou art thus incensed. Let him go, Gertrude.
125   Speak, man.
LAERTES: Where is my father?
KING: Dead.
QUEEN: But not by him.
KING: Let him demand his fill.
LAERTES: How came he dead? I'll not be juggled with.
To hell allegiance, vows to the blackest devil,
130   Conscience and grace to the profoundest pit!
I dare damnation. To this point I stand,
That both the worlds I give to negligence,
Let come what comes, only I'll be revenged
Most throughly for my father.
135   KING: Who shall stay you?
LAERTES: My will, not all the world's.
And for my means, I'll husband them so well
They shall go far with little.
KING: Good Laertes,
If you desire to know the certainty
Of your dear father, is't writ in your revenge
140   That, swoopstake, you will draw both friend and foe,
Winner and loser?
LAERTES: None but his enemies.

---

108 **counter** hunting backward on the trail   120 **fear** fear for
134 **throughly** thoroughly   140 **swoopstake** sweepstake, taking
all the stakes on the gambling table

KING: Will you know them, then?
LAERTES: To his good friends thus wide I'll ope my arms,
And like the kind life-rend'ring pelican,
Repast them with my blood.   145
KING: Why, now you speak
Like a good child and a true gentleman.
That I am guiltless of your father's death,
And am most sensibly in grief for it,
It shall as level to your judgement 'pear
As day does to your eye.   150

(A noise within: 'Let her come in.')

LAERTES: How now! what noise is that?

(Enter OPHELIA.*)*

O heat, dry up my brains! tears seven times salt
Burn out the sense and virtue of mine eye!
By heaven, thy madness shall be paid with weight
Till our scale turn the beam. O rose of May,   155
Dear maid, kind sister, sweet Ophelia!
O heavens! is 't possible a young maid's wits
Should be as mortal as an old man's life?
Nature is fine in love, and where 'tis fine
It sends some precious instance of itself   160
After the thing it loves.
OPHELIA: *(Song.)*

They bore him barefac'd on the bier;
Hey non nonny, nonny, hey nonny;
And in his grave rain'd many a tear—

Fare you well, my dove!   165
LAERTES: Hadst thou thy wits, and didst persuade revenge,
It could not move thus.
OPHELIA: You must sing 'A-down, a-down,' and you 'Call him
a-down-a.' O, how the wheel becomes it! It is the false stew
ard, that stole his master's daughter.   170
LAERTES: This nothing's more than matter.
OPHELIA: There's rosemary, that's for remembrance. Pray you,
love, remember. And there is pansies, that's for thoughts.
LAERTES: A document in madness, thoughts and remembrance
fitted.   175

---

144 **pelican** supposed to feed her young with her own blood
149 **level** plain   153 **virtue** power   159 **fine** refined to purity
169 **wheel** burden, refrain   172–80 Harold Jenkins in his
Arden edition of *Hamlet* (London and New York, 1982) 536–42,
suggests that Ophelia gives rosemary (emblematic of remembrance) and pansies (of thoughts) to Laertes; that she gives fennel
and columbines (both signifying marital infidelity) to the queen;
she gives rue (for repentance) to the king (keeping some for herself
as a sign of her sorrow, but noting that the king is to wear his rue
with a **difference**, an heraldic term designating a mark for distinguishing one branch of a family from another in a coat-of-arms.
The daisy, an emblem of love's victims, is given to the king as substitute for the absent Hamlet, whose absence he has caused. The
king would also be given the violets (emblems of faithfulness,
associated both with Ophelia's love for Hamlet, and Polonius's service to the state, both now lost) were these still available. Each gift
of flowers represents a symbolic reproach to the recipient.

OPHELIA: There's fennel for you, and columbines. There's rue
for you, and here's some for me. We may call it herb of grace
a Sundays. O, you must wear your rue with a difference.
There's a daisy. I would give you some violets, but they with
180   ered all when my father died. They say 'a made a good end,

(Sings.)   For bonny sweet Robin is all my joy.

LAERTES: Thought and affliction, passion, hell itself,
She turns to favor and to prettiness.

OPHELIA: (Song.)

            And will 'a not come again?
185   And will 'a not come again?
            No, no, he is dead:
            Go to thy death-bed:
            He never will come again.

            His beard was as white as snow,
            All flaxen was his poll:
190   He is gone, he is gone,
            And we cast away moan:
            God ha' mercy on his soul!

And of all Christian souls, I pray God. God buy you. (Exit.)
195 LAERTES: Do you see this, O God?
KING: Laertes, I must commune with your grief,
Or you deny me right. Go but apart,
Make choice of whom your wisest friends you will,
And they shall hear and judge 'twixt you and me.
200 If by direct or by collateral hand
They find us touched, we will our kingdom give,
Our crown, our life, and all that we call ours,
To you in satisfaction; but if not,
Be you content to lend your patience to us,
205 And we shall jointly labour with your soul
To give it due content.
LAERTES: Let this be so.
His means of death, his obscure funeral—
No trophy, sword, nor hatchment, o'er his bones,
No noble rite nor formal ostentation—
210 Cry to be heard, as 'twere from heaven to earth,
That I must call't in question.
KING: So you shall;
And where th' offence is let the great axe fall.
I pray you go with me.

(Exeunt.)

SCENE VI

Enter HORATIO *and* OTHERS.

HORATIO: What are they that would speak with me?
GENTLEMAN: Sea-faring men, sir. They say they have letters
for you.
HORATIO: Let them come in. (Exit GENTLEMAN.)
I do not know from what part of the world
5   I should be greeted, if not from Lord Hamlet.

(*Enter* SAILORS.)

---

190 **poll** head   208 **hatchment** coat of arms

SAILOR: God bless you, sir.
HORATIO: Let him bless thee too.
SAILOR: 'A shall sir, an't please him. There's a letter for you,
sir—it comes from th' ambassador that was bound for
England—if your name be Horatio, as I am let to know it is. 10
HORATIO: (*Reads.*) 'Horatio, when thou shalt have overlooked
this, give these fellows some means to the king. They have
letters for him. Ere we were two days old at sea, a pirate of
very warlike appointment gave us chase. Finding ourselves
too slow of sail, we put on a compelled valor, and in the 15
grapple I boarded them. On the instant they got clear of our
ship, so I alone became their prisoner. They have dealt with
me like thieves of mercy, but they knew what they did; I am
to do a good turn for them. Let the king have the letters I
have sent, and repair thou to me with as much speed as thou 20
wouldest fly death. I have words to speak in thine ear will
make thee dumb; yet are they much too light for the bore
of the matter. These good fellows will bring thee where I
am. Rosencrantz and Guildenstern hold their course for
England. Of them I have much to tell thee, Farewell. 25
                    'He that thou knowest thine, Hamlet.'
Come, I will give you way for these your letters,
And do't the speedier that you may direct me
To him from whom you brought them.

(*Exeunt.*)

SCENE VII

Enter KING *and* LAERTES.

KING: Now must your conscience my acquittance seal,
And you must put me in your heart for friend,
Sith you have heard, and with a knowing ear,
That he which hath your noble father slain
Pursued my life.   5
LAERTES: It well appears. But tell me
Why you proceeded not against these feats,
So criminal and so capital in nature,
As by your safety, wisdom, all things else,
You mainly were stirred up.
KING: O, for two special reasons,
Which may to you, perhaps, seem much unsinewed, 10
But yet to me th' are strong. The queen his mother
Lives almost by his looks, and for myself—
My virtue or my plague, be it either which—
She's so conjunctive to my life and soul
That, as the star moves not but in his sphere, 15
I could not but by her. The other motive,
Why to a public count I might not go,
Is the great love the general gender bear him,
Who, dipping all his faults in their affection,
Work, like the spring that turneth wood to stone, 20
Convert his gyves to graces; so that my arrows,
Too slightly timbered for so loud a wind,

IV.vi. 22 **bore** literally, caliber of a gun; hence, size, importance
IV.vii. 7 **capital** punishable by death   10 **unsinewed** weak   14
conjunctive closely joined   17 **count** reckoning   18 **general
gender** common people   21 **gyves** fetters

Would have reverted to my bow again,
And not where I had aimed them.
25 LAERTES: And so have I a noble father lost,
A sister driven into desp'rate terms,
Whose worth, if praises may go back again,
Stood challenger on mount of all the age
For her perfections. But my revenge will come.
30 KING: Break not your sleeps for that. You must not think
That we are made of stuff so flat and dull
That we can let our beard be shook with danger,
And think it pastime. You shortly shall hear more.
I loved your father, and we love our self,
35 And that, I hope, will teach you to imagine—

(Enter a MESSENGER *with letters.)*

MESSENGER: These to your majesty; this to the queen.
KING: From Hamlet! Who brought them?
MESSENGER: Sailors, my lord, they say. I saw them not.
They were given me by Claudio; he received them
40 Of him that brought them.
KING: Laertes, you shall hear them.—
Leave us. *(Exit* MESSENGER.*)*
(Reads.) 'High and mighty, you shall know I am set naked
on your kingdom. To-morrow shall I beg leave to see your
kingly eyes, when I shall, first asking your pardon, there-
45 unto recount the occasion of my sudden and more strange
return.   Hamlet.'
What should this mean? Are all the rest come back?
Or is it some abuse, and no such thing?
LAERTES: Know you the hand?
50 KING: 'Tis Hamlet's character. 'Naked!'
And in a postscript here, he says 'alone'.
Can you devise me?
LAERTES: I am lost in it, my lord. But let him come.
It warms the very sickness in my heart
55 That I shall live and tell him to his teeth
'Thus didst thou.'
KING: If it be so, Laertes—
As how should it be so, how otherwise?—
Will you be ruled by me?
LAERTES: Ay, my lord,
So you will not o'errule me to a peace.
60 KING: To thine own peace. If he be now returned,
As checking at his voyage, and that he means

No more to undertake it, I will work him
To an exploit now ripe in my device,
Under the which he shall not choose but fall;
And for his death no wind of blame shall breathe   65
But even his mother shall uncharge the practice
And call it accident.
LAERTES: My lord, I will be ruled;
The rather if you could devise it so
That I might be the organ.
KING: It falls right.
You have been talked of since your travel much,   70
And that in Hamlet's hearing, for a quality
Wherein they say you shine. Your sum of parts
Did not together pluck such envy from him
As did that one, and that, in my regard,
Of the unworthiest siege.   75
LAERTES: What part is that, my lord?
KING: A very riband in the cap of youth,
Yet needful too, for youth no less becomes
The light and careless livery that it wears
Than settled age his sables and his weeds,
Importing health and graveness. Two months since   80
Here was a gentleman of Normandy.
I have seen myself, and served against, the French,
And they can well on horseback, but this gallant
Had witchcraft in't. He grew unto his seat,
And to such wondrous doing brought his horse,   85
As had he been incorpsed and demi-natured
With the brave beast. So far he topped my thought
That I, in forgery of shapes and tricks,
Come short of what he did.
LAERTES: A Norman was't?
KING: A Norman.   90
LAERTES: Upon my life, Lamord.
KING: The very same.
LAERTES: I know him well. He is the brooch indeed
And gem of all the nation.
KING: He made confession of you,
And gave you such a masterly report   95
For art and exercise in your defence,
And for your rapier most especial,
That he cried out 'twould be a sight indeed
If one could match you. The scrimers of their nation,
He swore had neither motion, guard, nor eye,   100
If you opposed them. Sir, this report of his
Did Hamlet so envenom with his envy
That he could nothing do but wish and beg
Your sudden coming o'er, to play with you.
Now out of this—   105
LAERTES: What out of this, my lord?
KING: Laertes, was your father dear to you?
Or are you like the painting of a sorrow,
A face without a heart?
LAERTES: Why ask you this?

---

35 Following the entrance of the Messenger, the King says in *F*
"How now? What Newes?" and the Messenger replies, "Letters my
Lord from *Hamlet.*" Jenkins comments (*SB* 13.36): "In *Q* the King
is not told the letters come from Hamlet; he is left to find this out
as he reads, and his cry 'From *Hamlet*' betokens his astonishment
on doing so. I think Hamlet would not have approved of the *F*
messenger who robs his bomb of the full force of its explosion.
Shakespeare's messenger did not even know he carried such a
bomb, for the letters had reached him via sailors who were ignorant of their sender. They took him for 'th' Embassador that was
bound for *England*' (4.4.9). *F,* with its too knowledgeable messenger, by seeking to enhance the effect, destroys it"   52 **devise**
explain to   61 **checking at** turning aside from (like a falcon turning from its quarry for other prey)

---

66 **uncharge the practice** regard the deed as free from villainy
69 **organ** instrument   75 **siege** rank   79 **weeds** garments
86 **incorpsed** made one body; **demi-natured** like a centaur, half
man half horse   87 **topped** excelled   88 **forgery** invention
99 **scrimers** fencers (French *escrimeurs*)

KING: Not that I think you did not love your father,
110   But that I know love is begun by time,
         And that I see, in passages of proof,
         Time qualifies the spark and fire of it.
         There lives within the very flame of love
         A kind of wick or snuff that will abate it,
115   And nothing is at a like goodness still,
         For goodness, growing to a plurisy,
         Dies in his own too much. That we would do,
         We should do when we would; for this 'would' changes,
         And hath abatements and delays as many
120   As there are tongues, are hands, are accidents,
         And then this 'should' is like a spendthrift's sigh,
         That hurts by easing. But to the quick of th' ulcer—
         Hamlet comes back; what would you undertake
         To show yourself in deed your father's son
125   More than in words?
LAERTES: To cut his throat i' th' church.
KING: No place, indeed, should murder sanctuarize;
         Revenge should have no bounds. But good Laertes,
         Will you do this, keep close within your chamber;
         Hamlet returned shall know you are come home;
130   We'll put on those shall praise your excellence,
         And set a double varnish on the fame
         The Frenchman gave you, bring you in fine together,
         And wager on your heads. He, being remiss,
         Most generous, and free from all contriving,
135   Will not peruse the foils, so that with ease,
         Or with a little shuffling, you may choose
         A sword unbated, and in a pass of practice
         Requite him for your father.
LAERTES: I will do't,
         And for that purpose I'll anoint my sword.
140   I bought an unction of a mountebank
         So mortal that but dip a knife in it,
         Where it draws blood no cataplasm so rare,
         Collected from all simples that have virtue
         Under the moon, can save the thing from death
145   That is but scratched withal. I'll touch my point
         With this contagion, that if I gall him slightly,
         It may be death.
KING: Let's further think of this,
         Weigh what convenience both of time and means
         May fit us to our shape. If this should fail,
150   And that our drift look through our bad performance,
         'Twere better not assayed. Therefore this project
         Should have a back or second that might hold
         If this should blast in proof. Soft! let me see.
         We'll make a solemn wager on your cunnings—
155   I ha't.
         When in your motion you are hot and dry—

As make your bouts more violent to that end—
And that he calls for drink, I'll have preferred him
A chalice for the nonce, whereon but sipping,
If he by chance escape your venomed stuck,   160
Our purpose may hold there.—But stay, what noise?

(Enter QUEEN.)

QUEEN: One woe doth tread upon another's heel,
         So fast they follow. Your sister's drowned, Laertes.
LAERTES: Drowned! O, where?
QUEEN: There is a willow grows askant the brook   165
         That shows his hoar leaves in the glassy stream.
         Therewith fantastic garlands did she make
         Of crowflowers, nettles, daisies, and long purples
         That liberal shepherds give a grosser name,
         But our cold maids do dead men's fingers call them.   170
         There on the pendent boughs her crownet weeds
         Clamb'ring to hang, an envious sliver broke,
         When down her weedy trophies and herself
         Fell in the weeping brook. Her clothes spread wide,
         And mermaid-like awhile they bore her up,   175
         Which time she chanted snatches of old lauds,
         As one incapable of her own distress,
         Or like a creature native and indued
         Unto that element. But long it could not be
         Till that her garments, heavy with their drink,   180
         Pulled the poor wretch from her melodious lay
         To muddy death.
LAERTES: Alas, then, she is drowned?
QUEEN: Drowned, drowned.
LAERTES: Too much of water hast thou, poor Ophelia,
         And therefore I forbid my tears; but yet   185
         It is our trick; nature her custom holds,
         Let shame say what it will. When these are gone,
         The woman will be out. Adieu, my lord.
         I have a speech o' fire that fain would blaze
         But that this folly drowns it.   190

(Exit.)

KING: Let's follow, Gertrude.
         How much I had to do to calm his rage!
         Now fear I this will give it start again;
         Therefore let's follow.

(Exeunt.)

────── ACT FIVE ──────

SCENE I

Enter two CLOWNS.

---

111 **passages of proof** incidents of experience   112 **qualifies**
weakens   116 **plurisy** excess   122 **quick** sensitive flesh   126
sanctuarize give sanctuary to   133 **remiss** careless   135 **peruse**
inspect   137 **unbated** not blunted; **pass of practice** treacherous
thrust   142 **cataplasm** poultice   143 **simples** medicinal herbs
149 **shape** plan   150 **drift** scheme   152 **back or second** something in support   153 **blast in proof** burst during trial (like a
faulty cannon)   156 **motion** exertion

158 **preferred** offered to   159 **nonce** occasion   160 **stuck**
thrust   165 **askant** alongside   166 **hoar** gray   169 **liberal**
free-spoken, licentious   170 **cold** chaste   171 **crownet** coronet
172 **envious** malicious   176 **lauds** hymns   177 **incapable of**
insensible to   178 **indued** endowed   188 **woman** unmanly part
of nature
V.i. s.d. **clowns** rustics

CLOWN: Is she to be buried in Christian burial when she wilfully seeks her own salvation?

OTHER: I tell thee she is, therefore make her grave straight. The crowner hath sat on her, and finds it Christian burial.

5 CLOWN: How can that be, unless she drowned herself in her own defence?

OTHER: Why, 'tis found so.

CLOWN: It must be 'se offendendo', it cannot be else. For here lies the point: if I drown myself wittingly, it argues an act, 10 and an act hath three branches—it is to act, to do, and to perform; argal, she drowned herself wittingly.

OTHER: Nay, but hear you, Goodman Delver.

CLOWN: Give me leave. Here lies the water; good. Here stands the man; good. If the man go to this water and drown him-15 self, it is, will he, nill he, he goes—mark you that. But if the water come to him and drown him, he drowns not himself. Argal, he that is not guilty of his own death shortens not his own life.

OTHER: But is this law?

20 CLOWN: Ay, marry, is't; crowner's quest law.

OTHER: Will you ha' the truth on 't? If this had not been a gentlewoman, she should have been buried out o' Christian burial.

CLOWN: Why, there thou say'st. And the more pity that great 25 folk should have count'nance in this world to drown or hang themselves more than their even-Christen. Come, my spade. There is no ancient gentlemen but gard'ners, ditchers, and grave-makers. They hold up Adam's profession.

OTHER: Was he a gentleman?

30 CLOWN: 'A was the first that ever bore arms.

OTHER: Why, he had none.

CLOWN: What, art a heathen? How dost thou understand the Scripture? The Scripture says Adam digged. Could he dig without arms? I'll put another question to thee. If thou an-35 swerest me not to the purpose, confess thyself—

OTHER: Go to.

CLOWN: What is he that builds stronger than either the mason, the shipwright, or the carpenter?

OTHER: The gallows-maker for that frame outlives a thousand 40 tenants.

CLOWN: I like thy wit well, in good faith. The gallows does well. But how does it well? It does well to those that do ill. Now thou dost ill to say the gallows is built stronger than the church. Argal, the gallows may do well to thee. To't 45 again, come.

OTHER: 'Who builds stronger than a mason, a shipwright, or a carpenter?'

CLOWN: Ay tell me that, and unyoke.

OTHER: Marry, now I can tell.

50 CLOWN: To't.

OTHER: Mass, I cannot tell.

(Enter HAMLET and HORATIO afar off.)

---

4 **crowner** coroner   8 **se offendendo** the Clown's blunder for **se defendendo** ("in self-defense")   11 **argal** therefore (corrupt form of *ergo*)   20 **quest** inquest   26 **even-Christen** fellow Christian   48 **tell me that, and unyoke** answer the question and then you can relax

CLOWN: Cudgel thy brains no more about it, for your dull ass will not mend his pace with beating. And when you are asked this question next, say 'a grave-maker.' The houses he makes lasts till doomsday. Go, get thee in, and fetch me a 55 stoup of liquor. *(Exit OTHER CLOWN.)*

(HAMLET and HORATIO come forward as CLOWN digs and sings.)

(Song.)

> In youth, when I did love, did love,
>   Methought it was very sweet,
> To contract-O-the time, for-a-my behove,
>   O, methought, there-a-was nothing-a-meet.   60

HAMLET: Has this fellow no feeling of his business, that 'a sings at gravemaking?

HORATIO: Custom hath made it in him a property of easiness.

HAMLET: 'Tis e'en so. The hand of little employment hath the daintier sense.   65

CLOWN: *(Song.)*

> But age, with his stealing steps,
>   Hath clawed me in his clutch,
> And hath shipped me into the land,
>   As if I had never been such.

(Throws up a skull.)

HAMLET: That skull had a tongue in it, and could sing once. 70 How the knave jowls it to the ground, as if 'twere Cain's jawbone, that did the first murder! This might be the pate of a politician, which this ass now o'erreaches; one that would circumvent God, might it not?

HORATIO: It might, my lord.   75

HAMLET: Or of a courtier, which could say 'Good morrow, sweet lord! How dost thou, sweet lord?' This might be my Lord Such-a-one, that praised my Lord Such-a-one's horse, when 'a went to beg it, might it not?

HORANTIO: Ay, my lord.   80

HAMLET: Why, e'en so, and now my Lady Worm's, chopless, and knock'd about the mazzard with a sexton's spade. Here's fine revolution, an we had the trick to see't. Did these bones cost no more the breeding but to play at loggats with them? Mine ache to think on't.   85

CLOWN: *(Song.)*

> A pick-axe and a spade, a spade,
>   For and a shrouding sheet:
> O, a pit of clay for to be made
>   For such a guest is meet.

(Throws up another skull.)

HAMLET: There's another. Why may not that be the skull of a 90 lawyer? Where be his quiddities now, his quillets, his cases,

---

56 **stoup** tankard   59 **behove** benefit   59–60 The repeated *a* and *o* may represent the Clown's vocal embellishments, but more probably they represent his grunting as he takes breath in the course of his digging   63 **a property of easiness** a habit that comes easily to him   71 **jowls** hurls   74 **circumvent** cheat   81 **chopless** with lower jaw missing   82 **mazzard** head   84–85 **loggats** small logs of wood for throwing at a mark   91 **quiddities** subtle distinctions; **quillets** quibbles

his tenures, and his tricks? Why does he suffer this mad
knave now to knock him about the sconce with a dirty
shovel, and will not tell him of his action of battery? Hum!
95 This fellow might be in's time a great buyer of land, with
his statutes, his recognizances, his fines, his double vouchers, his recoveries. Is this the fine of his fines, and the recovery of his recoveries, to have his fine pate full of fine dirt?
Will his vouchers vouch him no more of his purchases, and
100 double ones too, than the length and breadth of a pair of
indentures? The very conveyances of his lands will scarcely
lie in this box, and must th' inheritor himself have no
more, ha?

HORATIO: Not a jot more, my lord.

105 HAMLET: Is not parchment made of sheepskins?

HORANTIO: Ay, my lord, and of calves' skins too.

HAMLET: They are sheep and calves which seek out assurance in
that. I will speak to this fellow. Whose grave's this, sirrah?

CLOWN: Mine, sir. *(Sings.)*

110   O, a pit of clay for to be made—

HAMLET: I think it be thine indeed, for thou liest in't.

CLOWN: You lie out on't, sir, and therefore 'tis not yours. For
my part, I do not lie in't, yet it is mine.

HAMLET: Thou dost lie in't, to be in't and say it is thine. 'Tis for
115 the dead, not for the quick; therefore thou liest.

CLOWN: 'Tis a quick lie, sir; 'twill away again from me to you.

HAMLET: What man dost thou dig it for?

CLOWN: For no man, sir.

HAMLET: What woman, then?

120 CLOWN: For none neither.

HAMLET: Who is to be buried in't?

CLOWN: One that was a woman, sir; but, rest her soul, she's
dead.

HAMLET: How absolute the knave is! We must speak by the
125 card, or equivocation will undo us. By the Lord, Horatio,
this three years I have took note of it, the age is grown so
picked that the toe of the peasant comes so near the heel of
the courtier, he galls his kibe. How long hast thou been a
grave-maker?

130 CLOWN: Of all the day i' th' year, I came to't that day that our
last King Hamlet overcame Fortinbras.

HAMLET: How long is that since?

CLOWN: Cannot you tell that? Every fool can tell that. It was
that very day that young Hamlet was born—he that is mad,
135 and sent into England.

HAMLET: Ay, marry, why was he sent into England?

CLOWN: Why, because 'a was mad. 'A shall recover his wits
there; or, if a do not, 'tis no great matter there.

HAMLET: Why?

140 CLOWN: 'Twill not be seen in him there. There the men are as
mad as he.

---

96 **recognizances** legal bonds, defining debts; **vouchers** persons
vouched or called on to warrant a title 97 **recoveries** legal
processes to break an entail 100–01 **pair of indentures** deed or
legal agreement in duplicate 101 **conveyances** deeds by which
property is transferred 124 **absolute** positive 125 **card** card
on which the points of the mariner's compass are marked (i.e.,
absolutely to the point) 127 **picked** fastidious 128 **kibe**
chilblain

HAMLET: How came he mad?

CLOWN: Very strangely, they say.

HAMLET: How strangely?

CLOWN: Faith, e'en with losing his wits.   145

HAMLET: Upon what ground?

CLOWN: Why, here in Denmark. I have been sexton here, man
and boy, thirty years.

HAMLET: How long will a man lie i' th' earth ere he rot?

CLOWN: Faith, if 'a be not rotten before 'a die—as we have 150
many pocky corses now-a-days that will scarce hold the
laying in—'a will last you some eight year or nine year. A
tanner will last you nine year.

HAMLET: Why he more than another?

CLOWN: Why, sir, his hide is so tanned with his trade that 'a 155
will keep out water a great while and your water is a sore
decayer of your whoreson dead body. Here's a skull now
hath lain you i' th' earth three and twenty years.

HAMLET: Whose was it?

CLOWN: A whoreson mad fellow's it was. Whose do you think 160
it was?

HAMLET: Nay, I know not.

CLOWN: A pestilence on him for a mad rogue! 'a poured a
flagon of Rhenish on my head once. This same skull, sir,
was, sir, Yorick's skull, the king's jester.   165

HAMLET: *(Takes the skull.)* This?

CLOWN: E'en That.

HAMLET: Alas, poor Yorick! I knew him, Horatio—a fellow of
infinite jest, of most excellent fancy. He hath bore me on his
back a thousand times, and now how abhorred in my imag- 170
ination it is! My gorge rises at it. Here hung those lips that
I have kissed I know not how oft. Where be your gibes now,
your gambols, your songs, your flashes of merriment that
were wont to set the table on a roar? Not one now to mock
your own grinning? Quite chop-fall'n? Now get you to my 175
lady's chamber, and tell her, let her paint an inch thick, to
this favour she must come. Make her laugh at that. Prithee,
Horatio, tell me one thing.

HORATIO: What's that, my lord?

HAMLET: Dost thou think Alexander looked o' this fashion i' 180
th' earth?

HORATIO: E'en so.

HAMLET: And smelt so? Pah!

(Throws down the skull.)

HORATIO: E'en so, my lord.

HAMLET: To what base uses we may return, Horatio! Why may 185
not imagination trace the noble dust of Alexander till 'a
find it stopping a bung-hole?

HORATIO: 'Twere to consider too curiously to consider so.

HAMLET: No, faith, not a jot, but to follow him thither with
modesty enough, and likelihood to lead it. Alexander died, 190
Alexander was buried, Alexander returneth to dust; the dust
is earth; of earth we make loam; and why of that loam
whereto he was converted might they not stop a beer-barrel?

       Imperious Caesar, dead and turned to clay,
       Might stop a hole to keep the wind away.   195

---

151 **pocky** infected with pox (syphilis) 164 **Rhenish** Rhine
wine 188 **too curiously** over ingenously

O, that that earth which kept the world in awe
Should patch a wall t'expel the winter's flaw!

But soft, but soft awhile! Here comes the king,
The queen, the courtiers.

(Enter KING, QUEEN, LAERTES, *and the Corse {with a Doctor of
Divinity as* PRIEST *and* LORDS *attendant}.)*

                       Who is this they follow?
200 And with such maimèd rites? This doth betoken
The corse they follow did with desperate hand
Fordo it own life. 'Twas of some estate.
Couch we awhile and mark.

(Retires with HORATIO.)

LAERTES: What ceremony else?
205 HAMLET: That is Laertes, a very noble youth. Mark.
LAERTES: What ceremony else?
DOCTOR: Her obsequies have been as far enlarged
As we have warranty. Her death was doubtful,
And but that great command o'ersways the order,
210 She should in ground unsanctified been lodged
Till the last trumpet. For charitable prayers,
Shards, flints and pebbles should be thrown on her.
Yet here she is allowed her virgin crants,
Her maiden strewments and the bringing home
215 Of bell and burial.
LAERTES: Must there no more be done?
DOCTOR: No more be done.
We should profane the service of the dead
To sing a requiem and such rest to her
As to peace-parted souls.
LAERTES: Lay her i' th' earth,
220 And from her fair and unpolluted flesh
May violets spring! I tell thee, churlish priest,
A minist'ring angel shall my sister be
When thou liest howling.
HAMLET: What, the fair Ophelia!
QUEEN: Sweets to the sweet. Farewell!

(Scatters flowers.)

225 I hoped thou shouldst have been my Hamlet's wife.
I thought thy bride-bed to have decked, sweet maid,
And not have strewed thy grave.
LAERTES: O treble woe
Fall ten times treble on that cursèd head,
Whose wicked deed thy most ingenious sense
230 Deprived thee of! Hold off the earth awhile,
Till I have caught her once more in mine arms.

(Leaps into the grave.)

Now pile your dust upon the quick and dead,
Till of this flat a mountain you have made

T' o'er-top old Pelion or the skyish head
Of blue Olympus.   235
HAMLET: *(Coming forward.)* What is he whose grief
Bears such an emphasis, whose phrase of sorrow
Conjures the wand'ring stars, and makes them stand
Like wonder-wounded hearers? This is I,
Hamlet the Dane.

*(*LAERTES *climbs out of the grave.)*

LAERTES: The devil take thy soul!   240

(Grappling with him.)

HAMLET: Thou pray'st not well.
I prithee take thy fingers from my throat,
For though I am not splenitive and rash,
Yet have I in me something dangerous,
Which let thy wisdom fear. Hold off thy hand.
KING: Pluck them asunder.   245
QUEEN: Hamlet! Hamlet!
ALL: Gentlemen!
HORATIO: Good my lord, be quiet.

(The ATTENDANTS *part them.)*

HAMLET: Why, I will fight with him upon this theme
Until my eyelids will no longer wag.   250
QUEEN: O my son, what theme?
HAMLET: I loved Ophelia. Forty thousand brothers
Could not with all their quantity of love
Make up my sum. What wilt thou do for her?
KING: O, he is mad, Laertes.   255
QUEEN: For love of God, forbear him.
HAMLET: 'Swounds, show me what thou't do.
Woo't weep, woo't fight, woo't fast, woo't tear thyself,
Woo't drink up eisel, eat a crocodile?
I'll do't. Dost come here to whine?   260
To outface me with leaping in her grave?
Be buried quick with her, and so will I,
And if thou prate of mountains, let them throw
Millions of acres on us, till our ground,
Singeing his pate against the burning zone,   265
Make Ossa like a wart! Nay, an thou'lt mouth,
I'll rant as well as thou.
QUEEN: This is mere madness;
And thus awhile the fit will work on him.
Anon, as patient as the female dove
When that her golden couplets are disclosed,   270
His silence will sit drooping.
HAMLET: Hear you, sir.
What is the reason that you use me thus?

---

197 **flaw** gust   202 **Fordo** destroy; **it** its   212 **Shards** bits of
broken pottery   213 **crants** garland   229 **most ingenious** of
quickest apprehension

234 **Pelion** a mountain in Thessaly, like Olympus, line 235, and
Ossa, line 266 (the allusion is to the war in which the Titans fought
the gods and, in their attempt to scale heaven, heaped Ossa and
Olympus on Pelion, or Pelion and Ossa on Olympus)   237 **such
an emphasis** so vehement an expression or display   242 **splenitive** fiery-tempered (from the spleen, seat of anger)   258 **Woo't**
wilt (thou)   259 **eisel** vinegar   270 **couplets** newly hatched pair

I loved you ever. But it is no matter.
Let Hercules himself do what he may,
275 The cat will mew, and dog will have his day.
KING: I pray thee, good Horatio, wait upon him.

(*Exit* HAMLET *and* HORATIO.)

(*To* LAERTES.) Strengthen your patience in our last night's
       speech.
We'll put the matter to the present push.—
Good Gertrude, set some watch over your son.—
280 This grave shall have a living monument.
An hour of quiet shortly shall we see;
Till then in patience our proceeding be.

(*Exeunt.*)

SCENE II

Enter HAMLET *and* HORATIO.

HAMLET: So much for this, sir; now shall you see the other.
       You do remember all the circumstance?
HORATIO: Remember it, my lord!
HAMLET: Sir, in my heart there was a kind of fighting
5   That would not let me sleep. Methought I lay
Worse than the mutines in the bilboes. Rashly,
And praised be rashness for it—let us know,
Our indiscretion sometime serves us well,
When our deep plots do pall; and that should learn us
10   There's a divinity that shapes our ends,
Rough-hew them how we will—
HORATIO: That is most certain.
HAMLET: Up from my cabin,
My sea-gown scarfed about me, in the dark
Groped I to find out them, had my desire,
15   Fingered their packet, and in fine withdrew
To mine own room again, making so bold,
My fears forgetting manners, to unseal
Their grand commission; where I found, Horatio—
Ah, royal knavery!—an exact command,
20   Larded with many several sorts of reasons
Importing Denmark's health and England's too,
With, ho! such bugs and goblins in my life,
That on the supervise, no leisure bated,
No, not to stay the grinding of the axe,
25   My head should be struck off.
HORATIO: Is't possible?
HAMLET: Here's the commission; read it at more leisure.
But will thou hear me how I did proceed?
HORATIO: I beseech you.
HAMLET: Being thus benetted round with villainies,
30   Or I could make a prologue to my brains,
They had begun the play. I sat me down,
Devised a new commission, wrote it fair.

I once did hold it, as our statists do,
A baseness to write fair, and laboured much
How to forget that learning; but sir, now   35
It did me yeoman's service. Wilt thou know
Th' effect of what I wrote?
HORATIO: Ay, good my lord.
HAMLET: An earnest conjuration from the king,
As England was his faithful tributary,
As love between them like the palm might flourish,   40
As peace should still her wheaten garland wear
And stand a comma 'tween their amities,
And many such like as's of great charge,
That on the view and knowing of these contents,
Without debatement further more or less,   45
He should the bearers put to sudden death,
Not shriving-time allowed.
HORATIO: How was this sealed?
HAMLET: Why, even in that was heaven ordinant,
I had my father's signet in my pursue,
Which was the model of that Danish seal,   50
Folded the writ up the form of th' other,
Subscribed it, gave't th' impression, placed it safely,
The changeling never known. Now the next day
Was our sea-fight, and what to this was sequent
Thou knowest already.   55
HORATIO: So Guildenstern and Rosencrantz go to't.
HAMLET: Why, man, they did make love to this employment.
They are not near my conscience; their defeat
Does by their own insinuation grow.
'Tis dangerous when the baser nature comes   60
Between the pass and fell incensèd points
Of mighty opposites.
HORATIO: Why, what a king is this!
HAMLET: Does it not, think thee, stand me now upon—
He that hath killed my king and whored my mother,
Popped in between th' election and my hopes,   65
Thrown out his angle for my proper life,
And with such coz'nage—is't not perfect conscience,
To quit him with this arm? And is't not to be damned
To let this canker of our nature come
In further evil?   70
HORATIO: It must be shortly known to him from England
What is the issue of the business there.
HAMLET: It will be short; the interim is mine.
And a man's life's no more than to say 'one.'
But I am very sorry, good Horatio,   75
That to Laertes I forgot myself;
For by the image of my cause I see
The portraiture of his. I'll court his favours.

V.ii. **6 mutines** mutineers; **bilboes** fetters **9 pall** fail **15 Fingered** filched **20 Larded** garnished **22 bugs and goblins** imaginary horrors (here, horrendous crimes attributed to Hamlet, and represented as dangers should he be allowed to live) **23 supervise** perusal; **bated** deducted, allowed **24 stay** await **30 Or ere**

33 statists statesmen **42 comma** a connective that also acknowledges separateness **43 charge** (1) importance (2) burden (the double meaning fits the play that makes "as's" into "asses") **48 ordinant** guiding **52 Subscribed** signed **59 insinuation** intrusion **61 pass** thrust; **fell** fierce **63 Does it not . . . stand me now upon** is it not incumbent upon me **65 election** i.e., to the kingship. Denmark being an elective monarchy **66 angle** fishing line; **proper** own **68 quit** repay

But sure the bravery of his grief did put me
80   Into a tow'ring passion.
HORATIO: Peace; who comes here?

(Enter [OSRIC] a courtier.)

OSRIC: Your lordship is right welcome back to Denmark.
HAMLET: I humbly thank you, sir. *(Aside to* HORATIO.*)* Dost
   know this water-fly?
HORATIO: *(Aside to* HAMLET.*)* No, my good lord.
85   HAMLET: *(Aside to* HORATIO.*)* Thy state is the more gracious, for
   'tis a vice to know him. He hath much land, and fertile. Let
   a beast be lord of beasts, and his crib shall stand at the
   king's mess. 'Tis a chough, but as I say, spacious in the possession of dirt.
90   OSRIC: Sweet lord, if your lordship were at leisure, I should impart a thing to you from his majesty.
HAMLET: I will receive it, sir, with all diligence of spirit. Put
   your bonnet to his right use. 'Tis for the head.
OSRIC: I thank you lordship, it is very hot.
95   HAMLET: No, believe me, 'tis very cold; the wind is northerly.
OSRIC: It is indifferent cold, my lord, indeed.
HAMLET: But yet methinks it is very sultry and hot for my
   complexion.
OSRIC: Exceedingly, my lord; it is very sultry, as 'twere—I can
100   not tell how. My lord, his majesty bade me signify to you
   that 'a has laid a great wager on your head. Sir, this is the
   matter—
HAMLET: I beseech you, remember.

(HAMLET moves him to put on his hat.)

OSRIC: Nay, good my lord; for my ease, in good faith. Sir, here
105   is newly come to court Laertes; believe me, an absolute gentleman, full of most excellent differences, of very soft society and great showing. Indeed, to speak feelingly of him, he
   is the card or calendar of gentry, for you shall find in him
   the continent of what part a gentleman would see.
110   HAMLET: Sir, his definement suffers, no perdition in you,
   though I know to divide him inventorially would dozy th'
   arithmetic of memory, and yet but yaw neither in respect of
   his quick sail. But in the verity of extolment, I take him to
   be a soul of great article, and his infusion of such dearth and
115   rareness as, to make true diction of him, his semblable is his
   mirror, and who else would trace him, his umbrage, nothing more.
OSRIC: Your lordship speaks most infallibly of him.
HAMLET: The concernancy, sir? Why do we wrap the gentleman
120   in our more rawer breath?
OSRIC: Sir?

HORATIO: It's not possible to understand in another tongue?
   You will to't, sir, really.
HAMLET: What imports the nomination of this gentleman?
OSRIC: Of Laertes?   125
HORATIO: *(Aside.)* His purse is empty already. All's golden
   words are spent.
HAMLET: Of him, sir.
OSRIC: I know you are not ignorant—
HAMLET: I would you did, sir; yet, in faith, if you did, it would   130
   not much approve me. Well, sir.
OSRIC: You are not ignorant of what excellence Laertes is—
HAMLET: I dare not confess that, lest I should compare with
   him in excellence; but to know a man well were to know
   himself.   135
OSRIC: I mean, sir, for his weapon; but in the imputation laid
   on him by them in his meed, he's unfellowed.
HAMLET: What's his weapon?
OSRIC: Rapier and dagger.
HAMLET: That's two of his weapons—but well.   140
OSRIC: The king, sir, hath wagered with him six Barbary
   horses, against the which he has impawned, as I take it, six
   French rapiers and poniards, with their assigns, as girdle,
   hangers, and so. Three of the carriages, in faith, are very
   dear to fancy, very responsive to the hilts, most delicate car- 145
   riages, and of very liberal conceit.
HAMLET: What call you the carriages?
HORATIO: *(Aside to* HAMLET.*)* I knew you must be edified by the
   margent ere you had done.
OSRIC: The carriages, sir, are the hangers.   150
HAMLET: The phrase would be more germane to the matter if
   we could carry cannon by our sides. I would it might be
   hangers till then. But on! Six Barbary horses against six
   French swords, their assigns, and three liberal conceited
   carriages; that's the French bet against the Danish. Why is   155
   this all impawned, as you call it?
OSRIC: The king, sir, hath laid, sir, that in a dozen passes between yourself and him he shall not exceed you three hits;
   he hath laid on twelve for nine, and it would come to immediate trial if your lordship would vouchsafe the answer.   160
HAMLET: How if I answer no?
OSRIC: I mean, my lord, the opposition of your person in trial.
HAMLET: Sir, I will walk here in the hall. If it please his majesty,
   it is the breathing time of day with me. Let the foils be
   brought, the gentleman willing, and the king hold his pur-   165
   pose; I will win for him an I can. If not, I will gain nothing
   but my shame and the odd hits.

---

79 **bravery** ostentatious display   88 **mess** table; **chough** jackdaw; thus, a chatterer   96 **indifferent** somewhat   98 **complexion** temperament   106 **differences** distinguishing qualities
107 **great showing** distinguished appearance   108 **card** map
109 **continent** all-containing embodiment   110 **definement** definition   111 **divide him inventorially** classify him in detail;
dozy dizzy   112 **yaw** hold to a course unsteadily like a ship that
steers wild   114 **article** scope, importance; **infusion** essence;
dearth scarcity   115 **semblable** likeness   116 **trace** (1) draw,
(2) follow; **umbrage** shadow   119 **concernancy** import, relevance

123 **to't** i.e., to get an understanding   124 **nomination** mention
131 **approve** commend   133 **compare** compete   137 **meed** pay;
unfellowed unequaled   142 **impawned** staked   143 **assigns** ap-
pendages   144 **carriages** an affected word for **hangers,** i.e., straps
from which the weapon was hung   146 **liberal conceit** elaborate
design   149 **margent** margin (where explanatory notes were
printed)   157–58 **in a dozen passes . . . he shall not exceed you
three hits** the odds the King proposes seem to be that in a match of
twelve bouts, Hamlet will win at least five. Laertes would need to
win by at least eight to four   159 **he hath laid on twelve for nine**
"he" apparently is Laertes, who has seemingly raised the odds
against himself by wagering that out of twelve bouts he will win
nine   164 **breathing time** time for taking exercise   166 **an if**

OSRIC: Shall I deliver you so?

HAMLET: To this effect, sir, after what flourish your nature will.

170 OSRIC: I commend my duty to your lordship.

HAMLET: Yours. *(Exit* OSRIC.*)* He does well to commend it himself; there are no tongues else for's turn.

HORATIO: This lapwing runs away with the shell on his head.

HAMLET: 'A did comply, sir, with his dug, before 'a sucked it.

175 Thus has he, and many more of the same bevy that I know the drossy age dotes on, only got the tune of the time; and out of an habit of encounter, a kind of yesty collection which carries them through and through the most fanned and winnowed opinions; and do but blow them to their

180 trial, the bubbles are out.

(Enter a LORD.*)*

LORD: My lord, his majesty commended him to you by young Osric, who brings back to him that you attend him in the hall. He sends to know if your pleasure hold to play with Laertes, or that you will take longer time.

185 HAMLET: I am constant to my purposes: they follow the king's pleasure. If his fitness speaks, mine is ready; now or whensoever, provided I be so able as now.

LORD: The king and queen and all are coming down.

HAMLET: In happy time.

190 LORD: The queen desires you to use some gentle entertainment to Laertes before you fall to play.

HAMLET: She well instructs me.

(Exit LORD.*)*

HORATIO: You will lose, my lord.

HAMLET: I do not think so. Since he went into France, I have

195 been in continual practice. I shall win at the odds. But thou wouldst not think how ill all's here about my heart. But it is no matter.

HORATIO: Nay, good my lord—

HAMLET: It is but foolery, but it is such a kind of gaingiving as

200 would perhaps trouble a woman.

HORATIO: If your mind dislike any thing, obey it. I will forestall their repair hither, and say you are not fit.

HAMLET: Not a whit, we defy augury. There is a special providence in the fall of a sparrow. If it be now, 'tis not to come;

205 if it be not to come, it will be now; if it be not now, yet it will come. The readiness is all. Since no man of aught he leaves knows, what is't to leave betimes? Let be.

(A table prepared. {Enter} trumpets, drums, and OFFICERS *with cushions;* KING, QUEEN, *{*OSRIC,*} and all the* STATE, *{with} foils, daggers, and* LAERTES.*)*

KING: Come, Hamlet, come, and take this hand from me.

---

173 **lapwing** a bird reputedly so precocious as to run as soon as hatched   174 **comply** observe the formalities of courtesy; **dug** mother's nipple   175 **bevy** a covey of quails or lapwings   176 **drossy** frivolous   177 **encounter** manner of address or accosting; **yesty collection** a frothy and superficial patchwork of terms from the conversation of others   179 **winnowed** tested, freed from inferior elements   186 **fitness** convenience, inclination   199 **gaingiving** misgiving

(The KING *puts* LAERTES' *hand into* HAMLET's.*)*

HAMLET: Give me your pardon, sir. I have done you wrong,
But pardon 't as you are a gentleman.   210
This presence knows, and you must needs have heard,
How I am punished with a sore distraction.
What I have done
That might your nature, honour, and exception,
Roughly awake, I here proclaim was madness.   215
Was 't Hamlet wronged Laertes? Never Hamlet.
If Hamlet from himself be ta'en away,
And when he's not himself does wrong Laertes,
Then Hamlet does it not. Hamlet denies it.
Who does it then? His madness. If't be so,   220
Hamlet is of the faction that is wronged;
His madness is poor Hamlet's enemy.
Sir, in this audience,
Let my disclaiming from a purposed evil
Free me so far in your most generous thoughts   225
That I have shot mine arrow o'er the house,
And hurt my brother.

LAERTES: I am satisfied in nature,
Whose motive in this case should stir me most
To my revenge. But in my terms of honor
I stand aloof, and will no reconcilement   230
Till by some elder masters of known honor,
I have a voice and precedent of peace
To keep my name ungored. But till that time
I do receive your offered love like love,
And will not wrong it.   235

HAMLET: I embrace if freely,
And will this brother's wager frankly play.
Give us the foils.

LAERTES: Come, one for me.

HAMLET: I'll be your foil, Laertes. In mine ignorance
Your skill shall, like a star i' th' darkest night,
Stick fiery off indeed.   240

LAERTES: You mock me, sir.

HAMLET: No, by this hand.

KING: Give them the foils, young Osric. Cousin Hamlet,
You know the wager?

HAMLET: Very well, my lord;
Your Grace has laid the odds o'th' weaker side.

KING: I do not fear it, I have seen you both;   245
But since he is bettered, we have therefore odds.

LAERTES: This is too heavy; let me see another.

HAMLET: This likes me well. These foils have all a length?

(They prepare to play.)

OSRIC: Ay, my good lord.

KING: Set me the stoups of wine upon that table.   250
If Hamlet give the first or second hit,
Or quit in answer of the third exchange,
Let all the battlements their ordnance fire.

---

232 **voice and precedent** authoritative statement justified by precedent   238 **foil** (1) setting for gem (2) weapon   246 **bettered** perfected through training   248 **have all a length** are all of the same length   252 **quit in answer** literally, give as good as he gets (i.e., if the third bout is a draw)

255   The king shall drink to Hamlet's better breath,
    And in the cup an union shall he throw,
    Richer than that which four successive kings
    In Denmark's crown have worn. Give me the cups,
    And let the kettle to the trumpet speak,
260   The trumpet to the cannoneer without,
    The cannons to the heavens, the heaven to earth,
    'Now the king drinks to Hamlet.' Come begin—

(Trumpets the while.)

    And you, the judges, bear a wary eye.
HAMLET: Come on, sir.
LAERTES: Come, my lord.

(They play.)

HAMLET: One.
LAERTES: No.
HAMLET: Judgment.
OSRIC: A hit, a very palpable hit.

(Drums, trumpets, and shot. Flourish; a piece goes off.)

265 LAERTES: Well, again.
    KING: Stay, give me drink. Hamlet, this pearl is thine.
    Here's to thy health. Give him the cup.
    HAMLET: I'll play this bout first; set it by awhile.
    Come.

(They play.)

270   Another hit; what say you?
    LAERTES: I do confess't.
    KING: Our son shall win.
    QUEEN: He's fat, and scant of breath.
    Here, Hamlet, take my napkin, rub thy brows.
    The queen carouses to thy fortune, Hamlet.
275 HAMLET: Good madam!
    KING: Gertrude, do not drink.
    QUEEN: I will, my lord; I pray you pardon me.
    KING: *(Aside.)* It is the poisoned cup; it is too late.
    HAMLET: I dare not drink yet, madam; by and by.
280 QUEEN: Come, let me wipe thy face.
    LAERTES: My lord, I'll hit him now.
    KING: I do not think't.
    LAERTES: *(Aside.)* And yet it is almost against my conscience.
    HAMLET: Come, for the third, Laertes. You but dally.
    I pray you pass with your best violence;
285   I am afeard you make a wanton of me.
    LAERTES: Say you so? come on.

(They play.)

OSRIC: Nothing, neither way.
LAERTES: Have at you now!

(LAERTES wounds HAMLET; then, in scuffling, they change rapiers.)

---

255 **union** pearl   272 **fat** out of training   285 **make a wanton of me** trifle with me

KING: Part them. They are incensed.
HAMLET: Nay, come again.   290

(HAMLET wounds LAERTES. The QUEEN falls.)

OSRIC: Look to the queen there, ho!
HORATIO: They bleed on both sides. How is it, my lord?
OSRIC: How is't Laertes?
LAERTES: Why, as a woodcock to mine own springe, Osric.
    I am justly killed with mine own treachery.   295
HAMLET: How does the queen?
KING: She swoons to see them bleed.
QUEEN: No, no, the drink, the drink! O my dear Hamlet!
    The drink, the drink! I am poisoned.

(Dies.)

HAMLET: O villany! Ho! let the door be locked.
    Treachery! Seek it out.   300

(LAERTES falls. Exit OSRIC.)

LAERTES: It is here, Hamlet. Hamlet, thou art slain;
    No med'cine in the world can do thee good.
    In thee there is not half an hour's life.
    The treacherous instrument is in thy hand,
    Unbated and envenomed. The foul practice   305
    Hath turned itself on me. Lo, here I lie,
    Never to rise again. Thy mother's poisoned.
    I can no more. The king, the king's to blame.
HAMLET: The point envenomed too!
    Then, venom, to thy work.   310

(Wounds the KING.)

ALL: Treason! treason!
KING: O, yet defend me, friends. I am but hurt.
HAMLET: Here, thou incestuous, murd'rous, damnèd Dane,
    Drink off this potion. Is thy union here?
    Follow my mother.   315

(KING dies.)

LAERTES: He is justly served.
    It is a poison tempered by himself.
    Exchange forgiveness with me, noble Hamlet.
    Mine and my father's death come not upon thee,
    Nor thine on me!

(Dies.)

HAMLET: Heaven make thee free of it! I follow thee.   320
    I am dead, Horatio. Wretched queen, adieu!
    You that look pale and tremble at this chance,
    That are but mutes or audience to this act,
    Had I but time, as this fell sergeant Death
    Is strict in his arrest, O, I could tell you—   325
    But let it be. Horatio, I am dead:

---

294 **springe** trap   305 **Unbated** unblunted; **practice** plot   324 **fell** cruel; **sergeant** an officer whose duty is to summon persons to appear before a court

Thou livest; report me and my cause aright
To the unsatisfied.
HORATIO: Never believe it:
I am more an antique Roman than a Dane.
330   Here's yet some liquor left.
HAMLET: As th'art a man,
Give me the cup. Let go. By heaven, I'll ha't.
O God, Horatio, what a wounded name,
Things standing thus unknown, shall live behind me!
If thou didst ever hold me in thy heart,
335   Absent thee from felicity awhile,
And in this harsh world draw thy breath in pain,
To tell my story.

(A march afar off.)

What warlike noise is this?

(Enter OSRIC.*)*

OSRIC: Young Fortinbras, with conquest come from Poland,
To th' ambassadors of England gives
340   This warlike volley.
HAMLET: O, I die, Horatio!
The potent poison quite o'er-crows my spirit.
I cannot live to hear the news from England,
But I do prophesy th' election lights
On Fortinbras. He has my dying voice.
345   So tell him, with th' occurrents, more and less,
Which have solicited—the rest is silence.

(Dies.)

HORATIO: Now cracks a noble heart. Good night, sweet prince,
And flights of angels sing thee to thy rest!

(March within.)

Why does the drum come hither?

(Enter FORTINBRAS, *with the* AMBASSADORS *{and with drum, colors,
and* ATTENDANTS*}.)*

350   FORTINBRAS: Where is this sight?
HORATIO: What is it you would see?
If aught of woe or wonder, cease your search.
FORTINBRAS: This quarry cries on havoc. O proud Death,
What feast is toward in thine eternal cell

That thou so many princes at a shot
So bloodily hast struck?   355
AMBASSADORS: The sight is dismal;
And our affairs from England come too late.
The ears are senseless that should give us hearing
To tell him his commandment is fulfilled,
That Rosencrantz and Guildenstern are dead.
Where should we have our thanks?   360
HORATIO: Not from his mouth,
Had it th' ability of life to thank you.
He never gave commandment for their death.
But since, so jump upon this bloody question,
You from the Polack wars, and you from England,
Are here arrived, give order that these bodies   365
High on a stage be placèd to the view,
And let me speak to th' yet unknowing world
How these things came about. So shall you hear
Of carnal, bloody, and unnatural acts;
Of accidental judgements, casual slaughters;   370
Of deaths put on by cunning and forced cause;
And, in this upshot, purposes mistook
Fall'n on th' inventors' heads. All this can I
Truly deliver.
FORTINBRAS: Let us haste to hear it.
And call the noblest to the audience.   375
For me, with sorrow I embrace my fortune.
I have some rights of memory in this kingdom,
Which now to claim my vantage doth invite me.
HORATIO: Of that I shall have also cause to speak,
And from his mouth whose voice will draw on more.   380
But let this same be presently performed,
Even while men's minds are wild, lest more mischance
On plots and errors happen.
FORTINBRAS: Let four captains
Bear Hamlet like a soldier to the stage,
For he was likely, had he been put on,   385
To have proved most royal; and for his passage
The soldier's music and the rite of war
Speak loudly for him.
Take up the bodies. Such a sight as this
Becomes the field, but here shows much amiss.   390
Go, bid the soldiers shoot.

(Exeunt {marching. A peal of ordnance shot off}.)

---

341 **o'er-crows** triumphs over   344 **voice** vote   345 **more and
less** great and small   346 **solicited** incited, prompted

---

352 **quarry** pile of dead   353 **toward** impending   363 **jump**
exactly   371 **put on** instigated; **forced cause** by reason of compulsion   385 **put on** set to perform in office   386 **passage** death

WILLIAM SHAKESPEARE

THE TEMPEST

The Tempest was staged at court in 1611. It is probably the last play that Shakespeare wrote without a collaborator, and generations of readers and audiences have taken Prospero as an image of Shakespeare himself: when Prospero puts aside his powerful, theatrical magic, Shakespeare may in a sense be making his farewell to the stage.

Renaissance audiences might have taken *The Tempest* as an example of a new kind of play becoming increasingly popular in the early seventeenth century: *tragicomedy*. Renaissance tragicomedy generally opens in the severe, disturbing mood of tragedy and builds to a moment of crisis; it then resolves into a comic finale of festivity, marriage, and harmony. That is, this version of "tragicomedy" concerns the play's plot structure, rather than its tone or mood. Shakespeare's company, the King's Men, had staged several plays by John Fletcher, one of the premier writers of tragicomedy, and it is inviting to see Shakespeare trying out his hand at the new genre late in his career in plays such as *Pericles, Cymbeline, The Winter's Tale,* and *The Tempest. The Tempest* begins as something like a revenge tragedy: Prospero plots to revenge himself on his usurping brother Antonio, and Sebastian's plot to murder Alonso also smacks of tragic intrigue. However, *The Tempest,* while raising the problems of tragedy, resolves them in the mode of comedy. Instead of murdering his brother, Prospero marries his daughter, Miranda, to Alonso's son, Ferdinand. The spirit Ariel prompts Prospero to discover that "The rarer action is / In virtue than in vengeance."

In other respects, *The Tempest* shares the forms and moods of Shakespearean comedy. In a plot reminiscent of many of Shakespeare's earlier comedies, Prospero's daughter, Miranda, falls instantly in love with Alonso's son, Ferdinand, for in *The Tempest,* virtue "naturally" recognizes virtue in others. The marriage also promises to heal the political rifts between Milan and Naples, and Prospero devises an elegant entertainment to lend the engagement an aura of sanctity. In its mythological characters, verse, song, and dance, Prospero's play resembles the masques frequently performed at court on such occasions. The romantic comedy of Ferdinand and Miranda is balanced by the play's more ironic treatment of Caliban, Stephano, and Trinculo. If the magical meeting of the lovers urges us to believe that the virtuous are drawn naturally together, the fact that Caliban takes the boozy Stephano and Trinculo for gods, and that the three of them try to overthrow Prospero from his second kingdom, suggests a parallel recognition—that bad nature also seeks itself out in others.

Although Prospero and Doctor Faustus—the title character in Christopher Marlowe's influential tragedy—may practice different kinds of magic, both are figures of the common desire to transcend nature through art. But much as Faustus is finally damned for his bargain with Mephostophilis, so Prospero learns that his own nature, and human nature generally, cannot be overcome. Prospero must learn to forgive in order to return to the world from his magic island-prison. Indeed, if the power of Prospero's artful magic is symbolized by the capable spirit Ariel, its limitations are suggested by Caliban. In some ways, Caliban represents a European imagination of human nature in its elemental form, an image of human nature that in the sixteenth and seventeenth centuries was often reinforced by European contacts with the indigenous peoples of the Americas and Africa. For although Prospero's island is located in the Mediterranean, many of its features—and the shipwreck motif—seem to be drawn from pamphlets describing the exploration of the New World. In 1609, a fleet of English ships bound for Virginia was wrecked by a storm in the Bermudas; and while many of the ships eventually reached Jamestown, one, the *Sea*

Adventure, remained lost for nearly a year. When the ship finally reached Virginia in May of 1610, the Englishmen's story of survival and their encounters with the natives of the "still-vexed Bermoothes" was widely published in pamphlets that Shakespeare seems to have read while writing the play.

The play's setting and sources have led critics to see *The Tempest* as a play not only about the state of human nature, but also about the conquest and subjection of the native peoples represented by Caliban. Caliban is clearly seen from the point of view of the European settlers: Prospero calls him a devil and a slave and uses him as a beast of burden; his language is simple; and instead of using the arts of romance on Miranda, as Ferdinand does, he tries to rape Miranda in an effort to people the island with Calibans. Caliban was the master of the island's nature, its "fresh springs, brine pits, barren place and fertile," but in attempting to civilize Caliban, Prospero has succeeded only in deforming him. Caliban is now neither "natural" nor civilized, but a parody of European "humanity": "You taught me language, and my profit on't / Is, I know how to curse."

Prospero's stagey magic, his ability to conjure storms and spectacles, is a glorious image of Renaissance "overreaching." As in *A Midsummer Night's Dream* or *Hamlet,* Shakespeare uses *The Tempest* to frame his final, most subtle imaging of the extraordinary powers of art—the arts of magic, of civilization, of the theater. At the same time, *The Tempest* also expresses the limitations of that art: neither Sebastian nor Antonio seems fundamentally changed by Prospero's magic. And much as Caliban has been changed, the play finally can find no voice, no language for Caliban to speak. In recent years, stage productions have sometimes taken the play as an opportunity to investigate the dynamics of colonialism. Lewis Baumander's production (Toronto, 1987) set the play on the Queen Charlotte Islands, off the coast of British Columbia, Canada, during the late eighteenth century, when these islands were being explored and settled by British seamen. Not only have other productions (Jonathan Miller's 1988 Tempest) more generally interrogated the questions of cultural and racial domination posed in Shakespeare's play, but many writers—Roberto Fernández Retamar, for example, in Caliban (1989)—have seen in Shakespeare's play an allegory of the West's continued representational power over its colonial and postcolonial subjects. Aimé Césaire's play *A Tempest* is perhaps the best-known dramatic response to *The Tempest,* and it is included in Unit 7.

The Tempest is also the subject of one of the most famous and experimental Shakespeare films of the 1990s, Peter Greenaway's *Prospero's Books* (1991).

THE TEMPEST

William Shakespeare

EDITED BY DAVID BEVINGTON

------ CHARACTERS ------

ALONSO, *King of Naples*
SEBASTIAN, *his brother*
PROSPERO, *the right Duke of Milan*
ANTONIO, *his brother, the usurping Duke of Milan*
FERDINAND, *son to the King of Naples*
GONZALO, *an honest old Counselor*
ADRIAN *and* ⎫
FRANCISCO ⎭ *Lords*
CALIBAN, *a savage and deformed Slave*
TRINCULO, *a Jester*
STEPHANO, *a drunken Butler*

MASTER *of a Ship*
BOATSWAIN
MARINERS
MIRANDA, *daughter to Prospero*
ARIEL, *an airy Spirit*
IRIS ⎫
CERES ⎪
JUNO ⎬ *{presented by}* SPIRITS
NYMPHS ⎪
REAPERS ⎭
{Other SPIRITS *attending on Prospero.}*

------ ACT ONE ------

SCENE I

An uninhabited island.

A tempestuous noise of thunder and lightning heard. Enter a SHIP-
MASTER *and a* BOATSWAIN.

MASTER: Boatswain!
BOATSWAIN: Here, master. What cheer?
MASTER: Good speak to th' mariners. Fall to 't, yarely, or we run
　　ourselves aground. Bestir, bestir.

(Exit.)

(Enter MARINERS.*)*

5　BOATSWAIN: Heigh, my hearts! Cheerly, cheerly, my hearts! Yare,
　　yare! Take in the topsail. Tend to th' master's whistle.—
　　Blow till thou burst thy wind, if room enough!

(Enter ALONSO, SEBASTIAN, ANTONIO, FERDINAND, GONZALO,
and others.)

ALONSO: Good boatswain, have care. Where's the master? Play
　　the men.
10　BOATSWAIN: I pray now, keep below.
ANTONIO: Where is the master, bos'n?
BOATSWAIN: Do you not hear him? You mar our labor. Keep
　　your cabins; you do assist the storm.
GONZALO: Nay, good, be patient.
15　BOATSWAIN: When the sea is. Hence! What cares these roarers
　　for the name of king? To cabin! Silence! Trouble us not.
GONZALO: Good, yet remember whom thou hast aboard.
BOATSWAIN: None that I more love than myself. You are a
　　counselor; if you can command these elements to silence,
20　and work the peace of the present, we will not hand a rope

more. Use your authority. If you cannot, give thanks you
have liv'd so long, and make yourself ready in your cabin for
the mischance of the hour, if it so hap.—Cheerly, good
hearts!—Out of our way, I say.

(Exit.)

GONZALO: I have great comfort from this fellow. Methinks he　25
hath no drowning mark upon him; his complexion is perfect gallows. Stand fast, good Fate, to his hanging! Make the
rope of his destiny our cable, for our own doth little advantage. If he be not born to be hang'd, our case is miserable.

(Exeunt.)

(Enter BOATSWAIN.*)*

BOATSWAIN: Down with the topmast! Yare! Lower, lower!　30
Bring her to try with main-course. *(A cry within.)* A plague
upon this howling! They are louder than the weather or our
office.

(Enter SEBASTIAN, ANTONIO, *and* GONZALO.*)*

Yet again? What do you here? Shall we give o'er and drown?
Have you a mind to sink?　35
SEBASTIAN: A pox o' your throat, you bawling, blasphemous,
incharitable dog!
BOATSWAIN: Work you then.
ANTONIO: Hang, cur! Hang, you whoreson, insolent noise-
maker! We are less afraid to be drown'd than thou art.　40
GONZALO: I'll warrant him for drowning, though the ship were
no stronger than a nutshell and as leaky as an unstanch'd
wench.

I.i. Location: On a ship at sea. 3 Good i.e., it's good you've
come; or, my good fellow; **yarely** nimbly **6 Tend** attend **7 Blow**
(addressed to the wind); **if room enough** as long as we have sea-
room enough **8–9 Play the men** act like men (?) ply, urge the men
to exert themselves (?) **15 roarers** waves or winds, or both; spoken
to as though they were "bullies" or "blusterers" **20 hand** handle

26–27 **complexion . . . gallows** appearance shows he was born to
be hanged (and therefore, according to the proverb, in no danger
of drowning) **28 our . . . advantage** i.e., our own cable is of little benefit **31 Bring . . . course** sail her close to the wind by
means of the mainsail **32 our office** i.e., the noise we make at
our work **41 warrant him for drowning** guarantee that he will
never be drowned **42 unstanch'd** insatiable, loose, unrestrained

BOATSWAIN: Lay her a-hold, a-hold! Set her two courses off to
45 sea again! Lay her off!

(Enter MARINERS *wet.)*

MARINERS: All lost! To prayers, to prayers! All lost!

(Exeunt.)

BOATSWAIN: What, must our mouths be cold?
GONZALO: The King and Prince at prayers! Let's assist them,
    For our case is as theirs.
SEBASTIAN: I am out of patience.
50 ANTONIO: We are merely cheated of our lives by drunkards.
    This wide-chopp'd rascal! Would thou mightst lie drowning
    The washing of ten tides!
GONZALO: He'll be hang'd yet,
    Though every drop of water swear against it
    And gape at wid'st to glut him.

(A confused noise within:)

                              "Mercy on us!"—
55 "We split, we split!"—"Farewell my wife and children!"–
    "Farewell, brother!"—"We split, we split, we split!"

(Exit BOATSWAIN*.)*

ANTONIO: Let's all sink wi' th' King.
SEBASTIAN: Let's take leave of him.

(Exit {with ANTONIO*}.)*

GONZALO: Now would I give a thousand furlongs of sea for an
60 acre of barren ground, long heath, brown furze, anything.
    The wills above be done! But I would fain die a dry death.

(Exit.)

SCENE II

Enter PROSPERO *{in his magic robes}* and MIRANDA.

MIRANDA: If by your art, my dearest father, you have
    Put the wild waters in this roar, allay them.
    The sky, it seems, would pour down stinking pitch,
    But that the sea, mounting to th' welkin's cheek,
5   Dashes the fire out. O, I have suffered
    With those that I saw suffer! A brave vessel,
    Who had, no doubt, some noble creature in her,
    Dash'd all to pieces. O, the cry did knock
    Against my very heart! Poor souls, they perish'd!

---

44 **a-hold** a-hull, close to the wind; **courses** sails, i.e., foresail as
well as mainsail, set in an attempt to get the ship back out into
open water   47 **must . . . cold** i.e., let us heat up our mouths with
liquor   50 **merely** quite   51 **wide-chopp'd** with mouth wide
open   51–52 **lie . . . tides** (Pirates were hanged on the shore and
left until three tides had come in.)   54 **glut** swallow   60 **heath**
uncultivated ground; heather; **furze** a weed growing on waste land
I.ii. Location: The island. Before Prospero's cell.   4 **welkin's
cheek** sky's face   6 **brave** gallant, splendid

Had I been any god of power, I would   10
Have sunk the sea within the earth or ere
It should the good ship so have swallow'd and
The fraughting souls within her.
PROSPERO: Be collected.
No more amazement. Tell your piteous heart
There's no harm done.   15
MIRANDA: O, woe the day!
PROSPERO: No harm.
I have done nothing but in care of thee,
Of thee, my dear one, thee, my daughter, who
Art ignorant of what thou art, nought knowing
Of whence I am, nor that I am more better
Than Prospero, master of a full poor cell,   20
And thy no greater father.
MIRANDA: More to know
Did never meddle with my thoughts.
PROSPERO: 'Tis time
I should inform thee farther. Lend thy hand,
And pluck my magic garment from me. So,

(Lays down his magic robe and staff.)

Lie there, my art. Wipe thou thine eyes; have comfort.   25
The direful spectacle of the wrack, which touch'd
The very virtue of compassion in thee,
I have with such provision in mine art
So safely ordered that there is no soul—
No, not so much perdition as an hair   30
Betid to any creature in the vessel
Which thou heard'st cry, which thou saw'st sink. Sit
    down;
For thou must now know farther.
MIRANDA: You have often
Begun to tell me what I am, but stopp'd
And left me to a bootless inquisition,   35
Concluding, "Stay, not yet."
PROSPERO: The hour's now come;
The very minute bids thee ope thine ear.
Obey and be attentive. Canst thou remember
A time before we came unto this cell?
I do not think thou canst, for then thou wast not   40
Out three years old.
MIRANDA: Certainly, sir, I can.
PROSPERO: By what? By any other house or person?
Of anything the image, tell me, that
Hath kept with thy remembrance.
MIRANDA: 'Tis far off,
And rather like a dream than an assurance   45
That my remembrance warrants. Had I not
Four or five women once that tended me?
PROSPERO: Thou hadst, and more, Miranda. But how is it
That this lives in thy mind? What seest thou else
In the dark backward and abysm of time?   50

---

11 **or ere** before   13 **fraughting** forming the cargo; **collected**
calm, composed   14 **amazement** consternation   20 **full**
very   30 **perdition** loss   31 **Betid** happened   35 **bootless inquisition** profitless inquiry   41 **Out** fully   45–46 **assurance . . .
warrants** certainty that my memory guarantees

If thou rememb'rest aught ere thou cam'st here,
How thou cam'st here thou mayst.
MIRANDA: But that I do not.
PROSPERO: Twelve year since, Miranda, twelve year since,
Thy father was the Duke of Milan and
55   A prince of power.
MIRANDA: Sir, are not you my father?
PROSPERO: Thy mother was a piece of virtue, and
She said thou wast my daughter; and thy father
Was Duke of Milan; and thou his only heir
And princess no worse issued.
MIRANDA: O the heavens!
60   What foul play had we, that we came from thence?
Or blessed was 't we did?
PROSPERO: Both, both, my girl.
By foul play, as thou say'st, were we heav'd thence,
But blessedly holp hither.
MIRANDA: O, my heart bleeds
To think o' th' teen that I have turn'd you to,
65   Which is from my remembrance! Please you, farther.
PROSPERO: My brother and thy uncle, call'd Antonio—
I pray thee mark me—that a brother should
Be so perfidious!—he whom next thyself
Of all the world I lov'd, and to him put
70   The manage of my state, as at that time
Through all the signories it was the first
And Prospero the prime duke, being so reputed
In dignity, and for the liberal arts
Without a parallel; those being all my study,
75   The government I cast upon my brother
And to my state grew stranger, being transported
And rapt in secret studies. Thy false uncle—
Dost thou attend me?
MIRANDA: Sir, most heedfully.
PROSPERO: Being once perfected how to grant suits,
80   How to deny them, who t' advance and who
To trash for overtopping, new created
The creatures that were mine, I say, or chang'd 'em,
Or else new form'd 'em; having both the key
Of officer and office, set all hearts i' th' state
85   To what tune pleas'd his ear, that now he was
The ivy which had hid my princely trunk,
And suck'd my verdure out on 't. Thou attend'st not.
MIRANDA: O, good sir, I do.
PROSPERO: I pray thee mark me.
I, thus neglecting worldly ends, all dedicated
90   To closeness and the bettering of my mind
With that which, but by being so retir'd,
O'er-priz'd all popular rate, in my false brother
Awak'd an evil nature; and my trust,

Like a good parent, did beget of him
A falsehood in its contrary as great   95
As my trust was, which had indeed no limit,
A confidence sans bound. He being thus lorded,
Not only with what my revenue yielded,
But what my power might else exact—like one
Who having into truth, by telling of it,   100
Made such a sinner of his memory
To credit his own lie—he did believe
He was indeed the Duke, out o' th' substitution,
And executing th' outward face of royalty,
With all prerogative. Hence his ambition growing—   105
Dost thou hear?
MIRANDA: Your tale, sir, would cure deafness.
PROSPERO: To have no screen between this part he play'd
And him he play'd it for, he needs will be
Absolute Milan. Me, poor man, my library
Was dukedom large enough. Of temporal royalties   110
He thinks me now incapable; confederates—
So dry he was for sway—wi' th' King of Naples
To give him annual tribute, do him homage,
Subject his coronet to his crown, and bend
The dukedom yet unbow'd—alas, poor Milan!—   115
To most ignoble stooping.
MIRANDA: O the heavens!
PROSPERO: Mark his condition and th' event, then tell me
If this might be a brother.
MIRANDA: I should sin
To think but nobly of my grandmother.
Good wombs have borne bad sons   120
PROSPERO: Now the condition.
This King of Naples, being an enemy
To me inveterate, hearkens my brother's suit,
Which was that he, in lieu o' th' premises
Of homage and I know not how much tribute,
Should presently extirpate me and mine   125
Out of the dukedom and confer fair Milan
With all the honors on my brother. Whereon,
A treacherous army levied, one midnight
Fated to th' purpose, did Antonio open
The gates of Milan, and, i' th' dead of darkness,   130
The ministers for th' purpose hurried thence
Me and thy crying self.
MIRANDA: Alack, for pity!
I, not rememb'ring how I cried out then,

---

56 **piece** masterpiece, exemplar   59 **issued** born, descended
63 **holp** helped   64 **teen . . . to** trouble I've caused you to remember, or put you to   65 **from** out of   71 **signories** i.e., city-
states of northern Italy   79 **perfected** grown skillful   81 **trash**
check a hound by tying a weight to its neck; **overtopping** running too far ahead of the pack; or, growing too tall   82 **creatures**
dependents; or either   83 **key** (1) key for unlocking (2) tool for
tuning stringed instruments   90 **closeness** retirement, seclu-
sion   91–92 **but . . . rate** except that it was done in retirement,
(would have) surpassed in value all popular estimate

---

94 **good parent** alludes to the proverb that good parents often bear
bad children; see also line 120   97 **sans** without; **lorded** raised
to lordship, with power and wealth   100–02 **Who . . . lie** i.e.,
who, by repeatedly telling the lie (that he was indeed Duke of
Milan), made his memory such a confirmed sinner against truth
that he began to believe his own lie   103 **out o'** as a result of   104
And . . . royalty and (as a result) his carrying out all the ceremonial
functions of royalty   108 **him** i.e., himself   109 **Absolute Milan**
unconditional Duke of Milan   110 **temporal royalties** practical
prerogatives and responsibilities of a sovereign   111 **confederates**
conspires, allies himself   112 **dry** thirsty   113 **him** i.e., the King
of Naples   114 **his . . . his** Antonio's . . . the King of Naples'   117
condition pact; **event** outcome   123 **in . . . premises** in return for
the stipulation   125 **presently extirpate** at once remove

Will cry it o'er again. It is a hint
135   That wrings mine eyes to 't.
PROSPERO: Hear a little further,
And then I'll bring thee to the present business
Which now's upon 's, without the which this story
Were most impertinent.
MIRANDA: Wherefore did they not
That hour destroy us?
PROSPERO: Well demanded, wench.
140   My tale provokes that question. Dear, they durst not,
So dear the love my people bore me, nor set
A mark so bloody on the business, but
With colors fairer painted their foul ends.
In few, they hurried us aboard a bark,
145   Bore us some leagues to sea, where they prepar'd
A rotten carcass of a butt, not rigg'd,
Nor tackle, sail, nor mast; the very rats
Instinctively have quit it. There they hoist us,
To cry to th' sea that roar'd to us, to sigh
150   To th' winds whose pity, sighing back again,
Did us but loving wrong.
MIRANDA: Alack, what trouble
Was I then to you!
PROSPERO: O, a cherubin
Thou wast that did preserve me. Thou didst smile,
Infused with a fortitude from heaven,
155   When I have deck'd the sea with drops full salt,
Under my burden groan'd, which rais'd in me
An undergoing stomach, to bear up
Against what should ensue.
MIRANDA: How came we ashore?
PROSPERO: By Providence divine.
160   Some food we had, and some fresh water, that
A noble Neapolitan, Gonzalo,
Out of his charity, who being then appointed
Master of this design, did give us, with
Rich garments, linens, stuffs, and necessaries,
165   Which since have steaded much. So, of his gentleness,
Knowing I lov'd my books, he furnish'd me
From mine own library with volumes that
I prize above my dukedom.
MIRANDA: Would I might
But ever see that man!
PROSPERO: Now I arise.

(Resumes his magic robes.)

170   Sit still, and hear the last of our sea-sorrow.
Here in this island we arriv'd; and here
Have I, thy schoolmaster, made thee more profit
Than other princess' can that have more time
For vainer hours and tutors not so careful.

MIRANDA: Heavens thank you for 't! And now, I pray you, sir,   175
For still 'tis beating in my mind, your reason
For raising this sea-storm?
PROSPERO: Know thus far forth.
By accident most strange, bountiful Fortune,
Now my dear lady, hath mine enemies
Brought to this shore; and by my prescience   180
I find my zenith doth depend upon
A most auspicious star, whose influence
If now I court not but omit, my fortunes
Will ever after droop. Here cease more questions.
Thou art inclin'd to sleep; 'tis a good dullness,   185
And give it way. I know thou canst not choose.

(MIRANDA sleeps.)

Come away, servant, come! I am ready now.
Approach, my Ariel, come.

(Enter ARIEL.)

ARIEL: All hail, great master! Grave sir, hail! I come
To answer thy best pleasure; be 't to fly,   190
To swim, to dive into the fire, to ride
On the curl'd clouds. To thy strong bidding, task
Ariel and all his quality.
PROSPERO: Hast thou, spirit,
Perform'd to point the tempest that I bade thee?
ARIEL: To every article.   195
I boarded the King's ship; now on the beak,
Now in the waist, the deck, in every cabin,
I flam'd amazement. Sometime I'd divide,
And burn in many places; on the topmast,
The yards, and boresprit, would I flame distinctly,   200
Then meet and join. Jove's lightnings, the precursors
O' th' dreadful thunder-claps, more momentary
And sight-outrunning were not; the fire and cracks
Of sulphurous roaring the most mighty Neptune
Seem to besiege and make his bold waves tremble,   205
Yea, his dread trident shake.
PROSPERO: My brave spirit!
Who was so firm, so constant, that this coil
Would not infect his reason?
ARIEL: Not a soul
But felt a fever of the mad and play'd
Some tricks of desperation. All but mariners   210
Plung'd in the foaming brine and quit the vessel;
Then all afire with me, the King's son, Ferdinand,
With hair up-staring—then like reeds, not hair—
Was the first man that leapt; cried, "Hell is empty,
And all the devils are here."   215

---

134 **hint** occasion   138 **impertinent** irrelevant   144 **few** few
words   146 **butt** cask, tub   151 **loving wrong** i.e., the winds
pitied Prospero and Miranda though of necessity they blew
them from shore   155 **deck'd** covered (with salt tears);
adorned   156 **which** i.e., the smile   157 **undergoing stomach**
courage to go on   165 **steaded much** been of much use   172
more profit profit more   173 **princess'** princesses

181 **zenith** height of fortune (astrological term)   182 **influence**
astrological power   187 **Come away** come   192 **task** make demands upon   193 **quality** (1) fellow-spirits (2) abilities   194 **to
point** to the smallest detail   196 **beak** prow   197 **waist** mid-
ships; **deck** poopdeck at the stern   198 **flam'd amazement**
struck terror in the guise of fire, i.e., St. Elmo's fire   200 **boresprit** bowsprit; **distinctly** in different places   207 **coil**
tumult   209 **of the mad** i.e., such as madmen feel   213 **up-
staring** standing on end

PROSPERO: Why, that's my spirit!
   But was not this nigh shore?
ARIEL: Close by, my master.
PROSPERO: But are they, Ariel, safe?
ARIEL: Not a hair perish'd.
   On their sustaining garments not a blemish,
   But fresher than before; and, as thou bad'st me,
220   In troops I have dispers'd them 'bout the isle.
   The King's son have I landed by himself,
   Whom I left cooling of the air with sighs
   In an odd angle of the isle and sitting,
   His arms in this sad knot.

(Folds his arms.)

PROSPERO: Of the King's ship,
225   The mariners, say how thou hast dispos'd,
   And all the rest o' th' fleet,
ARIEL: Safely in harbor
   Is the King's ship; in the deep nook, where once
   Thou call'dst me up at midnight to fetch dew
   From the still-vex'd Bermoothes, there she's hid;
230   The mariners all under hatches stow'd,
   Who, with a charm join'd to their suff'red labor,
   I have left asleep; and for the rest o' th' fleet,
   Which I dispers'd, they all have met again
   And are upon the Mediterranean flote
235   Bound sadly home for Naples,
   Supposing that they saw the King's ship wrack'd
   And his great person perish.
PROSPERO: Ariel, thy charge
   Exactly is perform'd. But there's more work.
   What is the time o' th' day?
ARIEL: Past the mid season.
240 PROSPERO: At least two glasses. The time 'twixt six and now
   Must by us both be spent most preciously.
ARIEL: Is there more toil? Since thou dost give me pains,
   Let me remember thee what thou hast promis'd,
   Which is not yet perform'd me.
PROSPERO: How now? Moody?
245   What is 't thou canst demand?
ARIEL: My liberty.
PROSPERO: Before the time be out? No more!
ARIEL: I prithee,
   Remember I have done thee worthy service,
   Told thee no lies, made thee no mistakings, serv'd
   Without or grudge or grumblings. Thou didst promise
250   To bate me a full year.
PROSPERO: Dost thou forget
   From what a torment I did free thee?
ARIEL: No.

---

218 **sustaining garments** garments that buoyed them up in the sea   223 **angle** corner   224 **sad knot** folded arms are indicative of melancholy   227 **nook** bay   229 **still-vex'd Bermoothes** ever stormy Bermudas. Perhaps refers to the then-recent Bermuda shipwreck; see Play Introduction   231 **with . . . labor** by means of a spell added to all the labor they have undergone   234 **flote** sea   239 **mid season** noon   240 **glasses** i.e., hourglasses   243 **remember** remind   250 **bate** remit, deduct

PROSPERO: Thou dost, and think'st it much to tread the ooze
   Of the salt deep,
   To run upon the sharp wind of the north,
   To do me business in the veins o' th' earth   255
   When it is bak'd with frost.
ARIEL: I do not, sir.
PROSPERO: Thou liest, malignant thing! Hast thou forgot
   The foul witch Sycorax, who with age and envy
   Was grown into a hoop? Hast thou forgot her?
ARIEL: No, sir.   260
PROSPERO: Thou hast. Where was she born? Speak. Tell me.
ARIEL: Sir, in Argier.
PROSPERO: O, was she so? I must
   Once in a month recount what thou hast been,
   Which thou forget'st. This damn'd witch Sycorax,
   For mischiefs manifold and sorceries terrible   265
   To enter human hearing, from Argier,
   Thou know'st, was banish'd; for one thing she did
   They would not take her life. Is not this true?
ARIEL: Ay, sir.
PROSPERO: This blue-ey'd hag was hither brought with child   270
   And here was left by th' sailors. Thou, my slave,
   As thou report'st thyself, was then her servant;
   And, for thou wast a spirit too delicate
   To act her earthy and abhorr'd commands,
   Refusing her grand hests, she did confine thee,   275
   By help of her more potent ministers,
   And in her most unmitigable rage,
   Into a cloven pine, within which rift
   Imprison'd thou didst painfully remain
   A dozen years; within which space she died   280
   And left thee there, where thou did'st vent thy groans
   As fast as mill-wheels strike. Then was this island—
   Save for the son that she did litter here,
   A freckled whelp hag-born—not honor'd with
   A human shape.   285
ARIEL: Yes, Caliban her son.
PROSPERO: Dull thing, I say so; he, that Caliban
   Whom now I keep in service. Thou best know'st
   What torment I did find thee in; thy groans
   Did make wolves howl and penetrate the breasts
   Of ever angry bears. It was a torment   290
   To lay upon the damn'd, which Sycorax
   Could not again undo. It was mine art,
   When I arriv'd and heard thee, that made gape
   The pine and let thee out.
ARIEL: I thank thee, master.
PROSPERO: If thou more murmur'st, I will rend an oak   295
   And peg thee in his knotty entrails till
   Thou hast howl'd away twelve winters.
ARIEL: Pardon, master;
   I will be correspondent to command
   And do my spriting gently.

---

258 **envy** malice   262 **Argier** Algiers   267 **one . . . did** perhaps a reference to her pregnancy, for which her life would be spared   270 **blue-ey'd** with dark circles under the eyes   273 **for** because   275 **hests** commands   296 **his** its   298 **correspondent** responsive, submissive

300 PROSPERO: Do so, and after two days
    I will discharge thee.
    ARIEL: That's my noble master!
    What shall I do? Say what? What shall I do?
    PROSPERO: Go make thyself like a nymph o' th' sea.
      Be subject
    To no sight but thine and mine, invisible
305   To every eyeball else. Go take this shape
    And hither come in 't. Go, hence with diligence!

(Exit {ARIEL}.)

    Awake, dear heart, awake! Thou hast slept well;
    Awake!
    MIRANDA: The strangeness of your story put
310   Heaviness in me.
    PROSPERO: Shake it off. Come on;
    We'll visit Caliban my slave, who never
    Yields us kind answer.
    MIRANDA: 'Tis a villain, sir,
    I do not love to look on.
    PROSPERO: But, as 'tis,
    We cannot miss him. He does make our fire,
315   Fetch in our wood, and serves in offices
    That profit us. What, ho! Slave! Caliban!
    Thou earth, thou! Speak.
    CALIBAN: *(Within.)*   There's wood enough within.
    PROSPERO: Come forth, I say! There's other business for thee.
    Come, thou tortoise! When?

(Enter ARIEL like a water-nymph.)

320   Fine apparition! My quaint Ariel,
    Hark in thine ear.

(Whispers.)

    ARIEL: My lord, it shall be done.

(Exit.)

    PROSPERO: Thou poisonous slave, got by the devil himself
    Upon thy wicked dam, come forth!

(Enter CALIBAN.)

    CALIBAN: As wicked dew as e'er my mother brush'd
325   With raven's feather from unwholesome fen
    Drop on you both! A south-west blow on ye
    And blister you all o'er!
    PROSPERO: For this, be sure, tonight thou shalt have cramps,
    Side-stitches that shall pen thy breath up; urchins
330   Shall, for that vast of night that they may work,
    All exercise on thee. Thou shalt be pinch'd

As thick as honeycomb, each pinch more stinging
Than bees that made 'em.
    CALIBAN: I must eat my dinner.
    This island's mine, by Sycorax my mother,
    Which thou tak'st from me. When thou cam'st first,   335
    Thou strok'st me and made much of me, wouldst
     give me
    Water with berries in 't, and teach me how
    To name the bigger light, and how the less,
    That burn by day and night; and then I lov'd thee
    And show'd thee all the qualities o' th' isle,   340
    The fresh springs, brine-pits, barren place and fertile.
    Curs'd be I that did so! All the charms
    Of Sycorax, toads, beetles, bats, light on you!
    For I am all the subjects that you have,
    Which first was mine own king; and here you sty me   345
    In this hard rock, whiles you do keep from me
    The rest o' th' island.
    PROSPERO: Thou most lying slave,
    Whom stripes may move, not kindness! I have us'd thee,
    Filth as thou art, with humane care, and lodg'd thee
    In mine own cell, till thou didst seek to violate   350
    The honor of my child.
    CALIBAN: O ho, O ho! Would't had been done!
    Thou didst prevent me; I had peopled else
    This isle with Calibans.
    MIRANDA: Abhorred slave,
    Which any print of goodness wilt not take,   355
    Being capable of all ill! I pitied thee,
    Took pains to make thee speak, taught thee each hour
    One thing or other. When thou didst not, savage,
    Know thine own meaning, but wouldst gabble like
    A thing most brutish, I endow'd thy purposes   360
    With words that made them known. But thy vile race,
    Though thou didst learn, had that in 't which good
     natures
    Could not abide to be with; therefore wast thou
    Deservedly confin'd into this rock,
    Who hadst deserv'd more than a prison.   365
    CALIBAN: You taught me language, and my profit on 't
    Is, I know how to curse. The red plague rid you
    For learning me your language!
    PROSPERO: Hag-seed, hence!
    Fetch us in fuel; and be quick, thou'rt best,
    To answer other business. Shrug'st thou, malice?   370
    If thou neglect'st or dost unwillingly
    What I command, I'll rack thee with old cramps,
    Fill all thy bones with aches, make thee roar
    That beasts shall tremble at thy din.
    CALIBAN: No, pray thee.
    (Aside.) I must obey. His art is of such pow'r,   375

---

314 **miss** do without   320 **quaint** ingenious   323 **wicked** mischievous, harmful   326 **south-west** i.e., wind thought to bring disease   329 **urchins** hedgehogs; here, suggesting goblins in the guise of hedgehogs   330 **vast** lengthy, desolate time; **that . . . work** malignant spirits were thought to be restricted to the hours of darkness

348 **stripes** lashes   354–65 **Abhorred . . . prison** sometimes assigned by editors to Prospero   360 **purposes** meanings, desires   361 **race** natural disposition; species, nature   367 **red plague** bubonic plague; **rid** destroy   368 **learning** teaching; **Hag-seed** offspring of a female demon   369 **thou'rt best** you'd be well advised   372 **old** such as old people suffer; or, plenty of   373 **aches** pronounced "aitches"

It would control my dam's god, Setebos,
And make a vassal of him.
PROSPERO: So, slave, hence!

(*Exit* CALIBAN.)

(*Enter* FERDINAND; *and* ARIEL, *invisible, playing and singing.*
{FERDINAND *does not see* PROSPERO *and* MIRANDA.})

(ARIEL'S *song.*)
                Come unto these yellow sands,
                    And then take hands.
380   Curtsied when you have and kiss'd,
                    The wild waves whist,
                Foot it featly here and there;
                And, sweet sprites, the burden bear.
                    Hark, hark!

(*Burden, dispersedly* {*within*}.)

385   Bow-wow.
                The watch-dogs bark.

(*Burden, dispersedly* {*within*}.)

                Bow-wow.
                Hark, hark! I hear
                The strain of strutting chanticleer
390   Cry, Cock-a-diddle-dow.

FERDINAND: Where should this music be? I' th' air or
    th' earth?
It sounds no more; and, sure, it waits upon
Some god o' th' island. Sitting on a bank,
Weeping again the King my father's wrack,
395 This music crept by me upon the waters,
Allaying both their fury and my passion
With its sweet air. Thence I have follow'd it,
Or it hath drawn me rather. But 'tis gone.
No, it begins again.

(ARIEL'S *song.*)
400   Full fathom five thy father lies;
                    Of his bones are coral made;
                Those are pearls that were his eyes.
                    Nothing of him that doth fade
                But doth suffer a sea-change
405   Into something rich and strange.
                Sea-nymphs hourly ring his knell:

(*Burden* {*within*}.)

                Ding-dong.
                Hark, now I hear them—Ding-dong,
                bell.

FERDINAND: The ditty does remember my drown'd father.
410 This is no mortal business, nor no sound
That the earth owes. I hear it now above me.

PROSPERO: The fringed curtains of thine eye advance
And say what thou seest yond.
MIRANDA: What is 't! A spirit!
Lord, how it looks about! Believe me, sir,
It carries a brave form. But 'tis a spirit.   415
PROSPERO: No, wench, it eats and sleeps and hath such senses
As we have, such. This gallant which thou seest
Was in the wrack; and, but he's something stain'd
With grief, that's beauty's canker, thou mightst call him
A goodly person. He hath lost his fellows   420
And strays about to find 'em.
MIRANDA: I might call him
A thing divine, for nothing natural
I ever saw so noble.
PROSPERO: (*Aside.*)   It goes on, I see,
As my soul prompts it. Spirit, fine spirit, I'll free thee
Within two days for this.   425
FERDINAND: (*Seeing* MIRANDA.) Most sure, the goddess
On whom these airs attend!—Vouchsafe my pray'r
May know if you remain upon this island,
And that you will some good instruction give
How I may bear me here. My prime request,
Which I do last pronounce, is, O you wonder!   430
If you be maid or no?
MIRANDA: No wonder, sir,
But certainly a maid.
FERDINAND: My language? Heavens!
I am the best of them that speak this speech,
Were I but where 'tis spoken.
PROSPERO: (*Coming forward.*)   How? The best?
What wert thou, if the King of Naples heard thee?   435
FERDINAND: A single thing, as I am now, that wonders
To hear thee speak of Naples. He does hear me;
And that he does I weep. Myself am Naples,
Who with mine eyes, never since at ebb, beheld
The King my father wrack'd.   440
MIRANDA: Alack, for mercy!
FERDINAND: Yes, faith, and all his lords, the Duke of Milan
And his brave son being twain.
PROSPERO: (*Aside.*)   The Duke of Milan
And his more braver daughter could control thee,
If now 'twere fit to do 't. At the first sight
They have chang'd eyes. Delicate Ariel,   445
I'll set thee free for this. (*To* FERDINAND.) A word, good sir.
I fear you have done yourself some wrong. A word!

---

381 **whist** being hushed   382 **featly** nimbly   383 **burden** refrain, undersong   384 s.d. **dispersedly** i.e., from all directions
409 **remember** commemorate   411 **owes** owns

412 **advance** raise   415 **brave** excellent   418 **but** except that; **something stain'd** somewhat disfigured   419 **canker** cankerworm (feeding on buds and leaves)   423 **It goes on** i.e., my plan works   427 **remain** dwell   429 **bear me** conduct myself; **prime** chief   433 **best** i.e., in birth   436 **single** (1) solitary (2) feeble   437–38 **He . . . weep** i.e., this man to whom I speak (Prospero) hears me as I hear him, proving to me I am indeed alive, not dreaming, and am in the sad plight I imagined (?)   438 **Naples** the King of Naples (also in line 437)   442 **son** the only reference in the play to a son of Antonio   443 **control** confute   445 **chang'd eyes** exchanged amorous glances   447 **done . . . wrong** i.e., spoken falsely

MIRANDA: *(Aside.)* Why speaks my father so ungently? This
Is the third man that e'er I saw, the first
450 That e'er I sigh'd for. Pity move my father
To be inclin'd my way!
FERDINAND: O, if a virgin,
And your affection not gone forth, I'll make you
The Queen of Naples.
PROSPERO: Soft, sir! One word more.
(Aside.) They are both in either's pow'rs; but this swift
business
455 I must uneasy make, lest too light winning
Make the prize light. *(To* FERDINAND.*)* One word more: I
charge thee
That thou attend me. Thou dost here usurp
The name thou ow'st not, and hast put thyself
Upon this island as a spy, to win it
460 From me, the lord on 't.
FERDINAND: No, as I am a man.
MIRANDA: There's nothing ill can dwell in such a temple.
If the ill spirit have so fair a house,
Good things will strive to dwell with 't.
PROSPERO: Follow me.—
Speak not you for him; he's a traitor.—Come,
465 I'll manacle thy neck and feet together.
Sea-water shalt thou drink; thy food shall be
The fresh-brook mussels, wither'd roots, and husks
Wherein the acorn cradled. Follow.
FERDINAND: No.
I will resist such entertainment till
470 Mine enemy has more pow'r.

(He draws, and is charmed from moving.)

MIRANDA: O dear father,
Make not too rash a trial of him, for
He's gentle, and not fearful.
PROSPERO: What, I say,
My foot my tutor?—Put thy sword up, traitor,
Who mak'st a show but dar'st not strike, thy conscience
475 Is so possess'd with guilt. Come, from thy ward,
For I can here disarm thee with this stick
And make thy weapon drop.

(Brandishes his staff.)

MIRANDA: *(Trying to hinder him.)* Beseech you, father.
PROSPERO: Hence! Hang not on my garments.
MIRANDA: Sir, have pity!
I'll be his surety.
PROSPERO: Silence! One word more
480 Shall make me chide thee, if not hate thee. What,
An advocate for an imposter? Hush!
Thou think'st there is no more such shapes as he,
Having seen but him and Caliban. Foolish wench,

To th' most of men this is a Caliban
And they to him are angels. 485
MIRANDA: My affections
Are then most humble; I have no ambition
To see a goodlier man.
PROSPERO: *(To* FERDINAND.*)* Come on, obey.
Thy nerves are in their infancy again
And have no vigor in them.
FERDINAND: So they are.
My spirits, as in a dream, are all bound up. 490
My father's loss, the weakness which I feel,
The wrack of all my friends, nor this man's threats
To whom I am subdu'd, are but light to me,
Might I put through my prison once a day
Behold this maid. All corners else o' th' earth 495
Let liberty make use of; space enough
Have I in such a prison.
PROSPERO: *(Aside.)* It works. *(To* FERDINAND.*)* Come on.—
Thou hast done well, fine Ariel! *(To* FERDINAND.*)* Follow
me.
(To ARIEL.*)* Hark what thou else shalt do me.
MIRANDA: *(To* FERDINAND.*)* Be of comfort.
My father's of a better nature, sir, 500
Than he appears by speech. This is unwonted
Which now came from him.
PROSPERO: *(To* ARIEL.*)* Thou shalt be as free
As mountain winds, but then exactly do
All points of my command.
ARIEL: To th' syllable.
PROSPERO: *(To* FERDINAND.*)* Come, follow. *(To* MIRANDA.*)* 505
Speak not for him.

(Exeunt.)

——— ACT TWO ———

SCENE I

Enter ALONSO, SEBASTIAN, ANTONIO, GONZALO, ADRIAN,
FRANCISCO, *and others.*

GONZALO: Beseech you, sir, be merry. You have cause,
So have we all, of joy, for our escape
Is much beyond our loss. Our hint of woe
Is common; every day some sailor's wife,
The masters of some merchant, and the merchant, 5
Have just our theme of woe; but for the miracle,
I mean our preservation, few in millions
Can speak like us. Then wisely, good sir, weigh
Our sorrow with our comfort.
ALONSO: Prithee, peace.
SEBASTIAN: *(To* ANTONIO.*)* He receives comfort like cold 10
porridge.

---

455 **uneasy** difficult   455–56 **light . . . light** easy . . . cheap
458 **ow'st** ownest   469 **entertainment** treatment   472 **gentle**
wellborn; **fearful** cowardly   473 **foot** subordinate (Miranda, the
foot, presumes to instruct Prospero, the head)   475 **ward** defen-
sive posture (in fencing)

---

484 **To** compared to   488 **nerves** sinews   499 **me** for me
II.i. Location: Another part of the island.   3 **hint of** occasion
for   5 **masters . . . the merchant** officers of some merchant vessel and the merchant himself, the owner   11 **porridge** with a pun
on *peace* and *pease,* a usual ingredient of porridge

ANTONIO: *(To* SEBASTIAN.*)* The visitor will not give him o'er
    so.

SEBASTIAN: Look, he's winding up the watch of his wit; by and
15   by it will strike.

GONZALO: Sir—

SEBASTIAN: *(To* ANTONIO.*)* One. Tell.

GONZALO: When every grief is entertain'd that's offer'd,
    Comes to th' entertainer—

20 SEBASTIAN: A dollar.

GONZALO: Dolor comes to him, indeed. You have spoken truer
    than you purpos'd.

SEBASTIAN: You have taken it wiselier than I meant you should.

GONZALO: Therefore, my lord—

25 ANTONIO: Fie, what a spendthrift is he of his tongue!

ALONSO: I prithee, spare.

GONZALO: Well, I have done. But yet—

SEBASTIAN: He will be talking.

ANTONIO: Which, of he or Adrian, for a good wager, first
30   begins to crow?

SEBASTIAN: The old cock.

ANTONIO: The cock'rel.

SEBASTIAN: Done. The wager?

ANTONIO: A laughter.

35 SEBASTIAN: A match!

ADRIAN: Though this island seem to be desert—

SEBASTIAN: Ha, ha, ha!

ANTONIO: So, you're paid.

ADRIAN: Uninhabitable and almost inaccessible—

40 SEBASTIAN: Yet—

ADRIAN: Yet—

ANTONIO: He could not miss 't.

ADRIAN: It must needs be of subtle, tender, and delicate
    temperance.

45 ANTONIO: Temperance was a delicate wench.

SEBASTIAN: Ay, and a subtle, as he most learnedly deliver'd.

---

12 **visitor** one taking nourishment and comfort to the sick, i.e.,
Gonzalo; **give him o'er** abandon him   17 **Tell** keep count   18–19
When . . . entertainer when every sorrow that presents itself is
accepted without resistance, there comes to the recipient   20 **dollar** widely circulated coin, the German *Thaler* and the Spanish *piece
of eight.* Sebastian puns on *entertainer* in the sense of *innkeeper;* to
Gonzalo, *dollar* suggests *dolor,* grief.   29–30 **Which . . . crow**
which of the two, Gonzalo or Adrian, do you bet will speak (crow)
first   31 **old cock** i.e., Gonzalo   32 **cock'rel** i.e., Adrian
34 **laughter** (1) burst of laughter (2) sitting of eggs. When
Adrian, the *cock'rel,* begins to speak two lines later, Sebastian loses
the bet. Some editors alter the speech prefixes in lines 37–38 so
that Antonio enjoys his laugh as the prize for winning, but possibly Sebastian pays for losing with a laugh   35 **A match** a bargain; agreed   42 **miss 't** (1) avoid saying "Yet" (2) miss the island
44 **temperance** climate   45 **Temperance** a girl's name; **delicate**
here it means *given to pleasure, voluptuous;* in line 43, *pleasant.* Antonio is evidently suggesting that "tender, and delicate temperance" sounds like a Puritan phrase, which Antonio then mocks by
applying the words to a woman rather than an island. He began
this bawdy comparison with a double entendre on *inaccessible,* line
39   46 **subtle** here it means *tricky;* in line 43, *delicate;* **deliver'd**
uttered. Sebastian joins in the Puritan baiting of Antonio with his
use of the pious cant phrase "learnedly deliver'd"

ADRIAN: The air breathes upon us here most sweetly.

SEBASTIAN: As if it had lungs, and rotten ones.

ANTONIO: Or as 'twere perfum'd by a fen.

GONZALO: Here is everything advantageous to life.   50

ANTONIO: True, save means to live.

SEBASTIAN: Of that there's none, or little.

GONZALO: How lush and lusty the grass looks! How green!

ANTONIO: The ground indeed is tawny.

SEBASTIAN: With an eye of green in 't.   55

ANTONIO: He misses not much.

SEBASTIAN: No; he doth but mistake the truth totally.

GONZALO: But the rarity of it is—which is indeed almost
    beyond credit—

SEBASTIAN: As many vouch'd rarities are.   60

GONZALO: That our garments, being, as they were, drench'd in
    the sea, hold notwithstanding their freshness and glosses,
    being rather new-dyed than stain'd with salt water.

ANTONIO: If but one of his pockets could speak, would it not
    say he lies?   65

SEBASTIAN: Ay, or very falsely pocket up his report.

GONZALO: Methinks our garments are now as fresh as when we
    put them on first in Afric, at the marriage of the King's fair
    daughter Claribel to the King of Tunis.

SEBASTIAN: 'Twas a sweet marriage, and we prosper well in our   70
    return.

ADRIAN: Tunis was never grac'd before with such a paragon to
    their queen.

GONZALO: Not since widow Dido's time.

ANTONIO: Widow! A pox o' that! How came that widow in?   75
    Widow Dido!

SEBASTIAN: What if he had said "widower Aeneas" too? Good
    Lord, how you take it!

ADRIAN: "Widow Dido" said you? You make me study of that.
    She was of Carthage, not of Tunis.   80

GONZALO: This Tunis, sir, was Carthage.

ADRIAN: Carthage?

GONZALO: A assure you, Carthage.

ANTONIO: His word is more than the miraculous harp.

SEBASTIAN: He hath rais'd the wall and houses too.   85

ANTONIO: What impossible matter will he make easy next?

SEBASTIAN: I think he will carry this island home in his pocket
    and give it his son for an apple.

ANTONIO: And, sowing the kernels of it in the sea, bring forth
    more islands.   90

GONZALO: Ay.

---

53 **lusty** healthy   54 **tawny** dull brown, yellowish   55 **eye** tinge,
or spot (perhaps with reference to Gonzalo's eye or judgment)
60 **vouch'd** certified   64 **pockets** i.e., because they are muddy
66 **pocket up** receive unprotestingly, fail to respond to a challenge   72 **to** for   74 **widow Dido** Queen of Carthage, deserted
by Aeneas. She was in fact a widow when Aeneas, a widower, met
her, but Antonio may be amused at the term "widow" to describe a
woman deserted by her lover   84 **miraculous harp** alludes to
Amphion's harp with which he raised the walls of Thebes; Gonzalo
has exceeded that deed by creating a modern Carthage—walls *and*
houses—mistakenly on the site of Tunis   91 **Ay** Gonzalo may be
reasserting his point about Carthage, or he may be responding ironically to Antonio who in turn answers sarcastically

ANTONIO: Why, in good time.

GONZALO: (*To* ALONSO.) Sir, we were talking that our garments
seem now as fresh as when we were at Tunis at the marriage
95 of your daughter, who is now queen.

ANTONIO: And the rarest that e'er came there.

SEBASTIAN: Bate, I beseech you, widow Dido.

ANTONIO: O, widow Dido? Ay, widow Dido.

GONZALO: Is not, sir, my doublet as fresh as the first day I wore
100 it? I mean, in a sort.

ANTONIO: That "sort" was well fish'd for.

GONZALO: When I wore it at your daughter's marriage?

ALONSO: You cram these words into mine ears against
The stomach of my sense. Would I had never
105 Married my daughter there! For, coming thence,
My son is lost and, in my rate, she too,
Who is so far from Italy removed
I ne'er again shall see her. O thou mine heir
Of Naples and of Milan, what strange fish
110 Hath made his meal on thee?

FRANCISCO: Sir, he may live.
I saw him beat the surges under him,
And ride upon their backs. He trod the water,
Whose enmity he flung aside, and breasted
The surge most swoll'n that met him. His bold head
115 'Bove the contentious waves he kept, and oared
Himself with his good arms in lusty stroke
To th' shore, that o'er his wave-worn basis bowed,
As stooping to relieve him. I not doubt
He came alive to land.

ALONSO: No, no, he's gone.

120 SEBASTIAN: Sir, you may thank yourself for this great loss,
That would not bless our Europe with your daughter,
But rather loose her to an African,
Where she at least is banish'd from your eye,
Who hath cause to wet the grief on 't.

ALONSO: Prithee, peace.

125 SEBASTIAN: You were kneel'd to and importun'd otherwise
By all of us, and the fair soul herself
Weigh'd between loathness and obedience, at
Which end o' th' beam should bow. We have lost your son,
I fear, for ever. Milan and Naples have
130 Moe widows in them of their business' making
Than we bring men to comfort them.
The fault's your own.

ALONSO: So is the dear'st o' th' loss.

GONZALO: My lord Sebastian,
The truth you speak doth lack some gentleness,

And time to speak it in. You rub the sore, 135
When you should bring the plaster.

SEBASTIAN: Very well.

ANTONIO: And most chirurgeonly.

GONZALO: It is foul weather in us all, good sir,
When you are cloudy.

SEBASTIAN: (*To* ANTONIO.) Foul weather?

ANTONIO: (*To* SEBASTIAN.) Very foul.

GONZALO: Had I plantation of this isle, my lord— 140

ANTONIO: He'd sow 't with nettle-seed.

SEBASTIAN: Or docks, or mallows.

GONZALO: And were the king on 't, what would I do?

SEBASTIAN: Scape being drunk for want of wine.

GONZALO: I' th' commonwealth I would by contraries
Execute all things; for no kind of traffic 145
Would I admit; no name of magistrate;
Letters should not be known; riches, poverty,
And use of service, none; contract, succession,
Bourn, bound of land, tilth, vineyard, none;
No use of metal, corn, or wine, or oil; 150
No occupation; all men idle, all,
And women too, but innocent and pure;
No sovereignty—

SEBASTIAN: Yet he would be king on 't.

ANTONIO: The latter end of his commonwealth forgets the
beginning.

GONZALO: All things in common nature should produce 155
Without sweat or endeavor. Treason, felony,
Sword, pike, knife, gun, or need of any engine,
Would I not have; but nature should bring forth,
Of it own kind, all foison, all abundance,
To feed my innocent people. 160

SEBASTIAN: No marrying 'mong his subjects?

ANTONIO: None, man; all idle—whores and knaves.

GONZALO: I would with such perfection govern, sir,
T' excel the golden age.

SEBASTIAN: Save his Majesty!

ANTONIO: Long live Gonzalo! 165

GONZALO: And—do you mark me, sir?

ALONSO: Prithee, no more. Thou dost talk nothing to me.

GONZALO: I do well believe your Highness, and did it to minister occasion to these gentlemen, who are of such sensible
and nimble lungs that they always use to laugh at nothing.

ANTONIO: 'Twas you we laugh'd at. 170

GONZALO: Who in this kind of merry fooling am nothing to
you; so you may continue and laugh at nothing still.

---

92 **in good time** an expression of ironical acquiescence or amazement; i.e., *sure, right away* 96 **rarest** most remarkable,
beautiful 97 **Bate** abate, except, leave out (i.e., don't forget Dido;
or, let's have no more talk of Dido) 100 **in a sort** in a way 104
stomach appetite 105 **Married** given in marriage 106 **rate** estimation, consideration 116 **lusty** vigorous 117 **that . . . bowed**
that hung out over its wave-worn foot 118 **As** as if 124 **Who**
which, i.e., the eye 126–28 **the fair . . . bow** i.e., Claribel herself
was poised uncertain between unwillingness to marry and obedience
to her father as to which end of the scale should sink, which should
prevail 130 **Moe** more 133 **dear'st** heaviest, most costly

135 **time** appropriate time 137 **chirurgeonly** like a skilled
surgeon. Antonio mocks Gonzalo's medical analogy of a *plaster*
applied curatively to a wound 140 **plantation** colonization
(with subsequent wordplay on the literal meaning) 141 **docks,**
mallows various weeds 144 **by contraries** by what is directly
opposite to usual custom 145 **traffic** trade 147 **Letters** learning 148 **use of service** custom of employing servants; **succes-**
sion holding of property by right of inheritance 149 **Bourn**
boundaries; **bound of land** landmarks; **tilth** tillage of soil 150
corn grain 157 **engine** instrument of warfare 159 **it** its; **foi-**
son plenty 164 **Save** God save 167–68 **minister occasion**
furnish opportunity 168 **sensible** sensitive

ANTONIO: What a blow was there given!

SEBASTIAN: An it had not fall'n flat-long.

175 GONZALO: You are gentlemen of brave mettle; you would lift
the moon out of her sphere, if she would continue in it five
weeks without changing.

(Enter ARIEL *{invisible} playing solemn music.)*

SEBASTIAN: We would so, and then go a-batfowling.

ANTONIO: Nay, good my lord, be not angry.

180 GONZALO: No, I warrant, you, I will not adventure my discretion so weakly. Will you laugh me asleep? For I am very
heavy.

ANTONIO: Go sleep, and hear us.

(All sleep except ALONSO, SEBASTIAN, *and* ANTONIO.)

ALONSO: What, all so soon asleep? I wish mine eyes

185 Would, with themselves, shut up my thoughts. I find
They are inclin'd to do so.

SEBASTIAN: Please you, sir,
Do not omit the heavy offer of it.
It seldom visits sorrow; when it doth,
It is a comforter.

ANTONIO: We two, my lord,

190 Will guard your person while you take your rest,
And watch your safety.

ALONSO: Thank you. Wondrous heavy.

(ALONSO sleeps. Exit ARIEL.)

SEBASTIAN: What a strange drowsiness possesses them!

ANTONIO: It is the quality o' th' climate.

SEBASTIAN: Why
Doth it not then our eyelids sink? I find not

195 Myself dispos'd to sleep.

ANTONIO: Nor I; my spirits are nimble.
They fell together all, as by consent;
They dropp'd, as by a thunder-stroke. What might,
Worthy Sebastian? O, what might—? No more—
And yet methinks I see it in thy face,

200 What thou shouldst be. Th' occasion speaks thee, and
My strong imagination sees a crown
Dropping upon thy head.

SEBASTIAN: What, art thou waking?

ANTONIO: Do you not hear me speak?

SEBASTIAN: I do; and surely
It is a sleepy language and thou speak'st

205 Out of thy sleep. What is it thou didst say?

This is a strange repose, to be asleep
With eyes wide open—standing, speaking, moving—
And yet so fast asleep.

ANTONIO: Noble Sebastian,
Thou let'st thy fortune sleep—die, rather; wink'st

210 Whiles thou art waking.

SEBASTIAN: Thou dost snore distinctly;
There's meaning in thy snores.

ANTONIO: I am more serious than my custom. You
Must be so too, if heed me; which to do
Trebles thee o'er.

SEBASTIAN: Well, I am standing water.

215 ANTONIO: I'll teach you how to flow.

SEBASTIAN: Do so. To ebb
Hereditary sloth instructs me.

ANTONIO: O,
If you but knew how you the purpose cherish
Whiles thus you mock it! How, in stripping it,
You more invest it! Ebbing men, indeed,

220 Most often do so near the bottom run
By their own fear or sloth.

SEBASTIAN: Prithee say on.
The setting of thine eye and cheek proclaim
A matter from thee, and a birth indeed
Which throes thee much to yield.

ANTONIO: Thus, sir:

225 Although this lord of weak remembrance, this,
Who shall be of as little memory
When he is earth'd, hath here almost persuaded—
For he's a spirit of persuasion, only
Professes to persuade—the King his son's alive,

230 'Tis as impossible that he's undrown'd
As he that sleeps here swims.

SEBASTIAN: I have no hope
That he's undrown'd.

ANTONIO: O, out of that "no hope"
What great hope have you! No hope that way is
Another way so high a hope that even

235 Ambition cannot pierce a wink beyond,

---

209 **wink'st** shut your eyes   214 **Trebles thee o'er** makes you
three times as great and rich; **standing water** water which neither
ebbs nor flows, at a standstill, indecisive   216 **Hereditary sloth**
natural laziness   217 **purpose** i.e., of being king; **cherish** i.e.,
make dear, enrich   219 **invest** clothe. Antonio's paradox is that
by sceptically stripping away illusions Sebastian can see the
essence of a situation and the opportunity it presents, or that by
disclaiming and deriding his purpose Sebastian shows how he values it   220 **the bottom** i.e., on which unadventurous men may go
aground and miss the tide of fortune   222 **setting** set expression
(of earnestness)   223 **matter** matter of importance   224 **throes**
causes pain, as in giving birth   225 **this lord** i.e., Gonzalo;
remembrance (1) power of remembering (2) being remembered
after his death   227 **earth'd** buried   228–29 **only . . .
persuade** i.e., whose whole function (as a privy councilor) is to
persuade   233 **that way** i.e., in regard to Ferdinand's being
saved   235–36 **Ambition . . . there** ambition itself cannot see
any further than that hope (of the crown), but is unsure of itself in
seeing even so far, is dazzled by daring to think so high

---

174 **An** if; **flat-long** with the flat of the sword, i.e., ineffectually.
(Cf. *fallen flat.*)   178 **a-batfowling** hunting birds at night with
lantern and stick; also, gulling a simpleton. Gonzalo is the simpleton, or fowl, and Sebastian will use the moon as his
lantern   180–81 **adventure . . . weakly** risk my reputation for
discretion for so trivial a cause (by getting angry at these sarcastic
fellows)   182 **heavy** sleep   183 **Go . . . us** let our laughing send
you to sleep, or, go to sleep and hear us laugh at you   187 **omit**
neglect; **heavy** drowsy   200 **speaks** calls upon; or, pronounces,
proclaims. Sebastian as usurper of Alonso's crown

But doubt discovery there. Will you grant with me
That Ferdinand is drown'd?
SEBASTIAN: He's gone.
ANTONIO: Then, tell me,
Who's the next heir of Naples?
SEBASTIAN: Claribel.
ANTONIO: She that is Queen of Tunis; she that dwells
240   Ten leagues beyond man's life; she that from Naples
Can have no note, unless the sun were post—
The man i' th' moon's too slow—till new-born chins
Be rough and razorable; she that from whom
We all were sea-swallow'd, though some cast again,
245   And by that destiny to perform an act
Whereof what's past is prologue, what to come
In yours and my discharge.
SEBASTIAN: What stuff is this? How say you?
'Tis true, my brother's daughter's Queen of Tunis;
250   So is she heir of Naples; 'twixt which regions
There is some space.
ANTONIO: A space whose ev'ry cubit
Seems to cry out, "How shall that Claribel
Measure us back to Naples? Keep in Tunis,
And let Sebastian wake." Say this were death
255   That now hath seiz'd them; why, they were no worse
Than now they are. There be that can rule Naples
As well as he that sleeps; lords that can prate
As amply and unnecessarily
As this Gonzalo; I myself could make
260   A chough of as deep chat. O, that you bore
The mind that I do! What a sleep were this
For your advancement! Do you understand me?
SEBASTIAN: Methinks I do.
ANTONIO: And how does your content
Tender your own good fortune?
SEBASTIAN: I remember
265   You did supplant your brother Prospero.
ANTONIO: True.
And look how well my garments sit upon me,
Much feater than before. My brother's servants
Were then my fellows; now they are my men.
SEBASTIAN: But, for your conscience?
270 ANTONIO: Ay, sir, where lies that? If 'twere a kibe,
'Twould put me to my slipper; but I feel not
This deity in my bosom. Twenty consciences,
That stand 'twixt me and Milan, candied be they
And melt ere they molest! Here lies your brother,
275   No better than the earth he lies upon,

If he were that which now he's like—that's dead,
Whom I, with this obedient steel, three inches of it,
Can lay to bed forever; whiles you, doing thus,
To the perpetual wink for aye might put
This ancient morsel, this Sir Prudence, who   280
Should not upbraid our course. For all the rest,
They'll take suggestion as a cat laps milk;
They'll tell the clock to any business that
We say befits the hour.
SEBASTIAN: Thy case, dear friend,
Shall be my precedent. As thou got'st Milan,   285
I'll come by Naples. Draw thy sword. One stroke
Shall free thee from the tribute which thou payest,
And I the king shall love thee.
ANTONIO: Draw together;
And when I rear my hand, do you the like,
To fall it on Gonzalo.   290

(They draw.)

SEBASTIAN: O, but one word.

(They talk apart.)

(Enter ARIEL {invisible}, with music and song.)

ARIEL: My master through his art foresees the danger
That you, his friend, are in, and sends me forth—
For else his project dies—to keep them living.

(Sings in GONZALO's ear.)

        While you here do snoring lie,
        Open-ey'd conspiracy   285 295
        His time doth take.
        If of life you keep a care,
        Shake off slumber, and beware.
        Awake, awake!

ANTONIO: Then let us both be sudden.   300
GONZALO: (Waking.) Now, good angels preserve the King!

(The others wake.)

ALONSO: Why, how now, ho, awake? Why are you drawn?
Wherefore this ghastly looking?
GONZALO: What's the matter?
SEBASTIAN: Whiles we stood here securing your repose,
Even now, we heard a hollow burst of bellowing   305
Like bulls, or rather lions. Did 't not wake you?
It struck mine ear most terribly.
ALONSO: I heard nothing.
ANTONIO: O, 'twas a din to fright a monster's ear,
To make an earthquake! Sure it was the roar
Of a whole herd of lions.   310
ALONSO: Heard you this, Gonzalo?
GONZALO: Upon mine honor, sir, I heard a humming,
And that a strange one too, which did awake me.

---

240 **Ten . . . life** i.e., it would take more than a lifetime to get there   241 **note** news, intimation; **post** messenger   243 **from on our voyage from**   244 **cast** were disgorged (with a pun on *casting* of parts for a play)   247 **discharge** performance   253 **Measure us** i.e., traverse the cubits, find her way   254 **wake** i.e., to his good fortune   259–60 **I . . . chat** I could teach a jackdaw to talk as wisely, or, be such a garrulous talker myself   263 **content** desire, inclination   264 **Tender** regard, look after   267 **feater** more becomingly, fittingly   270 **kibe** chilblain, sore on the heel   271 **put me to** oblige me to wear   273 **Milan** the dukedom of Milan; **candied** frozen, congealed in crystalline form

---

279 **wink** sleep, closing of eyes   283 **tell the clock** i.e., answer appropriately, chime   287 **tribute** (See 1.2.113–24)   296 **time** opportunity   304 **securing** standing guard over

I shak'd you, sir, and cried. As mine eyes open'd,
315   I saw their weapons drawn. There was a noise,
That's verily. 'Tis best we stand upon our guard,
Or that we quit this place. Let's draw our weapons.
ALONSO: Lead off this ground, and let's make further search
For my poor son.
GONZALO: Heavens keep him from these beasts!
320   For he is, sure, i' th' island.
ALONSO: Lead away.
ARIEL: *(Aside.)* Prospero my lord shall know what I have done.
So, King, go safely on to seek thy son.

(Exeunt {severally}.)

SCENE II

Enter CALIBAN *with a burden of wood. A noise of thunder heard.*

CALIBAN: All the infections that the sun sucks up
From bogs, fens, flats, on Prosper fall and make him
By inch-meal a disease! His spirits hear me,
And yet I needs must curse. But they'll nor pinch,
5   Fright me with urchin-shows, pitch me i' th' mire,
Nor lead me, like a firebrand, in the dark
Out of my way, unless he bid 'em; but
For every trifle are they set upon me;
Sometime like apes that mow and chatter at me
10   And after bite me, then like hedgehogs which
Lie tumbling in my barefoot way and mount
Their pricks at my footfall; sometime am I
All wound with adders who with cloven tongues
Do hiss me into madness.

(Enter TRINCULO.*)*

                Lo, now, lo!
15   Here comes a spirit of his, and to torment me
For bringing wood in slowly. I'll fall flat;
Perchance he will not mind me.

(Lies down.)

TRINCULO: Here's neither bush nor shrub, to bear off any
weather at all, and another storm brewing; I hear it sing i'
20   th' wind. Yond same black cloud, yond huge one, looks like
a foul bombard that would shed his liquor. If it should
thunder as it did before, I know not where to hide my head.
Yond same cloud cannot choose but fall by pailfuls. *(Sees*
CALIBAN.*)* What have we here? A man or a fish? Dead or
25   alive? A fish, he smells like a fish; a very ancient and fish-
like smell; a kind of not of the newest Poor-John. A strange
fish! Were I in England now, as once I was, and had but this
fish painted, not a holiday fool there but would give a piece

of silver. There would this monster make a man; any strange
beast there makes a man. When they will not give a doit to 30
relieve a lame beggar, they will lay out ten to see a dead Indian. Legg'd like a man! And his fins like arms! Warm, o'
my troth! I do now let loose my opinion, hold it no longer:
this is no fish, but an islander, that hath lately suffer'd by a
thunderbolt. *(Thunder.)* Alas, the storm is come again! My 35
best way is to creep under his gaberdine; there is no other
shelter hereabout. Misery acquaints a man with strange bedfellows. I will here shroud till the dregs of the storm be past.

(Creeps under CALIBAN's *garment.)*

(Enter STEPHANO, *singing, {a bottle in his hand}.)*

STEPHANO: "I shall no more to sea, to sea,
          Here shall I die ashore—"   40

This is a very scurvy tune to sing at a man's funeral.
Well, here's my comfort.

(Drinks.)

(Sings.)

   "The master, the swabber, the boatswain and I,
     The gunner and his mate
   Lov'd Mall, Meg, and Marian, and Margery,   45
     But none of us car'd for Kate;
     For she had a tongue with a tang,
     Would cry to a sailor, 'Go hang!'
   She lov'd not the savor of tar nor of pitch,
   Yet a tailor might scratch her where'er she did itch.   50
     Then to sea, boys, and let her go hang!"

This is a scurvy tune too; but here's my comfort.

(Drinks.)

CALIBAN: Do not torment me! Oh!
STEPHANO: What's the matter? Have we devils here? Do you
put tricks upon 's with savages and men of Ind, ha? I have 55
not scap'd drowning to be afeard now of your four legs; for
it hath been said, "As proper a man as ever went on four
legs cannot make him give ground"; and it shall be said so
again while Stephano breathes at' nostrils.
CALIBAN: This spirit torments me! Oh!   60
STEPHANO: This is some monster of the isle with four legs, who
hath got, as I take it, an ague. Where the devil should he
learn our language? I will give him some relief, if it be but
for that. If I can recover him and keep him tame and get to
Naples with him, he's a present for any emperor that ever 65
trod on neat's-leather.
CALIBAN: Do not torment me, prithee. I'll bring my wood
home faster.

II.ii. Location: Another part of the island.   3 **By inch-meal**
inch by inch 4 **nor** neither 5 **urchin-shows** apparitions
shaped like hedgehogs 6 **like a firebrand** in the guise of a will-
o'-the-wisp 9 **mow** make faces 17 **mind** notice 18 **bear off**
keep off 21 **foul bombard** dirty leathern bottle; **his** its 26
Poor-John salted hake, type of poor fare 28 **painted** i.e.,
painted on a sign set up outside a booth or tent at a fair

---

29 **make a man** make one's fortune 30 **doit** small coin 36
gaberdine cloak, loose upper garment 38 **shroud** take shelter;
dregs i.e., last remains 55 **Ind** India 57 **proper** handsome;
four legs the conventional phrase would supply *two legs* 59 **at'** at
the 64 **for that** i.e., for knowing our language; **recover**
restore 66 **neat's-leather** cowhide

STEPHANO: He's in his fit now and does not talk after the wis-
70 est. He shall taste of my bottle; if he have never drunk wine
afore, it will go near to remove his fit. If I can recover him
and keep him tame, I will not take too much for him; he
shall pay for him that hath him, and that soundly.

CALIBAN: Thou dost me yet but little hurt;
75 Thou wilt anon, I know it by thy trembling.
Now Prosper works upon thee.

STEPHANO: Come on your ways; open your mouth; here is that
which will give language to you, cat. Open your mouth;
this will shake your shaking, I can tell you, and that
80 soundly. (Gives CALIBAN drink.) You cannot tell who's your
friend. Open your chaps again.

TRINCULO: I should know that voice. It should be—but he is
drown'd; and these are devils. O defend me!

STEPHANO: Four legs and two voices; a most delicate monster!
85 His forward voice now is to speak well of his friend; his
backward voice is to utter foul speeches and to detract. If all
the wine in my bottle will recover him, I will help his ague.
Come. (Gives drink.) Amen! I will pour some in thy other
mouth.

90 TRINCULO: Stephano!

STEPHANO: Doth thy other mouth call me? Mercy, mercy! This
is a devil, and no monster. I will leave him; I have no long
spoon.

TRINCULO: Stephano! If thou beest Stephano, touch me and
95 speak to me; for I am Trinculo—be not afeard—thy good
friend Trinculo.

STEPHANO: If thou beest Trinculo, come forth. I'll pull thee by
the lesser legs. If any be Trinculo's legs, these are they. (Pulls
him out.) Thou art very Trinculo indeed! How cam'st thou to
100 be the siege of this moon-calf? Can he vent Trinculos?

TRINCULO: I took him to be kill'd with a thunder-stroke. But
art thou not drown'd, Stephano? I hope now thou art not
drown'd. Is the storm overblown? I hid me under the dead
moon-calf's gaberdine for fear of the storm. And art thou
105 living, Stephano? O Stephano, two Neapolitans scap'd!

STEPHANO: Prithee, do not turn me about; my stomach is not
constant.

CALIBAN: These be fine things, an if they be not sprites.
That's a brave god and bears celestial liquor.
110 I will kneel to him.

STEPHANO: How didst thou scape? How cam'st thou hither?
Swear by this bottle how thou cam'st hither. I escap'd upon
a butt of sack which the sailors heav'd o'erboard—by this
bottle, which I made of the bark of a tree with mine own
115 hands since I was cast ashore.

CALIBAN: (Kneeling.) I'll swear upon that bottle to be thy true
subject, for the liquor is not earthly.

STEPHANO: Here; swear then how thou escap'dst.

TRINCULO: Swum ashore, man, like a duck. I can swim like a
120 duck, I'll be sworn.

STEPHANO: Here, kiss the book. Though thou canst swim like
a duck, thou art made like a goose.

(Gives drink.)

TRINCULO: O Stephano, hast any more of this?

STEPHANO: The whole butt, man. My cellar is in a rock by the
125 sea-side where my wine is hid. How now, moon-calf? How
does thine ague?

CALIBAN: Hast thou not dropp'd from heaven?

STEPHANO: Out o' th' moon, I do assure thee. I was the man i'
th' moon when time was.

130 CALIBAN: I have seen thee in her and I do adore thee.
My mistress show'd me thee and thy dog and thy bush.

STEPHANO: Come, swear to that; kiss the book. I will furnish it
anon with new contents. Swear.

(Gives drink.)

TRINCULO: By this good light, this is a very shallow monster! I
135 afeard of him? A very weak monster! The man i' th' moon?
A most poor credulous monster! Well drawn, monster, in
good sooth!

CALIBAN: I'll show thee every fertile inch o' th' island;
And I will kiss thy foot. I prithee, by my god.

140 TRINCULO: By this light, a most perfidious and drunken monster! When's god's asleep, he'll rob his bottle.

CALIBAN: I'll kiss thy foot. I'll swear myself thy subject.

STEPHANO: Come on then; down, and swear.

(CALIBAN swears.)

TRINCULO: I shall laugh myself to death at this puppy-headed
145 monster. A most scurvy monster! I could find in my heart
to beat him—

STEPHANO: Come, kiss.

TRINCULO: But that the poor monster's in drink. An abominable monster!

150 CALIBAN: I'll show thee the best springs; I'll pluck thee berries;
I'll fish for thee and get thee wood enough.
A plague upon the tyrant that I serve!
I'll bear him no more sticks, but follow thee,
Thou wondrous man.

155 TRINCULO: A most ridiculous monster, to make a wonder of a
poor drunkard!

CALIBAN: I prithee, let me bring thee where crabs grow;
And I with my long nails will dig thee pig-nuts,
Show thee a jay's nest, and instruct thee how
160 To snare the nimble marmoset. I'll bring thee

---

72 **I will . . . much** i.e., no sum can be too much   73 **hath** possesses, receives   78 **cat . . . mouth** allusion to the proverb, "Good
liquor will make a cat speak"   81 **chaps** jaws   92–93 **long
spoon** allusion to the proverb, "He that sups with the devil has
need of a long spoon"   100 **siege** excrement; **moon-calf** monster,
abortion. Supposed to be caused by the influence of the moon;
vent emit   106–07 **not constant** unsteady   108 **an if** if   109
brave fine, magnificent   113 **butt of sack** barrel of Canary wine

121 **book** i.e., bottle   129 **when time was** once upon a
time   131 **dog . . . bush** the man in the moon was popularly
imagined to have with him a dog and a bush of thorn   134 **By
. . . light** by God's light, by this good light from heaven   136
Well drawn well pulled (on the bottle)   157 **crabs** crab
apples   158 **pig-nuts** peanuts   160 **marmoset** small monkey

To clust'ring filberts, and sometimes I'll get thee
Young scamels from the rock. Wilt thou go with me?
STEPHANO: I prithee now, lead the way without any more talk-
ing. Trinculo, the King and all our company else being
165 drown'd, we will inherit here. Here! Bear my bottle. Fellow
Trinculo, we'll fill him by and by again.
CALIBAN: (Sings drunkenly.)

       Farewell, master; farewell, farewell!

TRINCULO: A howling monster; a drunken monster!

CALIBAN: No more dams I'll make for fish,
170   Nor fetch in firing
          At requiring,
      Nor scrape trenchering, nor wash dish.
       'Ban, 'Ban, Ca-Caliban
      Has a new master, get a new man.
175   Freedom, high-day! High-day, freedom!
     Freedom, high-day, freedom!

STEPHANO: O brave monster! Lead the way.

(Exeunt.)

——— **ACT THREE** ———

SCENE I

Enter FERDINAND, *bearing a log.*

FERDINAND: There be some sports are painful, and their labor
Delight in them sets off; some kinds of baseness
Are nobly undergone; and most poor matters
Point to rich ends. This my mean task
5 Would be as heavy to me as odious, but
The mistress which I serve quickens what's dead
And makes my labors pleasures. O, she is
Ten times more gentle than her father's crabbed,
And he's compos'd of harshness. I must remove
10 Some thousands of these logs and pile them up,
Upon a sore injunction. My sweet mistress
Weeps when she sees me work, and says such baseness
Had never like executor. I forget;
But these sweet thoughts do even refresh my labors,
15 Most busy lest, when I do it.

(*Enter* MIRANDA; *and* PROSPERO {*at a distance, unseen*}.)

MIRANDA: Alas, now, pray you,
Work not so hard. I would the lightning had
Burnt up those logs that you are enjoin'd to pile!
Pray, set it down and rest you. When this burns,

---

162 **scamels** possibly "seamews," mentioned in Strachey's letter,
or shellfish; or perhaps from *squamelle,* furnished with little scales.
Contemporary French and Italian travel accounts report that the
natives of Patagonia in South America ate small fish described
as *fort scameux* and *squame* 165 **inherit** take possession 172
trenchering trenchers, wooden plates 175 **high-day** holiday (?)

III.i. Location: Before Prospero's cell. 2 **sets off** makes seem
greater by contrast 6 **quickens** gives life to 11 **sore injunction** severe command 15 **Most . . . it** i.e., least troubled by my labor when I think of her (?) The line may be in need of emendation

'Twill weep for having wearied you. My father
Is hard at study; pray now, rest yourself.   20
He's safe for these three hours.
FERDINAND: O most dear mistress,
The sun will set before I shall discharge
What I must strive to do.
MIRANDA: If you'll sit down,
I'll bear your logs the while. Pray give me that.
I'll carry it to the pile.   25
FERDINAND: No, precious creature,
I had rather crack my sinews, break my back,
Than you should such dishonor undergo
While I sit lazy by.
MIRANDA: It would become me
As well as it does you; and I should do it
With much more ease, for my good will is to it,   30
And yours it is against.
PROSPERO: (*Aside.*)   Poor worm, thou art infected!
This visitation shows it.
MIRANDA: You look wearily.
FERDINAND: No, noble mistress, 'tis fresh morning with me
When you are by at night. I do beseech you—
Chiefly that I might set it in my prayers—   35
What is your name?
MIRANDA: Miranda.—O my father,
I have broke your hest to say so.
FERDINAND: Admir'd Miranda!
Indeed the top of admiration! Worth
What's dearest to the world! Full many a lady
I have ey'd with best regard, and many a time   40
Th' harmony of their tongues hath into bondage
Brought my too diligent ear. For several virtues
Have I lik'd several women, never any
With so full soul but some defect in her
Did quarrel with the noblest grace she ow'd   45
And put it to the foil. But you, O you,
So perfect and so peerless, are created
Of every creature's best!
MIRANDA: I do not know
One of my sex; no woman's face remember,
Save, from my glass, mine own. Nor have I seen   50
More that I may call men than you, good friend,
And my dear father. How features are abroad,
I am skilless of; but, by my modesty,
The jewel in my dower, I would not wish
Any companion in the world but you,   55
Nor can imagination form a shape,
Besides yourself, to like of. But I prattle
Something too wildly, and my father's precepts
I therein do forget.
FERDINAND: I am in my condition
A prince, Miranda; I do think, a king—   60
I would, not so!—and would no more endure
This wooden slavery than to suffer
The flesh-fly blow my mouth. Hear my soul speak:

---

32 **visitation** (1) visit (2) visitation of the plague, i.e., infection of
love 37 **hest** command 45 **ow'd** owned 46 **put . . . foil** (1)
overthrew it (as in wrestling) (2) served as a "foil" or contrast to set
it off 53 **skilless** ignorant 63 **blow** befoul with fly-eggs

The very instant that I saw you, did
65 My heart fly to your service; there resides,
To make me slave to it; and for your sake
Am I this patient log-man.
MIRANDA: Do you love me?
FERDINAND: O heaven, O earth, bear witness to this sound,
And crown what I profess with kind event
70 If I speak true! If hollowly, invert
What best is boded me to mischief! I
Beyond all limit of what else i' th' world
Do love, prize, honor you.
MIRANDA: (Weeping.)   I am a fool
To weep at what I am glad of.
PROSPERO: (Aside.)   Fair encounter
75 Of two most rare affections! Heavens rain grace
On that which breeds between 'em!
FERDINAND: Wherefore weep you?
MIRANDA: At mine unworthiness, that dare offer
What I desire to give, and much less take
What I shall die to want. But this is trifling,
80 And all the more it seeks to hide itself
The bigger bulk it shows. Hence, bashful cunning,
And prompt me, plain and holy innocence!
I am your wife, if you will marry me;
If not, I'll die your maid. To be your fellow
85 You may deny me, but I'll be your servant,
Whether you will or no.
FERDINAND: My mistress, dearest,
And I thus humble ever.
MIRANDA: My husband, then?
FERDINAND: Ay, with a heart as willing
As bondage e'er of freedom. Here's my hand.
90 MIRANDA: And mine, with my heart in 't. And now farewell
Till half an hour hence.
FERDINAND: A thousand thousand!

(Exeunt {FERDINAND and MIRANDA severally}.)

PROSPERO: So glad of this as they I cannot be,
Who are surpris'd with all; but my rejoicing
At nothing can be more. I'll to my book,
95 For yet ere supper-time must I perform
Much business appertaining.

SCENE II

Enter CALIBAN, STEPHANO, *and* TRINCULO.

STEPHANO: Tell not me. When the butt is out, we will drink
water, not a drop before. Therefore bear up, and board 'em.
Servant-monster, drink to me.
TRINCULO: Servant-monster? The folly of this island! They say
5   there's but five upon this isle; we are three of them. If th'
other two be brain'd like us, the state totters.

---

69 **kind event** favorable outcome   70 **hollowly** insincerely, falsely
71 **boded** destined for   79 **want** lack   84 **fellow** mate, equal
III.ii. Location: Another part of the island.   1 **out** empty
2 **bear . . . 'em** Stephano uses the terminology of maneuvering at
sea and boarding a vessel under attack as a way of urging an assault
on the liquor supply

STEPHANO: Drink, servant-monster, when I bid thee. Thy
eyes are almost set in thy head.

(Gives drink.)

TRINCULO: Where should they be set else? He were a brave
monster indeed if they were set in his tail.   10
STEPHANO: My man-monster hath drown'd his tongue in sack.
For my part, the sea cannot drown me; I swam, ere I could
recover the shore, five and thirty leagues off and on. By this
light, thou shalt be my lieutenant, monster, or my standard.
TRINCULO: Your lieutenant, if you list; he's no standard.   15
STEPHANO: We'll not run, Monsieur Monster.
TRINCULO: Nor go neither, but you'll lie like dogs and yet say
nothing neither.
STEPHANO: Moon-calf, speak once in thy life, if thou beest a
good moon-calf.   20
CALIBAN: How does thy honor? Let me lick thy shoe.
I'll not serve him; he is not valiant.
TRINCULO: Thou liest, most ignorant monster, I am in case to
justle a constable. Why, thou debosh'd fish thou, was there
ever man a coward that hath drunk so much sack as I today?   25
Wilt thou tell a monstrous lie, being but half a fish and half
a monster?
CALIBAN: Lo, how he mocks me! Wilt thou let him, my lord?
TRINCULO: "Lord," quoth he? That a monster should be such a
natural!   30
CALIBAN: Lo, lo, again! Bite him to death, I prithee.
STEPHANO: Trinculo, keep a good tongue in your head. If you
prove a mutineer—the next tree! The poor monster's my
subject and he shall not suffer indignity.
CALIBAN: I thank my noble lord. Wilt thou be pleas'd   35
To hearken once again to the suit I made to thee?
STEPHANO: Marry, will I. Kneel and repeat it; I will stand, and
so shall Trinculo.

(CALIBAN kneels.)

(Enter ARIEL, invisible.)

CALIBAN: As I told thee before, I am subject to a tyrant,
A sorcerer, that by his cunning hath   40
Cheated me of the island.
ARIEL: Thou liest.
CALIBAN: Thou liest, thou jesting monkey, thou!
I would my valiant master would destroy thee.
I do not lie.
STEPHANO: Trinculo, if you trouble him any more in 's tale, by 45
this hand, I will supplant some of your teeth.

---

8 **set** fixed in a drunken stare; or sunk, like the sun   9 **brave** fine,
splendid   13 **recover** arrive at   14 **standard** standard-bearer,
ancient, i.e., ensign (as distinguished from *lieutenant*, line 15)   15
list prefer; **no standard** i.e., not able to stand up   16 **run** (1)
retreat (2) urinate (taking Trinculo's *standard* line 15, in the old
sense of *conduit*)   17 **go** walk; **lie** (1) tells lies (2) lie prostrate (3)
excret   23–24 **case . . . constable** i.e., in fit condition, made
valiant by drink, to taunt or challenge the police; **debosh'd** i.e.,
debauched   30 **natural** (1) idiot (2) natural as opposed to unnatural, monster-like   33 **the next tree** i.e., you'll hang   37 **Marry**
i.e., indeed (originally an oath by the Virgin Mary)

TRINCULO: Why, I said nothing.

STEPHANO: Mum, then, and no more.—Proceed.

CALIBAN: I say, by sorcery he got this isle;
50   From me he got it. If thy greatness will
      Revenge it on him—for I know thou dar'st,
      But this thing dare not—

STEPHANO: That's most certain.

CALIBAN: Thou shalt be lord of it, and I'll serve thee.

55   STEPHANO: How now shall this be compass'd? Canst thou
      bring me to the party?

CALIBAN: Yea, yea, my lord. I'll yield him thee asleep,
      Where thou mayst knock a nail into his head.

ARIEL: Thou liest; thou canst not.

60   CALIBAN: What a pied ninny's this! Thou scurvy patch!
      I do beseech thy greatness, give him blows
      And take his bottle from him. When that's gone
      He shall drink nought but brine, for I'll now show him
      Where the quick freshes are.

65   STEPHANO: Trinculo, run into no further danger. Interrupt the
      monster one word further, and, by this hand, I'll turn my
      mercy out o' doors and make a stock-fish of thee.

TRINCULO: Why, what did? I did nothing. I'll go farther off.

STEPHANO: Didst thou not say he lied?

70   ARIEL: Thou liest.

STEPHANO: Do I so? Take thou that. (Beats TRINCULO.) As you
      like this, give me the lie another time.

TRINCULO: I did not give the lie. Out o' your wits and hearing
      too? A pox o' your bottle! This can sack and drinking do. A
75   murrain on your monster, and the devil take your fingers!

CALIBAN: Ha, ha, ha!

STEPHANO: Now, forward with your tale.

(To TRINCULO.)

      Prithee, stand further off.

CALIBAN: Beat him enough. After a little time
80   I'll beat him too.

STEPHANO: Stand farther.—Come, proceed.

CALIBAN: Why, as I told thee, 'tis a custom with him
      I' th' afternoon to sleep. There thou mayst brain him,
      Having first seiz'd his books, or with a log
85   Batter his skull, or paunch him with a stake,
      Or cut his wezand with thy knife. Remember
      First to possess his books; for without them
      He's but a sot, as I am, nor hath not
      One spirit to command. They all do hate him
90   As rootedly as I. Burn but his books.
      He has brave utensils—for so he calls them—
      Which, when he has a house, he'll deck withal.
      And that most deeply to consider is
      The beauty of his daughter. He himself
95   Calls her a nonpareil. I never saw a woman,
      But only Sycorax my dam and she;

But she as far surpasseth Sycorax
      As great'st does least.

STEPHANO: Is it so brave a lass?

CALIBAN: Ay, lord; she will become thy bed, I warrant,   100
      And bring thee forth brave brood.

STEPHANO: Monster, I will kill this man. His daughter and I will
      be king and queen—save our Graces!—and Trinculo and
      thyself shall be viceroys. Dost thou like the plot, Trinculo?

TRINCULO: Excellent.   105

STEPHANO: Give me thy hand. I am sorry I beat thee; but, while
      thou liv'st, keep a good tongue in thy head.

CALIBAN: Within this half hour will he be asleep.
      Wilt thou destroy him then?

STEPHANO: Ay, on mine honor.   110

ARIEL: (Aside.) This will I tell my master.

CALIBAN: Thou mak'st me merry; I am full of pleasure.
      Let us be jocund. Will you troll the catch
      You taught me but while-ere?

STEPHANO: At thy request, monster, I will do reason, any rea-   115
      son. Come on, Trinculo, let us sing.

(Sings.)

                "Flout 'em and scout 'em
                And scout 'em and flout 'em!
                    Thought is free."

CALIBAN: That's not the tune.   120

(ARIEL plays the tune on a tabor and pipe.)

STEPHANO: What is this same?

TRINCULO: This is the tune of our catch, play'd by the picture
      of Nobody.

STEPHANO: If thou beest a man, show thyself in thy likeness. If
      thou beest a devil, take 't as thou list.   125

TRINCULO: O, forgive me my sins!

STEPHANO: He that dies pays all debts. I defy thee. Mercy
      upon us!

CALIBAN: Art thou afeard?

STEPHANO: No, monster, not I.   130

CALIBAN: Be not afeard. This isle is full of noises,
      Sounds and sweet airs, that give delight and hurt not.
      Sometimes a thousand twangling instruments
      Will hum about mine ears, and sometimes voices
      That, if I then had wak'd after long sleep,   135
      Will make me sleep again; and then, in dreaming,
      The clouds methought would open and show riches
      Ready to drop upon me, that, when I wak'd,
      I cried to dream again.

STEPHANO: This will prove a brave kingdom to me, where I   140
      shall have my music for nothing.

CALIBAN: When Prospero is destroy'd.

STEPHANO: That shall be by and by. I remember the story.

---

52 **this thing** i.e., Trinculo   60 **pied ninny** fool in motley; **patch**
fool   64 **quick freshes** running springs   67 **stock-fish** dried
cod beaten before cooking   72 **give me the lie** call me a liar to
my face   75 **murrain** plague (literally, a cattle disease)   85
paunch stab in the belly   86 **wezand** windpipe   88 **sot**
fool   91 **brave utensils** fine furnishings

---

113 **troll the catch** sing the round   114 **while-ere** a short time
ago   118 **scout** deride   s.d. **tabor** small drum   122–23 **picture of Nobody** (refers to a familiar figure with head, arms, and
legs, but no trunk   125 **take 't . . . list** i.e., take my defiance as
you please, as best you can

TRINCULO: The sound is going away. Let's follow it, and after
145   do our work.
STEPHANO: Lead, monster; we'll follow. I would I could see this
    taborer; he lays it on.
TRINCULO: Wilt come? I'll follow, Stephano.

(Exeunt {following ARIEL's *music}.)*

SCENE III

Enter ALONSO, SEBASTIAN, ANTONIO, GONZALO, ADRIAN,
FRANCISCO, *etc.*

GONZALO: By 'r lakin, I can go no further, sir;
    My old bones aches. Here's a maze trod indeed
    Through forth-rights and meanders! By your patience,
    I needs must rest me.
ALONSO: Old lord, I cannot blame thee,
5   Who am myself attach'd with weariness,
    To th' dulling of my spirits. Sit down, and rest.
    Even here I will put off my hope and keep it
    No longer for my flatterer. He is drown'd
    Whom thus we stray to find, and the sea mocks
10   Our frustrate search on land. Well, let him go.

*(*ALONSO *and* GONZALO *sit.)*

ANTONIO: *(Aside to* SEBASTIAN.*)* I am right glad that he's so
    out of hope.
    Do not, for one repulse, forego the purpose
    That you resolv'd t' effect.
SEBASTIAN: *(To* ANTONIO.*)*   The next advantage
    Will we take throughly.
ANTONIO: *(To* SEBASTIAN.*)* Let it be tonight,
15   For, now they are oppress'd with travail, they
    Will not, nor cannot, use such vigilance
    As when they are fresh.
SEBASTIAN: *(To* ANTONIO.*)* I say tonight. No more.

(Solemn and strange music; and PROSPERO *on the top, invisible.)*

ALONSO: What harmony is this? My good friends, hark!
GONZALO: Marvelous sweet music!

*(Enter several strange shapes, bringing in a banquet, and dance about
it with gentle actions of salutations; and, inviting* [ALONSO], *etc., to
eat, they depart.)*

20 ALONSO: Give us kind keepers, heavens! What were these?
SEBASTIAN: A living drollery. Now I will believe
    That there are unicorns, that in Arabia
    There is one tree, the phoenix' throne, one phoenix
    At this hour reigning there.

ANTONIO: I'll believe both;
    And what does else want credit, come to me, 25
    And I'll be sworn 'tis true. Travelers ne'er did lie,
    Though fools at home condemn 'em.
GONZALO: If in Naples
    I should report this now, would they believe me
    If I should say I saw such islanders?
    For, certes, these are people of the island, 30
    Who, though they are of monstrous shape, yet, note,
    Their manners are more gentle, kind, than of
    Our human generation you shall find
    Many, nay, almost any.
PROSPERO: *(Aside.)*   Honest lord,
    Thou hast said well; for some of you there present 35
    Are worse than devils.
ALONSO: I cannot too much muse
    Such shapes, such gesture, and such sound, expressing,
    Although they want the use of tongue, a kind
    Of excellent dumb discourse.
PROSPERO: *(Aside.)*   Praise in departing.
FRANCISCO: They vanish'd strangely. 40
SEBASTIAN: No matter, since
    They have left their viands behind; for we have stomachs.
    Will 't please you taste of what is here?
ALONSO: Not I.
GONZALO: Faith, sir, you need not fear. When we were boys,
    Who would believe that there were mountaineers
    Dew-lapp'd like bulls, whose throats had hanging at 'em 45
    Wallets of flesh? Or that there were such men
    Whose heads stood in their breasts? Which now we find
    Each putter-out of five for one will bring us
    Good warrant of.
ALONSO: I will stand to and feed,
    Although my last—no matter, since I feel 50
    The best is past. Brother, my lord the Duke,
    Stand to and do as we.

(They approach the table.)

(Thunder and lightning. Enter ARIEL, *like a harpy; claps his wings
upon the table; and, with a quaint device, the banquet vanishes.)*

ARIEL: You are three men of sin, whom Destiny,
    That hath to instrument this lower world
    And what is in 't, the never-surfeited sea 55

III.iii. Location: Another part of the island. 1 By 'r lakin
by our Ladykin, by our Lady 3 forth-rights and meanders
paths straight and crooked 5 attach'd seized 12 for because
of 14 throughly thoroughly 17 s.d. on the top at some high
point of the tiring-house or the theatre 20 kind keepers
guardian angels 21 drollery puppet show

25 want credit lack credence 30 certes certainly 36 muse
wonder at 39 Praise in departing i.e., save your praise until the
end of the performance 45 Dew-lapp'd having a dewlap, or fold
of skin hanging from the neck, like cattle 47 in their breasts
i.e., like the Anthropophagi described in *Othello* 48 putter-out . . .
one who invests money, or gambles on the risks of travel
on the condition that, if he returns safely, he is to receive five
times the amount deposited; hence, any traveler 49 stand to fall
to; take the risk 52 s.d. harpy a fabulous monster with a woman's
face and vulture's body, supposed to be a minister of divine
vengeance; quaint device ingenious stage contrivance; banquet
vanishes i.e., the food vanishes; the table remains until line 82
54 to i.e., as its

Hath caus'd to belch up you, and on this island
Where man doth not inhabit—you 'mongst men
Being most unfit to live. I have made you mad;
And even with such-like valor men hang and drown
60   Their proper selves.

(ALONSO, SEBASTIAN, and ANTONIO draw their swords.)

You fools! I and my fellows
Are ministers of Fate. The elements,
Of whom your swords are temper'd, may as well
Wound the loud winds, or with bemock'd-at stabs
65   Kill the still-closing waters, as diminish
One dowle that's in my plume. My fellow-ministers
Are like invulnerable. If you could hurt,
Your swords are now too massy for your strengths
And will not be uplifted. But remember—
For that's my business to you—that you three
70   From Milan did supplant good Prospero;
Expos'd unto the sea, which hath requit it,
Him and his innocent child; for which foul deed
The pow'rs, delaying, not forgetting, have
Incens'd the seas and shores, yea, all the creatures,
75   Against your peace. Thee of thy son, Alonso,
They have bereft; and do pronounce by me
Ling'ring perdition, worse than any death
Can be at once, shall step by step attend
You and your ways; whose wraths to guard you from—
80   Which here, in this most desolate isle, else falls
Upon your heads—is nothing but heart's sorrow
And a clear life ensuing.

*(He vanishes in thunder; then, to soft music, enter the shapes again,
and dance, with mocks and mows, and carrying out the table.)*

PROSPERO: Bravely the figure of this harpy hast thou
Perform'd, my Ariel; a grace it had devouring.
85   Of my instruction hast thou nothing bated
In what thou hadst to say. So, with good life
And observation strange, my meaner ministers
Their several kinds have done. My high charms work,
And these mine enemies are all knit up
90   In their distractions. They now are in my pow'r;
And in these fits I leave them, while I visit
Young Ferdinand, whom they suppose is drown'd,
And his and mine lov'd darling.

---

59 **such-like valor** i.e., the reckless valor derived from madness
60 **proper** own 62 **whom** which 64 **still-closing** always closing
again when parted 65 **dowle** soft, fine feather 66 **like** likewise,
similarly; **If** even if 71 **requit** requited, avenged 79 **whose**
refers to the heavenly powers s.d. **mocks and mows** mocking gestures and grimaces 83 **Bravely** finely, dashing 84 **a grace . . .**
devouring i.e., you gracefully caused the banquet to disappear as if
you had consumed it (with puns on *grace* meaning "gracefulness" and
"a blessing on the meal," and on *devouring* meaning "a literal eating"
and "an all-consuming or ravishing grace") 85 **bated** abated, diminished 86 **good life** faithful reproduction 87 **observation**
strange exceptional attention to detail; **meaner** i.e., subordinate to
Ariel 88 **several kinds** individual parts

(Exit above.)

GONZALO: I' th' name of something holy, sir, why stand you
In this strange stare?   95
ALONSO: O, it is monstrous, monstrous!
Methought the billows spoke and told me of it;
The winds did sing it to me, and the thunder,
That deep and dreadful organ-pipe, pronounc'd
The name of Prosper; it did bass my trespass.
Therefore my son i' th' ooze is bedded, and   100
I'll seek him deeper than e'er plummet sounded
And with him there lie mudded.

(Exit.)

SEBASTIAN: But one fiend at a time,
I'll fight their legions o'er.
ANTONIO: I'll be thy second.

(Exeunt [SEBASTIAN and ANTONIO].)

GONZALO: All three of them are desperate. Their great guilt,   105
Like poison given to work a great time after,
Now 'gins to bite the spirits. I do beseech you,
That are of suppler joints, follow them swiftly
And hinder them from what this ecstasy
May now provoke them to.   110
ADRIAN: Follow, I pray you.

(Exeunt omnes.)

——— ACT FOUR ———

SCENE I

Enter PROSPERO, FERDINAND, *and* MIRANDA.

PROSPERO: If I have too austerely punish'd you,
Your compensation makes amends, for I
Have given you here a third of mine own life,
Or that for which I live; who once again
I tender to thy hand. All thy vexations   5
Were but my trials of thy love, and thou
Hast strangely stood the test. Here, afore Heaven,
I ratify this my rich gift. O Ferdinand,
Do not smile at me that I boast her off,
For thou shalt find she will outstrip all praise   10
And make it halt behind her.
FERDINAND: I do believe it
Against an oracle.

---

94 **why** Gonzalo was not addressed in Ariel's speech to the "three
men of sin," line 53, and is not as they are in a maddened state; see
lines 105–07 95 **it** i.e., my sin 99 **bass my trespass** proclaim
my trespass like a bass note in music 104 **o'er** one after another
IV.i. Location: Before Prospero's cell. 3 **a third** i.e., Miranda,
into whose education Prospero has put a third of his life (?) or who
represents a large part of what he cares about, along with his dukedom and his learned study (?) 7 **strangely** extraordinarily 9
boast her off i.e., praise her so 11 **halt** limp 12 **Against an**
oracle i.e., even if an oracle should declare otherwise

PROSPERO: Then, as my gift and thine own acquisition
    Worthily purchas'd, take my daughter. But
15 If thou dost break her virgin-knot before
    All sanctimonious ceremonies may
    With full and holy rite be minist'red,
    No sweet aspersion shall the heavens let fall
    To make this contract grow; but barren hate,
20 Sour-ey'd disdain, and discord shall bestrew
    The union of your bed with weeds so loathly
    That you shall hate it both. Therefore take heed,
    As Hymen's lamps shall light you.
FERDINAND: As I hope
    For quiet days, fair issue, and long life,
25 With such love as 'tis now, the murkiest den,
    The most opportune place, the strong'st suggestion
    Our worser genius can, shall never melt
    Mine honor into lust, to take away
    The edge of that day's celebration
30 When I shall think or Phoebus' steeds are founder'd
    Or Night kept chain'd below.
PROSPERO: Fairly spoke.
    Sit then and talk with her; she is thine own.

(FERDINAND *and* MIRANDA *sit.*)

What, Ariel! My industrious servant, Ariel!

(*Enter* ARIEL.)

ARIEL: What would my potent master? Here I am.
35 PROSPERO: Thou and thy meaner fellows your last service
    Did worthily perform; and I must use you
    In such another trick. Go bring the rabble,
    O'er whom I give thee pow'r, here to this place.
    Incite them to quick motion, for I must
40 Bestow upon the eyes of this young couple
    Some vanity of mine art. It is my promise,
    And they expect it from me.
ARIEL: Presently?
PROSPERO: Ay, with a twink.
ARIEL: Before you can say "come" and "go,"
45   And breathe twice and cry "so, so,"
      Each one, tripping on his toe,
      Will be here with mop and mow.
      Do you love me, master? No?
PROSPERO: Dearly, my delicate Ariel. Do not approach
50 Till thou dost hear me call.
ARIEL: Well, I conceive.

(*Exit.*)

PROSPERO: Look thou be true; do not give dalliance
    Too much the rein. The strongest oaths are straw
    To th' fire i' th' blood. Be more abstemious,
    Or else good night your vow!
FERDINAND: I warrant you, sir;
    The white cold virgin snow upon my heart   55
    Abates the ardor of my liver.
PROSPERO: Well.
    Now come, my Ariel! Bring a corollary,
    Rather than want a spirit. Appear, and pertly!
    No tongue! All eyes! Be silent.

(*Soft music.*)

(*Enter* IRIS.)

IRIS: Ceres, most bounteous lady, thy rich leas   60
    Of wheat, rye, barley, vetches, oats, and pease;
    Thy turfy mountains, where live nibbling sheep,
    And flat meads thatch'd with stover, them to keep;
    Thy banks with pioned and twilled brims,
    Which spongy April at thy hest betrims,   65
    To make cold nymphs chaste crowns; and thy
      broom-groves,
    Whose shadow the dismissed bachelor loves,
    Being lass-lorn; thy pole-clipt vineyard;
    And thy sea-marge, sterile and rocky-hard,
    Where thou thyself dost air—the queen o' th' sky, 70
    Whose wat'ry arch and messenger am I,
    Bids thee leave these, and with her sovereign grace.

(JUNO *descends {slowly in her car}.*)

    Here on this grass-plot, in this very place,
    To come and sport. Her peacocks fly amain.
    Approach, rich Ceres, her to entertain.   75

(*Enter* CERES.)

CERES: Hail, many-color'd messenger, that ne'er
    Dost disobey the wife of Jupiter,
    Who with thy saffron wings upon my flow'rs
    Diffusest honey-drops, refreshing show'rs,
    And with each end of thy blue bow dost crown 80
    My bosky acres and my unshrubb'd down,

---

16 **sanctimonious** sacred   18 **aspersion** dew, shower   23 **Hymen's** Hymen was the Greek and Roman god of marriage   27 **worser genius** evil genius, or evil attendant spirit   30 **or** either; **founder'd** broken down, made lame (i.e., Ferdinand will wait impatiently for the bridal night)   37 **rabble** band, i.e., the *meaner fellows* of line 35   41 **vanity** illusion   47 **mop and mow** gestures and grimaces   50 **conceive** understand

---

56 **liver** as the presumed seat of the passions   57 **corollary** surplus, extra supply   58 **want** lack; **pertly** briskly   s.d. **Iris** goddess of the rainbow, and Juno's messenger   60 **Ceres** goddess of the generative power of nature; **leas** meadows   61 **vetches** plants for forage, fodder   63 **stover** winter fodder for cattle   64 **pioned and twilled** undercut by the swift current and protected by roots and branches woven into a mat (?)   66 **broom-groves** clumps of broom, gorse, yellow-flowered shrub   67 **dismissed bachelor** rejected male lover   68 **pole-clipt** hedged in with poles; or pruned   70 **queen o' th' sky** i.e., Juno   71 **wat'ry arch** rainbow   72 s.d. **Juno descends** i.e., starts her descent from the "heavens" above the stage (?)   74 **peacocks** birds sacred to Juno, and used to pull her chariot; **amain** with full speed   75 **entertain** receive   81 **bosky** wooded; **down** upland

Rich scarf to my proud earth; why hath thy Queen
Summon'd me hither, to this short-grass'd green?
IRIS: A contract of true love to celebrate,
85   And some donation freely to estate
       On the bless'd lovers.
       CERES: Tell me, heavenly bow,
       If Venus or her son, as thou dost know,
       Do now attend the Queen? Since they did plot
       The means that dusky Dis my daughter got,
90   Her and her blind boy's scandal'd company
       I have forsworn.
       IRIS: Of her society
       Be not afraid. I met her deity
       Cutting the clouds towards Paphos, and her son
       Dove-drawn with her. Here thought they to have done
95   Some wanton charm upon this man and maid,
       Whose vows are, that no bed-right shall be paid
       Till Hymen's torch be lighted; but in vain;
       Mars's hot minion is return'd again;
       Her waspish-headed son has broke his arrows,
100   Swears he will shoot no more, but play with sparrows
       And be a boy right out.

(JUNO alights.)

       CERES: Highest Queen of state,
       Great Juno, comes; I know her by her gait.
       JUNO: How does my bounteous sister? Go with me
       To bless this twain, that they may prosperous be
105   And honor'd in their issue.

(They sing.)

       JUNO: Honor, riches, marriage-blessing,
                 Long continuance, and increasing,
                 Hourly joys be still upon you!
                 Juno sings her blessings on you.

110   CERES: Earth's increase, foison plenty,
                 Barns and garners never empty,
                 Vines with clust'ring bunches growing,
                 Plants with goodly burden bowing;
                 Spring come to you at the farthest
115   In the very end of harvest!
                 Scarcity and want shall shun you;
                 Ceres' blessing so is on you.

       FERDINAND: This is a most majestic vision, and
       Harmonious charmingly. May I be bold
120   To think these spirits?
       PROSPERO: Spirits, which by mine art
       I have from their confines call'd to enact
       My present fancies.

FERDINAND: Let me live here ever;
So rare a wond'red father and a wife
Makes this place Paradise.

(JUNO and CERES whisper, and send IRIS on employment.)

PROSPERO: Sweet now, silence!
Juno and Ceres whisper seriously;   125
There's something else to do. Hush and be mute,
Or else our spell is marr'd.
IRIS: You nymphs, call'd Naiads, of the windring brooks,
With your sedg'd crowns and ever-harmless looks,
Leave your crisp channels, and on this green land   130
Answer your summons; Juno does command.
Come, temperate nymphs, and help to celebrate
A contract of true love; be not too late.

(Enter certain NYMPHS.)

You sunburnt sicklemen, of August weary,
Come hither from the furrow and be merry.   135
Make holiday; your rye-straw hats put on
And these fresh nymphs encounter every one
In country footing.

(Enter certain REAPERS, properly habited. They join with the NYMPHS in a graceful dance, towards the end whereof PROSPERO starts suddenly, and speaks; after which, to a strange, hollow, and confused noise, they heavily vanish.)

PROSPERO: (Aside.) I had forgot that foul conspiracy
Of the beast Caliban and his confederates   140
Against my life. The minute of their plot
Is almost come. (To the SPIRITS.) Well done! Avoid; no
       more!
FERDINAND: This is strange. Your father's in some passion
That works him strongly.
MIRANDA: Never till this day
Saw I him touch'd with anger so distemper'd.   145
PROSPERO: You do look, my son, in a mov'd sort,
As if you were dismay'd. Be cheerful, sir.
Our revels now are ended. These our actors,
As I foretold you, were all spirits and
Are melted into air, into thin air;   150
And, like the baseless fabric of this vision,
The cloud-capp'd tow'rs, the gorgeous palaces,
The solemn temples, the great globe itself,
Yea, all which it inherit, shall dissolve
And, like this insubstantial pageant faded,   155
Leave not a rack behind. We are such stuff
As dreams are made on, and our little life
Is rounded with a sleep. Sir, I am vex'd.
Bear with my weakness; my old brain is troubled.

---

85 **estate** bestow   87 **son** i.e., Cupid   89 **Dis . . . got** Pluto, or *Dis,* god of the infernal regions, carried off Persephone, daughter of Ceres, to be his bride in Hades   90 **Her** i.e., Venus; **scandal'd** scandalous   92 **her deity** i.e., her highness   93 **Paphos** place on the island of Cyprus, sacred to Venus   98 **Mars' hot minion** i.e., Venus, the beloved of Mars   99 **waspish-headed** fiery, hot-headed, peevish   100 **sparrows** supposed lustful, and sacred to Venus   101 **right out** outright   110 **foison plenty** plentiful harvest   111 **garners** granaries

---

123 **wond'red** wonder-performing, wondrous; **wife** sometimes emended to *wise*   128 **windring** wandering, winding (?)   130 **crisp** curled, rippled   132 **temperate** chaste   138 **country footing** country dancing; s.d. **heavily** slowly, dejectedly   142 **Avoid** depart, withdraw   146 **mov'd sort** troubled state, condition   148 **revels** entertainments, pageants   151 **baseless** without substance   154 **which it inherit** who occupy it   156 **rack** wisp of cloud   157 **on** of

160 Be not disturb'd with my infirmity.
If you be pleas'd, retire into my cell
And there repose. A turn or two I'll walk
To still my beating mind.
FERDINAND, MIRANDA: We wish your peace.

(Exeunt.)

PROSPERO: Come with a thought! I thank thee, Ariel. Come.

(Enter ARIEL.*)*

165 ARIEL: Thy thoughts I cleave to. What's thy pleasure?
PROSPERO: Spirit,
We must prepare to meet with Caliban.
ARIEL: Ay, my commander. When I presented Ceres,
I thought to have told thee of it, but I fear'd
Lest I might anger thee.
170 PROSPERO: Say again, where didst thou leave these varlets?
ARIEL: I told you, sir, they were red-hot with drinking,
So full of valor that they smote the air
For breathing in their faces; beat the ground
For kissing of their feet; yet always bending
175 Towards their project. Then I beat my tabor,
At which, like unback'd colts, they prick'd their ears,
Advanc'd their eyelids, lifted up their noses
As they smelt music. So I charm'd their ears
That calf-like they my lowing follow'd through
180 Tooth'd briers, sharp furzes, pricking goss, and thorns,
Which ent'red their frail shins. At last I left them
I' th' filthy-mantled pool beyond your cell,
There dancing up to th' chins, that the foul lake
O'erstunk their feet.
PROSPERO: This was well done, my bird.
185 Thy shape invisible retain thou still.
The trumpery in my house, go bring it hither,
For stale to catch these thieves.
ARIEL: I go, I go.

(Exit.)

PROSPERO: A devil, a born devil, on whose nature
Nurture can never stick; on whom my pains,
190 Humanely taken, all, all lost, quite lost!
And as with age his body uglier grows,
So his mind cankers. I will plague them all,
Even to roaring.

(Enter ARIEL, *loaden with glistering apparel, etc.)*

Come, hang them on this line.

*({*ARIEL *hangs up the showy finery;* PROSPERO *and* ARIEL *remain, invisible.} Enter* CALIBAN, STEPHANO, *and* TRINCULO, *all wet.)*

---

164 **with a thought** i.e., on the instant, or summoned by my thought, no sooner thought on than here   167 **presented** acted the part of, or introduced   176 **unback'd** unbroken, unridden   177 **Advanc'd** lifted up   180 **goss** gorse, a prickly shrub   182 **filthy-mantled** covered with a slimy coating   186 **trumpery** cheap goods, the *glistering apparel* mentioned in the following stage direction   187 **stale** (1) decoy (2) out of fashion garments (with possible further suggestions of *fit for a stale* or prostitute, *stale* meaning "horse-piss," line 198, and *steal*, pronounced like *stale*)   192 **cankers** festers, grows malignant   193 **line** lime tree or linden

CALIBAN: Pray you, tread softly, that the blind mole may not
Hear a foot fall. We now are near his cell.   195
STEPHANO: Monster, your fairy, which you say is a harmless
fairy, has done little better than play'd the Jack with us.
TRINCULO: Monster, I do smell all horse-piss, at which my nose
is in great indignation.
STEPHANO: So is mine. Do you hear, monster? If I should take   200
a displeasure against you, look you—
TRINCULO: Thou wert but a lost monster.
CALIBAN: Good my lord, give me thy favor still.
Be patient, for the prize I'll bring thee to
Shall hoodwink this mischance. Therefore speak softly.   205
All's hush'd as midnight yet.
TRINCULO: Ay, but to lose our bottles in the pool—
STEPHANO: There is not only disgrace and dishonor in that,
monster, but an infinite loss.
TRINCULO: That's more to me than my wetting. Yet this is your 210
harmless fairy, monster!
STEPHANO: I will fetch off my bottle, though I be o'er ears for
my labor.
CALIBAN: Prithee, my King, be quiet. See'st thou here,
This is the mouth o' th' cell. No noise, and enter.   215
Do that good mischief which may make this island
Thine own for ever, and I, thy Caliban,
For aye thy foot-licker.
STEPHANO: Give me thy hand. I do begin to have bloody
thoughts.   220
TRINCULO: *(Seeing the finery.)* O King Stephano! O peer! O wor-
thy Stephano! Look what a wardrobe here is for thee!
CALIBAN: Let it alone, thou fool! It is but trash.
TRINCULO: O, ho, monster! We know what belongs to a frip-
pery. O King Stephano! *(Takes a gown.)*   225
STEPHANO: Put off that gown, Trinculo. By this hand, I'll have
that gown.
TRINCULO: Thy Grace shall have it.
CALIBAN: The dropsy drown this fool! What do you mean
To dote thus on such luggage? Let's alone   230
And do the murder first. If he awake,
From toe to crown he'll fill our skins with pinches,
Make us strange stuff.
STEPHANO: Be you quiet, monster. Mistress line, is not this my
jerkin? *(Takes it down.)* Now is the jerkin under the line. 235
Now, jerkin, you are like to lose your hair and prove a bald
jerkin.
TRINCULO: Do, do! We steal by line and level, an 't like your
Grace.

---

197 **Jack** (1) Knave (2) will-o-the-wisp   205 **hoodwink** cover up, make you not see (a hawking term)   221 **King . . . peer** alludes to the old ballad beginning, "King Stephen was a worthy peer"   224 **frippery** place where cast-off clothes are sold   230 **luggage** cumbersome trash   235 **jerkin** jacket make of leather; **under the line** under the lime tree (with punning sense of being south of the equinoctial line or equator; sailors to the southern regions were popularly supposed to lose their hair from scurvy or other diseases. Stephano also quibbles bawdily on losing hair through syphilis, and in *Mistress* and *jerkin*)   238 **by line and level** i.e., by means of plumb-line and carpenter's level, methodically (with pun on *line*, "lime tree," line 235, and *steal* pronounced *stale*, i.e., prostitute, continuing Stephano's bawdy quibble); **an 't like** if it please

240 STEPHANO: I thank thee for that jest. Here's a garment for 't.
     (Gives a garment.) Wit shall not go unrewarded while I am
     king of this country. "Steal by line and level" is an excellent
     pass of pate. There's another garment for 't.
     TRINCULO: Monster, come, put some lime upon your fingers,
245 and away with the rest.
     CALIBAN: I have none on 't. We shall lose our time,
     And all be turn'd to barnacles, or to apes
     With foreheads villainous low.
     STEPHANO: Monster, lay to your fingers. Help to bear this away
250 where my hogshead of wine is, or I'll turn you out of my
     kingdom. Go to, carry this.
     TRINCULO: And this.
     STEPHANO: Ay, and this.

(They collect more and more garments.)

(A noise of hunters heard. Enter divers SPIRITS, *in shape of dogs and
hounds, hunting them about,* PROSPERO *and* ARIEL *setting them on.)*

     PROSPERO: Hey, Mountain, hey!
255 ARIEL: Silver! There it goes, Silver!
     PROSPERO: Fury, Fury! There, Tyrant, there! Hark! Hark!

*(*CALIBAN, STEPHANO, *and* TRINCULO *are driven out.)*

     Go charge my goblins that they grind their joints
     With dry convulsions, shorten up their sinews
     With aged cramps, and more pitch-spotted make them
260 Than pard or cat o' mountain.
     ARIEL: Hark, they roar!
     PROSPERO: Let them be hunted soundly. At this hour
     Lies at my mercy all mine enemies.
     Shortly shall all my labors end, and thou
     Shalt have the air at freedom. For a little
265 Follow, and do me service.

(Exeunt.)

———— ACT FIVE ————

SCENE I

Enter PROSPERO *in his magic robes, {with his staff,} and* ARIEL.

     PROSPERO: Now does my project gather to a head.
     My charms crack not, my spirits obey, and Time
     Goes upright with his carriage. How's the day?
     ARIEL: On the sixth hour; at which time, my lord,
5   You said our work should cease.

PROSPERO: I did say so,
     When first I rais'd the tempest. Say, my spirit,
     How fares the King and 's followers?
ARIEL: Confin'd together
     In the same fashion as you gave in charge,
     Just as you left them; all prisoners, sir,
     In the line-grove which weather-fends your cell.   10
     They cannot budge till your release. The King,
     His brother, and yours, abide all three distracted,
     And the remainder mourning over them,
     Brimful of sorrow and dismay; but chiefly
     Him that you term'd, sir, "The good old lord, Gonzalo." 15
     His tears runs down his beard like winter's drops
     From eaves of reeds. Your charm so strongly works 'em
     That if you now beheld them, your affections
     Would become tender.
PROSPERO: Dost thou think so, spirit?
ARIEL: Mine would, sir, were I human.   20
PROSPERO: And mine shall.
     Hast thou, which art but air, a touch, a feeling
     Of their afflictions, and shall not myself,
     One of their kind, that relish all as sharply,
     Passion as they, be kindlier mov'd than thou art?
     Though with their high wrongs I am struck to th' quick, 25
     Yet with my nobler reason 'gainst my fury
     Do I take part. The rarer action is
     In virtue than in vengeance. They being penitent,
     The sole drift of my purpose doth extend
     Not a frown further. Go release them, Ariel.   30
     My charms I'll break, their senses I'll restore,
     And they shall be themselves.
ARIEL: I'll fetch them, sir.

(Exit.)

*(*PROSPERO *traces a charmed circle with his staff.)*

PROSPERO: Ye elves of hills, brooks, standing lakes, and groves,
     And ye that on the sands with printless foot
     Do chase the ebbing Neptune, and do fly him   35
     When he comes back; you demi-puppets that
     By moonshine do the green sour ringlets make,
     Whereof the ewe not bites; and you whose pastime
     Is to make midnight mushrooms, that rejoice
     To hear the solemn curfew; by whose aid,   40
     Weak masters though ye be, I have bedimm'd
     The noontide sun, call'd forth the mutinous winds,
     And 'twixt the green sea and the azur'd vault
     Set roaring war; to the dread rattling thunder
     Have I given fire, and rifted Jove's stout oak   45

---

243 **pass of pate** sally of wit   244 **lime** birdlime, sticky substance (to give Caliban sticky fingers)   247 **barnacles** barnacle geese, formerly supposed to be hatched from seashells attached to trees and to fall thence into the water; here evidently used, like *apes,* as types of simpletons   248 **villainous** miserably   258 **dry** associated with age, arthritic (?); **convulsions** cramps   259 **aged** characteristic of old age   260 **pard** panther or leopard; **cat o' mountain** wildcat

V.i. Location: Before Prospero's cell.   3 **his carriage** its burden (i.e., Time is unstopped, runs smoothly)

---

10 **line-grove** grove of lime trees; **weather-fends** protects from the weather   11 **your release** you release them   17 **eaves of reeds** thatched roofs   23 **relish all** experience quite   24 **Passion** experience deep feeling   27 **rarer** nobler   33–50 **Ye . . . art** this famous passage is an embellished paraphrase of Golding's translation of Ovid's *Metamorphoses,* 7.197–219   36 **demi-puppets** puppets of half-size, i.e., elves and fairies   37 **green sour ringlets** fairy rings, circles in grass (actually produced by mushrooms)   44–45 **to . . . fire** I have discharged the dread rattling thunderbolt   45 **rifted** riven, split

With his own bolt; the strong-bas'd promontory
Have I made shake, and by the spurs pluck'd up
The pine and cedar; graves at my command
Have wak'd their sleepers, op'd, and let 'em forth
50 By my so potent art. But this rough magic
I here abjure, and, when I have requir'd
Some heavenly music, which even now I do,
To work mine end upon their senses that
This airy charm is for, I'll break my staff,
55 Bury it certain fathoms in the earth,
And deeper than did ever plummet sound
I'll drown my book.

(Solemn music.)

(Here enters ARIEL *before; then* ALONSO, *with a frantic gesture, attended by* GONZALO; SEBASTIAN *and* ANTONIO *in like manner, attended by* ADRIAN *and* FRANCISCO. *They all enter the circle which* PROSPERO *had made, and there stand charm'd; which* PROSPERO *observing, speaks:)*

A solemn air, and the best comforter
To an unsettled fancy, cure thy brains,
60 Now useless, boil'd within thy skull! There stand,
For you are spell-stopp'd.
Holy Gonzalo, honorable man,
Mine eyes, ev'n sociable to the show of thine,
Fall fellowly drops. The charm dissolves apace,
65 And as the morning steals upon the night,
Melting the darkness, so their rising senses
Begin to chase the ignorant fumes that mantle
Their clearer reason. O good Gonzalo,
My true preserver, and a loyal sir
70 To him thou follow'st! I will pay thy graces
Home both in word and deed. Most cruelly
Didst thou, Alonso, use me and my daughter.
Thy brother was a furtherer in the act.
Thou art pinch'd for 't now, Sebastian. Flesh and blood,
75 You, brother mine, that entertain'd ambition,
Expell'd remorse and nature, who, with Sebastian,
Whose inward pinches therefore are most strong,
Would here have kill'd your king, I do forgive thee,
Unnatural though thou art.—Their understanding
80 Begins to swell, and the approaching tide
Will shortly fill the reasonable shore
That now lies foul and muddy. Not one of them
That yet looks on me, or would know me. Ariel,
Fetch me the hat and rapier in my cell.

(ARIEL goes to the cell and returns immediately.)

85 I will discase me, and myself present
As I was sometime Milan. Quickly, spirit;
Thou shalt ere long be free.

(ARIEL sings and helps to attire him.)

ARIEL: Where the bee sucks, there suck I;
In a cowslip's bell I lie;
There I couch when owls do cry.   90
On the bat's back I do fly
After summer merrily.
Merrily, merrily shall I live now
Under the blossom that hangs on the bough.

PROSPERO: Why, that's my dainty Ariel! I shall miss thee;   95
But yet thou shalt have freedom. So, so, so.
To the King's ship, invisible as thou art!
There shalt thou find the mariners asleep
Under the hatches. The master and the boatswain
Being awake, enforce them to this place,   100
And presently, I prithee.
ARIEL: I drink the air before me, and return
Or ere your pulse twice beat. *(Exit.)*
GONZALO: All torment, trouble, wonder, and amazement
Inhabits here. Some heavenly power guide us   105
Out of this fearful country!
PROSPERO: Behold, sir King,
The wronged Duke of Milan, Prospero.
For more assurance that a living prince
Does now speak to thee, I embrace thy body;
And to thee and thy company I bid   110
A hearty welcome.

(Embraces him.)

ALONSO: Whe'er thou be'st he or no,
Or some enchanted trifle to abuse me,
As late I have been, I not know. Thy pulse
Beats as of flesh and blood; and, since I saw thee,
Th' affliction of my mind amends, with which,   115
I fear, a madness held me. This must crave,
An if this be at all, a most strange story.
Thy dukedom I resign, and do entreat
Thou pardon me my wrongs. But how should Prospero
Be living and be here?   120
PROSPERO: *(To* GONZALO.)   First, noble friend,
Let me embrace thine age, whose honor cannot
Be measur'd or confin'd.

(Embraces him.)

GONZALO: Whether this be
Or be not, I'll not swear.
PROSPERO: Yet do yet taste
Some subtleties o' th' isle, that will not let you
Believe things certain. Welcome, my friends all!   125
(Aside to SEBASTIAN *and* ANTONIO.) But you, my brace of
lords, were I so minded,

I here could pluck his Highness' frown upon you
And justify you traitors. At this time
I will tell no tales.
SEBASTIAN: The devil speaks in him.
PROSPERO: No.
130 For you, most wicked sir, whom to call brother
Would even infect my mouth, I do forgive
Thy rankest fault—all of them; and require
My dukedom of thee, which perforce I know
Thou must restore.
ALONSO: If thou be'st Prospero,
135 Give us particulars of thy preservation,
How thou hast met us here, who three hours since
Were wrack'd upon this shore; where I have lost—
How sharp the point of this remembrance is!—
My dear son Ferdinand.
PROSPERO: I am woe for 't, sir.
140 ALONSO: Irreparable is the loss, and Patience
Says it is past her cure.
PROSPERO: I rather think
You have not sought her help, of whose soft grace
For the like loss I have her sovereign aid
And rest myself content.
ALONSO: You the like loss?
145 PROSPERO: As great to me as late; and, supportable
To make the dear loss, have I means much weaker
Than you may call to comfort you, for I
Have lost my daughter.
ALONSO: A daughter?
150 O heavens, that they were living both in Naples,
The king and queen there! That they were, I wish
Myself were mudded in that oozy bed
Where my son lies. When did you lose your daughter?
PROSPERO: In this last tempest. I perceive these lords
155 At this encounter do so much admire
That they devour their reason and scarce think
Their eyes do offices of truth, their words
Are natural breath. But, howsoev'r you have
Been justled from your senses, know for certain
160 That I am Prospero and that very duke
Which was thrust forth of Milan, who most strangely
Upon this shore, where you were wrack'd, was landed,
To be the lord on 't. No more yet of this,
For 'tis a chronicle of day by day,
165 Not a relation for a breakfast nor
Befitting this first meeting. Welcome, sir;
This cell's my court. Here have I few attendants
And subjects none abroad. Pray you look in.
My dukedom since you have given me again,
170 I will requite you with as good a thing,
At least bring forth a wonder, to content ye
As much as me my dukedom.

(*Here* PROSPERO *discovers* FERDINAND *and* MIRANDA, *playing at chess.*)

MIRANDA: Sweet lord, you play me false.
FERDINAND: No, my dearest love,
I would not for the world.   175
MIRANDA: Yes, for a score of kingdoms you should wrangle,
And I would call it fair play.
ALONSO: If this prove
A vision of the island, one dear son
Shall I twice lose.
SEBASTIAN: A most high miracle!
FERDINAND: Though the seas threaten, they are merciful; 180
I have curs'd them without cause. (*Kneels.*)
ALONSO: Now all the blessings
Of a glad father compass thee about!
Arise, and say how thou cam'st here.
MIRANDA: O, wonder!
How many goodly creatures are there here!
How beauteous mankind is! O brave new world,   185
That has such people in 't!
PROSPERO: 'Tis new to thee.
ALONSO: What is this maid with whom thou wast at play?
Your eld'st acquaintance cannot be three hours.
Is she the goddess that hath sever'd us,
And brought us thus together?   190
FERDINAND: Sir, she is mortal;
But by immortal Providence she's mine.
I chose her when I could not ask my father
For his advice, nor thought I had one. She
Is daughter to this famous Duke of Milan,
Of whom so often I have heard renown,   195
But never saw before; of whom I have
Receiv'd a second life; and second father
This lady makes him to me.
ALONSO: I am hers.
But, O, how oddly will it sound that I
Must ask my child forgiveness!   200
PROSPERO: There, sir, stop.
Let us not burden our remembrances with
A heaviness that's gone.
GONZALO: I have inly wept
Or should have spoke ere this. Look down, you gods,
And on this couple drop a blessed crown!
For it is you that have chalk'd forth the way   205
Which brought us hither.
ALONSO: I say Amen, Gonzalo!
GONZALO: Was Milan thrust from Milan, that his issue
Should become kings of Naples? O, rejoice
Beyond a common joy, and set it down
With gold on lasting pillars: In one voyage   210
Did Claribel her husband find at Tunis,
And Ferdinand, her brother, found a wife

---

128 **justify you** prove you to be   139 **woe** sorry   145 **late** recent   155 **admire** wonder   156–58 **scarce . . . breath** scarcely
believe that their eyes inform them accurately what they see or
that their words are naturally spoken   172 s.d. **discovers** i.e., by
opening a curtain, presumably rear-stage

176–77 **Yes . . . play** i.e., yes, even if we were playing for twenty
kingdoms, something less than the whole world, you would still
contend mightily against me and play me false, and I would let
you do it as though it were fair play; or, if you were to play not
just for stakes but literally for kingdoms, my accusation of
false play would be out of order in that your "wrangling" would
be proper   185 **brave** splendid, gorgeously appareled, handsome   188 **eld'st** longest   207 **Was Milan** was the Duke of
Milan

Where he himself was lost; Prospero his dukedom
In a poor isle; and all of us ourselves
215   When no man was his own.
ALONSO: *(To* FERDINAND *and* MIRANDA.*)* Give me your hands.
Let grief and sorrow still embrace his heart
That doth not wish you joy!
GONZALO: Be it so! Amen!

(Enter ARIEL, *with the* MASTER *and* BOATSWAIN *amazedly following.)*

O, look, sir, look, sir! Here is more of us.
I prophesied, if a gallows were on land,
220   This fellow could not drown. Now, blasphemy,
That swear'st grace o'erboard, not an oath on shore?
Hast thou no mouth by land? What is the news?
BOATSWAIN: The best news is that we have safely found
Our King and company; the next, our ship—
225   Which, but three glasses since, we gave out split—
Is tight and yare and bravely rigg'd as when
We first put out to sea.
ARIEL: *(Aside to* PROSPERO.*)* Sir, all this service
Have I done since I went.
PROSPERO: *(Aside to* ARIEL.*)* My tricksy spirit!
ALONSO: These are not natural events; they strengthen
230   From strange to stranger. Say, how came you hither?
BOATSWAIN: If I did think, sir, I were well awake,
I'd strive to tell you. We were dead of sleep,
And—how we know not—all clapp'd under hatches;
Where but even now with strange and several noises
235   Of roaring, shrieking, howling, jingling chains,
And moe diversity of sounds, all horrible,
We were awak'd; straightway, at liberty;
Where we, in all her trim, freshly beheld
Our royal, good, and gallant ship, our master
240   Cap'ring to eye her. On a trice, so please you,
Even in a dream, were we divided from them
And were brought moping hither.
ARIEL: *(Aside to* PROSPERO.*)*   Was 't well done?
PROSPERO: *(Aside to* ARIEL.*)* Bravely, my diligence. Thou shalt
be free.
ALONSO: This is as strange a maze as e'er men trod,
245   And there is in this business more than nature
Was ever conduct of. Some oracle
Must rectify our knowledge.
PROSPERO: Sir, my liege,
Do not infest your mind with beating on
The strangeness of this business. At pick'd leisure,
250   Which shall be shortly, single I'll resolve you,
Which to you shall seem probable, of every
These happen'd accidents; till when, be cheerful
And think of each thing well. *(Aside to* ARIEL.*)* Come
hither, spirit.
Set Caliban and his companions free;

---

216 **still** always; **his** that man's   217 **That** who   225 **glasses**
i.e., hours; **gave out** reported   226 **yare** ready   240 **Cap'ring**
to eye dancing for joy to see   242 **moping** in a daze   246 **con-**
duct guide, leader   248 **infest** harass, disturb   249 **pick'd** chosen, convenient   250 **single** i.e., by my own human powers   252
accidents occurrences

Untie the spell. *(Exit* ARIEL.*)* How fares my gracious sir?   255
There are yet missing of your company
Some few odd lads that you remember not.

(Enter ARIEL, *driving in* CALIBAN, STEPHANO, *and* TRINCULO, *in
their stol'n apparel.)*

STEPHANO: Every man shift for all the rest, and let no man take
care of himself; for all is but fortune. Coragio, bully-monster,
coragio!   260
TRINCULO: If these be true spies which I wear in my head, here's
a goodly sight.
CALIBAN: O Setebos, these be brave spirits indeed!
How fine my master is! I am afraid
He will chastise me.   265
SEBASTIAN: Ha, ha!
What things are these, my lord, Antonio?
Will money buy 'em?
ANTONIO: Very like. One of them
Is a plain fish, and no doubt marketable.
PROSPERO: Mark but the badges of these men, my lords,   270
Then say if they be true. This misshapen knave,
His mother was a witch, and one so strong
That could control the moon, make flows and ebbs,
And deal in her command without her power.
These three have robb'd me; and this demi-devil—   275
For he's a bastard one—had plotted with them
To take my life. Two of these fellows you
Must know and own; this thing of darkness I
Acknowledge mine.
CALIBAN: I shall be pinch'd to death.
ALONSO: Is not this Stephano, my drunken butler?   280
SEBASTIAN: He is drunk now. Where had he wine?
ALONSO: And Trinculo is reeling ripe. Where should they
Find this grand liquor that hath gilded 'em?
How cam'st thou in this pickle?
TRINCULO: I have been in such a pickle since I saw you last that,   285
I fear me, will never out of my bones. I shall not fear fly-
blowing.
SEBASTIAN: Why, how now, Stephano?
STEPHANO: O, touch me not! I am not Stephano, but a cramp.   290
PROSPERO: You'd be king o' the isle, sirrah?
STEPHANO: I should have been a sore one then.
ALONSO: *(Pointing to* CALIBAN.*)* This is a strange thing as e'er
I look'd on.

---

259 **Coragio** courage; **bully-monster** gallant monster
(ironical)   264 **fine** splendidly attired   270 **badges** emblems of
cloth or silver worn on the arms of retainers. Prospero refers here
to the stolen clothes as emblems of their villainy   271 **true** honest   274 **deal . . . power** wield the moon's power, either without
her authority or beyond her influence   278 **own** recognize, admit
as belonging to you   283 **gilded** (1) flushed, made drunk (2) covered with gilt (suggesting the horse-urine)   284 **pickle** (1) fix,
predicament (2) pickling brine (in this case, horse urine)
286–87 **fly-blowing** i.e., being fouled by fly-eggs (from which he
is saved by being pickled)   291 **sirrah** Standard form of address
to an inferior   292 **sore** (1) tyrannical (2) wracked by pain

PROSPERO: He is as disproportion'd in his manners
295   As in his shape. Go, sirrah, to my cell;
       Take with you your companions. As you look
       To have my pardon, trim it handsomely.
CALIBAN: Ay, that I will; and I'll be wise hereafter
       And seek for grace. What a thrice-double ass
300   Was I to take this drunkard for a god
       And worship this dull fool!
PROSPERO: Go to; away!
ALONSO: Hence, and bestow your luggage where you found it.
SEBASTIAN: Or stole it, rather.

       (*Exeunt* CALIBAN, STEPHANO, *and* TRINCULO.)

PROSPERO: Sir, I invite your Highness and your train
305   To my poor cell, where you shall take your rest
       For this one night; which, part of it, I'll waste
       With such discourse as, I not doubt, shall make it
       Go quick away—the story of my life,
       And the particular accidents gone by
310   Since I came to this isle. And in the morn
       I'll bring you to your ship, and so to Naples,
       Where I have hope to see the nuptial
       Of these our dear-belov'd solemnized;
       And thence retire me to my Milan, where
315   Every third thought shall be my grave.
ALONSO: I long
       To hear the story of your life, which must
       Take the ear strangely.
PROSPERO: I'll deliver all;
       And promise you calm seas, auspicious gales,
       And sail so expeditious that shall catch
320   Your royal fleet far off. (*Aside to* ARIEL.) My Ariel, chick,

---

306 **waste** spend   309 **accidents** occurrences   317 **Take** take
effect upon, enchant; **deliver** declare, relate

That is thy charge. Then to the elements
Be free, and fare thou well!—Please you, draw near.

(*Exeunt omnes.*)

——— **EPILOGUE** ———

Spoken by PROSPERO.

Now my charms are all o'erthrown,
And what strength I have 's mine own,
Which is most faint. Now, 'tis true,
I must be here confin'd by you,
Or sent to Naples. Let me not,   5
Since I have my dukedom got
And pardon'd the deceiver, dwell
In this bare island by your spell,
But release me from my bands
With the help of your good hands.   10
Gentle breath of yours my sails
Must fill, or else my project fails,
Which was to please. Now I want
Spirits to enforce, art to enchant,
And my ending is despair,   15
Unless I be reliev'd by prayer,
Which pierces so that it assaults
Mercy itself and frees all faults.
As you from crimes would pardon'd be,
Let your indulgence set me free.   20

(*Exit.*)

---

322 **draw near** i.e., enter my cell

Epilogue   9 **bands** bonds   10 **hands** i.e., applause (the noise
of which would break the spell of silence)   13 **want** lack
16 **prayer** i.e., Prospero's petition to the audience   17 **assaults**
rightfully gains the attention of   18 **frees** obtains forgiveness
of   19 **crimes** sins

CRITICAL CONTEXTS

SIR PHILIP SIDNEY
(1554–1586)

from *Apology for Poetry*
(1598)

EDITED BY
FORREST G. ROBINSON

Philip Sidney was one of the preeminent courtiers of his day. He was a familiar figure at the court of Queen Elizabeth I, led an ill-fated military expedition to the Netherlands (where he was fatally wounded), wrote an important sonnet sequence, Astrophil and Stella, *and a prose romance,* Arcadia. *His* Apology for Poetry *develops a defense of poets and poetry based on their ability to offer a fictive "golden world," an idealized image of reality that can edify, entertain, and instruct.*

. . . There is no art delivered to mankind that hath not the works of nature for his principal object, without which they could not consist, and on which they so depend, as they become actors and players, as it were, of what nature will have set forth. So doth the astronomer look upon the stars, and by that he seeth, setteth down what order nature hath taken therein. So do the geometrician and arithmetician in their diverse sorts of quantities. So doth the musician in times tell you which by nature agree, which not. The natural philosopher thereon hath his name, and the moral philosopher standeth upon the natural virtues, vices, and passions of man; and follow nature (saith he) therein, and thou shalt not err. The lawyer saith what men have determined; the historian what men have done. The grammarian speaketh only of the rules of speech, and the rhetorician and logician, considering what in nature will soonest prove and persuade, thereon give artificial[1] rules, which still are compassed within the circle of a question, according to the proposed matter. The physician weigheth the nature of a man's body, and the nature of things helpful or hurtful unto it. And the metaphysic, though it be in the second and abstract notions, and therefore be counted supernatural, yet doth he indeed build upon the depth of nature. Only the poet, disdaining to be tied to any such subjection, lifted up with the vigor of his own invention, doth grow in effect another nature, in making things either better than nature bringeth forth, or quite anew, forms such as never were in nature, as the Heroes, Demigods, Cyclops, Chimeras, Furies, and such like; so as he goeth hand in hand with nature, not enclosed within the narrow warrant of her gifts, but freely ranging only within the zodiac of his own wit.

Nature never set forth the earth in so rich tapestry as divers poets have done, neither with pleasant rivers, fruitful trees, sweet smelling flowers, nor whatsoever else may make the too much loved earth more lovely. Her world is brazen, the poets only deliver a golden. . . .

Our tragedies and comedies (not without cause cried out against), observing rules neither of honest civility nor of skillful poetry, excepting *Gorboduc*[2] (again I say, of those that I have seen), which notwithstanding, as it is full of stately speeches and well sounding phrases, climbing to the height of Seneca his[3] style, and as full of notable morality, which it doth most delightfully teach, and so obtain the very end of poesy; yet in troth it is very defectious in the circumstances, which grieveth me, because it might not remain as an exact model of all tragedies. For it is faulty both in place and time, the two necessary companions of all corporal actions. For where the stage should always represent but one place, and the uttermost time presupposed in it should be, both by Aristotle's precept and common reason, but one day, there is both many days and many places inartificially[4] imagined.

---

[1]**artificial** humanly contrived, rather than natural
[2]***Gorboduc*** an early English play (first performed in 1562), modeled on the tragedies of Seneca
[3]**Seneca his** Seneca's
[4]**inartificially** artlessly

But if it be so in *Gorboduc,* how much more in all the rest? where you shall have Asia of the one side, and Afric of the other, and so many other under-kingdoms, that the player, when he cometh in, must ever begin with telling where he is, or else the tale will not be conceived. Now ye shall have three ladies walk to gather flowers, and then we must believe the stage to be a garden. By and by we hear news of shipwreck in the same place, and then we are to blame if we accept it not for a rock. Upon the back of that comes out a hideous monster with fire and smoke, and then the miserable beholders are bound to take it for a cave. While in the meantime two armies fly in, represented with four swords and bucklers, and then what hard heart will not receive it for a pitched field?

Now of time they are much more liberal, for ordinary it is that two young princes fall in love. After many traverses, she is got with child, delivered of a fair boy, he is lost, groweth a man, falls in love, and is ready to get another child, and all this in two hours' space: which, how absurd it is in sense, even sense may imagine, and art hath taught, and all ancient examples justified, and at this day, the ordinary players in Italy will not err in. Yet will some bring in an example of *Eunuchus* in Terence, that containeth matter of two days, yet far short of twenty years. True it is, and so was it to be played in two days, and so fitted to the time it set forth. And though Plautus hath in one place done amiss, let us hit with him, and not miss with him. But they will say, how then shall we set forth a story which containeth both many places and many times? And do they not know that a tragedy is tied to the laws of poesy, and not of history, not bound to follow the story, but having liberty, either to feign a quite new matter, or to frame the history to the most tragical conveniency? Again, many things may be told which cannot be showed, if they know the difference betwixt reporting and representing. . . .

Louis Montrose is an important American scholar of Shakespeare and Renaissance drama and culture, one of the first to be identified with the practice of NEW HISTORICISM. *In this chapter from* The Purpose of Playing: Shakespeare and the Cultural Politics of the Elizabethan Theatre, *Montrose provides an overview of Elizabethan attitudes toward the practice of theater.*

LOUIS MONTROSE

"Anatomies of Playing" (1996)

Throughout the course of Shakespeare's career in the theatre, the purpose of playing was much in dispute. In his *Treatise on Playe,* Sir John Harington defines the fundamental category of human activity called "playe" as "a spending of the tyme eyther in speeche or action, whose onely end ys a delyght of the mynd or the speryt."[1] Like such influential modern authors of treatises on play as Johan Huizinga and Roger Caillois, Harington stresses its nature as diversion or recreation, as a gratuitous and unproductive pastime, defined in antithesis to the practical realities of *negotium* that constitute everyday life.[2] However, Harington does not share the post-Kantian aesthetic perspective of his modern counterparts; he grounds his defense of gratuitous play in the values and prerogatives of the Renaissance courtier and gentleman. Nor will he celebrate all practices or practioners of play. "Stage-playes," along with "enterludes, tumblers, jesting fools, and scoffers, masking and dawncing," are included in the second of Harington's three "kyndes" of play—

---

[1]"A Treatise on Playe," which appears to have been written late in the reign of Queen Elizabeth, was first printed in John Harington, *Nugae Antiquae,* ed. Henry Harington, 3 vols. (1779; rpt. Hildesheim: Georg Olms, 1968), 2:154–208; quotation from 173. Subsequent page references are to volume two of this edition.

[2]See Johan Huizinga, *Homo ludens,* trans. (Boston: Beacon Press, 1955); Roger Caillois, *Man, Play, and Games,* trans. Meyer Barash (New York: Free Press, 1961); and, for an important critique of the ideological presuppositions of Huizinga and Caillois, Jacques Ehrmann, "Homo ludens revisited," in *Game, Play, Literature,* ed. Ehrmann (*Yale French Studies* 41 [1968]), 31–57.

namely, that consisting "of unseemly pleasures, provoking to wantonesse" (157). His condemnation appears to be directed at popular and public entertainments that appeal to the debased wits and wayward wills of the vulgar many. However, after having roundly condemned the drama in such conventionally antitheatrical terms, he adds that, in his own opinion, "in stage-playes may bee much good, in well penned comedies, and specially tragedies" (160). Those plays sufficiently learned and elevated to be able to "delyght . . . the mynd or the speryt" of courtly ladies and gentlemen are to be allowed. Harington's equivocation between the disapprobation and the defense of playing seems to be status-specific, whether the distinction be between base and gentle kinds of play or between the responses of vulgar and elite audiences to the same kinds of play. Harington's ambivalence is characteristic of courtly attitudes toward the drama.

Harington's conception of the purpose of playing may be usefully compared to the contemporaneous opinion of Shakespeare's Hamlet. As "the glass of fashion and the mold of form" (3.1.156), the paragon who fuses courtly grace and wit with university learning and introspection, Hamlet is Shakespeare's personification of the elite audience for his own plays. The learnedly antic prince invented by the public player-playwright is a connoisseur of plays, playing, and play-goers. For a taste of the first player's quality, he requests a speech that was "never acted, or if it was, not above once, for the play . . . pleased not the million; 'twas caviar to the general. But it was—as I received it, and others, whose judgments in such matters cried in the top of mine—an excellent play, well digested in the scenes, set down with as much modesty as cunning" (*Hamlet*, 2.2.435–40). Hamlet's description of this play implies that he knows it only as a text for readers—which is also the condition of our knowledge of *Hamlet*. Subsequently, he sees fit to instruct the players in their mystery: "Suit the action to the word, the word to the action, with this special observance, that you o'erstep not the modesty of nature. . . . Now, this overdone or come tardy off, though it makes the unskillful laugh, cannot but make the judicious grieve, the censure of the which one must in your allowance o'erweigh a whole theater of others" (3.2.17–19, 24–28); "And let those that play your clowns speak no more than is set down for them; for there be of them that will themselves laugh, to set on some quantity of barren spectators to laugh too, though in the meantime some necessary question of the play be then to be considered" (38–43). It is the elite perspective of the learned and courtly *reader* and *auditor*—rather than that of the popular *spectator*—that consistently characterizes Hamlet's tastes and his prejudices.

The Prince avers that "The purpose of playing . . . is, to hold as't were the mirror up to nature, to show virtue her feature, scorn her own image, and the very age and body of the time his form and pressure" (3.2.20–24). Because the stage play is both the product of a particular time and place and a circumscribed and reflexive space of representation, it may simultaneously exemplify and hold up to scrutiny the historically specific "nature" that it mirrors; it bears the pressure of the time's body but it may also clarify the form of the age. Hamlet implies that play can be serious and that jest can be earnest; that the seeming gratuitousness of play can mask its instrumentality. Through the persona of the Prince, the Elizabethan playwright voices the notion that theatrical fictions are forms of ethically and politically purposeful play. Plays that are well written and well performed imprint exemplary images of virtuous and vicious behavior upon the minds of their audiences, disposing them to emulate virtue and to repudiate vice. Thus, Hamlet defends the theatre upon the same high moral ground from which its enemies sought to destroy it.

However, Shakespeare's presentation of Hamlet's argument for drama's profound moral force is hardly unambiguous. By his reiterated disparagement of the vulgar majority of playgoers, the learned and courtly Hamlet implies that the theatre can work its ethical effect only upon those auditors with a prior disposition to attend to its "necessary question[s]" (3.2.42); those of "the groundlings, who . . . are capable of nothing but inexplicable dumb shows and noise" (10–12), those "barren spectators" to whom the extemporising clowns make their frivolous appeal, would appear to be impervious to the purpose of playing. Hamlet's vantage point on the theatre is not only limited but is surely intended to be so; it is not coterminous with that of the common player-playwright who has authored him, but is rather Shakespeare's characterization and dramatic internalization of the perspective of the elite segment within his own audience. Furthermore, the royal hero's own subsequent behavior and the actual outcome of the dramatist's play are far more equivocal—both ethically and politically—than the high theatrical principles espoused by Hamlet himself might lead us to expect. *Hamlet* incorporates Hamlet's desire for the drama to be ethically unequivocal in its purpose and force, and his wish that its actual performance proceed exactly as scripted, but *Hamlet* also continually and ironically undermines Hamlet's wishes and expectations. The playwright's perspective on the purpose of playing is more capacious, popular, and equivocal than that of the Prince. Playing at the Globe, Shakespeare and the Lord Chamberlain's Men seem to have sought out a *via media* between the plebian theatre of Henslowe and the elitism characteristic of the boys' companies and the private theatres. As Anthony Scoloker put it in his *Epistle to Daiphantus, or the Passions of Love* (1604), "Faith it should please all, like Prince *Hamlet.*"[3]

Like some Elizabethan apologists for poetry, and like Shakespeare's Hamlet, those few who defend the theatre in print do so by reversing the judgments of the theatre's detractors; nevertheless, their arguments remain constrained within the terms of the dominant antitheatrical discourse. In what is probably the most extended and informative of such defenses, *An Apology for Actors* (1612), Thomas Heywood argues that "playing is an ornament to the Citty"; that, thanks to playing and play-writing, "our *English* tongue . . . is now . . . continually refined"; and that "playes have made the ignorant more apprehensive, taught the unlearned the knowledge of many famous histories." Turning the oft-reiterated complaints of the civic magistrates inside out, Heywood proclaims that London's public and professional theatre is to be construed as a source of civic and national consciousness and pride, and as a most effective instrument for the inculcation of virtuous knowledge and the fashioning of obedient subjects. Enlarging upon the "true use" of plays based upon English chronicle histories—of which Shakespeare's form the largest and most celebrated corpus—Heywood maintains that these

> are writ with this ayme, and carryed with this methode, to teach the subjects obedience to their King, to shew the people the untimely ends of such as have moved tumults, commotions, and insurrections, to present them with the flourishing estate of such as live in obedience, exhorting them to allegeance, dehorting them from all trayterous and fellonious stratagems.[4]

Thus, according to Heywood, the intended effect of Elizabethan history plays was to exemplify in vivid word and action the moral lessons inscribed in the state homily "concernyng Good Ordre and Obedience to Rulers and Magistrates." Heywood embraces the terms dictated by the antitheatrical discourse and turns them to his own uses; he defends his profession by claiming that those "that are chaste, are by us extolled, and encouraged in their vertues. . . . The unchaste are by us shewed their errors" (*Apology,* GIV). Heywood's representation of the affective power of theatrical performance remains didactic and rigorously behavioristic. Although his defense is unequivocal, the terms in which it is framed do not fully comprehend the cultural practice that he is seeking to defend.

---

[3]Excerpt printed in E. K. Chambers, *William Shakespeare: A Study of Facts and Problems,* 2 vols. (Oxford: Clarendon Press, 1930), 2:214–15. On the unusually broad appeal of the Globe repertoire, see Gurr, *The Shakespearean Stage,* 230, and *Playgoing in Shakespeare's London,* 151, where Scoloker is also cited.

[4]Thomas Heywood, *An Apology for Actors* (1612) rpt. with I. G., *A Refutation of the Apology for Actors* (1615), facsimile ed. (New York: Garland, 1973), F3r-v.

In order to find an Elizabethan perspective that gives full weight to the affective power of theatrical performance, to its pleasures and its dangers, and that does so in a rhetorically compelling fashion, we must—ironically—look to those divines, magistrates, and putatively regenerate former players who attacked the theatre as an immoral force. The extensive antitheatrical discourse of Elizabethan and Jacobean pamphlets, sermons, and official documents provides a negative testimonial to the popularity and effectiveness of professional playing in the public playhouses. To take this discourse seriously is to respect the intelligence and sincerity of contemporary opponents, and also to appreciate that the Elizabethan theatre may have exercised a considerable but unauthorized and therefore deeply suspect affective power upon those Elizabethan subjects who experienced it. For example, consider the rhetoric of a letter from Edmund Grindal, then bishop of London, to Sir William Cecil. Writing early in the Elizabethan reign, and a dozen years before the opening of the Theatre, Grindal offers advice about measures to be taken against a recent outbreak of plague:

> Ther is no one thinge off late is more lyke to have renewed this contagion, then the practise off an idel sorte off people, which have ben infamouse in all goode common weales: I meane these Histriones, common playours; who now daylye, butt speciallye on holydayes, sett up bylles, wherunto the youthe resorteth excessively, & ther taketh infection: besides that goddes worde by theyr impure mowthes is prophaned, and turned into scoffes; for remedie wheroff in my judgement ye shulde do verie well to be a meane, that a proclamation wer sette furthe to inhibitte all playes for one whole yeare (and iff itt wer for ever, it wer nott amisse) within the Cittie, or 3, myles compasse, upon paynes aswell to the playours, as to the owners off the howses, wher they playe theyr lewde enterludes.[5]

One especially striking feature of the bishop's observation is the ambiguity in its epidemiology, the rhetorical force projected by its metaphorical identification of moral and medical discourses. The language of the letter suggests that the act of playgoing is itself the material source of the "contagion," that the youthful auditors quite literally take their "infection" from the "impure mouths" of the players. For Grindal, playing and plague are synonymous.

Hostility to plays, players, and playhouses varied enormously in source, motive, and intensity. There were some who did not oppose occasional dramatic performances by amateurs, and/or private dramatic performances by professionals that were intended exclusively for elite audiences in the royal court, noble households, inns of court, colleges, or guildhalls.[6] The Elizabethan antitheatrical prejudice was aimed most specifically and consistently at professional acting companies performing in public amphitheatres that

---

[5]Letter of 23 February 1564; excerpt printed in Chambers, *Elizabethan Stage,* 4:266–67.

[6]For example, the Act of Common Council of London of 6 December 1574, an unusually comprehensive attempt by the municipal authorities to regulate the texts and performances of plays, targeted those who owned venues suited to the performance of commercial entertainments:

> No Inkeper Tavernkeper nor other person whatsoever within the liberties of thys Cittie shall openlye shewe or playe, nor cawse or suffer to be openlye shewed or played, within the hous, yarde or anie other place within the Liberties of this Cyttie anie playe, enterlude, Commodye, Tragidie, matter, or shewe, which shall not be firste perused and Allowed . . . by suche persons as by the Lorde Maior and Courte of Aldermen . . . shalbe appoynted.

Explicitly excluded from the terms of this act were

> anie plaies, Enterludes, Comodies, Tragidies, or shewes to be played or shewed in the pryvate hous, dwellinge, or lodginge of anie nobleman, Citizen, or gentleman, which shall or will then have the same thear so played or shewed in his presence for the festyvitie of anie marriage, Assemblye of ffrendes, or otherlyke cawse withowte publique or Commen Collection of money of the Auditorie or beholders thereof. (Rpt. in Chambers, *Elizabethan Stage,* 4:273–76; quotations from 274, 276)

The Act made clear, however, that even plays performed for such private occasions were still to be held accountable for "the publishinge of unchaste, sedycious, and unmere matters."

charged for admission and whose audiences were largely although not exclusively composed of apprentices and servants, artisans and modest tradespeople.[7] However, even if the players were not adult professionals performing in a public playhouse, the social implications of *commercial* entertainment might alone be sufficiently alarming to provoke extreme measures.

A telling example comes from a resolution in the Accounts of the Master of the Merchant Taylors Company for 16 March 1574:

> Whereas at our comon playes and suche lyke exercises whiche be comonly exposed to be seene for money, everye lewd persone thinketh himself (for his penny) worthye of the chiefe and most comodious place without respecte of any other either for age or estimacion in the comon weale, whiche bringeth the youthe to such an impudente famyliaritie with theire betters that often tymes greite contempte of maisters, parents, and magistrates foloweth thereof, as experience of late in this our comon hall hath sufficyently declared, where by reason of the tumultuous disordered persones repayringe hither to see suche playes as by our schollers were here lately played, the Maisters of this Worshipful Companie and their deare ffrends could not have entertaynmente and convenyente place as they ought to have had, by no provision beinge made, notwithstandinge the spoyle of this howse, the charges of this Mystery, and theire juste authoritie which did reasonably require the contrary. Therefore . . . yt is ordeyned . . . that henceforthe theire shall be no more plays suffered to be played in this our Comon Hall, any use or custome heretofore to the contrary in anywise notwithstanding. (Quoted in Chambers, *Elizabethan Stage,* 2:75)

Here the occasion is a dramatic performance by the boys of the London Merchant Taylors School, founded in 1561 by Richard Mulcaster; and the venue is the Common Hall of the company itself. According to this account, the masters of the company were prepared to take the drastic step of forbidding the continuation of their own custom, not because of anything explicitly objectionable in the content of the boys' play or in the nature of their performance, but because of the composition and conduct of the audience that had been drawn to the event. Making payment of a penny the only criterion of admission had had the unintended consequence of levelling the hierarchical distinctions of honor and authority, the protocols of precedence and deference, upon which "this Worshipful Companie" and the social order at large were structured. If "everye lewd persone thinketh himself (for his penny) worthye of the chiefe and most comodious place without respecte of any other either for age or estimacion in the comon weale," then by the same token such persons might think their own judgments and opinions to be equally worthy of authority in the commonweal. Exchange value had subverted the principles of degree, priority, and place, leading inexorably from impudent familiarity to contempt, and from contempt to

[7]The classic work on the audiences of the Elizabethan theatres is Alfred Harbage, *Shakespeare's Audience* (New York: Columbia University Press, 1941). Harbage stresses the social heterogeneity and predominant commonality of the audiences in the public theatres. His conclusions are sharply challenged in Ann Jennalie Cook, *The Privileged Playgoers of Shakespeare's London, 1576–1642* (Princeton: Princeton University Press, 1981), who argues that even the public theatres of the period were predominantly the playground of the privileged few. In reaction against Harbage's fundamentally democratic Shakespeare, Cook produces an emphatically elitist Shakespeare that flies in the face of much statistical and anecdotal evidence. For critiques of Cook, and judicious reconsiderations of the whole question of the social composition of theatre audiences, see Martin Butler, *Theatre and Crisis 1632–1642* (Cambridge: Cambridge University Press, 1984), appendix 2, "Shakespeare's unprivileged playgoers," 293–306; and Gurr, *Playgoing in Shakespeare's London,* esp. 3–5, 49–79. Gurr's picture is more complex than those of Harbage and Cook, and takes into account variations among particular theatres and shifts over several decades. He suggests "that despite the infrequent reference to their presence citizens were the staple, at least of amphitheatre audiences, throughout the period. . . . Citizens . . . and their lesser neighbours the prosperous artisan class [were] a kind of silent majority in the playhouses" (64).

tumultuous disorder. The Masters of the Worshipful Company of the Merchant Taylors were appalled at the dire implications of the commodification of culture. At that very moment, however, other members of London's middling ranks were on the verge of institutionalizing such a culture industry in the public and professional amphitheatres sited in the liberties of London.

The public playhouses were attacked as the breeding ground of plague and vice, traffic congestion and mob violence, inefficient workers and dangerous ideas. In 1597, the Lord Mayor and aldermen of London petitioned the Privy Council to suppress stage plays, which they accused of causing numerous "inconveniences"; their petition is a compendium of the complaints that had been lodged against the performance of plays in the public theatres during the previous two decades. For example, they assert, with palpable alarm, that the plays performed in the commercial theatres

> are a speciall cause of corrupting . . . Youth, conteninge nothinge but unchaste matters . . . being so as that they impresse the very qualities & corruptions of manners which they represent. . . . Whereby such as frequent them, beinge of the base & refuze sort of people or such young gentlemen as have small regard of credit or conscience, drawe the same into imitacion and not to the avoidinge the like vices which they represent.[8]

These authoritative opponents represent plays, players, and playhouses as powerful agencies within Elizabethan society, and construe their power to be both utterly corrupt and utterly corrupting. The actors are believed to impress vicious images upon the minds of the most susceptible and dangerous groups in the general population, the lowly and the youthful. These impressions are here conceived of as material and absolute, and also as wholly malign: Unlike Thomas Heywood, the city fathers claim that theatrical images of vice always compel imitation, never aversion.[9] Those who attacked the theatre and those who defended it were agreed upon its compelling affective powers. Theatrical performance was thought to have the capacity to effect moral changes in its audience—whether for better or for worse. Plays might inspire, instruct, reform, delight, terrify, sadden, entrap, corrupt, infect, or incite—in any case, they might do far more than pass the time.

The 1597 petition continues by indicting the public playhouses as

> the ordinary places for vagrant persons, Maisterles men, thieves . . . contrivers of treason, and other idele and daungerous persons to meet together. . . .
>
> They maintaine idlenes in such persons as have no vocation & draw apprentices and other servauntes from theire ordinary workes and all sortes of people from the resort unto sermons and other Christian exercises, to the great hinderance of traides & prophanation of religion established by her highnes within this Realm.

---

[8]The Lord Mayor and Aldermen to the Privy Council, 28 July 1597; rpt. in Chambers, *Elizabethan Stage*, 4:322. Many of the complaints contained herein—and even some of the phrasing—are reproduced from a letter from the Lord Mayor to Lord Burghley, dated 3 November 1594, requesting support for the suppression of a planned new playhouse as well as "all other places, if possibly it may bee, whear the sayed playes ar shewed & frequented" (Chambers, *Elizabethan Stage*, 4:316–17).

[9]The 1597 petition of the Lord Mayor and Aldermen to the Privy Council reiterates not only the petition of 3 November 1594 but also that of 13 September 1595 (Chambers, *Elizabethan Stage*, 4:317–18). The latter appeal against "the common exercise of Stage Plaies" charges that they contain

> nothing but profane fables, Lascivious matters, cozonning devizes, & other unseemly & scurrilous behaviours, which ar so sett forthe, as that they move wholy to imitacion & not to the avoyding of those vyces which they represent, which wee verely think to bee the cheef cause aswell of many other disorders & lewd demeanors which appeer of late in young people of all degrees. (318)

The wording of this indictment seems to suggest that it is not merely the scurrilous content of the plays but the compelling manner of their performance ("which are so sett forthe") that endows them with the almost satanic power to "move wholy to imitacion."

To the extent that the Elizabethan church was a state institution through which the regime sought to shape and channel the spiritual lives of its subjects, the perceived threat to reformed religion posed by the theatres could also be construed as a political threat to the authority of the state. Thus, in their petition, London's city fathers appeal to the vital interests of the Queen with the charge that the theatres "draw . . . people from the resort unto sermons . . . to the . . . prophanation of religion *established by her highnes within this Realm*" (emphasis added). And in 1615, the author of *A Refutation of the Apology for Actors* gravely avers that "God onely gave authority of publique instruction and correction but to two sorts of men: to his Ecclesiasticall Ministers, and temporal Magistrates: hee never instituted a third authority of Players. . . . Playes were ordained by, & dedicated to the Divell, which is enemy to God and al goodnes."[10] The important point to be extracted from this polemic is that the theatre was perceived to have constituted itself as an alternative site of authority within contemporary society, an authority radically different in its sources, appeal, and potential effects from that which sanctioned the dominant institutions of church and state.

The apocalyptic tone in which the godly were apt to preach or write against the theatre might upon occasion modulate into something entirely more pragmatic. Consider, for example, a letter to the Queen's secretary, Sir Francis Walsingham, dated 25 January 1587, in which an anonymous correspondent bemoans "the daylie abuse of Stage Playes":

> Woe is me! the play howses are pestered, when churches are naked; at the one is not possible to gett a place, at the other voyde seates are plentie. . . . Yt is a wofull sight to see two hundred proude players jett in their silkes, wheare five hundred pore people sterve in the streets. But yf needes this mischief must be tollerated . . . yet for God's sake (Sir) lett every Stage in London pay a weekly pention to the pore, that *ex hoc malo proveniat aliquod bonum*. (Quoted in Chambers, *Elizabethan Stage*, 4:303–4)

The writer combines a charitable concern for the material welfare of the poor with a realistic assessment of the difficulty of suppressing so popular and profitable a vice as playing, and this leads him to his proposal that a part of those wicked profits might be put to virtuous use by the commonwealth.[11]

Such tacit recognition and acknowledgment of the degree to which the theatre was integrated into the urban socioeconomic fabric could also take less compromising forms. In 1603, Henry Crosse railed thus against the players: "These copper-lace gentlemen growe rich, purchase land by adulterous Playes, & not a fewe of them usurers and extortioners, which they exhaust out of the purses of their haunters."[12] The theatre and its personnel are here identified with the disruptive innovations of the marketplace. The players were not only attacked because the theatre was thought to be intrinsically immoral but also because the lowly and frequently disreputable practice of playing had suddenly become a means to relative affluence and upward social mobility—at least for those professionals who were sharers in licensed and liveried companies and had profits sufficient to acquire real estate and to engage in moneylending and other forms of financial speculation. Those who inveighed against the public and professional stage usually did so on

---

[10]I. G., *A Refutation of the Apology for Actors* (1615), facsimile ed., 57, 58.

[11]In this regard, see Ingram, *The Business of Playing,* 121–49, for extended discussion of the 6 December 1574 Act of the Common Council of London, and an argument that the chief intent of London's city fathers in asserting their regulatory authority was to find a new source of revenues to maintain the city's hospitals.

[12]Henry Crosse, *Vertues Common-wealth: Or the High-way to Honour* (1603), excerpt printed in Chambers, *Elizabethan Stage,* 4:247.

the grounds that it was an affront to godliness and a threat to the established social order. Depending upon specific circumstances and shifting contexts, however, they also seem to have been capable of viewing it as a potential source of municipal revenue or as a direct competitor for the leisure time of London's populace—and, perhaps, for their disposable income.[13] The purposes of antitheatricalism were no less diverse and divided than were the purposes of playing.

---

[13]That the players were not only luring audiences away from the preachers but were also stealing paying customers away from other kinds of commercial entertainments is suggested in the revealing comments of Thomas Nashe (1592) and Henry Chettle (1592), rpt. in Chambers, *Elizabethan Stage,* 4:239, 243. The economic basis of hostility to the Elizabethan stage is stressed in Russell Fraser, *The War against Poetry* (Princeton: Princeton University Press, 1970); and Alfred Harbage, "Copper into Gold," in *English Renaissance Drama,* ed. Standish Henning, Robert Kimbrough, and Richard Knowles (Carbondale: Southern Illinois University Press, 1976), 1–14.

iV

EARLY MODERN EUROPE

* * *

VI

✠ ✠ ✠

I N LONDON, PARIS, AND MADRID, THEATER AND DRAMA EXPERIENCED A SECOND "renaissance" in the later seventeenth century. In these cities, the theater came under the influence and protection of the king and his court, and the theaters of both London and Paris adapted Italian staging practices, as did the theaters of the Spanish court. As scenic technology became increasingly complex and spectacular, theater buildings achieved the form they would hold well into the nineteenth century, and the work of new playwrights and new dramatic designs invigorated the dramatic repertoire.

Yet for all their similarities, the theaters of Restoration England, of Louis XIV's France, and of the Spanish "Golden Age" were sustained by very different social and political climates. In France, Louis XIV declared *"L'état, c'est moi"*—"I am the state"—in 1660, confidently drawing all state authority into the person of the king and his magnificent court. The later seventeenth century in France was a period of royal absolutism, as the throne worked to consolidate its power. In England, conditions were very different, for 1660 brought the restoration of the monarchy. The Restoration period saw an ongoing negotiation between newly installed Charles II and Parliament for power, in which Parliament gradually gained control of many royal prerogatives. In both countries, the theater became associated with the throne and reflected the tensions animating social and political life.

THE POLITICAL CLIMATE

In France, a character in Molière's play *Tartuffe* drew the official portrait of the absolute monarch: "A Prince who sees into our inmost hearts, / And can't be fooled by any trickster's arts." Yet the authoritarian policies of the French government, the internecine competition among members of the court, and even the fortunes of the theater suggest that the king's claim of absolute power was challenged in a variety of ways. Under Louis XIII (reigned 1610–43) and Louis XIV (reigned 1643–1715), the Crown strove to centralize its power by crushing the claims of the landed nobility and by expanding French rule in a series of costly wars. Since Louis XIII came to the throne at the age of nine, when his father—Henry IV—was assassinated, much of this expansion was carried on by his chief minister, Cardinal Richelieu (1585–1642), and Richelieu's successor, Cardinal Mazarin (1602–61). The suppression of the traditional nobility was achieved largely through Richelieu's formation of a new bureaucracy loyal to the Crown, partly composed of politically active clergy and partly of commoners promoted over the heads of the nobility to critical positions in the government. Allowing these "new men" to buy aristocratic titles, the Crown raised money and further diluted the power of the nobility. The Crown's ravenous appetite for cash to pay for the lavish life of the court and for expensive building projects, such as the palace of Versailles (built by Louis XIV in 1673), further weakened the nobility and alienated the peasantry. Using tax-farmers, who paid a fixed sum to the government in exchange for the authority to collect taxes and pocket the excess as profit, the Crown squeezed the nobles' wealth directly into the royal coffers, impoverishing their lands and making the peasantry increasingly rebellious.

A poor and disaffected peasantry, a jealous aristocracy, an upstart bourgeoisie, and an increasingly authoritarian and isolated monarchy: this became the recipe for revolution. Although the French Revolution did not erupt until 1789, France suffered civil convulsions throughout the seventeenth century that dramatize the tension between Louis's absolutist rhetoric and the political realities of his reign. The nobles led a series of rebellions called the Fronde throughout the 1640s and 1650s, in an effort to unseat Louis and his powerful ministers. Louis defeated these uprisings and finally sealed the fate of his enemies when he required the nobility to attend him at Versailles, so he could keep his eye on their activities. However, the Fronde was part of a more pervasive unrest. Relentless taxation, economic stagnation, and repeated famines throughout the seventeenth century made the peasants angry as well, and peasant riots and rebellions took place in nearly every province of France in nearly every decade of the century. Finally, Louis XIV also had difficulty with the most volatile issue of seventeenth-century Europe—religious dissent. The close ties between the Crown and the church often resulted in the suppression of Protestant sects, particularly the Calvinist French Huguenots. Protestant rebellion had forced the enactment of the Edict of Nantes in 1598, granting the Huguenots considerable religious freedom. Louis XIV revoked the Edict in 1685, giving the government wider latitude to suppress increasingly energetic religious protest. Louis XIV carefully crafted the image of the "Le Roi Soleil"—the Sun King—whose absolute authority seemed almost a force of nature, not a fact of politics. Throughout his reign, though, Louis had to contend with recalcitrant factions who refused to accept completely his characterization of the king's power.

In England, resistance to royal authority had been much more successful. Between 1603 and 1642, the Stuart kings James I (reigned 1603–25) and his son, Charles I (reigned 1625–49), worked to limit the power of Parliament and to enforce increasingly strict religious laws that suppressed the Protestant Puritan sects and demanded conformity with the Church of England. In 1642, Parliament passed legislation limiting the powers of the throne, and Civil War between Parliamentary and Royalist forces erupted. Charles I was executed in 1649, while his wife and children (including the future king, Charles II) escaped to France. From 1653 to 1658, Oliver Cromwell served as Lord Protector of the realm, but Royalist sentiments eventually prevailed and established Charles II (reigned 1660–85) on the throne.

Although the monarchy was restored—the term *Restoration* refers generally to the period of Charles II's reign and the remainder of the seventeenth century—Charles II was in no position to command the nation, and English politics in the later seventeenth century mainly concerned the negotiation of power between the Crown and Parliament. Charles's death in 1685 spurred a crisis in that his brother James II (reigned 1685–88) was Catholic and threatened to compromise English religious and civil autonomy from the Catholic church and the Catholic states of Europe. In 1689, Parliament effectively deposed James, inviting his Protestant daughter Mary (reigned as Mary II, 1689–94) and her husband, William of Orange (reigned as William III, 1689–1702), to return to England and assume the throne. While Louis XIV increasingly insisted on the autonomous power of the throne in France, the Parliament in England finally achieved a lasting compromise with the Crown in the form of a constitutional monarchy. In bringing William and Mary into power, Parliament gained the authority of consent over royal succession, a power it confirmed in 1702 in naming James II's daughter Anne as successor (reigned as Queen Anne, 1702–14).

While in an important sense the gulf separating French and English culture has always been narrow and deep, like the English Channel, Spanish culture in the Renaissance arises from a very different history. Spain was occupied by the Moors in 711 and is still marked by its five centuries of Islamic culture. In 1479, Ferdinand of Aragon and Isabella of Castile were married, forming the alliance that gave rise to modern Spain; in 1480 they joined forces with the Catholic Inquisition, expelling Jews from the country. At the Conquest of Granada in 1492, the Moors were finally driven out of Spain.

Having formed a single state, the Spanish monarchy successfully expanded its reach into a global empire during the sixteenth century. Under Charles V, Spain's territory included its many New World colonies as well as the Netherlands and the Holy Roman Empire of central Europe, and the culture of the Spanish court was unrivaled in Europe: this is the era of Velásquez and El Greco. But during the reign of Philip II (1556–98), Spain's domination of Europe began to wane. Spain became involved in a brutal and expensive effort to keep control of the Netherlands, a hotbed of Protestant resistance. English soldiers—Sir Philip Sidney and Ben Jonson, among others—fought the Spanish in the Netherlands, and Philip tried in several ways to outmaneuver the English. He proposed marriage to Queen Elizabeth, but as with other suitors, she strung him along for political purposes and finally refused him. He also mounted a massive naval invasion of England, the Spanish Armada of 1588, which was surprisingly defeated. Spain continued to wane in the seventeenth century, eventually losing the Netherlands, and losing Portugal in 1657. By 1665, Spain was ruled by the last of the Hapsburg kings, the deformed imbecile Charles II (1665–1700). The death of Charles II drew all of Europe into the Wars of the Spanish Succession.

THEATER IN FRANCE, 1660—1700

Louis XIV's familiar sobriquet, "Le Roi Soleil," derives from a role he played in a court ballet devised for him in 1653. A fine dancer, Louis sponsored and took part in a wide variety of entertainments. Moreover, the centralization of power in the king and the court paralleled the increasing institutionalization of the arts under Louis XIV, as a means of advancing his own prestige and of keeping control over potentially seditious activities. The most famous of these institutions—the *ACADÉMIE FRANÇAISE*—was chartered in 1637, and used by Cardinal Richelieu to evaluate a critical controversy surrounding Pierre Corneille's play *The Cid*. Corneille's detractors had sharply attacked the play, and Richelieu urged the Académie to resolve whether *The Cid* could legitimately be described as effective tragedy in neoclassical terms (on *neoclassicism,* see page 279). In return, Richelieu promoted the Académie and its aims, the purification of French language and literature, and the advancement of official French culture. Louis XIV assumed the role of official protector of the Académie Française in 1672 and sponsored other institutions as ornaments to his reign: the Académie Royale de Musique (1672), the Académie Royale de Peinture et de Sculpture (1648), the Académie des Inscriptions (1663), the Académie des Sciences (1666), and the Académie de l'Architecture (1671). The institution of the stage was no exception. Theatrical companies had always needed the king's license to play in Paris, and Louis licensed several companies and named Molière's company as the *Troupe du roi.* After Molière's death in 1673, the leading tragic actress in Paris, Mademoiselle Champmeslé, joined with Molière's troupe and gained the king's patronage. The new company—THE COMÉDIE FRANÇAISE—opened in August of 1680. It held a MONOPOLY on the production of all spoken drama in French, and although this monopoly has long since vanished, the Comédie Française remains the principal company performing the French classical repertoire.

In Louis XIV's Paris, the institutions of art—including the theater—were identified with the prerogatives of the king and his court, though the structure of the theater had its roots in practices dating back to the Middle Ages. Throughout the later Middle Ages and into the sixteenth century, stage production in Paris was controlled by the Confrérie de la Passion, a guild-like corporation initially formed to stage religious drama. In 1545 the Confrérie purchased land in Paris from the Duke of Burgundy and erected the Hôtel de Bourgogne, at the time probably the only permanent theater building in Europe (*hôtel* in this case means "hall" or "large building"). Extensively remodeled in 1647, the Hôtel de Bourgogne served as the model for other theaters built in the seventeenth century: the Théâtre du Marais (built in a tennis court in 1629, rebuilt in 1644); the Palais-Cardinal

GROUND PLAN OF THE COMÉDIE FRANÇAISE THEATER

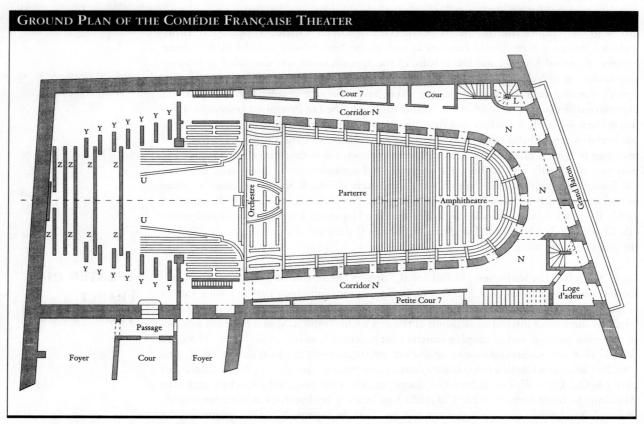

The Comédie Française had this basic design from 1689 to 1770. Note the open parterre, *the wings (marked Y), and the backdrops (Z). The benches on the stage were added during the eighteenth century.*

(built by Richelieu in 1640; later renamed the Palais-Royal); the Salle des Machines (1642), and the Comédie Française (1689).

The shape of these theaters owes something to the Hôtel de Bourgogne, and something to tennis courts as well, for tennis courts were often used as theaters. (In the sixteenth and seventeenth centuries, tennis courts were long indoor rooms with side galleries.) These theaters generally had deep, **RAKED STAGES** (40 feet deep, 45 feet wide at the Hôtel de Bourgogne) that faced an open **PIT** called the *PARTERRE* (literally, "on the ground") which was used for standing spectators. The auditorium had **BOXES** on three sides; **GALLERY** seating rose above the boxes opposite the stage; some patrons were also seated on the stage itself. The theaters were large—the Hôtel de Bourgogne initially held 1,600 spectators, the Comédie Française held 2,000—and many theaters made extensive use of stage scenery, sometimes concocting extraordinary spectacles. In a fantasy celebrating Louis XIV's wedding in 1662, the entire royal family and its entourage were "flown" by machines in the Salle des Machines; in a production in 1671, 300 deities were lifted aloft. The dramatic theaters—the Hôtel de Bourgogne, the Palais-Royal, the Comédie Française—tended to avoid such effects, using instead a single setting for each play, depending on the genre of the play. The theaters generally used a series of staggered **WINGS AND BACKDROP** to create the effect of perspective, adapting both scenic practices and scene-changing technology from Italian theaters.

Acting companies in Paris were organized as investment corporations requiring the patronage of the Crown and had long included women in their ranks. Louis XIV's reign saw a series of great actresses take the stage, Mademoiselle DuParc and Mademoiselle Champmeslé among them. Companies were comprised of twelve members (eight men, four women), who shared the company's profits. The company hired additional actors when necessary. The Comédie Française standardized this practice: its twelve main actors—called *SOCIÉTAIRES*—ran the company for twenty years, and new *sociétaires* could be recruited only after the retirement of current members. Actors in the Comédie Française received an annual subsidy from the Crown and a retirement pension if they completed their twenty years with the company. The company purchased plays, which were cast by the author. Throughout the 1650s and 1660s the major companies kept about 70 plays in repertoire and generally played three or four times per week. After the 1680s, the Comédie Française began daily performances, beginning at 5 P.M.

We should recall that life at court was itself a kind of performance, and that attending the theater provided ample opportunity for aristocrats, courtiers, and aspiring courtiers to display and preen themselves. In a milieu so dependent on the king's preference, we can easily imagine how stage seating and side boxes emphasized that the evening's entertainment included the audience's performances as well as the actors'. This sense of the reciprocity between court and stage is signaled more concretely by the fortunes of the Parisian theaters after Louis XIV moved the court to Versailles. Although five companies flourished in Paris while Louis kept court in the city, by 1700 only two remained.

THEATER IN ENGLAND, 1660–1737

At the outbreak of the English Civil War in 1642, Parliament closed the London theaters, putting a stop to dramatic performance. Some companies managed to mount secret productions between 1642 and 1660, but Parliament and city officials moved quickly to suppress them, sometimes by destroying the theater buildings. In the 1650s, however, William Davenant (1606–68), a Royalist supporter of Charles I and successor to Ben Jonson as writer of court masques, attempted to mount operas. In 1656 he succeeded in staging a production of *The Siege of Rhodes* at Rutland House, performing it again in 1658 and 1659 at the Cockpit theater and elsewhere in London.

The restoration of Charles II to the throne in 1660 inaugurated a period of renewed theatrical vitality. As in France—where Charles developed a taste for theater during his exile—the theater was closely associated with royal prerogatives. Upon his return, Charles rewarded PATENTS to William Davenant and Thomas Killegrew (1612–83) to open theaters under royal authority. These PATENT THEATERS (also called "theaters royal")—Davenant's Duke's company, and Killigrew's King's company—thus held a royal monopoly on the production of spoken English drama. Although they underwent huge modifications, the patent theaters dominated the legitimate theater until the mid-nineteenth century, when legislation was passed that finally broke their monopoly. Yet monopoly could not guarantee support. The two companies, unable to turn a profit, were united into a single company from 1682 to 1695.

When the theaters reopened in 1660, theatrical taste had changed significantly. Although a few of the older, pre-1642 theater buildings were still standing, they could not handle the new theater technology. For, as in the French theater, the English theater rapidly encouraged the development of scenic practices already well-known in Italy—a PROSCENIUM stage and moveable painted wings and backdrop used to create a visual setting for the play. Onstage, theaters used stock sets—one for classical tragedy, one for romantic comedy, and so on—that conformed to the dramatic genre of the play. In 1661, Davenant converted Lisle's Tennis Court to the Lincoln's Inn Fields Theater, which measured 30 by 70 feet; he replaced this theater with the Dorset Garden Theater in 1671.

CHRISTOPHER WREN'S THEATRE ROYAL, DRURY LANE

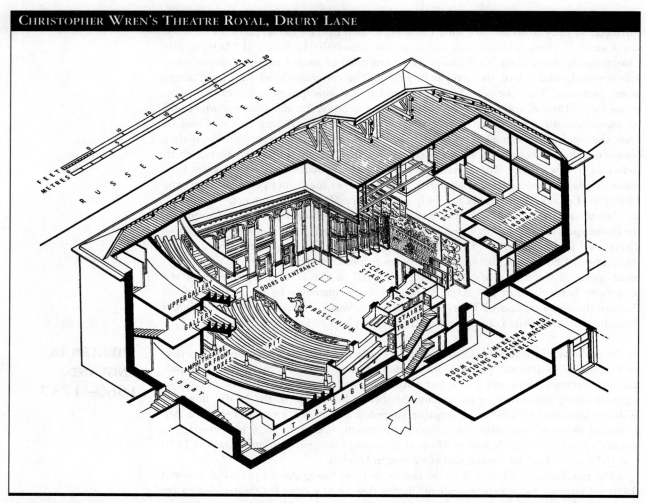

In 1674, Christopher Wren designed a new Theatre Royal, Drury Lane. Note that the acting area extends to the apron, in front of the wing and backdrop stage scenery. Pit seating, side boxes, and two galleries also are visible.

Killegrew erected his Theatre Royal in Bridges Street in 1663. When it burned in 1672, he built a new Theatre Royal in Drury Lane, which opened in 1674; a theater has occupied this site down to the present time.

The new English theaters were much smaller than the French theaters. The Drury Lane theater, for example, held 650–700 people, though it was expanded throughout the late seventeenth and eighteenth centuries and eventually held more than 2,000. Nonetheless, like the French theaters, the English houses also introduced new design and staging practices: a proscenium stage flanked by a large APRON, footlights to illuminate the stage, a raked pit with benches (the French *parterre* was flat and had no seats), side and rear box seats, and a rear gallery. This division of the house accorded with social and class distinctions in the audience, which was in any event a narrow selection of the English public, in part because the theater was recognized as the ornament of the privileged, and—not incidentally—because plays were produced in the afternoon, when working people could not easily attend. The entire auditorium was lighted by chandeliers, making the audience itself very much a part of the show: in an important sense the performance did not stop at the edge of the stage. Although the theaters were not at the court itself, they were frequently patronized by courtiers and the nobility, who preened and displayed themselves to the audience—sometimes from seats onstage. Charles II—who numbered the well-known actress Nell Gwynn (1650–87) among his many mistresses—was also frequently in the audience.

Companies were generally managed by one of the actors, and they avoided the need for lengthy casting and rehearsal by developing LINES OF BUSINESS, in which each actor would specialize in a particular type of character: heroic lead, comic lead, male heavy, female heavy, utility player, and so on. Acting style was relatively formal, and actors often played downstage on the apron directly to the audience; a famous speech—one of Hamlet's soliloquies, for example—would be delivered directly to the audience, something like an operatic aria today, a practice called POINTING. As the theater developed in the later seventeenth century, sharing companies were replaced by companies financed by outside investors, who paid the actors salaries and took a percentage of the profits. Companies were large and salaries low; actors were compensated by BENEFIT performances, in which the actor (on his or her benefit night) received the entire profit from a given evening's performance, minus the operating expenses of the house. The practice of supplementing salaries with benefit performances continued well into the nineteenth century, and although most benefit nights—after the house expenses were deducted—left the actors with little additional pay, benefits provided an excuse to keep actors' salaries low.

By far the greatest innovation in the English theater, though, was the introduction of actresses onstage. English comedies in this period were often frankly concerned with sexual intrigue, and the actresses who played in them—and in the new heroic tragedies, and in the plays by Shakespeare, Jonson, Fletcher, and other Renaissance playwrights who continued to hold the stage—also had a reputation for sexual licentiousness. Yet, while several actresses, like Nell Gwynne, were mistresses of the famous and powerful, the phenomenon of regarding actresses as sexual objects, of classing them with prostitutes, has more to do with the status and vulnerability of working women in a highly stratified and patriarchal society than it does with the immorality of the stage or its performers. Indeed, actresses' ongoing struggle to assert themselves as legitimate performers was born at this time as well, epitomized in the careers of Elizabeth Barry (1658–1713), Anne Bracegirdle (1663–1748), and many others.

THEATER IN SPAIN'S GOLDEN AGE, 1580—1680

As in medieval England and France, medieval Spanish theater was strongly influenced by the church, which saw in the drama a source of instruction and inspiration. Although there is some evidence for liturgical drama as early as the twelfth century, the principal form of medieval theater was the *AUTO SACRAMENTALE,* a form of allegorical religious drama initially devised to celebrate the feast of Corpus Christi. But while the mystery cycles were suppressed in Protestant England, the Spanish *autos* continued to be performed alongside the secular theater until they were banned in 1765. Like the English cycles, the *autos* were in civic hands, and by the late sixteenth century major cities would perform *autos* as many as three times per year, usually in the central city plaza before a gathering of citizens and civic officials. Professional actors were hired for the *autos* and were drawn through the city on wagons (*CARROS*); the *carros* were heavily decorated, and a prize was given for the most spectacular *carro*. Despite their abstract themes, the *autos* remained extremely popular and drew on the talents of the best playwrights of the era—between 1647 and 1681, for instance, all the *autos* performed in Madrid were written by Pedro Calderón de la Barca.

Philip II, Philip III, and Philip IV were all interested in theater and commissioned playwrights to devise entertainments; during the reign of Philip III, Spain developed an

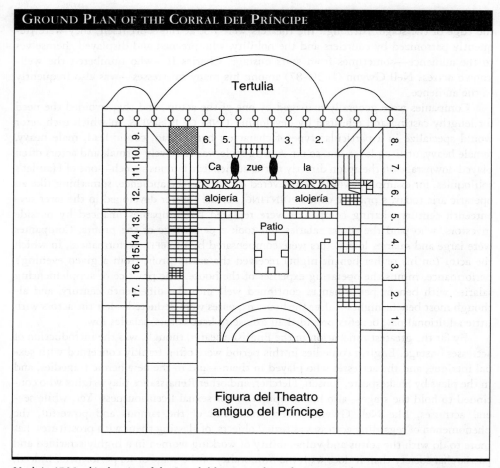

GROUND PLAN OF THE CORRAL DEL PRÍNCIPE

Tertulia

6. 5. 3. 2.

9.

11.|10.

Ca   zue   la

12.

alojería   alojería

13.

Patio

16.|15.|14.

17.

8.

7.

6.

5.

4.

3.

2.

1.

Figura del Theatro
antiguo del Príncipe

Made in 1730, this drawing of the Corral del Príncipe shows the important features of the theater: the patio, *the* alojería, *the* gradas, *and the* cazuela.

impressive court theater. Early in the seventeenth century, this court theater merely occupied a hall at the Alcázar palace, as Ben Jonson and Inigo Jones had done at Whitehall palace in England, and it produced a similar kind of entertainment: mythological dramas that required spectacular scenery, effects, and costumes. But by the 1630s, the center of court theater shifted to the new palace of Buen Retiro. Here, in 1640 Cosme Lotti (d. 1643) was retained to build a permanent theater that could perform the scenic effects of the Italian theater. This theater was roofed, but in its basic design resembled the most influential of Spanish theaters in the Golden Age, the public theater or *CORRAL.*

Although the Spanish public theater resembled the public theaters of Elizabethan London, it stood in a much different relationship to city life. While the English theaters were banned from the city proper and were erected across the Thames in Southwark, the Spanish theaters were public institutions. Since the medieval church held the rights to theatrical production, the public theaters were licensed by religious confraternities in the sixteenth century, which used the funds for various charitable purposes, including maintaining the general hospital of Madrid. By the early seventeenth century, these funds were paid directly to the city, and theaters continued to subsidize charities well into the

VIEW OF THE CORRAL DEL PRÍNCIPE

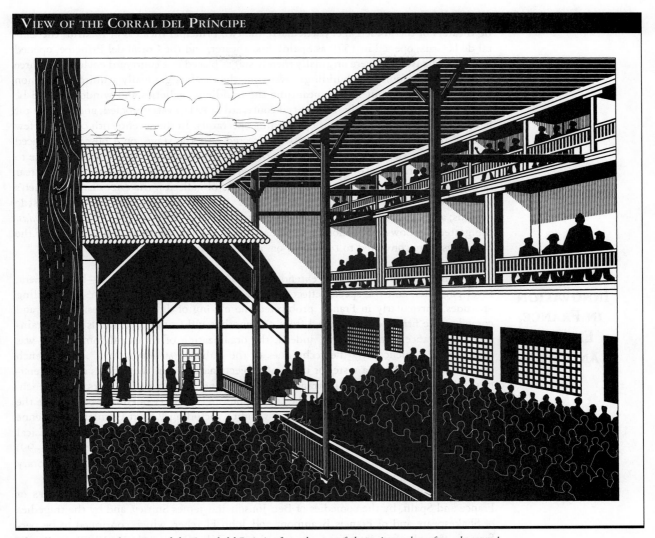

This illustration provides a view of the Corral del Príncipe from the rear of the patio, *perhaps from the* cazuela.

nineteenth century. Companies of actors were licensed to play in the city, and took a lease on a *corral* for a stated period of time. In general, Spanish companies toured major cities and towns, and only Seville and Madrid allowed two companies to perform at the same time. While playwrights were initially associated with individual companies, by the seventeenth century playwrights would sell their plays to the company: they were paid very well for an *auto,* and adequately for a regular play—about 500 reales, or about 10 times the daily wage of a laborer. Although companies were composed of men and boys until 1587, when women were allowed to appear onstage, the church issued a decree banning women from performing onstage in 1596. By 1599, however, a royal council ruled that actresses could be permitted, providing they were married to a member of the company; it also ruled against cross-dressing, so that when Rosaura appeared dressed as a man in Calderón's *Life Is a Dream,* the actress wore a man's costume only down to the waist with a skirt below.

The reciprocity between the city and the theater is also revealed in the design of public theaters of the golden age, particularly the two principal theaters of Madrid, the Corral de la Cruz, opened in 1579 as Spain's first theater, and the Corral del Príncipe, opened in 1583. The theaters were originally merely stages placed in a courtyard enclosed on three or four sides by four-story buildings; over time the theaters gradually acquired possession of these structures, but in the meantime the buildings' galleries and windows could be sold to spectators separately. The central courtyard or PATIO was unroofed, and like the pit of English theaters was occupied by standing spectators. In the seventeenth century, a few rows of benches (called *TABURETES*) were erected near the stage, on a raised and fenced dais. Along the sides of the *patio* rose the *GRADAS,* steeply raked rows of seats that rose to the second floor. The *ALOJERÍA,* a tavern, served refreshments, and was located at the rear of the *patio;* above the *alojería,* were several stories of galleries: the *CAZUELA,* or women's gallery, on the second floor; above it galleries for the City of Madrid and Council of Castile officials; and a gallery for intellectual and church officials, the *TERTULIA.* Above the *gradas,* the grated windows of the houses served as box seats. The third and fourth floors of the buildings were converted to *DESVANES* or "attics," small open galleries.

DRAMATIC INNOVATION IN FRANCE, ENGLAND, AND SPAIN

Although theatrical production extended into a number of other forms—ballet, opera, royal pageants, and the special-effects extravaganzas called MACHINE PLAYS—prevailing attitudes, particularly in France, prohibited the mixing of dramatic genres: tragedy and comedy were firmly discriminated from one another and from others kinds of entertainment. In France, comedy—and, indeed, the organization of theatrical companies—was particularly influenced by the techniques of the Italian *COMMEDIA DELL' ARTE.* French tragic drama inherited a taste for classical subject matter from the schools and universities, which had led Europe in translating Greek and Roman playwrights into French. Throughout the sixteenth century, the court sponsored a variety of efforts to classicize the theater, supporting several important playwrights, including Robert Garnier and Étienne Jodelle, who created highly wrought and refined tragedies based on the model of classical drama. The heroic tragedies of Pierre Corneille (1606–84) and Jean Racine (1639–99) epitomize this tradition while also turning it in a new direction, refracting contemporary moral, political, and philosophical issues through the lens of a classical style.

English drama in the Restoration also was affected by the HEROIC TRAGEDIES of France and Spain, by the comedies of Ben Jonson and James Shirley, and by the tragedies of Shakespeare and of Francis Beaumont and John Fletcher, which continued to be performed, though often in revised or adapted form. John Dryden (1631–1700), for example, not only adapted versions of *The Tempest* and *Antony and Cleopatra* (the latter as *All for Love,* 1677), but also wrote plays in the mode of heroic tragedy, such as *Aureng-Zebe* (1675) and *The Conquest of Granada* (1669). Heroic tragedy generally represents the idealized passions of characters forced to choose between love and personal honor. Comic drama took its inspiration both from European models—Molière's plays, for example—and from the earlier plays of Ben Jonson, but in the plays of William Wycherly (1640–1716), Sir George Etherege (1635–92), and William Congreve (1670–1729), English comedy rapidly developed its own original style. Restoration comedies are most often in the vein of COMEDY OF MANNERS, contemporary dramas in which witty aristocrats, city dupes and dandies, and dull country gentlemen are engaged in an elaborate adventure of sexual intrigue. Restoration comedy is often elegant and verbally polished, and obsessed with issues of class, privilege, manners, and sex. In addition, much as the Restoration theater witnessed the rise of actresses onstage, it also saw the first women to achieve success as playwrights: Aphra Behn (1640–89), Catharine Trotter (1679–1749), and Susanna Centlivre (1670–1723).

After the turn of the century, the risqué character of many plays spurred one of the perennial movements to restrain the theater as an immoral institution. Partly as a result of Jeremy Collier's diatribe *A Short View of the Immorality and Profaneness of the English Stage* (1698), and partly as a result of changing attitudes and social mores, English comedy after 1700—the plays of Sir Richard Steele (1672–1729), Colley Cibber (1671–1757), George Farquhar (1678–1707), Oliver Goldsmith (1728–74), and Richard Brinsley Sheridan (1751–1816), for instance—became more romantic and sentimental. Moreover, political satire in English theater was also sharply limited with the passing of the Stage Licensing Act of 1737. After 1737, all plays produced for public entertainment had to be submitted for censorship prior to production. The censor could require changes, delete words, passages, or scenes, or refuse to grant permission entirely. Confronting the Act by producing a nonlicensed play was to risk the fining and imprisonment of everyone involved in the production. While theaters found a variety of ways to subvert or sidestep the law, the censorship remained in effect—with some modifications—until 1968, inhibiting the possibility of dramatic innovation.

In the early sixteenth century, a Spanish theatrical manager may well have written his own plays and acted in them himself. Lope de Rueda (1510–65), for example, was a touring performer and the author of both *autos* and secular plays. But by the late sixteenth century, companies would pay a playwright for the play, and the theaters had made several genres popular: the *CAPA Y ESPADA* or heroic/romantic "cape and sword" play was very popular, as was the *RUIDO* or "noise" play. But the forms of Golden Age drama were in many ways determined by the extraordinary and prolific career of Lope Félix de Vega Carpio (1562–1635). Lope de Vega is frequently said to have written more than 1,500 plays—which points to the immense popularity of the theater and its constant need for new material—and more than 450 of his plays have survived. He is particularly associated with *COMEDIA NUEVA,* a genre mixing the tragic and the comic, high and low characters (including the *GRACIOSO,* a comic fool), and usually having a romantic plot. In the intervals between the acts of his plays, short interludes (*ENTREMESES*) were performed, which were coherent plays in themselves. Like other playwrights in this period, Lope de Vega also wrote *autos,* but his best-known work is *Fuente Ovejuna* (1614), a play about a vicious tyrant that critics have seen as an allegory on Portuguese independence.

Lope shared the stage with several equally brilliant playwrights, principally with Pedro Calderón de la Barca (1600–81), who succeeded Lope de Vega as Spain's most influential dramatist. Miguel de Cervantes (1547–1616), the author of *Don Quixote,* wrote about thirty plays, of which sixteen remain. Tirso de Molina (1584–1648) was a friar who had written more than 400 plays—eighty survive—before he was reprimanded by the Council of Castile; his best-known play, *El Burlador de Seville (The Trickster of Seville)* is the earliest play on the subject of Don Juan. The playwright Guillén de Castro (1569–1631) was a friend of Lope de Vega; his influence on the French theater is perhaps as marked as it was in Spain. Guillén de Castro wrote *Las Mocedades del Cid (The Youthful Adventures of the Cid),* which was adapted by Corneille as *Le Cid* and ignited a furious controversy about neoclassical esthetics.

NEOCLASSICISM, DRAMA, AND THEATER

In both France and England, the arts in general and drama in particular were closely regulated by the state, a state of affairs sustained by the rise of NEOCLASSICISM. Neoclassicism is, in the simplest sense, the revival of what was taken to be a "classical" ordering of the arts. The literature of classical Greece and Rome began to be recovered in the fourteenth and fifteenth centuries, first through the dissemination of texts preserved in monasteries and later through expanded contact with the Islamic world in the sixteenth and seventeenth centuries. Translating, imitating, and adapting classical texts, European writers in

THE TERM *COMMEDIA DELL' ARTE* MEANS the "comedy of the professional players," and *commedia* became popular throughout Europe in the sixteenth century. *Commedia* companies were itinerant (though one was established in Paris for part of Louis XIV's reign), organized around ten or twelve actors, men and women, each of whom played a stock character who could be easily recognized by typical and routine behavior. Although the characters were fixed, the plots that *commedia* companies played were generally improvised; the actor relied on the traits of his or her character and a core of

(ASIDE)

COMMEDIA DELL' ARTE

stage business from which to invent action and dialogue. The cast usually included one or two pairs of young lovers (the *INNAMORATO* and *INNAMORATA*), good-looking, aristocratic, or fashionable characters played without masks. The rest of the cast was masked and played more stereotypical roles: the *CAPITANO,* a military braggart and coward, played with sword and cape; the *PANTALONE,* an elderly dupe, often in love, played in stockings, breeches, and slippers; the *DOTTORE,* sometimes actually a doctor, but otherwise a pedantic friend of

the Pantalone; and a variety of comic parts called *ZANNI,* usually sly servants. The most familiar of these parts is *Arlecchino,* or *HARLEQUIN,* a cunning character who is usually an acrobat, wearing a patched costume (later refined to a diamond-shaped pattern), a black cap, and carrying his slapstick—the origin of our term "slapstick," which gives some idea of what *commedia* humor was like. *Commedia* was also popular in England, but it had fewer long-term effects on the comic drama than on the rise of English **PANTOMIME.** In England, plays were often followed by a short **AFTERPIECE,** which frequently led Harlequin into adventures with mythological characters. John Rich (1692–1761), taking the name Lun, was the most famous Harlequin of the early eighteenth-century English stage.

PANTALONE AND HARLEQUIN

Note the mask and breeches of the Pantalone (left), and the mask, slapstick, and diamond-shaped patches of the Harlequin (right).

the later seventeenth century appeared to "revive" the principles of classical art. In practice, however, neoclassicism offered an *interpretation* of the classics, emphasizing order, control, decorum, reason, and harmony.

In many respects, neoclassicism relied on the authority of Aristotle's *Poetics*, published first in Latin translation in 1498 and then in Italian in 1549, and on the series of critical commentaries written on Aristotle throughout the sixteenth century. Aristotle's *Poetics* is something of a naturalist's description of the several species of poetry and their characteristics, but readers in the sixteenth and seventeenth centuries fell under the influence of Aristotle's enormous authority and quickly transformed the *Poetics* into a prescription, a series of rules, for producing the most perfect and effective tragedies. Two central precepts of the *Poetics* regard the tragic hero's actions: those acts must seem both necessary and probable, and they should not entirely violate moral expectations. Neoclassical critics and playwrights schematized Aristotle's descriptions as necessary features of dramatic composition, arguing that a tragedy should be rigorously and causally plotted and should reveal the workings of providential justice through the actions of universalized or typical characters. These goals were transformed into the famous "unities" of neoclassicism: a play should take place within a single day (unity of time), in one location (unity of place), and consist of a single line of action, a single plot (unity of action). The action of neoclassical tragedy, therefore, is concentrated, maintaining a uniformity of tone and style called DECORUM. Plays in this mode maintain a single, narrow range of language and behavior; the action is either idealized (rather than realistic) in tragedy, or commonplace in comedy: tragic characters are classic and heroic, while comic characters are contemporary, even bourgeois; tragedy undertakes the conflict between the ideal passions of love and honor, while comedy takes its cue from more earthly desires—lust, greed, hypocrisy, and so on. Following the recovery of Vitruvius' *De Architectura* (15 BCE) in 1414, this neoclassical sensibility urged the modern stage to imitate Vitruvius' distinction between the proper stage settings of tragedy and comedy: classical architecture for tragedy, urban architecture for comedy. Especially in seventeenth-century Paris, theaters adjusted their stagecraft to these ideals of regularity and decorum, assigning a generalized palace setting to the elevated world of tragedy, and the *chambre à quatre portes*—the room with four doors—to the lower, contemporary world of comedy.

Writing later in the eighteenth century, the Englishman Thomas Davies characterized the differences between French and English audiences and suggests that neoclassical ideals did not take root as deeply in the English theater as they did in France:

> The Frenchman, when he goes to a play, seems to make his entertainment a matter of importance. The long speeches in the plays of Corneille, Racine, Crébillon, and Voltaire, which would disgust an English ear, are extremely pleasing to our light neighbours: they sit in silence, and enjoy the beauty of sentiment, and energy of language; and are taught habitually to cry at scenes of distress. The Englishman looks upon the theatre as a place of amusement; he does not expect to be alarmed with terror, or wrought upon by scenes of commiseration; but he is surprised into the feeling of those passions, and sheds tears because he cannot avoid it. The theatre, to most Englishmen, becomes a place of instruction by chance.

Davies, of course, betrays a common chauvinism of the English toward the French: while the French are pedantic and calculating, the English are spontaneous. But this distinction between English and French theaters—one for "art," one for "entertainment"; one tragic, one comic—conceals the fundamental likenesses between the two institutions and the plays they put on the stage. As the plays of Corneille, Racine, and Dryden suggest, neoclassical tragedy imposes severe and artificial forms on the irrepressible forces of the passions, which inevitably break through the formal speech and decorous behavior of the characters to destroy them and sometimes the state as well. Comedy of the period in England and in France reveals a cognate tension, as the formal acting styles and stereotyped characters common in Restoration comedy seem barely able to contain the bottomless appetites of the plays' heroes. To this extent, neoclassical decorum embodies a barely contained anxiety about the power of forms—forms of conduct, forms of art, forms of state—to prevent a revolution of unreason and disorder.

EARLY MODERN DRAMA IN PERFORMANCE AND HISTORY

In many respects, the theater of seventeenth-century Europe is continuous with our own. Given the fact that the European monarchies were rapidly expanding their political and mercantile influence around the globe, it's not surprising to find that their culture became exported as well, often to the cultivated elites of their new colonies. In Mexico, for example, the seventeenth-century nun Sor Juana Inés de la Cruz (1651–95) composed both *autos* and full-length dramas that echo—and, indeed, rival—the plays of the Spanish playwrights Calderón and Lope de Vega. The English drama of this period was exported as well; Farquhar's *The Recruiting Officer* was the first play to be performed in the penal colony of Australia. Moreover, the seventeenth century saw the institutionalization of theater as a commercial activity: in its architecture (indoor theaters, proscenium stages), in its greater appeal to a bourgeois audience, even in institutions like the Comédie Française (which, of course, continues to produce the plays of Molière and Racine), this theater is the direct forebear of the modern European theater, and in many ways the progenitor of its colonial theaters as well.

While the plays in this unit are all still in the classical repertory of modern theaters, these plays tend to pose particular problems to modern directors and actors. Although many plays of this period—*Tartuffe* or *The Rover,* for example—are given a contemporary setting, and concern themselves with relatively familiar characters, their language and characterization tends to be quite formal. Molière, for example, writes in a rich and fluid verse, even for the part of Tartuffe; Behn's cavaliers speak in prose, but their language is nonetheless dynamic and rhetorically complex. For modern actors, the elegance of this language often provides a point of entry to these characters, a way of seizing on the carefully discriminated social hierarchies at work in the cultures of these plays. Indeed, this verbal formality often becomes a kind of keynote to other aspects of performance as well, leading to a certain stateliness of physical movement and gesture, and an elegant balance of design elements as well. And yet in part because they are part of a classical repertoire, these plays have also inspired experiment and adaptation, a challenge to directors, designers, and actors to make it new.

PEDRO CALDERÓN DE LA BARCA

Like many of his contemporaries, Pedro Calderón de la Barca (1600–81) was a prolific playwright; he is thought to have written more than 200 plays, of which about 100 survive. Calderón was born in Madrid on January 17, 1600, the son of a minor court official. He was educated at a Jesuit "college," or preparatory school, before attending the University of Alcalá de Henares and the University of Salamanca. In 1620 he entered and won a poetry competition in honor of St. Isidore, which brought his writing to the attention of Lope de Vega, one of the judges of the contest. His first play, *Love, Honor, and Power,* was performed at court in 1623, but Calderón—who served intermittently in the military in the early 1620s—did not become established as a playwright until some time after 1626, when his plays were popular both at court and in the public theaters. With the death of Lope in 1635, Calderón became the most important playwright in Spain; he was knighted by Philip IV and became the principal court playwright in 1636.

Many of Calderón's plays in this period are either *capa y espada* plays, like *The Phantom Lady* (1629), or "love and honor" plays. *El alcalde de Zalamea* (*The Mayor of Zalamea,* 1642) is typical of the "love and honor" genre. In the play, a peasant's daughter is raped by a soldier; through a series of coincidences, the peasant becomes the mayor just as the soldier is apprehended, and he is torn between his desire for revenge, his obligation to enforce the process of law, and Christian charity. Calderón's most important play, *La vida es sueño* (*Life Is a Dream*) was produced in 1636. Throughout his career, Calderón also wrote *autos sacramentales,* but these became more significant later in his life. Calderón's mistress died in 1648, and Calderón entered the priesthood in 1651, possibly in grief over her loss; he also adopted and raised her child, who may have been his natural son. He was appointed priest of a Toledo parish, but the bishop objected to his playwriting, and Calderón devoted himself to *autos* thereafter; his *autos* were so popular that between 1647 and 1681 the only autos performed in Madrid were by Calderón. Calderón was made chaplain to the king in 1663 and died in retirement in 1681.

LIFE IS A DREAM

Life Is a Dream typifies the concerns of Calderón's mature drama: it is a play that tests the relationship between love and honor and conducts a searching meditation on human nature itself. The play is set in a mythological Poland, ruled by King Basil. Several years before the current action, it was predicted that if Basil's son, Segismund, were to succeed to the throne, he "would be the most outrageous / Of all men, the most cruel of all princes, / And impious of all monarchs, by whose acts / The kingdom would be torn up and divided." Basil, not willing to murder his son to save his country, has had Segismund removed from court and imprisoned in a cave, where he is attended only by the old courtier Clotaldo. This is where Rosaura—a well-born woman, also forsaken by her father—finds Segismund at the opening of the play.

Calderón begins his interrogation of human nature in the characterization of Segismund. Raised like a beast, Segismund is impulsive and untamed; though he opens the play complaining about his life of constant punishment, when he sees Rosaura (disguised as a man) watching him, he seizes and threatens to kill her. And yet when Rosaura kneels to him and begs for mercy, Segismund feels a strange sensation:

> Your voice has softened me, your presence halted me,
> And now, confusingly, I feel respect
> For you.

Living in captivity and isolation, Segismund is a "human monster": his behavior is ruled neither by reason nor by the conventions of polite society. Yet Segismund responds to Rosaura's plea for mercy as though some element of human sympathy were native to him. At the outset of the play, Calderón presents two contrasting views of human nature. In one perspective, human beings—like other animals—are ruled by their passions, which can only be governed by the civilizing force of law and reason; since Segismund has been raised without benefit of culture, he represents humanity in this unadorned state. Yet at the same time, Segismund's innate response to Rosaura suggests a second view of human nature, one in which sympathy, kindness, and morality are not imposed on human nature by education and society, but are somehow innate to humanity itself.

Just as Segismund relents toward Rosaura, Clotaldo suddenly bursts in and arrests her; Basil has decreed that even the existence of his son must remain a secret. But in arresting Rosaura, Clotaldo takes her sword, which he immediately recognizes as the sword he had left "fair Violante" years before: Rosaura—who has traveled to Poland disguised as a man for protection—must be Clotaldo's "son." Clotaldo is now caught in the classic "love-and-honor" bind. His duty to his king requires him to arrest and eventually execute anyone who spies Basil's secret son; yet to honor his bond to the king, he must betray the natural love he should show to his own child.

As the play proceeds, Clotaldo's effort to reclaim his son is paralleled by Basil's guilty desire to restore his own son to society. Basil hits on an experiment: he will put Segismund to sleep and awaken him at court; when he awakens, Segismund will be told that he is now the king. If his behavior is civilized and restrained, then Basil will know that the prophecy was wrong and will acknowledge Segismund as his heir; if his behavior is threatening, he will be sent back to prison. But Basil's plan has one flaw: having been raised in solitude, Segismund has no understanding of the elaborate conventions of courtly behavior. When he awakens as "king," he is rude to Prince Astolfo, offensively forward to Stella, and murderously impulsive to the servants who try to restrain and control his behavior. His behavior is so outrageous that he is again knocked unconscious and sent back to his prison.

Returned to captivity, Segismund can only understand his sojourn at court as a beautiful dream, a dream that becomes an image for the fleeting and illusory joys of life itself. But this recognition reforms Segismund, enables him to recognize that he can only assume his full humanity by governing his passions. In the play's final moments, Segismund is released from prison by a rebellious mob, who have come to release Segismund in order to overthrow Basil. When Segismund and his army confront Basil, the old king not only assumes that he has lost his kingdom, but that Segismund will kill him, in part to repay Basil for stealing the better part of his life. But Segismund now understands that although Basil's treatment has made him "savage" in his passions —an "inhuman monster"—the only way to regain his humanity is to govern his desire for revenge. So Segismund submits himself to Basil, who recognizes that his son has been reformed and gives him the kingdom: in conquering himself, Segismund wins the throne as well.

Calderón's drama is a deeply philosophical play, and the characters meditate extensively on the nature and meaning of their behavior. But *Life Is a Dream* is in some sense also a political play; its rich examination of "human nature" is conducted from a deeply aristocratic perspective. The only way that Segismund can demonstrate his humanity, after all, is to recognize and accept the conventions of courtly behavior as "natural." It is a sign of Segismund's acceptance of those values that his first act as king is to sentence the soldier who liberated him from prison to a life imprisonment of his own.

LIFE IS A DREAM

Pedro Calderón de la Barca

TRANSLATED BY ROY CAMPBELL

------ CHARACTERS ------

BASIL, *King of Poland*
SEGISMUND, *Prince*
ASTOLFO, *Duke of Muscovy*
CLOTALDO, *old man*
CLARION, *a comical servant*
ROSAURA, *a lady*

STELLA, *a princess*
SOLDIERS, GUARDS, MUSICIANS, SERVANTS, RETINUES, WOMEN

The scene is laid in the court of Poland, a nearby fortress, and the open country.

------ ACT ONE ------

On one side a craggy mountain: on the other a rude tower whose base serves as a prison for SEGISMUND. *The door facing the spectators is open. The action begins at nightfall.*

ROSAURA, *dressed as a man, appears on the rocks climbing down to the plain: behind her comes* CLARION.

ROSAURA: You headlong hippogriff who match the gale
In rushing to and fro, you lightning-flicker
Who give no light, you scaleless fish, you bird
Who have no coloured plumes, you animal
5 Who have no natural instinct, tell me whither
You lead me stumbling through this labyrinth
Of naked crags! Stay here upon this peak
And be a Phaëton to the brute-creation!
For I, pathless save only for the track
10 The laws of destiny dictate for me,
Shall, blind and desperate, descend this height
Whose furrowed brows are frowning at the sun.
How rudely, Poland, you receive a stranger
(Hardly arrived, but to be treated hardly)
15 And write her entry down in blood with thorns.
My plight attests this well, but after all,
Where did the wretchèd ever pity find?

CLARION: Say *two* so wretchèd. Don't you leave me out
When you complain! If we two sallied out
20 From our own country, questing high adventure,
And after so much madness and misfortune
Are still two here, and were two when we fell
Down those rough crags—shall I not be offended
To share the trouble yet forego the credit?

25 ROSAURA: I did not give you shares in my complaint
So as not to rob you of the right to sorrow
Upon your own account. There's such relief
In venting grief that a philosopher
Once said that sorrows should not be bemoaned
30 But sought for pleasure.

CLARION: Philosopher?
I call him a long-bearded, drunken sot
And would they'd cudgelled him a thousand blows
To give him something worth his while lamenting!
But, madam, what should we do, by ourselves,
35 On foot and lost at this late hour of day,
Here on this desert mountain far away—

The sun departing after fresh horizons?

ROSAURA: Clarion, how can I answer, being both
The partner of your plight and your dilemma?

CLARION: Would anyone believe such strange events? 40

ROSAURA: If there my sight is not deceived by fancy,
In the last timid light that yet remains
I seem to see a building.

CLARION: Either my hopes
Are lying or I see the signs myself.

ROSAURA: Between the towering crags, there stands so small 45
A royal palace that the lynx-eyed sun
Could scarce perceive it at midday, so rude
In architecture that it seems but one
Rock more down-toppled from the sun-kissed crags
That form the jaggèd crest.   Let's go closer, 50

CLARION: Let's go closer,
For we have stared enough: it would be better
To let the inmates makes us welcome.

ROSAURA: See:
The door, or, rather, that funereal gap,
Is yawning wide—whence night itself seems born,
Flowing out from its black, rugged centre. 55

(A sound of chains is heard.)

CLARION: Heavens! What's that I hear?

ROSAURA: I have become
A block immovable of ice and fire.

CLARION: Was that a little chain? Why, I'll be hanged
If that is not the clanking ghost of some
Past galley-slave—my terror proves it is! 60

SEGISMUND: Oh, miserable me! Unhappy me!

ROSAURA: How sad a cry that is! I fear new trials
And torments.

CLARION: It's a fearful sound.

ROSAURA: Oh, come,
My Clarion, let us fly from suffering!

CLARION: I'm in such sorry trim, I've not the spirit 65
Even to run away.

ROSAURA: And if you had,
You'd not have seen that door, not known of it.
When one's in doubt, the common saying goes
One walks between two lights.

CLARION: I'm the reverse.
It's not that way with me. 70

ROSAURA: What then disturbs you?

CLARION: I walk in doubt between two darknesses.

ROSAURA: Is not that feeble exhalation there
    A light? That pallid star whose fainting tremors,
    Pulsing a doubtful warmth of glimmering rays,
75   Make even darker with its spectral glow
    That gloomy habitation? Yes! because
    By its reflection (though so far away)
    I recognise a prison, grim and sombre,
    The sepulchre of some poor living carcase.
80   And, more to wonder at, a man lies there
    Clothed in the hides of savage beasts, with limbs
    Loaded with fetters, and a single lamp
    For company. So, since we cannot flee,
    Let us stay here and listen to his plaint
85   And what his sorrows are.

SEGISMUND: Unhappy me!
    Oh, miserable me! You heavens above,
    I try to think what crime I've done against you
    By being born. Although to have been born,
    I know, is an offence, and with just cause
90   I bear the rigours of your punishment:
    Since to be born is man's worst crime. But yet
    I long to know (to clarify my doubts)
    What greater crime, apart from being born,
    Can thus have earned my greater chastisement.
95   Aren't others born like me? And yet they seem
    To boast a freedom that I've never known.
    The bird is born, and in the hues of beauty
    Clothed with its plumes, yet scarce has it become
    A feathered posy—or a flower with wings—
100   When through ethereal halls it cuts its way,
    Refusing the kind shelter of its nest.
    And I, who have more soul than any bird,
    Must have less liberty?
    The beast is born, and with its hide bright-painted,
105   In lovely tints, has scarce become a spangled
    And starry constellation (thanks to the skilful
    Brush of the Painter) than its earthly needs
    Teach it the cruelty to prowl and kill,
    The monster of its labyrinth of flowers.
110   Yet I, with better instincts than a beast,
    Must have less liberty?
    The fish is born, the birth of spawn and slime,
    That does not even live by breathing air.
    No sooner does it feel itself a skiff
115   Of silver scales upon the wave than swiftly
    It roves about in all directions taking
    The measure of immensity as far
    As its cold blood's capacity allows.
    Yet I, with greater freedom of the will,
120   Must have less liberty?
    The brook is born, and like a snake unwinds
    Among the flowers. No sooner, silver serpent,
    Does it break through the blooms than it regales
    And thanks them with its music for their kindness,
125   Which opens to its course the majesty
    Of the wide plain. Yet I, with far more life,
    Must have less liberty?
    This fills me with such passion, I become
    Like the volcano Etna, and could tear

    Pieces of my own heart out of my breast!   130
    What law, justice, or reason can decree
    That man alone should never know the joys
    And be alone excepted from the rights
    God grants a fish, a bird, a beast, a brook?

ROSAURA: His words have filled me full of fear and pity.   135

SEGISMUND: Who is it overheard my speech? Clotaldo?

CLARION: Say "yes!"

ROSAURA: It's only a poor wretch, alas,
    Who in these cold ravines has overheard
    Your sorrows.

SEGISMUND: Then I'll kill you

(Seizes her.)

    So as to leave no witness of my frailty.   140
    I'll tear you into bits with these strong arms!

CLARION: I'm deaf. I wasn't able to hear that.

ROSAURA: If you were human born, it is enough
    That I should kneel to you for you to spare me.

SEGISMUND: Your voice has softened me, your presence   145
      halted me,
    And now, confusingly, I feel respect
    For you. Who are you? Though here I have learned
    So little of the world, since this grim tower
    Has been my cradle and my sepulchre;
    And though since I was born (if you can say   150
    I really have been born) I've only seen
    This rustic desert where in misery
    I dwell alone, a living skeleton,
    An animated corpse; and though till now,
    I never spoke, save to one man who hears   155
    My griefs and through whose converse I have heard
    News of the earth and of the sky; and though,
    To astound you more, and make you call me
    A human monster, I dwell here, and am
    A man of the wild animals, a beast   160
    Among the race of men; and though in such
    Misfortune, I have studied human laws,
    Instructed by the birds, and learned to measure
    The circles of the gentle stars, you only
    Have curbed my furious rage, amazed my vision,   165
    And filled with wonderment my sense of hearing.
    Each time I look at you, I feel new wonder!
    The more I see of you, the more I long
    To go on seeing more of you. I think
    My eyes are dropsical, to go on drinking   170
    What it is death for them to drink, because
    They go on drinking that which I am dying
    To see and that which, seen, will deal me death.
    Yet let me gaze on you and die, since I
    Am so bewitched I can no longer think   175
    What not seeing you would do to me—the sight
    Itself being fatal! that would be more hard
    Than dying, madness, rage, and fiercest grief:
    It would be life—worst fate of all because
    The gift of life to such a wretchèd man   180
    Would be the gift of death to happiness!

ROSAURA: Astonished as I look, amazed to hear,
    I know not what to say nor what to ask.

185 All I can say is that heaven guided me
     Here to be comforted, if it is comfort
     To see another sadder than oneself.
     They say a sage philosopher of old,
     Being so poor and miserable that he
     Lived on the few plain herbs he could collect,
190 One day exclaimed: "Could any man be poorer
     Or sadder than myself?"—when, turning round,
     He saw the very answer to his words.
     For there another sage philosopher
     Was picking up the scraps he'd thrown away.
195 I lived cursing my fortune in this world
     And asked within me: "Is there any other
     Suffers so hard a fate?" Now out of pity
     You've given me the answer. For within me
     I find upon reflection that my griefs
200 Would be as joys to you and you'd receive them
     To give you pleasure. So if they perchance
     In any measure may afford relief,
     Listen attentively to my misfortune
     And take what is left over for yourself.
205 I am . . .
     CLOTALDO: (Within.) Guards of the tower! You sluggards
     Or cowards, you have let two people pass
     Into the prison bounds . . .
     ROSAURA: Here's more confusion!
     SEGISMUND: That is Clotaldo, keeper of my prison.
     Are my misfortunes still not at an end?
210 CLOTALDO: Come. Be alert, and either seize or slay them
     Before they can resist!
     VOICES: (Within.)   Treason! Betrayal!
     CLARION: Guards of the tower who let us pass unhindered,
     Since there's a choice, to seize us would be simpler.

(Enter CLOTALDO with SOLDIERS. He holds a pistol and they all wear
masks.)

     CLOTALDO: (Aside to the SOLDIERS.) Cover your faces, all! It's a
          precaution
215 Imperative that nobody should know us
     While we are here.
     CLARION: What's this? A masquerade?
     CLOTALDO: O you, who ignorantly passed the bounds
     And limits of this region, banned to all—
     Against the king's decree which has forbidden
220 That any should find out the prodigy
     Hidden in these ravines—yield up your weapons
     Or else this pistol, like a snake of metal,
     Will spit the piercing venom of two shots
     With scandalous assault upon the air.
225 SEGISMUND: Tyrannic master, ere you harm these people
     Let my life be the spoil of these sad bonds
     In which (I swear it by Almighty God)
     I'll sooner rend myself with hands and teeth
     Amid these rocks than see them harmed and mourn
230 Their suffering.
     CLOTALDO: Since you know, Segismund,
     That your misfortunes are so huge that, even
     Before your birth, you died by heaven's decree,
     And since you know these walls and binding chains

Are but the brakes and curbs to your proud frenzies,
What use is it to bluster?   235

(To the GUARDS.)

                         Shut the door
Of this close prison! Hide him in its depths!
SEGISMUND: Ah, heavens, how justly you denied me freedom!
For like a Titan I would rise against you,
Pile jasper mountains high on stone foundations
And climb to burst the windows of the sun!   240
CLOTALDO: Perhaps you suffer so much pain today
Just to forestall that feat.
ROSAURA: Now that I see
How angry pride offends you, I'd be foolish
Not to plead humbly at your feet for life.
Be moved by me to pity. It would be   245
Notoriously harsh that neither pride
Nor humbleness found favour in your eyes!
CLARION: And if neither Humility nor Pride
Impress you (characters of note who act
And motivate a thousand mystery plays)   250
Let me, here, who am neither proud nor humble,
But merely something halfway in between,
Plead to you both for shelter and for aid.
CLOTALDO: Ho, there!
SOLDIER: Sir?
CLOTALDO: Take their weapons. Bind their eyes
So that they cannot see the way they're led.   255
ROSAURA: This is my sword. To nobody but you
I yield it, since you're, after all, the chief.
I cannot yield to one of meaner rank.
CLARION: My sword is such that I will freely give it
To the most mean and wretched.   260

(To one SOLDIER.)

                         Take it, you!
ROSAURA: And if I have to die, I'll leave it to you
In witness of your mercy. It's a pledge
Of great worth and may justly be esteemed
For someone's sake who wore it long ago.
CLOTALDO: (Apart.) Each moment seems to bring me new   265
     misfortune!
ROSAURA: Because of that, I ask you to preserve
This sword with care. Since if inconstant Fate
Consents to the remission of my sentence,
It has to win me honour. Though I know not
The secret that it carries, I do know   270
It has got one—unless I trick myself—
And prize it just as the sole legacy
My father left me.
CLOTALDO: Who then was your father?
ROSAURA: I never knew.
CLOTALDO: And why have you come here?
ROSAURA: I came to Poland to avenge a wrong.   275
CLOTALDO: (Apart.) Sacred heavens!

(On taking the sword he becomes very perturbed.)

                    What's this? Still worse and worse.
I am perplexed and troubled with more fears.

(Aloud.)

Tell me: who gave that sword to you?
ROSAURA: A woman.
CLOTALDO: Her name?
ROSAURA: A secret I am forced to keep.
280 CLOTALDO: What makes you think this sword contains a
        secret?
    ROSAURA: That she who gave it to me said: "Depart
        To Poland. There with subtlety and art
        Display it so that all the leading people
        And noblemen can see you wearing it,
285   And I know well that there's a lord among them
        Who will both shelter you and grant you favour."
        But, lest he should be dead, she did not name him.
    CLOTALDO: *(Aside.)* Protect me, heavens! What is this I hear?
        I cannot say if real or imagined
290   But here's the sword I gave fair Violante
        In token that, whoever in the future
        Should come from her to me wearing this sword,
        Would find in me a tender father's love.
        Alas, what can I do in such a pass,
295   When he who brings the sword to win my favour
        Brings it to find his own red death instead
        Arriving at my feet condemned already?
        What strange perplexity! How hard a fate!
        What an inconstant fortune to be plagued with!
300   This is my son not only by all signs
        But also by the promptings of my heart,
        Since, seeing him, my heart seems to cry out
        To him, and beat its wings, and, though unable
        To break the locks, behaves as one shut in,
305   Who, hearing noises in the street outside,
        Cranes from the window-ledge. Just so, not knowing
        What's really happening, but hearing sounds,
        My heart runs to my eyes which are its windows
        And out of them flows into bitter tears.
310   Protect me, heaven! What am I to do?
        To take him to the king is certain death.
        To hide him is to break my sacred oath
        And the strong law of homage. From one side
        Love of one's own, and from the other loyalty—
315   Call me to yield. Loyalty to my king
        (Why do I doubt?) comes before life and honour.
        Then live my loyalty, and let him die!
        When I remember, furthermore, he came
        To avenge an injury—a man insulted
320   And unavenged is in disgrace. My son
        Therefore he is not, nor of noble blood.
        But if some danger has mischanced, from which
        No one escapes, since honour is so fragile
        That any act can smash it, and it takes
325   A stain from any breath of air, what more
        Could any nobleman have done than he,
        Who, at the cost of so much risk and danger,
        Comes to avenge his honour? Since he's so brave
        He is my son, and my blood's in his veins.
330   And so betwixt the one doubt and the other,
        The most important mean between extremes
        Is to go to the king and tell the truth—

That he's my son, to kill, if so he wishes.
Perhaps my loyalty thus will move his mercy
And if I thus can merit a live son   335
I'll help him to avenge his injury.
But if the king prove constant in his rigour
And deal him death, he'll die in ignorance
That I'm his father.

(Aloud to ROSAURA *and* CLARION.*)*

                        Come then, strangers, come!
And do not fear that you have no companions   340
In your misfortunes, since, in equal doubt,
Tossed between life and death, I cannot guess
Which is the greater evil or the less.

A hall at the royal palace, in court.

Enter ASTOLFO *and* SOLDIERS *at one side: from the other side*
PRINCESS STELLA *and* [WOMEN]. *Military music and salvos.*

ASTOLFO: To greet your excellent bright beams
        As brilliant as a comet's rays,   345
        The drums and brasses mix their praise
        With those of fountains, birds, and streams.
        With sounds alike, in like amaze,
        Your heavenly face each voice salutes,
        Which puts them in such lively fettle,   350
        The trumpets sound like birds of metal,
        The songbirds play like feathered flutes.
        And thus they greet you, fair señora—
        The salvos, as their queen, the brasses,
        As to Minerva when she passes,   355
        The songbirds to the bright Aurora,
        And all the flowers and leaves and grasses
        As doing homage unto Flora,
        Because you come to cheat the day
        Which now the night has covered o'er—   360
        Aurora in your spruce array,
        Flora in peace, Pallas in war,
        But in my heart the queen of May.
STELLA: If human voice could match with acts
        You would have been unwise to say   365
        Hyperboles that a few facts
        May well refute some other day
        Confounding all this martial fuss
        With which I struggle daringly,
        Since flatteries you proffer thus   370
        Do not accord with what I see.
        Take heed that it's an evil thing
        And worthy of a brute accursed,
        Loud praises with your mouth to sing
        When in your heart you wish the worst.   375
ASTOLFO: Stella, you have been badly misinformed
        If you doubt my good faith. Here let me beg you
        To listen to my plea and hear me out.
        The third Eugtorgius died, the King of Poland.
        Basil, his heir, had two fair sisters who   380
        Bore you, my cousin, and myself. I would not
        Tire you with all that happened here. You know

Clorilene was your mother who enjoys,
Under a better reign, her starry throne.
385 She was the elder. Lovely Recisunda
(Whom may God cherish for a thousand years!)
The younger one, my mother and your aunt,
Was wed in Muscovy. Now to return:
Basil has yielded to the feebleness
390 Of age, loves learnèd study more than women,
Has lost his wife, is childless, will not marry.
And so it comes that you and I both claim
The heirdom of the realm. You claim that you
Were daughter to the elder daughter. I
395 Say that my being born a man, although
Son of the younger daughter, gives me title
To be preferred. We've told the king, our uncle,
Of both of our intentions. And he answered
That he would judge between our rival claims,
400 For which the time and place appointed was
Today and here. For the same reason I
Have left my native Muscovy. With that
Intent I come—not seeking to wage war
But so that you might thus wage war on me!
405 May Love, wise god, make true what people say
(Your "people" is a wise astrologer)
By settling this through your being chosen queen—
Queen and my consort, sovereign of my will;
My uncle crowning you, for greater honour;
410 Your courage conquering, as it deserves;
My love applauding you, its emperor!
STELLA: To such chivalrous gallantry, my breast
Cannot hold out. The imperial monarchy
I wish were mine only to make it yours—
415 Although my love is not quite satisfied
That you are to be trusted since your speech
Is somewhat contradicted by that portrait
You carry in the locket round your neck.
ASTOLFO: I'll give you satisfaction as to that.

(Drums.)

420 But these loud instruments will not permit it
That sound the arrival of the king and council.

(Enter KING BASIL *with his following.)*

STELLA: Wise Thales . . .
ASTOLFO: Learned Euclid . . .
STELLA: Among the signs . . .
ASTOLFO: Among the stars . . .
STELLA: Where you preside in power . . .
ASTOLFO: Where you reside . . .
425 STELLA: And plot their paths . . .
ASTOLFO: And trace their fiery trails . . .
STELLA: Describing . . .
ASTOLFO: . . . Measuring and judging them . . .
STELLA: Please read my stars that I, in humble bonds . . .
ASTOLFO: Please read them, so that I in soft embraces . . .
STELLA: May twine as ivy to this tree!
ASTOLFO: May find
430 Myself upon my knees before these feet!

BASIL: Come and embrace me, niece and nephew. Trust me,
Since you're both loyal to my loving precepts,
And come here so affectionately both—
In nothing shall I leave you cause to cavil,
And both of you as equals will be treated.   435
The gravity of what I have to tell
Oppresses me, and all I ask of you
Is silence: the event itself will claim
Your wonderment. So be attentive now,
Belovèd niece and nephew, illustrious courtiers,   440
Relatives, friends, and subjects! You all know
That for my learning I have merited
The surname of The Learnèd, since the brush
Of great Timanthes, and Lisippus' marbles—
Stemming oblivion (consequence of time)—   445
Proclaimed me to mankind Basil the Great.
You know the science that I most affect
And most esteem is subtle mathematics
(By which I forestall time, cheat fame itself)
Whose office is to show things gradually.   450
For when I look my tables up and see,
Present before me, all the news and actions
Of centuries to come, I gain on Time—
Since Time recounts whatever I have said
After I say it. Those snowflaking haloes,   455
Those canopies of crystal spread on high,
Lit by the sun, cut by the circling moon,
Those diamond orbs, those globes of radiant crystal
Which the bright stars adorn, on which the signs
Parade in blazing excellence, have been   460
My chiefest study all through my long years.
They are the volumes on whose adamantine
Pages, bound up in sapphire, heaven writes,
In lines of burnished gold and vivid letters,
All that is due to happen, whether adverse   465
Or else benign. I read them in a flash,
So quickly that my spirit tracks their movements—
Whatever road they take, whatever goal
They aim at. Would to heaven that before
My genius had been the commentary   470
Writ in their margins, or the index to
Their pages, that my life had been the rubble,
The ruin, and destruction of their wrath,
And that my tragedy in them had ended,
Because, to the unlucky, even their merit   475
Is like a hostile knife, and he whom knowledge
Injures is but a murderer to himself.
And this I say myself, though my misfortunes
Say it far better, which, to marvel at,
I beg once more for silence from you all.   480
With my late wife, the queen, I had a son,
Unhappy son, to greet whose birth the heavens
Wore themselves out in prodigies and portents.
Ere the sun's light brought him live burial
Out of the womb (for birth resembles death)   485
His mother many times, in the delirium
And fancies of her sleep, saw a fierce monster
Bursting her entrails in a human form,
Born spattered with her lifeblood, dealing death,
The human viper of this century!   490

The day came for his birth, and every presage
Was then fulfilled, for tardily or never
Do the more cruel ones prove false. At birth
His horoscope was such that the bright sun,
495   Stained in its blood, entered ferociously
Into a duel with the moon above.
The whole earth seemed a rampart for the strife
Of heaven's two lights, who—though not hand-to-hand—
Fought light-to-light to gain the mastery!
500   The worst eclipse the sun has ever suffered
Since Christ's own death horrified earth and sky.
The whole earth overflowed with conflagrations
So that it seemed the final paroxysm
Of existence. The skies grew dark. Buildings shook.
505   The clouds rained stones. The rivers ran with blood.
In this delirious frenzy of the sun,
Thus, Segismund was born into the world,
Giving a foretaste of his character
By killing his own mother, seeming to speak thus
510   By his ferocity: "I am a man,
Because I have begun now to repay
All kindnesses with evil." To my studies
I went forthwith, and saw in all I studied
That Segismund would be the most outrageous
515   Of all men, the most cruel of all princes,
And impious of all monarchs, by whose acts
The kingdom would be torn up and divided
So as to be a school of treachery
And an academy of vices. He,
520   Risen in fury, amidst crimes and horrors,
Was born to trample me (with shame I say it)
And make of my grey hairs his very carpet.
Who is there but believes an evil Fate?
And more if he discovers it himself,
525   For self-love lends its credit to our studies.
So I, believing in the Fates, and in
The havoc that their prophecies predestined,
Determined to cage up this newborn tiger
To see if on the stars we sages have
530   Some power. I gave out that the prince had died
Stillborn, and, well-forewarned, I built a tower
Amidst the cliffs and boulders of yon mountains
Over whose tops the light scarce finds its way,
So stubbornly their obelisks and crags
535   Defend the entry to them. The strict laws
And edicts that I published then (declaring
That nobody might enter the forbidden
Part of the range) were passed on that account.
There Segismund lives to this day, a captive,
540   Poor and in misery, where, save Clotaldo,
His guardian, none have seen or talked to him.
The latter has instructed him in all
Branches of knowledge and in the Catholic faith,
Alone the witness of his misery.
545   There are three things to be considered now:
Firstly, Poland, that I love you greatly,
So much that I would free you from the oppression
And servitude of such a tyrant king.
He would not be a kindly ruler who
550   Would put his realm and homeland in such danger.
The second fact that I must bear in mind

Is this: that to deny my flesh and blood
The rights which law, both human and divine,
Concedes, would not accord with Christian charity,
For no law says that, to prevent another   555
Being a tyrant, I may be one myself,
And if my son's a tyrant, to prevent him
From doing outrage, I myself should do it.
Now here's the third and last point I would speak of,
Namely, how great an error it has been   560
To give too much belief to things predicted,
Because, even if his inclination should
Dictate some headlong, rash precipitancies,
They may perhaps not conquer him entirely,
For the most accursèd destiny, the most   565
Violent inclination, the most impious
Planet—all can but influence, not force,
The free will which man holds direct from God.
And so, between one motive and another
Vacillating discursively, I hit   570
On a solution that will stun you all.
I shall tomorrow, but without his knowing
He is my son—your king—place Segismund
(For that's the name with which he was baptised)
Here on my throne, beneath my canopy,   575
Yes, in my very place, that he may govern you
And take command. And you must all be here
To swear him fealty as his loyal subjects.
Three things may follow from this test, and these
I'll set against the three which I proposed.   580
The first is that should the prince prove prudent,
Stable, and benign—thus giving the lie
To all that prophecy reports of him—
Then you'll enjoy in him your rightful ruler
Who was so long a courtier of the mountains   585
And neighbour to the beasts. Here is the second:
If he prove proud, rash, cruel, and outrageous,
And with a loosened rein gallop unheeding
Across the plains of vice, I shall have done
My duty, and fulfilled my obligation   590
Of mercy. If I then re-imprison him,
That's incontestably a kingly deed—
Not cruelty but merited chastisement.
The third thing's this: that if the prince should be
As I've described him, then—by the love I feel   595
For you, my vassals—I shall give you worthier
Rulers to wear the sceptre and the crown;
Because your king and queen will be my nephew
And niece, each with an equal right to rule,
Each gaining the inheritance he merits,   600
And joined in faith of holy matrimony.
This I command you as a king, I ask you
As a kind father, as a sage I pray you,
As an experienced old man I tell you,
And (if it's true, as Spanish Seneca   605
Says, that the king is slave unto his nation)
This, as a humble slave, I beg of you.
ASTOLFO: If it behoves me to reply (being
The person most involved in this affair)
Then, in the name of all, let Segismund   610
Appear! It is enough that he's your son!
ALL: Give us our prince: we want him for our king!

BASIL: Subjects, I thank you for your kindly favour.
    Accompany these, my two Atlases,
615   Back to their rooms. Tomorrow you shall see him.
ALL: Long live the great King Basil! Long live Basil!

(Exeunt all, accompanying STELLA *and* ASTOLFO. *The king remains.)*

(Enter CLOTALDO *with* ROSAURA *and* CLARION.*)*

CLOTALDO: May I have leave to speak, sire?
BASIL: Oh, Clotaldo!
    You're very welcome.
CLOTALDO: Thus to kneel before you
    Is always welcome, sire—yet not today
620   When sad and evil Fate destroys the joy
    Your presence normally concedes.
BASIL: What's wrong?
CLOTALDO: A great misfortune, sire, has come upon me
    Just when I should have met it with rejoicing.
BASIL: Continue.
CLOTALDO: Sire, this beautiful young man
625   Who inadvertently and daringly
    Came to the tower, wherein he saw the prince,
    Is my . . .
BASIL: Do not afflict yourself, Clotaldo.
    Had it not been just now, I should have minded,
    I must confess. But I've revealed the secret,
630   And now it does not matter if he knows it.
    Attend me afterwards. I've many things
    To tell you. You in turn have many things
    To do for me. You'll be my minister,
    I warn you, in the most momentous action
635   The world has ever seen. These prisoners, lest you
    Should think I blame your oversight, I'll pardon.

(Exit.)

CLOTALDO: Long may you live, great sire! A thousand years!

(Aside.)

    Heaven improves our fates. I shall not tell him
    Now that he is my son, since it's not needed
640   Till he's avenged.

(Aloud.)

    Strangers, you may go free.
ROSAURA: Humbly I kiss your feet.
CLARION: Whilst I'll just *miss* them—
    Old friends will hardly quibble at one letter.
ROSAURA: You've granted me my life, sir. I remain
645   Your servant and eternally your debtor.
CLOTALDO: No! It was not your life I gave you. No!
    Since any wellborn man who, unavenged,
    Nurses an insult does not live at all.
    And seeing you have told me that you came
650   For that sole reason, it was not life I spared—
    Life in disgrace is not a life at all.

(Aside.)

    I see this spurs him.
ROSAURA: Freely I confess it—
    Although you spared my life, it was no life.

    But I will wipe my honour's stain so spotless
    That after I have vanquished all my dangers
655   Life well may seem a shining gift from you.
CLOTALDO: Take here your burnished steel: 'twill be enough,
    Bathed in your enemies' red blood, to right you.
    For steel that once was mine (I mean of course
    Just for the time I've had it in my keeping)
660   Should know how to avenge you.
ROSAURA: Now, in your name I gird it on once more
    And on it I will swear to take revenge
    Although my foe were even mightier.
CLOTALDO: Is he so powerful?
ROSAURA: So much so that . . .
    Although I have no doubt in your discretion . . .
    I say no more because I'd not estrange
    Your clemency.
CLOTALDO: You would have won me had you told me, since
670   That would prevent me helping him.

(Aside.)

    If only I could discover who he is!
ROSAURA: So that you'll not think that I value lightly
    Such confidence, know that my adversary
    Is no less than Astolfo, Duke of Muscovy.
CLOTALDO: *(Aside.)* (I hardly can withstand the grief it
        gives me
    For it is worse than aught I could imagine!
    Let us inquire of him some further facts.)

(Aloud.)

    If you were born a Muscovite, your ruler
    Could never have affronted you. Go back
    Home to your country. Leave this headstrong valour.
    It will destroy you.
ROSAURA: Though he's been my prince,
    I know that he has done me an affront.
CLOTALDO: Even though he slapped your face, that's no
        affront.

(Aside.)

    O heavens!
ROSAURA: My insult was far deeper!
CLOTALDO: Tell it:
    Since nothing I imagine could be deeper.
ROSAURA: Yes. I will tell it, yet, I know not why,
    With such respect I look upon your face,
    I venerate you with such true affection,
    With such high estimation do I weigh you,
    That I scarce dare to tell you—these men's clothes
    Are an enigma, not what they appear.
    So now you know. Judge if it's no affront
    That here Astolfo comes to wed with Stella
    Although betrothed to me. I've said enough.

(Exeunt ROSAURA *and* CLARION.*)*

CLOTALDO: Here! Listen! Wait! What mazed confusion!
    It is a labyrinth wherein the reason
    Can find no clue. My family honour's injured.
    The enemy's all powerful. I'm a vassal

655

660

665

670

675

680

685

690

695

And she's a woman. Heavens! Show a path
700   Although I don't believe there is a way!
There's nought but evil bodings in the sky.
The whole world is a prodigy, say I.

——— ACT TWO ———

A hall in the royal palace.

Enter BASIL *and* CLOTALDO.

CLOTALDO: All has been done according to your orders.
BASIL: Tell me, Clotaldo, how it went?
CLOTALDO: Why, thus:
I took to Segismund a calming drug
Wherein are mixed herbs of especial virtue,
5   Tyrannous in their overpowering strength
Which seize and steal and alienate man's gift
Of reasoning, thus making a live corpse
Of him. His violence evaporated
With all his faculties and senses too.
10   There is no need to prove it's possible
Because experience teaches us that medicine
Is full of natural secrets, that there is no
Animal, plant, or stone that has not got
Appointed properties. If human malice
15   Explores a thousand poisons which deal death,
Who then can doubt, that being so, that other
Poisons, less violent, cause only sleep?
But (leaving that doubt aside, as proven false
By every evidence) hear then the sequel:
20   I went down into Segismund's close prison
Bearing the drink wherein, with opium,
Henbane and poppies had been mixed. With him
I talked a little while of the humanities,
In which dumb Nature has instructed him,
25   The mountains and the heavens and the stars,
In whose divine academies he learned
Rhetoric from the birds and the wild creatures.
To lift his spirit to the enterprise
Which you require of him, I chose for subject
30   The swiftness of a stalwart eagle, who,
Deriding the base region of the wind,
Rises into the sphere reserved for fire,
A feathered lightning, an untethered comet.
Then I extolled such lofty flight and said:
35   "After all, he's the king of birds, and so
Takes precedence, by right, over the rest."
No more was needful for, in taking up
Majesty for his subject, he discoursed
With pride and high ambition, as his blood
40   Naturally moves, incites, and spurs him on
To grand and lofty things, and so he said
That in the restless kingdom of the birds
There should be those who swear obedience, too!
"In this, my miseries console me greatly,
45   Because if I'm a vassal here, it's only
By force, and not by choice. Of my own will
I would not yield in rank to any man."
Seeing that he grew furious—since this touched
The theme of his own griefs—I gave the potion

And scarcely had it passed from cup to breast   50
Before he yielded all his strength to slumber.
A chill sweat ran through all his limbs and veins.
Had I not known that this was mere feigned death
I would have thought him dead. Then came the men
To whom you've trusted this experiment,   55
Who placed him in a coach and brought him here
To your own rooms, where all things were prepared
In royalty and grandeur as befitting
His person. In your own bed they have laid him
Where, when the torpor wanes, they'll do him service 60
As if he were Your Majesty himself.
All has been done as you have ordered it,
And if I have obeyed you well, my lord,
I'd beg a favour (pardon me this freedom)—
To know what your intention is in thus   65
Transporting Segismund here to the palace.
BASIL: Your curiosity is just, Clotaldo,
And yours alone I'll satisfy. The star
Which governs Segismund, my son, in life,
Threatens a thousand tragedies and woes.   70
And now I wish to see whether the stars
(Which never lie—and having shown to us
So many cruel signs seem yet more certain)
May yet be brought to moderate their sentence,
Whether by prudence charmed or valour won,   75
For man does have the power to rule his stars.
I would examine this, bringing him here
Where he may know he is my son, and make
Trial of his talent. If magnanimously
He conquers and controls himself, he'll reign,   80
But if he proves a tyrant and is cruel,
Back to his chains he'll go. Now, you will ask,
Why did we bring him sleeping in this manner
For the experiment? I'll satisfy you,
Down to the smallest detail, with my answer.   85
If he knows that he is my son today,
And if tomorrow he should find himself
Once more reduced to prison, to misery,
He would despair entirely, knowing truly
Who, and whose son, he is. What consolation   90
Could he derive, then, from his lot? So I
Contrive to leave an exit for such grief,
By making him believe it was a dream.
By these means we may learn two things at once:
First, his character—for he will really be   95
Awake in all he thinks and all his actions;
Second, his consolation—which would be
(If he should wake in prison on the morrow,
Although he saw himself obeyed today)
That he might understand he had been dreaming,   100
And he will not be wrong, for in this world,
Clotaldo, all who live are only dreaming.
CLOTALDO: I've proofs enough to doubt of your success,
But now it is too late to remedy it.
From what I can make out, I think he's awakened   105
And that he's coming this way, by the sound.
BASIL: I shall withdraw. You, as his tutor, go
And guide him through his new bewilderments
By answering his queries with the truth.

110 CLOTALDO: You give me leave to tell the truth of it?
    BASIL: Yes, because knowing all things, he may find
        Known perils are the easiest to conquer.

(Exit BASIL. Enter CLARION.)

    CLARION: It cost me four whacks to get here so quickly.
        I caught them from a red-haired halberdier
115   Sprouting a ginger beard over his livery,
        And I've come to see what's going on.
        No windows give a better view than those
        A man brings with him in his head, not asking
        For tickets of admission or paid seats,
120   Since at all functions, festivals, or feasts
        He looks out with the same nice self-composure.
    CLOTALDO: *(Aside.)* Here's Clarion who's the servant of that
        person—
        That trader in woes, importer from Poland
        Of my disgrace.

(Aloud.)

                    Come, Clarion, what news?
125 CLARION: Item the first: encouraged by the fact
        Your clemency's disposed to venge her insult,
        Rosaura has resumed her proper clothing.
    CLOTALDO: That's right: it's less indecorous and bold.
    CLARION: Item: she's changed her name, and given out
130   That she's your niece. And now they've made so much
        Of her that she's been raised to maid of honour
        To the unique and only princess, Stella.
    CLOTALDO: That's right: her honour stands to my account.
    CLARION: Indeed she merely bides the time till you
135   Will settle all accounts about her honour.
    CLOTALDO: Biding the time is wise, for in the end
        It's Time that's going to settle all accounts!
    CLARION: Item: that she's attended like a queen,
        Because they take her for your niece. Item:
140   That I, who trudged along with her, am dying
        Of hunger. Nobody remembers me,
        Nor yet remembers that I'm like my name
        And (should I sound my Clarion) could tell
        All to the king and Stella and Astolfo.
145   For I am both a Clarion and a servant—
        Two things which ill-accord with secrecy.
        If silence should, by chance, let slip my hand,
        Then there's a chorus which would fit me well:
        "Dawn-breaking Clarion plays no better tune!"
150 CLOTALDO: You've reason for complaint. I'll satisfy it
        If you'll but serve me . . .
    CLARION: Hush, here's Segismund!

(Enter MUSICIANS, singing, and SERVANTS arraying SEGISMUND, who seems amazed.)

    SEGISMUND: Heavens above! What's this that I am seeing?

        I wonder at it all, with naught of fear!
        But with a mighty doubt, I disbelieve it!
155   I?—in a sumptuous palace? I—encircled
        With rich brocades and silks? I—overwhelmed
        With servants in such brilliant liveries?

        I—to awake in such a gorgeous bed?
        I—in the middle of so many footmen
        Who clothe me in rich garments? I'm awake: 160
        It would be false to take this for a dream.
        Am I not Segismund? Heavens! disabuse me
        If I'm mistaken. Say, what could have happened
        In my imagination while I slept—
        That I should find myself in such a place?   165
        But why should I worry, whatever it was?
        I'll let myself be served and entertained—
        Befall what may.
    FIRST SERVANT: *(Aside to SECOND SERVANT and CLARION.)*
                    He's very melancholy!
    SECOND SERVANT: Who would not be, considering all that's
        happened
        To him?   170
    CLARION: I would not be!
    SECOND SERVANT: You, speak to him.
    FIRST SERVANT: Shall they begin to sing again?
    SEGISMUND: Why, no,
        I would not have them sing.
    SECOND SERVANT: You're so distraught,
        I wish you entertained.
    SEGISMUND: My griefs are such
        That no mere voices can amuse me now—
        Only the martial music pleased my mind.   175
    CLOTALDO: Your Highness, mighty prince, give me your hand
        To kiss. I'm glad to be the first to offer
        Obedience at your feet.
    SEGISMUND: *(Aside.)*   This is Clotaldo.
        How is it he, that tyrannised my thralldom,
        Should now be treating me with such respect?   180

(Aloud.)

        Tell me what's happening all round me here.
    CLOTALDO: With the perplexities of your new state,
        Your reason will encounter many doubts,
        But I shall try to free you from them all
        (If that may be) because you now must know   185
        You are hereditary Prince of Poland.
        If you have been withdrawn from public sight
        Under restraint, it was in strict obedience
        To Fate's inclemency, which will permit
        A thousand woes to fall upon this empire   190
        The moment that you wear the sovereign's crown.
        But trusting that you'll prudently defeat
        Your own malignant stars (since they can be
        Controlled by magnanimity) you've been
        Brought to this palace from the tower you knew   195
        Even while your soul was yielded up to sleep.
        My lord the king, your father, will be coming
        To see you, and from him you'll learn the rest.
    SEGISMUND: Then, vile, infamous traitor, what have I
        To know more than this fact of who I am,   200
        To show my pride and power from this day onward?
        How have you played your country such a treason
        As to deny me, against law and right,
        The rank which is my own?
    CLOTALDO: Unhappy me!

205 SEGISMUND: You were a traitor to the law, a flattering liar
       To your own king, and cruel to myself.
       And so the king, the law, and I condemn you,
       After such fierce misfortunes as I've borne,
       To die here by my hands.
    SECOND SERVANT: My lord!
    SEGISMUND: Let none
210   Get in the way. It is in vain. By God!
       If you intrude, I'll throw you through the window.
    SECOND SERVANT: Clotaldo, fly!
    CLOTALDO: Alas, poor Segismund!
       That you should show such pride, all unaware
       That you are dreaming this.

    (Exit.)

    SECOND SERVANT: Take care! Take care!
215 SEGISMUND: Get out!
    SECOND SERVANT: He was obeying the king's orders.
    SEGISMUND: In an injustice, no one should obey
       The king, and I'm his prince.
    SECOND SERVANT: He had no right
       To look into the rights and wrongs of it.
    SEGISMUND: You must be mad to answer back at me.
220 CLARION: The prince is right. It's you who're in the
              wrong!
    SECOND SERVANT: Who gave you right to speak?
    CLARION: I simply took it.
    SEGISMUND: And who are you?
    CLARION: I am the go-between,
       And in this art I think I am a master—
       Since I'm the greatest jackanapes alive.
225 SEGISMUND: *(To* CLARION.*)* In all this new world, you're the
              only one
       Of the whole crowd who pleases me.
    CLARION: Why, my lord,
       I am the best pleaser of Segismunds
       That ever was: ask anybody here!

    (Enter ASTOLFO.*)*

    ASTOLFO: Blessèd the day, a thousand times, my prince,
230   On which you landed here on Polish soil
       To fill with so much splendour and delight
       Our wide horizons, like the break of day!
       For you arise as does the rising sun
       Out of the rugged mountains, far away.
235   Shine forth then! And although so tardily
       You bind the glittering laurels on your brows,
       The longer may they last you still unwithered.
    SEGISMUND: God save you.
    ASTOLFO: That you do not know me, sir,
       Is some excuse for greeting me without
240   The honour due to me. I am Astolfo
       The Duke of Muscovy. You are my cousin.
       We are of equal rank.
    SEGISMUND: Then if I say,
       "God save you," do I not display good feeling?
       But since you take such note of who you are,
245   The next time that I see you, I shall say
       "God save you *not*," if you would like that better.

    SECOND SERVANT: *(To* ASTOLFO.*)* Your Highness, make
              allowance for his breeding
       Amongst the mountains. So he deals with all.

    (To SEGISMUND.*)*

       Astolfo does take precedence, Your Highness—
    SEGISMUND: I have no patience with the way he came   250
       To make his solemn speech, then put his hat on!
    SECOND SERVANT: He's a grandee!
    SEGISMUND: I'm grander than grandees!
    SECOND SERVANT: For all that, there should be respect between
              you,
       More than among the rest.
    SEGISMUND: And who told you
       To mix in my affairs?   255

    (Enter STELLA.*)*

    STELLA: Many times welcome to Your Royal Highness,
       Now come to grace the dais that receives him
       With gratitude and love. Long may you live
       August and eminent, despite all snares,
       And count your life by centuries, not years!   260
    SEGISMUND: *(Aside to* CLARION.*)* Now tell me, who's this
              sovereign deity
       At whose divinest feet Heaven lays down
       The fleece of its aurora in the east?
    CLARION: Sir, it's your cousin Stella.
    SEGISMUND: She were better
       Named "sun" than "star"!   265

    (To STELLA.*)*

                               Though your speech was fair,
       Just to have seen you and been conquered by you
       Suffices for a welcome in itself.
       To find myself so blessed beyond my merit
       What can I do but thank you, lovely Stella,
       For you could add more brilliance and delight   270
       To the most blazing star? When you get up
       What work is left the sun to do? O give me
       Your hand to kiss, from out whose cup of snow
       The solar horses drink the fires of day!
    STELLA: Be a more gentle courtier.   275
    ASTOLFO: I am lost.
    SECOND SERVANT: I know Astolfo's hurt. I must divert him.

    (To SEGISMUND.*)*

       Sir, you should know that thus to woo so boldly
       Is most improper. And, besides, Astolfo . . .
    SEGISMUND: Did I not tell you not to meddle with me?
    SECOND SERVANT: I only say what's just.   280
    SEGISMUND: All this annoys me.
       Nothing seems just to me but what I want.
    SECOND SERVANT: Why, sir, I heard you say that no obedience
       Or service should be lent to what's unjust.
    SEGISMUND: You also heard me say that I would throw
       Anyone who annoys me from that balcony.   285
    SECOND SERVANT: With men like me you cannot do such
              things.

SEGISMUND: No? Well, by God, I'll have to prove it then!

(He takes him in his arms and rushes out, followed by many, to return soon after.)

ASTOLFO: What on earth have I seen? Can it be true?

STELLA: Go, all, and stop him!

SEGISMUND: *(Returning.)*   From the balcony
290   He's fallen in the sea. How strange it seems!

ASTOLFO: Measure your acts of violence, my lord:
          From crags to palaces, the distance is
          As great as that between man and the beasts.

SEGISMUND: Well, since you are for speaking out so boldly,
295   Perhaps one day you'll find that on your shoulders
          You have no head to place your hat upon.

(Exit ASTOLFO. Enter BASIL.)

BASIL: What's happened here?

SEGISMUND: Nothing at all. A man
          Wearied me, so I threw him in the sea.

CLARION: *(To SEGISMUND.)* Be warned. That is the king.

BASIL: On the first day,
300   So soon, your coming here has cost a life?

SEGISMUND: He said I couldn't: so I won the bet.

BASIL: It grieves me, Prince, that, when I hoped to see you
          Forewarned, and overriding Fate, in triumph
          Over your stars, the first thing I should see
305   Should be such rigour—that your first deed here
          Should be a grievous homicide. Alas!
          With what love, now, can I offer my arms,
          Knowing your own have learned to kill already?
          Who sees a dirk, red from a mortal wound,
310   But does not fear it? Who can see the place
          Soaking in blood, where late a man was murdered,
          But even the strongest must respond to nature?
          So in your arms seeing the instrument
          Of death, and looking on a blood-soaked place,
315   I must withdraw myself from your embrace,
          And though I thought in loving bonds to bind
          Your neck, yet fear withholds me from your arms.

SEGISMUND: Without your loving arms I can sustain
          Myself as usual. That such a loving father
320   Could treat me with such cruelty, could thrust me
          From his side ungratefully, could rear me
          As a wild beast, could hold me for a monster,
          And pray that I were dead, that such a father
          Withholds his arms from winding round my neck,
325   Seems unimportant, seeing that he deprives
          Me of my very being as a man.

BASIL: Would to heaven I had never granted it,
          For then I never would have heard your voice,
          Nor seen your outrages.

SEGISMUND: Had you denied
330   Me being, then I would not have complained,
          But that you took it from me when you gave it—
          That is my quarrel with you. Though to give
          Is the most singular and noble action,
          It is the basest action if one gives
335   Only to take away.

BASIL: How well you thank me
          For being raised from pauper to a prince!

SEGISMUND: In this what is there I should thank you for?
          You tyrant of my will! If you are old
          And feeble, and you die, what can you give me
          More than what is my own by right of birth?   340
          You are my father and my king, therefore
          This grandeur comes to me by natural law.
          Therefore, despite my present state, I'm not
          Indebted to you, rather can I claim
          Account of all those years in which you robbed me   345
          Of life and being, liberty, and honour.
          You ought to thank me that I press no claim
          Since you're my debtor, even to bankruptcy.

BASIL: Barbarous and outrageous brute! The heavens
          Have now fulfilled their prophecy: I call   350
          Them to bear witness to your pride. Although
          You know now, disillusioned, who you are,
          And see yourself where you take precedence,
          Take heed of this I say: be kind and humble
          Since it may be that you are only dreaming,   355
          Although it seems to you you're wide-awake.

(Exit BASIL.)

SEGISMUND: Can I perhaps be dreaming, though I seem
          So wide-awake? No: I am not asleep,
          Since I can touch, and realise what I
          Have been before, and what I am today.   360
          And if you even now relented, Father,
          There'd be no cure since I know who I am
          And you cannot, for all your sighs and groans,
          Cheat me of my hereditary crown.
          And if I was submissive in my chains   365
          Before, then I was ignorant of what I am,
          Which I now know (and likewise know that I
          Am partly man but partly beast as well).

(Enter ROSAURA in woman's clothing.)

ROSAURA: *(Aside.)* I came in Stella's train. I am afraid
          Of meeting with Astolfo, since Clotaldo   370
          Says he must not know who I am, not see me,
          Because (he says) it touches on my honour.
          And well I trust Clotaldo since I owe him
          The safety of my life and honour both.

CLARION: What pleases you, and what do you admire   375
          Most, of the things you've seen here in the world?

SEGISMUND: Why, nothing that I could not have foreseen—
          Except the loveliness of women! Once,
          I read among the books I had out there
          That who owes God most grateful contemplation   380
          Is Man: who is himself a tiny world.
          But I think who owes God more grateful study
          Is Woman—since she is a tiny heaven,
          Having as much more beauty than a man
          As heaven than earth. And even more, I say,   385
          If she's the one that I am looking at.

ROSAURA: *(Aside.)* That is the prince. I'll go.

SEGISMUND: Stop! Woman! Wait!
          Don't join the sunset with the breaking day
          By fading out so fast. If east and west

390   Should clash like that, the day would surely suffer
    A syncope. But what is this I see?
ROSAURA: What I am looking at I doubt, and yet
    Believe.
SEGISMUND: *(Aside.)* This beauty I have seen before.
ROSAURA: *(Aside.)* This pomp and grandeur I have seen before
395   Cooped in a narrow dungeon.
SEGISMUND: *(Aside.)*   I have found
    My life at last.

(Aloud.)

              Woman (for that sole word
    Outsoars all wooing flattery of speech
    From one that is a man), woman, who are you?
    If even long before I ever saw you
400   You owed me adoration as your prince,
    How much the more should you be conquered by me
    Now I recall I've seen you once before!
    Who are you, beauteous woman?
ROSAURA: *(Aside.)*   I'll pretend.

(Aloud.)

    In Stella's train, I am a luckless lady.
405   SEGISMUND: Say no such thing. You are the sun from which
    The minor star that's Stella draws its life,
    Since she receives the splendour of your rays.
    I've seen how in the kingdom of sweet odours,
    Commander of the squadrons of the flowers,
410   The rose's deity presides, and is
    Their empress by divine right of her beauty.
    Among the precious stones which can be listed
    In the academy of mines, I've seen
    The diamond much preferred above the rest,
415   And crowned their emperor, for shining brightest.
    In the revolving empire of the stars
    The morning star takes pride among the others.
    In their perfected spheres, when the sun calls
    The planets to his council, he presides
420   And is the very oracle of day.
    Then if among stars, gems, planet, and flowers
    The fairest are exalted, why do you
    Wait on a lesser beauty than yourself
    Who are, in greater excellence and beauty,
425   The sun, the morning star, the diamond, and the rose!

(Enter CLOTALDO, *who remains by the stage-curtain.)*

CLOTALDO: *(Aside.)* I wish to curb him, since I brought
    him up.
    But, what is this?
ROSAURA: I reverence your favour,
    And yet reply, rhetorical, with silence,
    For when one's mind is clumsy and untaught,
430   He answers best who does not speak at all.
SEGISMUND: Stay! Do not go! How can you wish to go
    And leave me darkened by my doubts?
ROSAURA: Your Highness,
    I beg your leave to go.
SEGISMUND: To go so rudely
    Is not to beg my leave but just to take it.

ROSAURA: But if you will not grant it, I must take it.   435
SEGISMUND: That were to change my courtesy to rudeness.
    Resistance is like venom to my patience.
ROSAURA: But even if this deadly, raging venom
    Should overcome your patience, yet you dare not
    And could not treat me with dishonour, sir.   440
SEGISMUND: Why, just to see then if I can, and dare to—
    You'll make me lose the fear I bear your beauty,
    Since the impossible is always tempting
    To me. Why, only now I threw a man
    Over this balcony who said I couldn't: 445
    And so to find out if I can or not
    I'll throw your honour through the window too.
CLOTALDO: *(Aside.)* He seems determined in this course. Oh,
    heavens!
    What's to be done that for a second time
    My honour's threatened by a mad desire?   450
ROSAURA: Then with good reason it was prophesied
    Your tyranny would wreak this kingdom
    Outrageous scandals, treasons, crimes, and deaths.
    But what can such a creature do as you
    Who are not even a man, save in the name—   455
    Inhuman, barbarous, cruel, and unbending
    As the wild beasts amongst whom you were nursed?
SEGISMUND: That you should not insult me in this way
    I spoke to you most courteously, and thought
    I'd thereby get my way; but if you curse me thus   460
    Even when I am speaking gently, why,
    By the living God, I'll really give you cause.
    Ho there! Clear out, the lot of you, at once!
    Leave her to me! Close all the doors upon us.
    Let no one enter!   465

(Exeunt CLARION *and other* ATTENDANTS.*)*

ROSAURA: I am lost . . . I warn you . . .
SEGISMUND: I am a tyrant and you plead in vain.
CLOTALDO: *(Aside.)* Oh, what a monstrous thing! I must
    restrain him
    Even if I die for it.

(Aloud.)

             Sir! Wait! Look here!
SEGISMUND: A second time you have provoked my anger,
    You feeble, mad old man! Do you prize lightly   470
    My wrath and rigour that you've gone so far?
CLOTALDO: Brought by the accents of her voice, I came
    To tell you you must be more peaceful
    If still you hope to reign, and warn you that
    You should not be so cruel, though you rule—   475
    Since this, perhaps, is nothing but a dream.
SEGISMUND: When you refer to disillusionment
    You rouse me near to madness. Now you'll see,
    Here as I kill you, if it's truth or dreaming!

(As he tries to pull out his dagger, CLOTALDO *restrains him and throws himself on his knees before him.)*

CLOTALDO: It's thus I'd save my life: and hope to do so—   480
SEGISMUND: Take your presumptuous hand from off this steel.

CLOTALDO: Till people come to hold your rage and fury
   I shall not let you go.
ROSAURA: O heavens!
SEGISMUND: Loose it,

(They struggle.)

   I say, or else—you interfering fool—
485   I'll crush you to your death in my strong arms!
ROSAURA: Come quickly! Here's Clotaldo being killed!

(Exit.)

(ASTOLFO *appears as* CLOTALDO *falls on the floor, and the former
stands between* SEGISMUND *and* CLOTALDO.)

ASTOLFO: Why, what is this, most valiant prince? What?
      Staining
   Your doughty steel in such old, frozen blood?
   For shame! For shame! Sheathe your illustrious weapon!
490   SEGISMUND: When it is stained in his infamous blood!
ASTOLFO: At my feet here he has found sanctuary
   And there he's safe, for it will serve him well.
SEGISMUND: Then serve me well by dying, for like this
   I will avenge myself for your behaviour
495   In trying to annoy me first of all.
ASTOLFO: To draw in self-defence offends no king,
   Though in his palace.

(ASTOLFO *draws his sword and they fight.*)

CLOTALDO: *(To* ASTOLFO.) Do not anger him!

(Enter BASIL, STELLA, *and* ATTENDANTS.)

BASIL: Hold! Hold! What's this? Fighting with naked swords?
STELLA: *(Aside.)* It is Astolfo! How my heart misgives me!
500   BASIL: Why, what has happened here?
ASTOLFO: Nothing, my Lord,
   Since you've arrived.

(Both sheathe their swords.)

SEGISMUND: Much, though you *have* arrived.
   I tried to kill the old man.
BASIL: Had you no
   Respect for those white hairs?
CLOTALDO: Sire, since they're only
   Mine, as you well can see, it does not matter!
505   SEGISMUND: It is in vain you'd have me hold white hairs
   In such respect, since one day you may find
   Your own white locks prostrated at my feet
   For still I have not taken vengeance on you
   For the foul way in which you had me reared.

(Exit.)

510   BASIL: Before that happens you will sleep once more
   Where you were reared, and where what's happened may
   Seem just a dream (being mere earthly glory).

(All save ASTOLFO *and* STELLA *leave.*)

ASTOLFO: How seldom does prediction fail, when evil!
   How oft, foretelling good! Exact in harm,
   Doubtful in benefit! Oh, what a great   515
   Astrologer would be one who foretold
   Nothing but harms, since there's no doubt at all
   That they are always due! In Segismund
   And me the case is illustrated clearly.
   In him, crimes, cruelties, deaths, and disasters   520
   Were well predicted, since they all came true.
   But in my own case, to predict for me
   (As I foresaw beholding rays which cast
   The sun into the shade and outface heaven)
   Triumphs and trophies, happiness and praise,   525
   Was false—and yet was true: it's only just
   That when predictions start with promised favours
   They should end in disdain.
STELLA: I do not doubt
   Your protestations are most heartfelt; only
   They're not for me, but for another lady   530
   Whose portrait you were wearing round your neck
   Slung in a locket when you first arrived.
   Since it is so, she only can deserve
   These wooing flatteries. Let her repay you
   For in affairs of love, flatteries and vows   535
   Made for another are mere forged credentials.

(ROSAURA *enters but waits by the curtain.*)

ROSAURA: *(Aside.)* Thanks be to God, my troubles are near
      ended!
   To judge from what I see, I've naught to fear.
ASTOLFO: I will expel that portrait from my breast
   To make room for the image of your beauty   540
   And keep it there. For there where Stella is
   Can be no room for shade, and where the sun is
   No place for any star. I'll fetch the portrait.

(Aside.)

   Forgive me, beautiful Rosaura, that,
   When absent, men and women seldom keep   545
   More faith than this.

(Exit.)

(ROSAURA *comes forward.*)

ROSAURA: *(Aside.)*   I could not hear a word. I was afraid
   That they would see me.
STELLA: Oh, Astrea!
ROSAURA: My lady!
STELLA: I am delighted that you came. Because
   To you alone would I confide a secret.
ROSAURA: Thereby you greatly honour me, your servant.   550
STELLA: Astrea, in the brief time I have known you
   I've given you the latchkey of my will.
   For that, and being who you are, I'll tell you
   A secret which I've very often hidden
   Even from myself.   555
ROSAURA: I am your slave.
STELLA: Then, briefly:
   Astolfo, who's my cousin (the word cousin

Suffices, since some things are plainly said
Even by thinking them), is to wed me
If Fortune thus can wipe so many cares
560   Away with one great joy. But I am troubled
In that, the day he first came here, he carried
A portrait of a lady round his neck.
I spoke to him about it courteously.
He was most amiable, he loves me well,
565   And now he's gone for it. I am embarrassed
That he should give it me himself. Wait here,
And tell him to deliver it to you.
Do not say more. Since you're discreet and fair:
You'll surely know just what love is.

(Exit.)

ROSAURA: Great heavens!
570   How I wish that I did not! For who could be
So prudent or so skilful as would know
What to advise herself in such a case?
Lives there a person on this earth today
Who's more beset by the inclement stars,
575   Who has more cares besieging him, or fights
So many dire calamities at once?
What can I do in such bewilderment
Wherein it seems impossible to find
Relief or comfort? Since my first misfortune
580   No other thing has chanced or happened to me
But was a new misfortune. In succession
Inheritors and heirs of their own selves
(Just like the Phoenix, his own son and father)
Misfortunes reproduce themselves, are born,
585   And live by dying. In their sepulchre
The ashes they consume are hot forever.
A sage once said misfortunes must be cowards
Because they never dare to walk alone
But come in crowds. I say they are most valiant
590   Because they always charge so bravely on
And never turn their backs. Who charges with them
May dare all things because there is no fear
That they'll ever desert him; and I say it
Because in all my life I never once
595   Knew them to leave me, nor will they grow tired
Of me till, wounded and shot through and through
By Fate, I fall into the arms of death.
Alas, what can I do in this dilemma?
If I reveal myself, then old Clotaldo,
600   To whom I owe my life, may take offence,
Because he told me to await the cure
And mending of my honour in concealment.
If I don't tell Astolfo who I am
And he detects me, how can I dissimulate?
605   Since even if I say I am not I,
The voice, the language, and the eyes will falter,
Because the soul will tell them that they lie.
What shall I do? It is in vain to study
What I should do, when I know very well
610   That, whatsoever way I choose to act,
When the time comes I'll do as sorrow bids,
For no one has control over his sorrows.

Then since my soul dares not decide its actions
Let sorrow fill my cup and let my grief
Reach its extremity and, out of doubts   615
And vain appearances, once and for all
Come out into the light—and Heaven shield me!

(Enter ASTOLFO.)

ASTOLFO: Here, lady, is the portrait . . . but . . . great God!
ROSAURA: Why does Your Highness halt, and stare
      astonished?
ASTOLFO: Rosaura! Why, to see you here!   620
ROSAURA: Rosaura?
      Sir, you mistake me for some other lady.
      I am Astrea, and my humble station
      Deserves no perturbation such as yours.
ASTOLFO: Enough of this pretence, Rosaura, since
      The soul can never lie. Though as Astrea   625
      I see you now, I love you as Rosaura.
ROSAURA: Not having understood Your Highness' meaning
      I can make no reply except to say
      That Stella (who might be the star of Venus)
      Told me to wait here and to tell you from her   630
      To give to me the portrait you were fetching
      (Which seems a very logical request)
      And I myself will take it to my lady.
      Thus Stella bids: even the slightest things
      Which do me harm are governed by some star.   635
ASTOLFO: Even if you could make a greater effort
      How poorly you dissimulate, Rosaura!
      Tell your poor eyes they do not harmonise
      With your own voice, because they needs must jangle
      When the whole instrument is out of time.   640
      You cannot match the falsehood of your words
      With the sincerity of what you're feeling.
ROSAURA: All I can say is—that I want the portrait.
ASTOLFO: As you require a fiction, with a fiction
      I shall reply. Go and tell Stella this: 645
      That I esteem her so, it seems unworthy
      Only to send the counterfeit to her
      And that I'm sending her the original.
      And you, take the original along with you,
      Taking yourself to her.   650
ROSAURA: When a man starts
      Forth on a definite task, resolved and valiant,
      Though he be offered a far greater prize
      Than what he seeks, yet he returns with failure
      If he returns without his task performed.
      I came to get that portrait. Though I bear   655
      The original with me, of greater value,
      I would return in failure and contempt
      Without the copy. Give it me, Your Highness,
      Since I cannot return without it.
ASTOLFO: But
      If I don't give it you, how can you do so?   660
ROSAURA: Like this, ungrateful man! I'll take it from you.

(She tries to wrest it from him.)

ASTOLFO: It is in vain.

ROSAURA: By God, it shall not come
    Into another woman's hands!
ASTOLFO: You're terrifying!
ROSAURA: And you're perfidious!
ASTOLFO: Enough, my dear
665   Rosaura!
ROSAURA: I, your dear? You lie, you villain!

(They are both clutching the portrait.)

(Enter STELLA.*)*

STELLA: Astrea and Astolfo, what does this mean?
ASTOLFO: *(Aside.)* Here's Stella.
ROSAURA: *(Aside.)*   Love, grant me the strength to win
    My portrait.

(To STELLA.*)*

          If you want to know, my lady,
    What this is all about, I will explain.
670 ASTOLFO: *(To* ROSAURA, *aside.)* What do you mean?
ROSAURA: You told me to await
    Astolfo here and ask him for a portrait
    On your behalf. I waited here alone
    And as one thought suggests another thought,
    Thinking of portraits, I recalled my own
675   Was here inside my sleeve. When one's alone,
    One is diverted by a foolish trifle
    And so I took it out to look at it.
    It slipped and fell, just as Astolfo here,
    Bringing the portrait of the other lady,
680   Came to deliver it to you as promised.
    He picked my portrait up, and so unwilling
    Is he to give away the one you asked for,
    Instead of doing so, he seized upon
    The other portrait which is mine alone
685   And will not give it back though I entreated
    And begged him to return it. I was angry
    And tried to snatch it back. That's it he's holding,
    And you can see yourself if it's not mine.
STELLA: Let go the portrait.

(She snatches it from him.)

ASTOLFO: Madam!
STELLA: The draughtsman
690   Was not unkind to truth.
ROSAURA: Is it not mine?
STELLA: Why, who could doubt it?
ROSAURA: Ask him for the other.
STELLA: Here, take your own, Astrea. You may leave us.
ROSAURA: *(Aside.)* Now I have got my portrait, come what
    will.

(Exit.)

STELLA: Now give me up the portrait that I asked for
695   Although I'll see and speak to you no more.
    I do not wish to leave it in your power
    Having been once so foolish as to beg it.
ASTOLFO: *(Aside.)* Now how can I get out of this foul trap?

(To STELLA.*)*

    Beautiful Stella, though I would obey you,
    And serve you in all ways, I cannot give you   700
    The portrait, since . . .
STELLA: You are a crude, coarse villain
    And ruffian of a wooer. For the portrait—
    I do not want it now, since, if I had it,
    It would remind me I had asked you for it.

(Exit.)

ASTOLFO: Listen! Look! Wait! Let me explain!   705

(Aside.)

                  Oh, damn
    Rosaura! How the devil did she get
    To Poland for my ruin and her own?

The prison of SEGISMUND *in the tower.*

SEGISMUND *lying on the ground loaded with fetters and clothed in
skins as before.* CLOTALDO, *two* ATTENDANTS, *and* CLARION.

CLOTALDO: Here you must leave him—since his reckless pride
    Ends here today where it began.
ATTENDANT: His chain
    I'll rivet as it used to be before.   710
CLARION: O Prince, you'd better not awake too soon
    To find how lost you are, how changed your fate,
    And that your fancied glory of an hour
    Was but a shade of life, a flame of death!
CLOTALDO: For one who knows so well to wield his tongue   715
    It's fit a worthy place should be provided
    With lots of room and lots of time to argue.
    This is the fellow that you have to seize

(To the ATTENDANTS.*)*

    And that's the room in which you are to lock him.

(Points to the nearest cell.)

CLARION: Why me?   720
CLOTALDO: Because a Clarion who knows
    Too many secrets must be kept in gaol—
    A place where even clarions are silent.
CLARION: Have I, by chance, wanted to kill my father
    Or thrown an Icarus from a balcony?
    Am I asleep or dreaming? To what end   725
    Do you imprison me?
CLOTALDO: You're Clarion.
CLARION: Well, say I swear to be a cornet now,
    A silent one, a wretched instrument . . . ?

(They hustle him off. CLOTALDO *remains.)*

(Enter BASIL, *wearing a mask.)*

BASIL: Clotaldo.
CLOTALDO: Sire . . . and is it thus alone
    Your Majesty has come?   730

BASIL: Vain curiosity
  To see what happens here to Segismund.
CLOTALDO: See where he lies, reduced to misery!
BASIL: Unhappy prince! Born at a fatal moment!
  Come waken him, now he has lost his strength
735 With all the opium he's drunk.
CLOTALDO: He's stirring
  And talking to himself.
BASIL: What is he dreaming?
  Let's listen now.
SEGISMUND: He who chastises tyrants
  Is a most pious prince . . . Now let Clotaldo
  Die by my hand . . . my father kiss my feet . . .
740 CLOTALDO: He threatens me with death!
BASIL: And me with insult
  And cruelty.
CLOTALDO: He'd take my life away.
BASIL: And he'd humiliate me at his feet.
SEGISMUND: (Still in a dream.) Throughout the expanse of this
    world's theatre
  I'll show my peerless valour, let my vengeance
745 Be wreaked, and the Prince Segismund be seen
  To triumph—over his father . . . but, alas!

(Awakening.)

  Where am I?
BASIL: (To CLOTALDO.) Since he must not see me here,
  I'll listen further off. You know your cue.

(Retires to one side.)

SEGISMUND: Can this be I? Am I the same who, chained
750 And long imprisoned, rose to such a state?
  Are you not still my sepulchre and grave,
  You dismal tower? God! What things I have dreamed!
CLOTALDO: (Aside.) Now I must go to him to disenchant him.

(Aloud.)

  Awake already?
SEGISMUND: Yes: it was high time.
755 CLOTALDO: What? Do you have to spend all day asleep?
  Since I was following the eagle's flight
  With tardy discourse, have you still lain here
  Without awaking?
SEGISMUND: No. Nor even now
  Am I awake. It seems I've always slept,
760 Since, if I've dreamed what I've just seen and heard
  Palpably and for certain, then I am dreaming
  What I see now—nor is it strange I'm tired,
  Since what I, sleeping, see, tells me that I
  Was dreaming when I thought I was awake.
765 CLOTALDO: Tell me your dream.
SEGISMUND: That's if it *was* a dream!
  No, I'll not tell you what I dreamed; but what
  I lived and saw, Clotaldo, I *will* tell you.
  I woke up in a bed that might have been
  The cradle of the flowers, woven by Spring.
770 A thousand nobles, bowing, called me Prince,
  Attiring me in jewels, pomp, and splendour.
  My equanimity you turned to rapture

Telling me that I was the Prince of Poland.
CLOTALDO: I must have got a fine reward!
SEGISMUND: Not so:
  For as a traitor, twice, with rage and fury,   775
  I tried to kill you.
CLOTALDO: Such cruelty to me?
SEGISMUND: I was the lord of all, on all I took revenge,
  Except I loved one woman . . . I believe
  That *that* was true, though all the rest has faded.

(Exit BASIL.)

CLOTALDO: (Aside.) I see the king was moved, to hear him   780
  speak.

(Aloud.)

  Talking of eagles made you dream of empires,
  But even in your dreams it's good to honour
  Those who have cared for you and brought you up.
  For Segismund, even in dreams, I warn you
  Nothing is lost by trying to do good.   785

(Exit.)

SEGISMUND: That's true, and therefore let us subjugate
  The bestial side, this fury and ambition,
  Against the time when we may dream once more,
  As certainly we shall, for this strange world
  Is such that but to live here is to dream.   790
  And now experience shows me that each man
  Dreams what he is until he is awakened.
  The king dreams he's a king and in this fiction
  Lives, rules, administers with royal pomp.
  Yet all the borrowed praises that he earns   795
  Are written in the wind, and he is changed
  (How sad a fate!) by death to dust and ashes.
  What man is there alive who'd seek to reign
  Since he must wake into the dream that's death.
  The rich man dreams his wealth which is his care   800
  And woe. The poor man dreams his sufferings.
  He dreams who thrives and prospers in this life.
  He dreams who toils and strives. He dreams who injures,
  Offends, and insults. So that in this world
  Everyone dreams the thing he is, though no one   805
  Can understand it. I dream I am here,
  Chained in these fetters. Yet I dreamed just now
  I was in a more flattering, lofty station.
  What is this life? A frenzy, an illusion,
  A shadow, a delirium, a fiction.   810
  The greatest good's but little, and this life
  Is but a dream, and dreams are only dreams.

——— **ACT THREE** ———

The tower.

Enter CLARION.

CLARION: I'm held in an enchanted tower, because
  Of all I know. What would they do to me
  For all I don't know, since—for all I know—
  They're killing me by starving me to death.

5   O that a man so hungry as myself
      Should live to die of hunger while alive!
      I am so sorry for myself that others
      May well say "I can well believe it," since
      This silence ill accords with my name "Clarion,"
10   And I just can't shut up. My fellows here?
      Spiders and rats—fine feathered songsters those!
      My head's still ringing with a dream of fifes
      And trumpets and a lot of noisy humbug
      And long processions as of penitents
15   With crosses, winding up and down, while some
      Faint at the sight of blood besmirching others.
      But now to tell the truth, I am in prison.
      For knowing secrets, I am kept shut in,
      Strictly observed as if I were a Sunday,
20   And feeling sadder than a Tuesday, where
      I neither eat nor drink. They say a secret
      Is sacred and should be as strictly kept
      As any saint's day on the calendar.
      Saint Secret's Day for me's a working day
25   Because I'm never idle then. The penance
      I suffer here is merited, I say:
      Because being a lackey, I was silent,
      Which, in a servant, is a sacrilege.

(A noise of drums and trumpets.)

FIRST SOLDIER: *(Within.)* Here is the tower in which he is
         imprisoned.
30   Smash in the door and enter, everybody!
CLARION: Great God! They've come to seek me. That is
         certain
      Because they say I'm here. What can they want?

(Enter several SOLDIERS.*)*

FIRST SOLDIER: Go in.
SECOND SOLDIER: He's here!
CLARION: No, he's not here!
ALL THE SOLDIERS: Our lord!
CLARION: What, are they drunk?
FIRST SOLDIER: You are our rightful prince.
35   We do not want and never shall allow
      A stranger to supplant our trueborn prince.
      Give us your feet to kiss!
ALL THE SOLDIERS: Long live the prince!
CLARION: Bless me, if it's not real! In this strange kingdom
      It seems the custom, everyday, to take
40   Some fellow and to make him prince and then
      Shut him back in this tower. That *must* be it!
      So I must play my role.
ALL THE SOLDIERS: Give us your feet.
CLARION: I can't. They're necessary. After all
      What sort of use would be a footless prince?
45 SECOND SOLDIER: All of us told your father, as one man,
      We want no prince of Muscovy but you!
CLARION: You weren't respectful to my father? Shame!
FIRST SOLDIER: It was our loyalty that made us tell him.
CLARION: If it was loyalty, you have my pardon.
50 SECOND SOLDIER: Restore your empire. Long live Segismund!

CLARION: *(Aside.)* That is the name they seem to give to all
      These counterfeited princes.

(Enter SEGISMUND.*)*

SEGISMUND: Who called Segismund?
CLARION: *(Aside.)* I seem to be a hollow sort of prince.
FIRST SOLDIER: Which of you's Segismund?
SEGISMUND: I am.
SECOND SOLDIER: *(To* CLARION.*)*   Then why,
      Rash fool, did you impersonate the prince   55
      Segismund?
CLARION: What? I, Segismund? Yourselves
      Be-Segismunded me without request.
      All yours was both the rashness and the folly.
FIRST SOLDIER: Prince Segismund, whom we acclaim our lord,
      Your father, great King Basil, in his fear   60
      That heaven would fulfil a prophecy
      That one day he would kneel before your feet
      Wishes now to deprive you of the throne
      And give it to the Duke of Muscovy.
      For this he called a council, but the people   65
      Discovered his design and knowing, now,
      They have a native king, will have no stranger.
      So scorning the fierce threats of destiny,
      We've come to seek you in your very prison,
      That aided by the arms of the whole people,   70
      We may restore you to the crown and sceptre,
      Taking them from the tyrant's grasp. Come, then:
      Assembling here, in this wide desert region,
      Hosts of plebeians, bandits, and freebooters,
      Acclaim you king. Your liberty awaits you!   75
      Hark to its voice!

(Shouts within.)

                Long life to Segismund!
SEGISMUND: Once more, you heavens will that I should dream
      Of grandeur, once again, 'twixt doubts and shades,
      Behold the majesty of pomp and power
      Vanish into the wind, once more you wish   80
      That I should taste the disillusion and
      The risk by which all human power is humbled,
      Of which all human power should live aware.
      It must not be. I'll not be once again
      Put through my paces by my fortune's stars.   85
      And since I know this life is all a dream,
      Depart, vain shades, who feign, to my dead senses,
      That you have voice and body, having neither!
      I want no more feigned majesty, fantastic
      Display, nor void illusions, that one gust   90
      Can scatter like the almond tree in flower,
      Whose rosy buds, without advice or warning,
      Dawn in the air too soon and then, as one,
      Are all extinguished, fade, and fall, and wither
      In the first gust of wind that comes along!   95
      I know you well. I know you well by now.
      I know that all that happens in yourselves
      Happens as in a sleeping man. For me
      There are no more delusions and deceptions
      Since I well know this life is all a dream.   100

SECOND SOLDIER: If you think we are cheating, just sweep
    Your gaze along these towering peaks, and see
    The hosts that wait to welcome and obey you.
SEGISMUND: Already once before I've seen such crowds
105   Distinctly, quite as vividly as these:
    And yet it was a dream.
SECOND SOLDIER: No great event
    Can come without forerunners to announce it
    And this is the real meaning of your dream.
SEGISMUND: Yes, you say well. It was the fore-announcement
110   And just in case it was correct, my soul,
    (Since life's so short) let's dream the dream anew!
    But it must be attentively, aware
    That we'll awake from pleasure in the end.
    Forewarned of that, the shock's not so abrupt,
115   The disillusion's less. Evils anticipated
    Lose half their sting. And armed with this precaution—
    That power, even when we're sure of it, is borrowed
    And must be given back to its true owner—
    We can risk anything and dare the worst.
120   Subjects, I thank you for your loyalty.
    In me you have a leader who will free you,
    Bravely and skilfully, from foreign rule.
    Sound now to arms, you'll soon behold my valour.
    Against my father I must march and bring
125   Truth from the stars. Yes: he must kneel to me.

(Aside.)

    But yet, since I may wake before he kneels,
    Perhaps I'd better not proclaim what may not happen.
ALL: Long live Segismund!

(Enter CLOTALDO.*)*

CLOTALDO: Gracious heavens! What is
    This riot here?
SEGISMUND: Clotaldo!
CLOTALDO: Sir!

(Aside.)

                He'll prove
130   His cruelty on me.
CLARION: I bet he throws him
    Over the mountain.
CLOTALDO: At your royal feet
    I kneel, knowing my penalty is death.
SEGISMUND: Rise, rise, my foster father, from the ground,
    For you must be the compass and the guide
135   In which I trust. You brought me up, and I
    Know what I owe your loyalty. Embrace me!
CLOTALDO: What's that you say?
SEGISMUND: I know I'm in a dream,
    But I would like to act well, since good actions,
    Even in a dream, are not entirely lost.
140 CLOTALDO: Since doing good is now to be your glory,
    You will not be offended that I too
    Should do what's right. You march against your father!
    I cannot give you help against my king.
    Here at your feet, my lord, I plead for death.

SEGISMUND: *(Aloud.)* Villain!   145

(Aside.)

              But let us suffer this annoyance.
    Though my rage would slay him, yet he's loyal.
    A man does not deserve to die for that.
    How many angry passions does this leash
    Restrain in me, this curb of knowing well
    That I must wake and find myself alone!   150
SECOND SOLDIER: All this fine talk, Clotaldo, is a cruel
    Spurn of the public welfare. We are loyal
    Who wish our own prince to reign over us.
CLOTALDO: Such loyalty, after the king were dead,
    Would honour you. But while the king is living   155
    He is our absolute, unquestioned lord.
    There's no excuse for subjects who oppose
    His sovereignty in arms.
FIRST SOLDIER: We'll soon see well
    Enough, Clotaldo, what this loyalty
    Is worth.   160
CLOTALDO: You would be better if you had some.
    It is the greatest prize.
SEGISMUND: Peace, peace, I pray you.
CLOTALDO: My lord!
SEGISMUND: Clotaldo, if your feelings
    Are truly thus, go you, and serve the king;
    That's prudence, loyalty, and common sense.
    But do not argue here with anyone   165
    Whether it's right or wrong, for every man
    Has his own honour.
CLOTALDO: Humbly I take my leave.

(Exit.)

SEGISMUND: Now sound the drums and march in rank and
      order
    Straight to the palace.
ALL: Long live Segismund!
SEGISMUND: Fortune, we go to reign! Do not awake me   170
    If I am dreaming! Do not let me fall
    Asleep if it is true! To act with virtue
    Is what matters, since if this proves true,
    That truth's sufficient reason in itself;
    If not, we win us friends against the time   175
    When we at last awake.

A room in the royal palace.

Enter BASIL *and* ASTOLFO.

BASIL: Whose prudence can rein in a bolting horse?
    Who can restrain a river's pride, in spate?
    Whose valour can withstand a crag dislodged
    And hurtling downwards from a mountain peak?   180
    All these are easier by far than to hold back
    A crowd's proud fury, once it has been roused.
    It has two voices, both proclaiming war,
    And you can hear them echoing through the mountains,
    Some shouting "Segismund," others "Astolfo."   185

The scene I set for swearing of allegiance
Lends but an added horror to this strife:
It has become the back cloth to a stage
Where Fortune plays out tragedies in blood.

190 ASTOLFO: My lord, forget the happiness and wealth
You promised me from your most blessèd hand.
If Poland, which I hope to rule, refuses
Obedience to my right, grudging me honour,
It is because I've got to earn it first.

195 Give me a horse, that I with angry pride
May match the thunder in my voice and ride
To strike, like lightning, terror far and wide.

(Exit ASTOLFO.)

BASIL: No remedy for what's infallible!
What is foreseen is perilous indeed!
200 If something has to be, there's no way out;
In trying to evade it, you but court it.
This law is pitiless and horrible.
Thinking one can evade the risk, one meets it:
My own precautions have been my undoing,
205 And I myself have quite destroyed my kingdom.

(Enter STELLA.)

STELLA: If you, my lord, in person do not try
To curb the vast commotion that has started
In all the streets between the rival factions,
You'll see your kingdom, swamped in waves of crimson,
210 Swimming in its own blood, with nothing left
But havoc, dire calamity, and woe.
So frightful is the damage to your empire
That, seen, it strikes amazement; heard, despair.
The sun's obscured, the very winds are hindered.
215 Each stone is a memorial to the dead.
Each flower springs from a grave while every building
Appears a mausoleum, and each soldier
A premature and walking skeleton.

(Enter CLOTALDO.)

CLOTALDO: Praise be to God, I reach your feet alive!
220 BASIL: Clotaldo! What's the news of Segismund?
CLOTALDO: The crowd, a headstrong monster blind with rage,
Entered his dungeon tower and set him free.
He, now exalted for the second time,
Conducts himself with valour, boasting how
225 He will bring down the truth out of the stars.
BASIL: Give me a horse, that I myself, in person,
May vanquish such a base, ungrateful son!
For I, in the defence of my own crown,
Shall do by steel what science failed to do.

(Exit.)

230 STELLA: I'll be Bellona to your Sun, and try
To write my name next yours in history.
I'll ride as though I flew on outstretched wings
That I may vie with Pallas.

(Exit.)

(Enter ROSAURA, holding back CLOTALDO.)

ROSAURA: I know that all is war, Clotaldo, yet
Although your valour calls you to the front,   235
First hear me out. You know quite well that I
Arrived in Poland poor and miserable,
Where, shielded by your valour, I found mercy.
You told me to conceal myself, and stay
Here in the palace, hiding from Astolfo.   240
He saw me in the end, and so insulted
My honour that (although he saw me clearly)
He nightly speaks with Stella in the garden.
I have the key to it and I will show you
How you can enter there and end my cares.   245
Thus bold, resolved, and strong, you can recover
My honour, since you're ready to avenge me
By killing him.
CLOTALDO: It's true that I intended,
Since first I saw you (having heard your tale)
With my own life to rectify your wrongs.   250
The first step that I took was bid you dress
According to your sex, for fear Astolfo
Might see you as you were, and deem you wanton.
I was devising how we could recover
Your honour (so much did it weigh on me)   255
Even though we had to kill him. (A wild plan—
Though since he's not my king, I would not flinch
From killing him.) But then, when suddenly
Segismund tried to kill me, it was he
Who saved my life with his surpassing valour.   260
Consider: how can I requite Astolfo
With death for giving me my life so bravely,
And when my soul is full of gratitude?
So torn between the two of you I stand—
Rosaura, whose life I saved, and Astolfo,   265
Who saved my life. What's to be done? Which side
To take, and whom to help, I cannot judge.
What I owe you in that I gave you life
I owe to him in that he gave me life.
And so there is no course that I can take   270
To satisfy my love. I am a person
Who has to act, yet suffer either way.
ROSAURA: I should not have to tell so brave a man
That if it is nobility to give,
It's baseness to receive. That being so   275
You owe no gratitude to him, admitting
That it was he who gave you life, and you
Who gave me life, since he forced you to take
A meaner role, and through me you assumed
A generous role. So you should side with me: 280
My cause is so far worthier than his own
As giving is than taking.
CLOTALDO: Though nobility
Is with the giver, it is gratitude
That dwells with the receiver. As a giver
I have the name of being generous: 285
Then grant me that of being grateful too
And let me earn the title and be grateful,
As I am liberal, giving or receiving.
ROSAURA: You granted me my life, at the same time
Telling me it was worthless, since dishonoured,   290

And therefore was no life. Therefore from you
I have received no life at all. And since
You should be liberal first and grateful after
(Since so you said yourself) I now entreat you
295   Give me the life, the life you never gave me!
As giving magnifies the most, give first
And then be grateful after, if you will!
CLOTALDO: Won by your argument, I will be liberal.
Rosaura, I shall give you my estate
300   And you shall seek a convent, there to live.
This measure is a happy thought, for, see,
Fleeing a crime, you find a sanctuary.
For when the empire's threatened with disasters
And is divided thus, I, born a noble,
305   Am not the man who would augment its woes.
So with this remedy which I have chosen
I remain loyal to the kingdom, generous
To you, and also grateful to Astolfo.
And thus I choose the course that suits you best.
310   Were I your father, what could I do more?
ROSAURA: Were you my father, then I would accept
The insult. Since you are not, I refuse.
CLOTALDO: What do you hope to do then?
ROSAURA: Kill the duke!
CLOTALDO: A girl who never even knew her father
315   Armed with such courage?
ROSAURA: Yes.
CLOTALDO: What spurs you on?
ROSAURA: My good name.
CLOTALDO: In Astolfo you will find . . .
ROSAURA: My honour rides on him and strikes him down!
CLOTALDO: Your king, too, Stella's husband!
ROSAURA: Never, never
Shall that be, by almighty God, I swear!
320   CLOTALDO: Why, this is madness!
ROSAURA: Yes it is!
CLOTALDO: Restrain it.
ROSAURA: That I cannot.
CLOTALDO: Then you are lost forever!
ROSAURA: I know it!
CLOTALDO: Life and honour both together!
ROSAURA: I well believe it!
CLOTALDO: What do you intend?
ROSAURA: My death.
CLOTALDO: This is despair and desperation.
325   ROSAURA: It's honour.
CLOTALDO: It is nonsense.
ROSAURA: It is valour.
CLOTALDO: It's frenzy.
ROSAURA: Yes, it's anger! Yes, it's fury!
CLOTALDO: In short you cannot moderate your passion?
ROSAURA: No.
CLOTALDO: Who is there to help you?
ROSAURA: I, myself.
CLOTALDO: There is no cure?
ROSAURA: There is no cure!
CLOTALDO: Think well
330   If there's not some way out . . .
ROSAURA: Some other way
To do away with me . . .

(Exit.)

CLOTALDO: If you are lost,
My daughter, let us both be lost together!

In the country.

Enter SEGISMUND *clothed in skins.* SOLDIERS *marching.* CLARION.
Drums beating.

SEGISMUND: If Rome, today, could see me here, renewing
Her olden triumphs, she might laugh to see
A wild beast in command of mighty armies,   335
A wild beast, to whose fiery aspirations
The firmament were all too slight a conquest!
But stoop your flight, my spirit. Do not thus
Be puffed to pride by these uncertain plaudits
Which, when I wake, will turn to bitterness   340
In that I won them only to be lost.
The less I value them, the less I'll miss them.

(A trumpet sounds.)

CLARION: Upon a rapid courser (pray excuse me,
Since if it comes to mind I must describe it)
In which it seems an atlas was designed   345
Since if its body is earth, its soul is fire
Within its breast, its foam appears the sea,
The wind its breath, and chaos its condition,
Since in its soul, its foam, its breath and flesh,
It seems a monster of fire, earth, sea, and wind,   350
Upon the horse, all of a patchwork colour,
Dappled, and rushing forward at the will
Of one who plies the spur, so that it flies
Rather than runs—see how a woman rides
Boldly into your presence.   355
SEGISMUND: Her light blinds me.
CLARION: Good God! Why, here's Rosaura!
SEGISMUND: It is heaven
That has restored her to my sight once more.

(Enter ROSAURA *with sword and dagger in riding costume.)*

ROSAURA: Generous Segismund, whose majesty
Heroically rises in the lustre
Of his great deeds out of his night of shadows,   360
And as the greatest planet, in the arms
Of his aurora, lustrously returns
To plants and roses, over hills and seas,
When, crowned with gold, he looks abroad, dispersing
Radiance, flashing his rays, bathing the summits,   365
And broidering the fringes of the foam,
So may you dawn upon the world, bright sun
Of Poland, that a poor unhappy woman
May fall before your feet and beg protection
Both as a woman and unfortunate—   370
Two things that must oblige you, sire, as one
Who prizes yourself as valiant, each of them
More than suffices for your chivalry.

343–55 **Upon a . . . presence** Clarion's speech is a parody of
exaggerated style including Calderón's [R.C.]

Three times you have beheld me now, three times
375 Been ignorant of who I am, because
Three times you saw me in a different clothing.
The first time you mistook me for a man,
Within that rigorous prison, where your hardships
Made mine seem pleasure. Next time, as a woman,
380 You saw me, when your pomp and majesty
Were as a dream, a phantasm, a shade.
The third time is today when, as a monster
Of both the sexes, in a woman's costume
I bear a soldier's arms. But to dispose you
385 The better to compassion, hear my story.
My mother was a noble in the court
Of Moscow, who, since most unfortunate,
Must have been beautiful. Then came a traitor
And cast his eyes on her (I do not name him,
390 Not knowing who he is). Yet I deduce
That he was valiant too from my own valour,
Since he gave form to me—and I could wish
I had been born in pagan times, that I might
Persuade myself he was some god of those
395 Who rain in showers of gold, turn into swans
Or bulls, for Danaës, Ledas, or Europas.
That's strange: I thought I was just rambling on
By telling old perfidious myths, yet find
I've told you how my mother was cajoled.
400 Oh, she was beautiful as no one else
Has been, but was unfortunate like all.
He swore to wed her (that's an old excuse)
And this trick reached so nearly to her heart
That thought must weep, recalling it today.
405 The tyrant left her only with his sword
As Aeneas left Troy. I sheathed its blade here
Upon my thigh, and I will bare it too
Before the ending of this history.
Out of this union, this poor link which neither
410 Could bind the marriage nor handcuff the crime,
Myself was born, her image and her portrait,
Not in her beauty, but in her misfortune,
For mine's the same. That's all I need to say.
The most that I can tell you of myself
415 Is that the man who robbed me of the spoils
And trophies of my honour is Astolfo.
Alas! to name him my heart rages so
(As hearts will do when men name enemies).
Astolfo was my faithless and ungrateful
420 Lord, who (quite forgetful of our happiness,
Since of a past love even the memory fades)
Came here to claim the throne and marry Stella
For she's the star who rises as I set.
It's hard to credit that a star should sunder
425 Lovers the stars had made conformable!
So hurt was I, so villainously cheated,
That I became mad, brokenhearted, sick,
Half wild with grief, and like to die, with all
Hell's own confusion ciphered on my mind
430 Like Babel's incoherence. Mutely I told
My griefs (since woes and griefs declare themselves
Better than can the mouth, by their effects),
When, with my mother (we were by ourselves),

She broke the prison of my pent-up sorrows
And from my breast they all rushed forth in troops. 435
I felt no shyness, for in knowing surely
That one to whom one's errors are recounted
Has also been an ally in her own,
One finds relief and rest, since bad example
Can sometimes serve for a good purpose too. 440
She heard my plaint with pity, and she tried
To palliate my sorrows with her own.
How easily do judges pardon error
When they've offended too! An example,
A warning, in herself, she did not trust 445
To idleness, or the slow cure of time,
Nor try to find a remedy for her honour
In my misfortunes, but, with better counsel,
She bade me follow him to Poland here
And with prodigious gallantry persuade him 450
To pay the debt to honour that he owes me.
So that it would be easier to travel,
She bade me don male clothing, and took down
This ancient sword which I am wearing now.
Now it is time that I unsheathe the blade 455
As I was bid, for, trusting in its sign,
She said: "Depart to Poland, show this sword
That all the nobles may behold it well,
And it may be that one of them will take
Pity on you, and counsel you, and shield you." 460
I came to Poland and, you will remember,
Entered your cave. You looked at me in wonder.
Clotaldo passionately took my part
To plead for mercy to the king, who spared me,
Then, when he heard my story, bade me change 465
Into my own clothes and attend on Stella,
There to disturb Astolfo's love and stop
Their marriage. Again you saw me in woman's dress
And were confused by the discrepancy.
But let's pass to what's new: Clotaldo, now 470
Persuaded that Astolfo must, with Stella,
Come to the throne, dissuades me from my purpose,
Against the interests of my name and honour.
But seeing you, O valiant Segismund,
Are claiming your revenge, now that the heavens 475
Have burst the prison of your rustic tower,
(Wherein you were the tiger of your sorrows,
The rock of sufferings and direful pains)
And sent you forth against your sire and country,
I come to aid you, mingling Dian's silks 480
With the hard steel of Pallas. Now, strong Captain,
It well behoves us both to stop this marriage—
Me, lest my promised husband should be wed,
You, lest, when their estates are joined, they weigh
More powerfully against your victory. 485
I come, as a mere woman, to persuade you
To right my shame; but, as a man, I come
To help you battle for your crown. As woman,
To melt your heart, here at your feet I fall;
But, as a man, I come to serve you bravely 490
Both with my person and my steel, and thus,
If you today should woo me as a woman,
Then I should have to kill you as a man would

In honourable service of my honour;
495 Since I must be three things today at once—
     Passionate, to persuade you: womanly,
     To ply you with my woes: manly, to gain
     Honour in battle.
SEGISMUND: Heavens! If it is true I'm dreaming,
     Suspend my memory, for in a dream
500 So many things could not occur. Great heavens!
     If I could only come free of them all!
     Or never think of any! Who ever felt
     Such grievous doubts? If I but dreamed that triumph
     In which I found myself, how can this woman
505 Refer me to such sure and certain facts?
     Then all of it was true and not a dream.
     But if it be the truth, why does my past life
     Call it a dream? This breeds the same confusion.
     Are dreams and glories so alike, that fictions
510 Are held for truths, realities for lies?
     Is there so little difference in them both
     That one should question whether what one sees
     And tastes is true or false? What? Is the copy
     So near to the original that doubt
515 Exists between them? Then if that is so,
     And grandeur, power, majesty, and pomp,
     Must all evaporate like shades at morning,
     Let's profit by it, this time, to enjoy
     That which we only can enjoy in dreams.
520 Rosaura's in my power: my soul adores her beauty.
     Let's take the chance. Let love break every law
     On which she has relied in coming here
     And kneeling, trustful, prostrate at my feet.
     This is a dream. If so, dream pleasures now
525 Since they must turn to sorrows in the end!
     But with my own opinions, I begin
     Once again to convince myself. Let's think.
     If it is but vainglory and a dream,
     Who for mere human vainglory would lose
530 True glory? What past blessing is not merely
     A dream? Who has known heroic glories,
     That deep within himself, as he recalls them
     Has never doubted that they might be dreams?
     But if this all should end in disenchantment,
535 Seeing that pleasure is a lovely flame
     That's soon converted into dust and ashes
     By any wind that blows, then let us seek
     That which endures in thrifty, lasting fame
     In which no pleasures sleep, nor grandeurs dream.
540 Rosaura's without honour. In a prince
     It's worthier to restore it than to steal it.
     I shall restore it, by the living God,
     Before I win my throne! Let's shun the danger
     And fly from the temptation which is strong!
545 Then sound to arms!

     (To a SOLDIER.)

     Today I must give battle before darkness
     Buries the rays of gold in green-black waves!
ROSAURA: My lord! Alas, you stand apart, and offer
     No word of pity for my plight. How is it

You neither hear nor see me nor even yet   550
     Have turned your face on me?
SEGISMUND: Rosaura, for your honour's sake
     I must be cruel to you, to be kind.
     My voice must not reply to you because
     My honour must reply to you. I am silent
     Because my deeds must speak to you alone.   555
     I do not look at you since, in such straits,
     Having to see your honour is requited,
     I must not see your beauty.

(Exit with SOLDIERS.)

ROSAURA: What strange enigma's this? After such trouble
     Still to be treated with more doubtful riddles!   560

(Enter CLARION.)

CLARION: Madam, may you be visited just now?
ROSAURA: Why, Clarion, where have you been all this time?
CLARION: Shut in the tower, consulting cards
     About my death: "to be or not to be."
     And it was a near thing.   565
ROSAURA: Why?
CLARION: Because I know
     The secret who you are: in fact, Clotaldo . . .

(Drums.)

     But hush what noise is that?
ROSAURA: What can it be?
CLARION: From the beleaguered palace a whole squadron
     Is charging forth to harry and defeat
     That of fierce Segismund.   570
ROSAURA: Why, what a coward
     Am I, not to be at his side, the terror
     And scandal of the world, while such fierce strife
     Presses all round in lawless anarchy.

(Exit.)

VOICES OF SOME: Long live our king!
VOICES OF OTHERS: Long live our liberty!
CLARION: Long live both king and liberty. Yes, live!   575
     And welcome to them both! I do not worry.
     In all this pother, I behave like Nero
     Who never grieved at what was going on.
     If I had anything to grieve about
     It would be me, myself. Well hidden here   580
     Now, I can watch the sport that's going on.
     This place is safe and hidden between crags,
     And since death cannot find me here, two figs for death!

(He hides. Drums and the clash of arms are heard.)

(Enter BASIL, CLOTALDO, and ASTOLFO, fleeing.)

BASIL: Was ever king so hapless as myself
     Or father more ill used?   585
CLOTALDO: Your beaten army
     Rush down, in all directions, in disorder.
ASTOLFO: The traitors win!

BASIL: In battles such as these
      Those on the winning side are ever "loyal,"
      And traitors the defeated. Come, Clotaldo,
590   Let's flee from the inhuman cruelty
      Of my fierce son!

(Shots are fired within. CLARION *falls wounded.)*

CLARION: Heavens, save me!
ASTOLFO: Who is this
      Unhappy soldier bleeding at our feet?
CLARION: I am a most unlucky man who, wishing
      To guard myself from death, have sought it out
595   By fleeing from it. Shunning it, I found it,
      Because, to death, no hiding-place is secret.
      So you can argue that whoever shuns it
      Most carefully runs into it the quickest.
      Turn, then, once more into the thick of battle:
600   There is more safety there amidst the fire
      And clash of arms than here on this secluded
      Mountain, because no hidden path is safe
      From the inclemency of Fate; and so,
      Although you flee from death, yet you may find it
605   Quicker than you expect, if God so wills.

(He falls dead.)

BASIL: "If God so wills" . . . With what strange eloquence
      This corpse persuades our ignorance and error
      To better knowledge, speaking from the mouth
      Of its fell wound, where the red liquid flowing
610   Seems like a bloody tongue which teaches us
      That the activities of man are vain
      When they are pitted against higher powers.
      For I, who wished to liberate my country
      From murder and sedition, gave it up
615   To the same ills from which I would have saved it.
CLOTALDO: Though Fate, my lord, knows every path, and finds
      Him whom it seeks even in the midst of crags
      And thickets, it is not a Christian judgment
      To say there is no refuge from its fury.
620   A prudent man can conquer Fate itself.
      Though you are not exempted from misfortune,
      Take action to escape it while you can!
ASTOLFO: Clotaldo speaks as one mature in prudence,
      And I as one in valour's youthful prime.
625   Among the thickets of this mount is hidden
      A horse, the very birth of the swift wind.
      Flee on him, and I'll guard you in the rear.
BASIL: If it is God's will I should die, or if
      Death waits here for my coming, I will seek
630   Him out today, and meet him face to face.

(Enter SEGISMUND, STELLA, ROSAURA, SOLDIERS, *and their train.)*

A SOLDIER: Amongst the thickets of this mountain
      The king is hiding.
SEGISMUND: Seek him out at once!
      Leave no foot of the summit unexplored
      But search from stem to stem and branch to branch!
635 CLOTALDO: Fly, sir!

BASIL: What for?
ASTOLFO: What do you mean to do?
BASIL: Astolfo, stand aside!
CLOTALDO: What is your wish?
BASIL: To take a cure I've needed for sometime.

(To SEGISMUND.*)*

      If you have come to seek me, here I am.

(Kneeling.)

      Your father, prince, kneels humbly at your feet.
      The white snow of my hair is now your carpet.   640
      Tread on my neck and trample on my crown!
      Lay low and drag my dignity in dust!
      Take vengeance on my honour! Make a slave
      Of me and, after all I've done to thwart them,
      Let Fate fulfil its edict and claim homage   645
      And Heaven fulfil its oracles at last!
SEGISMUND: Illustrious court of Poland, who have been
      The witnesses of such unwonted wonders,
      Attend to me, and hear your prince speak out.
      What Heaven decrees and God writes with his finger   650
      (Whose prints and ciphers are the azure leaves
      Adorned with golden lettering of the stars)
      Never deceives nor lies. They only lie
      Who seek to penetrate the mystery
      And, having reached it, use it to ill purpose.   655
      My father, who is here to evade the fury
      Of my proud nature, made me a wild beast:
      So, when I, by my birth of gallant stock,
      My generous blood, and inbred grace and valour,
      Might well have proved both gentle and forbearing,   660
      The very mode of life to which he forced me,
      The sort of bringing up I had to bear
      Sufficed to make me savage in my passions.
      What a strange method of restraining them!
      If one were to tell any man: "One day   665
      You will be killed by an inhuman monster,"
      Would it be the best method he could choose
      To wake that monster when it was asleep?
      Or if they told him: "That sword which you're wearing
      Will be your death," what sort of cure were it   670
      To draw it forth and aim it at his breast?
      Or if they told him: "Deep blue gulfs of water
      Will one day be your sepulchre and grave
      Beneath a silver monument of foam,"
      He would be mad to hurl himself in headlong   675
      When the sea highest heaved its showy mountains
      And crystalline sierras plumed with spray.
      The same has happened to the king as to him
      Who wakes a beast which threatens death, to him
      Who draws a naked sword because he fears it,   680
      To him who dives into the stormy breakers.
      Though my ferocious nature (hear me now)
      Was like a sleeping beast, my inborn rage
      A sheathèd sword, my wrath a quiet ripple,
      Fate should not be coerced by man's injustice—   685
      This rouses more resentment. So it is
      That he who seeks to tame his fortune must

Resort to moderation and to measure.
He who foresees an evil cannot conquer it
690 Thus in advance, for though humility
Can overcome it, this it can do only
When the occasion's there, for there's no way
To dodge one's fate and thus evade the issue.
Let this strange spectacle serve as example—
695 This prodigy, this horror, and this wonder,
Because it is no less than one, to see,
After such measures and precautions taken
To thwart it, that a father should kneel
At his son's feet, a kingdom thus be shattered.
700 This was the sentence of the heavens above,
Which he could not evade, much though he tried.
Can I, younger in age, less brave, and less
In science than the king, conquer that fate?

(To the KING.*)*

Sire, rise, give me your hand, now that the heavens
705 Have shown you that you erred as to the method
To vanquish them. Humbly I kneel before you
And offer you my neck to tread upon.
BASIL: Son, such a great and noble act restores you
Straight to my heart. Oh, true and worthy prince!
710 You have won both the laurel and the palm.
Crown yourself with your deeds! For you *have* conquered!
ALL: Long live Segismund! Long live Segismund!
SEGISMUND: Since I have other victories to win,
The greatest of them all awaits me now:
715 To conquer my own self. Astolfo, give
Your hand here to Rosaura, for you know
It is a debt of honour and must be paid.
ASTOLFO: Although, it's true, I owe some obligations—
She does not know her name or who she is,
720 It would be base to wed a woman who . . .
CLOTALDO: Hold! Wait! Rosaura's of as noble stock
As yours, Astolfo. In the open field
I'll prove it with my sword. She is my daughter

And that should be enough.
ASTOLFO: What do you say?
CLOTALDO: Until I saw her married, righted, honoured, 725
I did not wish for it to be discovered.
It's a long story but she is my daughter.
ASTOLFO: That being so, I'm glad to keep my word.
SEGISMUND: And now, so that the princess Stella here
Will not remain disconsolate to lose 730
A prince of so much valour, here I offer
My hand to her, no less in birth and rank.
Give me your hand.
STELLA: I gain by meriting
So great a happiness.
SEGISMUND: And now, Clotaldo,
So long so loyal to my father, come 735
To my arms. Ask me anything you wish.
FIRST SOLDIER: If thus you treat a man who never served you,
What about me who led the revolution
And brought you from your dungeon in the tower?
What will you give me? 740
SEGISMUND: That same tower and dungeon
From which you never shall emerge till death.
No traitor is of use after his treason.
BASIL: All wonder at your wisdom!
ASTOLFO: What a change
Of character!
ROSAURA: How wise and prudent!
SEGISMUND: Why
Do you wonder? Why do you marvel, since 745
It was a dream that taught me and I still
Fear to wake up once more in my close dungeon?
Though that may never happen, it's enough
To dream it might, for thus I came to learn
That all our human happiness must pass 750
Away like any dream, and I would here
Enjoy it fully ere it glide away,
Asking (for noble hearts are prone to pardon)
Pardon for faults in the actors or the play.

MOLIÈRE

Jean-Baptiste Poquelin (1622–73) was born into a prosperous mercantile family with connections at court; his father, Jean Poquelin, secured the honor of *tapissier ordinaire du roi,* the upholsterer to the court, which carried an annual pension. Jean Poquelin also educated his son in the traditional disciplines of the humanities, philosophy, and the classics and must have intended a life at court for him. In 1643, Jean-Baptiste joined with the Illustre Théâtre, a theatrical company run by the Béjart family, took the stage name Molière, and after a brief period performing in Parisian tennis courts, left with the company to play in the provinces. In 1658, after several hard and impoverished years of touring, when Molière is thought to have mastered the techniques of *commedia dell' arte,* the company was invited to perform in Paris.

Molière's career was closely tied to the court. When his brother died in 1660, he received the position of court upholsterer and the income it provided. More important, Molière became an important playwright and both wrote and acted in a splendid series of plays that satirized the manners and morals of elegant society: *Les Précieuses Ridicules* (1659), *Sganarelle* (1660), *School for Husbands* (1661), *School for Wives* (1662), *Dom Juan* (1665), *The Misanthrope* (1666), *The Doctor in Spite of Himself* (1666), *The Miser* (1668), *The Learned Ladies* (1672), and *The Imaginary Invalid* (1673). Molière also prepared other entertainments at court, including many royal pageants, ballets, and machine plays devised by and for Louis XIV. In addition to being a great dramatist, Molière was a fine comic actor as well and performed in his own plays; he died shortly after playing the title role in the fourth performance of *The Imaginary Invalid.*

The fortunes of *Tartuffe* suggest Molière's importance at court. When Molière initially produced the first three acts of the play in 1664, the clergy protested and banned the play from production in Paris. Many of Molière's plays had excited controversy, and in this case Molière appealed to the king and proceeded to revise the play. Louis's attitude is perhaps revealed by the fact that he made Molière's company the *Troupe du roi* ("King's Company") in 1665, but even the throne could not prevent the clergy from censoring Molière's second version of the play in 1667, newly titled *The Impostor.* Molière finally produced the play to acclaim in 1669, and the record of his efforts is preserved in the series of letters and prefaces included here.

Molière's theatrical company was the most influential of its day. After his death, his young wife Amanda Béjart and the actress Mademoiselle Champmeslé—newly defected from the rival company at the Hôtel de Bourgogne—established a new company, the Comédie Française. Yet although Molière achieved extraordinary status at court, because he was an actor he remained stigmatized in ways that playwrights like Racine and Corneille were not. Following its standard practice, and perhaps because of *Tartuffe's* notoriety, the church refused to bury Molière in sacred ground. Louis XIV intervened, but was only able to persuade the Archbishop of Paris to bury Molière in a parish cemetery. The burial was conducted at night, by two priests, with no funeral ceremony.

TARTUFFE

The Catholic church criticized *Tartuffe* for its portrait of hypocritical piety, but the fact that Molière played the part of Orgon may suggest that the play is as much about Tartuffe's effect on that benighted householder as it is about the title character. For if Tartuffe is hypocritical, Orgon is obsessed, less with piety than with his own desire to achieve a kind of total power and authority in his household, a kind of domestic absolutism; he is, in a sense, a comic, bourgeois Louis XIV in miniature. Moreover, Tartuffe dupes Orgon not by tricking him, but by inviting Orgon to fulfill his own fantasy of autonomy and authority. As he brags to the sensible Cléante, under Tartuffe's teaching, "my soul's been freed / From earthly loves, and every human tie: / My mother, children, brother, and wife could die, / And I'd not feel a single moment's pain." Helping Orgon to realize this fantasy, Tartuffe transforms him into a kind of monster: Orgon comes near to selling his daughter, disinheriting his son, allowing his wife to be raped, and losing his family's property and fortune.

Tartuffe is very much a play of the world, a satiric comedy. Set in an urban landscape, the play insistently translates the idealized passions of tragedy and romantic comedy—love, honor, loyalty—into their ironic counterparts—lust, hypocrisy, betrayal. Molière peoples the play with individualized versions of the unchanging types of *commedia dell' arte* and the Roman comedy that inspired it: the reasonable and attractive heroes; an old, pedantic, self-absorbed dupe; a wily and conniving villain; a clever and witty servant. Yet Molière reinvents this range of stock characters, brilliantly turning his play toward an exploration of the folly of self-deception. For while we might take the neoclassical conflict between reason and the passions to be the hallmark of tragedy, it surges through this play as well. Orgon's passionate solipsism is, for all its ridiculousness, profound, troubling, and destructively obsessive, and his redemption by fiat of the king seems frighteningly arbitrary.

Since the characters cannot change in Molière's comedy, then change must happen to them. Molière's most brilliant device here arises in the person of the king's officer, who appears to apprehend Tartuffe and to restore Orgon and his family to their property: property is what establishes the position, the place, the social and individual identity of these characters. Although Molière's DEUS EX MACHINA might be regarded as an elegant (though somewhat clumsy) compliment to the king—and, perhaps, as a sly jab at the clerical critics who attacked *Tartuffe*—this device plays a subtle role in dramatizing the nature of royal authority. For in *Tartuffe,* the king has the power to assign every person to his or her proper place, to see into our inmost hearts, to structure the moral and social order of the world as the reflection of his own will and judgment: *"L'état, c'est moi."* In this sense, even though *Tartuffe* unleashes the uncontrollable power of self-delusion, and the power and destructive fantasies of absolute authority, it concludes by asserting the legitimacy of that absolute power. Molière's *deus ex machina* testifies both to the power and to the arbitrariness of the king's authority.

PREFACE[1]

TRANSLATED BY RICHARD WILBUR

Here is a comedy that has excited a good deal of discussion and that has been under attack for a long time; and the persons who are mocked by it have made it plain that they are more powerful in France than all whom my plays have satirized up to this time. Noblemen, ladies of fashion, cuckolds, and doctors all kindly consented to their presentation, which they themselves seemed to enjoy along with everyone else; but hypocrites do not understand banter: they became angry at once, and found it strange that I was bold enough to represent their actions and to care to describe a profession shared by so many good men. This is a crime for which they cannot forgive me, and they have taken up arms against my comedy in a terrible rage. They were careful not to attack it at the point that had wounded them: they are too crafty for that and too clever to reveal their true character. In keeping with their lofty custom, they have used the cause of God to mask their

---

[1]Molière added his three petitions to Louis XIV; they follow the preface.

private interests; and *Tartuffe,* they say, is a play that offends piety: it is filled with abominations from beginning to end, and nowhere is there a line that does not deserve to be burned. Every syllable is wicked, the very gestures are criminal, and the slightest glance, turn of the head, or step from right to left conceals mysteries that they are able to explain to my disadvantage. In vain did I submit the play to the criticism of my friends and the scrutiny of the public: all the corrections I could make, the judgment of the king and queen who saw the play,[2] the approval of great princes and ministers of state who honored it with their presence, the opinion of good men who found it worthwhile; all this did not help. They will not let go of their prey, and every day of the week they have pious zealots abusing me in public and damning me out of charity.

I would care very little about all they might say except that their devices make enemies of men whom I respect and gain the support of genuinely good men, whose faith they know and who, because of the warmth of their piety, readily accept the impressions that others present to them. And it is this which forces me to defend myself. Especially to the truly devout do I wish to vindicate my play, and I beg of them with all my heart not to condemn it before seeing it, to rid themselves of preconceptions, and not aid the cause of men dishonored by their actions.

If one takes the trouble to examine my comedy in good faith, he will surely see that my intentions are innocent throughout, and tend in no way to make fun of what men revere; that I have presented the subject with all the precautions that its delicacy imposes; and that I have used all the art and skill that I could to distinguish clearly the character of the hypocrite from that of the truly devout man. For that purpose I used two whole acts to prepare the appearance of my scoundrel. Never is there a moment's doubt about his character; he is known at once from the qualities I have given him; and from one end of the play to the other, he does not say a word, he does not perform an action which does not depict to the audience the character of a wicked man, and which does not bring out in sharp relief the character of the truly good man which I oppose to it.

I know full well that by way of reply, these gentlemen try to insinuate that it is not the role of the theater to speak of these matters; but with their permission, I ask them on what do they base this fine doctrine. It is a proposition they advance as no more than a supposition, for which they offer not a shred of proof; and surely it would not be difficult to show them that comedy, for the ancients, had its origin in religion and constituted a part of its ceremonies; that our neighbors, the Spaniards, have hardly a single holiday celebration in which a comedy is not a part; and that even here in France, it owes its birth to the efforts of a religious brotherhood who still own the Hôtel de Bourgogne, where the most important mystery plays of our faith were presented;[3] that you can still find comedies printed in gothic letters under the name of a learned doctor of the Sorbonne;[4] and without going so far, in our own day the religious dramas of Pierre Corneille[5] have been performed to the admiration of all France.

If the function of comedy is to correct men's vices, I do not see why any should be exempt. Such a condition in our society would be much more dangerous than the thing itself; and we have seen that the theater is admirably suited to provide correction. The most forceful lines of a serious moral statement are usually less powerful than those of satire; and

---

[2]Louis XIV was married to Marie Thérèse of Austria.

[3]A reference to the *Confrérie de la Passion et Résurrection de Notre-Seigneur* (the Fraternity of the Passion and Resurrection of Our Saviour), founded in 1402. The Hôtel de Bourgogne was a rival theater of Molière.

[4]Probably Maitre Jehán Michel, a medical doctor who wrote mystery plays.

[5]Pierre Corneille (1606–1684) and Racine were France's two greatest writers of classic tragedy. The two dramas Molière doubtlessly had in mind were *Polyeucte* (1643) and *Théodore, vierge et martyre* (1645).

nothing will reform most men better than the depiction of their faults. It is a vigorous blow to vices to expose them to public laughter. Criticism is taken lightly, but men will not tolerate satire. They are quite willing to be mean, but they never like to be ridiculed.

I have been attacked for having placed words of piety in the mouth of my impostor. Could I avoid doing so in order to represent properly the character of a hypocrite? It seemed to me sufficient to reveal the criminal motives which make him speak as he does, and I have eliminated all ceremonial phrases, which nonetheless he would not have been found using incorrectly. Yet some say that in the fourth act he sets forth a vicious morality; but is not this a morality which everyone has heard again and again? Does my comedy say anything new here? And is there any fear that ideas so thoroughly detested by everyone can make an impression on men's minds; that I make them dangerous by presenting them in the theater; that they acquire authority from the lips of a scoundrel? There is not the slightest suggestion of any of this; and one must either approve the comedy of *Tartuffe* or condemn all comedies in general.

This has indeed been done in a furious way for some time now, and never was the theater so much abused.[6] I cannot deny that there were Church Fathers who condemned comedy; but neither will it be denied me that there were some who looked on it somewhat more favorably. Thus authority, on which censure is supposed to depend, is destroyed by this disagreement; and the only conclusion that can be drawn from this difference of opinion among men enlightened by the same wisdom is that they viewed comedy in different ways, and that some considered it in its purity, while others regarded it in its corruption and confused it with all those wretched performances which have been rightly called performances of filth.

And in fact, since we should talk about things rather than words, and since most misunderstanding comes from including contrary notions in the same word, we need only to remove the veil of ambiguity and look at comedy in itself to see if it warrants condemnation. It will surely be recognized that as it is nothing more than a clever poem which corrects men's faults by means of agreeable lessons, it cannot be condemned without injustice. And if we listened to the voice of ancient times on this matter, it would tell us that its most famous philosophers have praised comedy—they who professed so austere a wisdom and who ceaselessly denounced the vices of their times. It would tell us that Aristotle spent his evenings at the theater[7] and took the trouble to reduce the art of making comedies to rules. It would tell us that some of its greatest and most honored men took pride in writing comedies themselves,[8] and that others did not disdain to recite them in public; that Greece expressed its admiration for this art by means of handsome prizes and magnificent theaters to honor it; and finally, that in Rome this same art also received extraordinary honors; I do not speak of Rome run riot under the license of the emperors, but of disciplined Rome, governed by the wisdom of the consuls, and in the age of the full vigor of Roman dignity.

I admit that there have been times when comedy became corrupt. And what do men not corrupt every day? There is nothing so innocent that men cannot turn it to crime; nothing so beneficial that its values cannot be reversed; nothing so good in itself that it

---

[6]Molière had in mind Nicole's two attacks on the theater: *Visionnaries* (1666) and *Traité de Comédie,* and the Prince de Condé's *Traité de Comédie* (1666).

[7]A reference to Aristotle's *Poetics* (composed between 335 and 322 BCE, the year of his death).

[8]The Roman consul and general responsible for the final destruction of Carthage in 146 BCE, Scipio Africanus Minor (c. 185–129 BCE), collaborated with the writer of comedies, Terence (Publius Terentius Afer, c. 195 or 185–c. 159 BCE).

cannot be put to bad uses. Medical knowledge benefits mankind and is revered as one of our most wonderful possessions; and yet there was a time when it fell into discredit, and was often used to poison men. Philosophy is a gift of Heaven; it has been given to us to bring us to the knowledge of a God by contemplating the wonders of nature; and yet we know that often it has been turned away from its function and has been used openly in support of impiety. Even the holiest of things are not immune from human corruption, and every day we see scoundrels who use and abuse piety, and wickedly make it serve the greatest of crimes. But this does not prevent one from making the necessary distinctions. We do not confuse in the same false inference the goodness of things that are corrupted with the wickedness of the corrupt. The function of an art is always distinguished from its misuse; and as medicine is not forbidden because it was banned in Rome,[9] nor philosophy because it was publicly condemned in Athens,[10] we should not suppress comedy simply because it has been condemned at certain times. This censure was justified then for reasons which no longer apply today; it was limited to what was then seen; and we should not seize on these limits, apply them more rigidly than is necessary, and include in our condemnation the innocent along with the guilty. The comedy that this censure attacked is in no way the comedy that we want to defend. We must be careful not to confuse the one with the other. There may be two persons whose morals may be completely different. They may have no resemblance to one another except in their names, and it would be a terrible injustice to want to condemn Olympia, who is a good woman, because there is also an Olympia who is lewd. Such procedures would make for great confusion everywhere. Everything under the sun would be condemned; now since this rigor is not applied to the countless instances of abuse we see every day, the same should hold for comedy, and those plays should be approved in which instruction and virtue reign supreme.

I know there are some so delicate that they cannot tolerate a comedy, who say that the most decent are the most dangerous, that the passions they present are all the more moving because they are virtuous, and that men's feelings are stirred by these presentations. I do not see what great crime it is to be affected by the sight of a generous passion; and this utter insensitivity to which they would lead us is indeed a high degree of virtue! I wonder if so great a perfection resides within the strength of human nature, and I wonder if it is not better to try to correct and moderate men's passions than to try to suppress them altogether. I grant that there are places better to visit than the theater; and if we want to condemn every single thing that does not bear directly on God and our salvation, it is right that comedy be included, and I should willingly grant that it be condemned along with everything else. But if we admit, as is in fact true, that the exercise of piety will permit interruptions, and that men need amusement, I maintain that there is none more innocent than comedy. I have dwelled too long on this matter. Let me finish with the words of a great prince on the comedy, *Tartuffe.*[11]

Eight days after it had been banned, a play called *Scaramouche the Hermit*[12] was performed before the court; and the king, on his way out, said to this great prince: "I should really like to know why the persons who make so much noise about Molière's comedy do not say a word about *Scaramouche.*" To which the prince replied, "It is because the comedy

---

[9]Pliny the Elder says that the Romans expelled their doctors at the same time that the Greeks did theirs.

[10]An allusion to Socrates' condemnation to death.

[11]One of Molière's benefactors who liked the play was the Prince de Condé; the Prince had *Tartuffe* read to him and also privately performed for him.

[12]A troupe of Italian comedians had just performed the licentious farce, where a hermit dressed as a monk makes love to a married woman, announcing that *questo e per mortificar la carne* ("this is to mortify the flesh").

of *Scaramouche* makes fun of Heaven and religion, which these gentlemen do not care about at all, but that of Molière makes fun of *them,* and that is what they cannot bear."

Molière

FIRST PETITION[13]
(PRESENTED TO THE KING ON THE COMEDY OF TARTUFFE)

Sire,

As the duty of comedy is to correct men by amusing them, I believed that in my occupation I could do nothing better than attack the vices of my age by making them ridiculous; and as hypocrisy is undoubtedly one of the most common, most improper, and most dangerous, I thought, Sire, that I would perform a service for all good men of your kingdom if I wrote a comedy which denounced hypocrites and placed in proper view all of the contrived poses of these incredibly virtuous men, all of the concealed villainies of these counterfeit believers who would trap others with a fraudulent piety and a pretended virtue.

I have written this comedy, Sire, with all the care and caution that the delicacy of the subject demands; and so as to maintain all the more properly the admiration and respect due to truly devout men, I have delineated my character as sharply as I could; I have left no room for doubt; I have removed all that might confuse good with evil, and have used for this painting only the specific colors and essential lines that make one instantly recognize a true and brazen hypocrite.

Nevertheless, all my precautions have been to no avail. Others have taken advantage of the delicacy of your feelings on religious matters, and they have been able to deceive you on the only side of your character which lies open to deception: your respect for holy things. By underhanded means, the Tartuffes have skillfully gained Your Majesty's favor, and the models have succeeded in eliminating the copy, no matter how innocent it may have been and no matter what resemblance was found between them.

Although the suppression of this work was a serious blow for me, my misfortune was nonetheless softened by the way in which Your Majesty explained his attitude on the matter; and I believed, Sire, that Your Majesty removed any cause I had for complaint, as you were kind enough to declare that you found nothing in this comedy that you would forbid me to present in public.

Yet, despite this glorious declaration of the greatest and most enlightened king in the world, despite the approval of the Papal Legate[14] and of most of our churchmen, all of whom, at private readings of my work, agreed with the views of Your Majesty, despite all this, a book has appeared by a certain priest[15] which boldly contradicts all of these noble judgments. Your Majesty expressed himself in vain, and the Papal Legate and churchmen gave their opinion to no avail: sight unseen, my comedy is diabolical, and so is my brain; I am a devil garbed in flesh and disguised as a man,[16] a libertine, a disbeliever who deserves a punishment that will set an example. It is not enough that fire expiate my crime in

---

[13]The first of the three *petitions* or *placets* to Louis XIV concerning the play. On May 12, 1664, *Tartuffe*—or at least the first three acts roughly as they now stand—was performed at Versailles. A cabal unfavorable to Molière, including the Archbishop of Paris, Hardouin de Péréfixe, Queen-Mother Anne of Austria, certain influential courtiers, and the Brotherhood or Company of the Holy Sacrament (formed in 1627 to enforce morality), arranged that the play be banned and Molière censured.

[14]Cardinal Legate Chigi, nephew to Pope Alexander VII, heard a reading of *Tartuffe* at Fontainebleau on August 4, 1664.

[15]Pierre Roullé, the curate of St. Barthélémy, who wrote a scathing attack on the play and sent his book to the king.

[16]Molière took some of these phrases from Roullé.

public, for that would be letting me off too easily: the generous piety of this good man will not stop there; he will not allow me to find any mercy in the sight of God; he demands that I be damned, and that will settle the matter.

This book, Sire, was presented to Your Majesty; and I am sure that you see for yourself how unpleasant it is for me to be exposed daily to the insults of these gentlemen, what harm these abuses will do my reputation if they must be tolerated, and finally, how important it is for me to clear myself of these false charges and let the public know that my comedy is nothing more than what they want it to be. I will not ask, Sire, for what I need for the sake of my reputation and the innocence of my work: enlightened kings such as you do not need to be told what is wished of them; like God, they see what we need and know better than we what they should give us. It is enough for me to place my interests in Your Majesty's hands, and I respectfully await whatever you may care to command.

(August, 1664)

SECOND PETITION[17]
(PRESENTED TO THE KING IN HIS CAMP BEFORE THE CITY OF LILLE, IN FLANDERS)

Sire,

It is bold indeed for me to ask a favor of a great monarch in the midst of his glorious victories; but in my present situation, Sire, where will I find protection anywhere but where I seek it, and to whom can I appeal against the authority of the power that crushes me,[18] if not to the source of power and authority, the just dispenser of absolute law, the sovereign judge and master of all?

My comedy, Sire, has not enjoyed the kindnesses of Your Majesty. All to no avail, I produced it under the title of *The Hypocrite* and disguised the principal character as a man of the world; in vain I gave him a little hat, long hair, a wide collar, a sword, and lace clothing,[19] softened the action and carefully eliminated all that I thought might provide even the shadow of grounds for discontent on the part of the famous models of the portrait I wished to present; nothing did any good. The conspiracy of opposition revived even at mere conjecture of what the play would be like. They found a way of persuading those who in all other matters plainly insist that they are not to be deceived. No sooner did my comedy appear than it was struck down by the very power which should impose respect; and all that I could do to save myself from the fury of this tempest was to say that Your Majesty had given me permission to present the play and I did not think it was necessary to ask this permission of others, since only Your Majesty could have refused it.

I have no doubt, Sire, that the men whom I depict in my comedy will employ every means possible to influence Your Majesty, and will use, as they have used already, those truly good men who are all the more easily deceived because they judge of others by themselves.[20] They know how to display all of their aims in the most favorable light; yet, no matter how pious they may seem, it is surely not the interests of God which stir them;

---

[17]On August 5, 1667, *Tartuffe* was performed at the Palais-Royal. The opposition—headed by the First President of Parliament—brought in the police, and the play was stopped. Since Louis was campaigning in Flanders, friends of Molière brought the second *placet* to Lille. Louis had always been favorable toward the playwright; in August 1665, Molière's company, the *Troupe de Monsieur* (nominally sponsored by Louis's brother Philippe, Duc d'Orléans) had become the *Troupe du Roi*.

[18]President de Lanvignon, in charge of the Paris police.

[19]There is evidence that in 1664 Tartuffe played his role dressed in a cassock, thus allying him more directly to the clergy.

[20]Molière apparently did not know that de Lanvignon had been affiliated with the Company of the Holy Sacrament for the previous ten years.

they have proven this often enough in the comedies they have allowed to be performed hundreds of times without making the least objection. Those plays attacked only piety and religion, for which they care very little; but this play attacks and makes fun of them, and that is what they cannot bear. They will never forgive me for unmasking their hypocrisy in the eyes of everyone. And I am sure that they will not neglect to tell Your Majesty that people are shocked by my comedy. But the simple truth, Sire, is that all Paris is shocked only by its ban, that the most scrupulous persons have found its presentation worthwhile, and men are astounded that individuals of such known integrity should show so great a deference to people whom everyone should abominate and who are so clearly opposed to the true piety which they profess.

I respectfully await the judgment that Your Majesty will deign to pronounce: but it's certain, Sire, that I need not think of writing comedies if the Tartuffes are triumphant, if they thereby seize the right to persecute me more than ever, and find fault with even the most innocent lines that flow from my pen.

Let your goodness, Sire, give me protection against their envenomed rage, and allow me, at your return from so glorious a campaign, to relieve Your Majesty from the fatigue of his conquests, give him innocent pleasures after such noble accomplishments, and make the monarch laugh who makes all Europe tremble!

(August, 1667)

THIRD PETITION
(PRESENTED TO THE KING)

Sire,

A very honest doctor[21] whose patient I have the honor to be, promises and will legally contract to make me live another thirty years if I can obtain a favor for him from Your Majesty. I told him of his promise that I do not deserve so much, and that I should be glad to help him if he will merely agree not to kill me. This favor, Sire, is a post of canon at your royal chapel of Vincennes, made vacant by death.

May I dare to ask for this favor from Your Majesty on the very day of the glorious resurrection of *Tartuffe*, brought back to life by your goodness? By this first favor I have been reconciled with the devout, and the second will reconcile me with the doctors.[22] Undoubtedly this would be too much grace for me at one time, but perhaps it would not be too much for Your Majesty, and I await your answer to my petition with respectful hope.

(February, 1669)

---

[21] A physician friend, M. de Mauvillain, who helped Molière with some of the medical details of *Le Malade imaginaire*.

[22] Doctors are ridiculed to varying degrees in earlier plays of Molière: *Dom Juan, L'Amour médecin,* and *Le Médecin malgré lui.*

TARTUFFE

Molière

TRANSLATED BY RICHARD WILBUR

------ **CHARACTERS** ------

MADAME PERNELLE, *Orgon's mother*
ORGON, *Elmire's husband*
ELMIRE, *Orgon's wife*
DAMIS, *Orgon's son, Elmire's stepson*
MARIANE, *Orgon's daughter, Elmire's stepdaughter, in love with Valère*
VALÈRE, *in love with Mariane*
CLÉANTE, *Orgon's brother-in-law*

TARTUFFE, *a hypocrite*
DORINE, *Mariane's lady's-maid*
M. LOYAL, *a bailiff*
A POLICE OFFICER
FLIPOTE, *Madame Pernelle's maid*

The scene throughout: Orgon's house in Paris

------ **ACT ONE** ------

SCENE I

MADAME PERNELLE *and* FLIPOTE, *her maid,* ELMIRE, MARIANE, DORINE, DAMIS, CLÉANTE

MADAME PERNELLE: Come, come, Flipote; it's time I left this
    place.
ELMIRE: I can't keep up, you walk at such a pace.
MADAME PERNELLE: Don't trouble, child; no need to show me
    out.
    It's not your manners I'm concerned about.
5 ELMIRE: We merely pay you the respect we owe.
    But, Mother, why this hurry? Must you go?
MADAME PERNELLE: I must. This house appals me. No one in it
    Will pay attention for a single minute.
    Children, I take my leave much vexed in spirit.
10   I offer good advice, but you won't hear it.
    You all break in and chatter on and on.
    It's like a madhouse with the keeper gone.
DORINE: If . . .
MADAME PERNELLE: Girl, you talk too much, and I'm afraid
    You're far too saucy for a lady's-maid.
15   You push in everywhere and have your say.
DAMIS: But . . .
MADAME PERNELLE: You, boy, grow more foolish every day.
    To think my grandson should be such a dunce!
    I've said a hundred times, if I've said it once,
    That if you keep the course on which you've started,
20   You'll leave your worthy father broken-hearted.
MARIANE: I think . . .
MADAME PERNELLE: And you, his sister, seem so pure,
    So shy, so innocent, and so demure.
    But you know what they say about still waters.
    I pity parents with secretive daughters.
25 ELMIRE: Now, Mother . . .
MADAME PERNELLE: And as for you, child, let me add
    That your behavior is extremely bad,
    And a poor example for these children, too.
    Their dear, dead mother did far better than you.
    You're much too free with money, and I'm distressed
30   To see you so elaborately dressed.
    When it's one's husband that one aims to please,
    One has no need of costly fripperies.
CLÉANTE: Oh, Madam, really . . .
MADAME PERNELLE: You are her brother, Sir,
    And I respect and love you; yet if I were
    My son, this lady's good and pious spouse, 35
    I wouldn't make you welcome in my house.
    You're full of worldly counsels which, I fear,
    Aren't suitable for decent folk to hear.
    I've spoken bluntly, Sir; but it behooves us
    Not to mince words when righteous fervor moves us. 40
DAMIS: Your man Tartuffe is full of holy speeches . . .
MADAME PERNELLE: And practises precisely what he preaches.
    He's a fine man, and should be listened to.
    I will not hear him mocked by fools like you.
DAMIS: Good God! Do you expect me to submit 45
    To the tyranny of that carping hypocrite?
    Must we forgo all joys and satisfactions
    Because that bigot censures all our actions?
DORINE: To hear him talk—and he talks all the time—
    There's nothing one can do that's not a crime. 50
    He rails at everything, your dear Tartuffe.
MADAME PERNELLE: Whatever he reproves deserves reproof.
    He's out to save your souls, and all of you
    Must love him, as my son would have you do.
DAMIS: Ah no, Grandmother, I could never take 55
    To such a rascal, even for my father's sake.
    That's how I feel, and I shall not dissemble.
    His every action makes me seethe and tremble
    With helpless anger, and I have no doubt
    That he and I will shortly have it out. 60
DORINE: Surely it is a shame and a disgrace
    To see this man usurp the master's place—
    To see this beggar who, when first he came,
    Had not a shoe or shoestring to his name
    So far forget himself that he behaves 65
    As if the house were his, and we his slaves.
MADAME PERNELLE: Well, mark my words, your souls would
    fare far better
    If you obeyed his precepts to the letter.
DORINE: You see him as a saint. I'm far less awed;
    In fact, I see right through him. He's a fraud. 70
MADAME PERNELLE: Nonsense!
DORINE: His man Laurent's the same, or worse;
    I'd not trust either with a penny purse.
MADAME PERNELLE: I can't say what his servant's morals may be;
    His own great goodness I can guarantee.

75   You all regard him with distaste and fear
        Because he tells you what you're loath to hear,
        Condemns your sins, points out your moral flaws,
        And humbly strives to further Heaven's cause.
    DORINE: If sin is all that bothers him, why is it
80   He's so upset when folk drop in to visit?
        Is Heaven so outraged by a social call
        That he must prophesy against us all?
        I'll tell you what I think: if you ask me,
        He's jealous of my mistress' company.
85 MADAME PERNELLE: Rubbish! (*To* ELMIRE.) He's not alone,
            child, in complaining
        Of all of your promiscuous entertaining.
        Why, the whole neighborhood's upset, I know,
        By all these carriages that come and go,
        With crowds of guests parading in and out
90   And noisy servants loitering about.
        In all of this, I'm sure there's nothing vicious;
        But why give people cause to be suspicious?
    CLÉANTE: They need no cause; they'll talk in any case.
        Madam, this world would be a joyless place
95   If, fearing what malicious tongues might say,
        We locked our doors and turned our friends away.
        And even if one did so dreary a thing,
        D'you think those tongues would cease their chattering?
        One can't fight slander; it's a losing battle;
100   Let us instead ignore their tittle-tattle.
        Let's strive to live by conscience' clear decrees,
        And let the gossips gossip as they please.
    DORINE: If there is talk against us, I know the source:
        It's Daphne and her little husband, of course.
105   Those who have greatest cause for guilt and shame
        Are quickest to besmirch a neighbor's name.
        When there's a chance for libel, they never miss it;
        When something can be made to seem illicit
        They're off at once to spread the joyous news,
110   Adding to fact what fantasies they choose.
        By talking up their neighbor's indiscretions
        They seek to camouflage their own transgressions,
        Hoping that others' innocent affairs
        Will lend a hue of innocence to theirs,
115   Or that their own black guilt will come to seem
        Part of a general shady color-scheme.
    MADAME PERNELLE: All that is quite irrelevant. I doubt
        That anyone's more virtuous and devout
        Than dear Orante; and I'm informed that she
120   Condemns your mode of life most vehemently.
    DORINE: Oh, yes, she's strict, devout, and has no taint
        Of worldliness; in short, she seems a saint.
        But it was time which taught her that disguise;
        She's thus because she can't be otherwise.
125   So long as her attractions could enthrall,
        She flounced and flirted and enjoyed it all,
        But now that they're no longer what they were
        She quits a world which fast is quitting her,
        And wears a veil of virtue to conceal
130   Her bankrupt beauty and her lost appeal.
        That's what becomes of old coquettes today:
        Distressed when all their lovers fall away,
        They see no recourse but to play the prude,

        And so confer a style on solitude.
        Thereafter, they're severe with everyone,   135
        Condemning all our actions, pardoning none,
        And claiming to be pure, austere, and zealous
        When, if the truth were known, they're merely jealous,
        And cannot bear to see another know
        The pleasures time has forced them to forgo.   140
    MADAME PERNELLE: (*Initially to* ELMIRE.) That sort of talk is
            what you like to hear;
        Therefore you'd have us all keep still, my dear,
        While Madam rattles on the livelong day.
        Nevertheless, I mean to have my say.
        I tell you that you're blest to have Tartuffe   145
        Dwelling, as my son's guest, beneath this roof;
        That Heaven has sent him to forestall its wrath
        By leading you, once more, to the true path;
        That all he reprehends is reprehensible,
        And that you'd better heed him, and be sensible.   150
        These visits, balls, and parties in which you revel
        Are nothing but inventions of the Devil.
        One never hears a word that's edifying:
        Nothing but chaff and foolishness and lying,
        As well as vicious gossip in which one's neighbor   155
        Is cut to bits with épée, foil, and saber.
        People of sense are driven half-insane
        At such affairs, where noise and folly reign
        And reputations perish thick and fast.
        As a wise preacher said on Sunday last,   160
        Parties are Towers of Babylon, because
        The guests all babble on with never a pause;
        And then he told a story which, I think . . .

    (*To* CLÉANTE.)

        I heard that laugh, Sir, and I saw that wink!
        Go find your silly friends and laugh some more!   165
        Enough; I'm going; don't show me to the door.
        I leave this household much dismayed and vexed;
        I cannot say when I shall see you next.

    (*Slapping* FLIPOTE.)

        Wake up, don't stand there gaping into space!
        I'll slap some sense into that stupid face.   170
        Move, move, you slut.

SCENE II

CLÉANTE, DORINE

CLÉANTE: I think I'll stay behind;
        I want no further pieces of her mind.
        How that old lady . . .
    DORINE: Oh, what wouldn't she say
        If she could hear you speak of her that way!
        She'd thank you for the *lady*, but I'm sure   5
        She'd find the *old* a little premature.
    CLÉANTE: My, what a scene she made, and what a din!
        And how this man Tartuffe has taken her in!
    DORINE: Yes, but her son is even worse deceived;
        His folly must be seen to be believed.   10
        In the late troubles, he played an able part

And served his king with wise and loyal heart,
But he's quite lost his senses since he fell
Beneath Tartuffe's infatuating spell.
15 He calls him brother, and loves him as his life,
Preferring him to mother, child, or wife.
In him and him alone will he confide;
He's made him his confessor and his guide;
He pets and pampers him with love more tender
20 Than any pretty mistress could engender,
Gives him the place of honor when they dine,
Delights to see him gorging like a swine,
Stuffs him with dainties till his guts distend,
And when he belches, cries "God bless you, friend!"
25 In short, he's mad; he worships him; he dotes;
His deeds he marvels at, his words he quotes,
Thinking each act a miracle, each word
Oracular as those that Moses heard.
Tartuffe, much pleased to find so easy a victim,
30 Has in a hundred ways beguiled and tricked him,
Milked him of money, and with his permission
Established here a sort of Inquisition.
Even Laurent, his lackey, dares to give
Us arrogant advice on how to live;
35 He sermonizes us in thundering tones
And confiscates our ribbons and colognes.
Last week he tore a kerchief into pieces
Because he found it pressed in a *Life of Jesus:*
He said it was a sin to juxtapose
40 Unholy vanities and holy prose.

SCENE III

ELMIRE, MARIANE, DAMIS, CLÉANTE, DORINE

ELMIRE: *(To* CLÉANTE.*)* You did well not to follow; she stood
    in the door
    And said *verbatim* all she'd said before.
    I saw my husband coming. I think I'd best
    Go upstairs now, and take a little rest.
5 CLÉANTE: I'll wait and greet him here; then I must go.
    I've really only time to say hello.
DAMIS: Sound him about my sister's wedding, please.
    I think Tartuffe's against it, and that he's
    Been urging Father to withdraw his blessing.
10 As you well know, I'd find that most distressing.
    Unless my sister and Valère can marry,
    My hopes to wed *his* sister will miscarry,
    And I'm determined . . .
DORINE: He's coming.

SCENE IV

ORGON, CLÉANTE, DORINE

ORGON: Ah, Brother, good-day.
CLÉANTE: Well, welcome back. I'm sorry I can't stay.
    How was the country? Blooming, I trust, and green?
ORGON: Excuse me, Brother; just one moment.

(To DORINE.*)*

                                    Dorine . . .

(To CLÉANTE.*)*

    To put my mind at rest, I always learn   5
    The household news the moment I return.

(To DORINE.*)*

    Has all been well, these two days I've been gone?
    How are the family? What's been going on?
DORINE: Your wife, two days ago, had a bad fever,
    And a fierce headache which refused to leave her.   10
ORGON: Ah. And Tartuffe?
DORINE: Tartuffe? Why, he's round and red,
    Bursting with health, and excellently fed.
ORGON: Poor fellow!
DORINE: That night, the mistress was unable
    To take a single bite at the dinner-table.
    Her headache-pains, she said, were simply hellish.   15
ORGON: Ah. And Tartuffe?
DORINE: He ate his meal with relish,
    And zealously devoured in her presence
    A leg of mutton and a brace of pheasants.
ORGON: Poor fellow!
DORINE: Well, the pains continued strong,
    And so she tossed and tossed the whole night long,   20
    Now icy-cold, now burning like a flame.
    We sat beside her bed till morning came.
ORGON: Ah. And Tartuffe?
DORINE: Why, having eaten, he rose
    And sought his room, already in a doze,
    Got into his warm bed, and snored away   25
    In perfect peace until the break of day.
ORGON: Poor fellow!
DORINE: After much ado, we talked her
    Into dispatching someone for the doctor.
    He bled her, and the fever quickly fell.
ORGON: Ah. And Tartuffe?   30
DORINE: He bore it very well.
    To keep his cheerfulness at any cost,
    And make up for the blood *Madame* had lost,
    He drank, at lunch, four beakers full of port.
ORGON: Poor fellow!
DORINE: Both are doing well, in short.
    I'll go and tell *Madame* that you've expressed   35
    Keen sympathy and anxious interest.

SCENE V

ORGON, CLÉANTE

CLÉANTE: That girl was laughing in your face, and though
    I've no wish to offend you, even so
    I'm bound to say that she had some excuse.
    How can you possibly be such a goose?
    Are you so dazed by this man's hocus-pocus   5
    That all the world, save him, is out of focus?
    You've given him clothing, shelter, food, and care;
    Why must you also . . .
ORGON: Brother, stop right there.
    You do not know the man of whom you speak.
CLÉANTE: I grant you that. But my judgment's not so weak   10
    That I can't tell, by his effect on others . . .

ORGON: Ah, when you meet him, you two will be like brothers!
    There's been no loftier soul since time began.
    He is a man who . . . a man who . . . an excellent man.
15 To keep his precepts is to be reborn,
    And view this dunghill of a world with scorn.
    Yes, thanks to him I'm a changed man indeed.
    Under his tutelage my soul's been freed
    From earthly loves, and every human tie:
20 My mother, children, brother, and wife could die,
    And I'd not feel a single moment's pain.
CLÉANTE: That's a fine sentiment, Brother; most humane.
ORGON: Oh, had you seen Tartuffe as I first knew him,
    Your heart, like mine, would have surrendered to him.
25 He used to come into our church each day
    And humbly kneel nearby, and start to pray.
    He'd draw the eyes of everybody there
    By the deep fervor of his heartfelt prayer;
    He'd sigh and weep, and sometimes with a sound
30 Of rapture he would bend and kiss the ground;
    And when I rose to go, he'd run before
    To offer me holy-water at the door.
    His serving-man, no less devout than he,
    Informed me of his master's poverty;
35 I gave him gifts, but in his humbleness
    He'd beg me every time to give him less.
    "Oh, that's too much," he'd cry, "too much by twice!
    I don't deserve it. The half, Sir, would suffice."
    And when I wouldn't take it back, he'd share
40 Half of it with the poor, right then and there.
    At length, Heaven prompted me to take him in
    To dwell with us, and free our souls from sin.
    He guides our lives, and to protect my honor
    Stays by my wife, and keeps an eye upon her;
45 He tells me whom she sees, and all she does,
    And seems more jealous than I ever was!
    And how austere he is! Why, he can detect
    A mortal sin where you would least suspect;
    In smallest trifles, he's extremely strict.
50 Last week, his conscience was severely pricked
    Because, while praying, he had caught a flea
    And killed it, so he felt, too wrathfully.
CLÉANTE: Good God, man! Have you lost your common sense—
    Or is this all some joke at my expense?
55 How can you stand there and in all sobriety . . .
ORGON: Brother, your language savors of impiety.
    Too much free-thinking's made your faith unsteady,
    And as I've warned you many times already,
    'Twill get you into trouble before you're through.
60 CLÉANTE: So I've been told before by dupes like you:
    Being blind, you'd have all others blind as well;
    The clear-eyed man you call an infidel,
    And he who sees through humbug and pretense
    Is charged, by you, with want of reverence.
65 Spare me your warnings, Brother; I have no fear
    Of speaking out, for you and Heaven to hear,
    Against affected zeal and pious knavery.
    There's true and false in piety, as in bravery,
    And just as those whose courage shines the most
70 In battle, are the least inclined to boast,
    So those whose hearts are truly pure and lowly
    Don't make a flashy show of being holy.

There's a vast difference, so it seems to me,
    Between true piety and hypocrisy:
    How do you fail to see it, may I ask?   75
    Is not a face quite different from a mask?
    Cannot sincerity and cunning art,
    Reality and semblance, be told apart?
    Are scarecrows just like men, and do you hold
    That a false coin is just as good as gold?   80
    Ah, Brother, man's a strangely fashioned creature
    Who seldom is content to follow Nature,
    But recklessly pursues his inclination
    Beyond the narrow bounds of moderation,
    And often, by transgressing Reason's laws,   85
    Perverts a lofty aim or noble cause.
    A passing observation, but it applies.
ORGON: I see, dear Brother, that you're profoundly wise;
    You harbor all the insight of the age.
    You are our one clear mind, our only sage,   90
    The era's oracle, its Cato too,
    And all mankind are fools compared to you.
CLÉANTE: Brother, I don't pretend to be a sage,
    Nor have I all the wisdom of the age.
    There's just one insight I would dare to claim: 95
    I know that true and false are not the same;
    And just as there is nothing I more revere
    Than a soul whose faith is steadfast and sincere,
    Nothing that I more cherish and admire
    Than honest zeal and true religious fire,   100
    So there is nothing that I find more base
    Than specious piety's dishonest face—
    Than these bold mountebanks, these histrios
    Whose impious mummeries and hollow shows
    Exploit our love of Heaven, and make a jest   105
    Of all that men think holiest and best;
    These calculating souls who offer prayers
    Not to their Maker, but as public wares,
    And seek to buy respect and reputation
    With lifted eyes and sighs of exaltation;   110
    These charlatans, I say, whose pilgrim souls
    Proceed, by way of Heaven, toward earthly goals,
    Who weep and pray and swindle and extort,
    Who preach the monkish life, but haunt the court,
    Who make their zeal the partner of their vice—   115
    Such men are vengeful, sly, and cold as ice,
    And when there is an enemy to defame
    They cloak their spite in fair religion's name,
    Their private spleen and malice being made
    To seem a high and virtuous crusade,   120
    Until, to mankind's reverent applause,
    They crucify their foe in Heaven's cause.
    Such knaves are all too common; yet, for the wise,
    True piety isn't hard to recognize,
    And, happily, these present times provide us   125
    With bright examples to instruct and guide us.
    Consider Ariston and Périandre;
    Look at Oronte, Alcidamas, Clitandre;
    Their virtue is acknowledged; who could doubt it?
    But you won't hear them beat the drum about it.   130
    They're never ostentatious, never vain,
    And their religion's moderate and humane;
    It's not their way to criticize and chide:

135   They think censoriousness a mark of pride,
And therefore, letting others preach and rave,
They show, by deeds, how Christians should behave.
They think no evil of their fellow man,
But judge of him as kindly as they can.
They don't intrigue and wangle and conspire;
140   To lead a good life is their one desire;
The sinner wakes no rancorous hate in them;
It is the sin alone which they condemn;
Nor do they try to show a fiercer zeal
For Heaven's cause than Heaven itself could feel.
145   These men I honor, these men I advocate
As models for us all to emulate.
Your man is not their sort at all, I fear:
And, while your praise of him is quite sincere,
I think that you've been dreadfully deluded.
150 ORGON: Now then, dear Brother, is your speech concluded?
CLÉANTE: Why, yes.
ORGON: Your servant, Sir.

(He turns to go.)

CLÉANTE: No, Brother; wait.
There's one more matter. You agreed of late
That young Valère might have your daughter's hand.
ORGON: I did.
CLÉANTE: And set the date, I understand.
155 ORGON: Quite so.
CLÉANTE: You've now postponed it; is that true?
ORGON: No doubt.
CLÉANTE: The match no longer pleases you?
ORGON: Who knows?
CLÉANTE: D'you mean to go back on your word?
ORGON: I won't say that.
CLÉANTE: Has anything occurred
Which might entitle you to break your pledge?
160 ORGON: Perhaps.
CLÉANTE: Why must you hem, and haw, and hedge?
The boy asked me to sound you in this affair . . .
ORGON: It's been a pleasure.
CLÉANTE: But what shall I tell Valère?
ORGON: Whatever you like.
CLÉANTE: But what have you decided?
What are your plans?
ORGON: I plan, Sir, to be guided
165   By Heaven's will.
CLÉANTE: Come, Brother, don't talk rot.
You've given Valère your word; will you keep it, or not?
ORGON: Good day.
CLÉANTE: This looks like poor Valère's undoing;
I'll go and warn him that there's trouble brewing.

———— ACT TWO ————

SCENE I

ORGON, MARIANE

ORGON: Mariane.
MARIANE: Yes, Father?
ORGON: A word with you; come here.
MARIANE: What are you looking for?
ORGON: *(Peering into a small closet.)*
               Eavesdroppers, dear.

I'm making sure we shan't be overheard.
Someone in there could catch our every word.
Ah, good, we're safe. Now, Mariane, my child,   5
You're a sweet girl who's tractable and mild,
Whom I hold dear, and think most highly of.
MARIANE: I'm deeply grateful, Father, for your love.
ORGON: That's well said, Daughter; and you can repay me
If, in all things, you'll cheerfully obey me.   10
MARIANE: To please you, Sir, is what delights me best.
ORGON: Good, good. Now, what d'you think of Tartuffe, our
  guest?
MARIANE: I, Sir?
ORGON: Yes. Weigh your answer; think it through.
MARIANE: Oh, dear. I'll say whatever you wish me to.
ORGON: That's wisely said, my Daughter. Say of him, then,   15
That he's the very worthiest of men,
And that you're fond of him, and would rejoice
In being his wife, if that should be my choice.
Well?
MARIANE: What?
ORGON: What's that?
MARIANE: I . . .
ORGON: Well?
MARIANE: Forgive me, pray.
ORGON: Did you not hear me?   20
MARIANE: Of *whom*, Sir, must I say
That I am fond of him, and would rejoice
In being his wife, if that should be your choice?
ORGON: Why, of Tartuffe.
MARIANE: But, Father, that's false, you know.
Why would you have me say what isn't so?
ORGON: Because I am resolved it shall be true.   25
That it's my wish should be enough for you.
MARIANE: You can't mean, Father . . .
ORGON: Yes, Tartuffe shall be
Allied by marriage to this family,
And he's to be your husband, is that clear?
It's a father's privilege . . .   30

SCENE II

DORINE, ORGON, MARIANE

ORGON: *(To* DORINE.*)*   What are you doing in here?
Is curiosity so fierce a passion
With you, that you must eavesdrop in this fashion?
DORINE: There's lately been a rumor going about—
Based on some hunch or chance remark, no doubt—   5
That you mean Mariane to wed Tartuffe.
I've laughed it off, of course, as just a spoof.
ORGON: You find it so incredible?
DORINE: Yes, I do.
I won't accept that story, even from you.
ORGON: Well, you'll believe it when the thing is done.   10
DORINE: Yes, yes, of course. Go on and have your fun.
ORGON: I've never been more serious in my life.
DORINE: Ha!
ORGON: Daughter, I mean it; you're to be his wife.
DORINE: No, don't believe your father; it's all a hoax.
ORGON: See here, young woman . . .   15
DORINE: Come, Sir, no more jokes;
You can't fool us.

ORGON: How dare you talk that way?
DORINE: All right, then: we believe you, sad to say.
     But how a man like you, who looks so wise
     And wears a moustache of such splendid size,
20   Can be so foolish as to . . .
ORGON: Silence, please!
     My girl, you take too many liberties.
     I'm master here, as you must not forget.
DORINE: Do let's discuss this calmly; don't be upset.
     You can't be serious, Sir, about this plan.
25   What should that bigot want with Mariane?
     Praying and fasting ought to keep him busy.
     And then, in terms of wealth and rank, what is he?
     Why should a man of property like you
     Pick out a beggar son-in-law?
ORGON: That will do.
30   Speak of his poverty with reverence.
     His is a pure and saintly indigence
     Which far transcends all worldly pride and pelf.
     He lost his fortune, as he says himself,
     Because he cared for Heaven alone, and so
35   Was careless of his interests here below.
     I mean to get him out of his present straits
     And help him to recover his estates—
     Which, in his part of the world, have no small fame.
     Poor though he is, he's a gentleman just the same.
40 DORINE: Yes, so he tells us; and, Sir, it seems to me
     Such pride goes very ill with piety.
     A man whose spirit spurns this dungy earth
     Ought not to brag of lands and noble birth;
     Such worldly arrogance will hardly square
45   With meek devotion and the life of prayer.
     . . . But this approach, I see, has drawn a blank;
     Let's speak, then, of his person, not his rank.
     Doesn't it seem to you a trifle grim
     To give a girl like her to a man like him?
50   When two are so ill-suited, can't you see
     What the sad consequences is bound to be?
     A young girl's virtue is imperilled, Sir,
     When such a marriage is imposed on her;
     For if one's bridegroom isn't to one's taste,
55   It's hardly an inducement to be chaste,
     And many a man with horns upon his brow
     Has made his wife the thing that she is now.
     It's hard to be a faithful wife, in short,
     To certain husbands of a certain sort,
60   And he who gives his daughter to a man she hates
     Must answer for her sins at Heaven's gates.
     Think, Sir, before you play so risky a role.
ORGON: This servant-girl presumes to save my soul!
DORINE: You would do well to ponder what I've said.
65 ORGON: Daughter, we'll disregard this dunderhead.
     Just trust your father's judgment. Oh, I'm aware
     That I once promised you to young Valère;
     But now I hear he gambles, which greatly shocks me;
     What's more, I've doubts about his orthodoxy.
70   His visits to church, I note, are very few.
DORINE: Would you have him go at the same hours as you,
     And kneel nearby, to be sure of being seen?
ORGON: I can dispense with such remarks, Dorine.

(To MARIANE.*)*

     Tartuffe, however, is sure of Heaven's blessing,
     And that's the only treasure worth possessing.   75
     This match will bring you joys beyond all measure;
     Your cup will overflow with every pleasure;
     You two will interchange your faithful loves
     Like two sweet cherubs, or two turtle-doves.
     No harsh word shall be heard, no frown be seen,   80
     And he shall make you happy as a queen.
DORINE: And she'll make him a cuckold, just wait and see.
ORGON: What language!
DORINE: Oh, he's a man of destiny;
     He's *made* for horns, and what the stars demand
     Your daughter's virtue surely can't withstand.   85
ORGON: Don't interrupt me further. Why can't you learn
     That certain things are none of your concern?
DORINE: It's for your own sake that I interfere.

(She repeatedly interrupts ORGON *just as he is turning to speak to his daughter.)*

ORGON: Most kind of you. Now, hold your tongue, d'you
          hear?
DORINE: If I didn't love you . . .   90
ORGON: Spare me your affection.
DORINE: I'll love you, Sir, in spite of your objection.
ORGON: Blast!
DORINE: I can't bear, Sir, for your honor's sake,
     To let you make this ludicrous mistake.
ORGON: You mean to go on talking?
DORINE: If I didn't protest
     This sinful marriage, my conscience couldn't rest.   95
ORGON: If you don't hold your tongue, you little shrew . . .
DORINE: What, lost your temper? A pious man like you?
ORGON: Yes! Yes! You talk and talk. I'm maddened by it.
     Once and for all, I tell you to be quiet.
DORINE: Well, I'll be quiet. But I'll be thinking hard.   100
ORGON: Think all you like, but you had better guard
     That saucy tongue of yours, or I'll . . .

(Turning back to MARIANE.*)*

                                   Now, child,
     I've weighed this matter fully.
DORINE: *(Aside.)*   It drives me wild
     That I can't speak.

*(*ORGON *turns his head, and she is silent.)*

ORGON: Tartuffe is no young dandy,
     But, still, his person . . .   105
DORINE: *(Aside.)*   Is as sweet as candy.
ORGON: Is such that, even if you shouldn't care
     For his other merits . . .

(He turns and stands facing DORINE, *arms crossed.)*

DORINE: *(Aside.)*   They'll make a lovely pair.
     If I were she, no man would marry me
     Against my inclination, and go scot-free.
     He'd learn, before the wedding-day was over,
     How readily a wife can find a lover.   110
ORGON: *(To* DORINE.*)* It seems you treat my orders as a joke.

DORINE: Why, what's the matter? 'Twas not to you I spoke.
ORGON: What *were* you doing?
DORINE: Talking to myself, that's all.
115 ORGON: Ah! *(Aside.)* One more bit of impudence and gall,
        And I shall give her a good slap in the face.

(He puts himself in position to slap her; DORINE, *whenever he glances
at her, stands immobile and silent.)*

        Daughter, you shall accept, and with good grace,
        The husband I've selected . . . Your wedding-day . . .

(To DORINE.*)*

        Why don't you talk to yourself?
        DORINE: I've nothing to say.
120 ORGON: Come, just one word.
        DORINE: No thank you, Sir. I pass.
        ORGON: Come, speak; I'm waiting.
        DORINE: I'd not be such an ass.
        ORGON: *(Turning to* MARIANE.*)* In short, dear Daughter, I
                mean to be obeyed,
            And you must bow to the sound choice I've made.
        DORINE: *(Moving away.)* I'd not wed such a monster, even in jest.

*(*ORGON *attempts to slap her, but misses.)*

125 ORGON: Daughter, that maid of yours is a thorough pest;
        She makes me sinfully annoyed and nettled.
        I can't speak further; my nerves are too unsettled.
        She's so upset me by her insolent talk,
        I'll calm myself by going for a walk.

Scene III

DORINE, MARIANE

DORINE: *(Returning.)* Well, have you lost your tongue, girl?
            Must I play
        Your part, and say the lines you ought to say?
        Faced with a fate so hideous and absurd,
        Can you not utter one dissenting word?
5 MARIANE: What good would it do? A father's power is great.
    DORINE: Resist him now, or it will be too late.
    MARIANE: But . . .
    DORINE: Tell him one cannot love at a father's whim;
        That you shall marry for yourself, not him;
        That since it's you who are to be the bride,
10   It's you, not he, who must be satisfied;
        And that if his Tartuffe is so sublime,
        He's free to marry him at any time.
    MARIANE: I've bowed so long to Father's strict control,
        I couldn't oppose him now, to save my soul.
15 DORINE: Come, come, Mariane. Do listen to reason, won't you?
        Valère has asked your hand. Do you love him, or don't you?
    MARIANE: Oh, how unjust of you! What can you mean
        By asking such a question, dear Dorine?
        You know the depth of my affection for him;
20   I've told you a hundred times how I adore him.
    DORINE: I don't believe in everything I hear;
        Who knows if your professions were sincere?
    MARIANE: They were, Dorine, and you do me wrong to doubt it;
        Heaven knows that I've been all too frank about it.

DORINE: You love him, then?   25
MARIANE: Oh, more than I can express.
DORINE: And he, I take it, cares for you no less?
MARIANE: I think so.
DORINE: And you both, with equal fire,
    Burn to be married?
MARIANE: That is our one desire.
DORINE: What of Tartuffe, then? What of your father's plan?
MARIANE: I'll kill myself, if I'm forced to wed that man.   30
DORINE: I hadn't thought of that recourse. How splendid!
    Just die, and all your troubles will be ended!
    A fine solution. Oh, it maddens me
    To hear you talk in that self-pitying key.
MARIANE: Dorine, how harsh you are! It's most unfair.   35
    You have no sympathy for my despair.
DORINE: I've none at all for people who talk drivel
    And, faced with difficulties, whine and snivel.
MARIANE: No doubt I'm timid, but it would be wrong . . .
DORINE: True love requires a heart that's firm and strong.   40
MARIANE: I'm strong in my affection for Valère,
    But coping with my father is his affair.
DORINE: But if your father's brain has grown so cracked
    Over his dear Tartuffe that he can retract
    His blessing, though your wedding-day was named,   45
    It's surely not Valère who's to be blamed.
MARIANE: If I defied my father, as you suggest,
    Would it not seem unmaidenly, at best?
    Shall I defend my love at the expense
    Of brazeness and disobedience?   50
    Shall I parade my heart's desires, and flaunt . . .
DORINE: No, I ask nothing of you. Clearly you want
    To be Madame Tartuffe, and I feel bound
    Not to oppose a wish so very sound.
    What right have I to criticize the match?   55
    Indeed, my dear, the man's a brilliant catch.
    Monsieur Tartuffe! Now, there's a man of weight!
    Yes, yes, Monsieur Tartuffe, I'm bound to state,
    Is quite a person; that's not to be denied.
    'Twill be no little thing to be his bride.   60
    The world already rings with his renown;
    He's a great noble—in his native town;
    His ears are red, he has a pink complexion,
    And all in all, he'll suit you to perfection.
MARIANE: Dear God!   65
DORINE: Oh, how triumphant you will feel
    At having caught a husband so ideal!
MARIANE: Oh, do stop teasing, and use your cleverness
    To get me out of this appalling mess.
    Advise me, and I'll do whatever you say.
DORINE: Ah no, a dutiful daughter must obey   70
    Her father, even if he weds her to an ape.
    You've a bright future; why struggle to escape?
    Tartuffe will take you back where his family lives,
    To a small town aswarm with relatives—
    Uncles and cousins whom you'll be charmed to meet.   75
    You'll be received at once by the elite,
    Calling upon the bailiff's wife, no less—
    Even, perhaps, upon the mayoress,
    Who'll sit you down in the *best* kitchen chair.
    Then, once a year, you'll dance at the village fair   80
    To the drone of bagpipes—two of them, in fact—

And see a puppet-show, or an animal act.
Your husband . . .
MARIANE: Oh, you turn my blood to ice!
  Stop torturing me, and give me your advice.
DORINE: (*Threatening to go.*)
85 Your servant, Madam.
MARIANE: Dorine, I beg of you . . .
DORINE: No, you deserve it; this marriage must go through.
MARIANE: Dorine!
DORINE: No.
MARIANE: Not Tartuffe! You know I think him . . .
DORINE: Tartuffe's your cup of tea, and you shall drink him.
MARIANE: I've always told you everything, and relied . . .
90 DORINE: No. You deserve to be tartuffified.
MARIANE: Well, since you mock me and refuse to care,
  I'll henceforth seek my solace in despair:
  Despair shall be my counsellor and friend,
  And help me bring my sorrows to an end.

(*She starts to leave.*)

95 DORINE: There now, come back; my anger has subsided.
  You do deserve some pity, I've decided.
MARIANE: Dorine, if Father makes me undergo
  This dreadful martyrdom, I'll die, I know.
DORINE: Don't fret; it won't be difficult to discover
100 Some plan of action . . . But here's Valère, your lover.

SCENE IV

VALÈRE, MARIANE, DORINE

VALÈRE: Madam, I've just received some wondrous news
  Regarding which I'd like to hear your views.
MARIANE: What news?
VALÈRE: You're marrying Tartuffe.
MARIANE: I find
  That Father does have such a match in mind.
5 VALÈRE: Your father, Madam . . .
MARIANE: . . . has just this minute said
  That it's Tartuffe he wishes me to wed.
VALÈRE: Can he be serious?
MARIANE: Oh, indeed he can;
  He's clearly set his heart upon the plan.
VALÈRE: And what position do you propose to take,
10 Madam?
MARIANE: Why—I don't know.
VALÈRE: For heaven's sake—
  You don't know?
MARIANE: No.
VALÈRE: Well, well!
MARIANE: Advise me, do.
VALÈRE: Marry the man. That's my advice to you.
MARIANE: That's your advice?
VALÈRE: Yes.
MARIANE: Truly?
VALÈRE: Oh, absolutely.
  You couldn't choose more wisely, more astutely.
15 MARIANE: Thanks for this counsel; I'll follow it, of course.
VALÈRE: Do, do; I'm sure 'twill cost you no remorse.
MARIANE: To give it didn't cause your heart to break.

VALÈRE: I gave it, Madam, only for your sake.
MARIANE: And it's for your sake that I take it, Sir.
DORINE: (*Withdrawing to the rear of the stage.*) Let's see which   20
  fool will prove the stubborner.
VALÈRE: So! I am nothing to you, and it was flat
  Deception when you . . .
MARIANE: Please, enough of that.
  You've told me plainly that I should agree
  To wed the man my father's chosen for me,
  And since you've deigned to counsel me so wisely,   25
  I promise, Sir, to do as you advise me.
VALÈRE: Ah, no, 'twas not by me that you were swayed.
  No, your decision was already made;
  Though now, to save appearances, you protest
  That you're betraying me at my behest.   30
MARIANE: Just as you say.
VALÈRE: Quite so. And I now see
  That you were never truly in love with me.
MARIANE: Alas, you're free to think so if you choose.
VALÈRE: I choose to think so, and here's a bit of news:
  You've spurned my hand, but I know where to turn   35
  For kinder treatment, as you shall quickly learn.
MARIANE: I'm sure you do. Your noble qualities
  Inspire affection . . .
VALÈRE: Forget my qualities, please.
  They don't inspire you overmuch, I find.
  But there's another lady I have in mind   40
  Whose sweet and generous nature will not scorn
  To compensate me for the loss I've borne.
MARIANE: I'm no great loss, and I'm sure that you'll transfer
  Your heart quite painlessly from me to her.
VALÈRE: I'll do my best to take it in my stride.   45
  The pain I feel at being cast aside
  Time and forgetfulness may put an end to.
  Or if I can't forget, I shall pretend to.
  No self-respecting person is expected
  To go on loving once he's been rejected.   50
MARIANE: Now, that's a fine, high-minded sentiment.
VALÈRE: One to which any sane man would assent.
  Would you prefer it if I pined away
  In hopeless passion till my dying day?
  Am I to yield you to a rival's arms   55
  And not console myself with other charms?
MARIANE: Go then: console yourself; don't hesitate.
  I wish you to; indeed, I cannot wait.
VALÈRE: You wish me to?
MARIANE: Yes.
VALÈRE: That's the final straw.
  Madam, farewell. Your wish shall be my law.   60

(*He starts to leave, and then returns: this repeatedly.*)

MARIANE: Splendid.
VALÈRE: (*Coming back again.*)
                This breach, remember, is of your making;
  It's you who've driven me to the step I'm taking.
MARIANE: Of course.
VALÈRE: (*Coming back again.*)
                Remember, too, that I am merely
  Following your example.
MARIANE: I see that clearly.

65 VALÈRE: Enough. I'll go and do your bidding, then.
MARIANE: Good.
VALÈRE: *(Coming back again.)*
                    You shall never see my face again.
MARIANE: Excellent.
VALÈRE: *(Walking to the door, then turning about.)*
                    Yes?
MARIANE: What?
VALÈRE: What's that? What did you say?
MARIANE: Nothing. You're dreaming.
VALÈRE: Ah. Well, I'm on my way.
    Farewell, *Madame.*

(He moves slowly away.)

MARIANE: Farewell.
DORINE: *(To MARIANE.)*   If you ask me,
70   Both of you are as mad as mad can be.
    Do stop this nonsense, now. I've only let you
    Squabble so long to see where it would get you.
    Whoa there, Monsieur Valère!

*(She goes and seizes VALÈRE by the arm; he makes a great show of
resistance.)*

VALÈRE: What's this, Dorine?
DORINE: Come here.
VALÈRE: No, no, my heart's too full of spleen.
75   Don't hold me back; her wish must be obeyed.
DORINE: Stop!
VALÈRE: It's too late now; my decision's made.
DORINE: Oh, pooh!
MARIANE: *(Aside.)*
                He hates the sight of me, that's plain.
    I'll go, and so deliver him from pain.
DORINE: *(Leaving VALÈRE, running after MARIANE.)* And now *you*
    run away! Come back.
MARIANE: No, no.
80   Nothing you say will keep me here. Let go!
VALÈRE: *(Aside.)* She cannot bear my presence, I perceive.
    To spare her further torment, I shall leave.
DORINE: *(Leaving MARIANE, running after VALÈRE.)* Again!
        You'll not escape, Sir; don't you try it.
    Come here, you two. Stop fussing, and be quiet.

*(She takes VALÈRE by the hand, then MARIANE, and draws them
together.)*

VALÈRE: *(To DORINE.)*
85   What do you want of me?
MARIANE: *(To DORINE.)*
                    What is the point of this?
DORINE: We're going to have a little armistice.

(To VALÈRE.)

    Now, weren't you silly to get so overheated?
VALÈRE: Didn't you see how badly I was treated?
DORINE: *(To MARIANE.)* Aren't you a simpleton, to have lost
    your head?
90 MARIANE: Didn't you hear the hateful things he said?

DORINE: *(To VALÈRE.)* You're both great fools. Her sole desire,
    Valère,
    Is to be yours in marriage. To that I'll swear.

(To MARIANE.)

    He loves you only, and he wants no wife
    But you, Mariane. On that I'll stake my life.
MARIANE: *(To VALÈRE.)* Then why you advised me so, I cannot see.   95
VALÈRE: *(To MARIANE.)* On such a question, why ask advice
    of *me?*
DORINE: Oh, you're impossible. Give me your hands, you two.

(To VALÈRE.)

    Yours first.
VALÈRE: *(Giving DORINE his hand.)*
                But why?
DORINE: *(To MARIANE.)*
                    And now a hand from you.
MARIANE: *(Also giving DORINE her hand.)*
    What are you doing?
DORINE: There: a perfect fit.
    You suit each other better than you'll admit.   100

*(VALÈRE and MARIANE hold hands for some time without looking at
each other.)*

VALÈRE: *(Turning toward MARIANE.)* Ah, come, don't be so
    haughty. Give a man
    A look of kindness, won't you, Mariane?

(MARIANE turns toward VALÈRE and smiles.)

DORINE: I tell you, lovers are completely mad!
VALÈRE: *(To MARIANE.)* Now come, confess that you were
    very bad
    To hurt my feelings as you did just now.   105
    I have a just complaint, you must allow.
MARIANE: *You* must allow that you were most unpleasant . . .
DORINE: Let's table that discussion for the present;
    Your father has a plan which must be stopped.
MARIANE: Advise us, then; what means must we adopt?   110
DORINE: We'll use all manner of means, and all at once.

(To MARIANE.)

    Your father's addled; he's acting like a dunce.
    Therefore you'd better humor the old fossil.
    Pretend to yield to him, be sweet and docile,
    And then postpone, as often as necessary,   115
    The day on which you have agreed to marry.
    You'll thus gain time, and time will turn the trick.
    Sometimes, for instance, you'll be taken sick,
    And that will seem good reason for delay;
    Or some bad omen will make you change the day—   120
    You'll dream of muddy water, or you'll pass
    A dead man's hearse, or break a looking-glass.
    If all else fails, no man can marry you
    Unless you take his ring and say "I do."
    But now, let's separate. If they should find   125
    Us talking here, our plot might be divined.

(To VALÈRE.*)*

  Go to your friends, and tell them what's occurred,
  And have them urge her father to keep his word.
  Meanwhile, we'll stir her brother into action,
130 And get Elmire, as well, to join our faction.
  Good-bye.
  VALÈRE: *(To* MARIANE.*)*
      Though each of us will do his best,
  It's your true heart on which my hopes shall rest.
  MARIANE: *(To* VALÈRE.*)* Regardless of what Father may decide,
  None but Valère shall claim me as his bride.
135 VALÈRE: Oh, how those words content me! Come what will . . .
  DORINE: Oh, lover, lovers! Their tongues are never still.
  Be off, now.
  VALÈRE: *(Turning to go, then turning back.)*
      One last word . . .
  DORINE: No time to chat:
  You leave by this door; and *you* leave by that.

*(*DORINE *pushes them, by the shoulders, toward opposing doors.)*

——— ACT THREE ———

SCENE I

DAMIS, DORINE

  DAMIS: May lightning strike me even as I speak,
  May all men call me cowardly and weak,
  If any fear or scruple holds me back
  From settling things, at once, with that great quack!
5 DORINE: Now, don't give way to violent emotion.
  Your father's merely talked about this notion,
  And words and deeds are far from being one.
  Much that is talked about is left undone.
  DAMIS: No, I must stop that scoundrel's machinations;
10 I'll go and tell him off; I'm out of patience.
  DORINE: Do calm down and be practical. I had rather
  My mistress dealt with him—and with your father.
  She has some influence with Tartuffe, I've noted.
  He hangs upon her words, seems most devoted,
15 And may, indeed, be smitten by her charm.
  Pray Heaven it's true! 'Twould do our cause no harm.
  She sent for him, just now, to sound him out
  On this affair you're so incensed about;
  She'll find out where he stands, and tell him, too,
20 What dreadful strife and trouble will ensue
  If he lends countenance to your father's plan.
  I couldn't get in to see him, but his man
  Says that he's almost finished with his prayers.
  Go, now. I'll catch him when he comes downstairs.
25 DAMIS: I want to hear this conference, and I will.
  DORINE: No, they must be alone.
  DAMIS: Oh, I'll keep still.
  DORINE: Not you. I know your temper. You'd start a brawl,
  And shout and stamp your foot and spoil it all.
  Go on.
  DAMIS: I won't; I have a perfect right . . .
30 DORINE: Lord, you're a nuisance! He's coming; get out of sight.

*(*DAMIS *conceals himself in a closet at the rear of the stage.)*

SCENE II

TARTUFFE, DORINE

  TARTUFFE: *(Observing* DORINE, *and calling to his manservant offstage.)*
  Hang up my hair-shirt, put my scourge in place,
  And pray, Laurent, for Heaven's perpetual grace.
  I'm going to the prison now, to share
  My last few coins with the poor wretches there.
  DORINE: *(Aside.)* Dear God, what affectation! What a fake! 5
  TARTUFFE: You wished to see me?
  DORINE: Yes . . .
  TARTUFFE: *(Taking a handkerchief from his pocket.)*
        For mercy's sake,
  Please take this handkerchief, before you speak.
  DORINE: What?
  TARTUFFE: Cover that bosom, girl. The flesh is weak,
  And unclean thoughts are difficult to control.
  Such sights as that can undermine the soul. 10
  DORINE: Your soul, it seems, has very poor defenses,
  And flesh makes quite an impact on your senses.
  It's strange that you're so easily excited;
  My own desires are not so soon ignited;
  And if I saw you naked as a beast, 15
  Not all your hide would tempt me in the least.
  TARTUFFE: Girl, speak more modestly; unless you do,
  I shall be forced to take my leave of you.
  DORINE: Oh, no, it's I who must be on my way;
  I've just one little message to convey. 20
  Madame is coming down, and begs you, Sir,
  To wait and have a word or two with her.
  TARTUFFE: Gladly.
  DORINE: *(Aside.)* That had a softening effect!
  I think my guess about him was correct.
  TARTUFFE: Will she be long? 25
  DORINE: No: that's her step I hear.
  Ah, here she is, and I shall disappear.

SCENE III

ELMIRE, TARTUFFE

  TARTUFFE: May Heaven, whose infinite goodness we adore,
  Preserve your body and soul forevermore,
  And bless your days, and answer thus the plea
  Of one who is its humblest votary.
  ELMIRE: I thank you for that pious wish. But please, 5
  Do take a chair and let's be more at ease.

(They sit down.)

  TARTUFFE: I trust that you are once more well and strong?
  ELMIRE: Oh, yes: the fever didn't last for long.
  TARTUFFE: My prayers are too unworthy, I am sure,
  To have gained from Heaven this most gracious cure; 10
  But lately, Madam, my every supplication
  Has had for object your recuperation.
  ELMIRE: You shouldn't have troubled so. I don't deserve it.
  TARTUFFE: Your health is priceless, Madam, and to preserve it
  I'd gladly give my own, in all sincerity. 15

ELMIRE: Sir, you outdo us all in Christian charity.
    You've been most kind. I count myself your debtor.
TARTUFFE: 'Twas nothing, Madam. I long to serve you better.
ELMIRE: There's a private matter I'm anxious to discuss.
20   I'm glad there's no one here to hinder us.
TARTUFFE: I too am glad; it floods my heart with bliss
    To find myself alone with you like this.
    For just this chance I've prayed with all my power—
    But prayed in vain, until this happy hour.
25 ELMIRE: This won't take long, Sir, and I hope you'll be
    Entirely frank and unconstrained with me.
TARTUFFE: Indeed, there's nothing I had rather do
    Than bare my inmost heart and soul to you.
    First, let me say that what remarks I've made
30   About the constant visits you are paid
    Were prompted not by any mean emotion,
    But rather by a pure and deep devotion,
    A fervent zeal . . .
ELMIRE: No need for explanation.
    Your sole concern, I'm sure, was my salvation.
TARTUFFE: (*Taking* ELMIRE's *hand and pressing her fingertips.*)
35   Quite so; and such great fervor do I feel . . .
ELMIRE: Ooh! Please! You're pinching!
TARTUFFE: 'Twas from excess of
    zeal.
    I never meant to cause you pain, I swear.
    I'd rather . . .

(*He places his hand on* ELMIRE's *knee.*)

ELMIRE: What can your hand be doing there?
TARTUFFE: Feeling your gown; what soft, fine-woven stuff!
40 ELMIRE: Please, I'm extremely ticklish. That's enough.

(*She draws her chair away;* TARTUFFE *pulls his after her.*)

TARTUFFE: (*Fondling the lace collar of her gown.*) My, my, what
    lovely lacework on your dress!
    The workmanship's miraculous, no less.
    I've not seen anything to equal it.
ELMIRE: Yes, quite. But let's talk business for a bit.
45   They say my husband means to break his word
    And give his daughter to you, Sir. Had you heard?
TARTUFFE: He did once mention it. But I confess
    I dream of quite a different happiness.
    It's elsewhere, Madam, that my eyes discern
50   The promise of that bliss for which I yearn.
ELMIRE: I see: you care for nothing here below.
TARTUFFE: Ah, well—my heart's not made of stone, you know.
ELMIRE: All your desires mount heavenward, I'm sure,
    In scorn of all that's earthly and impure.
55 TARTUFFE: A love of heavenly beauty does not preclude
    A proper love for earthly pulchritude;
    Our senses are quite rightly captivated
    By perfect works our Maker has created.
    Some glory clings to all that Heaven has made;
60   In you, all Heaven's marvels are displayed.
    On that fair face, such beauties have been lavished,
    The eyes are dazzled and the heart is ravished;
    How could I look on you, O flawless creature,
    And not adore the Author of all Nature,

    Feeling a love both passionate and pure   65
    For you, his triumph of self-portraiture?
    At first, I trembled lest that love should be
    A subtle snare that Hell had laid for me;
    I vowed to flee the sight of you, eschewing
    A rapture that might prove my soul's undoing;   70
    But soon, fair being, I became aware
    That my deep passion could be made to square
    With rectitude, and with my bounden duty.
    I thereupon surrendered to your beauty.
    It is, I know, presumptuous on my part   75
    To bring you this poor offering of my heart,
    And it is not my merit, Heaven knows,
    But your compassion on which my hopes repose.
    You are my peace, my solace, my salvation;
    On you depends my bliss—or desolation;   80
    I bide your judgment and, as you think best,
    I shall be either miserable or blest.
ELMIRE: Your declaration is most gallant, Sir,
    But don't you think it's out of character?
    You'd have done better to restrain your passion   85
    And think before you spoke in such a fashion.
    It ill becomes a pious man like you . . .
TARTUFFE: I may be pious, but I'm human too:
    With your celestial charms before his eyes,
    A man has not the power to be wise.   90
    I know such words sound strangely, coming from me,
    But I'm no angel, nor was meant to be,
    And if you blame my passion, you must needs
    Reproach as well the charms on which it feeds.
    Your loveliness I had no sooner seen   95
    Than you became my soul's unrivalled queen;
    Before your seraph glance, divinely sweet,
    My heart's defenses crumbled in defeat,
    And nothing fasting, prayer, or tears might do
    Could stay my spirit from adoring you.   100
    My eyes, my sighs have told you in the past
    What now my lips make bold to say at last,
    And if, in your great goodness, you will deign
    To look upon your slave, and ease his pain,—
    If, in compassion for my soul's distress,   105
    You'll stoop to comfort my unworthiness,
    I'll raise to you, in thanks for that sweet manna,
    An endless hymn, an infinite hosanna.
    With me, of course, there need be no anxiety.
    No fear of scandal or of notoriety.   110
    These young court gallants, whom all the ladies fancy,
    Are vain in speech, in action rash and chancy;
    When they succeed in love, the world soon knows it;
    No favor's granted them but they disclose it
    And by the looseness of their tongues profane   115
    The very altar where their hearts have lain.
    Men of my sort, however, love discreetly,
    And one may trust our reticence completely.
    My keen concern for my good name insures
    The absolute security of yours;   120
    In short, I offer you, my dear Elmire,
    Love without scandal, pleasure without fear.
ELMIRE: I've heard your well-turned speeches to the end,
    And what you urge I clearly apprehend.

125   Aren't you afraid that I may take a notion
        To tell my husband of your warm devotion,
        And that, supposing he were duly told,
        His feelings toward you might grow rather cold?
    TARTUFFE: I know, dear lady, that your exceeding charity
130   Will lead your heart to pardon my temerity;
        That you'll excuse my violent affection
        As human weakness, human imperfection;
        And that—O fairest!—you will bear in mind
        That I'm but flesh and blood, and am not blind.
135 ELMIRE: Some women might do otherwise, perhaps,
        But I shall be discreet about your lapse;
        I'll tell my husband nothing of what's occurred
        If, in return, you'll give your solemn word
        To advocate as forcefully as you can
140   The marriage of Valère and Mariane,
        Renouncing all desire to dispossess
        Another of his rightful happiness,
        And . . .

SCENE IV

DAMIS, ELMIRE, TARTUFFE

DAMIS: *(Emerging from the closet where he has been hiding.)*
            No! We'll not hush up this vile affair;
        I heard it all inside that closet there,
        Where Heaven, in order to confound the pride
        Of this great rascal, prompted me to hide.
5   Ah, now I have my long-awaited chance
        To punish his deceit and arrogance,
        And give my father clear and shocking proof
        Of the black character of his dear Tartuffe.
    ELMIRE: Ah no, Damis; I'll be content if he
10   Will study to deserve my leniency.
        I've promised silence—don't make me break my word;
        To make a scandal would be too absurd.
        Good wives laugh off such trifles, and forget them;
        Why should they tell their husbands, and upset them?
15 DAMIS: You have your reasons for taking such a course,
        And I have reasons, too, of equal force.
        To spare him now would be insanely wrong.
        I've swallowed my just wrath for far too long
        And watched this insolent bigot bringing strife
20   And bitterness into our family life.
        Too long he's meddled in my father's affairs,
        Thwarting my marriage-hopes, and poor Valère's.
        It's high time that my father was undeceived,
        And now I've proof that can't be disbelieved—
25   Proof that was furnished me by Heaven above.
        It's too good not to take advantage of.
        This is my chance, and I deserve to lose it
        If, for one moment, I hesitate to use it.
    ELMIRE: Damis . . .
    DAMIS: No, I must do what I think right.
30   Madam, my heart is bursting with delight,
        And, say whatever you will, I'll not consent
        To lose the sweet revenge on which I'm bent.
        I'll settle matters without more ado;
        And here, most opportunely, is my cue.

SCENE V

ORGON, DAMIS, TARTUFFE, ELMIRE

DAMIS: Father, I'm glad you've joined us. Let us advise you
        Of some fresh news which doubtless will surprise you.
        You've just now been repaid with interest
        For all your loving-kindness to our guest.
        He's proved his warm and grateful feelings toward you;   5
        It's with a pair of horns he would reward you.
        Yes, I surprised him with your wife, and heard
        His whole adulterous offer, every word.
        She, with her all too gentle disposition,
        Would not have told you of his proposition;   10
        But I shall not make terms with brazen lechery,
        And feel that not to tell you would be treachery.
    ELMIRE: And I hold that one's husband's peace of mind
        Should not be spoilt by tattle of this kind.
        One's honor doesn't require it: to be proficient   15
        In keeping men at bay is quite sufficient.
        These are my sentiments, and I wish, Damis,
        That you had heeded me and held your peace.

SCENE VI

ORGON, DAMIS, TARTUFFE

ORGON: Can it be true, this dreadful thing I hear?
    TARTUFFE: Yes, Brother, I'm a wicked man, I fear:
        A wretched sinner, all depraved and twisted,
        The greatest villain that has ever existed.
        My life's one heap of crimes, which grows each minute;   5
        There's naught but foulness and corruption in it;
        And I perceive that Heaven, outraged by me,
        Has chosen this occasion to mortify me.
        Charge me with any deed you wish to name;
        I'll not defend myself, but take the blame.   10
        Believe what you are told, and drive Tartuffe
        Like some base criminal from beneath your roof;
        Yes, drive me hence, and with a parting curse:
        I shan't protest, for I deserve far worse.
    ORGON: *(To* DAMIS.*)* Ah, you deceitful boy, how dare you try   15
        To stain his purity with so foul a lie?
    DAMIS: What! Are you taken in by such a bluff?
        Did you not hear . . . ?
    ORGON: Enough, you rogue, enough!
    TARTUFFE: Ah, Brother, let him speak: you're being unjust.
        Believe his story; the boy deserves your trust.   20
        Why, after all, should you have faith in me?
        How can you know what I might do, or be?
        Is it on my good actions that you base
        Your favor? Do you trust my pious face?
        Ah, no, don't be deceived by hollow shows;   25
        I'm far, alas, from being what men suppose;
        Though the world takes me for a man of worth,
        I'm truly the most worthless man on earth.

(To DAMIS.*)*

        Yes, my dear son, speak out now: call me the chief
        Of sinners, a wretch, a murderer, a thief;   30

Load me with all the names men most abhor;
I'll not complain; I've earned them all, and more;
I'll kneel here while you pour them on my head
As a just punishment for the life I've led.
ORGON: *(To* TARTUFFE.)
35   This is too much, dear Brother.

(To DAMIS.)

                          Have you no heart?
DAMIS: Are you so hoodwinked by this rascal's art. . . ?
ORGON: Be still, you monster.

(To TARTUFFE.)

                     Brother, I pray you, rise.

(To DAMIS.)

    Villain!
DAMIS: But . . .
ORGON: Silence!
DAMIS: Can't you realize. . . ?
ORGON: Just one word more, and I'll tear you limb from limb.
40 TARTUFFE: In God's name, Brother, don't be harsh with him.
    I'd rather far be tortured at the stake
    Than see him bear one scratch for my poor sake.
ORGON: *(To* DAMIS.)
    Ingrate!
TARTUFFE: If I must beg you, on bended knee,
    To pardon him . . .
ORGON: *(Falling to his knees, addressing* TARTUFFE.)
                 Such goodness cannot be!

(To DAMIS.)

45 Now, *there's* true charity!
DAMIS: What, you. . . ?
ORGON: Villain, be still!
    I know your motives; I know you wish him ill:
    Yes, all of you—wife, children, servants, all—
    Conspire against him and desire his fall,
    Employing every shameful trick you can
50 To alienate me from this saintly man.
    Ah, but the more you seek to drive him away,
    The more I'll do to keep him. Without delay,
    I'll spite this household and confound its pride
    By giving him my daughter as his bride.
55 DAMIS: You're going to force her to accept his hand?
ORGON: Yes, and this very night, d'you understand?
    I shall defy you all, and make it clear
    That I'm the one who gives the orders here.
    Come, wretch, kneel down and clasp his blessed feet,
60 And ask his pardon for your black deceit.
DAMIS: I ask that swindler's pardon? Why, I'd rather . . .
ORGON: So! You insult him, and defy your father!
    A stick! A stick! *(To* TARTUFFE.) No, no—release me, do.

(To DAMIS.)

    Out of my house this minute! Be off with you,
65 And never dare set foot in it again.
DAMIS: Well, I shall go, but . . .

ORGON: Well, go quickly, then.
    I disinherit you; an empty purse
    Is all you'll get from me—except my curse!

Scene VII

ORGON, TARTUFFE

ORGON: How he blasphemed your goodness! What a son!
TARTUFFE: Forgive him, Lord, as I've already done.

(To ORGON.)

    You can't know how it hurts when someone tries
    To blacken me in my dear Brother's eyes.
ORGON: Ahh!   5
TARTUFFE: The mere thought of such ingratitude
    Plunges my soul into so dark a mood . . .
    Such horror grips my heart . . . I gasp for breath,
    And cannot speak, and feel myself near death.
ORGON:

(He runs, in tears, to the door through which he has just driven his son.)

    You blackguard! Why did I spare you? Why did I not
    Break you in little pieces on the spot?   10
    Compose yourself, and don't be hurt, dear friend.
TARTUFFE: These scenes, these dreadful quarrels, have got to
      end.
    I've much upset your household, and I perceive
    That the best thing will be for me to leave.
ORGON: What are you saying!   15
TARTUFFE: They're all against me here;
    They'd have you think me false and insincere.
ORGON: Ah, what of that? Have I ceased believing in you?
TARTUFFE: Their adverse talk will certainly continue,
    And charges which you now repudiate
    You may find credible at a later date.   20
ORGON: No, Brother, never.
TARTUFFE: Brother, a wife can sway
    Her husband's mind in many a subtle way.
ORGON: No, no.
TARTUFFE: To leave at once is the solution;
    Thus only can I end their persecution.
ORGON: No, no, I'll not allow it; you shall remain.   25
TARTUFFE: Ah, well; 'twill mean much martyrdom and pain,
    But if you wish it . . .
ORGON: Ah!
TARTUFFE: Enough; so be it.
    But one thing must be settled, as I see it.
    For your dear honor, and for our friendship's sake,
    There's one precaution I feel bound to take.   30
    I shall avoid your wife, and keep away . . .
ORGON: No, you shall not, whatever they may say.
    It pleases me to vex them, and for spite
    I'd have them see you with her day and night.
    What's more, I'm going to drive them to despair   35
    By making you my only son and heir;
    This very day, I'll give to you alone
    Clear deed and title to everything I own.
    A dear, good friend and son-in-law-to-be

40   Is more than wife, or child, or kin to me.
        Will you accept my offer, dearest son?
TARTUFFE: In all things, let the will of Heaven be done.
ORGON: Poor fellow! Come, we'll go draw up the deed.
        Then let them burst with disappointed greed!

————— ACT FOUR —————

SCENE I

CLÉANTE, TARTUFFE

CLÉANTE: Yes, all the town's discussing it, and truly,
        Their comments do not flatter you unduly.
        I'm glad we've met, Sir, and I'll give my view
        Of this sad matter in a word or two.
5   As for who's guilty, that I shan't discuss;
        Let's say it was Damis who caused the fuss;
        Assuming, then, that you have been ill-used
        By young Damis, and groundlessly accused,
        Ought not a Christian to forgive, and ought
10   He not to stifle every vengeful thought?
        Should you stand by and watch a father make
        His only son an exile for your sake?
        Again I tell you frankly, be advised:
        The whole town, high and low, is scandalized;
15   This quarrel must be mended, and my advice is
        Not to push matters to a further crisis.
        No, sacrifice your wrath to God above,
        And help Damis regain his father's love.
TARTUFFE: Alas, for my part I should take great joy
20   In doing so. I've nothing against the boy.
        I pardon all, I harbor no resentment;
        To serve him would afford me much contentment.
        But Heaven's interest will not have it so:
        If he comes back, then I shall have to go.
25   After his conduct—so extreme, so vicious—
        Our further intercourse would look suspicious.
        God knows what people would think! Why, they'd describe
        My goodness to him as a sort of bribe;
        They'd say that out of guilt I made pretense
30   Of loving-kindness and benevolence—
        That, fearing my accuser's tongue, I strove
        To buy his silence with a show of love.
CLÉANTE: Your reasoning is badly warped and stretched,
        And these excuses, Sir, are most far-fetched.
35   Why put yourself in charge of Heaven's cause?
        Does Heaven need our help to enforce its laws?
        Leave vengeance to the Lord, Sir; while we live,
        Our duty's not to punish, but forgive;
        And what the Lord commands, we should obey
40   Without regard to what the world may say.
        What! Shall the fear of being misunderstood
        Prevent our doing what is right and good?
        No, no; let's simply do what Heaven ordains,
        And let no other thoughts perplex our brains.
45 TARTUFFE: Again, Sir, let me say that I've forgiven
        Damis, and thus obeyed the laws of Heaven;
        But I am not commanded by the Bible
        To live with one who smears my name with libel.

CLÉANTE: Were you commanded, Sir, to indulge the whim
        Of poor Orgon, and to encourage him   50
        In suddenly transferring to your name
        A large estate to which you have no claim?
TARTUFFE: 'Twould never occur to those who know me best
        To think I acted from self-interest.
        The treasures of this world I quite despise;   55
        Their specious glitter does not charm my eyes;
        And if I have resigned myself to taking
        The gift which my dear Brother insists on making,
        I do so only, as he well understands,
        Lest so much wealth fall into wicked hands,   60
        Lest those to whom it might descend in time
        Turn it to purposes of sin and crime,
        And not, as I shall do, make use of it.
        For Heaven's glory and mankind's benefit.
CLÉANTE: Forget these trumped-up fears. Your argument   65
        Is one the rightful heir might well resent;
        It *is* a moral burden to inherit
        Such wealth, but give Damis a chance to bear it.
        And would it not be worse to be accused
        Of swindling, than to see that wealth misused?   70
        I'm shocked that you allowed Orgon to broach
        This matter, and that you feel no self-reproach;
        Does true religion teach that lawful heirs
        May freely be deprived of what is theirs?
        And if the Lord has told you in your heart   75
        That you and young Damis must dwell apart,
        Would it not be the decent thing to beat
        A generous and honorable retreat,
        Rather than let the son of the house be sent,
        For your convenience, into banishment?   80
        Sir, if you wish to prove the honesty
        Of your intentions . . .
TARTUFFE: Sir, it is half-past three.
        I've certain pious duties to attend to,
        And hope my prompt departure won't offend you.
CLÉANTE: (*Alone.*) Damn.   85

SCENE II

ELMIRE, MARIANE, CLÉANTE, DORINE

DORINE: Stay, Sir, and help Mariane, for Heaven's sake!
        She's suffering so, I fear her heart will break.
        Her father's plan to marry her off tonight
        Has put the poor child in a desperate plight.
        I hear him coming. Let's stand together, now,   5
        And see if we can't change his mind, somehow,
        About this match we all deplore and fear.

SCENE III

ORGON, ELMIRE, MARIANE, CLÉANTE, DORINE

ORGON: Hah! Glad to find you all assembled here.

(*To* MARIANE.)

        This contract, child, contains your happiness,
        And what it says I think your heart can guess.
MARIANE: (*Falling to her knees.*) Sir, by that Heaven which sees
        me here distressed,

5   And by whatever else can move your breast,
      Do not employ a father's power, I pray you,
      To crush my heart and force it to obey you,
      Nor by your harsh commands oppress me so
      That I'll begrudge the duty which I owe—
10   And do not so embitter and enslave me
      That I shall hate the very life you gave me.
      If my sweet hopes must perish, if you refuse
      To give me to the one I've dared to choose,
      Spare me at least—I beg you, I implore—
15   The pain of wedding one whom I abhor;
      And do not, by a heartless use of force,
      Drive me to contemplate some desperate course.
      ORGON: *(Feeling himself touched by her.)* Be firm, my soul. No
         human weakness, now.
      MARIANE: I don't resent your love for him. Allow
20   Your heart free rein, Sir; give him your property,
      And if that's not enough, take mine from me;
      He's welcome to my money; take it, do,
      But don't, I pray, include my person too.
      Spare me, I beg you; and let me end the tale
25   Of my sad days behind a convent veil.
      ORGON: A convent! Hah! When crossed in their amours,
      All lovesick girls have the same thought as yours.
      Get up! The more you loathe the man, and dread him,
      The more ennobling it will be to wed him.
30   Marry Tartuffe, and mortify your flesh!
      Enough; don't start that whimpering afresh.
      DORINE: But why. . . ?
      ORGON: Be still, there. Speak when you're
         spoken to.
      Not one more bit of impudence out of you.
      CLÉANTE: If I may offer a word of counsel here . . .
35 ORGON: Brother, in counseling you have no peer;
      All your advice is forceful, sound, and clever;
      I don't propose to follow it, however.
      ELMIRE: *(To* ORGON.*)* I am amazed, and don't know what
         to say;
      Your blindness simply takes my breath away.
40   You are indeed bewitched, to take no warning
      From our account of what occurred this morning.
      ORGON: Madam, I know a few plain facts, and one
      Is that you're partial to my rascal son;
      Hence, when he sought to make Tartuffe the victim
45   Of a base lie, you dared not contradict him.
      Ah, but you underplayed your part, my pet;
      You should have looked more angry, more upset.
      ELMIRE: When men make overtures, must we reply
      With righteous anger and a battle-cry?
50   Must we turn back their amorous advances
      With sharp reproaches and with fiery glances?
      Myself, I find such offers merely amusing,
      And make no scenes and fusses in refusing;
      My taste is for good-natured rectitude,
55   And I dislike the savage sort of prude
      Who guards her virtue with her teeth and claws,
      And tears men's eyes out for the slightest cause;
      The Lord preserve me from such honor as that,
      Which bites and scratches like an alley-cat!
60   I've found that a polite and cool rebuff

Discourages a lover quite enough.
ORGON: I know the facts, and I shall not be shaken.
ELMIRE: I marvel at your power to be mistaken.
      Would it, I wonder, carry weight with you
      If I could *show* you that our tale was true?   65
ORGON: Show me?
ELMIRE: Yes.
ORGON: Rot.
ELMIRE: Come, what if I found a way
      To make you see the facts as plain as day?
ORGON: Nonsense.
ELMIRE: Do answer me; don't be absurd.
      I'm not now asking you to trust our word.
      Suppose that from some hiding-place in here   70
      You learned the whole sad truth by eye and ear—
      What would you say of your good friend, after that?
ORGON: Why, I'd say . . . nothing, by Jehoshaphat!
      It can't be true.
ELMIRE: You've been too long deceived,
      And I'm quite tired of being disbelieved.   75
      Come now: let's put my statements to the test,
      And you shall see the truth made manifest.
ORGON: I'll take that challenge. Now do your uttermost.
      We'll see how you make good your empty boast.
ELMIRE: *(To* DORINE.*)*
      Send him to me.   80
DORINE: He's crafty; it may be hard
      To catch the cunning scoundrel off his guard.
ELMIRE: No, amorous men are gullible. Their conceit
      So blinds them that they're never hard to cheat.
      Have him come down. *(To* CLÉANTE *and* MARIANE.*)* **Please
         leave us, for a bit.**

SCENE IV

ELMIRE, ORGON

ELMIRE: Pull up this table, and get under it.
ORGON: What?
ELMIRE: It's essential that you be well-hidden.
ORGON: Why there?
ELMIRE: Oh, Heavens! Just do as you are bidden
      I have my plans; we'll soon see how they fare.
      Under the table, now; and once you're there,   5
      Take care that you are neither seen nor heard.
ORGON: Well, I'll indulge you, since I gave my word
      To see you through this infantile charade.
ELMIRE: Once it is over, you'll be glad we played.

(To her husband, who is now under the table.)

      I'm going to act quite strangely, now, and you   10
      Must not be shocked at anything I do.
      Whatever I may say, you must excuse
      As part of that deceit I'm forced to use.
      I shall employ sweet speeches in the task
      Of making that impostor drop his mask;   15
      I'll give encouragement to his bold desires,
      And furnish fuel to his amorous fires.
      Since it's for your sake, and for his destruction,
      That I shall seem to yield to his seduction,

20 I'll gladly stop whenever you decide
That all your doubts are fully satisfied.
I'll count on you, as soon as you have seen
What sort of man he is, to intervene,
And not expose me to his odious lust
25 One moment longer than you feel you must.
Remember: you're to save me from my plight
Whenever . . . He's coming! Hush! Keep out of sight!

SCENE V

TARTUFFE, ELMIRE, ORGON

TARTUFFE: You wish to have a word with me, I'm told.
ELMIRE: Yes. I've a little secret to unfold.
Before I speak, however, it would be wise
To close that door, and look about for spies.

(TARTUFFE *goes to the door, closes it, and returns.*)

5 The very last thing that must happen now
Is a repetition of this morning's row.
I've never been so badly caught off guard.
Oh, how I feared for you! You saw how hard
I tried to make that troublesome Damis
10 Control his dreadful temper, and hold his peace.
In my confusion, I didn't have the sense
Simply to contradict his evidence;
But as it happened, that was for the best,
And all has worked out in our interest.
15 This storm has only bettered your position;
My husband doesn't have the least suspicion,
And now, in mockery of those who do,
He bids me be continually with you.
And that is why, quite fearless of reproof,
20 I now can be alone with my Tartuffe,
And why my heart—perhaps too quick to yield—
Feels free to let its passion be revealed.
TARTUFFE: Madam, your words confuse me. Not long ago,
You spoke in quite a different style, you know.
25 ELMIRE: Ah, Sir, if that refusal made you smart,
It's little that you know of woman's heart,
Or what that heart is trying to convey
When it resists in such a feeble way!
Always, at first, our modesty prevents
30 The frank avowal of tender sentiments;
However high the passion which inflames us,
Still, to confess its power somehow shames us.
Thus we reluct, at first, yet in a tone
Which tells you that our heart is overthrown,
35 That what our lips deny, our pulse confesses,
And that, in time, all noes will turn to yesses.
I fear my words are all too frank and free,
And a poor proof of woman's modesty;
But since I'm started, tell me, if you will—
40 Would I have tried to make Damis be still,
Would I have listened, calm and unoffended,
Until your lengthy offer of love was ended,
And been so very mild in my reaction,
Had your sweet words not given me satisfaction?
45 And when I tried to force you to undo

The marriage-plans my husband has in view,
What did my urgent pleading signify
If not that I admired you, and that I
Deplored the thought that someone else might own
Part of a heart I wished for mine alone?   50
TARTUFFE: Madam, no happiness is so complete
As when, from lips we love, come words so sweet;
Their nectar floods my every sense, and drains
In honeyed rivulets through all my veins.
To please you is my joy, my only goal;   55
Your love is the restorer of my soul;
And yet I must beg leave, now, to confess
Some lingering doubts as to my happiness
Might this not be a trick? Might not the catch
Be that you wish me to break off the match   60
With Mariane, and so have feigned to love me?
I shan't quite trust your fond opinion of me
Until the feelings you've expressed so sweetly
Are demonstrated somewhat more concretely,
And you have shown, by certain kind concessions,   65
That I may put my faith in your professions.
ELMIRE:

(*She coughs, to warn her husband.*)

Why be in such a hurry? Must my heart
Exhaust its bounty at the very start?
To make that sweet admission cost me dear,
But you'll not be content, it would appear,   70
Unless my store of favors is disbursed
To the last farthing, and at the very first.
TARTUFFE: The less we merit, the less we dare to hope,
And with our doubts, mere words can never cope.
We trust no promised bliss till we receive it;   75
Not till a joy is ours can we believe it.
I, who so little merit your esteem,
Can't credit this fulfillment of my dream,
And shan't believe it, Madam, until I savor
Some palpable assurance of your favor.   80
ELMIRE: My, how tyrannical your love can be,
And how it flusters and perplexes me!
How furiously you take one's heart in hand,
And make your every wish a fierce command!
Come, must you hound and harry me to death?   85
Will you not give me time to catch my breath?
Can it be right to press me with such force,
Give me no quarter, show me no remorse,
And take advantage, by your stern insistence,
Of the fond feelings which weaken my resistance?   90
TARTUFFE: Well, if you look with favor upon my love,
Why, then, begrudge me some clear proof thereof?
ELMIRE: But how can I consent without offense
To Heaven, toward which you feel such reverence?
TARTUFFE: If Heaven is all that holds you back, don't worry.   95
I can remove that hindrance in a hurry.
Nothing of that sort need obstruct our path.
ELMIRE: Must one not be afraid of Heaven's wrath?
TARTUFFE: Madam, forget such fears, and be my pupil,
And I shall teach you how to conquer scruple.   100
Some joys, it's true, are wrong in Heaven's eyes;

Yet Heaven is not averse to compromise;
There is a science, lately formulated,
Whereby one's conscience may be liberated,
105 And any wrongful act you care to mention
May be redeemed by purity of intention.
I'll teach you, Madam, the secrets of that science;
Meanwhile, just place on me your full reliance.
Assuage my keen desires, and feel no dread:
110 The sin, if any, shall be on my head.

(ELMIRE *coughs, this time more loudly.*)

You've a bad cough.
ELMIRE: Yes, yes. It's bad indeed.
TARTUFFE: (*Producing a little paper bag.*) A bit of licorice may
    be what you need.
ELMIRE: No, I've a stubborn cold, it seems. I'm sure it
    Will take much more than licorice to cure it.
115 TARTUFFE: How aggravating.
ELMIRE: Oh, more than I can say.
TARTUFFE: If you're still troubled, think of things this way:
    No one shall know our joys, save us alone,
    And there's no evil till the act is known;
    It's scandal, Madam, which makes it an offense,
120 And it's no sin to sin in confidence.
ELMIRE: (*Having coughed once more.*) Well, clearly I must do as
    you require,
    And yield to your importunate desire.
    It is apparent, now, that nothing less
    Will satisfy you, and so I acquiesce.
125 To go so far is much against my will;
    I'm vexed that it should come to this; but still,
    Since you are so determined on it, since you
    Will not allow mere language to convince you,
    And since you ask for concrete evidence, I
130 See nothing for it, now, but to comply.
    If this is sinful, if I'm wrong to do it,
    So much the worse for him who drove me to it.
    The fault can surely not be charged to me.
TARTUFFE: Madam, the fault is mine, if fault there be,
135 And . . .
ELMIRE: Open the door a little, and peek out;
    I wouldn't want my husband poking about.
TARTUFFE: Why worry about the man? Each day he grows
    More gullible; one can lead him by the nose.
    To find us here would fill him with delight,
140 And if he saw the worst, he'd doubt his sight.
ELMIRE: Nevertheless, do step out for a minute
    Into the hall, and see that no one's in it.

SCENE VI

ORGON, ELMIRE

ORGON: (*Coming out from under the table.*) That man's a perfect
    monster, I must admit!
    I'm simply stunned. I can't get over it.
ELMIRE: What, coming out so soon? How premature!
    Get back in hiding, and wait until you're sure.
5 Stay till the end, and be convinced completely;

We mustn't stop till things are proved concretely.
ORGON: Hell never harbored anything so vicious!
ELMIRE: Tut, don't be hasty. Try to be judicious.
    Wait, and be certain that there's no mistake.
    No jumping to conclusions, for Heaven's sake!   10

(*She places* ORGON *behind her, as* TARTUFFE *re-enters.*)

SCENE VII

TARTUFFE, ELMIRE, ORGON

TARTUFFE: (*Not seeing* ORGON.) Madam, all things have worked
    out to perfection;
    I've given the neighboring rooms a full inspection;
    No one's about; and now I may at last . . .
ORGON: (*Intercepting him.*) Hold on, my passionate fellow, not
    so fast!
    I should advise a little more restraint.   5
    Well, so you thought you'd fool me, my dear saint!
    How soon you wearied of the saintly life—
    Wedding my daughter, and coveting my wife!
    I've long suspected you, and had a feeling
    That soon I'd catch you at your double-dealing.   10
    Just now, you've given me evidence galore;
    It's quite enough; I have no wish for more.
ELMIRE: (*To* TARTUFFE.) I'm sorry to have treated you so slyly.
    But circumstances forced me to be wily.
TARTUFFE: Brother, you can't think . . .   15
ORGON: No more talk from
    you;
    Just leave this household, without more ado.
TARTUFFE: What I intended . . .
ORGON: That seems fairly clear.
    Spare me your falsehoods and get out of here.
TARTUFFE: No, I'm the master, and you're the one to go!
    This house belongs to me, I'll have you know,   20
    And I shall show you that you can't hurt *me*
    By this contemptible conspiracy,
    That those who cross me know not what they do,
    And that I've means to expose and punish you,
    Avenge offended Heaven, and make you grieve   25
    That ever you dared order me to leave.

SCENE VIII

ELMIRE, ORGON

ELMIRE: What was the point of all that angry chatter?
ORGON: Dear God, I'm worried. This is no laughing matter.
ELMIRE: How so?
ORGON: I fear I understood his drift.
    I'm much disturbed about that deed of gift.
ELMIRE: You gave him . . . ?   5
ORGON: Yes, it's all been drawn and
    signed.
    But one thing more is weighing on my mind.
ELMIRE: What's that?
ORGON: I'll tell you; but first let's see if there's
    A certain strong-box in his room upstairs.

——— ACT FIVE ———

Scene I

ORGON, CLÉANTE

CLÉANTE: Where are you going so fast?
ORGON: God knows!
CLÉANTE: Then wait;
    Let's have a conference, and deliberate
    On how this situation's to be met.
ORGON: That strong-box has me utterly upset;
5   This is the worst of many, many shocks.
CLÉANTE: Is there some fearful mystery in that box?
ORGON: My poor friend Argas brought that box to me
    With his own hands, in utmost secrecy;
    'Twas on the very morning of his flight.
10   It's full of papers which, if they came to light,
    Would ruin him—or such is my impression.
CLÉANTE: Then why did you let it out of your possession?
ORGON: Those papers vexed my conscience, and it seemed best
    To ask the counsel of my pious guest.
15   The cunning scoundrel got me to agree
    To leave the strong-box in his custody,
    So that, in case of an investigation,
    I could employ a slight equivocation
    And swear I didn't have it, and thereby,
20   At no expense to conscience, tell a lie.
CLÉANTE: It looks to me as if you're out on a limb.
    Trusting him with that box, and offering him
    That deed of gift, were actions of a kind
    Which scarcely indicate a prudent mind.
25   With two such weapons, he has the upper hand,
    And since you're vulnerable, as matters stand,
    You erred once more in bringing him to bay.
    You should have acted in some subtler way.
ORGON: Just think of it: behind that fervent face,
30   A heart so wicked, and a soul so base!
    I took him in, a hungry beggar, and then . . .
    Enough, by God! I'm through with pious men:
    Henceforth I'll hate the whole false brotherhood,
    And persecute them worse than Satan could.
35 CLÉANTE: Ah, there you go—extravagant as ever.
    Why can you not be rational? You never
    Manage to take the middle course, it seems,
    But jump, instead, between absurd extremes.
    You've recognized your recent grave mistake
40   In falling victim to a pious fake;
    Now, to correct that error, must you embrace
    An even greater error in its place,
    And judge our worthy neighbors as a whole
    By what you've learned of one corrupted soul?
45   Come, just because one rascal made you swallow
    A show of zeal which turned out to be hollow,
    Shall you conclude that all men are deceivers,
    And that, today, there are no true believers?
    Let atheists make that foolish inference;
50   Learn to distinguish virtue from pretense,
    Be cautious in bestowing admiration,
    And cultivate a sober moderation.

Don't humor fraud, but also don't asperse
True piety; the latter fault is worse,
And it is best to err, if err one must,   55
As you have done, upon the side of trust.

Scene II

DAMIS, ORGON, CLÉANTE

DAMIS: Father, I hear that scoundrel's uttered threats
    Against you; that he pridefully forgets
    How, in his need, he was befriended by you,
    And means to use your gifts to crucify you.
ORGON: It's true, my boy. I'm too distressed for tears.   5
DAMIS: Leave it to me, Sir; let me trim his ears.
    Faced with such insolence, we must not waver.
    I shall rejoice in doing you the favor
    Of cutting short his life, and your distress.
CLÉANTE: What a display of young hotheadedness!   10
    Do learn to moderate your fits of rage.
    In this just kingdom, this enlightened age,
    One does not settle things by violence.

Scene III

MADAME PERNELLE, MARIANE, ELMIRE, DORINE, DAMIS, ORGON,
CLÉANTE

MADAME PERNELLE: I hear strange tales of very strange events.
ORGON: Yes, strange events which these two eyes beheld.
    The man's ingratitude is unparalleled.
    I save a wretched pauper from starvation.
    House him, and treat him like a blood relation,   5
    Shower him every day with my largesse,
    Give him my daughter, and all that I possess;
    And meanwhile the unconscionable knave
    Tries to induce my wife to misbehave;
    And not content with such extreme rascality,   10
    Now threatens me with my own liberality,
    And aims, by taking base advantage of
    The gifts I gave him out of Christian love,
    To drive me from my house, a ruined man,
    And make me end a pauper, as he began.   15
DORINE: Poor fellow!
MADAME PERNELLE: No, my son, I'll never bring
    Myself to think him guilty of such a thing.
ORGON: How's that?
MADAME PERNELLE: The righteous always were maligned.
ORGON: Speak clearly, Mother. Say what's on your mind.
MADAME PERNELLE: I mean that I can smell a rat, my dear.   20
    You know how everybody hates him, here.
ORGON: That has no bearing on the case at all.
MADAME PERNELLE: I told you a hundred times, when you
        were small,
    That virtue in this world is hated ever;
    Malicious men may die, but malice never.   25
ORGON: No doubt that's true, but how does it apply?
MADAME PERNELLE: They've turned you against him by a
        clever lie.
ORGON: I've told you, I was there and saw it done.
MADAME PERNELLE: Ah, slanderers will stop at nothing, Son.

30 ORGON: Mother, I'll lose my temper . . . For the last time,
      I tell you I was witness to the crime.
   MADAME PERNELLE: The tongues of spite are busy night and noon
      And to their venom no man is immune.
   ORGON: You're talking nonsense. Can't you realize
35   I saw it; saw it; saw it with my eyes?
      Saw, do you understand me? Must I shout it
      Into your ears before you'll cease to doubt it?
   MADAME PERNELLE: Appearances can deceive, my son.
         Dear me,
      We cannot always judge by what we see.
40 ORGON: Drat! Drat!
   MADAME PERNELLE: One often interprets things awry;
      Good can seem evil to a suspicious eye.
   ORGON: Was I to see his pawing at Elmire
      As an act of charity?
   MADAME PERNELLE: Till his guilt is clear,
      A man deserves the benefit of the doubt.
45   You should have waited, to see how things turned out.
   ORGON: Great God in Heaven, what more proof did I need?
      Was I to sit there, watching, until he'd . . .
      You drive me to the brink of impropriety.
   MADAME PERNELLE: No, no, a man of such surpassing piety
50   Could not do such a thing. You cannot shake me.
      I don't believe it, and you shall not make me.
   ORGON: You vex me so that, if you weren't my mother,
      I'd say to you . . . some dreadful thing or other.
   DORINE: It's your turn now, Sir, not to be listened to;
55   You'd not trust us, and now she won't trust you.
   CLÉANTE: My friends, we're wasting time which should be spent
      In facing up to our predicament.
      I fear that scoundrel's threats weren't made in sport.
   DAMIS: Do you think he'd have the nerve to go to court?
60 ELMIRE: I'm sure he won't: they'd find it all too crude
      A case of swindling and ingratitude.
   CLÉANTE: Don't be too sure. He won't be at a loss
      To give his claims a high and righteous gloss;
      And clever rogues with far less valid cause
65   Have trapped their victims in a web of laws.
      I say again that to antagonize
      A man so strongly armed was most unwise.
   ORGON: I know it; but the man's appalling cheek
      Outraged me so, I couldn't control my pique.
70 CLÉANTE: I wish to Heaven that we could devise
      Some truce between you, or some compromise.
   ELMIRE: If I had known what cards he held, I'd not
      Have roused his anger by my little plot.
   ORGON: (To DORINE, as M. LOYAL enters.) What is that fellow
         looking for? Who is he?
75   Go talk to him—and tell him that I'm busy.

SCENE IV

MONSIEUR LOYAL, MADAME PERNELLE, ORGON, DAMIS, MARIANE,
DORINE, ELMIRE, CLÉANTE

MONSIEUR LOYAL: Good day, dear sister. Kindly let me see
      Your master.
   DORINE: He's involved with company,
      And cannot be disturbed just now, I fear.

MONSIEUR LOYAL: I hate to intrude; but what has brought me
         here
      Will not disturb your master, in any event.   5
      Indeed, my news will make him most content.
   DORINE: Your name?
   MONSIEUR LOYAL: Just say that I bring greetings from
      Monsieur Tartuffe, on whose behalf I've come.
   DORINE: (To ORGON.) Sir, he's a very gracious man, and bears
      A message from Tartuffe, which, he declares,   10
      Will make you most content.
   CLÉANTE: Upon my word,
      I think this man had best be seen, and heard.
   ORGON: Perhaps he has some settlement to suggest.
      How shall I treat him? What manner would be best?
   CLÉANTE: Control your anger, and if he should mention   15
      Some fair adjustment, give him your full attention.
   MONSIEUR LOYAL: Good health to you, good Sir. May Heaven
         confound
      Your enemies, and may your joys abound.
   ORGON: (Aside, to CLÉANTE.) A gentle salutation: it confirms
      My guess that he is here to offer terms.   20
   MONSIEUR LOYAL: I've always held your family most dear;
      I served your father, Sir, for many a year.
   ORGON: Sir, I must ask your pardon; to my shame,
      I cannot now recall your face or name.
   MONSIEUR LOYAL: Loyal's my name; I come from Normandy,   25
      And I'm a bailiff, in all modesty.
      For forty years, praise God, it's been my boast
      To serve with honor in that vital post,
      And I am here, Sir, if you will permit
      The liberty, to serve you with this writ . . .   30
   ORGON: To—what?
   MONSIEUR LOYAL: Now, please, Sir, let us have no friction:
      It's nothing but an order of eviction.
      You are to move your goods and family out
      And make way for new occupants, without
      Deferment or delay, and give the keys . . .   35
   ORGON: I? Leave this house?
   MONSIEUR LOYAL: Why yes, Sir, if you please.
      This house, Sir, from the cellar to the roof,
      Belongs now to the good Monsieur Tartuffe,
      And he is lord and master of your estate
      By virtue of a deed of present date,   40
      Drawn in due form, with clearest legal phrasing . . .
   DAMIS: Your insolence is utterly amazing!
   MONSIEUR LOYAL: Young man, my business here is not with
         you,
      But with your wise and temperate father, who,
      Like every worthy citizen, stands in awe   45
      Of justice, and would never obstruct the law.
   ORGON: But . . .
   MONSIEUR LOYAL: Not for a million, Sir, would you rebel
      Against authority; I know that well.
      You'll not make trouble, Sir, or interfere
      With the execution of my duties here.   50
   DAMIS: Someone may execute a smart tattoo
      On that black jacket of yours, before you're through.
   MONSIEUR LOYAL: Sir, bid your son be silent. I'd much regret
      Having to mention such a nasty threat
      Of violence, in writing my report.   55

DORINE: *(Aside.)* This man Loyal's a most disloyal sort!
MONSIEUR LOYAL: I love all men of upright character,
    And when I agreed to serve these papers, Sir,
    It was your feelings that I had in mind.
60   I couldn't bear to see the case assigned
    To someone else, who might esteem you less
    And so subject you to unpleasantness.
ORGON: What's more unpleasant than telling a man to leave
    His house and home?
MONSIEUR LOYAL: You'd like a short reprieve?
65   If you desire, Sir, I shall not press you,
    But wait until tomorrow to dispossess you.
    Splendid. I'll come and spend the night here, then,
    Most quietly, with half a score of men.
    For form's sake, you might bring me, just before
70   You go to bed, the keys to the front door.
    My men, I promise, will be on their best
    Behavior, and will not disturb your rest.
    But bright and early, Sir, you must be quick
    And move out all your furniture, every stick;
75   The men I've chosen are both young and strong,
    And with their help it shouldn't take you long.
    In short, I'll make things pleasant and convenient,
    And since I'm being so extremely lenient,
    Please show me, Sir, a like consideration,
80   And give me your entire cooperation.
ORGON: *(Aside.)* I may be all but bankrupt, but I vow
    I'd give a hundred louis, here and now,
    Just for the pleasure of landing one good clout
    Right on the end of that complacent snout.
85 CLÉANTE: Careful; don't make things worse.
DAMIS: My bootsole itches
    To give that beggar a good kick in the breeches.
DORINE: Monsieur Loyal, I'd love to hear the whack
    Of a stout stick across your fine broad back.
MONSIEUR LOYAL: Take care: a woman too may go to jail if
90   She uses threatening language to a bailiff.
CLÉANTE: Enough, enough, Sir. This must not go on.
    Give me that paper, please, and then begone.
MONSIEUR LOYAL: Well, *au revoir*. God give you all good
       cheer!
ORGON: May God confound you, and him who sent you here!

SCENE V

ORGON, CLÉANTE, MARIANE, ELMIRE, MADAME PERNELLE, DORINE, DAMIS

ORGON: Now, Mother, was I right or not? This writ
    Should change your notion of Tartuffe a bit.
    Do you perceive his villainy at last?
MADAME PERNELLE: I'm thunderstruck. I'm utterly aghast.
5 DORINE: Oh, come, be fair. You mustn't take offense
    At this new proof of his benevolence.
    He's acting out of selfless love, I know.
    Material things enslave the soul, and so
    He kindly has arranged your liberation
10   From all that might endanger your salvation.
ORGON: Will you not ever hold your tongue, you dunce?
CLÉANTE: Come, you must take some action, and at once.

ELMIRE: Go tell the world of the low trick he's tried.
    The deed of gift is surely nullified
    By such behavior, and public rage will not   15
    Permit the wretch to carry out his plot.

SCENE VI

VALÈRE, ORGON, CLÉANTE, ELMIRE, MARIANE, MADAME PERNELLE, DAMIS, DORINE

VALÈRE: Sir, though I hate to bring you more bad news,
    Such is the danger that I cannot choose.
    A friend who is extremely close to me
    And knows my interest in your family
    Has, for my sake, presumed to violate   5
    The secrecy that's due to things of state,
    And sends me word that you are in a plight
    From which your one salvation lies in flight.
    That scoundrel who's imposed upon you so
    Denounced you to the King an hour ago   10
    And, as supporting evidence, displayed
    The strong-box of a certain renegade
    Whose secret papers, so he testified,
    You had disloyally agreed to hide.
    I don't know just what charges may be pressed,   15
    But there's a warrant out for your arrest;
    Tartuffe has been instructed, furthermore,
    To guide the arresting officer to your door.
CLÉANTE: He's clearly done this to facilitate
    His seizure of your house and your estate.   20
ORGON: That man, I must say, is a vicious beast!
VALÈRE: Quick, Sir; you mustn't tarry in the least.
    My carriage is outside, to take you hence;
    This thousand louis should cover all expense.
    Let's lose no time, or you shall be undone;   25
    The sole defense, in this case, is to run.
    I shall go with you all the way, and place you
    In a safe refuge to which they'll never trace you.
ORGON: Alas, dear boy, I wish that I could show you
    My gratitude for everything I owe you.   30
    But now is not the time; I pray the Lord
    That I may live to give you your reward.
    Farewell, my dears; be careful . . .
CLÉANTE: Brother, hurry.
    We shall take care of things; you needn't worry.

SCENE VII

The OFFICER, TARTUFFE, VALÈRE, ORGON, ELMIRE, MARIANE, MADAME PERNELLE, DORINE, CLÉANTE, DAMIS

TARTUFFE: Gently, Sir, gently; stay right where you are.
    No need for haste; your lodging isn't far.
    You're off to prison, by order of the Prince.
ORGON: This is the crowning blow, you wretch; and since
    It means my total ruin and defeat,   5
    Your villainy is now at last complete.
TARTUFFE: You needn't try to provoke me; it's no use.
    Those who serve Heaven must expect abuse.
CLÉANTE: You are indeed most patient, sweet, and blameless.
DORINE: How he exploits the name of Heaven! It's shameless.   10

TARTUFFE: Your taunts and mockeries are all for naught;
  To do my duty is my only thought.
MARIANE: Your love of duty is more meritorious,
  And what you've done is little short of glorious.
15 TARTUFFE: All deeds are glorious, Madam, which obey
  The sovereign prince who sent me here today.
ORGON: I rescued you when you were destitute,
  Have you forgotten that, you thankless brute?
TARTUFFE: No, no, I well remember everything;
20 But my first duty is to serve my King.
  That obligation is so paramount
  That other claims, beside it, do not count;
  And for it I would sacrifice my wife,
  My family, my friend, or my own life.
25 ELMIRE: Hypocrite!
DORINE: All that we most revere, he uses
  To cloak his plots and camouflage his ruses.
CLÉANTE: If it is true that you are animated
  By pure and loyal zeal, as you have stated,
  Why was this zeal not roused until you'd sought
30 To make Orgon a cuckold, and been caught?
  Why weren't you moved to give your evidence
  Until your outraged host had driven you hence?
  I shan't say that the gift of all his treasure
  Ought to have damped your zeal in any measure;
35 But if he is a traitor, as you declare,
  How could you condescend to be his heir?
TARTUFFE: (To the OFFICER.) Sir, spare me all this clamor; it's
  growing shrill.
  Please carry out your orders, if you will.
OFFICER: Yes, I've delayed too long, Sir. Thank you kindly.
40 You're just the proper person to remind me.
  Come, you are off to join the other boarders
  In the King's prison, according to his orders.
TARTUFFE: Who? I, Sir?
OFFICER: Yes.
TARTUFFE: To prison? This can't be true!
OFFICER: I owe an explanation, but not to you.

  (To ORGON.)

45 Sir, all is well; rest easy, and be grateful.
  We serve a Prince to whom all sham is hateful,
  A Prince who sees into our inmost hearts,
  And can't be fooled by any trickster's arts.
  His royal soul, though generous and human,
50 Views all things with discernment and acumen;
  His sovereign reason is not lightly swayed,
  And all his judgments are discreetly weighed.
  He honors righteous men of every kind,
  And yet his zeal for virtue is not blind,
55 Nor does his love of piety numb his wits

And make him tolerant of hypocrites.
'Twas hardly likely that this man could cozen
A King who's foiled such liars by the dozen.
With one keen glance, the King perceived the whole
Perverseness and corruption of his soul,   60
And thus high Heaven's justice was displayed:
Betraying you, the rogue stood self-betrayed.
The King soon recognized Tartuffe as one
Notorious by another name, who'd done
So many vicious crimes that one could fill   65
Ten volumes with them, and be writing still.
But to be brief: our sovereign was appalled
By this man's treachery toward you, which he called
The last, worst villainy of a vile career,
And bade me follow the impostor here   70
To see how gross his impudence could be,
And force him to restore your property.
Your private papers, by the King's command,
I hereby seize and give into your hand.
The King, by royal order, invalidates   75
The deed which gave this rascal your estates,
And pardons, furthermore, your grave offense
In harboring an exile's documents.
By these decrees, our Prince rewards you for
Your loyal deeds in the late civil war,   80
And shows how heartfelt is his satisfaction
In recompensing any worthy action,
How much he prizes merit, and how he makes
More of men's virtues than of their mistakes.
DORINE: Heaven be praised!   85
MADAME PERNELLE: I breathe again, at last.
ELMIRE: We're safe.
MARIANE: I can't believe the danger's past.
ORGON: (To TARTUFFE.)
  Well, traitor, now you see . . .
CLÉANTE: Ah, Brother, please,
  Let's not descend to such indignities.
  Leave the poor wretch to his unhappy fate,
  And don't say anything to aggravate   90
  His present woes; but rather hope that he
  Will soon embrace an honest piety,
  And mend his ways, and by a true repentance
  Move our just King to moderate his sentence.
  Meanwhile, go kneel before your sovereign's throne   95
  And thank him for the mercies he has shown.
ORGON: Well said: let's go at once and, gladly kneeling,
  Express the gratitude which all are feeling.
  Then, when that first great duty has been done,
  We'll turn with pleasure to a second one,   100
  And give Valère, whose love has proven so true,
  The wedded happiness which is his due.

APHRA BEHN

Little is known about the early life of England's first female professional playwright, Aphra Behn (1640–89), who may have been born Eaffrey Johnson in Kent. She left England just after the restoration of Charles II for the South American colony of Surinam, where she lived from 1663 to 1664. Again, many of the details about her life there are unknown, though Surinam provided the setting for her great novel, *Oronooko: or, The Royal Slave,* published in 1688. Returning to England, she appears to have married someone named Behn; in *The Passionate Shepherdess: Aphra Behn 1640–89* (London: Jonathan Cape, 1977), Maureen Duffy accounts for several possible candidates, but also suggests that Aphra Behn's marriage may have been a legitimating fiction: "Mr. Behn, her putative husband, has less substance than any character she invented" (48). By the mid-1660s, however, Aphra Behn was serving Charles II as a spy in Antwerp, and seems to have been caught up in the politics surrounding the Dutch invasion of Surinam. When she returned to England penniless in 1667, she was sent to debtors' prison, and appealed to the government for her wages. Between 1670 and her death in 1689, however, Behn emerged as a famous and influential writer; in addition to her novel *Orinooko,* Behn had a successful career as a poet and celebrated playwright. She wrote fifteen plays, beginning with *The Forced Marriage: or, The Jealous Bridegroom* (1668), a tragicomedy produced by Thomas Betterton at Lincoln's Inn Fields. Behn's major plays are mainly in the mode of Restoration comedy, and were successful both in their day and well into the eighteenth century: her best-known plays today are *The Rover* (1677), *The Feigned Courtesans* (1679), which was dedicated to her friend and supporter (and the King's mistress) the actress Nell Gwynn, *The Second Part of The Rover* (1681), and *The City Heiress* (1682). Her novel *Oronooko* was dramatized by Thomas Southerne in 1695, and was popular onstage throughout the eighteenth century. Aphra Behn was part of the elite milieu of intellectual culture of her day, the friend of courtiers like Buckingham and Rochester, and of writers like Otway and Dryden. Although her work was, in a sense, recovered for modern readers by Virginia Woolf's famous essay *A Room of One's Own,* Behn's plays have been increasingly popular and successful in the theater. Aphra Behn is buried in Westminster Abbey.

THE ROVER

The Rover is a comedy of intrigue, set in Naples during the Carnival. The play concerns the sexual adventures of a band of Englishmen—Belvile, Willmore (the Rover), and Blunt—and their efforts to seduce the heroine Florinda and her sister Hellena. Like many Restoration comedies, *The Rover* takes a frank attitude toward sexual and financial negotiation, which are often paired in the play. The play opens with Hellena's rejection of a life in the convent and her decision to "provide my self this Carnival, if there be e'er a handsome proper fellow." In the course of the play, Hellena flirts with Willmore; Willmore wins the services (and, unfortunately, the love) of the courtesan Angelica, who eventually tries to murder him; Willmore and Blunt nearly rape Florinda on several occasions; and Blunt is tricked by a prostitute and turned out into the street in his shirt and underwear, "before consummation."

Yet despite the licentiousness of its action, the play clearly depends on a deeply ingrained sense of propriety, much of which operates through class distinctions. While it "would anger us vilely to be trussed up for a rape upon a maid of quality," one of the gentlemen declares, it seems otherwise acceptable to "ruffle a harlot." Morality, in *The Rover,* is in many ways determined by class and wealth. These distinctions are both troubled and confirmed by the important function of disguise and masking in the play. Since the action of *The Rover* takes place during Carnival, the main characters meet only in disguise. Masking enables the characters both to flirt without dishonoring themselves and to discover the truth about one another. In fact, masking in the play empowers the women, in that the temporary masking of the Carnival allows the women to escape their enforced lives at home and to meet men in public. Florinda and Hellena, for instance, can marry only with their brother Pedro's permission. He wants to marry his sisters to the wealthiest—and oldest—suitors, who will be able to settle large fortunes on them. However, the young Englishmen who attract the two sisters are Royalist supporters of Charles II, currently exiled from Cromwell's Protectorate because they support the Crown. As a result, although they are well-born, they are currently without funds and so are a poor match for Florinda and Hellena, at least in Pedro's eyes.

Masking also enables the women to escape Pedro's control, to act on their own behalf. Indeed, although the women are more modest than the Rover, they are equally devious in their pursuit of a lover—though the women insist on marriage as the price of their virginity. In Behn's brilliant comedy, the women emerge as the agents—as well as the objects—of the play's erotic intrigue.

In recent years, *The Rover* has received a number of excellent stage productions—at Minneapolis's Gothine Theater, the Royal Shakespeare Company, and on many university campuses.

THE ROVER

or The Banish'd Cavaliers

Aphra Behn

EDITED BY MONTAGUE SUMMERS

CHARACTERS

Don ANTONIO, *the Vice-Roy's Son*
Don PEDRO, *a Noble Spaniard, his Friend*
BELVILE, *an English Colonel in love with Florinda*
WILLMORE, *the Rover*
FREDERICK, *an English Gentleman, and Friend to Belvile and Blunt*
BLUNT, *an English Country Gentleman*
STEPHANO, *Servant to Don Pedro*
PHILIPPO, *Lucetta's Gallant*
SANCHO, *Pimp to Lucetta*
BISKEY *and* SEBASTIAN, *two Bravoes to Angelica*
DIEGO, *Page to Don Antonio*
PAGE *to Hellena*
BOY, *Page to Belvile*

Blunt's MAN
OFFICERS *and* SOLDIERS
FLORINDA, *Sister to Don Pedro*
HELLENA, *a gay young Woman design'd for a Nun, and Sister to Florinda*
VALERIA, *a Kinswoman to Florinda*
ANGELICA BIANCA, *a famous Curtezan*
MORETTA, *her Woman*
CALLIS, *Governess to Florinda and Hellena*
LUCETTA, *a jilting Wench*
SERVANTS, *other* MASQUERADERS, MEN *and* WOMEN

SCENE: *Naples, in Carnival-time.*

PROLOGUE

WRITTEN BY A PERSON OF QUALITY

WITS, like Physicians, never can agree,
When of a different Society;
And Rabel's Drops were never more cry'd down
By all the Learned Doctors of the Town,
5   Than a new Play, whose Author is unknown:
Nor can those Doctors with more Malice sue
(And powerful Purses) the dissenting Few,
Than those with an insulting Pride do rail
At all who are not of their own Cabal.
10   If a Young Poet hit your Humour right,
You judge him then out of Revenge and Spite;
So amongst Men there are ridiculous Elves,
Who Monkeys hate for being too like themselves:
So that the Reason of the Grand Debate,
15   Why Wit so oft is damn'd, when good Plays take,
Is, that you censure as you love or hate.
Thus, like a learned Conclave, Poets sit
Catholick Judges both of Sense and Wit,
And damn or save, as they themselves think fit.
20   Yet those who to others Faults are so severe,
Are not so perfect, but themselves may err.
Some write correct indeed, but then the whole
(Bating their own dull Stuff i'th' Play) is stole:
As Bees do suck from Flowers their Honey-dew,
25   So they rob others, striving to please you.
    Some write their Characters genteel and fine,
But then they do so toil for every Line,
That what to you does easy seem, and plain,
Is the hard issue of their labouring Brain.
30   And some th' Effects of all their Pains we see,
Is but to mimick good Extempore.
Others by long Converse about the Town,
Have Wit enough to write a leud Lampoon,

But their chief Skill lies in a Baudy Song.
In short, the only Wit that's now in Fashion   35
Is but the Gleanings of good Conversation.
As for the Author of this coming Play,
I ask'd him what he thought fit I should say,
In thanks for your good Company to day:
He call'd me Fool, and said it was well known,   40
You came not here for our sakes, but your own.
New Plays are stuff'd with Wits, and with Debauches,
That croud and sweat like Cits in *May*-day Coaches.

ACT ONE

SCENE I

A chamber.

Enter FLORINDA *and* HELLENA.

FLORINDA: What an impertient thing is a young Girl bred in a
    Nunnery! How full of Questions! Prithee no more, Hellena;
    I have told thee more than thou understand'st already.

HELLENA: The more's my Grief; I wou'd fain know as much as
    you, which makes me so inquisitive; nor is't enough to know   5
    you're a Lover, unless you tell me too, who 'tis you sigh for.

FLORINDA: When you are a Lover, I'll think you fit for a Secret
    of that nature.

HELLENA: 'Tis true, I was never a Lover yet—but I begin to
    have a shreud Guess, what 'tis to be so, and fancy it very   10
    pretty to sigh, and sing, and blush and wish, and dream and
    wish, and long and wish to see the Man; and when I do,
    look pale and tremble; just as you did when my Brother
    brought home the fine *English* Colonel to see you—what do
    you call him? Don *Belvile.*   15

FLORINDA: Fie, *Hellena.*

HELLENA: That Blush betrays you—I am sure 'tis so—or is it Don
    Antonio the Vice-Roy's Son?—or perhaps the rich old Don

Vincentio, whom my father designs for your Husband?—
20   Why do you blush again?

FLORINDA: With Indignation; and how near soever my Father
    thinks I am to marrying that hated Object, I shall let him
    see I understand better what's due to my Beauty, Birth and
    Fortune, and more to my Soul, than to obey those unjust
25   Commands.

HELLENA: Now hang me, if I don't love thee for that dear Dis-
    obedience. I love Mischief strangely, as most of our Sex do,
    who are come to love nothing else—But tell me, dear
    Florinda, don't you love that fine *Anglese?*—for I vow next
30   to loving him my self, 'twill please me most that you do so,
    for he is so gay and so handsom.

FLORINDA: *Hellena,* a Maid design'd for a Nun ought not to be
    so curious in a Discourse of Love.

HELLENA: And dost thou think that ever I'll be a Nun? Or at
35   least till I'm so old, I'm fit for nothing else. Faith no, Sister;
    and that which makes me long to know whether you love
    Belvile, is because I hope he has some mad Companion or
    other, that will spoil my Devotion; nay I'm resolv'd to pro-
    vide my self this Carnival, if there be e'er a handsom Fellow
40   of my Humour above Ground, tho I ask first.

FLORINDA: Prithee be not so wild.

HELLENA: Now you have provided your self with a Man, you
    take no Care for poor me—Prithee tell me, what dost thou
    see about me that is unfit for Love—have not I a world of
45   Youth? a Humour gay? a Beauty passable? a Vigour desir-
    able? well shap'd? clean limb'd? sweet breath'd? and Sense
    enough to know how all these ought to be employ'd to the
    best Advantage: yes, I do and will. Therefore lay aside your
    Hopes of my Fortune, by my being a Devotee, and tell me
50   how you came acquainted with this *Belvile;* for I perceive
    you knew him before he came to *Naples.*

FLORINDA: Yes, I knew him at the Siege of *Pampelona,* he was
    then a Colonel of *French* Horse, who when the Town was
    ransack'd, nobly treated my Brother and my self, preserving
55   us from all Insolencies; and I must own, (besides great
    Obligations) I have I know not what, that pleads kindly for
    him about my Heart, and will suffer no other to enter—But
    see my Brother.

(Enter Don PEDRO, STEPHANO, *with a Masquing Habit, and* CALLIS.*)*

PEDRO: Good morrow, Sister. Pray, when saw you your Lover
60   Don *Vincentio?*

FLORINDA: I know not, Sir—*Callis,* when was he here? for I
    consider it so little, I know not when it was.

PEDRO: I have a Command from my Father here to tell you, you
    ought not to despise him, a Man of so vast a Fortune, and
65   such a Passion for you—*Stephano,* my things—

(Puts on his Masquing Habit.)

FLORINDA: A Passion for me! 'tis more than e'er I saw, or had a
    desire should be known—I hate *Vincentio,* and I would not
    have a Man so dear to me as my Brother follow the ill Cus-
    toms of our Country, and make a Slave of his Sister—And
70   Sir, my Father's Will, I'm sure, you may divert.

---

52 **Siege of *Pampelona*** Pampluna, the strongly fortified capital
of Navarra and very frequently a center of military operations

PEDRO: I know not how dear I am to you, but I wish only to be
    rank'd in your Esteem, equal with the *English* Colonel
    Belvile—Why do you frown and blush? Is there any Guilt
    belongs to the Name of that Cavalier?

FLORINDA: I'll not deny I value *Belvile:* when I was expos'd to such   75
    Dangers as the licens'd Lust of common Soldiers threatned,
    when Rage and Conquest flew thro the City—then *Belvile,*
    this Criminal for my sake, threw himself into all Dangers to
    save my Honour, and will you not allow him my Esteem?

PEDRO: Yes, pay him what you will in Honour—but you must   80
    consider Don *Vincentio's* Fortune, and the Jointure he'll
    make you.

FLORINDA: Let him consider my Youth, Beauty and Fortune;
    which ought not to be thrown away on his Age and Jointure.

PEDRO: 'Tis true, he's not so young and fine a Gentleman as that   85
    Belvile—but what Jewels will that Cavalier present you
    with? those of his Eyes and Heart?

HELLENA: And are not those better than any Don *Vincentio* has
    brought from the *Indies?*

PEDRO: Why how now! Has your Nunnery-breeding taught   90
    you to understand the Value of Hearts and Eyes?

HELLENA: Better than to believe *Vincentio* deserves Value from
    any woman—He may perhaps encrease her Bags, but not
    her Family.

PEDRO: This is fine—Go up to your Devotion, you are not de-   95
    sign'd for the Conversation of Lovers.

HELLENA: *(Aside.)* Nor Saints yet a while I hope.
    Is't not enough you make a Nun of me, but you must cast
    my Sister away too, exposing her to a worse confinement
    than a religious Life?   100

PEDRO: The Girl's mad—Is it a Confinement to be carry'd into
    the Country, to an antient Villa belonging to the Family of
    the *Vincentio's* these five hundred Years, and have no other
    Prospect than that pleasing one of seeing all her own that
    meets her Eyes—a fine Air, large Fields and Gardens, where   105
    she may walk and gather Flowers?

HELLENA: When? By Moon-Light? For I'm sure she dares not
    encounter with the heat of the Sun; that were a Task only
    for Don *Vincentio* and his *Indian* Breeding, who loves it in
    the Dog-days—And if these be her daily Divertisements,   110
    what are those of the Night? to lie in a wide Moth-eaten
    Bed-Chamber with Furniture in Fashion in the Reign of
    King *Sancho* the First; the Bed that which his Forefathers
    liv'd and dy'd in.

PEDRO: Very well.   115

HELLENA: This Apartment (new furbisht and fitted out for the
    young Wife) he (out of Freedom) makes his Dressing-room;
    and being a frugal and a jealous Coxcomb, instead of a
    Valet to uncase his feeble Carcase, he desires you to do that
    Office—Signs of Favour, I'll assure you, and such as you   120
    must not hope for, unless your Woman be out of the way.

PEDRO: Have you done yet?

HELLENA: That Honour being past, the Giant stretches it self,
    yawns and sighs a Belch or two as loud as a Musket, throws

---

113 **King *Sancho* the First** Sancho I, 'the Fat,' of Castile and Leon,
reigned 955–67: Sancho I of Aragon 1067–94. But the phrase is
here only in a vague general sense to denote some musty and immemorial antiquity without any exact reference

125 himself into Bed, and expects you in his foul Sheets, and
e'er you can get your self undrest, calls you with a Snore or
two—And are not these fine Blessings to a young Lady?

PEDRO: Have you done yet?

HELLENA: And this man you must kiss, nay, you must kiss none
130 but him too—and nuzle thro his Beard to find his Lips—
and this you must submit to for threescore Years, and all for
a Jointure.

PEDRO: For all your Character of Don *Vincentio,* she is as like to
marry him as she was before.

135 HELLENA: Marry Don *Vincentio!* hang me, such a Wedlock would
be worse than Adultery with another Man: I had rather see
her in the *Hostel de Dieu,* to waste her Youth there in Vows,
and be a Handmaid to Lazers and Cripples, than to lose it
in such a Marriage.

140 PEDRO: You have consider'd, Sister, that *Belvile* has no Fortune
to bring you to, is banisht his Country, despis'd at home,
and pity'd abroad.

HELLENA: What then? the Vice-Roy's Son is better than that
Old Sir Fisty. Don *Vincentio!* Don *Indian!* he thinks he's
145 trading to *Gambo* still, and wou'd barter himself (that Bell
and Bawble) for your Youth and Fortune.

PEDRO: *Callis,* take her hence, and lock her up all this Carnival,
and at Lent she shall begin her everlasting Penance in a
Monastery.

150 HELLENA: I care not, I had rather be a Nun, than be oblig'd to
marry as you wou'd have me, if I were design'd for't.

PEDRO: Do not fear the Blessing of that Choice—you shall be
a Nun.

HELLENA: Shall I so? you may chance to be mistaken in my way
155 of Devotion—*(Aside.)* A Nun! yes I am like to make a fine
Nun! I have an excellent Humour for a Grate: No, I'll have
a Saint of my own to pray to shortly, if I like any that dares
venture on me.

PEDRO: *Callis,* make it your Business to watch this wild Cat. As
160 for you, *Florinda,* I've only try'd you all this while, and urg'd
my Father's Will; but mine is, that you would love *Antonio,*
he is brave and young, and all that can compleat the Happiness of a gallant Maid—This Absence of my Father will
give us opportunity to free you from *Vincentio,* by marrying
165 here, which you must do to morrow.

FLORINDA: To morrow!

PEDRO: To morrow, or 'twill be too late—'tis not my Friendship
to *Antonio,* which makes me urge this, but Love to thee, and
Hatred to *Vincentio*—therefore resolve upon't to morrow.

170 FLORINDA: Sir, I shall strive to do, as shall become your Sister.

PEDRO: I'll both believe and trust you—Adieu.

(Exeunt PEDRO *and* STEPHANO.*)*

HELLENA: As become his Sister!—That is, to be as resolved your
way, as he is his—

*(*HELLENA *goes to* CALLIS.*)*

FLORINDA: I ne'er till now perceiv'd my Ruin near,
175 I've no Defence against *Antonio's* Love,

---

137 *Hostel de Dieu* the first Spanish hospital was erected at
Granada by St. Juan de Dios before 1550   145 *Gambo* the Gam-
bia in West Africa has been a British Colony since 1664, when a
fort, now Fort James, was founded at the mouth of the river

For he has all the Advantages of Nature,
The moving Arguments of Youth and Fortune.

HELLENA: But hark you, *Callis,* you will not be so cruel to lock
me up indeed: will you?

CALLIS: I must obey the Commands I hate—besides, do you 180
consider what a Life you are going to lead?

HELLENA: Yes, *Callis,* that of a Nun: and till then I'll be indebted a World of Prayers to you, if you let me now see,
what I never did, the Divertisements of a Carnival.

CALLIS: What, go in Masquerade? 'twill be a fine farewell to the 185
World I take it—pray what wou'd you do there?

HELLENA: That which all the World does, as I am told, be as mad
as the rest, and take all innocent Freedom—Sister, you'll go
too, will you not? come prithee be not sad—We'll out-wit
twenty Brothers, if you'll be ruled by me—Come put off this 190
dull Humour with your Clothes, and assume one as gay, and
as fantastick as the Dress my Cousin *Valeria* and I have provided, and let's ramble.

FLORINDA: *Callis,* will you give us leave to go?

CALLIS: *(Aside.)* I have a youthful Itch of going my self. 195
—Madam, if I thought your Brother might not know it,
and I might wait on you, for by my troth I'll not trust
young Girls alone.

FLORINDA: Thou see'st my Brother's gone already, and thou
shalt attend and watch us. 200

(Enter STEPHANO.*)*

STEPHANO: Madam, the Habits are come, and your Cousin
Valeria is drest, and stays for you.

FLORINDA: 'Tis well—I'll write a Note, and if I chance to see
Belvile, and want an opportunity to speak to him, that shall
let him know what I've resolv'd in favour of him. 205

HELLENA: Come, let's in and dress us.

(Exeunt.)

SCENE II

A Long Street.

Enter BELVILE, *melancholy,* BLUNT *and* FREDERICK.

FREDERICK: Why, what the Devil ails the Colonel, in a time
when all the World is gay, to look like mere Lent thus? Hadst
thou been long enough in *Naples* to have been in love, I
should have sworn some such Judgment had befall'n thee.

BELVILE: No, I have made no new Amours since I came to 5
Naples.

FREDERICK: You have left none behind you in Paris.

BELVILE: Neither.

FREDERICK: I can't divine the Cause then; unless the old Cause,
the want of Mony. 10

BLUNT: And another old Cause, the want of a Wench—Wou'd
not that revive you?

BELVILE: You're mistaken, *Ned.*

BLUNT: Nay, 'Sheartlikins, then thou art past Cure.

FREDERICK: I have found it out; thou hast renew'd thy Ac- 15
quaintance with the Lady that cost thee so many Sighs at
the Siege of *Pampelona*—pox on't, what d'ye call her—her
Brother's a noble *Spaniard*—Nephew to the dead General—

---

14 *'Sheartlikins* by God's heart

20 *Florinda*—ay, *Florinda*—And will nothing serve thy turn but that damn'd virtuous Woman, whom on my Consicience thou lov'st in spite too, because thou seest little or no possibility of gaining her?

BELVILE: Thou art mistaken, I have Interest enough in that lovely Virgin's Heart, to make me proud and vain, were it
25 not abated by the Severity of a Brother, who perceiving my Happiness—

FREDERICK: Has civilly forbid thee the House?

BELVILE: 'Tis so, to make way for a powerful Rival, the Vice-Roy's Son, who has the advantage of me, in being a Man of Fortune,
30 a *Spaniard,* and her Brother's Friend; which gives him liberty to make his Court, whilst I have recourse only to Letters, and distant Looks from her Window, which are as soft and kind as those which Heav'n sends down on Penitents.

BLUNT: Hey day! 'Sheartlikins, Simile! by this Light the Man is
35 quite spoil'd—*Frederick,* what the Devil are we made of, that we cannot be thus concern'd for a Wench?—'Sheartlikins, our *Cupids* are like the Cooks of the Camp, they can roast or boil a Woman, but they have none of the fine Tricks to set 'em off, no Hogoes to make the Sauce pleasant, and
40 the Stomach sharp.

FREDERICK: I dare swear I have had a hundred as young, kind and handsom as this *Florinda;* and Dogs eat me, if they were not as troublesom to me i'th' Morning as they were welcome o'er night.

45 BLUNT: And yet, I warrant, he wou'd not touch another Woman, if he might have her for nothing.

BELVILE: That's thy Joy, a cheap Whore.

BLUNT: Why, 'dsheartlikins, I Love a frank Soul—When did you ever hear of an honest Woman that took a Man's Mony? I
50 warrant 'em good ones—But, Gentlemen, you may be free, you have been kept so poor with Parliaments and Protectors, that the little Stock you have is not worth preserving—but I thank my Stars, I have more Grace than to forfeit my Estate by Cavaliering.

55 BELVILE: Methinks only following the Court should be sufficient to entitle 'em to that.

BLUNT: 'Sheartlikins, they know I follow it to do it no good, unless they pick a hole in my Coat for lending you Mony now and then; which is a greater Crime to my Conscience,
60 Gentlemen, than to the Common-wealth.

(Enter WILLMORE.*)*

WILLMORE: Ha! dear *Belvile!* noble Colonel!

BELVILE: *Willmore!* welcome ashore, my dear Rover!—what happy Wind blew us this good Fortune?

WILLMORE: Let me salute you my dear *Fred,* and then command
65 me—How is't honest Lad?

FREDERICK: Faith, Sir, the old Complement, infinitely the better to see my dear mad *Willmore* again—Prithee why camest thou ashore? and where's the Prince?

WILLMORE: He's well, and reigns still Lord of the watery Ele-
70 ment—I must aboard again within a Day or two, and my Business ashore was only to enjoy my self a little this Carnival.

BELVILE: Pray know our new Friend, Sir, he's but bashful, a raw Traveller, but honest, stout, and one of us.

---

39 **Hogoes** Haut-goût, a relish

(Embraces BLUNT.*)*

WILLMORE: That you esteem him, gives him an Interest here.

BLUNT: Your Servant, Sir.   75

WILLMORE: But well—Faith I'm glad to meet you again in a warm Climate, where the kind Sun has its god-like Power still over the Wine and Woman.—Love and Mirth are my Business in *Naples;* and if I mistake not the Place, here's an excellent Market for Chapmen of my Humour.   80

BELVILE: See here be those kind Merchants of Love you look for.

(Enter several MEN *in masquing Habits, some playing on Musick, others dancing after;* WOMEN *drest like Curtezans, with Papers pin-n'd to their Breasts, and Baskets of Flowers in their Hands.)*

BLUNT: 'Sheartlikins, what have we here!

FREDERICK: Now the Game begins.

WILLMORE: Fine pretty Creatures! may a stranger have leave to   85 look and love?—What's here—*(Reads the Paper.) Roses for every Month!*

BLUNT: Roses for every Month! what means that?

BELVILE: They are, or wou'd have you think they're Curtezans, who here in *Naples* are to be hir'd by the Month.   90

WILLMORE: Kind and obliging to inform us—Pray where do these Roses grow? I would fain plant some of 'em in a Bed of mine.

WOMAN: Beware such Roses, Sir.

WILLMORE: A Pox of fear: I'll be bak'd with thee between a pair   95 of Sheets, and that's thy proper Still, so I might but strow such Roses over me and under me—Fair one, wou'd you wou'd give me leave to gather at your Bush this idle Month, I wou'd go near to make some Body smell of it all the Year after.   100

BELVILE: And thou hast need of such a Remedy, for thou stinkest of Tar and Rope-ends, like a Dock or Pesthouse.

(The WOMAN *puts her self into the Hands of a* MAN, *and Exit.)*

WILLMORE: Nay, nay, you shall not leave me so.

BELVILE: By all means use no Violence here.

WILLMORE: Death! just as I was going to be damnably in love,   105 to have her led off! I could pluck that Rose out of his Hand, and even kiss the Bed, the Bush it grew in.

FREDERICK: No Friend to Love like a long Voyage at Sea.

BLUNT: Except a Nunnery, *Frederick.*

WILLMORE: Death! but will they not be kind, quickly be kind?   110 Thou know'st I'm no tame Sigher, but a rampant Lion of the Forest.

(Two MEN *drest all over with Horns of several sorts, making Grimaces at one another, with Papers pinn'd on their Backs, advance from the farther end of the Scene.)*

BELVILE: Oh the fantastical Rogues, how they are dress'd! 'tis a Satir against the whole Sex.

WILLMORE: Is this a Fruit that grows in this warm Country?   115

BELVILE: Yes: 'Tis pretty to see these *Italian* start, swell, and stab at the Word *Cuckold,* and yet stumble at Horns on every Threshold.

WILLMORE: See what's on their Back—*(Reads.) Flowers for every Night.*—Ah Rogue! And more sweet than Roses of ev'ry   120 Month! This is a Gardiner of *Adam's* own breeding.

(They dance.)

BELVILE: What think you of those grave People?—is a Wake in *Essex* half so mad or extravagant?

WILLMORE: I like their sober grave way, 'tis a kind of legal au-
125   thoriz'd Fornication, where the Men are not chid for 't, nor
the Women despis'd, as amongst our dull *English;* even the
Monsieurs want that part of good Manners.

BELVILE: But here in *Italy* a Monsieur is the humblest best-bred
Gentleman—Duels are so baffled by Bravos that an age
130   shews not one, but between a *Frenchman* and a Hangman,
who is as much too hard for him on the Piazza, as they are
for a *Dutchman* on the new Bridge—But see another Crew.

(Enter FLORINDA, HELLENA, *and* VALERIA, *drest like Gipsies;* CALLIS
and STEPHANO, LUCETTA, PHILIPPO *and* SANCHO *in Masquerade.)*

HELLENA: Sister, there's your *Englishman,* and with him a handsome proper Fellow—I'll to him, and instead of telling him
135   his Fortune, try my own.

WILLMORE: Gipsies, on my Life—Sure these will prattle if a
Man cross their Hands. *(Goes to* HELLENA.*)*—Dear pretty
(and I hope) young Devil, will you tell an amorous Stranger
what Luck he's like to have?

140   HELLENA: Have a care how you venture with me, Sir, lest I pick
your Pocket, which will more vex your *English* Humour,
than an *Italian* Fortune will please you.

WILLMORE: How the Devil cam'st thou to know my Country
and Humour?

145   HELLENA: The first I guess by a certain forward Impudence,
which does not displease me at this time; and the Loss of
your Money will vex you, because I hope you have but very
little to lose.

WILLMORE: Egad Child, thou'rt i'th' right; it is so little, I dare
150   not offer it thee for a Kindness—But cannot you divine
what other things of more value I have about me, that I
would more willingly part with?

HELLENA: Indeed no, that's the Business of a Witch, and I am
but a Gipsy yet—Yet, without looking in your Hand, I
155   have a parlous Guess, 'tis some foolish Heart you mean, an
inconstant *English* Heart, as little worth stealing as your
Purse.

WILLMORE: Nay, then thou dost deal with the Devil, that's certain—Thou hast guess'd as right as if thou hadst been one
160   of that Number it has languisht for—I find you'll be better
acquainted with it; nor can you take it in a better time, for
I am come from Sea, Child; and *Venus* not being propitious
to me in her own Element, I have a world of Love in store—
Wou'd you would be good-natur'd, and take some on't off
165   my Hands.

HELLENA: Why—I could be inclin'd that way—but for a foolish Vow I am going to make—to die a Maid.

WILLMORE: Then thou art damn'd without Redemption; and as
I am a good Christian, I ought to charity to divert so
170   wicked a Design—therefore prithee, dear Creature, let me
know quickly when and where I shall begin to set a helping hand to so good a Work.

HELLENA: If you should prevail with my tender Heart (as I
begin to fear you will, for you have horrible loving Eyes)
175   there will be difficulty in't that you'll hardly undergo for
my sake.

WILLMORE: Faith, Child, I have been bred in Dangers, and wear
a Sword that has been employ'd in a worse Cause, than for
a handsom kind Woman—Name the Danger—let it be any
thing but a long Siege, and I'll undertake it.   180

HELLENA: Can you storm?

WILLMORE: Oh, most furiously.

HELLENA: What think you of a Nunnery-wall? for he that wins
me, must gain that first.

WILLMORE: A Nun! Oh how I love thee for't! there's no Sinner   185
like a young Saint—Nay, now there's no denying me: the
old Law had no Curse (to a Woman) like dying a Maid; witness *Jephtha's* Daughter.

HELLENA: A very good Text this, if well handled; and I perceive,
Father Captain, you would impose no severe Penance on her   190
who was inclin'd to console her self before she took Orders.

WILLMORE: If she be young and handsom.

HELLENA: Ay, there's it—but if she be not—

WILLMORE: By this Hand, Child, I have an implicit Faith, and
dare venture on thee with all Faults—besides, 'tis more   195
meritorious to leave the World when thou hast tasted and
prov'd the Pleasure on't; then 'twill be a Virtue in thee,
which now will be pure Ignorance.

HELLENA: I perceive, good Father Captain, you design only to
make me fit for Heaven—but if on the contrary you should   200
quite divert me from it, and bring me back to the World
again, I should have a new Man to seek I find; and what a
grief that will be—for when I begin, I fancy I shall love like
any thing: I never try'd yet.

WILLMORE: Egad, and that's kind—Prithee, dear Creature, give   205
me Credit for a Heart, for faith, I'm a very honest Fellow—
Oh, I long to come first to the Banquet of Love; and such a
swinging Appetite I bring—Oh, I'm impatient. Thy Lodging, Sweetheart, thy Lodging, or I'm a dead man.

HELLENA: Why must we be either guilty of Fornication or Mur-   210
der, if we converse with you Men?—And is there no difference between leave to love me, and leave to lie with me?

WILLMORE: Faith, Child, they were made to go together.

LUCETTA: *(Pointing to* BLUNT.*)* Are you sure this is the Man?

SANCHO: When did I mistake your Game?   215

LUCETTA: This is a stranger, I know by his gazing; if he be brisk
he'll venture to follow me; and then, if I understand my
Trade, he's mine: he's *English* too, and they say that's a sort
of good natur'd loving People, and have generally so kind
an opinion of themselves, that a Woman with any Wit may   220
flatter 'em into any sort of Fool she pleases.

BLUNT: 'Tis so—she is taken—I have Beauties which my false
Glass at home did not discover.

(She often passes by BLUNT *and gazes on him; he struts, and cocks, and
walks, and gazes on her.)*

FLORINDA: This Woman watches me so, I shall get no Opportunity to discover my self to him, and so miss the intent of   225
my coming—But as I was saying, Sir—*(Looking in his Hand.)*
by this Line you should be a Lover.

BELVILE: I thought how right you guess'd, all Men are in love,
or pretend to be so—Come, let me go, I'm weary of this
fooling.   230

(Walks away.)

FLORINDA: I will not, till you have confess'd whether the Passion that you have vow'd *Florinda* be true or false.

(She holds him, he strives to get from her.)

BELVILE: *Florinda!*

(Turns quick towards her.)

FLORINDA: Softly.

235 BELVILE: Thou hast nam'd one will fix me here for ever.

FLORINDA: She'll be disappointed then, who expects you this Night at the Garden-gate, and if you'll fail not—as let me see the other Hand—you will go near to do—she vows to die or make you happy.

(Looks on CALLIS, *who observes 'em.)*

240 BELVILE: What canst thou mean?

FLORINDA: That which I say—Farewell.

(Offers to go.)

BELVILE: Oh charming Sybil, stay, complete that Joy, which, as it is, will turn into Distraction!—Where must I be? at the Garden-gate? I know it—at night you say—I'll sooner for-
245 feit Heaven than disobey.

(Enter DON PEDRO and other Masquers, and pass over the Stage.)

CALLIS: Madam, your Brother's here.

FLORINDA: Take this to instruct you farther.

(Gives him a Letter, and goes off.)

FREDERICK: Have a care, Sir, what you promise; this may be a Trap laid by her Brother to ruin you.

250 BELVILE: Do not disturb my Happiness with Doubts.

(Opens the Letter.)

WILLMORE: My dear pretty Creature, a Thousand Blessings on thee; still in this Habit, you say, and after Dinner at this Place.

HELLENA: Yes, if you will swear to keep your Heart, and not bestow it between this time and that.

255 WILLMORE: By all the little Gods of Love I swear, I'll leave it with you; and if you run away with it, those Deities of Justice will revenge me.

(Exeunt all the WOMEN *except* LUCETTA.)

FREDERICK: Do you know the Hand?

BELVILE: 'Tis *Florinda's.*
260   All Blessings fall upon the virtuous Maid.

FREDERICK: Nay, no Idolatry, a sober Sacrifice I'll allow you.

BELVILE: Oh Friends! the welcom'st News, the softest Letter!—nay, you shall see it; and could you now be serious, I might be made the happiest Man the Sun shines on.

265 WILLMORE: The Reason of this mighty Joy.

BELVILE: See how kindly she invites me to deliver her from the threaten'd Violence of her Brother—will you not assist me?

WILLMORE: I know not what thou mean'st, but I'll make one at any Mischief where a Woman's concern'd—but she'll be
270 grateful to us for the Favour, will she not?

BELVILE: How mean you?

WILLMORE: How should I mean? Thou know'st there's but one way for a Woman to oblige me.

BELVILE: Don't prophane—the Maid is nicely virtuous.

WILLMORE: Who pox, then she's fit for nothing but a Husband; 275 let her e'en go, Colonel.

FREDERICK: Peace, she's the Colonel's Mistress, Sir.

WILLMORE: Let her be the Devil; if she be thy Mistress, I'll serve her—name the way.

BELVILE: Read here this Postscript.   280

(Gives him a Letter.)

WILLMORE: *(Reads.) At Ten at night—at the Garden-Gate—of which, if I cannot get the Key, I will contrive a way over the Wall—come attended with a Friend or two.*—Kind heart, if we three cannot weave a String to let her down a Garden-Wall, 'twere pity but the Hangman wove one for us all.   285

FREDERICK: Let her alone for that: your Woman's Wit, your fair kind Woman, will not out-trick a Brother or a Jew, and contrive like a Jesuit in Chains—but see, *Ned Blunt* is stoln out after the Lure of a Damsel.

(Exit BLUNT *and* LUCETTA.)

BELVILE: So he'll scarce find his way home again, unless we get 290 him cry'd by the Bell-man in the Market-place, and 'twou'd sound prettily—a lost *English* Boy of Thirty.

FREDERICK: I hope 'tis some common crafty Sinner, one that will fit him; it may be she'll sell him for *Peru*, the Rogue's sturdy and would work well in a Mine; at least I hope she'll 295 dress him for our Mirth; cheat him of all, then have him well-favour'dly bang'd, and turn'd out naked at Midnight.

WILLMORE: Prithee what Humour is he of, that you wish him so well?

BELVILE: Why, of an *English* Elder Brother's Humour, educated 300 in a Nursery, with a Maid to tend him till Fifteen, and lies with his Grand-mother till he's of Age; one that knows no Pleasure beyond riding to the next Fair, or going up to *London* with his right Worshipful Father in Parliament-time; wearing gay Clothes, or making honourable Love to his Lady 305 Mother's Landry-Maid; gets drunk at a Hunting-Match, and ten to one then gives some Proofs of his Prowess—A pox upon him, he's our Banker, and has all our Cash about him, and if he fail we are all broke.

FREDERICK: Oh let him alone for that matter, he's of a damn'd 310 stingy Quality, that will secure our Stock. I know not in what Danger it were indeed, if the Jilt should pretend she's in love with him, for 'tis a kind believing Coxcomb; otherwise if he part with more than a Piece of Eight—geld him: for which offer he may chance to be beaten, if she be a 315 Whore of the first Rank.

BELVILE: Nay the Rogue will not be easily beaten, he's stout enough; perhaps if they talk beyond his Capacity, he may chance to exercise his Courage upon some of them; else I'm sure they'll find it as difficult to beat as to please him.   320

WILLMORE: 'Tis a lucky Devil to light upon so kind a Wench!

FREDERICK: Thou hadst a great deal of talk with thy little Gipsy, coud'st thou do no good upon her? for mine was hard-hearted.

WILLMORE: Hang her, she was some damn'd honest Person of 325 Quality, I'm sure, she was so very free and witty. If her Face

---

314 **a Piece of Eight** a piastre, a coin of varying values in different countries

be but answerable to her Wit and Humour, I would be bound to Constancy this Month to gain her. In the mean time, have you made no kind Acquaintance since you came
330 to Town?—You do not use to be honest so long, Gentlemen.

FREDERICK: Faith Love has kept us honest, we have been all fir'd with a Beauty newly come to Town, the famous *Paduana Angelica Bianca.*

WILLMORE: What, the Mistress of the dead *Spanish* General?

335 BELVILE: Yes, she's now the only ador'd Beauty of all the Youth in *Naples,* who put on all their charms to appear lovely in her sight, their Coaches, Liveries, and themselves, all gay, as on a Monarch's Birth-Day, to attract the Eyes of this fair Charmer, while she has the Pleasure to behold all languish
340 for her that see her.

FREDERICK: 'Tis pretty to see with how much Love the Men regard her, and how much Envy the Women.

WILLMORE: What Gallant has she?

BELVILE: None, she's exposed to Sale, and four Days in the Week
345 she's yours—for so much a Month.

WILLMORE: The very Thought of it quenches all manner of Fire in me—yet prithee let's see her.

BELVILE: Let's first to Dinner, and after that we'll pass the Day as you please—but at Night ye must all be at my Devotion.

350 WILLMORE: I will not fail you.

(Exeunt.)

———— ACT TWO ————

SCENE I

The Long Street.

Enter BELVILE *and* FREDERICK *in Masquing-Habits, and* WILLMORE *in his own Clothes, with a Vizard in his Hand.*

WILLMORE: But why thus disguis'd and muzzl'd?

BELVILE: Because whatever Extravagances we commit in these Faces, our own may not be oblig'd to answer 'em.

WILLMORE: I should have chang'd my Eternal Buff too: but no
5 matter, my little Gipsy wou'd not have found me out then: for if she should change hers, it is impossible I should know her, unless I should hear her prattle—A Pox on't, I cannot get her out of my Head: Pray Heaven, if ever I do see her again, she prove damnable ugly, that I may fortify my self
10 against her Tongue.

BELVILE: Have a care of Love, for o' my conscience she was not of a Quality to give thee any hopes.

WILLMORE: Pox on 'em, why do they draw a Man in then? She has play'd with my Heart so, that 'twill never lie still till I
15 have met with some kind Wench, that will play the Game out with me—Oh for my Arms full of soft, white, kind—Woman! such as I fancy *Angelica.*

BELVILE: This is her House, if you were but in stock to get admittance; they have not din'd yet; I perceive the Picture is
20 not out.

(Enter BLUNT.*)*

WILLMORE: I long to see the Shadow of the fair Substance, a Man may gaze on that for nothing.

BLUNT: Colonel, thy Hand—and thine, *Frederick.* I have been an Ass, a deluded Fool, a very Coxcomb from my Birth till this Hour, and heartily repent my little Faith.   25

BELVILE: What the Devil's the matter with thee *Ned?*

BLUNT: Oh such a Mistress, *Frederick,* such a Girl!

WILLMORE: Ha! where? *Frederick.* Ay where!

BLUNT: So fond, so amorous, so toying and fine! and all for sheer Love, ye Rogue! Oh how she lookt and kiss'd! and sooth'd   30 my Heart from my Bosom. I cannot think I was awake, and yet methinks I see and feel her Charms still—*Frederick.*— Try if she have not left the Taste of her balmy Kisses upon my Lips—

(Kisses him.)

BELVILE: Ha, ha, ha! *Willmore.* Death Man, where is she?   35

BLUNT: What a Dog was I to stay in dull *England* so long— How have I laught at the Colonel when he sigh'd for Love! but now the little Archer has reveng'd him, and by his own Dart, I can guess at all his Joys, which then I took for Fancies, mere Dreams and Fables—Well, I'm resolved to sell all in   40 *Essex,* and plant here for ever.

BELVILE: What a Blessing 'tis, thou hast a Mistress thou dar'st boast of; for I know thy Humour is rather to have a proclaim'd Clap, than a secret Amour.

WILLMORE: Dost know her Name?   45

BLUNT: Her Name? No, 'sheartlikins: what care I for Names?— She's fair, young, brisk and kind, even to ravishment: and what a Pox care I for knowing her by another Title?

WILLMORE: Didst give her anything?

BLUNT: Give her!—Ha, ha, ha! why, she's a Person of Quality— 50 That's a good one, give her! 'sheartlikins dost think such Creatures are to be bought? Or are we provided for such a Purchase? Give her, quoth ye? Why she presented me with this Bracelet, for the Toy of a Diamond I us'd to wear: No, Gentlemen, *Ned Blunt* is not every Body—She expects me   55 again to night.

WILLMORE: Egad that's well; we'll all go.

BLUNT: Not a Soul: No, Gentlemen, you are Wits; I am a dull Country Rogue, I.

FREDERICK: Well, Sir, for all your Person of Quality, I shall be   60 very glad to understand your Purse be secure; 'tis our whole Estate at present, which we are loth to hazard in one Bottom: come, Sir, unload.

BLUNT: Take the necessary Trifle, useless now to me, that am belov'd by such a Gentlewoman—'sheartlikins Money!   65 Here take mine too.

FREDERICK: No, keep that to be cozen'd, that we may laugh.

WILLMORE: Cozen'd!—Death! wou'd I cou'd meet with one, that wou'd cozen me of all the Love I cou'd spare to night.

FREDERICK: Pox 'tis some common Whore upon my Life.   70

BLUNT: A Whore! yes with such Clothes! such Jewels! such a House! such Furniture, and so attended! a Whore!

BELVILE: Why yes, Sir, they are Whores, tho they'll neither entertain you with Drinking, Swearing, or Baudy; are Whores in all those gay Clothes, and right Jewels; are Whores with 75 great Houses richly furnisht with Velvet Beds, Store of Plate, handsome Attendance, and fine Coaches, are Whores and errant ones.

WILLMORE: Pox on't, where do these fine Whores live?

80 BELVILE: Where no Rogue in Office yclep'd Constables dare
give 'em laws, nor the Wine-inspired Bullies of the Town
break their Windows; yet they are Whores, tho this Essex
Calf believe them Persons of Quality.

BLUNT: 'Sheartlikins, y'are all Fools, there are things about this
85 *Essex* Calf, that shall take with the Ladies, beyond all your
Wits and Parts—This Shape and Size, Gentlemen, are not
to be despis'd; my Waste tolerably long, with other inviting Signs, that shall be nameless.

WILLMORE: Egad I believe he may have met with some Person
90 of Quality that may be kind to him.

BELVILE: Dost thou perceive any such tempting things about
him, should make a fine Woman, and of Quality, pick him
out from all Mankind, to throw away her Youth and Beauty
upon, nay, and her dear Heart too?—no, no, *Angelica* has
95 rais'd the Price too high.

WILLMORE: May she languish for Mankind till she die, and be
damn'd for that one Sin alone.

(*Enter two* BRAVOES, *and hang up a great Picture of* ANGELICA's,
against the Balcony, and two little ones at each side of the Door.)

BELVILE: See there the fair Sign to the Inn, where a Man may
lodge that's Fool enough to give her Price.

(WILLMORE *gazes on the Picture.*)

100 BLUNT: 'Sheartlikins, Gentlemen, what's this?

BELVILE: A famous Curtezan that's to be sold.

BLUNT: How! to be sold! nay then I have nothing to say to
her—sold! what Impudence is practis'd in this Country?—
With Order and Decency Whoring's established here by
105 virtue of the Inquisition—Come let's be gone, I'm sure
we're no Chapmen for this Commodity.

FREDERICK: Thou art none, I'm sure, unless thou could'st have
her in thy Bed at the Price of a Coach in the Street.

WILLMORE: How wondrous fair she is—a Thousand Crowns a
110 Month—by Heaven as many Kingdoms were too little. A
plague of this Poverty—of which I ne'er complain, but
when it hinders my Approach to Beauty, which Virtue ne'er
could purchase.

(*Turns from the Picture.*)

BLUNT: What's this?—(*Reads.*) *A Thousand Crowns a Month!*—
115 'Sheartlikins, here's a Sum! sure 'tis a mistake.—Hark you,
Friend, does she take or give so much by the Month!

FREDERICK: A Thousand Crowns! Why, 'tis a Portion for the
Infanta.

BLUNT: Hark ye, Friends, won't she trust?

120 BRAVO: This is a Trade, Sir, that cannot live by Credit.

(*Enter* DON PEDRO *in Masquerade, follow'd by* STEPHANO.)

BELVILE: See, here's more Company, let's walk off a while.

(PEDRO *reads. Exeunt English. Enter* ANGELICA *and* MORETTA *in
the Balcony, and draw a Silk Curtain.*)

PEDRO: Fetch me a Thousand Crowns, I never wish to buy this
Beauty at an easier Rate.

(*Passes off.*)

ANGELICA: Prithee what said those Fellows to thee?

BRAVO: Madam, the first were Admirers of Beauty only, but no 125
purchasers; they were merry with your Price and Picture,
laught at the Sum, and so past off.

ANGELICA: No matter, I'm not displeas'd with their rallying;
their Wonder feeds my Vanity, and he that wishes to buy,
gives me more Pride, than he that gives my Price can make 130
me Pleasure.

BRAVO: Madam, the last I knew thro all his disguises to be Don
Pedro, Nephew to the General, and who was with him in
Pampelona.

ANGELICA: Don *Pedro!* my old Gallant's Nephew! When his 135
Uncle dy'd, he left him a vast Sum of Money; it is he who
was so in love with me at *Padua,* and who us'd to make the
General so jealous.

MORETTA: Is this he that us'd to prance before our Window and
take such care to shew himself an amorous Ass? if I am not 140
mistaken, he is the likeliest Man to give your Price.

ANGELICA: The Man is brave and generous, but of an Humour
so uneasy and inconstant, that the victory over his Heart is as
soon lost as won; a Slave that can add little to the Triumph
of the Conqueror; but inconstancy's the Sin of all Mankind, 145
therefore I'm resolv'd that nothing but Gold shall charm
my Heart.

MORETTA: I'm glad on't; 'tis only interest that Women of our
Profession ought to consider: tho I wonder what has kept
you from that general Disease of our Sex so long, I mean 150
that of being in love.

ANGELICA: A kind, but sullen Star, under which I had the Happiness to be born; yet I have had no time for Love; the
bravest and noblest of Mankind have purchas'd my Favours
at so dear a Rate, as if no Coin but Gold were current with 155
our Trade—But here's Don *Pedro* again, fetch me my
Lute—for 'tis for him or Don *Antonio* the Vice-Roy's Son,
that I have spread my Nets.

(*Enter at one Door Don* PEDRO, *and* STEPHANO; *Don* ANTONIO *and*
DIEGO {*his page*}, *at the other Door, with people following him in
Masquerade, antickly attir'd, some with Musick: they both go up to
the Picture.*)

ANTONIO: A thousand Crowns! had not the Painter flatter'd
her, I should not think it dear. 160

PEDRO: Flatter'd her! by Heaven he cannot. I have seen the
Original, nor is there one Charm here more than adorns her
Face and Eyes; all this soft and sweet, with a certain lan-
guishing Air, that no Artist can represent.

ANTONIO: What I heard of her Beauty before had fir'd my Soul, 165
but this confirmation of it has blown it into a flame.

PEDRO: Ha!

PAGE: Sir, I have known you throw away a Thousand Crowns on
a worse Face, and tho y' are near your Marriage, you may
venture a little Love here; *Florinda*—will not miss it. 170

PEDRO: (*Aside.*) Ha! *Florinda!* Sure 'tis *Antonio.*

ANTONIO: *Florinda!* name not those distant Joys, there's not
one thought of her will check my Passion here.

PEDRO: Florinda scorn'd! and all my Hopes defeated of the Possession of Angelica! (*A noise of a Lute above. Antonio gazes up.*) 175
Her Injuries by Heaven he shall not boast of.

(*Song to a Lute above.*)

SONG

When *Damon* first began to love,
He languisht in a soft Desire,
And knew not how the Gods to move,
180   To lessen or increase his Fire,
For *Caelia* in her charming Eyes
    Wore all Love's Sweet, and all his Cruelties.

II

But as beneath a Shade he lay,
Weaving of Flow'rs for *Caelia's* Hair,
185 She chanc'd to lead her Flock that way,
And saw the am'rous Shepherd there.
She gaz'd around upon the Place,
  And saw the Grove (resembling Night)
To all the Joys of Love invite,
190   Whilst guilty Smiles and Blushes drest her Face.
At this the bashful Youth all Transport grew,
And with kind Force he taught the Virgin how
To yield what all his Sighs cou'd never do.

ANTONIO: By Heav'n she's charming fair!

(ANGELICA *throws open the Curtains, and bows to* ANTONIO, *who pulls off his Vizard, and bows and blows up Kisses.* PEDRO *unseen looks in his Face.*)

195 PEDRO: 'Tis he, the false *Antonio!*
ANTONIO: Friend, where must I pay my offering of Love?

(*To the bravo.*)

My Thousand Crowns I mean.
PEDRO: That offering I have design'd to make,
And yours will come too late.
200 ANTONIO: Prithee be gone, I shall grow angry else,
And then thou art not safe.
PEDRO: My Anger may be fatal, Sir, as yours;
And he that enters here may prove this Truth.
ANTONIO: I know not who thou art, but I am sure thou'rt
205 worth my killing, and aiming at *Angelica*.

(*They draw and fight.*)

(*Enter* WILLMORE *and* BLUNT, *who draw and part 'em.*)

BLUNT: 'Sheartlikins, here's fine doings.
WILLMORE: Tilting for the Wench I'm sure—nay gad, if that
wou'd win her, I have as good a Sword as the best of ye—
Put up—put up, and take another time and place, for this
210 is design'd for Lovers only.

(*They all put up.*)

PEDRO: We are prevented; dare you meet me to morrow on the
Molo?
For I've a Title to a better quarrel,
That of *Florinda*, in whose credulous Heart
Thou'st made an Int'rest, and destroy'd my Hopes.
215 ANTONIO: Dare?
I'll meet thee there as early as the Day.

PEDRO: We will come thus disguis'd, that whosoever chance to
get the better, he may escape unknown.
ANTONIO: It shall be so.

(*Exit* PEDRO *and* STEPHANO.)

Who shou'd this Rival be? unless the *English* Colonel, of 220
whom I've often heard Don *Pedro* speak; it must be he, and
time he were removed, who lays a Claim to all my Happiness.

(WILLMORE *having gaz'd all this while on the Picture, pulls down a little one.*)

WILLMORE: This posture's loose and negligent,
The sight on't wou'd beget a warm desire
In Souls, whom Impotence and Age had chill'd. 225
—This must along with me.
BRAVO: What means this rudeness, Sir?—restore the Picture.
ANTONIO: Ha! Rudeness committed to the fair *Angelica!*—
Restore the Picture, Sir.
WILLMORE: Indeed I will not, Sir. 230
ANTONIO: By Heav'n but you shall.
WILLMORE: Nay, do not shew your Sword; if you do, by this
dear Beauty—I will shew mine too.
ANTONIO: What right can you pretend to't?
WILLMORE: That of Possession which I will maintain—you per- 235
haps have 1000 Crowns to give for the Original.
ANTONIO: No matter, Sir, you shall restore the Picture.
ANGELICA: Oh, *Moretta!* what's the matter?

(ANGELICA *and* MORETTA *above.*)

ANTONIO: Or leave your Life behind.
WILLMORE: Death! you lye—I will do neither. 240
ANGELICA: Hold, I command you, if for me you fight.

(*They fight, the Spaniards join with* ANTONIO, BLUNT *laying on like mad. They leave off and bow.*)

WILLMORE: How heavenly fair she is!—ah Plague of her Price.
ANGELICA: You Sir in Buff, you that appear a Soldier, that first
began this Insolence.
WILLMORE: 'Tis true, I did so, if you call it Insolence for a Man 245
to preserve himself; I saw your charming Picture, and was
wounded: quite thro my Soul each pointed Beauty ran; and
wanting a Thousand Crowns to procure my Remedy, I laid
this little Picture to my Bosom—which if you cannot allow
me, I'll resign. 250
ANGELICA: No, you may keep the Trifle.
ANTONIO: You shall first ask my leave, and this.

(*Fight again as before.*)

(*Enter* BELVILE *and* FREDERICK *who join with the English.*)

ANGELICA: Hold; will you ruin me?—*Biskey, Sebastian,* part them.

(*The* SPANIARDS *are beaten off.*)

MORETTA: Oh Madam, we're undone, a pox upon that rude Fellow, he's set on to ruin us: we shall never see good days, till 255
all these fighting poor Rogues are sent to the Gallies.

(*Enter* BELVILE, BLUNT *and* WILLMORE, *with his shirt bloody.*)

BLUNT: 'Sheartlikins, beat me at this Sport, and I'll ne'er wear Sword more.

BELVILE: The Devil's in thee for a mad Fellow, thou art always
260   one at an unlucky Adventure.—Come, let's be gone whilst we're safe, and remember these are *Spaniards,* a sort of People that know how to revenge an Affront.

FREDERICK: *(To* WILLMORE.*)* You bleed; I hope you are not wounded.

265 WILLMORE: Not much:—a plague upon your Dons, if they fight no better they'll ne'er recover *Flanders.*—What the Devil was't to them that I took down the Picture?

BLUNT: Took it! 'Sheartlikins, we'll have the great one too; 'tis ours by Conquest.—Prithee, help me up, and I'll pull it
270   down.—

ANGELICA: Stay, Sir, and e'er you affront me further, let me know how you durst commit this Outrage—To you I speak, Sir, for you appear like a Gentleman.

WILLMORE: To me, Madam?—Gentlemen, your Servant.

(BELVILE stays him.)

275 BELVILE: Is the Devil in thee? Do'st know the danger of entring the house of an incens'd Curtezan?

WILLMORE: I thank you for your care—but there are other matters in hand, there are, tho we have no great Temptation.— Death! let me go.

280 FREDERICK: Yes, to your Lodging, if you will, but not in here.—Damn these gay Harlots—by this Hand I'll have as sound and hansome a Whore for a Patacoone.—Death, Man, she'll murder thee.

WILLMORE: Oh! fear me not, shall I not venture where a Beauty
285   calls? a lovely charming Beauty? for fear of danger! when by Heaven there's none so great as to long for her, whilst I want Money to purchase her.

FREDERICK: Therefore 'tis loss of time, unless you had the thousand Crowns to pay.

290 WILLMORE: It may be she may give a Favour, at least I shall have the pleasure of saluting her when I enter, and when I depart.

BELVILE: Pox, she'll as soon lie with thee, as kiss thee, and sooner stab than do either—you shall not go.

ANGELICA: Fear not, Sir, all I have to wound with, is my Eyes.

295 BLUNT: Let him go, 'Sheartlikins, I believe the Gentlewoman means well.

BELVILE: Well, take thy Fortune, we'll expect you in the next Street.—Farewell Fool,—farewell—

WILLMORE: B'ye Colonel—

(Goes in.)

300 FREDERICK: The Rogue's stark mad for a Wench.

(Exeunt.)

SCENE II

A Fine Chamber.

Enter WILLMORE, ANGELICA, *and* MORETTA.

ANGELICA: Insolent, Sir, how durst you pull down my Picture?
WILLMORE: Rather, how durst you set it up, to tempt poor

amorous Mortals with so much Excellence? which I find you have but too well consulted by the unmerciful price you set upon't.—Is all this Heaven of Beauty shewn to 5 move Despair in those that cannot buy? and can you think the effects of that Despair shou'd be less extravagant than I have shewn?

ANGELICA: I sent for you to ask my Pardon, Sir, not to aggravate your Crime.—I thought I shou'd have seen you at my 10 Feet imploring it.

WILLMORE: You are deceived, I came to rail at you, and talk such Truths, too, as shall let you see the Vanity of that Pride, which taught you how to set such a Price on Sin. For such it is, whilst that which is Love's due is meanly barter'd for. 15

ANGELICA: Ha, ha, ha, alas, good Captain, what pity 'tis your edifying Doctrine will do no good upon me—*Moretta,* fetch the Gentleman a Glass, and let him survey himself, to see what Charms he has,—*(Aside in a soft tone.)* and guess my Business. 20

MORETTA: He knows himself of old, I believe those Breeches and he have been acquainted ever since he was beaten at *Worcester.*

ANGELICA: Nay, do not abuse the poor Creature.—

MORETTA: Good Weather-beaten Corporal, will you march off? 25 we have no need of your Doctrine, tho you have of our Charity; but at present we have no Scraps, we can afford no kindness for God's sake; in fine, Sirrah, the Price is too high i'th' Mouth for you, therefore troop, I say.

WILLMORE: Here, good Fore-Woman of the Shop, serve me, and 30 I'll be gone.

MORETTA: Keep it to pay your Landress, your Linen stinks of the Gun-Room; for here's no selling by Retail.

WILLMORE: Thou hast sold plenty of thy stale Ware at a cheap Rate. 35

MORETTA: Ay, the more silly kind Heart I, but this is an Age wherein Beauty is at higher Rates.—In fine, you know the price of this.

WILLMORE: I grant you 'tis here set down a thousand Crowns a Month—Baud, take your black Lead and sum it up, that I 40 may have a Pistole-worth of these vain gay things, and I'll trouble you no more.

MORETTA: Pox on him, he'll fret me to Death:—abominable Fellow, I tell thee, we only sell by the whole Piece.

WILLMORE: 'Tis very hard, the whole Cargo or nothing—Faith, 45 Madam, my Stock will not reach it, I cannot be your Chapman.—Yet I have Countrymen in Town, Merchants of Love, like me; I'll see if they'll put for a share, we cannot lose much by it, and what we have no use for, we'll sell upon the *Friday's* Mart, at—*Who gives more?* I am studying, Madam, 50 how to purchase you, tho at present I am unprovided of Money.

ANGELICA: Sure, this from any other Man would anger me— nor shall he know the Conquest he has made—Poor angry Man, how I despise this railing. 55

WILLMORE: Yes, I am poor—but I'm a Gentleman,
And one that scorns this Baseness which you practise.
Poor as I am, I would not sell my self,
No, not to gain your charming high-priz'd Person.

---

282 **Patacoone** a Spanish coin

41 **Pistole** a gold coin

60   Tho I admire you strangely for your Beauty,
      Yet I contemn your Mind.
      —And yet I wou'd at any rate enjoy you;
      At your own rate—but cannot—See here
      The only Sum I can command on Earth;
65   I know not where to eat when this is gone:
      Yet such a Slave I am to Love and Beauty,
      This last reserve I'll sacrifice to enjoy you.
      —Nay, do not frown, I know you are to be bought,
      And wou'd be bought by me, by me,
70   For a mean trifling Sum, if I could pay it down.
      Which happy knowledge I will still repeat,
      And lay it to my Heart, it has a Virtue in't,
      And soon will cure those Wounds your Eyes have made.
      —And yet—there's something so divinely powerful there—
75   Nay, I will gaze—to let you see my Strength.

(Holds her, looks on her, and pauses and sighs.)

      By Heaven, bright Creature—I would not for the World
      Thy Fame were half so fair as thy Face.

(Turns her away from him.)

      ANGELICA: *(Aside.)* His words go thro me to the very Soul.
          —If you have nothing else to say to me.
80   WILLMORE: Yes, you shall hear how infamous you are—
          For which I do not hate thee:
          But that secures my Heart, and all the Flames it feels
          Are but so many Lusts,
          I know it by their sudden bold intrusion.
85   The Fire's impatient and betrays, 'tis false—
          For had it been the purer Flame of Love,
          I should have pin'd and languish'd at your Feet,
          E'er found the Impudence to have discover'd it.
          I now dare stand your Scorn, and your Denial.
90   MORETTA: Sure she's bewitcht, that you can stand thus tamely,
          and hear his saucy railing.—Sirrah, will you be gone?
      ANGELICA: How dare you take this liberty?—*(To* MORETTA.*)*
          Withdraw.—Pray, tell me, Sir, are not you guilty of the
          same mercenary Crime? When a Lady is proposed to you for
95   a Wife, you never ask, how fair, discreet, or virtuous she is;
          but what's her Fortune—which if but small, you cry—She
          will not do my business—and basely leave her, tho she lan-
          guish for you.—Say, is not this as poor?
      WILLMORE: It is a barbarous Custom, which I will scorn to de-
100   fend in our Sex, and do despise in yours.
      ANGELICA: Thou art a brave Fellow! put up thy Gold, and know
          That were thy Fortune large, as is thy Soul,
          Thou shouldst not buy my Love,
          Couldst thou forget those mean Effects of Vanity,
105   Which set me out to sale; and as a Lover, prize
          My yielding Joys.
          Canst thou believe they'l be entirely thine,
          Without considering they were mercenary?
      WILLMORE: *(Aside.)* I cannot tell, I must bethink me first—ha,
110   Death, I'm going to believe her.
      ANGELICA: Prithee, confirm that Faith—or if thou canst not—
          flatter me a little, 'twill please me from thy Mouth.
      WILLMORE: Curse on thy charming Tongue! dost thou return
          My feign'd Contempt with so much subtilty?

(Aside.)

      Thou'st found the easiest way into my Heart,   115
      Tho I yet know that all thou say'st is false.

(Turning from her in a Rage.)

ANGELICA: By all that's good 'tis real,
      I never lov'd before, tho oft a Mistress.
      —Shall my first Vows be slighted?
WILLMORE: *(Aside.)* What can she mean?   120
ANGELICA: *(In an angry tone.)* I find you cannot credit me.
WILLMORE: I know you take me for an errant Ass,
      An Ass that may be sooth'd into Belief,
      And then be us'd at pleasure.
      —But, Madam, I have been so often cheated   125
      By perjur'd, soft, deluding Hypocrites,
      That I've no Faith left for the cozening Sex,
      Especially for Women of your Trade.
ANGELICA: The low esteem you have of me, perhaps
      May bring my Heart again: 130
      For I have Pride that yet surmounts my Love.

(She turns with Pride, he holds her.)

WILLMORE: Throw off this Pride, this Enemy to Bliss,
      And shew the Power of Love: 'tis with those Arms
      I can be only vanquisht, made a Slave.
ANGELICA: Is all my mighty Expectation vanisht?   135
      —No, I will not hear thee talk,—thou hast a Charm
      In every word, that draws my Heart away.
      And all the thousand Trophies I design'd,
      Thou hast undone—Why are thou soft?
      Thy Looks are bravely rough, and meant for War.   140
      Could thou not storm on still?
      I then perhaps had been as free as thou.
WILLMORE: *(Aside.)* Death! how she throws her Fire about my
          Soul!
      —Take heed, fair Creature, how you raise my Hopes,
      Which once assum'd pretend to all Dominion.   145
      There's not a Joy thou hast in store
      I shall not then command:
      For which I'll pay thee back my Soul, my Life.
      Come, let's begin th' account this happy minute.
ANGELICA: And will you pay me then the Price I ask?   150
WILLMORE: Oh, why dost thou draw me from an awful
          Worship,
      By shewing thou art no Divinity?
      Conceal the Fiend, and shew me all the Angel;
      Keep me but ignorant, and I'll be devout,
      And pay my Vows for ever at this Shrine.   155

(Kneels, and kisses her Hand.)

ANGELICA: The Pay I mean is but thy Love for mine.—Can you
      give that?
WILLMORE: Intirely—come, let's withdraw: where I'll renew
      my vows,—and breathe 'em with such Ardour, thou shalt
      not doubt my Zeal.   160
ANGELICA: Thou hast a Power too strong to be resisted.

(Exit WILLMORE *and* ANGELICA.*)*

MORETTA: Now my Curse go with you—Is all our Project fallen to this? to love the only Enemy to our Trade? Nay, to love such a Shameroon, a very Beggar; nay, a Pirate-Beggar, whose Business is to rifle and be gone, a No-Purchase, No-Pay Tatterdemalion, an English Piccaroon; a Rogue that fights for daily Drink, and takes a Pride in being loyally lousy—Oh, I could curse now, if I durst—This is the Fate of most Whores.

Trophies, which from believing Fops we win,
Are Spoils to those who cozen us again.

──────── ACT THREE ────────

SCENE I

A Street.

Enter FLORINDA, VALERIA, HELLENA, *in Antick different Dresses from what they were in before,* CALLIS *attending.*

FLORINDA: I wonder what should make my Brother in so ill a Humour: I hope he has not found out our Ramble this Morning.

HELLENA: No, if he had, we should have heard on't at both Ears, and have been mew'd up this Afternoon; which I would not for the World should have happen'd—Hey ho! I'm sad as a Lover's Lute.

VALERIA: Well, methinks we have learnt this Trade of Gipsies as readily as if we had been bred upon the Road to *Loretto:* and yes I did so fumble, when I told the Stranger his Fortune, that I was afraid I should have told my own and yours by mistake—But methinks *Hellena* has been very serious ever since.

FLORINDA: I would give my Garters she were in love, to be reveng'd upon her, for abusing me—How is't, *Hellena?*

HELLENA: Ah!—would I had never seen my mad Monsieur—and yet for all your laughing I am not in love—and yet this small Acquaintance, o'my Conscience, will never out of my Head.

VALERIA: Ha, ha, ha—I laugh to think how thou art fitted with a Lover, a Fellow that, I warrant, loves every new Face he sees.

HELLENA: Hum—he has not kept his Word with me here—and may be taken up—that thought is not very pleasant to me—what the Duce should this be now that I feel?

VALERIA: What is't like?

HELLENA: Nay, the Lord knows—but if I should be hanged, I cannot chuse but be angry and afraid, when I think that mad Fellow should be in love with any Body but me—What to think of my self I know not—Would I could meet with some true damn'd Gipsy, that I might know my Fortune.

VALERIA: Know it! why there's nothing so easy; thou wilt love this wandering Inconstant till thou find'st thy self hanged about his Neck, and then be as mad to get free again.

FLORINDA: Yes, *Valeria;* we shall see her bestride his Baggage-horse, and follow him to the Campaign.

HELLENA: So, so; now you are provided for, there's no care taken of poor me—But since you have set my Heart a wishing, I am resolv'd to know for what. I will not die of the Pip, so I will not.

────────────

164 shameroon a trickster, a cozening rascal

FLORINDA: Art thou mad to talk so? Who will like thee well enough to have thee, that hears what a mad Wench thou art?

HELLENA: Like me! I don't intend every he that likes me shall have me, but he that I like: I shou'd have staid in the Nunnery still, if I had lik'd my Lady Abbess as well as she lik'd me. No, I came thence, not (as my wise Brother imagines) to take an eternal Farewel of the World, but to love and to be belov'd; and I will be belov'd, or I'll get one of your Men, so I will.

VALERIA: Am I put into the Number of Lovers?

HELLENA: You! my Couz, I know thou art too good natur'd to leave us in any Design: Thou wou't venture a Cast, tho thou comest off a Loser, especially with such a Gamester—I observ'd your Man, and your willing ears incline that way; and if you are not a Lover, 'tis an Art soon learnt—that I find.

(Sighs.)

FLORINDA: I wonder how you learnt to love so easily, I had a thousand Charms to meet my Eyes and Ears, e'er I cou'd yield; and 'twas the knowledge of *Belvile's* Merit, not the surprising Person, took my Soul—Thou art too rash to give a Heart at first sight.

HELLENA: Hang your considering Lover; I ne'er thought beyond the Fancy, that 'twas a very pretty, idle, silly kind of Pleasure to pass ones time with, to write little, soft, nonsensical Billets, and with great difficulty and danger receive Answers; in which I shall have my Beauty prais'd, my Wit admir'd (tho little or none) and have the Vanity and Power to know I am desirable; then I have the more Inclination that way, because I am to be a Nun, and so shall not be suspected to have any such earthly Thoughts about me—But when I walk thus—and sigh thus—they'll think my Mind's upon my Monastery, and cry, how happy 'tis she's so resolv'd!—But not a Word of Man.

FLORINDA: What a mad Creature's this!

HELLENA: I'll warrant, if my Brother hears either of you sigh, he cries (gravely)—I fear you have the Indiscretion to be in love, but take heed of the Honour of our House, and your own unspotted Fame; and so he conjures on till he has laid the soft-wing'd God in your Hearts, or broke the Birdsnest—But see here comes your Lover: but where's my inconstant? let's stop aside, and we may learn something.

(Go aside.)

(Enter BELVILE, FREDERICK, *and* BLUNT.*)*

BELVILE: What means this? the Picture's taken in.

BLUNT: It may be the Wench is good-natur'd, and will be kind *gratis.* Your Friend's a proper handsom Fellow.

BELVILE: I rather think she has cut his Throat and is fled: I am mad he should throw himself into Dangers—Pox on't, I shall want him to night—let's knock and ask for him.

HELLENA: My heart goes a-pit a-pat, for fear 'tis my Man they talk of.

(Knock, MORETTA *above.)*

MORETTA: What would you have?

BELVILE: Tell the Stranger that enter'd here about two Hours ago, that his Friends stay here for him.

90 MORETTA: A Curse upon him for *Moretta,* would he were at the Devil—but he's coming to you.

(Enter WILLMORE.*)*

HELLENA: I, I, 'tis he. Oh how this vexes me.

BELVILE: And how, and how, dear Lad, has Fortune smil'd? Are we to break her Windows, or raise up Altars to her! hah!

95 WILLMORE: Does not my Fortune sit triumphant on my Brow? dost not see the little wanton God there all gay and smil- ing? have I not an Air about my Face and Eyes, that distin- guish me from the Croud of common Lovers? By Heav'n, *Cupid's* Quiver has not half so many Darts as her Eyes—Oh

100 such a Bona Roba, to sleep in her Arms is lying in Fresco, all perfum'd Air about me.

HELLENA: *(Aside.)* Here's fine encouragement for me to fool on.

WILLMORE: Hark ye, where didst thou purchase that rich Canary we drank to-day? Tell me, that I may adore the Spigot, and

105 sacrifice to the Butt: the Juice was divine, into which I must dip my Rosary, and then bless all things that I would have bold and fortunate.

BELVILE: Well, Sir, let's go take a Bottle, and hear the Story of your Success.

110 FREDERICK: Would not *French* Wine do better?

WILLMORE: Damn the hungry Balderdash; cheerful Sack has a generous Virtue in't, inspiring a successful Confidence, gives Eloquence to the Tongue, and Vigour to the Soul; and has in a few Hours compleated all my Hopes and Wishes. There's

115 nothing left to raise a new Desire in me—Come let's be gay and wanton—and, Gentlemen, study, study what you want, for here are Friends,—that will supply, Gentlemen,—hark! what a charming sound they make—'tis he and she Gold whilst here, shall beget new Pleasures every moment.

120 BLUNT: But hark ye, Sir, you are not married, are you?

WILLMORE: All the Honey of Matrimony, but none of the Sting, Friend.

BLUNT: 'Sheartlikins, thou'rt a fortunate Rogue.

WILLMORE: I am so, Sir, let these inform you.—Ha, how

125 sweetly they chime! Pox of Poverty, it makes a Man a Slave, makes Wit and Honour sneak, my Soul grew lean and rusty for want of Credit.

BLUNT: 'Sheartlikins, this I like well, it looks like my lucky Bargain! Oh how I long for the Approach of my Squire, that

130 is to conduct me to her House again. Why! here's two pro- vided for.

FREDERICK: By this light y're happy Men.

BLUNT: Fortune is pleased to smile on us, Gentlemen,—to smile on us.

(Enter SANCHO, *and pulls* BLUNT *by the Sleeve. They go aside.)*

135 SANCHO: Sir, my Lady expects you—she has remov'd all that might oppose your Will and Pleasure—and is impatient till you come.

BLUNT: Sir, I'll attend you—Oh the happiest Rogue! I'll take no leave, lest they either dog me, or stay me.

(Exit with SANCHO.*)*

140 BELVILE: But then the little Gipsy is forgot?

WILLMORE: A Mischief on thee for putting her into my thoughts; I had quite forgot her else, and this Night's Debauch had drunk her quite down.

HELLENA: Had it so, good Captain?

(Claps him on the Back.)

WILLMORE: Ha! I hope she did not hear. 145

HELLENA: What, afraid of such a Champion!

WILLMORE: Oh! you're a fine Lady of your word, are you not? to make a Man languish a whole day—

HELLENA: In tedious search of me.

WILLMORE: Egad, Child, thou'rt in the right, hadst thou seen 150 what a melancholy Dog I have been ever since I was a Lover, how I have walkt the Streets like a *Capuchin,* with my Hands in my Sleeves—Faith, Sweetheart, thou wouldst pity me.

HELLENA: Now, if I should be hang'd, I can't be angry with him, he dissembles so heartily—Alas, good Captain, what 155 pains you have taken—Now were I ungrateful not to re- ward so true a Servant.

WILLMORE: Poor Soul! that's kindly said, I see thou bearest a Conscience—come then for a beginning shew me thy dear Face. 160

HELLENA: I'm afraid, my small Acquaintance, you have been staying that swinging stomach you boasted of this morn- ing; I remember then my little Collation would have gone down with you, without the Sauce of a handsom Face—Is your Stomach so quesy now? 165

WILLMORE: Faith long fasting, Child, spoils a Man's Appetite— yet if you durst treat, I could so lay about me still.

HELLENA: And would you fall to, before a Priest says Grace?

WILLMORE: Oh fie, fie, what an old out-of-fashion'd thing hast thou nam'd? Thou could'st not dash me more out of Coun- 170 tenance, shouldst thou shew me an ugly Face.

(Whilst he is seemingly courting HELLENA, *enter* ANGELICA, MORETTA, BISKEY, *and* SEBASTIAN, *all in Masquerade:* ANGELICA *sees* WILLMORE *and starts.)*

ANGELICA: Heavens, is't he? and passionately fond to see an- other Woman?

MORETTA: What cou'd you expect less from such a Swaggerer?

ANGELICA: Expect! as much as I paid him, a Heart intire, 175 Which I had pride enough to think when e'er I gave It would have rais'd the Man above the Vulgar, Made him all Soul, and that all soft and constant.

HELLENA: You see, Captain, how willing I am to be Friends with you, till Time and Ill-luck make us Lovers; and ask 180 you the Question first, rather than put your Modesty to the blush, by asking me: for alas, I know you Captains are such strict Men, severe Observers of your Vows to Chastity, that 'twill be hard to prevail with your tender Conscience to marry a young willing Maid. 185

WILLMORE: Do not abuse me, for fear I should take thee at thy word, and marry thee indeed, which I'm sure will be Re- venge sufficient.

HELLENA: O' my Conscience, that will be our Destiny, because we are both of one humour; I am as inconstant as you, for I 190 have considered, Captain, that a handsom Woman has a great deal to do whilst her Face is good, for then is our Harvest- time to gather Friends; and should I in these days of my Youth, catch a fit of foolish Constancy, I were undone; 'tis loitering by day-light in our great Journey: therefore declare, 195 I'll allow but one year for Love, one year for Indifference, and one year for Hate—and then—go hang your self—for I

profess myself the gay, the kind, and the inconstant—the
Devil's in't if this won't please you.

200 WILLMORE: Oh most damnably!—I have a Heart with a hole
quite thro it too, no Prison like mine to keep a Mistress in.

ANGELICA: *(Aside.)* Purjur'd Man! how I believe thee now!

HELLENA: Well, I see our Business as well as Humours are alike,
yours to cozen as many Maids as will trust you, and I as
205 many Men as have Faith—See if I have not as desperate a
lying look, as you can have for the heart of you.

(Pulls off her Vizard; he starts.)

—How do you like it, Captain?

WILLMORE: Like it! by Heav'n, I never saw so much Beauty. Oh
the Charms of those sprightly black Eyes, that strangely fair
210 Face, full of Smiles and Dimples! those soft round melting
cherry Lips! and small even white Teeth! not to be exprest,
but silently adored!—Oh one Look more, and strike me
dumb, or I shall repeat nothing else till I am mad.

(He seems to court her to pull off her Vizard: she refuses.)

ANGELICA: I can endure no more—nor is it fit to interrupt him;
215 for if I do, my Jealousy has so destroy'd my Reason,—I shall
undo him—Therefore I'll retire. And you *Sebastian (To one
of her bravoes.)* follow that Woman, and learn who 'tis; *(To
the other bravo.)* while you tell the Fugitive, I would speak to
him instantly.

(Exit.)

(This while FLORINDA *is talking to* BELVILE, *who stands sullenly.*
FREDERICK *courting* VALERIA.*)*

220 VALERIA: Prithee, dear Stranger, be not so sullen; for tho you
have lost your Love, you see my Friend frankly offers you
hers, to play with in the mean time.

BELVILE: Faith, Madam, I am sorry I can't play at her Game.

FREDERICK: Pray leave your Intercession, and mind your own
225 Affair, they'll better agree apart; he's a model Sigher in
Company, but alone no Woman escapes him.

FLORINDA: Sure he does but rally—yet if it should be true—I'll
tempt him farther—Believe me, noble Stranger, I'm no
common Mistress—and for a little proof on't—wear this
230 Jewel—nay, take it, Sir, 'tis right, and Bills of Exchange
may sometimes miscarry.

BELVILE: Madam, why am I chose out of all Mankind to be the
Object of your Bounty?

VALERIA: There's another civil Question askt.

235 FREDERICK: Pox of's Modesty, it spoils his own Markets, and
hinders mine.

FLORINDA: Sir, from my Window I have often seen you; and
Women of Quality have so few opportunities for Love, that
we ought to lose none.

240 FREDERICK: Ay, this is something! here's a Woman!—When
shall I be blest with so much kindness from your fair
Mouth? *(Aside to* BELVILE.*)* Take the Jewel, Fool.

BELVILE: You tempt me strangely, Madam, every way.

FLORINDA: *(Aside.)* So, if I find him false, my whole Repose is
245 gone.

BELVILE: And but for a Vow I've made to a very fine Lady, this
Goodness had subdu'd me.

FREDERICK: Pox on't be kind, in pity to me be kind, for I am to
thrive here but as you treat her Friend.

HELLENA: Tell me what did you in yonder House, and I'll un- 250
masque.

WILLMORE: Yonder House—oh—I went to—a—to—why,
there's a Friend of mine lives there.

HELLENA: What a she, or a he Friend?

WILLMORE: A Man upon my Honour! a Man—A she Friend! 255
no, no, Madam, you have done my Business, I thank you.

HELLENA: And was't your Man Friend, that had more Darts in's
Eyes than *Cupid* carries in a whole Budget of Arrows?

WILLMORE: So—

HELLENA: Ah such a *Bona Roba:* to be in her Arms is lying in 260
Fresco, all perfumed Air about me—Was this your Man
Friend too?

WILLMORE: So—

HELLENA: That gave you the He, and the She—Gold, that
begets young Pleasures. 265

WILLMORE: Well, well, Madam, then you see there are Ladies in
the World, that will not be cruel—there are, Madam, there
are—

HELLENA: And there be Men too as fine, wild, inconstant Fellows as your self, there be, Captain, there be, if you go to 270
that now—therefore I'm resolv'd—

WILLMORE: Oh!

HELLENA: To see your Face no more—

WILLMORE: Oh!

HELLENA: Till to morrow. 275

WILLMORE: Egad you frighted me.

HELLENA: Nor then neither, unless you'l swear never to see that
Lady more.

WILLMORE: See her!—why! never to think of Womankind
again? 280

HELLENA: Kneel, and swear.

(Kneels, she gives him her hand.)

WILLMORE: I do, never to think—to see—to love—nor lie with
any but thy self.

HELLENA: Kiss the Book.

WILLMORE: Oh, most religiously. 285

(Kisses her Hand.)

HELLENA: Now what a wicked Creature am I, to damn a proper
Fellow.

CALLIS: *(To* FLORINDA.*)* Madam, I'll stay no longer, 'tis e'en dark.

FLORINDA: However, Sir, I'll leave this with you—that when
I'm gone, you may repent the opportunity you have lost by 290
your modesty.

*(Gives him the Jewel, which is her Picture, and Exits. He gazes
after her.)*

WILLMORE: 'Twill be an Age till to morrow,—and till then I
will most impatiently expect you—Adieu, my dear pretty
Angel.

(Exeunt all the WOMEN.*)*

BELVILE: Ha! *Florinda's* Picture! 'twas she her self—what a dull 295
Dog was I? I would have given the World for one minute's
discourse with her.—

FREDERICK: This comes of your Modesty,—ah pox on your Vow,
'twas ten to one but we had lost the Jewel by't.

300 BELVILE: *Willmore!* the blessed'st Opportunity lost!—*Florinda,*
Friends, *Florinda!*
WILLMORE: Ah Rogue! such black Eyes, such a Face, such a
Mouth, such Teeth,—and so much Wit!
BELVILE: All, all, and a thousand Charms besides.
305 WILLMORE: Why, dost thou know her?
BELVILE: Know her! ay, ay, and a Pox take me with all my Heart
for being modest.
WILLMORE: But hark ye, Friend of mine, are you my Rival? and
have I been only beating the Bush all this while?
310 BELVILE: I understand thee not—I'm mad—see here—

(Shews the Picture.)

WILLMORE: Ha! whose Picture is this?—'tis a fine Wench.
FREDERICK: The Colonel's Mistress, Sir.
WILLMORE: Oh, oh, here—I thought it had been another
Prize—come, come, a Bottle will set thee right again.

(Gives the Picture back.)

315 BELVILE: I am content to try, and by that time 'twill be late
enough for our Design.
WILLMORE: Agreed.

Love does all day the Soul's great Empire keep,
But Wine at night lulls the soft God asleep.

(Exeunt.)

SCENE II

LUCETTA's House.

Enter BLUNT *and* LUCETTA *with a Light.*

LUCETTA: Now we are safe and free, no fears of the coming
home of my old jealous Husband, which made me a little
thoughtful when you came in first—but now Love is all the
business of my Soul.
5 BLUNT: *(Aside.)* I am transported—Pox on't, that I had but
some fine things to say to her, such as Lovers use—I was a
Fool not to learn of *Frederick* a little by Heart before I
came—something I must say.—'Sheartlikins, sweet Soul,
I am not us'd to complement, but I'm an honest Gentle-
10 man, and thy humble Servant.
LUCETTA: I have nothing to pay for so great a Favour, but such
a Love as cannot but be great, since at first sight of that
sweet Face and Shape it made me your absolute Captive.
BLUNT: *(Aside.)* Kind heart, how prettily she talks! Egad I'll
15 show her Husband a *Spanish* Trick; send him out of the
World, and marry her: she's damnably in love with me, and
will ne'er mind Settlements, and so there's that sav'd.
LUCETTA: Well, Sir, I'll go and undress me, and be with you
instantly.
20 BLUNT: Make haste then, for 'dsheartlikins, dear Soul, thou
canst not guess at the pain of a longing Lover, when his Joys
are drawn within the compass of a few minutes.
LUCETTA: You speak my Sense, and I'll make haste to provide it.

(Exit.)

BLUNT: 'Tis a rare Girl, and this one night's enjoyment with her 25
will be worth all the days I ever past in Essex.—Would she'd
go with me into *England,* tho' to say truth, there's plenty of
Whores there already.—But a pox on 'em they are such mer-
cenary prodigal Whores, that they want such a one as this,
that's free and generous, to give 'em good Examples:— 30
Why, what a House she has! how rich and fine!

(Enter SANCHO.*)*

SANCHO: Sir, my Lady has sent me to conduct you to her
Chamber.
BLUNT: Sir, I shall be proud to follow—Here's one of her Servants too: 'dsheartlikins, by his Garb and Gravity he might 35
be a Justice of Peace in *Essex,* and is but a Pimp here.

(Exeunt.)

(The Scene changes to a Chamber with an Alcove-Bed in it, a Table,
&c. LUCETTA *in Bed. Enter* SANCHO *and* BLUNT, *who takes the*
Candle of SANCHO *at the Door.)*

SANCHO: Sir, my Commission reaches no farther.
BLUNT: Sir, I'll excuse your Complement:—what, in Bed, my
sweet Mistress?
LUCETTA: You see, I still out-do you in kindness. 40
BLUNT: And thou shalt see what haste I'll make to quit scores—
oh the luckiest Rogue!

(Undresses himself.)

LUCETTA: Shou'd you be false or cruel now!
BLUNT: False, 'Sheartlikins, what dost thou take me for a *Jew?*
an insensible Heathen,—A Pox of thy old jealous Husband: 45
and he were dead, egad, sweet Soul, it shou'd be none of my
fault, if I did not marry thee.
LUCETTA: It never shou'd be mine.
BLUNT: Good Soul, I'm the fortunatest Dog!
LUCETTA: Are you not undrest yet? 50
BLUNT: As much as my Impatience will permit.

(Goes towards the Bed in his Shirt and Drawers.)

LUCETTA: Hold, Sir, put out the Light, it may betray us else.
BLUNT: Any thing, I need no other Light but that of thine
Eyes!—*(Aside.)* 'sheartlikins, there I think I had it.

(Puts out the Candle, the Bed descends, he gropes about to find it.)

—Why—why—where am I got? what, not yet?—where are 55
your sweetest?—ah, the Rogue's silent now—a pretty Love-
trick this—how she'll laugh at me anon!—you need not,
my dear Rogue! you need not! I'm all on a fire already—
come, come, now call me in for pity—Sure I'm enchanted!
I have been round the Chamber, and can find neither 60
Woman, nor Bed—I lockt the Door, I'm sure she cannot go
that way; or if she cou'd, the Bed cou'd not—Enough,
enough, my pretty Wanton, do not carry the Jest too far—
Ha, betray'd! Dogs! Rogues! Pimps! help! help!

(Lights on a Trap, and is let down. Enter LUCETTA, PHILIPPO, *and*
SANCHO *with a Light.)*

65 PHILIPPO: Ha, ha, ha, he's dispatcht finely.

LUCETTA: Now, Sir, had I been coy, we had mist of this Booty.

PHILIPPO: Nay when I saw 'twas a substantial Fool, I was mol-
lified; but when you doat upon a Serenading Coxcomb,
upon a Face, fine Clothes, and a Lute, it makes me rage.

70 LUCETTA: You know I never was guilty of that Folly, my dear
Philippo, but with your self—But come let's see what we
have got by this.

PHILIPPO: A rich Coat!—Sword and Hat!—these Breeches
too—are well lin'd!—see here a Gold Watch!—a Purse—

75 ha! Gold!—at least two hundred Pistoles! a bunch of Dia-
mond Rings; and one with the Family Arms!—a Gold
Box!—with a Medal of his King! and his Lady Mother's
Picture!—these were sacred Reliques, believe me!—see, the
Wasteband of his Breeches have a Mine of Gold!—Old

80 Queen *Bess's.* We have a Quarrel to her ever since Eighty
Eight, and may therefore justify the Theft, the Inquisition
might have committed it.

LUCETTA: See, a Bracelet of bow'd Gold, these his Sister ty'd
about his Arm at parting—but well—for all this, I fear his

85 being a Stranger may make a noise, and hinder our Trade
with them hereafter.

PHILIPPO: That's our security; he is not only a Stranger to us,
but to the Country too—the Common-Shore into which he
is descended, thou know'st, conducts him into another

90 Street, which this Light will hinder him from ever finding
again—he knows neither your Name, nor the Street where
your House is, nay, nor the way to his own Lodgings.

LUCETTA: And art not thou an unmerciful Rogue, not to afford
him one Night for all this?—I should not have been such

95 a *Jew.*

PHILIPPO: Blame me not, *Lucetta,* to keep as much of thee as I
can to my self—come, that thought makes me wanton,—
let's to Bed,—*Sancho,* lock up these.

This is the Fleece which Fools do bear,
100 *Design'd for witty Men to sheer.*

(Exeunt.)

(The Scene changes, and discovers BLUNT, *creeping out of a Common
Shore, his Face, &c., all dirty.)*

BLUNT: Oh Lord!

(Climbing up.)

I am got out at last, and (which is a Miracle) without a
Clue—and now to Damning and Cursing—but if that would
ease me, where shall I begin? with my Fortune, my self, or
105 the Quean that cozen'd me—What a dog was I to believe in
Women! Oh Coxcomb—ignorant conceited Coxcomb! to
fancy she cou'd be enamour'd with my Person, at the first
sight enamour'd—Oh, I'm a cursed Puppy, 'tis plain, Fool
was writ upon my Forehead, she perceiv'd it,—saw the *Essex*
110 Calf there—for what Allurements could there be in this
Countenance? which I can indure, because I'm acquainted
with it—Oh, dull silly Dog! to be thus sooth'd into a Cozening! Had I been drunk, I might fondly have credited the

---

83 **bow'd Gold** *bowed* is still used in the North of England for
bent: 'a bowed pin'

---

young Quean! but as I was in my right Wits, to be thus
cheated, confirms I am a dull believing *English* Country   115
Fop.—But my Comrades! Death and the Devil, there's the
worst of all—then a Ballad will be sung to Morrow on the
Prado, to a lousy Tune of the enchanted Squire, and the anni-
hilated Damsel—But *Frederick* that Rogue, and the Colonel,
will abuse me beyond all Christian patience—had she left me   120
my Clothes, I have a Bill of Exchange at home wou'd have
sav'd my Credit—but now all hope is taken from me—Well,
I'll home (if I can find the way) with this Consolation, that I
am not the first kind believing Coxcomb; but there are, Gallants, many such good Natures amongst ye.   125

And tho you've better Arts to hide your Follies,
Adsheartlikins y'are all as errant Cullies.

SCENE III

The Garden, in the Night.

Enter FLORINDA, *undress'd, with a Key, and a little Box.*

FLORINDA: Well, thus far I'm in my way to Happiness; I have got
my self free from *Callis;* my Brother too, I find by yonder
light, is gone into his Cabinet, and thinks not of me: I have
by good Fortune got the Key of the Garden Back-door,—I'll
open it, to prevent *Belvile's* knocking,—a little noise will   5
now alarm my Brother. Now am I as fearful as a young Thief.
(Unlocks the Door.)—Hark,—what noise is that?—Oh, 'twas
the Wind that plaid amongst the Boughs.—*Belvile* stays
long, methinks—it's time—stay—for fear of a surprize, I'll
hide these Jewels in yonder Jessamin.   10

(She goes to lay down the Box.)

(Enter WILLMORE *drunk.)*

WILLMORE: What the Devil is become of these Fellows, *Belvile*
and *Frederick?* They promis'd to stay at the next corner for
me, but who the Devil knows the corner of a full Moon?—
Now—whereabouts am I?—hah—what have we here? a
Garden!—a very convenient place to sleep in—hah—what   15
has God sent us here?—a Female—by this light, a Woman;
I'm a Dog if it be not a very Wench.—

FLORINDA: He's come!—hah—who's there?

WILLMORE: Sweet Soul, let me salute thy Shoe-string.

FLORINDA: 'Tis not my *Belvile*—good Heavens, I know him   20
not.—Who are you, and from whence come you!

WILLMORE: Prithee,—prithee, Child—not so many hard Questions—let it suffice I am here, Child—Come, come kiss me.

FLORINDA: Good Gods! what luck is mine?

WILLMORE: Only good luck, Child, parlous good luck.—Come   25
hither,—'tis a delicate shining Wench,—by this Hand she's
perfum'd, and smells like any Nosegay.—Prithee, dear Soul,
let's not play the Fool, and lose time,—precious time—for
as Gad shall save me, I'm as honest a Fellow as breathes, tho
I am a little disguis'd at present.—Come, I say,—why, thou   30
may'st be free with me, I'll be very secret. I'll not boast who
'twas oblig'd me, not I—for hang me if I know thy Name.

---

30 **disguis'd** a common phrase for drunk

FLORINDA: Heavens! what a filthy beast is this!

WILLMORE: I am so, and thou oughtst the sooner to lie with me
35   for that reason,—for look you, Child, there will be no Sin
in't, because 'twas neither design'd nor premeditated; 'tis
pure Accident on both sides—that's a certain thing now—
Indeed should I make love to you, and you vow Fidelity—
and swear and lye till you believ'd and yielded—Thou art
40   therefore (as thou art a good Christian) oblig'd in Conscience to deny me nothing. Now—come, be kind, without
any more idle prating.

FLORINDA: Oh, I am ruin'd—wicked Man, unhand me.

WILLMORE: Wicked! Egad, Child, a Judge, were he young and
45   vigorous, and saw those Eyes of thine, would know 'twas
they gave the first blow—the first provocation.—Come,
prithee let's lose no time, I say—this is a fine convenient
place.

FLORINDA: Sir, let me go, I conjure you, or I'll call out.

50 WILLMORE: Ay, ay, you were best to call Witness to see how
finely you treat me—do.—

FLORINDA: I'll cry Murder, Rape, or any thing, if you do not instantly let me go.

WILLMORE: A Rape! Come, come, you lye, you Baggage, you
55   lye: What, I'll warrant you would fain have the World believe now that you are not so forward as I. No, not you,—
why at this time of Night was your Cobweb-door set open,
dear Spider—but to catch Flies?—Hah come—or I shall be
damnably angry.—Why what a Coil is here.—

60 FLORINDA: Sir, can you think—

WILLMORE: That you'd do it for nothing? oh, oh, I find what
you'd be at—look here, here's a Pistole for you—here's a
work indeed—here—take it, I say.—

FLORINDA: For Heaven's sake, Sir, as you're a Gentleman—

65 WILLMORE: So—now—she would be wheedling me for more—
what, you will not take it then—you're resolv'd you will
not.—Come, come, take it, or I'll put it up again; for, look
ye, I never give more.—Why, how now, Mistress, are you so
high i'th' Mouth, a Pistole won't down with you?—hah—
70   why, what a work's here—in good time—come, no struggling, be gone—But an y'are good at a dumb Wrestle, I'm
for ye,—look ye,—I'm for ye.—

(She struggles with him.)

(Enter BELVILE *and* FREDERICK.)

BELVILE: The Door is open, a Pox of this mad Fellow, I'm angry
that we've lost him, I durst have sworn he had follow'd us.

75 FREDERICK: But you were so hasty, Colonel, to be gone.

FLORINDA: Help, help,—Murder!—help—oh, I'm ruin'd.

BELVILE: Ha, sure that's *Florinda's* Voice.

(Comes up to them.)

—A Man! Villain, let go that Lady.

(A noise.)

*(*WILLMORE *turns and draws,* FREDERICK *interposes.)*

FLORINDA: *Belvile!* Heavens! my Brother too is coming, and
80   'twill be impossible to escape.—*Belvile,* I conjure you to
walk under my Chamber-window, from whence I'll give

you some instructions what to do—This rude Man has
undone us.

(Exit.)

WILLMORE: *Belvile!*

(Enter PEDRO, STEPHANO, *and other Servants with Lights.)*

PEDRO: I'm betray'd; run, *Stephano,* and see if *Florinda* be safe. 85

(Exit STEPHANO.)

So who'er they be, all is not well, I'll to *Florinda's* Chamber.

(They fight, and PEDRO's *Party beats 'em out; going out, meets*
STEPHANO.)

STEPHANO: You need not, Sir, the poor Lady's fast asleep, and
thinks no harm: I wou'd not wake her, Sir, for fear of fright-
ning her with your danger.

PEDRO: I'm glad she's there—Rascals, how came the Garden- 90
Door open?

STEPHANO: That Question comes too late, Sir: some of my
Fellow-Servants Masquerading I'll warrant.

PEDRO: Masquerading! a leud Custom to debauch our
Youth—there's something more in this than I imagine. 95

(Exeunt.)

SCENE IV

Changes to the Street.

Enter BELVILE *in Rage,* FREDERICK *holding him, and* WILLMORE
melancholy.

WILLMORE: Why, how the Devil shou'd I know *Florinda?*

BELVILE: Ah plague of your ignorance! if it had not been
Florinda, must you be a Beast?—a Brute, a senseless
Swine?

WILLMORE: Well, Sir, you see I am endu'd with Patience—I can 5
bear—tho egad y're very free with me methinks,—I was in
good hopes the Quarrel wou'd have been on my side, for so
uncivilly interrupting me.

BELVILE: Peace, Brute, whilst thou'rt safe—oh, I'm distracted.

WILLMORE: Nay, nay, I'm an unlucky Dog, that's certain. 10

BELVILE: Ah curse upon the Star that rul'd my Birth! or whatsoever other Influence that makes me still so wretched.

WILLMORE: Thou break'st my Heart with these Complaints;
there is no Star in fault, no Influence but Sack, the cursed
Sack I drank. 15

FREDERICK: Why, how the Devil came you so drunk?

WILLMORE: Why, how the Devil came you so sober?

BELVILE: A curse upon his thin Skull, he was always before-hand
that way.

FREDERICK: Prithee, dear Colonel, forgive him, he's sorry for his 20
fault.

BELVILE: He's always so after he has done a mischief—a plague
on all such Brutes.

WILLMORE: By this Light I took her for an errant Harlot.

BELVILE: Damn your debaucht Opinion: tell me, Sot, hadst thou 25
so much sense and light about thee to distinguish her to be

a Woman, and could'st not see something about her Face
and Person, to strike an awful Reverence into thy Soul?

WILLMORE: Faith no, I consider'd her as mere a Woman as I
30   could wish.

BELVILE: 'Sdeath I have no patience—draw, or I'll kill you.

WILLMORE: Let that alone till to morrow, and if I set not all
right again, use your Pleasure.

BELVILE: To morrow, damn it.
35   The spiteful Light will lead me to no happiness.
To morrow is *Antonio's,* and perhaps
Guides him to my undoing;—oh that I could meet
This Rival, this powerful Fortunate.

WILLMORE: What then?

40   BELVILE: Let thy own Reason, or my Rage instruct thee.

WILLMORE: I shall be finely inform'd then, no doubt; hear
me, Colonel—hear me—shew me the Man and I'll do his
Business.

BELVILE: I know him no more than thou, or if I did, I should
45   not need thy aid.

WILLMORE: This you say is *Angelica's* House, I promis'd the
kind Baggage to lie with her to Night.

(Offers to go in.)

(Enter ANTONIO *and his Page.* ANTONIO *knocks on the Hilt of his
Sword.)*

ANTONIO: You paid the thousand Crowns I directed?

PAGE: To the Lady's old Woman, Sir, I did.

50   WILLMORE: Who the Devil have we here?

BELVILE: I'll now plant my self under *Florinda's* Window, and if
I find no comfort there, I'll die.

(Exit BELVILE *and* FREDERICK. *Enter* MORETTA.*)*

MORETTA: Page!

PAGE: Here's my Lord.

55   WILLMORE: How is this, a Piccaroon going to board my Frigate!
here's one Chase-Gun for you.

(Drawing his Sword, justles ANTONIO *who turns and draws. They
fight,* ANTONIO *falls.)*

MORETTA: Oh, bless us, we are all undone!

(Runs in, and shuts the Door.)

PAGE: Help, Murder!

*(*BELVILE *returns at the noise of fighting.)*

BELVILE: Ha, the mad Rogue's engag'd in some unlucky Ad-
60   venture again.

(Enter two or three MASQUERADERS.*)*

MASQUERADER: Ha, a Man kill'd!

WILLMORE: How! a Man kill'd! then I'll go home to sleep.

(Puts up, and reels out. Exeunt MASQUERADERS *another way.)*

BELVILE: Who shou'd it be! pray Heaven the Rogue is safe, for
all my Quarrel to him.

(As BELVILE *is groping about, enter an* OFFICER *and six*
SOLDIERS.*)*

SOLDIER: Who's there?   65

OFFICER: So, here's one dispatcht—secure the Murderer.

BELVILE: Do not mistake my Charity for Murder: I came to his
Assistance.

*(*SOLDIERS *sieze on* BELVILE.*)*

OFFICER: That shall be tried, Sir.—St. *Jago,* Swords drawn in
the Carnival time!   70

(Goes to ANTONIO.*)*

ANTONIO: Thy Hand prithee.

OFFICER: Ha, Don *Antonio!* look well to the Villain there.—
How is't, Sir?

ANTONIO: I'm hurt.

BELVILE: Has my Humanity made me a Criminal?   75

OFFICER: Away with him.

BELVILE: What a curst Chance is this!

(Exeunt SOLDIERS *with* BELVILE.*)*

ANTONIO: *(To the* OFFICER.*)* This is the Man that has set upon
me twice—carry him to my Apartment till you have further Orders from me.   80

(Exit. ANTONIO *led.)*

—————— ACT FOUR ——————

SCENE I

A fine Room.

Discovers BELVILE, *as by Dark alone.*

BELVILE: When shall I be weary of railing on Fortune, who is resolv'd never to turn with Smiles upon me?—Two such Defeats in one Night—none but the Devil and that mad
Rogue could have contriv'd to have plagued me with—I am
here a Prisoner—but where?—Heaven knows—and if there   5
be Murder done, I can soon decide the Fate of a Stranger in
a Nation without Mercy—Yet this is nothing to the Torture my Soul bows with, when I think of losing my fair, my
dear *Florinda.*—Hark—my Door opens—a Light—a Man—
and seems of Quality—arm'd too.—Now shall I die like a   10
Dog without defence.

(Enter ANTONIO *in a Night-Gown, with a Light; his Arm in a
Scarf, and a Sword under his Arm: He sets the Candle on the Table.)*

ANTONIO: Sir, I come to know what Injuries I have done you,
that could provoke you to so mean an Action, as to attack
me basely, without allowing time for my Defence.

BELVILE: Sir, for a Man in my Circumstances to plead Inno-   15
cence, would look like Fear—but view me well, and you
will find no marks of a Coward on me, nor any thing that
betrays that Brutality you accuse me of.

ANTONIO: In vain, Sir, you impose upon my Sense,
You are not only he who drew on me last Night,   20

But yesterday before the same House, that of *Angelica*.
Yet there is something in your Face and Mein—

BELVILE: I own I fought to day in the defence of a Friend of
mine, with whom you (if you're the same) and your

25   Party were first engag'd.
Perhaps you think this Crime enough to kill me,
But if you do, I cannot fear you'll do it basely.

ANTONIO: No, Sir, I'll make you fit for a Defence with this.

(Gives him the Sword.)

BELVILE: This Gallantry surprizes me—nor know I how to use

30   this Present, Sir, against a Man so brave.

ANTONIO: You shall not need;
For know, I come to snatch you from a Danger
That is decreed against you;
Perhaps your Life, or long Imprisonment:

35   And 'twas with so much Courage you offended,
I cannot see you punisht.

BELVILE: How shall I pay this Generosity?

ANTONIO: It had been safer to have kill'd another,
Than have attempted me:

40   To shew your Danger, Sir, I'll let you know my Quality;
And 'tis the Vice-Roy's Son whom you have wounded.

BELVILE: *(Aside.)* The Vice-Roy's Son!
Death and Confusion! was this Plague reserved
To compleat all the rest?—oblig'd by him!

45   The Man of all the World I would destroy.

ANTONIO: You seem disorder'd, Sir.

BELVILE: Yes, trust me, Sir, I am, and 'tis with pain
That Man receives such Bounties,
Who wants the pow'r to pay 'em back again.

50 ANTONIO: To gallant Spirits 'tis indeed uneasy;
—But you may quickly over-pay me, Sir.

BELVILE: Then I am well—*(Aside.)* kind Heaven! but set us
even,
That I may fight with him, and keep my Honour safe.
—Oh, I'm impatient, Sir, to be discounting

55   The mighty Debt I owe you; command me quickly—

ANTONIO: I have a Quarrel with a Rival, Sir,
About the Maid we love.

BELVILE: *(Aside.)* Death, 'tis *Florinda* he means—
That Thought destroys my Reason, and I shall kill him—

60 ANTONIO: My Rival, Sir,
Is one has all the Virtues Man can boast of.

BELVILE: Death! who shou'd this be?

ANTONIO: He challeng'd me to meet him on the *Molo*,
As soon as Day appear'd; but last Night's quarrel

65   Has made my Arm unfit to guide a Sword.

BELVILE: I apprehend you, Sir, you'd have me kill the Man
That lays a claim to the Maid you speak of.
—I'll do't—I'll fly to do it.

ANTONIO: Sir, do you know her?

70 BELVILE: —No, Sir, but 'tis enough she is admired by you.

ANTONIO: Sir, I shall rob you of the Glory on't,
For you must fight under my Name and Dress.

BELVILE: That Opinion must be strangely obliging that makes
You think I can personate the brave *Antonio*,

75   Whom I can but strive to imitate.

ANTONIO: You say too much to my Advantage.

Come, Sir, the Day appears that calls you forth.
Within, Sir, is the Habit.

(Exit ANTONIO.*)*

BELVILE: Fantastick Fortune, thou deceitful Light,
That cheats the wearied Traveller by Night,   80
Tho on a Precipice each step you tread,
I am resolv'd to follow where you lead.

(Exit.)

SCENE II

The Molo.

Enter FLORINDA *and* CALLIS *in Masques, with* STEPHANO.

FLORINDA: *(Aside.)* I'm dying with my fears; *Belvile's* not coming,
As I expected, underneath my Window,
Makes me believe that all those Fears are true.
—Canst thou not tell with whom my Brother fights?

STEPHANO: No, Madam, they were both in Masquerade, I was 5
by when they challeng'd one another, and they had decided
the Quarrel then, but were prevented by some Cavaliers;
which made 'em put it off till now—but I am sure 'tis
about you they fight.

FLORINDA: *(Aside.)* Nay then 'tis with *Belvile*, for what other 10
Lover have I that dares fight for me, except *Antonio?* and he
is too much in favour with my Brother—If it be he, for
whom shall I direct my Prayers to Heaven?

STEPHANO: Madam, I must leave you; for if my Master see me,
I shall be hang'd for being your Conductor.—I escap'd nar- 15
rowly for the Excuse I made for you last night i'th' Garden.

FLORINDA: And I'll reward thee for't—prithee no more.

(Exit STEPHANO.*)*

(Enter Don PEDRO *in his Masquing Habit.)*

PEDRO: *Antonio's* late to day, the place will fill, and we may be
prevented.

(Walks about.)

FLORINDA: (Aside.) Antonio! sure I heard amiss.   20

PEDRO: But who would not excuse a happy Lover.
When soft fair Arms comfine the yielding Neck;
And the kind Whisper languishingly breathes,
Must you be gone so soon?
Sure I had dwelt for ever on her Bosom.   25
—But stay, he's here.

(Enter BELVILE *drest in* ANTONIO's *Clothes.)*

FLORINDA: 'Tis not *Belvile*, half my Fears are vanisht.

PEDRO: *Antonio!*—

BELVILE: *(Aside.)* This must be he.
You're early, Sir,—I do not use to be out-done this way. 30

PEDRO: The wretched, Sir, are watchful, and 'tis enough
You have the advantage of me in *Angelica*.

BELVILE: *(Aside.)* Angelica!
Or I've mistook my Man! Or else *Antonio*,

35   Can he forget his Interest in *Florinda*,
        And fight for common Prize?
PEDRO: Come, Sir, you know our terms—
BELVILE: *(Aside.)* Be Heaven, not I.
        —No talking, I am ready, Sir.

(Offers to fight. FLORINDA *runs in.)*

40 FLORINDA: *(To* BELVILE.*)* Oh, hold! who'er you be, I do conjure
        you hold. If you strike here—I die—
PEDRO: *Florinda!*
BELVILE: *Florinda* imploring for my Rival!
PEDRO: Away, this Kindness is unseasonable.

(Puts her by, they fight; she runs in just as BELVILE *disarms* PEDRO.*)*

45 FLORINDA: Who are you, Sir, that dare deny my Prayers?
BELVILE: Thy Prayers destroy him; if thou wouldst preserve him.
        Do that thou'rt unacquainted with, and curse him.

(She holds him.)

FLORINDA: By all you hold most dear, by her you love,
        I do conjure you, touch him not.
50 BELVILE: By her I love!
        See—I obey—and at your Feet resign
        The useless Trophy of my Victory.

(Lays his sword at her Feet.)

PEDRO: *Antonio,* you've done enough to prove you love *Florinda.*
BELVILE: Love *Florinda!*
55   Does Heaven love Adoration, Pray'r, or Penitence?
        Love her! here Sir,—your Sword again.

(Snatches up the Sword, and gives it him.)

        Upon this Truth I'll fight my Life away.
PEDRO: No, you've redeem'd my Sister, and my Friendship.
BELVILE: Don *Pedro!*

(He gives him FLORINDA *and pulls off his Vizard to shew his Face,
and puts it on again.)*

60 PEDRO: Can you resign your Claims to other Women,
        And give your Heart intirely to *Florinda?*
BELVILE: Intire, as dying Saints Confessions are.
        I can delay my happiness no longer.
        This minute let me make *Florinda* mine:
65 PEDRO: This minute let it be—no time so proper,
        This Night my Father will arrive from *Rome,*
        And possibly may hinder what we propose.
FLORINDA: Oh Heavens! this Minute!

(Enter Masqueraders, and pass over.)

BELVILE: Oh, do not ruin me!
70 PEDRO: The place begins to fill; and that we may not be ob-
        serv'd, do you walk off to St. *Peter's* Church, where I will
        meet you, and conclude your Happiness.
BELVILE: I'll meet you there—*(Aside.)* if there be no more Saints
        Churches in *Naples.*

FLORINDA: Oh stay, Sir, and recall your hasty Doom: 75
        Alas I have not yet prepar'd my Heart
        To entertain so strange a Guest.
PEDRO: Away, this silly Modesty is assum'd too late.
BELVILE: Heaven, Madam! what do you do?
FLORINDA: Do! despise the Man that lays a Tyrant's Claim   80
        To what he ought to conquer by Submission.
BELVILE: You do not know me—move a little this way.

(Draws her aside.)

FLORINDA: Yes, you may even force me to the Altar,
        But not the holy Man that offers there
        Shall force me to be thine.   85

*(*PEDRO *talks to* CALLIS *this while.)*

BELVILE: Oh do not lose so blest an opportunity!
        See—'tis your *Belvile*—not *Antonio,*
        Whom your mistaken Scorn and Anger ruins.

(Pulls off his Vizard.)

FLORINDA: *Belvile!*
        Where was my Soul it cou'd not meet thy Voice,   90
        And take this knowledge in?

(As they are talking, enter WILLMORE *finely drest, and* FREDERICK.*)*

WILLMORE: No Intelligence! no News of *Belvile* yet—well I am
        the most unlucky Rascal in Nature—ha!—am I deceiv'd—
        or is it he—look, *Frederick*—'tis he—my dear *Belvile.*

(Runs and embraces him. BELVILE'S *Vizard falls out on's Hand.)*

BELVILE: Hell and Confusion seize thee!   95
PEDRO: Ha! *Belvile!* I beg your Pardon, Sir.

(Takes FLORINDA *from him.)*

BELVILE: Nay, touch her not, she's mine by Conquest, Sir.
        I won her by my Sword.
WILLMORE: Did'st thou so—and egad, Child, we'll keep her by
        the Sword.   100

(Draws on PEDRO, BELVILE *goes between.)*

BELVILE: Stand off.
        Thou'rt so profanely leud, so curst by Heaven,
        All Quarrels thou espousest must be fatal.
WILLMORE: Nay, an you be so hot, my Valour's coy,
        And shall be courted when you want it next.   105

(Puts up his Sword.)

BELVILE: You know I ought to claim a Victor's Right,

(To PEDRO.*)*

        But you're the Brother to divine *Florinda,*
        To whom I'm such a Slave—to purchase her,
        I durst not hurt the Man she holds so dear.
PEDRO: 'Twas by *Antonio's,* not by *Belvile's* Sword,   110
        This Question should have been decided, Sir:

I must confess much to your Bravery's due,
Both now, and when I met you last in Arms.
But I am nicely punctual in my word,
115   As Men of Honour ought, and beg your Pardon.

(Aside to FLORINDA *as they are going out.)*

—For this Mistake another Time shall clear.
—This was some Plot between you and *Belvile:*
But I'll prevent you.

*(*BELVILE *looks after her, and begins to walk up and down in a Rage.)*

WILLMORE: Do not be modest now, and lose the Woman: but if
120   we shall fetch her back, so—
BELVILE: Do not speak to me.
WILLMORE: Not speak to you!—Egad, I'll speak to you, and
       will be answered too.
BELVILE: Will you, Sir?
125   WILLMORE: I know I've done some mischief, but I'm so dull a
       Puppy, that I am the Son of a Whore, if I know how, or
       where—prithee inform my Understanding.—
BELVILE: Leave me I say, and leave me instantly.
WILLMORE: I will not leave you in this humour, nor till I know
130   my Crime.
BELVILE: Death, I'll tell you, Sir—

(Draws and runs at WILLMORE; *he runs out;* BELVILE *after him,*
FREDERICK *interposes.)*

(Enter ANGELICA, MORETTA, *and* SEBASTIAN.*)*

ANGELICA: Ha—*Sebastian*—Is not that *Willmore?* haste, haste,
       and bring him back.
FREDERICK: The Colonel's mad—I never saw him thus before;
135   I'll after 'em, lest he do some mischief, for I am sure *Will-
       more* will not draw on him.

(Exit.)

ANGELICA: I am all Rage! my first desires defeated
       For one, for ought he knows, that has no
       Other Merit than her Quality,—
140   Her being Don *Pedro's* Sister—He loves her:
       I know 'tis so—dull, dull, insensible—
       He will not see me now tho oft invited;
       And broke his Word last night—false perjur'd Man!
       —He that but yesterday fought for my Favours,
145   And would have made his Life a Sacrifice
       To've gain'd one Night with me,
       Must now be hired and courted to my Arms.
MORETTA: I told you what wou'd come on't, but *Moretta's* an
       old doating Fool—Why did you give him five hundred
150   Crowns, but to set himself out for other Lovers? You shou'd
       have kept him poor, if you had meant to have had any good
       from him.
ANGELICA: Oh, name not such mean Trifles.—Had I given him all
       My Youth has earn'd from Sin,
155   I had not lost a Thought nor Sigh upon't.
       But I have given him my eternal Rest,
       My whole Repose, my future Joys, my Heart;
       My Virgin Heart. *Moretta!* oh 'tis gone!

MORETTA: Curse on him, here he comes;
       How fine she has made him too!   160

(Enter WILLMORE *and* SEBASTIAN. ANGELICA *turns and walks away.)*

WILLMORE: How now, turn'd Shadow?
       Fly when I pursue, and follow when I fly!

(Sings.)

       Stay gentle Shadow of my Dove,
            And tell me e'er I go,
       Whether the Substance may not prove   165
            A fleeting Thing like you.

There's a soft kind Look remaining yet.

(As she turns she looks on him.)

ANGELICA: Well, Sir, you may be gay; all Happiness, all Joys
       pursue you still, Fortune's your Slave, and gives you every
       hour choice of new Hearts and Beauties, till you are cloy'd 170
       with the repeated Bliss, which others vainly languish for—
       But know, false Man, that I shall be reveng'd.

(Turns away in a Rage.)

WILLMORE: So, 'gad, there are of those faint-hearted Lovers,
       whom such a sharp Lesson next their Hearts would make as
       impotent as Fourscore—pox o' this whining—my Bus'ness 175
       is to laugh and love—a pox on't; I hate your sullen Lover, a
       Man shall lose as much time to put you in Humour now, as
       would serve to gain a new Woman.
ANGELICA: I scorn to cool that Fire I cannot raise,
       Or do the Drudgery of your virtuous Mistress.   180
WILLMORE: A virtuous Mistress! Death, what a thing thou hast
       found out for me! why what the Devil should I do with a
       virtuous Woman?—a sort of ill'natur'd Creatures, that take
       a Pride to torment a Lover. Virtue is but an Infirmity in
       Women, a Disease that renders even the handsom ungrate- 185
       ful; whilst the ill-favour'd, for want of Sollicitations and
       Address, only fancy themselves so.—I have lain with a
       Woman of Quality, who has all the while been railing at
       Whores.
ANGELICA: I will not answer for your Mistress's Virtue,   190
       Tho she be young enough to know no Guilt:
       And I could wish you would persuade my Heart,
       'Twas the two hundred thousand Crowns you courted.
WILLMORE: Two hundred thousand Crowns! what Story's
       this?—what Trick?—what Woman?—ha.   195
ANGELICA: How strange you make it! have you forgot the Crea-
       ture you entertain'd on the Piazza last night?
WILLMORE: Ha, my Gipsy worth two hundred thousand
       Crowns!—oh how I long to be with her—pox, I knew she
       was of Quality.   200
ANGELICA: False Man, I see my Ruin in thy Face.
       How many vows you breath'd upon my Bosom,
       Never to be unjust—have you forgot so soon?
WILLMORE: Faith no, I was just coming to repeat 'em—but
       here's a Humour indeed—would make a Man a Saint—   205
       (Aside.) Wou'd she'd be angry enough to leave me, and
       command me not to wait on her.

(Enter HELLENA, *drest in Man's Clothes.)*

HELLENA: This must be *Angelica,* I know it by her mumping
    Matron here—Ay, ay, 'tis she: my mad Captain's with her
210   too, for all his swearing—how this unconstant Humour
    makes me love him:—pray, good grave Gentlewoman, is
    not this *Angelica?*
MORETTA: My too young Sir, it is—I hope 'tis one from Don
    Antonio.

(Goes to ANGELICA.*)*

215 HELLENA: *(Aside.)* Well, something I'll do to vex him for this.
ANGELICA: I will not speak with him; am I in humour to receive
    a Lover?
WILLMORE: Not speak with him! why I'll be gone—and wait
    your idler minutes—Can I shew less Obedience to the
220   thing I love so fondly?

(Offers to go.)

ANGELICA: A fine Excuse this—stay—
WILLMORE: And hinder your Advantage: should I repay your
    Bounties so ungratefully?
ANGELICA: Come, hither, Boy,—that I may let you see
225   How much above the Advantages you name
    I prize one Minute's Joy with you.
WILLMORE: Oh, you destroy me with this Endearment.

(Impatient to be gone.)

    —Death, how shall I get away!—Madam, 'twill not be fit I
    should be seen with you—besides, it will not be conve-
230   nient—and I've a Friend—that's dangerously sick.
ANGELICA: I see you're impatient—yet you shall stay.
WILLMORE: And miss my Assignation with my Gipsy.

(Aside, and walks about impatiently. MORETTA *brings* HELLENA,
who addresses her self to ANGELICA.*)*

HELLENA: Madam, You'l hardly pardon my Intrusion,
    When you shall know my Business;
235   And I'm too young to tell my Tale with Art:
    But there must be a wondrous store of Goodness
    Where so much Beauty dwells.
ANGELICA: A pretty Advocate, whoever sent thee,
    —Prithee proceed—Nay, Sir, you shall not go.

(To WILLMORE *who is stealing off.)*

240 WILLMORE: Then shall I lose my dear Gipsy for ever.
    (Aside.)—Pox on't, she stays me out of spite.
HELLENA: I am related to a Lady, Madam,
    Young, rich, and nobly born, but has the fate
    To be in love with a young *English* Gentleman.
245   Strangely she loves him, at first sight she lov'd him,
    But did adore him when she heard him speak;
    For he, she said, had Charms in every word,
    That fail'd not to surprize, to wound, and conquer—
WILLMORE: *(Aside.)* Ha, Egad I hope this concerns me.
250 ANGELICA: 'Tis my false Man, he means—wou'd he were gone.
    This Praise will raise his Pride and ruin me—*(To* WILLMORE.*)*
    Well,

Since you are so impatient to be gone.
    I will release you, Sir.
WILLMORE: *(Aside.)* Nay, then I'm sure 'twas me he spoke of,
    this cannot be the Effects of Kindness in her.   255
    —No, Madam, I've consider'd better on't,
    And will not give you cause of Jealousy.
ANGELICA: But, Sir, I've—business, that—
WILLMORE: This shall not do, I know 'tis but to try me.
ANGELICA: *(Aside.)* Well, to your Story, Boy,—tho 'twill undo me. 260
HELLENA: With this Addition to his other Beauties,
    He won her unresisting tender Heart,
    He vow'd and sigh'd, and swore he lov'd her dearly;
    And she believ'd the cunning Flatterer,
    And thought her self the happiest Maid alive: 265
    To day was the appointed time by both,
    To consummate their Bliss;
    The Virgin, Altar, and the Priest were drest,
    And whilst she languisht for the expected Bridegroom,
    She heard, he paid his broken Vows to you.   270
WILLMORE: *(Aside.)* So, this is some dear Rogue that's in love
    with me, and this way lets me know it; or if it be not me,
    she means some one whose place I may supply.
ANGELICA: Now I perceive
    The cause of thy Impatience to be gone,   275
    And all the business of this glorious Dress.
WILLMORE: Damn the young Prater, I know not what he means.
HELLENA: Madam,
    In your fair Eyes I read too much concern
    To tell my farther Business.   280
ANGELICA: Prithee, sweet Youth, talk on, thou may'st perhaps
    Raise here a Storm that may undo my Passion,
    And then I'll grant thee any thing.
HELLENA: Madam, 'tis to intreat you, (oh unreasonable!)
    You wou'd not see this Stranger;   285
    For if you do, she vows you are undone,
    Tho Nature never made a Man so excellent;
    And sure he'ad been a God, but for Inconstancy.
WILLMORE: *(Aside.)* Ah, Rogue, how finely he's instructed!
    —'Tis plain some Woman that has seen me *en passant.* 290
ANGELICA: Oh, I shall burst with Jealousy! do you know the
    Man you speak of?—
HELLENA: Yes, Madam, he us'd to be in Buff and Scarlet.
ANGELICA: *(To* WILLMORE.*)* Thou, false as Hell, what canst thou
    say to this?   295
WILLMORE: By Heaven—
ANGELICA: Hold, do not damn thy self—
HELLENA: Nor hope to be believ'd.

(He walks about, they follow.)

ANGELICA: Oh, perjur'd Man!
    Is't thus you pay my generous Passion back?   300
HELLENA: Why wou'd you, Sir, abuse my Lady's Faith?
ANGELICA: And use me so unhumanly?
HELLENA: A Maid so young, so innocent—
WILLMORE: Ah, young Devil!
ANGELICA: Dost thou not know thy Life is in my Power?   305
HELLENA: Or think my Lady cannot be reveng'd?
WILLMORE: *(Aside.)* So, so, the Storm comes finely on.
ANGELICA: Now thou art silent, Guilt has struck thee dumb.

Oh, hadst thou still been so, I'd liv'd in safety.

(She turns away and weeps.)

310 WILLMORE: *(Aside to* HELLENA, *looks towards* ANGELICA *to watch
her turning; and as she comes towards them, he meets her.)* Sweetheart, the Lady's Name and House—quickly: I'm impatient
to be with her.—
HELLENA: *(Aside.)* So now is he for another Woman.
315 WILLMORE: The impudent'st young thing in Nature!
I cannot persuade him out of his Error, Madam.
ANGELICA: I know he's in the right,—yet thou'st a Tongue
That wou'd persuade him to deny his Faith.

(In Rage walks away.)

WILLMORE: *(Said softly to* HELLENA.*)* Her Name, her Name,
dear Boy—
320 HELLENA: Have you forgot it, Sir?
WILLMORE: *(Aside.)* Oh, I perceive he's not to know I am a
Stranger to his Lady.
—Yes, yes, I do know—but—I have forgot the—

*(*ANGELICA *turns.)*

—By Heaven, such early confidence I never saw.
ANGELICA: Did I not charge you with this Mistress, Sir?
325 Which you denied, tho I beheld your Perjury.
This little Generosity of thine has render'd back my Heart.

(Walks away.)

WILLMORE: So, you have made sweet work here, my little
mischief;
Look your Lady be kind and good-natur'd now, or
I shall have but a cursed Bargain on't.

*(*ANGELICA *turns towards them.)*

330 —The Rogue's bred up to Mischief,
Art thou so great a Fool to credit him?
ANGELICA: Yes, I do; and you in vain impose upon me.
—Come hither, Boy—Is not this he you speak of?
HELLENA: (HELLENA *looks in his Face, he gazes on her.)* I think—it
335 is; I cannot swear, but I vow he has just such another lying
Lover's look.
WILLMORE: *(Aside.)* Hah! do not I know that Face?—
By Heaven, my little Gipsy! what a dull Dog was I?
Had I but lookt that way, I'd known her.
340 Are all my hopes of a new Woman banisht?
—Egad, if I don't fit thee for this, hang me.
—Madam, I have found out the Plot.
HELLENA: Oh Lord, what does he say? am I discover'd now?
WILLMORE: Do you see this young Spark here?
345 HELLENA: He'll tell her who I am.
WILLMORE: Who do you think this is?
HELLENA: Ay, ay, he does know me.—Nay, dear Captain, I'm
undone if you discover me.
WILLMORE: Nay, nay, no cogging; she shall know what a pre-
350 cious Mistress I have.

------

349 **cogging** to cog = to trick, wheedle, or cajole

HELLENA: Will you be such a Devil?
WILLMORE: Nay, nay, I'll teach you to spoil sport you will not
make.—This small Ambassador comes not from a Person of
Quality, as you imagine, and he says; but from a very errant
Gipsy, the talkingst, pratingst, cantingst little Animal thou   355
ever saw'st.
ANGELICA: What news you tell me! that's the thing I mean.
HELLENA: *(Aside.)* Wou'd I were well off the place.—If ever I go
a Captain-hunting again.—
WILLMORE: Mean that thing? that Gipsy thing? thou may'st as   360
well be jealous of thy Monkey, or Parrot as her: a *German*
Motion were worth a dozen of her, and a Dream were a bet-
ter Enjoyment, a Creature of Constitution fitter for Heaven
than Man.
HELLENA: *(Aside.)* Tho I'm sure he lyes, yet this vexes me.   365
ANGELICA: You are mistaken, she's a *Spanish* Woman
Made up of no such dull Materials.
WILLMORE: Materials! Egad, and she be made of any that will ei-
ther dispense, or admit of Love, I'll be bound to continence.
HELLENA: *(Aside to him.)* Unreasonable Man, do you think so?   370
WILLMORE: You may Return, my little Brazen Head, and tell
your Lady, that till she be handsom enough to be belov'd,
or I dull enough to be religious, there will be small hopes
of me.
ANGELICA: Did you not promise then to marry her?   375
WILLMORE: Not I, by Heaven.
ANGELICA: You cannot undeceive my fears and torments, till
you have vow'd you will not marry her.
HELLENA: If he swears that, he'll be reveng'd on me indeed for
all my Rogueries.   380
ANGELICA: I know what Arguments you'll bring against me,
Fortune and Honour.
WILLMORE: Honour! I tell you, I hate it in your Sex; and those
that fancy themselves possest of that Foppery, are the most
impertinently troublesom of all Woman-kind, and will   385
transgress nine Commandments to keep one: and to satisfy
your Jealousy I swear—
HELLENA: *(Aside to him.)* Oh, no swearing, dear Captain—
WILLMORE: If it were possible I should ever be inclin'd to marry,
it should be some kind young Sinner, one that has Gen-   390
erosity enough to give a favour handsomely to one that can
ask it discreetly, one that has Wit enough to manage an
Intrigue of Love—oh, how civil such a Wench is, to a Man
than does her the Honour to marry her.
ANGELICA: By Heaven, there's no Faith in any thing he says.   395

(Enter SEBASTIAN.*)*

SEBASTIAN: Madam, *Don Antonio*—
ANGELICA: Come hither.
HELLENA: Ha, *Antonio!* he may be coming hither, and he'll cer-
tainly discover me, I'll therefore retire without a Ceremony.

(Exit HELLENA.*)*

ANGELICA: I'll see him, get my Coach ready.   400
SEBASTIAN: It waits you, Madam.
WILLMORE: This is lucky: what, Madam, now I may be gone
and leave you to the enjoyment of my Rival?
ANGELICA: Dull Man, that canst not see how ill, how poor
That false dissimulation looks—Be gone,   405
And never let me see thy cozening Face again,

Lest I relapse and kill thee.

WILLMORE: Yes, you can spare me now,—farewell till you are in
a better Humour—I'm glad of this release—
410 Now for my Gipsy:
For tho to worse we change, yet still we find
New Joys, New Charms, in a new Miss that's kind.

(Exit WILLMORE.)

ANGELICA: He's gone, and in this Ague of My Soul
The shivering Fit returns;
415 Oh with what willing haste he took his leave,
As if the long'd for Minute were arriv'd,
Of some blest Assignation.
In vain I have consulted all my Charms,
In vain this Beauty priz'd, in vain believ'd
420 My eyes cou'd kindle any lasting Fires.
I had forgot my Name, my Infamy,
And the Reproach that Honour lays on those
That dare pretend a sober passion here.
Nice Reputation, tho it leave behind
425 More Virtues than inhabit where that dwells,
Yet that once gone, those virtues shine no more.
—Then since I am not fit to belov'd,
I am resolv'd to think on a Revenge
On him that sooth'd me thus to my undoing.

(Exeunt.)

SCENE III

A Street.

Enter FLORINDA *and* VALERIA *in Habits different from what they
have been seen in.*

FLORINDA: We're happily escap'd, yet I tremble still.

VALERIA: A Lover and fear! why, I am but half a one, and yet I
have Courage for any Attempt. Would *Hellena* were here.
I wou'd fain have had her as deep in this Mischief as we,
5 she'll fare but ill else I doubt.

FLORINDA: She pretended a Visit to the *Augustine* Nuns, but I
believe some other design carried her out, pray Heavens we
light on her.

VALERIA: When I saw no reason wou'd go good on her, I fol-
10 low'd her into the Wardrobe, and as she was looking for
something in a great Chest, I tumbled her in by the Heels,
snatcht the Key of the Apartment where you were confin'd,
lockt her in, and left her bauling for help.

FLORINDA: 'Tis well you resolve to follow my Fortunes, for thou
15 darest never appear at home again after such an Action.

VALERIA: That's according as the young Stranger and I shall
agree—But to our business—I deliver'd your Letter, your
Note to *Belvile*, when I got out under pretence of going to
Mass, I found him at his Lodging, and believe me it came
20 seasonably; for never was Man in so desperate a Condition.
I told him of your Resolution of making your escape to day,
if your Brother would be absent long enough to permit you;
if not, die rather than be *Antonio's*.

FLORINDA: Thou shou'dst have told him I was confin'd to my
25 Chamber upon my Brother's suspicion, that the Business on
the *Molo* was a Plot laid between him and I.

VALERIA: I said all this, and told him your Brother was now
gone to his Devotion, and he resolves to visit every Church
till he find him; and not only undeceive him in that, but caress him so as shall delay his return home. 30

FLORINDA: Oh Heavens! he's here, and *Belvile* with him too.

(They put on their Vizards.)

(Enter Don PEDRO, BELVILE, WILLMORE; BELVILE *and Don* PEDRO
seeming in serious Discourse.)

VALERIA: Walk boldly by them, I'll come at a distance, lest he
suspect us.

(She walks by them, and looks back on them.)

WILLMORE: Ha! A Woman! and of an excellent Mien!

PEDRO: She throws a kind look back on you. 35

WILLMORE: Death, tis a likely Wench, and that kind look shall
not be cast away—I'll follow her.

BELVILE: Prithee do not.

WILLMORE: Do not! By Heavens to the Antipodes, with such an
Invitation. 40

(She goes out, and WILLMORE *follows her.)*

BELVILE: 'Tis a mad Fellow for a Wench.

(Enter FREDERICK.)

FREDERICK: Oh Colonel, such News.

BELVILE: Prithee what?

FREDERICK: News that will make you laugh in spite of Fortune.

BELVILE: What, *Blunt* has had some damn'd Trick put upon 45
him, cheated, bang'd, or clapt?

FREDERICK: Cheated, Sir, rarely cheated of all but his Shirt and
Drawers; the unconscionable Whore too turn'd him out before Consummation, so that traversing the Streets at Midnight, the Watch found him in this *Fresco,* and conducted 50
him home: By Heaven 'tis such a slight, and yet I durst as
well have been hang'd as laugh at him, or pity him; he
beats all that do but ask him a Question, and is in such an
Humour—

PEDRO: Who is't has met with this ill usage, Sir? 55

BELVILE: *(Aside.)* A Friend of ours, whom you must see for
Mirth's sake. I'll imploy him to give *Florinda* time for an
escape.

PEDRO: Who is he?

BELVILE: A young Countryman of ours, one that has been edu- 60
cated at so plentiful a rate, he yet ne'er knew the want of
Money, and 'twill be a great Jest to see how simply he'll
look without it. For my part I'll lend him none, and the
Rogue knows not how to put on a borrowing Face, and ask
first. I'll let him see how good 'tis to play our parts whilst 65
I play his—Prithee, *Frederick* do go home and keep him
in that posture till we come.

(Exeunt.)

(Enter FLORINDA *from the farther end of the Scene, looking behind her.)*

FLORINDA: I am follow'd still—hah—my Brother too advancing this way, good Heavens defend me from being seen by
him. 70

(She goes off.)

(Enter WILLMORE, *and after him* VALERIA, *at a little distance.)*

WILLMORE: Ah! There she sails, she looks back as she were willing to be boarded, I'll warrant her Prize.

(He goes out, VALERIA *following.)*

(Enter HELLENA, *just as he goes out, with a* PAGE.*)*

HELLENA: Hah, is not that my Captain that has a Woman in
chase?—'tis not *Angelica*. Boy, follow those People at a dis-
75 tance, and bring me an Account where they go in.—I'll find
his Haunts, and plague him every where.—ha—my
Brother!

(Exit PAGE. BELVILE, WILLMORE, *and* PEDRO *cross the Stage:* HELLENA
runs off.)

(Scene changes to another Street. Enter FLORINDA.*)*

FLORINDA: What shall I do, my Brother now pursues me. Will
no kind Power protect me from his Tyranny?—Hah, here's
80 a Door open, I'll venture in, since nothing can be worse
than to fall into his Hands, my Life and Honour are at
stake, and my Necessity has no choice.

(She goes in. Enter VALERIA, *and Hellena's* PAGE *peeping after*
FLORINDA.*)*

PAGE: Here she went in, I shall remember this House.

(Exit PAGE.*)*

VALERIA: This is *Belvile*'s Lodgings; she's gone in as readily as if
85 she knew it—hah—here's that mad Fellow again, I dare not
venture in—I'll watch my Opportunity.

(Goes aside. Enter WILLMORE, *gazing about him.)*

WILLMORE: I have lost her hereabouts—Pox on't she must not
scape me so.

(Goes out.)

(Scene changes to BLUNT's *chamber, discovers him sitting on a couch in
his shirt and drawers, reading.)*

BLUNT: So, now my Mind's a little at Peace, since I have re-
90 solv'd Revenge—A Pox on this Taylor tho, for not bringing
home the Clothes I bespoke; and a Pox of all poor Cavaliers,
a Man can never keep a spare Suit for 'em; and I shall have
these Rogues come in and find me naked; and then I'm
undone; but I'm resolv'd to arm my self—the Rascals shall
95 not insult over me too much.

(Puts on an old rusty Sword and Buff-Belt.)

—Now, how like a Morrice-Dancer I am equipt—a fine
Lady-like Whore to cheat me thus, without affording me a
Kindness for my Money, a Pox light on her, I shall never be
reconciled to the Sex more, she has made me as faithless as
100 a Physician, as uncharitable as a Churchman, and as ill-
natur'd as a Poet. O how I'll use all Womenkind hereafter!
what wou'd I give to have one of 'em within my reach now!

any Mortal thing in Petticoats, kind Fortune, send me; and
I'll forgive thy last Night's Malice—Here's a cursed Book
too, (a Warning to all young Travellers) that can instruct 105
me how to prevent such Mischiefs now 'tis too late. Well 'tis
a rare convenient thing to read a little now and then, as well
as hawk and hunt.

(Sits down again and reads.)

(Enter to him FLORINDA.*)*

FLORINDA: This House is haunted sure, 'tis well furnisht and no
living thing inhabits it—hah—a Man! Heavens how he's 110
attir'd! sure 'tis some Rope-dancer, or Fencing-Master; I
tremble now for fear, and yet I must venture now to speak
to him—Sir, if I may not interrupt your Meditations—

(He starts up and gazes.)

BLUNT: Hah—what's here? Are my wishes granted? and is not
that a she Creature? Adsheartlikins 'tis! what wretched 115
thing art thou—hah!

FLORINDA: Charitable Sir, you've told your self already what I
am; a very wretched Maid, forc'd by a strange unlucky Accident, to seek a safety here, and must be ruin'd, if you do
not grant it.   120

BLUNT: Ruin'd! Is there any Ruin so inevitable as that which
now threatens thee? Dost thou know, miserable Woman,
into what Den of Mischiefs thou art fall'n? what a Bliss of
Confusion?—hah—dost not see something in my looks
that frights thy guilty Soul, and makes thee wish to change 125
that Shape of Woman for any humble Animal, or Devil? for
those were safer for thee, and less mischievous.

FLORINDA: Alas, what mean you, Sir? I must confess your Looks
have something in 'em makes me fear; but I beseech you, as
you seem a Gentleman, pity a harmless Virgin, that takes 130
your House for Sanctuary.

BLUNT: Talk on, talk on, and weep too, till my faith return. Do,
flatter me out of my Senses again—a harmless Virgin with
a Pox, as much one as t'other, adsheartlikins. Why, what the
Devil can I not be safe in my House for you? not in my 135
Chamber? nay, even being naked too cannot secure me. This
is an Impudence greater than has invaded me yet.—Come,
no Resistance.

(Pulls her rudely.)

FLORINDA: Dare you be so cruel?

BLUNT: Cruel, adsheartlikins as a Gally-slave, or a *Spanish* 140
Whore: Cruel, yes, I will kiss and beat thee all over; kiss,
and see thee all over; thou shalt lie with me too, not that I
care for the Injoyment, but to let you see I have ta'en de-
liberated Malice to thee, and will be revenged on one
Whore for the Sins of another; I will smile and deceive thee, 145
flatter thee, and beat thee, kiss and swear, and lye to thee,
imbrace thee and rob thee, as she did me, fawn on thee,
and strip thee stark naked, then hang thee out at my Window by the Heels, with a Paper of scurvey Verses fasten'd to
thy Breast, in praise of damnable Women—Come, come 150
along.

FLORINDA: Alas, Sir, must I be sacrific'd for the Crimes of the most
infamous of my Sex? I never understood the Sins you name.

BLUNT: Do, persuade the Fool you love him, or that one of you
155   can be just or honest; tell me I was not an easy Coxcomb, or
any strange impossible Tale: it will be believ'd sooner than
thy false Showers or Protestations. A Generation of damn'd
Hypocrites, to flatter my very Clothes from my back! dis-
sembling Witches! are these the Returns you make an hon-
160   est Gentleman that trusts, believes, and loves you?—But if
I be not even with you—Come along, or I shall—

(Pulls her again.)

(Enter FREDERICK.)

FREDERICK: Hah, what's here to do?
BLUNT: Adsheartlikins, *Frederick* I am glad thou art come, to be
    a Witness of my dire Revenge.
165 FREDERICK: What's this, a Person of Quality too, who is upon
    the Ramble to supply the Defects of some grave impotent
    Husband?
BLUNT: No, this has another Pretence, some very unfortunate
    Accident brought her hither, to save a Life pursued by I
170   know not who, or why, and forc'd to take Sanctuary here at
    Fools Haven. Adsheartlikins to me of all Mankind for Pro-
    tection? Is the Ass to be cajol'd again, think ye? No, young
    one, no Prayers or Tears shall mitigate my Rage; therefore
    prepare for both my Pleasure of Enjoyment and Revenge,
175   for I am resolved to make up my Loss here on thy Body, I'll
    take it out in kindness and in beating.
FREDERICK: Now, Mistress of mine, what do you think of this?
FLORINDA: I think he will not—dares not be so barbarous.
FREDERICK: Have a care, *Blunt,* she fetch'd a deep Sigh, she is
180   inamour'd with thy Shirt and Drawers, she'll strip thee even
    of that. There are of her Calling such unconscionable Bag-
    gages, and such dexterous Thieves, they'll flea a Man, and
    he shall ne'er miss his Skin, till he feels the Cold. There was
    a Country-man of ours robb'd of a Row of Teeth whilst
185   he was sleeping, which the Jilt made him buy again when
    he wak'd—You see, Lady, how little Reason we have to
    trust you.
BLUNT: 'Dsheartlikins, why, this is most abominable.
FLORINDA: Some such Devils there may be, but by all that's
190   holy I am none such, I entered here to save a Life in danger.
BLUNT: For no goodness I'll warrant her.
FREDERICK: Faith, Damsel, you had e'en confess the plain
    Truth, for we are Fellows not to be caught twice in the same
    Trap: Look on that Wreck, a tight Vessel when he set out of
195   Haven, well trim'd and laden, and see how a Female Picca-
    roon of this Island of Rogues has shatter'd him, and canst
    thou hope for any Mercy?
BLUNT: No, no, Gentlewoman, come along, adsheartlikins we
    must be better acquainted—we'll both lie with her, and
200   then let me alone to bang her.
FREDERICK: I am ready to serve you in matters of Revenge, that
    has a double Pleasure in't.
BLUNT: Well said. You hear, little one, how you are condemn'd
    by publick Vote to the Bed within, there's no resisting your
205   Destiny, Sweetheart.

(Pulls her.)

FLORINDA: Stay, Sir, I have seen you with *Belvile,* an *English*
    Cavalier, for his sake use me kindly; you know how, Sir.

BLUNT: *Belvile!* why, yes, Sweeting, we do know *Belvile,* and
    wish he were with us now, he's a Cormorant at Whore and
    Bacon, he'd have a Limb or two of thee, my Virgin Pullet: 210
    but 'tis no matter, we'll leave him the Bones to pick.
FLORINDA: Sir, if you have any Esteem for that *Belvile,* I conjure
    you to treat me with more Gentleness; he'll thank you for
    the Justice.
FREDERICK: Hark ye, *Blunt,* I doubt we are mistaken in this 215
    matter.
FLORINDA: Sir, If you find me not worth *Belvile*'s Care, use me
    as you please; and that you may think I merit better treat-
    ment than you threaten—pray take this Present—

(Gives him a Ring: He looks on it.)

BLUNT: Hum—A Diamond! why, 'tis a wonderful Virtue now 220
    that lies in this Ring, a mollifying Virtue; adsheartlikins
    there's more persuasive Rhetorick in't, than all her Sex can
    utter.
FREDERICK: I begin to suspect something; and 'twou'd anger us
    vilely to be truss'd up for a Rape upon a Maid of Quality, 225
    when we only believe we ruffle a Harlot.
BLUNT: Thou art a credulous Fellow, but adsheartlikins I have
    no Faith yet; why, my Saint prattled as parlously as this
    does, she gave me a Bracelet too, a Devil on her: but I sent
    my Man to sell it to day for Necessaries, and it prov'd as 230
    counterfeit as her Vows of Love.
FREDERICK: However let it reprieve her till we see *Belvile.*
BLUNT: That's hard, yet I will grant it.

(Enter a SERVANT.)

SERVANT: Oh, Sir, the Colonel is just come with his new Friend
    and a *Spaniard* of Quality, and talks of having you to Din- 235
    ner with 'em.
BLUNT: 'Dsheartlikins, I'm undone—I would not see 'em for
    the World: Harkye, *Frederick* lock up the Wench in your
    Chamber.
FREDERICK: Fear nothing, Madam, whate'er he threatens, 240
    you're safe whilst in my Hands.

(Exit FREDERICK and FLORINDA.)

BLUNT: And, Sirrah—upon your Life, say—I am not at home—
    or that I am asleep—or—or any thing—away—I'll prevent
    them coming this way.

(Locks the Door and Exeunt.)

—— ACT FIVE ——

SCENE I

BLUNT's *Chamber.*

After a great knocking as at his Chamber-door, enter BLUNT *softly,
crossing the Stage in his Shirt and Drawers, as before.*

(Call within.) Ned, Ned Blunt, Ned Blunt.

BLUNT: The Rogues are up in Arms, 'dsheartlikins, this villain-
    ous *Frederick* has betray'd me, they have heard of my blessed
    Fortune.

(And knocking within.) Ned Blunt, Ned, Ned—

BELVILE: Why, he's dead, sir, without dispute dead, he has not
been seen to day; let's break open the Door—here—Boy—

BLUNT: Ha, break open the Door! 'dsheartlikins that mad Fellow will be as good as his word.

10 BELVILE: Boy, bring something to force the Door.

(A great noise within at the Door again.)

BLUNT: So, now must I speak in my own Defence, I'll try what
Rhetorick will do—hold—hold, what do you mean, Gentlemen, what do you mean?

BELVILE: Oh Rogue, art alive? prithee open the Door, and con-
15   vince us.

BLUNT: Yes, I am alive, Gentlemen—but at present a little busy.

BELVILE: *(Within.)* How! *Blunt* grown a man of Business! come,
come, open, and let's see this Miracle.

BLUNT: No, no, no, no, Gentlemen, 'tis no great Business—
20   but—I am—at—my Devotion,—'dsheartlikins, will you
not allow a man time to pray?

BELVILE: *(Within.)* Turn'd religious! a greater Wonder than the
first, therefore open quickly, or we shall unhinge, we shall.

BLUNT: This won't do—Why, hark ye, Colonel; to tell you the
25   plain Truth, I am about a necessary Affair of Life.—I have a
Wench with me—you apprehend me? the Devil's in't if
they be so uncivil as to disturb me now.

WILLMORE: How, a Wench! Nay, then we must enter and partake; no Resistance,—unless it be your Lady of Quality, and
30   then we'll keep our distance.

BLUNT: So, the Business is out.

WILLMORE: Come, come, lend more hands to the Door,—now
heave altogether—so, well done, my Boys—

(Breaks open the Door. Enter BELVILE, WILLMORE, FREDERICK,
PEDRO *and* BELVILE'S PAGE: BLUNT *looks simply, they all laugh at
him, he lays his hand on his Sword, and comes up to* WILLMORE.)

BLUNT: Hark ye, Sir, laugh out your laugh quickly, d'ye hear,
35   and be gone, I shall spoil your sport else; 'dsheartlikins, Sir,
I shall—the Jest has been carried on too long,—*(Aside.)* a
Plague upon my Taylor—

WILLMORE: 'Sdeath, how the Whore has drest him! Faith, Sir,
I'm sorry.

40 BLUNT: Are you so, Sir? keep't to your self then, Sir, I advise you,
d'ye hear? for I can as little endure your Pity as his Mirth.

(Lays his Hand on's Sword.)

BELVILE: Indeed, *Willmore,* thou wert a little too rough with *Ned
Blunt's* Mistress; call a Person of Quality Whore, and one so
young, so handsome, and so eloquent!—ha, ha, ha.

45 BLUNT: Hark ye, Sir, you know me, and know I can be angry;
have a care—for 'dsheartlikins I can fight too—I can, Sir,—
do you mark me—no more.

BELVILE: Why so peevish, good *Ned?* some Disappointments,
I'll warrant—What! did the jealous Count her Husband
50   return just in the nick?

(They laugh.)

BLUNT: Or the Devil, Sir,—d'ye laugh?
Look ye, settle me a good sober Countenance, and that
quickly too, or you shall know *Ned Blunt* is not—

BELVILE: Not every Body, we know that.

BLUNT: Not an Ass, to be laught at, Sir.   55

WILLMORE: Unconscionable Sinner, to bring a Lover so near his
Happiness, a vigorous passionate Lover, and then not only
cheat him of his Moveables, but his Desires too.

BELVILE: Ah, Sir, a Mistress is a Trifle with *Blunt,* he'll have a
dozen the next time he looks abroad; his Eyes have Charms   60
not to be resisted: There needs no more than to expose that
taking Person to the view of the Fair, and he leads 'em all
in Triumph.

PEDRO: Sir, tho I'm a stranger to you, I'm ashamed at the rudeness of my Nation; and could you learn who did it, would   65
assist you to make an Example of 'em.

BLUNT: Why, ay, there's one speaks sense now, and handsomly;
and let me tell you Gentlemen, I should not have shew'd my
self like a Jack-Pudding, thus to have made you Mirth, but
that I have revenge within my power; for know, I have got   70
into my possession a Female, who had better have fallen under any Curse, than the Ruin I design her: 'dsheartlikins, she
assaulted me here in my own Lodgings, and had doubtless
committed a Rape upon me, had not this Sword defended me.

FREDERICK: I knew not that, but o' my Conscience thou hadst   75
ravisht her, had she not redeem'd her self with a Ring—let's
see't, *Blunt.*

(BLUNT shews the Ring.)

BELVILE: *(Goes to whisper to him.)* Hah!—the Ring I gave
Florinda when we exchang'd our Vows!—hark ye, *Blunt*—

WILLMORE: No whispering, good Colonel, there's a Woman in   80
the case, no whispering.

BELVILE: Hark ye, Fool, be advis'd, and conceal both the Ring
and the Story, for your Reputation's sake; don't let People
know what despis'd Cullies we *English* are: to be cheated
and abus'd by one Whore, and another rather bribe thee   85
than be kind to thee, is an Infamy to our Nation.

WILLMORE: Come, come, where's the Wench! we'll see her, let
her be what she will, we'll see her.

PEDRO: Ay, ay, let us see her, I can soon discover whether she be
of Quality, or for your Diversion.   90

BLUNT: She's in *Frederick's* Custody.

WILLMORE: Come, come, the Key.

(To FREDERICK *who gives him the Key, they are going.)*

BELVILE: Death! what shall I do?—stay, Gentlemen—yet if I
hinder 'em, I shall discover all—hold, let's go one at once—
give me the Key.   95

WILLMORE: Nay, hold there, Colonel, I'll go first.

FREDERICK: Nay, no Dispute, *Ned* and I have the property of her.

WILLMORE: Damn Property—then we'll draw Cuts.

(BELVILE goes to whisper WILLMORE.)

Nay, no Corruption, good Colonel: come, the longest Sword
carries her.—   100

(They all draw, forgetting Don PEDRO, *being a Spaniard, had the
longest.)*

BLUNT: I yield up my Interest to you Gentlemen, and that will
be Revenge sufficient.

WILLMORE: The Wench is yours—*(To* PEDRO.) Pox of his *Toledo,*
I had forgot that.
105 FREDERICK: Come, Sir, I'll conduct you to the Lady.

(Exit FREDERICK *and* PEDRO.)

BELVILE: *(Aside.)* To hinder him will certainly discover—
Dost know, dull Beast, what Mischief thou hast done?

*(*WILLMORE *walking up and down out of Humour.)*

WILLMORE: Ay, ay, to trust our Fortune to Lots, a Devil on't,
'twas madness, that's the Truth on't.
110 BELVILE: Oh intolerable Sot!

(Enter FLORINDA, *running masqu'd,* PEDRO *after her,* WILLMORE
gazing round her.)

FLORINDA: *(Aside.)* Good Heaven, defend me from discovery.
PEDRO: 'Tis but in vain to fly me, you are fallen to my Lot.
BELVILE: Sure she is undiscover'd yet, but now I fear there is no
way to bring her off.
115 WILLMORE: Why, what a Pox is not this my Woman, the same
I follow'd but now?

*(*PEDRO *talking to* FLORINDA, *who walks up and down.)*

PEDRO: As if I did not know ye, and your Business here.
FLORINDA: *(Aside.)* Good Heaven! I fear he does indeed—
PEDRO: Come, pray be kind, I know you meant to be so when
120 you enter'd here, for these are proper Gentlemen.
WILLMORE: But, Sir—perhaps the Lady will not be impos'd
upon, she'll chuse her Man.
PEDRO: I am better bred, than not to leave her Choice free.

(Enter VALERIA, *and is surpriz'd at the Sight of Don* PEDRO.)

VALERIA: *(Aside.)* Don *Pedro* here! there's no avoiding him.
125 FLORINDA: *(Aside.)* *Valeria!* then I'm undone—
VALERIA: *(To* PEDRO, *running to him.)* Oh! have I found you,
Sir—
—The strangest Accident—if I had breath—to tell it.
PEDRO: Speak—is *Florinda* safe? *Hellena* well?
130 VALERIA: Ay, ay, Sir—*Florinda*—is safe—from any fears of you.
PEDRO: Why, where's *Florinda?*—speak.
VALERIA: Ay, where indeed, Sir? I wish I could inform you,—
But to hold you no longer in doubt—
FLORINDA: *(Aside.)* Oh, what will she say!
135 VALERIA: She's fled away in the Habit of one of her Pages, Sir—
but *Callis* thinks you may retrieve her yet, if you make
haste away; she'll tell you, Sir, the rest—*(Aside.)* if you can
find her out.
PEDRO: Dishonourable Girl, she has undone my Aim—Sir—
140 you see my necessity of leaving you, and I hope you'll pardon it: my Sister, I know, will make her flight to you; and
if she do, I shall expect she should be render'd back.
BELVILE: I shall consult my Love and Honour, Sir.

(Exit PEDRO.)

FLORINDA: *(To* VALERIA.) My dear Preserver, let me imbrace
145 thee.
WILLMORE: What the Devil's all this?

BLUNT: Mystery by this Light.
VALERIA: Come, come, make haste and get your selves married
quickly, for your Brother will return again.
BELVILE: I am so surpriz'd with Fears and Joys, so amaz'd to find 150
you here in safety, I can scarce persuade my Heart into a
Faith of what I see—
WILLMORE: Harkye, Colonel, is this that Mistress who has cost
you so many Sighs, and me so many Quarrels with you?
BELVILE: It is—*(To* FLORINDA.) Pray give him the Honour of 155
your Hand.
WILLMORE: Thus it must be receiv'd then.

(Kneels and kisses her Hand.)

And with it give your Pardon too.
FLORINDA: The Friend to *Belvile* may command me anything.
WILLMORE: *(Aside.)* Death, wou'd I might, 'tis a surprizing 160
Beauty.
BELVILE: Boy, run and fetch a Father instantly.

(Exit PAGE.)

FREDERICK: So, now do I stand like a Dog, and have not a Syllable to plead my own Cause with: by this Hand, Madam,
I was never thorowly confounded before, nor shall I ever 165
more dare look up with Confidence, till you are pleased to
pardon me.
FLORINDA: Sir, I'll be reconcil'd to you on one Condition, that
you'll follow the Example of your Friend, in marrying a
Maid that does not hate you, and whose Fortune (I believe) 170
will not be unwelcome to you.
FREDERICK: Madam, had I no Inclinations that way, I shou'd
obey your kind Commands.
BELVILE: Who, *Frederick* marry; he has so few Inclinations for
Womankind, that had he been possest of Paradise, he might 175
have continu'd there to this Day, if no Crime but Love cou'd
have disinherited him.
FREDERICK: Oh, I do not use to boast of my Intrigues.
BELVILE: Boast! why thou do'st nothing but boast; and I dare
swear, wer't thou as innocent from the Sin of the Grape, as 180
thou art from the Apple, thou might'st yet claim that right
in *Eden* which our first Parents lost by too much loving.
FREDERICK: I wish this Lady would think me so modest a Man.
VALERIA: She shou'd be sorry then, and not like you half so well,
and I shou'd be loth to break my Word with you; which 185
was, That if your Friend and mine are agreed, it shou'd be
a Match between you and I.

(She gives him her Hand.)

FREDERICK: Bear witness, Colonel, 'tis a Bargain.

(Kisses her Hand.)

BLUNT: *(To* FLORINDA.) I have a Pardon to beg too; but adsheartlikins I am so out of Countenance, that I am a Dog if 190
I can say any thing to purpose.
FLORINDA: Sir, I heartily forgive you all.
BLUNT: That's nobly said, sweet Lady—*Belvile,* prithee present
her her Ring again, for I find I have not Courage to approach her my self.   195

(Gives him the Ring, he gives it to FLORINDA. *Enter* BOY.)

BOY: Sir, I have brought the Father that you sent for.

BELVILE: 'Tis well, and now my dear *Florinda*, let's fly to compleat that mighty Joy we have so long wish'd and sigh'd for. Come, *Frederick* you'll follow?

200 FREDERICK: Your Example, Sir, 'twas ever my Ambition in War, and must be so in Love.

WILLMORE: And must not I see this juggling Knot ty'd?

BELVILE: No, thou shalt do us better Service, and be our Guard, lest Don *Pedro's* sudden Return interrupt the Ceremony.

205 WILLMORE: Content; I'll secure this Pass.

(Exit BELVILE, FLORINDA, FREDERICK, *and* VALERIA. *Enter* PAGE.)

BOY: *(To* WILLMORE.) Sir, there's a Lady without wou'd speak to you.

WILLMORE: Conduct her in, I dare not quit my Post.

BOY: And, Sir, your Taylor waits you in your Chamber.

210 BLUNT: Some comfort yet, I shall not dance naked at the Wedding.

(Exit BLUNT *and* BOY.)

(Enter again the BOY, *conducting in* ANGELICA *in a masquing Habit and a Vizard,* WILLMORE *runs to her.)*

WILLMORE: This can be none but my pretty Gipsy—Oh, I see you can follow as well as fly—Come, confess thy self the most malicious Devil in Nature, you think you have done 215 my Bus'ness with *Angelica*—

ANGELICA: Stand off, base Villain—

(She draws a Pistol and holds to his Breast.)

WILLMORE: Hah, 'tis not she: who art thou? and what's thy Business?

ANGELICA: One thou hast injur'd, and who comes to kill thee 220 for't.

WILLMORE: What the Devil canst thou mean?

ANGELICA: By all my Hopes to kill thee—

(Holds still the Pistol to his Breast, he going back, she following still.)

WILLMORE: Prithee on what Acquaintance? for I know thee not.

ANGELICA: Behold this Face!—so lost to thy Remembrance!

225 And then call all thy Sins about thy Soul,

(Pulls off her Vizard.)

And let them die with thee.

WILLMORE: *Angelica!*

ANGELICA: Yes, Traitor.

Does not thy guilty Blood run shivering thro thy Veins?

230 Hast thou no Horrour at this Sight, that tells thee,

Thou hast not long to boast thy shameful Conquest?

WILLMORE: Faith, no Child, my Blood keeps its old Ebbs and Flows still, and that usual Heat too, that cou'd oblige thee with a Kindness, had I but opportunity.

235 ANGELICA: Devil! dost wanton with my Pain—have at thy Heart.

WILLMORE: Hold, dear Virago! hold thy Hand a little,

I am not now at leisure to be kill'd—hold and hear me—

(Aside.) Death, I think she's in earnest.

ANGELICA: *(Aside, turning from him.)* Oh if I take not heed,

My coward Heart will leave me to his Mercy. 240

—What have you, Sir, to say?—but should I hear thee,

Thoud'st talk away all that is brave about me:

(Follows him with the Pistol to his Breast.)

And I have vow'd thy Death, by all that's sacred.

WILLMORE: Why, then, there's an end of a proper handsom Fellow, that might have liv'd to have done good Service yet:— 245 That's all I can say to't.

ANGELICA: *(Pausingly.)* Yet—I wou'd give thee—time for Penitence.

WILLMORE: Faith, Child, I thank God, I have ever took care to lead a good, sober, hopeful Life, and am of a Religion that teaches me to believe, I shall depart in Peace. 250

ANGELICA: So will the Devil: tell me

How many poor believing Fools thou hast undone;

How many Hearts thou hast betray'd to ruin!

—Yet, these are little Mischiefs to the Ills

Thou'st taught mine to commit: thou'st taught it Love. 255

WILLMORE: Egad, 'twas shrewdly hurt the while.

ANGELICA: —Love, that has robb'd it of its Unconcern,

Of all that Pride that taught me how to value it,

And in its room a mean submissive Passion was convey'd,

That made me humbly bow, which I ne'er did 260

To any thing but Heaven.

—Thou, perjur'd Man, didst this, and with thy Oaths,

Which on thy Knees thou didst devoutly make,

Soften'd my yielding Heart—And then, I was a Slave—

Yet still had been content to've worn my Chains, 265

Worn 'em with Vanity and Joy for ever,

Hadst thou not broke those Vows that put them on.

—'Twas then I was undone.

(All this while follows him with a Pistol to his Breast.)

WILLMORE: Broke my Vows! why, where hast thou lived?

Amongst the Gods! For I never heard of mortal Man, 270

That has not broke a thousand Vows.

ANGELICA: Oh, Impudence!

WILLMORE: *Angelica!* that Beauty has been too long tempting,

Not to have made a thousand Lovers languish,

Who in the amorous Favour, no doubt have sworn 275

Like me; did they all die in that Faith? still adoring?

I do not think they did.

ANGELICA: No, faithless Man: had I repaid their Vows, as I did thine, I wou'd have kill'd the ungrateful that had abandon'd me. 280

WILLMORE: This old General has quite spoil'd thee, nothing makes a Woman so vain, as being flatter'd; your old Lover ever supplies the Defects of Age, with intolerable Dotage, vast Charge, and that which you call Constancy; and attributing all this to your own Merits, you domineer, and 285 throw your Favours in's Teeth, upbraiding him still with the Defects of Age, and cuckold him as often as he deceives your Expectations. But the gay, young, brisk Lover, that brings his equal Fires, and can give you Dart for Dart, he'll be as nice as you sometimes. 290

ANGELICA: All this thou'st made me know, for which I hate thee.

Had I remain'd in innocent Security,
I shou'd have thought all Men were born my Slaves;
And worn my Pow'r like Lightning in my Eyes,
295 To have destroy'd at Pleasure when offended.
—But when Love held the Mirror, the undeceiving Glass
Reflected all the Weakness of my Soul, and made me
    know,
My richest Treasure being lost, my Honour,
All the remaining Spoil cou'd not be worth
300 The Conqueror's Care or Value.
—Oh how I fell like a long worship'd Idol,
Discovering all the Cheat!
Wou'd not the Incense and rich Sacrifice,
Which blind Devotion offer'd at my Altars,
305 Have fall'n to thee?
Why woud'st thou then destroy my fancy'd Power?
WILLMORE: By Heaven thou art brave, and I admire thee
    strangely.
I wish I were that dull, that constant thing,
Which thou woud'st have, and Nature never meant me:
310 I must, like chearful Birds, sing in all Groves,
And perch on every Bough,
Billing the next kind She that flies to meet me;
Yet after all cou'd build my Nest with thee,
Thither repairing when I'd lov'd my round,
315 And still reserve a tributary Flame.

(Offers her a Purse of Gold.)

—To gain your Credit, I'll pay you back your Charity,
And be oblig'd for nothing but for Love.
ANGELICA: Oh that thou wert in earnest!
So mean a Thought of me,
320 Wou'd turn my Rage to Scorn, and I shou'd pity thee,
And give thee leave to live;
Which for the publick Safety of our Sex,
And my own private Injuries, I dare not do.
Prepare—

(Follows still, as before.)

325 —I will no more be tempted with Replies.
WILLMORE: Sure—
ANGELICA: Another Word will damn thee! I've heard thee talk
    too long.

(She follows him with a Pistol ready to shoot: he retires still amaz'd.)

(Enter Don ANTONIO, *his Arm in a Scarf, and lays hold on the
Pistol.)*

ANTONIO: Hah! *Angelica!*
ANGELICA: *Antonio!* What Devil brought thee hither?
330 ANTONIO: Love and Curiosity, seeing your Coach at Door.
Let me disarm you of this unbecoming Instrument of
Death.—

(Takes away the Pistol.)

Amongst the Number of your Slaves, was there not one
worthy the Honour to have fought your Quarrel?
335 —Who are you, Sir, that are so very wretched

To merit Death from her?
WILLMORE: One, sir, that cou'd have made a better End of an
amorous Quarrel without you, than with you.
ANTONIO: Sure 'tis some Rival—hah—the very Man took down
her Picture yesterday—the very same that set on me last   340
night—Blest opportunity—

(Offers to shoot him.)

ANGELICA: Hold, you're mistaken, Sir.
ANTONIO: By Heaven the very same!
—Sir, what pretensions have you to this Lady?
WILLMORE: Sir, I don't use to be examin'd, and am ill at all   345
Disputes but this—

(Draws, ANTONIO *offers to shoot.)*

ANGELICA: *(To* WILLMORE.*)* Oh, hold! you see he's arm'd with
    certain Death:
—And you, *Antonio,* I command you hold,
By all the Passion you've so lately vow'd me.

(Enter Don PEDRO, *sees* ANTONIO, *and stays.)*

PEDRO: *(Aside.)* Hah, *Antonio!* and *Angelica!*   350
ANTONIO: When I refuse Obedience to your Will,
May you destroy me with your mortal Hate.
By all that's Holy I adore you so,
That even my Rival, who has Charms enough
To make him fall a Victim to my Jealousy,   355
Shall live, nay, and have leave to love on still.
PEDRO: *(Aside.)* What's this I hear?
ANGELICA: *(Pointing to* WILLMORE.*)* Ah thus, 'twas thus he
    talk'd, and I believ'd.
—*Antonio,* yesterday,
I'd not have sold my Interest in his Heart,   360
For all the Sword has won and lost in Battle.
—But now to show my utmost of Contempt,
I give thee Life—which if thou would'st preserve,
Live where my Eyes may never see thee more,
Live to undo some one, whose Soul may prove   365
So bravely constant to revenge my Love.

(Goes out, ANTONIO *follows, but* PEDRO *pulls him back.)*

PEDRO: *Antonio*—stay.
ANTONIO: Don *Pedro*—
PEDRO: What Coward Fear was that prevented thee
From meeting me this Morning on the *Molo?*   370
ANTONIO: Meet thee?
PEDRO: Yes me; I was the Man that dar'd thee to't.
ANTONIO: Hast thou so often seen me fight in War,
To find no better Cause to excuse my Absence?
—I sent my Sword and one to do thee Right,   375
Finding my self uncapable to use a Sword.
PEDRO: But 'twas *Florinda's* Quarrel that we fought,
And you to shew how little you esteem'd her,
Sent me your Rival, giving him your Interest.
—But I have found the Cause of this Affront,   380
But when I meet you fit for the Dispute,
—I'll tell you my Resentment.

ANTONIO: I shall be ready, Sir, e'er long to do your Reason.

(*Exit* ANTONIO.)

PEDRO: If I cou'd find *Florinda,* now whilst my Anger's high, I
385   think I shou'd be kind, and give her to *Belvile* in Revenge.

WILLMORE: Faith, Sir, I know not what you wou'd do, but I believe the Priest within has been so kind.

PEDRO: How! my Sister married?

WILLMORE: I hope by this time she is, and bedded too, or he has
390   not my longings about him.

PEDRO: Dares he do thus? Does he not fear my Pow'r?

WILLMORE: Faith not at all. If you will go in, and thank him
for the Favour he has done your Sister, so; if not, Sir, my
Power's greater in this House than yours; I have a damn'd
395   surly Crew here, that will keep you till the next Tide, and
then clap you an board my Prize; my Ship lies but a League
off the *Molo,* and we shall show your Donship a damn'd
Tramontana Rover's Trick.

(*Enter* BELVILE.)

BELVILE: This Rogue's in some new Mischief—hah, *Pedro* re-
400   turn'd!

PEDRO: Colonel *Belvile,* I hear you have married my Sister.

BELVILE: You have heard truth then, Sir.

PEDRO: Have I so? then, Sir, I wish you Joy.

BELVILE: How!

405 PEDRO: By this Embrace I do, and I glad on't.

BELVILE: Are you in earnest?

PEDRO: By our long Friendship and my Obligations to thee, I
am. The sudden Change I'll give you Reasons for anon.
Come lead me into my Sister, that she may know I now ap-
410   prove her Choice.

(*Exit* BELVILE *with* PEDRO. WILLMORE *goes to follow them. Enter*
HELLENA *as before in Boy's Clothes, and pulls him back.*)

WILLMORE: Ha! my Gipsy—Now a thousand Blessings on thee
for this Kindness. Egad, Child, I was e'en in despair of ever
seeing thee again; my Friends are all provided for within,
each Man his kind Woman.

415 HELLENA: Hah! I thought they had serv'd me some such Trick.

WILLMORE: And I was e'en resolv'd to go aboard, condemn my
self to my lone Cabin, and the Thoughts of thee.

HELLENA: And cou'd you have left me behind? wou'd you have
been so ill-natur'd?

420 WILLMORE: Why, 'twou'd have broke my Heart, Child—but
since we are met again, I defy foul Weather to part us.

HELLENA: And wou'd you be a faithful Friend now, if a Maid
shou'd trust you?

WILLMORE: For a Friend I cannot promise, thou art of a Form so
425   excellent, a Face and Humour too good for cold dull Friendship; I am parlously afraid of being in love, Child, and you
have not forgot how severely you have us'd me.

HELLENA: That's all one, such Usage you must still look for, to
find out all your Haunts, to rail at you to all that love you,

till I have made you love only me in your own Defence, be-   430
cause no body else will love.

WILLMORE: But hast thou no better Quality to recommend thy
self by?

HELLENA: Faith none, Captain—Why, 'twill be the greater
Charity to take me for thy Mistress, I am a lone Child, a   435
kind of Orphan Lover; and why I shou'd die a Maid, and in
a Captain's Hands too, I do not understand.

WILLMORE: Egad, I was never claw'd away with Broad-Sides
from any Female before, thou hast one Virtue I adore, good-
Nature; I hate a coy demure Mistress, she's as troublesom as   440
a Colt, I'll break none; no, give me a mad Mistress when
mew'd, and in flying on[e] I dare trust upon the Wing, that
whilst she's kind will come to the Lure.

HELLENA: Nay, as kind as you will, good Captain, whilst it
lasts, but let's lose no time.   445

WILLMORE: My time's as precious to me, as thine can be; therefore, dear Creature, since we are so well agreed, let's retire
to my Chamber, and if ever thou were treated with such savory Love—Come—My Bed's prepar'd for such a Guest, all
clean and sweet as thy fair self; I love to steal a Dish and a   450
Bottle with a Friend, and hate long Graces—Come, let's retire and fall to.

HELLENA: 'Tis but getting my Consent, and the Business is soon
done; let but old Gaffer *Hymen* and his Priest say Amen to't,
and I dare lay my Mother's Daughter by as proper a Fellow   455
as your Father's Son, without fear or blushing.

WILLMORE: Hold, hold, no Bugg Words, Child, Priest and *Hymen:*
prithee add Hangman to 'em to make up the Consort—No,
no, we'll have no Vows but Love, Child, nor Witness but
the Lover; the kind Diety injoins naught but love and enjoy.   460
Hymen and Priest wait still upon Portion, and Joynture; Love
and Beauty have their own Ceremonies. Marriage is as certain
a Bane to Love, as lending Money is to Friendship: I'll neither
ask nor give a Vow, tho I could be content to turn Gipsy, and
become a Left-hand Bridegroom, to have the Pleasure of   465
working that great Miracle of making a Maid a Mother, if you
durst venture; 'tis upse Gipsy that, and if I miss, I'll lose my
Labour.

HELLENA: And if you do not lose, what shall I get? A Cradle full
of Noise and Mischief, with a Pack of Repentance at my   470
Back? Can you teach me to weave Incle to pass my time
with? 'Tis upse Gipsy that too.

WILLMORE: I can teach thee to weave a true Love's Knot better.

HELLENA: So can my Dog.

WILLMORE: Well, I see we are both upon our Guard, and I see   475
there's no way to conquer good Nature, but by yielding—
here—give me thy Hand—one Kiss and I am thine—

HELLENA: One Kiss! How like my Page he speaks; I am resolv'd
you shall have none, for asking such a sneaking Sum—He
that will be satisfied with one Kiss, will never die of that   480
Longing; good Friend single-Kiss, is all your talking come
to this? A Kiss, a Caudle! farewel, Captain single-Kiss.

(*Going out he stays her.*)

---

398 **Tramontana** Italian and Spanish *tramontano* = from beyond
the mountains

467 **upse** *Op zijn* (Dutch) = in the fashion or manner of, *Upse
Gipsy* = like a gipsy   471 **Incle** linen thread or yarn which was
woven into a tape once very much in use

WILLMORE: Nay, if we part so, let me die like a Bird upon a Bough, at the Sheriff's Charge. By Heaven, both the *Indies*
485 shall not buy thee from me. I adore thy Humour and will marry thee, and we are so of one Humour, it must be a Bargain—give me thy Hand—

(Kisses her hand.)

And now let the blind ones (Love and Fortune) do their worst.
HELLENA: Why, God-a-mercy, Captain!
490 WILLMORE: But harkye—The Bargain is now made; but is it not fit we should know each other's Names? That when we have Reason to curse one another hereafter, and People ask me who 'tis I give to the Devil, I may at least be able to tell what Family you came of.
495 HELLENA: Good reason, Captain; and where I have cause, (as I doubt not but I shall have plentiful) that I may know at whom to throw my—Blessings—I beseech ye your Name.
WILLMORE: I am call'd *Robert the Constant.*
HELLENA: A very fine Name! pray was it your Faulkner or But-
500 ler that christen'd you? Do they not use to whistle when then call you?
WILLMORE: I hope you have a better, that a Man may name without crossing himself, you are so merry with mine.
HELLENA: I am call'd *Hellena the Inconstant.*

(Enter PEDRO, BELVILE, FLORINDA, FREDERICK, and VALERIA.)

505 PEDRO: Hah! *Hellena!*
FLORINDA: *Hellena!*
HELLENA: The very same—hah my Brother! now, Captain, shew your Love and Courage; stand to your Arms, and defend me bravely, or I am lost for ever.
510 PEDRO: What's this I hear? false Girl, how came you hither, and what's your Business? Speak.

(Goes roughly to her.)

WILLMORE: Hold off, Sir, you have leave to parly only.

(Puts himself between.)

HELLENA: I had e'en as good tell it, as you guess it. Faith, Brother, my Business is the same with all living Creatures
515 of my Age, to love, and be loved, and here's the Man.
PEDRO: Perfidious Maid, hast thou deceiv'd me too, deceiv'd thy self and Heaven?
HELLENA: 'Tis time enough to make my Peace with that: Be you but kind, let me alone with Heaven.
520 PEDRO: *Belvile,* I did not expect this false Play from you; was't not enough you'd gain *Florinda* (which I pardon'd) but your leud Friends too must be inrich'd with the Spoils of a noble Family?
BELVILE: Faith, Sir, I am as much surpriz'd at this as you can be:
525 Yet, Sir, my Friends are Gentlemen, and ought to be esteem'd for their Misfortunes, since they have the Glory to suffer with the best of Men and Kings; 'tis true, he's a Rover of Fortune, yet a Prince aboard his little wooden World.
PEDRO: What's this to the maintenance of a Woman or her
530 Birth and Quality?
WILLMORE: Faith, Sir, I can boast of nothing but a Sword which does me Right where-e'er I come, and has defended a worse

Cause than a Woman's: and since I lov'd her before I either knew her Birth or Name, I must pursue my Resolution, and marry her. 535
PEDRO: And is all your holy Intent of becoming a Nun debauch'd into a Desire of Man?
HELLENA: Why—I have consider'd the matter, Brother, and find the Three hundred thousand Crowns my Uncle left me (and you cannot keep from me) will be better laid out in 540 Love than in Religion, and turn to as good an Account—let most Voices carry it, for Heaven or the Captain?
ALL CRY: Captain, a Captain.
HELLENA: Look ye, Sir, 'tis a clear Case.
PEDRO: *(Aside.)* Oh I am mad—if I refuse, my Life's in Dan- 545 ger—Come—There's one motive induces me—take her—I shall now be free from the fear of her Honour; guard it you now, if you can, I have been a Slave to't long enough.

(Gives her to him.)

WILLMORE: Faith, Sir, I am of a Nation, that are of opinion a Woman's Honour is not worth guarding when she has a 550 mind to part with it.
HELLENA: Well said, Captain.
PEDRO: *(To VALERIA.)* This was your Plot, Mistress, but I hope you have married one that will revenge my Quarrel to you— 555
VALERIA: There's no altering Destiny, Sir.
PEDRO: Sooner than a Woman's Will, therefore I forgive you all—and wish you may get my Father's Pardon as easily; which I fear.

(Enter BLUNT drest in a Spanish Habit, looking very ridiculously; his MAN adjusting his Band.)

MAN: 'Tis very well, Sir. 560
BLUNT: Well, Sir, 'dsheartlikins I tell you 'tis damnable ill, Sir—a Spanish Habit, good Lord! cou'd the Devil and my Taylor devise no other Punishment for me, but the Mode of a Nation I abominate?
BELVILE: What's the matter, *Ned?* 565
BLUNT: Pray view me round, and judge—

(Turns round.)

BEVILE: I must confess thou art a kind of an odd Figure.
BLUNT: In a Spanish Habit with a Vengeance! I had rather be in the Inquisition for Judaism, than in this Doublet and Breeches; a Pillory were an easy Collar to this, three Hand- 570 fuls high; and these Shoes too are worse than the Stocks, with the Sole an Inch shorter than my Foot: In fine, Gentlemen, methinks I look altogether like a Bag of Bays stuff'd full of Fools Flesh.
BELVILE: Methinks 'tis well, and makes the look *en Cavalier:* 575 Come, Sir, settle your Face, and salute our Friends, Lady—
BLUNT: Hah! Say'st thou so, my little Rover?

(To HELLENA.)

Lady—(if you be one) give me leave to kiss your Hand, and tell you, adsheartlikins, for all I look so, I am your humble Servant—A Pox of my *Spanish* Habit. 580

WILLMORE: Hark—what's this?

(Musick is heard to Play. Enter BOY.*)*

BOY: Sir, as the Custom is, the gay People in Masquerade, who make every Man's House their own, are coming up.

(Enter several MEN *and* WOMEN *in masquing Habits, with Musick, they put themselves in order and dance.)*

BLUNT: Adsheartlikins, wou'd 'twere lawful to pull off their
585　false Faces, that I might see if my Doxy were not amongst 'em.

BELVILE: Ladies and Gentlemen, since you are come so *a propos,* you must take a small Collation with us.

(To the MASQUERADERS.*)*

WILLMORE: Whilst we'll to the Good Man within, who stays to
590　give us a Cast of his Office.

(To HELLENA.*)*

—Have you no trembling at the near approach?

HELLENA: No more than you have in an Engagement or a Tempest.

WILLMORE: Egad, thou'rt a brave Girl, and I admire thy Love
595　and Courage.
　　Lead on, no other Dangers they can dread,
　　Who venture in the Storms o'th' Marriage-Bed.

(Exeunt.)

───── **EPILOGUE** ─────

THE banisht Cavaliers! a Roving Blade!
A popish Carnival! a Masquerade!
The Devil's in't if this will please the Nation,
In these our blessed Times of Reformation,
5　When Conventicling is so much in Fashion.
And yet—
That mutinous Tribe less Factions do beget,
Than your continual differing in Wit;

Your Judgment's (as your Passions) a Disease:
Nor Muse nor Miss your Appetite can please;　　　10
You're grown as nice as queasy Consciences,
Whose each Convulsion, when the Spirit moves,
Damns every thing that Maggot disapproves.
　　With canting Rule you wou'd the Stage refine,
And to dull Method all our Sense confine.　　　15
With th' Insolence of Common-wealths you rule,
Where each gay Fop, and politick brave Fool
On Monarch Wit impose without controul.
As for the last who seldom sees a Play,
Unless it be the old Black-Fryers way,　　　20
Shaking his empty Noodle o'er *Bamboo,*
He crys—Good Faith, these Plays will never do.
—Ah, Sir, in my young days, what lofty Wit,
What high-strain'd Scenes of Fighting there were writ:
These are slight airy Toys. But tell me, pray,　　　25
What has the *House of Commons* done to day?
Then shews his Politicks, to let you see
Of State Affairs he'll judge as notably,
As he can do of Wit and Poetry.
　　The younger Sparks, who hither do resort,　　　30
Cry—
Pox o' your gentle things, give us more Sport;
—Damn me, I'm sure 'twill never please the Court.
　　Such Fops are never pleas'd, unless the Play
Be stuff'd with Fools, as brisk and dull as they:　　　35
Such might the Half-Crown spare, and in a Glass
At home behold a more accomplisht Ass,
Where they may set their Cravats, Wigs and Faces,
And practice all their Buffoonry Grimaces;
See how this—Huff becomes—this Dammy—flare—　　　40
Which they at home may act, because they dare,
But—must with prudent Caution do elsewhere.
Oh that our *Nokes,* or *Tony Lee* could show
A Fop but half so much to th' Life as you.

───────────────

43 *Nokes,* or *Tony Lee* James Nokes and Antony Leigh, the two famous actors, were the leading low comedians of the day

SOR JUANA INÉS DE LA CRUZ

Juana Inés de Asbaje y Ramírez de Santillana (1648/51–1695) was probably born in late November or early December of 1648, to the daughter of a wealthy landowner (Isabel Ramírez de Santillana) and an army officer (Pedro Manuel de Asbaje y Vargas Manchucha) serving in the Spanish new world colony of New Spain—present-day Mexico. Although her parents had two other children (Isabel Ramírez had three additional children with another officer), they were not married, and Juana Inés was born an illegitimate "daughter of the church." Raised in the provincial town of Panoyan, Juana had access to her grandfather's library and, by her own account, was a voracious reader, as she later wrote in her *Answer to Sor Filotea* (written 1691):

> When I was six or seven years old and already knew how to read and write, along with all the other skills like embroidery and sewing that women learn, I heard that in Mexico City there were a University and Schools where they studied sciences. As soon as I heard this I began to slay my poor mother with insistent and annoying pleas, begging her to dress me in men's clothes and send me to the capital, to the home of some relatives she had there, so that I could enter the University and study. She refused, and was right in doing so; but I quenched my desire by reading a great variety of books that belonged to my grandfather, and neither punishments nor scoldings could prevent me. And so when I did go to Mexico City, people marveled not so much at my intelligence as at my memory and the facts I knew at an age when it seemed I had scarcely had time to speak.[1]

Juana was sent to live with her mother's relatives in Mexico City in 1659. She lived with them for five years until she moved into the home of the viceroy, where she served in the court of the vicereine, doña Leonor Carreto, marquisa de Mancera.

Although she began to write on both religious and secular subjects while at court, Juana's career was closely tied to the church. In 1666 she joined the Carmelite convent of San José, but the penitential strictness of the order seems to have caused her health to suffer, and she left the convent after three months. Still eager to join a convent, she agreed to sit for an examination by the viceroy and forty scholars assembled to test the range of her knowledge, as a means to confirm her suitability for religious life. According to Diego Callega, a priest who wrote the first biography of Sor Juana, she performed like a "royal galleon attacked by canoes," and was admitted to the convent of Santa Paula in 1669, where she took the name Sor Juana Inés de la Cruz. (Illegitimate children were not admissible to convent life; at this time, Juana claimed that her parents had been married, and that her birthdate was November 12, 1651; a baptismal record for 1648—listing Juana's aunt and uncle as godparents of an infant "Inés"—is now usually taken as evidence for her birth in that year.)

Although the convent was cloistered, Sor Juana received money to support her servants and was able to receive guests, to study, and to write; she was also closely connected to the social life of New Spain's capital city. Although the Aztec city of Tenochtitlán had supported some 250,000 inhabitants before the conquest in 1520, Mexico City was a much smaller city in the seventeenth century. While war, disease, and enslavement drastically reduced the native population, the general population was augmented not only by the annual arrival of *peninsulares* (new inhabitants from Spain), but by an increasing population of *criollos* (people of European descent born in Mexico, like Sor Juana) and *mestizos,* as well as by a growing number of African slaves and immigrants from other Spanish colonies; in the 1800 census, for example, the population of Mexico City was 137,000, making it the largest city in the Americas. The church wielded extensive political power in Mexico (there

---

[1]See *The Answer/La Respuesta, Including a Selection of Poems,* Ed. And Trans. Electa Arenal and Amanda Powell (New York: Feminist Press, 1994).

were sixteen convents in Mexico City alone), and—as in Europe—the leaders of the church and of the state were often drawn from the same aristocratic families. In this sense, it's not surprising that throughout her life Sor Juana was an intimate acquaintance of aristocratic circles in Mexico City, particularly of the viceroys and vicereines.

One vicereine, Maria Luisa Manrique de Lara y Gonzaga (whose husband was viceroy 1680–86), was the inspiration of several of Sor Juana's poems and had her first volume, *Inundación Castálida,* published in Madrid in 1689 (the title refers to the nymph Castálida, who drowned herself rather than be seduced by Apollo); the title-page described Sor Juana as "the Tenth Muse." By 1690, Sor Juana was arguably the most accomplished secular and philosophical writer in the Americas: she mastered the baroque forms of secular Spanish poetry, writing not only sixty-five sonnets and many ballads and occasional poems, but two well-known comedies (including *Los empeños de una casa*) which were staged; she also wrote sixteen sets of VILLANCICOS, carols performed at the Mass (these often incorporate her understanding both of African dialects and of the indigenous Nahua language, and were performed at cathedrals throughout Mexico during her lifetime); she wrote three *auto sacramentales,* two of which were performed; thirty-two LOAS; a brilliant philosophical treatise *The First Dream* (1685); as well as a defense of women's claim to an intellectual and spiritual life, *Answer to Sor Filotea.*

Yet despite her fame, Sor Juana was under continual pressure from the church to conform to the more "feminine" role of quiet devotion and service. Early in her career she struggled with her confessor Antonio Núñez de Miranda, who regarded writing as improper for women, especially for women of the church. Although Sor Juana succeeded in dismissing him as her confessor, he continued to agitate for her silence with higher church officials, including the misogynist archbishop Francisco Aguian y Seijas. In 1690—shortly after her second volume of poetry had been published in Madrid, and her brilliant *auto The Divine Narcissus* had been published in Mexico—the church's opposition came to a head. During that year, Sor Juana wrote a theological critique of a sermon written forty years earlier, an essay clearly not intended for publication; her friend, the bishop of Puebla, Manuel Fernández de Santa Cruz, asked her to send it to him. Without her permission, he published Sor Juana's essay under the title *Carta atenagórica*—"Letter Worthy of Athena." Despite the praise implied in the title, the bishop was in fact eager to expose Sor Juana to censure and appended his own corrective letter to her treatise—from "Sor Filotea," "lover of God." This public rebuke spurred Sor Juana's brilliant *Answer to Sor Filotea de la Cruz,* a passionate defense of both her intellectual life and its contribution to her faith, written in 1691 but published only after her death in 1700. Despite her defense, however, Sor Juana acceded to the will of the church in 1692; her last set of *villancicos* was performed at the cathedral in Oaxaca; she sold both her musical instruments and her extensive library (among the largest private libraries in the Americas at the time), and in 1694 she signed—in blood—a new declaration of faith, vowing to give up secular studies as well. She died during an epidemic that swept Mexico City in April 1695.

Sor Juana's poetry, plays, and philosophical writings are well known in Spanish, and many have been published in English translations (see the Bibliography); the Mexican poet Octavio Paz has written a celebrated biography of Sor Juana: *Sor Juana, or, The Traps of Faith* (Trans. Margaret Sayers Peden [Cambridge: Harvard University Press, 1988]).

LOA TO THE DIVINE NARCISSUS

The Divine Narcissus is a full-length *auto sacramentale,* an allegorical drama on the subject of the Eucharist that Sor Juana wrote in 1687. She intended to submit it to be performed in Madrid as part of a competition for new *autos* following the death of Calderón, who had been the sole author of *autos* performed in the Spanish capital before his death in 1681.

Although the death of the queen in 1689 forced the cancellation of the festival, Sor Juana's *The Divine Narcissus* and its introductory *loa* remain among the most accomplished examples of this important genre of Spanish-language drama.

Although the *loa* can be used for either secular or sacred purposes, Sor Juana uses it here specifically to introduce the themes of the *auto,* which uses the Greek story of Echo and Narcissus to allegorize the theological doctrine of the Eucharist. However, to modern readers and audiences, the *loa* is perhaps more interesting for its staging of colonial conflict; through an allegorical conversation between Zeal (a *conquistador*), Religion (a Spanish lady), and the Aztec rulers (Occident and America), the short play also stages an allegory of the conquest of Mexico and its consequences. Although there is no record of the play being performed in Sor Juana's lifetime, it clearly records aspects of Aztec life—the opening dance and ritual worship of the God of the Seeds—that were legally prohibited in seventeenth-century New Spain, while staging a debate between the Aztec leaders and the Spanish invaders who insist on replacing the native religion with the practice of Christianity. While the bullheaded *conquistador,* Zeal, is on the point of murdering the defeated Aztecs, they are spared by Religion, who hears in their account of their religious rituals a profane version of the miracle of the Eucharist:

> What images,
> what dark designs, what shadowings
> of truths most sacred to our Faith
> do these lies seek to imitate?

Religion works to bring Christian salvation to Occident and America by pointing out the similarities between their religion and the mysteries of the Eucharist:

> a God composed
> of human blood, an offering
> of sacrifice, and in himself
> does He combine with bloody death
> the life-sustaining seeds of earth?

To instruct Occident and America, Religion decides to

> make for you a metaphor
> a concept clothed in rhetoric
> so colorful that what I show
> to you, your eyes will clearly see.

The *auto* that follows, *The Divine Narcissus,* is Religion's illustrative "metaphor," her way of explaining the Eucharist to the inhabitants of the New World.

Written by a *criolla,* as part of a competition to take place in Madrid, Sor Juana's play is in many ways a barometer of the situation of colonial writing; the final dialogue between Zeal and Religion considers whether such a play, written in the colony about colonial subjects, will be received in "the crown city of Madrid, / which is the center of the Faith, / the seat of Catholic majesty" as an act of "impropriety." Although written at the height of Spain's imperial expansion, and indeed in many ways written to celebrate that expansion, Sor Juana's *loa* to *The Divine Narcissus* deftly registers many of the tensions that typically inform colonial writing: between the colony and the capital, between the native population and their invaders, for instance. But particularly in the brittle relationship between Zeal and Religion, and the more charitable relationship between Religion and America, Sor Juana seems to open another kind of critique as well; Religion refuses, for example, to sanction the extermination, or even the subjugation, of Occident and America. While the *loa* testifies unambiguously to Sor Juana's confidence in the universality of her faith, it also seems to question some of the ways religion is used to advance Spain's political and economic mission in this new and distinct society.

LOA TO THE DIVINE NARCISSUS

Sor Juana Inés de la Cruz

TRANSLATED BY PATRICIA A. PETERS AND RENÉE DOMEIER, O. S. B.

———— CHARACTERS ————

OCCIDENT	RELIGION	AZTECS
AMERICA	MUSIC	DANCERS
ZEAL	SOLDIERS	

———— SCENE ONE ————

Enter OCCIDENT, *a gallant-looking Aztec, wearing a crown. By his side is* AMERICA, *an Aztec woman of poised self-possession. They are dressed in the mantas and huipiles worn for singing a tocotín. They seat themselves on two chairs. On each side, Aztec men and women dance with feathers and rattles in their hands, as is customary for those doing this dance. While they dance,* MUSIC *sings.*

MUSIC: O, Noble Mexicans,
whose ancient ancestry
comes forth from the clear light
and brilliance of the Sun,
5   since this, of all the year,
is your most happy feast
in which you venerate
your greatest deity,
come and adorn yourselves
10   with vestments of your rank;
let your holy fervor be
made one with jubilation;
and celebrate in festive pomp
the great God of the Seeds!

15 MUSIC: Since the abundance of
our native fields and farms
is owed to him alone
who gives fertility,
then offer him your thanks,
20   for it is right and just
to give from what has grown,
the first of the new fruits.
From your own veins, draw out
and give, without reserve,
25   the best blood, mixed with seed,
so that his cult be served,
and celebrate in festive pomp,
the great God of the Seeds!

(OCCIDENT *and* AMERICA *sit, and* MUSIC *ceases.*)

OCCIDENT: Of all the deities to whom
30   our rites demand I bend my knee—
among two thousand gods or more
who dwell within this royal city
and who require the sacrifice
of human victims still entreating
35   for life until their blood is drawn
and gushes forth from hearts still beating
and bowels still pulsing—I declare,
among all these, (it bears repeating),

whose ceremonies we observe,
the greatest is, surpassing all
this pantheon's immensity
40   the great God of the Seeds.

AMERICA: And you are right, since he alone
daily sustains our monarchy
because our lives depend on his
45   providing crops abundantly;
and since he gives us graciously
the gift from which all gifts proceed,
our fields rich with golden maize,
the source of life through daily bread,
50   we render him our highest praise.
Then how will it improve our lives
if rich America abounds
in gold from mines whose smoke deprives
the fields of their fertility
55   and with their clouds of filthy soot
will not allow the crops to grow
which blossom now so fruitfully
from seeded earth? Moreover, his
protection of our people far
60   exceeds our daily food and drink,
the body's sustenance. Indeed,
he feeds us with his very flesh
(first purified of every stain).
We eat his body, drink his blood,
65   and by this sacred meal are freed
and cleansed from all that is profane,
and thus, he purifies our soul.
And now, attentive to his rites,
together let us all proclaim:
70 OCCIDENT, AMERICA, DANCERS and MUSIC: We celebrate in
          festive pomp,
     the great God of the Seeds!

———— SCENE TWO ————

They exit dancing. Enter Christian RELIGION *as a Spanish lady,* ZEAL *as a Captain General in armor, and Spanish* SOLDIERS.

RELIGION: How, being Zeal, can you suppress
the flames of righteous Christian wrath
when here before your very eyes
idolatry, so blind with pride,
5   adores, with superstitious rites
an idol, leaving your own bride,
the holy faith of Christ disgraced?

ZEAL: Religion, trouble not your mind
or grieve my failure to attack,

10   complaining that my love is slack,
      for now the sword I wear is bared,
      its hilt in hand, clasped ready and
      my arm raised high to take revenge.
      Please stand aside and deign to wait
15   till I requite your grievances.

(Enter OCCIDENT *and* AMERICA *dancing, and accompanied by*
MUSIC, *who enters from the other side.)*

MUSIC: And celebrate in festive pomp,
      the great God of the Seeds!
ZEAL: Here they come! I will confront them.
RELIGION: And I, in peace, will also go
20   (before your fury lays them low)
      for justice must with mercy kiss;
      I shall invite them to arise
      from superstitious depths to faith.
ZEAL: Let us approach while they are still
25   absorbed in their lewd rituals.
MUSIC: And celebrate in festive pomp,
      the great God of the Seeds!

(ZEAL and RELIGION cross the stage.)

RELIGION: Great Occident, most powerful;
      America, so beautiful
30   and rich; you live in poverty
      amid the treasures of your land.
      Abandon this irreverent cult
      with which the demon has waylaid you.
      Open your eyes! Follow the path
35   that leads straightforwardly to truth,
      to which my love yearns to persuade you.
OCCIDENT: Who are these unknown people, so
      intrusive in my sight, who dare
      to stop us in our ecstasy?
40   Heaven forbid such infamy!
AMERICA: Who are these nations, never seen,
      that wish, by force, to pit themselves
      against my ancient power supreme?
OCCIDENT: Oh, you alien beauty fair;
45   oh, pilgrim woman from afar,
      who comes to interrupt my prayer,
      please speak and tell me who you are.
RELIGION: Christian Religion is my name,
      and I intend that all this realm
50   will make obeisance unto me.
OCCIDENT: An impossible concession!
AMERICA: Yours is but a mad obsession!
OCCIDENT: You will meet with swift repression.
AMERICA: Pay no attention; she is mad!
55   Let us go on with our procession.
MUSIC and AZTECS: And celebrate in festive pomp,
      the great God of the Seeds!
ZEAL: How is this, barbarous Occident?
      Can it be, sightless Idolatry,
60   that you insult Religion,
      the spouse I cherish tenderly?

Abomination fills your cup
and overruns the brim, but see
that God will not permit you to
continue drinking down delight,   65
and I am sent to deal your doom.
OCCIDENT: And who are you who frightens all
      who only look upon your face?
ZEAL: I am Zeal. Does that surprise you?
      Take heed! for when your excesses   70
      bring disgrace to fair Religion,
      then will Zeal arise to vengeance;
      for insolence I will chastise you.
      I am the minister of God,
      Who growing weary with the sight   75
      of overreaching tyrannies
      so sinful that they reach the height
      of error, practiced many years,
      has sent me forth to penalize you.
      And thus, these military hosts   80
      with flashing thunderbolts of steel,
      the ministers of His great wrath
      are sent, His anger to reveal.
OCCIDENT: What god? What sin? What tyranny?
      What punishment do you foresee?   85
      Your reasons make no sense to me,
      nor can I make the slightest guess
      who you might be with your insistence
      on tolerating no resistance,
      impeding us with rash persistence   90
      from lawful worship as we sing.
MUSIC: And celebrate with festive pomp,
      the great God of the Seeds!
AMERICA: Madman, blind, and barbarous,
      with mystifying messages   95
      you try to mar our calm and peace,
      destroying the tranquility
      that we enjoy. Your plots must cease,
      unless, of course, you wish to be
      reduced to ashes, whose existence   100
      even the winds will never sense.
      (To OCCIDENT.) And you, my spouse, and your cohort,
      close off your hearing and your sight
      to all their words; refuse to heed
      their fantasies of zealous might;   105
      proceed to carry out your rite.
      Do not concede to insolence
      from foreigners intent to dull
      our ritual's magnificence.
MUSIC: And celebrate with festive pomp,   110
      the great God of the Seeds!
ZEAL: Since our initial offering
      of peaceful terms, you held so cheap,
      the dire alternative of war,
      I guarantee you'll count more dear.   115
      Take up your arms! To war! To war!

(Drums and trumpets sound.)

OCCIDENT: What miscarriages of justice
      has heaven sent against me?

120   What are these weapons, blazing fire,
       before my unbelieving eyes?
       Get ready, guards! Aim well, my troops,
       Your arrows at this enemy!

       AMERICA: What lightening bolts does heaven send
125   to lay me low? What molten balls
          of burning lead so fiercely rain?
          What centaurs crush with monstrous force
          and cause my people such great pain?

       (Within.) To arms! To arms! War! War!

       ({Drums and trumpets} sound.)

       (Within.) Long life to Spain! Long live her king!

       *(The battle begins. Indians enter through one door and flee through
       another with the Spanish pursuing at their heels. From back stage,
       OCCIDENT backs away from RELIGION and AMERICA retreats before
       ZEAL's onslaught.)*

       ——— SCENE THREE ———

       RELIGION: Give up, arrogant Occident!
       OCCIDENT: I must bow to your aggression,
          but not before your arguments.
       ZEAL: Die, impudent America!
5   RELIGION: Desist! Do not give her to Death;
          her life is of some worth to us.
       ZEAL: How can you now defend this maid
          who has so much offended you?
       RELIGION: America has been subdued
10   because your valor won the strife,
          but now my mercy intervenes
          in order to preserve her life.
          It was your part to conquer her
          by force with military might;
15   mine is to gently make her yield,
          persuading her by reason's light.
       ZEAL: But you have seen the stubbornness
          with which these blind ones still abhor
          your creed; is it not better far
20   that they all die?
       RELIGION: Good Zeal, restrain
          your justice, and do not kill them.
          My gentle disposition deigns
          to forbear vengeance and forgive.
          I want them to convert and live.
25   AMERICA: If your petition for my life
          and show of Christian charity
          are motivated by the hope
          that you, at last, will conquer me,
          defeating my integrity
30   with verbal steel where bullets failed,
          then you are sadly self-deceived.
          A weeping captive, I may mourn
          for liberty, yet my will grows
          beyond these bonds; my heart is free,
35   and I will worship my own gods!
       OCCIDENT: Forced to surrender to your power,
          I have admitted my defeat,

       but still it must be clearly said
       that violence cannot devour
       my will, nor force constrain its right.   40
       Although in grief, I now lament,
       a prisoner, your cruel might
       has limits. You cannot prevent
       my saying here within my heart
       I worship the great God of Seeds!   45

       ——— SCENE FOUR ———

       RELIGION: Wait! What you perceive as force
          is not coercion, but affection.
          What god is this that you adore?
       OCCIDENT: The great God of the Seeds
          who causes fields to bring forth fruit.   5
          To him the lofty heavens bow;
          to him the rains obedience give;
          and when, at last, he cleanses us
          from stains of sin, then he invites
          us to the meal that he prepares.   10
          Consider whether you could find
          a god more generous and good
          who blesses more abundantly
          than he whom I describe to you.
       RELIGION: *(Aside.)* O God, help me! What images,   15
          what dark designs, what shadowings
          of truths most sacred to our Faith
          do these lies seek to imitate?
          O false, sly, and deceitful snake!
          O asp, with sting so venomous!   20
          O hydra, that from seven mouths
          pours noxious poisons, every one
          a passage to oblivion!
          To what extent, with this facade
          do you intend maliciously   25
          to mock the mysteries of God?
          Mock on! for with your own deceit,
          if God empowers my mind and tongue,
          I'll argue and impose defeat.
       AMERICA: Why do you find yourself perplexed?   30
          Do you not see there is no god
          other than ours who verifies
          with countless blessings his great works?
       RELIGION: In doctrinal disputes, I hold
          with the apostle Paul, for when   35
          he preached to the Athenians
          and found they had a harsh decree
          imposing death on anyone
          who tried to introduce new gods,
          since he had noticed they were free   40
          to worship at a certain shrine,
          an altar to "the Unknown God,"
          he said to them, "This Lord of mine
          is no new god, but one unknown
          that you have worshipped in this place,   45
          and it is He, my voice proclaims."
          And thus I—

       (OCCIDENT and AMERICA whisper to each other.)

Listen, Occident!
and hear me, blind Idolatry!
for all your happiness depends
50 on listening attentively.
These miracles that you recount,
these prodigies that you suggest,
these apparitions and these rays
of light in superstition dressed
55 are glimpsed but darkly through a veil.
These portents you exaggerate,
attributing to your false gods
effects that you insinuate,
but wrongly so, for all these works
60 proceed from our true God alone,
and of His Wisdom come to birth.
Then if the soil richly yields,
and if the fields bud and bloom,
if fruits increase and multiply,
65 if seeds mature in earth's dark womb,
if rains pour forth from leaden sky,
all is the work of His right hand;
for neither the arm that tills the soil
nor rains that fertilize the land
70 nor warmth that calls life from the tomb
of winter's death can make plants grow;
for they lack reproductive power
if Providence does not concur,
by breathing into each of them
75 a vegetative soul.
AMERICA: That might be so;
then tell me, is this God so kind—
this deity whom you describe—
that I might touch Him with my hands,
these very hands that carefully
80 create the idol, here before you,
an image made from seeds of earth
and innocent, pure human blood
shed only for this sacred rite?
RELIGION: Although the Essence of Divinity
85 is boundless and invisible,
because already It has been
eternally united with
our nature, He resembles us
so much in our humanity
90 that He permits unworthy priests
to take Him in their humble hands.
AMERICA: In this, at least, we are agreed,
for to my god no human hands
are so unstained that they deserve
95 to touch him; nonetheless, he gives
this honor graciously to those
who serve him with their priestly lives.
No others dare to touch the god,
nor in the sanctuary stand.
100 ZEAL: A reverence most worthily
directed to the one true God!
OCCIDENT: Whatever else you claim, now tell
me this: Is yours a God composed
of human blood, an offering
105 of sacrifice, and in Himself

does He combine with bloody death
the life-sustaining seeds of earth?
RELIGION: As I have said, His boundless
Majesty is insubstantial,
but in the Holy Sacrifice   110
of Mass, His blessed humanity
is placed unbloody under the
appearances of bread, which comes
from seeds of wheat and is transformed
into His Body and His Blood;   115
and this most holy Blood of Christ,
contained within a sacred cup,
is verily the offering
most innocent, unstained, and pure
that on the altar of the cross   120
was the redemption of the world.
AMERICA: Such miracles, unknown to us,
make me desire to believe;
but would the God that you reveal
offer Himself so lovingly   125
transformed for me into a meal
as does the god that I adore?
RELIGION: In truth, He does. For this alone
His Wisdom came upon the earth
to dwell among all humankind.   130
AMERICA: And so that I can be convinced,
may I not see this Deity?
OCCIDENT: And so that I can be made free
of old beliefs that shackle me?
RELIGION: Yes, you will see when you are bathed 135
in crystal waters from the font
of baptism.
OCCIDENT: And well I know,
in preparation to attend
a banquet, I must bathe, or else
our ancient custom I offend.   140
ZEAL: Your vain ablutions will not do
the cleansing that your stains require.
OCCIDENT: Then what?
RELIGION: There is a sacrament
of living waters, which can cleanse
and purify you of your sins.   145
AMERICA: Because you deluge my poor mind
with concepts of theology,
I've just begun to understand;
there is much more I want to see,
and my desire to know is now   150
by holy inspiration led.
OCCIDENT: And I desire more keenly still
to know about the life and death
of the God you say is in the bread.
RELIGION: Then come along with me, and I   155
shall make for you a metaphor,
a concept clothed in rhetoric
so colorful that what I show
to you, your eyes will clearly see;
for now I know that you require   160
objects of sight instead of words,
by which faith whispers in your ears
too deaf to hear; I understand,

for you necessity demands
165   that through the eyes, faith find her way
     to her reception in your hearts.
OCCIDENT: Exactly so. I do prefer
     to see the things you would impart.

——— SCENE FIVE ———

RELIGION: Then come.
ZEAL: Religion, answer me:
     what metaphor will you employ
     to represent these mysteries?
RELIGION: An *auto* will make visible
5   through allegory images
     of what America must learn
     and Occident implores to know
     about the questions that now burn
     within him so.
ZEAL: What will you call
10   this play in allegory cast?
RELIGION: *Divine Narcissus,* let it be,
     because if that unhappy maid
     adored an idol which disguised
     in such strange symbols the attempt
15   the demon made to counterfeit
     the great and lofty mystery
     of the most Blessed Eucharist,
     then there were also, I surmise,
     among more ancient pagans hints
20   of such high marvels symbolized.
ZEAL: Where will your drama be performed?
RELIGION: In the crown city of Madrid,
     which is the center of the Faith,
     the seat of Catholic majesty,
25   to whom the Indies owe their best
     beneficence, the blessed gift
     of Holy Writ, the Gospel light
     illuminating all the West.
ZEAL: That you should write in Mexico
30   for royal patrons don't you see
     to be an impropriety?
RELIGION: Is it beyond imagination
     that something made in one location
     can in another be of use?
35   Furthermore, my writing it
     comes, not of whimsical caprice,
     but from my vowed obedience
     to do what seems beyond my reach.
     Well, then, this work, however rough
40   and little polished it might be,
     results from my obedience,

and not from any arrogance.
ZEAL: Then answer me, Religion, how
     (before you leave the matter now),
     will you respond when you are chid   45
     for loading the whole Indies on
     a stage to transport to Madrid?
RELIGION: The purpose of my play can be
     none other than to glorify
     the Eucharistic Mystery;   50
     and since the cast of characters
     are no more than abstractions which
     depict the theme with clarity,
     then surely no one should object
     if they are taken to Madrid;   55
     distance can never hinder thought
     with persons of intelligence,
     nor seas impede exchange of sense.
ZEAL: Then, prostrate at his royal feet,
     beneath whose strength two worlds are joined   60
     we beg for pardon of the King;
RELIGION: and from her eminence, the Queen;
AMERICA: whose sovereign and anointed feet
     the humble Indies bow to kiss;
ZEAL: and from the Royal High Council;   65
RELIGION: and from the ladies, who bring light
     into their hemisphere;
AMERICA: and from
     their poets, I most humbly beg
     forgiveness for my crude attempt,
     desiring with these awkward lines   70
     to represent the Mystery.
OCCIDENT: Let's go, for anxiously I long to see
     exactly how this God of yours
     will give Himself as food to me.

(AMERICA, OCCIDENT, *and* ZEAL *sing:*)

     The Indies know   75
     and do concede
     who is the true
     God of the Seeds.
     In loving tears
     which joy prolongs   80
     we gladly sing
     our happy songs.
ALL: Blest be the day
     when I could see
     and worship the   85
     great God of Seeds.

(They all exit, dancing and singing.)

CRITICAL CONTEXTS

John Dryden is the most important English critic and poet of the late seventeenth century; he was appointed poet laureate and royal historiographer in 1668 and was also the author of many plays, both comedies and heroic tragedies. In 1679, he wrote an adaptation of Shakespeare's Troilus and Cressida, *and in his "Preface" to the play Dryden argues for neoclassical principles of unity and decorum.*

The poet Aeschylus was held in the same veneration by the Athenians of after ages as Shakespeare is by us; and Longinus has judged, in favor of him, that he had a noble bold-ness of expression, and that his imaginations were lofty and heroic; but, on the other side, Quintilian affirms that he was daring to extravagance. 'Tis certain that he affected pompous words, and that his sense too often was obscured by figures. Notwithstanding these imperfections, the value of his writings after his decease was such that his country-men ordained an equal reward to those poets who could alter his plays to be acted on the theater, with those whose productions were wholly new, and of their own. The case is not the same in England; though the difficulties of altering are greater, and our reverence for Shakespeare much more just, than that of the Grecians for Aeschylus. In the age of that poet, the Greek tongue was arrived to its full perfection; they had then amongst them an exact standard of writing and of speaking. The English language is not capable of such a certainty; and we are at present so far from it that we are wanting in the very foundation of it, a perfect grammar. Yet it must be allowed to the present age that the tongue in gen-eral is so much refined since Shakespeare's time that many of his words, and more of his phrases, are scarce intelligible. And of those which we understand, some are ungrammat-ical, others coarse; and his whole style is so pestered with figurative expressions, that it is as affected as it is obscure. 'Tis true, that in his later plays he had worn off somewhat of the rust; but the tragedy which I have undertaken to correct was, in all probability, one of his first endeavors on the stage.[1]

The original story was written by one Lollius, a Lombard, in Latin verse, and trans-lated by Chaucer into English; intended, I suppose, a satire on the inconstancy of women: I find nothing of it among the Ancients; not so much as the name Cressida once men-tioned. Shakespeare (as I hinted), in the apprenticeship of his writing, modeled it into that play which is now called by the name of *Troilus and Cressida;* but so lamely is it left to us, that it is not divided into acts; which fault I ascribe to the actors who printed it after Shakespeare's death; and that too so carelessly, that a more uncorrect copy I never saw. For the play itself, the author seems to have begun it with some fire; the characters of Pandarus and Thersites are promising enough; but as if he grew weary of his task, after an entrance or two, he lets 'em fall: and the later part of the tragedy is nothing but a confu-sion of drums and trumpets, excursions and alarms. The chief persons, who give name to the tragedy, are left alive; Cressida is false, and is not punished. Yet after all, because the play was Shakespeare's, and that there appeared in some places of it the admirable genius of the author, I undertook to remove that heap of rubbish under which many excellent thoughts lay wholly buried. Accordingly, I new modeled the plot; threw out many un-necessary persons; improved those characters which were begun and left unfinished: as Hector, Troilus, Pandarus, and Thersites; and added that of Andromache. After this I

JOHN DRYDEN
(1631–1700)

"Preface to *Troilus and Cressida,* Containing the Grounds of Criticism in Tragedy"
(1679)

**EDITED BY
ARTHUR C. KIRSCH**

---

[1] Actually, *Troilus and Cressida,* which was probably written around 1602, came at the midpoint of Shakespeare's career.

made, with no small trouble, an order and connection of all the scenes; removing them from the places where they were inartificially set; and though it was impossible to keep 'em all unbroken, because the scene must be sometimes in the city and sometimes in the camp, yet I have so ordered them that there is a coherence of 'em with one another, and a dependence on the main design: no leaping from Troy to the Grecian tents, and thence back again in the same act; but a due proportion of time allowed for every motion. I need not say that I have refined his language, which before was obsolete; but I am willing to acknowledge that as I have often drawn his English nearer to our times, so I have sometimes conformed my own to his; and consequently, the language is not altogether so pure as it is significant. The scenes of Pandarus and Cressida, of Troilus and Pandarus, of Andromache with Hector and the Trojans, in the second act, are wholly new; together with that of Nestor and Ulysses with Thersites, and that of Thersites with Ajax and Achilles. I will not weary my reader with the scenes which are added of Pandarus and the lovers, in the third; and those of Thersites, which are wholly altered; but I cannot omit the last scene in it, which is almost half the act, betwixt Troilus and Hector. The occasion of raising it was hinted to me by Mr. Betterton: the contrivance and working of it was my own. They who think to do me an injury by saying that it is an imitation of the scene betwixt Brutus and Cassius, do me an honor by supposing I could imitate the incomparable Shakespeare; but let me add that if Shakespeare's scene, or that faulty copy of it in *Amintor and Melantius,* had never been, yet Euripides had furnished me with an excellent example in his *Iphigenia,* between Agamemnon and Menelaus; and from thence, indeed, the last turn of it is borrowed.[2] The occasion which Shakespeare, Euripides, and Fletcher have all taken is the same; grounded upon friendship: and the quarrel of two virtuous men, raised by natural degrees to the extremity of passion, is conducted in all three to the declination of the same passion, and concludes with a warm renewing of their friendship. But the particular groundwork which Shakespeare has taken is incomparably the best; because he has not only chosen two of the greatest heroes of their age, but has likewise interested the liberty of Rome, and their own honors who were the redeemers of it, in this debate. And if he has made Brutus, who was naturally a patient man, to fly into excess at first, let it be remembered in his defense that, just before, he has received the news of Portia's death; whom the poet, on purpose neglecting a little chronology, supposes to have died before Brutus, only to give him an occasion of being more easily exasperated. Add to this that the injury he had received from Cassius had long been brooding in his mind; and that a melancholy man, upon consideration of an affront, especially from a friend, would be more eager in his passion than he who had given it, though naturally more choleric.

Euripides, whom I have followed, has raised the quarrel betwixt two brothers who were friends. The foundation of the scene was this: the Grecians were windbound at the port of Aulis, and the oracle had said that they could not sail, unless Agamemnon delivered up his daughter to be sacrificed: he refuses; his brother Menelaus urges the public safety; the father defends himself by arguments of natural affection, and hereupon they quarrel. Agamemnon is at last convinced, and promises to deliver up Iphigenia, but so passionately laments his loss that Menelaus is grieved to have been the occasion of it and, by a return of kindness, offers to intercede for him with the Grecians, that his daughter might not be sacrificed. But my friend Mr. Rymer has so largely, and with so much judgment, described this scene, in comparing it with that of Melantius and Amintor, that it is superfluous to say more of it; I only named the heads of it, that any reasonable man

---

[2]The comparison of the quarrels between Amintor and Melantius in Beaumont and Fletcher's *Maid's Tragedy* and Agamemnon and Menelaus in Euripides's *Iphigenia in Aulis* had already been made by Rymer in his *Tragedies of the Last Age* (1678), as Dryden acknowledges in the following paragraph.

might judge it was from thence I modeled my scene betwixt Troilus and Hector. I will conclude my reflections on it with a passage of Longinus, concerning Plato's imitation of Homer: "We ought not to regard a good imitation as a theft, but as a beautiful idea of him who undertakes to imitate, by forming himself on the invention and the work of another man; for he enters into the lists like a new wrestler, to dispute the prize with the former champion. This sort of emulation, says Hesiod, is honorable, 'this strife is wholesome to man,'[3] when we combat for victory with a hero, and are not without glory even in our overthrow. Those great men whom we propose to ourselves as patterns of our imitation serve us as a torch, which is lifted up before us to enlighten our passage; and often elevate our thoughts as high as the conception we have of our author's genius."[4]

I have been so tedious in three acts that I shall contract myself in the two last. The beginning scenes of the fourth act are either added or changed wholly by me; the middle of it is Shakespeare altered, and mingled with my own; three or four of the last scenes are altogether new. And the whole fifth act, both the plot and the writing, are my own additions.

But having written so much for imitation of what is excellent, in that part of the preface which related only to myself, methinks it would neither be unprofitable nor unpleasant to inquire how far we ought to imitate our own poets, Shakespeare and Fletcher, in their tragedies: and this will occasion another inquiry, how those two writers differ between themselves. But since neither of these questions can be solved unless some measures be first taken by which we may be enabled to judge truly of their writings, I shall endeavor, as briefly as I can, to discover the grounds and reason of all criticism, applying them in this place only to tragedy. Aristotle with his interpreters, and Horace, and Longinus, are the authors to whom I owe my lights; and what part soever of my own plans, or of this, which no mending could make regular, shall fall under the condemnation of such judges, it would be impudence in me to defend. . . .

Tragedy is thus defined by Aristotle (omitting what I thought unnecessary in his definition). 'Tis an imitation of one entire, great, and probable action; not told, but represented; which, by moving in us fear and pity, is conducive to the purging of those two passions in our minds. More largely thus, tragedy describes or paints an action, which action must have all the proprieties above named. First, it must be one or single, that is, it must not be a history of one man's life; suppose of Alexander the Great, or Julius Caesar, but one single action of theirs. This condemns all Shakespeare's historical plays, which are rather chronicles represented than tragedies, and all double action of plays. As to avoid a satire upon others, I will make bold with my own *Marriage à-la-Mode,* where there are manifestly two actions, not depending on one another: but in *Oedipus* there cannot properly be said to be two actions, because the love of Adrastus and Eurydice has a necessary dependence on the principal design, into which it is woven. The natural reason of rule is plain; for two different independent actions distract the attention and concernment of the audience, and consequently destroy the intention of the poet: if his business be to move terror and pity, and one of his actions be comical, the other tragical, the former will divert the people, and utterly make void his greater purpose. Therefore, as in perspective, so in tragedy, there must be a point of sight in which all the lines terminate; otherwise the eye wanders, and the work is false. This was the practice of the Grecian stage. But Terence made an innovation in the Roman: all his plays have double actions; for it was his custom to translate two Greek comedies, and to weave them into one of his, yet so that both the

THE GROUNDS OF CRITICISM IN TRAGEDY

---

[3] ἀγαθὴ δ' ἔρις ἐστὶ βροτοῖσιν (*Works and Days,* 1.24).
[4] *On the Sublime,* 13.4.

actions were comical, and one was principal, the other but secondary or subservient. And this has obtained on the English stage, to give us the pleasure of variety.

As the action ought to be one, it ought, as such, to have order in it, that is, to have a natural beginning, a middle, and an end. A natural beginning, says Aristotle, is that which could not necessarily have been placed after another thing, and so of the rest. This consideration will arraign all plays after the new model of Spanish plots, where accident is heaped upon accident, and that which is first might as reasonably be last: an inconvenience not to be remedied but by making one accident naturally produce another, otherwise 'tis a farce and not a play. Of this nature is the *Slighted Maid,*[5] where there is no scene in the first act which might not by as good reason be in the fifth. And if the action ought to be one, the tragedy ought likewise to conclude with the action of it. Thus in *Mustapha,*[6] the play should naturally have ended with the death of Zanger, and not have given us the grace cup after dinner of Solyman's divorce from Roxolana.

The following properties of the action are so easy that they need not my explaining. It ought to be great, and to consist of great persons, to distinguish it from comedy, where the action is trivial, and the persons of inferior rank. The last quality of the action is that it ought to be probable, as well as admirable and great. 'Tis not necessary that there should be historical truth in it; but always necessary that there should be a likeness of truth, something that is more than barely possible, *probable* being that which succeeds or happens oftener than it misses. To invent therefore a probability, and to make it wonderful, is the most difficult undertaking in the art of poetry; for that which is not wonderful is not great; and that which is not probable will not delight a reasonable audience. This action, thus described, must be represented and not told, to distinguish dramatic poetry from epic: but I hasten to the end or scope of tragedy, which is to rectify or purge our passions, fear and pity.

To instruct delightfully is the general end of all poetry. Philosophy instructs, but it performs its work by precept: which is not delightful, or not so delightful as example. To purge the passions by example is therefore the particular instruction which belongs to tragedy. Rapin, a judicious critic, has observed from Aristotle that pride and want of commiseration are the most predominant vices in mankind: therefore, to cure us of these two, the inventors of tragedy have chosen to work upon two other passions, which are fear and pity. We are wrought to fear by their setting before our eyes some terrible example of misfortune, which happened to persons of the highest quality; for such an action demonstrates to us that no condition is privileged from the turns of fortune; this must of necessity cause terror in us, and consequently abate our pride. But when we see that the most virtuous, as well as the greatest, are not exempt from such misfortunes, that consideration moves pity in us, and insensibly works us to be helpful to, and tender over, the distressed, which is the noblest and most god-like of moral virtues. Here 'tis observable that it is absolutely necessary to make a man virtuous, if we desire he should be pitied: we lament not, but detest, a wicked man; we are glad when we behold his crimes are punished, and that poetical justice[7] is done upon him. Euripides was censured by the critics of his time for making his chief characters too wicked: for example, Phaedra, though she loved her son-in-law with reluctancy, and that it was a curse upon her family for offending Venus, yet was thought too ill a pattern for the stage. Shall we therefore banish all characters of villainy? I confess I am not of that opinion; but it is necessary that the hero of the play be not a villain; that is, the characters which should move our pity ought to have virtuous inclinations, and degrees of moral goodness in them. As for a perfect character of virtue, it never was in nature, and therefore there can be no imitation of it; but there are allays of frailty to be allowed for the

---

[5]By Sir Robert Stapylton (1663).
[6]By Roger Boyle, Earl of Orrery (first performed in 1665).
[7]A phrase first coined by Rymer in *The Tragedies of the Last Age.*

chief persons, yet so that the good which is in them shall outweigh the bad, and consequently leave room for punishment on the one side, and pity on the other.

After all, if anyone will ask me whether a tragedy cannot be made upon any other grounds than those of exciting pity and terror in us, Bossu,[8] the best of modern critics, answers thus in general: that all excellent arts, and particularly that of poetry, have been invented and brought to perfection by men of a transcendent genius; and that therefore they who practice afterwards the same arts are obliged to tread in their footsteps, and to search in their writings the foundation of them; for it is not just that new rules should destroy the authority of the old. But Rapin writes more particularly thus:[9] that no passions in a story are so proper to move our concernment as fear and pity; and that it is from our concernment we receive our pleasure, is undoubted; when the soul becomes agitated with fear for one character, or hope for another, then it is that we are pleased in tragedy by the interest which we take in their adventures.

Here, therefore, the general answer may be given to the first question, how far we ought to imitate Shakespeare and Fletcher in their plots: namely, that we ought to follow them so far only as they have copied the excellencies of those who invented and brought to perfection dramatic poetry: those things only excepted which religion, customs of countries, idioms of languages, etc., have altered in the superstructures, but not in the foundation of the design.

How defective Shakespeare and Fletcher have been in all their plots, Mr. Rymer has discovered in his criticisms: neither can we who follow them be excused from the same or greater errors; which are the more unpardonable in us, because we want their beauties to countervail our faults. The best of their designs, the most approaching to antiquity, and the most conducing to move pity, is the *King and No King;* which, if the farce of Bessus were thrown away, is of that inferior sort of tragedies which end with a prosperous event. 'Tis probably derived from the story of Oedipus, with the character of Alexander the Great, in his extravagancies, given to Arbaces. The taking of this play, amongst many others, I cannot wholly ascribe to the excellency of the action; for I find it moving when it is read: 'tis true, the faults of the plot are so evidently proved that they can no longer be denied. The beauties of it must therefore lie either in the lively touches of the passion: or we must conclude, as I think we may, that even in imperfect plots there are less degrees of nature, by which some faint emotions of pity and terror are raised in us: as a less engine will raise a less proportion of weight, though not so much as one of Archimedes' making; for nothing can move our nature, but by some natural reason, which works upon passions. And since we acknowledge the effect, there must be something in the cause.

The difference between Shakespeare and Fletcher in their plotting seems to be this: that Shakespeare generally moves more terror, and Fletcher more compassion. For the first had a more masculine, a bolder and more fiery genius; the second, a more soft and womanish. In the mechanic beauties of the plot, which are the observation of the three unities, time, place, and action, they are both deficient; but Shakespeare most. Ben Jonson reformed those errors in his comedies, yet one of Shakespeare's was regular before him; which is, *The Merry Wives of Windsor.* For what remains concerning the design, you are to be referred to our English critic. That method which he has prescribed to raise it from mistake, or ignorance of the crime, is certainly the best, though 'tis not the only: for amongst all the tragedies of Sophocles, there is but one, *Oedipus,* which is wholly built after that model.

After the plot, which is the foundation of the play, the next thing to which we ought to apply our judgment is the manners, for now the poet comes to work above ground: the ground-work indeed is that which is most necessary, as that upon which depends the

[8]Le Bossu, author of *Traité du poème épique* (1675).
[9]In *Réflexions sur la poétique d'Aristote* (1674).

firmness of the whole fabric; yet it strikes not the eye so much as the beauties or imperfections of the manners, the thoughts, and the expressions.

The first rule which Bossu prescribes to the writer of an heroic poem, and which holds too by the same reason in all dramatic poetry, is to make the moral of the work, that is, to lay down to yourself what that precept of morality shall be, which you would insinuate into the people; as namely, Homer's (which I have copied in my *Conquest of Granada*) was, that union preserves a commonwealth, and discord destroys it; Sophocles, in his *Oedipus,* that no man is to be accounted happy before his death. 'Tis the moral that directs the whole action of the play to one center; and that action or fable is the example built upon the moral, which confirms the truth of it to our experience: when the fable is designed, then and not before, the persons are to be introduced with their manners, characters, and passions.

The manners in a poem are understood to be those inclinations, whether natural or acquired, which move and carry us to actions, good, bad, or indifferent, in a play; or which incline the persons to such or such actions. I have anticipated part of this discourse already, in declaring that a poet ought not to make the manners perfectly good in his best persons; but neither are they to be more wicked in any of his characters than necessity requires. To produce a villain, without other reason than a natural inclination to villainy is, in poetry, to produce an effect without a cause; and to make him more a villain than he has just reason to be, is to make an effect which is stronger than the cause.

The manners arise from many causes; and are either distinguished by complexion, as choleric and phlegmatic, or by the differences of age or sex, of climates, or quality of the persons, or their present condition. They are likewise to be gathered from the several virtues, vices, or passions, and many other commonplaces which a poet must be supposed to have learned from natural philosophy, ethics, and history; of all which whosoever is ignorant, does not deserve the name of poet.

But as the manners are useful in this art, they may be all comprised under these general heads: first, they must be apparent; that is, in every character of the play, some inclinations of the person must appear: and these are shown in the actions and discourse. Secondly, the manners must be suitable, or agreeing to the persons; that is, to the age, sex, dignity, and the other general heads of manners: thus, when a poet has given the dignity of a king to one of his persons, in all his actions and speeches, that person must discover majesty, magnanimity, and jealousy of power, because these are suitable to the general manners of a king. The third property of manners is resemblance; and this is founded upon the particular characters of men, as we have them delivered to us by relation or history; that is, when a poet has the known character of this or that man before him, he is bound to represent him such, at least not contrary to that which fame has reported him to have been. Thus, it is not a poet's choice to make Ulysses choleric, or Achilles patient, because Homer has described 'em quite otherwise. Yet this is a rock on which ignorant writers daily split; and the absurdity is as monstrous as if a painter should draw a coward running from a battle, and tell us it was the picture of Alexander the Great.

The last property of manners is that they be constant and equal, that is, maintained the same through the whole design: thus, when Virgil had once given the name of *pious* to Aeneas, he was bound to show him such, in all his words and actions through the whole poem. All these properties Horace has hinted to a judicious observer: "1. you must mark the manners of each age; 2. or follow tradition; 3. or create your own convention; 4. let each character remain constant and consistent with itself."[10]

---

[10]1. *notandi sunt tibi mores;* 2. *aut famam sequere;* 3. *aut sibi convenientia finge;* 4. *servetur ad imum, qualis ab incepto processerit, et sibi constet (Ars poetica,* 11.156, 119, 126–127).

From the manners, the characters of persons are derived; for indeed the characters are no other than the inclinations, as they appear in the several persons of the poem; a character being thus defined, that which distinguishes one man from another. Not to repeat the same things over again which have been said of the manners, I will only add what is necessary here. A character, or that which distinguishes one man from all others, cannot be supposed to consist of one particular virtue, or vice, or passion only; but 'tis a composition of qualities which are not contrary to one another in the same person; thus the same man may be liberal and valiant, but not liberal and covetous; so in a comical character, or humour (which is an inclination to this or that particular folly), Falstaff is a liar, and a coward, a glutton, and a buffoon, because all these qualities may agree in the same man; yet it is still to be observed that one virtue, vice, and passion ought to be shown in every man, as predominant over all the rest; as covetousness in Crassus, love of his country in Brutus; and the same in characters which are feigned.

The chief character or hero in a tragedy, as I have already shown, ought in prudence to be such a man who has so much more in him of virtue than of vice, that he may be left amiable to the audience, which otherwise cannot have any concernment for his sufferings; and 'tis on this one character that the pity and terror must be principally, if not wholly, founded—a rule which is extremely necessary, and which none of the critics that I know have fully enough discovered to us. For terror and compassion work but weakly when they are divided into many persons. If Creon had been the chief character in *Oedipus,* there had neither been terror nor compassion moved; but only detestation of the man and joy for his punishment; if Adrastus and Eurydice had been made more appealing characters, then the pity had been divided, and lessened on the part of Oedipus: but making Oedipus the best and bravest person, and even Jocasta but an underpart to him, his virtues and the punishment of his fatal crime drew both the pity and the terror to himself.

By what had been said of the manners, it will be easy for a reasonable man to judge whether the characters be truly or falsely drawn in a tragedy; for if there be no manners appearing in the characters, no concernment for the persons can be raised; no pity or horror can be moved, but by vice or virtue; therefore, without them, no person can have any business in the play. If the inclinations be obscure, 'tis a sign the poet is in the dark, and knows not what manner of man he presents to you; and consequently you can have no idea, or very imperfect, of that man; nor can judge what resolutions he ought to take; or what words or actions are proper for him. Most comedies made up of accidents or adventures are liable to fall into this error; and tragedies with many turns are subject to it; for the manners never can be evident where the surprises of fortune take up all the business of the stage; and where the poet is more in pain to tell you what happened to such a man than what he was. 'Tis one of the excellencies of Shakespeare that the manners of his persons are generally apparent, and you see their bent and inclinations. Fletcher comes far short of him in this, as indeed he does almost in everything: there are but glimmerings of manners in most of his comedies, which run upon adventures: and in his tragedies, *Rollo, Otto, A King and No King, Melantius,*[11] and many others of his best, are but pictures shown you in the twilight; you know not whether they resemble vice or virtue, and they are either good, bad, or indifferent, as the present scene requires it. But of all poets, this commendation is to be given to Ben Jonson, that the manners even of the most inconsiderable persons in his plays are everywhere apparent.

By considering the second quality of manners, which is that they be suitable to the age, quality, country, dignity, etc., of the character, we may likewise judge whether a poet has followed nature. In this kind, Sophocles and Euripides have more excelled among the

---

[11]Otto is Rollo's brother; Melantius is a character in *The Maid's Tragedy.*

Greeks than Aeschylus; and Terence more than Plautus among the Romans. Thus Sophocles gives to Oedipus the true qualities of a king, in both those plays which bear his name; but in the latter, which is the *Oedipus Colonæus,* he lets fall on purpose his tragic style; his hero speaks not in the arbitrary tone, but remembers, in the softness of his complaints, that he is an unfortunate blind old man, that he is banished from his country, and persecuted by his next relations. The present French poets are generally accused that wheresoever they lay the scene, or in whatsoever age, the manners of their heroes are wholly French. Racine's Bajazet is bred at Constantinople, but his civilities are conveyed to him, by some secret passage, from Versailles into the Seraglio. But our Shakespeare, having ascribed to Henry the Fourth the character of a king and of a father, gives him the perfect manners of each relation, when either he transacts with his son or with his subjects. Fletcher, on the other side, gives neither to Arbaces, nor to his King in the *Maid's Tragedy,* the qualities which are suitable to a monarch; though he may be excused a little in the latter, for the King there is not uppermost in the character; 'tis the lover of Evadne, who is King only in a second consideration; and though he be unjust, and has other faults which shall be nameless, yet he is not the hero of the play. 'Tis true, we find him a lawful prince (though I never heard of any King that was in Rhodes), and therefore Mr. Rymer's criticism stands good; that he should not be shown in so vicious a character. Sophocles has been more judicious in his *Antigone;* for though he represents in Creon a bloody prince, yet he makes him not a lawful king, but an usurper, and Antigona herself is the heroine of the tragedy. But when Philaster wounds Arethusa and the boy; and Perigot his mistress, in the *Faithful Shepherdess,* both these are contrary to the character of manhood. Nor is Valentinian managed much better, for though Fletcher has taken his picture truly, and shown him as he was, an effeminate, voluptuous man, yet he has forgotten that he was an Emperor, and has given him none of those royal marks which ought to appear in a lawful successor of the throne. If it be inquired what Fletcher should have done on this occasion: ought he not to have represented Valentinian as he was? Bossu shall answer this question for me, by an instance of the like nature: Mauritius, the Greek Emperor, was a prince far surpassing Valentinian, for he was endued with many kingly virtues; he was religious, merciful, and valiant, but withal he was noted of extreme covetousness, a vice which is contrary to the character of a hero, or a prince: therefore, says the critic, that emperor was no fit person to be represented in a tragedy, unless his good qualities were only to be shown, and his covetousness (which sullied them all) were slurred over by the artifice of the poet.[12] To return once more to Shakespeare: no man ever drew so many characters, or generally distinguished 'em better from one another, excepting only Jonson. I will instance but in one, to show the copiousness of his invention: 'tis that of Caliban, or the Monster in the *Tempest.* He seems there to have created a person which was not in nature, a boldness which at first sight would appear intolerable; for he makes him a species of himself, begotten by an incubus on a witch; but this, as I have elsewhere proved, is not wholly beyond the bounds of credibility, at least the vulgar still believe it. We have the separated notions of a spirit, and of a witch (and spirits, according to Plato, are vested with a subtle body; according to some of his followers, have different sexes); therefore, as from the distinct apprehensions of a horse, and of a man, imagination has formed a centaur; so from those of an incubus and a sorceress, Shakespeare has produced his monster. Whether or no his generation can be defended, I leave to philosophy; but of this I am certain, that the poet has most judiciously furnished him with a person, a language, and a character, which will suit him, both by father's and mother's side: he has all the discontents and malice of a witch, and of a devil, besides a convenient proportion of the deadly sins; gluttony,

---

[12]*Traité du poème épique,* 4.7.

sloth, and lust are manifest; the dejectedness of a slave is likewise given him, and the ignorance of one bred up in a desert island. His person is monstrous, as he is the product of unnatural lust; and his language is as hobgoblin as his person; in all things he is distinguished from other mortals. The characters of Fletcher are poor and narrow, in comparison of Shakespeare's; I remember not one which is not borrowed from him; unless you will except that strange mixture of a man in the *King and No King;* so that in this part Shakespeare is generally worth our imitation; and to imitate Fletcher is but to copy after him who was a copier.

Under this general head of manners, the passions are naturally included, as belonging to the characters. I speak not of pity and of terror, which are to be moved in the audience by the plot; but of anger, hatred, love, ambition, jealousy, revenge, etc., as they are shown in this or that person of the play. To describe these naturally, and to move them artfully, is one of the greatest commendations which can be given to a poet: to write pathetically, says Longinus, cannot proceed but from a lofty genius. A poet must be born with this quality; yet, unless he help himself by an acquired knowledge of the passions, what they are in their own nature, and by what springs they are to be moved, he will be subject either to raise them where they ought not to be raised, or not to raise them by the just degrees of nature, or to amplify them beyond the natural bounds, or not to observe the crisis and turns of them, in their cooling and decay: all which errors proceed from want of judgment in the poet, and from being unskilled in the principles of moral philosophy. Nothing is more frequent in a fanciful writer than to foil himself by not managing his strength; therefore, as in a wrestler, there is first required some measure of force, a well-knit body, and active limbs, without which all instruction would be vain; yet, these being granted, if he want the skill which is necessary to a wrestler, he shall make but small advantage of his natural robustuousness: so, in a poet, his inborn vehemence and force of spirit will only run him out of breath the sooner, if it be not supported by the help of art. The roar of passion indeed may please an audience, three parts of which are ignorant enough to think all is moving which is noise, and it may stretch the lungs of an ambitious actor, who will die upon the spot for a thundering clap; but it will move no other passion than indignation and contempt from judicious men. Longinus, whom I have hitherto followed, continues thus: *If the passions be artfully employed, the discourse becomes vehement and lofty: if otherwise, there is nothing more ridiculous than a great passion out of season:* and to this purpose he animadverts severely upon Aeschylus, who writ nothing in cold blood, but was always in a rapture, and in fury with his audience:[13] the inspiration was still upon him, he was ever tearing it upon the tripos;[14] or (to run off as madly as he does, from one similitude to another) he was always at high flood of passion, even in the dead ebb and lowest water-mark of the scene. He who would raise the passion of a judicious audience, says a learned critic, must be sure to take his hearers along with him; if they be in a calm, 'tis in vain for him to be in a huff: he must move them by degrees, and kindle with 'em; otherwise he will be in danger of setting his own heap of stubble on a fire, and of burning out by himself without warming the company that stand about him. They who would justify the madness of poetry from the authority of Aristotle have mistaken the text, and consequently the interpretation: I imagine it to be false read, where he says of poetry that it is εὐφνοῦς ἤ μανικοῦ, that it had always somewhat in it either of a genius, or of a madman. 'Tis more probable that the original ran thus, that poetry was εὐφνοῦς οὐ μανικοῦ, that it belongs to a witty man, but not to a madman.[15] Thus then the passions, as they are considered simply and in

[13]*On the Sublime,* 3.

[14]A reference to the tripod at Delphi on which the priestess of Apollo delivered her raving oracles.

[15]Aristotle, *Poetics,* 17.

themselves, suffer violence when they are perpetually maintained at the same height; for what melody can be made on that instrument, all whose strings are screwed up at first to their utmost stretch, and to the same sound? But this is not the worst: for the characters likewise bear a part in the general calamity, if you consider the passions embodied in them; for it follows of necessity that no man can be distinguished from another by his discourse, when every man is ranting, swaggering, and exclaiming with the same excess: as if it were the only business of all the characters to contend with each other for the prize at Billingsgate; or that the scene of the tragedy lay in Bet'lem.[16] Suppose the poet should intend this man to be choleric, and that man to be patient; yet when they are confounded in the writing, you cannot distinguish them from one another: for the man who was called patient and tame is only so before he speaks; but let his clack be set a-going, and he shall tongue it as impetuously, and as loudly, as the errantest hero in the play. By this means, the characters are only distinct in name; but, in reality, all the men and women in the play are the same person. No man should pretend to write who cannot temper his fancy with his judgment: nothing is more dangerous to a raw horseman than a hot-mouthed jade without a curb.

'Tis necessary therefore for a poet who would concern an audience by describing of a passion, first to prepare it, and not to rush upon it all at once. Ovid has judiciously shown the difference of these two ways, in the speeches of Ajax and Ulysses: Ajax, from the very beginning, breaks out into his exclamations, and is swearing by his Maker, "'By Jupiter,' he cried."[17] Ulysses, on the contrary, prepares his audience with all the submissiveness he can practice, and all the calmness of a reasonable man; he found his judges in a tranquillity of spirit, and therefore set out leisurely and softly with 'em, till he had warmed 'em by degrees; and then he began to mend his pace, and to draw them along with his own impetuousness: yet so managing his breath, that it might not fail him at his need, and reserving his utmost proofs of ability even to the last. The success, you see, was answerable; for the crowd only applauded the speech of Ajax:

and the applause of the crowd followed his closing words.[18]

But the judges awarded the prize for which they contended to Ulysses:

the assembly was very moved; and the power of eloquence was revealed, and the skillful orator carried off the hero's arms.[19]

The next necessary rule is to put nothing into the discourse which may hinder your moving of the passions. Too many accidents, as I have said, encumber the poet, as much as the arms of Saul did David; for the variety of passions which they produce are ever crossing and jostling each other out of the way. He who treats of joy and grief together is in a fair way of causing neither of those effects. There is yet another obstacle to be removed, which is pointed wit, and sentences affected out of season; these are nothing of kin to the violence of passion: no man is at leisure to make sentences and similes when his soul is in an agony. I the rather name this fault that it may serve to mind me of my former errors; neither will I spare myself, but give an example of this kind from my *Indian Emperor.* Montezuma, pursued by his enemies, and seeking sanctuary, stands parleying without the fort, and describing his danger to Cydaria, in a simile of six lines:

---

[16]Bedlam, a London hospital for the insane.

[17]*agimus, pro Jupiter, inquit* (*Metamorphoses*, 13.5).

[18]   *vulgique secutum*
ultima mumur erat.
      Ibid., 123.

[19]*mota manus procerum est; et quid facundia posset*
tum patuit, fortisque viri tulit arma disertus.
      Ibid., 282–83.

As on the sands the frighted traveller
Sees the high seas come rolling from afar, etc.[20]

My Indian potentate was well skilled in the sea for an inland prince, and well improved since the first act, when he sent his son to discover it. The image had not been amiss from another man, at another time: "but not now, in this place";[21] he destroyed the concernment which the audience might otherwise have had for him; for they could not think the danger near when he had the leisure to invent a simile.

If Shakespeare be allowed, as I think he must, to have made his characters distinct, it will easily be inferred that he understood the nature of the passions: because it has been proved already that confused passions make undistinguishable characters. Yet I cannot deny that he has his failings; but they are not so much in the passions themselves as in his manner of expression: he often obscures his meaning by his words, and sometimes makes it unintelligible. I will not say of so great a poet that he distinguished not the blown puffy style from true sublimity; but I may venture to maintain that the fury of his fancy often transported him beyond the bounds of judgment, either in coining of new words and phrases or racking words which were in use into the violence of a catachresis.[22] 'Tis not that I would explode[23] the use of metaphors from passions, for Longinus thinks 'em necessary to raise it: but to use 'em at every word, to say nothing without a metaphor, a simile, an image, or description, is I doubt to smell a little too strongly of the buskin. I must be forced to give an example of expressing passion figuratively; but that I may do it with respect to Shakespeare, it shall not be taken from anything of his: 'tis an exclamation against Fortune, quoted in his *Hamlet,* but written by some other poet:

Out, out, thou strumpet Fortune! all you gods,
In general synod, take away her power;
Break all the spokes and fellies from her wheel,
And bowl the round nave down the hill of Heav'n,
As low as to the fiends.

And immediately after, speaking of Hecuba, when Priam was killed before her eyes:

The mobled queen ran up and down,
Threatening the flame with bisson rheum; a clout about that head
Where late the diadem stood; and for a robe,
About her lank and all o'er-teemed loins,
A blanket in th' alarm of fear caught up.
Who this had seen, with tongue in venom steep'd
'Gainst Fortune's state would treason have pronounced;
But if the gods themselves did see her then,
When she saw Pyrrhus make malicious sport
In mincing with his sword her husband's limbs,
The instant burst of clamour that she made
(Unless things mortal move them not at all)
Would have made milch the burning eyes of Heaven,
And passion in the gods.[24]

---

[20]Act 5.

[21]*sed nunc non erat hisce locus* (*Ars poetica,* 1.19).

[22]A misuse of terms.

[23]Banish, reject.

[24]*Hamlet,* 2.2.475–79, 487–500. [Line numbers cited here are those in this anthology; the lines that Dryden quotes differ slightly from this anthology because of his use of another version of Shakespeare's play.—Editor]

What a pudder is here kept in raising the expression of trifling thoughts! Would not a man have thought that the poet had been bound prentice to a wheelwright, for his first rant? and had followed a ragman for the clout and blanket, in the second? Fortune is painted on a wheel, and therefore the writer, in a rage, will have poetical justice down upon every member of that engine: after this execution, he bowls the nave down hill, from Heaven to the fiends (an unreasonable long mark, a man would think); 'tis well there are no solid orbs to stop it in the way, or no element of fire to consume it: but when it came to the earth, it must be monstrous heavy, to break ground as low as to the center. His making milch the burning eyes of Heaven was a pretty tolerable flight too: and I think no man ever drew milk out of eyes before him: yet to make the wonder greater, these eyes were burning. Such a sight indeed were enough to have raised passion in the gods; but to excuse the effects of it, he tells you perhaps they did not see it. Wise men would be glad to find a little sense couched under all those pompous words; for bombast is commonly the delight of that audience which loves poetry, but understands it not: and as commonly has been the practice of those writers who, not being able to infuse a natural passion into the mind, have made it their business to ply the ears and to stun their judges by the noise. But Shakespeare does not often thus; for the passions in his scene between Brutus and Cassius are extremely natural, the thoughts are such as arise from the matter, and the expression of 'em not viciously figurative. I cannot leave this subject before I do justice to that divine poet by giving you one of his passionate descriptions: 'tis of Richard the Second when he was deposed, and led in triumph through the streets of London by Henry of Bolingbroke: the painting of it is so lively, and the words so moving, that I have scarce read anything comparable to it in any other language. Suppose you have seen already the fortunate usurper passing through the crowd, and followed by the shouts and acclamations of the people; and now behold King Richard entering upon the scene: consider the wretchedness of his condition, and his carriage in it; and refrain from pity if you can:

> As in a theater, the eyes of men,
> After a well-graced actor leaves the stage,
> Are idly bent on him that enters next,
> Thinking his prattle to be tedious:
> Even so, or with much more contempt, men's eyes
> Did scowl on Richard: no man cried, God save him:
> No joyful tongue gave him his welcome home,
> But dust was thrown upon his sacred head,
> Which with such gentle sorrow he shook off,
> His face still combating with tears and smiles
> (The badges of his grief and patience),
> That had not God (for some strong purpose) steel'd
> The hearts of men, they must perforce have melted,
> And barbarism itself have pitied him.[25]

To speak justly of this whole matter: 'tis neither height of thought that is discommended, nor pathetic vehemence, nor any nobleness of expression in its proper place; but 'tis a false measure of all these, something which is like 'em, and is not them; 'tis the Bristol-stone,[26] which appears like a diamond; 'tis an extravagant thought, instead of a sublime one; 'tis roaring madness, instead of vehemence; and a sound of words, instead of sense. If Shakespeare were stripped of all the bombast in his passions, and dressed in the most vulgar words, we should find the beauties of his thoughts remaining; if his embroideries were

---

[25]*Richard II*, 5.2.23–36.
[26]A rock crystal.

burnt down, there would still be silver at the bottom of the melting-pot: but I fear (at least let me fear it for myself) that we who ape his sounding words have nothing of his thought, but are all outside; there is not so much as a dwarf within our giant's clothes. Therefore, let not Shakespeare suffer for our sakes; 'tis our fault, who succeed him in an age which is more refined, if we imitate him so ill that we copy his failings only, and make a virtue of that in our writings which in his was an imperfection.

For what remains, the excellency of that poet was, as I have said, in the more manly passions; Fletcher's in the softer: Shakespeare writ better betwixt man and man; Fletcher, betwixt man and woman: consequently, the one described friendship better; the other love: yet Shakespeare taught Fletcher to write love: and Juliet, and Desdemona, are originals. 'Tis true, the scholar had the softer soul; but the master had the kinder. Friendship is both a virtue and a passion essentially; love is a passion only in its nature, and is not a virtue but by accident: good nature makes friendship, but effeminacy love. Shakespeare had an universal mind, which comprehended all characters and passions; Fletcher a more confined and limited: for though he treated love in perfection, yet honor, ambition, revenge, and generally all the stronger passions, he either touched not, or not masterly. To conclude all, he was a limb of Shakespeare.

I had intended to have proceeded to the last property of manners, which is that they must be constant, and the characters maintained the same from the beginning to the end; and from thence to have proceeded to the thoughts and expressions suitable to a tragedy: but I will first see how this will relish with the age. 'Tis, I confess, but cursorily written; yet the judgment which is given here is generally founded upon experience: but because many men are shocked at the name of rules, as if they were a kind of magisterial prescription upon poets, I will conclude with the words of Rapin, in his reflections on Aristotle's work of poetry: "If the rules be well considered, we shall find them to be made only to reduce nature into method, to trace her step by step, and not to suffer the least mark of her to escape us: 'tis only by these that probability in fiction is maintained, which is the soul of poetry. They are founded upon good sense, and sound reason, rather than on authority; for though Aristotle and Horace are produced, yet no man must argue that what they write is true because they writ it; but 'tis evident, by the ridiculous mistakes and gross absurdities which have been made by those poets who have taken their fancy only for their guide, that if this fancy be not regulated, 'tis a mere caprice, and utterly incapable to produce a reasonable and judicious poem."[27]

Katharine Eisaman Maus has written widely about seventeenth-century literature, including a book on the playwright Ben Jonson. In this essay, Maus explores the relationship between Restoration actresses, their reputation for sexual promiscuity, and the politics of gender in the Restoration theater and society.

KATHARINE EISAMAN MAUS

from "'Playhouse Flesh and Blood': Sexual Ideology and the Restoration Actress" (1979)

Sometime in the fall of 1660—no one is quite sure when or at which theater—the first professional English actress made her debut on the public stage. Her appearance was not entirely without precedents. In the first half of the seventeenth century, Queen Henrietta Maria and her ladies performed extensively in the English court theater. During the interregnum, when the theaters were officially closed, William D'Avenant used at least one woman—a Mrs. Edward Coleman—in his opera *The Siege of Rhodes*. On the Continent, women had been employed on the stage since the sixteenth century, and many royalists became familiar with the French custom when they followed Prince Charles into exile. However, women had never been used on the English stage in any regular or systematic way.

---

[27]*Réflexions*, 12.

Before the war, adolescent boys had performed the women's parts in the public theater. In November, 1629, when a French company with actresses came to London, Thomas Brand informed Archbishop Laud that "those women . . . giving just offense to all virtuous and well disposed persons in this town . . . were hissed, hooted, and pippin-pelted from the stage."[1] By the Restoration, though, attitudes toward women on the stage seem to have changed radically. The new actresses were accepted almost immediately into the life of the theater, and there was surprisingly little controversy over their suitability for the stage.

What caused this striking reversal of audience attitudes? Was it merely a case of English theater-goers belatedly relinquishing a set of absurd scruples? Discussions of seventeenth-century actresses have assumed that they succeeded on the stage because they could provide a more plausible portrayal of women characters than transvestite actors could.[2] There are two objections to this kind of explanation. For one thing, there is no evidence which implies that the female impersonators were incompetent. Female parts written by Shakespeare, Webster, Ford, Middleton, and others suggests no mean estimate by the playwrights of the boys' abilities; Elizabethan and Jacobean audiences applauded male Juliets, Rosalinds, and Cleopatras. The usual explanation of the actresses' success further assumes that naturalism is an obvious and desirable goal in theatrical representation—an assumption which is questionable to say the least. E. H. Gombrich has shown that standards of naturalism—what will seem "true to life" in a drawing or painting—vary from generation to generation depending upon the conventions which inform and have informed artistic production. What seems natural or conventional is not universal across time and space, but is historically and culturally conditioned.[3] There is no reason to suppose that naturalism in the theater is any less problematic than naturalism in the visual arts. Why should male impersonation of women seem more intolerable than other kinds of artificiality—extravagantly exotic sets, or a highly rhetorical acting style? The Restoration audience expected, and enjoyed, stage conventions which grievously ignore the demands of realism as understood by, say, Ibsen or Chekhov.

The orthodox explanation of the actresses' new acceptability is, if not entirely wrong, at least seriously insufficient. What is required is an examination of the issues in terms of the attitudes prevailing in Restoration culture. This examination logically begins with the contemporary accounts of the actresses, and inevitably widens to include analysis of Restoration attitudes toward women and the theater in general.

Unfortunately, there is very little comment upon the actresses in the years when they are first introduced, when the quality of contemporary response might best help illuminate

[1]John Payne Collier, *History of Dramatic Poetry to the Time of Shakespeare: And Annals of the Stage to the Restoration* (London: John Murray, 1831), II, pp. 23–24.

[2]e.g., Colley Cibber, *An Apology of the Life of Colley Cibber* (London, 1740), p. 55: "The characters of Women, on former Theatres, were perform'd by Boys, or young Men of the most effeminate Aspect. And what Grace, or Master-Stroke of Action, can we conceive such ungain Hoydens to have been capable of?"

Allardyce Nicoll, *The History of Restoration Drama 1660–1700* (Cambridge: Cambridge U P, 1928), p. 71: "the actresses certainly made possible a more charming presentation of Shakespearean tragedy and comedy, shedding a fresh light on the Desdemonas and Ophelias of the past."

Rosamund Gilder, *Enter the Actresses* (London: George C. Harrup, 1931), pp. 134–35: "In England the curtain of legal prohibition drops in 1642 on a stage peopled by squeaking Cleopatras, and rises eighteen years later on a rout of beautiful, witty, and accomplished actresses."

John Harold Wilson, *All the King's Ladies: Actresses of the Restoration* (Chicago: U Chicago Press, 1958), p. 90: "As creators of character there can be little doubt that the new actresses were superior to their juvenile predecessors . . . the stage life of the female impersonator was usually short, and his interpretation of a character could never be more than superficially correct."

[3]E. H. Gombrich, *Art and Illusion* (New York: Pantheon, 1960), esp. pp. 181–287.

the reasons for their professional success. Since no one seriously questioned women's fitness for the stage, the few attempts to account for the innovation involve no very elaborate process of justification. In 1660, the players and owners of theatrical companies were complaining that the hiatus in the theatrical tradition had created a dearth of well-trained female impersonators. The available actors were all too masculine-looking, they claimed, to excel in women's parts. As Thomas Jordan lamented in his preface to a revival of *Othello:*

> Our women are defective, and so siz'd
> You'ld think they were some of the guard disguis'd
> For to speak truth, men act that are between
> Forty and fifty, wenches of fifteen
> With bone so large and nerve so incompliant
> When you call Desdemona, enter Geant.[4]

According to this line of argument, the peculiar circumstances of the Restoration theater necessitated the employment of women. The closing of the theaters during the interregnum had interrupted the old system of apprenticeship, which had supplied the Elizabethan and Jacobean companies with adequately-trained female impersonators.

This explanation, even if true, would only reveal by what chance women arrived on the stage, and not how and why they were successful once they got there. Furthermore, the plight of the producers was not nearly so severe as Jordan represents it. According to John Downes in *Roscius Anglicanus,* the King's Company at its inception included four actors "Bred up from Boys, under the Master ACTORS."[5] The Duke's Company included six actors, who "commonly Acted Women's Parts"—notably Edward Kynaston, who "being young made a complete Femal Stage Beauty, performing his part so well . . . that it hath since been disputable among the Judicious, whether any Woman that succeeded him so sensibly touched the audience as he."[6] Pepys and Cibber, as well as Downes, comment upon the excellence of Kynaston's impersonations, as well as upon the more than passable abilities of the lesser actors.[7] Surely if the Restoration audience had greeted the women players with the hisses and orange pips of an earlier generation, the companies would have made do for a while with ungainly performances by untrained adolescent boys. The perceived unsuitability of male actors for female roles is really more a symptom than an explanation of changing attitudes.

As the theaters reopened, actors and producers urged yet another argument for the introduction of actresses, which seems at least in retrospect equally unsatisfactory as a real explanation. Initially some people hoped that the presence of women on the stage would eliminate the obscene and corrupt aspects of English drama, and encourage the adoption of purer standards for theatrical spectacle. The patents issued to William D'Avenant and Thomas Killigrew in 1660, and reissued in 1662, contain the following clause:

> forasmuch as many plays formerly acted, do conteine severall prophane, obscene, and scurrilous passages, and the women's parts therein have been acted by men in the habit of women, at which some have taken offense; for the preventing of these abuses for the future, we doe straitly charge, command, and enjoyn that henceforth no . . . play shall be acted by either of the said companies conteining any passages offensive to piety or good manners . . . And we

---

[4]Thomas Jordan, "A Prologue, to introduce the first Woman that came to act on the Stage, in the tragedy called The Moor of Venice," in *A Royal Arbour of Loyal Poesie* (London, 1664), p. 22.

[5]John Downes, *Roscius Anglicanus, or An Historical View of the Stage* (London, 1708), p. 2.

[6]Ibid., p. 19.

[7]Samuel Pepys, *The Diary of Samuel Pepys,* ed. R. Latham and W. Matthews (London: G. Bell, 1970), I, 224 (August 18, 1660) and II, 7 (January 7, 1660–61). Cibber, p. 71.

doe likewise permit and give leave that all the women's parts to be acted in either of the said two companies may be performed by women so long as these recreations, which by reason of the abuses aforesaid were scandalous and offensive, may by such reformation be esteemed not only harmlesse delight but useful instruction.[8]

By this account the actresses were introduced in order to help the dramatic arts exert a beneficial effect upon the community. Whether or not this apparently pious hope was initially a sincere one, it remained unrealized on the Restoration stage. Restoration drama, especially comedy, tends to be sexually more explicit and morally more subversive than the drama of earlier decades—and the sexual explicitness, at least, largely depends upon the physical presence of genuine women on the stage. "We can only conclude," writes a twentieth century critic, "that [the actresses'] chief effect on dramatic literature was to push it steadily in the direction of sex and sensuality."[9] The threat implied in the language of the patents—that the women's continued employment depended upon their moral efficacy—was of course never carried out. If women were now considered appropriate on the public stage, it was not for their purifying influence, any more than it was due to a shortage of teenage boys.

Since the overt attempts at contemporary justification seem inadequate, it is reasonable to suspect that the new acceptability of actresses is associated with ideological changes more fundamental or far-reaching than a mere modification of theatrical custom might indicate. The first such change which needs to be examined is the transformation in audience attitudes toward players in the latter part of the seventeenth century—a change which makes the success of the Restoration actress even more striking. Before the war, even the most appreciative playgoers seem not have been particularly interested in the offstage lives of Burbage, Kempe, or Alleyn. In the more intimate Restoration theater, though, the personalities of both male and female players intrigued the comparatively small and loyal audience. Actresses as well as actors were praised not for their ability to depict any character with equal skill, but for their ability to inform their dramatic portrayals with the force of their personal talent and idiosyncratic vision. In James Wright's *Historia Histrionica* (London, 1699), Truewit assumes that even in reading an old play one is curious about the personalities of the original actors:

I wish they had printed in the last age (so I call the times before the rebellion) the actors names over against the parts they acted, as they have done since the restoration: and thus one might have guess'd at the action of the men, by the parts which we now read in the old plays. (page 3)

Restoration theater did not really challenge the actor to submit himself to the demands of a fictional role; rather it provided, at least for the leading players, manifold opportunities for self-expression. In the case of women like Nell Gwynn, Elizabeth Barry, or Ann Bracegirdle, this kind of attention constituted a virtually unprecedented celebration of female personality—at least of middle- and lower-class female personality.

As Restoration playwrights worked very closely with the theatrical companies, they inevitably wrote with particular performers in mind. They were thus able to play upon the spectator's sense of the relationship between an actor's personality and the roles he was required to enact. Nell Gwynn and Charles Hart, lovers behind the scenes, played witty, amoral "mad couples" together—Florimel and Celadon in Dryden's *Secret Love,* Miridia and Philidor in Howard's *All Mistaken,* Jacintha and Wildblood in Dryden's *Evening's Love,* Olivia and Wildish in Sedley's *Mulberry Garden.* Ann Bracegirdle, who resisted the

---

[8]Nicoll, pp. 285–86n.
[9]Wilson, p. 107.

advances of enamored aristocrats throughout her career, and who was the object of a melo-dramatic rape attempt, became famous for her portrayal of chaste women in distress. She was applauded when, as Cordelia in the revised *Lear,* she described herself as "Arm'd in my Virgin Innocence"—although the promiscuous Mrs. Barry, "in the same part, more fam'd for her Stage Performance than the other, at the words, *Virgin Innocence,* has created a Horse-laugh . . . and the scene of generous Pity and Compassion at the close turn'd to Ridicule."[10]

Prologues and epilogues, with their ambiguous position between the fictional and the real, provided ideal opportunities to exploit the relation between the player and the part. The most extreme, and probably the funniest, example occurs at the end of Dryden's *Tyrannic Love.* Nell Gwynn, playing a doomed princess despite her generally recognized ineptitude in tragic roles, finally expires. Servants load her corpse onto a litter and are carrying it out when she suddenly sits bolt upright and exclaims, "Hold, are you mad? You damn'd confounded Dog! I am to rise, and speak the Epilogue!" She leaps off the bier and begins the final speech:

> I come, kind Gentlemen, strange news to tell ye
> I am the ghost of poor departed Nelly . . .
> To tell you truth, I walk because I die
> Out of my calling, in a Tragedy.
> O Poet, dam'd dull Poet, who could prove
> So senseless to make Nelly die for love! . . .
> As for my epitaph when I am gone,
> I'll trust no poet, but will write my own:
> "Here Nelly lies, who, though she liv'd a Slattern
> Yet dy'd a princess, acting in Saint Cathar'n."[11]

In *An Essay of Dramatic Poetry,* and *The Grounds of Criticism in Tragedy,* Dryden's qualified admiration for the French tradition testifies to his interest in and sensitivity to the requirements of theatrical decorum. But the demands of the tragic situation, even for Dryden, are overridden by the demands of Nell's personality.

It is tempting to think of the new acceptance of female assertiveness on the stage as part of a general revaluation of women's status—a reassessment that would eventually allow them to participate more fully in all aspects of public life. Certainly all the evidence suggests that although the actresses were never as numerous or as well-paid as their male colleagues, they participated extensively in the life of the companies to which they belonged. They were granted the same special privileges as the actors—most significantly a relative immunity from prosecution for debt. And with the formation of the Lincoln's Inn Fields Company in 1695, two actresses—Ann Bracegirdle and Mary Saunderson Betterton—became shareholders, with a right to a certain percentage of the company's profits.

The employment of actresses does not, however, coincide with a more general broadening of female participation in public life. In fact, during the second half of the seventeenth century women seem to have been losing rather than acquiring opportunities for gainful employment. Men were encroaching upon such traditionally female occupations as brewing, textile manufacture, dressmaking, and midwifery. Women were less and less likely to run businesses or enter trades independently of their husbands, to help their husbands in a family venture, or to continue such a venture when they were widowed. By the beginning of the eighteenth century, there were few alternatives for undowered,

---

[10]William Chetwood, *A General History of the Stage* (London, 1749), p. 28.
[11]John Dryden, *The Dramatic Works,* ed. Montague Summers (London: Nonesuch, 1931), II, p. 395.

unmarried women—or married women whose husbands could not support them—other than domestic service or prostitution.[12] The success of the actress has to be explained in ways which take into account the drastically different experience of women in other professions.

Actresses, in other words, seem to be anomalous rather than typical; the task is to isolate the factors that make their case so special. It is reasonable to look more closely to the audience's actual response to the women on the stage, in order to establish revealing patterns of assumptions. One such pattern is so obvious as to be unavoidable. Everyone from Dryden on has remarked upon the audience's extraordinarily lively, even obsessive, concern with the actresses' sexuality. John Downes, in *Roscius Angelicanus,* regales the reader with sly anecdotes:

> And all the Women's Parts admirably Acted: chiefly *Celia* [Moll Davis], a Shepherdess being Mad for Love; especially in Singing several Wild and Mad Songs. *My Lodging is on the Cold Ground,* etc. She perform'd that so Charmingly, that not long after, it Rais'd her from her Bed on the Cold Ground, to a Bed Royal.

> *Note, Mrs. Johnson in this Comedy, Dancing a Jigg so Charming Well, Love's power in a little time after Coerc'd her to Dance more Charming else where.*[13]

Others were less delicate. The anonymous author of "Satyr on Players" (London, ca. 1685), declares that actresses are "so lewd in every kind / You'd swear that Rogue and Whore had both combin'd," and goes on to support his claim in explicit detail:

> Sue Percival so long has known the Stage
> She grows in Lewdness faster, than in Age:
> From Eight or Nine she there has swiving been;
> So calls that Nature, which is truly Sin. (page 2)

Despite the difference in tone, Downes and the author of the "Satyr" both assume that the sexual exploits of the actress are an extension of her histrionic function rather than an irrelevant side-issue. Moll Davis's change of beds is described as the direct result of her fine performance; Mrs. Johnson gets invited to dance elsewhere because she has danced so well on the stage; Sue Percival's theatrical and sexual exploits coincide. Modern critics like John Harold Wilson and Allardyce Nicoll conclude that the presence of the actresses debased the theater, by lending it the atmosphere of a brothel.[14] . . .

No doubt the fuss is partly due to the fact that the actresses' sex lives really were fairly unorthodox. As Allardyce Nicoll primly declares, "very few of these women led chaste lives."[15] Elizabeth Barry was the mistress of John, Earl of Rochester; Elizabeth Hall the mistress of Sir Philip Howard; the Mrs. Johnson of Downes's anecdote the mistress of Henry, Earl of Peterborough. Margaret Hughes was the mistress of Prince Rupert, Susannah Hall the mistress of Sir Robert Howard, Ann Reeves the mistress of Dryden, Elizabeth Barry (again) of Otway, and Ann Bracegirdle (perhaps) of Congreve. Hester Davenport was irregularly married to the Earl of Oxford—when she refused to become his mistress he dressed up one of his servants as a parson, and had an invalid marriage ceremony

---

[12]The standard work on the subject is still Alice Clark's *Working Life of Women in the Seventeenth Century* (London: Routledge and Sons, 1919). Her conclusion—that women were progressively excluded from the job market during the seventeenth century—though not her Marxist analysis, has recently been supported by Roger Thompson, *Women In Stuart England and America* (London: Routledge and Kegan Paul, 1974), pp. 74–75.

[13]Downes, pp. 23–24, page 33.

[14]Wilson, *passim.;* Nic p. 72.

[15]Nicoll, p. 72.

performed. Nell Gwynn and Moll Davis went all the way to the top, and became mistresses of Charles II. Others, like Elizabeth Boutell and Rebecca Marshall, played the field.

Nonetheless, there were alternative models, like Mary Saunderson Betterton, who was the leading tragic actress before Mrs. Barry, and who seems to have led a faithful married life throughout her long career. An actress like Nell Gwynn, however, whose stage career lasted only five years, and whose histrionic talents were probably much smaller, seemed a much more exemplary specimen. When Ann Bracegirdle proved unexpectedly chaste, the audience did not divert its attention from her sexuality, but focused upon it all the more sharply.

> RAMBLE: And Mrs. Bracegirdle . . .
> CRITIC: Is a haughty conceited Woman, that has got more Money by dissembling her Lewdness, than others by professing it.
> SULLEN: But does that Romantick Virgin still keep up her great reputation?
> CRITIC: D'ye mean her Reputation for Acting?
> SULLEN: I mean her Reputation for not acting; you understand me.—[16]

By contrast, audience interest in the male players tended not to involve such an avid concern with their sex lives. Actors like Charles Hart, Edward Kynaston, and Cardell Goodman were "kept" by aristocratic ladies—in Goodman's case his connection with Lady Castlemaine obtained him a pardon after he had been convicted of highway robbery, a capital crime. But contemporary comment on their situation is muted; their sexuality is not considered part and parcel with their histrionic vocation. . . .

If hierarchical assumptions dominate conceptions of gender difference, boys and women occupy a similar position—they are inferior versions of mature men, *hommes manqués*. From one point of view, as *As You Like It*'s Rosalind-Ganymede knows, boys and women are cattle of the same color. The convention of the boy-actress has a certain logic; at any rate it does not pose a profound or necessary challenge to the audience's ideological convictions. If sexual difference is understood in terms of opposition, however, transvestite role-playing involves a much greater rupture of decorum—a rupture which may be ludicrous, implausible, or titillating depending upon the context. Boys no longer seem appropriate in women's tragic roles; a Cleopatra who shaves is the occasion for a jest.[17] The Restoration audience was more eager to see women in male disguise, but arguably this eagerness is rooted in the same attitudes which make the boy impersonators seem obsolete. John Harold Wilson has remarked upon the surprisingly "indelicate" methods by which women players in male disguise were unmasked in Restoration comedy.[18] Surely all the loosened hair, all the naked breasts in the fifth act are meant to heighten an incongruity of which the audience was already aware; the unmasking reinforces a histrionic appeal which depends upon the seductive appeal of female difference.

From this perspective one can see why the actresses appeared on the public stage for the first time at the Restoration; why their success could coincide with a more general withdrawal of women from public life; and also why their achievement took the specific forms that it did. It is not merely new attitudes toward women and the theater, but the persistence of old ones, which make possible the novel phenomenon of the Restoration actress, and which condition the highly selective enthusiasm of her audience.

---

[16]Anon. (sometimes ascribed to Charles Gildon), *A Comparison between The Two Stages* (London, 1702), p. 17.

[17]Cibber, p. 71.

[18]Wilson, p. 85.

✠ ✠ ✠

IN MANY WAYS THE WORLD WE LIVE IN TODAY WAS FORGED BETWEEN 1850 AND 1950. Since the mid-nineteenth century, enormous political changes have redrawn the map of the planet: two world wars; the rise of the United States and the rise and fall of the Union of Soviet Socialist Republics as world superpowers; revolutions in Russia and China; worldwide liberation from European colonial rule in Mexico, the Philippines, Latin America, Africa, India, and Southeast Asia. Political change was spurred by a series of industrial and technological revolutions. This is the century of the telephone, radio, film, and television; of the automobile and the highway; of the airplane and the rocket; of penicillin, anesthetics, vaccinations, and artificial organs; of the assembly line and mass production; of multinational corporations extending their markets and influence around the globe. The acceleration of technological change altered the fabric of daily life, creating new forms of living, working, and relating to one another, and new ways of measuring our lives: suburbs and housing developments, trade unions and public corporations, the time clock and the wristwatch, public education and compulsory retirement. It witnessed huge changes in the landscape of life: the growth of the modern cityscape, of modern slums, skyscrapers, subways, and even city streets; of massive public projects like the Panama and Suez canals, the Empire State Building, the Eiffel Tower, and their grim cousins—the gas chambers of Auschwitz and the nuclear bombing of Hiroshima and Nagasaki.

Political and social changes were rivaled by the intellectual and cultural revolutions that gave—or attempted to give—meaning to modern experience. This is the century of Darwin and the theory of evolution; of Marx and Lenin; of Gandhi's nonviolent resistance; of Einstein, Oppenheimer, and Teller, and a revolution in our understanding of the physical cosmos; of Freud's discovery of the unconscious; of Proust, Joyce, Stein, Eliot, and Woolf; of the Impressionist painters, and of Picasso, and Pollock; of Diaghilev and Nijinsky, of Fred Astaire and Ginger Rogers, of Isadora Duncan and Martha Graham; of Wagner, of Stravinsky and Schoenberg, of ragtime and jazz.

This complex of revolutions extends to the modern theater. Technological innovation, political developments, and two major wars encouraged an increasing internationalism across the arts of Europe, evident in the "international" style of architecture popularized by Le Corbusier, the Bauhaus, and their followers; in Cubist painting and sculpture; and in modernist writing and music. This internationalism, however, hardly fostered a single, monolithic sense of "modernism" in the arts. Instead, it gave rise to a series of fragmentary AVANT-GARDE movements—imagism, cubism, vorticism, futurism, symbolism, surrealism, Dada, and so on—each with its own ideals, esthetics, and audience, and usually with its own resistant posture toward society as well. The fragment—the poetic image, Joyce's "epiphanies," Schoenberg's twelve-tone row, montage in film—came to be valued as a means of expression in itself. Since the 1950s, a variety of social, political, and esthetic challenges have been made to modernism—usually under the general rubric of POST-MODERNISM. These challenges are discussed later in this essay.

Modernist art also developed a distinction between "high art" and the esthetics of mass culture that parallels the modern division of labor and implies a division between highbrow and lowbrow, the elite and the popular. In many respects, the modernist theater became definitive of "high art" as it was edged from the center of cultural life by other performance media—film, radio, and later television—which claimed greater immediacy and wider distribution. After the turn of the century, the modern theater and drama were increasingly pressed to define what is germane, special, essential to live dramatic performance.

Units 5, 6, and 7 survey the theater more widely than previous units, focusing not on a single city or site of performance, but instead on the broader developments of national and international movements. For although the theaters of Chekhov's Moscow, Shaw's London, and Brecht's Berlin reflected very different social dynamics, they were engaged in a common, distinctly modernist project: bringing the stage into a critical relation to the forms of modern life by taking an experimental attitude toward theatrical production. And many of these projects have a visible legacy in the work of their successors: in Beckett's sterile chambers, in Müller's assault on the dynamics of temporality and identity, in Churchill's parallel between sexual and colonial politics.

THE MODERN THEATER

Theatrical innovation always takes place on three fronts: as technology, as esthetics, and as ideology. The history of the modern theater is in one sense a history of new strategies and techniques for stage production: electric lighting, revolving stages, increasingly spectacular and illusionistic stage machinery, and new techniques of stage design, acting, and direction. What makes these changes meaningful is how they are used to represent and explain the world around us.

Reviewing the history of nineteenth-century drama, Brander Matthews—the first professor of dramatic literature in the United States—remarked in 1910 that modern drama owed its innovation more to Edison than to Ibsen, that the new drama was "the inevitable consequence of the incandescent bulb." The technological revolutions that brought engines and electricity to the public transformed theater throughout Europe and America: the replacement of candle lighting and gas lighting with more flexible electric lighting; the installation of the PROSCENIUM frame, emphasizing the pictorial coherence of the stage; the gradual disappearance of galleries and boxes in favor of seating the audience in darkened, fan-shaped theaters, emphasizing a perspective view of the proscenium; elevators to raise and lower sets; revolving stages on which several settings could be placed at one time. This technology could be put to a variety of uses, and the nineteenth-century theaters of Europe and America had an extraordinarily spectacular dimension, fostering a taste for EXTRAVAGANZAS, MELODRAMAS, NAUTICAL SHOWS, PANTOMIMES, and *TABLEAUX*. However, the apparatus of the modern theater came increasingly to be dominated by the notion of SCENIC UNITY, the idea that the stage set, the costumes, the behavior of the actors, and the dramatic action all should correspond to a single historical era and social milieu. Shakespeare's actors had mixed contemporary Elizabethan dress with "antique" costumes in the production of plays with classical settings. Throughout the eighteenth century, actors wore contemporary clothing regardless of the historical era of the play. By the late nineteenth century, however, following the example of Charles Kean and Henry Irving in England, the company of George II, the Duke of Saxe-Meiningen in Germany, and others, productions increasingly strove to establish a unified style on the stage, in which the dialogue, acting style, costumes, setting, and dramatic action all conformed to a single point-of-view.

The use of a unified theatrical style to assert a thorough VERISIMILITUDE, a photographic "slice of life" onstage, became the cornerstone of modern REALISM in drama and theater and of the movement called NATURALISM in which it began. In a series of essays calling for a "naturalism in the theater," published in the 1870s, the French novelist and playwright Émile Zola argued that the technology of the late nineteenth-century theater could be used to represent a more clinical or scientific attitude toward the world. He urged the stage to adopt a more lifelike and "naturalistic" style by adopting the "objective"

A PROSCENIUM STAGE: SHAKESPEARE MEMORIAL THEATRE

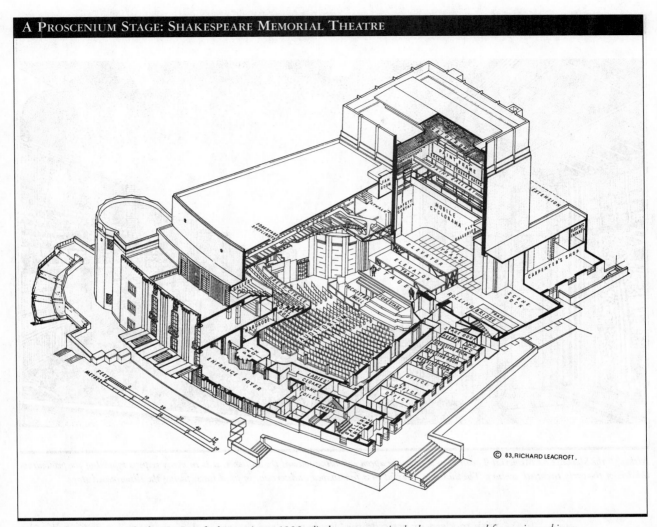

The Shakespeare Memorial Theatre, Stratford-upon-Avon, 1932, displays an extensive backstage area used for scenic machinery.

methods and perspective of the natural sciences. By filling the stage with objects—real doors, real walls, pictures, furniture, fireplaces—the theater could place men and women in their "environment" rather than in the idealized "setting" of the classical theater, and the characters could then be seen as influenced by that material environment. In contrast to the ideal heroes of earlier drama, the characters of modern plays would become part of that stage milieu, influenced by the forces of history, society, economy, and psychology. Naturalism, that is, uses the technology of the stage to claim a "scientific" attitude toward social problems, usually emphasizing the determining role that the social environment plays in the characters' actions. It organized the theater's new technology and the idea of scenic unity it made possible, and provided modern theater with a characteristic kind of meaning: the achievement of verisimilitude.

Naturalism and realism are notoriously difficult to distinguish; here we can describe them as two phases in the history of modern theater and drama. In this sense, naturalism provides the thematic inspiration and many of the dramatic techniques we now associate

SHAKESPEARE MEMORIAL THEATRE, INTERIOR VIEW

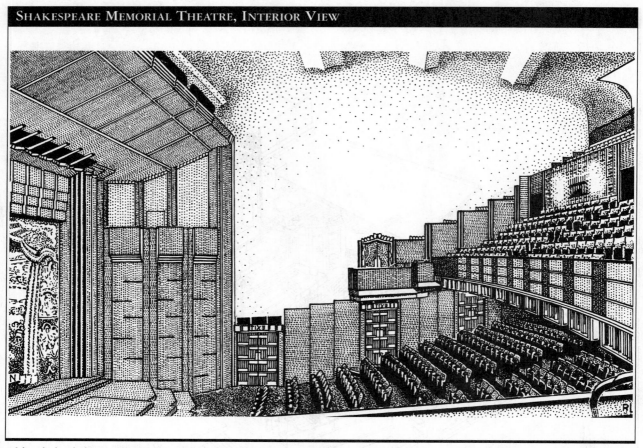

Although the Shakespeare Memorial Theatre has a forestage apron extending toward the audience, it is in many respects typical of the proscenium theaters of the early twentieth century. The audience is seated in a fan-shaped auditorium, in fixed seats, facing the illuminated stage.

with modern realistic drama. Realism in the theater is also committed to verisimilitude, but usually develops a wider range of style and a more problematic sense of the relationship of character and environment. While naturalistic plays tend to be preoccupied with the duplication of material reality onstage, realistic plays sometimes distort the verisimilitude of the stage picture in order to dramatize an inner, psychological truth. The domestic space of Tennessee Williams's *Glass Menagerie,* for instance, is at once a realistic tenement and the fluid space of memory. Realism extends and refines the techniques first explored by Zola's generation of playwrights, directors, and actors: a simple and direct speaking style that usually masks a SUBTEXT of subtle, unspoken motives; middle- or lower-class characters; action that revolves around the discovery of some past crime or indiscretion; a three-dimensional stage set, usually a domestic interior. Rather than using the play as a vehicle for a single "star" actor, realistic performance emphasizes the ensemble playing of the cast, so that each character becomes important in the overall action. Onstage, realism often treats the boundary of the proscenium as an invisible fourth wall dividing the environment onstage from the audience. The FOURTH WALL prevents the actors from playing to the audience and so from destroying the unity of illusion onstage.

Realism has become the dominant mode of dramatic performance today, so pervasive that it may be difficult for us to recapture its special excitement and danger when first introduced in the 1880s and 1890s. In the first blush of the modern era, the ability to picture an untheatrical, apparently "real" world on the stage was in itself a kind of spectacle, akin to the magic of the new, competing art of photography. Moreover, the first generation of realistic playwrights often adopted a critical posture toward the pieties of the middle-class audience whose attitudes were embodied in the "realistic" vision of the world. Plays like Ibsen's *Ghosts* and *A Doll House,* and even Glaspell's *Trifles,* raised the scandalous topics of sexual betrayal, marital discord, class conflict, sexual freedom, and gender politics in ways that challenged the conventional morality of the bourgeois audience.

The realistic theater developed many of the practices we are familiar with today: new sets for each production, rather than the same furniture recycled from show to show, in order to create the play's specific environment; the fourth wall; the darkened auditorium. Although realistic drama became pervasive, it first flourished in the small avant-garde theaters of the INDEPENDENT THEATER MOVEMENT at the turn of the century. Throughout Europe and the United States, playwrights and directors worked to carve a place for themselves outside the commercial mainstream, which often resisted and sometimes censored the controversial plays of the new realism. André Antoine founded the Théâtre Libre ("Free Theater") in Paris as a subscription theater in 1887; since the shows were open only to subscribers and not to the general public, he was able to avoid censorship and to produce plays like Ibsen's *Ghosts* and Strindberg's *The Father.* Antoine's work was paralleled by the German Freie Bühne ("Free Stage") in 1889. In England, the actress Janet Achurch mounted a production of Ibsen's *A Doll House* in 1889; J. T. Grein's Independent Theater opened in 1891 with a production of *Ghosts* and went on to produce plays by Ibsen, Shaw, and other contemporary playwrights. In Russia, Constantin Stanislavski and Vladimir Nemirovich-Danchenko founded the Moscow Art Theater in 1898, launching one of the most influential of modern theaters with their production of Chekhov's *The Seagull.* Independent theaters were often part of nationalist movements as well, especially in Norway, Sweden, Finland, Italy, and Ireland. In Ireland, W. B. Yeats, Lady Augusta Gregory, John Millington Synge, and a solid cast of amateur actors established a nationalist theater company in 1902 and opened The Abbey Theater in 1904. Here, the artistic resistance of the independent theater was allied to political resistance and national self-definition. The influence of these theaters was felt in the United States throughout the first decades of the twentieth century. David Belasco's minute fidelity to detail had firmly established a realistic idiom in the American theater, but it took the LITTLE THEATER MOVEMENT, inaugurated by Eugene O'Neill, Susan Glaspell, and the Provincetown Playhouse in 1915, to establish a repertoire of modern drama in the United States, and they were soon followed by other companies.

The rise of the independent theaters also points to the theater's fragmentation and its marginalization in modern society. The theater no longer commands the cultural centrality that it had in classical Athens or in London and Paris in the sixteenth and seventeenth centuries. Instead, it has become the site for a diverse, sometimes confusing array of artistic experiments. Naturalism and realism were the first dramatic modes to consider themselves not as expressing the dominant political and ideological order, but as criticizing the values and institutions of middle-class society. The major plays of the realistic canon often tend to criticize modern life, particularly its dehumanizing, exploitative routine. The major heroes of the realistic mode—Nora Helmer, Major Barbara, Laura Wingfield—are all characters whose desire for freedom, vitality, and life is threatened by the deadening, deceptive world in which they live. Because realistic drama usually sees that world as an all-embracing "environment," though, its social themes don't finally lead to a call for social change. Modern society may be a prison, but the liberation urged by realistic drama is imagined on the individual level; the characters' search for freedom, value, and meaning

FORMS OF MODERN DRAMA

leaves the world unchanged. Despite its critical stance toward modern society, realistic drama tacitly accepts the world and its values as an unchanging, and unchangeable, environment in which the characters live out their lives.

For this reason, realistic drama has often seemed an inadequate vehicle for a sustained critique of the forces of modern life, and almost from the moment of its inception in the 1880s and 1890s, realism inspired antagonistic forms of drama and theater. The history of modern drama is a series of reactions against bourgeois society and its values, and against the realistic drama that seemed to represent it and its vision of the world.

Although it was finally concerned with many of the same issues, the EXPRESSIONIST THEATER popular from the turn of the century through the 1930s marked an exciting stylistic departure from the realistic mode. Expressionist plays like Strindberg's *A Dream Play,* or American plays like Elmer Rice's *The Adding Machine,* Sophie Treadwell's *Machinal,* or Eugene O'Neill's *The Hairy Ape,* transformed the terms of realistic theater and drama. Rather than showing a character whose inner vitality is crushed by the bourgeois environment, expressionist plays try to show the mind and heart of the character visually, to express it directly in the objects and actions of the stage. The stage set becomes distorted, nearly dreamlike, and it is often peopled by characters who are exaggerated, mechanized, or fantastic, as a way of conveying the emotional coloring of the central character's experience. In O'Neill's *The Emperor Jones,* for instance, Jones is haunted by his "Little Formless Fears" when he flees into the forest; his flight is accompanied by the sound of a drum, which beats faster and louder as the play proceeds. More often, characters in expressionist drama are unnamed, like the Young Woman of *Machinal* or Mr. Zero of *The Adding Machine,* emphasizing that they have become cogs in the modern social and industrial machine. The action of expressionist drama is episodic and much like morality drama. Ernst Toller even named the scenes of his play *Transfiguration* "stations" to stress the play's likeness to a Christian passion play.

Thematically, expressionist theater resembles realism in its attention to character psychology and in its portrayal—however distorted or exaggerated—of the dehumanizing process of modern life. However, the style of expressionism also subverts realism in important ways, challenging both the logical, causal ordering of realistic dramatic action and the visual verisimilitude of the realistic theater. The SYMBOLIST THEATER also developed antirealistic attitudes toward drama and staging and extended the expressionist theater's repudiation of the drama of modern life. Written in prose or in verse, symbolic drama created a dim and mysterious other world, sometimes drawn from mythology or simply from the poet's imagination. The Belgian playwright Maurice Maeterlinck created a vogue for this kind of drama at the turn of the century, a drama which finds analogies in the work of Stéphane Mallarmé, August Strindberg, T. S. Eliot, W. B. Yeats, and Samuel Beckett. Yeats's mythological plays—such as *On Baile's Strand*—are typical of this special and influential mode. Relatively static in action, the plays rely on a densely figurative language to enlarge and energize the "poetic" meaning of events onstage.

Finally, an explicitly Marxist theory of the ideologically coercive dimension of realism —the sense that realism claims that its special perspective of the world is *natural,* that is, unavoidable and *real*—stands at the center of modern EPIC THEATER. Though usually associated with Bertolt Brecht, many of the techniques of epic theater were developed by Erwin Piscator in Berlin during the 1920s and early 1930s and by Vsevolod Meyerhold in his brilliant experiments with CONSTRUCTIVIST THEATER after the Russian Revolution of 1917. Brecht assimilated these techniques to a political purpose that he called epic theater. Rather than claiming to represent reality directly onstage by concealing the workings of the theater, epic theater alerts the audience to the ideological dimension of theater practice by constantly keeping the stage's "means of production" in view. Brecht developed the ALIENATION EFFECT as a way of alerting the audience to the constructed nature of stage events. While the realistic theater claims that the theater and drama, actor and character, stage and dramatic locale are the same, epic theater shows how they are different. In so doing, Brecht argued, the epic theater enables the audience to ask how—with what purpose, to what effect—stage practice is making this dramatic effect come about, and so leads the audience to take a more critical view of the process of the theater. Epic acting, then, comments on itself as "acting." The stage is not unified as a single dramatic locale, but always remains visibly a stage. Brecht also argued that epic drama should be structured differently than realistic plays. Instead of the apparently organic, "causal" action of realistic drama, Brecht's plays are written in a series of episodes. This technique, Brecht argued, allows the actors and the audience to reconsider the character's possibilities for action and change afresh in each scene. By calling the audience's attention to how the play comes into being onstage, epic theater encourages the audience to develop a dialectical sense of how social reality—in the theater and in the world at large—comes into being, how it is made through the interaction of individual and social forces and the interaction of material reality and IDEOLOGY. Epic theater has had an enormous influence on drama and theater around the world.

Stage practice has developed its own rich history, too—again often in reaction to realistic verisimilitude. Throughout the twentieth century, for instance, designers and architects have experimented with different ways of orienting the audience to the stage, in THEATER IN THE ROUND and in ENVIRONMENTAL THEATER, for instance. To see the dramatic action surrounded by spectators or to have the play take place among the audience members alters the audience's relationship to both the drama and its performance and changes how they can read the production. The Constructivist experiments of Vsevolod Meyerhold following the Russian Revolution placed a nonrepresentational "construction" onstage, a structure that the actors used as a "machine for acting" rather than as a realistic set. Similarly, experimental performance altered notions of what dramatic and theatrical representation could be like. Following World War I, writers like Tristan Tzara called for an art that was formless and irrational, a process rather than a product; such "Dada"—a nonsense term—poems, plays, and monologues were often given CABARET PERFORMANCE in Zurich, Berlin, and Paris. DADA and SURREALIST THEATER developed a kind of hallucinatory intimacy between stage and audience, laying the foundations for Artaud's THEATER OF CRUELTY. In all of these experiments, the theater worked to disperse the visual unity characteristic of the realistic stage in ways that led to new configurations of the relationship between the audience and the performers and to new interpretive perspectives on drama and the possibilities of theater.

Realism, expressionism, symbolist theater, and *epic theater*—these useful labels necessarily limit and categorize the rich variety of the stage in ways that are artificial and untrue to the dynamics of change in the modern theater, for new innovations tend to draw their techniques from several of these modes. Modern plays, for instance, often blend representational techniques as a way of challenging the audience's understanding of the drama and its implication in the world. Despite their "realistic" anchoring in a material, lifelike setting, for example, Chekhov's plays sometimes disturb the stability of that illusion with odd, almost "symbolic" effects—the breaking string in *The Cherry Orchard,* for instance. In Pirandello's *Six Characters in Search of an Author*—a play indebted in many ways to the "symbolist" theater—the Characters want the Actors to produce a play much in the manner of Ibsen's drama, a realistic drama of hidden crime and its discovery. These labels are useful in helping us to describe some of the outlines of a given play, but we should remember that many modern playwrights wrote in a variety of modes, and that each play is itself a kind of experiment.

ALTHOUGH MOST OF THE PLAYS IN-cluded in *The Harcourt Anthology of Drama,* Brief Edition, have been popular in the theater, they are all to some extent plays that have been canonized for their qualities as dramatic "literature": rich language and characterization, complex engagement with social and moral issues, deft and original use of dramatic convention, and so on. However, theater and drama pose special problems to the idea of a single literary canon. As popular entertainments, plays have not always been regarded as having "literary" merit. Plays were published only irregularly in Shakespeare's era partly for this reason, and even today few publishers have much commitment to keeping contemporary plays in print—which makes it particularly difficult for contemporary drama to become part of *any* literary canon. More important, plays are produced under very different conditions than novels and poems. Plays are made to be meaningful in a specific theater; their "literary" impact on readers is often secondary to their original purpose, which is to make a theatrical impact on a given body of spectators.

In late-eighteenth and nineteenth-century Europe—in part as a result of the relaxing of restrictions on theatrical performance, and in part as a reflection of a sense of "literature" as part of a circumscribed sphere of "high culture"—a variety of new dramatic genres became popular, of which the most important is MELODRAMA. The term was initially used to indicate plays in which music was used to accentuate the emotional coloring of the action; the term became more generally applied to plays with a conventionalized set of characters, a clear narrative structure, and a distinct moral cosmos. In the nineteenth-century theater, melodrama was an extremely popular genre, fusing the theater's increasing capacity for visual spectacle with a strongly colored and direct dramatic action. The world of melodrama is a world of clear-cut moral absolutes: the hero and heroine are thoroughly virtuous and are threatened by villains who are proportionately unscrupulous. The action is organized in a series of episodes, in each of which the hero/heroine's happiness, virtue, fortune, or life is threatened with destruction; each act of a melodrama usually ends with some striking crisis, often calling for an elaborate stage effect—an explosion, train wreck, or storm. The action of melodrama is often highly involved and

(A S I D E)

MELODRAMA

coincidental, yet usually works eventually toward a happy—or at least sentimental—ending. If the hero must die, he usually dies in the heroine's arms; more often, the couple are restored to one another and live happily ever after.

Melodrama is usually dated from the popularity of plays like Johann Christoph Friedrich von Schiller's (1759–1805) *The Robbers* (1782), August Friedrich Ferdinand von Kotzebue's (1761–1819) *Menschenhass und Reue* (1789), and René Charles Guilbert de Pixérécourt's (1773–1844) *Coelina* (1800); although Kotzebue and Pixérécourt are now rarely read, their plays were widely adapted throughout Europe. Thirty-six of Kotzebue's plays were translated into English, and several remained popular throughout the nineteenth century. Richard Brinsley Sheridan (1751–1816) adapted Kotzebue's *Der Spanier in Peru* as *Pizarro* in 1799, which became a brilliant success for the actor John Philip Kemble; Thomas Holcroft (1744–1809) adapted Pixérécourt's *Coelina* as *A Tale of Mystery* in 1802. While early nineteenth-century melodrama tended toward Gothic settings—mysterious castles, ghostly visitors, and the like—by later in the century melodrama's typical formal and moral patterns were applied to plays with local and contemporary settings. Pierce Egan's novel *Life in London* was adapted as *Tom and Jerry; or, Life in London* in 1821; Edward George Bulwer-Lytton's (1803–73) *Money* (1840)

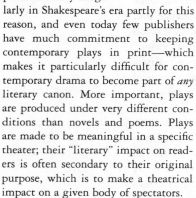

ACTING AND PERFORMANCE   The modern theater's radical redefinitions of the style and purpose of drama required similar redefinitions of acting and performance. At the turn of the century, a theatrical company would have been organized according to each actor's typical LINE OF BUSINESS. Something like the company in Pirandello's *Six Characters,* companies had a leading comic actor, a villain or "heavy," a leading man, a leading lady, a comic old man, a comic woman, and a variety of other parts. Unlike *commedia dell' arte,* actors each played a variety of different characters; nonetheless, each actor would have elaborated some relatively conventional "business" for acting the kind of character he or she usually played. The unity of illusion demanded by the realistic theater, however, required each character to be more finely individualized. Much as the stage designer provided a new set for each was one of several plays that held the stage through the end of the century.

Since melodrama drew a wide audience, and often centered on poor-but-virtuous heroes and heroines, it has sometimes been thought to articulate social resistance. For while early versions like Douglas Jerrold's (1803–57) hugely popular nautical melodrama *Black Ey'd Susan* (1829) emphasized the undying loyalty and patriotism of British navy sailors (or "tars"), the polarized moral ethos of melodrama could be turned into a vehicle for social critique. In the United States, melodrama became one vehicle for dramatizing ethnic and racial conflict. John Augustus Stone's (1800–34) *Metamora; or, The Last of the Wampanoags* (1829), dramatized a heroic Indian chief's losing battle to save the land of his ancestors from his rapacious white enemies. In *The Octoroon* (1859), Dion Boucicault (1820–90) staged the fatal love story between the octoroon Zoe, the virtuous plantation owner who loves her, and the wicked Yankee overseer, McCloskey, who threatens to buy her when it emerges that Zoe was never actually freed from slavery. But although these plays end with "tragic" consequences for their heroes and heroines, melodrama tends to locate its evils in the character of its villains, rather than in the structure of society itself: for this reason, melodrama is usually unable to develop a deeper analysis

---

MELODRAMA: *THE BELLS*

Sir Henry Irving's (1838–1905) performance in Leopold Lewis's melodrama The Bells *was one of his greatest roles. The illustration presents both the emotionally exaggerated quality of melodramatic acting and melodrama's use of special effects. In the play, Mathias (Irving's role) has murdered and concealed the body of a Polish Jew. Although many years have passed since the murder, Mathias is haunted by the sound of his victim's sleigh bells. In this scene, he staggers before a vision of the crime itself.*

of the social institutions—racism, for example—that afflict its characters' lives. When Bernard Shaw turned to melodrama as a vehicle for his own drama of social critique, he strategically inverted its patterns of characterization as a way of opening its social order to criticism: one way *Major Barbara,* for

example, attempts to jolt the audience into examining its attitudes about society at large is by casting Andrew Undershaft—so similar to the scheming and all-powerful industrialist villain of countless popular melodramas—as the moral "hero" of the play.

---

production and the costume designer provided clothing appropriate to the character and his or her setting, so the actors were forced to particularize their performances in new ways.

A second stimulus for this innovation was the drama itself. Playwrights like Ibsen and Chekhov typically created characters against the grain of theatrical stereotypes. Nora Helmer, for example, seems like a typical SOUBRETTE at the opening of *A Doll House,* the pert and clever young woman of light comedy. However, as the play develops, Ibsen challenges this convention and forces the actress to discover new ways of producing the character. Realistic plays frequently ask actors to work against the apparent "type" of the role, to discover the psychological subtext of will and desire beneath the spoken words that motivates the character's actions. Actors and actresses at the turn of the century frequently had difficulty reading the new realistic plays, precisely because they could not see how to represent the more indirect action and individualized characters through the kinds of stage behavior they had been trained to use.

A new kind of drama requires a new kind of acting, and companies throughout Europe developed ways of acting more behavioristically onstage. The most systematic approach to acting was undertaken by the actor and director Constantin Stanislavski at the Moscow Art Theater around the turn of the century. Although Stanislavski thought that his techniques could be applied to any play, he discovered the need for such acting largely in his work on Chekhov's plays. Chekhov's plays were frustrating to actors of the old school because the characters did not conform to traditional types and the action seemed so indirect and inconsequential, lacking familiar dramatic rhythms and climaxes. Stanislavski developed techniques for approaching each character as an individual, techniques that were later systematized as a "method" of actor-training. Stanislavski trained the actor to associate his or her personal history with the invented actions of the dramatic character so that the actor could tap that emotional spontaneity, a "life in art," as part of the performance. By using the MAGIC IF—imagining themselves *as* the character, rather than applying a stock line of business—and using their own EMOTION MEMORY to vivify the character's inner life, Stanislavski's actors were taught to bring authentic emotional experience into their performances. Of course, Stanislavski also emphasized the many other abilities that an actor must develop—physical training, vocal control, grace, concentration—but his real contribution to the modern stage is the emphasis on the actor's emotional reality in performance. The realistic theater uses real objects to create a persuasive material environment, and its characters come alive through the actor's real feeling. Stanislavski's work has been extremely influential, particularly in the United States, where it was adapted as the SCHOOL OF METHOD ACTING in the 1930s, and it remains—in very different and modified forms—at the center of much actor-training today.

Antirealistic drama also called for the development of new styles of performance. Meyerhold developed BIOMECHANICS as a way to make the actor's performance more physical, less directly concerned with the behavioral and psychological verisimilitude typical of Stanislavskian realistic acting. His work has analogies in the use of dance and ritualized performance in symbolist theater and in the nonrepresentational physicality of Antonin Artaud's Theater of Cruelty. Symbolist theater also repudiated the lifelike quality of realistic acting. It required a highly artificial and statuesque stillness from performers, allowing the actors to strike powerful but ethereal poses in order to deliver the densely poetic language of the play without interference. Yeats—whose antipathy to realism was profound—thought of training his actors in barrels, to keep them from moving and gesturing as they would do in everyday life: the art of the symbolist theater should be emphatically artificial, thoroughly apart from the conduct of life beyond the stage.

Brecht, again, voiced the most thorough critique of realistic acting. To Brecht, the problem of realistic acting was that it showed the "character" as a finished product, a commodity, rather than revealing *how* the character had come into being, both through the social forces described in the drama and through the decisions taken by the actor as part of the performance. Brecht argued that the actor should acknowledge that he or she both empathizes with the character and demonstrates the character to the audience, that acting is both feeling and showing at the same time. This dialectical approach invites the audience to see how the actor is making the "character" and allows the public to interpret both the process and the product of theater art, the dramatic "character" and the actor's labor.

Most readers of modern drama immediately note the prominence of women characters in the plays—Nora Helmer in *A Doll House,* Barbara in *Major Barbara,* Courage in *Mother Courage.* Playwrights frequently associated the political and social limitations of middle-class life with male characters and used female characters to pose subversive questions about that social order. However, in the drama, as in society, this subversive freedom sometimes emerges as illusory or problematic. Ibsen, for instance, enables Nora to recognize how she has been defined by the men in her life, but the world outside her home hardly seems inviting; is there really anywhere for her to go? Many of the women—the Stepdaughter of Pirandello's *Six Characters,* Major Barbara—are also assigned an erotic power opposed to the "reason" of their male antagonists. While this power, too, can be disruptive, it sometimes also reinforces traditional gender stereotypes. Feminine erotic power in the drama carries with it other ascribed values, defining women as more emotional, as more subject to the influence of the body, as closer to "nature." Men retain a pragmatic, "rational" authority that places them at the center of society, and that defines the arena of culture and civilization as an implicitly male domain. The apparent freedom of these stage women, that is, often signals their deeper captivity to the gendered economy of modern society, a captivity shared by actresses in the period as well. Although this is also a period in which actresses—Sarah Bernhardt, Eleonora Duse, or Ellen Terry, for example—could earn an international reputation, they worked in a theater in which men greatly outnumbered women in the audience and in which nearly all of the managers and producers were men. Women were also important playwrights throughout Europe in the first decades of the twentieth century: Elizabeth Robins's *Votes for Women!* brought the "woman question" to the English stage in 1907; Minna Canth was the leading playwright of the Finnish Theater (her portrait graces the proscenium of the National Theater today); Marieluise Fleisser's *Purgatory in Ingolstadt* (1924) in many ways rivaled Brecht's early vision of epic theater. In a male-dominated industry like the modern theater, it is not surprising that women onstage—both dramatic characters and performers—should reflect fundamentally masculine attitudes about the place of women in society.

To think of the history of theater and drama since Ibsen is to think of an increasingly large and problematic array of dramatic styles, modes of theatrical production, and conceptions of the audience and its world. Many of these innovations were local at first, responding to the social and theatrical conditions of a specific time and place: Brecht's Marxist theater arose in the cabaret culture of Berlin in the late 1920s; Pirandello's METATHEATER was part of the lively Italian avant-garde following World War I; Shaw's drama was informed by the progressive politics of the British Fabian Society and by dramatic conventions drawn from the popular plays of the late Victorian stage. The drama of modern Europe develops a posture of resistant inquiry toward the pieties of contemporary social life. It works both to represent that world and to change it, to affect our ideas about character and personality, about the political realities of our world, and even about the metaphysical certainties we have come to believe. But it is the impact of global political and cultural change that marks the theater of the second half of the twentieth century.

The impact of film and television has forced the theater to work to define what kinds of performance are specific to the stage, how live dramatic performances can offer something unique, something not already available in other performance media. For this reason, perhaps, theater and drama since 1950 have necessarily been "experimental," working to develop new kinds of plays, new practices of stage production, and new kinds of theatrical experience for their audiences. Much as the proscenium theaters of the early twentieth century have given way to other, more flexible kinds of theater spaces, so dramatic writing has become much more varied and experimental. Even stage realism—the mode of Ibsen

WOMEN IN MODERN DRAMA AND THEATER

THEATER AND CULTURE SINCE 1950

THEATER IN THE ROUND

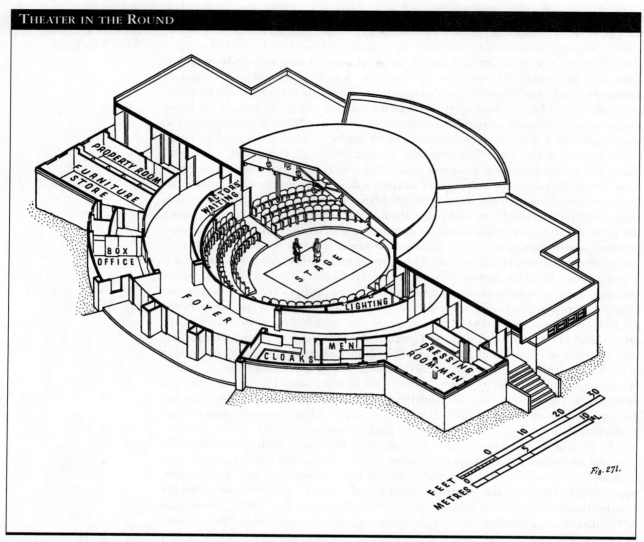

In a theater in the round, the audience surrounds the action, rather than facing the stage as in a proscenium theater. Theater space of this kind lends itself to greater immediacy and contact between the performers and the audience.

and Chekhov, Miller and Williams—has undergone an important reworking in the plays of Harold Pinter, Tony Kushner, Caryl Churchill, and others.

Here, we can identify three patterns of innovation as a way of organizing our thinking about the diversity of the contemporary stage. One strategy—inspired most directly by Antonin Artaud's THEATER OF CRUELTY—attacks the notion that the theater is essentially a *representational* medium, emphasizing instead the *experiential* aspect of theater. Rather than staging images of some fictive world to an audience of passive spectators, this kind of theater works to structure the *present experience* of the audience in new ways, as in the participatory and ritualistic theater experiments of the 1960s and 1970s. The influence of Artaud's assault on representation is evident in the contemporary theater in several ways: in absurdist drama, or in the emphasis on the performer's immediacy in performance art.

The second mode of innovation, THEATER OF THE ABSURD, originated as a new form of playwriting rather than as theatrical experimentation. The plays of Samuel Beckett, Slawomir Mrozek, Eugène Ionesco, Boris Vian, Edward Albee, Harold Pinter, and others create a strangely dislocated dramatic world, in which arbitrary or "absurd" events both confront and mystify the characters.

While Artaud inspired an existential or experiential theater, Bertolt Brecht—whose work became widely known and imitated only after World War II—inspired a different kind of assault on the conventions of realistic theater. Contemporary POLITICAL THEATER also criticizes the notion of "representation," but in different terms than Artaud or theater of the absurd, "representation" is a word with two senses; in "representing" a picture of the world, the arts necessarily claim that their images are "representative" in some way. Political theater frequently shows how a social or political order uses its power to "represent" others coercively—for example, by depicting those others through demeaning or limiting stereotypes. For this reason, political theater today is intent on using live performance to change the prejudicial attitudes concealed in conventional ideas of representation.

Of course, no plays fit easily or fully into these three categories, but to think of the drama of the postwar period as raising questions of our existential or our political relation to the theater—and so to the world—provides a useful and powerful way of opening that drama to our understanding. Each of these modes of theater creates a different relationship between the stage and its audience, and we should examine each of them in some detail.

The writings of Antonin Artaud, particularly the essays collected in the volume *The Theater and Its Double* (written in the late 1920s and 1930s, published in France in 1938, translated to English in 1958), have had an extraordinary impact on our sense of theater. Like many innovators of his generation—think of Brecht or Pirandello—Artaud worked to undermine the notion that the theater can only show its audiences realistic vignettes of daily life. Instead, Artaud argued that the theater should alter the balance between presentation—the actual, immediate activities of actors and audiences, their *presence* in the theater—and representation, the fictive "drama" that had seemed to define the purpose and scope of theater. Artaud—who used the term *theater of cruelty* for this project—advocated transforming the theater into an all-consuming spectacle, akin both to rituals like the Catholic Mass and to public festivals, in which the boundaries between acting and observing, actor and spectator, fiction and reality, conscious and unconscious would be broken or transgressed. The idea that the theater would "communicate," but not through rational means, is captured in one of Artaud's most powerful metaphors for this nearly unimaginable theater: the plague. Artaud envisioned a theater that would transmit its experiences corporeally, through the body, like disease, like mystical wisdom, alchemically transforming all of its participants. To avoid staging conventional dramas, Artaud called for a theater of "no more masterpieces," one that would use the dramatic text to transform the relations between stage and spectator by making the production a total experience—visual, auditory, gustatory, olfactory, tactile, physical—for the audience.

Stage director Peter Brook once remarked that "Artaud applied is Artaud betrayed," and it is true that Artaud's sense of theater is deeply metaphorical, a kind of theater experience that is almost unimaginable to us, and certainly not imaginable to us as theater. Artaud rarely offers a practical description of how this theater could come into being. Instead, the value and influence of Artaud's writing has been indirect and inspirational, bearing in a variety of tangential ways on kinds of theater that are not in any literal sense "Artaudian." In that Artaud imagines a theater of *presence*—not of representation—involving the audience in an experience rather than showing them a picture, his theater comes into contact with several very different kinds of innovation. Although the

ARTAUD AND
THE THEATER
OF CRUELTY

American experimental theater of the 1960s and 1970s is the most direct application—and betrayal—of Artaud, Artaud's conception of theater stands distantly behind a variety of more formally constructed plays: the dislocating imagery of Beckett and Parks; perhaps even the ritualized, hallucinatory violence of Pinter's plays. Of course, as *written* plays, "masterpieces," these plays are specifically opposed to the ideals of Artaud's unrealizable theater, while at the same time they explore part of the terrain opened by Artaud's vision.

THEATER OF THE ABSURD

Coined by the theater critic Martin Esslin in 1961, the phrase *theater of the absurd* tries to capture the special irrationality and unpredictability of a certain wave of dramatic writing of the late 1950s and 1960s, including the plays of Samuel Beckett and Harold Pinter, for example. Taking as his keynote Beckett's famous play *Waiting for Godot* (1953)—a play in which two Chaplinesque tramps wait for a mysterious man named Godot, who never arrives—Esslin finds the theater of the absurd to have certain stylistic and thematic characteristics. It rejects the sense of causality found in realistic plays, the sense that it is possible to find the causes for events either in the environment or in the psychological motives of the characters themselves. Instead, theater of the absurd tends to be about a world in which inexplicable, arbitrary, or irrational events happen. Although the events usually seem to be part of some kind of order or scheme, it is an order that the characters and their audience cannot quite grasp. As Hamm says in Beckett's play *Endgame,* "Something is taking its course," but neither the characters nor the audience are ever sure what that "something" is. In Eugène Ionesco's play *Rhinoceros* (1960), the inhabitants of a small French village begin to turn inexplicably into rhinoceroses. In each act of Boris Vian's *The Empire Builders* (1959), a family moves to a smaller room in an apartment building, always accompanied by a mysterious, bandaged figure. In Slawomir Mrozek's *Striptease* (1961), two men are commanded by a huge, silent finger to remove their clothes and don huge conical hats that conceal and blind them. As Esslin suggests, this drama insists that the fictions we use to make sense of our world—ideas of order, causality, rationality—are just that: fictions imposed on an arbitrary and mysterious reality, whose meanings remain fugitive and elusive.

Absurdist drama treats its audience somewhat differently than realistic plays do, rejecting the "dramatic irony" of the traditional theater, in which the audience understands more than the characters onstage. Instead, the theater of the absurd refuses to provide this privilege to its spectators. We are as baffled and frustrated by our attempts to make the events mean something as the characters are; "Mean something!" a character remarks in *Endgame,* "You and I, mean something! (*Brief laugh*)." Our *present* experience as an audience is structured and made significant by absurdist theatrical production. In the theater, we don't just observe the "absurd" drama onstage, we are forced to undergo it, to live it through. For this reason, both the drama onstage and the audience's experience in the theater are sometimes described as *existential.* We have to *decide* the meaning of our being in the theater, without the comfort, solace, or guidance of some transcendent, predetermined worldview.

POLITICAL THEATER

Much as theater of the absurd works to make the spectators' situation in the theater an extension of the characters' situation on the stage, political theater since Brecht has worked to make the audience's performance in the theater a recognizably political one. By fragmenting the stage space, by showing how the illusion is made rather than concealing its means of production, and by involving the audience more overtly in deciding the meaning of the play's events, the theater is shown to be a political instrument. Like television, newspapers, universities, the courts, and so on, the theater is an institution that produces the ideas and images with which we govern our lives. Both the example of Brecht's plays and his challenging theory of performance have been absorbed and redefined by the world theater. In common with theater of the absurd, political theater works to resist and complicate realistic representation, the "slice of life" of Ibsen, Chekhov, and Miller. Instead of staging an arbitrarily unreal and absurd world, political theater examines "representative" images of reality. Who makes those images? Who benefits from them? Who is injured, governed, or oppressed by them? How do they help to maintain the social *status quo?*

For this reason, much political theater connects representation onstage with representation in society, showing how various social groups—women, gay men, lesbians, ethnic and racial groups, the poor—have been staged in society and in the theater. A fundamental assumption of political theater is that these stereotypes are part of the larger system of discrimination that operates in society, and that they reveal the dominant attitudes of those who govern, control, or influence society from positions of power. In plays like Amiri Baraka's *Dutchman,* Suzan-Lori Parks's *America Play,* and Wole Soyinka's *Death and the King's Horseman,* the racial conflicts informing contemporary society and culture are explored in very different ways: in relation to colonialism, to the mythologies of American history, to women's experience. These plays are very different in style, ranging from a kind of realism in *Death and the King's Horseman* to the testifying monologues of Anna Deavere Smith. It is not a single point of view or a single dramatic style that defines political theater, but the use of theatrical representation itself as a way to analyze representation in society at large.

A similar approach to theater informs many of the modern plays gathered in this anthology, for many of them explore the issue of representation: how Asia is represented in the minds of the West in David Henry Hwang's *M. Butterfly,* how the English remapped and so represented the Irish in their own language and political system in Brian Friel's *Translations,* how African tribal traditions are tragically misunderstood by British imperialists in Wole Soyinka's *Death and the King's Horseman,* how the Chicano and Anglo cultures interact in Luis Valdez's *Los Vendidos.* Political theater sometimes seems highly message oriented and overtly didactic to readers and audiences used to the more subtle instruction offered by realistic plays. Yet the messages of contemporary political theater tend to be fused into the process of theater, so that the politics of the play come into being not in the prepared script of the play but in our experience as an audience. All of these plays disrupt the expectations, attitudes, and preconceptions of the empowered audience and invite the audience to develop different ways of reading their society as part of their involvement in the play.

On the contemporary stage, though, these modes of theater do not work in isolation from one another, but interact with one another, as part of the dynamic means the theater uses to engage its audiences in an understanding of the world. Indeed, to describe the contemporary theater in terms of its historical inheritance from the modernist theater of Brecht, Artaud, and the absurdists is in an important sense to overlook what is most significant about the stage today: its break from the traditions of modernism. If we look at the range of contemporary performance activity, much of it has little to do with traditional drama. Think of the performance-art monologues of Spalding Gray (one of his best-known, *Swimming to Cambodia,* was made into a film by Jonathan Demme) or Karen Finley (whose work was at the center of the 1990 censorship controversy at the National Endowment for the Arts); of the music of Laurie Anderson; of video art and film; of music television and advertising; of the disorienting stage spectacles of Robert Wilson; even of "plays" like Peter Handke's *Offending the Audience* and *The Ride Across Lake Constance,* or Heiner Müller's *Hamletmachine,* or Samuel Beckett's later work for the theater, *Not I, Footfalls,* and *Ohio Impromptu.*

DRAMA, THEATER, AND THE "POSTMODERN"

Theorists of culture and the arts have related these developments to innovations in the visual arts, in architecture, and in writing, characterizing their common features as POST-MODERN. The term itself is a difficult one, suggesting that these works often share some of the features of earlier, "modernist" art; the literary and cultural theorist Fredric Jameson suggests that the distinguishing feature of postmodern art is its attitude toward history. Jameson points out that postmodern works frequently invoke or appropriate the style of earlier historical periods, as in the use of neoclassical ornamentation in recent architecture, or the recollection of earlier film styles in more recent movies (FILM NOIR in *Chinatown* or *L.A. Confidential*). Jameson labels this technique PASTICHE. What is striking about these postmodern quotations of style, though, is not any systematic reinterpretation of tradition or any statement of value, but their tonelessness, their neutrality, the absence of the kind of moral and historical sense we might expect from the act of confronting history. In post-modern pastiche, the recollection of an earlier style does not provide a new understanding of the past, nor does it illuminate our contemporary historical situation. Instead, pastiche denatures that style by removing it from history, and history from it. Style becomes exactly that: simply another option. Hamm's many quotations from English literature in *Endgame* or the pastiche of Gilbert-and-Sullivan operetta in Churchill's *Cloud Nine* are perhaps part of this complex problem, for in each case the "past" is presented to the audience in terms of an artistic style that is largely emptied of its force as history.

Moreover, Jameson's discussion of pastiche also emphasizes the importance of the esthetic *surface* in postmodern art. Music video and advertising are sometimes taken as the paradigmatic postmodern forms, forms whose "message" lies almost exclusively in a rapidly changing, brilliantly seductive, series of images. Although this technique relates to the modernist use of MONTAGE in film and theater, it is different in several important ways. Modernist montage uses a series of images narratively, to tell a story. Although the camera cuts quickly from image to image, the audience assembles the images in a single complete narrative. Both the narrative and the interpreting spectator achieve a sense of wholeness. In contrast, postmodern images are juxtaposed in striking, sometimes contra-dictory combinations that resist our ability to impose a single narrative explanation, a sin-gle story line. Postmodern performance—on film or video or in the theater—is insistently fragmentary; it asserts the incompletion of the artistic object and the incomplete quality of the spectator's experience as well. Postmodern arts resist imposing a single explanatory interpretation that would both complete the narrative and confirm the audience's sense of wholeness, of self-integration. In this sense, postmodern arts are sometimes described as concerned with the "death of the subject." They question the possibility both of a com-prehensible world and of a comprehending individual. By disorienting language, frag-menting narrative, and dispensing with such organizing principles as "plot" and "character," postmodern art claims that we have entered a new age in which the complex disconnections of modern culture have made obsolete many of our beliefs about the world and our ways of representing the world and ourselves.

MODERN EUROPEAN DRAMA IN PERFORMANCE AND HISTORY

The understanding of theater that was inaugurated in the mid-nineteenth century is in many respects continuous with our own today: although various experiments—environ-mental theater, theater of cruelty, performance art—have contributed to a rich sense of the diversity of theatrical performance forms today, to many people "going to the theater" means going to a specially designated building, sitting in a darkened auditorium, and watching the events that take place on the stage. Of course, this activity is shaped today by social and economic forces still just emerging in the early-modern period: whereas ear-lier audiences usually had a small number of theaters to turn to for performance, perfor-mances are available today in a wide range of spaces—subsidized state and municipal theaters throughout Europe, commercial theaters like those in London's West End and New York's Broadway, college and university playhouses, festival theaters like the annual festival at Grahamstown in South Africa or the Shaw Festival in Stratford, Ontario, and many more. Theater in the twentieth century is characterized by its "optional" character: we choose theater from among a range of other forms of dramatic performance, like film and television; the theaters we attend are positioned in their ambient cultures in a much wider variety of ways; and the performances we see tend to value their "uniqueness" rather than their conventionality in typically modern ways.

Moreover, while the performance practices of earlier European theaters were highly conventionalized—masks and *cothurni* for tragedy in Athens, the phallus for comedy; a standard comic or tragic stage set in the neoclassical theaters of France and Italy—in the modern period, the style of dramatic production has become much more varied, not only as a sign of the director's and designer's artistic signature in the production, but also as part of what the play has to sell to its audiences. Indeed, the invention of the stage director in the late nineteenth century is symptomatic of a trend in modernist esthetics more generally, a trend from the polished deployment of convention to an emphasis on the artwork's originality—an originality that signals the individual creative presence of an author or *auteur*. In earlier theaters, of course, someone usually had the responsibility of organizing and rehearsing the actors: this was sometimes the playwright in classical Athenian theater, or the company's leading actor, like David Garrick, in the later eighteenth century. But in these theaters, performance practice was extremely conventionalized: actors, like Shakespeare's, who have a solid line of business, don't really need much rehearsal—an actor whose typical line of business is comic old men will more or less have an approach ready for characters like Polonius. In the modern theater, however, the director has the responsibility for shaping the diverse talents of the company—set, costume, and lighting designs; acting; music—into a single whole, one that seems to deploy the performance in a unique way. Much as we think of a film as embodying the director's vision, so too in the theater the performance is often understood as an expression of the director's ability to shape the play, the players, and the physical milieu of the stage into a uniquely expressive whole.

For this reason, the modern theater is often called the "director's theater," and in many respects the history of modern stage practice is the history of the innovations of brilliant directors. Although naturalistic or realistic drama—the plays of Ibsen and Chekhov and O'Neill—are duly appreciated for their striking departures from the standard practices of nineteenth-century playwriting, transforming these innovations from the page to the stage required a generation of brilliant directors: Antoine, Stanislavski, Meyerhold, Max Reinhardt. Indeed, at the end of the nineteenth century and the early decades of the twentieth, actors were frequently baffled by the new demands of these scripts; directors like Stanislavski helped them to discover new performance techniques to register the new demands of a new kind of drama. Similarly, when one thinks of the landmark theatrical productions of the twentieth-century European theater, they are always associated with the director: Stanislavski's productions of Chekhov at the turn of the century; Meyerhold's brilliant *Hedda Gabler,* with its white set and Hedda's brilliant, snakelike green dress; Piscator's work with Brecht in the 1920s, and Brecht's direction of the Berliner Ensemble in his own and others' plays after World War II; Peter Brook's use of the circus to realize the "magic" of Shakespeare's *A Midsummer Night's Dream* in 1970; Robert Wilson's visualization of Heiner Müller's *Hamletmachine* in the 1980s. As a consequence, one of the most energetic kinds of experiment in the later part of the century has been in the area of a more collaborative theater practice. Many contemporary theater companies are organized as collectives, in which responsibility for the "artistic" decisions is shared, rather than given over to a single person. But even in more conventional circumstances, companies often work to make the playwright's, actors', and designers' work have a more direct impact on the final stage of theater work. Caryl Churchill's play *Cloud Nine,* for example, arose from a series of workshops undertaken by members of the Joint Stock Company, in which the actors experimented by playing different gender, sexual, or racial roles in a variety of situations: Churchill wrote the text of the play out of the workshops, and director Max Stafford-Clark used the results of the workshops as a foundation for the play's theatrical performance. Given the increasing complexity of theatrical production—the use not only of complex technology backstage, but the inclusion of multimedia production as part of the performance itself—we can expect that this struggle to shape the authority of the stage will continue well into the future.

HENRIK IBSEN

At the turn of the century, Henrik Ibsen (1828–1906) was synonymous with modernity in the European theater; much of the territory of modern drama was first explored in Ibsen's work. Born into a mercantile family in provincial Norway, Ibsen had planned to study medicine; however, after failing to matriculate at the university, he turned to a career as a writer. From 1850 through 1864, Ibsen worked for the nationalist Norwegian Theater in Bergen and then for the Mollergate Theater in Christiania (now Oslo). As literary manager, stage manager, and assistant to the director, Ibsen learned the craft of practical theater firsthand. He also wrote a series of romantic history plays, some in prose and some in verse. Although his fame now rests on the realistic plays he wrote later in his career, in his own lifetime these history plays—such as *The Vikings at Helgeland* (1858)—were quite popular, especially in Norway.

In 1864, Ibsen left Norway and settled in Rome, where he wrote two pivotal plays, *Brand* (1866) and *Peer Gynt* (1867). The story of an idealistic minister, *Brand* established Ibsen as an important European writer and announced one of his central themes: the cost of moral idealism in the modern world. *Peer Gynt* is often taken as a companion-piece to *Brand,* for Peer's picaresque journey throughout Europe is undertaken simply for the purpose of his own self-satisfaction: while Brand's motto is "Be wholly what you are," Peer Gynt's is "To thine own self be . . . enough." In 1877, after extensive work on the Hegelian history drama *Emperor and Galilean,* Ibsen wrote *Pillars of Society,* a prose drama of modern life, inaugurating the stunning series of plays that made him famous and established the contours of modern realistic drama. In *A Doll House* (1879), *Ghosts* (1881), and *An Enemy of the People* (1882), Ibsen explored the conflict between the social and moral restrictions of bourgeois society and the psychological, often unconscious demands of individual freedom. Ibsen adapted the suspenseful, rigorously plotted form of the WELL-MADE PLAY (or *pièce bien faite*) popularized throughout Europe by French playwrights Eugène Scribe and Victorien Sardou and used it in plays of modern life critical of bourgeois morality and society. The well-made play is notoriously difficult to define, even though its features are familiar: a rigorously "causal" plot, a secret gradually revealed to the audience, a "necessary scene" (the *scène-à-faire*) in which the secret is revealed to the characters, a character (the *raisonneur*) who explains and moralizes the action to the others, and a predominance of coincidental events. In his earlier plays, Ibsen takes these formal conventions and makes them function as forces in the dramatic world. The world of the play comes to seem mechanistic, determined by a secret that will out, full of busybodies explaining and interpreting the action. The mechanics of the well-made play, that is, are identified with the deadening force of social convention, which painfully threatens to extinguish the vitality of the central characters. This conflict between deadening social convention and a mysterious inner vitality pervades Ibsen's mature plays as well, which increasingly moved away from the "well-made" form: *The Wild Duck* (1885), *Rosmersholm* (1887), *The Lady from the Sea* (1888), and *Hedda Gabler* (1890). Ibsen's last plays seem more poetic or symbolic, though they take place in the familiar milieu of the realistic stage: *The Master Builder* (1892), *Little Eyolf* (1894), *John Gabriel Borkman* (1896), and the unfinished *When We Dead Awaken* (1900). Ibsen suffered a paralyzing series of strokes in 1900 that left him unable to write. He died in 1906.

Ibsen's effect on his contemporaries and his influence on the course of modern drama were immediate and profound. His plays were rapidly translated into the major European languages, and stage productions—which often inaugurated the new "independent" theaters—frequently became the subject of sensation and controversy. Indeed, "Ibsenism" came to be a catchword for a variety of social causes, though Ibsen himself generally avoided politics. Although Ibsen's plays brought new issues to the stage, it was his practice as a playwright that proved truly revolutionary. Many playwrights had adopted the realistic theater's use of a material stage environment, its emphasis on the burden of the past, and its sense of a mechanized and constricting society. Ibsen not only used this material with powerful subtlety and resonance, he gave the stage its first distinctively modern characters: complex, contradictory individuals driven by a desire for something—the "joy of life," a sense of themselves—that they can barely recognize or name.

A DOLL HOUSE

A Doll House was inspired by a series of incidents that came to Ibsen's attention in 1878 when a woman named Laura Kieler contacted him. Kieler had signed a secret—and illegal—loan to raise money for a cure for her tubercular husband. She wrote to Ibsen asking him to recommend the novel she had written to his publisher, in hopes that the profits from its sale would allow her to repay the loan. Ibsen refused. Kieler forged a check and was caught. Her husband committed her to an asylum, had her charged as an unfit mother, and demanded a legal separation. When she was released from the asylum, however, the family remained together.

We can see the shaping power of Ibsen's imagination in his transformation of Laura Kieler's tragedy into the ironic masterpiece, *A Doll House*. The play—which by the turn of the century was a rallying point for international feminist demands for the vote and for other legal rights and protections for women—organizes the conflict between Nora and Helmer around a subtle set of contrasts: the childlike and protected Nora and the world-weary Mrs. Linde; the upright and protective Helmer and the shady—yet finally generous—Krogstad; the privations of the past and the financial freedom Nora sees on the horizon. However, as the play proceeds, the stable, bourgeois world that Helmer represents is revealed as a tissue of deception—the institutions of marriage, respectability, and social justice turn out to be fictions that the privileged use to manipulate their world. Nora comes to seem effective, efficient, worldly wise, and finally independent, while Helmer readily compromises his principles to save his reputation. The world of financial freedom Nora glimpses at the play's outset turns out to be a kind of prison and is replaced by another kind of freedom at the end of the play: the frightening freedom to cut herself loose from the bonds of marriage, family, and society.

Helmer had more authority with audiences in the 1880s and 1890s than he does today, and Nora was conventionally criticized as an "unwomanly woman" for taking the loan, deceiving her husband, and leaving her family. Indeed, the first English actress to be offered the part turned it down, because she didn't want audiences to think of her as the kind of woman who would desert her children. Yet the play tends to validate Nora's personal growth and her final decision to leave her family, and cannily uses the material environment of the stage setting to convey the suffocating situation in which Nora finds herself. The play takes place in one room: the drawing room where the upwardly mobile Helmers (deluxe books on the shelf, piano against the wall, framed art prints) receive their guests and conduct their lives. The room itself represents the Helmers' concern for social status and assumes a symbolic importance as well: it stands between the unseen privacy of the kitchen and bedroom—the domestic world of marriage and children—and the threatening public world beyond the front door, the world of Krogstad, of the dark and icy river, of Nora's final escape. The room becomes a kind of prison, a room in which Rank's declaration of love for Nora seems inappropriate, in which Helmer criticizes her dizzying tarantella—a Sicilian dance thought to imitate the death throes of someone bitten by a tarantula—as too abandoned, and in which Nora's final discussion with Helmer makes her submission to him impossible. That is, the room makes concrete the play's concern for the social constraints on a woman's life, becoming a visual image of how Helmer's masculine, bourgeois moral authority imprisons Nora. It is not entirely clear that Nora can survive in the harsh social and economic climate outside the comfortable parlor, but it is clear that escape from the parlor is her final alternative.

A Doll House was a successful—and a scandalous—play throughout Europe in the last decades of the nineteenth century, and it has remained in the repertoire ever since. Nora has always been associated with feminist politics, and several productions in the 1960s and 1970s saw in *A Doll House* an anticipatory allegory of the women's movement. Indeed, whereas Helmer appeared to 1880s audiences as a romantic leading man, the challenge for contemporary productions is to make him appear sympathetic, someone worth Nora's years of sacrifice, and someone she will have to struggle to leave.

A DOLL HOUSE

Henrik Ibsen

TRANSLATED BY ROLF FJELDE

———— CHARACTERS ————

TORVALD HELMER, *a lawyer*
NORA, *his wife*
DR. RANK
MRS. LINDE
NILS KROGSTAD, *a bank clerk*
THE HELMERS' THREE SMALL CHILDREN

ANNE-MARIE, *their nurse*
A MAID, *Helene*
A DELIVERY BOY

The action takes place in Helmer's residence.

———— ACT ONE ————

A comfortable room, tastefully but not expensively furnished. A door to the right in the back wall leads to the entryway; another to the left leads to HELMER's study. Between these doors, a piano. Midway in the left-hand wall a door, and further back a window. Near the window a round table with an armchair and a small sofa. In the right-hand wall, toward the rear, a door, and nearer the foreground a porcelain stove with two armchairs and a rocking chair beside it. Between the stove and the side door, a small table. Engravings on the walls. An etagère with china figures and other small art objects; a small bookcase with richly bound books; the floor carpeted; a fire burning in the stove. It is a winter day.

A bell rings in the entryway; shortly after we hear the door being unlocked. NORA comes into the room, humming happily to herself; she is wearing street clothes and carries an armload of packages, which she puts down on the table to the right. She has left the hall door open; and through it a DELIVERY BOY is seen, holding a Christmas tree and a basket, which he gives to the MAID who let them in.

NORA: Hide the tree well, Helene. The children mustn't get a glimpse of it till this evening, after it's trimmed. *(To the DELIVERY BOY, taking out her purse.)* How much?

DELIVERY BOY: Fifty, ma'am.

5 NORA: There's a crown. No, keep the change. *(The BOY thanks her and leaves. NORA shuts the door. She laughs softly to herself while taking off her street things. Drawing a bag of macaroons from her pocket, she eats a couple, then steals over and listens at her husband's study door.)* Yes, he's home. *(Hums again as she moves to the table right.)*

10 HELMER: *(From the study.)* Is that my little lark twittering out there?

NORA: *(Busy opening some packages.)* Yes, it is.

HELMER: Is that my squirrel rummaging around?

15 NORA: Yes!

HELMER: When did my squirrel get in?

NORA: Just now. *(Putting the macaroon bag in her pocket and wiping her mouth.)* Do come in, Torvald, and see what I've bought.

20 HELMER: Can't be disturbed. *(After a moment he opens the door and peers in, pen in hand.)* Bought, you say? All that there? Has the little spendthrift been out throwing money around again?

NORA: Oh, but Torvald, this year we really should let ourselves go a bit. It's the first Christmas we haven't had to economize.

25 HELMER: But you know we can't go squandering.

NORA: Oh yes, Torvald, we can squander a little now. Can't we? Just a tiny, wee bit. Now that you've got a big salary and are going to make piles and piles of money.

HELMER: Yes—starting New Year's. But then it's a full three 30 months till the raise comes through.

NORA: Pooh! We can borrow that long.

HELMER: Nora! *(Goes over and playfully takes her by the ear.)* Are your scatterbrains off again? What if today I borrowed a thousand crowns, and you squandered them over Christmas 35 week, and then on New Year's Eve a roof tile fell on my head, and I lay there—

NORA: *(Putting her hand on his mouth.)* Oh! Don't say such things!

HELMER: Yes, but what if it happened—then what? 40

NORA: If anything so awful happened, then it just wouldn't matter if I had debts or not.

HELMER: Well, but the people I'd borrowed from?

NORA: Them? Who cares about them! They're strangers.

HELMER: Nora, Nora, how like a woman! No, but seriously, 45 Nora, you know what I think about that. No debts! Never borrow! Something of freedom's lost—and something of beauty, too—from a home that's founded on borrowing and debt. We've made a brave stand up to now, the two of us; and we'll go right on like that the little while we have to. 50

NORA: *(Going toward the stove.)* Yes, whatever you say, Torvald.

HELMER: *(Following her.)* Now, now, the little lark's wings mustn't droop. Come on, don't be a sulky squirrel. *(Taking out his wallet.)* Nora, guess what I have here.

NORA: *(Turning quickly.)* Money! 55

HELMER: There, see. *(Hands her some notes.)* Good grief, I know how costs go up in a house at Christmastime.

NORA: Ten—twenty—thirty—forty. Oh, thank you, Torvald; I can manage no end on this.

HELMER: You really will have to. 60

NORA: Oh yes, I promise I will! But come here so I can show you everything I bought. And so cheap! Look, new clothes for Ivar here—and a sword. Here a horse and a trumpet for Bob. And a doll and a doll's bed here for Emmy; they're nothing much, but she'll tear them to bits in no time any 65 way. And here I have dress material and handkerchiefs for the maids. Old Anne-Marie really deserves something more.

HELMER: And what's in that package there?

NORA: *(With a cry.)* Torvald, no! You can't see that till tonight!

HELMER: I see. But tell me now, you little prodigal, what have 70 you thought of for yourself?

NORA: For myself? Oh, I don't want anything at all.

HELMER: Of course you do. Tell me just what—within reason—you'd most like to have.

75 NORA: I honestly don't know. Oh, listen, Torvald—

HELMER: Well?

NORA: (*Fumbling at his coat buttons, without looking at him.*) If you want to give me something, then maybe you could—you could—

80 HELMER: Come on, out with it.

NORA: (*Hurriedly.*) You could give me money, Torvald. No more than you think you can spare; then one of these days I'll buy something with it.

HELMER: But Nora—

85 NORA: Oh, please, Torvald darling, do that! I beg you, please. Then I could hang the bills in pretty gilt paper on the Christmas tree. Wouldn't that be fun?

HELMER: What are those little birds called that always fly through their fortunes?

90 NORA: Oh yes, spendthrifts; I know all that. But let's do as I say, Torvald; then I'll have time to decide what I really need most. That's very sensible, isn't it?

HELMER: (*Smiling.*) Yes, very—that is, if you actually hung onto the money I give you, and you actually used it to buy yourself something. But it goes for the house and for all sorts of

95 foolish things, and then I only have to lay out some more.

NORA: Oh, but Torvald—

HELMER: Don't deny it, my dear little Nora. (*Putting his arm around her waist.*) Spendthrifts are sweet, but they use up a

100 frightful amount of money. It's incredible what it costs a man to feed such birds.

NORA: Oh, how can you say that! Really, I save everything I can.

HELMER: (*Laughing.*) Yes, that's the truth. Everything you can.

105 But that's nothing at all.

NORA: (*Humming, with a smile of quiet satisfaction.*) Hm, if you only knew what expenses we larks and squirrels have, Torvald.

HELMER: You're an odd little one. Exactly the way your father

110 was. You're never at a loss for scaring up money; but the moment you have it, it runs right out through your fingers; you never know what you've done with it. Well, one takes you as you are. It's deep in your blood. Yes, these things are hereditary, Nora.

115 NORA: Ah, I could wish I'd inherited many of Papa's qualities.

HELMER: And I couldn't wish you anything but just what you are, my sweet little lark. But wait; it seems to me you have a very—what should I call it?—a very suspicious look today—

120 NORA: I do?

HELMER: You certainly do. Look me straight in the eye.

NORA: (*Looking at him.*) Well?

HELMER: (*Shaking an admonitory finger.*) Surely my sweet tooth hasn't been running riot in town today, has she?

125 NORA: No. Why do you imagine that?

HELMER: My sweet tooth really didn't make a little detour through the confectioner's?

NORA: No, I assure you, Torvald—

HELMER: Hasn't nibbled some pastry?

130 NORA: No, not at all.

HELMER: Not even munched a macaroon or two?

NORA: No, Torvald, I assure you, really—

HELMER: There, there now. Of course I'm only joking.

NORA: (*Going to the table, right.*) You know I could never think of going against you. 135

HELMER: No, I understand that; and you *have* given me your word. (*Going over to her.*) Well, you keep your little Christmas secrets to yourself, Nora darling. I expect they'll come to light this evening, when the tree is lit.

NORA: Did you remember to ask Dr. Rank? 140

HELMER: No. But there's no need for that; it's assumed he'll be dining with us. All the same, I'll ask him when he stops by here this morning. I've ordered some fine wine. Nora, you can't imagine how I'm looking forward to this evening.

NORA: So am I. And what fun for the children, Torvald! 145

HELMER: Ah, it's so gratifying to know that one's gotten a safe, secure job, and with a comfortable salary. It's a great satisfaction, isn't it?

NORA: Oh, it's wonderful!

HELMER: Remember last Christmas? Three whole weeks be- 150 fore, you shut yourself in every evening till long after midnight, making flowers for the Christmas tree, and all the other decorations to surprise us. Ugh, that was the dullest time I've ever lived through.

NORA: It wasn't at all dull for me. 155

HELMER: (*Smiling.*) But the outcome *was* pretty sorry, Nora.

NORA: Oh, don't tease me with that again. How could I help it that the cat came in and tore everything to shreds.

HELMER: No, poor thing, you certainly couldn't. You wanted so much to please us all, and that's what counts. But it's just 160 as well that the hard times are past.

NORA: Yes, it's really wonderful.

HELMER: Now I don't have to sit here alone, boring myself, and you don't have to tire your precious eyes and your fair little delicate hands— 165

NORA: (*Clapping her hands.*) No, is it really true, Torvald, I don't have to? Oh, how wonderfully lovely to hear! (*Taking his arm.*) Now I'll tell you just how I've thought we should plan things. Right after Christmas—(*The doorbell rings.*) Oh, the bell. (*Straightening the room up a bit.*) Somebody 170 would have to come. What a bore!

HELMER: I'm not at home to visitors, don't forget.

MAID: (*From the hall doorway.*) Ma'am, a lady to see you—

NORA: All right, let her come in.

MAID: (*To* HELMER.) And the doctor's just come too. 175

HELMER: Did he go right to my study?

MAID: Yes, he did.

(HELMER *goes into his room. The* MAID *shows in* MRS. LINDE, *dressed in traveling clothes, and shuts the door after her.*)

MRS. LINDE: (*In a dispirited and somewhat hesitant voice.*) Hello, Nora.

NORA: (*Uncertain.*) Hello— 180

MRS. LINDE: You don't recognize me.

NORA: No, I don't know—but wait, I think—(*Exclaiming.*) What! Kristine! Is it really you?

MRS. LINDE: Yes, it's me.

NORA: Kristine! To think I didn't recognize you. But then, how 185 could I? (*More quietly.*) How you've changed, Kristine!

MRS. LINDE: Yes, no doubt I have. In nine—ten long years.

NORA: Is it so long since we met! Yes, it's all of that. Oh, these last eight years have been a happy time, believe me. And so
190 now you've come in to town, too. Made the long trip in the winter. That took courage.

MRS. LINDE: I just got here by ship this morning.

NORA: To enjoy yourself over Christmas, of course. Oh, how lovely! Yes, enjoy ourselves, we'll do that. But take your
195 coat off. You're not still cold? (*Helping her.*) There now, let's get cozy here by the stove. No, the easy chair there! I'll take the rocker here. (*Seizing her hands.*) Yes, now you have your old look again; it was only in that first moment. You're a bit more pale, Kristine—and maybe a bit thinner.

200 MRS. LINDE: And much, much older, Nora.

NORA: Yes, perhaps a bit older; a tiny, tiny bit; not much at all. (*Stopping short; suddenly serious.*) Oh, but thoughtless me, to sit here, chattering away. Sweet, good Kristine, can you forgive me?

205 MRS. LINDE: What do you mean, Nora?

NORA: (*Softly.*) Poor Kristine, you've become a widow.

MRS. LINDE: Yes, three years ago.

NORA: Oh, I knew it, of course; I read it in the papers. Oh, Kristine, you must believe me; I often thought of writing
210 you then, but I kept postponing it, and something always interfered.

MRS. LINDE: Nora dear, I understand completely.

NORA: No, it was awful of me, Kristine. You poor thing, how much you must have gone through. And he left you
215 nothing?

MRS. LINDE: No.

NORA: And no children?

MRS. LINDE: No.

NORA: Nothing at all, then?

220 MRS. LINDE: Not even a sense of loss to feed on.

NORA: (*Looking incredulously at her.*) But Kristine, how could that be?

MRS. LINDE: (*Smiling wearily and smoothing her hair.*) Oh, sometimes it happens, Nora.

225 NORA: So completely alone. How terribly hard that must be for you. I have three lovely children. You can't see them now; they're out with the maid. But now you must tell me everything—

MRS. LINDE: No, no, no, tell me about yourself.

230 NORA: No, you begin. Today I don't want to be selfish. I want to think only of you today. But there *is* something I must tell you. Did you hear of the wonderful luck we had recently?

MRS. LINDE: No, what's that?

235 NORA: My husband's been made manager in the bank, just think!

MRS. LINDE: Your husband? How marvelous!

NORA: Isn't it? Being a lawyer is such an uncertain living, you know, especially if one won't touch any cases that aren't
240 clean and decent. And of course Torvald would never do that, and I'm with him completely there. Oh, we're simply delighted, believe me! He'll join the bank right after New Year's and start getting a huge salary and lots of commissions. From now on we can live quite differently—just as
245 we want. Oh, Kristine, I feel so light and happy! Won't it be lovely to have stacks of money and not a care in the world?

MRS. LINDE: Well, anyway, it would be lovely to have enough for necessities.

250 NORA: No, not just for necessities, but stacks and stacks of money!

MRS. LINDE: (*Smiling.*) Nora, Nora, aren't you sensible yet? Back in school you were such a free spender.

NORA: (*With a quiet laugh.*) Yes, that's what Torvald still says. (*Shaking her finger.*) But "Nora, Nora" isn't as silly as you all
255 think. Really, we've been in no position for me to go squandering. We've had to work, both of us.

MRS. LINDE: You too?

NORA: Yes, at odd jobs—needlework, crocheting, embroidery, and such—(*Casually.*) and other things too. You remember
260 that Torvald left the department when we were married? There was no chance of promotion in his office, and of course he needed to earn more money. But that first year he drove himself terribly. He took on all kinds of extra work that kept him going morning and night. It wore him down,
265 and then he fell deathly ill. The doctors said it was essential for him to travel south.

MRS. LINDE: Yes, didn't you spend a whole year in Italy?

NORA: That's right. It wasn't easy to get away, you know. Ivar had just been born. But of course we had to go. Oh, that
270 was a beautiful trip, and it saved Torvald's life. But it cost a frightful sum, Kristine.

MRS. LINDE: I can well imagine.

NORA: Four thousand, eight hundred crowns it cost. That's really a lot of money.
275

MRS. LINDE: But it's lucky you had it when you needed it.

NORA: Well, as it was, we got it from Papa.

MRS. LINDE: I see. It was just about the time your father died.

NORA: Yes, just about then. And, you know, I couldn't make that trip out to nurse him. I had to stay here, expecting Ivar
280 any moment, and with my poor sick Torvald to care for. Dearest Papa, I never saw him again, Kristine. Oh, that was the worst time I've known in all my marriage.

MRS. LINDE: I know how you loved him. And then you went off to Italy?
285

NORA: Yes. We had the means now, and the doctors urged us. So we left a month after.

MRS. LINDE: And your husband came back completely cured?

NORA: Sound as a drum!

MRS. LINDE: But—the doctor?
290

NORA: Who?

MRS. LINDE: I thought the maid said he was a doctor, the man who came in with me.

NORA: Yes, that was Dr. Rank—but he's not making a sick call. He's our closest friend, and he stops by at least once a day. 295
No, Torvald hasn't had a sick moment since, and the children are fit and strong, and I am, too. (*Jumping up and clapping her hands.*) Oh, dear God, Kristine, what a lovely thing to live and be happy! But how disgusting of me—I'm talking of nothing but my own affairs. (*Sits on a stool close by 300 KRISTINE, arms resting across her knees.*) Oh, don't be angry with me! Tell me, is it really true that you weren't in love with your husband? Why did you marry him, then?

MRS. LINDE: My mother was still alive, but bedridden and helpless—and I had my two younger brothers to look after. 305 In all conscience, I didn't think I could turn him down.

NORA: No, you were right there. But was he rich at the time?

MRS. LINDE: He was very well off, I'd say. But the business was shaky, Nora. When he died, it all fell apart, and nothing
310 was left.

NORA: And then——?

MRS. LINDE: Yes, so I had to scrape up a living with a little shop and a little teaching and whatever else I could find. The last three years have been like one endless workday without a
315 rest for me. Now it's over, Nora. My poor mother doesn't need me, for she's passed on. Nor the boys, either; they're working now and can take care of themselves.

NORA: How free you must feel—

MRS. LINDE: No—only unspeakably empty. Nothing to live for
320 now. (Standing up anxiously.) That's why I couldn't take it any longer out in that desolate hole. Maybe here it'll be easier to find something to do and keep my mind occupied. If I could only be lucky enough to get a steady job, some office work—

325 NORA: Oh, but Kristine, that's so dreadfully tiring, and you already look so tired. It would be much better for you if you could go off to a bathing resort.

MRS. LINDE: (Going toward the window.) I have no father to give me travel money, Nora.

330 NORA: (Rising.) Oh, don't be angry with me.

MRS. LINDE: (Going to her.) Nora dear, don't you be angry with me. The worst of my kind of situation is all the bitterness that's stored away. No one to work for, and yet you're always having to snap up your opportunities. You have to live; and
335 so you grow selfish. When you told me the happy change in your lot, do you know I was delighted less for your sakes than for mine?

NORA: How so? Oh, I see. You think maybe Torvald could do something for you.

340 MRS. LINDE: Yes, that's what I thought.

NORA: And he will, Kristine! Just leave it to me; I'll bring it up so delicately—find something attractive to humor him with. Oh, I'm so eager to help you.

MRS. LINDE: How very kind of you, Nora, to be so concerned
345 over me—doubly kind, considering you really know so little of life's burdens yourself.

NORA: I—? I know so little—?

MRS. LINDE: (Smiling.) Well, my heavens—a little needlework and such—Nora, you're just a child.

350 NORA: (Tossing her head and pacing the floor.) You don't have to act so superior.

MRS. LINDE: Oh?

NORA: You're just like the others. You all think I'm incapable of anything serious—

355 MRS. LINDE: Come now—

NORA: That I've never had to face the raw world.

MRS. LINDE: Nora dear, you've just been telling me all your troubles.

NORA: Hm! Trivia! (Quietly.) I haven't told you the big thing.
360 MRS. LINDE: Big thing? What do you mean?

NORA: You look down on me so, Kristine, but you shouldn't. You're proud that you worked so long and hard for your mother.

MRS. LINDE: I don't look down on a soul. But it is true: I'm
365 proud—and happy, too—to think it was given to me to make my mother's last days almost free of care.

NORA: And you're also proud thinking of what you've done for your brothers.

MRS. LINDE: I feel I've a right to be.

NORA: I agree. But listen to this, Kristine—I've also got some- 370 thing to be proud and happy for.

MRS. LINDE: I don't doubt it. But whatever do you mean?

NORA: Not so loud. What if Torvald heard! He mustn't, not for anything in the world. Nobody must know, Kristine. No one but you. 375

MRS. LINDE: But what is it, then?

NORA: Come here. (Drawing her down beside her on the sofa.) It's true—I've also got something to be proud and happy for. I'm the one who saved Torvald's life.

MRS. LINDE: Saved—? Saved how? 380

NORA: I told you about the trip to Italy. Torvald never would have lived if he hadn't gone south—

MRS. LINDE: Of course; your father gave you the means—

NORA: (Smiling.) That's what Torvald and all the rest think, but— 385

MRS. LINDE: But—?

NORA: Papa didn't give us a pin. I was the one who raised the money.

MRS. LINDE: You? That whole amount?

NORA: Four thousand, eight hundred crowns. What do you say 390 to that?

MRS. LINDE: But Nora, how was it possible? Did you win the lottery?

NORA: (Disdainfully.) The lottery? Pooh! No art to that.

MRS. LINDE: But where did you get it from then? 395

NORA: (Humming, with a mysterious smile.) Hmm, tra-la-la-la.

MRS. LINDE: Because you couldn't have borrowed it.

NORA: No? Why not?

MRS. LINDE: A wife can't borrow without her husband's consent.

NORA: (Tossing her head.) Oh, but a wife with a little business 400 sense, a wife who knows how to manage—

MRS. LINDE: Nora, I simply don't understand—

NORA: You don't have to. Whoever said I borrowed the money? I could have gotten it other ways. (Throwing herself back on the sofa.) I could have gotten it from some admirer or other. 405 After all, a girl with my ravishing appeal—

MRS. LINDE: You lunatic.

NORA: I'll bet you're eaten up with curiosity, Kristine.

MRS. LINDE: Now listen here, Nora—you haven't done something indiscreet? 410

NORA: (Sitting up again.) Is it indiscreet to save your husband's life?

MRS. LINDE: I think it's indiscreet that without his knowledge you—

NORA: But that's the point: he mustn't know! My Lord, can't 415 you understand? He mustn't ever know the close call he had. It was to me the doctors came to say his life was in danger—that nothing could save him but a stay in the south. Didn't I try strategy then! I began talking about how lovely it would be for me to travel abroad like other young 420 wives; I begged and I cried; I told him please to remember my condition, to be kind and indulge me; and then I dropped a hint that he could easily take out a loan. But at that, Kristine, he nearly exploded. He said I was frivolous, and it was his duty as man of the house not to indulge me 425 in whims and fancies—as I think he called them. Aha, I thought, now you'll just have to be saved—and that's when I saw my chance.

MRS. LINDE: And your father never told Torvald the money wasn't from him?

NORA: No, never. Papa died right about then. I'd considered bringing him into my secret and begging him never to tell. But he was too sick at the time—and then, sadly, it didn't matter.

MRS. LINDE: And you've never confided in your husband since?

NORA: For heaven's sake, no! Are you serious? He's so strict on that subject. Besides—Torvald, with all his masculine pride—how painfully humiliating for him if he ever found out he was in debt to me. That would just ruin our relationship. Our beautiful, happy home would never be the same.

MRS. LINDE: Won't you ever tell him?

NORA: (Thoughtfully, half smiling.) Yes—maybe sometime, years from now, when I'm no longer so attractive. Don't laugh! I only mean when Torvald loves me less than now, when he stops enjoying my dancing and dressing up and reciting for him. Then it might be wise to have something in reserve—(Breaking off.) How ridiculous! That'll never happen—Well, Kristine, what do you think of my big secret? I'm capable of something too, hm? You can imagine, of course, how this thing hangs over me. It really hasn't been easy meeting the payments on time. In the business world there's what they call quarterly interest and what they call amortization, and these are always so terribly hard to manage. I've had to skimp a little here and there, wherever I could, you know. I could hardly spare anything from my house allowance, because Torvald has to live well. I couldn't let the children go poorly dressed; whatever I got for them, I felt I had to use up completely—the darlings!

MRS. LINDE: Poor Nora, so it had to come out of your own budget, then?

NORA: Yes, of course. But I was the one most responsible, too. Every time Torvald gave me money for new clothes and such, I never used more than half; always bought the simplest, cheapest outfits. It was a godsend that everything looks so well on me that Torvald never noticed. But it did weigh me down at times, Kristine. It *is* such a joy to wear fine things. You understand.

MRS. LINDE: Oh, of course.

NORA: And then I found other ways of making money. Last winter I was lucky enough to get a lot of copying to do. I locked myself in and sat writing every evening till late in the night. Ah, I was tired so often, dead tired. But still it was wonderful fun, sitting and working like that, earning money. It was almost like being a man.

MRS. LINDE: But how much have you paid off this way so far?

NORA: That's hard to say, exactly. These accounts, you know, aren't easy to figure. I only know that I've paid out all I could scrape together. Time and again I haven't known where to turn. (Smiling.) Then I'd sit here dreaming of a rich old gentleman who had fallen in love with me—

MRS. LINDE: What! Who is he?

NORA: Oh, really! And that he'd died, and when his will was opened, there in big letters it said, "All my fortune shall be paid over in cash, immediately, to that enchanting Mrs. Nora Helmer."

MRS. LINDE: But Nora dear—who *was* this gentleman?

NORA: Good grief, can't you understand? The old man never existed; that was only something I'd dream up time and again whenever I was at my wits' end for money. But it makes no difference now; the old fossil can go where he pleases for all I care; I don't need him or his will—because now I'm free. (Jumping up.) Oh, how lovely to think of that, Kristine! Carefree! To know you're carefree, utterly carefree; to be able to romp and play with the children, and to keep up a beautiful, charming home—everything just the way Torvald likes it! And think, spring is coming, with big blue skies. Maybe we can travel a little then. Maybe I'll see the ocean again. Oh yes, it *is* so marvelous to live and be happy!

(The front doorbell rings.)

MRS. LINDE: (Rising.) There's the bell. It's probably best that I go.

NORA: No, stay. No one's expected. It must be for Torvald.

MAID: (From the hall doorway.) Excuse me, ma'am—there's a gentleman here to see Mr. Helmer, but I didn't know—since the doctor's with him—

NORA: Who is the gentleman?

KROGSTAD: (From the doorway.) It's me, Mrs. Helmer.

(MRS. LINDE *starts and turns away toward the window.*)

NORA: (Stepping toward him, tense, her voice a whisper.) You? What is it? Why do you want to speak to my husband?

KROGSTAD: Bank business—after a fashion. I have a small job in the investment bank, and I hear now your husband is going to be our chief—

NORA: In other words, it's—

KROGSTAD: Just dry business, Mrs. Helmer. Nothing but that.

NORA: Yes, then please be good enough to step into the study. (She nods indifferently as she sees him out by the hall door, then returns and begins stirring up the stove.)

MRS. LINDE: Nora—who was that man?

NORA: That was a Mr. Krogstad—a lawyer.

MRS. LINDE: Then it really was him.

NORA: Do you know that person?

MRS. LINDE: I did once—many years ago. For a time he was a law clerk in our town.

NORA: Yes, he's been that.

MRS. LINDE: How he's changed.

NORA: I understand he had a very unhappy marriage.

MRS. LINDE: He's a widower now.

NORA: With a number of children. There now, it's burning. (She closes the stove door and moves the rocker a bit to one side.)

MRS. LINDE: They say he has a hand in all kinds of business.

NORA: Oh? That may be true; I wouldn't know. But let's not think about business. It's so dull.

(DR. RANK *enters from* HELMER's *study.*)

RANK: (Still in the doorway.) No, no, really—I don't want to intrude, I'd just as soon talk a little while with your wife.

(Shuts the door, then notices MRS. LINDE.*)* Oh, beg pardon. I'm intruding here too.

NORA: No, not at all. *(Introducing him.)* Dr. Rank, Mrs. Linde.

RANK: Well now, that's a name much heard in this house. I
540   believe I passed the lady on the stairs as I came.

MRS. LINDE: Yes, I take the stairs very slowly. They're rather hard on me.

RANK: Uh-hm, some touch of internal weakness?

MRS. LINDE: More overexertion, I'd say.

545   RANK: Nothing else? Then you're probably here in town to rest up in a round of parties?

MRS. LINDE: I'm here to look for work.

RANK: Is that the best cure for overexertion?

MRS. LINDE: One has to live, Doctor.

550   RANK: Yes, there's a common prejudice to that effect.

NORA: Oh, come on, Dr. Rank—you really do want to live yourself.

RANK: Yes, I really do. Wretched as I am, I'll gladly prolong my torment indefinitely. All my patients feel like that.
555   And it's quite the same, too, with the morally sick. Right at this moment there's one of those moral invalids in there with Helmer—

MRS. LINDE: *(Softly.)* Ah!

NORA: Who do you mean?

560   RANK: Oh, it's a lawyer, Krogstad, a type you wouldn't know. His character is rotten to the root—but even he began chattering all-importantly about how he had to *live.*

NORA: Oh? What did he want to talk to Torvald about?

RANK: I really don't know. I only heard something about the
565   bank.

NORA: I didn't know that Krog—that this man Krogstad had anything to do with the bank.

RANK: Yes, he's gotten some kind of berth down there. *(To* MRS. LINDE.*)* I don't know if you also have, in your neck of the
570   woods, a type of person who scuttles about breathlessly, sniffing out hints of moral corruption, and then maneuvers his victim into some sort of key position where he can keep an eye on him. It's the healthy these days that are out in the cold.

575   MRS. LINDE: All the same, it's the sick who most need to be taken in.

RANK: *(With a shrug.)* Yes, there we have it. That's the concept that's turning society into a sanatorium.

*(*NORA, *lost in her thoughts, breaks out into quiet laughter and claps her hands.)*

RANK: Why do you laugh at that? Do you have any real idea of
580   what society is?

NORA: What do I care about dreary old society? I was laughing at something quite different—something terribly funny. Tell me, Doctor—is everyone who works in the bank dependent now on Torvald?

585   RANK: Is that what you find so terribly funny?

NORA: *(Smiling and humming.)* Never mind, never mind! *(Pacing the floor.)* Yes, that's really immensely amusing: that we—that Torvald has so much power now over all those people. *(Taking the bag out of her pocket.)* Dr. Rank, a little
590   macaroon on that?

RANK: See here, macaroons! I thought they were contraband here.

NORA: Yes, but these are some that Kristine gave me.

MRS. LINDE: What? I—?

NORA: Now, now, don't be afraid. You couldn't possibly know 595
that Torvald had forbidden them. You see, he's worried they'll ruin my teeth. But hmp! Just this once! Isn't that so, Dr. Rank? Help yourself! *(Puts a macaroon in his mouth.)* And you too, Kristine. And I'll also have one, only a little one— or two, at the most. *(Walking about again.)* Now I'm really 600
tremendously happy. Now there's just one last thing in the world that I have an enormous desire to do.

RANK: Well! And what's that?

NORA: It's something I have such a consuming desire to say so Torvald could hear.   605

RANK: And why can't you say it?

NORA: I don't dare. It's quite shocking.

MRS. LINDE: Shocking?

RANK: Well, then it isn't advisable. But in front of us you certainly can. What do you have such a desire to say so Torvald 610
could hear?

NORA: I have such a huge desire to say—to hell and be damned!

RANK: Are you crazy?

MRS. LINDE: My goodness, Nora!

RANK: Go on, say it. Here he is.   615

NORA: *(Hiding the macaroon bag.)* Shh, shh, shh!

*(*HELMER *comes in from his study, hat in hand, overcoat over his arm.)*

NORA: *(Going toward him.)* Well, Torvald dear, are you through with him?

HELMER: Yes, he just left.

NORA: Let me introduce you—this is Kristine, who's arrived 620
here in town.

HELMER: Kristine—? I'm sorry, but I don't know—

NORA: Mrs. Linde, Torvald dear. Mrs. Kristine Linde.

HELMER: Of course. A childhood friend of my wife's, no doubt?

MRS. LINDE: Yes, we knew each other in those days.   625

NORA: And just think, she made the long trip down here in order to talk with you.

HELMER: What's this?

MRS. LINDE: Well, not exactly—

NORA: You see, Kristine is remarkably clever in office work, 630
and so she's terribly eager to come under a capable man's supervision and add more to what she already knows—

HELMER: Very wise, Mrs. Linde.

NORA: And then when she heard that you'd become a bank manager—the story was wired out to the papers—then she 635
came in as fast as she could and—Really, Torvald, for my sake you can do a little something for Kristine, can't you?

HELMER: Yes, it's not at all impossible. Mrs. Linde, I suppose you're a widow?

MRS. LINDE: Yes.   640

HELMER: Any experience in office work?

MRS. LINDE: Yes, a good deal.

HELMER: Well, it's quite likely that I can make an opening for you—

NORA: *(Clapping her hands.)* You see, you see!   645

HELMER: You've come at a lucky moment, Mrs. Linde.

MRS. LINDE: Oh, how can I thank you?

HELMER: Not necessary. (*Putting his overcoat on.*) But today you'll have to excuse me—

650 RANK: Wait, I'll go with you. (*He fetches his coat from the hall and warms it at the stove.*)

NORA: Don't stay out long, dear.

HELMER: An hour; no more.

NORA: Are you going too, Kristine?

655 MRS. LINDE: (*Putting on her winter garments.*) Yes, I have to see about a room now.

HELMER: Then perhaps we can all walk together.

NORA: (*Helping her.*) What a shame we're so cramped here, but it's quite impossible for us to—

660 MRS. LINDE: Oh, don't even think of it! Good-bye, Nora dear, and thanks for everything.

NORA: Good-bye for now. Of course you'll be back this evening. And you too, Dr. Rank. What? If you're well enough? Oh, you've got to be! Wrap up tight now.

(*In a ripple of small talk the company moves out into the hall; children's voices are heard outside on the steps.*)

665 NORA: There they are! There they are! (*She runs to open the door. The* CHILDREN *come in with their nurse,* ANNE-MARIE.) Come in, come in! (*Bends down and kisses them.*) Oh, you darlings—! Look at them, Kristine. Aren't they lovely!

RANK: No loitering in the draft here.

670 HELMER: Come, Mrs. Linde—this place is unbearable now for anyone but mothers.

(DR. RANK, HELMER, *and* MRS. LINDE *go down the stairs.* ANNE-MARIE *goes into the living room with the* CHILDREN. NORA *follows, after closing the hall door.*)

NORA: How fresh and strong you look. Oh, such red cheeks you have! Like apples and roses. (*The* CHILDREN *interrupt her throughout the following.*) And it was so much fun? That's
675 wonderful. Really? You pulled both Emmy and Bob on the sled? Imagine, all together! Yes, you're a clever boy, Ivar. Oh, let me hold her a bit, Anne-Marie. My sweet little doll baby! (*Takes the smallest from* ANNE-MARIE *and dances with her.*) Yes, yes, Mama will dance with Bob as well. What? Did you
680 throw snowballs? Oh, if I'd only been there! No, don't bother, Anne-Marie—I'll undress them myself. Oh yes, let me. It's such fun. Go in and rest; you look half frozen. There's hot coffee waiting for you on the stove. (ANNE-MARIE *goes into the room to the left.* NORA *takes the* CHILDREN's *winter things off,*
685 *throwing them about, while the children talk to her all at once.*) Is that so? A big dog chased you? But it didn't bite? No, dogs never bite little, lovely doll babies. Don't peek in the packages, Ivar! What is it? Yes, wouldn't you like to know. No, no, it's an ugly something. Well? Shall we play? What
690 shall we play? Hide-and-seek? Yes, let's play hide-and-seek. Bob must hide first. I must? Yes, let me hide first. (*Laughing and shouting, she and the* CHILDREN *play in and out of the living room and the adjoining room to the right. At last* NORA *hides under the table. The* CHILDREN *come storming in, search, but*
695 *cannot find her, then hear her muffled laughter, dash over to the*

table, *lift the cloth up and find her. Wild shouting. She creeps forward as if to scare them. More shouts. Meanwhile, a knock at the hall door; no one has noticed it. Now the door half opens, and* KROGSTAD *appears. He waits a moment; the game goes on.*)

700 KROGSTAD: Beg pardon, Mrs. Helmer—

NORA: (*With a strangled cry, turning and scrambling to her knees.*) Oh! What do you want?

KROGSTAD: Excuse me. The outer door was ajar; it must be someone forgot to shut it—

705 NORA: (*Rising.*) My husband isn't home, Mr. Krogstad.

KROGSTAD: I know that.

NORA: Yes—then what do you want here?

KROGSTAD: A word with you.

NORA: With—? (*To the* CHILDREN, *quietly.*) Go in to Anne-Marie.
710 What? No, the strange man won't hurt Mama. When he's gone, we'll play some more. (*She leads the* CHILDREN *into the room to the left and shuts the door after them. Then, tense and nervous:*) You want to speak to me?

KROGSTAD: Yes, I want to.

715 NORA: Today? But it's not yet the first of the month—

KROGSTAD: No, it's Christmas Eve. It's going to be up to you how merry a Christmas you have.

NORA: What is it you want? Today I absolutely can't—

KROGSTAD: We won't talk about that till later. This is something else. You do have a moment to spare, I suppose?
720

NORA: Oh yes, of course—I do, except—

KROGSTAD: Good. I was sitting over at Olsen's Restaurant when I saw your husband go down the street—

NORA: Yes?

KROGSTAD: With a lady.
725

NORA: Yes. So?

KROGSTAD: If you'll pardon my asking: wasn't that lady a Mrs. Linde?

NORA: Yes.

KROGSTAD: Just now come into town?
730

NORA: Yes, today.

KROGSTAD: She's a good friend of yours?

NORA: Yes, she is. But I don't see—

KROGSTAD: I also knew her once.

NORA: I'm aware of that.
735

KROGSTAD: Oh? You know all about it. I thought so. Well, then let me ask you short and sweet: is Mrs. Linde getting a job in the bank?

NORA: What makes you think you can cross-examine me, Mr. Krogstad—you, one of my husband's employees? But since
740 you ask, you might as well know—yes, Mrs. Linde's going to be taken on at the bank. And I'm the one who spoke for her, Mr. Krogstad. Now you know.

KROGSTAD: So I guessed right.

NORA: (*Pacing up and down.*) Oh, one does have a tiny bit of
745 influence, I should hope. Just because I am a woman, don't think it means that—When one has a subordinate position, Mr. Krogstad, one really ought to be careful about pushing somebody who—hm—

KROGSTAD: Who has influence?
750

NORA: That's right.

KROGSTAD: (*In a different tone.*) Mrs. Helmer, would you be good enough to use your influence on my behalf?

NORA: What? What do you mean?

755 KROGSTAD: Would you please make sure that I keep my subordinate position in the bank?

NORA: What does that mean? Who's thinking of taking away your position?

KROGSTAD: Oh, don't play the innocent with me. I'm quite
760 aware that your friend would hardly relish the chance of running into me again; and I'm also aware now whom I can thank for being turned out.

NORA: But I promise you—

KROGSTAD: Yes, yes, yes, to the point: there's still time, and I'm
765 advising you to use your influence to prevent it.

NORA: But Mr. Krogstad, I have absolutely no influence.

KROGSTAD: You haven't? I thought you were just saying—

NORA: You shouldn't take me so literally. I! How can you believe that I have any such influence over my husband?

770 KROGSTAD: Oh, I've known your husband from our student days. I don't think the great bank manager's more steadfast than any other married man.

NORA: You speak insolently about my husband, and I'll show you the door.

775 KROGSTAD: The lady has spirit.

NORA: I'm not afraid of you any longer. After New Year's, I'll soon be done with the whole business.

KROGSTAD: *(Restraining himself.)* Now listen to me, Mrs. Helmer. If necessary, I'll fight for my little job in the bank
780 as if it were life itself.

NORA: Yes, so it seems.

KROGSTAD: It's not just a matter of income; that's the least of it. It's something else—All right, out with it! Look, this is the thing. You know, just like all the others, of course, that
785 once, a good many years ago, I did something rather rash.

NORA: I've heard rumors to that effect.

KROGSTAD: The case never got into court; but all the same, every door was closed in my face from then on. So I took up those various activities you know about. I had to grab hold
790 somewhere; and I dare say I haven't been among the worst. But now I want to drop all that. My boys are growing up. For their sakes, I'll have to win back as much respect as possible here in town. That job in the bank was like the first rung in my ladder. And now your husband wants to kick
795 me right back down in the mud again.

NORA: But for heaven's sake, Mr. Krogstad, it's simply not in my power to help you.

KROGSTAD: That's because you haven't the will to—but I have the means to make you.

800 NORA: You certainly won't tell my husband that I owe you money?

KROGSTAD: Hm—what if I told him that?

NORA: That would be shameful of you. *(Nearly in tears.)* This secret—my joy and my pride—that he should learn it in
805 such a crude and disgusting way—learn it from you. You'd expose me to the most horrible unpleasantness—

KROGSTAD: Only unpleasantness?

NORA: *(Vehemently.)* But go on and try. It'll turn out the worse for you, because then my husband will really see what a
810 crook you are, and then you'll *never* be able to hold your job.

KROGSTAD: I asked if it was just domestic unpleasantness you were afraid of?

NORA: If my husband finds out, then of course he'll pay what I owe at once, and then we'd be through with you for good.

KROGSTAD: *(A step closer.)* Listen, Mrs. Helmer—you've either 815 got a very bad memory, or else no head at all for business. I'd better put you a little more in touch with the facts.

NORA: What do you mean?

KROGSTAD: When your husband was sick, you came to me for a loan of four thousand, eight hundred crowns. 820

NORA: Where else could I go?

KROGSTAD: I promised to get you that sum—

NORA: And you got it.

KROGSTAD: I promised to get you that sum, on certain conditions. You were so involved in your husband's illness, and so 825 eager to finance your trip, that I guess you didn't think out all the details. It might just be a good idea to remind you. I promised you the money on the strength of a note I drew up.

NORA: Yes, and that I signed.

KROGSTAD: Right. But at the bottom I added some lines for 830 your father to guarantee the loan. He was supposed to sign down there.

NORA: Supposed to? He did sign.

KROGSTAD: I left the date blank. In other words, your father would have dated his signature himself. Do you remember 835 that?

NORA: Yes, I think—

KROGSTAD: Then I gave you the note for you to mail to your father. Isn't that so?

NORA: Yes. 840

KROGSTAD: And naturally you sent it at once—because only some five, six days later you brought me the note, properly signed. And with that, the money was yours.

NORA: Well, then; I've made my payments regularly, haven't I?

KROGSTAD: More or less. But—getting back to the point— 845 those were hard times for you then, Mrs. Helmer.

NORA: Yes, they were.

KROGSTAD: Your father was very ill, I believe.

NORA: He was near the end.

KROGSTAD: He died soon after? 850

NORA: Yes.

KROGSTAD: Tell me, Mrs. Helmer, do you happen to recall the date of your father's death? The day of the month, I mean.

NORA: Papa died the twenty-ninth of September.

KROGSTAD: That's quite correct; I've already looked into that. 855 And now we come to a curious thing—*(Taking out a paper.)* which I simply cannot comprehend.

NORA: Curious thing? I don't know—

KROGSTAD: This is the curious thing: that your father co-signed the note for your loan three days after his death. 860

NORA: How—? I don't understand.

KROGSTAD: Your father died the twenty-ninth of September. But look. Here your father dated his signature October second. Isn't that curious, Mrs. Helmer? *(NORA is silent.)* Can you explain it to me? *(NORA remains silent.)* It's also remark- 865 able that the words "October second" and the year aren't written in your father's hand, but rather in one that I think I know. Well, it's easy to understand. Your father forgot perhaps to date his signature, and then someone or other added it, a bit sloppily, before anyone knew of his death. 870 There's nothing wrong in that. It all comes down to the signature. And there's no question about *that,* Mrs. Helmer. It really *was* your father who signed his own name here, wasn't it?

875 NORA: (*After a short silence, throwing her head back and looking squarely at him.*) No, it wasn't. I signed Papa's name.

KROGSTAD: Wait, now—are you fully aware that this is a dangerous confession?

NORA: Why? You'll soon get your money.

880 KROGSTAD: Let me ask you a question—why didn't you send the paper to your father?

NORA: That was impossible. Papa was so sick. If I'd asked him for his signature, I also would have had to tell him what the money was for. But I couldn't tell him, sick as he was, that

885 my husband's life was in danger. That was just impossible.

KROGSTAD: Then it would have been better if you'd given up the trip abroad.

NORA: I couldn't possibly. The trip was to save my husband's life. I couldn't give that up.

890 KROGSTAD: But didn't you ever consider that this was a fraud against me?

NORA: I couldn't let myself be bothered by that. You weren't any concern of mine. I couldn't stand you, with all those cold complications you made, even though you knew how

895 badly off my husband was.

KROGSTAD: Mrs. Helmer, obviously you haven't the vaguest idea of what you've involved yourself in. But I can tell you this: it was nothing more and nothing worse that I once did—and it wrecked my whole reputation.

900 NORA: You? Do you expect me to believe that you ever acted bravely to save your wife's life?

KROGSTAD: Laws don't inquire into motives.

NORA: Then they must be very poor laws.

KROGSTAD: Poor or not—if I introduce this paper in court,

905 you'll be judged according to law.

NORA: This I refuse to believe. A daughter hasn't a right to protect her dying father from anxiety and care? A wife hasn't a right to save her husband's life? I don't know much about laws, but I'm sure that somewhere in the books these things

910 are allowed. And you don't know anything about it—you who practice the law? You must be an awful lawyer, Mr. Krogstad.

KROGSTAD: Could be. But business—the kind of business we two are mixed up in—don't you think I know about that?

915 All right. Do what you want now. But I'm telling you *this:* if I get shoved down a second time, you're going to keep me company. (*He bows and goes out through the hall.*)

NORA: (*Pensive for a moment, then tossing her head.*) Oh, really! Trying to frighten me! I'm not so silly as all that. (*Begins*

920 *gathering up the* CHILDREN*'s clothes, but soon stops.*) But—? No, but that's impossible! I did it out of love.

THE CHILDREN: (*In the doorway, left.*) Mama, that strange man's gone out the door.

NORA: Yes, yes, I know it. But don't tell anyone about the

925 strange man. Do you hear? Not even Papa!

THE CHILDREN: No, Mama. But now will you play again?

NORA: No, not now.

THE CHILDREN: Oh, but Mama, you promised.

NORA: Yes, but I can't now. Go inside; I have too much to do.

930 Go in, go in, my sweet darlings. (*She herds them gently back in the room and shuts the door after them. Settling on the sofa, she takes up a piece of embroidery and makes some stitches, but soon stops abruptly.*) No! (*Throws the work aside, rises, goes to the hall door and calls out.*) Helene! Let me have the tree in here.

(*Goes to the table, left, opens the table drawer, and stops again.*) 935 No, but that's utterly impossible!

MAID: (*With the Christmas tree.*) Where should I put it, ma'am?

NORA: There. The middle of the floor.

MAID: Should I bring anything else?

NORA: No, thanks. I have what I need. 940

(*The* MAID, *who has set the tree down, goes out.*)

NORA: (*Absorbed in trimming the tree.*) Candles here—and flowers here. That terrible creature! Talk, talk, talk! There's nothing to it at all. The tree's going to be lovely. I'll do anything to please you, Torvald. I'll sing for you, dance for you— 945

(HELMER *comes in from the hall, with a sheaf of papers under his arm.*)

NORA: Oh! You're back so soon?

HELMER: Yes. Has anyone been here?

NORA: Here? No.

HELMER: That's odd. I saw Krogstad leaving the front door.

NORA: So? Oh yes, that's true. Krogstad was here a moment. 950

HELMER: Nora, I can see by your face that he's been here, begging you to put in a good word for him.

NORA: Yes.

HELMER: And it was supposed to seem like your own idea? You were to hide it from me that he'd been here. He asked you 955 that, too, didn't he?

NORA: Yes, Torvald, but—

HELMER: Nora, Nora, and you could fall for that? Talk with that sort of person and promise him anything? And then in the bargain, tell me an untruth. 960

NORA: An untruth—?

HELMER: Didn't you say that no one had been here? (*Wagging his finger.*) My little songbird must never do that again. A songbird needs a clean beak to warble with. No false notes. (*Putting his arm about her waist.*) That's the way it should be, 965 isn't it? Yes, I'm sure of it. (*Releasing her.*) And so, enough of that. (*Sitting by the stove.*) Ah, how snug and cozy it is here. (*Leafing among his papers.*)

NORA: (*Busy with the tree, after a short pause.*) Torvald!

HELMER: Yes. 970

NORA: I'm so much looking forward to the Stenborgs' costume party, day after tomorrow.

HELMER: And I can't wait to see what you'll surprise me with.

NORA: Oh, that stupid business!

HELMER: What? 975

NORA: I can't find anything that's right. Everything seems so ridiculous, so inane.

HELMER: So my little Nora's come to *that* recognition?

NORA: (*Going behind his chair, her arms resting on its back.*) Are you very busy, Torvald? 980

HELMER: Oh—

NORA: What papers are those?

HELMER: Bank matters.

NORA: Already?

HELMER: I've gotten full authority from the retiring manage- 985 ment to make all necessary changes in personnel and procedure. I'll need Christmas week for that. I want to have everything in order by New Year's.

NORA: So that was the reason this poor Krogstad—

990 HELMER: Hm.

NORA: (*Still leaning on the chair and slowly stroking the nape of his neck.*) If you weren't so very busy, I would have asked you an enormous favor, Torvald.

HELMER: Let's hear. What is it?

995 NORA: You know, there isn't anyone who has your good taste—and I want so much to look well at the costume party. Torvald, couldn't you take over and decide what I should be and plan my costume?

HELMER: Ah, is my stubborn little creature calling for a life-
1000 guard?

NORA: Yes, Torvald, I can't get anywhere without your help.

HELMER: All right—I'll think it over. We'll hit on something.

NORA: Oh, how sweet of you. (*Goes to the tree again. Pause.*) Aren't the red flowers pretty—? But tell me, was it really
1005 such a crime that this Krogstad committed?

HELMER: Forgery. Do you have any idea what that means?

NORA: Couldn't he have done it out of need?

HELMER: Yes, or thoughtlessness, like so many others. I'm not so heartless that I'd condemn a man categorically for just
1010 one mistake.

NORA: No, of course not, Torvald!

HELMER: Plenty of men have redeemed themselves by openly confessing their crimes and taking their punishment.

NORA: Punishment—?

1015 HELMER: But now Krogstad didn't go that way. He got himself out by sharp practices, and that's the real cause of his moral breakdown.

NORA: Do you really think that would—?

HELMER: Just imagine how a man with that sort of guilt in him
1020 has to lie and cheat and deceive on all sides, has to wear a mask even with the nearest and dearest he has, even with his own wife and children. And with the children, Nora—that's where it's most horrible.

NORA: Why?

1025 HELMER: Because that kind of atmosphere of lies infects the whole life of a home. Every breath the children take in is filled with the germs of something degenerate.

NORA: (*Coming closer behind him.*) Are you sure of that?

HELMER: Oh, I've seen it often enough as a lawyer. Almost
1030 everyone who goes bad early in life has a mother who's a chronic liar.

NORA: Why just—the mother?

HELMER: It's usually the mother's influence that's dominant, but the father's works in the same way, of course. Every
1035 lawyer is quite familiar with it. And still this Krogstad's been going home year in, year out, poisoning his own children with lies and pretense; that's why I call him morally lost. (*Reaching his hands out toward her.*) So my sweet little Nora must promise me never to plead his cause. Your hand
1040 on it. Come, come, what's this? Give me your hand. There, now. All settled. I can tell you it'd be impossible for me to work alongside of him. I literally feel physically revolted when I'm anywhere near such a person.

NORA: (*Withdraws her hand and goes to the other side of the Christ-
1045 mas tree.*) How hot it is here! And I've got so much to do.

HELMER: (*Getting up and gathering his papers.*) Yes, and I have to think about getting some of these read through before dinner. I'll think about your costume, too. And something to

hang on the tree in gilt paper, I may even see about that. (*Putting his hand on her head.*) Oh you, my darling little 1050 songbird. (*He goes into his study and closes the door after him.*)

NORA: (*Softly, after a silence.*) Oh, really! it isn't so. It's impossible. It must be impossible.

ANNE-MARIE: (*In the doorway, left.*) The children are begging so hard to come in to Mama. 1055

NORA: No, no, no, don't let them in to me! You stay with them, Anne-Marie.

ANNE-MARIE: Of course, ma'am. (*Closes the door.*)

NORA: (*Pale with terror.*) Hurt my children—! Poison my home? (*A moment's pause; then she tosses her head.*) That's not 1060 true. Never. Never in all the world.

——— ACT TWO ———

Same room. Beside the piano the Christmas tree now stands stripped of ornament, burned-down candle stubs on its ragged branches. NORA's *street clothes lie on the sofa.* NORA, *alone in the room, moves restlessly about; at last she stops at the sofa and picks up her coat.*

NORA: (*Dropping the coat again.*) Someone's coming! (*Goes toward the door, listens.*) No—there's no one. Of course—nobody's coming today, Christmas Day—or tomorrow, either. But maybe—(*Opens the door and looks out.*) No, nothing in the mailbox. Quite empty. (*Coming forward.*) What nonsense! 5 He won't do anything serious. Nothing terrible could happen. It's impossible. Why, I have three small children.

(ANNE-MARIE, *with a large carton, comes in from the room to the left.*)

ANNE-MARIE: Well, at last I found the box with the masquerade clothes.

NORA: Thanks. Put it on the table. 10

ANNE-MARIE: (*Does so.*) But they're all pretty much of a mess.

NORA: Ahh! I'd love to rip them in a million pieces!

ANNE-MARIE: Oh, mercy, they can be fixed right up. Just a little patience.

NORA: Yes, I'll go get Mrs. Linde to help me. 15

ANNE-MARIE: Out again now? In this nasty weather? Miss Nora will catch cold—get sick.

NORA: Oh, worse things could happen—How are the children?

ANNE-MARIE: The poor mites are playing with their Christmas presents, but— 20

NORA: Do they ask for me much?

ANNE-MARIE: They're so used to having Mama around, you know.

NORA: Yes, but Anne-Marie, I *can't* be together with them as much as I was. 25

ANNE-MARIE: Well, small children get used to anything.

NORA: You think so? Do you think they'd forget their mother if she was gone for good?

ANNE-MARIE: Oh, mercy—gone for good!

NORA: Wait, tell me, Anne-Marie—I've wondered so often— 30 how could you ever have the heart to give your child over to strangers?

ANNE-MARIE: But I had to, you know, to become little Nora's nurse.

NORA: Yes, but how could you *do* it? 35

ANNE-MARIE: When I could get such a good place? A girl who's poor and who's gotten in trouble is glad enough for that.

Because that slippery fish, he didn't do a thing for me, you know.

40 NORA: But your daughter's surely forgotten you.

ANNE-MARIE: Oh, she certainly has not. She's written to me, both when she was confirmed and when she was married.

NORA: *(Clasping her about the neck.)* You old Anne-Marie, you were a good mother for me when I was little.

45 ANNE-MARIE: Poor little Nora, with no other mother but me.

NORA: And if the babies didn't have one, then I know that you'd—What silly talk! *(Opening the carton.)* Go in to them. Now I'll have to—Tomorrow you can see how lovely I'll look.

50 ANNE-MARIE: Oh, there won't be anyone at the party as lovely as Miss Nora. *(She goes off into the room, left.)*

NORA: *(Begins unpacking the box, but soon throws it aside.)* Oh, if I dared to go out. If only nobody would come. If only noth-
55 ing would happen here while I'm out. What craziness— nobody's coming. Just don't think. This muff—needs a brushing. Beautiful gloves, beautiful gloves. Let it go. Let it go! One, two, three, four, five, six—*(With a cry.)* Oh, there they are! *(Poises to move toward the door, but remains irresolutely standing.* MRS. LINDE *enters from the hall, where she has
60 removed her street clothes.)*

NORA: Oh, it's you, Kristine. There's no one else out there? How good that you've come.

MRS. LINDE: I hear you were up asking for me.

NORA: Yes, I just stopped by. There's something you really can
65 help me with. Let's get settled on the sofa. Look, there's going to be a costume party tomorrow evening at the Sten- borgs' right above us, and now Torvald wants me to go as a Neapolitan peasant girl and dance the tarantella that I learned in Capri.

70 MRS. LINDE: Really, are you giving a whole performance?

NORA: Torvald says yes, I should. See, here's the dress. Torvald had it made for me down there; but now it's all so tattered that I just don't know—

MRS. LINDE: Oh, we'll fix that up in no time. It's nothing more
75 than the trimmings—they're a bit loose here and there. Needle and thread? Good, now we have what we need.

NORA: Oh, how sweet of you!

MRS. LINDE: *(Sewing.)* So you'll be in disguise tomorrow, Nora. You know what? I'll stop by then for a moment and have a
80 look at you all dressed up. But listen, I've absolutely for- gotten to thank you for that pleasant evening yesterday.

NORA: *(Getting up and walking about.)* I don't think it was as pleasant as usual yesterday. You should have come to town a bit sooner, Kristine—Yes, Torvald really knows how to
85 give a home elegance and charm.

MRS. LINDE: And you do, too, if you ask me. You're not your father's daughter for nothing. But tell me, is Dr. Rank always so down in the mouth as yesterday?

NORA: No, that was quite an exception. But he goes around
90 critically ill all the time—tuberculosis of the spine, poor man. You know, his father was a disgusting thing who kept mistresses and so on—and that's why the son's been sickly from birth.

MRS. LINDE: *(Lets her sewing fall to her lap.)* But my dearest Nora,
95 how do you know about such things?

NORA: *(Walking more jauntily.)* Hmp! When you've had three children, then you've had a few visits from—from women

who know something of medicine, and they tell you this and that.

100 MRS. LINDE: *(Resumes sewing; a short pause.)* Does Dr. Rank come here every day?

NORA: Every blessed day. He's Torvald's best friend from child- hood, and *my* good friend, too. Dr. Rank almost belongs to this house.

105 MRS. LINDE: But tell me—is he quite sincere? I mean, doesn't he rather enjoy flattering people?

NORA: Just the opposite. Why do you think that?

MRS. LINDE: When you introduced us yesterday, he was pro- claiming that he'd often heard my name in this house; but
110 later I noticed that your husband hadn't the slightest idea who I really was. So how could Dr. Rank—?

NORA: But it's all true, Kristine. You see, Torvald loves me beyond words, and, as he puts it, he'd like to keep me all to himself. For a long time he'd almost be jealous if I even
115 mentioned any of my old friends back home. So of course I dropped that. But with Dr. Rank I talk a lot about such things, because he likes hearing about them.

MRS. LINDE: Now listen, Nora; in many ways you're still like a child. I'm a good deal older than you, with a little more
120 experience. I'll tell you something: you ought to put an end to all this with Dr. Rank.

NORA: What should I put an end to?

MRS. LINDE: Both parts of it, I think. Yesterday you said some- thing about a rich admirer who'd provide you with
125 money—

NORA: Yes, one who doesn't exist—worse luck. So?

MRS. LINDE: Is Dr. Rank well off?

NORA: Yes, he is.

MRS. LINDE: With no dependents?

130 NORA: No, no one. But—

MRS. LINDE: And he's over here every day?

NORA: Yes, I told you that.

MRS. LINDE: How can a man of such refinement be so grasping?

NORA: I don't follow you at all.

135 MRS. LINDE: Now don't try to hide it, Nora. You think I can't guess who loaned you the forty-eight hundred crowns?

NORA: Are you out of your mind? How could you think such a thing! A friend of ours, who comes here every single day. What an intolerable situation that would have been!

140 MRS. LINDE: Then it really wasn't him.

NORA: No, absolutely not. It never even crossed my mind for a moment—And he had nothing to lend in those days; his inheritance came later.

MRS. LINDE: Well, I think that was a stroke of luck for you,
145 Nora dear.

NORA: No, it never would have occurred to me to ask Dr. Rank—Still, I'm quite sure that if I had asked him—

MRS. LINDE: Which you won't, of course.

NORA: No, of course not. I can't see that I'd ever need to. But
150 I'm quite positive that if I talked to Dr. Rank—

MRS. LINDE: Behind your husband's back?

NORA: I've got to clear up this other thing; *that's* also behind his back. I've *got* to clear it all up.

MRS. LINDE: Yes, I was saying that yesterday, but—

155 NORA: *(Pacing up and down.)* A man handles these problems so much better than a woman—

MRS. LINDE: One's husband does, yes.

NORA: Nonsense. *(Stopping.)* When you pay everything you owe, then you get your note back, right?

160 MRS. LINDE: Yes, naturally.

NORA: And can rip it into a million pieces and burn it up— that filthy scrap of paper!

MRS. LINDE: *(Looking hard at her, laying her sewing aside, and rising slowly.)* Nora, you're hiding something from me.

165 NORA: You can see it in my face?

MRS. LINDE: Something's happened to you since yesterday morning. Nora, what is it?

NORA: *(Hurrying toward her.)* Kristine! *(Listening.)* Shh! Torvald's home. Look, go in with the children a while. Torvald can't

170 bear all this snipping and stitching. Let Anne-Marie help you.

MRS. LINDE: *(Gathering up some of the things.)* All right, but I'm not leaving here until we've talked this out. *(She disappears into the room, left, as* TORVALD [HELMER] *enters from the hall.)*

175 NORA: Oh, how I've been waiting for you, Torvald dear.

HELMER: Was that the dressmaker?

NORA: No, that was Kristine. She's helping me fix up my costume. You know, it's going to be quite attractive.

HELMER: Yes, wasn't that a bright idea I had?

180 NORA: Brilliant! But then wasn't I good as well to give in to you?

HELMER: Good—because you give in to your husband's judgment? All right, you little goose, I know you didn't mean it like that. But I won't disturb you. You'll want to have a

185 fitting, I suppose.

NORA: And you'll be working?

HELMER: Yes. *(Indicating a bundle of papers.)* See, I've been down to the bank. *(Starts toward his study.)*

NORA: Torvald.

190 HELMER: *(Stops.)* Yes.

NORA: If your little squirrel begged you, with all her heart and soul, for something—?

HELMER: What's that?

NORA: Then would you do it?

195 HELMER: First, naturally, I'd have to know what it was.

NORA: Your squirrel would scamper about and do tricks, if you'd only be sweet and give in.

HELMER: Out with it.

NORA: Your lark would be singing high and low in every

200 room—

HELMER: Come on, she does that anyway.

NORA: I'd be a wood nymph and dance for you in the moonlight.

HELMER: Nora—don't tell me it's that same business from this

205 morning?

NORA: *(Coming closer.)* Yes, Torvald, I beg you, please!

HELMER: And you actually have the nerve to drag that up again?

NORA: Yes, yes, you've got to give in to me; you *have* to let

210 Krogstad keep his job in the bank.

HELMER: My dear Nora, I've slated his job for Mrs. Linde.

NORA: That's awfully kind of you. But you could just fire another clerk instead of Krogstad.

HELMER: This is the most incredible stubbornness! Because you

215 go and give an impulsive promise to speak up for him, I'm expected to—

NORA: That's not the reason, Torvald. It's for your own sake. That man does writing for the worst papers; you said it yourself. He could do you any amount of harm. I'm scared to death of him— 220

HELMER: Ah, I understand. It's the old memories haunting you.

NORA: What do you mean by that?

HELMER: Of course, you're thinking about your father.

NORA: Yes, all right. Just remember how those nasty gossips wrote in the papers about Papa and slandered him so cru- 225 elly. I think they'd have had him dismissed if the department hadn't sent you up to investigate, and if you hadn't been so kind and open-minded toward him.

HELMER: My dear Nora, there's a notable difference between your father and me. Your father's official career was hardly 230 above reproach. But mine is; and I hope it'll stay that way as long as I hold my position.

NORA: Oh, who can ever tell what vicious minds can invent? We could be so snug and happy now in our quiet, carefree home—you and I and the children, Torvald! That's why I'm 235 pleading with you so—

HELMER: And just by pleading for him you make it impossible for me to keep him on. It's already known at the bank that I'm firing Krogstad. What if it's rumored around now that the new bank manager was vetoed by his wife— 240

NORA: Yes, what then—?

HELMER: Oh yes—as long as our little bundle of stubbornness gets her way—! I should go and make myself ridiculous in front of the whole office—give people the idea I can be swayed by all kinds of outside pressure. Oh, you can bet I'd 245 feel the effects of that soon enough! Besides—there's something that rules Krogstad right out at the bank as long as I'm the manager.

NORA: What's that?

HELMER: His moral failings I could maybe overlook if I had 250 to—

NORA: Yes, Torvald, why not?

HELMER: And I hear he's quite efficient on the job. But he was a crony of mine back in my teens—one of those rash friendships that crop up again and again to embarrass you later in 255 life. Well, I might as well say it straight out: we're on a firstname basis. And that tactless fool makes no effort at all to hide it in front of others. Quite the contrary—he thinks that entitles him to take a familiar air around me, and so every other second he comes booming out with his "Yes, 260 Torvald!" and "Sure thing, Torvald!" I tell you, it's been excruciating for me. He's out to make my place in the bank unbearable.

NORA: Torvald, you can't be serious about all this.

HELMER: Oh no? Why not? 265

NORA: Because these are such petty considerations.

HELMER: What are you saying? Petty? You think I'm petty!

NORA: No, just the opposite, Torvald dear. That's exactly why—

HELMER: Never mind. You call my motives petty; then I might 270 as well be just that. Petty! All right! We'll put a stop to this for good. *(Goes to the hall door and calls.)* Helene!

NORA: What do you want?

HELMER: *(Searching among his papers.)* A decision. *(The* MAID *comes in.)* Look here; take this letter; go out with it at once. 275

Get hold of a messenger and have him deliver it. Quick now. It's already addressed. Wait, here's some money.

MAID: Yes, sir. *(She leaves with the letter.)*

HELMER: *(Straightening his papers.)* There, now, little Miss 280 Willful.

NORA: *(Breathlessly.)* Torvald, what was that letter?

HELMER: Krogstad's notice.

NORA: Call it back, Torvald! There's still time. Oh, Torvald, call it back! Do it for my sake—for your sake, for the chil-285 dren's sake! Do you hear, Torvald; do it! You don't know how this can harm us.

HELMER: Too late.

NORA: Yes, too late.

HELMER: Nora dear, I can forgive you this panic, even though 290 basically you're insulting me. Yes, you are! Or isn't it an insult to think that *I* should be afraid of a courtroom hack's revenge? But I forgive you anyway, because this shows so beautifully how much you love me. *(Takes her in his arms.)* This is the way it should be, my darling Nora. Whatever 295 comes, you'll see: when it really counts, I have strength and courage enough as a man to take on the whole weight myself.

NORA: *(Terrified.)* What do you mean by that?

HELMER: The whole weight, I said.

300 NORA: *(Resolutely.)* No, never in all the world.

HELMER: Good. So we'll share it, Nora, as man and wife. That's as it should be. *(Fondling her.)* Are you happy now? There, there, there—not these frightened dove's eyes. It's nothing at all but empty fantasies—Now you should run through 305 your tarantella and practice your tambourine. I'll go to the inner office and shut both doors, so I won't hear a thing; you can make all the noise you like. *(Turning in the doorway.)* And when Rank comes, just tell him where he can find me. *(He nods to her and goes with his papers into the study, closing the 310 door.)*

NORA: *(Standing as though rooted, dazed with fright, in a whisper.)* He really could do it. He will do it. He'll do it in spite of everything. No, not that, never, never! Anything but that! Escape! A way out—*(The doorbell rings.)* Dr. Rank! Anything 315 but that! *Anything,* whatever it is! *(Her hands pass over her face, smoothing it; she pulls herself together, goes over and opens the hall door.* DR. RANK *stands outside, hanging his fur coat up. During the following scene, it begins getting dark.)*

NORA: Hello, Dr. Rank. I recognized your ring. But you mustn't 320 go in to Torvald yet; I believe he's working.

RANK: And you?

NORA: For you, I always have an hour to spare—you know that. *(He has entered, and she shuts the door after him.)*

RANK: Many thanks. I'll make use of these hours while I can.

325 NORA: What do you mean by that? While you can?

RANK: Does that disturb you?

NORA: Well, it's such an odd phrase. Is anything going to happen?

RANK: What's going to happen is what I've been expecting so 330 long—but I honestly didn't think it would come so soon.

NORA: *(Gripping his arm.)* What is it you've found out? Dr. Rank, you have to tell me!

RANK: *(Sitting by the stove.)* It's all over with me. There's nothing to be done about it.

NORA: *(Breathing easier.)* Is it you—then—? 335

RANK: Who else? There's no point in lying to one's self. I'm the most miserable of all my patients, Mrs. Helmer. These past few days I've been auditing my internal accounts. Bankrupt! Within a month I'll probably be laid out and rotting in the churchyard. 340

NORA: Oh, what a horrible thing to say.

RANK: The thing itself is horrible. But the worst of it is all the other horror before it's over. There's only one final examination left; when I'm finished with that, I'll know about when my disintegration will begin. There's something I want to 345 say. Helmer with his sensitivity has such a sharp distaste for anything ugly. I don't want him near my sickroom.

NORA: Oh, but Dr. Rank—

RANK: I won't have him in there. Under no condition. I'll lock my door to him—As soon as I'm completely sure of the 350 worst, I'll send you my calling card marked with a black cross, and you'll know then the wreck has started to come apart.

NORA: No, today you're completely unreasonable. And I wanted you so much to be in a really good humor. 355

RANK: With death up my sleeve? And then to suffer this way for somebody else's sins. Is there any justice in that? And in every single family, in some way or another, this inevitable retribution of nature goes on—

NORA: *(Her hands pressed over her ears.)* Oh, stuff! Cheer up! 360 Please—be gay!

RANK: Yes, I'd just as soon laugh at it all. My poor, innocent spine, serving time for my father's gay army days.

NORA: *(By the table, left.)* He was so infatuated with asparagus tips and *pâté de foie gras,* wasn't that it? 365

RANK: Yes—and with truffles.

NORA: Truffles, yes. And then with oysters, I suppose?

RANK: Yes, tons of oysters, naturally.

NORA: And then the port and champagne to go with it. It's so sad that all these delectable things have to strike at our bones. 370

RANK: Especially when they strike at the unhappy bones that never shared in the fun.

NORA: Ah, that's the saddest of all.

RANK: *(Looks searchingly at her.)* Hm.

NORA: *(After a moment.)* Why did you smile? 375

RANK: No, it was you who laughed.

NORA: No, it was you who smiled, Dr. Rank!

RANK: *(Getting up.)* You're even a bigger tease than I'd thought.

NORA: I'm full of wild ideas today.

RANK: That's obvious. 380

NORA: *(Putting both hands on his shoulders.)* Dear, dear Dr. Rank, you'll never die for Torvald and me.

RANK: Oh, that loss you'll easily get over. Those who go away are soon forgotten.

NORA: *(Looks fearfully at him.)* You believe that? 385

RANK: One makes new connections, and then—

NORA: Who makes new connections?

RANK: Both you and Torvald will when I'm gone. I'd say you're well under way already. What was that Mrs. Linde doing here last evening? 390

NORA: Oh, come—you can't be jealous of poor Kristine?

RANK: Oh yes, I am. She'll be my successor here in the house. When I'm down under, that woman will probably—

NORA: Shh! Not so loud. She's right in there.

395 RANK: Today as well. So you see.

NORA: Only to sew on my dress. Good gracious, how unreasonable you are. (*Sitting on the sofa.*) Be nice now, Dr. Rank. Tomorrow you'll see how beautifully I'll dance; and you can imagine then that I'm dancing only for you—yes, and of
400 course for Torvald, too—that's understood. (*Takes various items out of the carton.*) Dr. Rank, sit over here and I'll show you something.

RANK: (*Sitting.*) What's that?

NORA: Look here. Look.

405 RANK: Silk stockings.

NORA: Flesh-colored. Aren't they lovely? Now it's so dark here, but tomorrow—No, no, no, just look at the feet. Oh well, you might as well look at the rest.

RANK: Hm—

410 NORA: Why do you look so critical? Don't you believe they'll fit?

RANK: I've never had any chance to form an opinion on that.

NORA: (*Glancing at him a moment.*) Shame on you. (*Hits him lightly on the ear with the stockings.*) That's for you. (*Puts them
415 away again.*)

RANK: And what other splendors am I going to see now?

NORA: Not the least bit more, because you've been naughty. (*She hums a little and rummages among her things.*)

RANK: (*After a short silence.*) When I sit here together with you
420 like this, completely easy and open, then I don't know—I simply can't imagine—whatever would have become of me if I'd never come into this house.

NORA: (*Smiling.*) Yes, I really think you feel completely at ease with us.

425 RANK: (*More quietly, staring straight ahead.*) And then to have to go away from it all—

NORA: Nonsense, you're not going away.

RANK: (*His voice unchanged.*)—and not even be able to leave some poor show of gratitude behind, scarcely a fleeting regret—no
430 more than a vacant place that anyone can fill.

NORA: And if I asked you now for—? No—

RANK: For what?

NORA: For a great proof of your friendship—

RANK: Yes, yes?

435 NORA: No, I mean—for an exceptionally big favor—

RANK: Would you really, for once, make me so happy?

NORA: Oh, you haven't the vaguest idea what it is.

RANK: All right, then tell me.

NORA: No, but I can't, Dr. Rank—it's all out of reason. It's
440 advice and help, too—and a favor—

RANK: So much the better. I can't fathom what you're hinting at. Just speak out. Don't you trust me?

NORA: Of course. More than anyone else. You're my best and truest friend, I'm sure. That's why I want to talk to you. All
445 right, then, Dr. Rank: there's something you can help me prevent. You know how deeply, how inexpressibly dearly Torvald loves me; he'd never hesitate a second to give up his life for me.

RANK: (*Leaning close to her.*) Nora—do you think he's the only
450 one—

NORA: (*With a slight start.*) Who—?

RANK: Who'd gladly give up his life for you.

NORA: (*Heavily.*) I see.

RANK: I swore to myself you should know this before I'm gone. I'll never find a better chance. Yes, Nora, now you know. 455 And also you know now that you can trust me beyond anyone else.

NORA: (*Rising, natural and calm.*) Let me by.

RANK: (*Making room for her, but still sitting.*) Nora—

NORA: (*In the hall doorway.*) Helene, bring the lamp in. (*Goes over* 460 *to the stove.*) Ah, dear Dr. Rank, that was really mean of you.

RANK: (*Getting up.*) That I've loved you just as deeply as somebody else? Was *that* mean?

NORA: No, but that you came out and told me. That was quite unnecessary— 465

RANK: What do you mean? Have you known—?

(*The* MAID *comes in with the lamp, sets it on the table, and goes out again.*)

RANK: Nora—Mrs. Helmer—I'm asking you: have you known about it?

NORA: Oh, how can I tell what I know or don't know? Really, I don't know what to say—Why did you have to be so 470 clumsy, Dr. Rank! Everything was so good.

RANK: Well, in any case, you now have the knowledge that my body and soul are at your command. So won't you speak out?

NORA: (*Looking at him.*) After that? 475

RANK: Please, just let me know what it is.

NORA: You can't know anything now.

RANK: I have to. You mustn't punish me like this. Give me the chance to do whatever is humanly possible for you.

NORA: Now there's nothing you can do for me. Besides, actu- 480 ally, I don't need any help. You'll see—it's only my fantasies. That's what it is. Of course! (*Sits in the rocker, looks at him, and smiles.*) What a nice one you are, Dr. Rank. Aren't you a little bit ashamed, now that the lamp is here?

RANK: No, not exactly. But perhaps I'd better go—for good? 485

NORA: No, you certainly can't do that. You must come here just as you always have. You know Torvald can't do without you.

RANK: Yes, but *you?*

NORA: You know how much I enjoy it when you're here.

RANK: That's precisely what threw me off. You're a mystery to 490 me. So many times I've felt you'd almost rather be with me than with Helmer.

NORA: Yes—you see, there are some people that one loves most and other people that one would almost prefer being with.

RANK: Yes, there's something to that. 495

NORA: When I was back home, of course I loved Papa most. But I always thought it was so much fun when I could sneak down to the maids' quarters, because they never tried to improve me, and it was always so amusing, the way they talked to each other. 500

RANK: Aha, so it's *their* place that I've filled.

NORA: (*Jumping up and going to him.*) Oh, dear, sweet Dr. Rank, that's not what I meant at all. But you can understand that with Torvald it's just the same as with Papa—

(*The* MAID *enters from the hall.*)

MAID: Ma'am—please! (*She whispers to* NORA *and hands her a* 505 *calling card.*)

NORA: (*Glancing at the card.*) Ah! (*Slips it into her pocket.*)

RANK: Anything wrong?

NORA: No, no, not at all. It's only some—it's my new dress—

510 RANK: Really? But—there's your dress.

NORA: Oh, that. But this is another one—I ordered it—Torvald mustn't know—

RANK: Ah, now we have the big secret.

NORA: That's right. Just go in with him—he's back in the

515 inner study. Keep him there as long as—

RANK: Don't worry. He won't get away. *(Goes into the study.)*

NORA: *(To the* MAID.*)* And he's standing waiting in the kitchen?

MAID: Yes, he came up by the back stairs.

NORA: But didn't you tell him somebody was here?

520 MAID: Yes, but that didn't do any good.

NORA: He won't leave?

MAID: No, he won't go till he's talked with you, ma'am.

NORA: Let him come in, then—but quietly. Helene, don't breathe a word about this. It's a surprise for my husband.

525 MAID: Yes, yes, I understand—*(Goes out.)*

NORA: This horror—it's going to happen. No, no, no, it can't happen, it mustn't. *(She goes and bolts* HELMER'*s door. The* MAID *opens the hall door for* KROGSTAD *and shuts it behind him. He is dressed for travel in a fur coat, boots, and a fur cap.)*

530 NORA: *(Going toward him.)* Talk softly. My husband's home.

KROGSTAD: Well, good for him.

NORA: What do you want?

KROGSTAD: Some information.

NORA: Hurry up, then. What is it?

535 KROGSTAD: You know, of course, that I got my notice.

NORA: I couldn't prevent it, Mr. Krogstad. I fought for you to the bitter end, but nothing worked.

KROGSTAD: Does your husband's love for you run so thin? He knows everything I can expose you to, and all the same he

540 dares to—

NORA: How can you imagine he knows anything about this?

KROGSTAD: Ah, no—I can't imagine it either, now. It's not at all like my fine Torvald Helmer to have so much guts—

NORA: Mr. Krogstad, I demand respect for my husband!

545 KROGSTAD: Why, of course—all due respect. But since the lady's keeping it so carefully hidden, may I presume to ask if you're also a bit better informed than yesterday about what you've actually done?

NORA: More than you ever could teach me.

550 KROGSTAD: Yes, I *am* such an awful lawyer.

NORA: What is it you want from me?

KROGSTAD: Just a glimpse of how you are, Mrs. Helmer. I've been thinking about you all day long. A cashier, a night—court scribbler, a—well, a type like me also has a little of

555 what they call a heart, you know.

NORA: Then show it. Think of my children.

KROGSTAD: Did you or your husband ever think of mine? But never mind. I simply wanted to tell you that you don't need to take this thing too seriously. For the present, I'm not

560 proceeding with any action.

NORA: Oh no, really! Well—I knew that.

KROGSTAD: Everything can be settled in a friendly spirit. It doesn't have to get around town at all; it can stay just among us three.

565 NORA: My husband must never know anything of this.

KROGSTAD: How can you manage that? Perhaps you can pay me the balance?

NORA: No, not right now.

KROGSTAD: Or you know some way of raising the money in a

570 day or two?

NORA: No way that I'm willing to use.

KROGSTAD: Well, it wouldn't have done you any good, anyway. If you stood in front of me with a fistful of bills, you still couldn't buy your signature back.

575 NORA: Then tell me what you're going to do with it.

KROGSTAD: I'll just hold onto it—keep it on file. There's no outsider who'll even get wind of it. So if you've been thinking of taking some desperate step—

NORA: I have.

580 KROGSTAD: Been thinking of running away from home—

NORA: I have!

KROGSTAD: Or even of something worse—

NORA: How could you guess that?

KROGSTAD: You can drop those thoughts.

585 NORA: How could you guess I was thinking of *that?*

KROGSTAD: Most of us think about *that* at first. I thought about it too, but I discovered I hadn't the courage—

NORA: *(Lifelessly.)* I don't either.

KROGSTAD: *(Relieved.)* That's true, you haven't the courage? You

590 too?

NORA: I don't have it—I don't have it.

KROGSTAD: It would be terribly stupid, anyway. After that first storm at home blows out, why, then—I have here in my pocket a letter for your husband—

595 NORA: Telling everything?

KROGSTAD: As charitably as possible.

NORA: *(Quickly.)* He mustn't ever get that letter. Tear it up. I'll find some way to get money.

KROGSTAD: Beg pardon, Mrs. Helmer, but I think I just told

600 you—

NORA: Oh, I don't mean the money I owe you. Let me know how much you want from my husband, and I'll manage it.

KROGSTAD: I don't want any money from your husband.

605 NORA: What do you want, then?

KROGSTAD: I'll tell you what. I want to recoup, Mrs. Helmer; I want to get on in the world—and there's where your husband can help me. For a year and a half I've kept myself clean of anything disreputable—all that time

610 struggling with the worst conditions; but I was satisfied, working my way up step by step. Now I've been written right off, and I'm just not in the mood to come crawling back. I tell you, I want to move on. I want to get back in the bank—in a better position. Your husband can set up a

615 job for me—

NORA: He'll never do that!

KROGSTAD: He'll do it. I know him. He won't dare breathe a word of protest. And once I'm in there together with him, you just wait and see! Inside of a year, I'll be the manager's

620 righthand man. It'll be Nils Krogstad, not Torvald Helmer, who runs the bank.

NORA: You'll never see the day!

KROGSTAD: Maybe you think you can—

NORA: I have the courage now—for *that.*

625 KROGSTAD: Oh, you don't scare me. A smart, spoiled lady like you—

NORA: You'll see; you'll see!

KROGSTAD: Under the ice, maybe? Down in the freezing, coal-black water? There, till you float up in the spring, ugly, unrecognizable, with your hair falling out—

630 NORA: You don't frighten me.

KROGSTAD: Nor do you frighten me. One doesn't do these things, Mrs. Helmer. Besides, what good would it be? I'd still have him safe in my pocket.

635 NORA: Afterwards? When I'm no longer—?

KROGSTAD: Are you forgetting that *I'll* be in control then over your final reputation? (NORA *stands speechless, staring at him.*) Good; now I've warned you. Don't do anything stupid. When Helmer's read my letter, I'll be waiting for his reply.

640 And bear in mind that it's your husband himself who's forced me back to my old ways. I'll never forgive him for that. Good-bye, Mrs. Helmer. (*He goes out through the hall.*)

NORA: (*Goes to the hall door, opens it a crack, and listens.*) He's gone. Didn't leave the letter. Oh no, no, that's impossible too!

645 (*Opening the door more and more.*) What's that? He's standing outside—not going downstairs. He's thinking it over? Maybe he'll—? (*A letter falls in the mailbox; then* KROGSTAD's *footsteps are heard, dying away down a flight of stairs.* NORA *gives a muffled cry and runs over toward the sofa table. A short pause.*)

650 In the mailbox. (*Slips warily over to the hall door.*) It's lying there. Torvald, Torvald—now we're lost!

MRS. LINDE: (*Entering with the costume from the room, left.*) There now, I can't see anything else to mend. Perhaps you'd like to try—

655 NORA: (*In a hoarse whisper.*) Kristine, come here.

MRS. LINDE: (*Tossing the dress on the sofa.*) What's wrong? You look upset.

NORA: Come here. See that letter? *There!* Look—through the glass in the mailbox.

660 MRS. LINDE: Yes, yes, I see it.

NORA: That letter's from Krogstad—

MRS. LINDE: Nora—it's Krogstad who loaned you the money!

NORA: Yes, and now Torvald will find out everything.

MRS. LINDE: Believe me, Nora, it's best for both of you.

665 NORA: There's more you don't know. I forged a name.

MRS. LINDE: But for heaven's sake—?

NORA: I only want to tell you that, Kristine, so that you can be my witness.

MRS. LINDE: Witness? Why should I—?

670 NORA: If I should go out of my mind—it could easily happen—

MRS. LINDE: Nora!

NORA: Or anything else occurred—so I couldn't be present here—

MRS. LINDE: Nora, Nora, you aren't yourself at all!

675 NORA: And someone should try to take on the whole weight, all of the guilt, you follow me—

MRS. LINDE: Yes, of course, but why do you think—?

NORA: Then you're the witness that it isn't true, Kristine. I'm very much myself; my mind right now is perfectly clear;

680 and I'm telling you: nobody else has known about this; I alone did everything. Remember that.

MRS. LINDE: I will. But I don't understand all this.

NORA: Oh, how could you ever understand it? It's the miracle now that's going to take place.

685 MRS. LINDE: The miracle?

NORA: Yes, the miracle. But it's so awful, Kristine. It mustn't take place, not for anything in the world.

MRS. LINDE: I'm going right over and talk with Krogstad.

NORA: Don't go near him; he'll do you some terrible harm!

690 MRS. LINDE: There was a time once when he'd gladly have done anything for me.

NORA: He?

MRS. LINDE: Where does he live?

NORA: Oh, how do I know? Yes. (*Searches in her pocket.*) Here's his card. But the letter, the letter—!

695

HELMER: (*From the study, knocking on the door.*) Nora!

NORA: (*With a cry of fear.*) Oh! What is it? What do you want?

HELMER: Now, now, don't be so frightened. We're not coming in. You locked the door—are you trying on the dress?

NORA: Yes, I'm trying it. I'll look just beautiful, Torvald.

700

MRS. LINDE: (*Who has read the card.*) He's living right around the corner.

NORA: Yes, but what's the use? We're lost. The letter's in the box.

MRS. LINDE: And your husband has the key?

705

NORA: Yes, always.

MRS. LINDE: Krogstad can ask for his letter back unread; he can find some excuse—

NORA: But it's just this time that Torvald usually—

MRS. LINDE: Stall him. Keep him in there. I'll be back as quick 710 as I can. (*She hurries out through the hall entrance.*)

NORA: (*Goes to* HELMER's *door, opens it, and peers in.*) Torvald!

HELMER: (*From the inner study.*) Well—does one dare set foot in one's own living room at last? Come on, Rank, now we'll get a look—(*In the doorway.*) But what's this?

715

NORA: What, Torvald dear?

HELMER: Rank had me expecting some grand masquerade.

RANK: (*In the doorway.*) That was my impression, but I must have been wrong.

NORA: No one can admire me in my splendor—not till to-morrow.

720

HELMER: But Nora dear, you look so exhausted. Have you practiced too hard?

NORA: No, I haven't practiced at all yet.

HELMER: You know, it's necessary—

725

NORA: Oh, it's absolutely necessary, Torvald. But I can't get anywhere without your help. I've forgotten the whole thing completely.

HELMER: Ah, we'll soon take care of that.

NORA: Yes, take care of me, Torvald, please! Promise me that? 730 Oh, I'm so nervous. That big party—You must give up everything this evening for me. No business—don't even touch your pen. Yes? Dear Torvald, promise?

HELMER: It's a promise. Tonight I'm totally at your service—you little helpless thing. Hm—but first there's one thing I 735 want to—(*Goes toward the hall door.*)

NORA: What are you looking for?

HELMER: Just to see if there's any mail.

NORA: No, no, don't do that, Torvald!

HELMER: Now what?

740

NORA: Torvald, please. There isn't any.

HELMER: Let me look, though. (*Starts out.* NORA, *at the piano, strikes the first notes of the tarantella.* HELMER, *at the door, stops.*) Aha!

NORA: I can't dance tomorrow if I don't practice with you.

745

HELMER: (*Going over to her.*) Nora dear, are you really so frightened?

NORA: Yes, so terribly frightened. Let me practice right now; there's still time before dinner. Oh, sit down and play for me, Torvald. Direct me. Teach me, the way you always have.

HELMER: Gladly, if it's what you want. (*Sits at the piano.*)

NORA: (*Snatches the tambourine up from the box, then a long, varicolored shawl, which she throws around herself, whereupon she springs forward and cries out:*) Play for me now! Now I'll dance!

(HELMER *plays and* NORA *dances.* RANK *stands behind* HELMER *at the piano and looks on.*)

HELMER: (*As he plays.*) Slower. Slow down.

NORA: Can't change it.

HELMER: Not so violent, Nora!

NORA: Has to be just like this.

HELMER: (*Stopping.*) No, no, that won't do at all.

NORA: (*Laughing and swinging her tambourine.*) Isn't that what I told you?

RANK: Let me play for her.

HELMER: (*Getting up.*) Yes, go on. I can teach her more easily then.

(RANK *sits at the piano and plays;* NORA *dances more and more wildly.* HELMER *has stationed himself by the stove and repeatedly gives her directions; she seems not to hear them; her hair loosens and falls over her shoulders; she does not notice, but goes on dancing.* MRS. LINDE *enters.*)

MRS. LINDE: (*Standing dumbfounded at the door.*) Ah——!

NORA: (*Still dancing.*) See what fun, Kristine!

HELMER: But Nora darling, you dance as if your life were at stake.

NORA: And it is.

HELMER: Rank, stop! This is pure madness. Stop it, I say!

(RANK *breaks off playing, and* NORA *halts abruptly*).

HELMER: (*Going over to her.*) I never would have believed it. You've forgotten everything I taught you.

NORA: (*Throwing away the tambourine.*) You see for yourself.

HELMER: Well, there's certainly room for instruction here.

NORA: Yes, you see how important it is. You've got to teach me to the very last minute. Promise me that, Torvald?

HELMER: You can bet on it.

NORA: You mustn't, either today or tomorrow, think about anything else but me; you mustn't open any letters—or the mailbox—

HELMER: Ah, it's still the fear of that man—

NORA: Oh yes, yes, that too.

HELMER: Nora, it's written all over you—there's already a letter from him out there.

NORA: I don't know. I guess so. But you mustn't read such things now; there mustn't be anything ugly between us before it's all over.

RANK: (*Quietly to* HELMER.) You shouldn't deny her.

HELMER: (*Putting his arm around her.*) The child can have her way. But tomorrow night, after you've danced—

NORA: Then you'll be free.

MAID: (*In the doorway, right.*) Ma'am, dinner is served.

NORA: We'll be wanting champagne, Helene.

MAID: Very good, ma'am. (*Goes out.*)

HELMER: So—a regular banquet, hm?

NORA: Yes, a banquet—champagne till daybreak! (*Calling out.*) And some macaroons, Helene. Heaps of them—just this once.

HELMER: (*Taking her hands.*) Now, now, now—no hysterics. Be my own little lark again.

NORA: Oh, I will soon enough. But go on in—and you, Dr. Rank. Kristine, help me put up my hair.

RANK: (*Whispering, as they go.*) There's nothing wrong—really wrong, is there?

HELMER: Oh, of course not. It's nothing more than this childish anxiety I was telling you about. (*They go out, right.*)

NORA: Well?

MRS. LINDE: Left town.

NORA: I could see by your face.

MRS. LINDE: He'll be home tomorrow evening. I wrote him a note.

NORA: You shouldn't have. Don't try to stop anything now. After all, it's a wonderful joy, this waiting here for the miracle.

MRS. LINDE: What is it you're waiting for?

NORA: Oh, you can't understand that. Go in to them; I'll be along in a moment.

(MRS. LINDE *goes into the dining room.* NORA *stands a short while as if composing herself; then she looks at her watch.*)

NORA: Five. Seven hours to midnight. Twenty-four hours to the midnight after, and then the tarantella's done. Seven and twenty-four? Thirty-one hours to live.

HELMER: (*In the doorway, right.*) What's become of the little lark?

NORA: (*Going toward him with open arms.*) Here's your lark!

—————— ACT THREE ——————

Same scene. The table, with chairs around it, has been moved to the center of the room. A lamp on the table is lit. The hall door stands open. Dance music drifts down from the floor above. MRS. LINDE *sits at the table, absently paging through a book, trying to read, but apparently unable to focus her thoughts. Once or twice she pauses, tensely listening for a sound at the outer entrance.*

MRS. LINDE: (*Glancing at her watch.*) Not yet—and there's hardly any time left. If only he's not—(*Listening again.*) Ah, there he is. (*She goes out in the hall and cautiously opens the outer door. Quiet footsteps are heard on the stairs. She whispers:*) Come in. Nobody's here.

KROGSTAD: (*In the doorway.*) I found a note from you at home. What's back of all this?

MRS. LINDE: I just *had* to talk to you.

KROGSTAD: Oh? And it just *had* to be here in this house?

MRS. LINDE: At my place it was impossible; my room hasn't a private entrance. Come in; we're all alone. The maid's asleep, and the Helmers are at the dance upstairs.

KROGSTAD: (*Entering the room.*) Well, well, the Helmers are dancing tonight? Really?

MRS. LINDE: Yes, why not?

KROGSTAD: How true—why not?

MRS. LINDE: All right, Krogstad, let's talk.

KROGSTAD: Do we two have anything more to talk about?

MRS. LINDE: We have a great deal to talk about.

20 KROGSTAD: I wouldn't have thought so.

MRS. LINDE: No, because you've never understood me, really.

KROGSTAD: Was there anything more to understand—except what's all too common in life? A calculating woman throws over a man the moment a better catch comes by.

25 MRS. LINDE: You think I'm so thoroughly calculating? You think I broke it off lightly?

KROGSTAD: Didn't you?

MRS. LINDE: Nils—is that what you really thought?

KROGSTAD: If you cared, then why did you write me the way 30 you did?

MRS. LINDE: What else could I do? If I had to break off with you, then it was my job as well to root out everything you felt for me.

KROGSTAD: (Wringing his hands.) So that was it. And this—all 35 this, simply for money!

MRS. LINDE: Don't forget I had a helpless mother and two small brothers. We couldn't wait for you, Nils; you had such a long road ahead of you then.

KROGSTAD: That may be; but you still hadn't the right to aban- 40 don me for somebody else's sake.

MRS. LINDE: Yes—I don't know. So many, many times I've asked myself if I did have that right.

KROGSTAD: (More softly.) When I lost you, it was as if all the solid ground dissolved from under my feet. Look at me; I'm 45 a half-drowned man now, hanging onto a wreck.

MRS. LINDE: Help may be near.

KROGSTAD: It was near—but then you came and blocked it off.

MRS. LINDE: Without my knowing it, Nils. Today for the first time I learned that it's you I'm replacing at the bank.

50 KROGSTAD: All right—I believe you. But now that you know, will you step aside?

MRS. LINDE: No, because that wouldn't benefit you in the slightest.

KROGSTAD: Not "benefit" me, hm! I'd step aside anyway.

55 MRS. LINDE: I've learned to be realistic. Life and hard, bitter necessity have taught me that.

KROGSTAD: And life's taught me never to trust fine phrases.

MRS. LINDE: Then life's taught you a very sound thing. But you do have to trust in actions, don't you?

60 KROGSTAD: What does that mean?

MRS. LINDE: You said you were hanging on like a half-drowned man to a wreck.

KROGSTAD: I've good reason to say that.

MRS. LINDE: I'm also like a half-drowned woman on a wreck. 65 No one to suffer with; no one to care for.

KROGSTAD: You made your choice.

MRS. LINDE: There wasn't any choice then.

KROGSTAD: So—what of it?

MRS. LINDE: Nils, if only we two shipwrecked people could 70 reach across to each other.

KROGSTAD: What are you saying?

MRS. LINDE: Two on one wreck are at least better off than each on his own.

KROGSTAD: Kristine!

75 MRS. LINDE: Why do you think I came into town?

KROGSTAD: Did you really have some thought of me?

MRS. LINDE: I have to work to go on living. All my born days, as long as I can remember, I've worked, and it's been my best and my only joy. But now I'm completely alone in the world; it frightens me to be so empty and lost. To work for 80 yourself—there's no joy in that. Nils, give me something—someone to work for.

KROGSTAD: I don't believe all this. It's just some hysterical feminine urge to go out and make a noble sacrifice.

MRS. LINDE: Have you ever found me to be hysterical?   85

KROGSTAD: Can you honestly mean this? Tell me—do you know everything about my past?

MRS. LINDE: Yes.

KROGSTAD: And you know what they think I'm worth around here.   90

MRS. LINDE: From what you were saying before, it would seem that with me you could have been another person.

KROGSTAD: I'm positive of that.

MRS. LINDE: Couldn't it happen still?

KROGSTAD: Kristine—you're saying this in all seriousness? Yes, 95 you are! I can see it in you. And do you really have the courage, then—?

MRS. LINDE: I need to have someone to care for; and your children need a mother. We both need each other. Nils, I have faith that you're good at heart—I'll risk everything 100 together with you.

KROGSTAD: (Gripping her hands.) Kristine, thank you, thank you—Now I know I can win back a place in their eyes. Yes—but I forgot—

MRS. LINDE: (Listening.) Shh! The tarantella. Go now! Go on!   105

KROGSTAD: Why? What is it?

MRS. LINDE: Hear the dance up there? When that's over, they'll be coming down.

KROGSTAD: Oh, then I'll go. But—it's all pointless. Of course, you don't know the move I made against the Helmers.   110

MRS. LINDE: Yes, Nils, I know.

KROGSTAD: And all the same, you have the courage to—?

MRS. LINDE: I know how far despair can drive a man like you.

KROGSTAD: Oh, if I only could take it all back.

MRS. LINDE: You easily could—your letter's still lying in the   115 mailbox.

KROGSTAD: Are you sure of that?

MRS. LINDE: Positive. But—

KROGSTAD: (Looks at her searchingly.) Is that the meaning of it, then? You'll save your friend at any price. Tell me straight 120 out. Is that it?

MRS. LINDE: Nils—anyone who's sold herself for somebody else once isn't going to do it again.

KROGSTAD: I'll demand my letter back.

MRS. LINDE: No, no.   125

KROGSTAD: Yes, of course. I'll stay here till Helmer comes down; I'll tell him to give me my letter again—that it only involves my dismissal—that he shouldn't read it—

MRS. LINDE: No, Nils, don't call the letter back.

KROGSTAD: But wasn't that exactly why you wrote me to come   130 here?

MRS. LINDE: Yes, in that first panic. But it's been a whole day and night since then, and in that time I've seen such incredible things in this house. Helmer's got to learn everything; this dreadful secret has to be aired; those two have to come to a   135 full understanding; all these lies and evasions can't go on.

KROGSTAD: Well, then, if you want to chance it. But at least there's one thing I can do, and do right away—

MRS. LINDE: *(Listening.)* Go now, go, quick! The dance is over.
140   We're not safe another second.

KROGSTAD: I'll wait for you downstairs.

MRS. LINDE: Yes, please do; take me home.

KROGSTAD: I can't believe it; I've never been so happy. *(He leaves by way of the outer door; the door between the room and the hall*
145   *stays open.)*

MRS. LINDE: *(Straightening up a bit and getting together her street clothes.)* How different now! How different! Someone to work for, to live for—a home to build. Well, it is worth the try! Oh, if they'd only come! *(Listening.)* Ah, there they
150   are. Bundle up. *(She picks up her hat and coat.* NORA's *and* HELMER's *voices can be heard outside; a key turns in the lock, and* HELMER *brings* NORA *into the hall almost by force. She is wearing the Italian costume with a large black shawl about her; he has on evening dress, with a black domino open over it.)*

155   NORA: *(Struggling in the doorway.)* No, no, no, not inside! I'm going up again. I don't want to leave so soon.

HELMER: But Nora dear—

NORA: Oh, I beg you, please, Torvald. From the bottom of my heart, *please*—only an hour more!

160   HELMER: Not a single minute, Nora darling. You know our agreement. Come on, in we go; you'll catch cold out here. *(In spite of her resistance, he gently draws her into the room.)*

MRS. LINDE: Good evening.

NORA: Kristine!

165   HELMER: Why, Mrs. Linde—are you here so late?

MRS. LINDE: Yes, I'm sorry, but I did want to see Nora in costume.

NORA: Have you been sitting here, waiting for me?

MRS. LINDE: Yes. I didn't come early enough; you were all
170   upstairs; and then I thought I really couldn't leave without seeing you.

HELMER: *(Removing* NORA's *shawl.)* Yes, take a good look. She's worth looking at, I can tell you that, Mrs. Linde. Isn't she lovely?

175   MRS. LINDE: Yes, I should say—

HELMER: A dream of loveliness, isn't she? That's what everyone thought at the party, too. But she's horribly stubborn—this sweet little thing. What's to be done with her? Can you imagine, I almost had to use force to pry her away.

180   NORA: Oh, Torvald, you're going to regret you didn't indulge me, even for just a half hour more.

HELMER: There, you see. She danced her tarantella and got a tumultuous hand—which was well earned, although the performance may have been a bit too naturalistic—I mean
185   it rather overstepped the proprieties of art. But never mind—what's important is, she made a success, an overwhelming success. You think I could let her stay on after that and spoil the effect? Oh no; I took my lovely little Capri girl—my capricious little Capri girl, I should say—
190   took her under my arm; one quick tour of the ballroom, a curtsy to every side, and then—as they say in novels—the beautiful vision disappeared. An exit should always be effective, Mrs. Linde, but that's what I can't get Nora to grasp. Phew, it's hot in here. *(Flings the domino on a chair and*
195   *opens the door to his room.)* Why's it dark in here? Oh yes, of course. Excuse me. *(He goes in and lights a couple of candles.)*

NORA: *(In a sharp, breathless whisper.)* So?

MRS. LINDE: *(Quietly.)* I talked with him.

NORA: And—?

MRS. LINDE: Nora—you must tell your husband everything.   200

NORA: *(Dully.)* I knew it.

MRS. LINDE: You've got nothing to fear from Krogstad, but you have to speak out.

NORA: I won't tell.

MRS. LINDE: Then the letter will.   205

NORA: Thanks, Kristine. I know now what's to be done. Shh!

HELMER: *(Reentering.)* Well, then, Mrs. Linde—have you admired her?

MRS. LINDE: Yes, and now I'll say good night.

HELMER: Oh, come, so soon? Is this yours, this knitting?   210

MRS. LINDE: Yes, thanks. I nearly forgot it.

HELMER: Do you knit, then?

MRS. LINDE: Oh yes.

HELMER: You know what? You should embroider instead.

MRS. LINDE: Really? Why?   215

HELMER: Yes, because it's a lot prettier. See here, one holds the embroidery so, in the left hand, and then one guides the needle with the right—so—in an easy, sweeping curve—right?

MRS. LINDE: Yes, I guess that's—

HELMER: But, on the other hand, knitting—it can never be   220 anything but ugly. Look, see here, the arms tucked in, the knitting needles going up and down—there's something Chinese about it. Ah, that was really a glorious champagne they served.

MRS. LINDE: Yes, good night, Nora, and don't be stubborn any-   225 more.

HELMER: Well put, Mrs. Linde!

MRS. LINDE: Good night, Mr. Helmer.

HELMER: *(Accompanying her to the door.)* Good night, good night. I hope you get home all right. I'd be very happy   230 to—but you don't have far to go. Good night, good night. *(She leaves. He shuts the door after her and returns.)* There, now, at last we got her out the door. She's a deadly bore, that creature.

NORA: Aren't you pretty tired, Torvald?   235

HELMER: No, not a bit.

NORA: You're not sleepy?

HELMER: Not at all. On the contrary, I'm feeling quite exhilarated. But you? Yes, you really look tired and sleepy.

NORA: Yes, I'm very tired. Soon now I'll sleep.   240

HELMER: See! You see! I was right all along that we shouldn't stay longer.

NORA: Whatever you do is always right.

HELMER: *(Kissing her brow.)* Now my little lark talks sense. Say, did you notice what a time Rank was having tonight?   245

NORA: Oh, was he? I didn't get to speak with him.

HELMER: I scarcely did either, but it's a long time since I've seen him in such high spirits. *(Gazes at her a moment, then comes nearer her.)* Hm—it's marvelous, though, to be back home again—to be completely alone with you. Oh, you bewitch-   250 ingly lovely young woman!

NORA: Torvald, don't look at me like that!

HELMER: Can't I look at my richest treasure? At all that beauty that's mine, mine alone—completely and utterly.

NORA: *(Moving around to the other side of the table.)* You mustn't   255 talk to me that way tonight.

HELMER: *(Following her.)* The tarantella is still in your blood, I can see—and it makes you even more enticing. Listen. The

260   guests are beginning to go. (*Dropping his voice.*) Nora—it'll soon be quiet through this whole house.

NORA: Yes, I hope so.

HELMER: You do, don't you, my love? Do you realize—when I'm out at a party like this with you—do you know why I talk to you so little, and keep such a distance away; just
265   send you a stolen look now and then—you know why I do it? It's because I'm imagining then that you're my secret darling, my secret young bride-to-be, and that no one suspects there's anything between us.

NORA: Yes, yes; oh, yes, I know you're always thinking of me.

270 HELMER: And then when we leave and I place the shawl over those fine young rounded shoulders—over that wonderful curving neck—then I pretend that you're my young bride, that we're just coming from the wedding, that for the first time I'm bringing you into my house—that for the first
275   time I'm alone with you—completely alone with you, your trembling young beauty! All this evening I've longed for nothing but you. When I saw you turn and sway in the tarantella—my blood was pounding till I couldn't stand it—that's why I brought you down here so early—

280 NORA: Go away, Torvald! Leave me alone. I don't want all this.

HELMER: What do you mean? Nora, you're teasing me. You will, won't you? Aren't I your husband—?

(*A knock at the outside door.*)

NORA: (*Startled.*) What's that?

HELMER: (*Going toward the hall.*) Who is it?

285 RANK: (*Outside.*) It's me. May I come in a moment?

HELMER: (*With quiet irritation.*) Oh, what does he want now? (*Aloud.*) Hold on. (*Goes and opens the door.*) Oh, how nice that you didn't just pass us by!

RANK: I thought I heard your voice, and then I wanted so badly
290   to have a look in. (*Lightly glancing about.*) Ah, me, these old familiar haunts. You have it snug and cozy in here, you two.

HELMER: You seemed to be having it pretty cozy upstairs, too.

RANK: Absolutely. Why shouldn't I? Why not take in everything in life? As much as you can, anyway, and as long as
295   you can. The wine was superb—

HELMER: The champagne especially.

RANK: You noticed that too? It's amazing how much I could guzzle down.

NORA: Torvald also drank a lot of champagne this evening.

300 RANK: Oh?

NORA: Yes, and that always makes him so entertaining.

RANK: Well, why shouldn't one have a pleasant evening after a well-spent day?

HELMER: Well spent? I'm afraid I can't claim that.

305 RANK: (*Slapping him on the back.*) But I can, you see!

NORA: Dr. Rank, you must have done some scientific research today.

RANK: Quite so.

HELMER: Come now—little Nora talking about scientific
310   research!

RANK: Indeed you may.

NORA: Then they were good?

RANK: The best possible for both doctor and patient—certainty.

315 NORA: (*Quickly and searchingly.*) Certainty?

RANK: Complete certainty. So don't I owe myself a gay evening afterwards?

NORA: Yes, you're right, Dr. Rank.

HELMER: I'm with you—just so long as you don't have to suffer for it in the morning.
320

RANK: Well, one never gets something for nothing in life.

NORA: Dr. Rank—are you very fond of masquerade parties?

RANK: Yes, if there's a good array of odd disguises—

NORA: Tell me, what should we two go as at the next masquerade?
325

HELMER: You little featherhead—already thinking of the next!

RANK: We two? I'll tell you what: you must go as Charmed Life—

HELMER: Yes, but find a costume for *that!*

RANK: Your wife can appear just as she looks every day.
330

HELMER: That was nicely put. But don't you know what you're going to be?

RANK: Yes, Helmer, I've made up my mind.

HELMER: Well?

RANK: At the next masquerade I'm going to be invisible.
335

HELMER: That's a funny idea.

RANK: They say there's a hat—black, huge—have you never heard of the hat that makes you invisible? You put it on, and then no one on earth can see you.

HELMER: (*Suppressing a smile.*) Ah, of course.
340

RANK: But I'm quite forgetting what I came for. Helmer, give me a cigar, one of the dark Havanas.

HELMER: With the greatest pleasure. (*Holds out his case.*)

RANK: Thanks. (*Takes one and cuts off the tip.*)

NORA: (*Striking a match.*) Let me give you a light.
345

RANK: Thank you. (*She holds the match for him; he lights the cigar.*) And now good-bye.

HELMER: Good-bye, good-bye, old friend.

NORA: Sleep well, Doctor.

RANK: Thanks for that wish.
350

NORA: Wish me the same.

RANK: You? All right, if you like—Sleep well. And thanks for the light. (*He nods to them both and leaves.*)

HELMER: (*His voice subdued.*) He's been drinking heavily.

NORA: (*Absently.*) Could be. (HELMER *takes his keys from his pocket* 355
  and goes out in the hall.) Torvald—what are you after?

HELMER: Got to empty the mailbox; it's nearly full. There won't be room for the morning papers.

NORA: Are you working tonight?

HELMER: You know I'm not. Why—what's this? Someone's 360
  been at the lock.

NORA: At the lock—?

HELMER: Yes, I'm positive. What do you suppose—? I can't imagine one of the maids—? Here's a broken hairpin. Nora, it's yours— 365

NORA: (*Quickly.*) Then it must be the children—

HELMER: You'd better break them of that. Hm, hm—well, opened it after all. (*Takes the contents out and calls into the kitchen.*) Helene! Helene, would you put out the lamp in the hall. (*He returns to the room, shutting the hall door, then displays* 370
  the handful of mail.) Look how it's piled up. (*Sorting through them.*) Now what's this?

NORA: (*At the window.*) The letter! Oh, Torvald, no!

HELMER: Two calling cards—from Rank.

NORA: From Dr. Rank? 375

HELMER: (*Examining them.*) "Dr. Rank, Consulting Physician." They were on top. He must have dropped them in as he left.

NORA: Is there anything on them?

HELMER: There's a black cross over the name. See? That's a
380 gruesome notion. He could almost be announcing his own death.

NORA: That's just what he's doing.

HELMER: What! You've heard something? Something he's told you?

385 NORA: Yes. That when those cards came, he'd be taking his leave of us. He'll shut himself in now and die.

HELMER: Ah, my poor friend! Of course I knew he wouldn't be here much longer. But so soon—And then to hide himself away like a wounded animal.

390 NORA: If it has to happen, then it's best it happens in silence—don't you think so, Torvald?

HELMER: (*Pacing up and down.*) He'd grown right into our lives. I simply can't imagine him gone. He with his suffering and loneliness—like a dark cloud setting off our sunlit happi-
395 ness. Well, maybe it's best this way. For him, at least. (*Standing still.*) And maybe for us too, Nora. Now we're thrown back on each other, completely. (*Embracing her.*) Oh you, my darling wife, how can I hold you close enough? You know what, Nora—time and again I've wished you
400 were in some terrible danger, just so I could stake my life and soul and everything, for your sake.

NORA: (*Tearing herself away, her voice firm and decisive.*) Now you must read your mail, Torvald.

HELMER: No, no, not tonight. I want to stay with you, dearest.

405 NORA: With a dying friend on your mind?

HELMER: You're right. We've both had a shock. There's ugliness between us—these thoughts of death and corruption. We'll have to get free of them first. Until then—we'll stay apart.

NORA: (*Clinging about his neck.*) Torvald—good night! Good
410 night!

HELMER: (*Kissing her on the cheek.*) Good night, little songbird. Sleep well, Nora. I'll be reading my mail now. (*He takes the letters into his room and shuts the door after him.*)

NORA: (*With bewildered glances, groping about, seizing* HELMER's
415 *domino, throwing it around her, and speaking in short, hoarse, broken whispers.*) Never see him again. Never, never. (*Putting her shawl over her head.*) Never see the children either—them, too. Never, never. Oh, the freezing black water! The depths—down—Oh, I wish it were over—He has it now;
420 he's reading it—now. Oh no, no, not yet. Torvald, good-bye, you and the children—(*She starts for the hall; as she does,* HELMER *throws open his door and stands with an open letter in his hand.*)

HELMER: Nora!

425 NORA: (*Screams.*) Oh—!

HELMER: What is this? You know what's in this letter?

NORA: Yes, I know. Let me go! Let me out!

HELMER: (*Holding her back.*) Where are you going?

NORA: (*Struggling to break loose.*) You can't save me, Torvald!

430 HELMER: (*Slumping back.*) True! Then it's true what he writes? How horrible! No, no, it's impossible—it can't be true.

NORA: It *is* true. I've loved you more than all this world.

HELMER: Ah, none of your slippery tricks.

NORA: (*Taking one step toward him.*) Torvald—!

435 HELMER: What *is* this you've blundered into!

NORA: Just let me loose. You're not going to suffer for my sake. You're not going to take on my guilt.

HELMER: No more playacting. (*Locks the hall door.*) You stay right here and give me a reckoning. You understand what
440 you've done? Answer! You understand?

NORA: (*Looking squarely at him, her face hardening.*) Yes. I'm beginning to understand everything now.

HELMER: (*Striding about.*) Oh, what an awful awakening! In all these eight years—she who was my pride and joy—a hyp-
445 ocrite, a liar—worse, worse—a criminal! How infinitely disgusting it all is! The shame! (NORA *says nothing and goes on looking straight at him. He stops in front of her.*) I should have suspected something of the kind. I should have known. All your father's flimsy values—Be still! All your
450 father's flimsy values have come out in you. No religion, no morals, no sense of duty—Oh, how I'm punished for letting him off! I did it for your sake, and you repay me like this.

NORA: Yes, like this.

HELMER: Now you've wrecked all my happiness—ruined my
455 whole future. Oh, it's awful to think of. I'm in a cheap lit-tle grafter's hands; he can do anything he wants with me, ask for anything, play with me like a puppet—and I can't breathe a word. I'll be swept down miserably into the depths on account of a featherbrained woman.

460 NORA: When I'm gone from this world, you'll be free.

HELMER: Oh, quit posing. Your father had a mess of those speeches too. What good would that ever do me if you were gone from this world, as you say? Not the slightest. He can still make the whole thing known; and if he does, I could
465 be falsely suspected as your accomplice. They might even think that I was behind it—that I put you up to it. And all that I can thank you for—you that I've coddled the whole of our marriage. Can you see now what you've done to me?

NORA: (*Icily calm.*) Yes.

470 HELMER: It's so incredible, I just can't grasp it. But we'll have to patch up whatever we can. Take off the shawl. I said, take it off! I've got to appease him somehow or other. The thing has to be hushed up at any cost. And as for you and me, it's got to seem like everything between us is just as it
475 was—to the outside world, that is. You'll go right on liv-ing in this house, of course. But you can't be allowed to bring up the children; I don't dare trust you with them—Oh, to have to say this to someone I've loved so much, and that I still—! Well, that's done with. From now on happi-
480 ness doesn't matter; all that matters is saving the bits and pieces, the appearance—(*The doorbell rings.* HELMER *starts.*) What's that? And so late. Maybe the worst—? You think he'd—? Hide, Nora! Say you're sick. (NORA *remains stand-ing motionless.* HELMER *goes and opens the door.*)

485 MAID: (*Half dressed, in the hall.*) A letter for Mrs. Helmer.

HELMER: I'll take it. (*Snatches the letter and shuts the door.*) Yes, it's from him. You don't get it; I'm reading it myself.

NORA: Then read it.

HELMER: (*By the lamp.*) I hardly dare. We may be ruined, you
490 and I. But—I've got to know. (*Rips open the letter, skims through a few lines, glances at an enclosure, then cries out joy-fully.*) Nora! (NORA *looks inquiringly at him.*) Nora! Wait—better check it again—Yes, yes, it's true. I'm saved. Nora, I'm saved!

495 NORA: And I?

HELMER: You too, of course. We're both saved, both of us. Look. He's sent back your note. He says he's sorry and ashamed—that a happy development in his life—oh, who cares what he says! Nora, we're saved! No one can hurt you. Oh, Nora,

500   Nora—but first, this ugliness all has to go. Let me see—*(Takes a look at the note.)* No, I don't want to see it; I want the whole thing to fade like a dream. *(Tears the note and both letters to pieces, throws them into the stove and watches them burn.)* There—now there's nothing left—He wrote that since

505   Christmas Eve you—Oh, they must have been three terrible days for you, Nora.

NORA: I fought a hard fight.

HELMER: And suffered pain and saw no escape but—No, we're not going to dwell on anything unpleasant. We'll just be

510   grateful and keep on repeating: it's over now, it's over! You hear me, Nora? You don't seem to realize—it's over. What's it mean—that frozen look? Oh, poor little Nora, I understand. You can't believe I've forgiven you. But I have, Nora; I swear I have. I know that what you did, you did out

515   of love for me.

NORA: That's true.

HELMER: You loved me the way a wife ought to love her husband. It's simply the means that you couldn't judge. But you think I love you any the less for not knowing how to

520   handle your affairs? No, no—just lean on me; I'll guide you and teach you. I wouldn't be a man if this feminine helplessness didn't make you twice as attractive to me. You mustn't mind those sharp words I said—that was all in the first confusion of thinking my world had collapsed. I've for-

525   given you, Nora; I swear I've forgiven you.

NORA: My thanks for your forgiveness. *(She goes out through the door, right.)*

HELMER: No, wait—*(Peers in.)* What are you doing in there?

NORA: *(Inside.)* Getting out of my costume.

530 HELMER: *(By the open door.)* Yes, do that. Try to calm yourself and collect your thoughts again, my frightened little songbird. You can rest easy now; I've got wide wings to shelter you with. *(Walking about close by the door.)* How snug and nice our home is, Nora. You're safe here; I'll keep you like

535   a hunted dove I've rescued out of a hawk's claws. I'll bring peace to your poor, shuddering heart. Gradually it'll happen, Nora; you'll see. Tomorrow all this will look different to you; then everything will be as it was. I won't have to go on repeating I forgive you; you'll feel it for yourself. How

540   can you imagine I'd ever conceivably want to disown you—or even blame you in any way? Ah, you don't know a man's heart, Nora. For a man there's something indescribably sweet and satisfying in knowing he's forgiven his wife—and forgiven her out of a full and open heart. It's as if she

545   belongs to him in two ways now: in a sense he's given her fresh into the world again, and she's become his wife and his child as well. From now on that's what you'll be to me—you little, bewildered, helpless thing. Don't be afraid of anything, Nora; just open your heart to me, and I'll be con-

550   science and will to you both—*(NORA enters in her regular clothes.)* What's this? Not in bed? You've changed your dress?

NORA: Yes, Torvald, I've changed my dress.

HELMER: But why now, so late?

555 NORA: Tonight I'm not sleeping.

HELMER: But Nora dear—

NORA: *(Looking at her watch.)* It's still not so very late. Sit down, Torvald; we have a lot to talk over. *(She sits at one side of the table.)*

HELMER: Nora—what is this? That hard expression—   560

NORA: Sit down. This'll take some time. I have a lot to say.

HELMER: *(Sitting at the table directly opposite her.)* You worry me, Nora. And I don't understand you.

NORA: No, that's exactly it. You don't understand me. And I've never understood you either—until tonight. No, don't 565 interrupt. You can just listen to what I say. We're closing out accounts, Torvald.

HELMER: How do you mean that?

NORA: *(After a short pause.)* Doesn't anything strike you about our sitting here like this?   570

HELMER: What's that?

NORA: We've been married now eight years. Doesn't it occur to you that this is the first time we two, you and I, man and wife, have ever talked seriously together?

HELMER: What do you mean—seriously?   575

NORA: In eight whole years—longer even—right from our first acquaintance, we've never exchanged a serious word on any serious thing.

HELMER: You mean I should constantly go and involve you in problems you couldn't possibly help me with?   580

NORA: I'm not talking of problems. I'm saying that we've never sat down seriously together and tried to get to the bottom of anything.

HELMER: But dearest, what good would that ever do you?

NORA: That's the point right there: you've never understood 585 me. I've been wronged greatly, Torvald—first by Papa, and then by you.

HELMER: What! By us—the two people who've loved you more than anyone else?

NORA: *(Shaking her head.)* You never loved me. You've thought 590 it fun to be in love with me, that's all.

HELMER: Nora, what a thing to say!

NORA: Yes, it's true now, Torvald. When I lived at home with Papa, he told me all his opinions, so I had the same ones too; or if they were different I hid them, since he wouldn't 595 have cared for that. He used to call me his doll-child, and he played with me the way I played with my dolls. Then I came into your house—

HELMER: How can you speak of our marriage like that?

NORA: *(Unperturbed.)* I mean, then I went from Papa's hands 600 into yours. You arranged everything to your own taste, and so I got the same taste as you—or I pretended to; I can't remember. I guess a little of both, first one, then the other. Now when I look back, it seems as if I'd lived here like a beggar—just from hand to mouth. I've lived by doing 605 tricks for you, Torvald. But that's the way you wanted it. It's a great sin what you and Papa did to me. You're to blame that nothing's become of me.

HELMER: Nora, how unfair and ungrateful you are! Haven't you been happy here?   610

NORA: No, never. I thought so—but I never have.

HELMER: Not—not happy!

NORA: No, only lighthearted. And you've always been so kind to me. But our home's been nothing but a playpen. I've been your doll-wife here, just as at home I was Papa's 615 doll-child. And in turn the children have been my dolls. I thought it was fun when you played with me, just as they thought it fun when I played with them. That's been our marriage, Torvald.

620 HELMER: There's some truth in what you're saying—under all the raving exaggeration. But it'll all be different after this. Playtime's over; now for the schooling.

NORA: Whose schooling—mine or the children's?

HELMER: Both yours and the children's, dearest.

625 NORA: Oh, Torvald, you're not the man to teach me to be a good wife to you.

HELMER: And you can say that?

NORA: And I—how am I equipped to bring up children?

HELMER: Nora!

630 NORA: Didn't you say a moment ago that that was no job to trust me with?

HELMER: In a flare of temper! Why fasten on that?

NORA: Yes, but you were so very right. I'm not up to the job. There's another job I have to do first. I have to try to edu-

635 cate myself. You can't help me with that. I've got to do it alone. And that's why I'm leaving you now.

HELMER: (*Jumping up.*) What's that?

NORA: I have to stand completely alone, if I'm ever going to discover myself and the world out there. So I can't go on liv-

640 ing with you.

HELMER: Nora, Nora!

NORA: I want to leave right away. Kristine should put me up for the night—

HELMER: You're insane! You've no right! I forbid you!

645 NORA: From here on, there's no use forbidding me anything. I'll take with me whatever is mine. I don't want a thing from you, either now or later.

HELMER: What kind of madness is this!

NORA: Tomorrow I'm going home—I mean, home where I

650 came from. It'll be easier up there to find something to do.

HELMER: Oh, you blind, incompetent child!

NORA: I must learn to be competent, Torvald.

HELMER: Abandon your home, your husband, your children! And you're not even thinking what people will say.

655 NORA: I can't be concerned about that. I only know how essential this is.

HELMER: Oh, it's outrageous. So you'll run out like this on your most sacred vows.

NORA: What do you think are my most sacred vows?

660 HELMER: And I have to tell you that! Aren't they your duties to your husband and children?

NORA: I have other duties equally sacred.

HELMER: That isn't true. What duties are they?

NORA: Duties to myself.

665 HELMER: Before all else, you're a wife and a mother.

NORA: I don't believe in that anymore. I believe that, before all else, I'm a human being, no less than you—or anyway, I ought to try to become one. I know the majority thinks you're right, Torvald, and plenty of books agree with you,

670 too. But I can't go on believing what the majority says, or what's written in books. I have to think over these things myself and try to understand them.

HELMER: Why can't you understand your place in your own home? On a point like that, isn't there one everlasting

675 guide you can turn to? Where's your religion?

NORA: Oh, Torvald, I'm really not sure what religion is.

HELMER: What—?

NORA: I only know what the minister said when I was confirmed. He told me religion was this thing and that. When I get clear and away by myself, I'll go into that problem too. 680 I'll see if what the minister said was right, or, in any case, if it's right for me.

HELMER: A young woman your age shouldn't talk like that. If religion can't move you, I can try to rouse your conscience. You do have some moral feeling? Or, tell me—has that 685 gone too?

NORA: It's not easy to answer that, Torvald. I simply don't know. I'm all confused about these things. I just know I see them so differently from you. I find out, for one thing, that the law's not at all what I'd thought—but I can't get it 690 through my head that the law is fair. A woman hasn't a right to protect her dying father or save her husband's life! I can't believe that.

HELMER: You talk like a child. You don't know anything of the world you live in. 695

NORA: No, I don't. But now I'll begin to learn for myself. I'll try to discover who's right, the world or I.

HELMER: Nora, you're sick; you've got a fever. I almost think you're out of your head.

NORA: I've never felt more clearheaded and sure in my life. 700

HELMER: And—clearheaded and sure—you're leaving your husband and children?

NORA: Yes.

HELMER: Then there's only one possible reason.

NORA: What? 705

HELMER: You no longer love me.

NORA: No. That's exactly it.

HELMER: Nora! You can't be serious!

NORA: Oh, this is so hard, Torvald—you've been so kind to me always. But I can't help it. I don't love you anymore. 710

HELMER: (*Struggling for composure.*) Are you also clearheaded and sure about that?

NORA: Yes, completely. That's why I can't go on staying here.

HELMER: Can you tell me what I did to lose your love?

NORA: Yes, I can tell you. It was this evening when the mirac- 715 ulous thing didn't come—then I knew you weren't the man I'd imagined.

HELMER: Be more explicit; I don't follow you.

NORA: I've waited now so patiently eight long years—for, my Lord, I know miracles don't come every day. Then this cri- 720 sis broke over me, and such a certainty filled me: *now* the miraculous event would occur. While Krogstad's letter was lying out there, I never for an instant dreamed that you could give in to his terms. I was so utterly sure you'd say to him: go on, tell your tale to the whole wide world. And 725 when he'd done that—

HELMER: Yes, what then? When I'd delivered my own wife into shame and disgrace—!

NORA: When he'd done that, I was so utterly sure that you'd step forward, take the blame on yourself and say: I am the 730 guilty one.

HELMER: Nora—!

NORA: You're thinking I'd never accept such a sacrifice from you? No, of course not. But what good would my protests be against you? That was the miracle I was waiting for, in 735 terror and hope. And to stave that off, I would have taken my life.

HELMER: I'd gladly work for you day and night, Nora—and take on pain and deprivation. But there's no one who gives up honor for love.

NORA: Millions of women have done just that.

HELMER: Oh, you think and talk like a silly child.

NORA: Perhaps. But you neither think nor talk like the man I could join myself to. When your big fright was over—and it wasn't from any threat against me, only for what might damage you—when all the danger was past, for you it was just as if nothing had happened. I was exactly the same, your little lark, your doll, that you'd have to handle with double care now that I'd turned out so brittle and frail. *(Gets up.)* Torvald—in that instant it dawned on me that for eight years I've been living here with a stranger, and that I'd even conceived three children—oh, I can't stand the thought of it! I could tear myself to bits.

HELMER: *(Heavily.)* I see. There's a gulf that's opened between us—that's clear. Oh, but Nora, can't we bridge it somehow?

NORA: The way I am now, I'm no wife for you.

HELMER: I have the strength to make myself over.

NORA: Maybe—if your doll gets taken away.

HELMER: But to part! To part from you! No, Nora, no—I can't imagine it.

NORA: *(Going out, right.)* All the more reason why it has to be. *(She reenters with her coat and a small overnight bag, which she puts on a chair by the table.)*

HELMER: Nora, Nora, not now! Wait till tomorrow.

NORA: I can't spend the night in a strange man's room.

HELMER: But couldn't we live here like brother and sister—

NORA: You know very well how long that would last. *(Throws her shawl about her.)* Good-bye, Torvald. I won't look in on the children. I know they're in better hands than mine. The way I am now, I'm no use to them.

HELMER: But someday, Nora—someday—?

NORA: How can I tell? I haven't the least idea what'll become of me.

HELMER: But you're my wife, now and wherever you go.

NORA: Listen, Torvald—I've heard that when a wife deserts her husband's house just as I'm doing, then the law frees him from all responsibility. In any case, I'm freeing you from being responsible. Don't feel yourself bound, any more than I will. There has to be absolute freedom for us both. Here, take your ring back. Give me mine.

HELMER: That too?

NORA: That too.

HELMER: There it is.

NORA: Good. Well, now it's all over. I'm putting the keys here. The maids know all about keeping up the house—better than I do. Tomorrow, after I've left town, Kristine will stop by to pack up everything that's mine from home. I'd like those things shipped up to me.

HELMER: Over! All over! Nora, won't you ever think about me?

NORA: I'm sure I'll think of you often, and about the children and the house here.

HELMER: May I write you?

NORA: No—never. You're not to do that.

HELMER: Oh, but let me send you—

NORA: Nothing. Nothing.

HELMER: Or help you if you need it.

NORA: No. I accept nothing from strangers.

HELMER: Nora—can I never be more than a stranger to you?

NORA: *(Picking up the overnight bag.)* Ah, Torvald—it would take the greatest miracle of all—

HELMER: Tell me the greatest miracle!

NORA: You and I both would have to transform ourselves to the point that—Oh, Torvald, I've stopped believing in miracles.

HELMER: But I'll believe. Tell me! Transform ourselves to the point that—?

NORA: That our living together could be a true marriage. *(She goes out down the hall.)*

HELMER: *(Sinks down on a chair by the door, face buried in his hands.)* Nora! Nora! *(Looking about and rising.)* Empty. She's gone. *(A sudden hope leaps in him.)* The greatest miracle—?

(From below, the sound of a door slamming shut.)

ANTON CHEKHOV

The work of Anton Chekhov (1860–1904) is noted for its objectivity, its sympathetic yet almost clinical examination of turn-of-the-century Russian life. Born in the provincial town of Taganrog, Chekhov trained for a career in medicine and began practicing as a physician in the mid-1880s. At that time he also began to write his first short stories. In his fiction, as in his later plays, Chekhov adopted a mildly ironic attitude toward his subjects, one that resisted sensation and melodrama in favor of a more neutral stance; as he wrote in a letter, "It is necessary that on stage everything should be as complex and as simple as in life. People are having dinner, and while they're having it, their future happiness may be decided or their lives may be about to be shattered." Chekhov's life was shattered in just this way, simply, suddenly, and casually. In 1884 he coughed up blood, the sure sign that he had contracted tuberculosis. The disease could not be cured and required repeated periods of convalescence; an early death was a certainty.

Chekhov began writing plays in the 1880s as well, mainly short comic sketches he called "vaudevilles," among them *The Bear* (1888), *The Proposal* (1889), and *The Wedding* (1890). In 1896, the Alexandrinsky Theater in St. Petersburg performed his full-length drama *The Seagull*. The play's indirect plotting and its avoidance of the conventional climaxes of melodrama confused actors and audiences alike, and it failed. Chekhov was persuaded by Constantin Stanislavski and Vladimir Nemirovich-Danchenko to mount the play in their newly founded Moscow Art Theater (MAT) in 1898. Stanislavski's commitment to a restrained style of performance, emphasizing psychological complexity and balanced playing by the entire ensemble is generally credited with making the MAT production a success; a seagull became the company's signature. Chekhov produced three more major plays with the MAT. He revised *The Wood Demon* (1889) as *Uncle Vanya* in 1899 and then produced *Three Sisters* (1901) and *The Cherry Orchard* (1904). Chekhov married the actress Olga Knipper—who played leading roles in his plays, including Madame Ranevskaya in *The Cherry Orchard*—in 1901 and spent the final years of his life convalescing in Yalta.

THE CHERRY ORCHARD

The action of Chekhov's plays is usually indirect, not progressive and consequential in the manner of Ibsen's work. Instead, a Chekhov play generally opens with the arrival of some well-to-do characters in the provincial scene of the play and closes with their departure: Yelena and Serbryakov in *Uncle Vanya,* the regiment and its romantic Lieutenant Colonel Vershinin in Three Sisters, Madame Ranevskaya and her entourage in *The Cherry Orchard.* In between, we see how the lives of the characters are changed, and yet somehow remain the same, as though their interaction worked to reveal the fundamentally static condition of their lives.

More than Chekhov's earlier plays, perhaps, *The Cherry Orchard* also seems to prefigure the fall of a class: the leisured, ineffectual, yet attractive Madame Ranevskaya and her brother, who own the estate but are incapable of bringing it into the twentieth century. We are left with the final vision of the ancient servant Firs, himself a relic of the emancipation of the serfs half a century before, locked in the house while the orchard falls to the axes. The future seems to promise a brutal and sudden change which the main characters of the play are unable to face. The play takes, at best, an ironic attitude toward the fortunes of Lyubov and Gaev. Tragedies in Chekhov's plays occur in the momentary actions of daily life; they are casual and haphazard, almost accidental, and yet alter the course of life irrevocably. Varya and Lopakhin, for example, bumble their way through the long-expected scene of their engagement, but the scene doesn't come off. Lopakhin remains uncommitted and Varya remains a poor relation dependent on the charity of her family, soon to be sent away to work as a governess. For Varya, the misplayed scene has a bitter and tragic finality.

Chekhov calls the play a "comedy," and despite its mournful tone we might consider what he might have had in mind. Chekhov seems sympathetic to the tragedies of daily life, but often trains a skeptical eye on characters who assume the self-regarding accents of high tragedy, or whose sense of themselves verges on self-delusion, the solipsistic inability to see the world around them. Throughout *The Cherry Orchard,* some characters seem lost in a world of dreams: think of Gaev and his sister arriving in their childhood nursery, of Trofimov's vague and clumsy plans for the future, of kindly old Firs. Chekhov forces us to regard his characters with a certain distance, largely by weaving a texture of comedy into the fabric of the play. Everyone ridicules Gaev's sentimental apostrophe to the bookcase in act 1, and Chekhov adds a list of vaudeville tricks to his characters' performances: Lopakhin's "Ba-a-a" at the opening of the play, Yepikhodov crushing the hatbox with the suitcase in act 4, Trofimov tumbling down the stairs, Charlotta's music-hall turns, Firs's feeble efforts to keep everyone warm. The famous, inexplicable sound effect of act 2—the breaking string—may work in this way as well. It both underscores the mournful tone of the scene and interrupts the illusionistic surface of the action, forcing the audience out of a fully sympathetic engagement with Chekhov's sentimental characters. The play, in this light, seems "tragic" only if we accept the main characters' view of their predicament and accept their idle, self-absorbed fantasies as the stuff of tragedy.

Chekhov went to some lengths to keep the play's tone unsettled, in part because he knew that Stanislavski tended to regard his work as high tragedy. Chekhov suggested to Stanislavski that he play the part of Lopakhin: "When I was writing Lopakhin," he wrote in a letter to the actor, "I thought of it as a part for you. . . . Lopakhin is a merchant, of course, but he is a very decent person in every sense. He must behave with perfect decorum, like an educated man, with no petty ways or tricks of any sort, and it seemed to me that this part, the central one of the play, would come out brilliantly in your hands. . . . you must remember that Varya, a serious and religious girl, is in love with Lopakhin; she wouldn't be in love with a mere money-grubber." Describing Lopakhin in terms of Varya is typical of Chekhov's tendency to think of the ensemble as a whole, rather than in terms of individual characters; but we might also think that Chekhov has strategic designs on Stanislavski as well. Fearing that Stanislavski would want to play the part of Gaev, and would play the part too sympathetically, Chekhov tried to persuade him to train his talents on the comic part of Lopakhin. Imagining Stanislavski as Lopakhin, we begin to see the kind of drama Chekhov had imagined: had he taken the part (Stanislavski played Gaev after all), Stanislavski would have played against the grain of broad humor that underlies Lopakhin, humanizing the role, creating neither a fully sympathetic character nor a vulgar comedian, but something in between. Similarly, *The Cherry Orchard* as a whole strikes a balance somewhere between comedy and tragedy, in which comic and tragic possibilities strain against one another as ways of interpreting the play and the experience of our lives.

As it turned out, Stanislavski's direction emphasized the play's sombre tone, the sense of a generation falling before modern progress as the orchard falls to the axes. After the Russian Revolution in 1917, *The Cherry Orchard* came to be regarded as nearly a prophetic allegory of the progress of history, the displacing of the feudal past by the modern, industrial present.

A pronunciation guide for Russian names appears on page 470.

THE CHERRY ORCHARD

Anton Chekhov

TRANSLATED BY CAROL ROCAMORA

CHARACTERS

RANEVSKAYA, LYUBOV ANDREEVNA, *a landowner*
ANYA, *her daughter, age seventeen*
VARYA, *her adopted daughter, age twenty-four*
GAEV, *Leonid Andreevich, Ranevskaya's brother*
LOPAKHIN, *Yermolai Alekseevich, a merchant*
TROFIMOV, *Pyotr Sergeevich, a student*
SIMEONOV-PISHCHIK, *Boris Borisovich, a landowner*
CHARLOTTA IVANOVNA, *a governess*
YEPIKHODOV, *Semyon Panteleevich, a clerk*
DUNYASHA, *a maid*

FIRS, *a servant, an old man of eighty-seven*
YASHA, *a young servant*
A PASSERBY
A STATIONMASTER
A POST OFFICE CLERK
GUESTS, SERVANTS, CARRIAGE DRIVERS

The action takes place on the estate of Lyubov Andreevna Ranevskaya.

ACT ONE

A room, which is still called the nursery. One of the doors leads to ANYA's *room. It is dawn, just before sunrise. It is already May, the cherry trees are all in bloom, but outside it is still cold; there is an early morning frost in the orchard. The windows in the room are closed.*

Enter DUNYASHA *with a candle, and* LOPAKHIN *with a book in his hand.*

LOPAKHIN: The train's arrived, thank God. What time is it?
DUNYASHA: Almost two. *(Puts out the candle.)* It's already getting light out.
LOPAKHIN: So how late is the train, then? A couple of hours, at
5   least. *(Yawns and stretches.)* Well, I've made a fool of myself, then, haven't I! Hm? Came all the way out here, just to meet the train, and fell fast asleep . . . Sat here waiting and dozed right off. Annoying, isn't it . . . You should have woken me up.
10 DUNYASHA: I thought you'd already gone. *(Listens.)* Listen, I think they're here.
LOPAKHIN: *(Listens.)* No . . . They've got to get their baggage first, you know, that sort of thing . . .

(Pause.)

15 Lyubov Andreevna, she's been living abroad for five years, I don't know, I can't even imagine what's become of her now . . . She's a fine person, you know . . . a warm, kind person. I remember, once, when I was a boy, oh, about fifteen years old, say, and my father—he had a shop here in the village then—my father, he hit me in the face with his fist,
20 blood was pouring from my nose . . . We'd come out into the courtyard together, somehow, and he was drunk. And there was Lyubov Andreevna, I remember her so vividly, so young then, so graceful, so slender, she took me by the hand, brought me over to the washstand, right into this
25 very room, into the nursery. "Don't cry, little peasant," she said, "it will heal before your wedding day . . ."

(Pause.)

Little peasant . . . Yes, my father was a peasant, it's true enough, and here I am in a three-piece suit and fancy shoes. A silk purse from a sow's ear, or something like that,
30 isn't that how the expression goes . . . Yes . . . The only difference is, now I'm rich, I've got a lot of money, but don't look too closely, once a peasant . . . *(Leafs through the book.)* Look at me, I read through this entire book and didn't understand a word of it. Read it and dozed right off.

(Pause.)

DUNYASHA: The dogs didn't sleep at all last night, they can   35
sense their masters are coming home.
LOPAKHIN: What's wrong with you, Dunyasha . . .
DUNYASHA: My hands are trembling. I'm going to faint, I know I am.
LOPAKHIN: You're much too high-strung, Dunyasha. And look   40
at you, all dressed up like a young lady, hair done up, too. You mustn't do that. Remember who you are.

(Enter YEPIKHODOV *with a bouquet; he is wearing a jacket and highly polished boots, which squeak loudly; upon entering, he drops the bouquet.)*

YEPIKHODOV: *(Picks up the bouquet.)* Look what the gardener sent. Put them on the dining room table. That's what he said. *(Gives the bouquet to* DUNYASHA.)   45
LOPAKHIN: And bring me some kvass, will you?
DUNYASHA: Yes, sir. *(Leaves.)*
YEPIKHODOV: We have an early morning frost, we have three degrees below zero, and we have the cherry blossoms all in bloom. I don't approve of our climate. *(Sighs.)* Really, I   50
don't. Our climate doesn't work, it just doesn't work. It's not conducive. And would you like to hear more, Yermolai Alekseich, well, then you will, because the day before yesterday, I bought these boots, and, trust me, they squeak so much, that they are beyond hope. Now how can I oil them?   55
Tell me? How?
LOPAKHIN: Enough. You're getting on my nerves.
YEPIKHODOV: Every day some new disaster befalls me. A new day, a new disaster. But do I grumble, do I complain, no, I don't, I accept it, look, I'm smiling, even.   60

(DUNYASHA enters, gives LOPAKHIN *some kvass.)*

I'm going now. *(Stumbles against a chair, which falls down.)* There . . . *(As if vindicated.)* You see? I mean, that's the situation, and excuse me for saying so . . . Remarkable, even . . . isn't it! *(Exits.)*

65 DUNYASHA: Yermolai Alekseich, I have something to tell you . . . Yepikhodov has proposed to me.

LOPAKHIN: Ah!

DUNYASHA: But I don't know, really . . . He's a nice enough fel-
70 low, you know, quiet and all, it's just that whenever he starts to talk, I can't understand a word he's saying. I mean, it all sounds so sweet and sincere, only it just doesn't make any sense. I like him, I mean, I think I like him. And he? He adores me. But he's such an unfortunate fellow, you know, really, every day it's something else. They even have
75 a name for him, do you know what they call him: "Mister Disaster" . . .

LOPAKHIN: (Listens.) I think they're coming . . .

DUNYASHA: They're coming! What's happening to me . . . I'm freezing, look, I'm shivering all over.

80 LOPAKHIN: They're really coming! Let's go meet them. Will she recognize me? We haven't seen each other in five years.

DUNYASHA: (Agitated.) I'm going to faint, I know I am . . . Look, I'm fainting!

(Two carriages are heard pulling up to the house. LOPAKHIN and DUNYASHA exit quickly. The stage is empty. Then there is noise in the adjacent rooms. FIRS hurries across the stage to meet LYUBOV ANDREEVNA; he is leaning on a cane, and is dressed in old-fashioned livery and a high hat; he mutters something to himself, but it is impossible to make out a single word. The offstage noise crescendos. A voice calls out; "Let's go this way through here . . ." Enter LYUBOV ANDREEVNA, ANYA, and CHARLOTTA IVANOVNA with a little dog on a leash; they are all dressed in traveling clothes. Enter VARYA, wearing a coat and a shawl, GAEV, SIMEONOV-PISHCHIK, LOPAKHIN, DUNYASHA carrying a bundle and an umbrella, SER-VANTS carrying luggage—they all come through the room.)

ANYA: This way! Mama, do you remember what room this is?

85 LYUBOV ANDREEVNA: (Ecstatic, in tears.) The nursery!

VARYA: How cold it is, my hands are numb. (To LYUBOV ANDREEVNA.) Look, Mamochka, your rooms, violet and white, just as you left them.

LYUBOV ANDREEVNA: My nursery, my darling nursery, my beau-
90 tiful room . . . I slept here, when I was a child . . . (Weeps.) And now, I'm a child again . . . (Kisses her brother, VARYA, and her brother again.) And Varya looks the same as ever, just like a little nun. And Dunyasha I recognize, of course . . . (Kisses DUNYASHA.)

95 GAEV: The train was two hours late. How do you like that? How's that for efficiency!

CHARLOTTA: (To PISHCHIK.) My dog eats walnuts, too.

PISHCHIK: (Amazed.) Imagine that!

(They all exit, except for ANYA and DUNYASHA.)

DUNYASHA: We've been waiting forever . . . (Takes ANYA's coat
100 and hat.)

ANYA: I didn't sleep one moment the whole journey long, four whole nights . . . and now I'm absolutely frozen!

DUNYASHA: You left during Lent, we had snow then, and frost, and now! My darling! (Bursts out laughing, kisses her.) I've
105 waited forever for you, my precious, my joy . . . And I've got something to tell you, I can't wait one minute longer. . . .

ANYA: (Listlessly.) Now what . . .

DUNYASHA: Yepikhodov, the clerk, proposed to me just after Easter.

ANYA: Not again . . . (Adjusts her hair.) I've lost all my hair- 110
pins . . . (She is exhausted; she almost sways on her feet.)

DUNYASHA: No, really, I don't know what to think, any more. He adores me, God, how he adores me!

ANYA: (Gazes at the door to her room, tenderly.) My very own room, my windows, it's as if I never left. I'm home! And tomor- 115
row I'll wake up, and I'll run out into the orchard . . . Oh, if only I could rest! I'm so exhausted—I didn't sleep one moment the whole way, I was so worried.

DUNYASHA: Pyotr Sergeich arrived the day before yesterday.

ANYA: (Overjoyed.) Petya! 120

DUNYASHA: He's out in the bathhouse, asleep, that's where he's staying. "I'm afraid of being in the way," he said. (Glances at her pocket watch.) We ought to wake him up, but Varvara Mikhailovna gave us strict orders not to. "Don't you dare wake him up," she said. 125

(Enter VARYA, a bunch of keys hanging from her belt.)

VARYA: Dunyasha, go, quickly, bring the coffee . . . Mamochka wants coffee.

DUNYASHA: Right away. (Exits.)

VARYA: So, thank God, you're here. You're home at last! (Embracing her.) My darling's home! My angel is home! 130

ANYA: I've been through so much.

VARYA: I can imagine.

ANYA: I left during Holy Week, it was so cold then, remember? And Charlotta Ivanovna talked the whole way, talked and played card tricks. How could you have stuck me with 135
Charlotta! . . .

VARYA: You can't travel alone, darling. At seventeen!

ANYA: When we arrived in Paris, it was cold there, too, and snowing. My French is terrible. Mama lived on the fifth floor, and when I finally got there, the flat was filled with 140
all sorts of French people, ladies, an old Catholic priest with a little book, and, oh, it was so uncomfortable there, so stuffy, the room was filled with smoke. And suddenly I felt sorry for Mama, so very sorry, I threw my arms around her neck, I held her so tight, I couldn't let go. And Mama kept 145
clinging to me, and weeping . . .

VARYA: (In tears.) Enough, enough . . .

ANYA: She had already sold the dacha near Menton, she had nothing left, nothing at all. And neither did I, not a single kopek, we hardly had enough money to get home. And 150
Mama just doesn't understand it, still! There we are, sitting in the station restaurant, and she orders the most expensive thing on the menu, she gives the waiter a ruble tip for tea. Charlotta, too. And Yasha orders a complete dinner, it's simply terrible. Yasha is Mama's butler, you know. We 155
brought him with us . . .

VARYA: I'm seen him, the devil . . .

ANYA: So, tell me! Have we paid the interest yet?

VARYA: With what?

ANYA: Dear God, dear God . . . 160

VARYA: And in August, the estate will be sold . . .

ANYA: Dear God . . .

LOPAKHIN: (Peeks through the door and makes a 'bleating' sound.) Ba-a-a . . . (Exits.)

165 VARYA: *(In tears.)* I'd like to give him such a . . . *(Makes a threatening gesture with her fist.)*

ANYA: *(Embraces* VARYA, *softly.)* Varya, has he proposed yet? *(*VARYA *shakes her head "no.")* But he loves you, he does . . . Why don't you talk about it, what are you two
170 waiting for?

VARYA: I know nothing will ever come of it, nothing. He's so busy, he has no time for me, really . . . he pays no attention to me at all. Well, God bless him, but it's too painful for me even to look at him . . . Everyone talks about our wed-
175 ding, everyone congratulates us, but the fact is, there's absolutely nothing to it, it's all a dream . . . *(Changes tone.)* Your brooch looks just like a little bee.

ANYA: *(Sadly.)* Mama bought it. *(She goes to her room, speaking in a gay, child-like voice.)* And in Paris, I went up in a hot air
180 balloon!

VARYA: My darling's home! My angel is home!

*(*DUNYASHA *has already returned with the coffee pot and prepares the coffee.)*

(Stands by the doorway.) All day long, darling, I go about my business, I run the household, I do my chores, but all the time I'm thinking, dreaming. If only we could marry you
185 off to a rich man, then I'd find peace, I'd go to a cloister, and then on a pilgrimage to Kiev, to Moscow, and on and on, from one holy place to the next . . . on and on. A blessing!

ANYA: The birds are singing in the orchard. What time is it?

VARYA: After two, it must be . . . Time for you to sleep, darling.
190 *(Goes into* ANYA's *room.)* Yes, a blessing!

*(*YASHA *enters with a rug, and a traveling bag.)*

YASHA: *(Crosses the stage, discreetly.)* May I?

DUNYASHA: I wouldn't have recognized you, Yasha. How you've changed, since you've been abroad.

YASHA: Hm . . . And who are you?

195 DUNYASHA: When you left, I was about 'so' high . . . *(Indicates.)* Dunyasha, Fyodor Kozoedov's daughter. Don't you remember!

YASHA: Hm . . . Ripe as a cucumber! *(Glances around, and then grabs her and embraces her; she screams and drops a saucer.* YASHA
200 *exits quickly.)*

VARYA: *(In the doorway, displeased.)* What's going on here?

DUNYASHA: *(In tears.)* I broke a saucer . . .

VARYA: That means good luck.

ANYA: *(Coming out of her room.)* We'd better warn Mama: Petya's
205 here . . .

VARYA: I gave strict orders not to wake him up.

ANYA: *(Deep in thought.)* Father died six years ago, and one month later my little brother Grisha drowned in the river, a lovely little seven-year-old boy. Mama couldn't endure it,
210 she ran away, she ran away without once looking back . . . *(Shudders.)* How well I understand her, if only she knew!

(Pause.)

And Petya Trofimov was Grisha's tutor, he might remind her of it all . . .

(Enter FIRS, *in a jacket and white waistcoat.)*

FIRS: *(Goes to the coffee pot, anxiously.)* The mistress will take her coffee here . . . *(Puts on white gloves.)* Is the coffee ready? 215 *(Sternly, to* DUNYASHA.*)* You! Where is the cream?

DUNYASHA: Oh, my God . . . *(Rushes out.)*

FIRS: *(Fusses with the coffee pot.)* Pathetic fool . . . *(Mutters to himself under his breath.)* They've just returned from Paris . . . Now in the old days, the master used to go to Paris, too . . . 220 by horse and carriage . . . *(Bursts out laughing.)*

VARYA: What is it, Firs?

FIRS: Yes, and what may I do for you? *(Overjoyed.)* My mistress has come home! I've waited for so long! Now I can die . . . *(Weeps with joy.)* 225

(Enter LYUBOV ANDREEVNA, GAEV, LOPAKHIN, *and* SIMEONOV-PISHCHIK; SIMEONOV-PISHCHIK *wears a lightweight coat, fitted at the waist, and wide trousers. As he walks,* GAEV *gestures, as if he were playing a game of billiards.)*

LYUBOV ANDREEVNA: How does it go? Wait—don't tell me, let me think . . . "Yellow into the corner pocket! Double into the middle!"

GAEV: "Cut shot into the corner!" Once upon a time, sister dearest, we slept in this very room, you and I, and now I'm 230 fifty-one years old, strange, isn't? . . .

LOPAKHIN: Yes, time flies.

GAEV: Beg pardon?

LOPAKHIN: As I was saying, time flies.

GAEV: It smells of patchouli in here. 235

ANYA: I'm going to bed. Good night, Mama. *(Kisses her mother.)*

LYUBOV ANDREEVNA: My beloved child. *(Kisses her hands.)* Are you glad you're home? I simply can't get hold of myself.

ANYA: Good night, Uncle.

GAEV: *(Kisses her face, hands.)* God bless you. You are the image 240 of your mother! *(To his sister.)* Lyuba, you looked exactly like this at her age.

*(*ANYA *gives her hand to* LOPAKHIN *and* PISHCHIK; *she exits, and closes the door behind her.)*

LYUBOV ANDREEVNA: She's exhausted, really.

PISHCHIK: A tiring journey, no doubt.

VARYA: *(To* LOPAKHIN *and* PISHCHIK.*)* So, gentlemen? It's almost 245 three o'clock in the morning, let's not overstay our welcome.

LYUBOV ANDREEVNA: *(Laughs.)* You're the same as ever, Varya. *(Draws her close and kisses her.)* First I'll have my coffee, then we'll all go, yes?

*(*FIRS *places a cushion under her feet.)*

Thank you, dearest. I've gotten so used to coffee. I drink 250 it day and night. Thank you, my darling old man. *(Kisses* FIRS.*)*

VARYA: I'll go see if they've brought everything in . . . *(Exits.)*

LYUBOV ANDREEVNA: Am I really sitting here? *(Bursts out laughing.)* I feel like jumping up and down, and waving my arms 255 in the air! *(Covers her face with her hands.)* No, really, I must be dreaming! God knows, I love my country, I love it passionately, I couldn't even see out of the train window, I wept the whole way. *(In tears.)* Never mind, we must have our coffee. Thank you, Firs, thank you, my darling old man. I'm 260 so glad you're still alive.

FIRS: The day before yesterday.

GAEV: He's hard of hearing.

LOPAKHIN: I'd better be going; I leave for Kharkov at five this
265   morning. What a nuisance! I only wanted to see you, that's
all, to talk to you a little . . . You're as lovely as ever . . .

PISHCHIK: (*Sighs heavily.*) Even lovelier . . . All dressed up,
Parisian style . . . I'm head-over-heels, as they say!

LOPAKHIN: People like Leonid Andreich here, they say all sorts
270   of things about me, call me a boor, a kulak, but really, it
doesn't matter, I couldn't care less. Let them say whatever
they like. I only want you to believe in me, as you always
did, to look at me with those beautiful, soulful eyes, as you
used to, once. Merciful God! My father was a serf, he be-
275   longed to your grandfather and then to your father, but it
was you, yes, you, who did so much for me once, so much,
and I've forgotten everything now, I love you like my own
flesh and blood . . . more, even, than my own flesh and
blood.

280 LYUBOV ANDREEVNA: I can't sit still, I'm in such a state . . .
(*Jumps up and walks around the room, agitated.*) I simply can't
bear all this joy . . . Go ahead, laugh at me, I'm being foolish, I know it . . . My dear little bookcase . . . (*Kisses the bookcase.*) My own little table.

285 GAEV: Nanny died while you were gone.

LYUBOV ANDREEVNA: (*Sits and drinks coffee.*) Yes, God rest her
soul. They wrote me.

GAEV: Anastasy died, too. And cross-eyed Petrushka—you remember him—he ran away, he lives in town now, at the
290   district superintendent's. (*Takes a box of fruit drops out of his
pocket, pops one into his mouth.*)

PISHCHIK: My daughter, Dashenka . . . she sends her regards . . .

LOPAKHIN: I'd like to tell you some good news, if I may, some
cheerful news, all right? (*Looks at his watch.*) I've got to go,
295   there's no time to talk . . . so, very briefly, then. As you already know, your cherry orchard is being sold to pay off the
debts, the auction date has been set for the twenty-second of
August, but don't you worry, my dear, you don't have to lose
any sleep over this, rest assured, there is a way out . . . Here's
300   my plan. Your attention, please! Your estate is located only
thirteen miles from town, roughly, a railroad runs nearby, so
if the cherry orchard and the land along the river are divided
up into plots and then leased for summer homes, why then
you'll receive at least 25,000 in yearly income.

305 GAEV: Forgive me, but what nonsense!

LYUBOV ANDREEVNA: I don't quite understand you, Yermolai
Alekseich.

LOPAKHIN: You'll receive at least twenty-five rubles a year per
three acre plot from the summer tenants, and if you adver-
310   tise right away, I'll guarantee you, by autumn, there won't
be a single plot left, they'll all be bought up. In a word,
congratulations, you're saved. The site is marvelous, the
river is deep. Only, of course, you'll have to clear it out, get
rid of some things . . . for example, let us say, tear down all
315   the old buildings, and this house, too, which isn't much
good for anything any more, cut down the old cherry
orchard . . .

LYUBOV ANDREEVNA: Cut it down? Forgive me, my darling,
but you have no idea what you're talking about. If there is
320   one thing in the entire province that's of interest, that's remarkable, even, why it's our own cherry orchard.

LOPAKHIN: The only thing remarkable about this orchard is
that it's so big. There's a cherry crop once every two years,
and yes, there are a lot of them, but what good are they, nobody buys them.   325

GAEV: There is a reference to this cherry orchard in the Ency-
clopaedia.

LOPAKHIN: (*Looks at his watch.*) Unless we come up with a plan,
unless we reach a decision, then on the twenty-second of
August the cherry orchard and the entire estate will be auc- 330
tioned off. Make up your minds, will you, please! There is
no other way, I swear to you. None. Absolutely none.

FIRS: Once upon a time, forty—fifty years ago, they used to dry
the cherries, soak them, marinate them, preserve them, and
often . . .   335

GAEV: Hush, Firs.

FIRS: And often, they would send cart loads of dried cherries to
Moscow and Kharkov. Brought in heaps of money! And
those dried cherries, oh, how soft they were, soft, sweet,
plump, juicy, fragrant . . . They knew the recipe in those 340
days . . .

LYUBOV ANDREEVNA: Yes, where is that recipe now?

FIRS: Forgotten. No one remembers it any more.

PISHCHIK: (*To* LYUBOV ANDREEVNA.) Tell us! What is it like in
Paris? Did you eat frogs' legs?   345

LYUBOV ANDREEVNA: I ate crocodile.

PISHCHIK: Imagine that . . .

LOPAKHIN: Up until now, we've only had landowners and peasants living in our countryside, but now, the summer people
are starting to appear among us. All the towns, even the 350
smallest ones, are surrounded by summer homes now. And,
it's possible to predict that, in twenty years or so, the summer population will multiply beyond our wildest dreams.
Now they're just sitting out on their balconies, drinking
their tea, but just wait, soon it will come to pass, you'll see, 355
they'll start cultivating their little plots of land, and your
cherry orchard will bloom again with wealth, prosperity,
happiness . . .

GAEV: (*Indignant.*) What nonsense!

(*Enter* VARYA *and* YASHA.)

VARYA: Two telegrams came for you, Mamochka. (*Takes keys and* 360
unlocks the antique bookcase; the keys make a clinking sound.)
Here they are.

LYUBOV ANDREEVNA: From Paris. (*Rips them up, without reading
them.*) I'm through with Paris.

GAEV: And do you know, Lyuba, how old this bookcase is? 365
Only one week ago, I pull out the bottom drawer, I look,
and what do I see—a mark burned into it, a number. This
bookcase was built exactly one hundred years ago. How do
you like that? Eh? We may now celebrate the jubilee anniversary of this bookcase, ladies and gentlemen. Yes, it's an 370
inanimate object, of course, but nevertheless, it is still a *book*
case.

PISHCHIK: (*Amazed.*) One hundred years old. Imagine that! . . .

GAEV: Yes . . . a work of art . . . (*Touching the bookcase.*) O venerable bookcase! I salute thy existence. For over a century, 375
thou hast sought the pure ideals of truth and justice; thy
silent exhortation for fruitful labor has not yet faltered these
one hundred years, inspiring courage and hope for the

brightest future *(In tears.)* in generation after generation of
our kin, and fostering in us the noble ideals of charity and
good.

(Pause.)

LOPAKHIN: Yes . . .

LYUBOV ANDREEVNA: You haven't changed a bit, Lyonya.

GAEV: *(A bit embarrassed.)* "Off the ball . . . right-hand corner!
Cut shot into the middle."

LOPAKHIN: *(Glances at his watch.)* Time for me to go.

YASHA: *(Gives* LYUBOV ANDREEVNA *medicine.)* Perhaps you'll
take your pills now . . .

PISHCHIK: Why bother taking medicine, lovely lady . . .
doesn't do any harm, doesn't do any good either . . . Do let
me have them . . . dearest lady. *(Takes the pills, pours them into
the palm of his hand, blows on them, puts them in his mouth, and
washes them down with kvass.)* There!

LYUBOV ANDREEVNA: *(Frightened.)* You've gone mad!

PISHCHIK: Took them all.

LOPAKHIN: There's an appetite.

(Everyone laughs.)

FIRS: When he was here during Holy Week, he ate half a
bucket of cucumbers . . . *(Mutters to himself.)*

LYUBOV ANDREEVNA: What is he saying?

VARYA: He's been muttering like that for three years now.
We're used to it.

YASHA: Old age.

(Enter CHARLOTTA IVANOVNA *wearing a white dress; she is very thin
and tightly laced, with a lorgnette on her belt; she crosses the stage.)*

LOPAKHIN: Forgive me, Charlotta Ivanovna, I didn't have the
chance to greet you. *(Goes to kiss her hand.)*

CHARLOTTA IVANOVNA: *(Takes her hand away.)* If I let you kiss
my hand, next you'll want to kiss my elbow, then my
shoulder . . .

LOPAKHIN: Not my lucky day.

(Everyone laughs.)

So, Charlotta Ivanovna, show us a trick!

LYUBOV ANDREEVNA: Yes, Charlotta, show us a trick!

CHARLOTTA: I don't want to. I wish to sleep. *(Exits.)*

LOPAKHIN: We'll see each other again in three weeks. *(Kisses*
LYUBOV ANDREEVNA'S *hand.)* Farewell for now. Time to go.
(To GAEV.) A very good-bye to you. *(Kisses* PISHCHIK.) And
to you. *(Shakes hands with* VARYA, *then with* FIRS *and* YASHA.)
I don't feel like going. *(To* LYUBOV ANDREEVNA.) If you
make up your mind about the summer homes, if you decide
to proceed, just let me know, I'll lend you 50,000. Think
about it, seriously.

VARYA: *(Angrily.)* So go, then!

LOPAKHIN: I'm going, I'm going. . . . *(Exits.)*

GAEV: What a boor. Oh, wait, "pardon" . . . Our Varya's going
to marry him. That's our Varya's fiancé.

VARYA: Don't talk so much, Uncle.

LYUBOV ANDREEVNA: Why not, Varya, I'd be so pleased. He's a
good man.

PISHCHIK: And a most worthy man, as they say, truth be
told . . . Now my Dashenka . . . she also says, that . . . well,
she says a variety of things. *(Snores, then suddenly awakes with
a start.)* Nevertheless, dearest lady, oblige me, would you,
please . . . lend me two hundred and forty rubles . . . tomorrow I must pay off the interest on my mortgage.

VARYA: *(Startled.)* We have no money! None!

LYUBOV ANDREEVNA: As a matter of fact, I don't, I have nothing, really.

PISHCHIK: Some will turn up, you'll see! *(Bursts out laughing.)* I
never lose hope. There, I say to myself, all is lost, all is ruined, and then suddenly, what do you know—they build a
railroad right through my land, and . . . they pay me for it!
So just wait and see, something will happen, if not today,
then tomorrow. My Dashenka is going to win 200,000 . . .
she has a lottery ticket.

LYUBOV ANDREEVNA: The coffee's finished, now we can go to
bed.

FIRS: *(Brushes* GAEV'S *clothes, scolding him.)* And you've gone and
put on the wrong trousers again. What I am going to do
with you?

VARYA: *(Softly.)* Anya's sleeping. *(Quietly opens the window.)* The
sun is up now, it isn't cold any more. Look, Mamochka:
what glorious trees! My God, the air! And the starlings are
singing!

GAEV: *(Opens another window.)* The orchard is all in white. You
haven't forgotten, Lyuba, have you? Look—that long row of
trees stretching on and on, like a silver cord, on and on, do
you remember, how it gleams on moonlit nights? You
haven't forgotten, have you?

LYUBOV ANDREEVNA: *(Looks out the window onto the orchard.)* O,
my childhood, my innocence! Once I slept in this very nursery, I'd look out on the orchard, right from here, and happiness would awaken with me, every morning, every
morning, and look, it's all the same, nothing has changed.
(Laughs with joy.) White, all white! O, my orchard! After
the dark, dreary autumn, the cold winter, you're young
again, blooming with joy, the heavenly angels have not forsaken you . . . If only this terrible weight could be lifted
from my soul, if only I could forget my past!

GAEV: Yes, and the orchard will be sold to pay off our debts,
strange, isn't it . . .

LYUBOV ANDREEVNA: Look, there's my mother, walking
through the orchard . . . all in white! *(Laughs with joy.)*
There she is.

GAEV: Where?

VARYA: God bless you, Mamochka.

LYUBOV ANDREEVNA: There's no one there, I only dreamed
it . . . Look, to the right, on the way to the summer-house,
a white sapling, bowing low, I thought it was a woman . . .

*(TROFIMOV enters, wearing a shabby, threadbare student's uniform,
and spectacles.)*

What an astonishing orchard! Masses of white blossoms, radiant blue sky . . .

TROFIMOV: Lyubov Andreevna!

(She turns and looks at him.)

480 I only came to pay my respects, I'll go, right away. *(Kisses her hand passionately.)* They told me I had to wait till morning, but I couldn't bear it any longer . . .

(LYUBOV ANDREEVNA *looks at him with bewilderment.*)

VARYA: *(In tears.)* It's Petya Trofimov . . .

TROFIMOV: Petya Trofimov, former tutor to your Grisha . . .
485 Have I really changed that much?

(LYUBOV ANDREEVNA *embraces him and weeps softly.*)

GAEV: *(Embarrassed.)* Now, now, Lyuba.

VARYA: *(Weeps.)* You see, Petya, didn't I tell you to wait till tomorrow.

LYUBOV ANDREEVNA: My Grisha . . . my little boy . . .
490 Grisha . . . son . . .

VARYA: But what can we do, Mamochka. It's God's will.

TROFIMOV: *(Gently, in tears.)* There, there . . .

LYUBOV ANDREEVNA: *(Weeps softly.)* My little boy . . . lost . . . drowned . . . Why? Why, my friend? *(Softer.)* Anya's sleep-
495 ing, and here I am, raising my voice . . . carrying on . . . So, now, Petya, tell me! Why have you grown so ugly? And so old, too!

TROFIMOV: There was an old peasant woman on the train once, she called me "a shabby-looking gentleman."

500 LYUBOV ANDREEVNA: You were just a boy then, a sweet, young student, and now look at you, you're hair's gotten thin, you wear glasses . . . Don't tell me you're still a student? *(Goes to the door.)*

TROFIMOV: And I shall be an eternal student, so it seems.

505 LYUBOV ANDREEVNA: *(Kisses her brother, then* VARYA.*)* Better go to bed now . . . You've gotten old, too, Leonid.

PISHCHIK: *(Follows her.)* Yes, time for bed . . . Ach, this gout of mine . . . I'll stay the night with you . . . Lyubov Andreevna, lovely lady, tomorrow morning, if only you would . . . two
510 hundred and forty rubles . . .

GAEV: He never gives up.

PISHCHIK: Two hundred and forty rubles . . . to pay the interest on the mortgage.

LYUBOV ANDREEVNA: But I don't have any money, really, my
515 sweet, I don't.

PISHCHIK: I'll pay you back, charming lady . . . Such a small amount . . .

LYUBOV ANDREEVNA: Oh, all right, Leonid will give it to you . . . Give it to him, Leonid.
520 GAEV: I should give it to him? Don't hold your pockets open.

LYUBOV ANDREEVNA: Give it to him, what else can we do . . . He needs it . . . He'll pay it back.

(*Exeunt* LYUBOV ANDREEVNA, TROFIMOV, PISHCHIK, *and* FIRS. GAEV, VARYA, *and* YASHA *remain.*)

GAEV: My sister just can't seem to hold on to her money. *(To* YASHA.*)* Move away, good fellow, you smell like a chicken
525 coop.

YASHA: *(With a grin.)* And you, Leonid Andreich, you haven't changed a bit.

GAEV: Beg pardon? *(To* VARYA.*)* What did he say?

VARYA: *(To* YASHA.*)* Your mother's come from the village to see you, she's been waiting since yesterday in the servants' 530 quarters . . .

YASHA: Good for her!

VARYA: Shame on you!

YASHA: Who needs her? She could have waited till tomorrow to come. *(Exits.)* 535

VARYA: Mamochka's the same as she's always been, she hasn't changed at all. If she could, she'd give away everything.

GAEV: Yes . . .

(Pause.)

If there are many remedies offered for a disease, then that means the disease is incurable. Now, I've been thinking, 540 wracking my brain, and I've got lots of remedies, oh yes, lots and lots of remedies, and you know what that means, don't you, in essence, that means I don't have any. Wouldn't it be nice, for example, if we received a large inheritance from somebody or other, wouldn't it be nice to marry our Anya off 545 to a very rich fellow, wouldn't it be nice to go to Yaroslavl and try and get some money from our aunt, the countess. Our aunty's very very rich, you know.

VARYA: *(Weeps.)* If only God would help us.

GAEV: Stop weeping. The old lady's very rich, it's true, but the 550 fact is, she doesn't like us. For one thing, my dear sister went off and married a lawyer, and not a gentleman . . .

(ANYA *appears in the doorway.*)

She didn't marry a gentleman, and you can't really say she's led a particularly conventional life. I mean, she's a good, kind person, a splendid person, and I love her very very 555 much, of course, but, whatever the extenuating circumstances may have been, let's face it, she hasn't exactly been the model of virtue. Why, you can sense it in everything about her, her slightest gesture, her movements.

VARYA: *(In a whisper.)* Anya's standing in the doorway. 560

GAEV: Beg pardon?

(Pause.)

Amazing, there's something in my right eye . . . I can't see a thing. And on Thursday, when I was at the circuit court . . .

(ANYA *enters.*)

VARYA: Why aren't you in bed, Anya?

ANYA: I can't fall asleep. I just can't. 565

GAEV: My little one. *(Kisses* ANYA'S *face, hands.)* My child . . . *(In tears.)* You're not my niece, you're my angel, you're everything to me. Believe me, believe me . . .

ANYA: I believe you, Uncle, I do. Everyone loves you, everyone reveres you . . . but, darling Uncle, you must try to be 570 quiet, really, just be quiet. What were you saying just now about my Mama, about your own sister? Why would you say such a thing?

GAEV: Yes, yes . . . *(Covers his face with her hand.)* As a matter of fact, it's terrible! My God! My God, save me! And today, I 575 made a speech before a bookcase . . . how foolish of me! And it was only after I'd finished, that I realized how foolish it was.

VARYA: It's true, Uncle dear, you should try to be quiet. Just be
580   very quiet, that's all.

ANYA: And if you're quiet, you'll feel much better, really.

GAEV: I'll be quiet. *(Kisses* ANYA's *and* VARYA's *hands.)* I'll be
    quiet. Just one small matter. On Thursday I was at the cir-
    cuit court, and, well, some people got together and started
585   talking, you know, about this, that, the other thing, and so
    on and so on, and one thing led to another, and so it seems
    that a loan might be arranged, to pay off the interest to the
    bank.

VARYA: God willing!

590 GAEV: And, on Tuesday, I'm going to have another little talk
    with them again. *(To* VARYA.*)* Stop weeping. *(To* ANYA.*)*
    Your mama will have a word with Lopakhin; he won't
    refuse her, of course . . . As for you, as soon as you've had
    your rest, off you'll go to Yaroslavl to see the countess, your
595   great-aunt. So that way, we'll mount a three-pronged
    attack—and presto! it's in the bag. We'll pay off that inter-
    est, I'm sure of it . . . *(Pops a fruit drop into his mouth.)* On
    my honor, I swear to you, if you like, this estate will not be
    sold! *(Excited.)* I swear on my happiness! I give you my
600   hand, call me a worthless good-for-nothing, a dishonorable
    fellow, if I allow it to go up for auction! I swear on my en-
    tire being!

ANYA: *(She regains her composure: she is happy.)* How good you are,
    Uncle, how wise! *(Embraces her uncle.)* Now I'm content! I'm
605   content! I'm happy, now!

(Enter FIRS.*)*

FIRS: *(Reproachfully.)* Leonid Andreich, have you no fear of God
    in you? When are you going to bed?

GAEV: In a minute, in a minute. Go on, Firs. Yes, it's all right,
    I'm quite capable of undressing myself. So, children dear,
610   night-night . . . Details tomorrow, but now, it's time for
    bed. *(Kisses* ANYA *and* VARYA.*)* I am a man of the eighties . . .
    These are not laudable times, but nevertheless, I can say
    that I've suffered greatly for my convictions in this life. It's
    not without reason that the peasants love me. One must
615   give the peasant his due! Give him his due, for . . .

ANYA: You're off again, Uncle!

VARYA: Uncle, be quiet!

FIRS: *(Angrily.)* Leonid Andreich!

GAEV: I'm coming, I'm coming . . . And so, to bed. "Off two
620   cushions into the middle. Pocket the white . . . clean shot."
    (Exits, with FIRS *shuffling behind him.)*

ANYA: Now, I'm content. I don't want to go to Yaroslavl, not
    really, I don't like my great-aunt that much, but, all the
    same, I'm content. Thanks to Uncle. *(Sits.)*

625 VARYA: We must get to bed. I know I'm going to . . . Oh, an
    awful thing happened here while you were gone. You re-
    member the old servants' quarters, well, only the old ones
    live there now: you know, Yefimyushka, Polya, Yevstigney,
    oh, and don't forget Karp . . . Anyway, they started letting
630   some homeless folks stay the night with them—I didn't say
    anything at first. But then, I hear, they're spreading this ru-
    mor, that I'd been giving orders to feed them nothing but
    dried peas. Because I was being stingy, you see . . . And all
    this coming from Yevstigney . . . So I say to myself, fine. If
635   that's the way you want it, I say, just you wait and see. So I

call for Yevstigney . . . *(Yawns.)* And he comes in . . . And
I say to him, how dare you, Yevstigney . . . you're such a
fool . . . *(Looks at* ANYA.*)* Anechka!

(Pause.)

She's asleep! *(Takes* ANYA *by the arm.)* Come to bed . . .
Come ! . . . *(Leads her.)* My darling's sleeping! Come . . . 640

(They go.)

(Far beyond the orchard, a shepherd plays on a pipe. TROFIMOV *enters, crosses the stage, and, seeing* VARYA *and* ANYA, *stops.)*

VARYA: Shh . . . She's asleep . . . fast asleep . . . Come, my
    precious.

ANYA: *(Softly, half-asleep.)* I'm so tired . . . do you hear the
    bells . . . Dearest Uncle . . . Mama and Uncle . . .

VARYA: Come, my precious, come . . . *(Exits into* ANYA's *room.)* 645

TROFIMOV: *(Tenderly.)* My sunlight! My springtime!

——— ACT TWO ———

*A field. There is a small, dilapidated old chapel, long deserted, and
beside it, a well, an old bench, and several large stones, once apparently gravestones. The road to* GAEV's *country estate is visible. To the
side, towering poplar trees loom darkly, where the cherry orchard begins. In the distance, there is a row of telegraph poles, and far beyond
that, on the horizon, is the indistinct outline of a large town, visible
only in very clear, fine weather. Soon, it will be sunset.* CHARLOTTA,
YASHA, *and* DUNYASHA *sit on the bench;* YEPIKHODOV *stands nearby
and plays the guitar; all are lost in thought.* CHARLOTTA *is wearing
an old, peaked military cap; she removes the rifle from her shoulder and
adjusts the buckle on the rifle sling.*

CHARLOTTA: *(Deep in thought.)* I have no passport, no real
    one . . . no one ever told me how old I was, not really . . .
    but I always have this feeling that I'm still very young.
    When I was a little girl, Papa and Mama traveled in a cir-
    cus, they were acrobats, good ones. And I performed the 5
    "salto-mortale," the dive of death, and all kinds of tricks.
    And when Papa and Mama died, a German lady took me in,
    she raised me, gave me lessons. "Gut." I grew up, I became
    a governess. But where I am from, and who I am—I don't
    know . . . Who were my parents, were they ever married . . . 10
    I don't know. *(Takes a cucumber out of her pocket and eats it.)* I
    don't know anything.

(Pause.)

So now I feel like talking, but to whom . . . I have no one
to talk to.

YEPIKHODOV: *(Plays guitar and sings.)* "What care I for worldly 15
    woe, / What care I for friend and foe . . ." How pleasant it
    is to play upon the mandolin!

DUNYASHA: That's a guitar, not a mandolin. *(Looks in a little
    mirror and powders her nose.)*

YEPIKHODOV: For the man, who is mad with love, it's a man- 20
    dolin. *(Sings.)* "If my true love were requited, / It would set
    my heart aglow . . ."

*(*YASHA *joins in, harmonizing.)*

CHARLOTTA: These people sing terribly . . . Phooey! Like jackals.

25 DUNYASHA: (*To* YASHA.) How blissful, to have been abroad.

YASHA: Well, of course. I'm not going to disagree with you on that one. (*Yawns, then lights a cigar.*)

YEPIKHODOV: But we know that already. Everything abroad is very well organized, and has been so for a long long time.

30 YASHA: Right.

YEPIKHODOV: I am a man of the world. I am. I read many many remarkable books. But, speaking for myself, personally, I have no clue, no clue as to what direction I, personally, want my life to take, I mean: Do I want to live, or do I want to 35 shoot myself, in the head . . . So just in case, I always carry a revolver around with me. Here it is . . . (*Shows them a revolver.*)

CHARLOTTA: I'm finished. And now, I'm leaving. (*Puts on the rifle.*) You, Yepikhodov, you are a very intelligent man and 40 also a very dangerous one; women must be mad for you. Brrr! (*Starts to leave.*) These clever people, they're all such fools, no one for me to talk to . . . Alone, all alone, I have no one . . . and who I am, why I am on this earth, no one knows . . . (*Exits, without hurrying.*)

45 YEPIKHODOV: Now. Speaking for myself, personally, again, putting all else aside, that is, if I may, when it comes to me, I mean, personally, again, I ask myself: Does fate care? No, fate doesn't care, very much as a terrible storm doesn't care about a tiny boat upon the sea. Now. Let us assume I am 50 wrong in this regard, so then, tell me, would you, please, why is it that this morning, yes, this morning, I wake up, just to give you an example, I look up, and there, sitting right on my chest, is this huge and terrifying spider . . . About 'so' big. (*Indicates with both hands.*) And then, to give 55 you yet another example, I go to pick up a glass of kvass, you know, to drink it, I look inside it, and what do I see? Possibly the most offensive species on the face of this earth—like a cockroach.

(*Pause.*)

Have you ever read Buckle?

(*Pause.*)

60   May I trouble you, Avdotya Fyodorovna, for a word or two.

DUNYASHA: Speak.

YEPIKHODOV: It would be far more desirable to speak to you in private . . . (*Sighs.*)

DUNYASHA: (*Embarrassed.*) Oh, all right . . . only first, bring me 65 my cloak . . . I left it near the cupboard . . . it's a bit chilly out . . .

YEPIKHODOV: Of course . . . Right away . . . Of course. Now I know what to do with my revolver . . . (*Takes the guitar and exits, strumming.*)

70 YASHA: Mister Disaster! He's hopeless, just between you and me. (*Yawns.*)

DUNYASHA: God forbid he should shoot himself.

(*Pause.*)

I'm so nervous, I worry all the time. I was just a girl when they took me in, you know, I'm not used to the simple life

any more, look at my hands, how lily-white they are, like a 75 young lady's. Can't you see, I've become so delicate, so fragile, so . . . so sensitive, every little thing upsets me . . . It's just awful. And if you deceive me, Yasha, I just don't know what will happen to my nerves.

YASHA: (*Kisses her.*) My little cucumber! Of course, a girl should 80 know how to behave, I can't stand a girl who doesn't know how to behave.

DUNYASHA: I've fallen madly in love with you, you are so refined, you can talk about anything.

(*Pause.*)

YASHA: (*Yawns.*) Right! . . . Now, in my opinion, if a girl falls 85 in love, that means she's immoral.

(*Pause.*)

Nice, isn't it, to smoke a cigar in the fresh, open air . . . (*Listens.*) Someone's coming . . . It's the ladies and gentlemen . . .

(DUNYASHA *embraces him impetuously.*)

Go home, pretend you've gone for a swim in the river, take 90 that path there, or else they'll run into you and think I arranged this little rendezvous. I can't have that.

DUNYASHA: (*Coughs quietly.*) I've got a headache from all this cigar smoke . . . (*Exits.*)

(YASHA *remains; he sits by the chapel.* Enter LYUBOV ANDREEVNA, GAEV, *and* LOPAKHIN.)

LOPAKHIN: You must decide, once and for all—time waits for 95 no one. The question's quite simple, you know. Will you or won't you agree to lease your land for conversion into summer homes? Answer in one word: yes or no? One word, that's all!

LYUBOV ANDREEVNA: Who has been smoking those disgusting 100 cigars here . . . (*Sits.*)

GAEV: Since they've built the railroad, it's all become so convenient. (*Sits down.*) We took a little ride into town, we had our lunch . . . "yellow into the middle pocket!" Now, if only I'd gone home first, and played one little game . . . 105

LYUBOV ANDREEVNA: You'll have plenty of time.

LOPAHKIN: One word, that's all! (*Entreating.*) Give me your answer!

GAEV: (*Yawns.*) Beg pardon?

LYUBOV ANDREEVNA: (*Looks in her purse.*) Yesterday I had so 110 much money, and today I have hardly any at all. My poor, thrifty Varya feeds everyone milk soup, the old folks in the kitchen get nothing but dried peas to eat, and I manage to let money slip right through my fingers. (*Drops her purse, gold coins scatter.*) There, you see, now I've gone and spilled 115 it. . . (*She is annoyed.*)

YASHA: I'll get them, allow me. (*Collects the coins.*)

LYUBOV ANDREEVNA: Please do, Yasha. And why on earth did I go out to lunch . . . That ridiculous restaurant of yours with the music, and the tablecloths that smell of soap . . . And 120 why drink so much, Lyonya? Why eat so much? Why talk so much? Today in the restaurant you went on and on again,

on and on . . . About the seventies, about the decadents.
And to whom? Talking to the waiters about the decadents!

125 LOPAKHIN: Yes.

GAEV: (*Waves his hand.*) I'm incorrigible, it's obvious . . . (*Irritably, to* YASHA.) What is it with you, you're always disturbing my line of vision . . .

130 YASHA: (*Laughs.*) I can't hear the sound of your voice without laughing.

GAEV: (*To his sister.*) It's either him or me . . .

LYUBOV ANDREEVNA: Go away, Yasha, go on . . .

YASHA: (*Gives* LYUBOV ANDREEVNA *her purse.*) Right away.
(*Barely contains his laughter.*) At once . . . (*Exits.*)

135 LOPAKHIN: Your estate is going to be bought by that millionaire, Deriganov. He's coming to the auction himself, they say, in person.

LYUBOV ANDREEVNA: And where did you hear that?

LOPAKHIN: They were talking about it in town.

140 GAEV: Our aunty from Yaroslavl promised to send us something, but when and how much she will send, who knows . . .

LOPAKHIN: How much is she sending? One hundred thousand? Two hundred thousand?

LYUBOV ANDREEVNA: Oh, well, . . . ten–fifteen thousand, at
145   most, and that much we can be thankful for . . .

LOPAKHIN: Forgive me, but such frivolous people as you, my friends, such strange, impractical people, I have never before met in my entire life. I'm speaking to you in the Russian language, I'm telling you that your estate is about to be
150   sold, and you simply don't understand.

LYUBOV ANDREEVNA: But what on earth are we to do? Tell us, what?

LOPAKHIN: Every day I've been telling you. Every day I've been repeating the same thing, over and over again. The cherry
155   orchard and the land must be leased for summer homes, it must be done immediately, as soon as possible—the auction is imminent! Do you understand! As soon as you decide, once and for all, about the summer homes, you'll have as much money as you'll ever want, and then you will be
160   saved.

LYUBOV ANDREEVNA: Summer homes, summer people—forgive me, please, it all sounds so vulgar.

GAEV: I agree with you, absolutely.

LOPAKHIN: Either I'm going to burst out sobbing, or scream-
165   ing, or else I'm going to fall on the ground, right here in front of you. I can't stand it any more! You're driving me mad! (*To* GAEV.) And you, you act like an old woman!

GAEV: Beg pardon?

LOPAKHIN: An old woman! (*Wants to leave.*)

170 LYUBOV ANDREEVNA: (*Frightened.*) No, don't go, please, stay, dearest. I beg of you. Who knows, perhaps we'll think of something!

LOPAKHIN: What's there to think of!

LYUBOV ANDREEVNA: Don't go, I beg of you. It's so much more
175   cheerful when you're here . . .

(*Pause.*)

I keep waiting for something to happen, as if the house were going to tumble down on top of us.

GAEV: (*Deep in thought.*) "Double into the corner pocket . . .
Croisé into the middle . . ."

LYUBOV ANDREEVNA: How we have sinned . . .   180

LOPAKHIN: What are you talking about, what sins . . .

GAEV: (*Pops a fruit drop in his mouth.*) They say I've squandered a entire fortune on fruit drops . . . (*Laughs.*)

LYUBOV ANDREEVNA: O my sins, my sins . . . I've always thrown money around, uncontrollably, like a madwoman, and I   185
married a man, who did nothing but keep us in debt. My husband died from too much champagne—he drank himself to death,—then, for my next misfortune, I fell in love with another man, I began living with him . . . and just at that time, there came my first great punishment, and what   190
a blow it dealt me—right here in this river. . . my little boy drowned, and so I fled, abroad, I simply fled, never to return, never to see this river again . . . I closed my eyes and I ran, not knowing where I was going, what I was doing, and *he* following after . . . ruthlessly, relentlessly. I bought   195
a dacha near Menton, *he* had fallen ill there, and for three years I knew no rest, neither day nor night; his illness exhausted me, wasted me, my soul withered away. And then last year, when the dacha was sold to pay off the debts, I fled again, to Paris, and there he robbed me, he left me for an-   200
other woman, I tried to poison myself . . . How stupid, how shameful . . . And suddenly I felt drawn again to Russia, to my homeland, to my daughter . . . (*Wipes away her tears.*)
Dear God, dear God, be merciful, forgive me my sins! Don't punish me any longer! (*Pulls a telegram from her pocket.*) To-   205
day, I received this from Paris . . . He begs my forgiveness, beseeches me to return . . . (*Rips up the telegram.*) There's music playing, somewhere. (*Listens.*)

GAEV: It's our celebrated Jewish orchestra. Don't you remember, four violins, flute, and contrabass.   210

LYUBOV ANDREEVNA: Does it still exist? We ought to invite them sometime, plan a little soirée.

LOPAKHIN: (*Listens.*) I don't hear anything. (*Hums softly.*)

An enterprising man, the Prussian,
He'll make a Frenchman from a Russian!   215

(*Laughs.*) What a play I saw at the theatre last night, it was very funny, really.

LYUBOV ANDREEVNA: There probably wasn't anything funny about it. Why go to the theatre to see a play! Better to see yourselves more often. How grey your lives are, how end-   220
lessly you talk.

LOPAKHIN: It's the truth. And the truth must be told, our lives are foolish . . .

(*Pause.*)

My papa was a peasant, an ignorant fool, he understood nothing, taught me nothing, he only beat me when he was   225
drunk, and always with a stick. And the fact of the matter is, I'm the same kind of ignorant fool that he was. I never learned anything, I'm ashamed of my own handwriting, it's not even human, it's more like a hoof-mark than a signature.

LYUBOV ANDREEVNA: You ought to get married, my friend.   230

LOPAKHIN: Yes . . . It's the truth.

LYUBOV ANDREEVNA: Why not to our Varya? She's a good girl.

LOPAKHIN: Yes.

LYUBOV ANDREEVNA: She's of simple origin, she works all day long, but the important thing is, she loves you. And you've   235
been fond of her for a long time now.

LOPAKHIN: Well . . . I have nothing against it . . . She's a good girl.

(Pause.)

240 GAEV: They've offered me a job at the bank. 6,000 a year . . . Have you heard?

LYUBOV ANDREEVNA: You, in a bank! Stay where you are . . .

(FIRS enters; he is carrying a coat.)

FIRS: *(To GAEV.)* Please, sir, better put this on . . . it's chilly out.

GAEV: *(Puts on the coat.)* You get on my nerves, old man.

245 FIRS: Now, there's no need for that . . . You went out this morning, without telling anyone. *(Looks him over.)*

LYUBOV ANDREEVNA: How old you've grown, Firs!

FIRS: Yes, what may I do for you?

LOPAKHIN: She said: How old you've grown!

FIRS: Well, I've lived a long time. They were marrying me off,
250 and your papa wasn't even in this world yet . . . *(Laughs.)*
Then, when the emancipation came, I was already head
valet . . . I didn't want my freedom, so I stayed with my
masters . . .

(Pause.)

I remember how glad everyone was, but what they were
255 glad about, they didn't even know themselves.

LOPAKHIN: Ah yes, the good old days. At least there was flogging.

FIRS: *(Not hearing.)* I'll say. The servants belonged to the masters, the masters belonged to the servants, but now every-
260 thing's all mixed up, you can't tell one from the other.

GAEV: Hush, Firs. Tomorrow I've got to go to town. They've
promised to introduce me to some general, he might give
us a loan on a promissory note.

LOPAKHIN: Nothing will come of it. And you won't pay off the
265 interest, rest assured.

LYUBOV ANDREEVNA: He's delirious. There are no generals, they
don't exist.

(Enter TROFIMOV, ANYA, and VARYA.)

GAEV: Ah, here they come.

ANYA: Here's Mama.

270 LYUBOV ANDREEVNA: *(Tenderly.)* Come, come . . . My darling
children . . . *(Embraces ANYA and VARYA.)* If only you knew
how much I love you both. Sit here, right next to me.

(They all get settled.)

LOPAKHIN: Our eternal student is always in the company of the
young ladies.

275 TROFIMOV: Mind your own business.

LOPAKHIN: And when he's fifty, he'll still be a student.

TROFIMOV: Stop your foolish joking.

LOPAKHIN: You're such a peculiar fellow! Why are you so angry
with me, anyway?

280 TROFIMOV: Because you won't stop bothering me.

LOPAKHIN: *(Laughs.)* Permit me to ask you, if I may, what do
you think of me?

TROFIMOV: Here is what I think of you, Yermolai Alekseich:
You are a rich man, soon you'll be a millionaire. So, in the
general scheme of things, that is, according to the laws of 285
nature, we need you, we need predatory beasts, who devour
everything which stands in their path, so in that sense you
are a necessary evil.

(All laugh.)

VARYA: Petya, you do better when you talk about astronomy.

LYUBOV ANDREEVNA: No, let's continue yesterday's conversation. 290

TROFIMOV: What about?

GAEV: About pride. Pride in man.

TROFIMOV: That. We talked about that forever, but we did not
come to any conclusion. According to your way of thinking,
there is something mystical about the proud man, an aura, 295
almost. Perhaps you are correct in your beliefs, but if you
analyze the issue clearly, without complicating things, then
why does this pride even exist, what reason can there be for
pride, if a man is not physically distinguished, if the vast
majority of mankind is coarse, stupid, or profoundly miser- 300
able. There is no time for the admiration of self. There is
only time for work.

GAEV: We're all going to die, anyway, so what difference does
it make?

TROFIMOV: Who knows? And what does it really mean—to 305
die? For all we know, man is endowed with a hundred sensibilities, and when he dies, only the five known to us perish along with him, while the other ninety-five remain
alive.

LYUBOV ANDREEVNA: How intelligent you are, Petya! . . . 310

LOPAKHIN: *(Ironically.)* Yes, terribly!

TROFIMOV: Mankind marches onward, ever onward, strengthen-
ing his skills, his capacities. All that has up until now been
beyond his reach may one day be attainable, only he must
work, indeed, he must do everything in his power to help 315
those who seek the truth. In Russia, however, very few people actually do work. The vast majority of the intelligentsia,
as I know them, do nothing, pursue nothing, and, meanwhile, have no predisposition whatsoever to work, they're
completely incapable of it. They call themselves 'the intelli- 320
gentsia,' and yet they address their servants with disrespect,
they treat the peasants as if they were animals, they're dismal students, they're poorly educated, they never read serious literature, they're absolutely idle, they don't do a thing
except sit around talking about science and art, about which 325
they know nothing at all. And they're all so grim looking,
they have tense, taut faces, they only talk about 'important
things,' they spend all their time philosophizing, and meanwhile, right before their very eyes, the workers live atro-
ciously, eat abominably, sleep without bedding, thirty-forty 330
to a room, together with bedbugs, stench, dankness, depravity . . . And so it seems that all this lofty talk is simply
meant to conceal the truth from themselves and others.
Show me, please, where are the day nurseries, about which
they speak so much and so often, where are the public read- 335
ing rooms? They only write about them in novels, they
never become a reality, never. There is only filth, vulgarity,
barbarism . . . I dread their serious countenances, their serious conversations, I despise them. Better to be silent!

340 LOPAKHIN: You know, I get up before five every morning, I
work from dawn until night, I deal with money, constantly,
mine and others, and yes, I see how people really are. You
only have to try to get something done to realize how few
honest, decent people there are in this world. Sometimes,
345 when I can't fall asleep, I lie there thinking: "Dear Lord,
you have given us the vast forests, the boundless plains, the
endless horizons, and we who live here on this earth, we
should be true giants . . ."
LYUBOV ANDREEVNA: What good are giants . . . They're
350 very nice in fairy tales, you know, but in true life, they're
terrifying.

(YEPIKHODOV *crosses upstage, playing the guitar.*)

(*Pensively.*) There goes Yepikhodov.

ANYA: (*Pensively.*) There goes Yepikhodov.
GAEV: The sun has set, ladies and gentlemen.
355 TROFIMOV: Yes.
GAEV: (*Softly, as if reciting.*) O nature, wondrous nature, you
shine on, radiant and eternal, beauteous and indifferent,
you whom we call mother, you embody birth and death,
you create and you destroy, you . . .
360 VARYA: (*Imploring.*) Uncle, dear!
ANYA: Not again, Uncle!
TROFIMOV: You're better off "pocketing the yellow . . ."
GAEV: I'll be quiet, I'll be quiet.

(*All sit, deep in thought. Silence. Only* FIRS's *muttering can be heard.
Suddenly from far, far away, a sound is heard, as if coming from the
sky, the sound of a breaking string, dying away in the distance, a
mournful sound.*)

LYUBOV ANDREEVNA: What was that?
365 LOPAKHIN: Don't know. Somewhere far away, deep in the
mines, a bucket broke loose and fell . . . But somewhere
very far away.
GAEV: Or a bird of some kind . . . a heron, perhaps.
TROFIMOV: Or an owl . . .
370 LYUBOV ANDREEVNA: (*Shudders.*) Disturbing, somehow.

(*Pause.*)

FIRS: Right before the time of trouble, it was the same thing:
The owl screeched, and the samovar hissed, it never stopped.
GAEV: What time of trouble?
FIRS: Why, before the emancipation of the serfs.

(*Pause.*)

375 LYUBOV ANDREEVNA: Let's go, dear friends, shall we, it's get-
ting dark. (*To* ANYA.) You've got tears in your eyes . . .
What is it, my pet? (*Embraces her.*)
ANYA: I'm fine, Mama. It's nothing.
TROFIMOV: Someone's coming.

(*A* PASSERBY *appears in a shabby, white cap and a coat; he is slightly
drunk.*)

380 PASSERBY: Permit me to inquire, may I pass through here to get
to the train station?

GAEV: You may. Go down that road.
PASSERBY: I'm deeply grateful. (*Coughs.*) What superb weather
we're having . . . (*Recites.*) "My brother, my suffering
brother . . . Come down to the Volga, whose moan . . ." (*To* 385
VARYA.) Mademoiselle, please, give a poor starving Russian
thirty kopeks. . .

(VARYA *cries out in fear.*)

LOPAKHIN: (*Angrily.*) This has gone too far!
LYUBOV ANDREEVNA: (*Stunned.*) Here . . . take this . . . (*Searches
in her purse.*) I have no silver . . . Never mind, here's a gold 390
piece . . .
PASSERBY: I'm deeply grateful! (*Exits.*)

(*Laughter.*)

VARYA: (*Frightened.*) I'm leaving . . . I'm leaving . . . Oh,
Mamochka, the servants at home have nothing to eat, and
you gave him a gold piece. 395
LYUBOV ANDREEVNA: What are you going to do with me, I'm
such a silly fool! I'll give you everything I have. Yermolai
Alekseich, please, lend me some more money! . . .
LOPAKHIN: Yes, madam.
LYUBOV ANDREEVNA: Come, ladies and gentlemen, time to 400
go. Oh, yes, Varya, we've just made a match for you. Con-
gratulations.
VARYA: (*In tears.*) Mama, you musn't joke about that.
LOPAKHIN: "Oh-phel-i-a, get thee to a nunnery . . ."
GAEV: It's been so long since I've played a game of billiards, my 405
hands are shaking.
LOPAKHIN: "Oh-phel-i-a, o nymph, remember me in thy
prayers!"
LYUBOV ANDREEVNA: Come, ladies and gentlemen. It's almost
suppertime. 410
VARYA: How he frightened me. My heart is pounding.
LOPAKHIN: May I remind you, ladies and gentlemen: On the
twenty-second of August, the cherry orchard will be sold.
Think about it! Think! . . .

(*They all leave, except* TROFIMOV *and* ANYA.)

ANYA: (*Laughing.*) The stranger frightened Varya off, thank 415
goodness, now we're alone.
TROFIMOV: Varya's afraid we'll fall madly in love, she hasn't let
us out of her sight for days. She's so narrow-minded, she
can't understand we're above love. To overcome all obstacles, real and imagined, which stand in the path of freedom 420
and happiness,—that is our quest in life. Onward! We set
forth, undaunted, toward that star, burning bright in the
distance! Onward! Don't fall behind, my friends!
ANYA: (*Clasps her hands.*) How beautifully you talk!

(*Pause.*)

It's glorious here today! 425
TROFIMOV: Yes, the weather is amazing.
ANYA: What have you done to me, Petya, why don't I love the
cherry orchard, as I did, once? I loved it so tenderly, I
couldn't imagine any other place on earth more lovely than
our orchard. 430

TROFIMOV: All Russia is our orchard. The land is vast and beautiful, there are many marvelous places in it.

(Pause.)

Just think, Anya: Your grandfather, your great-grandfather,
and his forefathers before him, all were serf-owners, they all
435 owned living souls, so isn't it possible, then, that in every
blossom, every leaf, every tree trunk in the orchard, a human soul now gazes down upon us, can't you hear their
voices . . . To own human souls—can't you see how this has
transformed each and every one of us, those who have lived
440 before and those who live today, so that you, your mother,
your uncle, all of you, are no longer aware that you are alive
at the expense of others, at the expense of those whom you
would not even permit beyond your front hall . . . We have
fallen behind, by two hundred years or so, at least, we have
445 nothing left, absolutely nothing, no clear understanding of
the past, we only philosophize, complain about our boredom, or drink vodka. And it's all so clear, can't you see, that
to begin a new life, to live in the present, we must first redeem our past, put an end to it, and redeem it we shall, but
450 only with suffering, only with extraordinary, everlasting
toil and suffering. You must understand this, Anya.

ANYA: The house, in which we live, is no longer our house, and
I shall leave it, I give you my word.

TROFIMOV: If you have the key, throw it in the well and run,
455 run far, far away. Be free, like the wind.

ANYA: *(Ecstatic.)* How wonderfully you say it!

TROFIMOV: Believe me, Anya, believe me! I'm not even thirty
yet, I'm young, I'm still a student, and yet, I've endured so
much! Come winter, I'm hungry, sick, anxiety-ridden,
460 poverty-stricken, like a beggar, and wherever fate carries
me, there I shall be! And yet, all the while, every waking
moment, day and night, my soul is filled with an indescribable premonition, a vision. A vision of happiness,
Anya, I can see it now . . .

465 ANYA: *(Pensively.)* The moon is rising.

*(YEPIKHODOV is heard playing the guitar, the same melancholy song
as before. The moon is rising. Somewhere near the poplars, VARYA is
looking for ANYA and calling: "Anya! Where are you?")*

TROFIMOV: Yes, the moon is rising.

(Pause.)

Here comes happiness, here it comes, closer and closer, I can
already hear its footsteps. And if we don't see it, if we don't
recognize it, then what does it matter? Others will!

(VARYA's voice: "Anya! Where are you?")

470 Varya, again! *(Angrily.)* It's disgraceful!

ANYA: I know! Let's go down to the river. It's lovely there.

TROFIMOV: Let's go.

(They go.)

(VARYA's voice: "Anya! Anya!")

—— ACT THREE ——

*The drawing room, separated from the ballroom by an archway.
A chandelier burns brightly. A Jewish orchestra, the same one referred
to in Act II, is heard playing in the entrance hall. It is evening. In
the ballroom, the crowd is dancing the 'grand-rond.' The voice of
SIMEONOV-PISHCHIK is heard: "Promenade à une paire!" The couples
dance through the drawing room, as follows: first PISHCHIK and
CHARLOTTA IVANOVNA; then TROFIMOV and LYUBOV ANDREEVNA;
then ANYA and the POST OFFICE CLERK; then VARYA and the STATIONMASTER, and so on. VARYA is weeping quietly and wipes away
her tears as she dances. DUNYASHA is in the last couple. They dance
around the drawing room. PISHCHIK calls out: "Grand-rond, balancez!" and "Les cavaliers à genoux et remerciez vos dames!"*

FIRS, *wearing a tailcoat, carries a tray with seltzer water.* PISHCHIK
and TROFIMOV *enter the drawing room.*

PISHCHIK: I have high blood pressure, I've had two strokes already, it's difficult for me to dance, but, you know what
they say: "If you run in a pack, whether you bark or not,
you'd better wag your tail." Never you mind, I'm as healthy
as a horse. My dear departed father, joker that he was, God   5
rest his soul, always used to say, on the subject of our ancestry, that the Simeonov-Pishchiks are descended from the
same horse that Caligula appointed to the Senate . . . *(Sits.)*
The only trouble is: We don't have any money! And
you know what they say: "A hungry dog believes only in   10
meat . . ." *(Snores and suddenly wakes up.)* And that's my
problem . . . all I ever dream about is money . . .

TROFIMOV: As a matter of fact, you do bear some resemblance
to a horse.

PISHCHIK: And why not . . . a horse is a good animal . . . you   15
can get a very good price for a horse, you know . . .

(In the next room, the sound of a billiard game is heard. VARYA *appears in the archway to the ballroom.)*

TROFIMOV: *(Teasing.)* Madame Lopakhina! Madame Lopakhina! . . .

VARYA: *(Angrily.)* The shabby-looking gentleman!

TROFIMOV: Yes, I'm a shabby-looking gentleman, and proud   20
of it!

VARYA: *(Bitterly.)* We've gone and hired the musicians, now
how are we going to pay for them? *(Exits.)*

TROFIMOV: *(To* PISHCHIK.*)* Think about it: The energy you've
wasted your whole life through in search of money to pay   25
off the interest on your debts, if only you'd spent that energy elsewhere, then, no doubt, you could have changed the
world.

PISHCHIK: Nietzsche . . . the philosopher . . . the supreme, the
exalted . . . a man of the greatest genius, this man once said,   30
in his own writings, that it's all right to forge banknotes.

TROFIMOV: Have you ever read Nietzsche?

PISHCHIK: Well . . . Dashenka told me that one. And anyway,
given my situation, even if I could forge banknotes . . . Day
after tomorrow, I owe a payment of three hundred and ten   35
rubles . . . I've already scraped up one hundred and thirty
so far . . . *(Searches in his pockets, anxiously.)* My money's
gone! I've lost my money! *(In tears.)* Where is my money!

(*Overjoyed.*) Here it is, in the lining . . . Look, I even broke
40   into a sweat . . .

(*Enter* LYUBOV ANDREEVNA *and* CHARLOTTA IVANOVNA.)

LYUBOV ANDREEVNA: (*Humming the 'lezginka.'*) Why has Leonid
been gone so long? What is he doing in town? (*To*
DUNYASHA.) Dunyasha, offer the musicians some tea . . .
TROFIMOV: The auction didn't take place, in all probability.
45 LYUBOV ANDREEVNA: And of all times to invite the musicians
and give a ball . . . Oh well, never mind . . . (*Sits and hums
softly.*)
CHARLOTTA: (*Gives* PISHCHIK *a deck of cards.*) Here is a deck of
cards, think of a card, any card.
50 PISHCHIK: I've got one.
CHARLOTTA: Now shuffle the deck. Very good. Give it to me,
oh my dear Mr. Pishchik, Eins, zwei, drei! Now go look, it's
in your side pocket . . .
PISHCHIK: (*Takes a card from his side pocket.*) The eight of spades,
55   you're absolutely right! (*Amazed.*) Imagine that!
CHARLOTTA: (*Holds out the deck of cards in her palm to* TROFIMOV.)
Tell me, quickly, which card is the top card?
TROFIMOV: What? Oh, the queen of spades.
CHARLOTTA: Right! (*To* PISHCHIK.) So? Which card is the top
60   card?
PISHCHIK: The ace of hearts.
CHARLOTTA: Right! (*Claps her hands, and the deck of cards disap-
pears.*) My, what lovely weather we're having today!

(*A mysterious female voice answers her as if coming from underneath
the floor: "Oh yes, the weather is splendid, dear lady."*)

You are the image of perfection . . .

(*Voice: "And you I like very much too, dear lady."*)

65 STATIONMASTER: (*Applauds.*) Madame Ventriloquist, bravo!
PISHCHIK: (*Amazed.*) Imagine that! Most enchanting Charlotta
Ivanovna . . . I'm head-over-heels in love . . .
CHARLOTTA: In love? (*Shrugs her shoulders.*) How could you possibly be in love? "Guter Mensch, aber schlechter Musikant."
70 TROFIMOV: (*Claps* PISHCHIK *on the shoulder.*) Well done, old
horse . . .
CHARLOTTA: Your attention please, for one more trick. (*Gets a
lap robe from a chair.*) Here is a very lovely lap robe, I wish
to sell it . . . (*Shakes it.*) Doesn't anyone wish to buy it?
75 PISHCHIK: (*Amazed.*) Imagine that!
CHARLOTTA: Eins, zwei, drei! (*Quickly lifts the lap robe.*)

(ANYA *appears behind the lap robe; she curtsies, runs to her mother, embraces her, and runs out into the ballroom, amidst general delight.*)

LYUBOV ANDREEVNA: (*Applauds.*) Bravo, bravo! . . .
CHARLOTTA: Once more! Eins, zwei, drei! (*Lifts the lap robe.*)

(VARYA *appears behind the lap robe; she bows.*)

PISHCHIK: (*Amazed.*) Imagine that!
80 CHARLOTTA: The end! (*Throws the lap robe over* PISHCHIK, *curtsies,
and runs out into the ballroom.*)
PISHCHIK: (*Hurries after her.*) Sorceress . . . how did you do it?
How? (*Exits.*)

LYUBOV ANDREEVNA: And Leonid is still not back. What can he
be doing in town this long, I don't understand it! Surely 85
everything is over by now, either the estate has been sold or
else the auction never took place, one or the other, so why
must we be kept in the dark forever!
VARYA: (*Attempting to console her.*) Uncle has bought it, I'm sure
of it. 90
TROFIMOV: (*Sarcastically.*) Yes.
VARYA: Great-aunt sent him power of attorney to buy the estate
in her name and transfer the mortgage to her. She did it for
Anya. And Uncle will buy it, with God's help, I'm sure of it.
LYUBOV ANDREEVNA: Great-aunt in Yaroslavl sent 50,000 to 95
buy the estate in her name because she doesn't trust
us,—and that wasn't even enough to pay the interest. (*Covers her face with her hands.*) Today my destiny will be decided, my destiny . . .
TROFIMOV: (*Teasing* VARYA.) Madame Lopakhina! 100
VARYA: (*Angrily.*) The eternal student! Twice you've been expelled from the university.
LYUBOV ANDREEVNA: Why are you so angry, Varya? He's teasing you about Lopakhin, but what does it matter? If you
want to—marry Lopakhin, he's a fine man, a fascinating 105
man. And if you don't want to—don't; no one is forcing you
to, darling . . .
VARYA: I take this matter very seriously, Mamochka, I must tell
you. He is a good man, I like him, I do.
LYUBOV ANDREEVNA: Then marry him. What are you waiting 110
for, I don't understand!
VARYA: But Mamochka, I can't propose to him myself. For two
years now everyone's been talking to me about him, everyone, and either he says nothing, or else he jokes about it. I
understand. He's busy getting rich, he's preoccupied with 115
his affairs, he has no time for me. Oh, if only I had money,
only a little, a hundred rubles even, I'd give up everything,
I'd run away as far as I could. I'd enter a convent.
TROFIMOV: Blessings on you!
VARYA: (*To* TROFIMOV.) A student's supposed to be intelligent! 120
(*Gently, in tears.*) How ugly you've grown, Petya, and how
old, too! (*To* LYUBOV ANDREEVNA, *no longer crying.*) I simply
can't live without work, Mamochka. I must be doing something, every minute.

(*Enter* YASHA.)

YASHA: (*Hardly able to contain his laughter.*) Yepikhodov has bro- 125
ken a billiard cue! . . . (*Exits.*)
VARYA: Why is Yepikhodov here? Who allowed him to play
billiards? I don't understand these people . . . (*Exits.*)
LYUBOV ANDREEVNA: Don't tease her, Petya, can't you see how
miserable she is. 130
TROFIMOV: She's overbearing, that's what she is . . . always poking her nose into other people's business. She hasn't given
Anya and me a moment's peace all summer, she's afraid we
might fall in love. What business is it of hers, anyway? And
how could she even think that of me, I'm far beyond such 135
vulgarity. We are above love!
LYUBOV ANDREEVNA: And I suppose that means I must be beneath love. (*Tremendously agitated.*) Why isn't Leonid back
yet? I only want to know: Is the estate sold or isn't it? This
terrible business has gone too far, I don't know what to 140

think any more, I'm at my wits' end . . . I might scream any
minute . . . I might do something foolish. Save me, Petya.
Say something, anything . . .

TROFIMOV: Whether the estate is sold today or not—does it re-
145   ally matter? It's over, it's been so for a long time, there's no
turning back again, that path is long overgrown. Face it,
dear friend. You mustn't delude yourself any longer, for
once in your life you must look the truth straight in the eye.

LYUBOV ANDREEVNA: What truth? Oh, yes, of course, you see
150   what is true and what is not true, while I have lost my vision, I see nothing. You boldly solve all the problems of the
world, don't you, but tell me, my darling, isn't that because
you're still so young, because you haven't even suffered
through one of life's problems yet, not even one? You boldly
155   look to the future, but isn't that because you see nothing so
terrible lying ahead, because life is still safely hidden from
your young eyes? You have more courage, more character,
more honesty than any of us, so then why not have compassion, find it, somewhere in a corner of your heart, have
160   mercy on me. I was born here, my mother and father lived
here, my grandfather, too, I love this house, I can't comprehend a life without the cherry orchard, and if it must be
sold, then sell me with it . . . (Embraces TROFIMOV, kisses him
on the forehead.) My son drowned here . . . (Weeps.) Have pity
165   on me, my good, kind fellow.

TROFIMOV: You know I do, with all my heart.

LYUBOV ANDREEVNA: Yes, but there must be another way to say
it, another way . . . (Takes out a handkerchief, a telegram falls
on the floor.) My soul is so heavy today, you can't possibly
170   imagine. There is such a din here, I'm trembling with each
and every sound, trembling all over, but I can't be alone, the
silence would be terrifying. Don't judge me, Petya . . . I
love you, as if you were my own child. And I'd gladly let
you marry Anya, I would, I swear to you, only first you
175   must finish your education, darling, get your degree. You
don't do a thing, you just let fate carry you from place to
place, and that's such a strange way to live . . . Isn't it?
Well? And you simply must do something about that
beard, to make it grow, somehow . . . (Bursts out laughing.)
180   How funny-looking you are!

TROFIMOV: (Picks up the telegram.) I don't wish to be handsome.

LYUBOV ANDREEVNA: It's a telegram from Paris. Every day I receive one. Yesterday, and today, too. That terrible man is ill
again, he's in trouble again . . . He begs my forgiveness, he
185   beseeches me to return to him, I really ought to be going to
Paris, to be near him. You should see your face now, Petya,
so severe, so judgmental, but, really, what am I to do, darling, tell me, what can I do, he's ill, he's alone, unhappy,
and who will take care of him, who will keep him from
190   harm, who will nurse him through his illness? Oh, why
hide it, why keep silent, I love him, it's the truth. I love
him, I love him . . . He is the stone around my neck, and I
shall sink with him to the bottom, and how I love this
stone, I can't live without it! (Presses TROFIMOV's hand.)
195   Don't think ill of me, Petya, and don't speak, please, not a
word . . .

TROFIMOV: (In tears.) Forgive me for saying it, but for God's
sake: This man robbed you, he cleaned you out!

LYUBOV ANDREEVNA: No, no, no, you mustn't talk like that . . .
200   (Covers her ears.)

TROFIMOV: He's an absolute scoundrel, and you're the only one
who doesn't know it! A petty thief, a good-for-nothing . . .

LYUBOV ANDREEVNA: (With controlled anger.) And you're
twenty-six or twenty-seven years old, and still a schoolboy!

TROFIMOV: So be it!   205

LYUBOV ANDREEVNA: You're supposed to be a man, at your age
you're supposed to understand how lovers behave. Why
don't you know this by now . . . why haven't you fallen in
love yourself? (Angrily.) Yes, yes! You and all your talk
about purity . . . why, you're nothing but a prude, that's   210
what you are, an eccentric, a freak . . .

TROFIMOV: (Horrified.) What is she saying!

LYUBOV ANDREEVNA: "I am above love." You're not above love,
no, as Firs says, you're pathetic! At your age, not to have a
lover! . . .   215

TROFIMOV: (Horrified.) This is terrible! What is she saying?!
(Rushes out into the ballroom, holding his head.) This is terrible
. . . I can't bear it, I'm leaving . . . (Exits, but returns again
immediately.) It's all over between us! (Exits into the front
hall.)   220

LYUBOV ANDREEVNA: (Calls after him.) Petya, wait! Don't be
silly, I was only joking! Petya!

(In the front hall, someone is heard dashing down the stairs, and suddenly falling the rest of the way with a crash. ANYA and VARYA cry
out, but then, almost immediately, laughter is heard.)

What happened?

(ANYA runs in.)

ANYA: (Laughing.) Petya fell down the stairs! (Runs out.)

LYUBOV ANDREEVNA: What a peculiar fellow that Petya is . . .   225

(The STATIONMASTER stands in the middle of the ballroom, and starts
to recite a poem: 'The Fallen Woman' by Alexey Konstantinovich
Tolstoy. Everyone stops to listen, but after a few lines, the strains of a
waltz are heard coming from the front hall, and the recitation is interrupted. Everyone dances. TROFIMOV, ANYA, VARYA, and LYUBOV
ANDREEVNA pass through from the entrance hall.)

Petya . . . my pure Petya . . . I beg your forgiveness . . .
Come, dance with me . . . (Dances with him.)

(ANYA and VARYA dance together. FIRS enters, and places his cane near
the side door. YASHA also enters, and watches the dancing.)

YASHA: So, what's new, grandpa?

FIRS: I don't feel very well. In the old days, we used to have generals, barons, admirals dancing at our balls; nowadays we   230
have to send for the postal clerk and the stationmaster, and
even they come reluctantly. And I'm getting weaker, somehow. In the old days, when anyone of us fell ill, my old
master—that would be their grandfather—he would treat
us all with sealing wax. I've taken a dose of sealing wax   235
every day for twenty years now, even more, who knows; perhaps that's why I'm still alive.

YASHA: You get on my nerves, grandpa. (Yawns.) Maybe it's
time for you to kick the bucket.

FIRS: And you're a pathetic fool, that's what you are. (Mumbles.) 240

(TROFIMOV and LYUBOV ANDREEVNA *dance in the ballroom, and then in the drawing room.)*

LYUBOV ANDREEVNA: "Merci." Let me sit down . . . *(Sits.)* I'm exhausted.

(Enter ANYA.*)*

ANYA: *(Agitated.)* There's a man out in the kitchen, he was just saying that the cherry orchard was sold today.
245 LYUBOV ANDREEVNA: To whom?
ANYA: He didn't say. He left. *(Dances with* TROFIMOV.*)*

(Both exit into the ballroom.)

YASHA: Some old fellow jabbering, that's all. A stranger.
FIRS: And Leonid Andreich is still not here, he's still not back yet. All he has on is a lightweight overcoat, one for in-
250 between seasons, he's bound to catch cold. Oh, these young people nowadays!
LYUBOV ANDREEVNA: I think I'm going to die. Go, Yasha, hurry, find out to whom it was sold.
YASHA: Oh, he left a long time ago, that old fellow. *(Laughs.)*
255 LYUBOV ANDREEVNA: *(Slightly annoyed.)* And what are you laughing about? What's so funny?
YASHA: That Yepikhodov, he's a clown. The man is pitiful. "Mister Disaster."
LYUBOV ANDREEVNA: Firs, if the estate is sold, where will you
260 go?
FIRS: Wherever you tell me, that's where I'll go.
LYUBOV ANDREEVNA: Why do you look like that? Are you ill? You should be in bed, you know . . .
FIRS: Yes . . . *(With a grin.)* I'll go to bed, and who will serve,
265 who will manage everything? Hm? One servant for the whole household.
YASHA: *(To* LYUBOV ANDREEVNA.*)* Lyubov Andreevna! One small request, allow me, please! If you go to Paris again, take me with you, I beg of you. I can't stay here any more,
270 it's absolutely impossible. *(Looks around, in a low voice.)* What can I say, you see for yourself, this is an ignorant country, the people are immoral, and anyway, life here is boring, the food they give you in the kitchen is disgusting, and you have Firs wandering around everywhere, muttering
275 all kinds of nonsense. Take me with you, I beg of you!

(Enter PISHCHIK.*)*

PISHCHIK: May I have the pleasure . . . a little waltz, most charming lady . . .

*(*LYUBOV ANDREEVNA *joins him.)*

But, don't forget, one hundred eighty rubles, enchanting lady . . . That, I'll take . . . *(They dance.)* One hundred and
280 eighty sweet little rubles . . .

(They cross into the ballroom.)

YASHA: *(Sings softly.)* "O, do you know how my heart is yearning . . ."

(In the ballroom, a figure in a grey top hat and checkered trousers waves her hands and jumps up and down; there are cries of: "Bravo, Charlotta Ivanovna!")

DUNYASHA: *(Stops to powder her face.)* The mistress told me to dance—too many gentlemen, too few ladies,—but now my head is spinning from too much waltzing, my heart is pound- 285 ing, and, do you know what else, Firs Nikolaevich, the post-master just told me something that took my breath away.

(The music dies down.)

FIRS: What did he say?
DUNYASHA: "You," he said, "are like a little flower."
YASHA: *(Yawns.)* What ignorance . . . *(Exits.)*   290
DUNYASHA: "A little flower" . . . I'm such a sensitive young woman, you know, I adore a few tender words.
FIRS: You'll get yourself into a lot of trouble.

(Enter YEPIKHODOV.*)*

YEPIKHODOV: Avdotya Fyodorovna, you keep avoiding me . . . what am I, some sort of insect? *(Sighs.)* Ach, life!   295
DUNYASHA: Yes, what may I do for you?
YEPIKHODOV: And no doubt, probably, you're right. Of course. *(Sighs.)* Who can blame you. And yet, look at it from my point, of view, I mean, if I may say so myself, and I shall, so excuse me, but you have reduced me to a complete state of 300 mind. Now I know my destiny in life, every day some new disaster befalls me, and have I accepted this?—yes, I have, I look upon my fate with a smile. You have given me your word, and though . . .
DUNYASHA: Can we have our little talk later, please? Leave me 305 alone now. I'm in a fantasy. *(Plays with her fan.)*
YEPIKHODOV: A new day, a new disaster, and excuse me, I just keep smiling, I even laugh, sometimes.

(Enter VARYA *from the ballroom.)*

VARYA: You still haven't left yet, Semyon? Who do you think you are, really. *(To* DUNYASHA.*)* Get out of here, Dunyasha. 310 *(To* YEPIKHODOV.*)* First you play billiards and you break a cue, then you parade around the drawing room like a guest.
YEPIKHIDOV: You should not reprimand me. Excuse me.
VARYA: I'm not reprimanding you, I'm telling you. All you do is float from one place to the next, you don't do a blessed bit 315 of work. Why we keep you as clerk, God only knows.
YEPIKHODOV: *(Offended.)* Whether I work, or float, or eat, or play billiards, for that matter, excuse me, but that's a sub-ject of discussion only for our elders.
VARYA: How dare you speak to me like that! *(Enraged.)* How 320 dare you? Do you mean to tell me I don't know what I'm doing? Get out of here! This minute!
YEPIKHODOV: *(Cowering.)* Excuse me, may I ask that you ex-press yourself in a more delicate fashion?
VARYA: *(Besides herself.)* Get out, this minute! Out!   325

(He goes to the door, she follows him.)

"Mister Disaster!" Never set foot in here again, do you hear! I never want to lay eyes on you!

*(*YEPIKHODOV *has exited; from behind the door, his voice is heard: "I am going to file a complaint against you.")*

So, you're think you're coming back, eh? *(Grabs the cane, which* FIRS *has left by the door.)* Come on . . . come on . . .

330   come on, I'll show you . . . So, are you coming back? Are
you? This is for you, then . . . (Swings the cane.)

(Just at this moment LOPAKHIN enters.)

LOPAKHIN: I humbly thank you.
VARYA: (Angrily and sarcastically.) Sorry!
LOPAKHIN: Please, it's nothing. I'm most grateful for the warm
335   reception.
VARYA: Don't mention it. (She turns to go, then looks around and
asks, meekly.) I didn't hurt you, did I?
LOPAKHIN: No, of course not, it's nothing. Just a bump, an
enormous one, that's all.

(Voices in the ballroom: "Lopakhin has returned! Yermolai Alekseich!")

340   PISHCHIK: Well, well, well, and speaking of the devil! . . .
(Kisses LOPAKHIN.) I smell a touch of brandy, my dear,
good fellow, yes, I do! And we've been celebrating here,
too!

(Enter LYUBOV ANDREEVNA.)

LYUBOV ANDREEVNA: Yermolai Alekseich, you're back. Why
345   did it take you so long? Where is Leonid?
LOPAKHIN: Leonid Andreich returned with me, he's coming . . .
LYUBOV ANDREEVNA: (Upset.) So? Was there an auction? Tell me!
LOPAKHIN: (Disconcerted, afraid to reveal his excitement.) The auction was over at four o'clock . . . We missed the train, we
350   had to wait till nine-thirty. (Sighs heavily.) Oh! My head is
spinning . . .

(Enter GAEV. In his right hand he carries some packages; he wipes
away the tears with his left hand.)

LYUBOV ANDREEVNA: Lyonya, what is it? Lyonya? (Impatiently,
in tears.) Tell me, quickly, for God's sake . . .
GAEV: (Doesn't answer her, simply waves his hands; weeping, to FIRS.)
355   Here, take it . . . anchovies, and some kerch herring . . . I
haven't had a thing to eat all day . . . What I have lived
through!

(The door to the billiard room is open; the clicking of billiard balls is
heard, and YASHA's voice: "Seven and eighteen!" GAEV's expression
changes; he is no longer crying.)

I'm terribly tired. Help me change my clothes, Firs. (Exits
through the ballroom to his room, FIRS follows behind.)
360   PISHCHIK: What happened at the auction? Tell us! Please!
LYUBOV ANDREEVNA: Is the cherry orchard sold?
LOPAKHIN: It is sold.
LYUBOV ANDREEVNA: Who bought it?
LOPAKHIN: I bought it.

(Pause. LYUBOV ANDREEVNA is stunned; she might have fallen, were
she not standing near an armchair and table. VARYA takes the keys off
her belt, throws them on the floor in the middle of the drawing room,
and exits.)

365   I bought it! Wait, ladies and gentlemen, bear with me,
please, my head is spinning, I can't speak . . . (Laughs.) We
arrived at the auction, and Deriganov was already there.

Leonid Andreich only had 15,000, so right away Deriganov
bid 30,000 over and above the debt on the mortgage. I saw
how it was going, so I decided to take him on, I bid forty.   370
And he bid forty-five. Then I bid fifty-five. You see—he'd
raise it by five, I'd raise it by ten . . . And then, it was all
over. I bid ninety over and above the debt, and that was it,
it went to me. And now, the cherry orchard is mine! Mine!
(Roars with laughter.) My God, ladies and gentlemen, the   375
cherry orchard is mine! Tell me that I'm drunk, that I'm out
of my mind, that I've made it all up . . . (Stamps his feet.)
Don't you laugh at me! If only my father and my grandfather could get up from their graves and witness all these
events, how their Yermolai, their ignorant little Yermolai,   380
the one who was beaten, the one who ran barefoot in the
bitter winter, how this same little Yermolai bought the estate, the most beautiful estate in the world. I bought the estate, where my grandfather and my father were slaves,
where they were forbidden to set foot in the kitchen. No,   385
I'm dreaming, I'm hallucinating, it's only an illusion . . .
a figment of the imagination, shrouded in a cloak of mystery . . . (Picks up the keys, smiles tenderly.) She threw down
the keys, she's saying she's not the mistress of the house any
more . . . (Jingles the keys.) Ah, well, what does it matter.   390

(The orchestra can be heard tuning up.)

Eh, musicians, play, I want to hear you play! Everyone,
come and see, how Yermolai Lopakhin will take an axe out
into the cherry orchard, and all the trees will come crashing
to the ground! And we'll build summer homes, and our
grandchildren and great grandchildren will see a new   395
life . . . Let's have music, play!

(The music plays. LYUBOV ANDREEVNA lowers herself into a chair
and weeps bitterly.)

(Reproachfully.) Why, why didn't you listen to me? My,
poor, dear friend, you'll never get it back now, never. (In
tears.) Oh, the sooner all this is behind us, the sooner we can
change our chaotic lives, our absurd, unhappy lives.   400
PISHCHIK: (Takes him by the hand, in a low voice.) She is weeping.
Come into the ballroom, let's leave her alone . . . Come . . .
(Takes him by the hand and leads him into the ballroom.)
LOPAKHIN: What's going on here? Let there be music! Loud,
the way I want it! Let everything be the way I want it!   405
(With irony.) Here comes the new master, the owner of the
cherry orchard! (Accidentally shoves against a table, almost
turning over a candelabrum.) I can pay for it all, for every-
thing! (Exits with PISHCHIK.)

(There is no one left in the ballroom or the drawing room, except
LYUBOV ANDREEVNA, who is sitting, huddled over weeping bitterly.
The music plays softly. ANYA and TROFIMOV rush in. ANYA goes to
her mother and kneels before her. TROFIMOV stays at the entrance to
the ballroom.)

ANYA: Mama! . . . Mama, are you crying? My dear, good, kind   410
Mama, my beautiful Mama, I love you . . . I bless you. The
cherry orchard is sold, it's gone, it's true, it's true, but don't
cry, Mama, you still have your whole life before you to live,
and your pure and beautiful soul . . . Come with me, come,

415   my darling, away from here, come! . . . We'll plant a new
orchard, more glorious than this one, you'll see, you'll understand, and joy, a deep, peaceful, gentle joy will settle
into your soul, like the warm, evening sun, and you will
smile, Mama! Come, darling! Come! . . .

——— ACT FOUR ———

*The same setting as Act I. There are no curtains on the windows, no
pictures on the walls; only a few pieces of furniture remain, stacked in
a corner, as if for sale. There is a feeling of emptiness. There are suitcases, travel bags, etc. piled high upstage by the door leading to the outside. The door to stage left is open, from which the voices of* VARYA *and*
ANYA *can be heard.* LOPAKHIN *stands there, waiting.* YASHA *holds
a tray of glasses, filled with champagne. In the entrance hall,*
YEPIKHODOV *is packing a case. Offstage, voices are heard—the peasants have come to say good-bye.* GAEV's *voice is heard: "Thank you, my
friends, I thank you."*

YASHA: The peasants have come to say good-bye. Now here's
my opinion on that subject, Yermolai Alekseich: The people are good, but what do *they* know.

(The noise dies down. LYUBOV ANDREEVNA *and* GAEV *enter through
the entrance hall; she is no longer crying, but she is very pale: she is
trembling, and it is difficult for her to speak.)*

GAEV: You gave them everything in your purse, Lyuba. No!
5   You mustn't do that!
LYUBOV ANDREEVNA: I couldn't help it! I couldn't help it!

(Both exit.)

LOPAKHIN: *(At the door, following after them.)* Please, I humbly
beg you! A farewell toast! I didn't think to bring any from
town . . . and I could only find one bottle at the station.
10   Please!

(Pause.)

So, my friends! You don't want any? *(Steps away from the
door.)* If I'd known, I wouldn't have bought it. Never mind,
I won't have any, either.

(YASHA carefully places the tray on the table.)

Drink up, Yasha, why don't you.
15   YASHA: To those who are leaving! And to those who are staying
behind! *(Drinks.)* This isn't real champagne, that much I
can tell you.
LOPAKHIN: Eight rubles a bottle.

(Pause.)

Wickedly cold in here, isn't it.
20   YASHA: They didn't stoke up the stoves today, what's the point,
everybody's leaving. *(Laughs.)*
LOPAKHIN: What are you laughing about?
YASHA: I'm happy.
LOPAKHIN: It's October, but outside it's sunny and mild, like
25   summertime. Good weather for construction. *(Looks at his
watch, at the door.)* Ladies and gentlemen, bear in mind, only

forty-six minutes left until the train departs! That means
we have to leave for the station in twenty minutes. Hurry,
everyone!

(TROFIMOV enters from the outside, wearing a coat.)

TROFIMOV: I think it's time to go now. They've already brought   30
the horses around. Where are my galoshes, damn it!
They've disappeared. *(At the door.)* Anya, my galoshes aren't
here! I can't find them!
LOPAKHIN: And I've got to get to Kharkov. I'll go with you as
far as the station. I'm going to spend the winter in Kharkov.   35
Yes. Here I am, standing around, talking to you, I'm lost
when I'm not working. I can't live without work, I don't
know what to do with my hands; isn't it strange, look,
they're hanging there, as if they belonged to someone else.
TROFIMOV: We'll be leaving momentarily, and you'll return to   40
all your worthy enterprises.
LOPAKHIN: Have a glass with me.
TROFIMOV: I can't.
LOPAKHIN: So, it's off to Moscow, then?
TROFIMOV: Yes, that's right, I'll go with them into town, and   45
tomorrow, it's off to Moscow.
LOPAKHIN: Yes . . . Well, the professors haven't started their
lectures yet, no doubt they're all waiting for you!
TROFIMOV: That's none of your business.
LOPAKHIN: How many years is it, then, since you've been at the   50
university?
TROFIMOV: Think up something new, why don't you? That's a
stale and feeble joke, it's not funny any more. *(Searches for his
galoshes.)* It's very likely we may never see each other again,
you know, so allow me, please, to give you some parting ad-   55
vice: Don't wave your arms around so much! Try to get out of
the habit of waving your arms when you talk, if you can. All
this planning of yours, you know, building summer houses,
creating a new generation of independent landowners, and
so on and so forth,—why, that's just another form of waving   60
your arms . . . Oh, well, never mind, all things considered, I
like you . . . I do. You have delicate, sensitive fingers, the fingers of an artist . . . you have a delicate, sensitive soul . . .
LOPAKHIN: *(Embraces him.)* Good-bye, my friend. Thanks for
everything. Just in case, here, take some money for the   65
journey.
TROFIMOV: Why should I? I don't need it.
LOPAKHIN: But you don't have any!
TROFIMOV: Yes, I do, thank you very much. I've just received
some money for a translation. Here it is, right here, in my   70
pocket. *(Anxiously.)* Now where are my galoshes!
VARYA: *(From the other room.)* Here, take the filthy things! *(Tosses
a pair of rubber galoshes on the stage.)*
TROFIMOV: Why are you so angry, Varya? Hm . . . These are not
my galoshes!   75
LOPAKHIN: This spring I planted almost 3,000 acres of poppies,
and made a clean profit of 40,000. And when my poppies
bloomed, now what a sight that was! So, here's what I'm
saying, I've just made 40,000 rubles, and I'm offering you
a loan because I can afford to. Why do you look down your   80
nose at me? I'm a peasant . . . what do you expect?
TROFIMOV: Your father was a peasant, mine was a chemist, none
of it means a thing.

(LOPAKHIN *takes out his wallet.*)

85   Stop that, stop . . . Even if you were to give me 200,000, I
     wouldn't take it. I am a free man. And everything that is so
     sacred and dear to all of you, rich and poor alike, hasn't the
     slightest significance to me, it's all dust, adrift in the wind.
     I can survive without you, I can even surpass you, I am
90   proud and strong. Mankind is on a quest to seek the high-
     est truth, the greatest happiness possible on this earth, and
     I am in the front ranks!
LOPAKHIN: And will you reach your destination?
TROFIMOV: Yes, I shall.

(*Pause.*)

     I shall, or else I'll show others the way.

(*In the distance, the sound is heard of an axe falling on a tree.*)

95   LOPAKHIN: So, good-bye, my friend. Time to go. Here we are,
     looking down our noses at one another, and all the while,
     life goes on, in spite of any of us. When I work, for days on
     end, without any rest, that's when my thoughts come most
     clearly, that's when I know why I am on this earth, why I
100 exist. And how many of us are there in Russia, my friend,
     who still don't know why they exist. Ah well, what does it
     matter, that's not the point, is it. They say that Leonid
     Andreich has taken a position at a bank, 6,000 a year . . .
     He won't be able to keep it, though, he's too lazy . . .
105 ANYA: (*At the door.*) Mama asks you not to cut down the orchard
     till after she's gone.
     TROFIMOV: Isn't it possible to show some tact . . . (*Exits through
     the entrance hall.*)
     LOPAKHIN: Yes, yes, right away . . . Really.
110 ANYA: Have they sent Firs to the hospital yet?
     YASHA: I told them about it this morning. I'm sure they did.
     ANYA: (*To* YEPIKHODOV, *who is walking through the hall.*) Semyon
     Panteleich, please, go find out, would you, if they've taken
     Firs to the hospital yet.
115 YASHA: (*Offended.*) I told Yegor this morning. Why ask the
     same question over and over!
     YEPIKHODOV: The ancient Firs, in my final opinion, is beyond
     repair; he should return to his forefathers. And I can only
     envy him. (*Places the suitcase on a hat box, and crushes it.*) Oh,
120 well, of course. I knew it. (*Exits.*)
     YASHA: (*Mocking.*) "Mister Disaster" . . .
     VARYA: (*From behind the door.*) Have they taken Firs to the hos-
     pital?
     ANYA: Yes, they have.
125 VARYA: Why didn't they bring the letter to the doctor?
     ANYA: We'll just have to send it along . . . (*Exits.*)
     VARYA: (*From the adjacent room.*) Where's Yasha? Tell him his
     mother's here, she wants to say good-bye to him.
     YASHA: (*Waves his hand.*) I'm losing my patience.

(*During this,* DUNYASHA *has been busying herself with the luggage;
now that* YASHA *is alone, she goes up to him.*)

130 DUNYASHA: Just one last look, Yasha. You're leaving . . . you're
     abandoning me . . . (*Weeps and throws her arms around his
     neck.*)

YASHA: What's there to cry about? (*Drinks champagne.*) In six
     days, I'll be in Paris again. Tomorrow we'll board an express
     train, and off we'll go, that's the last you'll ever see of us. I   135
     just can't believe it. "Vive la France!" . . . This place is not
     for me, I can't live here . . . and that's all there is to it. I've
     seen a lot of ignorance—and I've had enough. (*Drinks cham-
     pagne.*) What's there to cry about? Behave yourself properly,
     then you won't cry so much.   140
DUNYASHA: (*Powders her face, looks at herself in the mirror.*) Send
     me a letter from Paris. You know much I have loved you,
     Yasha, I have loved you very, very much! I'm a sensitive
     creature, Yasha!
YASHA: They're coming. (*Busies himself with the luggage, hums*   145
     softly.)

(*Enter* LYUBOV ANDREEVNA, GAEV, ANYA, *and* CHARLOTTA
IVANOVNA.)

GAEV: We really ought to be going. There's hardly any time
     left. (*Looks at* YASHA.) Who smells of herring in here?
LYUBOV ANDREEVNA: In ten minutes time we'll be getting into
     the carriages . . . (*Glances around the room.*) Good-bye,   150
     beloved home, home of my forefathers. Winter will pass,
     spring will come, and you'll no longer be here, they will
     have destroyed you. How much these walls have seen!
     (*Kisses her daughter passionately.*) My treasure, you're radiant,
     your eyes are sparkling, like two diamonds. Are you happy?   155
     Very happy?
ANYA: Very! We're starting a new life, Mama!
GAEV: (*Cheerfully.*) Everything's turned out quite well, as a
     matter of fact, yes, indeed. Before the cherry orchard was
     sold, we were all upset, we suffered a great deal, but then,   160
     when everything was settled, once and for all, finally and ir-
     revocably, we all calmed down, we were even glad . . . And
     now I'm a bank official, a financier . . . "yellow into the
     middle pocket," and you, Lyuba, for all that we've been
     through, you're looking better than ever, no doubt about it.   165
LYUBOV ANDREEVNA: Yes, I'm calmer, it's true.

(*She is given her hat and coat.*)

     I can sleep better now. Take my things out, Yasha. It's time.
     (*To* ANYA.) My darling child, we shall see each other again,
     soon . . . I am going to Paris, I shall live there on the money
     your great-aunt from Yaroslavl sent to buy the estate—God   170
     bless great-aunt!—but that money won't last very long.
ANYA: You'll come home soon, Mama, soon . . . won't you? And
     I'll study, take my examinations, and then I'll work, I'll
     take care of you. And we'll read all sorts of marvelous books
     together, Mama . . . Won't we? (*Kisses her mother's hands.*)   175
     We'll read through the long autumn evenings, we'll read so
     many books, and a wonderful new world will open before us
     . . . (*Dreaming.*) Come home, Mama . . .
LYUBOV ANDREEVNA: I'll come, my jewel. (*Embraces her daughter.*)

(*Enter* LOPAKHIN, *and* CHARLOTTA, *who is softly humming a tune.*)

GAEV: Charlotta is happy: she's singing!   180
CHARLOTTA: (*Picks up a bundle, resembling an infant in swaddling
     clothes.*) "My sweet little baby, 'bye, 'bye . . ."

(The child's cry: "Wa, wa! . . ." can be heard.)

"Hushabye, baby, my sweet little boy."

(The child's cry: "Wa! . . . wa! . . .")

185 Poor baby! I feel so sorry for you! *(Throws the bundle down.)* Now, please, find me another job. I can't go on like this.

LOPAKHIN: We shall, Charlotta Ivanovna, don't worry.

GAEV: We're all being cast out, Varya's going away . . . suddenly no one needs us any more.

CHARLOTTA: There's nowhere for me to live in town. I must go 190 away . . . *(Hums.)* It doesn't matter . . .

(Enter PISHCHIK.)

LOPAKHIN: One of nature's wonders! . . .

PISHCHIK: *(Out of breath.)* Oy, let me catch my breath . . . I'm all worn out . . . Most honorable friends . . . Give me some water . . .

195 GAEV: Looking for money, by any chance? I remain your humble servant, but, forgive me, I really must avoid the temptation . . . *(Exits.)*

PISHCHIK: I haven't been here in such a long, long, time . . . loveliest lady . . . *(To LOPAKHIN.)* And you are here, too . . . 200 so good to see you . . . a man of the highest intelligence . . . here, take it . . . it's yours . . . *(Gives LOPAKHIN some money.)* Four hundred rubles . . . I still owe you eight hundred and forty . . .

LOPAKHIN: *(Shrugs his shoulders in amazement.)* I must be dreaming 205 . . . Where on earth did you get this?

PISHCHIK: Wait . . . So hot . . . Most extraordinary circumstances. Some Englishmen came to visit my estate, and what do you know, they found white clay in the earth . . . whatever that is . . . *(To LYUBOV ANDREEVNA.)* And here's 210 four hundred for you . . . elegant, exquisite lady . . . *(Gives her some money.)* The rest will come later. *(Drinks the water.)* Just now, a young man on the train was telling us about this great philosopher . . . how he's advising everyone to jump off the roof . . . "Jump!" —he says, and that will solve 215 everything. *(Amazed.)* Imagine that! Water!

LOPAKHIN: What Englishmen are you talking about?

PISHCHIK: I leased them a plot of the land with the white clay for twenty-four years . . . But now, forgive me, please, I've run out of time . . . a long ride ahead . . . I'm going to the 220 Znoykovs . . . to the Kardamonovs . . . I owe everybody . . . *(Drinks.)* Good day to you all . . . I'll drop by again on Thursday . . .

LYUBOV ANDREEVNA: We're just moving into town now, and tomorrow I'm going abroad . . .

225 PISHCHIK: What? *(Anxiously.)* Why to town? What's this I see . . . furniture . . . suitcases . . . Well, never mind . . . *(In tears.)* Never mind . . . Very very smart people, these Englishmen . . . people of the highest intelligence . . . Never mind . . . I wish you happiness . . . God will watch over you 230 . . . Never mind . . . Everything on this earth must come to an end . . . *(Kisses LYUBOV ANDREEVNA's hand.)* And when you hear the news that my own end has come, remember this good old horse, won't you, and say: "Once upon a time there lived an old so-and-so . . . Simeonov-Pishchik . . . God 235 rest his soul" . . . Magnificent weather we're having . . . Yes

. . . *(Exits in great confusion, and immediately returns and speaks from the doorway.)* Dashenka sends her regards! *(Exits.)*

LYUBOV ANDREEVNA: And now we can go. But I'm leaving with two worries. The first is Firs—he's ill. *(Looks at her watch.)* 240 We still have five minutes . . .

ANYA: Mama, they've already sent Firs to the hospital. Yasha sent him this morning.

LYUBOV ANDREEVNA: My second sorrow is Varya. She's used to getting up early and working, and now, without work, she's 245 like a fish out of water. She's grown thin and pale, she weeps all the time, poor thing . . .

(Pause.)

You know very well, Yermolai Alekseich, I have dreamed . . . that one day she would marry you, in fact, it was obvious to everyone that you would be married. *(She whispers to ANYA,* 250 *who motions to CHARLOTTA, and both exit.)* She loves you, you seem to be fond of her, and I don't know why, I simply don't know why it is that you go out of your way to avoid one other. I don't understand it!

LOPAKHIN: I don't understand it myself, to tell the truth. It's all 255 so strange, somehow . . . If there's still time, then I'm ready to do it now . . . Basta! Let's settle it once and for all; without you here, I don't think I could possibly propose to her.

LYUBOV ANDREEVNA: Excellent. It only takes a minute, you know. I'll call her in right away . . . 260

LOPAKHIN: Oh yes, and there's champagne, too. *(Looks at glasses.)* It's empty, someone drank it all up.

(YASHA coughs.)

Or, should I say, lapped it all up . . .

LYUBOV ANDREEVNA: *(Excited.)* Splendid. We're leaving . . . Yasha, "allez"! I'll call her . . . *(At the door.)* Varya, stop what 265 you're doing, and come here. Come! *(Exits with YASHA.)*

LOPAKHIN: *(Looks at his watch.)* Yes . . .

(Pause.)

(Muffled laughter and whispering is heard from behind the door; finally, VARYA enters.)

VARYA: *(In a lengthy search for something.)* That's strange, I can't find it anywhere . . .

LOPAKHIN: What are you looking for? 270

VARYA: I put it away myself, I can't remember where.

(Pause.)

LOPAKHIN: So where will you go now, Varvara Mikhailovna?

VARYA: Me? To the Ragulins' . . . I've agreed to work for them . . . you know . . . as a housekeeper.

LOPAKHIN: Aren't they in Yashnevo? That's about forty-five 275 miles from here.

(Pause.)

And so, life has come to an end in this house . . .

VARYA: *(Searching among the things.)* Where can it be . . . Perhaps I put it in the trunk . . . Yes, life has come to an end in this house . . . and will be no more . . . 280

LOPAKHIN: And I'm off to Kharkov now . . . on the same train. I've got a lot of business there. But I'm leaving Yepikhodov here to look after things . . . I've hired him, you know.

VARYA: Really!

285 LOPAKHIN: Last year at this time it was already snowing, if you remember, and now it's so sunny and calm. Only it's quite cold . . . Three degrees of frost, almost.

VARYA: I hadn't noticed.

(Pause.)

Anyway, our thermometer's broken . . .

(Pause.)

(A voice is heard calling from outside: "Yermolai Alekseich! . . .")

290 LOPAKHIN: *(As if he'd long been waiting for this call.)* Coming! *(He hurries out.)*

(VARYA sits on the floor, puts her head on a bundle of clothing, and sobs quietly. The door opens, and LYUBOV ANDREEVNA enters cautiously.)

LYUBOV ANDREEVNA: So?

(Pause.)

We'd better go.

VARYA: *(No longer weeping, wipes her eyes.)* Yes, Mamochka, it's
295   time. If I don't miss the train, I might even get to the Ragulins' today . . .

LYUBOV ANDREEVNA: *(At the door.)* Anya, put your coat on!

(Enter ANYA, then GAEV, CHARLOTTA IVANOVNA. GAEV is wearing a warm coat with a hood. The SERVANTS and CARRIAGE DRIVERS assemble. YEPIKHODOV is busy with the luggage.)

Now, we can be on our way.

ANYA: *(Overjoyed.)* We're on our way!

300 GAEV: My friends, my dear, kind friends! Upon leaving this house forever, how can I be silent, how can I refrain, upon this our departure, from expressing those feelings, which now fill my very being . . .

ANYA: *(Imploring.)* Uncle!

305 VARYA: Uncle, must you!

GAEV: *(Dejected.)* "Double the yellow into the middle . . ." I'll be quiet . . .

(Enter TROFIMOV, then LOPAKHIN.)

TROFIMOV: All right, ladies and gentlemen, time to depart!

LOPAKHIN: Yepikhodov, my coat!

310 LYUBOV ANDREEVNA: I want to sit for just one minute longer. I never really noticed before, what walls this house has, what ceilings, and now I look at them with such longing, with such tender love . . .

GAEV: I remember, when I was six, on Trinity Sunday, I sat at
315   this window and watched my father walking to church . . .

LYUBOV ANDREEVNA: Have they taken everything out?

LOPAKHIN: I think so. *(To YEPIKHODOV, who is putting on his coat.)* Yepikhodov, see to it that everything's been taken care of.

YEPIKHODOV: *(Speaking in a hoarse voice.)* Don't you worry,
320   Yermolai Alekseich.

LOPAKHIN: What's the matter with your voice?

YEPIKHODOV: I just drank some water, and I must have swallowed something.

YASHA: *(Contemptuously.)* What ignorance . . .

LYUBOV ANDREEVNA: We're leaving—and not a soul will be left   325
here . . .

LOPAKHIN: Until springtime.

VARYA: *(Pulls an umbrella out of a bundle—it appears as if she were about to strike someone; LOPAKHIN pretends to be frightened.)* What's wrong with you? . . . I wouldn't think of it . . .   330

TROFIMOV: Ladies and gentlemen, please, let's get into the carriages now . . . It's time to go! The train will arrive any minute!

VARYA: Petya, here they are, your galoshes, beside the suitcase. *(In tears.)* Look how old and muddy they are . . .   335

TROFIMOV: *(Putting on the galoshes.)* We're off, ladies and gentlemen!

GAEV: *(Very confused, afraid of bursting into tears.)* Train . . . station . . . "Croisé into the middle pocket, Double the white into the corner . . ."   340

LYUBOV ANDREEVNA: We're off!

LOPAKHIN: Is everyone here? No one left behind? *(Locks the side door stage left.)* There are some things stored in here, better lock up. We're off!

ANYA: Good-bye, house! Good-bye, old life!   345

TROFIMOV: Hello, new life . . . *(Exits with ANYA.)*

(VARYA glances around the room and exits without hurrying. Exit YASHA, and CHARLOTTA, with the little dog.)

LOPAKHIN: And so, until springtime. Come now, ladies and gentlemen, we'd better be going . . . Once more, a very good-bye!! . . . *(Exits.)*

(LYUBOV ANDREEVNA and GAEV are left alone together. It is as if they have been waiting for this moment; they throw themselves into each others' arms and sob quietly, with restraint, fearing they might be heard.)

GAEV: *(In despair.)* My sister, my sister . . .   350

LYUBOV ANDREEVNA: O my precious orchard, my sweet, lovely orchard! . . . My life, my youth, my happiness, farewell! . . . Farewell! . . .

(ANYA's voice calls out, merrily: "Mama! . . .")

(TROFIMOV's voice calls out, gaily, excitedly: "A-oo! . . .")

LYUBOV ANDREEVNA: For the last time, let me look at these walls, these windows . . . how my mother loved to walk   355
about this room . . .

GAEV: My sister, my sister! . . .

(ANYA's voice: "Mama! . . .")

(TROFIMOV's voice: "A-oo . . .")

LYUBOV ANDREEVNA: We're off! . . .

(They exit.)

(The stage is empty. There is the sound of all the doors being locked, and then of the carriages pulling away. It grows very still. Through the stillness comes the remote sound of the axe falling on a tree, a lonely,

melancholy sound. Footsteps are heard. FIRS *appears at the door, stage right. He is dressed, as always, in a jacket and a white waistcoat, with slippers on his feet. He is ill.)*

FIRS: *(Goes to the door, tries the handle.)* Locked. They've gone . . .
360   *(Sits on the sofa.)* They've forgotten about me . . . Never mind . . . I'll sit here for a just a bit . . . And Leonid Andreich, most likely, didn't put his fur coat on, went off wearing his light one . . . *(Sighs, anxiously.)* Just slipped my notice . . . These young people nowadays! *(Mutters something*

incomprehensible.) And life has passed by, somehow, as if I 365 never lived it at all. *(Lies down.)* I'll lie down for just a bit . . . Don't have too much strength left, now, do you, no, not much, not much at all . . . You pathetic old fool, you! . . . *(Lies there, immobile.)*

(A distant sound is heard, as if coming from the sky, the sound of a breaking string, dying away, a mournful sound. Silence falls, and all that is heard, far off in the orchard, is the sound of the axe falling on a tree.)

PRONUNCIATION GUIDE TO RUSSIAN NAMES

CAST OF CHARACTERS

Lyubov (Lyuba) Andreevna Ranevskaya, Lyoo-bof′ (Lyoo′-ba) An-drey′-ev-na Ra-nyef′-ska-ya
("drey" rhymes with the English word "grey")

Anya (Anechka), An′-ya (An′-yech-ka)

Varya (Varvara Mikhailovna), Va′-rya (Var-var′-a Mee-khai′-lov-na)
("khai" rhymes with the word "why")

Leonid (Lyonya) Andreevich (Andreich) Gaev, Le-o-need′ (Lyon′-ya) Andrey′-e-veech (An-drey′-eech) Ga′-yef

Yermolai Alekseevich (Alekseich) Lopakhin, Yer-mo-lai′ A-lek-syey′-e-veech (A-lek-sey′-eech) Lo-pa′-kheen
("lai" in "Yermolai" rhymes with the word "why")
("syey" rhymes with the word "grey")

Pyotr (Petya) Sergeevich (Sergeich) Trofimov, Pyo′-tr (Pye′-tya) Syer-gey′-e-veech (Syer-gey′-eech) Tro-fee′-mof

Boris Borisovich Simeonov-Pishchik, Bo-rees′ Bo-rees′-o-veech See-myon′-of-Peesh′-cheek

Charlotta Ivanovna, Shar-lo′-ta Ee-van′-ov-na

Semyon Panteleevich (Panteleich) Yepikhodov, Se-myon′ Pan-te-lyey′-e-veech (Pan-te-lyey′-eech) Ye-pee-khod′-of
("lyey" rhymes with the word "grey")

Dunyasha (Avdotya Fyodorovna), Doon-ya′-sha (Av-do′-tya Fyo′-do-rov-na)

Firs Nikolaevich, Feers Nee-ko-la′-ye-veech

Yasha, Ya′-sha

OTHER RUSSIAN NAMES APPEARING IN THE TEXT

Anastasy, A-na-sta′-see

Dashenka, Da′-shen-ka

Deriganov, Dye-ree-ga′-nof

Grisha, Gree′-sha

Kardamonov, Kar-da-mo′-nof

Karp, Karp

Kharkov, Khar′-kof

Kozoedov (Fyodor), Ko-zo-ye′-dof (Fyo′-dor)

Lopakhina, Lo-pa′-khee-na

Mama (Mamochka), Ma′-ma (Ma′-moch-ka)

Papa, Pa′-pa

Petrushka, Pye-troosh′-ka

Polya, Po′-lya

Ragulin, Ra-goo′-leen

Yaroslavl, Ya-ro-slavl′

Yashnevo, Yash′-nye-vo

Yefimyushka, Ye-fee′-myoosh-ka

Yegor, Ye-gor′

Yevstigney, Yev-steeg-nyey′
("nyey" rhymes with the word "grey")

Znoykov, Znoy′-kof

BERNARD SHAW

George Bernard Shaw (1856–1950)—Shaw disliked the name "George" and never used it, preferring the initials G. B. S.—was a man of wide-ranging passions and huge abilities. By his fortieth birthday he had written five novels, three volumes of classic music criticism, and three volumes of incendiary theater reviews; he had become visible in the influential socialist political organization, the FABIAN SOCIETY; he had written the first books in English on Wagner's operas and on Ibsen's plays; and he had just started his career as a dramatist, a career that would eventually include more than fifty plays.

Shaw was born in Dublin. Like Jonathan Swift and Richard Brinsley Sheridan before him, Shaw retained the satiric perspective of the Irish outsider in England. His mother was a music teacher and his sister was a promising singer when they left for London while Shaw was in his teens. He followed them to London in 1876. A shy and self-effacing young man, Shaw took a variety of jobs that brought him into contact with the public, and he used the opportunity of lecturing for the Fabian Society to develop the brilliantly articulate persona we recognize today as "G. B. S." Throughout the 1880s, Shaw worked with the Fabians, adopting their plan of gradual social reform in place of a more rigorously Marxist call for social revolution. The Fabians strove to change society through a strategy of permeation, working to get their members elected into prominent offices, where their educational and social reforms might be put into effect. Shaw was deeply influenced by the Fabians' gradualist scheme for social improvement—a scheme that underlies the utopian project of his greatest plays—for Fabian gradualism synchronized with Shaw's other passion, Creative Evolution. Appalled by what he regarded as the mindless mechanism of Darwinian natural selection, Shaw resisted the notion that human evolution followed a random and inevitable process. He urged instead that humanity take command of its future by willing itself to evolve in certain humane directions, and he advocated eugenics, capital punishment, and other ideas in the interest of the development of the species. Shaw attempted an uneasy synthesis of the Fabian socialist project of gradual social evolution with the individualist metaphysics of Creative Evolution: the improvement of society through the improvement of each of its members.

Shaw's friend William Archer once described seeing Shaw in the British Museum reading room simultaneously reading Marx's *Das Kapital* and the score of Wagner's *Ring of the Niebelung* cycle. The blending of political substance with a rich and deeply harmonized verbal music became a constant feature of Shaw's drama. Writing as a theater critic in the 1890s, Shaw became the champion of Ibsen in England. Vowing to lay siege to the conventions of the nineteenth-century theater, he touted Ibsen's plays and lambasted the corny tearjerkers, simplistic melodramas, and overstuffed Shakespearean productions that were the theater's common fare. Not incidentally, he worked to create a taste for his own plays, an operatic drama of the intellectual passions.

Shaw's career as a playwright falls into three main phases. Shaw's earliest plays— *Widowers' Houses* (1892) and *Mrs. Warren's Profession* (1893)—attacked specific social problems, like slum landlords and international prostitution. But Shaw more often linked social ills to the smug pieties of conventional morality. His plays generally work to disillusion his main characters—and his audience—from the ready acceptance of bourgeois ideology as a natural "reality." This process of disillusionment informs Shaw's lighter comedies of the 1890s, plays like *Arms and the Man* (1894), *Candida* (1894), and *Caesar and Cleopatra* (1898). After the turn of the century, however, Shaw entered on his maturity as a playwright, undertaking a series of major comedies that place this process of disillusionment directly in conflict with society's most important institutions: marriage and sexuality in *Man and Superman* (1903); British imperialism in Ireland in *John Bull's Other*

Island (1904); salvation, damnation, and raw power in *Major Barbara* (1905); medicine in *The Doctor's Dilemma* (1906); language and class in *Pygmalion* (1912). Several of these plays were first produced at the Court Theater, under the management of Shaw's close friend Harley Granville Barker, who originated the part of Cusins in *Major Barbara* and other Shavian roles. Under Barker and his partner J. E. Vedrenne, the Court Theater in 1904–07 became the most influential theater in London before World War I. Through its efforts, and Shaw's own energy as playwright, director, and advisor, the Court made Shaw's reputation as a major dramatist. With the coming of World War I, and the violent waste of civilization it brought with it, Shaw's confidence in the eventual perfection of humanity was deeply shaken, and the plays of his final half-century are much bleaker, more uncertain in tone: his magnificent "fantasia in the Russian manner on English themes," *Heartbreak House* (1919), modeled on Chekhov's *The Cherry Orchard; Saint Joan* (1923), perhaps his best-loved play; his five-play quintet on the origin and future of the species, *Back to Methuselah* (1921); and many others. In contrast to the confidence of Shaw's earlier plays, the later dramas generally seem to ask the question that Shaw gave to his Saint Joan, "O God that madest this beautiful earth, when will it be ready to receive Thy saints? How long, O Lord, how long?"

MAJOR BARBARA

Shaw was born before the publication of Darwin's *Origin of Species* in 1859, and he died after the dropping of the atomic bomb on Hiroshima. His major plays, like *Major Barbara,* treat the problems of the twentieth century in the dramatic vocabulary of Edwardian COMEDY OF MANNERS. *Major Barbara* is typical of the dialectical process of Shaw's plays. From the outset—when Stephen learns that his income is derived from his father's munitions empire—Shaw forces the audience and his characters to question the nature of their values, particularly the sense that good and evil, morality and economics, the power to save and the power to destroy can be easily or conveniently distinguished from one another. As a result, the play forces a deeply ironic experience on its characters and on the audience. For Shaw is interested in salvation, not simply the moralizing salvation promised by the Salvation Army, but a Nietzschean transvaluation of values, a salvation beyond the conventional abstractions of good and evil that he regards as necessary to the transformation of English society.

The play is structured dialectically, progressing from thesis, to antithesis, to a problematic synthesis. The "thesis" of act 1 concerns the values of Wilton Crescent: the comfortable morality of the English upper classes. As the scene proceeds, though, Shaw suggests that conventional morality, the innate knowledge of right and wrong, is in fact supported by Undershaft's money and gunpowder. The "antithesis" of act 2 offers the unconventional morality of the Salvation Army; Barbara's shelter in West Ham claims to provide true salvation by requiring a more sincere form of religious conviction. However, as it turns out, both Wilton Crescent and West Ham are equally in the grip of Bodger and Undershaft. The distiller and the munitions-maker determine the material realities on which society erects its illusory social "ideals" and calls them "reality." The Dionysian sacrifice of Barbara at the end of act 2—with its echoes of Christ's crucifixion as well—prepares us for her resurrection in the "synthesis" offered by act 3; in Perivale St Andrews, the spiritual Barbara and the intellectual Cusins are married with the blessing of the explosive Undershaft. We might be troubled, though, by the "synthesis" offered by the utopian factory town, for Undershaft's utopia hardly seems revolutionary. In many ways, Perivale St Andrews largely duplicates turn-of-the-century English class society and industrial capitalism, with the poverty and dirt cleaned up. The play's last act is often said to be unconvincing, and we might wonder whether that is in fact part of Shaw's purpose in *Major Barbara*. Once Shaw instructs us in the process of dialectical criticism, perhaps he invites us to scrutinize even Undershaft's bourgeois utopia, to see Perivale St Andrews as itself in need of further (r)evolution.

Shaw made Andrew Undershaft a magnificently melodramatic, attractive, amoral munitions-maker, whose creative ability is harnessed to the power to destroy. Moreover, Shaw drew a parallel between Undershaft and a crucial dramatic precursor, the Dionysus of Euripides' *The Bacchae.* The character of Cusins was modeled on Shaw's friend, the well-known classical scholar Gilbert Murray, and in the original production, Cusins was even played to resemble Murray. In act 2, Cusins quotes a brief passage adapted from Murray's translation of *The Bacchae,* part of the choral speech delivered just before Pentheus is led out to spy on the Bacchae and be killed. We might take this invocation of Dionysus as a final clue to the play's attitude. Much like Euripides, Shaw prevents his audience from sympathizing entirely with his hero, from readily accepting the terrible power necessary to change the world. Although the play ends with a ceremonial marriage characteristic of ROMANTIC COMEDY—symbolizing the union of intellect, spirit, and power—the fact that Dionysus Undershaft presides over this union should give us pause. Can the power he wields really be harnessed for our salvation?

Shaw, not surprisingly, had a systematic but unconventional approach to English spelling and punctuation, and insisted that publishers observe it when printing his plays; this edition of *Major Barbara* accordingly preserves Shaw's style.

MAJOR BARBARA

Bernard Shaw

——— CHARACTERS ———

STEPHEN UNDERSHAFT   ADOLPHUS CUSINS
LADY BRITOMART   CHARLES LOMAX
BARBARA UNDERSHAFT   RUMMY MITCHENS
SARAH UNDERSHAFT   SNOBBY PRICE
ANDREW UNDERSHAFT   PETER SHIRLEY
JENNY HILL   BILTON
BILL WALKER   MRS BAINES
MORRISON

——— ACT ONE ———

It is after dinner in January 1906, in the library in LADY BRITO-
MART UNDERSHAFT's *house in Wilton Crescent. A large and comfortable settee is in the middle of the room, upholstered in dark leather. A
person sitting on it (it is vacant at present) would have, on his right,*
LADY BRITOMART's *writing table, with the lady herself busy at it; a
smaller writing table behind him on his left; the door behind him on*
LADY BRITOMART's *side; and a window with a window seat directly
on his left. Near the window is an armchair.*

LADY BRITOMART *is a woman of fifty or thereabouts, well dressed and
yet careless of her dress, well bred and quite reckless of her breeding,
well mannered and yet appallingly outspoken and indifferent to the
opinion of her interlocutors, amiable and yet peremptory, arbitrary,
and high-tempered to the last bearable degree, and withal a very typical managing matron of the upper class, treated as a naughty child
until she grew into a scolding mother, and finally settling down with
plenty of practical ability and worldly experience, limited in the odd-
est way with domestic and class limitations, conceiving the universe exactly as if it were a large house in Wilton Crescent, though handling
her corner of it very effectively on that assumption, and being quite enlightened and liberal as to the books in the library, the pictures on the
walls, the music in the portfolios, and the articles in the papers.*

Her son, STEPHEN, *comes in. He is a gravely correct young man under
25, taking himself very seriously, but still in some awe of his mother,
from childish habit and bachelor shyness rather than from any weakness of character.*

STEPHEN: Whats the matter?
LADY BRITOMART: Presently, Stephen.

(STEPHEN *submissively walks to the settee and sits down. He takes up
a Liberal weekly called* The Speaker.)

LADY BRITOMART: Dont begin to read, Stephen. I shall require
    all your attention.
5 STEPHEN: It was only while I was waiting—
LADY BRITOMART: Dont make excuses, Stephen. (*He puts down*
    The Speaker.) Now! (*She finishes her writing; rises; and comes to
    the settee.*) I have not kept you waiting very long, I think.
STEPHEN: Not at all, mother.
10 LADY BRITOMART: Bring me my cushion. (*He takes the cushion
    from the chair at the desk and arranges it for her as she sits down*

on the settee.) Sit down. (*He sits down and fingers his tie ner-
vously.*) Dont fiddle with your tie, Stephen: there is nothing
the matter with it.
STEPHEN: I beg your pardon. (*He fiddles with his watch chain* 15
    instead.)
LADY BRITOMART: Now are you attending to me, Stephen?
STEPHEN: Of course, mother.
LADY BRITOMART: No: it's not of course. I want something
    much more than your everyday matter-of-course attention. 20
    I am going to speak to you very seriously, Stephen. I wish
    you would let that chain alone.
STEPHEN: (*Hastily relinquishing the chain.*) Have I done anything
    to annoy you, mother? If so, it was quite unintentional.
LADY BRITOMART: (*Astonished.*) Nonsense! (*With some remorse.*) 25
    My poor boy, did you think I was angry with you?
STEPHEN: What is it, then, mother? You are making me very
    uneasy.
LADY BRITOMART: (*Squaring herself at him rather aggressively.*)
    Stephen: may I ask how soon you intend to realize that you 30
    are a grown-up man, and that I am only a woman?
STEPHEN: (*Amazed.*) Only a—
LADY BRITOMART: Dont repeat my words, please: it is a most
    aggravating habit. You must learn to face life seriously,
    Stephen. I really cannot bear the whole burden of our fam- 35
    ily affairs any longer. You must advise me: you must assume
    the responsibility.
STEPHEN: I!
LADY BRITOMART: Yes, you, of course. You were 24 last June.
    Youve been at Harrow and Cambridge. Youve been to India 40
    and Japan. You must know a lot of things, now; unless you
    have wasted your time most scandalously. Well, advise me.
STEPHEN: (*Much perplexed.*) You know I have never interfered in
    the household—
LADY BRITOMART: No: I should think not. I dont want you to 45
    order the dinner.
STEPHEN: I mean in our family affairs.
LADY BRITOMART: Well, you must interfere now; for they are
    getting quite beyond me.
STEPHEN: (*Troubled.*) I have thought sometimes that perhaps I 50
    ought; but really, mother, I know so little about them; and
    what I do know is so painful! it is so impossible to mention
    some things to you—(*He stops, ashamed.*)
LADY BRITOMART: I suppose you mean your father.
STEPHEN: (*Almost inaudibly.*) Yes. 55

LADY BRITOMART: My dear: we cant go on all our lives not men-
     tioning him. Of course you were quite right not to open the
     subject until I asked you to; but you are old enough now to
     be taken into my confidence, and to help me to deal with
60   him about the girls.
STEPHEN: But the girls are all right. They are engaged.
LADY BRITOMART: *(Complacently.)* Yes: I have made a very good
     match for Sarah. Charles Lomax will be a millionaire at 35.
     But that is ten years ahead; and in the meantime his
65   trustees cannot under the terms of his father's will allow
     him more than £800 a year.
STEPHEN: But the will says also that if he increases his income
     by his own exertions, they may double the increase.
LADY BRITOMART: Charles Lomax's exertions are much more
70   likely to decrease his income than to increase it. Sarah will
     have to find at least another £800 a year for the next ten
     years; and even then they will be as poor as church mice.
     And what about Barbara? I thought Barbara was going to
     make the most brilliant career of all of you. And what does
75   she do? Joins the Salvation Army; discharges her maid; lives
     on a pound a week and walks in one evening with a profes-
     sor of Greek whom she has picked up in the street, and who
     pretends to be a Salvationist, and actually plays the big
     drum for her in public because he has fallen head over ears
80   in love with her.
STEPHEN: I was certainly rather taken aback when I heard they
     were engaged. Cusins is a very nice fellow, certainly: no-
     body would ever guess that he was born in Australia; but—
LADY BRITOMART: Oh, Adolphus Cusins will make a very good
85   husband. After all, nobody can say a word against Greek: it
     stamps a man at once as an educated gentleman. And my
     family, thank Heaven, is not a pig-headed Tory one. We are
     Whigs, and believe in liberty. Let snobbish people say what
     they please: Barbara shall marry, not the man they like, but
90   the man *I* like.
STEPHEN: Of course I was thinking only of his income. How-
     ever, he is not likely to be extravagant.
LADY BRITOMART: Dont be too sure of that, Stephen. I know
     your quiet, simple, refined, poetic people like Adolphus:
95   quite content with the best of everything! They cost more
     than your extravagant people, who are always as mean as
     they are second rate. No: Barbara will need at least £2000
     a year. You see it means two additional households. Besides,
     my dear, you must marry soon. I dont approve of the pre-
100 sent fashion of philandering bachelors and late marriages;
     and I am trying to arrange something for you.
STEPHEN: It's very good of you, mother; but perhaps I had bet-
     ter arrange that for myself.
LADY BRITOMART: Nonsense! you are much too young to begin
105 matchmaking: you would be taken in by some pretty little
     nobody. Of course I dont mean that you are not to be con-
     sulted: you know that as well as I do. (STEPHEN *closes his lips
     and is silent.*) Now dont sulk, Stephen.
STEPHEN: I am not sulking, mother. What has all this got to do
110 with—with—with my father?
LADY BRITOMART: My dear Stephen: where is the money to
     come from? It is easy enough for you and the other children
     to live on my income as long as we are in the same house;
     but I cant keep four families in four separate houses.
115 You know how poor my father is: he has barely seven

thousand a year now; and really, if he were not the Earl of
Stevenage, he would have to give up society. He can do
nothing for us. He says, naturally enough, that it is absurd
that he should be asked to provide for the children of a man
who is rolling in money. You see, Stephen, your father must   120
be fabulously wealthy, because there is always a war going
on somewhere.
STEPHEN: You need not remind me of that, mother. I have
     hardly ever opened a newspaper in my life without seeing
     our name in it. The Undershaft torpedo! The Undershaft   125
     quick firers! The Undershaft ten inch! the Undershaft dis-
     appearing rampart gun! the Undershaft submarine! and
     now the Undershaft aerial battleship! At Harrow they
     called me the Woolwich Infant. At Cambridge it was the
     same. A little brute at King's who was always trying to get   130
     up revivals, spoilt my Bible—your first birthday present to
     me—by writing under my name, "Son and heir to Under-
     shaft and Lazarus, Death and Destruction Dealers: address
     Christendom and Judea." But that was not so bad as the
     way I was kowtowed to everywhere because my father was   135
     making millions by selling cannons.
LADY BRITOMART: It is not only the cannons, but the war loans
     that Lazarus arranges under cover of giving credit for the
     cannons. You know, Stephen, it's perfectly scandalous.
     Those two men, Andrew Undershaft and Lazarus, positively   140
     have Europe under their thumbs. That is why your father is
     able to behave as he does. He is above the law. Do you think
     Bismarck or Gladstone or Disraeli could have openly defied
     every social and moral obligation all their lives as your fa-
     ther has? They simply wouldnt have dared. I asked   145
     Gladstone to take it up. I asked The Times to take it up. I
     asked the Lord Chamberlain to take it up. But it was just like
     asking them to declare war on the Sultan. They wouldnt.
     They said they couldnt touch him. I believe they were afraid.
STEPHEN: What could they do? He does not actually break   150
     the law.
LADY BRITOMART: Not break the law! He is always breaking the
     law. He broke the law when he was born: his parents were
     not married.
STEPHEN: Mother! Is that true?   155
LADY BRITOMART: Of course it's true: that was why we separated.
STEPHEN: He married without letting you know that!
LADY BRITOMART: *(Rather taken aback by this inference.)* Oh no.
     To do Andrew justice, that was not the sort of thing he did.
     Besides, you know the Undershaft motto: Unashamed.   160
     Everybody knew.
STEPHEN: But you said that was why you separated.
LADY BRITOMART: Yes, because he was not content with being a
     foundling himself: he wanted to disinherit you for another
     foundling. That was what I couldnt stand.   165
STEPHEN: *(Ashamed.)* Do you mean for—for—for—
LADY BRITOMART: Dont stammer, Stephen. Speak distinctly.
STEPHEN: But this is so frightful to me, mother. To have to
     speak to you about such things!
LADY BRITOMART: It's not pleasant for me, either, especially if   170
     you are still so childish that you must make it worse by a
     display of embarrassment. It is only in the middle classes,
     Stephen, that people get into a state of dumb helpless hor-
     ror when they find that there are wicked people in the
     world. In our class, we have to decide what is to be done   175

with wicked people; and nothing should disturb our self-possession. Now ask your question properly.

STEPHEN: Mother: have you no consideration for me? For Heaven's sake either treat me as a child, as you always do,
180 and tell me nothing at all or tell me everything and let me take it as best I can.

LADY BRITOMART: Treat you as a child! What do you mean? It is most unkind and ungrateful of you to say such a thing. You know I have never treated any of you as children. I have
185 always made you my companions and friends, and allowed you perfect freedom to do and say whatever you like, so long as you liked what I could approve of.

STEPHEN: (Desperately.) I daresay we have been the very imperfect children of a very perfect mother; but I do beg you to
190 let me alone for once, and tell me about this horrible business of my father wanting to set me aside for another son.

LADY BRITOMART: (Amazed.) Another son! I never said anything of the kind. I never dreamt of such a thing. This is what comes of interrupting me.

195 STEPHEN: But you said—

LADY BRITOMART: (Cutting him short.) Now be a good boy, Stephen, and listen to me patiently. The Undershafts are descended from a foundling in the parish of St Andrew Undershaft in the city. That was long ago, in the reign of
200 James the First. Well, this foundling was adopted by an armorer and gun-maker. In the course of time the foundling succeeded to the business; and from some notion of gratitude, or some vow or something, he adopted another foundling, and left the business to him. And that foundling
205 did the same. Ever since that, the cannon business has always been left to an adopted foundling named Andrew Undershaft.

STEPHEN: But did they never marry? Were there no legitimate sons?

210 LADY BRITOMART: Oh yes: they married just as your father did; and they were rich enough to buy land for their own children and leave them well provided for. But they always adopted and trained some foundling to succeed them in the business; and of course they always quarrelled with their
215 wives furiously over it. Your father was adopted in that way; and he pretends to consider himself bound to keep up the tradition and adopt somebody to leave the business to. Of course I was not going to stand that. There may have been some reason for it when the Undershafts could only marry
220 women in their own class, whose sons were not fit to govern great estates. But there could be no excuse for passing over my son.

STEPHEN: (Dubiously.) I am afraid I should make a poor hand of managing a cannon foundry.

225 LADY BRITOMART: Nonsense! you could easily get a manager and pay him a salary.

STEPHEN: My father evidently had no great opinion of my capacity.

LADY BRITOMART: Stuff, child! you were only a baby: it had noth-
230 ing to do with your capacity. Andrew did it on principle, just as he did every perverse and wicked thing on principle. When my father remonstrated, Andrew actually told him to his face that history tells us of only two successful institutions: one the Undershaft firm, and the other the Roman
235 Empire under the Antonines. That was because the Antonine

emperors all adopted their successors. Such rubbish! The Stevenages are as good as the Antonines, I hope; and you are a Stevenage. But that was Andrew all over. There you have the man! Always clever and unanswerable when he was defending nonsense and wickedness: always awkward and 240 sullen when he had to behave sensibly and decently!

STEPHEN: Then it was on my account that your home life was broken up, mother. I am sorry.

LADY BRITOMART: Well, dear, there were other differences. I really cannot bear an immoral man. I am not a Pharisee, I 245 hope; and I should not have minded his merely doing wrong things: we are none of us perfect. But your father didnt exactly do wrong things: he said them and thought them: that was what was so dreadful. He really had a sort of religion of wrongness. Just as one doesnt mind men prac- 250 tising immorality so long as they own that they are in the wrong by preaching morality; so I couldnt forgive Andrew for preaching immorality while he practised morality. You would all have grown up without principles, without any knowledge of right and wrong, if he had been in the house. 255 You know, my dear, your father was a very attractive man in some ways. Children did not dislike him; and he took advantage of it to put the wickedest ideas into their heads, and make them quite unmanageable. I did not dislike him myself: very far from it; but nothing can bridge over moral 260 disagreement.

STEPHEN: All this simply bewilders me, mother. People may differ about matters of opinion, or even about religion; but how can they differ about right and wrong? Right is right; and wrong is wrong; and if a man cannot distinguish them 265 properly, he is either a fool or a rascal: thats all.

LADY BRITOMART: (Touched.) Thats my own boy! (She pats his cheek.) Your father never could answer that: he used to laugh and get out of it under cover of some affectionate nonsense. And now that you understand the situation, what do you 270 advise me to do?

STEPHEN: Well, what can you do?

LADY BRITOMART: I must get the money somehow.

STEPHEN: We cannot take money from him. I had rather go and live in some cheap place like Bedford Square or even Hamp- 275 stead than take a farthing of his money.

LADY BRITOMART: But after all, Stephen, our present income comes from Andrew.

STEPHEN: (Shocked.) I never knew that.

LADY BRITOMART: Well, you surely didnt suppose your grand- 280 father had anything to give me. The Stevenages could not do everything for you. We gave you social position. Andrew had to contribute something. He had a very good bargain, I think.

STEPHEN: (Bitterly.) We are utterly dependent on him and his 285 cannons, then?

LADY BRITOMART: Certainly not: the money is settled. But he provided it. So you see it is not a question of taking money from him or not: it is simply a question of how much. I dont want any more for myself. 290

STEPHEN: Nor do I.

LADY BRITOMART: But Sarah does; and Barbara does. That is, Charles Lomax and Adolphus Cusins will cost them more. So I must put my pride in my pocket and ask for it, I suppose. That is your advice, Stephen, is it not? 295

STEPHEN: No.

LADY BRITOMART: (Sharply.) Stephen!

STEPHEN: Of course if you are determined—

300 LADY BRITOMART: I am not determined: I ask your advice; and I am waiting for it. I will not have all the responsibility thrown on my shoulders.

STEPHEN: (Obstinately.) I would die sooner than ask him for another penny.

305 LADY BRITOMART: (Resignedly.) You mean that I must ask him. Very well, Stephen: it shall be as you wish. You will be glad to know that your grandfather concurs. But he thinks I ought to ask Andrew to come here and see the girls. After all, he must have some natural affection for them.

STEPHEN: Ask him here!!!

310 LADY BRITOMART: Do not repeat my words, Stephen. Where else can I ask him?

STEPHEN: I never expected you to ask him at all.

LADY BRITOMART: Now dont tease, Stephen. Come! you see that it is necessary that he should pay us a visit, dont you?

315 STEPHEN: (Reluctantly.) I suppose so, if the girls cannot do without his money.

LADY BRITOMART: Thank you, Stephen: I knew you would give me the right advice when it was properly explained to you. I have asked your father to come this evening. (STEPHEN

320 bounds from his seat.) Dont jump, Stephen: it fidgets me.

STEPHEN: (In utter consternation.) Do you mean to say that my father is coming here tonight—that he may be here at any moment?

LADY BRITOMART: (Looking at her watch.) I said nine. (He gasps.

325 She rises.) Ring the bell, please. (STEPHEN goes to the smaller writing table; presses a button on it; and sits at it with his elbows on the table and his head in his hands, outwitted and overwhelmed.) It is ten minutes to nine yet; and I have to prepare the girls. I asked Charles Lomax and Adolphus to dinner on

330 purpose that they might be here. Andrew had better see them in case he should cherish any delusions as to their being capable of supporting their wives. (The butler enters: LADY BRITOMART goes behind the settee to speak to him.) Morrison: go up to the drawing room and tell everybody to come

335 down here at once. (MORRISON withdraws. LADY BRITOMART turns to STEPHEN.) Now remember, Stephen: I shall need all your countenance and authority. (He rises and tries to recover some vestige of these attributes.) Give me a chair, dear. (He pushes a chair forward from the wall to where she stands, near the

340 smaller writing table. She sits down; and he goes to the armchair, into which he throws himself.) I dont know how Barbara will take it. Ever since they made her a major in the Salvation Army she has developed a propensity to have her own way and order people about which quite cows me sometimes.

345 It's not ladylike: I'm sure I dont know where she picked it up. Anyhow, Barbara shant bully me; but still it's just as well that your father should be here before she has time to refuse to meet him or make a fuss. Dont look nervous, Stephen: it will only encourage Barbara to make difficulties.

350 I am nervous enough, goodness knows; but I dont shew it.

(SARAH and BARBARA come in with their respective young men, CHARLES LOMAX and ADOLPHUS CUSINS. SARAH is slender, bored, and mundane. BARBARA is robuster, jollier, much more energetic. SARAH is fashionably dressed: BARBARA is in Salvation Army uniform.)

LOMAX, a young man about town, is like many other young men about town. He is afflicted with a frivolous sense of humor which plunges him at the most inopportune moments into paroxysms of imperfectly suppressed laughter. CUSINS is a spectacled student, slight, thin haired, and sweet voiced, with a more complex form of LOMAX's complaint. His sense of humor is intellectual and subtle, and is complicated by an appalling temper. The lifelong struggle of a benevolent temperament and a high conscience against impulses of inhuman ridicule and fierce impatience has set up a chronic strain which has visibly wrecked his constitution. He is a most implacable, determined, tenacious, intolerant person who by mere force of character presents himself as—and indeed actually is—considerate, gentle, explanatory, even mild and apologetic, capable possibly of murder, but not of cruelty or coarseness. By the operation of some instinct which is not merciful enough to blind him with the illusions of love, he is obstinately bent on marrying BARBARA. LOMAX likes SARAH and thinks it will be rather a lark to marry her. Consequently he has not attempted to resist LADY BRITOMART's arrangements to that end.)

(All four look as if they had been having a good deal of fun in the drawing room. The girls enter first, leaving the swains outside. SARAH comes to the settee. BARBARA comes in after her and stops at the door.)

BARBARA: Are Cholly and Dolly to come in?

LADY BRITOMART: (Forcibly.) Barbara: I will not have Charles called Cholly: the vulgarity of it positively makes me ill.

BARBARA: It's all right, mother: Cholly is quite correct nowadays. Are they to come in?   355

LADY BRITOMART: Yes, if they will behave themselves.

BARBARA: (Through the door.) Come in, Dolly; and behave yourself.

(BARBARA comes to her mother's writing table. CUSINS enters smiling, and wanders towards LADY BRITOMART.)

SARAH: (Calling.) Come in, Cholly. (LOMAX enters, controlling his features very imperfectly, and places himself vaguely between   360 SARAH and BARBARA.)

LADY BRITOMART: (Peremptorily.) Sit down, all of you. (They sit. CUSINS crosses to the window and seats himself there. LOMAX takes a chair. BARBARA sits at the writing table and SARAH on the settee.) I dont in the least know what you are laughing at,   365 Adolphus. I am surprised at you, though I expected nothing better from Charles Lomax.

CUSINS: (In a remarkably gentle voice.) Barbara has been trying to teach me the West Ham Salvation March.

LADY BRITOMART: I see nothing to laugh at in that; nor should   370 you if you are really converted.

CUSINS: (Sweetly.) You were not present. It was really funny, I believe.

LOMAX: Ripping.

LADY BRITOMART: Be quiet, Charles. Now listen to me, chil-   375 dren. Your father is coming here this evening.

(General stupefaction. LOMAX, SARAH, and BARBARA rise: SARAH scared, and BARBARA amused and expectant.)

LOMAX: (Remonstrating.) Oh I say!

LADY BRITOMART: You are not called on to say anything, Charles.

SARAH: Are you serious, mother?   380

LADY BRITOMART: Of course I am serious. It is on your account, Sarah, and also on Charles's. (*Silence.* SARAH *sits, with a shrug.* CHARLES *looks painfully unworthy.*) I hope you are not going to object, Barbara.

385 BARBARA: I! why should I? My father has a soul to be saved like anybody else. He's quite welcome as far as I am concerned. (*She sits on the table, and softly whistles 'Onward, Christian Soldiers.'*)

LOMAX: (*Still remonstrant.*) But really, dont you know! Oh I say!

390 LADY BRITOMART: (*Frigidly.*) What do you wish to convey, Charles?

LOMAX: Well, you must admit that this is a bit thick.

LADY BRITOMART: (*Turning with ominous suavity to* CUSINS.) Adolphus: you are a professor of Greek. Can you translate

395 Charles Lomax's remarks into reputable English for us?

CUSINS: (*Cautiously.*) If I may say so, Lady Brit, I think Charles has rather happily expressed what we all feel. Homer, speaking of Autolycus, uses the same phrase. πυκινὸν δόμον ἐλθεῖν means a bit thick.

400 LOMAX: (*Handsomely.*) Not that I mind, you know, if Sarah dont. (*He sits.*)

LADY BRITOMART: (*Crushingly.*) Thank you. Have I your permission, Adolphus, to invite my own husband to my own house?

405 CUSINS: (*Gallantly.*) You have my unhesitating support in everything you do.

LADY BRITOMART: Tush! Sarah: have you nothing to say?

SARAH: Do you mean that he is coming regularly to live here?

LADY BRITOMART: Certainly not. The spare room is ready for

410 him if he likes to stay for a day or two and see a little more of you; but there are limits.

SARAH: Well, he cant eat us, I suppose. *I* dont mind.

LOMAX: (*Chuckling.*) I wonder how the old man will take it.

LADY BRITOMART: Much as the old woman will, no doubt,

415 Charles.

LOMAX: (*Abashed.*) I didnt mean—at least—

LADY BRITOMART: You didnt think, Charles. You never do; and the result is, you never mean anything. And now please attend to me, children. Your father will be quite a stranger

420 to us.

LOMAX: I suppose he hasnt seen Sarah since she was a little kid.

LADY BRITOMART: Not since she was a little kid, Charles, as you express it with that elegance of diction and refinement of thought that seem never to desert you. Accordingly—er—

425 (*Impatiently.*) Now I have forgotten what I was going to say. That comes of your provoking me to be sarcastic, Charles. Adolphus: will you kindly tell me where I was.

CUSINS: (*Sweetly.*) You were saying that as Mr Undershaft has not seen his children since they were babies, he will form

430 his opinion of the way you have brought them up from their behavior tonight, and that therefore you wish us all to be particularly careful to conduct ourselves well, especially Charles.

LADY BRITOMART: (*With emphatic approval.*) Precisely.

435 LOMAX: Look here, Dolly: Lady Brit didnt say that.

LADY BRITOMART: (*Vehemently.*) I did, Charles. Adolphus's recollection is perfectly correct. It is most important that you should be good; and I do beg you for once not to pair off into opposite corners and giggle and whisper while I am

440 speaking to your father.

BARBARA: All right, mother. We'll do you credit. (*She comes off the table, and sits in her chair with ladylike elegance.*)

LADY BRITOMART: Remember, Charles, that Sarah will want to feel proud of you instead of ashamed of you.

445 LOMAX: Oh I say! theres nothing to be exactly proud of, dont you know.

LADY BRITOMART: Well, try and look as if there was.

(MORRISON, *pale and dismayed, breaks into the room in unconcealed disorder.*)

MORRISON: Might I speak a word to you, my lady?

LADY BRITOMART: Nonsense! Shew him up.

450 MORRISON: Yes, my lady. (*He goes.*)

LOMAX: Does Morrison know who it is?

LADY BRITOMART: Of course. Morrison has always been with us.

LOMAX: It must be a regular corker for him, dont you know.

LADY BRITOMART: Is this a moment to get on my nerves,

455 Charles, with your outrageous expressions?

LOMAX: But this is something out of the ordinary, really—

MORRISON: (*At the door.*) The—er—Mr Undershaft. (*He retreats in confusion.*)

(ANDREW UNDERSHAFT *comes in. All rise.* LADY BRITOMART *meets him in the middle of the room behind the settee.*)

(ANDREW *is, on the surface, a stoutish, easygoing elderly man, with kindly patient manners, and an engaging simplicity of character. But he has a watchful, deliberate, waiting, listening face, and formidable reserves of power, both bodily and mental, in his capacious chest and long head. His gentleness is partly that of a strong man who has learnt by experience that his natural grip hurts ordinary people unless he handles them very carefully, and partly the mellowness of age and success. He is also a little shy in his present very delicate situation.*)

LADY BRITOMART: Good evening, Andrew.

460 UNDERSHAFT: How d'ye do, my dear.

LADY BRITOMART: You look a good deal older.

UNDERSHAFT: (*Apologetically.*) I am somewhat older. (*Taking her hand with a touch of courtship.*) Time has stood still with you.

465 LADY BRITOMART: (*Throwing away his hand.*) Rubbish! This is your family.

UNDERSHAFT: (*Surprised.*) Is it so large? I am sorry to say my memory is failing very badly in some things. (*He offers his hand with paternal kindness to* LOMAX.)

LOMAX: (*Jerkily shaking his hand.*) Ahdedoo.

470 UNDERSHAFT: I can see you are my eldest. I am very glad to meet you again, my boy.

LOMAX: (*Remonstrating.*) No, but look here dont you know— (*Overcome.*) Oh I say!

LADY BRITOMART: (*Recovering from momentary speechlessness.*) An-

475 drew: do you mean to say that you dont remember how many children you have?

UNDERSHAFT: Well, I am afraid I—. They have grown so much—er. Am I making any ridiculous mistake? I may as well confess: I recollect only one son. But so many things

480 have happened since, of course—er—

LADY BRITOMART: (*Decisively.*) Andrew: you are talking nonsense. Of course you have only one son.

UNDERSHAFT: Perhaps you will be good enough to introduce me, my dear.

485 LADY BRITOMART: That is Charles Lomax, who is engaged to
Sarah.

UNDERSHAFT: My dear sir, I beg your pardon.

LOMAX: Notatall. Delighted, I assure you.

LADY BRITOMART: This is Stephen.

490 UNDERSHAFT: (Bowing.) Happy to make your acquaintance, Mr
Stephen. Then (Going to CUSINS.) you must be my son. (Tak-
ing CUSINS' hands in his.) How are you, my young friend? (To
LADY BRITOMART) He is very like you, my love.

CUSINS: You flatter me, Mr Undershaft. My name is Cusins: en-
495 gaged to Barbara. (Very explicitly.) That is Major Barbara
Undershaft, of the Salvation Army. That is Sarah, your second daughter. This is Stephen Undershaft, your son.

UNDERSHAFT: My dear Stephen, I beg your pardon.

STEPHEN: Not at all.

500 UNDERSHAFT: Mr Cusins: I am much indebted to you for explaining so precisely. (Turning to SARAH.) Barbara, my
dear—

SARAH: (Prompting him.) Sarah.

UNDERSHAFT: Sarah, of course. (They shake hands. He goes over to
505 BARBARA.) Barbara—I am right this time, I hope?

BARBARA: Quite right. (They shake hands.)

LADY BRITOMART: (Resuming command.) Sit down, all of you. Sit
down, Andrew. (She comes forward and sits on the settee. CUSINS
also brings his chair forward on her left. BARBARA and STEPHEN
510 resume their seats. LOMAX gives his chair to SARAH and goes for
another.)

UNDERSHAFT: Thank you, my love.

LOMAX: (Conversationally, as he brings a chair forward between the
writing table and the settee, and offers it to UNDERSHAFT.) Takes
515 you some time to find out exactly where you are, dont it?

UNDERSHAFT: (Accepting the chair, but remaining standing.) That is
not what embarrasses me, Mr Lomax. My difficulty is that
if I play the part of a father, I shall produce the effect of an
intrusive stranger; and if I play the part of a discreet
520 stranger, I may appear a callous father.

LADY BRITOMART: There is no need for you to play any part at
all, Andrew. You had much better be sincere and natural.

UNDERSHAFT: (Submissively.) Yes, my dear: I daresay that will be
best. (He sits down comfortably.) Well, here I am. Now what
525 can I do for you all?

LADY BRITOMART: You need not do anything, Andrew. You are
one of the family. You can sit with us and enjoy yourself.

(A painfully conscious pause. BARBARA makes a face at LOMAX,
whose too long suppressed mirth immediately explodes in agonized
neighings.)

LADY BRITOMART: (Outraged.) Charles Lomax: if you can behave
yourself, behave yourself. If not, leave the room.

530 LOMAX: I'm awfully sorry, Lady Brit; but really you know, upon
my soul! (He sits on the settee between LADY BRITOMART and
UNDERSHAFT, quite overcome.)

BARBARA: Why dont you laugh if you want to, Cholly? It's
good for your inside.

535 LADY BRITOMART: Barbara: you have had the education of a
lady. Please let your father see that; and dont talk like a
street girl.

UNDERSHAFT: Never mind me, my dear. As you know, I am not
a gentleman; and I was never educated.

LOMAX: (Encouragingly.) Nobody'd know it, I assure you. You 540
look all right, you know.

CUSINS: Let me advise you to study Greek, Mr Undershaft.
Greek scholars are privileged men. Few of them know
Greek; and none of them know anything else; but their position is unchallengeable. Other languages are the qualifi- 545
cations of waiters and commercial travellers: Greek is to a
man of position what the hallmark is to silver.

BARBARA: Dolly: dont be insincere. Cholly: fetch your concertina and play something for us.

LOMAX: (Jumps up eagerly, but checks himself to remark doubtfully to 550
UNDERSHAFT.) Perhaps that sort of thing isnt in your line, eh?

UNDERSHAFT: I am particularly fond of music.

LOMAX: (Delighted.) Are you? Then I'll get it. (He goes upstairs
for the instrument.)

UNDERSHAFT: Do you play, Barbara?   555

BARBARA: Only the tambourine. But Cholly's teaching me the
concertina.

UNDERSHAFT: Is Cholly also a member of the Salvation Army?

BARBARA: No: he says it's bad form to be a dissenter. But I dont
despair of Cholly. I made him come yesterday to a meeting 560
at the dock gates, and take the collection in his hat.

UNDERSHAFT: (Looks whimsically at his wife.)!!

LADY BRITOMART: It is not my doing, Andrew. Barbara is old
enough to take her own way. She has no father to advise her.

BARBARA: Oh yes she has. There are no orphans in the Salvation 565
Army.

UNDERSHAFT: Your father there has a great many children and
plenty of experience, eh?

BARBARA: (Looking at him with quick interest and nodding.) Just
so. How did you come to understand that? (LOMAX is heard 570
at the door trying the concertina.)

LADY BRITOMART: Come in, Charles. Play us something at once.

LOMAX: Righto! (He sits down in his former place, and preludes.)

UNDERSHAFT: One moment, Mr Lomax. I am rather interested
in the Salvation Army. Its motto might be my own: Blood 575
and Fire.

LOMAX: (Shocked.) But not your sort of blood and fire, you
know.

UNDERSHAFT: My sort of blood cleanses: my sort of fire purifies.

BARBARA: So do ours. Come down tomorrow to my shelter— 580
the West Ham shelter—and see what we're doing. We're
going to march to a great meeting in the Assembly Hall at
Mile End. Come and see the shelter and then march with
us: it will do you a lot of good. Can you play anything?

UNDERSHAFT: In my youth I earned pennies, and even shillings 585
occasionally, in the streets and in public house parlors by
my natural talent for stepdancing. Later on, I became a
member of the Undershaft orchestral society, and performed
passably on the tenor trombone.

LOMAX: (Scandalized—putting down the concertina.) Oh I say!   590

BARBARA: Many a sinner has played himself into heaven on the
trombone, thanks to the Army.

LOMAX: (To BARBARA, still rather shocked.) Yes; but what about
the cannon business, dont you know? (To UNDERSHAFT.)
Getting into heaven is not exactly in your line, is it?   595

LADY BRITOMART: Charles!!!

LOMAX: Well; but it stands to reason, dont it? The cannon
business may be necessary and all that: we cant get on without cannons; but it isnt right, you know. On the other

600   hand, there may be a certain amount of tosh about the
      Salvation Army—I belong to the Established Church
      myself—but still you cant deny that it's religion; and you
      cant go against religion, can you? At least unless youre
      downright immoral, dont you know.

605   UNDERSHAFT: You hardly appreciate my position, Mr Lomax—
      LOMAX: (Hastily.) I'm not saying anything against you per-
      sonally—
      UNDERSHAFT: Quite so, quite so. But consider for a moment.
      Here I am, a profiteer in mutilation and murder. I find my-
610   self in a specially amiable humor just now because, this
      morning, down at the foundry, we blew twenty-seven
      dummy soldiers into fragments with a gun which formerly
      destroyed only thirteen.
      LOMAX: (Leniently.) Well, the more destructive war becomes,
615   the sooner it will be abolished, eh?
      UNDERSHAFT: Not at all. The more destructive war becomes the
      more fascinating we find it. No, Mr Lomax: I am obliged to
      you for making the usual excuse for my trade; but I am not
      ashamed of it. I am not one of those men who keep their
620   morals and their business in watertight compartments. All
      the spare money my trade rivals spend on hospitals, cathe-
      drals, and other receptacles for conscience money, I devote
      to experiments and researches in improved methods of de-
      stroying life and property. I have always done so; and I al-
625   ways shall. Therefore your Christmas card moralities of
      peace on earth and goodwill among men are of no use to
      me. Your Christianity, which enjoins you to resist not evil,
      and to turn the other cheek, would make me a bankrupt.
      My morality—my religion—must have a place for cannons
630   and torpedoes in it.
      STEPHEN: (Coldly—almost sullenly.) You speak as if there were
      half a dozen moralities and religions to choose from, instead
      of one true morality and one true religion.
      UNDERSHAFT: For me there is only one true morality; but it
635   might not fit you, as you do not manufacture aerial battle-
      ships. There is only one true morality for every man; but
      every man has not the same true morality.
      LOMAX: (Overtaxed.) Would you mind saying that again? I
      didnt quite follow it.
640   CUSINS: It's quite simple. As Euripides says, one man's meat is
      another man's poison morally as well as physically.
      UNDERSHAFT: Precisely.
      LOMAX: Oh, that! Yes, yes, yes. True. True.
      STEPHEN: In other words, some men are honest and some are
645   scoundrels.
      BARBARA: Bosh! There are no scoundrels.
      UNDERSHAFT: Indeed? Are there any good men?
      BARBARA: No. Not one. There are neither good men nor
      scoundrels: there are just children of one Father; and the
650   sooner they stop calling one another names the better. You
      neednt talk to me: I know them. I've had scores of them
      through my hands: scoundrels, criminals, infidels, philan-
      thropists, missionaries, county councillors, all sorts. Theyre
      all just the same sort of sinner; and theres the same salva-
655   tion ready for them all.
      UNDERSHAFT: May I ask have you ever saved a maker of cannons?
      BARBARA: No. Will you let me try?
      UNDERSHAFT: Well, I will make a bargain with you. If I go to
      see you tomorrow in your Salvation Shelter, will you come
660   the day after to see me in my cannon works?

      BARBARA: Take care. It may end in your giving up the cannons
      for the sake of the Salvation Army.
      UNDERSHAFT: Are you sure it will not end in your giving up the
      Salvation Army for the sake of the cannons?
665   BARBARA: I will take my chance of that.
      UNDERSHAFT: And I will take my chance of the other. (They
      shake hands on it.) Where is your shelter?
      BARBARA: In West Ham. At the sign of the cross. Ask anybody
      in Canning Town. Where are your works?
670   UNDERSHAFT: In Perivale St Andrews. At the sign of the sword.
      Ask anybody in Europe.
      LOMAX: Hadnt I better play something?
      BARBARA: Yes. Give us 'Onward, Christian Soldiers.'
      LOMAX: Well, thats rather a strong order to begin with, dont
675   you know. Suppose I sing 'Thourt passing hence, my
      brother.' It's much the same tune.
      BARBARA: It's too melancholy. You get saved, Cholly; and youll
      pass hence, my brother, without making such a fuss about it.
      LADY BRITOMART: Really, Barbara, you go on as if religion were
680   a pleasant subject. Do have some sense of propriety.
      UNDERSHAFT: I do not find it an unpleasant subject, my dear. It
      is the only one that capable people really care for.
      LADY BRITOMART: (Looking at her watch.) Well, if you are deter-
      mined to have it, I insist on having it in a proper and re-
      spectable way. Charles: ring for prayers.   685

      (General amazement. STEPHEN rises in dismay.)

      LOMAX: (Rising.) Oh I say!
      UNDERSHAFT: (Rising.) I am afraid I must be going.
      LADY BRITOMART: You cannot go now, Andrew: it would be
      most improper. Sit down. What will the servants think?
      UNDERSHAFT: My dear: I have conscientious scruples. May I   690
      suggest a compromise? If Barbara will conduct a little ser-
      vice in the drawing room, with Mr Lomax as organist, I will
      attend it willingly. I will even take part, if a trombone can
      be procured.
      LADY BRITOMART: Dont mock, Andrew.   695
      UNDERSHAFT: (Shocked—to BARBARA.) You dont think I am
      mocking, my love, I hope.
      BARBARA: No, of course not; and it wouldnt matter if you were:
      half the Army came to their first meeting for a lark. (Ris-
      ing.) Come along. (She throws her arm round her father and   700
      sweeps him out, calling to the others from the threshold.) Come,
      Dolly. Come, Cholly.

      (CUSINS rises.)

      LADY BRITOMART: I will not be disobeyed by everybody. Adol-
      phus: sit down. (He does not.) Charles: you may go. You are
      not fit for prayers: you cannot keep your countenance.   705
      LOMAX: Oh I say! (He goes out.)
      LADY BRITOMART: (Continuing.) But you, Adolphus, can behave
      yourself if you choose to. I insist on your staying.
      CUSINS: My dear Lady Brit: there are things in the family prayer
      book that I couldnt bear to hear you say.   710
      LADY BRITOMART: What things, pray?
      CUSINS: Well, you would have to say before all the servants that
      we have done things we ought not to have done, and left
      undone things we ought to have done, and that there is no
      health in us. I cannot bear to hear you doing yourself such   715
      an injustice, and Barbara such an injustice. As for myself, I

flatly deny it: I have done my best. I shouldnt dare to marry Barbara—I couldnt look you in the face—if it were true. So I must go to the drawing room.

720 LADY BRITOMART: (Offended.) Well, go. (He starts for the door.) And remember this, Adolphus (He turns to listen.): I have a very strong suspicion that you went to the Salvation Army to worship Barbara and nothing else. And I quite appreciate the very clever way in which you systematically hum-
725 bug me. I have found you out. Take care Barbara doesnt. Thats all.

CUSINS: (With unruffled sweetness.) Dont tell on me. (He steals out.)

LADY BRITOMART: Sarah: if you want to go, go. Anything's better than to sit there as if you wished you were a thousand
730 miles away.

SARAH: (Languidly.) Very well, mamma. (She goes.)

(LADY BRITOMART, with a sudden flounce, gives way to a little gust of tears.)

STEPHEN: (Going to her.) Mother: whats the matter?

LADY BRITOMART: (Swishing away her tears with her handkerchief.) Nothing. Foolishness. You can go with him, too, if you
735 like, and leave me with the servants.

STEPHEN: Oh, you mustnt think that, mother. I—I dont like him.

LADY BRITOMART: The others do. That is the injustice of a woman's lot. A woman has to bring up her children; and
740 that means to restrain them, to deny them things they want, to set them tasks, to punish them when they do wrong, to do all the unpleasant things. And then the father, who has nothing to do but pet them and spoil them, comes in when all her work is done and steals their affection from her.

745 STEPHEN: He has not stolen our affection from you. It is only curiosity.

LADY BRITOMART: (Violently.) I wont be consoled, Stephen. There is nothing the matter with me. (She rises and goes to-wards the door.)

750 STEPHEN: Where are you going, mother?

LADY BRITOMART: To the drawing room, of course. (She goes out. 'Onward, Christian Soldiers,' on the concertina, with tambourine accompaniment, is heard when the door opens.) Are you coming, Stephen?

755 STEPHEN: No. Certainly not. (She goes. He sits down on the settee, with compressed lips and an expression of strong dislike.)

——— ACT TWO ———

The yard of the West Ham shelter of the Salvation Army is a cold place on a January morning. The building itself, an old warehouse, is newly whitewashed. Its gabled end projects into the yard in the middle, with a door on the ground floor, and another in the loft above it without any balcony or ladder, but with a pulley rigged over it for hoisting sacks. Those who come from this central gable end into the yard have the gateway leading to the street on their left, with a stone horse-trough just beyond it, and, on the right, a penthouse shielding a table from the weather. There are forms at the table; and on them are seated a man and a woman, both much down on their luck, finishing a meal of bread (one thick slice each, with margarine and golden syrup) and diluted milk.

The man, a workman out of employment, is young, agile, a talker, a poser, sharp enough to be capable of anything in reason except honesty

or altruistic considerations of any kind. The woman is a commonplace old bundle of poverty and hard-worn humanity. She looks sixty and probably is forty-five. If they were rich people, gloved and muffed and well wrapped up in furs and overcoats, they would be numbed and miserable; for it is a grindingly cold raw January day; and a glance at the background of grimy warehouses and leaden sky visible over the whitewashed walls of the yard would drive any idle rich person straight to the Mediterranean. But these two, being no more troubled with visions of the Mediterranean than of the moon, and being compelled to keep more of their clothes in the pawnshop, and less on their persons, in winter than in summer, are not depressed by the cold: rather are they stung into vivacity, to which their meal has just now given an almost jolly turn. The man takes a pull at his mug, and then gets up and moves about the yard with his hands deep in his pockets, occasionally breaking into a stepdance.

THE WOMAN: Feel better arter your meal, sir?

THE MAN: No. Call that a meal! Good enough for you, praps; but wot is it to me, an intelligent workin man.

THE WOMAN: Workin man! Wot are you?

THE MAN: Painter.   5

THE WOMAN: (Sceptically.) Yus, I dessay.

THE MAN: Yus, you dessay! I know. Every loafer that cant do nothink calls itself a painter. Well, I'm a real painter: grainer, finisher, thirty-eight bob a week when I can get it.

THE WOMAN: Then why dont you go and get it?   10

THE MAN: I'll tell you why. Fust: I'm intelligent—fffff! it's rotten cold here (He dances a step or two.)—yes: intelligent beyond the station o life into which it has pleased the capitalists to call me; and they dont like a man that sees through em. Second, an intelligent bein needs a doo share 15 of appiness; so I drink somethink cruel when I get the chawnce. Third, I stand by my class and do as little as I can so's to leave arf the job for me fellow workers. Fourth, I'm fly enough to know wots inside the law and wots outside it; and inside it I do as the capitalists do: pinch wot I can lay 20 me ands on. In a proper state of society I am sober, industrious and honest: in Rome, so to speak, I do as the Romans do. Wots the consequence? When trade is bad—and it's rotten bad just now—and the employers az to sack arf their men, they generally start on me.   25

THE WOMAN: Whats your name?

THE MAN: Price. Bronterre O'Brien Price. Usually called Snobby Price, for short.

THE WOMAN: Snobby's a carpenter, aint it? You said you was a painter.   30

PRICE: Not that kind of snob, but the genteel sort. I'm too uppish, owing to my intelligence, and my father being a Chartist and a reading, thinking man: a stationer, too. I'm none of your common hewers of wood and drawers of water; and dont you forget it. (He returns to his seat at the table, and 35 takes up his mug.) Wots your name?

THE WOMAN: Rummy Mitchens, sir.

PRICE: (Quaffing the remains of his milk to her.) Your elth, Miss Mitchens.

RUMMY: (Correcting him.) Missis Mitchens.   40

PRICE: Wot! Oh Rummy, Rummy! Respectable married woman, Rummy, gittin rescued by the Salvation Army by pretendin to be a bad un. Same old game!

RUMMY: What am I to do? I cant starve. Them Salvation lasses is dear good girls; but the better you are, the worse they 45

likes to think you were before they rescued you. Why
shouldnt they av a bit o credit, poor loves? theyre worn to
rags by their work. And where would they get the money
to rescue us if we was to let on we're no worse than other
50 people? You know what ladies and gentlemen are.
PRICE: Thievin swine! Wish I ad their job, Rummy, all the
same. Wot does Rummy stand for? Pet name praps?
RUMMY: Short for Romola.
PRICE: For wot!?
55 RUMMY: Romola. It was out of a new book. Somebody me
mother wanted me to grow up like.
PRICE: We're companions in misfortune, Rummy. Both on us
got names that nobody cawnt pronounce. Consequently I'm
Snobby and youre Rummy because Bill and Sally wasnt
60 good enough for our parents. Such is life!
RUMMY: Who saved you, Mr Price? Was it Major Barbara?
PRICE: No: I come here on my own. I'm going to be Bronterre
O'Brien Price, the converted painter. I know wot they like.
I'll tell em how I blasphemed and gambled and wopped my
65 poor old mother—
RUMMY: (Shocked.) Used you to beat your mother?
PRICE: Not likely. She used to beat me. No matter: you come
and listen to the converted painter, and youll hear how she
was a pious woman that taught me me prayers at er knee,
70 an how I used to come home drunk and drag her out o bed
be er snow white airs, an lam into er with the poker.
RUMMY: Thats whats so unfair to us women. Your confessions
is just as big lies as ours: you dont tell what you really done
no more than us; but you men can tell your lies right out at
75 the meetins and be made much of for it; while the sort o
confessions we az to make az to be wispered to one lady at
a time. It aint right, spite of all their piety.
PRICE: Right! Do you spose the Army'd be allowed if it went
and did right? Not much. It combs our air and makes us
80 good little blokes to be robbed and put upon. But I'll play
the game as good as any of em. I'll see somebody struck by
lightnin, or hear a voice sayin 'Snobby Price: where will you
spend eternity?' I'll av a time of it, I tell you.
RUMMY: You wont be let drink, though.
85 PRICE: I'll take it out in gorspellin, then. I dont want to drink
if I can get fun enough any other way.

(JENNY HILL, a pale, overwrought, pretty Salvation lass of 18, comes
in through the yard gate, leading PETER SHIRLEY, a half hardened,
half worn-out elderly man, weak with hunger.)

JENNY: (Supporting him.) Come! pluck up. I'll get you something to eat. Youll be all right then.
PRICE: (Rising and hurrying officiously to take the old man off
90 JENNY's hands.) Poor old man! Cheer up, brother: youll find
rest and peace and appiness ere. Hurry up with the food,
miss: e's fair done. (JENNY hurries into the shelter.) Ere, buck
up, daddy! she's fetchin y'a thick slice o breadn treacle, an
a mug o skyblue. (He seats him at the corner of the table.)
95 RUMMY: (Gaily.) Keep up your old art! Never say die!
SHIRLEY: I'm not an old man. I'm only 46. I'm as good as ever
I was. The grey patch come in my hair before I was thirty.
All it wants is three pennorth o hair dye: am I to be turned
on the streets to starve for it? Holy God! I've worked ten to
100 twelve hours a day since I was thirteen, and paid my way all

through; and now am I to be thrown into the gutter and my
job given to a young man that can do it no better than me
because Ive black hair that goes white at the first change?
PRICE: (Cheerfully.) No good jawrin about it. Youre only a
jumped-up, jerked-off, orspittle-turned-out incurable of an 105
ole workin man: who cares about you? Eh? Make the
thievin swine give you a meal: theyve stole many a one from
you. Get a bit o your own back. (JENNY returns with the usual
meal.) There you are, brother. Awsk a blessin an tuck that
into you.   110
SHIRLEY: (Looking at it ravenously but not touching it, and crying
like a child.) I never took anything before.
JENNY: (Petting him.) Come, come! the Lord sends it to you: he
wasnt above taking bread from his friends; and why should
you be? Besides, when we find you a job you can pay us for 115
it if you like.
SHIRLEY: (Eagerly.) Yes, yes: thats true. I can pay you back: it's
only a loan. (Shivering.) O Lord! oh Lord! (He turns to the
table and attacks the meal ravenously.)
JENNY: Well, Rummy, are you more comfortable now?   120
RUMMY: God bless you, lovey! youve fed my body and saved my
soul, havnt you? (JENNY, touched, kisses her.) Sit down and
rest a bit: you must be ready to drop.
JENNY: Ive been going hard since morning. But theres more
work than we can do. I mustnt stop.   125
RUMMY: Try a prayer for just two minutes. Youll work all the
better after.
JENNY: (Her eyes lighting up.) Oh isnt it wonderful how a few
minutes prayer revives you! I was quite lightheaded at
twelve o'clock, I was so tired; but Major Barbara just sent   130
me to pray for five minutes; and I was able to go on as if I
had only just begun. (To PRICE.) Did you have a piece of
bread?
PRICE: (With unction.) Yes, miss; but Ive got the piece that I
value more; and thats the peace that passeth hall hanner-   135
stennin.
RUMMY: (Fervently.) Glory Hallelujah!

(BILL WALKER, a rough customer of about 25, appears at the yard gate
and looks malevolently at JENNY.)

JENNY: That makes me so happy. When you say that, I feel
wicked for loitering here. I must get to work again.

(She is hurrying to the shelter, when the new-comer moves quickly up
to the door and intercepts her. His manner is so threatening that she retreats as he comes at her truculently, driving her down the yard.)

BILL: Aw knaow you. Youre the one that took awy maw girl.   140
Youre the one that set er agen me. Well, I'm gowin to ev er
aht. Not that Aw care a carse for er or you: see? Bat Aw'll
let er knaow; and Aw'll let you knaow. Aw'm gowing to
give her a doin thatll teach er to cat awy from me. Nah in
wiv you and tell er to cam aht afore Aw cam in and kick er   145
aht. Tell er Bill Walker wants er. She'll knaow wot thet
means; and if she keeps me witin itll be worse. You stop to
jawr beck at me; and Aw'll stawt on you: d'ye eah? Theres
your wy. In you gow. (He takes her by the arm and slings her
towards the door of the shelter. She falls on her hand and knee.   150
RUMMY helps her up again.)

PRICE: *(Rising, and venturing irresolutely towards* BILL.*)* Easy there, mate. She aint doin you no arm.

BILL: Oo are you callin mite? *(Standing over him threateningly.)*
155 Youre gowin to stend ap for er, aw yer? Put ap your ends.

RUMMY: *(Running indignantly to him to scold him.)* Oh, you great brute—*(He instantly swings his left hand back against her face. She screams and reels back to the trough, where she sits down, cov-ering her bruised face with her hands and rocking herself and
160 moaning with pain.)*

JENNY: *(Going to her.)* Oh, God forgive you! How could you strike an old woman like that?

BILL: *(Seizing her by the hair so violently that she also screams, and tearing her away from the old woman.)* You Gawd forgimme
165 again an Aw'll Gawd forgive you one on the jawr thetll stop you pryin for a week. *(Holding her and turning fiercely on* PRICE.*)* Ev you ennything to sy agen it?

PRICE: *(Intimidated.)* No, matey: she aint anything to do with me.

170 BILL: Good job for you! Aw'd pat two meals into you and fawt you with one finger arter, you stawved cur. *(To* JENNY.*)* Nah are you gowin to fetch aht Mog Ebbijem; or em Aw to knock your fice off you and fetch her meself?

JENNY: *(Writhing in his grasp.)* Oh please someone go in and tell
175 Major Barbara—*(She screams again as he wrenches her head down; and* PRICE *and* RUMMY *flee into the shelter.)*

BILL: You want to gow in and tell your Mijor of me, do you?

JENNY: Oh please dont drag my hair. Let me go.

BILL: Do you or downt you? *(She stifles a scream.)* Yus or nao?

180 JENNY: God give me strength!

BILL: *(Striking her with his fist in the face.)* Gow an shaow her thet, and tell her if she wants one lawk it to cam and inter-fere with me. *(*JENNY, *crying with pain, goes into the shed. He goes to the form and addresses the old man.)* Eah: finish your
185 mess; an git aht o maw wy.

SHIRLEY: *(Springing up and facing him fiercely, with the mug in his hand.)* You take a liberty with me, and I'll smash you over the face with the mug and cut your eye out. Aint you satis-fied—young whelps like you—with takin the bread out o
190 the mouths of your elders that have brought you up and slaved for you, but you must come shovin and cheekin in here, where the bread o charity is sickenin in our stummicks?

BILL: *(Contemptuously, but backing a little.)* Wot good are you, you
195 aold palsy mag? Wot good are you?

SHIRLEY: As good as you and better. I'll do a day's work agen you or any fat young soaker of your age. Go and take my job at Horrockses, where I worked for ten year. They want young men there: they cant afford to keep men over forty-
200 five. Theyre very sorry—give you a character and happy to help you to get anything suited to your years—sure a steady man wont be long out of a job. Well, let em try you. Theyll find the differ. What do you know? Not as much as how to beeyave yourself—layin your dirty fist across the mouth of
205 a respectable woman!

BILL: Downt provowk me to ly it across yours: d'ye eah?

SHIRLEY: *(With blighting contempt.)* Yes: you like an old man to hit, dont you, when youve finished with the women. I aint seen you hit a young one yet.

210 BILL: *(Stung.)* You loy, you aold soupkitchener, you. There was a yang menn eah. Did Aw offer to itt him or did Aw not?

SHIRLEY: Was he starvin or was he not? Was he a man or only a crosseyed thief an a loafer? Would you hit my son-in-law's brother?

BILL: Oo's ee?   215

SHIRLEY: Todger Fairmile o Balls Pond. Him that won £20 off the Japanese wrastler at the music hall by standin out 17 minutes 4 seconds agen him.

BILL: *(Sullenly.)* Aw'm nao music awl wrastler. Ken he box?

SHIRLEY: Yes: an you cant.   220

BILL: Wot! Aw cawnt, cawnt Aw? Wots thet you sy *(Threaten-ing him.)*?

SHIRLEY: *(Not budging an inch.)* Will you box Todger Fairmile if I put him on to you? Say the word.

BILL: *(Subsiding with a slouch.)* Aw'll stend ap to enny menn   225
alawv, if he was ten Todger Fairmawls. But Aw dont set ap to be a perfeshnal.

SHIRLEY: *(Looking down on him with unfathomable disdain.)* You box! Slap an old woman with the back o your hand! You hadnt even the sense to hit her where a magistrate couldnt   230
see the mark of it, you silly young lump of conceit and ig-norance. Hit a girl in the jaw and ony make her cry! If Todger Fairmile'd done it, she wouldnt a got up inside o ten minutes, no more than you would if he got on to you. Yah! I'd set about you myself if I had a week's feedin in me   235
instead o two months' starvation. *(He turns his back on him and sits down moodily at the table.)*

BILL: *(Following him and stooping over him to drive the taunt in.)* You loy! youve the bread and treacle in you that you cam eah to beg.   240

SHIRLEY: *(Bursting into tears.)* Oh God! it's true: I'm only an old pauper on the scrap heap. *(Furiously.)* But youll come to it yourself; and then youll know. Youll come to it sooner than a teetotaller like me, fillin yourself with gin at this hour o the mornin!   245

BILL: Aw'm nao gin drinker, you oald lawr; bat wen Aw want to give my girl a bloomin good awdin Aw lawk to ev a bit o devil in me: see? An eah Aw emm, talkin to a rotten aold blawter like you sted o givin her wot for. *(Working himself into a rage.)* Aw'm gowin in there to fetch her aht. *(He makes   250
vengefully for the shelter door.)*

SHIRLEY: Youre going to the station on a stretcher, more likely; and theyll take the gin and the devil out of you there when they get you inside. You mind what youre about: the major here is the Earl o Stevenage's granddaughter.   255

BILL: *(Checked.)* Garn!

SHIRLEY: Youll see.

BILL: *(His resolution oozing.)* Well, Aw aint dan nathin to er.

SHIRLEY: Spose she said you did! who'd believe you?

BILL: *(Very uneasy, skulking back to the corner of the penthouse.)*   260
Gawd! theres no jastice in this cantry. To think wot them people can do! Aw'm as good as er.

SHIRLEY: Tell her so. It's just what a fool like you would do.

*(*BARBARA, *brisk and businesslike, comes from the shelter with a note book, and addresses herself to* SHIRLEY. BILL, *cowed, sits down in the corner on a form, and turns his back on them.)*

BARBARA: Good morning.

SHIRLEY: *(Standing up and taking off his hat.)* Good morning,   265
miss.

BARBARA: Sit down: make yourself at home. (*He hesitates; but she puts a friendly hand on his shoulder and makes him obey.*) Now then! since youve made friends with us, we want to know all about you. Names and addresses and trades.

SHIRLEY: Peter Shirley. Fitter. Chucked out two months ago because I was too old.

BARBARA: (*Not at all surprised.*) Youd pass still. Why didnt you dye your hair?

SHIRLEY: I did. Me age come out at a coroner's inquest on me daughter.

BARBARA: Steady?

SHIRLEY: Teetotaller. Never out of a job before. Good worker. And sent to the knackers like an old horse!

BARBARA: No matter: if you did your part God will do his.

SHIRLEY: (*Suddenly stubborn.*) My religion's no concern of anybody but myself.

BARBARA: (*Guessing.*) I know. Secularist?

SHIRLEY: (*Hotly.*) Did I offer to deny it?

BARBARA: Why should you? My own father's a Secularist, I think. Our Father—yours and mine—fulfils himself in many ways; and I daresay he knew what he was about when he made a Secularist of you. So buck up, Peter! we can always find a job for a steady man like you. (SHIRLEY, *disarmed and a little bewildered, touches his hat. She turns from him to* BILL.) Whats your name?

BILL: (*Insolently.*) Wots thet to you?

BARBARA: (*Calmly making a note.*) Afraid to give his name. Any trade?

BILL: Oo's afride to give is nime? (*Doggedly, with a sense of heroically defying the House of Lords in the person of Lord Stevenage.*) If you want to bring a chawge agen me, bring it. (*She waits, unruffled.*) Moy nime's Bill Walker.

BARBARA: (*As if the name were familiar: trying to remember how.*) Bill Walker? (*Recollecting.*) Oh, I know: you're the man that Jenny Hill was praying for inside just now. (*She enters his name in her note book.*)

BILL: Oo's Jenny Ill? And wot call as she to pry for me?

BARBARA: I dont know. Perhaps it was you that cut her lip.

BILL: (*Defiantly.*) Yus, it was me that cat her lip. Aw aint afride o you.

BARBARA: How could you be, since youre not afraid of God? Youre a brave man, Mr Walker. It takes some pluck to do our work here; but none of us dare lift our hand against a girl like that, for fear of her father in heaven.

BILL: (*Sullenly.*) I want nan o your kentin jawr. I spowse you think Aw cam eah to beg from you, like this demmiged lot eah. Not me. Aw downt want your bread and scripe and ketlep. Aw dont blieve in your Gawd, no more than you do yourself.

BARBARA: (*Sunnily apologetic and ladylike, as on a new footing with him.*) Oh, I beg your pardon for putting your name down, Mr Walker. I didnt understand. I'll strike it out.

BILL: (*Taking this as a slight, and deeply wounded by it.*) Eah! you let maw nime alown. Aint it good enaff to be in your book?

BARBARA: (*Considering.*) Well, you see, theres no use putting down your name unless I can do something for you, is there? Whats your trade?

BILL: (*Still smarting.*) Thets nao concern o yours.

BARBARA: Just so. (*Very businesslike.*) I'll put you down as (*Writing.*) the man who—struck—poor little Jenny Hill—in the mouth.

BILL: (*Rising threateningly.*) See eah. Awve ed enaff o this.

BARBARA: (*Quite sunny and fearless.*) What did you come to us for?

BILL: Aw cam for maw gel, see? Aw cam to tike her aht o this and to brike er jawr for er.

BARBARA: (*Complacently.*) You see I was right about your trade. (BILL, *on the point of retorting furiously, finds himself, to his great shame and terror, in danger of crying instead. He sits down again suddenly.*) Whats her name?

BILL: (*Dogged.*) Er nime's Mog Ebbijem: thets wot her nime is.

BARBARA: Mog Habbijam! Oh, she's gone to Canning Town, to our barracks there.

BILL: (*Fortified by his resentment of Mog's perfidy.*) Is she? (*Vindictively.*) Then Aw'm gowin to Kennintahn arter her. (*He crosses to the gate; hesitates; finally comes back at* BARBARA.) Are you loyin to me to git shat o me?

BARBARA: I dont want to get shut of you. I want to keep you here and save your soul. Youd better stay: youre going to have a bad time today, Bill.

BILL: Oo's gowin to give it to me? You, preps?

BARBARA: Someone you dont believe in. But youll be glad afterwards.

BILL: (*Slinking off.*) Aw'll gow to Kennintahn to be aht o reach o your tangue. (*Suddenly turning on her with intense malice.*) And if Aw downt fawnd Mog there, Aw'll cam beck and do two years for you, selp me Gawd if Aw downt!

BARBARA: (*A shade kindlier, if possible.*) It's no use, Bill. She's got another bloke.

BILL: Wot!

BARBARA: One of her own converts. He fell in love with her when he saw her with her soul saved, and her face clean, and her hair washed.

BILL: (*Surprised.*) Wottud she wash it for, the carroty slat? It's red.

BARBARA: It's quite lovely now, because she wears a new look in her eyes with it. It's a pity youre too late. The new bloke has put your nose out of joint, Bill.

BILL: Aw'll put his nowse aht o joint for him. Not that Aw care a carse for er, mawnd thet. But Aw'll teach her to drop me as if Aw was dirt. And Aw'll teach him to meddle with maw judy. Wots iz bleedin nime?

BARBARA: Sergeant Todger Fairmile.

SHIRLEY: (*Rising with grim joy.*) I'll go with him, miss. I want to see them two meet. I'll take him to the infirmary when it's over.

BILL: (*To* SHIRLEY, *with undissembled misgiving.*) Is thet im you was speakin on?

SHIRLEY: Thats him.

BILL: Im that wrastled in the music awl?

SHIRLEY: The competitions at the National Sportin Club was worth nigh a hundred a year to him. He's gev em up now for religion; so he's a bit fresh for want of the exercise he was accustomed to. He'll be glad to see you. Come along.

BILL: Wots is wight?

SHIRLEY: Thirteen four. (BILL's *last hope expires.*)

BARBARA: Go and talk to him, Bill. He'll convert you.

SHIRLEY: He'll convert your head into a mashed potato.

BILL: (*Sullenly.*) Aw aint afride of im. Aw aint afride of ennybody. Bat e can lick me. She's dan me. (*He sits down moodily on the edge of the horse trough.*)

SHIRLEY: You aint going. I thought not. (*He resumes his seat.*)

BARBARA: (*Calling.*) Jenny!

390 JENNY: (*Appearing at the shelter door with a plaster on the corner of her mouth.*) Yes, Major.

BARBARA: Send Rummy Mitchens out to clear away here.

JENNY: I think she's afraid.

BARBARA: (*Her resemblance to her mother flashing out for a moment.*) Nonsense! she must do as she's told.

395 JENNY: (*Calling into the shelter.*) Rummy: the Major says you must come.

(JENNY *comes to* BARBARA, *purposely keeping on the side next to* BILL, *lest he should suppose that she shrank from him or bore malice.*)

BARBARA: Poor little Jenny! Are you tired? (*Looking at the wounded cheek.*) Does it hurt?

JENNY: No: it's all right now. It was nothing.

400 BARBARA: (*Critically.*) It was as hard as he could hit, I expect. Poor Bill! You dont feel angry with him, do you?

JENNY: Oh no, no, no: indeed I dont, Major, bless his poor heart! (BARBARA *kisses her; and she runs away merrily into the shelter.* BILL *writhes with an agonizing return of his new and*

405 *alarming symptoms, but says nothing.* RUMMY MITCHENS *comes from the shelter.*)

BARBARA: (*Going to meet* RUMMY.) Now Rummy, bustle. Take in those mugs and plates to be washed; and throw the crumbs about for the birds.

(RUMMY *takes the three plates and mugs; but* SHIRLEY *takes back his mug from her, as there is still some milk left in it.*)

410 RUMMY: There aint any crumbs. This aint a time to waste good bread on birds.

PRICE: (*Appearing at the shelter door.*) Gentleman come to see the shelter, Major. Says he's your father.

BARBARA: All right. Coming. (SNOBBY [PRICE] *goes back into the*

415 *shelter, followed by* BARBARA.)

RUMMY: (*Stealing across to* BILL *and addressing him in a subdued voice, but with intense conviction.*) I'd av the lor of you, you flat eared pignosed potwalloper, if she'd let me. Youre no gentleman, to hit a lady in the face. (BILL, *with greater things*

420 *moving in him, takes no notice.*)

SHIRLEY: (*Following her.*) Here! in with you and dont get yourself into more trouble by talking.

RUMMY: (*With hauteur.*) I aint ad the pleasure o being hintroduced to you, as I can remember. (*She goes into the shelter with*

425 *the plates.*)

SHIRLEY: Thats the—

BILL: (*Savagely.*) Downt you talk to me, d'ye eah? You lea me alown, or Aw'll do you a mischief. Aw'm not dirt under your feet, ennywy.

430 SHIRLEY: (*Calmly.*) Dont you be afeerd. You aint such prime company that you need expect to be sought after. (*He is about to go into the shelter when* BARBARA *comes out, with* UNDERSHAFT *on her right.*)

BARBARA: Oh, there you are, Mr Shirley! (*Between them.*) This is

435 my father: I told you he was a Secularist, didnt I? Perhaps youll be able to comfort one another.

UNDERSHAFT: (*Startled.*) A Secularist! Not the least in the world: on the contrary, a confirmed mystic.

BARBARA: Sorry, I'm sure. By the way, papa, what is your reli-
440 gion? in case I have to introduce you again.

UNDERSHAFT: My religion? Well, my dear, I am a Millionaire. That is my religion.

BARBARA: Then I'm afraid you and Mr Shirley wont be able to comfort one another after all. Youre not a Millionaire, are
445 you, Peter?

SHIRLEY: No; and proud of it.

UNDERSHAFT: (*Gravely.*) Poverty, my friend, is not a thing to be proud of.

SHIRLEY: (*Angrily.*) Who made your millions for you? Me and
450 my like. Whats kep us poor? Keepin you rich. I wouldnt have your conscience, not for all your income.

UNDERSHAFT: I wouldnt have your income, not for all your conscience, Mr Shirley. (*He goes to the penthouse and sits down on a form.*)

455 BARBARA: (*Stopping* SHIRLEY *adroitly as he is about to retort.*) You wouldnt think he was my father, would you, Peter? Will you go into the shelter and lend the lasses a hand for a while: we're worked off our feet.

SHIRLEY: (*Bitterly.*) Yes: I'm in their debt for a meal, aint I?

460 BARBARA: Oh, not because youre in their debt, but for love of them, Peter, for love of them. (*He cannot understand, and is rather scandalized.*) There! dont stare at me. In with you; and give that conscience of yours a holiday (*Bustling him into the shelter.*)

465 SHIRLEY: (*As he goes in.*) Ah! it's a pity you never was trained to use your reason, miss. Youd have been a very taking lecturer on Secularism.

(BARBARA *turns to her father.*)

UNDERSHAFT: Never mind me, my dear. Go about your work; and let me watch it for a while.

470 BARBARA: All right.

UNDERSHAFT: For instance, whats the matter with that outpatient over there?

BARBARA: (*Looking at* BILL, *whose attitude has never changed, and whose expression of brooding wrath has deepened.*) Oh, we shall
475 cure him in no time. Just watch. (*She goes over to* BILL *and waits. He glances up at her and casts his eyes down again, uneasy, but grimmer than ever.*) It would be nice to just stamp on Mog Habbijam's face, wouldnt it, Bill?

BILL: (*Starting up from the trough in consternation.*) It's a loy: Aw
480 never said so. (*She shakes her head.*) Oo taold you wot was in moy mawnd?

BARBARA: Only your new friend.

BILL: Wot new friend?

BARBARA: The devil, Bill. When he gets round people they get
485 miserable, just like you.

BILL: (*With a heartbreaking attempt at devil-may-care cheerfulness.*) Aw aint miserable. (*He sits down again, and stretches his legs in an attempt to seem indifferent.*)

BARBARA: Well, if youre happy, why dont you look happy, as
490 we do?

BILL: (*His legs curling back in spite of him.*) Aw'm eppy enaff, Aw tell you. Woy cawnt you lea me alown? Wot ev I dan to you? Aw aint smashed your fice, ev Aw?

BARBARA: (*Softly: wooing his soul.*) It's not me thats getting at
495 you, Bill.

BILL: Oo else is it?

BARBARA: Somebody that doesnt intend you to smash women's faces, I suppose. Somebody or something that wants to make a man of you.

500 BILL: (*Blustering.*) Mike a menn o me! Aint Aw a menn? eh? Oo sez Aw'm not a menn?

BARBARA: Theres a man in you somewhere, I suppose. But why did he let you hit poor little Jenny Hill? That wasnt very manly of him, was it?

505 BILL: (*Tormented.*) Ev dan wiv it, Aw tell you. Chack it. Aw'm sick o your Jenny Ill and er silly little fice.

BARBARA: Then why do you keep thinking about it? Why does it keep coming up against you in your mind? Youre not getting converted, are you?

510 BILL: (*With conviction.*) Not ME. Not lawkly.

BARBARA: Thats right, Bill. Hold out against it. Put out your strength. Dont lets get you cheap. Todger Fairmile said he wrestled for three nights against his salvation harder than he ever wrestled with the Jap at the music hall. He gave in 515 to the Jap when his arm was going to break. But he didnt give in to his salvation until his heart was going to break. Perhaps youll escape that. You havnt any heart, have you?

BILL: Wot d'ye mean? Woy aint Aw got a awt the sime as ennybody else?

520 BARBARA: A man with a heart wouldnt have bashed poor little Jenny's face, would he?

BILL: (*Almost crying.*) Ow, will you lea me alown? Ev Aw ever offered to meddle with you, that you cam neggin and provowkin me lawk this? (*He writhes convulsively from his eyes 525 to his toes.*)

BARBARA: (*With a steady soothing hand on his arm and a gentle voice that never lets him go.*) It's your soul thats hurting you, Bill, and not me. Weve been through it all ourselves. Come with us, Bill. (*He looks wildly round.*) To brave manhood on earth 530 and eternal glory in heaven. (*He is on the point of breaking down.*) Come. (*A drum is heard in the shelter; and* BILL, *with a gasp, escapes from the spell as* BARBARA *turns quickly.* ADOLPHUS [CUSINS] *enters from the shelter with a big drum.*) Oh! there you are, Dolly. Let me introduce a new friend of mine, Mr Bill 535 Walker. This is my bloke, Bill: Mr Cusins. (CUSINS *salutes with his drumstick.*)

BILL: Gowin to merry im?

BARBARA: Yes.

BILL: (*Fervently.*) Gawd elp im! Gaw-aw-aw-awd elp im!

540 BARBARA: Why? Do you think he wont be happy with me?

BILL: Awve aony ed to stend it for a mawnin: e'll ev to stend it for a lawftawm.

CUSINS: That is a frightful reflection, Mr Walker. But I cant tear myself away from her.

545 BILL: Well, Aw ken. (*To* BARBARA.) Eah! do you knaow where Aw'm gowin to, and wot Aw'm gowin to do?

BARBARA: Yes: youre going to heaven; and youre coming back here before the week's out to tell me so.

BILL: You loy. Aw'm gowin to Kennintahn, to spit in Todger 550 Fairmawl's eye. Aw beshed Jenny Ill's fice; an nar Aw'll git me aown fice beshed and cam beck and shaw it to er. Ee'll itt me ardern Aw itt her. Thatll mike us square. (*To* ADOLPHUS [CUSINS].) Is thet fair or is it not? Youre a genlmn: you oughter knaow.

555 BARBARA: Two black eyes wont make one white one, Bill.

BILL: Aw didnt awst you. Cawnt you never keep your mahth shat? Oy awst the genlmn.

CUSINS: (*Reflectively.*) Yes: I think youre right, Mr Walker. Yes: I should do it. It's curious: it's exactly what an ancient Greek would have done.   560

BARBARA: But what good will it do?

CUSINS: Well, it will give Mr Fairmile some exercise; and it will satisfy Mr Walker's soul.

BILL: Rot! there aint nao sach a thing as a saoul. Ah kin you tell wevver Awve a saoul or not? You never seen it.   565

BARBARA: Ive seen it hurting you when you went against it.

BILL: (*With compressed aggravation.*) If you was maw gel and took the word aht o me mahth lawk thet, Aw'd give you sathink youd feel urtin, Aw would. (*To* CUSINS.) You tike maw tip, mite. Stop er jawr; or youll doy afoah your tawm (*With in- 570 tense expression.*) Wore aht: thets wot youll be: wore aht. (*He goes away through the gate.*)

CUSINS: (*Looking after him.*) I wonder!

BARBARA: Dolly! (*Indignant, in her mother's manner.*)

CUSINS: Yes, my dear, it's very wearing to be in love with you. 575 If it lasts, I quite think I shall die young.

BARBARA: Should you mind?

CUSINS: Not at all. (*He is suddenly softened, and kisses her over the drum, evidently not for the first time, as people cannot kiss over a big drum without practice.* UNDERSHAFT *coughs.*)   580

BARBARA: It's all right, papa, weve not forgotten you. Dolly: explain the place to papa: I havnt time. (*She goes busily into the shelter.*)

(UNDERSHAFT *and* ADOLPHUS [CUSINS] *now have the yard to themselves.* UNDERSHAFT, *seated on a form, and still keenly attentive, looks hard at* ADOLPHUS [CUSINS]. ADOLPHUS [CUSINS] *looks hard at him.*)

UNDERSHAFT: I fancy you guess something of what is in my mind, Mr Cusins. (CUSINS *flourishes his drumsticks as if in the 585 act of beating a lively rataplan, but makes no sound.*) Exactly so. But suppose Barbara finds you out!

CUSINS: You know, I do not admit that I am imposing on Barbara. I am quite genuinely interested in the views of the Salvation Army. The fact is, I am a sort of collector of reli- 590 gions; and the curious thing is that I find I can believe them all. By the way, have you any religion?

UNDERSHAFT: Yes.

CUSINS: Anything out of the common?

UNDERSHAFT: Only that there are two things necessary to 595 Salvation.

CUSINS: (*Disappointed, but polite.*) Ah, the Church Catechism. Charles Lomax also belongs to the Established Church.

UNDERSHAFT: The two things are—

CUSINS: Baptism and—   600

UNDERSHAFT: No. Money and gunpowder.

CUSINS: (*Surprised, but interested.*) That is the general opinion of our governing classes. The novelty is in hearing any man confess it.

UNDERSHAFT: Just so.   605

CUSINS: Excuse me: is there any place in your religion for honor, justice, truth, love, mercy and so forth?

UNDERSHAFT: Yes: they are the graces and luxuries of a rich, strong, and safe life.

610 CUSINS: Suppose one is forced to choose between them and
money or gunpowder?

UNDERSHAFT: Choose money and gunpowder; for without
enough of both you cannot afford the others.

CUSINS: That is your religion?

615 UNDERSHAFT: Yes.

(The cadence of this reply makes a full close in the conversation,
CUSINS *twists his face dubiously and contemplates* UNDERSHAFT.
UNDERSHAFT *contemplates him.)*

CUSINS: Barbara wont stand that. You will have to choose between your religion and Barbara.

UNDERSHAFT: So will you, my friend. She will find out that that
drum of yours is hollow.

620 CUSINS: Father Undershaft: you are mistaken: I am a sincere
Salvationist. You do not understand the Salvation Army. It
is the army of joy, of love, of courage: it has banished the
fear and remorse and despair of the old hell-ridden evangel-
ical sects: it marches to fight the devil with trumpet and
625 drum, with music and dancing, with banner and palm, as
becomes a sally from heaven by its happy garrison. It picks
the waster out of the public house and makes a man of him:
it finds a worm wriggling in a back kitchen, and lo! a
woman! Men and women of rank too, sons and daughters of
630 the Highest. It takes the poor professor of Greek, the most
artificial and self-suppressed of human creatures, from his
meal of roots, and lets loose the rhapsodist in him; reveals
the true worship of Dionysos to him; sends him down the
public street drumming dithyrambs *(He plays a thundering*
635 *flourish on the drum.)*

UNDERSHAFT: You will alarm the shelter.

CUSINS: Oh, they are accustomed to these sudden ecstasies.
However, if the drum worries you—*(He pockets the drum-
sticks; unhooks the drum; and stands it on the ground opposite the*
640 *gateway.)*

UNDERSHAFT: Thank you.

CUSINS: You remember what Euripides says about your money
and gunpowder?

UNDERSHAFT: No.

645 CUSINS: *(Declaiming.)*

> One and another
> In money and guns may outpass his brother;
> And men in their millions float and flow
> And seethe with a million hopes as leaven;
650 > And they win their will; or they miss their will;
> And their hopes are dead or are pined for still;
> > But who'er can know
> > As the long days go
> That to live is happy, has found his heaven.

655 My translation: what do you think of it?

UNDERSHAFT: I think, my friend, that if you wish to know, as
the long days go, that to live is happy, you must first acquire money enough for a decent life, and power enough to
be your own master.

660 CUSINS: You are damnably discouraging. *(He resumes his declamation.)*

> Is it so hard a thing to see
> That the spirit of God—whate'er it be—

> The law that abides and changes not, ages long,
> The Eternal and Nature-born: these things be strong? 665
> What else is Wisdom? What of Man's endeavor,
> Or God's high grace so lovely and so great?
> To stand from fear set free? to breathe and wait?
> To hold a hand uplifted over Fate?
> And shall not Barbara be loved for ever? 670

UNDERSHAFT: Euripides mentions Barbara, does he?

CUSINS: It is a fair translation. The word means Loveliness.

UNDERSHAFT: May I ask—as Barbara's father—how much a
year she is to be loved for ever on?

CUSINS: As for Barbara's father, that is more your affair than 675
mine. I can feed her by teaching Greek: that is about all.

UNDERSHAFT: Do you consider it a good match for her?

CUSINS: *(With polite obstinacy.)* Mr Undershaft: I am in many
ways a weak, timid, ineffectual person; and my health is far
from satisfactory. But whenever I feel that I must have any- 680
thing, I get it, sooner or later. I feel that way about Barbara.
I dont like marriage: I feel intensely afraid of it; and I dont
know what I shall do with Barbara or what she will do with
me. But I feel that I and nobody else must marry her. Please
regard that as settled.—Not that I wish to be arbitrary; but 685
why should I waste your time in discussing what is inevitable?

UNDERSHAFT: You mean that you will stick at nothing: not
even the conversion of the Salvation Army to the worship of
Dionysos. 690

CUSINS: The business of the Salvation Army is to save, not to
wrangle about the name of the pathfinder. Dionysos or another: what does it matter?

UNDERSHAFT: *(Rising and approaching him.)* Professor Cusins:
you are a young man after my own heart. 695

CUSINS: Mr Undershaft: you are, as far as I am able to gather, a
most infernal old rascal; but you appeal very strongly to my
sense of ironic humor.

(UNDERSHAFT mutely offers his hand. They shake.)

UNDERSHAFT: *(Suddenly concentrating himself.)* And now to
business. 700

CUSINS: Pardon me. We are discussing religion. Why go back to
such an uninteresting and unimportant subject as business?

UNDERSHAFT: Religion is our business at present, because it is
through religion alone that we can win Barbara.

CUSINS: Have you, too, fallen in love with Barbara? 705

UNDERSHAFT: Yes, with a father's love.

CUSINS: A father's love for a grown-up daughter is the most dangerous of all infatuations. I apologize for mentioning my
own pale, coy, mistrustful fancy in the same breath with it.

UNDERSHAFT: Keep to the point. We have to win her; and we 710
are neither of us Methodists.

CUSINS: That doesnt matter. The power Barbara wields here—
the power that wields Barbara herself—is not Calvinism,
not Presbyterianism, not Methodism—

UNDERSHAFT: Not Greek Paganism either, eh? 715

CUSINS: I admit that. Barbara is quite original in her religion.

UNDERSHAFT: *(Triumphantly.)* Aha! Barbara Undershaft would
be. Her inspiration comes from within herself.

CUSINS: How do you suppose it got there?

720 UNDERSHAFT: *(In towering excitement.)* It is the Undershaft inheritance. I shall hand on my torch to my daughter. She shall make my converts and preach my gospel—

CUSINS: What! Money and gunpowder!

UNDERSHAFT: Yes, money and gunpowder. Freedom and power.
725 Command of life and command of death.

CUSINS: *(Urbanely: trying to bring him down to earth.)* This is extremely interesting, Mr Undershaft. Of course you know that you are mad.

UNDERSHAFT: *(With redoubled force.)* And you?

730 CUSINS: Oh, mad as a hatter. You are welcome to my secret since I have discovered yours. But I am astonished. Can a madman make cannons?

UNDERSHAFT: Would anyone else than a madman make them? And now *(With surging energy.)* question for question. Can a
735 sane man translate Euripides?

CUSINS: No.

UNDERSHAFT: *(Seizing him by the shoulder.)* Can a sane woman make a man of a waster or a woman of a worm?

CUSINS: *(Reeling before the storm.)* Father Colossus—Mammoth
740 Millionaire—

UNDERSHAFT: *(Pressing him.)* Are there two mad people or three in this Salvation shelter today?

CUSINS: You mean Barbara is as mad as we are?

UNDERSHAFT: *(Pushing him lightly off and resuming his equanimity
745 suddenly and completely.)* Pooh, Professor! let us call things by their proper names. I am a millionaire; you are a poet; Barbara is a savior of souls. What have we three to do with the common mob of slaves and idolators? *(He sits down again with a shrug of contempt for the mob.)*

750 CUSINS: Take care! Barbara is in love with the common people. So am I. Have you never felt the romance of that love?

UNDERSHAFT: *(Cold and sardonic.)* Have you ever been in love with Poverty, like St Francis? Have you ever been in love with Dirt, like St Simeon! Have you ever been in love with
755 disease and suffering, like our nurses and philanthropists? Such passions are not virtues, but the most unnatural of all the vices. This love of the common people may please an earl's granddaughter and a university professor; but I have been a common man and a poor man; and it has no romance
760 for me. Leave it to the poor to pretend that poverty is a blessing: leave it to the coward to make a religion of his cowardice by preaching humility: we know better than that. We three must stand together above the common people: how else can we help their children to climb up beside
765 us? Barbara must belong to us, not to the Salvation Army.

CUSINS: Well, I can only say that if you think you will get her away from the Salvation Army by talking to her as you have been talking to me, you dont know Barbara.

UNDERSHAFT: My friend: I never ask for what I can buy.

770 CUSINS: *(In a white fury.)* Do I understand you to imply that you can buy Barbara?

UNDERSHAFT: No; but I can buy the Salvation Army.

CUSINS: Quite impossible.

UNDERSHAFT: You shall see. All religious organizations exist by
775 selling themselves to the rich.

CUSINS: Not the Army. That is the Church of the poor.

UNDERSHAFT: All the more reason for buying it.

CUSINS: I dont think you quite know what the Army does for the poor.

UNDERSHAFT: Oh yes I do. It draws their teeth: that is enough 780 for me as a man of business.

CUSINS: Nonsense! It makes them sober—

UNDERSHAFT: I prefer sober workmen. The profits are larger.

CUSINS: —honest—

UNDERSHAFT: Honest workmen are the most economical. 785

CUSINS: —attached to their homes—

UNDERSHAFT: So much the better: they will put up with anything sooner than change their shop.

CUSINS: —happy—

UNDERSHAFT: An invaluable safeguard against revolution. 790

CUSINS: —unselfish—

UNDERSHAFT: Indifferent to their own interests, which suits me exactly.

CUSINS: —with their thoughts on heavenly things—

UNDERSHAFT: *(Rising.)* And not on Trade Unionism nor Social- 795 ism. Excellent.

CUSINS: *(Revolted.)* You really are an infernal old rascal.

UNDERSHAFT: *(Indicating* PETER SHIRLEY, *who has just come from the shelter and strolled dejectedly down the yard between them.)* And this is an honest man! 800

SHIRLEY: Yes; and what av I got by it? *(He passes on bitterly and sits on the form, in the corner of the penthouse.)*

*(*SNOBBY PRICE, *beaming sanctimoniously, and* JENNY HILL, *with a tambourine full of coppers, come from the shelter and go to the drum, on which* JENNY *begins to count the money.)*

UNDERSHAFT: *(Replying to* SHIRLEY.*)* Oh, your employers must have got a good deal by it from first to last. *(He sits on the table, with one foot on the side form,* CUSINS, *overwhelmed, sits* 805 *down on the same form nearer the shelter.* BARBARA *comes from the shelter to the middle of the yard. She is excited and a little overwrought.)*

BARBARA: Weve just had a splendid experience meeting at the other gate in Cripps's lane. Ive hardly ever seen them so 810 much moved as they were by your confession, Mr Price.

PRICE: I could almost be glad of my past wickedness if I could believe that it would elp to keep hathers stright.

BARBARA: So it will, Snobby. How much, Jenny?

JENNY: Four and tenpence, Major. 815

BARBARA: Oh Snobby, if you had given your poor mother just one more kick, we should have got the whole five shillings!

PRICE: If she heard you say that, miss, she'd be sorry I didnt. But I'm glad. Oh what a joy it will be to her when she hears I'm saved! 820

UNDERSHAFT: Shall I contribute the odd twopence, Barbara? The millionaire's mite, eh? *(He takes a couple of pennies from his pocket.)*

BARBARA: How did you make that twopence?

UNDERSHAFT: As usual. By selling cannons, torpedoes, sub- 825 marines, and my new patent Grand Duke hand grenade.

BARBARA: Put it back in your pocket. You cant buy your salvation here for twopence: you must work it out.

UNDERSHAFT: Is twopence not enough? I can afford a little more, if you press me. 830

BARBARA: Two million millions would not be enough. There is bad blood on your hands; and nothing but good blood can cleanse them. Money is no use. Take it away. *(She turns to*

CUSINS.) Dolly: you must write another letter for me to the
835　papers. (He makes a wry face.) Yes: I know you dont like it;
but it must be done. The starvation this winter is beating
us: everybody is unemployed. The General says we must
close this shelter if we cant get more money. I force the col-
lections at the meetings until I am ashamed: dont I,
840　Snobby?

PRICE: It's a fair treat to see you work it, miss. The way you got
them up from three-and-six to four-and-ten with that
hymn, penny by penny and verse by verse, was a caution.
Not a Cheap Jack on Mile End Waste could touch you at it.

845　BARBARA: Yes; but I wish we could do without it. I am getting
at last to think more of the collection than of the people's
souls. And what are those hatfuls of pence and halfpence?
We want thousands! tens of thousands! hundreds of thousands! I want to convert people, not to be always begging
850　for the Army in a way I'd die sooner than beg for myself.

UNDERSHAFT: (In profound irony.) Genuine unselfishness is capable of anything, my dear.

BARBARA: (Unsuspectingly, as she turns away to take the money from
the drum and put it in a cash bag she carries.) Yes, isnt it?

855　(UNDERSHAFT looks sardonically at CUSINS.)

CUSINS: (Aside to UNDERSHAFT.) Mephistopheles! Machiavelli!

BARBARA: (Tears coming into her eyes as she ties the bag and pockets
it.) How are we to feed them? I cant talk religion to a man
with bodily hunger in his eyes. (Almost breaking down.) It's
860　frightful.

JENNY: (Running to her.) Major, dear—

BARBARA: (Rebounding.) No: dont comfort me. It will be all
right. We shall get the money.

UNDERSHAFT: How?

865　JENNY: By praying for it, of course. Mrs Baines says she prayed
for it last night; and she has never prayed for it in vain:
never once. (She goes to the gate and looks out into the street.)

BARBARA: (Who has dried her eyes and regained her composure.) By
the way, dad, Mrs Baines has come to march with us to our
870　big meeting this afternoon; and she is very anxious to meet
you, for some reason or other. Perhaps she'll convert you.

UNDERSHAFT: I shall be delighted, my dear.

JENNY: (At the gate: excitedly.) Major! Major! heres that man
back again.

875　BARBARA: What man?

JENNY: The man that hit me. Oh, I hope he's coming back to
join us.

(BILL WALKER, with frost on his jacket, comes through the gate, his
hands deep in his pockets and his chin sunk between his shoulders, like
a cleaned-out gambler. He halts between BARBARA and the drum.)

BARBARA: Hullo, Bill! Back already!

BILL: (Nagging at her.) Bin talkin ever sence, ev you?

880　BARBARA: Pretty nearly. Well, has Todger paid you out for poor
Jenny's jaw?

BILL: Nao e aint.

BARBARA: I thought your jacket looked a bit snowy.

BILL: Sao it is snaowy. You want to knaow where the snaow cam
885　from, downt you?

BARBARA: Yes.

BILL: Well, it cam from orf the grahnd in Pawkinses Corner in
Kennintahn. It got rabbed orf be maw shaoulders: see?

BARBARA: Pity you didnt rub some off with your knees, Bill!
That would have done you a lot of good.　890

BILL: (With sour mirthless humor.) Aw was sivin anather menn's
knees at the tawm. E was kneelin on moy ed, e was.

JENNY: Who was kneeling on your head?

BILL: Todger was. E was pryin for me: pryin camfortable wiv me
as a cawpet. Sow was Mog. Sao was the aol bloomin meetin.　895
Mog she sez 'Ow Lawd brike is stabborn sperrit; bat downt
urt is dear art.' Thet was wot she said. 'Downt urt is dear
art'! An er blowk—thirteen stun four!—kneelin wiv all is
wight on me. Fanny, aint it?

JENNY: Oh no. We're so sorry, Mr Walker.　900

BARBARA: (Enjoying it frankly.) Nonsense! of course it's funny.
Served you right, Bill! You must have done something to
him first.

BILL: (Doggedly.) Aw did wot Aw said Aw'd do. Aw spit in is
eye. E looks ap at the skoy and sez, 'Ow that Aw should be　905
fahnd worthy to be spit upon for the gospel's sike!' e sez; an
Mog sez 'Glaory Allelloolier!'; an then e called me Brad-
dher, an dahned me as if Aw was a kid and e was me mather
worshin me a Setterda nawt. Aw ednt jast nao shaow wiv im
at all. Arf the street pryed; an the tather arf larfed fit to split　910
theirselves. (To BARBARA.) There! are you settisfawd nah?

BARBARA: (Her eyes dancing.) Wish I'd been there, Bill.

BILL: Yus: youd a got in a hextra bit o talk on me, wouldnt you?

JENNY: I'm so sorry, Mr Walker.

BILL: (Fiercely.) Downt you gow being sorry for me: youve no　915
call. Listen eah. Aw browk your jawr.

JENNY: No, it didn't hurt me: indeed it didnt, except for a moment. It was only that I was frightened.

BILL: Aw downt want to be forgive be you, or be ennybody.
Wot Aw did Aw'll py for. Aw trawd to gat me aown jawr　920
browk to settisfaw you—

JENNY: (Distressed.) Oh no—

BILL: (Impatiently.) Tell y' Aw did: cawnt you listen to wots bein
taold you? All Aw got be it was bein mide a sawt of in the
pablic street for me pines. Well, if Aw cawnt settisfaw you　925
one wy, Aw ken anather. Listen eah! Aw ed two quid sived
agen the frost; an Awve a pahnd of it left. A mite o mawn
last week ed words with the judy e's gowing to merry. E
give er wot-for; an e's bin fawnd fifteen bob. E ed a rawt to
itt er cause they was gowin to be merrid; but Aw ednt nao　930
rawt to itt you; sao put anather fawv bob on an call it a
pahnd's worth. (He produces a sovereign.) Eahs the manney.
Tike it; and lets ev no more o your forgivin an pryin and
your Mijor jawrin me. Let wot Aw dan be dan an pide for;
and let there be a end of it.　935

JENNY: Oh, I couldnt take it, Mr Walker. But if you would give
a shilling or two to poor Rummy Mitchens! you really did
hurt her; and she's old.

BILL: (Contemptuously.) Not lawkly. Aw'd give her another as
soon as look at er. Let her ev the lawr o me as she threat-　940
ened! She aint forgiven me: not mach. Wot Aw dan to er is
not on me mawnd—wot she (Indicating BARBARA.) mawt
call on me conscience—no more than stickin a pig. It's this
Christian gime o yours that Aw wownt ev plyed agen me:
this bloomin forgivin an neggin an jawrin that mikes a　945
menn thet sore that iz lawf's a burdn to im. Aw wownt ev
it, Aw tell you; sao tike your manney and stop thraowin
your silly beshed fice hap agen me.

JENNY: Major: may I take a little of it for the Army?

950 BARBARA: No: the Army is not to be bought. We want your soul, Bill; and we'll take nothing less.

BILL: (*Bitterly.*) Aw knaow. Me an maw few shillins is not good enaff for you. Youre a earl's grendorter, you are. Nathink less than a andered pahnd for you.

955 UNDERSHAFT: Come, Barbara! you could do a great deal of good with a hundred pounds. If you will set this gentleman's mind at ease by taking his pound, I will give the other ninety-nine.

(BILL, *dazed by such opulence, instinctively touches his cap.*)

BARBARA: Oh, youre too extravagant, papa. Bill offers twenty
960 pieces of silver. All you need offer is the other ten. That will make the standard price to buy anybody who's for sale. I'm not; and the Army's not. (*To* BILL.) Youll never have another quiet moment, Bill, until you come round to us. You cant stand out against your salvation.

965 BILL: (*Sullenly.*) Aw cawnt stend aht agen music awl wrastlers and awtful tangued women. Awve offered to py. Aw can do no more. Tike it or leave it. There it is. (*He throws the sovereign on the drum, and sits down on the horse-trough. The coin fascinates* SNOBBY PRICE, *who takes an early opportunity of dropping*
970 *his cap on it.*)

(MRS BAINES *comes from the shelter. She is dressed as a Salvation Army Commissioner. She is an earnest looking woman of about 40, with a caressing, urgent voice, and an appealing manner.*)

BARBARA: This is my father, Mrs Baines. (UNDERSHAFT *comes from the table, taking his hat off with marked civility.*) Try what you can do with him. He wont listen to me, because he remembers what a fool I was when I was a baby. (*She leaves*
975 *them together and chats with* JENNY.)

MRS BAINES: Have you been shewn over the shelter, Mr Undershaft? You know the work we're doing, of course.

UNDERSHAFT: (*Very civilly.*) The whole nation knows it, Mrs Baines.

980 MRS BAINES: No, sir: the whole nation does not know it, or we should not be crippled as we are for want of money to carry our work through the length and breadth of the land. Let me tell you that there would have been rioting this winter in London but for us.

985 UNDERSHAFT: You really think so?

MRS BAINES: I know it. I remember 1886, when you rich gentlemen hardened your hearts against the cry of the poor. They broke the windows of your clubs in Pall Mall.

UNDERSHAFT: (*Gleaming with approval of their method.*) And the
990 Mansion House Fund went up next day from thirty thousand pounds to seventy-nine thousand! I remember quite well.

MRS BAINES: Well, wont you help me to get at the people? They wont break windows then. Come here, Price. Let me shew
995 you to this gentleman (PRICE *comes to be inspected.*) Do you remember the window breaking?

PRICE: My ole father thought it was the revolution, maam.

MRS BAINES: Would you break windows now?

PRICE: Oh no, maam. The windows of eaven av bin opened to
1000 me. I know now that the rich man is a sinner like myself.

RUMMY: (*Appearing above at the loft door.*) Snobby Price!

SNOBBY: Wot is it?

RUMMY: Your mother's askin for you at the other gate in Cripps's Lane. She's heard about your confession (PRICE *turns pale.*)

MRS BAINES: Go, Mr Price; and pray with her.   1005

JENNY: You can go through the shelter, Snobby.

PRICE: (*To* MRS BAINES.) I couldnt face her now, maam, with all the weight of my sins fresh on me. Tell her she'll find her son at ome, waitin for her in prayer. (*He skulks off through the gate, incidentally stealing the sovereign on his way out by picking* 1010 *up his cap from the drum.*)

MRS BAINES: (*With swimming eyes.*) You see how we take the anger and the bitterness against you out of their hearts, Mr Undershaft.

UNDERSHAFT: It is certainly most convenient and gratifying to 1015 all large employers of labor, Mrs Baines.

MRS BAINES: Barbara: Jenny: I have good news: most wonderful news. (JENNY *runs to her.*) My prayers have been answered. I told you they would, Jenny, didnt I?

JENNY: Yes, yes.   1020

BARBARA: (*Moving nearer to the drum.*) Have we got money enough to keep the shelter open?

MRS BAINES: I hope we shall have enough to keep all the shelters open. Lord Saxmundham has promised us five thousand pounds—   1025

BARBARA: Hooray!

JENNY: Glory!

MRS BAINES: —if—

BARBARA: 'If!' If what?

MRS BAINES: —if five other gentlemen will give a thousand 1030 each to make it up to ten thousand.

BARBARA: Who is Lord Saxmundham? I never heard of him.

UNDERSHAFT: (*Who has pricked up his ears at the peer's name, and is now watching* BARBARA *curiously.*) A new creation, my dear. You have heard of Sir Horace Bodger?   1035

BARBARA: Bodger! Do you mean the distiller? Bodger's whisky!

UNDERSHAFT: That is the man. He is one of the greatest of our public benefactors. He restored the cathedral at Hakington. They made him a baronet for that. He gave half a million to the funds of his party: they made him a baron for that. 1040

SHIRLEY: What will they give him for the five thousand?

UNDERSHAFT: There is nothing left to give him. So the five thousand, I should think, is to save his soul.

MRS BAINES: Heaven grant it may! Oh Mr Undershaft, you have some very rich friends. Cant you help us towards the other 1045 five thousand? We are going to hold a great meeting this afternoon at the Assembly Hall in the Mile End Road. If I could only announce that one gentleman had come forward to support Lord Saxmundham, others would follow. Dont you know somebody? couldnt you? wouldnt you? (*Her eyes* 1050 *fill with tears.*) oh, think of those poor people, Mr Undershaft: think of how much it means to them, and how little to a great man like you.

UNDERSHAFT: (*Sardonically gallant.*) Mrs Baines: you are irresistible. I cant disappoint you; and I cant deny myself the 1055 satisfaction of making Bodger pay up. You shall have your five thousand pounds.

MRS BAINES: Thank God!

UNDERSHAFT: You dont thank me?

MRS BAINES: Oh sir, dont try to be cynical: dont be ashamed of 1060 being a good man. The Lord will bless you abundantly; and our prayers will be like a strong fortification round you all the days of your life. (*With a touch of caution.*) You will let me have the cheque to shew at the meeting, wont you?

1065 Jenny: go in and fetch a pen and ink. (JENNY *runs to the shelter door.*)

UNDERSHAFT: Do not disturb Miss Hill: I have a fountain pen. (JENNY *halts. He sits at the table and writes the cheque.* CUSINS *rises to make room for him. They all watch him silently.*)

1070 BILL: (*Cynically, aside to* BARBARA, *his voice and accent horribly debased.*) Wot prawce selvytion nah?

BARBARA: Stop. (UNDERSHAFT *stops writing: they all turn to her in surprise.*) Mrs Baines: are you really going to take this money?

1075 MRS BAINES: (*Astonished.*) Why not, dear?

BARBARA: Why not! Do you know what my father is? Have you forgotten that Lord Saxmundham is Bodger the whisky man? Do you remember how we implored the County Council to stop him from writing Bodger's Whisky in let-
1080 ters of fire against the sky; so that the poor drink-ruined creatures on the Embankment could not wake up from their snatches of sleep without being reminded of their deadly thirst by that wicked sky sign? Do you know that the worst thing I have had to fight here is not the devil, but Bodger,
1085 Bodger, Bodger, with his whisky, his distilleries, and his tied houses? Are you going to make our shelter another tied house for him, and ask me to keep it?

BILL: Rotten dranken whisky it is too.

MRS BAINES: Dear Barbara: Lord Saxmundham has a soul to be
1090 saved like any of us. If heaven has found the way to make a good use of his money, are we to set ourselves up against the answer to our prayers?

BARBARA: I know he has a soul to be saved. Let him come down here; and I'll do my best to help him to his salvation. But
1095 he wants to send his cheque down to buy us, and go on being as wicked as ever.

UNDERSHAFT: (*With a reasonableness which* CUSINS *alone perceives to be ironical.*) My dear Barbara: alcohol is a very necessary article. It heals the sick—

1100 BARBARA: It does nothing of the sort.

UNDERSHAFT: Well, it assists the doctor: that is perhaps a less questionable way of putting it. It makes life bearable to millions of people who could not endure their existence if they were quite sober. It enables Parliament to do things at
1105 eleven at night that no sane person would do at eleven in the morning. Is it Bodger's fault that this inestimable gift is deplorably abused by less than one per cent of the poor? (*He turns again to the table; signs the cheque; and crosses it.*)

MRS BAINES: Barbara: will there be less drinking or more if all
1110 those poor souls we are saving come tomorrow and find the doors of our shelters shut in their faces? Lord Saxmundham gives us the money to stop drinking—to take his own business from him.

CUSINS: (*Impishly.*) Pure self-sacrifice on Bodger's part, clearly!
1115 Bless dear Bodger! (BARBARA *almost breaks down as* ADOLPHUS, *too, fails her.*)

UNDERSHAFT: (*Tearing out the cheque and pocketing the book as he rises and goes past* CUSINS *to* MRS BAINES.) I also, Mrs Baines, may claim a little disinterestedness. Think of my business!
1120 think of the widows and orphans! the men and lads torn to pieces with shrapnel and poisoned with lyddite! (MRS

BAINES *shrinks; but he goes on remorselessly.*) the oceans of blood, not one drop of which is shed in a really just cause! the ravaged crops! the peaceful peasants forced, women and men, to till their fields under the fire of opposing armies on
1125 pain of starvation! the bad blood of the fierce little cowards at home who egg on others to fight for the gratification of their national vanity! All this makes money for me: I am never richer, never busier than when the papers are full of it. Well, it is your work to preach peace on earth and good
1130 will to men. (MRS BAINES'S *face lights up again.*) Every convert you make is a vote against war. (*Her lips move in prayer.*) Yet I give you this money to help you to hasten my own commercial ruin. (*He gives her the cheque.*)

CUSINS: (*Mounting the form in an ecstasy of mischief.*) The millen-
1135 nium will be inaugurated by the unselfishness of Undershaft and Bodger. Oh be joyful! (*He takes the drum-sticks from his pocket and flourishes them.*)

MRS BAINES: (*Taking the cheque.*) The longer I live the more proof I see that there is an Infinite Goodness that turns
1140 everything to the work of salvation sooner or later. Who would have thought that any good could have come out of war and drink? And yet their profits are brought today to the feet of salvation to do its blessed work. (*She is affected to tears.*)
1145

JENNY: (*Running to* MRS BAINES *and throwing her arms round her.*) Oh dear! how blessed, how glorious it all is!

CUSINS: (*In a convulsion of irony.*) Let us seize this unspeakable moment. Let us march to the great meeting at once. Excuse me just an instant. (*He rushes into the shelter.* JENNY *takes her
1150 tambourine from the drum head.*)

MRS BAINES: Mr Undershaft: have you ever seen a thousand people fall on their knees with one impulse and pray? Come with us to the meeting. Barbara shall tell them that the Army is saved, and saved through you.
1155

CUSINS: (*Returning impetuously from the shelter with a flag and a trombone, and coming between* MRS BAINES *and* UNDERSHAFT.) You shall carry the flag down the first street, Mrs Baines. (*He gives her the flag.*) Mr Undershaft is a gifted trombonist: he shall intone an Olympian diapason to the West Ham
1160 Salvation March. (*Aside to* UNDERSHAFT, *as he forces the trombone on him.*) Blow, Machiavelli, blow.

UNDERSHAFT: (*Aside to him, as he takes the trombone.*) The trumpet in Zion! (CUSINS *rushes to the drum, which he takes up and puts on.* UNDERSHAFT *continues, aloud.*) I will do my best. I
1165 could vamp a bass if I knew the tune.

CUSINS: It is a wedding chorus from one of Donizetti's operas; but we have converted it. We convert everything to good here, including Bodger. You remember the chorus. 'For thee immense rejoicing—immenso giubilo—immenso giu-
1170 bilo.' (*With drum obbligato.*) Rum tum ti tum tum, tum tum ti ta—

BARBARA: Dolly: you are breaking my heart.

CUSINS: What is a broken heart more or less here? Dionysos Undershaft has descended. I am possessed.
1175

MRS BAINES: Come, Barbara: I must have my dear Major to carry the flag with me.

JENNY: Yes, yes, Major darling.

(CUSINS *snatches the tambourine out of* JENNY'S *hand and mutely offers it to* BARBARA.)

BARBARA: *(Coming forward a little as she puts the offer behind her*
1180   *with a shudder, whilst* CUSINS *recklessly tosses the tambourine back*
        to JENNY *and goes to the gate.)* I cant come.

JENNY: Not come!

MRS BAINES: *(With tears in her eyes.)* Barbara: do you think I am
        wrong to take the money?

1185 BARBARA: *(Impulsively going to her and kissing her.)* No, no: God
        help you, dear, you must: you are saving the Army. Go; and
        may you have a great meeting!

JENNY: But arnt you coming?

BARBARA: No. *(She begins taking off the silver S brooch from her*
1190   *collar.)*

MRS BAINES: Barbara: what are you doing?

JENNY: Why are you taking your badge off? You cant be going
        to leave us, Major.

BARBARA: *(Quietly.)* Father: come here.

1195 UNDERSHAFT: *(Coming to her.)* My dear! *(Seeing that she is going to*
        pin the badge on his collar, he retreats to the penthouse in some
        alarm.)

BARBARA: *(Following him.)* Dont be frightened. *(She pins the*
        badge on and steps back towards the table, shewing him to the oth-
1200   *ers.)* There! It's not much for £5000, is it?

MRS BAINES: Barbara: if you wont come and pray with us,
        promise me you will pray for us.

BARBARA: I cant pray now. Perhaps I shall never pray again.

MRS BAINES: Barbara!

1205 JENNY: Major!

BARBARA: *(Almost delirious.)* I cant bear any more. Quick
        march!

CUSINS: *(Calling to the procession in the street outside.)* Off we go.
        Play up, there! Immenso giubilo. *(He gives the time with his*
1210   *drum; and the band strikes up the march, which rapidly becomes*
        more distant as the procession moves briskly away.)

MRS BAINES: I must go, dear. Youre overworked: you will be all
        right tomorrow. We'll never lose you. Now Jenny: step out
        with the old flag. Blood and Fire! *(She marches out through the*
1215   *gate with her flag.)*

JENNY: Glory Hallelujah! *(Flourishing her tambourine and*
        marching.)

UNDERSHAFT: *(To CUSINS, as he marches out past him easing the slide*
        of his trombone.) 'My ducats and my daughter'!

1220 CUSINS: *(Following him out.)* Money and gunpowder!

BARBARA: Drunkenness and Murder! My God: why hast thou
        forsaken me?

(She sinks on the form with her face buried in her hands. The march
passes away into silence. BILL WALKER *steals across to her.)*

BILL: *(Taunting.)* Wot prawce selvytion nah?

SHIRLEY: Dont you hit her when she's down.

1225 BILL: She itt me wen aw wiz dahn. Waw shouldnt Aw git a bit
        o me aown beck?

BARBARA: *(Raising her head.)* I didnt take your money, Bill. *(She*
        crosses the yard to the gate and turns her back on the two men to
        hide her face from them.)

1230 BILL: *(Sneering after her.)* Naow, it warnt enaff for you. *(Turning*
        to the drum, he misses the money.) Ellow! If you aint took it
        sammun else ez. Weres it gorn? Bly me if Jenny Ill didnt
        tike it after all!

RUMMY: *(Screaming at him from the loft.)* You lie, you dirty black-
1235   guard! Snobby Price pinched it off the drum when he took
        up his cap. I was up here all the time an see im do it.

BILL: Wot! Stowl maw manney! Waw didnt you call thief on
        him, you silly aold macker you?

RUMMY: To serve you aht for ittin me acrost the fice. It's cost y'-
        pahnd, that az. *(Raising a pæan of squalid triumph.)* I done 1240
        you. I'm even with you. Uve ad it aht o y—(BILL *snatches*
        up SHIRLEY's *mug and hurls it at her. She slams the loft door*
        and vanishes. The mug smashes against the door and falls in
        fragments.)

BILL: *(Beginning to chuckle.)* Tell us, aol menn, wot o'clock this 1245
        mawnin was it wen im as they call Snobby Prawce was
        sived?

BARBARA: *(Turning to him more composedly, and with unspoiled*
        sweetness.) About half past twelve, Bill. And he pinched
        your pound at a quarter to two. *I* know. Well, you cant af- 1250
        ford to lose it. I'll send it to you.

BILL: *(His voice and accent suddenly improving.)* Not if Aw wiz to
        stawve for it. Aw aint to be bought.

SHIRLEY: Aint you? Youd sell yourself to the devil for a pint o
        beer; only there aint no devil to make the offer. 1255

BILL: *(Unashamed.)* Sao Aw would, mite, and often ev, cheerful.
        But she cawnt baw me. *(Approaching BARBARA.)* You wanted
        maw saoul, did you? Well, you aint got it.

BARBARA: I nearly got it, Bill. But weve sold it back to you for
        ten thousand pounds. 1260

SHIRLEY: And dear at the money!

BARBARA: No, Peter: it was worth more than money.

BILL: *(Salvationproof.)* It's nao good: you cawnt get rahnd me
        nah. Aw downt blieve in it; and Awve seen tody that Aw
        was rawt. *(Going.)* Sao long, aol soupkitchener! Ta, ta, Mi- 1265
        jor Earl's Grendorter! *(Turning at the gate.)* Wot prawce
        selvytion nah? Snobby Prawce! Ha! ha!

BARBARA: *(Offering her hand.)* Goodbye, Bill.

BILL: *(Taken aback, half plucks his cap off; then shoves it on again de-*
        fiantly.) Git aht. *(BARBARA drops her hand, discouraged. He has* 1270
        a twinge of remorse.) But thets aw rawt, you knaow. Nathink
        pasnl. Naow mellice. Sao long, Judy. *(He goes.)*

BARBARA: No malice. So long, Bill.

SHIRLEY: *(Shaking his head.)* You make too much of him, miss,
        in your innocence. 1275

BARBARA: *(Going to him.)* Peter: I'm like you now. Cleaned out,
        and lost my job.

SHIRLEY: Youve youth an hope. Thats two better than me.

BARBARA: I'll get you a job, Peter. Thats hope for you: the
        youth will have to be enough for me. *(She counts her money.)* 1280
        I have just enough left for two teas at Lockharts, a Rowton
        doss for you, and my tram and bus home. *(He frowns and*
        rises with offended pride. She takes his arm.) Dont be proud, Pe-
        ter: it's sharing between friends. And promise me youll talk
        to me and not let me cry. *(She draws him towards the gate.)* 1285

SHIRLEY: Well, I'm not accustomed to talk to the like of you—

BARBARA: *(Urgently.)* Yes, yes: you must talk to me. Tell me
        about Tom Paine's books and Bradlaugh's lectures. Come
        along.

SHIRLEY: Ah, if you would only read Tom Paine in the proper 1290
        spirit, miss! *(They go out through the gate together.)*

——— **ACT THREE** ———

Next day after lunch LADY BRITOMART *is writing in the library in*
Wilton Crescent. SARAH *is reading in the armchair near the window.*
BARBARA, *in ordinary fashionable dress, pale and brooding, is on the*

settee. CHARLES LOMAX *enters. He starts on seeing* BARBARA *fashionably attired and in low spirits.*

LOMAX: Youve left off your uniform!

(BARBARA *says nothing; but an expression of pain passes over her face.*)

LADY BRITOMART: (*Warning him in low tones to be careful.*) Charles!

5 LOMAX: (*Much concerned, coming behind the settee and bending sympathetically over* BARBARA.) I'm awfully sorry, Barbara. You know I helped you all I could with the concertina and so forth. (*Momentously.*) Still, I have never shut my eyes to the fact that there is a certain amount of tosh about the Salvation Army. Now the claims of the Church of England—

10 LADY BRITOMART: Thats enough, Charles. Speak of something suited to your mental capacity.

LOMAX: But surely the Church of England is suited to all our capacities.

BARBARA: (*Pressing his hand.*) Thank you for your sympathy,
15 Cholly. Now go and spoon with Sarah.

LOMAX: (*Dragging a chair from the writing table and seating himself affectionately by* SARAH's *side.*) How is my ownest today?

SARAH: I wish you wouldnt tell Cholly to do things, Barbara. He always comes straight and does them. Cholly: we're go-
20 ing to the works this afternoon.

LOMAX: What works?

SARAH: The cannon works.

LOMAX: What? your governor's shop!

SARAH: Yes.

25 LOMAX: Oh I say!

(CUSINS *enters in poor condition. He also starts visibly when he sees* BARBARA *without her uniform.*)

BARBARA: I expected you this morning, Dolly. Didnt you guess that?

CUSINS: (*Sitting down beside her.*) I'm sorry. I have only just breakfasted.

30 SARAH: But weve just finished lunch.

BARBARA: Have you had one of your bad nights?

CUSINS: No: I had rather a good night: in fact, one of the most remarkable nights I have ever passed.

BARBARA: The meeting?

35 CUSINS: No: after the meeting.

LADY BRITOMART: You should have gone to bed after the meeting. What were you doing?

CUSINS: Drinking.

LADY BRITOMART: ⎫   ⎧ Adolphus!
40 SARAH: ⎬   ⎨ Dolly!
BARBARA: ⎪   ⎪ Dolly!
LOMAX: ⎭   ⎩ Oh I say!

LADY BRITOMART: What were you drinking, may I ask?

CUSINS: A most devilish kind of Spanish burgundy, warranted
45 free from added alcohol: a Temperance burgundy in fact. Its richness in natural alcohol made any addition superfluous.

BARBARA: Are you joking, Dolly?

CUSINS: (*Patiently.*) No. I have been making a night of it with the nominal head of this household: that is all.

50 LADY BRITOMART: Andrew made you drunk!

CUSINS: No: he only provided the wine. I think it was Dionysos who made me drunk. (*To* BARBARA.) I told you I was possessed.

LADY BRITOMART: Youre not sober yet. Go home to bed at
55 once.

CUSINS: I have never before ventured to reproach you, Lady Brit; but how could you marry the Prince of Darkness?

LADY BRITOMART: It was much more excusable to marry him than to get drunk with him. That is a new accomplishment
60 of Andrew's, by the way. He usent to drink.

CUSINS: He doesnt now. He only sat there and completed the wreck of my moral basis, the rout of my convictions, the purchase of my soul. He cares for you, Barbara. That is what makes him so dangerous to me.

65 BARBARA: That has nothing to do with it, Dolly. There are larger loves and diviner dreams than the fireside ones. You know that, dont you?

CUSINS: Yes: that is our understanding. I know it. I hold to it. Unless he can win me on that holier ground he may amuse
70 me for a while; but he can get no deeper hold, strong as he is.

BARBARA: Keep to that; and the end will be right. Now tell me what happened at the meeting?

CUSINS: It was an amazing meeting. Mrs Baines almost died of emotion. Jenny Hill simply gibbered with hysteria. The
75 Prince of Darkness played his trombone like a madman: its brazen roarings were like the laughter of the damned. 117 conversions took place then and there. They prayed with the most touching sincerity and gratitude for Bodger, and for the anonymous donor of the £5000. Your father would
80 not let his name be given.

LOMAX: That was rather fine of the old man, you know. Most chaps would have wanted the advertisement.

CUSINS: He said all the charitable institutions would be down on him like kites on a battle-field if he gave his name.

85 LADY BRITOMART: Thats Andrew all over. He never does a proper thing without giving an improper reason for it.

CUSINS: He convinced me that I have all my life been doing improper things for proper reasons.

LADY BRITOMART: Adolphus: now that Barbara has left the Sal-
90 vation Army, you had better leave it too. I will not have you playing that drum in the streets.

CUSINS: Your orders are already obeyed, Lady Brit.

BARBARA: Dolly: were you ever really in earnest about it? Would you have joined if you had never seen me?

95 CUSINS: (*Disingenuously.*) Well—er—well, possibly, as a collector of religions—

LOMAX: (*Cunningly.*) Not as a drummer, though, you know. You are a very clearheaded brainy chap, Dolly; and it must have been apparent to you that there is a certain amount of
100 tosh about—

LADY BRITOMART: Charles: if you must drivel, drivel like a grown-up man and not like a schoolboy.

LOMAX: (*Out of countenance.*) Well, drivel is drivel, dont you know, whatever a man's age.

105 LADY BRITOMART: In good society in England, Charles, men drivel at all ages by repeating silly formulas with an air of wisdom. Schoolboys make their own formulas out of slang, like you. When they reach your age, and get political private secretaryships and things of that sort, they drop slang
110 and get their formulas out of the *Spectator* or *The Times.* You had better confine yourself to *The Times.* You will find that

there is a certain amount of tosh about *The Times;* but at least its language is reputable.

LOMAX: *(Overwhelmed.)* You are so awfully strong-minded, Lady
115 Brit—

LADY BRITOMART: Rubbish! (MORRISON *comes in.*) What is it?

MORRISON: If you please, my lady, Mr Undershaft has just drove up to the door.

LADY BRITOMART: Well, let him in. (MORRISON *hesitates.*) Whats
120 the matter with you?

MORRISON: Shall I announce him, my lady; or is he at home here, so to speak, my lady?

LADY BRITOMART: Announce him.

MORRISON: Thank you, my lady. You wont mind my asking, I
125 hope. The occasion is in a manner of speaking new to me.

LADY BRITOMART: Quite right. Go and let him in.

MORRISON: Thank you, my lady. *(He withdraws.)*

LADY BRITOMART: Children: go and get ready. (SARAH *and*
BARBARA *go upstairs for their out-of-door wraps.*) Charles: go
130 and tell Stephen to come down here in five minutes: you will find him in the drawing room. (CHARLES *goes.*) Adolphus: tell them to send round the carriage in about fifteen minutes. (ADOLPHUS [CUSINS] *goes.*)

MORRISON: *(At the door.)* Mr Undershaft.

(UNDERSHAFT comes in. MORRISON goes out.)

135 UNDERSHAFT: Alone! How fortunate!

LADY BRITOMART: *(Rising.)* Dont be sentimental, Andrew. Sit down. *(She sits on the settee: he sits beside her, on her left. She comes to the point before he has time to breathe.)* Sarah must have £800 a year until Charles Lomax comes into his property.
140 Barbara will need more, and need it permanently, because Adolphus hasnt any property.

UNDERSHAFT: *(Resignedly.)* Yes, my dear: I will see to it. Anything else? for yourself, for instance?

LADY BRITOMART: I want to talk to you about Stephen.

145 UNDERSHAFT: *(Rather wearily.)* Dont, my dear. Stephen doesnt interest me.

LADY BRITOMART: He does interest me. He is our son.

UNDERSHAFT: Do you really think so? He has induced us to bring him into the world; but he chose his parents very in-
150 congruously, I think. I see nothing of myself in him, and less of you.

LADY BRITOMART: Andrew: Stephen is an excellent son, and a most steady, capable, highminded young man. You are simply trying to find an excuse for disinheriting him.

155 UNDERSHAFT: My dear Biddy: the Undershaft tradition disinherits him. It would be dishonest of me to leave the cannon foundry to my son.

LADY BRITOMART: It would be most unnatural and improper of you to leave it to anyone else, Andrew. Do you suppose
160 this wicked and immoral tradition can be kept up for ever? Do you pretend that Stephen could not carry on the foundry just as well as all the other sons of the big business houses?

UNDERSHAFT: Yes: he could learn the office routine without un-
165 derstanding the business, like all the other sons; and the firm would go on by its own momentum until the real Undershaft—probably an Italian or a German—would invent a new method and cut him out.

LADY BRITOMART: There is nothing that any Italian or German could do that Stephen could not do. And Stephen at least 170 has breeding.

UNDERSHAFT: The son of a foundling! Nonsense!

LADY BRITOMART: My son, Andrew! And even you may have good blood in your veins for all you know.

UNDERSHAFT: True. Probably I have. That is another argument 175 in favour of a foundling.

LADY BRITOMART: Andrew: dont be aggravating. And dont be wicked. At present you are both.

UNDERSHAFT: This conversation is part of the Undershaft tradition, Biddy. Every Undershaft's wife has treated him to it 180 ever since the house was founded. It is mere waste of breath. If the tradition be ever broken it will be for an abler man than Stephen.

LADY BRITOMART: *(Pouting.)* Then go away.

UNDERSHAFT: *(Deprecatory.)* Go away! 185

LADY BRITOMART: Yes: go away. If you will do nothing for Stephen, you are not wanted here. Go to your foundling, whoever he is; and look after him.

UNDERSHAFT: The fact is, Biddy—

LADY BRITOMART: Dont call me Biddy. I dont call you Andy. 190

UNDERSHAFT: I will not call my wife Britomart: it is not good sense. Seriously, my love, the Undershaft tradition has landed me in a difficulty. I am getting on in years; and my partner Lazarus has at last made a stand and insisted that the succession must be settled one way or the other; and of course he is 195 quite right. You see, I havent found a fit successor yet.

LADY BRITOMART: *(Obstinately.)* There is Stephen.

UNDERSHAFT: Thats just it: all the foundlings I can find are exactly like Stephen.

LADY BRITOMART: Andrew!! 200

UNDERSHAFT: I want a man with no relations and no schooling: that is, a man who would be out of the running altogether if he were not a strong man. And I cant find him. Every blessed foundling nowadays is snapped up in his infancy by Barnardo homes, or School Board officers, or Boards of 205 Guardians; and if he shews the least ability he is fastened on by schoolmasters; trained to win scholarships like a racehorse; crammed with secondhand ideas; drilled and disciplined in docility and what they call good taste; and lamed for life so that he is fit for nothing but teaching. If you want 210 to keep the foundry in the family, you had better find an eligible foundling and marry him to Barbara.

LADY BRITOMART: Ah! Barbara! Your pet! You would sacrifice Stephen to Barbara.

UNDERSHAFT: Cheerfully. And you, my dear, would boil Bar- 215 bara to make soup for Stephen.

LADY BRITOMART: Andrew: this is not a question of our likings and dislikings: it is a question of duty. It is your duty to make Stephen your successor.

UNDERSHAFT: Just as much as it is your duty to submit to your 220 husband. Come, Biddy! these tricks of the governing class are of no use with me. I am one of the governing class myself; and it is waste of time giving tracts to a missionary. I have the power in this matter; and I am not to be humbugged into using it for your purposes. 225

LADY BRITOMART: Andrew: you can talk my head off; but you cant change wrong into right. And your tie is all on one side. Put it straight.

UNDERSHAFT: (*Disconcerted.*) It wont stay unless it's pinned (*He
230   fumbles at it with childish grimaces.*)—

(STEPHEN *comes in.*)

STEPHEN: (*At the door.*) I beg your pardon. (*About to retire.*)

LADY BRITOMART: No: come in, Stephen. (STEPHEN *comes forward
to his mother's writing table.*)

UNDERSHAFT: (*Not very cordially.*) Good afternoon.

235   STEPHEN: (*Coldly.*) Good afternoon.

UNDERSHAFT: (*To* LADY BRITOMART.) He knows all about the
tradition, I suppose?

LADY BRITOMART: Yes. (*To* STEPHEN.) It is what I told you last
night, Stephen.

240   UNDERSHAFT: (*Sulkily.*) I understand you want to come into the
cannon business.

STEPHEN: *I* go into trade! Certainly not.

UNDERSHAFT: (*Opening his eyes, greatly eased in mind and manner.*)
Oh! in that case—

245   LADY BRITOMART: Cannons are not trade, Stephen. They are
enterprise.

STEPHEN: I have no intention of becoming a man of business in
any sense. I have no capacity for business and no taste for it.
I intend to devote myself to politics.

250   UNDERSHAFT: (*Rising.*) My dear boy: this is an immense relief
to me. And I trust it may prove an equally good thing for
the country. I was afraid you would consider yourself dis-
paraged and slighted. (*He moves towards* STEPHEN *as if to
shake hands with him.*)

255   LADY BRITOMART: (*Rising and interposing.*) Stephen: I cannot allow you to throw away an enormous property like this.

STEPHEN: (*Stiffly.*) Mother: there must be an end of treating me
as a child, if you please. (LADY BRITOMART *recoils, deeply
wounded by his tone.*) Until last night I did not take your at-
260   titude seriously, because I did not think you meant it seriously. But I find now that you left me in the dark as to
matters which you should have explained to me years ago.
I am extremely hurt and offended. Any further discussion of
my intentions had better take place with my father, as be-
265   tween one man and another.

LADY BRITOMART: Stephen! (*She sits down again, her eyes filling
with tears.*)

UNDERSHAFT: (*With grave compassion.*) You see, my dear, it is
only the big men who can be treated as children.

270   STEPHEN: I am sorry, mother, that you have forced me—

UNDERSHAFT: (*Stopping him.*) Yes, yes, yes, yes: thats all right,
Stephen. She wont interfere with you any more: your independence is achieved: you have won your latchkey. Dont
rub it in; and above all, dont apologize. (*He resumes his seat.*)
275   Now what about your future, as between one man and another—I beg your pardon, Biddy: as between two men and
a woman.

LADY BRITOMART: (*Who has pulled herself together strongly.*) I quite
understand, Stephen. By all means go your own way if you
280   feel strong enough. (STEPHEN *sits down magisterially in the
chair at the writing table with an air of affirming his majority.*)

UNDERSHAFT: It is settled that you do not ask for the succession
to the cannon business.

STEPHEN: I hope it is settled that I repudiate the cannon business.

285   UNDERSHAFT: Come, come! dont be so devilishly sulky: it's
boyish. Freedom should be generous. Besides, I owe you a

fair start in life in exchange for disinheriting you. You cant
become prime minister all at once. Havnt you a turn for
something? What about literature, art, and so forth?

290   STEPHEN: I have nothing of the artist about me, either in faculty or character, thank Heaven!

UNDERSHAFT: A philosopher, perhaps? Eh?

STEPHEN: I make no such ridiculous pretension.

UNDERSHAFT: Just so. Well, there is the army, the navy, the
295   Church, the Bar. The Bar requires some ability. What about
the Bar?

STEPHEN: I have not studied law. And I am afraid I have not the
necessary push—I believe that is the name barristers give to
their vulgarity—for success in pleading.

300   UNDERSHAFT: Rather a difficult case, Stephen. Hardly anything
left but the stage, is there? (STEPHEN *makes an impatient movement.*) Well, come! is there anything you know or care for?

STEPHEN: (*Rising and looking at him steadily.*) I know the difference between right and wrong.

305   UNDERSHAFT: (*Hugely tickled.*) You dont say so! What! no capacity for business, no knowledge of law, no sympathy with
art, no pretension to philosophy; only a simple knowledge
of the secret that has puzzled all the philosophers, baffled all
the lawyers, muddled all the men of business, and ruined
310   most of the artists: the secret of right and wrong. Why,
man, youre a genius, a master of masters, a god! At twen-
tyfour, too!

STEPHEN: (*Keeping his temper with difficulty.*) You are pleased to
be facetious. I pretend to nothing more than any honorable
315   English gentleman claims as his birthright (*He sits down
angrily.*)

UNDERSHAFT: Oh, thats everybody's birthright. Look at poor
little Jenny Hill, the Salvation lassie! she would think you
were laughing at her if you asked her to stand up in the
320   street and teach grammar or geography or mathematics or
even drawing room dancing; but it never occurs to her to
doubt that she can teach morals and religion. You are all
alike, you respectable people. You cant tell me the bursting
strain of a ten-inch gun, which is a very simple matter; but
325   you all think you can tell me the bursting strain of a man
under temptation. You darent handle high explosives; but
youre all ready to handle honesty and truth and justice and
the whole duty of man, and kill one another at that game.
What a country! What a world!

330   LADY BRITOMART: (*Uneasily.*) What do you think he had better
do, Andrew?

UNDERSHAFT: Oh, just what he wants to do. He knows nothing
and he thinks he knows everything. That points clearly to a
political career. Get him a private secretaryship to someone
335   who can get him an Under Secretaryship; and then leave
him alone. He will find his natural and proper place in the
end on the Treasury Bench.

STEPHEN: (*Springing up again.*) I am sorry, sir, that you force me
to forget the respect due to you as my father. I am an Eng-
340   lishman and I will not hear the Government of my country
insulted. (*He thrusts his hands in his pockets, and walks angrily
across to the window.*)

UNDERSHAFT: (*With a touch of brutality.*) The government of
your country! *I* am the government of your country: I, and
345   Lazarus. Do you suppose that you and half a dozen amateurs
like you, sitting in a row in that foolish gabble shop, can

govern Undershaft and Lazarus? No, my friend: you will do
what pays us. You will make war when it suits us, and keep
peace when it doesnt. You will find out that trade requires
350   certain measures when we have decided on those measures.
When I want anything to keep my dividends up, you will
discover that my want is a national need. When other people want something to keep my dividends down, you will
call out the police and military. And in return you shall
355   have the support and applause of my newspapers, and the
delight of imagining that you are a great statesman. Government of your country! Be off with you, my boy, and play
with your caucuses and leading articles and historic parties
and great leaders and burning questions and the rest of your
360   toys. *I* am going back to my counting-house to pay the
piper and call the tune.
STEPHEN: (*Actually smiling, and putting his hand on his father's
shoulder with indulgent patronage.*) Really, my dear father, it is
impossible to be angry with you. You dont know how ab-
365   surd all this sounds to me. You are very properly proud of
having been industrious enough to make money; and it is
greatly to your credit that you have made so much of it. But
it has kept you in circles where you are valued for your
money and deferred to for it, instead of in the doubtless
370   very old-fashioned and behind-the-times public school and
university where I formed my habits of mind. It is natural
for you to think that money governs England; but you must
allow me to think I know better.
UNDERSHAFT: And what does govern England, pray?
375   STEPHEN: Character, father, character.
UNDERSHAFT: Whose character? Yours or mine?
STEPHEN: Neither yours nor mine, father, but the best elements
in the English national character.
UNDERSHAFT: Stephen: Ive found your profession for you. Youre
380   a born journalist. I'll start you with a high-toned weekly review. There!

(*Before* STEPHEN *can reply,* SARAH, BARBARA, LOMAX, *and* CUSINS
come in ready for walking. BARBARA *crosses the room to the window
and looks out.* CUSINS *drifts amiably to the armchair.* LOMAX *remains
near the door, whilst* SARAH *comes to her mother.*)

(STEPHEN *goes to the smaller writing table and busies himself with his
letters.*)

SARAH: Go and get ready, mamma: the carriage is waiting.
(LADY BRITOMART *leaves the room.*)
UNDERSHAFT: (*To* SARAH.) Good day, my dear. Good afternoon,
385   Mr Lomax.
LOMAX: (*Vaguely.*) Ahdedoo.
UNDERSHAFT: (*To* CUSINS.) Quite well after last night, Euripi-
des, eh?
CUSINS: As well as can be expected.
390   UNDERSHAFT: Thats right. (*To* BARBARA.) So you are coming to
see my death and devastation factory, Barbara?
BARBARA: (*At the window.*) You came yesterday to see my salva-
tion factory. I promised you a return visit.
LOMAX: (*Coming forward between* SARAH *and* UNDERSHAFT.) Youll
395   find it awfully interesting. Ive been through the Woolwich
Arsenal; and it gives you a ripping feeling of security, you
know, to think of the lot of beggars we could kill if it came

to fighting. (*To* UNDERSHAFT, *with sudden solemnity.*) Still, it
must be rather an awful reflection for you, from the reli-
gious point of view as it were. Youre getting on, you know,   400
and all that.
SARAH: You dont mind Cholly's imbecility, papa, do you?
LOMAX: (*Much taken aback.*) Oh I say!
UNDERSHAFT: Mr Lomax looks at the matter in a very proper
spirit, my dear.   405
LOMAX: Just so. Thats all I meant, I assure you.
SARAH: Are you coming, Stephen?
STEPHEN: Well, I am rather busy—er—(*Magnanimously.*) Oh
well, yes: I'll come. That is, if there is room for me.
UNDERSHAFT: I can take two with me in a little motor I am ex-   410
perimenting with for field use. You wont mind its being
rather unfashionable. It's not painted yet; but it's bullet
proof.
LOMAX: (*Appalled at the prospect of confronting Wilton Crescent in
an unpainted motor.*) Oh I say!   415
SARAH: The carriage for me, thank you. Barbara doesnt mind
what she's seen in.
LOMAX: I say, Dolly, old chap: do you really mind the car being
a guy? Because of course if you do I'll go in it. Still—
CUSINS: I prefer it.   420
LOMAX: Thanks awfully, old man. Come, my ownest. (*He hurries out to secure his seat in the carriage.* SARAH *follows him.*)
CUSINS: (*Moodily walking across to* LADY BRITOMART's *writing
table.*) Why are we two coming to this Works Department
of Hell? that is what I ask myself.   425
BARBARA: I have always thought of it as a sort of pit where lost
creatures with blackened faces stirred up smoky fires and
were driven and tormented by my father? Is it like that, dad?
UNDERSHAFT: (*Scandalized.*) My dear! It is a spotlessly clean and
beautiful hillside town.   430
CUSINS: With a Methodist chapel? Oh do say theres a
Methodist chapel.
UNDERSHAFT: There are two: a Primitive one and a sophisticated one. There is even an Ethical Society; but it is not
much patronized, as my men are all strongly religious. In   435
the High Explosives Sheds they object to the presence of
Agnostics as unsafe.
CUSINS: And yet they dont object to you!
BARBARA: Do they obey all your orders?
UNDERSHAFT: I never give them any orders. When I speak to   440
one of them it is 'Well, Jones, is the baby doing well? and
has Mrs Jones made a good recovery?' 'Nicely, thank you,
sir.' And thats all.
CUSINS: But Jones has to be kept in order. How do you maintain discipline among your men?   445
UNDERSHAFT: I dont. They do. You see, the one thing Jones
wont stand is any rebellion from the man under him, or any
assertion of social equality between the wife of the man
with 4 shillings a week less than himself, and Mrs Jones! Of
course they all rebel against me, theoretically. Practically,   450
every man of them keeps the man just below him in his
place. I never meddle with them. I never bully them. I dont
even bully Lazarus. I say that certain things are to be done;
but I dont order anybody to do them. I dont say, mind you,
that there is no ordering about and snubbing and even bul-   455
lying. The men snub the boys and order them about; the
carmen snub the sweepers; the artisans snub the unskilled

laborers; the foremen drive and bully both the laborers and
artisans; the assistant engineers find fault with the foremen;
460   the chief engineers drop on the assistants; the departmental
managers worry the chiefs; and the clerks have tall hats and
hymnbooks and keep up the social tone by refusing to associate on equal terms with anybody. The result is a colossal
profit, which comes to me.

465 CUSINS: (*Revolted.*) You really are a—well, what I was saying
yesterday.

BARBARA: What was he saying yesterday?

UNDERSHAFT: Never mind, my dear. He thinks I have made you
unhappy. Have I?

470 BARBARA: Do you think I can be happy in this vulgar silly
dress? I! who have worn the uniform. Do you understand
what you have done to me? Yesterday I had a man's soul in
my hand. I set him in the way of life with his face to salvation. But when we took your money he turned back to
475   drunkenness and derision. (*With intense conviction.*) I will
never forgive you that. If I had a child, and you destroyed
its body with your explosives—if you murdered Dolly with
your horrible guns—I could forgive you if my forgiveness
would open the gates of heaven to you. But to take a human
480   soul from me, and turn it into the soul of a wolf! that is
worse than any murder.

UNDERSHAFT: Does my daughter despair so easily? Can you
strike a man to the heart and leave no mark on him?

BARBARA: (*Her face lighting up.*) Oh, you are right: he can never
485   be lost now: where was my faith?

CUSINS: Oh, clever clever devil!

BARBARA: You may be a devil; but God speaks through you
sometimes. (*She takes her father's hands and kisses them.*) You
have given me back my happiness: I feel it deep down now,
490   though my spirit is troubled.

UNDERSHAFT: You have learnt something. That always feels at
first as if you had lost something.

BARBARA: Well, take me to the factory of death; and let me
learn something more. There must be some truth or other
495   behind all this frightful irony. Come, Dolly. (*She goes out.*)

CUSINS: My guardian angel! (*To* UNDERSHAFT.) Avaunt! (*He follows* BARBARA.)

STEPHEN: (*Quietly, at the writing table.*) You must not mind
Cusins, father. He is a very amiable good fellow; but he is a
500   Greek scholar and naturally a little eccentric.

UNDERSHAFT: Ah, quite so. Thank you, Stephen. Thank you.
(*He goes out.*)

(STEPHEN *smiles patronizingly; buttons his coat responsibly; and
crosses the room to the door.* LADY BRITOMART, *dressed for out-of-doors,
opens it before he reaches it. She looks round for others; looks at*
STEPHEN; *and turns to go without a word.*)

STEPHEN: (*Embarrassed.*) Mother—

LADY BRITOMART: Dont be apologetic, Stephen. And dont for-
505   get that you have outgrown your mother. (*She goes out.*)

(*Perivale St Andrews lies between two Middlesex hills, half climbing
the northern one. It is an almost smokeless town of white walls, roofs
of narrow green slates or red tiles, tall trees, domes, campaniles, and
slender chimney shafts, beautifully situated and beautiful in itself.
The best view of it is obtained from the crest of a slope about half a*
*mile to the east, where the high explosives are dealt with. The foundry
lies hidden in the depths between, the tops of its chimneys sprouting like
huge skittles into the middle distance. Across the crest runs an emplacement of concrete, with a firestep, and a parapet which suggests a
fortification, because there is a huge cannon of the obsolete Woolwich
Infant pattern peering across it at the town. The cannon is mounted on
an experimental gun carriage: possibly the original model of the Undershaft disappearing rampart gun alluded to by* STEPHEN. *The
firestep, being a convenient place to sit, is furnished here and there with
straw disc cushions; and at one place there is the additional luxury of
a fur rug.*)

(BARBARA *is standing on the firestep, looking over the parapet towards
the town. On her right is the cannon; on her left the end of a shed raised
on piles, with a ladder of three or four steps up to the door, which opens
outwards and has a little wooden landing at the threshold, with a fire
bucket in the corner of the landing. Several dummy soldiers more or less
mutilated, with straw protruding from their gashes, have been shoved
out of the way under the landing. A few others are nearly upright
against the shed; and one has fallen forward and lies, like a grotesque
corpse, on the emplacement. The parapet stops short of the shed, leaving
a gap which is the beginning of the path down the hill through the
foundry to the town. The rug is on the firestep near this gap. Down on
the emplacement behind the cannon is a trolley carrying a huge conical
bombshell with a red band painted on it. Further to the right is the
door of an office, which, like the sheds, is of the lightest possible construction.*)

(CUSINS *arrives by the path from the town.*)

BARBARA: Well?

CUSINS: Not a ray of hope. Everything perfect! wonderful! real!
It only needs a cathedral to be a heavenly city instead of a
hellish one.

BARBARA: Have you found out whether they have done any- 510
thing for old Peter Shirley?

CUSINS: They have found him a job as gatekeeper and time-
keeper. He's frightfully miserable. He calls the time-keep-
ing brainwork, and says he isnt used to it; and his gate
lodge is so splendid that he's ashamed to use the rooms, and 515
skulks in the scullery.

BARBARA: Poor Peter!

(STEPHEN *arrives from the town. He carries a fieldglass.*)

STEPHEN: (*Enthusiastically.*) Have you two seen the place? Why
did you leave us?

CUSINS: I wanted to see everything I was not intended to see; 520
and Barbara wanted to make the men talk.

STEPHEN: Have you found anything discreditable?

CUSINS: No. They call him Dandy Andy and are proud of his
being a cunning old rascal; but it's all horribly, frightfully,
immorally, unanswerably perfect. 525

(SARAH *arrives.*)

SARAH: Heavens! what a place! (*She crosses to the trolley.*) Did you
see the nursing home!? (*She sits down on the shell.*)

STEPHEN: Did you see the libraries and schools!?

SARAH: Did you see the ball room and the banqueting chamber
in the Town Hall!? 530

STEPHEN: Have you gone into the insurance fund, the pension fund, the building society, the various applications of cooperation!?

(UNDERSHAFT comes from the office, with a sheaf of telegrams in his hand.)

535 UNDERSHAFT: Well, have you seen everything? I'm sorry I was called away. *(Indicating the telegrams.)* Good news from Manchuria.

STEPHEN: Another Japanese victory?

UNDERSHAFT: Oh, I dont know. Which side wins does not concern us here. No: the good news is that the aerial battleship
540 is a tremendous success. At the first trial it has wiped out a fort with three hundred soldiers in it.

CUSINS: *(From the platform.)* Dummy soldiers?

UNDERSHAFT: *(Striding across to STEPHEN and kicking the prostrate dummy brutally out of his way.)* No: the real thing.

(CUSINS and BARBARA exchange glances. Then CUSINS sits on the step and buries his face in his hands. BARBARA gravely lays her hand on his shoulder. He looks up at her in whimsical desperation.)

545 UNDERSHAFT: Well, Stephen, what do you think of the place?

STEPHEN: Oh, magnificent. A perfect triumph of modern industry. Frankly, my dear father, I have been a fool: I had no idea of what it all meant: of the wonderful forethought, the power of organization, the administrative capacity, the fi
550 nancial genius, the colossal capital it represents. I have been repeating to myself as I came through your streets 'Peace hath her victories no less renowned than War.' I have only one misgiving about it all.

UNDERSHAFT: Out with it.

555 STEPHEN: Well, I cannot help thinking that all this provision for every want of your workmen may sap their independence and weaken their sense of responsibility. And greatly as we enjoyed our tea at that splendid restaurant—how they gave us all that luxury and cake and jam and cream for
560 threepence I really cannot imagine!—still you must remember that restaurants break up home life. Look at the continent, for instance! Are you sure so much pampering is really good for the men's characters?

UNDERSHAFT: Well you see, my dear boy, when you are orga
565 nizing civilization you have to make up your mind whether trouble and anxiety are good things or not. If you decide that they are, then, I take it, you simply dont organize civilization; and there you are, with trouble and anxiety enough to make us all angels! But if you decide the other
570 way, you may as well go through with it. However, Stephen, our characters are safe here. A sufficient dose of anxiety is always provided by the fact that we may be blown to smithereens at any moment.

SARAH: By the way, papa, where do you make the explosives?

575 UNDERSHAFT: In separate little sheds, like that one. When one of them blows up, it costs very little; and only the people quite close to it are killed.

*(STEPHEN, who is quite close to it, looks at it rather scaredly, and moves away quickly to the cannon. At the same moment the door of the shed is thrown abruptly open; and a foreman in overalls and list slip*pers comes out on the little landing and holds the door for LOMAX, who appears in the doorway.)*

LOMAX: *(With studied coolness.)* My good fellow: you neednt get into a state of nerves. Nothing's going to happen to you; and I suppose it wouldnt be the end of the world if any 580 thing did. A little bit of British pluck is what you want, old chap. *(He descends and strolls across to SARAH.)*

UNDERSHAFT: *(To the foreman.)* Anything wrong, Bilton?

BILTON: *(With ironic calm.)* Gentleman walked into the high explosives shed and lit a cigaret, sir: thats all. 585

UNDERSHAFT: Ah, quite so. *(Going over to LOMAX.)* Do you happen to remember what you did with the match?

LOMAX: Oh come! I'm not a fool. I took jolly good care to blow it out before I chucked it away.

BILTON: The top of it was red hot inside, sir. 590

LOMAX: Well, suppose it was! I didnt chuck it into any of your messes.

UNDERSHAFT: Think no more of it, Mr Lomax. By the way, would you mind lending me your matches.

LOMAX: *(Offering his box.)* Certainly. 595

UNDERSHAFT: Thanks. *(He pockets the matches.)*

LOMAX: *(Lecturing to the company generally.)* You know, these high explosives dont go off like gunpowder, except when theyre in a gun. When theyre spread loose, you can put a match to them without the least risk: they just burn qui 600 etly like a bit of paper. *(Warming to the scientific interest of the subject.)* Did you know that, Undershaft? Have you ever tried?

UNDERSHAFT: Not on a large scale, Mr Lomax. Bilton will give you a sample of gun cotton when you are leaving if you ask 605 him. You can experiment with it at home. *(BILTON looks puzzled.)*

SARAH: Bilton will do nothing of the sort, papa. I suppose it's your business to blow up the Russians and Japs; but you might really stop short of blowing up poor Cholly. *(BILTON 610 gives it up and retires into the shed.)*

LOMAX: My ownest, there is no danger. *(He sits beside her on the shell.)*

(LADY BRITOMART arrives from the town with a bouquet.)

LADY BRITOMART: *(Impetuously.)* Andrew: you shouldnt have let me see this place. 615

UNDERSHAFT: Why, my dear?

LADY BRITOMART: Never mind why: you shouldnt have: thats all. To think of all that *(Indicating the town.)* being yours! and that you have kept it to yourself all these years!

UNDERSHAFT: It does not belong to me. I belong to it. It is the 620 Undershaft inheritance.

LADY BRITOMART: It is not. Your ridiculous cannons and that noisy banging foundry may be the Undershaft inheritance; but all that plate and linen, all that furniture and those houses and orchards and gardens belong to us. They belong 625 to me: they are not a man's business. I wont give them up. You must be out of your senses to throw them all away; and if you persist in such folly, I will call in a doctor.

UNDERSHAFT: *(Stooping to smell the bouquet.)* Where did you get the flowers, my dear? 630

LADY BRITOMART: Your men presented them to me in your William Morris Labor Church.

CUSINS: Oh! It needed only that. A Labor Church! (*He mounts the firestep distractedly, and leans with his elbows on the parapet,*
635 *turning his back to them.*)

LADY BRITOMART: Yes, with Morris's words in mosaic letters ten feet high round the dome. NO MAN IS GOOD ENOUGH TO BE ANOTHER MAN'S MASTER. The cynicism of it!

UNDERSHAFT: It shocked the men at first, I am afraid. But now
640 they take no more notice of it than of the ten commandments in church.

LADY BRITOMART: Andrew: you are trying to put me off the subject of the inheritance by profane jokes. Well, you shant. I dont ask it any longer for Stephen: he has inherited far too
645 much of your perversity to be fit for it. But Barbara has rights as well as Stephen. Why should not Adolphus succeed to the inheritance? I could manage the town for him; and he can look after the cannons, if they are really necessary.

UNDERSHAFT: I should ask nothing better if Adolphus were a
650 foundling. He is exactly the sort of new blood that is wanted in English business. But he's not a foundling; and theres an end of it. (*He makes for the office door.*)

CUSINS: (*Turning to them.*) Not quite. (*They all turn and stare at him.*) I think—Mind! I am not committing myself in any
655 way as to my future course—but I think the foundling difficulty can be got over. (*He jumps down to the emplacement.*)

UNDERSHAFT: (*Coming back to him.*) What do you mean?

CUSINS: Well, I have something to say which is in the nature of a confession.

660 SARAH:
LADY BRITOMART: } Confession!
BARBARA:
STEPHEN:

LOMAX: Oh I say!

665 CUSINS: Yes, a confession. Listen, all. Until I met Barbara I thought myself in the main an honorable, truthful man, because I wanted the approval of my conscience more than I wanted anything else. But the moment I saw Barbara, I wanted her far more than the approval of my
670 conscience.

LADY BRITOMART: Adolphus!

CUSINS: It is true. You accused me yourself, Lady Brit, of joining the Army to worship Barbara; and so I did. She bought my soul like a flower at a street corner; but she bought it for
675 herself.

UNDERSHAFT: What! Not for Dionysos or another?

CUSINS: Dionysos and all the others are in herself. I adored what was divine in her, and was therefore a true worshipper. But I was romantic about her too. I thought she was a woman of
680 the people, and that a marriage with a professor of Greek would be far beyond the wildest social ambitions of her rank.

LADY BRITOMART: Adolphus!!

LOMAX: Oh I say!!!

CUSINS: When I learnt the horrible truth—

685 LADY BRITOMART: What do you mean by the horrible truth, pray?

CUSINS: That she was enormously rich; that her grandfather was an earl; that her father was the Prince of Darkness—

UNDERSHAFT: Chut!

690 CUSINS: —and that I was only an adventurer trying to catch a rich wife, then I stooped to deceive her about my birth.

BARBARA: (*Rising.*) Dolly!

LADY BRITOMART: Your birth! Now Adolphus, dont dare to make up a wicked story for the sake of these wretched can-
695 nons. Remember: I have seen photographs of your parents; and the Agent General for South Western Australia knows them personally and has assured me that they are most respectable married people.

CUSINS: So they are in Australia; but here they are outcasts. Their marriage is legal in Australia, but not in England.
700 My mother is my father's deceased wife's sister; and in this island I am consequently a foundling. (*Sensation.*)

BARBARA: Silly! (*She climbs to the cannon, and leans, listening, in the angle it makes with the parapet.*)

CUSINS: Is the subterfuge good enough, Machiavelli?
705

UNDERSHAFT: (*Thoughtfully.*) Biddy: this may be a way out of the difficulty.

LADY BRITOMART: Stuff! A man cant make cannons any the better for being his own cousin instead of his proper self (*She sits down on the rug with a bounce that expresses her downright
710 contempt for their casuistry.*)

UNDERSHAFT: (*To* CUSINS.) You are an educated man. That is against the tradition.

CUSINS: Once in ten thousand times it happens that the schoolboy is a born master of what they try to teach him. Greek
715 has not destroyed my mind: it has nourished it. Besides, I did not learn it at an English public school.

UNDERSHAFT: Hm! Well, I cannot afford to be too particular: you have cornered the foundling market. Let it pass. You are eligible, Euripides: you are eligible.
720

BARBARA: Dolly: yesterday morning, when Stephen told us all about the tradition, you became very silent; and you have been strange and excited ever since. Were you thinking of your birth then?

CUSINS: When the finger of Destiny suddenly points at a man in
725 the middle of his breakfast, it makes him thoughtful.

UNDERSHAFT: Aha! You have had your eye on the business, my young friend, have you?

CUSINS: Take care! There is an abyss of moral horror between me and your accursed aerial battleships.
730

UNDERSHAFT: Never mind the abyss for the present. Let us settle the practical details and leave your final decision open. You know that you will have to change your name. Do you object to that?

CUSINS: Would any man named Adolphus—any man called
735 Dolly!—object to be called something else?

UNDERSHAFT: Good. Now, as to money! I propose to treat you handsomely from the beginning. You shall start at a thousand a year.

CUSINS: (*With sudden heat, his spectacles twinkling with mischief.*) A
740 thousand! You dare offer a miserable thousand to the son-in-law of a millionaire! No, by Heavens, Machiavelli! you shall not cheat me. You cannot do without me; and I can do without you. I must have two thousand five hundred a year for two years. At the end of that time, if I am a failure, I go.
745 But if I am a success, and stay on, you must give me the other five thousand.

UNDERSHAFT: What other five thousand?

CUSINS: To make the two years up to five thousand a year. The two thousand five hundred is only half pay in case I should
750 turn out a failure. The third year I must have ten per cent on the profits.

UNDERSHAFT: *(Taken aback.)* Ten per cent! Why, man, do you know what my profits are?

755 CUSINS: Enormous, I hope: otherwise I shall require twenty-five per cent.

UNDERSHAFT: But, Mr Cusins, this is a serious matter of business. You are not bringing any capital into the concern.

CUSINS: What! no capital! Is my mastery of Greek no capital?
760 Is my access to the subtlest thought, the loftiest poetry yet attained by humanity, no capital? My character! my intellect! my life! my career! what Barbara calls my soul! are these no capital? Say another word; and I double my salary.

UNDERSHAFT: Be reasonable—

765 CUSINS: *(Peremptorily.)* Mr Undershaft: you have my terms. Take them or leave them.

UNDERSHAFT: *(Recovering himself.)* Very well. I note your terms; and I offer you half.

CUSINS: *(Disgusted.)* Half!

770 UNDERSHAFT: *(Firmly.)* Half.

CUSINS: You call yourself a gentleman; and you offer me half!!

UNDERSHAFT: I do not call myself a gentleman; but I offer you half.

CUSINS: This to your future partner! your successor! your son-
775 in-law!

BARBARA: You are selling your own soul, Dolly, not mine. Leave me out of the bargain, please.

UNDERSHAFT: Come! I will go a step further for Barbara's sake. I will give you three fifths; but that is my last word.

780 CUSINS: Done!

LOMAX: Done in the eye! Why, *I* get only eight hundred, you know.

CUSINS: By the way, Mac, I am a classical scholar, not an arithmetical one. Is three fifths more than half or less?

785 UNDERSHAFT: More, of course.

CUSINS: I would have taken two hundred and fifty. How you can succeed in business when you are willing to pay all that money to a University don who is obviously not worth a junior clerk's wages!—well! What will Lazarus say?

790 UNDERSHAFT: Lazarus is a gentle romantic Jew who cares for nothing but string quartets and stalls at fashionable theatres. He will be blamed for your rapacity in money matters, poor fellow! as he has hitherto been blamed for mine. You are a shark of the first order, Euripides. So much the
795 better for the firm!

BARBARA: Is the bargain closed, Dolly? Does your soul belong to him now?

CUSINS: No: the price is settled: that is all. The real tug of war is still to come. What about the moral question?

800 LADY BRITOMART: There is no moral question in the matter at all, Adolphus. You must simply sell cannons and weapons to people whose cause is right and just, and refuse them to foreigners and criminals.

UNDERSHAFT: *(Determinedly.)* No: none of that. You must keep
805 the true faith of an Armorer, or you dont come in here.

CUSINS: What on earth is the true faith of an Armorer?

UNDERSHAFT: To give arms to all men who offer an honest price for them, without respect of persons or principles: to aristocrat and republican, to Nihilist and Tsar, to Capitalist and Socialist, to Protestant and Catholic, to burglar and po-
810 liceman, to black man, white man and yellow man, to all sorts and conditions, all nationalities, all faiths, all follies,

all causes and all crimes. The first Undershaft wrote up in his shop IF GOD GAVE THE HAND, LET NOT MAN WITHHOLD THE SWORD. The second wrote up ALL HAVE THE RIGHT TO 815 FIGHT: NONE HAVE THE RIGHT TO JUDGE. The third wrote up TO MAN THE WEAPON: TO HEAVEN THE VICTORY. The fourth had no literary turn; so he did not write up anything; but he sold cannons to Napoleon under the nose of George the Third. The fifth wrote up PEACE SHALL NOT PREVAIL SAVE 820 WITH A SWORD IN HER HAND. The sixth, my master, was the best of all. He wrote up NOTHING IS EVER DONE IN THIS WORLD UNTIL MEN ARE PREPARED TO KILL ONE ANOTHER IF IT IS NOT DONE. After that, there was nothing left for the seventh to say. So he wrote up, simply, UNASHAMED. 825

CUSINS: My good Machiavelli, I shall certainly write something up on the wall; only, as I shall write it in Greek, you wont be able to read it. But as to your Armorer's faith, if I take my neck out of the noose of my own morality I am not going to put it into the noose of yours. I shall sell cannons to 830 whom I please and refuse them to whom I please. So there!

UNDERSHAFT: From the moment when you become Andrew Undershaft, you will never do as you please again. Dont come here lusting for power, young man.

CUSINS: If power were my aim I should not come here for it. 835 You have no power.

UNDERSHAFT: None of my own, certainly.

CUSINS: I have more power than you, more will. You do not drive this place: it drives you. And what drives the place?

UNDERSHAFT: *(Enigmatically.)* A will of which I am a part. 840

BARBARA: *(Startled.)* Father! Do you know what you are saying; or are you laying a snare for my soul?

CUSINS: Dont listen to his metaphysics, Barbara. The place is driven by the most rascally part of society, the money hunters, the pleasure hunters, the military promotion 845 hunters; and he is their slave.

UNDERSHAFT: Not necessarily. Remember the Armorer's Faith. I will take an order from a good man as cheerfully as from a bad one. If you good people prefer preaching and shirking to buying my weapons and fighting the rascals, dont blame 850 me. I can make cannons: I cannot make courage and conviction. Bah! you tire me, Euripides, with your morality mongering. Ask Barbara: she understands. *(He suddenly reaches up and takes* BARBARA's *hands, looking powerfully into her eyes.)* Tell him, my love, what power really means. 855

BARBARA: *(Hypnotized.)* Before I joined the Salvation Army, I was in my own power; and the consequence was that I never knew what to do with myself. When I joined it, I had not time enough for all the things I had to do.

UNDERSHAFT: *(Approvingly.)* Just so. And why was that, do you 860 suppose?

BARBARA: Yesterday I should have said, because I was in the power of God. *(She resumes her self-possession, withdrawing her hands from his with a power equal to his own.)* But you came and shewed me that I was in the power of Bodger and 865 Undershaft. Today I feel—oh! how can I put it into words? Sarah: do you remember the earthquake at Cannes, when we were little children?—how little the surprise of the first shock mattered compared to the dread and horror of waiting for the second? That is how I feel in this place today. I 870 stood on the rock I thought eternal; and without a word of warning it reeled and crumbled under me. I was safe with an infinite wisdom watching me, an army marching to Salvation with me; and in a moment, at a stroke of your pen in a cheque book, I stood alone; and the heavens were empty. That was the first shock of the earthquake: I am waiting for the second.

UNDERSHAFT: Come, come, my daughter! dont make too much of your little tinpot tragedy. What do we do here when we spend years of work and thought and thousands of pounds of solid cash on a new gun or an aerial battleship that turns out just a hairsbreadth wrong after all? Scrap it. Scrap it without wasting another hour or another pound on it. Well, you have made for yourself something that you call a morality or a religion or what not. It doesnt fit the facts. Well, scrap it. Scrap it and get one that does fit. That is what is wrong with the world at present. It scraps its obsolete steam engines and dynamos; but it wont scrap its old prejudices and its old moralities and its old religions and its old political constitutions. Whats the result? In machinery it does very well; but in morals and religion and politics it is working at a loss that brings it nearer bankruptcy every year. Dont persist in that folly. If your old religion broke down yesterday, get a newer and a better one for tomorrow.

BARBARA: Oh how gladly I would take a better one to my soul! But you offer me a worse one. (*Turning on him with sudden vehemence.*) Justify yourself: shew me some light through the darkness of this dreadful place, with its beautifully clean workshops, and respectable workmen, and model homes.

UNDERSHAFT: Cleanliness and respectability do not need justification, Barbara: they justify themselves. I see no darkness here, no dreadfulness. In your Salvation shelter I saw poverty, misery, cold and hunger. You gave them bread and treacle and dreams of heaven. I give from thirty shillings a week to twelve thousand a year. They find their own dreams; but I look after the drainage.

BARBARA: And their souls?

UNDERSHAFT: I save their souls just as I saved yours.

BARBARA: (*Revolted.*) You saved my soul! What do you mean?

UNDERSHAFT: I fed you and clothed you and housed you. I took care that you should have money enough to live handsomely—more than enough; so that you could be wasteful, careless, generous. That saved your soul from the seven deadly sins.

BARBARA: (*Bewildered.*) The seven deadly sins!

UNDERSHAFT: Yes, the deadly seven. (*Counting on his fingers.*) Food, clothing, firing, rent, taxes, respectability and children. Nothing can lift those seven millstones from Man's neck but money; and the spirit cannot soar until the millstones are lifted. I lifted them from your spirit. I enabled Barbara to become Major Barbara; and I saved her from the crime of poverty.

CUSINS: Do you call poverty a crime?

UNDERSHAFT: The worst of crimes. All the other crimes are virtues beside it: all the other dishonors are chivalry itself by comparison. Poverty blights whole cities; spreads horrible pestilences; strikes dead the very souls of all who come within sight, sound, or smell of it. What you call crime is nothing: a murder here and a theft there, a blow now and a curse then: what do they matter? they are only the accidents and illnesses of life: there are not fifty genuine professional criminals in London. But there are millions of poor people, abject people, dirty people, ill fed, ill clothed people. They poison us morally and physically: they kill the happiness of society: they force us to do away with our own liberties and to organize unnatural cruelties for fear they should rise against us and drag us down into their abyss. Only fools fear crime: we all fear poverty. Pah! (*Turning on* BARBARA.) you talk of your halfsaved ruffian in West Ham: you accuse me of dragging his soul back to perdition. Well, bring him to me here; and I will drag his soul back again to salvation for you. Not by words and dreams; but by thirty-eight shillings a week, a sound house in a handsome street, and a permanent job. In three weeks he will have a fancy waistcoat; in three months a tall hat and a chapel sitting; before the end of the year he will shake hands with a duchess at a Primrose League meeting, and join the Conservative Party.

BARBARA: And will he be the better for that?

UNDERSHAFT: You know he will. Dont be a hypocrite, Barbara. He will be better fed, better housed, better clothed, better behaved; and his children will be pounds heavier and bigger. That will be better than an American cloth mattress in a shelter, chopping firewood, eating bread and treacle, and being forced to kneel down from time to time to thank heaven for it: knee drill, I think you call it. It is cheap work converting starving men with a Bible in one hand and a slice of bread in the other. I will undertake to convert West Ham to Mahometanism on the same terms. Try your hand on my men: their souls are hungry because their bodies are full.

BARBARA: And leave the east end to starve?

UNDERSHAFT: (*His energetic tone dropping into one of bitter and brooding remembrance.*) I was an east ender. I moralized and starved until one day I swore that I would be a full-fed free man at all costs; that nothing should stop me except a bullet, neither reason nor morals nor the lives of other men. I said 'Thou shalt starve ere I starve'; and with that word I became free and great. I was a dangerous man until I had my will: now I am a useful, beneficent, kindly person. That is the history of most self-made millionaires, I fancy. When it is the history of every Englishman we shall have an England worth living in.

LADY BRITOMART: Stop making speeches, Andrew. This is not the place for them.

UNDERSHAFT: (*Punctured.*) My dear: I have no other means of conveying my ideas.

LADY BRITOMART: Your ideas are nonsense. You got on because you were selfish and unscrupulous.

UNDERSHAFT: Not at all. I had the strongest scruples about poverty and starvation. Your moralists are quite unscrupulous about both: they make virtues of them. I had rather be a thief than a pauper. I had rather be a murderer than a slave. I dont want to be either; but if you force the alternative on me, then, by Heaven, I'll choose the braver and more moral one. I hate poverty and slavery worse than any other crimes whatsoever. And let me tell you this. Poverty and slavery have stood up for centuries to your sermons and leading articles: they will not stand up to my machine guns. Dont preach at them: dont reason with them. Kill them.

BARBARA: Killing. Is that your remedy for everything?

UNDERSHAFT: It is the final test of conviction, the only lever strong enough to overturn a social system, the only way of saying Must. Let six hundred and seventy fools loose in the

995

streets; and three policemen can scatter them. But huddle them together in a certain house in Westminster; and let them go through certain ceremonies and call themselves certain names until at last they get the courage to kill; and your six hundred and seventy fools become a government. Your pious mob fills up ballot papers and imagines it is governing its masters; but the ballot paper that really governs is the paper that has a bullet wrapped up in it.

1000

CUSINS: That is perhaps why, like most intelligent people, I never vote.

UNDERSHAFT: Vote! Bah! When you vote, you only change the names of the cabinet. When you shoot, you pull down governments, inaugurate new epochs, abolish old orders and set up new. Is that historically true, Mr Learned Man, or is it not?

1005

CUSINS: It is historically true. I loathe having to admit it. I repudiate your sentiments. I abhor your nature. I defy you in every possible way. Still, it is true. But it ought not to be true.

1010

UNDERSHAFT: Ought! ought! ought! ought! ought! Are you going to spend your life saying ought, like the rest of our moralists? Turn your oughts into shalls, man. Come and make explosives with me. Whatever can blow men up can blow society up. The history of the world is the history of those who had courage enough to embrace this truth. Have you the courage to embrace it, Barbara?

1015

LADY BRITOMART: Barbara: I positively forbid you to listen to your father's abominable wickedness. And you, Adolphus, ought to know better than to go about saying that wrong things are true. What does it matter whether they are true if they are wrong?

1020

UNDERSHAFT: What does it matter whether they are wrong if they are true?

LADY BRITOMART: (Rising.) Children: come home instantly. Andrew: I am exceedingly sorry I allowed you to call on us. You are wickeder than ever. Come at once.

1025

BARBARA: (Shaking her head.) It's no use running away from wicked people, mamma.

LADY BRITOMART: It is every use. It shews your disapprobation of them.

1030

BARBARA: It does not save them.

LADY BRITOMART: I can see that you are going to disobey me. Sarah: are you coming home or are you not?

SARAH: I daresay it's very wicked of papa to make cannons; but I dont think I shall cut him on that account.

1035

LOMAX: (Pouring oil on the troubled waters.) The fact is, you know, there is a certain amount of tosh about this notion of wickedness. It doesnt work. You must look at facts. Not that I would say a word in favor of anything wrong; but then, you see, all sorts of chaps are always doing all sorts of things; and we have to fit them in somehow, dont you know. What I mean is that you cant go cutting everybody; and thats about what it comes to. (Their rapt attention to his eloquence makes him nervous.) Perhaps I dont make myself clear.

1040

1045

LADY BRITOMART: You are lucidity itself, Charles. Because Andrew is successful and has plenty of money to give to Sarah, you will flatter him and encourage him in his wickedness.

1050

LOMAX: (Unruffled.) Well, where the carcase is, there will the eagles be gathered, dont you know. (To UNDERSHAFT.) Eh? What?

UNDERSHAFT: Precisely. By the way, may I call you Charles?

LOMAX: Delighted. Cholly is the usual ticket.

UNDERSHAFT: (To LADY BRITOMART.) Biddy—

1055

LADY BRITOMART: (Violently.) Dont dare call me Biddy. Charles Lomax: you are a fool. Adolphus Cusins: you are a Jesuit. Stephen: you are a prig. Barbara: you are a lunatic. Andrew: you are a vulgar tradesman. Now you all know my opinion; and my conscience is clear, at all events. (She sits down with a vehemence that the rug fortunately softens.)

1060

UNDERSHAFT: My dear: you are the incarnation of morality. (She snorts.) Your conscience is clear and your duty done when you have called everybody names. Come, Euripides! it is getting late; and we all want to go home. Make up your mind.

1065

CUSINS: Understand this, you old demon—

LADY BRITOMART: Adolphus!

UNDERSHAFT: Let him alone, Biddy. Proceed, Euripides.

CUSINS: You have me in a horrible dilemma. I want Barbara.

UNDERSHAFT: Like all young men, you greatly exaggerate the difference between one young woman and another.

1070

BARBARA: Quite true, Dolly.

CUSINS: I also want to avoid being a rascal.

UNDERSHAFT: (With biting contempt.) You lust for personal righteousness, for self-approval, for what you call a good conscience, for what Barbara calls salvation, for what I call patronizing people who are not so lucky as yourself.

1075

CUSINS: I do not: all the poet in me recoils from being a good man. But there are things in me that I must reckon with. Pity—

UNDERSHAFT: Pity! The scavenger of misery.

1080

CUSINS: Well, love.

UNDERSHAFT: I know. You love the needy and the outcast: you love the oppressed races, the negro, the Indian ryot, the underdog everywhere. Do you love the Japanese? Do you love the French? Do you love the English?

1085

CUSINS: No. Every true Englishman detests the English. We are the wickedest nation on earth; and our success is a moral horror.

UNDERSHAFT: That is what comes of your gospel of love, is it?

CUSINS: May I not love even my father-in-law?

1090

UNDERSHAFT: Who wants your love, man? By what right do you take the liberty of offering it to me? I will have your due heed and respect, or I will kill you. But your love! Damn your impertinence!

CUSINS: (Grinning.) I may not be able to control my affections, Mac.

1095

UNDERSHAFT: You are fencing, Euripides. You are weakening: your grip is slipping. Come! try your last weapon. Pity and love have broken in your hand: forgiveness is still left.

CUSINS: No: forgiveness is a beggar's refuge. I am with you there: we must pay our debts.

1100

UNDERSHAFT: Well said. Come! you will suit me. Remember the words of Plato.

CUSINS: (Starting.) Plato! You dare quote Plato to me!

UNDERSHAFT: Plato says, my friend, that society cannot be saved until either the Professors of Greek take to making gunpowder, or else the makers of gunpowder become Professors of Greek.

1105

CUSINS: Oh, tempter, cunning tempter!

UNDERSHAFT: Come! choose, man, choose.

1110

CUSINS: But perhaps Barbara will not marry me if I make the wrong choice.

BARBARA: Perhaps not.

CUSINS: (Desperately perplexed.) You hear!

1115 BARBARA: Father: do you love nobody?

UNDERSHAFT: I love my best friend.

LADY BRITOMART: And who is that, pray?

UNDERSHAFT: My bravest enemy. That is the man who keeps me up to the mark.

1120 CUSINS: You know, the creature is really a sort of poet in his way. Suppose he is a great man, after all!

UNDERSHAFT: Suppose you stop talking and make up your mind, my young friend.

CUSINS: But you are driving me against my nature. I hate war.

1125 UNDERSHAFT: Hatred is the coward's revenge for being intimidated. Dare you make war on war? Here are the means: my friend Mr Lomax is sitting on them.

LOMAX: (Springing up.) Oh I say! You dont mean that this thing is loaded, do you? My ownest: come off it.

1130 SARAH: (Sitting placidly on the shell.) If I am to be blown up, the more thoroughly it is done the better. Dont fuss, Cholly.

LOMAX: (To UNDERSHAFT, strongly remonstrant.) Your own daughter, you know!

UNDERSHAFT: So I see! (To CUSINS.) Well, my friend, may we ex-
1135 pect you here at six tomorrow morning?

CUSINS: (Firmly.) Not on any account. I will see the whole establishment blown up with its own dynamite before I will get up at five. My hours are healthy, rational hours: eleven to five.

1140 UNDERSHAFT: Come when you please: before a week you will come at six and stay until I turn you out for the sake of your health. (Calling.) Bilton! (He turns to LADY BRITOMART, who rises.) My dear: let us leave these two young people to themselves for a moment. (BILTON comes from the shed.) I am going
1145 to take you through the gun cotton shed.

BILTON: (Barring the way.) You cant take anything explosive in here, sir.

LADY BRITOMART: What do you mean? Are you alluding to me?

BILTON: (Unmoved.) No, maam. Mr Undershaft has the other
1150 gentleman's matches in his pocket.

LADY BRITOMART: (Abruptly.) Oh! I beg your pardon. (She goes into the shed.)

UNDERSHAFT: Quite right, Bilton, quite right: here you are. (He gives BILTON the box of matches.) Come, Stephen. Come,
1155 Charles. Bring Sarah. (He passes into the shed.)

(BILTON opens the box and deliberately drops the matches into the fire-bucket.)

LOMAX: Oh! I say (BILTON stolidly hands him the empty box.) Infernal nonsense! Pure scientific ignorance! (He goes in.)

SARAH: Am I all right, Bilton?

BILTON: Youll have to put on list slippers, miss: thats all. Weve
1160 got em inside. (She goes in.)

STEPHEN: (Very seriously to CUSINS.) Dolly, old fellow, think. Think before you decide. Do you feel that you are a sufficiently practical man? It is a huge undertaking, an enormous responsibility. All this mass of business will be Greek
1165 to you.

CUSINS: Oh, I think it will be much less difficult than Greek.

STEPHEN: Well, I just want to say this before I leave you to yourselves. Dont let anything I have said about right and wrong prejudice you against this great chance in life. I have

satisfied myself that the business is one of the highest char- 1170 acter and a credit to our country. (Emotionally.) I am very proud of my father. I—(Unable to proceed, he presses CUSINS' hand and goes hastily into the shed, followed by BILTON.)

(BARBARA and CUSINS, left alone together, look at one another silently.)

CUSINS: Barbara: I am going to accept this offer.

BARBARA: I thought you would.   1175

CUSINS: You understand, dont you, that I had to decide without consulting you. If I had thrown the burden of the choice on you, you would sooner or later have despised me for it.

BARBARA: Yes: I did not want you to sell your soul for me any more than for this inheritance.   1180

CUSINS: It is not the sale of my soul that troubles me: I have sold it too often to care about that. I have sold it for a professorship. I have sold it for an income. I have sold it to escape being imprisoned for refusing to pay taxes for hangmen's ropes and unjust wars and things that I abhor. 1185 What is all human conduct but the daily and hourly sale of our souls for trifles? What I am now selling it for is neither money nor position nor comfort, but for reality and for power.

BARBARA: You know that you will have no power, and that he 1190 has none.

CUSINS: I know. It is not for myself alone. I want to make power for the world.

BARBARA: I want to make power for the world too; but it must be spiritual power.   1195

CUSINS: I think all power is spiritual: these cannons will not go off by themselves. I have tried to make spiritual power by teaching Greek. But the world can never be really touched by a dead language and a dead civilization. The people must have power; and the people cannot have Greek. Now the 1200 power that is made here can be wielded by all men.

BARBARA: Power to burn women's houses down and kill their sons and tear their husbands to pieces.

CUSINS: You cannot have power for good without having power for evil too. Even mother's milk nourishes murderers as well 1205 as heroes. This power which only tears men's bodies to pieces has never been so horribly abused as the intellectual power, the imaginative power, the poetic, religious power that can enslave men's souls. As a teacher of Greek I gave the intellectual man weapons against the common man. I 1210 now want to give the common man weapons against the intellectual man. I love the common people. I want to arm them against the lawyers, the doctors, the priests, the literary men, the professors, the artists, and the politicians, who, once in authority, are more disastrous and tyrannical than 1215 all the fools, rascals, and impostors. I want a power simple enough for common men to use, yet strong enough to force the intellectual oligarchy to use its genius for the general good.

BARBARA: Is there no higher power than that? (Pointing to the 1220 shell.)

CUSINS: Yes; but that power can destroy the higher powers just as a tiger can destroy a man: therefore Man must master that power first. I admitted this when the Turks and Greeks were last at war. My best pupil went out to fight for Hellas. 1225

My parting gift to him was not a copy of Plato's Republic, but a revolver and a hundred Undershaft cartridges. The blood of every Turk he shot—if he shot any—is on my head as well as on Undershaft's. That act committed me to this place for ever. Your father's challenge has beaten me. Dare I make war on war? I must. I will. And now, is it all over between us?

1230

BARBARA: (*Touched by his evident dread of her answer.*) Silly baby Dolly! How could it be!

1235 CUSINS: (*Overjoyed.*) Then you—you—you—Oh for my drum! (*He flourishes imaginary drumsticks.*)

BARBARA: (*Angered by his levity.*) Take care, Dolly, take care. Oh, if only I could get away from you and from father and from it all! if I could have the wings of a dove and fly away to heaven!

1240

CUSINS: And leave me!

BARBARA: Yes, you, and all the other naughty mischievous children of men. But I cant. I was happy in the Salvation Army for a moment. I escaped from the world into a paradise of enthusiasm and prayer and soul saving; but the moment our money ran short, it all came back to Bodger: it was he who saved our people: he, and the Prince of Darkness, my papa. Undershaft and Bodger: their hands stretch everywhere: when we feed a starving fellow creature, it is with their bread, because there is no other bread; when we tend the sick, it is in the hospitals they endow; if we turn from the churches they build, we must kneel on the stones of the streets they pave. As long as that lasts, there is no getting away from them. Turning our backs on Bodger and Undershaft is turning our backs on life.

1245

1250

1255

CUSINS: I thought you were determined to turn your back on the wicked side of life.

BARBARA: There is no wicked side: life is all one. And I never wanted to shirk my share in whatever evil must be endured, whether it be sin or suffering. I wish I could cure you of middle-class ideas, Dolly.

1260

CUSINS: (*Gasping.*) Middle cl——! A snub! A social snub to me! from the daughter of a foundling!

BARBARA: That is why I have no class, Dolly: I come straight out of the heart of the whole people. If I were middle-class I should turn my back on my father's business; and we should both live in an artistic drawing room, with you reading the reviews in one corner, and I in the other at the piano, playing Schumann: both very superior persons, and neither of us a bit of use. Sooner than that, I would sweep out the guncotton shed, or be one of Bodger's barmaids. Do you know what would have happened if you had refused papa's offer?

1265

1270

CUSINS: I wonder!

1275 BARBARA: I should have given you up and married the man who accepted it. After all, my dear old mother has more sense than any of you. I felt like her when I saw this place—felt that I must have it—that never, never, never could I let it go; only she thought it was the houses and the kitchen ranges and the linen and china, when it was really all the human souls to be saved: not weak souls in starved bodies, sobbing with gratitude for a scrap of bread and treacle, but fullfed, quarrelsome, snobbish, uppish creatures, all standing on their little rights and dignities, and thinking that my father ought to be greatly obliged to them for making so much money for him—and so he ought. That is where salvation is really wanted. My father shall never throw it in my teeth again that my converts were bribed with bread. (*She is transfigured.*) I have got rid of the bribe of bread. I have got rid of the bribe of heaven. Let God's work be done for its own sake: the work he had to create us to do because it cannot be done except by living men and women. When I die, let him be in my debt, not I in his; and let me forgive him as becomes a woman of my rank.

1280

1285

1290

CUSINS: Then the way of life lies through the factory of death? 1295

BARBARA: Yes, through the raising of hell to heaven and of man to God, through the unveiling of an eternal light in the Valley of The Shadow. (*Seizing him with both hands.*) Oh, did you think my courage would never come back? did you believe that I was a deserter? that I, who have stood in the streets, and taken my people to my heart, and talked of the holiest and greatest things with them, could ever turn back and chatter foolishly to fashionable people about nothing in a drawing room? Never, never, never, never: Major Barbara will die with the colors. Oh! and I have my dear little Dolly boy still; and he has found me my place and my work. Glory Hallelujah! (*She kisses him.*)

1300

1305

CUSINS: My dearest: consider my delicate health. I cannot stand as much happiness as you can.

BARBARA: Yes: it is not easy work being in love with me, is it? But it's good for you. (*She runs to the shed, and calls, childlike.*) Mamma! Mamma! (BILTON *comes out of the shed, followed by* UNDERSHAFT.) I want Mamma.

1310

UNDERSHAFT: She is taking off her list slippers, dear. (*He passes on to* CUSINS.) Well? What does she say? 1315

CUSINS: She has gone right up into the skies.

LADY BRITOMART: (*Coming from the shed and stopping on the steps, obstructing* SARAH, *who follows with* LOMAX. BARBARA *clutches like a baby at her mother's skirt.*) Barbara: when will you learn to be independent and to act and think for yourself? I know as well as possible what that cry of 'Mamma, Mamma,' means. Always running to me!

1320

SARAH: (*Touching* LADY BRITOMART's *ribs with her finger tips and imitating a bicycle horn.*) Pip! pip!

LADY BRITOMART: (*Highly indignant.*) How dare you say Pip! pip! to me, Sarah? You are both very naughty children. What do you want, Barbara?

1325

BARBARA: I want a house in the village to live in with Dolly. (*Dragging at the skirt.*) Come and tell me which one to take.

UNDERSHAFT: (*To* CUSINS.) Six o'clock tomorrow morning, Euripides.

1330

BERTOLT BRECHT

Bertolt Brecht (1898–1956) changed the course of the modern European theater—and theater around the world—more than any playwright since Ibsen. However, Brecht's sphere of influence extends beyond his career as a playwright. As a dramatist, he wrote an unsurpassed body of plays; as a theoretician, Brecht's conception of "alienation" in the epic theater opened the way for sweeping innovation in our understanding of the possibilities of the stage; as a director, Brecht's work with his company, the Berliner Ensemble, made it the most influential and important theater in postwar Europe. The challenge of understanding Brecht is to understand the dialectical interplay between theory and practice that informs his assault on stage realism, and on the bourgeois theater itself.

Eugen Berthold Brecht (he later changed his name to Bertolt) was born in Augsburg, Bavaria, in 1898 to a prosperous family. In 1917, he enrolled at Munich University in the natural sciences and worked as a drama critic on the side. He also began work on several plays, including *Baal* (1917). In 1918 he was conscripted into military service for the remainder of World War I and worked in a military hospital. He returned briefly to the university after the war, but soon turned his attention full time to the theater. He moved to Berlin—Germany's theatrical capital at the time—and had the good fortune to work with two influential directors, Max Reinhardt and Erwin Piscator. Piscator advocated the use of new technologies in the theater, as a way of developing a kind of performance more responsive to the mechanized and accelerated routines of modern life. Brecht acknowledged that many of his own staging techniques were derived from his work with Piscator in the 1920s. Throughout the 1920s and early 1930s, Brecht wrote a series of plays that brought him notoriety, largely for their satire of the bourgeois establishment: *Drums in the Night* (1919), *In the Jungle of Cities* (1921), *Man Is Man* (1926), and the musical plays he wrote in collaboration with the composer Kurt Weill, *The Threepenny Opera* (1928) and *The Rise and Fall of the City of Mahagonny* (1930). In the 1920s, Brecht also began to collaborate with Margarete Steffin, one of several women—including Elisabeth Hauptmann and Ruth Berlau—with whom he collaborated as playwright.

Brecht also began his serious reading of Marx in the 1920s, and it was his application of Marxist dialectic to the process of theater that gave rise to his most powerful and original ideas for the stage. From Marx, Brecht adopted a revolutionary posture, not only toward the class struggle, but toward the stage of bourgeois "realism." To Brecht, the realistic theater was not an unbiased window on social reality. Instead, Brecht argued that realistic theater presented a particular political vision, a view of society as inevitably determined by history and evolution, and therefore not susceptible to change. In order to displace "realism," and to demonstrate these hidden politics, Brecht redefined Marx's conception of "alienation" as a theatrical practice. In *Das Kapital,* Marx argues that the division of labor in modern industrial production has altered the relationship between mankind and the world. In modern industry, workers sell their labor in order to produce commodities. These commodities, Marx contends, then seem "alien" in that they appear to have arisen magically. Capitalist production conceals the signs of how they were produced, so that commodities come to have a "natural" life of their own. Yet, even as commodities seem to come alive, the workers become dehumanized, incorporated into the machinery of production. In the world of capital, where everything is for sale, all human relations, lives, and desires become commodified. The prevailing view of the world—in which commodities confront workers as something natural and entirely separate from their makers—is, to Marx, a *false* view, perpetuated within the bourgeois social order to the political advantage of the ruling classes.

Brecht's theater works to provide its audience with ways of regarding bourgeois reality—including realistic theater and drama—as "unnatural," as a political vision, as an ideological view of the world produced in the interest of profit. Brecht's theater, that is, works to "alienate" or "estrange" the audience from the commonplace "realities" of daily life—which we have unreflectively come to regard as "natural" and "inevitable"—in order to train us to question the world made by modern capitalism and the society it sustains. As he wrote in "The Modern Theater Is the Epic Theater," his theater is based on a "radical separation of the elements" of production, rather than on the scenic unity typical of realism. The seamless illusion of the realistic stage is that theater's most seductive commodity: it constantly and subliminally urges the audience to accept its "picture" of reality as a natural, apolitical image of the world as it is. Brecht's theater, in contrast, always shows both the dramatic illusion (the character, the setting, the action) and the process of its making (the work of the actor, the machinery of the theater, the activities of the stage). Brecht works to show the "means of production" in his theater, as a way of suggesting that stage realism, like social reality outside the theater, is *made,* not given.

Brecht called this theater by a variety of names, including EPIC THEATER, the term now generally used for Brecht's body of theory and technique. Brecht's plays tend to be episodic, a disconnected, open-ended MONTAGE of scenes: The audience must arrive at its own understanding of how the events are linked together, rather than being given an apparently inevitable narrative. Brecht generally left the stage bare in his productions, as a way of preventing the audience from seeing a complete illusion of some fictional dramatic locale. He exposed the lights above the stage, so the audience could see how lights influence the mood of the scene and so influence the audience's judgment. Brecht fragmented the "realistic" unity of the setting in other ways, too. Films could be projected on screens above the stage, forcing the audience to hold the drama in counterpoint to more recent events; placards onstage described the action to take place before the scene began. Finally, Brecht also urged his actors not to empathize entirely with the characters they played, but to strike a balance between a Stanislavskian identification with the character (being "in character," acting the character entirely from his or her point of view) and a more demonstrative attitude, one that enables the actor to represent the character from a variety of perspectives. Through these means, Brecht worked to involve the audience in the process of the play's production. Rather than being seduced by a commodified illusion of reality, the audience of epic theater is invited to consider, and enjoy, how the theater makes its fictions—as a way of teaching the audience to adopt a more critical, "alienated" way of seeing life outside the theater.

Brecht used many of these devices in *The Threepenny Opera* and in the series of plays he wrote in exile. Forced to flee Germany by Nazi purges of left-wing writers in 1933, Brecht spent the greater part of his creative life on the run, living briefly in Sweden, in Finland, and finally in Santa Monica, California, from 1941 to 1947. Although he had drafted *Life of Galileo* in 1938, Brecht continued to work on the play in California, collaborating on an English version with the actor Charles Laughton. He was also questioned by the House Un-American Activities Committee in 1947, as part of its infamous investigation of communism in the entertainment industry. Brecht was not charged and left the United States the following day to return to Europe and Germany. Living in exile, with no theater and little support, Brecht wrote his major plays: *Life of Galileo* (1938), *The Good Person of Szechwan* (1939), *Mother Courage and Her Children* (1939), *The Caucasian Chalk Circle* (1944). He also wrote his most important theoretical essays, including *A Short Organum for the Theater,* written in Zurich, Switzerland in 1947, but published in 1948 after Brecht returned to Germany.

Brecht returned to East Berlin in 1947 and established his company, the Berliner Ensemble. Brecht's antirealist plays had long been the source of conflict with the SOCIAL REALISM advocated by the Communist Party, and even after the war Brecht had to work with a wary eye on the East German authorities. Nonetheless, the Berliner Ensemble—under Brecht's guidance and with the talents of his wife, Helene Weigel—became the leading European production company of the 1950s, sowing the seeds of innovation in every country they visited. Brecht died in August of 1956, just before the Berliner Ensemble's stunning visit to London, but the influence of his conception of theater has become worldwide, visible in plays from Luis Valdez's *Los Vendidos* to Caryl Churchill's *Cloud 9* to Tony Kushner's *Angels in America*.

MOTHER COURAGE AND HER CHILDREN

Mother Courage and Her Children is typical of Brecht's innovative approach to theater and to "political theater" as well. Rather than presenting a thesis, the play works to question the audience's attitudes about a variety of social institutions: warfare, business, motherhood, morality. In a parable-like series of scenes reminiscent both of expressionist theater and of morality drama, *Mother Courage and Her Children* invites the audience to estrange, and so reconsider, its ways of mapping the world.

In his model-book of the play, Brecht wrote that he wanted to show that "war, which is a continuation of business by other means, makes the human virtues fatal to their possessors." The play considers this problem in a variety of challenging ways. Although it is perhaps tempting to see Courage—Why is she called Courage? Was she courageous?—as a tragic heroine, the play relentlessly questions her "heroic" survival, and our own attitudes about the distinctions between war, business, and morality. As scene 1 demonstrates, war and business create an all-embracing market in which everything is commodified, that is, for sale. Mother Courage sells a belt buckle and loses a son as part of the same transaction.

Much of the play's power onstage arises through its use of physical space and a few significant properties. The wagon—Courage's home, her means of survival, her mode of production—becomes in a sense the play's central "character." Placing it on a turntable, most productions convey the sense that the wagon is almost always in motion, yet never actually getting anywhere, much as Courage herself enters the play and leaves it singing the same song. Courage's fortunes are emblematized by the wagon as well. Loaded with goods and pulled by her two strong sons in the first scene, it is battered, barren, and empty in the last, pulled by Mother Courage herself as she struggles to catch up with the army. Brecht was attracted to the idea of using the wagon, the play's economic and material "base," so to speak, to elucidate some of the play's symbolic or moral themes. He used Courage's wash-line to link the wagon to the cannon at the opening of scene 3, tying warfare, the economy, and the domestic sphere together. He raised the harness-poles to form a kind of crucifix after the death of her son Swiss Cheese. Many of the most ironic moments of the Berliner Ensemble production of the play were Weigel's invention: as Mother Courage, she bit the coin in scene 1 and slowly measured her pennies out of her purse when she paid the peasants to bury Kattrin at the end of the play. This is the kind of moment that Brecht worked—in theory, as a playwright, in directing productions—to make happen in the theater, a moment when a single gesture forces the audience to consider the scene in a new light, to question the relationship between its ideas of identity and morality and the society that gives them shape and meaning.

MOTHER COURAGE AND HER CHILDREN
A Chronicle of the Thirty Years' War

Bertolt Brecht

TRANSLATED BY JOHN WILLETT

─────── CHARACTERS ───────

MOTHER COURAGE	A CLERK
KATTRIN, *her dumb daughter*	A YOUNG SOLDIER
EILIF, *the elder son*	AN OLDER SOLDIER
SWISS CHEESE, *the younger son*	A PEASANT
THE RECRUITER	THE PEASANT'S WIFE
THE SERGEANT	THE YOUNG MAN
THE COOK	THE OLD WOMAN
THE GENERAL	ANOTHER PEASANT
THE CHAPLAIN	HIS WIFE
THE ARMOURER	THE YOUNG PEASANT
YVETTE POTTIER	THE ENSIGN
THE MAN WITH THE PATCH	SOLDIERS
ANOTHER SERGEANT	A VOICE
THE ANCIENT COLONEL	

─────── SCENE ONE ───────

Spring 1624. The Swedish Commander-in-Chief Count Oxenstierna is raising troops in Dalecarlia for the Polish campaign. The canteen woman Anna Fierling, known under the name of Mother Courage, loses one son.

Country road near a town.

A SERGEANT *and a* RECRUITER *stand shivering.*

RECRUITER: How can you muster a unit in a place like this? I've been thinking about suicide, sergeant. Here am I, got to find our commander four companies before the twelfth of the month, and people round here are so nasty I can't sleep
5   nights. S'pose I get hold of some bloke and shut my eye to his pigeon chest and varicose veins, I get him proper drunk, he signs on the line, I'm just settling up, he goes for a piss, I follow him to the door because I smell a rat; bob's your uncle, he's off like a flea with the itch. No notion of word
10   of honour, loyalty, faith, sense of duty. This place has shattered my confidence in the human race, sergeant.
SERGEANT: It's too long since they had a war here; stands to reason. Where's their sense of morality to come from? Peace—that's just a mess; takes a war to restore order. Peacetime,
15   the human race runs wild. People and cattle get buggered about, who cares? Everyone eats just as he feels inclined, a hunk of cheese on top of his nice white bread, and a slice of fat on top of the cheese. How many young blokes and good horses in that town there, nobody knows; they never
20   thought of counting. I been in places ain't seen a war for nigh seventy years: folks hadn't got names to them, couldn't tell one another apart. Takes a war to get proper nominal rolls and inventories—shoes in bundles and corn in bags, and man and beast properly numbered and carted
25   off, cause it stands to reason: no order, no war.
RECRUITER: Too true.

SERGEANT: Same with all good things, it's a job to get a war going. But once it's blossomed out there's no holding it; folk start fighting shy of peace like punters what can't stop for fear of having to tot up what they lost. Before that it's war 30 they're fighting shy of. It's something new to them.
RECRUITER: Hey, here's a cart coming. Two tarts with two young fellows. Stop her, sergeant. If this one's a flop I'm not standing around in your spring winds any longer, I can tell you. 35

(Sound of a jew's-harp. Drawn by two young fellows, a covered cart rolls in. On it sit MOTHER COURAGE *and her dumb daughter* KATTRIN.)

MOTHER COURAGE: Morning, sergeant.
SERGEANT: *(Blocking the way.)* Morning, all. And who are you?
MOTHER COURAGE: Business folk. *(Sings.)*

> You captains, tell the drums to slacken
> And give your infanteers a break: 40
> It's Mother Courage with her waggon
> Full of the finest boots they make.
> With crawling lice and looted cattle
> With lumbering guns and straggling kit—
> How can you flog them into battle 45
> Unless you get them boots that fit?
>   The new year's come. The watchmen shout.
>   The thaw sets in. The dead remain.
>   Whatever life has not died out
>   It staggers to its feet again. 50

> Captains, how can you make them face it—
> Marching to death without a brew?
> Courage has rum with which to lace it
> And boil their souls and bodies through.
> Their musket primed, their stomach hollow— 55
> Captains, your men don't look so well.
> So feed them up and let them follow

While you command them into hell.
The new year's come. The watchmen shout.
60   The thaw sets in. The dead remain.
Wherever life has not died out
It staggers to its feet again.

SERGEANT: Halt! Who are you with, you trash?
THE ELDER SON: Second Finnish Regiment.
65 SERGEANT: Where's your papers?
MOTHER COURAGE: Papers?
THE YOUNGER SON: What, mean to say you don't know Mother
    Courage?
SERGEANT: Never heard of her. What's she called Courage for?
70 MOTHER COURAGE: Courage is the name they gave me because
    I was scared of going broke, sergeant, so I drove me cart
    right through the bombardment of Riga with fifty loaves of
    bread aboard. They were going mouldy, it was high time,
    hadn't any choice really.
75 SERGEANT: Don't be funny with me. Your papers.
MOTHER COURAGE: (*Pulling a bundle of papers from a tin box and
    climbing down off the cart.*) That's all my papers, sergeant.
    You'll find a whole big missal from Altötting in Bavaria for
    wrapping gherkins in, and a road map of Moravia, the Lord
80   knows when I'll ever get there, might as well chuck it away,
    and here's a stamped certificate that my horse hasn't got
    foot-and-mouth, only he's dead worse luck, cost fifteen
    florins he did—not me luckily. That enough paper for you?
SERGEANT: You pulling my leg? I'll knock that sauce out of
85   you. S'pose you know you got to have a licence.
MOTHER COURAGE: Talk proper to me, do you mind, and don't
    you dare say I'm pulling your leg in front of my unsullied
    children, 'tain't decent, I got no time for you. My honest
    face, that's me licence with the Second Regiment, and if it's
90   too difficult for you to read there's nowt I can do about it.
    Nobody's putting a stamp on that.
RECRUITER: Sergeant, methinks I smell insubordination in this
    individual. What's needed in our camp is obedience.
MOTHER COURAGE: Sausage, if you ask me.
95 SERGEANT: Name.
MOTHER COURAGE: Anna Fierling.
SERGEANT: You all called Fierling then?
MOTHER COURAGE: What d'you mean? It's me's called Fierling,
    not them.
100 SERGEANT: Aren't all this lot your children?
MOTHER COURAGE: You bet they are, but why should they all
    have to be called the same, eh? (*Pointing to her elder son.*) For
    instance, that one's called Eilif Nojocki—Why? his father
    always claimed he was called Kojocki or Mojocki or some-
105   thing. The boy remembers him clearly, except that the one
    he remembers was someone else, a Frenchie with a little
    beard. Aside from that he's got his father's wits; that man
    knew how to snitch a peasant's pants off his bum without
    him noticing. This way each of us has his own name, see.
110 SERGEANT: What, each one different?
MOTHER COURAGE: Don't tell me you ain't never come across
    that.
SERGEANT: So I s'pose he's a Chinaman? (*Pointing to the younger
    son.*)
115 MOTHER COURAGE: Wrong. Swiss.
SERGEANT: After the Frenchman?

MOTHER COURAGE: What Frenchman? I never heard tell of no
    Frenchman. You keep muddling things up, we'll be hang-
    ing around here till dark. A Swiss, but called Fejos, and the
    name has nowt to do with his father. He was called some-   120
    thing quite different and was a fortifications engineer, only
    drunk all the time.

(SWISS CHEESE *beams and nods; dumb* KATTRIN *too is amused.*)

SERGEANT: How in hell can he be called Fejos?
MOTHER COURAGE: I don't like to be rude, sergeant, but you
    ain't got much imagination, have you? Course he's called   125
    Fejos, because when he arrived I was with a Hungarian,
    very decent fellow, had terrible kidney trouble though he
    never touched a drop. The boy takes after him.
SERGEANT: But he wasn't his father . . .
MOTHER COURAGE: Took after him just the same. I call him   130
    Swiss Cheese. (*Pointing to her daughter.*) And that's Kattrin
    Haupt, she's half German.
SERGEANT: Nice family, I must say.
MOTHER COURAGE: Aye, me cart and me have seen the world.
SERGEANT: I'm writing all this down. (*He writes.*) And you're   135
    from Bamberg in Bavaria; how d'you come to be here?
MOTHER COURAGE: Can't wait till war chooses to visit Bam-
    berg, can I?
RECRUITER: (*To* EILIF.) You two should be called Jacob Ox and
    Esau Ox, pulling the cart like that. I s'pose you never get   140
    out of harness?
EILIF: Ma, can I clobber him one? I wouldn't half like to.
MOTHER COURAGE: And I says you can't; just you stop where
    you are. And now two fine officers like you, I bet you could
    use a good pistol, or a belt buckle, yours is on its last legs,   145
    sergeant.
SERGEANT: I could use something else. Those boys are healthy
    as young birch trees, I observe: chests like barrels, solid leg
    muscles. So why are they dodging their military service,
    may I ask?   150
MOTHER COURAGE: (*Quickly.*) Nowt doing, sergeant. Yours is
    no trade for my kids.
RECRUITER: But why not? There's good money in it, glory too.
    Flogging boots is women's work. (*To* EILIF.) Come here, let's
    see if you've muscles in you or if you're a chicken.   155
MOTHER COURAGE: He's a chicken. Give him a fierce look, he'll
    fall over.
RECRUITER: Killing a young bull that happens to be in his way.
    (*Wants to lead him off.*)
MOTHER COURAGE: Let him alone, will you? He's nowt for you   160
    folk.
RECRUITER: He was crudely offensive and talked about clob-
    bering me. The two of us are going to step into that field
    and settle it man to man.
EILIF: Don't you worry, mum, I'll fix him.   165
MOTHER COURAGE: Stop there! You varmint! I know you, nowt
    but fights. There's a knife down his boot. A slasher, that's
    what he is.
RECRUITER: I'll draw it out of him like a milk-tooth. Come
    along, sonny.   170
MOTHER COURAGE: Sergeant, I'll tell the colonel. He'll have
    you both in irons. The lieutenant's going out with my
    daughter.

SERGEANT: No rough stuff, chum. *(To* MOTHER COURAGE.*)*
175   What you got against military service? Wasn't his own father a soldier? Died a soldier's death, too? Said it yourself.
MOTHER COURAGE: He's nowt but a child. You want to take
him off to slaughterhouse, I know you lot. They'll give you
five florins for him.
180 RECRUITER: First he's going to get a smart cap and boots, eh?
EILIF: Not from you.
MOTHER COURAGE: Let's both go fishing, said angler to worm.
(To SWISS CHEESE.*)* Run off, call out they're trying to kidnap
your brother. *(She pulls a knife.)* Go on, you kidnap him, just
185   try. I'll slit you open, trash. I'll teach you to make war with
him. We're doing an honest trade in ham and linen, and
we're peaceable folk.
SERGEANT: Peaceable I don't think; look at your knife. You
should be ashamed of yourself; put that knife away, you old
190   harridan. A minute back you were admitting you live off
the war, how else should you live, what from? But how's
anyone to have war without soldiers?
MOTHER COURAGE: No need for it to be my kids.
SERGEANT: Oh, you'd like war to eat the pips but spit out the
195   apple? It's to fatten up your kids, but you won't invest in it.
Got to look after itself, eh? And you called Courage, fancy
that. Scared of the war that keeps you going? Your sons
aren't scared of it, I can see that.
EILIF: Take more than a war to scare me.
200 SERGEANT: And why? Look at me: has army life done all that
badly by me? Joined up at seventeen.
MOTHER COURAGE: Still got to reach seventy.
SERGEANT: I don't mind waiting.
MOTHER COURAGE: Under the sod, eh?
205 SERGEANT: You trying to insult me, saying I'll die?
MOTHER COURAGE: S'pose it's true? S'pose I can see the mark's
on you? S'pose you look like a corpse on leave to me? Eh?
SWISS CHEESE: She's got second sight, Mother has.
RECRUITER: Go ahead, tell the sergeant's fortune, might amuse
210   him.
MOTHER COURAGE: Gimme helmet. *(He gives it to her.)*
SERGEANT: It don't mean a bloody sausage. Anything for a
laugh though.
MOTHER COURAGE: *(Taking out a sheet of parchment and tearing it up.)*
215   Eilif, Swiss Cheese and Kattrin, may all of us be torn apart like
this if we lets ourselves get too mixed up in the war. *(To the*
SERGEANT.*)* Just for you I'm doing it for free. Black's for death.
I'm putting a big black cross on this slip of paper.
SWISS CHEESE: Leaving the other one blank, see?
220 MOTHER COURAGE: Then I fold them across and shake them.
All of us is jumbled together like this from our mother's
womb, and now draw a slip and you'll know. *(The* SERGEANT
hesitates.)
RECRUITER: *(To* EILIF.*)* I don't take just anybody, they all know
225   I'm choosey, but you got the kind of fire I like to see.
SERGEANT: *(Fishing in the helmet.)* Too silly. Load of eyewash.
SWISS CHEESE: Drawn a black cross, he has. Write him off.
RECRUITER: They're having you on; not everybody's name's on
a bullet.
230 SERGEANT: *(Hoarsely.)* You've put me in the shit.
MOTHER COURAGE: Did that yourself the day you became a soldier. Come along, let's move on now. 'Tain't every day we
have a war, I got to get stirring.

SERGEANT: God damn it, you can't kid me. We're taking that
bastard of yours for a soldier.   235
EILIF: Swiss Cheese'd like to be a soldier too.
MOTHER COURAGE: First I've heard of that. You'll have to draw
too, all three of you. *(She goes to the rear to mark crosses on further slips.)*
RECRUITER: *(To* EILIF.*)* One of the things they say against us is that   240
it's all holy-holy in the Swedish camp; but that's a malicious
rumour to do us down. There's no hymn-singing but Sundays,
just a single verse, and then only for those got voices.
MOTHER COURAGE: *(Coming back with the slips, which she drops
into the* SERGEANT's *helmet.)* Trying to get away from their   245
ma, the devils, off to war like calves to salt-lick. But I'm
making you draw lots, and that'll show you the world is no
vale of joys with 'Come along, son, we need a few more generals'. Sergeant, I'm so scared they won't get through the
war. Such dreadful characters, all three of them. *(She hands*   250
the helmet to EILIF.*)* Hey, come on, fish out your slip. *(He fishes
one out, unfolds it. She snatches it from him.)* There you are, it's
a cross. Oh, wretched mother that I am, o pain-racked giver
of birth! Shall he die? Aye, in the springtime of life he is
doomed. If he becomes a soldier he shall bite the dust, it's   255
plain to see. He is too foolhardy, like his dad was. And if he
ain't sensible he'll go the way of all flesh, his slip proves it.
(Shouts at him.) You going to be sensible?
EILIF: Why not?
MOTHER COURAGE: Sensible thing is stay with your mother,   260
never mind if they poke fun at you and call you chicken, just
you laugh.
RECRUITER: If you're pissing in your pants I'll make do with
your brother.
MOTHER COURAGE: I told you laugh. Go on, laugh. Now you   265
draw, Swiss Cheese. I'm not so scared on your account,
you're honest. *(He fishes in the helmet.)* Oh, why look at your
slip in that strange way? It's got to be a blank. There can't
be any cross on it. Surely I'm not going to lose *you*. *(She takes
the slip.)* A cross? What, you too? Is that because you're so   270
simple, perhaps? O Swiss Cheese, you too will be sunk if
you don't stay utterly honest all the while, like I taught you
from childhood when you brought the change back from
the baker's. Else you can't save yourself. Look, sergeant,
that's a black cross, ain't it?   275
SERGEANT: A cross, that's right. Can't think how I come to get
one. I always stay in the rear. *(To the* RECRUITER.*)* There's no
catch. Her own family get it too.
SWISS CHEESE: I get it too. But I listen to what I'm told.
MOTHER COURAGE: *(To* KATTRIN.*)* And now you're the only one   280
I know's all right, you're a cross yourself; got a kind heart
you have. *(Holds the helmet up to her on the cart, but takes the
slip out herself.)* No, that's too much. That can't be right;
must have made a mistake shuffling. Don't be too kind-
hearted, Kattrin, you'll have to give it up, there's a cross   285
above your path too. Lie doggo, girl, it can't be that hard
once you're born dumb. Right, all of you know now. Look
out for yourselves, you'll need to. And now up we get and
on we go. *(She climbs on to the cart.)*
RECRUITER: *(To the* SERGEANT.*)* Do something.   290
SERGEANT: I don't feel very well.
RECRUITER: Must of caught a chill taking your helmet off in
that wind. Involve her in a deal. *(Aloud.)* Might as well have

295 a look at that belt-buckle, sergeant. After all, our friends here have to live by their business. Hey, you people, the sergeant wants to buy that belt-buckle.

MOTHER COURAGE: Half a florin. Two florins is what a belt like that's worth. (*Climbs down again.*)

300 SERGEANT: 'Tain't new. Let me get out of this damned wind and have a proper look at it. (*Goes behind the cart with the buckle.*)

MOTHER COURAGE: Ain't what I call windy.

SERGEANT: I s'pose it might be worth half a florin, it's silver.

MOTHER COURAGE: (*Joining him behind the cart.*) It's six solid ounces.

305 RECRUITER: (*To* EILIF.) And then we men'll have one together. Got your bounty money here, come along. (EILIF *stands undecided.*)

MOTHER COURAGE: Half a florin it is.

SERGEANT: It beats me. I'm always at the rear. Sergeant's the
310 safest job there is. You can send the others up front, cover themselves with glory. Me dinner hour's properly spoiled. Shan't be able to hold nowt down, I know.

MOTHER COURAGE: Mustn't let it prey on you so's you can't eat. Just stay at the rear. Here, take a swig of brandy, man.
315 (*Gives him a drink.*)

RECRUITER: (*Has taken* EILIF *by the arm and is leading him away up stage.*) Ten florins bounty money, then you're a gallant fellow fighting for the king and women'll be after you like flies. And you can clobber me for free for insulting you.

(*Exeunt both.*)

(*Dumb* KATTRIN *leans down from the cart and makes hoarse noises.*)

320 MOTHER COURAGE: All right, Kattrin, all right. Sergeant's just paying. (*Bites the half-florin.*) I got no faith in any kind of money. Burnt child, that's me, sergeant. This coin's good, though. And now let's get moving. Where's Eilif?

SWISS CHEESE: Went off with the recruiter.

325 MOTHER COURAGE: (*Stands quite still, then.*) You simpleton. (*To* KATTRIN.) 'Tain't your fault, you can't speak, I know.

SERGEANT: Could do with a swig yourself, ma. That's life. Plenty worse things than being a soldier. Want to live off war, but keep yourself and family out of it, eh?

330 MOTHER COURAGE: You'll have to help your brother pull now, Kattrin.

(*Brother and sister hitch themselves to the cart and start pulling.* MOTHER COURAGE *walks alongside. The cart rolls on.*)

SERGEANT: (*Looking after them.*)
Like the war to nourish you?
Have to feed it something too.

──────── SCENE TWO ────────

In the years 1625 and 1626 Mother Courage crosses Poland in the train of the Swedish armies. Before the fortress of Wallhof she meets her son again. Successful sale of a capon and heyday of her dashing son.

The GENERAL'S *tent.*

Beside it, his kitchen. Thunder of cannon. The COOK *is arguing with* MOTHER COURAGE, *who wants to sell him a capon.*

THE COOK: Sixty hellers for a miserable bird like that?

MOTHER COURAGE: Miserable bird? This fat brute? Mean to say some greedy old general—and watch your step if you got nowt for his dinner—can't afford sixty hellers for him?

THE COOK: I can get a dozen like that for ten hellers just down 5 the road.

MOTHER COURAGE: What, a capon like this you can get just down the road? In time of siege, which means hunger that tears your guts. A rat you might get: 'might' I say because they're all being gobbled up, five men spending best part of 10 day chasing one hungry rat. Fifty hellers for a giant capon in time of siege!

THE COOK: But it ain't us having the siege, it's t'other side. We're conducting the siege, can't you get that in your head?

MOTHER COURAGE: But we got nowt to eat too, even worse than 15 them in the town. Took it with them, didn't they? They're having a high old time, everyone says. And look at us! I been to the peasants, there's nowt there.

THE COOK: There's plenty. They're sitting on it.

MOTHER COURAGE: (*Triumphantly.*) They ain't. They're bust, 20 that's what they are. Just about starving. I saw some, were grubbing up roots from sheer hunger, licking their fingers after they boiled some old leather strap. That's way it is. And me got a capon here and supposed to take forty hellers for it. 25

THE COOK: Thirty, not forty. I said thirty.

MOTHER COURAGE: Here, this ain't just any old capon. It was such a gifted beast, I been told, it could only eat to music, had a military march of its own. It could count, it was that intelligent. And you say forty hellers is too much? General 30 will make mincemeat of you if there's nowt on his table.

THE COOK: See what I'm doing? (*He takes a piece of beef and puts his knife to it.*) Here I got a bit of beef, I'm going to roast it. Make up your mind quick.

MOTHER COURAGE: Go on, roast it. It's last year's. 35

THE COOK: Last night's. That animal was still alive and kicking, I saw him myself.

MOTHER COURAGE: Alive and stinking, you mean.

THE COOK: I'll cook him five hours if need be. I'll just see if he's still tough. (*He cuts into it.*) 40

MOTHER COURAGE: Put plenty of pepper on it so his lordship the general don't smell the pong.

(*The* GENERAL, *a* CHAPLAIN *and* EILIF *enter the tent.*)

THE GENERAL: (*Slapping* EILIF *on the shoulder.*) Now then, Eilif my son, into your general's tent with you and sit thou at my right hand. For you accomplished a deed of heroism, like a 45 pious cavalier; and doing what you did for God, and in a war of religion at that, is something I commend in you most highly, you shall have a gold bracelet as soon as we've taken this town. Here we are, come to save their souls for them, and what do those insolent dung-encrusted yokels go 50 and do? Drive their beef away from us. They stuff it into those priests of theirs all right, back and front, but you taught 'em manners, ha! So here's a pot of red wine for you, the two of us'll knock it back at one gulp. (*They do so.*) Piss all for the chaplain, the old bigot. And now, what would 55 you like for dinner, my darling?

EILIF: A bit of meat, why not?

THE GENERAL: Cook! Meat!

THE COOK: And then he goes and brings guests when there's
60   nowt there.

(MOTHER COURAGE *silences him so she can listen.*)

EILIF: Hungry job cutting down peasants.

MOTHER COURAGE: Jesus Christ, it's my Eilif.

THE COOK: Your what?

MOTHER COURAGE: My eldest boy. It's two years since I lost
65   sight of him, they pinched him from me on the road, must
think well of him if the general's asking him to dinner, and
what kind of a dinner can you offer? Nowt. You heard what
the visitor wishes to eat: meat. Take my tip, you settle for
the capon, it'll be a florin.

70   THE GENERAL: (*Has sat down with* EILIF, *and bellows.*) Food,
Lamb, you foul cook, or I'll have your hide.

THE COOK: Give it over, dammit, this is blackmail.

MOTHER COURAGE: Didn't someone say it was a miserable bird?

THE COOK: Miserable; give it over, and a criminal price, fifty
75   hellers.

MOTHER COURAGE: A florin, I said. For my eldest boy, the general's guest, no expense is too great for me.

THE COOK: (*Gives her the money.*) You might at least pluck it
while I see to the fire.

80   MOTHER COURAGE: (*Sits down to pluck the fowl.*) He won't half be
surprised to see me. He's my dashing clever son. Then I got
a stupid one too, he's honest though. The girl's nowt. One
good thing, she don't talk.

THE GENERAL: Drink up, my son, this is my best Falernian;
85   only got a barrel or two left, but that's nothing to pay for a
sign that's there's still true faith to be found in my army. As
for that shepherd of souls he can just look on, because all he
does is preach, without the least idea how it's to be carried
out. And now, my son Eilif, tell us more about the neat way
90   you smashed those yokels and captured the twenty oxen.
Let's hope they get here soon.

EILIF: A day or two at most.

MOTHER COURAGE: Thoughtful of our Eilif not to bring the
oxen in till tomorrow, else you lot wouldn't have looked
95   twice at my capon.

EILIF: Well, it was like this, see. I'd heard peasants had been
driving the oxen they'd hidden, out of the forest into one
particular wood, on the sly and mostly by night. That's
where people from the town were s'posed to come and pick
100   them up. So I holds off and lets them drive their oxen together, reckoning they'd be better than me at finding 'em.
I had my blokes slavering after the meat, cut their emergency rations even further for a couple of days till their
mouths was watering at the least sound of any word begin-
105   ning with 'me-', like 'measles' say.

THE GENERAL: Very clever of you.

EILIF: Possibly. The rest was a piece of cake. Except that the
peasants had cudgels and outnumbered us three to one and
made a murderous attack on us. Four of 'em shoved me into
110   a thicket, knocked my sword from my hand and bawled out
'Surrender!' What's the answer, I wondered; they're going
to make mincemeat of me.

THE GENERAL: What did you do?

EILIF: I laughed.

115   THE GENERAL: You did what?

EILIF: Laughed. So we got talking. I put it on a business footing from the start, told them 'Twenty florins a head's too
much. I'll give you fifteen'. As if I was meaning to pay. That
threw them, and they began scratching their heads. In a
flash I'd picked up my sword and was hacking 'em to pieces.   120
Necessity's the mother of invention, eh, sir?

THE GENERAL: What is your view, pastor of souls?

THE CHAPLAIN: That phrase is not strictly speaking in the
Bible, but when Our Lord turned the five loaves into five
hundred there was no war on and he could tell people to   125
love their neighbours as they'd had enough to eat. Today it's
another story.

THE GENERAL: (*Laughs.*) Quite another story. You can have a
swig after all for that, you old Pharisee. (*To* EILIF.) Hacked
'em to pieces, did you, so my gallant lads can get a proper   130
bite to eat? What do the Scriptures say? 'Whatsoever thou
doest for the least of my brethren, thou doest for me'. And
what did you do for them? Got them a good square meal of
beef, because they're not accustomed to mouldy bread, the
old way was to fix a cold meal of rolls and wine in your hel-   135
met before you went out to fight for God.

EILIF: Aye, in a flash I'd picked up my sword and was hacking
them to pieces.

THE GENERAL: You've the makings of a young Caesar. You
ought to see the King.   140

EILIF: I have from a distance. He kind of glows. I'd like to
model myself on him.

THE GENERAL: You've got something in common already. I appreciate soldiers like you, Eilif, men of courage. Somebody
like that I treat as I would my own son. (*He leads him over to*   145
the map.) Have a look at the situation, Eilif; it's a long haul
still.

MOTHER COURAGE: (*Who has been listening and now angrily plucks*
the fowl.) That must be a rotten general.

THE COOK: He's ravenous all right, but why rotten?   150

MOTHER COURAGE: Because he's got to have men of courage,
that's why. If he knew how to plan a proper campaign what
would he be needing men of courage for? Ordinary ones
would do. It's always the same; whenever there's a load of
special virtues around it means something stinks.   155

THE COOK: I thought it meant things is all right.

MOTHER COURAGE: No, that they stink. Look, s'pose some general or king is bone stupid and leads his men up shit creek,
then those men've got to be fearless, there's another virtue
for you. S'pose he's stingy and hires too few soldiers, then   160
they got to be a crowd of Hercules's. And s'pose he's slap-
dash and don't give a bugger, then they got to be clever as
monkeys else their number's up. Same way they got to
show exceptional loyalty each time he gives them impossible jobs. Nowt but virtues no proper country and no   165
decent king or general would ever need. In decent countries
folk don't have to have virtues, the whole lot can be perfectly ordinary, average intelligence, and for all I know
cowards.

THE GENERAL: I'll wager your father was a soldier.   170

EILIF: A great soldier, I been told. My mother warned me about
it. There's a song I know.

THE GENERAL: Sing it to us. (*Roars.*) When's that dinner
coming?

EILIF: It's called The Song of the Girl and the Soldier. (*He sings*   175
it, dancing a war dance with his sabre.)

The guns blaze away, and the bay'nit'll slay
And the water can't hardly be colder.
What's the answer to ice? Keep off's my advice!
180   That's what the girl told the soldier.
Next thing the soldier, wiv' a round up the spout
Hears the band playing and gives a great shout:
Why, it's marching what makes you a soldier!
So it's down to the south and then northwards once more:
185   See him catching that bay'nit in his naked paw!
That's what his comrades done told her.

Oh, do not despise the advice of the wise
Learn wisdom from those that are older
And don't try for things that are out of your reach—
190   That's what the girl told the soldier.
Next thing the soldier, his bay'nit in place
Wades into the river and laughs in her face
Though the water comes up to his shoulder.
When the shingle roof glints in the light o' the moon
195   We'll be wiv' you again, not a moment too soon!
That's what his comrades done told her.

MOTHER COURAGE: *(Takes up the song in the kitchen, beating on a pot with her spoon.)*

You'll go out like a light! And the sun'll take flight
200   For your courage just makes us feel colder.
Oh, that vanishing light! May God see that it's right!—
That's what the girl told the soldier.

EILIF: What's that?
MOTHER COURAGE: *(Continues singing.)*

205   Next thing the soldier, his bay'nit in place
Was caught by the current and went down without trace
And the water couldn't hardly be colder.
Then the shingle roof froze in the light o' the moon
As both soldier and ice drifted down to their doom—
210   And d'you know what his comrades done told her?

He went out like a light. And the sunshine took flight
For his courage just made 'em feel colder.
Oh, do not despise the advice of the wise!
That's what the girl told the soldier.

215 THE GENERAL: The things they get up to in my kitchen these days.
EILIF: *(Has gone into the kitchen. He flings his arms round his mother.)* Fancy seeing you again, ma! Where's the others?
MOTHER COURAGE: *(In his arms.)* Snug as a bug in a rug. They
220   made Swiss Cheese paymaster of the Second Finnish; any road he'll stay out of fighting that way, I couldn't keep him out altogether.
EILIF: How's the old feet?
MOTHER COURAGE: Bit tricky getting me shoes on of a morning.
225 THE GENERAL: *(Has joined them.)* So you're his mother, I hope you've got plenty more sons for me like this one.
EILIF: Ain't it my lucky day? You sitting out there in the kitchen, ma, hearing your son commended . . .
MOTHER COURAGE: You bet I heard. *(Slaps his face.)*
230 EILIF: *(Holding his cheek.)* What's that for? Taking the oxen?
MOTHER COURAGE: No. Not surrendering when those four went for you and wanted to make mincemeat of you. Didn't I say you should look after yourself? You Finnish devil!

(The GENERAL and the CHAPLAIN stand in the doorway laughing.)

——— SCENE THREE ———

Three years later Mother Courage is taken prisoner along with elements of a Finnish regiment. She manages to save her daughter, likewise her covered cart, but her honest son is killed.

Military camp.

Afternoon. A flagpole with the regimental flag. From her cart, festooned now with all kinds of goods, MOTHER COURAGE *has stretched a washing line to a large cannon, across which she and* KATTRIN *are folding the washing. She is bargaining at the same time with an* ARMOURER *over a sack of shot.* SWISS CHEESE, *now wearing a paymaster's uniform, is looking on.*

A comely person, YVETTE POTTIER, *is sewing a gaily coloured hat, a glass of brandy before her. She is in her stockinged feet, having laid aside her red high-heeled boots.*

THE ARMOURER: I'll let you have that shot for a couple of florins. It's cheap at the price, I got to have the money because the colonel's been boozing with his officers since two days back, and the drink's run out.
MOTHER COURAGE: That's troops' munitions. They catch me 5 with that, I'm for court-martial. You crooks flog the shot, and troops got nowt to fire at enemy.
THE ARMOURER: Have a heart, can't you; you scratch my back and I'll scratch yours.
MOTHER COURAGE: I'm not taking army property. Not at that 10 price.
THE ARMOURER: You can sell it on the q.t. tonight to the Fourth Regiment's armourer for five florins, eight even, if you let him have a receipt for twelve. He's right out of ammunition. 15
MOTHER COURAGE: Why not you do it?
THE ARMOURER: I don't trust him, he's a pal of mine.
MOTHER COURAGE: *(Takes the sack.)* Gimme. *(To* KATTRIN.*)* Take it away and pay him a florin and a half. *(The* ARMOURER *protests.)* I said a florin and a half. *(*KATTRIN *drags the sack up-* 20 *stage, the* ARMOURER *following her.* MOTHER COURAGE *addresses* SWISS CHEESE.*)* Here's your woollies, now look after them, it's October and autumn may set in any time. I ain't saying it's got to, cause I've learned nowt's got to come when you think it will, not even seasons of the year. But your regi- 25 mental accounts got to add up right, come what may. Do they add up right?
SWISS CHEESE: Yes, mother.
MOTHER COURAGE: Don't you forget they made you paymaster cause you was honest, not dashing like your brother, and 30 above all so stupid I bet you ain't even thought of clearing off with it, no not you. That's a big consolation to me. And don't lose those woollies.
SWISS CHEESE: No, mother, I'll put them under my mattress. *(Begins to go.)* 35
THE ARMOURER: I'll go along with you, paymaster.
MOTHER COURAGE: And don't you start learning him none of your tricks.

(The ARMOURER *leaves with* SWISS CHEESE *without any farewell gesture.)*

YVETTE: *(Waving to him.)* No reason not to say goodbye, armourer.

40 MOTHER COURAGE: *(To* YVETTE.*)* I don't like to see them together. He's wrong company for our Swiss Cheese. Oh well, war's off to a good start. Easily take four, five years before all countries are in. A bit of foresight, don't do nothing silly, and business'll flourish. Don't you know you ain't s'posed to

45 drink before midday with your complaint?

YVETTE: Complaint, who says so, it's a libel.

MOTHER COURAGE: They all say so.

YVETTE: Because they're all telling lies, Mother Courage, and me at my wits' end cause they're all avoiding me like some-

50 thing the cat brought in thanks to those lies, what the hell am I remodelling my hat for? *(She throws it away.)* That's why I drink before midday. Never used to, gives you crows' feet, but now what the hell? All the Second Finnish know me. Ought to have stayed at home when my first fellow did

55 me wrong. No good our sort being proud. Eat shit, that's what you got to do, or down you go.

MOTHER COURAGE: Now don't you start up again about that Pieter of yours and how it all happened, in front of my innocent daughter too.

60 YVETTE: She's the one should hear it, put her off love.

MOTHER COURAGE: Nobody can put 'em off that.

YVETTE: Then I'll go on, get it off my chest. It all starts with yours truly growing up in lovely Flanders, else I'd never of seen him and wouldn't be stuck here now in Poland, cause

65 he was an army cook, fair-haired, a Dutchman but thin for once. Kattrin, watch out for the thin ones, only in those days I didn't know that, or that he'd got a girl already, or that they all called him Puffing Piet cause he never took his pipe out of his mouth when he was on the job, it meant that

70 little to him. *(She sings the Song of Fraternisation.)*

> When I was only sixteen
> The foe came into our land.
> He laid aside his sabre
> And with a smile he took my hand.
75   After the May parade
> The May light starts to fade.
> The regiment dressed by the right
> The drums were beaten, that's the drill.
> The foe took us behind the hill
80   And fraternised all night.
>
> There were so many foes then
> But mine worked in the mess.
> I loathed him in the daytime.
> At night I loved him none the less.
85   After the May parade
> The May light starts to fade.
> The regiment dressed by the right
> The drums were beaten, that's the drill.
> The foe took us behind the hill
90   And fraternised all night.
>
> The love which came upon me
> Was wished on me by fate.
> My friends could never grasp why
> I found it hard to share their hate.
95   The fields were wet with dew
> When sorrow first I knew.

> The regiment dressed by the right
> The drums were beaten, that's the drill.
> And then the foe, my lover still
> Went marching out of sight.   100

I followed him, fool that I was, but I never found him, and that was five years back. *(She walks unsteadily behind the cart.)*

MOTHER COURAGE: You left your hat here.

YVETTE: Anyone wants it can have it.

MOTHER COURAGE: Let that be a lesson, Kattrin. Don't you 105 start anything with them soldiers. Love makes the world go round, I'm warning you. Even with fellows not in the army it's no bed of roses. He says he'd like to kiss the ground your feet walk on—reminds me, did you wash them yesterday?—and after that you're his skivvy. Be thankful you're 110 dumb, then you can't contradict yourself and won't be wanting to bite your tongue off for speaking the truth; it's a godsend, being dumb is. And here comes the general's cook, now what's he after?

(Enter the COOK *and the* CHAPLAIN.*)*

THE CHAPLAIN: I have a message for you from your son Eilif, 115 and the cook has come along because you made such a profound impression on him.

THE COOK: I just came along to get a bit of air.

MOTHER COURAGE: That you can always do here if you behave yourself, and if you don't I can deal with you. What does he 120 want? I got no spare cash.

THE CHAPLAIN: Actually I had a message for his brother the paymaster.

MOTHER COURAGE: He ain't here now nor anywhere else neither. He ain't his brother's paymaster. He's not to lead him 125 into temptation nor be clever at his expense. *(Giving him money from the purse slung round her.)* Give him this, it's a sin, he's banking on mother's love and ought to be ashamed of himself.

THE COOK: Not for long, he'll have to be moving off with the 130 regiment, might be to his death. Give him a bit extra, you'll be sorry later. You women are tough, then later on you're sorry. A little glass of brandy wouldn't have been a problem, but it wasn't offered and, who knows, a bloke may lie beneath the green sod and none of you people will ever 135 be able to dig him up again.

THE CHAPLAIN: Don't give way to your feelings, cook. To fall in battle is a blessing, not an inconvenience, and why? It is a war of faith. None of your common wars but a special one, fought for the faith and therefore pleasing to God. 140

THE COOK: Very true. It's a war all right in one sense, what with requisitioning, murder and looting and the odd bit of rape thrown in, but different from all the other wars because it's a war of faith; stands to reason. But it's thirsty work at that, you must admit. 145

THE CHAPLAIN: *(To* MOTHER COURAGE, *indicating the* COOK.*)* I tried to stop him, but he says he's taken a shine to you, you figure in his dreams.

THE COOK: *(Lighting a stumpy pipe.)* Just want a glass of brandy from a fair hand, what harm in that? Only I'm groggy already cause the chaplain here's been telling such jokes all 150 the way along you bet I'm still blushing.

MOTHER COURAGE: Him a clergyman too. I'd best give the pair of you a drink or you'll start making me immoral sugges-
155 tions cause you've nowt else to do.

THE CHAPLAIN: Behold a temptation, said the court preacher, and fell. (*Turning back to look at* KATTRIN *as he leaves.*) And who is this entrancing young person?

MOTHER COURAGE: That ain't an entrancing but a decent young
160 person. (*The* CHAPLAIN *and the* COOK *go behind the cart with* MOTHER COURAGE. KATTRIN *looks after them, then walks away from her washing towards the hat. She picks it up and sits down, pulling the red boots towards her.* MOTHER COURAGE *can be heard in the background talking politics with the* CHAPLAIN *and the*
165 COOK.)

MOTHER COURAGE: Those Poles here in Poland had no business sticking their noses in. Right, our king moved in on them, horse and foot, but did they keep the peace? no, went and stuck their noses into their own affairs, they did, and fell on
170 king just as he was quietly clearing off. They committed a breach of peace, that's what, so blood's on their own head.

THE CHAPLAIN: All our king minded about was freedom. The emperor had made slaves of them all, Poles and Germans alike, and the king had to liberate them.

175 THE COOK: Just what I say, your brandy's first rate, I weren't mistaken in your face, but talk of the king, it cost the king dear trying to give freedom to Germany, what with giving Sweden the salt tax, what cost the poor folk a bit, so I've heard, on top of which he had to have the Germans
180 locked up and drawn and quartered cause they wanted to carry on slaving for the emperor. Course the king took a serious view when anybody didn't want to be free. He set out by just trying to protect Poland against bad people, particularly the emperor, then it started to become a habit
185 till he ended up protecting the whole of Germany. They didn't half kick. So the poor old king's had nowt but trouble for all his kindness and expenses, and that's something he had to make up for by taxes of course, which caused bad blood, not that he'd let a little matter like that depress
190 him. One thing he had on his side, God's word, that was a help. Because otherwise folk would of been saying he done it all for himself and to make a bit on the side. So he's always had a good conscience, which was the main point.

195 MOTHER COURAGE: Anyone can see you're no Swede or you wouldn't be talking that way about the Hero King.

THE CHAPLAIN: After all he provides the bread you eat.

THE COOK: I don't eat it, I bake it.

MOTHER COURAGE: They'll never beat him, and why, his men
200 got faith in him. (*Seriously.*) To go by what the big shots say, they're waging war for almighty God and in the name of everything that's good and lovely. But look closer, they ain't so silly, they're waging it for what they can get. Else little folk like me wouldn't be in it at all.

205 THE COOK: That's the way it is.

THE CHAPLAIN: As a Dutchman you'd do better to glance at the flag above your head before venting your opinions here in Poland.

MOTHER COURAGE: All good Lutherans here. Prosit!

(KATTRIN *has put on* YVETTE's *hat and begun strutting around in imitation of her way of walking.*)

(*Suddenly there is a noise of cannon fire and shooting. Drums.* MOTHER COURAGE, *the* COOK *and the* CHAPLAIN *rush out from behind the cart, the two last-named still carrying their glasses. The* ARMOURER *and another* SOLDIER *run up to the cannon and try to push it away.*)

MOTHER COURAGE: What's happening? Wait till I've taken my 210 washing down, you louts! (*She tries to rescue her washing.*)

THE ARMOURER: The Catholics! Broken through. Don't know if we'll get out of here. (*To the* SOLDIER.) Get that gun shifted! (*Runs on.*)

THE COOK: God, I must find the general. Courage, I'll drop by 215 in a day or two for another talk.

MOTHER COURAGE: Wait, you forgot your pipe.

THE COOK: (*In the distance.*) Keep it for me. I'll be needing it.

MOTHER COURAGE: Would happen just as we're making a bit of money. 220

THE CHAPLAIN: Ah well, I'll be going too. Indeed, if the enemy is so close that it might be dangerous. Blessèd are the peacemakers is the motto in wartime. If only I had a cloak to cover me.

MOTHER COURAGE: I ain't lending no cloaks, not on your life. I 225 been had too often.

THE CHAPLAIN: But my faith makes it particularly dangerous for me.

MOTHER COURAGE: (*Gets him a cloak.*) Goes against my con-science, this does. Now you run along. 230

THE CHAPLAIN: Thank you, dear lady, that's very generous of you, but I think it might be wiser for me to remain seated here; it could arouse suspicion and bring the enemy down on me if I were seen to run.

MOTHER COURAGE: (*To the* SOLDIER.) Leave it, you fool, who's 235 going to pay you for that? I'll look after it for you, you're risking your neck.

THE SOLDIER: (*Running away.*) You can tell 'em I tried.

MOTHER COURAGE: Cross my heart. (*Sees her daughter with the hat.*) What you doing with that strumpet's hat? Take that 240 lid off, you gone crazy? And the enemy arriving any minute! (*Pulls the hat off* KATTRIN's *head.*) Want 'em to pick you up and make a prostitute of you? And she's gone and put those boots on, whore of Babylon! Off with those boots! (*Tries to tug them off her.*) Jesus Christ, chaplain, gimme a 245 hand, get those boots off her, I'll be right back. (*Runs to the cart.*)

YVETTE: (*Arrives, powdering her face.*) Fancy that, the Catholics are coming. Where's my hat? Who's been kicking it around? I can't go about looking like this if the Catholics 250 are coming. What'll they think of me? No mirror either. (*To the* CHAPLAIN.) How do I look? Too much powder?

THE CHAPLAIN: Exactly right.

YVETTE: And where are them red boots? (*Fails to find them as* KATTRIN *hides her feet under her skirt.*) I left them here 255 all right. Now I'll have to get to me tent barefoot. It's an outrage.

(*Exit.*)

(SWISS CHEESE *runs in carrying in a small box.*)

MOTHER COURAGE: (*Arrives with her hands full of ashes. To* KAT-TRIN.) Here some ashes. (*To* SWISS CHEESE.) What's that you're carrying? 260

SWISS CHEESE: Regimental cash box.

MOTHER COURAGE: Chuck it away. No more paymastering for you.

SWISS CHEESE: I'm responsible. *(He goes to the rear.)*

265 MOTHER COURAGE: *(To the* CHAPLAIN.*)* Take your clerical togs off, padre, or they'll spot you under that cloak. *(She rubs* KATTRIN's *face with ash.)* Keep still, will you? There you are, a bit of muck and you'll be safe. What a disaster. Sentries
270 were drunk. Hide your light under a bushel, it says. Take a soldier, specially a Catholic one, add a clean face, and there's your instant whore. For weeks they get nowt to eat, then soon as they manage to get it by looting they're falling on anything in skirts. That ought to do. Let's have a look. Not
275 bad. Looks like you been grubbing in muckheap. Stop trembling. Nothing'll happen to you like that. *(To* SWISS CHEESE.*)* Where d'you leave cash box?

SWISS CHEESE: Thought I'd put it in cart.

MOTHER COURAGE: *(Horrified.)* What, my cart? Sheer criminal idiocy. Only take me eyes off you one instant. Hang us all
280 three, they will.

SWISS CHEESE: I'll put it somewhere else then, or clear out with it.

MOTHER COURAGE: You sit on it, it's too late now.

THE CHAPLAIN: *(Who is changing his clothes downstage.)* For
285 heaven's sake, the flag!

MOTHER COURAGE: *(Hauls down the regimental flag.)* Bozhe moi! I'd given up noticing it were there. Twenty-five years I've had it.

(The thunder of cannon intensifies.)

(A morning three days later. The cannon has gone. MOTHER COURAGE, KATTRIN, *the* CHAPLAIN *and* SWISS CHEESE *are sitting gloomily over a meal.)*

SWISS CHEESE: That's three days I been sitting around with
290 nowt to do, and sergeant's always been kind to me but any moment now he'll start asking where's Swiss Cheese with the pay box?

MOTHER COURAGE: You thank your stars they ain't after you.

THE CHAPLAIN: What can I say? I can't even hold a service here,
295 it might make trouble for me. Whosoever hath a full heart, his tongue runneth over, it says, but heaven help me if mine starts running over.

MOTHER COURAGE: That's how it goes. Here they sit, one with his faith and the other with his cash box. Dunno which is
300 more dangerous.

THE CHAPLAIN: We are all of us in God's hands.

MOTHER COURAGE: Oh, I don't think it's as bad as that yet, though I must say I can't sleep nights. If it weren't for you, Swiss Cheese, things'd be easier. I think I got meself
305 cleared. I told 'em I didn't hold with Antichrist, the Swedish one with horns on, and I'd observed left horn was a bit unserviceable. Half way through their interrogation I asked where I could get church candles not too dear. I knows the lingo cause Swiss Cheese's dad were Catholic, of-ten used to make jokes about it, he did. They didn't believe
310 me all that much, but they ain't got no regimental canteen lady. So they're winking an eye. Could turn out for the best, you know. We're prisoners, but same like fleas on dog.

THE CHAPLAIN: That's good milk. But we'll need to cut down our Swedish appetites a bit. After all, we've been defeated. 315

MOTHER COURAGE: Who's been defeated? Look, victory and defeat ain't bound to be same for the big shots up top as for them be-low, not by no means. Can be times the bottom lot find a de-feat really pays them. Honour's lost, nowt else. I remember once up in Livonia our general took such a beating from en- 320 emy I got a horse off our baggage train in the confusion, pulled me cart seven months, he did, before we won and they checked up. As a rule you can say victory and defeat both come expensive to us ordinary folk. Best thing for us is when politics get bogged down solid. *(To* SWISS CHEESE.*)* Eat up. 325

SWISS CHEESE: Got no appetite for it. What's sergeant to do when pay day comes round?

MOTHER COURAGE: They don't have pay days on a retreat.

SWISS CHEESE: It's their right, though. They needn't retreat if they don't get paid. Needn't stir a foot. 330

MOTHER COURAGE: Swiss Cheese, you're that conscientious it makes me quite nervous. I brought you up to be honest, you not being clever, but you got to know where to stop. Chaplain and me, we're off now to buy Catholic flag and some meat. Dunno anyone so good at sniffing meat, like 335 sleepwalking it is, straight to target. I'd say he can pick out a good piece by the way his mouth starts watering. Well, thank goodness they're letting me go on trading. You don't ask tradespeople their faith but their prices. And Lutheran trousers keep cold out too. 340

THE CHAPLAIN: What did the mendicant say when he heard the Lutherans were going to turn everything in town and coun-try topsy-turvy? 'They'll always need beggars'. (MOTHER COURAGE *disappears into the cart.)* So she's still worried about the cash box. So far they've taken us all for granted as part 345 of the cart, but how long for?

SWISS CHEESE: I can get rid of it.

THE CHAPLAIN: That's almost more dangerous. Suppose you're seen. They have spies. Yesterday a fellow popped up out of the ditch in front of me just as I was relieving myself first 350 thing. I was so scared I only just suppressed an ejaculatory prayer. That would have given me away all right. I think what they'd like best is to go sniffing people's excrement to see if they're Protestants. The spy was a little runt with a patch over one eye. 355

MOTHER COURAGE: *(Clambering out of the cart with a basket.)* What have I found, you shameless creature? *(She holds up the red boots in triumph.)* Yvette's red high-heeled boots! Coolly went and pinched them, she did. Cause you put it in her head she was an enchanting young person. *(She lays them in* 360 *the basket.)* I'm giving them back. Stealing Yvette's boots! She's wrecking herself for money. That's understandable. But you'd do it for nothing, for pleasure. What did I tell you: you're to wait till it's peace. No soldiers for you. You're not to start exhibiting yourself till it's peacetime. 365

THE CHAPLAIN: I don't find she exhibits herself.

MOTHER COURAGE: Too much for my liking. Let her be like a stone in Dalecarlia, where there's nowt else, so folk say 'Can't see that cripple', that's how I'd lief have her. Then nowt'll happen to her. *(To* SWISS CHEESE.*)* You leave that box 370 where it is, d'you hear? And keep an eye on your sister, she needs it. The pair of you'll have me in grave yet. Sooner be minding a bagful of fleas.

(She leaves with the CHAPLAIN. KATTRIN *clears away the dishes.)*

SWISS CHEESE: Won't be able to sit out in the sun in shirt-
375 sleeves much longer. (KATTRIN *points at a tree.*) Aye, leaves
turning yellow. (KATTRIN *asks by gestures if he wants a drink.*)
Don't want no drink. I'm thinking. *(Pause.)* Said she can't
sleep. Best if I got rid of that box, found a good place for it.
All right, let's have a glass. (KATTRIN *goes behind the cart.*) I'll
380 stuff it down the rat-hole by the river for the time being.
Probably pick it up tonight before first light and take it to
Regiment. How far can they have retreated in three days?
Bet sergeant's surprised. I'm agreeably disappointed in you,
Swiss Cheese, he'll say. I make you responsible for the cash,
385 and you go and bring it back.

(As KATTRIN *emerges from behind the cart with a full glass in her
hand, two men confront her. One is a* SERGEANT, *the other doffs his
hat to her. He has a patch over one eye.)*

THE MAN WITH THE PATCH: God be with you, mistress. Have
you seen anyone round here from Second Finnish Regimental Headquarters?

*(*KATTRIN, *badly frightened, runs downstage, spilling the brandy.
The two men look at one another, then withdraw on seeing* SWISS
CHEESE *sitting there.)*

SWISS CHEESE: *(Interrupted in his thoughts.)* You spilt half of it.
390 What are those faces for? Jabbed yourself in eye? I don't get
it. And I'll have to be off, I've thought it over, it's the only
way. *(He gets up. She does everything possible to make him realise
the danger. He only shrugs her off.)* Wish I knew what you're
trying to say. Sure you mean well, poor creature, just can't
395 get words out. What's it matter your spilling my brandy,
I'll drink plenty more glasses yet, what's one more or less?
(He gets the box from the cart and takes it under his tunic.) Be
back in a moment. Don't hold me up now, or I'll be angry.
I know you mean well. Too bad you can't speak.

*(As she tries to hold him back he kisses her and tears himself away.
Exit. She is desperate, running hither and thither uttering little noises.
The* CHAPLAIN *and* MOTHER COURAGE *return.* KATTRIN *rushes to
her mother.)*

400 MOTHER COURAGE: What's all this? Pull yourself together, love.
They done something to you? Where's Swiss Cheese? Tell it
me step by step, Kattrin. Mother understands you. What,
so that bastard did take the box? I'll wrap it round his ears,
the little hypocrite. Take your time and don't gabble, use
405 your hands, I don't like it when you howl like a dog, what'll
his reverence say? Makes him uncomfortable. What, a one-
eyed man came along?
THE CHAPLAIN: That one-eyed man is a spy. Have they arrested
Swiss Cheese? (KATTRIN *shakes her head, shrugs her shoulders.*)
410 We're done for.
MOTHER COURAGE: *(Fishes in her basket and brings out a Catholic
flag, which the* CHAPLAIN *fixes to the mast.)* Better hoist new
flag.
THE CHAPLAIN: *(Bitterly.)* All good Catholics here.

(Voices are heard from the rear. The two men bring in SWISS CHEESE.)*

SWISS CHEESE: Let me go, I got nowt. Don't twist my shoulder,   415
I'm innocent.
SERGEANT: Here's where he came from. You know each other.
MOTHER COURAGE: Us? How?
SWISS CHEESE: I don't know her. Got no idea who she is, had
nowt to do with them. I bought me dinner here, ten hellers   420
it cost. You might have seen me sitting here, it was too
salty.
SERGEANT: Who are you people, eh?
MOTHER COURAGE: We're law-abiding folk. That's right, he
bought a dinner. Said it was too salty.   425
SERGEANT: Trying to pretend you don't know each other,
that it?
MOTHER COURAGE: Why should I know him? Can't know
everyone. I don't go asking 'em what they're called and are
they a heretic; if he pays he ain't a heretic. You a heretic?   430
SWISS CHEESE: Go on.
THE CHAPLAIN: He sat there very properly, never opening his
mouth except when eating. Then he had to.
SERGEANT: And who are you?
MOTHER COURAGE: He's just my potboy. Now I expect you gen-   435
tlemen are thirsty, I'll get you a glass of brandy, you must
be hot and tired with running.
SERGEANT: No brandy on duty. *(To* SWISS CHEESE.*)* You were carrying something. Must have hidden it by the river. Was a
bulge in your tunic when you left here.   440
MOTHER COURAGE: You sure it was him?
SWISS CHEESE: You must be thinking of someone else. I saw
someone bounding off with a bulge in his tunic. I'm the
wrong man.
MOTHER COURAGE: I'd say it was a misunderstanding too, such   445
things happen. I'm a good judge of people, I'm Courage,
you heard of me, everyone knows me, and I tell you that's
an honest face he has.
SERGEANT: We're on the track of the Second Finnish Regiment's cash box. We got the description of the fellow re-   450
sponsible for it. Been trailing him two days. It's you.
SWISS CHEESE: It's not me.
SERGEANT: And you better cough it up, or you're a goner, you
know. Where is it?
MOTHER COURAGE: *(Urgently.)* Of course he'd give it over rather   455
than be a goner. Right out he'd say: I got it, here it is,
you're too strong. He ain't all that stupid. Speak up, stupid
idiot, here's the sergeant giving you a chance.
SWISS CHEESE: S'pose I ain't got it.
SERGEANT: Then come along. We'll get it out of you. *(They lead*   460
him off.)
MOTHER COURAGE: *(Calls after them.)* He'd tell you. He's not
that stupid. And don't you twist his shoulder! *(Runs after
them.)*

(Evening of the same day. The CHAPLAIN *and dumb* KATTRIN *are
cleaning glasses and polishing knives.)*

THE CHAPLAIN: Cases like that, where somebody gets caught,   465
are not unknown in religious history. It reminds me of the
Passion of Our Lord and Saviour. There's an old song about
that. *(He sings the Song of the Hours.)*

---

469 **Song of the Hours** translated by Ralph Manheim

In the first hour Jesus mild
470   Who had prayed since even
Was betrayed and led before
Pontius the heathen.

Pilate found him innocent
475   Free from fault and error
Therefore, having washed his hands
Sent him to King Herod.

In the third hour he was scourged
Stripped and clad in scarlet
And a plaited crown of thorns
480   Set upon his forehead.

On the Son of Man they spat
Mocked him and made merry.
Then the cross of death was brought
Given him to carry.

485   At the sixth hour with two thieves
To the cross they nailed him
And the people and the thieves
Mocked him and reviled him.

This is Jesus King of Jews
490   Cried they in derision
Till the sun withdrew its light
From that awful vision.

At the ninth hour Jesus wailed
Why hast thou me forsaken?
495   Soldiers brought him vinegar
Which he left untaken.

Then he yielded up the ghost
And the earth was shaken.
Rended was the temple's veil
500   And the saints were wakened.

Soldiers broke the two thieves' legs
As the night descended.
Thrust a spear in Jesus' side
When his life had ended.

505   Still they mocked, as from his wound
Flowed the blood and water
And blasphemed the Son of Man
With their cruel laughter.

MOTHER COURAGE: (*Entering excitedly.*) It's touch and go. They
510   say sergeant's open to reason though. Only we mustn't let on
it's Swiss Cheese else they'll say we helped him. It's a matter
of money, that's all. But where's money to come from?
Hasn't Yvette been round? I ran into her, she's got her hooks
on some colonel, maybe he'd buy her a canteen business.
515   THE CHAPLAIN: Do you really wish to sell?
MOTHER COURAGE: Where's money for sergeant to come from?
THE CHAPLAIN: What'll you live on, then?
MOTHER COURAGE: That's just it.

(YVETTE POTTIER *arrives with an extremely ancient* COLONEL.)

YVETTE: (*Embracing* MOTHER COURAGE.) My dear Courage,
520   fancy seeing you so soon. (*Whispers.*) He's not unwilling.

(*Aloud.*) This is my good friend who advises me in business
matters. I happened to hear you wanted to sell your cart on
account of circumstances. I'll think it over.
MOTHER COURAGE: Pledge it, not sell, just not too much hurry,
tain't every day you find a cart like this in wartime.   525
YVETTE: (*Disappointed.*) Oh, pledge. I thought it was for sale.
I'm not so sure I'm interested. (*To the* COLONEL.) How do
you feel about it?
THE COLONEL: Just as you feel, pet.
MOTHER COURAGE: I'm only pledging it.   530
YVETTE: I thought you'd got to have the money.
MOTHER COURAGE: (*Firmly.*) I got to have it, but sooner run
myself ragged looking for a bidder than sell outright. And
why? The cart's our livelihood. It's a chance for you, Yvette;
who knows when you'll get another like it and have a spe-   535
cial friend to advise you, am I right?
YVETTE: Yes, my friend thinks I should clinch it, but I'm not
sure. If it's only a pledge . . . so you agree we ought to buy
outright?
THE COLONEL: I agree, pet.   540
MOTHER COURAGE: Best look and see if you can find anything
for sale then; maybe you will if you don't rush it, take your
friend along with you, say a week or fortnight, might find
something suits you.
YVETTE: Then let's go looking. I adore going around looking   545
for things, I adore going around with you, Poldi, it's such
fun, isn't it? No matter if it takes a fortnight. How soon
would you pay the money back if you got it?
MOTHER COURAGE: I'd pay back in two weeks, maybe one.
YVETTE: I can't make up my mind, Poldi chéri, you advise me.   550
(*Takes the* COLONEL *aside.*) She's got to sell, I know, no problem there. And there's that ensign, you know, the fair-
haired one, he'd be glad to lend me the money. He's crazy
about me, says there's someone I remind him of. What do
you advise?   555
THE COLONEL: You steer clear of him. He's no good. He's only
making use of you. I said I'd buy you something, didn't I,
pussykins?
YVETTE: I oughtn't to let you. Of course if you think the ensign
might try to take advantage . . . Poldi, I'll accept it from you. 560
THE COLONEL: That's how I feel too.
YVETTE: Is that your advice?
THE COLONEL: That is my advice.
YVETTE: (*To* COURAGE *once more.*) My friend's advice would be to
accept. Make me out a receipt saying the cart's mine once   565
two weeks are up, with all its contents, we'll check it now,
I'll bring the two hundred florins later. (*To the* COLONEL.)
You go back to the camp, I'll follow, I got to check it all and
see there's nothing missing from my cart. (*She kisses him. He
leaves. She climbs up on the cart.*) Not all that many boots, are 570
there?
MOTHER COURAGE: Yvette, it's no time for checking your cart,
s'posing it is yours. You promised you'd talk to sergeant
about Swiss Cheese, there ain't a minute to lose, they say in
an hour he'll be courtmartialled.   575
YVETTE: Just let me count the shirts.
MOTHER COURAGE: (*Pulling her down by the skirt.*) You bloody
vampire. Swiss Cheese's life's at stake. And not a word about
who's making the offer, for God's sake, pretend it's your
friend, else we're all done for cause we looked after him.   580

YVETTE: I fixed to meet that one-eyed fellow in the copse, he should be there by now.

THE CHAPLAIN: It doesn't have to be the whole two hundred either, I'd go up to a hundred and fifty, that may be enough.

585 MOTHER COURAGE: Since when has it been your money? You kindly keep out of this. You'll get your hotpot all right, don't worry. Hurry up and don't haggle, it's life or death. *(Pushes* YVETTE *off.)*

THE CHAPLAIN: Far be it from me to interfere, but what are we

590 going to live on? You're saddled with a daughter who can't earn her keep.

MOTHER COURAGE: I'm counting on regimental cash box, Mr. Clever. They'll allow it as his expenses.

THE CHAPLAIN: But will she get the message right?

595 MOTHER COURAGE: It's her interest I should spend her two hundred so she gets the cart. She's set on that, God knows how long that colonel of hers'll last. Kattrin, polish the knives, there's the pumice. And you, stop hanging round like Jesus on Mount of Olives, get moving, wash them glasses, we'll

600 have fifty or more of cavalry in tonight and I don't want to hear a lot of 'I'm not accustomed to having to run about, oh my poor feet, we never ran in church'. Thank the Lord they're corruptible. After all, they ain't wolves, just humans out for money. Corruption in humans is same as compassion

605 in God. Corruption's our only hope. Long as we have it there'll be lenient sentences and even an innocent man'll have a chance of being let off.

YVETTE: *(Comes in panting.)* They'll do it for two hundred. But it's got to be quick. Soon be out of their hands. Best thing

610 is I go right away to my colonel with the one-eyed man. He's admitted he had the box, they put the thumb-screws on him. But he chucked it in the river soon as he saw they were on his track. The box is a write-off. I'll go and get the money from my colonel, shall I?

615 MOTHER COURAGE: Box is a write-off? How'm I to pay back two hundred then?

YVETTE: Oh, you thought you'd get it from the box, did you? And I was to be Joe Soap I suppose? Better not count on that. You'll have to pay up if you want Swiss Cheese back,

620 or would you sooner I dropped the whole thing so's you can keep your cart?

MOTHER COURAGE: That's something I didn't allow for. Don't worry, you'll get your cart, I've said goodbye to it, had it seventeen years, I have. I just need a moment to think, it's

625 bit sudden, what'm I to do, two hundred's too much for me, pity you didn't beat 'em down. Must keep a bit back, else any Tom, Dick and Harry'll be able to shove me in ditch. Go and tell them I'll pay hundred and twenty florins, else it's all off, either way I'm losing me cart.

630 YVETTE: They won't do it. That one-eyed man's impatient already, keeps looking over his shoulder, he's so worked up. Hadn't I best pay them the whole two hundred?

MOTHER COURAGE: *(In despair.)* I can't pay that. Thirty years I been working. She's twenty-five already, and no husband. I

635 got her to think of too. Don't push me, I know what I'm doing. Say a hundred and twenty, or it's off.

YVETTE: It's up to you. *(Rushes off.)*

(Without looking at either the CHAPLAIN *or her daughter,* MOTHER COURAGE *sits down to help* KATTRIN *polish knives.)*

MOTHER COURAGE: Don't smash them glasses, they ain't ours now. Watch what you're doing, you'll cut yourself. Swiss Cheese'll be back, I'll pay two hundred if it comes to the 640 pinch. You'll get your brother, love. For eighty florins we could fill a pack with goods and start again. Plenty of folk has to make do.

THE CHAPLAIN: The Lord will provide, it says.

MOTHER COURAGE: See they're properly dry. *(She cleans knives in* 645 *silence.* KATTRIN *suddenly runs behind the cart, sobbing.)*

YVETTE: *(Comes running in.)* They won't do it. I told you so. The one-eyed man wanted to leave right away, said there was no point. He says he's just waiting for the drum-roll; that means sentence has been pronounced. I offered a hundred 650 and fifty. He didn't even blink. I had to convince him to stay there so's I could have another word with you.

MOTHER COURAGE: Tell him I'll pay the two hundred. Hurry! *(*YVETTE *runs off. They sit in silence. The* CHAPLAIN *has stopped polishing the glasses.)* I reckon I bargained too long. 655

(In the distance drumming is heard. The CHAPLAIN *gets up and goes to the rear.* MOTHER COURAGE *remains seated. It grows dark. The drumming stops. It grows light once more.* MOTHER COURAGE *is sitting exactly as before.)*

YVETTE: *(Arrives, very pale.)* Well, you got what you asked for, with your haggling and trying to keep your cart. Eleven bullets they gave him, that's all. You don't deserve I should bother any more about you. But I did hear they don't believe the box really is in the river. They've an idea it's here 660 and anyhow that you're connected with him. They're going to bring him here, see if you gives yourself away when you sees him. Thought I'd better warn you so's you don't recognise him, else you'll all be for it. They're right on my heels, best tell you quick. Shall I keep Kattrin away? *(*MOTHER 665 COURAGE *shakes her head.)* Does she know? She mayn't have heard the drumming or know what it meant.

MOTHER COURAGE: She knows. Get her.

*(*YVETTE *fetches* KATTRIN, *who goes to her mother and stands beside her.* MOTHER COURAGE *takes her hand. Two lansequenets come carrying a stretcher with something lying on it covered by a sheet. The* SERGEANT *marches beside them. They set down the stretcher.)*

SERGEANT: Here's somebody we dunno the name of. It's got to be listed, though, so everything's shipshape. He had a meal 670 here. Have a look, see if you know him. *(He removes the sheet.)* Know him? *(*MOTHER COURAGE *shakes her head.)* What, never see him before he had that meal here? *(*MOTHER COURAGE *shakes her head.)* Pick him up. Chuck him in the pit. He's got nobody knows him. *(They carry him away.)* 675

——— SCENE FOUR ———

| Mother Courage sings the Song of the Grand Capitulation. |

Outside an officer's tent.

MOTHER COURAGE *is waiting. A* CLERK *looks out of the tent.*

THE CLERK: I know you. You had a paymaster from the Lutherans with you, what was in hiding. I'd not complain if I were you.

MOTHER COURAGE: But I got a complaint to make. I'm innocent, would look as how I'd a bad conscience if I let this
pass. Slashed everything in me cart to pieces with their
sabres, they did, then wanted I should pay five taler fine for
nowt, I tell you, nowt.

THE CLERK: Take my tip, better shut up. We're short of can-
teens, so we let you go on trading, specially if you got a bad
conscience and pay a fine now and then.

MOTHER COURAGE: I got a complaint.

THE CLERK: Have it your own way. Then you must wait till the
captain's free. (*Withdraws inside the tent.*)

YOUNG SOLDIER: (*Enters aggressively.*) Bouque la Madonne!
Where's that bleeding pig of a captain what's took my reward money to swig with his tarts? I'll do him.

OLDER SOLDIER: (*Running after him.*) Shut up. They'll put you in
irons.

YOUNG SOLDIER: Out of there, you thief! I'll slice you into pork
chops, I will. Pocketing my prize money after I'd swum the
river, only one in the whole squadron, and now I can't even
buy meself a beer. I'm not standing for that. Come on out
there so I can cut you up!

OLDER SOLDIER: Blessed Mother of God, he's asking for trouble.

MOTHER COURAGE: Is it some reward he weren't paid?

YOUNG SOLDIER: Lemme go, I'll slash you too while I'm
at it.

OLDER SOLDIER: He rescued the colonel's horse and got no reward for it. He's young yet, still wet behind the ears.

MOTHER COURAGE: Let him go, he ain't a dog you got to chain
up. Wanting your reward is good sound sense. Why be a
hero otherwise?

YOUNG SOLDIER: So's he can sit in there and booze. You're shit-
scared, the lot of you. I done something special and I want
my reward.

MOTHER COURAGE: Don't you shout at me, young fellow. Got
me own worries, I have; any road you should spare your
voice, be needing it when captain comes, else there he'll be
and you too hoarse to make a sound, which'll make it hard
for him to clap you in irons till you turn blue. People what
shouts like that can't keep it up ever; half an hour, and they
have to be rocked to sleep, they're so tired.

YOUNG SOLDIER: I ain't tired and to hell with sleep. I'm hungry. They make our bread from acorns and hemp-seed, and
they even skimp on that. He's whoring away my reward and
I'm hungry. I'll do him.

MOTHER COURAGE: Oh I see, you're hungry. Last year that general of yours ordered you all off roads and across fields so
corn should be trampled flat; I could've got ten florins for a
pair of boots s'pose I'd had boots and s'pose anyone'd been
able to pay ten florins. Thought he'd be well away from that
area this year, he did, but here he is, still there, and hunger
is great. I see what you're angry about.

YOUNG SOLDIER: I won't have it, don't talk to me, it ain't fair
and I'm not standing for that.

MOTHER COURAGE: And you're right; but how long? How long
you not standing for unfairness? One hour, two hours?
Didn't ask yourself that, did you, but it's the whole point,
and why, once you're in irons it's too bad if you suddenly
finds you can put up with unfairness after all.

YOUNG SOLDIER: What am I listening to you for, I'd like to
know? Bouque la Madonne, where's that captain?

MOTHER COURAGE: You been listening to me because you
knows it's like what I say, your anger has gone up in smoke
already, it was just a short one and you needed a long one,
but where you going to get it from?

YOUNG SOLDIER: Are you trying to tell me asking for my reward is wrong?

MOTHER COURAGE: Not a bit. I'm just telling you your anger
ain't long enough, it's good for nowt, pity. If you'd a long
one I'd be trying to prod you on. Cut him up, the swine,
would be my advice to you in that case; but how about if
you don't cut him up cause you feels your tail going between your legs? Then I'd look silly and captain'd take it
out on me.

OLDER SOLDIER: You're perfectly right, he's just a bit crazy.

YOUNG SOLDIER: Very well, let's see if I don't cut him up.
(*Draws his sword.*) When he arrives I'm going to cut him up.

THE CLERK: (*Looks out.*) The captain'll be here in one minute.
Sit down.

(*The* YOUNG SOLDIER *sits down.*)

MOTHER COURAGE: He's sitting now. See, what did I say?
You're sitting now. Ah, how well they know us, no one need
tell 'em how to go about it. Sit down! and, bingo, we're sitting. And sitting and sedition don't mix. Don't try to stand
up, you won't stand the way you was standing before. I
shouldn't worry about what I think; I'm no better, not one
moment. Bought up all our fighting spirit, they have. Eh?
S'pose I kick back, might be bad for business. Let me tell
you a thing or two about the Grand Capitulation. (*She sings
the Song of the Grand Capitulation.*)

Back when I was young, I was brought to realise
What a very special person I must be
(Not just any old cottager's daughter, what with my looks
      and my talents and my urge towards Higher Things)
And insisted that my soup should have no hairs in it.
No one makes a sucker out of me!
(All or nothing, only the best is good enough, each man
      for himself, nobody's telling *me* what to do.)
Then I heard a tit
Chirp: Wait a bit!
      And you'll be marching with the band
      In step, responding to command
      And striking up your little dance:
      Now we advance.
      And now: parade, form square!
      Then men swear God's there—
      Not the faintest chance!

In no time at all anyone who looked could see
That I'd learned to take my medicine with good grace.
(Two kids on my hands and look at the price of bread, and
      things they expect of you!)
When they finally came to feel that they were through
      with me
They'd got me grovelling on my face.
(Takes all sorts to make a world, you scratch my back and
      I'll scratch yours, no good banging your head against a
      brick wall.)
Then I heard that tit

Chirp: Wait a bit!

115 And you'll be marching with the band
In step, responding to command
And striking up your little dance:
Now they advance.
And now: parade, form square!

120 Then men swear God's there—
Not the faintest chance!

I've known people tried to storm the summits:
There's no star too bright or seems too far away.
(Dogged does it, where there's a will there's a way, by
hook or by crook.)

125 As each peak disclosed fresh peaks to come, it's
Strange how much a plain straw hat could weigh.
(You have to cut your coat according to your cloth.)
Then I hear the tit
Chirp: Wait a bit!

130 And they'll be marching with the band
In step, responding to command
And striking up their little dance:
Now they advance
And now: parade, form square!

135 Then men swear God's there—
Not the faintest chance!

MOTHER COURAGE: (To the YOUNG SOLDIER.) That's why I
reckon you should stay there with your sword drawn if
you're truly set on it and your anger's big enough, because

140 you got grounds, I agree, but if your anger's a short one best
leave right away.
YOUNG SOLDIER: Oh stuff it. (He staggers off with the OLDER SOL-
DIER following.)
THE CLERK: (Sticks his head out.) Captain's here now. You can

145 make your complaint.
MOTHER COURAGE: I changed me mind. I ain't complaining.
(Exit.)

——— SCENE FIVE ———

Two years have gone by. The war is spreading to new areas. Ceaselessly on the move, Courage's little cart crosses
Poland, Moravia, Bavaria, Italy, then Bavaria again.
1631. Tilly's victory at Magdeburg costs Mother
Courage four officers' shirts.

MOTHER COURAGE's cart has stopped in a badly shot-up village.
Thin military music in the distance. Two SOLDIERS at the bar being
served by KATTRIN and MOTHER COURAGE. One of them has a lady's
fur coat over his shoulders.

MOTHER COURAGE: Can't pay, that it? No money, no schnapps.
They give us victory parades, but catch them giving men
their pay.
FIRST SOLDIER: I want my schnapps. I missed the looting. That

5 double-crossing general only allowed an hour's looting in
the town. He ain't an inhuman monster, he said. Town
must of paid him.
THE CHAPLAIN: (Stumbles in.) There are people still lying in that
yard. The peasant's family. Somebody give me a hand. I

10 need linen.

(The SECOND SOLDIER goes off with him. KATTRIN becomes very excited and tries to make her mother produce linen.)

MOTHER COURAGE: I got none. All my bandages was sold to
regiment. I ain't tearing up my officer's shirts for that lot.
THE CHAPLAIN: (Calling back.) I need linen, I tell you.
MOTHER COURAGE: (Blocking KATTRIN's way into the cart by sit-
ting on the step.) I'm giving nowt. They'll never pay, and   15
why, nowt to pay with.
THE CHAPLAIN: (Bending over a woman he has carried in.) Why
d'you stay around during the gunfire?
PEASANT WOMAN: (Feebly.) Farm.
MOTHER COURAGE: Catch them abandoning anything. But now   20
I'm s'posed to foot the bill. I won't do it.
FIRST SOLDIER: Those are Protestants. What they have to be
Protestants for?
MOTHER COURAGE: They ain't bothering about faith. They lost
their farm.   25
SECOND SOLDIER: They're no Protestants. They're Catholics
like us.
FIRST SOLDIER: No way of sorting 'em out in a bombardment.
A PEASANT: (Brought in by the CHAPLAIN.) My arm's gone.
THE CHAPLAIN: Where's that linen?   30
MOTHER COURAGE: I can't give nowt. What with expenses,
taxes, loan interest and bribes. (Making guttural noises,
KATTRIN raises a plank and threatens her mother with it.) You
gone plain crazy? Put that plank away or I'll paste you one,
you cow. I'm giving nowt, don't want to, got to think of   35
meself. (The CHAPLAIN lifts her off the steps and sets her on the
ground, then starts pulling out shirts and tearing them into strips.)
My officers' shirts! Half a florin apiece! I'm ruined. (From the
house comes the cry of a child in pain.)
THE PEASANT: The baby's in there still. (KATTRIN dashes in.)   40
THE CHAPLAIN: (To the woman.) Don't move. They'll get it out.
MOTHER COURAGE: Stop her, roof may fall in.
THE CHAPLAIN: I'm not going back in there.
MOTHER COURAGE: (Torn both ways.) Don't waste my precious
linen.   45

(KATTRIN brings a baby out of the ruins.)

MOTHER COURAGE: How nice, found another baby to cart
around? Give it to its ma this instant, unless you'd have me
fighting for hours to get it off you, like last time, d'you
hear? (To the SECOND SOLDIER.) Don't stand there gawping,
you go back and tell them cut out that music, we can see   50
it's a victory with our own eyes. All your victories mean to
me is losses.
THE CHAPLAIN: (Tying a bandage.) Blood's coming through.

(KATTRIN is rocking the baby and making lullaby noises.)

MOTHER COURAGE: Look at her, happy as a queen in all this
misery; give it back at once, its mother's coming round.   55
(She catches the FIRST SOLDIER, who has been attacking the drinks
and is trying to make off with one of the bottles.) Psia krew!
Thought you'd score another victory, you animal? Now pay.
FIRST SOLDIER: I got nowt.
MOTHER COURAGE: (Pulling the fur coat off his back.) Then leave   60
that coat, it's stolen any road.
THE CHAPLAIN: There's still someone under there.

——— SCENE SIX ———

Outside the Bavarian town of Ingolstadt Courage participates in the funeral of the late Imperial commander Tilly. Discussions are held about war heroes and the war's duration. The Chaplain complains that his talents are lying fallow, and dumb Kattrin gets the red boots. The year is 1632.

Inside a canteen tent.

It has a bar towards the rear. Rain. Sound of drums and Funeral music. The CHAPLAIN *and the regimental* CLERK *are playing a board game.* MOTHER COURAGE *and her daughter are stocktaking.*

THE CHAPLAIN: Now the funeral procession will be moving off.

MOTHER COURAGE: Too bad about commander in chief—twenty-two pairs those socks—he fell by accident, they say. Mist over fields, that was the trouble. General had just been

5   haranguing a regiment saying they must fight to last man and last round, he was riding back when mist made him lose direction so he was up front and a bullet got him in midst of battle—only four hurricane lamps left. (*A whistle from the rear. She goes to the bar.*) You scrimshankers, dodging

10   your commander in chief's funeral, scandal I call it. (*Pours drinks.*)

THE CLERK: They should never of paid troops out before the funeral. Instead of going now they're all getting pissed.

THE CHAPLAIN: (*To the* CLERK.) Aren't you supposed to go to the

15   funeral?

THE CLERK: Dodged it cause of the rain.

MOTHER COURAGE: It's different with you, your uniform might get wet. I heard they wanted to toll bells for funeral as usual, except it turned out all churches had been blown to

20   smithereens by his orders, so poor old commander in chief won't be hearing no bells as they let the coffin down. They're going to let off three salvoes instead to cheer things up—seventeen belts.

SHOUTS: (*From the bar.*) Hey, Missis, a brandy!

25   MOTHER COURAGE: Let's see your money. No, I ain't having you in my tent with your disgusting boots. You can drink outside, rain or no rain. (*To the* CLERK.) I'm only letting in sergeants and up. Commander in chief had been having his worries, they say. S'posed to have been trouble with Second

30   Regiment cause he stopped their pay, said it was a war of faith and they should do it for free. (*Funeral march. All look to the rear.*)

THE CHAPLAIN: Now they'll be filing past the noble corpse.

MOTHER COURAGE: Can't help feeling sorry for those generals

35   and emperors, there they are maybe thinking they're doing something extra special what folk'll talk about in years to come, and earning a public monument, like conquering the world for instance, that's a fine ambition for a general, how's he to know any better? I mean, he plagues hisself to death,

40   then it all breaks down on account of ordinary folk what just wants their beer and bit of a chat, nowt higher. Finest plans get bolloxed up by the pettiness of them as should be carrying them out, because emperors can't do nowt themselves, they just counts on soldiers and people to back 'em

45   up whatever happens, am I right?

THE CHAPLAIN: (*Laughs.*) Courage, you're right, aside from the soldiers. They do their best. Give me that lot outside there, for instance, drinking their brandy in the rain, and I'd guarantee to make you one war after another for a hundred years if need be, and I'm no trained general.

50

MOTHER COURAGE: You don't think war might end, then?

THE CHAPLAIN: What, because the commander in chief's gone? Don't be childish. They're two a penny, no shortage of heroes.

MOTHER COURAGE: Ee, I'm not asking for fun of it, but because I'm thinking whether to stock up, prices are low now, but   55
if war's going to end it's money down the drain.

THE CHAPLAIN: I realise it's a serious question. There've always been people going round saying 'the war can't go on for ever'. I tell you there's nothing to stop it going on for ever. Of course there can be a bit of a breathing space. The war   60
may need to get its second wind, it may even have an accident so to speak. There's no guarantee against that; nothing's perfect on this earth of ours. A perfect war, the sort you might say couldn't be improved on, that's something we shall probably never see. It can suddenly come to a   65
standstill for some quite unforeseen reason, you can't allow for everything. A slight case of negligence, and it's bogged down up to the axles. And then it's a matter of hauling the war out of the mud again. But emperor and kings and popes will come to its rescue. So on the whole it has nothing seri-   70
ous to worry about, and will live to a ripe old age.

A SOLDIER: (*Sings at the bar.*)

A schnapps, landlord, you're late!
A soldier cannot wait
To do his emperor's orders.   75

Make it a double, this is a holiday.

MOTHER COURAGE: S'pose I went by what you say . . .

THE CHAPLAIN: Think it out for yourself. What's to compete with the war?

THE SOLDIER: (*At the rear.*)

Your breast, my girl, you're late!   80
A soldier cannot wait
To ride across the borders.

THE CLERK: (*Unexpectedly.*) And what about peace? I'm from Bohemia and I'd like to go home some day.

THE CHAPLAIN: Would you indeed? Ah, peace. Where is the   85
hole once the cheese has been eaten?

THE SOLDIER: (*At the rear.*)

Lead trumps, my friend, you're late!
A soldier cannot wait.
His emperor needs him badly.

Your blessing, priest, you're late!   90
A soldier cannot wait.
Must lay his life down gladly.

THE CLERK: In the long run life's impossible if there's no peace.

THE CHAPLAIN: I'd say there's peace in war too; it has its peaceful moments. Because war satisfies all requirements, peace-   95
able ones included, they're catered for, and it would simply fizzle out if they weren't. In war you can do a crap like in the depths of peacetime, then between one battle and the next you can have a beer, then even when you're moving up

100   you can lay your head on your arms and have a bit of shut-
eye in the ditch, it's entirely possible. During a charge you
can't play cards maybe, but nor can you in the depths of
peacetime when you're ploughing, and after a victory there
are various openings. You may get a leg blown off, then you
105   start by making a lot of fuss as though it were serious, but
afterwards you calm down or get given a schnapps, and you
end up hopping around and the war's no worse off than before. And what's to stop you being fruitful and multiplying
in the middle of all the butchery, behind a barn or some-
110   thing, in the long run you can't be held back from it, and
then the war will have your progeny and can use them to
carry on with. No, the war will always find an outlet, mark
my words. Why should it ever stop?

(KATTRIN *has ceased working and is staring at the* CHAPLAIN.)

MOTHER COURAGE: I'll buy fresh stock then. If you say so.
115   (KATTRIN *suddenly flings a basket full of bottles to the ground and
runs off.*) Kattrin! (*Laughs.*) Damn me if she weren't waiting
for peace. I promised her she'd get a husband soon as peace
came. (*Hurries after her.*)
THE CLERK: (*Standing up.*) I won. You been talking too much.
120   Pay up.
MOTHER COURAGE: (*Returning with* KATTRIN.) Don't be silly,
war'll go on a bit longer, and we'll make a bit more money,
and peacetime'll be all the nicer for it. Now you go into
town, that's ten minutes' walk at most, fetch things from
125   Golden Lion, the expensive ones, we can fetch rest in cart
later, it's all arranged, regimental clerk here will go with
you. Nearly everybody's attending commander in chief's funeral, nowt can happen to you. Careful now, don't let them
steal nowt, think of your dowry.

(KATTRIN *puts a cloth over her head and leaves with the* CLERK.)

130   THE CHAPLAIN: Is that all right to let her go with the clerk?
MOTHER COURAGE: She's not that pretty they'd want to ruin her.
THE CHAPLAIN: I admire the way you run your business and always win through. I see why they called you Courage.
MOTHER COURAGE: Poor folk got to have courage. Why, they're
135   lost. Simply getting up in morning takes some doing in their
situation. Or ploughing a field, and in a war at that. Mere
fact they bring kids into world shows they got courage, cause
there's no hope for them. They have to hang one another and
slaughter one another, so just looking each other in face must
140   call for courage. Being able to put up with emperor and pope
shows supernatural courage, cause those two cost 'em their
lives. (*She sits down, takes a little pipe from her purse and smokes.*)
You might chop us a bit of kindling.
THE CHAPLAIN: (*Reluctantly removing his coat and preparing to chop
145   up sticks.*) I happen to be a pastor of souls, not a woodcutter.
MOTHER COURAGE: I got no soul, you see. Need firewood,
though.
THE CHAPLAIN: Where's that stumpy pipe from?
MOTHER COURAGE: Just a pipe.
150   THE CHAPLAIN: What d'you mean, 'just', it's a quite particular
pipe, that.
MOTHER COURAGE: Aha?
THE CHAPLAIN: That stumpy pipe belongs to the Oxenstierna
Regiment's cook.

MOTHER COURAGE: If you know that already why ask, Mr   155
Clever?
THE CHAPLAIN: Because I didn't know if you were aware what
you're smoking. You might just have been rummaging
around in your things, come across some old pipe or other,
and used it out of sheer absence of mind.   160
MOTHER COURAGE: And why not?
THE CHAPLAIN: Because you didn't. You're smoking that deliberately.
MOTHER COURAGE: And why shouldn't I?
THE CHAPLAIN: Courage, I'm warning you. It's my duty. Prob-   165
ably you'll never clap eyes on the gentleman again, and
that's no loss but your good fortune. He didn't make at all
a reliable impression on me. Quite the opposite.
MOTHER COURAGE: Really? Nice fellow that.
THE CHAPLAIN: So he's what you would call a nice fellow? I   170
wouldn't. Far be it from me to bear him the least ill-will,
but nice is not what I would call him. More like one of
those Don Juans, a slippery one. Have a look at that pipe if
you don't believe me. You must admit it tells you a good
deal about his character.   175
MOTHER COURAGE: Nowt that I can see. Worn out, I'd call it.
THE CHAPLAIN: Practically bitten through, you mean. A man of
wrath. That is the pipe of an unscrupulous man of wrath;
you must see that if you have any discrimination left.
MOTHER COURAGE: Don't chop my chopping block in two.   180
THE CHAPLAIN: I told you I'm not a woodcutter by trade. I
studied to be a pastor of souls. My talent and abilities are
being abused in this place, by manual labour. My Godgiven
endowments are denied expression. It's a sin. You have
never heard me preach. One sermon of mine can put a reg-   185
iment in such a frame of mind it'll treat the enemy like a
flock of sheep. Life to them is a smelly old foot-cloth which
they fling away in a vision of final victory. God has given me
the gift of speech. I can preach so you'll lose all sense of
sight and hearing.   190
MOTHER COURAGE: I don't wish to lose my sense of sight and
hearing. Where'd that leave me?
THE CHAPLAIN: Courage, I have often thought that your dry
way of talking conceals more than just a warm heart. You
too are human and need warmth.   195
MOTHER COURAGE: Best way for us to get this tent warm is have
plenty of firewood.
THE CHAPLAIN: Don't change the subject. Seriously, Courage, I
sometimes ask myself what it would be like if our relationship were to become somewhat closer. I mean, given that   200
the whirlwind of war has so strangely whirled us together.
MOTHER COURAGE: I'd say it was close enough. I cook meals for
you and you run around and chop firewood for instance.
THE CHAPLAIN: (*Coming closer.*) You know what I mean by
closer; it's not a relationship founded on meals and wood-   205
chopping and other such base necessities. Let your head
speak, harden thyself not.
MOTHER COURAGE: Don't you come at me with that axe. That'd
be too close a relationship.
THE CHAPLAIN: You shouldn't make a joke of it. I'm a serious   210
person and I've thought about what I'm saying.
MOTHER COURAGE: Be sensible, padre. I like you. I don't want
to row you. All I'm after is get myself and children through
all this with my cart. I don't see it as mine, and I ain't in

215   the mood for private affairs. Right now I'm taking a gamble, buying stores just when commander in chief's fallen
and all the talk's of peace. Where d'you reckon you'd turn
if I'm ruined? Don't know, do you? You chop us some kindling wood, then we can keep warm at night, that's quite
220   something these times. What's this? (*She gets up. Enter* KAT-
TRIN, *out of breath, with a wound above her eye. She is carrying
a variety of stuff: parcels, leather goods, a drum and so on.*)
MOTHER COURAGE: What happened, someone assault you? On
way back? She was assaulted on her way back. Bet it was that
225   trooper was getting drunk here. I shouldn't have let you go,
love. Drop that stuff. Not too bad, just a flesh wound you
got. I'll bandage it and in a week it'll be all right. Worse
than wild beasts, they are. (*She ties up the wound.*)
THE CHAPLAIN: It's not them I blame. They never went raping
230   back home. The fault lies with those that start wars, it
brings humanity's lowest instincts to the surface.
MOTHER COURAGE: Calm down. Didn't clerk come back with
you? That's because you're respectable, they don't bother.
Wound ain't a deep one, won't leave no mark. There you are,
235   all bandaged up. You'll get something, love, keep calm.
Something I put aside for you, wait till you see. (*She delves
into a sack and brings out* YVETTE's *red high-heeled boots.*) Made
you open your eyes, eh? Something you always wanted.
They're yours. Put 'em on quick, before I change me mind.
240   Won't leave no mark, and what if it does? Ones I'm really
sorry for's the ones they fancy. Drag them around till they're
worn out, they do. Those they don't care for they leaves
alive. I seen girls before now had pretty faces, then in no
time looking fit to frighten a hyaena. Can't even go behind
245   a bush without risking trouble, horrible life they lead. Same
like with trees, straight well-shaped ones get chopped down
to make beams for houses and crooked ones live happily ever
after. So it's a stroke of luck for you really. Them boots'll be
all right, I greased them before putting them away.

(KATTRIN *leaves the boots where they are and crawls into the cart.*)

250   THE CHAPLAIN: Let's hope she's not disfigured.
MOTHER COURAGE: She'll have a scar. No use her waiting for
peacetime now.
THE CHAPLAIN: She didn't let them steal the things.
MOTHER COURAGE: Maybe I shouldn't have dinned that into her
255   so. Wish I knew what went on in that head of hers. Just
once she stayed out all night, once in all those years. Afterwards she went around like before, except she worked
harder. Couldn't get her to tell what had happened. Worried me quite a while, that did. (*She collects the articles brought
260   by* KATTRIN, *and sorts them angrily.*) That's war for you. Nice
way to get a living!

(*Sound of cannon fire.*)

THE CHAPLAIN: Now they'll be burying the commander in
chief. This is a historic moment.
MOTHER COURAGE: What I call a historic moment is them
265   bashing my daughter over the eye. She's half wrecked already, won't get no husband now, and her so crazy about
kids; any road she's only dumb from war, soldier stuffed
something in her mouth when she was little. As for Swiss
Cheese I'll never see him again, and where Eilif is God alone
270   knows. War be damned.

──────── **SCENE SEVEN** ────────

Mother Courage at the peak of her business career

High road.

The CHAPLAIN, MOTHER COURAGE *and* KATTRIN *are pulling the
cart, which is hung with new wares.* MOTHER COURAGE *is wearing
a necklace of silver coins.*

MOTHER COURAGE: I won't have you folk spoiling my war for
me. I'm told it kills off the weak, but they're write-off in
peacetime too. And war gives its people a better deal. (*She
sings.*)

> And if you feel your forces fading   5
> You won't be there to share the fruits.
> But what is war but private trading
> That deals in blood instead of boots?

And what's the use of settling down? Them as does are first
to go. (*Sings.*)   10

> Some people think to live by looting
> The goods some others haven't got.
> You think it's just a line they're shooting
> Until you hear they have been shot.

> And some I saw dig six feet under   15
> In haste to lie down and pass out.
> Now they're at rest perhaps they wonder
> Just what was all their haste about.

(*They pull it further.*)

──────── **SCENE EIGHT** ────────

The same year sees the death of the Swedish king Gus-
tavus Adolphus at the battle of Lützen. Peace threatens
to ruin Mother Courage's business. Courage's dashing
son performs one heroic deed too many and comes to a
sticky end.

Camp.

A summer morning. In front of the cart stand an OLD WOMAN *and
her son. The son* [YOUNG MAN] *carries a large sack of bedding.*

MOTHER COURAGE'S VOICE: (*From inside the cart.*) Does it need to
be this ungodly hour?
THE YOUNG MAN: We walked twenty miles in the night and
got to be back today.
MOTHER COURAGE'S VOICE: What am I to do with bedding?   5
Folk've got no houses.
THE YOUNG MAN: Best have a look first.
THE OLD WOMAN: This place is no good either. Come on.
THE YOUNG MAN: What, and have them sell the roof over our
head for taxes? She might pay three florins if you throw in   10
the bracelet. (*Bells start ringing.*) Listen, mother.
VOICES: (*From the rear.*) Peace! Swedish king's been killed.
MOTHER COURAGE: (*Sticks her head out of the cart. She has not yet
done her hair.*) What's that bell-ringing about in mid-week?
THE CHAPLAIN: (*Crawling out from under the cart.*) What are they 15
shouting? Peace?

MOTHER COURAGE: Don't tell me peace has broken out just after I laid in new stock.

THE CHAPLAIN: (Calling to the rear.) That true? Peace?

20 VOICES: Three weeks ago, they say, only no one told us.

THE CHAPLAIN: (To COURAGE.) What else would they be ringing the bells for?

VOICES: A whole lot of Lutherans have driven into town, they brought the news.

25 THE YOUNG MAN: Mother, it's peace. What's the matter?

(The OLD WOMAN has collapsed.)

MOTHER COURAGE: (Speaking into the cart.) Holy cow! Kattrin, peace! Put your black dress on, we're going to church. Least we can do for Swiss Cheese. Is it true, though?

THE YOUNG MAN: The people here say so. They've made peace.
30 Can you get up? (The OLD WOMAN stands up dumbfounded.) I'll get the saddlery going again, I promise. It'll all work out. Father will get his bedding back. Can you walk? (To the CHAPLAIN.) She came over queer. It's the news. She never thought there'd be peace again. Father always said so. We're
35 going straight home. (They go off.)

MOTHER COURAGE'S VOICE: Give her a schnapps.

THE CHAPLAIN: They've already gone.

MOTHER COURAGE'S VOICE: What's up in camp?

THE CHAPLAIN: They're assembling. I'll go on over. Shouldn't I
40 put on my clerical garb?

MOTHER COURAGE'S VOICE: Best check up before parading yourself as heretic. I'm glad about peace, never mind if I'm ruined. Any road I'll have got two of me children through the war. Be seeing Eilif again now.

45 THE CHAPLAIN: And who's that walking down the lines? Bless me, the army commander's cook.

THE COOK: (Somewhat bedraggled and carrying a bundle.) What do I behold? The padre!

THE CHAPLAIN: Courage, we've got company.

(MOTHER COURAGE clambers out.)

50 THE COOK: I promised I'd drop over for a little talk soon as I had the time. I've not forgotten your brandy, Mrs Fierling.

MOTHER COURAGE: Good grief, the general's cook! After all these years! Where's my eldest boy Eilif?

THE COOK: Hasn't he got here? He left before me, he was on his
55 way to see you too.

THE CHAPLAIN: I shall don my clerical garb, just a moment.

(Goes off behind the cart.)

MOTHER COURAGE: Then he may be here any minute. (Calls into the cart.) Kattrin, Eilif's on his way. Get cook a glass of brandy, Kattrin! (KATTRIN does not appear.) Drag your hair
60 down over it, that's all right. Mr Lamb's no stranger. (Fetches the brandy herself.) She don't like to come out, peace means nowt to her. Took too long coming, it did. They gave her a crack over one eye, you barely notice it now but she thinks folks are staring at her.

65 THE COOK: Ah yes. War. (He and MOTHER COURAGE sit down.)

MOTHER COURAGE: Cooky, you caught me at bad moment. I'm ruined.

THE COOK: What? That's hard.

MOTHER COURAGE: Peace'll wring my neck. I went and took Chaplain's advice, laid in fresh stocks only t'other day. And 70 now they're going to demobilise and I'll be left sitting on me wares.

THE COOK: What d'you want to go and listen to padre for? If I hadn't been in such a hurry that time, the Catholics arriving so quickly and all, I'd warned you against that man. All 75 piss and wind, he is. So he's the authority around here, eh?

MOTHER COURAGE: He's been doing washing-up for me and helping pull.

THE COOK: Him pull! I bet he told you some of those jokes of his too, I know him, got a very unhealthy view of women, 80 he has, all my good influence on him went for nowt. He ain't steady.

MOTHER COURAGE: You steady then?

THE COOK: Whatever else I ain't, I'm steady. Mud in your eye!

MOTHER COURAGE: Steady, that's nowt. I only had one steady 85 fellow, thank God. Hardest I ever had to work in me life; he flogged the kids' blankets soon as autumn came, and he called me mouth-organ an unchristian instrument. Ask me, you ain't saying much for yourself admitting you're steady.

THE COOK: Still tough as nails, I see; but that's what I like 90 about you.

MOTHER COURAGE: Now don't tell me you been dreaming of me nails.

THE COOK: Well, well, here we are, along with armistice bells and your brandy like what nobody else ever serves, it's fa- 95 mous, that is.

MOTHER COURAGE: I don't give two pins for your armistice bells just now. Can't see 'em handing out all the back pay what's owing, so where does that leave me with my famous brandy? Had your pay yet? 100

THE COOK: (Hesitantly.) Not exactly. That's why we all shoved off. If that's how it is, I thought, I'll go and visit friends. So here I am sitting with you.

MOTHER COURAGE: Other words you got nowt.

THE COOK: High time they stopped that bloody clanging. 105 Wouldn't mind getting into some sort of trade. I'm fed up being cook to that lot. I'm s'posed to rustle them up meals out of tree roots and old bootsoles, then they fling the hot soup in my face. Cook these days is a dog's life. Sooner do war service, only of course it's peacetime now. (He sees the 110 CHAPLAIN reappearing in his old garments.) More about that later.

THE CHAPLAIN: It's still all right, only had a few moths in it.

THE COOK: Can't see why you bother. You won't get your old job back, who are you to inspire now to earn his pay hon- 115 ourably and lay down his life? What's more I got a bone to pick with you, cause you advised this lady to buy a lot of unnecessary goods saying war would go on for ever.

THE CHAPLAIN: (Heatedly.) I'd like to know what concern that is of yours. 120

THE COOK: Because it's unscrupulous, that sort of thing is. How dare you meddle in other folks' business arrangements with your unwanted advice?

THE CHAPLAIN: Who's meddling? (To COURAGE.) I never knew this gentleman was such an intimate you had to account to 125 him for everything.

MOTHER COURAGE: Keep your hair on, cook's only giving his personal opinion and you can't deny your war was a flop.

THE CHAPLAIN: You should not blaspheme against peace,
130   Courage. You are a hyaena of the battlefield.
MOTHER COURAGE: I'm what?
THE COOK: If you're going to insult this lady you'll have to settle with me.
THE CHAPLAIN: It's not you I'm talking to. Your intentions are
135   only too transparent. (To COURAGE.) But when I see you
   picking up peace betwixt your finger and your thumb like
   some dirty old snot-rag, then my humanity feels outraged;
   for then I see that you don't want peace but war, because
   you profit from it; in which case you shouldn't forget the
140   ancient saying that whosoever sups with the devil needs a
   long spoon.
MOTHER COURAGE: I got no use for war, and war ain't got much
   use for me. But I'm not being called no hyaena, you and
   me's through.
145 THE CHAPLAIN: Then why grumble about peace when everybody's breathing sighs of relief? Because of some old junk
   in your cart?
MOTHER COURAGE: My goods ain't old junk but what I lives by,
   and you too up to now.
150 THE CHAPLAIN: Off war, in other words. Aha.
THE COOK: (To the CHAPLAIN.) You're old enough to know it's
   always a mistake offering advice. (To COURAGE.) Way things
   are, your best bet's to get rid of certain goods quick as you
   can before prices hit rock-bottom. Dress yourself and get
155   moving, not a moment to lose.
MOTHER COURAGE: That ain't bad advice. I'll do that, I guess.
THE CHAPLAIN: Because cooky says it.
MOTHER COURAGE: Why couldn't you say it? He's right, I'd
   best go off to market. (Goes inside the cart.)
160 THE COOK: That's one to me, padre. You got no presence of
   mind. What you should of said was: what, me offer advice,
   all I done was discuss politics. Better not take me on. Cock-
   fighting don't suit that get-up.
THE CHAPLAIN: If you don't stop your gob I'll murder you, get-
165   up or no get-up.
THE COOK: (Pulling off his boots and unwrapping his foot-cloths.)
   Pity the war made such a godless shit of you, else you'd easily get another parsonage now it's peacetime. Cooks won't
   be needed, there's nowt to cook, but faith goes on just the
170   same, nowt changed in that direction.
THE CHAPLAIN: Mr Lamb, I'm asking you not to elbow me out.
   Since I came down in the world I've become a better person. I couldn't preach to anyone now.

(Enter YVETTE POTTIER in black, dressed up to the nines, carrying a
cane. She is much older and fatter, and heavily powdered. She is followed by a manservant.)

YVETTE: Hullo there, everybody. Is this Mother Courage's
175   establishment?
THE CHAPLAIN: It is. And with whom have we the honour . . .?
YVETTE: With the Countess Starhemberg, my good man.
   Where's Courage?
THE CHAPLAIN: (Calls into the cart.) The Countess Starhemberg
180   wishes to speak to you.
MOTHER COURAGE'S VOICE: Just coming.
YVETTE: It's Yvette.
MOTHER COURAGE'S VOICE: Oh, Yvette!

YVETTE: Come to see how you are. (Sees the COOK turn round
   aghast.) Pieter!   185
THE COOK: Yvette!
YVETTE: Well I never! How d'you come to be here?
THE COOK: Got a lift.
THE CHAPLAIN: You know each other then? Intimately?
YVETTE: I should think so. (She looks the COOK over.) Fat.   190
THE COOK: Not all that skinny yourself.
YVETTE: All the same I'm glad to see you, you shit. Gives me a
   chance to say what I think of you.
THE CHAPLAIN: You say it, in full; but don't start till Courage
   is out here.   195
MOTHER COURAGE: (Coming out with all kinds of goods.) Yvette!
   (They embrace.) But what are you in mourning for?
YVETTE: Suits me, don't it? My husband the colonel died a few
   years back.
MOTHER COURAGE: That old fellow what nearly bought the cart? 200
YVETTE: His elder brother.
MOTHER COURAGE: Then you're sitting pretty. Nice to find
   somebody what's made it in this war.
YVETTE: Up and down and up again, that's the way it went.
MOTHER COURAGE: I'm not hearing a word against colonels, 205
   they make a mint of money.
THE CHAPLAIN: I would put my boots back on if I were you. (To
   YVETTE.) You promised you would say what you think of
   the gentleman.
THE COOK: Don't kick up a stink here, Yvette.   210
MOTHER COURAGE: Yvette, this is a friend of mine.
YVETTE: That's old Puffing Piet.
THE COOK: Let's drop the nicknames. I'm called Lamb.
MOTHER COURAGE: (Laughs.) Puffing Piet! Him as made all the
   women crazy! Here, I been looking after your pipe for you. 215
THE CHAPLAIN: Smoking it, too.
YVETTE: What luck I can warn you against him. Worst of the
   lot, he was, rampaging along the whole Flanders coastline.
   Got more girls in trouble than he has fingers.
THE COOK: That's all a long while ago. Tain't true anyhow.   220
YVETTE: Stand up when a lady brings you into the conversa-
   tion! How I loved this man! All the time he had a little
   dark girl with bandy legs, got her in trouble too of course.
THE COOK: Got you into high society more like, far as I can see.
YVETTE: Shut your trap, you pathetic remnant! Better watch 225
   out for him, though; fellows like that are still dangerous
   even when on their last legs.
MOTHER COURAGE: (To YVETTE.) Come along, got to get rid of
   my stuff afore prices start dropping. You might be able to
   put a word in for me at regiment, with your connections. 230
   (Calls into the cart.) Kattrin, church is off, I'm going to market instead. When Eilif turns up, one of you give him a
   drink. (Exit with YVETTE.)
YVETTE: (As she leaves.) Fancy a creature like that ever making
   me leave the straight and narrow path. Thank my lucky 235
   stars I managed to reach the top all the same. But I've
   cooked your goose, Puffing Piet, and that's something
   that'll be credited to me one day in the world to come.
THE CHAPLAIN: I would like to take as a text for our little talk
   'The mills of God grind slowly'. Weren't you complaining 240
   about my jokes?
THE COOK: Dead out of luck, I am. It's like this, you see: I
   thought I might get a hot meal. Here am I starving, and

now they'll be talking about me and she'll get quite a
245 wrong picture. I think I'll clear out before she's back.
THE CHAPLAIN: I think so too.
THE COOK: Padre, I'm fed up already with this bloody peace.
Human race has to go through fire and sword cause it's sin-
ful from the cradle up. I wish I could be roasting a fat capon
250 once again for the general, wherever he's got to, in mustard
sauce with a carrot or two.
THE CHAPLAIN: Red cabbage. Red cabbage for a capon.
THE COOK: You're right, but carrots was what he had to have.
THE CHAPLAIN: No sense of what's fitting.
255 THE COOK: Not that it stopped you guzzling your share.
THE CHAPLAIN: With misgivings.
THE COOK: Anyway you must admit those were the days.
THE CHAPLAIN: I might admit it if pressed.
THE COOK: Now you've called her a hyaena your days here are
260 finished. What you staring at?
THE CHAPLAIN: Eilif! (EILIF *arrives, followed by* SOLDIERS *with
pikes. His hands are fettered. His face is chalky-white.*) What's
wrong?
EILIF: Where's mother?
265 THE CHAPLAIN: Gone into town.
EILIF: I heard she was around. They've allowed me to come and
see her.
THE COOK: (*To the* SOLDIERS.) What you doing with him?
A SOLDIER: Something not nice.
270 THE CHAPLAIN: What's he been up to?
THE SOLDIER: Broke into a peasant's place. The wife's dead.
THE CHAPLAIN: How could you do a thing like that?
EILIF: It's what I did last time, ain't it?
THE COOK: Aye, but it's peace now.
275 EILIF: Shut up. All right if I sit down till she comes?
THE SOLDIER: We've no time.
THE CHAPLAIN: In wartime they recommended him for that, sat
him at the general's right hand. Dashing, it was, in those
days. Any chance of a word with the provost-marshal?
280 THE SOLDIER: Wouldn't do no good. Taking some peasant's cat-
tle, what's dashing about that?
THE COOK: Dumb, I call it.
EILIF: If I'd been dumb you'd of starved, clever bugger.
THE COOK: But as you were clever you're going to be shot.
285 THE CHAPLAIN: We'd better fetch Kattrin out anyhow.
EILIF: Sooner have a glass of schnapps, could do with that. 290
THE SOLDIER: No time, come along.
THE CHAPLAIN: And what shall we tell your mother?
EILIF: Tell her it wasn't any different, tell her it was the same
290 thing. Or tell her nowt. (*The* SOLDIERS *propel him away.*)
THE CHAPLAIN: I'll accompany you on your grievous journey.
EILIF: Don't need any bloody parsons.
THE CHAPLAIN: Wait and see. (*Follows him.*)
THE COOK: (*Calls after them.*) I'll have to tell her, she'll want to
295 see him.
THE CHAPLAIN: I wouldn't tell her anything. At most that he
was here and will come again, maybe tomorrow. By then I'll
be back and can break it to her. (*Hurries off.*)

(*The* COOK *looks after him, shaking his head, then walks restlessly
around. Finally he comes up to the cart.*)

THE COOK: Hoy! Don't you want to come out? I can understand
300 you hiding away from peace. Like to do the same myself.

Remember me, I'm general's cook? I was wondering if
you'd a bit of something to eat while I wait for your mum.
I don't half feel like a bit of pork, or bread even, just to fill
the time. (*Peers inside.*) Head under blanket. (*Sound of gunfire off.*) 305
MOTHER COURAGE: (*Runs in, out of breath and with all her goods
still.*) Cooky, peacetime's over. War's been on again three
days now. Heard news before selling me stuff, thank God.
They're having a shooting match with Lutherans in town.
We must get cart away at once. Kattrin, pack up! What you 310
in the dumps for? What's wrong?
THE COOK: Nowt.
MOTHER COURAGE: Something is. I see it way you look.
THE COOK: Cause war's starting up again, I s'pose. Looks as if
it'll be tomorrow night before I get next hot food inside me. 315
MOTHER COURAGE: You're lying, cooky.
THE COOK: Eilif was here. Had to leave almost at once, though.
MOTHER COURAGE: Was he now? Then we'll be seeing him on
march. I'm joining our side this time. How's he look?
THE COOK: Same as usual. 320
MOTHER COURAGE: Oh, he'll never change. Take more than war
to steal him from me. Clever, he is. You going to help me
get packed? (*Begins to pack up.*) What's his news? Still in
general's good books? Say anything about his deeds of
valour? 325
THE COOK: (*Glumly.*) Repeated one of them, I'm told.
MOTHER COURAGE: Tell it me later, we got to move off.
(KATTRIN *appears.*) Kattrin, peacetime's finished now. We're
moving on. (*To the* COOK.) How about you?
THE COOK: Have to join up again. 330
MOTHER COURAGE: Why don't you . . . Where's padre?
THE COOK: Went into town with Eilif.
MOTHER COURAGE: Then you come along with us a way. Need
somebody to help me.
THE COOK: That business with Yvette, you know . . . 335
MOTHER COURAGE: Done you no harm in my eyes. Opposite.
Where there's smoke there's fire, they say. You coming
along?
THE COOK: I won't say no.
MOTHER COURAGE: The Twelfth moved off already. Take the 340
shaft. Here's a bit of bread. We must get round behind to
Lutherans. Might even be seeing Eilif tonight. He's my
favourite one. Short peace, wasn't it? Now we're off again.
(*She sings as the* COOK *and* KATTRIN *harness themselves up.*)

From Ulm to Metz, from Metz to Munich 345
Courage will see the war gets fed.
The war will show a well-filled tunic
Given its daily shot of lead.
But lead alone can hardly nourish
It must have soldiers to subsist. 350
It's you it needs to make it flourish.
The war's still hungry. So enlist!

——— SCENE NINE ———

It is the seventeenth year of the great war of faith. Germany has lost more than half her inhabitants. Those who
survive the bloodbath are killed off by terrible epidemics. Once fertile areas are ravaged by famine, wolves
roam the burnt-out towns. In autumn 1634 we find

Courage in the Fichtelgebirge, off the main axis of the
Swedish armies. The winter this year is early and harsh.
Business is bad, so that there is nothing to do but beg.
The cook gets a letter from Utrecht and is sent packing.

Outside a semi-dilapidated parsonage.

Grey morning in early winter. Gusts of wind. MOTHER COURAGE
and the COOK *in shabby sheepskins, drawing the cart.*

THE COOK: It's all dark, nobody up yet.
MOTHER COURAGE: Except it's parson's house. Have to crawl
    out of bed to ring bells. Then he'll have hot soup.
THE COOK: What from when whole village is burnt, we
5   seen it.
MOTHER COURAGE: It's lived in, though, dog was barking.
THE COOK: S'pose parson's got, he'll give nowt.
MOTHER COURAGE: Maybe if we sing. . . .
THE COOK: I've had enough. *(Abruptly.)* Got a letter from
10   Utrecht saying mother died of cholera and inn's mine.
    Here's letter if you don't believe me. No business of yours
    the way aunty goes on about my mode of existence, but
    have a look.
MOTHER COURAGE: *(Reads the letter.)* Lamb, I'm tired too of al-
15   ways being on the go. I feel like butcher's dog, dragging
    meat round customers and getting nowt off it. I got nowt
    left to sell, and folk got nowt left to buy nowt with. Saxony
    a fellow in rags tried landing me a stack of old books for two
    eggs, Württemberg they wanted to swap their plough for
20   a titchy bag of salt. What's to plough for? Nowt growing no
    more, just brambles. In Pomerania villages are s'posed to
    have started in eating the younger kids, and nuns have been
    caught sticking folk up.
THE COOK: World's dying out.
25 MOTHER COURAGE: Sometimes I sees meself driving through
    hell with me cart selling brimstone, or across heaven with
    packed lunches for hungry souls. Give me my kids what's
    left, let's find some place they ain't shooting, and I'd like a
    few more years undisturbed.
30 THE COOK: You and me could get that inn going, Courage,
    think it over. Made up me mind in the night, I did: back to
    Utrecht with or without you, and starting today.
MOTHER COURAGE: Have to talk to Kattrin. That's a bit quick
    for me; I'm against making decisions all freezing cold and
35   nowt inside you. Kattrin! (KATTRIN *climbs out of the cart.*)
    Kattrin, got something to tell you. Cook and I want to go
    to Utrecht. He's been left an inn there. That'd be a settled
    place for you, let you meet a few people. Lots of 'em respect
    somebody mature, looks ain't everything. I'd like it too. I
40   get on with cook. Say one thing for him, got a head for
    business. We'd have our meals for sure, not bad, eh? And
    your own bed too; like that, wouldn't you? Road's no life re-
    ally. God knows how you might finish up. Lousy already,
    you are. Have to make up our minds, see, we could move
45   with the Swedes, up north, they're somewhere up that way.
    (She points to the left.) Reckon that's fixed, Kattrin.
THE COOK: Anna, I got something private to say to you.
MOTHER COURAGE: Get back in cart, Kattrin.

(KATTRIN *climbs back.*)

THE COOK: I had to interrupt, cause you don't understand, far
    as I can see. I didn't think there was need to say it, sticks   50
    out a mile. But if it don't, then let me tell you straight, no
    question of taking her along, not on your life. You get
    me, eh.

(KATTRIN *sticks her head out of the cart behind them and listens.*)

MOTHER COURAGE: You mean I'm to leave Kattrin back here?
THE COOK: Use your imagination. Inn's got no room. It ain't   55
    one of the sort got three bar parlours. Put our backs in it we
    two'll get a living, but not three, no chance of that. She can
    keep cart.
MOTHER COURAGE: Thought she might find husband in
    Utrecht.   60
THE COOK: Go on, make me laugh. Find a husband, how?
    Dumb and that scar on top of it. And at her age?
MOTHER COURAGE: Don't talk so loud.
THE COOK: Loud or soft, no getting over facts. And that's an-
    other reason why I can't have her in the inn. Customers   65
    don't want to be looking at that all the time. Can't blame
    them.
MOTHER COURAGE: Shut your big mouth. I said not so loud.
THE COOK: Light's on in parson's house. We can try singing.
MOTHER COURAGE: Cooky, how's she to pull the cart on her   70
    own? War scares her. She'll never stand it. The dreams she
    must have . . . I hear her nights groaning. Mostly after a
    battle. What's she seeing in those dreams, I'd like to know.
    She's got a soft heart. Lately I found she'd got another
    hedgehog tucked away what we'd run over.   75
THE COOK: Inn's too small. *(Calls out.)* Ladies and gentlemen,
    domestic staff and other residents! We are now going to
    give you a song concerning Solomon, Julius Caesar and
    other famous personages what had bad luck. So's you can see
    we're respectable folk, which makes it difficult to carry on,   80
    particularly in winter. *(They sing.)*

    You saw sagacious Solomon
    You know what came of him.
    To him complexities seemed plain.
    He cursed the hour that gave birth to him   85
    And saw that everything was vain.
    How great and wise was Solomon!
    The world however didn't wait
    But soon observed what followed on.
    It's wisdom that had brought him to this state—   90
    How fortunate the man with none!

Yes, the virtues are dangerous stuff in this world, as this fine
song proves, better not to have them and have a pleasant life
and breakfast instead, hot soup for instance. Look at me: I
haven't any but I'd like some. I'm a serving soldier but what   95
good did my courage do me in all them battles, nowt, here
I am starving and better have been shit-scared and stayed at
home. For why?

    You saw courageous Caesar next
    You know what he became.   100
    They deified him in his life
    Then had him murdered just the same.
    And as they raised the fatal knife
    How loud he cried: You too, my son!

105   The world however didn't wait
       But soon observed what followed on.
       It's courage that had brought him to that state.
       How fortunate the man with none!

       (Sotto voce.) Don't even look out. (Aloud.) Ladies and gentle-
110   men, domestic staff and other inmates! All right, you may
       say, gallantry never cooked a man's dinner, what about try-
       ing honesty? You can eat all you want then, or anyhow not
       stay sober. How about it?

           You heard of honest Socrates
115   The man who never lied:
           They weren't so grateful as you'd think
           Instead the rulers fixed to have him tried
           And handed him the poisoned drink.
           How honest was the people's noble son!
120   The world however didn't wait
           But soon observed what followed on.
           It's honesty that brought him to that state.
           How fortunate the man with none!

       Ah yes, they say, be unselfish and share what you've got, but
125   how about if you got nowt? It's all very well to say the do-
       gooders have a hard time, but you still got to have some-
       thing. Aye, unselfishness is a rare virtue, cause it just don't
       pay.

           Saint Martin couldn't bear to see
130   His fellows in distress.
           He met a poor man in the snow
           And shared his cloak with him, we know.
           Both of them therefore froze to death.
           His place in Heaven was surely won!
135   The world however didn't wait
           But soon observed what followed on.
           Unselfishness had brought him to that state.
           How fortunate the man with none!

       That's how it is with us. We're respectable folk, stick to-
140   gether, don't steal, don't murder, don't burn places down.
       And all the time you might say we're sinking lower and
       lower, and it's true what the song says, and soup is few and
       far between, and if we weren't like this but thieves and
       murderers I dare say we'd be eating our fill. For virtues
145   aren't their own reward, only wickednesses are, that's how
       the world goes and it didn't ought to.

           Here you can see respectable folk
           Keeping to God's own laws.
           So far he hasn't taken heed.
150   You who sit safe and warm indoors
           Help to relieve our bitter need!
           How virtuously we had begun!
           The world however didn't wait
           But soon observed what followed on.
155   It's fear of God that brought us to that state.
           How fortunate the man with none!

       VOICE: (From above.) Hey, you there! Come on up! There's hot
           soup if you want.
       MOTHER COURAGE: Lamb, me stomach won't stand nowt.
160   'Tain't that it ain't sensible, what you say, but is that your
       last word? We got on all right.

THE COOK: Last word. Think it over.
MOTHER COURAGE: I've nowt to think. I'm not leaving her here.
THE COOK: That's proper senseless, nothing I can do about it
    though. I'm not a brute, just the inn's a small one. So now   165
    we better get on up, or there'll be nowt here either and
    wasted time singing in the cold.
MOTHER COURAGE: I'll get Kattrin.
THE COOK: Better bring a bit back for her. Scare them if they
    sees three of us coming. (Exeunt both.)   170

(KATTRIN climbs out of the cart with a bundle. She looks around to see
if the other two have gone. Then she takes an old pair of trousers of the
COOK's and a skirt of her mother's, and lays them side by side on one
of the wheels, so that they are easily seen. She has finished and is picking up her bundle to go, when MOTHER COURAGE comes back from the
house.)

MOTHER COURAGE: (With a plate of soup.) Kattrin! Will you stop
    there? Kattrin! Where you off to with that bundle? Has
    devil himself taken you over? (She examines the bundle.) She's
    packed her things. You been listening? I told him nowt do-
    ing, Utrecht, his rotten inn, what'd we be up to there? You   175
    and me, inn's no place for us. Still plenty to be got out of
    war. (She sees the trousers and the skirt.) You're plain stupid.
    S'pose I'd seen that, and you gone away? (She holds KATTRIN
    back as she tries to break away.) Don't you start thinking it's
    on your account I given him the push. It was cart, that's it.   180
    Catch me leaving my cart I'm used to, it ain't you, it's for
    cart. We'll go off in t'other direction, and we'll throw cook's
    stuff out so he finds it, silly man. (She climbs in and throws
    out a few other articles in the direction of the trousers.) There, he's
    out of our business now, and I ain't having nobody else in,   185
    ever. You and me'll carry on now. This winter will pass,
    same as all the others. Get hitched up, it looks like snow.

(They both harness themselves to the cart, then wheel it round and drag
it off. When the COOK arrives he looks blankly at his kit.)

─────── SCENE TEN ───────

During the whole of 1635 Mother Courage and her
daughter Kattrin travel over the highroads of central
Germany, in the wake of the increasingly bedraggled
armies.

High road.

MOTHER COURAGE and KATTRIN are pulling the cart. They pass a
PEASANT's house inside which there is a voice singing.

THE VOICE: The roses in our arbour
           Delight us with their show:
           They have such lovely flowers
           Repaying all our labour
           After the summer showers.   5
           Happy are those with gardens now:
           They have such lovely flowers.

           When winter winds are freezing
           As through the woods they blow
           Our home is warm and pleasing.   10
           We fixed the thatch above it

With straw and moss we wove it.
Happy are those with shelter now
When winter winds are freezing.

(MOTHER COURAGE *and* KATTRIN *pause to listen, then continue pulling.*)

——— **SCENE ELEVEN** ———

January 1636. The emperor's troops are threatening the Protestant town of Halle. The stone begins to speak. Mother Courage loses her daughter and trudges on alone. The war is a long way from being over.

The cart is standing, much the worse for wear, alongside a PEASANT'*s house with a huge thatched roof, backing on a wall of rock. It is night.*

An ENSIGN *and* THREE SOLDIERS *in heavy armour step out of the wood.*

THE ENSIGN: I want no noise now. Anyone shouts, shove your pike into him.
FIRST SOLDIER: Have to knock them up, though, if we're to find a guide.
5 THE ENSIGN: Knocking sounds natural. Could be a cow bumping the stable wall.

(*The* SOLDIERS *knock on the door of the house. The* PEASANT'*s* WIFE *opens it. They stop her mouth.* TWO SOLDIERS *go in.*)

MAN'S VOICE: (*Within.*) What is it?

(*The* SOLDIERS *bring out the* PEASANT *and his son* [THE YOUNG PEASANT]*.*)

THE ENSIGN: (*Pointing at the cart, where* KATTRIN'*s head has appeared.*) There's another one. (*A* SOLDIER *drags her out.*) Any-
10 one else live here beside you lot?
THE PEASANTS: This is our son. And she's dumb. Her mother's gone into town to buy stuff. For their business, cause so many people's getting out and selling things cheap. They're just passing through. Canteen folk.
15 THE ENSIGN: I'm warning you, keep quiet, or if there's the least noise you get a pike across your nut. Now I want someone to come with us and show us the path to the town. (*Points to the* YOUNG PEASANT.) Here, you.
THE YOUNG PEASANT: I don't know no path.
20 SECOND SOLDIER: (*Grinning.*) He don't know no path.
THE YOUNG PEASANT: I ain't helping Catholics.
THE ENSIGN: (*To the* SECOND SOLDIER.) Stick your pike in his ribs.
THE YOUNG PEASANT: (*Forced to his knees, with the pike threatening*
25 *him.*) I won't do it, not to save my life.
FIRST SOLDIER: I know what'll change his mind. (*Goes towards the stable.*) Two cows and an ox. Listen, you: if you're not reasonable I'll chop up your cattle.
THE YOUNG PEASANT: No, not that!
30 THE PEASANT'S WIFE: (*Weeps.*) Please spare our cattle, captain, it'd be starving us to death.
THE ENSIGN: They're dead if he goes on being obstinate.
FIRST SOLDIER: I'm taking the ox first.
THE YOUNG PEASANT: (*To his father.*) Have I got to? (*The* WIFE
35 *nods.*) Right.

THE PEASANT'S WIFE: And thank you kindly, captain, for sparing us, for ever and ever, Amen.

(*The* PEASANT *stops his* WIFE *from further expressions of gratitude.*)

FIRST SOLDIER: I knew the ox was what they minded about most, was I right?

(*Guided by the* YOUNG PEASANT, *the* ENSIGN *and his* SOLDIERS *continue on their way.*)

THE PEASANT: What are they up to, I'd like to know. Nowt good.   40
THE PEASANT'S WIFE: Perhaps they're just scouting. What you doing?
THE PEASANT: (*Putting a ladder against the roof and climbing up it.*) Seeing if they're on their own. (*From the top.*) Something moving in the wood. Can see something down by the   45
quarry. And there are men in armour in the clearing. And a gun. That's at least a regiment. God's mercy on the town and everyone in it!
THE PEASANT'S WIFE: Any lights in the town?
THE PEASANT: No. They'll all be asleep. (*Climbs down.*) If those   50
people get in they'll butcher the lot.
THE PEASANT'S WIFE: Sentries're bound to spot them first.
THE PEASANT: Sentry in the tower up the hill must have been killed, or he'd have blown his bugle.
THE PEASANT'S WIFE: If only there were more of us.   55
THE PEASANT: Just you and me and that cripple.
THE PEASANT'S WIFE: Nowt we can do, you'd say. . . .
THE PEASANT: Nowt.
THE PEASANT'S WIFE: Can't possibly run down there in the blackness.   60
THE PEASANT: Whole hillside's crawling with 'em. We could give a signal.
THE PEASANT'S WIFE: What, and have them butcher us too?
THE PEASANT: You're right, nowt we can do.
THE PEASANT'S WIFE: (*To* KATTRIN.) Pray, poor creature, pray!   65
Nowt we can do to stop bloodshed. You can't talk, maybe, but at least you can pray. He'll hear you if no one else can. I'll help you. (*All kneel,* KATTRIN *behind the two* PEASANTS.) Our Father, which art in Heaven, hear Thou our prayer, let not the town be destroyed with all what's in it sound asleep   70
and suspecting nowt. Arouse Thou them that they may get up and go to the walls and see how the enemy approacheth with picks and guns in the blackness across fields below the slope. (*Turning to* KATTRIN.) Guard Thou our mother and ensure that the watchman sleepeth not but wakes up, or it   75
will be too late. Succour our brother-in-law also, he is inside there with his four children, spare Thou them, they are innocent and know nowt. (*To* KATTRIN, *who gives a groan.*) One of them's not two yet, the eldest's seven. (KATTRIN *stands up distractedly.*) Our Father, hear us, for only Thou   80
canst help; we look to be doomed, for why, we are weak and have no pike and nowt and can risk nowt and are in Thy hand along with our cattle and all the farm, and same with the town, it too is in Thy hand and the enemy is before the walls in great strength.   85

(*Unobserved,* KATTRIN *has slipped away to the cart and taken from it something which she hides beneath her apron; then she climbs up the ladder on to the stable roof.*)

THE PEASANT'S WIFE: Forget not the children, what are in danger, the littlest ones especially, the old folk what can't move, and every living creature.

THE PEASANT: And forgive us our trespasses as we forgive them
90   that trespass against us. Amen.

(Sitting on the roof, KATTRIN *begins to beat the drum which she has pulled out from under her apron.)*

THE PEASANT'S WIFE: Jesus Christ, what's she doing?

THE PEASANT: She's out of her mind.

THE PEASANT'S WIFE: Quick, get her down.

(The PEASANT *hurries to the ladder, but* KATTRIN *pulls it up on to the roof.)*

THE PEASANT'S WIFE: She'll do us in.

95   THE PEASANT: Stop drumming at once, you cripple!

THE PEASANT'S WIFE: Bringing the Catholics down on us!

THE PEASANT: *(Looking for stones to throw.)* I'll stone you.

THE PEASANT'S WIFE: Where's your feelings? Where's your heart? We're done for if they come down on us. Slit our
100   throats, they will.

*(*KATTRIN *stares into the distance towards the town and carries on drumming.)*

THE PEASANT'S WIFE: *(To her husband.)* I told you we shouldn't have allowed those vagabonds on to farm. What do they care if our last cows are taken?

THE ENSIGN: *(Runs in with his* SOLDIERS *and the* YOUNG PEAS-
105   ANT.) I'll cut you to ribbons, all of you!

THE PEASANT'S WIFE: Please, sir, it's not our fault, we couldn't help it. It was her sneaked up there. A foreigner.

THE ENSIGN: Where's the ladder?

THE PEASANT: There.

110   THE ENSIGN: *(Calls up.)* I order you, throw that drum down.

*(*KATTRIN *goes on drumming.)*

THE ENSIGN: You're all in this together. It'll be the end of you.

THE PEASANT: They been cutting pine trees in that wood. How about if we got one of the trunks and poked her off. . . .

FIRST SOLDIER: *(To the* ENSIGN.) Permission to make a sugges-
115   tion, sir! *(He whispers something in the* ENSIGN'*s ear.)* Listen, we got a suggestion could help you. Get down off there and come into town with us right away. Show us which your mother is and we'll see she ain't harmed.

*(*KATTRIN *goes on drumming.)*

THE ENSIGN: *(Pushes him roughly aside.)* She doesn't trust you;
120   with a mug like yours it's not surprising. *(Calls up.)* Suppose I gave you my word? I can give my word of honour as an officer.

*(*KATTRIN *drums harder.)*

THE ENSIGN: Is nothing sacred to her?

THE YOUNG PEASANT: There's more than her mother involved, sir.

125   FIRST SOLDIER: This can't go on much longer. They're bound to hear in the town.

THE ENSIGN: We'll have somehow to make a noise that's louder than her drumming. What can we make a noise with?

FIRST SOLDIER: Thought we weren't s'posed to make no noise.

THE ENSIGN: A harmless one, you fool. A peaceful one.   130

THE PEASANT: I could chop wood with my axe.

THE ENSIGN: Good: you chop. *(The* PEASANT *fetches his axe and attacks a tree-trunk.)* Chop harder! Harder! You're chopping for your life.

*(*KATTRIN *has been listening, drumming less loudly the while. She now looks wildly round, and goes on drumming.)*

THE ENSIGN: Not loud enough. *(To the* FIRST SOLDIER.) You chop   135 too.

THE PEASANT: Only got the one axe. *(Stops chopping.)*

THE ENSIGN: We'll have to set the farm on fire. Smoke her out, that's it.

THE PEASANT: It wouldn't help, captain. If the townspeople see   140 a fire here they'll know what's up.

*(*KATTRIN *has again been listening as she drums. At this point she laughs.)*

THE ENSIGN: Look at her laughing at us. I'm not having that. I'll shoot her down, and damn the consequences. Fetch the harquebus.

*(*THREE SOLDIERS *hurry off.* KATTRIN *goes on drumming.)*

THE PEASANT'S WIFE: I got it, captain. That's their cart. If we   145 smash it up she'll stop. Cart's all they got.

THE ENSIGN: *(To the* YOUNG PEASANT.) Smash it up. *(Calls up.)* We're going to smash up your cart if you don't stop drumming. *(The* YOUNG PEASANT *gives the cart a few feeble blows.)*

THE PEASANT'S WIFE: Stop it, you animal!   150

(Desperately looking towards the cart, KATTRIN *emits pitiful noises. But she goes on drumming.)*

THE ENSIGN: Where are those clodhoppers with the harquebus?

FIRST SOLDIER: Can't have heard nowt in town yet, else we'd be hearing their guns.

THE ENSIGN: *(Calls up.)* They can't hear you at all. And now we're going to shoot you down. For the last time: throw   155 down that drum!

THE YOUNG PEASANT: *(Suddenly flings away his plank.)* Go on drumming! Or they'll all be killed! Go on, go on. . . .

(The FIRST SOLDIER *knocks him down and beats him with his pike.* KATTRIN *starts to cry, but she goes on drumming.)*

THE PEASANT'S WIFE: Don't strike his back! For God's sake, you're beating him to death!   160

(The SOLDIERS *hurry in with the arquebus.)*

SECOND SOLDIER: Colonel's frothing at the mouth, sir. We're all for court-martial.

THE ENSIGN: Set it up! Set it up! *(Calls up while the gun is being erected.)* For the very last time: stop drumming! *(*KATTRIN, *in tears, drums as loud as she can.)* Fire! *(The* SOLDIERS *fire.* KAT-   165 TRIN *is hit, gives a few more drumbeats and then slowly crumples.)*

THE ENSIGN: That's the end of that.

(But KATTRIN's *last drumbeats are taken up by the town's cannon. In the distance can be heard a confused noise of tocsins and gunfire.)*

FIRST SOLDIER: She's made it.

——— **SCENE TWELVE** ———

Before first light. Sound of the fifes and drums of troops marching off into the distance.

In front of the cart MOTHER COURAGE *is squatting by her daughter. The peasant family are standing near her.*

THE PEASANTS: *(With hostility.)* You must go, missis. There's only one more regiment behind that one. You can't go on your own.

MOTHER COURAGE: I think she's going to sleep. *(She sings.)*

5   Lullaby baby
           What's that in the hay?
           Neighbours' kids grizzle
           But my kids are gay.
           Neighbours' are in tatters
10   And you're dressed in lawn
           Cut down from the raiment an
           Angel has worn.
           Neighbours' kids go hungry
           And you shall eat cake
15   Suppose it's too crumbly
           You've only to speak.
           Lullaby baby
           What's that in the hay?
           The one lies in Poland
20   The other—who can say?

Better if you'd not told her nowt about your brother-in-law's kids.

THE PEASANT: If you'd not gone into town to get your cut it might never of happened.

25 MOTHER COURAGE: Now she's asleep.

THE PEASANT'S WIFE: She ain't asleep. Can't you see she's passed over?

THE PEASANT: And it's high time you got away yourself. There are wolves around and, what's worse, marauders.

MOTHER COURAGE: Aye.   30

(She goes and gets a tarpaulin to cover the dead girl with.)

THE PEASANT'S WIFE: Ain't you got nobody else? What you could go to?

MOTHER COURAGE: Aye, one left. Eilif.

THE PEASANT: *(As* MOTHER COURAGE *covers the dead girl.)* Best look for him, then. We'll mind her, see she gets proper burial. Don't you worry about that.   35

MOTHER COURAGE: Here's money for expenses.

(She counts out coins into the PEASANT's *hands. The* PEASANT *and his* SON *shake hands with her and carry* KATTRIN *away.)*

THE PEASANT'S WIFE: *(As she leaves.)* I'd hurry.

MOTHER COURAGE: *(Harnessing herself to the cart.)* Hope I can pull cart all right by meself. Be all right, nowt much inside   40
it. Got to get back in business again.

(Another regiment with its fifes and drums marches past in the background.)

MOTHER COURAGE: *(Tugging the cart.)* Take me along!

(Singing is heard from offstage.)

           With all its luck and all its danger
           The war is dragging on a bit
           Another hundred years or longer   45
           The common man won't benefit.
           Filthy his food, no soap to shave him
           The regiment steals half his pay.
           But still a miracle may save him:
           Tomorrow is another day!   50
               The new year's come. The watchmen shout.
               The thaw sets in. The dead remain.
               Wherever life has not died out
               It staggers to its feet again.

SAMUEL BECKETT

Samuel Beckett (1906–89) is the most influential European dramatist of the postwar period. Born near Dublin, Ireland, Beckett was educated at Trinity College, Dublin, where he studied modern languages. Taking his B.A. in 1928, Beckett received an appointment as *lecteur* at l'École Normale Supérieure in Paris. While in Paris, Beckett met the Irish novelist James Joyce. Beckett assisted Joyce (who was nearly blind) in a variety of ways and became a close friend. Joyce also exerted a profound influence on Beckett's writing. In 1929, Beckett contributed an essay entitled "Dante . . . Bruno . Vico . . Joyce" to a volume on Joyce's *Finnegans Wake.* Throughout the 1930s, Beckett was associated with Joyce and with a variety of avant-garde movements in Paris. He wrote a series of poems—including the prize-winning "Whoroscope"—as well as a study of Proust (1931), the volume of short stories *More Pricks than Kicks* (1934), and the novel *Murphy* (1938). Although Beckett returned briefly to Ireland on a few occasions, he had settled permanently in Paris. During World War II, Beckett served in the French Resistance. He was discovered by the Nazis and forced to flee Paris in 1942. He worked in the unoccupied zone of southern France for the remainder of the war, where he wrote the novel *Watt* (1953). After the war, Beckett received the Croix de Guerre and the Médaille de la Résistance for his services. He began to write exclusively in French, starting work on a major trilogy of novels—*Molloy* (1951), *Malone Dies* (1951), and *The Unnameable* (1953).

Beckett had experimented with drama during the 1930s and 1940s, but his first staged play, *Waiting for Godot* (first written in French, as *En attendant Godot*), produced at the tiny Théâtre de Babylone in January of 1953, impelled him in a new direction. Although Beckett continued to write fiction—including *From an Abandoned Work* (1956), *How It Is* (1964), *Imagination Dead Imagine* (1965), and *Company* (1979)—his major writing of the 1960s, 1970s, and 1980s was for the theater. His second play, *Endgame,* also written in French, was produced in 1957 and was followed by a series of challenging works for the stage: *Krapp's Last Tape* (1958), *Happy Days* (1962), *Play* (1963), *Not I* (1972), *Footfalls* (1975), *Rockaby* (1981), and *Catastrophe* (1982). For his extraordinarily diverse and influential body of work, Beckett won the Nobel Prize for Literature in 1970. Beckett also wrote several plays for radio and television, as well as a film starring Buster Keaton, *Film* (1965). Beginning in the mid-1960s, Beckett directed productions of his plays, and several productions he directed in France and in Germany now have the status of classics—something like Elia Kazan's productions of Tennessee Williams's plays, or Stanislavski's productions of Chekhov.

Beckett's impact on the contemporary theater can hardly be overestimated and can be seen in the work of Sam Shepard, Harold Pinter, and many others. *Waiting for Godot* signaled new possibilities for stage action—or inaction—and developed the implications of Chekhov's static stage in a more symbolic direction. Each of Beckett's plays explores the nature and limitations of its medium in new and challenging ways. *Endgame* refigures the claustral box of realistic drama, for its characters are trapped in a room of endless—or possibly ending—routine. In *Play,* Beckett puts three urns onstage, from which three heads emerge to deliver, more or less simultaneously, a jarring, repetitive monologue of seduction and betrayal. Once the play has finished, Beckett directs his performers—and his audience—to "Repeat play," and so calls the relationship between actors and spectators, theater and reality into question: If we cannot leave the theater when the play is over, is it possible that there is no way out of the purgatory on the stage and in the auditorium? This sense that the self is always in flight is the theme of several of Beckett's later plays. In *Not I,* for instance, all that the audience sees is a Mouth eight feet above the stage, reciting an endless narrative in which she avoids claiming the speech as her own. In *Ohio*

Impromptu (1981), an identical reader and listener relate a painful narrative of loss, in which it is unclear whether they are two individuals or parts of a single person. The power of Beckett's spare, minimalist theater, the beauty of his sculptural use of actors and stage space, and the harsh exigency of the action of his plays have transformed the stage of our time.

ENDGAME

Endgame is Beckett's second full-length play to reach the stage; although its simplicity and repetitiveness are in some ways reminiscent of *Waiting for Godot,* the tone of *Endgame* is bleaker, harsher. As Beckett wrote to Alan Schneider, the play's first American director, *Endgame's* power is "the power of the text to claw."

The "endgame" of a chess match is the final portion of the game, at which either a checkmate or a stalemate has become inevitable. In *Endgame,* Beckett literalizes the uncertainty of the endgame—will the tortuous nothingness of the characters' lives continue indefinitely, move after move, or will it somehow end? Although some critics have taken the "shelter" and the empty landscape outside as an indication that the play takes place in a bomb shelter after a nuclear bombing, *Endgame* seems to present a microcosm of postmodern life, in which the futile search for fugitive "meanings" raises the despairing feeling that our lives are meaningless, "absurd" after all. Hamm is a kind of ham actor and recalls Shakespeare's Richard III ("My kingdom for a nightman") and Prospero ("Our revels now are ended"), as well as perhaps King Lear and Hamlet in his performance. Hamm is perhaps the first POSTMODERN dramatic hero, less a full "character" than a *pastiche* of dramatic roles and possibilities, which exist now only in bits and pieces, recollected fragments (on PASTICHE, see Fredric Jameson's essay). Hamm's blindness also recalls both Oedipus—who also struggled with his father—and Ham the son of Noah, who was blinded when he saw his father naked. Hamm continually reminds us that his performance —it's full of asides, a "last soliloquy," and many self-regarding comments on Hamm's success or failure—is an attempt to impose meaning on the process of the play's action. This recollection of the dramatic and literary tradition also points to the problematic place— or absence—of history in *Endgame.* If there is a kind of past ("Once!") in *Endgame,* it is recalled most clearly by Hamm's parents. Nagg and Nell, legless in their garbage cans, describe an earlier, more sentimental or romantic era, when couples rode tandems in the Ardennes and rowed on Lake Como. Overall, though, time seems to be an endless present moment in *Endgame,* a moment disconnected from the past that once gave it meaning, and from the future which gave it closure. It may be that the play is post-nuclear (though Beckett's draft manuscripts suggest that the inspiration was really a war hospital), but this setting is less important than the sense of time that this tiny world contains. For *Endgame* is finally about time and its passing, the painfully slow passage of moment to moment, and its finality once it is past.

Endgame was originally written in French as *Fin de partie,* and was rewritten into English by Beckett himself; there are several small differences in dialogue and action between the two versions.

ENDGAME

Samuel Beckett

────── CHARACTERS ──────

NAGG   HAMM
NELL   CLOV

─────────────────────────────

Bare interior.

Grey light.

Left and right back, high up, two small windows, curtains drawn.

Front right, a door. Hanging near door, its face to wall, a picture.

Front left, touching each other, covered with an old sheet, two ashbins.

Center, in an armchair on castors, covered with an old sheet, HAMM.

Motionless by the door, his eyes fixed on HAMM, CLOV. *Very red face.*

Brief tableau.

CLOV *goes and stands under window left. Stiff, staggering walk. He looks up at window left. He turns and looks at window right. He goes and stands under window right. He looks up at window right. He turns and looks at window left. He goes out, comes back immediately with a small step-ladder, carries it over and sets it down under window left, gets up on it, draws back curtain. He gets down, takes six steps (for example) towards window right, goes back for ladder, carries it over and sets it down under window right, gets up on it, draws back curtain. He gets down, takes three steps towards window left, goes back for ladder, carries it over and sets it down under window left, gets up on it, looks out of window. Brief laugh. He gets down, takes one step towards window right, goes back for ladder, carries it over and sets it down under window right, gets up on it, looks out of window. Brief laugh. He gets down, goes with ladder towards ashbins, halts, turns, carries back ladder and sets it down under window right, goes to ashbins, removes sheet covering them, folds it over his arm. He raises one lid, stoops and looks into bin. Brief laugh. He closes lid. Same with other bin. He goes to* HAMM, *removes sheet covering him, folds it over his arm. In a dressing-gown, a stiff toque on his head, a large blood-stained handkerchief over his face, a whistle hanging from his neck, a rug over his knees, thick socks on his feet,* HAMM *seems to be asleep.* CLOV *looks him over. Brief laugh. He goes to door, halts, turns towards auditorium.*

CLOV: *(Fixed gaze, tonelessly.)* Finished, it's finished, nearly finished, it must be nearly finished.

(Pause.)

Grain upon grain, one by one, and one day, suddenly, there's a heap, a little heap, the impossible heap.

(Pause.)

5   I can't be punished any more.

(Pause.)

I'll go now to my kitchen, ten feet by ten feet by ten feet, and wait for him to whistle me.

(Pause.)

Nice dimensions, nice proportions, I'll lean on the table, and look at the wall, and wait for him to whistle me.

(He remains a moment motionless, then goes out. He comes back immediately, goes to window right, takes up the ladder and carries it out. Pause. HAMM *stirs. He yawns under the handkerchief. He removes the handkerchief from his face. Very red face. Black glasses.)*

HAMM: Me—   10
(He yawns.)
      —to play.
(He holds the handkerchief spread out before him.)
      Old stancher!
(He takes off his glasses, wipes his eyes, his face, the glasses, puts them on again, folds the handkerchief and puts it back neatly in the breast-pocket of his dressing-gown. He clears his throat, joins the tips of his fingers.)
      Can there be misery—
(He yawns.)
      —loftier than mine? No doubt. Formerly. But now?
(Pause.)
      My father?   15
(Pause.)
      My mother?
(Pause.)
      My . . . dog?
(Pause.)
      Oh I am willing to believe they suffer as much as such creatures can suffer. But does that mean their sufferings equal mine? No doubt.   20
(Pause.)
      No, all is a—
(He yawns.)
      —bsolute,
(Proudly.)
      the bigger a man is the fuller he is.
(Pause. Gloomily.)
      And the emptier.
(He sniffs.)
      Clov!   25
(Pause.)
      No, alone.
(Pause.)
      What dreams! Those forests!
(Pause.)
      Enough, it's time it ended, in the shelter too.
(Pause.)
      And yet I hesitate, I hesitate to . . . to end. Yes, there it is, it's time it ended and yet I hesitate to—   30
(He yawns.)
      —to end.
(Yawns.)
      God, I'm tired, I'd be better off in bed.
(He whistles. Enter CLOV *immediately. He halts beside the chair.)*

You pollute the air!

(*Pause.*)

Get me ready, I'm going to bed.

35   CLOV: I've just got you up.

HAMM: And what of it?

CLOV: I can't be getting you up and putting you to bed every
five minutes, I have things to do.

(*Pause.*)

HAMM: Did you ever see my eyes?

40   CLOV: No.

HAMM: Did you never have the curiosity, while I was sleeping,
to take off my glasses and look at my eyes?

CLOV: Pulling back the lids?

(*Pause.*)

No.

45   HAMM: One of these days I'll show them to you.

(*Pause.*)

It seems they've gone all white.

(*Pause.*)

What time is it?

CLOV: The same as usual.

HAMM: (*Gesture towards window right.*) Have you looked?

50   CLOV: Yes.

HAMM: Well?

CLOV: Zero.

HAMM: It'd need to rain.

CLOV: It won't rain.

(*Pause.*)

55   HAMM: Apart from that, how do you feel?

CLOV: I don't complain.

HAMM: You feel normal?

CLOV: (*Irritably.*) I tell you I don't complain.

HAMM: I feel a little queer.

(*Pause.*)

60   Clov!

CLOV: Yes.

HAMM: Have you not had enough?

CLOV: Yes!

(*Pause.*)

Of what?

65   HAMM: Of this . . . this . . . thing.

CLOV: I always had.

(*Pause.*)

Not you?

HAMM: (*Gloomily.*) Then there's no reason for it to change.

CLOV: It may end.

(*Pause.*)

70   All life long the same questions, the same answers.

HAMM: Get me ready.

(CLOV *does not move.*)

Go and get the sheet.

(CLOV *does not move.*)

Clov!

CLOV: Yes.

75   HAMM: I'll give you nothing more to eat.

CLOV: Then we'll die.

HAMM: I'll give you just enough to keep you from dying. You'll
be hungry all the time.

CLOV: Then we won't die.

(*Pause.*)

I'll go and get the sheet.   80

(*He goes towards the door.*)

HAMM: No!

(CLOV *halts.*)

I'll give you one biscuit per day.

(*Pause.*)

One and a half.

(*Pause.*)

Why do you stay with me?

CLOV: Why do you keep me?   85

HAMM: There's no one else.

CLOV: There's nowhere else.

(*Pause.*)

HAMM: You're leaving me all the same.

CLOV: I'm trying.

HAMM: You don't love me.   90

CLOV: No.

HAMM: You loved me once.

CLOV: Once!

HAMM: I've made you suffer too much.

(*Pause.*)

Haven't I?   95

CLOV: It's not that.

HAMM: (*Shocked.*) I haven't made you suffer too much?

CLOV: Yes!

HAMM: (*Relieved.*) Ah you gave me a fright!

(*Pause. Coldly.*)

Forgive me.   100

(*Pause. Louder.*)

I said, Forgive me.

CLOV: I heard you.

(*Pause.*)

Have you bled?

HAMM: Less.

(*Pause.*)

Is it not time for my pain-killer?   105

CLOV: No.

(*Pause.*)

HAMM: How are your eyes?

CLOV: Bad.

HAMM: How are your legs?

CLOV: Bad.   110

HAMM: But you can move.

CLOV: Yes.

HAMM: (*Violently.*) Then move!

(CLOV *goes to back wall, leans against it with his forehead and
hands.*)

Where are you?

CLOV: Here.   115

HAMM: Come back!

(CLOV *returns to his place beside the chair.*)

Where are you?
CLOV: Here.
HAMM: Why don't you kill me?
120 CLOV: I don't know the combination of the cupboard.

(Pause.)

HAMM: Go and get two bicycle-wheels.
CLOV: There are no more bicycle-wheels.
HAMM: What have you done with your bicycle?
CLOV: I never had a bicycle.
125 HAMM: The thing is impossible.
CLOV: When there were still bicycles I wept to have one. I crawled at your feet. You told me to go to hell. Now there are none.
HAMM: And your rounds? When you inspected my paupers. Al-
130 ways on foot?
CLOV: Sometimes on horse.
(The lid of one of the bins lifts and the hands of NAGG appear, gripping the rim. Then his head emerges. Nightcap. Very white face. NAGG yawns, then listens.)
I'll leave you, I have things to do.
HAMM: In your kitchen?
CLOV: Yes.
135 HAMM: Outside of here it's death.
(Pause.)
All right, be off.
(Exit CLOV. Pause.)
We're getting on.
NAGG: Me pap!
HAMM: Accursed progenitor!
140 NAGG: Me pap!
HAMM: The old folks at home! No decency left! Guzzle, guzzle, that's all they think of.
(He whistles. Enter CLOV. He halts beside the chair.)
Well! I thought you were leaving me.
CLOV: Oh not just yet, not just yet.
145 NAGG: Me pap!
HAMM: Give him his pap.
CLOV: There's no more pap.
HAMM: (To NAGG.) Do you hear that? There's no more pap. You'll never get any more pap.
150 NAGG: I want me pap!
HAMM: Give him a biscuit.
(Exit CLOV.)
Accursed fornicator! How are your stumps?
NAGG: Never mind me stumps.

(Enter CLOV with biscuit.)

CLOV: I'm back again, with the biscuit.

(He gives biscuit to NAGG who fingers it, sniffs it.)

155 NAGG: (Plaintively.) What is it?
CLOV: Spratt's medium.
NAGG: (As before.) It's hard! I can't!
HAMM: Bottle him!

(CLOV pushes NAGG back into the bin, closes the lid.)

CLOV: (Returning to his place beside the chair.) If age but knew!
160 HAMM: Sit on him!
CLOV: I can't sit.

HAMM: True. And I can't stand.
CLOV: So it is.
HAMM: Every man his speciality.
(Pause.)
No phone calls? 165
(Pause.)
Don't we laugh?
CLOV: (After reflection.) I don't feel like it.
HAMM: (After reflection.) Nor I.
(Pause.)
Clov!
CLOV: Yes. 170
HAMM: Nature has forgotten us.
CLOV: There's no more nature.
HAMM: No more nature! You exaggerate.
CLOV: In the vicinity.
HAMM: But we breathe, we change! We lose our hair, our teeth! 175
Our bloom! Our ideals!
CLOV: Then she hasn't forgotten us.
HAMM: But you say there is none.
CLOV: (Sadly.) No one that ever lived ever thought so crooked as we. 180
HAMM: We do what we can.
CLOV: We shouldn't.

(Pause.)

HAMM: You're a bit of all right, aren't you?
CLOV: A smithereen.

(Pause.)

HAMM: This is slow work. 185
(Pause.)
Is it not time for my pain-killer?
CLOV: No.
(Pause.)
I'll leave you, I have things to do.
HAMM: In your kitchen?
CLOV: Yes. 190
HAMM: What, I'd like to know.
CLOV: I look at the wall.
HAMM: The wall! And what do you see on your wall? Mene, mene? Naked bodies?
CLOV: I see my light dying. 195
HAMM: Your light dying! Listen to that! Well, it can die just as well here, your light. Take a look at me and then come back and tell me what you think of your light.

(Pause.)

CLOV: You shouldn't speak to me like that.

(Pause.)

HAMM: (Coldly.) Forgive me. 200
(Pause. Louder.)
I said, Forgive me.
CLOV: I heard you.

(The lid of NAGG's bin lifts. His hands appear, gripping the rim. Then his head emerges. In his mouth the biscuit. He listens.)

HAMM: Did your seeds come up?

CLOV: No.

205 HAMM: Did you scratch round them to see if they had sprouted?

CLOV: They haven't sprouted.

HAMM: Perhaps it's still too early.

CLOV: If they were going to sprout they would have sprouted. *(Violently.)*

They'll never sprout!

(Pause. NAGG takes biscuit in his hand.)

210 HAMM: This is not much fun.

(Pause.)

But that's always the way at the end of the day, isn't it, Clov?

CLOV: Always.

HAMM: It's the end of the day like any other day, isn't it, Clov?

215 CLOV: Looks like it.

(Pause.)

HAMM: *(Anguished.)* What's happening, what's happening?

CLOV: Something is taking its course.

(Pause.)

HAMM: All right, be off.

(He leans back in his chair, remains motionless. CLOV does not move, heaves a great groaning sigh. HAMM sits up.)

I thought I told you to be off.

220 CLOV: I'm trying.

(He goes to door, halts.)

Ever since I was whelped.

(Exit CLOV.)

HAMM: We're getting on.

(He leans back in his chair, remains motionless. NAGG knocks on the lid of the other bin. Pause. He knocks harder. The lid lifts and the hands of NELL appear, gripping the rim. Then her head emerges. Lace cap. Very white face.)

NELL: What is it, my pet?

(Pause.)

Time for love?

225 NAGG: Were you asleep?

NELL: Oh no!

NAGG: Kiss me.

NELL: We can't.

NAGG: Try.

(Their heads strain towards each other, fail to meet, fall apart again.)

230 NELL: Why this farce, day after day?

(Pause.)

NAGG: I've lost me tooth.

NELL: When?

NAGG: I had it yesterday.

NELL: *(Elegiac.)* Ah yesterday!

(They turn painfully towards each other.)

NAGG: Can you see me?   235

NELL: Hardly. And you?

NAGG: What?

NELL: Can you see me?

NAGG: Hardly.

NELL: So much the better, so much the better.   240

NAGG: Don't say that.

(Pause.)

Our sight has failed.

NELL: Yes.

(Pause. They turn away from each other.)

NAGG: Can you hear me?

NELL: Yes. And you?   245

NAGG: Yes.

(Pause.)

Our hearing hasn't failed.

NELL: Our what?

NAGG: Our hearing.

NELL: No.   250

(Pause.)

Have you anything else to say to me?

NAGG: Do you remember—

NELL: No.

NAGG: When we crashed on our tandem and lost our shanks.

(They laugh heartily.)

NELL: It was in the Ardennes.   255

(They laugh less heartily.)

NAGG: On the road to Sedan.

(They laugh still less heartily.)

Are you cold?

NELL: Yes, perished. And you?

NAGG: *(Pause.)* I'm freezing.

(Pause.)

Do you want to go in?   260

NELL: Yes.

NAGG: Then go in.

(NELL does not move.)

Why don't you go in?

NELL: I don't know.

(Pause.)

NAGG: Has he changed your sawdust?   265

NELL: It isn't sawdust.

(Pause. Wearily.)

Can you not be a little accurate, Nagg?

NAGG: Your sand then. It's not important.

NELL: It is important.

(Pause.)

NAGG: It was sawdust once.   270

NELL: Once!

NAGG: And now it's sand.

(Pause.)

From the shore.

(Pause. Impatiently.)

Now it's sand he fetches from the shore.

275 NELL: Now it's sand.

NAGG: Has he changed yours?

NELL: No.

NAGG: Nor mine.

(Pause.)

I won't have it!

(Pause. Holding up the biscuit.)

280 Do you want a bit?

NELL: No.

(Pause.)

Of what?

NAGG: Biscuit. I've kept you half.

(He looks at the biscuit. Proudly.)

Three quarters. For you. Here.

(He proffers the biscuit.)

285 No?

(Pause.)

Do you not feel well?

HAMM: *(Wearily.)* Quiet, quiet, you're keeping me awake.

(Pause.)

Talk softer.

(Pause.)

If I could sleep I might make love. I'd go into the woods.

290 My eyes would see . . . the sky, the earth. I'd run, run, they
wouldn't catch me.

(Pause.)

Nature!

(Pause.)

There's something dripping in my head.

(Pause.)

A heart, a heart in my head.

(Pause.)

295 NAGG: *(Soft.)* Do you hear him? A heart in his head!

(He chuckles cautiously.)

NELL: One mustn't laugh at those things, Nagg. Why must you
always laugh at them?

NAGG: Not so loud!

NELL: *(Without lowering her voice.)* Nothing is funnier than un-
300 happiness, I grant you that. But—

NAGG: *(Shocked.)* Oh!

NELL: Yes, yes, it's the most comical thing in the world. And
we laugh, we laugh, with a will, in the beginning. But it's
always the same thing. Yes, it's like the funny story we have
305 heard too often, we still find it funny, but we don't laugh
any more.

(Pause.)

Have you anything else to say to me?

NAGG: No.

NELL: Are you quite sure?

(Pause.)

310 Then I'll leave you.

NAGG: Do you not want your biscuit?

(Pause.)

I'll keep it for you.

(Pause.)

I thought you were going to leave me.

NELL: I am going to leave you.

NAGG: Could you give me a scratch before you go?   315

NELL: No.

(Pause.)

Where?

NAGG: In the back.

NELL: No.

(Pause.)

Rub yourself against the rim.   320

NAGG: It's lower down. In the hollow.

NELL: What hollow?

NAGG: The hollow!

(Pause.)

Could you not?

(Pause.)

Yesterday you scratched me there.   325

NELL: *(Elegiac.)* Ah yesterday!

NAGG: Could you not?

(Pause.)

Would you like me to scratch you?

(Pause.)

Are you crying again?

NELL: I was trying.   330

(Pause.)

HAMM: Perhaps it's a little vein.

(Pause.)

NAGG: What was that he said?

NELL: Perhaps it's a little vein.

NAGG: What does that mean?

(Pause.)

That means nothing.   335

(Pause.)

Will I tell you the story of the tailor?

NELL: No.

(Pause.)

What for?

NAGG: To cheer you up.

NELL: It's not funny.   340

NAGG: It always made you laugh.

(Pause.)

The first time I thought you'd die.

NELL: It was on Lake Como.

(Pause.)

One April afternoon.

(Pause.)

Can you believe it?   345

NAGG: What?

NELL: That we once went out rowing on Lake Como.

(Pause.)

One April afternoon.

NAGG: We had got engaged the day before.

NELL: Engaged!   350

NAGG: You were in such fits that we capsized. By rights we
should have been drowned.

NELL: It was because I felt happy.

NAGG: (*Indignant.*) It was not, it was not, it was my story and
355 nothing else. Happy! Don't you laugh at it still? Every time
I tell it. Happy!

NELL: It was deep, deep. And you could see down to the bottom. So white. So clean.

NAGG: Let me tell it again.

(*Raconteur's voice.*)
360 An Englishman, needing a pair of striped trousers in a
hurry for the New Year festivities, goes to his tailor who
takes his measurements.

(*Tailor's voice.*)
"That's the lot, come back in four days, I'll have it ready."
Good. Four days later.

(*Tailor's voice.*)
365 "So sorry, come back in a week, I've made a mess of the
seat." Good, that's all right, a neat seat can be very ticklish.
A week later.

(*Tailor's voice.*)
"Frightfully sorry, come back in ten days, I've made a hash
of the crotch." Good, can't be helped, a snug crotch is al-
370 ways a teaser. Ten days later.

(*Tailor's voice.*)
"Dreadfully sorry, come back in a fortnight, I've made a balls
of the fly." Good, at a pinch, a smart fly is a stiff proposition.

(*Pause. Normal voice.*)
I never told it worse.

(*Pause. Gloomy.*)
I tell this story worse and worse.

(*Pause. Raconteur's voice.*)
375 Well, to make it short, the bluebells are blowing and he
ballockses the buttonholes.

(*Customer's voice.*)
"God damn you to hell, Sir, no, it's indecent, there are limits! In six days, do you hear me, six days, God made the
world. Yes Sir, no less Sir, the WORLD! And you are not
380 bloody well capable of making me a pair of trousers in three
months!"

(*Tailor's voice, scandalized.*)
"But my dear Sir, my dear Sir, look—

(*Disdainful gesture, disgustedly.*)
—at the world—

(*Pause.*)
and look—

(*Loving gesture, proudly.*)
385 —at my TROUSERS!"

(*Pause. He looks at* NELL *who has remained impassive, her eyes unsee-
ing, breaks into a high forced laugh, cuts it short, pokes his head towards* NELL, *launches his laugh again.*)

HAMM: Silence!

(NAGG *starts, cuts short his laugh.*)

NELL: You could see down to the bottom.

HAMM: (*Exasperated.*) Have you not finished? Will you never
finish?

(*With sudden fury.*)
390 Will this never finish?

(NAGG *disappears into his bin, closes the lid behind him.* NELL *does
not move. Frenziedly.*)

My kingdom for a nightman!

(*He whistles. Enter* CLOV.)
Clear away this muck! Chuck it in the sea!

(CLOV *goes to bins, halts.*)

NELL: So white.

HAMM: What? What's she blathering about?

(CLOV *stoops, takes* NELL's *hand, feels her pulse.*)

NELL: (*To* CLOV.) Desert! 395

(CLOV *lets go her hand, pushes her back in the bin, closes the lid.*)

CLOV: (*Returning to his place beside the chair.*) She has no pulse.

HAMM: What was she drivelling about?

CLOV: She told me to go away, into the desert.

HAMM: Damn busybody! Is that all?

CLOV: No. 400

HAMM: What else?

CLOV: I didn't understand.

HAMM: Have you bottled her?

CLOV: Yes.

HAMM: Are they both bottled? 405

CLOV: Yes.

HAMM: Screw down the lids.

(CLOV *goes towards door.*)
Time enough.

(CLOV *halts.*)
My anger subsides, I'd like to pee.

CLOV: (*With alacrity.*) I'll go and get the catheter. 410

(*He goes towards door.*)

HAMM: Time enough.

(CLOV *halts.*)
Give me my pain-killer.

CLOV: It's too soon.

(*Pause.*)
It's too soon on top of your tonic, it wouldn't act.

HAMM: In the morning they brace you up and in the evening 415
they calm you down. Unless it's the other way round.

(*Pause.*)
That old doctor, he's dead naturally?

CLOV: He wasn't old.

HAMM: But he's dead?

CLOV: Naturally. 420

(*Pause.*)
You ask *me* that?

(*Pause.*)

HAMM: Take me for a little turn.

(CLOV *goes behind the chair and pushes it forward.*)
Not too fast!

(CLOV *pushes chair.*)
Right round the world!

(CLOV *pushes chair.*)
Hug the walls, then back to the center again. 425

(CLOV *pushes chair.*)
I was right in the center, wasn't I?

CLOV: (*Pushing.*) Yes.
HAMM: We'd need a proper wheel-chair. With big wheels. Bicycle wheels!
(*Pause.*)
430   Are you hugging?
CLOV: (*Pushing.*) Yes.
HAMM: (*Groping for wall.*) It's a lie! Why do you lie to me?
CLOV: (*Bearing closer to wall.*) There! There!
HAMM: Stop!
(CLOV *stops chair close to back wall.* HAMM *lays his hand against wall.*)
435   Old wall!
(*Pause.*)
    Beyond is the . . . other hell.
(*Pause. Violently.*)
    Closer! Closer! Up against!
CLOV: Take away your hand.
(HAMM *withdraws his hand.* CLOV *rams chair against wall.*)
    There!

(HAMM *leans towards wall, applies his ear to it.*)

440 HAMM: Do you hear?
(*He strikes the wall with his knuckles.*)
    Do you hear? Hollow bricks!
(*He strikes again.*)
    All that's hollow!
(*Pause. He straightens up. Violently.*)
    That's enough. Back!
CLOV: We haven't done the round.
445 HAMM: Back to my place!
(CLOV *pushes chair back to center.*)
    Is that my place?
CLOV: Yes, that's your place.
HAMM: Am I right in the center?
CLOV: I'll measure it.
450 HAMM: More or less! More or less!
CLOV: (*Moving chair slightly.*) There!
HAMM: I'm more or less in the center?
CLOV: I'd say so.
HAMM: You'd say so! Put me right in the center!
455 CLOV: I'll go and get the tape.
HAMM: Roughly! Roughly!
(CLOV *moves chair slightly.*)
    Bang in the center!
CLOV: There!

(*Pause.*)

HAMM: I feel a little too far to the left.
(CLOV *moves chair slightly.*)
460   Now I feel a little too far to the right.
(CLOV *moves chair slightly.*)
    I feel a little too far forward.
(CLOV *moves chair slightly.*)
    Now I feel a little too far back.
(CLOV *moves chair slightly.*)
    Don't stay there,
(*i.e., Behind the chair.*)
    you give me the shivers.

(CLOV *returns to his place beside the chair.*)

CLOV: If I could kill him I'd die happy.   465

(*Pause.*)

HAMM: What's the weather like?
CLOV: As usual.
HAMM: Look at the earth.
CLOV: I've looked.
HAMM: With the glass?   470
CLOV: No need of the glass.
HAMM: Look at it with the glass.
CLOV: I'll go and get the glass.

(*Exit* CLOV.)

HAMM: No need of the glass!

(*Enter* CLOV *with telescope.*)

CLOV: I'm back again, with the glass.   475
(*He goes to window right, looks up at it.*)
    I need the steps.
HAMM: Why? Have you shrunk?
(*Exit* CLOV *with telescope.*)
    I don't like that, I don't like that.

(*Enter* CLOV *with ladder, but without telescope.*)

CLOV: I'm back again, with the steps.
(*He sets down ladder under window right, gets up on it, realizes he has not the telescope, gets down.*)
    I need the glass.   480

(*He goes towards door.*)

HAMM: (*Violently.*) But you have the glass!
CLOV: (*Halting, violently.*) No, I haven't the glass!

(*Exit* CLOV.)

HAMM: This is deadly.

(*Enter* CLOV *with telescope. He goes towards ladder.*)

CLOV: Things are livening up.
(*He gets up on ladder, raises the telescope, lets it fall.*)
    I did it on purpose.   485
(*He gets down, picks up the telescope, turns it on auditorium.*)
    I see . . . a multitude . . . in transports . . . of joy.
(*Pause.*)
    That's what I call a magnifier.
(*He lowers the telescope, turns towards* HAMM.)
    Well? Don't we laugh?
HAMM: (*After reflection.*) I don't.
CLOV: (*After reflection.*) Nor I.   490
(*He gets up on ladder, turns the telescope on the without.*)
    Let's see.
(*He looks, moving the telescope.*)
    Zero . . .
(*He looks.*)
    . . . zero . . .
(*He looks.*)
    . . . and zero.

495   HAMM: Nothing stirs. All is—
CLOV: Zer—
HAMM: (*Violently.*) Wait till you're spoken to!
(*Normal voice.*)
   All is . . . all is . . . all is what?
(*Violently.*)
   All is what?
500   CLOV: What all is? In a word? Is that what you want to know?
   Just a moment.
(*He turns the telescope on the without, looks, lowers the telescope, turns towards* HAMM.)
   Corpsed.
(*Pause.*)
   Well? Content?
HAMM: Look at the sea.
505   CLOV: It's the same.
HAMM: Look at the ocean!

(CLOV *gets down, takes a few steps towards window left, goes back for ladder, carries it over and sets it down under window left, gets up on it, turns the telescope on the without, looks at length. He starts, lowers the telescope, examines it, turns it again on the without.*)

CLOV: Never seen anything like that!
HAMM: (*Anxious.*) What? A sail? A fin? Smoke?
CLOV: (*Looking.*) The light is sunk.
510   HAMM: (*Relieved.*) Pah! We all knew that.
CLOV: (*Looking.*) There was a bit left.
HAMM: The base.
CLOV: (*Looking.*) Yes.
HAMM: And now?
515   CLOV: (*Looking.*) All gone.
HAMM: No gulls?
CLOV: (*Looking.*) Gulls!
HAMM: And the horizon? Nothing on the horizon?
CLOV: (*Lowering the telescope, turning towards* HAMM, *exasperated.*)
520   What in God's name could there be on the horizon?

(*Pause.*)

HAMM: The waves, how are the waves?
CLOV: The waves?
(*He turns the telescope on the waves.*)
   Lead.
HAMM: And the sun?
525   CLOV: (*Looking.*) Zero.
HAMM: But it should be sinking. Look again.
CLOV: (*Looking.*) Damn the sun.
HAMM: Is it night already then?
CLOV: (*Looking.*) No.
530   HAMM: Then what is it?
CLOV: (*Looking.*) Gray.
(*Lowering the telescope, turning towards* HAMM, *louder.*)
   Gray!
(*Pause. Still louder.*)
   GRRAY!

(*Pause. He gets down, approaches* HAMM *from behind, whispers in his ear.*)

HAMM: (*Starting.*) Gray! Did I hear you say gray?

CLOV: Light black. From pole to pole.   535
HAMM: You exaggerate.
(*Pause.*)
   Don't stay there, you give me the shivers.

(CLOV *returns to his place beside the chair.*)

CLOV: Why this farce, day after day?
HAMM: Routine. One never knows.
(*Pause.*)
   Last night I saw inside my breast. There was a big sore.   540
CLOV: Pah! You saw your heart.
HAMM: No, it was living.
(*Pause. Anguished.*)
   Clov!
CLOV: Yes.
HAMM: What's happening?   545
CLOV: Something is taking its course.

(*Pause.*)

HAMM: Clov!
CLOV: (*Impatiently.*) What is it?
HAMM: We're not beginning to . . . to . . . mean something?   550
CLOV: Mean something! You and I, mean something!
(*Brief laugh.*)
   Ah that's a good one!
HAMM: I wonder.
(*Pause.*)
   Imagine if a rational being came back to earth, wouldn't he be liable to get ideas into his head if he observed us long enough.   555
(*Voice of rational being.*)
   Ah, good, now I see what it is, yes, now I understand what they're at!
(CLOV *starts, drops the telescope and begins to scratch his belly with both hands. Normal voice.*)
   And without going so far as that, we ourselves . . .
(*With emotion.*)
   . . . we ourselves . . . at certain moments . . .
(*Vehemently.*)
   To think perhaps it won't all have been for nothing!   560
CLOV: (*Anguished, scratching himself.*) I have a flea!
HAMM: A flea! Are there still fleas?
CLOV: On me there's one.
(*Scratching.*)
   Unless it's a crablouse.
HAMM: (*Very perturbed.*) But humanity might start from there   565
   all over again! Catch him, for the love of God!
CLOV: I'll go and get the powder.

(*Exit* CLOV.)

HAMM: A flea! This is awful! What a day!

(*Enter* CLOV *with a sprinkling-tin.*)

CLOV: I'm back again, with the insecticide.
HAMM: Let him have it!   570

(CLOV loosens the top of his trousers, pulls it forward and shakes powder into the aperture. He stoops, looks, waits, starts, frenziedly shakes more powder, stoops, looks, waits.)

CLOV: The bastard!

HAMM: Did you get him?

CLOV: Looks like it.

(He drops the tin and adjusts his trousers.)

    Unless he's laying doggo.

575 HAMM: Laying! Lying you mean. Unless he's *lying* doggo.

CLOV: Ah? One says lying? One doesn't say laying?

HAMM: Use your head, can't you. If he was laying we'd be bitched.

CLOV: Ah.

(Pause.)

580   What about that pee?

HAMM: I'm having it.

CLOV: Ah that's the spirit, that's the spirit!

(Pause.)

HAMM: *(With ardour.)* Let's go from here, the two of us! South! You can make a raft and the currents will carry us away, far

585   away, to other . . . mammals!

CLOV: God forbid!

HAMM: Alone, I'll embark alone! Get working on that raft immediately. Tomorrow I'll be gone for ever.

CLOV: *(Hastening towards door.)* I'll start straight away.

590 HAMM: Wait!

(CLOV halts.)

    Will there be sharks, do you think?

CLOV: Sharks? I don't know. If there are there will be.

(He goes towards door.)

HAMM: Wait!

(CLOV halts.)

    Is it not yet time for my pain-killer?

595 CLOV: *(Violently.)* No!

(He goes towards door.)

HAMM: Wait!

(CLOV halts.)

    How are your eyes?

CLOV: Bad.

HAMM: But you can see.

600 CLOV: All I want.

HAMM: How are your legs?

CLOV: Bad.

HAMM: But you can walk.

CLOV: I come . . . and go.

605 HAMM: In my house.

(Pause. With prophetic relish.)

    One day you'll be blind, like me. You'll be sitting there, a speck in the void, in the dark, for ever, like me.

(Pause.)

    One day you'll say to yourself, I'm tired, I'll sit down, and you'll go and sit down. Then you'll say, I'm hungry, I'll get

610   up and get something to eat. But you won't get up. You'll say, I shouldn't have sat down, but since I have I'll sit on a

little longer, then I'll get up and get something to eat. But you won't get up and you won't get anything to eat.

(Pause.)

    You'll look at the wall a while, then you'll say, I'll close my eyes, perhaps have a little sleep, after that I'll feel better, 615 and you'll close them. And when you open them again there'll be no wall any more.

(Pause.)

    Infinite emptiness will be all around you, all the resurrected dead of all the ages wouldn't fill it, and there you'll be like a little bit of grit in the middle of the steppe. 620

(Pause.)

    Yes, one day you'll know what it is, you'll be like me, except that you won't have anyone with you, because you won't have had pity on anyone and because there won't be anyone left to have pity on.

(Pause.)

CLOV: It's not certain. 625

(Pause.)

    And there's one thing you forget.

HAMM: Ah?

CLOV: I can't sit down.

HAMM: *(Impatiently.)* Well you'll lie down then, what the hell! Or you'll come to a standstill, simply stop and stand still, 630 the way you are now. One day you'll say, I'm tired, I'll stop. What does the attitude matter?

(Pause.)

CLOV: So you all want me to leave you.

HAMM: Naturally.

CLOV: Then I'll leave you. 635

HAMM: You can't leave us.

CLOV: Then I won't leave you.

(Pause.)

HAMM: Why don't you finish us?

(Pause.)

    I'll tell you the combination of the cupboard if you promise to finish me. 640

CLOV: I couldn't finish you.

HAMM: Then you won't finish me.

(Pause.)

CLOV: I'll leave you, I have things to do.

HAMM: Do you remember when you came here?

CLOV: No. Too small, you told me. 645

HAMM: Do you remember your father.

CLOV: *(Wearily.)* Same answer.

(Pause.)

    You've asked me these questions millions of times.

HAMM: I love the old questions.

(With fervour.)

    Ah the old questions, the old answers, there's nothing like 650 them!

(Pause.)

    It was I was a father to you.

CLOV: Yes.
(*He looks at* HAMM *fixedly.*)
   You were that to me.
655   HAMM: My house a home for you.
CLOV: Yes.
(*He looks about him.*)
   This was that for me.
HAMM: (*Proudly.*) But for me,
(*Gesture towards himself.*)
   no father. But for Hamm,
(*Gesture towards surroundings.*)
660   no home.

(*Pause.*)

CLOV: I'll leave you.
HAMM: Did you ever think of one thing?
CLOV: Never.
HAMM: That here we're down in a hole.
(*Pause.*)
665   But beyond the hills? Eh? Perhaps it's still green. Eh?
(*Pause.*)
   Flora! Pomona!
(*Ecstatically.*)
   Ceres!
(*Pause.*)
   Perhaps you won't need to go very far.
CLOV: I can't go very far.
(*Pause.*)
670   I'll leave you.
HAMM: Is my dog ready?
CLOV: He lacks a leg.
HAMM: Is he silky?
CLOV: He's a kind of Pomeranian.
675   HAMM: Go and get him.
CLOV: He lacks a leg.
HAMM: Go and get him!
(*Exit* CLOV.)
   We're getting on.

(*Enter* CLOV *holding by one of its three legs a black toy dog.*)

CLOV: Your dogs are here.

(*He hands the dog to* HAMM *who feels it, fondles it.*)

680   HAMM: He's white, isn't he?
CLOV: Nearly.
HAMM: What do you mean, nearly? Is he white or isn't he? 940
CLOV: He isn't.

(*Pause.*)

HAMM: You've forgotten the sex.
685   CLOV: (*Vexed.*) But he isn't finished. The sex goes on at the end.

(*Pause.*)

HAMM: You haven't put on his ribbon.
CLOV: (*Angrily.*) But he isn't finished, I tell you! First you finish your dog and then you put on his ribbon!

(*Pause.*)

HAMM: Can he stand?
CLOV: I don't know.   690
HAMM: Try.
(*He hands the dog to* CLOV *who places it on the ground.*)
   Well?
CLOV: Wait!

(*He squats down and tries to get the dog to stand on its three legs, fails, lets it go. The dog falls on its side.*)

HAMM: (*Impatiently.*) Well?
CLOV: He's standing.   695
HAMM: (*Groping for the dog.*) Where? Where is he?

(CLOV *holds up the dog in a standing position.*)

CLOV: There.

(*He takes* HAMM's *hand and guides it towards the dog's head.*)

HAMM: (*His hand on the dog's head.*) Is he gazing at me?
CLOV: Yes.
HAMM: (*Proudly.*) As if he were asking me to take him for a   700
   walk?
CLOV: If you like.
HAMM: (*As before.*) Or as if he were begging me for a bone.
(*He withdraws his hand.*)
   Leave him like that, standing there imploring me.

(CLOV *straightens up. The dog falls on its side.*)

CLOV: I'll leave you.   705
HAMM: Have you had your visions?
CLOV: Less.
HAMM: Is Mother Pegg's light on?
CLOV: Light! How could anyone's light be on?
HAMM: Extinguished!   710
CLOV: Naturally it's extinguished. If it's not on it's extinguished.
HAMM: No, I mean Mother Pegg.
CLOV: But naturally she's extinguished!
(*Pause.*)
   What's the matter with you today?   715
HAMM: I'm taking my course.
(*Pause.*)
   Is she buried?
CLOV: Buried! Who would have buried her?
HAMM: You.
CLOV: Me! Haven't I enough to do without burying people?   720
HAMM: But you'll bury me.
CLOV: No I won't bury you.

(*Pause.*)

HAMM: She was bonny once, like a flower of the field.
(*With reminiscent leer.*)
   And a great one for the men!
CLOV: We too were bonny—once. It's a rare thing not to have   725
   been bonny—once.

(*Pause.*)

HAMM: Go and get the gaff.

(CLOV goes to door, halts.)

CLOV: Do this, do that, and I do it. I never refuse. Why?
HAMM: You're not able to.
730 CLOV: Soon I won't do it any more.
HAMM: You won't be able to any more.
(Exit CLOV.)
    Ah the creatures, the creatures, everything has to be explained to them.

(Enter CLOV with gaff.)

CLOV: Here's your gaff. Stick it up.

(He gives the gaff to HAMM who, wielding it like a puntpole, tries to move his chair.)

735 HAMM: Did I move?
CLOV: No.

(HAMM throws down the gaff.)

HAMM: Go and get the oilcan.
CLOV: What for?
HAMM: To oil the castors.
740 CLOV: I oiled them yesterday.
HAMM: Yesterday! What does that mean? Yesterday!
CLOV: *(Violently.)* That means that bloody awful day, long ago, before this bloody awful day. I use the words you taught me. If they don't mean anything any more, teach me others.
745   Or let me be silent.

(Pause.)

HAMM: I once knew a madman who thought the end of the world had come. He was a painter—and engraver. I had a great fondness for him. I used to go and see him, in the asylum. I'd take him by the hand and drag him to the window.
750   Look! There! All that rising corn! And there! Look! The sails of the herring fleet! All that loveliness!
(Pause.)
    He'd snatch away his hand and go back into his corner. Appalled. All he had seen was ashes.
(Pause.)
    He alone had been spared.
(Pause.)
755   Forgotten.
(Pause.)
    It appears the case is . . . was not so . . . so unusual.
CLOV: A madman? When was that?
HAMM: Oh way back, way back, you weren't in the land of the living.
760 CLOV: God be with the days!

(Pause. HAMM raises his toque.)

HAMM: I had a great fondness for him.
(Pause. He puts on his toque again.)
    He was a painter—and engraver.
CLOV: There are so many terrible things.

HAMM: No, no, there are not so many now.
(Pause.)
    Clov!   765
CLOV: Yes.
HAMM: Do you not think this has gone on long enough?
CLOV: Yes!
(Pause.)
    What?
HAMM: This . . . this . . . thing.   770
CLOV: I've always thought so.
(Pause.)
    You not?
HAMM: *(Gloomily.)* Then it's a day like any other day.
CLOV: As long as it lasts.
(Pause.)
    All life long the same inanities.   775
HAMM: I can't leave you.
CLOV: I know. And you can't follow me.

(Pause.)

HAMM: If you leave me how shall I know?
CLOV: *(Briskly.)* Well you simply whistle me and if I don't come running it means I've left you.   780

(Pause.)

HAMM: You won't come and kiss me goodbye?
CLOV: Oh I shouldn't think so.

(Pause.)

HAMM: But you might be merely dead in your kitchen.
CLOV: The result would be the same.
HAMM: Yes, but how would I know, if you were merely dead in   785
your kitchen?
CLOV: Well . . . sooner or later I'd start to stink.
HAMM: You stink already. The whole place stinks of corpses.
CLOV: The whole universe.
HAMM: *(Angrily.)* To hell with the universe.   790
(Pause.)
    Think of something.
CLOV: What?
HAMM: An idea, have an idea.
(Angrily.)
    A bright idea!
CLOV: Ah good.   795
(He starts pacing to and fro, his eyes fixed on the ground, his hands behind his back. He halts.)
    The pains in my legs! It's unbelievable! Soon I won't be able to think any more.
HAMM: You won't be able to leave me.
(CLOV resumes his pacing.)
    What are you doing?
CLOV: Having an idea.   800
(He paces.)
    Ah!

(He halts.)

HAMM: What a brain!
(Pause.)

Well?

CLOV: Wait!

(He meditates. Not very convinced.)

805   Yes . . .

(Pause. More convinced.)

Yes!

(He raises his head.)

I have it! I set the alarm.

(Pause.)

HAMM: This is perhaps not one of my bright days, but frankly—

810   CLOV: You whistle me. I don't come. The alarm rings. I'm gone. It doesn't ring. I'm dead.

(Pause.)

HAMM: Is it working?

(Pause. Impatiently.)

The alarm, is it working?

CLOV: Why wouldn't it be working?

815   HAMM: Because it's worked too much.

CLOV: But it's hardly worked at all.

HAMM: (Angrily.) Then because it's worked too little!

CLOV: I'll go and see.

(Exit CLOV. Brief ring of alarm off. Enter CLOV with alarm-clock. He holds it against HAMM's ear and releases alarm. They listen to it ringing to the end. Pause.)

Fit to wake the dead! Did you hear it?

820   HAMM: Vaguely.

CLOV: The end is terrific!

HAMM: I prefer the middle.

(Pause.)

Is it not time for my pain-killer?

CLOV: No!

(He goes to door, turns.)

825   I'll leave you.

HAMM: It's time for my story. Do you want to listen to my story.

CLOV: No.

HAMM: Ask my father if he wants to listen to my story.

(CLOV goes to bins, raises the lid of NAGG's, stoops, looks into it. Pause. He straightens up.)

830   CLOV: He's asleep.

HAMM: Wake him.

(CLOV stoops, wakes NAGG with the alarm. Unintelligible words. CLOV straightens up.)

CLOV: He doesn't want to listen to your story.

HAMM: I'll give him a bon-bon.

(CLOV stoops. As before.)

CLOV: He wants a sugar-plum.

835   HAMM: He'll get a sugar-plum.

(CLOV stoops. As before.)

CLOV: It's a deal.

(He goes towards door. NAGG's hands appear, gripping the rim. Then the head emerges. CLOV reaches door, turns.)

Do you believe in the life to come?

HAMM: Mine was always that.

(Exit CLOV.)

Got him that time!

NAGG: I'm listening.   840

HAMM: Scoundrel! Why did you engender me?

NAGG: I didn't know.

HAMM: What? What didn't you know?

NAGG: That it'd be you.

(Pause.)

You'll give me a sugar-plum?   845

HAMM: After the audition.

NAGG: You swear?

HAMM: Yes.

NAGG: On what?

HAMM: My honor.   850

(Pause. They laugh heartily.)

NAGG: Two.

HAMM: One.

NAGG: One for me and one for—

HAMM: One! Silence!

(Pause.)

Where was I?   855

(Pause. Gloomily.)

It's finished, we're finished.

(Pause.)

Nearly finished.

(Pause.)

There'll be no more speech.

(Pause.)

Something dripping in my head, ever since the fontanelles.

(Stifled hilarity of NAGG.)

Splash, splash, always on the same spot.   860

(Pause.)

Perhaps it's a little vein.

(Pause.)

A little artery.

(Pause. More animated.)

Enough of that, it's story time, where was I?

(Pause. Narrative tone.)

The man came crawling towards me, on his belly. Pale, wonderfully pale and thin, he seemed on the point of—   865

(Pause. Normal tone.)

No, I've done that bit.

(Pause. Narrative tone.)

I calmly filled my pipe—the meerschaum, lit it with . . . let us say a vesta, drew a few puffs. Aah!

(Pause.)

Well, what is it you want?

(Pause.)

It was an extra-ordinarily bitter day, I remember, zero by   870 the thermometer. But considering it was Christmas Eve there was nothing . . . extra-ordinary about that. Seasonable weather, for once in a way.

(Pause.)

Well, what ill wind blows you my way? He raised his face to me, black with mingled dirt and tears.   875

(Pause. Normal tone.)

That should do it.

(*Narrative tone.*)

No no, don't look at me, don't look at me. He dropped his eyes and mumbled something, apologies I presume.

(*Pause.*)

880 I'm a busy man, you know, the final touches, before the festivities, you know what it is.

(*Pause. Forcibly.*)

Come on now, what is the object of this invasion?

(*Pause.*)

It was a glorious bright day, I remember, fifty by the heliometer, but already the sun was sinking down into the . . . down among the dead.

(*Normal tone.*)

885 Nicely put, that.

(*Narrative tone.*)

Come on now, come on, present your petition and let me resume my labors.

(*Pause. Normal tone.*)

There's English for you. Ah well . . .

(*Narrative tone.*)

It was then he took the plunge. It's my little one, he said.

890 Tsstss, a little one, that's bad. My little boy, he said, as if the sex mattered. Where did he come from? He named the hole. A good half-day, on horse. What are you insinuating? That the place is still inhabited? No no, not a soul, except himself and the child—assuming he existed. Good. I en-

895 quired about the situation at Kov, beyond the gulf. Not a sinner. Good. And you expect me to believe you have left your little one back there, all alone, and alive into the bargain? Come now!

(*Pause.*)

It was a howling wild day, I remember, a hundred by the

900 anenometer. The wind was tearing up the dead pines and sweeping them . . . away.

(*Pause. Normal tone.*)

A bit feeble, that.

(*Narrative tone.*)

Come on, man, speak up, what is it you want from me, I have to put up my holly.

(*Pause.*)

905 Well to make it short it finally transpired that what he wanted from me was . . . bread for his brat? Bread? But I have no bread, it doesn't agree with me. Good. Then perhaps a little corn?

(*Pause. Normal tone.*)

That should do it.

(*Narrative tone.*)

Corn, yes, I have corn, it's true, in my granaries. But use

910 your head. I give you some corn, a pound, a pound and a half, you bring it back to your child and you make him— if he's still alive—a nice pot of porridge,

(NAGG *reacts.*)

a nice pot and a half of porridge, full of nourishment. Good. The colors come back into his little cheeks—perhaps. And

915 then?

(*Pause.*)

I lost patience.

(*Violently.*)

Use your head, can't you, use your head, you're on earth, there's no cure for that!

(*Pause.*)

It was an exceedingly dry day, I remember, zero by the hy-

920 grometer. Ideal weather, for my lumbago.

(*Pause. Violently.*)

But what in God's name do you imagine? That the earth will awake in spring? That the rivers and seas will run with fish again? That there's manna in heaven still for imbeciles like you?

(*Pause.*)

Gradually I cooled down, sufficiently at least to ask him 925 how long he had taken on the way. Three whole days. Good. In what condition he had left the child. Deep in sleep.

(*Forcibly.*)

But deep in what sleep, deep in what sleep already?

(*Pause.*)

Well to make it short I finally offered to take him into my service. He had touched a chord. And then I imagined al- 930 ready that I wasn't much longer for this world.

(*He laughs. Pause.*)

Well?

(*Pause.*)

Well? Here if you were careful you might die a nice natural death, in peace and comfort.

(*Pause.*)

Well? 935

(*Pause.*)

In the end he asked me would I consent to take in the child as well—if he were still alive.

(*Pause.*)

It was the moment I was waiting for.

(*Pause.*)

Would I consent to take in the child . . .

(*Pause.*)

I can see him still, down on his knees, his hands flat on the 940 ground, glaring at me with his mad eyes, in defiance of my wishes.

(*Pause. Normal tone.*)

I'll soon have finished with this story.

(*Pause.*)

Unless I bring in other characters.

(*Pause.*)

But where would I find them? 945

(*Pause.*)

Where would I look for them?

(*Pause. He whistles. Enter* CLOV.)

Let us pray to God.

NAGG: Me sugar-plum!

CLOV: There's a rat in the kitchen!

HAMM: A rat! Are there still rats? 950

CLOV: In the kitchen there's one.

HAMM: And you haven't exterminated him?

CLOV: Half. You disturbed us.

HAMM: He can't get away?

CLOV: No. 955

HAMM: You'll finish him later. Let us pray to God.

CLOV: Again!

NAGG: Me sugar-plum!

HAMM: God first!

(*Pause.*)

Are you right? 960

CLOV: (*Resigned.*) Off we go.

HAMM: (*To* NAGG.) And you?

NAGG: (*Clasping his hands, closing his eyes, in a gabble.*) Our Father which art—

965 HAMM: Silence! In silence! Where are your manners?

(*Pause.*)

Off we go.

(*Attitudes of prayer. Silence. Abandoning his attitude, discouraged.*)

Well?

CLOV: (*Abandoning his attitude.*) What a hope! And you?

HAMM: Sweet damn all!

(*To* NAGG.)

970 And you?

NAGG: Wait!

(*Pause. Abandoning his attitude.*)

Nothing doing!

HAMM: The bastard! He doesn't exist!

CLOV: Not yet.

975 NAGG: Me sugar-plum!

HAMM: There are no more sugar-plums!

(*Pause.*)

NAGG: It's natural. After all I'm your father. It's true if it hadn't been me it would have been someone else. But that's no excuse.

(*Pause.*)

980 Turkish Delight, for example, which no longer exists, we all know that, there is nothing in the world I love more. And one day I'll ask you for some, in return for a kindness, and you'll promise it to me. One must live with the times.

(*Pause.*)

Whom did you call when you were a tiny boy, and were

985 frightened, in the dark? Your mother? No. Me. We let you cry. Then we moved you out of earshot, so that we might sleep in peace.

(*Pause.*)

I was asleep, as happy as a king, and you woke me up to have me listen to you. It wasn't indispensable, you didn't

990 really need to have me listen to you.

(*Pause.*)

I hope the day will come when you'll really need to have me listen to you, and need to hear my voice, any voice.

(*Pause.*)

Yes, I hope I'll live till then, to hear you calling me like when you were a tiny boy, and were frightened, in the dark,

995 and I was your only hope.

(*Pause.* NAGG *knocks on lid of* NELL's *bin. Pause.*)

Nell!

(*Pause. He knocks louder. Pause. Louder.*)

Nell!

(*Pause.* NAGG *sinks back into his bin, closes the lid behind him. Pause.*)

HAMM: Our revels now are ended.

(*He gropes for the dog.*)

The dog's gone.

1000 CLOV: He's not a real dog, he can't go.

HAMM: (*Groping.*) He's not there.

CLOV: He's lain down.

HAMM: Give him up to me.

(CLOV *picks up the dog and gives it to* HAMM. HAMM *holds it in his arms. Pause.* HAMM *throws away the dog.*)

Dirty brute!

(CLOV *begins to pick up the objects lying on the ground.*)

What are you doing?   1005

CLOV: Putting things in order.

(*He straightens up. Fervently.*)

I'm going to clear everything away!

(*He starts picking up again.*)

HAMM: Order!

CLOV: (*Straightening up.*) I love order. It's my dream. A world where all would be silent and still and each thing in its last 1010 place, under the last dust.

(*He starts picking up again.*)

HAMM: (*Exasperated.*) What in God's name do you think you are doing?

CLOV: (*Straightening up.*) I'm doing my best to create a little order.   1015

HAMM: Drop it!

(CLOV *drops the objects he has picked up.*)

CLOV: After all, there or elsewhere.

(*He goes towards door.*)

HAMM: (*Irritably.*) What's wrong with your feet?

CLOV: My feet?

HAMM: Tramp! Tramp!   1020

CLOV: I must have put on my boots.

HAMM: Your slippers were hurting you?

(*Pause.*)

CLOV: I'll leave you.

HAMM: No!

CLOV: What is there to keep me here?   1025

HAMM: The dialogue.

(*Pause.*)

I've got on with my story.

(*Pause.*)

I've got on with it well.

(*Pause. Irritably.*)

Ask me where I've got to.

CLOV: Oh, by the way, your story?   1030

HAMM: (*Surprised.*) What story?

CLOV: The one you've been telling yourself all your days.

HAMM: Ah you mean my chronicle?

CLOV: That's the one.

(*Pause.*)

HAMM: (*Angrily.*) Keep going, can't you, keep going!   1035

CLOV: You've got on with it, I hope.

HAMM: (*Modestly.*) Oh not very far, not very far.

(*He sighs.*)

There are days like that, one isn't inspired.

(Pause.)
    Nothing you can do about it, just wait for it to come.
(Pause.)
1040   No forcing, no forcing, it's fatal.
(Pause.)
    I've got on with it a little all the same.
(Pause.)
    Technique, you know.
(Pause. Irritably.)
    I say I've got on with it a little all the same.
CLOV: *(Admiringly.)* Well I never! In spite of everything you
1045   were able to get on with it!
HAMM: *(Modestly.)* Oh not very far, you know, not very far, but
    nevertheless, better than nothing.
CLOV: Better than nothing! Is it possible?
HAMM: I'll tell you how it goes. He comes crawling on his
1050   belly—
CLOV: Who?
HAMM: What?
CLOV: Who do you mean, he?
HAMM: Who do I mean! Yet another.
1055 CLOV: Ah him! I wasn't sure.
HAMM: Crawling on his belly, whining for bread for his brat.
    He's offered a job as gardener. Before—
(CLOV bursts out laughing.)
    What is there so funny about that?
CLOV: A job as gardener!
1060 HAMM: Is that what tickles you?
CLOV: It must be that.
HAMM: It wouldn't be the bread?
CLOV: Or the brat.

(Pause.)

HAMM: The whole thing is comical, I grant you that. What
1065   about having a good guffaw the two of us together?
CLOV: *(After reflection.)* I couldn't guffaw again today.
HAMM: *(After reflection.)* Nor I.
(Pause.)
    I continue then. Before accepting with gratitude he asks if
    he may have his little boy with him.
1070 CLOV: What age?
HAMM: Oh tiny.
CLOV: He would have climbed the trees.
HAMM: All the little odd jobs.
CLOV: And then he would have grown up.
1075 HAMM: Very likely.

(Pause.)

CLOV: Keep going, can't you, keep going!
HAMM: That's all. I stopped there.

(Pause.)

CLOV: Do you see how it goes on.
HAMM: More or less.
1080 CLOV: Will it not soon be the end?
HAMM: I'm afraid it will.
CLOV: Pah! You'll make up another.
HAMM: I don't know.

(Pause.)
    I feel rather drained.
(Pause.)
    The prolonged creative effort.   1085
(Pause.)
    If I could drag myself down to the sea! I'd make a pillow of
    sand for my head and the tide would come.
CLOV: There's no more tide.

(Pause.)

HAMM: Go and see is she dead.

(CLOV goes to bins, raises the lid of NELL's, stoops, looks into it. Pause.)

CLOV: Looks like it.   1090

(He closes the lid, straightens up. HAMM raises his toque. Pause. He puts it on again.)

HAMM: *(With his hand to his toque.)* And Nagg?

(CLOV raises lid of NAGG's bin, stoops, looks into it. Pause.)

CLOV: Doesn't look like it.

(He closes the lid, straightens up.)

HAMM: *(Letting go his toque.)* What's he doing?

(CLOV raises lid of NAGG's bin, stoops, looks into it. Pause.)

CLOV: He's crying.

(He closes lid, straightens up.)

HAMM: Then he's living.   1095
(Pause.)
    Did you ever have an instant of happiness?
CLOV: Not to my knowledge.

(Pause.)

HAMM: Bring me under the window.
(CLOV goes towards chair.)
    I want to feel the light on my face.
(CLOV pushes chair.)
    Do you remember, in the beginning, when you took me for 1100
    a turn? You used to hold the chair too high. At every step
    you nearly tipped me out.
(With senile quaver.)
    Ah great fun, we had, the two of us, great fun.
(Gloomily.)
    And then we got into the way of it.
(CLOV stops the chair under window right.)
    There already?   1105
(Pause. He tilts back his head.)
    Is it light?
CLOV: It isn't dark.
HAMM: *(Angrily.)* I'm asking you is it light.
CLOV: Yes.

(Pause.)

1110 HAMM: The curtain isn't closed?
CLOV: No.
HAMM: What window is it?
CLOV: The earth.
HAMM: I knew it!
(*Angrily.*)
1115   But there's no light there! The other!
(CLOV *pushes chair towards window left.*)
        The earth!
(CLOV *stops the chair under window left.* HAMM *tilts back his head.*)
        That's what I call light!
(*Pause.*)
        Feels like a ray of sunshine.
(*Pause.*)
        No?
1120 CLOV: No.
HAMM: It isn't a ray of sunshine I feel on my face?
CLOV: No.

(*Pause.*)

HAMM: Am I very white?
(*Pause. Angrily.*)
        I'm asking you am I very white!
1125 CLOV: Not more so than usual.

(*Pause.*)

HAMM: Open the window.
CLOV: What for?
HAMM: I want to hear the sea.
CLOV: You wouldn't hear it.
1130 HAMM: Even if you opened the window?
CLOV: No.
HAMM: Then it's not worth while opening it?
CLOV: No.
HAMM: (*Violently.*) Then open it!
(CLOV *gets up on the ladder, opens the window. Pause.*)
1135   Have you opened it?
CLOV: Yes.

(*Pause.*)

HAMM: You swear you've opened it?
CLOV: Yes.

(*Pause.*)

HAMM: Well . . . !
(*Pause.*)
1140   It must be very calm.
(*Pause. Violently.*)
        I'm asking you is it very calm!
CLOV: Yes.
HAMM: It's because there are no more navigators.
(*Pause.*)
        You haven't much conversation all of a sudden. Do you not
1145 feel well?
CLOV: I'm cold.
HAMM: What month are we?
(*Pause.*)

Close the window, we're going back.
(CLOV *closes the window, gets down, pushes the chair back to its place, remains standing behind it, head bowed.*)
        Don't stay there, you give me the shivers!
(CLOV *returns to his place beside the chair.*)
        Father!   1150
(*Pause. Louder.*)
        Father!
(*Pause.*)
        Go and see did he hear me.

(CLOV *goes to* NAGG's *bin, raises the lid, stoops. Unintelligible words.*
CLOV *straightens up.*)

CLOV: Yes.
HAMM: Both times?

(CLOV *stoops. As before.*)

CLOV: Once only.   1155
HAMM: The first time or the second?

(CLOV *stoops. As before.*)

CLOV: He doesn't know.
HAMM: It must have been the second.
CLOV: We'll never know.

(*He closes lid.*)

HAMM: Is he still crying?   1160
CLOV: No.
HAMM: The dead go fast.
(*Pause.*)
        What's he doing?
CLOV: Sucking his biscuit.
HAMM: Life goes on.   1165
(CLOV *returns to his place beside the chair.*)
        Give me a rug, I'm freezing.
CLOV: There are no more rugs.

(*Pause.*)

HAMM: Kiss me.
(*Pause.*)
        Will you not kiss me?
CLOV: No.   1170
HAMM: On the forehead.
CLOV: I won't kiss you anywhere.

(*Pause.*)

HAMM: (*Holding out his hand.*) Give me your hand at least.
(*Pause.*)
        Will you not give me your hand?
CLOV: I won't touch you.   1175

(*Pause.*)

HAMM: Give me the dog.
(CLOV *looks round for the dog.*)
        No!

CLOV: Do you not want your dog?

HAMM: No.

1180 CLOV: Then I'll leave you.

HAMM: (*Head bowed, absently.*) That's right.

(CLOV *goes to door, turns.*)

CLOV: If I don't kill that rat he'll die.

HAMM: (*As before.*) That's right.

(*Exit* CLOV. *Pause.*)

Me to play.

(*He takes out his handkerchief, unfolds it, holds it spread out before him.*)

1185　We're getting on.

(*Pause.*)

You weep, and weep, for nothing, so as not to laugh, and little by little . . . you begin to grieve.

(*He folds the handkerchief, puts it back in his pocket, raises his head.*)

All those I might have helped.

(*Pause.*)

Helped!

(*Pause.*)

1190　Saved.

(*Pause.*)

Saved!

(*Pause.*)

The place was crawling with them!

(*Pause. Violently.*)

Use your head, can't you, use your head, you're on earth, there's no cure for that!

(*Pause.*)

1195　Get out of here and love one another! Lick your neighbor as yourself!

(*Pause. Calmer.*)

When it wasn't bread they wanted it was crumpets.

(*Pause. Violently.*)

Out of my sight and back to your petting parties!

(*Pause.*)

All that, all that!

(*Pause.*)

1200　Not even a real dog!

(*Calmer.*)

The end is in the beginning and yet you go on.

(*Pause.*)

Perhaps I could go on with my story, end it and begin another.

(*Pause.*)

Perhaps I could throw myself out on the floor.

(*He pushes himself painfully off his seat, falls back again.*)

1205　Dig my nails into the cracks and drag myself forward with my fingers.

(*Pause.*)

It will be the end and there I'll be, wondering what can have brought it on and wondering what can have . . .

(*He hesitates.*)

. . . why it was so long coming.

(*Pause.*)

1210　There I'll be, in the old shelter, alone against the silence and . . .

(*He hesitates.*)

. . . the stillness. If I can hold my peace, and sit quiet, it will be all over with sound, and motion, all over and done with.

(*Pause.*)

I'll have called my father and I'll have called my . . .

(*He hesitates.*)

. . . my son. And even twice, or three times, in case they 1215 shouldn't have heard me, the first time, or the second.

(*Pause.*)

I'll say to myself, He'll come back.

(*Pause.*)

And then?

(*Pause.*)

And then?

(*Pause.*)

He couldn't, he has gone too far. 1220

(*Pause.*)

And then?

(*Pause. Very agitated.*)

All kinds of fantasies! That I'm being watched! A rat! Steps! Breath held and then . . .

(*He breathes out.*)

Then babble, babble, words, like the solitary child who turns himself into children, two, three, so as to be together, 1225 and whisper together, in the dark.

(*Pause.*)

Moment upon moment, pattering down, like the millet grains of . . .

(*He hesitates.*)

. . . that old Greek, and all life long you wait for that to mount up to a life. 1230

(*Pause. He opens his mouth to continue, renounces.*)

Ah let's get it over!

(*He whistles. Enter* CLOV *with alarm-clock. He halts beside the chair.*)

What? Neither gone nor dead?

CLOV: In spirit only.

HAMM: Which?

CLOV: Both. 1235

HAMM: Gone from me you'd be dead.

CLOV: And vice versa.

HAMM: Outside of here it's death!

(*Pause.*)

And the rat?

CLOV: He's got away. 1240

HAMM: He can't go far.

(*Pause. Anxious.*)

Eh?

CLOV: He doesn't need to go far.

(*Pause.*)

HAMM: Is it not time for my pain-killer?

CLOV: Yes. 1245

HAMM: Ah! At last! Give it to me! Quick!

(*Pause.*)

CLOV: There's no more pain-killer.

(*Pause.*)

HAMM: (*Appalled.*) Good . . . !

(Pause.)
No more pain-killer!
1250 CLOV: No more pain-killer. You'll never get any more pain-killer.

(Pause.)

HAMM: But the little round box. It was full!
CLOV: Yes. But now it's empty.

(Pause. CLOV starts to move about the room. He is looking for a place to put down the alarm-clock.)

HAMM: *(Soft.)* What'll I do?
(Pause. In a scream.)
1255   What'll I do?
(CLOV sees the picture, takes it down, stands it on the floor with its face to the wall, hangs up the alarm-clock in its place.)
What are you doing?
CLOV: Winding up.
HAMM: Look at the earth.
CLOV: Again!
1260 HAMM: Since it's calling to you.
CLOV: Is your throat sore?
(Pause.)
Would you like a lozenge?
(Pause.)
No.
(Pause.)
Pity.

(CLOV goes, humming, towards window right, halts before it, looks up at it.)

1265 HAMM: Don't sing.
CLOV: *(Turning towards HAMM.)* One hasn't the right to sing any more?
HAMM: No.
CLOV: Then how can it end?
1270 HAMM: You want it to end?
CLOV: I want to sing.
HAMM: I can't prevent you.

(Pause. CLOV turns towards window right.)

CLOV: What did I do with that steps?
(He looks around for ladder.)
You didn't see that steps?
(He sees it.)
1275   Ah, about time.
(He goes towards window left.)
Sometimes I wonder if I'm in my right mind. Then it passes over and I'm as lucid as before.
(He gets up on ladder, looks out of window.)
Christ, she's under water!
(He looks.)
How can that be?
(He pokes forward his head, his hand above his eyes.)
1280   It hasn't rained.
(He wipes the pane, looks. Pause.)
Ah what a fool I am! I'm on the wrong side!

(He gets down, takes a few steps towards window right.)
Under water!
(He goes back for ladder.)
What a fool I am!
(He carries ladder towards window right.)
Sometimes I wonder if I'm in my right senses. Then it passes off and I'm as intelligent as ever.   1285
(He sets down ladder under window right, gets up on it, looks out of window. He turns towards HAMM.)
Any particular sector you fancy? Or merely the whole thing?
HAMM: Whole thing.
CLOV: The general effect? Just a moment.

(He looks out of window. Pause.)

HAMM: Clov.   1290
CLOV: *(Absorbed.)* Mmm.
HAMM: Do you know what it is?
CLOV: *(As before.)* Mmm.
HAMM: I was never there.
(Pause.)
Clov!   1295
CLOV: *(Turning towards HAMM, exasperated.)* What is it?
HAMM: I was never there.
CLOV: Lucky for you.

(He looks out of window.)

HAMM: Absent, always. It all happened without me. I don't know what's happened.   1300
(Pause.)
Do you know what's happened?
(Pause.)
Clov!
CLOV: *(Turning towards HAMM, exasperated.)* Do you want me to look at this muckheap, yes or no?
HAMM: Answer me first.   1305
CLOV: What?
HAMM: Do you know what's happened?
CLOV: When? Where?
HAMM: *(Violently.)* When! What's happened? Use your head, can't you! What has happened?   1310
CLOV: What for Christ's sake does it matter?

(He looks out of window.)

HAMM: I don't know.

(Pause. CLOV turns towards HAMM.)

CLOV: *(Harshly.)* When old Mother Pegg asked you for oil for her lamp and you told her to get out to hell, you knew what was happening then, no?   1315
(Pause.)
You know what she died of, Mother Pegg? Of darkness.
HAMM: *(Feebly.)* I hadn't any.
CLOV: *(As before.)* Yes, you had.

(Pause.)

HAMM: Have you the glass?

1320 CLOV: No, it's clear enough as it is.
HAMM: Go and get it.

(*Pause.* CLOV *casts up his eyes, brandishes his fists. He loses balance, clutches on to the ladder. He starts to get down, halts.*)

CLOV: There's one thing I'll never understand.
(*He gets down.*)
  Why I always obey you. Can you explain that to me?
HAMM: No. . . . Perhaps it's compassion.
(*Pause.*)
1325 A kind of great compassion.
(*Pause.*)
  Oh you won't find it easy, you won't find it easy.

(*Pause.* CLOV *begins to move about the room in search of the telescope.*)

CLOV: I'm tired of our goings on, very tired.
(*He searches.*)
  You're not sitting on it?

(*He moves the chair, looks at the place where it stood, resumes his search.*)

HAMM: (*Anguished.*) Don't leave me there!
(*Angrily* CLOV *restores the chair to its place.*)
1330 Am I right in the center?
CLOV: You'd need a microscope to find this—
(*He sees the telescope.*)
  Ah, about time.

(*He picks up the telescope, gets up on the ladder, turns the telescope on the without.*)

HAMM: Give me the dog.
CLOV: (*Looking.*) Quiet!
1335 HAMM: (*Angrily.*) Give me the dog!

(CLOV *drops the telescope, clasps his hands to his head. Pause. He gets down precipitately, looks for the dog, sees it, picks it up, hastens towards* HAMM *and strikes him violently on the head with the dog.*)

CLOV: There's your dog for you!

(*The dog falls to the ground. Pause.*)

HAMM: He hit me!
CLOV: You drive me mad, I'm mad!
HAMM: If you must hit me, hit me with the axe.
(*Pause.*)
1340 Or with the gaff, hit me with the gaff. Not with the dog.
  With the gaff. Or with the axe.

(CLOV *picks up the dog and gives it to* HAMM *who takes it in his arms.*)

CLOV: (*Imploringly.*) Let's stop playing!
HAMM: Never!
(*Pause.*)
  Put me in my coffin.
1345 CLOV: There are no more coffins.
HAMM: Then let it end!
(CLOV *goes towards ladder.*)

  With a bang!
(CLOV *gets up on ladder, gets down again, looks for telescope, sees it, picks it up, gets up ladder, raises telescope.*)
  Of darkness! And me? Did anyone ever have pity on me?
CLOV: (*Lowering the telescope, turning towards* HAMM.) What?
(*Pause.*)
  Is it me you're referring to? 1350
HAMM: (*Angrily.*) An aside, ape! Did you never hear an aside before?
(*Pause.*)
  I'm warming up for my last soliloquy.
CLOV: I warn you. I'm going to look at this filth since it's an order. But it's the last time. 1355
(*He turns the telescope on the without.*)
  Let's see.
(*He moves the telescope.*)
  Nothing . . . nothing . . . good . . . good . . . nothing . . . goo—
(*He starts, lowers the telescope, examines it, turns it again on the without. Pause.*)
  Bad luck to it!
HAMM: More complications!
(CLOV *gets down.*)
  Not an underplot, I trust. 1360

(CLOV *moves ladder nearer window, gets up on it, turns telescope on the without.*)

CLOV: (*Dismayed.*) Looks like a small boy!
HAMM: (*Sarcastic.*) A small . . . boy!
CLOV: I'll go and see.
(*He gets down, drops the telescope, goes towards door, turns.*)
  I'll take the gaff.

(*He looks for the gaff, sees it, picks it up, hastens towards door.*)

HAMM: No! 1365

(CLOV *halts.*)

CLOV: No? A potential procreator?
HAMM: If he exists he'll die there or he'll come here. And if he doesn't . . .

(*Pause.*)

CLOV: You don't believe me? You think I'm inventing?

(*Pause.*)

HAMM: It's the end, Clov, we've come to the end. I don't need 1370
  you any more.

(*Pause.*)

CLOV: Lucky for you.

(*He goes towards door.*)

HAMM: Leave me the gaff.

(CLOV *gives him the gaff, goes towards door, halts, looks at alarm-clock, takes it down, looks round for a better place to put it, goes to bins, puts it on lid of* NAGG's *bin. Pause.*)

CLOV: I'll leave you.

(He goes towards door.)

1375   HAMM: Before you go . . .
(CLOV halts near door.)
    . . . say something.
CLOV: There is nothing to say.
HAMM: A few words . . . to ponder . . . in my heart.
CLOV: Your heart!
1380   HAMM: Yes.
(Pause. Forcibly.)
    Yes!
(Pause.)
    With the rest, in the end, the shadows, the murmurs, all
    the trouble, to end up with.
(Pause.)
    Clov. . . . He never spoke to me. Then, in the end, before he
1385   went, without my having asked him, he spoke to me. He
    said . . .
CLOV: *(Despairingly.)* Ah . . . !
HAMM: Something . . . from your heart.
CLOV: My heart!
1390   HAMM: A few words . . . from your heart.

(Pause.)

CLOV: *(Fixed gaze, tonelessly, towards auditorium.)* They said to
    me, That's love, yes, yes, not a doubt, now you see how—
HAMM: Articulate!
CLOV: *(As before.)* How easy it is. They said to me, That's friend-
1395   ship, yes, yes, no question, you've found it. They said to me,
    Here's the place, stop, raise your head and look at all that
    beauty. That order! They said to me, Come now, you're not
    a brute beast, think upon these things and you'll see how all
    becomes clear. And simple! They said to me, What skilled
1400   attention they get, all these dying of their wounds.
HAMM: Enough!
CLOV: *(As before.)* I say to myself—sometimes, Clov, you must
    learn to suffer better than that if you want them to weary of
    punishing you—one day. I say to myself—sometimes, Clov,
1405   you must be there better than that if you want them to let
    you go—one day. But I feel too old, and too far, to form new
    habits. Good, it'll never end, I'll never go.
(Pause.)
    Then one day, suddenly, it ends, it changes, I don't under-
    stand, it dies, or it's me, I don't understand, that either. I
1410   ask the words that remain—sleeping, waking, morning,
    evening. They have nothing to say.
(Pause.)
    I open the door of the cell and go. I am so bowed I only see
    my feet, if I open my eyes, and between my legs a little trail
    of black dust. I say to myself that the earth is extinguished,
1415   though I never saw it lit.
(Pause.)
    It's easy going.
(Pause.)
    When I fall I'll weep for happiness.

(Pause. He goes towards door.)

HAMM: Clov!
(CLOV halts, without turning.)
    Nothing.
(CLOV moves on.)
    Clov!   1420

(CLOV halts, without turning.)

CLOV: This is what we call making an exit.
HAMM: I'm obliged to you, Clov. For your services.
CLOV: *(Turning, sharply.)* Ah pardon, it's I am obliged to you.
HAMM: It's we are obliged to each other.
(Pause. CLOV goes towards door.)
    One thing more.   1425
(CLOV halts.)
    A last favor.
(Exit CLOV.)
    Cover me with the sheet.
(Long pause.)
    No? Good.
(Pause.)
    Me to play.
(Pause. Wearily.)
    Old endgame lost of old, play and lose and have done with   1430
    losing.
(Pause. More animated.)
    Let me see.
(Pause.)
    Ah yes!
*(He tries to move the chair, using the gaff as before. Enter CLOV,
dressed for the road. Panama hat, tweed coat, raincoat over his arm,
umbrella, bag. He halts by the door and stands there, impassive and
motionless, his eyes fixed on HAMM, till the end. HAMM gives up.)*
    Good.
(Pause.)
    Discard.   1435
*(He throws away the gaff, makes to throw away the dog, thinks bet-
ter of it.)*
    Take it easy.
(Pause.)
    And now?
(Pause.)
    Raise hat.
(He raises his toque.)
    Peace to our . . . arses.
(Pause.)
    And put on again.   1440
(He puts on his toque.)
    Deuce.
(Pause. He takes off his glasses.)
    Wipe.
*(He takes out his handkerchief and, without unfolding it, wipes his
glasses.)*
    And put on again.
(He puts on his glasses, puts back the handkerchief in his pocket.)
    We're coming. A few more squirms like that and I'll call.
(Pause.)
    A little poetry.   1445
(Pause.)
    You prayed—

(Pause. He corrects himself.)

You CRIED for night; it comes—

(Pause. He corrects himself.)

It FALLS: now cry in darkness.

(He repeats, chanting.)

You cried for night; it falls: now cry in darkness.

(Pause.)

1450   Nicely put, that.

(Pause.)

And now?

(Pause.)

Moments for nothing, now as always, time was never and time is over, reckoning closed and story ended.

(Pause. Narrative tone.)

If he could have his child with him. . . .

(Pause.)

1455   It was the moment I was waiting for.

(Pause.)

You don't want to abandon him? You want him to bloom while you are withering? Be there to solace your last million last moments?

(Pause.)

He doesn't realize, all he knows is hunger, and cold, and

1460   death to crown it all. But you! You ought to know what the earth is like, nowadays. Oh I put him before his responsibilities!

(Pause. Normal tone.)

Well, there we are, there I am, that's enough.

(He raises the whistle to his lips, hesitates, drops it. Pause.)

Yes, truly!

(He whistles. Pause. Louder. Pause.)

1465   Good.

(Pause.)

Father!

(Pause. Louder.)

Father!

(Pause.)

Good.

(Pause.)

We're coming.

(Pause.)

And to end up with?   1470

(Pause.)

Discard.

(He throws away the dog. He tears the whistle from his neck.)

With my compliments.

(He throws whistle towards auditorium. Pause. He sniffs. Soft.)

Clov!

(Long pause.)

No? Good.

(He takes out the handkerchief.)

Since that's the way we're playing it . . .   1475

(He unfolds handkerchief.)

. . . let's play it that way . . .

(He unfolds.)

. . . and speak no more about it . . .

(He finishes unfolding.)

. . . speak no more.

(He holds handkerchief spread out before him.)

Old stancher!

(Pause.)

You . . . remain.   1480

(Pause. He covers his face with handkerchief, lowers his arms to armrests, remains motionless.)

(Brief tableau.)

CARYL CHURCHILL

Caryl Churchill (b. 1938) was born in England and began her education in Canada during World War II; she returned to study at Oxford University, taking her B.A. in 1960. At Oxford, Churchill began her career as a playwright, producing several plays: *Downstairs* (1958), *Having a Wonderful Time* (1960), and *Early Death* (1962). During the 1960s, she wrote a series of brilliant radio plays. She also studied radical politics and returned to the theater in the 1970s with a series of striking political dramas: *Owners* (1972), *Objections to Sex and Violence* (1975), and *A Light Shining in Buckinghamshire* (1976). In the mid-1970s, Churchill began to work more closely with experimental theater companies, collaborating with actors and directors in the writing of her plays. Working with the feminist theater company Monstrous Regiment (the name alludes to the Calvinist preacher John Knox's 1558 diatribe against Queen Mary of England, "The First Blast of the Trumpet against the Monstrous Regiment of Women"), she wrote *Vinegar Tom* (1976), a play about witchcraft and sexual politics in seventeenth-century England. With the Joint Stock company, she investigated the politics of sexuality more extensively in *Cloud Nine* (1979), a pastiche of melodrama, Gilbert-and-Sullivan operetta, and modern realistic theater that uses CROSS-DRESSING and ROLE-DOUBLING to explore the relationship between colonial and sexual oppression in the nineteenth century and today. The history of gender oppression and the options for contemporary women are the subject of *Top Girls* (1982), and Churchill has continued to write challenging plays on the relationship between class, race, and gender in British social life, including *Fen* (1983), *Serious Money* (1987), and *Three More Sleepless Nights* (1995). *Mad Forest* (1990) concerns the revolution in Romania and *Skryker* (1994) was developed from Lancashire folk-tales. Churchill's most recent play, *Blue Heart* (1997), was written after Churchill collaborated on several music-theater pieces, including *Lives of the Great Poisoners* (1993) and *Hotel* (1997).

CLOUD NINE

Onstage, the most exciting and interesting device in *Cloud Nine* is its use of cross-dressing and role-doubling. In the first act, for instance, Betty must be played by a man, Joshua by a white man, and Edward by a woman. By "alienating" actors from the characters they play, Churchill clearly intends to raise the questions of gender, sexual orientation, and race as ideological issues, for in each of these cases the difference between the performer and the role marks what Clive wants to see as real. Betty is played by a man because Clive—and his patriarchal society—cannot envision women's identity; women are constructed on the model of male attitudes. Joshua is played by a white man because imperial and racist culture reduces African identity to the construction of white, European attitudes. Edward is played by a woman to express the impossibility of Edward's conforming to Clive's heterosexual standards. In all three cases, the "identity" of the character is compromised or even erased, to be filled-in and embodied by the attitudes that Clive and his society want them to hold. This performative dimension of the play's politics is echoed by the play's doubling of parts—each of the actors in act 1 takes a part in act 2, inviting the audience to draw comparisons between the two characters. Although other doubling patterns are possible, Churchill has suggested doubling Harry Bagley, the explorer, with Martin, the superficially liberated man; Clive, the father, with Cathy, the child; Betty with Edward; and so on. Doubling and cross-dressing are familiar conventions in the theater, but in *Cloud Nine* they have a specific dramatic purpose in developing the themes of the play. By denaturalizing the categories of gender, race, and sexuality, *Cloud Nine* undertakes a typically postmodern inquiry into the construction of social reality, asking what meanings are created by these categories, and how they work to structure the relationship between self and society.

AUTHOR'S NOTE

Cloud Nine was written for Joint Stock Theatre Group in 1978–79. The company's usual work method is to set up a workshop in which the writer, director and actors research a particular subject. The writer then goes away to write the play, before returning to the company for a rehearsal and rewrite period. In the case of *Cloud Nine* the workshop lasted for three weeks, the writing period for twelve, and the rehearsal for six.

The workshop for *Cloud Nine* was about sexual politics. This meant that the starting point for our research was to talk about ourselves and share our very different attitudes and experiences. We also explored stereotypes and role reversals in games and improvisations, read books and talked to other people. Though the play's situations and characters were not developed in the workshop, it draws deeply on this material, and I wouldn't have written the same play without it.

When I came to write the play, I returned to an idea that had been touched on briefly in the workshop—the parallel between colonial and sexual oppression, which Genet calls "the colonial or feminine mentality of interiorised repression." So the first act of *Cloud Nine* takes place in Victorian Africa, where Clive, the white man, imposes his ideals on his family and the natives. Betty, Clive's wife, is played by a man because she wants to be what men want her to be, and, in the same way, Joshua, the black servant, is played by a white man because he wants to be what whites want him to be. Betty does not value herself as a woman, nor does Joshua value himself as a black. Edward, Clive's son, is played by a woman for a different reason—partly to do with the stage convention of having boys played by women (Peter Pan, radio plays, etc.) and partly with highlighting the way Clive tries to impose traditional male behaviour on him. Clive struggles throughout the act to maintain the world he wants to see—a faithful wife, a manly son. Harry's homosexuality is reviled, Ellen's is invisible. Rehearsing the play for the first time, we were initially taken by how funny the first act was and then by the painfulness of the relationships—which then became more funny than when they had seemed purely farcical.

The second act is set in London in 1979—this is where I wanted the play to end up, in the changing sexuality of our own time. Betty is middle-aged, Edward and Victoria have grown up. A hundred years have passed, but for the characters only twenty-five years. There were two reasons for this. I felt the first act would be stronger set in Victorian times, at the height of colonialism, rather than in Africa during the 1950s. And when the company talked about their childhoods and the attitudes to sex and marriage that they had been given when they were young, everyone felt that they had received very conventional, almost Victorian expectations and that they had made great changes and discoveries in their lifetimes.

The first act, like the society it shows, is male dominated and firmly structured. In the second act, more energy comes from the women and the gays. The uncertainties and changes of society, and a more feminine and less authoritarian feeling, are reflected in the looser structure of the act. Betty, Edward and Victoria all change from the rigid positions they had been left in by the first act, partly because of their encounters with Gerry and Lin.

In fact, all the characters in this act change a little for the better. If men are finding it hard to keep control in the first act, they are finding it hard to let go in the second: Martin dominates Victoria, despite his declarations of sympathy for feminism, and the bitter end of colonialism is apparent in Lin's soldier brother, who dies in Northern Ireland. Betty is now played by a woman, as she gradually becomes real to herself. Cathy is played by a man, partly as a simple reversal of Edward being played by a woman, partly because the size and presence of a man on stage seemed appropriate to the emotional force of young children, and partly, as with Edward, to show more clearly the issues involved in learning what is considered correct behaviour for a girl.

It is essential for Joshua to be played by a white, Betty (I) by a man, Edward (I) by a woman, and Cathy by a man. The soldier should be played by the actor who plays Cathy. The doubling of Mrs Saunders and Ellen is not intended to make a point so much as for sheer fun—and of course to keep the company to seven in each act. The doubling can be done in any way that seems right for any particular production. The first production went Clive-Cathy, Betty-Edward, Edward-Betty, Maud-Victoria, Mrs Saunders/Ellen-Lin, Joshua-Gerry, Harry-Martin. When we did the play again, at the Royal Court in 1980, we decided to try a different doubling: Clive-Edward, Betty-Gerry, Edward-Victoria, Maud-Lin, Mrs Saunders/Ellen-Betty, Joshua-Cathy, Harry-Martin. I've a slight preference for the first way because I like seeing Clive become Cathy, and enjoy the Edward-Betty connections. Some doublings aren't practicable, but any way of doing the doubling seems to set up some interesting resonances between the two acts.

C.C. 1983

THE TEXT

The first edition of *Cloud Nine* (Pluto/Joint Stock 1979) went to press before the end of rehearsal. Further changes were made within the first week or two of production, and these were incorporated in the Pluto/Joint Stock/Royal Court edition (1980). This edition also went to press during rehearsal, so although it may include some small changes made for that production, others don't turn up till the Pluto Plays edition (1983), which also includes a few changes from the American production, a few lines cut here or reinstated there. Other changes for the American production can be found in French's American acting edition—the main ones are the position of Betty's monologue and some lines of the 'ghosts'. For the Fireside Bookclub and Methuen Inc. (1984) in America I did another brushing up, not very different from Pluto '83, and I have kept almost the same text for this edition. The scenes I tinker with most are the flogging scene and Edward's and Gerry's last scene—I no longer know what's the final version except by looking at the text.

There's a problem with the Maud and Ellen reappearances in Act Two. If Ellen is doubled with Betty, obviously only Maud can appear. Equally Maud-Betty would mean only Ellen could, though that seems a dull doubling. This text gives both Maud and Ellen. In the production at the Court in 1981 only Maud appeared and she has some extra lines so she can talk about sex as well as work; they can be found in Pluto (1983).

C.C. 1984

CLOUD NINE

Caryl Churchill

——— CHARACTERS ———

ACT ONE

CLIVE, *a colonial administrator*
BETTY, *his wife, played by a man*
JOSHUA, *his black servant, played by a white*
EDWARD, *his son, played by a woman*
VICTORIA, *his daughter, a dummy*
MAUD, *his mother-in-law*
ELLEN, *Edward's governess*
HARRY BAGLEY, *an explorer*
MRS SAUNDERS, *a widow*

ACT TWO

BETTY
EDWARD, *her son*

VICTORIA, *her daughter*
MARTIN, *Victoria's husband*
LIN
CATHY, *Lin's daughter, age 5, played by a man*
GERRY, *Edward's lover*

Except for CATHY, characters in Act Two are played by actors of their own sex.

Act One takes place in a British colony in Africa in Victorian times.

Act Two takes place in London in 1979. But for the characters it is twenty-five years later.

——— ACT ONE ———

SCENE I

Low bright sun. Verandah. Flagpole with union jack. The Family—
CLIVE, BETTY, EDWARD, VICTORIA, MAUD, ELLEN, JOSHUA

ALL: *(Sing.)*

    Come gather, sons of England, come gather in your pride.
    Now meet the world united, now face it side by side;
    Ye who the earth's wide corners, from veldt to prairie,
        roam.
    From bush and jungle muster all who call old England
        "home."
5   Then gather round for England,
    Rally to the flag,
    From North and South and East and West
    Come one and all for England!

CLIVE: This is my family. Though far from home
10   We serve the Queen wherever we may roam
    I am a father to the natives here,
    And father to my family so dear.

(He presents BETTY. She is played by a man.)

    My wife is all I dreamt a wife should be,
    And everything she is she owes to me.
15 BETTY: I live for Clive. The whole aim of my life
    Is to be what he looks for in a wife.
    I am a man's creation as you see,
    And what men want is what I want to be.

(CLIVE presents JOSHUA. He is played by a white.)

CLIVE: My boy's a jewel. Really has the knack.
20   You'd hardly notice that the fellow's black.
JOSHUA: My skin is black but oh my soul is white.
    I hate my tribe. My master is my light.
    I only live for him. As you can see,
    What white men want is what I want to be.

(CLIVE presents EDWARD. He is played by a woman.)

CLIVE: My son is young. I'm doing all I can   25
    To teach him to grow up to be a man.
EDWARD: What father wants I'd dearly like to be.
    I find it rather hard as you can see.

(CLIVE presents VICTORIA, who is a dummy, MAUD, and ELLEN.)

CLIVE: No need for any speeches by the rest.
    My daughter, mother-in-law, and governess.   30
ALL: *(Sing.)*

    O'er countless numbers she, our Queen,
    Victoria reigns supreme;
    O'er Africa's sunny plains, and o'er
    Canadian frozen stream;
    The forge of war shall weld the chains of brotherhood   35
        secure;
    So to all time in ev'ry clime our Empire shall endure.
    Then gather round for England,
    Rally to the flag,
    From North and South and East and West
    Come one and all for England!   40

(All go except BETTY. CLIVE comes.)

BETTY: Clive?
CLIVE: Betty. Joshua!

(JOSHUA comes with a drink for CLIVE.)

BETTY: I thought you would never come. The day's so long
    without you.
CLIVE: Long ride in the bush.   45
BETTY: Is anything wrong? I heard drums.
CLIVE: Nothing serious. Beauty is a damned good mare. I must
    get some new boots sent from home. These ones have never
    been right. I have a blister.
BETTY: My poor dear foot.   50
CLIVE: It's nothing.

BETTY: Oh but it's sore.

CLIVE: We are not in this country to enjoy ourselves. Must have ridden fifty miles. Spoke to three different headmen who
55 would all gladly chop off each other's heads and wear them round their waists.

BETTY: Clive!

CLIVE: Don't be squeamish, Betty, let me have my joke. And what has my little dove done today?

60 BETTY: I've read a little.

CLIVE: Good. Is it good?

BETTY: It's poetry.

CLIVE: You're so delicate and sensitive.

BETTY: And I played the piano. Shall I send for the children?

65 CLIVE: Yes, in a minute. I've a piece of news for you.

BETTY: Good news?

CLIVE: You'll certainly think it's good. A visitor.

BETTY: From home?

CLIVE: No. Well of course originally from home.

70 BETTY: Man or woman?

CLIVE: Man.

BETTY: I can't imagine.

CLIVE: Something of an explorer. Bit of a poet. Odd chap but brave as a lion. And a great admirer of yours.

75 BETTY: What do you mean? Whoever can it be?

CLIVE: With an H and a B. And does conjuring tricks for little Edward.

BETTY: That sounds like Mr Bagley.

CLIVE: Harry Bagley.

80 BETTY: He certainly doesn't admire me, Clive, what a thing to say. How could I possibly guess from that. He's hardly explored anything at all, he's just been up a river, he's done nothing at all compared to what you do. You should have said a heavy drinker and a bit of a bore.

85 CLIVE: But you like him well enough. You don't mind him coming?

BETTY: Anyone at all to break the monotony.

CLIVE: But you have your mother. You have Ellen.

BETTY: Ellen is a governess. My mother is my mother.

90 CLIVE: I hoped when she came to visit she would be company for you.

BETTY: I don't think mother is on a visit. I think she lives with us.

CLIVE: I think she does.

95 BETTY: Clive you are so good.

CLIVE: But are you bored my love?

BETTY: It's just that I miss you when you're away. We're not in this country to enjoy ourselves. If I lack society that is my form of service.

100 CLIVE: That's a brave girl. So today has been all right? No fainting? No hysteria?

BETTY: I have been very tranquil.

CLIVE: Ah what a haven of peace to come home to. The coolth, the calm, the beauty.

105 BETTY: There is one thing, Clive, if you don't mind.

CLIVE: What can I do for you, my dear?

BETTY: It's about Joshua.

CLIVE: I wouldn't leave you alone here with a quiet mind if it weren't for Joshua.

110 BETTY: Joshua doesn't like me.

CLIVE: Joshua has been my boy for eight years. He has saved my life. I have saved his life. He is devoted to me and to mine. I have said this before.

BETTY: He is rude to me. He doesn't do what I say. Speak to him.

CLIVE: Tell me what happened.   115

BETTY: He said something improper.

CLIVE: Well, what?

BETTY: I don't like to repeat it.

CLIVE: I must insist.

BETTY: I had left my book inside on the piano. I was in the 120
hammock. I asked him to fetch it.

CLIVE: And did he not fetch it?

BETTY: Yes, he did eventually.

CLIVE: And what did he say?

BETTY: Clive—   125

CLIVE: Betty.

BETTY: He said Fetch it yourself. You've got legs under that dress.

CLIVE: Joshua!

(JOSHUA comes.)

Joshua, madam says you spoke impolitely to her this afternoon. 130

JOSHUA: Sir?

CLIVE: When she asked you to pass her book from the piano.

JOSHUA: She has the book, sir.

BETTY: I have the book now, but when I told you—

CLIVE: Betty, please, let me handle this. You didn't pass it at 135
once?

JOSHUA: No sir, I made a joke first.

CLIVE: What was that?

JOSHUA: I said my legs were tired, sir. That was funny because the book was very near, it would not make my legs tired to 140
get it.

BETTY: That's not true.

JOSHUA: Did madam hear me wrong?

CLIVE: She heard something else.

JOSHUA: What was that, madam?   145

BETTY: Never mind.

CLIVE: Now Joshua, it won't do you know. Madam doesn't like that kind of joke. You must do what madam says, just do what she says and don't answer back. You know your place, Joshua. I don't have to say any more.   150

JOSHUA: No sir.

BETTY: I expect an apology.

JOSHUA: I apologise, madam.

CLIVE: There now. It won't happen again, my dear. I'm very shocked Joshua, very shocked.   155

(CLIVE winks at JOSHUA, unseen by BETTY. JOSHUA goes.)

CLIVE: I think another drink, and send for the children, and isn't that Harry riding down the hill? Wave, wave. Just in time before dark. Cuts it fine, the blighter. Always a hot-head, Harry.

BETTY: Can he see us?   160

CLIVE: Stand further forward. He'll see your white dress. There, he waved back.

BETTY: Do you think so? I wonder what he saw. Sometimes sunset is so terrifying I can't bear to look.

165 CLIVE: It makes me proud. Elsewhere in the empire the sun is
     rising.
     BETTY: Harry looks so small on the hillside.

(ELLEN comes.)

ELLEN: Shall I bring the children?
BETTY: Shall Ellen bring the children?
170 CLIVE: Delightful.
     BETTY: Yes, Ellen, make sure they're warm. The night air is de-
     ceptive. Victoria was looking pale yesterday.
     CLIVE: My love.

(MAUD comes from inside the house.)

MAUD: Are you warm enough Betty?
175 BETTY: Perfectly.
     MAUD: The night air is deceptive.
     BETTY: I'm quite warm. I'm too warm.
     MAUD: You're not getting a fever, I hope? She's not strong, you
     know, Clive. I don't know how long you'll keep her in this
180 climate.
     CLIVE: I look after Her Majesty's domains. I think you can trust
     me to look after my wife.

*(ELLEN comes carrying VICTORIA, age 2. EDWARD, age 9, lags
behind.)*

BETTY: Victoria, my pet, say good evening to papa.

(CLIVE takes VICTORIA on his knee.)

CLIVE: There's my sweet little Vicky. What have we done today?
185 BETTY: She wore Ellen's hat.
     CLIVE: Did she wear Ellen's big hat like a lady? What a pretty.
     BETTY: And Joshua gave her a piggy back. Tell papa. Horsy
     with Joshy?
     ELLEN: She's tired.
190 CLIVE: Nice Joshy played horsy. What a big strong Joshy. Did
     you have a gallop? Did you make him stop and go? Not
     very chatty tonight are we?
     BETTY: Edward, say good evening to papa.
     CLIVE: Edward my boy. Have you done your lessons well?
195 EDWARD: Yes papa.
     CLIVE: Did you go riding?
     EDWARD: Yes papa.
     CLIVE: What's that you're holding?
     BETTY: It's Victoria's doll. What are you doing with it, Edward?
200 EDWARD: Minding her.
     BETTY: Well I should give it to Ellen quickly. You don't want
     papa to see you with a doll.
     CLIVE: No, we had you with Victoria's doll once before, Edward.
     ELLEN: He's minding it for Vicky. He's not playing with it.
205 BETTY: He's not playing with it, Clive. He's minding it for
     Vicky.
     CLIVE: Ellen minds Victoria, let Ellen mind the doll.
     ELLEN: Come, give it to me.

(ELLEN takes the doll.)

EDWARD: Don't pull her about. Vicky's very fond of her. She
210 likes me to have her.

BETTY: He's a very good brother.
CLIVE: Yes, it's manly of you Edward, to take care of your little
     sister. We'll say no more about it. Tomorrow I'll take you
     riding with me and Harry Bagley. Would you like that?
EDWARD: Is he here?   215
CLIVE: He's just arrived. There Betty, take Victoria now. I must
     go and welcome Harry.

(CLIVE tosses VICTORIA to BETTY, who gives her to ELLEN.)

EDWARD: Can I come, papa?
BETTY: Is he warm enough?
EDWARD: Am I warm enough?   220
CLIVE: Never mind the women, Ned. Come and meet Harry.

(They go. The women are left. There is a silence.)

MAUD: I daresay Mr Bagley will be out all day and we'll see
     nothing of him.
BETTY: He plays the piano. Surely he will sometimes stay at
     home with us.   225
MAUD: We can't expect it. The men have their duties and we
     have ours.
BETTY: He won't have seen a piano for a year. He lives a very
     rough life.
ELLEN: Will it be exciting for you, Betty?   230
MAUD: Whatever do you mean, Ellen?
ELLEN: We don't have very much society.
BETTY: Clive is my society.
MAUD: It's time Victoria went to bed.
ELLEN: She'd like to stay up and see Mr Bagley.   235
MAUD: Mr Bagley can see her tomorrow.

(ELLEN goes.)

MAUD: You let that girl forget her place, Betty.
BETTY: Mother, she is governess to my son. I know what her
     place is. I think my friendship does her good. She is not
     very happy.   240
MAUD: Young women are never happy.
BETTY: Mother, what a thing to say.
MAUD: Then when they're older they look back and see that
     comparatively speaking they were ecstatic.
BETTY: I'm perfectly happy.   245
MAUD: You are looking very pretty tonight. You were such a
     success as a young girl. You have made a most fortunate
     marriage. I'm sure you will be an excellent hostess to Mr
     Bagley.
BETTY: I feel quite nervous at the thought of entertaining. 250
MAUD: I can always advise you if I'm asked.
BETTY: What a long time they're taking. I always seem to be
     waiting for the men.
MAUD: Betty you have to learn to be patient. I am patient. My
     mama was very patient.   255

(CLIVE approaches, supporting CAROLINE SAUNDERS.)

CLIVE: It is a pleasure. It is an honour. It is positively your duty
     to seek my help. I would be hurt, I would be insulted by
     any show of independence. Your husband would have been
     one of my dearest friends if he had lived. Betty, look who

260   has come, Mrs Saunders. She has ridden here all alone,
      amazing spirit. What will you have? Tea or something
      stronger? Let her lie down, she is overcome. Betty, you will
      know what to do.

(MRS SAUNDERS *lies down.*)

      MAUD: I knew it. I heard drums. We'll be killed in our beds.
265   CLIVE: Now, please, calm yourself.
      MAUD: I am perfectly calm. I am just outspoken. If it comes to
            being killed I shall take it as calmly as anyone.
      CLIVE: There is no cause for alarm. Mrs Saunders has been alone
            since her husband died last year, amazing spirit. Not sur-
270   prisingly, the strain has told. She has come to us as her near-
            est neighbours.
      MAUD: What happened to make her come?
      CLIVE: This is not an easy country for a woman.
      MAUD: Clive, I heard drums. We are not children.
275   CLIVE: Of course you heard drums. The tribes are constantly at
            war, if the term is not too grand to grace their squabbles.
            Not unnaturally Mrs Saunders would like the company of
            white women. The piano. Poetry.
      BETTY: We are not her nearest neighbours.
280   CLIVE: We are among her nearest neighbours and I was a dear
            friend of her late husband. She knows that she will find a
            welcome here. She will not be disappointed. She will be
            cared for.
      MAUD: Of course we will care for her.
285   BETTY: Victoria is in bed. I must go and say goodnight. Mother,
            please, you look after Mrs Saunders.
      CLIVE: Harry will be here at once.

(BETTY *goes.*)

      MAUD: How rash to go out after dark without a shawl.
      CLIVE: Amazing spirit. Drink this.
290   MRS SAUNDERS: Where am I?
      MAUD: You are quite safe.
      MRS SAUNDERS: Clive? Clive? Thank God. This is very kind.
            How do you do? I am sorry to be a nuisance. Charmed.
            Have you a gun? I have a gun.
295   CLIVE: There is no need for guns I hope. We are all friends here.
      MRS SAUNDERS: I think I will lie down again.

(HARRY BAGLEY *and* EDWARD *have approached.*)

      MAUD: Ah, here is Mr Bagley.
      EDWARD: I gave his horse some water.
      CLIVE: You don't know Mrs Saunders, do you Harry? She has at
300   present collapsed, but she is recovering thanks to the good
            offices of my wife's mother who I think you've met before.
            Betty will be along in a minute. Edward will go home to
            school shortly. He is quite a young man since you saw him.
      HARRY: I hardly knew him.
305   MAUD: What news have you for us, Mr Bagley?
      CLIVE: Do you know Mrs Saunders, Harry? Amazing spirit.
      EDWARD: Did you hardly know me?
      HARRY: Of course I knew you. I mean you have grown.
      EDWARD: What do you expect?
310   HARRY: That's quite right, people don't get smaller.
      MAUD: Edward. You should be in bed.

      EDWARD: No, I'm not tired, I'm not tired am I Uncle Harry?
      HARRY: I don't think he's tired.
      CLIVE: He is overtired. It is past his bedtime. Say goodnight.
      EDWARD: Goodnight, sir.   315
      CLIVE: And to your grandmother.
      EDWARD: Goodnight, grandmother.

(EDWARD *goes.*)

      MAUD: Shall I help Mrs Saunders indoors? I'm afraid she may
            get a chill.
      CLIVE: Shall I give her an arm?   320
      MAUD: How kind of you Clive. I think I am strong enough.

(MAUD *helps* MRS SAUNDERS *into the house.*)

      CLIVE: Not a word to alarm the women.
      HARRY: Absolutely.
      CLIVE: I did some good today I think. Kept up some alliances.
            There's a lot of affection there.   325
      HARRY: They're affectionate people. They can be very cruel of
            course.
      CLIVE: Well they are savages.
      HARRY: Very beautiful people many of them.
      CLIVE: Joshua! (*To* HARRY.) I think we should sleep with guns. 330
      HARRY: I haven't slept in a house for six months. It seems ex-
            tremely safe.

(JOSHUA *comes.*)

      CLIVE: Joshua, you will have gathered there's a spot of bother.
            Rumours of this and that. You should be armed I think.
      JOSHUA: There are many bad men, sir. I pray about it. Jesus will 335
            protect us.
      CLIVE: He will indeed and I'll also get you a weapon. Betty,
            come and keep Harry company. Look in the barn, Joshua,
            every night.

(CLIVE *and* JOSHUA *go.* BETTY *comes.*)

      HARRY: I wondered where you were.   340
      BETTY: I was singing lullabies.
      HARRY: When I think of you I always think of you with Edward
            in your lap.
      BETTY: Do you think of me sometimes then?
      HARRY: You have been thought of where no white woman has   345
            ever been thought of before.
      BETTY: It's one way of having adventures. I suppose I will never
            go in person.
      HARRY: That's up to you.
      BETTY: Of course it's not. I have duties.   350
      HARRY: Are you happy, Betty?
      BETTY: Where have you been?
      HARRY: Built a raft and went up the river. Stayed with some
            people. The king is always very good to me. They have a lot
            of skulls around the place but not white men's I think. I   355
            made up a poem one night. If I should die in this forsaken
            spot, There is a loving heart without a blot, Where I will
            live—and so on.
      BETTY: When I'm near you it's like going out into the jungle.
            It's like going up the river on a raft. It's like going out in 360
            the dark.

HARRY: And you are safety and light and peace and home.
BETTY: But I want to be dangerous.
HARRY: Clive is my friend.
365 BETTY: I am your friend.
HARRY: I don't like dangerous women.
BETTY: Is Mrs Saunders dangerous?
HARRY: Not to me. She's a bit of an old boot.

(JOSHUA comes, unobserved.)

BETTY: Am I dangerous?
370 HARRY: You are rather.
BETTY: Please like me.
HARRY: I worship you.
BETTY: Please want me.
HARRY: I don't want to want you. Of course I want you.
375 BETTY: What are we going to do?
HARRY: I should have stayed on the river. The hell with it.

(He goes to take her in his arms, she runs away into the house. HARRY stays where he is. He becomes aware of JOSHUA.)

HARRY: Who's there?
JOSHUA: Only me sir.
HARRY: Got a gun now have you?
380 JOSHUA: Yes sir.
HARRY: Where's Clive?
JOSHUA: Going round the boundaries sir.
HARRY: Have you checked there's nobody in the barns?
JOSHUA: Yes sir.
385 HARRY: Shall we go in a barn and fuck? It's not an order.
JOSHUA: That's all right, yes.

(They go off.)

SCENE II

An open space some distance from the house. MRS SAUNDERS *alone, breathless. She is carrying a riding crop.* CLIVE *arrives.*

CLIVE: Why? Why?
MRS SAUNDERS: Don't fuss, Clive, it makes you sweat.
CLIVE: Why ride off now? Sweat, you would sweat if you were in love with somebody as disgustingly capricious as you are.
5   You will be shot with poisoned arrows. You will miss the picnic. Somebody will notice I came after you.
MRS SAUNDERS: I didn't want you to come after me. I wanted to be alone.
CLIVE: You will be raped by cannibals.
10 MRS SAUNDERS: I just wanted to get out of your house.
CLIVE: My God, what women put us through. Cruel, cruel. I think you are the sort of woman who would enjoy whipping somebody. I've never met one before.
MRS SAUNDERS: Can I tell you something, Clive?
15 CLIVE: Let me tell you something first. Since you came to the house I have had an erection twenty-four hours a day except for ten minutes after the time we had intercourse.
MRS SAUNDERS: I don't think that's physically possible.
CLIVE: You are causing me appalling physical suffering. Is this
20   the way to treat a benefactor?

MRS SAUNDERS: Clive, when I came to your house the other night I came because I was afraid. The cook was going to let his whole tribe in through the window.
CLIVE: I know that, my poor sweet. Amazing—
MRS SAUNDERS: I came to you although you are not my nearest   25
neighbour—
CLIVE: Rather than to the old major of seventy-two.
MRS SAUNDERS: Because the last time he came to visit me I had to defend myself with a shotgun and I thought you would take no for an answer.   30
CLIVE: But you've already answered yes.
MRS SAUNDERS: I answered yes once. Sometimes I want to say no.
CLIVE: Women, my God. Look the picnic will start, I have to go to the picnic. Please Caroline—   35
MRS SAUNDERS: I think I will have to go back to my own house.
CLIVE: Caroline, if you were shot with poisoned arrows do you know what I'd do? I'd fuck your dead body and poison myself. Caroline, you smell amazing. You terrify me. You are dark like this continent. Mysterious. Treacherous. When   40
you rode to me through the night. When you fainted in my arms. When I came to you in your bed, when I lifted the mosquito netting, when I said let me in, let me in. Oh don't shut me out, Caroline, let me in.

(He has been caressing her feet and legs. He disappears completely under her skirt.)

MRS SAUNDERS: Please stop. I can't concentrate. I want to go   45
home. I wish I didn't enjoy the sensation because I don't like you, Clive. I do like living in your house where there's plenty of guns. But I don't like you at all. But I do like the sensation. Well I'll have it then. I'll have it, I'll have it—

(Voices are heard singing The First Noël.*)*

Don't stop. Don't stop.   50

(CLIVE comes out from under her skirt.)

CLIVE: The Christmas picnic. I came.
MRS SAUNDERS: I didn't.
CLIVE: I'm all sticky.
MRS SAUNDERS: What about me? Wait.
CLIVE: All right, are you? Come on. We mustn't be found.   55
MRS SAUNDERS: Don't go now.
CLIVE: Caroline, you are so voracious. Do let go. Tidy yourself up. There's a hair in my mouth.

(CLIVE and MRS SAUNDERS go off. BETTY and MAUD come, with JOSHUA carrying hamper.)

MAUD: I never would have thought a guinea fowl could taste so like a turkey.   60
BETTY: I had to explain to the cook three times.
MAUD: You did very well dear.

(JOSHUA sits apart with gun. EDWARD and HARRY with VICTORIA on his shoulder, singing The First Noël. *MAUD and BETTY are unpacking the hamper. CLIVE arrives separately.)*

MAUD: This tablecloth was one of my mama's.

BETTY: Uncle Harry playing horsy.
65 EDWARD: Crackers crackers.
BETTY: Not yet, Edward.
CLIVE: And now the moment we have all been waiting for.

(CLIVE *opens champagne. General acclaim.*)

CLIVE: Oh dear, stained my trousers, never mind.
EDWARD: Can I have some?
70 MAUD: Oh no Edward, not for you.
CLIVE: Give him half a glass.
MAUD: If your father says so.
CLIVE: All rise please. To Her Majesty Queen Victoria, God
    bless her, and her husband and all her dear children.
75 ALL: The Queen.
EDWARD: Crackers crackers.

(*General cracker pulling, hats.* CLIVE *and* HARRY *discuss champagne.*)

HARRY: Excellent, Clive, wherever did you get it?
CLIVE: I know a chap in French Equatorial Africa.
EDWARD: I won, I won mama.

(ELLEN *arrives.*)

80 BETTY: Give a hat to Joshua, he'd like it.

(EDWARD *takes hat to* JOSHUA. BETTY *takes a ball from the hamper
and plays catch with* ELLEN. *Murmurs of surprise and congratulations
from the men whenever they catch the ball.*)

EDWARD: Mama, don't play. You know you can't catch a ball.
BETTY: He's perfectly right. I can't throw either.

(BETTY *sits down.* ELLEN *has the ball.*)

EDWARD: Ellen, don't you play either. You're no good. You
    spoil it.

(EDWARD *takes* VICTORIA *from* HARRY *and gives her to* ELLEN. *He
takes the ball and throws it to* HARRY. HARRY, CLIVE *and* EDWARD
play ball.)

85 BETTY: Ellen come and sit with me. We'll be spectators and
    clap.

(EDWARD *misses the ball.*)

CLIVE: Butterfingers.
EDWARD: I'm not.
HARRY: Throw straight now.
90 EDWARD: I did, I did.
CLIVE: Keep your eye on the ball.
EDWARD: You can't throw.
CLIVE: Don't be a baby.
EDWARD: I'm not, throw a hard one, throw a hard one—
95 CLIVE: Butterfingers. What will Uncle Harry think of you?
EDWARD: It's your fault. You can't throw. I hate you.

(*He throws the ball wildly in the direction of* JOSHUA.)

CLIVE: Now you've lost the ball. He's lost the ball.
EDWARD: It's Joshua's fault. Joshua's butterfingers.

CLIVE: I don't think I want to play any more. Joshua, find the
    ball will you?   100
EDWARD: Yes, please play. I'll find the ball. Please play.
CLIVE: You're so silly and you can't catch. You'll be no good at
    cricket.
MAUD: Why don't we play hide and seek?
EDWARD: Because it's a baby game.   105
BETTY: You've hurt Edward's feelings.
CLIVE: A boy has no business having feelings.
HARRY: Hide and seek. I'll be it. Everybody must hide. This is
    the base, you have to get home to base.
EDWARD: Hide and seek, hide and seek.   110
HARRY: Can we persuade the ladies to join us?
MAUD: I'm playing. I love games.
BETTY: I always get found straight away.
ELLEN: Come on, Betty, do. Vicky wants to play.
EDWARD: You won't find me ever.   115

(*They all go except* CLIVE, HARRY, JOSHUA.)

HARRY: It is safe, I suppose?
CLIVE: They won't go far. This is very much my territory and
    it's broad daylight. Joshua will keep an open eye.
HARRY: Well I must give them a hundred. You don't know
    what this means to me, Clive. A chap can only go on so long   120
    alone. I can climb mountains and go down rivers, but
    what's it for? For Christmas and England and games and
    women singing. This is the empire, Clive. It's not me
    putting a flag in new lands. It's you. The empire is one big
    family. I'm one of its black sheep, Clive. And I know you   125
    think my life is rather dashing. But I want you to know I
    admire you. This is the empire, Clive, and I serve it. With
    all my heart.
CLIVE: I think that's about a hundred.
HARRY: Ready or not, here I come!   130

(*He goes.*)

CLIVE: Harry Bagley is a fine man, Joshua. You should be proud
    to know him. He will be in history books.
JOSHUA: Sir, while we are alone.
CLIVE: Joshua of course, what is it? You always have my ear.
    Any time.   135
JOSHUA: Sir, I have some information. The stable boys are not
    to be trusted. They whisper. They go out at night. They
    visit their people. Their people are not my people. I do not
    visit my people.
CLIVE: Thank you, Joshua. They certainly look after Beauty. I'll   140
    be sorry to have to replace them.
JOSHUA: They carry knives.
CLIVE: Thank you, Joshua.
JOSHUA: And, sir.
CLIVE: I appreciate this, Joshua, very much.   145
JOSHUA: Your wife.
CLIVE: Ah, yes.
JOSHUA: She also thinks Harry Bagley is a fine man.
CLIVE: Thank you, Joshua.
JOSHUA: Are you going to hide?   150
CLIVE: Yes, yes I am. Thank you. Keep your eyes open Joshua.
JOSHUA: I do, sir.

(CLIVE goes. JOSHUA goes. HARRY and BETTY race back to base.)

BETTY: I can't run, I can't run at all.
HARRY: There, I've caught you.
155 BETTY: Harry, what are we going to do?
HARRY: It's impossible, Betty.
BETTY: Shall we run away together?

(MAUD comes.)

MAUD: I give up. Don't catch me. I have been stung.
HARRY: Nothing serious I hope.
160 MAUD: I have ointment in my bag. I always carry ointment. I
shall just sit down and rest. I am too old for all this fun.
Hadn't you better be seeking, Harry?

*(HARRY goes. MAUD and BETTY are alone for some time. They don't
speak. HARRY and EDWARD race back.)*

EDWARD: I won, I won, you didn't catch me.
HARRY: Yes I did.
165 EDWARD: Mama, who was first?
BETTY: I wasn't watching. I think it was Harry.
EDWARD: It wasn't Harry. You're no good at judging. I won,
didn't I grandma?
MAUD: I expect so, since it's Christmas.
170 EDWARD: I won, Uncle Harry. I'm better than you.
BETTY: Why don't you help Uncle Harry look for the others?
EDWARD: Shall I?
HARRY: Yes, of course.
BETTY: Run along then. He's just coming.

(EDWARD goes.)

175   Harry, I shall scream.
HARRY: Ready or not, here I come.

(HARRY runs off.)

BETTY: Why don't you go back to the house, mother, and rest
your insect-bite?
MAUD: Betty, my duty is here. I don't like what I see. Clive
180   wouldn't like it, Betty. I am your mother.
BETTY: Clive gives you a home because you are my mother.

(HARRY comes back.)

HARRY: I can't find anyone else. I'm getting quite hot.
BETTY: Sit down a minute.
HARRY: I can't do that. I'm he. How's your sting?
185 MAUD: It seems to be swelling up.
BETTY: Why don't you go home and rest? Joshua will go with
you. Joshua!
HARRY: I could take you back.
MAUD: That would be charming.
190 BETTY: You can't go. You're he.

(JOSHUA comes.)

    Joshua, my mother wants to go back to the house. Will you
    go with her please.
JOSHUA: Sir told me I have to keep an eye.

BETTY: I am telling you to go back to the house. Then you can
come back here and keep an eye.   195
MAUD: Thank you Betty. I know we have our little differences,
but I always want what is best for you.

(JOSHUA and MAUD go.)

HARRY: Don't give way. Keep calm.
BETTY: I shall kill myself.
HARRY: Betty, you are a star in my sky. Without you I would   200
have no sense of direction. I need you, and I need you where
you are, I need you to be Clive's wife. I need to go up rivers
and know you are sitting here thinking of me.
BETTY: I want more than that. Is that wicked of me?
HARRY: Not wicked, Betty. Silly.   205

(EDWARD calls in the distance.)

EDWARD: Uncle Harry, where are you?
BETTY: Can't we ever be alone?
HARRY: You are a mother. And a daughter. And a wife.
BETTY: I think I shall go and hide again.

*(BETTY goes. HARRY goes. CLIVE chases MRS SAUNDERS across the
stage. EDWARD and HARRY call in the distance.)*

EDWARD: Uncle Harry!   210
HARRY: Edward!

(EDWARD comes.)

EDWARD: Uncle Harry!

(HARRY comes.)

    There you are. I haven't found anyone have you?
HARRY: I wonder where they all are.
EDWARD: Perhaps they're lost forever. Perhaps they're dead. 215
There's trouble going on isn't there, and nobody says be-
cause of not frightening the women and children.
HARRY: Yes, that's right.
EDWARD: Do you think we'll be killed in our beds?
HARRY: Not very likely.   220
EDWARD: I can't sleep at night. Can you?
HARRY: I'm not used to sleeping in a house.
EDWARD: If I'm awake at night can I come and see you? I won't
wake you up. I'll only come in if you're awake.
HARRY: You should try to sleep.   225
EDWARD: I don't mind being awake because I make up adventures. Once we were on a raft going down to the rapids.
We've lost the paddles because we used them to fight off the
crocodiles. A crocodile comes at me and I stab it again and
again and the blood is everywhere and it tips up the raft and 230
it has you by the leg and it's biting your leg right off and I
take my knife and stab it in the throat and rip open its
stomach and it lets go of you but it bites my hand but it's
dead. And I drag you onto the river bank and I'm almost
fainting with pain and we lie there in each other's arms.   235
HARRY: Have I lost my leg?
EDWARD: I forgot about the leg by then.
HARRY: Hadn't we better look for the others?
EDWARD: Wait. I've got something for you. It was in mama's
box but she never wears it.   240

(EDWARD *gives* HARRY *a necklace.*)

You don't have to wear it either but you might like it to
look at.

HARRY: It's beautiful. But you'll have to put it back.

EDWARD: I wanted to give it to you.

245   HARRY: You did. It can go back in the box. You still gave it to
me. Come on now, we have to find the others.

EDWARD: Harry, I love you.

HARRY: Yes I know. I love you too.

EDWARD: You know what we did when you were here before. I

250   want to do it again. I think about it all the time. I try to do
it to myself but it's not as good. Don't you want to any more?

HARRY: I do, but it's a sin and a crime and it's also wrong.

EDWARD: But we'll do it anyway won't we?

HARRY: Yes of course.

255   EDWARD: I wish the others would all be killed. Take it out now
and let me see it.

HARRY: No.

EDWARD: Is it big now?

HARRY: Yes.

260   EDWARD: Let me touch it.

HARRY: No.

EDWARD: Just hold me.

HARRY: When you can't sleep.

EDWARD: We'd better find the others then. Come on.

265   HARRY: Ready or not, here we come.

(*They go out with whoops and shouts.* BETTY *and* ELLEN *come.*)

BETTY: Ellen, I don't want to play any more.

ELLEN: Nor do I, Betty.

BETTY: Come and sit here with me. Oh Ellen, what will become
of me?

270   ELLEN: Betty, are you crying? Are you laughing?

BETTY: Tell me what you think of Harry Bagley.

ELLEN: He's a very fine man.

BETTY: No, Ellen, what you really think.

ELLEN: I think you think he's very handsome.

275   BETTY: And don't you think he is? Oh Ellen, you're so good and
I'm so wicked.

ELLEN: I'm not so good as you think.

(EDWARD *comes.*)

EDWARD: I've found you.

ELLEN: We're not hiding Edward.

280   EDWARD: But I found you.

ELLEN: We're not playing, Edward, now run along.

EDWARD: Come on, Ellen, do play. Come on, mama.

ELLEN: Edward, don't pull your mama like that.

BETTY: Edward, you must do what your governess says. Go and

285   play with Uncle Harry.

EDWARD: Uncle Harry!

(EDWARD *goes.*)

BETTY: Ellen, can you keep a secret?

ELLEN: Oh yes, yes please.

BETTY: I love Harry Bagley. I want to go away with him. There,

290   I've said it, it's true.

ELLEN: How do you know you love him?

BETTY: I kissed him.

ELLEN: Betty.

BETTY: He held my hand like this. Oh I want him to do it
again. I want him to stroke my hair.   295

ELLEN: Your lovely hair. Like this, Betty?

BETTY: I want him to put his arm around my waist.

ELLEN: Like this, Betty?

BETTY: Yes, oh I want him to kiss me again.

ELLEN: Like this Betty?   300

(ELLEN *kisses* BETTY.)

BETTY: Ellen, whatever are you doing? It's not a joke.

ELLEN: I'm sorry, Betty. You're so pretty. Harry Bagley doesn't
deserve you. You wouldn't really go away with him?

BETTY: Oh Ellen, you don't know what I suffer. You don't know
what love is. Everyone will hate me, but it's worth it for 305
Harry's love.

ELLEN: I don't hate you, Betty, I love you.

BETTY: Harry says we shouldn't go away. But he says he worships me.

ELLEN: I worship you Betty.   310

BETTY: Oh Ellen, you are my only friend.

(*They embrace. The others have all gathered together.* MAUD *has re-
joined the party, and* JOSHUA.)

CLIVE: Come along everyone, you mustn't miss Harry's conjuring trick.

(BETTY *and* ELLEN *go to join the others.*)

MAUD: I didn't want to spoil the fun by not being here.

HARRY: What is it that flies all over the world and is up my   315
sleeve?

(HARRY *produces a union jack from up his sleeve. General acclaim.*)

CLIVE: I think we should have some singing now. Ladies, I rely
on you to lead the way.

ELLEN: We have a surprise for you. I have taught Joshua a
Christmas carol. He has been singing it at the piano but I'm 320
sure he can sing it unaccompanied, can't you, Joshua?

JOSHUA: In the deep midwinter
                 Frosty wind made moan,
                 Earth stood hard as iron,
                 Water like a stone.   325
                 Snow had fallen snow on snow
                 Snow on snow,
                 In the deep midwinter
                 Long long ago.

                 What can I give him   330
                 Poor as I am?
                 If I were a shepherd
                 I would bring a lamb.
                 If I were a wise man
                 I would do my part   335
                 What can I give him,
                 Give my heart.

A theater which, abandoning psychology, recounts the extraordinary, stages natural conflicts, natural and subtle forces, and presents itself first of all as an exceptional power of redirection. A theater that induces trance, as the dances of Dervishes induce trance, and that addresses itself to the organism by precise instruments, by the same means as those of certain tribal music cures which we admire on records but are incapable of originating among ourselves.

There is a risk involved, but in the present circumstances I believe it is a risk worth running. I do not believe we have managed to revitalize the world we live in, and I do not believe it is worth the trouble of clinging to; but I do propose something to get us out of our marasmus, instead of continuing to complain about it, and about the boredom, inertia, and stupidity of everything.

✠ ✠ ✠

SOCIAL AND TECHNOLOGICAL CHANGE TRANSFORMED THE WORLD IN THE LATE NINE-teenth and early twentieth centuries. Between 1860 and 1999, the United States emerged from a crippling civil war and then two world wars to become a dominant global power. However, despite the nation's emergence as a major player on the world stage, the arts in the United States were shaped by divided and contradictory impulses. The desire to imitate European models competed with a desire to bring distinctively American arts into being. Even as the Civil War threatened to destroy the nation itself, writers such as Walt Whitman, Ralph Waldo Emerson, Henry David Thoreau, and others gave voice to a national literature that both incorporated and redefined European traditions. With the global expansion of U.S. influence, especially after World War I, the question of an "American culture" became a pressing one; after World War II, certain forms of culture became one of the United States' most significant exports.

In the theater, the modern era has brought with it the search for a quintessentially "American" drama, in which theme, setting, and characterization explore American experience, often by invoking and then discarding styles and attitudes derived from the European stage. In a sense, American drama in the twentieth century translates the idea of American political freedom into more abstract, metaphorical, even Romantic terms, as a conflict between individual freedom and the pressures of confining social realities such as economic hardship, social class, gender, and race. The search for an American idiom in the theater absorbs the stylistic experiments of European modernism and reshapes them, bending the formal innovation of the European theater to American issues and concerns.

The democratic experience and populist rhetoric of American public life has generally resisted the idea of a national culture emanating from a single center like New York City or Washington, D.C. For this reason, perhaps, the dream of a national theater has repeatedly failed. In the nineteenth century, westward expansion brought theater from New York, Philadelphia, and Boston to the midwestern cities of Chicago, St. Louis, and Kansas City, and then to Los Angeles and San Francisco, and to scores of smaller towns between the Mississippi and the Pacific. The theater was a widely dispersed, local affair. Towns often boasted theaters that could be used for opera, drama, or vaudeville, and that supported local companies while also catering to touring shows with stars drawn from New York and Europe. Although a lively local theater thrived throughout the country, offering melodrama, classical plays, comedies, and other entertainments, the appetite for touring shows created a demand for organizations capable of handling scheduling problems for local theaters and regional booking agencies.

In 1896 a group of theatrical entrepreneurs headed by Charles Frohman formed a nationwide organization of booking agents called the SYNDICATE. In a sense, they created the first model of how a national theater might work in the United States. The Syndicate offered theater managers a full season of touring shows—provided that the manager contracted to deal only with the Syndicate. By gaining exclusive control over theaters on key travel routes, the Syndicate thwarted competition from other touring producers and often even denied local companies the use of local theaters. At its height, the Syndicate had exclusive rights to more than 700 theaters. It could blackball non-Syndicate performers from

"THE" AMERICAN THEATER?

working by threatening producers who hired them, and it could withdraw Syndicate support from any manager who booked non-Syndicate shows or performers.

The effects of the Syndicate were profound and shaped the American theater for the next half-century. The Syndicate's grip on the theater effectively extinguished major professional theater outside New York as a source of new plays and productions; it also influenced playwriting, since the Syndicate developed plays only as commercial properties that could be successfully marketed to a general audience coast-to-coast. Although the Syndicate's power was resisted by a few famous actors and powerful producers, its approach was imitated by other groups. The parochial interests of the New York stage—where the shows of such organizations originated—became in practice the interests of the American theater, and New York became the center of theatrical production and theatrical investment. The revival of significant, professional "regional" theaters as centers of new productions—Margo Jones's Theater 47 in Dallas, the Alley Theater of Houston, the Arena Stage in Washington, D.C., the Actors Workshop of San Francisco, the Guthrie Theater in Minneapolis—had to wait until the 1940s and 1950s. The Syndicate's fortunes also point out the fallacy inherent in the notion of *an* American theater. Throughout its history, the American theater has embraced a range of dynamic and contradictory attitudes toward the stage and its place in society: New York versus the "provinces," mainstream versus elite, conventional versus experimental, commercial versus artistic. Theatrical innovation has been spurred primarily by theaters outside the commercial mainstream, especially by small, amateur "little theaters," by university and college theaters, by community theaters, and by ethnic theaters.

EUROPEAN INFLUENCE AND AMERICAN INNOVATION

The growth of American drama and theater was decisively shaped by the commercial climate of the stage, and also by the United States' isolation from the energetic traditions of European theater. Although turn-of-the-century Broadway developed a homegrown version of theatrical realism—epitomized by writer/producer David Belasco's *The Governor's Lady* (1912), which reproduced the interior of a familiar theater district restaurant onstage—European experimentation made its impact on America in more indirect ways, usually only after those experiments had crystallized into a body of theatrical practices and conventions. Many major companies toured the United States. The Abbey Theater came with John Millington Synge's *The Playboy of the Western World* in 1911–12, and the German producer Max Reinhardt brought his spectacular productions to the United States in 1912, 1914, 1924, and 1927–28. The British director Harley Granville Barker, who sponsored Shaw's plays and had gained fame as an innovative director of Shakespeare, directed in New York in 1915; the Ballets Russes toured in 1916; and the Moscow Art Theater—whose disciples Richard Boleslavsky and Maria Ouspenskaya founded the American Laboratory Theater in 1923—performed in 1923–24.

Many of these companies—the Abbey and the Moscow Art Theater in particular—had begun as small, independent, amateur theaters, and their work was most directly implemented in the United States by similar groups. Some innovation came from the new college and university programs in drama, George Pierce Baker's famous playwriting course at Harvard University in the first decades of the century (taken by Eugene O'Neill, among many others) and Montgomery T. Gregory's program for black writers and performers at Howard University in the 1920s were only the beginning of a concerted effort to bring theater and drama into the university curriculum and to develop a greater awareness of progressive theater. However, it largely fell to the LITTLE THEATER MOVEMENT to assimilate this new work and redirect it toward particularly American concerns. Innovation in the American theater came largely from these small companies, committed to mounting new and uncommercial work. The Chicago Little Theater, the Toy Theater of

Boston, the Neighborhood Playhouse and the Washington Square Playhouse of New York, and Detroit's Arts and Crafts Theater were all in operation by 1917, and the Little Negro Theater Movement was producing plays in Harlem and Washington, D.C., as well.

The Provincetown Playhouse provides a model of the "little theaters" and their fortunes in the early twentieth century. Founded in 1915 in Provincetown, Massachusetts—an artists' retreat at the tip of Cape Cod—the company was initially a group of young amateurs intent on theater, including the playwright Susan Glaspell; her husband, George Cram Cook; and, later, Eugene O'Neill. In the first year, the players produced plays in their summer homes. In 1916 they converted an old wharf building into a small theater and produced, among other plays, O'Neill's *Bound East for Cardiff*. In the autumn, the players returned to New York and opened a small theater in Greenwich Village. The company could hardly afford complex and expensive sets and turned its efforts instead toward a simple and realistic kind of performance. Eugene O'Neill's early plays were produced by the Provincetown company, and after he became a successful Broadway playwright, he continued to open many of his plays there. Like all of the "little theaters," the Provincetown had difficulty managing the transition from a small amateur company to the larger demands of a self-sustaining professional company. It went through a series of transformations before closing in 1929, having introduced O'Neill to the stage and having staged plays by John Reed, Edna St. Vincent Millay, Susan Glaspell, Djuna Barnes, Edmund Wilson, Paul Green, Wallace Stevens, Theodore Dreiser, August Strindberg, and many others.

In the United States, the freedom to make theater has always been qualified by the need to make it pay. The trials of sustaining artistic ambition in the commercial environment of the theater is the central narrative of the most innovative theatrical companies of the modern era. The ideal of an American theater remained tantalizing yet elusive and was often pursued in several ways, usually by developing a distinctive repertoire of plays, or by trying to define a typically American performance idiom. "Little theaters" like the Provincetown emphasized the production of American drama. Other theaters tried to produce American drama, the new European drama, and the classics for a larger audience than the "little theaters" could reach. The Theater Guild, for example, was organized in 1919 in New York as a subscription company specifically for the purpose of producing noncommercial plays. In the course of the next decade, the Guild staged plays by Shaw, Pirandello, Ibsen, and Strindberg, as well as plays by Americans like O'Neill and Elmer Rice. The Guild succeeded in incorporating American plays like O'Neill's *Strange Interlude* (1928) and Rice's *The Adding Machine* (1923) into the repertoire of serious modern drama and in bringing it to a significant public. However, following the stock market crash of 1929 and the economic depression that ensued, the Guild invested in a less adventuresome repertoire in the hopes of drawing a larger audience and so lost its original mission.

Although it sponsored an innovative selection of plays, the Theater Guild did not develop an original style of production. In 1931, several Guild members began a spin-off company—called simply the Group—for the purpose of investigating different kinds of drama and different approaches to performance. Eventually including Harold Clurman, Cheryl Crawford, Lee Strasberg, Elia Kazan, Sanford Meisner, and many others, the Group at first worked on plays examining the social ferment of the 1930s and the hardship of the Great Depression. Much as Chekhov became the centerpiece of Stanislavski's Moscow Art Theater, so the plays of Clifford Odets became the Group's standards: *Awake and Sing!*, *Waiting for Lefty*, and *Golden Boy*. However, the Group's most extensive contribution to the American theater was its systematic importation of Stanislavskian acting techniques. In the Group, and later in the Actors Studio, actors were trained in Stanislavski's approach to EMOTION MEMORY and GIVEN CIRCUMSTANCES, laying the groundwork for what became a distinctly "American" style of acting, acting that was emotionally spontaneous, grounded in subtext, psychologically realistic and nuanced. Nonetheless, the Group, the Studio, and the training they devised produced a generation of actors ready to meet the challenges of the burgeoning American drama of the 1940s and 1950s: Marlon Brando, Ben Gazzara, Karl Malden, Geraldine Page, Kim Stanley, Maureen Stapleton, and many others.

The impact of this acting can be seen in the great stage productions of the post-war period. The 1940s and early 1950s saw the development of a distinctively American approach to stage realism, balancing nuanced characterization with a concern for the social environment. Arthur Miller's *Death of a Salesman* and *The Crucible,* Tennessee Williams's *A Streetcar Named Desire* and *The Glass Menagerie,* and Eugene O'Neill's *The Iceman Cometh* and *Long Day's Journey into Night* demanded the subtle realism that became the hallmark of American acting and of American drama in the world repertoire. These plays—and their descendants, like the plays of Beth Henley, David Mamet, Maria Irene Fornes, August Wilson, or Sam Shepard—succeeded by criticizing American ideals and institutions while at the same time exploring the psyche of the American character. Indeed, in these plays the American character often seems to be thwarted precisely by the process of American society. The fragile beauty of Tennessee Williams's Southern belles is usually crushed by the sordid realities of modern urban life; the limitless horizon of hope that fuels the "American dream" is nearly undone by the dynamics of American racism in August Wilson's *Fences.*

POSTWAR EXPERIMENTS

After World War II, the most significant innovations in American theater have come from small "experimental" theater companies. In part through the influence of Antonin Artaud's conception of a THEATER OF CRUELTY (see Unit 5), and the several tours of Jerzy Grotowski's Lab Theater of Poland, experimental theater in the 1960s and 1970s tended to reject the esthetic of stage realism in favor of producing an immediate, quintessentially *theatrical* experience for its audiences. As a result, many productions in the 1960s and 1970s—the Living Theater's *Paradise Now,* the Performance Group's *Dionysus in 69,* the Open Theater's *The Serpent,* the work of the Bread and Puppet Theater, of the San Francisco Mime Troup, of Mabou Mines, and many others—incorporated the audience as participants in the action. Many of these experiments also led to new forms of playwriting, in which classical notions of representation also were broken down. Moreover, these experiments not only led to the incorporation of a more immediate, physical esthetic into American drama (visible, too, in performance art), but also to the exploration of Brechtian epic theater: experiments with narrative (Parks's *America Play*), with an episodic epic form (Kushner's *Angels in America*), or with a more politicized performance of "character" (Anna Deavere Smith's monologues).

Indeed, American drama continued to strike a compromise with the innovations of the European theater after World War II. Eric Bentley—a brilliant scholar, director, playwright, and translator—worked indefatigably to bring Bertolt Brecht to the attention of the American theater. Brecht became particularly important in the United States as the Vietnam War and widespread civil and social discontent spurred the theater in more agitational, political directions. Feminist theater, ethnic theater, and gay and lesbian theater have all at times availed themselves of Brecht's theater theory and practice. The work of Luis Valdez and El Teatro Campesino in California in the 1960s and 1970s is a direct extension of Brecht's sense of theater. Bringing a flatbed truck to farmworkers' strikes, Teatro Campesino produced its short, political dramas to an active, involved audience and became part of the process of social change. "Absurdist" playwrights like Samuel Beckett, Harold Pinter, and Eugène Ionesco were also both produced and imitated in the United States, influencing the work of American playwrights like Edward Albee, Maria Irene Fornes, Jack Gelber, Adrienne Kennedy, David Mamet, and Sam Shepard. Indeed, in plays like Amiri Baraka's *Dutchman* or Sam Shepard's *True West,* we can see the inflections of THEATER OF THE ABSURD in plays that are recognizably "American" in style and subject matter.

In 1935, an act of Congress established the Federal Theater Project, as a way to employ workers left unemployed by the Depression (see Aside). The Federal Theater Project also sponsored a Negro Unit, directed by John Houseman and Orson Welles, which operated in ten cities around the United States; two of its productions, an all-black *Macbeth* and *The Swing Mikado,* were among the Federal Theater's most successful productions. The fact of a separate Negro Unit points to a different crisis in the idea of an American theater. How could a theater largely in the hands of the white, Anglo, male, middle class adequately represent the diversity of the nation's experience, particularly the experience of the oppressed? As the poet and playwright Langston Hughes observed in "Notes on Commercial Theater," published in 1940, the stage had in many ways appropriated African-American culture, systematically absorbing it into its own dominant values:

> Yep, you done taken my blues and gone.
> You also took my spirituals and gone.
> You put me in Macbeth and Carmen Jones
> And all kinds of Swing Mikados
> And in everything but what's about me—
> But someday somebody'll
> Stand up and talk about me,
> And write about me—
> Black and beautiful—

Far from representing authentic black experience in America, such theater more often confirmed the discriminatory fantasies already prominent on the stage and in society. Such stereotypes as the boozy Irishman, the dull Swede, the sunny and/or murderous Italian, and the greedy Jew—appearing even in "realistic" plays like Rice's *Street Scene* (1929)—work to reinforce the "normative" perspective of dominant culture, reflecting the attitudes, behavior, and social practices that oppress such groups in the world outside the theater. It is not surprising, then, that throughout the history of the United States, ethnic theaters have played a prominent part in maintaining the cultural identity of America's minority populations: the Yiddish theater of New York, Polish theaters in Chicago, Scandinavian theaters throughout the Midwest, a thriving circuit of Spanish-language theaters shared by Mexico and Southwestern states from Texas to California, Cuban-influenced theater in Florida, and Puerto Rican theater in New York. Some of these theaters produced versions of classic European plays in their own accents, but most developed their own dramatic forms, as ways of maintaining themselves in the face of a brutally exclusive "American" culture.

The experience of slavery places African-Americans in a different position vis-à-vis the culture of the United States, and the black theater has had a profound impact on the course of the American stage. Although an African Theater Company was founded in New York in 1821—sponsoring, among others, the brilliant Shakespearean actor Ira Aldridge (1807–67) who left the United States for a distinguished career in Europe—in the main, African Americans had little direct access to the theater before the twentieth century. Black characters had long figured as stage villains and comic buffoons in American drama. Played by white actors in blackface makeup, these abusive types literally enacted white attitudes toward racial difference. "Jim Crow" was first popularized by the white song-and-dance man T. D. Rice in the 1830s, and more "sympathetic" characters, like Tom in the hugely popular stage adaptations of Harriet Beecher Stowe's *Uncle Tom's Cabin* (1832), were devised by white authors and played by white actors. The minstrel troupes that

AFRICAN-AMERICAN DRAMA AND THEATER

IF THE GROUP THEATER AND THE Actors Studio created an identifiably "American" approach to acting, the Federal Theater Project succeeded—briefly—in creating a truly national theater. An act of Congress established the Federal Theater Project in 1935 under the Works Projects Administration, with Hallie Flanagan Davis (1890–1969) as director. Like other WPA projects, the Federal Theater was designed both to employ workers idled by the Depression and to provide service to the community. It was an enormous undertaking; in New York City alone, half the theaters were closed by 1933 and half its population of actors unemployed. Given the mission of providing employment by hiring large casts and supporting personnel, and a commitment to dramatizing contemporary social issues, the Federal Theater developed its most notable genre, the Living Newspaper. Living Newspapers incorporated dialogue taken from newspapers and other public media into a series of vignettes, readings, films, and other techniques to a problem in current national and world affairs: the farm crisis in *Triple A Plowed Under* (1936), housing in *One-Third of a Nation* (1938), rural electrification in *Power* (1937). At its height, the Federal Theater had branches in forty states; these branches staged productions devised by the project's directors, using their own local resources, and often developed their own material. In 1936, for instance, a stage adaptation of Sinclair Lewis's *It Can't Happen Here*

(ASIDE)

THE FEDERAL THEATER PROJECT

opened simultaneously in twenty-one theaters around the country, including black-cast and Yiddish productions. The Federal Theater ran for four full seasons before being terminated by Congress in 1939: it financed twelve hundred productions of 830 major works, at times employing more than ten thousand people, most of whom had been unemployed. Admission to its shows was inexpensive, and in an average week five hundred thousand people saw its productions; over its four years of production, its audiences numbered more than thirty million people. In New York alone, more than twelve million people saw its productions. However, in an era of labor unrest and the pervasive fear of outside agitation, the Newspapers were seen by the Project's enemies in government—many of whom opposed the WPA altogether—as too left-wing for government support.

Despite its demise, the United State's only truly national theater had significant influence on the course of

became popular after the Civil War for depicting romanticized vignettes of plantation life were also first performed by white actors. Later, black performers—in minstrel troupes, or in the newly popular "Negro musicals"—often had little choice other than to enact these stereotypes themselves, for such roles were the only openings available on the stage (even black theaters were usually financed and operated by white entrepreneurs). Despite small inroads like the Lafayette Theater (founded in Harlem in 1915), representing black experience to America at large was almost exclusively the prerogative of white actors, producers, playwrights, and performers. In this regard, the theater—like the institutions of literature, the press, the legal system, and state and federal government—denied African Americans their own voice.

Spurred in part by successful plays by white dramatists that self-consciously attempted to "humanize" black characters for white audiences—O'Neill's *The Emperor Jones* (1920) and *All God's Chillun Got Wings* (1924), Marc Connelly's *The Green Pastures* (1930), Paul Green's *In Abraham's Bosom* (1926), and Dubose and Dorothy Heyward's *Porgy* (1920; transformed into the Gershwin musical *Porgy and Bess* in 1935)—black actors and writers became galvanized to "stand up and talk" about themselves. Throughout the 1920s the LITTLE NEGRO THEATER MOVEMENT sponsored plays of black life largely for black audiences. The Lafayette Theater, for example, opened Willis Richardson's *The Chipwoman's Fortune* in 1923; it later became the first play by a black playwright to reach Broadway. In the 1920s and 1930s, black drama increasingly addressed the politics of racism in the United States, while also depicting the effect of racism in daily life. Several organizations worked to sponsor African-

American theater and drama. Not only did the Federal Theater have huge audiences, but it brought new audiences into the theater: 65 percent of its audiences were seeing a stage play for the first time. The Living Newspapers developed a home-grown adaptation of the techniques of European experimental theater (including Brechtian epic theater) in the United States. In this sense, the Federal Theater inspired the work of several distinguished theater companies that survived its demise, notably John Houseman's (1915–85) Mercury Theater, which produced Mark Blitzstein's *The Cradle Will Rock,* and a distinguished series of productions of modern and classic plays—by Shaw, Büchner, Shakespeare, and others. In addition, the Negro Units of the Federal Theater operated in Seattle, Hartford, Philadelphia, Newark, Los Angeles, Boston, Birmingham, Raleigh, San Francisco, and Chicago, employing more than 800 people and staging seventy-five productions in the pro-

LIVING NEWSPAPER

The Federal Theater Project dramatizes news events in the New York production of 1935.

ject's four years of operation. Most importantly, the Federal Theater enabled a generation of actors, designers, directors, and playwrights to survive the Depression, and it brought the theater powerfully into the national scene.

American drama and theater. W. E. B. DuBois, a founder of the National Association for the Advancement of Colored People (NAACP), used his *Crisis* magazine—in collaboration with the National Urban League's *Opportunity*—to give a series of prizes to promising black playwrights; winners included Eulalie Spence's *Foreign Mail* (1926), Zora Neale Hurston's *Colorstruck* and *Spears* (1925), and Georgia Douglas Johnson's *Blue Blood* (1926). The NAACP also sponsored the production of plays, including Angelina Weld Grimke's influential drama of a young woman's reaction to the lynching of her father and brother, *Rachel* (1916). *Rachel* was one of the first of a series of plays about lynching. How this important genre of black theater—and a crucial element of black experience in the United States—was both overlooked and distorted by white theater is the subject of Alice Childress's brilliant play *Trouble in Mind,* which opened off-Broadway in 1955. Finally, black colleges, universities, and even high schools also became centers for a new dramatic repertoire. In 1921, Montgomery T. Gregory formed a department of Dramatic Arts at Howard University in Washington, D.C., and with Alain Locke developed an influential program in acting, playwriting, and theatrical production, offering the first institutionalized training for black writers and performers in the United States.

In a 1926 playbill for Harlem's Krigwa Players, W. E. B. DuBois described the goals of a black theater:

> The plays of a real Negro theater must be: *One: About us.* That is, they must have plots which reveal Negro life as it is. *Two: By us.* That is, they must be written by Negro authors who understand from birth and continual association just what it means to be a Negro today.

Three: For us. That is, the theater must cater primarily to Negro audiences and be supported and sustained by their entertainment and approval. *Fourth: Near us.* The theater must be in a Negro neighborhood near the mass of ordinary Negro people.

Throughout the 1930s and 1940s, African-American playwrights and actors came into increasing national prominence, both by developing DuBois's agenda and by working to bring an authentic black drama to a wider audience. Langston Hughes wrote a number of plays in the 1930s, including the well-known *Mulatto* (1935); the Federal Theater Project produced W. E. B. DuBois's *Haiti* at the Lafayette Theater; and playwrights trained at Howard were produced in New York and elsewhere. The founding of the companies like the American Negro Theater in 1939, the Negro Playwrights Company in 1940, and the Negro Ensemble Company in 1957 began to meet DuBois's charge, developing the actors, the production experience, and the financing that would sustain the explosive growth of black American drama after World War II. When Lorraine Hansberry's *A Raisin in the Sun* opened in 1959, it was the first play written by a black woman to reach Broadway, the first directed by a black director (Lloyd Richards), and the first financed predominantly by African Americans. The success of *Raisin* foretold the success of black theater in the coming decades, as black playwrights—Amiri Baraka, Adrienne Kennedy, Charles Gordone, Ed Bullins, Charles Fuller, Ntozake Shange, August Wilson, Anna Deavere Smith, Suzan-Lori Parks, and many others—came to shape the American theater.

POPULAR THEATER AND MASS CULTURE

The tension between commercial viability and dramatic achievement is perhaps best symbolized by Broadway itself, the American theater's "magnificent invalid," where even the greatest American plays can hardly compare in terms of commercial and popular success with Broadway's most uniquely American genre: the musical. Musical theater has a long history in the United States, and in many respects its fortunes parallel those of the dramatic theater. Musical theater also witnessed the tyranny of national producing syndicates, the impact of European innovation, and the powerful contributions of black and ethnic cultures. However, the integration of song and dance, orchestral music, and (usually) a romantic plot characteristic of the Broadway musical really dates to the period of World War II, probably to Richard Rodgers and Oscar Hammerstein's *Oklahoma!* (1943), which ran for 2,248 performances (*Death of a Salesman,* in contrast, ran for 742). *Oklahoma!* provided the model not only for other Rodgers and Hammerstein hits—*Carousel* (1945), *South Pacific* (1949), *The King and I* (1951)—but for other musicals as well: Alan Jay Lerner and Frederick Loewe's updating of Shaw's *Pygmalion* in *My Fair Lady* (1956), Frank Loesser's *Guys and Dolls* (1950), and Leonard Bernstein, Stephen Sondheim, and Arthur Laurents's *West Side Story* (1957). Although the form of the Broadway musical underwent significant changes in the 1970s and 1980s, its popularity points to one of the ways that the theater has sought to recapture an audience from film and television: by emphasizing the unique excitement of a dazzling live spectacle. This is as true of recent Broadway hits like *High Society* (1997), which used the Cole Porter music from the 1956 film of the same name, as it is of several musicals adapted from animated films—notably *The Lion King* (1997). The musical theater also points to the fundamental conditions of the Broadway theatrical economy as well. Musicals remain popular with producers because the huge financial investment required to mount a musical can repay much larger returns for investors than any "straight" play.

Throughout the history of the stage in the West, important theaters have succeeded both in creating innovative drama and in creating a public. However, the American theater —if there is *an* American theater—is a different entity altogether from the citizens' theater of classical Athens, the courtly theater of Racine and Molière, or even the educated circle of subscribers to Shaw's Court Theater. In a sense, this difference can be traced to the fact that the American theater first came into force only in the twentieth century, at just the moment when other dramatic media—film and television—began to compete with it. The American theater has had to define itself in the environment of modern mass culture. Not only are film and television more accessible to most people, but the technology and distribution of such mass media have fundamentally altered our understanding both of drama and performance, and of what an audience *is*. "The American theater" has always been a critical fiction, homogenizing the diversity of stage activity in the United States, writing some forms of drama—chiefly American realistic plays—into history, and writing others out of it. Today, it may be equally artificial to separate live theater from other forms of dramatic production, forms that have massively changed the terrain where dramatic performance takes place.

With the global expansion of the United States in the first two thirds of the twentieth century, the development of new modes of commerce and trade in the 1960s and 1970s (notably the multinational corporation), and especially with the breakup of the Soviet Union and its satellite states symbolized by the fall of the Berlin Wall in 1989, "American" culture has become a widely exported commodity. Much as American culture has absorbed both immigrant and conquered cultures as part of the development of the United States, so now the image of "America" is projected around the world, on T-shirts, in cartoons, in the imagery of Mickey Mouse and Michael Jordan, in television programs, in films.

Drama and theater are also part of that projected image, and American drama has rapidly become part of a global canon of modern theater: plays such as *Death of a Salesman* and *Fences* have been performed in the People's Republic of China; *Angels in America* was produced in London before it opened in New York, and has since been produced around the world. One of the most challenging aspects of American theater, however, is what might be called its *diversity*, the way different playwrights have worked to challenge a monolithic notion of "American" culture, and the values—white, masculinist, heterosexual, middle-class, English-speaking—it asserts as definitive. This diversity emerges in several ways, not only through a writer's or a company's decision to make their own alternative perspective *count*—as Luis Valdez and El Teatro Campesino do in *Los Vendidos*—but to use theatrical production to mark, make visible, "alienate" in Brecht's sense the ways the normative values of "American" culture are produced, and the kinds of work those values do.

For this reason, while there remains a large "mainstream" of stage style, much of the most adventurous work in the American theater has experimented with new, alternative ways of representing drama on the stage, and new ways of engaging its audience. The "rep and rev" of Suzan-Lori Parks's plays, the ways they "repeat and revise" a single gesture in order to highlight the *constructedness* of the body and the ways it represents itself culturally is one of these techniques; Anna Deavere Smith's effort to imitate the gestural conventions of her interview subjects does a similar kind of work, implying that those gestures are part of a common cultural repertoire, an individual act of expression that uses social means. This "alienating" of the ways "identity" is produced onstage extends to a wide range of contemporary performance. In 1983, for example, the Wooster Group's *L.S.D.—Just the High Point*s set portions of Arthur Miller's *The Crucible* as a trial, literalizing the parallel with the McCarthy hearings that the play was widely thought to allegorize; in *Routes 1 & 9,* the company integrated scenes from Thornton Wilder's *Our Town* into a blackface minstrel show, in effect staging the racist attitudes that "our town"—white America in this case—has both produced and disowned.

This use of the stage to expose dominant or oppressive attitudes that are concealed within the monuments of American culture is also characteristic of performance works

AMERICAN DRAMA IN PERFORMANCE AND HISTORY

SINCE THE MID 1960s, A VARIETY OF nondramatic performance modes have developed in Western theater that are commonly known by the generic label of "performance art." Although it is difficult to generalize about this wide range of performances, most performance art works share certain features: many (though certainly not all) are solo works, in which a performer (or performers) relates directly to an audience; although the performer(s) may be working from a plan or script, the performance is not a traditional "drama," enacting a fictitious narrative of the deeds of a fictitious "character" through "acting." Instead, in performance art, the performer uses a variety of means—monologue, physical performance, music, dance—to produce a spectacle that is "really happening" between him/herself and the spectators.

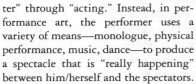

(ASIDE)

PERFORMANCE ART

Many performance-art works of the 1970s and 1980s used the performers' bodies to explore the limits of "theater." Chris Burden, for example, staged several events in which he wounded himself before an audience: in one 1970 work, he shot himself in the arm with a pistol; in another, he was crucified on top of a Volkswagen. In one of Carolee Schneeman's works, she unwinds a long scroll from her vagina, reading it to the audience. Annie Sprinkle, once a pornographic film star, openly objectifies her body onstage for a visible audience of men (and women), as she had once done in the more covert and coercive scene of pornography; in one performance, she invites the audience onstage while she conducts her own cervical examination. Many performance art works take place outside theatrical venues, so that the performance becomes part of the everyday "performance" of street life. Linda Montano spent one year connected by a short rope to Teching Tsieh; the artists'

lack of privacy was constantly on display in the streets of New York. In one of her early performances, Laurie Anderson stood on a large block of ice on a New York City street, playing her violin until the ice melted.

Several performance artists have become well-known for their monologue-performances, which range widely in technique and strategy. Anna Deavere Smith's works—such as *Fires in the Mirror: Crown Heights, Brooklyn and Other Identities* and *Twilight—Los Angeles, 1992*—differ from many performance art monologues in that Smith impersonates and represents a range of speakers; yet both in the brilliance of her individual performance, and in her effort to perform the speakers faithfully (rather than "act" them in a theatrical sense), Smith's work touches on the "authentic" aspect of performance art. This emphasis on the "authentic," the "real," enables several performance artists to explore the relationship between identity politics and performance. In *Memory Tricks,* Marga Gomez, daughter of a Cuban theater impresario and a Puerto Rican "exotic dancer," recalls her family and childhood to interrogate the formation of Latina identity in the United States. David Drake's *The Night Larry Kramer Kissed Me* dramatizes the performer's understanding and exploration of his gay sexuality from the time of his sixth birthday, on the night of the 1969 Stonewall Riots in New York's Greenwich Village—in which gay men and lesbians protested abusive treatment by the police—through the AIDS crisis of the 1980s and 1990s.

Many artists use performance to foreground and criticize the everyday racist, sexist, and/or homophobic "performance" commonly accepted as "normal behavior" in U.S. society, and to

bring into view other ways of performing identity. Adrian Piper, a light-skinned African-American woman, sometimes hands out business cards to people who "ignore" her race:

I am black. I am sure that you did not realize this when you made/ laughed at/agreed with that racist remark. In the past, I have attempted to alert white people to my racial identity in advance. Unfortunately, this invariably causes them to react to me as pushy, manipulative, or socially inappropriate. Therefore, my policy is to assume that white people do not make these remarks, even when they believe there are no black people present, and to distribute this card when they do. I regret any discomfort my presence is causing you, just as I am sure you regret the discomfort your racism is causing me.

Lesbian playwright Holly Hughes had written several plays—notably *The Well of Horniness, The Lady Dick,* and *Dress Suits for Hire,* which was performed by Peggy Shaw and Lois Weaver at the WOW Cafe—before developing her well-known performance piece *World Without End* in 1989. In *My Queer Body,* Tim Miller narrates the history of his sexual experience and the formation of his identity as a gay man; he undresses during the performance and performs part of *My Queer Body* in the nude, sometimes moving about the audience. Karen Finley's performances often express her outrage at the implicit and explicit violence against women in American culture; in monologues like *Constant State of Desire* and *We Keep Our Victims Ready,* she uses her body to enact and physicalize the "obscenity" of such violence. In a section of *We Keep Our Victims Ready* entitled "St. Valentine's Massacre," Finley examines the way patriarchal culture encodes a subtle hatred of women, one that women can self-destructively internalize. In performance, while Finley monologues, "My life is worth nothing but shit," she smears her naked body with chocolate pudding and studs it with sperm-like bean sprouts, a stunning and physical image of the sexualization of violence; as the performance continues, though, she layers herself with tinsel and red candies, transforming her abjection into a strange beauty. Such performances purposefully transgress the boundaries of decorous social behavior, in part to dramatize the kind of oppression that lurks in "everyday" performance. By all accounts, audiences who have seen Finley's or Miller's performances have found them powerful and moving; but to some critics (who often proudly claim that they have not seen the performance), such performance verges on "obscenity." In 1990, conservative politicians led by Senator Jesse Helms (R-North Carolina) pressured the National Endowment for the Arts to withdraw funding from four performance artists who had been recommended by the peer-review process for support. Not only were Tim Miller, Karen Finley, Holly Hughes, and John Fleck denied funding, but the Endowment's head, John Frohnmayer, subsequently resigned, and a "general standards of decency" restriction of dubious constitutionality was required of subsequent recipients of NEA support.

Perhaps the best-known autobiographical performer, however, is Spalding Gray. Gray began his career with The Performance Group, an avant-garde company working with **ENVIRONMENTAL THEATER** in the late 1960s and 1970s. With Elizabeth LeCompte and other members of the group, Gray collaborated on a series of performances, collectively called *The Rhode Island Trilogy—Sakonnet Point* (1975), *Rumstick Road* (1977), and *Nyatt School* (1978), followed by an epilogue, *Point Judith* (1979). The Performance Group was committed to authentic "performance" (in which the actors behave as themselves, rather than "acting" in a theatrical sense), and Gray found a sequence of *Rumstick Road*—in which he narrated events of his life to the audience—to be a particularly fertile ground for contin-

PERFORMANCE ART

Anna Deavere Smith portrays Angela King at the world premier of Smith's Twilight—Los Angeles, 1992.

ued exploration. In the course of the next several years, Gray developed a series of autobiographical performances. In some of these works, Gray structures a certain degree of randomness in the performance: in *India and After (America)* (1979), for example, he randomly chooses words from a dictionary to key part of his monologue; in *A Personal History of the American Theatre* (1980), he shuffles a collection of index cards with play titles on them and uses the series to direct his performance. Gray's more recent work has been made into films, and so has become known to a wider audience. The film versions of *Swimming to Cambodia* (1984) and *Monster in a Box* (1990) preserve much of the ambience of Gray's performance. In the opening sequence of *Swimming to*

Cambodia, for example, we see Gray walking through the streets of the Village, entering the Performance Garage, seating himself onstage at a long table, and opening the notebook that seems to provide the score for his performance. Gray addresses the camera and, as in his stage performances, seems to occupy a startling and fascinating middle ground between acting and being: he is clearly shaping the story, representing and constructing the narrative of his life as a kind of fiction, while at the same time claiming that quasi-fictive narrative as his own, as himself. Like other postmodern art forms, performance art evocatively explores the edge between representation and "reality," refusing to demarcate a fixed difference between them.

like Coco Fusco and Guillermo Gómez-Peña's *Two Undiscovered Amerindians Visit . . . ,* (which has been filmed as *The Couple in the Cage*). In the early 1990s, Gómez-Peña (a performance artist born in Mexico) and Fusco (a Cuban-American) devised a performance in which they portrayed "native" or "indigenous" inhabitants of the (fictitious) Carribean island of Guatinaui. Wearing deeply layered costumes—basketball sneakers, feathered headdresses, sunglasses, bottle-cap–studded vests—Fusco and Gómez-Peña were displayed in a cage, as anthropological "discoveries." During the course of the performance, which was produced in several art museums around the United States, as well as in the Field Museum of Natural History in Chicago, and on a plaza in Madrid, Gómez-Peña and Fusco exhibited behavior: they watched TV, they ate, for a fee they had their photo taken with spectators, or danced, and so on. The purpose of the production, however, was less to portray an exoticized native "other," than it was to *stage* the attitudes of their audiences to the spectacle of these imprisoned, displayed people. Although we might think this an extreme or at least a special case, it might be said that what Gómez-Peña and Fusco did here—stage the audience—is a task that stretches back to Valdez's work in the 1960s, and has become one of the principal innovations of contemporary American performance.

SUSAN GLASPELL

Susan Glaspell (1882–1948) was born in Iowa, studied at Drake University in Des Moines and at the University of Chicago, and then briefly pursued a career as a journalist. With her husband, George Cram Cook, she founded the Provincetown Playhouse and wrote many of the plays it produced: *Suppressed Desires* (1914, written with Cook), a spoof of the vogue for psychoanalysis among New York's intellectual elite; *Trifles* (1916); *Close the Book* (1917); *A Woman's Honor* (1918); and *Tickless Time* (1918, again written with Cook). After the reorganization of the Provincetown in 1921, Glaspell wrote a series of full-length, often experimental, plays: *Inheritors* (1920), *The Verge* (1921), and *Alison's House* (1930). *Alison's House,* based loosely on the life of Emily Dickinson and her family, won Glaspell the Pulitzer Prize in 1930. Glaspell then retired from playwriting and largely from the theater as well, returning briefly to serve as the director of the Mid-West Play Bureau for the Federal Theater Project.

TRIFLES

Trifles is an important play in the development of American realism. It poses a distinct contrast to Eugene O'Neill's early plays, with which it shared the Provincetown stage. O'Neill's realistic plays attempt to filter an abstract, metaphysical longing into the drab world of his down-and-out drifters and sailors. Glaspell's drama more directly examines the values and behavior of the society she brings to the stage. In *Trifles*—and in the short story "A Jury of Her Peers," which she adapted from the play the following year—Glaspell considers the relationship between truth, power, and gender. The play is a murder mystery. A local man, John Wright, has been found dead, and his wife, Minnie, is suspected of killing him. Called to investigate, County Attorney George Henderson, Sheriff Henry Peters, and neighbor Lewis Hale readily assume a masculine prerogative to discover the truth of John Wright's murder, telling their wives to remain in the kitchen out of the way. However, the truth of the crime is in fact concealed *in* the kitchen, and only the women are able to discover it. Glaspell shows the audience that the "trifles" of the women's world are the signs of a reality wholly unreadable to the men, precisely because it is a world they regard as feminine, and therefore unimportant and uninteresting. *Trifles,* that is, works to subvert out notions of reality and truth by suggesting how such ideas are constructed within a specific social order—the masculine order of modern society.

TRIFLES

A PLAY IN ONE ACT
Susan Glaspell

——— **CHARACTERS** ———

COUNTY ATTORNEY, *George Henderson*
SHERIFF, *Henry Peters*
LEWIS HALE, *A Neighboring Farmer*
MRS. PETERS

MRS. HALE

THE SETTING: *The kitchen in the now abandoned farmhouse of John Wright*

SCENE: *The kitchen in the now abandoned farmhouse of John Wright, a gloomy kitchen, and left without having been put in order— unwashed pans under the sink, a loaf of bread outside the breadbox, a dish towel on the table—other signs of incompleted work. At the rear the outer door opens and the* SHERIFF *comes in followed by the* COUNTY ATTORNEY *and* HALE. *The* SHERIFF *and* HALE *are men in middle life, the* COUNTY ATTORNEY *is a young man; all are much bundled up and go at once to the stove. They are followed by the two women—the* SHERIFF's *wife first; she is a slight wiry woman, a thin nervous face.* MRS. HALE *is larger and would ordinarily be called more comfortable looking, but she is disturbed now and looks fearfully about as she enters. The women have come in slowly, and stand close together near the door.*

COUNTY ATTORNEY: (*Rubbing his hands.*) This feels good. Come up to the fire, ladies.

MRS. PETERS: (*After taking a step forward.*) I'm not—cold.

SHERIFF: (*Unbuttoning his overcoat and stepping away from the stove*
5 *as if to mark the beginning of official business.*) Now, Mr. Hale, before we move things about, you explain to Mr. Henderson just what you saw when you came here yesterday morning.

COUNTY ATTORNEY: By the way, has anything been moved?
10 Are things just as you left them yesterday?

SHERIFF: (*Looking about.*) It's just the same. When it dropped below zero last night I thought I'd better send Frank out this morning to make a fire for us—no use getting pneumonia with a big case on, but I told him not to touch any-
15 thing except the stove—and you know Frank.

COUNTY ATTORNEY: Somebody should have been left here yesterday.

SHERIFF: Oh—yesterday. When I had to send Frank to Morris Center for that man who went crazy—I want you to know
20 I had my hands full yesterday, I knew you could get back from Omaha by today and as long as I went over everything here myself—

COUNTY ATTORNEY: Well, Mr. Hale, tell just what happened when you came here yesterday morning.

25 HALE: Harry and I had started to town with a load of potatoes. We came along the road from my place and as I got here I said, "I'm going to see if I can't get John Wright to go in with me on a party telephone." I spoke to Wright about it once before and he put me off, saying folks talked too much
30 anyway, and all he asked was peace and quiet—I guess you know about how much he talked himself; but I thought maybe if I went to the house and talked about it before his wife, though I said to Harry that I didn't know as what his wife wanted made much difference to John—

COUNTY ATTORNEY: Let's talk about that later, Mr. Hale. I do 35 want to talk about that, but tell now just what happened when you got to the house.

HALE: I didn't hear or see anything; I knocked at the door, and still it was all quiet inside. I knew they must be up, it was past eight o'clock. So I knocked again, and I thought I 40 heard somebody say, "Come in." I wasn't sure, I'm not sure yet, but I opened the door—this door (*Indicating the door by which the two women are still standing.*) and there in that rocker—(*Pointing to it.*) sat Mrs. Wright.

(*They all look at the rocker.*)

COUNTY ATTORNEY: What—was she doing? 45

HALE: She was rockin' back and forth. She had her apron in her hand and was kind of—pleating it.

COUNTY ATTORNEY: And how did she—look?

HALE: Well, she looked queer.

COUNTY ATTORNEY: How do you mean—queer? 50

HALE: Well, as if she didn't know what she was going to do next. And kind of done up.

COUNTY ATTORNEY: How did she seem to feel about your coming?

HALE: Why, I don't think she minded—one way or other. She didn't pay much attention. I said, "How do, Mrs. Wright, 55 it's cold, ain't it?" And she said, "Is it?"—and went on kind of pleating at her apron. Well, I was surprised; she didn't ask me to come up to the stove, or to set down, but just sat there, not even looking at me, so I said, "I want to see John." And then she—laughed. I guess you would call it a 60 laugh. I thought of Harry and the team outside, so I said a little sharp: "Can't I see John?" "No," she says, kind o' dull like. "Ain't he home?" says I. "Yes," says she, "he's home." "Then why can't I see him?" I asked her, out of patience. "'Cause he's dead," says she. "*Dead?*" says I. She just nodded 65 her head, not getting a bit excited, but rockin' back and forth. "Why—where is he?" says I, not knowing what to say. She just pointed upstairs—like that (*Himself pointing to the room above.*) I got up, with the idea of going up there. I walked from there to here—then I says, "Why, what did he 70 die of?" "He died of a rope round his neck," says she, and just went on pleatin' at her apron. Well, I went out and called Harry. I thought I might—need help. We went upstairs and there he was lyin'—

COUNTY ATTORNEY: I think I'd rather have you go into that up- 75 stairs, where you can point it all out. Just go on now with the rest of the story.

HALE: Well, my first thought was to get that rope off. It looked . . . (*Stops, his face twitches.*) . . . but Harry, he went up to

632

80   him, and he said, "No, he's dead all right, and we'd better
     not touch anything." So we went back down stairs. She was
     still sitting that same way. "Has anybody been notified?" I
     asked. "No," says she, unconcerned. "Who did this, Mrs.
     Wright?" said Harry. He said it businesslike—and she
85   stopped pleatin' of her apron. "I don't know," she says. "You
     don't *know?*" says Harry. "No," says she. "Weren't you
     sleepin' in the bed with him?" says Harry. "Yes," says she,
     "but I was on the inside." "Somebody slipped a rope round
     his neck and strangled him and you didn't wake up?" says
90   Harry. "I didn't wake up," she said after him. We must 'a
     looked as if we didn't see how that could be, for after a
     minute she said, "I sleep sound." Harry was going to ask
     her more questions but I said maybe we ought to let her tell
     her story first to the coroner, or the sheriff, so Harry went
95   fast as he could to Rivers' place, where there's a telephone.
COUNTY ATTORNEY: And what did Mrs. Wright do when you
     knew that you had gone for the coroner?
HALE: She moved from that chair to this one over here (*Point-
     ing to a small chair in the corner.*) and just sat there with her
100 hands held together and looking down. I got a feeling that
     I ought to make some conversation, so I said I had come in
     to see if John wanted to put in a telephone, and at that she
     started to laugh, and then she stopped and looked at me—
     scared. (*The* COUNTY ATTORNEY, *who has had his notebook out,
105 makes a note.*) I dunno, maybe it wasn't scared. I wouldn't
     like to say it was. Soon Harry got back, and then Dr. Lloyd
     came, and you, Mr. Peters, and so I guess that's all I know
     that you don't.
COUNTY ATTORNEY: (*Looking around.*) I guess we'll go upstairs
110 first—and then out to the barn and around there. (*To the*
     SHERIFF.) You're convinced that there was nothing impor-
     tant here—nothing that would point to any motive.
SHERIFF: Nothing here but kitchen things.

(*The* COUNTY ATTORNEY *after again looking around the kitchen,
opens the door of a cupboard closet. He gets up on a chair and looks on
a shelf. Pulls his hand away, sticky.*)

COUNTY ATTORNEY: Here's a nice mess.

(*The women draw nearer.*)

115 MRS. PETERS: (*To the other woman.*) Oh, her fruit; it did freeze.
     (*To the* COUNTY ATTORNEY.) She worried about that when it
     turned so cold. She said the fire'd go out and her jars would
     break.
SHERIFF: Well, can you beat the women! Held for murder and
120 worryin' about her preserves.
COUNTY ATTORNEY: I guess before we're through she may have
     something more serious than preserves to worry about.
HALE: Well, women are used to worrying over trifles.

(*The two women move a little closer together.*)

COUNTY ATTORNEY: (*With the gallantry of a young politician.*)
125 And yet, for all their worries, what would we do without
     the ladies? (*The women do not unbend. He goes to the sink, takes
     a dipperful of water from the pail and pouring it into a basin,
     washes his hands. Starts to wipe them on the roller towel, turns it
     for a cleaner place.*) Dirty towels! (*Kicks his foot against the pans*

under the sink.) Not much of a housekeeper, would you say,   130
ladies?
MRS. HALE: (*Stiffly.*) There's a great deal of work to be done on
     a farm.
COUNTY ATTORNEY: To be sure. And yet (*With a little bow to her.*)
     I know there are some Dickson county farmhouses which do   135
     not have such roller towels.

(*He gives it a pull to expose its full length again.*)

MRS. HALE: Those towels get dirty awful quick. Men's hands
     aren't always as clean as they might be.
COUNTY ATTORNEY: Ah, loyal to your sex, I see. But you and
     Mrs. Wright were neighbors. I suppose you were friends,   140
     too.
MRS. HALE: (*Shaking her head.*) I've not seen much of her of late
     years. I've not been in this house—it's more than a year.
COUNTY ATTORNEY: And why was that? You didn't like her?
MRS. HALE: I liked her all well enough. Farmers' wives have   145
     their hands full, Mr. Henderson. And then—
COUNTY ATTORNEY: Yes—?
MRS. HALE: (*Looking about.*) It never seemed a very cheerful place.
COUNTY ATTORNEY: No—it's not cheerful. I shouldn't say she
     had the homemaking instinct.   150
MRS. HALE: Well, I don't know as Wright had, either.
COUNTY ATTORNEY: You mean that they didn't get on very well?
MRS. HALE: No, I don't mean anything. But I don't think a
     place'd be any cheerfuller for John Wright's being in it.
COUNTY ATTORNEY: I'd like to talk more of that a little later. I   155
     want to get the lay of things upstairs now.

(*He goes to the left, where three steps lead to a stair door.*)

SHERIFF: I suppose anything Mrs. Peters does'll be all right. She
     was to take in some clothes for her, you know, and a few lit-
     tle things. We left in such a hurry yesterday.
COUNTY ATTORNEY: Yes, but I would like to see what you take,   160
     Mrs. Peters, and keep an eye out for anything that might be
     of use to us.
MRS. PETERS: Yes, Mr. Henderson.

(*The women listen to the men's steps on the stairs, then look about
the kitchen.*)

MRS. HALE: I'd hate to have men coming into my kitchen,
     snooping around and criticising.   165

(*She arranges the pans under sink which the* COUNTY ATTORNEY *had
shoved out of place.*)

MRS. PETERS: Of course it's no more than their duty.
MRS. HALE: Duty's all right, but I guess that deputy sheriff that
     came out to make the fire might have got a little of this on.
     (*Gives the roller towel a pull.*) Wish I'd thought of that
     sooner. Seems mean to talk about her for not having things   170
     slicked up when she had to come away in such a hurry.
MRS. PETERS: (*Who has gone to a small table in the left rear corner of
     the room, and lifted one end of a towel that covers a pan.*) She had
     bread set.

(*Stands still.*)

175 MRS. HALE: (*Eyes fixed on a loaf of bread beside the breadbox, which is on a low shelf at the other side of the room. Moves slowly toward it.*) She was going to put this in there. (*Picks up loaf, then abruptly drops it. In a manner of returning to familiar things.*) It's a shame about her fruit. I wonder if it's all gone. (*Gets*

180 *up on the chair and looks.*) I think there's some here that's all right, Mrs. Peters. Yes—here; (*Holding it toward the window.*) this is cherries, too. (*Looking again.*) I declare I believe that's the only one. (*Gets down, bottle in her hand. Goes to the sink and wipes it off on the outside.*) She'll feel awful bad after

185 all her hard work in the hot weather. I remember the afternoon I put up my cherries last summer.

(*She puts the bottle on the big kitchen table, center of the room. With a sigh, is about to sit down in the rocking-chair. Before she is seated realizes what chair it is; with a slow look at it, steps back. The chair which she has touched rocks back and forth.*)

MRS. PETERS: Well, I must get those things from the front room closet. (*She goes to the door at the right, but after looking into the other room, steps back.*) You coming with me, Mrs. Hale? You

190 could help me carry them.

(*They go in the other room; reappear,* MRS. PETERS *carrying a dress and skirt,* MRS. HALE *following with a pair of shoes.*)

MRS. PETERS: My, it's cold in there.

(*She puts the clothes on the big table, and hurries to the stove.*)

MRS. HALE: (*Examining the skirt.*) Wright was close. I think maybe that's why she kept so much to herself. She didn't even belong to the Ladies Aid. I suppose she felt she couldn't do

195 her part, and then you don't enjoy things when you feel shabby. She used to wear pretty clothes and be lively, when she was Minnie Foster, one of the town girls singing in the choir. But that—oh, that was thirty years ago. This all you was to take in?

200 MRS. PETERS: She said she wanted an apron. Funny thing to want, for there isn't much to get you dirty in jail, goodness knows. But I suppose just to make her feel more natural. She said they was in the top drawer in this cupboard. Yes, here. And then her little shawl that always hung behind the

205 door. (*Opens stair door and looks.*) Yes, here it is.

(*Quickly shuts door leading upstairs.*)

MRS. HALE: (*Abruptly moving toward her.*) Mrs. Peters?
MRS. PETERS: Yes, Mrs. Hale?
MRS. HALE: Do you think she did it?
MRS. PETERS: (*In a frightened voice.*) Oh, I don't know.
210 MRS. HALE: Well, I don't think she did. Asking for an apron and her little shawl. Worrying about her fruit.
MRS. PETERS: (*Starts to speak, glances up, where footsteps are heard in the room above. In a low voice.*) Mr. Peters says it looks bad for her. Mr. Henderson is awful sarcastic in a speech and he'll
215 make fun of her sayin' she didn't wake up.
MRS. HALE: Well, I guess John Wright didn't wake when they was slipping that rope under his neck.
MRS. PETERS: No, it's strange. It must have been done awful crafty and still. They say it was such a—funny way to kill a
220 man, rigging it all up like that.

MRS. HALE: That's just what Mr. Hale said. There was a gun in the house. He says that's what he can't understand.
MRS. PETERS: Mr. Henderson said coming out that what was needed for the case was a motive; something to show anger, or—sudden feeling. 225
MRS. HALE: (*Who is standing by the table.*) Well, I don't see any signs of anger around here. (*She puts her hand on the dish towel which lies on the table, stands looking down at table, one half of which is clean, the other half messy.*) It's wiped to here. (*Makes a move as if to finish work, then turns and looks at loaf of bread* 230 *outside the breadbox. Drops towel. In that voice of coming back to familiar things.*) Wonder how they are finding things upstairs. I hope she had it a little more red-up up there. You know, it seems kind of *sneaking.* Locking her up in town and then coming out here and trying to get her own house to 235 turn against her!
MRS. PETERS: But Mrs. Hale, the law is the law.
MRS. HALE: I s'pose 'tis. (*Unbuttoning her coat.*) Better loosen up your things, Mrs. Peters. You won't feel them when you go out. 240

(MRS. PETERS *takes off her fur tippet, goes to hang it on hook at back of room, stands looking at the under part of the small corner table.*)

MRS. PETERS: She was piecing a quilt.

(*She brings the large sewing basket and they look at the bright pieces.*)

MRS. HALE: It's log cabin pattern. Pretty, isn't it? I wonder if she was goin' to quilt it or just knot it?

(*Footsteps have been heard coming down the stairs. The* SHERIFF *enters followed by* HALE *and the* COUNTY ATTORNEY.)

SHERIFF: They wonder if she was going to quilt it or just knot it!

(*The men laugh; the women look abashed.*)

COUNTY ATTORNEY: (*Rubbing his hands over the stove.*) Frank's fire 245 didn't do much up there, did it? Well, let's go out to the barn and get that cleared up.

(*The men go outside.*)

MRS. HALE: (*Resentfully.*) I don't know as there's anything so strange, our takin' up our time with little things while we're waiting for them to get the evidence. (*She sits down at* 250 *the big table smoothing out a block with decision.*) I don't see as it's anything to laugh about.
MRS. PETERS: (*Apologetically.*) Of course they've got awful important things on their minds.

(*Pulls up a chair and joins* MRS. HALE *at the table.*)

MRS. HALE: (*Examining another block.*) Mrs. Peters, look at this 255 one. Here, this is the one she was working on, and look at that sewing! All the rest of it has been so nice and even. And look at this! It's all over the place! Why, it looks as if she didn't know what she was about!

(*After she has said this they look at each other, then start to glance back at the door. After an instant* MRS. HALE *has pulled at a knot and ripped the sewing.*)

260 MRS. PETERS: Oh, what are you doing, Mrs. Hale?

MRS. HALE: (*Mildly.*) Just pulling out a stitch or two that's not sewed very good. (*Threading a needle.*) Bad sewing always made me fidgety.

MRS. PETERS: (*Nervously.*) I don't think we ought to touch things.

265 MRS. HALE: I'll just finish up this end. (*Suddenly stopping and leaning forward.*) Mrs. Peters?

MRS. PETERS: Yes, Mrs. Hale?

MRS. HALE: What do you suppose she was so nervous about?

MRS. PETERS: Oh—I don't know. I don't know as she was ner-
270 vous. I sometimes sew awful queer when I'm just tired. (MRS. HALE *starts to say something, looks at* MRS. PETERS, *then goes on sewing.*) Well, I must get these things wrapped up. They may be through sooner than we think. (*Putting apron and other things together.*) I wonder where I can find a piece of
275 paper, and string.

MRS. HALE: In that cupboard, maybe.

MRS. PETERS: (*Looking in cupboard.*) Why, here's a birdcage. (*Holds it up.*) Did she have a bird, Mrs. Hale?

MRS. HALE: Why, I don't know whether she did or not—I've
280 not been here for so long. There was a man around last year selling canaries cheap, but I don't know as she took one; maybe she did. She used to sing real pretty herself.

MRS. PETERS: (*Glancing around.*) Seems funny to think of a bird here. But she must have had one, or why would she have a
285 cage? I wonder what happened to it.

MRS. HALE: I s'pose maybe the cat got it.

MRS. PETERS: No, she didn't have a cat. She's got that feeling some people have about cats—being afraid of them. My cat got in her room and she was real upset and asked me to take it out.

290 MRS. HALE: My sister Bessie was like that. Queer, ain't it?

MRS. PETERS: (*Examining the cage.*) Why, look at this door. It's broke. One hinge is pulled apart.

MRS. HALE: (*Looking too.*) Looks as if someone must have been rough with it.

295 MRS. PETERS: Why, yes.

(*She brings the cage forward and puts it on the table.*)

MRS. HALE: I wish if they're going to find any evidence they'd be about it. I don't like this place.

MRS. PETERS: But I'm awful glad you came with me, Mrs. Hale. It would be lonesome for me sitting here alone.

300 MRS. HALE: It would, wouldn't it? (*Dropping her sewing.*) But I tell you what I do wish, Mrs. Peters. I wish I had come over sometimes when *she* was here. I—(*Looking around the room.*)—wish I had.

MRS. PETERS: But of course you were awful busy, Mrs. Hale—
305 your house and your children.

MRS. HALE: I could've come. I stayed away because it weren't cheerful—and that's why I ought to have come. I—I've never liked this place. Maybe because it's down in a hollow and you don't see the road. I dunno what it is, but it's a
310 lonesome place and always was. I wish I had come over to see Minnie Foster sometimes. I can see now—

(*Shakes her head.*)

MRS. PETERS: Well you mustn't reproach yourself, Mrs. Hale. Somehow we just don't see how it is with other folks until—something comes up.

MRS. HALE: Not having children makes less work—but it 315 makes a quiet house, and Wright out to work all day, and no company when he did come in. Did you know John Wright, Mrs. Peters?

MRS. PETERS: Not to know him; I've seen him in town. They say he was a good man. 320

MRS. HALE: Yes—good; he didn't drink, and kept his word as well as most, I guess, and paid his debts. But he was a hard man, Mrs. Peters. Just to pass the time of day with him—(*Shivers.*) Like a raw wind that gets to the bone. (*Pauses, her eye falling on the cage.*) I should think she would 'a wanted a 325 bird. But what do you suppose went with it?

MRS. PETERS: I don't know, unless it got sick and died.

(*She reaches over and swings the broken door, swings it again. Both women watch it.*)

MRS. HALE: You weren't raised round here, were you? (MRS. PETERS *shakes her head.*) You didn't know—her?

MRS. PETERS: Not till they brought her yesterday. 330

MRS. HALE: She—come to think of it, she was kind of like a bird herself—real sweet and pretty, but kind of timid and—fluttery. How—she—did—change. (*Silence; then as if struck by a happy thought and relieved to get back to every day things.*) Tell you what, Mrs. Peters, why don't you take the quilt in 335 with you? It might take up her mind.

MRS. PETERS: Why, I think that's a real nice idea, Mrs. Hale. There couldn't possibly be any objection to it, could there? Now, just what would I take? I wonder if her patches are in here—and her things. 340

(*They look in the sewing basket.*)

MRS. HALE: Here's some red. I expect this has got sewing things in it. (*Brings out a fancy box.*) What a pretty box. Looks like something somebody would give you. Maybe her scissors are in here. (*Opens box. Suddenly puts her hand to her nose.*) Why—(MRS. PETERS *bends nearer, then turns her face away.*) 345 There's something wrapped up in this piece of silk.

MRS. PETERS: Why, this isn't her scissors.

MRS. HALE: (*Lifting the silk.*) Oh, Mrs. Peters—its—

(MRS. PETERS *bends closer.*)

MRS. PETERS: It's the bird.

MRS. HALE: (*Jumping up.*) But, Mrs. Peters—look at it! Its neck! 350 Look at its neck! It's all—other side *to.*

MRS. PETERS: Somebody—wrung—its—neck.

(*Their eyes meet. A look of growing comprehension, of horror. Steps are heard outside.* MRS. HALE *slips box under quilt pieces, and sinks into her chair. Enter* SHERIFF *and* COUNTY ATTORNEY. MRS. PETERS *rises.*)

COUNTY ATTORNEY: (*As one turning from serious things to little pleasantries.*) Well, ladies, have you decided whether she was going to quilt it or knot it? 355

MRS. PETERS: We think she was going to—knot it.

COUNTY ATTORNEY: Well, that's interesting, I'm sure. (*Seeing the birdcage.*) Has the bird flown?

MRS. HALE: (*Putting more quilt pieces over the box.*) We think the—cat got it. 360

COUNTY ATTORNEY: *(Preoccupied.)* Is there a cat?

(MRS. HALE glances in a quick covert way at MRS. PETERS.)

MRS. PETERS: Well, not *now.* They're superstitious, you know. They leave.

365 COUNTY ATTORNEY: *(To SHERIFF PETERS continuing an interrupted conversation.)* No sign at all of anyone having come from the outside. Their own rope. Now let's go up again and go over it piece by piece. *(They start upstairs.)* It would have to have been someone who knew just the—

(MRS. PETERS sits down. The two women sit there not looking at one another, but as if peering into something and at the same time holding back. When they talk now it is in the manner of feeling their way over strange ground, as if afraid of what they are saying, but as if they cannot help saying it.)

370 MRS. HALE: She liked the bird. She was going to bury it in that pretty box.

MRS. PETERS: *(In a whisper.)* When I was a girl—my kitten—there was a boy took a hatchet, and before my eyes—and before I could get there—*(Covers her face an instant.)* If they hadn't held me back I would have—*(Catches herself, looks up-*
375 *stairs where steps are heard, falters weakly.)*—hurt him.

MRS. HALE: *(With a slow look around her.)* I wonder how it would seem never to have had any children around. *(Pause.)* No, Wright wouldn't like the bird—a thing that sang. She used to sing. He killed that, too.

380 MRS. PETERS: *(Moving uneasily.)* We don't know who killed the bird.

MRS. HALE: I knew John Wright.

MRS. PETERS: It was an awful thing was done in this house that night, Mrs. Hale. Killing a man while he slept, slipping a
385 rope around his neck that choked the life out of him.

MRS. HALE: His neck. Choked the life out of him.

(Her hand goes out and rests on the birdcage.)

MRS. PETERS: *(With rising voice.)* We don't know who killed him. We don't know.

MRS. HALE: *(Her own feeling not interrupted.)* If there'd been years
390 and years of nothing, then a bird to sing to you, it would be awful—still, after the bird was still.

MRS. PETERS: *(Something within her speaking.)* I know what still-ness is. When we homesteaded in Dakota, and my first baby died—after he was two years old, and me with no other
395 then—

MRS. HALE: *(Moving.)* How soon do you suppose they'll be through, looking for the evidence?

MRS. PETERS: I know what stillness is. *(Pulling herself back.)* The law has got to punish crime, Mrs. Hale.

400 MRS. HALE: *(Not as if answering that.)* I wish you'd seen Minnie Foster when she wore a white dress with blue ribbons and stood up there in the choir and sang. *(A look around the room.)* Oh, I *wish* I'd come over here once in a while! That was a crime! That was a crime! Who's going to punish that?

405 MRS. PETERS: *(Looking upstairs.)* We mustn't—take on.

MRS. HALE: I might have known she needed help! I know how things can be—for women. I tell you, it's queer, Mrs. Peters. We live close together and we live far apart. We all go

through the same things—it's all just a different kind of the
410 same thing. *(Brushes her eyes; noticing the bottle of fruit, reaches out for it.)* If I was you I wouldn't tell her her fruit was gone. Tell her it *ain't.* Tell her it's all right. Take this in to prove it to her. She—she may never know whether it was broke or not.

MRS. PETERS: *(Takes the bottle, looks about for something to wrap it*
415 *in, takes petticoat from the clothes brought from the other room, very nervously begins winding this around the bottle. In a false voice.)* My, it's a good thing the men couldn't hear us. Wouldn't they just laugh! Getting all stirred up over a little thing like a—dead canary. As if that could have anything to do with—with—wouldn't they *laugh!*
420

(The men are heard coming down stairs.)

MRS. HALE: *(Under her breath.)* Maybe they would—maybe they wouldn't.

COUNTY ATTORNEY: No, Peters, it's all perfectly clear except a reason for doing it. But you know juries when it comes to
425 women. If there was some definite thing. Something to show—something to make a story about—a thing that would connect up with this strange way of doing it—

(The women's eyes meet for an instant. Enter HALE from outer door.)

HALE: Well, I've got the team around. Pretty cold out there.

COUNTY ATTORNEY: I'm going to stay here a while by myself. *(To the SHERIFF.)* You can send Frank out for me, can't you? I want
430 to go over everything. I'm not satisfied that we can't do better.

SHERIFF: Do you want to see what Mrs. Peters is going to take in?

(The COUNTY ATTORNEY goes to the table, picks up the apron, laughs.)

COUNTY ATTORNEY: Oh, I guess they're not very dangerous things the ladies have picked out. *(Moves a few things about, disturbing the quilt pieces which cover the box. Steps back.)* No,
435 Mrs. Peters doesn't need supervising. For that matter, a sheriff's wife is married to the law. Ever think of it that way, Mrs. Peters?

MRS. PETERS: Not—just that way.

SHERIFF: *(Chuckling.)* Married to the law. *(Moves toward the other*
440 *room.)* I just want you to come in here a minute, George. We ought to take a look at these windows.

COUNTY ATTORNEY: *(Scoffingly.)* Oh, windows!

SHERIFF: We'll be right out, Mr. Hale.

(HALE goes outside. The SHERIFF follows the COUNTY ATTORNEY into the other room. Then MRS. HALE rises, hands tight together, looking in-tensely at MRS. PETERS, whose eyes make a slow turn, finally meeting MRS. HALE's. A moment MRS. HALE holds her, then her own eyes point the way to where the box is concealed. Suddenly MRS. PETERS throws back quilt pieces and tries to put the box in the bag she is wearing. It is too big. She opens box, starts to take bird out, cannot touch it, goes to pieces, stands there helpless. Sound of a knob turning in the other room. MRS. HALE snatches the box and puts it in the pocket of her big coat. Enter COUNTY ATTORNEY and SHERIFF.)

COUNTY ATTORNEY: *(Facetiously.)* Well, Henry, at least we
445 found out that she was not going to quilt it. She was going to—what is it you call it, ladies?

MRS. HALE: *(Her hand against her pocket.)* We call it—knot it, Mr. Henderson.

TENNESSEE WILLIAMS

Like Amanda Wingfield in *The Glass Menagerie,* Tennessee Williams (1911–83) regarded himself as a product of the Old South and its genteel, rural, and—finally—obsolete traditions. Born Thomas Lanier Williams to a traveling shoe salesman and his wife, Williams was raised in Mississippi before moving to the tenements of St. Louis. As a child, Williams contracted diphtheria, which briefly paralyzed his legs and left him frail and homebound for some time. During his convalescence, Williams read and wrote avidly and published his first story at the age of sixteen. After high school, he briefly attended the University of Missouri, but withdrew when his poor health prevented him from passing the ROTC course. He then worked for three years in a shoe factory, then tried Washington University in St. Louis, but again dropped out. He finally took his degree in playwriting from the University of Iowa in 1938, when he changed his name to "Tennessee." In the 1930s, Williams's embattled relation to the world was deepened by the "loss" of his beloved sister Rose. Rose became chronically depressed, and Williams's mother, unable to cope with her erratic and wild behavior, consented to having a lobotomy performed. Rose was left docile but inert and became the prototype of several of Williams's most memorable dramatic characters, women whose inner beauty is too delicate to be disclosed to the world. At this time Williams also recognized his own homosexuality, a recognition that deepened his sense of the threatening conformity imposed by mainstream American society.

Coming of age in the Great Depression was formative for Williams's drama, particularly the range of themes associated with his mature work: a sexual tension surging beneath the surface of the characters' lives, the collapse of a sustaining family and social order, the attraction of misfits destroyed by a world that will not accept them. Williams wrote several now-lost plays in the late 1930s, and *Battle of Angels* (1940; later revised as *Orpheus Descending* in 1957) was produced by the Theater Guild in Boston, where it failed. Williams scored a major success with his next play, *The Glass Menagerie* (1944). He continued his success with a series of important dramas: *Summer and Smoke* (1947), *A Streetcar Named Desire* (1947), *The Rose Tattoo* (1951), *Camino Real* (1953), *Cat on a Hot Tin Roof* (1955), *Sweet Bird of Youth* (1959), *Night of the Iguana* (1961). In his later years, Williams's drama became increasingly gothic and sensational, and his personal life suffered as well; Williams became an alcoholic and was institutionalized on several occasions. He continued to write plays to the end of his life, developing his characteristic strengths: a feel for the nuances of character, and a flair for dramatizing the victims of an unfeeling world.

THE GLASS MENAGERIE

First performed in 1944, *The Glass Menagerie* looks back to the 1930s. Its characters are reminiscent of Williams and his family, and their grinding poverty recalls the depression-era plays of Elmer Rice and Clifford Odets. In many ways, *The Glass Menagerie* is a play in the realistic tradition. Laura's menagerie recalls how Ibsen, Chekhov, and Strindberg used stage objects (Nora's Christmas tree in *A Doll House,* the cherry orchard, Miss Julie's bird) to evoke and symbolize the characters' motives and sensibilities. However, Williams also uses the device of the "memory play" to disrupt the linearity of realistic drama. Tom constructs the scene and the characters for the audience, and slide projections of phrases and images often illustrate the action as it takes place. These devices lend *The Glass Menagerie* the flavor of symbolist theater. Moreover, Tom's anticipation of the Spanish Civil War and World War II sets the play in a larger social and political context that looms forebodingly over the fragile and self-absorbed characters. Amanda and Laura seem doomed never to escape the drab apartment, and even Tom, wandering the world, finally cannot escape it either. Deeply personal, *The Glass Menagerie* also provides a kind of study for Williams's later plays, for it includes a typical panoply of Williams's characters: the blunt, sexually aggressive, emotionally stunted Jim; Amanda, the faded Southern belle; Laura, more crippled emotionally than physically; and Tom, who falls in love with long distance yet never succeeds in escaping his past or in finding his future.

PRODUCTION NOTES

Being a "memory play," *The Glass Menagerie* can be presented with unusual freedom of convention. Because of its considerably delicate or tenuous material, atmospheric touches and subtleties of direction play a particularly important part. Expressionism and all other unconventional techniques in drama have only one valid aim, and that is a closer approach to truth. When a play employs unconventional techniques, it is not, or certainly shouldn't be, trying to escape its responsibility of dealing with reality, or interpreting experience, but is actually or should be attempting to find a closer approach, a more penetrating and vivid expression of things as they are. The straight realistic play with its genuine Frigidaire and authentic ice-cubes, its characters who speak exactly as its audience speaks, corresponds to the academic landscape and has the same virtue of a photographic likeness. Everyone should know nowadays the unimportance of the photographic in art: that truth, life, or reality is an organic thing which the poetic imagination can represent or suggest, in essence, only through transformation, through changing into other forms than those which were merely present in appearance.

These remarks are not meant as a preface only to this particular play. They have to do with a conception of a new, plastic theatre which must take the place of the exhausted theatre of realistic conventions if the theatre is to resume vitality as a part of our culture.

THE SCREEN DEVICE: There is *only one important difference between the original and the acting version of the play* and that is the *omission* in the latter of the device that I tentatively included in my *original* script. This device was the use of a screen on which were projected magic-lantern slides bearing images or titles. I do not regret the omission of this device from the original Broadway production. The extraordinary power of Miss Taylor's performance made it suitable to have the utmost simplicity in the physical production. But I think it may be interesting to some readers to see how this device was conceived. So I am putting it into the published manuscript. These images and legends, projected from behind, were cast on a section of wall between the front-room and dining-room areas, which should be indistinguishable from the rest when not in use.

The purpose of this will probably be apparent. It is to give accent to certain values in each scene. Each scene contains a particular point (or several) which is structurally the most important. In an episodic play, such as this, the basic structure or narrative line may be obscured from the audience; the effect may seem fragmentary rather than architectural. This may not be the fault of the play so much as a lack of attention in the audience. The legend or image upon the screen will strengthen the effect of what is merely allusion in the writing and allow the primary point to be made more simply and lightly than if the entire responsibility were on the spoken lines. Aside from this structural value, I think the screen will have a definite emotional appeal, less definable but just as important. An imaginative producer or director may invent many other uses for this device than those indicated in the present script. In fact the possibilities of the device seem much larger to me than the instance of this play can possibly utilize.

THE MUSIC: Another extra-literary accent in this play is provided by the use of music. A single recurring tune, "The Glass Menagerie," is used to give emotional emphasis to suitable passages. This tune is like circus music, not when you are on the grounds or in the immediate vicinity of the parade, but when you are at some distance and very likely thinking of something else. It seems under those circumstances to continue almost interminably and it weaves in and out of your preoccupied consciousness; then it is the lightest, most delicate music in the world and perhaps the saddest. It expresses the surface vivacity of life with the underlying strain of immutable and inexpressible sorrow. When you look at a piece of delicately spun glass you think of two things: how beautiful it is and how easily it can be broken. Both of those ideas should be woven into the recurring tune, which dips in and out of the play as if it were carried on a wind that changes. It serves as a thread of connection and allusion between the narrator with his separate point in time and space and the subject of his story. Between each episode it returns as reference to the emotion, nostalgia, which is the first condition of the play. It is primarily Laura's music and therefore comes out most clearly when the play focuses upon her and the lovely fragility of glass which is her image.

THE LIGHTING: The lighting in the play is not realistic. In keeping with the atmosphere of memory, the stage is dim. Shafts of light are focused on selected areas or actors, sometimes in contradistinction to what is the apparent center. For instance, in the quarrel scene between Tom and Amanda, in which Laura has no active part, the clearest pool of light is on her figure. This is also true of the supper scene, when her silent figure on the sofa should remain the visual center. The light upon Laura should be distinct from the others, having a peculiar pristine clarity such as light used in early religious portraits of female saints or madonnas. A certain correspondence to light in religious paintings, such as El Greco's, where the figures are radiant in atmosphere that is relatively dusky, could be effectively used throughout the play. (It will also permit a more effective use of the screen.) A free, imaginative use of light can be of enormous value in giving a mobile, plastic quality to plays of a more or less static nature.

Tennessee Williams

THE GLASS MENAGERIE

Tennessee Williams

——— CHARACTERS ———

AMANDA WINGFIELD *(the mother), a little woman of great but confused vitality clinging frantically to another time and place. Her characterization must be carefully created, not copied from type. She is not paranoiac, but her life is paranoia. There is much to admire in Amanda, and as much to love and pity as there is to laugh at. Certainly she has endurance and a kind of heroism, and though her foolishness makes her unwittingly cruel at times, there is tenderness in her slight person.*

LAURA WINGFIELD *(her daughter), Amanda, having failed to establish contact with reality, continues to live vitally in her illusions, but Laura's situation is even graver. A childhood illness has left her crippled, one leg slightly shorter than the other, and held in a brace. This defect need not be more than suggested on the stage. Stemming from this, Laura's separation increases till she is like a piece of her own glass collection, too exquisitely fragile to move from the shelf.*

TOM WINGFIELD *(her son), and the narrator of the play. A poet with a job in a warehouse. His nature is not remorseless, but to escape from a trap he has to act without pity.*

JIM O'CONNOR *(the gentleman caller), a nice, ordinary, young man.*

SCENE: *An Alley in St. Louis*

Part I   Preparation for a Gentleman Caller.
Part II The Gentlemen calls.

TIME: *Now and the Past.*

——— SCENE ONE ———

The Wingfield apartment is in the rear of the building, one of those vast hive-like conglomerations of the cellular living-units that flower as warty growths in overcrowded urban centers of lower middle-class population and are symptomatic of the impulse of this largest and fundamentally enslaved section of American society to avoid fluidity and differentiation and to exist and function as one interfused mass of automatism.

The apartment faces an alley and is entered by a fire escape, a structure whose name is a touch of accidental poetic truth, for all of these huge buildings are always burning with the slow and implacable fires of human desperation. The fire escape is part of what we see—that is, the landing of it and steps descending from it.

The scene is memory and is therefore nonrealistic. Memory takes a lot of poetic license. It omits some details; others are exaggerated, according to the emotional value of the articles it touches, for memory is seated predominantly in the heart. The interior is therefore rather dim and poetic.

At the rise of the curtain, the audience is faced with the dark, grim rear wall of the Wingfield tenement. This building is flanked on both sides by dark, narrow alleys which run into murky canyons of tangled clotheslines, garbage cans, and the sinister latticework of neighboring fire escapes. It is up and down these side alleys that exterior entrances and exits are made during the play. At the end of TOM's *opening commentary, the dark tenement wall slowly becomes transparent and reveals the interior of the ground-floor Wingfield apartment.*

Nearest the audience is the living room, which also serves as a sleeping room for LAURA, *the sofa unfolding to make her bed. Just beyond, separated from the living room by a wide arch or second proscenium with transparent faded portieres (or second curtain), is the dining room. In an old-fashioned whatnot in the living room are seen scores of transparent glass animals. A blown-up photograph of the father hangs on the wall of the living room, to the left of the archway. It is the face of a very handsome young man in a doughboy's First World War cap. He is gallantly smiling, ineluctably smiling, as if to say "I will be smiling forever."*

Also hanging on the wall, near the photograph, are a typewriter keyboard chart and a Gregg shorthand diagram. An upright typewriter on a small table stands beneath the charts.

The audience hears and sees the opening scene in the dining room through both the transparent fourth wall of the building and the transparent gauze portieres of the dining-room arch. It is during this revealing scene that the fourth wall slowly ascends, out of sight. This transparent exterior wall is not brought down again until the very end of the play, during TOM's *final speech.*

The narrator is an undisguised convention of the play. He takes whatever license with dramatic convention is convenient to his purposes.

TOM *enters, dressed as a merchant sailor, and strolls across to the fire escape. There he stops and lights a cigarette. He addresses the audience.*

TOM: Yes, I have tricks in my pocket, I have things up my sleeve. But I am the opposite of a stage magician. He gives you illusion that has the appearance of truth. I give you truth in the pleasant disguise of illusion.

To begin with, I turn back time. I reverse it to that 5 quaint period, the thirties, when the huge middle class of America was matriculating in a school for the blind. Their eyes had failed them, or they had failed their eyes, and so they were having their fingers pressed forcibly down on the fiery Braille alphabet of a dissolving economy. 10

In Spain there was revolution. Here there was only shouting and confusion. In Spain there was Guernica. Here there were disturbances of labor, sometimes pretty violent, in otherwise peaceful cities such as Chicago, Cleveland, Saint Louis . . . This is the social background of the play. 15

(Music begins to play.)

The play is memory. Being a memory play, it is dimly lighted, it is sentimental, it is not realistic. In memory everything seems to happen to music. That explains the fiddle in the wings.

I am the narrator of the play, and also a character in it. 20
The other characters are my mother, Amanda, my sister,

Laura, and a gentleman caller who appears in the final scenes.
He is the most realistic character in the play, being an emissary from a world of reality that we were somehow set apart
25 from. But since I have a poet's weakness for symbols, I am
using this character also as a symbol; he is the long-delayed
but always expected something that we live for.

There is a fifth character in the play who doesn't appear
except in this larger-than-life-size photograph over the
30 mantel. This is our father who left us a long time ago. He
was a telephone man who fell in love with long distances; he
gave up his job with the telephone company and skipped
the light fantastic out of town . . .

The last we heard of him was a picture postcard from
35 Mazatlan, on the Pacific coast of Mexico, containing a message of two words: "Hello—Goodbye!" and no address.
I think the rest of the play will explain itself. . . .

(AMANDA's voice becomes audible through the portieres.)

(Legend on screen: "Ou sont les neiges.")

*(TOM divides the portieres and enters the dining room. AMANDA and
LAURA are seated at a drop-leaf table. Eating is indicated by gestures
without food or utensils. AMANDA faces the audience. TOM and LAURA
are seated in profile. The interior has lit up softly and through the
scrim we see AMANDA and LAURA seated at the table.)*

AMANDA: *(Calling.)* Tom?
TOM: Yes, Mother.
40 AMANDA: We can't say grace until you come to the table!
TOM: Coming, Mother. *(He bows slightly and withdraws, reappearing a few moments later in his place at the table.)*
AMANDA: *(To her son.)* Honey, don't *push* with your *fingers.* If you
have to push with something, the thing to push with is a
45 crust of bread. And chew—chew! Animals have secretions
in their stomachs which enable them to digest food without mastication, but human beings are supposed to chew
their food before they swallow it down. Eat food leisurely,
son, and really enjoy it. A well-cooked meal has lots of deli-
50 cate flavors that have to be held in the mouth for appreciation. So chew your food and give your salivary glands a
chance to function!

*(TOM deliberately lays his imaginary fork down and pushes his chair
back from the table.)*

TOM: I haven't enjoyed one bite of this dinner because of your
constant directions on how to eat it. It's you that make me
55 rush through meals with your hawklike attention to every
bite I take. Sickening—spoils my appetite—all this discussion of—animals' secretion—salivary glands—mastication!
AMANDA: *(Lightly.)* Temperament like a Metropolitan star!

(TOM rises and walks toward the living room.)

You're not excused from the table.
60 TOM: I'm getting a cigarette.
AMANDA: You smoke too much.

(LAURA rises.)

LAURA: I'll bring in the blanc mange.

(TOM remains standing with his cigarette by the portieres.)

AMANDA: *(Rising.)* No, sister, no, sister—you be the lady this
time and I'll be the darky.
LAURA: I'm already up.   65
AMANDA: Resume your seat, little sister—I want you to stay
fresh and pretty—for gentlemen callers!
LAURA: *(Sitting down.)* I'm not expecting any gentlemen callers.
AMANDA: *(Crossing out to the kitchenette, airily.)* Sometimes they
come when they are least expected! Why, I remember one 70
Sunday afternoon in Blue Mountain—

(She enters the kitchenette.)

TOM: I know what's coming!
LAURA: Yes. But let her tell it.
TOM: Again?
LAURA: She loves to tell it.   75

(AMANDA returns with a bowl of dessert.)

AMANDA: One Sunday afternoon in Blue Mountain—your
mother received—*seventeen!*—gentlemen callers! Why, sometimes there weren't chairs enough to accommodate them
all. We had to send the nigger over to bring in folding
chairs from the parish house.   80
TOM: *(Remaining at the portieres.)* How did you entertain those
gentlemen callers?
AMANDA: I understood the art of conversation!
TOM: I bet you could talk.
AMANDA: Girls in those days *knew* how to talk, I can tell you.   85
TOM: Yes?

(Image on screen: AMANDA as a girl on a porch, greeting callers.)

AMANDA: They knew how to entertain their gentlemen callers.
It wasn't enough for a girl to be possessed of a pretty face
and a graceful figure—although I wasn't slighted in either
respect. She also needed to have a nimble wit and a tongue 90
to meet all occasions.
TOM: What did you talk about?
AMANDA: Things of importance going on in the world! Never
anything coarse or common or vulgar.

*(She addresses TOM as though he were seated in the vacant chair at the
table though he remains by the portieres. He plays this scene as though
reading from a script.)*

My callers were gentlemen—all! Among my callers were 95
some of the most prominent young planters of the Mississippi Delta—planters and sons of planters!

*(TOM motions for music and a spot of light on AMANDA. Her eyes lift,
her face glows, her voice becomes rich and elegiac.)*

(Screen legend: "Ou sont les neiges d'antan?")

There was young Champ Laughlin who later became vice-
president of the Delta Planters Bank. Hadley Stevenson
who was drowned in Moon Lake and left his widow one 100
hundred and fifty thousand in Government bonds. There
were the Cutrere brothers, Wesley and Bates. Bates was one
of my bright particular beaux! He got in a quarrel with that

wild Wainwright boy. They shot it out on the floor of Moon
105   Lake Casino. Bates was shot through the stomach. Died in
the ambulance on his way to Memphis. His widow was also
well provided-for, came into eight or ten thousand acres,
that's all. She married him on the rebound—never loved
her—carried my picture on him the night he died! And
110   there was that boy that every girl in the Delta had set her
cap for! That beautiful, brilliant young Fitzhugh boy from
Greene County!

TOM: What did he leave his widow?

AMANDA: He never married! Gracious, you talk as though all
115   of my old admirers had turned up their toes to the daisies!

TOM: Isn't this the first you've mentioned that still survives?

AMANDA: That Fitzhugh boy went North and made a fortune—came to be known as the Wolf of Wall Street! He
had the Midas touch, whatever he touched turned to gold!
120   And I could have been Mrs. Duncan J. Fitzhugh, mind you!
But—I picked your *father!*

LAURA: (*Rising.*) Mother, let me clear the table.

AMANDA: No, dear, you go in front and study your typewriter
chart. Or practice your shorthand a little. Stay fresh and
125   pretty!—It's almost time for our gentlemen callers to start
arriving. (*She flounces girlishly toward the kitchenette.*) How many
do you suppose we're going to entertain this afternoon?

(TOM *throws down the paper and jumps up with a groan.*)

LAURA: (*Alone in the dining room.*) I don't believe we're going to
receive any, Mother.

130 AMANDA: (*Reappearing, airily.*) What? No one—not one? You
must be joking!

(LAURA *nervously echoes her laugh. She slips in a fugitive manner
through the half-open portieres and draws them gently behind her. A
shaft of very clear light is thrown on her face against the faded tapestry of the curtains. Faintly the music of "The Glass Menagerie" is
heard as she continues, lightly.*)

Not one gentleman caller? It can't be true! There must be a
flood, there must have been a tornado!

LAURA: It isn't a flood, it's not a tornado, Mother. I'm just not
135   popular like you were in Blue Mountain. . . .

(TOM *utters another groan.* LAURA *glances at him with a faint, apologetic smile. Her voice catches a little.*)

Mother's afraid I'm going to be an old maid.

(*The scene dims out with the "Glass Menagerie" music.*)

—————— **SCENE TWO** ——————

*On the dark stage the screen is lighted with the image of blue roses.
Gradually* LAURA's *figure becomes apparent and the screen goes out.
The music subsides.*

LAURA *is seated in the delicate ivory chair at the small claw-foot
table. She wears a dress of soft violet material for a kimono—her hair
is tied back from her forehead with a ribbon. She is washing and polishing her collection of glass.* AMANDA *appears on the fire escape steps.
At the sound of her ascent,* LAURA *catches her breath, thrusts the bowl
of ornaments away, and seats herself stiffly before the diagram of the*

*typewriter keyboard as though it held her spellbound. Something has
happened to* AMANDA. *It is written in her face as she climbs to the
landing: a look that is grim and hopeless and a little absurd. She has
on one of those cheap or imitation velvety-looking cloth coats with imitation fur collar. Her hat is five or six years old, one of those dreadful cloche hats that were worn in the late Twenties, and she is clutching
an enormous black patent-leather pocketbook with nickel clasps and
initials. This is her full-dress outfit, the one she usually wears to the
D.A.R. Before entering she looks through the door. She purses her lips,
opens her eyes very wide, rolls them upward and shakes her head. Then
she slowly lets herself in the door. Seeing her mother's expression* LAURA
touches her lips with a nervous gesture.

LAURA: Hello, Mother, I was—(*She makes a nervous gesture toward
the chart on the wall.* AMANDA *leans against the shut door and
stares at* LAURA *with a martyred look.*)

AMANDA: Deception? Deception? (*She slowly removes her hat and
gloves, continuing the sweet suffering stare. She lets the hat and* 5
gloves fall on the floor—a bit of acting.)

LAURA: (*Shakily.*) How was the D.A.R. meeting?

(AMANDA *slowly opens her purse and removes a dainty white handkerchief which she shakes out delicately and delicately touches to her
lips and nostrils.*)

Didn't you go to the D.A.R. meeting, Mother?

AMANDA: (*Faintly, almost inaudibly.*) —No.—No. (*Then more
forcibly.*) I did not have the strength—to go to the D.A.R. 10
In fact, I did not have the courage! I wanted to find a hole
in the ground and hide myself in it forever! (*She crosses slowly
to the wall and removes the diagram of the typewriter keyboard.
She holds it in front of her for a second, staring at it sweetly and
sorrowfully—then bites her lips and tears it into two pieces.*) 15

LAURA: (*Faintly.*) Why did you do that, Mother?

(AMANDA *repeats the same procedure with the chart of the Gregg
Alphabet.*)

Why are you—

AMANDA: Why? Why? How old are you, Laura?

LAURA: Mother, you know my age.

AMANDA: I thought that you were an adult; it seems that I was 20
mistaken. (*She crosses slowly to the sofa and sinks down and
stares at* LAURA.)

LAURA: Please don't stare at me, Mother.

(AMANDA *closes her eyes and lowers her head. There is a ten-second
pause.*)

AMANDA: What are we going to do, what is going to become of
us, what is the future? 25

(*There is another pause.*)

LAURA: Has something happened, Mother?

(AMANDA *draws a long breath, takes out the handkerchief again, goes
through the dabbing process.*)

Mother, has—something happened?

AMANDA: I'll be all right in a minute, I'm just bewildered—
(*She hesitates.*)—by life. . . .

30 LAURA: Mother, I wish that you would tell me what's happened!
AMANDA: As you know, I was supposed to be inducted into my office at the D.A.R. this afternoon.

(*Screen image:* A swarm of typewriters.)

But I stopped off at Rubicam's Business College to speak to your teachers about your having a cold and ask them what
35 progress they thought you were making down there.
LAURA: Oh . . . .
AMANDA: I went to the typing instructor and introduced myself as your mother. She didn't know who you were. "Wingfield," she said, "We don't have any such student
40 enrolled at the school!"
I assured her she did, that you had been going to classes since early in January.
"I wonder," she said, "If you could be talking about that terribly shy little girl who dropped out of school after only
45 a few days' attendance?"
"No," I said, "Laura, my daughter, has been going to school every day for the past six weeks!"
"Excuse me," she said. She took the attendance book out and there was your name, unmistakably printed, and all
50 the dates you were absent until they decided that you had dropped out of school.
I still said, "No, there must have been some mistake! There must have been some mix-up in the records!"
And she said, "No—I remember her perfectly now. Her
55 hands shook so that she couldn't hit the right keys! The first time we gave a speed test, she broke down completely—was sick at the stomach and almost had to be carried into the wash room! After that morning she never showed up any more. We phoned the house but never got any an-
60 swer"—While I was working at Famous-Barr, I suppose, demonstrating those—

(*She indicates a brassiere with her hands.*)

Oh! I felt so weak I could barely keep on my feet! I had to sit down while they got me a glass of water! Fifty dollars' tuition, all of our plans—my hopes and ambitions for you—
65 just gone up the spout, just gone up the spout like that.

(LAURA *draws a long breath and gets awkwardly to her feet. She crosses to the Victrola and winds it up.*)

What are you doing?
LAURA: Oh! (*She releases the handle and returns to her seat.*)
AMANDA: Laura, where have you been going when you've gone out pretending that you were going to business college?
70 LAURA: I've just been going out walking.
AMANDA: That's not true.
LAURA: It is. I just went walking.
AMANDA: Walking? Walking? In winter? Deliberately courting pneumonia in that light coat? Where did you walk to, Laura?
75 LAURA: All sorts of places—mostly in the park.
AMANDA: Even after you'd started catching that cold?
LAURA: It was the lesser of two evils, Mother.

(*Screen image:* Winter scene in a park.)

I couldn't go back there. I—threw up—on the floor!

AMANDA: From half past seven till after five every day you mean to tell me you walked around in the park, because you 80 wanted to make me think that you were still going to Rubicam's Business College?
LAURA: It wasn't as bad as it sounds. I went inside places to get warmed up.
AMANDA: Inside where? 85
LAURA: I went in the art museum and the bird houses at the Zoo. I visited the penguins every day! Sometimes I did without lunch and went to the movies. Lately I've been spending most of my afternoons in the Jewel Box, that big glass house where they raise the tropical flowers. 90
AMANDA: You did all this to deceive me, just for deception? (LAURA *looks down.*) Why?
LAURA: Mother, when you're disappointed, you get that awful suffering look on your face, like the picture of Jesus' mother in the museum! 95
AMANDA: Hush!
LAURA: I couldn't face it.

(*There is a pause. A whisper of strings is heard. Legend on screen: "The Crust of Humility."*)

AMANDA: (*Hopelessly fingering the huge pocketbook.*) So what are we going to do the rest of our lives? Stay home and watch the parades go by? Amuse ourselves with the glass menagerie, 100 darling? Eternally play those worn-out phonograph records your father left as a painful reminder of him? We won't have a business career—we've given that up because it gave us nervous indigestion! (*She laughs wearily.*) What is there left but dependency all our lives? I know so well what be- 105 comes of unmarried women who aren't prepared to occupy a position. I've seen such pitiful cases in the South—barely tolerated spinsters living upon the grudging patronage of sister's husband or brother's wife!—stuck away in some little mousetrap of a room—encouraged by one in-law to visit 110 another—little birdlike women without any nest—eating the crust of humility all their life!
Is that the future that we've mapped out for ourselves? I swear it's the only alternative I can think of! (*She pauses.*) It isn't a very pleasant alternative, is it? (*She pauses again.*) Of 115 course—some girls *do* marry.

(LAURA *twists her hands nervously.*)

Haven't you ever liked some boy?
LAURA: Yes. I liked one once. (*She rises.*) I came across his picture a while ago.
AMANDA: (*With some interest.*) He gave you his picture? 120
LAURA: No, it's in the yearbook.
AMANDA: (*Disappointed.*) Oh—a high school boy.

(*Screen image:* JIM as the high school hero bearing a silver cup.)

LAURA: Yes. His name was Jim. (*She lifts the heavy annual from the claw-foot table.*) Here he is in *The Pirates of Penzance.*
AMANDA: (*Absently.*) The what? 125
LAURA: The operetta the senior class put on. He had a wonderful voice and we sat across the aisle from each other Mondays, Wednesdays and Fridays in the Aud. Here he is with the silver cup for debating! See his grin?

130 AMANDA: (*Absently.*) He must have had a jolly disposition.
LAURA: He used to call me—Blue Roses.

(*Screen image:* Blue roses.)

AMANDA: Why did he call you such a name as that?
LAURA: When I had that attack of pleurosis—he asked me what
     was the matter when I came back. I said pleurosis—he
135   thought that I said Blue Roses! So that's what he always
     called me after that. Whenever he saw me, he'd holler,
     "Hello, Blue Roses!" I didn't care for the girl that he went
     out with. Emily Meisenbach. Emily was the best-dressed girl
     at Soldan. She never struck me, though, as being sincere . . .
140 It says in the Personal Section—they're engaged. That's—six
     years ago! They must be married by now.
AMANDA: Girls that aren't cut out for business careers usually
     wind up married to some nice man. (*She gets up with a spark
     of revival.*) Sister, that's what you'll do!

(LAURA *utters a startled, doubtful laugh. She reaches quickly for a
piece of glass.*)

145 LAURA: But, Mother—
AMANDA: Yes? (*She goes over to the photograph.*)
LAURA: (*In a tone of frightened apology.*) I'm—crippled!
AMANDA: Nonsense! Laura, I've told you never, never to use
     that word. Why, you're not crippled, you just have a little
150   defect—hardly noticeable, even! When people have some
     slight disadvantage like that, they cultivate other things to
     make up for it—develop charm—and vivacity—and—
     charm! That's all you have to do! (*She turns again to the pho-
     tograph.*) One thing your father had *plenty of*—was *charm!*

(*The scene fades out with music.*)

——— SCENE THREE ———

Legend on screen: "After the fiasco—"

TOM *speaks from the fire escape landing.*

TOM: After the fiasco at Rubicam's Business College, the idea
     of getting a gentleman caller for Laura began to play a more
     and more important part in Mother's calculations. It be-
5   came an obsession. Like some archetype of the universal
     unconscious, the image of the gentleman caller haunted our
     small apartment. . . .

(*Screen image:* A young man at the door of a house with flowers.)

An evening at home rarely passed without some allusion to
this image, this specter, this hope . . . Even when he wasn't
mentioned, his presence hung in Mother's preoccupied look
10 and in my sister's frightened, apologetic manner—hung
like a sentence passed upon the Wingfields!
     Mother was a woman of action as well as words. She be-
gan to take logical steps in the planned direction. Late that
winter and in the early spring—realizing that extra money
15 would be needed to properly feather the nest and plume the
bird—she conducted a vigorous campaign on the telephone,
roping in subscribers to one of those magazines for matrons
called *The Homemaker's Companion,* the type of journal that

features the serialized sublimations of ladies of letters who
think in terms of delicate cuplike breasts, slim, tapering 20
waists, rich, creamy thighs, eyes like wood smoke in autumn, fingers that soothe and caress like strains of music,
bodies as powerful as Etruscan sculpture.

(*Screen image:* The cover of a glamor magazine.)

(AMANDA *enters with the telephone on a long extension cord. She is
spotlighted in the dim stage.*)

AMANDA: Ida Scott? This is Amanda Wingfield! We *missed*
     you at the D.A.R. last Monday! I said to myself: She's prob- 25
     ably suffering with that sinus condition! How is that sinus
     condition?
          Horrors! Heaven have mercy!—You're a Christian mar-
     tyr, yes, that's what you are, a Christian martyr!
          Well, I just now happened to notice that your subscrip- 30
     tion to the *Companion*'s about to expire! Yes, it expires with
     the next issue, honey!—just when that wonderful new serial
     by Bessie Mae Hopper is getting off to such an exciting start.
     Oh, honey, it's something that you can't miss! You remember
     how *Gone with the Wind* took everybody by storm? You sim- 35
     ply couldn't go out if you hadn't read it. All everybody *talked*
     was Scarlett O'Hara. Well, this is a book that critics already
     compare to *Gone with the Wind.* It's the *Gone with the Wind* of
     the post–World War generation!—What?—Burning?—Oh,
     honey, don't let them burn, go take a look in the oven and I'll 40
     hold the wire! Heavens—I think she's hung up!

(*The scene dims out.*)

(*Legend on screen:* "You think I'm in love with Continental
Shoemakers?")

(*Before the lights come up again, the violent voices of* TOM *and*
AMANDA *are heard. They are quarreling behind the portieres. In front
of them stands* LAURA *with clenched hands and panicky expression. A
clear pool of light is on her figure throughout this scene.*)

TOM: What in Christ's name am I—
AMANDA: (*Shrilly.*) Don't you use that—
TOM: —supposed to do!
AMANDA: —expression! Not in my—   45
TOM: Ohhh!
AMANDA: —presence! Have you gone out of your senses?
TOM: I have, that's true, *driven* out!
AMANDA: What is the matter with you, you—big—big—
     IDIOT!   50
TOM: Look!—I've got *no thing,* no single thing—
AMANDA: Lower your voice!
TOM: —in my life here that I can call my OWN! Everything is—
AMANDA: Stop that shouting!
TOM: Yesterday you confiscated my books! You had the nerve 55
     to—
AMANDA: I took that horrible novel back to the library—yes!
     That hideous book by that insane Mr. Lawrence.

(TOM *laughs wildly.*)

I cannot control the output of diseased minds or people who
cater to them—   60

(TOM *laughs still more wildly.*)

BUT I WON'T ALLOW SUCH FILTH BROUGHT INTO MY HOUSE! No, no, no, no, no!

TOM: House, house! Who pays rent on it, who makes a slave of himself to—

65 AMANDA: *(Fairly screeching.)* Don't you DARE to—

TOM: No, no, I mustn't say things! *I've* got to just—

AMANDA: Let me tell you—

TOM: I don't want to hear any more!

(He tears the portieres open. The dining-room area is lit with a turgid smoky red glow. Now we see AMANDA; her hair is in metal curlers and she is wearing a very old bathrobe, much too large for her slight figure, a relic of the faithless Mr. Wingfield. The upright typewriter now stands on the drop-leaf table, along with a wild disarray of manuscripts. The quarrel was probably precipitated by AMANDA's interruption of TOM's creative labor. A chair lies overthrown on the floor. Their gesticulating shadows are cast on the ceiling by the fiery glow.)

AMANDA: You *will* hear more, you—

70 TOM: No, I won't hear more, I'm going out!

AMANDA: You come right back in—

TOM: Out, out, out! Because I'm—

AMANDA: Come back here, Tom Wingfield! I'm not through talking to you!

75 TOM: Oh, go—

LAURA: *(Desperately.)*—Tom!

AMANDA: You're going to listen, and no more insolence from you! I'm at the end of my patience!

(He comes back toward her.)

TOM: What do you think I'm at? Aren't I supposed to have any
80   patience to reach the end of, Mother? I know, I know. It seems unimportant to you, what I'm *doing*—what I *want* to do—having a little *difference* between them! You don't think that—

AMANDA: I think you've been doing things that you're ashamed
85   of. That's why you act like this. I don't believe that you go every night to the movies. Nobody goes to the movies night after night. Nobody in their right minds goes to the movies as often as you pretend to. People don't go to the movies at nearly midnight, and movies don't let out at two A.M. Come
90   in stumbling. Muttering to yourself like a maniac! You get three hours' sleep and then go to work. Oh, I can picture the way you're doing down there. Moping, doping, because you're in no condition.

TOM: *(Wildly.)* No, I'm in no condition!

95 AMANDA: What right have you got to jeopardize your job? Jeopardize the security of us all? How do you think we'd manage if you were—

TOM: Listen! You think I'm crazy about the *warehouse?* (He bends fiercely toward her slight figure.) You think I'm in love
100   with the Continental Shoemakers? You think I want to spend fifty-five *years* down there in that—*celotex interior!* with—*fluorescent*—*tubes!* Look! I'd rather somebody picked up a crowbar and battered out my brains—than go back mornings! I *go!* Every time you come in yelling that God-
105   damn *"Rise and Shine!"* "Rise and Shine!" I say to myself, "How *lucky dead* people are!" But I get up. I *go!* For sixty-five dollars a month I give up all that I dream of doing and

being *ever!* And you say self—*self's* all I ever think of. Why, listen, if self is what I thought of, Mother, I'd be where he is—GONE! *(He points to his father's picture.)* As far as the sys- 110 tem of transportation reaches! *(He starts past her. She grabs his arm.)* Don't grab at me, Mother!

AMANDA: Where are you going?

TOM: I'm going to the *movies!*

AMANDA: I don't believe that lie!   115

(TOM *crouches toward her, overtowering her tiny figure. She backs away, gasping.*)

TOM: I'm going to opium dens! Yes, opium dens, dens of vice and criminals' hangouts, Mother. I've joined the Hogan Gang, I'm a hired assassin, I carry a tommy gun in a violin case! I run a string of cat houses in the Valley! They call me Killer, Killer Wingfield, I'm leading a double-life, a simple, 120 honest warehouse worker by day, by night a dynamic *czar* of the *underworld, Mother.* I go to gambling casinos, I spin away fortunes on the roulette table! I wear a patch over one eye and a false mustache, sometimes I put on green whiskers. On those occasions they call me—*El Diablo!* Oh, I could tell 125 you many things to make you sleepless! My enemies plan to dynamite this place. They're going to blow us all sky-high some night! I'll be glad, very happy, and so will you! You'll go up, up on a broomstick, over Blue Mountain with seventeen gentlemen callers! You ugly—babbling old—*witch* . . . 130 (He goes through a series of violent, clumsy movements, seizing his overcoat, lunging to the door, pulling it fiercely open. The women watch him, aghast. His arm catches in the sleeve of the coat as he struggles to pull it on. For a moment he is pinioned by the bulky garment. With an outraged groan he tears the coat off again, split- 135 ting the shoulder of it, and hurls it across the room. It strikes against the shelf of LAURA's glass collection, and there is a tinkle of shattering glass. LAURA cries out as if wounded.)

(Music.)

(Screen legend: "The Glass Menagerie.")

LAURA: *(Shrilly.)* My glass!—menagerie . . . (She covers her face and turns away.)   140

(But AMANDA is still stunned and stupefied by the "ugly witch" so that she barely notices this occurrence. Now she recovers her speech.)

AMANDA: *(In an awful voice.)* I won't speak to you—until you apologize!

(She crosses through the portieres and draws them together behind her. TOM *is left with* LAURA. LAURA *clings weakly to the mantel with her face averted.* TOM *stares at her stupidly for a moment. Then he crosses to the shelf. He drops awkwardly on his knees to collect the fallen glass, glancing at* LAURA *as if he would speak but couldn't.*)

("The Glass Menagerie" music steals in as the scene dims out.)

──────── SCENE FOUR ────────

The interior of the apartment is dark. There is a faint light in the alley. A deep-voiced bell in a church is tolling the hour of five.

TOM *appears at the top of the alley. After each solemn boom of the bell in the tower, he shakes a little noisemaker or rattle as if to express the tiny spasm of man in contrast to the sustained power and dignity of the Almighty. This and the unsteadiness of his advance make it evident that he has been drinking. As he climbs the few steps to the fire escape landing light steals up inside.* LAURA *appears in the front room in a nightdress. She notices that* TOM's *bed is empty.* TOM *fishes in his pockets for his door key, removing a motley assortment of articles in the search, including a shower of movie ticket stubs and an empty bottle. At last he finds the key, but just as he is about to insert it, it slips from his fingers. He strikes a match and crouches below the door.*

TOM: (*Bitterly.*) One crack—and it falls through!

(LAURA *opens the door.*)

LAURA: Tom! Tom, what are you doing?

TOM: Looking for a door key.

LAURA: Where have you been all this time?

5   TOM: I have been to the movies.

LAURA: All this time at the movies?

TOM: There was a very long program. There was a Garbo picture and a Mickey Mouse and a travelogue and a newsreel and a preview of coming attractions. And there was an organ solo

10   and a collection for the Milk Fund—simultaneously—which ended up in a terrible fight between a fat lady and an usher!

LAURA: (*Innocently.*) Did you have to stay through everything?

TOM: Of course! And, oh, I forgot! There was a big stage

15   show! The headliner on this stage show was Malvolio the Magician. He performed wonderful tricks, many of them, such as pouring water back and forth between pitchers. First it turned to wine and then it turned to beer and then it turned to whisky. I know it was whisky it finally turned

20   into because he needed somebody to come up out of the audience to help him, and I came up—both shows! It was Kentucky Straight Bourbon. A very generous fellow, he gave souvenirs. (*He pulls from his back pocket a shimmering rainbow-colored scarf.*) He gave me this. This is his magic

25   scarf. You can have it, Laura. You wave it over a canary cage and you get a bowl of goldfish. You wave it over the goldfish bowl and they fly away canaries . . . But the wonderfullest trick of all was the coffin trick. We nailed him into a coffin and he got out of the coffin without remov-

30   ing one nail. (*He has come inside.*) There is a trick that would come in handy for me—get me out of this two-by-four situation! (*He flops onto the bed and starts removing his shoes.*)

LAURA: Tom—shhh!

35   TOM: What're you shushing me for?

LAURA: You'll wake up Mother.

TOM: Goody, goody! Pay 'er back for all those "Rise an' Shines." (*He lies down, groaning.*) You know it don't take much intelligence to get yourself into a nailed-up coffin, Laura. But

40   who in hell ever got himself out of one without removing one nail?

(*As if in answer, the father's grinning photograph lights up. The scene dims out.*)

(*Immediately following, the church bell is heard striking six. At the sixth stroke the alarm clock goes off in* AMANDA's *room, and after a few moments we hear her calling: "Rise and Shine! Rise and Shine!* LAURA, *go tell your brother to rise and shine!"*)

TOM: (*Sitting up slowly.*) I'll rise—but I won't shine.

(*The light increases.*)

AMANDA: Laura, tell your brother his coffee is ready.

(LAURA *slips into the front room.*)

LAURA: Tom!—It's nearly seven. Don't make Mother nervous.

(*He stares at her stupidly.*)

(*Beseechingly.*) Tom, speak to Mother this morning. Make up   45
with her, apologize, speak to her!

TOM: She won't to me. It's her that started not speaking.

LAURA: If you just say you're sorry she'll start speaking.

TOM: Her not speaking—is that such a tragedy?

LAURA: Please—please!   50

AMANDA: (*Calling from the kitchenette.*) Laura, are you going to do what I asked you to do, or do I have to get dressed and go out myself?

LAURA: Going, going—soon as I get on my coat!

(*She pulls on a shapeless felt hat with a nervous, jerky movement, pleadingly glancing at* TOM. *She rushes awkwardly for her coat. The coat is one of* AMANDA's, *inaccurately made-over, the sleeves too short for* LAURA.)

Butter and what else?   55

AMANDA: (*Entering from the kitchenette.*) Just butter. Tell them to charge it.

LAURA: Mother, they make such faces when I do that.

AMANDA: Sticks and stones can break our bones, but the expression on Mr. Garfinkel's face won't harm us! Tell your   60
brother his coffee is getting cold.

LAURA: (*At the door.*) Do what I asked you, will you, will you, Tom?

(*He looks sullenly away.*)

AMANDA: Laura, go now or just don't go at all!

LAURA: (*Rushing out.*) Going—going!   65

(*A second later she cries out.* TOM *springs up and crosses to the door.* TOM *opens the door.*)

TOM: Laura?

LAURA: I'm all right. I slipped, but I'm all right.

AMANDA: (*Peering anxiously after her.*) If anyone breaks a leg on those fire-escape steps, the landlord ought to be sued for every cent he possesses! (*She shuts the door. Now she remembers*   70
she isn't speaking to TOM *and returns to the other room.*)

(*As* TOM *comes listlessly for his coffee, she turns her back to him and stands rigidly facing the window on the gloomy gray vault of the areaway. Its light on her face with its aged but childish features is cruelly sharp, satirical as a Daumier print.*)

(*The music of "Ave Maria" is heard softly.*)

(TOM *glances sheepishly but sullenly at her averted figure and slumps at the table. The coffee is scalding hot; he sips it and gasps and spits it back in the cup. At his gasp,* AMANDA *catches her breath and half turns. Then she catches herself and turns back to the window.* TOM *blows on his coffee, glancing sidewise at his mother. She clears her throat.* TOM *clears his. He starts to rise, sinks back down again, scratches his head, clears his throat again.* AMANDA *coughs.* TOM *raises his cup in both hands to blow on it, his eyes staring over the rim of it at his mother for several moments. Then he slowly sets the cup down and awkwardly and hesitantly rises from the chair.*)

TOM: *(Hoarsely.)* Mother. I—I apologize, Mother.

(AMANDA *draws a quick, shuddering breath. Her face works grotesquely. She breaks into childlike tears.*)

I'm sorry for what I said, for everything that I said, I didn't mean it.

75 AMANDA: *(Sobbingly.)* My devotion has made me a witch and so I make myself hateful to my children!

TOM: *No, you* don't.

AMANDA: I worry so much, don't sleep, it makes me nervous!

TOM: *(Gently.)* I understand that.

80 AMANDA: I've had to put up a solitary battle all these years. But you're my right-hand bower! Don't fall down, don't fail!

TOM: *(Gently.)* I try, Mother.

AMANDA: *(With great enthusiasm.)* Try and you will *succeed!* (*The notion makes her breathless.*) Why, you—you're just *full* of

85 natural endowments! Both of my children—they're *un-usual* children! Don't you think I know it? I'm so—*proud!* Happy and—feel I've—so much to be thankful for but—promise me one thing, son!

TOM: What, Mother?

90 AMANDA: Promise, son, you'll—never be a drunkard!

TOM: *(Turns to her grinning.)* I will never be a drunkard, Mother.

AMANDA: That's what frightened me so, that you'd be drinking! Eat a bowl of Purina!

TOM: Just coffee, Mother.

95 AMANDA: Shredded wheat biscuit?

TOM: No. No, Mother, just coffee.

AMANDA: You can't put in a day's work on an empty stomach. You've got ten minutes—don't gulp! Drinking too-hot liquids makes cancer of the stomach . . . Put cream in.

100 TOM: No, thank you.

AMANDA: To cool it.

TOM: No! No, thank you, I want it black.

AMANDA: I know, but it's not good for you. We have to do all that we can to build ourselves up. In these trying times we

105 live in, all that we have to cling to is—each other . . . That's why it's so important to—Tom, I—sent out your sister so I could discuss something with you. If you hadn't have spoken I would have spoken to you. *(She sits down.)*

TOM: *(Gently.)* What is it, Mother, that you want to discuss?

110 AMANDA: *Laura!*

(TOM *puts his cup down slowly.*)

(*Legend on screen:* "Laura." *Music:* "The Glass Menagerie.")

TOM: —Oh.—Laura . . .

AMANDA: *(Touching his sleeve.)* You know how Laura is. So quiet but—still water runs deep! She notices things and I think she—broods about them.

(TOM *looks up.*)

A few days ago I came in and she was crying.   115

TOM: What about?

AMANDA: You.

TOM: Me?

AMANDA: She has an idea that you're not happy here.

TOM: What gave her that idea?   120

AMANDA: What gives her any idea? However, you do act strangely. I—I'm not criticizing, understand *that!* I know your ambitions do not lie in the warehouse, that like everybody in the whole wide world—you've had to—make sacrifices, but—Tom—Tom—life's not easy, it calls for—   125 Spartan endurance! There's so many things in my heart that I cannot describe to you! I've never told you but I—*loved* your father. . . .

TOM: *(Gently.)* I know that, Mother.

AMANDA: And you—when I see you taking after his ways! Stay-   130 ing out late—and—well, you *had* been drinking the night you were in that—terrifying condition! Laura says that you hate the apartment and that you go out nights to get away from it! Is that true, Tom?

TOM: No. You say there's so much in your heart that you can't   135 describe to me. That's true of me, too. There's so much in my heart that I can't describe to *you!* So let's respect each other's—

AMANDA: But, why—*why,* Tom—are you always so *restless?* Where do you *go* to, nights?   140

TOM: I—go to the movies.

AMANDA: Why do you go to the movies so much, Tom?

TOM: I go to the movies because—I like adventure. Adventure is something I don't have much of at work, so I go to the movies.   145

AMANDA: But, Tom, you go to the movies *entirely* too *much!*

TOM: I like a lot of adventure.

(AMANDA *looks baffled, then hurt. As the familiar inquisition resumes,* TOM *becomes hard and impatient again.* AMANDA *slips back into her querulous attitude toward him.*)

(*Image on screen:* A sailing vessel with Jolly Roger.)

AMANDA: Most young men find adventure in their careers.

TOM: Then most young men are not employed in a warehouse.

AMANDA: The world is full of young men employed in ware-   150 houses and offices and factories.

TOM: Do all of them find adventure in their careers?

AMANDA: They do or they do without it! Not everybody has a craze for adventure.

TOM: Man is by instinct a lover, a hunter, a fighter, and none of   155 those instincts are given much play at the warehouse!

AMANDA: Man is by instinct! Don't quote instinct to me! Instinct is something that people have got away from! It belongs to animals! Christian adults don't want it!

TOM: What do Christian adults want, then, Mother?   160

AMANDA: Superior things! Things of the mind and the spirit! Only animals have to satisfy instincts! Surely your aims are somewhat higher than theirs! Than monkeys—pigs—

TOM: I reckon they're not.

AMANDA: You're joking. However, that isn't what I wanted to   165 discuss.

TOM: *(Rising.)* I haven't much time.

AMANDA: (*Pushing his shoulders.*) Sit down.

TOM: You want me to punch in red at the warehouse, Mother?

170   AMANDA: You have five minutes. I want to talk about Laura.

(*Screen legend:* "Plans and Provisions.")

TOM: All right! What about Laura?

AMANDA: We have to be making some plans and provisions for her. She's older than you, two years, and nothing has happened. She just drifts along doing nothing. It frightens me

175   terribly how she just drifts along.

TOM: I guess she's the type that people call home girls.

AMANDA: There's no such type, and if there is, it's a pity! That is unless the home is hers, with a husband!

TOM: What?

180   AMANDA: Oh, I can see the handwriting on the wall as plain as I see the nose in front of my face! It's terrifying! More and more you remind me of your father! He was out all hours without explanation!—Then *left!* Goodbye! And me with the bag to hold. I saw that letter you got from the Merchant

185   Marine. I know what you're dreaming of. I'm not standing here blindfolded. (*She pauses.*) Very well, then. Then *do* it! But not till there's somebody to take your place.

TOM: What do you mean?

AMANDA: I mean that as soon as Laura has got somebody to

190   take care of her, married, a home of her own, independent—why, then you'll be free to go wherever you please, on land, on sea, whichever way the wind blows you! But until that time you've got to look out for your sister. I don't say me because I'm old and don't matter! I say for your sister be-

195   cause she's young and dependent.

I put her in business college—a dismal failure! Frightened her so it made her sick at the stomach. I took her over to the Young People's League at the church. Another fiasco. She spoke to nobody, nobody spoke to her. Now all she does

200   is fool with those pieces of glass and play those worn-out records. What kind of a life is that for a girl to lead?

TOM: What can I do about it?

AMANDA: Overcome selfishness! Self, self, self is all that you ever think of!

(TOM *springs up and crosses to get his coat. It is ugly and bulky. He pulls on a cap with earmuffs.*)

205   Where is your muffler? Put your wool muffler on!

(*He snatches it angrily from the closet, tosses it around his neck and pulls both ends tight.*)

Tom! I haven't said what I had in mind to ask you.

TOM: I'm too late to—

AMANDA: (*Catching his arm—very importunately; then shyly.*) Down at the warehouse, aren't there some—nice young

210   men?

TOM: No!

AMANDA: There *must* be—some. . . .

TOM: Mother—(*He gestures.*)

AMANDA: Find out one that's clean-living—doesn't drink and

215   ask him out for sister!

TOM: What?

AMANDA: For *sister!* To *meet!* Get *acquainted!*

TOM: (*Stamping to the door.*) Oh, my go-*osh!*

AMANDA: Will you?

(*He opens the door. She says, imploringly:*)

Will you?   220

(*He starts down the fire escape.*)

Will you? *Will* you, dear?

TOM: (*Calling back.*) Yes!

(AMANDA *closes the door hesitantly and with a troubled but faintly hopeful expression.*)

(*Screen image:* The cover of a glamor magazine.)

(*The spotlight picks up* AMANDA *at the phone.*)

AMANDA: Ella Cartwright? This is Amanda Wingfield! How are you, honey? How is that kidney condition?   225

(*There is a five-second pause.*)

Horrors!

(*There is another pause.*)

You're a Christian martyr, yes, honey, that's what you are, a Christian martyr! Well, I just now happened to notice in my little red book that your subscription to the *Companion* has just run out! I knew that you wouldn't want to miss out on   230 the wonderful serial starting in this new issue. It's by Bessie Mae Hopper, the first thing she's written since *Honeymoon for Three.* Wasn't that a strange and interesting story? Well, this one is even lovelier, I believe. It has a sophisticated, society background. It's all about the horsey set on Long Island!   235

(*The light fades out.*)

──────── SCENE FIVE ────────

Legend on the screen: "Annunciation."

Music is heard as the light slowly comes on.

It is early dusk of a spring evening. Supper has just been finished in the Wingfield apartment. AMANDA *and* LAURA, *in light-colored dresses, are removing dishes from the table in the dining room, which is shadowy, their movements formalized almost as a dance or ritual, their moving forms as pale and silent as moths.* TOM, *in white shirt and trousers, rises from the table and crosses toward the fire escape.*

AMANDA: (*As he passes her.*) Son, will you do me a favor?

TOM: What?

AMANDA: Comb your hair! You look so pretty when your hair is combed!

(TOM *slouches on the sofa with the evening paper. Its enormous headline reads:* "Franco Triumphs.")

There is only one respect in which I would like you to emu-   5 late your father.

TOM: What respect is that?

AMANDA: The care he always took of his appearance. He never allowed himself to look untidy.

(*He throws down the paper and crosses to the fire escape.*)

10   Where are you going?

TOM: I'm going out to smoke.

AMANDA: You smoke too much. A pack a day at fifteen cents a pack. How much would that amount to in a month? Thirty times fifteen is how much, Tom? Figure it out and you will
15   be astounded at what you could save. Enough to give you a night-school course in accounting at Washington U! Just think what a wonderful thing that would be for you, son!

(TOM *is unmoved by the thought.*)

TOM: I'd rather smoke. (*He steps out on the landing, letting the screen door slam.*)

20   AMANDA: (*Sharply.*) I know! That's the tragedy of it. . . . (*Alone, she turns to look at her husband's picture.*)

(*Dance music:* "The World Is Waiting for the Sunrise!")

TOM: (*To the audience.*) Across the alley from us was the Paradise Dance Hall. On evenings in spring the windows and doors were open and the music came outdoors. Sometimes the
25   lights were turned out except for a large glass sphere that hung from the ceiling. It would turn slowly about and filter the dusk with delicate rainbow colors. Then the orchestra played a waltz or a tango, something that had a slow and sensuous rhythm. Couples would come outside, to the rela-
30   tive privacy of the alley. You could see them kissing behind ash pits and telephone poles. This was the compensation for lives that passed like mine, without any change or adventure. Adventure and change were imminent in this year. They were waiting around the corner for all these kids. Sus-
35   pended in the mist over Berchtesgaden, caught in the folds of Chamberlain's umbrella. In Spain there was Guernica! But here there was only hot swing music and liquor, dance halls, bars, and movies, and sex that hung in the gloom like a chandelier and flooded the world with brief, deceptive
40   rainbows. . . . All the world was waiting for bombardments!

(AMANDA *turns from the picture and comes outside.*)

AMANDA: (*Sighing.*) A fire escape landing's a poor excuse for a porch. (*She spreads a newspaper on a step and sits down, gracefully and demurely as if she were settling into a swing on a Mississippi veranda.*) What are you looking at?

45   TOM: The moon.

AMANDA: Is there a moon this evening?

TOM: It's rising over Garfinkel's Delicatessen.

AMANDA: So it is! A little silver slipper of a moon. Have you made a wish on it yet?

50   TOM: Um-hum.

AMANDA: What did you wish for?

TOM: That's a secret.

AMANDA: A secret, huh? Well, I won't tell mine either. I will be just as mysterious as you.

55   TOM: I bet I can guess what yours is.

AMANDA: Is my head so transparent?

TOM: You're not a sphinx.

AMANDA: No, I don't have secrets. I'll tell you what I wished for on the moon. Success and happiness for my precious children! I wish for that whenever there's a moon, and when   60
there isn't a moon, I wish for it, too.

TOM: I thought perhaps you wished for a gentleman caller.

AMANDA: Why do you say that?

TOM: Don't you remember asking me to fetch one?

AMANDA: I remember suggesting that it would be nice for your   65
sister if you brought home some nice young man from the warehouse. I think that I've made that suggestion more than once.

TOM: Yes, you have made it repeatedly.

AMANDA: Well?   70

TOM: We are going to have one.

AMANDA: *What?*

TOM: A gentleman caller!

(*The annunciation is celebrated with music.*)

(AMANDA *rises.*)

(*Image on screen:* A caller with a bouquet.)

AMANDA: You mean you have asked some nice young man to come over?

TOM: Yep. I've asked him to dinner.   75

AMANDA: You really did?

TOM: I did!

AMANDA: You did, and did he—*accept?*

TOM: He did!   80

AMANDA: Well, well—well, well! That's—lovely!

TOM: I thought that you would be pleased.

AMANDA: It's definite then?

TOM: Very definite.

AMANDA: Soon?   85

TOM: Very soon.

AMANDA: For heaven's sake, stop putting on and tell me some things, will you?

TOM: What things do you want me to tell you?

AMANDA: *Naturally* I would like to know when he's *coming!*   90

TOM: He's coming tomorrow.

AMANDA: *Tomorrow?*

TOM: Yep. Tomorrow.

AMANDA: But, Tom!

TOM: Yes, Mother?   95

AMANDA: Tomorrow gives me no time!

TOM: Time for what?

AMANDA: Preparations! Why didn't you phone me at once, as soon as you asked him, the minute that he accepted? Then don't you see, I could have been getting ready!   100

TOM: You don't have to make any fuss.

AMANDA: Oh, Tom, Tom, Tom, of course I have to make a fuss! I want things nice, not sloppy! Not thrown together. I'll certainly have to do some fast thinking, won't I?

TOM: I don't see why you have to think at all.   105

AMANDA: You just don't know. We can't have a gentleman caller in a pigsty! All my wedding silver has to be polished, the monogrammed table linen ought to be laundered! The

windows have to be washed and fresh curtains put up. And
110   how about clothes? We have to *wear* something, don't we?

TOM: Mother, this boy is no one to make a fuss over!

AMANDA: Do you realize he's the first young man we've introduced to your sister? It's terrible, dreadful, disgraceful that
poor little sister has never received a single gentleman
115   caller! Tom, come inside! *(She opens the screen door.)*

TOM: What for?

AMANDA: I want to ask you some things.

TOM: If you're going to make such a fuss, I'll call it off, I'll tell
him not to come!

120   AMANDA: You certainly won't do anything of the kind. Nothing offends people worse than broken engagements. It simply means I'll have to work like a Turk! We won't be
brilliant, but we will pass inspection. Come on inside.

(TOM follows her inside, groaning.)

Sit down.

125   TOM: Any particular place you would like me to sit?

AMANDA: Thank heavens I've got that new sofa! I'm also making payments on a floor lamp I'll have sent out! And put the
chintz covers on, they'll brighten things up! Of course I'd
hoped to have these walls re-papered. . . . What is the young
130   man's name?

TOM: His name is O'Connor.

AMANDA: That, of course, means fish—tomorrow is Friday! I'll
have that salmon loaf—with Durkee's dressing! What does
he do? He works at the warehouse?

135   TOM: Of course! How else would I—

AMANDA: Tom, he—doesn't drink?

TOM: Why do you ask me that?

AMANDA: Your father *did!*

TOM: Don't get started on that!

140   AMANDA: He *does* drink, then?

TOM: Not that I know of!

AMANDA: Make sure, be certain! The last thing I want for my
daughter's a boy who drinks!

TOM: Aren't you being a little bit premature? Mr. O'Connor
145   has not yet appeared on the scene!

AMANDA: But will tomorrow. To meet your sister, and what do
I know about his character? Nothing! Old maids are better
off than wives of drunkards!

TOM: Oh, my God!

150   AMANDA: Be still!

TOM: *(Leaning forward to whisper.)* Lots of fellows meet girls
whom they don't marry!

AMANDA: Oh, talk sensibly, Tom—and don't be sarcastic! *(She
has gotten a hairbrush.)*

155   TOM: What are you doing?

AMANDA: I'm brushing that cowlick down! *(She attacks his hair
with the brush.)* What is this young man's position at the
warehouse?

TOM: *(Submitting grimly to the brush and the interrogation.)* This
160   young man's position is that of a shipping clerk, Mother.

AMANDA: Sounds to me like a fairly responsible job, the sort of
a job *you* would be in if you just had more *get-up.* What is
his salary? Have you any idea?

TOM: I would judge it to be approximately eighty-five dollars
165   a month.

AMANDA: Well—not princely, but—

TOM: Twenty more than I make.

AMANDA: Yes, how well I know! But for a family man, eighty-
five dollars a month is not much more than you can just get
by on. . . .   170

TOM: Yes, but Mr. O'Connor is not a family man.

AMANDA: He might be, mightn't he? Some time in the future?

TOM: I see. Plans and provisions.

AMANDA: You are the only young man that I know of who ignores the fact that the future becomes the present, the pre-   175
sent the past, and the past turns into everlasting regret if
you don't plan for it!

TOM: I will think that over and see what I can make of it.

AMANDA: Don't be supercilious with your mother! Tell me
some more about this—what do you call him?   180

TOM: James D. O'Connor. The D. is for Delaney.

AMANDA: Irish on *both* sides! *Gracious!* And doesn't drink?

TOM: Shall I call him up and ask him right this minute?

AMANDA: The only way to find out about those things is to
make discreet inquiries at the proper moment. When I was   185
a girl in Blue Mountain and it was suspected that a young
man drank, the girl whose attentions he had been receiving,
if any girl *was,* would sometimes speak to the minister of
his church, or rather her father would if her father was living, and sort of feel him out on the young man's character. 190
That is the way such things are discreetly handled to keep
a young woman from making a tragic mistake!

TOM: Then how did you happen to make a tragic mistake?

AMANDA: That innocent look of your father's had everyone
fooled! He *smiled*—the world was *enchanted!* No girl can do   195
worse than put herself at the mercy of a handsome appearance! I hope that Mr. O'Connor is not too good-looking.

TOM: No, he's not too good-looking. He's covered with freckles and hasn't too much of a nose.

AMANDA: He's not right-down homely, though?   200

TOM: Not right-down homely. Just medium homely, I'd say.

AMANDA: Character's what to look for in a man.

TOM: That's what I've always said, Mother.

AMANDA: You've never said anything of the kind and I suspect
you would never give it a thought.   205

TOM: Don't be so suspicious of me.

AMANDA: At least I hope he's the type that's up and coming.

TOM: I think he really goes in for self-improvement.

AMANDA: What reason have you to think so?

TOM: He goes to night school.   210

AMANDA: *(Beaming.)* Splendid! What does he do, I mean study?

TOM: Radio engineering and public speaking!

AMANDA: Then he has visions of being advanced in the world!
Any young man who studies public speaking is aiming to
have an executive job some day! And radio engineering? A   215
thing for the future! Both of these facts are very illuminating. Those are the sort of things that a mother should know
concerning any young man who comes to call on her daughter. Seriously or—not.

TOM: One little warning. He doesn't know about Laura. I didn't   220
let on that we had dark ulterior motives. I just said, why
don't you come and have dinner with us? He said okay and
that was the whole conversation.

AMANDA: I bet it was! You're eloquent as an oyster. However,
he'll know about Laura when he gets here. When he sees   225

how lovely and sweet and pretty she is, he'll thank his lucky
stars he was asked to dinner.

TOM: Mother, you mustn't expect too much of Laura.

AMANDA: What do you mean?

230 TOM: Laura seems all those things to you and me because she's
ours and we love her. We don't even notice she's crippled
any more.

AMANDA: Don't say crippled! You know that I never allow that
word to be used!

235 TOM: But face facts, Mother. She is and—that's not all—

AMANDA: What do you mean "not all"?

TOM: Laura is very different from other girls.

AMANDA: I think the difference is all to her advantage.

TOM: Not quite all—in the eyes of others—strangers—she's
240 terribly shy and lives in a world of her own and those things
make her seem a little peculiar to people outside the house.

AMANDA: Don't say peculiar.

TOM: Face the facts. She is.

*(The dance hall music changes to a tango that has a minor and some-
what ominous tone.)*

245 AMANDA: In what way is she peculiar—may I ask?

TOM: *(Gently.)* She lives in a world of her own—a world of
little glass ornaments, Mother. . . .

(He gets up. AMANDA *remains holding the brush, looking at him,
troubled.)*

She plays old phonograph records and—that's about all—
(He glances at himself in the mirror and crosses to the door.)

AMANDA: *(Sharply.)* Where are you going?

250 TOM: I'm going to the movies. *(He goes out the screen door.)*

AMANDA: Not to the movies, every night to the movies! *(She
follows quickly to the screen door.)* I don't believe you always go
to the movies!

(He is gone. AMANDA *looks worriedly after him for a moment. Then
vitality and optimism return and she turns from the door, crossing to
the portieres.)*

Laura! Laura!

(LAURA answers from the kitchenette.)

255 LAURA: Yes, Mother.

AMANDA: Let those dishes go and come in front!

(LAURA appears with a dish towel. AMANDA *speaks to her gaily.)*

Laura, come here and make a wish on the moon!

(Screen image: The Moon.)

LAURA: *(Entering.)* Moon—moon?

AMANDA: A little silver slipper of a moon. Look over your left
260 shoulder, Laura, and make a wish!

(LAURA looks faintly puzzled as if called out of sleep. AMANDA *seizes
her shoulders and turns her at an angle by the door.)*

Now! Now, darling, *wish!*

LAURA: What shall I wish for, Mother?

AMANDA: *(Her voice trembling and her eyes suddenly filling with
tears.)* Happiness! Good fortune!

(The sound of the violin rises and the stage dims out.)

——— SCENE SIX ———

The light comes up on the fire escape landing. TOM *is leaning against
the grill, smoking.*

Screen image: The high school hero.

TOM: And so the following evening I brought Jim home to dinner. I had known Jim slightly in high school. In high school
Jim was a hero. He had tremendous Irish good nature and
vitality with the scrubbed and polished look of white chi-
naware. He seemed to move in a continual spotlight. He   5
was a star in basketball, captain of the debating club, president of the senior class and the glee club and he sang the
male lead in the annual light operas. He was always running or bounding, never just walking. He seemed always at
the point of defeating the law of gravity. He was shooting   10
with such velocity through his adolescence that you would
logically expect him to arrive at nothing short of the White
House by the time he was thirty. But Jim apparently ran
into more interference after his graduation from Soldan.
His speed had definitely slowed. Six years after he left high 15
school he was holding a job that wasn't much better than
mine.

(Screen image: The Clerk.)

He was the only one at the warehouse with whom I was on
friendly terms. I was valuable to him as someone who could
remember his former glory, who had seen him win basket-   20
ball games and the silver cup in debating. He knew of my
secret practice of retiring to a cabinet of the washroom to
work on poems when business was slack in the warehouse.
He called me Shakespeare. And while the other boys in the
warehouse regarded me with suspicious hostility, Jim took   25
a humorous attitude toward me. Gradually his attitude affected the others, their hostility wore off and they also began to smile at me as people smile at an oddly fashioned
dog who trots across their path at some distance.
    I knew that Jim and Laura had known each other at   30
Soldan, and I had heard Laura speak admiringly of his voice.
I didn't know if Jim remembered her or not. In high school
Laura had been as unobtrusive as Jim had been astonishing.
If he did remember Laura, it was not as my sister, for when
I asked him to dinner, he grinned and said, "You know,   35
Shakespeare, I never thought of you as having folks!"
    He was about to discover that I did. . . .

(Legend on screen: "The accent of a coming foot.")

(The light dims out on TOM *and comes up in the Wingfield living
room—a delicate lemony light. It is about five on a Friday evening of
late spring which comes "scattering poems in the sky.")*

*(AMANDA has worked like a Turk in preparation for the gentleman
caller. The results are astonishing. The new floor lamp with its rose*

silk shade is in place, a colored paper lantern conceals the broken light fixture in the ceiling, new billowing white curtains are at the windows, chintz covers are on the chairs and sofa, a pair of new sofa pillows make their initial appearance. Open boxes and tissue paper are scattered on the floor.)

(LAURA stands in the middle of the room with lifted arms while AMANDA crouches before her, adjusting the hem of a new dress, devout and ritualistic. The dress is colored and designed by memory. The arrangement of LAURA's hair is changed; it is softer and more becoming. A fragile, unearthly prettiness has come out in LAURA: she is like a piece of translucent glass touched by light, given a momentary radiance, not actual, not lasting.)

AMANDA: *(Impatiently.)* Why are you trembling?
LAURA: Mother, you've made me so nervous!
40 AMANDA: How have I made you nervous?
LAURA: By all this fuss! You make it seem so important!
AMANDA: I don't understand you, Laura. You couldn't be satisfied with just sitting home, and yet whenever I try to arrange something for you, you seem to resist it. *(She gets up.)* Now
45 take a look at yourself. No, wait! Wait just a moment— I have an idea!
LAURA: What is it now?

(AMANDA produces two powder puffs which she wraps in handkerchiefs and stuffs in LAURA's bosom.)

LAURA: Mother, what are you doing?
AMANDA: They call them "Gay Deceivers"!
50 LAURA: I won't wear them!
AMANDA: You will!
LAURA: Why should I?
AMANDA: Because, to be painfully honest, your chest is flat.
LAURA: You make it seem like we were setting a trap.
55 AMANDA: All pretty girls are a trap, a pretty trap, and men expect them to be.

(Legend on screen: "A pretty trap.")

Now look at yourself, young lady. This is the prettiest you will ever be! *(She stands back to admire LAURA.)* I've got to fix myself now! You're going to be surprised by your mother's
60 appearance!

(AMANDA crosses through the portieres, humming gaily. LAURA moves slowly to the long mirror and stares solemnly at herself. A wind blows the white curtains inward in a slow, graceful motion and with a faint, sorrowful sighing.)

AMANDA: *(From somewhere behind the portieres.)* It isn't dark enough yet.

(LAURA turns slowly before the mirror with a troubled look.)

(Legend on screen: "This is my sister: Celebrate her with strings!" Music plays.)

AMANDA: *(Laughing, still not visible.)* I'm going to show you something. I'm going to make a spectacular appearance!
65 LAURA: What is it, Mother?

AMANDA: Possess your soul in patience—you will see! Something I've resurrected from that old trunk! Styles haven't changed so terribly much after all. . . . *(She parts the portieres.)* Now just look at your mother! *(She wears a girlish frock of yellowed voile with a blue silk sash. She carries a bunch of jon-* 70 *quils—the legend of her youth is nearly revived. Now she speaks feverishly.)* This is the dress in which I led the cotillion. Won the cakewalk twice at Sunset Hill, wore one Spring to the Governor's Ball in Jackson! See how I sashayed around the ballroom, Laura? *(She raises her skirt and does a mincing* 75 *step around the room.)* I wore it on Sundays for my gentlemen callers! I had it on the day I met your father. . . . I had malaria fever all that Spring. The change of climate from East Tennessee to the Delta—weakened resistance. I had a little temperature all the time—not enough to be serious— 80 just enough to make me restless and giddy! Invitations poured in—parties all over the Delta! "Stay in bed," said Mother, "you have a fever!"—but I just wouldn't. I took quinine but kept on going, going! Evenings, dances! Afternoons, long, long rides! Picnics—lovely! So lovely, that 85 country in May—all lacy with dogwood, literally flooded with jonquils! That was the spring I had the craze for jonquils. Jonquils became an absolute obsession. Mother said, "Honey, there's no more room for jonquils." And still I kept on bringing in more jonquils. Whenever, wherever I saw 90 them, I'd say "Stop! Stop! I see jonquils!" I made the young men help me gather the jonquils! It was a joke, Amanda and her jonquils! Finally there were no more vases to hold them, every available space was filled with jonquils. No vases to hold them? All right, I'll hold them myself! And 95 then I—*(She stops in front of the picture. Music plays.)* met your father! Malaria fever and jonquils and then—this—boy. . . . *(She switches on the rose-colored lamp.)* I hope they get here before it starts to rain. *(She crosses the room and places the jonquils in a bowl on the table.)* I gave your brother a little extra 100 change so he and Mr. O'Connor could take the service car home.
LAURA: *(With an altered look.)* What did you say his name was?
AMANDA: O'Connor.
LAURA: What is his first name? 105
AMANDA: I don't remember. Oh, yes, I do. It was—Jim!

(LAURA sways slightly and catches hold of a chair.)

(Legend on screen: "Not Jim!")

LAURA: *(Faintly.)* Not—Jim!
AMANDA: Yes, that was it, it was Jim! I've never known a Jim that wasn't nice!

(The music becomes ominous.)

LAURA: Are you sure his name is Jim O'Connor? 110
AMANDA: Yes. Why?
LAURA: Is he the one that Tom used to know in high school?
AMANDA: He didn't say so. I think he just got to know him at the warehouse.
LAURA: There was a Jim O'Connor we both knew in high 115 school—*(Then, with effort.)* If that is the one that Tom is bringing to dinner—you'll have to excuse me, I won't come to the table.

AMANDA: What sort of nonsense is this?

120 LAURA: You asked me once if I'd ever liked a boy. Don't you remember I showed you this boy's picture?

AMANDA: You mean the boy you showed me in the yearbook?

LAURA: Yes, that boy.

AMANDA: Laura, Laura, were you in love with that boy?

125 LAURA: I don't know, Mother. All I know is I couldn't sit at the table if it was him!

AMANDA: It won't be him! It isn't the least bit likely. But whether it is or not, you will come to the table. You will not be excused.

130 LAURA: I'll have to be, Mother.

AMANDA: I don't intend to humor your silliness, Laura. I've had too much from you and your brother, both! So just sit down and compose yourself till they come. Tom has forgotten his key so you'll have to let them in, when they arrive.

135 LAURA: (Panicky.) Oh, Mother—you answer the door!

AMANDA: (Lightly.) I'll be in the kitchen—busy!

LAURA: Oh, Mother, please answer the door, don't make me do it!

AMANDA: (Crossing into the kitchenette.) I've got to fix the dress-
140 ing for the salmon. Fuss, fuss—silliness!—over a gentle-man caller!

(The door swings shut. LAURA is left alone.)

(Legend on screen: "Terror!")

(She utters a low moan and turns off the lamp—sits stiffly on the edge of the sofa, knotting her fingers together.)

(Legend on screen: "The Opening of a Door!")

(TOM and JIM appear on the fire escape steps and climb to the landing. Hearing their approach, LAURA rises with a panicky gesture. She retreats to the portieres. The doorbell rings. LAURA catches her breath and touches her throat. Low drums sound.)

AMANDA: (Calling.) Laura, sweetheart! The door!

(LAURA stares at it without moving.)

JIM: I think we just beat the rain.

TOM: Uh-huh. (He rings again, nervously. JIM whistles and fishes for
145 a cigarette.)

AMANDA: (Very, very gaily.) Laura, that is your brother and Mr. O'Connor! Will you let them in, darling?

(LAURA crosses toward the kitchenette door.)

LAURA: (Breathlessly.) Mother—you go to the door!

(AMANDA steps out of the kitchenette and stares furiously at LAURA. She points imperiously at the door.)

LAURA: Please, please!

150 AMANDA: (In a fierce whisper.) What is the matter with you, you silly thing?

LAURA: (Desperately.) Please, you answer it, please!

AMANDA: I told you I wasn't going to humor you, Laura. Why have you chosen this moment to lose your mind?

155 LAURA: Please, please, please, you go!

AMANDA: You'll have to go to the door because I can't!

LAURA: (Despairingly.) I can't either!

AMANDA: Why?

LAURA: I'm sick!

AMANDA: I'm sick, too—of your nonsense! Why can't you 160 and your brother be normal people? Fantastic whims and behavior!

(TOM gives a long ring.)

Preposterous goings on! Can you give me one reason—(She calls out lyrically.) Coming! Just one second!—why you should be afraid to open a door? Now you answer it, Laura! 165

LAURA: Oh, oh, oh . . . (She returns through the portieres, darts to the Victrola, winds it frantically and turns it on.)

AMANDA: Laura Wingfield, you march right to that door!

LAURA: Yes—yes, Mother!

(A faraway, scratchy rendition of "Dardanella" softens the air and gives her strength to move through it. She slips to the door and draws it cautiously open. TOM enters with the caller, JIM O'CONNOR.)

TOM: Laura, this is Jim. Jim, this is my sister, Laura. 170

JIM: (Stepping inside.) I didn't know that Shakespeare had a sister!

LAURA: (Retreating, stiff and trembling, from the door.) How—how do you do?

JIM: (Heartily, extending his hand.) Okay!

(LAURA touches it hesitantly with hers.)

JIM: Your hand's cold, Laura! 175

LAURA: Yes, well—I've been playing the Victrola. . . .

JIM: Must have been playing classical music on it! You ought to play a little hot swing music to warm you up!

LAURA: Excuse me—I haven't finished playing the Victrola . . . (She turns awkwardly and hurries into the front room. She pauses 180 a second by the Victrola. Then she catches her breath and darts through the portieres like a frightened deer.)

JIM: (Grinning.) What was the matter?

TOM: Oh—with Laura? Laura is—terribly shy.

JIM: Shy, huh? It's unusual to meet a shy girl nowadays. I don't 185 believe you ever mentioned you had a sister.

TOM: Well, now you know. I have one. Here is the Post Dis-patch. You want a piece of it?

JIM: Uh-huh.

TOM: What piece? The comics? 190

JIM: Sports! (He glances at it.) Ole Dizzy Dean is on his bad behavior.

TOM: (Uninterested.) Yeah? (He lights a cigarette and goes over to the fire-escape door.)

JIM: Where are you going? 195

TOM: I'm going out on the terrace.

JIM: (Going after him.) You know, Shakespeare—I'm going to sell you a bill of goods!

TOM: What goods?

JIM: A course I'm taking. 200

TOM: Huh?

JIM: In public speaking! You and me, we're not the warehouse type.

TOM: Thanks—that's good news. But what has public speak-ing got to do with it? 205

JIM: It fits you for—executive positions!

TOM: Awww.

JIM: I tell you it's done a helluva lot for me.

(Image on screen: Executive at his desk.)

TOM: In what respect?

210   JIM: In every! Ask yourself what is the difference between you
an' me and men in the office down front? Brains?—No!—
Ability?—No! Then what? Just one little thing—

TOM: What is that one little thing?

JIM: Primarily it amounts to—social poise! Being able to

215   square up to people and hold your own on any social level!

AMANDA: *(From the kitchenette.)* Tom?

TOM: Yes, Mother?

AMANDA: Is that you and Mr. O'Connor?

TOM: Yes, Mother.

220   AMANDA: Well, you just make yourselves comfortable in there.

TOM: Yes, Mother.

AMANDA: Ask Mr. O'Connor if he would like to wash his
hands.

JIM: Aw, no—no—thank you—I took care of that at the ware-

225   house. Tom—

TOM: Yes?

JIM: Mr. Mendoza was speaking to me about you.

TOM: Favorably?

JIM: What do you think?

230   TOM: Well—

JIM: You're going to be out of a job if you don't wake up.

TOM: I am waking up—

JIM: You show no signs.

TOM: The signs are interior.

(Image on screen: The sailing vessel with the Jolly Roger again.)

235   TOM: I'm planning to change. *(He leans over the fire-escape rail,
speaking with quiet exhilaration. The incandescent marquees and
signs of the first-run movie houses light his face from across the
alley. He looks like a voyager.)* I'm right at the point of committing myself to a future that doesn't include the ware-

240   house and Mr. Mendoza or even a night-school course in
public speaking.

JIM: What are you gassing about?

TOM: I'm tired of the movies.

JIM: Movies!

245   TOM: Yes, movies! Look at them—*(A wave toward the marvels of
Grand Avenue.)* All of those glamorous people—having adventures—hogging it all, gobbling the whole thing up! You
know what happens? People go to the *movies* instead of
moving! Hollywood characters are supposed to have all the

250   adventures for everybody in America, while everybody in
America sits in a dark room and watches them have them!
Yes, until there's a war. That's when adventure becomes
available to the masses! *Everyone's* dish, not only Gable's!
Then the people in the dark room come out of the dark

255   room to have some adventures themselves—goody, goody!
It's our turn now, to go to the South Sea Island—to make a
safari—to be exotic, far-off! But I'm not patient. I don't
want to wait till then. I'm tired of the *movies* and I am *about
to move!*

260   JIM: *(Incredulously.)* Move?

TOM: Yes.

JIM: When?

TOM: Soon!

JIM: Where? Where?

(The music seems to answer the question, while TOM *thinks it over. He
searches in his pockets.)*

265   TOM: I'm starting to boil inside. I know I seem dreamy, but inside—well, I'm boiling! Whenever I pick up a shoe, I shudder a little thinking how short life is and what I am doing!
Whatever that means, I know it doesn't mean shoes—
except as something to wear on a traveler's feet! *(He finds

270   what he has been searching for in his pockets and holds out a
paper to Jim.)* Look—

JIM: What?

TOM: I'm a member.

JIM: *(Reading.)* The Union of Merchant Seamen.

275   TOM: I paid my dues this month, instead of the light bill.

JIM: You will regret it when they turn the lights off.

TOM: I won't be here.

JIM: How about your mother?

TOM: I'm like my father. The bastard son of a bastard! Did you

280   notice how he's grinning in his picture in there? And he's
been absent going on sixteen years!

JIM: You're just talking, you drip. How does your mother feel
about it?

TOM: Shhh! Here comes Mother! Mother is not acquainted

285   with my plans!

AMANDA: *(Coming through the portieres.)* Where are you all?

TOM: On the terrace, Mother.

(They start inside. She advances to them. TOM *is distinctly shocked at
her appearance. Even* JIM *blinks a little. He is making his first contact with girlish Southern vivacity and in spite of the night-school
course in public speaking is somewhat thrown off the beam by the unexpected outlay of social charm. Certain responses are attempted by* JIM
but are swept aside by AMANDA's *gay laughter and chatter.* TOM *is
embarrassed but after the first shock* JIM *reacts very warmly. He grins
and chuckles, is altogether won over.)*

(Image on screen: AMANDA *as a girl.)*

AMANDA: *(Coyly smiling, shaking her girlish ringlets.)* Well, well,
well, so this is Mr. O'Connor. Introductions entirely unnec-

290   essary. I've heard so much about you from my boy. I finally
said to him, Tom—good gracious!—why don't you bring
this paragon to supper? I'd like to meet this nice young
man at the warehouse!—instead of just hearing him sing
your praises so much! I don't know why my son is so stand-

295   offish—that's not Southern behavior!
    Let's sit down and—I think we could stand a little more
air in here! Tom, leave the door open. I felt a nice fresh
breeze a moment ago. Where has it gone to? Mmm, so
warm already! And not quite summer, even. We're going to

300   burn up when summer really gets started. However, we're
having—we're having a very light supper. I think light
things are better fo' this time of year. The same as light
clothes are. Light clothes an' light food are what warm
weather calls fo'. You know our blood gets so thick during

305   th' winter—it takes a while fo' us to *adjust* ou'selves!—when

the season changes . . . It's come so quick this year. I wasn't prepared. All of a sudden—heavens! Already summer! I ran to the trunk an' pulled out this light dress—terribly old! Historical almost! But feels so good—so good an' co-ol, y' know. . . .

310 TOM: Mother—

AMANDA: Yes, honey?

TOM: How about—supper?

AMANDA: Honey, you go ask Sister if supper is ready! You know that Sister is in full charge of supper! Tell her you hungry
315 boys are waiting for it. *(To* JIM.*)* Have you met Laura?

JIM: She—

AMANDA: Let you in? Oh, good, you've met already! It's rare for a girl as sweet an' pretty as Laura to be domestic! But Laura
320 is, thank heavens, not only pretty but also very domestic. I'm not at all. I never was a bit. I never could make a thing but angel-food cake. Well, in the South we had so many servants. Gone, gone, gone. All vestige of gracious living! Gone completely! I wasn't prepared for what the future
325 brought me. All of my gentlemen callers were sons of planters and so of course I assumed that I would be married to one and raise my family on a large piece of land with plenty of servants. But man proposes—and woman accepts the proposal! To vary that old, old saying a little bit—I
330 married no planter! I married a man who worked for the telephone company! That gallantly smiling gentleman over there! *(She points to the picture.)* A telephone man who—fell in love with long-distance! Now he travels and I don't even know where! But what am I going on for about my—tribu-
335 lations? Tell me yours—I hope you don't have any! Tom?

TOM: *(Returning.)* Yes, Mother?

AMANDA: Is supper nearly ready?

TOM: It looks to me like supper is on the table.

AMANDA: Let me look—*(She rises prettily and looks through the*
340 *portieres.)* Oh, lovely! But where is Sister?

TOM: Laura is not feeling well and she says that she thinks she'd better not come to the table.

AMANDA: What? Nonsense! Laura? Oh, Laura!

LAURA: *(From the kitchenette, faintly.)* Yes, Mother.

345 AMANDA: You really must come to the table. We won't be seated until you come to the table! Come in, Mr. O'Connor. You sit over there, and I'll . . . .Laura? Laura Wingfield! You're keeping us waiting, honey! We can't say grace until you come to the table!

(The kitchenette door is pushed weakly open and LAURA *comes in. She is obviously quite faint, her lips trembling, her eyes wide and staring. She moves unsteadily toward the table.)*

(Screen legend: "Terror!")

(Outside a summer storm is coming on abruptly. The white curtains billow inward at the windows and there is a sorrowful murmur from the deep blue dusk.)

(LAURA suddenly stumbles; she catches at a chair with a faint moan.)

350 TOM: Laura!

AMANDA: Laura!

(There is a clap of thunder.)

(Screen legend: "Ah!")

(Despairingly.) Why, Laura, you *are* ill, darling! Tom, help your sister into the living room, dear! Sit in the living room, Laura—rest on the sofa. Well! *(to* JIM *as* TOM *helps his*
355 *sister to the sofa in the living room.)* Standing over the hot stove made her ill! I told her that it was just too warm this evening, but—

(TOM comes back to the table.)

Is Laura all right now?

TOM: Yes.

AMANDA: What *is* that? Rain? A nice cool rain has come up!
360 *(She gives* JIM *a frightened look.)* I think we may—have grace—now . . . (TOM *looks at her stupidly.)* Tom, honey— you say grace!

TOM: Oh . . . "For these and all thy mercies—"

(They bow their heads, AMANDA *stealing a nervous glance at* JIM. *In the living room* LAURA, *stretched on the sofa, clenches her hand to her lips, to hold back a shuddering sob.)*

God's Holy Name be praised— 365

(The scene dims out.)

──────── SCENE SEVEN ────────

It is half an hour later. Dinner is just being finished in the dining room, LAURA *is still huddled upon the sofa, her feet drawn under her, her head resting on a pale blue pillow, her eyes wide and mysteriously watchful. The new floor lamp with its shade of rose-colored silk gives a soft, becoming light to her face, bringing out the fragile, unearthly prettiness which usually escapes attention. From outside there is a steady murmur of rain, but it is slackening and soon stops; the air outside becomes pale and luminous as the moon breaks through the clouds. A moment after the curtain rises, the lights in both rooms flicker and go out.*

JIM: Hey, there, Mr. Light Bulb!

(AMANDA laughs nervously.)

(Legend on screen: "Suspension of a public service.")

AMANDA: Where was Moses when the lights went out? Ha-ha. Do you know the answer to that one, Mr. O'Connor?

JIM: No, Ma'am, what's the answer?

AMANDA: In the dark! 5

(JIM laughs appreciatively.)

Everybody sit still. I'll light the candles. Isn't it lucky we have them on the table? Where's a match? Which of you gentlemen can provide a match?

JIM: Here.

AMANDA: Thank you, Sir.

JIM: Not at all, Ma'am! 10

AMANDA: *(As she lights the candles.)* I guess the fuse has burnt out. Mr. O'Connor, can you tell a burnt-out fuse? I know I can't and Tom is a total loss when it comes to mechanics.

(They rise from the table and go into the kitchenette, from where their voices are heard.)

15   Oh, be careful you don't bump into something. We don't want our gentleman caller to break his neck. Now wouldn't that be a fine howdy-do?

JIM: Ha-ha! Where is the fuse-box?

AMANDA: Right here next to the stove. Can you see anything?

20   JIM: Just a minute.

AMANDA: Isn't electricity a mysterious thing? Wasn't it Benjamin Franklin who tied a key to a kite? We live in such a mysterious universe, don't we? Some people say that science clears up all the mysteries for us. In my opinion it only cre-

25   ates more! Have you found it yet?

JIM: No, Ma'am. All these fuses look okay to me.

AMANDA: Tom!

TOM: Yes, Mother?

AMANDA: That light bill I gave you several days ago. The one I

30   told you we got the notices about?

(Legend on screen: "Ha!")

TOM: Oh—yeah.

AMANDA: You didn't neglect to pay it by any chance?

TOM: Why, I—

AMANDA: Didn't! I might have known it!

35   JIM: Shakespeare probably wrote a poem on that light bill, Mrs. Wingfield.

AMANDA: I might have known better than to trust him with it! There's such a high price for negligence in this world!

JIM: Maybe the poem will win a ten-dollar prize.

40   AMANDA: We'll just have to spend the remainder of the evening in the nineteenth century, before Mr. Edison made the Mazda lamp!

JIM: Candlelight is my favorite kind of light.

AMANDA: That shows you're romantic! But that's no excuse for

45   Tom. Well, we got through dinner. Very considerate of them to let us get through dinner before they plunged us into everlasting darkness, wasn't it, Mr. O'Connor?

JIM: Ha-ha!

AMANDA: Tom, as a penalty for your carelessness you can help

50   me with the dishes.

JIM: Let me give you a hand.

AMANDA: Indeed you will not!

JIM: I ought to be good for something.

AMANDA: Good for something? *(Her tone is rhapsodic.)* You?

55   Why, Mr. O'Connor, nobody, *nobody's* given me this much entertainment in years—as you have!

JIM: Aw, now, Mrs. Wingfield!

AMANDA: I'm not exaggerating, not one bit! But Sister is all by her lonesome. You go keep her company in the parlor! I'll

60   give you this lovely old candelabrum that used to be on the altar at the Church of the Heavenly Rest. It was melted a little out of shape when the church burnt down. Lightning struck it one spring. Gypsy Jones was holding a revival at the time and he intimated that the church was destroyed

65   because the Episcopalians gave card parties.

JIM: Ha-ha.

AMANDA: And how about you coaxing Sister to drink a little wine? I think it would be good for her! Can you carry both at once?

JIM: Sure. I'm Superman!   70

AMANDA: Now, Thomas, get into this apron!

*(*JIM *comes into the dining room, carrying the candelabrum, its candles lighted, in one hand and a glass of wine in the other. The door of the kitchenette swings closed on* AMANDA'S *gay laughter; the flickering light approaches the portieres.* LAURA *sits up nervously as* JIM *enters. She can hardly speak from the almost intolerable strain of being alone with a stranger.)*

(Screen legend: "I don't suppose you remember me at all!")

(At first, before JIM'S *warmth overcomes her paralyzing shyness,* LAURA'S *voice is thin and breathless, as though she had just run up a steep flight of stairs.* JIM'S *attitude is gently humorous. While the incident is apparently unimportant, it is to* LAURA *the climax of her secret life.)*

JIM: Hello there, Laura.

LAURA: *(Faintly.)* Hello.

(She clears her throat.)

JIM: How are you feeling now? Better?

LAURA: Yes. Yes, thank you.   75

JIM: This is for you. A little dandelion wine. *(He extends the glass toward her with extravagant gallantry.)*

LAURA: Thank you.

JIM: Drink it—but don't get drunk!

(He laughs heartily. LAURA *takes the glass uncertainly; she laughs shyly.)*

Where shall I set the candles?   80

LAURA: Oh—oh, anywhere. . . .

JIM: How about here on the floor? Any objections?

LAURA: No.

JIM: I'll spread a newspaper under to catch the drippings. I like to sit on the floor. Mind if I do?   85

LAURA: Oh, no.

JIM: Give me a pillow?

LAURA: What?

JIM: A pillow!

LAURA: Oh . . . *(She hands him one quickly.)*   90

JIM: How about you? Don't you like to sit on the floor?

LAURA: Oh—yes.

JIM: Why don't you, then?

LAURA: I—will.

JIM: Take a pillow!   95

    *(*LAURA *does. She sits on the floor on the other side of the candelabrum.* JIM *crosses his legs and smiles engagingly at her.)* I can't hardly see you sitting way over there.

LAURA: I can—see you.

JIM: I know, but that's not fair, I'm in the limelight.   100

*(*LAURA *moves her pillow closer.)*

Good! Now I can see you! Comfortable?

LAURA: Yes.

JIM: So am I. Comfortable as a cow! Will you have some gum?

LAURA: No, thank you.

105 JIM: I think that I will indulge, with your permission. *(He musingly unwraps a stick of gum and holds it up.)* Think of the fortune made by the guy that invented the first piece of chewing gum. Amazing, huh? The Wrigley Building is one of the sights of Chicago—I saw it when I went up to the

110 Century of Progress. Did you take in the Century of Progress?

LAURA: No, I didn't.

JIM: Well, it was quite a wonderful exposition. What impressed me most was the Hall of Science. Gives you an idea of what

115 the future will be in America, even more wonderful than the present time is! *(There is a pause. JIM smiles at her.)* Your brother tells me you're shy. Is that right, Laura?

LAURA: I—don't know.

JIM: I judge you to be an old-fashioned type of girl. Well, I

120 think that's a pretty good type to be. Hope you don't think I'm being too personal—do you?

LAURA: *(Hastily, out of embarrassment.)* I believe I *will* take a piece of gum, if you—don't mind. *(Clearing her throat.)* Mr. O'Connor, have you—kept up with your singing?

125 JIM: Singing? Me?

LAURA: Yes. I remember what a beautiful voice you had.

JIM: When did you hear me sing?

(LAURA does not answer, and in the long pause which follows a man's voice is heard singing offstage.)

VOICE: O blow, ye winds, heigh-ho,
        A-roving I will go!
130   I'm off to my love
          With a boxing glove—
          Ten thousand miles away!

JIM: You say you've heard me sing?

LAURA: Oh, yes! Yes, very often . . . I—don't suppose—you re-

135 member me—at all?

JIM: *(Smiling doubtfully.)* You know I have an idea I've seen you before. I had that idea soon as you opened the door. It seemed almost like I was about to remember your name. But the name that I started to call you—wasn't a name!

140 And so I stopped myself before I said it.

LAURA: Wasn't it—Blue Roses?

JIM: *(Springing up, grinning.)* Blue Roses! My gosh, yes—Blue Roses! That's what I had on my tongue when you opened the door! Isn't it funny what tricks your memory plays? I

145 didn't connect you with high school somehow or other. But that's where it was; it was high school. I didn't even know you were Shakespeare's sister! Gosh, I'm sorry.

LAURA: I didn't expect you to. You—barely knew me!

JIM: But we did have a speaking acquaintance, huh?

150 LAURA: Yes, we—spoke to each other.

JIM: When did you recognize me?

LAURA: Oh, right away!

JIM: Soon as I came in the door?

LAURA: When I heard your name I thought it was probably you.

155 I knew that Tom used to know you a little in high school. So when you came in the door—well, then I was—sure.

JIM: Why didn't you *say* something, then?

LAURA: *(Breathlessly.)* I didn't know what to say, I was—too surprised!

160 JIM: For goodness' sakes! You know, this sure is funny!

LAURA: Yes! Yes, isn't it, though. . . .

JIM: Didn't we have a class in something together?

LAURA: Yes, we did.

JIM: What class was that?

165 LAURA: It was—singing—chorus!

JIM: Aw!

LAURA: I sat across the aisle from you in the Aud.

JIM: Aw.

LAURA: Mondays, Wednesdays, and Fridays.

170 JIM: Now I remember—you always came in late.

LAURA: Yes, it was so hard for me, getting upstairs. I had that brace on my leg—it clumped so loud!

JIM: I never heard any clumping.

LAURA: *(Wincing at the recollection.)* To me it sounded like—

175 thunder!

JIM: Well, well, well, I never even noticed.

LAURA: And everybody was seated before I came in. I had to walk in front of all those people. My seat was in the back row. I had to go clumping all the way up the aisle with

180 everyone watching!

JIM: You shouldn't have been self-conscious.

LAURA: I know, but I was. It was always such a relief when the singing started.

JIM: Aw, yes, I've placed you now! I used to call you Blue Roses.

185 How was it that I got started calling you that?

LAURA: I was out of school a little while with pleurosis. When I came back you asked me what was the matter. I said I had pleurosis—you thought I said *Blue Roses*. That's what you always called me after that!

190 JIM: I hope you didn't mind.

LAURA: Oh, no—I liked it. You see, I wasn't acquainted with many—people. . . .

JIM: As I remember you sort of stuck by yourself.

LAURA: I—I—never have had much luck at—making friends.

195 JIM: I don't see why you wouldn't.

LAURA: Well, I—started out badly.

JIM: You mean being—

LAURA: Yes, it sort of—stood between me—

JIM: You shouldn't have let it!

200 LAURA: I know, but it did, and—

JIM: You were shy with people!

LAURA: I tried not to be but never could—

JIM: Overcome it?

LAURA: No, I—I never could!

205 JIM: I guess being shy is something you have to work out of kind of gradually.

LAURA: *(Sorrowfully.)* Yes—I guess it—

JIM: Takes time!

LAURA: Yes—

210 JIM: People are not so dreadful when you know them. That's what you have to remember! And everybody has problems, not just you, but practically everybody has got some problems. You think of yourself as having the only problems, as being the only one who is disappointed. But just look

215 around you and you will see lots of people as disappointed as you are. For instance, I hoped when I was going to high school that I would be further along at this time, six years later, than I am now. You remember that wonderful write-up I had in *The Torch?*

220 LAURA: Yes! *(She rises and crosses to the table.)*
JIM: It said I was bound to succeed in anything I went into!

(LAURA returns with the high school yearbook.)

Holy Jeez! *The Torch!*

(He accepts it reverently. They smile across the book with mutual wonder. LAURA crouches beside him and they begin to turn the pages. LAURA's shyness is dissolving in his warmth.)

LAURA: Here you are in *The Pirates of Penzance!*
JIM: *(Wistfully.)* I sang the baritone lead in that operetta.
225 LAURA: *(Raptly.)* So—*beautifully!*
JIM: *(Protesting.)* Aw—
LAURA: Yes, yes—beautifully—beautifully!
JIM: You heard me?
LAURA: All three times!
230 JIM: No!
LAURA: Yes!
JIM: All three performances?
LAURA: *(Looking down.)* Yes.
JIM: Why?
235 LAURA: I—wanted to ask you to—autograph my program. *(She takes the program from the back of the yearbook and shows it to him.)*
JIM: Why didn't you ask me to?
LAURA: You were always surrounded by your own friends so much that I never had a chance to.
240 JIM: You should have just—
LAURA: Well, I—thought you might think I was—
JIM: Thought I might think you was—what?
LAURA: Oh—
JIM: *(With reflective relish.)* I was beleaguered by females in those
245 days.
LAURA: You were terribly popular!
JIM: Yeah—
LAURA: You had such a—friendly way—
JIM: I was spoiled in high school.
250 LAURA: Everybody—liked you!
JIM: Including you?
LAURA: I—yes, I—did, too—*(She gently closes the book in her lap.)*
JIM: Well, well, well! Give me that program, Laura.

(She hands it to him. He signs it with a flourish.)

There you are—better late than never!
255 LAURA: Oh, I—what a—surprise!
JIM: My signature isn't worth very much right now. But some day—maybe—it will increase in value! Being disappointed is one thing and being discouraged is something else. I am disappointed but I am not discouraged. I'm twenty-three
260 years old. How old are you?
LAURA: I'll be twenty-four in June.
JIM: That's not old age!
LAURA: No, but—
JIM: You finished high school?
265 LAURA: *(With difficulty.)* I didn't go back.
JIM: You mean you dropped out?
LAURA: I made bad grades in my final examinations. *(She rises and replaces the book and the program on the table. Her voice is strained.)* How is—Emily Meisenbach getting along?

JIM: Oh, that kraut-head! 270
LAURA: Why do you call her that?
JIM: That's what she was.
LAURA: You're not still—going with her?
JIM: I never see her.
LAURA: It said in the "Personal" section that you were— 275
engaged!
JIM: I know, but I wasn't impressed by that—propaganda!
LAURA: It wasn't—the truth?
JIM: Only in Emily's optimistic opinion!
LAURA: Oh— 280

(Legend: "What have you done since high school?")

(JIM lights a cigarette and leans indolently back on his elbows smiling at LAURA with a warmth and charm which lights her inwardly with altar candles. She remains by the table, picks up a piece from the glass menagerie collection, and turns it in her hands to cover her tumult.)

JIM: *(After several reflective puffs on his cigarette.)* What have you done since high school?

(She seems not to hear him.)

Huh?

(LAURA looks up.)

I said what have you done since high school, Laura?
LAURA: Nothing much. 285
JIM: You must have been doing something these six long years.
LAURA: Yes.
JIM: Well, then, such as what?
LAURA: I took a business course at business college—
JIM: How did that work out? 290
LAURA: Well, not very—well—I had to drop out, it gave me—
indigestion—

(JIM laughs gently.)

JIM: What are you doing now?
LAURA: I don't do anything—much. Oh, please don't think I sit around doing nothing! My glass collection takes up a 295
good deal of time. Glass is something you have to take good care of.
JIM: What did you say—about glass?
LAURA: Collection I said—I have one—*(She clears her throat and turns away again, acutely shy.)* 300
JIM: *(Abruptly.)* You know what I judge to be the trouble with you? Inferiority complex! Know what that is? That's what they call it when someone low-rates himself! I understand it because I had it, too. Although my case was not so aggravated as yours seems to be. I had it until I took up public speaking, developed my voice, and learned that I had an 305
aptitude for science. Before that time I never thought of myself as being outstanding in any way whatsoever! Now I've never made a regular study of it, but I have a friend who says I can analyze people better than doctors that make 310
a profession of it. I don't claim that to be necessarily true, but I can sure guess a person's psychology, Laura! *(He takes out his gum.)* Excuse me, Laura. I always take it out when the flavor is gone. I'll use this scrap of paper to wrap it in.

315   I know how it is to get it stuck on a shoe. (*He wraps the gum in paper and puts it in his pocket.*) Yep—that's what I judge to be your principal trouble. A lack of confidence in yourself as a person. You don't have the proper amount of faith in yourself. I'm basing that fact on a number of your remarks

320   and also on certain observations I've made. For instance that clumping you thought was so awful in high school. You say that you even dreaded to walk into class. You see what you did? You dropped out of school, you gave up an education because of a clump, which as far as I know was practically

325   non-existent! A little physical defect is what you have. Hardly noticeable even! Magnified thousands of times by imagination! You know what my strong advice to you is? Think of yourself as *superior* in some way!
      LAURA: In what way would I think?

330   JIM: Why, man alive, Laura! Just look about you a little. What do you see? A world full of common people! All of 'em born and all of 'em going to die! Which of them has one-tenth of your good points! Or mine! Or anyone else's, as far as that goes—gosh! Everybody excels in some one thing. Some in

335   many! (*He unconsciously glances at himself in the mirror.*) All you've got to do is discover in *what!* Take me, for instance. (*He adjusts his tie at the mirror.*) My interest happens to lie in electro-dynamics. I'm taking a course in radio engineering at night school, Laura, on top of a fairly responsible job at

340   the warehouse. I'm taking that course and studying public speaking.
      LAURA: Ohhhh.
      JIM: Because I believe in the future of television! (*Turning his back to her.*) I wish to be ready to go up right along with it.

345   Therefore I'm planning to get in on the ground floor. In fact I've already made the right connections and all that remains is for the industry itself to get under way! Full steam—(*His eyes are starry.*) Knowledge—Zzzzzp! Money—Zzzzzp!— Power! That's the cycle democracy is built on!

(*His attitude is convincingly dynamic.* LAURA *stares at him, even her shyness eclipsed in her absolute wonder. He suddenly grins.*)

350   I guess you think I think a lot of myself!
      LAURA: No—o-o-o, I—
      JIM: Now how about you? Isn't there something you take more interest in than anything else?
      LAURA: Well, I do—as I said—have my—glass collection—

(*A peal of girlish laughter rings from the kitchenette.*)

355   JIM: I'm not right sure I know what you're talking about. What kind of glass is it?
      LAURA: Little articles of it, they're ornaments mostly! Most of them are little animals made out of glass, the tiniest little animals in the world. Mother calls them a glass menagerie!

360   Here's an example of one, if you'd like to see it! This one is one of the oldest. It's nearly thirteen.

(*Music: "The Glass Menagerie."*)

(*He stretches out his hand.*)

Oh, be careful—if you breathe, it breaks!
JIM: I'd better not take it. I'm pretty clumsy with things.

LAURA: Go on, I trust you with him! (*She places the piece in his palm.*) There now—you're holding him gently! Hold him   365 over the light, he loves the light! You see how the light shines through him?
JIM: It sure does shine!
LAURA: I shouldn't be partial, but he is my favorite one.
JIM: What kind of a thing is this one supposed to be?   370
LAURA: Haven't you noticed the single horn on his forehead?
JIM: A unicorn, huh?
LAURA: Mmmm-hmmm!
JIM: Unicorns—aren't they extinct in the modern world?
LAURA: I know!   375
JIM: Poor little fellow, he must feel sort of lonesome.
LAURA: (*Smiling.*) Well, if he does, he doesn't complain about it. He stays on a shelf with some horses that don't have horns and all of them seem to get along nicely together.
JIM: How do you know?   380
LAURA: (*Lightly.*) I haven't heard any arguments among them!
JIM: (*Grinning.*) No arguments, huh? Well, that's a pretty good sign! Where shall I set him?
LAURA: Put him on the table. They all like a change of scenery once in a while!   385
JIM: Well, well, well, well—(*He places the glass piece on the table, then raises his arms and stretches.*) Look how big my shadow is when I stretch!
LAURA: Oh, oh, yes—it stretches across the ceiling!
JIM: (*Crossing to the door.*) I think it's stopped raining. (*He opens   390 the fire-escape door and the background music changes to a dance tune.*) Where does the music come from?
LAURA: From the Paradise Dance Hall across the alley.
JIM: How about cutting the rug a little, Miss Wingfield?
LAURA: Oh, I—   395
JIM: Or is your program filled up? Let me have a look at it. (*He grasps an imaginary card.*) Why, every dance is taken! I'll just have to scratch some out.

(*Waltz music: "La Golondrina."*)

Ahhh, a waltz! (*He executes some sweeping turns by himself, then holds his arms toward* LAURA.)   400
LAURA: (*Breathlessly.*) I—can't dance!
JIM: There you go, that inferiority stuff!
LAURA: I've never danced in my life!
JIM: Come on, try!
LAURA: Oh, but I'd step on you!   405
JIM: I'm not made out of glass.
LAURA: How—how—how do we start?
JIM: Just leave it to me. You hold your arms out a little.
LAURA: Like this?
JIM: (*Taking her in his arms.*) A little bit higher. Right. Now   410 don't tighten up, that's the main thing about it—relax.
LAURA: (*Laughing breathlessly.*) It's hard not to.
JIM: Okay.
LAURA: I'm afraid you can't budge me.
JIM: What do you bet I can't? (*He swings her into motion.*)   415
LAURA: Goodness, yes, you can!
JIM: Let yourself go, now, Laura, just let yourself go.
LAURA: I'm—
JIM: Come on!
LAURA: —trying!   420

JIM: Not so stiff—easy does it!

LAURA: I know but I'm—

JIM: Loosen th' backbone! There now, that's a lot better.

LAURA: Am I?

425   JIM: Lots, lots better! *(He moves her about the room in a clumsy waltz.)*

LAURA: Oh, my!

JIM: Ha-ha!

LAURA: Oh, my goodness!

430   JIM: Ha-ha-ha!

(They suddenly bump into the table, and the glass piece on it falls to the floor. JIM *stops the dance.)*

What did we hit on?

LAURA: Table.

JIM: Did something fall off it? I think—

LAURA: Yes.

435   JIM: I hope that it wasn't the little glass horse with the horn!

LAURA: Yes. *(She stoops to pick it up.)*

JIM: Aw, aw, aw. Is it broken?

LAURA: Now it is just like all the other horses.

JIM: It's lost its—

440   LAURA: Horn! It doesn't matter. Maybe it's a blessing in disguise.

JIM: You'll never forgive me. I bet that that was your favorite piece of glass.

LAURA: I don't have favorites much. It's no tragedy, Freckles.

445   Glass breaks so easily. No matter how careful you are. The traffic jars the shelves and things fall off them.

JIM: Still I'm awfully sorry that I was the cause.

LAURA: *(Smiling.)* I'll just imagine he had an operation. The horn was removed to make him feel less—freakish!

(They both laugh.)

450   Now he will feel more at home with the other horses, the ones that don't have horns. . . .

JIM: Ha-ha, that's very funny! *(Suddenly he is serious.)* I'm glad to see that you have a sense of humor. You know—you're— well—very different! Surprisingly different from anyone

455   else I know! *(His voice becomes soft and hesitant with a genuine feeling.)* Do you mind me telling you that?

*(*LAURA *is abashed beyond speech.)*

I mean it in a nice way—

*(*LAURA *nods shyly, looking away.)*

You make me feel sort of—I don't know how to put it! I'm usually pretty good at expressing things, but—this is

460   something that I don't know how to say!

*(*LAURA *touches her throat and clears it—turns the broken unicorn in her hands. His voice becomes softer.)*

Has anyone ever told you that you were pretty?

(There is a pause, and the music rises slightly. LAURA *looks up slowly, with wonder, and shakes her head.)*

Well, you are! In a very different way from anyone else. And all the nicer because of the difference, too.

(His voice becomes low and husky. LAURA *turns away, nearly faint with the novelty of her emotions.)*

I wish that you were my sister. I'd teach you to have some confidence in yourself. The different people are not like 465
other people, but being different is nothing to be ashamed of. Because other people are not such wonderful people. They're one hundred times one thousand. You're one times one! They walk all over the earth. You just stay here. They're common as—weeds, but—you—well, you're— 470
Blue Roses!

(Image on screen: Blue Roses.)

(The music changes.)

LAURA: But blue is wrong for—roses. . . .

JIM: It's right for you! You're—pretty!

LAURA: In what respect am I pretty?

JIM: In all respects—believe me! Your eyes—your hair—are 475
pretty! Your hands are pretty! *(He catches hold of her hand.)* You think I'm making this up because I'm invited to din- ner and have to be nice. Oh, I could do that! I could put on an act for you, Laura, and say lots of things without being very sincere. But this time I am. I'm talking to you sin- 480
cerely. I happened to notice you had this inferiority com- plex that keeps you from feeling comfortable with people. Somebody needs to build your confidence up and make you proud instead of shy and turning away and—blushing. Somebody—ought to—*kiss* you, Laura! 485

(His hand slips slowly up her arm to her shoulder as the music swells tumultuously. He suddenly turns her about and kisses her on the lips. When he releases her, LAURA *sinks on the sofa with a bright, dazed look.* JIM *backs away and fishes in his pocket for a cigarette.)*

(Legend on screen: "A souvenir.")

Stumblejohn!

(He lights the cigarette, avoiding her look. There is a peal of girlish laughter from AMANDA *in the kitchenette.* LAURA *slowly raises and opens her hand. It still contains the little broken glass animal. She looks at it with a tender, bewildered expression.)*

Stumblejohn! I shouldn't have done that—that was way off the beam. You don't smoke, do you?

(She looks up, smiling, not hearing the question. He sits beside her rather gingerly. She looks at him speechlessly—waiting. He coughs decorously and moves a little farther aside as he considers the situation and senses her feelings, dimly, with perturbation. He speaks gently.)

Would you—care for a—mint?

(She doesn't seem to hear him but her look grows brighter even.)

Peppermint? Life Saver? My pocket's a regular drugstore— 490
wherever I go . . . *(He pops a mint in his mouth. Then he gulps

and decides to make a clean breast of it. He speaks slowly and
gingerly.) Laura, you know, if I had a sister like you, I'd
do the same thing as Tom. I'd bring out fellows and—
495 introduce her to them. The right type of boys—of a type
to—appreciate her. Only—well—he made a mistake about
me. Maybe I've got no call to be saying this. That may not
have been the idea in having me over. But what if it was?
There's nothing wrong about that. The only trouble is that
500 in my case—I'm not in a situation to—do the right thing.
I can't take down your number and say I'll phone. I can't
call up next week and—ask for a date. I thought I had better explain the situation in case you—misunderstood it
and—I hurt your feelings. . . .

(There is a pause. Slowly, very slowly, LAURA's *look changes, her eyes*
returning slowly from his to the glass figure in her palm. AMANDA
utters another gay laugh in the kitchenette.)

505 LAURA: *(Faintly.)* You—won't—call again?
JIM: No, Laura. I can't. *(He rises from the sofa.)* As I was just explaining, I've—got strings on me. Laura, I've—been going
steady! I go out all the time with a girl named Betty. She's
a home-girl like you, and Catholic, and Irish, and in a great
510 many ways we—get along fine. I met her last summer on a
moonlight boat trip up the river to Alton, on the *Majestic.*
Well—right away from the start it was—love!

(Legend: "Love!")

*(*LAURA *sways slightly forward and grips the arm of the sofa. He fails*
to notice, now enrapt in his own comfortable being.)

Being in love has made a new man of me!

(Leaning stiffly forward, clutching the arm of the sofa, LAURA *strug-*
gles visibly with her storm. But JIM *is oblivious; she is a long way off.)*

The power of love is really pretty tremendous! Love is
515 something that—changes the whole world, Laura!

(The storm abates a little and LAURA *leans back. He notices her*
again.)

It happened that Betty's aunt took sick, she got a wire
and had to go to Centralia. So Tom—when he asked me to
dinner—I naturally just accepted the invitation, not knowing that you—that he—that I—*(He stops awkwardly.)*
520 Huh—I'm a stumblejohn!

(He flops back on the sofa. The holy candles on the altar of LAURA's
face have been snuffed out. There is a look of almost infinite desolation.
JIM *glances at her uneasily.)*

I wish that you would—say something.

(She bites her lip which was trembling and then bravely smiles. She
opens her hand again on the broken glass figure. Then she gently takes
his hand and raises it level with her own. She carefully places the uni-
corn in the palm of his hand, then pushes his fingers closed upon it.)

What are you—doing that for? You want me to have him?
Laura?

(She nods.)

What for?
LAURA: A—souvenir. . . .   525

(She rises unsteadily and crouches beside the Victrola to wind
it up.)

(Legend on screen: "Things have a way of turning out so badly!"
Or image: Gentleman caller waving goodbye—gaily.)

(At this moment AMANDA *rushes brightly back into the living room.*
She bears a pitcher of fruit punch in an old-fashioned cut-glass pitcher,
and a plate of macaroons. The plate has a gold border and poppies
painted on it.)

AMANDA: Well, well, well! Isn't the air delightful after the
shower? I've made you children a little liquid refreshment.
(She turns gaily to JIM.*)* Jim, do you know that song about
lemonade?

"Lemonade, lemonade   530
Made in the shade and stirred with a spade—
Good enough for any old maid!"

JIM: *(Uneasily.)* Ha-ha! No—I never heard it.
AMANDA: Why, Laura! You look so serious!
JIM: We were having a serious conversation.   535
AMANDA: Good! Now you're better acquainted!
JIM: *(Uncertainly.)* Ha-ha! Yes.
AMANDA: You modern young people are much more serious-
minded than my generation. I was so gay as a girl!
JIM: You haven't changed, Mrs. Wingfield.   540
AMANDA: Tonight I'm rejuvenated! The gaiety of the occasion,
Mr. O'Connor! *(She tosses her head with a peal of laughter,*
spilling some lemonade.) Oooo! I'm baptizing myself!
JIM: Here—let me—
AMANDA: *(Setting the pitcher down.)* There now. I discovered we 545
had some maraschino cherries. I dumped them in, juice
and all!
JIM: You shouldn't have gone to that trouble, Mrs. Wingfield.
AMANDA: Trouble, trouble? Why, it was loads of fun! Didn't
you hear me cutting up in the kitchen? I bet your ears were 550
burning! I told Tom how outdone with him I was for keeping you to himself so long a time! He should have brought
you over much, much sooner! Well, now that you've found
your way, I want you to be a very frequent caller! Not just
occasional but all the time. Oh, we're going to have a lot of 555
gay times together! I see them coming! Mmm, just breathe
that air! So fresh, and the moon's so pretty! I'll skip back
out—I know where my place is when young folks are having a—serious conversation!
JIM: Oh, don't go out, Mrs. Wingfield. The fact of the matter 560
is I've got to be going.
AMANDA: Going, now? You're joking! Why, it's only the shank
of the evening, Mr. O'Connor!
JIM: Well, you know how it is.
AMANDA: You mean you're a young workingman and have to 565
keep workingmen's hours. We'll let you off early tonight.
But only on the condition that next time you stay later.
What's the best night for you? Isn't Saturday night the best
night for you workingmen?

570 JIM: I have a couple of time-clocks to punch, Mrs. Wingfield. One at morning, another one at night!

AMANDA: My, but you *are* ambitious! You work at night, too?

JIM: No, Ma'am, not work but—Betty!

(He crosses deliberately to pick up his hat. The band at the Paradise Dance Hall goes into a tender waltz.)

AMANDA: Betty? Betty? Who's—Betty!

(There is an ominous cracking sound in the sky.)

575 JIM: Oh, just a girl. The girl I go steady with!

(He smiles charmingly. The sky falls.)

(Legend: "The Sky Falls.")

AMANDA: *(A long-drawn exhalation.)* Ohhhh . . . Is it a serious romance, Mr. O'Connor?

JIM: We're going to be married the second Sunday in June.

AMANDA: Ohhhh—how nice! Tom didn't mention that you 580 were engaged to be married.

JIM: The cat's not out of the bag at the warehouse yet. You know how they are. They call you Romeo and stuff like that. *(He stops at the oval mirror to put on his hat. He carefully shapes the brim and the crown to give a discreetly dashing effect.)* 585 It's been a wonderful evening, Mrs. Wingfield. I guess this is what they mean by Southern hospitality.

AMANDA: It really wasn't anything at all.

JIM: I hope it don't seem like I'm rushing off. But I promised Betty I'd pick her up at the Wabash depot, an' by the time 590 I get my jalopy down there her train'll be in. Some women are pretty upset if you keep 'em waiting.

AMANDA: Yes, I know—the tyranny of women! *(She extends her hand.)* Goodbye, Mr. O'Connor. I wish you luck—and happiness—and success! All three of them, and so does 595 Laura! Don't you, Laura?

LAURA: Yes!

JIM: *(Taking LAURA's hand.)* Goodbye, Laura. I'm certainly going to treasure that souvenir. And don't you forget the good advice I gave you. *(He raises his voice to a cheery shout.)* So 600 long, Shakespeare! Thanks again, ladies. Good night!

(He grins and ducks jauntily out. Still bravely grimacing, AMANDA closes the door on the gentleman caller. Then she turns back to the room with a puzzled expression. She and LAURA don't dare to face each other. LAURA crouches beside the Victrola to wind it.)

AMANDA: *(Faintly.)* Things have a way of turning out so badly. I don't believe that I would play the Victrola. Well, well—well! Our gentleman caller was engaged to be married! *(She raises her voice.)* Tom!

605 TOM: *(From the kitchenette.)* Yes, Mother?

AMANDA: Come in here a minute. I want to tell you something awfully funny.

TOM: *(Entering with a macaroon and a glass of the lemonade.)* Has the gentleman caller gotten away already?

610 AMANDA: The gentleman caller has made an early departure. What a wonderful joke you played on us!

TOM: How do you mean?

AMANDA: You didn't mention that he was engaged to be married.

TOM: Jim? Engaged? 615

AMANDA: That's what he just informed us.

TOM: I'll be jiggered! I didn't know about that.

AMANDA: That seems very peculiar.

TOM: What's peculiar about it?

AMANDA: Didn't you call him your best friend down at the 620 warehouse?

TOM: He is, but how did I know?

AMANDA: It seems extremely peculiar that you wouldn't know your best friend was going to be married!

TOM: The warehouse is where I work, not where I know things 625 about people!

AMANDA: You don't know things anywhere! You live in a dream; you manufacture illusions!

(He crosses to the door.)

Where are you going?

TOM: I'm going to the movies. 630

AMANDA: That's right, now that you've had us make such fools of ourselves. The effort, the preparations, all the expense! The new floor lamp, the rug, the clothes for Laura! All for what? To entertain some other girl's fiancé! Go to the movies, go! Don't think about us, a mother deserted, an 635 unmarried sister who's crippled and has no job! Don't let anything interfere with your selfish pleasure! Just go, go, go—to the movies!

TOM: All right, I will! The more you shout about my selfishness to me the quicker I'll go, and I won't go to the movies! 640

AMANDA: Go, then! Go to the moon—you selfish dreamer!

(TOM smashes his glass on the floor. He plunges out on the fire escape, slamming the door. LAURA screams in fright. The dance-hall music becomes louder. TOM stands on the fire escape, gripping the rail. The moon breaks through the storm clouds, illuminating his face.)

(Legend on screen: "And so goodbye . . .")

(TOM's closing speech is timed with what is happening inside the house. We see, as though through soundproof glass, that AMANDA appears to be making a comforting speech to LAURA, who is huddled upon the sofa. Now that we cannot hear the mother's speech, her silliness is gone and she has dignity and tragic beauty. LAURA's hair hides her face until, at the end of the speech, she lifts her head to smile at her mother. AMANDA's gestures are slow and graceful, almost dancelike, as she comforts her daughter. At the end of her speech she glances a moment at the father's picture—then withdraws through the portieres. At the close of TOM's speech, LAURA blows out the candles, ending the play.)

TOM: I didn't go to the moon, I went much further—for time is the longest distance between two places. Not long after that I was fired for writing a poem on the lid of a shoe-box. I left Saint Louis. I descended the steps of this fire escape for 645 a last time and followed, from then on, in my father's footsteps, attempting to find in motion what was lost in space. I traveled around a great deal. The cities swept about me like dead leaves, leaves that were brightly colored but torn away from the branches. I would have stopped, but I was 650 pursued by something. It always came upon me unawares, taking me altogether by surprise. Perhaps it was a familiar bit of music. Perhaps it was only a piece of transparent glass. Perhaps I am walking along a street at night, in some strange city, before I have found companions. I pass the lighted window of a shop where perfume is sold. The window is filled with pieces of colored glass, tiny transparent bottles in delicate colors, like bits of a shattered rainbow. Then all at once my sister touches my shoulder. I turn around and look into her eyes. Oh, Laura, Laura, I tried to leave you behind me, but I am more faithful than I intended to be! I reach for a cigarette, I cross the street, I run into the movies or a bar, I buy a drink, I speak to the nearest stranger—anything that can blow your candles out!

(LAURA bends over the candles.)

For nowadays the world is lit by lightning! Blow out your candles, Laura—and so goodbye. . . .

(She blows the candles out.)

LUIS VALDEZ

AND EL TEATRO CAMPESINO

Luis Valdez (b. 1940) was born and raised the son of farmworkers in Delano, California. He majored in drama at San Jose State College, taking his B.A. in 1964, and then joined the San Francisco Mime Troup, an important experimental theater company. In 1965, when farm workers at the Delano grape plantations went on strike, Valdez formed El Teatro Campesino ("The Farmworkers' Theater"). Valdez and Teatro Campesino devised two dramatic forms: ACTOS, short, satirical plays dramatizing the oppression of the field-workers, and MITOS, poetic, lyrical plays on Chicano life. *Actos* were improvised by members of El Teatro Campesino playing "stock" characters (the farmworker, the boss, etc.); because they were improvised for each production and each community, *actos* varied considerably from performance to performance. The final versions published by Valdez were written down much later. El Teatro Campesino became one of several important Chicano theater companies that performed throughout the Southwest and in urban areas of the Midwest and Northeast, drawing on both American and European dramatic traditions, as well as traditions of Mexican and Spanish-language theater in the United States that date to the seventeenth century. In the late 1960s and 1970s, Teatro Campesino toured the United States and Europe and gained an international reputation. Valdez's other *actos* with Teatro Campesino include *Las Dos Caras del Patroncito* (1965), *No Saco Nada de la Escuela* (1969), and *Vietnam Campesino* (1970). Valdez produced the stage play *Zoot Suit* in 1978, which was released as a film in 1981. In 1980, Valdez transformed El Teatro Campesino into a production company, a marked shift from its collaborative and activist origins. This version of El Teatro Campesino hired "professional" actors, abandoning the collective esthetic characteristic of the company's earlier work. Valdez developed several new projects in connection with the company's new theater in San Juan Bautista (built in 1981), notably *Bandido!* (1981), *Corridos* (1992), and *I Don't Have to Show You No Stinking Badges* (1990). His film *La Bamba* was released in 1987, and Valdez filmed *Pastorelas* for PBS TV in 1990. Valdez has held academic appointments at the University of California, Berkeley, and at the University of California, Santa Cruz. He is teaching at the new campus of the California State University at Monterey.

LOS VENDIDOS

One of Teatro Campesino's best and most popular *actos, Los Vendidos*—"The Sellouts"—is reminiscent both of Brechtian political theater and more generally of popular satire. In its brief sketch of Honest Sancho's Used Mexican Lot, the play dramatizes a range of stereotypes applied by Anglo culture (represented by the Anglicized Mexican-American, Miss JIM-enez) to Chicano experience: farmworkers, Johnny Pachuco, the *revolucionario,* and the "new 1970 Mexican-American" yuppie. In the play's surprising finale, though, the yuppie turns on Miss JIM-enez, and the "used Mexicans" turn out to run the shop: Honest Sancho is *their* front.

The play clearly engages conflicting attitudes toward social experience, as emblematized by its title. For the title can mean both "those who are sold"—like the "used Mexicans" on Sancho's lot—and "the sellouts," presumably Honest Sancho and Miss JIM-enez. This duplicity is also inflected by the play's language, its mixture of Spanish and English, the two languages Chicano culture uses to define itself and to engage the Anglo world. The play works at the border between two cultures, where language is part of the complex social and political negotiation that characterizes Mexican-American life today.

LOS VENDIDOS

Luis Valdez and El Teatro Campesino

—— CHARACTERS ——

HONEST SANCHO
SECRETARY
FARM WORKER
JOHNNY
REVOLUCIONARIO
MEXICAN-AMERICAN

SCENE: *Honest Sancho's Used Mexican Lot and Mexican Curio Shop. Three models are on display in Honest Sancho's shop: to the right, there is a* REVOLUCIONARIO, *complete with sombrero, carrilleras, and carabina 30–30. At center, on the floor, there is the* FARM WORKER, *under a broad straw sombrero. At stage left is,* JOHNNY, *the Pachuco, filero in hand.*

HONEST SANCHO *is moving among his models, dusting them off and preparing for another day of business.*

SANCHO: Bueno, bueno, mis monos, vamos a ver a quien vendemos ahora, ¿no? *(To audience.)* ¡Quihubo! I'm Honest Sancho and this is my shop. Antes fui contratista pero ahora logré tener mi negocito. All I need now is a customer. *(A*
5 *bell rings offstage.)* Ay, a customer!
SECRETARY: *(Entering.)* Good morning, I'm Miss Jiménez from—
SANCHO: ¡Ah, una chicana! Welcome, welcome Señorita Jiménez.
10 SECRETARY: *(Anglo pronunciation.)* JIM-enez.
SANCHO: ¿Qué?
SECRETARY: My name is Miss JIM-enez. Don't you speak English? What's wrong with you?
SANCHO: Oh, nothing, Señorita JIM-enez. I'm here to help you.
15 SECRETARY: That's better. As I was starting to say, I'm a secretary from Governor Reagan's office, and we're looking for a Mexican type for the administration.
SANCHO: Well, you come to the right place, lady. This is Honest Sancho's Used Mexican lot, and we got all types here.
20 Any particular type you want?
SECRETARY: Yes, we were looking for somebody suave—
SANCHO: Suave.
SECRETARY: Debonair.
SANCHO: De buen aire.
25 SECRETARY: Dark.
SANCHO: Prieto.
SECRETARY: But of course not too dark.
SANCHO: No muy prieto.
SECRETARY: Perhaps, beige.
30 SANCHO: Beige, just the tone. Así como cafecito con leche, ¿no?
SECRETARY: One more thing. He must be hard-working.
SANCHO: That could only be one model. Step right over here to the center of the shop, lady. *(They cross to the* FARM WORKER.) This is our standard farm worker model. As you can see, in
35 the words of our beloved Senator George Murphy, he is "built close to the ground." Also take special notice of his

four-ply Goodyear huaraches, made from the rain tire. This wide-brimmed sombrero is an extra added feature—keeps off the sun, rain, and dust.
SECRETARY: Yes, it does look durable.   40
SANCHO: And our farm worker model is friendly. Muy amable. Watch. *(Snaps his fingers.)*
FARM WORKER: *(Lifts up head.)* Buenos días, señorita. *(His head drops.)*
SECRETARY: My, he's friendly.   45
SANCHO: Didn't I tell you? Loves his patrones! But his most attractive feature is that he's hard-working. Let me show you. *(Snaps fingers.* FARM WORKER *stands.)*
FARM WORKER: ¡El jale! *(He begins to work.)*
SANCHO: As you can see, he is cutting grapes.   50
SECRETARY: Oh, I wouldn't know.
SANCHO: He also picks cotton. *(Snap.* FARM WORKER *begins to pick cotton.)*
SECRETARY: Versatile isn't he?
SANCHO: He also picks melons. *(Snap.* FARM WORKER *picks mel-*   55
ons.) That's his slow speed for late in the season. Here's his fast speed. *(Snap.* FARM WORKER *picks faster.)*
SECRETARY: ¡Chihuahua! . . . I mean, goodness, he sure is a hard worker.
SANCHO: *(Pulls the* FARM WORKER *to his feet.)* And that isn't the   60
half of it. Do you see these little holes on his arms that appear to be pores? During those hot sluggish days in the field, when the vines or the branches get so entangled, it's almost impossible to move; these holes emit a certain grease that allow our model to slip and slide right through the   65
crop with no trouble at all.
SECRETARY: Wonderful. But is he economical?
SANCHO: Economical? Señorita, you are looking at the Volkswagen of Mexicans. Pennies a day is all it takes. One plate of beans and tortillas will keep him going all day. That, and   70
chile. Plenty of chile. Chile jalapenos, chile verde, chile colorado. But, of course, if you do give him chile *(Snap.* FARM WORKER *turns left face. Snap.* FARM WORKER *bends over.)* then you have to change his oil filter once a week.
SECRETARY: What about storage?   75
SANCHO: No problem. You know these new farm labor camps our Honorable Governor Reagan has built out by Parlier or Raisin City? They were designed with our model in mind. Five, six, seven, even ten in one of those shacks will give you no trouble at all. You can also put him in old barns, old   80

Scene **carrilleras** literally chin straps, but may refer to cartridge belts   **Pachuco** Chicano slang for 1940s zoot suiter   **filero** blade   1–2 **Bueno, bueno, . . .** Quihubo "Good, good, my cute ones, let's see who we can sell now, O.K.?"   3–4 **Antes fui . . . negocito** "I used to be a contractor, but now I've succeeded in having my little business."   30 **Así como . . . leche** like coffee with milk

---

41 **Muy amable** very friendly   49 **El jale** the job

cars, river banks. You can even leave him out in the field overnight with no worry!

SECRETARY: Remarkable.

SANCHO: And here's an added feature: Every year at the end of the season, this model goes back to Mexico and doesn't return, automatically, until next Spring.

SECRETARY: How about that. But tell me: does he speak English?

SANCHO: Another outstanding feature is that last year this model was programmed to go out on STRIKE! (*Snap.*)

FARM WORKER: ¡HUELGA! ¡HUELGA! Hermanos, sálganse de esos files. (*Snap. He stops.*)

SECRETARY: No! Oh no, we can't strike in the State Capitol.

SANCHO: Well, he also scabs. (*Snap.*)

FARM WORKER: Me vendo barato, ¿y qué? (*Snap.*)

SECRETARY: That's much better, but you didn't answer my question. Does he speak English?

SANCHO: Bueno . . . no pero he has other—

SECRETARY: No.

SANCHO: Other features.

SECRETARY: NO! He just won't do!

SANCHO: Okay, okay pues. We have other models.

SECRETARY: I hope so. What we need is something a little more sophisticated.

SANCHO: Sophisti—¿qué?

SECRETARY: An urban model.

SANCHO: Ah, from the city! Step right back. Over here in this corner of the shop is exactly what you're looking for. Introducing our new 1969 JOHNNY PACHUCO model! This is our fast-back model. Streamlined. Built for speed, low-riding, city life. Take a look at some of these features. Mag shoes, dual exhausts, green chartreuse paint-job, dark-tint windshield, a little poof on top. Let me just turn him on. (*Snap.* JOHNNY *walks to stage center with a pachuco bounce.*)

SECRETARY: What was that?

SANCHO: That, señorita, was the Chicano shuffle.

SECRETARY: Okay, what does he do?

SANCHO: Anything and everything necessary for city life. For instance, survival: He knife fights. (*Snap.* JOHNNY *pulls out switch blade and swings at secretary.*)

(SECRETARY *screams.*)

SANCHO: He dances. (*Snap.*)

JOHNNY: (*Singing.*) "Angel Baby, my Angel Baby . . ." (*Snap.*)

SANCHO: And here's a feature no city model can be without. He gets arrested, but not without resisting, of course. (*Snap.*)

JOHNNY: ¡En la madre, la placa! I didn't do it! I didn't do it!

(JOHNNY *turns and stands up against an imaginary wall, legs spread out, arms behind his back.*)

SECRETARY: Oh no, we can't have arrests! We must maintain law and order.

SANCHO: But he's bilingual!

SECRETARY: Bilingual?

SANCHO: Simón que yes. He speaks English! Johnny, give us some English. (*Snap.*)

JOHNNY: (*Comes downstage.*) Fuck-you!

SECRETARY: (*Gasps.*) Oh! I've never been so insulted in my whole life!

SANCHO: Well, he learned it in your school.

SECRETARY: I don't care where he learned it.

SANCHO: But he's economical!

SECRETARY: Economical?

SANCHO: Nickels and dimes. You can keep JOHNNY running on hamburgers, Taco Bell tacos, Lucky Lager beer, Thunderbird wine, yesca—

SECRETARY: Yesca?

SANCHO: Mota.

SECRETARY: Mota?

SANCHO: Leños . . . Marijuana. (*Snap.* JOHNNY *inhales on an imaginary joint.*)

SECRETARY: That's against the law!

JOHNNY: (*Big smile, holding his breath.*) Yeah.

SANCHO: He also sniffs glue. (*Snap.* JOHNNY *inhales glue, big smile.*)

JOHNNY: Tha's too much man, ése.

SECRETARY: No, Mr. Sancho, I don't think this—

SANCHO: Wait a minute, he has other qualities I know you'll love. For example, an inferiority complex. (*Snap.*)

JOHNNY: (*To* SANCHO.) You think you're better than me, huh ése? (*Swings switch blade.*)

SANCHO: He can also be beaten and he bruises, cut him and he bleeds; kick him and he—(*He beats, bruises and kicks* PACHUCO.) would you like to try it?

SECRETARY: Oh, I couldn't.

SANCHO: Be my guest. He's a great scapegoat.

SECRETARY: No, really.

SANCHO: Please.

SECRETARY: Well, all right. Just once. (*She kicks* PACHUCO.) Oh, he's so soft.

SANCHO: Wasn't that good? Try again.

SECRETARY: (*Kicks* PACHUCO.) Oh, he's so wonderful! (*She kicks him again.*)

SANCHO: Okay, that's enough, lady. You ruin the merchandise. Yes, our Johnny Pachuco model can give you many hours of pleasure. Why, the L.A.P.D. just bought twenty of these to train their rookie cops on. And talk about maintenance. Señorita, you are looking at an entirely self-supporting machine. You're never going to find our Johnny Pachuco model on the relief rolls. No, sir, this model knows how to liberate.

SECRETARY: Liberate?

SANCHO: He steals. (*Snap.* JOHNNY *rushes the* SECRETARY *and steals her purse.*)

JOHNNY: ¡Dame esa bolsa, vieja! (*He grabs the purse and runs. Snap by* SANCHO. *He stops.*)

(SECRETARY *runs after* JOHNNY *and grabs purse away from him, kicking him as she goes.*)

SECRETARY: No, no, no! We can't have any *more* thieves in the State Administration. Put him back.

90–91 **¡HUELGA! ¡HUELGA! . . . esos files** "Strike! Strike! Brothers, leave those rows." 94 **Me vendo . . . qué** "I come cheap, so what?" 97 **Bueno . . . no pero** "Well, no, but . . ." 124 **En la . . . placa** "Wow, the police!" 131 **Simón . . . yes** yeah, sure

146 **Leños** "joints" of marijuana 181 **Dame esa . . . , vieja** "Gimme that bag, old lady!"

185 SANCHO: Okay, we still got other models. Come on, Johnny, we'll sell you to some old lady. (SANCHO *takes* JOHNNY *back to his place.*)

SECRETARY: Mr. Sancho, I don't think you quite understand what we need. What we need is something that will attract the

190 women voters. Something more traditional, more romantic.

SANCHO: Ah, a lover. (*He smiles meaningfully.*) Step right over here, señorita. Introducing our standard Revolucionario and/or Early California Bandit type. As you can see he is well-built, sturdy, durable. This is the International Harvester of Mexicans.

195 SECRETARY: What does he do?

SANCHO: You name it, he does it. He rides horses, stays in the mountains, crosses deserts, plains, rivers, leads revolutions, follows revolutions, kills, can be killed, serves as a martyr, hero, movie star—did I say movie star? Did you ever see *Viva*

200 *Zapata? Viva Villa? Villa Rides? Pancho Villa Returns? Pancho Villa Goes Back? Pancho Villa Meets Abbot and Costello—*

SECRETARY: I've never seen any of those.

SANCHO: Well, he was in all of them. Listen to this. (*Snap.*)

REVOLUCIONARIO: (*Scream.*) ¡VIVA VILLAAAAA!

205 SECRETARY: That's awfully loud.

SANCHO: He has a volume control. (*He adjusts volume. Snap.*)

REVOLUCIONARIO: (*Mousey voice.*) ¡Viva Villa!

SECRETARY: That's better.

SANCHO: And even if you didn't see him in the movies, perhaps

210 you saw him on TV. He makes commercials. (*Snap.*)

REVOLUCIONARIO: Is there a Frito Bandito in your house?

SECRETARY: Oh yes, I've seen that one!

SANCHO: Another feature about this one is that he is economical. He runs on raw horsemeat and tequila!

215 SECRETARY: Isn't that rather savage?

SANCHO: Al contrario, it makes him a lover. (*Snap.*)

REVOLUCIONARIO: (*To* SECRETARY.) ¡Ay, mamasota, cochota, ven pa'ca! (*He grabs* SECRETARY *and folds her back—Latin-lover style.*)

SANCHO: (*Snap.* REVOLUCIONARIO *goes back upright.*) Now wasn't

220 that nice?

SECRETARY: Well, it was rather nice.

SANCHO: And finally, there is one outstanding feature about this model I KNOW the ladies are going to love: He's a GENUINE antique! He was made in Mexico in 1910!

225 SECRETARY: Made in Mexico?

SANCHO: That's right. Once in Tijuana, twice in Guadalajara, three times in Cuernavaca.

SECRETARY: Mr. Sancho, I thought he was an American product.

SANCHO: No, but—

230 SECRETARY: No, I'm sorry. We can't buy anything but American-made products. He just won't do.

SANCHO: But he's an antique!

SECRETARY: I don't care. You still don't understand what we need. It's true we need Mexican models such as these, but

235 it's more important that he be *American.*

SANCHO: American?

SECRETARY: That's right, and judging from what you've shown me, I don't think you have what we want. Well, my lunch hour's almost over; I better—

240 SANCHO: Wait a minute! Mexican but American?

SECRETARY: That's correct.

---

216 **Al contrario** on the contrary

SANCHO: Mexican but . . . (*A sudden flash.*) AMERICAN! Yeah, I think we've got exactly what you want. He just came in today! Give me a minute. (*He exits. Talks from backstage.*) Here he is in the shop. Let me just get some papers off. 245 There. Introducing our new 1970 Mexican-American! Ta-ra-ra-ra-ra-ra-RA-RAAA!

(SANCHO *brings out the* MEXICAN-AMERICAN *model, a clean-shaven middle-class type in business suit, with glasses.*)

SECRETARY: (*Impressed.*) Where have you been hiding this one?

SANCHO: He just came in this morning. Ain't he a beauty? Feast your eyes on him! Sturdy US Steel frame, streamlined, 250 modern. As a matter of fact, he is built exactly like our Anglo models except that he comes in a variety of darker shades: naugahyde, leather, or leatherette.

SECRETARY: Naugahyde.

SANCHO: Well, we'll just write that down. Yes, señorita, this model 255 represents the apex of American engineering! He is bilingual, college educated, ambitious! Say the word "acculturate" and he accelerates. He is intelligent, well-mannered, clean—did I say clean? (*Snap.* MEXICAN-AMERICAN *raises his arm.*) Smell.

SECRETARY: (*Smells.*) Old Sobaco, my favorite. 260

SANCHO: (*Snap.* MEXICAN-AMERICAN *turns toward* SANCHO.) Eric! (*To* SECRETARY.) We call him Eric Garcia. (*To* ERIC.) I want you to meet Miss JIM-enez, Eric.

MEXICAN-AMERICAN: Miss JIM-enez, I am delighted to make your acquaintance. (*He kisses her hand.*) 265

SECRETARY: Oh, my, how charming!

SANCHO: Did you feel the suction? He has seven especially engineered suction cups right behind his lips. He's a charmer all right!

SECRETARY: How about boards? Does he function on boards? 270

SANCHO: You name them, he is on them. Parole boards, draft boards, school boards, taco quality control boards, surf boards, two-by-fours.

SECRETARY: Does he function in politics?

SANCHO: Señorita, you are looking at a political MACHINE. 275 Have you ever heard of the OEO, EOC, COD, WAR ON POVERTY? That's our model! Not only that, he makes political speeches.

SECRETARY: May I hear one?

SANCHO: With pleasure. (*Snap.*) Eric, give us a speech. 280

MEXICAN-AMERICAN: Mr. Congressman, Mr. Chairman, members of the board, honored guests, ladies and gentlemen. (SANCHO *and* SECRETARY *applaud.*) Please, please, I come before you as a Mexican-American to tell you about the problems of the Mexican. The problems of the Mexican 285 stem from one thing and one thing alone: He's stupid. He's uneducated. He needs to stay in school. He needs to be ambitious, forward-looking, harder-working. He needs to think American, American, American, AMERICAN, AMERICAN, AMERICAN. GOD BLESS AMERICA! 290 GOD BLESS AMERICA!! (*He goes out of control.*)

(SANCHO *snaps frantically and the* MEXICAN-AMERICAN *finally slumps forward, bending at the waist.*)

SECRETARY: Oh my, he's patriotic too!

SANCHO: Sí, señorita, he loves his country. Let me just make a little adjustment here. (*Stands* MEXICAN-AMERICAN *up.*)

SECRETARY: What about upkeep? Is he economical? 295

SANCHO: Well, no, I won't lie to you. The Mexican-American costs a little bit more, but you get what you pay for. He's worth every extra cent. You can keep him running on dry martinis, Langendorf bread.

300 SECRETARY: Apple pie?

SANCHO: Only Mom's. Of course, he's also programmed to eat Mexican food on ceremonial functions, but I must warn you: an overdose of beans will plug up his exhaust.

SECRETARY: Fine! There's just one more question: How much do
305 you want for him?

SANCHO: Well, I tell you what I'm gonna do. Today and today only, because you've been so sweet, I'm gonna let you steal this model from me! I'm gonna let you drive him off the lot for the simple price of—let's see taxes and license included—
310 $15,000.

SECRETARY: Fifteen thousand DOLLARS? For a MEXICAN!

SANCHO: Mexican? What are you talking, lady? This is a Mexican-AMERICAN! We had to melt down two pachucos, a farm worker and three gabachos to make this model!
315 You want quality, but you gotta pay for it! This is no cheap run-about. He's got class!

SECRETARY: Okay, I'll take him.

SANCHO: You will?

SECRETARY: Here's your money.

320 SANCHO: You mind if I count it?

SECRETARY: Go right ahead.

SANCHO: Well, you'll get your pink slip in the mail. Oh, do you want me to wrap him up for you? We have a box in the back.

SECRETARY: No, thank you. The Governor is having a luncheon
325 this afternoon, and we need a brown face in the crowd. How do I drive him?

SANCHO: Just snap your fingers. He'll do anything you want.

(SECRETARY snaps. MEXICAN-AMERICAN steps forward.)

MEXICAN-AMERICAN: RAZA QUERIDA, ¡VAMOS LEVAN-
TANDO ARMAS PARA LIBERARNOS DE ESTOS
330 DESGRACIADOS GABACHOS QUE NOS EXPLOTAN! VAMOS.

SECRETARY: What did he say?

SANCHO: Something about lifting arms, killing white people, etc.

SECRETARY: But he's not supposed to say that!

335 SANCHO: Look, lady, don't blame me for bugs from the factory. He's your Mexican-American; you bought him, now drive him off the lot!

SECRETARY: But he's broken!

SANCHO: Try snapping another finger.

(SECRETARY snaps. MEXICAN-AMERICAN comes to life again.)

329–32 **RAZA QUERIDA, . . . VAMOS** "Beloved Raza, let's pick up arms to liberate ourselves from those damned whites that exploit us! Let's go."   340–44 **ESTA GRAN . . . CHICANO POWER** "This great mass of humanity has said enough! And it begins to march! Enough! Enough! Long live La Raza! Long live the Cause! Long live the strike! Long live the Brown Berets! Long live the students! Chicano Power!"

MEXICAN-AMERICAN: ¡ESTA GRAN HUMANIDAD HA 340 DICHO BASTA! Y SE HA PUESTO EN MARCHA! ¡BASTA! ¡BASTA! ¡VIVA LA RAZA! ¡VIVA LA CAUSA! ¡VIVA LA HUELGA! ¡VIVAN LOS BROWN BERETS! ¡VIVAN LOS ESTUDIANTES! ¡CHICANO POWER!

(The MEXICAN-AMERICAN turns toward the SECRETARY, who gasps and backs up. He keeps turning toward the PACHUCO, FARM WORKER, and REVOLUCIONARIO, snapping his fingers and turning each of them on, one by one.)

PACHUCO: *(Snap. To SECRETARY.)* I'm going to get you, baby! 345 ¡Viva La Raza!

FARM WORKER: *(Snap. To SECRETARY.)* ¡Viva la huelga! ¡Viva la Huelga! ¡VIVA LA HUELGA!

REVOLUCIONARIO: *(Snap. To SECRETARY.)* ¡Viva la revolución! ¡VIVA LA REVOLUCIÓN! 350

REVOLUCIONARIO: *(Snap. To SECRETARY.)* ¡Viva la revolución! ¡VIVA LA REVOLUCIÓN!

(The three models join together and advance toward the SECRETARY who backs up and runs out of the shop screaming. SANCHO is at the other end of the shop holding his money in his hand. All freeze. After a few seconds of silence, the PACHUCO moves and stretches, shaking his arms and loosening up. The FARM WORKER and REVOLUCIONARIO do the same. SANCHO stays where he is, frozen to his spot.)

JOHNNY: Man, that was a long one, ése. *(Others agree with him.)*

FARM WORKER: How did we do?

JOHNNY: Perty good, look all that lana, man! *(He goes over to 355 SANCHO and removes the money from his hand. SANCHO stays where he is.)*

REVOLUCIONARIO: En la madre, look at all the money.

JOHNNY: We keep this up, we're going to be rich.

FARM WORKER: They think we're machines. 360

REVOLUCIONARIO: Burros.

JOHNNY: Puppets.

MEXICAN-AMERICAN: The only thing I don't like is—how come I always got to play the goddamn Mexican-American?

JOHNNY: That's what you get for finishing high school. 365

FARM WORKER: How about our wages, ése?

JOHNNY: Here it comes right now. $3,000 for you, $3,000 for you, $3,000 for you, and $3,000 for me. The rest we put back into the business.

MEXICAN-AMERICAN: Too much, man. Heh, where you vatos 370 going tonight?

FARM WORKER: I'm going over to Concha's. There's a party.

JOHNNY: Wait a minute, vatos. What about our salesman? I think he needs an oil job.

REVOLUCIONARIO: Leave him to me. 375

(The PACHUCO, FARM WORKER, and MEXICAN-AMERICAN exit, talking loudly about their plans for the night. The REVOLUCIONARIO goes over to SANCHO, removes his derby hat and cigar, lifts him up and throws him over his shoulder. SANCHO hangs loose, lifeless.)

REVOLUCIONARIO: *(To audience.)* He's the best model we got! ¡Ajúa! *(Exit.)*

AUGUST WILSON

August Wilson was born in 1945 and raised on "The Hill," the black ghetto of Pittsburgh. He dropped out of school in the ninth grade, but supported himself with odd jobs while he continued his self-education, reading and studying; he also began to write poems and stories on the changing problems of race relations in America. He founded a theater in Pittsburgh in the mid-1960s, and then founded Black Horizons Theater Company there in 1968. His first play, *Jitney,* was staged in 1978. Wilson then applied to study playwriting at the Eugene O'Neill Theater Center's National Playwrights' Conference, where he submitted the text of *Ma Rainey's Black Bottom,* which was read by the eminent African-American stage director Lloyd Richards, who had brought Lorraine Hansberry's *A Raisin in the Sun* to Broadway in 1959. Richards read the play and produced it at the Yale Repertory Theater in 1984 before bringing it to Broadway. *Ma Rainey's Black Bottom* is the first of several plays examining African-American history in the twentieth century, many of them using jazz as a musical idiom; it was followed by *Fences* (1985)—which won the Pulitzer Prize—*Joe Turner's Come and Gone* (1986), *The Piano Lesson* (1987), and *Two Trains Running* (1991). His most recent play, *Seven Guitars,* opened in Chicago in 1995.

FENCES

Set in 1957, the action of *Fences* sits on the brink of the civil rights movement and outlines the challenges facing African-Americans whose legal freedoms had yet to become a social reality. The play is—as its final funeral scene implies—deeply reminiscent of Arthur Miller's *Death of a Salesman,* and suggests that realism is in many way still the dominant mode of American theater. Like Miller's play, it is about a hardworking man whose responsibilities to his family fall athwart his dreams of happiness, a conflict that finally costs him both. However, while Miller's Willy Loman is victimized by his belief in the "American Dream," Wilson's Troy Maxson lives his life on the underside of that dream. Thrown out of his home at fourteen by his father, Troy moved north to Pittsburgh; unable to find work, he made a living through petty crime until he was caught and sentenced to fifteen years' imprisonment. On his release, he found his wife and child and began a career in baseball, playing in the Negro Leagues. Integration came to baseball, and by 1957 Jackie Robinson, Hank Aaron, and a young Roberto Clemente are all playing in the major leagues—but it is too late for Troy. He is now working as a trash collector, fighting the company to let African-Americans drive the garbage trucks as well as pick up the trash.

Like Willy Loman, Troy, too, is a family man. The family is Troy's refuge from the racism and defeat of his daily life, and his proudest accomplishment as well: he has forced himself to shoulder the responsibility of providing for his children and of loving his wife, a responsibility that lends his life purpose and direction. As he says to Rose in act 1, "Woman . . . I do the best I can do. . . . We go upstairs in that room at night . . . and I fall down on you and try to blast a hole into forever. I get up Monday morning . . . find my lunch on the table. I go out. Make my way. Find my strength to carry me through to the next Friday." However, as Rose notes, the world is changing around Troy, and these changes threaten the life that he has made. His son Cory is being recruited on a football scholarship. Troy, his own exploitation by the white-dominated sports industry still in mind, forces Cory to quit the team, and so to pass up the scholarship—and the chance to go to college. Nor does Troy shoulder the rest of his family life easily. He cares for his mentally handicapped brother Gabriel, but eventually has him committed to a mental hospital in order to get half of his government pension. Despite his love for and gratitude to Rose, he has an affair with another woman, who dies delivering their daughter. Although family life has been Troy's salvation, it also has hemmed him in—in the dead-end jobs, the constant poverty, the fence he builds at the end of the play. He risks it all for the chance of some happiness with Alberta and loses; Rose takes in Troy's daughter: "From right now . . . this child got a mother. But you a womanless man." He fights Cory, and much as his own father had thrown him out of the house, he forces his own son to leave as well.

The joyous, mournful conclusion of *Fences*—when Gabriel dances Troy's soul into heaven—perhaps provides the best commentary on the life of Troy Maxson. Suffering the indignities and humiliation of racism throughout his life, Troy built a stable home for himself, a life. As a defense against the world, perhaps, that life was bound to crumble, particularly as pressure of social change forced Troy to deal with a future he had never imagined. In Wilson's final image, however, Troy's life is celebrated, a thing of rough and rugged beauty, demanding our attention and respect.

FENCES

August Wilson

——— CHARACTERS ———

TROY MAXSON
JIM BONO, *Troy's friend*
ROSE, *Troy's wife*
LYONS, *Troy's oldest son by previous marriage*
GABRIEL, *Troy's brother*
CORY, *Troy and Rose's son*
RAYNELL, *Troy's daughter*

> When the sins of our fathers visit us
> We do not have to play host.
> We can banish them with forgiveness
> As God, in His Largeness and Laws.
> —AUGUST WILSON

SETTING: *The setting is the yard which fronts the only entrance to the Maxson household, an ancient two-story brick house set back off a small alley in a big-city neighborhood. The entrance to the house is gained by two or three steps leading to a wooden porch badly in need of paint.*

A relatively recent addition to the house and running its full width, the porch lacks congruence. It is a sturdy porch with a flat roof. One or two chairs of dubious value sit at one end where the kitchen window opens onto the porch. An old-fashioned icebox stands silent guard at the opposite end.

The yard is a small dirt yard, partially fenced, except for the last scene, with a wooden sawhorse, a pile of lumber, and other fence-building equipment set off to the side. Opposite is a tree from which hangs a ball made of rags. A baseball bat leans against the tree. Two oil drums serve as garbage receptacles and sit near the house at right to complete the setting.

THE PLAY: *Near the turn of the century, the destitute of Europe sprang on the city with tenacious claws and an honest and solid dream. The city devoured them. They swelled its belly until it burst into a thousand furnaces and sewing machines, a thousand butcher shops and bakers' ovens, a thousand churches and hospitals and funeral parlors and moneylenders. The city grew. It nourished itself and offered each man a partnership limited only by his talent, his guile, and his willingness and capacity for hard work. For the immigrants of Europe, a dream dared and won true.*

The descendants of African slaves were offered no such welcome or participation. They came from places called the Carolinas and the Virginias, Georgia, Alabama, Mississippi, and Tennessee. They came strong, eager, searching. The city rejected them and they fled and settled along the riverbanks and under bridges in shallow, ramshackle houses made of sticks and tar-paper. They collected rags and wood. They sold the use of their muscles and their bodies. They cleaned houses and washed clothes, they shined shoes, and in quiet desperation and vengeful pride, they stole, and lived in pursuit of their own dream. That they could breathe free, finally, and stand to meet life with the force of dignity and whatever eloquence the heart could call upon.

By 1957, the hard-won victories of the European immigrants had solidified the industrial might of America. War had been confronted and won with new energies that used loyalty and patriotism as its fuel. Life was rich, full, and flourishing. The Milwaukee Braves won the World Series, and the hot winds of change that would make the sixties a turbulent, racing, dangerous, and provocative decade had not yet begun to blow full.

——— ACT ONE ———

SCENE I

It is 1957. TROY *and* BONO *enter the yard, engaged in conversation.* TROY *is fifty-three years old, a large man with thick, heavy hands; it is this largeness that he strives to fill out and make an accommodation with. Together with his blackness, his largeness informs his sensibilities and the choices he has made in his life.*

Of the two men, BONO *is obviously the follower. His commitment to their friendship of thirty-odd years is rooted in his admiration of* TROY's *honesty, capacity for hard work, and his strength, which* BONO *seeks to emulate.*

It is Friday night, payday, and the one night of the week the two men engage in a ritual of talk and drink. TROY *is usually the most talkative and at times he can be crude and almost vulgar, though he is capable of rising to profound heights of expression. The men carry lunch buckets and wear or carry burlap aprons and are dressed in clothes suitable to their jobs as garbage collectors.*

BONO: Troy, you ought to stop that lying!

TROY: I ain't lying! The nigger had a watermelon this big.

(He indicates with his hands.)

Talking about . . . "What watermelon, Mr. Rand?" I liked to fell out! "What watermelon, Mr. Rand?" . . . And it sitting there big as life. 5

BONO: What did Mr. Rand say?

TROY: Ain't said nothing. Figure if the nigger too dumb to know he carrying a watermelon, he wasn't gonna get much sense out of him. Trying to hide that great big old watermelon under his coat. Afraid to let the white man see him carry it home. 10

BONO: I'm like you . . . I ain't got no time for them kind of people.

TROY: Now what he look like getting mad cause he see the man from the union talking to Mr. Rand?

BONO: He come to me talking about . . . "Maxson gonna get us 15 fired." I told him to get away from me with that. He walked away from me calling you a troublemaker. What Mr. Rand say?

TROY: Ain't said nothing. He told me to go down the Commissioner's office next Friday. They called me down there to 20 see them.

BONO: Well, as long as you got your complaint filed, they can't fire you. That's what one of them white fellows tell me.

671

TROY: I ain't worried about them firing me. They gonna fire me
25 cause I asked a question? That's all I did. I went to
Mr. Rand and asked him, "Why? Why you got the white
mens driving and the colored lifting?" Told him, "what's
the matter, don't I count? You think only white fellows got
sense enough to drive a truck. That ain't no paper job! Hell,
30 anybody can drive a truck. How come you got all whites
driving and the colored lifting?" He told me "take it to the
union." Well, hell, that's what I done! Now they wanna
come up with this pack of lies.

BONO: I told Brownie if the man come and ask him any ques-
35 tions . . . just tell the truth! It ain't nothing but something
they done trumped up on you cause you filed a complaint
on them.

TROY: Brownie don't understand nothing. All I want them to
do is change the job description. Give everybody a chance
40 to drive the truck. Brownie can't see that. He ain't got that
much sense.

BONO: How you figure he be making out with that gal be up
at Taylors' all the time . . . that Alberta gal?

TROY: Same as you and me. Getting just as much as we is.
45 Which is to say nothing.

BONO: It is, huh? I figure you doing a little better than me . . .
and I ain't saying what I'm doing.

TROY: Aw, nigger, look here . . . I know you. If you had got
anywhere near that gal, twenty minutes later you be look-
50 ing to tell somebody. And the first one you gonna tell . . .
that you gonna want to brag to . . . is gonna be me.

BONO: I ain't saying that. I see where you be eyeing her.

TROY: I eye all the women. I don't miss nothing. Don't never
let nobody tell you Troy Maxson don't eye the women.

55 BONO: You been doing more than eyeing her. You done bought
her a drink or two.

TROY: Hell yeah, I bought her a drink! What that mean? I
bought you one, too. What that mean cause I buy her a
drink? I'm just being polite.

60 BONO: It's alright to buy her one drink. That's what you call
being polite. But when you wanna be buying two or
three . . . that's what you call eyeing her.

TROY: Look here, as long as you known me . . . you ever known
me to chase after women?

65 BONO: Hell yeah! Long as I done known you. You forgetting I
knew you when.

TROY: Naw, I'm talking about since I been married to Rose?

BONO: Oh, not since you been married to Rose. Now, that's the
truth, there. I can say that.

70 TROY: Alright then! Case closed.

BONO: I see you be walking up around Alberta's house. You
supposed to be at Taylors' and you be walking up around
there.

TROY: What you watching where I'm walking for? I ain't
75 watching after you.

BONO: I seen you walking around there more than once.

TROY: Hell, you liable to see me walking anywhere! That don't
mean nothing cause you see me walking around there.

BONO: Where she come from anyway? She just kinda showed
80 up one day.

TROY: Tallahassee. You can look at her and tell she one of them
Florida gals. They got some big healthy women down
there. Grow them right up out the ground. Got a little bit

of Indian in her. Most of them niggers down in Florida got
some Indian in them.   85

BONO: I don't know about that Indian part. But she damn sure
big and healthy. Woman wear some big stockings. Got
them great big old legs and hips as wide as the Mississippi
River.

TROY: Legs don't mean nothing. You don't do nothing but   90
push them out of the way. But them hips cushion the ride!

BONO: Troy, you ain't got no sense.

TROY: It's the truth! Like you riding on Goodyears!

(ROSE *enters from the house. She is ten years younger than* TROY, *her
devotion to him stems from her recognition of the possibilities of her life
without him: a succession of abusive men and their babies, a life of
partying and running the streets, the Church, or aloneness with its
attendant pain and frustration. She recognizes* TROY's *spirit as a fine
and illuminating one and she either ignores or forgives his faults, only
some of which she recognizes. Though she doesn't drink, her presence is
an integral part of the Friday night rituals. She alternates between the
porch and the kitchen, where supper preparations are under way.*)

ROSE: What you all out here getting into?

TROY: What you worried about what we getting into for? This   95
is men talk, woman.

ROSE: What I care what you all talking about? Bono, you gonna
stay for supper?

BONO: No, I thank you, Rose. But Lucille say she cooking up a
pot of pigfeet.   100

TROY: Pigfeet! Hell, I'm going home with you! Might even
stay the night if you got some pigfeet. You got something
in there to top them pigfeet, Rose?

ROSE: I'm cooking up some chicken. I got some chicken and
collard greens.   105

TROY: Well, go on back in the house and let me and Bono finish what we was talking about. This is men talk. I got some
talk for you later. You know what kind of talk I mean. You
go on and powder it up.

ROSE: Troy Maxson, don't you start that now!   110

TROY: (*Puts his arm around her.*) Aw, woman . . . come here. Look
here, Bono . . . when I met this woman . . . I got out that
place, say, "Hitch up my pony, saddle up my mare . . .
there's a woman out there for me somewhere. I looked here.
Looked there. Saw Rose and latched on to her." I latched on 115
to her and told her—I'm gonna tell you the truth—I told
her, "Baby, I don't wanna marry, I just wanna be your man."
Rose told me . . . tell him what you told me, Rose.

ROSE: I told him if he wasn't the marrying kind, then move out
the way so the marrying kind could find me.   120

TROY: That's what she told me. "Nigger, you in my way. You
blocking the view! Move out the way so I can find me a husband." I thought it over two or three days. Come back—

ROSE: Ain't no two or three days nothing. You was back the
same night.   125

TROY: Come back, told her . . . "Okay, baby . . . but I'm gonna
buy me a banty rooster and put him out there in the back-
yard . . . and when he sees a stranger come, he'll flap his
wings and crow . . ." Look here, Bono, I could watch the front
door by myself . . . it was that back door I was worried about. 130

ROSE: Troy, you ought not talk like that. Troy ain't doing nothing but telling a lie.

TROY: Only thing is . . . when we first got married . . . forget the rooster . . . we ain't had no yard!

135 BONO: I hear you tell it. Me and Lucille was staying down there on Logan Street. Had two rooms with the outhouse in the back. I ain't mind the outhouse none. But when that god-damn wind blow through there in the winter . . . that's what I'm talking about! To this day I wonder why in the

140 hell I ever stayed down there for six long years. But see, I didn't know I could do no better. I thought only white folks had inside toilets and things.

ROSE: There's a lot of people don't know they can do no better than they doing now. That's just something you got to

145 learn. A lot of folks still shop at Bella's.

TROY: Ain't nothing wrong with shopping at Bella's. She got fresh food.

ROSE: I ain't said nothing about if she got fresh food. I'm talk-ing about what she charge. She charge ten cents more than

150 the A&P.

TROY: The A&P ain't never done nothing for me. I spends my money where I'm treated right. I go down to Bella, say, "I need a loaf of bread, I'll pay you Friday." She give it to me. What sense that make when I got money to go and spend

155 it somewhere else and ignore the person who done right by me? That ain't in the Bible.

ROSE: We ain't talking about what's in the Bible. What sense it make to shop there when she overcharge?

TROY: You shop where you want to. I'll do my shopping where

160 the people been good to me.

ROSE: Well, I don't think it's right for her to overcharge. That's all I was saying.

BONO: Look here . . . I got to get on. Lucille going be raising all kind of hell.

165 TROY: Where you going, nigger? We ain't finished this pint. Come here, finish this pint.

BONO: Well, hell, I am . . . if you ever turn the bottle loose.

TROY: (Hands him the bottle.) The only thing I say about the A&P is I'm glad Cory got that job down there. Help him take care

170 of his school clothes and things. Gabe done moved out and things getting tight around here. He got that job . . . He can start to look out for himself.

ROSE: Cory done went and got recruited by a college football team.

175 TROY: I told that boy about that football stuff. The white man ain't gonna let him get nowhere with that football. I told him when he first come to me with it. Now you come telling me he done went and got more tied up in it. He ought to go and get recruited in how to fix cars or some-

180 thing where he can make a living.

ROSE: He ain't talking about making no living playing foot-ball. It's just something the boys in school do. They gonna send a recruiter by to talk to you. He'll tell you he ain't talking about making no living playing football. It's a

185 honor to be recruited.

TROY: It ain't gonna get him nowhere. Bono'll tell you that.

BONO: If he be like you in the sports . . . he's gonna be alright. Ain't but two men ever played baseball as good as you. That's Babe Ruth and Josh Gibson. Them's the only two

190 men ever hit more home runs than you.

TROY: What it ever get me? Ain't got a pot to piss in or a win-dow to throw it out of.

ROSE: Times have changed since you was playing baseball, Troy. That was before the war. Times have changed a lot since then. 195

TROY: How in hell they done changed?

ROSE: They got lots of colored boys playing ball now. Baseball and football.

BONO: You right about that, Rose. Times have changed, Troy. You just come along too early. 200

TROY: There ought not never have been no time called too early! Now you take that fellow . . . what's that fellow they had playing right field for the Yankees back then? You know who I'm talking about, Bono. Used to play right field for the Yankees. 205

ROSE: Selkirk?

TROY: Selkirk! That's it! Man batting .269, understand? .269. What kind of sense that make? I was hitting .432 with thirty-seven home runs! Man batting .269 and playing right field for the Yankees! I saw Josh Gibson's daughter 210 yesterday. She walking around with raggedy shoes on her feet. Now I bet you Selkirk's daughter ain't walking around with raggedy shoes on her feet! I bet you that!

ROSE: They got a lot of colored baseball players now. Jackie Robinson was the first. Folks had to wait for Jackie 215 Robinson.

TROY: I done seen a hundred niggers play baseball better than Jackie Robinson. Hell, I know some teams Jackie Robinson couldn't even make! What you talking about Jackie Robinson. Jackie Robinson wasn't nobody. I'm talking 220 about if you could play ball then they ought to have let you play. Don't care what color you were. Come telling me I come along too early. If you could play . . . then they ought to have let you play.

(TROY takes a long drink from the bottle.)

ROSE: You gonna drink yourself to death. You don't need to be 225 drinking like that.

TROY: Death ain't nothing. I done seen him. Done wrassled with him. You can't tell me nothing about death. Death ain't nothing but a fastball on the outside corner. And you know what I'll do to that! Lookee here, Bono . . . am I 230 lying? You get one of them fastballs, about waist high, over the outside corner of the plate where you can get the meat of the bat on it . . . and good god! You can kiss it goodbye. Now, am I lying?

BONO: Naw, you telling the truth there. I seen you do it. 235

TROY: If I'm lying . . . that 450 feet worth of lying!

(Pause.)

That's all death is to me. A fastball on the outside corner.

ROSE: I don't know why you want to get on talking about death.

TROY: Ain't nothing wrong with talking about death. That's 240 part of life. Everybody gonna die. You gonna die, I'm gonna die. Bono's gonna die. Hell, we all gonna die.

ROSE: But you ain't got to talk about it. I don't like to talk about it.

TROY: You the one brought it up. Me and Bono was talking 245 about baseball . . . you tell me I'm gonna drink myself to death. Ain't that right, Bono? You know I don't drink this but one night out of the week. That's Friday night. I'm gonna drink just enough to where I can handle it. Then I cuts it loose. I leave it alone. So don't you worry about me drinking myself to death. 'Cause I ain't worried about Death. I done seen him. I done wrestled with him.

Look here, Bono . . . I looked up one day and Death was marching straight at me. Like Soldiers on Parade! The Army of Death was marching straight at me. The middle of July, 1941. It got real cold just like it be winter. It seem like Death himself reached out and touched me on the shoulder. He touch me just like I touch you. I got cold as ice and Death standing there grinning at me.

ROSE: Troy, why don't you hush that talk.

TROY: I say . . . What you want, Mr. Death? You be wanting me? You done brought your army to be getting me? I looked him dead in the eye. I wasn't fearing nothing. I was ready to tangle. Just like I'm ready to tangle now. The Bible say be ever vigilant. That's why I don't get but so drunk. I got to keep watch.

ROSE: Troy was right down there in Mercy Hospital. You remember he had pneumonia? Laying there with a fever talking plumb out of his head.

TROY: Death standing there staring at me . . . carrying that sickle in his hand. Finally he say, "You want bound over for another year?" See, just like that . . . "You want bound over for another year?" I told him, "Bound over hell! Let's settle this now!"

It seem like he kinda fell back when I said that, and all the cold went out of me. I reached down and grabbed that sickle and threw it just as far as I could throw it . . . and me and him commenced to wrestling.

We wrestled for three days and three nights. I can't say where I found the strength from. Every time it seemed like he was gonna get the best of me, I'd reach way down deep inside myself and find the strength to do him one better.

ROSE: Every time Troy tell that story he find different ways to tell it. Different things to make up about it.

TROY: I ain't making up nothing. I'm telling you the facts of what happened. I wrestled with Death for three days and three nights and I'm standing here to tell you about it.

(Pause.)

Alright. At the end of the third night we done weakened each other to where we can't hardly move. Death stood up, throwed on his robe . . . had him a white robe with a hood on it. He threw on that robe and went off to look for his sickle. Say, "I'll be back." Just like that. "I'll be back." I told him, say, "Yeah, but . . . you gonna have to find me!" I wasn't no fool. I wasn't going looking for him. Death ain't nothing to play with. And I know he's gonna get me. I know I got to join his army . . . his camp followers. But as long as I keep my strength and see him coming . . . as long as I keep up my vigilance . . . he's gonna have to fight to get me. I ain't going easy.

BONO: Well, look here, since you got to keep up your vigilance . . . let me have the bottle.

TROY: Aw hell, I shouldn't have told you that part. I should have left out that part.

ROSE: Troy be talking that stuff and half the time don't even know what he be talking about.

TROY: Bono know me better than that.

BONO: That's right. I know you. I know you got some Uncle Remus in your blood. You got more stories than the devil got sinners.

TROY: Aw hell, I done seen him too! Done talked with the devil.

ROSE: Troy, don't nobody wanna be hearing all that stuff.

(LYONS enters the yard from the street. Thirty-four years old, TROY's son by a previous marriage, he sports a neatly trimmed goatee, sport coat, white shirt, tieless and buttoned at the collar. Though he fancies himself a musician, he is more caught up in the rituals and "idea" of being a musician than in the actual practice of the music. He has come to borrow money from TROY, and while he knows he will be successful, he is uncertain as to what extent his lifestyle will be held up to scrutiny and ridicule.)

LYONS: Hey, Pop.

TROY: What you come "Hey, Popping" me for?

LYONS: How you doing, Rose?

(He kisses her.)

Mr. Bono. How you doing?

BONO: Hey, Lyons . . . how you been?

TROY: He must have been doing alright. I ain't seen him around here last week.

ROSE: Troy, leave your boy alone. He come by to see you and you wanna start all that nonsense.

TROY: I ain't bothering Lyons.

(Offers him the bottle.)

Here . . . get you a drink. We got an understanding. I know why he come by to see me and he know I know.

LYONS: Come on, Pop . . . I just stopped by to say hi . . . see how you was doing.

TROY: You ain't stopped by yesterday.

ROSE: You gonna stay for supper, Lyons? I got some chicken cooking in the oven.

LYONS: No, Rose . . . thanks. I was just in then neighborhood and thought I'd stop by for a minute.

TROY: You was in the neighborhood alright, nigger. You telling the truth there. You was in the neighborhood cause it's my payday.

LYONS: Well, hell, since you mentioned it . . . let me have ten dollars.

TROY: I'll be damned! I'll die and go to hell and play blackjack with the devil before I give you ten dollars.

BONO: That's what I wanna know about . . . that devil you done seen.

LYONS: What . . . Pop done seen the devil? You too much, Pops.

TROY: Yeah, I done seen him. Talked to him too!

ROSE: You ain't seen no devil. I done told you that man ain't had nothing to do with the devil. Anything you can't understand, you want to call it the devil.

TROY: Look here, Bono . . . I went down to see Hertzberger about some furniture. Got three rooms for two-ninety-eight. That what it say on the radio. "Three rooms . . . two-ninety-eight."

350 Even made up a little song about it. Go down there . . . man tell me I can't get no credit. I'm working every day and can't get no credit. What to do? I got an empty house with some raggedy furniture in it. Cory ain't got no bed. He's sleeping on a pile of rags on the floor. Working every day and can't
355 get no credit. Come back here—Rose'll tell you—madder than hell. Sit down . . . try to figure what I'm gonna do. Come a knock on the door. Ain't been living here but three days. Who know I'm here? Open the door . . . devil standing there bigger than life. White fellow . . . got on good
360 clothes and everything. Standing there with a clipboard in his hand. I ain't had to say nothing. First words come out of his mouth was . . . "I understand you need some furniture and can't get no credit." I liked to fell over. He say "I'll give you all the credit you want, but you got to pay the in-
365 terest on it." I told him, "Give me three rooms worth and charge whatever you want." Next day a truck pulled up here and two men unloaded them three rooms. Man what drove the truck give me a book. Say send ten dollars, first of every month to the address in the book and everything
370 will be alright. Say if I miss a payment the devil was coming back and it'll be hell to pay. That was fifteen years ago. To this day . . . the first of the month I send my ten dollars, Rose'll tell you.

ROSE: Troy lying.

375 TROY: I ain't never seen that man since. Now you tell me who else that could have been but the devil? I ain't sold my soul or nothing like that, you understand. Naw, I wouldn't have truck with the devil about nothing like that. I got my furniture and pays my ten dollars the first of the month just
380 like clockwork.

BONO: How long you say you been paying this ten dollars a month?

TROY: Fifteen years!

BONO: Hell, ain't you finished paying for it yet? How much the
385 man done charged you.

TROY: Aw hell, I done paid for it. I done paid for it ten times over! The fact is I'm scared to stop paying it.

ROSE: Troy lying. We got that furniture from Mr. Glickman. He ain't paying no ten dollars a month to nobody.

390 TROY: Aw hell, woman. Bono know I ain't that big a fool.

LYONS: I was just getting ready to say . . . I know where there's a bridge for sale.

TROY: Look here, I'll tell you this . . . it don't matter to me if he was the devil. It don't matter if the devil give credit.
395 Somebody has got to give it.

ROSE: It ought to matter. You going around talking about having truck with the devil . . . God's the one you gonna have to answer to. He's the one gonna be at the Judgment.

LYONS: Yeah, well, look here, Pop . . . let me have that ten
400 dollars. I'll give it back to you. Bonnie got a job working at the hospital.

TROY: What I tell you, Bono? The only time I see this nigger is when he wants something. That's the only time I see him.

LYONS: Come on, Pop, Mr. Bono don't want to hear all that. Let
405 me have the ten dollars. I told you Bonnie working.

TROY: What that mean to me? "Bonnie working." I don't care if she working. Go ask her for the ten dollars if she working. Talking about "Bonnie working." Why ain't you working?

LYONS: Aw, Pop, you know I can't find no decent job. Where 410 am I gonna get a job at? You know I can't get no job.

TROY: I told you I know some people down there. I can get you on the rubbish if you want to work. I told you that the last time you came by here asking me for something.

LYONS: Naw, Pop . . . thanks. That ain't for me. I don't wanna 415 be carrying nobody's rubbish. I don't wanna be punching nobody's time clock.

TROY: What's the matter, you too good to carry people's rubbish? Where you think that ten dollars you talking about come from? I'm just supposed to haul people's rubbish and 420 give my money to you cause you too lazy to work. You too lazy to work and wanna know why you ain't got what I got.

ROSE: What hospital Bonnie working at? Mercy?

LYONS: She's down at Passavant working in the laundry.

TROY: I ain't got nothing as it is. I give you that ten dollars and 425 I got to eat beans the rest of the week. Naw . . . you ain't getting no ten dollars here.

LYONS: You ain't got to be eating no beans. I don't know why you wanna say that.

TROY: I ain't got no extra money. Gabe done moved over to 430 Miss Pearl's paying her the rent and things done got tight around here. I can't afford to be giving you every payday.

LYONS: I ain't asked you to give me nothing. I asked you to loan me ten dollars. I know you got ten dollars.

TROY: Yeah, I got it. You know why I got it? Cause I don't 435 throw my money away out there in the streets. You living the fast life . . . wanna be a musician . . . running around in them clubs and things . . . then, you learn to take care of yourself. You ain't gonna find me going and asking nobody for nothing. I done spent too many years without. 440

LYONS: You and me is two different people, Pop.

TROY: I done learned my mistake and learned to do what's right by it. You still trying to get something for nothing. Life don't owe you nothing. You owe it to yourself. Ask Bono. He'll tell you I'm right. 445

LYONS: You got your way of dealing with the world . . . I got mine. The only thing that matters to me is the music.

TROY: Yeah, I can see that! It don't matter how you gonna eat . . . where your next dollar is coming from. You telling the truth there. 450

LYONS: I know I got to eat. But I got to live too. I need something that gonna help me to get out of the bed in the morning. Make me feel like I belong in the world. I don't bother nobody. I just stay with my music cause that's the only way I can find to live in the world. Otherwise there ain't no 455 telling what I might do. Now I don't come criticizing you and how you live. I just come by to ask you for ten dollars. I don't wanna hear all that about how I live.

TROY: Boy, your mama did a hell of a job raising you.

LYONS: You can't change me, Pop. I'm thirty-four years old. If 460 you wanted to change me, you should have been there when I was growing up. I come by to see you . . . ask for ten dollars and you want to talk about how I was raised. You don't know nothing about how I was raised.

ROSE: Let the boy have ten dollars, Troy. 465

TROY: (To LYONS.) What the hell you looking at me for? I ain't got no ten dollars. You know what I do with my money.

(To ROSE.)

Give him ten dollars if you want him to have it.

ROSE: I will. Just as soon as you turn it loose.

470 TROY: (*Handing* ROSE *the money.*) There it is. Seventy-six dollars and forty-two cents. You see this, Bono? Now, I ain't gonna get but six of that back.

ROSE: You ought to stop telling that lie. Here, Lyons.

(*She hands him the money.*)

LYONS: Thanks, Rose. Look . . . I got to run . . . I'll see you later.

475 TROY: Wait a minute. You gonna say, "thanks, Rose" and ain't gonna look to see where she got that ten dollars from? See how they do me, Bono?

LYONS: I know she got it from you, Pop. Thanks. I'll give it back to you.

480 TROY: There he go telling another lie. Time I see that ten dollars . . . he'll be owing me thirty more.

LYONS: See you, Mr. Bono.

BONO: Take care, Lyons!

LYONS: Thanks, Pop. I'll see you again.

(LYONS *exits the yard.*)

485 TROY: I don't know why he don't go and get him a decent job and take care of that woman he got.

BONO: He'll be alright, Troy. The boy is still young.

TROY: The *boy* is thirty-four years old.

ROSE: Let's not get off into all that.

490 BONO: Look here . . . I got to be going. I got to be getting on. Lucille gonna be waiting.

TROY: (*Puts his arm around* ROSE.) See this woman, Bono? I love this woman. I love this woman so much it hurts. I love her so much . . . I done run out of ways of loving her. So I got

495 to go back to basics. Don't you come by my house Monday morning talking about time to go to work . . . 'cause I'm still gonna be stroking!

ROSE: Troy! Stop it now!

BONO: I ain't paying him no mind, Rose. That ain't nothing

500 but gin-talk. Go on, Troy. I'll see you Monday.

TROY: Don't you come by my house, nigger! I done told you what I'm gonna be doing.

(*The lights go down to black.*)

SCENE II

The lights come up on ROSE *hanging up clothes. She hums and sings softly to herself. It is the following morning.*

ROSE: (*Sings.*)

Jesus, be a fence all around me every day.
Jesus, I want you to protect me as I travel on my way.
Jesus, be a fence all around me every day.

(TROY *enters from the house.*)

ROSE: (*Continues.*)

Jesus, I want you to protect me
5   As I travel on my way.

(*To* TROY.)

'Morning. You ready for breakfast? I can fix it soon as I finish hanging up these clothes?

TROY: I got the coffee on. That'll be alright. I'll just drink some of that this morning.

ROSE: That 651 hit yesterday. That's the second time this 10 month. Miss Pearl hit for a dollar . . . seem like those that need the least always get lucky. Poor folks can't get nothing.

TROY: Them numbers don't know nobody. I don't know why you fool with them. You and Lyons both.

ROSE: It's something to do. 15

TROY: You ain't doing nothing but throwing your money away.

ROSE: Troy, you know I don't play foolishly. I just play a nickel here and a nickel there.

TROY: That's two nickels you done thrown away.

ROSE: Now I hit sometimes . . . that makes up for it. It always 20 comes in handy when I do hit. I don't hear you complaining then.

TROY: I ain't complaining now. I just say it's foolish. Trying to guess out of six hundred ways which way the number gonna come. If I had all the money niggers, these Negroes, throw 25 away on numbers for one week—just one week—I'd be a rich man.

ROSE: Well, you wishing and calling it foolish ain't gonna stop folks from playing numbers. That's one thing for sure. Besides . . . some good things come from playing numbers. 30 Look where Pope done bought him that restaurant off of numbers.

TROY: I can't stand niggers like that. Man ain't had two dimes to rub together. He walking around with his shoes all run over bumming money for cigarettes. Alright. Got lucky 35 there and hit the numbers . . .

ROSE: Troy, I know all about it.

TROY: Had good sense, I'll say that for him. He ain't throwed his money away. I seen niggers hit the numbers and go through two thousand dollars in four days. Man bought 40 him that restaurant down there . . . fixed it up real nice . . . and then didn't want nobody to come in it! A Negro go in there and can't get no kind of service. I seen a white fellow come in there and order a bowl of stew. Pope picked all the meat out the pot for him. Man ain't had nothing but a bowl 45 of meat! Negro come behind him and ain't got nothing but the potatoes and carrots. Talking about what numbers do for people, you picked a wrong example. Ain't done nothing but make a worser fool out of him than he was before.

ROSE: Troy, you ought to stop worrying about what happened 50 at work yesterday.

TROY: I ain't worried. Just told me to be down there at the Commissioner's office on Friday. Everybody think they gonna fire me. I ain't worried about them firing me. You ain't got to worry about that. 55

(*Pause.*)

Where's Cory? Cory in the house? (*Calls.*) Cory?

ROSE: He gone out.

TROY: Out, huh? He gone out 'cause he know I want him to help me with this fence. I know how he is. That boy scared of work. 60

(GABRIEL *enters. He comes halfway down the alley and, hearing* TROY's *voice, stops.*)

TROY: (Continues.) He ain't done a lick of work in his life.

ROSE: He had to go to football practice. Coach wanted them to get in a little extra practice before the season start.

TROY: I got his practice . . . running out of here before he get his chores done.

ROSE: Troy, what is wrong with you this morning? Don't nothing set right with you. Go on back in there and go to bed . . . get up on the other side.

TROY: Why something got to be wrong with me? I ain't said nothing wrong with me.

ROSE: You got something to say about everything. First it's the numbers . . . then it's the way the man runs his restaurant . . . then you done got on Cory. What's it gonna be next? Take a look up there and see if the weather suits you . . . or is it gonna be how you gonna put up the fence with the clothes hanging in the yard.

TROY: You hit the nail on the head then.

ROSE: I know you like I know the back of my hand. Go on in there and get you some coffee . . . see if that straighten you up. 'Cause you ain't right this morning.

(TROY starts into the house and sees GABRIEL. GABRIEL starts singing. TROY's brother, he is seven years younger than TROY. Injured in World War II, he has a metal plate in his head. He carries an old trumpet tied around his waist and believes with every fiber of his being that he is the Archangel Gabriel. He carries a chipped basket with an assortment of discarded fruits and vegetables he has picked up in the strip district and which he attempts to sell.)

GABRIEL: (Singing.)

> Yes, ma'am, I got plums
> You ask me how I sell them
> Oh ten cents apiece
> Three for a quarter
> Come and buy now
> 'Cause I'm here today
> And tomorrow I'll be gone

(GABRIEL enters.)

Hey, Rose!

ROSE: How you doing, Gabe?

GABRIEL: There's Troy . . . Hey, Troy!

TROY: Hey, Gabe.

(Exit into kitchen.)

ROSE: (To GABRIEL.) What you got there?

GABRIEL: You know what I got, Rose. I got fruits and vegetables.

ROSE: (Looking in basket.) Where's all these plums you talking about?

GABRIEL: I ain't got no plums today, Rose. I was just singing that. Have some tomorrow. Put me in a big order for plums. Have enough plums tomorrow for St. Peter and everybody.

(TROY re-enters from kitchen, crosses to steps.)

(To ROSE.)

Troy's mad at me.

TROY: I ain't mad at you. What I got to be mad at you about? You ain't done nothing to me.

GABRIEL: I just moved over to Miss Pearl's to keep out from in your way. I ain't mean no harm by it.

TROY: Who said anything about that? I ain't said anything about that.

GABRIEL: You ain't mad at me, is you?

TROY: Naw . . . I ain't mad at you, Gabe. If I was mad at you I'd tell you about it.

GABRIEL: Got me two rooms. In the basement. Got my own door too. Wanna see my key?

(He holds up a key.)

That's my own key! Ain't nobody else got a key like that. That's my key! My two rooms!

TROY: Well, that's good, Gabe. You got your own key . . . that's good.

ROSE: You hungry, Gabe? I was just fixing to cook Troy his breakfast.

GABRIEL: I'll take some biscuits. You got some biscuits? Did you know when I was in heaven . . . every morning me and St. Peter would sit down by the gate and eat some big fat biscuits? Oh, yeah! We had us a good time. We'd sit there and eat us them biscuits and then St. Peter would go off to sleep and tell me to wake him up when it's time to open the gates for the judgment.

ROSE: Well, come on . . . I'll make up a batch of biscuits.

(ROSE exits into the house.)

GABRIEL: Troy . . . St. Peter got your name in the book. I seen it. It say . . . Troy Maxson. I say . . . I know him! He got the same name like what I got. That's my brother!

TROY: How many times you gonna tell me that, Gabe?

GABRIEL: Ain't got my name in the book. Don't have to have my name. I done died and went to heaven. He got your name though. One morning St. Peter was looking at his book . . . marking it for the judgment . . . and he let me see your name. Got it in there under M. Got Rose's name . . . I ain't seen it like I seen yours . . . but I know it's in there. He got a great big book. Got everybody's name what was ever been born. That's what he told me. But I seen your name. Seen it with my own eyes.

TROY: Go on in the house there. Rose going to fix you something to eat.

GABRIEL: Oh, I ain't hungry. I done had breakfast with Aunt Jemimah. She come by and cooked me up a whole mess of flapjacks. Remember how we used to eat them flapjacks.

TROY: Go on in the house and get you something to eat now.

GABRIEL: I got to go sell my plums. I done sold some tomatoes. Got me two quarters. Wanna see?

(He shows TROY his quarters.)

I'm gonna save them and buy me a new horn so St. Peter can hear me when it's time to open the gates.

(GABRIEL stops suddenly. Listens.)

Hear that? That's the hellhounds. I got to chase them out of here. Go on get out of here! Get out!

(GABRIEL *exits singing.*)

> Better get ready for the judgment
> Better get ready for the judgment
> My Lord is coming down

(ROSE *enters from the house.*)

TROY: He gone off somewhere.

GABRIEL: (*Offstage.*)

155
> Better get ready for the judgment
> Better get ready for the judgment morning
> Better get ready for the judgment
> My God is coming down

ROSE: He ain't eating right. Miss Pearl say she can't get him to
160   eat nothing.

TROY: What you want me to do about it, Rose? I done did
everything I can for the man. I can't make him get well.
Man got half his head blown away . . . what you expect?

ROSE: Seem like something ought to be done to help him.

165 TROY: Man don't bother nobody. He just mixed up from that
metal plate he got in his head. Ain't no sense for him to go
back into the hospital.

ROSE: Least he be eating right. They can help him take care of
himself.

170 TROY: Don't nobody wanna be locked up, Rose. What you
wanna lock him up for? Man go over there and fight the
war . . . messin' around with them Japs, get half his head
blown off . . . and they give him a lousy three thousand
dollars. And I had to swoop down on that.

175 ROSE: Is you fixing to go into that again?

TROY: That's the only way I got a roof over my head . . . cause
of that metal plate.

ROSE: Ain't no sense you blaming yourself for nothing. Gabe
wasn't in no condition to manage that money. You done
180   what was right by him. Can't nobody say you ain't done
what was right by him. Look how long you took care of
him . . . till he wanted to have his own place and moved
over there with Miss Pearl.

TROY: That ain't what I'm saying, woman! I'm just stating the
185   facts. If my brother didn't have that metal plate in his
head . . . I wouldn't have a pot to piss in or a window to
throw it out of. And I'm fifty-three years old. Now see if
you can understand that!

(TROY *gets up from the porch and starts to exit the yard.*)

ROSE: Where you going off to? You been running out of here
190   every Saturday for weeks. I thought you was gonna work on
this fence?

TROY: I'm gonna walk down to Taylors'. Listen to the ball
game. I'll be back in a bit. I'll work on it when I get back.

(*He exits the yard. The lights go to black.*)

SCENE III

The lights come up on the yard. It is four hours later. ROSE *is taking down the clothes from the line.* CORY *enters carrying his football
equipment.*

ROSE: Your daddy like to had a fit with you running out of here
this morning without doing your chores.

CORY: I told you I had to go to practice.

ROSE: He say you were supposed to help him with this fence.

CORY: He been saying that the last four or five Saturdays, and   5
then he don't never do nothing, but go down to Taylors'.
Did you tell him about the recruiter?

ROSE: Yeah, I told him.

CORY: What he say?

ROSE: He ain't said nothing too much. You get in there and get   10
started on your chores before he gets back. Go on and scrub
down them steps before he gets back here hollering and carrying on.

CORY: I'm hungry. What you got to eat, Mama?

ROSE: Go on and get started on your chores. I got some meat   15
loaf in there. Go on and make you a sandwich . . . and don't
leave no mess in there.

(CORY *exits into the house.* ROSE *continues to take down the clothes.*
TROY *enters the yard and sneaks up and grabs her from behind.*)

Troy! Go on, now. You liked to scared me to death. What
was the score of the game? Lucille had me on the phone and
I couldn't keep up with it.   20

TROY: What I care about the game? Come here, woman.

(*He tries to kiss her.*)

ROSE: I thought you went down Taylors' to listen to the game.
Go on, Troy! You supposed to be putting up this fence.

TROY: (*Attempting to kiss her again.*) I'll put it up when I finish
with what is at hand.   25

ROSE: Go on, Troy. I ain't studying you.

TROY: (*Chasing after her.*) I'm studying you . . . fixing to do my
homework!

ROSE: Troy, you better leave me alone.

TROY: Where's Cory? That boy brought his butt home yet?   30

ROSE: He's in the house doing his chores.

TROY: (*Calling.*) Cory! Get your butt out here, boy!

(ROSE *exits into the house with the laundry.* TROY *goes over to the pile
of wood, picks up a board, and starts sawing.* CORY *enters from the
house.*)

TROY: You just now coming in here from leaving this morning?

CORY: Yeah, I had to go to football practice.

TROY: Yeah, what?   35

CORY: Yessir.

TROY: I ain't but two seconds off you noway. The garbage sitting in there overflowing . . . you ain't done none of your
chores . . . and you come in here talking about "Yeah."

CORY: I was just getting ready to do my chores now, Pop . . .   40

TROY: Your first chore is to help me with this fence on Saturday. Everything else come after that. Now get that saw and
cut them boards.

(CORY *takes the saw and begins cutting the boards.* TROY *continues
working. There is a long pause.*)

CORY: Hey, Pop . . . why don't you buy a TV?

TROY: What I want with a TV? What I want one of them for?   45

CORY: Everybody got one. Earl, Ba Bra . . . Jesse!

TROY: I ain't asked you who had one. I say what I want with one?

CORY: So you can watch it. They got lots of things on TV. Base-
50 ball games and everything. We could watch the World Series.

TROY: Yeah . . . and how much this TV cost?

CORY: I don't know. They got them on sale for around two hundred dollars.

55 TROY: Two hundred dollars, huh?

CORY: That ain't that much, Pop.

TROY: Naw, it's just two hundred dollars. See that roof you got over your head at night? Let me tell you something about that roof. It's been over ten years since that roof was last
60 tarred. See now . . . the snow come this winter and sit up there on that roof like it is . . . and it's gonna seep inside. It's just gonna be a little bit . . . ain't gonna hardly notice it. Then the next thing you know, it's gonna be leaking all over the house. Then the wood rot from all that water and
65 you gonna need a whole new roof. Now, how much you think it cost to get that roof tarred?

CORY: I don't know.

TROY: Two hundred and sixty-four dollars . . . cash money. While you thinking about a TV, I got to be thinking about
70 the roof . . . and whatever else go wrong around here. Now if you had two hundred dollars, what would you do . . . fix the roof or buy a TV?

CORY: I'd buy a TV. Then when the roof started to leak . . . when it needed fixing . . . I'd fix it.

75 TROY: Where you gonna get the money from? You done spent it for a TV. You gonna sit up and watch the water run all over your brand new TV.

CORY: Aw, Pop. You got money. I know you do.

TROY: Where I got it at, Huh?

80 CORY: You got it in the bank.

TROY: You wanna see my bankbook? You wanna see that seventy-three dollars and twenty-two cents I got sitting up in there.

CORY: You ain't got to pay for it all at one time. You can put a
85 down payment on it and carry it on home with you.

TROY: Not me. I ain't gonna owe nobody nothing if I can help it. Miss a payment and they come and snatch it right out your house. Then what you got? Now, soon as I get two hundred dollars clear, then I'll buy a TV. Right now, as soon
90 as I get two hundred and sixty-four dollars, I'm gonna have this roof tarred.

CORY: Aw . . . Pop!

TROY: You go on and get you two hundred dollars and buy one if ya want it. I got better things to do with my money.

95 CORY: I can't get no two hundred dollars. I ain't never seen two hundred dollars.

TROY: I'll tell you what . . . you get you a hundred dollars and I'll put the other hundred with it.

CORY: Alright, I'm gonna show you.

100 TROY: You gonna show me how you can cut them boards right now.

(CORY *begins to cut the boards. There is a long pause.*)

CORY: The Pirates won today. That makes five in a row.

TROY: I ain't thinking about the Pirates. Got an all-white team. Got that boy . . . that Puerto Rican boy . . . Clemente. Don't even half-play him. That boy could be something if 105
they give him a chance. Play him one day and sit him on the bench the next.

CORY: He gets a lot of chances to play.

TROY: I'm talking about playing regular. Playing every day so you can get your timing. That's what I'm talking about. 110

CORY: They got some white guys on the team that don't play every day. You can't play everybody at the same time.

TROY: If they got a white fellow sitting on the bench . . . you can bet your last dollar he can't play! The colored guy got to be twice as good before he get on the team. That's why I 115
don't want you to get all tied up in them sports. Man on the team and what it get him? They got colored on the team and don't use them. Same as not having them. All them teams the same.

CORY: The Braves got Hank Aaron and Wes Covington. Hank 120
Aaron hit two home runs today. That makes forty-three.

TROY: Hank Aaron ain't nobody. That's what you supposed to do. That's how you supposed to play the game. Ain't nothing to it. It's just a matter of timing . . . getting the right follow-through. Hell, I can hit forty-three home runs right 125
now!

CORY: Not off no major-league pitching, you couldn't.

TROY: We had better pitching in the Negro leagues. I hit seven home runs off of Satchel Paige. You can't get no better than that! 130

CORY: Sandy Koufax. He's leading the league in strikeouts.

TROY: I ain't thinking of no Sandy Koufax.

CORY: You got Warren Spahn and Lew Burdette. I bet you couldn't hit no home runs off of Warren Spahn.

TROY: I'm through with it now. You go on and cut them 135
boards.

(*Pause.*)

Your mama tell me you done got recruited by a college football team? Is that right?

CORY: Yeah. Coach Zellman say the recruiter gonna be coming by to talk to you. Get you to sign the permission papers. 140

TROY: I thought you supposed to be working down there at the A&P. Ain't you suppose to be working down there after school?

CORY: Mr. Stawicki say he gonna hold my job for me until after the football season. Say starting next week I can work 145
weekends.

TROY: I thought we had an understanding about this football stuff? You suppose to keep up with your chores and hold that job down at the A&P. Ain't been around here all day on a Saturday. Ain't none of your chores done . . . and now 150
you telling me you done quit your job.

CORY: I'm gonna be working weekends.

TROY: You damn right you are! And ain't no need for nobody coming around here to talk to me about signing nothing.

CORY: Hey, Pop . . . you can't do that. He's coming all the way 155
from North Carolina.

TROY: I don't care where he coming from. The white man ain't gonna let you get nowhere with that football noway. You go on and get your book-learning so you can work yourself up

160 in that A&P or learn how to fix cars or build houses or something, get you a trade. That way you have something can't nobody take away from you. You go on and learn how to put your hands to some good use. Besides hauling peo-ple's garbage.

165 CORY: I get good grades, Pop. That's why the recruiter wants to talk with you. You got to keep up your grades to get recruited. This way I'll be going to college. I'll get a chance . . .

TROY: First you gonna get your butt down there to the A&P
170 and get your job back.

CORY: Mr. Stawicki done already hired somebody else 'cause I told him I was playing football.

TROY: You a bigger fool than I thought . . . to let somebody take away your job so you can play some football. Where
175 you gonna get your money to take out your girlfriend and whatnot? What kind of foolishness is that to let somebody take away your job?

CORY: I'm still gonna be working weekends.

TROY: Naw . . . naw. You getting your butt out of here and
180 finding you another job.

CORY: Come on, Pop! I got to practice. I can't work after school and play football too. The team needs me. That's what Coach Zellman say . . .

TROY: I don't care what nobody else say. I'm the boss . . . you
185 understand? I'm the boss around here. I do the only saying what counts.

CORY: Come on, Pop!

TROY: I asked you . . . did you understand?

CORY: Yeah . . .
190 TROY: What?!

CORY: Yessir.

TROY: You go on down there to that A&P and see if you can get your job back. If you can't do both . . . then you quit the football team. You've got to take the crookeds with the
195 straights.

CORY: Yessir.

(Pause.)

Can I ask you a question?

TROY: What the hell you wanna ask me? Mr. Stawicki the one
200 you got the questions for.

CORY: How come you ain't never liked me?

TROY: Liked you? Who the hell say I got to like you? What law is there say I got to like you? Wanna stand up in my face and ask a damn fool-ass question like that. Talking about liking somebody. Come here boy, when I talk to you.

(CORY comes over to where TROY is working. He stands slouched over and TROY shoves him on his shoulder.)

205 Straighten up, goddammit! I asked you a question . . . what law is there say I got to like you?

CORY: None.

TROY: Well, alright then! Don't you eat every day?

(Pause.)

Answer me when I talk to you! Don't you eat every day?
210 CORY: Yeah.

TROY: Nigger, as long as you in my house, you put that sir on the end of it when you talk to me!

CORY: Yes . . . sir.

TROY: You eat every day.

CORY: Yessir!   215

TROY: Got a roof over your head.

CORY: Yessir!

TROY: Got clothes on your back.

CORY: Yessir.

TROY: Why you think that is?   220

CORY: Cause of you.

TROY: Aw, hell I know it's 'cause of me . . . but why do you think that is?

CORY: *(Hesitant.)* Cause you like me.

TROY: Like you? I go out of here every morning . . . bust my 225
butt . . . putting up with them crackers every day . . . cause I like you? You about the biggest fool I ever saw.

(Pause.)

It's my job. It's my responsibility! You understand that? A man got to take care of his family. You live in my house . . . sleep you behind on my bedclothes . . . fill you belly up 230
with my food . . . cause you my son. You my flesh and blood. Not 'cause I like you! Cause it's my duty to take care of you. I owe a responsibility to you! Let's get this straight right here . . . before it go along any further . . . I ain't got to like you. Mr. Rand don't give me my money come pay- 235
day cause he likes me. He gives me cause he owe me. I done give you everything I had to give you. I gave you your life! Me and your mama worked that out between us. And lik-ing your black ass wasn't part of the bargain. Don't you try and go through life worrying about if somebody like you or 240
not. You best be making sure they doing right by you. You understand what I'm saying, boy?

CORY: Yessir.

TROY: Then get the hell out of my face, and get on down to that A&P.   245

(ROSE has been standing behind the screen door for much of the scene. She enters as CORY exits.)

ROSE: Why don't you let the boy go ahead and play football, Troy? Ain't no harm in that. He's just trying to be like you with the sports.

TROY: I don't want him to be like me! I want him to move as far away from my life as he can get. You the only decent 250
thing that ever happened to me. I wish him that. But I don't wish him a thing else from my life. I decided seven-teen years ago that boy wasn't getting involved in no sports. Not after what they did to me in the sports.

ROSE: Troy, why don't you admit you was too old to play in the 255
major leagues? For once . . . why don't you admit that?

TROY: What do you mean too old? Don't come telling me I was too old. I just wasn't the right color. Hell, I'm fifty-three years old and can do better than Selkirk's .269 right now!

ROSE: How's was you gonna play ball when you were over 260
forty? Sometimes I can't get no sense out of you.

TROY: I got good sense, woman. I got sense enough not to let my boy get hurt over playing no sports. You been mother-ing that boy too much. Worried about if people like him.

265 ROSE: Everything that boy do . . . he do for you. He wants you to say "Good job, son." That's all.

TROY: Rose, I ain't got time for that. He's alive. He's healthy. He's got to make his own way. I made mine. Ain't nobody gonna hold his hand when he get out there in that world.

270 ROSE: Times have changed from when you was young, Troy. People change. The world's changing around you and you can't even see it.

TROY: (Slow, methodical.) Woman . . . I do the best I can do. I come in here every Friday. I carry a sack of potatoes and a

275 bucket of lard. You all line up at the door with your hands out. I give you the lint from my pockets. I give you my sweat and my blood. I ain't got no tears. I done spent them. We go upstairs in that room at night . . . and I fall down on you and try to blast a hole into forever. I get up Monday

280 morning . . . find my lunch on the table. I go out. Make my way. Find my strength to carry me through to the next Friday.

(Pause.)

That's all I got, Rose. That's all I got to give. I can't give nothing else.

(TROY exits into the house. The lights go down to black.)

SCENE IV

It is Friday. Two weeks later. CORY starts out of the house with his football equipment. The phone rings.

CORY: (Calling.) I got it!

(He answers the phone and stands in the screen door talking.)

Hello? Hey, Jesse. Naw . . . I was just getting ready to leave now.

ROSE: (Calling.) Cory!

5 CORY: I told you, man, them spikes is all tore up. You can use them if you want, but they ain't no good. Earl got some spikes.

ROSE: (Calling.) Cory!

CORY: (Calling to ROSE.) Mam? I'm talking to Jesse.

(Into phone.)

10 When she say that. (Pause.) Aw, you lying, man. I'm gonna tell her you said that.

ROSE: (Calling.) Cory, don't you go nowhere!

CORY: I got to go to the game, Ma!

(Into the phone.)

Yeah, hey, look, I'll talk to you later. Yeah, I'll meet you

15 over Earl's house. Later. Bye, Ma. ——

(CORY exits the house and starts out the yard.)

ROSE: Cory, where you going off to? You got that stuff all pulled out and thrown all over your room.

CORY: (In the yard.) I was looking for my spikes. Jesse wanted to borrow my spikes.

ROSE: Get up there and get that cleaned up before your daddy 20 get back in here.

CORY: I got to go to the game! I'll clean it up when I get back.

(CORY exits.)

ROSE: That's all he need to do is see that room all messed up.

(ROSE exits into the house. TROY and BONO enter the yard. TROY is dressed in clothes other than his work clothes.)

BONO: He told him the same thing he told you. Take it to the union. 25

TROY: Brownie ain't got that much sense. Man wasn't thinking about nothing. He wait until I confront them on it . . . then he wanna come crying seniority.

(Calls.)

Hey, Rose!

BONO: I wish I could have seen Mr. Rand's face when he told 30 you.

TROY: He couldn't get it out of his mouth! Liked to bit his tongue! When they called me down there to the Commissioner's office . . . he thought they was gonna fire me. Like everybody else. 35

BONO: I didn't think they was gonna fire you. I thought they was gonna put you on the warning paper.

TROY: Hey, Rose!

(To BONO.)

Yeah, Mr. Rand like to bit his tongue.

(TROY breaks the seal on the bottle, takes a drink, and hands it to BONO.)

BONO: I see you run right down to Taylors' and told that 40 Alberta gal.

TROY: (Calling.) Hey Rose! (To BONO.) I told everybody. Hey, Rose! I went down there to cash my check.

ROSE: (Entering from the house.) Hush all that hollering, man! I know you out here. What they say down there at the 45 Commissioner's office?

TROY: You supposed to come when I call you, woman. Bono'll tell you that.

(To BONO.)

Don't Lucille come when you call her?

ROSE: Man, hush your mouth. I ain't no dog . . . talk about 50 "come when you call me."

TROY: (Puts his arm around ROSE.) You hear this, Bono? I had me an old dog used to get uppity like that. You say, "C'mere, Blue!" . . . and he just lay there and look at you. End up getting a stick and chasing him away trying to make him 55 come.

ROSE: I ain't studying you and your dog. I remember you used to sing that old song.

TROY: (He sings.) Hear it ring! Hear it ring! I had a dog his name was Blue. 60

ROSE: Don't nobody wanna hear you sing that old song.

TROY: *(Sings.)* You know Blue was mighty true.

ROSE: Used to have Cory running around here singing that song.

BONO: Hell, I remember that song myself.

TROY: *(Sings.)*

65   You know Blue was a good old dog.
          Blue treed a possum in a hollow log.

That was my daddy's song. My daddy made up that song.

ROSE: I don't care who made it up. Don't nobody wanna hear you sing it.

70 TROY: *(Makes a song like calling a dog.)* Come here, woman.

ROSE: You come in here carrying on, I reckon they ain't fired you. What they say down there at the Commissioner's office?

TROY: Look here, Rose . . . Mr. Rand called me into his office today when I got back from talking to them people down

75   there . . . it come from up top . . . he called me in and told me they was making me a driver.

ROSE: Troy, you kidding!

TROY: No I ain't. Ask Bono.

ROSE: Well, that's great, Troy. Now you don't have to hassle

80   them people no more.

(LYONS enters from the street.)

TROY: Aw hell, I wasn't looking to see you today. I thought you was in jail. Got it all over the front page of the *Courier* about them raiding Sefus' place . . . where you hanging out with all them thugs?

85 LYONS: Hey, Pop . . . that ain't got nothing to do with me. I don't go down there gambling. I go down there to sit in with the band. I ain't got nothing to do with the gambling part. They got some good music down there.

TROY: They got some rogues . . . is what they got.

90 LYONS: How you been, Mr. Bono? Hi, Rose.

BONO: I see where you playing down at the Crawford Grill tonight.

ROSE: How come you ain't brought Bonnie like I told you. You should have brought Bonnie with you, she ain't been over

95   in a month of Sundays.

LYONS: I was just in the neighborhood . . . thought I'd stop by.

TROY: Here he come . . .

BONO: Your daddy got a promotion on the rubbish. He's gonna be the first colored driver. Ain't got to do nothing but sit

100   up there and read the paper like them white fellows.

LYONS: Hey, Pop . . . if you knew how to read you'd be alright.

BONO: Naw . . . naw . . . you mean if the nigger knew how to *drive* he'd be all right. Been fighting with them people about driving and ain't even got a license. Mr. Rand know

105   you ain't got no driver's license?

TROY: Driving ain't nothing. All you do is point the truck where you want it to go. Driving ain't nothing.

BONO: Do Mr. Rand know you ain't got no driver's license? That's what I'm talking about. I ain't asked if driving

110   was easy. I asked if Mr. Rand know you ain't got no driver's license.

TROY: He ain't got to know. The man ain't got to know my business. Time he find out, I have two or three driver's licenses.

LYONS: *(Going into his pocket.)* Say, look here, Pop . . .

115 TROY: I knew it was coming. Didn't I tell you, Bono? I know what kind of "Look here, Pop" that was. The nigger fixing

to ask me for some money. It's Friday night. It's my payday. All them rogues down there on the avenue . . . the ones that ain't in jail . . . and Lyons is hopping in his shoes to get down there with them.   120

LYONS: See, Pop . . . if you give somebody else a chance to talk sometime, you'd see that I was fixing to pay you back your ten dollars like I told you. Here . . . I told you I'd pay you when Bonnie got paid.

TROY: Naw . . . you go ahead and keep that ten dollars. Put it   125
in the bank. The next time you feel like you wanna come by here and ask me for something . . . you go on down there and get that.

LYONS: Here's your ten dollars, Pop. I told you I don't want you to give me nothing. I just wanted to borrow ten dollars.   130

TROY: Naw . . . you go on and keep that for the next time you want to ask me.

LYONS: Come on, Pop . . . here go your ten dollars.

ROSE: Why don't you go on and let the boy pay you back, Troy?

LYONS: Here you go, Rose. If you don't take it I'm gonna have   135
to hear about it for the next six months.

(He hands her the money.)

ROSE: You can hand yours over here too, Troy.

TROY: You see this, Bono. You see how they do me.

BONO: Yeah, Lucille do me the same way.

(GABRIEL is heard singing offstage. He enters.)

GABRIEL: Better get ready for the Judgment! Better get ready   140
for . . . Hey! . . . Hey! . . . There's Troy's boy!

LYONS: How you doing, Uncle Gabe?

GABRIEL: Lyons . . . The King of the Jungle! Rose . . . hey, Rose. Got a flower for you.

(He takes a rose from his pocket.)

        Picked it myself. That's the same rose like you is!   145

ROSE: That's right nice of you, Gabe.

LYONS: What you been doing, Uncle Gabe?

GABRIEL: Oh, I been chasing hellhounds and waiting on the time to tell St. Peter to open the gates.

LYONS: You been chasing hellhounds, huh? Well . . . you doing   150
the right thing, Uncle Gabe. Somebody got to chase them.

GABRIEL: Oh, yeah . . . I know it. The devil's strong. The devil ain't no pushover. Hellhounds snipping at everybody's heels. But I got my trumpet waiting on the judgment time.

LYONS: Waiting on the Battle of Armageddon, huh?   155

GABRIEL: Ain't gonna be too much of a battle when God get to waving that Judgment sword. But the people's gonna have a hell of a time trying to get into heaven if them gates ain't open.

LYONS: *(Putting his arm around GABRIEL.)* You hear this, Pop.   160
Uncle Gabe, you alright!

GABRIEL: *(Laughing with LYONS.)* Lyons! King of the Jungle.

ROSE: You gonna stay for supper, Gabe. Want me to fix you a plate?

GABRIEL: I'll take a sandwich, Rose. Don't want no plate. Just   165
wanna eat with my hands. I'll take a sandwich.

ROSE: How about you, Lyons? You staying? Got some short ribs cooking.

LYONS: Naw, I won't eat nothing till after we finished playing.

(Pause.)

170   You ought to come down and listen to me play, Pop.

TROY: I don't like that Chinese music. All that noise.

ROSE: Go on in the house and wash up, Gabe . . . I'll fix you a sandwich.

GABRIEL: *(To LYONS, as he exits.)* Troy's mad at me.

175 LYONS: What you mad at Uncle Gabe for, Pop.

ROSE: He thinks Troy's mad at him cause he moved over to Miss Pearl's.

TROY: I ain't mad at the man. He can live where he want to live at.

180 LYONS: What he move over there for? Miss Pearl don't like nobody.

ROSE: She don't mind him none. She treats him real nice. She just don't allow all that singing.

TROY: She don't mind that rent he be paying . . . that's what

185   she don't mind.

ROSE: Troy, I ain't going through that with you no more. He's over there cause he want to have his own place. He can come and go as he please.

TROY: Hell, he could come and go as he please here. I wasn't

190   stopping him. I ain't put no rules on him.

ROSE: It ain't the same thing, Troy. And you know it.

(GABRIEL comes to the door.)

Now, that's the last I wanna hear about that. I don't wanna hear nothing else about Gabe and Miss Pearl. And next week . . .

195 GABRIEL: I'm ready for my sandwich, Rose.

ROSE: And next week . . . when that recruiter come from that school . . . I want you to sign that paper and go on and let Cory play football. Then that'll be the last I have to hear about that.

200 TROY: *(To ROSE as she exits into the house.)* I ain't thinking about Cory nothing.

LYONS: What . . . Cory got recruited? What school he going to?

TROY: That boy walking around here smelling his piss . . . thinking he's grown. Thinking he's gonna do what he want,

205   irrespective of what I say. Look here, Bono . . . I left the Commissioner's office and went down to the A&P . . . that boy ain't working down there. He lying to me. Telling me he got his job back . . . telling me he working weekends . . . telling me he working after school . . . Mr. Stawicki tell me

210   he ain't working down there at all!

LYONS: Cory just growing up. He's just busting at the seams trying to fill out your shoes.

TROY: I don't care what he's doing. When he get to the point where he wanna disobey me . . . then it's time for him to

215   move on. Bono'll tell you that. I bet he ain't never disobeyed his daddy without paying the consequences.

BONO: I ain't never had a chance. My daddy came on through . . . but I ain't never knew him to see him . . . or what he had on his mind or where he went. Just moving on

220   through. Searching out the New Land. That's what the old folks used to call it. See a fellow moving around from place to place . . . woman to woman . . . called it searching out

the New Land. I can't say if he ever found it. I come along, didn't want no kids. Didn't know if I was gonna be in one place long enough to fix on them right as their daddy. I fig- 225 ured I was going searching too. As it turned out I been hooked up with Lucille near about as long as your daddy been with Rose. Going on sixteen years.

TROY: Sometimes I wish I hadn't known my daddy. He ain't cared nothing about no kids. A kid to him wasn't nothing. 230 All he wanted was for you to learn how to walk so he could start you to working. When it come time for eating . . . he ate first. If there was anything left over, that's what you got. Man would sit down and eat two chickens and give you the wing. 235

LYONS: You ought to stop that, Pop. Everybody feed their kids. No matter how hard times is . . . everybody care about their kids. Make sure they have something to eat.

TROY: The only thing my daddy cared about was getting them bales of cotton into Mr. Lubin. That's the only thing that 240 mattered to him. Sometimes I used to wonder why he was living. Wonder why the devil hadn't come and got him. "Get them bales of cotton in to Mr. Lubin" and find out he owe him money . . .

LYONS: He should have just went on and left when he saw he 245 couldn't get nowhere. That's what I would have done.

TROY: How he gonna leave with eleven kids? And where he gonna go? He ain't knew how to do nothing but farm. No, he was trapped and I think he knew it. But I'll say this for him . . . he felt a responsibility toward us. Maybe he ain't 250 treated us the way I felt he should have . . . but without that responsibility he could have walked off and left us . . . made his own way.

BONO: A lot of them did. Back in those days what you talking about . . . they walk out their front door and just take on 255 down one road or another and keep on walking.

LYONS: There you go! That's what I'm talking about.

BONO: Just keep on walking till you come to something else. Ain't you never heard of nobody having the walking blues? Well, that's what you call it when you just take off like that. 260

TROY: My daddy ain't had them walking blues! What you talking about? He stayed right there with his family. But he was just as evil as he could be. My mama couldn't stand him. Couldn't stand that evilness. She run off when I was about eight. She sneaked off one night after he had gone to 265 sleep. Told me she was coming back for me. I ain't never seen her no more. All his women run off and left him. He wasn't good for nobody.

When my turn come to head out, I was fourteen and got to sniffing around Joe Canewell's daughter. Had us an old 270 mule we called Greyboy. My daddy sent me out to do some plowing and I tied up Greyboy and went to fooling around with Joe Canewell's daughter. We done found us a nice lit- tle spot, got real cozy with each other. She about thirteen and we done figured we was grown anyway . . . so we down 275 there enjoying ourselves . . . ain't thinking about nothing. We didn't know Greyboy had got loose and wandered back to the house and my daddy was looking for me. We down there by the creek enjoying ourselves when my daddy come up on us. Surprised us. He had them leather straps off the 280 mule and commenced to whupping me like there was no tomorrow. I jumped up, mad and embarrassed. I was scared

of my daddy. When he commenced to whupping on me . . .
quite naturally I run to get out of the way.

(Pause.)

285 Now I thought he was mad cause I ain't done my work. But
I see where he was chasing me off so he could have the gal
for himself. When I see what the matter of it was, I lost all
fear of my daddy. Right there is where I become a man . . .
at fourteen years of age.

(Pause.)

290 Now it was my turn to run him off. I picked up them same
reins that he had used on me. I picked up them reins and
commenced to whupping on him. The gal jumped up and
run off . . . and when my daddy turned to face me, I could
295 see why the devil had never come to get him . . . cause
he was the devil himself. I don't know what happened.
When I woke up, I was laying right there by the creek, and
Blue . . . this old dog we had . . . was licking my face. I
thought I was blind. I couldn't see nothing. Both my eyes
300 were swollen shut. I layed there and cried. I didn't know
what I was gonna do. The only thing I knew was the time
had come for me to leave my daddy's house. And right there
the world suddenly got big. And it was a long time before
I could cut it down to where I could handle it.

305 Part of that cutting down was when I got to the place
where I could feel him kicking in my blood and knew that
the only thing that separated us was the matter of a few years.

(GABRIEL enters from the house with a sandwich.)

LYONS: What you got there, Uncle Gabe?
GABRIEL: Got me a ham sandwich. Rose gave me a ham
sandwich.
310 TROY: I don't know what happened to him. I done lost touch
with everybody except Gabriel. But I hope he's dead. I hope
he found some peace.
LYONS: That's a heavy story, Pop. I didn't know you left home
when you was fourteen.
315 TROY: And didn't know nothing. The only part of the world I
knew was the forty-two acres of Mr. Lubin's land. That's all
I knew about life.
LYONS: Fourteen's kinda young to be out on your own. *(Phone
rings.)* I don't even think I was ready to be out on my own
320 at fourteen. I don't know what I would have done.
TROY: I got up from the creek and walked on down to Mobile.
I was through with farming. Figured I could do better in
the city. So I walked the two hundred miles to Mobile.
LYONS: Wait a minute . . . you ain't walked no two hundred
325 miles, Pop. Ain't nobody gonna walk no two hundred
miles. You talking about some walking there.
BONO: That's the only way you got anywhere back in them days.
LYONS: Shhh. Damn if I wouldn't have hitched a ride with
somebody!
330 TROY: Who you gonna hitch it with? They ain't had no cars and
things like they got now. We talking about 1918.
ROSE: *(Entering.)* What you all out here getting into?
TROY: *(To ROSE.)* I'm telling Lyons how good he got it. He
don't know nothing about this I'm talking.

ROSE: Lyons, that was Bonnie on the phone. She say you sup- 335
posed to pick her up.
LYONS: Yeah, okay, Rose.
TROY: I walked on down to Mobile and hitched up with some
of them fellows that was heading this way. Got up here
and found out . . . not only couldn't you get a job . . . you 340
couldn't find no place to live. I thought I was in freedom.
Shhh. Colored folks living down there on the riverbanks
in whatever kind of shelter they could find for themselves.
Right down there under the Brady Street Bridge. Living
in shacks made of sticks and tarpaper. Messed around 345
there and went from bad to worse. Started stealing. First
it was food. Then I figured, hell, if I steal money I can buy
me some food. Buy me some shoes too! One thing led to
another. Met your mama. I was young and anxious to be a
man. Met your mama and had you. What I do that for? 350
Now I got to worry about feeding you and her. Got to
steal three times as much. Went out one day looking for
somebody to rob . . . that's what I was, a robber. I'll tell
you the truth. I'm ashamed of it today. But it's the truth.
Went to rob this fellow . . . pulled out my knife . . . and 355
he pulled out a gun. Shot me in the chest. It felt just like
somebody had taken a hot branding iron and laid it on
me. When he shot me I jumped at him with my knife.
They told me I killed him and they put me in the peni-
tentiary and locked me up for fifteen years. That's where I 360
met Bono. That's where I learned how to play baseball.
Got out that place and your mama had taken you and
went on to make life without me. Fifteen years was a long
time for her to wait. But that fifteen years cured me of
that robbing stuff. Rose'll tell you. She asked me when I 365
met her if I had gotten all that foolishness out of my system. And I told her, "Baby, it's you and baseball all what
count with me." You hear me, Bono? I meant it too. She
say, "Which one comes first?" I told her, "Baby, ain't no
doubt it's baseball . . . but you stick and get old with me 370
and we'll both outlive this baseball." Am I right, Rose?
And it's true.
ROSE: Man, hush your mouth. You ain't said no such thing.
Talking about, "Baby, you know you'll always be number
one with me." That's what you was talking. 375
TROY: You hear that, Bono. That's why I love her.
BONO: Rose'll keep you straight. You get off the track, she'll
straighten you up.
ROSE: Lyons, you better get on up and get Bonnie. She waiting
on you. 380
LYONS: *(Gets up to go.)* Hey, Pop, why don't you come on down
to the Grill and hear me play?
TROY: I ain't going down there. I'm too old to be sitting around
in them clubs.
BONO: You got to be good to play down at the Grill. 385
LYONS: Come on, Pop . . .
TROY: I got to get up in the morning.
LYONS: You ain't got to stay long.
TROY: Naw, I'm gonna get my supper and go on to bed.
LYONS: Well, I got to go. I'll see you again. 390
TROY: Don't you come around my house on my payday.
ROSE: Pick up the phone and let somebody know you coming.
And bring Bonnie with you. You know I'm always glad to
see her.

395 LYONS: Yeah, I'll do that, Rose. You take care now. See you,
          Pop. See you, Mr. Bono. See you, Uncle Gabe.
     GABRIEL: Lyons! King of the Jungle!

(LYONS *exits.*)

     TROY: Is supper ready, woman? Me and you got some business
          to take care of. I'm gonna tear it up too.
400 ROSE: Troy, I done told you now!
     TROY: (*Puts his arm around* BONO.) Aw hell, woman . . . this is
          Bono. Bono like family. I done known this nigger since . . .
          how long I done know you?
     BONO: It's been a long time.
405 TROY: I done known this nigger since Skippy was a pup. Me
          and him done been through some times.
     BONO: You sure right about that.
     TROY: Hell, I done know him longer than I known you. And
          we still standing shoulder to shoulder. Hey, look here,
410   Bono . . . a man can't ask for no more than that.

(*Drinks to him.*)

     I love you, nigger.
     BONO: Hell, I love you too . . . but I got to get home see my
          woman. You got yours in hand. I got to go get mine.

(BONO *starts to exit as* CORY *enters the yard, dressed in his football
uniform. He gives* TROY *a hard, uncompromising look.*)

     CORY: What you do that for, Pop?

(*He throws his helmet down in the direction of* TROY.)

415 ROSE: What's the matter? Cory . . . what's the matter?
     CORY: Papa done went up to the school and told Coach Zellman
          I can't play football no more. Wouldn't even let me play the
          game. Told him to tell the recruiter not to come.
     ROSE: Troy . . .
420 TROY: What you Troying me for? Yeah, I did it. And the boy
          know why I did it.
     CORY: Why you wanna do that to me? That was the one chance
          I had.
     ROSE: Ain't nothing wrong with Cory playing football, Troy.
425 TROY: The boy lied to me. I told the nigger if he wanna play
          football . . . to keep his chores and hold down that job at
          the A&P. That was the conditions. Stopped down there to
          see Mr. Stawicki . . .
     CORY: I can't work after school during the football season, Pop!
430   I tried to tell you that Mr. Stawicki's holding my job for
          me. You don't never want to listen to nobody. And then you
          wanna go and do this to me!
     TROY: I ain't done nothing to you. You done it to yourself.
     CORY: Just cause you didn't have a chance! You just scared I'm
435   gonna be better than you, that's all.
     TROY: Come here.
     ROSE: Troy . . .

(CORY *reluctantly crosses over to* TROY.)

     TROY: Alright! See. You done made a mistake.
     CORY: I didn't even do nothing!

     TROY: I'm gonna tell you what your mistake was. See . . . you 440
          swung at the ball and didn't hit it. That's strike one. See,
          you in the batter's box now. You swung and you missed.
          That's strike one. Don't you strike out!

(*Lights fade to black.*)

──────── ACT TWO ────────

SCENE I

The following morning. CORY *is at the tree hitting the ball with the
bat. He tries to mimic* TROY, *but his swing is awkward, less sure.*
ROSE *enters from the house.*

     ROSE: Cory, I want you to help me with this cupboard.
     CORY: I ain't quitting the team. I don't care what Poppa say.
     ROSE: I'll talk to him when he gets back. He had to go see
          about your Uncle Gabe. The police done arrested him. Say
          he was disturbing the peace. He'll be back directly. Come   5
          on in here and help me clean out the top of this cupboard.

(CORY *exits into the house.* ROSE *sees* TROY *and* BONO *coming down
the alley.*)

     Troy . . . what they say down there?
     TROY: Ain't said nothing. I give them fifty dollars and they let
          him go. I'll talk to you about it. Where's Cory?
     ROSE: He's in there helping me clean out these cupboards.   10
     TROY: Tell him to get his butt out here.

(TROY *and* BONO *go over to the pile of wood.* BONO *picks up the saw
and begins sawing.*)

     TROY: (*To* BONO.) All they want is the money. That makes six
          or seven times I done went down there and got him. See me
          coming they stick out their hands.
     BONO: Yeah. I know what you mean. That's all they care   15
          about . . . that money. They don't care about what's right.

(*Pause.*)

     Nigger, why you got to go and get some hard wood? You
     ain't doing nothing but building a little old fence. Get you
     some soft pine wood. That's all you need.
     TROY: I know what I'm doing. This is outside wood. You put   20
          pine wood inside the house. Pine wood is inside wood. This
          here is outside wood. Now you tell me where the fence is
          gonna be?
     BONO: You don't need this wood. You can put it up with pine
          wood and it's stand as long as you gonna be here look-   25
          ing at it.
     TROY: How you know how long I'm gonna be here, nigger?
          Hell, I might just live forever. Live longer than old man
          Horsely.
     BONO: That's what Magee used to say.   30
     TROY: Magee's a damn fool. Now you tell me who you ever
          heard of gonna pull their own teeth with a pair of rusty
          pliers.
     BONO: The old folks . . . my granddaddy used to pull his teeth
          with pliers. They ain't had no dentists for the colored folks 35
          back then.

TROY: Get clean pliers! You understand? Clean pliers! Sterilize them! Besides we ain't living back then. All Magee had to do was walk over to Doc Goldblums.

40 BONO: I see where you and that Tallahassee gal . . . that Alberta . . . I see where you all done got tight.

TROY: What you mean "got tight"?

BONO: I see where you be laughing and joking with her all the time.

45 TROY: I laughs and jokes with all of them, Bono. You know me.

BONO: That ain't the kind of laughing and joking I'm talking about.

(CORY enters from the house.)

CORY: How you doing, Mr. Bono?

TROY: Cory? Get that saw from Bono and cut some wood. He
50 talking about the wood's too hard to cut. Stand back there, Jim, and let that young boy show you how it's done.

BONO: He's sure welcome to it.

(CORY takes the saw and begins to cut the wood.)

Whew-e-e! Look at that. Big old strong boy. Look like Joe Louis. Hell, must be getting old the way I'm watching that
55 boy whip through that wood.

CORY: I don't see why Mama want a fence around the yard noways.

TROY: Damn if I know either. What the hell she keeping out with it? She ain't got nothing nobody want.

60 BONO: Some people build fences to keep people out . . . and other people build fences to keep people in. Rose wants to hold on to you all. She loves you.

TROY: Hell, nigger, I don't need nobody to tell me my wife loves me, Cory . . . go on in the house and see if you can find
65 that other saw.

CORY: Where's it at?

TROY: I said find it! Look for it till you find it!

(CORY exits into the house.)

What's that supposed to mean? Wanna keep us in?

BONO: Troy . . . I done known you seem like damn near my
70 whole life. You and Rose both. I done know both of you all for a long time. I remember when you met Rose. When you was hitting them baseball out the park. A lot of them old gals was after you then. You had the pick of the litter. When you picked Rose, I was happy for you. That was the
75 first time I knew you had any sense. I said . . . My man Troy knows what he's doing . . . I'm gonna follow this nigger . . . he might take me somewhere. I been following you too. I done learned a whole heap of things about life watching you. I done learned how to tell where the shit lies. How to
80 tell it from the alfalfa. You done learned me a lot of things. You showed me how to not make the same mistakes . . . to take life as it comes along and keep putting one foot in front of the other.

(Pause.)

Rose a good woman, Troy.

85 TROY: Hell, nigger, I know she a good woman. I been married to her for eighteen years. What you got on your mind, Bono?

BONO: I just say she a good woman. Just like I say anything. I ain't got to have nothing on my mind.

TROY: You just gonna say she a good woman and leave it hang-
90 ing out there like that? Why you telling me she a good woman?

BONO: She loves you, Troy. Rose loves you.

TROY: You saying I don't measure up. That's what you trying to say. I don't measure up cause I'm seeing this other gal. I
95 know what you trying to say.

BONO: I know what Rose means to you, Troy. I'm just trying to say I don't want to see you mess up.

TROY: Yeah, I appreciate that, Bono. If you was messing around on Lucille I'd be telling you the same thing.

100 BONO: Well, that's all I got to say. I just say that because I love you both.

TROY: Hell, you know me . . . I wasn't out there looking for nothing. You can't find a better woman than Rose. I know that. But seems like this woman just stuck onto me where
105 I can't shake her loose. I done wrestled with it, tried to throw her off me . . . but she just stuck on tighter. Now she's stuck on for good.

BONO: You's in control . . . that's what you tell me all the time. You responsible for what you do.

110 TROY: I ain't ducking the responsibility of it. As long as it sets right in my heart . . . then I'm okay. Cause that's all I listen to. It'll tell me right from wrong every time. And I ain't talking about doing Rose no bad turn. I love Rose. She done carried me a long ways and I love and respect her
115 for that.

BONO: I know you do. That's why I don't want to see you hurt her. But what you gonna do when she find out? What you got then? If you try and juggle both of them . . . sooner or later you gonna drop one of them. That's common sense.

120 TROY: Yeah, I hear what you saying, Bono. I been trying to fig- ure a way to work it out.

BONO: Work it out right, Troy. I don't want to be getting all up between you and Rose's business . . . but work it so it come out right.

125 TROY: Aw hell, I get all up between you and Lucille's business. When you gonna get that woman that refrigerator she been wanting? Don't tell me you ain't got no money now. I know who your banker is. Mellon don't need that money bad as Lucille want that refrigerator. I'll tell you that.

130 BONO: Tell you what I'll do . . . when you finish building this fence for Rose . . . I'll buy Lucille that refrigerator.

TROY: You done stuck your foot in your mouth now!

(TROY grabs up a board and begins to saw. BONO starts to walk out the yard.)

Hey, nigger . . . where you going?

BONO: I'm going home. I know you don't expect me to help
135 you now. I'm protecting my money. I wanna see you put that fence up by yourself. That's what I want to see. You'll be here another six month without me.

TROY: Nigger, you ain't right.

BONO: When it comes to my money . . . I'm right as fireworks
140 on the Fourth of July.

TROY: Alright, we gonna see now. You better get out your bankbook.

(BONO *exits, and* TROY *continues to work.* ROSE *enters from the house.*)

ROSE: What they say down there? What's happening with Gabe?

145 TROY: I went down there and got him out. Cost me fifty dollars. Say he was disturbing the peace. Judge set up a hearing for him in three weeks. Say to show cause why he shouldn't be re-committed.

ROSE: What was he doing that cause them to arrest him?

150 TROY: Some kids was teasing him and he run them off home. Say he was howling and carrying on. Some folks seen him and called the police. That's all it was.

ROSE: Well, what's you say? What'd you tell the judge?

TROY: Told him I'd look after him. It didn't make no sense to
155 recommit the man. He stuck out his big greasy palm and told me to give him fifty dollars and take him on home.

ROSE: Where's he at now? Where'd he go off to?

TROY: He's gone on about his business. He don't need nobody to hold his hand.

160 ROSE: Well, I don't know. Seem like that would be the best place for him if they did put him into the hospital. I know what you're gonna say. But that's what I think would be best.

TROY: The man done had his life ruined fighting for what? And
165 they wanna take and lock him up. Let him be free. He don't bother nobody.

ROSE: Well, everybody got their own way of looking at it I guess. Come on and get your lunch. I got a bowl of lima beans and some cornbread in the oven. Come on get some-
170 thing to eat. Ain't no sense you fretting over Gabe.

(ROSE *turns to go into the house.*)

TROY: Rose . . . got something to tell you.

ROSE: Well, come on . . . wait till I get this food on the table.

TROY: Rose!

(*She stops and turns around.*)

I don't know how to say this.

(*Pause.*)

175 I can't explain it none. It just sort of grows on you till it gets out of hand. It starts out like a little bush . . . and the next thing you know it's a whole forest.

ROSE: Troy . . . what is you talking about?

TROY: I'm talking, woman, let me talk. I'm trying to find a way
180 to tell you . . . I'm gonna be a daddy. I'm gonna be somebody's daddy.

ROSE: Troy . . . you're not telling me this? You're gonna be . . . what?

TROY: Rose . . . now . . . see . . .

185 ROSE: You telling me you gonna be somebody's daddy? You telling your *wife* this?

(GABRIEL *enters from the street. He carries a rose in his hand.*)

GABRIEL: Hey, Troy! Hey, Rose!

ROSE: I have to wait eighteen years to hear something like this.

GABRIEL: Hey, Rose . . . I got a flower for you.

(*He hands it to her.*)

That's a rose. Same rose like you is.   190

ROSE: Thanks, Gabe.

GABRIEL: Troy, you ain't mad at me is you? Them bad mens come and put me away. You ain't mad at me is you?

TROY: Naw, Gabe, I ain't mad at you.

ROSE: Eighteen years and you wanna come with this.   195

GABRIEL: (*Takes a quarter out of his pocket.*) See what I got? Got a brand new quarter.

TROY: Rose . . . it's just . . .

ROSE: Ain't nothing you can say, Troy. Ain't no way of explaining that.   200

GABRIEL: Fellow that give me this quarter had a whole mess of them. I'm gonna keep this quarter till it stop shining.

ROSE: Gabe, go on in the house there. I got some watermelon in the frigidaire. Go on and get you a piece.

GABRIEL: Say, Rose . . . you know I was chasing hellhounds and 205
them bad mens come and get me and take me away. Troy helped me. He come down there and told them they better let me go before he beat them up. Yeah, he did!

ROSE: You go on and get you a piece of watermelon, Gabe. Them bad mens is gone now.   210

GABRIEL: Okay, Rose . . . gonna get me some watermelon. The kind with the stripes on it.

(GABRIEL *exits into the house.*)

ROSE: Why, Troy? Why? After all these years to come dragging this in to me now. It don't make no sense at your age. I could have expected this ten or fifteen years ago, but not 215
now.

TROY: Age ain't got nothing to do with it, Rose.

ROSE: I done tried to be everything a wife should be. Everything a wife could be. Been married eighteen years and I got to live to see the day you tell me you been seeing an- 220
other woman and done fathered a child by her. And you know I ain't never wanted no half nothing in my family. My whole family is half. Everybody got different fathers and mothers . . . my two sisters and my brother. Can't hardly tell who's who. Can't never sit down and talk about Papa 225
and Mama. It's your papa and your mama and my papa and my mama . . .

TROY: Rose . . . stop it now.

ROSE: I ain't never wanted that for none of my children. And now you wanna drag your behind in here and tell me some- 230
thing like this.

TROY: You ought to know. It's time for you to know.

ROSE: Well, I don't want to know, goddamn it!

TROY: I can't just make it go away. It's done now. I can't wish the circumstance of the thing away.   235

ROSE: And you don't want to either. Maybe you want to wish me and my boy away. Maybe that's what you want? Well, you can't wish us away. I've got eighteen years of my life invested in you. You ought to have stayed upstairs in my bed where you belong.   240

TROY: Rose . . . now listen to me . . . we can get a handle on this thing. We can talk this out . . . come to an understanding.

ROSE: All of a sudden it's "we." Where was "we" at when you was down there rolling around with some godforsaken

245 woman? "We" should have come to an understanding be-
     fore you started making a damn fool of yourself. You're a
     day late and a dollar short when it comes to an understand-
     ing with me.

     TROY: It's just . . . She gives me a different idea . . . a different
250 understanding about myself. I can step out of this house
     and get away from the pressures and problems . . . be a dif-
     ferent man. I ain't got to wonder how I'm gonna pay the
     bills or get the roof fixed. I can just be a part of myself that
     I ain't never been.

255 ROSE: What I want to know . . . is do you plan to continue see-
     ing her. That's all you can say to me.

     TROY: I can sit up in her house and laugh. Do you understand
     what I'm saying. I can laugh out loud . . . and it feels good.
     It reaches all the way down to the bottom of my shoes.

     (Pause.)

260 Rose, I can't give that up.

     ROSE: Maybe you ought to go on and stay down there with
     her . . . if she a better woman than me.

     TROY: It ain't about nobody being a better woman or nothing.
     Rose, you ain't the blame. A man couldn't ask for no
265 woman to be a better wife than you've been. I'm responsi-
     ble for it. I done locked myself into a pattern trying to take
     care of you all that I forgot about myself.

     ROSE: What the hell was I there for? That was my job, not
     somebody else's.

270 TROY: Rose, I done tried all my life to live decent . . . to live a
     clean . . . hard . . . useful life. I tried to be a good husband
     to you. In every way I knew how. Maybe I come into the
     world backwards, I don't know. But . . . you born with two
     strikes on you before you come to the plate. You got to
275 guard it closely . . . always looking for the curve-ball on the
     inside corner. You can't afford to let none get past you. You
     can't afford a call strike. If you going down . . . you going
     down swinging. Everything lined up against you. What you
     gonna do. I fooled them, Rose. I bunted. When I found you
280 and Cory and a halfway decent job . . . I was safe. Couldn't
     nothing touch me. I wasn't gonna strike out no more. I
     wasn't going back to the penitentiary. I wasn't gonna lay in
     the streets with a bottle of wine. I was safe. I had me a family.
     A job. I wasn't gonna get that last strike. I was on first look-
285 ing for one of them boys to knock me in. To get me home.

     ROSE: You should have stayed in my bed, Troy.

     TROY: Then when I saw that gal . . . she firmed up my back-
     bone. And I got to thinking that if I tried . . . I just might
     be able to steal second. Do you understand after eighteen
290 years I wanted to steal second.

     ROSE: You should have held me tight. You should have grabbed
     me and held on.

     TROY: I stood on first base for eighteen years and I thought . . .
     well, goddamn it . . . go on for it!

295 ROSE: We're not talking about baseball! We're talking about
     you going off to lay in bed with another woman . . . and
     then bring it home to me. That's what we're talking about.
     We ain't talking about no baseball.

     TROY: Rose, you're not listening to me. I'm trying the best I
300 can to explain it to you. It's not easy for me to admit that
     I been standing in the same place for eighteen years.

ROSE: I been standing with you! I been right here with you,
     Troy. I got a life too. I gave eighteen years of my life to
     stand in the same spot with you. Don't you think I ever
     wanted other things? Don't you think I had dreams and   305
     hopes? What about my life? What about me? Don't you
     think it ever crossed my mind to want to know other men?
     That I wanted to lay up somewhere and forget about my
     responsibilities? That I wanted someone to make me laugh
     so I could feel good? You not the only one who's got wants   310
     and needs. But I held on to you, Troy. I took all my feelings,
     my wants and needs, my dreams . . . and I buried them
     inside you. I planted a seed and watched and prayed over it.
     I planted myself inside you and waited to bloom. And it
     didn't take me no eighteen years to find out the soil was   315
     hard and rocky and it wasn't never gonna bloom.

     But I held on to you, Troy. I held you tighter. You was
     my husband. I owed you everything I had. Every part of me
     I could find to give you. And upstairs in that room . . . with
     the darkness falling in on me . . . I gave everything I had to   320
     try and erase the doubt that you wasn't the finest man in the
     world. And wherever you was going . . . I wanted to be
     there with you. Cause you was my husband. Cause that's the
     only way I was gonna survive as your wife. You always talk-
     ing about what you give . . . and what you don't have to   325
     give. But you take too. You take . . . and don't even know
     nobody's giving!

(ROSE *turns to exit into the house;* TROY *grabs her arm.*)

TROY: You say I take and don't give!
ROSE: Troy! You're hurting me!
TROY: You say I take and don't give.   330
ROSE: Troy . . . you're hurting my arm! Let go!
TROY: I done give you everything I got. Don't you tell that lie
     on me.
ROSE: Troy!
TROY: Don't you tell that lie on me!   335

(CORY *enters from the house.*)

CORY: Mama!
ROSE: Troy. You're hurting me.
TROY: Don't you tell me about no taking and giving.

(CORY *comes up behind* TROY *and grabs him.* TROY, *surprised, is
thrown off balance just as* CORY *throws a glancing blow that
catches him on the chest and knocks him down.* TROY *is stunned, as
is* CORY.)

ROSE: Troy. Troy. No!

(TROY *gets to his feet and starts at* CORY.)

     Troy . . . no. Please! Troy!   340

(ROSE *pulls on* TROY *to hold him back.* TROY *stops himself.*)

TROY: (*To* CORY.) Alright. That's strike two. You stay away
     from around me, boy. Don't you strike out. You living with
     a full count. Don't you strike out.

(TROY *exits out the yard as the lights go down.*)

SCENE II

It is six months later, early afternoon. TROY *enters from the house and starts to exit the yard.* ROSE *enters from the house.*

ROSE: Troy, I want to talk to you.

TROY: All of a sudden, after all this time, you want to talk to me, huh? You ain't wanted to talk to me for months. You ain't wanted to talk to me last night. You ain't wanted no
5   part of me then. What you wanna talk to me about now?

ROSE: Tomorrow's Friday.

TROY: I know what day tomorrow is. You think I don't know tomorrow's Friday? My whole life I ain't done nothing but look to see Friday coming and you got to tell me it's Friday.

10 ROSE: I want to know if you're coming home.

TROY: I always come home, Rose. You know that. There ain't never been a night I ain't come home.

ROSE: That ain't what I mean . . . and you know it. I want to know if you're coming straight home after work.

15 TROY: I figure I'd cash my check . . . hang out at Taylors' with the boys . . . maybe play a game of checkers . . .

ROSE: Troy, I can't live like this. I won't live like this. You livin' on borrowed time with me. It's been going on six months now you ain't been coming home.

20 TROY: I be here every night. Every night of the year. That's 365 days.

ROSE: I want you to come home tomorrow after work.

TROY: Rose . . . I don't mess up my pay. You know that now. I take my pay and I give it to you. I don't have no money but
25 what you give me back. I just want to have a little time to myself . . . a little time to enjoy life.

ROSE: What about me? When's my time to enjoy life?

TROY: I don't know what to tell you, Rose. I'm doing the best I can.

30 ROSE: You ain't been home from work but time enough to change your clothes and run out . . . and you wanna call that the best you can do?

TROY: I'm going over to the hospital to see Alberta. She went into the hospital this afternoon. Look like she might have
35 the baby early. I won't be gone long.

ROSE: Well, you ought to know. They went over to Miss Pearl's and got Gabe today. She said you told them to go ahead and lock him up.

TROY: I ain't said no such thing. Whoever told you that is telling
40 a lie. Pearl ain't doing nothing but telling a big fat lie.

ROSE: She ain't had to tell me. I read it on the papers.

TROY: I ain't told them nothing of the kind.

ROSE: I saw it right there on the papers.

TROY: What it say, huh?

45 ROSE: It said you told them to take him.

TROY: Then they screwed that up, just the way they screw up everything. I ain't worried about what they got on the paper.

ROSE: Say the government send part of his check to the hospi-
50 tal and the other part to you.

TROY: I ain't got nothing to do with that if that's the way it works. I ain't made up the rules about how it work.

ROSE: You did Gabe just like you did Cory. You wouldn't sign the paper for Cory . . . but you signed for Gabe. You signed
55 that paper.

(The telephone is heard ringing inside the house.)

TROY: I told you I ain't signed nothing, woman! The only thing I signed was the release form. Hell, I can't read, I don't know what they had on that paper! I ain't signed nothing about sending Gabe away.

ROSE: I said send him to the hospital . . . you said let him be   60
free . . . now you done went down there and signed him to the hospital for half his money. You went back on yourself, Troy. You gonna have to answer for that.

TROY: See now . . . you been over there talking to Miss Pearl. She done got mad cause she ain't getting Gabe's rent   65
money. That's all it is. She's liable to say anything.

ROSE: Troy, I seen where you signed the paper.

TROY: You ain't seen nothing I signed. What she doing got papers on my brother anyway? Miss Pearl telling a big fat lie. And I'm gonna tell her about it too! You ain't seen nothing   70
I signed. Say . . . you ain't seen nothing I signed.

*(*ROSE *exits into the house to answer the telephone. Presently she returns.)*

ROSE: Troy . . . that was the hospital. Alberta had the baby.

TROY: What she have? What is it?

ROSE: It's a girl.

TROY: I better get on down to the hospital to see her.   75

ROSE: Troy . . .

TROY: Rose . . . I got to go see her now. That's only right . . . what's the matter . . . the baby's alright, ain't it?

ROSE: Alberta died having the baby.

TROY: Died . . . you say she's dead? Alberta's dead?   80

ROSE: They said they done all they could. They couldn't do nothing for her.

TROY: The baby? How's the baby?

ROSE: They say it's healthy. I wonder who's gonna bury her.

TROY: She had family, Rose. She wasn't living in the world by   85
herself.

ROSE: I know she wasn't living in the world by herself.

TROY: Next thing you gonna want to know if she had any insurance.

ROSE: Troy, you ain't got to talk like that.   90

TROY: That's the first thing that jumped out your mouth. "Who's gonna bury her?" Like I'm fixing to take on that task for myself.

ROSE: I am your wife. Don't push me away.

TROY: I ain't pushing nobody away. Just give me some space.   95
That's all. Just give me some room to breathe.

*(*ROSE *exits into the house.* TROY *walks about the yard.)*

TROY: *(With a quiet rage that threatens to consume him.)* Alright . . . Mr. Death. See now . . . I'm gonna tell you what I'm gonna do. I'm gonna take and build me a fence around this yard. See? I'm gonna build me a fence around what belongs to me.   100
And then I want you to stay on the other side. See? You stay over there until you're ready for me. Then you come on. Bring your army. Bring your sickle. Bring your wrestling clothes. I ain't gonna fall down on my vigilance this time. You ain't gonna sneak up on me no more. When you ready   105
for me . . . when the top of your list say Troy Maxson . . . that's when you come around here. You come up and knock

on the front door. Ain't nobody else got nothing to do with this. This is between you and me. Man to man. You stay on
110   the other side of that fence until you ready for me. Then you come up and knock on the front door. Anytime you want. I'll be ready for you.

(The lights go down to black.)

Scene III

The lights come up on the porch. It is late evening three days later. ROSE *sits listening to the ball game waiting for* TROY. *The final out of the game is made and* ROSE *switches off the radio.* TROY *enters the yard carrying an infant wrapped in blankets. He stands back from the house and calls.*

ROSE *enters and stands on the porch. There is a long, awkward silence, the weight of which grows heavier with each passing second.*

TROY: Rose . . . I'm standing here with my daughter in my arms. She ain't but a wee bittie little old thing. She don't know nothing about grownups' business. She innocent . . . and she ain't got no mama.
5 ROSE: What you telling me for, Troy?

(She turns and exits into the house.)

TROY: Well . . . I guess we'll just sit out here on the porch.

(He sits down on the porch. There is an awkward indelicateness about the way he handles the baby. His largeness engulfs and seems to swallow it. He speaks loud enough for ROSE *to hear.)*

A man's got to do what's right for him. I ain't sorry for nothing I done. It felt right in my heart.

(To the baby.)

What you smiling at? Your daddy's a big man. Got these
10 great big old hands. But sometimes he's scared. And right now your daddy's scared cause we sitting out here and ain't got no home. Oh, I been homeless before. I ain't had no little baby with me. But I been homeless. You just be out on the road by your lonesome and you see one of them trains
15 coming and you just kinda go like this . . .

(He sings as a lullaby.)

Please, Mr. Engineer let a man ride the line
Please, Mr. Engineer let a man ride the line
I ain't got no ticket please let me ride the blinds

*(ROSE *enters from the house.* TROY *hearing her steps behind him, stands and faces her.)*

She's my daughter, Rose. My own flesh and blood. I can't
20 deny her no more than I can deny them boys.

(Pause.)

You and them boys is my family. You and them and this child is all I got in the world. So I guess what I'm saying is . . . I'd appreciate it if you'd help take care of her.

ROSE: Okay, Troy . . . you're right. I'll take care of your baby for you . . . cause . . . like you say . . . she's innocent . . . and 25 you can't visit the sins of the father upon the child. A motherless child has got a hard time.

(She takes the baby from him.)

From right now . . . this child got a mother. But you a womanless man.

*(ROSE *turns and exits into the house with the baby. Lights go down to black.)*

Scene IV

It is two months later. LYONS *enters from the street. He knocks on the door and calls.*

LYONS: Hey, Rose! *(Pause.)* Rose!
ROSE: *(From inside the house.)* Stop that yelling. You gonna wake up Raynell. I just got her to sleep.
LYONS: I just stopped by to pay Papa this twenty dollars I owe him. Where's Papa at? 5
ROSE: He should be here in a minute. I'm getting ready to go down to the church. Sit down and wait on him.
LYONS: I got to go pick up Bonnie over her mother's house.
ROSE: Well, sit it down there on the table. He'll get it.
LYONS: *(Enters the house and sets the money on the table.)* Tell Papa 10 I said thanks. I'll see you again.
ROSE: Alright, Lyons. We'll see you.

*(LYONS *starts to exit as* CORY *enters.)*

CORY: Hey, Lyons.
LYONS: What's happening, Cory. Say man, I'm sorry I missed your graduation. You know I had a gig and couldn't get 15 away. Otherwise, I would have been there, man. So what you doing?
CORY: I'm trying to find a job.
LYONS: Yeah I know how that go, man. It's rough out here. Jobs are scarce. 20
CORY: Yeah, I know.
LYONS: Look here, I got to run. Talk to Papa . . . he know some people. He'll be able to help get you a job. Talk to him . . . see what he say.
CORY: Yeah . . . alright, Lyons. 25
LYONS: You take care. I'll talk to you soon. We'll find some time to talk.

*(LYONS *exits the yard.* CORY *wanders over to the tree, picks up the bat and assumes a batting stance. He studies an imaginary pitcher and swings. Dissatisfied with the result, he tries again.* TROY *enters. They eye each other for a beat.* CORY *puts the bat down and exits the yard.* TROY *starts into the house as* ROSE *exits with* RAYNELL. *She is carrying a cake.)*

TROY: I'm coming in and everybody's going out.
ROSE: I'm taking this cake down to the church for the bakesale. Lyons was by to see you. He stopped by to pay you 30 your twenty dollars. It's laying in there on the table.
TROY: *(Going into his pocket.)* Well . . . here go this money.
ROSE: Put it in there on the table, Troy. I'll get it.

TROY: What time you coming back?

35 ROSE: Ain't no use in you studying me. It don't matter what time I come back.

TROY: I just asked you a question, woman. What's the matter . . . can't I ask you a question?

ROSE: Troy, I don't want to go into it. Your dinner's in there on 40 the stove. All you got to do is heat it up. And don't you be eating the rest of them cakes in there. I'm coming back for them. We having a bakesale at the church tomorrow.

(ROSE *exits the yard.* TROY *sits down on the steps, takes a pint bottle from his pocket, opens it and drinks. He begins to sing.*)

TROY: Hear it ring! Hear it ring!
    Had an old dog his name was Blue
45   You know Blue was mighty true
    You know Blue as a good old dog
    Blue trees a possum in a hollow log
    You know from that he was a good old dog

(BONO *enters the yard.*)

BONO: Hey, Troy.

50 TROY: Hey, what's happening, Bono?

BONO: I just thought I'd stop by to see you.

TROY: What you stop by and see me for? You ain't stopped by in a month of Sundays. Hell, I must owe you money or something.

55 BONO: Since you got your promotion I can't keep up with you. Used to see you everyday. Now I don't even know what route you working.

TROY: They keep switching me around. Got me out in Greentree now . . . hauling white folks' garbage.

60 BONO: Greentree, huh? You lucky, at least you ain't got to be lifting them barrels. Damn if they ain't getting heavier. I'm gonna put in my two years and call it quits.

TROY: I'm thinking about retiring myself.

BONO: You got it easy. You can *drive* for another five years.

65 TROY: It ain't the same, Bono. It ain't like working the back of the truck. Ain't got nobody to talk to . . . feel like you working by yourself. Naw, I'm thinking about retiring. How's Lucille?

BONO: She alright. Her arthritis get to acting up on her some-70 time. Saw Rose on my way in. She going down to the church, huh?

TROY: Yeah, she took up going down there. All them preachers looking for somebody to fatten their pockets.

(*Pause.*)

    Got some gin here.

75 BONO: Naw, thanks. I just stopped by to say hello.

TROY: Hell, nigger . . . you can take a drink. I ain't never known you to say no to a drink. You ain't got to work tomorrow.

BONO: I just stopped by. I'm fixing to go over to Skinner's. 80 We got us a domino game going over his house every Friday.

TROY: Nigger, you can't play no dominoes. I used to whup you four games out of five.

BONO: Well, that learned me. I'm getting better.

TROY: Yeah? Well, that's alright. 85

BONO: Look here . . . I got to be getting on. Stop by sometime, huh?

TROY: Yeah, I'll do that, Bono. Lucille told Rose you bought her a new refrigerator.

BONO: Yeah, Rose told Lucille you had finally built your 90 fence . . . so I figured we'd call it even.

TROY: I knew you would.

BONO: Yeah . . . okay. I'll be talking to you.

TROY: Yeah, take care, Bono. Good to see you. I'm gonna stop over. 95

BONO: Yeah. Okay, Troy.

(BONO *exits.* TROY *drinks from the bottle.*)

TROY: Old Blue died and I dig his grave
    Let him down with a golden chain
    Every night when I hear old Blue bark
    I know Blue treed a possum in Noah's Ark. 100
    Hear it ring! Hear it ring!

(CORY *enters the yard. They eye each other for a beat.* TROY *is sitting in the middle of the steps.* CORY *walks over.*)

CORY: I got to get by.

TROY: Say what? What's you say?

CORY: You in my way. I got to get by.

TROY: You got to get by where? This is my house. Bought and 105 paid for. In full. Took me fifteen years. And if you wanna go in my house and I'm sitting on the steps . . . you say excuse me. Like your mama taught you.

CORY: Come on, Pop . . . I got to get by.

(CORY *starts to maneuver his way past* TROY. TROY *grabs his leg and shoves him back.*)

TROY: You just gonna walk over top of me? 110

CORY: I live here too!

TROY: (*Advancing toward him.*) You just gonna walk over top of me in my own house?

CORY: I ain't scared of you.

TROY: I ain't asked if you was scared of me. I asked you if you 115 was fixing to walk over top of me in my own house? That's the question. You ain't gonna say excuse me? You just gonna walk over top of me?

CORY: If you wanna put it like that.

TROY: How else am I gonna put it? 120

CORY: I was walking by you to go into the house cause you sitting on the steps drunk, singing to yourself. You can put it like that.

TROY: Without saying excuse me???

(CORY *doesn't respond.*)

    I asked you a question. Without saying excuse me??? 125

CORY: I ain't got to say excuse me to you. You don't count around here no more.

TROY: Oh, I see . . . I don't count around here no more. You ain't got to say excuse me to your daddy. All of a sudden you done got so grown that your daddy don't count around here 130 no more . . . Around here in his own house and yard that he

done paid for with the sweat of his brow. You done got so grown to where you gonna take over. You gonna take over my house. Is that right? You gonna wear my pants. You
135 gonna go in there and stretch out on my bed. You ain't got to say excuse me cause I don't count around here no more. Is that right?

CORY: That's right. You always talking this dumb stuff. Now, why don't you just get out my way.

140 TROY: I guess you got someplace to sleep and something to put in your belly. You got that, huh? You got that? That's what you need. You got that, huh?

CORY: You don't know what I got. You ain't got to worry about what I got.

145 TROY: You right! You one hundred percent right! I done spent the last seventeen years worrying about what you got. Now it's your turn, see? I'll tell you what to do. You grown . . . we done established that. You a man. Now, let's see you act like one. Turn your behind around and walk out this yard.
150 And when you get out there in the alley . . . you can forget about this house. See? Cause this is my house. You go on and be a man and get your own house. You can forget about this. Cause this is mine. You go on and get yours cause I'm through with doing for you.

155 CORY: You talking about what you did for me . . . what'd you ever give me?

TROY: Them feet and bones! That pumping heart, nigger! I give you more than anybody else is ever gonna give you.

CORY: You ain't never gave me nothing! You ain't never done
160 nothing but hold me back. Afraid I was gonna be better than you. All you ever did was try and make me scared of you. I used to tremble every time you called my name. Every time I heard your footsteps in the house. Wondering all the time . . . what's Papa gonna say if I do this? . . .
165 What's he gonna say if I do that? . . . What's Papa gonna say if I turn on the radio? And Mama, too . . . she tries . . . but she's scared of you.

TROY: You leave your mama out of this. She ain't got nothing to do with this.

170 CORY: I don't know how she stand you . . . after what you did to her.

TROY: I told you to leave your mama out of this!

(He advances toward CORY.*)*

CORY: What you gonna do . . . give me a whupping? You can't whup me no more. You're too old. You just an old man.
175 TROY: *(Shoves him on his shoulder.)* Nigger! That's what you are. You just another nigger on the street to me!

CORY: You crazy! You know that?

TROY: Go on now! You got the devil in you. Get on away from me!

180 CORY: You just a crazy old man . . . talking about I got the devil in me.

TROY: Yeah, I'm crazy! If you don't get on the other side of that yard . . . I'm gonna show you how crazy I am! Go on . . . get the hell out of my yard.

185 CORY: It ain't your yard. You took Uncle Gabe's money he got from the army to buy this house and then you put him out.

TROY: *(*TROY *advances on* CORY.*)* Get your black ass out of my yard!

*(*TROY's *advance backs* CORY *up against the tree.* CORY *grabs up the bat.)*

CORY: I ain't going nowhere! Come on . . . put me out! I ain't
190 scared of you.

TROY: That's my bat!

CORY: Come on!

TROY: Put my bat down!

CORY: Come on, put me out.

*(*CORY *swings at* TROY, *who backs across the yard.)*

What's the matter? You so bad . . . put me out!
195

*(*TROY *advances toward* CORY.*)*

CORY: *(Backing up.)* Come on! Come on!

TROY: You're gonna have to use it! You wanna draw that bat back on me . . . you're gonna have to use it.

CORY: Come on! . . . Come on!

*(*CORY *swings the bat at* TROY *a second time. He misses.* TROY *continues to advance toward him.)*

TROY: You're gonna have to kill me! You wanna draw that bat
200 back on me. You're gonna have to kill me.

*(*CORY, *backed up against the tree, can go no farther.* TROY *taunts him. He sticks out his head and offers him a target.)*

Come on! Come on!

*(*CORY *is unable to swing the bat.* TROY *grabs it.)*

TROY: Then I'll show you.

*(*CORY *and* TROY *struggle over the bat. The struggle is fierce and fully engaged.* TROY *ultimately is the stronger, and takes the bat from* CORY *and stands over him ready to swing. He stops himself.)*

Go on and get away from around my house.

*(*CORY, *stung by his defeat, picks himself up, walks slowly out of the yard and up the alley.)*

CORY: Tell Mama I'll be back for my things.
205

TROY: They'll be on the other side of that fence.

*(*CORY *exits.)*

TROY: I can't taste nothing. Helluljah! I can't taste nothing no more. *(*TROY *assumes a batting posture and begins to taunt Death, the fastball in the outside corner.)* Come on! It's between you and me now! Come on! Anytime you want! Come on! I
210 be ready for you . . . but I ain't gonna be easy.

(The lights go down on the scene.)

SCENE V

The time is 1965. The lights come up in the yard. It is the morning of TROY's *funeral. A funeral plaque with a light hangs beside the door. There is a small garden plot off to the side. There is noise and activity in the house as* ROSE, LYONS *and* BONO *have gathered. The door opens and* RAYNELL, *seven years old, enters dressed in a flannel nightgown. She crosses to the garden and pokes around with a stick.* ROSE *calls from the house.*

ROSE: Raynell!
RAYNELL: Mam?
ROSE: What you doing out there?
RAYNELL: Nothing.

(ROSE *comes to the door.*)

5   ROSE: Girl, get in here and get dressed. What you doing?
RAYNELL: Seeing if my garden growed.
ROSE: I told you it ain't gonna grow overnight. You got to wait.
RAYNELL: It don't look like it never gonna grow. Dag!
ROSE: I told you a watched pot never boils. Get in here and get
10   dressed.
RAYNELL: This ain't even no pot, Mama.
ROSE: You just have to give it a chance. It'll grow. Now you
    come on and do what I told you. We got to be getting ready.
    This ain't no morning to be playing around. You hear me?
15   RAYNELL: Yes, mam.

(ROSE *exits into the house.* RAYNELL *continues to poke at her garden with a stick.* CORY *enters. He is dressed in a Marine corporal's uniform, and carries a duffel bag. His posture is that of a military man, and his speech has a clipped sternness.*)

CORY: (*To* RAYNELL.) Hi.

(*Pause.*)

    I bet your name is Raynell.
RAYNELL: Uh huh.
CORY: Is your mama home?

(RAYNELL *runs up on the porch and calls through the screen door.*)

20   RAYNELL: Mama . . . there's some man out here. Mama?

(ROSE *comes to the door.*)

ROSE: Cory? Lord have mercy! Look here, you all!

(ROSE *and* CORY *embrace in a tearful reunion as* BONO *and* LYONS *enter from the house dressed in funeral clothes.*)

BONO: Aw, looka here . . .
ROSE: Done got all grown up!
CORY: Don't cry, Mama. What you crying about?
25   ROSE: I'm just so glad you made it.
CORY: Hey Lyons. How you doing, Mr. Bono.

(LYONS *goes to embrace* CORY.)

LYONS: Look at you, man. Look at you. Don't he look good,
    Rose. Got them Corporal stripes.
ROSE: What took you so long.
30   CORY: You know how the Marines are, Mama. They got to
    get all their paperwork straight before they let you do
    anything.
ROSE: Well, I'm sure glad you made it. They let Lyons come.
    Your Uncle Gabe's still in the hospital. They don't know if

they gonna let him out or not. I just talked to them a little   35
while ago.
LYONS: A Corporal in the United States Marines.
BONO: Your daddy knew you had it in you. He used to tell me
    all the time.
LYONS: Don't he look good, Mr. Bono?   40
BONO: Yeah, he remind me of Troy when I first met him.

(*Pause.*)

    Say, Rose, Lucille's down at the church with the choir. I'm
    gonna go down and get the pallbearers lined up. I'll be back
    to get you all.
ROSE: Thanks, Jim.   45
CORY: See you, Mr. Bono.
LYONS: (*With his arm around* RAYNELL.) Cory . . . look at
    Raynell. Ain't she precious? She gonna break a whole lot
    of hearts.
ROSE: Raynell, come and say hello to your brother. This is your 50
    brother, Cory. You remember Cory.
RAYNELL: No, Mam.
CORY: She don't remember me, Mama.
ROSE: Well, we talk about you. She heard us talk about you. (*To*
    RAYNELL.) This is your brother, Cory. Come on and say   55
    hello.
RAYNELL: Hi.
CORY: Hi. So you're Raynell. Mama told me a lot about you.
ROSE: You all come on into the house and let me fix you some
    breakfast. Keep up your strength.   60
CORY: I ain't hungry, Mama.
LYONS: You can fix me something, Rose. I'll be in there in a
    minute.
ROSE: Cory, you sure you don't want nothing. I know they ain't
    feeding you right.   65
CORY: No, Mama . . . thanks. I don't feel like eating. I'll get
    something later.
ROSE: Raynell . . . get on upstairs and get that dress on like I
    told you.

(ROSE *and* RAYNELL *exit into the house.*)

LYONS: So . . . I hear you thinking about getting married.   70
CORY: Yeah, I done found the right one, Lyons. It's about time.
LYONS: Me and Bonnie been split up about four years now.
    About the time Papa retired. I guess she just got tired of all
    them changes I was putting her through.

(*Pause.*)

    I always knew you was gonna make something out yourself. 75
    Your head was always in the right direction. So . . . you
    gonna stay in . . . make it a career . . . put in your twenty
    years?
CORY: I don't know. I got six already, I think that's enough.
LYONS: Stick with Uncle Sam and retire early. Ain't nothing   80
    out here. I guess Rose told you what happened with me.
    They got me down the workhouse. I thought I was being
    slick cashing other people's checks.
CORY: How much time you doing?
LYONS: They give me three years. I got that beat now. I ain't got 85
    but nine more months. It ain't so bad. You learn to deal

with it like anything else. You got to take the crookeds
with the straights. That's what Papa used to say. He used to
say that when he struck out. I seen him strike out three
90   times in a row . . . and the next time up he hit the ball over
the grandstand. Right out there in Homestead Field. He
wasn't satisfied hitting in the seats . . . he want to hit it over
everything! After the game he had two hundred people
standing around waiting to shake his hand. You got to take
95   the crookeds with the straights. Yeah, papa was something
else.
CORY: You still playing?
LYONS: Cory . . . you know I'm gonna do that. There's some fellows down there we got us a band . . . we gonna try and stay
100   together when we get out . . . but yeah, I'm still playing. It
still helps me to get out of bed in the morning. As long as
it do that I'm gonna be right there playing and trying to
make some sense out of it.
ROSE: (Calling.) Lyons, I got these eggs in the pan.
105   LYONS: Let me go on and get these eggs, man. Get ready to go
bury Papa.

(Pause.)

How you doing? You doing alright?

(CORY nods. LYONS touches him on the shoulder and they share a moment of silent grief. LYONS exits into the house. CORY wanders about
the yard. RAYNELL enters.)

RAYNELL: Hi.
CORY: Hi.
110   RAYNELL: Did you used to sleep in my room?
CORY: Yeah . . . that used to be my room.
RAYNELL: That's what Papa call it. "Cory's room." It got your
football in the closet.

(ROSE comes to the door.)

ROSE: Raynell, get in there and get them good shoes on.
115   RAYNELL: Mama, can't I wear these. Them other ones hurt my feet.
ROSE: Well, they just gonna have to hurt your feet for a while.
You ain't said they hurt your feet when you went down to
the store and got them.
RAYNELL: They didn't hurt then. My feet done got bigger.
120   ROSE: Don't you give me no backtalk now. You get in there and
get them shoes on.

(RAYNELL exits into the house.)

Ain't too much changed. He still got that piece of rag tied
to that tree. He was out here swinging that bat. I was just
ready to go back in the house. He swung that bat and then
125   he just fell over. Seem like he swung it and stood there with
this grin on his face . . . and then he just fell over. They carried him on down to the hospital, but I knew there wasn't
no need . . . why don't you come on in the house?
CORY: Mama . . . I got something to tell you. I don't know
130   how to tell you this . . . but I've got to tell you . . . I'm not
going to Papa's funeral.
ROSE: Boy, hush your mouth. That's your daddy you talking
about. I don't want hear that kind of talk this morning. I

done raised you to come to this? You standing there all
healthy and grown talking about you ain't going to your   135
daddy's funeral.
CORY: Mama . . . listen . . .
ROSE: I don't want to hear it, Cory. You just get that thought
out of your head.
CORY: I can't drag Papa with me everywhere I go. I've got to   140
say no to him. One time in my life I've got to say no.
ROSE: Don't nobody have to listen to nothing like that. I know
you and your daddy ain't seen eye to eye, but I ain't got to
listen to that kind of talk this morning. Whatever was between you and your daddy . . . the time has come to put it   145
aside. Just take it and set it over there on the shelf and forget about it. Disrespecting your daddy ain't gonna make
you a man, Cory. You got to find a way to come to that on
your own. Not going to your daddy's funeral ain't gonna
make you a man.   150
CORY: The whole time I was growing up . . . living in his
house . . . Papa was like a shadow that followed you everywhere. It weighed on you and sunk into your flesh. It would
wrap around you and lay there until you couldn't tell which
one was you anymore. That shadow digging in your flesh.   155
Trying to crawl in. Trying to live through you. Everywhere
I looked, Troy Maxson was staring back at me . . . hiding
under the bed . . . in the closet. I'm just saying I've got to
find a way to get rid of that shadow, Mama.
ROSE: You just like him. You got him in you good.   160
CORY: Don't tell me that, Mama.
ROSE: You Troy Maxson all over again.
CORY: I don't want to be Troy Maxson. I want to be me.
ROSE: You can't be nobody but who you are, Cory. That shadow
wasn't nothing but you growing into yourself. You either   165
got to grow into it or cut it down to fit you. But that's all
you got to make life with. That's all you got to measure
yourself against that world out there. Your daddy wanted
you to be everything he wasn't . . . and at the same time he
tried to make you into everything he was. I don't know if   170
he was right or wrong . . . but I do know he meant to do
more good than he meant to do harm. He wasn't always
right. Sometimes when he touched he bruised. And sometimes when he took me in his arms he cut.
When I first met your daddy I thought . . . Here is a man   175
I can lay down with and make a baby. That's the first thing
I thought when I seen him. I was thirty years old and had
done seen my share of men. But when he walked up to me
and said, "I can dance a waltz that'll make you dizzy," I
thought, Rose Lee, here is a man that you can open yourself   180
up to and be filled to bursting. Here is a man that can
fill all them empty spaces you been tipping around the edges
of. One of them empty spaces was being somebody's mother.
I married your daddy and settled down to cooking his
supper and keeping clean sheets on the bed. When your   185
daddy walked through the house he was so big he filled it up.
That was my first mistake. Not to make him leave some
room for me. For my part in the matter. But at that time I
wanted that. I wanted a house that I could sing in. And that's
what your daddy gave me. I didn't know to keep up his   190
strength I had to give up little pieces of mine. I did that. I
took on his life as mine and mixed up the pieces so that you
couldn't hardly tell which was which anymore. It was my

195 choice. It was my life and I didn't have to live it like that. But that's what life offered me in the way of being a woman and I took it. I grabbed hold of it with both hands.

By the time Raynell came into the house, me and your daddy had done lost touch with one another. I didn't want to make my blessing off of nobody's misfortune . . . but I 200 took on to Raynell like she was all them babies I had wanted and never had.

(The phone rings.)

Like I'd been blessed to relive a part of my life. And if the Lord see fit to keep up my strength . . . I'm gonna do her just like your daddy did you . . . I'm gonna give her the best 205 of what's in me.

RAYNELL: *(Entering, still with her old shoes.)* Mama . . . Reverend Tollivier on the phone.

(ROSE exits into the house.)

RAYNELL: Hi.
CORY: Hi.
210 RAYNELL: You in the Army or the Marines?
CORY: Marines.
RAYNELL: Papa said it was the Army. Did you know Blue?
CORY: Blue? Who's Blue?
RAYNELL: Papa's dog what he sing about all the time.
CORY: *(Singing.)*

215   Hear it ring! Hear it ring!
        I had a dog his name was Blue
        You know Blue was mighty true
        You know Blue was a good old dog
        Blue treed a possum in a hollow log
220   You know from that he was a good old dog.
        Hear it ring! Hear it ring!

(RAYNELL joins in singing.)

CORY and RAYNELL: Blue treed a possum out on a limb
        Blue looked at me and I looked at him
        Grabbed that possum and put him in a sack
225   Blue stayed there till I came back
        Old Blue's feets was big and round
        Never allowed a possum to touch the ground.
        Old Blue died and I dug his grave
        I dug his grave with a silver spade
230   Let him down with a golden chain
        And every night I call his name
        Go on Blue, you good dog you
        Go on Blue, you good dog you
RAYNELL: Blue laid down and died like a man
235   Blue laid down and died . . .

BOTH: Blue laid down and died like a man
        Now he's treeing possums in the Promised Land
        I'm gonna tell you this to let you know
        Blue's gone where the good dogs go
        When I hear old Blue bark   240
        When I hear old Blue bark
        Blue treed a possum in Noah's Ark
        Blue treed a possum in Noah's Ark.

(ROSE comes to the screen door.)

ROSE: Cory, we gonna be ready to go in a minute.
CORY: *(To RAYNELL.)* You go on in the house and change them 245
shoes like Mama told you so we can go to Papa's funeral.
RAYNELL: Okay, I'll be back.

(RAYNELL exits into the house. CORY gets up and crosses over to the tree. ROSE stands in the screen door watching him. GABRIEL enters from the alley.)

GABRIEL: *(Calling.)* Hey, Rose!
ROSE: Gabe?
GABRIEL: I'm here, Rose. Hey Rose, I'm here!   250

(ROSE enters from the house.)

ROSE: Lord . . . Look here, Lyons!
LYONS: See, I told you, Rose . . . I told you they'd let him come.
CORY: How you doing, Uncle Gabe?
LYONS: How you doing, Uncle Gabe?   255
GABRIEL: Hey, Rose. It's time. It's time to tell St. Peter to open the gates. Troy, you ready? You ready, Troy. I'm gonna tell St. Peter to open the gates. You get ready now.

(GABRIEL, with great fanfare, braces himself to blow. The trumpet is without a mouthpiece. He puts the end of it into his mouth and blows with great force, like a man who has been waiting some twenty-odd years for this single moment. No sound comes out of the trumpet. He braces himself and blows again with the same result. A third time he blows. There is a weight of impossible description that falls away and leaves him bare and exposed to a frightful realization. It is a trauma that a sane and normal mind would be unable to withstand. He begins to dance. A slow, strange dance, eerie and lifegiving. A dance of atavistic signature and ritual. LYONS attempts to embrace him. GABRIEL pushes LYONS away. He begins to howl in what is an attempt at song, or perhaps a song turning back into itself in an attempt at speech. He finishes his dance and the gates of heaven stand open as wide as God's closet.)

That's the way that go!

(Blackout.)   260

DAVID HENRY HWANG

David Henry Hwang was born in Los Angeles in 1957. He graduated with a B.A. in English from Stanford University in 1979 and studied at the Yale School of Drama 1980–81. In the 1980s, Hwang wrote a series of powerful plays concerning the cultural and political experience of Asian-Americans in the United States. His first play, *F.O.B.* ("fresh off the boat"), dramatizes the tensions that arise between Chinese immigrants to the United States and their assimilated friends and relatives. The play won an Obie award in 1980. Hwang addressed similar issues in *The Dance of the Railroad* (1981) and in *Rich Relations* (1986), and he collaborated with composer Philip Glass on *1000 Airplanes on the Roof* (1988). Hwang's Tony Award–winning *M. Butterfly* (1988) is a brilliant critique of Western attitudes toward Asia, epitomized by one of Western culture's most powerful and seductive images of the Orient: Puccini's opera, *Madame Butterfly*. His recent plays include *Trying to Find Chinatown* (1996) and *Bondage* (1996).

M. BUTTERFLY

In *M. Butterfly,* Hwang traces the relationship between the "Orient" of the Western imagination and the political realities that such images help to foster. The play's central character, the diplomat Gallimard, conducts his relationship with China in terms of Puccini's *Madame Butterfly.* In Puccini's 1904 opera, based on the 1900 play by David Belasco, the naval officer Pinkerton marries the Japanese geisha girl Butterfly. He leaves for the United States, promising to return, and Butterfly waits for him, meanwhile bearing his child. When Pinkerton returns with his wife from America to collect his child, Butterfly realizes that he will never return to her. She commits suicide.

As Hwang has remarked, Butterfly has become a cultural stereotype of East-West relations—"speaking of an Asian woman, we would sometimes say, 'She's pulling a Butterfly,' which meant playing the submissive Oriental number." This sexist and racist stereotype, Hwang argues, pervades not only Western men's fantasies about Asian women—as the mail-order business in Asian wives suggests, Western men see Asian women as obedient, submissive, and sexually self-sacrificing—but also conditions the political relationship between Asia and the West as well.

M. Butterfly fuses this erotic and political desire for domination in the character of Gallimard, a French diplomat who falls in love with Song Liling, an opera singer whom he first sees singing the death aria from *Madame Butterfly.* However, the play develops a fascinating twist, for Song is in fact a man, who plays female roles in the Beijing Opera, and who—as a woman—develops a love affair with Gallimard in order to spy for the Chinese government. *M. Butterfly* compacts a complex reading of the politics of race, gender, and sexuality in a brilliantly theatrical drama.

M. BUTTERFLY

David Henry Hwang

——— CHARACTERS ———

KUROGO

RENE GALLIMARD

SONG LILING

MARC

MAN 2

CONSUL SHARPLESS

RENEE

WOMAN AT PARTY

PINUP GIRL

COMRADE CHIN

SUZUKI

SHU-FANG

HELGA

M. TOULON

MAN 1

JUDGE

The action of the play takes place in a Paris prison in the present, and in recall, during the decade 1960 to 1970 in Beijing, and from 1966 to the present in Paris.

——— ACT ONE ———

SCENE I

M. GALLIMARD's *prison cell. Paris. Present.*

Lights fade up to reveal RENE GALLIMARD, *65, in a prison cell. He wears a comfortable bathrobe, and looks old and tired. The sparsely furnished cell contains a wooden crate upon which sits a hot plate with a kettle, and a portable tape recorder.* GALLIMARD *sits on the crate staring at the recorder, a sad smile on his face.*

Upstage SONG, *who appears as a beautiful woman in traditional Chinese garb, dances a traditional piece from the Peking Opera, surrounded by the percussive clatter of Chinese music.*

Then, slowly, lights and sound cross-fade; the Chinese opera music dissolves into a Western opera, the "Love Duet" from Puccini's Madame Butterfly. SONG *continues dancing, now to the Western accompaniment. Though her movements are the same, the difference in music now gives them a balletic quality.*

GALLIMARD *rises, and turns upstage towards the figure of* SONG, *who dances without acknowledging him.*

GALLIMARD: Butterfly, Butterfly . . .

(He forces himself to turn away, as the image of SONG *fades out, and talks to us.)*

GALLIMARD: The limits of my cell are as such: four-and-a-half meters by five. There's one window against the far wall; a door, very strong, to protect me from autograph hounds.
5 I'm responsible for the tape recorder, the hot plate, and this charming coffee table.
    When I want to eat, I'm marched off to the dining room—hot, steaming slop appears on my plate. When I want to sleep, the light bulb turns itself off—the work of
10 fairies. It's an enchanted space I occupy. The French—we know how to run a prison.
    But, to be honest, I'm not treated like an ordinary prisoner. Why? Because I'm a celebrity. You see, I make people laugh.
15   I never dreamed this day would arrive. I've never been considered witty or clever. In fact, as a young boy, in an informal poll among my grammar school classmates, I was voted

"least likely to be invited to a party." It's a title I managed to hold onto for many years. Despite some stiff competition.
    But now, how the tables turn! Look at me: the life of 20 every social function in Paris. Paris? Why be modest? My fame has spread to Amsterdam, London, New York. Listen to them! In the world's smartest parlors. I'm the one who lifts their spirits!

(With a flourish, GALLIMARD *directs our attention to another part of the stage.)*

SCENE II

A party. Present.

Lights go up on a chic-looking parlor, where a well-dressed trio, two men and one woman, make conversation. GALLIMARD *also remains lit; he observes them from his cell.*

WOMAN: And what of Gallimard?

MAN 1: Gallimard?

MAN 2: Gallimard!

GALLIMARD: *(To us.)* You see? They're all determined to say my name, as if it were some new dance. 5

WOMAN: He still claims not to believe the truth.

MAN 1: What? Still? Even since the trial?

WOMAN: Yes. Isn't it mad?

MAN 2: *(Laughing.)* He says . . . it was dark . . . and she was very modest! 10

(The trio break into laughter.)

MAN 1: So—what? He never touched her with his hands?

MAN 2: Perhaps he did, and simply misidentified the equipment. A compelling case for sex education in the schools.

WOMAN: To protect the National Security—the Church can't argue with that. 15

MAN 1: That's impossible! How could he not know?

MAN 2: Simple ignorance.

MAN 1: For twenty years?

MAN 2: Time flies when you're being stupid.

WOMAN: Well, I thought the French were ladies' men. 20

MAN 2: It seems Monsieur Gallimard was overly anxious to live up to his national reputation.

WOMAN: Well, he's not very good-looking.

MAN 1: No, he's not.
25 MAN 2: Certainly not.
WOMAN: Actually, I feel sorry for him.
MAN 2: A toast! To Monsieur Gallimard!
WOMAN: Yes! To Gallimard!
MAN 1: To Gallimard!
30 MAN 2: Vive la différence!

(*They toast, laughing. Lights down on them.*)

SCENE III

M. GALLIMARD's *cell.*

GALLIMARD: (*Smiling.*) You see? They toast me. I've become patron saint of the socially inept. Can they really be so foolish? Men like that—they should be scratching at my door,
begging to learn my secrets! For I, Rene Gallimard, you see,
5   I have known, and been loved by . . . the Perfect Woman.
Alone in this cell, I sit night after night, watching our
story play through my head, always searching for a new ending, one which redeems my honor, where she returns at last to
my arms. And I imagine you—my ideal audience—who
10   come to understand and even, perhaps just a little, to envy me.

(*He turns on his tape recorder. Over the house speakers, we hear the
opening phrases of* Madame Butterfly.)

GALLIMARD: In order for you to understand what I did and why,
I must introduce you to my favorite opera: *Madame Butterfly.*
By Giacomo Puccini. First produced at La Scala, Milan, in
1904, it is now beloved throughout the Western world.

(*As* GALLIMARD *describes the opera, the tape segues in and out to sections he may be describing.*)

15 GALLIMARD: And why not? Its heroine, Cio-Cio-San, also known
as Butterfly, is a feminine ideal, beautiful and brave. And its
hero, the man for whom she gives up everything, is—(*He
pulls out a naval officer's cap from under his crate, pops it on his
head, and struts about.*)—not very good-looking, not too
20   bright, and pretty much a wimp: Benjamin Franklin
Pinkerton of the U.S. Navy. As the curtain rises, he's just
closed on two great bargains: one on a house, the other on a
woman—call it a package deal.
Pinkerton purchased the rights to Butterfly for one hun-
25   dred yen—in modern currency, equivalent to about . . .
sixty-six cents. So, he's feeling pretty pleased with himself
as Sharpless, the American consul, arrives to witness the
marriage.

(MARC, *wearing an official cap to designate* SHARPLESS, *enters and
plays the character.*)

SHARPLESS/MARC: Pinkerton!
30 PINKERTON/GALLIMARD: Sharpless! How's it hangin'? It's a
great day, just great. Between my house, my wife, and the
rickshaw ride in from town, I've saved nineteen cents just
this morning.
SHARPLESS: Wonderful. I can see the inscription on your tomb-
35   stone already: "I saved a dollar, here I lie." (*He looks around.*)
Nice house.

PINKERTON: It's artistic. Artistic, don't you think? Like the way
the shoji screens slide open to reveal the wet bar and disco
mirror ball? Classy, huh? Great for impressing the chicks.
SHARPLESS: "Chicks"? Pinkerton, you're going to be a married   40
man!
PINKERTON: Well, sort of.
SHARPLESS: What do you mean?
PINKERTON: This country—Sharpless, it is okay. You got all
these geisha girls running around—   45
SHARPLESS: I know! I live here!
PINKERTON: Then, you know the marriage laws, right? I split
for one month, it's annulled!
SHARPLESS: Leave it to you to read the fine print. Who's the
lucky girl?   50
PINKERTON: Cio-Cio-San. Her friends call her Butterfly.
Sharpless, she eats out of my hand!
SHARPLESS: She's probably very hungry.
PINKERTON: Not like American girls. It's true what they say
about Oriental girls. They want to be treated bad!   55
SHARPLESS: Oh, please!
PINKERTON: It's true!
SHARPLESS: Are you serious about this girl?
PINKERTON: I'm marrying her, aren't I?
SHARPLESS: Yes—with generous trade-in terms.   60
PINKERTON: When I leave, she'll know what it's like to have
loved a real man. And I'll even buy her a few nylons.
SHARPLESS: You aren't planning to take her with you?
PINKERTON: Huh? Where?
SHARPLESS: Home!   65
PINKERTON: You mean, America? Are you crazy? Can you see
her trying to buy rice in St. Louis?
SHARPLESS: So, you're not serious.

(*Pause.*)

PINKERTON/GALLIMARD: (*As* PINKERTON.) Consul, I am a sailor
in port. (*As* GALLIMARD.) They then proceed to sing the   70
famous duet, "The Whole World Over."

(*The duet plays on the speakers.* GALLIMARD, *as* PINKERTON, *lip-
syncs his lines from the opera.*)

GALLIMARD: To give a rough translation: "The whole world
over, the Yankee travels, casting his anchor wherever he
wants. Life's not worth living unless he can win the hearts
of the fairest maidens, then hotfoot it off the premises   75
ASAP." (*He turns towards* MARC.) In the preceding scene, I
played Pinkerton, the womanizing cad, and my friend Marc
from school . . . (MARC *bows grandly for our benefit.*) played
Sharpless, the sensitive soul of reason. In life, however, our
positions were usually—no, always—reversed.   80

SCENE IV

Ecole Nationale. Aix-en-Provence. 1947.

GALLIMARD: No, Marc, I think I'd rather stay home.
MARC: Are you crazy?! We are going to Dad's condo in Marseille!
You know what happened last time?
GALLIMARD: Of course I do.
MARC: Of course you don't! You never know. . . . They stripped,   5
Rene!

GALLIMARD: Who stripped?

MARC: The girls!

GALLIMARD: Girls? Who said anything about girls?

10 MARC: Rene, we're a buncha university guys goin' up to the woods. What are we gonna do—talk philosophy?

GALLIMARD: What girls? Where do you get them?

MARC: Who cares? The point is, they come. On trucks. Packed in like sardines. The back flips open, babes hop out, we're

15 ready to roll.

GALLIMARD: You mean, they just—?

MARC: Before you know it, every last one of them—they're stripped and splashing around my pool. There's no moon out, they can't see what's going on, their boobs are flapping,

20 right? You close your eyes, reach out—it's grab bag, get it? Doesn't matter whose ass is between whose legs, whose teeth are sinking into who. You're just in there, going at it, eyes closed, on and on for as long as you can stand. (Pause.) Some fun, huh?

25 GALLIMARD: What happens in the morning?

MARC: In the morning, you're ready to talk some philosophy. (Beat.) So how 'bout it?

GALLIMARD: Marc, I can't . . . I'm afraid they'll say no—the girls. So I never ask.

30 MARC: You don't have to ask! That's the beauty—don't you see? They don't have to say yes. It's perfect for a guy like you, really.

GALLIMARD: You go ahead . . . I may come later.

MARC: Hey, Rene—it doesn't matter that you're clumsy and

35 got zits—they're not looking!

GALLIMARD: Thank you very much.

MARC: Wimp.

(MARC walks over to the other side of the stage, and starts waving and smiling at women in the audience.)

GALLIMARD: (To us.) We now return to my version of Madame Butterfly and the events leading to my recent conviction for

40 treason.

(GALLIMARD notices MARC making lewd gestures.)

Marc, what are you doing?

MARC: Huh? (Sotto voce.) Rene, there're a lotta great babes out there. They're probably lookin' at me and thinking, "What a dangerous guy."

45 GALLIMARD: Yes—how could they help but be impressed by your cool sophistication?

(GALLIMARD pops the SHARPLESS cap on MARC's head, and points him offstage. MARC exits, leering.)

SCENE V

M. GALLIMARD's cell.

GALLIMARD: Next, Butterfly makes her entrance. We learn her age—fifteen . . . but very mature for her years.

(Lights come up on the area where we saw SONG dancing at the top of the play. She appears there again, now dressed as MADAME BUTTERFLY, moving to the "Love Duet." GALLIMARD turns upstage slightly to watch, transfixed.)

GALLIMARD: But as she glides past him, beautiful, laughing softly behind her fan, don't we who are men sigh with hope? We, who are not handsome, nor brave, nor powerful, 5 yet somehow believe, like Pinkerton, that we deserve a Butterfly. She arrives with all her possessions in the folds of her sleeves, lays them all out, for her man to do with as he pleases. Even her life itself—she bows her head as she whispers that she's not even worth the hundred yen he paid for 10 her. He's already given too much, when we know he's really had to give nothing at all.

(Music and lights on SONG out. GALLIMARD sits at his crate.)

GALLIMARD: In real life, women who put their total worth at less than sixty-six cents are quite hard to find. The closest we come is in the pages of these magazines. (He reaches into 15 his crate, pulls out a stack of girlie magazines, and begins flipping through them.) Quite a necessity in prison. For three or four dollars, you get seven or eight women.

   I first discovered these magazines at my uncle's house. One day, as a boy of twelve. The first time I saw them in his 20 closet . . . all lined up—my body shook. Not with lust— no, with power. Here were women—a shelful—who would do exactly as I wanted.

(The "Love Duet" creeps in over the speakers. Special comes up, revealing, not SONG this time, but a PINUP GIRL in a sexy negligee, her back to us. GALLIMARD turns upstage and looks at her.)

GIRL: I know you're watching me.

GALLIMARD: My throat . . . it's dry.   25

GIRL: I leave my blinds open every night before I go to bed.

GALLIMARD: I can't move.

GIRL: I leave my blinds open and the lights on.

GALLIMARD: I'm shaking. My skin is hot, but my penis is soft. Why?   30

GIRL: I stand in front of the window.

GALLIMARD: What is she going to do?

GIRL: I toss my hair, and I let my lips part . . . barely.

GALLIMARD: I shouldn't be seeing this. It's so dirty. I'm so bad.   35

GIRL: Then, slowly, I lift off my nightdress.

GALLIMARD: Oh, god. I can't believe it. I can't—

GIRL: I toss it to the ground.

GALLIMARD: Now, she's going to walk away. She's going to—

GIRL: I stand there, in the light, displaying myself.   40

GALLIMARD: No. She's—why is she naked?

GIRL: To you.

GALLIMARD: In front of a window? This is wrong. No—

GIRL: Without shame.

GALLIMARD: No, she must . . . like it.   45

GIRL: I like it.

GALLIMARD: She . . . she wants me to see.

GIRL: I want you to see.

GALLIMARD: I can't believe it! She's getting excited!

GIRL: I can't see you. You can do whatever you want.   50

GALLIMARD: I can't do a thing. Why?

GIRL: What would you like me to do . . . next?

(Lights go down on her. Music off. Silence, as GALLIMARD puts away his magazines. Then he resumes talking to us.)

GALLIMARD: Act Two begins with Butterfly staring at the ocean. Pinkerton's been called back to the U.S., and he's
55 given his wife a detailed schedule of his plans. In the column marked "return date," he's written "when the robins nest." This failed to ignite her suspicions. Now, three years have passed without a peep from him. Which brings a response from her faithful servant, Suzuki.

(COMRADE CHIN enters, playing SUZUKI.)

60 SUZUKI: Girl, he's a loser. What'd he ever give you? Nineteen cents and those ugly Day-Glo stockings? Look, it's finished! Kaput! Done! And you should be glad! I mean, the guy was a woofer! He tried before, you know—before he met you, he went down to geisha central and plunked down his spare
65 change in front of the usual candidates—everyone else gagged! These are hungry prostitutes, and they were not interested, get the picture? Now, stop slathering when an American ship sails in, and let's make some bucks—I mean, yen! We are broke!
70   Now, what about Yamadori? Hey, hey—don't look away—the man is a prince—figuratively, and, what's even better, literally. He's rich, he's handsome, he says he'll die if you don't marry him—and he's even willing to overlook the little fact that you've been deflowered all over the place by
75 a foreign devil. What do you mean, "But he's Japanese?" You're Japanese! You think you've been touched by the whitey god? He was a sailor with dirty hands!

(SUZUKI stalks offstage.)

GALLIMARD: She's also visited by Consul Sharpless, sent by Pinkerton on a minor errand.

(MARC enters, as SHARPLESS.)

80 SHARPLESS: I hate this job.
GALLIMARD: This Pinkerton—he doesn't show up personally to tell his wife he's abandoning her. No, he sends a government diplomat . . . at taxpayer's expense.
SHARPLESS: Butterfly? Butterfly? I have some bad—I'm going
85 to be ill. Butterfly, I came to tell you—
GALLIMARD: Butterfly says she knows he'll return and if he doesn't she'll kill herself rather than go back to her own people. (Beat.) This causes a lull in the conversation.
SHARPLESS: Let's put it this way . . .
90 GALLIMARD: Butterfly runs into the next room, and returns holding—

(Sound cue: a baby crying. SHARPLESS, "seeing" this, backs away.)

SHARPLESS: Well, good. Happy to see things going so well. I suppose I'll be going now. Ta ta. Ciao. (He turns away. Sound cue out.) I hate this job. (He exits.)
95 GALLIMARD: At that moment, Butterfly spots in the harbor an American ship—the Abramo Lincoln!

(Music cue: "The Flower Duet." SONG, still dressed as BUTTERFLY, changes into a wedding kimono, moving to the music.)

GALLIMARD: This is the moment that redeems her years of waiting. With Suzuki's help, they cover the room with flowers—

(CHIN, as SUZUKI, trudges onstage and drops a lone flower without much enthusiasm.)

GALLIMARD: —and she changes into her wedding dress to prepare for Pinkerton's arrival.   100

(SUZUKI helps BUTTERFLY change. HELGA enters, and helps GALLIMARD change into a tuxedo.)

GALLIMARD: I married a woman older than myself—Helga.
HELGA: My father was ambassador to Australia. I grew up among criminals and kangaroos.
GALLIMARD: Hearing that brought me to the altar—

(HELGA exits.)

GALLIMARD: —where I took a vow renouncing love. No fantasy 105 woman would ever want me, so, yes, I would settle for a quick leap up the career ladder. Passion, I banish, and in its place—practicality!
    But my vows had long since lost their charm by the time we arrived in China. The sad truth is that all men want a 110 beautiful woman, and the uglier the man, the greater the want.

(SUZUKI makes final adjustments of BUTTERFLY's costume, as does GALLIMARD of his tuxedo.)

GALLIMARD: I married late, at age thirty-one. I was faithful to my marriage for eight years. Until the day when, as a junior-level diplomat in puritanical Peking, in a parlor at the 115 German ambassador's house, during the "Reign of a Hundred Flowers," I first saw her . . . singing the death scene from Madame Butterfly.

(SUZUKI runs offstage.)

SCENE VI

German ambassador's house. Beijing. 1960.

The upstage special area now becomes a stage. Several chairs face upstage, representing seating for some twenty guests in the parlor. A few "diplomats"—RENEE, MARC, TOULON—in formal dress enter and take seats.

GALLIMARD also sits down, but turns towards us and continues to talk. Orchestral accompaniment on the tape is now replaced by a simple piano. SONG picks up the death scene from the point where BUTTERFLY uncovers the hara-kiri knife.

GALLIMARD: The ending is pitiful. Pinkerton, in an art of great courage, stays home and sends his American wife to pick up Butterfly's child. The truth, long deferred, has come up to her door.

(SONG, playing BUTTERFLY, sings the lines from the opera in her own voice—which, though not classical, should be decent.)

SONG: "Con onor muore/ chi non puo serbar/ vita con onore."   5
GALLIMARD: (Simultaneously.) "Death with honor / Is better than life / Life with dishonor."

(The stage is illuminated; we are now completely within an elegant diplomat's residence. SONG *proceeds to play out an abbreviated death scene. Everyone in the room applauds.* SONG, *shyly, takes her bows. Others in the room rush to congratulate her.* GALLIMARD *remains with us.)*

GALLIMARD: They say in opera the voice is everything. That's probably why I'd never before enjoyed opera. Here . . . here
10   was a Butterfly with little or no voice—but she had the grace, the delicacy . . . I believed this girl. I believed her suffering. I wanted to take her in my arms—so delicate, even I could protect her, take her home, pamper her until she smiled.

(Over the course of the preceding speech, SONG *has broken from the upstage crowd and moved directly upstage of* GALLIMARD.*)*

SONG: Excuse me. Monsieur . . . ?

*(*GALLIMARD *turns upstage, shocked.)*

15 GALLIMARD: Oh! Gallimard. Mademoiselle . . . ? A beautiful . . .
SONG: Song Liling.
GALLIMARD: A beautiful performance.
SONG: Oh, please.
GALLIMARD: I usually—
20 SONG: You make me blush. I'm no opera singer at all.
GALLIMARD: I usually don't like *Butterfly.*
SONG: I can't blame you in the least.
GALLIMARD: I mean, the story—
SONG: Ridiculous.
25 GALLIMARD: I like the story, but . . . what?
SONG: Oh, you like it?
GALLIMARD: I . . . what I mean is, I've always seen it played by huge women in so much bad makeup.
SONG: Bad makeup is not unique to the West.
30 GALLIMARD: But, who can believe them?
SONG: And you believe me?
GALLIMARD: Absolutely. You were utterly convincing. It's the first time—
SONG: Convincing? As a Japanese woman? The Japanese used
35   hundreds of our people for medical experiments during the war, you know. But I gather such an irony is lost on you.
GALLIMARD: No! I was about to say, it's the first time I've seen the beauty of the story.
SONG: Really?
40 GALLIMARD: Of her death. It's a . . . a pure sacrifice. He's unworthy, but what can she do? She loves him . . . so much. It's a very beautiful story.
SONG: Well, yes, to a Westerner.
GALLIMARD: Excuse me?
45 SONG: It's one of your favorite fantasies, isn't it? The submissive Oriental woman and the cruel white man.
GALLIMARD: Well, I didn't quite mean . . .
SONG: Consider it this way: what would you say if a blonde homecoming queen fell in love with a short Japanese busi-
50   nessman? He treats her cruelly, then goes home for three years, during which time she prays to his picture and turns down marriage from a young Kennedy. Then, when she learns he has remarried, she kills herself. Now, I believe you would consider this girl to be a deranged idiot, correct? But
55   because it's an Oriental who kills herself for a Westerner—ah!—you find it beautiful.

(Silence.)

GALLIMARD: Yes . . . well . . . I see your point . . .
SONG: I will never do Butterfly again, Monsieur Gallimard. If you wish to see some real theatre, come to the Peking Opera sometime. Expand your mind.   60

*(*SONG *walks offstage.)*

GALLIMARD: *(To us.)* So much for protecting her in my big Western arms.

SCENE VII

M. GALLIMARD'S *apartment. Beijing. 1960.*

GALLIMARD *changes from his tux into a casual suit.* HELGA *enters.*

GALLIMARD: The Chinese are an incredibly arrogant people.
HELGA: They warned us about that in Paris, remember?
GALLIMARD: Even Parisians consider them arrogant. That's a switch.
HELGA: What is it that Madame Su says? "We are a very old 5
    civilization." I never know if she's talking about her country or herself.
GALLIMARD: I walk around here, all I hear every day, everywhere is how *old* this culture is. The fact that "old" may be synonymous with "senile" doesn't occur to them. 10
HELGA: You're not going to change them. "East is east, west is west, and . . ." whatever that guy said.
GALLIMARD: It's just that—silly. I met . . . at Ambassador Koening's tonight—you should've been there.
HELGA: Koening? Oh god, no. Did he enchant you all again 15
    with the history of Bavaria?
GALLIMARD: No. I met, I suppose, the Chinese equivalent of a diva. She's a singer in the Chinese opera.
HELGA: They have an opera, too? Do they sing in Chinese? Or maybe—in Italian? 20
GALLIMARD: Tonight, she did sing in Italian.
HELGA: How'd she manage that?
GALLIMARD: She must've been educated in the West before the Revolution. Her French is very good also. Anyway, she sang the death scene from *Madame Butterfly.* 25
HELGA: *Madame Butterfly!* Then I should have come. *(She begins humming, floating around the room as if dragging long kimono sleeves.)* Did she have a nice costume? I think it's a classic piece of music.
GALLIMARD: That's what *I* thought, too. Don't let her hear you 30
    say that.
HELGA: What's wrong?
GALLIMARD: Evidently the Chinese hate it.
HELGA: She hated it, but she performed it anyway? Is she perverse? 35
GALLIMARD: They hate it because the white man gets the girl. Sour grapes if you ask me.
HELGA: Politics again? Why can't they just hear it as a piece of beautiful music? So, what's in their opera?
GALLIMARD: I don't know. But, whatever it is, I'm sure it must 40
    be *old.*

*(*HELGA *exits.)*

SCENE VIII

Chinese opera house and the streets of Beijing. 1960.

The sound of gongs clanging fills the stage.

GALLIMARD: My wife's innocent question kept ringing in my ears. I asked around, but no one knew anything about the Chinese opera. It took four weeks, but my curiosity overcame my cowardice. This Chinese diva—this unwilling
5   Butterfly—what did she do to make her so proud?
      The room was hot, and full of smoke. Wrinkled faces, old women, teeth missing—a man with a growth on his neck, like a human toad. All smiling, pipes falling from their mouths, cracking nuts between their teeth, a live
10   chicken pecking at my foot—all looking, screaming, gawking . . . at her.

(The upstage area is suddenly hit with a harsh white light. It has become the stage for the Chinese opera performance. Two dancers enter, along with SONG. GALLIMARD *stands apart, watching.* SONG *glides gracefully amidst the two dancers. Drums suddenly slam to a halt.* SONG *strikes a pose, looking straight at* GALLIMARD. *Dancers exit. Light change. Pause, then* SONG *walks right off the stage and straight up to* GALLIMARD.)

SONG: Yes. You. White man. I'm looking straight at you.
GALLIMARD: Me?
SONG: You see any other white men? It was too easy to spot
15   you. How often does a man in my audience come in a tie?

*(*SONG *starts to remove her costume. Underneath, she wears simple baggy clothes. They are now backstage. The show is over.)*

SONG: So, you are an adventurous imperialist?
GALLIMARD: I . . . thought it would further my education.
SONG: It took you four weeks. Why?
GALLIMARD: I've been busy.
20   SONG: Well, education has always been undervalued in the West, hasn't it?
GALLIMARD: *(Laughing.)* I don't think it's true.
SONG: No, you wouldn't. You're a Westerner. How can you objectively judge your own values?
25   GALLIMARD: I think it's possible to achieve some distance.
SONG: Do you? *(Pause.)* It stinks in here. Let's go.
GALLIMARD: These are the smells of your loyal fans.
SONG: I love them for being my fans, I hate the smell they leave behind. I too can distance myself from my people.
30   *(She looks around, then whispers in his ear.)* "Art for the masses" is a shitty excuse to keep artists poor. *(She pops a cigarette in her mouth.)* Be a gentleman, will you? And light my cigarette.

*(*GALLIMARD *fumbles for a match.)*

GALLIMARD: I don't . . . smoke.
35   SONG: *(Lighting her own.)* Your loss. Had you lit my cigarette, I might have blown a puff of smoke right between your eyes. Come.

(They start to walk about the stage. It is a summer night on the Beijing streets. Sounds of the city play on the house speakers.)

SONG: How I wish there were even a tiny cafe to sit in. With cappuccinos, and men in tuxedos and bad expatriate jazz.
GALLIMARD: If my history serves me correctly, you weren't even 40 allowed into the clubs in Shanghai before the Revolution.
SONG: Your history serves you poorly, Monsieur Gallimard. True, there were signs reading "No dogs and Chinamen." But a woman, especially a delicate Oriental woman—we always go where we please. Could you imagine it other- 45 wise? Clubs in China filled with pasty, big-thighed white women, while thousands of slender lotus blossoms wait just outside the door? Never. The clubs would be empty. *(Beat.)* We have always held a certain fascination for you Caucasian men, have we not? 50
GALLIMARD: But . . . that fascination is imperialist, or so you tell me.
SONG: Do you believe everything I tell you? Yes. It is always imperialist. But sometimes . . . sometimes, it is also mutual. Oh—this is my flat. 55
GALLIMARD: I didn't even—
SONG: Thank you. Come another time and we will further expand your mind.

*(*SONG *exits.* GALLIMARD *continues roaming the streets as he speaks to us.)*

GALLIMARD: What was that? What did she mean, "Sometimes. . . it is mutual?" Women do not flirt with me. And 60 I normally can't talk to them. But tonight, I held up my end of the conversation.

SCENE IX

GALLIMARD's *bedroom. Beijing. 1960.*

HELGA *enters.*

HELGA: You didn't tell me you'd be home late.
GALLIMARD: I didn't intend to. Something came up.
HELGA: Oh! Like what?
GALLIMARD: I went to the . . . to the Dutch ambassador's home.
HELGA: Again? 5
GALLIMARD: There was a reception for a visiting scholar. He's writing a six-volume treatise on the Chinese revolution. We all gathered that meant he'd have to live here long enough to actually write six volumes, and we all expressed our deepest sympathies. 10
HELGA: Well, I had a good night too. I went with the ladies to a martial arts demonstration. Some of those men—when they break those thick boards—*(She mimes fanning herself.)* whoo-whoo!

*(*HELGA *exits. Lights dim.)*

GALLIMARD: I lied to my wife. Why? I've never had any reason 15 to lie before. But what reason did I have tonight? I didn't do anything wrong. That night, I had a dream. Other people, I've been told, have dreams where angels appear. Or dragons, or Sophia Loren in a towel. In my dream, Marc from school appeared. 20

*(*MARC *enters, in a nightshirt and cap.)*

MARC: Rene! You met a girl!

(GALLIMARD *and* MARC *stumble down the Beijing streets. Night sounds over the speakers.*)

GALLIMARD: It's not that amazing, thank you.
MARC: No! It's so monumental, I heard about it halfway around the world in my sleep!
25 GALLIMARD: I've met girls before, you know.
MARC: Name one. I've come across time and space to congratulate you. (*He hands* GALLIMARD *a bottle of wine.*)
GALLIMARD: Marc, this is expensive.
MARC: On those rare occasions when you become a formless
30   spirit, why not steal the best?

(MARC *pops open the bottle, begins to share it with* GALLIMARD.)

GALLIMARD: You embarrass me. She . . . there's no reason to think she likes me.
MARC: "Sometimes, it is mutual"?
GALLIMARD: Oh.
35 MARC: "Mutual"? "Mutual"? What does that mean?
GALLIMARD: You heard!
MARC: It means the money is in the bank, you only have to write the check!
GALLIMARD: I am a married man!
40 MARC: And an excellent one too. I cheated after . . . six months. Then again and again, until now—three hundred girls in twelve years.
GALLIMARD: I don't think we should hold that up as a model.
MARC: Of course not! My life—it is disgusting! Phooey!
45   Phooey! But, you—you are the model husband.
GALLIMARD: Anyway, it's impossible. I'm a foreigner.
MARC: Ah, yes. She cannot love you, it is taboo, but something deep inside her heart . . . she cannot help herself . . . she must surrender to you. It is her destiny.
50 GALLIMARD: How do you imagine all this?
MARC: The same way you do. It's an old story. It's in our blood. They fear us, Rene. Their women fear us. And their men— their men hate us. And, you know something? They are all correct.

(*They spot a light in a window.*)

55 MARC: There! There, Rene!
GALLIMARD: It's her window.
MARC: Late at night—it burns. The light—it burns for you.
GALLIMARD: I won't look. It's not respectful.
MARC: We don't have to be respectful. We're foreign devils.

(*Enter* SONG, *in a sheer robe. The "One Fine Day" aria creeps in over the speakers. With her back to us,* SONG *mimes attending to her toilette. Her robe comes loose, revealing her white shoulders.*)

60 MARC: All your life you've waited for a beautiful girl who would lay down for you. All your life you've smiled like a saint when it's happened to every other man you know. And you see them in magazines and you see them in movies. And you wonder, what's wrong with me? Will anyone
65   beautiful ever want me? As the years pass, your hair thins and you struggle to hold onto even your hopes. Stop struggling, Rene. The wait is over. (*He exits.*)

GALLIMARD: Marc? Marc?

(*At that moment,* SONG, *her back still towards us, drops her robe. A second of her naked back, then a sound cue: a phone ringing, very loud. Blackout, followed in the next beat by a special up on the bedroom area, where a phone now sits.* GALLIMARD *stumbles across the stage and picks up the phone. Sound cue out. Over the course of his conversation, area lights fill in the vicinity of his bed. It is the following morning.*)

GALLIMARD: Yes? Hello?
SONG: (*Offstage.*) Is it very early?   70
GALLIMARD: Why, yes.
SONG: (*Offstage.*) How early?
GALLIMARD: It's . . . it's 5:30. Why are you—?
SONG: (*Offstage.*) But it's light outside. Already.
GALLIMARD: It is. The sun must be in confusion today.   75

(*Over the course of* SONG'S *next speech, her upstage special comes up again. She sits in a chair, legs crossed, in a robe, telephone to her ear.*)

SONG: I waited until I saw the sun. That was as much discipline as I could manage for one night. Do you forgive me?
GALLIMARD: Of course . . . for what?
SONG: Then I'll ask you quickly. Are you really interested in the opera?   80
GALLIMARD: Why, yes. Yes I am.
SONG: Then come again next Thursday. I am playing *The Drunken Beauty.* May I count on you?
GALLIMARD: Yes. You may.
SONG: Perfect. Well, I must be getting to bed. I'm exhausted. 85 It's been a very long night for me.

(SONG *hangs up; special on her goes off.* GALLIMARD *begins to dress for work.*)

Scene X

SONG LILING'S *apartment. Beijing. 1960.*

GALLIMARD: I returned to the opera that next week, and the week after that . . . she keeps our meetings so short—perhaps fifteen, twenty minutes at most. So I am left each week with a thirst which is intensified. In this way, fifteen weeks have gone by. I am starting to doubt the words of my friend Marc. 5 But no, not really. In my heart, I know she has . . . an interest in me. I suspect this is her way. She is outwardly bold and outspoken, yet her heart is shy and afraid. It is the Oriental in her at war with her Western education.
SONG: (*Offstage.*) I will be out in an instant. Ask the servant for 10 anything you want.
GALLIMARD: Tonight, I have finally been invited to enter her apartment. Though the idea is almost beyond belief, I believe she is afraid of me.

(GALLIMARD *looks around the room. He picks up a picture in a frame, studies it. Without his noticing,* SONG *enters, dressed elegantly in a black gown from the twenties. She stands in the doorway looking like Anna May Wong.*)

SONG: That is my father.   15
GALLIMARD: (*Surprised.*) Mademoiselle Song . . .

(She glides up to him, snatches away the picture.)

SONG: It is very good that he did not live to see the Revolution. They would, no doubt, have made him kneel on broken glass. Not that he didn't deserve such a punishment. But he
20   is my father. I would've hated to see it happen.
GALLIMARD: I'm very honored that you've allowed me to visit your home.

(SONG curtsys.)

SONG: Thank you. Oh! Haven't you been poured any tea?
GALLIMARD: I'm really not—
25   SONG: *(To her offstage servant.)* Shu-Fang! Cha! Kwai-lah! *(To*
            GALLIMARD.*)* I'm sorry. You want everything to be perfect—
GALLIMARD: Please.
SONG: —and before the evening even begins—
GALLIMARD: I'm really not thirsty.
30   SONG: —it's ruined.
GALLIMARD: *(Sharply.)* Mademoiselle Song!

(SONG sits down.)

SONG: I'm sorry.
GALLIMARD: What are you apologizing for now?

(Pause; SONG starts to giggle.)

SONG: I don't know!

(GALLIMARD laughs.)

35   GALLIMARD: Exactly my point.
SONG: Oh, I am silly. Lightheaded. I promise not to apologize for anything else tonight, do you hear me?
GALLIMARD: That's a good girl!

(SHU-FANG, a servant girl, comes out with a tea tray and starts to pour.)

SONG: *(To SHU-FANG.)* No! I'll pour myself for the gentleman!

(SHU-FANG, staring at GALLIMARD, exits.)

40   SONG: No, I . . . I don't even know why I invited you up.
GALLIMARD: Well, I'm glad you did.

(SONG looks around the room.)

SONG: There is an element of danger to your presence.
GALLIMARD: Oh?
SONG: You must know.
45   GALLIMARD: It doesn't concern me. We both know why I'm here.
SONG: It doesn't concern me either. No . . . well perhaps . . .
GALLIMARD: What?
SONG: Perhaps I am slightly afraid of scandal.
50   GALLIMARD: What are we doing?
SONG: I'm entertaining you. In my parlor.
GALLIMARD: In France, that would hardly—
SONG: France. France is a country living in the modern era. Perhaps even ahead of it. China is a nation whose soul is firmly
55   rooted two thousand years in the past. What I do, even

pouring the tea for you now . . . it has . . . implications. The walls and windows say so. Even my own heart, strapped inside this Western dress . . . even it says things—things I don't care to hear.

(SONG hands GALLIMARD a cup of tea. GALLIMARD puts his hand over both the teacup and SONG's hand.)

GALLIMARD: This is a beautiful dress.   60
SONG: Don't.
GALLIMARD: What?
SONG: I don't even know if it looks right on me.
GALLIMARD: Believe me—
SONG: You are from France. You see so many beautiful women.   65
GALLIMARD: France? Since when are the European women—?
SONG: Oh! What am I trying to do, anyway?!

(SONG runs to the door, composes herself, then turns towards GALLI-MARD.)

SONG: Monsieur Gallimard, perhaps you should go.
GALLIMARD: But . . . why?
SONG: There's something wrong about this.   70
GALLIMARD: I don't see what.
SONG: I feel . . . I am not myself.
GALLIMARD: No. You're nervous.
SONG: Please. Hard as I try to be modern, to speak like a man, to hold a Western woman's strong face up to my own . . . in   75
     the end, I fail. A small, frightened heart beats too quickly and gives me away. Monsieur Gallimard, I'm a Chinese girl. I've never . . . never invited a man up to my flat before. The forwardness of my actions makes my skin burn.
GALLIMARD: What are you afraid of? Certainly not me, I hope.   80
SONG: I'm a modest girl.
GALLIMARD: I know. And very beautiful. *(He touches her hair.)*
SONG: Please—go now. The next time you see me, I shall again be myself.
GALLIMARD: I like you the way you are right now.   85
SONG: You are a cad.
GALLIMARD: What do you expect? I'm a foreign devil.

(GALLIMARD walks downstage. SONG exits.)

GALLIMARD: *(To us.)* Did you hear the way she talked about Western women? Much differently than the first night. She does—she feels inferior to them—and to me.   90

SCENE XI

The French embassy. Beijing. 1960.

GALLIMARD *moves towards a desk.*

GALLIMARD: I determined to try an experiment. In *Madame Butterfly*, Cio-Cio-San fears that the Western man who catches a butterfly will pierce its heart with a needle, then leave it to perish. I began to wonder: had I, too, caught a butterfly who would writhe on a needle?   5

(MARC enters, dressed as a bureaucrat, holding a stack of papers. As GALLIMARD speaks, MARC hands papers to him. He peruses, then signs, stamps or rejects them.)

GALLIMARD: Over the next five weeks, I worked like a dynamo. I stopped going to the opera, I didn't phone or write her. I knew this little flower was waiting for me to call, and, as I wickedly refused to do so, I felt for the first time that rush of power—the absolute power of a man.

(MARC continues acting as the bureaucrat, but he now speaks as himself.)

MARC: Rene! It's me!

GALLIMARD: Marc—I hear your voice everywhere now. Even in the midst of work.

MARC: That's because I'm watching you—all the time.

GALLIMARD: You were always the most popular guy in school.

MARC: Well, there's no guarantee of failure in life like happiness in high school. Somehow I knew I'd end up in the suburbs working for Renault and you'd be in the Orient picking exotic women off the trees. And they say there's no justice.

GALLIMARD: That's why you were my friend?

MARC: I gave you a little of my life, so that now you can give me some of yours. *(Pause.)* Remember Isabelle?

GALLIMARD: Of course I remember! She was my first experience.

MARC: We all wanted to ball her. But she only wanted me.

GALLIMARD: I had her.

MARC: Right. You balled her.

GALLIMARD: You were the only one who ever believed me.

MARC: Well, there's a good reason for that. *(Beat.)* C'mon. You must've guessed.

GALLIMARD: You told me to wait in the bushes by the cafeteria that night. The next thing I knew, she was on me. Dress up in the air.

MARC: She never wore underwear.

GALLIMARD: My arms were pinned to the dirt.

MARC: She loved the superior position. A girl ahead of her time.

GALLIMARD: I looked up, and there was this woman . . . bouncing up and down on my loins.

MARC: Screaming, right?

GALLIMARD: Screaming, and breaking off the branches all around me, and pounding my butt up and down into the dirt.

MARC: Huffing and puffing like a locomotive.

GALLIMARD: And in the middle of all this, the leaves were getting into my mouth, my legs were losing circulation, I thought, "God. So this is *it?*"

MARC: You thought that?

GALLIMARD: Well, I was worried about my legs falling off.

MARC: You didn't have a good time?

GALLIMARD: No, that's not what I—I had a great time!

MARC: You're sure?

GALLIMARD: Yeah. Really.

MARC: 'Cuz I wanted you to have a good time.

GALLIMARD: I did.

(Pause.)

MARC: Shit. *(Pause.)* When all is said and done, she was kind of a lousy lay, wasn't she? I mean, there was a lot of energy there, but you never knew what she was doing with it. Like when she yelled "I'm coming!"—hell, it was so loud, you wanted to go "Look, it's not that big a deal."

GALLIMARD: I got scared. I thought she meant someone was actually coming. *(Pause.)* But, Marc?

MARC: What?

GALLIMARD: Thanks.

MARC: Oh, don't mention it.

GALLIMARD: It was my first experience.

MARC: Yeah. You got her.

GALLIMARD: I got her.

MARC: Wait! Look at that letter again!

(GALLIMARD picks up one of the papers he's been stamping, and rereads it.)

GALLIMARD: *(To us.)* After six weeks, they began to arrive. The letters.

(Upstage special on SONG, as MADAME BUTTERFLY. The scene is underscored by the "Love Duet.")

SONG: Did we fight? I do not know. Is the opera no longer of interest to you? Please come—my audiences miss the white devil in their midst.

(GALLIMARD looks up from the letter, towards us.)

GALLIMARD: *(To us.)* A concession, but much too dignified. *(Beat; he discards the letter.)* I skipped the opera again that week to complete a position paper on trade.

(The bureaucrat hands him another letter.)

SONG: Six weeks have passed since last we met. In this your practice—to leave friends in the lurch? Sometimes I hate you, sometimes I hate myself, but always I miss you.

GALLIMARD: *(To us.)* Better, but I don't like the way she calls me "friend." When a woman calls a man her "friend," she's calling him a eunuch or a homosexual. *(Beat; he discards the letter.)* I was absent from the opera for the seventh week, feeling a sudden urge to clean out my files.

(Bureaucrat hands him another letter.)

SONG: Your rudeness is beyond belief. I don't deserve this cruelty. Don't bother to call. I'll have you turned away at the door.

GALLIMARD: *(To us.)* I didn't. *(He discards the letter; bureaucrat hands him another.)* And then finally, the letter that concluded my experiment.

SONG: I am out of words. I can hide behind dignity no longer. What do you want? I have already given you my shame.

(GALLIMARD gives the letter back to MARC, slowly. Special on SONG fades out.)

GALLIMARD: *(To us.)* Reading it, I became suddenly ashamed. Yes, my experiment had been a success. She was turning on my needle. But the victory seemed hollow.

MARC: Hollow? Are you crazy?

GALLIMARD: Nothing, Marc. Please go away.

MARC: *(Exiting, with papers.)* Haven't I taught you anything?

GALLIMARD: "I have already given you my shame." I had to attend a reception that evening. On the way, I felt sick. If there is a God, surely he would punish me now. I had finally gained power over a beautiful woman, only to abuse it cruelly. There must be justice in the world. I had the strange feeling that the ax would fall this very evening.

SCENE XII

AMBASSADOR TOULON's *residence. Beijing. 1960.*

Sound cue: party noises. Light change. We are now in a spacious residence. TOULON, *the French ambassador, enters and taps* GALLIMARD *on the shoulder.*

TOULON: Gallimard? Can I have a word? Over here.

GALLIMARD: *(To us.)* Manuel Toulon. French ambassador to China. He likes to think of us all as his children. Rather like God.

5 TOULON: Look, Gallimard, there's not much to say. I've liked you. From the day you walked in. You were no leader, but you were tidy and efficient.

GALLIMARD: Thank you, sir.

TOULON: Don't jump the gun. Okay, our needs in China are

10 changing. It's embarrassing that we lost Indochina. Someone just wasn't on the ball there. I don't mean you personally, of course.

GALLIMARD: Thank you, sir.

TOULON: We're going to be doing a lot more information-

15 gathering in the future. The nature of our work here is changing. Some people are just going to have to go. It's nothing personal.

GALLIMARD: Oh.

TOULON: Want to know a secret? Vice-Consul LeBon is being

20 transferred.

GALLIMARD: *(To us.)* My immediate superior!

TOULON: And most of his department.

GALLIMARD: *(To us.)* Just as I feared! God has seen my evil heart—

25 TOULON: But not you.

GALLIMARD: *(To us.)*—and he's taking her away just as . . . *(To* TOULON.*)* Excuse me, sir?

TOULON: Scare you? I think I did. Cheer up, Gallimard. I want you to replace LeBon as vice-consul.

30 GALLIMARD: You—? Yes, well, thank you, sir.

TOULON: Anytime.

GALLIMARD: I . . . accept with great humility.

TOULON: Humility won't be part of the job. You're going to co-ordinate the revamped intelligence division. Want to know

35 a secret? A year ago, you would've been out. But the past few months, I don't know how it happened, you've become this new aggressive confident . . . thing. And they also tell me you get along with the Chinese. So I think you're a lucky man, Gallimard. Congratulations.

(They shake hands. TOULON *exits. Party noises out.* GALLIMARD *stumbles across a darkened stage.)*

40 GALLIMARD: Vice-consul? Impossible! As I stumbled out of the party, I saw it written across the sky: There is no God. Or, no—say that there is a God. But that God . . . understands. Of course! God who creates Eve to serve Adam, who blesses Solomon with his harem but ties Jezebel to a burning

45 bed—that God is a man. And he understands! At age thirty-nine, I was suddenly initiated into the way of the world.

SCENE XIII

SONG LILING's *apartment. Beijing. 1960.*

SONG *enters, in a sheer dressing gown.*

SONG: Are you crazy?

GALLIMARD: Mademoiselle Song—

SONG: To come here—at this hour? After . . . after eight weeks?

GALLIMARD: It's the most amazing—

SONG: You bang on my door? Scare my servants, scandalize the 5
neighbors?

GALLIMARD: I've been promoted. To vice-consul.

(Pause.)

SONG: And what is that supposed to mean to me?

GALLIMARD: Are you my Butterfly?

SONG: What are you saying? 10

GALLIMARD: I've come tonight for an answer: are you my Butterfly?

SONG: Don't you know already?

GALLIMARD: I want you to say it.

SONG: I don't want to say it. 15

GALLIMARD: So, that is your answer?

SONG: You know how I feel about—

GALLIMARD: I do remember one thing.

SONG: What?

GALLIMARD: In the letter I received today. 20

SONG: Don't.

GALLIMARD: "I have already given you my shame."

SONG: It's enough that I even wrote it.

GALLIMARD: Well, then—

SONG: I shouldn't have it splashed across my face. 25

GALLIMARD: —if that's all true—

SONG: Stop!

GALLIMARD: Then what is one more short answer?

SONG: I don't want to!

GALLIMARD: Are you my Butterfly? *(Silence; he crosses the room* 30
and begins to touch her hair.) I want from you honesty. There should be nothing false between us. No false pride.

(Pause.)

SONG: Yes, I am. I am your Butterfly.

GALLIMARD: Then let me be honest with you. It is because of you that I was promoted tonight. You have changed my life 35
forever. My little Butterfly, there should be no more secrets: I love you.

(He starts to kiss her roughly. She resists slightly.)

SONG: No . . . no . . . gently . . . please, I've never . . .

GALLIMARD: No?

SONG: I've tried to appear experienced, but . . . the truth 40
is . . . no.

GALLIMARD: Are you cold?

SONG: Yes. Cold.

GALLIMARD: Then we will go very, very slowly.

(He starts to caress her; her gown begins to open.)

45 SONG: No . . . let me . . . keep my clothes . . .
GALLIMARD: But . . .
SONG: Please . . . it all frightens me. I'm a modest Chinese girl.
GALLIMARD: My poor little treasure.
SONG: I am your treasure. Though inexperienced, I am not . . .
50   ignorant. They teach us things, our mothers, about pleasing
  a man.
GALLIMARD: Yes?
SONG: I'll do my best to make you happy. Turn off the lights.

(GALLIMARD *gets up and heads for a lamp.* SONG, *propped up on one elbow, tosses her hair back and smiles.*)

SONG: Monsieur Gallimard?
55 GALLIMARD: Yes, Butterfly?
SONG: "Vieni, vieni!"
GALLIMARD: "Come, darling."
SONG: "Ah! Dolce notte!"
GALLIMARD: "Beautiful night."
60 SONG: "Tutto estatico d'amor ride il ciel!"
GALLIMARD: "All ecstatic with love, the heavens are filled with
  laughter."

(*He turns off the lamp. Blackout.*)

──────── ACT TWO ────────

SCENE I

M. GALLIMARD's *cell. Paris. Present.*

Lights up on GALLIMARD. *He sits in his cell, reading from a leaflet.*

GALLIMARD: This, from a contemporary critic's commentary on
  Madame Butterfly: "Pinkerton suffers from . . . being an obnoxious bounder whom every man in the audience itches to
  kick." Bully for us men in the audience! Then, in the same
5   note: "Butterfly is the most irresistibly appealing of Puccini's
  'Little Women.' Watching the succession of her humiliations
  is like watching a child under torture." (*He tosses the pamphlet
  over his shoulder.*) I suggest that, while we men may all want
  to kick Pinkerton, very few of us would pass up the oppor-
10   tunity to be Pinkerton.

(GALLIMARD *moves out of his cell.*)

SCENE II

GALLIMARD *and* BUTTERFLY's *flat. Beijing. 1960.*

We are in a simple but well-decorated parlor. GALLIMARD *moves to sit on a sofa, while* SONG, *dressed in a chong sam, enters and curls up at his feet.*

GALLIMARD: (*To us.*) We secured a flat on the outskirts of
  Peking. Butterfly, as I was calling her now, decorated our
  "home" with Western furniture and Chinese antiques. And
  there, on a few stolen afternoons or evenings each week,
5   Butterfly commenced her education.
SONG: The Chinese men—they keep us down.
GALLIMARD: Even in the "New Society"?
SONG: In the "New Society," we are all kept ignorant equally.
  That's one of the exciting things about loving a Western man.
10   I know you are not threatened by a woman's education.

GALLIMARD: I'm no saint, Butterfly.
SONG: But you come from a progressive society.
GALLIMARD: We're not always reminding each other how "old"
  we are, if that's what you mean.
SONG: Exactly. We Chinese—once, I suppose, it is true, we   15
  ruled the world. But so what? How much more exciting to
  be part of the society ruling the world today. Tell me—
  what's happening in Vietnam?
GALLIMARD: Oh, Butterfly—you want me to bring my work
  home?   20
SONG: I want to know what you know. To be impressed by my
  man. It's not the particulars so much as the fact that you're
  making decisions which change the shape of the world.
GALLIMARD: Not the world. At best, a small corner.

(TOULON *enters, and sits at a desk upstage.*)

SCENE III

French embassy. Beijing. 1961.

GALLIMARD *moves downstage, to* TOULON's *desk.* SONG *remains upstage, watching.*

TOULON: And a more troublesome corner is hard to imagine.
GALLIMARD: So, the Americans plan to begin bombing?
TOULON: This is very secret, Gallimard: yes. The Americans
  don't have an embassy here. They're asking us to be their
  eyes and ears. Say Jack Kennedy signed an order to bomb   5
  North Vietnam, Laos. How would the Chinese react?
GALLIMARD: I think the Chinese will squawk—
TOULON: Uh-huh.
GALLIMARD: —but, in their hearts, they don't even like Ho
  Chi Minh.   10

(*Pause.*)

TOULON: What a bunch of jerks. Vietnam was *our* colony. Not
  only didn't the Americans help us fight to keep them, but
  now, seven years later, they've come back to grab the territory for themselves. It's very irritating.
GALLIMARD: With all due respect, sir, why, should the Ameri-   15
  cans have won our war for us back in '54 if we didn't have
  the will to win it ourselves?
TOULON: You're kidding, aren't you?

(*Pause.*)

GALLIMARD: The Orientals simply want to be associated with
  whoever shows the most strength and power. You live with   20
  the Chinese, sir. Do you think they like Communism?
TOULON: I live in China. Not with the Chinese.
GALLIMARD: Well, I—
TOULON: *You* live with the Chinese.
GALLIMARD: Excuse me?   25
TOULON: I can't keep a secret.
GALLIMARD: What are you saying?
TOULON: Only that I'm not immune to gossip. So, you're keep-
  ing a native mistress. Don't answer. It's none of my busi-
  ness. (*Pause.*) I'm sure she must be gorgeous.   30
GALLIMARD: Well . . .

TOULON: I'm impressed. You have the stamina to go out into the streets and hunt one down. Some of us have to be content with the wives of the expatriate community.

35　GALLIMARD: I do feel . . . fortunate.

TOULON: So, Gallimard, you've got the inside knowledge—what *do* the Chinese think?

GALLIMARD: Deep down, they miss the old days. You know, cappuccinos, men in tuxedos—

40　TOULON: So what do we tell the Americans about Vietnam?

GALLIMARD: Tell them there's a natural affinity between the West and the Orient.

TOULON: And that you speak from experience?

GALLIMARD: The Orientals are people too. They want the good

45　things we can give them. If the Americans demonstrate the will to win, the Vietnamese will welcome them into a mutually beneficial union.

TOULON: I don't see how the Vietnamese can stand up to American firepower.

50　GALLIMARD: Orientals will always submit to a greater force.

TOULON: I'll note your opinions in my report. The Americans always love to hear how "welcome" they'll be. (*He starts to exit.*)

GALLIMARD: Sir?

55　TOULON: Mmmm?

GALLIMARD: This . . . rumor you've heard.

TOULON: Uh-huh?

GALLIMARD: How . . . widespread do you think it is?

TOULON: It's only widespread within this embassy. Where nobody

60　talks because everybody is guilty. We were worried about you, Gallimard. We thought you were the only one here without a secret. Now you go and find a lotus blossom . . . and top us all. (*He exits.*)

GALLIMARD: (*To us.*) Toulon knows! And he approves! I was

65　learning the benefits of being a man. We form our own clubs, sit behind thick doors, smoke—and celebrate the fact that we're still boys. (*He starts to move downstage, towards* SONG.) So, over the—

(*Suddenly* COMRADE CHIN *enters.* GALLIMARD *backs away.*)

GALLIMARD: (*To* SONG.) No! Why does she have to come in?

70　SONG: Rene, be sensible. How can they understand the story without her? Now, don't embarrass yourself.

(GALLIMARD *moves down center.*)

GALLIMARD: (*To us.*) Now, you will see why my story is so amusing to so many people. Why they snicker at parties in disbelief. Please—try to understand it from my point of

75　view. We are all prisoners of our time and place. (*He exits.*)

Scene IV

GALLIMARD *and* BUTTERFLY'S *flat. Beijing. 1961.*

SONG: (*To us.*) 1961. The flat Monsieur Gallimard rented for us. An evening after he has gone.

CHIN: Okay, see if you find out when the Americans plan to start bombing Vietnam. If you can find out what cities,

5　even better.

SONG: I'll do my best, but I don't want to arouse his suspicions.

CHIN: Yeah, sure, of course. So, what else?

SONG: The Americans will increase troops in Vietnam to 170,000 soldiers with 120,000 militia and 11,000 American advisors.

10

CHIN: (*Writing.*) Wait, wait. 120,000 militia and —

SONG: —11,000 American—

CHIN: —American advisors. (*Beat.*) How do you remember so much?

SONG: I'm an actor.

15

CHIN: Yeah. (*Beat.*) Is that how come you dress like that?

SONG: Like what, Miss Chin?

CHIN: Like that dress! You're wearing a dress. And every time I come here, you're wearing a dress. Is that because you're an actor? Or what?

20

SONG: It's a . . . disguise, Miss Chin.

CHIN: Actors, I think they're all weirdos. My mother tells me actors are like gamblers or prostitutes or —

SONG: It helps me in my assignment.

(*Pause.*)

CHIN: You're not gathering information in any way that violates Communist Party principles, are you?

25

SONG: Why would I do that?

CHIN: Just checking. Remember: when working for the Great Proletarian State, you represent our Chairman Mao in every position you take.

30

SONG: I'll try to imagine the Chairman taking my positions.

CHIN: We all think of him this way. Good-bye, comrade. (*She starts to exit.*) Comrade?

SONG: Yes?

CHIN: Don't forget: there is no homosexuality in China!

35

SONG: Yes, I've heard.

CHIN: Just checking. (*She exits.*)

SONG: (*To us.*) What passes for a woman in modern China.

(GALLIMARD *sticks his head out from the wings.*)

GALLIMARD: Is she gone?

SONG: Yes, Rene. Please continue in your own fashion.

40

Scene V

Beijing. 1961–63.

GALLIMARD *moves to the couch where* SONG *still sits. He lies down in her lap, and she strokes his forehead.*

GALLIMARD: (*To us.*) And so, over the years 1961, '62, '63, we settled into our routine, Butterfly and I. She would always have prepared a light snack and then, ever so delicately, and only if I agreed, she would start to pleasure me. With her hands, her mouth . . . too many ways to explain, and too 5 sad, given my present situation. But mostly we would talk. About my life. Perhaps there is nothing more rare than to find a woman who passionately listens.

(SONG *remains upstage, listening, as* HELGA *enters and plays a scene downstage with* GALLIMARD.)

HELGA: Rene, I visited Dr. Bolleart this morning.

GALLIMARD: Why? Are you ill?

10

HELGA: No, no. You see, I wanted to ask him . . . that question we've been discussing.

GALLIMARD: And I told you, it's only a matter of time. Why did you bring a doctor into this? We just have to keep trying—like a crapshoot, actually.

HELGA: I went, I'm sorry. But listen: he says there's nothing wrong with me.

GALLIMARD: You see? Now, will you stop—?

HELGA: Rene, he says he'd like you to go in and take some tests.

GALLIMARD: Why? So he can find there's nothing wrong with both of us?

HELGA: Rene, I don't ask for much. One trip! One visit! And then, whatever you want to do about it—you decide.

GALLIMARD: You're assuming he'll find something defective!

HELGA: No! Of course not! Whatever he finds—if he finds nothing, we decide what to do about nothing! But go!

GALLIMARD: If he finds nothing, we keep trying. Just like we do now.

HELGA: But at least we'll know! (Pause.) I'm sorry. (She starts to exit.)

GALLIMARD: Do you really want me to see Dr. Bolleart?

HELGA: Only if you want a child, Rene. We have to face the fact that time is running out. Only if you want a child. (She exits.)

GALLIMARD: (To SONG.) I'm a modern man, Butterfly. And yet, I don't want to go. It's the same old voodoo. I feel like God himself is laughing at me if I can't produce a child.

SONG: You men of the West—you're obsessed by your odd desire for equality. Your wife can't give you a child, and you're going to the doctor?

GALLIMARD: Well, you see, she's already gone.

SONG: And because this incompetent can't find the defect, you now have to subject yourself to him? It's unnatural.

GALLIMARD: Well, what is the "natural" solution?

SONG: In Imperial China, when a man found that one wife was inadequate, he turned to another—to give him his son.

GALLIMARD: What do you—? I can't . . . marry you, yet.

SONG: Please. I'm not asking you to be my husband. But I am already your wife.

GALLIMARD: Do you want to . . . have my child?

SONG: I thought you'd never ask.

GALLIMARD: But, your career . . . your—

SONG: Phooey on my career! That's your Western mind, twisting itself into strange shapes again. Of course I love my career. But what would I love most of all? To feel something inside me—day and night—something I know is yours. (Pause.) Promise me . . . you won't go to this doctor. Who is this Western quack to set himself as judge over the man I love? I know who is a man, and who is not. (She exits.)

GALLIMARD: (To us.) Dr. Bolleart? Of course I didn't go. What man would?

SCENE VI

Beijing. 1963.

Party noises over the house speakers. RENEE *enters, wearing a revealing gown.*

GALLIMARD: 1963. A party at the Austrian embassy. None of us could remember the Austrian ambassador's name, which seemed somehow appropriate. (To RENEE.) So, I tell the Americans, Diem must go. The U.S. wants to be respected by the Vietnamese, and yet they're propping up this nobody seminarian as her president. A man whose claim to fame is his sister-in-law imposing fanatic "moral order" campaigns? Oriental women—when they're good, they're very good, but when they're bad, they're Christians.

RENEE: Yeah.

GALLIMARD: And what do you do?

RENEE: I'm a student. My father exports a lot of useless stuff to the Third World.

GALLIMARD: How useless?

RENEE: You know. Squirt guns, confectioner's sugar, hula hoops . . .

GALLIMARD: I'm sure they appreciate the sugar.

RENEE: I'm here for two years to study Chinese.

GALLIMARD: Two years?

RENEE: That's what everybody says.

GALLIMARD: When did you arrive?

RENEE: Three weeks ago.

GALLIMARD: And?

RENEE: I like it. It's primitive, but . . . well, this is the place to learn Chinese, so here I am.

GALLIMARD: Why Chinese?

RENEE: I think it'll be important someday.

GALLIMARD: You do?

RENEE: Don't ask me when, but . . . that's what I think.

GALLIMARD: Well, I agree with you. One hundred percent. That's very farsighted.

RENEE: Yeah. Well of course, my father thinks I'm a complete weirdo.

GALLIMARD: He'll thank you someday.

RENEE: Like when the Chinese start buying hula hoops?

GALLIMARD: There're a billion bellies out there.

RENEE: And if they end up taking over the world—well, then I'll be lucky to know Chinese too, right?

(Pause.)

GALLIMARD: At this point, I don't see how the Chinese can possibly take—

RENEE: You know what I *don't* like about China?

GALLIMARD: Excuse me? No—what?

RENEE: Nothing to do at night.

GALLIMARD: You come to parties at embassies like everyone else.

RENEE: Yeah, but they get out at ten. And then what?

GALLIMARD: I'm afraid the Chinese idea of a dance hall is a dirt floor and a man with a flute.

RENEE: Are you married?

GALLIMARD: Yes. Why?

RENEE: You wanna . . . fool around?

(Pause.)

GALLIMARD: Sure.

RENEE: I'll wait for you outside. What's your name?

GALLIMARD: Gallimard. Rene.

RENEE: Weird. I'm Renee too. (She exits.)

GALLIMARD: (To us.) And so, I embarked on my first extra-extramarital affair. Renee was picture perfect. With a body like those girls in the magazines. If I put a tissue paper over

my eyes, I wouldn't have been able to tell the difference.
60 And it was exciting to be with someone who wasn't afraid
to be seen completely naked. But is it possible for a woman
to be *too* uninhibited, *too* willing, so as to seem almost too . . .
masculine?

(Chuck Berry blares from the house speakers, then comes down in volume as RENEE *enters, toweling her hair.)*

RENEE: You have a nice weenie.
65 GALLIMARD: What?
RENEE: Penis. You have a nice penis.
GALLIMARD: Oh. Well, thank you. That's very . . .
RENEE: What—can't take a compliment?
GALLIMARD: No, it's very . . . reassuring.
70 RENEE: But most girls don't come out and say it, huh?
GALLIMARD: And also . . . what did you call it?
RENEE: Oh. Most girls don't call it a "weenie," huh?
GALLIMARD: It sounds very—
RENEE: Small, I know.
75 GALLIMARD: I was going to say, "young."
RENEE: Yeah. Young, small, same thing. Most guys are pretty,
uh, sensitive about that. Like, you know, I had a boyfriend
back home in Denmark. I got mad at him once and called
him a little weeniehead. He got so mad! He said at least I
80 should call him a great big weeniehead.
GALLIMARD: I suppose I just say "penis."
RENEE: Yeah. That's pretty clinical. There's "cock," but that
sounds like a chicken. And "prick" is painful, and "dick" is
like you're talking about someone who's not in the room.
85 GALLIMARD: Yes. It's a . . . bigger problem than I imagined.
RENEE: I—I think maybe it's because I really don't know what
to do with them—that's why I call them "weenies."
GALLIMARD: Well, you did quite well with . . . mine.
RENEE: Thanks, but I mean, really *do* with them. Like, okay,
90 have you ever looked at one? I mean, really?
GALLIMARD: No, I suppose when it's part of you, you sort of
take it for granted.
RENEE: I guess. But, like, it just hangs there. This little . . . flap
of flesh. And there's so much fuss that we make about it.
95 Like, I think the reason we fight wars is because we wear
clothes. Because no one knows—between the men, I
mean—who has the bigger . . . weenie. So, if I'm a guy with
a small one, I'm going to build a really big building or take
over a really big piece of land or write a really long book so
100 the other men don't know, right? But, see, it never really
works, that's the problem. I mean, you conquer the country,
or whatever, but you're still wearing clothes, so there's no
way to prove absolutely whose is bigger or smaller. And
that's what we call a civilized society. The whole world run
105 by a bunch of men with pricks the size of pins. *(She exits.)*
GALLIMARD: *(To us.)* This was simply not acceptable.

(A high-pitched chime rings through the air. SONG, *dressed as
Butterfly, appears in the upstage special. She is obviously distressed.
Her body swoons as she attempts to clip the stems of flowers she's ar-
ranging in a vase.)*

GALLIMARD: But I kept up our affair, wildly, for several months.
Why? I believe because of Butterfly. She knew the secret
I was trying to hide. But, unlike a Western woman, she

didn't confront me, threaten, even pout. I remembered the 110
words of Puccini's *Butterfly:*
SONG: "Noi siamo gente avvezza / alle piccole cose / umili e
silenziose."
GALLIMARD: "I come from a people / Who are accustomed to
little / Humble and silent." I saw Pinkerton and Butterfly, 115
and what she would say if he were unfaithful . . . nothing. She
would cry, alone, into those wildly soft sleeves, once full of
possessions, now empty to collect her tears. It was her tears
and her silence that excited me, every time I visited Renee.
TOULON: *(Offstage.)* Gallimard! 120

*(*TOULON *enters.* GALLIMARD *turns towards him. During the next section,* SONG, *up center, begins to dance with the flowers. It is a drunken
dance, where she breaks small pieces off the stems.)*

TOULON: They're killing him.
GALLIMARD: Who? I'm sorry? What?
TOULON: Bother you to come over at this late hour?
GALLIMARD: No . . . of course not.
TOULON: Not after you hear my secret. Champagne? 125
GALLIMARD: Um . . . thank you.
TOULON: You're surprised. There's something that you've
wanted, Gallimard. No, not a promotion. Next time.
Something in the world. You're not aware of this, but
there's an informal gossip circle among intelligence agents. 130
And some of ours heard from some of the Americans—
GALLIMARD: Yes?
TOULON: That the U.S. will allow the Vietnamese generals to
stage a coup . . . and assassinate President Diem.

(The chime rings again. TOULON *freezes.* GALLIMARD *turns upstage
and looks at* SONG, *who slowly and deliberately clips a flower off its
stem.* GALLIMARD *turns back towards* TOULON.)*

GALLIMARD: I think . . . that's a very wise move! 135

*(*TOULON *unfreezes.)*

TOULON: It's what you've been advocating. A toast?
GALLIMARD: Sure. I consider this a vindication.
TOULON: Not exactly. "To the test. Let's hope you pass."

(They drink. The chime rings again. TOULON *freezes.* GALLIMARD
turns upstage, and SONG *clips another flower.)*

GALLIMARD: *(To* TOULON.*)* The test?
TOULON: *(Unfreezing.)* It's a test of everything you've been say- 140
ing. I personally think the generals probably will stop the
Communists. And you'll be a hero. But if anything goes
wrong, then your opinions won't be worth a pig's ear. I'm
sure that won't happen. But sometimes it's easier when they
don't listen to you. 145
GALLIMARD: They're your opinions too, aren't they?
TOULON: Personally, yes.
GALLIMARD: So we agree.
TOULON: But my opinions aren't on that report. Yours are. Cheers.

*(*TOULON *turns away from* GALLIMARD *and raises his glass. At that
instant* SONG *picks up the vase and hurls it to the ground. It shatters.*
SONG *sinks down amidst the shards of the vase, in a calm, childlike
trance. She sings softly, as if reciting a child's nursery rhyme.)*

150 SONG: *(Repeat as necessary.)* "The whole world over, the white man travels, setting anchor, wherever he likes. Life's not worth living, unless he finds, the finest maidens, of every land . . ."

(GALLIMARD turns downstage towards us. SONG continues singing.)

GALLIMARD: I shook as I left his house. That coward! That worm! To put the burden for his decisions on my shoulders!
155   I started for Renee's. But no, that was all I needed. A schoolgirl who would question the role of the penis in modern society. What I wanted was revenge. A vessel to contain my humiliation. Though I hadn't seen her in several weeks, I headed for Butterfly's.

(GALLIMARD enters SONG's apartment.)

160 SONG: Oh! Rene . . . I was dreaming!
GALLIMARD: You've been drinking?
SONG: If I can't sleep, then yes, I drink. But then, it gives me these dreams which—Rene, it's been almost three weeks since you visited me last.
165 GALLIMARD: I know. There's been a lot going on in the world.
SONG: Fortunately I am drunk. So I can speak freely. It's not the world, it's you and me. And an old problem. Even the softest skin becomes like leather to a man who's touched it too often. I confess I don't know how to stop it. I don't know
170   how to become another woman.
GALLIMARD: I have a request.
SONG: Is this a solution? Or are you ready to give up the flat?
GALLIMARD: It may be a solution. But I'm sure you won't like it.
SONG: Oh well, that's very important. "Like it?" Do you think
175   I "like" lying here alone, waiting, always waiting for your return? Please—don't worry about what I may not "like."
GALLIMARD: I want to see you . . . naked.

(Silence.)

SONG: I thought you understood my modesty. So you want me to—what—strip? Like a big cowboy girl? Shiny pasties
180   on my breasts? Shall I fling my kimono over my head and yell "ya-hoo" in the process? I thought you respected my shame!
GALLIMARD: I believe you gave me your shame many years ago.
SONG: Yes—and it is just like a white devil to use it against me. I can't believe it. I thought myself so repulsed by the
185   passive Oriental and the cruel white man. Now I see—we are always most revolted by the things hidden within us.
GALLIMARD: I just mean—
SONG: Yes?
GALLIMARD: —that it will remove the only barrier left be-
190   tween us.
SONG: No, Rene. Don't couch your request in sweet words. Be yourself—a cad—and know that my love is enough, that I submit—submit to the worst you can give me. *(Pause.)* Well, come. Strip me. Whatever happens, know that you have
195   willed it. Our love, in your hands. I'm helpless before my man.

(GALLIMARD starts to cross the room.)

GALLIMARD: Did I not undress her because I knew, somewhere deep down, what I would find? Perhaps. Happiness is so rare that our mind can turn somersaults to protect it.

At the time, I only knew that I was seeing Pinkerton 200
stalking towards his Butterfly, ready to reward her love with his lecherous hands. The image sickened me, pulled me to my knees, so I was crawling towards her like a worm. By the time I reached her, Pinkerton . . . had vanished from my heart. To be replaced by something new, something un- 205
natural, that flew in the face of all I'd learned in the world—something very close to love.

(He grabs her around the waist; she strokes his hair.)

GALLIMARD: Butterfly, forgive me.
SONG: Rene . . .
GALLIMARD: For everything. From the start.   210
SONG: I'm . . .
GALLIMARD: I want to—
SONG: I'm pregnant. *(Beat.)* I'm pregnant. *(Beat.)* I'm pregnant.

(Beat.)

GALLIMARD: I want to marry you!

SCENE VII

GALLIMARD *and* BUTTERFLY's *flat. Beijing. 1963.*

Downstage, SONG *paces as* COMRADE CHIN *reads from her notepad. Upstage,* GALLIMARD *is still kneeling. He remains on his knees throughout the scene, watching it.*

SONG: I need a baby.
CHIN: *(From pad.)* He's been spotted going to a dorm.
SONG: I need a baby.
CHIN: At the Foreign Language Institute.
SONG: I need a baby.   5
CHIN: The room of a Danish girl . . . What do you mean, you need a baby?!
SONG: Tell Comrade Kang—last night, the entire mission, it could've ended.
CHIN: What do you mean?   10
SONG: Tell Kang—he told me to strip.
CHIN: *Strip?!*
SONG: Write!
CHIN: I tell you, I don't understand nothing about this case anymore. Nothing.   15
SONG: He told me to strip, and I took a chance. Oh, we Chinese, we know how to gamble.
CHIN: *(Writing.)* " . . . told him to strip."
SONG: My palms were wet, I had to make a split-second decision.
CHIN: Hey! Can you slow down?!   20

(Pause.)

SONG: You write faster, I'm the artist here. Suddenly, it hit me—"All he wants is for her to submit. Once a woman submits, a man is always ready to become 'generous.'"
CHIN: You're just gonna end up with rough notes.
SONG: And it worked! He gave in! Now, if I can just present 25
him with a baby. A Chinese baby with blond hair—he'll be mine for life!
CHIN: Kang will never agree! The trading of babies has to be a counterrevolutionary act.

30 SONG: Sometimes, a counterrevolutionary act is necessary to counter a counterrevolutionary act.

(Pause.)

CHIN: Wait.
SONG: I need one . . . in seven months. Make sure it's a boy.
35 CHIN: This doesn't sound like something the Chairman would do. Maybe you'd better talk to Comrade Kang yourself.
SONG: Good. I will.

(CHIN gets up to leave.)

SONG: Miss Chin? Why, in the Peking Opera, are women's roles played by men?
CHIN: I don't know. Maybe, a reactionary remnant of male—
40 SONG: No. *(Beat.)* Because only a man knows how a woman is supposed to act.

(CHIN exits. SONG turns upstage, towards GALLIMARD.)

GALLIMARD: *(Calling after CHIN.)* Good riddance! *(To SONG.)* I could forget all that betrayal in an instant, you know. If you'd just come back and become Butterfly again.
45 SONG: Fat chance. You're here in prison, rotting in a cell. And I'm on a plane, winging my way back to China. Your President pardoned me of our treason, you know.
GALLIMARD: Yes, I read about that.
SONG: Must make you feel . . . lower than shit.
50 GALLIMARD: But don't you, even a little bit, wish you were here with me?
SONG: I'm an artist, Rene. You were my greatest . . . acting challenge. *(She laughs.)* It doesn't matter how rotten I answer, does it? You still adore me. That's why I love you,
55 Rene. *(She points to us.)* So—you were telling your audience about the night I announced I was pregnant.

(GALLIMARD puts his arms around SONG's waist. He and SONG are in the positions they were in at the end of Scene 6.)

SCENE VIII

Same.

GALLIMARD: I'll divorce my wife. We'll live together here, and then later in France.
SONG: I feel so . . . ashamed.
GALLIMARD: Why?
5 SONG: I had begun to lose faith. And now, you shame me with your generosity.
GALLIMARD: Generosity? No, I'm proposing for very selfish reasons.
SONG: Your apologies only make me feel more ashamed. My
10 outburst a moment ago!
GALLIMARD: Your outburst? What about my request?!
SONG: You've been very patient dealing with my . . . eccentricities. A Western man, used to women freer with their bodies—
15 GALLIMARD: It was sick! Don't make excuses for me.
SONG: I have to. You don't seem willing to make them for yourself.

(Pause.)

GALLIMARD: You're crazy.
SONG: I'm happy. Which often looks like crazy.
GALLIMARD: Then make me crazy. Marry me. 20

(Pause.)

SONG: No.
GALLIMARD: What?
SONG: Do I sound silly, a slave, if I say I'm not worthy?
GALLIMARD: Yes. In fact you do. No one has loved me like you.
SONG: Thank you. And no one ever will. I'll see to that. 25
GALLIMARD: So what is the problem?
SONG: Rene, we Chinese are realists. We understand rice, gold, and guns. You are a diplomat. Your career is skyrocketing. Now, what would happen if you divorced your wife to marry a Communist Chinese actress? 30
GALLIMARD: That's not being realistic. That's defeating yourself before you begin.
SONG: We must conserve our strength for the battles we can win.
GALLIMARD: That sounds like a fortune cookie!
SONG: Where do you think fortune cookies come from? 35
GALLIMARD: I don't care.
SONG: You do. So do I. And we should. That is why I say I'm not worthy. I'm worthy to love and even to be loved by you. But I am not worthy to end the career of one of the West's most promising diplomats. 40
GALLIMARD: It's not that great a career! I made it sound like more than it is!
SONG: Modesty will get you nowhere. Flatter yourself, and you flatter me. I'm flattered to decline your offer. *(She exits.)*
GALLIMARD: *(To us.)* Butterfly and I argued all night. And, in 45 the end, I left, knowing I would never be her husband. She went away for several months—to the countryside, like a small animal. Until the night I received her call.

(A baby's cry from offstage. SONG enters, carrying a child.)

He looks like you.
GALLIMARD: Oh! *(Beat; he approaches the baby.)* Well, babies are 50 never very attractive at birth.
SONG: Stop!
GALLIMARD: I'm sure he'll grow more beautiful with age. More like his mother.
SONG: "Chi vide mai / a bimbo del Giappon . . ." 55
GALLIMARD: "What baby, I wonder, was ever born in Japan"— or China, for that matter—
SONG: ". . . occhi azzurrini?"
GALLIMARD: "With azure eyes"—they're actually sort of brown, wouldn't you say? 60
SONG: "E il labbro."
GALLIMARD: "And such lips!" *(He kisses SONG.)* And such lips.
SONG: "E i ricciolini d'oro schietto?"
GALLIMARD: "And such a head of golden"—if slightly patchy— "curls?" 65
SONG: I'm going to call him "Peepee."
GALLIMARD: Darling, could you repeat that because I'm sure a rickshaw just flew by overhead.
SONG: You heard me.
GALLIMARD: "Song Peepee"? May I suggest Michael, or Stephan, 70 or Adolph?

SONG: You may, but I won't listen.

GALLIMARD: You can't be serious. Can you imagine the time this child will have in school?

75 SONG: In the West, yes.

GALLIMARD: It's worse than naming him Ping Pong or Long Dong or—

SONG: But he's never going to live in the West, is he?

(Pause.)

GALLIMARD: That wasn't my choice.

80 SONG: It is mine. And this is my promise to you: I will raise him, he will be our child, but he will never burden you outside of China.

GALLIMARD: Why do you make these promises? I want to be burdened! I want a scandal to cover the papers!

85 SONG: *(To us.)* Prophetic.

GALLIMARD: I'm serious.

SONG: So am I. His name is as I registered it. And he will never live in the West.

(SONG exits with the child.)

GALLIMARD: *(To us.)* It is possible that her stubbornness only
90 made me want her more. That drawing back at the moment of my capitulation was the most brilliant strategy she could have chosen. It is possible. But it is also possible that by this point she could have said, could have done . . . anything, and I would have adored her still.

SCENE IX

Beijing. 1966.

A driving rhythm of Chinese percussion fills the stage.

GALLIMARD: And then, China began to change. Mao became very old, and his cult became very strong. And, like many old men, he entered his second childhood. So he handed over the reins of state to those with minds like his own.
5 And children ruled the Middle Kingdom with complete caprice. The doctrine of the Cultural Revolution implied continuous anarchy. Contact between Chinese and foreigners became impossible. Our flat was confiscated. Her fame and my money now counted against us.

(Two dancers in Mao suits and red-starred caps enter, and begin crudely mimicking revolutionary violence, in an agitprop fashion.)

10 GALLIMARD: And somehow the American war went wrong too. Four hundred thousand dollars were being spent for every Viet Cong killed; so General Westmoreland's remark that the Oriental does not value life the way Americans do was oddly accurate. Why weren't the Vietnamese people giving in?
15 Why were they content instead to die and die and die again?

(TOULON enters.)

TOULON: Congratulations, Gallimard.

GALLIMARD: Excuse me, sir?

TOULON: Not a promotion. That was last time. You're going home.

GALLIMARD: What?   20

TOULON: Don't say I didn't warn you.

GALLIMARD: I'm being transferred . . . because I was wrong about the American war?

TOULON: Of course not. We don't care about the Americans. We care about your mind. The quality of your analysis. In   25
general, everything you've predicted here in the Orient . . . just hasn't happened.

GALLIMARD: I think that's premature.

TOULON: Don't force me to be blunt. Okay, you said China was ready to open to Western trade. The only thing they're   30
trading out there are Western heads. And, yes, you said the Americans would succeed in Indochina. You were kidding, right?

GALLIMARD: I think the end is in sight.

TOULON: Don't be pathetic. And don't take this personally. You   35
were wrong. It's not your fault.

GALLIMARD: But I'm going home.

TOULON: Right. Could I have the number of your mistress? *(Beat.)* Joke! Joke! Eat a croissant for me.

(TOULON exits. SONG, wearing a Mao suit, is dragged in from the wings as part of the upstage dance. They "beat" her, then lampoon the acrobatics of the Chinese opera, as she is made to kneel onstage.)

GALLIMARD: *(Simultaneously.)* I don't care to recall how Butter-   40
fly and I said our hurried farewell. Perhaps it was better to end our affair before it killed her.

(GALLIMARD exits. COMRADE CHIN walks across the stage with a banner reading: "The Actor Renounces His Decadent Profession!" She reaches the kneeling SONG. Percussion stops with a thud. Dancers strike poses.)

CHIN: Actor-oppressor, for years you have lived above the common people and looked down on their labor. While the farmer ate millet—   45

SONG: I ate pastries from France and sweetmeats from silver trays.

CHIN: And how did you come to live in such an exalted position?

SONG: I was a plaything for the imperialists!

CHIN: What did you do?   50

SONG: I shamed China by allowing myself to be corrupted by a foreigner . . .

CHIN: What does this mean? The People demand a full confession!

SONG: I engaged in the lowest perversions with China's enemies!

CHIN: What perversions? Be more clear!   55

SONG: I let him put it up my ass!

(Dancers look over, disgusted.)

CHIN: Aaaa-ya! How can you use such sickening language?!

SONG: My language . . . is only as foul as the crimes I committed . . .

CHIN: Yeah. That's better. So—what do you want to do now?   60

SONG: I want to serve the people.

(Percussion starts up, with Chinese strings.)

CHIN: What?

SONG: I want to serve the people!

(Dancers regain their revolutionary smiles, and begin a dance of victory.)

CHIN: What?!

65 SONG: I want to serve the people!

(Dancers unveil a banner: "The Actor Is Rehabilitated!" SONG *remains kneeling before* CHIN, *as the dancers bounce around them, then exit. Music out.)*

SCENE X

A commune. Hunan Province. 1970.

CHIN: How you planning to do that?

SONG: I've already worked four years in the fields of Hunan, Comrade Chin.

CHIN: So? Farmers work all their lives. Let me see your hands.

(SONG holds them out for her inspection.)

5   CHIN: Goddamn! Still so smooth! How long does it take to turn you actors into good anythings? Hunh. You've just spent too many years in luxury to be any good to the Revolution.

SONG: I served the Revolution.

CHIN: Serve the Resolution? Bullshit! You wore dresses! Don't
10   tell me—I was there. I saw you! You and your white vice-consul! Stuck up there in your flat, living off the People's Treasury! Yeah, I knew what was going on! You two . . . homos! Homos! Homos! *(Pause; she composes herself.)* Ah! Well . . . you will serve the people, all right. But not with
15   the Revolution's money. This time, you use your own money.

SONG: I have no money.

CHIN: Shut up! And you won't stink up China anymore with your pervert stuff. You'll pollute the place where pollution
20   begins—the West.

SONG: What do you mean?

CHIN: Shut up! You're going to France. Without a cent in your pocket. You find your consul's house, you make him pay your expenses—

25   SONG: No.

CHIN: And you give us weekly reports! Useful information!

SONG: That's crazy. It's been four years.

CHIN: Either that, or back to rehabilitation center!

SONG: Comrade Chin, he's not going to support me! Not in
30   France! He's a white man! I was just his plaything—

CHIN: Oh yuck! Again with the sickening language. Where's my stick?

SONG: You don't understand the mind of a man.

(Pause.)

CHIN: Oh no? No I don't? Then how come I'm married, huh?
35   How come I got a man? Five, six years ago, you always tell me those kinds of things, I felt very bad. But not now! Because what does the Chairman say? He tells us *I'm* now the smart one, you're now the nincompoop! *You're* the black-head, the harebrain, the nitwit! You think you're so smart?
40   You understand "The Mind of a Man"? Good! Then *you* go to France and be a pervert for Chairman Mao!

(CHIN and SONG exit in opposite directions.)

SCENE XI

Paris. 1968–70.

GALLIMARD *enters.*

GALLIMARD: And what was waiting for me back in Paris? Well, better Chinese food than I'd eaten in China. Friends and relatives. A little accounting, regular schedule, keeping track of traffic violations in the suburbs. . . . And the indignity of students shouting the slogans of Chairman Mao at me—in   5
French.

HELGA: Rene? Rene? *(She enters, soaking wet.)* I've had a . . . a problem. *(She sneezes.)*

GALLIMARD: You're wet.

HELGA: Yes, I . . . coming back from the grocer's. A group of   10
students, waving red flags, they—

(GALLIMARD fetches a towel.)

HELGA: —they ran by, I was caught up along with them. Before I knew what was happening—

(GALLIMARD gives her the towel.)

HELGA: Thank you. The police started firing water cannons at us. I tried to shout, to tell them I was the wife of a diplo-   15
mat, but—you know how it is . . . *(Pause.)* Needless to say, I lost the groceries. Rene, what's happening to France?

GALLIMARD: What's—? Well, nothing, really.

HELGA: Nothing? The storefronts are in flames, there's glass in the streets, buildings are toppling—and I'm wet!   20

GALLIMARD: Nothing! . . . that I care to think about.

HELGA: And is that why you stay in this room?

GALLIMARD: Yes, in fact.

HELGA: With the incense burning? You know something? I hate incense. It smells so sickly sweet.   25

GALLIMARD: Well, I hate the French. Who just smell—period!

HELGA: And the Chinese were better?

GALLIMARD: Please—don't start.

HELGA: When we left, this exact same thing, the riots—

GALLIMARD: No, no . . .   30

HELGA: Students screaming slogans, smashing down doors—

GALLIMARD: Helga—

HELGA: It was all going on in China, too. Don't you remember?!

GALLIMARD: Helga! Please! *(Pause.)* You have never understood China, have you? You walk in here with these ridiculous   35
ideas, that the West is falling apart, that China was spitting in our faces. You come in, dripping of the streets, and you leave water all over my floor. *(He grabs* HELGA's *towel, begins mopping up the floor.)*

HELGA: But it's the truth!   40

GALLIMARD: Helga, I want a divorce.

(Pause; GALLIMARD *continues, mopping the floor.)*

HELGA: I take it back. China is . . . beautiful. Incense, I like incense.

GALLIMARD: I've had a mistress.

HELGA: So?   45

GALLIMARD: For eight years.

HELGA: I knew you would. I knew you would the day I married you. And now what? You want to marry her?

GALLIMARD: I can't. She's in China.

50 HELGA: I see. You want to leave. For someone who's not here, is that right?

GALLIMARD: That's right.

HELGA: You can't live with her, but still you don't want to live with me.

55 GALLIMARD: That's right.

(Pause.)

HELGA: Shit. How terrible that I can figure that out. *(Pause.)* I never thought I'd say it. But, in China, I was happy. I knew, in my own way, I knew that you were not everything you pretended to be. But the pretense—going on your arm to

60 the embassy ball, visiting your office and the guards saying, "Good morning, good morning, Madame Gallimard"—the pretense . . . was very good indeed. *(Pause.)* I hope everyone is mean to you for the rest of your life. *(She exits.)*

GALLIMARD: *(To us.)* Prophetic.

(MARC enters with two drinks.)

65 GALLIMARD: *(To MARC.)* In China, I was different from all other men.

MARC: Sure. You were white. Here's your drink.

GALLIMARD: I felt . . . touched.

MARC: In the head? Rene, I don't want to hear about the Ori-

70 ental love goddess. Okay? One night—can we just drink and throw up without a lot of conversation?

GALLIMARD: You still don't believe me, do you?

MARC: Sure I do. She was the most beautiful, et cetera, et cetera, blasé blasé.

(Pause.)

75 GALLIMARD: My life in the West has been such a disappointment.

MARC: Life in the West is like that. You'll get used to it. Look, you're driving me away. I'm leaving. Happy, now? *(He exits, then returns.)* Look, I have a date tomorrow night. You wanna come? I can fix you up with—

80 GALLIMARD: Of course. I would love to come.

(Pause.)

MARC: Uh—on second thought, no. You'd better get ahold of yourself first.

(He exits; GALLIMARD nurses his drink.)

GALLIMARD: *(To us.)* This is the ultimate cruelty, isn't it? That I can talk and talk and to anyone listening, it's only air—

85 too rich a diet to be swallowed by a mundane world. Why can't anyone understand? That in China, I once loved, and was loved by, very simply, the Perfect Woman.

(SONG enters, dressed as Butterfly in wedding dress.)

GALLIMARD: *(To SONG.)* Not again. My imagination is hell. Am I asleep this time? Or did I drink too much?

90 SONG: Rene?

GALLIMARD: God, it's too painful! That you speak?

SONG: What are you talking about? Rene—touch me.

GALLIMARD: Why?

SONG: I'm real. Take my hand.

GALLIMARD: Why? So you can disappear again and leave me 95 clutching at the air? For the entertainment of my neighbors who—?

(SONG touches GALLIMARD.)

SONG: Rene?

(GALLIMARD takes SONG's hand. Silence.)

GALLIMARD: Butterfly? I never doubted you'd return.

SONG: You hadn't . . . forgotten—? 100

GALLIMARD: Yes, actually, I've forgotten everything. My mind, you see—there wasn't enough room in this hard head—not for the world *and* for you. No, there was only room for one. *(Beat.)* Come, look. See? Your bed has been waiting, with the Klimt poster you like, and—see? The xiang lu [incense 105 burner] you gave me?

SONG: I . . . I don't know what to say.

GALLIMARD: There's nothing to say. Not at the end of a long trip. Can I make you some tea?

SONG: But where's your wife? 110

GALLIMARD: She's by my side. She's by my side at last.

(GALLIMARD reaches to embrace SONG. SONG sidesteps, dodging him.)

GALLIMARD: Why?

SONG: *(To us.)* So I did return to Rene in Paris. Where I found—

GALLIMARD: Why do you run away? Can't we show them how 115 we embraced that evening?

SONG: Please. I'm talking.

GALLIMARD: You have to do what I say! I'm conjuring you up in *my* mind!

SONG: Rene, I've never done what you've said. Why should it 120 be any different in your mind? Now split—the story moves on, and I must change.

GALLIMARD: I welcomed you into my home! I didn't have to, you know! I could've left you penniless on the streets of Paris! But I took you in! 125

SONG: Thank you.

GALLIMARD: So . . . please . . . don't change.

SONG: You know I have to. You know I will. And anyway, what difference does it make? No matter what your eyes tell you, you can't ignore the truth. You already know too much. 130

(GALLIMARD exits. SONG turns to us.)

SONG: The change I'm going to make requires about five minutes. So I thought you might want to take this opportunity to stretch your legs, enjoy a drink, or listen to the musicians. I'll be here, when you return, right where you left me. 135

(SONG goes to a mirror in front of which is a wash basin of water. She starts to remove her makeup as stagelights go to half and houselights come up.)

——— **ACT THREE** ———

SCENE I

A courthouse in Paris. 1986.

As he promised, SONG *has completed the bulk of his transformation onstage by the time the houselights go down and the stagelights come up full. He removes his wig and kimono, leaving them on the floor. Underneath, he wears a well-cut suit.*

SONG: So I'd done my job better than I had a right to expect. Well, give him some credit, too. He's right—I was in a fix when I arrived in Paris. I walked from the airport into town, then I located, by blind groping, the Chinatown dis-
5   trict. Let me make one thing clear: whatever else may be said about the Chinese, they are stingy! I slept in doorways three days until I could find a tailor who would make me this kimono on credit. As it turns out, maybe I didn't even need it. Maybe he would've been happy to see me in a sim-
10   ple shift and mascara. But . . . better safe than sorry.
    That was 1970, when I arrived in Paris. For the next fif-teen years, yes, I lived in a very comfy life. Some relief, believe me, after four years on a fucking commune in Nowheresville, China. Rene supported the boy and me, and
15   I did some demonstrations around the country as part of my "cultural exchange" cover. And then there was the spying.

(SONG moves upstage, to a chair. TOULON *enters as a* JUDGE, *wearing the appropriate wig and robes. He sits near* SONG. *It's 1986, and* SONG *is testifying in a courtroom.)*

SONG: Not much at first. Rene had lost all his high-level con-tacts. Comrade Chin wasn't very interested in parking-ticket statistics. But finally, at my urging, Rene got a job as
20   a courier, handling sensitive documents. He'd photograph them for me, and I'd pass them on to the Chinese embassy.
JUDGE: Did he understand the extent of his activity?
SONG: He didn't ask. He knew that I needed those documents, and that was enough.
25 JUDGE: But he must've known he was passing classified information.
SONG: I can't say.
JUDGE: He never asked what you were going to do with them?
SONG: Nope.

(Pause.)

30 JUDGE: There is one thing that the court—indeed, that all of France—would like to know.
SONG: Fire away.
JUDGE: Did Monsieur Gallimard know you were a man?
SONG: Well, he never saw me completely naked. Ever.
35 JUDGE: But surely, he must've . . . how can I put this?
SONG: Put it however you like. I'm not shy. He must've felt around?
JUDGE: Mmmmm.
SONG: Not really. I did all the work. He just laid back. Of
40   course we did enjoy more . . . complete union, and I sup-pose he *might* have wondered why I was always on my stom-ach, but. . . . But what you're thinking is, "Of course a wrist must've brushed . . . a hand hit . . . over twenty years!"

Yeah. Well, Your Honor, it was my job to make him think I was a woman. And chew on this: it wasn't all that hard.   45
See, my mother was a prostitute along the Bundt before the Revolution. And, uh, I think it's fair to say she learned a few things about Western men. So I borrowed her knowl-edge. In service to my country.
JUDGE: Would you care to enlighten the court with this secret   50
knowledge? I'm sure we're all very curious.
SONG: I'm sure you are. *(Pause.)* Okay, Rule One is: Men always believe what they want to hear. So a girl can tell the most obnoxious lies and the guys will believe them every time— "This is my first time"—"That's the biggest I've ever   55
seen"—or *both,* which, if you really think about it, is not possible in a single lifetime. You've maybe heard those phrases a few times in your own life, yes, Your Honor?
JUDGE: It's not my life, Monsieur Song, which is on trial today.
SONG: Okay, okay, just trying to lighten up the proceedings.   60
Tough room.
JUDGE: Go on.
SONG: Rule Two: As soon as a Western man comes into contact with the East—he's already confused. The West has sort of an international rape mentality towards the East. Do you   65
know rape mentality?
JUDGE: Give us your definition, please.
SONG: Basically, "Her mouth says no, but her eyes say yes." The West thinks of itself as masculine—big guns, big in-dustry, big money—so the East is feminine—weak, deli-   70
cate, poor . . . but good at art, and full of inscrutable wisdom—the feminine mystique.
    Her mouth says no, but her eyes say yes. The West be-lieves the East, deep down, *wants* to be dominated—because a woman can't think for herself.   75
JUDGE: What does this have to do with my question?
SONG: You expect Oriental countries to submit to your guns, and you expect Oriental women to be submissive to your men. That's why you say they make the best wives.
JUDGE: But why would that make it possible for you to fool   80
Monsieur Gallimard? Please—get to the point.
SONG: One, because when he finally met his fantasy woman, he wanted more than anything to believe that she was, in fact, a woman. And second, I am an Oriental. And being an Oriental, I could never be completely a man.   85

(Pause.)

JUDGE: Your armchair political theory is tenuous, Monsieur Song.
SONG: You think so? That's why you'll lose in all your dealings with the East.
JUDGE: Just answer my question: did he know you were a man?   90

(Pause.)

SONG: You know, your Honor, I never asked.

SCENE II

Same.

Music from the "Death Scene" from Butterfly *blares over the house speakers. It is the loudest thing we've heard in this play.*

GALLIMARD *enters, crawling towards* SONG's *wig and kimono.*

GALLIMARD: Butterfly? Butterfly?

*(*SONG *remains a man, in the witness box, delivering a testimony we do not hear.)*

GALLIMARD: *(To us.)* In my moment of greatest shame, here, in this courtroom—with that . . . person up there, telling the world. . . . What strikes me especially is how shallow he is,
5 how glib and obsequious . . . completely . . . without substance! The type that prowls around discos with a gold medallion stinking of garlic. So little like my Butterfly.
      Yet even in this moment my mind remains agile, flip-flopping like a man on a trampoline. Even now, my picture
10 dissolves, and I see that . . . witness . . . talking to me.

*(*SONG *suddenly stands staight up in his witness box, and looks at* GALLIMARD.)*

SONG: Yes. You. White man.

*(*SONG *steps out of the witness box, and moves downstage towards* GALLIMARD. *Light change.)*

GALLIMARD: *(To* SONG.) Who? Me?
SONG: Do you see any other white men?
GALLIMARD: Yes. There're white men all around. This is a
15 French courtroom.
SONG: So you are an adventurous imperialist. Tell me, why did it take you so long? To come back to this place?
GALLIMARD: What place?
SONG: This theatre in China. Where we met many years ago.
20 GALLIMARD: *(To us.)* And once again, against my will, I am transported.

(Chinese opera music comes up on the speakers. SONG *begins to do opera moves, as he did the night they met.)*

SONG: Do you remember? The night you gave your heart?
GALLIMARD: It was a long time ago.
SONG: Not long enough. A night that turned your world up-
25 side down.
GALLIMARD: Perhaps.
SONG: Oh, be honest with me. What's another bit of flattery when you've already given me twenty years' worth? It's a wonder my head hasn't swollen to the size of China.
30 GALLIMARD: Who's to say it hasn't?
SONG: Who's to say? And what's the shame? In pride? You think I could've pulled this off if I wasn't already full of pride when we met? No, not just pride. Arrogance. It takes arrogance, really—to believe you can will, with your eyes and your
35 lips, the destiny of another. *(He dances.)* C'mon. Admit it. You still want me. Even in slacks and a button-down collar.
GALLIMARD: I don't see what the point of—
SONG: You don't? Well maybe, Rene, just maybe—I want you.
GALLIMARD: You do?
40 SONG: Then again, maybe I'm just playing with you. How can you tell? *(Reprising his feminine character, he sidles up to* GALLIMARD.) "How I wish there were even a small cafe to sit in. With men in tuxedos, and cappuccinos, and bad expatriate jazz." Now you want to kiss me, don't you?

GALLIMARD: *(Pulling away.)* What makes you—?   45
SONG: —so sure? See? I take the words from your mouth. Then I wait for you to come and retrieve them. *(He reclines on the floor.)*
GALLIMARD: Why? Why do you treat me so cruelly?
SONG: Perhaps I *was* treating you cruelly. But now—I'm being 50 nice. Come here, my little one.
GALLIMARD: I'm not your little one!
SONG: My mistake. It's I who am *your* little one, right?
GALLIMARD: Yes, I—
SONG: So come get your little one. If you like. I may even let 55 you strip me.
GALLIMARD: I mean, you were! Before . . . but not like this!
SONG: I was? Then perhaps I still am. If you look hard enough. *(He starts to remove his clothes.)*
GALLIMARD: What—what are you doing?   60
SONG: Helping you to see through my act.
GALLIMARD: Stop that! I don't want to! I don't—
SONG: Oh, but you asked me to strip, remember?
GALLIMARD: What? That was years ago! And I took it back!
SONG: No. You postponed it. Postponed the inevitable. Today, 65 the inevitable has come calling.

(From the speakers, cacophony: Butterfly *mixed in with Chinese gongs.)*

GALLIMARD: No! Stop! I don't want to see!
SONG: Then look away.
GALLIMARD: You're only in my mind! All this is in my mind! I order you! To stop!   70
SONG: To what? To strip? That's just what I'm—
GALLIMARD: No! Stop! I want you—!
SONG: You want me?
GALLIMARD: To stop!
SONG: You know something, Rene? Your mouth says no, but 75 your eyes say yes. Turn them away. I dare you.
GALLIMARD: I don't have to! Every night, you say you're going to strip, but then I beg you and you stop!
SONG: I guess tonight is different.
GALLIMARD: Why? Why should that be?   80
SONG: Maybe I've become frustrated. Maybe I'm saying "Look at me, you fool!" Or maybe I'm just feeling . . . sexy. *(He is down to his briefs.)*
GALLIMARD: Please. This is unnecessary. I know what you are.
SONG: Do you? What am I?   85
GALLIMARD: A—a man.
SONG: You don't really believe that.
GALLIMARD: Yes I do! I knew all the time somewhere that my happiness was temporary, my love a deception. But my mind kept the knowledge at bay. To make the wait bearable.   90
SONG: Monsieur Gallimard—the wait is over.

*(*SONG *drops his briefs. He is naked. Sound cue out. Slowly, we and* SONG *come to the realization that what we had thought to be* GALLIMARD's *sobbing is actually his laughter.)*

GALLIMARD: Oh god! What an idiot! Of course!
SONG: Rene—what?
GALLIMARD: Look at you! You're a man! *(He bursts into laughter again.)*   95
SONG: I fail to see what's so funny!

GALLIMARD: "You fail to see—!" I mean, you never did have much of a sense of humor, did you? I just think it's ridiculously funny that I've wasted so much time on just a man!

100 SONG: Wait. I'm not "just a man."

GALLIMARD: No? Isn't that what you've been trying to convince me of?

SONG: Yes, but what I mean—

GALLIMARD: And now, I finally believe you, and you tell me
105 it's not true? I think you must have some kind of identity problem.

SONG: Will you listen to me?

GALLIMARD: Why?! I've been listening to you for twenty years. Don't I deserve a vacation?

110 SONG: I'm not just any man!

GALLIMARD: Then, what exactly are you?

SONG: Rene, how can you ask—? Okay, what about this?

(He picks up Butterfly's robes, starts to dance around. No music.)

GALLIMARD: Yes, that's very nice. I have to admit.

(SONG holds out his arm to GALLIMARD.)

SONG: It's the same skin you've worshiped for years. Touch it.
115 GALLIMARD: Yes, it does feel the same.

SONG: Now—close your eyes.

(SONG covers GALLIMARD's eyes with one hand. With the other, SONG draws GALLIMARD's hand up to his face. GALLIMARD, like a blind man, lets his hands run over SONG's face.)

GALLIMARD: This skin, I remember. The curve of her face, the softness of her cheek, her hair against the back of my hand . . .
120 SONG: I'm your Butterfly. Under the robes, beneath everything, it was always me. Now, open your eyes and admit it—you adore me. *(He removes his hand from GALLIMARD's eyes.)*

GALLIMARD: You, who knew every inch of my desires—how could you, of all people, have made such a mistake?
125 SONG: What?

GALLIMARD: You showed me your true self. When all I loved was the lie. A perfect lie, which you let fall to the ground—and now, it's old and soiled.

SONG: So—you never really loved me? Only when I was play-
130 ing a part?

GALLIMARD: I'm a man who loved a woman created by a man. Everything else—simply falls short.

(Pause.)

SONG: What am I supposed to do now?

GALLIMARD: You were a fine spy, Monsieur Song, with an even
135 finer accomplice. But now I believe you should go. Get out of my life!

SONG: Go where? Rene, you can't live without me. Not after twenty years.

GALLIMARD: I certainly can't live with you—not after twenty
140 years of betrayal.

SONG: Don't be so stubborn! Where will you go?

GALLIMARD: I have a date . . . with my Butterfly.

SONG: So, throw away your pride. And come . . .

GALLIMARD: Get away from me! Tonight, I've finally learned to tell fantasy from reality. And, knowing the difference, I   145
choose fantasy.

SONG: *I'm* your fantasy!

GALLIMARD: You? You're as real as hamburger. Now get out! I have a date with my Butterfly and I don't want your body polluting the room! *(He tosses SONG's suit at him.)* Look at   150
these—you dress like a pimp.

SONG: Hey! These are Armani slacks and—! *(He puts on his briefs and slacks.)* Let's just say . . . I'm disappointed in you, Rene. In the crush of your adoration, I thought you'd become something more. More like . . . a woman.   155

But no. Men. You're like the rest of them. It's all in the way we dress, and make up our faces, and bat our eyelashes. You really have so little imagination!

GALLIMARD: You, Monsieur Song? Accuse me of too little imagination? You, if anyone, should know—I am pure imagina-   160
tion. And in imagination I will remain. Now get out!

(GALLIMARD bodily removes SONG from the stage, taking his kimono.)

SONG: Rene! I'll never put on those robes again! You'll be sorry!

GALLIMARD: *(To SONG.)* I'm already sorry! *(Looking at the kimono in his hands.)* Exactly as sorry . . . as a Butterfly.

SCENE III

M. GALLIMARD's *prison cell. Paris. Present.*

GALLIMARD: I've played out the events of my life night after night, always searching for a new ending to my story, one where I leave this cell and return forever to my Butterfly's arms.

Tonight I realize my search is over. That I've looked all   5
along in the wrong place. And now, to you, I will prove that my love was not in vain—by returning to the world of fantasy where I first met her.

(He picks up the kimono; dancers enter.)

GALLIMARD: There is a vision of the Orient that I have. Of slender women in chong sams and kimonos who die for the   10
love of unworthy foreign devils. Who are born and raised to be the perfect women. Who take whatever punishment we give them, and bounce back, strengthened by love, unconditionally. It is a vision that has become my life.

(Dancers bring the wash basin to him and help him make up his face.)

GALLIMARD: In public, I have continued to deny that Song Liling   15
is a man. This brings me headlines, and is a source of great embarrassment to my French colleagues, who can now be sent into a coughing fit by the mere mention of Chinese food. But alone, in my cell, I have long since faced the truth.

And the truth demands a sacrifice. For mistakes made over   20
the course of a lifetime. My mistakes were simple and absolute—the man I loved was a cad, a bounder. He deserved nothing but a kick in the behind, and instead I gave him . . . all my love.

Yes—love. Why not admit it all? That was my undo-   25
ing, wasn't it? Love warped my judgment, blinded my eyes,

rearranged the very lines on my face . . . until I could look in the mirror and see nothing but . . . a woman.

(Dancers help him put on the Butterfly wig.)

GALLIMARD: I have a vision. Of the Orient. That, deep within
30   its almond eyes, there are still women. Women willing to sacrifice themselves for the love of a man. Even a man whose love is completely without worth.

(Dancers assist GALLIMARD in donning the kimono. They hand him a knife.)

GALLIMARD: Death with honor is better than life . . . life with dishonor. (He sets himself center stage, in a seppuku posi-
35   tion.) The love of a Butterfly can withstand many things—unfaithfulness, loss, even abandonment. But how can it face the one sin that implies all others? The devastating

knowledge that, underneath it all, the object of her love was nothing more, nothing less than . . . a man. (He sets the tip of the knife against his body.) It is 19___. And I 40 have found her at last. In a prison on the outskirts of Paris. My name is Rene Gallimard—also known as Madame Butterfly.

(GALLIMARD turns upstage and plunges his knife into his body, as music from the "Love Duet" blares over the speakers. He collapses into the arms of the dancers, who lay him reverently on the floor. The image holds for several beats. Then a tight special up on SONG, who stands as a man, staring at the dead GALLIMARD. He smokes a cigarette; the smoke filters up through the lights. Two words leave his lips.)

SONG: Butterfly? Butterfly?

(Smoke rises as lights fade slowly to black.)

TONY KUSHNER

Born in 1956, Tony Kushner first came to international prominence with *Angels in America* (1991), a two-part play that was an enormous success both in London and in Los Angeles before moving to New York in 1993. Kushner's "gay fantasia on national themes" is, in a sense, a displaced autobiography: the displaced narrative of his own growing up as a gay man in the American era of Roy Cohn, the decline of the Communist menace, the onset of the AIDS epidemic, and the rise of the conservative political agenda that dominated American politics in the 1980s. Kushner was born in New York, but his family soon moved to New Orleans, where his parents were musicians in the New Orleans Philharmonic. When he was two, the family moved to Lake Charles, Louisiana; his mother, once a prominent New York bassoonist, devoted herself to educating the children in literature, music, and the arts; she also acted in the Lake Charles theater company. Kushner knew that he was gay but concealed it from his parents; when he went to college at Columbia University, he spent some time in psychoanalysis trying to alter his sexual orientation. However, by his mid-twenties, Kushner was able to accept his sexuality and came out. After taking his B.A. at Columbia, he studied theater at New York University. His first play, *A Bright Room Called Day* (1985), was written while he worked as a switchboard operator; it concerns the collapse of the political left and the rise of fascism during the German Weimar Republic; Kushner also adapted a translation of Corneille's play *The Illusion*. *Angels in America* is his second play. *Slavs* opened in New York in 1994, and an early play *Hydriotaphia* opened in 1998.

ANGELS IN AMERICA, PART I:
MILLENIUM APPROACHES

The first part of *Angels in America* (the second part is entitled *Perestroika*), *Millennium Approaches* is a complete play in its own right. Kushner began writing the play in 1988 when Oskar Eustis, who had directed his first play for the Eureka Theater Company in San Francisco, asked Kushner for another play. Subtitled "A Gay Fantasia on National Themes," *Millennium Approaches* is at once a deeply personal look at the lives of two couples— Joe and Harper, a young Mormon couple transplanted to New York; Louis and Prior, a gay couple facing (and not facing) the onset of AIDS—and a political "fantasia" in the manner of Shaw's *Heartbreak House* or *The Apple Cart*. Kushner sets the characters' struggles against the background of conservative politics and the increasing power of the conservative right in 1980s America; as Martin remarks in act 2: ". . . we'll get our way on just about everything: abortion, defense, Central America, protecting the family, a live investment climate. . . . It's really the end of Liberalism. The end of New Deal Socialism. The end of ipso facto secular humanism."

While Kushner's play takes aim at the policies of the Republican administration, the play's politics extend deeply into the politics of personal action. The emphasis on individualism, on self-sufficiency, on destroying the liberal consensus, and on eliminating social programs characteristic of the Reagan administration has consequences in the private sphere as well, where freedom looks alternately like selfishness and chaos. Roy Cohn— famous for his anticommunist activities and for prosecuting (and winning) the death sentence for Julius and Ethel Rosenberg for selling secret information to the Soviet Union—in many ways exemplifies this linkage in the play. Unable to give up his view of political power ("the game . . . of being alive"), Cohn refuses to be treated for AIDS because it would mean a public admission that he is gay, something generally known but not acknowledged. Louis, unable to bring himself to care for Prior during his horrifying illness, finds both emptiness and freedom in deserting his lover. Harper, whose valium-induced fantasies summon the cosmic travel agent Mr. Lies (who whisks her off to Antarctica) is in the throes of a nervous breakdown, a literalized response to the decaying world in which she lives, where "everywhere, things are collapsing, lies surfacing, systems of defense giving way."

The hallucinatory style of *Millennium Approaches* enables Kushner to bring this blending of public and private, the grand sweep of history and the narrower compass of individual suffering, into a close juxtaposition. *Millennium Approaches* ends when Prior's ancestors—a medieval monk and a seventeenth-century dandy—appear to announce the coming of a mysterious angel, whose voice is heard intermittently throughout the play. The Angel's arrival is heralded in a number of ways: Prior regards his first lesion of Karposi's Syndrome as the mark of the angel of death; a feather drops from above and the voice is heard at the end of Harper's/Prior's intertwined dream-hallucination in act 1; Joe alludes to Jacob wrestling with his angel, an image of Joe's fight to recognize and admit his own homosexuality. The Angel is a figure of release and redemption from the isolation in which the characters find themselves.

However, the Angel also has a public, historical significance as well. Kushner has suggested that the Angel alludes to a comment made by the German cultural critic Walter Benjamin. In "Theses on the Philosophy of History," Benjamin makes the following remark on the process of history:

> A Klee painting named "Angelus Novus" shows an angel looking as though he is about to move away from something he is fixedly contemplating. His eyes are staring, his mouth is open, his wings are spread. This is how one pictures the angel of history. His face is turned toward the past. Where we perceive a chain of events, he sees one single catastrophe which keeps piling wreckage upon wreckage and hurls it in front of his feet. The angel would like to stay, awaken the dead, and make whole what has been smashed. But a storm is blowing from Paradise; it has got caught in his wings with such violence that the angel can no longer close them. This storm irresistibly propels him into the future to which his back is turned, while the pile of debris before him grows skyward. This storm is what we call progress.

The Angel is, to Kushner as to Benjamin, a figure for the dialectical force of history, the way that history moves into the future both in antithesis to the past, and yet bearing the past along with it. In *Angels in America*, Tony Kushner provides a sense of how it is we live today, in the midst of this "storm . . . we call progress."

ANGELS IN AMERICA, PART I: MILLENNIUM APPROACHES

Tony Kushner

—— CHARACTERS ——

ROY M. COHN, *a successful New York lawyer and unofficial power broker*

JOSEPH (JOE) PORTER PITT, *chief clerk for Justice Theodore Wilson of the Federal Court of Appeals, Second Circuit*

HARPER AMATY PITT, *Joe's wife, an agoraphobic with a mild Valium addiction*

LOUIS IRONSON, *a word processor working for the Second Circuit Court of Appeals*

PRIOR WALTER, *Louis's boyfriend. Occasionally works as a club designer or caterer, otherwise lives very modestly but with great style off a small trust fund*

HANNAH PORTER PITT, *Joe's mother, currently residing in Salt Lake City, living off her deceased husband's army pension*

BELIZE, *a former drag queen and former lover of Prior's: A registered nurse. Belize's name was originally Norman Arriaga; Belize is a drag name that stuck*

THE ANGEL, *four divine emanations, Fluor, Phosphor, Lumen and Candle; manifest in One: the Continental Principality of America. She has magnificent steel-gray wings*

RABBI ISIDOR CHEMELWITZ, *an orthodox Jewish rabbi, played by the actor playing Hannah*

MR. LIES, *Harper's imaginary friend, a travel agent, who in style of dress and speech suggests a jazz musician; he always wears a large lapel badge emblazoned "IOTA" (The International Order of Travel Agents). He is played by the actor playing Belize*

THE MAN IN THE PARK, *played by the actor playing Prior*

THE VOICE, *the voice of The Angel*

HENRY, *Roy's doctor, played by the actor playing Hannah*

EMILY, *a nurse, played by the actor playing The Angel*

MARTIN HELLER, *a Reagan Administration Justice Department flackman, played by the actor playing Harper*

SISTER ELLA CHAPTER, *a Salt Lake City real-estate saleswoman, played by the actor playing The Angel*

PRIOR 1, *the ghost of a dead Prior Walter from the 13th century, played by the actor playing Joe. He is a blunt, gloomy medieval farmer with a gutteral Yorkshire accent*

PRIOR 2, *the ghost of a dead Prior Walter from the 17th century, played by the actor playing Roy. He is a Londoner, sophisticated, with a High British accent*

THE ESKIMO, *played by the actor playing Joe*

THE WOMAN IN THE SOUTH BRONX, *played by the actor playing The Angel*

ETHEL ROSENBERG, *played by the actor playing Hannah*

—— PLAYWRIGHT'S NOTES ——

A DISCLAIMER: *Roy M. Cohn, the character, is based on the late Roy M. Cohn (1927–1986), who was all too real; for the most part the acts attributed to the character Roy, such as his illegal conferences with Judge Kaufmann during the trial of Ethel Rosenberg, are to be found in the historical record. But this Roy is a work of dramatic fiction; his words are my invention, and liberties have been taken.*

A NOTE ABOUT THE STAGING: *The play benefits from a pared-down style of presentation, with minimal scenery and scene shifts done rapidly (no blackouts!), employing the cast as well as stagehands—which makes for an actor-driven event, as this must be. The moments of magic—the appearance and disappearance of Mr. Lies and the ghosts, the Book hallucination, and the ending—are to be fully realized, as bits of wonderful theatrical illusion—which means it's OK if the wires show, and maybe it's good that they do, but the magic should at the same time be thoroughly amazing.*

> . . . In a murderous time
> the heart breaks and breaks
> and lives by breaking.
>
> —STANLEY KUNITZ
> "THE TESTING-TREE"

—— ACT ONE ——

BAD NEWS
OCTOBER–NOVEMBER 1985

SCENE I

The last days of October. RABBI ISODOR CHEMELWITZ *alone onstage with a small coffin. It is a rough pine box with two wooden pegs, one at the foot and one at the head, holding the lid in place. A prayer shawl embroidered with a Star of David is draped over the lid, and by the head a yarzheit candle is burning.*

RABBI ISIDOR CHEMELWITZ: *(He speaks sonorously, with a heavy Eastern European accent, unapologetically consulting a sheet of notes for the family names.)* Hello and good morning. I am Rabbi Isidor Chemelwitz of the Bronx Home for Aged Hebrews.

We are here this morning to pay respects at the passing of Sarah Ironson, devoted wife of Benjamin Ironson, also deceased, loving and caring mother of her sons Morris, Abraham, and Samuel, and her daughters Esther and Rachel; beloved grandmother of Max, Mark, Louis, Lisa, Maria . . . uh . . . Lesley, Angela, Doris, Luke and Eric. *(Looks more closely at paper.)* Eric? This is a Jewish name? *(Shrugs.)* Eric. A large and loving family. We assemble that we may mourn collectively this good and righteous woman.

(He looks at the coffin.)

This woman. I did not know this woman. I cannot accurately describe her attributes, nor do justice to her dimensions. She was. . . . Well, in the Bronx Home of Aged Hebrews are many like this, the old, and to many I speak but not to be frank with this one. She preferred silence. So I do not know her and yet I know her. She was . . .

(He touches the coffin.)

20   . . . not a person but a whole kind of person, the ones who crossed the ocean, who brought with us to America the villages of Russia and Lithuania—and how we struggled, and how we fought, for the family, for the Jewish home, so that you would not grow up *here,* in this strange
25 place, in the melting pot where nothing melted. Descendants of this immigrant woman, you do not grow up in America, you and your children and their children with the goyische names. You do not live in America. No such place exists. Your clay is the clay of some Litvak shtetl,
30 your air the air of the steppes—because she carried the old world on her back across the ocean, in a boat, and she put it down on Grand Concourse Avenue, or in Flatbush, and she worked that earth into your bones, and you pass it to your children, this ancient, ancient culture and
35 home.

(Little pause.)

You can never make that crossing that she made, for such Great Voyages in this world do not any more exist. But every day of your lives the miles that voyage between that place and this one you cross. Every day. You understand
40 me? In you that journey is.

      So . . .

      She was the last of the Mohicans, this one was. Pretty soon . . . all the old will be dead.

SCENE II

Same day. ROY *and* JOE *in* ROY's *office.* ROY *at an impressive desk, bare except for a very elaborate phone system, rows and rows of flashing buttons which bleep and beep and whistle incessantly, making chaotic music underneath* ROY's *conversations.* JOE *is sitting, waiting.* ROY *conducts business with great energy, impatience and sensual abandon: gesticulating, shouting, cajoling, crooning, playing the phone, receiver and hold button with virtuosity and love.*

ROY: *(Hitting a button.)* Hold. *(To* JOE.) I wish I was an octopus, a fucking octopus. Eight loving arms and all those suckers. Know what I mean?

JOE: No, I . . .

5 ROY: *(Gesturing to a deli platter of little sandwiches on his desk.)* You want lunch?

JOE: No, that's OK really I just . . .

ROY: *(Hitting a button.)* Ailene? Roy Cohn. Now what kind of a greeting is. . . . I thought we were friends, Ai. . . . Look
10 Mrs. Soffer you don't have to get. . . . You're upset. You're yelling. You'll aggravate your condition, you shouldn't yell, you'll pop little blood vessels in your face if you yell. . . . No that was a joke, Mrs. Soffer, I was joking. . . . I already apologized sixteen times for that, Mrs. Soffer, you . . .
15 *(While she's fulminating,* ROY *covers the mouthpiece with his hand and talks to* JOE.) This'll take a minute, *eat* already, what is this tasty sandwich here it's—(*He takes a bite of a sandwich.*) Mmmmm, liver or some. . . . Here.

(He pitches the sandwich to JOE, *who catches it and returns it to the platter.)*

ROY: *(Back to Mrs. Soffer.)* Uh huh, uh huh. . . . No, I already told you, it wasn't a vacation, it was business. Mrs. Soffer, I 20 have clients in Haiti, Mrs. Soffer, I. . . . Listen, Ailene, YOU THINK I'M THE ONLY GODDAM LAWYER IN HISTORY EVER MISSED A COURT DATE? Don't make such a big fucking. . . . Hold. *(He hits the hold button.)* You HAG! 25

JOE: If this is a bad time . . .

ROY: *Bad* time? This is a *good* time! *(Button.)* Baby doll, get me. . . . Oh fuck, wait . . . *(Button, button.)* Hello? Yah. Sorry to keep you holding, Judge Hollins, I. . . . Oh *Mrs.* Hollins, sorry dear deep voice you got. Enjoying your visit? *(Hand* 30 *over mouthpiece, to* JOE.) She sounds like a truckdriver and he sounds like Kate Smith, very confusing. Nixon appointed him, all the geeks are Nixon appointees . . . *(To Mrs. Hollins.)* Yeah yeah right good so how many tickets dear? Seven. For what, *Cats, 42nd Street,* what? No you wouldn't 35 like *La Cage,* trust me, I know. Oh for godsake. . . . Hold. *(Button, button.)* Baby doll, seven for *Cats* or something, anything hard to get, I don't give a fuck what and neither will they. *(Button; to* JOE.) You see *La Cage?*

JOE: No, I . . . 40

ROY: Fabulous. Best thing on Broadway. Maybe ever. *(Button.)* Who? Aw, Jesus H. Christ, Harry, *no,* Harry, Judge John Francis Grimes, Manhattan Family Court. Do I have to do every goddam thing myself? *Touch* the bastard, Harry, and don't call me on this line again, I told you not to . . . 45

JOE: *(Starting to get up.)* Roy, uh, should I wait outside or . . .

ROY: *(To* JOE.) Oh sit. *(To* HARRY.) You hold. I pay you to hold fuck you Harry you jerk. *(Button.)* Half-wit dick-brain. *(Instantly philosophical.)* I see the universe, Joe, as a kind of sandstorm in outer space with winds of mega-hurricane 50 velocity, but instead of grains of sand it's shards and splinters of glass. You ever feel that way? Ever have one of those days?

JOE: I'm not sure I . . .

ROY: So how's life in Appeals? How's the Judge? 55

JOE: He sends his best.

ROY: He's a good man. Loyal. Not the brightest man on the bench, but he has manners. And a nice head of silver hair.

JOE: He gives me a lot of responsibility.

ROY: Yeah, like writing his decisions and signing his name. 60

JOE: Well . . .

ROY: He's a nice guy. And you cover admirably.

JOE: Well, thanks, Roy, I . . .

ROY: *(Button.)* Who is *this?* Well who the fuck are *you?* Hold— *(Button.)* Harry? Eighty-seven grand, something like that. 65 Fuck him. Eat me. New Jersey, chain of porno film stores in, uh, Weehawken. That's—Harry, that's the beauty of the law. *(Button.)* So, baby doll, what? *Cats?* Bleah. *(Button.)* Cats! It's about cats. Singing cats, you'll love it. Eight o'clock, the theatre's always at eight. *(Button.)* Fucking tourists. *(Button,* 70 *then to* JOE.) Oh live a little, Joe, *eat* something for Christ sake—

JOE: Um, Roy, could you . . .

ROY: What? *(To* HARRY.) Hold a minute. *(Button.)* Mrs. Soffer? Mrs. . . . *(Button.)* God-fucking-dammit to hell, where 75 is . . .

JOE: (*Overlapping.*) Roy, I'd really appreciate it if . . .
ROY: (*Overlapping.*) Well she was here a minute ago, baby doll, see if . . .

(*The phone starts making three different beeping sounds, all at once.*)

80   ROY: (*Smashing buttons.*) Jesus fuck this goddam thing . . .
JOE: (*Overlapping.*) I really wish you wouldn't . . .
ROY: (*Overlapping.*) Baby doll? Ring the *Post* get me Suzy see if . . .

(*The phone starts whistling loudly.*)

ROY: CHRIST!
85   JOE: *Roy.*
ROY: (*Into receiver.*) Hold. (*Button; to* JOE.) What?
JOE: Could you please not take the Lord's name in vain?

(*Pause.*)

I'm sorry. But please. At least while I'm . . .
ROY: (*Laughs, then.*) Right. Sorry. Fuck.
90   Only in America. (*Punches a button.*) Baby doll, tell 'em all to fuck off. Tell 'em I died. You handle Mrs. Soffer. Tell her it's on the way. Tell her I'm schtupping the judge. I'll call her back. I *will* call her. I *know* how much I borrowed. She's got four hundred times that stuffed up her. . . . Yeah, tell
95   her I said that. (*Button. The phone is silent.*)
     So, Joe.
JOE: I'm sorry Roy, I just . . .
ROY: No no no no, principles count, I respect principles, I'm not religious but I like God and God likes me. Baptist,
100   Catholic?
JOE: Mormon.
ROY: Mormon. Delectable. Absolutely. Only in America. So, Joe. Whattya think?
JOE: It's . . . well . . .
105   ROY: Crazy life.
JOE: Chaotic.
ROY: Well but God bless chaos. Right?
JOE: Ummm . . .
ROY: Huh. Mormons. I knew Mormons, in, um, Nevada.
110   JOE: Utah, mostly.
ROY: No, these Mormons were in Vegas.
     So. So, how'd you like to go to Washington and work for the Justice Department?
JOE: Sorry?
115   ROY: How'd you like to go to Washington and work for the Justice Department? All I gotta do is pick up the phone, talk to Ed, and you're in.
JOE: In . . . what, exactly?
ROY: Associate Assistant Something Big. Internal Affairs, heart
120   of the woods, something nice with clout.
JOE: Ed . . . ?
ROY: Meese. The Attorney General.
JOE: Oh.
ROY: I just have to pick up the phone . . .
125   JOE: I have to think.
ROY: Of course.

(*Pause.*)

It's a great time to be in Washington, Joe.
JOE: Roy, it's incredibly exciting . . .
ROY: And it would mean something to me. You understand?

(*Little pause.*)

JOE: I . . . can't say how much I appreciate this Roy, I'm sort   130
of . . . well, stunned, I mean. . . . Thanks, Roy. But I have to give it some thought. I have to ask my wife.
ROY: Your wife. Of course.
JOE: But I really appreciate . . .
ROY: Of course. Talk to your wife.   135

SCENE III

Later that day. HARPER *at home, alone. She is listening to the radio and talking to herself, as she often does. She speaks to the audience.*

HARPER: People who are lonely, people left alone, sit talking nonsense to the air, imagining . . . beautiful systems dying, old fixed orders spiraling apart . . .
     When you look at the ozone layer, from outside, from a spaceship, it looks like a pale blue halo, a gentle, shimmer-   5
ing aureole encircling the atmosphere encircling the earth. Thirty miles above our heads, a thin layer of three-atom oxygen molecules, product of photosynthesis, which ex-plains the fussy vegetable preference for visible light, its re-jection of darker rays and emanations. Danger from   10
without. It's a kind of gift, from God, the crowning touch to the creation of the world: guardian angels, hands linked, make a spherical net, a blue-green nesting orb, a shell of safety for life itself. But everywhere, things are collapsing, lies surfacing, systems of defense giving way. . . . This is   15
why, Joe, this is why I shouldn't be left alone.

(*Little pause.*)

I'd like to go traveling. Leave you behind to worry. I'll send postcards with strange stamps and tantalizing messages on the back. "Later maybe." "Nevermore . . ."

(MR. LIES, *a travel agent, appears.*)

HARPER: Oh! You startled me!   20
MR. LIES: Cash, check or credit card?
HARPER: I remember you. You're from Salt Lake. You sold us the plane tickets when we flew here. What are you doing in Brooklyn?
MR. LIES: You said you wanted to travel . . .   25
HARPER: And here you are. How thoughtful.
MR. LIES: Mr. Lies. Of the International Order of Travel Agents. We mobilize the globe, we set people adrift, we stir the populace and send nomads eddying across the planet. We are adepts of motion, acolytes of the flux. Cash, check or   30
credit card. Name your destination.
HARPER: Antarctica, maybe. I want to see the hole in the ozone. I heard on the radio . . .
MR. LIES: (*He has a computer terminal in his briefcase.*) I can arrange a guided tour. Now?   35
HARPER: Soon. Maybe soon. I'm not safe here you see. Things aren't right with me. Weird stuff happens . . .
MR. LIES: Like?

HARPER: Well, like you, for instance. Just appearing. Or last
40   week . . . well never mind.
      People are like planets, you need a thick skin. Things get to
      me, Joe stays away and now. . . . Well look. My dreams are
      talking back to me.
MR. LIES: It's the price of rootlessness. Motion sickness. The
45   only cure: to keep moving.
HARPER: I'm undecided. I feel . . . that something's going to
      give. It's 1985. Fifteen years till the third millennium.
      Maybe Christ will come again. Maybe seeds will be planted,
      maybe there'll be harvests then, maybe early figs to eat,
50   maybe new life, maybe fresh blood, maybe companionship
      and love and protection, safety from what's outside, maybe
      the door will hold, or maybe . . . maybe the troubles will
      come, and the end will come, and the sky will collapse and
      there will be terrible rains and showers of poison light, or
55   maybe my life is really fine, maybe Joe loves me and I'm
      only crazy thinking otherwise, or maybe not, maybe it's
      even worse than I know, maybe . . . I want to know, maybe
      I don't. The suspense, Mr. Lies, it's killing me.
MR. LIES: I suggest a vacation.
60 HARPER: (Hearing something.) That was the elevator. Oh God, I
      should fix myself up, I. . . . You have to go, you shouldn't
      be here . . . you aren't even real.
MR. LIES: Call me when you decide . . .
HARPER: Go!

(The travel agent [MR. LIES] vanishes as JOE enters.)

65 JOE: Buddy?
      Buddy? Sorry I'm late. I was just . . . out. Walking. Are
      you mad?
HARPER: I got a little anxious.
JOE: Buddy kiss.

(They kiss.)

70   Nothing to get anxious about.
      So. So how'd you like to move to Washington?

SCENE IV

Same day. LOUIS *and* PRIOR *outside the funeral home, sitting on a
bench, both dressed in funereal finery, talking. The funeral service for
Sarah Ironson has just concluded and* LOUIS *is about to leave for the
cemetery.*

LOUIS: My grandmother actually saw Emma Goldman speak. In
      Yiddish. But all Grandma could remember was that she
      spoke well and wore a hat.
      What a weird service. That rabbi . . .
5 PRIOR: A definite find. Get his number when you go to the
      graveyard. I want him to bury me.
LOUIS: Better head out there. Everyone gets to put dirt on the
      coffin once it's lowered in.
PRIOR: Oooh. Cemetery fun. Don't want to miss that.
10 LOUIS: It's an old Jewish custom to express love. Here,
      Grandma, have a shovelful. Latecomers run the risk of find-
      ing the grave completely filled.
      She was pretty crazy. She was up there in that home for
      ten years, talking to herself. I never visited. She looked too
15   much like my mother.

PRIOR: (*Hugs him.*) Poor Louis. I'm sorry your grandma is
      dead.
LOUIS: Tiny little coffin, huh?
      Sorry I didn't introduce you to. . . . I always get so
      closety at these family things.   20
PRIOR: Butch. You get butch. (*Imitating.*) "Hi Cousin Doris,
      you don't remember me I'm Lou, Rachel's boy." Lou, not
      Louis, because if you say Louis they'll hear the sibilant S.
LOUIS: I don't have a . . .
PRIOR: I don't blame you, hiding. Bloodlines. Jewish curses are 25
      the worst. I personally would dissolve if anyone ever looked me
      in the eye and said "Feh." Fortunately WASPs don't say
      "Feh." Oh and by the way, darling, cousin Doris is a dyke.
LOUIS: No.
      Really?   30
PRIOR: You don't notice anything. If I hadn't spent the last four
      years fellating you I'd swear you were straight.
LOUIS: You're in a pissy mood. Cat still missing?

(*Little pause.*)

PRIOR: Not a furball in sight. It's your fault.
LOUIS: It is?   35
PRIOR: I warned you, Louis. Names are important. Call an ani-
      mal "Little Sheba" and you can't expect it to stick around.
      Besides, it's a dog's name.
LOUIS: I wanted a dog in the first place, not a cat. He sprayed
      my books.   40
PRIOR: He was a female cat.
LOUIS: Cats are stupid, high-strung predators. Babylonians
      sealed them up in bricks. Dogs have brains.
PRIOR: Cats have intuition.
LOUIS: A sharp dog is as smart as a really dull two-year-old   45
      child.
PRIOR: Cats know when something's wrong.
LOUIS: Only if you stop feeding them.
PRIOR: They know. That's why Sheba left, because she knew.
LOUIS: Knew what?   50

(*Pause.*)

PRIOR: I did my best Shirley Booth this morning, floppy slip-
      pers, housecoat, curlers, can of Little Friskies; "Come back,
      little Sheba, come back. . . ." To no avail. Le chat, elle ne
      reviendra jamais, jamais . . .

(*He removes his jacket, rolls up his sleeve, shows* LOUIS *a dark purple
spot on the underside of his arm near the shoulder.*)

      See.   55
LOUIS: That's just a burst blood vessel.
PRIOR: Not according to the best medical authorities.
LOUIS: What?

(*Pause.*)

      Tell me.
PRIOR: K.S., baby. Lesion number one. Lookit. The wine-dark   60
      kiss of the angel of death.
LOUIS: (*Very softly, holding* PRIOR*'s arm.*) Oh please . . .
PRIOR: I'm a lesionnaire. The Foreign Lesion. The American
      Lesion. Lesionnaire's disease.

65 LOUIS: Stop.

PRIOR: My troubles are lesion.

LOUIS: Will you *stop.*

PRIOR: Don't you think I'm handling this well? I'm going to die.

70 LOUIS: Bullshit.

PRIOR: Let go of my arm.

LOUIS: No.

PRIOR: Let go.

LOUIS: *(Grabbing* PRIOR, *embracing him ferociously.)* No.

75 PRIOR: I can't find a way to spare you baby. No wall like the wall of hard scientific fact. K.S. Wham. Bang your head on that.

LOUIS: Fuck you. *(Letting go.)* Fuck you fuck you fuck you.

PRIOR: Now that's what I like to hear. A mature reaction.

80   Let's go see if the cat's come home.
        Louis?

LOUIS: When did you find this?

PRIOR: I couldn't tell you.

LOUIS: Why?

85 PRIOR: I was scared, Lou.

LOUIS: Of what?

PRIOR: That you'll leave me.

LOUIS: Oh.

(Little pause.)

PRIOR: Bad timing, funeral and all, but I figured as long as

90 we're on the subject of death . . .

LOUIS: I have to go bury my grandma.

PRIOR: Lou?

(Pause.)

    Then you'll come home?

LOUIS: Then I'll come home.

SCENE V

Same day, later on. Split scene: JOE *and* HARPER *at home;* LOUIS *at the cemetery with* RABBI ISIDOR CHEMELWITZ *and the little coffin.*

HARPER: Washington?

JOE: It's an incredible honor, buddy, and . . .

HARPER: I have to think.

JOE: Of course.

5 HARPER: Say no.

JOE: You said you were going to think about it.

HARPER: I don't want to move to Washington.

JOE: Well I do.

HARPER: It's a giant cemetery, huge white graves and mau-

10 soleums everywhere.

JOE: We could live in Maryland. Or Georgetown.

HARPER: We're happy here.

JOE: That's not really true, buddy, we . . .

HARPER: Well happy enough! Pretend-happy. That's better

15 than nothing.

JOE: It's time to make some changes, Harper.

HARPER: No changes. Why?

JOE: I've been chief clerk for four years. I make twenty-nine thousand dollars a year. That's ridiculous. I graduated fourth

in my class and I make less than anyone I know. And I'm 20

. . . I'm tired of being a clerk, I want to go where something good is happening.

HARPER: Nothing good happens in Washington. We'll forget church teachings and buy furniture at . . . at *Conran's* and become yuppies. I have too much to do here. 25

JOE: Like what?

HARPER: I *do* have things . . .

JOE: What things?

HARPER: I have to finish painting the bedroom.

JOE: You've been painting in there for over a year. 30

HARPER: I know, I. . . . It just isn't done because I never get time to finish it.

JOE: Oh that's . . . that doesn't make sense. You have all the time in the world. You could finish it when I'm at work.

HARPER: I'm afraid to go in there alone. 35

JOE: Afraid of what?

HARPER: I heard someone in there. Metal scraping on the wall. A man with a knife, maybe.

JOE: There's no one in the bedroom, Harper.

HARPER: Not now. 40

JOE: Not this morning either.

HARPER: How do you know? You were at work this morning. There's something creepy about this place. Remember *Rosemary's Baby?*

JOE: *Rosemary's Baby?* 45

HARPER: Our apartment looks like that one. Wasn't that apartment in Brooklyn?

JOE: No, it was . . .

HARPER: Well, it looked like this. It did.

JOE: Then let's move. 50

HARPER: Georgetown's worse. *The Exorcist* was in Georgetown.

JOE: The devil, everywhere you turn, huh, buddy.

HARPER: Yeah. Everywhere.

JOE: How many pills today, buddy?

HARPER: None. One. Three. Only three. 55

LOUIS: *(Pointing at the coffin.)* Why are there just two little wooden pegs holding the lid down?

RABBI ISIDOR CHEMELWITZ: So she can get out easier if she wants to.

LOUIS: I hope she stays put. 60

    I pretended for years that she was already dead. When they called to say she had died it was a surprise. I abandoned her.

RABBI ISIDOR CHEMELWITZ: "Sharfer vi di tson fun a shlang iz an umdankbar kind!" 65

LOUIS: I don't speak Yiddish.

RABBI ISIDOR CHEMELWITZ: Sharper than the serpent's tooth is the ingratitude of children. Shakespeare. *Kenig Lear.*

LOUIS: Rabbi, what does the Holy Writ say about someone who abandons someone he loves at a time of great need? 70

RABBI ISIDOR CHEMELWITZ: Why would a person do such a thing?

LOUIS: Because he has to.

    Maybe because this person's sense of the world, that it will change for the better with struggle, maybe a person 75

who has this neo-Hegelian positivist sense of constant historical progress towards happiness or perfection or something, who feels very powerful because he feels connected to

these forces, moving uphill all the time . . . maybe that per-
80 son can't, um, incorporate sickness into this sense of how
things are supposed to go. Maybe vomit . . . and sores and
disease . . . really frighten him, maybe . . . he isn't so good
with death.
RABBI ISIDOR CHEMELWITZ: The Holy Scriptures have nothing
85 to say about such a person.
LOUIS: Rabbi, I'm afraid of the crimes I may commit.
RABBI ISIDOR CHEMELWITZ: Please, mister. I'm a sick old rabbi
facing a long drive home to the Bronx. You want to confess,
better you should find a priest.
90 LOUIS: But I'm not a Catholic, I'm a Jew.
RABBI ISIDOR CHEMELWITZ: Worse luck for you, bubbulah.
Catholics believe in forgiveness. Jews believe in Guilt. (He
pats the coffin tenderly.)
LOUIS: You just make sure those pegs are in good and tight.
95 RABBI ISIDOR CHEMELWITZ: Don't worry, mister. The life she
had, she'll stay put. She's better off.

JOE: Look, I know this is scary for you. But try to understand
what it means to me. Will you try?
HARPER: Yes.
100 JOE: Good. Really try.
    I think things are starting to change in the world.
HARPER: But I don't want . . .
JOE: Wait. For the good. Change for the good. America has re-
discovered itself. Its sacred position among nations. And
105 people aren't ashamed of that like they used to be. This is a
great thing. The truth restored. Law restored. That's what
President Reagan's done, Harper. He says "Truth exists and
can be spoken proudly." And the country responds to him.
We become better. More good. I need to be a part of that,
110 I need something big to lift me up. I mean, six years ago the
world seemed in decline, horrible, hopeless, full of unsolv-
able problems and crime and confusion and hunger and . . .
HARPER: But it still seems that way. More now than before.
They say the ozone layer is . . .
115 JOE: Harper . . .
HARPER: And today out the window on Atlantic Avenue there
was a schizophrenic traffic cop who was making these . . .
JOE: Stop it! I'm trying to make a point.
HARPER: So am I.
120 JOE: You aren't even making sense, you . . .
HARPER: My point is the world seems just as . . .
JOE: It only seems that way to you because you never go out in
the world, Harper, and you have emotional problems.
HARPER: I do so get out in the world.
125 JOE: You don't. You stay in all day, fretting about imaginary . . .
HARPER: I get out. I do. You don't know what I do.
JOE: You don't stay in all day.
HARPER: No.
JOE: Well. . . . Yes you do.
130 HARPER: That's what you think.
JOE: Where do you go?
HARPER: Where do you go? When you walk.
    (Pause, then angrily.) And I DO NOT have emotional
problems.
135 JOE: I'm sorry.
HARPER: And if I do have emotional problems it's from living
with you. Or . . .

JOE: I'm sorry buddy, I didn't mean to . . .
HARPER: Or if you do think I do then you should never have
married me. You have all these secrets and lies.   140
JOE: I want to be married to you, Harper.
HARPER: You shouldn't. You never should.

(Pause.)

    Hey buddy. Hey buddy.
JOE: Buddy kiss . . .

(They kiss.)

HARPER: I heard on the radio how to give a blowjob.   145
JOE: What?
HARPER: You want to try?
JOE: You really shouldn't listen to stuff like that.
HARPER: Mormons can give blowjobs.
JOE: Harper.   150
HARPER: (Imitating his tone.) Joe.
    It was a little Jewish lady with a German accent.
    This is a good time. For me to make a baby.

(Little pause. JOE turns away.)

HARPER: Then they went on to a program about holes in the
ozone layer. Over Antarctica. Skin burns, birds go blind,   155
icebergs melt. The world's coming to an end.

SCENE VI

First week of November. In the men's room of the offices of the Brooklyn
Federal Court of Appeals; LOUIS is crying over the sink; JOE enters.

JOE: Oh, um. . . . Morning.
LOUIS: Good morning, counselor.
JOE: (He watches LOUIS cry.) Sorry, I . . . I don't know your name.
LOUIS: Don't bother. Word processor. The lowest of the low.
JOE: (Holding out hand.) Joe Pitt. I'm with Justice Wilson . . .   5
LOUIS: Oh, I know that. Counselor Pitt. Chief Clerk.
JOE: Were you . . . are you OK?
LOUIS: Oh, yeah. Thanks. What a nice man.
JOE: Not so nice.
LOUIS: What?   10
JOE: Not so nice. Nothing. You sure you're . . .
LOUIS: Life sucks shit. Life . . . just sucks shit.
JOE: What's wrong?
LOUIS: Run in my nylons.
JOE: Sorry . . . ?   15
LOUIS: Forget it. Look, thanks for asking.
JOE: Well . . .
LOUIS: I mean it really is nice of you.

(He starts crying again.)

    Sorry, sorry, sick friend . . .
JOE: Oh, I'm sorry.   20
LOUIS: Yeah, yeah, well, that's sweet.
    Three of your colleagues have preceded you to this bale-
ful sight and you're the first one to ask. The others just
opened the door, saw me, and fled. I hope they had to pee
real bad.   25

JOE: *(Handing him a wad of toilet paper.)* They just didn't want to intrude.

LOUIS: Hah. Reaganite heartless macho asshole lawyers.

JOE: Oh, that's unfair.

30 LOUIS: What is? Heartless? Macho? Reaganite? Lawyer?

JOE: I voted for Reagan.

LOUIS: You did?

JOE: Twice.

LOUIS: Twice? Well, oh boy. A Gay Republican.

35 JOE: Excuse me?

LOUIS: Nothing.

JOE: I'm not . . .
Forget it.

LOUIS: Republican? Not Republican? Or . . .

40 JOE: What?

LOUIS: What?

JOE: Not gay. I'm not gay.

LOUIS: Oh. Sorry. *(Blows his nose loudly.)* It's just . . .

JOE: Yes?

45 LOUIS: Well, sometimes you can tell from the way a person sounds that . . . I mean you *sound* like a . . .

JOE: No I don't. Like what?

LOUIS: Like a Republican.

(Little pause. JOE *knows he's being teased;* LOUIS *knows he knows.* JOE *decides to be a little brave.)*

JOE: *(Making sure no one else is around.)* Do I? Sound like a . . . ?

50 LOUIS: What? Like a . . . ? Republican, or . . . ? Do *I?*

JOE: Do you what?

LOUIS: Sound like a . . . ?

JOE: Like a . . . ?
I'm confused.

55 LOUIS: Yes.
My name is Louis. But all my friends call me Louise. I work in Word Processing. Thanks for the toilet paper.

*(*LOUIS *offers* JOE *his hand,* JOE *reaches,* LOUIS *feints and pecks* JOE *on the cheek, then exits.)*

SCENE VII

A week later. Mutual dream scene. PRIOR *is at a fantastic makeup table, having a dream, applying the face.* HARPER *is having a pill-induced hallucination. She has these from time to time. For some reason,* PRIOR *has appeared in this one. Or* HARPER *has appeared in* PRIOR*'s dream. It is bewildering.*

PRIOR: *(Alone, putting on makeup, then examining the results in the mirror; to the audience.)* "I'm ready for my closeup, Mr. DeMille."
5 One wants to move through life with elegance and grace, blossoming infrequently but with exquisite taste, and perfect timing, like a rare bloom, a zebra orchid. . . . One wants. . . . But one so seldom gets what one wants, does one? No. One does not. One gets fucked. Over. One . . . dies at thirty, robbed of . . . decades of majesty.
10 Fuck this shit. Fuck this shit.

(He almost crumbles; he pulls himself together; he studies his handiwork in the mirror.)

I look like a corpse. A corpsette. Oh my queen; you know you've hit rock-bottom when even drag is a drag.

*(*HARPER *appears.)*

HARPER: Are you. . . . Who are you?

PRIOR: Who are you?

HARPER: What are you doing in my hallucination?   15

PRIOR: I'm not in your hallucination. You're in my dream.

HARPER: You're wearing makeup.

PRIOR: So are you.

HARPER: But you're a man.

PRIOR: *(Feigning dismay, shock, he mimes slashing his throat with* 20 *his lipstick and dies, fabulously tragic. Then.)* The hands and feet give it away.

HARPER: There must be some mistake here. I don't recognize you. You're not. . . . Are you my . . . some sort of imaginary friend?   25

PRIOR: No. Aren't you too old to have imaginary friends?

HARPER: I have emotional problems. I took too many pills. Why are you wearing makeup?

PRIOR: I was in the process of applying the face, trying to make myself feel better—I swiped the new fall colors at the 30 Clinique counter at Macy's. *(Showing her.)*

HARPER: You stole these?

PRIOR: I was out of cash; it was an emotional emergency!

HARPER: Joe will be so angry. I promised him. No more pills.

PRIOR: These pills you keep alluding to?   35

HARPER: Valium. I take Valium. Lots of Valium.

PRIOR: And you're dancing as fast as you can.

HARPER: I'm not *addicted.* I don't believe in addiction, and I never . . . well, I *never* drink. And I *never* take drugs.

PRIOR: Well, smell *you,* Nancy Drew.   40

HARPER: Except Valium.

PRIOR: Except Valium; in wee fistfuls.

HARPER: It's terrible. Mormons are not supposed to be addicted to anything. I'm a Mormon.

PRIOR: I'm a homosexual.   45

HARPER: Oh! In my church we don't believe in homosexuals.

PRIOR: In my church we don't believe in Mormons.

HARPER: What church do . . . oh! *(She laughs.)* I get it.
I don't understand this. If I didn't ever see you before and I don't think I did then I don't think you should be 50 here, in this hallucination, because in my experience the mind, which is where hallucinations come from, shouldn't be able to make up anything that wasn't there to start with, that didn't enter it from experience, from the real world. Imagination can't create anything new, can it? It only recy- 55 cles bits and pieces from the world and reassembles them into visions. . . . Am I making sense right now?

PRIOR: Given the circumstances, yes.

HARPER: So when we think we've escaped the unbearable ordinariness and, well, untruthfulness of our lives, it's really 60 only the same old ordinariness and falseness rearranged into the appearance of novelty and truth. Nothing unknown is knowable. Don't you think it's depressing?

PRIOR: The limitations of the imagination?

HARPER: Yes.   65

PRIOR: It's something you learn after your second theme party: It's All Been Done Before.

HARPER: The world. Finite. Terribly, terribly. . . . Well . . . This is the most depressing hallucination I've ever had.

70 PRIOR: Apologies. I do try to be amusing.

HARPER: Oh, well, don't apologize, you. . . . I can't expect someone who's really sick to entertain me.

PRIOR: How on earth did you know . . .

HARPER: Oh that happens. This is the very threshhold of reve-
75   lation sometimes. You can see things . . . how sick you are. Do you see anything about me?

PRIOR: Yes.

HARPER: What?

PRIOR: You are amazingly unhappy.

80 HARPER: Oh big deal. You meet a Valium addict and you fig-
ure out she's unhappy. That doesn't count. Of course I. . . . Something else. Something surprising.

PRIOR: Something surprising.

HARPER: Yes.

85 PRIOR: Your husband's a homo.

(Pause.)

HARPER: Oh, ridiculous.

(Pause, then very quietly.)

    Really?

PRIOR: *(Shrugs.)* Threshhold of revelation.

HARPER: Well I don't like your revelations. I don't think you
90   intuit well at all. Joe's a very normal man, he . . .
        Oh God. Oh God. He. . . . Do homos take, like, lots of long walks?

PRIOR: Yes. We do. In stretch pants with lavender coifs. I just looked at you, and there was . . .

95 HARPER: A sort of blue streak of recognition.

PRIOR: Yes.

HARPER: Like you knew me incredibly well.

PRIOR: Yes.

HARPER: Yes.
100   I have to go now, get back, something just . . . fell apart. Oh God, I feel so sad . . .

PRIOR: I . . . I'm sorry. I usually say, "Fuck the truth," but mostly, the truth fucks you.

HARPER: I see something else about you . . .

105 PRIOR: Oh?

HARPER: Deep inside you, there's a part of you, the most inner part, entirely free of disease. I can see that.

PRIOR: Is that. . . . That isn't true.

HARPER: Threshhold of revelation.
110   Home . . .

(She vanishes.)

PRIOR: People come and go so quickly here . . .
        (To himself in the mirror.) I don't think there's any unin-
fected part of me. My heart is pumping polluted blood. I feel dirty.

(He begins to wipe makeup off with his hands, smearing it around. A large gray feather falls from up above. PRIOR stops smearing the makeup and looks at the feather. He goes to it and picks it up.)

115 THE VOICE: *(It is an incredibly beautiful voice.)* Look up!

PRIOR: *(Looking up, not seeing anyone.)* Hello?

THE VOICE: Look up!

PRIOR: Who is that?

THE VOICE: Prepare the way!

PRIOR: I don't see any . . .   120

(There is a dramatic change in lighting, from above.)

A VOICE: Look up, look up,
    prepare the way
    the infinite descent
    A breath in air
    floating down   125
    Glory to . . .

(Silence.)

PRIOR: Hello? Is that it? Helloooo!
        What the fuck . . . ? *(He holds himself.)*
        Poor me. Poor poor me. Why me? Why poor poor me?
        Oh I don't feel good right now. I really don't.   130

SCENE VIII

That night. Split scene: HARPER *and* JOE *at home;* PRIOR *and* LOUIS *in bed.*

HARPER: Where were you?

JOE: Out.

HARPER: Where?

JOE: Just out. Thinking.

HARPER: It's late.   5

JOE: I had a lot to think about.

HARPER: I burned dinner.

JOE: Sorry.

HARPER: Not my dinner. My dinner was fine. Your dinner. I put it back in the oven and turned everything up as high as   10
it could go and I watched till it burned black. It's still hot. Very hot. Want it?

JOE: You didn't have to do that.

HARPER: I know. It just seemed like the kind of thing a mentally deranged sex-starved pill-popping housewife would do.   15

JOE: Uh huh.

HARPER: So I did it. Who knows anymore what I have to do?

JOE: How many pills?

HARPER: A bunch. Don't change the subject.

JOE: I won't talk to you when you . . .   20

HARPER: No. No. Don't do that! I'm . . . fine, pills are not the problem, not our problem, I WANT TO KNOW WHERE YOU'VE BEEN! I WANT TO KNOW WHAT'S GOING ON!

JOE: Going on with what? The job?   25

HARPER: Not the job.

JOE: I said I need more time.

HARPER: Not the job!

JOE: Mr. Cohn, I talked to him on the phone, he said I had to hurry . . .   30

HARPER: Not the . . .

JOE: But I can't get you to talk sensibly about anything so . . .

HARPER: SHUT UP!

JOE: Then what?

35   HARPER: Stick to the subject.
     JOE: I don't know what that is. You have something you want
          to ask me? Ask me. Go.
     HARPER: I . . . can't. I'm scared of you.
     JOE: I'm tired, I'm going to bed.
40   HARPER: Tell me without making me ask. Please.
     JOE: This is crazy, I'm not . . .
     HARPER: When you come through the door at night your face
          is never exactly the way I remembered it. I get surprised by
          something . . . mean and hard about the way you look. Even
45   the weight of you in the bed at night, the way you breathe
          in your sleep seems unfamiliar.
          You terrify me.
     JOE: (Cold.) I know who you are.
     HARPER: Yes. I'm the enemy. That's easy. That doesn't change.
50   You think you're the only one who hates sex; I do; I hate it
          with you; I do. I dream that you batter away at me till all
          my joints come apart, like wax, and I fall into pieces. It's
          like a punishment. It was wrong of me to marry you. I knew
          you . . . (She stops herself.) It's a sin, and it's killing us both.
55   JOE: I can always tell when you've taken pills because it makes
          you red-faced and sweaty and frankly that's very often why
          I don't want to . . .
     HARPER: Because . . .
     JOE: Well, you aren't pretty. Not like this.
60   HARPER: I have something to ask you.
     JOE: Then ASK! ASK! What in hell are you . . .
     HARPER: Are you a homo?

     (Pause.)

     Are you? If you try to walk out right now I'll put your din-
65   ner back in the oven and turn it up so high the whole build-
     ing will fill with smoke and everyone in it will asphyxiate.
     So help me God I will.
          Now answer the question.
     JOE: What if I . . .

     (Small pause.)

     HARPER: Then tell me, please. And we'll see.
70   JOE: No. I'm not.
          I don't see what difference it makes.

     LOUIS: Jews don't have any clear textual guide to the afterlife;
          even that it exists. I don't think much about it. I see it as a
          perpetual rainy Thursday afternoon in March. Dead leaves.
75   PRIOR: Eeeugh. Very Greco-Roman.
     LOUIS: Well for us it's not the verdict that counts, it's the act of
          judgment. That's why I could never be a lawyer. In court all
          that matters is the verdict.
     PRIOR: You could never be a lawyer because you are oversexed.
80   You're too distracted.
     LOUIS: Not distracted, abstracted. I'm trying to make a point:
     PRIOR: Namely:
     LOUIS: It's the judge in his or her chambers, weighing, books
          open, pondering the evidence, ranging freely over cate-
85   gories: good, evil, innocent, guilty; the judge in the cham-
          ber of circumspection, not the judge on the bench with the
          gavel. The shaping of the law, not its execution.
     PRIOR: The point, dear, the point . . .

     LOUIS: That it should be the questions and shape of a life, its
          total complexity gathered, arranged and considered, which   90
          matters in the end, not some stamp of salvation or damna-
          tion which disperses all the complexity in some unsatisfy-
          ing little decision—the balancing of the scales . . .
     PRIOR: I like this; very zen; it's . . . reassuringly incomprehen-
          sible and useless. We who are about to die thank you.   95
     LOUIS: You are not about to die.
     PRIOR: It's not going well, really . . . two new lesions. My leg
          hurts. There's protein in my urine, the doctor says, but who
          knows what the fuck that portends. Anyway it shouldn't be
          there, the protein. My butt is chapped from diarrhea and   100
          yesterday I shat blood.
     LOUIS: I really hate this. You don't tell me . . .
     PRIOR: You get too upset, I wind up comforting you. It's
          easier . . .
     LOUIS: Oh thanks.   105
     PRIOR: If it's bad I'll tell you.
     LOUIS: Shitting blood sounds bad to me.
     PRIOR: And I'm telling you.
     LOUIS: And I'm handling it.
     PRIOR: Tell me some more about justice.   110
     LOUIS: I am not handling it.
     PRIOR: Well Louis you win Trooper of the Month.

     (LOUIS starts to cry.)

     PRIOR: I take it back. You aren't Trooper of the Month.
          This isn't working . . .
          Tell me some more about justice.   115
     LOUIS: You are not about to die.
     PRIOR: Justice . . .
     LOUIS: . . . is an immensity, a confusing vastness. Justice is
          God. Prior?
     PRIOR: Hmmm?   120
     LOUIS: You love me.
     PRIOR: Yes.
     LOUIS: What if I walked out on this?
          Would you hate me forever?

     (PRIOR kisses LOUIS on the forehead.)

     PRIOR: Yes.   125

     JOE: I think we ought to pray. Ask God for help. Ask him
          together . . .
     HARPER: God won't talk to me. I have to make up people to
          talk to me.
     JOE: You have to keep asking.   130
     HARPER: I forgot the question.
          Oh yeah. God, is my husband a . . .
     JOE: (Scary.) Stop it. Stop it. I'm warning you.
          Does it make any difference? That I might be one thing
          deep within, no matter how wrong or ugly that thing is, so   135
          long as I have fought, with everything I have, to kill it.
          What do you want from me? What do you want from me,
          Harper? More than that? For God's sake, there's nothing
          left, I'm a shell. There's nothing left to kill.
          As long as my behavior is what I know it has to be.   140
     Decent. Correct. That alone in the eyes of God.

HARPER: No, no, not that, that's Utah talk, Mormon talk, I hate it, Joe, tell me, say it . . .

JOE: All I will say is that I am a very good man who has worked very hard to become good and you want to destroy that. You want to destroy me, but I am not going to let you do that.

(Pause.)

HARPER: I'm going to have a baby.

JOE: Liar.

HARPER: You liar.

A baby born addicted to pills. A baby who does not dream but who hallucinates, who stares up at us with big mirror eyes and who does not know who we are.

(Pause.)

JOE: Are you really . . .

HARPER: No. Yes. No. Yes. Get away from me.

Now we both have a secret.

PRIOR: One of my ancestors was a ship's captain who made money bringing whale oil to Europe and returning with immigrants—Irish mostly, packed in tight, so many dollars per head. The last ship he captained foundered off the coast of Nova Scotia in a winter tempest and sank to the bottom. He went down with the ship—la Grande Geste—but his crew took seventy women and kids in the ship's only long-boat, this big, open rowboat, and when the weather got too rough, and they thought the boat was overcrowded, the crew started lifting people up and hurling them into the sea. Until they got the ballast right. They walked up and down the longboat, eyes to the waterline, and when the boat rode low in the water they'd grab the nearest passenger and throw them into the sea. The boat was leaky, see; seventy people; they arrived in Halifax with nine people on board.

LOUIS: Jesus.

PRIOR: I think about that story a lot now. People in a boat, waiting, terrified, while implacable, unsmiling men, irresistibly strong, seize . . . maybe the person next to you, maybe you, and with no warning at all, with time only for a quick intake of air you are pitched into freezing, turbulent water and salt and darkness to drown.

I like your cosmology, baby. While time is running out I find myself drawn to anything that's suspended, that lacks an ending—but it seems to me that it lets you off scot-free.

LOUIS: What do you mean?

PRIOR: No judgment, no guilt or responsibility.

LOUIS: For me.

PRIOR: For anyone. It was an editorial "you."

LOUIS: Please get better. Please.

Please don't get any sicker.

SCENE IX

Third week in November. ROY *and* HENRY, *his doctor, in* HENRY's *office.*

HENRY: Nobody knows what causes it. And nobody knows how to cure it. The best theory is that we blame a retrovirus, the Human Immunodeficiency Virus. Its presence is made known to us by the useless antibodies which appear in reaction to its entrance into the bloodstream through a cut, or an orifice. The antibodies are powerless to protect the body against it. Why, we don't know. The body's immune system ceases to function. Sometimes the body even attacks itself. At any rate it's left open to a whole horror house of infections from microbes which it usually defends against.

Like Kaposi's sarcomas. These lesions. Or your throat problem. Or the glands.

We think it may also be able to slip past the blood-brain barrier into the brain. Which is of course very bad news. And it's fatal in we don't know what percent of people with suppressed immune responses.

(Pause)

ROY: This is very interesting, Mr. Wizard, but why the fuck are you telling me this?

(Pause.)

HENRY: Well, I have just removed one of three lesions which biopsy results will probably tell us is a Kaposi's sarcoma lesion. And you have a pronounced swelling of glands in your neck, groin, and armpits—lymphadenopathy is another sign. And you have oral candidiasis and maybe a little more fungus under the fingernails of two digits on your right hand. So that's why . . .

ROY: This disease . . .

HENRY: Syndrome.

ROY: Whatever. It afflicts mostly homosexuals and drug addicts.

HENRY: Mostly. Hemophiliacs are also at risk.

ROY: Homosexuals and drug addicts. So why are you implying that I . . .

(Pause.)

What are you implying, Henry?

HENRY: I don't . . .

ROY: I'm not a drug addict.

HENRY: Oh come on Roy.

ROY: What, what, come on Roy what? Do you think I'm a junkie, Henry, do you see tracks?

HENRY: This is absurd.

ROY: Say it.

HENRY: Say what?

ROY: Say, "Roy Cohn, you are a . . . "

HENRY: Roy.

ROY: "You are a . . . ." Go on. Not "Roy Cohn you are a drug fiend." "Roy Marcus Cohn, you are a . . . "

Go on, Henry, it starts with an "H."

HENRY: Oh I'm not going to . . .

ROY: *With an "H,"* Henry, and it isn't "Hemophiliac." Come on . . .

HENRY: What are you doing, Roy?

ROY: No, say it. I mean it. Say: "Roy Cohn, you are a homosexual."

(Pause.)

And I will proceed, systemically, to destroy your reputation and your practice and your career in New York State, Henry. Which you know I can do.

(Pause.)

55　HENRY: Roy, you have been seeing me since 1958. Apart from the facelifts I have treated you for everything from syphilis . . .

ROY: From a whore in Dallas.

HENRY: From syphilis to venereal warts. In your rectum. Which you may have gotten from a whore in Dallas, but it
60　wasn't a female whore.

(Pause.)

ROY: So say it.

HENRY: Roy Cohn, you are . . .

　　You have had sex with men, many many times, Roy, and one of them, or any number of them, has made you very
65　sick. You have AIDS.

ROY: AIDS.

　　Your problem, Henry, is that you are hung up on words, on labels, that you believe they mean what they seem to mean. AIDS. Homosexual. Gay. Lesbian. You think these
70　are names that tell you who someone sleeps with, but they don't tell you that.

HENRY: No?

ROY: No. Like all labels they tell you one thing and one thing only: where does an individual so identified fit in the food
75　chain, in the pecking order? Not ideology, or sexual taste, but something much simpler: clout. Not who I fuck or who fucks me, but who will pick up the phone when I call, who owes me favors. This is what a label refers to. Now to someone who does not understand this, homosexual is what I am
80　because I have sex with men. But really this is wrong. Homosexuals are not men who sleep with other men. Homosexuals are men who in fifteen years of trying cannot get a pissant antidiscrimination bill through City Council. Homosexuals are men who know nobody and who nobody knows.
85　Who have zero clout. Does this sound like me, Henry?

HENRY: No.

ROY: No. I have clout. A lot. I can pick up this phone, punch fifteen numbers, and you know who will be on the other end in under five minutes, Henry?

90　HENRY: The President.

ROY: Even better, Henry. His wife.

HENRY: I'm impressed.

ROY: I don't want you to be impressed. I want you to understand. This is not sophistry. And this is not hypocrisy. This
95　is reality. I have sex with men. But unlike nearly every other man of whom this is true, I bring the guy I'm screwing to the White House and President Reagan smiles at us and shakes his hand. Because *what* I am is defined entirely by *who* I am. Roy Cohn is not a homosexual. Roy Cohn is a
100　heterosexual man, Henry, who fucks around with guys.

HENRY: OK, Roy.

ROY: And what is my diagnosis, Henry?

HENRY: You have AIDS, Roy.

ROY: No, Henry, no. AIDS is what homosexuals have. I have
105　liver cancer.

(Pause.)

HENRY: Well, whatever the fuck you have, Roy, it's very serious, and I haven't got a damn thing for you. The NIH in Bethesda has a new drug called AZT with a two-year

waiting list that not even I can get you onto. So get on the phone, Roy, and dial the fifteen numbers, and tell the First　110 Lady you need in on an experimental treatment for liver cancer, because you can call it any damn thing you want, Roy, but what it boils down to is very bad news.

────── ACT TWO ──────

IN VITRO
DECEMBER 1985–JANUARY 1986

SCENE I

Night, the third week in December. PRIOR *alone on the floor of his bedroom; he is much worse.*

PRIOR: Louis, Louis, please wake up, oh God.

*(*LOUIS *runs in.)*

PRIOR: I think something horrible is wrong with me I can't breathe . . .

LOUIS: *(Starting to exit.)* I'm calling the ambulance.

PRIOR: No, wait, I . . .　　　　　　　　　　　　　　　　　5

LOUIS: *Wait?* Are you fucking crazy? Oh God you're on fire, your head is on fire.

PRIOR: It hurts, it hurts . . .

LOUIS: I'm calling the ambulance.

PRIOR: I don't want to go to the hospital, I don't want to go to　10 the hospital please let me lie here, just . . .

LOUIS: No, no, God, Prior, stand up . . .

PRIOR: DON'T TOUCH MY LEG!

LOUIS: We have to . . . oh God this is so crazy.

PRIOR: I'll be OK if I just lie here Lou, really, if I can only sleep　15 a little . . .

*(*LOUIS *exits.)*

PRIOR: Louis?

　　NO! NO! Don't call, you'll send me there and I won't come back, please, please Louis I'm begging, baby, please . . . *(Screams.)* LOUIS!!　　　　　　　　　　　　　　　20

LOUIS: *(From off; hysterical.)* WILL YOU SHUT THE FUCK UP!

PRIOR: *(Trying to stand.)* Aaaah. I have . . . to go to the bathroom. Wait. Wait, just . . . oh. Oh God. *(He shits himself.)*

LOUIS: *(Entering.)* Prior? They'll be here in . . . Oh my God.　25

PRIOR: I'm sorry, I'm sorry.

LOUIS: What did . . . ? What?

PRIOR: I had an accident.

*(*LOUIS *goes to him.)*

LOUIS: This is blood.

PRIOR: Maybe you shouldn't touch it . . . me. . . . I . . . *(He*　30 *faints.)*

LOUIS: *(Quietly.)* Oh help. Oh help. Oh God oh God oh God help me I can't I can't I can't.

SCENE II

Same night. HARPER *is sitting at home, all alone, with no lights on. We can barely see her.* JOE *enters, but he doesn't turn on the lights.*

JOE: Why are you sitting in the dark? Turn on the light.

HARPER: *No.* I heard the sounds in the bedroom again. I know someone was in there.

JOE: No one was.

HARPER: Maybe actually in the bed, under the covers with a knife.

Oh, boy. Joe. I, um, I'm thinking of going away. By which I mean: I think I'm going off again. You . . . you know what I mean?

JOE: Please don't. Stay. We can fix it. I pray for that. This is my fault, but I can correct it. You have to try too . . .

(He turns on the light. She turns it off again.)

HARPER: When you pray, what do you pray for?

JOE: I pray for God to crush me, break me up into little pieces and start all over again.

HARPER: Oh. Please. Don't pray for that.

JOE: I had a book of Bible stories when I was a kid. There was a picture I'd look at twenty times every day: Jacob wrestles with the angel. I don't really remember the story, or why the wrestling—just the picture. Jacob is young and very strong. The angel is . . . a beautiful man, with golden hair and wings, of course. I still dream about it. Many nights. I'm. . . . It's me. In that struggle. Fierce, and unfair. The angel is not human, and it holds nothing back, so how could anyone human win, what kind of a fight is that? It's not just. Losing means your soul thrown down in the dust, your heart torn out from God's. But you can't not lose.

HARPER: In the whole entire world, you are the only person, the only person I love or have ever loved. And I love you terribly. Terribly. That's what's so awfully, irreducibly real. I can make up anything but I can't dream that away.

JOE: Are you . . . are you really going to have a baby?

HARPER: It's my time and there's no blood. I don't really know. I suppose it wouldn't be a great thing. Maybe I'm just not bleeding because I take too many pills. Maybe I'll give birth to a pill. That would give a new meaning to pill-popping, huh?

I think you should go to Washington. Alone. Change, like you said.

JOE: I'm not going to leave you, Harper.

HARPER: Well maybe not. But I'm going to leave you.

SCENE III

One a.m., the next morning. LOUIS *and a nurse,* EMILY, *are sitting in* PRIOR's *room in the hospital.*

EMILY: He'll be all right now.

LOUIS: No he won't.

EMILY: No. I guess not. I gave him something that makes him sleep.

LOUIS: Deep asleep?

EMILY: Orbiting the moons of Jupiter.

LOUIS: A good place to be.

EMILY: Anyplace better than here. You his . . . uh?

LOUIS: Yes. I'm his uh.

EMILY: This must be hell for you.

LOUIS: It is. Hell. The After Life. Which is not at all like a rainy afternoon in March, by the way, Prior. A lot more vivid than I'd expected. Dead leaves, but the crunchy kind. Sharp, dry air. The kind of long, luxurious dying feeling that breaks your heart.

EMILY: Yeah, well we all get to break our hearts on this one. He seems like a nice guy. Cute.

LOUIS: Not like this.

Yes, he is. Was. Whatever.

EMILY: Weird name. Prior Walter. Like, "The Walter before this one."

LOUIS: Lots of Walters before this one. Prior is an old old family name in an old old family. The Walters go back to the Mayflower and beyond. Back to the Norman Conquest. He says there's a Prior Walter stitched into the Bayeux tapestry.

EMILY: Is that impressive?

LOUIS: Well, it's old. Very old. Which in some circles equals impressive.

EMILY: Not in my circle. What's the name of the tapestry?

LOUIS: The Bayeux tapestry. Embroidered by La Reine Mathilde.

EMILY: I'll tell my mother. She embroiders. Drives me nuts.

LOUIS: Manual therapy for anxious hands.

EMILY: Maybe you should try it.

LOUIS: Mathilde stitched while William the Conqueror was off to war. She was capable of . . . more than loyalty. Devotion. She waited for him, she stitched for years. And if he had come back broken and defeated from war, she would have loved him even more. And if he had returned mutilated, ugly, full of infection and horror, she would still have loved him; fed by pity, by a sharing of pain, she would love him even more, and even more, and she would never, never have prayed to God, please let him die if he can't return to me whole and healthy and able to live a normal life. . . . If he had died, she would have buried her heart with him.

So what the fuck is the matter with me?

(Little pause.)

Will he sleep through the night?

EMILY: At least.

LOUIS: I'm going.

EMILY: It's one A.M. Where do you have to go at . . .

LOUIS: I know what time it is. A walk. Night air, good for the. . . . The park.

EMILY: Be careful.

LOUIS: Yeah. Danger.

Tell him, if he wakes up and you're still on, tell him goodbye, tell him I had to go.

SCENE IV

An hour later. Split scene: JOE *and* ROY *in a fancy (straight) bar;* LOUIS *and a* MAN *in the Rambles in Central Park.* JOE *and* ROY *are sitting at the bar; the place is brightly lit.* JOE *has a plate of food in front of him but he isn't eating.* ROY *occasionally reaches over the table and forks small bites off* JOE's *plate.* ROY *is drinking heavily,* JOE *not at all.* LOUIS *and the* MAN *are eyeing each other, each alternating interest and indifference.*

JOE: The pills were something she started when she miscarried or . . . no, she took some before that. She had a really bad time at home, when she was a kid, her home was really bad. I think a lot of drinking and physical stuff. She doesn't talk about that, instead she talks about . . . the sky falling down, people with knives hiding under sofas. Monsters. Mormons.

Everyone thinks Mormons don't come from homes like that, we aren't supposed to behave that way, but we do. It's not lying, or being two-faced. Everyone tries very hard to
10   live up to God's strictures, which are very . . . um . . .

ROY: Strict.

JOE: I shouldn't be bothering you with this.

ROY: No, please. Heart to heart. Want another. . . . What is that, seltzer?

15 JOE: The failure to measure up hits people very hard. From such a strong desire to be good they feel very far from goodness when they fail.

    What scares me is that maybe what I really love in her is the part of her that's farthest from the light, from God's
20   love; maybe I was drawn to that in the first place. And I'm keeping it alive because I need it.

ROY: Why would you need it?

JOE: There are things. . . . I don't know how well we know ourselves. I mean, what if? I know I married her because she . . .
25   because I loved it that she was always wrong, always doing something wrong, like one step out of step. In Salt Lake City that stands out. I never stood out, on the outside, but inside, it was hard for me. To pass.

ROY: Pass?

30 JOE: Yeah.

ROY: Pass as what?

JOE: Oh. Well. . . . As someone cheerful and strong. Those who love God with an open heart unclouded by secrets and struggles are cheerful; God's easy simple love for them
35   shows in how strong and happy they are. The saints.

ROY: But you had secrets? Secret struggles . . .

JOE: I wanted to be one of the elect, one of the Blessed. You feel you ought to be, that the blemishes are yours by choice, which of course they aren't. Harper's sorrow, that really
40   deep sorrow, she didn't choose that. But it's there.

ROY: You didn't put it there.

JOE: No.

ROY: You sound like you think you did.

JOE: I am responsible for her.

45 ROY: Because she's your wife.

JOE: That. And I do love her.

ROY: Whatever. She's your wife. And so there are obligations. To her. But also to yourself.

JOE: She'd fall apart in Washington.

50 ROY: Then let her stay here.

JOE: She'll fall apart if I leave her.

ROY: Then bring her to Washington.

JOE: I just can't, Roy. She needs me.

ROY: Listen, Joe. I'm the best divorce lawyer in the business.

(Little pause.)

55 JOE: Can't Washington wait?

ROY: You do what you need to do, Joe. What *you* need. *You.* Let her life go where it wants to go. You'll both be better for that. *Somebody* should get what they want.

MAN: What do you want?

60 LOUIS: I want you to fuck me, hurt me, make me bleed.

MAN: I want to.

LOUIS: Yeah?

MAN: I want to hurt you.

LOUIS: Fuck me.

MAN: Yeah?   65

LOUIS: Hard.

MAN: Yeah? You been a bad boy?

(Pause. LOUIS *laughs, softly.)*

LOUIS: Very bad. Very bad.

MAN: You need to be punished, boy?

LOUIS: Yes. I do.   70

MAN: Yes what?

(Little pause.)

LOUIS: Um, I . . .

MAN: Yes *what,* boy?

LOUIS: Oh. Yes sir.

MAN: I want you to take me to your place, boy.   75

LOUIS: No, I can't do that.

MAN: No *what?*

LOUIS: No sir, I can't, I . . .
    I don't live alone, sir.

MAN: Your lover know you're out with a man tonight, boy?   80

LOUIS: No sir, he . . .
    My lover doesn't know.

MAN: Your lover know you . . .

LOUIS: Let's change the subject, OK? Can we go to your place?

MAN: I live with my parents.   85

LOUIS: Oh.

ROY: Everyone who makes it in this world makes it because somebody older and more powerful takes an interest. The most precious asset in life, I think, is the ability to be a good son. You have that, Joe. Somebody who can be a good   90
son to a father who pushes them farther than they would otherwise go. I've had many fathers, I owe my life to them, powerful, powerful men. Walter Winchell, Edgar Hoover. Joe McCarthy most of all. He valued me because I am a good lawyer, but he loved me because I was and am a good   95
son. He was a very difficult man, very guarded and cagey; I brought out something tender in him. He would have died for me. And me for him. Does this embarrass you?

JOE: I had a hard time with my father.

ROY: Well sometimes that's the way. Then you have to find   100
other fathers, substitutes, I don't know. The father-son relationship is central to life. Women are for birth, beginning, but the father is continuance. The son offers the father his life as a vessel for carrying forth his father's dream. Your father's living?   105

JOE: Um, dead.

ROY: He was . . . what? A difficult man?

JOE: He was in the military. He could be very unfair. And cold.

ROY: But he loved you.

JOE: I don't know.   110

ROY: No, no, Joe, he did, I know this. Sometimes a father's love has to be very, very hard, unfair even, cold to make his son grow strong in a world like this. This isn't a good world.

MAN: Here, then.

LOUIS: I. . . . Do you have a rubber?   115

MAN: I don't use rubbers.

LOUIS: You should. (*He takes one from his coat pocket.*) Here.

MAN: I don't use them.

LOUIS: Forget it, then. (*He starts to leave.*)

120 MAN: No, wait.

Put it on me. Boy.

LOUIS: Forget it, I have to get back. Home. I must be going crazy.

MAN: Oh come on please he won't find out.

LOUIS: It's cold. Too cold.

125 MAN: It's never too cold, let me warm you up. Please?

(*They begin to fuck.*)

MAN: Relax.

LOUIS: (*A small laugh.*) Not a chance.

MAN: It . . .

LOUIS: What?

130 MAN: I think it broke. The rubber. You want me to keep going?
(*Little pause.*) Pull out? Should I . . .

LOUIS: Keep going.

Infect me.

I don't care. I don't care.

(*Pause. The* MAN *pulls out.*)

135 MAN: I . . . um, look, I'm sorry, but I think I want to go.

LOUIS: Yeah.

Give my best to mom and dad.

(*The* MAN *slaps him.*)

LOUIS: Ow!

(*They stare at each other.*)

LOUIS: It was a joke.

(*The* MAN *leaves.*)

140 ROY: How long have we known each other?

JOE: Since 1980.

ROY: Right. A long time. I feel close to you, Joe. Do I advise
you well?

JOE: You've been an incredible friend, Roy, I . . .

145 ROY: I want to be family. Familia, as my Italian friends call it.
La Familia. A lovely word. It's important for me to help
you, like I was helped.

JOE: I owe practically everything to you, Roy.

ROY: I'm dying, Joe. Cancer.

150 JOE: Oh my God.

ROY: Please. Let me finish.

Few people know this and I'm telling you this only
because. . . . I'm not afraid of death. What can death bring
that I haven't faced? I've lived; life is the worst. (*Gently*
155 *mocking himself.*) Listen to me, I'm a philosopher.

Joe. You must do this. You must must must. Love; that's
a trap. Responsibility; that's a trap too. Like a father to a
son I tell you this: Life is full of horror; nobody escapes,
nobody; save yourself. Whatever pulls on you, whatever
160 needs from you, threatens you. Don't be afraid; people are
so afraid; don't be afraid to live in the raw wind, naked,
alone. . . . Learn at least this: What you are capable of. Let
nothing stand in your way.

SCENE V

Three days later. PRIOR *and* BELIZE *in* PRIOR'*s hospital room.* PRIOR
is very sick but improving. BELIZE *has just arrived.*

PRIOR: Miss Thing.

BELIZE: Ma cherie bichette.

PRIOR: Stella.

BELIZE: Stella for star. Let me see. (*Scrutinizing* PRIOR.) You look
like shit, why yes indeed you do, comme la merde!   5

PRIOR: Merci.

BELIZE: (*Taking little plastic bottles from his bag, handing them to*
PRIOR.) Not to despair, Belle Reeve. Lookie! Magic goop!

PRIOR: (*Opening a bottle, sniffing.*) Pooh! What kinda crap is that?

BELIZE: Beats me. Let's rub it on your poor blistered body and   10
see what it does.

PRIOR: This is not Western medicine, these bottles . . .

BELIZE: Voodoo cream. From the botanica 'round the block.

PRIOR: And you a registered nurse.

BELIZE: (*Sniffing it.*) Beeswax and cheap perfume. Cut with Jer-   15
gen's Lotion. Full of good vibes and love from some little
black Cubana witch in Miami.

PRIOR: Get that trash away from me. I am immune-suppressed.

BELIZE: I *am* a health professional. I *know* what I'm doing.

PRIOR: It stinks. Any word from Louis?   20

(*Pause.* BELIZE *starts giving* PRIOR *a gentle massage.*)

PRIOR: Gone.

BELIZE: He'll be back. I know the type. Likes to keep a girl on
edge.

PRIOR: It's been . . .

(*Pause*)

BELIZE: (*Trying to jog his memory.*) How long?   25

PRIOR: I don't remember.

BELIZE: How long have you been here?

PRIOR: (*Getting suddenly upset.*) I don't remember, I don't give a
fuck. I want Louis. I want my fucking boyfriend, where the
fuck is he? I'm dying, I'm dying, where's Louis?   30

BELIZE: Shhhh, shhh . . .

PRIOR: This is a very strange drug, this drug. Emotional labil-
ity, for starters.

BELIZE: Save a tab or two for me.

PRIOR: Oh no, not this drug, ce n'est pas pour la joyeux noël et   35
la bonne année, this drug she is serious poisonous chem-
istry, ma pauvre bichette.

And not just disorienting. I hear things. Voices.

BELIZE: Voices.

PRIOR: A voice.   40

BELIZE: Saying what?

(*Pause.*)

PRIOR: I'm not supposed to tell.

BELIZE: You better tell the doctor. Or I will.

PRIOR: No no don't. Please. I want the voice; it's wonderful. It's
all that's keeping me alive. I don't want to talk to some   45
intern about it.

You know what happens? When I hear it, I get hard.

BELIZE: Oh my.

PRIOR: Comme ça. (*He uses his arm to demonstrate.*) And you
50   know I am slow to rise.

BELIZE: My jaw aches at the memory.

PRIOR: And would you deny me this little solace—betray my
    concupiscence to Florence Nightingale's storm troopers?

BELIZE: Perish the thought, ma bébé.

55 PRIOR: They'd change the drug just to spoil the fun.

BELIZE: You and your boner can depend on me.

PRIOR: Je t'adore, ma belle nègre.

BELIZE: All this girl-talk shit is politically incorrect, you know.
    We should have dropped it back when we gave up drag.

60 PRIOR: I'm sick, I get to be politically incorrect if it makes me
    feel better. You sound like Lou.

(*Little pause.*)

    Well, at least I have the satisfaction of knowing he's in an-
    guish somewhere. I loved his anguish. Watching him stick
    his head up his asshole and eat his guts out over some rela-
65   tively minor moral conundrum—it was the best show in
    town. But Mother warned me; if they get overwhelmed by
    the little things . . .

BELIZE: They'll be belly-up bustville when something big
    comes along.

70 PRIOR: Mother warned me.

BELIZE: And they do come along.

PRIOR: But I didn't listen.

BELIZE: No. (*Doing Hepburn.*) Men are beasts.

PRIOR: (*Also Hepburn.*) The absolute lowest.

75 BELIZE: I have to go. If I want to spend my whole lonely life
    looking after white people I can get underpaid to do it.

PRIOR: You're just a Christian martyr.

BELIZE: Whatever happens, baby, I will be here for you.

PRIOR: Je t'aime.

80 BELIZE: Je t'aime. Don't go crazy on me, girlfriend, I already
    got enough crazy queens for one lifetime. For two. I can't be
    bothering with dementia.

PRIOR: I promise.

BELIZE: (*Touching him; softly.*) Ouch.

85 PRIOR: Ouch. Indeed.

BELIZE: Why'd they have to pick on you?
    And eat more, girlfriend, you really do look like shit.

(BELIZE *leaves.*)

PRIOR: (*After waiting a beat.*) He's gone.
    Are you still . . .

90 VOICE: I can't stay. I will return.

PRIOR: Are you one of those "Follow me to the other side" voices?

VOICE: No. I am no nightbird. I am a messenger . . .

PRIOR: You have a beautiful voice, it sounds . . . like a viola,
    like a perfectly tuned, tight string, balanced, the truth. . . .
95   Stay with me.

THE VOICE: Not now. Soon I will return, I will reveal myself to you;
    I am glorious, glorious; my heart, my countenance and my
    message. You must prepare.

PRIOR: For what? I don't want to . . .

100 THE VOICE: No death, no:
    A marvelous work and a wonder we undertake, an edifice
    awry we sink plumb and straighten, a great Lie we abolish,

a great error correct, with the rule, sword and broom of
Truth!

PRIOR: What are you talking about, I . . .   105

THE VOICE: I am on my way; when I am manifest, our Work begins;
    Prepare for the parting of the air,
    The breath, the ascent,
    Glory to . . .

SCENE VI

The second week of January. MARTIN, ROY *and* JOE *in a fancy Manhattan restaurant.*

MARTIN: It's a revolution in Washington, Joe. We have a new
    agenda and finally a real leader. They got back the Senate
    but we have the courts. By the nineties the Supreme Court
    will be block-solid Republican appointees, and the Federal
    bench—Republican judges like land mines, everywhere, 5
    everywhere they turn. Affirmative action? Take it to court.
    Boom! Land mine. And we'll get our way on just about
    everything: abortion, defense, Central America, family val-
    ues, a live investment climate. We have the White House
    locked till the year 2000. And beyond. A permanent fix on 10
    the Oval Office? It's possible. By '92 we'll get the Senate
    back, and in ten years the South is going to give us the
    House. It's really the end of Liberalism. The end of New
    Deal Socialism. The end of ipso facto secular humanism.
    The dawning of a genuinely American political personality. 15
    Modeled on Ronald Wilson Reagan.

JOE: It sounds great, Mr. Heller.

MARTIN: Martin. And Justice is the hub. Especially since Ed
    Meese took over. He doesn't specialize in Fine Points of
    the Law. He's a flatfoot, a cop. He reminds me of Teddy 20
    Roosevelt.

JOE: I can't wait to meet him.

MARTIN: Too bad, Joe, he's been dead for sixty years!

(*There is a little awkwardness.* JOE *doesn't respond.*)

MARTIN: Teddy Roosevelt. You said you wanted to. . . . Little
    joke. It reminds me of the story about the . . .   25

ROY: (*Smiling, but nasty.*) Aw shut the fuck up Martin.
    (*To* JOE.) You see that? Mr. Heller here is one of the
    mighty, Joseph, in D.C. he sitteth on the right hand of the
    man who sitteth on the right hand of The Man. And yet
    I can say "shut the fuck up" and he will take no offense. 30
    Loyalty. He . . . Martin?

MARTIN: Yes, Roy?

ROY: Rub my back.

MARTIN: Roy . . .

ROY: No no really, a sore spot, I get them all the time now, 35
    these. . . . Rub it for me darling, would you do that for me?

(MARTIN *rubs* ROY's *back. They both look at* JOE.)

ROY: (*To* JOE.) How do you think a handful of Bolsheviks
    turned St. Petersburg into Leningrad in one afternoon?
    Comrades. Who do for each other. Marx and Engels. Lenin
    and Trotsky. Josef Stalin and Franklin Delano Roosevelt. 40

(MARTIN *laughs.*)

ROY: *Comrades,* right Martin?

MARTIN: This man, Joe, is a Saint of the Right.

JOE: I know, Mr. Heller, I . . .

ROY: And you see what I mean, Martin? He's special, right?

45 MARTIN: Don't embarrass him, Roy.

ROY: Gravity, decency, smarts! His strength is as the strength of ten because his heart is pure! *And* he's a Royboy, one hundred percent.

MARTIN: We're on the move, Joe. On the move.

50 JOE: Mr. Heller, I . . .

MARTIN: *(Ending backrub.)* We can't wait any longer for an answer.

(Little pause.)

JOE: Oh. Um, I . . .

ROY: Joe's a married man, Martin.

MARTIN: Aha.

55 ROY: With a wife. She doesn't care to go to D.C., and so Joe cannot go. And keeps us dangling. We've seen that kind of thing before, haven't we? These men and their wives.

MARTIN: Oh yes. Beware.

JOE: I really can't discuss this under . . .

60 MARTIN: Then *don't* discuss. Say yes, Joe.

ROY: Now.

MARTIN: Say yes I will.

ROY: Now.

   Now. I'll hold my breath till you do, I'm turning blue

65 waiting. . . . *Now,* goddammit!

MARTIN: Roy, calm down, it's not . . .

ROY: Aw, fuck it. *(He takes a letter from his jacket pocket, hands it to* JOE.*)*

   Read. Came today.

*(*JOE *reads the first paragraph, then looks up.)*

70 JOE: Roy. This is . . . Roy, this is terrible.

ROY: You're telling me.

   A letter from the New York State Bar Association, Martin. They're gonna try and disbar me.

MARTIN: Oh my.

75 JOE: Why?

ROY: Why, Martin?

MARTIN: Revenge.

ROY: The whole Establishment. Their little rules. Because I know no rules. Because I don't see the Law as a dead and ar-

80 bitrary collection of antiquated dictums, thou shall, thou shalt not, because, because I know the Law's a pliable, breathing, sweating . . . *organ,* because, because . . .

MARTIN: Because he borrowed half a million from one of his clients.

85 ROY: Yeah, well, there's that.

MARTIN: *And* he forgot to *return* it.

JOE: Roy, that's. . . . You borrowed money from a client?

ROY: I'm deeply ashamed.

(Little pause.)

JOE: *(Very sympathetic.)* Roy, you know how much I admire you.

90 Well I mean I know you have unorthodox ways, but I'm sure you only did what you thought at the time you needed to do. And I have faith that . . .

ROY: Not so damp, please. I'll deny it was a loan. She's got no paperwork. Can't prove a fucking thing.

(Little pause. MARTIN *studies the menu.)*

JOE: *(Handing back the letter, more official in tone.)* Roy I really 95 appreciate your telling me this, and I'll do whatever I can to help.

ROY: *(Holding up a hand, then, carefully.)* I'll tell you what you can do.

   I'm about to be tried, Joe, by a jury that is not a jury of 100 my peers. The disbarment committee: genteel gentleman Brahmin lawyers, country-club men. I offend them, to these men . . . I'm what, Martin, some sort of filthy little Jewish troll?

MARTIN: Oh well, I wouldn't go so far as . . . 105

ROY: Oh well I would.

   Very fancy lawyers, these disbarment committee lawyers, fancy lawyers with fancy corporate clients and complicated cases. Antitrust suits. Deregulation. Environmental control. Complex cases like these need Justice De- 110 partment cooperation like flowers need the sun. Wouldn't you say that's an accurate assessment, Martin?

MARTIN: I'm not here, Roy. I'm not hearing any of this.

ROY: No. Of course not.

   Without the light of the sun, Joe, these cases, and the 115 fancy lawyers who represent them, will wither and die.

   A well-placed friend, someone in the Justice Department, say, can turn off the sun. Cast a deep shadow on my behalf. Make them shiver in the cold. If they overstep. They would fear that. 120

(Pause.)

JOE: Roy. I don't understand.

ROY: You do.

(Pause.)

JOE: You're not asking me to . . .

ROY: Ssshhhh. Careful.

JOE: *(A beat, then.)* Even if I said yes to the job, it would be 125 illegal to interfere. With the hearings. It's unethical. No. I can't.

ROY: Un-ethical.

   Would you excuse us, Martin?

MARTIN: Excuse you? 130

ROY: Take a walk, Martin. For real.

*(*MARTIN *leaves.)*

ROY: Un-ethical. Are you trying to embarrass me in front of my friend?

JOE: Well it is unethical, I can't . . .

ROY: Boy, you are really something. What the fuck do you 135 think this is, Sunday School?

JOE: No, but Roy this is . . .

ROY: This is . . . this is gastric juices churning, this is enzymes and acids, this is intestinal is what this is, bowel movement and blood-red meat—this stinks, this is *politics,* Joe, the 140 game of being alive. And you think you're. . . . What?

Above that? Above alive is what? Dead! In the clouds!
You're on earth, goddammit! Plant a foot, stay a while.
    I'm sick. They smell I'm weak. They want blood this time.
145 I must have eyes in Justice. In Justice you will protect me.
JOE: Why can't Mr. Heller . . .
ROY: Grow up, Joe. The administration can't get involved.
JOE: But I'd be part of the administration. The same as him.
ROY: Not the same. Martin's Ed's man. And Ed's Reagan's man.
150 So Martin's Reagan's man.
    And you're mine.

(Little pause. He holds up the letter.)

This will never be. Understand me?

(He tears the letter up.)

I'm gonna be a lawyer, Joe, I'm gonna be a lawyer, Joe, I'm
gonna be a goddam motherfucking legally licensed member
155 of the bar lawyer, just like my daddy was, till my last bitter day on earth, Joseph, until the day I die.

(MARTIN returns.)

ROY: Ah, Martin's back.
MARTIN: So are we agreed?
ROY: Joe?

(Little pause.)

160 JOE: I will think about it.
        (To ROY.) I will.
ROY: Huh.
MARTIN: It's the fear of what comes after the doing that makes
    the doing hard to do.
165 ROY: Amen.
MARTIN: But you can almost always live with the consequences.

SCENE VII

*That afternoon. On the granite steps outside the Hall of Justice,
Brooklyn. It is cold and sunny. A Sabrett wagon is selling hot dogs.
LOUIS, in a shabby overcoat, is sitting on the steps contemplatively
eating one. JOE enters with three hot dogs and a can of Coke.*

JOE: Can I . . . ?
LOUIS: Oh sure. Sure. Crazy cold sun.
JOE: *(Sitting.)* Have to make the best of it.
    How's your friend?
5 LOUIS: My . . . ? Oh. He's worse. My friend is worse.
JOE: I'm sorry.
LOUIS: Yeah, well. Thanks for asking. It's nice. You're nice. I
    can't believe you voted for Reagan.
JOE: I hope he gets better.
10 LOUIS: Reagan?
JOE: Your friend.
LOUIS: He won't. Neither will Reagan.
JOE: Let's not talk politics, OK?
LOUIS: *(Pointing to JOE's lunch.)* You're eating three of those?
15 JOE: Well . . . I'm . . . hungry.
LOUIS: They're really terrible for you. Full of rat-poo and beetle
    legs and wood shavings 'n' shit.

JOE: Huh.
LOUIS: And . . . um . . . irridium, I think. Something toxic.
JOE: You're eating one. 20
LOUIS: Yeah, well, the shape, I can't help myself, plus I'm *trying*
    to commit suicide, what's your excuse?
JOE: I don't have an excuse. I just have Pepto-Bismol.

*(JOE takes a bottle of Pepto-Bismol and chugs it. LOUIS shudders
audibly.)*

JOE: Yeah I know but then I wash it down with Coke.

*(He does this. LOUIS mimes barfing in JOE's lap. JOE pushes LOUIS's
head away.)*

JOE: Are you *always* like this? 25
LOUIS: I've been worrying a lot about his kids.
JOE: Whose?
LOUIS: Reagan's. Maureen and Mike and little orphan Patti and
    Miss Ron Reagan Jr., the you-should-pardon-the-expression
    heterosexual. 30
JOE: Ron Reagan Jr. is *not* . . . You shouldn't just make these
    assumptions about people. How do you know? About him?
    What he is? You don't know.
LOUIS: *(Doing Tallulah.)* Well darling he never sucked *my* cock
    but . . . 35
JOE: Look, if you're going to get vulgar . . .
LOUIS: No no really I mean. . . . What's it like to be the child
    of the Zeitgeist? To have the American Animus as your
    dad? It's not really a *family,* the Reagans, I read *People,* there
    aren't any connections there, no love, they don't ever even 40
    speak to each other except through their agents. So what's
    it like to be Reagan's kid? Enquiring minds want to know.
JOE: You can't believe everything you . . .
LOUIS: *(Looking away.)* But . . . I think we all know what that's
    like. Nowadays. No connections. No responsibilities. All of 45
    us . . . falling through the cracks that separate what we owe
    to our selves and . . . and what we owe to love.
JOE: You just. . . . Whatever you feel like saying or doing, you
    don't care, you just . . . do it.
LOUIS: Do what? 50
JOE: It. Whatever. Whatever it is you want to do.
LOUIS: Are you trying to tell me something?

(Little pause, sexual. They stare at each other. JOE looks away.)

JOE: No, I'm just observing that you . . .
LOUIS: Impulsive.
JOE: Yes, I mean it must be scary, you . . . 55
LOUIS: *(Shrugs.)* Land of the free. Home of the brave. Call me
    irresponsible.
JOE: It's kind of terrifying.
LOUIS: Yeah, well, freedom is. Heartless, too.
JOE: Oh you're not heartless. 60
LOUIS: You don't know.
    Finish your weenie.

(He pats JOE on the knee, starts to leave.)

JOE: Um . . .

(LOUIS turns, looks at him. JOE searches for something to say.)

JOE: Yesterday was Sunday but I've been a little unfocused recently and I thought it was Monday. So I came here like I was going to work. And the whole place was empty. And at first I couldn't figure out why, and I had this moment of incredible . . . fear and also. . . . It just flashed through my mind: The whole Hall of Justice, it's empty, it's deserted, it's gone out of business. Forever. The people that make it run have up and abandoned it.

LOUIS: (*Looking at the building.*) Creepy.

JOE: Well yes but. I felt that I was going to scream. Not because it was creepy, but because the emptiness felt so *fast.* And . . . well, good. A . . . happy scream.

I just wondered what a thing it would be . . . if overnight everything you owe anything to, justice, or love, had really gone away. Free.

It would be . . . heartless terror. Yes. Terrible, and . . .

Very great. To shed your skin, every old skin, one by one and then walk away, unencumbered, into the morning.

(*Little pause. He looks at the building.*)

I can't go in there today.

LOUIS: Then don't.

JOE: (*Not really hearing* LOUIS.) I can't go in, I need . . .

(*He looks for what he needs. He takes a swig of Pepto-Bismol.*)

I can't *be* this anymore. I need . . . a change, I should just . . .

LOUIS: (*Not a come-on, necessarily; he doesn't want to be alone.*) Want some company? For whatever?

(*Pause.* JOE *looks at* LOUIS *and looks away, afraid.* LOUIS *shrugs.*)

LOUIS: Sometimes, even if it scares you to death, you have to be willing to break the law. Know what I mean?

(*Another little pause.*)

JOE: Yes.

(*Another little pause.*)

LOUIS: I moved out. I moved out on my . . .
I haven't been sleeping well.

JOE: Me neither.

(LOUIS *goes up to* JOE, *licks his napkin and dabs at* JOE'*s mouth.*)

LOUIS: Antacid moustache.
(*Points to the building.*) Maybe the court won't convene. Ever again. Maybe we are free. To do whatever.
Children of the new morning, criminal minds. Selfish and greedy and loveless and blind. Reagan's children.
You're scared. So am I. Everybody is in the land of the free. God help us all.

SCENE VIII

Late that night. JOE *at a payphone phoning* HANNAH *at home in Salt Lake City.*

JOE: Mom?

HANNAH: Joe?

JOE: Hi.

HANNAH: You're calling from the street. It's . . . it must be four in the morning. What's happened?

JOE: Nothing, nothing, I . . .

HANNAH: It's Harper. Is Harper. . . . Joe? Joe?

JOE: Yeah, hi. No, Harper's fine. Well, no, she's . . . not fine. How are you, Mom?

HANNAH: What's happened?

JOE: I just wanted to talk to you. I, uh, wanted to try something out on you.

HANNAH: Joe, you haven't . . . have you been drinking, Joe?

JOE: Yes ma'am. I'm drunk.

HANNAH: That isn't like you.

JOE: No. I mean, who's to say?

HANNAH: Why are you out on the street at four A.M.? In that crazy city. It's dangerous.

JOE: Actually, Mom, I'm not on the street. I'm near the boathouse in the park.

HANNAH: What park?

JOE: Central Park.

HANNAH: CENTRAL PARK! Oh my Lord. What on earth are you doing in Central Park at this time of night? Are you . . . Joe, I think you ought to go home right now. Call me from home.

(*Little pause.*)

Joe?

JOE: I come here to watch, Mom. Sometimes. Just to watch.

HANNAH: Watch what? What's there to watch at four in the . . .

JOE: Mom, did Dad love me?

HANNAH: What?

JOE: Did he?

HANNAH: You ought to go home and call from there.

JOE: Answer.

HANNAH: Oh now really. This is maudlin. I don't like this conversation.

JOE: Yeah, well, it gets worse from here on.

(*Pause.*)

HANNAH: Joe?

JOE: Mom. Momma. I'm a homosexual, Momma.
Boy, did that come out awkward.

(*Pause.*)

Hello? Hello?
I'm a homosexual.

(*Pause.*)

Please, Momma, Say something.

HANNAH: You're old enough to understand that your father didn't love you without being ridiculous about it.

JOE: What?

HANNAH: You're ridiculous. You're being ridiculous.

JOE: I'm . . .
What?

HANNAH: You really ought to go home now to your wife. I need to go to bed. This phone call. . . . We will just forget this phone call.

JOE: Mom.

HANNAH: No more talk. Tonight. This . . .

155   *(Suddenly very angry.)* Drinking is a sin! A sin! I raised
    you better than that. *(She hangs up.)*

SCENE IX

The following morning, early. Split scene: HARPER *and* JOE *at home;*
LOUIS *and* PRIOR *in* PRIOR'S *hospital room.* JOE *and* LOUIS *have just
entered. This should be fast and obviously furious; overlapping is fine;
the proceedings may be a little confusing but not the final results.*

HARPER: Oh God. Home. The moment of truth has arrived.

JOE: Harper.

LOUIS: I'm going to move out.

PRIOR: The fuck you are.

5 JOE: Harper. Please listen. I still love you very much. You're
    still my best buddy; I'm not going to leave you.

HARPER: No, I don't like the sound of this. I'm leaving.

LOUIS: I'm leaving.
    I already have.

10 JOE: Please listen. Stay. This is really hard. We have to talk.

HARPER: We are talking. Aren't we. Now please shut up.
    OK?

PRIOR: Bastard. Sneaking off while I'm flat out here, that's low.
    If I could get up now I'd beat the holy shit out of you.

15 JOE: Did you take pills? How many?

HARPER: No pills. Bad for the . . . *(Pats stomach.)*

JOE: You aren't pregnant. I called your gynecologist.

HARPER: I'm seeing a new gynecologist.

PRIOR: You have no right to do this.

20 LOUIS: Oh, that's ridiculous.

PRIOR: No right. It's criminal.

JOE: Forget about that. Just listen. You want the truth. This is
    the truth.
    I knew this when I married you. I've known this I guess

25   for as long as I've known anything, but . . . I don't know, I
    thought maybe that with enough effort and will I could
    change myself . . . but I can't . . .

PRIOR: Criminal.

LOUIS: There oughta be a law.

30 PRIOR: There is a law. You'll see.

JOE: I'm losing ground here, I go walking, you want to know
    where I walk, I . . . go to the park, or up and down 53rd
    Street, or places where. . . . And I keep swearing I won't go
    walking again, but I just can't.

35 LOUIS: I need some privacy.

PRIOR: That's new.

LOUIS: Everything's new, Prior.

JOE: I try to tighten my heart into a knot, a snarl, I try to learn
    to live dead, just numb, but then I see someone I want, and

40   it's like a nail, like a hot spike right through my chest, and
    I know I'm losing.

PRIOR: Apartment too small for three? Louis and Prior comfy
    but not Louis and Prior and Prior's disease?

LOUIS: Something like that.

45   I won't be judged by you. This isn't a crime, just—the
    inevitable consequence of people who run out of—whose
    limitations . . .

PRIOR: Bang bang bang. The court will come to order.

LOUIS: I mean let's talk practicalities, schedules; I'll come over
    if you want, spend nights with you when I can, I can . . .   50

PRIOR: Has the jury reached a verdict?

LOUIS: I'm doing the best I can.

PRIOR: Pathetic. Who cares?

JOE: My whole life has conspired to bring me to this place, and
    I can't despise my whole life. I think I believed when I met 55
    you I could save you, you at least if not myself, but . . . I
    don't have any sexual feelings for you, Harper. And I don't
    think I ever did.

(Little pause.)

HARPER: I think you should go.

JOE: Where?   60

HARPER: Washington. Doesn't matter.

JOE: What are you talking about?

HARPER: Without me.
    Without me, Joe. Isn't that what you want to hear?

(Little pause.)

JOE: Yes.   65

LOUIS: You can love someone and fail them. You can love some-
    one and not be able to . . .

PRIOR: You *can*, theoretically, yes. A person can, maybe an
    editorial "you" can love, Louis, but not *you*, specifically you,
    I don't know, I think you are excluded from that general   70
    category.

HARPER: You were going to save me, but the whole time you
    were spinning a lie. I just don't understand that.

PRIOR: A person could theoretically love and maybe many do
    but we both know now you can't.   75

LOUIS: I do.

PRIOR: You can't even say it.

LOUIS: I love you, Prior.

PRIOR: I repeat. Who cares?

HARPER: This is so scary, I want this to stop, to go back . . .   80

PRIOR: We have reached a verdict, your honor. This man's heart
    is deficient. He loves, but his love is worth nothing.

JOE: Harper . . .

HARPER: Mr. Lies, I want to get away from here. Far away. Right
    now. Before he starts talking again. Please, please . . .   85

JOE: As long as I've known you Harper you've been afraid of . . .
    of men hiding under the bed, men hiding under the sofa,
    men with knives.

PRIOR: *(Shattered; almost pleading; trying to reach him.)* I'm dying!
    You stupid fuck! Do you know what that is! Love! Do you   90
    know what love means? We lived together four-and-a-half
    years, you animal, you idiot.

LOUIS: I have to find some way to save myself.

JOE: Who are these men? I never understood it. Now I know.

HARPER: What?   95

JOE: It's me.

HARPER: It is?

PRIOR: GET OUT OF MY ROOM!

JOE: I'm the man with the knives.

HARPER: You are?   100

PRIOR: If I could get up now I'd kill you. I would. Go away. Go
    away or I'll scream.

HARPER: Oh God . . .

JOE: I'm sorry . . .

105 HARPER: It is you.

LOUIS: Please don't scream.

PRIOR: Go.

HARPER: I recognize you now.

LOUIS: Please . . .

110 JOE: Oh. Wait, I. . . . Oh!

(He covers his mouth with his hand, gags, and removes his hand, red with blood.)

I'm bleeding.

(PRIOR screams.)

HARPER: Mr. Lies.

MR. LIES: *(Appearing, dressed in antarctic explorer's apparel.)* Right here.

115 HARPER: I want to go away. I can't see him anymore.

MR. LIES: Where?

HARPER: Anywhere. Far away.

MR. LIES: Absolutamento.

(HARPER and MR. LIES vanish. JOE looks up, sees that she's gone.)

PRIOR: *(Closing his eyes.)* When I open my eyes you'll be gone.

(LOUIS leaves.)

120 JOE: Harper?

PRIOR: *(Opening his eyes.)* Huh. It worked.

JOE: *(Calling.)* Harper?

PRIOR: I hurt all over. I wish I was dead.

Scene X

The same day, sunset. HANNAH *and* SISTER ELLA CHAPTER, *a real-estate saleswoman,* HANNAH PITT's *closest friend, in front of* HANNAH's *house in Salt Lake City.*

SISTER ELLA CHAPTER: Look at that view! A view of heaven. Like the living city of heaven, isn't it, it just fairly glimmers in the sun.

HANNAH: Glimmers.

5 SISTER ELLA CHAPTER: Even the stone and brick it just glimmers and glitters like heaven in the sunshine. Such a nice view you get, perched up on a canyon rim. Some kind of beautiful place.

HANNAH: It's just Salt Lake, and you're selling the house *for*
10 me, not *to* me.

SISTER ELLA CHAPTER: I like to work up an enthusiasm for my properties.

HANNAH: Just get me a good price.

SISTER ELLA CHAPTER: Well, the market's off.

15 HANNAH: At least fifty.

SISTER ELLA CHAPTER: Forty'd be more like it.

HANNAH: Fifty.

SISTER ELLA CHAPTER: Wish you'd wait a bit.

HANNAH: Well I can't.

20 SISTER ELLA CHAPTER: Wish you would. You're about the only friend I got.

HANNAH: Oh well now.

SISTER ELLA CHAPTER: Know why I decided to like you? I decided to like you 'cause you're the only unfriendly Mormon
25 I ever met.

HANNAH: Your wig is crooked.

SISTER ELLA CHAPTER: Fix it.

(HANNAH straightens SISTER ELLA's wig.)

SISTER ELLA CHAPTER: New York City. All they got there is tiny rooms.

I always thought: People ought to stay put. That's why
30 I got my license to sell real estate. It's a way of saying: Have a house! Stay put! It's a way of saying traveling's no good. Plus I needed the cash. *(She takes a pack of cigarettes out of her purse, lights one, offers pack to HANNAH.)*

HANNAH: Not out here, anyone could come by.
35 There's been days I've stood at this ledge and thought about stepping over.

It's a hard place, Salt Lake: baked dry. Abundant energy; not much intelligence. That's a combination that can wear a body out. No harm looking someplace else. I don't need
40 much room.

My sister-in-law Libby thinks there's radon gas in the basement.

SISTER ELLA CHAPTER: Is there gas in the . . .

HANNAH: Of course not. Libby's a fool.
45 SISTER ELLA CHAPTER: 'Cause I'd have to include that in the description.

HANNAH: There's no gas, Ella. *(Little pause.)* Give a puff. *(She takes a furtive drag of ELLA's cigarette.)* Put it away now.

SISTER ELLA CHAPTER: So I guess it's goodbye.
50 HANNAH: You'll be all right, Ella, I wasn't ever much of a friend.

SISTER ELLA CHAPTER: I'll say something but don't laugh, OK? This is the home of saints, the godliest place on earth, they say, and I think they're right. That means there's no evil
55 here? No. Evil's everywhere. Sin's everywhere. But this . . . is the spring of sweet water in the desert, the desert flower. Every step a Believer takes away from here is a step fraught with peril. I fear for you, Hannah Pitt, because you are my friend. Stay put. This is the right home of saints.

HANNAH: Latter-day saints.
60
SISTER ELLA CHAPTER: Only kind left.

HANNAH: But still. Late in the day . . . for saints and everyone. That's all. That's all.

Fifty thousand dollars for the house, Sister Ella Chapter;
65 don't undersell. It's an impressive view.

—— ACT THREE ——

NOT-YET-CONSCIOUS, FORWARD DAWNING
JANUARY 1986

Scene I

Late night, three days after the end of Act Two. The stage is completely dark. PRIOR *is in bed in his apartment, having a nightmare. He wakes up, sits up and switches on a nightlight. He looks at his clock. Seated by the table near the bed is a man dressed in the clothing of a 13th-century British squire.*

PRIOR: *(Terrified.)* Who are you?

PRIOR 1: My name is Prior Walter.

(Pause.)

PRIOR: My name is Prior Walter.

PRIOR 1: I know that.

5   PRIOR: Explain.

PRIOR 1: You're alive. I'm not. We have the same name. What do you want me to explain?

PRIOR: A ghost?

PRIOR 1: An ancestor.

10 PRIOR: Not *the* Prior Walter? The Bayeux tapestry Prior Walter?

PRIOR 1: His great-great grandson. The fifth of the name.

PRIOR: I'm the thirty-fourth, I think.

PRIOR 1: Actually the thirty-second.

PRIOR: Not according to Mother.

15 PRIOR 1: She's including the two bastards, then; I say leave them out. I say no room for bastards. The little things you swallow . . .

PRIOR: Pills.

PRIOR 1: Pills. For the pestilence. I too . . .

20 PRIOR: Pestilence. . . . You too what?

PRIOR 1: The pestilence in my time was much worse than now. Whole villages of empty houses. You could look outdoors and see Death walking in the morning, dew dampening the ragged hem of his black robe. Plain as I see you now.

25 PRIOR: You died of the plague.

PRIOR 1: The spotty monster. Like you, alone.

PRIOR: I'm not alone.

PRIOR 1: You have no wife, no children.

PRIOR: I'm gay.

30 PRIOR 1: So? Be gay, dance in your altogether for all I care, what's that to do with not having children?

PRIOR: Gay homosexual, not bonny, blithe and . . . never mind.

PRIOR 1: I had twelve. When I died.

(The second ghost appears, this one dressed in the clothing of an elegant 17th-century Londoner.)

PRIOR 1: *(Pointing to* PRIOR 2.*)* And I was three years younger
35   than him.

*(*PRIOR *sees the new ghost, screams.)*

PRIOR: Oh God another one.

PRIOR 2: Prior Walter. Prior to you by some seventeen others.

PRIOR 1: He's counting the bastards.

PRIOR: Are we having a convention?

40 PRIOR 2: We've been sent to declare her fabulous incipience. They love a well-paved entrance with lots of heralds, and . . .

PRIOR 1: The messenger come. Prepare the way. The infinite descent, a breath in air . . .

45 PRIOR 2: They chose us, I suspect, because of the mortal affinities. In a family as long-descended as the Walters there are bound to be a few carried off by plague.

PRIOR 1: The spotty monster.

PRIOR 2: Black Jack. Came from a water pump, half the city
50   of London, can you imagine? His came from fleas. Yours, I understand, is the lamentable consequence of venery . . .

PRIOR 1: Fleas on rats, but who knew that?

PRIOR: Am I going to die?

PRIOR 2: We aren't allowed to discuss . . .

PRIOR 1: When you do, you don't get ancestors to help you   55
through it. You may be surrounded by children but you die alone.

PRIOR: I'm afraid.

PRIOR 1: You should be. There aren't even torches, and the path's rocky, dark and steep.   60

PRIOR 2: Don't alarm him. There's good news before there's bad.
    We two come to strew rose petal and palm leaf before the triumphal procession. Prophet. Seer. Revelator. It's a great honor for the family.   65

PRIOR 1: He hasn't got a family.

PRIOR 2: I meant for the Walters, for the family in the larger sense.

PRIOR: *(Singing.)*

        All I want is a room somewhere,
        Far away from the cold night air . . .   70

PRIOR 2: *(Putting a hand on* PRIOR*'s forehead.)* Calm, calm, this is no brain fever . . .

*(*PRIOR *calms down, but keeps his eyes closed. The lights begin to change. Distant Glorious Music.)*

PRIOR 1: *(Low chant.)* Adonai, Adonai,
    Olam ha-yichud,
    Zefirot, Zazahot,   75
    Ha-adam, ha-gadol
    Daughter of Light,
    Daughter of Splendors,
    Fluor! Phosphor!
    Lumen! Candle!   80

PRIOR 2: *(Simultaneously.)* Even now,
    From the mirror-bright halls of heaven,
    Across the cold and lifeless infinity of space,
    The Messenger comes
    Trailing orbs of light,   85
    Fabulous, incipient,
    Oh Prophet,
    To you . . .

PRIOR 1 and PRIOR 2: Prepare, prepare,
    The Infinite Descent,   90
    A breath, a feather,
    Glory to . . .

(They vanish.)

SCENE II

The next day. Split scene: LOUIS *and* BELIZE *in a coffee shop.* PRIOR *is at the outpatient clinic at the hospital with* EMILY, *the nurse; she has him on a pentamidine IV drip.*

LOUIS: Why has democracy succeeded in America? Of course by succeeded I mean comparatively, not literally, not in the present, but what makes for the prospect of some sort of radical democracy spreading outward and growing up? Why does the power that was once so carefully preserved at   5
the top of the pyramid by the original framers of the Constitution seem drawn inexorably downward and outward in spite of the best effort of the Right to stop this? I mean it's

10 the really hard thing about being Left in this country, the American Left can't help but trip over all these petrified little fetishes: freedom, that's the worst; you know, *Jeane Kirkpatrick* for God's sake will go on and on about freedom and so what does that mean, the word freedom, when she talks 15 about it, or human rights; you have Bush talking about human rights, and so what are these people talking about, they might as well be talking about the mating habits of Venusians, these people don't begin to know what, ontologically, freedom is or human rights, like they see these bourgeois property-based Rights-of-Man-type rights but 20 that's not enfranchisement, not democracy, not what's implicit, what's potential within the idea, not the idea with blood in it. That's just liberalism, the worst kind of liberalism, really, bourgeois tolerance, and what I think is that what AIDS shows us is the limits of tolerance, that it's not 25 enough to be tolerated, because when the shit hits the fan you find out how much tolerance is worth. Nothing. And underneath all the tolerance is intense, passionate hatred.

BELIZE: Uh huh.

LOUIS: Well don't you think that's true?

30 BELIZE: Uh huh. It is.

LOUIS: *Power* is the object, not being tolerated. Fuck assimilation. But I mean in spite of all this the thing about America, I think, is that ultimately we're different from every other nation on earth, in that, with people here of every 35 race, we can't. . . . Ultimately what defines us isn't race, but politics. Not like any European country where there's an insurmountable fact of a kind of racial, or ethnic, monopoly, or monolith, like all Dutchmen, I mean Dutch people, are well, Dutch, and the Jews of Europe were never Euro- 40 peans, just a small problem. Facing the monolith. But here there are so many small problems, it's really just a collection of small problems, the monolith is missing. Oh, I mean, of course I suppose there's the monolith of White America. White Straight Male America.

45 BELIZE: Which is not unimpressive, even among monoliths.

LOUIS: Well, no, but when the race thing gets taken care of, and I don't mean to minimize how major it is, I mean I know it is, this is a really, really incredibly racist country but it's like, well, the British. I mean, all these blue-eyed pink peo- 50 ple. And it's just weird, you know, I mean I'm not all that Jewish-looking, or . . . well, maybe I am but, you know, in New York, everyone is . . . well, not everyone, but so many are but so but in England, in London I walk into bars and I feel like Sid the Yid, you know I mean like Woody Allen 55 in *Annie Hall,* with the payess and the gabardine coat, like never, never anywhere so much—I mean, not actively despised, not like they're Germans, who I think are still terribly anti-Semitic, and racist too, I mean black-racist, they pretend otherwise but, anyway, in London, there's just . . . 60 and at one point I met this black gay guy from Jamaica who talked with a lilt but he said his family'd been living in London since before the Civil War—the American one— and how the English never let him forget for a minute that he wasn't blue-eyed and pink and I said yeah, me too, these 65 people are anti-Semites and he said yeah but the British Jews have the clothing business all sewed up and blacks there can't get a foothold. And it was an incredibly awkward moment of just. . . . I mean here we were, in this bar that was gay but it was a *pub,* you know, the beams and the 70 plaster and those horrible little, like, two-day-old fish and egg sandwiches—and just so British, so *old,* and I felt, well, there's no way out of this because both of us are, right now, too much immersed in this history, hope is dissolved in the sheer age of this place, where race is what counts and there's no real hope of change—it's the racial destiny of the Brits 75 that matters to them, not their political destiny, whereas in America . . .

BELIZE: Here in America race doesn't count.

LOUIS: No, no, that's not. . . . I mean you *can't* be hearing that . . . 80

BELIZE: I . . .

LOUIS: It's—look, race, yes, but ultimately race here is a political question, right? Racists just try to use race here as a tool in a political struggle. It's not really about race. Like the spiritualists try to use that stuff, are you enlightened, 85 are you centered, channeled, whatever, this reaching out for a spiritual past in a country where no indigenous spirits exist—only the Indians, I mean Native American spirits and we killed them off so now, there are no gods here, no ghosts and spirits in America, there are no angels in Amer- 90 ica, no spiritual past, no racial past, there's only the political, and the decoys and the ploys to maneuver around the inescapable battle of politics, the shifting downwards and outwards of political power to the people . . .

BELIZE: POWER to the People! AMEN! *(Looking at his watch.)* 95 *OH MY GOODNESS!* Will you look at the time, I gotta . . .

LOUIS: Do you. . . . You think this is, what, racist or naive or something?

BELIZE: Well it's certainly *something.* Look, I just remembered I have an appointment . . . 100

LOUIS: What? I mean I really don't want to, like, speak from some position of privilege and . . .

BELIZE: I'm sitting here, thinking, eventually he's *got* to run out of steam, so I let you rattle on and on saying about maybe seven or eight things I find really offensive. 105

LOUIS: What?

BELIZE: But I know you, Louis, and I know the guilt fueling this peculiar tirade is obviously already swollen bigger than your hemorrhoids.

LOUIS: I don't have hemorrhoids. 110

BELIZE: I hear different. May I finish?

LOUIS: Yes, but I don't have hemorrhoids.

BELIZE: So finally, when I . . .

LOUIS: Prior told you, he's an asshole, he shouldn't have . . .

BELIZE: You promised, Louis. Prior is not a subject. 115

LOUIS: You brought him up.

BELIZE: I brought up hemorrhoids.

LOUIS: So it's indirect. Passive-aggressive.

BELIZE: Unlike, I suppose, banging me over the head with your theory that America doesn't have a race problem. 120

LOUIS: Oh be fair I never said that.

BELIZE: Not exactly, but . . .

LOUIS: I said . . .

BELIZE: . . . but it was close enough, because if it'd been that blunt I'd've just walked out and . . . 125

LOUIS: You deliberately misinterpreted! I . . .

BELIZE: Stop interrupting! I haven't been able to . . .

LOUIS: Just let me . . .

130 BELIZE: NO! What, *talk?* You've been running your mouth nonstop since I got here, yaddadda yaddadda blah blah blah, up the hill, down the hill, playing with your MONOLITH . . .

LOUIS: *(Overlapping)* Well, you could have joined in at any time instead of . . .

135 BELIZE: *(Continuing over LOUIS.)* . . . and girlfriend it is truly an *awesome* spectacle but I got better things to do with my time than sit here listening to this racist bullshit just because I feel sorry for you that . . .

LOUIS: I am not a racist!

140 BELIZE: Oh come on . . .

LOUIS: So maybe I am a racist but . . .

BELIZE: Oh I really hate that! It's no fun picking on you Louis; you're so guilty, it's like throwing darts at a glob of jello, there's no satisfying hits, just quivering, the darts just blop

145 in and vanish.

LOUIS: I just think when you are discussing lines of oppression it gets very complicated and . . .

BELIZE: Oh is that a fact? You know, we black drag queens have a rather intimate knowledge of the complexity of the lines

150 of . . .

LOUIS: *Ex*-black drag queen.

BELIZE: Actually ex-ex.

LOUIS: You're doing drag again?

BELIZE: I don't. . . . Maybe. I don't have to tell you. Maybe.

155 LOUIS: I think it's sexist.

BELIZE: I didn't ask you.

LOUIS: Well it is. The gay community, I think, has to adopt the same attitude towards drag as black women have to take towards black women blues singers.

160 BELIZE: Oh my we *are* walking dangerous tonight.

LOUIS: Well, it's all internalized oppression, right, I mean the masochism, the stereotypes, the . . .

BELIZE: Louis, are you deliberately trying to make me hate you?

165 LOUIS: No, I . . .

BELIZE: I mean, are you deliberately transforming yourself into an arrogant, sexual-political Stalinist-slash-racist flag-waving thug for my benefit?

(Pause.)

LOUIS: You know what I think?

170 BELIZE: What?

LOUIS: You hate me because I'm a Jew.

BELIZE: I'm leaving.

LOUIS: It's true.

BELIZE: You have no basis except your . . .

175 Louis, it's good to know you haven't changed; you are still an honorary citizen of the Twilight Zone, and after your pale, pale white polemics on behalf of racial insensitivity you have a flaming *fuck* of a lot of nerve calling me an anti-Semite. Now I really gotta go.

180 LOUIS: You called me Lou the Jew.

BELIZE: That was a joke.

LOUIS: I didn't think it was funny. It was hostile.

BELIZE: It was three years ago.

LOUIS: So?

185 BELIZE: You just called yourself Sid the Yid.

LOUIS: That's not the same thing.

BELIZE: Sid the Yid is different from Lou the Jew.

LOUIS: Yes.

BELIZE: Someday you'll have to explain that to me, but right

190 now . . . *You* hate me because you hate black people.

LOUIS: I do not. But I do think most black people are anti-Semitic.

BELIZE: "Most black people." *That's* racist, Louis, and *I* think

195 most Jews . . .

LOUIS: Louis Farrakhan.

BELIZE: Ed Koch.

LOUIS: Jesse Jackson.

BELIZE: Jackson. Oh really, Louis, this is . . .

200 LOUIS: Hymietown! Hymietown!

BELIZE: Louis, you voted for Jesse Jackson. You send checks to the Rainbow Coalition.

LOUIS: I'm ambivalent. The checks bounced.

BELIZE: All your checks bounce, Louis; you're ambivalent about

205 everything.

LOUIS: What's that supposed to mean?

BELIZE: You may be dumber than shit but I refuse to believe you can't figure it out. Try.

LOUIS: I was never ambivalent about Prior. I love him. I do. I

210 really do.

BELIZE: Nobody said different.

LOUIS: Love and ambivalence are. . . . Real love isn't ambivalent.

BELIZE: "Real love isn't ambivalent." I'd swear that's a line from my favorite bestselling paperback novel, *In Love with the*

215 *Night Mysterious,* except I don't think you ever read it.

(Pause.)

LOUIS: I never read it, no.

BELIZE: You ought to. Instead of spending the rest of your life trying to get through *Democracy in America.* It's about this white woman whose Daddy owns a plantation in the Deep

220 South in the years before the Civil War—the American one—and her name is Margaret, and she's in love with her Daddy's number-one slave, and his name is Thaddeus, and she's married but her white slave-owner husband has AIDS: Antebellum Insufficiently Developed Sexorgans.

225 And there's a lot of hot stuff going down when Margaret and Thaddeus can catch a spare torrid ten under the cotton-picking moon, and then of course the Yankees come, and they set the slaves free, and the slaves string up old Daddy, and so on. Historical fiction. Somewhere in there I recall

230 Margaret and Thaddeus find the time to discuss the nature of love; her face is reflecting the flames of the burning plantation—you know, the way white people do—and his black face is dark in the night and she says to him, "Thaddeus, real love isn't ever ambivalent."

235

(Little pause. EMILY enters and turns off IV drip.)

BELIZE: Thaddeus looks at her; he's contemplating her thesis; and he isn't sure he agrees.

EMILY: *(Removing IV drip from PRIOR's arm.)* Treatment number . . . *(Consulting chart.)* four.

240 PRIOR: Pharmaceutical miracle. Lazarus breathes again.
LOUIS: Is he. . . . How bad is he?
BELIZE: You want the laundry list?
EMILY: Shirt off, let's check the . . .

(PRIOR takes his shirt off. She examines his lesions.)

BELIZE: There's the weight problem and the shit problem and
245 the morale problem.
EMILY: Only six. That's good. Pants.

(He drops his pants. He's naked. She examines.)

BELIZE: And. He thinks he's going crazy.
EMILY: Looking good. What else?
PRIOR: Ankles sore and swollen, but the leg's better. The nau-
250 sea's mostly gone with the little orange pills. BM's pure
liquid but not bloody anymore, for now, my eye doctor
says everything's OK, for now, my dentist says "Yuck!"
when he sees my fuzzy tongue, and now he wears little
condoms on his thumb and forefinger. And a mask. So
255 what? My dermatologist is in Hawaii and my mother . . .
well leave my mother out of it. Which is usually where
my mother is, out of it. My glands are like walnuts, my
weight's holding steady for week two, and a friend died
two days ago of bird tuberculosis; bird tuberculosis; that
260 scared me and I didn't go to the funeral today because he
was an Irish Catholic and it's probably open casket and
I'm afraid of . . . something, the bird TB or seeing him
or. . . . So I guess I'm doing OK. Except for of course I'm
going nuts.
265 EMILY: We ran the toxoplasmosis series and there's no
indication . . .
PRIOR: I know, I know, but I feel like something terrifying is
on its way, you know, like a missile from outer space, and
it's plummeting down towards the earth, and I'm ground
270 zero, and . . . I am generally known where I am known as
one cool, collected queen. And I am ruffled.
EMILY: There's really nothing to worry about. I think that
shochen bamromim hamtzeh menucho nechono al kanfey
haschino.
275 PRIOR: What?
EMILY: Everything's fine. Bemaalos k'doshim ut'horim kezohar
horokeea mazhirim . . .
PRIOR: Oh I don't understand what you're . . .
EMILY: Es nishmas Prior sheholoch leolomoh, baavur shenodvoo
280 z'dokoh b'ad hazkoras nishmosoh.
PRIOR: Why are you doing that?! Stop it! Stop it!
EMILY: Stop what?
PRIOR: You were just . . . weren't you just speaking in Hebrew
or something.
285 EMILY: *Hebrew? (Laughs.)* I'm basically Italian-American. No. I
didn't speak in Hebrew.
PRIOR: Oh no, oh God please I really think I . . .
EMILY: Look, I'm sorry, I have a waiting room full of. . . . I
think you're one of the lucky ones, you'll live for years,
290 probably—you're pretty healthy for someone with no immune system. Are you seeing someone? Loneliness is a
danger. A therapist?
PRIOR: No, I don't need to see anyone, I just . . .

EMILY: Well think about it. You aren't going crazy. You're just
under a lot of stress. No wonder . . . *(She starts to write in his* 295
chart.)

*(Suddenly there is an astonishing blaze of light, a huge chord sounded
by a gigantic choir, and a great book with steel pages mounted atop a
molten-red pillar pops up from the stage floor. The book opens; there is
a large Aleph inscribed on its pages, which bursts into flames. Immediately the book slams shut and disappears instantly under the floor as
the lights become normal again. EMILY notices none of this, writing.
PRIOR is agog.)*

EMILY: *(Laughing, exiting.)* Hebrew . . .

(PRIOR flees.)

LOUIS: Help me.
BELIZE: I beg your pardon?
LOUIS: You're a nurse, give me something, I . . . don't know 300
what to do anymore, I. . . . Last week at work I screwed
up the Xerox machine like permanently and so I . . . then
I tripped on the subway steps and my glasses broke and
I cut my forehead, here, see, and now I can't see much and
my forehead . . . it's like the Mark of Cain, stupid, right, 305
but it won't heal and every morning I see it and I think,
Biblical things, Mark of Cain, Judas Iscariot and his silver and his noose, people who . . . in betraying what they
love betray what's truest in themselves, I feel . . . nothing
but cold for myself, just cold, and every night I miss him, 310
I miss him so much but then . . . those sores, and the
smell and . . . where I thought it was going. . . . I could
be . . . I could be sick too, maybe I'm sick too. I don't
know.
    Belize. Tell him I love him. Can you do that? 315
BELIZE: I've thought about it for a very long time, and I still
don't understand what love is. Justice is simple. Democracy
is simple. Those things are unambivalent. But love is very
hard. And it goes bad for you if you violate the hard law
of love. 320
LOUIS: I'm dying.
BELIZE: He's dying. You just wish you were. Oh cheer up,
Louis. Look at that heavy sky out there.
LOUIS: Purple.
BELIZE: *Purple?* Boy, what kind of a homosexual are you, any- 325
way? That's not purple, Mary, that color up there is *(Very
grand.)* mauve.
    All day today it's felt like Thanksgiving. Soon, this . . .
ruination will be blanketed white. You can smell it—can
you smell it? 330
LOUIS: Smell what?
BELIZE: Softness, compliance, forgiveness, grace.
LOUIS: No . . .
BELIZE: I can't help you learn that. I can't help you, Louis.
You're not my business. *(He exits.)* 335

*(LOUIS puts his head in his hands, inadvertently touching his cut
forehead.)*

LOUIS: Ow FUCK! *(He stands slowly, looks towards where BELIZE
exited.)* Smell what? *(He looks both ways to be sure no one is
watching, then inhales deeply, and is surprised.)* Huh. Snow.

SCENE III

Same day. HARPER *in a very white, cold place, with a brilliant blue sky above; a delicate snowfall. She is dressed in a beautiful snowsuit. The sound of the sea, faint.*

HARPER: Snow! Ice! Mountains of ice! Where am I? I . . . feel better, I do, I . . . feel better. There are ice crystals in my lungs, wonderful and sharp. And the snow smells like cold, crushed peaches. And there's something . . . some current of blood in the wind, how strange, it has that iron taste.

MR. LIES: Ozone.

HARPER: Ozone! Wow! Where am I?

MR. LIES: The Kingdom of Ice, the bottommost part of the world.

HARPER: (*Looking around, then realizing.*) Antarctica. This is Antarctica!

MR. LIES: Cold shelter for the shattered. No sorrow here, tears freeze.

HARPER: Antarctica, Antarctica, oh boy oh boy, LOOK at this, I. . . . Wow, I must've really snapped the tether, huh?

MR. LIES: Apparently . . .

HARPER: That's great. I want to stay here forever. Set up camp. Build things. Build a city, an enormous city made up of frontier forts, dark wood and green roofs and high gates made of pointed logs and bonfires burning on every street corner. I should build by a river. Where are the forests?

MR. LIES: No timber here. Too cold. Ice, no trees.

HARPER: Oh details! I'm sick of details! I'll plant them and grow them. I'll live off caribou fat, I'll melt it over the bonfires and drink it from long, curved goat-horn cups. It'll be great. I want to make a new world here. So that I never have to go home again.

MR. LIES: As long as it lasts. Ice has a way of melting . . .

HARPER: No. Forever. I can have anything I want here—maybe even companionship, someone who has . . . desire for me. You, maybe.

MR. LIES: It's against the by-laws of the International Order of Travel Agents to get involved with clients. Rules are rules. Anyway, I'm not the one you really want.

HARPER: There isn't anyone . . . maybe an Eskimo. Who could ice-fish for food. And help me build a nest for when the baby comes.

MR. LIES: There are no Eskimo in Antarctica. And you're not really pregnant. You made that up.

HARPER: Well all of this is made up. So if the snow feels cold I'm pregnant. Right? Here, I can be pregnant. And I can have any kind of a baby I want.

MR. LIES: This is a retreat, a vacuum, its virtue is that it lacks everything; deep-freeze for feelings. You can be numb and safe here, that's what you came for. Respect the delicate ecology of your delusions.

HARPER: You mean like no Eskimo in Antarctica.

MR. LIES: Correcto. Ice and snow, no Eskimo. Even hallucinations have laws.

HARPER: Well then who's that?

(*The* ESKIMO *appears.*)

MR. LIES: An Eskimo.

HARPER: An antarctic Eskimo. A fisher of the polar deep.

MR. LIES: There's something wrong with this picture.

(*The* ESKIMO *beckons.*)

HARPER: I'm going to like this place. It's my own National Geographic Special! Oh! Oh! (*She holds her stomach.*) I think . . . I think I felt her kicking. Maybe I'll give birth to a baby covered with thick white fur, and that way she won't be cold. My breasts will be full of hot cocoa so she doesn't get chilly. And if it gets really cold, she'll have a pouch I can crawl into. Like a marsupial. We'll mend together. That's what we'll do; we'll mend.

SCENE IV

Same day. An abandoned lot in the South Bronx. A homeless WOMAN *is standing near an oil drum in which a fire is burning. Snowfall. Trash around.* HANNAH *enters dragging two heavy suitcases.*

HANNAH: Excuse me? I said excuse me? Can you tell me where I am? Is this Brooklyn? Do you know a Pineapple Street? Is there some sort of bus or train or . . . ?

I'm lost, I just arrived from Salt Lake. City. Utah? I took the bus that I was told to take and I got off—well it was the very last stop, so I had to get off, and I *asked* the driver was this Brooklyn but he nodded yes but he was from one of those foreign countries where they think it's good manners to nod at everything even if you have no idea what it is you're nodding at, and in truth I think he spoke no English at all, which I think would make him ineligible for employment on public transportation. The public being English-speaking, mostly. Do you speak English?

(*The* WOMAN *nods.*)

HANNAH: I was supposed to be met at the airport by my son. He didn't show and I don't wait more than three and three-quarters hours for *anyone*. I should have been patient, I guess, I. . . . Is this . . .

WOMAN: Bronx.

HANNAH: Is that. . . . The *Bronx?* Well how in the name of Heaven did I get to the Bronx when the bus driver said . . .

WOMAN: (*Talking to herself.*) Slurp slurp slurp will you STOP that disgusting slurping! YOU DISGUSTING SLURPING FEEDING ANIMAL! Feeding yourself, just feeding yourself, what would it matter, to you or to ANYONE, if you just stopped. Feeding. And DIED?

(*Pause.*)

HANNAH: Can you just tell me where I . . .

WOMAN: Why was the Kosciusko Bridge named after a Polack?

HANNAH: I don't know what you're . . .

WOMAN: That was a joke.

HANNAH: Well what's the punchline?

WOMAN: I don't know.

HANNAH: (*Looking around desperately.*) Oh for pete's sake, is there anyone else who . . .

WOMAN: (*Again, to herself.*) Stand further off you fat loathsome whore, you can't have any more of this soup, slurp slurp slurp you animal, and the—I know you'll just go pee it all away and where will you do that? Behind what bush? It's FUCKING COLD out here and I . . .

Oh that's right, because it was supposed to have been a tunnel!

That's not very funny.

Have you read the prophecies of Nostradamus?

HANNAH: Who?

WOMAN: Some guy I went out with once somewhere, Nos-
45 tradamus. Prophet, outcast, eyes like. . . . Scary shit, he . . .

HANNAH: Shut up. Please. Now I want you to stop jabbering
for a minute and pull your wits together and tell me how to
get to Brooklyn. Because you know! And you are going to
tell me! Because there is no one else around to tell me and
50 I am wet and cold and I am very angry! So I am sorry you're
psychotic but just make the effort—take a deep breath—
DO IT!

(HANNAH *and* WOMAN *breathe together.*)

HANNAH: That's good. Now exhale.

(*They do.*)

HANNAH: Good. Now how do I get to Brooklyn?

55 WOMAN: Don't know. Never been. Sorry. Want some soup?

HANNAH: Manhattan? Maybe you know . . . I don't suppose you
know the location of the Mormon Visitor's . . .

WOMAN: 65th and Broadway.

HANNAH: How do you . . .

60 WOMAN: Go there all the time. Free movies. Boring, but you
can stay all day.

HANNAH: Well. . . . So how do I . . .

WOMAN: Take the D Train. Next block make a right.

HANNAH: Thank you.

65 WOMAN: Oh yeah. In the new century I think we will all be
insane.

SCENE V

Same day. JOE *and* ROY *in the study of* ROY's *brownstone.* ROY *is
wearing an elegant bathrobe. He has made a considerable effort to look
well. He isn't well, and he hasn't succeeded much in looking it.*

JOE: I can't. The answer's no. I'm sorry.

ROY: Oh, well, apologies . . .

I can't see that there's anyone asking for apologies.

(*Pause.*)

JOE: I'm sorry, Roy.

5 ROY: Oh, well, apologies.

JOE: My wife is missing, Roy. My mother's coming from Salt
Lake to . . . to help look, I guess. I'm supposed to be at the
airport now, picking her up but. . . . I just spent two days
in a hospital, Roy, with a bleeding ulcer, I was spitting up
10 blood.

ROY: Blood, huh? Look, I'm very busy here and . . .

JOE: It's just a job.

ROY: A job? A *job? Washington!* Dumb Utah Mormon hick
shit!

15 JOE: Roy . . .

ROY: *WASHINGTON!* When Washington called me I was
younger than you, you think I said "Aw fuck no I can't go
I got two fingers up my asshole and a little moral nosebleed
to boot!" When Washington calls you my pretty young
20 punk friend you go or you can go fuck yourself sideways
'cause the train has pulled out of the station, and you are

out, nowhere, out in the cold. Fuck you, Mary Jane, get
outta here.

JOE: Just let me . . .

ROY: Explain? Ephemera. You broke my heart. Explain that. 25
Explain that.

JOE: I love you. Roy.

There's so much that I want, to be . . . what you see in
me, I want to be a participant in the world, in your world,
Roy, I want to be capable of that, I've tried, really I have but 30
. . . I can't do this. Not because I don't believe in you, but
because I believe in you so much, in what you stand for, at
heart, the order, the decency. I would give anything to protect you, but. . . . There are laws I can't break. It's too ingrained. It's not me. There's enough damage I've already 35
done.

Maybe you were right, maybe I'm dead.

ROY: You're not dead, boy, you're a sissy.

You love me; that's moving, I'm moved. It's nice to be
loved. I warned you about her, didn't I, Joe? But you don't 40
listen to me, why, because you say Roy is smart and Roy's a
friend but Roy . . . well, he isn't nice, and you wanna be
nice. Right? A nice, nice man!

(*Little pause.*)

You know what my greatest accomplishment was, Joe, in
my life, what I am able to look back on and be proudest of? 45
And I have helped make Presidents and unmake them and
mayors and more goddam judges than anyone in NYC
ever—AND several million dollars, tax-free—and what do
you think means the most to me?

You ever hear of Ethel Rosenberg? Huh, Joe, huh? 50

JOE: Well, yeah, I guess I. . . . Yes.

ROY: Yes. Yes. You have heard of Ethel Rosenberg. Yes. Maybe
you even read about her in the history books.

If it wasn't for me, Joe, Ethel Rosenberg would be alive
today, writing some personal-advice column for *Ms.* maga- 55
zine. She isn't. Because during the trial, Joe, I was on the
phone every day, talking with the judge . . .

JOE: Roy . . .

ROY: Every day, doing what I do best, talking on the telephone, making sure that timid Yid nebbish on the bench 60
did his duty to America, to history. That sweet unprepos-
sessing woman, two kids, boo-hoo-hoo, reminded us all of
our little Jewish mamas—she came this close to getting
life; I pleaded till I wept to put her in the chair. Me. I did
that. I would have fucking pulled the switch if they'd have 65
let me. Why? Because I fucking hate traitors. Because I
fucking hate communists. Was it legal? Fuck legal. Am I
a nice man? Fuck nice. They say terrible things about me
in the *Nation.* Fuck the *Nation.* You want to be Nice, or
you want to be Effective? Make the law, or subject to it. 70
Choose. Your wife chose. A week from today, she'll be
back. SHE knows how to get what SHE wants. Maybe I
ought to send *her* to Washington.

JOE: I don't believe you.

ROY: Gospel. 75

JOE: You can't possibly mean what you're saying.

Roy, you were the Assistant United States Attorney on
the Rosenberg case, ex-parte communication with the judge
during the trial would be . . . censurable, at least, probably

80 conspiracy and . . . in a case that resulted in execution, it's . . .
ROY: What? Murder?
JOE: You're not well is all.
ROY: What do you mean, not well? Who's not well?

(Pause.)

85 JOE: You said . . .
ROY: No I didn't. I said what?
JOE: Roy, you have cancer.
ROY: No I don't.

(Pause.)

JOE: You told me you were dying.
90 ROY: What the fuck are you talking about, Joe? I never said that. I'm in perfect health. There's not a goddam thing wrong with me.

(He smiles.)

Shake?

(JOE hesitates. He holds out his hand to ROY. ROY pulls JOE into a close, strong clinch.)

ROY: *(More to himself than to JOE.)* It's OK that you hurt me
95 because I love you, baby Joe. That's why I'm so rough on you.

(ROY releases JOE. JOE backs away a step or two.)

ROY: Prodigal son. The world will wipe its dirty hands all over you.
JOE: It already has, Roy.
100 ROY: Now go.

(ROY shoves JOE hard. JOE turns to leave. ROY stops him, turns him around.)

ROY: *(Smoothing JOE's lapels, tenderly.)* I'll always be here, waiting for you . . .

(Then again, with sudden violence, he pulls JOE close, violently.)

What did you want from me, what was all this, what do you want, treacherous ungrateful little . . .

(JOE, very close to belting ROY, grabs him by the front of his robe, and propels him across the length of the room. He holds ROY at arm's length, the other arm ready to hit.)

105 ROY: *(Laughing softly, almost pleading to be hit.)* Transgress a little, Joseph.

(JOE releases ROY.)

ROY: There are so many laws; find one you can break.

(JOE hesitates, then leaves, backing out. When JOE has gone, ROY doubles over in great pain, which he's been hiding throughout the scene with JOE.)

ROY: Ah, Christ . . .
Andy! Andy! Get in here! Andy!

(The door opens, but it isn't ANDY. A small Jewish Woman dressed modestly in a fifties hat and coat stands in the doorway. The room darkens.)

ROY: Who the fuck are you? The new nurse? 110

(The figure in the doorway says nothing. She stares at ROY. A pause. ROY looks at her carefully, gets up, crosses to her. He crosses back to the chair, sits heavily.)

ROY: Aw, fuck. Ethel.
ETHEL ROSENBERG: *(Her manner is friendly, her voice is ice-cold.)* You don't look good, Roy.
ROY: Well, Ethel. I don't feel good.
ETHEL ROSENBERG: But you lost a lot of weight. That suits you. 115 You were heavy back then. Zaftig, mit hips.
ROY: I haven't been that heavy since 1960. We were all heavier back then, before the body thing started. Now I look like a skeleton. They stare.
ETHEL ROSENBERG: The shit's really hit the fan, huh, Roy? 120

(Little pause. ROY nods.)

ETHEL ROSENBERG: Well the fun's just started.
ROY: What is this, Ethel, Halloween? You trying to scare me?

(ETHEL says nothing.)

ROY: Well you're wasting your time! I'm scarier than you any day of the week! So beat it, Ethel! BOOO! BETTER DEAD THAN RED! Somebody trying to shake me up? HAH 125 HAH! From the throne of God in heaven to the belly of hell, you can all fuck yourselves and then go jump in the lake because I'M NOT AFRAID OF YOU OR DEATH OR HELL OR ANYTHING!
ETHEL ROSENBERG: Be seeing you soon, Roy. Julius sends his 130 regards.
ROY: Yeah, well send this to Julius!

(He flips the bird in her direction, stands and moves towards her. Halfway across the room he slumps to the floor, breathing laboriously, in pain.)

ETHEL ROSENBERG: You're a very sick man, Roy.
ROY: Oh God . . . ANDY!
ETHEL ROSENBERG: Hmmm. He doesn't hear you, I guess. We 135 should call the ambulance.

(She goes to the phone.)

Hah! Buttons! Such things they got now.
What do I dial, Roy?

(Pause. ROY looks at her, then:)

ROY: 911.
ETHEL ROSENBERG: *(Dials the phone.)* It sings! 140
(Imitating dial tones.) La la la . . .
Huh.
Yes, you should please send an ambulance to the home of Mister Roy Cohn, the famous lawyer.

145　　　　What's the address, Roy?

ROY: (A beat, then.) 244 East 87th.

ETHEL ROSENBERG: 244 East 87th Street. No apartment number, he's got the whole building.

　　　　My name? (A beat.) Ethel Greenglass Rosenberg.

150　　　(Small smile.) Me? No I'm not related to Mr. Cohn. An old friend.

(She hangs up.)

　　　They said a minute.

ROY: I have all the time in the world.

ETHEL ROSENBERG: You're immortal.

155 ROY: I'm immortal. Ethel. (He forces himself to stand.)

　　　I have *forced* my way into history. I ain't never gonna die.

ETHEL ROSENBERG: (A little laugh, then.) History is about to crack wide open. Millennium approaches.

SCENE VI

Late that night. PRIOR's *bedroom.* PRIOR 1 *watching* PRIOR *in bed, who is staring back at him, terrified. Tonight* PRIOR 1 *is dressed in weird alchemical robes and hat over his historical clothing and he carries a long palm-leaf bundle.*

PRIOR 1: Tonight's the night! Aren't you excited? Tonight she arrives! Right through the roof! Ha-adam, Ha-gadol . . .

PRIOR 2: (Appearing, similarly attired.) Lumen! Phosphor! Fluor! Candle! An unending billowing of scarlet and . . .

5 PRIOR: Look. Garlic. A mirror. Holy water. A crucifix. FUCK OFF! Get the fuck out of my room! GO!

PRIOR 1: (To PRIOR 2.) Hard as a hickory knob, I'll bet.

PRIOR 2: We all tumesce when they approach. We wax full, like moons.

10 PRIOR 1: Dance.

PRIOR: Dance?

PRIOR 1: Stand up, dammit, give us your hands, dance!

PRIOR 2: Listen . . .

(A lone oboe begins to play a little dance tune.)

PRIOR 2: Delightful sound. Care to dance?

15 PRIOR: Please leave me alone, please just let me sleep . . .

PRIOR 2: Ah, he wants someone familiar. A partner who knows his steps. (To PRIOR.) Close your eyes. Imagine . . .

PRIOR: I don't . . .

PRIOR 2: Hush. Close your eyes.

(PRIOR does.)

20 PRIOR 2: Now open them.

(PRIOR does. LOUIS appears. He looks gorgeous. The music builds gradually into a full-blooded, romantic dance tune.)

PRIOR: Lou.

LOUIS: Dance with me.

PRIOR: I can't, my leg, it hurts at night . . .

　　　Are you . . . a ghost, Lou?

25 LOUIS: No. Just spectral. Lost to myself. Sitting all day on cold park benches. Wishing I could be with you. Dance with me, babe . . .

(PRIOR stands up. The leg stops hurting. They begin to dance. The music is beautiful.)

PRIOR 1: (To PRIOR 2.) Hah. Now I see why he's got no children. He's a sodomite.

PRIOR 2: Oh be quiet, you medieval gnome, and let them 30 dance.

PRIOR 1: I'm not interfering, I've done my bit. Hooray, hooray, the messenger's come, now I'm blowing off. I don't like it here.

(PRIOR 1 vanishes.)

PRIOR 2: The twentieth century. Oh dear, the world has gotten 35 so terribly, terribly old.

(PRIOR 2 vanishes. LOUIS and PRIOR waltz happily. Lights fade back to normal. LOUIS vanishes.)

(PRIOR dances alone.)

(Then suddenly, the sound of wings fills the room.)

SCENE VII

Split scene: PRIOR *alone in his apartment;* LOUIS *alone in the park.*

Again, a sound of beating wings.

PRIOR: Oh don't come in here don't come in . . . LOUIS!! No. My name is Prior Walter, I am . . . the scion of an ancient line, I am . . . abandoned I . . . no, my name is . . . is . . . Prior and I live . . . *here and now,* and . . . in the dark, in the dark, the Recording Angel opens its hundred eyes and 5 snaps the spine of the Book of Life and . . . hush! Hush! I'm talking nonsense, I . . .

　　　No more mad scene, hush, hush . . .

(LOUIS in the park on a bench. JOE approaches, stands at a distance. They stare at each other, then LOUIS turns away.)

LOUIS: Do you know the story of Lazarus?

JOE: Lazarus?　　　　　　　　　　　　　　　　　　　　　　10

LOUIS: Lazarus. I can't remember what happens, exactly.

JOE: I don't. . . . Well, he was dead, Lazarus, and Jesus breathed life into him. He brought him back from death.

LOUIS: Come here often?

JOE: No. Yes. Yes.　　　　　　　　　　　　　　　　　　　15

LOUIS: Back from the dead. You believe that really happened?

JOE: I don't know anymore what I believe.

LOUIS: This is quite a coincidence. Us meeting.

JOE: I followed you.

　　　From work. I . . . followed you here.　　　　　　　　20

(Pause.)

LOUIS: You followed me.

　　　You probably saw me that day in the washroom and thought: there's a sweet guy, sensitive, cries for friends in trouble.

JOE: Yes.　　　　　　　　　　　　　　　　　　　　　　25

LOUIS: You thought maybe I'll cry for you.

JOE: Yes.

LOUIS: Well I fooled you. Crocodile tears. Nothing . . . *(He touches his heart, shrugs.)*

(JOE reaches tentatively to touch LOUIS's face.)

30 LOUIS: *(Pulling back.)* What are you doing? Don't do that.
JOE: *(Withdrawing his hand.)* Sorry. I'm sorry.
LOUIS: I'm . . . just not . . . I think, if you touch me, your hand might fall off or something. Worse things have happened to people who have touched me.
35 JOE: Please.
   Oh, boy . . .
   Can I . . .
   I . . . want . . . to touch you. Can I please just touch you . . . um, here?

(He puts his hand on one side of LOUIS's face. He holds it there.)

40   I'm going to hell for doing this.
LOUIS: Big deal. You think it could be any worse than New York City?
      (He puts his hand on JOE's hand. He takes JOE's hand away from his face, holds it for a moment, then.) Come on.
45 JOE: Where?
LOUIS: Home. With me.
JOE: This makes no sense. I mean I don't know you.
LOUIS: Likewise.
JOE: And what you do know about me you don't like.
50 LOUIS: The Republican stuff?
JOE: Yeah, well for starters.
LOUIS: I don't not like that. I *hate* that.
JOE: So why on earth should we . . .

(LOUIS goes to JOE and kisses him.)

LOUIS: Strange bedfellows. I don't know. I never made it with
55   one of the damned before.
      I would really rather not have to spend tonight alone.
JOE: I'm a pretty terrible person, Louis.
LOUIS: Lou.
JOE: No, I really really am. I don't think I deserve being loved.
60 LOUIS: There? See? We already have a lot in common.

(LOUIS stands, begins to walk away. He turns, looks back at JOE. JOE follows. They exit.)

(PRIOR listens. At first no sound, then once again, the sound of beating wings, frighteningly near.)

PRIOR: That sound, that sound, it. . . . What is that, like birds or something, like a *really* big bird, I'm frightened, I . . . no, no fear, find the anger, find the . . . anger, my blood is clean, my brain is fine, I can handle pressure, I am a gay man and I am used to pressure, to trouble, I am tough and 65 strong and. . . . Oh. Oh my goodness. I . . . *(He is washed over by an intense sexual feeling.)* Ooohhhh. . . . I'm hot, I'm . . . so . . . aw Jeez what is going on here I . . . must have a fever I . . .

(The bedside lamp flickers wildly as the bed begins to roll forward and back. There is a deep bass creaking and groaning from the bedroom ceiling, like the timbers of a ship under immense stress, and from above a fine rain of plaster dust.)

PRIOR: OH!   70
      PLEASE, OH PLEASE! Something's coming in here, I'm scared, I don't like this at all, something's approaching and I. . . . OH!

(There is a great blaze of triumphal music, heralding. The light turns an extraordinary harsh, cold, pale blue, then a rich, brilliant warm golden color, then a hot, bilious green, and then finally a spectacular royal purple. Then silence.)

PRIOR: *(An awestruck whisper.)* God almighty . . .
      Very Steven Spielberg.   75

(A sound, like a plummeting meteor, tears down from very, very far above the earth, hurtling at an incredible velocity towards the bedroom; the light seems to be sucked out of the room as the projectile approaches; as the room reaches darkness, we hear a terrifying CRASH as something immense strikes earth; the whole building shudders and a part of the bedroom ceiling, lots of plaster and lathe and wiring, crashes to the floor. And then in a shower of unearthly white light, spreading great opalescent gray-silver wings, the ANGEL descends into the room and floats above the bed.)

ANGEL: Greetings, Prophet;
      The Great Work begins:
      The Messenger has arrived.

(Blackout.)

SUZAN-LORI PARKS

Suzan-Lori Parks (b. 1963) is among the best known African-American playwrights writing today; her work is characterized by brilliant language and elegant and powerful imagery onstage. She is the author of *Betting on the Dust Commander* (1987), *Imperceptible Mutabilities in the Third Kingdom* (1989), *The Death of the Last Black Man in the Whole Entire World* (1990), *The America Play* (1994), and *Venus* (1995). She has won a range of awards for her playwriting, collaborated on the script for the Spike Lee film *Girl 6,* and is an Associate Artist of the Yale School of Drama.

THE AMERICA PLAY

The America Play, for all its formal and verbal complexity, is a play about history, a play about how the construction of history takes place over time, and implicates our action in the present. Like many of Parks's plays, *The America Play* doesn't quite proceed along the lines of an Aristotelian, causal plot, one event seeming to "cause" another. Instead, Parks's plays proceed through what she calls "rep and rev"—repetition and revision, akin to the conventions of African-American oral and song traditions—and this patterning pervades both the verbal texture of the play and its physical and temporal organization on the stage, as well. The dominant image of the play is a kind of theme park, "A great hole. In the middle of nowhere. The hole is an exact replica of the Great Hole of History." In the park, the central character The Foundling Father has a kind of vaudeville act: "his act would now consist of a single chair, a rocker, in a dark box. The public was invited to pay a penny, choose from the selection of provided pistols, enter the darkened box and 'Shoot Mr. Lincoln.'" Throughout the first half of *The America Play,* the Foundling Father performs his act, with a variety of different beards, and a variety of different people arriving to play John Wilkes Booth. In act 2, Lucy and Brazil dig in the replica of the Great Hole, hoping to find the echo of the Foundling Father's act.

On the horizon of contemporary American drama, there are few playwrights whose work is as challenging and rewarding as Parks's. Reminiscent in some respects of the formal difficulty of Adrienne Kennedy's plays, such as *Funnyhouse of a Negro* or *A Movie Star Has to Star in Black and White, The America Play* undertakes a searching interrogation of the space of African-American history. One way into thinking about the play is to consider how theme parks work. Despite creating a visible, concrete appearance to the contrary, theme parks don't claim to produce the *real* historical event: Plimoth Plantation in Massachusetts, Colonial Williamsburg in Virginia, even Shakespeare's Globe in London, construct a contemporary "image" of history, a place—with whatever signs of authenticity—in which we can reenact, perform, imagine the past, always recognizing that that "past" is a past we make today, in the present, and as the present. Parks's play concerns a history that is at once a "whole"—something fixed, agreed-upon, monolithic, like "American History," or "the Assassination of President Lincoln"—and a "hole," a place where things are lost, absent, like much of the history of African-Americans in the United States. *The America Play* enacts a double displacement of history: we don't have access to it directly, but only via its reenactment, in the theme park that is "an exact replica" of the w/hole of history.

On the page and on the stage, Parks's interrogation of history works through a challenging process of metaphor and analogy. Much as the Foundling Father has moved his replica to the west, we might imagine that *The America Play* figures the course of westward expansion; yet the museum-hole brings with it its founding mythologies, as though what fashions the nation is the process of the Foundling Father's act: "Fakin was your Daddys callin but diggin was his livelihood." The nation is produced as a "nation" through an ongoing process of "fakin," reenacting—with whatever beard, with whatever slogans, seem appropriate—the founding imagery of the nation. Like the Foundling Father himself, an African-American man with a collection of Lincolnesque beards, we can only perform our sense of national origin—fakin and diggin at the same time, so to speak—by recognizing that origin, that *founding* moment as something we are always orphaned by, *foundlings*.

THE AMERICA PLAY

Suzan-Lori Parks

IN THE BEGINNING, ALL THE WORLD WAS AMERICA

—JOHN LOCKE

——— CHARACTERS ———

ACT ONE

THE FOUNDLING FATHER, AS ABRAHAM LINCOLN
A VARIETY OF VISITORS

ACT TWO

LUCY
BRAZIL
THE FOUNDLING FATHER, AS ABRAHAM LINCOLN
2 ACTORS

The Visitors in Act One are played by the 2 ACTORS *who assume the roles in the passages from* Our American Cousin *in Act Two.*

PLACE: *A great hole. In the middle of nowhere. The hole is an exact replica of The Great Hole of History.*

——— SYNOPSIS OF ACTS AND SCENES ———

Act I   Lincoln Act
Act II The Hall of Wonders
    A. Big Bang
    B. Echo
    C. Archeology
    D. Echo
    E. Spadework
    F. Echo
    G. The Great Beyond

Brackets in the text indicate optional cuts for production.

——— ACT ONE ———

LINCOLN ACT

A great hole. In the middle of nowhere. The hole is an exact replica of the Great Hole of History.

THE FOUNDLING FATHER, AS ABRAHAM LINCOLN: "To stop too fearful and too faint to go."

(Rest.)

"He digged the hole and the whole held him."

(Rest.)

"I cannot dig, to beg I am ashamed."

(Rest.)

5 "He went to the theatre but home went she."

(Rest.)

Goatee. Goatee. What he sported when he died. Its not my favorite.

(Rest.)

"He digged the hole and the whole held him." Huh.

(Rest.)

10 There was once a man who was told that he bore a strong resemblance to Abraham Lincoln. He was tall and thinly built just like the Great Man. His legs were the longer part just like the Great Mans legs. His hands and feet were large as the Great Mans were large. The Lesser Known had several beards which he carried around in a box. The beards were his al-

15 though he himself had not grown them on his face but since he'd secretly bought the hairs from his barber and arranged their beard shapes and since the procurement and upkeep of his beards took so much work he figured that the beards were completely his. Were as authentic as he was, so to speak. His

20 beard box was of cherry wood and lined with purple velvet. He had the initials "A.L." tooled in gold on the lid.

(Rest.)

While the Great Mans livelihood kept him in Big Town the Lesser Knowns work kept him in Small Town. The Great Man by trade was a President. The Lesser Known was a

25 Digger by trade. From a family of Diggers. Digged graves. He was known in Small Town to dig his graves quickly and neatly. This brought him a steady business.

(Rest.)

A wink to Mr. Lincolns pasteboard cutout. *(Winks at Lincoln's pasteboard cutout.)*

(Rest.)

30 It would be helpful to our story if when the Great Man died in death he were to meet the Lesser Known. It would be helpful to our story if, say, the Lesser Known were summoned to Big Town by the Great Mans wife: "*Emergency* oh, *Emergency,* please put the Great Man in the ground" (they

35 say the Great Mans wife was given to hysterics: one young son dead others sickly: even the Great Man couldnt save them: a war on then off and surrendered to: "Play Dixie I always liked that song": the brother against the brother: a new nation all conceived and ready to be hatched: the Great

40 Man takes to guffawing guffawing at thin jokes in bad plays: "You sockdologizing old man-trap!" haw haw haw because he wants so very badly to laugh at something and one moment guffawing and the next moment the Great Man is gunned down. In his rocker. "Useless. Useless." And

45 there were bills to pay.) "*Emergency,* oh *Emergency* please put the Great Man in the ground."

(Rest.)

1–2 "**To stop . . . go**" an example of chiasmus, by Oliver Goldsmith, cited under "chiasmus" in *Webster's Ninth New Collegiate Dictionary* (Springfield, MA: Merriam-Webster, Inc., 1983) p. 232. Notes 2 and 3 also refer to examples of chiasmus   4 "**I . . . ashamed**" *A Dictionary of Modern English Usage,* H.W. Fowler (New York: Oxford University Press, 1983) p. 86   5 "**He . . . she**" *The New American Heritage Dictionary of the English Language,* William Morris, ed. (Boston: Houghton Mifflin Co., 1981) p. 232

33–34 "**Emergency . . . ground**" possibly the words of Mary Todd Lincoln after the death of her husband   37–38 "**Play . . . song**" at the end of the Civil War, President Lincoln told his troops to play "Dixie," the song of the South, in tribute to the Confederacy   41 "**You . . . man-trap**" a very funny line from the play *Our American Cousin.* As the audience roared with laughter, Booth entered Lincoln's box and shot him dead   44 "**Useless Useless.**" the last words of President Lincoln's assassin, John Wilkes Booth

It is said that the Great Mans wife did call out and it is said
that the Lesser Known would [sneak away from his digging
and stand behind a tree where he couldnt be seen or get up
and] leave his wife and child after the blessing had been said
and [the meat carved during the distribution of the vegetables it is said that he would leave his wife and his child and]
standing in the kitchen or sometimes out in the yard [be-
tween the right angles of the house] stand out there where
he couldnt be seen standing with his ear cocked. "*Emergency,*
oh *Emergency,* please put the Great Man in the ground."
(*Rest.*)
It would help if she had called out and if he had been summoned been given a ticket all bought and paid for and
boarded a train in his look-alike black frock coat bought on
time and already exhausted. Ridiculous. If he had been
summoned. [Been summoned between the meat and the
vegetables and boarded a train to Big Town where he would
line up and gawk at the Great Mans corpse along with the
rest of them.] But none of this was meant to be.
(*Rest.*)
A nod to the bust of Mr. Lincoln. (*Nods to the bust of Lincoln.*)
But none of this was meant to be. For the Great Man had
been murdered long before the Lesser Known had been born.
Howuhboutthat. [So that any calling that had been done he
couldnt hear, any summoning he had hoped for he couldnt
answer but somehow not even unheard and unanswered because he hadnt even been there] although you should note
that he talked about the murder and the mourning that followed as if he'd been called away on business at the time and
because of the business had missed it. Living regretting he
hadnt arrived sooner. Being told from birth practically that
he and the Great Man were dead ringers, more or less, and
knowing that he, if he had been in the slightest vicinity
back then, would have had at least a chance at the great
honor of digging the Great Mans grave.
(*Rest.*)
This beard I wear for the holidays. I got shoes to match.
Rarely wear em together. Its a little *much.*
(*Rest.*)
[His son named in a fit of meanspirit after the bad joke
about fancy nuts and old mens toes his son looked like a nobody. Not Mr. Lincoln or the father or the mother either for
that matter although the father had assumed the superior-
ity of his own blood and hadnt really expected the mother
to exert any influence.]
(*Rest.*)
Sunday. Always slow on Sunday. I'll get thuh shoes. Youll
see. A wink to Mr. Lincolns pasteboard cutout. (*Winks at
Lincoln's cutout.*)
(*Rest.*)
Everyone who has ever walked the earth has a shape around
which their entire lives and their posterity shapes itself. The
Great Man had his log cabin into which he was born, the
distance between the cabin and Big Town multiplied by
the half-life, the staying power of his words and image, being the true measurement of the Great Mans stature. The
Lesser Known had a favorite hole. A chasm, really. Not a
hole he had digged but one he'd visited. Long before the
son was born. When he and his Lucy were newly wedded.
Lucy kept secrets for the dead. And they figured what with
his digging and her Confidence work they could build a

mourning business. The son would be a weeper. Such a long
time uhgo. So long uhgo. When he and his Lucy were newly
wedded and looking for some postnuptial excitement: A Big
Hole. A theme park. With historical parades. The size of
the hole itself was enough to impress any Digger but it
was the Historicity of the place the order and beauty of
the pageants which marched by them the Greats on parade
in front of them. From the sidelines he'd be calling
"Ohwayohwhyohwayoh" and "Hello" and waving and saluting. The Hole and its Historicity and the part he played in
it all gave a shape to the life and posterity of the Lesser
Known that he could never shake.
(*Rest.*)
Here they are. I wont put them on. I'll just hold them up.
See. Too much. Told ya. Much much later when the Lesser
Known had made a name for himself he began to record his
own movements. He hoped he'd be of interest to posterity.
As in the Great Mans footsteps.
(*Rest.*)
Traveling home again from the honeymoon at the Big Hole
riding the train with his Lucy: wife beside him the Reconstructed Historicities he has witnessed continue to march
before him in his minds eye as they had at the Hole. Cannons wicks were lit and the rockets did blare and the enemy
was slain and lay stretched out and smoldering for dead and
rose up again to take their bows. On the way home again the
histories paraded again on past him although it wasnt on
past him at all it wasnt something he could expect but
again like Lincolns life not "on past" but *past. Behind him.*
Like an echo in his head.
(*Rest.*)
When he got home again he began to hear the summoning.
At first they thought it only an echo. Memories sometimes
stuck like that and he and his Lucy had both seen visions.
But after a while it only called to him. And it became louder
not softer but louder louder as if he were moving toward it.
(*Rest.*)
This is my fancy beard. Yellow. Mr. Lincolns hair was dark
so I dont wear it much. If you deviate too much they wont
get their pleasure. Thats my experience. Some inconsistencies are perpetuatable because theyre good for business. But
not the yellow beard. Its just my fancy. Ev-ery once and a
while. Of course, his hair was dark.
(*Rest.*)
The Lesser Known left his wife and child and went out West
finally. [Between the meat and the vegetables. A monumentous journey. Enduring all the elements. Without a friend in
the world. And the beasts of the forest took him in. He got
there and he got his plot he staked his claim he tried his
hand at his own Big Hole.] As it had been back East everywhere out West he went people remarked on his likeness to
Lincoln. How, in a limited sort of way, taking into account
of course his natural God-given limitations, how he was
identical to the Great Man in gait and manner how his legs
were long and torso short. The Lesser Known had by this
time taken to wearing a false wart on his cheek in remembrance of the Great Mans wart. When the Westerners noted
his wart they pronounced the 2 men in virtual twinship.
(*Rest.*)
Goatee. Huh. Goatee.
(*Rest.*)

"He digged the Hole and the Whole held him."
(*Rest.*)
     "I cannot dig, to beg I am ashamed."
(*Rest.*)
     The Lesser Known had under his belt a few of the Great
Mans words and after a day of digging, in the evenings,
160 would stand in his hole reciting. But the Lesser Known was
a curiosity at best. None of those who spoke of his virtual
twinship with greatness would actually pay money to watch
him be that greatness. One day he tacked up posters inviting them to come and throw old food at him while he
165 spoke. This was a moderate success. People began to save
their old food "for Mr. Lincoln" they said. He took to traveling playing small towns. Made money. And when someone remarked that he played Lincoln so well that he ought
to be shot, it was as if the Great Mans footsteps had been
170 suddenly revealed:
     (*Rest.*)
     The Lesser Known returned to his hole and, instead of
speeching, his act would now consist of a single chair, a
rocker, in a dark box. The public was invited to pay a
penny, choose from the selection of provided pistols, enter
175 the darkened box and "Shoot Mr. Lincoln." The Lesser
Known became famous overnight.

(A MAN, *as John Wilkes Booth, enters. He takes a gun and "stands in
position": at the left side of the* FOUNDLING FATHER, *as* ABRAHAM
LINCOLN, *pointing the gun at the* FOUNDLING FATHER'*s head.*)

A MAN: Ready.
THE FOUNDLING FATHER: Haw Haw Haw Haw
(*Rest.*)
     HAW HAW HAW HAW

(*Booth shoots.* LINCOLN *"slumps in his chair." Booth jumps.*)

180 A MAN: (*Theatrically.*) "Thus to the tyrants!"
(*Rest.*)
     Hhhh. (*Exits.*)
THE FOUNDLING FATHER: Most of them do that, thuh "Thus to
the tyrants!"—what they say the killer said. "Thus to the
tyrants!" The killer was also heard to say "The South is
185 avenged!" Sometimes they yell that.

(A MAN, *the same man as before, enters again, again as John Wilkes
Booth. He takes a gun and "stands in position": at the left side of the*
FOUNDLING FATHER, AS ABRAHAM LINCOLN, *pointing the gun at
the* FOUNDLING FATHER'*s head.*)

A MAN: Ready.
THE FOUNDLING FATHER: Haw Haw Haw Haw
(*Rest.*)
     HAW HAW HAW HAW

(*Booth shoots.* LINCOLN *"slumps in his chair." Booth jumps.*)

---

180 "**Thus . . . tyrants!**" or "Sic semper tyrannis." Purportedly,
Booth's words after he slew Lincoln and leapt from the presidential box to the stage of Ford's Theatre in Washington, D.C. on 14
April 1865, not only killing the President but also interrupting a
performance of *Our American Cousin*, starring Miss Laura Keene
184–85 "**The South . . . avenged**" allegedly, Booth's words

A MAN: (*Theatrically.*) "The South is avenged!"
(*Rest.*)
     Hhhh.   190
(*Rest.*)
     Thank you.
THE FOUNDLING FATHER: Pleasures mine.
A MAN: Till next week.
THE FOUNDLING FATHER: Till next week.

(A MAN *exits.*)

THE FOUNDLING FATHER: Comes once a week that one. Always 195
chooses the Derringer although we've got several styles he
always chooses the Derringer. Always "The tyrants" and then
"The South avenged." The ones who choose the Derringer are
the ones for History. He's one for History. As it Used to Be.
Never wavers. No frills. By the book. Nothing excessive.   200
(*Rest.*)
     A nod to Mr. Lincolns bust. (*Nods to Lincoln's bust.*)
(*Rest.*)
     I'll wear this one. He sported this style in the early war
years. Years of uncertainty. When he didnt know if the war
was right when it could be said he didnt always know which
side he was on not because he was a stupid man but because 205
it was sometimes not 2 different sides at all but one great
side surging toward something beyond either Northern or
Southern. A beard of uncertainty. The Lesser Known meanwhile living his life long after all this had happened and not
knowing much about it until he was much older [(as a boy   210
"The Civil War" was an afterschool game and his folks didnt
mention the Great Mans murder for fear of frightening
him)] knew only that he was a dead ringer in a family of
Diggers and that he wanted to grow and have others think
of him and remove their hats and touch their hearts and look 215
up into the heavens and say something about the freeing of
the slaves. That is, he wanted to make a great impression as
he understood Mr. Lincoln to have made.
(*Rest.*)
     And so in his youth the Lesser Known familiarized himself
with all aspects of the Great Mans existence. What inter-   220
ested the Lesser Known most was the murder and what was
most captivating about the murder was the 20 feet—

(A WOMAN, *as Booth, enters.*)

A WOMAN: Excuse me.
THE FOUNDLING FATHER: Not at all.

(A WOMAN, *as Booth, "stands in position."*)

THE FOUNDLING FATHER: Haw Haw Haw Haw   225
(*Rest.*)
     HAW HAW HAW HAW

(*Booth shoots.* LINCOLN *"slumps in his chair." Booth jumps.*)

A WOMAN: "Strike the tent." (*Exits.*)
THE FOUNDLING FATHER: What interested the Lesser Known most
about the Great Mans murder was the 20 feet which separated

---

227 "**Strike the tent**" the last words of General Robert E. Lee,
Commander of the Confederate Army

230 the presidents box from the stage. In the presidents box sat the president his wife and their 2 friends. On the stage that night was *Our American Cousin* starring Miss Laura Keene. The plot of this play is of little consequence to our story. Suffice it to say that it was thinly comedic and somewhere in the 3rd Act a
235 man holds a gun to his head—something about despair—
(Rest.)

Ladies and Gentlemen: *Our American Cousin*—

(B WOMAN, as Booth, enters. She "stands in position.")

B WOMAN: Go ahead.
THE FOUNDLING FATHER: Haw Haw Haw Haw
(Rest.)
        HAW HAW HAW HAW

(Booth shoots. LINCOLN *"slumps in his chair." Booth jumps.)*

240 B WOMAN: *(Rest.)* LIES!
(Rest.)
        LIIIIIIIIIIIIIIIIIIIIIIIIIIIES!
(Rest.)
        LIIIIIIIIIIIIIIIIIIIIIIARRRRRRRRRRRRRRRRRS!
(Rest.)
        Lies.
(Rest. Exits. Reenters. Steps downstage. Rest.)
        LIES!
(Rest.)
245   LIIIIIIIIIIIIIIIIIIIIIIIIIIIES!
(Rest.)
        LIIIIIIIIIIIIIIIIIIIIIARRRRRRRRRRRRRRRRRS!
(Rest.)
        Lies
(Rest. Exits.)
THE FOUNDLING FATHER: *(Rest.)* I think I'll wear the yellow one. Variety. Works like uh tonic.
(Rest.)
250 Some inaccuracies are good for business. Take the stovepipe hat! Never really worn indoors but people dont like their Lincoln hatless.
(Rest.)
        Mr. Lincoln my apologies. *(Nods to the bust and winks to the cutout.)*
(Rest.)
255 [Blonde. Not bad if you like a stretch. Hmmm. Let us pretend for a moment that our beloved Mr. Lincoln was a blonde. "The sun on his fair hair looked like the sun itself." Now. What interested our Mr. Lesser Known most was those feet between where the Great *Blonde* Man sat, in his rocker,
260 the stage, the time it took the murderer to cross that expanse, and how the murderer crossed it. He jumped. Broke his leg in the jumping. It was said that the Great Mans wife then began to scream. (She was given to hysterics several years afterward in fact declared insane did you know she ran around Big
265 Town poor desperate for money trying to sell her clothing? On that sad night she begged her servant: "Bring in Taddy,

---

257 **"The sun . . . itself"** from "The Sun," a composition by The Foundling Father, unpublished   266 **"Bring . . . Taddy"** Mary Todd Lincoln, wanting her dying husband to speak to their son Tad, might have said this that night

Father will speak to Taddy." But Father died instead unconscious. And she went mad from grief. Off her rocker. Mad Mary claims she hears her dead men. Summoning. The older son, Robert, he locked her up: "*Emergency*, oh, *Emergency* 270 please put the Great Man in the ground.")

(Enter B MAN, as Booth. He "stands in position.")

THE FOUNDLING FATHER: Haw Haw Haw Haw
(Rest.)
        HAW HAW HAW HAW

(Booth shoots. LINCOLN *"slumps in his chair." Booth jumps.)*

B MAN: "Now he belongs to the ages."
(Rest.)
        Blonde?   275
THE FOUNDLING FATHER: (I only talk with the regulars.)
B MAN: He wasnt blonde. *(Exits.)*
THE FOUNDLING FATHER: A slight deafness in this ear other than that there are no side effects.
(Rest.)
        Hhh. Clean-shaven for a while. The face needs air. Clean- 280 shaven as in his youth. When he met his Mary.—. Hhh. Blonde.
(Rest.)
        6 feet under is a long way to go. Imagine. When the Lesser Known left to find his way out West he figured he had dug over 7 hundred and 23 graves. 7 hundred and 23. Exclud- 285 ing his Big Hole. Excluding the hundreds of shallow holes he later digs the hundreds of shallow holes he'll use to bury his faux-historical knickknacks when he finally quits this business. Not including those. 7 hundred and 23 graves.

(C MAN and C WOMAN enter.)

C MAN: You allow 2 at once?   290
THE FOUNDLING FATHER
(Rest.)
C WOMAN: We're just married. You know: newlyweds. We hope you dont mind. Us both at once.
THE FOUNDLING FATHER
(Rest.)
C MAN: We're just married.   295
C WOMAN: Newlyweds.
THE FOUNDLING FATHER
(Rest.)
(Rest.)

(They "stand in position." Both hold one gun.)

C MAN and C WOMAN: Shoot.
THE FOUNDLING FATHER: Haw Haw Haw Haw
(Rest.)
        HAW HAW HAW HAW   300
(Rest.)
(Rest.)
        HAW HAW HAW HAW

---

274 **"Now . . . ages"** the words of Secretary of War Edwin Stanton, as Lincoln died

(They shoot. LINCOLN *"slumps in his chair." They jump.)*

C MAN: Go on.

C WOMAN: *(Theatrically.)* "They've killed the president!"

(Rest. They exit.)

THE FOUNDLING FATHER: Theyll have children and theyll bring
their children here. A slight deafness in this ear other than
that there are no side effects. Little ringing in the ears.
Slight deafness. I cant complain.

(Rest.)

The passage of time. The crossing of space. [The Lesser
Known recorded his every movement.] He'd hoped he'd be
of interest in his posterity. [Once again riding in the Great
Mans footsteps.] A nod to the presidents bust. *(Nods.)*

(Rest.)

(Rest.)

The Great Man lived in the past that is was an inhabitant
of time immemorial and the Lesser Known out West alive
a resident of the present. And the Great Mans deeds had
transpired during the life of the Great Man somewhere in
past-land that is somewhere "back there" and all this while
the Lesser Known digging his holes bearing the burden of
his resemblance all the while trying somehow to equal the
Great Man in stature, word and deed going forward with
his lesser life trying somehow to follow in the Great Mans
footsteps footsteps that were of course behind him. The
Lesser Known trying somehow to catch up to the Great
Man all this while and maybe running too fast in the wrong
direction. Which is to say that maybe the Great Man had
to catch him. Hhhh. Ridiculous.

(Rest.)

Full fringe. The way he appears on the money.

(Rest.)

A wink to Mr. Lincolns pasteboard cutout. A nod to Mr.
Lincolns bust.

(Rest. Time passes. Rest.)

When someone remarked that he played Lincoln so well
that he ought to be shot it was as if the Great Mans footsteps had been suddenly revealed: instead of making
speeches his act would now consist of a single chair, a
rocker, in a dark box. The public was cordially invited to
pay a penny, choose from a selection of provided pistols enter the darkened box and "Shoot Mr. Lincoln." The Lesser
Known became famous overnight.

(A MAN, *as John Wilkes Booth, enters. He takes a gun and "stands in
position": at the left side of the* FOUNDLING FATHER, *as Abraham
Lincoln, pointing the gun at the* FOUNDLING FATHER'S *head.)*

THE FOUNDLING FATHER: Mmm. Like clockwork.

A MAN: Ready.

THE FOUNDLING FATHER: Haw Haw Haw Haw

(Rest.)

HAW HAW HAW HAW

(Booth shoots. LINCOLN *"slumps in his chair." Booth jumps.)*

---

303 **"They've . . . president!"** the words of Mary Todd, just after
Lincoln was shot

A MAN: *(Theatrically.)* "Thus to the tyrants!"

(Rest.)

Hhhh.

LINCOLN

BOOTH

LINCOLN   345

BOOTH

LINCOLN

BOOTH

LINCOLN

BOOTH   350

LINCOLN

*(*BOOTH *jumps.)*

A MAN: *(Theatrically.)* "The South is avenged!"

(Rest.)

Hhhh.

(Rest.)

Thank you.

THE FOUNDLING FATHER: Pleasures mine.   355

A MAN: Next week then. *(Exits.)*

THE FOUNDLING FATHER: Little ringing in the ears. Slight deafness.

(Rest.)

Little ringing in the ears.

(Rest.)

A wink to the Great Mans cutout. A nod to the Great Mans
bust. *(Winks and nods.)* Once again striding in the Great 360
Mans footsteps. Riding on in. Riding to the rescue the way
they do. They both had such long legs. Such big feet. And
the Greater Man had such a lead although of course somehow
still "back there." If the Lesser Known had slowed down
stopped moving completely gone in reverse died maybe the 365
Greater Man could have caught up. Woulda had a chance.
Woulda sneaked up behind him the Greater Man would have
sneaked up behind the Lesser Known unbeknownst and
wrestled him to the ground. Stabbed him in the back. In revenge. "Thus to the tyrants!" Shot him maybe. The Lesser 370
Known forgets who he is and just crumples. His bones cannot be found. The Greater Man continues on.

(Rest.)

"Emergency, oh *Emergency,* please put the Great Man in the
ground."

(Rest.)

Only a little ringing in the ears. Thats all. Slight deafness. 375

(Rest.)

Huh. Whatdoyou say I wear the blonde.

(Rest.)

(A gunshot echoes. Softly. And echoes.)

——— ACT TWO ———

THE HALL OF WONDERS

*A gunshot echoes. Loudly. And echoes. They are in a great hole. In the
middle of nowhere. The hole is an exact replica of The Great Hole of
History. A gunshot echoes. Loudly. And echoes.* LUCY *with ear trumpet circulates.* BRAZIL *digs.*

A. BIG BANG

LUCY: Hear that?

BRAZIL: Zit him?

LUCY: No.

BRAZIL: Oh.

(A gunshot echoes. Loudly. And echoes.)

5 LUCY: Hear?

BRAZIL: Zit him?!

LUCY: Nope. Ssuhecho.

BRAZIL: Ssuhecho.

LUCY: Uh echo uh huhn. Of gunplay. Once upon uh time some-
10   body had uh little gunplay and now thuh gun goes on play-
      ing: *KER-BANG!* KERBANG-Kerbang-kerbang-(kerbang)-
      ((kerbang)).

BRAZIL: Thuh echoes.

(Rest.)

(Rest.)

LUCY: Youre stopped.

15 BRAZIL: Mmlistenin.

LUCY: Dig on, Brazil. Cant stop diggin till you dig up some-
      thin. Your Daddy was uh Digger.

BRAZIL: Uh huhnnn.

LUCY

20 BRAZIL

*(A gunshot echoes. Loudly. And echoes. Rest. A gunshot echoes.
Loudly. And echoes. Rest.)*

[LUCY: Itssalways been important in my line to distinguish.
      Tuh know thuh difference. Not like your Fathuh. Your
      Fathuh became confused. His lonely death and lack of
      proper burial is our embarrassment. Go on: dig. Now me I
25   need tuh know thuh real thing from thuh echo. Thuh truth
      from thuh hearsay.

(Rest.)

      Bram Price for example. His dear ones and relations told me
      his dying words but Bram Price hisself of course told me
      something quite different.

30 BRAZIL: I wept forim.

LUCY: Whispered his true secrets to me and to me uhlone.

BRAZIL: Then he died.

LUCY: Then he died.

(Rest.)

      Thuh things he told me I will never tell. Mr. Bram Price.
35   Huh.

(Rest.)

      Dig on.

BRAZIL

LUCY

BRAZIL

40 LUCY: Little Bram Price Junior.

BRAZIL: Thuh fat one?

LUCY: Burned my eardrums. Just like his Dad did.

BRAZIL: I wailed forim.

LUCY: Ten days dead wept over and buried and that boy comes
45   back. Not him though. His echo. Sits down tuh dinner and
      eats up everybodys food just like he did when he was livin.

(Rest.)

(Rest.)

      Little Bram Junior. Burned my eardrums. Miz Penny Price
      his mother. Thuh things she told me I will never tell.

(Rest.)

      You remember her.

BRAZIL: Wore red velvet in August.   50

LUCY: When her 2 Brams passed she sold herself, son.

BRAZIL: O.

LUCY: Also lost her mind.—. She finally went. Like your
      Fathuh went, perhaps. Foul play.

BRAZIL: I gnashed for her.   55

LUCY: You did.

BRAZIL: Couldnt choose between wailin or gnashin. Weepin
      sobbin or moanin. Went for gnashing. More to it. Gnashed
      for her and hers like I have never gnashed. I woulda tore at
      my coat but thats extra. Chipped uh tooth. One in thuh   60
      front.

LUCY: You did your job son.

BRAZIL: I did my job.

LUCY: Confidence. Huh. Thuh things she told me I will never
      tell. Miz Penny Price. Miz Penny Price.   65

(Rest.)

      Youre stopped.

BRAZIL: Mmlistenin.

LUCY: Dig on, Brazil.

BRAZIL

LUCY   70

BRAZIL: We arent from these parts.

LUCY: No. We're not.

BRAZIL: Daddy iduhnt either.

LUCY: Your Daddy iduhnt either.

(Rest.)

      Dig on, son.—. Cant stop diggin till you dig up somethin. 75
      You dig that something up you brush that something off
      you give that something uh designated place. Its own place.
      Along with thuh other discoveries. In thuh Hall of Wonders.
      Uh place in the Hall of Wonders right uhlong with thuh
      rest of thuh Wonders hear?   80

BRAZIL: Uh huhn.

(Rest.)

LUCY: Bram Price Senior, son. Bram Price Senior was not thuh
      man he claimed tuh be. Huh. Nope. Was not thuh man he
      claimed tuh be atall. You ever see him in his stocking feet?
      Or barefoot? Course not. I guessed before he told me. He   85
      told me then he died. He told me and I havent told no one.
      I'm uh good Confidence. As Confidences go. Huh. One of
      thuh best. As Confidence, mmonly contracted tuh keep
      quiet 12 years. After 12 years nobody cares. For 19 years I
      have kept his secret. In my bosom.   90

(Rest.)

      He wore lifts in his shoes, son.

BRAZIL: Lifts?

LUCY: Lifts. Made him seem taller than he was.

BRAZIL: Bram Price Senior?

LUCY: Bram Price Senior wore lifts in his shoes yes he did,   95
      Brazil. I tell you just as he told me with his last breaths on
      his dying bed: "Lifts." Thats all he said. Then he died. I put
      thuh puzzle pieces in place. I put thuh puzzle pieces in
      place. Couldnt tell no one though. Not even your Pa.
      "Lifts." I never told no one son. For 19 years I have kept 100
      Brams secret in my bosom. Youre thuh first tuh know.
      Hhh! Dig on. Dig on.

BRAZIL: Dig on.

LUCY

BRAZIL   105

LUCY

(A gunshot echoes. Loudly. And echoes.)

BRAZIL: *(Rest.)* Ff Pa was here weud find his bones.

LUCY: Not always.

110 BRAZIL: Thereud be his bones and thereud be thuh Wonders
surrounding his bones.

LUCY: Ive heard of different.

BRAZIL: Thereud be thuh Wonders surrounding his bones and
thereud be his Whispers.

LUCY: Maybe.

115 BRAZIL: Ffhe sspast like they say he'd of parlayed to uh
Confidence his last words and dying wishes. His secrets and
his dreams.

LUCY: Thats how we pass back East. They could pass different
out here.

120 BRAZIL: We got Daddys ways Daddyssgot ours. When theres
no Confidence available we just dribble thuh words out. In
uh whisper.

LUCY: Sometimes.

BRAZIL: Thuh Confidencell gather up thuh whispers when she

125 arrives.

LUCY: Youre uh prize, Brazil. Uh prize.]

BRAZIL

LUCY

BRAZIL

130 LUCY

BRAZIL

LUCY

BRAZIL: You hear him then? His whispers?

LUCY: Not exactly.

135 BRAZIL: He wuduhnt here then.

LUCY: He was here.

BRAZIL: Ffyou dont hear his whispers he wuduhnt here.

LUCY: Whispers dont always come up right away. Takes time
sometimes. Whispers could travel different out West than

140 they do back East. Maybe slower. Maybe. Whispers are secrets and often shy. We aint seen your Pa in 30 years. That
could be part of it. We also could be experiencing some sort
of interference. Or some sort of technical difficulty. Ssard
tuh tell.

(Rest.)

145 So much to live for.

BRAZIL: So much to live for.

LUCY: Look on thuh bright side.

BRAZIL: Look on thuh bright side. Look on thuh bright side.
Look onnnnn thuhhhh briiiiiiiight siiiiiiiide!!!!

150 LUCY: DIIIIIIIIIIG!

BRAZIL: Dig.

LUCY

BRAZIL

LUCY: Helloooo!—. Hellooooo!

155 BRAZIL

LUCY

BRAZIL: [We're from out East. We're not from these parts.

(Rest.)

My foe-father, her husband, my Daddy, her mate, her man,
my Pa come out here. Out West.

(Rest.)

160 Come out here all uhlone. Cleared thuh path tamed thuh

wilderness dug this whole Hole with his own 2 hands and
et cetera.

(Rest.)

Left his family behind. Back East. His Lucy and his child.
He waved "Goodbye." Left us tuh carry on. I was only 5.

(Rest.)

My Daddy was uh Digger. Shes whatcha call uh Confidence.   165
I did thuh weepin and thuh moanin.

(Rest.)

His lonely death and lack of proper burial is our embarrassment.

(Rest.)

Diggin was his livelihood but fakin was his callin. Ssonly
natural heud come out here and combine thuh 2. Back East
he was always diggin. He was uh natural. Could dig uh hole   170
for uh body that passed like no one else. Digged em quick
and they looked good too. This Hole here—this large
one—sshis biggest venture to date. So says hearsay.

(Rest.)

Uh exact replica of thuh Great Hole of History!

LUCY: Sshhhhhht.   175

BRAZIL: *(Rest.)* Thuh original ssback East. He and Lucy they
honeymooned there. At thuh original Great Hole. Its uh
popular spot. He and Her would sit on thuh lip and watch
everybody who was ever anybody parade on by. Daily parades! Just like thuh Tee Vee. Mr. George Washington, for   180
example, thuh Fathuh of our Country hisself, would rise up
from thuh dead and walk uhround and cross thuh Delaware
and say stuff!! Right before their very eyes!!!!

LUCY: Son?

BRAZIL: Huh?   185

LUCY: That iduhnt how it went.

BRAZIL: Oh.

LUCY: Thuh Mr. Washington me and your Daddy seen was uh
lookuhlike of thuh Mr. Washington of history-fame, son.

BRAZIL: Oh.   190

LUCY: Thuh original Mr. Washingtonssbeen long dead.

BRAZIL: O.

LUCY: That Hole back East was uh theme park son. Keep your
story to scale.

BRAZIL: K.   195

(Rest.)

Him and Her would sit by thuh lip uhlong with thuh others
all in uh row cameras clickin and theyud look down into that
Hole and see—ooooo—you name it. Ever-y-day you could
look down that Hole and see—ooooo you name it. Amerigo
Vespucci hisself made regular appearances. Marcus Garvey.   200
Ferdinand and Isabella. Mary Queen of thuh Scots! Tarzan
King of thuh Apes! Washington Jefferson Harding and
Millard Fillmore. Mistufer Columbus even. Oh they saw all
thuh greats. Parading daily in thuh Great Hole of History.

(Rest.)

My Fathuh did thuh living and thuh dead. Small-town and   205
big-time Mr. Lincoln was of course his favorite.

(Rest.)

Not only Mr. Lincoln but Mr. Lincolns last show. His last
deeds. His last laughs.

(Rest.)

Being uh Digger of some renown Daddy comes out here
tuh build uh like attraction. So says hearsay. Figures theres 210
people out here who'll enjoy amusements such as them

amusements He and Her enjoyed. We're all citizens of one
country afterall.
(Rest.)
    Mmrestin.

(A gunshot echoes. Loudly. And echoes.)

215   BRAZIL: Woooo! *(Drops dead.)*
    LUCY: Youre fakin Mr. Brazil.
    BRAZIL: Uh uhnnn.
    LUCY: Tryin tuh get you some benefits.
    BRAZIL: Uh uhnnnnnnnn.
220   LUCY: I know me uh faker when I see one. Your Father was uh
    faker. Huh. One of thuh best. There wuduhnt nobody your
    Fathuh couldnt do. Did thuh living and thuh dead.
    Small-town and big-time. Made-up and historical. Fakin was
    your Daddys callin but diggin was his livelihood. Oh, back
225   East he was always diggin. Was uh natural. Could dig uh hole
    for uh body that passed like no one else. Digged em quick and
    they looked good too. You dont remember of course you dont.
    BRAZIL: I was only 5.
    LUCY: You were only 5. When your Fathuh spoke he'd quote
230   thuh Greats. Mister George Washington. Thuh Misters
    Roosevelt. Mister Millard Fillmore. Huh. All thuh greats.
    You dont remember of course you dont.
    BRAZIL: I was only 5—
    LUCY: —only 5. Mr. Lincoln was of course your Fathuhs fa-
235   vorite. Wuz. Huh. Wuz. Huh. Heresay says he's past. Your
    Daddy. Digged this hole then he died. So says hearsay.
(Rest.)
    Dig, Brazil.
    BRAZIL: My paw—
    LUCY: Ssonly natural that heud come out here tuh dig out one
240   of his own. He loved that Great Hole so. He'd stand at thuh
    lip of that Great Hole: "OHWAYOHWHYOHWAYOH!"
    BRAZIL: "OHWAYOHWHYOHWAYOH!"
    LUCY: "OHWAYOHWHYOHWAYOH!" You know: hole talk.
    Ohwayohwhyohwayoh, just tuh get their attention, then:
245   "Hellooo!" He'd shout down to em. Theyd call back
    "Hellllooooo!" and wave. He loved that Great Hole so.
    Came out here. Digged this lookuhlike.
    BRAZIL: Then he died?
    LUCY: Then he died. Your Daddy died right here. Huh. Oh, he
250   was uh faker. Uh greaaaaat biiiiig faker too. He was your
    Fathuh. Thats thuh connection. You take after him.
    BRAZIL: I do?
    LUCY: Sure. Put your paw back where it belongs. Go on—back
    on its stump.—. Poke it on out of your sleeve son. There
255   you go. I'll draw uh X for you. See? Heresuh X. Huh. Dig
    here.
(Rest.)
    DIG!
    BRAZIL
    LUCY
260   BRAZIL
    LUCY: Woah! Woah!
    BRAZIL: Whatchaheard?!
    LUCY: No tellin, son. Cant say.

(BRAZIL digs. LUCY circulates.)

BRAZIL: *(Rest. Rest.)* On thuh day he claimed to be the 100th
anniversary of the founding of our country the Father took   265
the Son out into the yard. The Father threw himself down
in front of the Son and bit into the dirt with his teeth. His
eyes leaked. "This is how youll make your mark, Son" the
Father said. The Son was only 2 then. "This is the Wail,"
the Father said. "There's money init," the Father said. The   270
Son was only 2 then. Quiet. On what he claimed was the
101st anniversary the Father showed the Son "the Weep"
"the Sob" and "the Moan." How to stand just so what to do
with the hands and feet (to capitalize on what we in the
business call "the Mourning Moment"). Formal stances the   275
Fatherd picked up at the History Hole. The Son studied
night and day. By candlelight. No one could best him. The
money came pouring in. On the 102nd anniversary the Son
was 5 and the Father taught him "the Gnash." The day af-
ter that the Father left for out West. To seek his fortune. In   280
the middle of dinnertime. The Son was eating his peas.
LUCY
BRAZIL
LUCY
BRAZIL   285
LUCY: Helloooo! Helloooo!
(Rest.)
BRAZIL
LUCY
BRAZIL: HO! *(Unearths something.)*
LUCY: Whatcha got?   290
BRAZIL: Uh Wonder!
LUCY: Uh Wonder!
BRAZIL: Uh Wonder: Ho!
LUCY: Dust it off and put it over with thuh rest of thuh Wonders.
BRAZIL: Uh bust.   295
LUCY: Whose?
BRAZIL: Says "A. Lincoln." A. Lincolns bust. —. Abraham
    Lincolns bust!!!
LUCY: Howuhboutthat!
(Rest.)
(Rest.)
    Woah! Woah!   300
BRAZIL: Whatchaheard?
LUCY: Uh—. Cant say.
BRAZIL: Whatchaheard?!!
LUCY: SSShhhhhhhhhhhhhhhhhhht!
(Rest.)
    dig!   305

B. ECHO

THE FOUNDLING FATHER: Ladies and Gentlemen: *Our American
    Cousin,* Act III, scene 5:
MR. TRENCHARD: Have you found it?
MISS KEENE: I find no trace of it. *(Discovering.)* What is this?!   5
MR. TRENCHARD: This is the place where father kept all the old
    deeds.
MISS KEENE: Oh my poor muddled brain! What can this
    mean?!

—————————————

278 **anniversary** hearsay

MR. TRENCHARD: *(With difficulty.)* I cannot survive the downfall
10   of my house but choose instead to end my life with a pistol
    to my head!

(Applause.)

THE FOUNDLING FATHER: OHWAYOHWHYOHWAYOH!
(Rest.)
(Rest.)
    Helllooooooo!
(Rest.)
    Helllooooooo!
(Rest. Waves.)

C. ARCHEOLOGY

BRAZIL: You hear im?
LUCY: Echo of thuh first sort: thuh sound. (E.g. thuh gunplay.)
(Rest.)
    Echo of thuh 2nd sort: thuh words. Type A: thuh words
    from thuh dead. Category: Unrelated.
(Rest.)
5   Echo of thuh 2nd sort, Type B: words less fortunate: thuh
    Disembodied Voice. Also known as "Thuh Whispers."
    Category: Related. Like your Fathuhs.
(Rest.)
    Echo of thuh 3rd sort: thuh body itself.
(Rest.)
BRAZIL: You hear im.
10 LUCY: Cant say. Cant say, son.
BRAZIL: My faux-father. Thuh one who comed out here before
    us. Thuh one who left us behind. Tuh come out here all
    uhlone. Tuh do his bit. All them who comed before us—my
    Daddy. He's one of them.
15 LUCY
(Rest.)
(Rest.)
[BRAZIL: He's one of them. All of them who comed before
    us—my Daddy.
(Rest.)
    I'd say thuh creation of thuh world must uh been just like
    thuh clearing off of this plot. Just like him diggin his Hole.
20   I'd say. Must uh been just as dug up. And unfair.
(Rest.)
    Peoples (or thuh what-was), just had tuh hit thuh road. In
    thuh beginning there was one of those voids here and then
    "bang" and then *voilà!* And here we is.
(Rest.)
    But where did those voids that was here before *we* was here
25   go off to? Hmmm. In thuh beginning there were some of
    them voids here and then: KERBANG-KERBLAMMO!
    And now it all belongs tuh us.
LUCY
(Rest.)
(Rest.)
BRAZIL: This Hole is our inheritance of sorts. My Daddy died
30   and left it to me and Her. And when She goes, Shes gonna
    give it all to me!!
LUCY: Dig, son.
BRAZIL: I'd rather dust and polish. *(Puts something on.)*
LUCY: Dust and polish then.——. You dont got tuh put on that
35   tuh do it.

BRAZIL: It helps. Uh Hehm. *Uh Hehm.* WELCOME WEL-
COME WELCOME TUH THUH HALL OF—
LUCY: Sssht.
BRAZIL
LUCY   40
BRAZIL
LUCY
BRAZIL
LUCY
BRAZIL   45
LUCY
BRAZIL: (welcome welcome welcome to thuh hall. of.
    wonnndersss: To our right A Jewel Box made of cherry
    wood, lined in velvet, letters "A. L." carved in gold on thuh
    lid: the jewels have long escaped. Over here one of Mr. 50
    Washingtons bones, right pointed so they say; here is his
    likeness and here: his wooden teeth. Yes, uh top and bottom
    pair of nibblers: nibblers, lookin for uh meal. Nibblin. I
    iduhnt your lunch. Quit nibblin. Quit that nibblin you.
    Quit that nibblin you nibblers you nibblin nibblers you.) 55
LUCY: Keep it tuh scale.
BRAZIL: (Over here our newest Wonder: uh bust of Mr. Lincoln
    carved of marble lookin like he looked in life. Right heress
    thuh bit from thuh mouth of thuh mount on which some
    great Someone rode tuh thuh rescue. This is all thats left. 60
    Uh glass tradin bead—one of thuh first. Here are thuh
    lick-ed boots. Here, uh dried scrap of whales blubber. Uh
    petrified scrap of uh great blubberer, servin to remind us
    that once this land was covered with sea. And blubberers
    were Kings. In this area here are several documents: peace 65
    pacts, writs, bills of sale, treaties, notices, handbills and cir-
    culars, freein papers, summonses, declarations of war, ad-
    dresses, title deeds, obits, long lists of dids. And thuh
    medals: for bravery and honesty; for trustworthiness and for
    standing straight; for standing tall; for standing still. For 70
    advancing and retreating. For makin do. For skills in whit-
    tlin, for skills in painting and drawing, for uh knowledge of
    sewin, of handicrafts and building things, for leather tannin,
    blacksmithery, lacemakin, horseback riding, swimmin, cro-
    quet and badminton. Community Service. For cookin and for 75
    cleanin. For bowin and scrapin. Uh medal for fakin? Huh.
    This could uh been his Zsis his? This is his! This is his!!!
LUCY: Keep it tuh scale, Brazil.
BRAZIL: This could be his!
LUCY: May well be. 80
BRAZIL: *(Rest.)* Whaddyahear?
LUCY: Bits and pieces.
BRAZIL: This could be his.
LUCY: Could well be.
BRAZIL: *(Rest. Rest.)* waaaaaahhhhhhhhhHHHHHHHHHHHH! 85
    HUH HEE HUH HEE HUH HEE HUH.
LUCY: There there, Brazil. Dont weep.
BRAZIL: WAHHHHHHHHHHH!—imissim—WAHHHHH-
    HHHHHHH!
LUCY: It is an honor to be of his line. He cleared this plot for 90
    us. He was uh Digger.
BRAZIL: Huh huh huh. Uh Digger.
LUCY: Mr. Lincoln was his favorite.
BRAZIL: I was only 5.
LUCY: He dug this whole Hole. 95
BRAZIL: Sssnuch. This whole Hole.

LUCY: This whole Hole.

(Rest.)

BRAZIL

LUCY

100 BRAZIL

LUCY

BRAZIL

LUCY: I couldnt never deny him nothin.
    I gived intuh him on everything.
105 Thuh moon. Thuh stars.
    Thuh bees knees. Thuh cats pyjamas.

(Rest.)

BRAZIL

LUCY

BRAZIL: Anything?

110 LUCY: Stories too horrible tuh mention.

BRAZIL: His stories?

LUCY: Nope.

(Rest.)

BRAZIL

LUCY

115 BRAZIL

LUCY

BRAZIL: Mama Lucy?

LUCY: Whut.

BRAZIL: —Imissim—.

120 LUCY: Hhh. ((dig.))

D. ECHO

THE FOUNDLING FATHER: Ladies and Gentlemen: *Our American
    Cousin,* Act III, scene 2:

MR. TRENCHARD: You crave affection, *you* do. Now I've no for-
    tune, but I'm biling over with affections, which I'm ready
5   to pour out to all of you, like apple sass over roast pork.

AUGUSTA: Sir, your American talk do woo me.

THE FOUNDLING FATHER: *(As Mrs. Mount.)* Mr. Trenchard, you
    will please recollect you are addressing my daughter and in
    my presence.

10 MR. TRENCHARD: Yes, I'm offering her my heart and hand just
    as she wants them, with nothing in 'em.

THE FOUNDLING FATHER: *(As Mrs. Mount.)* Augusta dear, to
    your room.

AUGUSTA: Yes, Ma, the nasty beast.

15 THE FOUNDLING FATHER: *(As Mrs. Mount.)* I am aware, Mr.
    Trenchard, that you are not used to the manners of good so-
    ciety, and that, alone, will excuse the impertinence of which
    you have been guilty.

MR. TRENCHARD: Don't know the manners of good society, eh?
20   Wal, I guess I know enough to turn you inside out, old
    gal—you sockdologizing old man-trap.

(Laughter. Applause.)

THE FOUNDLING FATHER: Thanks. Thanks so much. Snyder has
    always been a very special very favorite town uh mine.
    Thank you thank you so very much. Loverly loverly evening
25   loverly tuh be here loverly tuh be here with you with all of
    you thank you very much.

(Rest.)

Uh Hehm. I *only* do thuh greats.

(Rest.)

A crowd pleaser: 4score and 7 years ago our fathers brought
forth upon this continent a new nation conceived in Liberty
and dedicated to the proposition that all men are created 30
equal!

(Applause.)

Observe!: Indiana? Indianapolis. Louisiana? Baton Rouge.
Concord? New Hampshire. Pierre? South Dakota. Honolulu?
Hawaii. Springfield? Illinois. Frankfort? Kentucky. Lincoln?
Nebraska Ha! Lickety split!   35

(Applause.)

And now, the centerpiece of the evening!!

(Rest.)

Uh Hehm. The Death of Lincoln!:—. The watching of the
play, the laughter, the smiles of Lincoln and Mary Todd,
the slipping of Booth into the presidential box unseen, the
freeing of the slaves, the pulling of the trigger, the bullets 40
piercing above the left ear, the bullets entrance into the
great head, the bullets lodging behind the great right eye,
the slumping of Lincoln, the leaping onto the stage of Booth,
the screaming of Todd, the screaming of Todd, the screaming of Keene, the leaping onto the stage of Booth; the 45
screaming of Todd, the screaming of Keene; the shouting of
Booth "Thus to the tyrants!," the death of Lincoln!—And
the silence of the nation.

(Rest.)

Yes.—. The year was way back when. The place: our nations
capitol 4score, back in the olden days, and Mr. Lincolns 50
great head. The the-a-ter was "Fords." The wife "Mary
Todd." Thuh freeing of the slaves and thuh great black hole
that thuh fatal bullet bored. And how that great head was
bleedin. Thuh body stretched crossways acrosst thuh bed.
Thuh last words. Thuh last breaths. And how thuh nation 55
mourned.

(Applause.)

E. SPADEWORK

LUCY: Thats uh hard nut tuh crack uh hard nut tuh crack
    indeed.

BRAZIL: Alaska—?

LUCY: Thats uh hard nut tuh crack. Thats uh hard nut tuh
    crack indeed. —. Huh. Juneau.   5

BRAZIL: Good!

LUCY: Go uhgain.

BRAZIL: —. Texas?

LUCY: —. Austin. Wyoming?

BRAZIL: —. —. Cheyenne. Florida?   10

LUCY: Tallahassee.

(Rest.)

Ohio.

BRAZIL: Oh. Uh. Well: Columbus. Louisiana?

LUCY: Baton Rouge. Arkansas.

BRAZIL: Little Rock. Jackson.   15

LUCY: Mississippi. Spell it.

BRAZIL: M-i-s-s-i-s-s-i-p-p-i!

LUCY: Huh. Youre good. Montgomery.

BRAZIL: Alabama.

20   LUCY: Topeka.

BRAZIL: Kansas?

LUCY: Kansas.

BRAZIL: Boise, Idaho?

LUCY: Boise, Idaho.

25   BRAZIL: Huh. Nebraska.

LUCY: Nebraska. Lincoln.

(Rest.)

Thuh year was way back when. Thuh place: our nations capitol.

(Rest.)

Your Fathuh couldnt get that story out of his head: Mr. Lin-

30   colns great head. And thuh hole thuh fatal bullet bored. I low that great head was bleedin. Thuh body stretched crossways acrosst thuh bed. Thuh last words. Thuh last breaths. And how thuh nation mourned. Huh. Changed your Fathuhs life.

(Rest.)

Couldnt get that story out of his head. Whuduhnt my fa-

35   vorite page from thuh book of Mr. Lincolns life, me myself now I prefer thuh part where he gets married to Mary Todd and she begins to lose her mind (and then of course where he frees all thuh slaves) but shoot, he couldnt get that story out of his head. Hhh. Changed his life.

(Rest.)

40   BRAZIL: (wahhhhhhhh—)

LUCY: There there, Brazil.

BRAZIL: (wahhhhhh—)

LUCY: Dont weep. Got somethin for ya.

BRAZIL: (o)?

45   LUCY: Spade.—. Dont scrunch up your face like that, son. Go on. Take it.

BRAZIL: Spade?

LUCY: Spade. He woulda wanted you tuh have it.

BRAZIL: Daddys diggin spade? Ssnnuch.

50   LUCY: I swannee you look more and more and more and more like him ever-y day.

BRAZIL: His chin?

LUCY: You got his chin.

BRAZIL: His lips?

55   LUCY: You got his lips.

BRAZIL: His teeths?

LUCY: Top and bottom. In his youth. He had some. Just like yours. His frock coat. Was just like that. He had hisself uh stovepipe hat which you lack. His medals—yours are for

60   weepin his of course were for diggin.

BRAZIL: And I got his spade.

LUCY: And now you got his spade.

BRAZIL: We could say I'm his spittin image.

LUCY: We could say that.

65   BRAZIL: We could say I just may follow in thuh footsteps of my foe-father.

LUCY: We could say that.

BRAZIL: Look on thuh bright side!

LUCY: Look on thuh bright side!

70   BRAZIL: So much tuh live for!

LUCY: So much tuh live for! Sweet land of—! Sweet land of—?

BRAZIL: Of liberty!

LUCY: Of liberty! Thats it thats it and "Woah!" Lets say I hear his words!

BRAZIL: And you could say?   75

LUCY: And I could say.

BRAZIL: Lets say you hear his words!

LUCY: Woah!

BRAZIL: Whatwouldhesay?!

LUCY: He'd say: "Hello." He'd say. —. "Hope you like your   80
spade."

BRAZIL: Tell him I do.

LUCY: He'd say: "My how youve grown!" He'd say: "Hows your weepin?" He'd say: —. "Ha! He's running through his states and capitals! Licketysplit!"   85

BRAZIL: Howuhboutthat!

LUCY: He'd say: "Uh house divided cannot stand!" He'd say: "4score and 7 years uhgoh." Say: "Of thuh people by thuh people and for thuh people." Say: "Malice toward none and charity toward all." Say: "Cheat some of thuh people some   90
of thuh time." He'd say: (and this is only to be spoken be- tween you and me and him—)

BRAZIL: K.

LUCY: Lean in. Ssfor our ears and our ears uhlone.

(Rest.)

BRAZIL: O.   95

LUCY: Howuhboutthat. And here he comes. Striding on in striding on in and he surveys thuh situation. And he nods tuh what we found cause he knows his Wonders. And he smiles. And he tells us of his doins all these years. And he does his Mr. Lincoln for us. Uh great page from thuh great   100
mans great life! And you n me llsmile, cause then we'll know, more or less, exactly where he is.

(Rest.)

BRAZIL: Lucy? Where is he?

LUCY: Lincoln?

BRAZIL: Papa.   105

LUCY: Close by, I guess. Huh. Dig.

(BRAZIL digs. Times passes.)

Youre uh Digger. Youre uh Digger. Your Daddy was uh Digger and so are you.

BRAZIL: Ho!

LUCY: I couldnt never deny him nothin.   110

BRAZIL: Wonder: Ho! Wonder: Ho!

LUCY: I gived intuh him on everything.

BRAZIL: Ssuhtrumpet.

LUCY: Gived intuh him on everything.

BRAZIL: Ssuhtrumpet, Lucy.   115

LUCY: Howboutthat.

BRAZIL: Try it out.

LUCY: How uh-bout that.

BRAZIL: Anythin?

LUCY: Cant say, son. Cant say.   120

(Rest.)

I couldnt never deny him nothin.

I gived intuh him on everything.

Thuh moon. Thuh stars.

BRAZIL: Ho!

LUCY: Thuh bees knees. Thuh cats pyjamas.   125

BRAZIL: Wonder: Ho! Wonder: Ho!

(Rest.)

Howuhboutthat: Uh bag of pennies. Money, Lucy.

LUCY: Howuhboutthat.
(Rest.)
130   Thuh bees knees.
      Thuh cats pyjamas.
      Thuh best cuts of meat.
      My baby teeth.
BRAZIL: Wonder: Ho! Wonder: HO!
135 LUCY: Thuh apron from uhround my waist.
      Thuh hair from off my head.
BRAZIL: Huh. Yellow fur.
LUCY: My mores and my folkways.
BRAZIL: Oh. Uh beard. Howuhboutthat.
(Rest.)
140 LUCY: WOAH. WOAH!
BRAZIL: Whatchaheard?
LUCY
(Rest.)
(Rest.)
BRAZIL: Whatchaheard?!
LUCY: You dont wanna know.
145 BRAZIL
LUCY
BRAZIL
LUCY
BRAZIL: Wonder: Ho! Wonder: HO! WONDER: HO!
150 LUCY: Thuh apron from uhround my waist.
      Thuh hair from off my head.
BRAZIL: Huh: uh Tee-Vee.
LUCY: Huh.
BRAZIL: I'll hold ontooit for uh minit.
(Rest.)
155 LUCY: Thuh apron from uhround my waist.
      Thuh hair from off my head.
      My mores and my folkways.
      My rock and my foundation.
BRAZIL
160 LUCY
BRAZIL
LUCY: My re-memberies—you know—thuh stuff out of my
      head.

(The TV comes on. The FOUNDING FATHER's *face appears.)*

BRAZIL: (ho! ho! wonder: ho!)
165 LUCY: My spare buttons in their envelopes.
      Thuh leftovers from all my unmade meals.
      Thuh letter R.
      Thuh key of G.
BRAZIL: (ho! ho! wonder: ho!)
170 LUCY: All my good jokes. All my jokes that fell flat.
      Thuh way I walked, cause you liked it so much.
      All my winnin dance steps.
      My teeth when yours runned out.
      My smile.
175 BRAZIL: (ho! ho! wonder: ho!)
LUCY: Sssssht.
(Rest.)
      Well. Its him.

F. ECHO

A gunshot echoes. Loudly. And echoes.

G. THE GREAT BEYOND

LUCY *and* BRAZIL *watch the TV: a replay of "The Lincoln Act." The*
FOUNDING FATHER *has returned. His coffin awaits him.*

LUCY: Howuhboutthat!
BRAZIL: They just gunned him down uhgain.
LUCY: Howuhboutthat.
BRAZIL: He's dead but not really.
LUCY: Howuhboutthat.   5
BRAZIL: Only fakin. Only fakin. See? Hesupuhgain.
LUCY: What-izzysayin?
BRAZIL: Sound duhnt work.
LUCY: Zat right.
(Rest.)
THE FOUNDING FATHER: I believe this is the place where I do   10
      the Gettysburg Address, I believe.
BRAZIL
THE FOUNDING FATHER
LUCY
BRAZIL: Woah!   15
LUCY: Howuhboutthat.
BRAZIL: Huh. Well.
(Rest.)
      Huh. Zit him?
LUCY: Its him.
BRAZIL: He's dead?   20
LUCY: He's dead.
BRAZIL: Howuhboutthat.
(Rest.)
      Shit.
LUCY
BRAZIL   25
LUCY
BRAZIL: Mail the in-vites?
LUCY: I did.
BRAZIL: Think theyll come?
LUCY: I do. There are hundreds upon thousands who knew of   30
      your Daddy, glorified his reputation, and would like to pay
      their respects.
THE FOUNDING FATHER: Howuhboutthat.
BRAZIL: Howuhboutthat!
LUCY: Turn that off, son.   35
(Rest.)
      You gonna get in now or later?
THE FOUNDING FATHER: I'd like tuh wait uhwhile.
LUCY: Youd like tuh wait uhwhile.
BRAZIL: Mmgonna gnash for you. You know: teeth in thuh dirt,
      hands like this, then jump up rip my clothes up, you know,   40
      you know go all out.
THE FOUNDING FATHER: Howuhboutthat. Open casket or
      closed?
LUCY: —. Closed.
(Rest.)
      Turn that off, son.   45
BRAZIL: K.
THE FOUNDING FATHER: Hug me.
BRAZIL: Not yet.
THE FOUNDING FATHER: You?
LUCY: Gimmieuhminute.   50

(A gunshot echoes. Loudly. And echoes.)

LUCY
BRAZIL
THE FOUNDLING FATHER
LUCY
55 BRAZIL
THE FOUNDLING FATHER
LUCY: That gunplay. Wierdiduhntit. Comes. And goze.

(They ready his coffin. He inspects it.)

At thuh Great Hole where we honeymooned—son, at thuh
Original Great Hole, you could see thuh whole world
60 without goin too far. You could look intuh that Hole and
see your entire life pass before you. Not your own life but
someones life from history, you know, [someone who'd done
somethin of note, got theirselves known somehow, uh
President or] somebody who killed somebody important, uh
65 face on uh postal stamp, you know, someone from History.
Like you, but *not* you. You know: *Known.*
THE FOUNDLING FATHER: "*Emergency,* oh, *Emergency,* please put
the Great Man in the ground."
LUCY: Go on. Get in. Try it out. Ssnot so bad. See? Sstight, but
70 private. Bought on time but we'll manage. And you got
enough height for your hat.
(Rest.)
THE FOUNDLING FATHER: Hug me.
LUCY: Not yet.
THE FOUNDLING FATHER: You?
75 BRAZIL: Gimmieuhminute.
(Rest.)
LUCY: He loved that Great Hole so. Came out here. Digged this
lookuhlike.
BRAZIL: Then he died?
LUCY: Then he died.
80 THE FOUNDLING FATHER
BRAZIL
LUCY
THE FOUNDLING FATHER
BRAZIL
85 LUCY
THE FOUNDLING FATHER: A monumentous occasion. I'd like
to say a few words from the grave. Maybe a little conver-
sation: Such a long story. Uhhem. I quit the business. And
buried all my things. I dropped anchor: Bottomless. Your
turn.
90 LUCY
BRAZIL
THE FOUNDLING FATHER
LUCY: *(Rest.)* Do your Lincoln for im.
THE FOUNDLING FATHER: Yeah?
95 LUCY: He was only 5.
THE FOUNDLING FATHER: Only 5. *Uh Hehm.* So very loverly to be
here so very very loverly to be here the town of—Wonderville
has always been a special favorite of mine always has been
a very very special favorite of mine. Now, I *only* do thuh
100 greats. Uh hehm: I was born in a log cabin of humble
parentage. But I picked up uh few things. Uh Hehm:
4score and 7 years ago our fathers—ah you know thuh rest.

Lets see now. Yes. Uh house divided cannot stand! You can
fool some of thuh people some of thuh time! Of thuh people by thuh people and for thuh people! Malice toward none   105
and charity toward all! Ha! The Death of Lincoln!
(Highlights): Haw Haw Haw Haw
(Rest.)
HAW HAW HAW HAW

(A gunshot echoes. Loudly. And echoes. The FOUNDLING FATHER
"*slumps in his chair.*")

THE FOUNDLING FATHER
LUCY
BRAZIL   110
LUCY
THE FOUNDLING FATHER
BRAZIL: [Izzy dead?
LUCY: Mmlistenin.
BRAZIL: Anything?   115
LUCY: Nothin.
BRAZIL: *(Rest.)* As a child it was her luck tuh be in thuh same
room with her Uncle when he died. Her family wanted to
know what he had said. What his last words had been.
Theyre hadnt been any. Only screaming. Or, you know,   120
breath. Didnt have uh shape to it. Her family thought she
was holding on to thuh words. For safe-keeping. And they
proclaimed thuh girl uh Confidence. At the age of 8. Sworn
tuh secrecy. She picked up thuh tricks of thuh trade as she
went uhlong.]   125
(Rest.)
Should I gnash now?
LUCY: Better save it for thuh guests. I guess.
(Rest.)
Well. Dust and polish, son. I'll circulate.
BRAZIL: Welcome Welcome Welcome to thuh hall. Of. Wonders.
(Rest.)
To our right A Jewel Box of cherry wood, lined in velvet,   130
letters "A.L." carved in gold on thuh lid. Over here one of
Mr. Washingtons bones and here: his wooden teeth. Over
here: uh bust of Mr. Lincoln carved of marble lookin like he
looked in life.—More or less. And thuh medals: for bravery
and honesty; for trustworthiness and for standing straight; 135
for standing tall; for standing still. For advancing and retreating. For makin do. For skills in whittlin, for skills in
painting and drawing, for uh knowledge of sewin, of hand-
icrafts and building things, for leather tannin, black-
smithery, lacemakin, horseback riding, swimmin, croquet   140
and badminton. Community Service. For cookin and for
cleanin. For bowin and scrapin. Uh medal for fakin.
(Rest.)
To my right: our newest Wonder: One of thuh greats Hisself! Note: thuh body sitting propped upright in our great
Hole. Note the large mouth opened wide. Note the top hat 145
and frock coat, just like the greats. Note the death wound:
thuh great black hole—thuh great black hole in thuh great
head.—And how this great head is bleedin.—Note: thuh
last words.—And thuh last breaths.—And how thuh nation
mourns—   150

(Takes his leave.)

CRITICAL CONTEXTS

**ARTHUR
MILLER**

"Tragedy and the
Common Man"
(1949)

Arthur Miller wrote this essay for the New York Times *shortly after the opening of* Death of a Salesman. *In the essay, Miller develops a reading of the tragic hero that both contests and modifies Aristotle's description of the form and style of tragic drama. He also identifies his own presiding interests in the dynamics of tragic character.*

In this age few tragedies are written. It has often been held that the lack is due to a paucity of heroes among us, or else that modern man has had the blood drawn out of his organs of belief by the skepticism of science, and the heroic attack on life cannot feed on an attitude of reserve and circumspection. For one reason or another, we are often held to be below tragedy—or tragedy above us. The inevitable conclusion is, of course, that the tragic mode is archaic, fit only for the very highly placed, the kings or the kingly, and where this admission is not made in so many words it is most often implied.

I believe that the common man is as apt a subject for tragedy in its highest sense as kings were. On the face of it this ought to be obvious in the light of modern psychiatry, which bases its analysis upon classic formulations, such as the Oedipus and Orestes complexes, for instances, which were enacted by royal beings, but which apply to everyone in similar emotional situations.

More simply, when the question of tragedy in art is not at issue, we never hesitate to attribute to the well-placed and the exalted the very same mental processes as the lowly. And finally, if the exaltation of tragic action were truly a property of the high-bred character alone, it is inconceivable that the mass of mankind should cherish tragedy above all other forms, let alone be capable of understanding it.

As a general rule, to which there may be exceptions unknown to me, I think the tragic feeling is evoked in us when we are in the presence of a character who is ready to lay down his life, if need be, to secure one thing—his sense of personal dignity. From Orestes to Hamlet, Medea to Macbeth, the underlying struggle is that of the individual attempting to gain his "rightful" position in his society.

Sometimes he is one who has been displaced from it, sometimes one who seeks to attain it for the first time, but the fateful wound from which the inevitable events spiral is the wound of indignity, and its dominant force is indignation. Tragedy, then, is the consequence of a man's total compulsion to evaluate himself justly.

In the sense of having been initiated by the hero himself, the tale always reveals what has been called his "tragic flaw," a failing that is not peculiar to grand or elevated characters. Nor is it necessarily a weakness. The flaw, or crack in the character, is really nothing—and need be nothing—but his inherent unwillingness to remain passive in the face of what he conceives to be a challenge to his dignity, his image of his rightful status. Only the passive, only those who accept their lot without active retaliation, are "flawless." Most of us are in that category.

But there are among us today, as there always have been, those who act against the scheme of things that degrades them, and in the process of action everything we have accepted out of fear or insensitivity or ignorance is shaken before us and examined, and from this total onslaught by an individual against the seemingly stable cosmos surrounding us—from this total examination of the "unchangeable" environment—comes the terror and the fear that is classically associated with tragedy.

More important, from this total questioning of what has previously been unquestioned, we learn. And such a process is not beyond the common man. In revolutions around the world, these past thirty years, he has demonstrated again and again this inner dynamic of all tragedy.

Insistence upon the rank of the tragic hero, or the so-called nobility of his character, is really but a clinging to the outward forms of tragedy. If rank or nobility of character was indispensable, then it would follow that the problems of those with rank were the particular problems of tragedy. But surely the right of one monarch to capture the domain from another no longer raises our passions, nor are our concepts of justice what they were to the mind of an Elizabethan king.

The quality in such plays that does shake us, however, derives from the underlying fear of being displaced, the disaster inherent in being torn away from our chosen image of what and who we are in this world. Among us today this fear is as strong, and perhaps stronger, than it ever was. In fact, it is the common man who knows this fear best.

Now, if it is true that tragedy is the consequence of a man's total compulsion to evaluate himself justly, his destruction in the attempt posits a wrong or an evil in his environment. And this is precisely the morality of tragedy and its lesson. The discovery of the moral law, which is what the enlightenment of tragedy consists of, is not the discovery of some abstract or metaphysical quantity.

The tragic right is a condition of life, a condition in which the human personality is able to flower and realize itself. The wrong is the condition which suppresses man, perverts the flowing out of his love and creative instinct. Tragedy enlightens—and it must, in that it points the heroic finger at the enemy of man's freedom. The thrust for freedom is the quality in tragedy which exalts. The revolutionary questioning of the stable environment is what terrifies. In no way is the common man debarred from such thoughts or such actions.

Seen in this light, our lack of tragedy may be partially accounted for by the turn which modern literature has taken toward the purely psychiatric view of life, or the purely sociological. If all our miseries, our indignities, are born and bred within our minds, then all action, let alone the heroic action, is obviously impossible.

And if society alone is responsible for the cramping of our lives, then the protagonist must needs be so pure and faultless as to force us to deny his validity as a character. From neither of these views can tragedy derive, simply because neither represents a balanced concept of life. Above all else, tragedy requires the finest appreciation by the writer of cause and effect.

No tragedy can therefore come about when its author fears to question absolutely everything, when he regards any institution, habit or custom as being either everlasting, immutable or inevitable. In the tragic view the need of man to wholly realize himself is the only fixed star, and whatever it is that hedges his nature and lowers it is ripe for attack and examination. Which is not to say that tragedy must preach revolution.

The Greeks could probe the very heavenly origin of their ways and return to confirm the rightness of laws. And Job could face God in anger, demanding his right and end in submission. But for a moment everything is in suspension, nothing is accepted, and in this stretching and tearing apart of the cosmos, in the very action of so doing, the character gains "size," the tragic stature which is spuriously attached to the royal or the highborn in our minds. The commonest of men may take on that stature to the extent of his willingness to throw all he has into the contest, the battle to secure his rightful place in his world.

There is a misconception of tragedy with which I have been struck in review after review, and in many conversations with writers and readers alike. It is the idea that tragedy is of necessity allied to pessimism. Even the dictionary says nothing more about the word than that it means a story with a sad or unhappy ending. This impression is so firmly fixed

768 UNIT VI ◆ THE UNITED STATES

that I almost hesitate to claim that in truth tragedy implies more optimism in its author than does comedy, and that its final result ought to be the reinforcement of the onlooker's brightest opinions of the human animal.

For, if it is true to say that in essence the tragic hero is intent upon claiming his whole due as a personality, and if this struggle must be total and without reservation, then it automatically demonstrates the indestructible will of man to achieve his humanity.

The possibility of victory must be there in tragedy. Where pathos rules, where pathos is finally derived, a character has fought a battle he could not possibly have won. The pathetic is achieved when the protagonist is, by virtue of his witlessness, his insensitivity or the very air he gives off, incapable of grappling with a much superior force.

Pathos truly is the mode for the pessimist. But tragedy requires a nicer balance between what is possible and what is impossible. And it is curious, although edifying, that the plays we revere, century after century, are the tragedies. In them, and in them alone, lies the belief—optimistic, if you will, in the perfectibility of man.

It is time, I think, that we who are without kings, took up this bright thread of our history and followed it to the only place it can possibly lead in our time—the heart and spirit of the average man.

HENRY LOUIS GATES JR.

"Beyond the Culture Wars"
(1994)

Henry Louis Gates Jr. is the W. E. B. Du Bois Professor of the Humanities at Harvard University and is one of the most distinguished critics of African-American literature and culture writing in the United States today. His many books include Figures in Black: Words, Signs, and the "Racial" Self, Loose Canons: Notes on the Culture Wars, *and* The Signifying Monkey: A Theory of Afro-American Literary Criticism. *In "Beyond the Culture Wars," Gates examines the relationship between the movement for multiculturalism in education, the discourse of identity politics, and the formation of "race."*

MULTICULTURALISM
AT THE LIMIT

What is this crazy thing called multiculturalism? As an overview of the current debate suggests, a salient difficulty raised by the variety of uses to which the term has been put is that multiculturalism itself has certain imperial tendencies. Its boundaries have not been easy to establish. We are told that it is concerned with the representation of difference—but whose differences? which differences?

Almost all differences in which we take an interest express themselves in cultural ways: many, perhaps most, are exhausted by their cultural manifestations. To assert this claim is, in most cases, to assert a tautology. Narrowing the terms of argument, we might say that multiculturalism is concerned with the representation, not of difference as such, but of cultural identities. But which ones are those? Indeed, if we ask what sort of identities are helpfully modeled by multiculturalism, the answer is less than obvious. Gender identity, sexual identity, racial identity: if all these things are socially inflected and produced, rather than unmediatedly natural, why won't they fit into the culturalist model? (I use the slippery term *culturalist* here, somewhat anomalously, as a back-formation from *multicultural*.) Or will they?

We can probably agree, for example, that gender identity and sexual identity are hard to reduce to the model of cultural difference, even though the meaning of these categories is culturally specific. First, we can discuss the categories in a transcultural, transhistorical manner, if only to elaborate on their transcultural and transhistorical disparities. (Try that with "Basque" or "Catalan.") Second, the culturalist model normally imagines its constituent elements as cultural bubbles that may collide but that usually could, in principle, exist in splendid isolation from one another: hence the rubric of "cultural diversity." This sort of cultural externalism—required by a model of cultural distance or disparity—does not work so well with gender identity or sexual identity. What we call "sexual difference" is a difference within, something culturally intrinsic. Why won't the culturalist reduction work? As Jonathan Dollimore and others point out about sexual difference, homophobia in our culture is part of the structure of sexuality itself: it's not out there; it's in here. Sexism, perhaps even more obviously, is also part of our conventional gender identities. Othering starts in the home.

I do not mean to deny the existence of subcultural differentiae in particular social contexts, wherein sexual difference seems to become "ethnicized" and a sexual ethnicity is forged. At the same time, the relation between the sexual and the cultural is necessarily contingent. Obviously, we can't assume that Ronald Firbank and Sophocles—or, for that matter, Marcel Proust and Michelangelo—would recognize their putative fraternity.

And yet it has sometimes seemed to me that what really explains the fervor of some of the Afro-centrist preoccupation with Egypt is an unexpressed belief that deep continuities supervene on skin color. Beyond the heartfelt claim that Cleopatra was "black" is the lurking conviction that if you traveled back in time and dropped the needle on a James Brown album, Cleo would instantly break out into the camel walk. The belief that we cherish is not so much a proposition about melanin and physiognomy; it's the proposition that, through the mists of history, Cleopatra was a *sister*.

For obvious reasons, sexual dimorphism is a basic aspect of human experience. Racial difference is certainly less so; understanding its significance always requires a particular engagement with a specific historical trajectory. There is no master key. But what emerges, again, is that despite the complex interrelations between race and culture—a matter that takes a sinister turn in the racialization of culture in the nineteenth century—no ready conversion factor connects the two, only the vagaries of history.

As the critic John Brenkman notes, blacks have been inscribed in the American matrix in a particular way; they are not just missing or absent or elsewhere: "[B]lacks were historically not merely excluded from the American polity; they were inscribed within it as *nonparticipants*." He continues:

> The forms of that negating inscription have varied through a complex history of legal and political designations. These set the conditions of the African-American discourse on identity and citizenship, and the meaning of that discourse would in turn have to be interpreted in light of those conditions and of the strategies embedded in its response to them. (98)

What good are roots, Gertrude Stein once asked, if you can't take them with you? But a number of critics now suggest that the contemporary model of ethnicity sometimes fails us by its historically foreshortened perspective, its inability to grasp the roots as well as the branches of cultural identity. In a recent book, the theorist E. San Juan, Jr., harshly decries what he calls the "cult of ethnicity and the fetish of pluralism" and launches probably the most thoroughgoing critique of multiculturalism from a radical perspective that we have. San Juan writes:

> With the gradual academicization of Ethnic Studies, "the cult of ethnicity" based on the paradigm of European immigrant success became the orthodox doctrine. The theoretical aggrandizement of ethnicity systematically erased from the historical frame of reference any perception of race and racism as causal factors in the making of the political and economic structures of the United States. (132)

In a similar vein, Hazel Carby has proposed a perspective that "[b]y insisting that 'culture' denotes antagonistic relations of domination and subordination . . . undermines the pluralistic notion of compatibility inherent in *multi*culturalism. . . ." She continues:

> The paradigm of multiculturalism actually excludes the concept of dominant and subordinate cultures—either indigenous or migrant—and fails to recognize that the existence of racism relates to the possession and exercise of politico-economic control and authority and also to forms of resistance to the power of dominant social groups. (64–65)

The issues that radical critics such as San Juan and Carby raise are important, but they have received little hearing because liberal multiculturalism has generally failed to engage with leftist critiques of this sort. Those familiar with multiculturalism only through its right-wing opponents are sometimes surprised to discover that these broad-gauge radical critiques even exist. Consequently, the extended face-off with conservatism has had a deforming effect, encouraging multiculturalism to know what it is against but not what it is for. So even if we finally demur to aspects of the radical critique, we will be better off for having sorted through some of its arguments. In what follows, I want to examine the paradoxes of pluralism and consider some of the limitations of multiculturalism—that is, of multi*culturalism*—as a model for the range of phenomena it has often been required to subsume. I also raise questions about the historically recent triumph of "ethnicity" as a paradigm or master code for human difference. I conclude with an appeal for pluralism, but it is a pluralism, let me serve fair notice, of a singularly banal and uninspiring variety, conducing to a vision of society, and of the university, as a place of what one philosopher calls "constrained disagreement" (MacIntyre 231). Here, then, are two cheers for multiculturalism.

How does the vocabulary of multiculturalism occlude race? You may have noticed that *multiculturalism* is frequently used in the popular media as a substitute for the earlier designation *multiracial*. Typically, a column on advertising will describe a Benetton-style ad with, say, black and white and Asian children together as "multicultural." Do these children—presumably supplied by the Ford Model Agency and in all likelihood hailing from exotic Westchester County—in fact represent different cultures? That, of course, is the one thing you cannot tell from a photograph of this sort. But you will find that in almost every instance where the older form *multiracial* would have been used, the newer lexeme *multicultural* is employed instead, even where cultural traits, as opposed to physiognomic traits, are obviously undiscoverable or irrelevant.

I want to be clear. In many cases, the shift from race to ethnicity is a salutary one, a necessary move away from the essentialist biologizing of a previous era. The emphasis on the social construction of race may be a familiar one, but it remains an imperative one for all that. And yet we ought to consider the correlative danger of essentializing culture when we blithely allow *culture* to substitute for *race* without affecting the basic circulation of the term. The conventional multicultural vision suggests that for every insult there is a culture: that is, if I can be denigrated as an X, I can be affirmed as an X. This mechanism of remediation is perhaps not the most sophisticated, but the intentions are good.

So far, we've seen the ethnicity paradigm faulted for a tendency to leave out history, power relations, and, of course, the history of power relations. But its perplexities do not end here. We might bear in mind that the ascent of the vocabulary of ethnicity is, as Werner Sollors has emphasized, largely a postwar phenomenon, the very term having been coined by W. Lloyd Warner in 1941. The most conservative aspect of some populist versions of multiculturalism may be an understanding of group identity and group rights that borrows whole hog a reified conception of cultural membership derived from the social sciences of mid-century. What's new is that cultural survival—the preservation of cultural differentiae—is assigned an almost medical sense of urgency. And if the delimitation of cultural identity borrows from the social sciences, the interpretation of its products sometimes seems to court the gaze of anthropology; in place of hermeneutics, it would seem, some might prefer ethnography. That is, under the sign of multiculturalism, literary readings are often guided by the desire to elicit, first and foremost, indices of ethnic particularity, especially those that can be construed as oppositional, transgressive, subversive.

Then there's another paradox. In a critique of liberal individualism, we debunk the supposed "stability" of the individual as a category, and yet we sometimes reconstitute and recuperate the same essential stability in the form of an ethnos that allegedly exhibits all the regularities and uniformities we could not locate in the individual subject. Conversely, as John Guillory writes, "The critique of the canon responds to the disunity of the culture as a whole, as a *fragmented* whole, by constituting new cultural unities at the level of gender, race, or more recently, ethnic subcultures, or gay or lesbian subcultures" (34). Skepticism about the status of the individual is surely chastening, but there may be a danger in a too easy invocation of the correlative group, the status of which may be problematic in another way.

Finally, to complete our overview of the limits of culturalism, we should take account of the critique of multiculturalism put forward by the influential French anthropologist Jean-Loup Amselle, who contends that the very notion of discrete ethnicities is an artifact of his discipline. Warning against what he dubs ethnic or cultural fundamentalism, Amselle maintains that the notion of a multicultural society, "far from being an instrument of tolerance and of liberation of minorities, as its partisans affirm, manifests, to the contrary, all the hallmarks of ethnological reason, and that is why it has been taken up in France by the New Right" (35). But Amselle's concerns are not merely political; they are ontological as well. "Cultures aren't situated one by the other like Leibniz's windowless monads," he argues. Rather, "the very definition of a given culture is in fact the result of intercultural relations of forces" (55). On the face of it, Amselle's considerations are yet another blow against what I've referred to as the bubble model of cultures. Insofar as this idea is a necessary feature of the culturalism promoted by multiculturalism, it might have to be discarded.

**IDENTITY
VERSUS
POLITICS**

While the discourses of identity politics and of liberation are often conflated, they may be in mortal combat on a more fundamental level. Identity politics, in its purest form, must be concerned with the survival of an identity. By contrast, the utopian agenda of liberation pursues what it takes to be the objective interests of its subjects, but it may be little concerned with its cultural continuity or integrity. More than that, the discourse of liberation often looks forward to the birth of a transformed subject, the creation of a new identity, which is, by definition, the surcease of the old. And that, at least in theory, is the rub.

Consider an example I have touched on in "Critical Fanonism." If colonialism inscribes itself on the psyche of the colonized, if it is part of the process of colonial subject formation, then doesn't this inscription establish limits to the very intelligibility of liberation? This critique, more or less, is the one that the Tunisian philosopher Albert Memmi makes about Frantz Fanon's anticolonial rhetoric. How are we to prize apart the discourse of the colonized and the discourse of the colonizer? Memmi suggests that Fanon, for all his ambivalences, somehow believed that "the day oppression ceases, the new man is supposed to appear before our eyes immediately." But, says Memmi, "this is not the way it happens." The utopian moment that Memmi decries in Fanon is the depiction of decolonization as engendering "a kind of tabula rasa," as "quite simply the replacing of a certain 'species' of men by another 'species' of men" so that the fear that we will continue to be "overdetermined from without" is never reconciled with Fanon's political vision of emancipation (qtd. in Gates 469). Certainly it would be hard to reconcile with any recognizable version of identitarian politics.

We can easily retrieve a lesson from the hot sands of Algeria. Any discourse of emancipation, insofar as it retains a specifically cultural cast, must contend with similar issues. That is the paradox entailed by a politics conducted on behalf of cultural identities when those identities are in part defined by the structural or positional features that the politics aims to dismantle.

Return, for a moment, to Carby's insistence that the "paradigm of multiculturalism actually excludes the concept of dominant and subordinate cultures." In what sense is this statement true? I think that Guillory, whose work on the canon debate is plainly the best of its kind, provides a helpful gloss when he writes that

> . . . a culturalist politics, though it glances worriedly at the phenomenon of class, has in prac-
> tice never devised a politics that would arise from a class "identity." For while it is easy
> enough to conceive of a self-affirmative racial or sexual identity, it makes very little sense to
> posit an affirmative lower-class identity, as such an identity would have to be grounded in
> the experience of deprivation per se, [the affirmation of which is] hardly incompatible with
> a program for the abolition of want. (13)

And yet class may provide a particularly stark instance of a more general limitation. Obviously, if being subordinate is a constitutive aspect of an identity, then a liberation politics would foreclose an identity politics and vice versa. This situation is stipulatively true for Guillory's example of a "lower-class identity." But might it not, at least contingently, prove true for a host of other putatively cultural identities as well?

The point is that identity politics cannot be understood as a politics in the harness of a pregiven identity. The "identity" half of the catchall phrase "identity politics" must be conceived as being just as labile and dynamic as the "politics" half is. The two terms must be in dialogue, as it were, or we should be prepared for the phrase to be revealed as an oxymoron.

MULTI-CULTURALISM AND DEMOCRACY

We might then ask how identity and politics are best reconciled. Can multiculturalism—often depicted as a slippery slope to anarchy and tribal war—support the sort of civil society one might want?

In a recent essay, the distinguished historian John Higham complained that

> . . . multiculturalism has remained for two decades a stubbornly practical enterprise, jus-
> tified by immediate demands rather than long range goals: a movement without an overall
> theory. . . . Still, it is troubling that twenty years after those convulsive beginnings, multi-
> culturalism has suddenly become a policy issue in America's colleges, universities, and sec-
> ondary schools without yet proposing a vision of the kind of society it wants. (204)

Multiculturalism may or may not have political consequences, in Higham's rather persuasive diagnosis, but it does not have a political vision.

In a provocative and unusual attempt to connect the multicultural agenda to the program of democracy, Brenkman takes up Higham's challenge. He argues:

> Citizens can *freely* enter the field of political persuasion and decision only insofar as they draw
> on the contingent vocabularies of their own identities. Democracy needs participants who are
> conversant with the images, symbols, stories, and vocabularies that have evolved across the
> whole of the history. . . . By the same token, democracy also requires citizens who are fluent
> enough in one another's vocabularies and histories to share the forums of political delibera-
> tion and decision on an equal footing. (89)

I find this formulation attractive and heartening, though in its instrumental conception of cultural knowledge it may have unsuspected affinities with E. D. Hirsch. But I want to make two points here. First, a caveat: to say that "[c]itizens can freely enter the field of political persuasion and decision"—that is, the field of politics, *tout court*—"only insofar as they draw on the contingent vocabularies of their own identities" is to suppose that one exists, in some sense, as a cultural atom, that one's identity exists anterior to one's engagement in the field of the political. It is to suppose that one arrives at this field already constituted, already culturally whole, rather than to acknowledge that the political might create or contour one's cultural or ethnic identity. Second, this formulation does not entail what we might call "group" multiculturalism, which devotes itself to the empow-erment of crisply delimited cultural units and conceives society as a sort of federation of officially recognized cultural sovereignties. We've already registered the sorts of criticisms that have been raised against that model, but they needn't arise just yet.

Brenkman is no Pangloss: he remarks a tension between multiculturalism and democ-racy but proposes a tradition of civic republicanism or civic humanism by which the ten-sion might be resolved. The emphasis of this tradition, which was of particular influence in the early history of the United States, is on civic participation over liberalism's pri-vatism; individual development (here he cites the British historian J. G. A. Pocock) is seen as intrinsically linked to the individual's participation as a citizen of an "autonomous decision-making community, a polis or republic." Even so, Brenkman concedes:

> [C]ivic humanism also always assumed the homogeneity of those who enjoyed citizenship. As Michael Warner has shown, for example, the republican representation of citizenship in revo-lutionary America tacitly depended upon the exclusion of women, African slaves, and Native Americans from the forms of literacy that were the emblem and the means of the patriots' equality. To evoke the republican tradition in the context of multicultural societies quickly ex-poses those elements of civic humanism that run directly counter to diversity and plurality. (95)

The charge that this civic humanism depended on the homogeneity of its citizenry is easily supported, but is *cultural* homogeneity precisely the issue? As I noted earlier, the exclusion of women is not, at least customarily, depicted as a matter of cultural distance. And while both Native Americans and African slaves would doubtless be marked by cul-tural differentiae, what Brenkman criticizes here is the perpetuation of such differences by the patriots' withholding the tools of assimilation, namely, English literacy. What is at stake is not the eradication of difference—by, for example, the unwanted imposition of English literacy, which is a grievance that has arisen in some non-Western settings. We cannot, then, conclude that cultural distance motivated the exclusion of Native Americans and African slaves; on the contrary, their exclusion was achieved by the patriots' enforcing the cultural distance. And so what we come up against, once again, are the limits of the culturalist model, its tendency to occlude the categories of race.

However symptomatic these slippages—and I cite them as cautionary—I believe that Brenkman's elaborated vision of the "modern polity [as] a dynamic space in which citi-zenship is always being contested rather than the fixed space of the premodern ideal of a republic" is a signal contribution to the debate surrounding multiculturalism (99).

One last obstacle remains to the articulation of a multicultural polity: the specter of rela-tivism, which haunts many of multiculturalism's friends and outrages its enemies. For the cultural conservatives, from William Kristol to Roger Kimball, it has totemic signifi-cance, a one-word encapsulation of all that is wrong with their progressive counterparts. If all difference deserves respect, how can morality survive and governance be maintained? Progressives find the doctrine equally unsettling: the righting of wrongs, after all, de-mands a recognition of them as wrongs. And the classic 1965 handbook by Herbert Marcuse, Barrington Moore, and Robert Paul Wolff, *A Critique of Pure Tolerance,* should remind us that critiques from the left are far from exceptional. Indeed, it seems scarcely plausible that relativism has anything like the currency that some critics have imputed to it. "'Relativism,'" Richard Rorty has stated, "is the view that every belief on a certain topic, or perhaps about *any* topic is as good as every other. No one holds this view," he says flatly, except "the occasional cooperative freshman" (166). Alas, this is surely an over-statement, though in the present climate probably a salutary one.

Certainly, relativism comes in many different flavors—moral and aesthetic as well as epistemological—and what actually follows from relativism of any particular variety is

MULTI-CULTURALISM VERSUS RELATIVISM

seldom clear. But one kind of relativism—the epistemological or cognitive—has achieved a certain limited currency among some anthropologists, whose business is culture, and might be supposed to make an occasional appearance in the multicultural context.

The Wittgensteinian Peter Winch, for example, in his classic book *The Idea of a Social Science and Its Relation to Philosophy,* has argued that "our idea of what belongs to the realm of reality is given to us in the language that we use" (15). John Beattie has decried a similar cognitive relativism in, for example, F. Allan Hanson's *Meaning in Culture* and Roy Wagner's *The Invention of Culture.* For Winch, there is no reality independent of our conceptual schemes, which may differ in incommensurable ways.

This is a curious view, one that has been rebutted most vigorously by intellectuals from just those non-Western cultures that relativism would consign to hermetic isolation. As the distinguished Ghanaian philosopher Kwasi Wiredu writes:

> [R]elativism . . . falsely denied the existence of inter-personal criteria of rationality. That is what the denial of objectivity amounts to. Unless at least the basic canons of rational think-ing were common to men, they could not even communicate among themselves. Thus, in seeking to foreclose rational discussion, the relativist view is in effect seeking to undermine the foundations of human community. (220–21)

The general problem with relativism of this sort is that it makes the project of cross-cultural understanding unintelligible. (Martin Hollis observes that "without assumptions about reality and rationality we cannot translate anything and no translation could show the assumptions to be wrong" [240].)

So let me put the argument at its strongest: if relativism is right, then multicultur-alism is impossible. Relativism, far from conducing to multiculturalism, would rescind its very conditions of possibility.

PLURALISM REDUX

By way of a return to politics and a rounding out of my critical overview, I wish to enlist Isaiah Berlin, whom we might describe as the paterfamilias of liberal pluralism and whose banishment from the current debate is a matter of puzzlement, unless the fear is that ad-ducing Berlin's lifelong argument would compromise our claims to novelty. Berlin stresses that "relativism is not the only alternative to what Lovejoy called uninformitarianism" ("Relativism" 85). In what Berlin distinguishes as pluralism, "[w]e are free to criticize the values of other cultures, to condemn them, but we cannot pretend not to understand them at all, or to regard them simply as subjective, the product of creatures in different cir-cumstances with different tastes from our own, which do not speak to us at all" ("Pursuit" 11). He writes:

> What is clear is that values can clash—that is why civilizations are incompatible. They can be incompatible between cultures, or groups in the same culture, or between you and me. . . . Values may easily clash within the breast of a single individual; and it does not follow that, if they do some must be true and others false. [Indeed], these collisions of values are of the essence of what they are and what we are. ("Pursuit" 12–13).

Berlin's pluralism is radically anti-utopian. Perhaps it is not the sort of thing likely to in-spire one to risk one's life or the lives of others. But I don't think it is a flaccid or unde-manding faith for all that. And, in the essay from which I've been reading, entitled "The Pursuit of the Ideal," Berlin anticipates the complaint:

> Of course social or political collisions will take place; the mere conflict of positive values alone makes this unavoidable. Yet they can, I believe, be minimized by promoting and pre-serving an uneasy equilibrium, which is constantly threatened and in need of repair—that alone, I repeat, is the precondition for decent societies and morally acceptable behavior; otherwise we are bound to lose our way. A little dull as a solution, you will say? Not the

stuff of which calls to heroic action by inspired leaders are made? Yet if there is some truth in this view, perhaps that is sufficient. (19)

The vision here, if it is a vision, is one of the central themes of Berlin's corpus, but we can find it promulgated elsewhere with a range of inflections. It warns us off final solutions of all sorts, admonishes us that the search for purity—whether we speak of "ethnic cleansing" or of primordial "cultural authenticity"—poses a greater threat to civil order, and human decency, than does the messy affair of cultural variegation. It lets us remember that identities are always in dialogue, that they exist (as Amselle expatiates) only in relation to one another, and that they are, like everything else, sites of contest and negotiation, self-fashioning and refashioning. (As Higham observes, "[A]n adequate theory of American culture will have to address the reality of assimilation as well as the persistence of differences" [209]). And it suggests, finally, that a multiculturalism that can accept its limitations might be one worth working for.

WORKS CITED

Amselle, Jean-Loup. *Logiques métisses.* Paris: Payot, 1990.

Beattie, John M. "Objectivity and Social Anthropology." *Objectivity and Cultural Divergence.* Ed. S. C. Brown. Cambridge: Cambridge UP, 1984. 1–20.

Berlin, Isaiah. "Alleged Relativism in Eighteenth-Century European Thought." *Crooked Timber* 70–90.

———. *The Crooked Timber of Humanity: Chapters in the History of Ideas.* New York: Knopf, 1991.

———. "The Pursuit of the Ideal." *Crooked Timber* 1–19.

Brenkman, John. "Multiculturalism and Criticism." *English Inside and Out.* Ed. Susan Gubar and Jonathan Kamholtz. New York: Routledge, 1993. 87–101.

Carby, Hazel. "Multi-culture." *Screen* 34 (1980): 62–70.

Dollimore, Jonathan. "Homophobia and Sexual Difference." *Oxford Literary Review* 8. 1-2 (1986): 5–12.

Gates, Henry Louis, Jr. "Critical Fanonism." *Critical Inquiry* 17 (1991): 457–70.

Guillory, John. *Cultural Capital: The Problem of Literary Canon Formation.* Chicago: U of Chicago P, 1993.

Higham, John. "Multiculturalism and Universalism: A History and Critique." *American Quarterly* 45 (1993): 195–219.

Hollis, Martin. "Reason and Ritual." *Philosophy* 43 (1968): 231–47.

MacIntyre, Alasdair. *Three Rival Versions of Moral Enquiry.* Notre Dame: U of Notre Dame P, 1990.

Marcuse, Herbert, Barrington Moore, and Robert Paul Wolff. *A Critique of Pure Tolerance.* Boston: Beacon, 1965.

Rorty, Richard. "Pragmatism, Relativism, Irrationalism." *Consequences of Pragmatism.* Minneapolis: U of Minnesota P, 1982. 160–75.

San Juan, E., Jr. *Racial Formations/Critical Transformations: Articulations of Power in Ethnic and Racial Studies in the United States.* Atlantic Highlands: Humanities, 1992.

Sollors, Werner. "E Pluribus Unus." Unpublished essay.

Winch, Peter. *The Idea of a Social Science and Its Relation to Philosophy.* London: Routledge, 1958.

Wiredu, Kwasi. *Philosophy and an African Culture.* Cambridge: Cambridge UP, 1980.

✠ ✠ ✠

A GLOBAL THEATER?

Historic social, political, and technological changes have reshaped the world since 1950, with a consequential impact on the theater. The aftermath of World War II has seen the remapping of the planet: the independence of India, Pakistan, and many Asian and African nations from colonial rule; the founding of Israel and the displacement of the Palestinians; and wars in Korea, Indochina, the Middle East, Africa, and the Persian Gulf. Those decades also witnessed bitter civil strife and the glimmering of peace in Northern Ireland, Argentina, Chile, the United States, Europe, and elsewhere; the Cuban missile crisis, the death of Francisco Franco in Spain, and the dismantling of the Berlin Wall; independence movements in the former Soviet Union and in Eastern Europe; the collapse of Yugoslavia and protracted war in Bosnia; the civil rights movement in the United States and the waning of apartheid in South Africa.

With the rise of global communications, a global economy, and global political and military interests, such social and political revolutions immediately become the world's business. They reshape the world we live in even as we watch the changes unfold on our television screens. Television, fortunately, has not really transformed the world's diverse cultures into a single "global village," but local cultures all feel the impact of events around the world. Think of the global effects of environmental disasters like the Chernobyl nuclear meltdown and the deforestation of the rain forests of the Amazon; of medical advances like vaccination and of epidemics like AIDS; of the international effects of social movements like nuclear disarmament, human rights, Amnesty International, feminism, and the peace movement, or, more horrifyingly, of anti-Semitism, racism, homophobia, and "ethnic cleansing."

Drama requires the collaboration of playwrights, actors, and audiences; the public structure of a theater site or building; and the social and political incentives and protections that make theatergoing attractive—it is an art deeply woven into the social fabric of a given culture and its history. Although we can still speak of the "London theater" or of "American drama," terms like these have become in our era a critical convenience for reducing the dynamic variety of contemporary theater to the fictional boundaries of a single "national" culture. Although the theater still requires the support, work, and energy of its local community, today's dramatic repertoire is a global one. American playwright Sam Shepard first produced several of his plays in London. British playwright Edward Bond is more widely produced in Germany than in the United Kingdom. Many Eastern European and Latin American playwrights have been forced by censorship and political persecution to smuggle their plays to Europe or the United States to be staged. South African playwright Athol Fugard has premiered several plays in the United States. Nigerian Wole Soyinka is regularly produced throughout the world. These playwrights are deeply implicated in the working of their native cultures, but their plays have rapidly become part of the world repertoire.

Unit 7 presents a different perspective on drama and theater than other units in *The Harcourt Anthology of Drama,* Brief Edition. Earlier units have been organized around a distinctive moment in the history of a relatively discrete culture: Athens in the fifth century BCE, Japan in the early shogunate; late medieval England and Renaissance London; late seventeenth-century London, Paris, and Madrid; twentieth-century Europe and the United States. In many respects, this book is organized around undergraduate college teaching in the United States today, which emphasizes the historical development of Western theater practices and dramatic literatures. This unit takes a broadly "postcolonial" perspective on contemporary drama, establishing some continuities with Western traditions while bringing other traditions of world theater and drama into view.

POSTCOLONIAL PERSPECTIVES

In the past several decades all areas of the humanities and cultural studies have come to challenge a narrowly Eurocentric vision of the contemporary world. These challenges have arisen from a wide range of causes: worldwide national independence movements, such as those in India in 1947, and on the African continent throughout the 1950s and 1960s; international involvement in South Africa's struggle with apartheid; global media and economic interconnections, that make business activity in Asia have an immediate impact on Wall Street; the fall of the Berlin wall in 1989, the breakup of the Soviet Union, and of the new relations between Eastern and Western Europe, and between the republics of formerly Soviet Central Asia; the return of Islam as a political, social, and military force in the West; oil crises and the war in the Persian Gulf; the challenges to "national" identity reflected in Québec's ongoing separatist movement in Canada; the various anxieties about language and immigration in the United States; racial tensions in Britain, France, Germany, and elsewhere in Europe; the ongoing political and social crisis in Northern Ireland; the emergence of Japan, South Korea, and China as economic powers; the struggles of many Latin American countries—often against both local military dictatorships and the international finance they receive—to achieve the promise of their nineteenth-century wars of liberation. In many places, these changes have not only had to overcome the military and political power of European governments—the Latin American revolutions against Spain; African and Indian independence movements—but have forced crucial challenges to the model of European culture itself, dramatizing the often oppressive entailments of the culture of "enlightenment" that was imposed on much of the world in the "civilizing" process of colonization.

In 1900, the sun never set on Britain's colonies around the world, and the legacy of three centuries of European expansion are still felt throughout the world: England, France, Spain, Portugal, the Netherlands, Italy, and Belgium all had extensive colonial holdings in Africa, Asia, and the New World. In many cases, of course, colonization was undertaken largely as a means of extracting wealth, in the form of slaves, precious metals, and/or raw materials, that could be sent back to enrich the capital: this was the model of Spanish colonization in the New World, in which Spain prevented trading between colonial cities in Mexico, Peru, Argentina, and elsewhere, in order to have all trade proceed directly to Madrid. Even though very different patterns of colonization were practiced throughout the world, colonization always brought with it European institutions, such as Catholic and Protestant churches, legal practices and courts, schools and universities, and other aspects of European culture as well—sports and games, fashion and foods, and literature, drama, and theater. In many places, the colonial language was rapidly imposed as the language of government, education, and the law. Much as England banned Gaelic in Ireland in the eighteenth century (Gaelic is now taught in school in the Republic of Ireland, but not in state-supported schools in Northern Ireland), so in the twentieth century postcolonial politics are often centered in the politics of language. In Latin America, for example, there has been a significant movement to reestablish various native languages—Quechua in Peru, Nahua in Mexico—as part of literary and public discourse; in Mexico, for example, many Precolumbian architectural sites have guide materials in at least one native language, as well as in Spanish. Writers like Aimé Césaire, in French-speaking Martinique, or Wole Soyinka, growing up in pre-independence Nigeria, were schooled on European writers like Molière and Shakespeare, and have used this education as part of their critical representation of the cultural politics of colonial and postcolonial rule: Césaire in his adaptation of Shakespeare's *The Tempest* to a Caribbean setting; Soyinka in the dialogue between English and Yoruba culture that informs many of his plays, including *Death and the King's Horseman.*

Language is never neutral; as Stephen Dedalus notices when talking to an English clergyman in James Joyce's *A Portrait of the Artist as a Young Man,* language encodes an entire system of social and political values—the words "Christ," "ale," and "master" mean something different to the English than they do to the Irish, much as terms like "white," "free," "citizen," or "nation" are obvious flashpoints, places where words reveal the political work language performs. Like language itself, the values exported to the colonies often have traced within them a powerfully oppressive dynamic. For in regarding itself as bearing "civilization" into the wilderness—as though North and South America, Africa, and parts of Asia were not only uninhabited, but as though the highly developed cultures the Europeans found there were negligible—European culture often regards the colonized as "other," and as inferior. The indigenous cultures of Africa, Latin America, and Asia were usually defined in antithesis to the values that justified the brutalities of occupation and exploitation: in opposition to the values of civilization, of a rich literary language, of an important and dynamic culture, indigenous cultures were seen as noncivil, their languages nonliterary, their cultures noncultivated, their (nonwhite) peoples nonpeople. Given this history, the cultural sphere—the sphere of theater and drama, of music and the visual arts, of literature, of film—has also been an important area of revolution as well. As the Kenyan novelist and playwright Ngũgĩ wa Thiong'o has argued, the practices of culture are in many ways more forceful than the more visible structures of the law or politics in maintaining a sense of "colonized" identity. He suggests that "decolonizing the mind" means decolonizing the tools that the mind thinks with, language, visual imagery, patterns of narrative and storytelling, everything used to make sense of the world:

> The oppressed and the exploited of the earth maintain their defiance: liberty from theft. But the biggest weapon wielded and actually daily unleashed by imperialism against that collective defiance is the cultural bomb. The effect of a cultural bomb is to annihilate a people's belief in their names, in their languages, in their environment, in their heritage of struggle, in their unity, in their capacities and ultimately in themselves. It makes them see their past as one wasteland of nonachievement and it makes them want to distance themselves from that wasteland. It makes them want to identify with that which is farthest removed from themselves; for instance, with other peoples' languages rather than their own.[1]

In their introduction to British postcolonial literatures, *The Empire Writes Back,* Bill Ashcroft, Gareth Griffiths, and Helen Tiffin "use the term 'post-colonial' . . . to cover all the culture affected by the imperial process from the moment of colonization to the present day" (2). Although several of the playwrights and theaters presented here—Wole Soyinka from Nigeria, Maishe Maponya from South Africa, Aimé Césaire from the French island of Martinique—are readily understood within the context of national liberation movements, others point to a different, though analogous, understanding of the global politics of culture today. The Northern Irish playwright Brian Friel writes in a place where the politics of "nation"—Northern Ireland is physically part of Ireland, but politically a province of the United Kingdom—are still unresolved. Beyond that, in the twentieth century the dynamics of a kind of imperialism are not restricted to politics: a former colony—the United States—has emerged as a prodigiously powerful influence on many areas of

[1]Ngũgĩ wa Thiong'o, *Decolonising the Mind: The Politics of Language in African Literature* (Portsmouth: Heinemann, 1986), 3.

economic and cultural life around the world, in ways that are frequently experienced as a kind of colonialism. While France, for instance, continues to struggle with the legacy of its colonization of North Africa, it also is engaged in a protracted trade controversy with the United States, protecting the French film industry—and, by extension, "French" culture— by sharply limiting the distribution of American films. This sense, that American culture, American values, American money, and American military power have become so pervasive as to threaten the political, economic, and cultural autonomy even of powerful countries— like France or Canada—informs a broader resistance to "imported" or Western or American culture. This resistance to a form of cultural imperialism animates some aspects of contemporary Asian theater, for instance; it is also a theme in contemporary Canadian arts, in Mexico, and elsewhere. Finally, many indigenous peoples—the aboriginal peoples of Australia, the native peoples of North and South America—were not really "colonized"; instead they were both decimated and isolated on reservations, and often stand in a quite different relationship to cultural formation in the state.

POSTCOLONIAL DRAMA IN PERFORMANCE AND HISTORY

The remainder of this introduction briefly traces some connections between the dramatic, theatrical, and cultural history informing the work of playwrights presented later in the unit. This discussion—like the collection of plays assembled here—is by no means "representative": Japan's role in Asia, and the theater traditions that have developed there are very different from the energetic performance traditions of Indonesia, or Malaysia, and from both the traditional and contemporary theater of India; although their histories are quite different, the energetic theatrical life of South Africa and Nigeria in the past four decades hardly spans the range of African dramatic and nondramatic performance, especially the performance traditions of North African countries like Algeria or Egypt; Argentina's orientation toward northern Europe, and the relatively sparse population of indigenous peoples in Argentina during the conquest period make its theater quite different from the flourishing theaters of Mexico and Brazil. In each of these places, however, drama and theater have come to be one of the ways in which public discourse is conducted, an esthetic engagement with the changing status of the "nation" and its peoples.

CANADA

Theater in Canada, like the culture of Canada itself, has been largely defined by its two dominant European settler cultures—English and French. Until the American Revolution, much of the eastern third of North America was contested by English and French explorers and traders: Jacques Cartier sailed down the St. Lawrence River, past the sites of Québec and Montréal in the 1530s; Samuel de Champlain's extensive explorations in the first quarter of the seventeenth century helped to define important fur-trading routes. By the mid-seventeenth century, however, Louis XIV declared New France a royal province, and throughout the remainder of the seventeenth and eighteenth centuries, France and Britain vied for control of Canada. The British had several strongholds in the maritime provinces, and to the west, in present-day Ontario; the exodus of British loyalists from the American colonies during the revolution—many of whom went into French Canada— enabled Britain to gain control of Canada; the 1791 Constitutional Act recognizes British legal and civil institutions, and the increasing British dominance of the important fur trade as well. In 1841, the United Provinces of Canada, in an effort to "assimilate" French Canada more effectively, gave a plurality of seats in the parliament to the British provinces. Although Canada was united as a Dominion in 1867, and gained its autonomy in 1931, the tensions between British and French Canada remain very much alive today: the separatist Parti Québécois and its charismatic leader René Levesque came to prominence in the early 1970s, and in several recent plebiscites, the citizens of Québec have voted to remain in Canada by only a narrow margin.

Although there are records of garrison performances in English Canada—an English version of Molière's *The Misanthrope* in January of 1744, in Nova Scotia—the earliest European performances in Canada are in French Canada. At Port-Royal, in Arcadia, Marc Lescarbot's aquatic pageant *Le Théâtre de Neptune en la Nouvelle-France* was performed (in war canoes!) to honor visiting French dignitaries in November, 1606, and until a production of Molière's *Tartuffe* aroused the ire of the Catholic bishop—who forbade public theater in Québec in 1694—many performances of neoclassical French playwrights, including Corneille, Racine, and Molière were given in Québec. By the early nineteenth century, however, the Amateur Canada Dramatic Society had formed in Montréal (1835), and the church came to see that modest and moral stage performance could promote Catholic values. In 1898 it sanctioned the first lay company of actors, *Les Soirées de Famille* ("Family Evenings"). By this time, however, two permanent French-speaking theaters had been built in Montréal: the Monument National (1894) and Le Théâtre des Nouveautés (1898), serving a thriving trade in both touring companies from France and in the work of French-Canadian playwrights, such as Louis-Honoré Fréchette (1839–1908), whose sensational patriotic drama *Félix Porré* opened in 1862.

Theater in English Canada was stimulated in part by the American Revolution; many British loyalists fled the revolution to the eastern provinces of Canada. The five-hundred–seat Grand Playhouse was built in Halifax in 1789, and by the early nineteenth century, Toronto and other cities had major theaters on the European model. Nonetheless, much of the theatrical activity in the nineteenth century was by touring companies. However, much as in Europe, several smaller amateur companies developed, both to stage the new drama, and to support Canadian playwrights. The most significant of these companies was founded in 1919 by Roy Mitchell, at the University of Toronto—the Hart House Theatre. The Hart House was responsible for importing a number of experimental European playwrights, as well as for supporting the production of Canadian playwrights, including Dora Smith Conover, and Marjorie Price; Herman Voaden's expressionistic plays of the 1930s were produced at the Play Workshop. Other art theaters were formed in other cities as well; Martha Allan returned from working at the Pasadena Playhouse to her native Montréal to found the Montréal Repertory theater in 1930; the Toronto Workers Theater was active in the 1930s as well; and the establishment of the Canadian Broadcasting Company in 1936 brought radio drama throughout the nation.

The postwar period was the first real period for the growth of Canadian drama and theater. In part spurred by the Vincent Massey Report on the Arts of 1951 and the development of the Canada Council in 1957, both English and French Canada witnessed a flowering of new theater in the 1960s and 1970s. Several institutions—notably the Dora Mavor Moore New Play Society of Toronto (1946)—worked to develop Canadian plays and playwrights, like John Coulter's epic of the Métis rebellion in western Canada, *Riel* (1950); the founding in 1960 of a National Theatre School in Montréal. Both the Stratford Festival (established in 1953) and the Shaw Festival (1962) became showcases for Canadian actors, and by the mid-1960s a range of important theaters often working with new Canadian material had been founded: the Jupiter Theatre (1951); Tarragon Theatre (1971) in Toronto; L'équipe (1943), the Rideau Vert (1948), the Théâtre du Nouveau Monde (1961), the Théâtre des Cuisines (1973) and the Théâtre Expérimental des Femmes (1979) in Montréal; the Manitoba Theatre Center (1958), the Vancouver Playhouse (1962), the Neptune Theatre in Halifax (1962).

Although Gratien Gélinas (b. 1908) is usually described as the instigator of postwar French-Canadian drama—his play *Tit-Coq* (1948) about a soldier returning to Québec after the war is a modern classic—the drama of contemporary Canada was given an important impetus by the 1967 Dominion Drama Festival. Within the year a series of important plays were produced throughout Canada as part of its Centennial celebrations—Gelinas's *Yesterday the Children Were Dancing* (in English Translation), George Ryga's (1932–67) *The Ecstasy of Rita Joe* among them. In 1968 Michel Tremblay's (b. 1942) groundbreaking play of working-class life in Québec, *Les Belles Soeurs* was produced; the play is also notable for being written in *joual,* the characteristic dialect of the city. Many plays, such as Sharon Pollock's *Walsh* (1973) attempt to reinterpret Canadian history; this play dramatizes the relationship between Major James Walsh, who commanded the North West Mounted Police in the 1870s and Sitting Bull, chief of the Hunkpapa Sioux. Since throughout much of the history of Canada, the French-speaking minority of Québec has been dominated by an English-speaking majority, it's not surprising that the agitation in support of Québécois independence is reflected in a variety of plays as well. Indeed, the past three decades have seen a range of plays interrogating the Québec situation—not only the well-known plays of Michel Tremblay, but plays like Jean Barbeau's *Le chemin de lacroix* (1970) about a bill permitting Anglophone Québec parents to send their children to English-language schools in violation of Québec's bilingual policy, or Jean-Claude Germain's *A Canadian Play/Une plaie canadienne* (1979) about the mythology of a unified Canada. More recently, Marianne Ackerman's *L'Affaire Tartuffe,* or, *The Garrison Officers Rehearse Molière* (1993) takes a production of *Tartuffe* at the moment of Québec's incorporation into English Canada in 1774 as a turning point in the imagining of a nation. Much as Canadian drama—in different ways in English and French plays, in English and French theaters—considers the dynamics of Canadian nationalism, so the more recent work of Native playwrights like Tomson Highway, Monique Mojica—author of *Princess Pocahontas and the Blue Spots* (1990)—and others engage the position and representation of Native Canadians today.

IRELAND AND NORTHERN IRELAND

English involvement in Ireland dates to the twelfth-century "conquest" of Ireland—Henry VIII assumed the title of "King of Ireland" in 1541—and the relationship between England and Ireland has been contested ever since. In the late sixteenth and early seventeenth century, Hugh O'Neill led a series of uprisings against English immigrants, who were establishing plantations in the northern areas of Ulster; later, during the English Civil War (1641–42), the forces that Charles I raised in Ireland were eventually defeated, and Oliver Cromwell enacted a series of brutal massacres in Ireland in retribution, confiscating lands as well. When Charles II took the English throne in 1660, the Act of Settlement confirmed the landowning claims then in place in Ireland: Catholics who had been evicted from their property were unable to regain it. In 1688 the Catholic heir, James II, ascended the English throne; when Parliament invited William of Orange (who was married to Mary Stuart, a Protestant heir) to assume the throne, James fled to Ireland: his forces were defeated at the Battle of the Boyne in 1690 and he fled to France; his Irish supporters were defeated in 1691 at Aughrim.

William's victories inaugurated a prolonged period of Irish misery: the displacement of Catholics from land and property, restrictions of their rights to education, to bear arms, to pass property to their heirs, or to vote. Although some of these laws lost force in the later eighteenth century, they provided the backdrop for political unrest in the period, particularly Wolfe Tone's mobilization of the Dublin United Irishmen in support of a French-supplied invasion. Although the French did send naval forces, and rebellions in Leinster, Ulster, and elsewhere looked promising, Tone was captured in 1798 and committed suicide in prison. In 1809, the Act of Union brought Ireland into the United Kingdom, effectively ending aspirations to nationhood. Nonetheless, throughout the nineteenth century, several movements worked for independence: Daniel O'Connell fought to repeal the Union, and Michael Davitt won security for tenants following the crop failures of 1879. Yet famine and immigration cut the Irish population in half between 1840 and 1900, and the Union's free-trade legislation turned Ireland into an impoverished supplier of raw material and labor to English factories. In the later nineteenth century, nationalism was pursued on two fronts: by the desire for "home rule" led by Charles Stewart Parnell, and by a new sense of Irish cultural identity, fostered by the Gaelic league and other cultural institutions.

Although Dublin and Ulster had supported theaters, these theaters were driven by an English repertoire: the only Irish characters to play on the stage were comic, drunken, buffoons, "Stage Irishmen." It was this sense of cultural nationalism that gave rise to the first burst of Irish theater, the founding of the Irish Literary Theater—later the Abbey Theatre—in 1899 by the poet/playwright W. B. Yeats (1865–1939), and the playwrights Lady Augusta Gregory (1852–1932) and John Millington Synge (1871–1909). The ambition of this company was to "build up a Celtic and Irish school of dramatic literature," and in the next thirty years, the Abbey succeeded not only in producing a wide range of plays on national subjects—peasant dramas about rural life like Synge's *The Playboy of the Western World* (1907); plays exhuming Irish mythology, like Yeats's cycle on Cuchulain; or realistic dramas of working-class urban life like Sean O'Casey's *The Plough and the Stars* (1926)—but establishing both an Irish style of performance, and the materials of a national theater as well. The Abbey remains a leading theater in the Republic of Ireland, and several leading playwrights have had major productions there: Tom Murphy, Ann Devlin, and Frank McGuinness among many others.

The aborted revolution of Easter 1916 was a precursor of things to come: by 1917, Eamonn De Valera was elected president of Sinn Féin, and campaigned for an independent Ireland rather than merely achieving Home Rule as a province of Britain; in 1919, Ireland's war of independence was under way. In 1922, Sinn Féin succeeded in negotiating a treaty with the United Kingdom for independence, but the Free State was not to include the counties of Northern Ireland, which remained a British province. Although there have been various periods of tension between Northern Ireland and the Republic of Ireland, and between Ireland and the U.K., these tensions came to a head in the late 1960s. In Northern Ireland, sharp divisions between rich and poor, the politically powerful and the oppressed, have often fallen across religious divisions as well, separating Protestant Anglo-Irish from Catholics. Throughout the 1960s, Catholic and Protestant groups rioted in the Northern cities of Belfast and Derry (then, Londonderry); British soldiers were summoned to protect Protestant marchers. In 1972, the "Bloody Sunday" riots resulted in thirteen dead, and a newly mobilized Provisional Irish Republican Army began a series of retaliatory campaigns; the British Embassy was burned in Dublin, and the British secretary of state suspended the Northern Irish parliament and instigated direct rule.

The history of Northern Ireland for the past thirty years is the history of this conflict: the hunger strikes by Catholic prisoners in the Maze prison who claimed the right to be treated as political prisoners rather than criminals; the increasing insurgency of Protestant paramilitary forces, inspired by the nationalist rhetoric of Ian Paisley; Gerry Adams and Sinn Féin's efforts to gain and remain in a position to be part of the bargaining for peace. The IRA cease-fire of 1994 was part of that bargain, and while violence has erupted since then, the current round of peace talks seems promising.

One of the most difficult aspects of the situation in Northern Ireland is the challenge to ideas of "national identity." Although Northern Ireland is physically part of Ireland, many of its citizens—even those who do not wish to be part of the United Kingdom—feel distinct from the Republic of Ireland; similarly, the long traditions of English rule have instilled a feeling of identification with England, one strengthened (for some) by the pro-Irish violence of the IRA. In many respects the theater of Northern Ireland has had to negotiate this vexed sense of nationalism. The Field Day Theatre Company was founded in 1980, for example, by the playwright Brian Friel, the poet Tom Paulin, the actor Stephen Rea, and the poet Seamus Heaney: the purpose of the company was to develop a new theater, a new dramatic literature of the North, one that attempted to identify the distinctiveness of Northern Ireland. In plays like Friel's *Translations* or Thomas Kilroy's (b. 1934) *The Double Cross* (1986), or even in translations like Tom Paulin's version of *Antigone, The Riot Act,* Field Day attempted to bring a specifically Northern Irish culture into dialogue with a wider world. But the work of Field Day should be seen in the context of other playwrights, some of whom, such as Christina Reid (b. 1942), see the problems of contemporary urban life in cities like Belfast to be "political" in ways that extend well beyond the problems of national identification, into areas of gender and economic exploitation. Although Field Day—which toured its productions throughout Northern Ireland—has ceased producing plays, it has published a widely read anthology of Irish writing, and has sponsored a series of essays on questions of national and postcolonial art and culture.

JAPAN   The introductory essay of Unit 2 traced the development of the classical forms of Japanese theater—Noh, Kabuki, and Doll Theater—through the period of the Tokugawa shogunate (1603–1868). In 1868, the last of the Tokugawa shoguns was defeated and replaced by the Meiji Emperor, who wanted to open political, social, and cultural relations with the West, while at the same time disentangling Japan from a series of restrictive and exploitative trade relations with Europe. Indeed, throughout the 1880s and 1890s, Japan developed an aggressive military presence throughout the northern Asian Pacific, and both fought with China over the control of Korea, and skirmished with Russia over the control of several of its islands. By the 1930s, Japan was a major military presence in the region. Taking advantage of political disorganization in China, Japan invaded Manchuria, and by 1938 had occupied parts of Mongolia and Kiangsu. Before drawing the United States into the Pacific theater with the bombing of its naval base at Pearl Harbor in Hawai'i, Japan had gained control of a huge territory, including all of Southeast Asia, Burma, the Philippines, and parts of New Guinea. Although the Western allies were unprepared for a Pacific war—after Pearl Harbor, the Japanese Navy greatly outnumbered the U.S. Navy—and suffered great casualties, the tide of the war was turned by one of the decisive events of the twentieth century: dropping the first atomic bombs on Hiroshima and Nagasaki. It is fair to say that life in Japan—and in different ways, in the rest of the world—was forever changed in that instant.

The new Meiji cultural connections to the West put different kinds of pressure on the traditional forms of Japanese theater. The Noh theater had been the special province of the *samurai* classes, and in the newly competitive theater marketplace was rapidly threatened with extinction. Several Noh actors—notably Umewaka Minoru (1828–1909)—worked to establish the Noh as a special part of Japan's cultural inheritance, an elite entertainment funded by the state (something like the "state opera" in many Western countries today), and today there are five Noh and two kyōgen schools operating in Japan. Kabuki and Bunraku (the only form of Doll Theater still active) were more readily assimilated by the more open Japanese culture of the late nineteenth and early twentieth centuries, in large part because they had always been popular entertainments. Although there has been considerable modernization of Kabuki in the past century—contemporary Kabuki is not usually the daylong affair of the eighteenth-century theater; and to some extent Kabuki's reputation for lasciviousness has been replaced by a more "classical" orientation—the Kabuki and Bunraku theaters did not need to look for a new audience after 1868, and in many respects are a continuous performance tradition.

The history of modern Japanese theater is the history of Japan's negotiation of Western modes of playwriting and performance. The *SHIMPA* theater of the turn of the century adapted Western plays—Shakespearean tragedies and popular melodramas alike—to Japanese settings; it was a significant also for introducing actresses to the stage. Of greater consequence was the *SHINGEKI* theater. *Shingeki* ("new theater") imported both European plays in the realistic mode—Ibsen, Chekhov, Gorky, for example—and stimulated a new "realistic" style of drama among Japanese playwrights of the 1920s, 1930s, and 1940s. As it had in Europe in the 1880s, and in the United States in the 1910s and 1920s, this new dramaturgy was associated with a little theater movement. The most influential theater—the Tsukiji Little Theater of Tokyo—produced only Western playwrights in its first two years of operation, under the influence of its director Osanai Kaoru (1881–1928), who admired the work of Stanislavski and the Moscow Art Theater. Thereafter, the Tsukiji and other theaters like it tended toward social realism, plays such as Kubo Sakae's (1900–58) splendid Marxist-inspired drama, *The Land of Volcanic Ash,* which traces the social and economic upheaval of the 1930s in a rural Japanese village on the colonial island of Hokkaido, and was first performed by the Shinyo Troupe at the Tsukiji Little Theater in 1938. Although *shingeki* performance was banned during the war, it became the predominant movement of the immediate postwar period, and Kubo's play was not only among the first plays to be staged after the war, but the play—and especially its central character, the radical agricultural scientist Kubo Amamiya—provided a model for postwar playwrights as well.

After World War II, the rebuilding of Japan was heavily financed by the United States, which also exerted considerable censorship control as well. Yet while "modern" Japanese theater had developed largely through the importation of European dramatic models, after the war, many writers worked to revive more traditional Japanese literary, dramatic, and theatrical forms. In some cases—Mishima Yukio (1925–70) is a good example—this revival was part of an intense and conservative nationalist movement, the sense that "true" Japan was embodied in the prewar values of an imperial culture; but in other cases, it was part of a broader resistance to being culturally absorbed by the United States. A more experimental approach to blending foreign and indigenous dramatic modes arose, for instance, as part of the energetic protest against the U.S.-Japan Mutual Security Treaty in 1960. Many Japanese refused to participate in a "nuclear umbrella" agreement with the United States after the bombings of Hiroshima and Nagasaki (nearly a million demonstrated in Tokyo alone in 1959–60), and the demonstrations around the treaty catalyzed a new introspection into the shape and meaning of Japanese culture, with its unique, deeply scarred relation to the postnuclear era. Hotta Kiyomi's (b. 1922) *The Island* (1955) was the first play about the bombings, and in the wake of the 1960 protests, a range of new kinds of theater and drama emerged: the backlash against Western dominance of Japan in the postwar period often appeared as a rejection of *shingeki* and of the Marxist politics that sustained its socialist realist esthetics. Kobo Abe's (1924–93) plays, for example, often resonate with the THEATER OF THE ABSURD, but develop—as in the play *Slave Hunting* (1955)—a critique of spiritual poverty of postwar Japan. As David Goodman argues in his book *Japanese Drama and Culture in the 1960s: The Return of the Gods* (Armonk, NY: East Gate, 1988), playwrights like Fukuda Yoshiyuki (b. 1931) and Satoh Makoto (b. 1943) responded to the social and spiritual crisis of the post-1960 period in two ways: departing from *shingeki* conventions, they tend to use at least one godlike or archetypal character, and develop plays concerned "with the interrelated questions of personal redemption (salvation of the individual) and social revolution (salvation of the world)" (10).

This new style of playwriting demanded a new style of performance, and some of the most powerful innovations of the Japanese theater in the past twenty years have involved performance style. The director Suzuki Tadashi (b. 1939) has been very influential in this regard. Suzuki's production of Satoh's play *The Black Tent* seemed to call for a "new realism";

Suzuki formed an experimental company SCOT (Suzuki Company of Toga), in which he developed some exercises from Noh training toward a kind of performance emphasizing the actor's physicality. Suzuki's work has become well known to American audiences through his collaborations with Anne Bogart and the Saratoga International Theater Institute's productions (see Unit 6). The spiritual scars of Hiroshima and Nagasaki are perhaps more literally visible in the emergence of *BUTOH* (the word means simply "dance") performance. In *butoh,* the dancers are naked, shaven, and dusted with a white powder; their performance style demands a ferocious discipline, for their movements are exceptionally slow. Devised originally by Ohno Kazuo (b. 1966) and Tatsumi Hijikata (1928–86), *butoh* is famous for the sense of ghostly apparitions that its dancers become onstage, enacting what Tatsumi called "the gestures of the dead."

MARTINIQUE

Christopher Columbus stopped at the island of Martinique in 1502; it was an inhospitable island, dominated by the fierce Caribs. Although both Spain and England briefly established outposts on the island, it was settled in 1658 as a French colony, soon of some six thousand settlers. As happened throughout the Caribbean, the native population was exterminated by violence and disease. But the Compagnie de Sénégal, a French slave-trading company, made frequent stops at Martinique on its way to the larger island of Guadeloupe; the French imported slaves to the island, especially after the introduction of coffee in 1723. But a series of slave uprisings (1789, 1815, 1822), and an ongoing conflict with the English over the slave trade, led France to abolish slavery in Martinique in 1848; as a result, plantation owners frequently had to import workers from India and China, and the population of Martinique today is descended from these various groups. Martinique was made a crown colony in 1674; control of the island passed briefly to the English several times in the late eighteenth and early nineteenth century. Since the 1840s, however, Martinique has been governed by France: first as a colony, then as a *département* (1946), and since 1974 as a region.

All of the colonial powers brought theaters to the Caribbean—the first theater was built in Jamaica in 1682, and a production of John Gay's *The Beggar's Opera* was staged there in 1733. Since the 1950s, Aimé Césaire—Martinique's most famous poet, playwright, and essayist—has been critical to the public life of Martinique, and indeed to the theory of postcolonial development more widely. For Césaire has played an important part in the public life of Martinique, beginning a long term of service as a deputy to the French National Assembly in 1945, and then leading his Progressive party into power in 1957.

NIGERIA

With ninety million people, Nigeria is Africa's most populous country; of its twenty language groups, four—Yoruba, Ibo, Hausa, and Fulani—predominate. In the precolonial period, Nigeria was home to several rich cultures. In the northern region adjacent to Lake Chad, ninth-century Arab writers described a flourishing culture, organized around a series of walled cities along Saharan trade routes between Egypt and western Africa. With the introduction of Islam from Mali in the fourteenth century, the Hausa and Fulani peoples became Muslim; in the nineteenth century, several emirs led a massive *jihad* or holy war against religious and civil authorities, and established a new center of power in Sokoto. Yoruba culture emanated from the southwestern region of Nigeria, centered around the city of Ife (11th–15th centuries); this Old Oyo culture—from which contemporary Yoruba culture descends—was a complex monarchial society, spread through several important cities; this is the kingdom that the Portuguese discovered when they arrived in the city of Benin in the fifteenth century. Ibo culture was less centrally organized, and stretched in a series of villages through the southeastern part of Nigeria.

European colonization of Nigeria began around the slave trade. The Portuguese slave trade of the seventeenth and eighteenth centuries was centered in Benin; the Portuguese transported slaves to their New World colonies, and deep strains of Yoruba can be found in many New World–African cultures, particularly in Brazil. The expansion of Islamic Fulani emirates in northern Nigeria in the nineteenth century intruded into the Old Oyo empire, driving the Yoruba south, instigating a series of wars, and—by displacing a large population—stimulating the slave trade.

The British Royal Niger Company established trade with various Ibo and Yoruba leaders in the 1840s, but only established an administrative headquarters in Lagos in 1886. Although initially making contact as traders, the British presence rapidly developed from trade and missionary work into a more conventional colonial profile: consolidating territory, developing a legal apparatus, deporting local leaders who resisted, including the northern emirs, who were conquered in 1903. Originally divided into northern and southern colonies, Britain formed the Colony and Protectorate of Nigeria under a governor-general in 1914. Nigeria gained independence in 1960, but the strains between various regions and ethnic groups have not been readily resolved; in 1967 General Odumegwu Ojukwu declared a secession of the eastern states (Biafra), and despite marching successfully on Benin City, and nearly taking Lagos, surrendered in 1970. Although an initial constitution placed a legislature in each region, Nigeria has been beset by a series of brutal military regimes—the first coup in 1966 established a pattern for the 1970s, 1980s, and 1990s. In 1999, the government of Nigeria was returned to civilian control, with free elections.

The area now known as Nigeria was the home of a variety of cultures prior to becoming a British colony, and many of the performance practices of these cultures are visible in contemporary Nigerian theater and drama. Best known is the festival of *EGUNGEN;* this festival, which has been performed at least since the fourteenth century, attempts to establish a communion between the living and the dead. In it, masked and costumed celebrants proceed to a sacred grove, where the accumulated troubles of the village are removed by a "carrier." The persistence of this ritual is acknowledged by Wole Soyinka's play *Death and the King's Horseman,* which in various direct and indirect ways engages with the *egungen* narrative. Yoruba ritual is also known for the dynamic character of its gods—Obatala, the god of creation; Ogun, the god of creativity; Sango, the god of lightning—and for the use of masquerade as a central feature of ritual. One of the most popular theatrical forms in Nigeria is the Yoruba Traveling Theater; first developed by Hubert Ogunde (1916–90), these performances generally concern a contemporary social issue, such as the exploitation of workers in his 1945 *Strike and Hunger.* Rather than a formal "drama," though, this form of theater takes the shape of a series of short skits, involving both dialogue and song, framed by a musical opening and closing number. In part because his company frequently satirized the colonial government (and was censored), Ogunde's work became widely known and imitated, and gave rise to a large number of companies practicing this narrative/dramatic/musical genre. Recently, Yoruba Traveling Theater has become almost exclusively a film genre.

In part because of the English presence—an English-language theater first opened in Lagos in 1899—in education, drama and theater played a large part in colonial Nigeria. D. A. Oloyede's play *King Elejigbo and Princess Abeje* (1904)—the first play in English by a Nigerian author—was written for a church group, and both reading and playing in the plays of the European tradition—Shakespeare, Molière, Shaw, Chekhov—formed part of the education of the generation of Nigerian writers and intellectuals who came of age with the independence. Wole Soyinka's plays often stage a rich dialogue between colonial and indigenous culture, drawing on the ritual and religious beliefs of the Yoruba. An Ibo playwright, John Pepper Clark (b. 1936) has dramatized the tales of the *ozidi* sagas—long stories that required several years to prepare and were performed by an entire village—and since the 1980s has directed his own professional theater. Femi Osofisan (b. 1946) is well known for taking a more critical, and politically engaged view of the problems of contemporary Nigerian society.

SOUTH AFRICA   Contemporary theater and drama in South Africa has been marked, as have all areas of South African life, by the imposition of racial *apartheid*—the legal separation and discrimination of various "racial" and ethnic groups—in 1948, laws which were only lifted with the election of Nelson Mandela as president in 1994. Apartheid can be seen as a politically conservative response to the social and racial situation that has developed in South Africa over the past four hundred years, in which the Portuguese, British, and Dutch vied with one another for control of the land, while at the same time being hugely outnumbered—South Africa today has about five million white inhabitants and thirty million black inhabitants—by an oppressed indigenous population.

In 1487, Bartholomeu Dias, a Portuguese explorer, reached Mossel Bay, opening a sea route from Europe to Asia; over the course of the next three centuries, the port at the Cape of Good Hope gained enormous strategic and military value. In 1652, the Dutch East India Company established a station there to supply water, food, and supplies to trade ships. Dutch settlers—called "Afrikaners" (or "Boers")—expanded from the immediate Cape region, conquering the Khoisan tribes, and importing slaves from Indonesia, India, Ceylon, Madagascar, and Mozambique. Throughout the eighteenth century, however, important colonies of British settlers developed in the region as well: after a series of battles and broken treaties, Britain gained control of the Cape Colony in 1806. Yet by gaining control of the region, the British were faced with two opponents: the indigenous tribes, and the Afrikaners, who resisted the imposition of British rule. The nineteenth century then witnessed two kinds of struggle. The conflict between British and Afrikaner settlers intensified when the British emancipated the colonial slaves in 1834. The years 1835–40 saw the "Great Trek," the departure of Afrikaners and their "clients"—slaves—from the Cape Colony northward, where they settled the Transvaal and Orange Free State as independent republics in 1852 and 1854 (the Trek is part of the consciousness of Afrikaner culture, and is frequently reenacted). However, the discovery of diamonds in 1867 and of gold in 1886 led to renewed conflict, as Britain attempted to annex the Afrikaner republics. The "War Between the Whites"—the Boer War of 1899–1902—led to British control of all three republics, which were united in 1910 as the Union of South Africa. The Union gained its independence from Britain in 1931, and became the Republic of South Africa in 1961, when it left the British Commonwealth.

Competing with one another for land and resources, the British and Afrikaners also had large and powerful indigenous populations to contend with, and despite the British policy against slavery, both parties systematically subjugated the black populations of South Africa. The most important of these groups were the Zulu; their leader Shaka defeated other African tribes, organized the Zulu as a kingdom in the 1820s, and was killed in 1828. In a series of conflicts—the British war with the Xhosa in 1834–40, the Afrikaner defeat of a Zulu force at the Battle of Blood River in 1838, and the final British defeat of the Zulu in 1879—the white population gained control of the land and its people.

In many respects, the political history of modern South Africa is the history of the white minority's efforts to subordinate and control this populace. The discovery of gold and diamonds led—after the Boer War—to an increasing demand for mine laborers; although 64,000 Chinese workers were imported in 1904–07, the bulk of these laborers were Africans, who were increasingly segregated from the white population. When the Union of South Africa was formed in 1910, only whites were enfranchised; in 1911, the

Mine and Works Act, the first of a series of laws restricting African workers to laboring work stipulated that skilled labor in the mines could only be performed by whites; in 1913, the Natives Land Act enacted the first of a series of segregation laws, by limiting African land ownership to certain reserves. Eventually, Africans were restricted to "townships," large, impoverished cities close enough to major cities to provide a constant labor supply. Moreover, the conflicts between British and Afrikaner South Africans were hardly resolved by the Union. Although South Africa participated in World War I as a dominion of the British Empire, the rise of Afrikaner nationalism in the 1930s led not only to considerable support for Germany in the country, but finally to the election of the Afrikaner National party in 1948.

The Afrikaner government installed apartheid as the law of the land in South Africa. Based on the notion that South Africa was comprised of four "racial" groups—White, Colored, Indian, and African—these laws legitimated White South Africans as the "nation," with the power to govern all other groups. Apartheid legislation was rapidly passed, and pervasive in its structuring of South African society: the Pass Laws of 1948 required one to carry a passbook at all times; the Population Registration Act of 1950 classified each person by race; the Group Areas Act forced people to live in racially segregated areas; in 1949 the Prohibition of Mixed Marriages Act passed; and in 1950 the Immorality Amendment Act prohibited sex between white and "nonwhite" persons. Property once "reserved" for ownership by Africans was claimed by whites: the segregated area of Sophiatown west of Johannesburg—where, since 1923, some African and Colored people owned land—was summarily converted into a White area, "Triomf" ("Triumph"). In the 1953 Bantu Education Act, the government assumed control of all schools—including missionary schools and colleges that had formerly educated Africans—and prohibited any instruction counter to the aims of the government; the 1959 Extension of University Education Act prohibited universities from admitting African students except with the permission of a cabinet minister.

The South African Native National Congress was founded in 1912 to advance the cause of Africans in South Africa: renamed the African National Congress, it responded swiftly to the imposition of apartheid: it organized a passive resistance campaign in 1952, and other acts of resistance throughout the 1950s. In 1959 a more radical group—the Pan African Congress, which included only Africans as members—split from the ANC; both were banned by the State of Emergency declared in 1960, after an uprising in Sharpeville when sixty Africans were shot by police during a peaceful protest. Although national and international opposition to apartheid was intense, it remained in force throughout the tumult of the 1960s, 1970s, and 1980s: the imprisonment of Nelson Mandela in 1962; the rise of the Black Consciousness Movement sponsored by Steve Biko and Barney Pityana in the late 1960s; the 1976 uprising in Soweto, a black township of one million people; the government's efforts to release the pressure on apartheid by forming black "homelands" in Transkei, Bophuthatswana, Venda, and Ciskei. By the mid-1980s, however, South Africa's isolation led to some political change: A new constitution in 1984 giving Colored, Asian, and Indian populations separate houses of parliament; the repeal of some pass laws in 1986; the release of Mandela in 1990, and the negotiations for a new constitution.

In all respects, theater in South Africa has been marked by this history. As a rough-and-tumble port, Cape Town did not support a legitimate theater until 1801, with the building of the African Theater, though performances of plays were given occasionally elsewhere (Beaumarchais's *Barber of Seville* was performed in Cape Town in 1783). By the early twentieth century, though, diamonds and gold were able to finance theater building, and every large city had several good theaters, performing European plays to white audiences. Since there was no repertory in Afrikaans, Afrikaners were particularly concerned to develop a "literary" culture: the first Afrikaans play was *Magrita Prinslo,* written by S. J. du Toit in 1897. Afrikaner theater flourished in the 1920s and 1930s, and continues today. Indeed, because the English-language theaters could rely on the traditional repertoire and touring companies, dramatic writing in English emerged much later in South Africa. Although the traditional forms of performance predate the colonial period, black theater in South Africa originates with Herbert Dhlomo (1903–56), who studied at a mission school and became a teacher and journalist, and the author of twenty-four plays. In 1933 the Bantu Drama Society at the Bantu Men's Social Center performed his play *The Girl Who Killed to Save,* the first play by a black South African to be published in English, in 1936. Nonetheless, despite producing Dhlomo's play, the repertoire of the Bantu Drama Society was very much a European repertoire: Dhlomo himself played in Sheridan's comedy *She Stoops to Conquer.* Throughout the 1920s and 1930s, several companies—the Lucky Stars, the Syco Fans—worked to develop black drama.

The production of theater, like everything else in South African society, was segregated. In 1947 the government began funding a National Theater. Although the theater supported two companies—one in English, one in Afrikaans—they used no black actors, and included South African plays in their European repertoire only if they were written by white authors. In the 1940s, Es'kia Mphahlele and Khoti Mngoma founded the Syndicate of African Artists, but were refused government funding as long as they insisted on performing to mixed racial audiences: they were disbanded in 1956 after years of police harassment. The Union of South African Artists was organized in the 1950s to protect black artists' royalties, and engineered the production of the massively successful musical review about a boxer, *King Kong,* in 1959. Although the organization was white run, and showcased black talent to white audiences, it also performed successfully to mixed audiences, and sponsored mixed-cast shows: the Union produced Athol Fugard's *No-Good Friday* in 1958, at the Bantu Men's Social Center in Johannesburg, with a cast including Fugard, Zakes Mokae, Bloke Modisane, and Stephen Moloi. When the show moved to the Brooke Theater, however, Fugard had to be replaced by a black actor—Lewis Nkosi— because segregated venues (the Brooke was an all-white theater) required segregated casts.

The principal challenge to resistant theater offered by the apartheid laws in the 1960s was the Group Areas Act, which prohibited the association of different races in clubs, cinemas, and restaurants; while mixed casts could perform to these segregated audiences, this loophole was closed in 1965: segregated audiences, segregated casts. In 1961, Fugard's *The Blood Knot*—about half brothers, one black (played by Mokae), one passing as white (played by Fugard)—could not be played in a legitimate theater, but gained good audiences in Dorkay House, and was shortly produced in London and New York. In 1963, Fugard began to work with the Serpent Players of Port Elizabeth, a black company, on adaptations of European playwrights—Büchner, Chekhov, Brecht, and Sophocles' *Antigone.* At the same time, however, a more improvisational, storytelling mode of theater was being developed in the townships, in plays such as Gibson Kente's *Manana, the Jazz Prophet* (1963). Kente's performances were popular and influential; in their use of narrative, mime, music, and dance to dramatize township life, they provided the form for later works like Barney Simon, Mbongeni Ngema, and Percy Mtwa's *Woza Albert!* (1981). Despite their popularity, these township playwrights had difficulty getting published; the South African Performing Arts Councils received large subsidies, but produced European plays mainly for white audiences, while the township theaters performed under poor circumstances to huge audiences, often sponsored by the Union.

The 1970s saw the real flowering of resistance theater in South Africa: Athol Fugard's collaboration with John Kani and Winston Ntshona (from the Serpent Players) led to *Sizwe Bansi Is Dead* (1972), which they performed (while the police looked on) as a mixed cast;

subsequent performances were canceled. When they attempted to perform the play at the University of Witwatersrand, the security police arrested both the cast and the audience. Kente's performances became more politically inflected, in township plays like *How Long* (1973) and *Too Late* (1981), and inspired many other township works: Sol Rachilos's *The Township Wife* (1972), Sidney Sepamia's *Cry Yesterday* (1972), the Theater Work-shop of Durban's *Umabatha* (the Zulu Macbeth, revived in London and the U.S. in 1997). The 1970s also saw the forming of several influential theater groups, including the Market Theater of Johannesburg in 1976, which produced Kente's *Mama and the Load* in 1980; Simon, Ngema, and Mtwa's *Woza Albert!* in 1981; Maishe Maponya's Gangsters in 1984; Ngema's *Asinamali;* and Mtwa's *Bhopa!* in 1985. The Market Theater has been influential outside South Africa as well, as many of its plays have been exported to Europe and the United States, and many of its playwrights—Fugard and Maponya, for instance—have since produced plays outside South Africa. With the lifting of apartheid, race emerges as a different kind of issue in South African drama.

In part because postcolonial drama emerges out of the complex historical dynamics of global expansion, intercultural contact, political controversy, and sometimes unfamiliar artistic traditions, analyzing and discussing this material presents unique challenges. One approach to postcolonial culture attempts to develop a "national" or "regional" model, isolating themes (apartheid in South Africa, for instance), historical questions (plays that respond to the 1960 treaty controversy in Japan), or local features of dramatic style (the prevalence of domestic realism in American drama; the use of a trickster figure by Native Canadian playwrights) to assess the relationship between theater and the place of its production. This model can also lead to productive kinds of comparative study: in what ways does it make sense to frame a dialogue, say, between the writing of Aboriginal Australian writers like Jack Davis, and Native Canadian writers like Tomson Highway?

A second model recognizes the importance that ideas of "race" have had in mapping literary study, in drawing out political affinities between African, African-American, and Caribbean writers, for example. This model interrogates the ways in which "race" informs ideas of identity across national boundaries; it might place the ideas of W. E. B. DuBois or Amiri Baraka (see Unit 6) alongside the writings of Aimé Césaire and the Senegalese poet Leopold Senghor or the black Algerian psychiatrist Frantz Fanon's incendiary and brilliant book, *The Wretched of the Earth* (1961). In these writings, "race" emerges often as a cultural construct rather than a biological "fact," though its consequences are nonetheless powerful; and theorists of the production of "race" have often found a searching model in dramatic performance, both in plays in which "race" is a conscious issue—Soyinka's *Death and the King's Horseman,* or Baraka's *Dutchman*—as well as those in which it seems to be part of the play's unconscious politics, O'Neill's *The Hairy Ape,* for example, or Pinter's *The Homecoming.* Indeed, the constructedness of "race" or "ethnicity" can be a powerful weapon for *forging* a political consciousness: while the term "Latino" or "Latina" is relatively meaningless outside the Anglo-affiliated cultures of North America (people from Latin American countries tend to identify *nationally,* much as North Americans do; they think of themselves as Mexicans, Peruvians, Cubans), it has become an important way for people experiencing *ethnic* discrimination in the United States to organize in a common effort.

One of the most powerful ways of considering postcolonial culture—its art, music, literature, drama, and performance—is to consider the formal properties of its artworks. Postcolonial critics, however, have resisted merely imposing the critical categories of Western literary study—tragic and comic form, for example, or verbal as opposed to music drama—on postcolonial arts, largely because such works often seem designed both to resist those categories, and to dramatize their implication in a wider politics. Wole Soyinka's early play

ANALYZING
POSTCOLONIAL
THEATER AND
DRAMA

The Lion and the Jewel, for example, is at once a play using the familiar stereotypes of Western comedy since Plautus—a pedantic schoolteacher, a cantankerous aging king, a pretty young girl—and interrogating them as well. As the play proceeds, it seems to ask whether this way of representing African village life—comedy—is complicit with the other ways that African village life is represented in the play: in magazine pictures, as a site for a railroad station, as the "dark continent" of the schoolteacher's textbooks. In other words, the play brings about a collision between the Western dramatic traditions Soyinka learned in Lagos, Leeds, and London, and the indigenous traditions—the social routines of the village, the songs, the marriage rituals—he blends into the texture of the play. This practice of blending both "indigenous" and "colonizing" literary or performance styles is generally called **HYBRIDIZATION,** and considering plays, poems, novels, films, and music in terms of their "hybrid" blending of cultural traditions is an important way of recognizing the cultural work that artworks do. Some writers (Ngũgĩ might be an example here) call for postcolonial art to resist and replace the inauthentic and oppressive means of "colonial" art—writing in the colonial language, using colonial forms, like tragedy, the novel, the pop song—as a way to locate a new and authentic space of liberation. Others (Soyinka and Homi Bhabha, for example) tend to see hybrid forms as a useful tool, an instrument for exposing the dynamics of oppression at the heart of the colonizing culture itself. Reading or listening for hybridity—the collision between the tragedy of Steve Biko and Samuel Beckett's absurdist play *Catastrophe* in Maponya's *Gangsters* for instance—involves the subtle and delicate task of putting these forms into dialogue with one another, listening for how they shape and qualify one another, open the possibility of new meanings.

One of the most challenging aspects of performance today has to do with the relative ease with which cultures now come into contact with one another, use—or steal—one another's forms of art and this hybridizing tendency is often visible in the plays in Unit 7. The interpenetration of different musical idioms has become a standard aspect of contemporary pop music, for instance: reggae and ska and mambo and tango and high-life and many other musical languages once local to a given culture now filter in and out of many American pop songs. And while the music industry has worked to sell this variety by copying the restaurant industry—as "World Music"—we might wonder whether the analogy with the variety of "ethnic" or "international" cuisine in the pricey restaurant districts of major cities (or even the new interest in Asian and Mexican foods shown by McDonald's and Burger King) isn't more to the point: have the products of other cultures, their music, their food, their plays, become empty commodities, consumed by a kind of global consumer elite?

In the past two decades, this kind of controversy has animated "intercultural performance," a kind of performance that attempts to bridge the differences between two different cultures not so much by erasing or occluding them as by concocting artworks in which these boundaries become visible and meaningful. Ariane Mnouchkine's productions of Shakespearean or classical Greek dramas using Eastern movement

(ASIDE)

INTERCULTURAL PERFORMANCE

and dance techniques is one well-known example; another is Peter Brook's famous staging of the Indian epic, *The Mahabharata* at the Avignon Festival in 1985, and then on tour in the following years, which used fundamentally Western theatrical techniques to stage the narrative. In 1989, David McRuvie and Annette Leday collaborated with the Kerala State Arts Academy on a production of Shakespeare's *King Lear,* adapted to the extraordinarily complex conventions of the *kathakali*—an Indian form of masked dance-drama. Unlike the hybrid works of playwrights like Maponya or Luis Valdez, this intercultural strategy does not arise from the blending of cultural materials already present in a given culture—in the way Luis Valdez's *actos* draw from both Mexican and Anglo performance traditions visible in California in the 1960s. Instead, they work to bring about a dialogue between cultures that are distant from one another in space and time.

As Marvin Carlson suggests in a careful anatomy of contemporary intercultural performances, there is not only a long tradition of intercultural performance, but a variety of ways of imagining the relationship between cultural forms that performance brings about.[1] He lists seven possibilities: a performance in a tradition foreign to the audience, such as a Noh company or the Comédie Française visiting New York; the complete assimilation of foreign elements (does anyone really hear a reggae beat as "foreign" to American pop anymore?); the assimilation of an entire foreign structure, such as Yeats's writing of Noh plays, or Maponya's work with Brechtian epic theater; making the foreign into a new blend with familiar elements (Molière's absorption of Italian *commedia dell' arte*); assimilating an entire foreign genre, such as Westerns in Japan; using some foreign elements within familiar structures, such as the dance sequences in Hwang's *M. Butterfly,* or perhaps the *egungen* costumes in Soyinka's *Death and the King's Horseman;* importing an entire performance from another culture as something distinctly unfamiliar, such as *butoh.*

This list clarifies the extent to which intercultural performance is a highly charged, contestatory activity: Brook was widely criticized, despite the evident elegance of *The Mahabharata,* for transforming something like the national conscience of India into a piece of slick theater; similarly, while McRuvie and Leday's *Kathakali King Lear* framed an ambitious attempt to chart how far one kind of theater might be translated into the traditions of another culture, its reception was often relatively simplistic: British reviewers complained that the "true" *King Lear* was lost in the translation. As we move into the next millennium, we can certainly expect kind of theatrical and dramatic experimentation to continue, and to be challenged to think about the kind of cultural work it performs.

---

[1] Marvin Carlson, "Brook and Mnouchkine: Passages to India?" *The Intercultural Performance Reader,* ed. Patrice Pavis (London: Routledge, 1996), 82–83.

AIMÉ CÉSAIRE

Aimé Césaire, one of the most prominent and influential theorists of postcolonial culture, was born in Martinique, West Indies, in 1913; he was educated there, and in Paris at L'École Normale Supérieur, and in 1934 began *L'Étudiant Noir* with Leopold Senghor and Léon Damas. Since 1946, Césaire has served as deputy from Martinique in the French National Assembly, and was a founding member of the Parti Progressiste Martiniquais, which came to power in 1950. Throughout the 1950s and 1960s, Césaire laid the foundations for the theory of postcolonial culture, and was closely associated with the Négritude movement: the assertion of black history, culture, and identity in the face of oppressive European culture. Césaire's cultural criticism—*Discourse on Colonialism* (1950), *Toussaint L'Ouverture: The French Revolution and the Colonial Problem* (1960), *Culture and Colonization* (1978)—were accompanied by several volumes of poetry and four plays: And the *Dogs Were Quiet* (1956), *The Tragedy of King Christophe* (1964), *A Season in the Congo* (1966), and *A Tempest* (1969).

A TEMPEST

Césaire's *A Tempest* is one of many works written in the past forty years taking Shakespeare's play as a site for revising colonial experience: O. Mannoni's psychoanalytic study, *Prospero and Caliban: The Psychology of Colonization* (1950); Max Dorsinville's *Caliban without Prospero* (1974); the Cuban critic Roberto Fernández Retamar's brilliant essay, *Caliban* (1974); and David Malouf's dramatic resetting of the play to contemporary Australia, *Blood Relations* (1987), to name only a few. Shakespeare's *The Tempest* was based in part on accounts of a shipwreck in the Americas (see Unit 3), and although Prospero's island seems to be at once in the Bermudas and the Mediterranean, most commentators have seen in *The Tempest* Shakespeare's representation of contact between European and New World peoples. Prospero, for example, both exploits Caliban's knowledge of the island and enslaves him and Ariel, a clear symmetry with European behavior throughout Africa and the Americas. For this reason, invoking Caliban as a kind of guiding spirit, or rewriting *The Tempest* to bring this dynamic more to the surface, has become an important strategy for evoking the relations between colonizer and colonized.

Aimé Césaire's *The Tempest* makes several uses of Shakespeare's play, taking both a more colloquial and more clearly political perspective on the action. When Prospero is forced into exile by his brother and the Inquisition, he is trying to conceal a secret "empire" that he has discovered, ripe for conquest; when Alonso sets sail to find it, Prospero uses his magic to divert him to the island, so as to save the empire for later exploitation. We also get some idea of what kind of king Prospero might be from his treatment of Caliban and Ariel, who themselves demonstrate a range of attitudes held by colonized subjects. While Caliban refuses, like many African-Americans, to continue using his "slave name" and wants to be called simply "X," like a man "whose name has been stolen," Ariel serves Prospero as a kind of overseer, and identifies his interests with him.

Césaire develops a resistant reading of Shakespeare in a number of ways: showing how Prospero's power divides rather than unites Ariel and Caliban; depicting how manual labor is fit only for the indigenous Caliban, not for the European Ferdinand; summoning Eshu to invade Prospero's masque of the classical goddesses; staging Caliban's overwhelming desire for revolution. Césaire's rewriting of Shakespeare, and his critique of European colonial representation, is focused in the final scene of *A Tempest,* which enacts a striking reversal of *The Tempest.* In Césaire's version, Prospero finds the pleasures of colonial rule so irresistible, he refuses to return to Europe.

TRANSLATOR'S NOTE

The translation of Aimé Césaire's *Une Tempête* presented more challenges than usually arise in the transfer of a play from one language into another (differences in cultural background, tone, milieu and so on). Although Césaire has denied attempting any linguistic echo of Shakespeare, the transposition of his play into English inevitably calls up such echoes, for the literate English/American playgoer cannot help but "hear," behind the language of the play, the original text resounding in all its well-known beauty, its familiarity. For the translator, therefore, the temptation to quote the Ariel songs, for example, or to paraphrase them, was strong. When Césaire has his Ariel sing of something "proche et étrange," for example, Shakespeare's "rich and strange" must, inevitably, sound in the translator's mind.

I have attempted to avoid temptation (there is, if I recall, only one instance of direct quotation in the prose text, but it fell so aptly into place that I was unable to resist); in the main I have left the (slightly altered) song for Ariel with its Shakespearean references unchanged. In an appendix I have now added a "literal" translation of Césaire's text to give a better notion of the imagery he uses for the character. As for the other songs in the text, the options indicated are extremely free adaptations or indications of what I felt to be the substance of the originals or (as in the case of "Oh, Susannah" and "Blow the Man Down") songs familiar to an English-speaking audience that I thought reflected something of the spirit and possible familiarity of the originals.

For this revised edition, I have also included, as an appendix, a "literal" translation of these songs as they occur in French.

Then there is the question of over-all tone of voice, taken for granted in *The Tempest,* where social classes, the real and the spirit worlds, are a given. In *A Tempest,* with its Caribbean (and therefore colonial) setting and its consecration to a black theater, it is essential, I feel, for the director and the actors to decide what accents, what "classes," they wish the various characters to reflect. In my own head, I have heard Ariel's song, for example, as vaguely calypso; others will have other ideas. The director may also wish to emphasize the "political" aspects of the play, in which case the accents employed by the actors would tend to serve that purpose. In any event, in translating the play I have not tried to indicate accent (other than in the Ariel song) and where slang or obscenities have been employed, the emphasis to be given will be set by the director or actor in the way that will best reflect and enhance the tone and style of the particular production.

—Richard Miller

A TEMPEST

Aimé Césaire

TRANSLATED BY RICHARD MILLER

——— CHARACTERS ———

ARIEL	FERDINAND	GODS *and* GODDESSES (CERES, JUNO)
TRINCULO/CAPTAIN	ALONSO	BOATSWAIN
CALIBAN	ESHU/MASTER OF CEREMONIES	SAILORS
STEPHANO	MIRANDA	THE FRIAR
GONZALO	SEBASTIAN	ELVES
PROSPERO	ANTONIO	NYMPHS

Ambiance of a psychodrama. The actors enter singly, at random, and each chooses for himself a mask at his leisure.

MASTER OF CEREMONIES: Come gentlemen, help yourselves. To each his character, to each character his mask. You, Prospero? Why not? He has reserves of will power he's not even aware of himself. You want Caliban? Well, that's re-
5 vealing. Ariel? Fine with me. And what about Stephano, Trinculo? No takers? Ah, just in time! It takes all kinds to make a world.

    And after all, they aren't the worst characters. No problem about the juvenile leads, Miranda and Ferdinand. You,
10 okay. And there's no problem about the villains either: you, Antonio; you, Alonso, perfect! Oh, Christ! I was forgetting the Gods. Eshu will fit you like a glove. As for the other parts, just take what you want and work it out among yourselves. But make up your minds . . . Now, there's one part I
15 have to pick out myself: you! It's for the part of the Tempest, and I need a storm to end all storms . . . I need a really big guy to do the wind. Will you do that? Fine! And then someone strong for Captain of the ship. Good, now let's go. Ready? Begin. Blow, winds! Rain and lightning *ad lib!*

——— ACT ONE ———

SCENE I

GONZALO: Of course, we're only straws tossed on the raging sea . . . but all's not lost, Gentlemen. We just have to try to get to the eye of the storm.
ANTONIO: We might have known this old fool would nag us to
5 death!
SEBASTIAN: To the bitter end!
GONZALO: Try to understand what I'm telling you: imagine a huge cylinder like the chimney of a lamp, fast as a galloping horse, but in the center as still and unmoving as Cy-
10 clop's eye. That's what we're talking about when we say "the eye of the storm" and that's where we have to get.
ANTONIO: Oh, great! Do you really mean that the cyclone or Cyclops, if he can't see the beam in his own eye, will let us escape! Oh, that's very illuminating!
15 GONZALO: It's a clever way of putting it, at any rate. Literally false, but yet quite true. But what's the fuss going on up there? The Captain seems worried. *(Calling.)* Captain!
CAPTAIN: *(With a shrug.)* Boatswain!
BOATSWAIN: Aye, sir!

CAPTAIN: We're coming round windward of the island. At this 20 speed we'll run aground. We've got to turn her around. Heave to! *(Exits.)*
BOATSWAIN: Come on, men! Heave to! To the topsail; man the ropes. Pull! Heave ho, heave ho!
ALONSO: *(Approaching.)* Well, Boatswain, how are things go- 25 ing? Where are we?
BOATSWAIN: If you ask me, you'd all be better off below, in your cabins.
ANTONIO: *He* doesn't seem too happy. We'd better ask the Captain. Where's the Captain, Boatswain? He was here just a 30 moment ago, and now he's gone off.
BOATSWAIN: Get back below where you belong! We've got work to do!
GONZALO: My dear fellow, I can quite understand your being nervous, but a man should be able to control himself in any 35 situation, even the most upsetting.
BOATSWAIN: Shove it! If you want to save your skins, you'd better get yourselves back down below to those first-class cabins of yours.
GONZALO: Now, now, my good fellow, you don't seem to know 40 to whom you're speaking. *(Making introductions.)* The King's brother, the King's son and myself, the King's counsellor.
BOATSWAIN: King! King! Well, there's someone who doesn't give a fuck more about the kind that he does about you or 45 me, and he's called the Gale. His Majesty the Gale! And right now, he's in control and we're all his subjects.
GONZALO: He might just as well be pilot on the ferry to hell . . . his mouth's foul enough!
ANTONIO: In a sense, the fellow *regales* me, as you might say. 50 We'll pull through, you'll see, because he looks to me more like someone who'll end up on the gallows, not beneath the billows.
SEBASTIAN: The end result is the same. The fish will get us and the crows will get him. 55
GONZALO: He did irritate me, rather. However, I take the attenuating circumstances into account . . . and, you must admit, he lacks neither courage nor wit.
BOATSWAIN: *(Returning.)* Pull in the stud sails. Helmsman, into the wind! Into the wind! 60

(Enter SEBASTIAN, ANTONIO, GONZALO.)

BOATSWAIN: You again! If you keep bothering us and don't get below and say your prayers I'll give up and let you sail the

ship! You can't expect me to be the go-between for your
souls and Beelzebub!

65 ANTONIO: It's really too much! The fellow is taking advantage
of the situation . . .

BOATSWAIN: Windward! Windward! Heave into the wind!

(Thunder, lightning.)

SEBASTIAN: Ho! Ho!

GONZALO: Did you see that? There, at the top of the masts, in
70   the rigging, that glitter of blue fire, flashing, flashing?
They're right when they call these magic lands, so different
from our homes in Europe . . . Look, even the lightning is
different!

ANTONIO: Maybe its a foretaste of the hell that awaits us.

75 GONZALO: You're too pessimistic. Anyway, I've always kept
myself in a state of grace, ready to meet my maker.

(SAILORS enter.)

SAILORS: Shit! We're sinking!

(The passengers can be heard singing "Nearer, my God, to Thee . . .")

BOATSWAIN: To leeward! To leeward!

FERDINAND: *(Entering.)* Alas! There's no one in hell . . . all the
80   devils are here!

(The ship sinks.)

SCENE II

MIRANDA: Oh God! Oh God! A sinking ship! Father, help!

PROSPERO: *(Enters hurriedly carrying a megaphone.)* Come daughter, calm yourself! It's only a play. There's really nothing
wrong. Anyway, everything that happens is for our own
5   good. Trust me, I won't say any more.

MIRANDA: But such a fine ship, and so many fine, brave lives
sunk, drowned, laid waste to wrack and ruin . . . A person
would have to have a heart of stone not to be moved . . .

PROSPERO: Drowned . . . hmmm. That remains to be seen. But
10   draw near, dear Princess. The time has come.

MIRANDA: You're making fun of me, father. Wild as I am, you
know I am happy—like a queen of the wildflowers, of the
streams and paths, running barefoot through thorns and
flowers, spared by one, caressed by the other.

15 PROSPERO: But you are a Princess . . . for how else does one address the daughter of a Prince? I cannot leave you in ignorance any longer. Milan is the city of your birth, and the
city where for many years I was the Duke.

MIRANDA: Then how did we come here? And tell me, too, by
20   what ill fortune did a prince turn into the reclusive hermit
you are now, here, on this desert isle? Was it because you
found the world distasteful, or through the perfidy of some
enemy? Is our island a prison or a hermitage? You've hinted
at some mystery so many times and aroused my curiosity,
25   and today you shall tell me all.

PROSPERO: In a way, it is because of all the things you mention.
First, it is because of political disagreements, because of the
intrigues of my ambitious younger brother. Antonio is his
name, your uncle, and Alonso the name of the envious King
30   of Naples. How their ambitions were joined, how my

brother became the accomplice of my rival, how the latter
promised the former his protection and my throne . . . the
devil alone knows how all that came about. In any event,
when they learned that through my studies and experiments I had managed to discover the exact location of these 35
lands for which many had sought for centuries and that I
was making preparations to set forth to take possession of
them, they hatched a scheme to steal my as-yet-unborn empire from me. They bribed my people, they stole my charts
and documents and, to get rid of me, they denounced me to 40
the Inquisition as a magician and sorcerer. To be brief, one
day I saw arriving at the palace men to whom I had never
granted audience: the priests of the Holy Office.

*(Flashback: Standing before PROSPERO, who is wearing his ducal
robes, we see a FRIAR reading from a parchment scroll.)*

THE FRIAR: The Holy Inquisition for the preservation and integrity of the Faith and the pursuit of heretical perversion, 45
acting through the special powers entrusted to it by the
Holy Apostolic See, informed of the errors you profess, insinuate and publish against God and his Creation with regard to the shape of the Earth and the possibility of discovering other lands, notwithstanding the fact that the Prophet 50
Isaiah stated and taught that the Lord God is seated upon
the circle of the Earth and in its center is Jerusalem and that
around the world lies inaccessible Paradise, convinced that it
is through wickedness that to support your heresy you quote
Strabus, Ptolemy and the tragic author Seneca, thereby lend- 55
ing credence to the notion that profane writings can aspire
to an authority equal to that of the most profound of the
Holy Scriptures, given your notorious use by both night and
day of Arabic calculations and scribblings in Hebrew, Syrian
and other demonic tongues and, lastly, given that you have 60
hitherto escaped punishment owing to your temporal authority and have, if not usurped, then transformed that authority and made it into a tyranny, doth hereby strip you of
your titles, positions and honors in order that it may then
proceed against you according to due process through a full 65
and thorough examination, under which authority we require that you accompany us.

PROSPERO: *(Back in the present.)* And yet, the trial they said they
were going to hold never took place. Such creatures of darkness are too much afraid of the light. To be brief: instead of 70
killing me they chose—even worse—to maroon me here
with you on this desert island.

MIRANDA: How terrible, and how wicked the world is! How
you must have suffered!

PROSPERO: In all this tale of treason and felony there is but one 75
honorable name: Gonzalo, counsellor to the King of Naples
and fit to serve a better master. By furnishing me with food
and clothing, by supplying me with my books and instruments, he has done all in his power to make my exile in this
disgusting place bearable. And now, through a singular 80
turn, Fortune has brought to these shores the very men involved in the plot against me. My prophetic science had of
course already informed me that they would not be content
merely with seizing my lands in Europe and that their
greed would win out over their cowardice, that they would 85
confront the sea and set out for those lands my genius had

discovered. I couldn't let them get away with that, and since I was able to stop them, I did so, with the help of Ariel. We brewed up the storm you have just witnessed, thereby saving my possessions overseas and bringing the scoundrels into my power at the same time.

(Enter ARIEL.)

PROSPERO: Well, Ariel?

ARIEL: Mission accomplished.

PROSPERO: Bravo; good work! But what seems to be the matter? I give you a compliment and you don't seem pleased? Are you tired?

ARIEL: Not tired; disgusted. I obeyed you but—well, why not come out with it?—I did so most unwillingly. It was a real pity to see that great ship go down, so full of life.

PROSPERO: Oh, so you're upset, are you! It's always like that with you intellectuals! Who cares! What interests me is not your moods, but your deeds. Let's split: I'll take the zeal and you can keep your doubts. Agreed?

ARIEL: Master, I must beg you to spare me this kind of labour.

PROSPERO: *(Shouting.)* Listen, and listen good! There's a task to be performed, and I don't care how it gets done!

ARIEL: You've promised me my freedom a thousand times, and I'm still waiting.

PROSPERO: Ingrate! And who freed you from Sycorax, may I ask? Who rent the pine in which you had been imprisoned and brought you forth?

ARIEL: Sometimes I almost regret it . . . After all, I might have turned into a real tree in the end . . . Tree: that's a word that really gives me a thrill! It often springs to mind: palm tree—springing into the sky like a fountain ending in nonchalant, squid-like elegance. The baobab—twisted like the soft entrails of some monster. Ask the calao bird that lives a cloistered season in its branches. Or the Ceiba tree—spread out beneath the proud sun. O bird, o green mansions set in the living earth!

PROSPERO: Stuff it! I don't like talking trees. As for your freedom, you'll have it when I'm good and ready. In the meanwhile, see to the ship. I'm going to have a few words with Master Caliban. I've been keeping my eye on him, and he's getting a little too emancipated. *(Calling.)* Caliban! Caliban! *(He sighs.)*

(Enter CALIBAN.)

CALIBAN: Uhuru!

PROSPERO: What did you say?

CALIBAN: I said, Uhuru!

PROSPERO: Mumbling your native language again! I've already told you, I don't like it. You could be polite, at least; a simple "hello" wouldn't kill you.

CALIBAN: Oh, I forgot . . . But make that as froggy, waspish, pustular and dung-filled "hello" as possible. May today hasten by a decade the day when all the birds of the sky and beasts of the earth will feast upon your corpse!

PROSPERO: Gracious as always, you ugly ape! How can anyone be so ugly?

CALIBAN: You think I'm ugly . . . well, I don't think you're so handsome yourself. With that big hooked nose, you look just like some old vulture. *(Laughing.)* An old vulture with a scrawny neck!

PROSPERO: Since you're so fond of invective, you could at least thank me for having taught you to speak at all. You, a savage . . . a dumb animal, a beast I educated, trained, dragged up from the bestiality that still clings to you.

CALIBAN: In the first place, that's not true. You didn't teach me a thing! Except to jabber in your own language so that I could understand your orders: chop the wood, wash the dishes, fish for food, plant vegetables, all because you're too lazy to do it yourself. And as for your learning, did you ever impart any of *that* to me? No, you took care not to. All your science you keep for yourself alone, shut up in those big books.

PROSPERO: What would you be without me?

CALIBAN: Without you? I'd be the king, that's what I'd be, the King of the Island. The king of the island given me by my mother, Sycorax.

PROSPERO: There are some family trees it's better not to climb! She's a ghoul! A witch from whom—and may God be praised—death has delivered us.

CALIBAN: Dead or alive, she was my mother, and I won't deny her! Anyhow, you only think she's dead because you think the earth itself is dead . . . It's so much simpler that way! Dead, you can walk on it, pollute it, you can tread upon it with the steps of a conqueror. I respect the earth, because I know that it is alive, and I know that Sycorax is alive.

Sycorax. Mother.
Serpent, rain, lightning.
And I see thee everywhere!
In the eye of the stagnant pool which stares back at me, through the rushes,
in the gesture made by twisted root and its awaiting thrust.
In the night, the all-seeing blinded night,
the nostril-less all-smelling night!
. . . Often, in my dreams, she speaks to me and warns me . . . Yesterday, even, when I was lying by the stream on my belly lapping at the muddy water, when the Beast was about to spring upon me with that huge stone in his hand . . .

PROSPERO: If you keep on like that even your magic won't save you from punishment!

CALIBAN: That's right, that's right! In the beginning, the gentleman was all sweet talk: dear Caliban here, my little Caliban there! And what do you think you'd have done without me in this strange land? Ingrate! I taught you the trees, fruits, birds, the seasons, and now you don't give a damn . . . Caliban the animal, Caliban the slave! I know that story! Once you've squeezed the juice from the orange, you toss the rind away!

PROSPERO: Oh!

CALIBAN: Do I lie? Isn't it true that you threw me out of your house and made me live in a filthy cave. The ghetto!

PROSPERO: It's easy to say "ghetto"! It wouldn't be such a ghetto if you took the trouble to keep it clean! And there's something you forgot, which is that what forced me to get rid of you was your lust. Good God, you tried to rape my daughter!

200 CALIBAN: Rape! Rape! Listen, you old goat, you're the one that put those dirty thoughts in my head. Let me tell you something: I couldn't care less about your daughter, or about your cave, for that matter. If I gripe, it's on principle, because I didn't like living with you at all, as a matter of fact.
205 Your feet stink!

PROSPERO: I did not summon you here to argue. Out! Back to work! Wood, water, and lots of both! I'm expecting company today.

CALIBAN: I've had just about enough. There's already a pile of
210 wood that high . . .

PROSPERO: Enough! Careful, Caliban! If you keep grumbling you'll be whipped. And if you don't step lively, if you keep dragging your feet or try to strike or sabotage things, I'll beat you. Beating is the only language you really under-
215 stand. So much the worse for you: I'll speak it, loud and clear. Get a move on!

CALIBAN: All right, I'm going . . . but this is the last time. It's the last time, do you hear me? Oh . . . I forgot: I've got something important to tell you.
220 PROSPERO: Important? Well, out with it.

CALIBAN: It's this: I've decided I don't want to be called Caliban any longer.

PROSPERO: What kind of rot is that? I don't understand.

CALIBAN: Put it this way: I'm *telling* you that from now on I
225 won't answer to the name Caliban.

PROSPERO: Where did you get that idea?

CALIBAN: Well, because Caliban *isn't* my name. It's as simple as that.

PROSPERO: Oh, I suppose it's mine!
230 CALIBAN: It's the name given me by your hatred, and everytime it's spoken it's an insult.

PROSPERO: My, aren't we getting sensitive! All right, suggest something else . . . I've got to call you something. What will it be? Cannibal would suit you, but I'm sure you
235 wouldn't like that, would you? Let's see . . . what about Hannibal? That fits. And why not . . . they all seem to like historical names.

CALIBAN: Call me X. That would be best. Like a man without a name. Or, to be more precise, a man whose name has been
240 stolen. You talk about history . . . well, that's history, and everyone knows it! Every time you summon me it reminds me of a basic fact, the fact that you've stolen everything from me, even my identity! Uhuru! *(He exits.)*

(Enter ARIEL *as a sea-nymph.)*

PROSPERO: My dear Ariel, did you see how he looked at me,
245 that glint in his eye? That's something new. Well, let me tell you, Caliban is the enemy. As for those people on the boat, I've changed my mind about them. Give them a scare, but for God's sake don't touch a hair of their heads! You'll answer to me if you do.
250 ARIEL: I've suffered too much myself for having made them suffer not to be pleased at your mercy. You can count on me, Master.

PROSPERO: Yes, however great their crimes, if they repent you can assure them of my forgiveness. They are men of my race,
255 and of high rank. As for me, at my age one must rise above disputes and quarrels and think about the future. I have a daughter. Alonso has a son. If they were to fall in love, I would give my consent. Let Ferdinand marry Miranda, and may their marriage bring us harmony and peace. That is my plan. I want it executed. As for Caliban, does it matter what 260 that villain plots against me? All the nobility of Italy, Naples and Milan henceforth combined, will protect me bodily. Go!

ARIEL: Yes, Master. Your orders will be fully carried out.

*(*ARIEL *sings:)*

Sandy seashore, deep blue sky,   265
Surf is rising, sea birds fly
Here the lover finds delight,
Sun at noontime, moon at night.
Join hands lovers, join the dance,
Find contentment, find romance.   270

Sandy seashore, deep blue sky,
Cares will vanish . . . so can I . . .

FERDINAND: What is this music? It has led me here and now it stops . . . No, there it is again . . .

ARIEL: *(Singing.)*

Waters move, the ocean flows,   275
Nothing comes and nothing goes . . .
Strange days are upon us . . .

Oysters stare through pearly eyes
Heart-shaped corals gently beat
In the crystal undersea   280

Waters move and ocean flows,
Nothing comes and nothing goes . . .
Strange days are upon us . . .

FERDINAND: What is this that I see before me? A goddess? A mortal?   285

MIRANDA: I know what *I'm* seeing: a flatterer. Young man, your ability to pay compliments in the situation in which you find yourself at least proves your courage. Who are you?

FERDINAND: As you see, a poor shipwrecked soul.

MIRANDA: But one of high degree!   290

FERDINAND: In other surroundings I might be called "Prince," "son of the King" . . . But, no, I was forgetting . . . not "Prince" but "King," alas . . . "King" because my father has just perished in the shipwreck.

MIRANDA: Poor young man! Here, you'll be received with hos- 295 pitality and we'll support you in your misfortune.

FERDINAND: Alas, my father . . . Can it be that I am an unnatural son? Your pity would make the greatest of sorrows seem sweet.

MIRANDA: I hope you'll like it here with us. The island is 300 pretty. I'll show you the beaches and the forests, I'll tell you the names of fruits and flowers, I'll introduce you to a whole world of insects, of lizards of every hue, of birds . . . Oh, you cannot imagine! The birds! . . .

PROSPERO: That's enough, daughter! I find your chatter irritat- 305 ing . . . and let me assure you, it's not at all fitting. You are doing too much honor to an impostor. Young man, you are a traitor, a spy, and a woman-chaser to boot! No sooner has he escaped the perils of the sea than he's sweet-talking the

310 first girl he meets! You won't get round me that way. Your arrival is convenient, because I need more manpower: you shall be my house servant.

FERDINAND: Seeing the young lady, more beautiful than any wood-nymph, I might have been Ulysses on Nausicaa's isle.
315 But hearing you, Sir, I now understand my fate a little better . . . I see I have come ashore on the Barbary Coast and am in the hands of a cruel pirate. (*Drawing his sword.*) However, a gentleman prefers death to dishonor! I shall defend my life with my freedom!

320 PROSPERO: Poor fool: your arm is growing weak, your knees are trembling! Traitor! I could kill you now . . . but I need the manpower. Follow me.

ARIEL: It's no use trying to resist, young man. My master is a sorcerer: neither your passion nor your youth can prevail
325 against him. Your best course would be to follow and obey him.

FERDINAND: Oh God! What sorcery is this? Vanquished, a captive—yet far from rebelling against my fate, I am finding my servitude sweet. Oh, I would be imprisoned for life if
330 only heaven will grant me a glimpse of my sun each day, the face of my own sun. Farewell, Nausicaa.

(*They exit.*)

——— ACT TWO ———

SCENE I

CALIBAN's *cave.* CALIBAN *is singing as he works when* ARIEL *enters. He listens to him for a moment.*

CALIBAN: (*Singing.*)

May he who eats his corn heedless of Shango
Be accursed! May Shango creep beneath
His nails and eat into his flesh!
Shango, Shango ho!

5 Forget to give him room if you dare!
He will make himself at home on your nose!

Refuse to have him under your roof at your own risk!
He'll tear off your roof and wear it as a hat!
Whoever tries to mislead Shango
10 Will suffer for it!
Shango, Shango ho!

ARIEL: Greetings, Caliban. I know you don't think much of me, but after all we *are* brothers, brothers in suffering and slavery, but brothers in hope as well. We both want our free-
15 dom. We just have different methods.

CALIBAN: Greetings to you. But you didn't come to see me just to make that profession of faith. Come on, Alastor! The old man sent you, didn't he? A great job: carrying out the Master's fine ideas, his great plans.

20 ARIEL: No, I've come on my own. I came to warn you. Prospero is planning horrible acts of revenge against you. I thought it my duty to alert you.

CALIBAN: I'm ready for him.

ARIEL: Poor Caliban, you're doomed. You know that you aren't
25 the stronger, you'll never be the stronger. What good will it do you to struggle?

CALIBAN: And what about you? What good has your obedience done you, your Uncle Tom patience and your sucking up to him. The man's just getting more demanding and despotic
30 day by day.

ARIEL: Well, I've at least achieved one thing: he's promised me my freedom. In the distant future, of course, but it's the first time he's actually committed himself.

CALIBAN: Talk's cheap! He'll promise you a thousand times and
35 take it back a thousand times. Anyway, tomorrow doesn't interest me. What I want is (*Shouting.*) "Freedom now!"

ARIEL: Okay. But you know you're not going to get it out of him "now," and that he's stronger than you are. I'm in a good position to know just what he's got in his arsenal.

40 CALIBAN: The stronger? How do you know that? Weakness always has a thousand means and cowardice is all that keeps us from listing them.

ARIEL: I don't believe in violence.

CALIBAN: What *do* you believe in, then? In cowardice? In giv-
45 ing up? In kneeling and groveling? That's it, someone strikes you on the right cheek and you offer the left. Someone kicks you on the left buttock and you turn the right . . . that way there's no jealousy. Well, that's not Caliban's way . . .

50 ARIEL: You know very well that that's not what I mean. No violence, no submission either. Listen to me: Prospero is the one we've got to change. Destroy his serenity so that he's finally forced to acknowledge his own injustice and put an end to it.

55 CALIBAN: Oh sure . . . that's a good one! Prospero's conscience! Prospero is an old scoundrel who has no conscience.

ARIEL: Exactly—that's why it's up to us to give him one. I'm not fighting just for *my* freedom, for *our* freedom, but for Prospero too, so that Prospero can acquire a conscience.
60 Help me, Caliban.

CALIBAN: Listen, kid, sometimes I wonder if you aren't a little bit nuts. So that Prospero can acquire a conscience? You might as well ask a stone to grow flowers.

ARIEL: I don't know what to do with you. I've often had this in-
65 spiring, uplifting dream that one day Prospero, you, me, we would all three set out, like brothers, to build a wonderful world, each one contributing his own special thing: patience, vitality, love, will-power too, and rigor, not to mention the dreams without which mankind would perish.

70 CALIBAN: You don't understand a thing about Prospero. He's not the collaborating type. He's a guy who only feels something when he's wiped someone out. A crusher, a pulveriser, that's what he is! And you talk about brotherhood!

ARIEL: So then what's left? War? And you know that when it
75 comes to that, Prospero is invincible.

CALIBAN: Better death than humiliation and injustice. Anyhow, I'm going to have the last word. Unless nothingness has it. The day when I begin to feel that everything's lost, just let me get hold of a few barrels of your infernal powder and as
80 you fly around up there in your blue skies you'll see this island, my inheritance, my work, all blown to smithereens . . . and, I trust, Prospero and me with it. I hope you'll like the fireworks display—it'll be signed Caliban.

ARIEL: Each of us marches to his own drum. You follow yours.
85 I follow the beat of mine. I wish you courage, brother.

CALIBAN: Farewell, Ariel, my brother, and good luck.

SCENE II

GONZALO: A magnificent country! Bread hangs from the trees and the apricots are bigger than a woman's full breast.

SEBASTIAN: A pity that it's so wild and uncultivated . . . here and there.

5 GONZALO: Oh, that's nothing. If there were anything poisonous, an antidote would never be far away, for nature is intrinsically harmonious. I've even read somewhere that guano is excellent compost for sterile ground.

SEBASTIAN: Guano? What kind of animal is that? Are you sure 10 you don't mean iguana?

GONZALO: Young man, if I say guano, I mean guano. Guano is the name for bird-droppings that build up over centuries, and it is by far the best fertilizer known. You dig it out of caves . . . If you want my opinion, I think we should inves-15 tigate all the caves on this island one by one to see if we find any, and if we do, this island, if wisely exploited, will be richer than Egypt with its Nile.

ANTONIO: Let me understand: your guano cave contains a river of dried bird-shit.

20 GONZALO: To pick up your image, all we need to do is channel that river, use it to irrigate, if I may use the term, the fields with this wonderful fecal matter, and everything will bloom.

SEBASTIAN: But we'll still need manpower to farm it. Is the is-25 land even inhabited?

GONZALO: That's the problem, of course. But if it is, it must be by wonderful people. It's obvious: a wondrous land can only contain wonderful creatures.

ANTONIO: Yes!

30   Men whose bodies are wiry and strong
       And women whose eyes are open and frank . . .
       creatures in it! . . .

GONZALO: Something like that! I see you know your literature. But in that case, watch out: it will all mean new responsi-35 bilities for us!

SEBASTIAN: How do you get that?

GONZALO: I mean that if the island is inhabited, as I believe, and if we colonize it, as is my hope, then we have to take every precaution not to import our shortcomings, yes, what 40 we call civilization. They must stay as they are: savages, noble and good savages, free, without any complexes or complications. Something like a pool granting eternal youth where we periodically come to restore our aging, citified souls.

45 ALONSO: Sir Gonzalo, when will you shut up?

GONZALO: Ah, Your Majesty, if I am boring you, I apologize. I was only speaking as I did to distract you and to turn our sad thoughts to something more pleasant. There, I'll be silent. Indeed, these old bones have had it. Oof! Let me sit 50 down . . . with your permission, of course.

ALONSO: Noble Old Man, even though younger than you, we are all in the same fix.

GONZALO: In other words, dead tired and dying of hunger.

ALONSO: I have never pretended to be above the human 55 condition.

(*A strange, solemn music is heard.*)

. . . Listen, listen! Did you hear that?

GONZALO: Yes, it's an odd melody!

(PROSPERO *enters invisible. Other strange figures enter as well, bearing a laden table. They dance and graciously invite the* KING *and his company to eat, then they disappear.*)

ALONSO: Heaven protect us! Live marionettes!

GONZALO: Such grace! Such music! Hum. The whole thing is most peculiar.   60

SEBASTIAN: Gone! Faded away! But what does that matter, since they've left their food behind! No meal was ever more welcome. Gentlemen, to table!

ALONSO: Yes, let us partake of this feast, even though it may be our last.   65

(*They prepare to eat, but* ELVES *enter and, with much grimacing and many contortions, carry off the table.*)

GONZALO: Ah! that's a fine way to behave!

ALONSO: I have the distinct feeling that we have fallen under the sway of powers that are playing at cat and mouse with us. It's a cruel way to make us aware of our dependent status.

GONZALO: The way things have been going it's not surprising, 70 and it will do us no good to protest.

(*The* ELVES *return, bringing the food with them.*)

ALONSO: Oh no, this time I won't bite!

SEBASTIAN: I'm so hungry that I don't care, I'll abandon my scruples.

GONZALO: (*To* ALONSO) Why not try? Perhaps the Powers con-75 trolling us saw how disappointed we were and took pity on us. After all, even though disappointed a hundred times, Tantalus still tried a hundred times.

ALONSO: That was also his torture. I won't touch that food.

PROSPERO: (*Invisible.*) Ariel, I don't like his refusing. Harass 80 them until they eat.

ARIEL: Why should we go to any trouble for them? If they won't eat, they can die of hunger.

PROSPERO: No, I *want* them to eat.

ARIEL: That's despotism. A while ago you made me snatch it 85 away just when they were about to gobble it up, and now that they don't want it you are ready to force feed them.

PROSPERO: Enough hairsplitting! My mood has changed! They insult me by not eating. They must be made to eat out of my hand like chicks. That is a sign of submission I insist 90 they give me.

ARIEL: It's evil to play with their hunger as you do with their anxieties and their hopes.

PROSPERO: That is how power is measured. I am Power.

(ALONSO *and his group eat.*)

ALONSO: Alas, when I think . . .   95

GONZALO: That's your trouble, Sire: you think too much.

ALONSO: And thus I should not even think of my lost son! My throne! My country!

GONZALO: (*Eating.*) Your son! What's to say we won't find him again! As for the rest of it . . . Look, Sire, this filthy hole is 100 now our entire world. Why seek further? If your thoughts are too vast, cut them down to size.

(They eat.)

ALONSO: So be it! But I would prefer to sleep. To sleep and to
forget.

105 GONZALO: Good idea! Let's put up our hammocks!

(They sleep.)

Scene III

ANTONIO: Look at those leeches, those slugs! Wallowing in
their slime and their snot: Idiots, slime—they're like
beached jellyfish.

SEBASTIAN: Shhh! It's the King. And that old graybeard is his
5   venerable counsellor.

ANTONIO: The King is he who watches over his flock when they
sleep. That one isn't watching over anything. Ergo, he's not
the King. *(Brusquely.)* You're really a bloodless lily-liver if
you can see a king asleep without getting certain ideas . . .

10 SEBASTIAN: I mustn't have any blood, only water.

ANTONIO: Don't insult water. Every time I look at myself I
think I'm more handsome, more *there.* My inner juices have
always given me my greatness, my true greatness . . . not
the greatness men grant me.

15 SEBASTIAN: All right, so I'm stagnant water.

ANTONIO: Water is never stagnant. It works, it works in us. It
is what gives man his dimension, his true one. Believe me,
you're mistaken if you don't grab the opportunity when it's
offered you. It may never come again.

20 SEBASTIAN: What are you getting at? I have a feeling I can guess.

ANTONIO: Guess, guess! Look at that tree swaying in the wind.
It's called a coconut palm. My dear Sebastian, in my opinion it's time to shake the coconut palm.

SEBASTIAN: Now I really don't understand.

25 ANTONIO: What a dope! Consider my position: I'm Duke of
Milan. Well, I wasn't always . . . I had an older brother.
That was Duke Prospero. And if I'm now Duke Antonio,
it's because I knew when to shake the coconut palm.

SEBASTIAN: And Prospero?

30 ANTONIO: What do you mean by that? When you shake a tree,
someone is bound to fall. And obviously it wasn't me who
fell, because here I am: to assist and serve you, Majesty!

SEBASTIAN: Enough! He's my brother! My scruples won't allow
me to . . . You take care of him while I deal with the old
35   Counsellor.

(They draw their swords.)

ARIEL: Stop, ruffians! Resistance is futile: your swords are enchanted and falling from your hands!

ANTONIO, SEBASTIAN: Alas! Alas!

ARIEL: Sleepers, awake! Awake, I say! Your life depends on it.
40   With these fine fellows with their long teeth and swords
around, anyone who sleeps too soundly risks sleeping forever.

(ALONSO and GONZALO awaken.)

ALONSO: *(Rubbing his eyes.)* What's happening? I was asleep, and
I was having a terrible dream!

ARIEL: No, you were not dreaming. These fine lords here are
45   criminals who were about to perpetrate the most odious of
crimes upon you. Yes, Alonso, you may well marvel that a god
should fly to your aid. Were to heaven you deserved it more!

ALONSO: I have never been wanting in respect for the
divinity . . .

ARIEL: I don't know what effect my next piece of news will have 50
on you: The name of him who has sent me to you is
Prospero.

ALONSO: Prospero! God save us! *(He falls to his knees.)*

ARIEL: I understand your feelings. He lives. It is he who reigns
over this isle, as he reigns over the spirits of the air you 55
breathe . . . But rise . . . You need fear no longer. He has not
saved your lives to destroy them. Your repentance will suffice, for I can see that it is deep and sincere. *(To ANTONIO
and SEBASTIAN.)* As for you, Gentlemen, my master's pardon
extends to you as well, on the condition that you renounce 60
your plans, knowing them to be vain.

SEBASTIAN: *(To ANTONIO.)* We could have got worse!

ANTONIO: If it were men we were up against, no one could
make me withdraw, but when it's demons and magic there's
no shame in giving in. *(To ARIEL.)* . . . We are the Duke's 65
most humble and obedient servants. Please beg him to accept our thanks.

GONZALO: Oh, how ignoble! How good of you to just wipe the
slate clean! No surface repentance . . . not only do you want
attrition, you want contrition as well! Why look at me as 70
though you didn't know what I was talking about? *Attrition:* A selfish regret for offending God, caused by a fear of
punishment. *Contrition:* An unselfish regret growing out of
sorrow at displeasing God.

ARIEL: Honest Gonzalo, thank you for your clarification. Your 75
eloquence has eased my mission and your pedagogical skill
has abbreviated it, for in a few short words you have expressed my master's thought. May your words be heard!
Therefore, let us turn the page. To terminate this episode, I
need only convoke you all, on my master's behalf, to the cel- 80
ebrations that this very day will mark the engagement of his
daughter, Miranda. Alonso, that's good news for you . . .

ALONSO: What—my son?

ARIEL: Correct. Saved by my master from the fury of the waves.

ALONSO: *(Falling to his knees.)* God be praised for this blessing 85
more than all the rest. Rank, fortune, throne, I am prepared
to forgo all if my son is returned to me . . .

ARIEL: Come, Gentlemen, follow me.

——— ACT THREE ———

Scene I

FERDINAND: *(Hoeing and singing.)*

> How life has changed
> Now, hoe in hand
> I work away all day . . .
>
> Hoeing all the day,
> I go my weary way . . .   5

CALIBAN: Poor kid! What would he say if he was Caliban! He
works night and day, and when he sings, it's

> Oo-en-day, Oo-en-day, Oo-en-day, Macaya . . .

And no pretty girl to console him! *(Sees MIRANDA approaching.)* Aha! Let's listen to this!   10

FERDINAND: (*Singing.*)

> How life has changed
> Now, hoe in hand
> I work away all day . . .

MIRANDA: Poor young man! Can I help you? You don't look
15   like you were cut out for this kind of work!

FERDINAND: One word from you would be more help to me
than anything in the world.

MIRANDA: One word? From me? I must say, I . . .

FERDINAND: Your name—that's all: What is your name?

20 MIRANDA: That, I cannot do! It's impossible. My father has expressly forbidden it!

FERDINAND: It is the only thing I long for.

MIRANDA: But I can't, I tell you; it's forbidden!

CALIBAN: (*Taking advantage of* MIRANDA's *momentary distraction,*
25   *he whispers her name to* FERDINAND.) Mi-ran-da!

FERDINAND: All right then, I shall christen you with a name of
my own. I will call you Miranda.

MIRANDA: That's too much! What a low trick! You must have
heard my father calling me . . . Unless it was that awful Cal-
30   iban who keeps pursuing me and calling out my name in
his stupid dreams!

FERDINAND: No, Miranda . . . I had only to allow my eyes to
speak, as you your face.

MIRANDA: Sssh! My father's coming! He'd better not catch you
35   trying to sweet talk me . . .

FERDINAND: (*Goes back to work, singing.*)

> But times have changed
> Now, hoeing all the day,
> I go my weary way . . .

PROSPERO: That's fine, young man! You've managed to accom-
40   plish a good deal for a beginning! I see I've misjudged you.
But you won't be the loser if you serve me well. Listen, my
young friend, there are three things in life: Work, Patience,
Continence, and the world is yours . . . Hey, Caliban, I'm
taking this boy away with me. He's done enough for one
45   day. But since the job is urgent, see that it gets finished.

CALIBAN: Me?

PROSPERO: Yes, you! You've cheated me enough with your loafing
and fiddling around, so you can work a double shift for once!

CALIBAN: I don't see why I should do someone else's job!

50 PROSPERO: Who's the boss here? You or me? Listen, monster: if
you don't like work, I'll see to it you change your mind!

(PROSPERO *and* FERDINAND *move away.*)

CALIBAN: Go on, go on . . . I'll get you one day, you bastard!
(*He sets to work, singing.*)

> "O-o-en-day, Oo-en-day, Oo-en-day, Macaya . . ."

55   Shit, now it's raining! As if things weren't bad enough . . . (*Suddenly, at the sound of a voice,* CALIBAN *stiffens.*) Do you hear that,
boy? That voice through the storm. Bah! It's Ariel. No, that's
not his voice. Whose, then? With an old coot like Prospero . . .
One of his cops, probably. Oh, fine! Now, I'm for it. Men and
60   the elements both against me. Well, the hell with it . . . I'm
used to it. Patience! I'll get them yet. In the meantime better make myself scarce! Let Prospero and his storm and his
cops go by . . . let the seven maws of Malediction bay!

SCENE II

Enter TRINCULO.

TRINCULO: (*Singing.*)

> Oh Susannah . . . oh don't you cry for me . . . (Etc.)

You can say that again! My dearest Susannah . . . trust Trin-
culo, we've had all the roaring storms we need, and more! I
swear: the whole crew wiped out, liquidated . . . Nothing!
Nothing left . . . ! Nothing but poor wandering and wailing 5
Trinculo! No question about it, it'll be a while before anyone
persuades me to depart from affectionate women and friendly
towns to go off to brave roaring storms! How it's raining!
(*Notices* CALIBAN *underneath the wheelbarrow.*) Ah, an Indian!
Dead or alive? You never know with these tricky races. 10
Yukkk! Anyhow, this will do me fine. If he's dead, I can use
his clothes for shelter, for a coat, a tent, a covering. If he's
alive I'll make him my prisoner and take him back to Europe
and then, by golly, my fortune will be made! I'll sell him to
a carnival. No! I'll show him myself at fairs! What a stroke of 15
luck! I'll just settle in here where it's warm and let the storm
rage! (*He crawls under cover, back to back with* CALIBAN.)

(*Enter* STEPHANO.)

STEPHANO: (*Singing.*)

> Blow the man down, hearties,
> Blow the man down . . . (Etc.)

(*Takes a swig of his bottle and continues.*)

> Blow, blow, blow the man down . . . (Etc.)   20

Fortunately, there's still a little wine left in this bottle . . .
enough to give me courage! Be of good cheer, Stephano,
where there's life there's thirst . . . and vice versa! (*Suddenly
spies* CALIBAN's *head sticking out of the cover.*) My God, on
Stephano's word, it looks like a Nindian! (*Comes nearer.*) 25
And that's just what it is! A Nindian. That's neat. I really
am lucky. There's money to be made from a Nindian like
that. If you showed him at a carnival . . . along with the
bearded lady and the flea circus, a real Nindian! An authentic Nindian from the Caribbean! That means real 30
dough, or I'm the last of the idiots! (*Touching* CALIBAN.) But
he's ice cold! I don't know what the body temperature of a
Nindian is, but this one seems pretty cold to me! Let's hope
he's not going to croak! How's that for bad luck: You find a
Nindian and he dies on you! A fortune slips through your fin- 35
gers! But wait, I've got an idea . . . a good swig of this booze
between his lips, that'll warm him up. (*He gives* CALIBAN *a
drink.*) Look . . . he's better already. The little glutton even
wants some more! Just a second, just a second! (*He walks
around the wheelbarrow and sees* TRINCULO's *head sticking out from* 40
under the covering.) Jeez! I must be seeing things! A Nindian
with two heads! Shit! If I have to pour drink down *two* gul-
lets I won't have much left for myself! Well, never mind.
It's incredible . . . your everyday Nindian is already something, but one with two heads . . . a Siamese-twin Nindian, 45
a Nindian with two heads and eight paws, that's really something! My fortune is made. Come on, you wonderful monster,
you . . . let's get a look at your other head! (*He draws nearer*

to TRINCULO.*)* Hello! That face reminds me of something!
50   That nose that shines like a lighthouse . . .

TRINCULO: That gut . . .

STEPHANO: That nose looks familiar . . .

TRINCULO: That gut—there can't be two of them in this lousy
world!

55   STEPHANO: Oh-my-gawd, oh-my-gawd, oh-my-gawd . . . *that's*
it . . . it's that crook Trinculo!

TRINCULO: Good lord! It's Stephano!

STEPHANO: So, Trinculo, you were saved too . . . It almost
makes you believe God looks after drunks . . .

60   TRINCULO: Huh! God . . . Bacchus, maybe. As a matter of fact,
I reached these welcoming shores by floating on a barrel . . .

STEPHANO: And I by floating on my stomach . . . it's nearly the
same thing. But what kind of creature is this? Isn't it a
Nindian?

65   TRINCULO: That's just what I was thinking . . . Yes, by God, it's
a Nindian. That's a piece of luck . . . he'll be our guide.

STEPHANO: Judging from the way he can swill it down, he
doesn't seem to be stupid. I'll try to civilize him. Oh . . .
not too much, of course. But enough so that he can be of
70   some use.

TRINCULO: Civilize him! Shee-it! Does he even know how to talk?

STEPHANO: I couldn't get a word out of him, but I know a way
to loosen his tongue. *(He takes a bottle from his pocket.)*

TRINCULO: *(Stopping him.)* Look here, you're not going to waste
75   that nectar on the first savage that comes along, are you?

STEPHANO: Selfish! Back off! Let me perform my civilizing mission. *(Offering the bottle to* CALIBAN.*)* Of course, if he was
cleaned up a bit he'd be worth more to both of us. Okay?
We'll exploit him together? It's a deal? *(To* CALIBAN.*)* Drink
80   up, pal. You. Drink . . . Yum-yum botty botty! *(*CALIBAN
drinks.) You, drink more. *(*CALIBAN *refuses.)* You no more
thirsty? *(*STEPHANO *drinks.)* Me always thirsty! *(*STEPHANO
and TRINCULO *drink.)*

STEPHANO: Trinculo, you know I used to be prejudiced against
85   shipwrecks, but I was wrong. They're not bad at all.

TRINCULO: That's true. It seems to make things taste better
afterwards . . .

STEPHANO: Not to mention the fact that it's got rid of a lot of
old farts that were always keeping the world down! May
90   they rest in peace! But then, you liked them, didn't you, all
those kings and dukes, all those noblemen! Oh, I served
them well enough, you've got to earn your drink somehow . . . But I could never stand them, ever—understand?
Never. Trinculo, my friend, I'm a long-time believer in the
95   republic . . . you might as well say it: I'm a died-in-
the-wool believer in the people first, a republican in my
guts! Down with tyrants!

TRINCULO: Which reminds me . . . If, as it would seem, the
King and the Duke are dead, there's a crown and a throne
100 up for grabs around here . . .

STEPHANO: By God, you're right! Smart thinking, Trinculo! So,
I appoint myself heir . . . I crown myself king of the island.

TRINCULO: *(Sarcastically.)* Sure you do! And why you, may I
ask? I'm the one who thought of it first, that crown!

105 STEPHANO: Look, Trinculo, don't be silly! I mean, really: just
take a look at yourself! What's the first thing a king needs?
Bearing. Presence. And if I've got anything, it's that.
Which isn't true for everyone. So, I am the King!

CALIBAN: Long live the King!

STEPHANO: It's a miracle . . . he can talk! And what's more, he   110
talks sense! O brave savage! *(He embraces* CALIBAN.*)* You see,
my dear Trinculo, the people has spoken! Vox populi, vox Dei
. . . But please, don't be upset. Stephano is magnanimous and
will never abandon his friend Trinculo, the friend who stood
by him in his trials. Trinculo, we've eaten rough bread to-   115
gether, we've drunk rot-gut wine together. I want to do something for you. I shall appoint you Marshal. But we're forgetting our brave savage . . . It's a scientific miracle! He can talk!

CALIBAN: Yes, Sire. My enthusiasm has restored my speech.
Long live the King! But beware the usurper!   120

STEPHANO: Usurper? Who? Trinculo?

CALIBAN: No, the other one . . . Prospero!

STEPHANO: Prospero? Don't know him.

CALIBAN: Well, you see, this island used to belong to me, except that a man named Prospero cheated me of it. I'm per-   125
fectly willing to give you my right to it, but the only thing
is, you'll have to fight Prospero for it.

STEPHANO: That is of no matter, brave savage. It's a bargain! I'll
get rid of this Prospero for you in two shakes.

CALIBAN: Watch out, he's powerful.   130

STEPHANO: My dear savage, I eat a dozen Prosperos like that for
breakfast every day. But say no more, say no more! Trinculo,
take command of the troops! Let us march upon the foe!

TRINCULO: Yes, forward march! But first, a drink. We will need
all our strength and vigor.   135

CALIBAN: Let's drink, my new-found friends, and let us sing.
Let us sing of winning the day and of an end to tyranny.

(Singing.)

> Black pecking creature of the savannas
> The quetzal measures out the new day
>   solid and lively   140
>   in its haughty armor.
> Zing! the determined hummingbird
>   revels in the flower's depths,
>   going crazy, getting drunk,
>   a lyrebird gathers up our ravings,   145
> Freedom hi-day! Freedom hi-day!

STEPHANO and TRINCULO: *(Together.)* Freedom hi-day! Freedom
hi-day!

CALIBAN:

> The ringdove dallies amid the trees,
>   wandering the islands, here it rests—   150
> The white blossoms of the miconia
> Mingle with the violet blood of ripe berries
> And blood stains your plumage,
>   traveller!
> Lying here after a weary day   155
> We listen to it:
> Freedom hi-day! Freedom hi-day!

STEPHANO: Okay, monster . . . enough crooning. Singing
makes a man thirsty. Let's drink instead. Here, have some
more . . . spirits create higher spirits . . . *(Filling a glass.)*   160
Lead the way, O bountiful wine! Soldiers, forward march!
Or rather . . . no: At ease! Night is falling, the fireflies twinkle, the crickets chirp, all nature makes its brek-ke-ke-kek!

165 And since night has fallen, let us take advantage of it to gather our forces and regain our strength, which has been sorely tried by the unusually . . . copious emotions of the day. And tomorrow, at dawn, with a new spring in our step, we'll have the tyrant's hide. Good night, gentlemen. (*He falls asleep and begins to snore.*)

SCENE III

PROSPERO'S *cave.*

PROSPERO: So then, Ariel! Where are the gods and goddesses? They'd better get a move on! And all of them! I want all of them to take part in the entertainment I have planned for our dear children. Why do I say "entertainment"? Because
5 starting today I want to inculcate in them the spectacle of tomorrow's world: logic, beauty, harmony, the foundations for which I have laid down by my own will-power. Unfortunately, alas, at my age it's time to stop thinking of deeds and to begin thinking of passing on . . . Enter, then!

(GODS *and* GODDESSES *enter.*)

10 JUNO: Honor and riches to you! Long continuance and increasing long life and honored issue! Juno sings to you her blessings!
CERES: May scarcity and want shun you! That is Ceres' blessing on you.
IRIS: (*Beckoning to the* NYMPHS.) Nymphs, come help to celebrate
15 here a contact of true love.

(NYMPHS *enter and dance.*)

PROSPERO: My thanks, Goddesses, and my thanks to you, Iris. Thank you for your good wishes.

(GODS *and* GODDESSES *continue their dance.*)

FERDINAND: What a splendid and majestic vision! May I be so bold to think these spirits?
20 PROSPERO: Yes, spirits which by my art I have from their confines called to greet you and to bless you.

(*Enter* ESHU.)

MIRANDA: But who is that? He doesn't look very benevolent! If I weren't afraid of blaspheming, I'd say he was a devil rather than a god.
25 ESHU: (*Laughing.*) You are not mistaken, fair lady. God to my friends, the Devil to my enemies! And lots of laughs for all!
PROSPERO: (*Softly.*) Ariel must have made a mistake. Is my magic getting rusty? (*Aloud.*) What are you doing here? Who invited you? I don't like such loose behavior, even
30 from a god!
ESHU: But that's just the point . . . no one invited me . . . And that wasn't very nice! Nobody remembered poor Eshu! So poor Eshu came anyway. Hihihi! So how about something to drink? (*Without waiting for a reply, he pours a drink.*) . . .
35 Your liquor's not bad. However, I must say I prefer dogs! (*Looking at* IRIS.) I see that shocks the little lady, but to each his own. Some prefer chickens, others prefer goats. I'm not too fond of chickens, myself. But if you're talking about a black dog . . . think of poor Eshu!

40 PROSPERO: Get out! Go away! We will have none of your grimaces and buffoonery in this noble assembly. (*He makes a magic sign.*)
ESHU: I'm going, boss, I'm going . . . But not without a little song in honor of the bride and the noble company, as you say.

Eshu can play many tricks, 45
Give him twenty dogs!
You will see his dirty tricks.

Eshu plays a trick on the Queen
And makes her so upset that she runs
Naked into the street 50

Eshu plays a trick on a bride,
And on the day of the wedding
She gets into the wrong bed!

Eshu can throw a stone yesterday
And kill a bird today. 55
He can make a mess out of order and vice-versa.
Ah, Eshu is a wonderful bad joke.
Eshu is not the man to carry a heavy load.
His head comes to a point. When he dances
He doesn't move his shoulders . . . 60
Oh, Eshu is a merry elf!

Eshu is a merry elf,
And he can whip you with his dick,
He can whip you,
He can whip you . . . 65

CERES: My dear Iris, don't you find that song quite obscene?
JUNO: It's disgusting! It's quite intolerable . . . if he keeps on, I'm leaving!
IRIS: It's like Liber, or Priapus!
JUNO: Don't mention that name in my presence! 70
ESHU: (*Continuing to sing.*)

. . . with his dick
He can whip you, whip you . . .

JUNO: Oh! Can't someone get rid of him? I'm not staying here!
ESHU: Okay, okay . . . Eshu will go. Farewell, my dear colleagues!

(GODS *and* GODDESSES *exit.*)

PROSPERO: He's gone . . . what a relief! But alas, the harm is 75
done! I am perturbed . . . My old brain is confused. Power!
Power! Alas! All this will one day fade, like foam, like a
cloud, like all the world. And what is power, if I cannot
calm my own fears? But come! My power has gone cold.
(*Calling.*) Ariel! 80
ARIEL: (*Runs in.*) What is it, Sire?
PROSPERO: Caliban is alive, he is plotting, he is getting a guerrilla force together and you—you don't say a word! Well, take care of him. Snakes, scorpions, porcupines, all stinging poisonous creatures, he is to be spared nothing! His pun- 85
ishment must be exemplary. Oh, and don't forget the mud and mosquitoes!
ARIEL: Master, let me intercede for him and beg your indulgence. You've got to understand: he's a rebel.
PROSPERO: By his insubordination he's calling into question the 90
whole order of the world. Maybe the Divinity can afford to let him get away with it, but I have a sense of responsibility!

ARIEL: Very well, Master.

95 PROSPERO: But a thought: arrange some glass trinkets, some trumpery and some second-hand clothes too . . . but colorful ones . . . by the side of the road along which General Caliban and his troops are travelling. Savages adore loud, gaudy clothes . . .

ARIEL: Master . . .

100 PROSPERO: You're going to make me angry. There's nothing to understand. There is a punishment to be meted out. I will not compromise with evil. Hurry! Unless you want to be the next to feel my wrath.

SCENE IV

In the wild; night is drawing to a close; the murmurings of the spirits of the tropical forest are heard.

VOICE I: Fly!

VOICE II: Here!

VOICE I: Ant!

VOICE II: Here.

5 VOICE I: Vulture!

VOICE II: Here.

VOICE I: Soft-shelled crab, calao, crab, hummingbird!

VOICES: Here. Here. Here.

VOICE I: Cramp, crime, fang, opossum!

10 VOICE II: Kra. Kra. Kra.

VOICE I: Huge hedgehog, you will be our sun today. Shaggy, taloned, stubborn. May it burn! Moon, my fat spider, my big dreamcat, go to sleep, my velvet one.

VOICES: *(Singing.)*

> King-ay
15 > King-ay
> Von-von
> Maloto
> Vloom-vloom!

(The sun rises. ARIEL's *band vanishes.* CALIBAN *stands for a moment, rubbing his eyes.)*

CALIBAN: *(Rises and searches the bushes.)* Have to think about get-
20 ting going again. Away, snakes, scorpions, porcupines! All stinging, biting, sticking beasts! Sting, fever, venom, away! Or if you really want to lick me, do it with a gentle tongue, like the toad whose pure drool soothes me with sweet dreams of the future. For it is for you, for all of us, that I go
25 forth today to face the common enemy. Yes, hereditary and common. Look, a hedgehog! Sweet little thing . . . How can any animal—any natural animal, if I may put it that way—go against me on the day I'm setting forth to conquer Prospero! Unimaginable! Prospero is the Anti-Nature! And I
30 say, down with Anti-Nature! And does the porcupine bristle his spines at that? No, he smoothes them down! That's nature! It's kind and gentle, in a word. You've just got to know how to deal with it. So come on, the way is clear! Off we go!

(The band sets out. CALIBAN *marches forward singing his battle song:)*

35 > Shango carries a big stick,
> He strikes and money expires!

> He strikes and lies expire!
> He strikes and larceny expires!
> Shango, Shango ho!
40 > Shango is the gatherer of the rain,
> He passes, wrapped in his fiery cloak,
> His horse's hoofs strike lighting
> On the pavements of the sky!
> Shango is a great knight!
45 > Shango, Shango ho!

(The roar of the sea can be heard.)

STEPHANO: Tell me, brave savage, what is that noise? It sounds like the roaring of a beast at bay.

CALIBAN: Not a bay . . . more like on the prow! . . . Don't worry, it's a pal of mine.

50 STEPHANO: You are very closemouthed about the company you keep.

CALIBAN: And yet it helps me breathe. That's why I call it a pal. Sometimes it sneezes, and a drop falls on my forehead and cools me with its salt, or blesses me . . .

55 STEPHANO: I don't understand. You aren't drunk, are you?

CALIBAN: Come on! It's that howling impatient thing that suddenly appears in a clap of thunder like some God and hits you in the face, that rises up out of the very depths of the abyss and smites you with its fury! It's the sea!

60 STEPHANO: Odd country! And an odd baptism!

CALIBAN: But the best is still the wind and the songs it sings . . . its dirty sigh when it rustles through the bushes, or its triumphant chant when it passes by breaking trees, remnants of their terror in its beard.

65 STEPHANO: The savage is delirious, he's raving mad! Tough luck, Trinculo, our savage is playing without a full deck!

TRINCULO: I'm kind of shuffling myself . . . In other words, I'm exhausted. I never knew such hard going! Savage, even your mud is muddier.

70 CALIBAN: That isn't mud . . . it's something Prospero's dreamed up.

TRINCULO: There's a savage for you . . . everything's always caused by someone. The sun is Prospero's smile. The rain is the tear in Prospero's eye . . . And I suppose the mud is
75 Prospero's shit. And what about the mosquitoes? What are they, may I ask? Zzzzzz, Zzzzzz . . . do you hear them? My face is being eaten off!

CALIBAN: Those aren't mosquitoes. It's some kind of gas that stings your nose and throat and makes you itch. It's another
80 of Prospero's tricks. It's part of his arsenal.

STEPHANO: What do you mean by that?

CALIBAN: I mean his anti-riot arsenal! He's got a lot of gadgets like these . . . gadgets to make you deaf, to blind you, to make you sneeze, to make you cry . . .

85 TRINCULO: And to make you slip! Shit! This is some fix you've got us in! I can't take anymore . . . I'm going to sit down!

STEPHANO: Come on, Trinculo, show a little courage! We're engaged in a mobile ground manoeuvre here, and you know what that means: drive, initiatives, split-second decisions to
90 meet new eventualities, and—above all—mobility. Let's go! Up you get! Mobility!

TRINCULO: But my feet are bleeding!

STEPHANO: Get up or I'll knock you down! (TRINCULO *begins to walk again.)* But tell me, my good savage, this usurper of

95 yours seems very well protected. It might be dangerous to
    attack him!
    CALIBAN: You mustn't underestimate him. You mustn't overes-
    timate him, either . . . he's showing his power, but he's do-
    ing it mostly to impress us.
100 STEPHANO: No matter. Trinculo, we must take precautions. Ax-
    iom: never underestimate the enemy. Here, pass me that
    bottle. I can always use it as a club.

(Highly colored clothing is seen, hanging from a rope.)

    TRINCULO: Right, Stephano. On with the battle. Victory means
    loot. And there's a foretaste of it . . . look at that fine
105 wardrobe! Trinculo, my friend, methinks you are going to
    put on those britches . . . they'll replace your torn trousers.
    STEPHANO: Look out, Trinculo . . . one move and I'll knock you
    down. As your lord and master I have the first pick, and
    with those britches I'm exercising my feudal rights . . .
110 TRINCULO: I saw them first!
    STEPHANO: The King gets first pick in every country in the world.
    TRINCULO: That's tyranny, Stephano. I'm not going to let you
    get away with it.

(They fight.)

    CALIBAN: Let it alone, fool. I tell you about winning your dig-
115 nity, and you start fighting over hand-me-downs! *(To him-
    self.)* To think I'm stuck with these jokers! What an idiot I
    am! How could I ever have thought I could create the Rev-
    olution with swollen guts and fat faces! Oh well! History
    won't blame me for not having been able to win my free-
120 dom all by myself. It's you and me, Prospero! *(Weapon in
    hand, he advances on PROSPERO who has just appeared.)*
    PROSPERO: *(Bares his chest to him.)* Strike! Go on, strike! Strike
    your Master, your benefactor! Don't tell me you're going to
    spare him!

(CALIBAN raises his arm, but hesitates.)

125 Go on! You don't dare! See, you're nothing but an animal . . .
    you don't know how to kill.
    CALIBAN: Defend yourself! I'm not a murderer.
    PROSPERO: *(Very calm.)* The worse for you. You've lost your
    chance. Stupid as a slave! And now, enough of this farce.
130 *(Calling.)* Ariel! *(To ARIEL.)* Ariel, take charge of the pris-
    oners!

(CALIBAN, TRINCULO, and STEPHANO are taken prisoners.)

SCENE V

PROSPERO's cave. MIRANDA and FERDINAND are playing chess.

    MIRANDA: Sir, I think you're cheating.
    FERDINAND: And what if I told you that I would not do so for
    twenty kingdoms?
    MIRANDA: I would not believe a word of it, but I would forgive
5   you. Now, be honest . . . you did cheat!
    FERDINAND: I'm pleased that you were able to tell. *(Laughing.)*
    That makes me less worried at the thought that soon you
    will be leaving your innocent flowery kingdom for my
    less-innocent world of men.

    MIRANDA: Oh, you know that, hitched to your star, I would 10
    brave the demons of hell!

(The NOBLES enter.)

    ALONSO: My son! This marriage! The thrill of it has struck me
    dumb! The thrill and the joy!
    GONZALO: A happy ending to a most opportune shipwreck!
    ALONSO: A unique one, indeed, for it can legitimately be de- 15
    scribed as such.
    GONZALO: Look at them! Isn't it wonderful! I've been too
    choked up to speak, or I would have already told these chil-
    dren all the joy my old heart feels at seeing them living
    love's young dream and cherishing each other so tenderly. 20
    ALONSO: *(To FERDINAND and MIRANDA.)* My children, give me
    your hands. May the Lord bless you.
    GONZALO: Amen! Amen!

(Enter PROSPERO.)

    PROSPERO: Thank you, Gentlemen, for having agreed to join in
    this little family party. Your presence has brought us com- 25
    fort and joy. However, you must now think of getting some
    rest. Tomorrow morning, you will recover your vessels—
    they are undamaged—and your men, who I can guarantee
    are safe, hale and hearty. I shall return with you to Europe,
    and I can promise you—I should say: promise us—a rapid 30
    sail and propitious winds.
    GONZALO: God be praised! We are delighted . . . delighted
    and overcome! What a happy, what a memorable day! With
    one voyage Antonio has found a brother, his brother has
    found a dukedom, his daughter has found a husband. 35
    Alonso has regained his son and gained a daughter. And
    what else? . . . Anyway, I am the only one whose emotion
    prevents him from knowing what he's saying . . .
    PROSPERO: The proof of that, my fine Gonzalo, is that you are
    forgetting someone: Ariel, my loyal servant. *(Turning to* 40
    ARIEL.) Yes, Ariel, today you will be free. Go, my sweet. I
    hope you will not be bored.
    ARIEL: Bored! I fear that the days will seem all too short!
    There, where the Cecropia gloves its impatient hands with
    silver,
    Where the ferns free the stubborn black stumps 45
    from their scored bodies with a green cry—
    There where the intoxicating berry ripens the visit
    of the wild ring-dove
    through the throat of that musical bird
    I shall let fall 50
    one by one,
    each more pleasing than the last
    four notes so sweet that the last
    will give rise to a yearning
    in the heart of the most forgetful slaves 55
    yearning for freedom.
    PROSPERO: Come, come. All the same, you are not going to set
    my world on fire with your music, I trust!
    ARIEL: *(With intoxication.)* Or on some stony plane
    perched on an agave stalk 60
    I shall be the thrush that launches
    its mocking cry
    to the benighted field-hand

"Dig, nigger! Dig, nigger!"
65   and the lightened agave will
straighten from my flight,
a solemn flag.
PROSPERO: That is a very unsettling agenda! Go! Scram! Before
I change my mind!

(Enter STEPHANO, TRINCULO, CALIBAN.*)*

70   GONZALO: Sire, here are your people.
PROSPERO: Oh no, not all of them! Some are yours.
ALONSO: True. There's that fool Trinculo and that unspeakable
Stephano.
STEPHANO: The very ones, Sire, in person. We throw ourselves
75   at your merciful feet.
ALONSO: What became of you?
STEPHANO: Sire, we were walking in the forest—no, it was in
the fields—when we saw some perfectly respectable clothing blowing in the wind. We thought it only right to col-
80   lect them and we were returning them to their rightful
owner when a frightful adventure befell us . . .
TRINCULO: Yes, we were mistaken for thieves and treated accordingly.
STEPHANO: Yes, Sire, it is the most dreadful thing that could
85   happen to an honest man: victims of a judicial error, a mis-
carriage of justice!
PROSPERO: Enough! Today is a day to be benevolent, and it will
do no good to try to talk sense to you in the state you're
in . . . Leave us. Go sleep it off, drunkards. We raise sail
90   tomorrow.
TRINCULO: Raise sail! But that's what we do all the time, Sire,
Stephano and I . . . at least, we raise our glasses, from dawn
till dusk till dawn. The hard part is putting them down,
landing, as you might say.
95   PROSPERO: Scoundrels! If only life could bring you to the safe
harbors of Temperance and Sobriety!
ALONSO: *(Indicating* CALIBAN.*)* That is the strangest creature
I've ever seen!
PROSPERO: And the most devilish too!
100   GONZALO: What's that? Devilish! You've reprimanded him,
preached at him, you've ordered and made him obey and
you say he is still indomitable!
PROSPERO: Honest Gonzalo, it is as I have said.
GONZALO: Well—and forgive me, Counsellor, if I give
105   counsel—on the basis of my long experience the only
thing left is exorcism. "Begone, unclean spirit, in the
name of the Father, of the Son and of the Holy Ghost."
That's all there is to it!

*(*CALIBAN *bursts out laughing.)*

GONZALO: You were absolutely right! And more so that you
110   thought . . . He's not just a rebel, he's a real tough customer! *(To* CALIBAN.*)* So much the worse for you, my friend.
I have tried to save you. I give up. I leave you to the secular arm!
PROSPERO: Come here, Caliban. Have you got anything to say
115   in your own defence? Take advantage of my good humor.
I'm in a forgiving mood today.
CALIBAN: I'm not interested in defending myself. My only regret is that I've failed.

PROSPERO: What were you hoping for?
CALIBAN: To get back my island and regain my freedom.   120
PROSPERO: And what would you do all alone here on this is-
land, haunted by the devil, tempest tossed?
CALIBAN: First of all, I'd get rid of you! I'd spit you out, all your
works and pomps! Your "white" magic!
PROSPERO: That's a fairly negative program . . .   125
CALIBAN: You don't understand it . . . I say I'm going to spit
you out, and that's very positive . . .
PROSPERO: Well, the world is really upside down . . . We've
seen everything now: Caliban as a dialectician! However, in
spite of everything I'm fond of you, Caliban. Come, let's   130
make peace. We've lived together for ten years and worked
side by side! Ten years count for something, after all! We've
ended up by becoming compatriots!
CALIBAN: You know very well that I'm not interested in peace.
I'm interested in being free! Free, you hear?   135
PROSPERO: It's odd . . . no matter what you do, you won't succeed in making me believe that I'm a tyrant!
CALIBAN: Understand what I say, Prospero:
For years I bowed my head
for years I took it, all of it—   140
your insults, your ingratitude . . .
and worst of all, more degrading than all the rest,
your condescension.
But now, it's over!
Over, do you hear?   145
Of course, at the moment
You're still stronger than I am.
But I don't give a damn for your power
or for your dogs or your police or your inventions!
And do you know why?   150
It's because I know I'll get you.
I'll impale you! And on a stake that you've sharpened
yourself!
You'll have impaled yourself!
Prospero, you're a great magician: 155
you're an old hand at deception.
And you lied to me so much,
about the world, about myself,
that you ended up by imposing on me
an image of myself: 160
underdeveloped, in your words, undercompetent
that's how you made me see myself!
And I hate that image . . . and it's false!
But now I know you, you old cancer,
And I also know myself!   165
And I know that one day
my bare fist, just that,
will be enough to crush your world!
The old world is crumbling down!

Isn't it true? Just look!
It even bores you to death.   170

And by the way . . . you have a chance to get it over with:
You can pick up and leave.
You can go back to Europe.
But the hell you will!
I'm sure you won't leave.   175
You make me laugh with your "mission"!

Your "vocation"!
Your vocation is to hassle me.
And that's why you'll stay,
180   just like those guys who founded the colonies
and who now can't live anywhere else.
You're just an old addict, that's what you are!
PROSPERO: Poor Caliban! You know that you're headed towards
your own ruin. You're sliding towards suicide! You know
185   I will be the stronger, and stronger all the time. I pity you!
CALIBAN: And I hate you!
PROSPERO: Beware! My generosity has its limits.
CALIBAN: (Shouting.)

        Shango marches with strength
        along his path, the sky!
190   Shango is a fire-bearer,
        his steps shake the heavens
        and the earth
        Shango, Shango, ho!

PROSPERO: I have uprooted the oak and raised the sea,
195   I have caused the mountain to tremble and have bared my
        chest to adversity.
With Jove I have traded thunderbolt for thunderbolt.
Better yet—from a brutish monster I have made man!
But ah! To have failed to find the path to man's heart . . .
if that be where man is.
200   (To CALIBAN.) Well, I hate you as well!
For it is you who have made me
doubt myself for the first time.
(To the NOBLES.) . . . My friends, come near. We must say
farewell . . . I shall not be going with you. My fate is here:
205   I shall not run from it.
ANTONIO: What, Sire?
PROSPERO: Hear me well.
I am not in any ordinary sense a master,
as this savage thinks,
210   but rather the conductor of a boundless score:
this isle,
summoning voices, I alone,
and mingling them at my pleasure,
arranging out of confusion
215   one intelligible line.
Without me, who would be able to draw music from all that?
This isle is mute without me.
My duty, thus, is here,
and here I shall stay.

GONZALO: Oh day full rich in miracles!   220
PROSPERO: Do not be distressed. Antonio, be you the lieutenant of
my goods and make use of them as procurator until that time
when Ferdinand and Miranda may take effective possession of
them, joining them with the Kingdom of Naples. Nothing of
that which has been set for them must be postponed: Let their   225
marriage be celebrated at Naples with all royal splendor. Honest Gonzalo, I place my trust in your word. You shall stand as
father to our princess at this ceremony.
GONZALO: Count on me, Sire.
PROSPERO: Gentlemen, farewell.   230

(They exit.)

And now, Caliban, it's you and me!
What I have to tell you will be brief:
Ten times, a hundred times, I've tried to save you,
        above all from yourself.
But you have always answered me with wrath   235
        and venom,
like the opossum that pulls itself up by its own tail
the better to bite the hand that tears it from the darkness.
Well, my boy, I shall set aside my indulgent nature
and henceforth I will answer your violence   240
with violence!

(Time passes, symbolized by the curtain's being lowered halfway and
reraised. In semi-darkness PROSPERO appears, aged and weary. His
gestures are jerky and automatic, his speech weak, toneless, trite.)

PROSPERO: Odd, but for some time now we seem to be overrun
with opossums. They're everywhere. Peccarys, wild boar, all
this unclean nature! But mainly opossums. Those eyes! The
vile grins they have! It's as though the jungle was laying   245
siege to the cave . . . But I shall stand firm . . . I shall not let
my work perish! (Shouting.) I shall protect civilization! (He
fires in all directions.) They're done for! Now, this way I'll be
able to have some peace and quiet for a while. But it's cold.
Odd how the climate's changed. Cold on this island . . .   250
Have to think about making a fire . . . Well, Caliban, old fellow, it's just us two now, here on the island . . . only you and
me. You and me. You-me . . . me-you! What in the hell is
he up to? (Shouting.) Caliban!

(In the distance, above the sound of the surf and the chirping of birds,
we hear snatches of CALIBAN's song:)

        FREEDOM HI-DAY, FREEDOM HI-DAY!   255

APPENDIX

LITERAL TRANSLATIONS OF SONGS
ARIEL'S SONG
(Act I, Scene 2)

Chestnut horses of the sand
They bite out the place
Where the waves expire in
Pure languor.

Where the waves die
Here come all,
Join hands
And dance.

Blond sands,
What fire!
Languorous waves,
Pure expiration.
Here lips lick and lick again
Our wounds.

The waves make a waterline . . .
Nothing is, all is becoming . . .
The season is close and strange

The eye is a fine pearl
The heart of coral, the bone of coral,
There, at the waterline
As the sea swells within us.

TRINCULO'S SONG
(Act III, Scene 2)

Virginia, with tears in my eyes
I bid you farewell.
We're off to Mexico,
Straight into the setting sun.

With sails unfurled, my dear love,
It torments me to leave you,
A tempest is brewing
Some storm is howling
That will carry off the entire crew!

STEPHANO'S SONG
(Act III, Scene 2)

(Obviously an old sea chanty or Césaire's adaptation of one.)

Bravely on, guys, step it lively,
bravely on, farewell Bordeaux,
To Cape Horn, it won't be hot,
Off to hunt the whale.

More than one of us will lose his skin
Farewell misery, farewell ship.
The ones who return with all flags flying
Will be the first-rate sailors . . .

WOLE SOYINKA

Wole Soyinka was born in 1934 in Abeokuta, Nigeria. Educated at Government College in Ibadan, Soyinka then studied at Leeds University in England, where he worked with the notable Shakespearian scholar and actor G. Wilson Knight and took his B.A. in English in 1957. He remained in England working as play reader for the Royal Court Theater before returning to Nigeria in 1959, where his first play, *The Lion and the Jewel,* was produced. In the course of the next decade, Soyinka wrote an important body of dramatic work, including the plays *The Invention* (1959), *A Dance of the Forests* (1960), *The Trials of Brother Jero* (1960), *Camwood on the Leaves* (radio play, 1960), *The Strong Breed* (1964), *Kongi's Harvest* (1964), and *The Road* (1965). He also taught at the universities of Ibadan, Ife, and Lagos, and founded two important theaters, the Orisun Theater (1964) and the Masks Theater (1960). Much of Soyinka's work is critical of authoritarian politics; he was arrested in 1967 and held as a political prisoner until 1969. Soyinka's memoir of imprisonment, *The Man Died,* was published in 1972 and was cited for excellence by Amnesty International. In the 1970s, Soyinka continued to write plays examining the tensions of tribal life in modern Africa: *Madmen and Specialists* (1970) and *Death and the King's Horseman* (1976). He also wrote plays more directly examining contemporary African politics: his rewriting of Brecht's *Threepenny Opera* as *Opera Wonyosi* (1977), and *A Play of Giants* (1985). He also wrote an adaptation of Euripides' *The Bacchae* (1973), placing the Greek narrative in a more explicitly tribal and ritualistic setting. Soyinka was awarded the Nobel Prize in 1986, the first African writer to receive the prize for literature.

DEATH AND THE KING'S HORSEMAN

Soyinka is sometimes criticized by other African writers for being too oriented toward Europe. Not only are some of his plays adaptations or imitations of European works, but Soyinka has continued to write in English—the language of the colonial power, after all—rather than writing in his native language, Yoruba. It is precisely this tension between village and metropolis, between Africa and Europe, that provides the springboard for some of Soyinka's greatest work and dramatizes the challenges of cross-cultural interaction in the complex contemporary political environment.

Death and the King's Horseman is based on events that took place in the Yoruba city of Oyo in 1946. The play opens on the day the local African king is to be buried. According to custom, his Horseman, Elesin Oba, will die on this day as well, following his master in death as he followed him in life. It is clear from the scene in the marketplace that this ritual death is, however, a celebration. The village enacts a festive and playful marriage between Elesin and a new, young bride, so that he can procreate before he dies, bringing new life into the world even as he passes out of it, but fatefully delaying his required sacrifice.

In *Death and the King's Horseman,* indigenous African culture operates within the more restricted sphere of Britain's colonial values, laws, and institutions. The region's colonial administrator, Simon Pilkings, who is on his way to a masquerade to celebrate the arrival of the Prince, acts to stop Elesin's death. However, Pilkings and his wife are wearing African ceremonial costumes of the dead to the English masquerade, a decision that is not only offensive and irreligious to the Africans they meet, but that marks their complete incomprehension of the complex situation in which they find themselves. Wearing the costume also marks the Pilkingses, and the colonial British as a whole, as figures of death, in contrast to the paradoxical life celebrated by Elesin. Pilkings "saves" Elesin and brings about the play's tragic catastrophe. Elesin's son Olunde—studying medicine in Britain—returns to perform funeral rites for his father. However, when Elesin is prevented from dying, it becomes clear that colonial intervention has destroyed what it attempted to protect. Olunde, too, is dishonored when his father remains alive and takes the only possible course of action.

In his note to the play, Soyinka criticizes the phrase "clash of cultures" to describe his work, for it "presupposes a potential equality in every given situation of the alien culture and the indigenous." In *Death and the King's Horseman,* the power vested in the colonial administration signals its ability to destroy the indigenous culture it claims, ironically, to govern.

AUTHOR'S NOTE

This play is based on events which took place in Oyo, ancient Yoruba city of Nigeria, in 1946. That year, the lives of Elesin (Olori Elesin), his son, and the Colonial District Officer intertwined with the disastrous results set out in the play. The changes I have made are in matters of detail, sequence and of course characterisation. The action has also been set back two or three years to while the war was still on, for minor reasons of dramaturgy.

The factual account still exists in the archives of the British Colonial Administration. It has already inspired a fine play in Yoruba (Oba Wàjà) by Duro Ladipo. It has also misbegotten a film by some German television company.

The bane of themes of this genre is that they are no sooner employed creatively than they acquire the facile tag of 'clash of cultures', a prejudicial label which, quite apart from its frequent misapplication, presupposes a potential equality *in every given situation* of the alien culture and the indigenous, on the actual soil of the latter. (In the area of misapplication, the overseas prize for illiteracy and mental conditioning undoubtedly goes to the blurb-writer for the American edition of my novel *Season of Anomy* who unblushingly declares that this work portrays the 'clash between old values and new ways, between western methods and African traditions'!) It is thanks to this kind of perverse mentality that I find it necessary to caution the would-be producer of this play against a sadly familiar reductionist tendency, and to direct his vision instead to the far more difficult and risky task of eliciting the play's threnodic essence.

One of the more obvious alternative structures of the play would be to make the District Officer the victim of a cruel dilemma. This is not to my taste and it is not by chance that I have avoided dialogue or situation which would encourage this. No attempt should be made in production to suggest it. The Colonial Factor is an incident, a catalytic incident merely. The confrontation in the play is largely metaphysical, contained in the human vehicle which is Elesin and the universe of the Yoruba mind—the world of the living, the dead and the unborn, and the numinous passage which links all: transition. *Death and the King's Horseman* can be fully realised only through an evocation of music from the abyss of transition.

Wole Soyinka

DEATH AND THE KING'S HORSEMAN

Wole Soyinka

——— CHARACTERS ———

PRAISE-SINGER
ELESIN, *Horseman of the King*
IYALOJA, *'Mother' of the market*
SIMON PILKINGS, *District Officer*
JANE PILKINGS, *his wife*
SERGEANT AMUSA
JOSEPH, *houseboy to the Pilkingses*
BRIDE

H.R.H. THE PRINCE
THE RESIDENT
AIDE-DE-CAMP
OLUNDE, *eldest son of Elesin*
DRUMMERS, WOMEN, YOUNG GIRLS, DANCERS AT THE BALL

The play should run without an interval. For rapid scene changes, one adjustable outline set is very appropriate.

——— ACT ONE ———

A passage through a market in its closing stages. The stalls are being emptied, mats folded. A few women pass through on their way home, loaded with baskets. On a cloth-stand, bolts of cloth are taken down, display pieces folded and piled on a tray. ELESIN OBA *enters along a passage before the market, pursued by his* DRUMMERS *and* PRAISE-SINGERS. *He is a man of enormous vitality, speaks, dances and sings with that infectious enjoyment of life which accompanies all his actions.*

PRAISE-SINGER: Elesin O! Elesin Oba! Howu! What tryst is this the cockerel goes to keep with such haste that he must leave his tail behind?

ELESIN: *(Slows down a bit, laughing.)* A tryst where the cockerel
5   needs no adornment.

PRAISE-SINGER: O-oh, you hear that my companions? That's the way the world goes. Because the man approaches a brand-new bride he forgets the long faithful mother of his children.

ELESIN: When the horse sniffs the stable does he not strain at
10   the bridle? The market is the long-suffering home of my spirit and the women are packing up to go. That Esu-harassed day slipped into the stewpot while we feasted. We ate it up with the rest of the meat. I have neglected my women.

15 PRAISE-SINGER: We know all that. Still it's no reason for shedding your tail on this day of all days. I know the women will cover you in damask and *alari* but when the wind blows cold from behind, that's when the fowl knows his true friends.

20 ELESIN: Olohun-iyo!

PRAISE-SINGER: Are you sure there will be one like me on the other side?

ELESIN: Olohun-iyo!

PRAISE-SINGER: Far be it for me to belittle the dwellers of that
25   place but, a man is either born to his art or he isn't. And I don't know for certain that you'll meet my father, so who is going to sing these deeds in accents that will pierce the deafness of the ancient ones. I have prepared my going—just tell me: Olohun-iyo, I need you on this journey and I
30   shall be behind you.

Note to this edition: Certain Yoruba words which appear in italics in the text are explained in a brief glossary at the end of the play.

ELESIN: You're like a jealous wife. Stay close to me, but only on this side. My fame, my honour are legacies to the living; stay behind and let the world sip its honey from your lips.

PRAISE-SINGER: Your name will be like the sweet berry a child places under his tongue to sweeten the passage of food. The 35 world will never spit it out.

ELESIN: Come then. This market is my roost. When I come among the women I am a chicken with a hundred mothers. I become a monarch whose palace is built with tenderness and beauty. 40

PRAISE-SINGER: They love to spoil you but beware. The hands of women also weaken the unwary.

ELESIN: This night I'll lay my head upon their lap and go to sleep. This night I'll touch feet with their feet in a dance that is no longer of this earth. But the smell of their flesh, 45 their sweat, the smell of indigo on their cloth, this is the last air I wish to breathe as I go to meet my great forebears.

PRAISE-SINGER: In their time the world was never tilted from its groove, it shall not be in yours.

ELESIN: The gods have said No. 50

PRAISE-SINGER: In their time the great wars came and went, the little wars came and went; the white slavers came and went, they took away the heart of our race, they bore away the mind and muscle of our race. The city fell and was rebuilt; the city fell and our people trudged through mountain and forest to 55 found a new home but—Elesin Oba do you hear me?

ELESIN: I hear your voice Olohun-iyo.

PRAISE-SINGER: Our world was never wrenched from its true course.

ELESIN: The gods have said No. 60

PRAISE-SINGER: There is only one home to the life of a river-mussel; there is only one home to the life of a tortoise; there is only one shell to the soul of man: there is only one world to the spirit of our race. If that world leaves its course and smashes on boulders of the great void, whose world will 65 give us shelter?

ELESIN: It did not in the time of my forebears, it shall not in mine.

PRAISE-SINGER: The cockerel must not be seen without his feathers. 70

ELESIN: Nor will the Not-I bird be much longer without his nest.

PRAISE-SINGER: *(Stopped in his lyric stride.)* The Not-I bird, Elesin?

ELESIN: I said, the Not-I bird. 75

PRAISE-SINGER: All respect to our elders but, is there really such
a bird?

ELESIN: What! Could it be that he failed to knock on your door?

PRAISE-SINGER: (*Smiling.*) Elesin's riddles are not merely the nut
80   in the kernel that breaks human teeth; he also buries the
kernel in hot embers and dares a man's fingers to draw it out.

ELESIN: I am sure he called on you, Olohun-iyo. Did you hide in
the loft and push out the servant to tell him you were out?

(ELESIN *executes a brief, half-taunting dance. The* DRUMMER *moves
in and draws a rhythm out of his steps.* ELESIN *dances towards the
market-place as he chants the story of the Not-I bird, his voice changing dexterously to mimic his characters. He performs like a born raconteur, infecting his retinue with his humour and energy. More women
arrive during his recital, including* IYALOJA.)

Death came calling.
85   Who does not know his rasp of reeds?
A twilight whisper in the leaves before
The great araba falls? Did you hear it?
'Not I!' swears the farmer. He snaps
His fingers round his head, abandons
90   A hard-won harvest and begins
A rapid dialogue with his legs.

'Not I,' shouts the fearless hunter, 'but—
It's getting dark, and this night-lamp
Has leaked out all its oil. I think
95   It's best to go home and resume my hunt
Another day.' But now he pauses, suddenly
Lets out a wail: 'Oh foolish mouth, calling
Down a curse on your own head! Your lamp
Has leaked out all its oil, has it?'
100   Forwards or backwards now he dare not move.
To search for leaves and make *etutu*
On that spot? Or race home to the safety
Of his hearth? Ten market-days have passed
My friends, and still he's rooted there
105   Rigid as the plinth of Orayan.

The mouth of the courtesan barely
Opened wide enough to take a ha' penny *robo*
When she wailed: 'Not I.' All dressed she was
To call upon my friend the Chief Tax Officer.
110   But now she sends her go-between instead:
'Tell him I'm ill: my period has come suddenly
But not—I hope—my time.'

Why is the pupil crying?
His hapless head was made to taste
115   The knuckles of my friend the Mallam:
'If you were then reciting the Koran
Would you have ears for idle noises
Darkening the trees, you child of ill omen?'
He shuts down school before its time
120   Runs home and rings himself with amulets.
And take my good kinsman Ifawomi.
His hands were like a carver's, strong
And true. I saw them
Tremble like wet wings of a fowl
125   One day he cast his time-smoothed *opele*
Across the divination board. And all because

The suppliant looked him in the eye and asked,
'Did you hear that whisper in the leaves?'
'Not I,' was his reply; 'perhaps I'm growing deaf—
Good-day.' And Ifa spoke no more that day   130
The priest locked fast his doors,
Sealed up his leaking roof—but wait!
This sudden care was not for Fawomi
But for Osanyin, courier-bird of Ifa's
Heart of wisdom. I did not know a kite   135
Was hovering in the sky
And Ifa now a twittering chicken in
The brood of Fawomi the Mother Hen.

Ah, but I must not forget my evening
Courier from the abundant palm, whose groan   140
Became 'Not I,' as he constipated down
A wayside bush. He wonders if Elegbara
Has tricked his buttocks to discharge
Against a sacred grove. Hear him
Mutter spells to ward off penalties   145
For an abomination he did not intend.
If any here
Stumbles on a gourd of wine, fermenting
Near the road, and nearby hears a stream
Of spells issuing from a crouching form.   150
Brother to a *sigidi*, bring home my wine,
Tell my tapper I have ejected
Fear from home and farm. Assure him,
All is well.

PRAISE-SINGER: In your time we do not doubt the peace of farm- 155
stead and home, the peace of road and hearth, we do not
doubt the peace of the forest.

ELESIN: There was fear in the forest too.
Not-I was lately heard even in the lair
Of beasts. The hyena cackled loud 'Not I,'   160
The civet twitched his fiery tail and glared:
Not I. Not-I became the answering-name
Of the restless bird, that little one
Whom Death found nesting in the leaves
When whisper of his coming ran   165
Before him on the wind. 'Not-I'
Has long abandoned home. This same dawn
I heard him twitter in the gods' abode.
Ah, companions of this living world
What a thing this is, that even those   170
We call immortal
Should fear to die.

IYALOJA: But you, husband of multitudes?

ELESIN: I, when that Not-I bird perched
Upon my roof, bade him seek his nest again,   175
Safe, without care or fear. I unrolled
My welcome mat for him to see. Not-I
Flew happily away, you'll hear his voice
No more in this lifetime—You all know
What I am.   180

PRAISE-SINGER: That rock which turns its open lodes
Into the path of lightning. A gay
Thoroughbred whose sudden disdains
To falter though an adder reared
Suddenly in his path.   185

ELESIN: My rein is loosened.
    I am master of my Fate. When the hour comes
    Watch me dance along the narrowing path
    Glazed by the soles of my great precursors.
190   My soul is eager. I shall not turn aside.
WOMEN: You will not delay?
ELESIN: Where the storm pleases, and when, it directs
    The giants of the forest. When friendship summons
    Is when the true comrade goes.
195 WOMEN: Nothing will hold you back?
ELESIN: Nothing. What! Has no one told you yet?
    I go to keep my friend and master company.
    Who says the mouth does not believe in
    'No, I have chewed all that before?' I say I have.
200   The world is not a constant honey-pot.
    Where I found little I made do with little.
    Where there was plenty I gorged myself.
    My master's hands and mine have always
    Dipped together and, home or sacred feast,
205   The bowl was beaten bronze, the meats
    So succulent our teeth accused us of neglect.
    We shared the choicest of the season's
    Harvest of yams. How my friend would read
    Desire in my eyes before I knew the cause—
210   However rare, however precious, it was mine.
WOMEN: The town, the very land was yours.
ELESIN: The world was mine. Our joint hands
    Raised houseposts of trust that withstood
    The siege of envy and the termites of time.
215   But the twilight hour brings bats and rodents—
    Shall I yield them cause to foul the rafters?
PRAISE-SINGER: Elesin Oba! Are you not that man who
    Looked out of doors that stormy day
    The god of luck limped by, drenched
220   To the very lice that held
    His rags together? You took pity upon
    His sores and wished him fortune.
    Fortune was footloose this dawn, he replied,
    Till you trapped him in a heartfelt wish
225   That now returns to you. Elesin Oba!
    I say you are that man who
    Chanced upon the calabash of honour
    You thought it was palm wine and
    Drained its contents to the final drop.
230 ELESIN: Life has an end. A life that will outlive
    Fame and friendship begs another name.
    What elder takes his tongue to his plate,
    Licks it clean of every crumb? He will encounter
    Silence when he calls on children to fulfill
235   The smallest errand! Life is honour.
    It ends when honour ends.
WOMEN: We know you for a man of honour.
ELESIN: Stop! Enough of that!
WOMEN: (*Puzzled, they whisper among themselves, turning mostly to*
240 IYALOJA.) What is it? Did we say something to give offense?
    Have we slighted him in some way?
ELESIN: Enough of that sound I say. Let me hear no more in that
    vein. I've heard enough.
IYALOJA: We must have said something wrong. (*Comes forward*
245 *a little.*) Elesin Oba, we ask forgiveness before you speak.

ELESIN: I am bitterly offended.
IYALOJA: Our unworthiness has betrayed us. All we can do is
    ask your forgiveness. Correct us like a kind father.
ELESIN: This day of all days . . .
IYALOJA: It does not bear thinking. If we offend you now we 250
    have mortified the gods. We offend heaven itself. Father of
    us all, tell us where we went astray. (*She kneels, the other*
    women follow.)
ELESIN: Are you not ashamed? Even a tear-veiled
    Eye preserves its function of sight. 255
    Because my mind was raised to horizons
    Even the boldest man lowers his gaze
    In thinking of, must my body here
    Be taken for a vagrant's?
IYALOJA: Horseman of the King, I am more baffled than ever. 260
PRAISE-SINGER: The strictest father unbends his brow when the
    child is penitent, Elesin. When time is short, we do not
    spend it prolonging the riddle. Their shoulders are bowed
    with the weight of fear lest they have marred your day be-
    yond repair. Speak now in plain words and let us pursue the 265
    ailment to the home of remedies.
ELESIN: Words are cheap. 'We know you for
    A man of honour.' Well tell me, is this how
    A man of honour should be seen?
    Are these not the same clothes in which 270
    I came among you a full half-hour ago?

(*He roars with laughter and the* WOMEN, *relieved, rise and rush into*
stalls to fetch rich cloths.)

WOMAN: The gods are kind. A fault soon remedied is soon for-
    given. Elesin Oba, even as we match our words with deed,
    let your heart forgive us completely.
ELESIN: You who are breath and giver of my being 275
    How shall I dare refuse you forgiveness
    Even if the offence were real.
IYALOJA: (*Dancing round him. Sings.*)

        He forgives us. He forgives us.
        What a fearful thing it is when
        The voyager sets forth 280
        But a curse remains behind.

WOMEN: For a while we truly feared
    Our hands had wrenched the world adrift
    In emptiness.
IYALOJA: Richly, richly, robe him richly 285
    The cloth of honour is *alari*
    Sanyan is the band of friendship
    Boa-skin makes slippers of esteem.
WOMEN: For a while we truly feared
    Our hands had wrenched the world adrift 290
    In emptiness.
PRAISE-SINGER: He who must, must voyage forth
    The world will not roll backwards
    It is he who must, with one
    Great gesture overtake the world. 295
WOMEN: For a while we truly feared
    Our hands had wrenched the world
    In emptiness.
PRAISE-SINGER: The gourd you bear is not for shirking.
    The gourd is not for setting down 300

At the first crossroad or wayside grove.
Only one river may know its contents.
WOMEN: We shall all meet at the great market
We shall all meet at the great market
305   He who goes early takes the best bargains
But we shall meet, and resume our banter.

(ELESIN *stands resplendent in rich clothes, cap, shawl, etc. His sash is
of a bright red* alari *cloth. The* WOMEN *dance round him. Suddenly,
his attention is caught by an object off-stage.*)

ELESIN: The world I know is good.
WOMEN: We know you'll leave it so.
ELESIN: The world I know is the bounty
310   Of hives after bees have swarmed.
No goodness teems with such open hands
Even in the dreams of deities.
WOMEN: And we know you'll leave it so.
ELESIN: I was born to keep it so. A hive
315   Is never known to wander. An anthill
Does not desert its roots. We cannot see
The still great womb of the world—
No man beholds his mother's womb—
Yet who denies it's there? Coiled
320   To the navel of the world is that
Endless cord that links us all
To the great origin. If I lose my way
The trailing cord will bring me to the roots.
WOMEN: The world is in your hands.

(*The earlier distraction, a beautiful young girl, comes along the passage through which* ELESIN *first made his entry.*)

325   ELESIN: I embrace it. And let me tell you, women—
I like this farewell that the world designed,
Unless my eyes deceive me, unless
We are already parted, the world and I,
And all that breeds desire is lodged
330   Among our tireless ancestors. Tell me friends,
Am I still earthed in that beloved market
Of my youth? Or could it be my will
Has outleapt the conscious act and I have come
Among the great departed?
335   PRAISE-SINGER: Elesin-Oba why do your eyes roll like a bush-
rat who sees his fate like his father's spirit, mirrored in the
eye of a snake? And all these questions! You're standing on
the same earth you've always stood upon. This voice you
hear is mine, Oluhun-iyo, not that of an acolyte in heaven.
340   ELESIN: How can that be? In all my life
As Horseman of the King, the juiciest
Fruit on every tree was mine. I saw,
I touched, I wooed, rarely was the answer No.
The honour of my place, the veneration I
345   Received in the eye of man or woman
Prospered my suit and
Played havoc with my sleeping hours.
And they tell me my eyes were a hawk
In perpetual hunger. Split an iroko tree
350   In two, hide a woman's beauty in its heartwood
And seal it up again—Elesin, journeying by,
Would make his camp beside that tree
Of all the shades in the forest.

PRAISE-SINGER: Who would deny your reputation, snake-on-
the-loose in dark passages of the market! Bed-bug who   355
wages war on the mat and receives the thanks of the vanquished! When caught with his bride's own sister he
protested—but I was only prostrating myself to her as becomes a grateful in-law. Hunter who carries his powder-horn
on the hips and fires crouching or standing! Warrior who   360
never makes that excuse of the whining coward—but how
can I go to battle without my trousers?—trouserless or shirt-
less it's all one to him. Oka-rearing-from-a-camouflage-of-
leaves, before he strikes the victim is already prone! Once
they told him, Howu, a stallion does not feed on the grass   365
beneath him: he replied, true, but surely he can roll on it!
WOMEN: Ba-a-a-ba O!
PRAISE-SINGER: Ah, but listen yet. You know there is the leaf-
knibbling grub and there is the cola-chewing beetle; the
leaf-nibbling grub lives on the leaf, the cola-chewing bee-   370
tle lives in the colanut. Don't we know what our man feeds
on when we find him cocooned in a woman's wrapper?
ELESIN: Enough, enough, you all have cause
To know me well. But, if you say this earth
Is still the same as gave birth to those songs,   375
Tell me who was that goddess through whose lips
I saw the ivory pebbles of Oya's river-bed.
Iyaloja, who is she? I saw her enter
Your stall; all your daughters I know well.
No, not even Ogun-of-the-farm toiling   380
Dawn till dusk on his tuber patch
Not even Ogun with the finest hoe he ever
Forged at the anvil could have shaped
That rise of buttocks, not though he had
The richest earth between his fingers.   385
Her wrapper was no disguise
For thighs whose ripples shamed the river's
Coils around the hills of Ilesi. Her eyes
Were new-laid eggs glowing in the dark.
Her skin . . .   390
IYALOJA: Elesin Oba . . .
ELESIN: What! Where do you all say I am?
IYALOJA: Still among the living.
ELESIN: And that radiance which so suddenly
Lit up this market I could boast   395
I knew so well?
IYALOJA: Has one step already in her husband's home. She is
betrothed.
ELESIN: (*Irritated.*) Why do you tell me that?

(IYALOJA *falls silent. The* WOMEN *shuffle uneasily.*)

IYALOJA: Not because we dare give you offence Elesin. Today is   400
your day and the whole world is yours. Still, even those who
leave town to make a new dwelling elsewhere like to be re-
membered by what they leave behind.
ELESIN: Who does not seek to be remembered?
Memory is Master of Death, the chink   405
In his armour of conceit. I shall leave
That which makes my going the sheerest
Dream of an afternoon. Should voyagers
Not travel light? Let the considerate traveller
Shed, of his excessive load, all   410
That may benefit the living.

WOMEN: *(Relieved.)* Ah Elesin Oba, we knew you for a man of honour.

ELESIN: Then honour me. I deserve a bed of honour to lie upon.

415   IYALOJA: The best is yours. We know you for a man of honour.
You are not one who eats and leaves nothing on his plate for children. Did you not say it yourself? Not one who blights the happiness of others for a moment's pleasure.

ELESIN: Who speaks of pleasure? O women, listen!

420   Pleasure palls. Our acts should have meaning.
The sap of the plantain never dries.
You have seen the young shoot swelling
Even as the parent stalk begins to wither.
Women, let my going be likened to

425   The twilight hour of the plantain.

WOMEN: What does he mean Iyaloja? This language is the language of our elders, we do not fully grasp it.

IYALOJA: I dare not understand you yet Elesin.

ELESIN: All you who stand before the spirit that dares

430   The opening of the last door of passage,
Dare to rid my going of regrets! My wish
Transcends the blotting out of thought
In one mere moment's tremor of the senses.
Do me credit. And do me honour.

435   I am girded for the route beyond
Burdens of waste and longing.
Then let me travel light. Let
Seed that will not serve the stomach
On the way remain behind. Let it take root

440   In the earth of my choice, in this earth
I leave behind.

IYALOJA: *(Turns to* WOMEN.*)* The voice I hear is already touched by the waiting fingers of our departed. I dare not refuse.

WOMAN: Buy Iyaloja . . .

445   IYALOJA: The matter is no longer in our hands.

WOMAN: But she is betrothed to your own son. Tell him.

IYALOJA: My son's wish is mine. I did the asking for him, the loss can be remedied. But who will remedy the blight of closed hands on the day when all should be openness and light? Tell

450   him, you say! You wish that I burden him with knowledge that will sour his wish and lay regrets on the last moments of his mind. You pray to him who is your intercessor to the other world—don't set this world adrift in your own time; would you rather it was my hand whose sacrilege wrenched it loose?

455   WOMAN: Not many men will brave the curse of a dispossessed husband.

IYALOJA: Only the curses of the departed are to be feared. The claims of one whose foot is on the threshold of their abode surpasses even the claims of blood. It is impiety even to

460   place hindrances in their ways.

ELESIN: What do my mothers say? Shall I step
Burdened into the unknown?

IYALOJA: Not we, but the very earth says No. The sap in the plantain does not dry. Let grain that will not feed the voy-

465   ager at his passage drop here and take root as he steps beyond this earth and us. Oh you who fill the home from hearth to threshold with the voices of children, you who now bestride the hidden gulf and pause to draw the right foot across and into the resting-home of the great forebears,

470   it is good that your loins be drained into the earth we know, that your last strength be ploughed back into the womb that gave you being.

PRAISE-SINGER: Iyaloja, mother of multitudes in the teeming market of the world, how your wisdom transfigures you!

IYALOJA: *(Smiling broadly, completely reconciled.)* Elesin, even at   475
the narrow end of the passage I know you will look back and sigh a last regret for the flesh that flashed past your spirit in flight. You always had a restless eye. Your choice has my blessing. *(To the* WOMEN.*)* Take the good news to our daughter and make her ready. *(Some* WOMEN *go off.)*   480

ELESIN: Your eyes were clouded at first.

IYALOJA: Not for long. It is those who stand at the gateway of the great change to whose cry we must pay heed. And then, think of this—it makes the mind tremble. The fruit of such a union is rare. It will be neither of this world nor of the   485
next. Nor of the one behind us. As if the timelessness of the ancestor world and the unborn have joined spirits to wring an issue of the elusive being of passage . . . Elesin!

ELESIN: I am here. What is it?

IYALOJA: Did you hear all I said just now?   490

ELESIN: Yes.

IYALOJA: The living must eat and drink. When the moment comes, don't turn the food to rodents' droppings in their mouth. Don't let them taste the ashes of the world when they step out at dawn to breathe the morning dew.   495

ELESIN: This doubt is unworthy of you Iyaloja.

IYALOJA: Eating the awusa nut is not so difficult as drinking water afterwards.

ELESIN: The waters of the bitter stream are honey to a man
Whose tongue has savoured all.   500

IYALOJA: No one knows when the ants desert their home; they leave the mound intact. The swallow is never seen to peck holes in its nest when it is time to move with the season. There are always throngs of humanity behind the leave-taker. The rain should not come through the roof for them,   505
the wind must not blow through the walls at night.

ELESIN: I refuse to take offence.

IYALOJA: You wish to travel light. Well, the earth is yours. But be sure the seed you leave in it attracts no curse.

ELESIN: You really mistake my person Iyaloja.   510

IYALOJA: I said nothing. Now we must go prepare your bridal chamber. Then these same hands will lay your shrouds.

ELESIN: *(Exasperated.)* Must you be so blunt? *(Recovers.)* Well, weave your shrouds, but let the fingers of my bride seal my eyelids with earth and wash my body.   515

IYALOJA: Prepare yourself Elesin.

(She gets up to leave. At that moment the women return, leading the BRIDE. ELESIN's *face glows with pleasure. He flicks the sleeves of his agbada with renewed confidence and steps forward to meet the group. As the girl kneels before* IYALOJA, *lights fade out on the scene.)*

––––––– **ACT TWO** –––––––

The verandah of the District Officer's bungalow. A tango is playing from an old hand-cranked gramophone and, glimpsed through the wide windows and doors which open onto the forestage verandah are the shapes of SIMON PILKINGS *and his wife,* JANE, *tangoing in and out of shadows in the living-room. They were wearing what is immediately apparent as some form of fancy-dress. The dance goes on for some moments and then the figure of a 'Native Administration' policeman emerges and climbs up the steps onto the verandah. He peeps through and observes the dancing couple, reacting with what is obviously a long-standing bewilderment. He stiffens suddenly, his expression changes to one of disbelief and horror. In his excitement he upsets a flower-pot and attracts the attention of the couple. They stop dancing.*

PILKINGS: Is there anyone out there?

JANE: I'll turn off the gramophone.

PILKINGS: *(Approaching the verandah.)* I'm sure I heard something fall over. *(The constable retreats slowly, open-mouthed as*
5   PILKINGS *approaches the verandah.)* Oh it's you Amusa. Why didn't you just knock instead of knocking things over?

AMUSA: *(Stammers badly and points a shaky finger at his dress.)* Mista Pirinkin . . . Mista Pirinkin . . .

PILKINGS: What is the matter with you?

10 JANE: *(Emerging.)* Who is it dear? Oh, Amusa . . .

PILKINGS: Yes it's Amusa, and acting most strangely.

AMUSA: *(His attention now transferred to* MRS PILKINGS.*)* Mammadam . . . you too!

PILKINGS: What the hell is the matter with you man!

15 JANE: Your costume darling. Our fancy dress.

PILKINGS: Oh hell, I'd forgotten all about that. *(Lifts the face mask over his head showing his face. His wife follows suit.)*

JANE: I think you've shocked his big pagan heart bless him.

PILKINGS: Nonsense, he's a Moslem. Come on Amusa, you don't
20 believe in all this nonsense do you? I thought you were a good Moslem.

AMUSA: Mista Pirinkin, I beg you sir, what you think you do with that dress? It belong to dead cult, not for human being.

PILKINGS: Oh Amusa, what a let down you are. I swear by you
25 at the club when you know—thank God for Amusa, he doesn't believe in any mumbo-jumbo. And now look at you!

AMUSA: Mista Pirinkin, I beg you, take it off. Is not good for man like you to touch that cloth.

PILKINGS: Well, I've got it on. And what's more Jane and I have
30 bet on it we're taking first prize at the ball. Now, if you can just pull yourself together and tell me what you wanted to see me about . . .

AMUSA: Sir, I cannot talk this matter to you in that dress. I no fit.

35 PILKINGS: What's that rubbish again?

JANE: He is dead earnest too Simon. I think you'll have to handle this delicately.

PILKINGS: Delicately my. . . ! Look here Amusa, I think this little joke has gone far enough hm? Let's have some sense. You
40 seem to forget that you are a police officer in the service of His Majesty's Government. I order you to report your business at once or face disciplinary action.

AMUSA: Sir, it is a matter of death. How can man talk against death to person in uniform of death? Is like talking against
45 government to person in uniform of police. Please sir, I go and come back.

PILKINGS: *(Roars.)* Now! *(*AMUSA *switches his gaze to the ceiling suddenly, remains mute.)*

JANE: Oh Amusa, what is there to be scared of in the costume?
50 You saw it confiscated last month from those *egungun* men who were creating trouble in town. You helped arrest the cult leaders yourself—if the juju didn't harm you at the time how could it possibly harm you now? And merely by looking at it?

55 AMUSA: *(Without looking down.)* Madam, I arrest the ringleaders who make trouble but me I no touch *egungun.* That

egungun inself, I no touch. And I no abuse 'am. I arrest ringleader but I treat *egungun* with respect.

PILKINGS: It's hopeless. We'll merely end up missing the best part of the ball. When they get this way there is nothing 60
you can do. It's simply hammering against a brick wall. Write your report or whatever it is on that pad Amusa and take yourself out of here. Come on Jane. We only upset his delicate sensibilities by remaining here.

*(*AMUSA *waits for them to leave, then writes in the notebook, somewhat laboriously. Drumming from the direction of the town wells up.* AMUSA *listens, makes a movement as if he wants to recall* PILKINGS *but changes his mind. Completes his note and goes. A few moments later* PILKINGS *emerges, picks up the pad and reads.)*

PILKINGS: Jane!   65

JANE: *(From the bedroom.)* Coming darling. Nearly ready.

PILKINGS: Never mind being ready, just listen to this.

JANE: What is it?

PILKINGS: Amusa's report. Listen. 'I have to report that it come to my information that one prominent chief, namely, the 70
Elesin Oba, is to commit death tonight as a result of native custom. Because this is criminal offence I await further instruction at charge office. Sergeant Amusa.'

*(*JANE *comes out onto the verandah while he is reading.)*

JANE: Did I hear you say commit death?

PILKINGS: Obviously he means murder.   75

JANE: You mean a ritual murder?

PILKINGS: Must be. You think you've stamped it all out but it's always lurking under the surface somewhere.

JANE: Oh. Does it mean we are not getting to the ball at all?

PILKINGS: No-o. I'll have the man arrested. Everyone remotely in- 80
volved. In any case there may be nothing to it. Just rumours.

JANE: Really? I thought you found Amusa's rumours generally reliable.

PILKINGS: That's true enough. But who knows what may have been giving him the scare lately. Look at his conduct 85
tonight.

JANE: *(Laughing.)* You have to admit he had his own peculiar logic. *(Deepens her voice.)* How can man talk against death to person in uniform of death? *(Laughs.)* Anyway, you can't go into the police station dressed like that.   90

PILKINGS: I'll send Joseph with instructions. Damn it, what a confounded nuisance!

JANE: But don't you think you should talk first to the man, Simon?

PILKINGS: Do you want to go to the ball or not?   95

JANE: Darling, why are you getting rattled? I was only trying to be intelligent. It seems hardly fair just to lock up a man—and a chief at that—simply on the er . . . what is that legal word again?—uncorroborated word of a sergeant.

PILKINGS: Well, that's easily decided. Joseph!   100

JOSEPH: *(From within.)* Yes master.

PILKINGS: You're quite right of course, I am getting rattled. Probably the effect of those bloody drums. Do you hear how they go on and on?

JANE: I wondered when you'd notice. Do you suppose it has 105
something to do with this affair?

PILKINGS: Who knows? They always find an excuse for making a noise . . . *(Thoughtfully.)* Even so . . .

JANE: Yes Simon?

110 PILKINGS: It's different Jane. I don't think I've heard this particular—sound—before. Something unsettling about it.

JANE: I thought all bush drumming sounded the same.

PILKINGS: Don't tease me now Jane. This may be serious.

JANE: I'm sorry. *(Gets up and throws her arms around his neck.*
115 *Kisses him. The houseboy enters, retreats and knocks.)*

PILKINGS: *(Wearily.)* Oh, come in Joseph! I don't know where you pick up all these elephantine notions of tact. Come over here.

JOSEPH: Sir?

PILKINGS: Joseph, are you a christian or not?

120 JOSEPH: Yessir.

PILKINGS: Does seeing me in this outfit bother you?

JOSEPH: No sir, it has no power.

PILKINGS: Thank God for some sanity at last. Now Joseph, answer me on the honour of a christian—what is supposed to
125 be going on in town tonight?

JOSEPH: Tonight sir? You mean that chief who is going to kill himself?

PILKINGS: What?

JANE: What do you mean, kill himself?

130 PILKINGS: You do mean he is going to kill somebody don't you?

JOSEPH: No master. He will not kill anybody and no one will kill him. He will simply die.

JANE: But why Joseph?

JOSEPH: It is native law and custom. The King die last month.
135 Tonight is his burial. But before they can bury him, the Elesin must die so as to accompany him to heaven.

PILKINGS: I seem to be fated to clash more often with that man than with any of the other chiefs.

JOSEPH: He is the King's Chief Horseman.

140 PILKINGS: *(In a resigned way.)* I know.

JANE: Simon, what's the matter?

PILKINGS: It would have to be him!

JANE: Who is he?

PILKINGS: Don't you remember? He's that chief with whom I
145 had a scrap some three or four years ago. I helped his son get to a medical school in England, remember? He fought tooth and nail to prevent it.

JANE: Oh now I remember. He was that very sensitive young man. What was his name again?

150 PILKINGS: Olunde. Haven't replied to his last letter come to think of it. The old pagan wanted him to stay and carry on some family tradition or the other. Honestly I couldn't understand the fuss he made. I literally had to help the boy escape from close confinement and load him onto the next
155 boat. A most intelligent boy, really bright.

JANE: I rather thought he was much too sensitive you know. The kind of person you feel should be a poet munching rose petals in Bloomsbury.

PILKINGS: Well, he's going to make a first-class doctor. His
160 mind is set on that. And as long as he wants my help he is welcome to it.

JANE: *(After a pause.)* Simon.

PILKINGS: Yes?

JANE: This boy, he was his eldest son wasn't he?

165 PILKINGS: I'm not sure. Who could tell with that old ram?

JANE: Do you know, Joseph?

JOSEPH: Oh yes madam. He was the eldest son. That's why Elesin cursed master good and proper. The eldest son is not supposed to travel away from the land.

JANE: *(Giggling.)* Is that true Simon? Did he really curse you 170 good and proper?

PILKINGS: By all accounts I should be dead by now.

JOSEPH: Oh no, master is white man. And good christian. Black man juju can't touch master.

JANE: If he was his eldest, it means that he would be the Elesin 175 to the next king. It's a family thing isn't it, Joseph?

JOSEPH: Yes madam. And if this Elesin had died before the King, his eldest son must take his place.

JANE: That would explain why the old chief was so mad you took the boy away. 180

PILKINGS: Well it makes me all the more happy I did.

JANE: I wonder if he knew.

PILKINGS: Who? Oh, you mean Olunde?

JANE: Yes. Was that why he was so determined to get away? I wouldn't stay if I knew I was trapped in such a horrible 185 custom.

PILKINGS: *(Thoughtfully.)* No, I don't think he knew. At least he gave no indication. But you couldn't really tell with him. He was rather close you know, quite unlike most of them. Didn't give much away, not even to me. 190

JANE: Aren't they all rather close, Simon?

PILKINGS: These natives here? Good gracious. They'll open their mouths and yap with you about their family secrets before you can stop them. Only the other day . . .

JANE: But Simon, do they really give anything away? I mean, 195 anything that really counts. This affair for instance, we didn't know they still practised that custom did we?

PILKINGS: Ye-e-es, I suppose you're right there. Sly, devious bastards.

JOSEPH: *(Stiffly.)* Can I go now master? I have to clean the kitchen. 200

PILKINGS: What? Oh, you can go. Forgot you were still here.

(JOSEPH goes.)

JANE: Simon, you really must watch your language. Bastard isn't just a simple swear-word in these parts, you know.

PILKINGS: Look, just when did you become a social anthropologist, that's what I'd like to know. 205

JANE: I'm not claiming to know anything. I just happen to have overheard quarrels among the servants. That's how I know they consider it a smear.

PILKINGS: I thought the extended family system took care of all that. Elastic family, no bastards. 210

JANE: *(Shrugs.)* Have it your own way.

(Awkward silence. The drumming increases in volume. JANE gets up suddenly, restless.)

That drumming Simon, do you think it might really be connected with this ritual? It's been going on all evening.

PILKINGS: Let's ask our native guide. Joseph! Just a minute Joseph. *(JOSEPH re-enters.)* What's the drumming about? 215

JOSEPH: I don't know master.

PILKINGS: What do you mean you don't know? It's only two years since your conversion. Don't tell me all that holy water nonsense also wiped out your tribal memory.

220 JOSEPH: (*Visibly shocked.*) Master!

JANE: Now you've done it.

PILKINGS: What have I done now?

JANE: Never mind. Listen Joseph, just tell me this. Is that drumming connected with dying or anything of that nature?

225 JOSEPH: Madam, this is what I am trying to say: I am not sure.
It sounds like the death of a great chief and then, it sounds
like the wedding of a great chief. It really mix me up.

PILKINGS: Oh get back to the kitchen. A fat lot of help you are.

JOSEPH: Yes master. (*Goes.*)

230 JANE: Simon . . .

PILKINGS: Alright, alright. I'm in no mood for preaching.

JANE: It isn't my preaching you have to worry about, it's the
preaching of the missionaries who preceded you here.
When they make converts they really convert them. Calling

235 holy water nonsense to our Joseph is really like insulting
the Virgin Mary before a Roman Catholic. He's going to
hand in his notice tomorrow you mark my word.

PILKINGS: Now you're being ridiculous.

JANE: Am I? What are you willing to bet that tomorrow we are

240 going to be without a steward-boy? Did you see his face?

PILKINGS: I am more concerned about whether or not we will
be one native chief short by tomorrow. Christ! Just listen to
those drums. (*He strides up and down, undecided.*)

JANE: (*Getting up.*) I'll change and make up some supper.

245 PILKINGS: What's that?

JANE: Simon, it's obvious we have to miss this ball.

PILKINGS: Nonsense. It's the first bit of real fun the European
club has managed to organise for over a year, I'm damned if
I'm going to miss it. And it is a rather special occasion.

250 Doesn't happen every day.

JANE: You know this business has to be stopped Simon. And
you are the only man who can do it.

PILKINGS: I don't have to stop anything. If they want to throw
themselves off the top of a cliff or poison themselves for the

255 sake of some barbaric custom what is that to me? If it were
ritual murder or something like that I'd be duty-bound to
do something. I can't keep an eye on all the potential suicides in this province. And as for that man—believe me it's
good riddance.

260 JANE: (*Laughs.*) I know you better than that Simon. You are going to have to do something to stop it—after you've finished blustering.

PILKINGS: (*Shouts after her.*) And suppose after all it's only a
wedding. I'd look a proper fool if I interrupted a chief on

265 his honeymoon, wouldn't I? (*Resumes his angry stride, slows
down.*) Ah well, who can tell what those chiefs actually do
on their honeymoon anyway? (*He takes up the pad and scrib-
bles rapidly on it.*) Joseph! Joseph! Joseph! (*Some moments later
JOSEPH puts in a sulky appearance.*) Did you hear me call you?

270 Why the hell didn't you answer?

JOSEPH: I didn't hear master.

PILKINGS: You didn't hear me! How come you are here then?

JOSEPH: (*Stubbornly.*) I didn't hear master.

PILKINGS: (*Controls himself with an effort.*) We'll talk about it in

275 the morning. I want you to take this note directly to
Sergeant Amusa. You'll find him at the charge office. Get
on your bicycle and race there with it. I expect you back in
twenty minutes exactly. Twenty minutes, is that clear?

JOSEPH: Yes master. (*Going.*)

PILKINGS: Oh er . . . Joseph. 280

JOSEPH: Yes master?

PILKINGS: (*Between gritted teeth.*) Er . . . forget what I said just
now. The holy water is not nonsense. *I* was talking nonsense.

JOSEPH: Yes master. (*Goes.*)

JANE: (*Pokes her head round the door.*) Have you found him? 285

PILKINGS: Found who?

JANE: Joseph. Weren't you shouting for him?

PILKINGS: Oh yes, he turned up finally.

JANE: You sounded desperate. What was it all about?

PILKINGS: Oh nothing. I just wanted to apologise to him. As- 290
sure him that the holy water isn't really nonsense.

JANE: Oh? And how did he take it?

PILKINGS: Who the hell gives a damn! I had a sudden vision of
our Very Reverend Macfarlane drafting another letter of
complaint to the Resident about my unchristian language 295
towards his parishioners.

JANE: Oh I think he's given up on you by now.

PILKINGS: Don't be too sure. And anyway, I wanted to make
sure Joseph didn't 'lose' my note on the way. He looked sufficiently full of the holy crusade to do some such thing. 300

JANE: If you've finished exaggerating, come and have something to eat.

PILKINGS: No, put it all way. We can still get to the ball.

JANE: Simon . . .

PILKINGS: Get your costume back on. Nothing to worry 305
about. I've instructed Amusa to arrest the man and lock
him up.

JANE: But that station is hardly secure Simon. He'll soon get
his friends to help him escape.

PILKINGS: A-ah, that's where I have out-thought you. I'm not 310
having him put in the station cell. Amusa will bring him
right here and lock him up in my study. And he'll stay with
him till we get back. No one will dare come here to incite
him to anything.

JANE: How clever of you darling. I'll get ready. 315

PILKINGS: Hey.

JANE: Yes darling.

PILKINGS: I have a surprise for you. I was going to keep it until
we actually got to the ball.

JANE: What is it? 320

PILKINGS: You know the Prince is on a tour of the colonies don't
you? Well, he docked in the capital only this morning but
he is already at the Residency. He is going to grace the ball
with his presence later tonight.

JANE: Simon! Not really. 325

PILKINGS: Yes he is. He's been invited to give away the prizes
and he has agreed. You must admit old Engleton is the best
Club Secretary we ever had. Quick off the mark that lad.

JANE: But how thrilling.

PILKINGS: The other provincials are going to be damned envious. 330

JANE: I wonder what he'll come as.

PILKINGS: Oh I don't know. As a coat-of-arms perhaps. Anyway
it won't be anything to touch this.

JANE: Well that's lucky. If we are to be presented I won't have
to start looking for a pair of gloves. It's all sewn on. 335

PILKINGS: (*Laughing.*) Quite right. Trust a woman to think of
that. Come on, let's get going.

JANE: (*Rushing off.*) Won't be a second. (*Stops.*) Now I see
why you've been so edgy all evening. I thought you weren't

340   handling this affair with your usual brilliance—to begin
      with that is.
      PILKINGS: *(His mood is much improved.)* Shut up woman and get
         your things on.
      JANE: Alright boss, coming.

*(PILKINGS suddenly begins to hum the tango to which they were danc-
ing before. Starts to execute a few practice steps. Lights fade.)*

─────── ACT THREE ───────

*A swelling, agitated hum of women's voices rises immediately in the
background. The lights come on and we see the frontage of a converted
cloth stall in the market. The floor leading up to the entrance is covered in rich velvets and woven cloth. The* WOMEN *come on stage, borne
backwards by the determined progress of Sergeant* AMUSA *and his two
constables who already have their batons out and use them as a pressure against the* WOMEN. *At the edge of the cloth-covered floor however
the* WOMEN *take a determined stand and block all further progress of
the* MEN. *They begin to tease them mercilessly.*

AMUSA: I am tell you women for last time to commot my road.
   I am here on official business.
WOMAN: Official business you white man's eunuch? Official
   business is taking place where you want to go and it's a
5 business you wouldn't understand.
WOMAN: *(Makes a quick tug at the constable's baton.)* That doesn't
   fool anyone you know. It's the one you carry under your
   government knickers that counts. *(She bends low as if to peep
   under the baggy shorts. The embarrassed constable quickly puts his
10 knees together. The* WOMEN *roar.)*
WOMAN: You mean there is nothing there at all?
WOMAN: Oh there was something. You know that handbell
   which the whiteman uses to summon his servants . . . ?
AMUSA: *(He manages to preserve some dignity throughout.)* I hope
15 you women know that interfering with officer in execution
   of his duty is criminal offence.
WOMAN: Interfere? He says we're interfering with him. You
   foolish man we're telling you there's nothing there to interfere with.
20 AMUSA: I am order you now to clear the road.
WOMAN: What road? The one your father built?
WOMAN: You are a Policeman not so? Then you know what
   they call trespassing in court. Or—*(Pointing to the cloth-lined
   steps.)*—do you think that kind of road is built for every
25 kind of feet.
WOMAN: Go back and tell the white man who sent you to come
   himself.
AMUSA: If I go I will come back with reinforcement. And we
   will all return carrying weapons.
30 WOMAN: Oh, now I understand. Before they can put on those
   knickers the white man first cuts off their weapons.
WOMAN: What a cheek! You mean you come here to show
   power to women and you don't even have a weapon.
AMUSA: *(Shouting above the laughter.)* For the last time I warn you
35 women to clear the road.
WOMAN: To where?
AMUSA: To that hut. I know he dey dere.
WOMAN: Who?
AMUSA: The chief who call himself Elesin Oba.

WOMAN: You ignorant man. It is not he who calls himself   40
   Elesin Oba, it is his blood that says it. As it called out to
   his father before him and will to his son after him. And that
   is in spite of everything your white man can do.
WOMAN: Is it not the same ocean that washes this land and the
   white man's land? Tell your white man he can hide our son   45
   away as long as he likes. When the time comes for him, the
   same ocean will bring him back.
AMUSA: The government say dat kin' ting must stop.
WOMAN: Who will stop it? You? Tonight our husband and fa-
   ther will prove himself greater than the laws of strangers.   50
AMUSA: I tell you nobody go prove anyting tonight or anytime.
   Is ignorant and criminal to prove dat kin' prove.
IYALOJA: *(Entering, from the hut. She is accompanied by a group of*
   YOUNG GIRLS *who have been attending the* BRIDE.*)* What is it
   Amusa? Why do you come here to disturb the happiness of   55
   others.
AMUSA: Madame Iyaloja, I glad you come. You know me. I no
   like trouble but duty is duty. I am here to arrest Elesin for
   criminal intent. Tell these women to stop obstructing me in
   the performance of my duty.   60
IYALOJA: And you? What gives you the right to obstruct our
   leader of men in the performance of his duty.
AMUSA: What kin' duty be dat one Iyaloja.
IYALOJA: What kin' duty? What kin' duty does a man have to
   his new bride?   65
AMUSA: *(Bewildered, looks at the* WOMEN *and at the entrance to the
   hut.)* Iyaloja, is it wedding you call dis kin' ting?
IYALOJA: You have wives haven't you? Whatever the white man
   has done to you he hasn't stopped you having wives. And if
   he has, at least he is married. If you don't know what a mar- 70
   riage is, go and ask him to tell you.
AMUSA: This no to wedding.
IYALOJA: And ask him at the same time what he would have
   done if anyone had come to disturb him on his wedding
   night.   75
AMUSA: Iyaloja, I say dis no to wedding.
IYALOJA: You want to look inside the bridal chamber? You want
   to see for yourself how a man cuts the virgin knot?
AMUSA: Madam . . .
WOMAN: Perhaps his wives are still waiting for him to learn.   80
AMUSA: Iyaloja, make you tell dese women make den no insult
   me again. If I hear dat kin' insult once more . . .
GIRL: *(Pushing her way through.)* You will do what?
GIRL: He's out of his mind. It's our mothers you're talking to,
   do you know that? Not to any illiterate villager you can   85
   bully and terrorise. How dare you intrude here anyway?
GIRL: What a cheek, what impertinence!
GIRL: You've treated them too gently. Now let them see what
   it is to tamper with the mothers of this market.
GIRLS: Your betters dare not enter the market when the women 90
   say no!
GIRL: Haven't you learnt that yet, you jester in khaki and
   starch?
IYALOJA: Daughters . . .
GIRL: No no Iyaloja, leave us to deal with him. He no longer   95
   knows his mother, we'll teach him.

*(With a sudden movement they snatch the batons of the two constables.
They begin to hem them in.)*

GIRL: What next? We have your batons? What next? What are you going to do?

(With equally swift movements they knock off their hats.)

100   GIRL: Move if you dare. We have your hats, what will you do about it? Didn't the white man teach you to take off your hats before women?

IYALOJA: It's a wedding night. It's a night of joy for us. Peace . . .

GIRL: Not for him. Who asked him here?

GIRL: Does he dare go to the Residency without an invitation?

105   GIRL: Not even where the servants eat the left-overs.

GIRLS: *(In turn. In an 'English' accent.)* Well well it's Mister Amusa. Were you invited? *(Play-acting to one another. The older* WOMEN *encourage them with their titters.)*
—Your invitation card please?

110   —Who are you? Have we been introduced?
—And who did you say you were?
—Sorry, I didn't quite catch your name.
—May I take your hat?
—If you insist. May I take yours? *(Exchanging the police-*

115   *man's hats.)*
—How very kind of you.
—Not at all. Won't you sit down?
—After you.
—Oh no.

120   —I insist.
—You're most gracious.
—And how do you find the place?
—The natives are alright.
—Friendly?

125   —Tractable.
—Not a teeny-weeny bit restless?
—Well, a teeny-weeny bit restless.
—One might even say, difficult?
—Indeed one might be tempted to say, difficult.

130   —But you do manage to cope?
—Yes indeed I do. I have a rather faithful ox called Amusa.
—He's loyal?
—Absolutely.
—Lay down his life for you what?

135   —Without a moment's thought.
—Had one like that once. Trust him with my life.
—Mostly of course they are liars.
—Never known a native tell the truth.
—Does it get rather close around here?

140   —It's mild for this time of the year.
—But the rains may still come.
—They are late this year aren't they?
—They are keeping African time.
—Ha ha ha ha

145   —Ha ha ha ha
—The humidity is what gets me.
—It used to be whisky.
—Ha ha ha ha
—Ha ha ha ha

150   —What's your handicap old chap?
—Is there racing by golly?
—Splendid golf course, you'll like it.
—I'm beginning to like it already.

—And a European club, exclusive.
—You've kept the flag flying.   155
—We do our best for the old country.
—It's a pleasure to serve.
—Another whisky old chap?
—You are indeed too too kind.
—Not at all sir. Where is that boy? *(With a sudden bellow.)*   160
Sergeant!

AMUSA: *(Snaps to attention.)* Yessir!

(The WOMEN *collapse with laughter.)*

GIRL: Take your men out of here.

AMUSA: *(Realising the trick, he rages from loss of face.)* I'm give you   165
warning . . .

GIRL: Alright then. Off with his knickers! *(They surge slowly forward.)*

IYALOJA: Daughters, please.

AMUSA: *(Squaring himself for defence.)* The first woman wey touch   170
me . . .

IYALOJA: My children, I beg of you . . .

GIRL: Then tell him to leave this market. This is the home of our mothers. We don't want the eater of white left-overs at the feast their hands have prepared.

IYALOJA: You heard them Amusa. You had better go.   175

GIRLS: Now!

AMUSA: *(Commencing his retreat.)* We dey go now, but make you no say we no warn you.

GIRL: Before we read the riot act—you should know all about that.   180

AMUSA: Make we go. *(They depart, more precipitately.)*

(The WOMEN *strike their palms across in the gesture of wonder.)*

WOMEN: Do they teach you all that school?

WOMAN: And to think I nearly kept Apinke away from the place.

WOMAN: Did you hear them? Did you see how they mimicked   185
the white man?

WOMAN: The voices exactly. Hey, there are wonders in this world!

IYALOJA: Well, our elders have said it: Dada may be weak, but he has a younger sibling who is truly fearless.   190

WOMAN: The next time the white man shows his face in this market I will set Wuraola on his tail.

(A WOMAN *bursts into song and dance of euphoria—'Tani l'awa o l'ogbeja? Kayi! A l'ogbeja. Omo Kekere l'ogbeja.' {'Who says we haven't a defender? Silence! We have our defenders. Little children are our champions.'} The rest of the* WOMEN *join in, some placing the* GIRLS *on their back like infants, other dancing round them. The dance becomes general, mounting in excitement.* ELESIN *appears, in wrapper only. In his hands a white velvet cloth folded loosely as if it held some delicate object. He cries out.)*

ELESIN: Oh you mothers of beautiful brides! *(The dancing stops. They turn and see him, and the object in his hands.* IYALOJA *approaches and gently takes the cloth from him.)* Take it. It is no   195
mere virgin stain, but the union of life and the seeds of passage. My vital flow, the last from this flesh is intermingled with the promise of future life. All is prepared. Listen! *(A*

steady drum-beat from the distance.) Yes. It is nearly time. The
200 King's dog has been killed. The King's favourite horse is
about to follow his master. My brother chiefs know their
task and perform it well. (*He listens again.*)

(*The* BRIDE *emerges, stands shyly by the door. He turns to her.*)

Our marriage is not yet wholly fulfilled. When earth and
passage wed, the consummation is complete only when
205 there are grains of earth on the eyelids of passage. Stay by
me till then. My faithful drummers, do me your last service.
This is where I have chosen to do my leave-taking, in this
heart of life, this hive which contains the swarm of the
world in its small compass. This is where I have known love
210 and laughter away from the palace. Even the richest food
cloys when eaten days on end; in the market, nothing ever
cloys. Listen. (*They listen to the drums.*) They have begun to
seek out the heart of the King's favourite horse. Soon it will
ride in its bolt of raffia with the dog at its feet. Together
215 they will ride on the shoulders of the King's grooms
through the pulse centres of the town. They know it is here
I shall await them. I have told them. (*His eyes appear to cloud.
He passes his hand over them as if to clear his sight. He gives a
faint smile.*) It promises well; just then I felt my spirit's ea-
220 gerness. The kite makes for wide spaces and the wind creeps
up behind its tail; can the kite say less than—thank you,
the quicker the better? But wait a while my spirit. Wait.
Wait for the coming of the courier of the King. Do you
know friends, the horse is born to this one destiny, to bear
225 the burden that is man upon its back. Except for this night,
this night alone when the spotless stallion will ride in triumph on the back of man. In the time of my father I witnessed the strange sight. Perhaps tonight also I shall see it
for the last time. If they arrive before the drums beat for me,
230 I shall tell him to let the Alafin know I follow swiftly. If
they come after the drums have sounded, why then, all is
well for I have gone ahead. Our spirits shall fall in step
along the great passage. (*He listens to the drums. He seems
again to be falling into a state of semi-hypnosis; his eyes scan the
235 sky but it is in a kind of daze. His voice is a little breathless.*) The
moon has fed, a glow from its full stomach fills the sky and
air, but I cannot tell where is that gateway through which
I must pass. My faithful friends, let our feet touch together
this last time, lead me into the other market with sounds
240 that cover my skin with down yet make my limbs strike
earth like a thoroughbred. Dear mothers, let me dance into
the passage even as I have lived beneath your roofs. (*He comes
down progressively among them. They make a way for him, the*
DRUMMERS *playing. His dance is one of solemn, regal motions,
245 each gesture of the body is made with a solemn finality. The*
WOMEN *join him, their steps a somewhat more fluid version of his.
Beneath the* PRAISE-SINGER's *exhortations the* WOMEN *dirge 'Alẹ
lẹ lẹ', awo mi lọ'.*)
PRAISE-SINGER: Elesin Alafin, can you hear my voice?
250 ELESIN: Faintly, my friend, faintly.
PRAISE-SINGER: Elesin Alafin, can you hear my call?
ELESIN: Faintly my king, faintly.
PRAISE-SINGER: Is your memory sound Elesin?
Shall my voice be a blade of grass and
255 Tickle the armpit of the past?

ELESIN: My memory needs no prodding but
What do you wish to say to me?
PRAISE-SINGER: Only what has been spoken. Only what concerns
The dying wish of the father of all.
ELESIN: It is buried like seed-yam in my mind   260
This is the season of quick rains, the harvest
Is this moment due for gathering.
PRAISE-SINGER: If you cannot come, I said, swear
You'll tell my favourite horse. I shall
Ride on through the gates alone.   265
ELESIN: Elesin's message will be read
Only when his loyal heart no longer beats.
PRAISE-SINGER: If you cannot come Elesin, tell my dog.
I cannot stay the keeper too long
At the gate.   270
ELESIN: A dog does not outrun the hand
That feeds it meat. A horse that throws its rider
Slows down to a stop. Elesin Alafin
Trusts no beasts with messages between
A king and his companion.   275
PRAISE-SINGER: If you get lost my dog will track
The hidden path to me.
ELESIN: The seven-way crossroads confuses
Only the stranger. The Horseman of the King
Was born in the recesses of the house.   280
PRAISE-SINGER: I know the wickedness of men. If there is
Weight on the loose end of your sash, such weight
As no mere man can shift; if your sash is earthed
By evil minds who mean to part us at the last . . .
ELESIN: My sash is of the deep purple *alari*;   285
It is no tethering-rope. The elephant
Trails no tethering-rope; that king
Is not yet crowned who will peg an elephant—
Not even you my friend and King.
PRAISE-SINGER: And yet this fear will not depart from me   290
The darkness of this new abode is deep—
Will your human eyes suffice?
ELESIN: In a night which falls before our eyes
However deep, we do not miss our way.
PRAISE-SINGER: Shall I now not acknowledge I have stood   295
Where wonders met their end? The elephant deserves
Better than that we say 'I have caught
A glimpse of something.' If we see the tamer
Of the forest let us say plainly, we have seen
An elephant.   300
ELESIN: (*His voice is drowsy.*) I have freed myself of earth and now
It's getting dark. Strange voices guide my feet.
PRAISE-SINGER: The river is never so high that the eyes
Of a fish are covered. The night is not so dark
That the albino fails to find his way. A child   305
Returning homewards craves no leading by the hand.
Gracefully does the mask regain his grove at the end of
the day . . .
Gracefully. Gracefully does the mask dance
Homeward at the end of day, gracefully . . .

(ELESIN's *trance appears to be deepening, his steps heavier.*)

IYALOJA: It is the death of war that kills the valiant,   310
Death of water is how the swimmer goes

It is the death of markets that kills the trader
And death of indecision takes the idle away
The trade of the cutlass blunts its edge
315 And the beautiful die the death of beauty.
It takes an Elesin to die the death of death . . .
Only Elesin . . . dies the unknowable death of death . . .
Gracefully, gracefully does the horseman regain
The stables at the end of day, gracefully . . .

320 PRAISE-SINGER: How shall I tell what my eyes have seen? The
Horseman gallops on before the courier, how shall I tell
what my eyes have seen? He says a dog may be confused by
new scents of beings he never dreamt of, so he must precede
the dog to heaven. He says a horse may stumble on strange
325 boulders and be lamed, so he races on before the horse to
heaven. It is best, he says, to trust no messenger who may
falter at the outer gate; oh how shall I tell what my ears
have heard? But do you hear me still Elesin, do you hear
your faithful one?

(ELESIN *in his motions appears to feel for a direction of sound, subtly,
but he only sinks deeper into his trance-dance.*)

330 Elesin Alafin, I no longer sense your flesh. The drums are
changing now but you have gone far ahead of the world. It
is not yet noon in heaven; let those who claim it is begin
their own journey home. So why must you rush like an impatient bride: why do you race to desert your Olohun-iyo?

(ELESIN *is now sunk fully deep in his trance, there is no longer sign of
any awareness of his surroundings.*)

335 Does the deep voice of *gbedu* cover you then, like the passage of royal elephants? Those drums that brook no rivals,
have they blocked the passage to your ears that my voice
passes into wind, a mere leaf floating in the night? Is your
flesh lightened Elesin, is that lump of earth I slid between
340 your slippers to keep you longer slowly sifting from your
feet? Are the drums on the other side now tuning skin to
skin with ours in *osugbo?* Are there sounds there I cannot
hear, do footsteps surround you which pound the earth like
gbedu, roll like thunder round the dome of the world? Is the
345 darkness gathering in your head Elesin? Is there now a
streak of light at the end of the passage, a light I dare not
look upon? Does it reveal whose voices we often heard,
whose touches we often felt, whose wisdoms come suddenly
into the mind when the wisest have shaken their heads and
350 murmured: It cannot be done? Elesin Alafin, don't think I
do not know why your lips are heavy, why your limbs are
drowsy as palm oil in the cold of harmattan. I would call
you back but when the elephant heads for the jungle, the
tail is too small a handhold for the hunter that would pull
355 him back. The sun that heads for the sea no longer heeds
the prayers of the farmer. When the river begins to taste the
salt of the ocean, we no longer know what deity to call on,
the river-god or Olokun. No arrow flies back to the string,
the child does not return through the same passage that
360 gave it birth. Elesin Oba, can you hear me at all? Your eyelids are glazed like a courtesan's, is it that you see the dark
groom and master of life? And will you see my father? Will
you tell him that I stayed with you tothe last? Will my
voice ring in your ears awhile, will you remember Olohun-

iyo even if the music on the other side surpasses his mortal 365
craft? But will they know you over there? Have they eyes to
gauge your worth, have they the heart to love you, will they
know what thoroughbred prances towards them in ca-
parisons of honour? If they do not Elesin, if any there cuts
your yam with a small knife, or pours you wine in a small 370
calabash, turn back and return to welcoming hands. If the
world were not greater than the wishes of Olohun-iyo, I
would not let you go . . .

(*He appears to break down.* ELESIN *dances on, completely in a trance.
The dirge wells up louder and stronger.* ELESIN's *dance does not lose its
elasticity but his gestures become, if possible, even more weighty. Lights
fade slowly on the scene.*)

——— ACT FOUR ———

*A Masque. The front side of the stage is part of a wide corridor around
the great hall of the Residency extending beyond vision into the rear
and wings. It is redolent of the tawdry decadence of a far-flung but key
imperial frontier. The couples in a variety of fancy-dress are ranged
around the walls, gazing in the same direction. The guest-of-honour is
about to make an appearance. A portion of the local police brass band
with its white conductor is just visible. At last, the entrance of Royalty. The band plays 'Rule Britannia', badly, beginning long before
he is visible. The couples bow and curtsey as he passes by them. Both
he and his companions are dressed in seventeenth century European costume. Following behind are the* RESIDENT *and his partner similarly
attired. As they gain the end of the hall where the orchestra dais begins the music comes to an end. The* PRINCE *bows to the guests. The
band strikes up a Viennese waltz and the* PRINCE *formally opens the
floor. Several bars later the* RESIDENT *and his companion follow suit.
Others follow in appropriate pecking order. The orchestra's waltz rendition is not of the highest musical standard.*

Some time later the PRINCE *dances again into view and is settled into
a corner by the* RESIDENT *who then proceeds to select couples as they
dance past for introduction, sometimes threading his way through the
dancers to tap the lucky couple on the shoulder. Desperate efforts from
many to ensure that they are recognised in spite of, perhaps, their costume. The ritual of introductions soon takes in* PILKINGS *and his wife.
The* PRINCE *is quite fascinated by their costume and they demonstrate
the adaptations they have made to it, pulling down the mask to demonstrate how the egungun normally appears, then showing the various
press-button controls they have innovated for the face flaps, the sleeves,
etc. They demonstrate the dance steps and the guttural sounds made by
the egungun, harass other dancers in the hall,* MRS PILKINGS *playing the 'restrainer' to* PILKINGS' *manic darts. Everyone is highly en-
tertained, the Royal Party especially who lead the applause.*

*At this point a liveried footman comes in with a note on a salver and
is intercepted almost absent-mindedly by the* RESIDENT *who takes the
note and reads it. After polite coughs he succeeds in excusing the* PILK-
INGSES *from the* PRINCE *and takes them aside. The* PRINCE *consider-
ately offers the* RESIDENT's *wife his hand and dancing is resumed.*

On their way out the RESIDENT *gives an order to his* AIDE-DE-CAMP.
They come into the side corridor where the RESIDENT *hands the note to*
PILKINGS.

RESIDENT: As you see it says 'emergency' on the outside. I took
the liberty of opening it because His Highness was obviously

enjoying the entertainment. I didn't want to interrupt unless
really necessary.

5 PILKINGS: Yes, yes of course sir.

RESIDENT: Is it really as bad as it says? What's it all about?

PILKINGS: Some strange custom they have sir. It seems because the
King is dead some important chief has to commit suicide.

RESIDENT: The King? Isn't it the same one who died nearly a
10   month ago?

PILKINGS: Yes sir.

RESIDENT: Haven't they buried him yet?

PILKINGS: They take their time about these things sir. The pre-
burial ceremonies last nearly thirty days. It seems tonight is
15   the final night.

RESIDENT: But what has it got to do with the market women?
Why are they rioting? We've waived that troublesome tax
haven't we?

PILKINGS: We don't quite know that they are exactly rioting yet
20   sir. Sergeant Amusa is sometimes prone to exaggerations.

RESIDENT: He sounds desperate enough. That comes out even in
his rather quaint grammar. Where is the man anyway? I
asked my aide-de-camp to bring him here.

PILKINGS: They are probably looking in the wrong verandah.
25   I'll fetch him myself.

RESIDENT: No no you stay here. Let your wife go and look for
them. Do you mind my dear . . . ?

JANE: Certainly not, your Excellency. (Goes.)

RESIDENT: You should have kept me informed Pilkings. You re-
30   alise how disastrous it would have been if things had
erupted while His Highness was here.

PILKINGS: I wasn't aware of the whole business until tonight sir.

RESIDENT: Nose to the ground Pilkings, nose to the ground. If
we all let these little things slip past us where would the
35   empire be eh? Tell me that. Where would we all be?

PILKINGS: (Low voice.) Sleeping peacefully at home I bet.

RESIDENT: What did you say Pilkings?

PILKINGS: It won't happen again sir.

RESIDENT: It mustn't Pilkings. It mustn't. Where is that
40   damned sergeant? I ought to get back to His Highness as
quickly as possible and offer him some plausible explanation for my rather abrupt conduct. Can you think of one
Pilkings?

PILKINGS: You could tell him the truth sir.

45 RESIDENT: I could? No no no no no Pilkings, that would never do.
What! Go and tell him there is a riot just two miles away
from him? This is supposed to be a secure colony of His
Majesty, Pilkings.

PILKINGS: Yes sir.

50 RESIDENT: Ah, there they are. No, these are not our native police. Are these the ring-leaders of the riot?

PILKINGS: Sir, these are my police officers.

RESIDENT: Oh, I beg your pardon officers. You do look a
little . . . I say, isn't there something missing in their uni-
55   forms? I think they used to have some rather colourful
sashes. If I remember rightly I recommended them myself
in my young days in the service. A bit of colour always appeals to the natives, yes. I remember putting that in my report. Well well well, where are we? Make your report man.

60 PILKINGS: (Moves close to AMUSA, between his teeth.) And let's have
no more superstitious nonsense from you Amusa or I'll
throw you in the guardroom for a month and feed you pork!

RESIDENT: What's that? What has pork to do with it?

PILKINGS: Sir, I was just warning him to be brief. I'm sure you
are most anxious to hear his report.   65

RESIDENT: Yes yes yes of course. Come on man, speak up. Hey,
didn't we give them some colourful fez hats with all those
wavy things, yes, pink tassells . . .

PILKINGS: Sir, I think if he was permitted to make his report we
might find that he lost his hat in the riot.   70

RESIDENT: Ah yes indeed. I'd better tell His Highness that. Lost
his hat in the riot, ha ha. He'll probably say well, as long as
he didn't lost his head. (Chuckles to himself.) Don't forget to
send me a report first thing in the morning young Pilkings.

PILKINGS: No sir.   75

RESIDENT: And whatever you do, don't let things get out of
hand. Keep a cool head and—nose to the ground Pilkings.
(Wanders off in the general direction of the hall.)

PILKINGS: Yes sir.

AIDE-DE-CAMP: Would you be needing me sir?   80

PILKINGS: No thanks Bob. I think His Excellency's need of you
is greater than ours.

AIDE-DE-CAMP: We have a detachment of soldiers from the capital sir. They accompanied His Highness up here.

PILKINGS: I doubt if it will come to that but, thanks, I'll bear   85
it in mind. Oh, could you send an orderly with my cloak.

AIDE-DE-CAMP: Very good sir. (Goes.)

PILKINGS: Now Sergeant.

AMUSA: Sir . . . (Makes an effort, stops dead. Eyes to the ceiling.)

PILKINGS: Oh, not again.   90

AMUSA: I cannot against death to dead cult. This dress get
power of dead.

PILKINGS: Alright, let's go. You are relieved of all further duty
Amusa. Report to me first thing in the morning.

JANE: Shall I come Simon?   95

PILKINGS: No, there's no need for that. If I can get back later I
will. Otherwise get Bob to bring you home.

JANE: Be careful Simon . . . I mean, be clever.

PILKINGS: Sure I will. You two, come with me. (As he turns to
go, the clock in the Residency begins to chime. PILKINGS looks at his   100
watch then turns, horror-stricken, to stare at his wife. The same
thought clearly occurs to her. He swallows hard. An ORDERLY
brings his cloak.) It's midnight. I had no idea it was that late.

JANE: But surely . . . they don't count the hours the way we do.
The moon, or something.   105

PILKINGS: I am . . . not so sure.

(He turns and breaks into a sudden run. The two constables follow,
also at a run. AMUSA, who has kept his eyes on the ceiling throughout
waits until the last of the footsteps has faded out of hearing. He salutes
suddenly, but without once looking in the direction of the woman.)

AMUSA: Goodnight madam.

JANE: Oh. (She hesitates.) Amusa . . . (He goes off without seeming
to have heard.) Poor Simon . . . (A figure emerges from the shadows, a young black man dressed in a sober western suit. He peeps   110
into the hall, trying to make out the figures of the dancers.) Who
is that?

OLUNDE: (Emerging into the light.) I didn't mean to startle you
madam. I am looking for the District Officer.

JANE: Wait a minute . . . don't I know you? Yes, you are   115
Olunde, the young man who . . .

OLUNDE: Mrs Pilkings! How fortunate. I came here to look for your husband.

JANE: Olunde! Let's look at you. What a fine young man you've become. Grand but solemn. Good God, when did you return? Simon never said a word. But you do look well Olunde. Really!

OLUNDE: You are . . . well, you look quite well yourself Mrs Pilkings. From what little I can see of you.

JANE: Oh, this. It's caused quite a stir I assure you, and not all of it very pleasant. You are not shocked I hope?

OLUNDE: Why should I be? But don't you find it rather hot in there? Your skin must find it difficult to breathe.

JANE: Well, it is a little hot I must confess, but it's all in a good cause.

OLUNDE: What cause Mrs Pilkings?

JANE: All this. The ball. And His Highness being here in person and all that.

OLUNDE: (Mildly.) And that is the good cause for which you desecrate an ancestral mask?

JANE: Oh, so you are shocked after all. How disappointing.

OLUNDE: No I am not shocked Mrs Pilkings. You forget that I have now spent four years among your people. I discovered that you have no respect for what you do not understand.

JANE: Oh. So you've returned with a chip on your shoulder. That's a pity Olunde. I am sorry.

(An uncomfortable silence follows.)

I take it then that you did not find your stay in England altogether edifying.

OLUNDE: I don't say that. I found your people quite admirable in many ways, their conduct and courage in this war for instance.

JANE: Ah yes the war. Here of course it is all rather remote. From time to time we have a black-out drill just to remind us that there is a war on. And the rare convoy passes through on its way somewhere or on manoeuvres. Mind you there is the occasional bit of excitement like that ship that was blown up in the harbour.

OLUNDE: Here? Do you mean through enemy action?

JANE: Oh no, the war hasn't come that close. The captain did it himself. I don't quite understand it really. Simon tried to explain. The ship had to be blown up because it had become dangerous to the other ships, even to the city itself. Hundreds of the coastal population would have died.

OLUNDE: Maybe it was loaded with ammunition and had caught fire. Or some of those lethal gases they've been experimenting on.

JANE: Something like that. The captain blew himself up with it. Deliberately. Simon said someone had to remain on board to light the fuse.

OLUNDE: It must have been a very short fuse.

JANE: (Shrugs.) I don't know much about it. Only that there was no other way to save lives. No time to devise anything else. The captain took the decision and carried it out.

OLUNDE: Yes . . . I quite believe it. I met men like that in England.

JANE: Oh just look at me! Fancy welcoming you back with such morbid news. Stale too. It was at least six months ago.

OLUNDE: I don't find it morbid at all. I find it rather inspiring. It is an affirmative commentary on life.

JANE: What is?

OLUNDE: That captain's self-sacrifice.

JANE: Nonsense. Life should never be thrown deliberately away.

OLUNDE: And the innocent people round the harbour?

JANE: Oh, how does one know? The whole thing was probably exaggerated anyway.

OLUNDE: That was a risk the captain couldn't take. But please Mrs Pilkings, do you think you could find your husband for me? I have to talk to him.

JANE: Simon? Oh. (As she recollects for the first time the full significance of OLUNDE's presence.) Simon is . . . there is a little problem in town. He was sent for. But . . . when did you arrive? Does Simon know you're here?

OLUNDE: (Suddenly earnest.) I need your help Mrs Pilkings. I've always found you somewhat more understanding than your husband. Please find him for me and when you do, you must help me talk to him.

JANE: I'm afraid I don't quite . . . follow you. Have you seen my husband already?

OLUNDE: I went to your house. Your houseboy told me you were here. (He smiles.) He even told me how I would recognise you and Mr Pilkings.

JANE: Then you must know what my husband is trying to do for you.

OLUNDE: For me?

JANE: For you. For your people. And to think he didn't even know you were coming back! But how do you happen to be here? Only this evening we were talking about you. We thought you were still four thousand miles away.

OLUNDE: I was sent a cable.

JANE: A cable? Who did? Simon? The business of your father didn't begin till tonight.

OLUNDE: A relation sent it weeks ago, and it said nothing about my father. All it said was, Our King is dead. But I knew I had to return home at once so as to bury my father. I understood that.

JANE: Well, thank God you don't have to go through that agony. Simon is going to stop it.

OLUNDE: That's why I want to see him. He's wasting his time. And since he has been so helpful to me I don't want him to incur the enmity of our people. Especially over nothing.

JANE: (Sits down open-mouthed.) You . . . you Olunde!

OLUNDE: Mrs Pilkings, I came home to bury my father. As soon as I heard the news I booked my passage home. In fact we were fortunate. We travelled in the same convoy as your Prince, so we had excellent protection.

JANE: But you don't think your father is also entitled to whatever protection is available to him?

OLUNDE: How can I make you understand? He has protection. No one can undertake what he does tonight without the deepest protection the mind can conceive. What can you offer him in place of his peace of mind, in place of the honour and veneration of his own people? What would you think of your Prince if he had refused to accept the risk of losing his life on this voyage? This . . . showing-the-flag tour of colonial possessions.

JANE: I see. So it isn't just medicine you studied in England.

OLUNDE: Yet another error into which your people fall. You believe that everything which appears to make sense was learnt from you.

235 JANE: Not so fast Olunde. You have learnt to argue I can tell
       that, but I never said you made sense. However cleverly you
       try to put it, it is still a barbaric custom. It is even worse—
       it's feudal! The king dies and a chieftain must be buried
       with him. How feudalistic can you get!

240 OLUNDE: (*Waves his hand towards the background. The* PRINCE *is
       dancing past again—to a different step—and all the guests are
       bowing and curtseying as he passes.*) And this? Even in the
       midst of a devastating war, look at that. What name would
       you give to that?

245 JANE: Therapy, British style. The preservation of sanity in the
       midst of chaos.

     OLUNDE: Others would call it decadence. However, it doesn't
       really interest me. You white races know how to survive;
       I've seen proof of that. By all logical and natural laws this
250   war should end with all the white races wiping out one an-
       other, wiping out their so-called civilisation for all time and
       reverting to a state of primitivism the like of which has so
       far only existed in your imagination when you thought of
       us. I thought all that at the beginning. Then I slowly re-
255   alised that your greatest art is the art of survival. But at
       least have the humility to let others survive in their own
       way.

     JANE: Through ritual suicide?

     OLUNDE: Is that worse than mass suicide? Mrs Pilkings, what
260   do you call what those young men are sent to do by their
       generals in this war? Of course you have also mastered the
       art of calling things by names which don't remotely de-
       scribe them.

     JANE: You talk! You people with your long-winded, round-
265   about way of making conversation.

     OLUNDE: Mrs Pilkings, whatever we do, we never suggest that
       a thing is the opposite of what it really is. In your newsreels
       I heard defeats, thorough, murderous defeats described as
       strategic victories. No wait, it wasn't just on your news-
270   reels. Don't forget I was attached to hospitals all the time.
       Hordes of your wounded passed through those wards. I
       spoke to them. I spent long evenings by their bedside while
       they spoke terrible truths of the realities of that war. I know
       now how history is made.

275 JANE: But surely, in a war of this nature, for the morale of the
       nation you must expect . . .

     OLUNDE: That a disaster beyond human reckoning be spoken of
       as a triumph? No. I mean, is there no mourning in the
       home of the bereaved that such blasphemy is permitted?

280 JANE: (*After a moment's pause.*) Perhaps I can understand you
       now. The time we picked for you was not really one for see-
       ing us at our best.

     OLUNDE: Don't think it was just the war. Before that even
       started I had plenty of time to study your people. I saw
285   nothing, finally, that gave you the right to pass judgement
       on other peoples and their ways. Nothing at all.

     JANE: (*Hesitantly.*) Was it the . . . colour thing? I know there is
       some discrimination.

     OLUNDE: Don't make it so simple, Mrs Pilkings. You make it
290   sound as if when I left, I took nothing at all with me.

     JANE: Yes . . . and to tell the truth, only this evening, Simon
       and I agreed that we never really knew what you left with.

     OLUNDE: Neither did I. But I found out over there. I am grate-
       ful to your country for that. And I will never give it up.

295 JANE: Olunde, please . . . promise me something. Whatever
       you do, don't throw away what you have started to do. You
       want to be a doctor. My husband and I believe you will
       make an excellent one, sympathetic and competent. Don't
       let anything make you throw away your training.

300 OLUNDE: (*Genuinely surprised.*) Of course not. What a strange
       idea. I intend to return and complete my training. Once the
       burial of my father is over.

     JANE: Oh, please . . . !

     OLUNDE: Listen! Come outside. You can't hear anything against
       that music.   305

     JANE: What is it?

     OLUNDE: The drums. Can you hear the change? Listen.

(*The drums come over, still distant but more distinct. There is a change
of rhythm, it rises to a crescendo and then, suddenly, it is cut off. After a silence, a new beat begins, slow and resonant.*)

       There. It's all over.

     JANE: You mean he's . . .

     OLUNDE: Yes Mrs Pilkings, my father is dead. His will-power   310
       has always been enormous; I know he is dead.

     JANE: (*Screams.*) How can you be so callous! So unfeeling! You
       announce your father's own death like a surgeon looking
       down on some strange . . . stranger's body! You're just a sav-
       age like all the rest.   315

     AIDE-DE-CAMP: (*Rushing out.*) Mrs Pilkings. Mrs Pilkings. (*She
       breaks down, sobbing.*) Are you alright, Mrs Pilkings?

     OLUNDE: She'll be alright. (*Turns to go.*)

     AIDE-DE-CAMP: Who are you? And who the hell asked your
       opinion?   320

     OLUNDE: You're quite right, nobody. (*Going.*)

     AIDE-DE-CAMP: What the hell! Did you hear me ask you who
       you were?

     OLUNDE: I have business to attend to.

     AIDE-DE-CAMP: I'll give you business in a moment you impu-   325
       dent nigger. Answer my question!

     OLUNDE: I have a funeral to arrange. Excuse me. (*Going.*)

     AIDE-DE-CAMP: I said stop! Orderly!

     JANE: No no, don't do that. I'm alright. And for heaven's sake
       don't act so foolishly. He's a family friend.   330

     AIDE-DE-CAMP: Well he'd better learn to answer civil questions
       when he's asked them. These natives put a suit on and they
       get high opinions of themselves.

     OLUNDE: Can I go now?

     JANE: No no don't go. I must talk to you. I'm sorry about what 335
       I said.

     OLUNDE: It's nothing Mrs Pilkings. And I'm really anxious to
       go. I couldn't see my father before, it's forbidden for me, his
       heir and successor to set eyes on him from the moment of
       the king's death. But now . . . I would like to touch his   340
       body while it is still warm.

     JANE: You will. I promise I shan't keep you long. Only, I
       couldn't possibly let you go like that. Bob, please excuse us.

     AIDE-DE-CAMP: If you're sure . . .

     JANE: Of course I'm sure. Something happened to upset me just   345
       then, but I'm alright now. Really.

(*The* AIDE-DE-CAMP *goes, somewhat reluctantly.*)

     OLUNDE: I mustn't stay long.

JANE: Please, I promise not to keep you. It's just that . . . oh you saw yourself what happens to one in this place. The
350 Resident's man thought he was being helpful, that's the way we all react. But I can't go in among that crowd just now and if I stay by myself somebody will come looking for me. Please, just say something for a few moments and then you can go. Just so I can recover myself.

355 OLUNDE: What do you want me to say?

JANE: Your calm acceptance for instance, can you explain that? It was so unnatural. I don't understand that at all. I feel a need to understand all I can.

OLUNDE: But you explained it yourself. My medical training
360 perhaps. I have seen death too often. And the soldiers who returned from the front, they died on our hands all the time.

JANE: No. It has to be more than that. I feel it has to do with the many things we don't really grasp about your people.
365 At least you can explain.

OLUNDE: All these things are part of it. And anyway, my father has been dead in my mind for nearly a month. Ever since I learnt of the King's death. I've lived with my bereavement so long now that I cannot think of him alive. On that jour-
370 ney on the boat, I kept my mind on my duties as the one who must perform the rites over his body. I went through it all again and again in my mind as he himself had taught me. I didn't want to do anything wrong, something which might jeopardise the welfare of my people.

375 JANE: But he had disowned you. When you left he swore pub-licly you were no longer his son.

OLUNDE: I told you, he was a man of tremendous will. Some-times that's another way of saying stubborn. But among our people, you don't disown a child just like that. Even if I had
380 died before him I would still be buried like his eldest son. But it's time for me to go.

JANE: Thank you. I feel calmer. Don't let me keep you from your duties.

OLUNDE: Goodnight Mrs Pilkings.

385 JANE: Welcome home. (*She holds out her hand. As he takes it foot-steps are heard approaching the drive. A short while later a woman's sobbing is also heard.*)

PILKINGS: (*Off.*) Keep her there till I get back. (*He strides into view, reacts at the sight of* OLUNDE *but turns to his wife.*)
390 Thank goodness you're still here.

JANE: Simon, what happened?

PILKINGS: Later Jane, please. Is Bob still here?

JANE: Yes, I think so. I'm sure he must be.

PILKINGS: Try and get him out here as quietly as you can. Tell
395 him it's urgent.

JANE: Of course. Oh Simon, you remember . . .

PILKINGS: Yes yes. I can see who it is. Get Bob out here. (*She runs off.*) At first I thought I was seeing a ghost.

OLUNDE: Mr Pilkings, I appreciate what you tried to do. I want
400 you to believe that. I can only tell you it would have been a terrible calamity if you'd succeeded.

PILKINGS: (*Opens his mouth several times, shuts it.*) You . . . said what?

OLUNDE: A calamity for us, the entire people.

405 PILKINGS: (*Sighs.*) I see. Hm.

OLUNDE: And now I must go. I must see him before he turns cold.

PILKINGS: Oh ah . . . em . . . but this is a shock to see you. I mean er thinking all this while you were in England and thanking God for that.
410

OLUNDE: I came on the mail boat. We travelled in the Prince's convoy.

PILKINGS: Ah yes, a-ah, hm . . . er well . . .

OLUNDE: Goodnight. I can see you are shocked by the whole business. But you must know by now there are things you 415 cannot understand—or help.

PILKINGS: Yes. Just a minute. There are armed policemen that way and they have instructions to let no one pass. I suggest you wait a little. I'll er . . . yes, I'll give you an escort.

OLUNDE: That's very kind of you. But do you think it could be 420 quickly arranged.

PILKINGS: Of course. In fact, yes, what I'll do is send Bob over with some men to the er . . . place. You can go with them. Here he comes now. Excuse me a minute.

AIDE-DE-CAMP: Anything wrong sir? 425

PILKINGS: (*Takes him to one side.*) Listen Bob, that cellar in the disused annexe of the Residency, you know, where the slaves were stored before being taken down to the coast . . .

AIDE-DE-CAMP: Oh yes, we use it as a storeroom for broken furniture. 430

PILKINGS: But it's still got the bars on it?

AIDE-DE-CAMP: Oh yes, they are quite intact.

PILKINGS: Get the keys please. I'll explain later. And I want a strong guard over the Residency tonight.

AIDE-DE-CAMP: We have that already. The detachment from the 435 coast . . .

PILKINGS: No, I don't want them at the gates of the Residency. I want you to deploy them at the bottom of the hill, a long way from the main hall so they can deal with any situation long before the sound carries to the house. 440

AIDE-DE-CAMP: Yes of course.

PILKINGS: I don't want His Highness alarmed.

AIDE-DE-CAMP: You think the riot will spread here?

PILKINGS: It's unlikely but I don't want to take a chance. I made them believe I was going to lock the man up in my house, 445 which was what I had planned to do in the first place. They are probably assailing it by now. I took a roundabout route here so I don't think there is any danger at all. At least not before dawn. Nobody is to leave the premises of course—the native employees I mean. They'll soon smell something 450 is up and they can't keep their mouths shut.

AIDE-DE-CAMP: I'll give instructions at once.

PILKINGS: I'll take the prisoner down myself. Two policemen will stay with him throughout the night. Inside the cell.

AIDE-DE-CAMP: Right sir. (*Salutes and goes off at the double.*) 455

PILKINGS: Jane. Bob is coming back in a moment with a de-tachment. Until he gets back please stay with Olunde.

(*He makes an extra warning gesture with his eyes.*)

OLUNDE: Please Mr Pilkings . . .

PILKINGS: I hate to be stuffy old son, but we have a crisis on our hands. It has to do with your father's affair if you must 460 know. And it happens also at a time when we have His Highness here. I am responsible for security so you'll sim-ply have to do as I say. I hope that's understood. (*Marches off quickly, in the direction from which he made his first appearance.*)

465 OLUNDE: What's going on? All this can't be just because he
        failed to stop my father killing himself.
    JANE: I honestly don't know. Could it have sparked off a riot?
    OLUNDE: No. If he'd succeeded that would be more likely to
        start the riot. Perhaps there were other factors involved.
470   Was there a chieftancy dispute?
    JANE: None that I know of.
    ELESIN: (An animal bellow from off.) Leave me alone! Is it not
        enough that you have covered me in shame! White man,
        take your hand from my body!

    (OLUNDE stands frozen on the spot. JANE understanding at last, tries
    to move him.)

475 JANE: Let's go in. It's getting chilly out here.
    PILKINGS: (Off.) Carry him.
    ELESIN: Give me back the name you have taken away from me
        you ghost from the land of the nameless!
    PILKINGS: Carry him! I can't have a disturbance here. Quickly!
480   stuff up his mouth.
    JANE: Oh God! Let's go in. Please Olunde. (OLUNDE does not move.)
    ELESIN: Take your albino's hand from me you . . .

    (Sounds of a struggle. His voice chokes as he is gagged.)

    OLUNDE: (Quietly.) That was my father's voice.
    JANE: Oh you poor orphan, what have you come home to?

    (There is a sudden explosion of rage from off-stage and powerful steps
    come running up the drive.)

485 PILKINGS: You bloody fools, after him!

    (Immediately ELESIN, in handcuffs, comes pounding in the direction of
    JANE and OLUNDE, followed some moments afterwards by PILKINGS
    and the constables. ELESIN confronted by the seeming statue of his son,
    stops dead. OLUNDE stares above his head into the distance. The con-
    stables try to grab him. JANE screams at them.)

    JANE: Leave him alone! Simon, tell them to leave him alone.
    PILKINGS: All right, stand aside you. (Shrugs.) Maybe just as
        well. It might help to calm him down.

    (For several moments they hold the same position. ELESIN moves a few
    steps forward, almost as if he's still in doubt.)

    ELESIN: Olunde? (He moves his head, inspecting him from side to
490   side.) Olunde! (He collapses slowly at OLUNDE's feet.) Oh son,
        don't let the sight of your father turn you blind!
    OLUNDE: (He moves for the first time since he heard his voice, brings
        his head slowly down to look on him.) I have no father, eater of
        left-overs.

    (He walks slowly down the way his father had run. Light fades out
    on ELESIN, sobbing into the ground.)

    ———— ACT FIVE ————

    A wide iron-barred gate stretches almost the whole width of the cell in
    which ELESIN is imprisoned. His wrists are encased in thick iron
    bracelets, chained together; he stands against the bars, looking out.
    Seated on the ground to one side on the outside is his recent BRIDE, her

eyes bent perpetually to the ground. Figures of the two guards can be
seen deeper inside the cell, alert to every movement ELESIN makes. PILK-
INGS now in a police officer's uniform enters noiselessly, observes him for
a while. Then he coughs ostentatiously and approaches. Leans against
the bars near a corner, his back to ELESIN. He is obviously trying to
fall in mood with him. Some moments' silence.

PILKINGS: You seem fascinated by the moon.
ELESIN: (After a pause.) Yes, ghostly one. Your twin-brother up
    there engages my thoughts.
PILKINGS: It is a beautiful night.
ELESIN: Is that so?   5
PILKINGS: The light on the leaves, the peace of the night . . .
ELESIN: The night is not at peace, District Officer.
PILKINGS: No? I would have said it was. You know, quiet . . .
ELESIN: And does quiet mean peace for you?
PILKINGS: Well, nearly the same thing. Naturally there is a   10
    subtle difference . . .
ELESIN: The night is not at peace ghostly one. The world is not
    at peace. You have shattered the peace of the world for ever.
    There is no sleep in the world tonight.
PILKINGS: It is still a good bargain if the world should lose one 15
    night's sleep as the price of saving a man's life.
ELESIN: You did not save my life District Officer. You destroyed
    it.
PILKINGS: Now come on . . .
ELESIN: And not merely my life but the lives of many. The end   20
    of the night's work is not over. Neither this year nor the
    next will see it. If I wished you well, I would pray that you
    do not stay long enough on our land to see the disaster you
    have brought upon us.
PILKINGS: Well, I did my duty as I saw it. I have no regrets.   25
ELESIN: No. The regrets of life always come later.

(Some moments' pause.)

    You are waiting for dawn white man. I hear you saying to
    yourself: only so many hours until dawn and then the dan-
    ger is over. All I must do is keep him alive tonight. You
    don't quite understand it all but you know that tonight is   30
    when what ought to be must be brought about. I shall ease
    your mind even more, ghostly one. It is not an entire night
    but a moment of the night, and that moment is past. The
    moon was my messenger and guide. When it reached a cer-
    tain gateway in the sky, it touched that moment for which   35
    my whole life has been spent in blessings. Even I do not
    know the gateway. I have stood here and scanned the sky for
    a glimpse of that door but, I cannot see it. Human eyes are
    useless for a search of this nature. But in the house of osugbo,
    those who keep watch through the spirit recognised the   40
    moment, they sent word to me through the voice of our sa-
    cred drums to prepare myself. I heard them and I shed all
    thoughts of earth. I began to follow the moon to the abode
    of gods . . . servant of the white king, that was when you
    entered my chosen place of departure on feet of desecration. 45
PILKINGS: I'm sorry, but we all see our duty differently.
ELESIN: I no longer blame you. You stole from me my first-
    born, sent him to your country so you could turn him into
    something in your own image. Did you plan it all before-
    hand? There are moments when it seems part of a larger   50

plan. He who must follow my footsteps is taken from me, sent across the ocean. Then, in my turn, I am stopped from fulfilling my destiny. Did you think it all out before, this plan to push our world from its course and sever the cord
55   that links us to the great origin?

PILKINGS: You don't really believe that. Anyway, if that was my intention with your son, I appear to have failed.

ELESIN: You did not fail in the main thing ghostly one. We know the roof covers the rafters, the cloth covers blemishes;
60   who would have known that the white skin covered our future, preventing us from seeing the death our enemies had prepared for us. The world is set adrift and its inhabitants are lost. Around them, there is nothing but emptiness.

PILKINGS: Your son does not take so gloomy a view.

65   ELESIN: Are you dreaming now white man? Were you not present at my reunion of shame? Did you not see when the world reversed itself and the father fell before his son, asking forgiveness?

PILKINGS: That was in the heat of the moment. I spoke to him
70   and . . . if you want to know, he wishes he could cut out his tongue for uttering the words he did.

ELESIN: No. What he said must never be unsaid. The contempt of my own son rescued something of my shame at your hands. You may have stopped me in my duty but I know
75   now that I did give birth to a son. Once I mistrusted him for seeking the companionship of those my spirit knew as enemies of our race. Now I understand. One should seek to obtain the secrets of his enemies. He will avenge my shame, white one. His spirit will destroy you and yours.

80   PILKINGS: That kind of talk is hardly called for. If you don't want my consolation . . .

ELESIN: No white man, I do not want your consolation.

PILKINGS: As you wish. Your son anyway, sends his consolation. He asks your forgiveness. When I asked him not to despise
85   you his reply was: I cannot judge him, and if I cannot judge him, I cannot despise him. He wants to come to you to say goodbye and to receive your blessing.

ELESIN: Goodbye? Is he returning to your land?

PILKINGS: Don't you think that's the most sensible thing for
90   him to do? I advised him to leave at once, before dawn, and he agrees that is the right course of action.

ELESIN: Yes, it is best. And even if I did not think so, I have lost the father's place of honour. My voice is broken.

PILKINGS: Your son honours you. If he didn't he would not ask
95   your blessing.

ELESIN: No. Even a thoroughbred is not without pity for the turf he strikes with his hoof. When is he coming?

PILKINGS: As soon as the town is a little quieter. I advised it.

ELESIN: Yes white man, I am sure you advised it. You advise all
100   our lives although on the authority of what gods, I do not know.

PILKINGS: (Opens his mouth to reply, then appears to change his mind. Turns to go. Hesitates and stops again.) Before I leave you, may I ask just one thing of you?

105   ELESIN: I am listening.

PILKINGS: I wish to ask you to search the quiet of your heart and tell me—do you not find great contradictions in the wisdom of your own race?

ELESIN: Make yourself clear, white one.

110   PILKINGS: I have lived among you long enough to learn a saying or two. One came to my mind tonight when I stepped into the market and saw what was going on. You were surrounded by those who egged you on with song and praises. I thought, are these not the same people who say: the elder grimly approaches heaven and you ask him to bear your   115
greetings yonder; do you really think he makes the journey willingly? After that, I did not hesitate.

(A pause. ELESIN sighs. Before he can speak a sound of running feet is heard.)

JANE: (Off.) Simon! Simon!

PILKINGS: What on earth . . . ! (Runs off.)

(ELESIN turns to his new wife, gazes on her for some moments.)

ELESIN: My young bride, did you hear the ghostly one? You sit   120
and sob in your silent heart but say nothing to all this. First I blamed the white man, then I blamed my gods for deserting me. Now I feel I want to blame you for the mystery of the sapping of my will. But blame is a strange peace offering for a man to bring a world he has deeply wronged, and   125
to its innocent dwellers. Oh little mother, I have taken countless women in my life but you were more than a desire of the flesh. I needed you as the abyss across which my body must be drawn, I filled it with earth and dropped my seed in it at the moment of preparedness for my crossing. You   130
were the final gift of the living to their emissary to the land of the ancestors, and perhaps your warmth and youth brought new insights of this world to me and turned my feet leaden on this side of the abyss. For I confess to you, daughter, my weakness came not merely from the abomination of   135
the white man who came violently into my fading presence, there was also a weight of longing on my earth-held limbs. I would have shaken it off, already my foot had begun to lift but then, the white ghost entered and all was defiled.

(Approaching voices of PILKINGS and his wife.)

JANE: Oh Simon, you will let her in won't you?   140

PILKINGS: I really wish you'd stop interfering.

(They come in view. JANE is in a dressing-gown. PILKINGS is holding a note to which he refers from time to time.)

JANE: Good gracious, I didn't initiate this. I was sleeping quietly, or trying to anyway, when the servant brought it. It's not my fault if one can't sleep undisturbed even in the Residency.   145

PILKINGS: He'd have done the same if we were sleeping at home so don't sidetrack the issue. He knows he can get round you or he wouldn't send you the petition in the first place.

JANE: Be fair Simon. After all he was thinking of your own interests. He is grateful you know, you seem to forget that. He feels he owes you something.   150

PILKINGS: I just wish they'd leave this man alone tonight, that's all.

JANE: Trust him Simon. He's pledged his word it will all go peacefully.   155

PILKINGS: Yes, and that's the other thing. I don't like being threatened.

JANE: Threatened? (Takes the note.) I didn't spot any threat.

PILKINGS: It's there. Veiled, but it's there. The only way to prevent serious rioting tomorrow—what a cheek!   160

JANE: I don't think he's threatening you Simon.

PILKINGS: He's picked up the idiom alright. Wouldn't surprise me if he's been mixing with commies or anarchists over there. The phrasing sounds too good to be true. Damn! If only the Prince hadn't picked this time for his visit.

JANE: Well, even so Simon, what have you got to lose? You don't want a riot on your hands, not with the Prince here.

PILKINGS: (Going up to ELESIN.) Let's see what he has to say. Chief Elesin, there is yet another person who wants to see you. As she is not a next-of-kin I don't really feel obliged to let her in. But your son sent a note with her, so it's up to you.

ELESIN: I know who that must be. So she found out your hiding-place. Well, it was not difficult. My stench of shame is so strong, it requires no hunter's dog to follow it.

PILKINGS: If you don't want to see her, just say so and I'll send her packing.

ELESIN: Why should I not want to see her? Let her come. I have no more holes in my rag of shame. All is laid bare.

PILKINGS: I'll bring her in. (Goes off.)

JANE: (Hesitates, then goes to ELESIN.) Please, try and understand. Everything my husband did was for the best.

ELESIN: (He gives her a long strange stare, as if he is trying to understand who she is.) You are the wife of the District Officer?

JANE: Yes. My name, is Jane.

ELESIN: That is my wife sitting down there. You notice how still and silent she sits? My business is with your husband.

(PILKINGS returns with IYALOJA.)

PILKINGS: Here she is. Now first I want your word of honour that you will try nothing foolish.

ELESIN: Honour? White one, did you say you wanted my word of honour?

PILKINGS: I know you to be an honourable man. Give me your word of honour you will receive nothing from her.

ELESIN: But I am sure you have searched her clothing as you would never dare touch your own mother. And there are these two lizards of yours who roll their eyes even when I scratch.

PILKINGS: And I shall be sitting on that tree trunk watching even how you blink. Just the same I want your word that you will not let her pass anything to you.

ELESIN: You have my honour already. It is locked up in that desk in which you will put away your report of this night's events. Even the honour of my people you have taken already; it is tied together with those papers of treachery which make you masters in this land.

PILKINGS: Alright. I am trying to make things easy but if you must bring in politics we'll have to do it the hard way. Madam, I want you to remain along this line and move no nearer to that cell door. Guards! (They spring to attention.) If she moves beyond this point, blow your whistle. Come on Jane. (They go off.)

IYALOJA: How boldly the lizard struts before the pigeon when it was the eagle itself he promised us he would confront.

ELESIN: I don't ask you to take pity on me Iyaloja. You have a message for me or you would not have come. Even if it is the curses of the world, I shall listen.

IYALOJA: You made so bold with the servant of the white king who took your side against death. I must tell your brother chiefs when I return how bravely you waged war against him. Especially with words.

ELESIN: I more than deserve your scorn.

IYALOJA: (With sudden anger.) I warned you, if you must leave a seed behind, be sure it is not tainted with the curses of the world. Who are you to open a new life when you dared not open the door to a new existence? I say who are you to make so bold? (The BRIDE sobs and IYALOJA notices her. Her contempt noticeably increases as she turns back to ELESIN.) Oh you self-vaunted stem of the plantain, how hollow it all proves. The pith is gone in the parent stem, so how will it prove with the new shoot? How will it go with that earth that bears it? Who are you to bring this abomination on us!

ELESIN: My powers deserted me. My charms, my spells, even my voice lacked strength when I made to summon the powers that would lead me over the last measure of earth into the land of the fleshless. You saw it, Iyaloja. You saw me struggle to retrieve my will from the power of the stranger whose shadow fell across the doorway and left me floundering and blundering in a maze I had never before encountered. My senses were numbed when the touch of cold iron came upon my wrists. I could do nothing to save myself.

IYALOJA: You have betrayed us. We fed you sweetmeats such as we hoped awaited you on the other side. But you said No, I must eat the world's left-overs. We said you were the hunter who brought the quarry down; to you belonged the vital portions of the game. No, you said, I am the hunter's dog and I shall eat the entrails of the game and the faeces of the hunter. We said you were the hunter returning home in triumph, a slain buffalo pressing down on his neck, you said wait, I first must turn up this cricket hole with my toes. We said yours was the doorway at which we first spy the tapper when he comes down from the tree, yours was the blessing of the twilight wine, the purl that brings night spirits out of doors to steal their portion before the light of day. We said yours was the body of wine whose burden shakes the tapper like a sudden gust on his perch. You said, No, I am content to lick the dregs from each calabash when the drinkers are done. We said, the dew on earth's surface was for you to wash your feet along the slopes of honour. You said No, I shall step in the vomit of cats and the droppings of mice; I shall fight them for the left-overs of the world.

ELESIN: Enough Iyaloja, enough.

IYALOJA: We called you leader and oh, how you led us on. What we have no intention of eating should not be held to the nose.

ELESIN: Enough, enough. My shame is heavy enough.

IYALOJA: Wait. I came with a burden.

ELESIN: You have more than discharged it.

IYALOJA: I wish I could pity you.

ELESIN: I need neither your pity nor the pity of the world. I need understanding. Even I need to understand. You were present at my defeat. You were part of the beginnings. You brought about the renewal of my tie to earth, you helped in the binding of the cord.

IYALOJA: I gave you warning. The river which fills up before our eyes does not sweep us away in its flood.

ELESIN: What were warnings beside the moist contact of living earth between my fingers? What were warnings beside the renewal of famished embers lodged eternally in the heart of man. But even that, even if it overwhelmed one with a thousandfold temptations to linger a little while, a man could overcome it. It is when the alien hand pollutes the source of will, when a stranger force of violence shatters the

mind's calm resolution, this is when a man is made to commit the awful treachery of relief, commit in his thought the
unspeakable blasphemy of seeing the hand of the gods in
this alien rupture of his world. I know it was this thought
285 that killed me, sapped my powers and turned me into an infant in the hands of unnamable strangers. I made to utter
my spells anew but my tongue merely rattled in my mouth.
I fingered hidden charms and the contact was damp; there
was no spark left to sever the life-strings that should stretch
290 from every finger-tip. My will was squelched in the spittle
of an alien race, and all because I had committed this blasphemy of thought—that there might be the hand of the
gods in a stranger's intervention.
IYALOJA: Explain it how you will, I hope it brings you peace of
295 mind. The bush-rat fled his rightful cause, reached the market and set up a lamentation. 'Please save me!'—are these
fitting words to hear from an ancestral mask? 'There's a
wild beast at my heels' is not becoming language from a
hunter.
300 ELESIN: May the world forgive me.
IYALOJA: I came with a burden I said. It approaches the gates
which are so well guarded by those jackals whose spittle
will from this day on be your food and drink. But first, tell
me, you who were once Elesin Oba, tell me, you who know
305 so well the cycle of the plantain: is it the parent shoot which
withers to give sap to the younger or, does your wisdom see
it running the other way?
ELESIN: I don't see your meaning Iyaloja?
IYALOJA: Did I ask you for a meaning? I asked a question.
310 Whose trunk withers to give sap to the other? The parent
shoot or the younger?
ELESIN: The parent.
IYALOJA: Ah. So you do know that. There are sights in this
world which say different Elesin. There are some who
315 choose to reverse this cycle of our being. Oh you emptied
bark that the world once saluted for a pith-laden being,
shall I tell you what the gods have claimed of you?

(In her agitation she steps beyond the line indicated by PILKINGS *and
the air is rent by piercing whistles. The two* GUARDS *also leap forward
and place safe-guarding hands on* ELESIN. IYALOJA *stops, astonished.*
PILKINGS *comes racing, followed by* JANE.)

PILKINGS: What is it? Did they try something?
GUARD: She stepped beyond the line.
320 ELESIN: *(In a broken voice.)* Let her alone. She meant no harm.
IYALOJA: Oh Elesin, see what you've become. Once you had no
need to open your mouth in explanation because evil-
smelling goats, itchy of hand and foot had lost their senses.
And it was a brave man indeed who dared lay hands on you
325 because Iyaloja stepped from one side of the earth onto
another. Now look at the spectacle of your life. I grieve
for you.
PILKINGS: I think you'd better leave. I doubt you have done him
much good by coming here. I shall make sure you are not
330 allowed to see him again. In any case we are moving him to
a different place before dawn, so don't bother to come back.
IYALOJA: We foresaw that. Hence the burden I trudged here to
lay beside your gates.
PILKINGS: What was that you said?

IYALOJA: Didn't our son explain? Ask that one. He knows what 335
it is. At least we hope the man we once knew as Elesin remembers the lesser oaths he need not break.
PILKINGS: Do you know what she is talking about?
ELESIN: Go to the gates, ghostly one. Whatever you find there,
bring it to me. 340
IYALOJA: Not yet. It drags behind me on the slow, weary feet of
women. Slow as it is Elesin, it has long overtaken you. It
rides ahead of your laggard will.
PILKINGS: What is she saying now? Christ! Must your people
forever speak in riddles? 345
ELESIN: It will come white man, it will come. Tell your men at
the gates to let it through.
PILKINGS: *(Dubiously.)* I'll have to see what it is.
IYALOJA: You will. *(Passionately.)* But this is one oath he cannot
shirk. White one, you have a king here, a visitor from your 350
land. We know of his presence here. Tell me, were he to die
would you leave his spirit roaming restlessly on the surface
of earth? Would you bury him here among those you consider less than human? In your land have you no ceremonies
of the dead? 355
PILKINGS: Yes. But we don't make our chiefs commit suicide to
keep him company.
IYALOJA: Child, I have not come to help your understanding.
(Points to ELESIN.) This is the man whose weakened understanding holds us in bondage to you. But ask him if you 360
wish. He knows the meaning of a king's passage; he was not
born yesterday. He knows the peril to the race when our
dead father, who goes as intermediary, waits and waits and
knows he is betrayed. He knows when the narrow gate was
opened and he knows it will not stay for laggards who drag 365
their feet in dung and vomit, whose lips are reeking of the
left-overs of lesser men. He knows he has condemned our
king to wander in the void of evil with beings who are enemies of life.
PILKINGS: Yes er . . . but look here . . . 370
IYALOJA: What we ask is little enough. Let him release our
King so he can ride on homewards alone. The messenger is
on his way on the backs of women. Let him send word
through the heart that is folded up within the bolt. It is the
least of all his oaths, it is the easiest fulfilled. 375

(The AIDE-DE-CAMP *runs in.)*

PILKINGS: Bob?
AIDE-DE-CAMP: Sir, there's a group of women chanting up the
hill.
PILKINGS: *(Rounding on* IYALOJA.) If you people want trouble . . .
JANE: Simon, I think that's what Olunde referred to in his letter. 380
PILKINGS: He knows damned well I can't have a crowd here!
Damn it, I explained the delicacy of my position to him. I
think it's about time I got him out of town. Bob, send a car
and two or three soldiers to bring him in. I think the sooner
he takes his leave of his father and gets out the better. 385
IYALOJA: Save your labour white one. If it is the father of your
prisoner you want, Olunde, he who until this night we
knew as Elesin's son, he comes soon himself to take his
leave. He has sent the women ahead, so let them in.

*(*PILKINGS *remains undecided.)*

390 AIDE-DE-CAMP: What do we do about the invasion? We can still
stop them far from here.
PILKINGS: What do they look like?
AIDE-DE-CAMP: They're not many. And they seem quite peaceful.
PILKINGS: No men?
395 AIDE-DE-CAMP: Mm, two or three at the most.
JANE: Honestly, Simon, I'd trust Olunde. I don't think he'll deceive you about their intentions.
PILKINGS: He'd better not. Alright, let them in Bob. Warn
them to control themselves. Then hurry Olunde here. Make
400 sure he brings his baggage because I'm not returning him
into town.
AIDE-DE-CAMP: Very good sir. *(Goes.)*
PILKINGS: *(To* IYALOJA.*)* I hope you understand that if anything
goes wrong it will be on your head. My men have orders to
405 shoot at the first sign of trouble.
IYALOJA: To prevent one death you will actually make other
deaths? Ah, great is the wisdom of the white race. But have
no fear. Your Prince will sleep peacefully. So at long last will
ours. We will disturb you no further, servant of the white
410 king. Just let Elesin fulfil his oath and we will retire home
and pay homage to our King.
JANE: I believe her Simon, don't you?
PILKINGS: Maybe.
ELESIN: Have no fear ghostly one. I have a message to send my
415 King and then you have nothing more to fear.
IYALOJA: Olunde would have done it. The chiefs asked him to
speak the words but he said no, not while you lived.
ELESIN: Even from the depths to which my spirit has sunk, I
find some joy that this little has been left to me.

(The WOMEN *enter, intoning the dirge 'Alę lę lę' and swaying from
side to side. On their shoulders is borne a longish object roughly like a
cylindrical bolt, covered in cloth. They set it down on the spot where*
IYALOJA *had stood earlier, and form a semicircle round it. The*
PRAISE-SINGER *and* DRUMMER *stand on the inside of the semicircle
but the drum is not used at all. The* DRUMMER *intones under the*
PRAISE-SINGER*'s invocations.)*

420 PILKINGS: *(As they enter.)* What is *that?*
IYALOJA: The burden you have made white one, but we bring it
in peace.
PILKINGS: I said *what* is it?
ELESIN: White man, you must let me out. I have a duty to per-
425 form.
PILKINGS: I most certainly will not.
ELESIN: There lies the courier of my King. Let me out so I can
perform what is demanded of me.
PILKINGS: You'll do what you need to do from inside there or
430 not at all. I've gone as far as I intend to with this business.
ELESIN: The worshipper who lights a candle in your church to
bear a message to his god bows his head and speaks in a
whisper to the flame. Have I not seen it ghostly one? His
voice does not ring out to the world. Mine are no words for
435 anyone's ears. They are not words even for the bearers of this
load. They are words I must speak secretly, even as my father
whispered them in my ears and I in the ears of my first-born.
I cannot shout them to the wind and the open night-sky.
JANE: Simon . . .
440 PILKINGS: Don't interfere. Please!

IYALOJA: They have slain the favourite horse of the king and
slain his dog. They have borne them from pulse to pulse centre of the land receiving prayers for their king. But the rider
has chosen to stay behind. Is it too much to ask that he speak
his heart to heart of the waiting courier? *(*PILKINGS *turns his* 445
back on her.) So be it. Elesin Oba, you see how even the mere
leavings are denied you. *(She gestures to the* PRAISE-SINGER.*)*
PRAISE-SINGER: Elesin Oba! I call you by that name only this last
time. Remember when I said, if you cannot come, tell my
horse. *(Pause.)* What? I cannot hear you? I said, if you can- 450
not come, whisper in the ears of my horse. Is your tongue
severed from the roots Elesin? I can hear no response. I said,
if there are boulders you cannot climb, mount my horse's
back, this spotless black stallion, he'll bring you over them.
(Pauses.) Elesin Oba, once you had a tongue that darted like 455
a drummer's stick. I said, if you get lost my dog will track a
path to me. My memory fails me but I think you replied: My
feet have found the path, Alafin.

(The dirge rises and falls.)

I said at the last, if evil hands hold you back, just tell my
horse there is weight on the hem of your smock. I dare not 460
wait too long.

(The dirge rises and falls.)

There lies the swiftest ever messenger of a king, so set me
free with the errand of your heart. There lie the head and
heart of the favourite of the gods, whisper in his ears. Oh my
companion, if you had followed when you should, we would 465
not say that the horse preceded its rider. If you had followed
when it was time, we would not say the dog has raced beyond and left his master behind. If you had raised your will
to cut the thread of life at the summons of the drums, we
would not say your mere shadow fell across the gateway and 470
took its owner's place at the banquet. But the hunter, laden
with a slain buffalo, stayed to root in the cricket's hole with
his toes. What now is left? If there is a dearth of bats, the pigeon must serve us for the offering. Speak the words over
your shadow which must now serve in your place. 475
ELESIN: I cannot approach. Take off the cloth. I shall speak my
message from heart to heart of silence.
IYALOJA: *(Moves forward and removes the coverings.)* Your courier
Elesin, cast your eyes on the favoured companion of the King.

*(Rolled up in the mat, his head and feet showing at either end is the
body of* OLUNDE.*)*

There lies the honour of your household and of our race. Be- 480
cause he could not bear to let honour fly out of doors, he
stopped it with his life. The son has proved the father
Elesin, and there is nothing left in your mouth to gnash but
infant gums.
PRAISE-SINGER: Elesin, we placed the reins of the world in your 485
hands yet you watched it plunge over the edge of the bitter
precipice. You sat with folded arms while evil strangers
tilted the world from its course and crashed it beyond the
edge of emptiness—you muttered, there is little that one
man can do, you left us floundering in a blind future. Your 490
heir has taken the burden on himself. What the end will be,

we are not gods to tell. But this young shoot has poured its sap into the parent stalk, and we know this is not the way of life. Our world is tumbling in the void of strangers, Elesin.

(ELESIN has stood rock-still, his knuckles taut on the bars, his eyes glued to the body of his son. The stillness seizes and paralyses everyone, including PILKINGS who has turned to look. Suddenly ELESIN flings one arm round his neck, once, and with the loop of the chain, strangles himself in a swift, decisive pull. The guards rush forward to stop him but they are only in time to let his body down. PILKINGS has leapt to the door at the same time and struggles with the lock. He rushes within, fumbles with the handcuffs and unlocks them, raises the body to a sitting position while he tries to give resuscitation. The WOMEN continue their dirge, unmoved by the sudden event.)

495   IYALOJA: Why do you strain yourself? Why do you labour at tasks for which no one, not even the man lying there would give you thanks? He is gone at last into the passage but oh, how late it all is. His son will feast on the meat and throw him bones. The passage is clogged with droppings from the
500   King's stallion; he will arrive all stained in dung.
      PILKINGS: *(In a tired voice.)* Was this what you wanted?
      IYALOJA: No child, it is what you brought to be, you who play with strangers' lives, who even usurp the vestments of our

dead, yet believe that the stain of death will not cling to you. The gods demanded only the old expired plantain but 505 you cut down the sap-laden shoot to feed your pride. There is your board, filled to overflowing. Feast on it. *(She screams at him suddenly, seeing that PILKINGS is about to close ELESIN's staring eyes.)* Let him alone! However sunk he was in debt he is no pauper's carrion abandoned on the road. Since when 510 have strangers donned clothes of indigo before the bereaved cries out his loss?

(She turns to the BRIDE who has remained motionless throughout.)

Child.

(The girl takes up a little earth, walks calmly into the cell and closes ELESIN's eyes. She then pours some earth over each eyelid and comes out again.)

Now forget the dead, forget even the living. Turn your mind only to the unborn. 515

(She goes off, accompanied by the BRIDE. The dirge rises in volume and the WOMEN continue their sway. Lights fade to a black-out.)

GLOSSARY

alari, a rich, woven cloth, brightly coloured

egungun, ancestral masquerade

etutu, placatory rites or medicine

gbedu, a deep-timbred royal drum

opele, string of beads used in Ifa divination

osugbo, secret 'executive' cult of the Yoruba; its meeting place

robo, a delicacy made from crushed melon seeds, fried in tiny balls

sanyan, a richly valued woven cloth

sigidi, a squat, carved figure, endowed with the powers of an incubus

BRIAN FRIEL

Brian Friel (b. 1929) is perhaps the most prominent living Irish playwright, the heir of Ireland's brilliant modern dramatic tradition, the tradition of William Butler Yeats, John Millington Synge, and Sean O'Casey. Unlike these predecessors, who worked for the independence of the Republic of Ireland, Friel works in Northern Ireland, still a part of the United Kingdom. Educated in Derry and Belfast, Friel's concerns as a playwright have spanned the "troubles" of Northern Ireland, the poverty and depression of Derry in the 1930s, 1940s, and 1950s, and the installation of a British military presence and the open street warfare of the 1960s, 1970s, and 1980s. From his earliest success, *Philadelphia, Here I Come!* (1964), about a man's divided feelings concerning his emigration to the United States, Friel's drama has centered on the problems of Irish identity in the face of British rule. Many of his early plays and stories—*The Loves of Cass McGuire* (1966), *The Lovers* (1967)—are portraits of Irish life in the manner of Synge, and Friel's dramatization of the personal consequences of contemporary Irish life remains a prominent feature of fine plays like *Living Quarters* (1977) and *Faith Healer* (1979). However, Friel's drama has increasingly become more satirical—in *The Mundy Scheme* (1969) and *The Gentle Island* (1971)—and more politically concerned. In *The Freedom of the City* (1973), Friel dramatizes the fate of three people caught and killed by British soldiers in the 1972 "Bloody Sunday" riots in Derry. In *Volunteers* (1975), a crew of political prisoners are forced to work on an archaeological site, recovering the history of Celtic Ireland even as they are oppressed by British rule. In *Making History* (1988), Friel returns to the origins of Ireland's subjection to the British in the seventeenth and eighteenth centuries. In 1980, Friel and Stephen Rea founded the Field Day Theatre Company in Derry, and its first production was the play generally taken to be Friel's masterpiece, *Translations*. Friel's more recent plays include *Dancing at Lughnasa* (1990), *Wonderful Tennessee* (1992), and *Give Me Your Answer, Do!* (1997). Friel has also recently adapted two plays—Turgenev's *A Month in the Country* (1992) and *London Vertigo,* by the eighteenth-century actor Charles Macklin (1992).

TRANSLATIONS

Translations is set in early nineteenth-century Ireland and concerns the mapping—both actual and cultural—of Ireland by the British. The play takes place at a local hedge-school, a subscription school run by a local master and attended by a variety of children and adults. This Ireland is already threatened by the British culture to the east: a national school—where, presumably, English will be the required language—is about to open, and the British army surveyors have arrived to map the region, part of the 1833 Ordnance Survey of Ireland.

The play's politics are largely conveyed through the politics of language. Jimmy's Homeric Greek, for example, draws a parallel between Ireland and another lost civilization. The romance between Yolland and Maire bridges the barrier of language. They learn to communicate across this barrier, while the British army works to tear it down and destroy Irish cultural identity in the process. In mapping Ireland, the British convert local place names into English, either by translating them directly or by inventing some equivalent. As the relationship between the Irish Owen and his British officers makes clear, English is the language of power; to map the landscape with English names is a figure for rewriting Ireland and its culture into submission and, finally, into nonexistence.

Although *Translations* may seem only indirectly about contemporary Irish politics, it dramatizes a struggle for national and cultural identity that continues to embroil Northern Ireland today. Throughout the play, for example, the mysterious and unseen Donnelly twins move around the edges of the action, guerrillas hindering the British progress through the country. Finally, when Yolland is missing, we learn the true consequences of the British mapping of Ireland. Mapping the land in English is the prelude to its occupation, as the army systematically destroys the village and countryside that they have made their own. At the play's close, we scent the sickly sweet smell of blighted potatoes, the sign of the impending famine that would weaken and disperse rural Ireland.

TRANSLATIONS

Brian Friel

The action takes place in a hedge-school in the townland of Baile Beag/Ballybeg, an Irish-speaking community in County Donegal.

------ ACT ONE ------

The hedge-school is held in a disused barn or hay-shed or byre. Along the back wall are the remains of five or six stalls—wooden posts and chains—where cows were once milked and bedded. A double door left, large enough to allow a cart to enter. A window right. A wooden stairway without a banister leads to the upstairs living-quarters (off) of the schoolmaster and his son. Around the room are broken and forgotten implements: a cart-wheel, some lobster-pots, farming tools, a battle of hay, a churn, etc. There are also the stools and bench-seats which the pupils use and a table and chair for the master. At the door a pail of water and a soiled towel. The room is comfortless and dusty and functional—there is no trace of a woman's hand.

When the play opens, MANUS *is teaching* SARAH *to speak. He kneels beside her. She is sitting on a low stool, her head down, very tense, clutching a slate on her knees. He is coaxing her gently and firmly and—as with everything he does—with a kind of zeal.*

MANUS *is in his late twenties/early thirties; the master's older son. He is pale-faced, lightly built, intense, and works as an unpaid assistant—a monitor—to his father. His clothes are shabby; and when he moves we see that he is lame.*

SARAH's *speech defect is so bad that all her life she has been considered locally to be dumb and she has accepted this: when she wishes to communicate, she grunts and makes unintelligible nasal sounds. She has a waiflike appearance and could be any age from seventeen to thirty-five.*

JIMMY JACK CASSIE—*known as the Infant Prodigy—sits by himself, contentedly reading Homer in Greek and smiling to himself. He is a bachelor in his sixties, lives alone, and comes to these evening classes partly for the company and partly for the intellectual stimulation. He is fluent in Latin and Greek but is in no way pedantic—to him it is perfectly normal to speak these tongues. He never washes. His clothes—heavy top coat, hat, mittens, which he wears now—are filthy and he lives in them summer and winter, day and night. He now reads in a quiet voice and smiles in profound satisfaction. For* JIMMY *the world of the gods and the ancient myths is as real and as immediate as everyday life in the townland of Baile Beag.*

MANUS *holds* SARAH's *hands in his and he articulates slowly and distinctly into her face.*

MANUS: We're doing very well. And we're going to try it once more—just once more. Now—relax and breathe in . . . deep . . . and out . . . in . . . and out . . .

*(*SARAH *shakes her head vigorously and stubbornly.)*

MANUS: Come on, Sarah. This is our secret.

(Again vigorous and stubborn shaking of SARAH's *head.)*

MANUS: Nobody's listening. Nobody hears you.   5
JIMMY: *'Ton d'emeibet epeita thea glaukopis Athene . . .'*
MANUS: Get your tongue and your lips working. 'My name—' Come on. One more try. 'My name is—' Good girl.
SARAH: My . . .
MANUS: Great. 'My name—'   10
SARAH: My . . . my . . .
MANUS: Raise your head. Shout it out. Nobody's listening.
JIMMY: *'. . . alla hekelos estai en Atreidao domois . . .'*
MANUS: Jimmy, please! Once more—just once more—'My name—' Good girl. Come on now. Head up. Mouth open. 15
SARAH: My . . .
MANUS: Good.
SARAH: My . . .
MANUS: Great.
SARAH: My name . . .   20
MANUS: Yes?
SARAH: My name is . . .
MANUS: Yes?

*(*SARAH *pauses. Then in a rush.)*

SARAH: My name is Sarah.
MANUS: Marvellous! Bloody marvellous!   25

*(*MANUS *hugs* SARAH. *She smiles in shy, embarrassed pleasure.)*

Did you hear that, Jimmy?—'My name is Sarah'—clear as a bell. *(To* SARAH.*)* The Infant Prodigy doesn't know what we're at. *(*SARAH *laughs at this.* MANUS *hugs her again and stands up.)* Now we're really started! Nothing'll stop us now! Nothing in the wide world!   30

I. 6 *Ton . . . Athene* But the grey-eyed goddess Athene then replied to him (from Homer, *Odyssey*, 13.420) 13 *alla . . . domois . . .* but he sits at ease in the halls of the Sons of Athens . . . (from Homer, *Odyssey*, 13.423–24)

(JIMMY, *chuckling at his text, comes over to them.*)

JIMMY: Listen to this, Manus.

MANUS: Soon you'll be telling me all the secrets that have been in that head of yours all these years. Certainly, James—what is it? (*To* SARAH.) Maybe you'd set out the stools?

(MANUS *runs up the stairs.*)

35 JIMMY: Wait till you hear this, Manus.

MANUS: Go ahead. I'll be straight down.

JIMMY: '*Hos ara min phamene rabdo epemassat Athene—*' 'After Athene had said this, she touched Ulysses with her wand. She withered the fair skin of his supple limbs and destroyed

40 the flaxen hair from off his head and about his limbs she put the skin of an old man . . .'! The divil! The divil!

(MANUS *has emerged again with a bowl of milk and a piece of bread.*)

JIMMY: And wait till you hear! She's not finished with him yet!

(As MANUS *descends the stairs he toasts* SARAH *with his bowl.*)

JIMMY: '*Knuzosen de oi osse—*' 'She dimmed his two eyes that were so beautiful and clothed him in a vile ragged cloak be-

45 grimed with filthy smoke . . .'! D'you see! Smoke! Smoke! D'you see! Sure look at what the same turf-smoke has done to myself! (*He rapidly removes his hat to display his bald head.*) Would you call that flaxen hair?

MANUS: Of course I would.

50 JIMMY: 'And about him she cast the great skin of a filthy hind, stripped of the hair, and into his hand she thrust a staff and a wallet'! Ha-ha-ha! Athene did that to Ulysses! Made him into a tramp! Isn't she the tight one?

MANUS: You couldn't watch her, Jimmy.

55 JIMMY: You know what they call her?

MANUS: '*Glaukopis Athene.*'

JIMMY: That's it! The flashing-eyed Athene! By God, Manus, sir, if you had a woman like that about the house, it's not stripping a turf-bank you'd be thinking about—eh?

60 MANUS: She was a goddess, Jimmy.

JIMMY: Better still. Sure isn't our own Grania a class of a goddess and—

MANUS: Who?

JIMMY: Grania—Grania—Diarmuid's Grania.

65 MANUS: Ah.

JIMMY: And sure she can't get her fill of men.

MANUS: Jimmy, you're impossible.

JIMMY: I was just thinking to myself last night: if you had the choosing between Athene and Artemis and Helen of

70 Troy—all three of them Zeus's girls—imagine three powerful-looking daughters like that all in the one parish of Athens!—now, if you had the picking between them, which would you take?

MANUS: (*To* SARAH.) Which should I take, Sarah?

JIMMY: No harm to Helen; and no harm to Artemis; and indeed   75
no harm to our own Grania, Manus. But I think I've no choice but to go bull-straight for Athene. By God, sir, them flashing eyes would fair keep a man jigged up constant!

(*Suddenly and momentarily, as if in spasm,* JIMMY *stands to attention and salutes, his face raised in pained ecstasy.* MANUS *laughs. So does* SARAH. JIMMY *goes back to his seat, and his reading.*)

MANUS: You're a dangerous bloody man, Jimmy Jack.

JIMMY: 'Flashing-eyed'! Hah! Sure Homer knows it all, boy.   80
Homer knows it all.

(MANUS *goes to the window and looks out.*)

MANUS: Where the hell has he got to?

(SARAH *goes to* MANUS *and touches his elbow. She mimes rocking a baby.*)

MANUS: Yes, I know he's at the christening; but it doesn't take them all day to put a name on a baby, does it?

(SARAH *mimes pouring drinks and tossing them back quickly.*)

MANUS: You may be sure. Which pub?   85

(SARAH *indicates.*)

MANUS: Gracie's?

(*No. Further away.*)

MANUS: Con Connie Tim's?

(*No. To the right of there.*)

MANUS: Anna na mBreag's?

(*Yes. That's it.*)

MANUS: Great. She'll fill him up. I suppose I may take the class then.   90

(MANUS *begins to distribute some books, slates and chalk, texts, etc., beside the seats.* SARAH *goes over to the straw and produces a bunch of flowers she has hidden there. During this:*)

JIMMY: '*Autar o ek limenos prosebe—*' 'But Ulysses went forth from the harbour and through the woodland to the place where Athene had shown him he could find the good swineherd who—'*o oi biotoio malista kedeto*'—what's that, Manus?

MANUS: 'Who cared most for his substance'.   95

JIMMY: That's it! 'The good swineherd who cared most for his substance above all the slaves that Ulysses possessed . . .'

---

37 *Hos . . . Athene* as she spoke Athene touched him with her wand (from Homer, *Odyssey,* 13.429)   43 *Knuzosen . . . osse* she dimmed his eyes (from Homer, *Odyssey,* 13.433)   56 *Glaukopis Athene* flashing-eyed Athene

---

91 *Autar . . . prosebe* but he went forth from the harbour (from Homer, *Odyssey,* 14.1)   94 *o . . . kedeto* he cared very much for his substance (from Homer, *Odyssey,* 14.3–4)

(SARAH *presents the flowers to* MANUS.)

MANUS: Those are lovely, Sarah.

(*But* SARAH *has fled in embarrassment to her seat and has her head buried in a book.* MANUS *goes to her.*)

MANUS: Flow-ers.

(*Pause.* SARAH *does not look up.*)

100 MANUS: Say the word: flow-ers. Come on—flow-ers.
SARAH: Flowers.
MANUS: You see?—you're off!

(MANUS *leans down and kisses the top of* SARAH's *head.*)

MANUS: And they're beautiful flowers. Thank you.

(MAIRE *enters, a strong-minded, strong-bodied woman in her twenties with a head of curly hair. She is carrying a small can of milk.*)

MAIRE: Is this all's here? Is there no school this evening?
105 MANUS: If my father's not back, I'll take it.

(MANUS *stands awkwardly, having been caught kissing* SARAH *and with the flowers almost formally at his chest.*)

MAIRE: Well now, isn't that a pretty sight. There's your milk. How's Sarah?

(SARAH *grunts a reply.*)

MANUS: I saw you out at the hay.

(MAIRE *ignores this and goes to* JIMMY.)

MAIRE: And how's Jimmy Jack Cassie?
110 JIMMY: Sit down beside me, Maire.
MAIRE: Would I be safe?
JIMMY: No safer man in Donegal.

(MAIRE *flops on a stool beside* JIMMY.)

MAIRE: Ooooh. The best harvest in living memory, they say; but I don't want to see another like it. (*Showing* JIMMY *her
115   hands.*) Look at the blisters.
JIMMY: *Esne fatigata?*
MAIRE: *Sum fatigatissima.*
JIMMY: *Bene! Optime!*
MAIRE: That's the height of my Latin. Fit me better if I had
120   even that much English.
JIMMY: English? I thought you had some English?
MAIRE: Three words. Wait—there was a spake I used to have off by heart. What's this it was? (*Her accent is strange because she is speaking a foreign language and because she does not understand
125   what she is saying.*) 'In Norfolk we besport ourselves around the maypoll.' What about that!

---

116 *Esne fatigata?* are you tired?   117 *Sum fatigatissima* I am very tired   118 *Bene! Optime!* good! Excellent!

MANUS: Maypole.

(*Again* MAIRE *ignores* MANUS.)

MAIRE: God have mercy on my Aunt Mary—she taught me that when I was about four, whatever it means. Do you know what it means, Jimmy?   130
JIMMY: Sure you know I have only Irish like yourself.
MAIRE: And Latin. And Greek.
JIMMY: I'm telling you a lie: I know one English word.
MAIRE: What?
JIMMY: Bo-som.   135
MAIRE: What's a bo-som?
JIMMY: You know—(*He illustrates with his hands.*)—bo-som— bo-som—you know—Diana, the huntress, she has two powerful bosom.
MAIRE: You may be sure that's the one English word you would 140
know. (*Rises.*) Is there a drop of water about?

(MANUS *gives* MAIRE *his bowl of milk.*)

MANUS: I'm sorry I couldn't get up last night.
MAIRE: Doesn't matter.
MANUS: Biddy Hanna sent for me to write a letter to her sister in Nova Scotia. All the gossip of the parish. 'I brought the 145
cow to the bull three times last week but no good. There's nothing for it now but Big Ned Frank.'
MAIRE: (*Drinking.*) That's better.
MANUS: And she got so engrossed in it that she forgot who she was dictating to: 'The aul drunken schoolmaster and that 150
lame son of his are still footering about in the hedge-school, wasting people's good time and money.'

(MAIRE *has to laugh at this.*)

MAIRE: She did not!
MANUS: And me taking it all down. 'Thank God one of them new national schools is being built above at Poll na 155
gCaorach.' It was after midnight by the time I got back.
MAIRE: Great to be a busy man.

(MAIRE *moves away.* MANUS *follows.*)

MANUS: I could hear music on my way past but I thought it was too late to call.
MAIRE: (*To* SARAH.) Wasn't your father in great voice last night? 160

(SARAH *nods and smiles.*)

MAIRE: It must have been near three o'clock by the time you got home?

(SARAH *holds up four fingers.*)

MAIRE: Was it four? No wonder we're in pieces.
MANUS: I can give you a hand at the hay tomorrow.
MAIRE: That's the name of a hornpipe, isn't it?—'The Scholar 165
In The Hayfield'—or is it a reel?
MANUS: If the day's good.
MAIRE: Suit yourself. The English soldiers below in the tents, them sapper fellas, they're coming up to give us a hand. I don't know a word they're saying, nor they me; but sure 170
that doesn't matter, does it?

MANUS: What the hell are you so crabbed about?!

(DOALTY *and* BRIDGET *enter noisily. Both are in their twenties.* DOALTY *is brandishing a surveyor's pole. He is an open-minded, open-hearted, generous and slightly thick young man.* BRIDGET *is a plump, fresh young girl, ready to laugh, vain, and with a countrywoman's instinctive cunning.* DOALTY *enters doing his imitation of the master.*)

DOALTY: Vesperal salutations to you all.

BRIDGET: He's coming down past Carraig na Ri and he's as full
175   as a pig!

DOALTY: *Ignari, stulti, rustici*—pot-boys and peasant whelps—semi-literates and illegitimates.

BRIDGET: He's been on the batter since this morning; he sent the wee ones home at eleven o'clock.

180   DOALTY: Three questions. Question A—Am I drunk? Question B—Am I sober? (*Into* MAIRE's *face.*) *Responde—responde!*

BRIDGET: Question C, Master—When were you last sober?

MAIRE: What's the weapon, Doalty?

BRIDGET: I warned him. He'll be arrested one of these days.

185   DOALTY: Up in the bog with Bridget and her aul fella, and the Red Coats were just across at the foot of Croc na Mona, dragging them aul chains and peeping through that big machine they lug about everywhere with them—you know the name of it, Manus?

190   MAIRE: Theodolite.

BRIDGET: How do you know?

MAIRE: They leave it in our byre at night sometimes if it's raining.

JIMMY: Theodolite—what's the etymology of that word, Manus?

195   MANUS: No idea.

BRIDGET: Get on with the story.

JIMMY: *Theo—theos*—something to do with a god. Maybe *thea*—a goddess! What shape's the yoke?

DOALTY: 'Shape!' Will you shut up, you aul eejit you! Anyway,
200   every time they'd stick one of these poles into the ground and move across the bog, I'd creep up and shift it twenty or thirty paces to the side.

BRIDGET: God!

DOALTY: Then they'd come back and stare at it and look at their
205   calculations and stare at it again and scratch their heads. And cripes, d'you know what they ended up doing?

BRIDGET: Wait till you hear!

DOALTY: They took the bloody machine apart!

(*And immediately he speaks in gibberish—an imitation of two very agitated and confused sappers in rapid conversation.*)

BRIDGET: That's the image of them!

210   MAIRE: You must be proud of yourself, Doalty.

DOALTY: What d'you mean?

MAIRE: That was a very clever piece of work.

MANUS: It was a gesture.

MAIRE: What sort of gesture?

MANUS: Just to indicate . . . a presence.   215

MAIRE: Hah!

BRIDGET: I'm telling you—you'll be arrested.

(*When* DOALTY *is embarrassed—or pleased—he reacts physically. He now grabs* BRIDGET *around the waist.*)

DOALTY: What d'you make of that for an implement, Bridget? Wouldn't that make a great aul shaft for your churn?

BRIDGET: Let go of me, you dirty brute! I've a headline to do   220
before Big Hughie comes.

MANUS: I don't think we'll wait for him. Let's get started.

(*Slowly, reluctantly they begin to move to their seats and specific tasks.* DOALTY *goes to the bucket of water at the door and washes his hands.* BRIDGET *sets up a hand-mirror and combs her hair.*)

BRIDGET: Nellie Ruadh's baby was to be christened this morning. Did any of yous hear what she called it? Did you, Sarah?

(SARAH *grunts:* No.)

BRIDGET: Did you, Maire?   225

MAIRE: No.

BRIDGET: Our Seamus says she was threatening she was going to call it after its father.

DOALTY: Who's the father?

BRIDGET: That's the point, you donkey you!   230

DOALTY: Ah.

BRIDGET: So there's a lot of uneasy bucks about Baile Beag this day.

DOALTY: She told me last Sunday she was going to call it Jimmy.

BRIDGET: You're a liar, Doalty.   235

DOALTY: Would I tell you a lie? Hi, Jimmy, Nellie Ruadh's aul fella's looking for you.

JIMMY: For me?

MAIRE: Come on, Doalty.

DOALTY: Someone told him . . .   240

MAIRE: Doalty!

DOALTY: He heard you know the first book of the Satires of Horace off by heart . . .

JIMMY: That's true.

DOALTY: . . . and he wants you to recite it for him.   245

JIMMY: I'll do that for him certainly, certainly.

DOALTY: He's busting to hear it.

(JIMMY *fumbles in his pockets.*)

JIMMY: I came across this last night—this'll interest you—in Book Two of Virgil's *Georgics*.

DOALTY: Be God, that's my territory alright.   250

BRIDGET: You clown you! (*To* SARAH.) Hold this for me, would you? (*Her mirror.*)

JIMMY: Listen to this, Manus. '*Nigra fere et presso pinguis sub vomere terra . . .*'

DOALTY: Steady on now—easy, boys, easy—don't rush me, boys—   255

---

176 *Ignari, stulti, rustici* ignoramuses, fools, peasants   181 *Responde—responde!* answer—answer   197 *theos* a god   198 *thea* a goddess

---

253–54 *Nigra . . . terra* land that is black and rich beneath the pressure of the plough

(He mimes great concentration.)

JIMMY: Manus?

MANUS: 'Land that is black and rich beneath the pressure of the plough . . .'

DOALTY: Give *me* a chance!

260 JIMMY: 'And with *cui putre*—with crumbly soil—is in the main best for corn.' There you are!

DOALTY: There you are.

JIMMY: 'From no other land will you see more wagons wending homeward behind slow bullocks.' Virgil! There!

265 DOALTY: 'Slow bullocks'!

JIMMY: Isn't that what I'm always telling you? Black soil for corn. *That's* what you should have in that upper field of yours—corn, not spuds.

DOALTY: Would you listen to that fella! Too lazy be Jasus to
270 wash himself and he's lecturing me on agriculture! Would you go and take a running race at yourself, Jimmy Jack Cassie! *(Grabs* SARAH.*)* Come away out of this with me, Sarah, and we'll plant some corn together.

MANUS: All right—all right. Let's settle down and get some
275 work done. I know Sean Beag isn't coming—he's at the salmon. What about the Donnelly twins? *(To* DOALTY.*)* Are the Donnelly twins not coming any more?

*(*DOALTY *shrugs and turns away.)*

Did you ask them?

DOALTY: Haven't seen them. Not about these days.

*(*DOALTY *begins whistling through his teeth. Suddenly the atmosphere is silent and alert.)*

280 MANUS: Aren't they at home?

DOALTY: No.

MANUS: Where are they then?

DOALTY: How would I know?

BRIDGET: Our Seamus says two of the soldiers' horses were
285 found last night at the foot of the cliffs at Machaire Buidhe and . . . *(She stops suddenly and begins writing with chalk on her slate.)* D'you hear the whistles of this aul slate? Sure nobody could write on an aul slippery thing like that.

MANUS: What headline did my father set you?

290 BRIDGET: 'It's easier to stamp out learning than to recall it.'

JIMMY: Book Three, the *Agricola* of Tacitus.

BRIDGET: God but you're a dose.

MANUS: Can you do it?

BRIDGET: There. Is it bad? Will he ate me?

295 MANUS: It's very good. Keep your elbow in closer to your side. Doalty?

DOALTY: I'm at the seven-times table. I'm perfect, skipper.

*(*MANUS *moves to* SARAH.*)*

MANUS: Do you understand those sums?

*(*SARAH *nods:* Yes. MANUS *leans down to her ear.)*

----

260 *cui putre* crumbly soil

MANUS: My name is Sarah.

*(*MANUS *goes to* MAIRE. *While he is talking to her the others swop books, talk quietly, etc.)*

MANUS: Can I help you? What are you at?   300

MAIRE: Map of America. *(Pause.)* The passage money came last Friday.

MANUS: You never told me that.

MAIRE: Because I haven't seen you since, have I?

MANUS: You don't want to go. You said that yourself.   305

MAIRE: There's ten below me to be raised and no man in the house. What do you suggest?

MANUS: Do you want to go?

MAIRE: Did you apply for that job in the new national school?

MANUS: No.   310

MAIRE: You said you would.

MANUS: I said I might.

MAIRE: When it opens, this is finished: nobody's going to pay to go to a hedge-school.

MANUS: I know that and I . . . *(He breaks off because he sees* SARAH, 315
obviously listening, at his shoulder. She moves away again.) I was thinking that maybe I could . . .

MAIRE: It's £56 a year you're throwing away.

MANUS: I can't apply for it.

MAIRE: You *promised* me you would.   320

MANUS: My father has applied for it.

MAIRE: He has not!

MANUS: Day before yesterday.

MAIRE: For God's sake, sure you know he'd never—

MANUS: I couldn't—I can't go in against him.   325

*(*MAIRE *looks at him for a second. Then:—)*

MAIRE: Suit yourself. *(To* BRIDGET.*)* I saw your Seamus heading off to the Port fair early this morning.

BRIDGET: And wait till you hear this—I forgot to tell you this. He said that as soon as he crossed over the gap at Cnoc na Mona—just beyond where the soldiers are making the 330
maps—the sweet smell was everywhere.

DOALTY: You never told me that.

BRIDGET: It went out of my head.

DOALTY: He saw the crops in Port?

BRIDGET: Some.   335

MANUS: How did the tops look?

BRIDGET: Fine—I think.

DOALTY: In flower?

BRIDGET: I don't know. I think so. He didn't say.

MANUS: Just the sweet smell—that's all?   340

BRIDGET: They say that's the way it snakes in, don't they? First the smell; and then one morning the stalks are all black and limp.

DOALTY: Are you stupid? It's the rotting stalks makes the sweet smell for God's sake. That's what the smell is—rotting 345
stalks.

MAIRE: Sweet smell! Sweet smell! Every year at this time some-body comes back with stories of the sweet smell. Sweet God, did the potatoes ever fail in Baile Beag? Well, did they ever—ever? Never! There was never blight here. 350
Never. Never. But we're always sniffing about for it, aren't

we?—looking for disaster. The rents are going to go up again—the harvest's going to be lost—the herring have gone away for ever—there's going to be evictions. Honest to God, some of you people aren't happy unless you're miserable and you'll not be right content until you're dead!

DOALTY: Bloody right, Maire. And sure St Colmcille prophesied there'd never be blight here. He said:

> The spuds will bloom in Baile Beag
> Till rabbits grow an extra lug.

And sure that'll never be. So we're all right. Seven threes are twenty-one; seven fours are twenty-eight; seven fives are forty-nine—Hi, Jimmy, do you fancy my chances as boss of the new national school?

JIMMY: What's that?—what's that?

DOALTY: Agh, g'way back home to Greece, son.

MAIRE: You ought to apply, Doalty.

DOALTY: D'you think so? Cripes, maybe I will. Hah!

BRIDGET: Did you know that you start at the age of six and you have to stick at it until you're twelve at least—no matter how smart you are or how much you know.

DOALTY: Who told you that yarn?

BRIDGET: And every child from every house has to go all day, every day, summer or winter. That's the law.

DOALTY: I'll tell you something—nobody's going to go near them—they're not going to take on—law or no law.

BRIDGET: And everything's free in them. You pay for nothing except the books you use; that's what our Seamus says.

DOALTY: 'Our Seamus'. Sure your Seamus wouldn't pay anyway. She's making this all up.

BRIDGET: Isn't that right, Manus?

MANUS: I think so.

BRIDGET: And from the very first day you go, you'll not hear one word of Irish spoken. You'll be taught to speak English and every subject will be taught through English and everyone'll end up as cute as the Buncrana people.

(SARAH suddenly grunts and mimes a warning that the master is coming. The atmosphere changes. Sudden business. Heads down.)

DOALTY: He's here, boys. Cripes, he'll make yella meal out of me for those bloody tables.

BRIDGET: Have you any extra chalk, Manus?

MAIRE: And the atlas for me.

(DOALTY goes to MAIRE who is sitting on a stool at the back.)

DOALTY: Swop you seats.

MAIRE: Why?

DOALTY: There's an empty one beside the Infant Prodigy.

MAIRE: I'm fine here.

DOALTY: Please, Maire. I want to jouk in the back here.

(MAIRE rises.)

God love you. *(Aloud.)* Anyone got a bloody table-book? Cripes, I'm wrecked.

(SARAH gives him one.)

God, I'm dying about you.

(In his haste to get to the back seat, DOALTY bumps into BRIDGET who is kneeling on the floor and writing laboriously on a slate resting on top of a bench-seat.)

BRIDGET: Watch where you're going, Doalty!

(DOALTY gooses BRIDGET. She squeals. Now the quiet hum of work: JIMMY reading Homer in a low voice; BRIDGET copying her headline; MAIRE studying the atlas; DOALTY, his eyes shut tight, mouthing his tables; SARAH doing sums. After a few seconds:—)

BRIDGET: Is this 'g' right, Manus? How do you put a tail on it?

DOALTY: Will you shut up! I can't concentrate!

(A few more seconds of work. Then DOALTY opens his eyes and looks around.)

False alarm, boys. The bugger's not coming at all. Sure the bugger's hardly fit to walk.

(And immediately HUGH enters. A large man, with residual dignity, shabbily dressed, carrying a stick. He has, as always, a large quantity of drink taken, but he is by no means drunk. He is in his early sixties.)

HUGH: *Adsum*, Doalty, *adsum*. Perhaps not in *sobrietate perfecta* but adequately *sobrius* to overhear your quip. Vesperal salutations to you all.

(Various responses.)

JIMMY: *Ave*, Hugh.

HUGH: James. *(He removes his hat and coat and hands them and his stick to MANUS, as if to a footman.)* Apologies for my late arrival: we were celebrating the baptism of Nellie Ruadh's baby.

BRIDGET: *(Innocently.)* What name did she put on it, Master?

HUGH: Was it Eamon? Yes, it was Eamon.

BRIDGET: Eamon Donal from Tor! Cripes!

HUGH: And after the *caerimonia nominationis*—Maire?

MAIRE: The ritual of naming.

HUGH: Indeed—we then had a few libations to mark the occasion. Altogether very pleasant. The derivation of the word 'baptize'?—where are my Greek scholars? Doalty?

DOALTY: Would it be—ah—ah—

HUGH: Too slow. James?

JIMMY: 'Baptizein'—to dip or immerse.

HUGH: Indeed—our friend Pliny Minor speaks of the 'baptisterium'—the cold bath.

DOALTY: Master.

HUGH: Doalty?

DOALTY: I suppose you could talk then about baptizing a sheep at sheep-dipping, could you?

(Laughter. Comments.)

---

404 *adsum* I am present; *sobrietate perfecta* with complete sobriety 405 *sobrius* sober 407 *Ave* hail 415 *caerimonia nominationis* ceremony of naming 422 *baptizein* to dip or immerse 423 *baptisterium* a cold bath, swimming pool

HUGH: Indeed—the precedent is there—the day you were ap-
430   propriately named Doalty—seven nines?
DOALTY: What's that, Master?
HUGH: Seven times nine?
DOALTY: Seven nines—seven nines—seven times nine—seven
     times nine are—cripes, it's on the tip of my tongue, Mas-
435   ter—I knew it for sure this morning—funny that's the only
     one that foxes me—
BRIDGET: (Prompt.) Sixty-three.
DOALTY: What's wrong with me: sure seven nines are fifty-
     three, Master.
440 HUGH: Sophocles from Colonus would agree with Doalty Dan
     Doalty from Tulach Alainn: 'To know nothing is the sweet-
     est life.' Where's Sean Beag?
MANUS: He's at the salmon.
HUGH: And Nora Dan?
445 MAIRE: She says she's not coming back any more.
HUGH: Ah. Nora Dan can now write her name—Nora Dan's
     education is complete. And the Donnelly twins?

(Brief pause. Then:—)

BRIDGET: They're probably at the turf. (She goes to HUGH.)
     There's the one-and-eight I owe you for last quarter's arith-
450   metic and there's my one-and-six for this quarter's writing.
HUGH: Gratias tibi ago. (He sits at his table.) Before we com-
     mence our studia I have three items of information to im-
     part to you—(To MANUS.) A bowl of tea, strong tea, black—

(MANUS leaves.)

     Item A: on my perambulations today—Bridget? Too slow.
455   Maire?
MAIRE: Perambulare—to walk about.
HUGH: Indeed—I encountered Captain Lancey of the Royal En-
     gineers who is engaged in the ordnance survey of this area.
     He tells me that in the past few days two of his horses have
460   strayed and some of his equipment seems to be mislaid. I
     expressed my regret and suggested he address you himself
     on these matters. He then explained that he does not speak
     Irish. Latin? I asked. None. Greek? Not a syllable. He
     speaks—on his own admission—only English; and to his
465   credit he seemed suitably verecund—James?
JIMMY: Verecundus—humble.
HUGH: Indeed—he voiced some surprise that we did not speak
     his language. I explained that a few of us did, on occasion—
     outside the parish of course—and then usually for the pur-
470   poses of commerce, a use to which his tongue seemed par-
     ticularly suited—(Shouts.) and a slice of soda bread—and I
     went on to propose that our own culture and the classical
     tongues made a happier conjugation—Doalty?
DOALTY: Conjugo—I join together.

(DOALTY is so pleased with himself that he prods and winks at
BRIDGET.)

HUGH: Indeed—English, I suggested, couldn't really express   475
     us. And again to his credit he acquiesced to my logic.
     Acquiesced—Maire?

(MAIRE turns away impatiently. HUGH is unaware of the gesture.)

     Too slow. Bridget?
BRIDGET: Acquiesco.
HUGH: Procede.   480
BRIDGET: Acquiesco, acquiescere, acquievi, acquietum.
HUGH: Indeed—and Item B . . .
MAIRE: Master.
HUGH: Yes?

(MAIRE gets to her feet uneasily but determinedly. Pause.)

     Well, girl?   485
MAIRE: We should all be learning to speak English. That's what
     my mother says. That's what I say. That's what Dan O'Con-
     nell said last month in Ennis. He said the sooner we all
     learn to speak English the better.

(Suddenly several speak together.)

JIMMY: What's she saying? What? What?   490
DOALTY: It's Irish he uses when he's travelling around scroung-
     ing votes.
BRIDGET: And sleeping with married women. Sure no woman's
     safe from that fella.
JIMMY: Who-who-who? Who's this? Who's this?   495
HUGH: Silentium! (Pause.) Who is she talking about?
MAIRE: I'm talking about Daniel O'Connell.
HUGH: Does she mean that little Kerry politician?
MAIRE: I'm talking about the Liberator, Master, as you well
     know. And what he said was this: 'The old language is a bar- 500
     rier to modern progress.' He said that last month. And he's
     right. I don't want Greek. I don't want Latin. I want English.

(MANUS reappears on the platform above.)

     I want to be able to speak English because I'm going to
     America as soon as the harvest's all saved.

(MAIRE remains standing. HUGH puts his hand into his pocket and
produces a flask of whiskey. He removes the cap, pours a drink into it,
tosses it back, replaces the cap, puts the flask back into his pocket.
Then:—)

HUGH: We have been diverted—diverto—divertere—Where   505
     were we?
DOALTY: Three items of information, Master. You're at Item B.
HUGH: Indeed—Item B—Item B—yes—On my way to the
     christening this morning I chanced to meet Mr George
     Alexander, Justice of the Peace. We discussed the new na- 510
     tional school. Mr Alexander invited me to take charge of it
     when it opens. I thanked him and explained that I could do

---

451 *Gratias tibi ago* I thank you   452 *studia* studies   456 *perambulare* to walk through   466 *verecundus* shame-faced, modest
474 *conjugo* I join together

481 *acquiesco, acquiescere* to rest, to find comfort in   480 *procede* proceed   496 *Silentium!* silence!   505 *diverto, divertere*
to turn away

that only if I were free to run it as I have run this hedge-
school for the past thirty-five years—filling what our friend
515   Euripides calls the 'aplestos pithos'—James?
JIMMY: 'The cask that cannot be filled'.
HUGH: Indeed—and Mr Alexander retorted courteously and
emphatically that he hopes that is how it will be run.

(MAIRE now sits.)

Indeed. I have had a strenuous day and I am weary of you
520   all. (He rises.) Manus will take care of you.

(HUGH goes towards the steps. OWEN enters. OWEN is the younger son,
a handsome, attractive young man in his twenties. He is dressed
smartly—a city man. His manner is easy and charming: everything
he does is invested with consideration and enthusiasm. He now stands
framed in the doorway, a travelling bag across his shoulder.)

OWEN: Could anybody tell me is this where Hugh Mor
O'Donnell holds his hedge-school?
DOALTY: It's Owen—Owen Hugh! Look, boys—it's Owen
Hugh!

(OWEN enters. As he crosses the room he touches and has a word for
each person.)

525   OWEN: Doalty! (Playful punch.) How are you, boy? Jacobe, quid
agis? Are you well?
JIMMY: Fine. Fine.
OWEN: And Bridget! Give us a kiss. Aaaaaah!
BRIDGET: You're welcome, Owen.
530   OWEN: It's not—? Yes, it is Maire Chatach! God! A young
woman.
MAIRE: How are you, Owen?

(OWEN is now in front of HUGH. He puts his two hands on his FA-
THER's shoulders.)

OWEN: And how's the old man himself?
HUGH: Fair—fair.
535   OWEN: Fair? For God's sake you never looked better! Come
here to me. (He embraces HUGH warmly and genuinely.) Great
to see you, Father. Great to be back.

(HUGH's eyes are moist—partly joy, partly the drink.)

HUGH: I—I'm—I'm—pay no attention to—
OWEN: Come on—come on—come on—(He gives HUGH his
540   handkerchief.) Do you know what you and I are going to do
tonight? We are going to go up to Anna na mBreag's . . .
DOALTY: Not there, Owen.
OWEN: Why not?
DOALTY: Her poteen's worse than ever.
545   BRIDGET: They say she puts frogs in it!
OWEN: All the better. (To HUGH.) And you and I are going to
get footless drunk. That's arranged.

_____

515 aplestos pithos unfillable cask   525–26 Jacobe, quid agis?
James, how are you?

(OWEN sees MANUS coming down the steps with tea and soda bread.
They meet at the bottom.)

And Manus!
MANUS: You're welcome, Owen.
OWEN: I know I am. And it's great to be here. (He turns round,   550
arms outstretched.) I can't believe it. I come back after six
years and everything's just as it was! Nothing's changed!
Not a thing! (Sniffs.) Even that smell—that's the same
smell this place always had. What is it anyway? Is it the
straw?   555
DOALTY: Jimmy Jack's feet.

(General laughter. It opens little pockets of conversation round the
room.)

OWEN: And Doalty Dan Doalty hasn't changed either!
DOALTY: Bloody right, Owen.
OWEN: Jimmy, are you well?
JIMMY: Dodging about.   560
OWEN: Any word of the big day?

(This is greeted with 'ohs' and 'ahs'.)

Time enough, Jimmy. Homer's easier to live with, isn't he?
MAIRE: We heard stories that you own ten big shops in
Dublin—is it true?
OWEN: Only nine.   565
BRIDGET: And you've twelve horses and six servants.
OWEN: Yes—that's true. God Almighty, would you listen to
them—taking a hand at me!
MANUS: When did you arrive?
OWEN: We left Dublin yesterday morning, spent last night in   570
Omagh and got here half an hour ago.
MANUS: You're hungry then.
HUGH: Indeed—get him food—get him a drink.
OWEN: Not now, thanks; later. Listen—am I interrupting you
all?   575
HUGH: By no means. We're finished for the day.
OWEN: Wonderful. I'll tell you why. Two friends of mine are
waiting outside the door. They'd like to meet you and I'd
like you to meet them. May I bring them in?
HUGH: Certainly. You'll all eat and have . . .   580
OWEN: Not just yet, Father. You've seen the sappers working in
this area for the past fortnight, haven't you? Well, the older
man is Captain Lancey . . .
HUGH: I've met Captain Lancey.
OWEN: Great. He's the cartographer in charge of this whole   585
area. Cartographer—James?

(OWEN begins to play this game—his father's game—partly to involve his classroom audience, partly to show he has not forgotten it, and
indeed partly because he enjoys it.)

JIMMY: A maker of maps.
OWEN: Indeed—and the younger man that I travelled with
from Dublin, his name is Lieutenant Yolland and he is at-
tached to the toponymic department—Father?—responde—   590
responde!
HUGH: He gives names to places.
OWEN: Indeed—although he is in fact an orthographer—
Doalty?—too slow—Manus?

595 MANUS: The correct spelling of those names.
    OWEN: Indeed—indeed!

(OWEN laughs and claps his hands. Some of the others join in.)

Beautiful! Beautiful! Honest to God, it's such a delight to be back here with you all again—'civilized' people. Any-how—may I bring them in?
600 HUGH: Your friends are our friends.
    OWEN: I'll be straight back.

(There is general talk as OWEN goes towards the door. He stops beside SARAH.)

OWEN: That's a new face. Who are you?

(A very brief hesitation. Then:—)

SARAH: My name is Sarah.
OWEN: Sarah who?
605 SARAH: Sarah Johnny Sally.
    OWEN: Of course! From Bun na hAbhann! I'm Owen—Owen Hugh Mor. From Baile Beag. Good to see you.

(During this OWEN—SARAH exchange.)

HUGH: Come on now. Let's tidy this place up. *(He rubs the top of his table with his sleeve.)* Move, Doalty—lift those books off
610 the floor.
    DOALTY: Right, Master; certainly, Master; I'm doing my best, Master.

(OWEN stops at the door.)

OWEN: One small thing, Father.
HUGH: *Silentium!*
615 OWEN: I'm on their pay-roll.

(SARAH, very elated at her success, is beside MANUS.)

SARAH: I said it, Manus!

(MANUS ignores SARAH. He is much more interested in OWEN now.)

MANUS: You haven't enlisted, have you?!

(SARAH moves away.)

OWEN: Me a soldier? I'm employed as a part-time, underpaid, civilian interpreter. My job is to translate the quaint, ar-
620 chaic tongue you people persist in speaking into the King's good English.

(He goes out.)

HUGH: Move—move—move! Put some order on things! Come on, Sarah—hide that bucket. Whose are these slates? Some-body take these dishes away. *Festinate! Festinate!*

(MANUS goes to MAIRE who is busy tidying.)

————————————
624 *Festinate!* hurry!

MANUS: You didn't tell me you were definitely leaving. 625
MAIRE: Not now.
HUGH: Good girl, Bridget. That's the style.
MANUS: You might at least have told me.
HUGH: Are these your books, James?
JIMMY: Thank you. 630
MANUS: Fine! Fine! Go ahead! Go ahead!
MAIRE: You talk to me about getting married—with neither a roof over your head nor a sod of ground under your foot. I suggest you go for the new school; but no—'My father's in for that.' Well now he's got it and now this is finished and 635 now you've nothing.
MANUS: I can always . . .
MAIRE: What? Teach classics to the cows? Agh—

(MAIRE moves away from MANUS. OWEN enters with LANCEY and YOLLAND. CAPTAIN LANCEY is middle-aged; a small, crisp officer, ex-pert in his field as cartographer but uneasy with people—especially civilians, especially these foreign civilians. His skill is with deeds, not words. LIEUTENANT YOLLAND is in his late twenties/early thirties. He is tall and thin and gangling, blond hair, a shy, awkward man-ner. A soldier by accident.)

OWEN: Here we are. Captain Lancey—my father.
LANCEY: Good evening. 640

(HUGH becomes expansive, almost courtly, with his visitors.)

HUGH: You and I have already met, sir.
LANCEY: Yes.
OWEN: And Lieutenant Yolland—both Royal Engineers—my father.
HUGH: You're very welcome, gentlemen. 645
YOLLAND: How do you do.
HUGH: *Gaudeo vos hic adesse.*
OWEN: And I'll make no other introductions except that these are some of the people of Baile Beag and—what?—well you're among the best people in Ireland now. *(He pauses to 650 allow LANCEY to speak. LANCEY does not.)* Would you like to say a few words, Captain?
HUGH: What about a drop, sir?
LANCEY: A what?
HUGH: Perhaps a modest refreshment? A little sampling of our 655 *aqua vitae?*
LANCEY: No, no.
HUGH: Later perhaps when—
LANCEY: I'll say what I have to say, if I may, and as briefly as possible. Do they speak *any* English, Roland? 660
OWEN: Don't worry. I'll translate.
LANCEY: I see. *(He clears his throat. He speaks as if he were address-ing children—a shade too loudly and enunciating excessively.)* You may have seen me—seen me—working in this section—section?—working. We are here—here—in this place—you 665 understand?—to make a map—a map—a map and—
JIMMY: *Nonne Latine loquitur?*

————————————
647 *Gaudeo . . . adesse* welcome   667 *Nonne Latine loquitur?* does he not speak Latin?

(HUGH *holds up a restraining hand.*)

HUGH: James.
LANCEY: *(To* JIMMY.*)* I do not speak Gaelic, sir.

(He looks at OWEN.*)*

670   OWEN: Carry on.
LANCEY: A map is a representation on paper—a picture—you understand picture?—a paper picture—showing, representing this country—yes?—showing your country in miniature—a scaled drawing on paper of—of—of—

(Suddenly DOALTY *sniggers. Then* BRIDGET. *Then* SARAH. OWEN *leaps in quickly.*)

675   OWEN: It might be better if you *assume* they understand you—
LANCEY: Yes?
OWEN: And I'll translate as you go along.
LANCEY: I see. Yes. Very well. Perhaps you're right. Well. What we are doing is this. *(He looks at* OWEN. OWEN *nods reassur-*
680   *ingly.)* His Majesty's government has ordered the first ever comprehensive survey of this entire country—a general triangulation which will embrace detailed hydrographic and topographic information and which will be executed to a scale of six inches to the English mile.
685   HUGH: *(Pouring a drink.)* Excellent—excellent.

*(*LANCEY *looks at* OWEN.*)*

OWEN: A new map is being made of the whole country.

*(*LANCEY *looks to* OWEN: *Is that all?* OWEN *smiles reassuringly and indicates to proceed.*)

LANCEY: This enormous task has been embarked on so that the military authorities will be equipped with up-to-date and accurate information on every corner of this part of the Empire.
690   OWEN: The job is being done by soldiers because they are skilled in this work.
LANCEY: And also so that the entire basis of land valuation can be reassessed for purposes of more equitable taxation.
OWEN: This new map will take the place of the estate agent's
695   map so that from now on you will know exactly what is yours in law.
LANCEY: In conclusion I wish to quote two brief extracts from the white paper which is our governing charter: *(Reads)* 'All former surveys of Ireland originated in forfeiture and vio-
700   lent transfer of property; the present survey has for its object the relief which can be afforded to the proprietors and occupiers of land from unequal taxation.'
OWEN: The captain hopes that the public will cooperate with the sappers and that the new map will mean that taxes are
705   reduced.
HUGH: A worthy enterprise—*opus honestrum!* And Extract B?
LANCEY: 'Ireland is privileged. No such survey is being undertaken in England. So this survey cannot but be received as

---

706 *opus honestrum* an honourable task

proof of the disposition of this government to advance the interests of Ireland.' My sentiments, too.   710
OWEN: This survey demonstrates the government's interest in Ireland and the captain thanks you for listening so attentively to him.
HUGH: Our pleasure, Captain.
LANCEY: Lieutenant Yolland?   715
YOLLAND: I—I—I've nothing to say—really—
OWEN: The captain is the man who actually makes the new map. George's task is to see that the place-names on this map are . . . correct. *(To* YOLLAND.*)* Just a few words— they'd like to hear you. *(To class.)* Don't you want to hear   720
George, too?
MAIRE: Has he anything to say?
YOLLAND: *(To* MAIRE.*)* Sorry—sorry?
OWEN: She says she's dying to hear you.
YOLLAND: *(To* MAIRE.*)* Very kind of you—thank you . . . *(To*   725
class.) I can only say that I feel—I feel very foolish to—to— to be working here and not to speak your language. But I intend to rectify that—with Roland's help—indeed I do.
OWEN: He wants me to teach him Irish!
HUGH: You are doubly welcome, sir.   730
YOLLAND: I think your countryside is—is—is—is very beautiful. I've fallen in love with it already. I hope we're not too— too crude an intrusion on your lives. And I know that I'm going to be happy, very happy, here.
OWEN: He is already a committed Hibernophile—   735
JIMMY: He loves!
OWEN: All right, Jimmy—we know—he loves Baile Beag; and he loves you all.
HUGH: Please . . . May I . . . ?

*(*HUGH *is now drunk. He holds on to the edge of the table.*)

OWEN: Go ahead, Father. *(Hands up for quiet.)* Please—please.   740
HUGH: And we, gentlemen, we in turn are happy to offer you our friendship, our hospitality, and every assistance that you may require. Gentlemen—welcome!

(A few desultory claps. The formalities are over. General conversation. The soldiers meet the locals. MANUS *and* OWEN *meet down stage.*)

OWEN: Lancey's a bloody ramrod but George's all right. How are you anyway?   745
MANUS: What sort of a translation was that, Owen?
OWEN: Did I make a mess of it?
MANUS: You weren't saying what Lancey was saying!
OWEN: 'Uncertainty in meaning is incipient poetry'—who said that?   750
MANUS: There was nothing uncertain about what Lancey said: it's a bloody military operation, Owen! And what's Yolland's function? What's 'incorrect' about the place-names we have here?
OWEN: Nothing at all. They're just going to be standardized.   755
MANUS: You mean changed into English?
OWEN: Where there's ambiguity, they'll be Anglicized.
MANUS: And they call you Roland! They both call you Roland!
OWEN: Shhhhh. Isn't it ridiculous? They seemed to get it wrong from the very beginning—or else they can't pronounce   760
Owen. I was afraid some of you bastards would laugh.

MANUS: Aren't you going to tell them?
OWEN: Yes—yes—soon—soon.
MANUS: But they . . .
765 OWEN: Easy, man, easy. Owen—Roland—what the hell. It's
       only a name. It's the same me, isn't it? Well, isn't it?
MANUS: Indeed it is. It's the same Owen.
OWEN: And the same Manus. And in a way we complement
       each other. (*He punches* MANUS *lightly, playfully and turns to*
770   *join the others. As he goes.*) All right—who has met whom?
       Isn't this a job for the go-between?

(MANUS *watches* OWEN *move confidently across the floor, taking*
MAIRE *by the hand and introducing her to* YOLLAND. HUGH *is try-*
ing to negotiate the steps. JIMMY *is lost in a text.* DOALTY *and* BRID-
GET *are reliving their giggling.* SARAH *is staring at* MANUS.)

ACT TWO

SCENE I

The sappers have already mapped most of the area. YOLLAND'*s official*
task, which OWEN *is now doing, is to take each of the Gaelic names—*
every hill, stream, rock, even every patch of ground which possessed its
own distinctive Irish name—and Anglicize it, either by changing it
into its approximate English sound or by translating it into English
words. For example, a Gaelic name like Cnoc Ban *could become*
Knockban *or—directly translated—*Fair Hill. *These new standard-*
ized names were entered into the Name-Book, and when the new maps
appeared they contained all these new Anglicized names. OWEN'*s offi-*
cial function as translator is to pronounce each name in Irish and then
provide the English translation.

The hot weather continues. It is late afternoon some days later.

Stage right: an improvised clothes-line strung between the shafts of the
cart and a nail in the wall; on it are some shirts and socks.

A large map—one of the new blank maps—is spread out on the floor.
OWEN *is on his hands and knees, consulting it. He is totally engrossed*
in his task which he pursues with great energy and efficiency.

YOLLAND'*s hesitancy has vanished—he is at home here now. He is sit-*
ting on the floor, his long legs stretched out before him, his back resting
against a creel, his eyes closed. His mind is elsewhere. One of the refer-
ence books—a church registry—lies open on his lap.

Around them are various reference books, the Name-Book, a bottle of
poteen, some cups, etc.

OWEN *completes an entry in the Name-Book and returns to the map*
on the floor.

OWEN: Now. Where have we got to? Yes—the point where that
       stream enters the sea—that tiny little beach there. George!
YOLLAND: Yes. I'm listening. What do you call it? Say the Irish
       name again?
5 OWEN: Bun na hAbhann.
YOLLAND: Again.
OWEN: Bun na hAbhann.
YOLLAND: Bun na hAbhann.
OWEN: That's terrible, George.
10 YOLLAND: I know. I'm sorry. Say it again.

OWEN: Bun na hAbbann.
YOLLAND: Bun na hAbbann.
OWEN: That's better. Bun is the Irish word for bottom. And
       Abha means river. So it's literally the mouth of the river.
YOLLAND: Let's leave it alone. There's no English equivalent for   15
       a sound like that.
OWEN: What is it called in the church registry?

(*Only now does* YOLLAND *open his eyes.*)

YOLLAND: Let's see . . . Banowen.
OWEN: That's wrong. (*Consults text.*) The list of freeholders calls
       it Owenmore—that's completely wrong: Owenmore's the   20
       big river at the west end of the parish. (*Another text.*) And
       in the grand jury lists it's called—God!—Binhone!—wher-
       ever they got that. I suppose we could Anglicize it to
       Bunowen; but somehow that's neither fish nor flesh.

(YOLLAND *closes his eyes again.*)

YOLLAND: I give up.   25
OWEN: (*At map.*) Back to first principles. What are we trying
       to do?
YOLLAND: Good question.
OWEN: We are trying to denominate and at the same time de-
       scribe that tiny area of soggy, rocky, sandy ground where   30
       that little stream enters the sea, an area known locally as
       Bun na hAbhann . . . Burnfoot! What about Burnfoot?
YOLLAND: (*Indifferently.*) Good, Roland, Burnfoot's good.
OWEN: George, my name isn't . . .
YOLLAND: B-u-r-n-f-o-o-t?   35
OWEN: Are you happy with that?
YOLLAND: Yes.
OWEN: Burnfoot it is then. (*He makes the entry into the Name-*
       Book.) Bun na hAbhann—B-u-r-n-
YOLLAND: You're becoming very skilled at this.   40
OWEN: We're not moving fast enough.
YOLLAND: (*Opens eyes again.*) Lancey lectured me again last
       night.
OWEN: When does he finish here?
YOLLAND: The sappers are pulling out at the end of the week.   45
       The trouble is, the maps they've completed can't be printed
       without these names. So London screams at Lancey and
       Lancey screams at me. But I wasn't intimidated.

(MANUS *emerges from upstairs and descends.*)

       'I'm sorry, sir,' I said, 'But certain tasks demand their own
       tempo. You cannot rename a whole country overnight.'   50
       Your Irish air has made me bold. (*To* MANUS.) Do you want
       us to leave?
MANUS: Time enough. Class won't begin for another half-hour.
YOLLAND: Sorry—sorry?
OWEN: Can't you speak English?   55

(MANUS *gathers the things off the clothes-line.* OWEN *returns to the*
map.)

OWEN: We now come across that beach . . .
YOLLAND: Tra—that's the Irish for beach. (*To* MANUS.) I'm
       picking up the odd word, Manus.

MANUS: So.

60 OWEN: . . . on past Burnfoot; and there's nothing around here that has any name that I know of until we come down here to the south end, just about here . . . and there should be a ridge of rocks there . . . Have the sappers marked it? They have. Look, George.

65 YOLLAND: Where are we?

OWEN: There.

YOLLAND: I'm lost.

OWEN: Here. And the name of that ridge is Druim Dubh. Put English on that, Lieutenant.

70 YOLLAND: Say it again.

OWEN: Druim Dubh.

YOLLAND: Dubh means black.

OWEN: Yes.

YOLLAND: And Druim means . . . what? a fort?

75 OWEN: We met it yesterday in Druim Luachra.

YOLLAND: A ridge! The Black Ridge! (To MANUS.) You see, Manus?

OWEN: We'll have you fluent at the Irish before the summer's over.

80 YOLLAND: Oh, I wish I were. (To MANUS as he crosses to go back upstairs.) We got a crate of oranges from Dublin today. I'll send some up to you.

MANUS: Thanks. (To OWEN.) Better hide that bottle. Father's just up and he'd be better without it.

85 OWEN: Can't you speak English before your man?

MANUS: Why?

OWEN: Out of courtesy.

MANUS: Doesn't he want to learn Irish? (To YOLLAND.) Don't you want to learn Irish?

90 YOLLAND: Sorry—sorry? I—I—

MANUS: I understand the Lanceys perfectly but people like you puzzle me.

OWEN: Manus, for God's sake!

MANUS: (Still to YOLLAND.) How's the work going?

95 YOLLAND: The work?—the work? Oh, it's—it's staggering along—I think—(To OWEN.)—isn't it? But we'd be lost without Roland.

MANUS: (Leaving.) I'm sure. But there are always the Rolands, aren't there?

(He goes upstairs and exits.)

100 YOLLAND: What was that he said?—something about Lancey, was it?

OWEN: He said we should hide that bottle before Father gets his hands on it.

YOLLAND: Ah.

105 OWEN: He's always trying to protect him.

YOLLAND: Was he lame from birth?

OWEN: An accident when he was a baby: Father fell across his cradle. That's why Manus feels so responsible for him.

YOLLAND: Why doesn't he marry?

110 OWEN: Can't afford to, I suppose.

YOLLAND: Hasn't he a salary?

OWEN: What salary? All he gets is the odd shilling Father throws him—and that's seldom enough. I got out in time, didn't I?

(YOLLAND is pouring a drink.)

Easy with that stuff—it'll hit you suddenly. 115

YOLLAND: I like it.

OWEN: Let's get back to the job. Druim Dubh—what's it called in the jury lists? (Consults texts.)

YOLLAND: Some people here resent us.

OWEN: Dramduff—wrong as usual. 120

YOLLAND: I was passing a little girl yesterday and she spat at me.

OWEN: And it's Drimdoo here. What's it called in the registry?

YOLLAND: Do you know the Donnelly twins?

OWEN: Who? 125

YOLLAND: The Donnelly twins.

OWEN: Yes. Best fishermen about here. What about them?

YOLLAND: Lancey's looking for them.

OWEN: What for?

YOLLAND: He wants them for questioning. 130

OWEN: Probably stolen somebody's nets. Dramduffy! Nobody ever called it Dramduffy. Take your pick of those three.

YOLLAND: My head's addled. Let's take a rest. Do you want a drink?

OWEN: Thanks. Now, every Dubh we've come across we've 135 changed to Duff. So if we're to be consistent, I suppose Druim Dubh has to become Dromduff.

(YOLLAND is now looking out the window.)

You can see the end of the ridge from where you're standing. But D-r-u-m- or D-r-o-m-? (Name-Book.) Do you remember—which did we agree on for Druim Luachra? 140

YOLLAND: That house immediately above where we're camped—

OWEN: Mm?

YOLLAND: The house where Maire lives.

OWEN: Maire? Oh, Maire Chatach. 145

YOLLAND: What does that mean?

OWEN: Curly-haired; the whole family are called the Chatachs. What about it?

YOLLAND: I hear music coming from that house almost every night. 150

OWEN: Why don't you drop in?

YOLLAND: Could I?

OWEN: Why not? We used D-r-o-m then. So we've got to call it D-r-o-m-d-u-f-f—all right?

YOLLAND: Go back up to where the new school is being built 155 and just say the names again for me, would you?

OWEN: That's a good idea. Poolkerry, Ballybeg—

YOLLAND: No, no; as they still are—in your own language.

OWEN: Poll na gCaorach,

(YOLLAND repeats the names silently after him.)

Baile Beag, Ceann Balor, Lis Maol, Machaire Buidhe, Baile 160 na gGall, Carraig na Ri, Mullach Dearg—

YOLLAND: Do you think I could live here?

OWEN: What are you talking about?

YOLLAND: Settle down here—live here.

OWEN: Come on, George. 165

YOLLAND: I mean it.

OWEN: Live on what? Potatoes? Buttermilk?

YOLLAND: It's really heavenly.

OWEN: For God's sake! The first hot summer in fifty years and
170   you think it's Eden. Don't be such a bloody romantic. You
      wouldn't survive a mild winter here.
YOLLAND: Do you think not? Maybe you're right.

(DOALTY *enters in a rush.*)

DOALTY: Hi, boys, is Manus about?
OWEN: He's upstairs. Give him a shout.
175   DOALTY: Manus! The cattle's going mad in that heat—Cripes,
      running wild all over the place. (*To* YOLLAND.) How are you
      doing, skipper?

(MANUS *appears.*)

YOLLAND: Thank you for—I—I'm very grateful to you for—
DOALTY: Wasting your time. I don't know a word you're saying.
180   Hi, Manus, there's two bucks down the road there asking
      for you.
MANUS: (*Descending.*) Who are they?
DOALTY: Never clapped eyes on them. They want to talk to you.
MANUS: What about?
185   DOALTY: They wouldn't say. Come on. The bloody beasts'll end
      up in Loch an Iubhair if they're not capped. Good luck, boys!

(DOALTY *rushes off.* MANUS *follows him.*)

OWEN: Good luck! What were you thanking Doalty for?
YOLLAND: I was washing outside my tent this morning and he
      was passing with a scythe across his shoulder and he came up
190   to me and pointed to the long grass and then cut a pathway
      round my tent and from the tent down to the road—so that
      my feet won't get wet with the dew. Wasn't that kind of
      him? And I have no words to thank him . . . I suppose you're
      right: I suppose I couldn't live here . . . Just before Doalty
195   came up to me this morning, I was thinking that at that mo-
      ment I might have been in Bombay instead of Ballybeg. You
      see, my father was at his wits end with me and finally he got
      me a job with the East India Company—some kind of a
      clerkship. That was ten, eleven months ago. So I set off for
200   London. Unfortunately I—I—I missed the boat. Literally.
      And since I couldn't face Father and hadn't enough money
      to hang about until the next sailing, I joined the army. And
      they stuck me into the Engineers and posted me to Dublin.
      And Dublin sent me here. And while I was washing this
205   morning and looking across the Tra Bhan, I was thinking
      how very, very lucky I am to be here and not in Bombay.
OWEN: Do you believe in fate?
YOLLAND: Lancey's so like my father. I was watching him last
      night. He met every group of sappers as they reported in.
210   He checked the field kitchens. He examined the horses. He
      inspected every single report—even examining the texture
      of the paper and commenting on the neatness of the hand-
      writing. The perfect colonial servant: not only must the job
      be done—it must be done with excellence. Father has that
215   drive, too; that dedication; that indefatigable energy. He
      builds roads—hopping from one end of the Empire to the
      other. Can't sit still for five minutes. He says himself the
      longest time he ever sat still was the night before Waterloo
      when they were waiting for Wellington to make up his
220   mind to attack.

OWEN: What age is he?
YOLLAND: Born in 1789—the very day the Bastille fell. I've of-
      ten thought maybe that gave his whole life its character. Do
      you think it could? He inherited a new world the day he
      was born—The Year One. Ancient time was at an end. The   225
      world had cast off its old skin. There were no longer any
      frontiers to man's potential. Possibilities were endless and
      exciting. He still believes that. The Apocalypse is just
      about to happen . . . I'm afraid I'm a great disappointment
      to him. I've neither his energy, nor his coherence, nor his   230
      belief. Do I believe in fate? The day I arrived in Ballybeg—
      no, Baile Beag—the moment you brought me in here, I had
      a curious sensation. It's difficult to describe. It was a mo-
      mentary sense of discovery; no—not quite a sense of dis-
      covery—a sense of recognition, of confirmation of some-   235
      thing I half knew instinctively; as if I had stepped . . .
OWEN: Back into ancient time?
YOLLAND: No, no. It wasn't an awareness of *direction* being
      changed but of experience being of a totally different order.
      I had moved into a consciousness that wasn't striving nor   240
      agitated, but at its ease and with its own conviction and as-
      surance. And when I heard Jimmy Jack and your father
      swapping stories about Apollo and Cuchulainn and Paris
      and Ferdia—as if they lived down the road—it was then
      that I thought—I knew—perhaps I could live here . . .   245
      (*Now embarrassed.*) Where's the pot-een?
OWEN: Poteen.
YOLLAND: Poteen—poteen—poteen. Even if I did speak Irish
      I'd always be an outsider here, wouldn't I? I may learn the
      password but the language of the tribe will always elude   250
      me, won't it? The private core will always be . . . hermetic,
      won't it?
OWEN: You can learn to decode us.

(HUGH *emerges from upstairs and descends. He is dressed for the road.
Today he is physically and mentally jaunty and alert—almost self-
consciously jaunty and alert. Indeed, as the scene progresses, one has the
sense that he is deliberately parodying himself. The moment* HUGH *gets
to the bottom of the steps* YOLLAND *leaps respectfully to his feet.*)

HUGH: (*As he descends.*)
      Quantumvis cursum longum fessumque moratur   255
      Sol, sacro tandem carmine vesper adest.
      I dabble in verse, Lieutenant, after the style of Ovid. (*To*
      OWEN.) A drop of that to fortify me.
YOLLAND: You'll have to translate it for me.
HUGH: Let's see—   260
      No matter how long the sun may linger on his long and
          weary journey
      At length evening comes with its sacred song.
YOLLAND: Very nice, sir.
HUGH: English succeeds in making it sound . . . plebeian.
OWEN: Where are you off to, Father?   265

II.i. 255–56 *Quantumvis . . . adest* no matter how long the sun
delays on his long weary course / At length evening comes with its
sacred song

HUGH: An *expeditio* with three purposes. Purpose A: to acquire a testimonial from our parish priest—(*To* YOLLAND.) a worthy man but barely literate; and since he'll ask me to write it myself, how in all modesty can I do myself justice? (*To* OWEN.) Where did this *{drink}* come from?

270 OWEN: Anna na mBreag's.

HUGH: (*To* YOLLAND.) In that case address yourself to it with circumspection. (*And* HUGH *instantly tosses the drink back in one gulp and grimaces.*) Aaaaaaagh! (*Holds out his glass for a refill.*) Anna na mBreag means Anna of the Lies. And Purpose

275 B: to talk to the builders of the new school about the kind of living accommodation I will require there. I have lived too long like a journeyman tailor.

YOLLAND: Some years ago we lived fairly close to a poet—well,

280 about three miles away.

HUGH: His name?

YOLLAND: Wordsworth—William Wordsworth.

HUGH: Did he speak of me to you?

YOLLAND: Actually I never talked to him. I just saw him out

285 walking—in the distance.

HUGH: Wordsworth? . . . No. I'm afraid we're not familiar with your literature, Lieutenant. We feel closer to the warm Mediterranean. We tend to overlook your island.

YOLLAND: I'm learning to speak Irish, sir.

290 HUGH: Good.

YOLLAND: Roland's teaching me.

HUGH: Splendid.

YOLLAND: I mean—I feel so cut off from the people here. And I was trying to explain a few minutes ago how remarkable

295 a community this is. To meet people like yourself and Jimmy Jack who actually converse in Greek and Latin. And your place names—what was the one we came across this morning?—Termon, from Terminus, the god of boundaries. It—it—it's really astonishing.

300 HUGH: We like to think we endure around truths immemorially posited.

YOLLAND: And your Gaelic literature—you're a poet yourself—

HUGH: Only in Latin, I'm afraid.

YOLLAND: I understand it's enormously rich and ornate.

305 HUGH: Indeed, Lieutenant. A rich language. A rich literature. You'll find, sir, that certain cultures expend on their vocabularies and syntax acquisitive energies and ostentations entirely lacking in their material lives. I suppose you could call us a spiritual people.

310 OWEN: (*Not unkindly; more out of embarrassment before* YOLLAND.) Will you stop that nonsense, Father.

HUGH: Nonsense? What nonsense?

OWEN: Do you know where the priest lives?

HUGH: At Lis na Muc, over near . . .

315 OWEN: No, he doesn't. Lis na Muc, the Fort of the Pigs, has become Swinefort. (*Now turning the pages of the Name-Book—a page per name.*) And to get to Swinefort you pass through Greencastle and Fair Head and Strandhill and Gort and Whiteplains. And the new school isn't at Poll na gCao-

320 rach—it's at Sheepsrock. Will you be able to find your way?

---

266 *expeditio* an expedition

(HUGH *pours himself another drink. Then:—*)

HUGH: Yes, it is a rich language, Lieutenant, full of the mythologies of fantasy and hope and self-deception—a syntax opulent with tomorrows. It is our response to mud cabins and a diet of potatoes; and our only method of replying 325 to . . . inevitabilities. (*To* OWEN.) Can you give me the loan of half-a-crown? I'll repay you out of the subscriptions I'm collecting for the publication of my new book. (*To* YOLLAND.) It is entitled: 'The Pentaglot Preceptor or Elementary Institute of the English, Greek, Hebrew, Latin and 330 Irish Languages; Particularly Calculated for the Instruction of Such Ladies and Gentlemen as may Wish to Learn without the Help of a Master'.

YOLLAND: (*Laughs.*) That's a wonderful title!

HUGH: Between ourselves—the best part of the enterprise. Nor 335 do I, in fact, speak Hebrew. And that last phrase—'without the Help of a Master'—that was written before the new national school was thrust upon me—do you think I ought to drop it now? After all you don't dispose of the cow just because it has produced a magnificent calf, do you?   340

YOLLAND: You certainly do not.

HUGH: The phrase goes. And I'm interrupting work of moment. (*He goes to the door and stops there.*) To return briefly to that other matter, Lieutenant. I understand your sense of exclusion, of being cut off from a life here; and I trust you 345 will find access to us with my son's help. But remember that words are signals, counters. They are not immortal. And it can happen—to use an image you'll understand—it can happen that a civilization can be imprisoned in a linguistic contour which no longer matches the landscape 350 of . . . fact. Gentlemen. (*He leaves.*)

OWEN: 'An *expeditio* with three purposes': the children laugh at him: he always promises three points and he never gets beyond A and B.

YOLLAND: He's an astute man.   355

OWEN: He's bloody pompous.

YOLLAND: But so astute.

OWEN: And he drinks too much. Is it astute not to be able to adjust for survival? Enduring around truths immemorially posited—hah!   360

YOLLAND: He knows what's happening.

OWEN: What is happening?

YOLLAND: I'm not sure. But I'm concerned about my part in it. It's an eviction of sorts.

OWEN: We're making a six-inch map of the country. Is there 365 something sinister in that?

YOLLAND: Not in—

OWEN: And we're taking place-names that are riddled with confusion and—

YOLLAND: Who's confused? Are the people confused?   370

OWEN: —and we're standardizing those names as accurately and as sensitively as we can.

YOLLAND: Something is being eroded.

OWEN: Back to the romance again. All right! Fine! Fine! Look where we've got to. (*He drops on his hands and knees and stabs* 375 *a finger at the map.*) We've come to this crossroads. Come here and look at it, man! Look at it! And we call that crossroads Tobair Vree. And why do we call it Tobair Vree? I'll tell you why. Tobair means a well. But what does Vree

380 mean? It's a corruption of Brian—(*Gaelic pronunciation.*) Brian—an erosion of Tobair Bhriain. Because a hundred-and-fifty years ago there used to be a well there, not at the crossroads, mind you—that would be too simple—but in a field close to the crossroads. And an old man called Brian,
385 whose face was disfigured by an enormous growth, got it into his head that the water in that well was blessed; and every day for seven months he went there and bathed his face in it. But the growth didn't go away; and one morning Brian was found drowned in that well. And ever since that
390 crossroads is known as Tobair Vree—even though that well has long since dried up. I know the story because my grand-father told it to me. But ask Doalty—or Maire—or Bridget—even my father—even Manus—why it's called Tobair Vree; and do you think they'll know? I know they don't
395 know. So the question I put to you, Lieutenant, is this: what do we do with a name like that? Do we scrap Tobair Vree altogether and call it—what?—The Cross? Crossroads? Or do we keep piety with a man long dead, long forgotten, his name 'eroded' beyond recognition, whose trivial little story
400 nobody in the parish remembers?

YOLLAND: Except you.

OWEN: I've left here.

YOLLAND: You remember it.

OWEN: I'm asking you: what do we write in the Name-Book?

405 YOLLAND: Tobair Vree.

OWEN: Even though the well is a hundred yards from the ac-tual crossroads—and there's no well anyway—and what the hell does Vree mean?

YOLLAND: Tobair Vree.

410 OWEN: That's what you want?

YOLLAND: Yes.

OWEN: You're certain?

YOLLAND: Yes.

OWEN: Fine. Fine. That's what you'll get.

415 YOLLAND: That's what you want, too, Roland.

(*Pause.*)

OWEN: (*Explodes.*) George! For God's sake! *My name is not Roland!*

YOLLAND: What?

OWEN: (*Softly.*) My name is Owen.

(*Pause.*)

YOLLAND: Not Roland?

420 OWEN: Owen.

YOLLAND: You mean to say—?

OWEN: Owen.

YOLLAND: But I've been—

OWEN: O-w-e-n.

425 YOLLAND: Where did Roland come from?

OWEN: I don't know.

YOLLAND: It was never Roland?

OWEN: Never.

YOLLAND: O my God!

(*Pause. They stare at one another. Then the absurdity of the situation strikes them suddenly. They explode with laughter.* OWEN *pours drinks. As they roll about, their lines overlap.*)

YOLLAND: Why didn't you tell me?   430

OWEN: Do I look like a Roland?

YOLLAND: Spell Owen again.

OWEN: I was getting fond of Roland.

YOLLAND: O my God!

OWEN: O-w-e-n.   435

YOLLAND: What'll we write—

OWEN: —in the Name-Book?!

YOLLAND: R-o-w-e-n!

OWEN: Or what about Ol-

YOLLAND: Ol-what?   440

OWEN: Oland!

(*And again they explode.* MANUS *enters. He is very elated.*)

MANUS: What's the celebration?

OWEN: A christening!

YOLLAND: A baptism!

OWEN: A hundred christenings!   445

YOLLAND: A thousand baptisms! Welcome to Eden!

OWEN: Eden's right! We name a thing and—bang!—it leaps into existence!

YOLLAND: Each name a perfect equation with its roots.

OWEN: A perfect congruence with its reality. (*To* MANUS.) Take   450 a drink.

YOLLAND: Poteen—beautiful.

OWEN: Lying Anna's poteen.

YOLLAND: Anna na mBreag's poteen.

OWEN: Excellent, George.   455

YOLLAND: I'll decode you yet.

OWEN: (*Offers drink.*) Manus?

MANUS: Not if that's what it does to you.

OWEN: You're right. Steady—steady—sober up—sober up.

YOLLAND: Sober as a judge, Owen.   460

(MANUS *moves beside* OWEN.)

MANUS: I've got good news! Where's Father?

OWEN: He's gone out. What's the good news?

MANUS: I've been offered a job.

OWEN: Where? (*Now aware of* YOLLAND.) Come on, man—speak in English.   465

MANUS: For the benefit of the colonist?

OWEN: He's a decent man.

MANUS: Aren't they all at some level?

OWEN: Please.

(MANUS *shrugs.*)

He's been offered a job.   470

YOLLAND: Where?

OWEN: Well—tell us!

MANUS: I've just had a meeting with two men from Inis Mead-hon. They want me to go there and start a hedge-school. They're giving me a free house, free turf, and free milk; a   475 rood of standing corn; twelve drills of potatoes; and—

(*He stops.*)

OWEN: And what?

MANUS: A salary of £42 a year!

OWEN: Manus, that's wonderful!

480 MANUS: You're talking to a man of substance.

OWEN: I'm delighted.

YOLLAND: Where's Inis Meadhon?

OWEN: An island south of here. And they came looking for you?

485 MANUS: Well, I mean to say . . .

(OWEN punches MANUS.)

OWEN: Aaaaagh! This calls for a real celebration.

YOLLAND: Congratulations.

MANUS: Thank you.

OWEN: Where are you, Anna?

490 YOLLAND: When do you start?

MANUS: Next Monday.

OWEN: We'll stay with you when we're there. *(To YOLLAND.)* How long will it be before we reach Inis Meadhon?

YOLLAND: How far south is it?

495 MANUS: About fifty miles.

YOLLAND: Could we make it by December?

OWEN: We'll have Christmas together. *(Sings.)* 'Christmas Day on Inis Meadhon . . .'

YOLLAND: *(Toast.)* I hope you're very content there, Manus.

500 MANUS: Thank you.

(YOLLAND holds out his hand. MANUS takes it. They shake warmly.)

OWEN: *(Toast.)* Manus.

MANUS: *(Toast.)* To Inis Meadhon.

(He drinks quickly and turns to leave.)

OWEN: Hold on—hold on—refills coming up.

MANUS: I've got to go.

505 OWEN: Come on, man; this is an occasion. Where are you rushing to?

MANUS: I've got to tell Maire.

(MAIRE enters with her can of milk.)

MAIRE: You've got to tell Maire what?

OWEN: He's got a job!

510 MAIRE: Manus?

OWEN: He's been invited to start a hedge-school in Inis Meadhon.

MAIRE: Where?

MANUS: Inis Meadhon—the island! They're giving me £42 a

515 year and . . .

OWEN: A house, fuel, milk, potatoes, corn, pupils, what-not!

MANUS: I start on Monday.

OWEN: You'll take a drink. Isn't it great?

MANUS: I want to talk to you for—

520 MAIRE: There's your milk. I need the can back.

(MANUS takes the can and runs up the steps.)

MANUS: *(As he goes.)* How will you like living on an island?

OWEN: You know George, don't you?

MAIRE: We wave to each other across the fields.

YOLLAND: Sorry-sorry?

525 OWEN: She says you wave to each other across the fields.

YOLLAND: Yes, we do; oh, yes; indeed we do.

MAIRE: What's he saying?

OWEN: He says you wave to each other across the fields.

MAIRE: That's right. So we do.

YOLLAND: What's she saying?

530 OWEN: Nothing—nothing—nothing. *(To MAIRE.)* What's the news?

(MAIRE moves away, touching the text books with her toe.)

MAIRE: Not a thing. You're busy, the two of you.

OWEN: We think we are.

MAIRE: I hear the Fiddler O'Shea's about. There's some talk of 535 a dance tomorrow night.

OWEN: Where will it be?

MAIRE: Maybe over the road. Maybe at Tobair Vree.

YOLLAND: Tobair Vree!

MAIRE: Yes. 540

YOLLAND: Tobair Vree! Tobair Vree!

MAIRE: Does he know what I'm saying?

OWEN: Not a word.

MAIRE: Tell him then.

OWEN: Tell him what? 545

MAIRE: About the dance.

OWEN: Maire says there may be a dance tomorrow night.

YOLLAND: *(To OWEN.)* Yes? May I come? *(To MAIRE.)* Would anybody object if I came?

MAIRE: *(To OWEN.)* What's he saying? 550

OWEN: *(To YOLLAND.)* Who would object?

MAIRE: *(To OWEN.)* Did you tell him?

YOLLAND: *(To MAIRE.)* Sorry-sorry?

OWEN: *(To MAIRE.)* He says may he come?

YOLLAND: *(To OWEN.)* What does she say? 555

OWEN: *(To YOLLAND.)* She says—

YOLLAND: *(To MAIRE.)* What-what?

MAIRE: *(To OWEN.)* Well?

YOLLAND: *(To OWEN.)* Sorry-sorry? 560

OWEN: *(To YOLLAND.)* Will you go?

YOLLAND: *(To MAIRE.)* Yes, yes, if I may.

MAIRE: *(To OWEN.)* What does he say?

YOLLAND: *(To OWEN.)* What is she saying?

OWEN: Oh for God's sake! *(To MANUS who is descending with the 565 empty can.)* You take on this job, Manus.

MANUS: I'll walk you up to the house. Is your mother at home? I want to talk to her.

MAIRE: What's the rush? *(To OWEN.)* Didn't you offer me a drink?

OWEN: Will you risk Anna na mBreag? 570

MAIRE: Why not.

(YOLLAND is suddenly intoxicated. He leaps up on a stool, raises his glass and shouts.)

YOLLAND: Anna na mBreag! Baile Beag! Inis Meadhon! Bombay! Tobair Vree! Eden! And poteen—correct, Owen?

OWEN: Perfect.

YOLLAND: And bloody marvellous stuff it is, too. I love it! 575 Bloody, bloody, bloody marvellous!

(Simultaneously with his final 'bloody marvellous' bring up very loud the introductory music of the reel. Then immediately go to black. Retain the music throughout the very brief interval.)

SCENE II

The following night.

This scene may be played in the schoolroom, but it would be preferable to lose—by lighting—as much of the schoolroom as possible, and to play the scene down front in a vaguely 'outside' area.

The music rises to a crescendo. Then in the distance we hear MAIRE *and* YOLLAND *approach—laughing and running. They run on, hand-in-hand. They have just left the dance. Fade the music to distant background. Then after a time it is lost and replaced by guitar music.* MAIRE *and* YOLLAND *are now down front, still holding hands and excited by their sudden and impetuous escape from the dance.*

MAIRE: O my God, that leap across the ditch nearly killed me.
YOLLAND: I could scarcely keep up with you.
MAIRE: Wait till I get my breath back.
YOLLAND: We must have looked as if we were being chased.

(They now realize they are alone and holding hands—the beginnings of embarrassment. The hands disengage. They begin to drift apart. Pause.)

5 MAIRE: Manus'll wonder where I've got to.
YOLLAND: I wonder did anyone notice us leave.

(Pause. Slightly further apart.)

MAIRE: The grass must be wet. My feet are soaking.
YOLLAND: Your feet must be wet. The grass is soaking.

(Another pause. Another few paces apart. They are now a long distance from one another.)

YOLLAND: *(Indicating himself.)* George.

(MAIRE nods: Yes-yes. Then:—)

10 MAIRE: Lieutenant George.
YOLLAND: Don't call me that. I never think of myself as Lieutenant.
MAIRE: What-what?
YOLLAND: Sorry-sorry? *(He points to himself again.)* George.

(MAIRE nods: Yes-yes. Then points to herself.)

15 MAIRE: Maire.
YOLLAND: Yes, I know you're Maire. Of course I know you're Maire. I mean I've been watching you night and day for the past—
MAIRE: *(Eagerly.)* What-what?
20 YOLLAND: *(Points.)* Maire. *(Points.)* George. *(Points both.)* Maire and George.

(MAIRE nods: Yes-yes-yes.)

I—I—I—
MAIRE: Say anything at all. I love the sound of your speech.
YOLLAND: *(Eagerly.)* Sorry-sorry?

(In acute frustration he looks around, hoping for some inspiration that will provide him with communicative means. Now he has a thought:

he tries raising his voice and articulating in a staccato style and with equal and absurd emphasis on each word.)

Every-morning-I-see-you-feeding-brown-hens-and-giving- 25
meal-to-black-calf—*(The futility of it.)*—Oh my God.

(MAIRE smiles. She moves towards him. She will try to communicate in Latin.)

MAIRE: *Tu es centurio in—in—in exercitu Britannico—*
YOLLAND: Yes-yes? Go on—go on—say anything at all—I love the sound of your speech.
MAIRE: —*et es in castris quae—quae—quae sunt in agro—(The fu-* 30
tility of it.)—O my God. *(YOLLAND smiles. He moves towards her. Now for her English words.)* George—water.
YOLLAND: 'Water'? Water! Oh yes—water—water—very good—water—good—good.
MAIRE: Fire. 35
YOLLAND: Fire—indeed—wonderful—fire, fire, fire—splendid—splendid!
MAIRE: Ah . . . ah . . .
YOLLAND: Yes? Go on.
MAIRE: Earth. 40
YOLLAND: 'Earth'?
MAIRE: Earth. Earth. *(YOLLAND still does not understand.* MAIRE *stoops down and picks up a handful of clay. Holding it out.)* Earth.
YOLLAND: Earth! Of course—earth! Earth. Earth. Good Lord, 45
Maire, your English is perfect!
MAIRE: *(Eagerly.)* What-what?
YOLLAND: Perfect English. English perfect.
MAIRE: George—
YOLLAND: That's beautiful—oh, that's really beautiful. 50
MAIRE: George—
YOLLAND: Say it again—say it again—
MAIRE: Shhh. *(She holds her hand up for silence—she is trying to remember her one line of English. Now she remembers it and she delivers the line as if English were her language—easily, fluidly,* 55
conversationally.) George, 'In Norfolk we besport ourselves around the maypoll.'
YOLLAND: Good God, do you? That's where my mother comes from—Norfolk. Norwich actually. Not exactly Norwich town but a small village called Little Walsingham close be- 60
side it. But in our own village of Winfarthing we have a maypole too and every year on the first of May—*(He stops abruptly, only now realizing. He stares at her. She in turn misunderstands his excitement.)*
MAIRE: *(To herself.)* Mother of God, my Aunt Mary wouldn't 65
have taught me something dirty, would she?

(Pause. YOLLAND *extends his hand to* MAIRE. *She turns away from him and moves slowly across the stage.)*

YOLLAND: Maire.

II.ii. 27 *Tu . . . Britannico* you are a centurion in the British Army   30 *et . . . agro* and you are in the camp in the field

(She still moves away.)

    Maire Chatach.

(She still moves away.)

70   Bun na hAbhann? *(He says the name softly, almost privately, very tentatively, as if he were searching for a sound she might respond to. He tries again.)* Druim Dubh?

(MAIRE stops. She is listening. YOLLAND is encouraged.)

    Poll na gCaorach. Lis Maol.

(MAIRE turns towards him.)

    Lis na nGall.
MAIRE: Lis na nGradh.

(They are now facing each other and begin moving—almost imperceptibly—towards one another.)

75   MAIRE: Carraig an Phoill.
YOLLAND: Carraig na Ri. Loch na nEan.
MAIRE: Loch an Iubhair. Machaire Buidhe.
YOLLAND: Machaire Mor. Cnoc na Mona.
MAIRE: Cnoc na nGabhar.
80   YOLLAND: Mullach.
MAIRE: Port.
YOLLAND: Tor.
MAIRE: Lag.

(She holds out her hands to YOLLAND. He takes them. Each now speaks almost to himself/herself.)

YOLLAND: I wish to God you could understand me.
85   MAIRE: Soft hands; a gentleman's hands.
YOLLAND: Because if you could understand me I could tell you how I spend my days either thinking of you or gazing up at your house in the hope that you'll appear even for a second.
MAIRE: Every evening you walk by yourself along the Tra Bhan
90   and every morning you wash yourself in front of your tent.
YOLLAND: I would tell you how beautiful you are, curly-headed Maire. I would so like to tell you how beautiful you are.
MAIRE: Your arms are long and thin and the skin on your shoulders is very white.
95   YOLLAND: I would tell you . . .
MAIRE: Don't stop—I know what you're saying.
YOLLAND: I would tell you how I want to be here—to live here—always—with you—always, always.
MAIRE: 'Always'? What is that word—'always'?
100 YOLLAND: Yes-yes; always.
MAIRE: You're trembling.
YOLLAND: Yes, I'm trembling because of you.
MAIRE: I'm trembling, too.

(She holds his face in her hand.)

YOLLAND: I've made up my mind . . .
105 MAIRE: Shhhh.
YOLLAND: I'm not going to leave here . . .
MAIRE: Shhhh—listen to me. I want you, too, soldier.

YOLLAND: Don't stop—I know what you're saying.
MAIRE: I want to live with you—anywhere—anywhere at all—always—always.   110
YOLLAND: 'Always'? What is that word—'always'?
MAIRE: Take me away with you, George.

(Pause. Suddenly they kiss. SARAH enters. She sees them. She stands shocked, staring at them. Her mouth works. Then almost to herself.)

SARAH: Manus . . . Manus!

(SARAH runs off. Music to crescendo.)

————— **ACT THREE** —————

The following evening. It is raining.

SARAH *and* OWEN *alone in the schoolroom.* SARAH, *more waif-like than ever, is sitting very still on a stool, an open book across her knee. She is pretending to read but her eyes keep going up to the room upstairs.* OWEN *is working on the floor as before, surrounded by his reference books, map, Name-Book, etc. But he has neither concentration nor interest; and like* SARAH *he glances up at the upstairs room.*

After a few seconds MANUS *emerges and descends, carrying a large paper bag which already contains his clothes. His movements are determined and urgent. He moves around the classroom, picking up books, examining each title carefully, and choosing about six of them which he puts into his bag. As he selects these books:—*

OWEN: You know that old limekiln beyond Con Connie Tim's pub, the place we call The Murren?—do you know why it's called The Murren?

(MANUS does not answer.)

I've only just discovered: it's a corruption of Saint Muranus. It seems Saint Muranus had a monastery somewhere about   5
there at the beginning of the seventh century. And over the years the name became shortened to the Murren. Very unattractive name, isn't it? I think we should go back to the original—Saint Muranus. What do you think? The original's Saint Muranus. Don't you think we should go back to that?   10

(No response. OWEN *begins writing the name into the Name-Book.* MANUS *is now rooting about among the forgotten implements for a piece of rope. He finds a piece. He begins to tie the mouth of the flimsy, overloaded bag—and it bursts, the contents spilling out on the floor.)*

MANUS: Bloody, bloody, bloody hell!

(His voice breaks in exasperation: he is about to cry. OWEN *leaps to his feet.)*

OWEN: Hold on. I've a bag upstairs.

(He runs upstairs. SARAH *waits until* OWEN *is off. Then:—)*

SARAH: Manus . . . Manus, I . . .

*(MANUS *hears* SARAH *but makes no acknowledgement. He gathers up his belongings.* OWEN *reappears with the bag he had on his arrival.)*

OWEN: Take this one—I'm finished with it anyway. And it's supposed to keep out the rain.   15

(MANUS *transfers his few belongings.* OWEN *drifts back to his task. The packing is now complete.*)

MANUS: You'll be here for a while? For a week or two anyhow?
OWEN: Yes.
MANUS: You're not leaving with the army?
OWEN: I haven't made up my mind. Why?
20 MANUS: Those Inis Meadhon men will be back to see why I haven't turned up. Tell them—tell them I'll write to them as soon as I can. Tell them I still want the job but that it might be three or four months before I'm free to go.
OWEN: You're being damned stupid, Manus.
25 MANUS: Will you do that for me?
OWEN: Clear out now and Lancey'll think you're involved somehow.
MANUS: Will you do that for me?
OWEN: Wait a couple of days even. You know George—he's a
30 bloody romantic—maybe he's gone out to one of the islands and he'll suddenly reappear tomorrow morning. Or maybe the search party'll find him this evening lying drunk somewhere in the sandhills. You've seen him drinking that poteen—doesn't know how to handle it. Had he drink on him
35 last night at the dance?
MANUS: I had a stone in my hand when I went out looking for him—I was going to fell him. The lame scholar turned violent.
OWEN: Did anybody see you?
40 MANUS: (*Again close to tears.*) But when I saw him standing there at the side of the road—smiling—and her face buried in his shoulder—I couldn't even go close to them. I just shouted something stupid—something like, 'You're a bastard, Yolland.' If I'd even said it in English . . . 'cos he kept saying
45 'Sorry-sorry?' The wrong gesture in the wrong language.
OWEN: And you didn't see him again?
MANUS: 'Sorry?'
OWEN: Before you leave tell Lancey that—just to clear yourself.
MANUS: What have I to say to Lancey? You'll give that message
50 to the islandmen?
OWEN: I'm warning you: run away now and you're bound to be—
MANUS: (*To* SARAH.) Will you give that message to the Inis Meadhon men?
55 SARAH: I will.

(MANUS *picks up an old sack and throws it across his shoulders.*)

OWEN: Have you any idea where you're going?
MANUS: Mayo, maybe. I remember Mother saying she had cousins somewhere away out in the Erris Peninsula. (*He picks up his bag.*) Tell Father I took only the Virgil and the
60 Caesar and the Aeschylus because they're mine anyway—I bought them with the money I got for that pet lamb I reared—do you remember that pet lamb? And tell him that Nora Dan never returned the dictionary and that she still owes him two-and-six for last quarter's reading—he always
65 forgets those things.
OWEN: Yes.
MANUS: And his good shirt's ironed and hanging up in the press and his clean socks are in the butter-box under the bed.
OWEN: All right.

MANUS: And tell him I'll write.   70
OWEN: If Maire asks where you've gone . . . ?
MANUS: He'll need only half the amount of milk now, won't he? Even less than half—he usually takes his tea black.(*Pause.*) And when he comes in at night—you'll hear him; he makes a lot of noise—I usually come down and give him a hand 75 up. Those stairs are dangerous without a banister. Maybe before you leave you'd get Big Ned Frank to put up some sort of a handrail. (*Pause.*) And if you can bake, he's very fond of soda bread.
OWEN: I can give you money. I'm wealthy. Do you know what 80 they pay me? Two shillings a day for this—this—this—

(MANUS *rejects the offer by holding out his hand.*)

Goodbye, Manus.

(MANUS *and* OWEN *shake hands. Then* MANUS *picks up his bag briskly and goes towards the door. He stops a few paces beyond* SARAH, *turns, comes back to her. He addresses her as he did in Act One but now without warmth or concern for her.*)

MANUS: What is your name? (*Pause.*) Come on. What is your name?
SARAH: My name is Sarah.   85
MANUS: Just Sarah? Sarah what? (*Pause.*) Well?
SARAH: Sarah Johnny Sally.
MANUS: And where do you live? Come on.
SARAH: I live in Bun na hAbhann.

(*She is now crying quietly.*)

MANUS: Very good, Sarah Johnny Sally. There's nothing to stop 90 you now—nothing in the wide world. (*Pause. He looks down at her.*) It's all right—it's all right—you did no harm—you did no harm at all.

(*He stoops over her and kisses the top of her head—as if in absolution. Then briskly to the door and off.*)

OWEN: Good luck, Manus!
SARAH: (*Quietly.*) I'm sorry . . . I'm sorry . . . I'm so sorry, 95 Manus . . .

(OWEN *tries to work but cannot concentrate. He begins folding up the map. As he does:—*)

OWEN: Is there a class this evening?

(SARAH *nods: Yes.*)

I suppose Father knows. Where is he anyhow?

(SARAH *points.*)

Where?

(SARAH *mimes rocking a baby.*)

I don't understand—where?   100

(SARAH *repeats the mime and wipes away tears.* OWEN *is still puzzled.*)

It doesn't matter. He'll probably turn up.

(BRIDGET and DOALTY enter, sacks over their heads against the rain. They are self-consciously noisier, more ebullient, more garrulous than ever—brimming over with excitement and gossip and brio.)

DOALTY: You're missing the crack, boys! Cripes, you're missing the crack! Fifty more soldiers arrived an hour ago!

105 BRIDGET: And they're spread out in a big line from Sean Neal's over to Lag and they're moving straight across the fields towards Cnoc na nGabhar!

DOALTY: Prodding every inch of the ground in front of them with their bayonets and scattering animals and hens in all directions!

110 BRIDGET: And tumbling everything before them—fences, ditches, haystacks, turf-stacks!

DOALTY: They came to Barney Petey's field of corn—straight through it be God as if it was heather!

BRIDGET: Not a blade of it left standing!

115 DOALTY: And Barney Petey just out of his bed and running after them in his drawers: 'You hoors you! Get out of my corn, you hoors you!'

BRIDGET: First time he ever ran in his life.

DOALTY: Too lazy, the wee get, to cut it when the weather was

120 good.

(SARAH begins putting out the seats.)

BRIDGET: Tell them about Big Hughie.

DOALTY: Cripes, if you'd seen your aul fella, Owen.

BRIDGET: They were all inside in Anna na mBreag's pub—all the crowd from the wake—

125 DOALTY: And they hear the commotion and they all come out to the street—

BRIDGET: Your father in front; the Infant Prodigy footless behind him!

DOALTY: And your aul fella, he sees the army stretched across

130 the countryside—

BRIDGET: O my God!

DOALTY: And Cripes he starts roaring at them!

BRIDGET: 'Visigoths! Huns! Vandals!'

DOALTY: 'Ignari! Stulti! Rustici!'

135 BRIDGET: And wee Jimmy Jack jumping up and down and shouting, 'Thermopylae! Thermopylae!'

DOALTY: You never saw crack like it in your life, boys. Come away on out with me, Sarah, and you'll see it all.

BRIDGET: Big Hughie's fit to take no class. Is Manus about?

140 OWEN: Manus is gone.

BRIDGET: Gone where?

OWEN: He's left—gone away.

DOALTY: Where to?

OWEN: He doesn't know. Mayo, maybe.

145 DOALTY: What's on in Mayo?

OWEN: *(To BRIDGET.)* Did you see George and Maire Chatach leave the dance last night?

BRIDGET: We did. Didn't we, Doalty?

OWEN: Did you see Manus following them out?

150 BRIDGET: I didn't see him going out but I saw him coming in by himself later.

OWEN: Did George and Maire come back to the dance?

BRIDGET: No.

OWEN: Did you see them again?

BRIDGET: He left her home. We passed them going up the back   155
road—didn't we, Doalty?

OWEN: And Manus stayed till the end of the dance?

DOALTY: We know nothing. What are you asking us for?

OWEN: Because Lancey'll question me when he hears Manus's
gone. *(Back to BRIDGET.)* That's the way George went home?   160
By the back road? That's where you saw him?

BRIDGET: Leave me alone, Owen. I know nothing about Yolland.
If you want to know about Yolland, ask the Donnelly twins.

(Silence. DOALTY moves over to the window.)

(To SARAH.) He's a powerful fiddler, O'Shea, isn't he? He
told our Seamus he'll come back for a night at Hallowe'en.   165

(OWEN goes to DOALTY who looks resolutely out the window.)

OWEN: What's this about the Donnellys? *(Pause.)* Were they
about last night?

DOALTY: Didn't see them if they were.

(Begins whistling through his teeth.)

OWEN: George is a friend of mine.

DOALTY: So.   170

OWEN: I want to know what's happened to him.

DOALTY: Couldn't tell you.

OWEN: What have the Donnelly twins to do with it? *(Pause.)*
Doalty!

DOALTY: I know nothing, Owen—nothing at all—I swear to   175
God. All I know is this: on my way to the dance I saw their
boat beached at Port. It wasn't there on my way home, after
I left Bridget. And that's all I know. As God's my judge.
The half-dozen times I met him I didn't know a word he
said to me; but he seemed a right enough sort . . . *(With sud-*   180
den excessive interest in the scene outside.) Cripes, they're crawling all over the place! Cripes, there's millions of them!
Cripes, they're levelling the whole land!

*(OWEN moves away. MAIRE enters. She is bareheaded and wet from the
rain; her hair in disarray. She attempts to appear normal but she is in
acute distress, on the verge of being distraught. She is carrying the
milk-can.)*

MAIRE: Honest to God, I must be going off my head. I'm
halfway here and I think to myself, 'Isn't this can very   185
light?' and I look into it and isn't it empty.

OWEN: It doesn't matter.

MAIRE: How will you manage for tonight?

OWEN: We have enough.

MAIRE: Are you sure?   190

OWEN: Plenty, thanks.

MAIRE: It'll take me no time at all to go back up for some.

OWEN: Honestly, Maire.

MAIRE: Sure it's better you have it than that black calf that's . . .
that . . . *(She looks around.)* Have you heard anything?   195

OWEN: Nothing.

MAIRE: What does Lancey say?

OWEN: I haven't seen him since this morning.

MAIRE: What does he *think*?

200 OWEN: We really didn't talk. He was here for only a few seconds.

MAIRE: He left me home, Owen. And the last thing he said to me—he tried to speak in Irish—he said, 'I'll see you yesterday'—he meant to say 'I'll see you tomorrow.' And I laughed that much he pretended to get cross and he said

205 'Maypoll! Maypoll!' because I said that word wrong. And off he went, laughing—laughing, Owen! Do you think he's all right? What do *you* think?

OWEN: I'm sure he'll turn up, Maire.

MAIRE: He comes from a tiny wee place called Winfarthing.

210 *(She suddenly drops on her hands and knees on the floor—where OWEN had his map a few minutes ago—and with her finger traces out an outline map.)* Come here till you see. Look. There's Winfarthing. And there's two other wee villages right beside it; one of them's called Barton Bendish—it's there; and

215 the other's called Saxingham Nethergate—it's about there. And there's Little Walsingham—that's his mother's townland. Aren't they odd names? Sure they make no sense to me at all. And Winfarthing's near a big town called Norwich. And Norwich is in a county called Norfolk. And

220 Norfolk is in the east of England. He drew a map for me on the wet strand and wrote the names on it. I have it all in my head now: Winfarthing—Barton Bendish—Saxingham Nethergate—Little Walsingham—Norwich—Norfolk. Strange sounds, aren't they? But nice sounds; like Jimmy Jack recit-

225 ing his Homer. *(She gets to her feet and looks around; she is almost serene now. To SARAH.)* You were looking lovely last night, Sarah. Is that the dress you got from Boston? Green suits you. *(To OWEN.)* Something very bad's happened to him, Owen. I know. He wouldn't go away without telling

230 me. Where is he, Owen? You're his friend—where is he? *(Again she looks around the room; then sits on a stool.)* I didn't get a chance to do my geography last night. The master'll be angry with me. *(She rises again.)* I think I'll go home now. The wee ones have to be washed and put to bed and

235 that black calf has to be fed . . . My hands are that rough; they're still blistered from the hay. I'm ashamed of them. I hope to God there's no hay to be saved in Brooklyn. *(She stops at the door.)* Did you hear? Nellie Ruadh's baby died in the middle of the night. I must go up to the wake. It didn't

240 last long, did it?

(MAIRE leaves. Silence. Then:)

OWEN: I don't think there'll be any class. Maybe you should . . .

(OWEN begins picking up his texts. DOALTY goes to him.)

DOALTY: Is he long gone?—Manus?

OWEN: Half an hour.

DOALTY: Stupid bloody fool.

245 OWEN: I told him that.

DOALTY: Do they know he's gone?

OWEN: Who?

DOALTY: The army.

OWEN: Not yet.

250 DOALTY: They'll be after him like bloody beagles. Bloody, bloody fool, limping along the coast. They'll overtake him before night for Christ's sake.

(DOALTY returns to the window. LANCEY enters—now the commanding officer.)

OWEN: Any news? Any word?

(LANCEY moves into the centre of the room, looking around as he does.)

LANCEY: I understood there was a class. Where are the others?

OWEN: There was to be a class but my father—   255

LANCEY: This will suffice. I will address them and it will be their responsibility to pass on what I have to say to every family in this section.

(LANCEY indicates to OWEN to translate. OWEN hesitates, trying to assess the change in LANCEY's manner and attitude.)

I'm in a hurry, O'Donnell.

OWEN: The captain has an announcement to make.   260

LANCEY: Lieutenant Yolland is missing. We are searching for him. If we don't find him, or if we receive no information as to where he is to be found, I will pursue the following course of action. *(He indicates to OWEN to translate.)*

OWEN: They are searching for George. If they don't find him—   265

LANCEY: Commencing twenty-four hours from now we will shoot all livestock in Ballybeg.

(OWEN stares at LANCEY.)

At once.

OWEN: Beginning this time tomorrow they'll kill every animal in Baile Beag—unless they're told where George is.   270

LANCEY: If that doesn't bear results, commencing forty-eight hours from now we will embark on a series of evictions and levelling of every abode in the following selected areas—

OWEN: You're not—!

LANCEY: Do your job. Translate.   275

OWEN: If they still haven't found him in two days time they'll begin evicting and levelling every house starting with these townlands.

(LANCEY reads from his list.)

LANCEY: Swinefort.

OWEN: Lis na Muc.   280

LANCEY: Burnfoot.

OWEN: Bun na hAbhann.

LANCEY: Dromduff.

OWEN: Druim Dubh.

LANCEY: Whiteplains.   285

OWEN: Machaire Ban.

LANCEY: Kings Head.

OWEN: Cnoc na Ri.

LANCEY: If by then the lieutenant hasn't been found, we will proceed until a complete clearance is made of this entire   290 section.

OWEN: If Yolland hasn't been got by then, they will ravish the whole parish.

LANCEY: I trust they know exactly what they've got to do. *(Pointing to BRIDGET.)* I know you. I know where you live.   295 *(Pointing to SARAH.)* Who are you? Name!

(SARAH's mouth opens and shuts, opens and shuts. Her face becomes contorted.)

What's your name?

(Again SARAH *tries frantically.)*

OWEN: Go on, Sarah. You can tell him.

(But SARAH *cannot. And she knows she cannot. She closes her mouth. Her head goes down.)*

OWEN: Her name is Sarah Johnny Sally.
300 LANCEY: Where does she live?
OWEN: Bun na hAbhann.
LANCEY: Where?
OWEN: Burnfoot.
LANCEY: I want to talk to your brother—is he here?
305 OWEN: Not at the moment.
LANCEY: Where is he?
OWEN: He's at a wake.
LANCEY: What wake?

*(*DOALTY, *who has been looking out the window all through* LANCEY'S *announcements, now speaks—calmly, almost casually.)*

DOALTY: Tell him his whole camp's on fire.
310 LANCEY: What's your name? *(To* OWEN.*)* Who's that lout?
OWEN: Doalty Dan Doalty.
LANCEY: Where does he live?
OWEN: Tulach Alainn.
LANCEY: What do we call it?
315 OWEN: Fair Hill. He says your whole camp is on fire.

*(*LANCEY *rushes to the window and looks out. Then he wheels on* DOALTY.)*

LANCEY: I'll remember you, Mr Doalty. *(To* OWEN.*)* You carry a big responsibility in all this.

(He goes off.)

BRIDGET: Mother of God, does he mean it, Owen?
OWEN: Yes, he does.
320 BRIDGET: We'll have to hide the beasts somewhere—our Seamus'll know where. Maybe at the back of Lis na nGradh—or in the caves at the far end of Tra Bhan. Come on, Doalty! Come on! Don't be standing about there!

*(*DOALTY *does not move.* BRIDGET *runs to the door and stops suddenly. She sniffs the air. Panic.)*

325 The sweet smell! Smell it! It's the sweet smell! Jesus, it's the potato blight!
DOALTY: It's the army tents burning, Bridget.
BRIDGET: Is it? Are you sure? Is that what it is? God, I thought we were destroyed altogether. Come on! Come on!

(She runs off. OWEN *goes to* SARAH *who is preparing to leave.)*

OWEN: How are you? Are you all right?

*(*SARAH *nods:* Yes.*)*

330 OWEN: Don't worry. It will come back to you again.

*(*SARAH *shakes her head.)*

OWEN: It will. You're upset now. He frightened you. That's all's wrong.

(Again SARAH *shakes her head, slowly, emphatically, and smiles at* OWEN. *Then she leaves.* OWEN *busies himself gathering his belongings.* DOALTY *leaves the window and goes to him.)*

DOALTY: He'll do it, too.
OWEN: Unless Yolland's found.
DOALTY: Hah!   335
OWEN: Then he'll certainly do it.
DOALTY: When my grandfather was a boy they did the same thing. *(Simply, altogether without irony.)* And after all the trouble you went to, mapping the place and thinking up new names for it. *(*OWEN *busies himself. Pause.* DOALTY *almost* 340 *dreamily.)* I've damned little to defend but he'll not put me out without a fight. And there'll be others who think the same as me.
OWEN: That's a matter for you.
DOALTY: If we'd all stick together. If we knew how to defend 345 ourselves.
OWEN: Against a trained army.
DOALTY: The Donnelly twins know how.
OWEN: If they could be found.
DOALTY: If they could be found. *(He goes to the door.)* Give me a 350 shout after you've finished with Lancey. I might know something then.

(He leaves.)

*(*OWEN *picks up the Name-Book. He looks at it momentarily, then puts it on top of the pile he is carrying. It falls to the floor. He stoops to pick it up—hesitates—leaves it. He goes upstairs. As* OWEN *ascends,* HUGH *and* JIMMY JACK *enter. Both wet and drunk.* JIMMY *is very unsteady. He is trotting behind* HUGH, *trying to break in on* HUGH'S *declamation.* HUGH *is equally drunk but more experienced in drunkenness: there is a portion of his mind which retains its clarity.)*

HUGH: There I was, appropriately dispositioned to proffer my condolences to the bereaved mother . . .
JIMMY: Hugh—   355
HUGH: . . . and about to enter the *domus lugubris*—Maire Chatach?
JIMMY: The wake house.
HUGH: Indeed—when I experience a plucking at my elbow: Mister George Alexander, Justice of the Peace. 'My tidings 360 are infelicitous,' said he—Bridget? Too slow. Doalty?
JIMMY: *Infelix*—unhappy.
HUGH: Unhappy indeed. 'Master Bartley Timlin has been appointed to the new national school.' 'Timlin? Who is Timlin?' 'A schoolmaster from Cork. And he will be a major as- 365 set to the community: he is also a very skilled bacon-curer!'
JIMMY: Hugh—
HUGH: Ha-ha-ha-ha-ha! The Cork bacon-curer! *Barbarus hic ego sum quia non intelligor ulli*—James?

III. 356 *domus lugubris* house of mourning   362 *infelix* unlucky, unhappy   368–69 *Barbarus . . . ulli* I am a barbarian here because I am not understood by anyone

370 JIMMY: Ovid.
HUGH: *Procede.*
JIMMY: 'I am a barbarian in this place because I am not under-
stood by anyone.'
HUGH: Indeed—(*Shouts.*) Manus! Tea! I will compose a satire
375 on Master Bartley Timlin, schoolmaster and bacon-curer.
But it will be too easy, won't it? (*Shouts.*) Strong tea! Black!

(*The only way* JIMMY *can get* HUGH's *attention is by standing in front
of him and holding his arms.*)

JIMMY: Will you listen to me, Hugh!
HUGH: James. (*Shouts.*) And a slice of soda bread.
JIMMY: I'm going to get married.
380 HUGH: Well!
JIMMY: At Christmas.
HUGH: Splendid.
JIMMY: To Athene.
HUGH: Who?
385 JIMMY: Pallas Athene.
HUGH: *Glaukopis Athene?*
JIMMY: Flashing-eyed, Hugh, flashing-eyed!

(*He attempts the gesture he has made before: standing to attention, the
momentary spasm, the salute, the face raised in pained ecstasy—but
the body does not respond efficiently this time. The gesture is grotesque.*)

HUGH: The lady has assented?
JIMMY: She asked *me*—I assented.
390 HUGH: Ah. When was this?
JIMMY: Last night.
HUGH: What does her mother say?
JIMMY: Metis from Hellespont? Decent people—good stock.
HUGH: And her father?
395 JIMMY: I'm meeting Zeus tomorrow. Hugh, will you be my best
man?
HUGH: Honoured, James; profoundly honoured.
JIMMY: You know what I'm looking for, Hugh, don't you? I
mean to say—you know—I—I—I joke like the rest of
400 them—you know?—(*Again he attempts the pathetic routine but
abandons it instantly.*) You know yourself, Hugh—don't
you?—you know all that. But what I'm really looking for,
Hugh—what I really want—companionship, Hugh—at
my time of life, companionship, company, someone to talk
405 to. Away up in Beann na Gaoithe—you've no idea how
lonely it is. Companionship—correct, Hugh? Correct?
HUGH: Correct.
JIMMY: And I always liked her, Hugh. Correct?
HUGH: Correct, James.
410 JIMMY: Someone to talk to.
HUGH: Indeed.
JIMMY: That's all, Hugh. The whole story. You know it all now,
Hugh. You know it all.

(*As* JIMMY *says those last lines he is crying, shaking his head, trying
to keep his balance, and holding a finger up to his lips in absurd gestures of secrecy and intimacy. Now he staggers away, tries to sit on a
stool, misses it, slides to the floor, his feet in front of him, his back
against the broken cart. Almost at once he is asleep.* HUGH *watches all
of this. Then he produces his flask and is about to pour a drink when
he sees the Name-Book on the floor. He picks it up and leafs through*

it, pronouncing the strange names as he does. Just as he begins, OWEN
emerges and descends with two bowls of tea.)

HUGH: Ballybeg. Burnfoot. King's Head. Whiteplains. Fair
Hill. Dunboy. Green Bank.   415

(OWEN *snatches the book from* HUGH.)

OWEN: I'll take that. (*In apology.*) It's only a catalogue of names.
HUGH: I know what it is.
OWEN: A mistake—my mistake—nothing to do with us. I
hope that's strong enough {*tea*}. (*He throws the book on the
table and crosses over to* JIMMY.) Jimmy. Wake up, Jimmy.   420
Wake up, man.
JIMMY: What—what-what?
OWEN: Here. Drink this. Then go on away home. There may
be trouble. Do you hear me, Jimmy? There may be trouble.
HUGH: (*Indicating Name-Book.*) We must learn those new   425
names.
OWEN: (*Searching around.*) Did you see a sack lying about?
HUGH: We must learn where we live. We must learn to make
them our own. We must make them our new home.

(OWEN *finds a sack and throws it across his shoulders.*)

OWEN: I know where I live.   430
HUGH: James thinks he knows, too. I look at James and three
thoughts occur to me: A—that it is not the literal past, the
'facts' of history, that shape us, but images of the past embodied in language. James has ceased to make that discrimination.   435
OWEN: Don't lecture me, Father.
HUGH: B—we must never cease renewing those images; because once we do, we fossilize. Is there no soda bread?
OWEN: And C, Father—one single, unalterable 'fact': if Yolland
is not found, we are all going to be evicted. Lancey has is-   440
sued the order.
HUGH: Ah. *Edictum imperatoris.*
OWEN: You should change out of those wet clothes. I've got to
go. I've got to see Doalty Dan Doalty.
HUGH: What about?   445
OWEN: I'll be back soon.

(*As* OWEN *exits.*)

HUGH: Take care, Owen. To remember everything is a form of
madness. (*He looks around the room, carefully, as if he were about
to leave it forever. Then he looks at* JIMMY, *asleep again.*) The
road to Sligo. A spring morning. 1798. Going into battle.   450
Do you remember, James? Two young gallants with pikes
across their shoulders and the *Aeneid* in their pockets.
Everything seemed to find definition that spring—a congruence, a miraculous matching of hope and past and present and possibility. Striding across the fresh, green land.   455
The rhythms of perception heightened. The whole enterprise of consciousness accelerated. We were gods that morning, James; and I had recently married *my* goddess, Caitlin

---

442 *edictum imperatoris* the decree of the commander

460 Dubh Nic Reactainn, may she rest in peace. And to leave her and my infant son in his cradle—that was heroic, too. By God, sir, we were magnificent. We marched as far as—where was it?—Glenties! All of twenty-three miles in one day. And it was there, in Phelan's pub, that we got home-465 sick for Athens, just like Ulysses. The *desiderium nostrorum*—the need for our own. Our *pietas*, James, was for older, quieter things. And that was the longest twenty-three miles back I ever made. *(Toasts* JIMMY.) My friend, confusion is not an ignoble condition.

(MAIRE enters.)

470 MAIRE: I'm back again. I set out for somewhere but I couldn't remember where. So I came back here.
HUGH: Yes, I will teach you English, Maire Chatach.
MAIRE: Will you, Master? I must learn it. I need to learn it.
HUGH: Indeed you may well be my only pupil.

(He goes towards the steps and begins to ascend.)

MAIRE: When can we start?
475 HUGH: Not today. Tomorrow, perhaps. After the funeral. We'll begin tomorrow. *(Ascending.)* But don't expect too much. I will provide you with the available words and the available grammar. But will that help you to interpret between privacies? I have no idea. But it's all we have. I have no idea at all.

(He is now at the top.)

480 MAIRE: Master, what does the English word 'always' mean?
HUGH: *Semper—per omnia saecula*. The Greeks called it '*aei*'. It's not a word I'd start with. It's a silly word, girl.

(He sits. JIMMY *is awake. He gets to his feet.* MAIRE *sees the Name-Book, picks it up, and sits with it on her knee.)*

464–65 *desiderium nostrorum* longing/need for our things/people 465 *pietas* piety 481 *Semper . . . saecula* always—for all time; *aei* always

MAIRE: When he comes back, this is where he'll come to. He told me this is where he was happiest.

(JIMMY sits beside MAIRE.)

JIMMY: Do you know the Greek word *endogamein*? It means to 485 marry within the tribe. And the word *exogamein* means to marry outside the tribe. And you don't cross those borders casually—both sides get very angry. Now, the problem is this: Is Athene sufficiently mortal or am I sufficiently god-like for the marriage to be acceptable to her people and to 490 my people? You think about that.
HUGH: *Urbs antiqua fuit*—there was an ancient city which, 'tis said, Juno loved above all the lands. And it was the god-dess's aim and cherished hope that here should be the capi-tal of all nations—should the fates perchance allow that. 495 Yet in truth she discovered that a race was springing from Trojan blood to overthrow some day these Tyrian towers—a people *late regem belloque superbum*—kings of broad realms and proud in war who would come forth for Libya's down-fall—such was—such was the course—such was the course 500 ordained—ordained by fate . . . What the hell's wrong with me? Sure I know it backwards. I'll begin again. *Urbs antiqua fuit*—there was an ancient city which, 'tis said, Juno loved above all the lands.

(Begin to bring down the lights.)

And it was the goddess's aim and cherished hope that here 505 should be the capital of all nations—should the fates per-chance allow that. Yet in truth she discovered that a race was springing from Trojan blood to overthrow some day these Tyrian towers—a people kings of broad realms and proud in war who would come forth for Libya's downfall . . . 510

(Blackout.)

---

485 *endogamein* to marry within the tribe 486 *exogamein* to marry outside the tribe 492 *Urbs antiqua fuit* there was an an-cient city 498 *late . . . superbum* kings of broad realms and proud in war, from Virgil's *Aeneid*, book I.

MAISHE MAPONYA

Maishe Maponya (b. 1951) is one of South Africa's best-known playwrights. Born in the Alexandra township near Johannesburg, Maponya moved to Soweto when his family was forcibly resettled there in 1962. He worked as an insurance clerk, writing plays in his spare time; he also worked with the Medupi Writers Association (banned in 1977), and was cofounder of the Bahumutsi Drama Group in 1977. The Bahumutsi Group produced many of his plays, but Maponya is also an accomplished poet and oral performer, and worked with the Allahpoets in the townships as well. Maponya had written two plays— *The Cry* (1976) and *Peace and Forgive* (1978)—when he won a British Council grant to study in England. There, he read Bertolt Brecht's classic "learning play" *The Measures Taken,* which inspired his own play, *The Hungry Earth,* about labor conditions in South Africa (1978). Brecht emphasized a socially engaged drama episodic in structure, and revealing its characters' social implications through a dramatic gesture, the gest: Maponya adapts, extends, and redirects these principles in several plays, notably *Umongikazi* (1982), a play about the working conditions of nurses, *Dirty Work* (1984), about the security police, and *Gangsters* (1984), about the detention and murder of activists like Steve Biko. Maponya teaches in the Drama Department of Witwatersrand University, and has written several other plays, including *Jika* (1986) and *Valley of the Blind* (1987).

GANGSTERS

Although it's possible to read *Gangsters* as a purely political allegory—on the model of Samuel Beckett's play *Catastrophe,* which it both invokes and challenges—the play in fact responds to a series of laws that came into force in South Africa in the 1980s. As Ian Steadman remarks in "The Theatre of Maishe Maponya," the play engages the South African Internal Security Act of 1982, which allowed the minister of Justice to detain individuals suspected of supporting communism or otherwise endangering the state.[1] The minister was given broad powers, and could seize any publication (and its author) that appeared to challenge "law and order," to advocate communism, to be published by or agree with the views of any banned organization, or appearing to "encourage or foment feelings of hostility between different population groups." The character Masechaba—in the original version of *Gangsters* a male poet named Rasechaba and played by Maponya—is detained under the act and subjected to a series of increasingly brutal interrogations, until she is killed.

Much as Brecht's *The Measures Taken* provided a kind of inspiration for *The Hungry Earth, Gangsters* clearly invokes—indeed, literally transcribes—the action of Beckett's *Catastrophe.* Beckett's play, which was written to protest the incarceration of Czech playwright—later, president of the Czech Republic—Vaclav Havel, is a kind of metadramatic allegory: a nameless Protagonist is put on a pedestal, while a Director orders his Assistant to pose and re-pose the figure, whitening his flesh, revealing his skin, bowing his head, in order to provide a kind of perfect image of the suffering victim. Maponya had been asked by the novelist Nadine Gordimer to direct *Catastrophe,* but he found the play not only too abstract from his own experience, but too remote from the more concrete experience of apartheid. In this sense, then, as in Césaire's *A Tempest,* we might consider *Gangsters* as a kind of resistant writing, a play that invokes a familiar document of European culture—here, both Beckett's play and perhaps the entire absurdist tradition it embodies—to suggest its role in the politics of oppression. Is there a sense, for example, in

---

[1]In Maishe Maponya, *Doing Plays for a Change* (Johannesburg: Witwatersrand UP, 1995).

which "the absurd" is something like the condition of arbitrary violence that was the condition of everyday life for black South Africans before the ending of apartheid? Is there a sense in which "the absurd" is not only the instrument of apartheid, but in some way part of its rationale, its justification?

When *Gangsters* was to be produced at Johannesburg's Market Theater in 1984, the theater was notified that the play verged on violating the 1974 Publications Act. Yet rather than censoring the play outright, the government merely stipulated that it could only be performed in small theaters, and that any future productions in a different venue would need to be approved. Since 1984, however, *Gangsters* has been performed successfully not only in South Africa, but throughout the world.

GANGSTERS

Maishe Maponya

—————— CHARACTERS ——————

MAJOR WHITEBEARD, *a white Security Police Officer*
JONATHAN, *a black Security Policeman*
MASECHABA, *a poet*

SETTING: *The stage is divided into two acting areas, stage left and stage right, by lighting or other means. Stage right is a security cell. Stage left represents Major Whitebeard's office and various settings. Additional lighting needed is a blue cover (for the recitation of poems) and a special, used twice only. The transitions between these states are marked in the text.*

PROPS: *Slab or stretcher, table, two chairs, cell window bars, blanket (black), rope (two metres), two tape recorders (one small, one large), note pad and pen, one Bible, a briefcase, books, papers, two photographs, a gun and holster, handcuffs. Uniforms for Jonathan and Whitebeard, veil for Masechaba, clothes and gown (mourning) for Masechaba.*

SOUND: *A taped hymn.*

—————— PROLOGUE ——————

House lights off. Stage lights off. House lights slowly come up to 50 per cent as MASECHABA *enters the auditorium.*

The recitation of the first three poems should take place in the auditorium suggesting a public performance by the poet. The reading must not be in a rigid stationary position, the poet must move in any direction she wishes, through the seats of the auditorium, walking and sometimes running, depending on the mood in each poem. It is also important to note that the tempo varies from one poem to the other and therefore requires the poet to be flexible.

MASECHABA: Kutheni na mawethu
    that you leave the evil fires
    from Europe to spread through Afrika!

    Sisi Phithiphithi!
5   Our children lie dead in the streets
    whilst their fathers die
    digging the gold
    they will never smell.

    Sisi Wiliwili!
10   Gugulethu is no longer ours
    Sophiatown is no more
    e-Mgababa ziya phel'izindlu ngo mlilo

    There are no roads e-Crossroads
    And our heroes
15   Are buried in Sharpeville.

    Izwe liya nyikima!
    Zi ya phel'ingane nga-mabhunu
    They still refuse to swallow Bantu Education
    Ncedani Mawethu
20   They are your children.

    Izwe liya shukuma!
    Nobody can buy apartheid
    Rent is going up!
    Food is also expensive
25   Asinamali we cannot afford it.

(Lights come up to 30 per cent on Major WHITEBEARD's *office revealing* WHITEBEARD *on a chair at a table and* JONATHAN *adjacent to* WHITEBEARD. *They are both reading newspapers.)*

Kutheni na mawethu
That you leave the stranger
To beat the drums of war
In your own backyards!
Hlanganani mawethu!   30
Lelethu!

(She pauses as she contemplates the audience and then continues with another poem.)

Ugly brown canvas uniform
Have you had lunch today?
I have seen
Your contorted face   35
Behind an ugly brown truck
In Sharpeville again

Ugly brown canvas uniform
I thought I saw your cousin
Behind an ugly brown truck   40
That roams the streets
By day in Mamelodi

My brother wrote me a letter
And told me about a mean looking face
In Nyanga   45
Behind an ugly brown truck
And I bet you
It sounds like your brother

Other people too
In Katlehong   50
In Huhudi
In Leandra
Say they live in fear of
Ugly brown canvas uniforms
Behind ugly brown trucks   55

And when at night
I smell cyanide in the air
I twitch my nose
Helplessly acknowledging
The announcement of the air   60
'Life must be short for others'

And in the morning
When I walk the same streets

865

In Sharpeville again
65 I see mothers kneeling beside bodies
Riddled with bullets
And I mutter to myself
The ugly brown truck
Drives a maneater
70 Dressed in ugly brown canvas uniform

(She pauses, then continues with a third poem.)

You puzzle me Mister Gunslinger
To think you will be strong enough
To rid your conscience
Of the days you made our lives ugly

75 With torture
With blood
With massacre

Mister Gunslinger
Are you really sure
80 You understand why you suppress
Our aspirations
And our dreams
Into nightmares

Mister Gunslinger
85 Are you aware of the deeds
Of your settler-forebears
With their wagon-wheels
Running
And crushing
90 The blooming lives
Cuddled with hope

You with your brown bombers
Ugly as ever
Parading the streets
95 Like it is the bush
Instilling fears into old folks
Cannot do the same
To the young determined
Azanians

100 Grandmothers!
Daughters of the living cradle
Summon your gods
In all Afrika
And let it be known
105 The realities of history are today

Settler child
You defended your
Vile interests
With the blood of my brother
110 You broom-flying witch
Afrika knows your kind

All ye black shadows
Very darkness of
The gunslingers' high noon
115 Awake and break open
The gates of the Azanian morning

Grope dear children
Waggle your fingers
Grab the pole
And raise the flag   120
Drenched in blood
And give us a song
For this victory!

(With her hands raised and fists clenched in a black power salute she shouts her last lines as she walks backwards out of the auditorium.)

Amandla to the people!
Amandla to the people!   125

———— FIRST ENCOUNTER ————

Lights at full on WHITEBEARD's *office.* WHITEBEARD *and* JONATHAN *are still seated in the same positions.*

WHITEBEARD: Jonathan!

JONATHAN: Yes sir!

WHITEBEARD: Has someone gone to fetch the poet?

JONATHAN: Yes sir, Sergeant Ngobese has gone to fetch her.

WHITEBEARD: All right. *(Pause. He pages through the newspaper to* 5
the end.)
    I see Kaizer Chiefs are playing Orlando Pirates on
Saturday—who do you think is going to win?

JONATHAN: Of course it goes without saying, it will be Orlando
Pirates all the way—it's like I see it happening again. Ex-   10
actly what happened in 1973 when they collected all the
titles. They are the darlings of our soccer in black and white.
(He throws down the paper, excitedly and mimics.) Nang'u Rhee!
Nang'u Jomo Sono! There's Rhee and Jomo Sono is close
behind him . . . Rhee dribbles past two defenders . . . one   15
man lies sprawling on the ground! Rhee passes the ball to
Jomo Sono . . . walibamba umfana wa likhahlela! *(Kicks with
one leg.)* Laduma! It's a goal!

WHITEBEARD: *(Interrupting.)* Jonathan!

JONATHAN: *(Freezes, leg still in the air.)* Yes sir!   20

WHITEBEARD: Fetch the poet.

JONATHAN: Yes sir! *(Shouts out* MASECHABA's *name.* MASECHABA
walks in slowly. She notes the tape recorder on WHITEBEARD's
desk. She stops.)

WHITEBEARD: *(Folds the newspaper and stands up.)* Miss Masechaba?   25
(He mispronounces the name.)

MASECHABA: *(Correcting him.)* Masechaba is my name.

WHITEBEARD: Oh, I'm sorry Miss Masechaba—Major Whitebeard
is my name . . . security. *(Produces an identification document.)*

MASECHABA: Yes, what can I do for you?   30

WHITEBEARD: Miss Masechaba, we in the branch are a little
worried about your poetry. We feel it's inflammatory.

MASECHABA: Can you explain yourself? What do you mean?

WHITEBEARD: I don't have to explain myself. All I have to do is
to play one of the cassettes that we've got of you reciting   35
those poems—particularly the one called . . . *(Recalling.)*
"The Spirit of Nation." All I have to do is play one of the
video tapes we've made of you doing your poetry at Regina
Mundi commemorative services. That's explanation enough
of what I mean. Oh, I'm forgetting my manners, please sit   40
down. *(Offers her a seat.)* Let me get one thing clear for myself. Do you write as well as perform these poems?

MASECHABA: Yes I do.

WHITEBEARD: Don't you feel they are inflammatory?
45 MASECHABA: They're not.
WHITEBEARD: They're not inflammatory?
MASECHABA: No.
WHITEBEARD: So Miss Masechaba, when you stand in front of a
hall full of people, and you've just recited one of your po-
50 ems and the people start screaming and waving their fists in
the air . . . you don't feel it's your poetry that's caused them
to react like that?
MASECHABA: No.
WHITEBEARD: That interests me. It interests me . . . (He looks at
55 JONATHAN.) I don't think we need you any longer Jonathan.
Why don't you get yourself a cup of coffee. (JONATHAN
leaves. WHITEBEARD switches off the tape.)
MASECHABA: So you have been taping all this?
WHITEBEARD: Regulations, I'm afraid. That's why I got rid of
60 Jonathan. I wanted to have an off-the-record chat with you
and I didn't want him to report me upstairs for breaking
the rules.
    But Miss Masechaba, it really interests me that a woman
as obviously intelligent and sensitive as you, can actually
65 believe that your poetry and the reaction it evokes are unrelated? How does the whole thing work?
MASECHABA: You see Major, the manner in which I write my poetry is decided by the situation and inspiration at a given
time. Major, when a poet pens anything on paper and the
70 spirit of nature moves within her, she will write about nature.
If the spirit of the nation moves within her, she will write
about the nation. She will talk about botho, humanness,
she'll talk about pain and she'll talk about that which moves
the people at a given time. If her people live in happiness,
75 this happiness will be seen in her works; and that will be
evidence to the world of how marvellous the lives of her people are. If I don't feel anything, I don't write anything.
WHITEBEARD: Very interesting Miss Masechaba, but that doesn't
explain the militant style that you've chosen.
80 MASECHABA: Major, a poet sees things not in the manner that
you and your colleagues see them. You may regard their
world as fantasy, but it is in that abstract frame of mind that
things start to take a certain shape and form, and that shape
is influenced by the material that inspires the poet; hence
85 the manner that I express myself in my poetry.
WHITEBEARD: Very good and very informative. (Sighs.) But unfortunately as you yourself put it, my colleagues and I see
things differently from you and your people. We live in a
different world; far from your abstract frames of mind. So
90 what interests us is not so much the creative process as the
effect that your poetry has on ordinary people; people who
don't have the insight and understanding that you and I
have, and therefore there can be no doubt Miss Masechaba
that your poems have made a lot of people feel very angry,
95 even violent and it is my job to put a stop to that sort of
thing. So I called you in to have a friendly chat with you
and to warn you . . .
MASECHABA: But you talk about violence! I think it's your
frame of mind. Maybe it's guilt.
100 WHITEBEARD: But your poetry is responsible for the creation of
a violent frame of mind in the people who hear it . . .
MASECHABA: I am not responsible for the creation of the squat-
ters. I am not responsible for the starvation of millions of

children because their parents have been forced into arid
homelands. I did not create the humiliating laws, and I 105
never created the racial barriers in this land. Who do you
expect me to blame when life becomes unfair to a black
soul?

(No response. Lights fade leaving MASECHABA covered by blue light
for poem.)

    When life becomes unfair to a black soul
    Who is to blame? 110
    When a child leaves home for school never to come back
    When a mother hides the cracks on her face created by
        years of crying.
    When a brother dashes in fear to seek refuge in the
        wilderness
    We are all taken by surprise!
    When life becomes unfair to a black soul 115
    Who is to blame?
    When a child throws a stone in anger and dies!
    When a family takes a brazier into a shack and dies!
    We are all taken by surprise.
    But God is not at all taken by surprise! 120

(Blue light fades as general lights come up. MASECHABA turns chal-
lengingly to the major.)

    Who do you expect me to blame?
WHITEBEARD: Okay, Miss Masechaba, for the purposes of this
discussion I will agree that things are not perfect with your
people, and this government is doing everything within realistic terms to improve their situation. But you as a poet 125
have a responsibility to your people. I don't know why you
choose to depress them by concentrating on the negative aspects of their life. Why don't you cheer them up by talking
about the good things that surround them—by telling
them of the natural beauty that surrounds them. I'm not an 130
expert of course but I had to learn one poem at school which
has stuck in my mind. It goes something like this:

(He recites any Afrikaans poem about flowers or nature. At the end of
his recitation, he goes to lean on the table directly opposite MASECHABA
and challenges her.)

    Now that sort of poem Miss Masechaba has a beautiful
melody to it and it makes me feel good inside not violent
and angry. 135
MASECHABA: Of course I could write about flowers. But where
are the flowers in Winterveld for me to write about? What
kind of flowers will ever grow in Crossroads? (Daringly
walks to the table, leans on it in the same position as his.)
    If that poet of yours lived in Alexandra he would write 140
about the stagnant pools of water and the smell of shit filtering through the streets at night because there is no
drainage system! He would write about the buckets of faeces placed in the streets at night as if families are bragging
which family eats more to shit more! 145
WHITEBEARD: I don't think we need that kind of language Miss
Masechaba!
MASECHABA: And my people don't need that kind of life Major
Whitebeard.

(There is tension as they look each other in the eye.)

150 WHITEBEARD: All right. Let's get back to your poetry. *(MASECHABA goes back to her seat.)*

Can't you see that you are inciting people to violence with your poetry. When you use lines like "the barbed wire mentality of a good-looking Afrikaner" you are insulting
155 the Afrikaner people. When you write about the "trigger-happy fingers" it shouldn't surprise you when the people respond by raising their fists in the air and shouting "Amandla Ngawethu!"

MASECHABA: *(Standing to make her point.)* But you have just di-
160 rected your . . .

WHITEBEARD: Yes Miss Masechaba! *(Points to the chair. Then softer.)* It's been a very interesting discussion. But the fact remains that I have a job to do and that job is to warn you. *(Goes to stand behind the chair on which* MASECHABA *is seated.)*
165 You are playing with fire. And remember my friend that people who play with fire must expect to get burned. If you want to continue playing with fire, don't blame anyone when you get those poetry-writing fingers of yours burned. Well, thank you very much for coming to this chat with
170 me. You may go.

(There is tension as MASECHABA *stands to leave the room.)*

WHITEBEARD: *(Calls out.)* Jonathan!
JONATHAN: *(Comes in.)* Yes sir!
WHITEBEARD: Give me the tape. *(JONATHAN goes to some corner in the office and produces a small tape recorder which he passes to him.*
175 WHITEBEARD *makes a mark on the tape and puts it away.)*

I want you to keep an eye on Masechaba. This means, Jonathan, that you do not go to Ellis Park to watch the soccer match on Saturday. I want you to do a good job. Do you hear me Jonathan?
180 JONATHAN: *(Disappointed.)* Yes sir.

(The church. A hymn. Suggest that Bach or Mozart should be played softly during this scene. Suggest the acting area should be downstage centre. MASECHABA *enters dressed for church. She crosses herself, finds a place and goes to kneel down. Hymn continues.* JONATHAN *enters, Bible in hand. Finds a place and kneels. Crosses himself and looks about. He sees her and shuffles about to get closer to her. She sees him. He kneels immediately behind her. A little later she challenges him. They talk in whispers.)*

MASECHABA: Jonathan, is there anywhere one can go without you following one?
JONATHAN: *(Sarcastically.)* Yes. The toilet.
MASECHABA: No Jonathan, this is serious. I am getting irritated
185 at the manner in which you keep following me. What is it you want from me?
JONATHAN: *(Amused.)* You must be exaggerating. What makes you such an expert on the Special Branch? Anyway, what would I find to do here besides attending the church
190 service?
MASECHABA: You should be ashamed of yourself coming to church every Sunday and knowing that your job is to help the white man preserve an ungodly status quo.
JONATHAN: Remember Masechaba that I'm doing a job like
195 any other person who wakes up in the morning to go to

work for a white man in town. On Friday when that person gets his salary I also get my salary.
MASECHABA: But the difference is that your salary is dirty. It is enveloped with the blood of your own brothers!
BOTH: *(Responding loudly to the priest at the altar.)* Amen!   200

(Different hymn, softer. MASECHABA *rises to go to the front to receive the sacrament. As she kneels,* JONATHAN *follows her and kneels beside her. She opens her mouth.)*

MASECHABA: Amen! *(Crosses herself.)*
JONATHAN: *(Receives the communion.)* Amen!

(She goes back to her previous position. A little later he follows. Then he challenges her as the hymn goes softer.)

JONATHAN: How many children die of malnutrition because their parents cannot find jobs? I have mouths to feed. *(Makes sure he is not heard by other congregants.)* I have my   205
children's school fees to attend to. Do you know that since I took up this job things have changed for the better for me. I'm also convinced that we must stand aloof from politics. We are servants of God and God does not wish us to enter the political arena.   210
MASECHABA: I've had enough of this senseless talk. The sermon delivered by the priest is enough. I'm not going to listen to a sell-out sermon from you Jonathan, you are a bloodsucker. You have no conscience. You are dead inside.
JONATHAN: What do you mean I'm dead? I'm alive. I've the   215
same feelings as you.
MASECHABA: *(Shifting away from him slightly.)* I knew you wouldn't understand me.
By dead *(Blue light comes up, simultaneously general light fades down.)*
I mean the smile you put on when the enemy grins at you.   220
Death is when the colour of your skin turns against you and you don't know where you stand as others decide your fate.
Death is the smile you put on when the enemy grins at you.
Death is when you stop being you! And above all,

(General lights come up whilst the blue fades down.)

Death, is when you start to hate to be black!

(A closing hymn.)

JONATHAN: Masechaba you are too hasty to condemn me before   225
you understand my situation better. Maybe we are not so different after all.
MASECHABA: Ag fuck off you are a sellout! *(She moves away.)*
JONATHAN: *(Humiliated and disregarding the congregants.)* Hey Masechaba you ridicule me in the presence of all these   230
people—that is nice for you.

(MASECHABA heads for the door and he calls after her.)

But one day you'll know who I am. Then you'll know what death is. Mcundu wakho! Lentombi iyandigezela, masemb'akho! Shit! Bastard! *(Realises the Bible is still in his hand. Quickly crosses himself as he exits.)*   235

Oh! I'm sorry Lord!

(Blackout.)

──────── **SECOND ENCOUNTER** ────────

WHITEBEARD *is sorting out some documents at the table.*

WHITEBEARD: Jonathan, where are those poems of Masechaba's that the Soweto Business Association is complaining about?
JONATHAN: Which ones are those sir?
WHITEBEARD: The ones I gave you to photostat.
5 JONATHAN: *(To himself as he goes through his bag.)* My driver's licence, my insurance contract. O sir look, my daughter turned two years yesterday, this is her picture taken last night.
WHITEBEARD: *(Businesslike.)* Later Jonathan. Bring me the
10 poems. (JONATHAN *gives him the poems.*)
Now call the poet inside.
JONATHAN: *(Opens the door and calls out.)* Masechaba!

(She walks in and stops. JONATHAN *stands at the door.)*

WHITEBEARD: Miss Masechaba, you disappoint me. When I had you in here the last time I thought we'd come to some un-
15 derstanding. But when I read these poems I'm not sure. Sit down please, and listen objectively to these poems of yours. I'm going to read them the way you do . . .
MASECHABA: No. If they have to be read I'll read them for you, I wrote them.
20 WHITEBEARD: No! I want you to hear the way they sound.

*(*MASECHABA *stands to take the page from* WHITEBEARD *but* JONATHAN *quickly steps in and looks at her threateningly.* MASECHABA *stops, realises the risk and sits down.* JONATHAN *walks back to his previous position.* WHITEBEARD *starts to read the poem out loud with agitation.)*

Look deep into the ghetto
And see the modernised graves,
Where only the living-dead exist
Manacled with chains
25 So as not to resist.
Look deep into the ghetto
And see streets dividing the graves
Streets with pavements
Dyed with blood
30 Blood of the innocent.
Look deep into the ghetto
And see yourself silenced
By a ninety-nine year lease
Thus creating a class struggle
35 Within a struggle for survival
Look the ghetto over
You will see smog hover
And dust choking the lifeless living dead
Can you hear the beasts hell
40 And creatures evil
Howling and brawling
As they rush to devour you
and suck the last drop of blood

From your emaciated corpse . . .
MASECHABA: That is not the way the poem is . . .   45
WHITEBEARD: I haven't finished yet. *(Pause.)* Now, "class struggle," that is Marxist talk. It is dangerous talk Miss Masechaba. Don't you feel that Marxism and Africanism are contradictory?
MASECHABA: No. They are not contradictory.   50
WHITEBEARD: Oh! So you admit that you are a Marxist.
MASECHABA: I didn't say that.
WHITEBEARD: I'm glad you didn't say that. Because if you had you wouldn't be here with me. Miss Masechaba you're fortunate that you're here with me tonight because some of my   55
colleagues would have dealt with you firmly.

(Slight pause.)

You puzzle me Miss Masechaba. You claim to be an Africanist and yet when one of your people goes out to improve his or her living conditions and when some of them participate in the political organs made available to them   60
you attack them.
Can't you see that places like Crossroads and Mogopa are a health hazard? Can't you see that the proliferation of shacks and shanties in the townships are a drawback to those blacks who want to live a better life? What is your   65
Black Consciousness motto? "Black man you are on your own." Why then do you try and belittle the black men who are trying to go on their own by owning businesses and improving their living conditions? It seems you in your poetry attack them.   70
MASECHABA: You have spoken about two groups of people. Besides you know that I am not attacking those who are caught in the capitalists' spider's web . . .
WHITEBEARD: Who do you attack then? You go about attacking your own people and then you tell me there are two   75
groups. I want you to tell me here and now who your attack is aimed at? *(No response.)*
I asked you a question. Who do you attack?

(General lights fade, blue comes up.)

MASECHABA: *(Standing on a chair.)* On the wings of the storm of liberation
Waving black tickets in their hands   80
Degrees hanging like monuments of heroes
In their glass houses
Sit the cheese and wine drinkers
Of our struggle.

Others are undegreed   85
Unread, underpaid
And deprived of the right to quench
Their education thirst.
Pity, they too are caught in the web.

The motto reads thus!   90
"Divide and rule"
A new dispensation
Is the name of the game.
The ghetto is fast becoming a suburb
Beverly Hills   95
Selection Park

Prestige Park
Monument Park

100 "Who cares
"It's my sweat
"It's my money
"You're just wasting your time
"Damn it. I'm going out
105 "To have a swim."

105 Hats off for the Master's plan!
We salute you Soweto Homemakers' Festival!
Thank you Urban Foundation!
Thank you Gough Cooper!
Thank you Mr Constructive Engagement!
110 Thank you "Iron Lady"
Voetsek! You have messed up our struggle!

(General lights come up, blue light fades.)

WHITEBEARD: I asked you a question—who do you attack?
MASECHABA: *(Seemingly inattentive and still seated.)* The cheese
and wine drinkers of our struggle.
115 WHITEBEARD: Always a poet. That rings a bell—here in this
poem you write "silenced by a ninety-nine year lease . . .
Selection Park, Monument Park . . ." It seems to me Miss
Masechaba that these people who go and live in these better suburbs are worthy of your contempt?
120 MASECHABA: Everything I feel is in the poem and the poem says
it all . . .
WHITEBEARD: Would I be correct in assuming that organisa-
tions like for example the Soweto Business Association are
targets of your attack?
125 MASECHABA: You can make up your mind on that.
WHITEBEARD: *(Tension as their eyes lock. Pause.)* I'll do that! You
may go. *(Before* MASECHABA *reaches the door.)*
One more thing before you go. *(*MASECHABA *stops.)* It
might interest you Miss Masechaba, to know that a lot of
130 people give us information. Normally we don't want to
share it but sometimes we do. Every Thursday night for
the past four weeks you've been going to these rent boy-
cott meetings and reciting your poetry in support of those
leaders of yours who've been saying to the people "Don't
135 go and live in Selection Park, don't go to that petit-bour-
geois place." It might interest you to know that those
very same people have applied for bigger and better
houses in Beverley Hills and Prestige Park. Would you
like to see their names? *(He tries to pass a book to her. She is
140 not interested.)*
I thought not. What about those Black Consciousness,
Afrika for the Africans leaders of yours who send their children secretly to white schools to get a white education—
would you like to see their names?
145 MASECHABA: Every struggle has its betrayers. My leader is the
people.
WHITEBEARD: The people? *(Disappointed.)* I'll try and remember
that. *(Gestures with finger to dismiss her and then remembers
something. This action is intended deliberately to torment her.)*
150 Oh, just before you go, I have a poem of yours which
seems to be written in some ethnic language. Would you tell
me what it means? It's called Hoy, Hoy, Hoy-in-a-Hoyini . . .

(General light fades. Blue light comes up.)

MASECHABA: Hoyina!!
Nivile nga maculo
Esizwe sintsundu e-Azania   155
Ethetha ngokuthi asifikanga apha
We have no history of arrival
Kuya mangalisa
Asihlalanga ngoxolo ezweni lethu
Simile kodwa ngomlenz'omnye   160
Siphandliwe simana siyalila
Sovuthelwa ngubanina
Namhlanje siyagxothwa
Ngomso siyabotshwa
Hayi ngenyimini siyazilwela   165
We fight back
Unzima lomthwalo womzabalazo

Abanye bayathengisa
Abanye bayathengiswa
Kuvuthumlilo   170
Ithayela lityumtu
Kwenze njanina sizwe' sintsundu
Aqhubeka njalo
Amaculo esizwe sintsundu e-Azania
Igcwele imigaqo ngabasebenzi   175
Bayazabalaza nabo
Baqhubeka phambili
Abantwana bayalishukumisa ilizwe
Baculela phezulu
Bazama ngapha nangapha   180
Bayalinyikimisa
Bayalizongomisa
Ngomso ngenene sophumelela

Abasetyhini bayalilizela
Sengathi kumnandi kowethu   185
Kanti thina siyazi
It is the African
Way of doing things
Even the revolution!

(Blue light fades, general light comes up.)

WHITEBEARD: It's called "Hoyina." Would you care to tell me 190
what it means?
MASECHABA: *(Immediately.)* No! I'm sure you have translators in
here who would be happy to do it for you.

*(She walks out angrily. As she pulls the door open, she's pushed back
into the room by* JONATHAN *who's been standing outside the door. He
walks a few steps towards her as she steps backwards.)*

WHITEBEARD: *(Angrily.)* Masechaba. *(Points to a chair.* MASECHABA
sits down.)   195
Jonathan, it seems you are going to get a chance to read
this after all. *(Hands him a written page.)* Read clauses four,
five and six out loud.
JONATHAN: Clause Four: You are to report at your nearest police
station daily before eight o'clock every evening. Clause Five: 200
You are not to attend any gathering and note that talking to
more than one person at a time will be a contravention of

your banning order. Clause Six: This banning order is imposed on you for the next three years.

205 WHITEBEARD: I warned you, and you chose to ignore my friendly advice. You asked for it. Jonathan explain the full implications of that document to our Soweto poet laureate.

(He makes a move for the door.)

MASECHABA: *(Standing.)* Just before you go, Major! *(WHITEBEARD*
210 *returns and stands in front of her. He is obviously shocked at her nerve in calling him back as he called her back. There is more tension as she addresses him.)* Mr William Shakespeare wrote some very wonderful lines about you which go:

Man proud man,
Dressed in a little brief authority
215 Plays such fantastic tricks before high heaven
As makes the angels weep.

WHITEBEARD: *(Chuckling.)* You really amuse me. What did you expect me to answer? Who is this Shakespeare? What political organisation does he belong to? *(Softer, but hard.)* We
220 are not as stupid as you might think. *(He leaves.* MASECHABA *sits down. She is obviously shattered by the banning order.)*

JONATHAN: Ya Masechaba, poet of the people! Where are all the people you were preaching poetry to? Do you think the people will eat your poetry when they starve? Let me tell you
225 something. I can't be led by a bastard like you! I know your kind. Showing off all the time with your name on the front pages of newspapers. All you know is jet-setting from time to time, and then you think you can fool us with your petty politics. Ha! You think we are impressed by your behaviour
230 in your two-piece costumes—carrying an executive bag when you go and talk to the same white people that you criticise. Ah! but when you read your poetry you put on African dresses, use revolutionary language and then you think you can fool everybody. *(Laughs.)* Bigmouth, I'm talking to you.
235 Talk! You've just earned yourself a banning order!

MASECHABA: *(Grabs the banning order, crumples it and throws it away.)* This is just a piece of paper—I'm still myself. My conscience is clear . . . The people out there are waiting for me—Masechaba, Mother of the Nation . . . That's what the
240 name means if you don't know. If they have to wait for you, it will only be to tear you apart! They will scorn you, they'll reject you!

JONATHAN: C'mon enjoy yourself for this is your last poetry session . . .
245 MASECHABA: Yes, they can ban me here but they won't ban the spirit of the nation. For as long as those millions of people are still thirsty the march will continue. I respect the convictions of my people and they respect my beliefs. I will help them carry the cross . . .
250 JONATHAN: Don't give me this shit about "your people." I know your kind . . .

MASECHABA: You don't know for you have no conscience.

JONATHAN: It's easy for you because you get your money from the World Council of Churches. You have nothing to lose,
255 because you have no mouths to feed . . .

MASECHABA: And so that is what makes you sell your people out? Why don't you stand up and pull up your pants and tell the white man it's enough—your face against his; tell him you've had enough . . .

JONATHAN: You are dreaming, for the white man is in power— 260 can't you see?

MASECHABA: *(Changes mood.)* Jonathan, you don't understand. You are black and I'm black . . .

JONATHAN: And then?

MASECHABA: In the beginning it was you and me. The land be- 265 longed to us. We tilled it. We shared everything equally. Then came the white man with his own thoughts. He put us asunder; put us against each other and while this was going on, he fenced us around and then moved about freely declaring our land his land—no man's land. Did you not 270 seen those boards along the road as you came from home this morning, saying: "In front of you, behind you and all around you is a Rand Mines Property?" Have you bothered to ask yourself "where did Rand Mines get our land from? Who did he buy it from?" He took it with the gun. Do you 275 know what the white man is doing today? He is sharing every little bit of our soil equally with his own brother. *(JONATHAN is torn apart.)*

The system is so planned that we don't realise these tricks easily. *(Her voice builds up.)* Why should we let the 280 white man decide our fate? Are we not matured to know and understand the world around us? *(She hoists his hand and fits her palm into his.)* The white man is aware that your clenched fist together with mine is the dawning of a new era. And when that dawn comes, no amount of machinery 285 will put us apart. This is the spirit of the nation! And this is what moves the people today!

WHITEBEARD: *(Bursting in.)* Masechaba! *(JONATHAN pulls his hand away and stands a distance away from her.)* You have overstayed your welcome! *(Picks up the crumpled banning or- 290 der and puts it into* MASECHABA's *pocket.* MASECHABA *exits.)*

JONATHAN: *(Guilty.)* Major, what she was saying to me—there is sense in her talk . . .

WHITEBEARD: Do you think she makes sense?

JONATHAN: I . . . I . . . I think . . . 295

WHITEBEARD: Let me make some sense to you. How many children have you got?

JONATHAN: Four, Major.

WHITEBEARD: Where are they being educated?

JONATHAN: Waterford, in Swaziland. 300

WHITEBEARD: And who pays for their education?

JONATHAN: You do, sir, as a benefit for me.

WHITEBEARD: Am I making sense Jonathan. Am I making sense?

JONATHAN: *(Embarrassed.)* Yes Sir! 305

WHITEBEARD: Now, I'm detaching you from normal duties. I want you to organise a team of four men to follow her wherever she goes. I want to know who she meets. I want her telephone tapped and mail screened. I have a suspicion that since the bastard is banned she is going to pursue her ac- 310 tivities underground. I want you to do a good job . . . Hear me Jonathan?

JONATHAN: Yes sir. *(Slight pause.)* By the way Major, you promised that I could take the blue Mercedes Benz home for the weekend. 315

WHITEBEARD: Yes. The keys are in the key-box.

JONATHAN: *(Excited.)* Thank you sir!

(Blackout.)

(Back in the township MASECHABA *continues to read her poetry in public, defying the banning order. The following poem can be read from any part of the stage as long as the position will not confuse the location. Blue light comes on.)*

MASECHABA: Apartheid!
    You maintained yourself
320   By keeping us separate
    You were father of many
    Like Suppression of Communism Act

    Who killed many
    Who hanged many
325   Who maimed many

    And when later you realised
    He was not doing you good
    You killed him

    Amongst your sons
330   Bantu Education
    Stripped many
    Of their brains

    Made them docile
    Killed many
335   Maimed many
    Jailed many

    And now you realise
    He is not doing you good
    You want to kill him

340   I remember your other son
    Old and notorious
    Pass-Law
    Never smiled
    Just locked millions
345   And I heard yesterday
    He died
    And millions are beginning to smile
    I hope he is not resurrected underground
    As for you
350   I heard your bodyguard Botha say
    You are outdated
    And wants to send you to the grave
    But he defended you
    By sending many of us to their graves

355   I think we must bring him to trial
    Like all Nazi war criminals
    How's that?

(Blue light fades.)

——— THIRD ENCOUNTER ———

MASECHABA *is arrested. Special light comes up on* MASECHABA'*s face behind bars. She is dressed in her nightgown and her feet are bare. This part can also be depicted by light—no specific stage area.*

MASECHABA: They broke one window first
    Then on all windows played sounds
    Made by the drums of wars
    Both doors joined the chorus

    The front emitting quick soprano notes   5
    The back a slow dub-dub-dub

    It all happened in minutes
    The vocalists shouted
    The notes one after the other
    Like they'd never rehearsed before   10
    Vula! Vula! Bulang man!
    Open up! The lyrics went
    The timing was bad.

    This is the music
    That has become notorious   15
    It plays at the first hour of the day
    When your name rings
    To be registered in the books
    Of those messengers of darkness
    You jump to your feet   20

    Try to say something you think makes sense
    You take all your poems
    Hide all manuscripts
    Throw some into the stove
    To destroy the creation   25
    rather than see it defiled by them
    With their dirty hands.

    If you are the poet's sister
    "Don't open they are thugs!"
    And then the poet will follow   30
    "We won't open you are thugs!"
    To give herself time to destroy
    Everything and quickly relay messages
    To the family.

    But then the door has to be opened   35
    Delaying tactics won't last forever
    You saw it in Zimbabwe
    The back door is kicked open
    While you open the front
    Within seconds   40

    The musicians spit their songs into every room
    While others guard the doors for escapers.
    Torches flashing all over!
    And the poet is taken.

*(*JONATHAN *comes to take her out of the cell and pushes her into the interrogation room. She falls on her knees.)*

MASECHABA: *(Exhausted and still handcuffed.)* I could not say no   45
to them. Does the impala say no to the lion? Could the Star
of David say no to the jackboot? I could not say no.

*(*JONATHAN *walks behind her.* WHITEBEARD *bursts in. He switches on the tape. Tension.* MASECHABA *stands up to challenge him.)*

    And why do all this to me . . .
WHITEBEARD: Shut up! If I want you to talk I'll order you! Miss
Masechaba, spirit of the nation, poet, word merchant, what   50
is the protector of the state? *(No response.)* I asked you a
question. What is the protector of the state? Jonathan, will
you tell Miss Masechaba what the protector of the state is?

JONATHAN: Yes. The law.

55 WHITEBEARD: And you Miss Masechaba have chosen to break that law . . .

MASECHABA: I have not . . .

WHITEBEARD: Shut up! Six months ago I had you in my office, I talked to you person-to-person. One intelligence to what

60 I thought was another intelligence. I said to you Miss Masechaba, your poetry is inciting the people. Please, I said to you, you are a woman of reason, stop this! You are treading on a dangerous path. You wouldn't listen to me. Three months later, I bring you in here again. I say to you, I'm

65 sorry, justice has to prevail everywhere. I don't want to do this to you, I respect you, but the law has decided, here is your banning order for your own protection. That too is not good enough for Miss Masechaba . . .

MASECHABA: But . . .

70 WHITEBEARD: Shut up! Miss Masechaba has to ignore the provisions of her banning order. She has to go out into the halls and she has to say to the people, "you see my banning order. This is what I do to my banning order!" *(He raises his hand and shows his palm to the audience. He spits on it.)* I could live

75 with that Miss Masechaba, I could just live with it. But then yesterday something happened. I have a press release which is going out this afternoon . . . *(First he goes to wipe his hand on her shoulder, then goes to his table, produces a document and reads it out to her.)*

80 "Yesterday evening patrol police spotted four men who they suspected were part of the fifty cadres that crossed the border into the country and when the terrorists realised they were being followed they opened fire on the police who responded by killing all four men. None of the police was

85 injured. Large quantities of arms and ammunition and literature were captured."

Now Miss Masechaba, amongst the AK47s, Scorpions and limpet mines; among the T5s and T7s; amongst those instruments of terror that were going to sow discord and

90 violence among your people as well as mine, among them was a book of your poetry with the inscription inside *(He produces the book.)* "To LMA—solidarity and strength my comrades—Masechaba."

MASECHABA: I have signed lots of autographs in my poetry

95 books. When people bring them to me to sign what do I do? Do I refuse? As for LMA, I don't know who he is . . .

WHITEBEARD: Who is LMA?

MASECHABA: I said I do not know.

WHITEBEARD: *(Going closer to her and punching her in the stomach.)*

100 I asked you a question. Who is LMA?

MASECHABA: *(Writhing in pain.)* How must I talk to convince you that I do not know? Are you ever going to understand my language?

WHITEBEARD: *(Making as if to punch her again.)* I have no desire

105 to understand your language. *(Sarcastic assurance.)* You don't need to be scared of me, remember we are friends. *(He rushes to the table.)* I have a confession to make to a friend. Yes, Miss Masechaba, you have been followed night and day. Yes you have been watched. *(Indicating from a list in his hands.)* This

110 is a known terrorist hideout, that is a known terrorist hideout. That is a shebeen where terrorists are known to congregate. Is it coincidence that you visited these places on your poetic pilgrimage? What organisation do you belong to?

MASECHABA: I do not belong to any organisation.

WHITEBEARD: Isn't the African Poets of Azania an organisation? 115 Is that not an organisation?

MASECHABA: It is a cultural body. It's a traditional African ensemble . . .

WHITEBEARD: Is it not an organisation?

MASECHABA: Yes it is. 120

WHITEBEARD: Are you not their member?

MASECHABA: Yes I am.

(WHITEBEARD presses the tape to play back MASECHABA's denials: "I do not belong to any organisation.")

WHITEBEARD: Now you tell me you do. Do you know what that means Miss Masechaba? That means my friend that you are lying to me and I don't like that. You've just told me one 125 lie, how do I know how many other lies you have told me? I think I must give you a chance to decide whether you want to continue lying to me. *(He pulls her by the handcuffs.)* Jonathan, will you teach Miss Masechaba what we do to people who tell lies. *(Walks out.)* 130

(JONATHAN takes out a rope and hooks it to the handcuffed hands and then orders her to squat while he relaxes. This continues until he falls asleep. The lights fade to a blackout. She continues to squat until she falls down. Lights come up.)

(WHITEBEARD comes back. JONATHAN jumps to his feet.)

WHITEBEARD: Poor Miss Masechaba has been treated so badly. Jonathan, what have you done? *(JONATHAN does not respond. He knows WHITEBEARD's tricks during interrogations. WHITEBEARD changes moods.)*

Weren't you taught manners, kaffir, that when you're in 135 the presence of the white man you must stand up? *(He kicks her.)* Up! Up! I can't talk to a grown woman on the floor. Up! *(MASECHABA stands.)* Who is LMA?

MASECHABA: I said I do not know.

WHITEBEARD: *(Taking some documents from the drawers of his table.)* 140 These are all the names and addresses of people you communicated with regularly—have you anything to say?

MASECHABA: I have communicated with lots of friends in the past, some of them are fellow writers. Do you expect me to live in isolation? I'm human. 145

WHITEBEARD: There you are, agreeing that you have something in common with the people on our lists.

MASECHABA: Whatever my friends do because of their convictions has nothing to do with me. I'm a simple poet.

WHITEBEARD: Yes, a poet you are, but I don't think you are that 150 simple. I have here photographs of two of your best friends who've skipped the country and received training in Moscow and in Africa. How do you respond to your friends doing that?

MASECHABA: Your government sells diamonds to Moscow. It is 155 known to be getting arms from Bulgaria. How do you respond to your friends doing that?

WHITEBEARD: Did you hear that Jonathan? Our poet friend fancies herself as a foreign policy analyst. Now you listen very carefully. You see these hands. They are clean, unsoiled and 160 they look friendly. Every day when these hands get home, they lift up a one-year-old bundle called David and they

throw him into the air and they catch him, they tickle him
and hold him steady as he threatens to fall over with pure
165 enjoyment. But Miss Masechaba, in order to protect that
little boy from you and your Marxist friends, to stop your
violence and terror from changing that little boy's joy to
tears, these hands will do anything, (*Hits her with both
hands.*) anything! And the blood will wash off very easily.
170 Do you understand me? I asked you a question. Do you understand me? Well my friend, seeing that you don't understand my words maybe you'll understand my actions. (*He
throttles her and throws her to the floor.* MASECHABA *falls and
writhes in pain. He kicks her in the stomach. Pause.*) Is there
175 anything that you don't understand?

MASECHABA: (*On her knees boldly faces* WHITEBEARD.) So deep is
my love for my land that those who fail to understand seek
to destroy me.

(*She stands up slowly.*)

Perhaps, finally at the very end
180 When the curtain falls
On the last act of your pillage
You will come to understand
How deeply
We loved this land
185 And cared for all its people

(*Upright and facing forward.*)

White and black
Free and unfree

(*There is silence and tension.*)

WHITEBEARD: Jonathan, will you deal with Masechaba as you
deem fit and if you have to teach her that electricity has
190 other uses than providing light you must do it!

JONATHAN: (*In a dilemma.*) But sir, it seems from the look of
things she does not know who this LMA is. Besides, she's
an ordinary poet.

WHITEBEARD: (*Angrily.*) Do I have to start wondering where
195 your loyalties lie Jonathan?

JONATHAN: No sir!

WHITEBEARD: Then do it! (WHITEBEARD *exits leaving the two
behind. A little later* JONATHAN *takes off his jacket to start the
torture of* MASECHABA *as lights fade to blackout.*)

——— FOURTH ENCOUNTER ———

Lights come up instantly on the cell area. MASECHABA's *body is lying
on a slab covered with a blanket. A hood covers her head.* WHITEBEARD
stands to the left of the slab with JONATHAN *opposite him. The atmosphere is tense.* JONATHAN *puts on his jacket.* WHITEBEARD *begins to
walk nervously round the slab.* JONATHAN *does the same to make way
for* WHITEBEARD.

WHITEBEARD: So, this is what you did?

JONATHAN: Yes my lord.

WHITEBEARD: How long has she been like this?

JONATHAN: My lord knows.

5 WHITEBEARD: I forget!

JONATHAN: One week!

WHITEBEARD: So, so! (*Pause.*) This is serious! I'll have to see
what I can do. Why the slab?

JONATHAN: So that you can see her well!

WHITEBEARD: Why the blanket? 10

JONATHAN: To have her covered!

WHITEBEARD: Why the hood?

JONATHAN: To help hide the head!

WHITEBEARD: What?

JONATHAN: It is common practice my lord that when detainees 15
are in this state, we cover their heads.

WHITEBEARD: It is a stupid procedure to have them covered all
the time! She was healthier when I last saw her!

(*Blackout.*)

——— FIFTH ENCOUNTER ———

In the cell a few hours later. The slab is positioned in a different place.
WHITEBEARD *and* JONATHAN *walk round it.*

WHITEBEARD: How's the head?

JONATHAN: As before.

WHITEBEARD: I forget! (JONATHAN *moves towards* MASECHABA *to
show her head.*)
Say it! (JONATHAN *stops.*) 5

JONATHAN: Septic.

WHITEBEARD: Colour?

JONATHAN: Red and pink.

WHITEBEARD: Put calamine lotion on head.

JONATHAN: Okay my lord. I make a note. Calamine lotion on 10
head.

(*He takes out pad and pencil and makes notes. A piece of rope protrudes
from his pocket.*)

WHITEBEARD: And why the rope?

JONATHAN: Used during interrogation.

WHITEBEARD: Unnecessary evidence!

JONATHAN: I make a note. 15
(*Writes again.*) Rope to discard. (*Slowly, with a sad look on
his face.*) Rope to discard.

WHITEBEARD: What is wrong now Jonathan?

JONATHAN: I remember seeing her hands many times in
church. 20

WHITEBEARD: Remember, you had a job to do.

JONATHAN: Yes my lord.

——— SIXTH ENCOUNTER ———

In the cell a few hours later. The slab has been removed. MASECHABA's
body lies sprawled on the floor.

WHITEBEARD: What will you tell the court?

JONATHAN: I'll say she threw herself out of the window in an
attempt to escape . . .

WHITEBEARD: No good. The interrogation room is on the
ground floor! 5

JONATHAN: No, no, it's simple. We called her in to have breakfast with us—she was so hungry that she ate her food so fast
that it choked her . . .

10 WHITEBEARD: Not convincing. We never have breakfast with detainees in our rooms.

JONATHAN: (*Tries again.*) All right, I'll say she was on a hunger strike since we took her in.

WHITEBEARD: No! Jonathan when last did you check your record books? We gave that excuse some time ago!

15 JONATHAN: (*Still panicking.*) How about saying she hanged herself with her gown-strap, that's right! (*Excited.*) Suicide!

WHITEBEARD: Not convincing. There's nothing in the cell to hang herself from!

JONATHAN: (*A bit hopeless but tries . . . to himself.*) Seems like
20 nothing is convincing. I'll try one more time . . . (*Hilarious with excitement.*) She slipped on a piece of soap . . . !

WHITEBEARD: You can't fool the public with that one again!

JONATHAN: (*Defeated.*) My lord knows all . . .

WHITEBEARD: Maybe we should look back at our history with
25 her. Maybe that will give us a clue.

JONATHAN: Yes my lord. Maybe that will give us an idea. (*JONATHAN exits.*)

(*Blackout.*)

───── **SEVENTH ENCOUNTER** ─────

In the cell one day later. WHITEBEARD *and* JONATHAN *are among huge piles of files.* MASECHABA's *body is in the same position as before.* JONATHAN *drops the files on the floor one after the other.*

JONATHAN: (*Apologetic.*) Some pages are missing sir . . .

WHITEBEARD: (*Authoritative.*) Confidential to The Party!

(*A pause as* JONATHAN *continues his search through the files.*)

JONATHAN: When will the pathologist see her sir?

WHITEBEARD: That too is confidential to The Party. Be here on
5 Sunday. Eight o'clock. Write your statement in full.

JONATHAN: Should I make up anything?

WHITEBEARD: No! That's important. He has to know what direction to channel his finding. Let him know it. What happened. Where. When it happened and who was present.

10 JONATHAN: I'll remember. I make a note. (*Louder.*) Details of torture in full . . . !

WHITEBEARD: Shhh! Walls have ears. I pray they don't have a private pathologist.

JONATHAN: Will you allow it sir . . . ?

15 WHITEBEARD: Sometimes we have to show off our democratic processes. Now let's take a closer look at her.

JONATHAN: Why my lord?

WHITEBEARD: Don't be stupid we must make our own study.

JONATHAN: Fine. Orders taken.

20 WHITEBEARD: Remove the hood, the blanket. (*JONATHAN is slow.*) Snap to it! I have a meeting with the pathologist!

JONATHAN: Like to see her naked?

WHITEBEARD: (*Irritated.*) Quick! The court will order it. This looks horrible—cover her up!

25   (*JONATHAN covers the body.*) Calamine all visible wounds.

WHITEBEARD: The gown, why did you do it when she had it on?

JONATHAN: She refused to change into different clothes when I ordered her to.

(*Another long pause.*)

WHITEBEARD: Now bring back the slab. Move it to the right.
(*JONATHAN does as instructed.*) More. Pick up the body 30 and put it back on the slab. Higher. Make sure that we see all parts of her body before we make the first press statements.

JONATHAN: Why my lord?

WHITEBEARD: Don't be stupid, the family may order a public 35 enquiry!

JONATHAN: Fine. Orders taken.

WHITEBEARD: Remove the blanket again. Bare the chest. (*JONATHAN unbuttons the gown and steps back.*) Now let's go to the legs. (*He rolls the gown up.*) Higher. Put calamine on 40 chest and legs.

JONATHAN: I make a note. Calamine chest and legs.

(WHITEBEARD *and* JONATHAN *take a final look at* MASECHABA *as in the opening scene.*)

JONATHAN: What if we were to clothe her in prison attire?

WHITEBEARD: That's stupid! This is detention. She hasn't been to prison yet.   45

JONATHAN: (*Humiliated.*) My lord knows everything.

(*More contemplation of* MASECHABA.)

WHITEBEARD: That's enough for the day and remember whatever happens DON'T PANIC! You've proved your loyalty and I'll do everything to protect you!

(*He puts his arm around* JONATHAN *as they walk away and freeze at some point with their faces looking down as if shying away from the public eye.*)

(*General lights fade as Special comes up on* MASECHABA's *head and shoulders. Slow fade to semi-darkness on* WHITEBEARD *and* JONATHAN *so that their shadows can be seen.* MASECHABA's *voice can be heard reciting her last poem.*)

───── **EPILOGUE** ─────

(ON TAPE)

When the parricidal mania
That grips the uncrowned villains
Roams free
And the streets are
Dyed with blood   5
They would seek me out to pray together
At the altar
For they would have come to realise
That I was against their own destruction
And clung frantically   10
On the frail hope
That they would be brought to sanity

Perhaps finally
They would be calling me out
To rebuke the storms   15
But all hope and understanding
Shall have gone by then

(*Slow fade both positions to blackout.*)

TOMSON HIGHWAY

Since the production of his two most celebrated plays, *The Rez Sisters* (1986) and *Dry Lips Oughta Move to Kapuskasing* (1989), Tomson Highway has become perhaps the best-known of the many Native playwrights now working in North America. Tomson Highway was born in 1951, the eleventh of twelve children, on a trapline in a Native reserve (the Canadian term for what is called a "reservation" in the United States) in northern Manitoba, Canada. Until the age of six, Highway lived a nomadic life with his family. His first language was Cree, and he did not begin to learn English until he was sent to a Roman Catholic boarding school. Like many Native children, Highway attended boarding school, visiting his family only during the summer. After graduating from high school in Winnipeg, Highway studied piano at the University of Manitoba Faculty of Music, and then studied in London before returning to Canada. He graduated with a bachelor's degree in music from the University of Western Ontario in 1975 and is an accomplished concert pianist. He remained at the university for an additional year, however, to complete a bachelor's degree in English.

After college, Highway worked at The Native Peoples' Resource Centre in London, Ontario, and at the Ontario Federation of Indian Friendship Centres in Toronto. Highway traveled to reserves across Canada, working with Native people in schools, prisons, and other institutions. He also began writing plays about Native life, many of which were performed on reserves and in Native community centers. He first worked on *The Rez Sisters* with the De-ba-jeh-mu-jig Theatre Company of Manitoulin Island, Ontario, in 1986. Like many Native theater companies, De-ba-jeh-mu-jig is devoted to the production of new plays by Native playwrights and produces an increasing number of its plays in Native languages. As artistic director of the Native Earth Performing Arts Company, Highway produced *The Rez Sisters* again in Toronto in December of 1986, where it won the Dora Mavor Moore Award for the best new play of the season and was runner-up for outstanding Canadian play of the year. The play was produced in 1993 in New York by the American Indian Community House and the New York Theater Workshop.

Highway's next play, *Dry Lips Oughta Move to Kapuskasing* was first produced in Toronto in 1989 by the Native Earth Performing Arts Company. It was later moved to the Royal Alexandra Theatre in Toronto, one of the very few Canadian plays—and the first by a Native playwright—to receive a full-scale production by a commercial theater. Highway continues to work as artistic director of Native Earth Performing Arts, one of many important Native theater companies now working in Canada and the United States (others include Four Winds Theatre, Native Theatre School, Ondinnok, Takwakin Theatre, Awasikan Theatre, and A-Maize Theatre in Canada; Spiderwoman Theater, Institute of American Indian Arts, American Indian Theater Company, Minneapolis American Indian AIDS Task Force, and Off the Beaten Path in the United States). Though Highway is gay, his central aims as a playwright to date have been to make Native narrative and mythological traditions more central to contemporary Native—and non-Native—arts.

DRY LIPS OUGHTA MOVE TO KAPUSKASING

Like *The Rez Sisters*, *Dry Lips Oughta Move to Kapuskasing* concerns life on the fictional Wasaychigan Hill reserve and is written in a mixture of English, Cree, and Ojibway. However, while *The Rez Sisters* concerns a group of Native women who travel to Toronto for the "World's Biggest Bingo," *Dry Lips* is a much darker and more violent play, concerning the men of the reserve. In some respects, the poverty of life on the reserve is made evident in the play's opening scene, the run-down living room of the reserve house shared by Big Joey and Gazelle Nataways, and is developed through the men's interrupted plans to improve life on the "rez." While the women have formed a hockey team (the importance of hockey is epitomized in Pierre's mantra, "Hockey. Life. Hockey. Life."), the men squabble about their plans: Zachary Jeremiah Keechigeesik's bakery, Big Joey's radio station, and Pierre St. Pierre's new job as referee for the women's games. In some ways, the men seem threatened by the women's independence and by their brash appropriation of hockey, and this anxiety seems to imply a more generalized impotence: seedy Creature Nataways does Big Joey's bidding, even though his wife Gazelle has moved in with Big Joey; Simon Starblanket is absorbed in an endlessly aborted effort at cultural revival; Dickie Bird Halked, born with fetal alcohol syndrome, is at once shy and explosive, violently raping Patsy Pegahmagahbow with a crucifix. Even Pierre St. Pierre has a hard time finding his other skate.

Hanging around, drinking beer, complaining about the women—in many ways the Native men seem to epitomize "Canadian hoser culture," in the words of one Native critic of the play. Yet the men continually blame the women for the state of their lives, as Big Joey does in act 2: "I hate them fuckin' bitches. Because they—our own women—took the fuckin' power away from us faster than the FBI ever did." Big Joey's tirade points up the play's most controversial element, which centers on the performance of the Trickster figure Nanabush. The play begins and ends with Zachary awakening on the floor of Big Joey's house; we don't discover until the end of the play that the action has been a kind of dream, maybe a nightmare. Throughout, Nanabush occupies an elevated stage, sometimes watching the action, sometimes participating in it. In Native mythology, Nanabush is capable of changing shape and gender; neither explicitly male nor female, the Trickster uses his/her wiles in a range of legendary escapades. In *Dry Lips,* however, Nanabush takes "female" shape in a number of ways—assuming outsized breasts to play Gazelle Nataways, a large rear-end to play Patsy ("Big-Bum") Pegahmagahbow, and so on. In one reading of the play—a dream play, after all—Nanabush here enacts the men's phobias and fantasies about women, and so offers an implied critique of their sexist attitudes. From another perspective, though, one shared by many Native women who saw the play, the way Nanabush is characterized *as* a woman—her appearance (a version of the derogatory "squaw" stereotype), the "stripper" scene, the rape scene, the loss of the hockey puck in Gazelle/Nanabush's enormous breasts—merely reinforces the fundamentally misogynistic attitudes of the men in the play. In this sense, *Dry Lips Oughta Move to Kapuskasing* seems poised on the razor's edge of political theater: readers, audiences, and producers of the play must consider whether it criticizes the sexist and possibly misogynist ways women are presented in the play, or whether it merely reinforces such attitudes.

PRODUCTION NOTES

The set for the original production of *Dry Lips Oughta Move to Kapuskasing* contained certain elements which I think are essential to the play.

First of all, it was designed on two levels, the lower of which was the domain of the "real" Wasaychigan Hill. This lower level contained, on stage-left, Big Joey's living room/kitchen, with its kitchen counter at the back and, facing down-stage, an old brown couch with a television set a few feet in front of it. This television set could be made to double as a smaller rock for the forest scenes. Stage-right had Spooky Lacroix's kitchen, with its kitchen counter (for which Big Joey's kitchen counter could double) and its table and chairs.

In front of all this was an open area, the floor of which was covered with Teflon, a material which looks like ice and on which one can actually skate, using real ice skates; this was the rink for the hockey arena scenes. With lighting effects, this area could also be turned into "the forest" surrounding the village of Wasaychigan Hill, with its leafless winter trees. The only other essential element here was a larger jutting rock beside which, for instance, Zachary Jeremiah Keechigeesik and Simon Starblanket meet, a rock which could be made to glow at certain key points. Pierre's "little boot-leg joint" in Act Two, with its "window," was also created with lighting effects.

The upper level of the set was almost exclusively the realm of Nanabush. The principal element here was her perch, located in the very middle of this area. The perch was actually an old jukebox of a late 60's/early 70's make, but it was semi-hidden throughout most of the play, so that it was fully revealed as this fabulous jukebox only at those few times when it was needed; the effect sought after here is of this magical, mystical jukebox hanging in the night air, like a haunting and persistent memory, high up over the village of Wasaychigan Hill. Over and behind this perch was suspended a huge full moon whose glow came on, for the most part, only during the outdoor scenes, which all take place at nighttime. All other effects in this area were accomplished with lighting. The very front of this level, all along its edge, was also utilized as the "bleachers" area for the hockey arena scenes.

Easy access was provided for between the lower and the upper levels of this set.

The "sound-scape" of *Dry Lips Oughta Move to Kapuskasing* was mostly provided for by a musician playing, live, on harmonica, off to the side. It is as though the "dream-scape" of the play were laced all the way through with Zachary Jeremiah Keechigeesik's "idealized" form of harmonica playing, permeated with a definite "blues" flavor. Although Zachary ideally should play his harmonica, and not too well, in those few scenes where it is called for, the sound of this harmonica is most effectively used to underline and highlight the many magical appearances of Nanabush in her various guises.

Spooky Lacroix's baby, towards the end of Act Two, can, and should, be played by a doll wrapped in a blanket. But for greatest effect, Zachary's baby, at the very end of the play, should be played by a real baby, preferably about five months of age.

Finally, both Cree and Ojibway are used freely in this text for the reasons that these two languages, belonging to the same linguistic family, are very similar and that the fictional reserve of Wasaychigan Hill has a mixture of both Cree and Ojibway residents.

A NOTE ON NANABUSH

The dream world of North American Indian mythology is inhabited by the most fantastic creatures, beings and events. Foremost among these beings is the "Trickster," as pivotal and important a figure in our world as Christ is in the realm of Christian mythology. "Weesageechak" in Cree, "Nanabush" in Ojibway, "Raven" in others, "Coyote" in still others, this Trickster goes by many names and many guises. In fact, he can assume any guise he chooses. Essentially a comic, clownish sort of character, his role is to teach us about the nature and the meaning of existence on the planet Earth; he straddles the consciousness of man and that of God, the Great Spirit.

The most explicit distinguishing feature between the North American Indian languages and the European languages is that in Indian (e.g., Cree, Ojibway), there is no gender. In Cree, Ojibway, etc., unlike English, French, German, etc., the male-female-neuter hierarchy is entirely absent. So that by this system of thought, the central hero figure from our mythology—theology, if you will—is theoretically neither exclusively male nor exclusively female, or is both simultaneously. Therefore, where in *The Rez Sisters,* Nanabush was male, in this play—"flip-side" to *The Rez Sisters*—Nanabush is female.

Some say that Nanabush left this continent when the white man came. We believe she/he is still here among us—albeit a little the worse for wear and tear—having assumed other guises. Without the continued presence of this extraordinary figure, the core of Indian culture would be gone forever.

Tomson Highway

DRY LIPS OUGHTA MOVE TO KAPUSKASING

Tomson Highway

—— CHARACTERS ——

NANABUSH (*as the spirit of Gazelle Nataways, Patsy
    Pegahmagahbow and Black Lady Halked*)
ZACHARY JEREMIAH KEECHIGEESIK—*41 years old*
BIG JOEY—*39*
CREATURE NATAWAYS—*39*
DICKIE BIRD HALKED—*17*
PIERRE ST. PIERRE—*53*
SPOOKY LACROIX—*39*

SIMON STARBLANKET—*20*
HERA KEECHIGEESIK—*39*

TIME: *Between Saturday, February 3, 1990, 11 P.M., and
Saturday, February 10, 1990, 11 A.M.*

PLACE: *The Wasaychigan Hill Indian Reserve, Manitoulin Island,
Ontario*

—— ACT ONE ——

*The set for this first scene is the rather shabby and very messy living
room/kitchen of the reserve house* BIG JOEY *and* GAZELLE NATAWAYS
*currently share. Prominently displayed on one wall is a life-size pin-
up poster of Marilyn Monroe. The remains of a party are obvious. On
the worn-out old brown couch, with its back towards the entrance, lies*
ZACHARY JEREMIAH KEECHIGEESIK, *a very handsome Indian man.
He is naked, passed out. The first thing we see when the light comes
up—a very small "spot," precisely focussed—is* ZACHARY's *bare,
naked bum. Then, from behind the couch, we see a woman's leg, sliding languorously into a nylon stocking and right over Zachary's bum.
It is* NANABUSH, *as the spirit of* GAZELLE NATAWAYS, *dressing to
leave. She eases herself luxuriously over the couch and over Zachary's
bum and then reaches under Zachary's sleeping head, from where she
gently pulls a gigantic pair of false, rubberized breasts. She proceeds to
put these on over her own bare breasts. Then* NANABUSH/GAZELLE
NATAWAYS *sashays over to the side of the couch, picks a giant hockey
sweater up off the floor and shimmies into it. The sweater has a huge,
plunging neck-line, with the capital letter "W" and the number "1"
prominently sewn on. Then she sashays back to the couch and behind
it. Pleasurably and mischievously, she leans over and plants a kiss on
Zachary's bum, leaving behind a gorgeous, luminescent lip-stick mark.
The last thing she does before she leaves is to turn the television on.
This television sits facing the couch that* ZACHARY *lies on.*
NANABUSH/GAZELLE *does not use her hand for this, though; instead,
she turns the appliance on with one last bump of her voluptuous hips.
"Hockey Night in Canada" comes on. The sound of this hockey game
is on only slightly, so that we hear it as background "music" all the
way through the coming scene. Then* NANABUSH/GAZELLE *exits, to sit
on her perch on the upper level of the set. The only light left on stage is
that coming from the television screen, giving off its eery glow. Beat.*

The kitchen door bangs open, the "kitchen light" flashes on and BIG
JOEY *and* CREATURE NATAWAYS *enter,* CREATURE *carrying a case of
beer on his head. At first, they are oblivious to* ZACHARY's *presence.
Also at about this time, the face of* DICKIE BIRD HALKED *emerges from
the shadows at the "kitchen window." Silently, he watches the rest of
the proceedings, taking a particular interest—even fascination—in
the movements and behavior of* BIG JOEY.

BIG JOEY: (*Calling out for* GAZELLE *who, of course, is not home.*) Hey,
    bitch!

Keechigeesik means "heaven" or "great sky" in Cree   **Wasaychigan** means "window" in Ojibway

CREATURE: (*As he, at regular intervals, bangs the beer case down on
    the kitchen counter, rips it open, pops bottles open, throws one to* BIG
    JOEY, *all noises that serve to "punctuate" the rat-a-tat rhythm of* 5
    his frenetic speech.) Batman oughta move to Kapuskasing,
    nah, Kap's too good for Batman, right, Big Joey? I tole you
    once I tole you twice he shouldna done it he shouldna done
    what he went and did goddawful Batman Manitowabi the
    way he went and crossed that blue line with the puck, man, 10
    he's got the flippin' puck right in the palm of his flippin'
    hand and only a minute-and-a-half to go he just about gave
    me the shits the way Batman Manitowabi went and crossed
    that blue line right in front of that brick shithouse of a
    whiteman why the hell did that brick shit-house of a white- 15
    man have to be there . . .
ZACHARY: (*Talking in his sleep.*) No!
CREATURE: Hey!

(BIG JOEY *raises a finger signaling* CREATURE *to shut up.*)

ZACHARY: I said no!
CREATURE: (*In a hoarse whisper.*) That's not a TV kind of sound. 20
BIG JOEY: Shhh!
ZACHARY: . . . goodness sakes, Hera, you just had a baby . . .
CREATURE: That's a real life kind of sound, right, Big Joey? (BIG
    JOEY *and* CREATURE *slowly come over to the couch.*)
ZACHARY: . . . women playing hockey . . . damn silliest thing I 25
    heard in my life . . .
BIG JOEY: Well, well . . .
CREATURE: Ho-leee! (*Whispering.*) Hey, what's that on his arse
    look like lip marks.
ZACHARY: . . . Simon Starblanket, that's who's gonna help me 30
    with my bakery . . .
CREATURE: He's stitchless, he's nude, he's gonna pneumonia . . .
BIG JOEY: Shut up.
CREATURE: Get the camera. Chris'sakes, take a picture.

(CREATURE *scrambles for the Polaroid, which he finds under one end
of the couch.*)

ZACHARY: . . . Simon! (*Jumps up.*) What the?! 35
CREATURE: Surprise! (*Camera flashes.*)
ZACHARY: Put that damn thing away. What are you doing here?
    Where's my wife? Hera!

(*He realizes he's naked, grabs a cast iron frying pan and slaps it over
his crotch, almost castrating himself in the process.*)

Ooof!

40 BIG JOEY: *(Smiling.)* Over easy or sunny side up, Zachary Jeremiah Keechigeesik?

ZACHARY: Get outa my house.

CREATURE: This ain't your house. This is Big Joey's house, right, Big Joey?

45 BIG JOEY: Shut up.

ZACHARY: Creature Nataways. Get outa here. Gimme that camera.

CREATURE: Come and geeeet it!

(Grabs ZACHARY's *pants from the floor.)*

ZACHARY: Cut it out. Gimme them goddamn pants.

50 CREATURE: *(Singing.)* Lipstick on your arshole, tole da tale on you-hoo.

ZACHARY: What? *(Straining to see his bum.)* Oh lordy, lordy, lordy gimme them pants.

(As he tries to wipe the stain off.)

CREATURE: Here doggy, doggy. Here poochie, poochie woof
55 woof! *(*ZACHARY *grabs the pants. They rip almost completely in half.* CREATURE *yelps.)* Yip!

(Momentary light up on NANABUSH/GAZELLE, *up on her perch, as she gives a throaty laugh.* BIG JOEY *echoes this,* CREATURE *tittering away in the background.)*

ZACHARY: Hey, this is not my doing, Big Joey. *(As he clumsily puts on what's left of his pants.* CREATURE *manages to get in one more shot with the camera.)* We were just having a nice quiet drink
60 over at Andy Manigitogan's when Gazelle Nataways shows up. She brought me over here to give me the recipe for her bannock apple pie cuz, goodness sakes, Simon Starblanket was saying it's the best, that pie was selling like hot cakes at the bingo and he knows I'm tryna establish this reserve's first
65 pie-making business gimme that camera.

*(*BIG JOEY *suddenly makes a lunge at* ZACHARY *but* ZACHARY *evades him.)*

CREATURE: *(In the background, like a little dog.)* Yah, yah.

BIG JOEY: *(Slowly stalking* ZACHARY *around the room.)* You know, Zach, there's a whole lotta guys on this rez been slippin' my old lady the goods but there ain't but a handful been stupid
70 enough to get caught by me. *(He snaps his fingers and, as always,* CREATURE *obediently scurries over. He hands* BIG JOEY *the picture of* ZACHARY *naked on the couch.* BIG JOEY *shows the picture to* ZACHARY, *right up to his face.)* Kinda em-bare-ass-in' for a hoity-toity educated community pillar like you, eh
75 Zach?

*(*ZACHARY *grabs for the picture but* BIG JOEY *snaps it away.)*

ZACHARY: What do you want?

BIG JOEY: What's this I hear about you tellin' the chief I can wait for my radio station?

ZACHARY: *(As he proceeds with looking around the room to collect and
80 put on what he can find of his clothes.* BIG JOEY *and* CREATURE *follow him around, obviously enjoying his predicament.)* I don't know where the hell you heard that from.

BIG JOEY: Yeah, right. Well, Lorraine Manigitogan had a word or two with Gazelle Nataways the other night. When you presented your initial proposal at the band office, you said: 85 "Joe can wait. He's only got another three months left in the hockey season."

ZACHARY: I never said no such thing.

BIG JOEY: Bullshit.

ZACHARY: W-w-w-what I said was that employment at this bak- 90 ery of mine would do nothing but add to those in such places as those down at the arena. I never mentioned your name once. And I said it only in passing reference to the fact . . .

BIG JOEY: . . . that this radio idea of mine doesn't have as much long-term significance to the future of this community as 95 this fancy bakery idea of yours, Mr. Pillsbury dough-boy, right?

ZACHARY: If that's what you heard, then you didn't hear it from Lorraine Manigitogan. You got it from Gazelle Nataways and you know yourself she's got a bone to pick with . . . 100

BIG JOEY: You know, Zach, you and me, we work for the same cause, don't we?

ZACHARY: Never said otherwise.

BIG JOEY: We work for the betterment and the advancement of this community, don't we? And seeing as we're about the 105 only two guys in this whole hell-hole who's got the get-up-and-go to do something . . .

ZACHARY: That's not exactly true, Joe. Take a look at Simon Starblanket . . .

BIG JOEY: . . . we should be working together, not against. 110 What do you say you simply postpone that proposal to the Band Council . . .

ZACHARY: I'm sorry. Can't do that.

BIG JOEY: *(Cornering* ZACHARY.) Listen here, bud. You turned your back on me when everybody said I was responsible for 115 that business in Espanola seventeen years ago and you said nothin'. I overlooked that. Never said nothin'. *(*ZACHARY *remembers his undershorts and proceeds, with even greater desperation, to look for them, zeroing in on the couch and under it.* BIG JOEY *catches the drift and snaps his fingers, signaling* CREATURE 120 *to look for the shorts under the couch.* CREATURE *jumps for the couch. Without missing a beat,* BIG JOEY *continues.)* You turned your back on me when you said you didn't want nothin' to do with me from that day on. I overlooked that. Never said nothin'. You gave me one hell of a slap in the face when 125 your wife gave my Gazelle that kick in the belly. I overlooked that. Never said nothin'. *(*CREATURE, *having found the shorts among the junk under the couch just split seconds before* ZACHARY *does, throws them to* BIG JOEY. BIG JOEY *holds the shorts up to* ZACHARY, *smiling with satisfaction.)* That, how- 130 ever, was the last time . . .

ZACHARY: That wasn't my fault, Joe. It's that witch woman of yours Gazelle Nataways provoked that fight between her and Hera and you know yourself Hera tried to come and sew up her belly again . . . 135

BIG JOEY: Zach. I got ambition . . .

ZACHARY: Yeah, right.

BIG JOEY: I aim to get that radio station off the ground, starting with them games down at my arena.

ZACHARY: Phhhh! 140

BIG JOEY: I aim to get a chain of them community radio stations not only on this here island but beyond as well . . .

ZACHARY: Dream on, Big Joey, dream on . . .

BIG JOEY: . . . and I aim to prove this broadcasting of games
145   among the folks is one sure way to get some pride . . .

ZACHARY: Bullshit! You're in it for yourself.

BIG JOEY: . . . some pride and dignity back so you just get your
ass on out of my house and you go tell that Chief your
Band Council Resolution can wait until next fiscal year or
150   else . . .

ZACHARY: I ain't doing no such thing, Joe, no way. Not when
I'm this close.

BIG JOEY: (As he eases himself down onto the couch, twirling the shorts
with his fore-finger.) . . . or else I get my Gazelle Nataways to
155   wash these skivvies of yours, put them in a box all nice and
gussied up, your picture on top, show up at your door-stop
and hand them over to your wife. (Silence.)

ZACHARY: (Quietly, to BIG JOEY.) Gimme them shorts. (No answer. Then to CREATURE.) Gimme them snapshots. (Still no
160   response.)

BIG JOEY: (Dead calm.) Get out.

ZACHARY: (Seeing he can't win for the moment, prepares to exit.) You
may have won this time, Joe, but . . .

BIG JOEY: (Like a steel trap.) Get out.

(Silence. Finally ZACHARY exits, looking very humble. Seconds before
ZACHARY's exit, DICKIE BIRD HALKED, to avoid being seen by ZACHARY,
disappears from the "window." The moment ZACHARY is gone, CREATURE
scurries to the kitchen door, shaking his fist in the direction of the already-
departed ZACHARY.)

165   CREATURE: Damn rights! (Then strutting like a cock, he turns to BIG
JOEY.) Zachary Jeremiah Keechigeesik never shoulda come
in your house, Big Joey. Thank god, Gazelle Nataways ain't
my wife no more . . . (BIG JOEY merely has to throw a glance
in CREATURE's direction to intimidate him. At once, CREATURE
170   reverts back to his usual nervous self.) . . . not really, she's yours
now, right, Big Joey? It's you she's livin' with these days,
not me.

BIG JOEY: (As he sits on the couch with his beer, mostly ignoring CREA-
TURE and watching the hockey game on television.) Don't make
175   her my wife.

CREATURE: But you live together, you sleep together, you eat
ooops!

BIG JOEY: Still don't make her my wife.

CREATURE: (As he proceeds to try to clean up the mess around the
180   couch, mostly shoving everything back under it.) I don't mind,
Big Joey, I really don't. I tole you once I tole you twice she's
yours now. It's like I loaned her to you, I don't mind. I can
take it. We made a deal, remember? The night she threw
the toaster at me and just about broke my skull, she tole
185   me: "I had enough, Creature Nataways, I had enough from
you. I had your kids and I had your disease and that's all I
ever want from you, I'm leavin'." And then she grabbed her
suitcase and she grabbed the kids, no, she didn't even grab
the kids, she grabbed the TV and she just sashayed herself
190   over here. She left me. It's been four years now, Big Joey, I
know, I know. Oh, it was hell, it was hell at first but you
and me we're buddies since we're babies, right? So I
thought it over for about a year . . . then one day I swallowed
my pride and I got up off that chesterfield and I walked over
195   here, I opened your door and I shook your hand and I said:

"It's okay, Big Joey, it's okay." And then we went and played
darts in Espanola except we kinda got side-tracked, remember, Big Joey, we ended up on that three-day bender?

BIG JOEY: Creature Nataways?

CREATURE: What?   200

BIG JOEY: You talk too much.

CREATURE: I tole you once I tole you twice I don't mind . . .

(But PIERRE ST. PIERRE comes bursting in, in a state of great excitement.)

PIERRE: (Addressing the case of beer directly.) Hallelujah! Have you
heard the news?

CREATURE: Pierre St. Pierre. Chris'sakes, knock. You're walkin'   205
into a civilized house.

PIERRE: The news. Have you heard the news?

CREATURE: I'll tell you a piece of news. Anyways, we come in
the door and guess who . . .

BIG JOEY: (To CREATURE.) Sit down.   210

PIERRE: Gimme a beer.

CREATURE: (To PIERRE.) Sit down.

PIERRE: Gimme a beer.

BIG JOEY: Give him a fuckin' beer. (But PIERRE has already
grabbed, opened and is drinking a beer.)   215

CREATURE: Have a beer.

PIERRE: (Talking out the side of his mouth, as he continues drinking.)
Tank you.

BIG JOEY: Talk.

PIERRE: (Putting his emptied bottle down triumphantly and grabbing   220
another beer.) Toast me.

BIG JOEY: Spit it out.

CREATURE: Chris'sakes.

PIERRE: Toast me.

CREATURE: Toast you? The hell for?   225

PIERRE: Shut up. Just toast me.

CREATURE/BIG JOEY: Toast.

PIERRE: Tank you. You just toasted "The Ref."

CREATURE: (To PIERRE.) The ref? (To BIG JOEY.) The what?

PIERRE: "The Ref!"   230

CREATURE: The ref of the what?

PIERRE: The ref. I'm gonna be the referee down at the arena.
Big Joey's arena. The Wasaychigan Hill Hippodrome.

CREATURE: We already got a referee.

PIERRE: Yeah, but this here's different, this here's special.   235

BIG JOEY: I'd never hire a toothless old bootlegger like you.

PIERRE: They play their first game in just a coupla days.
Against the Canoe Lake Bravettes. And I got six teeth left
so you just keep your trap shut about my teeth.

CREATURE: The Canoe Lake Bravettes?   240

BIG JOEY: Who's "they"?

PIERRE: Haven't you heard?

BIG JOEY: Who's "they"?

PIERRE: I don't believe this.

BIG JOEY: Who's "they"?   245

PIERRE: I don't believe this. (BIG JOEY bangs PIERRE on the head.)
Oww, you big bully! The Wasaychigan Hill Wailerettes, of
course. I'm talkin' about the Wasy Wailerettes, who else
geez.

CREATURE: The Wasy Wailerettes? Chris'sakes . . .   250

PIERRE: Dominique Ladouche, Black Lady Halked, that terrible Dictionary woman, Fluffy Sainte-Marie, Dry Lips

Manigitogan, Leonarda Lee Starblanket, Annie Cook, June Bug McLeod, Big Bum Pegahmagahbow, all twenty-seven of 'em. Them women from right here on this reserve, a whole batch of 'em, they upped and they said: "Bullshit! Ain't nobody on the face of this earth's gonna tell us us women's got no business playin' hockey. That's bullshit!" That's what they said: "Bullshit!" So. They took matters into their own hands. And, holy shit la marde, I almost forgot to tell you my wife Veronique St. Pierre, she went and made up her mind she's joinin' the Wasy Wailerettes, only the other women wouldn't let her at first on account she never had no babies—cuz, you see, you gotta be pregnant or have piles and piles of babies to be a Wasy Wailerette—but my wife, she put her foot down and she says: "Zhaboonigan Peterson may be just my adopted daughter and she may be retarded as a doormat but she's still my baby." That's what she says to 'em. And she's on and they're playin' hockey and the Wasy Wailerettes, they're just a-rarin' to go, who woulda thunk it, huh?

CREATURE: Ho-leee!

PIERRE: God's truth . . .

BIG JOEY: They never booked the ice.

PIERRE: Ha! Booked it through Gazelle Nataways. Sure as I'm alive and walkin' these treacherous icy roads . . .

BIG JOEY: Hang on.

PIERRE: . . . god's truth in all its naked splendor. (As he pops open yet another beer.) I kid you not, gentlemen, not for one slippery goddamn minute. Toast!

BIG JOEY: (Grabbing the bottle right out of PIERRE's mouth.) Where'd you sniff out all this crap?

PIERRE: From my wife, who else? My wife, Veronique St. Pierre, she told me. She says to me: "Pierre St. Pierre, you'll eat your shorts but I'm playin' hockey and I don't care what you say. Or think." And she left. No. First, she cleaned out my wallet, (Grabs his beer back from BIG JOEY's hand.) grabbed her big brown rosaries from off the wall. Then she left. Just slammed the door and left. Period. I just about ate my shorts. Toast!

CREATURE: Shouldn't we . . . shouldn't we stop them?

PIERRE: Phhht! . . . (CREATURE just misses getting spat on.)

CREATURE: Ayoah!

PIERRE: . . . Haven't seen hide nor hair of 'em since. Gone to Sudbury. Every single last one of 'em. Piled theirselves into seven cars and just took off. Them back wheels was squealin' and rattlin' like them little jinger bells. Just past tea-time. Shoppin'. Hockey equipment. Phhht! (Again, CREATURE just misses getting spat on.)

CREATURE: Ayoah! It's enough to give you the shits every time he opens his mouth.

PIERRE: And they picked me. Referee.

BIG JOEY: And why, may I ask?

PIERRE: (Faking humility.) Oh, I don't know. Somethin' about the referee here's too damn perschnickety. That drum-bangin' young whipperschnapper, Simon Starblanket, (Grabbing yet another beer.) he's got the rules all mixed up or somethin' like that, is what they says. They kinda wanna play it their own way. So they picked me. Toast me.

CREATURE: Toast.

PIERRE: To the ref.

CREATURE: To the ref.

PIERRE: Tank you. (They both drink.) Ahhh. (Pause. To BIG JOEY.) So. I want my skates.

CREATURE: Your skates?

PIERRE: My skates. I want 'em back.

CREATURE: The hell's he talkin' about now?

PIERRE: They're here. I know they're here. I loaned 'em to you, remember?

BIG JOEY: Run that by me again?

PIERRE: I loaned 'em to you. That Saturday night Gazelle Nataways came in that door with her TV and her suitcase and you and me we were sittin' right there on that old chesterfield with Lalala Lacroix sittin' between us and I loaned you my skates in return for that forty-ouncer of rye and Gazelle Nataways plunked her TV down, marched right up to Lalala Lacroix, slapped her in the face and chased her out the door. But we still had time to make the deal whereby if I wanted my skates back you'd give 'em back to me if I gave you back your forty-ouncer, right? Right. (Produces the bottle from under his coat.) Ta-da! Gimme my skates.

BIG JOEY: You sold them skates. They're mine.

PIERRE: Never you mind, Big Joey, never you mind. I want my skates. Take this. Go on. Take it.

(BIG JOEY fishes one skate out from under the couch.)

CREATURE: (To himself, as he sits on the couch.) Women playin' hockey. Ho-leee!

(BIG JOEY and PIERRE exchange bottle and skate.)

PIERRE: Tank you. (He makes a triumphant exit. BIG JOEY merely sits there and waits knowingly. Silence. Then PIERRE suddenly re-enters.) There's only one. (Silence.) Well, where the hell's the other one? (Silence. PIERRE nearly explodes with indignation.) Gimme back my bottle! Where's the other one?

BIG JOEY: You got your skate. I got my bottle.

PIERRE: Don't talk backwards at me. I'm your elder.

CREATURE: It's gone.

PIERRE: Huh?

CREATURE: Gone. The other skate's gone, right, Big Joey?

PIERRE: Gone? Where?

CREATURE: My wife Gazelle Nataways . . .

PIERRE: . . . your ex-wife . . .

CREATURE: . . . she threw it out the door two years ago the night Spooky Lacroix went crazy in the head and tried to come and rip Gazelle Nataways' door off for cheatin' at the bingo. Just about killed Spooky Lacroix too, right, Big Joey?

PIERRE: So where's my other skate?

CREATURE: At Spooky Lacroix's, I guess.

PIERRE: Aw, shit la marde, you guys don't play fair.

BIG JOEY: You go over to Spooky Lacroix's and you tell him I told you you could have your skate back.

PIERRE: No way, José. Spooky Lacroix's gonna preach at me.

BIG JOEY: Preach back.

PIERRE: You come with me. You used to be friends with Spooky Lacroix. You talk to Spooky Lacroix. Spooky Lacroix likes you.

BIG JOEY: He likes you too.

PIERRE: Yeah, but he likes you better. Oh, shit la marde! (*As he takes another beer out of the case.*) And I almost forgot to tell you they decided to make Gazelle Nataways captain of the
370 Wasy Wailerettes. I mean, she kind of . . . decided on her own, if you know what I mean.

BIG JOEY: Spooky Lacroix's waitin' for you.

PIERRE: How do you know?

BIG JOEY: God told me.

375 PIERRE: (*Pause.* PIERRE *actually wonders to himself. Then:*) Aw, bullshit.

(*Exits. Silence. Then* BIG JOEY *and* CREATURE *look at each other, break down and laugh themselves into prolonged hysterical fits. After a while, they calm down and come to a dead stop. They sit and think. They look at the hockey game on the television. Then, dead serious, they turn to each other.*)

CREATURE: Women . . . Gazelle Nataways . . . hockey? Ho-leee . . .

BIG JOEY: (*Still holding* PIERRE's *bottle of whiskey.*) Chris'-sakes . . .

(*Fade-out.*)

(*From this darkness emerges the sound of* SPOOKY LACROIX's *voice, singing with great emotion. As he sings, the lights fade in on his kitchen, where* DICKIE BIRD HALKED *is sitting across the table from* SPOOKY LACROIX. DICKIE BIRD *is scribbling on a piece of paper with a pencil.* SPOOKY *is knitting (pale blue baby booties). A bible sits on the table to the left of* SPOOKY, *a knitting pattern to his right. The place is covered with knitted doodads: knitted doilies, tea cozy, a tacky picture of "The Last Supper" with knitted frame and, on the wall, as subtly conspicuous as possible, a crucifix with pale blue knitted baby booties covering each of its four extremities. Throughout this scene,* SPOOKY *periodically consults the knitting pattern, wearing tiny little reading glasses, perched "just so" on the end of his nose. He knits with great difficulty and, therefore, with great concentration, sometimes, in moments of excitement, getting the bible and the knitting pattern mixed up with each other. He has tremendous difficulty getting the "disturbed"* DICKIE BIRD *to sit still and pay attention.*)

SPOOKY: (*Singing.*) Everybody oughta know. Everybody oughta
380 know. Who Jesus is. (*Speaking.*) This is it. This is the end. Igwani eeweepoonaskeewuk. ("The end of the world is at hand.") Says right here in the book. Very, very, very important to read the book. If you want the Lord to come into your life, Dickie Bird Halked, you've got to read the book.
385 Not much time left. Yessiree. 1990. The last year. This will be the last year of our lives. Clear as a picture. The end of the world is here. At last. About time too, with the world going crazy, people shooting, killing each other left, right
390 and center. Jet planes full of people crashing into the bushes, lakes turning black, fish choking to death. Terrible. Terrible. (DICKIE BIRD *shoves a note he's been scribbling over to* SPOOKY.) What's this? (SPOOKY *reads, with some difficulty.*) "How . . . do . . . you . . . make . . . babies?" (*Shocked.*) Dickie Bird Halked? At your age? Surely. Anyway. That
395 young Starblanket boy who went and shot himself. Right here. Right in the einsteins. Bleeding from the belly, all this white mushy stuff come oozing out. Yuch! Brrr! I guess there's just nothing better to do for the young people on this reserve these days than go around shooting their ein-
400 steins out from inside their bellies. But the Lord has had

enough. He's sick of it. No more, he says, no more. This is it. (DICKIE BIRD *shoves another note over.* SPOOKY *pauses to read. And finishes.*) Why, me and Lalala, we're married. And we're gonna have a baby. Period. Now. When the world comes to an end? The sky will open up. The clouds will part. And 405 the Lord will come down in a holy vapor. And only those who are born-again Christian will go with him when he goes back up. And the rest? You know what's gonna happen to the rest? They will die. Big Joey, for instance, they will go to hell and they will burn for their wicked, whorish 410 ways. But we will be taken up into the clouds to spend eternity surrounded by the wondrous and the mystical glory of god. Clear as a picture, Dickie Bird Halked, clear as a picture. So I'm telling you right now, you've got to read the book. Very, very, very important. (DICKIE BIRD *shoves a* 415 *third note over to* SPOOKY. SPOOKY *reads and finishes.*) Why, Wellington Halked's your father, Dickie Bird Halked. Don't you be asking questions like that. My sister, Black Lady Halked, that's your mother. Right? And because Wellington Halked is married to Black Lady Halked, he is 420 your father. And don't you ever let no one tell you different.

(*Black-out. From the darkness of the theater emerges the magical flickering of a luminescent powwow dancing bustle. As it moves gradually towards the downstage area, a second—and larger—bustle appears on the upper level of the set, also flickering magically and moving about. The two bustles "play" with each other, almost affectionately, looking like two giant fire flies. The smaller bustle finally reaches the downstage area and from behind it emerges the face of* SIMON STARBLANKET. *He is dancing and chanting in a forest made of light and shadows. The larger bustle remains on the upper level; behind it is the entire person of* NANABUSH *as the spirit of* PATSY PEGAHMAGAHBOW, *a vivacious young girl of eighteen with a very big bum (i.e., an over-sized prosthetic bum). From this level,* NANABUSH/PATSY *watches and "plays" with the proceedings on the lower level. The giant full moon is in full bloom behind her. From the very beginning of all this, and in counterpoint to* SIMON's *chanting, also emerges the sound of someone playing a harmonica, a sad, mournful tune. It is* ZACHARY JEREMIAH KEECHIGEESIK, *stuck in the bush in his embarrassing state, playing his heart out. Then the harmonica stops and, from the darkness, we hear* ZACHARY's *voice.*)

ZACHARY: Hey. (SIMON *hears this, looks behind, but sees nothing and continues his chanting and dancing.* SIMON *chants and dances as though he were desperately trying to find the right chant and dance. Then:*) Pssst! 425

SIMON: Awinuk awa? ("Who's this?")

ZACHARY: (*In a hoarse whisper.*) Simon Starblanket.

SIMON: Neee, Zachary Jeremiah Keechigeesik. Awus! ("Go away!") Katha peeweestatooweemin. ("Don't come bothering me [with your words].") 430

(*Finally,* ZACHARY *emerges from the shadows and from behind a large rock, carrying his harmonica in one hand and holding his torn pants together as best he can with the other.* SIMON *ignores him and continues with his chanting and dancing.*)

I. 428 **Neee** probably the most common Cree expression, meaning something like "Oh, you," or "My goodness"

ZACHARY: W-w-w-what's it cost to get one of them dough-making machines?

SIMON: *(Not quite believing his ears.)* What?

ZACHARY: Them dough-making machines. What's it cost to
435 buy one of them?

SIMON: A Hobart?

ZACHARY: A what?

SIMON: Hobart. H-O-B-A-R-T. Hobart.

ZACHARY: *(To himself.)* Hobart. Hmmm.

440 SIMON: *(Amused at the rather funny-looking ZACHARY.)* Neee,
machi ma-a, ("Oh you, but naturally,") Westinghouse for
refrigerators, Kellogg's for corn flakes igwa ("and") Hobart
for dough-making machines. Kinsitootawin na? ("Get it?")
Brand name. Except we used to call it "the pig" because it
445 had this . . . piggish kind of motion to it. But never mind.
Awus. Don't bother me.

ZACHARY: What's it cost to get this . . . pig?

SIMON: *(Laughing.)* Neee, Zachary Jeremiah, here you are, one
of Wasy's most respected citizens, standing in the middle of
450 the bush on a Saturday night in February freezing your
buns off and you want to know how much a pig costs?

ZACHARY: *(Vehemently.)* I promised Hera I'd have all this information by tonight we were supposed to sit down and discuss
the budget for this damn bakery tonight and here I went and
455 messed it all up thank god I ran into you because now you're
the only person left on this whole reserve who might have
the figures I need what's this damn dough-making machine
cost come on now tell me!

SIMON: *(A little cowed.)* Neee, about four thousand bucks.
460 Maybe five.

ZACHARY: You don't know for sure? But you worked there.

SIMON: I was only the dishwasher, Zachary Jeremiah, I didn't
own the place. Mama Louisa was a poor woman. She had really old equipment, most of which she dragged over herself
465 all the way from Italy after the Second World War. It
wouldn't cost the same today.

ZACHARY: Five thousand dollars for a Mobart, hmmm . . .

SIMON: Hobart.

ZACHARY: I wish I had a piece of paper to write all this down,
470 sheesh. You got a piece of paper on you?

SIMON: No. Just . . . this. *(Holding the dancing bustle up.)* Why
are you holding yourself like that?

ZACHARY: I was . . . standing on the road down by Andy
Manigitogan's place when this car came by and wooof!
475 My pants ripped. Ripped right down the middle. And
my shorts, well, they just . . . took off. How do you like
that, eh?

SIMON: Nope. I don't like it. Neee, awus. Kigithaskin. ("You're
lying to me.")

480 ZACHARY: W-w-w-why would I pull your leg for? I don't really
mind it except it is damn cold out here.

*(At this point, NANABUSH/PATSY, on the upper level, scurries closer to get
a better look, her giant powwow dancing bustle flickering magically in the
half-light. SIMON's attention is momentarily pulled away by this fleeting
vision.)*

SIMON: Hey! Did you see that?

(But ZACHARY, too caught up with his own dilemma, does not notice.)

ZACHARY: I'm very, very upset right now . . .

SIMON: . . . I thought I just saw Patsy Pegahmagahbow . . .
with this . . .   485

ZACHARY: *(As he looks, perplexed, in the direction SIMON indicates.)*
. . . do you think . . . my two ordinary convection ovens . . .

SIMON: *(Calling out.)* Patsy? . . . *(Pause. Then, slowly, he turns back
to ZACHARY.)* . . . like . . . she made this for me, eh? *(Referring
to the bustle.)* She and her step-mother, Rosie Kakapetum,   490
back in September, after my mother's funeral. Well, I was out
here thinking, if this . . . like, if this . . . dance didn't come
to me real natural, like from deep inside of me, then I was
gonna burn it. *(Referring to the bustle.)* Right here on this spot.
Cuz then . . . it doesn't mean anything real to me, does it?   495
Like, it's false . . . it's driving me crazy, this dream where
Indian people are just dropping off like flies . . .

*(NANABUSH/PATSY begins to "play" with the two men, almost as if with
the help of the winter night's magic and the power of the full moon, she
were weaving a spell around SIMON and ZACHARY.)*

ZACHARY: *(Singing softly to himself.)* Hot cross buns. Hot cross
buns. One a penny, two a penny, hot cross buns . . .

SIMON: . . . something has to be done . . .   500

ZACHARY: *(Speaking.)* . . . strawberry pies . . .

SIMON: . . . in this dream . . .

ZACHARY: . . . so fresh and flakey they fairly bubble over with
the cream from the very breast of Mother Nature herself . . .

SIMON: . . . the drum has to come back, mistigwuskeek ("the   505
drum") . . .

ZACHARY: . . . bran muffins, cherry tarts . . .

SIMON: . . . the medicine, the power, this . . .

(Holding the bustle up in the air.)

ZACHARY: . . . butter tarts . . .

SIMON: . . . has to come back. We've got to learn to dance again. 510

ZACHARY: . . . tarts tarts tarts upside-down cakes cakes cakes
and not to forget, no, never, ever to forget that Black Forest
Cake . . .

SIMON: . . . Patsy Pegahmagahbow . . .

ZACHARY: . . . cherries jubilee . . .   515

SIMON: . . . her step-mother, Rosie Kakapetum, the medicine
woman . . .

ZACHARY: . . . lemon meringue pie . . .

SIMON: . . . the power . . .

ZACHARY: . . . baked Alaska . . .   520

SIMON: . . . Nanabush! . . .

ZACHARY: *(Then suddenly, with bitterness.)* . . . Gazelle Nataways.
K'skanagoos! ("The female dog!")

*(All of a sudden, from the darkness of the winter night, emerges a strange,
eery sound; whether it is wolves howling or women wailing, we are not sure
at first. And whether this sound comes from somewhere deep in the forest,
from the full moon or where, we are not certain. But there is definitely a
"spirit" in the air. The sound of this wailing is under-cut by the sound of
rocks hitting boards, or the sides of houses, echoing, as in a vast empty
chamber. Gradually, as SIMON speaks, ZACHARY—filled with confusing
emotion as he is—takes out his harmonica, sits down on the large rock and
begins to play, a sad, mournful melody, tinged, as always, with a touch
of the blues.)*

SIMON: . . . I have my arms around this rock, this large black
525   rock sticking out of the ground, right here on this spot.
And then I hear this baby crying, from inside this rock. The
baby is crying out my name. As if I am somehow responsible for it being caught inside that rock. I can't move.
My arms, my whole body, stuck to this rock. Then this . . .
530   eagle . . . lands beside me, right over there. But this bird
has three faces, three women. And the eagle says to me: "the
baby is crying, my grand-child is crying to hear the drum
again." (NANABUSH/PATSY, *her face surrounded by the brilliant*
feathers of her bustle, so that she looks like some fantastic, mysteri-
535   *ous bird, begins to wail, her voice weaving in and out of the other*
wailing voices.) There's this noise all around us, as if rocks are
hitting the sides of houses—echoing and echoing like in a
vast empty room—and women are wailing. The whole
world is filled with this noise. (*Then* SIMON, *too, wails, a*
540   *heart-searing wail. From here on, all the wailing begins to fade.*)
Then the eagle is gone and the rock cracks and this mass of
flesh, covered with veins and blood, comes oozing out and
a woman's voice somewhere is singing something about
angels and god and angels and god . . .

(*The wailing has now faded into complete silence.* ZACHARY *finally*
rises from his seat on the rock.)

545 ZACHARY: . . . I dreamt I woke up at Gazelle Nataways' place
with no shorts on. And I got this nagging suspicion them
shorts are still over there. If you could just go on over there
now . . . I couldn't have been over there. I mean, there's my
wife Hera. And there's my bakery. And this bakery could do
550   a lot for the Indian people. Economic development. Jobs.
Bread. Apple pie. So you see, there's an awful lot that's
hanging on them shorts. This is a good chance for you to do
something for your people, Simon, if you know what I
mean . . .
555 SIMON: I'm the one who has to bring the drum back. And it's
Patsy's medicine power, that stuff she's learning from her
step-mother Rosie Kakapetum that . . . helps me . . .
ZACHARY: I go walking into my house with no underwear,
pants ripped right down the middle, not a shred of budget
560   in sight and wooof! . . .

(PIERRE ST. PIERRE *comes bursting in on the two men with his one*
skate in hand, taking them completely by surprise. NANABUSH/PATSY
disappears.)

ZACHARY: Pierre St. Pierre! Just the man . . .
PIERRE: No time. No time. Lalala Lacroix's having a baby any
minute now so I gotta get over to Spook's before she pops.
SIMON: I can go get Rosie Kakapetum.
565 PIERRE: Too old. Too old. She can't be on the team.
SIMON: Neee, what team? Rosie Kakapetum's the last mid-wife
left in Wasy, Pierre St. Pierre, of course she can't be on a
team.
ZACHARY: (*To* PIERRE.) You know that greasy shit-brown
570   chesterfield over at Gazelle Nataways?
SIMON: (*To* ZACHARY.) Mind you, if there was a team of mid-
wives, chee-i? ("eh?") Wha!
PIERRE: Gazelle Nataways? Hallelujah, haven't you heard the
news?
575 ZACHARY: What? . . . you mean . . . it's out already?

PIERRE: All up and down Wasaychigan Hill . . .
ZACHARY: (*Thoughtfully, to himself, as it dawns on him.*) The
whole place knows.
PIERRE: . . . clean across Manitoulin Island and right to the out-
skirts of Sudbury . . . 580
ZACHARY: Lordy, lordy, lordy . . .
PIERRE: Gazelle Nataways, Dominique Ladouche, Black Lady
Halked, that terrible Dictionary woman, Fluffy Sainte-Marie,
Dry Lips Manigitogan, Leonarda Lee Starblanket, Annie
Cook, June Bug McLeod, Big Bum Pegahmagahbow . . . 585
SIMON: Patsy Pegahmagahbow. Get it straight . . .
PIERRE: Quiet! I'm not finished . . . all twenty-seven of 'em . . .
SIMON: Neee, Zachary Jeremiah, your goose is cooked.
PIERRE: Phhht! Cooked and burnt right down to a nice crispy
pitch black cinder because your wife Hera Keechigeesik is 590
in on it too.

(ZACHARY, *reeling from the horror of it all, finally sits back down on*
the rock.)

SIMON: Patsy Pegahmagahbow is pregnant, Pierre St. Pierre.
She can't go running around all over Manitoulin Island
with a belly that's getting bigger by the . . .
SIMON: Aw, they're all pregnant, them women, or have piles 595
and piles of babies and I'll be right smack dab in the middle of it all just a-blowin' my whistle and a-throwin' that
dirty little black thingie around . . .
ZACHARY: (*Rising from the rock.*) Now you listen here, Pierre St.
Pierre. I may have lost my shorts under Gazelle Nataways' 600
greasy shit-brown chesterfield not one hour ago and I may
have lost my entire life, not to mention my bakery, as a result of that one very foolish mistake but I'll have you know
that my shorts, they are clean as a whistle, I change them
every day, my favorite color is light blue and black and 605
crusted with shit my shorts most certainly are not!
SIMON: (*Surprised and thrilled at* ZACHARY'S *renewed "fighting"*
spirit.) Wha!
PIERRE: Whoa! Easy, Zachary Jeremiah, easy there. Not one
stitch of your shorts has anything whatsoever to do with the 610
revolution.
SIMON: Pierre St. Pierre, what revolution are you wheezing and
snorting on about?
PIERRE: The puck. I'm talkin' about the puck.
ZACHARY: The puck? 615
SIMON: The puck?
PIERRE: Yes, the puck. The puck, the puck, the puck and nothin'
but the goddam puck they're playin' hockey, them women
from right here on this reserve, they're playin' hockey and
nothin', includin' Zachary Jeremiah Keechigeesik's bright 620
crispy undershorts, is gonna stop 'em.
SIMON: Women playing hockey. Neee, watstagatch! ("Good
grief!")
PIERRE: "Neee, watstagatch" is right because they're in Sudbury, as I speak, shoppin' for hockey equipment, and I'm 625
the referee! Outa my way! Or the Lacroixs will pop before I
get there.

(*He begins to exit.*)

ZACHARY: Pierre St. Pierre, get me my shorts or I'll report your
bootleg joint to the police.

630 PIERRE: No time. No time.

(Exits.)

ZACHARY: *(Calling out.)* Did Hera go to Sudbury, too? *(But* PIERRE *is gone.)*

SIMON: *(Thoughtfully to himself, as he catches another glimpse of* NANABUSH/PATSY *and her bustle.)* . . . rocks hitting boards . . .

635 ZACHARY: *(To himself.)* What in God's name is happening to Wasaychigan Hill . . .

SIMON: . . . women wailing . . .

ZACHARY: *(With even greater urgency.)* Do you think those two or-dinary convection ovens are gonna do the job or should I

640 get one of them great big pizza ovens right away?

SIMON: . . . pucks . . .

ZACHARY: Simon, I'm desperate!

SIMON: *(Finally, snapping out of his speculation and looking straight into* ZACHARY's *face.)* Neee, Zachary Jeremiah. Okay. Goes

645 like this. *(Then, very quickly:)* It depends on what you're gonna bake, eh? Like if you're gonna bake bread and, like, lots of it, you're gonna need one of them great big ovens but if you're gonna bake just muffins . . .

ZACHARY: *(In the background.)* . . . muffins, nah, not just

650 muffins . . .

SIMON: . . . then all you need is one of them ordinary little ovens but like I say, I was only the dishwasher . . .

ZACHARY: How many employees were there in your bakery?

SIMON: . . . it depends on how big a community you're gonna

655 serve, Zachary Jeremiah . . .

ZACHARY: . . . nah, Wasy, just Wasy, to start with . . .

SIMON: . . . like, we had five, one to make the dough—like, mix the flour and the water and the yeast and all that— like, this guy had to be at work by six A.M., that's gonna

660 be hard here in Wasy, Zachary Jeremiah, I'm telling you that right now . . .

ZACHARY: . . . nah, I can do that myself, no problem . . .

SIMON: . . . then we had three others to roll the dough and knead and twist and punch and pound it on this great big

665 wooden table . . .

ZACHARY: . . . I'm gonna need a great big wooden table? . . .

SIMON: . . . hard wood, Zachary Jeremiah, not soft wood. And then one to actually bake the loaves, like, we had these long wooden paddles, eh? . . .

670 ZACHARY: . . . paddles . . .

SIMON: . . . yeah, paddles, Zachary Jeremiah, real long ones. It was kinda neat, actually . . .

ZACHARY: . . . go on, go on . . .

SIMON: Listen here, Zachary Jeremiah, I'm going to Sudbury

675 next Saturday, okay? And if you wanna come along, I can take you straight to Mama Louisa's Pasticerria myself. I'll introduce you to the crusty old girl and you can take a good long look at her rubbery old Hobart, how's that? You can even touch it if you want, neee . . .

680 ZACHARY: . . . really? . . .

SIMON: Me? I'm asking Patsy Pegahmagahbow to marry me . . .

ZACHARY: . . . Simon, Simon . . .

SIMON: . . . and we're gonna hang two thousand of these things *(Referring to his dancing bustle.)* all over Manitoulin Island,

685 me and Patsy and our baby. And me and Patsy and our baby and this Nanabush character, we're gonna be dancing up

and down Wasaychigan Hill like nobody's business cuz I'm gonna go out there and I'm gonna bring that drum back if it kills me.

ZACHARY: *(Pause. Then, quietly.)* Get me a safety pin. 690

SIMON: *(Pause.)* Neee, okay. And you, Zachary Jeremiah Keechigeesik, you're gonna see a Hobart such as you have never seen one before in your entire life!

SIMON/ZACHARY: *(Smiling, almost laughing, at each other.)* Neee . . .

(Black-out.)

(Lights up on the upper level, where we see this bizarre vision of NANABUSH, *now in the guise of* BLACK LADY HALKED, *nine months pregnant (i.e., wearing a huge, out-sized prosthetic belly). Over this, she wears a maternity gown and, pacing the floor slowly, holds a huge string of rosary beads. She recites the rosary quietly to herself. She is also drinking a beer and, obviously, is a little unsteady on her feet be-cause of this.)*

(Fade-in on the lower level into SPOOKY LACROIX's *kitchen.* DICKIE BIRD HALKED *is on his knees, praying fervently to this surrealistic, miraculous vision of "the Madonna" (i.e., his own mother), which he actually sees inside his own mind. Oblivious to all this,* SPOOKY LACROIX *sits at his table, still knitting his baby booties and preach-ing away.)*

SPOOKY: Dickie Bird Halked? I want you to come to heaven 695 with me. I insist. But before you do that, you take one of them courses in sign language, help me prepare this reserve for the Lord. Can't you just see yourself, standing on that podium in the Wasaychigan Hill Hippodrome, talking sign language to the people? Talking about the Lord and 700 how close we are to the end? I could take a break. And these poor people with their meaningless, useless . . .

*(*PIERRE ST. PIERRE *comes bursting in and marches right up to* SPOOKY. *The vision of* NANABUSH/BLACK LADY HALKED *disappears.)*

PIERRE: Alright. Hand it over.

SPOOKY: *(Startled out of his wits.)* Pierre St. Pierre! You went and mixed up my booty! 705

PIERRE: I know it's here somewhere.

SPOOKY: Whatever it is you're looking for, you're not getting it until you bring the Lord into your life.

PIERRE: My skate. Gimme my skate.

SPOOKY: I don't have no skate. Now listen to me. 710

PIERRE: My skate. The skate Gazelle Nataways threw at you and just about killed you.

SPOOKY: What the hell are you gonna do with a skate at this hour of the night?

PIERRE: Haven't you heard the news? 715

SPOOKY: *(Pauses to think.)* No, I haven't heard any news.

*(*DICKIE BIRD *gets up and starts to wander around the kitchen. He looks around at random, first out the window, as if to see who has been chanting, then, eventually, he zeroes in on the crucifix on the wall and stands there looking at it. Finally, he takes it off the wall and plays with its cute little booties.)*

PIERRE: The women. I'm gonna be right smack dab in the mid-dle of it all. The revolution. Right here in Wasaychigan Hill.

SPOOKY: The Chief or the priest. Which one are they gonna
720   revolution?
PIERRE: No, no, no. Dominique Ladouche, Black Lady Halked,
        that terrible Dictionary woman, that witch Gazelle Nataways,
        Fluffy Sainte-Marie, Dry Lips Manigitogan, Leonarda Lee
        Starblanket, Annie Cook, June Bug McLeod, Big Bum
725   Pegahmagahbow, all twenty-seven of 'em. Even my wife,
        Veronique St. Pierre, she'll be right smack dab in the
        middle of it all. Defense.
SPOOKY: Defense? The Americans. We're being attacked. Is the
        situation that serious?
730 PIERRE: No, no, no, for Chris'sakes. They're playin' hockey.
        Them women are playin' hockey. Dead serious they are too.
SPOOKY: No.
PIERRE: Yes.
SPOOKY: Thank the Lord this is the last year!
735 PIERRE: Don't you care to ask?
SPOOKY: Thank the Lord the end of the world is coming this
        year!

(Gasping, he marches up to DICKIE BIRD.)

PIERRE: I'm the referee, dammit.
SPOOKY: Watch your language.

(Grabbing the crucifix from DICKIE BIRD.)

740 PIERRE: That's what I mean when I say I'm gonna be right
        smack dab in the middle of it all. You don't listen to me.
SPOOKY: *(As he proceeds to put the little booties back on the crucifix.)*
        But you're not a woman.
PIERRE: You don't have to be. To be a referee these days, you can
745   be anything, man or woman, don't matter which away. So
        gimme my skate.
SPOOKY: What skate?
PIERRE: The skate Gazelle Nataways just about killed you with
        after the bingo that time.
750 SPOOKY: Oh, that. I hid it in the basement. *(PIERRE opens a door,*
        falls in and comes struggling out with a mouse trap stuck to a
        finger.) Pierre St. Pierre, what the hell are you doing in
        Lalala's closet?
PIERRE: Well, where the hell's the basement?

(He frees his finger.)

755 SPOOKY: Pierre St. Pierre, you drink too much. You gotta have
        the Lord in your life.
PIERRE: I don't need the Lord in my life, for god's sake, I need
        my skate. I gotta practice my figure eights.
SPOOKY: *(As he begins to put the crucifix back up on the wall.)* You
760   gotta promise me before I give you your skate.
PIERRE: I promise.
SPOOKY: *(Unaware, he threatens* PIERRE *with the crucifix, holding it*
        up against his neck.) You gotta have the Lord come into your
        life.
765 PIERRE: Alright, alright.
SPOOKY: For how long?
PIERRE: My whole life. I promise I'm gonna bring the Lord into
        my life and keep him there right up until the day I die just
        gimme my goddamn skate.
770 SPOOKY: Cross my heart.

PIERRE: Alright? Cross your heart.

(Neither man makes a move, until SPOOKY, *finally catching on, throws*
PIERRE *a look.* PIERRE *crosses himself.)*

SPOOKY: Good.

(Exits to the basement.)

PIERRE: *(Now alone with* DICKIE BIRD, *half-whispering to him. As*
        PIERRE *speaks,* DICKIE BIRD *again takes the crucifix off the wall*
        and returns with it to his seat and there takes the booties off in 775
        haphazard fashion.) Has he been feedin' you this crappola,
        too? Don't you be startin' that foolishness. That Spooky
        Lacroix's so fulla shit he wouldn't know a two thousand
        year-old Egyptian Sphinxter if he came face to face with
        one. He's just preachifyin' at you because you're the one 780
        person on this reserve who can't argue back. You listen to
        me. I was there in the same room as your mother when she
        gave birth to you. So I know well who you are and where
        you come from. I remember the whole picture. Even
        though we were all in a bit of a fizzy . . . I remember. Do 785
        you know, Dickie Bird Halked, that you were named after
        that bar? Anyone ever tell you that? *(DICKIE BIRD starts to*
        shake. PIERRE *takes fright.)* Spooky Lacroix, move that holy
        ass of yours, for fuck's sakes! *(DICKIE BIRD laughs. PIERRE*
        makes a weak attempt to laugh along.) And I'll never forgive 790
        your father, Big Joey oops . . . *(DICKIE BIRD reacts.)* . . . I
        mean, Wellington Halked, for letting your mother do that
        to you. "It's not good for the people of this world," I says to
        him "it's not good for 'em to have the first thing they see
        when they come into the world is a goddamn jukebox." 795
        That's what I says to him. Thank god, you survived, Dickie
        Bird Halked, thank god, seventeen years later you're sittin'
        here smack-dab in front of me, hail and hearty as cake. Ex-
        cept for your tongue. Talk, Dickie Bird Halked, talk. Say
        somethin'. Come on. Try this: "Daddy, daddy, daddy." 800
        (DICKIE BIRD shakes his head.) Come on. Just this once.
        Maybe it will work. *(Takes* DICKIE BIRD *by the cheeks with one*
        hand.) "Daddy, daddy, daddy, daddy." *(DICKIE BIRD jumps up*
        and attacks PIERRE, *looking as though he were about to shove the*
        crucifix down PIERRE's *throat.* PIERRE *is genuinely terrified. Just* 805
        then, SPOOKY *reenters with the skate.)* Whoa, whoa. Easy. Easy
        now, Dickie Bird. Easy.
SPOOKY: *(Gasping again at the sight of* DICKIE BIRD *man-handling*
        the crucifix, he makes a bee-line for the boy.) Dickie Bird
        Halked? Give me that thing. *(And grabs the crucifix with a* 810
        flourish. Then he turns to PIERRE *and holds the skate out with his*
        other hand.) Promise.
PIERRE: Cross my heart. *(Crosses himself.)*
SPOOKY: *(Replacing the crucifix on the wall and pointing at* PIERRE.)
        The Lord. 815
PIERRE: The Lord.

(SPOOKY hands the skate over to PIERRE. *Just then,* CREATURE NATAWAYS
stumbles in, now visibly drunk.)

CREATURE: The Lord!

(Picking on the hapless DICKIE BIRD, CREATURE *roughly shoves the boy*
down to a chair.)

PIERRE: (*Holding up both his skates.*) I got 'em both. See? I got 'em.

820 CREATURE: Hallelujah! Now all you gotta do is learn how to skate.

SPOOKY: Creature Nataways, I don't want you in my house in that condition. Lalala is liable to pop any minute now and I don't want my son to see the first thing he sees when he 825 comes into the world is a drunk.

PIERRE: Damn rights!

SPOOKY: . . . you too, Pierre St. Pierre.

CREATURE: Aw! William Lacroix, don't give me that holier than-me, poker-up-the-bum spiritual bull crap . . .

830 SPOOKY: . . . say wha? . . .

CREATURE: Are you preachin' to this boy, William Lacroix? Are you usin' him again to practice your preachy-preachy? Don't do that, William, the boy is helpless. If you wanna practice, go practice on your old buddy, go preach on Big 835 Joey. He's the one who needs it.

SPOOKY: You're hurting again, aren't you, Creature Nataways.

CREATURE: Don't listen to Spooky Lacroix, Dickie Bird. You follow Spooky Lacroix and you go right down to the dogs, I'm tellin' you that right now. Hair spray, Lysol, vanilla ex-840 tract, shoe polish, Xerox machine juice, he's done it all, this man. If you'd given William Lacroix the chance, he'd have sliced up the Xerox machine and ate it . . .

PIERRE: (*Mockingly, in the background.*) No!

CREATURE: . . . He once drank a Kitty Wells record. He lied to 845 his own mother and he stole her record and he boiled it and swallowed it right up . . .

PIERRE: Good heavens!

(BIG JOEY *enters and stands at the door unseen.*)

CREATURE: . . . Made the Globe and Mail, too. He's robbed, he's cheated his best friend . . .

850 SPOOKY: Alphonse Nataways? Why are you doing this, may I ask?

CREATURE: Oh, he was bad, Dickie Bird Halked, he was bad. Fifteen years. Fifteen years of his life pukin' his guts out on sidewalks from here to Sicamous, B.C., this man . . .

SPOOKY: Shush!

855 CREATURE: . . . and this is the same man . . .

BIG JOEY: (*Speaking suddenly and laughing, he takes everyone by surprise. They gasp. And practically freeze in their tracks.*) . . . who's yellin' and preachin' about "the Lord!" They oughta retire the beaver and put this guy on the Canadian nickel, 860 he's become a national goddamn symbol, that what you're sayin', Creature Nataways? This the kind of man you wanna become, that what you're sayin' to the boy, Creature Nataways? (*Close up to* DICKIE BIRD.) A man who couldn't get a hard-on in front of a woman if you paid him a two 865 dollar bill?

SPOOKY: (*Stung to the quick.*) And is this the kind of man you wanna become, Dickie Bird Halked, this MAN who can't take the sight of blood least of all woman's blood, this MAN who, when he sees a woman's blood, chokes up, 870 pukes and faints, how do you like that?

(PIERRE, *sensing potential violence, begins to sneak out.*)

BIG JOEY: (*Pulls a bottle out of his coat.*) Spooky Lacroix, igwani eeweepoonaskeewuk. ("The end of the world is at hand.")

(PIERRE, *seeing the bottle, retraces his steps and sits down again, grabbing a tea-cup en route, ready for a drink.*)

SPOOKY: (*Shocked.*) Get that thing out of my house!

BIG JOEY: Tonight, we're gonna celebrate my wife, Spooky Lacroix, we're gonna celebrate because my wife, the fabu- 875 lous, the incredible Gazelle Delphina Nataways has been crowned Captain of the Wasy Wailerettes. The Rez is makin' history, Spooky Lacroix. The world will never be the same. Come on, it's on me, it's on your old buddy, the old, old buddy you said you'd never, ever forget. 880

SPOOKY: I told you a long time ago, Big Joey, after what you went and done to my sister, this here boy's own mother, you're no buddy of mine. Get out of my house. Get!

BIG JOEY: (*Handing the bottle of whiskey to* CREATURE.) Creature Nataways, celebrate your wife. 885

CREATURE: (*Raising the bottle in a toast.*) To my wife!

PIERRE: (*Holding his cup out to the bottle.*) Your ex-wife.

BIG JOEY: (*Suddenly quiet and intimate.*) William. William. You and me. You and me, we used to be buddies, kigiskisin? ("Remember?") Wounded Knee. South Dakota. Spring of 890 '73. We parked my van over by that little lake, we swam across, you almost didn't make it and nothin' could get you to swim back. Kigiskisin? So here we're walkin' back through the bush, all the way around this small lake, nothin' on but bare feet and wet undershorts and this black 895 bear come up behind you, kigiskisin? And you freaked out.

(*Laughs.* PIERRE *tries, as best he can, to create a party atmosphere, to little avail.* CREATURE *nervously watches* BIG JOEY *and* SPOOKY. DICKIE BIRD *merely sits there, head down, rocking back and forth.*)

SPOOKY: (*Obviously extremely uncomfortable.*) You freaked out too, ha-ha, ha-ha.

BIG JOEY: That bear gave you a real spook, huh? (*Pause. Then, suddenly, he jumps at the other men.*) Boo! (*The other men, in-* 900 *cluding* SPOOKY, *jump, splashing whiskey all over the place.* BIG JOEY *laughs. The other men pretend to laugh.*) That's how you got your name, you old Spook . . .

SPOOKY: You were scared too, ha-ha, ha-ha.

BIG JOEY: . . . we get back to the camp and there's Creature and 905 Eugene and Zach and Roscoe, bacon and eggs all ready for us. Christ, I never laughed so hard in my life. But here you were, not laughin' and we'd say: "What's the matter, Spook, you don't like our jokes?" And you'd say: "That's good, yeah, that's good." I guess you were laughin' from a different part 910 of yourself, huh? You were beautiful . . .

SPOOKY: That's good, yeah, that's good.

BIG JOEY: (*Getting the bottle back from* CREATURE *and* PIERRE.) So tonight, Bear-who-went-and-gave-you-a-real-Spooky Lacroix, we're gonna celebrate another new page in our lives. 915 Wounded Knee Three! Women's version!

PIERRE: Damn rights.

BIG JOEY: (*Raising the bottle up in a toast.*) To my wife!

SPOOKY: Ha! Get that thing away from me.

PIERRE: Spooky Lacroix, co-operate. Co-operate for once. The 920 women, the women are playin' hockey.

CREATURE: To my wife!

PIERRE: Your ex-wife.

CREATURE: Shut up you toothless old bugger.

SPOOKY: Big Joey, you're not my friend no more. 925

BIG JOEY: *(Finally grabbing* SPOOKY *roughly by the throat.* CREATURE *jumps to help hold* SPOOKY *still.)* You never let a friend for life go, William Hector Lacroix, not even if you turn your back on your own father, Nicotine Lacroix's spiritual teachings and
930 pretend like hell to be this born-again Christian.

SPOOKY: Let go, Creature Nataways, let go of me! *(To* BIG JOEY.*)* For what you did to this boy at that bar seventeen years ago, Joseph Jeremiah McLeod, you are going to hell. To hell! *(*BIG JOEY *baptizes* SPOOKY *with the remainder of the bottle's con-*
935 *tents. Breaking free,* SPOOKY *grabs* DICKIE BIRD *and shoves him toward* BIG JOEY.*)* Look at him. He can't even talk. He hasn't talked in seventeen years! *(*DICKIE BIRD *cries out, breaks free, grabs the crucifix from off the wall and runs out the door, crying.* SPOOKY *breaks down, falls to the floor and weeps.* BIG JOEY *at-*
940 *tempts to pick him up gently, but* SPOOKY *kicks him away.)* Let go of me! Let go!

CREATURE: *(Lifting the empty bottle, laughing and crying at the same time.)* To my wife, to my wife, to my wife, to my wife, to my wife . . .

*(*BIG JOEY *suddenly lifts* SPOOKY *off the floor by the collar and lifts a fist to punch his face. Black-out.)*

(Out of this black-out emerges the eery, distant sound of women wailing and pucks hitting boards, echoing and echoing as in a vast empty chamber. The lights come up on DICKIE BIRD HALKED *and* SIMON STARBLANKET, *standing beside each other in the "bleachers" of the hockey arena, watching the "ice" area (i.e., looking out over the audi- ence). The "bleachers" area is actually on the upper level of the set, in a straight line directly in front of* NANABUSH's *perch.* DICKIE BIRD *is still holding* SPOOKY's *crucifix and* SIMON *is still holding his danc- ing bustle.)*

945 SIMON: Your grandpa, Nicotine Lacroix, was a medicine man. Hell of a name, but he was a medicine man. Old priest here, Father Boucher, years ago—oh, he was a terrible man—he went and convinced the people old Nicotine Lacroix talked to the devil. That's not true. Nicotine Lacroix was a good
950 man. That's why I want you for my best man. Me and Patsy are getting married a couple of months from now. It's de- cided. We're gonna have a baby. Then we're going down to South Dakota and we're gonna dance with the Rosebud Sioux this summer. *(Sings as he stomps his foot in the rhythm of*
955 *a powwow drum.)* " . . . and me I don't wanna go to the moon, I'm gonna leave that moon alone. I just wanna dance with the Rosebud Sioux this summer, yeah, yeah, yeah . . . "

(And he breaks into a chant. DICKIE BIRD *watches, fascinated, par- ticularly by the bustle* SIMON *holds up in the air.)*

(At this point, ZACHARY JEREMIAH KEECHIGEESIK *approaches timidly from behind a beam, his pants held flimsily together with a huge safety pin. The sound of women wailing and pucks hitting boards now shifts into the sound of an actual hockey arena, just before a big game.)*

ZACHARY: *(To* SIMON.*)* Hey! *(But* SIMON *doesn't hear and continues chanting.)* Pssst!
960 SIMON: Zachary Jeremiah. Neee, watstagatch!
ZACHARY: Is Hera out there?
SIMON: *(Indicating the "ice.")* Yup. There she is.

ZACHARY: Lordy, lordy, lordy . . .
SIMON: Just kidding. She's not out there . . .
ZACHARY: Don't do that to me!   965
SIMON: . . . yet.
ZACHARY: *(Finally coming up to join the young men at the "bleach- ers.")* You know that Nanabush character you were telling me about a couple of nights ago? What do you say I give his name over to them little gingerbread cookie men I'm 970 gonna be making? For starters. Think that would help any?
SIMON: Neee . . .

(Just then, BIG JOEY *enters and proceeds to get a microphone stand ready for broadcasting the game.* ZACHARY *recoils and goes to stand as far away from him as possible.)*

ZACHARY: *(Looking out over the "ice.")* It's almost noon. They're late getting started.
BIG JOEY: *(Yawning luxuriously.)* That's right. Me and Gazelle 975 Nataways . . . slept in.

*(*CREATURE NATAWAYS *comes scurrying in.)*

CREATURE: *(Still talking to himself.)* . . . I tole you once I tole you twice . . . *(Then to the other men.)* Chris' sakes! Are they re- ally gonna do it? Chris'sakes!

*(*SPOOKY LACROIX *enters wearing a woolen scarf he obviously knitted himself. He is still knitting, this time a pale blue baby sweater. He also now sports a black eye and band-aide on his face. All the men, except* PIERRE ST. PIERRE, *are now in the "bleachers," standing in a straight line facing the audience, with* DICKIE BIRD *in the center area,* SIMON *and* SPOOKY *to his immediate right and left, respectively.)*

SPOOKY: It's bad luck to start late. I know. I read the interview 980 with Gay Lafleur in last week's Expositor. They won't get far. *(He sees* GAZELLE NATAWAYS *entering the "rink," unseen by the audience. {All the hockey players on the "ice" are unseen by the audience; it is only the men who can actually "see" them.})* Look! Gazelle Nataways went and got her sweater trimmed in the 985 chest area!

(Wild cat calls from the men.)

CREATURE: Trimmed it? She's got it plunging down to her oot- see. ("belly button.")
ZACHARY: Ahem. Smokes too much. Lung problems.
BIG JOEY: Nah. More like it's got somethin' to do with the un- 990 dershorts she's wearin' today.
ZACHARY: *(Fast on the up-take.)* Fuck you!
BIG JOEY: *(Blowing* ZACHARY *a kiss.)* Poosees. ("Pussy cat." [Zachary's childhood nickname.])
SPOOKY: Terrible. Terrible. Tsk, tsk, tsk.   995

*(*PIERRE ST. PIERRE *enters on the lower level, teetering dangerously on his skates towards the "ice" area downstage. He wears a referee's top and a whistle around his neck.)*

PIERRE: *(Checking the names off as he reads from a clipboard.)* Dominique Ladouche, Black Lady Halked, Annie Cook, June Bug McLeod, Big Bum Pegahmagahbow . . .
SIMON: *(Calling out.)* Patsy Pegahmagahbow, turkey.

1000 PIERRE: Shut up. I'm workin' here. . . . Leonarda Lee Starblanket, that terrible Dictionary woman, Fluffy Sainte-Marie, Chicken Lips Pegahmagahbow, Dry Lips Manigitogan, Little Hand Manigitogan, Little Girl Manitowabi, Victoria Manitowabi, Belinda Nickikoosimeenicaning, Martha Two-Axe Early-in-

1005 the-Morning, her royal highness Gazelle Delphina Nataways, Delia Opekokew, Barbra Nahwegahbow, Gloria May Eshkibok, Hera Keechigeesik, Tall Mary Ann Patchnose, Short Mary Ann Patchnose, Queen Elizabeth Patchnose, the triplets Marjorie Moose, Maggie May Moose, Mighty Moose and, of course, my

1010 wife, Veronique St. Pierre. Yup. They're all there, I hope, and the world is about to explode!

SPOOKY: That's what I've been trying to tell you!

(PIERRE ST. PIERRE, *barely able to stand on his skates, hobbles about, obviously getting almost trampled by the hockey players at various times.*)

BIG JOEY: (*Now speaking on the microphone. The other men watch the women on the "ice"; some are cheering and whistling, some calling*

1015 *down the game.*) Welcome, ladies igwa gentlemen, welcome one and all to the Wasaychigan Hill Hip-hip-hippodrome. This is your host for the big game, Big Joey—and they don't call me Big Joey for nothin'—Chairman, CEO and Proprietor of the Wasaychigan Hill Hippodrome, bringin'

1020 you a game such as has never been seen ever before on the ice of any hockey arena anywhere on the island of Manitoulin, anywhere on the face of this country, anywhere on the face of this planet. And there . . .

CREATURE: . . . there's Gazelle Nataways, number one . . .

1025 BIG JOEY: . . . they are, ladies . . .

SPOOKY: . . . terrible, terrible . . .

BIG JOEY: . . . igwa gentlemen . . .

CREATURE: . . . Chris'sakes, that's my wife, Chris'sakes . . .

BIG JOEY: . . . there they are, the most beautiful . . .

1030 SIMON: . . . give 'em hell, Patsy Pegahmagahbow, give 'em hell . . .

BIG JOEY: . . . daring, death- . . .

SIMON: (*To* ZACHARY.) . . . there's Hera Keechigeesik, number nine . . .

1035 BIG JOEY: . . . defying Indian women . . .

SPOOKY: . . . terrible, terrible . . .

BIG JOEY: . . . in the world . . .

ZACHARY: . . . that's my wife . . .

BIG JOEY: . . . the Wasy Wailerettes . . .

(*Clears his throat and tests the microphone by tapping it gently.*)

1040 ZACHARY: . . . lordy, lordy, lordy . . .

CREATURE: Hey, Gazelle Nataways and Hera Keechigeesik are lookin' at each other awful funny. Something bad's gonna happen, I tole you once I tole you twice, something bad's gonna happen . . .

1045 SPOOKY: This is sign from the Lord. This is THE sign . . .

BIG JOEY: Number One Gazelle Nataways, Captain of the Wasy Wailerettes, facing off with Number Nine, Flora McDonald, Captain of the Canoe Lake Bravettes. And referee Pierre St. Pierre drops the puck and takes off like a herd of wild

1050 turtles . . .

SIMON: Aw, Spooky Lacroix, eat my shitty shorts, neee . . .

BIG JOEY: . . . Hey, aspin Number Six Dry Lips Manigitogan, right-winger for the Wasy Wailerettes . . .

ZACHARY: . . . look pretty damn stupid, if you ask me. Fifteen thousand dollars for all that new equipment . . . 1055

BIG JOEY: . . . eemaskamat Number Thirteen of the Canoe Lake Bravettes anee-i puck . . .

CREATURE: . . . Cancel the game! Cancel the game! Cancel the game! . . .

(*Etc.*)

BIG JOEY: . . . igwa aspin sipweesinskwataygew. Hey, k'see 1060 goochin! (*Off microphone.*) Creature Nataways. Shut up. (*To the other men.*) Get this asshole out of here. . . .

SIMON: Yay, Patsy Pegahmagahbow! Pat-see! Pat-see! Pat-see! . . .

(*Etc.*)

BIG JOEY: (*Back on microphone.*) . . . How, Number Six Dry Lips Manigitogan, right-winger for the Wasy Wailerettes, 1065 soogi pugamawew igwa anee-i puck igwa aspin center-line ispathoo ana puck . . .

CREATURE: (*To* SIMON.) Shut up. Don't encourage them . . .

BIG JOEY: . . . ita Number Nine Hera Keechigeesik, left-winger for . . . 1070

SIMON: (*To* CREATURE.) Aw, lay off! Pat-see! Pat-see! Pat-see! . . . (*Etc.*)

BIG JOEY: . . . the Wasy Wailerettes, kagatchitnat. How, Number Nine Hera Keechigeesik . . .

(*He continues uninterrupted.*)

CREATURE: . . . Stop the game! Stop the game! Stop the game! . . . 1075 (*Etc.*)

ZACHARY: Goodness sakes, there's gonna be a fight out there!

(CREATURE *continues his "stop the game,"* ZACHARY *repeats "goodness sakes, there's gonna be a fight out there,"* SIMON'*s "Pat-see!" has now built up into a full chant, his foot pounding on the floor so that it sounds like a powwow drum, his dancing bustle held aloft like a shield.* SPOOKY *finally grabs the crucifix away from* DICKIE BIRD, *holds it aloft and begins to pray, loudly, as in a ceremony.* DICKIE BIRD, *caught between Simon's chanting and* SPOOKY'*s praying, blocks his ears with his hands and looks with growing consternation at "the game."* PIERRE *blows his whistle and skates around like a puppet gone mad.*)

SPOOKY: The Lord is my shepherd; I shall not want. He maketh me to lie down in green pastures; he leadeth me beside the still waters. He restoreth my soul; he leadeth me in the 1080 paths of righteousness for his name's sake. Yea, though I walk through the valley of the shadow of death, I will fear no evil; for thou art with me. Yea, though I walk through the valley of the shadow of death, I will fear no evil; for thou art with me . . . 1085

(*He repeats this last phrase over and over again. Finally,* DICKIE BIRD *freaks out, screams and runs down to the "ice" area.*)

1052 . . . Hey, . . . The following hockey commentary by Big Joey (pages 1389–1390) is translated on page 1402.

BIG JOEY: (*Continuing uninterrupted above all the other men's voices.*) . . . igwa ati-ooteetum blue line ita Number One Gazelle Nataways, Captain of the Wasy Wailerettes, kagagweemaskamat anee-i puck, ma-a Number Nine Hera Keechigeesik mawch weemeethew anee-i puck. Wha! "Hooking," itwew referee Pierre St. Pierre, Gazelle Nataways isa keehookiwatew her own team-mate Hera Keechigeesikwa, wha! How, Number One Gazelle Nataways, Captain of the Wasy Wailerettes, face-off igwa meena itootum asichi Number Nine Flora McDonald, Captain of the Canoe Lake Bravettes igwa Flora McDonald soogi pugamawew anee-i puck, ma-a Number Thirty-seven Big Bum Pegahmagahbow, defense-woman for the Wasy Wailerettes, stops the puck and passes it to Number Eleven Black Lady Halked, also defense-woman for the Wasy Wailerettes, but Gazelle Nataways, Captain of the Wasy Wailerettes, soogi body check meethew her own team-mate Black Lady Halked woops! She falls, ladies igwa gentlemen, Black Lady Halked hits the boards and Black Lady Halked is singin' the blues, ladies igwa gentlemen, Black Lady Halked sings the blues. (*Off microphone, to the other men.*) What the hell is goin' on down there? Dickie Bird, get off the ice! (*Back on microphone.*) Wha! Number Eleven Black Lady Halked is up in a flash igwa seemak n'taymaskamew Gazelle Nataways anee-i puck, holy shit! The ailing but very, very furious Black Lady Halked skates back, turns and takes aim, it's gonna be a slap shot, ladies igwa gentlemen, slap shot keetnatch taytootum Black Lady Halked igwa Black Lady Halked shootiwoo anee-i puck, wha! She shoots straight at her very own captain, Gazelle Nataways and holy shit, holy shit, holy fuckin' shit!

(*All hell breaks loose; it is as though some bizarre dream has entered the arena. We hear the sound of women wailing and pucks hitting boards, echoing and echoing as in a vast empty chamber. The men are all screaming at the same time, from the "bleachers," re-calling* BLACK LADY HALKED's *legendary fall of seventeen years ago.*)

BIG JOEY: (*Dropping his microphone in horror.*) Holy Christ! If there is a devil in this world, then he has just walked into this room. Holy Christ! . . . (*He says this over and over again.*)

ZACHARY: Do something about her, goodness sakes, I told you guys to do something about her seventeen years ago, but you wouldn't do fuck-all. So go out there now and help her . . . (*Repeated.*)

CREATURE: Never mind, Chris'sakes, don't bother her. Let me out of here. Chris'sakes, let me out of here! . . . (*Repeated.*)

SPOOKY: . . . Yea, though I walk through the valley of the shadow of death, I will fear no evil; for thou art with me . . .

(*Repeated. While* SIMON *continues chanting and stomping.*)

PIERRE: (*From the "ice" area.*) Never you mind, Zachary Jeremiah, never you mind. She'll be okay. No she won't. Zachary Jeremiah, go out there and help her. No. She'll be okay. No she won't. Yes. No. Yes. No. Help! Where's the puck? Can't do nothin' without the goddamn puck. Where's the puck?! Where's the puck?! Where's the puck?! . . .

(*He repeats this last phrase over and over again. Center- and down-stage, on the "ice" area,* DICKIE BIRD *is going into a complete "freak-out," breaking into a grotesque, fractured version of a Cree chant. Gradually,* BIG

JOEY, ZACHARY *and* CREATURE *join* PIERRE's *refrain of "where's the puck?!", with which they all, including the chanting* SIMON *and the praying* SPOOKY, *scatter and come running down to the "ice" area. As they reach the lower level and begin to approach the audience, their movements break down into slow motion, as though they were trying to run through the sticky, gummy substance of some horrible, surrealistic nightmare.*)

PIERRE/BIG JOEY/ZACHARY/CREATURE: (*Slower and slower, as on a record that is slowing down gradually to a stop.*) Where's the puck?! Where's the puck?! Where's the puck?! . . . (*Etc.*)

(SIMON *continues chanting and stomping,* SPOOKY *continues intoning the last phrase of his prayer and* DICKIE BIRD *continues his fractured chant. Out of this fading "sound collage" emerges the sound of a jukebox playing the introduction to Kitty Wells' "It Wasn't God Who Made Honky Tonk Angels," as though filtered through memory. At this point, on the upper level, a giant luminescent hockey stick comes seemingly out of nowhere and, in very slow motion, shoots a giant luminescent puck. On the puck, looking like a radiant but damaged "Madonna-with-child," sits* NANABUSH, *as the spirit of* BLACK LADY HALKED, *naked, nine months pregnant, drunk almost senseless and barely able to hold a bottle of beer up to her mouth. All the men freeze in their standing positions facing the audience, except for* DICKIE BIRD *who continues his fractured chanting and whimpering, holding his arms up towards* NANABUSH/BLACK LADY HALKED. *The giant luminescent puck reaches and stops at the edge of the upper level.* NANABUSH/BLACK LADY HALKED *struggles to stand and begins staggering toward her perch. She reaches it and falls with one arm on top of it. The magical, glittering lights flare on and, for the first time, the jukebox is revealed.* NANABUSH/BLACK LADY HALKED *staggers laboriously up to the top of the jukebox and stands there in profile, one arm lifted to raise her beer as she pours it over her belly. Behind her, the full moon begins to glow, blood red. And from the jukebox, Kitty Wells sings.*)

As I sit here tonight, the jukebox playing,
That tune about the wild side of life;
As I listen to the words you are saying,
It brings memories when I was a trusting wife.

It wasn't God who made honky tonk angels,
As you said in the words of your song;
Too many times married men think they're still single,
That has caused many a good girl to go wrong.

(*During the "instrumental break" of the song here,* DICKIE BIRD *finally explodes and shrieks out towards the vision of* NANABUSH/BLACK LADY HALKED.)

DICKIE BIRD: Mama! Mama! Katha paksini. Katha paksini. Kanawapata wastew. Kanawapataw wastew. Michimina. Michimina. Katha pagitina. Kaweechee-ik nipapa. Kaweechee-ik nipapa. Nipapa. Papa. Papa. Papa. Papa. Papa. Papa! Mommy! Mommy! Don't fall. Don't fall. Look at the light. Look at the light. Hold on to it. Hold on to it. Don't let it go. My daddy will help you. My daddy will help you. My daddy. Daddy. Daddy. . . . (*Etc.*)

(*He crumples to the floor and freezes. Kitty Wells sings.*)

It's a shame that all the blame is on us women,
It's not true that only you men feel the same;
From the start most every heart that's ever broken,
Was because there always was a man to blame.

It wasn't God who made honky tonk angels;
As you said in the words of your song;
Too many times married men think they're still single,
That has caused many a good girl to go wrong.

(As the song fades, the final tableau is one of DICKIE BIRD *collapsed on the floor between* SIMON, *who is holding aloft his bustle, and* SPOOKY, *who is holding aloft his crucifix, directly in front of and at the feet of* BIG JOEY *and, above* BIG JOEY, *the pregnant* NANABUSH/BLACK LADY HALKED, *who is standing on top of the flashing jukebox, in silhouette against the full moon, bottle held up above her mouth.* ZACHARY, CREATURE *and* PIERRE *are likewise frozen, standing off to the side of this central grouping. Slow fade-out.)*

——— **ACT TWO** ———

When the lights come up, DICKIE BIRD HALKED *is standing on a rock in the forest, his clothes and hair all askew. He holds* SPOOKY's *crucifix, raised with one hand up to the night sky; he is trying, as best he can, to chant, after* SIMON STARBLANKET's *fashion. As he does,* NANABUSH *appears in the shadows a distance behind him (as the spirit of* GAZELLE NATAWAYS, *minus the gigantic breasts, but dressed, this time, as a stripper). She lingers and watches with interest. Slowly,* DICKIE BIRD *climbs off the rock and walks off-stage, his quavering voice fading into the distance. The full moon glows. Fade-out.*

Fade-in on SPOOKY LACROIX's *kitchen, where* SPOOKY *is busy pinning four little pale blue baby booties on the wall where the crucifix used to be, the booties that, in Act One, covered the four extremities of the crucifix. At the table are* PIERRE ST. PIERRE *and* ZACHARY JEREMIAH KEECHIGEESIK. PIERRE *is stringing pale blue yarn around* ZACHARY's *raised, parted hands. Then* SPOOKY *joins them at the table and begins knitting again, this time, a baby bonnet, also pale blue.* ZACHARY *sits removed through most of this scene, pre-occupied with the problem of his still missing shorts, his bakery and his wife. The atmosphere is one of fear and foreboding, almost as though the men were constantly resisting the impulse to look over their shoulders. On the upper level, in a soft, dim light,* NANABUSH/GAZELLE *can be seen sitting up on her perch, waiting impatiently for "the boys" to finish their talk.*

PIERRE: *(In a quavering voice.)* The Wasy Wailerettes are dead. Gentlemen, my job is disappeared from underneath my feet.
SPOOKY: And we have only the Lord to thank for that.
5 PIERRE: Gazelle Nataways, she just sashayed herself off that ice, behind swayin' like a walrus pudding. That game, gentlemen, was what I call a real apostrophe . . .
ZACHARY: Catastrophe.
PIERRE: That's what I said, dammit. . . .
10 SPOOKY: . . . tsk . . .
PIERRE: . . . didn't even get to referee more than ten minutes. But you have to admit, gentlemen, that slap shot . . .
SPOOKY: . . . that's my sister, Black Lady Halked, that's my sister . . .
15 PIERRE: . . . did you see her slap shot? Fantastic! Like a bullet, like a killer shark. Unbelievable!
ZACHARY: *(Uncomfortable.)* Yeah, right.
PIERRE: When Black Lady Halked hit Gazelle Nataways with that puck. Them Nataways eyes. Big as plates!
20 SPOOKY: Bigger than a ditch!

PIERRE: Them mascara stretch marks alone was a perfectly frightful thing to behold. Holy shit la marde! But you know, they couldn't find that puck.
SPOOKY: *(Losing his cool and laughing, falsely and nervously.)* Did you see it? It fell . . . it fell . . . that puck went splat on her 25
chest . . . and it went . . . it went . . . plummety plop . . .
PIERRE: . . . plummety plop to be sure . . .
SPOOKY: . . . down her . . . down her . . .
PIERRE: Down the crack. Right down that horrendous, scarifyin' Nataways bosom crack. 30

(The "kitchen lights" go out momentarily and, to the men, inexplicably. Then they come back on. The men look about them, perplexed.)

SPOOKY: Serves . . . her . . . right for trimming her hockey sweater in the chest area, is what I say.
PIERRE: They say that puck slid somewhere deep, deep into the folds of her fleshy, womanly juices . . .
ZACHARY: . . . there's a lot of things they're saying about that 35
puck . . .
PIERRE: . . . and it's lost. Disappeared. Gone. Phhht! Nobody can find that puck.

(At this point, SPOOKY *gets up to check the light switch. The lights go out.)*

ZACHARY: *(In the darkness.)* Won't let no one come near her, is what they say. Not six inches. 40
PIERRE: I gotta go look for that puck. *(Lights come back on.* PIERRE *inexplicably appears sitting in another chair.)* Gentlemen, I gotta go jiggle that woman.

(Lights out again.)

ZACHARY: *(From the darkness.)* What's the matter, Spook?
SPOOKY: *(Obviously quite worried.)* Oh, nothing, nothing . . . 45
(Lights come back on. PIERRE *appears sitting back in his original chair. The men are even more mystified, but try to brighten up anyway.)* . . . just . . . checking the lights . . . Queen of the Indians, that's what she tried to look like, walking off that ice. 50
PIERRE: Queen of the Indians, to be sure. That's when them women went and put their foot down and made up their mind, on principle, no holds barred . . .

(A magical flash of lavender light floods the room very briefly, establishing a connection between SPOOKY's *kitchen and* NANABUSH's *perch, where* NANABUSH/GAZELLE *is still sitting, tapping her fingers impatiently, looking over her shoulder periodically, as if to say: "come on, boys, get with it."* PIERRE's *speech momentarily goes into slow motion.)*

. . . no . . . way . . . they're . . . takin' up . . . them hockey sticks again until that particular puck is found. "The particular puck," that's what they call it. Gentlemen, the Wasy 55
Wailerettes are dead. My job is disappeared. Gone. Kaput kaput. Phhht!
SPOOKY: Amen.

(Pause. Thoughtful silence for a beat or two.)

ZACHARY: W-w-w-where's that nephew of yours, Spook? 60
SPOOKY: Dickie Bird Halked?

PIERRE: My wife, Veronique St. Pierre, she informs me that Dickie Bird Halked, last he was seen, was pacin' the bushes in the general direction of the Pegahmagahbow acreage near Buzwah, lookin' for all the world like he had lost his mind, poor boy.

65

ZACHARY: Lordy, lordy, lordy, I'm telling you right now, Spooky Lacroix, if you don't do something about that nephew of yours, he's liable to go out there and kill someone next time.

70

SPOOKY: I'd be out there myself pacing the bushes with him except my wife Lalala's liable to pop any minute now and I gotta be ready to zip her up to Sudbury General.

PIERRE: Bah. Them folks of his, they don't care. If it's not hockey, it's bingo she's out playin' every night of the week, that Black Lady of a mother of his.

75

ZACHARY: Went and won the jackpot again last night, Black Lady Halked did. All fifty pounds of it . . .

PIERRE: Beat Gazelle Nataways by one number!

80

ZACHARY: . . . if it wasn't for her, I'd have mastered that apple pie recipe by now. I was counting on all that lard. Fifty pounds, goodness sakes.

SPOOKY: This little old kitchen? It's yours, Zachary Jeremiah, anytime, anytime. Lalala's got tons of lard.

85

PIERRE: Ha! She better have. Zachary Jeremiah hasn't dared go nowhere near his own kitchen in almost a week.

ZACHARY: Four nights! It's only Wednesday night, Pierre St. Pierre. Don't go stretching the truth just cuz you were too damn chicken to go get me my shorts.

90

PIERRE: Bah!

SPOOKY: (To ZACHARY.) Your shorts?

ZACHARY: (Evading the issue.) I just hope that Black Lady Halked's out there looking after her boy cuz if she isn't, we're all in a heap of trouble, I have a funny feeling. (Suddenly, he throws the yarn down and rises.) Achh! I've got to cook!

95

(He goes behind the kitchen counter, puts an apron on and begins the preparations for making pie pastry.)

SPOOKY: (To PIERRE, half-whispering.) His shorts?

(PIERRE merely shrugs, indicating ZACHARY's pants, which are still held together with a large safety pin. SPOOKY and PIERRE laugh nervously. SPOOKY looks concernedly at the four little booties on the wall where the crucifix used to be. Beat.)

(Suddenly, PIERRE slaps the table with one hand and leans over to SPOOKY, all set for an argument, an argument they've obviously had many times before. Through all this, ZACHARY is making pie pastry at the counter and SPOOKY continues knitting. The atmosphere of "faked" jocular camaraderie grows, particularly as the music gets louder later on. NANABUSH/GAZELLE is now getting ready for her strip in earnest, standing on her perch, spraying perfume on, stretching her legs, etc. The little tivoli lights in the jukebox begin to twinkle little by little.)

PIERRE: Queen of Hearts.

SPOOKY: Belvedere.

PIERRE: Queen of Hearts.

100

SPOOKY: The Belvedere.

PIERRE: I told you many times, Spooky Lacroix, it was the Queen of Hearts. I was there. You were there. Zachary Jeremiah, Big Joey, Creature Nataways, we were all there.

(From here on, the red/blue/purple glow of the jukebox (i.e., NANABUSH's perch) becomes more and more apparent.)

SPOOKY: And I'm telling you it was the Belvedere Hotel, before it was even called the Belvedere Hotel, when it was still called . . .

105

PIERRE: Spooky Lacroix, don't contribute your elder. Big Joey, may he rot in hell, he was the bouncer there that night, he was right there the night it happened.

ZACHARY: Hey, Spook. Where do you keep your rolling pin?

110

SPOOKY: Use my salami.

PIERRE: (To SPOOKY.) He was there.

ZACHARY: Big Joey was never the bouncer, he was the janitor.

SPOOKY: At the Belvedere Hotel.

PIERRE: Never you mind, Spooky Lacroix, never you mind. Black Lady Halked was sittin' there in her corner of the bar for three weeks . . .

115

SPOOKY: Three weeks?! It was more like three nights. Aw, you went and mixed up my baby's cap. (Getting all tangled up with his knitting.)

120

ZACHARY: Got any cinnamon?

SPOOKY: I got chili powder. Same color as cinnamon.

(Faintly, the strip music from the jukebox begins to play.)

PIERRE: . . . the place was so jam-packed with people drinkin' beer and singin' and smokin' cigarettes and watchin' the dancin' girl . . .

125

SPOOKY: . . . Gazelle Nataways, she was the dancing girl . . .

(The music is now on full volume and NANABUSH/GAZELLE's strip is in full swing. She dances on top of the jukebox, which is now a riot of sound and flashing lights. SPOOKY's kitchen is bathed in a gorgeous lavender light. BIG JOEY and CREATURE NATAWAYS appear at SPOOKY's table, each drinking a bottle of beer. The strip of seventeen years ago is fully recreated, the memory becoming so heated that NANABUSH/GAZELLE magically appears dancing right on top of SPOOKY's kitchen table. The men are going wild, applauding, laughing, drinking, all in slow motion and in mime. In the heat of the moment, as NANABUSH/GAZELLE strips down to silk tassels and G-string, they begin tearing their clothes off.)

(Suddenly, SIMON STARBLANKET appears at SPOOKY's door: NANABUSH/GAZELLE disappears, as do BIG JOEY and CREATURE. And SPOOKY, PIERRE and ZACHARY are caught with their pants down. The jukebox music fades.)

SIMON: Spooky Lacroix. (The lavender light snaps off, we are back to "reality" and SPOOKY, PIERRE and ZACHARY stand there, embarrassed. In a panic, they begin putting their clothes back on and reclaim the positions they had before the strip. SPOOKY motions SIMON to take a seat at the table. SIMON does so.) Spooky Lacroix. Rosie Kakapetum expresses interest in coming here to birth Lalala's baby when the time comes.

130

SPOOKY: Rosie Kakapetum? No way some witch is gonna come and put her witchy little fingers on my baby boy.

135

SIMON: Rosie Kakapetum's no witch, Spooky Lacroix. She's Patsy Pegahmagahbow's step-mother and she's Wasy's only surviving medicine woman and mid-wife . . .

SPOOKY: Hogwash!

140

PIERRE: Ahem. Rosie Kakapetum says it's a cryin' shame the Wasy Wailerettes is the only team that's not in the Ontario Hockey League.

ZACHARY: Ontario Hockey League?

145 PIERRE: Absolutely. The OHL. Indian women's OHL. All the Indian women in Ontario's playin' hockey now. It's like a fever out there.

ZACHARY: Shoot. (*Referring to his pastry.*) I hope this new recipe works for me.

150 PIERRE: Well, it's not exactly new without the cinnamon.

SPOOKY: (*To* SIMON.) My son will be born at Sudbury General Hospital . . .

SIMON: You know what they do to them babies in them city hospitals?

155 SPOOKY: . . . Sudbury General, Simon Starblanket, like any good Christian boy . . .

PIERRE: (*Attempting to diffuse the argument.*) Ahem. We got to get them Wasy Wailerettes back on that ice again.

SIMON: (*Refusing to let go of* SPOOKY.) They pull them away right
160 from their own mother's breast the minute they come into this world and they put them behind these glass cages together with another two hundred babies like they were some kind of scientific specimens . . .

PIERRE: . . . like two hundred of them little monsters . . .

165 ZACHARY: Hamsters!

PIERRE: . . . that's what I said dammit . . .

SPOOKY: . . . tsk . . .

PIERRE: . . . you can't even tell which hamster belongs to which mother. You take Lalala to Sudbury General, Spooky
170 Lacroix, and your hamster's liable to end up stuck to some French lady's tit.

SIMON: . . . and they'll hang Lalala up in metal stirrups and your baby's gonna be born going up instead of dropping down which is the natural way. You were born going up in-
175 stead of dropping down like you should have . . .

PIERRE: Yup. You were born at Sudbury General, Spooky Lacroix, that's why you get weirder and weirder as the days get longer, that's why them white peoples is so weird they were all born going up . . .

180 SIMON: . . . instead of dropping down . . .

ZACHARY: (*Sprinkling flour in* SPOOKY's *face, with both hands, and laughing.*) . . . to the earth, Spooky Lacroix, to the earth . . .

SPOOKY: Pooh!

PIERRE: . . . but we got to find that puck, Simon Starblanket,
185 them Wasy Wailerettes have got to join the OHL . . .

SPOOKY: (*To* SIMON.) If Rosie Kakapetum is a medicine woman, Simon Starblanket, then how come she can't drive the madness from my nephew's brain, how come she can't make him talk, huh?

190 SIMON: Because the medical establishment and the church establishment and people like you, Spooky Lacroix, have effectively put an end to her usefulness and the usefulness of people like her everywhere, that's why Spooky Lacroix.

SPOOKY: Phooey!

195 SIMON: Do you or your sister even know that your nephew hasn't been home in two days, since that incident at the hockey game, Spooky Lacroix? Do you even care? Why can't you and that thing . . . (*Pointing at the bible that sits beside* SPOOKY.) and all it stands for cure your nephew's
200 madness, as you call it, Spooky Lacroix? What has this

thing . . . (*The bible again.*) done to cure the madness of this community and communities like it clean across this country, Spooky Lacroix? Why didn't "the Lord" as you call him, come to your sister's rescue at that bar seventeen years ago, huh, Spooky Lacroix? (*Pause. Tense silence.*) Rosie 205 Kakapetum is gonna be my mother-in-law in two months, Spooky Lacroix, and if Patsy and I are gonna do this thing right, if we're gonna work together to make my best man, Dickie Bird Halked, well again, then Rosie Kakapetum has got to birth that baby. (*He begins to exit.*) 210

SPOOKY: (*In hard, measured cadence.*) Rosie Kakapetum works for the devil.

(SIMON *freezes in his tracks. Silence. Then he turns, grabs a chair violently, bangs it down and sits determinedly.*)

SIMON: Fine. I'll sit here and I'll wait.

SPOOKY: Fine. You sit there and you wait.

(*Silence.* SIMON *sits silent and motionless, his back to the other men.*)

PIERRE: Ahem. Never you mind, Spooky Lacroix, never you 215 mind. Now as I was sayin', Black Lady Halked was nine months pregnant when she was sittin' in that corner of the Queen of Hearts.

SPOOKY: The Belvedere!

PIERRE: Three weeks, Black Lady Halked was sittin' there 220 drinkin' beer. They say she got the money by winnin' the jackpot at the Espanola bingo just three blocks down the street. Three weeks, sure as I'm alive and walkin' these treacherous icy roads, three weeks she sat there in that dark corner by herself. They say the only light you could see her 225 by was the light from the jukebox playin' "Rim of Fire" by Johnny Cash . . .

ZACHARY: "Rim of Fire." Yeah, right, Pierre St. Pierre.

SPOOKY: Kitty Wells! Kitty Wells!

(*The sound of the jukebox playing "It Wasn't God Who Made Honky Tonk Angels" can be heard faintly in the background.*)

PIERRE: . . . the place was so jam-packed with people drinkin' 230 and singin' and smokin' cigarettes and watchin' the dancin' girl . . .

SPOOKY: . . . Gazelle Nataways, she was the dancing girl, Lord save her soul . . .

PIERRE: . . . until Black Lady Halked collapsed . . . 235

(SPOOKY, PIERRE *and* ZACHARY *freeze in their positions, looking in horror at the memory of seventeen years ago.*)

(*On the upper level,* NANABUSH, *back in her guise as the spirit of* BLACK LADY HALKED, *sits on the jukebox, facing the audience, legs out directly in front. Nine months pregnant and naked, she holds a bottle of beer up in the air and is drunk almost senseless. The song, "It Wasn't God Who Made Honky Tonk Angels," rises to full volume, the lights from the jukebox flashing riotously. The full moon glows blood red. Immediately below* NANABUSH/BLACK LADY HALKED, DICKIE BIRD HALKED *appears, kneeling, naked, arms raised toward his mother.* NANABUSH/BLACK LADY HALKED *begins to writhe and scream, laughing and crying hysterically at the same time and, as she does, her water breaks.* DICKIE BIRD, *drenched, rises slowly from the floor, arms still raised, and screams.*)

DICKIE BIRD: Mama! Mama!

(And from here on, the lights and the sound on this scene begin to fade slowly, as the scene on the lower level resumes.)

PIERRE: . . . she kind of oozed down right then and there, right
down to the floor of the Queen of Hearts Tavern. And Big
Joey, may he rot in hell, he was the bouncer there that
240 night, when he saw the blood, he ran away and puked over
on the other side of the bar, the sight of all that woman's
blood just scared the shit right out of him. And that's when
Dickie Bird Halked, as we know him, came ragin' out from
his mother's womb, Spooky Lacroix, in between beers, right
245 there on the floor, under a table, by the light of the jukebox, on a Saturday night, at the Queen of Hearts . . .

SPOOKY: They went and named him after the bar, you crusted
old fossil! That bar, which is now called the Belvedere
Hotel, used to be called the Dickie Bird Tavern . . .

250 SIMON: (Suddenly jumping out of his chair and practically lunging at
SPOOKY.) It doesn't matter what the fuck the name of that
fucking bar was! (The lights and sound on NANABUSH and the
jukebox have now faded completely.) The fact of the matter is,
it never should have happened, that kind of thing should
255 never be allowed to happen, not to us Indians, not to anyone living and breathing on the face of God's green earth.
(Pause. Silence. Then, dead calm.) You guys have given up,
haven't you? You and your generation. You gave up a long
time ago. You'd rather turn your back on the whole thing
260 and pretend to laugh, wouldn't you? (Silence.) Well, not me.
Not us. (Silence.) This is not the kind of Earth we want to
inherit. (He begins to leave, but turns once more.) I'll be back.
With Patsy. And Rosie.

(He exits. Another embarrassed silence.)

SPOOKY: (Unwilling to face up to the full horror of it, he chooses, in-
265 stead, to do exactly what SIMON said: turn his back and pretend to
laugh.) That bar, which is now called the Belvedere Hotel,
used to be called the Dickie Bird Tavern. That's how Dickie
Bird Halked got his name. And that's why he goes hay-wire
every now and again and that's why he doesn't talk. Fetal Al-
270 cohol something-something, Pierre St. Pierre . . .

ZACHARY: (From behind the counter, where he is still busy making pie
crust.) Fetal Alcohol Syndrome.

SPOOKY: . . . that's the devil that stole the baby's tongue because Dickie Bird Halked was born drunk and very, very
275 mad. At the Dickie Bird Tavern in downtown Espanola seventeen years ago and that's a fact.

PIERRE: Aw, shit la marde. Fuck you, Spooky Lacroix, I'm
gonna go get me my rest.

(Throws the yarn in SPOOKY's face, jumps up and exits. SPOOKY sits
there with a pile of yarn stuck to his face, caught on his glasses.)

ZACHARY: (Proudly holding up the pie crust in its plate.) It worked!

(Black-out)

(On the upper level, in a dim light away from her perch, NANABUSH/
BLACK LADY HALKED is getting ready to go out for the evening, combing
her hair in front of a mirror, putting on her clothes, etc. DICKIE BIRD is

with her, naked, getting ready to go to bed. SPOOKY's crucifix sits on a
night-table to his side. In DICKIE BIRD's mind, he is at home with his
mother.)

DICKIE BIRD: Mama. Mama. N'tagoosin. ("I'm sick.")   280
NANABUSH/BLACK LADY: Say your prayers.
DICKIE BIRD: Achimoostawin nimoosoom. ("Tell me about my
grandpa.")
NANABUSH/BLACK LADY: Go to bed. I'm going out soon.
DICKIE BIRD: Mawch. Achimoostawin nimoosoom. ("No. Tell 285
me about my grandpa.")
NANABUSH/BLACK LADY: You shouldn't talk about him.
DICKIE BIRD: Tapweechee eegeemachipoowamit nimoosoom?
("Is it true my grandpa had bad medicine?")
NANABUSH/BLACK LADY: They say he met the devil once. Your 290
grandpa talked to the devil. Don't talk about him.
DICKIE BIRD: Eegeemithoopoowamit nimoosoom, eetweet
Simon Starblanket. ("Simon Starblanket says he had good
medicine.")
NANABUSH/BLACK LADY: Ashhh! Simon Starblanket.   295
DICKIE BIRD: Mawch eemithoosit awa aymeewatik keetnanow
kichi, eetweet Simon Starblanket. ("Simon Starblanket says
that this cross is not right for us.") (He grabs the crucifix from
the night-table and spits on it.)
NANABUSH/BLACK LADY: (Grabbing the crucifix from DICKIE BIRD, 300
she attempts to spank him but DICKIE BIRD evades her.) Dickie
Bird! Kipasta-oon! ("You're committing a mortal sin!") Say
ten Hail Marys and two Our Fathers.
DICKIE BIRD: Mootha apoochiga taskootch nimama keetha.
Mootha apoochiga m'tanawgatch kisagee-in. ("You're 305
even like my mother. You don't even love me at all.")
NANABUSH/BLACK LADY: Dickie Bird. Shut up. I'll say them with
you. "Hail Mary, full of grace, the Lord is with thee . . . "
Hurry up. I have to go out. (As NANABUSH/BLACK LADY
HALKED now prepares to leave.) "Hail Mary, full of grace, the 310
Lord is with thee . . . " (She gives up.) Ashhh! Your father
should be home soon. (Exits.)
DICKIE BIRD: (Speaking out to the now absent NANABUSH/BLACK
LADY.) Mootha nipapa ana. ("He's not my father.") (He grabs
his clothes and the crucifix and runs out, down to the lower level 315
and into the forest made of light and shadows.) Tapwee anima
ka-itweechik, chee-i? Neetha ooma kimineechagan, chee-i?
("It's true what they say, isn't it? I'm a bastard, aren't I?")
(He is now sitting on the rock, where SIMON and ZACHARY first
met in Act One.) Nipapa ana . . . Big Joey . . . (To himself, 320
quietly.) . . . nipapa ana . . . Big Joey . . . ("My father is . . .
Big Joey.")

(Silence.)

(A few moments later, NANABUSH comes bouncing into the forest, as
the spirit of the vivacious, young PATSY PEGAHMAGAHBOW, complete
with very large, oversized bum. The full moon glows.)

NANABUSH/PATSY: (To herself, as she peers into the shadows.) Oooh,
my poor bum. I fell on the ice four days ago, eh? And it still
hurts, oooh. (She finally sees DICKIE BIRD huddling on the rock, 325
barely dressed.) There you are. I came out to look for you.
What happened to your clothes? It's freezing out here. Put
them on. Here. (She starts to help dress him.) What happened

330 at the arena? You were on the ice, eh? You feel like talking?
In Indian? How, weetamawin. ("Come on, tell me.")

(BIG JOEY and CREATURE NATAWAYS *enter a distance away. They
are smoking a joint and* BIG JOEY *carries a gun. They stop and watch
from the shadows.*)

CREATURE: Check her out.
NANABUSH/PATSY: Why do you always carry that crucifix? I
don't believe that stuff. I traded mine in for sweetgrass.
Hey. You wanna come to Rosie's and eat fry bread with me?
335 Simon will be there, too. Simon and me, we're getting married, eh? We're gonna have a baby . . .
CREATURE: What's she trying to do?
NANABUSH/PATSY: . . . Rosie's got deer meat, too, come on, you
like my Mom's cooking, eh? (*She attempts to take the crucifix
340 away from* DICKIE BIRD.) But you'll have to leave that here
because Rosie can't stand the Pope . . .

(DICKIE BIRD *grabs the crucifix back.*)

CREATURE: What's he trying to do?
NANABUSH/PATSY: . . . give it to me . . . Dickie . . . come on . . .
CREATURE: He's weird, Big Joey, he's weird.
345 NANABUSH/PATSY: . . . leave it here . . . it will be safe here . . .
we'll bury it in the snow . . .

(*Playfully, she tries to get the crucifix away from* DICKIE BIRD.)

CREATURE: Hey, don't do that, don't do that, man, he's ticklish.
NANABUSH/PATSY: (*As* DICKIE BIRD *begins poking her playfully
with the crucifix and laughing,* NANABUSH/PATSY *gradually
350 starts to get frightened.*) . . . don't look at me that way . . .
Dickie Bird, what's wrong? . . . ya, Dickie Bird, awus . . .

(DICKIE BIRD *starts to grab at* NANABUSH/PATSY.)

CREATURE: Hey, don't you think, don't you think . . . he's getting kind of carried away?
NANABUSH/PATSY: . . . awus . . .
355 CREATURE: We gotta do something, Big Joey, we gotta do
something. (BIG JOEY *stops* CREATURE.) Let go! Let go!
NANABUSH/PATSY: (*Now in a panic.*) . . . Awus! Awus! Awus! . . .

(DICKIE BIRD *grabs* NANABUSH/PATSY *and throws her violently to the
ground, he lifts her skirt and shoves the crucifix up against her.*)

BIG JOEY: (*To* CREATURE.) Shut up.
NANABUSH/PATSY: (*Screams and goes into hysteria.*) . . . Simon! . . .

(DICKIE BIRD *rapes* NANABUSH/PATSY *with the crucifix. A heartbreaking, very slow, sensuous tango breaks out on off-stage harmonica.*)

360 CREATURE: (*To* BIG JOEY.) No! Let me go. Big Joey, let me go,
please! (BIG JOEY *suddenly grabs* CREATURE *violently by the collar.*)
BIG JOEY: Get out. Get the fuck out of here. You're nothin' but
a fuckin' fruit. Fuck off. (CREATURE *collapses.*) I said fuck off.

(CREATURE *flees.* BIG JOEY *just stands there, paralyzed, and watches.*)

(NANABUSH/PATSY, *who has gradually been moving back and back,
is now standing up on her perch again (i.e., the "mound"/jukebox
which no longer looks like a jukebox). She stands there, facing the*

audience, *and slowly gathers her skirt, in agony, until she is holding
it up above her waist. A blood stain slowly spreads across her panties
and flows down her leg. At the same time,* DICKIE BIRD *stands downstage beside the rock, holding the crucifix and making violent jabbing
motions with it, downward. All this happens in slow motion. The crucifix starts to bleed. When* DICKIE BIRD *lifts the crucifix up, his arms
and chest are covered with blood. Finally,* NANABUSH/PATSY *collapses
to the floor of her platform and slowly crawls away. Lights fade on her.
On the lower level,* BIG JOEY, *in a state of shock, staggers, almost
faints and vomits violently. Then he reels over to* DICKIE BIRD *and,
not knowing what else to do, begins collecting his clothes and calming
him down.*)

BIG JOEY: How, Dickie Bird, How, astum. Igwa. Mootha nantow. Mootha nantow. Shhh. Shhh. ("Come on, Dickie Bird. 365
Come. Let's go. It's okay. It's okay. Shhh. Shhh . . .") (*Barely
able to bring himself to touch it, he takes the crucifix from* DICKIE
BIRD *and drops it quickly on the rock. Then he begins wiping the
blood off* DICKIE BIRD.) How, mootha nantow. Mootha nantow. How, astum, keeyapitch upisees ootee. Igwani. Igwani. 370
Poonimatoo. Mootha nantow. Mootha nantow. ("Come on,
it's okay. It's okay. Come on, a little more over here. That's
all. That's all. Stop crying. It's okay. It's okay . . .") (DICKIE
BIRD, *shaking with emotion, looks questioningly into* BIG JOEY'*s
face.*) Eehee. Nigoosis keetha. Mootha Wellington Halked 375
kipapa. Neetha . . . kipapa. ("Yes. You are my son. Wellington
Halked is not your father. I'm . . . your father.")

(*Silence. They look at each other.* DICKIE BIRD *grabs* BIG JOEY *and
clings to him,* BIG JOEY *reacting tentatively, at first, and then passionately, with* DICKIE BIRD *finally bursting out into uncontrollable
sobs. Fade-out.*)

(*Out of this darkness, gunshots explode. And we hear a man's voice
wailing, in complete and utter agony. Then comes violent pounding at
a door. Finally, still in the darkness, we hear* SIMON STARBLANKET'*s
speaking voice.*)

SIMON: Open up! Pierre St. Pierre, open up! I know you're in
there!
PIERRE: (*Still in the darkness.*) Whoa! Easy now. Easy on that 380
goddamn door. Must you create such a carpostrophe smack
dab in the middle of my rest period? (*When the lights come
up, we are outside the "window" to* PIERRE ST. PIERRE'*s little boot-
leg joint.* PIERRE *pokes his head out, wearing his night clothes,
complete with pointy cap.*) Go home. Go to bed. Don't be dis- 385
turbin' my rest period. My wife, Veronique St. Pierre, she
tells me there's now not only a OHL but a NHL, too. Indian women's National Hockey League. All the Indian
women on every reserve in Canada, all the Indian women in
Canada is playin' hockey now. It's like a fever out there. 390
That's why I gotta get my rest. First thing tomorrow
mornin', I go jiggle that puck out of Gazelle Nataways. Listen to me. I'm your elder.

(SIMON *shoots the gun into the house, just missing* PIERRE'*s head.*)

SIMON: (*Dead calm.*) One, you give me a bottle. Two, I report
your joint to the Manitowaning police. Three, I shoot your 395
fucking head off.

PIERRE: Alright. Alright. (*He pops in for a bottle of whiskey and hands it out to* SIMON.) Now you go on home with this. Go have yourself a nice quiet drink. (SIMON *begins to exit.* PIERRE *calls out.*) What the hell are you gonna do with that gun?

SIMON: (*Calling back.*) I'm gonna go get that mute. Little bastard raped Patsy Pegahmagahbow. (*Exits.*)

(*Pause.*)

PIERRE: Holy shit la marde! (*Pause.*) I gotta warn him. No. I need my rest. No. I gotta warn that boy. No. I gotta find that puck. No. Dickie Bird's life. No. The puck. No. Dickie Bird. No. Hockey. No. His life. No. Hockey. No. Life. Hockey. Life. Hockey. Life. Hockey. Life. Hockey. Life . . .

(*Fade-out.*)

(*Lights up on* SPOOKY LACROIX's *kitchen.* CREATURE NATAWAYS *is sitting at the table, silent, head propped up in his hands.* SPOOKY *is knitting, with obvious haste, a white christening gown, of which a large crucifix is the center-piece.* SPOOKY's *bible still sits on the table beside him.*)

SPOOKY: Why didn't you do something? (*Silence.*) Creature. (*Silence. Finally,* SPOOKY *stops knitting and looks up.*) Alphonse Nataways, why didn't you stop him? (*Silence.*) You're scared of him, aren't you? You're scared to death of Big Joey. Admit it.

(*Silence.*)

CREATURE: (*Quietly and calmly.*) I love him, Spooky.

SPOOKY: Say wha?!

CREATURE: I love him.

SPOOKY: You love him? What do you mean? How? How do you love him?

CREATURE: I love him.

SPOOKY: Lord have mercy on Wasaychigan Hill!

CREATURE: (*Rising suddenly.*) I love the way he stands. I love the way he walks. The way he laughs. The way he wears his cowboy boots . . .

SPOOKY: You're kidding me.

CREATURE: . . . the way his tight blue jeans fall over his ass. The way he talks so smart and tough. The way women fall at his feet. I wanna be like him. I always wanted to be like him, William. I always wanted to have a dick as big as his.

SPOOKY: Creature Alphonse Nataways? You know not what you say.

CREATURE: I don't care.

SPOOKY: I care.

CREATURE: I don't care. I can't stand it anymore.

SPOOKY: Shut up. You're making me nervous. Real nervous.

CREATURE: Come with me.

SPOOKY: Come with you where?

CREATURE: To his house.

SPOOKY: Whose house?

CREATURE: Big Joey.

SPOOKY: Are you crazy?

CREATURE: Come with me.

SPOOKY: No.

CREATURE: Yes.

SPOOKY: No.

CREATURE: (*Suddenly and viciously grabbing* SPOOKY *by the throat.*) Cut the goddamn bull crap, Spooky Lacroix! (SPOOKY *tries desperately to save the christening gown.*) I seen you crawl in the mud and shit so drunk you were snortin' like a pig.

SPOOKY: I changed my ways, thank you.

CREATURE: Twenty one years. Twenty one years ago. You, me, Big Joey, Eugene Starblanket, that goddamn Zachary Jeremiah Keechigeesik. We were eighteen. We cut our wrists. Your own father's huntin' knife. We mixed blood. Swore we'd be friends for life. Frontenac Hotel. Twenty one years ago. You got jumped by seven white guys. Broken beer bottle come straight at your face. If it wasn't for me, you wouldn't be here today, wavin' that stinkin' bible in my face like it was a slab of meat. I'm not a dog. I'm your buddy. Your friend.

SPOOKY: I know that.

(CREATURE *tightens his hold on* SPOOKY's *throat. The two men are staring straight into each other's eyes, inches apart. Silence.*)

CREATURE: William. Think of your father. Remember the words of Nicotine Lacroix.

(*Finally,* SPOOKY *screams, throwing the christening gown, knitting needles and all, over the bible on the table.*)

SPOOKY: You goddamn, fucking son-of-a-bitch!

(*Black-out. Gunshots in the distance.*)

(*Lights up on* BIG JOEY's *living room/kitchen.* BIG JOEY *is sitting, silent and motionless, on the couch, staring straight ahead, as though he were in a trance. His hunting rifle rests on his lap.* DICKIE BIRD HALKED *stands directly in front of and facing the life-size pin-up poster of Marilyn Monroe, also as though he were in a trance. Then his head drops down in remorse.* BIG JOEY *lifts the gun, loads it and aims it out directly in front. When* DICKIE BIRD *hears the snap of the gun being loaded, he turns to look. Then he slowly walks over to* BIG JOEY, *kneels down directly in front of the barrel of the gun, puts it in his mouth and then slowly reaches over and gently, almost lovingly, moves* BIG JOEY's *hand away from the trigger, caressing the older man's hand as he does.* BIG JOEY *slowly looks up at* DICKIE BIRD's *face, stunned.* DICKIE BIRD *puts his own thumb on the trigger and pulls. Click. Nothing. In the complete silence, the two men are looking directly into each other's eyes. Complete stillness. Fade-out. Split seconds before complete black-out, Marilyn Monroe farts, courtesy of* MS. NANABUSH: *a little flag reading "poot" pops up out of Ms. Monroe's derrier, as on a play gun. We hear a cute little "poot" sound.*)

(*Out of this black-out emerges the sound of a harmonica; it is* ZACHARY JEREMIAH KEECHIGEESIK *playing his heart out. Fade-in on* PIERRE ST. PIERRE, *still in his night-clothes but also wearing his winter coat and hat over them, rushing all over the "forest" ostensibly rushing to* BIG JOEY's *house to warn* DICKIE BIRD HALKED *about the gun-toting* SIMON STARBLANKET. *He mutters to himself as he goes.*)

PIERRE: . . . Hockey. Life. Hockey. Life. Hockey. Life . . .

(ZACHARY *appears in the shadows and sees* PIERRE.)

ZACHARY: Hey!

PIERRE: (*Not hearing* ZACHARY.) . . . Hockey. Life. Hockey. Life . . .

ZACHARY: Pssst!

PIERRE: (*Still not hearing* ZACHARY.) . . . Hockey. Life. Hockey. Life. (*Pause.*) Hockey life!

ZACHARY: (*Finally yelling.*) Pierre St. Pierre!

(PIERRE *jumps.*)

470 PIERRE: Hallelujah! Have you heard the news?

ZACHARY: The Band Council went and okayed Big Joey's radio station.

PIERRE: All the Indian women in the world is playin' hockey now! World Hockey League, they call themselves. Aborig-
475 inal Women's WHL. My wife, Veronique St. Pierre, she just got the news. Eegeeweetamagoot fax machine. ("Fax machine told her.") It's like a burnin', ragin', blindin' fever out there. Them Cree women in Saskatchewan, them Blood women in Alberta, them Yakima, them Heidis out in the
480 middle of your Specific Ocean, them Kickapoo, Chickasaw, Cherokee, Chipewyan, Choctaw, Chippewa, Wichita, Kiowa down in Oklahoma, them Seminole, Navajo, Onondaga, Tuscarora, Winnebago, Mimac-paddy-wack-why-it's-enough-to-give-your-dog-a-bone! . . .

(*As, getting completely carried away, he grabs his crotch.*)

485 ZACHARY: Pierre. Pierre.

PIERRE: . . . they're turnin' the whole world topsy-turkey right before our very eyes and the Prime Minister's a-shittin' grape juice . . . (*A gunshot explodes in the near distance.* PIERRE *suddenly lays low and changes tone completely.*) Holy shit la
490 marde! He's after Dickie Bird. There's a red-eyed, crazed devil out there and he's after Dickie Bird Halked and he's gonna kill us all if we don't stop him right this minute.

ZACHARY: Who? Who's gonna kill us?

PIERRE: Simon Starblanket. Drunk. Power mad. Half-crazed on
495 whiskey and he's got a gun.

ZACHARY: Simon?

PIERRE: He's drunk and he's mean and he's out to kill. (*Another gunshot.*) Hear that?

ZACHARY: (*To himself.*) That's Simon? I thought . . .

500 PIERRE: When he heard about the Pegahmagahbow rape . . .

ZACHARY: Pegahmagahbow what?

PIERRE: Why, haven't you heard? Dickie Bird Halked raped Patsy Pegahmagahbow in most brutal fashion and Simon Starblanket is out to kill Dickie Bird Halked so I'm on my
505 way to Big Joey's right this minute and I'm takin' that huntin' rifle of his and I'm sittin' next to that Halked boy right up until the cows come home.

(*Exits.*)

ZACHARY: (*To himself.*) Simon Starblanket. Patsy . . .

(*Black-out.*)

(*Out of this black-out come the gunshots, much louder this time, and* SIMON's *wailing voice.*)

SIMON: Aieeeeee-yip-yip! Nanabush! . . . (*Fade-in on* SIMON, *in
510 the forest close by the large rock, still carrying his hunting rifle.* SIMON *is half-crazed by this time, drunk out of his skull. The full moon glows.*) . . . Weesageechak! Come back! Rosie!

Rosie Kakapetum, tell him to come back, not to run away, cuz we need him . . .

(NANABUSH/PATSY PEGAHMAGAHBOW's *voice comes filtering out of the darkness on the upper level. It is as though* SIMON *were hearing a voice from inside his head.*)

NANABUSH/PATSY: . . . her . . .   515

SIMON: . . . him . . .

NANABUSH/PATSY: . . . her . . .

(*Slow fade-in on* NANABUSH/PATSY, *standing on the upper level, look-ing down at* SIMON. *She still wears her very large bum.*)

SIMON: . . . weetha ("him/her"—i.e., no gender) . . . Christ! What is it? Him? Her? Stupid fucking language, fuck you, da Englesa. Me no speakum no more da goodie Englesa, in 520 Cree we say "weetha," not "him" or "her" Nanabush, come back! (*Speaks directly to* NANABUSH, *as though he/she were there, directly in front of him; he doesn't see* NANABUSH/PATSY *standing on the upper level.*) Aw, boozhoo how are ya? Me good. Me berry, berry good. I seen you! I just seen you jumping jack- 525 ass thisa away . . .

NANABUSH/PATSY: (*As though she/he were playing games behind* SIMON's *back.*) . . . and thataway . . .

SIMON: . . . and thisaway and . . .

NANABUSH/PATSY: . . . thataway . . .   530

SIMON: . . . and thisaway and . . .

NANABUSH/PATSY: . . . thataway . . .

SIMON: . . . and thisaway and . . .

NANABUSH/PATSY: . . . thataway . . .

SIMON: . . . etcetra, etcetra, etcetra . . .   535

NANABUSH/PATSY: . . . etcetERA. (*Pause.*) She's here! She's here!

SIMON: . . . Nanabush! Weesageechak! . . . (NANABUSH/PATSY *peals out with a silvery, magical laugh that echoes and echoes.*) . . . Dey shove dis . . . whach-you-ma-call-it . . . da crucifix up your holy cunt ouch, eh? Ouch, eh? (SIMON *sees the bloody* 540 *crucifix sitting on the rock and slowly approaches it. He kneels directly before it.*) Nah . . . (*Laughs a long mad, hysterical laugh that ends with hysterical weeping.*) . . . yesssss . . . noooo . . . oh, noooo! Crucifix! (*Spits violently on the crucifix.*) Fucking goddamn crucifix yesssss . . . God! You're a man. You're a 545 woman. You're a man? You're a woman? You see, nineethoo-wan poogoo neetha ("I speak only Cree") . . .

NANABUSH/PATSY: . . . ohhh . . .

SIMON: . . . keetha ma-a? ("How about you?") . . . Nah. Da En-glesa him . . .   550

NANABUSH/PATSY: . . . her . . .

SIMON: . . . him . . .

NANABUSH/PATSY: . . . her . . .

SIMON: . . . him! . . .

NANABUSH/PATSY: . . . her! . . .   555

SIMON: . . . all da time . . .

NANABUSH/PATSY: . . . all da time . . .

SIMON: . . . tsk, tsk, tsk . . .

NANABUSH/PATSY: . . . tsk, tsk, tsk.

SIMON: If God, you are a woman/man in Cree but only a man 560 in da Englesa, then how come you still got a cun . . .

NANABUSH/PATSY: . . . a womb.

(*With this,* SIMON *finally sees* NANABUSH/PATSY. *He calls out to her.*)

SIMON: Patsy! Big Bum Pegahmagahbow, you flying across da ice on world's biggest puck. Patsy, look what dey done to your puss . . . (NANABUSH/PATSY *lifts her skirt and displays the blood stain on her panties. She then finally takes off the prosthetic that is her huge bum and holds it in one arm.*) Hey! (*And* NANABUSH/PATSY *holds an eagle feather up in the air, ready to dance.* SIMON *stomps on the ground, rhythmically, and sings.*) " . . . and me I don't wanna go to the moon, I'm gonna leave that moon alone. I just wanna dance with the Rosebud Sioux this summer, yeah, yeah, yeah . . . " (SIMON *chants and he and* NANABUSH/PATSY *dance, he on the lower level with his hunting rifle in the air, she on the upper level with her eagle feather.*) How, astum, Patsy, kiam. N'tayneemeetootan. ("Come on, Patsy, never mind. Let's go dance.")

(*We hear* ZACHARY JEREMIAH KEECHIGEESIK's *voice calling from the darkness a distance away.*)

ZACHARY: Hey!

(*But* SIMON *and* NANABUSH/PATSY *pay no heed.*)

NANABUSH/PATSY: . . . n'tayneemeetootan South Dakota? . . .
SIMON: . . . how, astum, Patsy. N'tayneemeetootan South Dakota. Hey, Patsy Pegahmagahbow. . . .

(*As he finally approaches her and holds his hand out.*)

NANABUSH/PATSY: (*As she holds her hand out toward his.*) . . . Simon Starblanket . . .
SIMON/NANABUSH/PATSY: . . . eenpaysagee-itan ("I love you to death") . . .

(ZACHARY *finally emerges tentatively from the shadows. He is holding a beautiful, fresh pie.* NANABUSH/PATSY *disappears.*)

ZACHARY: (*Calling out over the distance.*) Hey! You want some pie?
SIMON: (*Silence. Calling back.*) What?!

(*Not seeing* ZACHARY, *he looks around cautiously.*)

ZACHARY: I said. You want some pie?
SIMON: (*Calling back, after some confused thought.*) What?
ZACHARY: (*He approaches* SIMON *slowly.*) Do you want some pie?
SIMON: (*Silence. Finally, he sees* ZACHARY *and points the gun at him.*) What kind?
ZACHARY: Apple. I just made some. It's still hot.
SIMON: (*Long pause.*) Okay.

(*Slowly,* NANABUSH/PATSY *enters the scene and comes up behind* SIMON, *holding* SIMON's *dancing bustle in front of her, as in a ceremony.*)

ZACHARY: Okay. But you gotta give me the gun first. (*The gun goes off accidentally, just missing* ZACHARY's *head.*) I said, you gotta give me the gun first.

(*Gradually, the dancing bustle begins to shimmer and dance in* NANABUSH/PATSY's *hands.*)

SIMON: Patsy. I gotta go see Patsy.
ZACHARY: You and me and Patsy and Hera. We're gonna go have some pie. Fresh, hot apple pie. Then, we go to Sudbury and have a look at that Mobart, what do you say?

(*The shimmering movements of the bustle balloon out into these magical, dance-like arches, as* NANABUSH/PATSY *maneuvers it directly in front of* SIMON, *hiding him momentarily. Behind this,* SIMON *drops the base of the rifle to the ground, causing it to go off accidentally. The bullet hits* SIMON *in the stomach. He falls to the ground.* ZACHARY *lets go of his pie and runs over to him. The shimmering of the bustle dies off into the darkness of the forest and disappears,* NANABUSH/PATSY *maneuvering it.*)

ZACHARY: Simon! Simon! Oh, lordy, lordy, lordy . . . Are you alright? Are you okay? Simon. Simon. Talk to me. Goodness sakes, talk to me Simon. Ayumi-in! ("Talk to me!")
SIMON: (*Barely able to speak, as he sinks slowly to the ground beside the large rock.*) Kamoowanow . . . apple . . . pie . . . patima . . . neetha . . . igwa Patsy . . . n'gapeetootanan . . . patima . . . apple . . . pie . . . neee. ("We'll eat . . . apple . . . pie . . . later . . . me . . . and Patsy . . . we'll come over . . . later . . . apple . . . pie . . . neee.")

(*He dies.*)

ZACHARY: (*As he kneels over* SIMON's *body, the full moon glowing even redder.*) Oh, lordy, lordy . . . Holy shit! Holy shit! What's happening? What's become of this place? What's happening to this place? What's happening to these people? My people. He didn't have to die. He didn't have to die. That's the goddamn most stupid . . . no reason . . . this kind of living has got to stop. It's got to stop! (*Talking and then just shrieking at the sky.*) Aieeeeeee-Lord! God! God of the Indian! God of the Whiteman! God-Al-fucking-mighty! Whatever the fuck your name is. Why are you doing this to us? Why are you doing this to us? Are you up there at all? Or are you some stupid, drunken shit, out-of-your-mind-passed out under some great beer table up there in your stupid fucking clouds? Come down! Astum oota! ("Come down here!") Why don't you come down? I dare you to come down from your high-falutin' fuckin' shit-throne up there, come down and show us you got the guts to stop this stupid, stupid, stupid way of living. It's got to stop. It's got to stop. It's got to stop. It's got to stop. It's got to stop. It's got to stop . . .

(*He collapses over* SIMON's *body and weeps. Fade-out. Towards the end of this speech, a light comes up on* NANABUSH. *Her perch (i.e., the jukebox) has swivelled around and she is sitting on a toilet having a good shit. He/she is dressed in an old man's white beard and wig, but also wearing sexy, elegant women's high-heeled pumps. Surrounded by white, puffy clouds, she/he sits with her legs crossed, nonchalantly filing his/her fingernails. Fade-out.*)

(*Fade-in on* BIG JOEY's *living room/kitchen.* BIG JOEY, DICKIE BIRD HALKED, CREATURE NATAWAYS, SPOOKY LACROIX *and* PIERRE ST. PIERRE *are sitting and standing in various positions, in complete silence. A hush pervades the room for about twenty beats.* DICKIE BIRD *is holding* BIG JOEY's *hunting rifle. Suddenly,* ZACHARY JEREMIAH KEECHIGEESIK *enters; in a semi-crazed state.* DICKIE BIRD *starts and points the rifle straight at* ZACHARY's *head.*)

CREATURE: Zachary Jeremiah! What are you doing here?
BIG JOEY: Lookin' for your shorts, Zach?

(*From his position on the couch, he motions* DICKIE BIRD *to put the gun down.* DICKIE BIRD *does so.*)

ZACHARY: *(To* BIG JOEY.*)* You're unbelievable. You're fucking unbelievable. You let this young man, you let your own son get away with this inconceivable act . . .

635 CREATURE: Don't say that to him, Zachary Jeremiah, don't say that . . .

ZACHARY: *(Ignoring* CREATURE.*)* You know he did it and you're hiding him what in God's name is wrong with you?

SPOOKY: Zachary Jeremiah, you're not yourself . . .

640 PIERRE: Nope. Not himself. Talkin' wild.

(Sensing potential violence, he sneaks out the door.)

BIG JOEY: *(To* ZACHARY.*)* He don't even know he done anything.

ZACHARY: Bull shit! They're not even sure the air ambulance will get Patsy Pegahmagahbow to Sudbury in time. Simon Starblanket just shot himself and this boy is responsible . . .

*(*SIMON *rises slowly from the ground and "sleep walks" right through this scene and up to the upper level, towards the full moon. The men are only vaguely aware of his passing.)*

645 BIG JOEY: He ain't responsible for nothin'.

ZACHARY: Simon Starblanket was on his way to South Dakota where he could have learned a few things and made something of himself, same place you went and made a total asshole of yourself seventeen years ago . . .

650 CREATURE: Shush, Zachary Jeremiah, that's the past . . .

SPOOKY: . . . the past . . .

CREATURE: . . . Chris'sakes . . .

ZACHARY: What happened to all those dreams you were so full of for your people, the same dreams this young man just

655 died for?

SPOOKY: *(To* BIG JOEY, *though not looking at him.)* And my sister, Black Lady Halked, seventeen years ago at that bar, Big Joey, you could have stopped her drinking, you could have sent her home and this thing never would have happened.

660 That was your son inside her belly.

CREATURE: He didn't do nothing. He wouldn't let me do nothing. He just stood there and watched the whole thing . . .

SPOOKY: Creature Nataways!

CREATURE: I don't care. I'm gonna tell. He watched this little

665 bastard do that to Patsy Pegahmagahbow . . .

BIG JOEY: *(Suddenly turning on* CREATURE.*)* You little cocksucker!

*(*DICKIE BIRD *hits* CREATURE *on the back with the butt of the rifle, knocking him unconscious.)*

SPOOKY: Why, Big Joey, why did you do that?

(Silence.)

ZACHARY: Yes, Joe. Why?

(Long silence. All the men look at BIG JOEY.*)*

BIG JOEY: *(Raising his arms, as for a battle cry.)* "This is the end

670 of the suffering of a great nation!" That was me. Wounded Knee, South Dakota, Spring of '73. The FBI. They beat us to the ground. Again and again and again. Ever since that spring, I've had these dreams where blood is spillin' out from my groin, nothin' there but blood and emptiness. It's

675 like . . . I lost myself. So when I saw this baby comin' out

of Caroline, Black Lady . . . Gazelle dancin' . . . all this blood . . . and I knew it was gonna come . . . I . . . I tried to stop it . . . I freaked out. I don't know what I did . . . and I knew it was mine . . .

680 ZACHARY: Why? Why did you let him do it? Why? Why did you let him do it? Why? Why did you let him do it? Why? Why did you let him do it? *(Finally grabbing* BIG JOEY *by the collar.)* Why?! Why did you let him do it?!

BIG JOEY: *(Breaking free from* ZACHARY's *hold.)* Because I hate them! I hate them fuckin' bitches. Because they—our own

685 women—took the fuckin' power away from us faster than the FBI ever did.

SPOOKY: *(Softly, in the background.)* They always had it.

(Silence.)

BIG JOEY: There. I said it. I'm tired. Tired.

(He slumps down on the couch and cries.)

ZACHARY: *(Softly.)* Joe. Joe.   690

(Fade-out.)

(Out of this darkness emerges the sound of SIMON STARBLANKET's *chanting voice. Away up over* NANABUSH's *perch, the moon begins to glow, fully and magnificently. Against it, in silhouette, we see* SIMON *wearing his powwow bustle.* SIMON STARBLANKET *is dancing in the moon. Fade-out.)*

(Fade-in on the "ice" at the hockey arena, where PIERRE ST. PIERRE, *in full referee regalia, is gossiping with* CREATURE NATAWAYS *and* SPOOKY LACROIX. CREATURE *is knitting, with great difficulty, pink baby booties.* SPOOKY *is holding his new baby, wrapped in a pale blue knit blanket. We hear the sound of a hockey arena, just before a big game.)*

PIERRE: . . . she says to me: "did you know, Pierre St. Pierre, that Gazelle Nataways found Zachary Jeremiah Keechigeesik's undershorts under her chesterfield and washed them and put them in a box real nice, all folded up and even sprinkled her perfume all over them and sashayed 695 herself over to Hera Keechigeesik's house and handed the box over to her? I just about had a heart attack," she says to me. "And what's more," she says to me, "when Hera Keechigeesik opened that box, there was a picture sittin' on top of them shorts, a color picture of none other than our 700 very own Zachary Jeremiah Keechigeesik . . . *(Unseen by* PIERRE, ZACHARY *approaches the group, wearing a baker's hat and carrying a rolling pin.)* . . . wearin' nothin' but the suit God gave him. That's when Hera Keechigeesik went wild, like a banshee tigger, and she tore the hair out of Gazelle 705 Nataways which, as it turns out, was a wig . . . " Imagine. After all these years. " . . . and she beat Gazelle Nataways to a cinder, right there into the treacherous icy door-step. And that's when 'the particular puck' finally came squishin' out of them considerable Nataways bosoms." And gentle- 710 men? The Wasy Wailerettes are on again!

CREATURE: Ho-leee!

SPOOKY: Holy fuck!

PIERRE: And I say shit la ma . . . *(Finally seeing* ZACHARY, *who is standing there, listening to all this.)* . . . oh my . . . *(*PIERRE 715 *turns quickly to* SPOOKY's *baby.)* . . . hello there, koochie-koochie-koo, welcome to the world!

SPOOKY: It's not koochie-koochie-koo, Pierre St. Pierre. Her name's "Kichigeechacha." Rhymes with Lalala. Ain't she purdy?

720

(Up in the "bleachers," BIG JOEY *enters and prepares his microphone stand.* DICKIE BIRD *enters with a big sign saying: "WASY-FM" and hangs it proudly up above the microphone stand.)*

PIERRE: Aw, she'll be readin' that ole holy bible before you can go: "Phhht! Phhht!"

*(*PIERRE *accidentally spits in the baby's face.* SPOOKY *shoos him away.)*

SPOOKY: "Phhht! Phhht!" to you too, Pierre St. Pierre.

CREATURE: Spooky Lacroix. Lalala. They never made it to Sudbury General.

725

SPOOKY: I was busy helping Eugene Starblanket out with Simon . . .

SPOOKY/PIERRE: . . . may he rest in peace . . .

ZACHARY: Good old Rosie Kakapetum. "Stand and deliver," they said to her. And stand and deliver she did. How's the knitting going there, Creature Nataways?

730

CREATURE: Kichigeechacha, my god-daughter, she's wearin' all the wrong colors. I gotta work like a dog.

PIERRE: *(Calling up to* DICKIE BIRD HALKED.*)* Don't you worry a wart about that court appearance, Dickie Bird Halked. I'll be right there beside you tellin' that ole judge a thing or two about that goddamn jukebox.

735

SPOOKY: *(To* CREATURE.*)* Come on. Let's go watch Lalala play her first game.

(He and CREATURE *go up to the "bleachers" on the upper level, directly in front of* NANABUSH's *perch, to watch the big "game.")*

PIERRE: *(Reading from his clip-board and checking off the list.)* Now then, Dominique Ladouche, Black Lady Halked, Annie Cook, June Bug Mcleod . . .

740

(He stops abruptly for BIG JOEY's *announcement, as do the other men.)*

BIG JOEY: *(On the microphone.)* Patsy Pegahmagahbow, who is recuperating at Sudbury General Hospital, sends her love and requests that the first goal scored by the Wasy Wailerettes be dedicated to the memory of Simon Starblanket . . .

745

*(*CREATURE *and* SPOOKY, *with knitting and baby, respectively, are now up in the "bleachers" with* DICKIE BIRD *and* BIG JOEY, *who are standing beside each other at the microphone stand.* PIERRE ST. PIERRE *is again skating around on the "ice" in his own inimitable fashion, "warming up."* ZACHARY JEREMIAH KEECHIGEESIK, *meanwhile, now has his apple pie, as well as his rolling pin, in hand, still wearing his baker's hat. At this point, the hockey arena sounds shift abruptly to the sound of women wailing and pucks hitting boards, echoing and echoing as in a vast empty chamber. As this "hockey game sequence" progresses, the spectacle of the men watching, cheering, etc., becomes more and more dream-like, all the men's movements imperceptibly breaking down into slow motion, until they fade, later, into the darkness.* ZACHARY *"sleep walks" through the whole lower level of the set, almost as though he were retracing his steps back through the whole*

play. Slowly, he takes off his clothes item by item, until, by the end, he is back lying naked on the couch where he began the play, except that, this time, it will be his own couch he is lying on. BIG JOEY *continues uninterrupted.)*

. . . And there they are, ladies igwa gentlemen, there they are, the most beautiful, daring, death-defying Indian women in the world, the Wasy Wailerettes! How, Number Nine Hera Keechigeesik, CAPTAIN of the Wasy Wailerettes, face-off igwa itootum asichi Number Nine Flora McDonald, Captain of the Canoe Lake Bravettes. Hey, soogi pagichee-ipinew "particular puck" referee Pierre St. Pierre . . .

750

CREATURE: Go Hera go! Go Hera go! Go Hera go! . . .

*(Repeated all the way through—and under—*BIG JOEY's *commentary.)*

BIG JOEY: . . . igwa seemak wathay g'waskootoo like a herd of wild turtles . . .

755

SPOOKY: Wasy once. Wasy twice. Holy jumping Christ! Rim ram. God damn. Fuck, son-of-a-bitch, shit!

(Repeated in time to CREATURE's *cheer, all the way through—and under—*BIG JOEY's *commentary.)*

BIG JOEY: . . . Hey, aspin Number Six Dry Lips Manigitogan, right-winger for the Wasy Wailerettes, eemaskamat Number Thirteen of the Canoe Lake Bravettes anee-i "particular puck" . . . *(*DICKIE BIRD *begins chanting and stomping his foot in time to* CREATURE's *and* SPOOKY's *cheers. Bits and pieces of* NANABUSH/GAZELLE NATAWAYS' *"strip music" and Kitty Wells' "It Wasn't God Who Made Honky Tonk Angels" begin to weave in and out of this "sound collage," a collage which now has a definite "pounding" rhythm to it. Over it all soars the sound of* ZACHARY's *harmonica, swooping and diving brilliantly, recalling many of* NANABUSH's *appearances throughout the play.* BIG JOEY *continues uninterrupted.)* . . . igwa aspin sipweesinskwataygew. Hey, k'seegoochin! How, Number Six Dry Lips Manigitogan igwa soogi pugamawew anee-i "particular puck" ita Number Twenty-six Little Girl Manitowabi, left-winger for the Wasy Wailerettes, katee-ooteetuk blue line ita Number Eleven Black Lady Halked, wha! defensewoman for the Wasy Wailerettes, kagatchitnat anee-i "particular puck" igwa seemak kapassiwatat Captain Hera Keechigeesikwa igwa Hera Keechigeesik mitooni eepimithat, hey, kwayus graceful Hera Keechigeesik, mitooni Russian ballerina eesinagoosit. Captain Hera Keechigeesik bee-line igwa itootum straight for the Canoe Lake Bravettes' net igwa shootiwatew anee-i "particular puck" igwa she shoots, she scores . . . almost! Wha! Close one, ladies igwa gentlemen, kwayus close one. But Number Six Dry Lips Manigitogan, right-winger for the Wasy Wailerettes, accidentally tripped and blocked the shot . . . *(*BIG JOEY's *voice begins to trail off as, at this point,* CREATURE NATAWAYS *marches over and angrily grabs the microphone away from him.)* . . . How, Number Nine Flora McDonald, Captain of the Canoe Lake Bravettes, igwa ooteetinew anee-i "particular puck" igwa skate-oo-oo behind the net igwa

760

765

770

775

780

785

790

747 . . . **And** . . . The following hockey commentary by Big Joey (pages 1400–1401) is translated on page 1402.

soogi heading along the right side of the rink ita Number
Twenty-one Annie Cook . . .

CREATURE: *(Off microphone, as he marches over to it.)* Aw shit! Aw
795   shit! . . . *(He grabs the microphone and, as he talks into it, the
sound of all the other men's voices, including the entire "sound
collage," begins to fade.)* . . . That Dry Lips Manigitogan,
she's no damn good, Spooky Lacroix, I tole you once I
tole you twice she shouldna done it she shouldna done
800   what she went and did goddawful Dry Lips Manigitogan
they shouldna let her play, she's too fat, she's gotten positively blubbery lately, I tole you once I tole you twice that
Dry Lips Manigitogan oughta move to Kapuskasing, she really oughta, Spooky Lacroix. I tole you once I tole you twice
805   she oughta move to Kapuskasing, Dry Lips oughta move to
Kapuskasing! Dry Lips oughta move to Kapuskasing! Dry
Lips oughta move to Kapuskasing! Dry Lips oughta move to
Kapuskasing Dry Lips oughta move to Kapuskasing Dry
Lips oughta move to Kapuskasing Dry Lips oughta move to
810   Kapuskasing Dry Lips oughta move to Kapuskasing Dry
Lips oughta move to Kapuskasing . . .

*(And this, too, fades into, first a whisper, magnified on tape to "other-
worldly" proportions, then into a slow kind of heavy breathing. On top
of this we hear* SPOOKY's *baby crying. Complete fade-out on all this
(lights and sound), except for the baby's crying and the heavy breathing, which continue in the darkness. When the lights come up again,
we are in* ZACHARY's *own living room (i.e., what was all along* BIG
JOEY's *living room/kitchen, only much cleaner). The couch* ZACHARY
*lies on is now covered with a "starblanket" and over the pin-up poster
of Marilyn Monroe now hangs what was, earlier on,* NANABUSH's
*large powwow dancing bustle. The theme from "The Smurfs" television
show bleeds in.* ZACHARY *is lying on the couch face down, naked, sleeping and snoring. The television in front of the couch comes on and "The
Smurfs" are playing merrily away.* ZACHARY's *wife, the "real"* HERA
KEECHIGEESIK, *enters carrying their baby, who is covered completely
with a blanket.* HERA *is soothing the crying baby.)*

ZACHARY: *(Talking in his sleep.)* . . . Dry Lips . . . oughta move
to . . . Kapus . . .
HERA: Poosees.
815   ZACHARY: . . . kasing . . . damn silliest thing I heard in my
life . . .
HERA: Honey.

(Bends over the couch and kisses ZACHARY *on the bum.)*

ZACHARY: . . . goodness sakes, Hera, you just had a baby . . .
(Suddenly, he jumps up and falls off the couch.) Simon!
820   HERA: Yoah! Keegatch igwa kipageecheep'skawinan. ("Yoah!
You almost knocked us down.")
ZACHARY: Hera! Where's my shorts?!

HERA: Neee, kigipoochimeek awus-chayees. ("Neee, just a
couple of inches past the rim of your ass-hole.")
ZACHARY: Neee, chimagideedoosh. ("Neee, you unfragrant   825
kozy": Ojibway.)

(He struggles to a sitting position on the couch.)

HERA: *(Correcting him and laughing.)* "ChimagideeDEESH."
("You unfragrant KOOZIE.")
ZACHARY: Alright. "ChimagideeDEESH."
HERA: And what were you dreaming abou . . .   830
ZACHARY: *(Finally seeing the television.)* Hey, it's the Smurfs! And
they're not playing hockey de Englesa.
HERA: Neee, machi ma-a tatoo-Saturday morning Smurfs.
Mootha meena weegatch hockey meetaweewuk weethawow
Smurfs. ("Well, of course, the Smurfs are on every Saturday   835
morning. But they never play hockey, those Smurfs.") Here,
you take her. *(She hands the baby over to* ZACHARY *and goes to
sit beside him.)* Boy, that full moon last night. Ever look particularly like a giant puck, eh? Neee . . .

(Silence. ZACHARY *plays with the baby.)*

ZACHARY: *(To* HERA.) Hey, cup-cake. You ever think of playing   840
hockey?
HERA: Yeah, right. That's all I need is a flying puck right in the
left tit, neee . . . *(But she stops to speculate.)* . . . hockey,
hmmm . . .
ZACHARY: *(To himself.)* Lordy, lordy, lordy . . . *(*HERA *fishes   845
*ZACHARY's *undershorts, which are pale blue in color, from un-
der a cushion and hands them to him.* ZACHARY *gladly grabs
them.)* Neee, magawa nipeetawitoos . . . ("Neee, here's my
sharts . . . ")
HERA: *(Correcting him and laughing.)* "NipeetawiTAS." ("My   850
SHORTS")
ZACHARY: Alright. "NipeetawiTAS." *(Dangles the shorts up to the
baby's face with thumb and fore-finger and laughs. Sing-songy,
bouncing the baby on his lap:)* Magawa nipeetawitas.
Nipeetawitas. Nipeetawitas. Nipeetawitas . . .   855

*(The baby finally gets "dislodged" from the blanket and emerges,
naked. And the last thing we see is this beautiful naked Indian man
lifting his naked baby Indian girl up in the air, his wife sitting beside them watching and laughing. Slow fade-out. Split seconds before
complete black-out,* HERA *peals out with this magical, silvery*
NANABUSH *laugh, which is echoed and echoed by one last magical
arpeggio on the harmonica, from off-stage. Finally, in the darkness,
the last sound we hear is the baby's laughing voice, magnified on tape
to fill the entire theater. And this, too, fades into complete silence.)*

(End of play.)

TRANSLATION OF BIG JOEY'S HOCKEY COMMENTARIES

Translation from the Cree of Big Joey's hockey commentary, Act One, pages 1389–1390.

. . . Hey, and there goes Number Six Dry Lips Manigitogan, right-winger for the Wasy Wailerettes . . . and steals the puck from Number Thirteen of the Canoe Lake Bravettes . . . and skates off. Hey, is she ever flying . . . *(Off microphone.)* Creature Nataways. Shut up. *(To the other men.)* Get this ass-hole out of here. *(Back on microphone.)* Now, Number Six Dry Lips Manigitogan, right-winger for the Wasy Wailerettes, shoots the puck and the puck goes flying over towards the center-line . . . where Number Nine Hera Keechigeesik, left-winger for . . . the Wasy Wailerettes, catches it. Now, Number Nine Hera Keechigeesik . . . approaching the blue line where Number One Gazelle Nataways, Captain of the Wasy Wailerettes, tries to get the puck off her, but Number Nine Hera Keechigeesik won't give it to her. Wha! "Hooking," says referee Pierre St. Pierre, Gazelle Nataways has apparently hooked her own team-mate Hera Keechigeesik, wha! Now, Number One Gazelle Nataways, Captain of the Wasy Wailerettes, facing off once again with Number Nine Flora McDonald, Captain of the Canoe Lake Bravettes and Flora McDonald shoots the puck, but Number Thirty-seven Big Bum Pegahmagahbow, defense-woman for the Wasy Wailerettes, stops the puck and passes it to Number Eleven Black Lady Halked, also defense-woman for the Wasy Wailerettes, but Gazelle Nataways, Captain of the Wasy Wailerettes, gives a mean body check to her own team-mate Black Lady Halked woops! She falls, ladies and gentlemen, Black Lady Halked hits the boards and Black Lady Halked is singin' the blues, ladies and gentlemen, Black Lady sings the blues. *(Off microphone.)* What the hell is going on down there? Dickie Bird, get off the ice! *(Back on microphone.)* Wha! Number Eleven Black Lady Halked is up in a flash and grabs the puck from Gazelle Nataways, holy shit! The ailing but very, very furious Black Lady Halked skates back, turns and takes aim, it's gonna be a slap shot, ladies and gentlemen, Black Lady Halked is gonna take a slap shot for sure and Black Lady Halked shoots the puck, wha! She shoots straight at her very own captain, Gazelle Nataways and holy shit, holy shit, holy fuckin' shit!

Translation from the Cree of Big Joey's hockey commentary, Act Two, pages 1400–1401.

. . . And there they are, ladies and gentlemen, there they are, the most beautiful, daring, death-defying Indian women in the world, the Wasy Wailerettes! Now, Number Nine HeraKeechigeesik, CAPTAIN of the Wasy Wailerettes, facing off with Number Nine Flora McDonald, Captain of the Canoe Lake Bravettes. Hey, and referee Pierre St. Pierre drops the "particular puck" . . . and takes off like a herd of wild turtles . . . Hey, and there goes Dry Lips Manigitogan, right-winger for the Wasy Wailerettes, and steals the "particular puck" from Number Thirteen of the Canoe Lake Bravettes . . . and skates off. Hey, is she ever flying. Now, Number Six Dry Lips Manigitogan shoots the "particular puck" towards where Number Twenty-six Little Girl Manitowabi, left-winger for the Wasy Wailerettes, is heading straight for the blue line where Number Eleven Black Lady Halked, wha! defense-woman for the Wasy Wailerettes, catches the "particular puck" and straight-way passes it to Captain Hera Keechigeesik and Hera Keechi-geesik is just a-flyin', hey, is she graceful or what, that Hera Keechigeesik, she looks just like a Russian ballerina. Captain Hera Keechigeesik now makes a bee-line straight for the Canoe Lake Bravettes' net and shoots the "particular puck" and she shoots, she scores . . . almost! Wha! Close one, ladies and gentlemen, real close one. But Number Six Dry Lips Man-itigotan, right-winger for the Wasy Wailerettes, accidentally tripped and blocked the shot . . . *(CREATURE NATAWAYS grabs the microphone away from* BIG JOEY.*)* . . . Now, Number Nine Flora McDonald, Captain of the Canoe Lake Bravettes, grabs the "particular puck" and skates behind the net and now heading along the right side of the rink where Number Twenty-one Annie Cook . . .

ATHOL FUGARD

Born in 1932, the South African playwright Athol Fugard began his career in the theater in the 1950s, working with the Circle Players of Cape Town. As a mixed-race company, the Circle Players worked in violation of South Africa's apartheid laws, and brought the issue of apartheid to a head when Fugard—a white man—collaborated with Zakes Mokae in the play *The Blood Knot* (1961), a play about two brothers, one of whom is light-skinned enough to "pass" for white. The play's powerful indictment of apartheid and the performances of Fugard and Mokae were widely admired and gained Fugard a reputation as a dramatist outside South Africa. Yet, despite its notoriety, the play could hardly remove apartheid itself: Fugard and Mokae were still forced to travel separately, and could not perform the play together before all-white segregated audiences.

By the 1970s, Fugard had written several of his best-known plays—*Hello and Goodbye* (1965), *Boesman and Lena* (1969)—when he became frustrated with his method of writing plays and decided to work collaboratively with a different company, the Serpent Players. Two of his collaborators, John Kani and Winston Ntshona, were prominent black actors in South Africa's township theaters, and had suffered from the limitations of apartheid throughout their lives. When they began to work with Fugard, they could perform legally only by being registered as his employees. Yet the plays they devised—*Sizwe Bansi is Dead* (1972) and *The Island* (1973)—are fully collaborative, for the three men improvised a variety of possible performances before setting them down in a final design, and drew much of their material from Kani and Ntshona's township performance work. Fugard has gone on to write a number of plays about the effects of apartheid and racism on South African life, including *Master Harold . . . and the Boys* (1982), *My Children! My Africa!* (1989), and *Playland* (1993). *Valley Song* (1996) is his first play of the postapartheid era.

VALLEY SONG

Valley Song is set in the Afrikaner farmlands of South Africa and is very much a play about the land and its meanings in the postapartheid era. Despite its simplicity as a two-hander, *Valley Song* develops a reflexive double plot: one concerns Abraam Jonkers ("Buks"), an elderly "colored"—the "official" term for mixed-race South Africans—tenant farmer, and his granddaughter Veronica; he is eager for her to remain in the country, perhaps working as a maid, while she wants to go to Johannesburg to become a singer. The second plot concerns an anonymous Author, who buys the old Landman house, and the property that Buks and his family have farmed for four generations. The crisis in national identity posed by the end of apartheid remains just offstage in *Valley Song;* lifting apartheid is what enables Veronica to go to the city legally in the first place; it's also what makes the Landman house attractive to the Author, who can move back to the country now that much of the civil strife has ended. It also animates the social relationships in the play, particularly the formality with which Buks treats the Author: the social habits of a lifetime die hard, for both men. In the course of the play, while the Author recognizes Veronica's desire to leave for a career in Johannesburg, he's also possessed by his own feelings about the land, and the "traditional" ways of life there, and in the final scene of the play, the Author describes going out into the fields to plant pumpkins with Buks, an image of "colored" and white South Africans returning to plant their common soil.

Valley Song's deep nostalgia for "the land" and perhaps for an idealized vision of pre-apartheid farming life are offset in the play by its casting: not only are Buks and the Author played by the same actor, but in the original production of the play, both roles were played by Fugard. This role doubling has a number of potential consequences in performance, for both Buks and the Author are shown in the play to be haunted by a nostalgia for a way of life that the new South Africa will no longer, and should no longer, support. The role doubling has the effect of bringing these attitudes into alignment, make them appear to spring from the same source in the actor's performance: the Author's desire for a "land" free of its political history, and Buks's desire to maintain the forms of farm life, not to gamble on the changes offered by the new era. Indeed, having a white actor play both roles lends this dynamic a more subtle politics as well, dramatizing how both attitudes stem from fundamentally "white" attitudes toward the land and its people; it will take time, the play seems to argue, for the minds and habits of South Africans to be fully "decolonized." While Fugard has written several plays that take a sharp and incisive critique of racial politics, *Valley Song* takes a more lyrical perspective on the problems of national identity in the new South Africa, and their implication in common attitudes toward the idea of the nation, the country, and the land itself.

VALLEY SONG

Athol Fugard

To the Memory of Barney Simon

—— CHARACTERS ——

THE AUTHOR, *in his early sixties*

ABRAAM JONKERS, *also known as* BUKS *and* OUPA; *a colored tenant farmer in his seventies*

VERONICA JONKERS, *Abraam's granddaughter; seventeen years old*

TIME: *The present*

AUTHOR'S NOTE: *The role of the* AUTHOR *and* ABRAAM JONKERS *must be played by the same actor.*

—— NOTES ——

KAROO: *A vast semi-desert region in the heart of South Africa. "Karoo" is a Khoi word meaning "place of little water." Several mountain ranges dot the Karoo, among them the Sneeuberg (Snow Mountains) in the southeast, whose highest peak (6300 feet) is the Kompassberg. Few plants grow on the dry mountains, but farms thrive in the valleys and lowlands. Most of the inhabitants of the Karoo are either white Afrikaners or coloreds.*

THE VALLEY: *A fertile valley deep in the Sneeuberg; fruits, vegetables and alfalfa are produced there. At this time, all of the farmland is still owned by whites.*

THE VILLAGE: *The small town of Nieu-Bethesda. Resident white population: 65; colored population: 950. Like most rural South African villages, Nieu-Bethesda is still essentially divided into two areas: the white town and the outlying "location" populated by coloreds and blacks.*

COLOREDS: *One of four official racial categories (along with whites, blacks and Asians) of the "old" South Africa. Colored is defined as anyone of mixed racial descent. The Colored population of South Africa is approximately 4.5 million; their language is Afrikaans.*

A bare stage. Enter THE AUTHOR. *He comes down and speaks directly to the audience.*

AUTHOR: (*A handful of pumpkin seeds.*) Pumpkin seeds, ladies and gentlemen . . . genuine Karoo pumpkin seeds. I can vouch for that. I grew the pumpkin myself last summer, cut it open, scooped out the seeds and dried them under a hot Karoo
5 sun. This is the so-called "Flat White Boer" variety. That's the actual name, Flat White Boer pumpkin. I don't think I've ever seen that sort here in America. As the name tells you, its flat, about five or six inches deep, round, on an average about twelve to eighteen inches across, white . . . and
10 delicious eating! But only as a vegetable. We unfortunately don't have a pumpkin pie tradition in South Africa. Anyway, this is how they start out . . . one of these together with a little prayer for rain in a hole in the ground, and in a good year, when you get that rain, this little handful could easily
15 give you up to a hundred of those beauties.

    In my little Village in the Sneeuberg Mountains spring is now well underway and everyone has already planted their pumpkin seeds. The seasons are of course reversed down there and by the time you reach November the dan-
20 ger of a late frost is past. With any luck the Valley has had its first rain and that wonderful smell of damp Karoo earth is mingled with the fragrance of roses and pine trees. After its long winter sleep that little world is wide awake once again and rowdy with birdsong and bleating lambs and
25 noisy children.

    Imagine a day like that, a glorious Karoo spring day! and these seeds in the hands of old Abraam Jonkers—in the Village we all just call him "ou Buks." He's out there in his akkers behind the derelict old Landman house with his
30 spade, planting—a little stab at the ground and then a seed, stab at the ground and a seed—it's a well-rehearsed action. He's planted a lot of pumpkin seeds in the course of his seventy-six years. And there's nothing haphazard about what he's doing either. When the young plants come up he

wants to see them standing shoulder to shoulder in lines as 35 straight as those the Sergeant Major drilled them into on the Sonderwater Parade Ground during the Second World War. Buks was a corporal in that famous old colored regiment, the Cape Corps, and was stationed up in the Transvaal guarding Italian prisoners of war. He's in fact thinking 40 about those days as he drops the seeds into the ground. One of the prisoners became a good friend of his and taught him a couple of Italian songs. He's trying very hard to remember one of them—they are now the only souvenirs he's got left of that time. Everything else—badges and brass but- 45 tons, discharge papers and scraps of his old uniform, even his old army kitbag—are either lost or disintegrated with time. Only the song is left and even that has moldered away to only half the memory it used to be. It went something like this: 50

(*In the course of the song he moves into the character of* BUKS.)

BUKS:

          Lae donder mobili
          En soo moretsa
          da da de da da da . . .

(VERONICA *enters. She carries* BUKS's *lunch: bottle of tea, sandwiches and an enamel mug.*)

VERONICA: Oupa! Oupa!
BUKS: (*Ignoring her and trying again.*)

          Lae donder mobili 55
          En soo moretsa
          da da de da da da . . .

VERONICA: Oupa! Are you deaf!
BUKS: (*Turning to her and bellowing out in good Sergeant-Major style.*) A . . . ten . . . tion! 60

(VERONICA *obeys.*)

By the left—Quick March! Left-right, left-right, left-right . . .

(VERONICA *marches.*)

Plato-o-o-n halt!

(VERONICA *stops, staying rigidly "at Attention" while* BUKS *carries out an inspection.*)

What do you want Private?
VERONICA: It's lunch time Corporal. (*She salutes.*)
65 BUKS: No Veronica . . . your other arm!
VERONICA: Sorry Corporal. (*She salutes again.*)
BUKS: That's better. Platoon dismissed!
VERONICA: Tell me the truth now Oupa, were you a real soldier?
BUKS: I don't know. What's a "real" soldier. I was just a ordi-
70 nary soldier.
VERONICA: You know, Oupa, like on TV, with a gun and all that.
BUKS: I had a gun. When I went on guard duty I had a real gun
with real bullets . . . and all that.
VERONICA: But did you ever shoot anybody with it?
75 BUKS: No. I've told you before I was guarding Italian prisoners
and none of them tried to escape.
VERONICA: Well then you certainly didn't win the war did you.
BUKS: No. I certainly didn't. The other men did that—the ones
up north. I just marched up and down the fence with my
80 gun on my shoulder and Carlo Tucci on the other side trying to teach me the words of Italian songs.

(*Another attempt at his Italian song.*)

VERONICA: What's it mean?
BUKS: I don't know. He told me but I've forgotten.
VERONICA: I'm going to make a song about you. I'll call it "The
85 Army Man."
BUKS: Good. I like that. But you must remember in your song
that I was a corporal . . . two stripes!
VERONICA: (*Singing.*)

My Oupa was a corporal
Left, Left-right Left-right.

90 BUKS: Come. Give me some tea.

(VERONICA *lays out lunch—pours tea into an enamel mug.*)

VERONICA: (*A recitative mixture of song and speech.*) Nearly fresh
brown bread and delicious first-grade Langeberg Koop-
erasie Smooth Apricot Jam.
BUKS: Who says so?
95 VERONICA: The jam tin label says so. Eerste Graad. Langeberg
Kooperasie.
BUKS: (*Tasting his tea.*) How much sugar did you put in?
VERONICA: The usual Oupa. Three spoons for every mug.
BUKS: (*He tastes again.*) What is happening to all the sweetness
100 in the world?
VERONICA: What do you mean Oupa?
BUKS: I don't know. I don't know what I mean. But put in an
extra spoon tomorrow. That whiteman was back here again
early this morning looking at the house and the land . . .
105 our akkers.
VERONICA: So?
BUKS: I'm just saying. That's three times now.

VERONICA: That doesn't mean anything. Stop worrying about
it Oupa. Every few months there's another car full of white
people driving around the Village and looking at the old 110
houses and talking about buying, and what happens? . . .
They drive away in the dust and we never see them again.
You watch and see: It will be just the same with this lot . . .
nothing will happen!
BUKS: This one looks serious my child. He even had the keys to 115
get into the house.
VERONICA: Did he say anything to you?
BUKS: No. Just greeted me. Then walked around—like a
whiteman!—and looked at everything.
VERONICA: Well I still say you are worrying for nothing. 120
BUKS: Anyway, worry or not there's nothing we can do about it,
hey. If he buys the land he can tell me take my spade and
my wheelbarrow and go and that's the end of the story.
VERONICA: Don't say that Oupa! That will make it come true!
BUKS: You're right. Let's talk about something else. 125
So what mischief were you up to this morning my girl?
VERONICA: Nothing Oupa.
Nothing . . . nothing . . . nothing . . . nothing! There's
no good mischief left in this place. I've used it all up. Any-
way, I'm not looking for mischief anymore. 130
BUKS: I see. So what are you looking for then?
VERONICA: Adventure and Romance!
BUKS: That's now something new. Since when is this?
VERONICA: Since a long time Oupa.
BUKS: Well I don't know how much adventure and . . . what 135
was it?
VERONICA: Romance.
BUKS: I don't know how much of that you are going to find
around here.
VERONICA: So then what Oupa? 140
BUKS: What do you mean?
VERONICA: What is there for me? I'm bored.
BUKS: Open your eyes and look around you.
VERONICA: They're open Oupa . . . wide open . . . and what do I see?
Always just the same old story. Nothing happens here Oupa. 145
BUKS: Nothing happens? Haai, you young people!

(*Out of a pocket comes a handful of pumpkin seeds.*)

Veronica. Come here. What are these?
VERONICA: Pumpkin seeds.
BUKS: No. That's what people call them but that is not what
they really are. They are miracles. A handful of miracles, 150
Veronica!
Every year, in these akkers . . . thousands of miracles.
And you say nothing happens here?
VERONICA: Ja, I know all that Oupa, but a girl can't make ad-
venture and romance out of pumpkin seeds. 155
BUKS: Veronica! Veronica! What's got into you lately?
You're as restless as a little dwarrelwindjie out there in the
veld. What's the matter with you?
VERONICA: I don't know Oupa. Yes, I do.
I'm Veronica Jonkers and I want to sing! 160
BUKS: So?
VERONICA: So Oupa asked me and I'm telling you. I want to sing.
BUKS: So sing. Nobody is stopping you.
VERONICA: No. Oupa doesn't understand.

165 BUKS: Then you must explain to me.

VERONICA: I want to sing to lots of people.

BUKS: But you already do that. In church. At the school concert. You know how much everybody likes your singing and all the nice songs you make.

170 VERONICA: That's not enough.

BUKS: Not enough? I hear you. The whole Village hears you. God hears you. And that is not enough?

VERONICA: I don't mean it that way Oupa. But I don't just want to sing hymns and the same old school songs to the

175 same old people . . . over and over again.

BUKS: But you don't. Every time I listen there's a new song coming out of you.

VERONICA: You mean the ones I make up myself?

BUKS: Ja. And let me tell you my girl, those are the best songs

180 I ever heard.

VERONICA: Oupa is just saying that to make me happy.

BUKS: If it makes you happy that's good—but I'm saying it because it's the truth.

VERONICA: I made a new one this morning when I was clean-

185 ing the house.

BUKS: There you see! That's what I mean.

VERONICA: So do you want to hear it?

BUKS: But of course.

VERONICA: Are you ready?

190 BUKS: *("Getting ready"—putting down his mug and folding his arms.)* Yes.

VERONICA: It's called: "Railway Bus O Railway Bus."

BUKS: "Railway Bus?"

VERONICA: Yes. But you must say it two times with a "O" in

195 between. "Railway Bus O Railway Bus."

BUKS: The Railway Bus that used to come from Graaff-Reinet?

VERONICA: Yes yes yes!

Wait for the song Oupa. Then you'll understand.

(Singing.)

Railway Bus O Railway Bus

200 Why don't you come no more

I want to travel fast

On the smooth tar road

Far away, Far away.

Railway Bus O Railway Bus

205 I want to climb on board

I want to see Big Cities

And strange places

Far away, Far away.

(Breaking off abruptly when she sees that her song is disturbing her Oupa.)

What's the matter Oupa?

210 BUKS: No. I don't want to hear it.

VERONICA: Why?

BUKS: Because I don't like it. Don't sing it to me again.

VERONICA: But why? What's wrong with it.

BUKS: The Railway Bus is not a nice thing for a song.

215 Sing me one of your other songs . . . about the school or our house, or that nice one about when it rains. Ja. Sing me that one.

VERONICA: I don't feel like singing that song Oupa.

(A hurt, estranged silence settles in between the two of them. VERONICA *starts to leave.)*

I'm going now Oupa.

BUKS: Veronica . . . 220

VERONICA: Yes Oupa?

BUKS: Come back. Come sit here.

(She returns to his side.)

I'm not cross with you my child. I'm not cross with your song. I'm not even cross with the old Railway Bus . . . but it brings back memories . . . memories of things I've tried 225 all these years to forget. That is why your song upset me.

VERONICA: Are they memories about my mother, Oupa.

BUKS: Ja . . . about her mostly. If that Railway Bus hadn't been there and made it so easy for her, who knows? Maybe she would still be alive and sitting here with us today. That is 230 how she ran away.

And that is how you came back—in your Ouma's arms, wrapped in a blanket. Haai!

VERONICA: Oupa has told me so little.

BUKS: Because I've tried so hard to forget. 235

VERONICA: You promised you would tell me everything one day when I was old enough. I think I'm old enough now Oupa.

BUKS: I was working here on the akkers when I got a message that your Ouma had phoned from Graaff-Reinet to say I 240 must meet the bus. I thought she was bringing back your mother you see. We didn't know anything about there being a baby. After she ran away we waited and waited but we didn't hear anything for a whole year. Then when the hospital in Johannesburg phoned they just said we must come 245 quickly because your mother was very sick. So your Ouma went. I waited here. Then I got the message that I must meet the bus and like I said I thought she was bringing Caroline back. But instead it was you. By the time your Ouma got to the hospital, your mother was already dead. 250 Betty never saw her daughter again.

VERONICA: She ran away with her boyfriend didn't she.

BUKS: Who told you that?

VERONICA: Other children Oupa. They hear what their parents say about me. 255

BUKS: What else do you know?

VERONICA: His name, Harry Ruiters.

BUKS: That's right.

VERONICA: Is he my father?

BUKS: No! 260

(Pause.) I don't know.

(Pause.) Maybe he is.

VERONICA: What was he like?

BUKS: Don't think about him Veronica! He was a rubbish, a good for nothing rubbish who led your mother into sin. He 265 made trouble in the Village from the day he was born— fighting and stealing. Ja. The first time they caught him breaking into the shop he was too young to go before the magistrate so they gave him a good hiding at the police station and sent him home. It didn't help anything. A few 270 years later they caught him again and this time he was old enough to go to court. They were waiting for his case to come up when he ran away with your mother.

VERONICA: And my mother? Tell me about her.

275　BUKS: It hurts me to talk about her.

VERONICA: I'm sorry Oupa but it feels like I know nothing about her.

BUKS: What did you want to know?

VERONICA: Anything. You say she looked like me?

280　BUKS: Oh yes. So much it almost frightens me.

VERONICA: Why "frighten" Oupa?

BUKS: No, that's the wrong word. Surprise. I meant to say surprise.

VERONICA: Did she like singing?

285　BUKS: Yes, but not like you . . . (*A small smile and a shake of the head.*) . . . definitely not like you.

VERONICA: (*Eagerly.*) You remember something else?

BUKS: Yes, but it's not about Caroline, it's about you.

　　　After your Ouma got off the bus and we were walking

290　home—I was carrying her suitcase and she was carrying you—you started to cry. And I thought . . . Oh heavens, this child is going to be difficult, I can hear that right now. And I said so to your Ouma. But she said: No Buks. She's not crying. She's singing.

295　VERONICA: Ouma said that?

BUKS: She did. She's singing Buks, she said. Look for yourself. And I did . . . and so waar! . . . I could see she was right. You know the way a baby squashes and wrinkles up its face when it's crying, like a dirty old handkerchief you've been

300　sneezing in the whole summer, well that wasn't what I saw. Your eyes were open, your face was smooth and this funny little noise was coming out of your mouth . . . Betty was right! You were singing.

(VERONICA *laughs and claps her hands with happiness.*)

　　　And so it was from then on. Your Ouma always used to say

305　to me: If that child ever stops singing, Abraam Yonkers, then you must know there is something wrong with the world. That was your Ouma. Betty Bruintjies. She loved you my girl.

VERONICA: I haven't got a picture of her in my head. All I can

310　remember is a soft voice and a pair of strong hands . . . beautiful hands! . . . I think they're Ouma's.

BUKS: Of course they're hers. After she died the only other hands that washed you and fed you were mine, and they're not beautiful.

315　VERONICA: Yes they are!

(*It is a moment of deep union between the old man and the young girl.*)

VERONICA: Oupa, I'm not going to sing that song again.

BUKS: No. Sing it if it makes you happy.

VERONICA: No. I'm not going to if it upsets you.

BUKS: What will upset me is if you don't have a nice supper

320　waiting for me tonight when I get home. What have you got?

VERONICA: (*More recitative.*) Glenryck Maalvis Chilli-chilli en Sneeuberge aartappel en wortels . . .

BUKS: So what are you doing sitting here? Go home and cook.

325　VERONICA: Right Corporal. (*She salutes.*)

BUKS: The other arm Veronica!

VERONICA: (*She salutes again and then goes marching off, singing her latest song.*)

My Oupa was a soldier
But he didn't win the war
Put a pampoen on the
Left-right left-right left-right.　　　330

He had a gun and bullets
But he didn't know what for
Put a pampoen on the
'Left-right left-right left-right.

BUKS: So Betty . . . what do you think?　　　335
　　　(*A pause . . . he remembers.*) Speak woman, I can see there are thoughts in your head!
　　　(*Shakes his head.*) Ja, if only it was still like that and we could sit down at the kitchen table tonight and talk about things the way we used to. More and more I feel so useless　340
. . . so by myself! . . . There's nobody I want to talk to anymore—only Veronica and I can't put my worries on those young shoulders, specially when she is one of them.
　　　Am I saying the right things to her, Betty? Doing the right things?　　　345
　　　You can see for yourself she is happy. She is singing more than ever—even making her own songs now. And obedient. She listens to me. When I tell her to do something she does it. But I can also see she is starting to get restless. She's nearly as old now as Caroline was when she ran away. And　350
she looks so much like her, Betty, it really does frighten me. Just yesterday she was standing in the street laughing and teasing a young man, her hands on her hips just the way her mother used to do it. I thought I was seeing a ghost. Because it was Caroline standing there! So waar! I nearly called her　355
name. Sometimes it happens in the house as well, when she's sweeping, or doing the washing . . . I see Caroline! But then she starts singing and I remember . . . No! It's Veronica. It's my grandchild.
　　　And now there is also this whiteman looking at the　360
house and the land. He is going to buy Betty, I know it. And then what do I do? I know what you want to say . . . Have faith in the Lord, Abraam Jonkers . . . and I do . . . it's just that He's asking for a lot of it these days. And He's not making me any younger! I feel too old now for all these wor-　365
ries. Every day there's a new one. I don't know anymore . . . is it me or is it the world that's gone so skeef. I wake up in the morning and I lie there and listen to the birds and Veronica singing, or I can smell the rain that fell in the night, and I think to myself . . . Ja! This is now going to be　370
a good day and my heart fills up with happiness again the way it used to when you were lying there next to me . . . but there's a leak somewhere, Betty, because at the end of it . . . there's nothing left . . . it's all gone.
　　　(*Shaking his head.*) Anyway Betty . . . where was I? Ja! I　375
got the pumpkin seed in, I led water to the potatoes—those onions also need some but there wasn't any left for them. I'll get Veronica to say a little prayer for rain tonight—her prayers are very strong! And if you want to give us some help up there, Betty, that would also be very nice.　　　380

VERONICA: (*Coming forward and speaking to the audience.*) So like my Oupa said I must, I go home and cook supper. I also see that there is hot water ready for him to wash himself when he comes home. And a clean shirt. He always wears a clean shirt for supper. Then we eat and after I wash the　385

dishes we go for a walk and visit somebody or maybe somebody comes and visits us and if it's summertime we take the kitchen chairs and go sit outside under the blue gum tree where it's nice and cool and we talk and talk. The last thing
390 that happens is that we go and sit at the table again and I read to my Oupa from the Bible. Oupa can't read. He only went as far as Standard One in school. Then we say good night because now it's supposed to be bedtime you see. Night Oupa, Moenie vergeet om die kers dood te blaas nie.
395 I say "supposed to be" because I got other ideas. As soon as I hear my Oupa snoring—he sleeps in the bedroom and I sleep in the kitchen—I get up and go quietly out of the house and when I'm outside I run like hell to old Mrs.
400 Jooste's house—the big white one there on the corner in Martin Street. That old Boerevrou doesn't know it but she's my best friend. You see she drinks whiskey and watches TV until late, late at night. And she's always got the curtains open so if I stand on a box or something I can look over her head and see the whole TV. But the best thing of all is that
405 that old Boerevrou likes music—doesn't matter what kind— fast slow, hop skip en jump, Boeremusik, tiekie-draai—but that's what she looks for! . . .

(She grabs her apple box and standing on it gives us the scene . . . mimicking the pop star she sees on the TV. Mike in hand, she sings to an audience of thousands . . . She pretends to be singing loudly, but her voice is very soft. At the end of her song there is a small round of applause from THE AUTHOR *who has been watching from the shadows.* VERONICA *gets a fright, grabs her apple box and starts to run away.)*

AUTHOR: Don't run away!
VERONICA: You gave me a fright Master!
410 AUTHOR: I'm sorry. I didn't mean to.
VERONICA: How long has Master been watching?
AUTHOR: A long time.
VERONICA: So?
AUTHOR: So what?
415 VERONICA: So did you like what you heard?
AUTHOR: Yes. Very much.
VERONICA: Then why didn't you show it?
AUTHOR: But I did. I clapped.
VERONICA: That's not enough.
420 *(Showing him how to do it.)* You must clap your hands and stamp your feet and shout and scream . . . Veronica! Veronica! . . . and then I come out again you see and sing some more.
That's the way they're going to do it one day.
425 AUTHOR: When you're famous.
VERONICA: That's right. In Johannesburg and Durban and Cape Town . . . Veronica! Veronica! Give us more! We want to hear Veronica!
AUTHOR: So then come on. Sing some more.
430 VERONICA: Just like that?
AUTHOR: Why not?
VERONICA: *(To the audience.)* Listen to him! He wants the famous Veronica to sing for him just like that?
(Back to Author.) It will cost you a lot of money Master.
435 AUTHOR: How much?
VERONICA: For one ticket?
AUTHOR: Yes.

VERONICA: *(Taking a chance.)* Twenty-five rand. If you bring your girlfriend you must to pay fifty rand.

(Laughter.)

You laugh now but wait and see. One day it will happen. 440
AUTHOR: Go on. I want to hear more.
VERONICA: I'll be on TV. Ja. Then you can stand here on the stoep and loer through the window and watch me singing. I'll be wearing a beautiful shiny green dress—that's my color—and green shoes with high, high heels and long 445 gloves that go all the way up to my elbow and a fancy hair style with sparkles in it. You wait and see my boy. You wait and see.
AUTHOR: So that's your dream.
VERONICA: Yes. Anything wrong with it? 450
AUTHOR: No. But it's a big one.
VERONICA: Of course. That's the only way to do it.
AUTHOR: Really?
VERONICA: Oh yes. What's the use of a little dream. A dream must be big and special. It much be the most special thing 455 you can imagine for yourself in the whole world. Don't you have dreams like that?
AUTHOR: Not anymore, but I used to.
VERONICA: There you see. You've got to dream big. It's like my friend Alfred Witbooi—he told me he's dreaming about 460 getting a job so that he can buy a bicycle. So I straight away saw this big, black, shiny, new bicycle with a loud ringatin-galing bell and all that, but he said: No, he just wanted to buy Baasie Koopman's old second-hand bicycle. I was so cross with him! No Alfred! I said. Wake up! You're not 465 dreaming properly—it must be a brand new bicycle with a bell and a lamp and a pump and a red light in the back and everything else.
AUTHOR: I think Alfred is being sensible.
VERONICA: No. Alfred's a bangbroek. 470
AUTHOR: Come on Veronica. That's not fair. You know how hard it is to find work here in the Valley. If he tries to save up enough for a new bicycle he could spend the rest of his life waiting for it.
VERONICA: No he won't. If he dreams properly he'll get it. 475
AUTHOR: How do you dream "properly?"
VERONICA: You must see it and believe it. Alfred must see the bicycle like he was watching it on TV, he must see himself sitting on it and riding around the Village ringing the bell and waving at everybody and then he must believe that 480 is what is going to happen. He must believe that as hard as he can.
AUTHOR: It doesn't always work that way Veronica.
VERONICA: Yes it does!
AUTHOR: A lot of my big dreams didn't come true and I saw 485 them very clearly.
VERONICA: Then that's because you didn't believe them hard enough.
AUTHOR: I think I did.
VERONICA: No you didn't . . . otherwise they would have come 490 true. Anyway I don't want to argue anymore. Don't spoil it for me!
AUTHOR: Okay, okay. I'll stop.
VERONICA: So them come on. I want to dream some more.

495   Come on!

       (Clapping her hands and stamping her feet, etc.) I showed you how to do it.

AUTHOR: *(Clapping his hands and stamping his feet, etc.)* Veronica! Veronica!! We want Veronica!

500 VERONICA: *(Once again, mike in hand, and talking to an audience of thousands.)* Thank you . . . thank you . . . and now all you beautiful people I am going to sing you one of my very own songs . . . number one on the hit parade! . . . "Wake Up and Dream Properly, Alfred Witbooi."

(Singing.)

505   Wake up and dream properly Alfred Witbooi
      Don't waste your life on a second-hand dream
      Dream it now
      Dream it new
      That bicycle
510   Was meant for you
      Wake up and dream properly Alfred Witbooi.

AUTHOR: *(To the audience.)* "The Earth is the Lord's and the fullness thereof; the world and they that dwell there in.

515   For He hath founded it upon the seas, and established it upon the floods.

    Who shall ascend into the hill of the Lord? or who shall stand in his holy place?

    He that hath clean hands and a pure heart, who hath not lifted his soul into vanity, nor sworn deceitfully.

520   He shall receive the blessing from the Lord and righteousness from the God of his salvation." Psalm 24.

(BUKS and VERONICA stand side by side and sing a hymn. VERONICA's voice rings out pure and clear.)

BUKS and VERONICA:

      Die Heiland is gebore!
      —so klink die Aengelstem;
      en sang van hemelskare
525   ruis soet oor Betlehem
      Uit liefde tot die wereld
      Het God sy Seun gegee;
      wie in Hom glo—sal lewe,
      want Hy bring heil en vree
530   Amen.

(At the end of the hymn VERONICA positions the apple box for her Oupa in the shade of the old blue gum tree outside their house.)

VERONICA: *(With all the conviction she can muster.)* I don't believe it! It's not going to happen!

    Come on now Oupa. I can't do it by myself. You must also be strong. So say it with me: I don't believe it! It's not
535 going to happen! Oupa!!

BUKS: It doesn't work like that Veronica. If we want to believe it or not, that is what Stella said. She says she heard him say so with her own two ears. She came by this way specially to tell me. She said she was cleaning there in the municipal of-
540 fice on Friday afternoon when the whiteman came in and spoke to Mrs. Kruger. She heard him say: "I want to buy the old Landman house and the land." Those were his words.

VERONICA: Well then maybe she heard wrong.

BUKS: Stella hear wrong? She's got the biggest ears in the whole Village . . . specially when she's listening to someone else's 545 business.

VERONICA: Well even if she is right, none of our people is going to try and push in there with him. Everybody knows those are your akkers.

BUKS: It's not our people I'm worried about, it's him, the 550 whiteman. If he buys the house and the land he's going to get a piece of paper that tells him those akkers are his. He can tell me to go anytime he likes and get somebody else to work for him.

VERONICA: It makes me so mad. It's just not right. 555

BUKS: Come now Veronica . . .

VERONICA: No Oupa! You mustn't accept it just like that.

BUKS: There's nothing we can do.

VERONICA: Yes there is.

BUKS: What? 560

VERONICA: We can tell the Government.

BUKS: What do you mean?

VERONICA: A petition Oupa. We write a petition.

BUKS: What's that?

VERONICA: It's like a letter Oupa. And in it we tell the Gov- 565 ernment just how things are with us here in the Valley. And we must get all of our people to sign it.

BUKS: And then what happens?

VERONICA: Then the Government comes here and changes things. They're doing it in lots of other places now Oupa— 570 taking the land and giving it back to the people.

BUKS: You think those groot Kokkedoore are going to worry about me and my few akkers? Anyway I don't think they even know where the Village is. You told me yourself that you couldn't find us on the map. 575

VERONICA: That was the school map Oupa! Don't be silly now. The Government doesn't sit down with a school map and try to find all the places where it must do things. It already knows where everybody is. We had the elections here didn't we? . . . Just like all the other places in the country. 580

BUKS: No! Leave the Government out of it. Every time they stick their nose in your business you got to pay something. I know what I'm talking about my child. Government is trouble. I'll be very happy if they don't know where we are.

VERONICA: Well God certainly knows where the Village is so 585 I'm going to pray to Him to do something.

BUKS: That's better . . . but God also helps those who help themselves. I think maybe I must go try to speak to the whiteman myself. I see his car is still standing there in front of the guest house. 590

VERONICA: What are you going to say to him Oupa?

BUKS: Tell him about myself and those akkers—if he'll listen. Ask him—nicely!—if I can carry on there.

VERONICA: I hate to see Oupa like this.

BUKS: Like what? 595

VERONICA: Like you are now. All worried and down and . . . I don't know . . . upset.

BUKS: I also don't like it, but what can I do?

    Anyway he doesn't look so bad. He greeted me nicely the last time when they came to look at the house. And as 600 Stella said maybe there is also a good side to this business. If he does buy the house and fixes it up and comes to live here in the Village, who knows, maybe there's a chance for you in there.

605 VERONICA: *(Alarmed.)* What do you mean Oupa?

BUKS: Work my girl. For you. Ja! Stella is right. They're going to need somebody to clean the house and do the washing.

VERONICA: No Oupa!

BUKS: No? I think you are old enough for it now Veronica.

610 VERONICA: *(Panic.)* Yes, I know I am but . . . No no no!

(A few seconds of surprised silence at her outburst. She is desperate and flustered.)

I know Oupa means good for me . . . and I'm very grateful . . . but No! . . . Oupa mustn't just . . . decide like that . . . what I mean is you promised Oupa that when the time came we would talk about these things first . . . yes you did! . . .

615 BUKS: Veronica?

VERONICA: What I'm trying to say Oupa is that I also got ideas . . . other ideas about what I want to do . . . about my future and everything . . . so Oupa mustn't decide just like that . . .

620 BUKS: You're talking too fast for me. I don't understand what you are saying. Speak so that I can understand you.

VERONICA: I don't want to do housework Oupa.

BUKS: But you do it in here very day Veronica.

VERONICA: This is different Oupa. This is our house. I'm doing
625 it for us. I don't want to do it for other people. I don't want to do it for a living. Specially that house.

BUKS: What is wrong with getting work there? Your Ouma cleaned that house.

VERONICA: Exactly Oupa! That's what I been trying to say.
630 Isn't it supposed to be different now.

BUKS: What must be different?

VERONICA: Everything. Our lives and . . . and everything. Isn't that why there was an election. Oupa mos voted in it . . . and all that talk that was going on about how things was going
635 to change and be different from now on. Well this doesn't look like it. Here we are carrying on and talking just like the "klomp arme ou Kleurlinge" we've always been, frightened of the whiteman, ready to crawl and beg him and be happy and grateful if we can scrub his floors . . .

640 BUKS: Veronica? Where does all this nonsense come from? Who's been giving you these ideas?

VERONICA: Nobody. I don't need other people to give me ideas. They're my own. And it's not nonsense Oupa . . .

BUKS: Veronica!
645 *(It takes him a few seconds to control his anger before he can speak coherently.)* Okay—now you listen to me very carefully my child. I've never talked to you like this before and I don't ever want to talk to you like this again. You wouldn't be alive today, standing there insulting the memory of your
650 Ouma . . .

VERONICA: No! I didn't!

BUKS: *(Ignoring her.)* . . . insulting the memory of your Ouma, if that "arme ou kleurling" hadn't gone to the city and rescued you. Ja. You would most probably be lying in the
655 same grave as your mother if Betty Bruintjies hadn't climbed into that vervloekte railway bus and found you and brought you back here. Broken hearted as she was, she nursed you and gave you a start in life. Ja, it's true she scrubbed floors in that Landman house, went down on her

hands and knees and scrubbed and polished, but if you can
660 walk through your life with even half of the pride that that woman had in herself and her life, then you will be a very lucky girl. As for this "arme ou kleurling" . . . you're right—I've done a lot of crawling and begging in my life and I am ready to do it again for those few akkers. You want
665 to know why Veronica? So that I can grow food there for you to eat, just as I grew food there for your mother and your Ouma to eat, and as my father grew food there for me to eat.

VERONICA: *(Struggling to hold back tears.)* I'm sorry Oupa.
670

(THE AUTHOR leaves the role of BUKS and talks to the audience.)

AUTHOR: Stella was being a little premature in telling Buks that the whiteman had decided to buy the Landman house and land. At that point I was still only thinking about it. The price wasn't bad but the house itself, like all the other
675 derelict and abandoned old houses in the Village, was in a terrible condition with plaster falling off the walls, rotten floorboards, broken windows, a roof that leaked in a dozen places. I could see that it would cost quite a bit to have it made habitable once again. But at the same time the thought of owning a little piece of the Karoo—where I was
680 born—complete with vegetable akkers, vines at the kitchen door, an established orchard and a real working windmill, was very appealing.

On that Sunday I was loading up my car for the drive back to Port Elizabeth when the old man—still in his Sun-
685 day suit—came down the road pushing his wheelbarrow. It was piled high with vegetables—half a dozen pumpkins, beetroot, potatoes, a small sack of walnuts . . .

He parked it in front of me, took off his hat and spoke . . . "nicely" . . .
690

BUKS: Morning Master . . .

Master remembers me? . . . . At the Landman house . . .

That's right Master . . . that's right . . .

Abraam Jonkers . . . Jonkers . . . that's right Master, but everybody here in the Village just calls me Buks . . .
695

Seventy-six Master this next birthday . . .

No no that's not old, not here by us. I still do a full day's work . . . yes Master . . . I'm out there on the lands before sunrise and if Master doesn't believe me here is my evidence . . . look . . . *(The barrow load of vegetables.)*
700

Ja, the earth is like a woman, Master, and it's us old men that know how to make her happy . . . Ja, if you look after her she will feed you . . .

No . . . I'm not selling them . . . they are for you Master . . . yes . . .
705

Master! . . . I hear that Master is going to buy the Land-man house . . . that's what I heard . . .

Oh I see . . . Master is still thinking about it . . .

I was just asking because if Master does buy it I was wondering what the Master's plans was going to be and if I
710 could carry on there with my few akkers.

I see Master . . . yes I see . . . but if Master does decide . . .

All right Master . . . we'll talk then because I was also going to tell Master that if Master does buy it and fixes up the house nicely and comes to live here in the Village I got
715 a young granddaughter who . . .

Okay . . . Okay Master . . . we'll talk then.

Where does Master want me to put the vegetables . . . there by the car? Okay Master. Thank you Master.

720 AUTHOR: That wheelbarrow load of vegetables did it. I mean, come on now, how could I pass up the chance to own a piece of my native Karoo earth that would allow me to brag and boast about "my own pumpkins," "my own beetroot," "my own potatoes." And the timing was perfect! I had ended up
725 sick and tired of the madness and desperate scramble of my life in the make-believe world of theatre. I wanted to return to "essentials," to the "real" world and here was my chance to do it. During the three-and-a-half-hour drive back to PE, a vision of a new life unfolded before me. I could see my-
730 self sitting on my stoep after a day of good writing—all prose now, no more nonsense from actors and producers and critics—sitting there on my stoep watching the sun set and admiring my land, finally at peace with myself. In my imagination Buks's little peace offering of vegetables grew
735 into a huge stack of pumpkins, little mountains of beetroot and onions, sacks of the famous Sneeuberg potatoes. By the time I reached home I had made up my mind. I wrote out a check for the modest sum they wanted for the house and land, and after the usual formalities between lawyers, I fi-
740 nally had it in my hand . . . The Title Deed! The land was mine!

Or was it?

Had my few thousand rand really bought me ownership of that land? Remember the psalm? "The Earth is the Lord's
745 and the fullness thereof . . ."

I would have felt a lot better if God had countersigned that Title Deed. Because you see, Buks put his first seed into that soil when he was only a few years old . . . when his father went to work for old Landman. Jaap Jonkers. That
750 was his father's name. And it was Landman himself who told Jaap that he must lay a few akkers for himself and grow vegetables there for his family.

That old house that was standing there empty and falling apart when I first saw it, Landman and Jaap built
755 it with their own hands. Just the two of them! And then when Jaap died in the great flu epidemic, the young Buks stepped into his father's shoes and husbanded that land. And that's how it has been ever since. His life is rooted now as deeply in that soil as the old walnut tree next to
760 the windmill. When it's like that between you and a piece of land, you end up being a part of it. Your soul wilts and withers with the young plants during the droughts. You feel the late frosts as if it was your skin that had been burnt black. And when it rains you rejoice
765 and your heart swells with sweetness like the fruit on the trees. But Buks doesn't have a piece of paper with his name on it which says all these things, and so he has to come begging to me because I've got a piece of paper with my name on it which said that those akkers are
770 mine.

VERONICA: (To the audience. Her mood is dark and defiant.) I hate those akkers. Yes. Hate them.

I know that's a big sin—to hate the Earth what God created—but I can't help it. That's the way I feel and
775 that's what I want to say. If I was my Oupa I would rather let us go hungry than plant another seed in that ground. I mean it.

It gives us food, but it takes our lives. Oh yes it does! That's why my mother ran away. I just know it. She didn't want her life to be buried in that old house the
780 way my Ouma's was. If ever anybody sees a spook in that house it will be my Ouma . . . scrubbing the floors. And my Oupa also—he'll spook those akkers one day. You'll see.

He's like a slave now to that little piece of land. That's
785 all he lives for, and it's not even his. He talks about nothing else, worries about nothing else, prays for nothing else . . . "Come Veronica, let us hold hands and pray for rain." "Come Veronica, let us hold hands and pray that there is no late frost." "Come Veronica, let us hold hands and pray that
790 the bees don't sting the young pumpkins."

Well, what about me? I'm also a living thing you know. I also want to grow. What about: "Come everybody, let us hold hands and pray that the bees don't sting the young Veronica."
795

(She grabs her apple box and jumps onto it ready to launch into another TV session.)

AUTHOR: No, Veronica!
VERONICA: Why not? I want to dream.
AUTHOR: I know you do but . . . haven't you heard? She's dead. Look! The curtains are closed. The house is in dark-
800 ness. Yes. Dead. Sophie Jacobs found her lying on the kitchen floor when she came to clean the house. She was lying there stiff and cold with a broken whiskey glass in her hand. Sister Pienaar thinks it was a heart attack and that she was lying there the whole night. They called the
805 ambulance from Graaff-Reinet but it was too late. She was dead.

(VERONICA is stunned.)

Another white spook in the Village. There's supposed to be quite a few of them already you know. Do you believe in ghosts? I'm not sure if I do or if I don't. I must admit I get a little scared when I walk around late at night. I almost
810 imagine I can see them—at the windows of the old houses—pale, frightened white faces looking out at a world that doesn't belong to them anymore. I'm going to be one of them one day.

So Veronica Jonkers, it looks like your dreaming times
815 in Martin Street are over, doesn't it.
VERONICA: No.
AUTHOR: They're not?
VERONICA: No.
AUTHOR: How are you going to do it? Wait for her ghost to
820 open the curtains and turn on the TV set for you?
VERONICA: There are other ways.
AUTHOR: So you're not going to stop?
VERONICA: No.
AUTHOR: But the same dream?
825
VERONICA: Yes!
AUTHOR: You're famous! You're a TV star!
VERONICA: (Defiant.) Yes! Yes! All of that. And more . . . I'm also rich and I'm beautiful! . . . Why don't you want me to dream?
830
AUTHOR: I don't want to stop you dreaming but I also don't want you to be hurt.

VERONICA: By what?

AUTHOR: Your dreams.

835 VERONICA: They can't hurt me.

AUTHOR: Oh yes they can. Believe me I know what I'm talking about. It's a very special hurt—the big dream that didn't come true. It's like your friend Alfred and that old second-hand bicycle he wants to buy. If he doesn't get it, it won't
840 be too bad. The world is full of old second-hand bicycles. There'll be another chance one day. But if he takes your advice and starts dreaming—hard!—about a shiny brand-new one and believes—with all his might—that he is going to get it, and then doesn't because the only work he can find
845 are occasional odd jobs that don't even pay enough for him to feed his family . . . That's a recipe for bitterness.

And you're not dreaming about bicycles Veronica. You're dreaming about your life!

VERONICA: That's right, and that life isn't over like yours
850 maybe is.

If your dreams didn't come true that's your bad luck not mine. Maybe you are ready to be a ghost, I am not. You can't see into the future. You don't know what is going to happen to me.

855 AUTHOR: That's true. I don't. But what I do know is that dreams don't do well in this Valley. Pumpkins yes, but not dreams—and you've already seen enough of life to know that as well.

Listen to me Veronica. Take your apple box and go
860 home, and dream about something that has a chance of happening—a wonderful year for your Oupa on his akkers with hundreds of pumpkins. Or dream that you meet a handsome young man with a good job . . .

VERONICA: You're wasting your breath.

865 AUTHOR: Okay, let's leave it at that. But for your sake I hope you don't remember tonight and what I've said to you, in ten years time, if like all the other women in the Village you are walking barefoot into the veld every day with a baby on your back to collect firewood.

870 VERONICA: Never!

AUTHOR: Because you know what you'll be dreaming about then don't you? . . . that I've given you a job scrubbing and polishing the floors of my nicely renovated old Landman house.

875 VERONICA: Never! Now you listen to me. I swear on the Bible, on my Ouma's grave, that you will never see me walk barefoot with firewood on my head and a baby on my back—you will never see me on my knees scrubbing a whiteman's floor.

(VERONICA *leaves the scene. With a demure smile she comes forward and talks to the audience.*)

Môre Meneer. Môre Mevrou. My name is Veronica and I
880 live here in the Village. Would you like to hear a very nice song? I made it myself. Yes, I promise you it's a very, very nice song. It's called; "The Windmill Is Turning Around and Around." Can I sing it for you?

(*Composes herself and sings.*)

The wind is blowing
885 And the windmill is turning
Around and around
Around and around.

The water is flowing
And everything is growing
In the ground in the ground 890
In the ground in the ground.

Tomatoes and onions
Cabbages and beans
Quinces and peaches
That's what summer means. 895

Potatoes and carrots
Pumpkins and peas
Apples and walnuts
As much as you please.

(*With one final smile of innocence and purity she holds out her hand for a reward.*)

Dankie Mevrou. 900

(*She gets it and pockets it and then turns around and walks into a scene with her Oupa. There is a bucket of water and a towel for* BUKS *to wash himself. This is a scene of secrets.*)

VERONICA: Oupa hear about the business at the Post Office?

BUKS: No. Tell me.

VERONICA: There was a bad argument between Mrs. Oliphant and old Brigadier Pelser.

BUKS: What happened? 905

VERONICA: It was already past twelve o'clock you see and Mrs. Oliphant was closing up the Post Office when the Brigadier walked in to do some business there. So Mrs. Oliphant said to him: No, he must come back tomorrow because now the Post Office is closed. But the Brigadier 910 said how can the Post Office be closed because the door was open and she was behind the counter. So Mrs. Oliphant said, "Look at your watch and you will see that it is past twelve o'clock which is closing time." But he just stood there and said he wasn't going until he had done his busi- 915 ness. So Mrs. Oliphant said to him, "This is no longer the old South Africa, Brigadier." And she went next door to the police station and got the Police Sergeant to go back with her and tell the Brigadier to leave. By now there was a lot of our people waiting outside to see what would hap- 920 pen and when the Police Sergeant came out with the Brigadier they all clapped their hands and laughed at him. He got into his bakkie and slammed the door and drove away very fast like it was a racing car. People had to jump out of the way! 925

BUKS: And then?

VERONICA: That's all Oupa.

BUKS: Who told you all this?

VERONICA: I heard it first from Rosie but then Mrs. Oliphant told me the whole story herself. 930

BUKS: I see. Were you at the Post Office?

VERONICA: Yes.

(*Pause.*) Oupa?

BUKS: Yes.

VERONICA: Mrs. Oliphant also said that Oupa's got a letter for 935 me. She says she gave it to you yesterday.

BUKS: That's right. She came past this way to ask me to go and look at her windmill. It's not throwing water the way it

940 should. And she said there was a letter for you. Have you been writing letters?

VERONICA: Just to my friend Priscilla.

BUKS: That's nice. Why didn't you tell me about it?

VERONICA: I didn't think Oupa would be interested. It wasn't an important letter. Just silly talk you know and news
945 about the Village.

(She waits.) So can I have it please Oupa? (BUKS takes the letter out of a jacket pocket and hands it to her.) It's open.

BUKS: That's right.

VERONICA: Who opened it?

950 BUKS: I did.

VERONICA: Why Oupa?

BUKS: I wanted to know what it said.

VERONICA: But Oupa can't read

BUKS: I asked JanMei to read it for me.

955 VERONICA: What does the letter say, Oupa?

OUPA: I don't know—JanMei couldn't read it. He said the writing was too hard for him to read.

You tell me what it says Veronica.

VERONICA: (Stalling while she scans the letter quickly.) Yes, it's from
960 Priscilla. You remember her, Oupa—Priscilla Meintjies—she was at school with me. We used to play together. Oupa always said you liked her. Then her father died in that motor-car accident and she and her mother and her brothers left the Village and went to Johannesburg.

965 BUKS: Ja, I remember them. Read the letter Veronica.

VERONICA: (Trying to fabricate an "innocent" letter.) Dear Veronica, How are you keeping? I hope you and your Oupa are happy and well. Please send him our love from all of us. I miss you and all my friends very much. Johannesburg is a
970 very nice place . . . (She falters and stops. She is too terrified and ashamed to keep up the lie.)

BUKS: Veronica I think you are lying to me. That isn't what the letter says is it? Answer me child.

VERONICA: I'm not a child anymore Oupa.

975 BUKS: Just answer me! Look me in the eye Veronica! I don't think that is what the letter says.

VERONICA: Yes

BUKS: Yes what?

VERONICA: Yes, I am lying to you Oupa.

(Her dishonesty leaves BUKS speechless for a few seconds.)

980 I'm sorry. Please forgive me Oupa. I didn't mean to tell Oupa a lie but I got frightened . . . and suddenly it was coming out . . . and I couldn't stop myself . . .
(Nothing from BUKS.) I said I'm sorry Oupa!
(Still no response.) Anyway, Oupa had no right to open it.

985 BUKS: Don't try to tell me about my rights Veronica! This is my house. I got all the rights I need in here. For as long as you sleep under this roof and eat my food . . .

VERONICA: Okay Oupa, then here—take it. (She holds out the letter.) You can have it. Go back to Mrs. Oliphant and ask her
990 to read it for you. Or the school principal. Or the Dominee when he comes on Sunday. Let the whole Village see how you open my letters and spy on me. Take it Oupa!

BUKS: Veronica? What has happened to you? Why are you doing this to me?

995 VERONICA: (Ashamed of herself, she relents, opens the letter again and this time reads it truthfully.) "Dear Veronica, I got your letter

and goodness gracious what a surprise it was! Anyway I asked my mother like you said and she said I must write and tell you that you can certainly come and stay here with us. I sleep on a double pull-out sofa in the lounge so there 1000 is plenty of room for you as well. So come quickly. You will like Eldorado Park. It's a crazy place. There are a lot of crazy things here in Johannesburg and I will show them to you. And you don't have to worry about finding work here also. There's plenty of jobs here in Johannesburg, specially for a 1005 clever and good-looker like you. Are you still so crazy about singing? Write me another letter and tell me when you are coming. Give my love to everybody, specially Diedericks. Is he still so handsome as ever? Totsiens for now. Your ever loving friend Priscilla." 1010

BUKS: You've been making plans to go to Johannesburg?

VERONICA: Please try to understand Oupa.

BUKS: You also want to run away from me like your mother?

VERONICA: Please Oupa . . . please listen! I was going to tell Oupa, but first I wanted to know where I was going and 1015 that there was somewhere I could stay so that Oupa wouldn't worry about me. I wasn't going to just run away and disappear.

BUKS: I knew it! I knew there was something going on behind my back. 1020

VERONICA: You're not listening to me Oupa.

BUKS: That's right. I'm not listening to you because you tell me lies Veronica. That's how it started with your mother. Lies and Secrets. And then stealing.

VERONICA: No. 1025

BUKS: Yes. Your mother. From me—her own father. You keep asking me about her, well here's the truth. She was a thief. Ja, my own daughter but I must say it . . . a thief! She knew where I had my money and then one day, without even so much as a goodbye to your Ouma, she took it all and ran 1030 away to Johannesburg.

I promised your Ouma that I would never tell you, but she didn't know that one day you would be like that as well.

VERONICA: No! No! I would never steal from Oupa. Never! Never! 1035

BUKS: So how were you going to Johannesburg?

VERONICA: I got my own money.

BUKS: Your own money?

(VERONICA is silent.) What do you mean your own money?

VERONICA: Money I save Oupa. 1040

BUKS: From where?

VERONICA: From what the white people give me.

BUKS: You ask them for money?

VERONICA: No. I earned it. I sing my songs for them and they pay me. 1045

(Misinterpreting BUKS's silence and thinking she can bring him over to her side.) It's true. They all like my singing. They say I got a good voice and that I must go somewhere where there is a singing teacher so that I can take lessons and make it better. That's why I wrote to Priscilla. And 1050 you heard what she said in her letter Oupa . . . there's plenty of jobs in Johannesburg so I'll be able to get work and pay for my singing lessons—because if I become a very good singer Oupa I can make lots of money. People who sing on the TV and the radio get paid a lot of money. 1055 Just think Oupa! You can even come up there as well then if you want to . . . forget about those old Landman akkers and come and live in Johannesburg in a proper house with a big garden . . .

(She takes a chance, fetching the tin with her savings, opening it and placing it trustingly on the table in front of her Oupa.)

1060 Look Oupa—I nearly got half the price of a train ticket already.

I'm doing it because I want Oupa to be proud of me. I want to give you something back for all you've given me. But I can't do that if I stay here. There's nothing for me in 1065 this Valley. Please try to understand what it is like for me. I'll die if I got to live my whole life here.

(BUKS's devastation turns to rage. He grabs the tin and hurls it out into the night.)

No Oupa! No! It's mine!

BUKS: Devil's money.

VERONICA: It's not. I earned it. I earned it properly.

1070 BUKS: I'm telling you it's Devil's money! That's where it comes from. Devil's money. He's trying to get you the way he got your mother. But this time I'm ready for him.

Now you listen to me very carefully Veronica. Don't let me ever catch you begging money from the white people 1075 again. And you can also forget all about Johannesburg.

This family has already got one grave up there. There won't be another one. Whatever you might think, you are still a child and I am your Oupa. If you try to run away I'll have the police after you. I mean it. And I'll tell them to 1080 lock you up until you come to your senses.

AUTHOR: *(To the audience.)* The psalm in church the next Sunday was number one hundred and twenty-one.

"I will lift up mine eyes unto the hills from whence cometh my help.

1085 My help cometh from the Lord, which made heaven and earth.

He will not suffer thy foot to be moved: He that keepeth thee will not slumber.

The Lord is thy Keeper: The Lord is thy shade upon the 1090 right hand.

The sun shall not smite thee by day nor the moon by night.

The Lord shall preserve thee from all evil: He shall preserve thy soul.

The Lord shall preserve thy going out and thy coming 1095 in from this time forth, and even for evermore."

(A darkly silent VERONICA comes and stands beside her Oupa for the church service, but this time she doesn't sing. BUKS doggedly sings the hymn through to the end.)

BUKS: *(Singing.)*

Ek sal die Here loof
Ek sal his Here loof
Met al my hart
Sal ek hom Loof.

1100 Ek sal die here dien
Ek sal die here dien
Met al my hart
Sal ek hom dien.

Ek sal die here dank
1105 Ek sal die here dank

Met al my hart
Sal ek hom dank.

(They separate.)

BUKS: You didn't sing.

VERONICA: No.

BUKS: Did you pray? 1110

VERONICA: No.

BUKS: Why? Is it because of me? *(She doesn't answer.)*

Are you trying to hurt me? *(She still doesn't answer.)*

Did you listen to the psalm in church Veronica? "I will lift up mine eyes unto the hills . . ." Come do that with me. 1115 Look at them . . . all around us, and Spitskop over there waiting for the first snow of winter. Do you see it?

VERONICA: I see it.

BUKS: And? Is that all? Do you just "see it?" Look again.

VERONICA: I'm looking. 1120

BUKS: Don't you sometimes stop and stand still and look at all of them and think how small you are?

I do. And then I think: God made them. Ja! All these mountains that stand around and guard the Village, HE put them down here. That's how big HE is. Everything . . . 1125 everything you can see with your eyes, or touch with your hands . . . HE made it.

The blue gum tree where we sit for shade when the house is too hot, the pretty flowers you like so much, the rain that falls, the birds that sing . . . and your voice, so that 1130 you can also sing . . . all of it comes from God. That's how full of love he is for us.

Our church is His house—that is where God lives and that is where we thank Him for all the love He gives us.

What you do in there has got nothing to do with me or 1135 Alfred or Rosie or Mrs. Oliphant or anybody else. It's for HIM. HE wants to hear that beautiful voice he gave you. HE wants to hear you sing and listen to your prayers.

VERONICA: *(Shaking her head.)* I can't Oupa.

You've killed the song in me. I can't sing. I can't pray. 1140 *(Pause.)* Is Oupa finished?

(BUKS doesn't answer. He stands very still. VERONICA waits a few more seconds then leaves.)

AUTHOR: *(To the audience.)* Another late night walk in the Village.

This time it is winter—A Sneeuberg winter! . . . bitterly cold and deathly still. Not even a location dog is barking. 1145 A full moon has flooded the Valley with light—it is almost as bright as day. I can see everything around me—and very clearly! Trees, houses, fences, the mountains in the distance—but they are all cold and colorless, drained of their life as if that world has bled to death. I see a figure coming 1150 down the road toward me. I step into the shadows of a pine tree. It is Buks! His little woollen cap is pulled down low over his ears, his hands buried deep in the pockets of his old jacket as he shuffles slowly past. That is what he has been reduced to . . . walking those roads late at night like a 1155 ghost. After all, what is there left of his life? First he lost Caroline—his only child—buried somewhere in an unmarked grave. He would have made a simple wooden cross for it if she had died in the Village. Then he lost Betty—he made a cross for that grave. He might also lose his land. 1160

And now Veronica—her love and her songs—her beautiful valley songs that filled their little house and his life with laughter and music—they are now as silent as a grave.

All he's got left is one last little question: What did I do
1165   wrong?

It leads him back, all the way back to the memory of a day when he was still a young boy. He and his father were working together on the land. It was very hot and they had sat down in the shade of a tree to eat a bunch of grapes which
1170   his father had picked. It was late summer. They were the sweetest grapes he had ever tasted, and he said so. His father, Jaap Jonkers, laughed and then asked the little boy "Do you know who made the grapes so sweet for us?" Little Abraam knew the answer: "The Almighty did." Jaap patted his son
1175   proudly on the back. "That's right Abraam, and if you grow up to be a good man, then God will make the days of your life even sweeter than those juicy korrels in your mouth." They went back to work, but it was so hot it wasn't long before they had to sit down in the shade again. This time the
1180   young boy had a question. "What must I do to be a good man Pa?" Jaap thought about this question for a long time, so long in fact his son was beginning to think his father hadn't heard him, but then he finally spoke. "You will live your life in three places Abraam—these akkers, our house
1185   and the church. The rest is unimportant. Here, on the land, you must work, and work hard my boy, in your house you must love, love everybody who lives under that roof with you and also your neighbor, and in the church you must have faith and worship the Almighty and thank Him for all His
1190   blessings and then you will grow up to be a good man."

His father's words come back to him again and again now as he haunts the sleeping Village.

A sense of injustice, of betrayal, begins to rankle and fester in his soul. He was given a promise of days as sweet as
1195   hanepoot grapes, but instead they have ended up as bitter as aloe juice.

Because he has tried—Every day!—Just as his father had said he must, he has tried to be "a good man." And Betty is his witness. She shared twenty-five years of that life with
1200   him. She saw! When Caroline was born he came running home from the akkers where he was planting and she saw him go down on his knees next to her bed, and thank God for the blessing of a child. They had waited seven years for it. When his prayer was finished he made the little bundle
1205   in Betty's arms a promise: "You will never want for food or love in this house."

(THE AUTHOR *moves into the character of* BUKS. VERONICA *comes forward and stands listening to her Oupa.*)

BUKS: "You will never want for food or love in this house." And did I not keep that promise Betty? Was there even one day
1210   that she went hungry under this roof? And not just food. Everything else. I sweated my life into those akkers so that she could have everything she needed.

I tried to teach her what is right and what is wrong the way my father taught me. We stood together in church on Sunday and praised the Lord and thanked Him for his blessings.
1215   And I love her. Oh Betty . . . there is so much love for her inside me I don't know what to do with it.

VERONICA: Oupa?

(*He now sees* VERONICA.)

BUKS: Caroline? . . .
VERONICA: No . . .
BUKS: You've come back?   1220
VERONICA: No! . . .
BUKS: Betty! Betty! She's come back!
VERONICA: No . . . no! . . .
BUKS: Please . . . don't go! . . . I must talk to you. Please—I must know—Why? What did I do wrong? Help me Caroline—   1225
    that's all I want, just to know what I did wrong?
VERONICA: No Oupa! It's me . . . Veronica . . .

(BUKS *stops.*)

. . . your grandchild. Caroline is dead Oupa. Ouma is also dead. Yes, both of them. Dead a long time ago.
There is just you and me left . . . Oupa and Veronica.   1230

(*Desperate to help him back to reality, she breaks her silence and sings.*)

        You plant seeds
        And I sing songs
        We're Oupa and Veronica
        Yes, Oupa and Veronica.

        You work hard   1235
        And I dream dreams
        That's Oupa and Veronica
        Yes, Oupa and Veronica.

        Summer into autumn
        Winter into spring   1240
        Planting seeds and singing songs
        It's Oupa and Veronica
        Yes, Oupa and Veronica.

BUKS: Veronica? . . .
VERONICA: That's right. Say it again Oupa.   1245
BUKS: Veronica. I thought . . .
VERONICA: I know Oupa—you thought I was Caroline.
BUKS: I thought she had come back.
VERONICA: She can't Oupa. She's dead.
BUKS: That's right. My child is dead.   1250

We waited for her. Everyday. Right up to the day when we got the message from the hospital, we waited for her to come back—Betty here in the house, me on the akkers— waiting. Sometimes I would stop working and go to the gate and look down the road and I imagined I could see her   1255 coming with my bottle of tea and bread.

At night we sat in here and went on waiting. There was a deep shame between us—your Ouma and me—I could see it in her eyes and she saw it in mine . . . the same question: What did we do wrong? Every night, in this room, at this   1260 table, trying to live with that question. And when your Ouma had cried herself to sleep I used to get up and go out and walk and ask it again . . . What did we do wrong? Because we loved her.

VERONICA: I know that Oupa. I know she knew it to.   1265
You didn't do anything wrong Oupa. You didn't do any-

thing wrong with me either . . . but I know my time is also coming.

BUKS: What do you mean?

1270 VERONICA: You must let me go, Oupa, otherwise I will also run away from you.

BUKS: No! You mustn't do that! I will let you go. But explain it to me. I want to understand.

VERONICA: Can Oupa explain to me how a little seed becomes a big pumpkin?

BUKS: No.

VERONICA: You said to me once it was a miracle.

BUKS: That's right.

VERONICA: You give it water and skoffel out the weeds and it just grows. Isn't that so?

BUKS: Yes, that is so.

VERONICA: I think it is like that with me and my singing Oupa. I also can't tell you how it happens. All I know is that when I sing, I'm alive. My singing is my life. I must look after it the way Oupa looks after his vegetables. I know that if I stay here in the Valley it will die.

Does Oupa understand now?

BUKS: No . . . but that doesn't matter.

I'm frightened for you.

1290 VERONICA: I'm not.

BUKS: It's a bad world out there Veronica. Ja. Look at what happened to your mother.

VERONICA: It won't happen to me Oupa. You have made me strong. All that you have taught me has made me strong.

1295 Will you give me your blessing Oupa?

BUKS: Come here.

(She does.) God bless you my child.

VERONICA: I love you Oupa.

(She leaves her Oupa and then sings.)

1300
You're breaking my heart
Valley that I love
You're breaking my heart
When I say Goodbye.

1305
You gave me a start
Valley that I love
but now we must part
'Cause I'm on my way.

I'll sing all your songs
Valley that I love
So that people will know
1310 How beautiful you are.

The dream I've got
Is leading me away
But Valley that I love
I'll come back one day.

1315 AUTHOR: So you're going to do it.

VERONICA: Yes.

AUTHOR: Johannesburg?

VERONICA: Yes. The school principal is giving me a lift to Bellevue. Then I catch the train.

1320 AUTHOR: Are you excited?

VERONICA: Yes! But I'm also a little frightened. And sad.

I had a big cry when I said goodbye to my Oupa. So did he.

AUTHOR: So then don't go.

VERONICA: No!

1325 AUTHOR: Come on Veronica. Think of your poor Oupa. He's only got a few years left. Make them happy ones. Go back and tell him that you've changed your mind . . .

VERONICA: No, I can't do that! It isn't something I can change my mind about. I have to go.

1330 AUTHOR: You make it sound like an order: "Go To Johannesburg Veronica Jonkers . . . And Sing!"

VERONICA: Yes! Don't laugh at me. That is what it feels like.

AUTHOR: I know. I wasn't laughing at you, I was laughing at myself.

1335 VERONICA: Then you understand?

AUTHOR: Oh yes.

VERONICA: My Oupa didn't. I tried to explain it to him but he didn't understand.

1340 AUTHOR: I would have been surprised if he had. You are all he's got left in the world. How can he understand losing that?

VERONICA: He's not losing me! I told him I'm going to write to him every week. And the school principal promised he will read my letters to him. And I'll come back to visit him whenever I can.

1345 AUTHOR: And did that cheer him up?

VERONICA: No.

AUTHOR: I always had a feeling that you would do it you know.

VERONICA: I don't believe you.

AUTHOR: No. It's true. The very first time I saw you dreaming on your apple box I had a feeling that one day you would be 1350 saying goodbye to the Valley.

VERONICA: Then why did you make it so hard for me? Always laughing and teasing me and trying to stop me? You're still doing it.

AUTHOR: I was testing you. 1355

VERONICA: Testing me?

AUTHOR: Yes.

VERONICA: Like in the tests at school?

AUTHOR: Sort of.

VERONICA: And did I pass? 1360

AUTHOR: Oh yes. You're strong. I think you've got what it takes.

But I must be honest with you, there's a selfish part of me that wanted you to fail that test.

VERONICA: Why? 1365

AUTHOR: A lot of reasons.

VERONICA: Such as?

AUTHOR: Like your Oupa, I don't want to see you go. It means the Valley is changing and that selfish part of me doesn't want that to happen. It wants it to stay the unspoilt, inno- 1370 cent little world it was when I first discovered it. On all the late-night walks that are left in my life, I want to find lit- tle Veronica Jonkers dreaming on her apple box outside Mrs. Jooste's house. You see the truth is that I am not as brave about change as I would like to be. It involves letting 1375 go of things and I've discovered that that is a lot harder than I thought it was.

And then on top of all that, I am also jealous.

VERONICA: Of what?

AUTHOR: You. Your youth. Your dreams. The future belongs to 1380 you now. There was a time when it was mine, when I dreamt about it the way you do, but not anymore. I've just about used up all of the "Glorious Future" that I once had. But it isn't something you give up easily. I'm trying to hold 1385 onto it the way your Oupa wanted to hold onto you.

VERONICA: *(Shaking her head.)* You old men!

AUTHOR: That's right. And take my advice . . . Be careful of us!

VERONICA: It's time for me to go.

AUTHOR: Good luck.

(She starts to leave.)

1390 AUTHOR: Wait!
   Can you hear it?

VERONICA: What?

AUTHOR: Listen.
   "Veronica. Veronica. We want Veronica!"

1395 VERONICA: Now I'm excited again.

(She leaves the stage.)

AUTHOR: And Buks? How do we leave him? Slumped in defeat and misery as we last saw him? I don't think so. That is what Buks himself would describe as a dishonorable discharge from life and Buks is an honorable old soldier. The truth is 1400 there was enough life left in him to yield to one last temptation . . . and I was the devil who did it!

I found him in his house, sitting at the little kitchen table. He asked me "nicely" to sit down but I said: "No, I'm in a hurry . . . and so should you be!"

Come on, Buks. Onto your legs. Didn't you hear the rain 1405 last night? I'm telling you man, down at my end of the Village it came down so hard it sounded like that Sonderwater Military Band of yours was practicing on the tin roof.

Think of it Buks. Another spring has come and we are still here! Still strong enough to go out there and plant! 1410

Tell me the truth now Buks, think back to your young days and tell me . . . Did a woman ever smell as good as the Karoo earth after a good rain? Or feel as good? *(A sly laugh.)*

Ja, the ground is soft and wet and waiting. And look what I've got for you! *(A handful of shiny, white pumpkin* 1415 *seeds.)* Pumpkin seeds! Imagine it Buks. An akker full of shiny, Flat White Boer pumpkins as big as donkey-cart wheels!

(THE AUTHOR laughs; starts to leave.)

Come . . .
(Looks back and beckons once more.) Come . . . that's it! . . . 1420
COME!

CRITICAL CONTEXTS

Frantz Fanon was perhaps the seminal theoretician of postcolonial politics, culture, and identity; his two major books, Black Skin, White Masks *(1952) and* The Wretched of the Earth *(1961), have been widely read and have provided an important inspiration for liberation movements around the world. Born in Martinique, Fanon studied medicine in Paris, and became a psychiatrist in Algeria during its wars of liberation from France. "The Fact of Blackness" is Fanon's celebrated essay describing the consciousness of "black" subjects in a world of "white" power.*

FRANTZ FANON
(1925–61)

"The Fact of Blackness"
(1952)

"Dirty nigger!" Or simply, "Look, a Negro!"

I came into the world imbued with the will to find a meaning in things, my spirit filled with the desire to attain to the source of the world, and then I found that I was an object in the midst of other objects.

Sealed into that crushing objecthood, I turned beseechingly to others. Their attention was a liberation, running over my body suddenly abraded into nonbeing, endowing me once more with an agility that I had thought lost, and by taking me out of the world, restoring me to it. But just as I reached the other side, I stumbled, and the movements, the attitudes, the glances of the other fixed me there, in the sense in which a chemical solution is fixed by a dye. I was indignant; I demanded an explanation. Nothing happened. I burst apart. Now the fragments have been put together again by another self.

As long as the black man is among his own, he will have no occasion, except in minor internal conflicts, to experience his being through others. There is of course the moment of "being for others," of which Hegel speaks, but every ontology is made unattainable in a colonized and civilized society. It would seem that this fact has not been given sufficient attention by those who have discussed the question. In the *Weltanschauung* of a colonized people there is an impurity, a flaw that outlaws any ontological explanation. Someone may object that this is the case with every individual, but such an objection merely conceals a basic problem. Ontology—once it is finally admitted as leaving existence by the wayside—does not permit us to understand the being of the black man. For not only must the black man be black; he must be black in relation to the white man. Some critics will take it on themselves to remind us that this proposition has a converse. I say that this is false. The black man has no ontological resistance in the eyes of the white man. Overnight the Negro has been given two frames of reference within which he has had to place himself. His metaphysics, or, less pretentiously, his customs and the sources on which they were based, were wiped out because they were in conflict with a civilization that he did not know and that imposed itself on him.

The black man among his own in the twentieth century does not know at what moment his inferiority comes into being through the other. Of course I have talked about the black problem with friends, or, more rarely, with American Negroes. Together we protested, we asserted the equality of all men in the world. In the Antilles there was also that little gulf that exists among the almost-white, the mulatto, and the nigger. But I was satisfied with an intellectual understanding of these differences. It was not really dramatic. And then. . . .

And then the occasion arose when I had to meet the white man's eyes. An unfamiliar weight burdened me. The real world challenged my claims. In the white world the man of color encounters difficulties in the development of his bodily schema. Consciousness of the body is solely a negating activity. It is a third-person consciousness. The body is surrounded by an atmosphere of certain uncertainty. I know that if I want to smoke, I shall have to reach out my right arm and take the pack of cigarettes lying at the other end of the table. The matches, however, are in the drawer on the left, and I shall have to lean back slightly. And all these movements are made not out of habit but out of implicit knowledge. A slow composition of my *self* as a body in the middle of a spatial and temporal world—such seems to be the schema. It does not impose itself on me; it is, rather, a definitive structuring of the self and of the world—definitive because it creates a real dialectic between my body and the world.

For several years certain laboratories have been trying to produce a serum for "denegrification"; with all the earnestness in the world, laboratories have sterilized their test tubes, checked their scales, and embarked on researches that might make it possible for the miserable Negro to whiten himself and thus to throw off the burden of that corporeal malediction. Below the corporeal schema I had sketched a historico-racial schema. The elements that I used had been provided for me not by "residual sensations and perceptions primarily of a tactile, vestibular, kinesthetic, and visual character,"[1] but by the other, the white man, who had woven me out of a thousand details, anecdotes, stories. I thought that what I had in hand was to construct a physiological self, to balance space, to localize sensations, and here I was called on for more.

"Look, a Negro!" It was an external stimulus that flicked over me as I passed by. I made a tight smile.

"Look, a Negro!" It was true. It amused me.

"Look, a Negro!" The circle was drawing a bit tighter. I made no secret of my amusement.

"Mama, see the Negro! I'm frightened!" Frightened! Frightened! Now they were beginning to be afraid of me. I made up my mind to laugh myself to tears, but laughter had become impossible.

I could no longer laugh, because I already knew that there were legends, stories, history, and above all *historicity,* which I had learned about from Jaspers. Then, assailed at various points, the corporeal schema crumbled, its place taken by a racial epidermal schema. In the train it was no longer a question of being aware of my body in the third person but in a triple person. In the train I was given not one but two, three places. I had already stopped being amused. It was not that I was finding febrile coordinates in the world. I existed triply: I occupied space. I moved toward the other . . . and the evanescent other, hostile but not opaque, transparent, not there, disappeared. Nausea. . . .

I was responsible at the same time for my body, for my race, for my ancestors. I subjected myself to an objective examination, I discovered my blackness, my ethnic characteristics; and I was battered down by tom-toms, cannibalism, intellectual deficiency, fetishism, racial defects, slave-ships, and above all else, above all: "Sho' good eatin'."

On that day, completely dislocated, unable to be abroad with the other, the white man, who unmercifully imprisoned me, I took myself far off from my own presence, far indeed, and made myself an object. What else could it be for me but an amputation, an excision, a hemorrhage that spattered my whole body with black blood? But I did not want this revision, this thematization. All I wanted was to be a man among other men. I wanted to come lithe and young into a world that was ours and to help to build it together.

But I rejected all immunization of the emotions. I wanted to be a man, nothing but a man. Some identified me with ancestors of mine who had been enslaved or lynched: I decided to accept this. It was on the universal level of the intellect that I understood this inner kinship— I was the grandson of slaves in exactly the same way in which President Lebrun was the grandson of tax-paying, hard-working peasants. In the main, the panic soon vanished.

---

[1] Jean Lhermitte, *L'Image de notre corps* (Paris: Nouvelle Revue critique, 1939), p. 17.

In America, Negroes are segregated. In South America, Negroes are whipped in the streets, and Negro strikers are cut down by machine-guns. In West Africa, the Negro is an animal. And there beside me, my neighbor in the university, who was born in Algeria, told me: "As long as the Arab is treated like a man, no solution is possible."

"Understand, my dear boy, color prejudice is something I find utterly foreign. . . . But of course, come in, sir, there is no color prejudice among us. . . . Quite, the Negro is a man like ourselves. . . . It is not because he is black that he is less intelligent than we are. . . . I had a Senegalese buddy in the army who was really clever. . . ."

Where am I to be classified? Or, if you prefer, tucked away?

"A Martinican, a native of 'our' old colonies."

Where shall I hide?

"Look at the nigger! . . . Mama, a Negro! . . . Hell, he's getting mad. . . . Take no notice, sir, he does not know that you are as civilized as we. . . ."

My body was given back to me sprawled out, distorted, recolored, clad in mourning in that white winter day. The Negro is an animal, the Negro is bad, the Negro is mean, the Negro is ugly; look, a nigger, it's cold, the nigger is shivering, the nigger is shivering because he is cold, the little boy is trembling because he is afraid of the nigger, the nigger is shivering with cold, that cold that goes through your bones, the handsome little boy is trembling because he thinks that the nigger is quivering with rage, the little white boy throws himself into his mother's arms: Mama, the nigger's going to eat me up.

All round me the white man, above the sky tears at its navel, the earth rasps under my feet, and there is a white song, a white song. All this whiteness that burns me. . . .

I sit down at the fire and I become aware of my uniform. I had not seen it. It is indeed ugly. I stop there, for who can tell me what beauty is?

Where shall I find shelter from now on? I felt an easily identifiable flood mounting out of the countless facets of my being. I was about to be angry. The fire was long since out, and once more the nigger was trembling.

"Look how handsome that Negro is! . . ."

"Kiss the handsome Negro's ass, madame!"

Shame flooded her face. At last I was set free from my rumination. At the same time I accomplished two things: I identified my enemies and I made a scene. A grand slam. Now one would be able to laugh.

The field of battle having been marked out, I entered the lists.

What? While I was forgetting, forgiving, and wanting only to love, my message was flung back in my face like a slap. The white world, the only honorable one, barred me from all participation. A man was expected to behave like a man. I was expected to behave like a black man—or at least like a nigger. I shouted a greeting to the world and the world slashed away my joy. I was told to stay within bounds, to go back where I belonged.

They would see, then! I had warned them, anyway. Slavery? It was no longer even mentioned, that unpleasant memory. My supposed inferiority? A hoax that it was better to laugh at. I forgot it all, but only on condition that the world not protect itself against me any longer. I had incisors to test. I was sure they were strong. And besides. . . .

What! When it was I who had every reason to hate, to despise, I was rejected? When I should have been begged, implored, I was denied the slightest recognition? I resolved, since it was impossible for me to get away from an *inborn complex,* to assert myself as a BLACK MAN. Since the other hesitated to recognize me, there remained only one solution: to make myself known.

In *Anti-Semite and Jew* (p. 95), Sartre says: "They [the Jews] have allowed themselves to be poisoned by the stereotype that others have of them, and they live in fear that their acts will correspond to this stereotype. . . . We may say that their conduct is perpetually overdetermined from the inside."

All the same, the Jew can be unknown in his Jewishness. He is not wholly what he is. One hopes, one waits. His actions, his behavior are the final determinant. He is a white man, and, apart from some rather debatable characteristics, he can sometimes go unnoticed. He belongs to the race of those who since the beginning of time have never known cannibalism. What an idea, to eat one's father! Simple enough, one has only not to be a nigger. Granted, the Jews are harassed—what am I thinking of? They are hunted down, exterminated, cremated. But these are little family quarrels. The Jew is disliked from the moment he is tracked down. But in my case everything takes on a *new* guise. I am given no chance. I am overdetermined from without. I am the slave not of the "idea" that others have of me but of my own appearance.

I move slowly in the world, accustomed now to seek no longer for upheaval. I progress by crawling. And already I am being dissected under white eyes, the only real eyes. I am *fixed*. Having adjusted their microtomes, they objectively cut away slices of my reality. I am laid bare. I feel, I see in those white faces that it is not a new man who has come in, but a new kind of man, a new genus. Why, it's a Negro!

I slip into corners, and my long antennae pick up the catch-phrases strewn over the surface of things—nigger underwear smells of nigger—nigger teeth are white—nigger feet are big—the nigger's barrel chest—I slip into corners, I remain silent, I strive for anonymity, for invisibility. Look, I will accept the lot, as long as no one notices me!

"Oh, I want you to meet my black friend. . . . Aimé Césaire, a black man and a university graduate. . . . Marian Anderson, the finest of Negro singers. . . . Dr. Cobb, who invented white blood, is a Negro. . . . Here, say hello to my friend from Martinique (be careful, he's extremely sensitive). . . ."

Shame. Shame and self-contempt. Nausea. When people like me, they tell me it is in spite of my color. When they dislike me, they point out that it is not because of my color. Either way, I am locked into the infernal circle.

I turn away from these inspectors of the Ark before the Flood and I attach myself to my brothers, Negroes like myself. To my horror, they too reject me. They are almost white. And besides they are about to marry white women. They will have children faintly tinged with brown. Who knows, perhaps little by little. . . .

I had been dreaming.

"I want you to understand, sir, I am one of the best friends the Negro has in Lyon."

The evidence was there, unalterable. My blackness was there, dark and unarguable. And it tormented me, pursued me, disturbed me, angered me.

Negroes are savages, brutes, illiterates. But in my own case I knew that these statements were false. There was a myth of the Negro that had to be destroyed at all costs. The time had long since passed when a Negro priest was an occasion for wonder. We had physicians, professors, statesmen. Yes, but something out of the ordinary still clung to such cases. "We have a Senegalese history teacher. He is quite bright. . . . Our doctor is colored. He is very gentle."

It was always the Negro teacher, the Negro doctor; brittle as I was becoming, I shivered at the slightest pretext. I knew, for instance, that if the physician made a mistake it would be the end of him and of all those who came after him. What could one expect, after all, from a Negro physician? As long as everything went well, he was praised to the skies, but look out, no nonsense, under any conditions! The black physician can never be sure how close he is to disgrace. I tell you, I was walled in: No exception was made for my refined manners, or my knowledge of literature, or my understanding of the quantum theory.

I requested, I demanded explanations. Gently, in the tone that one uses with a child, they introduced me to the existence of a certain view that was held by certain people, but, I was always told, "We must hope that it will very soon disappear." What was it? Color prejudice.

> It [colour prejudice] is nothing more than the unreasoning hatred of one race for another, the contempt of the stronger and richer peoples for those whom they consider inferior to themselves and the bitter resentment of those who are kept in subjection and are so frequently insulted. As colour is the most obvious outward manifestation of race it has been made the criterion by which men are judged, irrespective of their social or educational attainments. The light-skinned races have come to despise all those of a darker colour, and the dark-skinned peoples will no longer accept without protest the inferior position to which they have been relegated.[2]

I had read it rightly. It was hate; I was hated, despised, detested, not by the neighbor across the street or my cousin on my mother's side, but by an entire race. I was up against something unreasoned. The psychoanalysts say that nothing is more traumatizing for the young child than his encounters with what is rational. I would personally say that for a man whose only weapon is reason there is nothing more neurotic than contact with unreason.

I felt knife blades open within me. I resolved to defend myself. As a good tactician, I intended to rationalize the world and to show the white man that he was mistaken.

In the Jew, Jean-Paul Sartre says, there is

> a sort of impassioned imperialism of reason: for he wishes not only to convince others that he is right; his goal is to persuade them that there is an absolute and unconditioned value to rationalism. He feels himself to be a missionary of the universal; against the universality of the Catholic religion, from which he is excluded, he asserts the "catholicity" of the rational, an instrument by which to attain to the truth and establish a spiritual bond among men.[3]

And, the author adds, though there may be Jews who have made intuition the basic category of their philosophy, their intuition

> has no resemblance to the Pascalian subtlety of spirit, and it is this latter—based on a thousand imperceptible perceptions—which to the Jew seems his worst enemy. As for Bergson, his philosophy offers the curious appearance of an anti-intellectualist doctrine constructed entirely by the most rational and most critical of intelligences. It is through argument that he establishes the existence of pure duration, of philosophic intuition; and that very intuition which discovers duration or life, is itself universal, since anyone may practice it, and it leads toward the universal, since its objects can be named and conceived.[4]

With enthusiasm I set to cataloguing and probing my surroundings. As times changed, one had seen the Catholic religion at first justify and then condemn slavery and prejudices. But by referring everything to the idea of the dignity of man, one had ripped prejudice to shreds. After much reluctance, the scientists had conceded that the Negro was a human being; *in vivo* and *in vitro* the Negro had been proved analogous to the white man: the same morphology, the same histology. Reason was confident of victory on every level. I put all the parts back together. But I had to change my tune.

That victory played cat and mouse; it made a fool of me. As the other put it, when I was present, it was not; when it was there, I was no longer. In the abstract there was agreement: The Negro is a human being. That is to say, amended the less firmly convinced, that

---

[2]Sir Alan Burns, *Colour Prejudice* (London: Allen and Unwin, 1948), p. 16.
[3]*Anti-Semite and Jew* (New York: Grove Press, 1960), pp. 112–13.
[4]Ibid., p. 115.

like us he has his heart on the left side. But on certain points the white man remained intractable. Under no conditions did he wish any intimacy between the races, for it is a truism that "crossings between widely different races can lower the physical and mental level. . . . Until we have a more definite knowledge of the effect of race-crossings we shall certainly do best to avoid crossings between widely different races."[5]

For my own part, I would certainly know how to react. And in one sense, if I were asked for a definition of myself, I would say that I am one who waits; I investigate my surroundings, I interpret everything in terms of what I discover, I become sensitive.

In the first chapter of the history that the others have compiled for me, the foundation of cannibalism has been made eminently plain in order that I may not lose sight of it. My chromosomes were supposed to have a few thicker or thinner genes representing cannibalism. In addition to the *sex-linked,* the scholars had now discovered the *racial-linked.*[6] What a shameful science!

But I understand this "psychological mechanism." For it is a matter of common knowledge that the mechanism is only psychological. Two centuries ago I was lost to humanity, I was a slave forever. And then came men who said that it all had gone on far too long. My tenaciousness did the rest; I was saved from the civilizing deluge. I have gone forward.

Too late. Everything is anticipated, thought out, demonstrated, made the most of. My trembling hands take hold of nothing; the vein has been mined out. Too late! But once again I want to understand.

Since the time when someone first mourned the fact that he had arrived too late and everything had been said, a nostalgia for the past has seemed to persist. Is this that lost original paradise of which Otto Rank speaks? How many such men, apparently rooted to the womb of the world, have devoted their lives to studying the Delphic oracles or exhausted themselves in attempts to plot the wanderings of Ulysses! The pan-spiritualists seek to prove the existence of a soul in animals by using this argument: A dog lies down on the grave of his master and starves to death there. We had to wait for Janet to demonstrate that the aforesaid dog, in contrast to man, simply lacked the capacity to liquidate the past. We speak of the glory of Greece, Artaud says; but, he adds, if modern man can no longer understand the *Choephoroi* of Aeschylus, it is Aeschylus who is to blame. It is tradition to which the anti-Semites turn in order to ground the validity of their "point of view." It is tradition, it is that long historical past, it is that blood relation between Pascal and Descartes, that is invoked when the Jew is told, "There is no possibility of your finding a place in society." Not long ago, one of those good Frenchmen said in a train where I was sitting: "Just let the real French virtues keep going and the race is safe. Now more than ever, national union must be made a reality. Let's have an end of internal strife! Let's face up to the foreigners (here he turned toward my corner) no matter who they are."

It must be said in his defense that he stank of cheap wine; if he had been capable of it, he would have told me that my emancipated-slave blood could not possibly be stirred by the name of Villon or Taine.

An outrage!

The Jew and I: Since I was not satisfied to be racialized, by a lucky turn of fate I was humanized. I joined the Jew, my brother in misery.

An outrage!

At first thought it may seem strange that the anti-Semite's outlook should be related to that of the Negro-phobe. It was my philosophy professor, a native of the Antilles, who

---

[5]Jon Alfred Mjoen, "Harmonic and Disharmonic Race-crossings," The Second International Congress of Eugenics (1921), *Eugenics in Race and State,* vol. 2, p. 60, quoted in Sir Alan Burns, op. cit., p. 120.

[6]In English in the original (*Translator's note*).

recalled the fact to me one day: "Whenever you hear anyone abuse the Jews, pay attention, because he is talking about you." And I found that he was universally right—by which I meant that I was answerable in my body and in my heart for what was done to my brother. Later I realized that he meant, quite simply, an anti-Semite is inevitably anti-Negro.

You come too late, much too late. There will always be a world—a white world—between you and us. . . . The other's total inability to liquidate the past once and for all. In the face of this affective ankylosis of the white man, it is understandable that I could have made up my mind to utter my Negro cry. Little by little, putting out pseudopodia here and there, I secreted a race. And that race staggered under the burden of a basic element. What was it? *Rhythm!* Listen to our singer, Léopold Senghor:

> It is the thing that is most perceptible and least material. It is the archetype of the vital element. It is the first condition and the hallmark of Art, as breath is of life: breath, which accelerates or slows, which becomes even or agitated according to the tension in the individual, the degree and the nature of his emotion. This is rhythm in its primordial purity, this is rhythm in the masterpieces of Negro art, especially sculpture. It is composed of a theme—sculptural form—which is set in opposition to a sister theme, as inhalation is to exhalation, and that is repeated. It is not the kind of symmetry that gives rise to monotony; rhythm is alive, it is free. . . . This is how rhythm affects what is least intellectual in us, tyrannically, to make us penetrate to the spirituality of the object; and that character of abandon which is ours is itself rhythmic.[7]

Had I read that right? I read it again with redoubled attention. From the opposite end of the white world a magical Negro culture was hailing me. Negro sculpture! I began to flush with pride. Was this our salvation?

I had rationalized the world and the world had rejected me on the basis of color prejudice. Since no agreement was possible on the level of reason, I threw myself back toward unreason. It was up to the white man to be more irrational than I. Out of the necessities of my struggle I had chosen the method of regression, but the fact remained that it was an unfamiliar weapon; here I am at home; I am made of the irrational; I wade in the irrational. Up to the neck in the irrational. And now how my voice vibrates!

> Those who invented neither gunpowder nor the compass
> Those who never learned to conquer steam or electricity
> Those who never explored the seas or the skies
> But they know the farthest corners of the land of anguish
> Those who never knew any journey save that of abduction
> Those who learned to kneel in docility
> Those who were domesticated and Christianized
> Those who were injected with bastardy. . . .

Yes, all those are my brothers—a "bitter brotherhood" imprisons all of us alike. Having stated the minor thesis, I went overboard after something else.

> . . . But those without whom the earth would not be the earth
> Tumescence all the more fruitful
> than
> the empty land
> still more the land
> Storehouse to guard and ripen all
> on earth that is most earth
> My blackness is no stone, its deafness
> hurled against the clamor of the day
> My blackness is no drop of lifeless water

[7]"Ce que l'homme noir apporte," in Claude Nordey, *L'Homme de couleur* (Paris: Plon, 1939), pp. 309–10.

on the dead eye of the world
My blackness is neither a tower nor a cathedral
It thrusts into the red flesh of the sun
It thrusts into the burning flesh of the sky
It hollows through the dense dismay of its own pillar of patience.[8]

Eyah! the tom-tom chatters out the cosmic message. Only the Negro has the capacity to convey it, to decipher its meaning, its import. Astride the world, my strong heels spurring into the flanks of the world, I stare into the shoulders of the world as the celebrant stares at the midpoint between the eyes of the sacrificial victim.

But they abandon themselves, possessed, to the essence of all things, knowing nothing of externals but possessed by the movement of all things

uncaring to subdue but playing the play of the world
truly the eldest sons of the world
open to all the breaths of the world
meeting-place of all the winds of the world
undrained bed of all the waters of the world
spark of the sacred fire of the World
flesh of the flesh of the world, throbbing with the very movement of the world.[9]

Blood! Blood! . . . Birth! Ecstasy of becoming! Three-quarters engulfed in the confusions of the day, I feel myself redden with blood. The arteries of all the world, convulsed, torn away, uprooted, have turned toward me and fed me.

"Blood! Blood! All our blood stirred by the male heart of the sun."[10]

Sacrifice was a middle point between the creation and myself—now I went back no longer to sources but to The Source. Nevertheless, one had to distrust rhythm, earth-mother love, this mystic, carnal marriage of the group and the cosmos.

In *La vie sexuelle en Afrique noire,* a work rich in perceptions, De Pédrals implies that always in Africa, no matter what field is studied, it will have a certain magico-social structure. He adds:

All these are the elements that one finds again on a still greater scale in the domain of secret societies. To the extent, moreover, to which persons of either sex, subjected to circumcision during adolescence, are bound under penalty of death not to reveal to the uninitiated what they have experienced, and to the extent to which initiation into a secret society always excites to acts of *sacred love,* there is good ground to conclude by viewing both male and female circumcision and the rites that they embellish as constitutive of minor secret societies.[11]

I walk on white nails. Sheets of water threaten my soul on fire. Face to face with these rites, I am doubly alert. Black magic! Orgies, witches' sabbaths, heathen ceremonies, amulets. Coitus is an occasion to call on the gods of the clan. It is a sacred act, pure, absolute, bringing invisible forces into action. What is one to think of all these manifestations, all these initiations, all these acts? From very direction I am assaulted by the obscenity of dances and of words. Almost at my ear there is a song:

First our hearts burned hot
Now they are cold
All we think of now is Love
When we return to the village
When we see the great phallus

[8]Aimé Césaire, *Cahier d'un retour au pays natal* (Paris: Présence Africaine, 1956), pp. 77–78.

[9]Ibid., p. 78.

[10]Ibid., p. 79.

[11]De Pédrals, *La vie sexuelle en Afrique noire* (Paris: Payot), p. 83.

Ah how then we will make Love
For our parts will be dry and clean.[12]

The soil, which only a moment ago was still a tamed steed, begins to revel. Are these virgins, these nymphomaniacs? Black Magic, primitive mentality, animism, animal eroticism, it all floods over me. All of it is typical of peoples that have not kept pace with the evolution of the human race. Or, if one prefers, this is humanity at its lowest. Having reached this point, I was long reluctant to commit myself. Aggression was in the stars. I had to choose. What do I mean? I had no choice. . . .

Yes, we are—we Negroes—backward, simple, free in our behavior. That is because for us the body is not something opposed to what you call the mind. We are in the world. And long live the couple, Man and Earth! Besides, our men of letters helped me to convince you; your white civilization overlooks subtle riches and sensitivity. Listen:

Emotive sensitivity. *Emotion is completely Negro as reason is Greek.*[13] Water rippled by every breeze? Unsheltered soul blown by every wind, whose fruit often drops before it is ripe? Yes, in one way, the Negro today is richer *in gifts than in works.*[14] But the tree thrusts its roots into the earth. The river runs deep, carrying precious seeds. And, the Afro-American poet, Langston Hughes, says:

I have known rivers
ancient dark rivers
my soul has grown deep
like the deep rivers.

The very nature of the Negro's emotion, of his sensitivity, furthermore, explains his attitude toward the object perceived with such basic intensity. It is an abandon that becomes need, an active state of communion, indeed of identification, however negligible the action—I almost said the personality—of the object. A rhythmic attitude: The adjective should be kept in mind.[15]

So here we have the Negro rehabilitated, "standing before the bar," ruling the world with his intuition, the Negro recognized, set on his feet again, sought after, taken up, and he is a Negro—no, he is not a Negro but the Negro, exciting the fecund antennae of the world, placed in the foreground of the world, raining his poetic power on the world, "open to all the breaths of the world." I embrace the world! I am the world! The white man has never understood this magic substitution. The white man wants the world; he wants it for himself alone. He finds himself predestined master of this world. He enslaves it. An acquisitive relation is established between the world and him. But there exist other values that fit only my forms. Like a magician, I robbed the white man of "a certain world," forever after lost to him and his. When that happened, the white man must have been rocked backward by a force that he could not identify, so little used as he is to such reactions. Somewhere beyond the objective world of farms and banana trees and rubber trees, I had subtly brought the real world into being. The essence of the world was my fortune. Between the world and me a relation of coexistence was established. I had discovered the primeval One. My "speaking hands" tore at the hysterical throat of the world. The white man had the anguished feeling that I was escaping from him and that I was taking something with me. He went through my pockets. He thrust probes into the least circumvolution of my brain. Everywhere he found only the obvious. So it was obvious that I had a secret. I was interrogated; turning away with an air of mystery, I murmured:

---

[12]A. M. Vergiat, *Les rites secrets des primitifs de l'Oubangui* (Paris: Payot, 1951), p. 113.

[13]My italics—F.F.

[14]My italics—F.F.

[15]Léopold Senghor, "Ce que l'homme noir apporte," in Nordey, op. cit., p. 205.

Tokowaly, uncle, do you remember the nights gone by
When my head weighed heavy on the back of your patience or
Holding my hand your hand led me by shadows and signs
The fields are flowers of glowworms, stars hang on the bushes, on the trees
Silence is everywhere
Only the scents of the jungle hum, swarms of reddish bees that overwhelm the crickets'
    shrill sounds,
And covered tom-tom, breathing in the distance of the night.
You, Tokowaly, you listen to what cannot be heard, and you explain to me what the
    ancestors are saying in the liquid calm of the constellations,
The bull, the scorpion, the leopard, the elephant, and the fish we know,
And the white pomp of the Spirits in the heavenly shell that has no end,
But now comes the radiance of the goddess Moon and the veils of the shadows fall.
Night of Africa, my black night, mystical and bright, black and shining.[16]

I made myself the poet of the world. The white man had found a poetry in which there was nothing poetic. The soul of the white man was corrupted, and, as I was told by a friend who was a teacher in the United States, "The presence of the Negroes beside the whites is in a way an insurance policy on humanness. When the whites feel that they have become too mechanized, they turn to the men of color and ask them for a little human sustenance." At last I had been recognized, I was no longer a zero.

I had soon to change my tune. Only momentarily at a loss, the white man explained to me that, genetically, I represented a stage of development: "Your properties have been exhausted by us. We have had earth mystics such as you will never approach. Study our history and you will see how far this fusion has gone." Then I had the feeling that I was repeating a cycle. My originality had been torn out of me. I wept a long time, and then I began to live again. But I was haunted by a galaxy of erosive stereotypes: the Negro's *sui generis* odor . . . the Negro's *sui generis* good nature . . . the Negro's *sui generis* gullibility. . . .

I had tried to flee myself through my kind, but the whites had thrown themselves on me and hamstrung me. I tested the limits of my essence; beyond all doubt there was not much of it left. It was here that I made my most remarkable discovery. Properly speaking, this discovery was a rediscovery.

I rummaged frenetically through all the antiquity of the black man. What I found there took away my breath. In his book *L'abolition de l'esclavage* Schoelcher presented us with compelling arguments. Since then, Frobenius, Westermann, Delafosse—all of them white—had joined the chorus: Ségou, Djenné, cities of more than a hundred thousand people; accounts of learned blacks (doctors of theology who went to Mecca to interpret the Koran). All of that, exhumed from the past, spread with its insides out, made it possible for me to find a valid historic place. The white man was wrong, I was not a primitive, not even a half-man, I belonged to a race that had already been working in gold and silver two thousand years ago. And too there was something else, something else that the white man could not understand. Listen:

What sort of men were these, then, who had been torn away from their families, their countries, their religions, with a savagery unparalleled in history?

Gentle men, polite, considerate, unquestionably superior to those who tortured them—that collection of adventurers who slashed and violated and spat on Africa to make the stripping of her the easier.

The men they took away knew how to build houses, govern empires, erect cities, cultivate fields, mine for metals, weave cotton, forge steel.

---

[16]Léopold Senghor, *Chants d'ombre* (Paris: Editions du Seuil, 1945).

Their religion had its own beauty, based on mystical connections with the founder of the city. Their customs were pleasing, built on unity, kindness, respect for age.

No coercion, only mutual assistance, the joy of living, a free acceptance of discipline.

Order—Earnestness—Poetry and Freedom.

From the untroubled private citizen to the almost fabulous leader there was an unbroken chain of understanding and trust. No science? Indeed yes; but also, to protect them from fear, they possessed great myths in which 'the most subtle observation and the most daring imagination were balanced and blended. No art? They had their magnificent sculpture, in which human feeling erupted so unrestrained yet always followed the obsessive laws of rhythm in its organization of the major elements of a material called upon to capture, in order to redistribute, the most secret forces of the universe. . . .[17]

Monuments in the very heart of Africa? Schools? Hospitals? Not a single good burgher of the twentieth century, no Durand, no Smith, no Brown even suspects that such things existed in Africa before the Europeans came. . . .

But Schoelcher reminds us of their presence, discovered by Caillé, Mollien, the Cander brothers. And, though he nowhere reminds us that when the Portuguese landed on the banks of the Congo in 1498, they found a rich and flourishing state there and that the courtiers of Ambas were dressed in robes of silk and brocade, at least he knows that Africa had brought itself up to a juridical concept of the state, and he is aware, living in the very flood of imperialism, that European civilization, after all, is only one more civilization among many—and not the most merciful.[18]

I put the white man back into his place; growing bolder, I jostled him and told him point-blank, "Get used to me, I am not getting used to anyone." I shouted my laughter to the stars. The white man, I could see, was resentful. His reaction time lagged interminably. . . . I had won. I was jubilant.

"Lay aside your history, your investigations of the past, and try to feel yourself into our rhythm. In a society such as ours, industrialized to the highest degree, dominated by scientism, there is no longer room for your sensitivity. One must be tough if one is to be allowed to live. What matters now is no longer playing the game of the world but subjugating it with integers and atoms. Oh, certainly, I will be told, now and then when we are worn out by our lives in big buildings, we will turn to you as we do to our children—to the innocent, the ingenuous, the spontaneous. We will turn to you as to the childhood of the world. You are so real in your life—so funny, that is. Let us run away for a little while from our ritualized, polite civilization and let us relax, bend to those heads, those adorably expressive faces. In a way, you reconcile us with ourselves."

Thus my unreason was countered with reason, my reason with "real reason." Every hand was a losing hand for me. I analyzed my heredity. I made a complete audit of my ailment. I wanted to be typically Negro—it was no longer possible. I wanted to be white—that was a joke. And, when I tried, on the level of ideas and intellectual activity, to reclaim my negritude, it was snatched away from me. Proof was presented that my effort was only a term in the dialectic:

But there is something more important: The Negro, as we have said, creates an anti-racist racism for himself. In no sense does he wish to rule the world: He seeks the abolition of all ethnic privileges, wherever they come from; he asserts his solidarity with the oppressed of all colors. At once the subjective, existential, ethnic idea of *negritude* "passes," as Hegel puts it,

---

[17]Aimé Césaire, Introduction to Victor Schoelcher, *Esclavage et colonisation* (Paris: Presses Universitaires de France, 1948), p. 7.

[18]Ibid., p. 8.

into the objective, positive, exact idea of *proletariat*. "For Césaire," Senghor says, "the white man is the symbol of capital as the Negro is that of labor. . . . Beyond the black-skinned men of his race it is the battle of the world proletariat that is his song."

That is easy to say, but less easy to think out. And undoubtedly it is no coincidence that the most ardent poets of negritude are at the same time militant Marxists.

But that does not prevent the idea of race from mingling with that of class: The first is concrete and particular, the second is universal and abstract; the one stems from what Jaspers calls understanding and the other from intellection; the first is the result of a psychobiological syncretism and the second is a methodical construction based on experience. In fact, negritude appears as the minor term of a dialectical progression: The theoretical and practical assertion of the supremacy of the white man is its thesis; the position of negritude as an antithetical value is the moment of negativity. But this negative moment is insufficient by itself, and the Negroes who employ it know this very well; they know that it is intended to prepare the synthesis or realization of the human in a society without races. Thus negritude is the root of its own destruction, it is a transition and not a conclusion, a means and not an ultimate end.[19]

When I read that page, I felt that I had been robbed of my last chance. I said to my friends, "The generation of the younger black poets has just suffered a blow that can never be forgiven." Help had been sought from a friend of the colored peoples, and that friend had found no better response than to point out the relativity of what they were doing. For once, that born Hegelian had forgotten that consciousness has to lose itself in the night of the absolute, the only condition to attain to consciousness of self. In opposition to rationalism, he summoned up the negative side, but he forgot that this negativity draws its worth from an almost substantive absoluteness. A consciousness committed to experience is ignorant, has to be ignorant, of the essences and the determinations of its being.

Orphée Noir is a date in the intellectualization of the *experience* of being black. And Sartre's mistake was not only to seek the source of the source but in a certain sense to block that source:

Will the source of Poetry be dried up? Or will the great black flood, in spite of everything, color the sea into which it pours itself? It does not matter: Every age has its own poetry; in every age the circumstances of history choose a nation, a race, a class to take up the torch by creating situations that can be expressed or transcended only through Poetry; sometimes the poetic impulse coincides with the revolutionary impulse, and sometimes they take different courses. Today let us hail the turn of history that will make it possible for the black men to utter "the great Negro cry with a force that will shake the pillars of the world" (Césaire).[20]

And so it is not I who make a meaning for myself, but it is the meaning that was already there, pre-existing, waiting for me. It is not out of my bad nigger's misery, my bad nigger's teeth, my bad nigger's hunger that I will shape a torch with which to burn down the world, but it is the torch that was already there, waiting for that turn of history.

In terms of consciousness, the black consciousness is held out as an absolute density, as filled with itself, a stage preceding any invasion, any abolition of the ego by desire. Jean-Paul Sartre, in this work, has destroyed black zeal. In opposition to historical becoming, there had always been the unforeseeable. I needed to lose myself completely in negritude. One day, perhaps, in the depths of that unhappy romanticism. . . .

In any case I *needed* not to know. This struggle, this new decline had to take on an aspect of completeness. Nothing is more unwelcome than the commonplace: "You'll change, my boy; I was like that too when I was young . . . you'll see, it will all pass."

The dialectic that brings necessity into the foundation of my freedom drives me out of myself. It shatters my unreflected position. Still in terms of consciousness, black

---

[19]Jean-Paul Sartre, *Orphée Noir*, preface to *Anthologie de la nouvelle poésie nègre et malgache* (Paris: Presses Universitaires de France, 1948), pp. xl ff.

[20]Ibid., p. xliv.

consciousness is immanent in its own eyes. I am not a potentiality of something, I am wholly what I am. I do not have to look for the universal. No probability has any place inside me. My Negro consciousness does not hold itself out as a lack. It *is*. It is its own follower.

But, I will be told, your statements show a misreading of the processes of history. Listen then:

> Africa I have kept your memory Africa
> you are inside me
> Like the splinter in the wound
> like a guardian fetish in the center of the village
> make me the stone in your sling
> make my mouth the lips of your wound
> make my knees the broken pillars of your abasement
> AND YET
> I want to be of your race alone
> workers peasants of all lands . . .
> . . . white worker in Detroit black peon in Alabama
> uncountable nation in capitalist slavery
> destiny ranges us shoulder to shoulder
> repudiating the ancient maledictions of blood taboos
> we roll away the ruins of our solitudes
> If the flood is a frontier
> we will strip the gully of its endless
> covering flow
> If the Sierra is a frontier
> we will smash the jaws of the volcanoes
> upholding the Cordilleras
> and the plain will be the parade ground of the dawn
> where we regroup our forces sundered
> by the deceits of our masters
> As the contradiction among the features
> creates the harmony of the face
> we proclaim the oneness of the suffering
> and the revolt
> of all the peoples on all the face of the earth
> and we mix the mortar of the age of brotherhood
> out of the dust of idols.[21]

Exactly, we will reply, Negro experience is not a whole, for there is not merely *one* Negro, there are *Negroes*. What a difference, for instance, in this other poem:

> The white man killed my father
> Because my father was proud
> The white man raped my mother
> Because my mother was beautiful
> The white man wore out my brother in the hot sun of the roads
> Because my brother was strong
> Then the white man came to me
> His hands red with blood
> Spat his contempt into my black face
> Out of his tyrant's voice:
> "Hey boy, a basin, a towel, water."[22]

---

[21]Jacques Roumain, "Bois d'Ebène," Prelude, in *Anthologie de la nouvelle poésie nègre et malgache,* p. 113.
[22]David Diop, "Le temps du martyre," in ibid., p. 174.

Or this other one:

> My brother with teeth that glisten at the compliments of hypocrites
> My brother with gold-rimmed spectacles
> Over eyes that turn blue at the sound of the Master's voice
> My poor brother in dinner jacket with its silk lapels
> Clucking and whispering and strutting through the drawing rooms of Condescension
> How pathetic you are
> The sun of your native country is nothing more now than a shadow
> On your composed civilized face
> And your grandmother's hut
> Brings blushes into cheeks made white by years of abasement and *Mea culpa*
> But when regurgitating the flood of lofty empty words
> Like the load that presses on your shoulders
> You walk again on the rough red earth of Africa
> These words of anguish will state the rhythm of your uneasy gait
> I feel so alone, so alone here![23]

From time to time one would like to stop. To state reality is a wearing task. But, when one has taken it into one's head to try to express existence, one runs the risk of finding only the nonexistent. What is certain is that, at the very moment when I was trying to grasp my own being, Sartre, who remained The Other, gave me a name and thus shattered my last illusion. While I was saying to him

> My negritude is neither a tower nor a cathedral,
> it thrusts into the red flesh of the sun,
> it thrusts into the burning flesh of the sky,
> it hollows through the dense dismay of its own pillar of patience . . .

while I was shouting that, in the paroxysm of my being and my fury, he was reminding me that my blackness was only a minor term. In all truth, in all truth I tell you, my shoulders slipped out of the framework of the world, my feet could no longer feel the touch of the ground. Without a Negro past, without a Negro future, it was impossible for me to live my Negrohood. Not yet white, no longer wholly black, I was damned. Jean-Paul Sartre had forgotten that the Negro suffers in his body quite differently from the white white man.[24] Between the white man and me the connection was irrevocably one of transcendence.[25]

But the constancy of my love had been forgotten. I defined myself as an absolute intensity of beginning. So I took up my negritude, and with tears in my eyes I put its machinery together again. What had been broken to pieces was rebuilt, reconstructed by the intuitive lianas of my hands.

My cry grew more violent: I am a Negro, I am a Negro, I am a Negro. . . .

And there was my poor brother—living out his neurosis to the extreme and finding himself paralyzed:

THE NEGRO: I can't, ma'am.
LIZZIE: Why not?
THE NEGRO: I can't shoot white folks.

---

[23]David Diop, "Le Renégat."

[24]Though Sartre's speculations on the existence of The Other may be correct (to the extent, we must remember, to which *Being and Nothingness* describes an alienated consciousness), their application to a black consciousness proves fallacious. That is because the white man is not only The Other but also the master, whether real or imaginary.

[25]In the sense in which the word is used by Jean Wahl in *Existence humaine et transcendance* (Neuchâtel: La Baconnière, 1944).

LIZZIE: Really! That would bother them, wouldn't it?

THE NEGRO: They're white folks, ma'am.

LIZZIE: So what? Maybe they got a right to bleed you like a pig just because they're white?

THE NEGRO: But they're white folks.

A feeling of inferiority? No, a feeling of nonexistence. Sin is Negro as virtue is white. All those white men in a group, guns in their hands, cannot be wrong. I am guilty. I do not know of what, but I know that I am no good.

THE NEGRO: That's how it goes, ma'am. That's how it always goes with white folks.

LIZZIE: You too? You feel guilty?

THE NEGRO: Yes, ma'am.[26]

It is Bigger Thomas—he is afraid, he is terribly afraid. He is afraid, but of what is he afraid? Of himself. No one knows yet who he is, but he knows that fear will fill the world when the world finds out. And when the world knows, the world always expects something of the Negro. He is afraid lest the world know, he is afraid of the fear that the world would feel if the world knew. Like that old woman on her knees who begged me to tie her to her bed:

"I just know, Doctor: Any minute that thing will take hold of me."

"What thing?"

"The wanting to kill myself. Tie me down, I'm afraid."

In the end, Bigger Thomas acts. To put an end to his tension, he acts, he responds to the world's anticipation.[27]

So it is with the character in *If He Hollers Let Him Go*[28]—who does precisely what he did not want to do. That big blonde who was always in his way, weak, sensual, offered, open, fearing (desiring) rape, became his mistress in the end.

The Negro is a toy in the white man's hands; so, in order to shatter the hellish cycle, he explodes. I cannot go to a film without seeing myself. I wait for me. In the interval, just before the film starts, I wait for me. The people in the theater are watching me, examining me, waiting for me. A Negro groom is going to appear. My heart makes my head swim.

The crippled veteran of the Pacific war says to my brother, "Resign yourself to your color the way I got used to my stump; we're both victims."[29]

Nevertheless with all my strength I refuse to accept that amputation. I feel in myself a soul as immense as the world, truly a soul as deep as the deepest of rivers, my chest has the power to expand without limit. I am a master and I am advised to adopt the humility of the cripple. Yesterday, awakening to the world, I saw the sky turn upon itself utterly and wholly. I wanted to rise, but the disemboweled silence fell back upon me, its wings paralyzed. Without responsibility, straddling Nothingness and Infinity, I began to weep.

Helen Gilbert and Joanne Tompkins are both well known for their studies of postcolonial theater and drama, and teach at the University of Queensland, Australia. In this selection from their recent book Post-Colonial Drama, *Gilbert and Tompkins discuss the ways in which the body can be made to represent the impact of gender, racial, or sexualizing ideologies, and so become a site for social critique in performance.*

HELEN GILBERT AND JOANNE TOMPKINS,

from
Post-Colonial Drama
(1996)

---

[26]Jean-Paul Sartre, *The Respectful Prostitute*, in *Three Plays* (New York: Knopf, 1949), pp. 189, 191. Originally, *La Putain respectueuse* (Paris: Gallimard, 1947). See also *Home of the Brave*, a film by Mark Robson.

[27]Richard Wright, *Native Son* (New York: Harper, 1940).

[28]By Chester Himes (Garden City: Doubleday, 1945).

[29]*Home of the Brave*, op. cit.

> The body is the inscribed surface of events (traced by language and dissolved by ideas), the locus of a dissociated self (adopting the illusion of substantial unity), and a volume of disintegration.
>
> —Foucault (1977): 148

Foucault's definition of the body omits a crucial performative fact: the body also *moves*. In the theatre, the actor's body is the major physical symbol; it is distinguished from other such symbols by its capacity to offer a multifarious complex of meanings. The body signifies through both its appearance and its actions. As well as indicating such categories as race and gender, the performing body can also express place and narrative through skilful mime and/or movement. Moreover, it interacts with all other stage signifiers—notably costume, set, and dialogue—and, crucially, with the audience. It is not surprising, then, that the body functions as one of the most charged sites of theatrical representation.

The colonised subject's body, as Elleke Boehmer explains, has been an object of the coloniser's fascination and repulsion (and, in effect, possession) in sexual, pseudo-scientific, and political terms:

> In colonial representation, exclusion or suppression can often literally be seen as 'embodied'. From the point of view of the colonizer specifically, fears and curiosities, sublimated fascinations with the strange or the 'primitive', are expressed in concrete physical and anatomical images. . . . [T]he Other is cast as corporeal, carnal, untamed, instinctual, raw, and therefore also open to mastery, available for use, for husbandry, for numbering, branding, cataloging, description or possession.

Paying attention to the body can be a highly useful (and even essential) strategy for reconstructing post-colonial subjectivity because imperialist discourse has been both insidious and persuasive in its construction of the colonised subject as an inscribed object of knowledge. As Elizabeth Grosz argues, the body is never simply a passive object upon which regimes of power are played out:

> If the body is the strategic target of systems of codification, supervision and constraint, it is also because the body and its energies and capacities exert an uncontrollable, unpredictable threat to a regular, systematic mode of social organisation. As well as being the site of knowledge-power, the body is thus a site of *resistance*, for it exerts a recalcitrance, and always entails the possibility of a counter-strategic reinscription, for it is capable of being self-marked, self-represented in alternative ways.

The ways in which the reinscription and self-representation of colonised bodies translate into performative strategies is obviously a key issue for post-colonial theatre. Hence, current movements towards cultural decolonisation involve not just a verbal/textual counter-discourse but a reviewing of the body and its signifying practices. Whereas narrative writing tends to erase the gender and race of its authors and protagonists through its production as an artefact of predominantly western cultures, performance centralises the physical and socio-cultural specificities of its participants. It follows that post-colonial theatre (much like feminist theatre) finds in the body more than mere 'actor function' or 'actor vehicle'. The body's ability to move, cover up, reveal itself, and even 'fracture' on stage provides it with many possible sites for decolonisation.

In general, the post-colonial body disrupts the constrained space and signification left to it by the colonisers and becomes a site for resistant inscription. For instance, the Kathakali actor's stylised facial expressions signify the history of specific Indian acting traditions and communicate the carefully preserved systems of meaning through the actor's body. The colonial subject's body contests its stereotyping and representation by others to insist on self-representation by its physical presence on the stage. Corporeal signifiers quickly become politicised when a black actor appears in a traditionally 'white' role, or when a West Indian cast stages, say, a Shakespearian play; such choices, as well as colour-blind casting, contribute to the development of an identity independent from the imposed colonial one of inadequacy, subordination, and often barbarity. Because the body is open to multifarious inscriptions which produce it as a dialogic, ambivalent, and unstable signifier rather than a single, independent, and discrete entity, it is not surprising that the production of some sort of personal or cultural subjectivity via the body is complex indeed.

The post-colonial subject is often preoccupied with refusing colonially determined labels and definitions, especially those which operate in the name of race and gender. Part of the project of redefining staged identity is to affix the *colonised*'s choice of signification to the body rather than to maintain the limited tropes traditionally assigned to it. This oppositional process of *embodiment* whereby the colonised creates his/her own subjectivity ascribes more flexible, culturally laden, and multivalent delineations to the body, rather than circumscribing it within an imposed, imperialist calculation of otherness. The post-colonial stage offers opportunities to recuperate the colonised subject's body—especially when it has been maimed or otherwise rendered 'incomplete'—and to transform its signification and its subjectivity. This chapter explores the process of recuperation by examining some of the basic performative elements of the post-colonial body: how it looks, what it does, how it is seen, and, most importantly, how it presents itself.

As *visual* markers of 'identity', race and gender are particularly significant in theatrical contexts even if their connotations are sometimes highly unstable. It is crucial to remember, however, that such markers are inscribed on the body through discourse—visual, verbal, or otherwise—rather than simply being unmediated or objectively given. In other words, the perceived (constructed) binary categories of male/female and white/black are never merely biologically determined but are also historically and ideologically conditioned. Moreover, as our earlier discussion of various feminisms indicates, race and gender are distinct, albeit sometimes intersecting and/or overlapping, factors which cannot be collapsed under the conceptual umbrella of marginalisation. It follows, then, that there can be neither an unproblematically essentialised 'black', 'female', or any other kind of body nor, conversely, can there be a universalised body which categorically avoids these markers of difference. If post-colonial theory has long rejected the idealised undifferentiated body of the other that is characteristic of imperialist discourse, representational practice—especially in largely iconic art-forms such as theatre—still faces the problem of how to avoid essentialist constructions of race and gender while recognising the irreducible specificity of their impact on subject formation. One possible solution is to conceptualise all markers of identity/difference as partial, provisional, and likely to change depending upon the context or the signifying system in which they operate at any particular time. This notion avoids a single (biological) origin for race or gender but leaves open the possibility of what Spivak calls 'strategic essentialism'—the foregrounding of 'pure' difference for particular political purposes.

RACE

Since one of the key features of colonialism has been the exertion of European authority over non-white peoples, it is not surprising that an emphasis on race is widespread in post-colonial drama, particularly when the projected audience includes a high proportion of white (or otherwise dominant) viewers. Two parallel, if apparently contradictory, strategies are evident: to emphasise racial difference as part of a 'scrupulously visible political interest' (Spivak) designed to recuperate marginalised subjects, or, alternatively, to dismantle all racial categories by showing their constructedness. Some plays adopt both of these approaches simultaneously, a manoeuvre which often results in a dialectical tension that further destabilises 'race' as a signifying code. A case in point is Chi and Kuckles's *Bran*

Nue Dae, which highlights the presence of a large cast of Australian Aboriginal characters/ actors while at the same time insisting that race is less a colour than an attitude. In this context, it becomes artistically plausible that even several 'white' characters (played by non-Aborigines) eventually discover their Aboriginality. The play participates in current debates in Australia about the construction of Aboriginal identity and notions of authenticity based primarily on skin colour.

The physical stage presence of black, indigenous, or otherwise 'coloured' actors cannot be undervalued in discussing the counter-discursive possibilities of the body in performance, even if what constitutes race is neither fixed nor objectively measurable. On one level, staging the visibility of imperialism's racial other is in itself a subversive act since Anglo-European theatre has a long history of excluding non-white actors while maintaining *representations* of racial difference, usually constructed through costume, make-up, and/or mask. The Othello of Shakespeare's day, for example, was played by a white actor who 'blacked up' and donned a curly-haired wig, a tradition which varied little for centuries. Not just a trope in popular entertainment (epitomised by Al Jolson's blackface performances in the early part of this century), blackface was used by Sir Laurence Olivier's version of *Othello* even as recently as the 1960s. When racially marked characters are played in this way, the resistance potential of the fictionalised black/coloured body is compromised by the 'wayward signification' of the actor's whiteness (Goldie). Matching the race (and/or gender) of the actor with that of the character does not mean, however, that the performing body completely escapes the web of imperial inscription. Rather, the body is inevitably 'read' through multiple codes and contexts and shaped not only by the narrative structures of a play itself but also by its audience. Historically, this has meant that when the nonwhite actor performed on western stages, his/her body generally carried a kind of mystique that both heightened and detracted from its significance. Another mode of *mis*representation consistent with colonial attempts to figure racial others as inferior and/or subordinate was thus conventionalised.

Whereas much western culture constructs the female body on stage as a passive to-be-looked-at object rather than as an active subject, the racially distinct body is often designed to be *overlooked* (in two senses of the word: to be examined more fully than other signifiers as an object of curiosity *and* to be rendered invisible as an object of disregard). Until quite recently, many post-colonial plays devised by whites fell into this representational trap by depicting sentimentalised or exoticised versions of racial difference. Terry Goldie's study of settler drama in Canada, Australia, and New Zealand demonstrates the ways in which images of the indigene have been circumscribed by a semiotic field that is limited to seven signifiers: orality, mysticism, violence, nature, sexuality, historicity, and an imitation of indigenous 'forms' of communication. Often moved on or off stage to create a particular atmosphere and/or elicit laughter, indigenous characters have functioned as stage properties, as fragments of the setting, and, at times, as foils against which the normative values of white society can be defined. Likewise, roles for blacks in the wider field of western drama have been constituted within racist discourses, with perhaps even more emphasis on their supposed violence and sexuality. In these prescribed spaces, imperialism's colonised subject is denied its full humanity; it performs an imposed representational function rather than being a focal point in its own right. And while some roles can be subverted in performance, there is little scope in such plays for significant interrogation of dominant assumptions about race.

When indigenous and black playwrights depict themselves on stage, the body is one of the first theatrical elements to take on new iconic possibilities. One text that manipulates the body's signification for political purposes is Monique Mojica's *Princess Pocahontas and the Blue Spots,* which deconstructs the semiotic field of 'Indianness'—to use Daniel

Francis's concept of the term (1992)—by staging its common inscriptions in juxtaposition to alternative (and generally more empowering) expressions of native North American subjectivity. Conflicting images/identities are held in tension through the performing body of Contemporary Woman #1, who plays (with) the white-defined stereotypes presented, as well as transforming herself into various native characters. In this way, Mojica provides a critical rereading of the ways in which indigenous women have characteristically been coded and constrained by North and South American history, culture, and literature. The women's bodies contort to create images of imposed signifying codes; they also depict the scenery, including a volcano, thereby critiquing the conventional use of indigenous bodies to suggest the geographical landscape and/or to provide an apparently authentic atmosphere. The play employs an overabundance of clichéd Hollywood and explorer/pioneer depictions of the 'Indian' in order to demonstrate their emptiness as representations: the sheer number of represented 'Indian' and 'native' bodies destabilises the power of the imposed depictions. Such figures as the Cigar Store Squaw, the Storybook Princess, and Princess Buttered-on-Both-Sides are effectively meaningless, having been overdetermined by and within white discourse. More specifically, Pocahontas, Christianised and re-named Lady Rebecca, is 'stuck [and] girdled' in the costume of the 'good Indian' even if it is clearly an uncomfortable fit. These 'museum exhibits' contrast sharply with the two contemporary women and with others recuperated from the margins of imperial representation: Matoaka (the younger persona of Pocahontas), Malinche, and the three Métis women who demand that their stories be told. The Storybook Princess and the Cigar Store Squaw are predictably wooden in personality and in their movements on the stage, whereas Matoaka and Malinche, in particular, embody sexualities that cannot be contained within the virgin/whore paradigm imposed upon them by the British and the Spaniards.

Mojica's interest in countering the semiotic codes of cinema and television is shared by other native Canadian writers such as Margo Kane, Daniel David Moses, and Tomson Highway, all of whom have dramatised characters/events that rework the stereotype of the Hollywood Indian. In Australia, the project of reconstructing an indigenous subjectivity is slightly different in so far as Aborigines have been less often mythologised in/through popular representation than simply ignored, especially in visual media. In some ways, then, the conventional Aboriginal body is underdetermined because of its systematic erasure, rather than overdetermined as a result of repeated exposure. This is not to suggest that Aborigines escape the designation of 'other', but to argue that this particular other is often less well-delineated in imperial discourse than is the 'Indian'. Nevertheless, Aboriginal inscriptions of corporeality—as opposed to European constructions of Aboriginality or a generic and even less specific otherness—function to embody in Aborigines on stage a different, more culturally accurate, subjectivity. Jack Davis's plays address the blind spots of settler history and literature on a number of levels, bringing the black body into acute visibility via individual characters (often dancers) and also through group interaction (especially across colour lines). *Kullark,* for example, inverts imperialism's racial norms in a comic depiction of first contact when Mitjitjiroo responds to Captain Stirling's proffered hand by rubbing its skin vigorously to see if the white stain can be removed. This gesture, along with the Aborigines' astonishment at the strange appearance of the Europeans, denaturalises the white body as the dominant sign of humanity. In a related manoeuvre, the play points to the *in*humanity of the invaders when they decapitate Yagan and skin him in order to remove his tribal markings for a souvenir. Here, Davis suggests that the mutilated black body functions within the colonising culture as a fetishised object. His overall project is to reinstate the corporeal presence of the Aborigines in history—and, on a metatheatrical level, in theatre—at the same time as he details the colonisers' attempts to annihilate all signs of difference. Reference to such atrocities does not mean, however, that *Kullark* simply stereotypes its characters according to race, reassigning the connotations of 'black' and 'white' in the process; rather, this play, like Davis's other works, carefully stages the misunderstandings brought about by discourses of racial otherness in a context where it is possible for conceptual gaps to be bridged. . . .

GENDER The South African plays discussed demonstrate the constructedness of racial categories at the same time as they attempt to (re)claim strategic, if negotiable, race-inflected identities. For many post-colonial dramatists, particularly women, a parallel project is to recuperate female subjectivities while showing that gender is an ideology mapped across the body in and through representation. It seems, however, that the imperative is less to deconstruct the category of female (or male) than to intervene in the discourses that naturalise gender hierarchies. This pattern is possibly related to the perceived fixity of the gender binary. White/black classifications are quickly broken down by racial hybridity—indeed the threat of miscegenation is precisely that it produces visible signs of the permeability of racial boundaries. Gender classifications, in contrast, most often admit androgyny as merely as hypothetical category which can be dissolved into male *or* female when the biological markers of sex are known. Some writers and practitioners do share Anglo-American feminism's interest in destabilising gender binaries, whether through 'sex-radical' performance or through visually recorded (transvestite) bodies, but most are more concerned with demarcating areas of women's subjugation under imperialism. Accordingly, gender is less likely to function alone as a category of discrimination in post-colonial plays than in combination with other factors such as race, class, and/or cultural background. An additional factor complicating the delineation of a gender-specific body politics is the metaphorical link between woman and the land, a powerful trope in imperial discourse and one which is reinforced, consciously or not, in much post-colonial drama, particularly by male writers. In some instances, women's bodies are not only exploited by the colonisers but also reappropriated by the colonised patriarchy as part of a political agenda which may not fully serve the interests of the women in question.

Rape is a prominent signifier in a number of plays, particularly in countries where settlers' annexation of so-called 'unoccupied territories' disrupted not only the culture but also the livelihoods of indigenous peoples. Both native and non-native dramatists have featured inter-racial rape as an analogue for the colonisers' violation of the land, and also for related forms of economic and political exploitation. Often such representations are designed to reveal less about the experiences of the oppressed than about the rape mentality of the oppressors. In the chilling final moments of Canadian George Ryga's *The Ecstasy of Rita Joe,* for example, the rape and murder of the central protagonist by three white men provides a graphic depiction of the widespread brutality of the colonial/judicial system. This play figures Rita Joe as the site on and through which the disciplinary inscriptions of imperial patriarchy are played out as her body is progressively marked by capture, assault, and sexual penetration. Politically, she functions less as an individual than as an emblem of native cultures in Canada; hence, her death signals the grim triumph of the imperial project. As Gary Boire argues, Ryga's text can be read as a 'Foucaultian allegory' which foregrounds the sexually fragmented body of Rita Joe in order to chart the systems of power that instigate and maintain the settler/invader society's dominance over indigenous groups.

Depending on how they are staged, theatrical images of sexual violence can have more than merely illustrative functions; in some instances, they also challenge the voyeuristic gaze of the white spectator, inviting him/her to admit complicity in that violence. Janis Balodis's *Too Young for Ghosts* critiques white invasion of indigenous land/culture in Australia in a complex 'cross-over' scene in which the same actors play Aboriginal and Latvian women almost simultaneously. The scene collapses the rapes of two Aboriginal women with the sexual assault of their Latvian counterparts in a displaced persons camp after World War Two. This visual conflation—achieved through doubling roles and overlaying theatrical time and space—is a performative technique intended to elicit both empathy for the Aboriginal women and outrage against the colonial regime, here constructed as a more local 'war' for control over native land/bodies. Throughout the composite rape scene, the audience's perspective is further manipulated by the presence of Karl, whose position as a callous observer reminds the viewers of their own non-intervention. By collapsing chronological and spatial frameworks, Balodis is able to use the bodies of white characters/actors to stand in for black ones without appropriating Aboriginal figures in service of a narrative about migrant experience. Instead, by refusing to display the violation of the black women, the performance text frustrates the libidinal economy of inter-racial rape while still harnessing this trope's metaphorical power to express the colonisers' attitudes and actions. Using different strategies for a similar effect, Dorothy Hewett's *The Man From Mukinupin* (1979) stages the 'rape' of Aboriginal women through a savagely ironic song which details the settlers' attempts to conquer the recalcitrant landscape, a project explicitly figured as the male penetration of female space. Hewett's call for the doubling of her one Aboriginal character with the female heroine, presumably played by a white actor, effectively highlights the ways in which all women have been discursively merged with each other and with the landscape.

The treatment of rape in texts by native dramatists who recognise the significant intersections of race and gender takes on slightly different inflections, especially when local mythologies inform the wider play. Tomson Highway's *The Rez Sisters,* for example, stages rape as a violation not only of the land but also of the very spirit of native culture. In a brief but visually haunting scene, the mentally disabled Zhaboonigan reveals that a gang of white boys penetrated her vagina with a screwdriver. While she details the event with the casual disinterest of a child who has only limited understanding of what has happened, the Ojibway trickster spirit, Nanabush, *embodies* her trauma by performing the 'agonising contortions' of the rape victim. Zhaboonigan's assault thus accrues wider significance, though her own body remains relatively unmarked because the trickster absorbs and transforms her experience. Moreover, the conventional gender paradigms of such a scene are somewhat complicated by the fact that Nanabush—a spirit who adopts the forms of either and both genders simultaneously—is played by a male dancer. In what is to some extent a mirror image of *The Rez Sisters'* rape scene, Highway's controversial companion play, *Dry Lips Oughta Move to Kapuskasing,* enacts a native youth's sexual assault of a young native woman, Patsy Pegahmagahbow. That the rape is performed with a crucifix by a victim of foetal alcohol syndrome suggests that Christian imperialism is at least partly responsible for the current schism between native men and women. On a performative level, this scene also points to the desecration of indigenous land/culture by the colonising forces, a resonance achieved in a series of stylised movements in which Dickie Bird Halked repeatedly stabs his crucifix into the earth while Nanabush, here played by a woman, lifts her skirt to reveal the blood which slowly spreads down her legs. In *Dry Lips,* Nanabush and Patsy are embodied by the same ever-transforming actor who variously functions as the *idea* of the 'real' women referred to in the play *and* as the female trickster who again absorbs Patsy's experience. Although Highway has been accused of displaying sexism and gratuitous violence, it could be argued that *Dry Lips,* like *The Rez Sisters,* actually refuses the power of rape by subsuming it within the mythological frameworks invoked, since Nanabush is, above all, the great survivor and healer. Once again, the trickster's body—operating in this text as a sign of native women/culture/land that refigures the imperial collapsing of these categories—absorbs and transforms the forces which would leave it vulnerable and degraded. After the rape, Nanabush is visibly marked but still all-powerful as she reappears in various guises throughout the rest of the dream play, and then enters the 'real' action in a final triumphant moment with the baby that foreshadows a hopeful future for the Rez.

As all these images of sexual violence suggest, women's bodies often function in post-colonial theatre as the spaces on and through which larger territorial or cultural battles are being fought. In a similar fashion, representations of fertility, pregnancy, and motherhood frequently take on political inflections, a fact which is not surprising, given that imperialism's will to power over its (female) subjects also extended to the control of many aspects of reproduction. The slave trade, in which women were bought and sold for their 'breeding' capacities, is the most obvious example of a political economy based on the institutionalised commodification of the female body. Dennis Scott takes up this particular subject in one of the historical scenes of *An Echo in the Bone,* foregrounding the processes by which slavery reduced the female body to its sexual and reproductive functions. The setting is an early nineteenth-century auctioneer's office where three slaves are being inspected by a regular customer while the black middleman lists their attributes in turn, lingering over the two women:

> Now this—*(To* BRIGIT.*)* please make note, the wide hips, the breasts just fulling out. No off-spring yet. Do you wish to see proof of virginity—perhaps you'll wish to see for yourself—indeed, that's hardly necessary, we have a long association of trust, don't we, sir. Calves well muscled, exceedingly well turned, you will notice. . . . The other. . . . Here is the doctor's certificate, equally untouched. Notice the nipples. Fire in this one sir, you'll forgive my saying so. But the clear eyes show how easily she can be taught. All kinds of things.

With their bodies anatomised by the imperial gaze, the women are positioned as merchandise and are thus denied all sense of subjectivity. At the same time, they are constructed as sex objects *and* as passive children ripe for the expert tutelage (read exploitation) of the white master. Further degradation follows when Stone puts on a glove to examine the 'goods', inspecting one of the women's teeth and then running his hand up between her thighs, as if at a livestock sale. While the male slave is also commodified, he is not described in corporeal terms; indeed, his best selling feature is that he 'can read, write and reckon like a schoolmaster'. This scene exemplifies gender's impact on slavery: women's bodies are marked for consumption within imperialism's particular brand of patriarchy. The added focus on the middleman's ingratiating 'sales talk' also gives weight to the theory that in patriarchal systems women function in a symbolic exchange which cements the relationships between men—in this case between the white slave owner and the black agent who acts as proxy for the buyer.

Whereas the bodies of black women were commandeered in some colonies to breed a slave class to fulfil the demands of imperialism's labour market, white women's bodies were often appropriated to preserve the racial (and moral) integrity of the ruling class. In Africa and India, as well as in the Caribbean, the colonial woman/wife was expected, indeed compelled, to offer her sexual, social, and reproductive labours in the service of the Empire. Where the goal was settlement rather than rule, white women were even more crucial to the imperial project because of the imperative to (re)populate newly conquered lands. Jill Shearer's quasi-historical play, *Catherine* (1978), demonstrates how the body of the Australian settler woman functioned as part of the physical terrain upon which colonial expansion was mapped, both literally and symbolically. A large section of this metatheatrical text details the shipment of the first convict women to Botany Bay and makes abundantly clear the fact that such 'cargo' was designed to 'balance the imbalance' of the colony—that is, to prevent the male settlers' deviant sexual behaviour (with indigenous women or other men) and to provide progeny for the successful peopling of the nation. The main character, Catherine, becomes pregnant by the ship's surgeon but will not be allowed to keep her child, who has been earmarked as the first of a new generation of Australians whose ignominious heritage must be suppressed. The proposed management of Catherine's pregnancy—she will be taken care of only until she can safely deliver the baby into its father's hands—highlights the transplanted society's complete disregard for women themselves. While much of the play's narrative content critiques the convict system by exposing the ways in which it facilitated institutional control over the female body, the performance text insists on staging women's subjectivity: its structure as a play-within-a-play enables the recuperation of Catherine's body as a group of contemporary actors continually rehearse and re-interpret the fragments of her history to provide a wider comment on gender oppression.

If the settler woman's reproductive labour was harnessed in the interests of expanding the Empire, the indigenous woman's fertility presented a threat to the colonisers and was often suppressed. Eva Johnson's *Murras* (1988) addresses this issue in Australia by referring to the deliberate and systematic sterilisation of pubescent Aboriginal girls who are duped into taking medication that renders them infertile. *Murras* illustrates ways in which native women's bodies become sites of conquest in the imperial regime and how they are permanently marked by its various administrative systems, even those which purport to be benevolent. As Ruby says of her daughter in the closing scene, 'She carries the scars of the *wudjella*'s [whitefellow's] medicine'. While generally much less harmful than the enforced sterilisation detailed in *Murras,* medical management of pregnancy and childbirth also has the effect, if not the intention, of bringing the bodies of indigenous women under control. Sistren Theatre Collective's *Bellywoman Bangarang* (1978) takes up the issue of western medicine as part of its focus on teenage pregnancy in Jamaica, and attempts to reclaim the birthing process through the use of African-based rituals which emphasise female power. The play's opening image features three masked interlocking figures as the mother-woman, a healer and protector who mimes a traditional labour before transforming herself into a modern-day doctor in a movement which indicates the medicalisation of childbirth. After the stories of the four pregnant girls have been told, the mother-woman returns at the end of the play to oversee the births. She guides Marie through a difficult labour and also frees her from the ropes (symbols of fear and self-loathing) which have entangled her since her rape. Like the trickster in Highway's plays, the mother-woman is a regenerative force/spirit who disperses the effects of trauma, restoring the colonised body to physical and spiritual health.

Imperialism's attempt to exercise authority over the reproductive processes of its female subjects is sometimes paralleled with more local tendencies to reduce women to functions of gender and/or fertility. Some post-colonial drama invests female fertility with great symbolic importance but none the less subordinates women to the interests of the colonised patriarchy. In India and Africa in particular, male writers are inclined to image the land as a mother and to present the truly-fecund woman as a signifier of nationhood. Giving birth thus becomes largely metaphorical, particularly in plays concerning independence from colonial rule, where the birth of a child mirrors the birth of the new nation. This trope, also common to Caribbean drama, occurs in Michael Gilkes's *Couvade* (1972) which invokes an Amerindian birthing ritual to articulate the play's complex dream-vision of a unified post-independent Guyana. The custom of *couvade* requires the father-to-be to undertake a trial or ordeal while his wife is in labour. This tradition is designed to affirm the connection between the unborn child and its father and to ensure a successful birth. *Couvade,* recently revised for Guyana's 1993 independence anniversary celebrations, uses the ritual to chart the psychological and spiritual 'rebirth' of the protagonist, Lionel, who, along with his new-born child, becomes emblematic of the nation.

While the choice of ritual is apt for Gilkes's political vision, it shifts the focus of the birth from the woman (and the child) to the man and the community. Such paradigms figure the paternal body as much more significant than the maternal counterpart; thus, possible representations of the female post-colonial subject are often limited to the merely practical.

The maternal body is also compromised by her child in several plays when, for instance, stalled or uncertain progress towards decolonisation is figured by some kind of failure in the reproductive process. The unborn, stillborn, or otherwise incomplete child has special significance in this respect and often features in several signifying capacities: as well as representing the specific and local community, this child also acts as a site of struggle between competing political groups, especially in cultures that acknowledge the presence of ancestral spirits. The *abiku* or Half-Child in Soyinka's *A Dance of the Forests* (1960), a play about and for Nigeria's independence, represents the contemporary Nigerian world of spiritual transition, matching the political and social transition of the country. *A Dance of the Forests* is a cautionary rather than a purely celebratory play in so far as it recognises the difficulties inherent in attempts to unite the variety of forces that would impact on an independent Nigeria. The uncertain location of the *abiku* in this text also points to some of the dilemmas Nigerians would face in the following decades. Just as the *abiku* is neither living nor dead, neither body nor spirit, neither recognised nor forgotten, Nigeria's independence augurs an ambivalent future. A more hopeful treatment of the spirit child occurs in Walcott's *Ti-Jean and His Brothers* where the *bolum,* a disfigured foetus who represents the Caribbean people under the tyranny of colonialism, is eventually wrested from the clutches of the devil/plantation owner and reborn into full human life. In both of these plays, the female body is once again completely removed from the (potential) birthing process: the *abiku*'s 'mother', the Dead Woman, has no say in the life or role of her half-child while the *bolum* is restored to the human world as a result of Ti-Jean's victory over the devil. On a performative level, the incomplete child-figure simply transforms from the spirit state as if birthing itself independently of any mother figure. This process was imaged through costuming codes in one recent video production of *Ti-Jean* where the *bolum* was encased in a huge egg-shell which it broke upon 'hatching'.

Examples such as these suggest that male playwrights are primarily interested in childbirth as a symbolic, often unifying trope. Women, on the other hand, have a vested interest in refusing the gender-specific roles/images that circumscribe their representation. One of the most important achievements of recent women's post-colonial writing is its refusal to endorse the traditional signifiers of gender, particularly those linked to reproduction and mothering. When motherhood is invoked, it frequently becomes a very mixed 'blessing', much as it is in Buchi Emecheta's ironically titled novel, *The Joys of Motherhood.* Interestingly, with a few exceptions, post-colonial plays by women tend not to centralise birth, perhaps in an attempt to fracture the concept of 'Mother Earth', an idealistic notion that denies women full humanity and compromises their ability to change, to choose, and to be individuated. The Canadian playwright, Judith Thompson, *does* frequently foreground pregnancies—in *The Crackwalker* (1980), *Tornado* (1987), and *I am Yours* (1987)— but these imminent births tend not to represent a bright hope for the future. Instead, they symbolise evil or a social cancer; regardless of the baby's health, pregnancy is a metaphor for dis-ease in Thompson's work. Likewise, Sistren's *Bellywoman Bangarang* and Shearer's *Catherine* construct the pregnant body in terms of disorder and/or pathology rather than invoking traditional images of fruition.

Our discussion of the gendered body supports Ketu Katrak's argument that 'the traditions most oppressive for women [in colonised societies] are specifically located within the arena of female sexuality: fertility/infertility, motherhood and the sexual division of labour'. While women as narrative subjects are characteristically erased in imperial and patriarchal discourses, their corporeal presence is often intensified through a focus on factors such as sexuality and reproduction. This habit can be just as limiting as the neglect of gender-specific issues. As Peggy Phelan argues, 'In excessively marking the boundaries of the woman's *body,* in order to make it thoroughly visible, patriarchal culture subjects it to legal, artistic, and psychic surveillance. This, in turn, reinforces the idea that she *is* her body'. The challenge for post-colonial dramatists—both male and female—is to refuse such body politics while re-inscribing all theatricalised bodies with more enabling markers of gender. Yet, as Monique Mojica makes clear in *Princess Pocahontas and the Blue Spots,* women as a group cannot claim a collective victim status when they have been—and continue to be—complicit in the colonisation, appropriation, and denigration of other women. In this play, Contemporary Woman #1 refuses the feminist label because its collectivity tries to override her individuality as a subject who happens to be native and who happens to be female. The contemporary characters (and actors) present to their audience transforming, individuated bodies that refuse collectivity of any type if it does not also recognise the rights of the singular subject. Contemporary Woman #1 rejects the International Women's Day march until 'feminist shoes' manage to accommodate her 'wide, square, brown feet' and so allow her to 'feel the earth through their soles'. Refusing to be both the token 'Indian' and to represent all natives, this woman demands, in Gloria Anzaldua's words, 'the freedom to carve and chisel [her] own face', thus maintaining the individuality of her body *among* groups (mis)identified solely by race or gender. . . .

APPENDIX:
WRITING ABOUT DRAMA AND THEATER

✠ ✠ ✠

✠ ✠ ✠

I N MOST WAYS, WRITING ABOUT DRAMA AND THEATER IS LIKE OTHER KINDS OF analytical and argumentative writing. The best work is clear in its claims, tenacious in its analysis, rich and skillful in its discussion of detail. This section presents a brief outline of some of the techniques and practices of effective writing and some of the special concerns particular to writing about drama.

WHY WRITE?

On one level, the question, Why write? is easy to answer. You are writing because the instructor has assigned a paper as one of the requirements of the class. Most instructors assign papers—rather than merely assigning quizzes or examinations—because they believe that writing plays a unique role in teaching and in learning. Writing is active, a means of producing learning. When you write, you explore a particular problem or issue: thinking about it in a variety of ways, and teaching yourself something about it in the process. By writing, you also present an argument that attempts to persuade your audience to view the problem in the way that you do. In effect, you become a teacher yourself. Writing forces you to make the subject your own. It forces you to explore it and to consider how you can best represent the results of your thinking. Indeed, in the act of writing you may well discover what it is you have to say.

THE WRITING PROCESS

Most college-level writing about drama asks you to construct an interpretation of some aspect of a play or plays. The kind of interpretation you will perform, though, has much in common with persuasive argument—your paper should make an assertion about the play, a *claim* that you will develop in the course of the essay. First, a good claim is not simply a description of the work, a statement of what's already self-evident. To say, for example, that Ibsen's play *A Doll House* is about conflicted gender and marital relations is merely to state the obvious; it leaves you nothing to argue. Nor is a good claim merely a personal opinion about the work, a statement that invites agreement without persuasion or evidence. To say that *A Doll House* is a bad play, or that Nora is an unbelievable character, is an opinion-statement of this kind. Argumentative writing requires you to consider a fundamentally *problematic* issue, a question about which there could be some important disagreement—disagreement regarding the interpretation of the play itself. Writing is, after all, a form of communication. It is important that you have something worthwhile to say and that your way of saying it can be made persuasive to others.

For most people, writing an effective analytical argument has three basic phases that work to transform thoughts into an effective piece of writing. The first phase is the *invention* phase, when you consider the issues you want to raise. This is the time to ask yourself very general and stimulating questions that will lead to a commitment—a *claim*—about the work. If the choice of the paper is up to you, you might ask which of the plays you have read you liked the most. What aspects of the play seem most important, impressive, or unusual to you? If a paper topic has been assigned, you still need to make it your own. You might ask yourself how the topic seems to interpret the play, what problems or questions the topic seems to raise about your understanding of the play. It is at this point that most students come up with the *topic* of their papers, but a topic is only a first step. In order for a topic to be transformed into an argumentative claim, you have to think about it as a *problem*. A topic is inert while a problem is controversial—an idea about which there can be disagreement. For example, this is a topic: "Nora Helmer is a good mother in *A Doll House*." Although this statement does make a claim, the claim is vague and under-developed. Its importance and consequences are not yet made clear. To transform the topic into a problem, we might ask how this claim could be seen as controversial, to involve us in a specific kind of interpretation of the play. One way to transform this topic into a problem is to imply an alternative perspective as part of the claim: "Although Nora Helmer leaves her children at the end of the play, she is really a good mother." This is a more problematic claim, precisely because it raises the possibility that Nora could be seen in two ways. This claim could be made more effective by suggesting how resolving this problem is central to an understanding of the play: "Although Nora Helmer leaves her children at the end of *A Doll House,* the play presents her as a good mother. Nora herself must become a free adult, must discover who she really is, before she can raise her children." This claim raises several complex issues and suggests a particular perspective on them. Your audience would expect you to discuss Nora's accomplishments as a mother in the play and relate those accomplishments to her difficult decision to leave her family at the end of the play.

This process—transforming a topic into a problem—usually marks the end of the first phase of writing, at which you come up with the major claim of your paper, a provisional *thesis.* This claim is still only provisional, because you will probably have to modify it in the next phase of the writing process: organizing your argument, developing your evidence, and drafting the paper. Now that you have a sense of what you want to claim in the essay, you will want to consider how to present your claim effectively. This usually means choosing some elements of the play to examine in detail. In this case, for instance, you might choose to discuss the scenes in which Nora interacts with her children; or the scenes in which she refuses to see them; or the scenes in which she discusses her children with others, like Mrs. Linde and Torvald. Of course, none of these scenes explicitly answers your claim: Ibsen never tells his audience "Nora is a good mother in this scene." It's your task to *interpret* the scene, suggest how we—your audience—should look at it in order to see it as you do. Generating detail of this kind—scenes, characters, speeches, language—to discuss is often one of the most challenging parts of the writing process. One way to help yourself here (and as a writer) is to take some notes on the play after you have read it. What scenes do you think are important or memorable? Why? What do you make of the major characters? These notes can help to provide some of the initial material you will discuss as part of your drafting of the essay.

Having considered what aspects of the play you want to address, you will want to make an outline, a map of your approach. Most students learn to make a formal outline—with major headings, subheadings, and so on—in high school, and some college and university classes require you to submit the outline as part of your writing process. Most writers use a more informal outlining strategy; they make a list of the issues or evidence they want to treat in the paper, as a way of putting main points and main pieces of evidence in order. Once you begin writing, you may well need to revise your outline, as what you have already written suggests new directions for the rest of the essay. Having outlined your approach, the next step is the writing itself. Instead of trying to get everything right in the first draft, most writers use the writing process to generate ideas and develop some prose. There will be plenty of opportunity to shape, develop, and revise the writing later. So, when you begin the paper, do your best to get your argument into a clear order. Write as much as it occurs to you to say on each point, giving yourself a lot of leeway to improvise ideas that may need to be clarified in revision. If important new evidence occurs to you, put it down in the draft, making a note to return to it. The important factor at this stage is to get as many of your thoughts down in order as you can.

The final phase—or phases, since most good papers take several revisions—is the process of revision. Revising is where the process of your thinking is transformed into an effective argument. Through revision your thinking is reshaped to become effective written communication. Written communication is sequential; your audience can only process information one piece at a time. For that reason, it's important to clarify your claims at the outset, tell your audience where the argument is going, and why. It's also important to tell the audience how each section of the argument is helping to substantiate that claim, and why it is important that we've accompanied you so far. A major objective of revision is to make the outlines of the argument—its major phases—explicit in this way. When revising, one useful trick is to read over your text—a paragraph, for instance—and then ask yourself, "What's the point of this paragraph? How does it contribute to my overall argument?" If you cannot answer that question, then you need to consider whether the paragraph—in this form—belongs in the paper at all. If you can answer it, then look to see that your answer is actually written down in the paragraph somewhere, made explicit to your readers, who, after all, are probably not thinking about the problem in exactly the way that you are.

Of course, these are the large-scale revisions; you will also want to ask similar questions of more local matters. Have I presented enough evidence on this point? Have I interpreted the evidence fully for the reader? How are my mechanics—sentence clarity, structure, variety, spelling?

APPROACHES TO WRITING

Writing about drama and theater is not essentially different from writing about other literary, historical, or cultural subjects, and the skills and habits of effective writing will serve well in writing about drama, too. However, writing about drama and theater also follows some of its own conventions. First, papers are generally written in the present verb tense, as though the play were actually taking place now, in front of us. It's up to you, of course, whether you want to write from the point of view of the reader or the point of view of the theater audience, but you will have to adopt a consistent perspective throughout and recognize that each perspective can help to make certain features of the play more clearly visible.

Second, many papers about drama begin by taking issue with one of Aristotle's categories of dramatic structure: the play's plot (how does its sequence of events contribute to its overall meaning?), its characters (how are the characters constructed; how do the conventions of characterization represent "real" people?), its thought or themes (how does the play generate its "themes"?), its language (are there patterns of language, images, or ways of speaking that contribute to your sense of its action?), and its spectacle (are there explicit features of its action onstage that help to realize the play's meaning?). These topics can be expanded through reference to the specific forms of drama in a given period or theater. To talk about the plot structure of a Shakespearean play, after all, is to talk about something very different from the plot of a Beckett play. It's important to realize that these features of the drama can provide a good starting point for your discussion, but that each will need to be specified in terms of your particular argument.

Another approach that's often useful in thinking about drama is to consider the play's staging, either in terms of effects that are described or made explicit in the text (the times that Prospero appears "aloft" in *The Tempest;* the confining single room of *A Doll House*), or in terms of the actual production choices made in a given staging. Thinking about how a production you have seen interpreted the text and how it used acting, movement, set design, and costuming to provide the audience with a given perspective on the play is another standard approach to writing about drama and theater.

CITATION AND DOCUMENTATION

There are a few mechanical conventions specific to writing about drama. As you can see from the essays included in this volume, there are several forms you can use for citing secondary sources. The two main approaches are to use footnotes for all citations (see Louis Montrose's article in Unit 3), or to put the page numbers in parentheses in the text and add a list of Works Cited at the end of the paper, saving notes only for further explanation (see Henry Louis Gates's article in Unit 6). Your instructor may well have a preference here and will help you to use secondary citations. The purpose of citing secondary works you may use in writing your essay is twofold: first, to give credit to your sources, to the other writers whose work you may have used in coming to your own conclusions; second, to direct your readers to other material that may be interesting or helpful to them. At most colleges and universities, plagiarism—submitting someone else's work as your own—is an extremely serious offense, and careful attention to citations protects you as well as informing your readers.

Writing about drama uses several conventions to identify quotations from plays. Classical Greek plays are usually cited by line number, and the citation follows the quotation:

> Clytaemnestra's effect on Agamemnon is complete when he steps on to the blood-red-carpet, saying, "I feel such shame / to tread the life of the house" (ll. 945–46).

Notice that "ll." is the abbreviation for the word "lines" and is used to identify the line numbers of the quotation, and that the citation follows the close-quotation mark and precedes the period. The citation is part of the sentence, so it's included inside the sentence, before the period.

A different convention is followed for plays from the Renaissance, Restoration, and Neoclassical periods, which are commonly written in verse and usually are divided into

---

Although many literature and theater students tend to write about the action, characters, language, or themes of plays as literary works, different kinds of issues often emerge when a play is considered in performance. While a more "literary" essay necessarily focuses considerable attention on developing evidence suggestively from the text of the play, writing about performance negotiates between the prescriptions of the text and their engagement by live performers, actual men and women onstage, moving and behaving in a specific environment.

Two papers recently written by university students dramatize some of the consequences of writing about drama-as-literature or drama-in-the-theater. Both papers are about Caryl Churchill's play Cloud Nine, *in which questions of text-and-performance are central to thinking about the play's action. The first paper, written by Kimberly Gordon, a Theater major at*

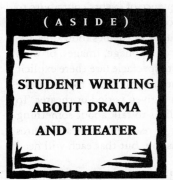

(ASIDE)

STUDENT WRITING ABOUT DRAMA AND THEATER

Northwestern University, considers the play's representation of women, and particularly its characterization of Betty, as part of its critique of the effects of the sexual revolution on the lives of women today. The second paper, written by Charles Heath, an English and Political Science major at the University of California at Davis, responds directly to a performance of Cloud Nine, *staged by the Department of Theater and Dance at UC Davis in 1998. Heath concentrates his attention on the ways different roles were performed in this production, and comes to some surprising conclusions about how this production represented the play's sexual politics. Both Kimberly Gordon and Charles Heath graduated in 1998.*

Kimberly Gordon
Professor Worthen
Introduction to Modern Drama
Fall 1994

BETTY IN BONDAGE

Choices, respect, and new possibilities were all to have been characteristic of the post-sexual revolution. Many people believed that an entirely new place in history for women would be born. Caryl Churchill, England's most noted feminist playwright, would laugh at such a notion. In all her works, she portrays women as "stuck" and unsatisfied. The relationships of Churchill's women and their positions in them, have been predefined by their male counterparts. A woman's adherence to these man-made molds forces her to give precedence to society's demands over her own desires; this trap is exemplified in Churchill's play, *Cloud Nine.* In this play Churchill employs the character Betty to illustrate the subordinate role of the woman in a male-dominated world. This "subordination" is addressed by the character's desire for something more, her views on marriage, her ingrained, warped perception that a woman must be "bad" in order to be happy, and the punishment she faces if she dares to disobey man's guidelines.

acts and scenes. Here, the citation includes act, scene, and line numbers, separated by a period. Some people prefer using Roman numerals (IV.iii.21–22)—for act 4, scene 3, lines 21–22—but many people now use Arabic numerals (4.3.21–22) as follows:

> Prospero finally accepts his own role in creating Caliban at the end of *The Tempest,* when he says, "this thing of darkness I / Acknowledge mine" (5.1.278–79).

When the play is written in verse, the lineation of the original text is preserved with a slash (/) between the lines, and the capitalization of each new line is preserved as above. Usually, quotations of more than three lines are set off as a separate quotation.

Since modern plays are not consistently divided into acts and scenes, and are usually not written in verse lines, it's common to identify the section (act and scene) of the play you are discussing as part of your prose, and then to cite the page number:

> The most chilling moment in Shaw's *Major Barbara* occurs at the end of the second act of the play, when Cusins claims, "Dionysus Undershaft has descended. I am possessed!" (491).

The mechanics of quotation are easy to learn and lend your work an air of competence and credibility. For additional information, ask your instructor to recommend a handbook, or consult *The MLA Handbook for Writers of Research Papers*. It contains extensive material on how and when to use footnotes, the preparation of works cited, and more specialized questions of style and mechanics.

Cloud Nine opens in Victorian Africa with the colonist Clive's introduction of his family. When he speaks of Betty, his wife, he admits, "My wife is all I dreamt a wife to be / and everything she is she owes to me" (Churchill 559). The first words Betty utters confirm Clive's remark: "I live for Clive. The whole aim of my life / Is to be what he looks for in a wife. / I am a man's creation as you see, / And what men want is what I want to be" (559). Betty has become a "man's creation" by patterning her behavior and actions to fit her husband's desires. Churchill emphasizes the inequalities in this relationship by using role reversal. In the first act of the play, Betty and others are portrayed by actors of the opposite sex. This information layers the interpretation of the first scene. The audience watches a man play Betty, literalizing the idea that a man helped create her role; the viewer witnesses Betty through the male creator's eyes.

Regarding the issue of cross-dressing, Elin Diamond reminds the reader, "The point is not that the male is feminized but that the female is absent" (97). Betty, who in thought and action is represented as the "token female," is presented, not as a woman, but rather as the illusion of one. A man in a woman's costume produces a greater presence of masculinity and reduction of physical femininity. The absence Diamond speaks of also reflects on women's character—they must be content with being discontent, with having their desires denied. This attitude is established by the male characters and later fostered through the women. When Betty acknowledges her dissatisfaction with the expectations imposed upon her, for example, Harry, an old friend of the family, proves discouraging:

> HARRY: [. . .] I need you, and I need you where you are, I need you to be Clive's wife. I need to go up rivers and know that you are still here thinking of me.
>
> BETTY: I want more than that. Is that wicked of me?
>
> HARRY: Not wicked Betty, silly. (565)

Betty's wanting more is irrelevant. Harry trivializes her plea by calling her "silly," an adjective implying a lack of power more frequently used to describe women and children than men.

Perhaps more damaging than the implications made by the men, are the ways in which they are passed down by the women. This masculine legacy occurs frequently in the mother-daughter relationship, and is seen in the following dialogue between Betty and Maud:

> MAUD: Young women are never happy.
>
> BETTY: Mother, what a thing to say.
>
> MAUD: Then when they're older they look back and see that comparatively speaking they were ecstatic. (561)

In this scene, a mother is guilty of perpetuating the void and emptiness in her daughter. As Betty hints of interests outside the domestic range, Maud smothers this curiosity by instructing Betty of her place as a wife and daughter. When Betty asks for information about

Continued

the tribes and floggings taking place on their property, Maud reminds her, "I don't think it's up to us to wonder. [. . .] You would not want to be told about it, Betty. It is enough for you to know that Clive knows what is happening. Clive will know what to do. Your father always knew what to do" (567). Betty is not taught to be a self-sufficient woman. Maud helps to create and reinforce Betty's dependency on men. As with any mother, Maud means no malice. In act 2, Maud lets her daughter know that all her actions were out of love. She confesses, "I know we have our little differences but I always want what is best for you" (582). Betty's mother, like all mothers, wants her daughter to fit the mold of society. Unfortunately, following Maud's advice robs Betty of her identity as an independent woman.

Betty has been taught to understand the protection she receives by conforming to society's ideals, and reproduces those ideals in her own relationships with other women. She convinces the governess of her children, Ellen, to disregard her own desires and marry for the sole purpose of fulfilling her obligations as a woman:

BETTY: If you go back to England you might get married, Ellen. You're quite pretty, you shouldn't despair of getting a husband.
ELLEN: I don't want a husband. I want you.
BETTY: Children of your own, Ellen, think.
ELLEN: I don't want children [. . .]
BETTY: [. . . W]omen have their duties as soldiers have. You must be a mother if you can. (570)

Ellen agrees to marry Harry, and just moments after the wedding Betty reminds her friend that she is, "not getting married to enjoy herself" (571).

Not only are the women portrayed as inferior, and prevented from living life as they please, they are also made to feel "bad" and "weak." In the exchange between Betty and Harry, Betty questions whether she is innately "wicked." Betty refers to being made "better," implying that she feels there is something wrong with her present condition. Churchill reinforces the widespread acceptance of these qualities in women when Clive confronts Betty about her kissing Harry. Betty automatically finds fault in her actions and confesses:

BETTY: There is something wicked in me, Clive.
CLIVE: I have never thought of you as having the weakness of your sex, only good qualities.
BETTY: I am bad, bad, bad—
CLIVE: You are thoughtless, Betty, that's all. Women can be treacherous and evil. They are darker and more dangerous than men [. . .] It was a moment of passion such as women are too weak to resist. (568)

The key words "bad," "wicked," "weak," and "treacherous" become not merely the ways in which the men perceive the women, but more dangerously, the characteristics women attribute to themselves. Betty learns to equate sin with happiness, and is punished accordingly.

When women stray from the alleged "social norm" in thought or behavior, the men discipline them to correct their actions. After Clive blames the female sex for Betty's weakness with Harry, he goes on to explain the severe consequences that might have followed had he not shown his wife mercy. He threatens, "It would hurt me to cast you off. That would be my duty [. . .] If I shot you every British man and woman would applaud me [. . .]" (568). Clive's warning carries with it a double standard. He reprimands Betty for being an unfaithful wife while he is currently having an affair with the widow Mrs. Saunders.

As act 2 of *Cloud Nine* begins, the audience encounters an entirely new setting and an entirely new Betty. Act 2 jumps seventy-five years into the future (although the characters age only twenty-five years) and Churchill switches continents as well. It is London, 1979, and Betty has undergone an enormous transformation. During the transition she has become more comfortable with her own sexuality and herself, and her role is now appropriately played by an actress.

The Betty of act 2 leaves her husband, seeks and finds employment, and starts to define herself as her own person. As she begins to disregard her conventional definitions of the roles of wife and mother, she is able to escape her self-implemented boundaries. Betty comes to the realization, "You appreciate the weekend when you're working. [. . .] And the money, I feel like a child with the money, Clive always paid everything but I do understand it perfectly well" (581). She enjoys work and the strength derived from the ability to support herself.

Betty's new self-possession is complemented by her rediscovery of her sexuality at the end of the show. She confides:

I touched my face, it was there, my arm, my breast and my hand went down where I thought it shouldn't, and I thought well there is somebody there [. . .] and I felt angry with Clive and angry with my mother and I went on defying them. [. . .] Afterwards I thought I'd betrayed Clive. My mother would kill me. But then I felt triumphant because I was a separate person from them. And I cried because I didn't want to be. But I don't cry anymore. Sometimes I do it three times in one night and it really is great fun. (582)

Where Betty finds success in living alone, the adjustment is not an easy one. It is hard to break old habits, such as making tea for two. She discovers that, "It's strange not having a man in the house. You don't know how to do things for yourself" (577). The Betty in act 2 is still lonely and struggles with some reluctance to accept the new ideals and lifestyles presented by the generations of her children and grandchildren.

By the play's close, Betty does begin to embrace a more independent future. This action is visually demonstrated as Churchill instructs that the Bettys from each act appear on stage together and embrace as the last action of the play. This hug implies both a sympathetic understanding of their shared past, and an appreciation for the genuine efforts to ensure a happier future. Betty is on the right path to freeing herself from remaining "stuck" in the outline man has provided her. But she has just begun the challenge. For now, Betty and all of Churchill's women, are still a long way from being on "Cloud Nine."

Works Cited

Churchill, Caryl. *Cloud Nine. The Harcourt Anthology of Drama.* Brief ed. Ed. W. B. Worthen. Fort Worth: Harcourt, 2002. 559–83.

Diamond, Elin. "Refusing the Romanticism of Identity." *Performing Feminisms: Feminist Critical Theory and Theatre.* Ed. Sue-Ellen Case. Baltimore: Johns Hopkins UP, 1990. 92–105.

Charles Heath
Professor Worthen
Modern Drama
Winter 1998

THE VALUE OF SUBTLE CROSS-DRESSING

What everyone remembers after seeing a performance of *Cloud Nine* are the cross-dressing characters and the stark difference between the first and second acts. The performance of the cross-dressing characters and the staging changes between acts can be manipulated to produce a multitude of effects on the audience. If the director opts to have the cross-dressing characters of Betty, Edward, and Cathy be flamboyant and exaggerated in their portrayal of the opposite sex, a highly funny yet probing production ensues. This performance choice produces a strong Brechtian alienation effect on the audience. The flamboyant performance examines what outwardly expressed symbols define us as men and women. Seeing a woman playing a man clearly delineates between actor and character, drawing out the methodology employed by the actor to perform the "stock male," drawing the audience's attention to how speech, physical movements, interaction among characters, construct "masculine" behavior. When the audience sees these gestures performed in an exaggerated way, it becomes possible to recognize that they too employ this socially constructed system to label themselves "male" or "female." Witnessing exaggerated gender construction alienates audience members from their own practices of gender construction and the identities that accompany those constructions. Once alienated, having stepped back from this "identity," the spectator can scrutinize and examine it. The flamboyant method of performing *Cloud Nine* is visually appetizing, producing a colorful spectacle on stage as it communicates what Churchill clearly wants us to take from the play: that our identities are a social construction, and that construction is inextricably linked to the power hierarchies of our society and history.

The current production of *Cloud Nine* at UC Davis accomplishes very different goals. To say it accomplishes different goals is not to say it does not embody the themes of a more flamboyant production, but that it emphasizes a different set of effects available to a director of Churchill's rich text. The cross-dressing Davis actors are far from flamboyant in their portrayals of the opposite sex; they at times seem gender neutral, almost to "disappear" in a realistic way into the roles they play. Despite Craig Swogger's elevated voice and occasional fluttering of a Victorian-era fan, he rarely makes overtly feminine gestures in his performance of Betty in act 1. Similarly, he never adds masculine gestures to the performance. Rather than highlighting his own gender, or flamboyantly exaggerating Betty's, Swogger instead remains gender neutral, allowing the wig, dress, and Churchill's brilliant lines to convey the character's femininity and trapped masculinity. Similarly, Nancy Stone's portrayal of Edward is not flamboyantly masculine, nor does she allow her femininity to show through. Again Churchill's dialogue and the young Victorian boy's outfit contrast against her clearly female appearance to stage a problem of frustrated identity in a low-key, realistic manner.

While this way of performing *Cloud Nine* takes away from the audience's examination of the socially constructed male and female as exaggerated by an actor, it does allow the audience to see Churchill's characters in more psychological terms, struggling between their inner selves and their social circumstances. The theme of this production is entrapment. The inner self, as symbolized by the gender of the actor playing the role, is not allowed to express itself because it is trapped inside the social role of the character, be it Betty, Edward, or Cathy. Instead of commenting on what it means to be a man or a woman in some essential way, this production looks more at what it means to want to live the socially constructed life of a man or woman, and the consequences that arise from the imposed conformity to norms of gender and sexuality.

What we find out, through the course of the play, is that men and women are quite capable of crossing gender barriers, once oppressive males are out of the way. Mrs. Saunders in act 1 seemingly lives the life Betty desires: to break out of the constricted female role of a Victorian wife and satisfy her desires for sexual and personal independence. Mrs. Saunders is liberated because her husband is dead. Betty, too, is able to dislodge the yoke of patriarchy by leaving her husband in

Continued

act 2, and subsequently satisfies her own needs. Edward seems to come to terms with his sexuality once on his own, out from under the scrutinizing and demanding reign of his father. In act 2, with a sense of liberation, Edward's repressed homosexuality (construed as femininity in act 1) flourishes; even the "male," self-determining side of Betty appears. In act 2 Betty and Edward are no longer confined in the roles their characters were subjected to in act 1. Liberated from repression, the innate person and his or her outward identity are reconciled, which is the point of having actors play same-sex characters in act 2.

What the Davis performance does particularly well is to emphasize *Cloud Nine* as metatheater, as a play that examines the practice of drama. Act 1 is a more or less realist Victorian drama. The stage has an elaborate Victorian verandah with white wicker furniture and a Union Jack flying above. The characters wear elaborate period costumes and even though the theater has a thrust stage (surrounded on three sides by the audience), the stage is brightly lit, marking out the familiar, proscenium-like "realistic" division between stage and audience. The story of act 1 unfolds organically as we learn about the characters' pasts in order to understand the present conflict that drives the drama. When the audience returns from the intermission, though, they find a dimly lit stage with the Victorian plantation home removed. In the plantation's place is an ominous wrought iron fence and some children's play furniture. The dark stage blends almost seamlessly with the auditorium, providing no buffer between drama onstage, and the world of the audience. Further breaking down the space between the characters and the audience, the characters often speak directly to the audience, in addition to using traditional methods of dialogue at other times. The plot of the play becomes very fragmented and episodic. The links between the individual episodes are left to be made by the audience. Despite the over-130-year gap between Victorian colonialism and late 1970s London, the characters have only aged twenty-five years. This deconstruction of time compresses modern English history into a short representative mode that conveys the process of modernization in a single setting.

The multitude of marked changes between act 1 and act 2 shows the evolution of theater from the conventional Victorian stage, contemporary with the act 1 characters, to the postmodern stage contemporary with the act 2 characters and the audience. David Moon's scenic and lighting design accentuate the period-specific differences between the acts to make the audience member aware of the dramatic methodology being employed. Nancy Stone and Jon Jackson, as Betty and Gerry, respectively, deliver highly provocative monologues describing their sexual liberation, leaving the audience member convinced that the modern dramatic conventions applied in *Cloud Nine* are the only suitable means of representation for the contemporary world. A more traditional realistic rendering could not adequately convey the intimate details of Nancy and Gerry's sex lives that the intimate dialogue between character and audience made clear. The "realistic" separation of stage and audience in act 1 both protects the audience and provides a feeling of omniscience; breaking down the proscenium in act 2 puts the audience more into the middle of the action, where we look for our bearings in the confusion of the present, much like the characters. The production's synthesis of history becomes overtly clear when certain characters of act 1 come onto the modern stage and clash with act 2 characters who remain in contemporary apparel, and clash with the dark and sparse set. The contrast looks unnatural and the characters of the past look foreign or alien. The production shows at once how alien Victorian England is within the realm of modernity, and how those characters nonetheless form the past's very presence on the modern stage, demonstrating how that colonial and patriarchal history lingers and influences the modern day.

A production of *Cloud Nine* forces actors, director, and designers to make many very important decisions. The impressions of the audience can be swayed immensely by the handling of the play's abundant complexities. The UC Davis production uses a rather conservative production style for a potentially outrageous play. The conservative line does compromise the play's spectacular qualities. However, to downplay the visual feast is to evoke the more subtle qualities in Churchill's text. What the play loses in flamboyant performance it recovers in simplicity. Costuming, scenery and lighting are dead-on throughout the play, picking up on and exploiting Churchill's toying with notions of time, modernization and representation. Churchill's text is meant to reach out and probe each audience member's conception of his or her identity; the UC Davis performance aptly violates its viewing audience.

Absurd *See* Theater of the Absurd.

Académie Française An academy founded by Cardinal Richelieu in 1635 to resolve the critical debate surrounding Corneille's play *The Cid,* and to regularize the French language.

actos Short satirical plays devised by Luis Valdez and El Teatro Campesino in the late 1960s to dramatize the conditions of farmworkers in California.

afterpiece A short play—usually a pantomime or farce—that followed the main play on the evening's bill; common in England in the eighteenth and nineteenth centuries.

agora The marketplace in ancient Greek towns; the *agora* was often used for dramatic performance.

alienation effect A stage technique developed by Bertolt Brecht in the 1920s and 1930s for "estranging" the action of the play. By making characters and their actions seem remarkable, alien, or unusual, Brecht encouraged the audience to question the social realities that produced such events, the political and ideological background of the drama and of its stage production.

allegory A literary or dramatic technique that uses actual characters, places, and actions to represent more abstract political, moral, or religious ideas. *See Everyman* in Unit 3.

alojería The tavern at the rear of the *patio* in a Spanish Golden Age theater, or *corral.*

amphitheater A semicircular theater design, consisting of a playing area faced by rising tiers of seats; often used outdoors, this was the design of classical Greek theaters.

anachronism Using people, places, or things that are chronologically out of keeping with the rest of the fictive world of a play or narrative; for example, using medieval English shepherds to attend the birth of Christ in medieval cycle plays.

anagnorisis Greek term for a character's "recognition" of something previously not known in the play. In the *Poetics,* Aristotle links *anagnorisis* with *peripeteia,* the "reversal" in the action of the play.

antagonist The force or character that opposes the main character (**protagonist**) of a play.

antimasque A scene of misrule, usually involving witches, goblins, demons, or savages, who are transformed magically into princes, gods and goddesses, or virtues in a Jacobean **masque.**

antiphonal performance Alternative or responsive singing between individuals or groups; in the Middle Ages, it commonly involved two choirs.

archon A magistrate in classical Athens; each year, an *archon* was assigned the responsibility for organizing the City Dionysia.

apron The section of the stage that extends toward the auditorium beyond the **proscenium.**

Atellan farce Improvised comic skits featuring stock characters performed by masked actors in ancient Rome.

atoza Upstage area in a **Noh** theater in which the musicians are seated.

auto sacramentale Elaborate Spanish religious dramas originally devised as part of the feast of Corpus Christi. *Autos* continued to be performed in Spain until 1765.

avant-garde Literally the "advance guard," the term usually refers to the most innovative, experimental, or unorthodox artists in a given historical period. Used almost exclusively of late nineteenth- and twentieth-century movements.

backcloth   A painted cloth lowered at the rear of the stage to represent a dramatic location.

Beijing Opera   Elaborate form of Chinese theater involving an onstage orchestra, ornate costumes, music, and dance.

benefit   In the English theater of the seventeenth, eighteenth, and nineteenth centuries, a performance whose profits were assigned to a single performer or to the playwright.

biomechanics   An experimental technique for actor training and performance devised by the Russian director Vsevolod Meyerhold after the Russian Revolution (1917). The technique emphasized the actor's physical training, stressing acrobatic and choreographic elements in production.

bhava   A stageable emotion in **Sanskrit drama,** related to the play's principal *rasa* or mood.

biwa   Four-stringed, plucked instrument used to accompany spoken narration in medieval Japan.

blank verse   An English verse meter consisting of unrhymed **iambic pentameter** lines (ten syllables with alternating stress, the first stress falling on the second syllable).

box   Box seating first appeared in theaters in the late seventeenth century; boxes were arranged around the side of the stage and the sides of the auditorium for the private accommodation of small numbers of people. Boxes were more expensive than **pit** or **gallery** seats.

box set   First devised in the 1830s, a set consisting of three practical walls enclosing the stage in a room-like way.

bunraku   The term used for modern Japanese doll theater, derived from the eighteenth-century master Uemura Bunrakuken.

butai   The acting area, or stage proper, of a **Noh** theater.

butoh   A powerful form of dance developed in the post-Hiroshima era in Japan; it features nude actors, covered in white powder, whose movements are slow and ethereal.

cabaret performance   Stage performances in restaurants serving food and drink; especially popular in Europe after World War I, cabarets often were used for innovative kinds of performance.

canon   An authorized body of texts, such as the "canon" of Shakespeare's known plays; also commonly used to mean a "traditional" body of texts.

capa y espada   Literally "cape and sword" plays, swashbuckling romances in the Spanish Golden Age theater.

Capitano   The braggart soldier of *commedia dell' arte.*

carro   Wagon used for performance of Spanish *auto sacramentale.*

catastrophe   The turning point in the plot of a classical tragedy.

catharsis   Literally, the "purging" that Aristotle discusses as the effect of tragedy in his *Poetics.* Catharsis has been variously described as an emotional release on the part of the spectators, or as the recognition and purging of wrongdoing in the action of the play.

cazuela   The women's gallery above the *alojería* in a Spanish Golden Age theater, or *corral.*

character   A fictional "person" appearing in a play or other work of fiction; usually conventionalized to some degree.

chonin   Japanese term for townsmen.

choregos   An important citizen in ancient Athens given the responsibility for financing, assembling, and training the chorus of Greek tragedy.

chorus   A masked group of young men who sang and danced as a group in Greek tragedy and comedy; larger choruses also performed *dithyrambs.*

City Dionysia   Annual spring festival honoring the god Dionysus; one of four festivals held between December and April. Sometimes called the "Great Dionysia," it was the site of dramatic competitions and other public displays and rituals.

comedia nueva   Mixed mode form of drama associated with Lope de Vega.

Comédie Française   The official national theater of France, devoted to the staging of the classics. Founded and chartered by Louis XIV in 1680 when Molière's company and the Marais company were united.

comedy   Traditionally a humorous literary form, comedy typically concerns the trials of love, and/or ridicules the failings of certain members of society. *See* **comedy of manners, new comedy, old comedy, romantic comedy.**

comedy of manners   Comic drama that takes the manners of high society as its subject; in comedy of manners, the dialogue is often witty or epigrammatic.

commedia dell' arte   Improvised comic plays performed by itinerant companies; it originated in Italy in the sixteenth century and then spread throughout Europe. Actors each played a stock character type and improvised the action according to a shared outline plot.

Constructivist theater   A movement in the Soviet theater after World War I, and often associated with the director Vsevolod Meyerhold. Adapted from the visual arts, constructivist theater resisted the use of representational sets, using more abstract "constructions" onstage.

corral   Open-air Spanish theater of the sixteenth and seventeenth centuries, constructed within an open courtyard.

cross-dressing   One of the conventions of cross-gendered acting, in which women play male characters in male costume, and men play female characters in women's clothing.

cycle plays   A series of plays dramatizing Christian history from the Creation to the Last Judgment, devised and performed in the Middle Ages by craft guilds called "mysteries"; the cycles are sometimes also called "mystery cycles" or "mystery plays." Performed outside the church on the Feast of Corpus Christi.

Dada   A nonsense term adopted as the name of a literary and theatrical movement in Europe after World War I; Dada developed an esthetic of random and irrational art. Dada performances became popular in cabarets of Paris, Zurich, and Berlin in the 1920s.

daimyo   Feudal lord of Japan, member of the *samurai* class of warriors, and owing duty to the *shogun.*

decorum   The notion, associated with neoclassicism, that the action and subject matter (idealized), language (heightened), and moral propriety (elevated), should be stylistically integrated and unified.

deme   A neighborhood in classical Athens; the root of the modern word "democracy."

demonstration   Describing the "**alienation effect,**" Bertolt Brecht urged his actors to "demonstrate" the roles they played, rather than identifying with them in the mode of Stanislavskian acting. Acting-as-demonstration keeps the audience aware of both the actor *and* the "character" at the same time.

dengaku-no   Form of dance, role-playing, and acrobatics popular in Japan in the eleventh and twelfth centuries; said to be one of the progenitors of Noh theater.

desvanes   Small open galleries on the third and fourth storeys in a Spanish Golden Age theater, or *corral.*

deus ex machina   Literally the "god from the machine," the term refers to the practice of using a crane to lower the character of a god to the stage at the end of a classical Greek tragedy, usually to resolve the action of the play. Modern usage takes the term to refer to any dramatic device that suddenly resolves the action of a play.

dithyramb Choral hymns sung and danced to honor Dionysus as part of the City Dionysia. Choruses of fifty men or fifty boys drawn from each tribe performed dithyrambs prior to the tragedy competition; Aristotle thought tragedy to have originated in these dithyrambic performances.

dokekata Comic roles in **Kabuki** theater.

doll theater Form of Japanese theater originating in the seventeenth century; doll theater uses elaborate dolls, operated by three visible puppeteers, and combines music and narration. The most prominent form of doll theater today is called *bunraku.*

Dottore The "doctor" or old pedant of *commedia dell' arte;* usually a friend of **Pantalone.**

drama A literary composition, usually in dialogue form, and centering on the actions of fictional characters.

Egungen Festival common among the Yoruba peoples of Nigeria involving masks and costumes for communication with the dead.

ekkyklema A low platform used to roll objects or bodies from the *skene* doors onto the stage in classical Greek theater.

emotion memory A term developed by the Russian director Constantin Stanislavski to describe an actor's "work on himself" in acting. After considering a character's circumstances in the play, and his past life leading up to the action of the play, the actor tries to connect the character's situation with important events in his or her own life: this emotional or affectual connection can make the character's display of emotion onstage seem realistic and immediate.

entremeses Short plays performed as interludes between acts of Golden Age dramas.

environmental theater A term coined by Richard Schechner in the late 1960s to describe performances that do not distinguish between the playing area and the audience; the performance takes place throughout the theatrical environment.

epic theater A term associated with the German director Erwin Piscator and theorized by Bertolt Brecht in the late 1920s and 1930s, epic theater uses episodic dramatic action, nonrepresentational staging, and the **alienation effect,** to demonstrate the political, social, and economic factors governing the lives of the dramatic characters. In the theater, Brecht advocated the use of placards to announce the action, visible lighting, filmscreens on the stage, and other devices to produce this epic effect.

episode Originally, a dramatic scene in a classical Greek tragedy, as distinct from the choral odes; now, usually refers to any incident or event in a play. Plays that are episodic tend not to subordinate episodes to a causal plot, but simply to arrange them in a series.

exodos The final scene and exit of the characters and chorus in a classical Greek play.

expressionist theater An early twentieth-century movement challenging the **verisimilitude** of realistic theater by staging individual emotional, unconscious states of mind directly. In expressionist plays, the action is usually abrupt and intense; the characters are usually generalized; the plot is typically symbolic or allegorical.

extravaganza Visual spectacle popular in nineteenth-century theater.

Fabian society A late nineteenth-century English socialist political society; Marxist in its orientation to social change, the Fabian society advocated a policy of gradual reform rather than revolution.

farce Usually a short comic play, often relying on a highly coincidental plot.

film noir A genre of black-and-white detective films popular in the 1940s, which frequently used shadowy, nighttime settings to establish an aura of menace and foreboding.

folio   A large-format printed volume, in which only four pages (two per side) are printed on each sheet of paper; the paper is folded once to form four pages.

fourth wall   Refers to the style of realistic theater since the late nineteenth century, in which the stage is treated as a room with one wall missing. The audience is not acknowledged or addressed by the actors, but overlooks the scene as a silent, invisible observer.

fuebashira   Flute-player's pillar in a **Noh** theater, the upstage right pillar where the flute-player is positioned during the performance.

gallery   In seventeenth-, eighteenth-, and nineteenth-century theaters, ascending rows of bench seating usually located opposite the stage on the third level of the auditorium; generally the most inexpensive seats in the theater.

geisha   In Japan, a hired female companion valued for artistic accomplishment; legally not classed as a prostitute.

genre   Literally, "kind" or "type," *genre* in literary and dramatic studies refers to the main types of literary form, principally tragedy and comedy. The term can also refer to forms that are more specific to a given historical era, such as **revenge tragedy** or to more specific subgenres of **tragedy** and **comedy**, such as **comedy of manners.**

given circumstances   Term used by Constantin Stanislavski to describe the situation a character finds himself or herself in at the opening of the play, which the actor must construct as his first step in building the character toward performance.

gracioso   The comic fool of Spanish Golden Age drama, popularized in part by Lope de Vega.

gradas   The steeply raked side seats along the side of the *patio* in a Spanish Golden Age theater, or *corral.*

grave trap   A trap door in the floor of the stage, often in the center.

hamartia   A term used by Aristotle in the *Poetics* to describe the tragic hero's decisive act, the "error" or "mistake" that brings about the tragedy. Sometimes mistranslated as "tragic flaw," a translation that mistakenly changes the meaning of the term from the description of an action to a feature of the character's moral makeup or personality.

hanamichi   Elevated gangway extending from the rear of **Kabuki** theater to the stage; major characters use this bridge for their entrances and some scenes are played here as well.

Harlequin   The main character of *commedia dell' arte,* and later of English pantomime. Usually a wily schemer, Harlequin was originally played in a patched costume, which became conventionalized as the familiar diamond-covered costume. Harlequin was usually masked and carried a flat bat or paddle.

hashigakari   The long bridge from the **mirror room** to the stage of a **Noh** theater.

heroic tragedy   A seventeenth-century genre, usually on the theme of love vs. honor; associated with Dryden in England, Corneille in France, and Calderón de la Barca in Spain.

hon kyōgen   The main play of a **Kabuki** performance, originally lasting from about 7 A.M. until dusk when the theater closed.

hurry door   The small door leading offstage from the *atoza,* or upstage area of a **Noh** theater; used by the chorus, the stage assistants, and by dead characters.

hybridization   In the theory of **postcolonial** literatures, the use of several styles— typically elements of indigenous or colonized and colonial cultures—in one work, typically to dramatize the cultural politics engrained in colonial habits of representation.

iambic pentameter   English verse meter consisting of ten-syllable lines with alternating stressed and unstressed syllables, the first stress falling on the second syllable.

ideology A complex term first used in the eighteenth century to categorize political beliefs and attitudes. Used to mean 1) a body of beliefs, a doctrine; 2) a body of illusory beliefs, a false doctrine; 3) a socially grounded system for producing beliefs and values, a way of producing meanings or doctrines.

Independent Theater Movement A late-nineteenth-century movement in Europe, in which small theaters gambled on the production of new and unconventional plays— by Ibsen, Shaw, Chekhov—to a small audience, usually outside the theatrical mainstream.

Innamorata/o The attractive young lovers of *commedia dell' arte;* played without masks.

interlude A short play, usually comic, performed during courtly feasts at the English court in the sixteenth century.

jidaimono The four- to six-act "history" section of a **Kabuki** performance.

jōruri Performance of narrative and dialogue to the accompaniment of a *samisen* in Japanese theater; these elements absorbed into **doll theater.**

Kabuki Form of Japanese popular theater originating in the early seventeenth century. Kabuki tends to encompass both comic and serious elements in elaborate and conventional performances that originally lasted from ten to twelve hours; it includes live acting, narration, music, and singing.

kamyonguk Dance-drama form practiced in Korea, using colorful costumes, masked actors, and musical accompaniment.

katakiyaku Villain role in **Kabuki** theater.

komos A procession and dance in ancient Greece, sometimes thought to be the origin of comic drama.

kyōgen Brief farcical play performed as interludes between **Noh** plays.

language One of the six constituent elements of drama defined by Aristotle in the *Poetics.*

line of business A conventional or stock "character" type that is the specialty of a given actor; his or her "line of business" might be old men, heavy villains, comic heroines, etc.

Little Negro Theater Movement A movement in U.S. theater in the 1920s to develop theaters owned and operated by African-Americans, playing a dramatic repertory by African-American writers.

Little Theater Movement A movement in the American theater in the early twentieth century akin to the **Independent Theater Movement** in Europe. Little Theaters offered new or noncommercial plays to smaller audiences.

liturgical drama Short dramatized sections of the Catholic Mass performed as part of the service; may have inspired the more elaborate, non-liturgical **cycle plays.**

loa a short, typically allegorical play used to introduce a comedy or religious play in Spanish Golden Age theater.

machina The Greek term for the crane used in the ancient theater to raise and lower characters, particularly the gods.

machine plays Term used principally in seventeenth-century French theater to describe spectacular special-effects extravaganzas, in which the dramatic action—usually drawn from mythological subjects—was merely a pretext for the use of stage machinery.

magic if Term developed by Constantin Stanislavski to describe the actor's attitude toward a role; to play "as if I were in this situation."

mansions Structures placed at several locations inside medieval churches as settings for liturgical plays.

masque   A brief, usually symbolic, mythological, or allegorical play, with elaborate scenic effects performed at the English court during the sixteenth and seventeenth centuries; performed both by actors and by courtiers.

melodrama   First used in the late eighteenth century, the term originally referred to highly charged, popular plays using music to reinforce their clear-cut moral action; now refers more generally to plays with a schematic opposition between good and evil, in which good usually prevails.

metatheater   A term used to describe plays that self-consciously comment on the process of theater, or treat the process of theater as a metaphor for off-stage reality. Such plays sometimes use the play-within-the-play device.

Method acting   A technique of acting developed by Constantin Stanislavski at the turn of the twentieth century, which teaches actors to use **emotion memory** to enact the character's feelings persuasively and realistically in performance; method acting became especially popular in the United States in the 1930s, 1940s, and 1950s.

metsukebashira   The "gazing pillar" in a **Noh** theater, where the *shite* looks when delivering his first speech. It is the downstage right pillar.

mie   Exaggerated pose struck for expressive effect by actors in **Kabuki** theater.

mimesis   Greek word for "imitation" used by Aristotle in *Poetics* to describe the function of art.

mirror room   The waiting room of a **Noh** theater, where actors in costume contemplate their characterization.

mise-en-scène   The "putting onstage" of a play, including the setting, scenery, direction, and action.

mitos   Lyrical plays on Mexican-American life devised by Luis Valdez and El Teatro Campesino in the late 1960s and 1970s.

monopoly   The right to exclusive production of the drama.

montage   A technique used in film consisting of a rapid sequence of images.

morality drama   A late-medieval dramatic form using allegorical characters to dramatize moral and ethical problems involved in leading a Christian life.

music   A constituent element of drama as defined by Aristotle in the *Poetics;* Aristotle refers to the flute music that accompanied performance in the ancient Greek theater.

mystery cycles   *See* **cycle plays.**

naturalism   A late nineteenth-century movement that attempted to achieve an objective **verisimilitude** in art—chiefly in theater and literature—by adopting a "scientific" attitude toward its subject matter. Thematically, naturalism emphasizes the role of society, history, and personality in determining the actions of its characters, usually expressed as a conflict between the characters and their environment.

nautical shows   A type of melodrama popular in England in the eighteenth and nineteenth centuries on seafaring subjects; in aquatic dramas, the stage was actually flooded.

neoclassical drama   Drama written under the influence of **neoclassicism.**

neoclassicism   A movement throughout Europe in the sixteenth to eighteenth centuries to revive the forms and values of art exemplified by ancient literature; associated with the recovery of Aristotle's *Poetics* and its translation into prescriptions for the stage.

new comedy   A form originating in the fourth and third centuries BCE, first in Greece and then in Rome. In the plays of Plautus, for instance, new comedy generally concerns a romantic plot involving a conflict between young lovers, an old man, and a tricky servant.

Noh   Japanese classical theater dating from the fourteenth century; the plays are highly poetic dramas given extremely formal production onstage. Noh drama was admired by Yeats and by other modern playwrights.

ode   In Greek drama, a song performed by the chorus while dancing.

old comedy   Satiric social comedy of fifth-century BCE Athens; Aristophanes' plays are the only surviving examples.

onnagata   Women's roles in **Kabuki** theater, all of which are played by men.

onna kabuki   Literally, "women's Kabuki," an early name for **Kabuki** companies, which were composed mainly of women.

orchestra   Literally, the "dancing place," the circular area before the **skene** where the chorus performed in ancient Greek theater.

pageant master   The guild officer responsible for gathering funds to finance medieval mystery pageants.

pageant wagons   Wagons carrying the sets for productions of medieval **cycle plays**, on which the plays were performed.

Pantalone   Foolish old man in *commedia dell' arte;* played masked.

pantomime   In general, silent acting using gesture and facial expression. English pantomime—or "panto"—is a spoken form, in which spectacular fairy-tale extravaganzas are performed with music and dance during the Christmas holidays.

parabasis   A choral speech in ancient Greek comedy in which the **chorus** comments on contemporary social issues.

parodos   The entrance song of the **chorus** in Greek tragedy.

parterre   The standing area in the auditorium of late seventeenth-century Parisian theaters; the **pit**.

pastiche   Term used by Fredric Jameson to describe the toneless quotation of earlier artistic styles in contemporary (or postmodern) works.

patents   Licenses given by the crown permitting a company to give dramatic performances; often, a patent would give a company or a small number of companies a **monopoly** on dramatic performance.

patent theaters   Theaters given **patents** (or licenses) by the crown for dramatic performance, sometimes holding a monopoly on performance. Charles II of England granted two patents and gave their owners a monopoly on dramatic performance.

patio   The flat central courtyard of a Spanish Golden Age theater, or *corral.*

peripeteia   A term used by Aristotle in the *Poetics* to describe the "reversal" in the action of a **tragedy**.

phallus   A leather phallus worn by male characters in Greek comedy.

pit   Floor area immediately in front of the stage in seventeenth- and eighteenth-century theaters.

plot   The sequence of events in a play or narrative; differs from the "story," which encompasses earlier events. Some works have several plots.

pointing   Common practice in the eighteenth-century theater of delivering a famous speech directly to the audience from a downstage position; to "make a point."

polis   A city-state in ancient Greece.

political theater   In conventional usage, theater that seems to question the inequities and injustices of contemporary society. Bertolt Brecht developed a more searching critique of political theater, however, in which the ideology of theatrical representation itself could be seen as the theater's "politics."

postcolonial   While referring specifically to the cultures of a nation that has gained independence, the term postcolonial is generally applied more broadly, referring to cultures still negotiating for political freedom, to internally colonized cultures, and to cultures that experience economic or cultural imperialism, even though they may be part of an independent nation-state.

postmodern   A term used to characterize the complex relationship between some contemporary works of art and their modernist forebears. Postmodern works are generally characterized by stylistic "quotation," an invocation and disengagement from history, and the fragmentation of artistic surface.

Prakit The everyday, prose dialect spoken in **Sanskrit drama,** usually reserved for comic characters, women, and children.

private theaters In Renaissance England, indoor theaters serving a more privileged audience. Often located on lands within the city limits that were not under city jurisdiction, such as Blackfriars.

prologue In Greek drama, an introductory scene preceding the entrance of the **chorus.** In later usage, an introductory scene not directly part of the main action.

proscenium An arch over the front of the stage. First used in European theaters in the Renaissance; throughout the eighteenth and nineteenth centuries, theater design gradually eliminated the **apron** that extended in front of the proscenium and decorated the proscenium arch itself, emphasizing its frame-like quality.

protagonist Literally the "first contestant" in the ancient Greek theater, the term referred to the "first" or main actor competing for a prize. In modern usage, refers to the play's main character.

public theaters In Renaissance England, large outdoor theaters, usually polygonal in shape, consisting of three-storey galleries surrounding an open standing pit and a thrust stage.

quarto A small-size book format, in which eight pages are printed on a single sheet of paper; the paper is folded twice to make eight pages.

raked stage A stage that is elevated in the back and lower in the front; common in Europe after the seventeenth century. The raked stage gave rise to the terms "upstage" (toward the back, which was higher) and "downstage" (toward the front, which was lower).

rasa An impersonal mood or attitude of contemplation in Hindu philosophy; in **Sanskrit drama,** the play is designed to produce one of eight *rasas* in the audience: erotic, comic, pathetic, furious, heroic, terrible, odious, or marvelous. The basic *rasa* of each play is related to its *bhava,* or stageable emotion.

realism A literary and theatrical practice valuing direct imitation or **verisimilitude.** Often associated with **naturalism,** modern realism is sometimes described as the inheritor of naturalism. In practice, realism is usually more concerned with psychological motives, the "inner reality," and less committed to achieving a superficial verisimilitude alone.

repertory A company that performs several plays in rotation throughout a season is a repertory company; the term also refers to a set of plays.

revenge tragedy A tragic genre popular in English Renaissance, usually involving a complicated intrigue plot in which the hero is forced to commit murder in order to avenge himself; madness and supernatural agents (ghosts) are also a common feature. Shakespeare's Hamlet is the best-known example.

role-doubling The practice of using one actor to play more than one part.

romance A modern term used to define idealized narratives and sometimes applied to the idealized comedies written by Shakespeare late in his career, especially *The Winter's Tale* and *The Tempest.*

romantic comedy Comic form centering on the romance between two lovers, or between several sets of lovers. Romantic comedy typically begins with some unreasonable impediment to the lovers' union, and when after a complicated series of events the obstacle is overcome, the play ends in marriage.

rōnin *Samurai* warriors who have been disgraced and outcast from society; "men adrift."

ruido A "noise" play or violent comedy in Spanish Golden Age theater.

Rupaka The "major drama" of classical **Sanskrit** theater.

sainete   Deriving from the *genero chico* of Spain, a short, sometimes satirical play often used for interludes or *entremeses,* it was widely used for plays on regional or local-color themes in Argentina in the nineteenth century.

samisen   Three-stringed instrument that is both plucked and struck as accompaniment to narration in *jōruri.* In the late sixteenth century, became instrumental in the **doll theater.**

samurai   Warrior class of feudal Japan; *samurai* lords both patronized **Noh** playwrights and companies, and provided the code of conduct informing many **Noh, doll theater,** and **Kabuki** plays.

Sanskrit   An ancient Indo-European language; once a spoken language, by the modern era it had become mainly a written language reserved for academic and religious purposes. In **Sanskrit drama,** Sanskrit is reserved for elevated scenes and characters, while **Prakrit,** the everyday dialect, is spoken by other characters.

Sanskrit drama   The drama of ancient India, particularly the plays of its "Golden Age" (second to ninth centuries).

sarugaku-no   Form of dance, role-playing, and acrobatics popular in Japan in the eleventh and twelfth centuries; said to be the progenitor of **Noh** theater.

saruwaka   Comic roles in **Kabuki** theater, performed by men.

satyr play   A brief, rugged comedy performed by actors in satyr costumes (half-man, half-goat) after the performance of a tragic **trilogy** at the **City Dionysia;** usually on mythological subjects.

scaena   Three-storey stage house behind the stage in the Roman theater, facing the audience. Elaborately decorated with columns, panels, and porticos.

scenic unity   The practice of harmonizing acting style, costumes, and sets to create the illusion of a single, unified environment on the stage.

sewamono   "Domestic plays" of the Japanese **doll theater.**

sharers   Actors and playwrights in the English Renaissance theater who, as investors in the company, took a share of the profits; they were responsible for building or leasing a theater and were legally liable for the company's actions.

shimpa   A movement in Japanese theater beginning in the late nineteenth century to adapt European drama to Japanese style and subject matter.

shingeki   A movement in twentieth-century Japanese theater to import the style and techniques of European realistic theater into the Japanese theater.

shite   Principal actor in **Noh** theater.

shitebashira   The upstage right pillar in a **Noh** theater, near the *hashigakari,* where the *shite* delivers his opening speech.

shogun   Hereditary military leader of Japan from the twelfth through the nineteenth centuries; the *shogun* was the most important of the *samurai* (warrior) class, composed of *daimyo* (feudal lords) and lesser *samurai.*

skene   A low building behind the **orchestra** in the Greek theater facing the audience; possibly used for changing costumes or storage.

social realism   A form of modern realistic drama emphasizing social messages and themes; social realism was the official genre approved by the Communist party in the Soviet Union after the revolution.

sociétaires   Leading actors and shareholders in the Comédie Française; upon serving twenty years, *sociétaires* were entitled to a pension.

soliloquy   A speech delivered by a character alone onstage, speaking to himself or herself, or to the audience.

soubrette   A stock character in drama: a young, pert female character.

spectacle   Aristotle's term for the visual element of theatrical performance in the *Poetics.*

subtext   A term first elaborated by Constantin Stanislavski, "subtext" refers to the unspoken motive for a given line or speech, what the character wants to get or to do by saying the line. It is sometimes now used more generally to suggest a text's underlying sense or meaning.

surrealist theater   A movement originating in Paris in the 1920s attempting to represent subconscious experience directly in art.

symbolist theater   A European movement of the later nineteenth and early twentieth centuries in reaction to **realism** and **naturalism**. Symbolist theater attempted to dramatize more poetic or metaphorical situations, often using unusual stage settings and ethereal dramatic action and language.

syndicate   A group of investors who developed a massive organization for theatrical production in the United States in the late nineteenth century.

tableau/tableaux (pl.)   A motionless grouping of actors to represent a "picture" of a dramatic scene; sometimes called *tableau vivant,* a "living picture."

tableaux vivants   *See* **tableau;** *tableaux vivants* is the plural form of *tableau vivant.*

taburetes   The raised and fenced rows of benches near the stage in a Spanish Golden Age theater, or *corral.*

tachiyaku   Leading male role in **Kabuki** theater.

tertulia   An upper gallery occupied by church officials and intellectuals in a Spanish Golden Age theater, or *corral.*

theater   A structure built for the performance of drama; also refers to the institution of dramatic performance.

theater in the round   The presentation of a play in an arena setting, in which the audience sits on all sides of the stage area, but is separate from the playing space itself.

Theater of Cruelty   Term used by Antonin Artaud to describe his nonrepresentational, mystical, mythological theater.

Theater of the Absurd   A type of late twentieth-century theater and drama, characterized by a relatively abstract setting, and arbitrary and illogical action. It is sometimes said to express the "human condition" in a basic or "existential" way. The term was first coined by Martin Esslin.

theme   A term used to describe a consistent kind of meaning asserted by a work of literature.

tiring house   A structure at the rear of the stage in the Renaissance English public theater, where actors would change costumes (attire themselves), and from which they would enter the stage.

tragedy   Originating in the classical Greek theater, tragedy generally refers to serious drama, taking a central character's conflict with himself or herself, with society, or with god as its subject. Aristotle first described tragedy in his *Poetics,* and tragedy has undergone almost continual redefinition.

tragicomedy   In the English Renaissance, a term describing a dramatic form: a play beginning like a tragedy, but ending happily, like a comedy. In modern usage, the term refers most often to a play's tone or attitude: a play that is ironic, both serious and absurd, leaning toward black comedy or tragic farce.

traveling song   Song sung in **Noh** theater by the *waki* during his first entrance; it announces who the *waki* is, and where he is going.

trilogy   Three tragedies produced in sequence as part of the tragic competition in the **City Dionysia** of ancient Greece. Plays were not necessarily on the same subject.

trope   An enlargement on Catholic liturgy, through song or dramatic performance.

tsure   Followers of the *shite* and *waki* in **Noh** theater.

Upa-rupaka   The "minor drama" of classical **Sanskrit** theater.

verisimilitude   Refers to the extent to which the drama or stage setting appears to copy the superficial appearance of life offstage.

villancicos   Religious songs, like English carols, performed in Spain and its colonies.

wakashugata   Adolescent male roles in **Kabuki** theater.

wakashu kabuki   Literally, "boys' Kabuki," the term refers to **Kabuki** companies composed mainly of adolescent boys, many of whom were prostitutes; banned by the Tokugawa shogunate in 1652.

waki   The secondary actor in **Noh** theater, who responds to the *shite.*

wakibashira   The downstage left pillar in a **Noh** theater, where the *waki* is usually positioned at the opening of the play.

waki-za   A narrow stage area along the stage-left side of a **Noh** theater stage used for seating the chorus.

wayang kulit   Shadow-puppet theater of Java concerning characters and events drawn from the *Ramayana* and *Mahabharata,* the epic poems of classical India. Performances generally begin early in the evening and last until dawn; audiences sit on both sides of a screen, against which puppeteers cast the shadows of elaborate, flat puppets, whose actions are accompanied by dialogue, narration, song, and music.

well-made play   A form of drama popularized in the nineteenth century, especially in France. The plot usually turns on the revelation of a secret and includes a character who explains and moralizes the action of the play to others; the plot is often relentlessly coincidental, often mechanically so.

wings and backdrop   Scenic practice developed in Italy and exported to France and England in the seventeenth century, using staggered painted flats in a receding series, and a painted central backcloth to depict the setting of the play.

yaro kabuki   The "adult male Kabuki" common in Japan today that replaced the boys' and women's **Kabuki** that were popular before such companies were banned in the early seventeenth century.

yugen   The Japanese term for the mysterious beauty, grace, and repose that are the goal of **Noh** performance.

Yūgo   Professional prostitute in classical Japan; distinct from *geisha,* a hired companion valued for artistic accomplishment.

Yūgo kabuki   Literally, "prostitutes' Kabuki," an early term for **Kabuki** companies, which were composed mainly of women.

Zanni   Wily and clever comic characters, usually clowns or servants, in *commedia dell' arte;* played masked.

zen   Term in Buddhist thought for a contemplative attitude that is disengaged from worldly desire

BIBLIOGRAPHY

Barish, Jonas. *The Antitheatrical Prejudice.* Berkeley, CA: U of California P, 1981.

Beckerman, Bernard. *Dynamics of Drama.* New York: Drama Book Specialists, 1979.

Bennett, Susan. *Theatre Audiences: A Theory of Production and Reception.* London: Routledge, 1990.

Bentley, Eric. *The Life of the Drama.* New York: Atheneum, 1964.

Brockett, Oscar G. *History of the Theatre.* Boston: Allyn & Bacon, 1987.

Carlson, Marvin. *Theories of the Theatre: A Historical and Critical Survey, from the Greeks to the Present.* Ithaca, NY: Cornell UP, 1984.

Case, Sue-Ellen. *Feminism and Theatre.* New York: Methuen, 1988.

———, ed. *Performing Feminisms: Feminist Critical Theory and Theatre.* Baltimore: Johns Hopkins UP, 1990.

Clark, Barrett H. *European Theories of the Drama.* New York: Crown, 1965.

Dukore, Bernard F. *Dramatic Theory and Criticism: Greeks to Grotowski.* New York: Holt, Rinehart and Winston, 1974.

Elam, Keir. *The Semiotics of Theatre and Drama.* London: Methuen, 1980.

Frye, Northrop. *Anatomy of Criticism,* Princeton, NJ: Princeton UP, 1957.

Goldman, Michael. *The Actor's Freedom.* New York: Viking, 1975.

Leacroft, Richard, and Helen Leacroft. *Theatre and Playhouse: An Illustrated Survey of Theatre Building from Ancient Greece to the Present Day.* New York: Methuen, 1984.

Nagler, Alois M. *Sources of Theatrical History.* New York: Dover, 1952.

States, Bert O. *Great Reckonings in Little Rooms: On the Phenomenology of Theater.* Berkeley, CA: U of California P, 1985.

———. *Irony and Drama.* Ithaca, NY: Cornell UP, 1971.

Turner, Victor. *From Ritual to Theatre: The Human Seriousness of Play.* New York: Performing Arts Journal Publications, 1982.

Worthen, William B. *The Idea of the Actor: Drama and the Ethics of Performance.* Princeton, NJ: Princeton UP, 1984.

Arnott, Peter D. *Greek Scenic Conventions in the Fifth Century, B.C.* Oxford, England: Oxford UP, 1962.

Beare, William. *The Roman Stage.* London: Methuen, 1969.

Bieber, Margarete. *The History of the Greek and Roman Theatre.* Princeton, NJ: Princeton UP, 1961.

Else, Gerald F. *The Origin and Early Form of Greek Tragedy.* New York: Norton, 1972.

Hamilton, Edith. *The Greek Way.* New York: Norton, 1983.

Knox, Bernard M. *Word and Action: Essays on the Ancient Theater.* Baltimore: Johns Hopkins UP, 1979.

Konstan, David. *Roman Comedy.* Ithaca, NY: Cornell UP, 1983.

Pickard-Cambridge, A. W. *Dithyramb, Tragedy, and Comedy.* Oxford, England: Oxford UP, 1962.

———. *The Dramatic Festivals of Athens.* Oxford, England: Oxford UP, 1968.

———. *The Theatre of Dionysus in Athens.* Oxford, England: Oxford UP, 1945.

Segal, Erich, ed. *Greek Tragedy: Modern Essays in Criticism.* New York: Harper & Row, 1983.

Taplin, Oliver. *Greek Tragedy in Action.* Berkeley, CA: U of California P, 1978.

READINGS ON DRAMA AND THEATER

UNIT 1: CLASSICAL ATHENS

Vince, Ronald W. *Ancient and Medieval Theatre: A Historiographical Handbook.* Westport, CT: Greenwood, 1984.

Webster, T. B. L. *Greek Theater Production.* London: Methuen, 1970.

Winkler, John J., and Froma I. Zeitlin, eds. *Nothing to Do with Dionysus? Athenian Drama in Its Social Context.* Princeton, NJ: Princeton UP, 1990.

ARISTOPHANES

Deardon, C. W. *The Stage of Aristophanes.* London: Athlone, 1976.

Dover, K. J. *Aristophanic Comedy.* Berkeley, CA: U of California P, 1972.

Harriott, Rosemary. *Aristophanes: Poet and Dramatist.* Baltimore: Johns Hopkins UP, 1986.

Ussher, Robert Glenn. *Aristophanes.* Oxford, England: Oxford UP, 1979.

EURIPIDES

Dodds, E. R. *The Greeks and the Irrational.* Berkeley, CA: U of California P, 1951.

Foley, Helene P. *Ritual Irony: Poetry and Sacrifice in Euripides.* Ithaca, NY: Cornell UP, 1985.

Michelini, Ann N. *Euripides and the Tragic Tradition.* Madison, WI: U of Wisconsin P, 1987.

SOPHOCLES

Dodds, E. R., "On Misunderstanding the Oedipus Rex." *Greek Tragedy: Modern Essays in Criticism.* Ed. Erich Segal. New York: Harper & Row, 1983.

Fergusson, Francis. *The Idea of a Theater.* Princeton, NJ: Princeton UP, 1947.

Knox, B. M. W. *Oedipus at Thebes.* New York: Norton, 1971.

Segal, Charles. *Tragedy and Civilization: An Interpretation of Sophocles.* Cambridge, MA: Harvard UP, 1981.

Whitman, C. H. *Sophocles: A Study in Heroic Humanism.* Cambridge, England: Cambridge UP, 1951.

Winnington-Ingram, R. P. *Sophocles: An Interpretation.* New York: Cambridge UP, 1980.

UNIT 2: CLASSICAL JAPAN

Arnott, Peter D. *The Theatres of Japan.* New York: St. Martin's Press, 1969.

Bowers, Faubion. *Japanese Theatre.* New York: Hermitage House, 1952.

Brandon, James R. *Theatre in Southeast Asia.* Cambridge, MA: Harvard UP, 1967.

———, ed. *Traditional Asian Plays.* New York: Hill and Wang, 1972.

Dunn, Charles James, and Bunzo Torigoe, trans. and eds. *The Actors' Analects: Yakusha Rongo.* New York: Columbia UP, 1969.

Malm, William P. *Japanese Music and Musical Instruments.* Rutland, VT: Tuttle, 1963.

Samson, G. B. *A Short Cultural History of Japan.* London: Cresset Press, 1952.

DOLL THEATER AND KABUKI THEATER

Brandon, James R., ed. *Chūshingura: Studies in Kabuki and the Puppet Theater.* Honolulu: U of Hawai'i P, 1982.

———, trans. *Kabuki: Five Classic Plays.* Cambridge, MA: Harvard UP, 1975.

Ernst, Earle. *The Kabuki Theatre.* Rev. ed. Honolulu: U of Hawaii P, 1974.

Halford, Aubrey S. and Giovanna M. Halford. *The Kabuki Handbook.* Tokyo: Tuttle, 1952.

Kawatake Toshio. *A History of Japanese Theatre, II: Bunraku and Kabuki.* Tokyo: Kokusai Bunka Shinkokai, 1971.

Keene, Donald. *Chūshingura: The Treasury of Loyal Retainers.* New York: Columbia UP, 1971.

———, trans. *Major Plays of Chikamatsu.* New York: Columbia UP, 1961.

Rimer, J. Thomas, and Yamazaki Masakazu, trans. *On the Art of the Nō Drama: The Major Treatises of Zeami.* Princeton, NJ: Princeton UP, 1984.

Scott, Adolphe Clarence. *The Kabuki Theatre of Japan.* London: George Allen and Unwin, 1955.

Araki, James T. *The Ballad-Drama of Medieval Japan.* Berkeley, CA: U of California P, 1964.

Brower, Robert H., and Earl Miner. *Japanese Court Poetry.* Stanford, CA: Stanford UP, 1961.

Ernst, Earle. *Three Japanese Plays from the Traditional Theatre.* London: Oxford UP, 1959.

Fenollosa, Ernest, and Ezra Pound. *The Classic Noh Theatre of Japan.* New York: New Directions, 1959.

Keene, Donald. *Nō, the Classical Theatre of Japan.* Tokyo and Palo Alto, CA: Kodansha International, 1966.

———, ed. *Twenty Plays of the Nō Theatre.* New York: Columbia UP, 1970.

Komparo Kunio. *The Noh Theater: Principles and Perspectives.* Trans. Jane Corddry and Stephen Comeo. Tokyo and New York: Weatherhill, 1983.

Waley, Arthur. *The Nō Plays of Japan.* London: George Allen and Unwin, 1921.

Yasuda, Kenneth. *Masterworks of the Nō Theater.* Bloomington, IN: Indiana UP, 1989.

Baumer, Rachel V., and James R. Brandon. *Sanskrit Drama in Performance.* Honolulu: U of Hawai'i P, 1981.

Bharata. *Natyasastra.* Trans. P. S. R. Appa Rao. Hyderabad, India: Naatyd Maala, 1967.

Keith, A. B. *Sanskrit Drama: Its Origins, Development, Theory and Practice.* Oxford, England: Oxford UP, 1924.

Tarlekar, G. H. *Studies in the Natyasastra, with Special Reference to the Sanskrit Drama in Performance.* Delhi, 1975.

Wells, Henry W. *Six Sanskrit Plays.* London and Bombay: Asia Publishing House, 1964.

Bentley, Gerald Eades. *The Jacobean and Caroline Stage.* 5 vols. Oxford, England: Oxford UP, 1941–1956.

———. *The Profession of Dramatist in Shakespeare's Time, 1590–1642.* Princeton, NJ: Princeton UP, 1971.

———. *The Profession of Player in Shakespeare's Time, 1590–1642.* Princeton, NJ: Princeton UP, 1984.

Bevington, David. *From Mankind to Marlowe: Growth in Structure in the Popular Drama of Tudor England.* Cambridge, MA: Harvard UP, 1962.

———. *Medieval Drama.* Boston: Houghton, 1975.

Chambers, E. K. *The Elizabethan Stage.* 4 vols. Oxford, England: Oxford UP, 1923.

———. *The Medieval Stage.* 2 vols. London: Oxford UP, 1967.

Cox, John D., and David Scott Kastan, eds. *A New History of Early English Drama.* New York: Columbia UP, 1997.

Greenblatt, Stephen, ed. *Representing the English Renaissance.* Berkeley, CA: U of California P, 1988.

Gurr, Andrew. *The Shakespearean Stage, 1574–1642.* Cambridge, England: Cambridge UP, 1970.

Hardison, O. B., Jr. *Christian Rite and Christian Drama in the Middle Ages.* Baltimore: Johns Hopkins UP, 1965.

Kolve, V. A. *The Play Called Corpus Christi.* Stanford, CA: Stanford UP, 1966.

Orgel, Stephen. *The Illusion of Power: Political Theatre in the English Renaissance.* Berkeley, CA: U of California P, 1975.

Vince, Ronald W. *Ancient and Medieval Theatre: A Historiographical Handbook.* Westport, CT: Greenwood, 1984.

Wickham, Glynne. *The Medieval Theatre.* New York: Cambridge UP, 1987.

Woolf, Rosemary. *The English Mystery Plays.* Berkeley, CA: U of California P, 1972.

EVERYMAN

Bevington, David. *From Mankind to Marlowe: Growth in Structure in the Popular Drama of Tudor England.* Cambridge, MA: Harvard UP, 1962.

Garner, Stanton B., Jr. "Theatricality in Mankind and Everyman." *Studies in Philology,* 84 (1987): 272–85.

WILLIAM SHAKESPEARE

Bamber, Linda. *Comic Women, Tragic Men: A Study of Gender and Genre in Shakespeare.* Stanford, CA: Stanford UP, 1982.

Barber, C. L. *Shakespeare's Festive Comedy.* Princeton, NJ: Princeton UP, 1968.

Barker, Francis, and Peter Hulme. "Nymphs and Reapers Heavily Vanish: The Discursive Contexts of The Tempest." *Alternative Shakespeares.* Ed. John Drakakis. New York: Methuen, 1985.

Bennett, Susan. *Performing Nostalgia: Shifting Shakespeare and the Contemporary Past.* London: Routledge, 1996.

Boose, Lynda E., and Richard Burt, eds. *Shakespeare the Movie: Popularizing the Plays on Film, TV, and Video.* London: Routledge, 1997.

Booth, Stephen. "On the Value of Hamlet." *Reinterpretations of Elizabethan Drama: Selected Papers from the English Institute.* Ed. Norman Rabkin. New York: Columbia UP, 1969. 137–76.

Brown, Paul. "This Thing of Darkness I Acknowledge Mine: The Tempest and the Discourse of Colonialism." *Political Shakespeare: New Essays in Cultural Materialism.* Ed. Jonathan Dollimore and Alan Sinfield. Ithaca, NY: Cornell UP, 1985.

Bullough, Geoffrey, ed. *Narrative and Dramatic Sources of Shakespeare.* 8 vols. New York: Columbia UP, 1957–75.

Bulman, James, ed. *Shakespeare, Theory, and Performance.* London: Routledge, 1996.

Cerasano, S. P., and Marion Wynne-Davies, eds. *Renaissance Drama by Women: Texts and Documents.* London: Routledge, 1996.

Dollimore, Jonathan, and Alan Sinfield, eds. *Political Shakespeare: New Essays in Cultural Materialism.* Ithaca, NY: Cornell UP, 1985.

Drakakis, John, ed. *Alternative Shakespeares.* New York: Methuen, 1985.

Fergusson, Francis. *The Idea of a Theatre.* Princeton, NJ: Princeton UP, 1947.

Forker, Charles R. "Shakespeare's Theatrical Symbolism and Its Function in Hamlet." *Shakespeare Quarterly* 14 (1963): 215–29.

Goldman, Michael. *Shakespeare and the Energies of Drama.* Princeton, NJ: Princeton UP, 1970.

Greenblatt, Stephen. *Shakespearean Negotiations.* Berkeley, CA: U of California P, 1988.

Hendricks, Margo, and Patricia Parker, eds. *Women, "Race," and Writing in the Early Modern Period.* London: Routledge, 1994.

Howard, Jean E., and Marion F. O'Connor, eds. *Shakespeare Reproduced: The Text in History and Ideology.* London: Methuen, 1987.

Jardine, Lisa. *Still Harping on Daughters: Women and Drama in the Age of Shakespeare.* Totowa, NJ: Barnes & Noble, 1983.

Kernan, Alvin B., ed. *Modern Shakespeare Criticism.* New York: Harcourt, Brace & World, 1970.

———. *The Playwright as Magician.* New Haven, CT: Yale UP, 1979.

Mack, Maynard. "The World of Hamlet." *Yale Review* 41 (1952): 502–23.

Orgel, Stephen. "Prospero's Wife." *Representing the English Renaissance.* Ed. Stephen Greenblatt. Berkeley, CA: U of California P, 1988.

Parker, Patricia, and Geoffrey Hartmenn, eds. *Shakespeare and the Question of Theory.* London: Methuen, 1985.

Schoenbaum, S. *Shakespeare: A Documentary Life.* New York: Oxford UP, 1975.

Schwartz, Murray M., and Coppélia Kahn, eds. *Representing Shakespeare: New Psychoanalytic Essays.* Baltimore: Johns Hopkins UP, 1981.

Thompson, Marvin, and Ruth Thompson, eds. *Shakespeare and the Sense of Performance.* Newark, DE: U of Delaware P, 1989.

Worthen, W. B. *Shakespeare and the Authority of Performance.* Cambridge: Cambridge UP, 1997.

Allen, John. *The Reconstruction of a Spanish Golden Age Playhouse: El Corral del Principe, 1583–1744.* Gainesville: U of Florida P, 1983.

Holland, Norman N. *The First Modern Comedies: The Significance of Etheredge, Wycherly, and Congreve.* Cambridge, MA: Harvard UP, 1959.

Kirsch, Arthur C. *Dryden's Heroic Drama.* Princeton, NJ: Princeton UP, 1965.

Lancaster, H. C. *A History of French Dramatic Literature in the Seventeenth Century.* 5 vols. Baltimore: Johns Hopkins UP, 1929–42.

Loftis, John. *The Politics of Drama in Augustan England.* Oxford, England: Oxford UP, 1963.

Loftis, John, Richard Southern, Marion Jones, and A. H. Scouten, eds. *The Revels History of Drama in English.* Volume 5: 1660–1750. London: Methuen, 1976.

McKendrick, Melveena. *Theatre in Spain, 1490–1700.* Cambridge, England: Cambridge UP, 1989.

Staves, Susan. *Players' Scepters: Fictions of Authority in the Restoration.* Lincoln, NE: U of Nebraska P, 1979.

Styan, J. L. *Restoration Comedy in Performance.* Cambridge, England: Cambridge UP, 1986.

Waith, Eugene, *The Herculean Hero.* New York: Columbia UP, 1962.

———. *Ideas of Greatness.* London: Routledge & Kegan Paul, 1971.

Wiley, W. L. *The Early Public Theatre in France.* Cambridge, MA: Harvard UP, 1920.

Wilson, Margaret. *Spanish Drama of the Golden Age.* New York, 1989.

Diamond, Elin. "Gestus and Signature in Aphra Behn's *The Rover.*" *ELH* 56 (1989): 519–39.

Duffy, Maureen. *The Passionate Shepherdess: Aphra Behn, 1640–89.* London: Methuen, 1977.

Goreau, Angeline. *Reconstructing Aphra: A Social Biography of Aphra Behn.* New York: Dial, 1980.

Armas, F. A., D. M. Gitlitz, J. A. Madrigal, eds. *Critical Perspectives on Calderón de la Barca.* Lincoln, NE: U of Nebraska P, 1981.

Honig, Edwin. *Calderón and the Seizures of Honor.* Cambridge, MA: Harvard UP, 1972.

Maraniss, James A. *On Calderón.* Columbia, MO: U of Missouri P, 1977.

Campion, John, trans. *El Sueño.* Austin: Thorp Springs, 1983.

Flores, Angel, and Kate Flores, eds. *The Defiant Muse: Hispanic Feminist Poems from the Middle Ages to the Present, A Bilingual Anthology.* New York: Feminist Press, 1986.

Paz, Octavio. *Sor Juana, or, The Traps of Faith.* Trans. Margaret Sayers Peden. Cambridge, MA: Harvard UP, 1988.

Peden, Margaret, trans. *Sor Juana Inés de la Cruz: Poems.* Binghamton, NY: Bilingual Rev. 1985.

Peters, Patricia, and Renée Domeier, O. S. B., trans. *The Divine Narcissus/El Divino Narciso.* Albuquerque: U of New Mexico P, 1998.

Plancarte, Alfonso Méndez, and Alberto G. Salceda, eds. *Obras Completas de Sor Juana Inés de la Cruz,* 4 vols. Mexico City: Fondo de Cultura Económica, 1976.

UNIT 4: EARLY MODERN EUROPE

APHRA BEHN

PEDRO CALDERÓN DE LA BARCA

SOR JUANA INÉS DE LA CRUZ

Tavard, George H. *Juana Inés de la Cruz and the Theology of Beauty: The First Mexican Theology.* Notre Dame: U of Notre Dame P, 1991.

Trueblood, Alan S., ed. and trans. *A Sor Juana Anthology.* Cambridge, MA: Harvard UP, 1988.

MOLIÈRE

Gaines, James F. *Molière's Theater.* Columbus, OH: Ohio State UP, 1984.

Gossman, L. *Men and Masks: A Study of Molière.* Baltimore: Johns Hopkins UP, 1963.

Gross, Nathan. *From Gesture to Idea: Esthetics and Ethics in Molière's Comedy.* New York: Columbia UP, 1982.

Guicharnaud, Jacques. *Molière: A Collection of Critical Essays.* Englewood Cliffs, NJ: Prentice-Hall, 1964.

UNIT 5: MODERN EUROPE

Antoine, André. *Memories of the Théâtre Libre.* Trans. Marvin Carlson. Coral Gables FL: U of Miami P, 1964.

Artaud, Antonin. *The Theater and Its Double.* Trans. Mary Caroline Richards. New York: Grove, 1958.

Bennett, Benjamin. *Modern Drama and German Classicism: Renaissance from Lessing to Brecht.* Ithaca: Cornell UP, 1979.

———. *Theater as Problem: Modern Drama and Its Place in Literature.* Ithaca: Cornell UP, 1990.

Bentley, Eric. *The Playwright as Thinker: A Study of Drama in Modern Times.* New York: Harcourt Brace, 1946.

Bigsby, C. W. E. "The Language of Crisis in British Theatre: The Drama of Cultural Pathology." *Contemporary English Drama.* Ed. C. W. E. Bigsby. New York: Holmes and Meier, 1981.

Blau, Herbert. *Eye of the Prey: Subversions of the Postmodern.* Bloomington: Indiana UP, 1987.

Bradby, David. *Modern French Drama, 1940–1980.* New York: Grove, 1984.

Brater, Enoch, ed. *Feminine Focus: The New Women Playwrights.* New York: Oxford UP, 1989.

Braun, Edward. *Meyerhold on Theater.* New York: Hill and Wang, 1969.

Brockett, Oscar G., and Robert R. Findlay. *Century of Innovation: A History of European and American Theatre and Drama Since 1870.* Englewood Cliffs: Prentice-Hall, 1973.

Brook, Peter. *The Empty Space.* New York: Avon, 1968.

Brustein, Robert. *The Theater of Revolt.* Boston: Little, Brown, 1964.

Chaudhuri, Una. *Staging Place: The Geography of Modern Drama.* Ann Arbor: U of Michigan P, 1995.

Cohn, Ruby. *From Desire to Godot: Pocket Theater of Postwar Paris.* Berkeley: U of California P, 1987.

Cole, Toby, ed. *Directors on Directing.* Indianapolis: Bobbs-Merrill, 1963.

———. *Playwrights on Playwriting.* New York: Hill and Wang, 1960.

Davis, Tracy C. *Actresses as Working Women: Their Social Identity in Victorian Culture.* London: Routledge, 1991.

Dolan, Jill. *The Feminist Spectator as Critic.* Ann Arbor: UMI Research Press, 1988.

Driver, Tom. *Romantic Quest and Modern Query: A History of Modern Theatre.* New York: Delacorte, 1970.

Elsom, John. *Post-War British Theatre.* London: Routledge and Kegan Paul, 1976.

Esslin, Martin. *The Theatre of the Absurd.* New York: Doubleday, 1969.

Finney, Gail. *Women in Modern Drama: Freud, Feminism, and European Theater at the Turn of the Century.* Ithaca: Cornell UP, 1989.

Garner, Stanton B., Jr. *Bodied Spaces: Phenomenology and Performance in Contemporary Drama.* Ithaca: Cornell UP, 1994.

Gilman, Richard. *The Making of Modern Drama.* New York: Farrar, Straus and Giroux, 1974.

Grotowski, Jerzy. *Towards a Poor Theatre.* New York: Simon & Schuster, 1968.

Hunt, Hugh, et al. *The Revels History of Drama in English.* Vol. 7: *1880 to the Present Day.* London: Methuen, 1979.

Jones, David Richard. *Great Directors at Work.* Berkeley: U of California P, 1986.

Kelly, Katherine E., ed. *Modern Drama by Women 1880s–1930s: An International Anthology.* London: Routledge, 1996.

Peter, John. *Vladimir's Carrot: Modern Drama and the Modern Imagination.* Chicago: U of Chicago P, 1987.

Quigley, Austin. *The Modern Stage and Other Worlds.* London: Methuen, 1985.

Rosen, Carol. *Plays of Impasse: Contemporary Drama Set in Confining Institutions.* Princeton, NJ: Princeton UP, 1983.

Schechner, Richard. *Environmental Theater.* New York: Hawthorn, 1973.

Seltzer, Daniel, ed. *The Modern Theatre: Readings and Documents.* Boston: Little, Brown, 1967.

Stanislavski, Constantin. *An Actor Prepares.* Trans. Elizabeth Reynolds Hapgood. New York: Theatre Arts, 1936.

———. *Building a Character.* Trans. Elizabeth Reynolds Hapgood. New York: Theatre Arts, 1949.

———. *Creating a Role.* Trans. Elizabeth Reynolds Hapgood. New York: Theatre Arts, 1961.

———. *My Life in Art.* Trans. J. J. Robbins. Boston: Little, Brown, 1924.

Styan, J. L. *The Dark Comedy.* Cambridge, England: Cambridge UP, 1968.

———. *Modern Drama in Theory and Practice.* 3 vols. Cambridge, England: Cambridge UP, 1980.

Taylor, John Russell. *Anger and After.* London: Methuen, 1969.

———. *The Second Wave: British Drama of the Sixties.* London: Eyre Methuen, 1978.

Whitaker, Thomas R. *Fields of Play in Modern Drama.* Princeton: Princeton UP, 1977.

Wiles, Timothy J. *The Theater Event: Modern Theories of Performance.* Chicago: U of Chicago P, 1980.

Williams, Raymond. *Drama from Ibsen to Brecht.* London: Hogarth, 1987.

———. *Modern Tragedy.* Stanford, CA: Stanford UP, 1966.

Worth, Katharine. *Revolutions in Modern English Drama.* London: G. Bell and Sons, 1972.

Worthen, W. B. *Modern Drama and the Rhetoric of Theater.* Berkeley: U of California P, 1992.

SAMUEL BECKETT

Acheson, James, and Kateryna Arthur, eds. *Beckett's Later Fiction and Drama: Texts for Company.* New York: St. Martin's Press, 1987.

Bair, Deirdre. *Samuel Beckett: A Biography.* New York: Harcourt Brace Jovanovich, 1978.

Beckett, Samuel. *Happy Days: The Production Notebook of Samuel Beckett.* Ed. James Knowlson. New York: Grove, 1985.

Brater, Enoch, ed. *Beckett at 80/Beckett in Context.* Oxford, England: Oxford UP, 1986.

———. *Beyond Minimalism: Beckett's Late Style in the Theater.* Oxford, England: Oxford UP, 1987.

Cohn, Ruby. *Just Play: Beckett's Theater.* Princeton, NJ: Princeton UP, 1980.

———. *Samuel Beckett: The Comic Gamut.* New Brunswick, NJ: Rutgers UP, 1962.

Gontarski, S. E. *Beckett's Happy Days: A Manuscript Study.* Columbus, OH: Ohio University Libraries, 1977.

————. *On Beckett: Essays and Criticism.* New York: Grove, 1986.

Graver, Lawrence, and Raymond Federman, eds. *Samuel Beckett: The Critical Heritage.* London: Routledge & Kegan Paul, 1979.

Kalb, Jonathan. *Beckett in Performance.* Cambridge, England: Cambridge UP, 1989.

Kenner, Hugh. *Samuel Beckett.* Berkeley, CA: U of California P, 1968.

Worth, Katharine. *The Irish Drama of Europe from Yeats to Beckett.* London: Athlone, 1978.

BERTOLT BRECHT

Benjamin, Walter. *Understanding Brecht.* Trans. Anna Bostock. London: NLB, 1973.

Bentley, Eric. *The Brecht Commentaries 1943–1980.* New York: Grove, 1981.

Brecht, Bertolt. *Brecht on Theatre: The Development of an Aesthetic.* Ed. and trans. John Willett. New York: Hill and Wang, 1964.

————. *The Messingkauf Dialogues.* Trans. John Willett. London: Methuen, 1965.

Dickson, Keith A. *Towards Utopia: A Study of Brecht.* Oxford, England: Oxford UP, 1978.

Esslin, Martin. *Brecht: The Man and His Work.* Garden City, NJ: Doubleday, 1971.

Ewen, Frederick. *Bertolt Brecht: His Life, His Art and His Times.* New York: Citadel, 1967.

Fuegi, John. *Bertolt Brecht: Chaos According to Plan.* Cambridge, England: Cambridge UP, 1987.

————. *Brecht and Company.* New York: Grove, 1994.

Lyon, James K. *Bertolt Brecht in America.* Princeton, NJ: Princeton UP, 1980.

Wright, Elizabeth. *Postmodern Brecht: A Re-Presentation.* London: Routledge, 1989.

ANTON CHEKHOV

Chekhov, Anton. *Letters of Anton Chekhov.* Trans. Michael Henry Heim and Simon Karlinsky. New York: Harper & Row, 1973.

Gottleib, Vera. *Chekhov and the Vaudeville.* Cambridge, England: Cambridge UP, 1982.

Hingley, Ronald. *Chekhov: A Biographical and Critical Study.* New York: Barnes & Noble, 1966.

Magarshack, David. *Chekhov the Dramatist.* New York: Hill and Wang, 1960.

Peace, Richard. *Chekhov: A Study of the Four Major Plays.* New Haven, CT: Yale UP, 1983.

Pitcher, Henry. *The Chekhov Play.* London: Chatto and Windus, 1973.

Rayfield, Donald. *Chekhov: The Evolution of His Art.* London: Paul Elek, 1975.

Styan, J. L. *Chekhov in Performance.* Cambridge, England: Cambridge UP, 1971.

CARYL CHURCHILL

Churchill, Caryl. "The Common Imagination and the Individual Voice." *New Theatre Quarterly* 4 (February 1988): 3–16.

Diamond, Elin. "Brechtian Theory/Feminist Criticism: Toward a Gestic Feminist Criticism." *TDR—Drama Review* 32.1 (1988): 82–94.

————. "(In)Visible Bodies in Churchill's Theatre." *Theatre Journal* 40 (1988): 188–204.

————. "Refusing the Romanticism of Identity: Narrative Interventions in Churchill, Benmussa, Duras." *Theatre Journal* 37 (1985): 273–86.

Harding, James M. "Cloud Cover: (Re)Dressing Desire and Comfortable Subversions in Caryl Churchill's *Cloud Nine.*" *PMLA* 113 (1998): 258–72

Quigley, Austin E. "Stereotype and Prototype: Character in the Plays of Caryl Churchill." *Feminine Focus: The New Women Playwrights.* Ed. Enoch Brater. New York: Oxford UP, 1989.

Randall, Phyllis R., ed. *Caryl Churchill: A Casebook.* New York: Garland, 1989.

HENRIK IBSEN

Cima, Gay Gibson. "Discovering Signs: The Emergence of the Critical Actor in Ibsen." *Theatre Journal* 35 (1983): 5–22.

Egan, Michael, ed. *Ibsen: The Critical Heritage.* London: Routledge & Kegan Paul, 1972.

Hardwick, Elizabeth. "A Doll's House." In *Seduction and Betrayal.* New York: Random House, 1970.

Lyons, Charles R. *Henrik Ibsen: The Divided Consciousness.* Carbondale, IL: Southern Illinois UP, 1972.

Marker, Frederick J., and Lise-Lone Marker. *Ibsen's Lively Art: A Performance Study of the Major Plays.* Cambridge, England: Cambridge UP, 1989.

Meyer, Michael. *Henrik Ibsen: A Biography.* Garden City, NJ: Doubleday, 1971.

Northam, John. *Ibsen: A Critical Study.* Cambridge, England: Cambridge UP, 1973.

————. *Ibsen's Dramatic Method: A Study of the Prose Dramas.* London: Faber & Faber, 1953.

Shaw, Bernard. *The Quintessence of Ibsenism.* New York: Hill and Wang, 1957.

Sprinchorn, Evert, ed. *Ibsen: Letters and Speeches.* New York: Hill and Wang, 1964.

Bentley, Eric. *Bernard Shaw.* New York: Norton, 1976.

Berst, Charles A. *Bernard Shaw and the Art of Drama.* Urbana, IL: U of Illinois P, 1973.

Compton, Louis. *Shaw the Dramatist.* Lincoln, NE: U of Nebraska P, 1969.

Evans, T. F., ed. *Shaw: The Critical Heritage.* London: Routledge & Kegan Paul, 1976.

Goldman, Michael. "Shaw and the Marriage in Dionysus." *The Play and Its Critic: Essays for Eric Bentley.* Ed. Michael Bertin. New York: UP of America, 1986.

Holroyd, Michael. *Bernard Shaw.* 3 vols. New York: Random House, 198891.

Meisel, Martin. *Shaw and the Nineteenth-Century Theater.* Princeton, NJ: Princeton UP, 1963.

Peters, Margot. *Bernard Shaw and the Actresses.* Garden City, NJ: Doubleday, 1980.

Turco, Alfred, Jr. *Shaw's Moral Vision: The Self and Salvation.* Ithaca, NY: Cornell UP, 1976.

Wisenthal, J. L. *The Marriage of Contraries: Bernard Shaw's Middle Plays.* Cambridge, MA: Harvard UP, 1974.

BERNARD SHAW

Betsko, Kathleen, and Rachel Koenig, eds. *Interviews with Contemporary Women Playwrights.* New York: Beech Tree, 1987.

Bigsby, C. W. E. *A Critical Introduction to Twentieth-Century American Drama.* 3 vols. Cambridge, England: Cambridge UP, 1982–85.

Bronner, Edwin, ed. *The Encyclopedia of the American Theatre 1900–1975.* New York: A. S. Barnes, 1980.

Case, Sue-Ellen. "Toward a Butch-Femme Aesthetic." *Making a Spectacle: Feminist Essays on Contemporary Women's Theatre.* Ed. Lynda Hart. Ann Arbor: U of Michigan P, 1989.

Case, Sue-Ellen, Philip Brett, and Susan Leigh Foster, eds. *Cruising the Performative: Interventions into the Representation of Ethnicity, Nationality, and Sexuality.* Bloomington: Indiana UP, 1995.

Chinoy, Helen Krich, and Linda Walsh Jenkins, eds. *Women in American Theatre.* New York: Crown, 1981.

Clurman, Harold. *The Fervent Years: The Story of the Group Theatre and the Thirties.* New York: Knopf, 1945.

Cohn, Ruby. *New American Dramatists, 1960–1980.* New York: Grove, 1982.

Coven, Brenda, ed. *American Women Dramatists of the Twentieth Century: A Bibliography.* Metuchen, NJ: Scarecrow, 1982.

Diamond, Elin. *Unmaking Mimesis: Essays on Feminism and Theater.* London: Routledge, 1997.

Downer, Alan S. *American Drama and Its Critics.* Chicago: U of Chicago P, 1965.

Elam, Harry J., Jr. *Taking It to the Streets: The Social Protest Theater of Luis Valdez and Amiri Baraka.* Ann Arbor: U of Michigan P, 1997.

UNIT 6: THE UNITED STATES

Flanagan, Hallie. *Arena.* New York: Duell, Sloan and Pearce, 1949.

Garza, Roberto, ed. *Contemporary Chicano Theatre.* Notre Dame: U of Notre Dame P, 1996.

Harrison, Paul Carter. *The Drama of Nommo.* New York: Grove, 1972.

Hart, Lynda, ed. *Making a Spectacle: Feminist Essays on Contemporary Women's Theatre.* Ann Arbor: U of Michigan P, 1989.

Hatch, James V., ed. *Black Theatre USA: Forty-Five Plays by Black Americans, 1847–1974.* New York: Macmillan, 1974.

Hill, Errol, ed. *The Theatre of Black Americans.* 2 vols. Englewood Cliffs: Prentice-Hall, 1980.

Houston, Velina Hasu, ed. *But Still, Like Air, I'll Rise: New Asian American Plays.* Philadelphia: Temple UP, 1997.

Huerta, Jorge A. *Chicano Theater: Themes and Forms.* Ypsilanti, MI: Bilingual Press, 1982.

Kanellos, Nicolás. *Hispanic Theatre in the United States.* Houston: Arte Público Press, 1984.

Lee, Josephine. *Performing Asian America: Race and Ethnicity and the Contemporary Stage.* Philadelphia: Temple UP, 1997.

Marker, Lise-Lone. *David Belasco: Naturalism in the American Theatre.* Princeton, NJ: Princeton UP, 1975.

Marranca, Bonnie, ed. *The Theatre of Images.* New York: Drama Book Specialists, 1977.

Perkins, Kathy A. *Black Female Playwrights: An Anthology of Plays before 1950.* Bloomington: Indiana UP, 1989.

Perkins, Kathy A., and Roberta A. Uno, eds. *Contemporary Plays by Women of Color.* London: Routledge, 1996.

Rabkin, Gerald. *Drama and Commitment: Politics in the American Theatre of the Thirties.* Bloomington: Indiana UP, 1964.

Roach, Joseph. *Cities of the Dead: Circum-Atlantic Performances.* New York: Columbia UP, 1996.

Savran, David. *Taking It Like a Man: White Masculinity, Masochism, and Contemporary American Culture.* Princeton, NJ: Princeton UP, 1998.

Schneider, Rebecca. *The Explicit Body in Performance.* London: Routledge, 1997.

Shank, Ted. *American Alternative Theatres.* New York: Grove, 1982.

Shewey, Don, ed. *Out Front: Contemporary Gay and Lesbian Plays.* New York: Grove, 1988.

SUSAN GLASPELL

Ben-Zvi, Linda. "Susan Glaspell's Contributions to Contemporary Women Playwrights." *Feminine Focus: The New Women Playwrights.* Ed. Enoch Brater. New York: Oxford UP, 1989.

Dymkowski, Christine. "On the Edge: The Plays of Susan Glaspell." *Modern Drama* 31 (1988): 91–105.

Kolodny, Annette. "A Map for Rereading: Gender and the Interpretation of Literary Texts." *The New Feminist Criticism: Essays on Women, Literature, and Theory.* Ed. Elaine Showalter. New York: Pantheon, 1985.

Stein, Karen F. "The Women's World of Glaspell's *Trifles.*" *Women in American Theatre.* Ed. Helen Krich Chinoy and Linda Walsh Jenkins. New York: Crown, 1981.

DAVID HENRY HWANG

Garber, Majorie. *Vested Interests: Cross-Dressing and Cultural Anxiety.* London: Routledge, 1992.

Hwang, David Henry. Afterword. *M. Butterfly.* New York: New American Library, 1988.

———. *F. O. B.* in *New Plays USA 1.* New York: Theatre Communications Group, 1982.

Moy, James S. "David Henry Hwang's *M. Butterfly* and Philip Kan Gotanda's *Yankee Dawg You Die:* Repositioning Chinese American Marginality on the American Stage." *Theatre Journal* 42 (1990): 48–56.

Cheever, Susan. Interview with Tony Kushner. *New York Times* 13 September 1992: II, 7.

Geis, Deborah R., and Steven F. Kruger, eds. *Approaching the Millennium: Essays on Angels in America.* Ann Arbor: U of Michigan P, 1997.

Savran, David. "Ambivalence, Utopia, and a Queer Sort of Materialism: How Angels in America Reconstructs the Nation." *Theatre Journal* 47(1995): 207–28.

TONY KUSHNER

Diamond, Liz. "Perceptible Mutability in the Word Kingdom." *Theatre* 24.3 (1993): 86–87.

Drunkman, Steven. "Suzan-Lori Parks and Liz Diamond: Doo-a-diddly-dit-dit." *TDR— The Drama Review* 39.3 (1995): 56–75.

Parks, Suzan-Lori. *The America Play and Other Works.* New York: TCG, 1995.

Pearce, Michele. "Alien Nation: An Interview with the Playwright Suzan-Lori Parks." *American Theatre* March 1994: 26–28.

Rayner, Alice, and Harry J. Elam, Jr. "Unfinished Business: Reconfiguring History in Suzan-Lori Parks's *The Death of the Last Black Man in the Whole Entire World.*" *Theatre Journal* 46 (1994): 447–62.

SUZAN-LORI PARKS

Broyles-González, Yolanda. *El Teatro Campesino: Theater in the Chicano Movement.* Austin, Texas, U of Texas P, 1994.

———. "Toward a Re-Vision of Chicano Theatre History: The Women of El Teatro Campesino." *Making a Spectacle: Feminist Essays on Contemporary Women's Theatre.* Ed. Lynda Hart. Ann Arbor, MI: U of Michigan P, 1989.

Huerta, Jorge A. *Chicano Theater: Themes and Forms.* Ypsilanti, MI: Bilingual Press, 1982.

Kanellos, Nicolás. *Hispanic Theatre in the United States.* Houston: Arte Público, 1984.

Morton, Carlos. "The Teatro Campesino." *Tulane Drama Review* 18.4 (1974): 71–76.

Valdez, Luis. *Pensamiento Serpentino.* El Centro Campesino Cultural, CA: Cucaracha, 1973.

Valdez, Luis, and El Teatro Campesino. *Actos.* San Juan Bautista, CA: Menyah Productions, 1971.

von Bardeleben, Renate, ed. *Missions in Conflict: Essays on U.S.-Mexican Relations and Chicano Culture.* Tübingen, Germany: G. Narr, 1986.

LUIS VALDEZ

Boxill, Roger. *Tennessee Williams.* New York: St. Martin's Press, 1987.

Devlin, Albert J., ed. *Conversations with Tennessee Williams.* Jackson, MS: U of Mississippi P, 1986.

Leavitt, Richard Freeman, ed. *The World of Tennessee Williams.* New York: Putnam, 1978.

Spoto, Donald. *The Kindness of Strangers: The Life of Tennessee Williams.* Boston: Little, Brown, 1985.

Stanton, Stephen, ed. *Tennessee Williams: A Collection of Critical Essays.* Englewood Cliffs, NJ: Prentice-Hall, 1977.

Williams, Tennessee. *Memoirs.* Garden City, NJ: Doubleday, 1975.

TENNESSEE WILLIAMS

Ching, Mei-Ling. "Wrestling against History." *Theater/Yale* 19.3 (1988): 70–71.

Henderson, Heather. "Building Fences: An Interview with Mary Alice and James Earl Jones." *Theater/Yale* 16.3 (1985): 67–70.

Shannon, Sandra G. "The Long Wait: August Wilson's *Ma Rainey's Black Bottom.*" *Black American Literature Forum* 25.1 (1991): 135–45.

Wilde, Lisa. "Reclaiming the Past: Narrative and Memory in August Wilson's *Two Trains Running.*" *Theatre/Yale* 22.1 (1991): 73–74.

AUGUST WILSON

UNIT 7: WORLD STAGES

Allison, H. *Sistren Song: Popular Theatre in Jamaica.* London: War on Want, 1986.

Alston, J. B. *Yoruba Drama in English: Interpretation and Production.* Lewiston, NY: Mellen, 1989.

Appiah, Kwame Anthony. "Is the Post- in Postmodernism the Post- in Postcolonial?" *Critical Inquiry* 17 (1991): 336–57.

————. *In My Father's House: Africa in the Philosophy of Culture.* London: Methuen, 1992.

Ashcroft, Bill, Gareth Griffiths, and Helen Tiffin. *The Empire Writes Back: Theory and Practice in Post-Colonial Literatures.* London: Routledge, 1989.

————. *The Post-Colonial Studies Reader.* London: Routledge, 1995.

Bennett, Susan. "Who Speaks? Representations of Native Women in Some Canadian Plays." *Canadian Journal of Drama and Theatre* 1.2 (1991): 13–25.

Bhabha, Homi K. *The Location of Culture.* London: Routledge, 1993.

Bharucha, Rustom. *Theatre and the World: Performance and the Politics of Culture.* London: Routledge, 1993.

Black, S. "'What Kind of Society Can Develop Under Corrugated Iron?': Glimpses of New Zealand History in New Zealand Plays." *Australasian Drama Studies* 3.1 (1984): 31–52.

Boal, Augusto. *The Theatre of the Oppressed.* Trans. C. A. McBride and M. L. McBride. New York TCG, 1979.

Boon, Richard, and Jane Plaistow, eds. *Theatre Matters: Performance and Culture on the World Stage.* Cambridge, England: Cambridge UP, 1998.

Carlson, Marvin. *Performance: A Critical Introduction.* London: Routledge, 1996.

Chinwezu, Onwuchekwa Jemie, and Ihechukwu Madubuike. *Toward the Decolonization of African Literature.* Vol. 1. Washington, DC: Howard UP, 1983.

Coplan, David. *In Township Tonight! South Africa's Black City Music and Theatre.* London: Longman, 1985.

Crow, Brian, and Chris Canfield. *An Introduction to Post-Colonial Theatre.* Cambridge: Cambridge UP, 1996.

Drewal, Margaret T. *Yoruba Ritual: Performers, Play, Agency.* Bloomington: Indiana UP, 1992.

Dunton, C. *"Make Man Talk True": Nigerian Drama in English Since 1970.* London: Hans Zell, 1992.

Emberley, J. V. *Thresholds of Difference: Feminist Critique, Native Women's Writing, Postcolonial Theory.* Toronto: U of Toronto P, 1993.

Fanon, Frantz. *Black Skin, White Masks.* Trans. C. L. Markmann. New York: Grove, 1967.

Filewod, Alan. "Between Empires: Post-Imperialism and Canadian Theatre." *Essays in Theatre/Études Théâtrales* 11.1 (1992): 3–15.

Fuchs, A. *Playing the Market: The Market Theatre, Johannesburg 1976–1980.* London: Harwood, 1990.

Gargi, B. *Folk Theater of India.* Calcutta: Rupa, 1991.

Gilbert, Helen, and Joanne Tompkins. *Post-Colonial Drama: Theory, Practice, Politics.* London: Routledge, 1996.

Glissant, Edouard. *Caribbean Discourse: Selected Essays.* Charlottesville: UP of Virginia, 1989.

Goldie, T. *Fear and Temptation: The Image of the Indigene in Canadian, Australian, and New Zealand Literatures.* Kingston, Ontario: McGill-Queen's UP, 1989.

Holloway, P., ed. *Contemporary Australian Drama: Perspectives Since 1955.* Sydney: Currency Press, 1987.

Hulme, Peter. *Colonial Encounters: Europe and the Native Caribbean 1492–1797.* London: Routledge, 1986.

Kavangh, Robert Mshengu. *Theatre and Cultural Struggle in South Africa.* London: Zed, 1985.

Mead, P., and Campbell, M., eds. *Shakespeare's Books: Contemporary Cultural Politics and the Persistence of Empire.* Melbourne: U of Melbourne English Department, 1993.

Ndlovu, Duma. *Woza Afrika! An Anthology of South African Plays.* New York: Braziller, 1986.

Ngũgĩ wa Thiong'o. *Decolonising the Mind: The Politics of Language in African Literature.* London: James Currey, 1986.

Olaniyan, Tejumola. *Scars of Conquest/Masks of Resistance.* New York: Oxford UP, 1995.

Orkin, Martin. *Drama and the South African State.* Manchester: Manchester UP, 1991.

Pavis, Patrice, ed. *The Intercultural Performance Reader.* London: Routledge, 1996.

Phelan, Peggy. *Unmarked: The Politics of Performance.* London: Routledge, 1992.

Retamar, Roberto Fernández. *Caliban and Other Essays.* Trans. E. Baker. Minneapolis: U of Minnesota P, 1989.

Rock, David. *Argentina, 1516–1987: From Spanish Colonization to Alfonsín.* Berkeley: U of California P, 1987.

Said, Edward. *Culture and Imperialism.* London: Chatto and Windus, 1993.

Salter, Denis. "On Native Ground: Canadian Theatre Historiography and the Postmodernism/Postcolonial Axis." *Theatre Research in Canada* 13.12 (1992): 134–43.

Savigliano, Marta E. *Tango and the Political Economy of Passion.* Boulder: Westview, 1995.

Spivak, Gayatri Chakravorty. *In Other Worlds: Essays in Cultural Politics.* New York: Methuen, 1988.

Taylor, Diana. *Disappearing Acts: Spectacles of Gender and Nationalism in Argentina's "Dirty War."* Durham: Duke UP, 1997.

———. *Theatre of Crisis: Drama and Politics in Latin America.* Lexington: U of Kentucky P, 1991.

Taylor, Diana, and Juan Villegas, eds. *Negotiating Performance: Gender, Sexuality, and Theatricality in Latin/o America.* Durham: Duke UP, 1994.

Trinh, T. Minh-ha. *Woman, Native, Other.* Bloomington: Indiana UP, 1989.

Versényi, Adam. *Theatre in Latin America: Religion, Politics and Culture from Cortés to the 1980s.* Cambridge, England: Cambridge UP, 1993.

Zarrilli, Phillip. *The Kathakali Complex: Actor, Performance and Structure.* New Delhi: Abhinav, 1984.

AIMÉ CÉSAIRE

Arnold, A. James. *Modernism and Negritude: The Poetry and Poetics of Aimé Césaire.* Cambridge, MA: Harvard UP, 1981.

Balme, Chris. "The Aboriginal Theater of Jack Davis: Prolegomena to a Theory of Syncretic Theatre." *Crisis and Creativity in New Literatures in English.* Eds. G. Davis and H. Maes-Jelinek. Amsterdam: Rodopi, 1990. 401–17.

Davis, Gregson. *Aimé Césaire.* Cambridge, England: Cambridge UP, 1997.

Dawborn, Charles. *Makers of New France.* New York: Pott, 1951.

Frutkin, Susan. *Aimé Césaire: Black between Worlds.* Coral Gables, FL: U of Miami P, 1973.

BRIAN FRIEL

Dantanus, Ulf. *Brian Friel: A Study.* London: Faber & Faber, 1988.

Deane, Seamus. *Celtic Revivals: Essays in Modern Irish Literature, 1880–1900.* Winston-Salem, NC: Wake Forest UP, 1987.

Maxwell, D. E. S. *Brian Friel.* Lewisburg, PA: Bucknell UP, 1973.

O'Brien, Lance. *Brian Friel.* Boston: Twayne, 1990.

Pine, Richard. *The Diviner: The Art of Brian Friel.* Mullingar, Ireland: Lilliput Press, 1988.

Richtarik, Marilyn. *Acting Between the Lines: The Field Day Company and Irish Cultural Politics, 1980–1984.* Oxford, England: Clarendon Press, 1994.

ATHOL FUGARD

Benson, Mary. *Athol Fugard and Barney Simon.* Randburg: Ravan, 1997.

Fuchs, Anne. *Playing the Market: The Market Theatre, Johannesburg, 1976–1986.* New York: Harwood, 1990.

Fugard, Athol. *Notebooks 1960–1977.* Johannesburg: Ad. Donker, 1983.

Gray, Stephen. *Athol Fugard.* New York: McGraw-Hill, 1992.

———. *File on Fugard.* London: Methuen, 1991.

Vandenbroucke, Russell. *Truths the Hand Can Touch: The Theatre of Athol Fugard.* New York: TCG, 1985.

Walder, Dennis. *Athol Fugard.* New York: Grove, 1995.

TOMSON HIGHWAY

Baker, Marie Annharte. "An Old Indian Trick Is To Laugh." *Canadian Theatre Review* 68 (Fall 1991): 48–49.

———. "Angry Enough to Spit But with *Dry Lips* It Hurts More Than You Know." *Canadian Theatre Review* 68 (Fall 1991): 88–89.

Dahlquist, Gordon. "I Did It—Highway." *Native Playwrights' Newsletter* (Winter 1994): 22–23.

Filewod, Alan. "Receiving Aboriginality: Tomson Highway and the Crisis of Cultural Authenticity." *Theatre Journal* 46 (1994): 363–73.

Loucks, Bryan. "Another Glimpse: Excerpts from a Conversation with Tomson Highway." *Canadian Theatre Review* 68 (Fall 1991): 9–11.

Rabillard, Sheila. "Absorption, Elimination, and the Hybrid: Some Impure Questions of Gender and Culture in the Trickster Drama of Tomson Highway." *Essays in Theatre/ Études Théàtrales* 12.1 (1993): 3–27.

Wilson, Ann. "Tomson Highway." *Other Solitudes: Canadian Multicultural Fictions.* Eds. Linda Hutcheon and Marion Richmond. Toronto: Oxford UP, 1990.

WOLE SOYINKA

Gibbs, James. *Wole Soyinka.* London: Macmillan, 1986.

———, ed. *Critical Perspectives on Wole Soyinka.* Washington, DC: Three Continents, 1980.

Gibbs, James, Ketu H. Katrak, and Henry Louis Gates Jr., eds. *Wole Soyinka: A Bibliography of Primary and Secondary Sources.* Westport, CT: Greenwood, 1986.

Gugelberger, Georg M., ed. *Marxism and African Literature.* London: James Currey, 1985.

Jones, Eldred Durosimi. *The Writings of Wole Soyinka.* London: James Currey, 1988.

Nazareth, Peter. *An African View of Literature.* Evanston, IL: Northwestern UP, 1974.

Ogunba, Oyin. *The Movement of Transition: A Study of the Plays of Wole Soyinka.* Ibadan, Nigeria: Ibadan UP, 1975.

Soyinka, Wole. "The Fourth Stage." *The Morality of Art: Essays Presented to G. Wilson Knight by his Colleagues and Friends.* Ed. D. W. Jefferson, New York: Barnes & Noble, 1969.

———. *The Man Died.* London: Rex Collings, 1972.

Aristophanes, *Lysistrata*
>   VHS. 1987. Distributed by Insight Media.
>   Sound Recording. 1966. Director: Howard Sackler. Cast includes Hermione Gingold and Stanley Holloway. Caedmon Records.

Euripides, *Medea*
>   VHS. 1970. Director: Pier Paolo Passolini. Cast includes Maria Callas, Guiseppi Gentile, and Laurent Tarzieff.
>   VHS. 1979. Cast includes Marina Goderdzishvili and Vladimir Julukhadze.
>   VHS. 1979. Director: Pier Paolo Passolini. Cast includes Maria Callas and Guiseppi Gentile.
>   VHS. 1982. Cast includes Zoe Caldwell and Judith Anderson. Films for the Humanities.
>   Sound Recording. Cast includes Judith Anderson and Anthony Quayle. Caedmon Records.

Sophocles, *Oedipus the King*
>   VHS. 1957. Deaf actors' performance. Gallaudet University Library.
>   VHS. 1957. Director: Tyrone Guthrie. Cast includes Douglas Campbell, Douglas Rain, Eric House, and Eleanor Stuart.
>   VHS. 1959. *Oedipus Rex: Age of Sophocles, I.* Distributed by Encyclopedia Britannica Educational Corp.
>   VHS. 1967. Director: Philip Saville. Cast includes Donald Sutherland, Christopher Plummer, Lilli Palmer, Orson Welles, and Cyril Cusack.
>   VHS. 1975. *The Rise of Greek Tragedy.* Director: Howard Mantell. Cast includes James Mason, Claire Bloom. Set in outdoor amphitheater, using masks. Films for the Humanities, 1982.
>   VHS. 1987. Cast includes John Gielgud, Michael Pennington, and Claire Bloom. Films for the Humanities.
>   Sound Recording. Cast includes Douglas Campbell and Eric House. Caedmon Records.
>   Sound Recording. Cast includes Bernard Mayes. Mind's Eye.

Anonymous, *Everyman*
>   Film. 1971. Distributed by Paul Lewison.
>   VHS. 1991. Distributed by Insight Media.
>   Sound Recording. Cast includes Burgess Meredith. Caedmon Records.

William Shakespeare, *Hamlet*
>   Film. 1948. Director: Laurence Olivier. Cast includes Olivier.
>   Film. 1954. *Prince of Players.* Cast includes Richard Burton and Eva LeGallienne.
>   Film. 1963. *The Bad Sleep Well.* Director: Akira Kurosawa.
>   Film. 1966. Russian with English subtitles. Cast includes Innokenti Smoktunovsky and Mikhail Nazvanov.
>   VHS. 1969. Director: Tony Richardson. Cast includes Nicol Williamson.

UNIT 1

UNIT 3

Film. 1969. Cast includes Nicol Williamson, Gordon Jackson, Judy Parfitt, and Marianne Faithful.

VHS. 1979. Director: Derek Jacobi. Time-Life Video.

VHS. 1980. Director: Rodney Bennett. BBC.

Film. 1982. Director: Robert Nelson.

VHS. 1983. The BBC-TV Shakespeare Plays. Cast includes Derek Jacobi.

VHS. 1985. Director: Douglas Fisher. Classics on Video series.

VHS. 1989. Director: Melvyn Bragg.

VHS. 1990. Director: Franco Zeffirelli. Cast includes Mel Gibson and Glenn Close.

VHS. 1996. Director: Kenneth Branagh. Cast includes Branagh, Derek Jacobi, Julie Christie, and Kate Winslet.

Sound Recording. Cast includes John Gielgud. Durkin Hayes Publishing.

Sound Recording. 1985. Michael Redgrave.

Sound Recording. 1988. Cast includes Ronald Pickup and Angela Pleasance. BBC Audio Collection.

William Shakespeare, *The Tempest*

Film. 1959. Cast includes Van Heflin and Silvano Mangano.

VHS. 1960. Hallmark Hall of Fame. Cast includes Richard Burton.

Film. 1961. Michigan Media.

VHS. 1963. Director: George Schaefer. Cast includes Maurice Evans, Roddy McDowall, Richard Burton, and Lee Remick. Films for the Humanities.

Film. 1968. Director: Peter Brook.

Film. 1969. *Tempest: O Brave New World.* National Broadcasting Co.

VHS. 1973. Yale Repertory Theatre production recorded for Television. LCL TOFT.

VHS. 1980. Director: Derek Jarman. Cast includes Heathcote Williams and Karl Johnson. World Northal.

VHS. 1980. Director: Audrey E. Stanley. Berkeley Shakespeare Festival.

VHS. 1982. Director: Paul Mazursky. Cast includes John Cassavetes, Gena Rowlands, Susan Sarandon, Vittorio Gassman, and Raul Julia.

VHS. 1983. The BBC-TV Shakespeare Plays. Cast includes Michael Hordern.

VHS. 1983. Director: William Woodman. Cast includes Efrem Zimbalist Jr., William H. Basset, Ted Sorrel, and Kay E. Kuter.

VHS. 1986. Director: Julie Taymor. Theatre for a New Audience.

VHS. 1992. *Prospero's Books.* Director: Peter Greenaway. Cast includes John Gielgud, Erland Josephson, and Michael Clark.

Sound Recording. Cast includes Michael Redgrave and Vanessa Redgrave. Caedmon Records.

UNIT 4

Pedro Calderón de la Barca, *Life Is a Dream*

Film. 1988. Director: Raul Ruiz. Cast includes Sylvain Thirolle and Roch Leibovici. French with English subtitles.

Molière, *Tartuffe*

VHS. *Molière and the Comédie Française.* Director: Jacques Charon.

Sound Recording. 1968. Director: Jean Gascon. Stratford National Theatre of Canada. Caedmon Records.

Henrik Ibsen, *A Doll House*
> VHS. 1959. Director: Barry A. Brown. Cast includes Christopher Plummer, Julie Harris, and Richard Thomas.
> VHS. 1973. Director: Joseph Losey. Cast includes Jane Fonda and Trevor Howard.
> VHS. 1973. Director: Patrick Garland. Cast includes Claire Bloom and Anthony Hopkins.
> VHS. 1977. Cast includes Claire Bloom.
> Sound Recording. Cast includes Claire Bloom and Donald Madden. Caedmon Records.

Bernard Shaw, *Major Barbara*
> VHS. 1941. Director: Gabriel Pascal, in consultation with George Bernard Shaw. Cast includes Wendy Hiller, Rex Harrison, and Sybil Thorndike.
> Sound Recording. Cast includes Maggie Smith and Robert Morley. Caedmon Records.

David Henry Hwang, *M. Butterfly*
> VHS. 1993. Director: David Cronenberg. Cast includes Jeremy Irons, John Lone, and Barbara Sukowa.

Tennessee Williams, *The Glass Menagerie*
> Film. 1950. Director: Irving Rippen. Cast includes Jane Wyman, Kirk Douglas, and Arthur Kennedy.
> Film. 1973. Director: Anthony Harvey. Cast includes Katharine Hepburn, Sam Waterston, Joanna Miles, and Michael Moriarty.
> VHS. 1987. Director: Paul Newman. Cast includes John Malkovich, Joanne Woodward, and Karen Allen.
> Sound Recording. 1980. Cast includes Helen Hayes and Montgomery Clift. Mind's Eye.
> Sound Recording. Cast includes Montgomery Clift and Julie Harris. Caedmon Records.
> Sound Recording. *Tennessee Williams Reads "The Glass Menagerie" and Others.* Cast includes Tennessee Williams. Caedmon Records.

UNIT 5

UNIT 6

ARISTOPHANES *Lysistrata*, translated by Donald Sutherland. Copyright 1959, 1961 by the Chandler Publishing Company. Used by permission of Addison-Wesley Publishers.

ARISTOTLE Selection from *The Poetics* from Aristotle's *Poetics*, translated by Gerald F. Else. Copyright 1967 by The University of Michigan Press. Reprinted by permission of the publisher.

ANTONIN ARTAUD Selection from *The Theatre and Its Double*, translated by Mary Caroline Richard. English translation copyright 1958 by Grove Press, Inc. Used by permission of Grove/Atlantic, Inc.

CALDERÓN DE LA BARCA *Life is a Dream* from *Life is a Dream and Other Spanish Classics*, edited by Eric Bentley and translated by Roy Campbell. Copyright 1959, 1958 by Eric Bentley. Reprinted by permission of Applause Theatre Book Publishers.

SAMUEL BECKETT *Endgame*. Copyright 1958 by Grove Press, Inc.; renewed copyright 1986 by Samuel Beckett. Reprinted by permission of Grove/Atlantic, Inc.

APHRA BEHN *The Rover*, edited by Montague Summers. This version published 1915.

BERTOLT BRECHT *Mother Courage and Her Children*. Original work *Mutter Courage and ihre Kinder*. Copyright 1940 by Arvid Englind Teaterforlag, a.b., renewed June 1967 by Stefan S. Brecht; copyright 1949 by Suhrkamp Verlag, Frankfurt am Main. John Willett's translation of *Mother Courage and Her Children* and texts by Brecht. Copyright 1980 by Stefan S. Brecht. Reprinted from *Mother Courage and Her Children*, translated by John Willett and edited by John Willett and Ralph Manheim, published by Arcade Publishing, New York, NY. Used with permission.

BERTOLT BRECHT "Theatre for Pleasure or Theater for Instruction" from *Brecht on Theatre: The Development of an Aesthetic* by Bertolt Brecht, edited and translated by John Willett. Translation copyright 1964 and renewed 1992 by John Willett. Reprinted by permission of Hill & Wang, a division of Farrar, Straus & Giroux, Inc.

A. C. CAWLEY *Everyman*, with footnotes by A. C. Cawley, from *Everyman and Medieval Miracle Plays*, edited by A. C. Cawley, Everyman's Library edition, 1974. Reprinted by permission of David Campbell Publishers, Ltd.

AIMÉ CÉSAIRE *A Tempest*, translated by Richard Miller. Copyright 1992 by Richard Miller. Originally published in French as *Une Tempete* by Editions du Seuil, Paris. Copyright 1969 by Editions du Seuil. Reprinted by permission of Georges Borchardt, Inc.

ANTON CHEKHOV *The Cherry Orchard* from *Chekhov: Four Plays*, translated by Carol Rocamora. Copyright 1996 by Carol Rocamora. Reprinted by permission of Smith & Kraus Publishers, POB 127, Lyme, NH 03768. All inquiries concerning rights should be addressed to Smith & Kraus Publishers.

CARYL CHURCHILL *Cloud Nine*. Copyright 1979, 1980, 1983, 1984, 1985 by Caryl Churchill. Reprinted by permission with Nick Hern Books, London.

CHŪSHINGURA *The Forty-Seven Samurai: A Kabuki Version of Chūshingura*, adapted by Nakamura Matagorō II and James R. Brandon, from *Chūshingura: Studies in Kabuki and the Puppet Theater*, edited by James R. Brandon, Junko Berberich, and Michael Feldman. Copyright 1982 by James R. Brandon. Reprinted with permission.

JOHN DRYDEN "Preface to *Troilus and Cressida*, Containing the Grounds of Criticism in Tragedy" from *Literary Criticism of John Dryden*, edited by Arthur C. Kirsch. Copyright 1966 by the University of Nebraska Press. Copyright renewed 1994 by the University of Nebraska Press. Reprinted by permission of the publisher.

EURIPIDES *Medea*, translated by Rex Warner (Dover Thrift Editions), edited by Stanley Appelbaum. This Dover edition first published in 1993 is an unabridged republication of the Rex Warner translation originally published by John Lane, The Bodley Head Limited, London, 1944.

FRANTZ FANON Selection from "The Fact of Blackness" from *Black Skin, White Masks*, translated by Charles Lam Markmann. Copyright 1967 by Grove Press, Inc. Used by permission of Grove/Atlantic, Inc.

BRIAN FRIEL *Translations* from *Selected Plays of Brian Friel*, published by Faber & Faber, Ltd. Copyright 1984 by Catholic University of America Press. Reprinted by permission of the publisher.

ATHOL FUGARD *Valley Song*. Copyright 1996 by Athol Fugard. Published by Theatre Communications Group. Used by permission of Theatre Communications Group.

HENRY LOUIS GATES JR. "Beyond the Culture Wars: Identities in Dialogue" from *Profession 93*. Copyright 1993 by The Modern Language Association of America. Reprinted by permission of The Modern Language Association of America.

HELEN GILBERT and JOANNE TOMPKINS "Body Politics," selection from *Post-Colonial Drama: Theory, Practice, Politics*. Copyright 1996 by Gilbert and Tompkins. Reprinted by permission of Routledge.

SUSAN GLASPELL *Trifles*, first published in 1916.

TOMSON HIGHWAY *Dry Lips Oughta Move to Kapuskasing*, published by Fifth House Publishers, 1989. Copyright 1989 by Tomson Highway. Reprinted by permission of Fifth House, Ltd., Calgary, Canada. CAUTION: All rights reserved. No part of this play may be reproduced in any form or by any means, electronic or mechanical, without permission in writing from the publisher.

DAVID HENRY HWANG *M. Butterfly*. Copyright 1986, 1987, 1988 by David Henry Hwang. Used by permission of Dutton Signet, a division of Penguin Putnam, Inc.

HENRIK IBSEN *A Doll House* from *The Complete Major Prose Plays of Henrik Ibsen*, translated by Rolf Fjelde. Translation copyright 1965, 1970, 1978 by Rolf Fjelde. Used by permission of Dutton Signet, a division of Penguin Putnam, Inc.

KAN'AMI KIYOTSUGU *Matsukaze*, translated by Royall Tyler in *Twenty Plays of the Nō Theatre*, edited by Donald Keene. Copyright 1970 by Columbia University Press. Reprinted by permission of the publisher.

TONY KUSHNER *Angels in America, Part I: Millennium Approaches*, first published in *American Theatre*, July/August 1992, published by Theatre Communications Group, 1993. Copyright 1992, 1993 by Tony Kushner. Reprinted by permission of Theatre Communications Group.

MAISHE MAPONYA *Gangsters* from *Doing Plays For a Change: Five Works Introduced by Ian Steadman* by Maishe Maponya. Copyright 1995 by Witwatersrand University Press. Reprinted by permission of Witwatersrand University Press on behalf of Maishe Maponya. Applications to perform this work should be addressed to Dramatic and Literary Rights Organization (DALRO): fax 27-11-404-1934.

KATHERINE EISAMAN MAUS Selection from "'Playhouse Flesh and Blood': Sexual Ideology and the Restoration Actress," in *Elh Journal*, 1979, published by Johns Hopkins University Press. Reprinted by permission of Johns Hopkins University Press.

ARTHUR MILLER "Tragedy and the Common Man" from *The Theater Essays of Arthur Miller* by Arthur Miller, edited by Robert A. Martin.

—— ILLUSTRATIONS ——

Italicized page numbers refer to texts included in this volume.